C. Lukomski
8-97
Staines,

CHAMBERS

Giant Paperback

ENGLISH THESAURUS

CHAMBERS

Giant Paperback ENGLISH THESAURUS

Managing Editor
Catherine Schwarz

Editors
Anne Seaton
George Davidson
John Simpson

CHAMBERS

CHAMBERS
An imprint of Larousse plc
43-45 Annandale Street
Edinburgh EH7 4AZ

First published as *Chambers Paperback Thesaurus* 1992
10 9 8 7 6 5 4 3 2

We have made every effort to mark as such all words which we believe to be trademarks. We should also like to make it clear that the presence of a word in the dictionary, whether marked or unmarked, in no way affects its legal status as a trademark.

A catalogue record for this book is available from the British Library

ISBN 0 550 10595 6

Typeset by Hewer Text Composition Services, Edinburgh
Printed in England by Clays Ltd, St Ives plc

CONTENTS

PREFACE

Chambers Giant Paperback English Thesaurus reflects the recent benefits gained by the English language from the vocabulary of varied medical, scientific and technical advances, of national and international politics, of widening cultural horizons, and even of war.

These and many other areas have contributed to the Chambers English language database, on which this *Giant Paperback Thesaurus* is based. The *Thesaurus* is up-to-date and authoritative, comprehensive and accessible, and is essential for everyone who wants to use the English language proficiently and imaginatively.

The scope and versatility of *Chambers Giant Paperback Thesaurus* will be enhanced by using it in conjunction with a dictionary — *Chambers Giant Paperback Dictionary* (1995), the standard *Chambers Concise Dictionary* (1991), or the fuller *Chambers Dictionary* (1993).

How to use this thesaurus

Little explanation is needed, as the arrangement is deliberately simple. To take the word **ailment** as an example: the part of speech, *n,* is given, and then a list of related and synonymous words in straightforward alphabetical order — affliction, complaint, disability, disease, disorder, illness, indisposition, infection, infirmity, malady, sickness, weakness. If none of the synonyms will do, many (in this case all) have entries of their own, providing further alternatives. It is the same with the antonyms: at **abiding** the word 'transient' is supplied as an antonym; the entry **transient** will give further opposites to 'abiding'.

Separate parts of speech have separate lists of synonyms: thus at **act**, two distinct lists are provided for the word as noun and as verb; the list for each new part of speech begins on a new line.

There is coverage of phrases too: again at **act**, there are the sub-entries **act up** and **act upon**, each with its list of synonymous expressions. Some phrases occur as independent entries rather than as sub-entries, and are ordered according to their first word. This means that all the phrases beginning with the word **in**, for example, will be found in an alphabetically arranged group *before* the word **inability**, and the phrase **de trop** must be looked for *before* the word **dead**.

Among the listed synonyms the user will find the occasional abstruse or colourfully unusual word, reflecting the broad coverage of *The Chambers Dictionary*. At **aftermath**, for instance, the words 'lattermath' and 'rowen', which correspond to the original meaning of aftermath (a second crop of grass), are included in the synonym list. As a general policy, however, the editors have excluded dialect and obsolete terms, unless such terms make an appearance in, say, a well-known song, poem or play.

The simple alphabetical arrangement of synonyms means that there is no classification of meanings within an entry, but many words that have strongly distinct senses are given two or more entries. For example, **bear** (carry . . . endure . . . sustain . . . transport . . . weather, etc) and **bear** (breed . . . engender . . . give birth to . . . produce . . . propagate, etc) have been entered as **bear**[1] and **bear**[2].

The editors hope that the readers will get as much enjoyment out of using this thesaurus as they have had in compiling it, and that it will be found to live up to the definition of **thesaurus** in *The Chambers Dictionary* — 'a treasury, a storehouse of knowledge'.

Acknowledgement

The publishers would like to thank Peter Schwarz for the invaluable contribution in time and technical expertise that he has made to this project.

A

abandon *v* abdicate, back-pedal, cede, chuck, desert, desist, discontinue, ditch, drop, evacuate, forgo, forsake, give up, jilt, leave, leave behind, leave in the lurch, quit, relinquish, renounce, repudiate, resign, scrap, sink, surrender, vacate, waive, withdraw from, yield.

antonyms continue, persist, support.

n dash, recklessness, unrestraint, wantonness, wildness.

antonym restraint.

abandoned *adj* cast aside, cast away, cast out, corrupt, debauched, depraved, derelict, deserted, desolate, discarded, dissipated, dissolute, dropped, forlorn, forsaken, jilted, left, neglected, outcast, profligate, rejected, relinquished, reprobate, scorned, sinful, unoccupied, vacant, wanton, wicked.

antonyms cherished, restrained.

abandonment *n* apostasy, cession, decampment, dereliction, desertion, desistance, discontinuance, discontinuation, dropping, evacuation, forsaking, giving up, jilting, leaving, neglect, relinquishment, renegation, renunciation, resignation, sacrifice, scrapping, surrender, waiver.

abase *v* belittle, cast down, debase, degrade, demean, discredit, disgrace, dishonour, downgrade, humble, humiliate, lower, malign, mortify, reduce, vitiate.

antonyms elevate, honour.

abasement *n* belittlement, debasement, degradation, demotion, depravation, deterioration, disgrace, dishonour, downgrading, humbling, humiliation, lowering, mortification, reduction, shame, vitiation.

antonyms elevation, promotion.

abashed *adj* affronted, ashamed, astounded, bewildered, chagrined, confounded, confused, cowed, discomfited, discomposed, disconcerted, discountenanced, discouraged, dismayed, dum(b)founded, embarrassed, floored, humbled, humiliated, mortified, nonplussed, perturbed, shamefaced, taken aback.

antonyms at ease, audacious, composed.

abate *v* alleviate, appease, attenuate, bate, decline, decrease, deduct, diminish, discount, dull, dwindle, ease, ebb, fade, faik, fall off, lessen, let up, mitigate, moderate, mollify, pacify, quell, rebate, reduce, relieve, remit, sink, slacken, slake, slow, subside, subtract, taper off, wane, weaken.

antonyms increase, strengthen.

abatement *n* alleviation, allowance, assuagement, attenuation, cessation, decline, decrease, deduction, diminution, discount, dulling, dwindling, easing, ebb, extenuation, fading, fall-off, lessening, let-up, mitigation, moderation, mollification, palliation, quelling, rebatement, reduction, relief, remission, slackening, slowing, softening, subsidence, subtraction, tapering off, tempering, waning, weakening.

antonyms crescendo, increase.

abbey *n* abbacy, cloister, convent, friary, monastery, nunnery, priory, seminary.

abbot *n* abbe, archimandrite, general, head, prior, superior.

abbreviate *v* abridge, abstract, clip, compress, condense, contract, curtail, cut, digest, epitomise, lessen, precis, reduce, shorten, shrink, summarise, trim, truncate.

antonyms amplify, extend.

abbreviation *n* abridgement, abstract, abstraction, clipping, compendium, compression, condensation, conspectus, contraction, curtailment, digest, epitome, precis, reduction, resume, shortening, summarisation, summary, summation, synopsis, trimming, truncation.

antonyms expansion, extension.

abdicate *v* abandon, abjure, abnegate, cede, demit, forgo, give up, quit, relinquish, renounce, repudiate, resign, retire, surrender, vacate, yield.

abdication *n* abandonment, abjuration, abnegation, cession, giving up, quitting, relinquishment, renunciation, resignation, retiral, retirement, surrender.

abdomen *n* belly, bread-basket, corporation, guts, hind-body, midriff, paunch, pot, stomach, tum, tummy, venter.

abdominal *adj* coeliac, gastric, intestinal, stomachic(al), ventral, ventricular, visceral.

abduct *v* abduce, appropriate, carry off, kidnap, lay hold of, make off with, rape, run away with, run off with, seduce, seize, snatch, spirit away.

abducted *adj* appropriated, enleve, kidnapped, seduced, seized, snatched, stolen.

abduction *n* appropriation, enlevement, kidnap, rape, seduction, seizure, theft.

aberrant *adj* abnormal, anomalous, atypical, corrupt, corrupted, defective, degenerate, depraved, deviant, different, divergent, eccentric, egregious, erroneous, incongruous, irregular, odd, peculiar, perverse, perverted, queer, quirky, rambling, roving, straying, untypical, wandering, wrong.

antonyms normal, straight.

aberration *n* aberrancy, abnormality, anomaly, defect, delusion, deviation, divergence, eccentricity, freak, hallucination, illusion, irregularity, lapse, nonconformity, oddity, peculiarity, quirk, rambling, rogue, straying, vagary, wandering.

antonym conformity.

abet *v* aid, assist, back, condone, connive, egg on, encourage, goad, help, incite, promote, prompt, sanction, second, spur, succour, support, sustain, uphold, urge.

antonym discourage.

abettor *n* accessory, accomplice, assistant, associate, backer, confederate, conniver, co-operator, encourager, fautor, fomenter, goad, helper, henchman, inciter, instigator, particeps criminis, prompter, second, supporter.

abeyance *n* adjournment, deferral, discontinuation, inactivity, intermission, lull, postponement, recess, remission, reservation, suspension, waiting.

antonyms activity, continuation.

abhor *v* abominate, despise, detest, execrate, hate, loathe, recoil from, shrink from, shudder at, spurn.

antonyms adore, love.

abhorrence *n* abomination, animosity, aversion, despite, detestation, disgust, distaste, enmity, execration, hate, hatred, horror, loathing, malice, odium, repugnance, revulsion.

antonyms adoration, love.

abhorrent *adj* abominable, absonant, despiteful, detestable, disgusting, distasteful, execrable, hated, hateful, heinous, horrible, horrid, loathsome, nauseating, obnoxious, odious, offensive, repellent, repugnant, repulsive, revolting.

antonym attractive.

abide *v* accept, bear, brook, continue, endure, last, outlive, persist, put up with, remain, stand, stay, stomach, submit to, suffer, survive, tarry, tolerate.

antonyms dispute, quit.

abide by acknowledge, acquiesce in, adhere to, agree to, carry out, comply with, conform to, discharge, follow, fulfil, go along with, hold to, keep to, obey, observe, stand by, submit to.

abiding *adj* constant, continual, continuing, continuous, durable, enduring, eternal, everlasting, fast, firm, immortal, immutable, indissoluble, lasting, permanent, persistent, persisting, stable, steadfast, surviving, tenacious, unchangeable, unchanging, unending.

antonyms ephemeral, transient.

ability *n* adeptness, adroitness, aptitude, capability, capacity, competence, competency, deftness, dexterity, endowment, energy, expertise, expertness, facility, faculty, flair, forte, genius, gift, knack, know-how, long suit, nous, potentiality, power, proficiency, qualification, savoir-faire, savvy, skill, strength, talent, touch.

antonyms inability, incompetence.

abject *adj* base, contemptible, cringing, debased, degenerate, degraded, deplorable, despicable, dishonourable, execrable, fawning, forlorn, grovelling, hopeless, humiliating, ignoble, ignominious, low, mean, miserable, outcast, pathetic, pitiable, servile, slavish, sordid, submissive, vile, worthless, wretched.

antonym exalted.

abjuration *n* abnegation, abstention, denial, disavowal, disclaiming, disclamation, eschewal, forswearing, recantation, refusal, rejection, relinquishment, renunciation, retraction, self-denial.

antonyms agreement, assent, support.

abjure *v* abandon, abnegate, abstain from, deny, disavow, discard, disclaim, disown, eschew, forsake, forswear, give up, recant, refrain from, reject, relinquish, renegue on, renounce, retract.

antonyms agree, assent, support.

ablaze *adj* afire, aflame, aglow, alight, angry, aroused, blazing, brilliant, burning, enthusiastic, excited, exhilarated, fervent, fiery, flaming, flashing, frenzied, fuming, furious, glaring, gleaming, glowing, ignited, illuminated, impassioned, incandescent, incensed, lighted, luminous, on fire, passionate, radiant, raging, sparkling, stimulated.

able *adj* accomplished, adept, adequate, adroit, capable, clever, competent, deft, dexterous, effective, efficient, experienced, expert, fere, fit, fitted, gifted, ingenious, masterful, masterly, powerful, practised, proficient, qualified, skilful, skilled, strong, talented.

antonyms incapable, incompetent.

able-bodied *adj* firm, fit, hale, hardy, healthy, hearty, lusty, powerful, robust, sound, stalwart, staunch, stout, strapping, strong, sturdy, tough, vigorous.

antonyms delicate, infirm.

ablution *n* bath, bathing, cleansing, lavation, purgation, purging, purification, shower, wash, washing.

abnegate *v* abandon, abdicate, abjure, abstain from, acquiesce, concede, decline, deny, disallow, eschew, forbear, forgo, forsake, give up, refrain from, reject, relinquish, renounce, sacrifice, submit, surrender, yield.

abnegation *n* abandonment, abjuration, abstinence, acquiescence, continence, disallowance, eschewal, forbearance, giving up, refusal, rejection, relinquishment, renunciation, sacrifice, self-denial, submission, surrender, temperance.

antonyms acceptance, support.

abnormal *adj* aberrant, anomalous, atypical, curious, deviant, different, divergent, eccentric, erratic, exceptional, extraordinary, irregular, monstrous, odd, paranormal, peculiar, queer, singular, strange, uncanny, uncommon, unexpected, unnatural, untypical, unusual, wayward, weird.

antonyms normal, straight.

abnormality *n* aberration, anomaly, atypicalness, bizarreness, deformity, deviation, difference, divergence, dysfunction, eccentricity, exception, flaw, irregularity, monstrosity, oddity, peculiarity, queerness, singularity, strangeness, uncommonness, unexpectedness, unnaturalness, untypicalness, unusualness, weirdness.

antonym normality.

abode *n* domicile, dwelling, dwelling-place, habitat, habitation, home, house, lodging, pad, place, quarters, residence.

abolish *v* abrogate, annihilate, annul, blot out, cancel, destroy, do away with, eliminate, end, eradicate, expunge, exterminate, extinguish, extirpate, get rid of, invalidate, kibosh, nullify, obliterate, overthrow, overturn, put an end to, put the kibosh on, quash, repeal, repudiate, rescind, revoke, sink, stamp out, subvert, suppress, terminate, vitiate, void, wipe out.

antonyms continue, retain.

abolition *n* abolishment, abrogation, annihilation, annulment, cancellation, destruction, dissolution, elimination, end, ending, eradication, expunction, extermination, extinction, extirpation, invalidation, nullification, obliteration, overthrow, overturning, quashing, repeal, repudiation, rescission, revocation, subversion, suppression, termination, vitiation, voiding, withdrawal.

antonyms continuance, retention.

abominable *adj* abhorrent, accursed, appalling, atrocious, base, beastly, contemptible, despicable, detestable, disgusting, execrable, foul, hateful, heinous, hellish, horrible, horrid, loathsome, nauseating, nauseous, nefandous, nefast, obnoxious, odious, repellent, reprehensible, repugnant, repulsive, revolting, terrible, vile, villainous, wretched.

antonyms delightful, desirable.

abominate *v* abhor, condemn, despise, detest, execrate, hate, loathe.

antonyms adore, esteem, love.

abomination *n* abhorrence, anathema, animosity, animus, antipathy, aversion, bête noire, bugbear, curse, detestation, disgrace, disgust, distaste, evil, execration, hate, hatred, horror, hostility, loathing, odium, offence, plague, repugnance, revulsion, torment.

antonyms adoration, delight.

aboriginal *adj* ancient, autochthonic, autochthonous, domestic, earliest, enchorial, endemic, first, indigenous, native, original, primal, primary, primeval, primitive, primordial, pristine.

aborigine *n* aboriginal, autochthon, indigene, native, warragal.

antonyms immigrant, incomer.

abort *v* arrest, call off, check, end, fail, frustrate, halt, miscarry, nullify, stop, terminate, thwart.

antonym continue.

abortion *n* aborticide, disappointment, failure, fiasco, foeticide, freak, frustration, misadventure, misbirth, miscarriage, monster, monstrosity, termination, thwarting.

antonyms continuation, success.

abortive *adj* barren, bootless, failed, failing, fruitless, futile, idle, ineffective, ineffectual, misborn, miscarried, sterile, unavailing, unproductive, unsuccessful, useless, vain.

antonym successful.

abound *v* be plentiful, brim over, crowd, exuberate, flourish, increase, infest, luxuriate, overflow, proliferate, run riot, superabound, swarm, swell, teem, thrive.

antonym be in short supply.

abounding *adj* abundant, bountiful, copious, filled, flourishing, flowing, flush, full, lavish, luxuriant, overflowing, plenteous, plentiful, prodigal, profuse, prolific, rank, replete, rich, superabundant, teeming, unstinting.

antonym lacking.

about *prep* adjacent to, all over, anent, around, as regards, beside, busy with, circa, close to, concerned with, concerning, connected with, encircling, encompassing, engaged on, in respect to, in the matter of, near, nearby, of, on, over, re, referring to, regarding, relating to, relative to, respecting, round, surrounding, through, throughout, touching, with reference to, with regard to, with respect to.

adv active, almost, approaching, approximately, around, astir, close to, from place to place, here and there, hither and thither, in motion, in the region of, more or less, nearing, nearly, present, roughly, stirring, to and fro.

about to all but, intending to, on the point of, on the verge of, preparing to, ready to.

about-turn *n* about-face, apostasy, backtrack, enantiodromia, reversal, right-about (face), turnabout, turn(a)round, uey, U-turn, volte-face.

above *prep* atop, before, beyond, exceeding, higher than, in excess of, on top of, over, prior to, superior to, surpassing, upon.

antonyms below, under.

adv aloft, atop, earlier, heavenwards, in heaven, on high, overhead, supra.

antonym below.

adj above-mentioned, above-stated, aforementioned, aforesaid, earlier, foregoing, preceding, previous, prior.

above suspicion above reproach, blameless, guiltless, honourable, innocent, irreproachable, pure, sinless, unimpeachable, virtuous.

above-board *adj* candid, fair, fair and square, forthright, frank, guileless, honest, honourable, legitimate, on the level, open, overt, reputable, square, straight, straightforward, true, trustworthy, truthful, upright, veracious.

antonyms shady, underhand.

abrade *v* chafe, erase, erode, file, grind, levigate, rub off, scour, scrape, triturate, wear away, wear down, wear off.

abrasion *n* abrading, chafe, chafing, erosion, friction, grating, graze, grinding, levigation, rubbing, scouring, scrape, scraping, scratch, scratching, scuff, scuffing, trituration, wearing away, wearing down.

abrasive *adj* abradant, annoying, attritional, biting, caustic, chafing, erodent, erosive, frictional, galling, grating, hurtful, irritating, nasty, rough, scraping, scratching, scratchy, scuffing, sharp, unpleasant.

antonyms pleasant, smooth.

abreast *adj* acquainted, au courant, au fait, conversant, familiar, in the picture, in touch, informed, knowledgeable, on the ball, up to date.

antonyms out of touch, unaware.

abridge *v* abbreviate, abstract, circumscribe, clip, compress, concentrate, condense, contract, curtail, cut, cut down, decrease, digest, diminish, dock, epitomise, lessen, lop, precis, prune, reduce, shorten, summarise, synopsise, trim, truncate.

antonyms amplify, pad.

abridgement *n* abbreviation, abrege, abstract, compendium, compression, concentration, condensation, conspectus, contraction, curtailment, cutting, decrease, digest, diminishing, diminution, epitome, lessening, limitation, outline, precis, pruning, reduction, restriction, resume, shortening, summary, synopsis, truncation.

antonyms expansion, padding.

abroad *adv* about, at large, away, circulating, current, elsewhere, extensively, far, far and wide, forth, in circulation, in foreign parts, out, out of the country, out-of-doors, outside, overseas, publicly, widely.

abrogate *v* abolish, annul, cancel, countermand, disannul, discontinue, disenact, dissolve, end, invalidate, nullify, override, overrule, quash, recall, repeal, repudiate, rescind, retract, reverse, revoke, scrap, set aside, terminate, void, withdraw.

antonyms establish, institute.

abrogation *n* abolition, annulling, annulment, cancellation, countermanding, defeasance, disannulment, discontinuation, ending, invalidation, nullification, overriding, overruling, quashing, repeal, repudiation, rescission, retraction, reversal, revocation, scrapping, setting aside, termination, voiding, withdrawal.

antonyms continuation, retention.

abrupt *adj* blunt, brief, brisk, broken, brusque, curt, direct, disconnected, discontinuous, discourteous, gruff, hasty, headlong, hurried, impolite, irregular, jerky, precipitate, precipitous, prerupt, quick, rapid, rough, rude, sharp, sheer, short, snappy, steep, sudden, surprising, swift, terse, unannounced, unceremonious, uncivil, uneven, unexpected, unforeseen, ungracious.

antonyms ceremonious, expansive, leisurely.

abscond *v* absquatulate, beat it, bolt, clear out, decamp, disappear, do a bunk, escape, flee, flit, fly, hightail it, levant, make off, quit, run off, scram, skedaddle, skive, take French leave, vamoose.

absconder *n* absentee, bolter, escapee, levanter, quitter, truant.

absence *n* absenteeism, absent-mindedness, abstraction, dearth, default, defect, deficiency, distraction, inattention, lack, need, non-appearance, non-attendance, non-existence, omission, paucity, preoccupation, privation, reverie, scarcity, truancy, unavailability, vacancy, vacuity, want.

antonyms existence, presence.

absent *adj* absent-minded, absorbed, abstracted, away, bemused, blank, day-dreaming, distracted, distrait(e), dreamy, elsewhere, empty, faraway, gone, heedless, inattentive, lacking, missing, musing, non-existent, not present, oblivious, out, preoccupied, truant, unavailable, unaware, unconscious, unheeding, unthinking, vacant, vague, wanting, withdrawn, wool-gathering.

antonyms aware, present.

absent-minded *adj* absent, absorbed, abstracted, bemused, distracted, distrait(e), dreaming, dreamy, engrossed, faraway, forgetful, heedless, impractical, inattentive, musing, oblivious, otherwordly, pensive, preoccupied, scatterbrained, unaware, unconscious, unheeding, unthinking, withdrawn, wool-gathering.

antonyms matter-of-fact, attentive, practical.

absent-mindedness *n* absence, absorption, abstraction, distraction, dreaminess, forgetfulness, heedlessness, inattention, muse, preoccupation, unawareness, vacancy, vagueness.

antonym alertness.

absolute *adj* absolutist, actual, almighty, arbitrary, autarchical, autocratic, autonomous, categorical, certain, complete, conclusive, consummate, decided, decisive, definite, definitive, despotic, dictatorial, downright, entire, exact, exhaustive, final, flawless, free, full, genuine, independent, indubitable, infallible, omnipotent, out-and-out, outright, peremptory, perfect, positive, precise, pure, sheer, sovereign, supreme, sure, terminative, thorough, total, totalitarian, tyrannical, unadulterated, unalloyed, unambiguous, unbounded, unconditional, uncontrolled, undivided, unequivocal, unlimited, unmitigated, unmixed, unqualified, unquestionable, unrestrained, unrestricted, utter.

antonyms conditional, partial.

absolutely *adv* actually, arbitrarily, autocratically, autonomously, bang, categorically, certainly, completely, conclusively, consummately, dead, decidedly, decisively, definitely, despotically, diametrically, dictatorially, entirely, exactly, exhaustively, finally, fully, genuinely, indubitably, infallibly, peremptorily, perfectly, positively, precisely, purely, sovereignly, supremely, surely, thoroughly, totally, truly, tyrannically, unambiguously, unconditionally, unequivocally, unmitigatedly, unquestionably, unrestrainedly, utterly, wholly.

absolution *n* acquittal, acquittance, amnesty, compurgation, deliverance, discharge, dispensation, emancipation, exculpation, exemption, exoneration, forgiveness, forgiving, freeing, indulgence, liberation, mercy, pardon, purgation, redemption, release, remission, shriving, vindication.

antonym condemnation.

absolve *v* acquit, clear, deliver, discharge, emancipate, exculpate, excuse, exempt, exonerate, forgive, free, justify, let off, liberate, loose, pardon, ransom, redeem, release, remit, set free, shrive, vindicate.

antonym charge.

absorb *v* adsorb, apprehend, assimilate, captivate, consume, co-opt, devour, digest, drink in, engage, engross, engulf, enthral(l), enwrap, exhaust, fascinate, fill (up), fix, grip, hold, imbibe, immerse, incorporate, ingest, involve, monopolise, occupy, osmose, preoccupy, receive, retain, rivet, soak up, sorb, submerge, suck up, take in, understand, utilise.

antonyms dissipate, exude.

absorbed *adj* captivated, concentrating, engaged, engrossed, enthralled, fascinated, fixed, gripped, held, immersed, intent, involved, lost, obsessed, occupied, preoccupied, rapt, riveted, wrapped up.

antonyms bored, distracted.

absorbent *adj* absorptive, assimilative, blotting, penetrable, permeable, pervious, porous, receptive, resorbent, retentive, sorbefacient, sorbent, spongy.

antonym impermeable.

absorbing *adj* amusing, arresting, captivating, compulsive, diverting, engrossing, entertaining, enthralling, fascinating, gripping, interesting, intriguing, preoccupying, riveting, spellbinding, unputdownable.

antonyms boring, off-putting.

absorption *n* adsorption, assimilation, attentiveness, captivation, concentration, consumption, digestion, engagement, exhaustion, fascination, holding, imbibition, immersion, incorporation, ingestion, intentness, involvement, occupation, osmosis, preoccupation, raptness, soaking up, sucking up.

abstain *v* avoid, cease, decline, deny, desist, eschew, forbear, forgo, give up, keep from, refrain, refuse, reject, renounce, resist, shun, stop, swear off, withhold.

antonym indulge.

abstemious *adj* abstinent, ascetic, austere, continent, disciplined, frugal, moderate, restrained, self-denying, self-disciplined, sober, sparing, temperate.

antonyms gluttonous, intemperate, luxurious.

abstention *n* abstaining, abstinence, avoidance, continence, desistance, eschewal, forbearance, frugality, nephalism, non-indulgence, refraining, refusal, restraint, self-control, self-denial, self-discipline, self-restraint, sobriety.

abstinence *n* abstemiousness, abstinency, asceticism, avoidance, continence, forbearance, frugality, moderation, nephalism, non-indulgence, refraining, self-denial, self-discipline, self-restraint, soberness, sobriety, teetotalism, temperance.

antonym self-indulgence.

abstinent *adj* abstaining, abstemious, continent, disciplined, forbearing, frugal, moderate, self-controlled, self-denying, self-disciplined, self-restrained, sober, temperate.

antonyms self-indulgent, voluptuous, wanton.

abstract *adj* abstruse, academic, arcane, complex, conceptual, deep, discrete, general, generalised, hypothetical, indefinite, intellectual, metaphysical, non-concrete, occult, philosophical, profound, recondite, separate, subtle, theoretic, theoretical, unpractical, unrealistic.

antonym concrete.

n abbreviation, abridgement, abstractive, compendium, compression, condensation, conspectus, digest, epitome, essence, outline, precis, recapitulation, resume, summary, synopsis.

v abbreviate, abridge, compress, condense, detach, digest, dissociate, epitomise, extract, isolate, outline, precis, purloin, remove, separate, shorten, steal, summarise, withdraw.

antonyms expand, insert.

abstracted *adj* absent, absent-minded, bemused, distrait(e), dreamy, faraway, inattentive, pensive, preoccupied, remote, withdrawn, wool-gathering.

antonyms alert, on the ball.

abstraction *n* absence, absent-mindedness, absorption, bemusedness, concept, conception, dissociation, distraction, dream, dreaminess, formula, generalisation, generality, hypothesis, idea, inattention, notion, pensiveness, preoccupation, remoteness, separation, theorem, theory, thought, withdrawal, wool-gathering.

abstruse *adj* abstract, arcane, complex, cryptic, dark, deep, devious, difficult, enigmatic, esoteric, hermetic, hidden, incomprehensible, mysterious, mystical, obscure, occult, perplexing, profound, puzzling, recondite, subtle, tortuous, unfathomable, unobvious, vague.

antonyms concrete, obvious.

absurd *adj* anomalous, comical, crazy, daft, derisory, fantastic, farcical, foolish, funny, humorous, idiotic, illogical, implausible, incongruous, irrational, laughable, ludicrous, meaningless, nonsensical, paradoxical, preposterous, ridiculous, risible, senseless, silly, stupid, unreasonable, untenable.

antonyms logical, rational, sensible.

absurdity *n* comicality, craziness, daftness, farce, farcicality, farcicalness, fatuity, fatuousness, folly, foolery, foolishness, idiocy, illogicality, illogicalness, incongruity, irrationality, joke, ludicrousness, meaninglessness, nonsense, nonsensicality, preposterousness, ridiculousness, senselessness, silliness, stupidity, unreasonableness.

abundance *n* affluence, ampleness, amplitude, bonanza, bounty, copiousness, exuberance, fortune, fullness, glut, heap, lavishness, luxuriance, luxuriancy, milk and honey, munificence, oodles, opulence, plenitude, plenteousness, plenty, pleroma, plethora, prodigality, profusion, riches, richness, routh, uberty, wealth.

antonyms dearth, scarcity.

abundant *adj* ample, bounteous, bountiful, copious, exuberant, filled, full, generous, in plenty, lavish, luxuriant, overflowing, plenteous, plentiful, prodigal, profuse, rank, rich, superabundant, teeming, uberous, unstinted, well-provided, well-supplied.

antonyms scarce, sparse.

abuse *v* batter, calumniate, castigate, curse, damage, deceive, defame, denigrate, disparage, exploit, harm, hurt, ill-treat, impose on, injure, insult, inveigh against, libel, malign, maltreat, manhandle, mar, misapply, miscall, misemploy, misuse, molest, objurgate, oppress, oppugn, revile, scold, slander, slate, smear, spoil, swear at, take advantage of, traduce, upbraid, vilify, violate, vituperate, wrong.

antonyms cherish, compliment, praise.

n affront, blame, calumniation, calumny, castigation, censure, contumely, curses, cursing, damage, defamation, denigration, derision, diatribe, disparagement, execration, exploitation, flyting, harm, hurt, ill-treatment, imposition, injury, insults, invective, libel, malediction, maltreatment, manhandling, misapplication, misconduct, misdeed, misuse, obloquy, offence, oppression, opprobrium, reproach, revilement, scolding, sin, slander, spoiling, swearing, tirade, traducement, upbraiding, vilification, violation, vitriol, vituperation, wrong, wrong-doing.

antonyms attention, care.

abusive *adj* brutal, calumniating, calumnious, castigating, censorious, contumelious, cruel, defamatory, denigrating, derisive, derogatory, destructive, disparaging, harmful, hurtful, injurious, insulting, invective, libellous, maligning, objurgatory, offensive, opprobrious, pejorative, reproachful, reviling, rough, rude, scathing, scolding, slanderous, traducing, upbraiding, vilifying, vituperative.

antonym complimentary.

abut *v* adjoin, border, conjoin, connect, impinge, join, meet, touch, verge.

abysmal *adj* abyssal, bottomless, boundless, complete, deep, endless, extreme, immeasurable, incalculable, infinite, profound, thorough, unending, unfathomable, vast, yawning.

abyss *n* abysm, Avernus, barathrum, canyon, chasm, crater, crevasse, depth, fissure, gorge, gulf, pit, profound, swallow, void.

academic *adj* abstract, bookish, collegiate, conjectural, donnish, educational, erudite, highbrow, hypothetical, impractical, instructional, learned, lettered, literary, notional, pedagogical, scholarly, scholastic, speculative, studious, theoretical, well-read.

n academe, academician, don, fellow, lecturer, man of letters, master, pedant, professor, pundit, savant, scholar, scholastic, schoolman, student, tutor.

accede *v* accept, acquiesce, admit, agree, assent, assume, attain, capitulate, comply, concede, concur, consent, defer, endorse, grant, inherit, submit, succeed (to), yield.

antonyms demur, object.

accelerate *v* advance, antedate, dispatch, expedite, facilitate, festinate, forward, further, hasten, hurry, pick up speed, precipitate, promote, quicken, speed, speed up, spur, step on the gas, step on the juice, step up, stimulate.

antonyms delay, slow down.

accent *n* accentuation, arsis, articulation, beat, cadence, emphasis, enunciation, force, ictus, inflection, intensity, intonation, modulation, pitch, pronunciation, pulsation, pulse, rhythm, stress, thesis, timbre, tonality, tone.

v accentuate, emphasise, stress, underline, underscore.

accentuate *v* accent, deepen, emphasise, highlight, intensify, italicise, spotlight, strengthen, stress, underline, underscore.

antonyms play down, weaken.

accept *v* abide by, accede, acknowledge, acquiesce, acquire, admit, adopt, affirm, agree to, approve, assume, avow, bear, believe, bow to, brook, concur with, consent to, co-operate with, defer to, gain, get, have, jump at, obtain, put up with, receive, recognise, secure, stand, stomach, submit to, suffer, swallow, take, take on, tolerate, undertake, wear, yield to.

antonyms demur, reject.

acceptable *adj* adequate, admissible, agreeable, all right, conventional, correct, delightful, desirable, done, grateful, gratifying, moderate, passable, pleasant, pleasing, satisfactory, standard, suitable, tolerable, U, unexceptionable, unobjectionable, welcome.

antonyms unsatisfactory, unwelcome.

acceptance *n* accedence, accepting, accession, acknowledgement, acquiescence, acquiring, admission, adoption, affirmation, agreement, approbation, approval, assent, belief, compliance, concession, concurrence, consent, credence, gaining, getting, having, obtaining, OK, permission, ratification, receipt, recognition, seal of approval, securing, stamp of approval, taking, tolerance, toleration, undertaking.

antonyms dissent, refusal.

accepted *adj* acceptable, acknowledged, admitted, agreed, agreed upon, approved, authorised, common, confirmed, consuetudinary, conventional, correct, customary, established, normal, ratified, received, recognised, regular, sanctioned, standard, time-honoured, traditional, universal, unwritten, usual.

antonym unorthodox.

access *n* adit, admission, admittance, approach, avenue, course, door, entering, entrance, entree, entry, gateway, increase, ingress, key, onset, passage, passageway, path, road, upsurge, upsurgence.

antonyms egress, outlet.

accessible *adj* achievable, affable, approachable, at hand, attainable, available, come-at-able, conversable, cordial, exposed, friendly, get-at-able, handy, informal, liable, near, nearby, obtainable, on hand, open, possible, procurable, reachable, ready, sociable, subject, susceptible, user-friendly, vulnerable, wide-open.

antonym inaccessible.

accession *n* accedence, acceptance, acquiescence, acquisition, addition, agreement, assumption, attaining, attainment, augmentation, concurrence, consent, enlargement, entering upon, extension, increase, installation, purchase, submission, succession, taking over, yielding.

accessory *n* abettor, accompaniment, accomplice, addition, adjunct, adjuvant, adornment, aid, appendage, assistant, associate, attachment, colleague, component, confederate, conniver, convenience, decoration, embellishment, extension, extra, frill, help, helper, particeps criminis, partner, supplement, trim, trimming.

adj abetting, additional, adjuvant, adventitious, aiding, ancillary, assisting, auxiliary, contributory, extra, incidental, secondary, subordinate, subsidiary, supplemental, supplementary.

accident *n* blow, calamity, casualty, chance, collision, contingency, contretemps, crash, disaster, fate, fluke, fortuity, fortune, happenstance, hazard, luck, misadventure, miscarriage, mischance, misfortune, mishap, pile-up, prang, serendipity, shunt.

accidental *adj* adventitious, adventive, casual, chance, contingent, fluky, fortuitous, haphazard, inadvertent, incidental, random, serendipitous, unanticipated, uncalculated, uncertain, unexpected, unforeseen, unintended, unintentional, unlooked-for, unplanned, unpremeditated, unwitting.

antonyms intentional, premeditated.

accidentally *adv* adventitiously, bechance, by accident, by chance, by mistake, casually, fortuitously, haphazardly, inadvertently, incidentally, involuntarily, randomly, serendipitously, unconsciously, undesignedly, unexpectedly, unintentionally, unwittingly.

antonym intentionally.

acclaim *v* announce, applaud, approve, celebrate, cheer, clap, commend, crown, declare, eulogise, exalt, extol, fanfare, hail, honour, laud, praise, salute, welcome.

antonym demean.

n acclamation, applause, approbation, approval, celebration, cheering, clapping, commendation, eulogising, eulogy, exaltation, fanfare, honour, laudation, ovation, plaudits, praise, welcome.

antonyms brickbats, criticism, vituperation.

acclamation *n* acclaim, adulation, applause, approbation, bravos, cheer, cheering, cheers, commendation, declaration, eclat, endorsement, enthusiasm, extolment, homage, laudation, ovation, paean, panegyric, plaudit, praise, salutation, shouting, tribute.

antonym disapproval.

acclimatise *v* accommodate, acculturate, accustom, adapt, adjust, attune, conform, familiarise, find one's legs, get used to, habituate, inure, naturalise.

acclivity *n* ascent, gradient, hill, rise, rising ground, slope.

accolade *n* award, honour, kudos, laurels, praise.

accommodate *v* acclimatise, accustom, adapt, adjust, afford, aid, assist, attune, billet, board, cater for, comply, compose, conform, domicile, entertain, fit, furnish, harbour, harmonise, help, house, lodge, modify, oblige, provide, put up, quarter, reconcile, serve, settle, shelter, supply.

accommodating *adj* complaisant, considerate, co-operative, friendly, helpful, hospitable, indulgent, kind, obliging, polite, sympathetic, unselfish, willing.

antonym disobliging.

accommodation[1] *n* adaptation, adjustment, assistance, compliance, composition, compromise, conformity, fitting, harmonisation, harmony, help, modification, reconciliation, settlement.

accommodation[2] *n* bed and breakfast, billet, board, digs, domicile, dwelling, harbouring, house, housing, lodgings, quartering, quarters, residence, shelter, sheltering.

accompaniment *n* accessory, attendance, background, back-up, complement, concomitant, obligato, support, vamp.

accompany *v* attend, belong to, chaperon, co-exist, coincide, complement, conduct, consort, convoy, escort, follow, go with, occur with, squire, supplement, usher.

accompanying *adj* accessory, added, additional, appended, associate, associated, attached, attendant, background, complementary, concomitant, concurrent, connected, fellow, joint, related, subsidiary, supplemental, supplementary.

accomplice *n* abettor, accessory, ally, assistant, associate, coadjutor, collaborator, colleague, confederate, conspirator, helper, helpmate, henchman, mate, particeps criminis, participator, partner, practisant, shill.

accomplish *v* achieve, attain, bring about, bring off, carry out, compass, complete, conclude, consummate, discharge, do, effect, effectuate, engineer, execute, finish, fulfil, manage, obtain, perform, produce, realise.

accomplished *adj* adept, adroit, consummate, cultivated, expert, facile, gifted, masterly, polished, practised, professional, proficient, skilful, skilled, talented.

antonym inexpert.

accomplishment *n* ability, achievement, act, aptitude, art, attainment, capability, carrying out, completion, conclusion, consummation, coup, deed, discharge, doing, effecting, execution, exploit, faculty, feat, finishing, forte, fruition, fulfilment, futurition, gift, management, perfection, performance, production, proficiency, realisation, skill, stroke, talent, triumph.

accord *v* agree, allow, assent, bestow, concede, concur, confer, conform, correspond, endow, fit, give, grant, harmonise, jibe, match, present, render, suit, tally, tender, vouchsafe.

antonym disagree.

n accordance, agreement, assent, concert, concurrence, conformity, congruence, congruity, consort, correspondence, harmony, rapport, symmetry, sympathy, unanimity, unity.

antonym discord.

accordance *n* accord, agreement, assent, concert, concurrence, conformity, congruence, consistency, consonance, correspondence, harmony, rapport, sympathy, unanimity.

accordingly *adv* appropriately, as a result, as requested, consequently, correspondingly, ergo, fitly, hence, in accord with, in accordance, in consequence, properly, so, suitably, therefore, thus.

according to after, after the manner of, agreeably to, commensurate with, consistent with, in accordance with, in compliance with, in conformity with, in keeping with, in line with, in obedience to, in proportion, in relation, in the light of, in the manner of, obedient to.

accost *v* address, approach, button-hole, confront, detain, greet, hail, halt, importune, salute, solicit, stop, waylay.

account[1] *n* advantage, basis, battels, benefit, cause, cnronicle, communique, concern, consequence, consideration, description, detail, distinction, esteem, estimation, explanation, ground, grounds, history, honour, import, importance, interest, memoir, merit, motive, narration, narrative, note, performance, portrayal, presentation, profit, rank, reason, recital, record, regard, relation, report, reputation, repute, sake, score, significance, sketch, standing, statement, story, tale, use, value, version, worth, write-up.

v adjudge, appraise, assess, believe, consider, count, deem, esteem, estimate, explain, gauge, hold, judge, rate, reckon, regard, think, value, weigh.

account for answer for, clarify, clear up, destroy, elucidate, explain, illuminate, incapacitate, justify, kill, put paid to, rationalise, vindicate.

account[2] *n* balance, battels, bill, book, books, charge, check, computation, inventory, invoice, ledger, reckoning, register, score, statement, tab, tally, tick.

accountability *n* amenability, answerability, blamableness, blameworthiness, chargeability, liability, responsibility.

accountable *adj* amenable, answerable, blamable, bound, charged with, liable, obligated, obliged, responsible.

accoutrements *n* adornments, apparel, appurtenances, array, attire, caparison, clothes, clothing, decorations, dress, equipage, equipment, fittings, fixtures, furnishings, garb, gear, habiliments, kit, ornamentation, outfit, paraphernalia, tackle, trappings, traps, trimmings.

accredit *v* appoint, approve, ascribe, assign, attribute, authorise, certificate, certify, commission, credit, depute, empower, enable, endorse, entrust, guarantee, license, okay, qualify, recognise, sanction, vouch for.

accredited *adj* appointed, approved, attested, authorised, certificated, certified, commissioned, deputed, deputised, empowered, endorsed, guaranteed, licensed, official, qualified, recognised, sanctioned, vouched for.

antonym unauthorised.

accretion *n* accession, accrual, accumulation, addition, amplification, augmentation, coherence, cohesion, enlargement, fusion, growth, increase, increment, supplement.

antonyms decrease, deduction.

accrue *v* accumulate, amass, arise, be added, build up, collect, emanate, enlarge, ensue, fall due, flow, follow, gather, grow, increase, issue, proceed, redound, result, spring up.

accumulate *v* accrue, agglomerate, aggregate, amass, assemble, build up, collect, cumulate, gather, grow, hoard, increase, multiply, pile up, stash, stockpile, store.

antonyms diffuse, disseminate.

accumulation *n* accretion, aggregation, assemblage, augmentation, backlog, build-up, collection, conglomeration, gathering, growth, heap, hoard, increase, mass, pile, reserve, stack, stock, stockpile, store.

accuracy *n* accurateness, actuality, authenticity, carefulness, closeness, correctness, exactitude, exactness, faithfulness, faultlessness, fidelity, meticulousness, minuteness, niceness, nicety, precision, rigorousness, scrupulosity, scrupulousness, strictness, truth, truthfulness, veracity, veridicality, verity.

antonym inaccuracy.

accurate *adj* authentic, careful, close, correct, exact, factual, faithful, faultless, just, letter-perfect, mathematical, meticulous, minute, nice, perfect, precise, proper, regular, right, rigorous, scrupulous, sound, spot-on, strict, true, truthful, unerring, veracious, veridical, well-aimed, well-directed, well-judged, word-perfect.

antonyms inaccurate, wrong.

accursed *adj* abominable, anathematised, bedevilled, bewitched, blighted, condemned, cursed, damned, despicable, detestable, doomed, execrable, foredoomed, hateful, hellish, hopeless, horrible, ill-fated, ill-omened, jinxed, luckless, maledict, ruined, star-crossed, undone, unfortunate, unholy, unlucky, wretched.

antonym blessed.

accusation *n* accusal, allegation, arraignment, attribution, charge, citation, complaint, crimination, delation, denunciation, gravamen, impeachment, imputation, incrimination, indictment, plaint, recrimination, threap.

accuse *v* allege, arraign, attaint, attribute, blame, censure, charge, cite, criminate, delate, denounce, impeach, impugn, impute, incriminate, indict, inform against, recriminate, tax.

accustom *v* acclimatise, acculturate, acquaint, adapt, adjust, discipline, exercise, familiarise, habituate, harden, inure, season, train.

accustomed *adj* acclimatised, acquainted, adapted, common, confirmed, consuetudinary, conventional, customary, disciplined, established, everyday, exercised, expected, familiar, familiarised, fixed, general, given to, habitual, habituated, in the habit of, inured, normal, ordinary, prevailing, regular, routine, seasoned, set, traditional, trained, used, usual, wonted.

antonym unaccustomed.

ace *n* adept, champion, dab hand, dabster, expert, genius, maestro, master, nonpareil, star, talent, virtuoso, winner, wizard.

antonyms colt, novice.

adj brilliant, champion, excellent, expert, fine, first-class, great, hell of a, masterly, matchless, nonpareil, outstanding, superb, superlative, tiptop, virtuoso.

acerbic *adj* abrasive, acid, acidulous, acrid, acrimonious, astringent, bitter, brusque, caustic, churlish, corrosive, harsh, incisive, mordant, nasty, rancorous, rude, sarcastic, severe, sharp, sour, stern, tart, trenchant, unfriendly, unkind.

antonym mild.

acerbity *n* acidity, acidulousness, acridity, acridness, acrimoniousness, acrimony, asperity, astringency, bitterness, brusqueness, causticity, churlishness, harshness, mordacity, mordancy, nastiness, rancour, rudeness, severity, sharpness, sourness, sternness, tartness, trenchancy, unfriendliness, unkindness.

antonym mildness.

ache *v* agonise, covet, crave, desire, grieve, hanker, hunger, hurt, itch, long, mourn, need, pain, pine, pound, rack, smart, sorrow, suffer, throb, twinge, yearn.

n anguish, craving, desire, grief, hankering, hunger, hurt, itch, longing, misery, mourning, need, pain, pang, pining, pounding, smart, smarting, soreness, sorrow, suffering, throb, throbbing, yearning.

achieve *v* accomplish, acquire, attain, bring about, carry out, compass, complete, consummate, do, earn, effect, effectuate, execute, finish, fulfil, gain, get, manage, obtain, perform, procure, produce, reach, realise, score, strike, succeed, win.

antonyms fail, miss.

achievement *n* accomplishment, acquirement, act, attainment, completion, deed, effort, execution, exploit, feat, fruition, fulfilment, magnum opus, performance, production, qualification, realisation, stroke, success.

achiever *n* doer, goer, go-getter, performer, succeeder.

acid *adj* acerbic, acidulous, acrid, astringent, biting, bitter, caustic, corrosive, cutting, harsh, hurtful, ill-natured, incisive, mordant, morose, pungent, sharp, sour, stinging, tart, trenchant, vinegarish, vinegary, vitriolic.

acid test experimentum crucis, proof of the pudding.

acidity *n* acerbity, acidulousness, acridity, acridness, asperity, astringency, bitterness, causticity, causticness, corrosiveness, harshness, hurtfulness, incisiveness, mordancy, pungency, sharpness, sourness, tartness, trenchancy, vinegariness, vinegarishness.

acidulous *adj* acerbic, acid, astringent, biting, bitter, caustic, cutting, harsh, incisive, pungent, sharp, sour, tart, vinegarish, vinegary.

antonyms saccharine, sugary, sweet.

acknowledge *v* accede, accept, acquiesce, address, admit, affirm, agnise, allow, answer, attest, avouch, concede, confess, confirm, declare, endorse, grant, greet, hail, notice, own, profess, react to, recognise, reply to, respond to, return, salute, vouch for, witness, yield.

acknowledged *adj* accepted, accredited, admitted, affirmed, answered, approved, attested, avowed, conceded, confessed, declared, endorsed, professed, recognised, returned.

acknowledgement *n* acceptance, accession, acquiescence, addressing, admission, affirmation, allowing, answer, appreciation, confession, credit, declaration, endorsement, gratitude, greeting, hail, hailing, honour, notice, profession, reaction, realisation, recognition, recompense, reply, response, return, salutation, salute, thanks, tribute, yielding.

acme *n* apex, apogee, climax, crest, crown, culmination, height, high point, maximum, optimum, peak, pinnacle, sublimation, sublimity, summit, top, vertex, zenith.

antonym nadir.

acolyte *n* acolyth, adherent, admirer, altar boy, assistant, attendant, follower, helper, lackey, slave.

acoustic *adj* audile, auditory, aural.

acquaint *v* accustom, advise, announce, apprise, brief, disclose, divulge, enlighten, familiarise, inform, notify, reveal, tell.

acquaintance *n* associate, association, awareness, chum, cognisance, colleague, companionship, confrère, consociate, contact, conversance, conversancy, experience, familiarity, fellowship, intimacy, knowledge, relationship, understanding.

acquainted *adj* abreast, conversant, familiar, in the know, informed.

acquiesce *v* accede, accept, agree, allow, approve, assent, comply, concur, conform, consent, defer, give in, submit, yield.

antonyms disagree, object.

acquiescence *n* acceptance, accession, agreement, approval, assent, compliance, concurrence, conformity, consent, deference, giving in, obedience, sanction, submission, yielding.

antonyms disagreement, rebelliousness.

acquiescent *adj* acceding, accepting, agreeable, amenable, approving, assenting, biddable, complaisant, compliant, concurrent, conforming, consenting, docile, obedient, submissive, yielding.

acquire *v* achieve, amass, appropriate, attain, buy, collect, cop, earn, gain, gather, get, net, obtain, pick up, procure, realise, receive, secure, win.

antonyms forfeit, forgo, relinquish.

acquirements *n* accomplishments, achievements, acquisitions, attainments, attributes, culture, erudition, knowledge, learning, mastery, qualifications, skills.

acquisition *n* accession, achievement, acquest, acquirement, appropriation, attainment, buy, gain, gaining, learning, obtainment, possession, prize, procurement, property, purchase, pursuit, securing, take-over.

acquisitive *adj* avaricious, avid, covetous, grabbing, grasping, greedy, insatiable, mercenary, possessive, predatory, rapacious, voracious.

antonym generous.

acquisitiveness *n* avarice, avidity, avidness, covetousness, graspingness, greed, predatoriness, rapaciousness, rapacity, voracity.

acquit *v* absolve, bear, behave, clear, comport, conduct, deliver, discharge, dismiss, exculpate, excuse, exonerate, free, fulfil, liberate, pay, pay off, perform, release, relieve, repay, reprieve, satisfy, settle, vindicate.

antonym convict.

acquittal *n* absolution, clearance, compurgation, deliverance, discharge, dismissal, dispensation, exculpation, excusing, exoneration, freeing, liberation, release, relief, reprieve, vindication.

antonym conviction.

acquittance *n* discharge, dispensation, payment, quittance, release, satisfaction, settlement.

acrid *adj* acerbic, acid, acrimonious, astringent, biting, bitter, burning, caustic, cutting, empyreumatic, harsh, incisive, irritating, malicious, mordant, nasty, pungent, sarcastic, sardonic, sharp, stinging, trenchant, venomous, virulent, vitriolic.

acridity *n* acidity, acrimoniousness, acrimony, astringency, bitterness, causticity, empyreuma, harshness, mordancy, sharpness, trenchancy.

acrimonious *adj* abusive, acerbic, astringent, atrabilious, biting, bitter, caustic, censorious, churlish, crabbed, cutting, ill-tempered, irascible, mordant, peevish, petulant, pungent, rancorous, sarcastic, severe, sharp, spiteful, splenetic, tart, testy, trenchant, virulent, waspish.

antonyms irenic, kindly, peaceable.

acrimony *n* acerbity, asperity, astringency, bitterness, churlishness, gall, harshness, ill-temper, ill-will, irascibility, mordancy, peevishness, petulance, rancour, resentment, sarcasm, spleen, tartness, trenchancy, virulence, waspishness.

acrobat *n* aerialist, balancer, contortionist, equilibrist, funambulist, gymnast, somersaulter, stunt-girl, stuntman, tumbler, voltigeur.

act *n* accomplishment, achievement, action, affectation, attitude, bill, blow, counterfeit, decree, deed, dissimulation, doing, edict, enactment, enterprise, execution, exertion, exploit, fake, feat, feigning, front, gest, gig, law, make-believe, manoeuvre, measure, move, operation, ordinance, performance, pose, posture, pretence, proceeding, resolution, routine, sham, show, sketch, spiel, stance, statute, step, stroke, transaction, turn, undertaking.

v acquit, act out, affect, assume, bear, behave, carry, carry out, characterise, comport, conduct, counterfeit, dissimulate, do, enact, execute, exert, feign, function, go about, imitate, impersonate, make, mime, mimic, move, operate, perform, personate, personify, play, portray, pose, posture, pretend, put on, react, represent, seem, serve, sham, simulate, strike, take effect, undertake, work.

act up carry on, cause trouble, give bother, give trouble, horse around, make waves, malfunction, mess about, misbehave, muck about, play up, rock the boat.

act (up)on affect, alter, carry out, change, comply with, conform to, execute, follow, fulfil, heed, influence, modify, obey, sway, transform, yield to.

acting *adj* interim, pro tem, provisional, reserve, stand-by, stop-gap, substitute, supply, surrogate, temporary.

n affectation, assuming, bluff, characterisation, counterfeiting, dissimulation, dramatics, enacting, feigning, histrionicism, histrionics, histrionism, imitating, imitation, impersonation, imposture, melodrama, performance, performing, play-acting, playing, portrayal, portraying, posing, posturing, pretence, pretending, putting on, seeming, shamming, stagecraft, theatre, theatricals.

action *n* accomplishment, achievement, act, activity, affray, agency, battle, case, cause, clash, combat, conflict, contest, deed, effect, effort, encounter, endeavour, energy, engagement, enterprise, exercise, exertion, exploit, feat, fight, fighting, force, fray, functioning, influence, lawsuit, litigation, liveliness, mechanism, motion, move, movement, operation, performance, power, proceeding, process, prosecution, skirmish, sortie, spirit, stop, stroke, suit, undertaking, vigour, vim, vitality, warfare, work, working, works.

actions *n* address, air, bearing, behaviour, comportment, conduct, demeanour, deportment, manners, mein, port, ways.

activate *v* actuate, animate, arouse, bestir, energise, excite, fire, galvanise, impel, initiate, mobilise, motivate, move, prompt, propel, rouse, set in motion, set off, start, stimulate, stir, switch on, trigger.

antonyms arrest, deactivate, stop.

active *adj* acting, activist, aggressive, agile, alert, ambitious, animated, assertive, assiduous, astir, bustling, busy, committed, deedy, devoted, diligent, doing, effectual, energetic, engaged, enterprising, enthusiastic, forceful, forward, full, functioning, hard-working, in force, in operation, industrious, involved, light-footed, live, lively, militant, moving, nimble, occupied, on the go, on the move, operate, quick, running, sedulous, spirited, sprightly, spry, stirabout, stirring, strenuous, through-going, vibrant, vigorous, vital, vivacious, working, zealous.

antonyms dormant, inactive, inert, passive.

activity *n* act, action, activeness, animation, avocation, bustle, commotion, deed, endeavour, enterprise, exercise, exertion, hobby, hurly-burly, hustle, industry, interest, job, kerfuffle, labour, life, liveliness, motion, movement, occupation, pastime, project, pursuit, scheme, stir, task, undertaking, venture, work.

actor *n* actress, agent, artist, comedian, doer, executor, factor, functionary, guiser, ham, hamfatter, histrio, histrion, impersonator, masquerader, mime, mummer, operative, operator, participant, participator, performer, perpetrator, personator, play-actor, player, practitioner, Roscius, Thespian, tragedian, trouper, worker.

actual *adj* absolute, authentic, bona fide, categorical, certain, concrete, confirmed, corporeal, current, de facto, definite, existent, extant, factual, genuine, indisputable, indubitable, legitimate, live, living, material, physical, positive, present, present-day, prevailing, real, realistic, substantial, tangible, thingy, true, truthful, unquestionable, verified, veritable.

antonyms apparent, imaginary, theoretical.

actuality *n* corporeality, fact, factuality, historicity, materiality, reality, realness, substance, substantiality, truth, verity.

actually *adv* absolutely, as a matter of fact, de facto, essentially, in fact, in reality, in truth, indeed, literally, really, truly, verily, veritably.

actuate *v* activate, animate, arouse, cause, circulate, dispose, drive, excite, impel, incite, induce, influence, inspire, instigate, lead, mobilise, motivate, move, prod, prompt, propel, quicken, rouse, spur, stimulate, stir, urge.

acumen *n* acuteness, astuteness, cleverness, discernment, discrimination, gumption, ingenuity, insight, intelligence, intuition, judgement, judiciousness, keenness, penetration, perception, perceptiveness, percipience, perspicacity, perspicuity, quickness, sagacity, sapience, sharpness, shrewdness, smartness, wisdom, wit.

antonym obtuseness.

acute[1] *adj* astute, canny, clever, critical, crucial, cutting, dangerous, decisive, discerning, discriminating, distressing, essential, excruciating, exquisite, extreme, fierce, grave, important, incisive, ingenious, insightful, intense, intuitive, judicious, keen, lancinating, observant, overpowering, overwhelming, penetrating, perceptive, percipient, perspicacious, piercing, poignant, pointed, powerful, racking, sagacious, sapient, sensitive, serious, severe, sharp, shooting, shrewd, shrill, smart, stabbing, subtle, sudden, urgent, violent, vital.

antonyms chronic, mild, obtuse.

acute[2] *adj* acicular, apiculate, cuspate, cuspidate, needle-shaped, peaked, pointed, sharp, sharpened.

antonym obtuse.

acuteness *n* acuity, astuteness, canniness, cleverness, criticality, danger, dangerousness, discernment, discrimination, fierceness, gravity, importance, ingenuity, insight, intensity, intuition, intuitiveness, keenness, perception, perceptiveness, percipience, perspicacity, poignancy, powerfulness, sagacity, sapience, sensitivity, seriousness, severity, sharpness, shrewdness, shrillness, smartness, subtlety, suddenness, urgency, violence, wit.

adage *n* aphorism, apophthegm, axiom, byword, dictum, gnome, maxim, motto, paroemia, precept, proverb, saw, saying, sentence.

adamant *adj* adamantine, determined, firm, fixed, flinty, hard, immovable, impenetrable, indestructible, inexorable, inflexible, infrangible, insistent, intransigent, obdurate, resolute, rigid, rock-like, rocky, set, steely, stiff, stony, stubborn, tough, unbending, unbreakable, uncompromising, unrelenting, unshakable, unyielding.

antonyms flexible, pliant, yielding.

adapt *v* acclimatise, accommodate, adjust, alter, apply, attemper, change, comply, conform, contemper, convert, customise, familiarise, fashion, fit, habituate, harmonise, match, metamorphose, modify, prepare, proportion, qualify, refashion, remodel, shape, suit, tailor.

adaptable *adj* adjustable, alterable, amenable, changeable, compliant, conformable, convertible, easy-going, flexible, malleable, modifiable, plastic, pliant, resilient, tractable, variable, versatile.

antonyms inflexible, refractory.

adaptation *n* acclimatisation, accommodation, accustomedness, adaption, adjustment, alteration, change, conversion, familiarisation, habituation, modification, naturalisation, refashioning, refitting, remodelling, reshaping, reworking, shift, transformation, variation, version.

add *v* adjoin, affix, amplify, annex, append, attach, augment, combine, compute, count, include, join, reckon, subjoin, sum up, superimpose, supplement, tack on, tot up, total.

antonym subtract.

add up add, amount, be consistent, be plausible, be reasonable, come to, compute, count, count up, hang together, hold water, imply, indicate, make sense, mean, reckon, reveal, ring true, signify, stand to reason, sum up, tally, tot up, total.

added *adj* additional, adjective, adjunct, extra, fresh, further, increased, new, supplementary.

addendum *n* addition, adjunct, affix, allonge, appendage, appendix, attachment, augmentation, codicil, endorsement, epilogue, extension, extra, postscript, supplement.

addict *n* acid-head, adherent, buff, devotee, dope-fiend, enthusiast, fan, fiend, follower, freak, head, hop-head, junkie, mainliner, nut, pillhead, pillpopper, pot-head, tripper, user.

addicted *adj* absorbed, accustomed, dedicated, dependent, devoted, disposed, enslaved, fond, habituated, hooked, inclined, obsessed, prone, spaced out.

addiction *n* a monkey on one's back, craving, dependence, enslavement, habit, monkey, obsession.

addition *n* accession, accessory, accretion, addend, addendum, adding, additament, additive, adjoining, adjunct, adjunction, affix, affixing, amplification, annexation, annexure, appendage, appendix, appurtenance, attachment, augmentation, computation, counting, enlargement, extension, extra, gain, inclusion, increase, increasing, increment, inpouring, reckoning, summation, summing-up, supplement, totalling, totting-up.

additional *adj* added, additive, adscititious, adventitious, adventive, affixed, appended, excrescent, extra, fresh, further, increased, more, new, other, spare, supplementary.

addled *adj* bad, bamboozled, befuddled, bewildered, confused, flustered, foolish, gone bad, mixed-up, muddled, off, perplexed, putrid, rancid, rotten, silly, turned, unbalanced.

antonyms clear, fresh.

address[1] *n* abode, department, direction, domicile, dwelling, home, house, inscription, location, lodging, place, residence, situation, superscription, whereabouts.

address[2] *n* adroitness, air, allocution, application, art, bearing, declamation, deftness, dexterity, discourse, discretion, dispatch, disquisition, dissertation, expedition, expertise, expertness, facility, harangue, ingenuity, lecture, manner, oration, sermon, skilfulness, skill, speech, tact, talk.

v accost, address (oneself) to, apostrophise, apply (oneself) to, approach, attend to, bespeak, button-hole, concentrate on, devote (oneself) to, discourse, engage in, focus on, greet, hail, harangue, invoke, lecture, orate, salute, sermonise, speak, speak to, take care of, talk, talk to, turn to, undertake.

addresses *n* advances, approaches, attentions, courting, courtship, lovemaking, proposals, wooing.

adept *adj* able, accomplished, ace, adroit, deft, dexterous, experienced, expert, masterful, masterly, nimble, polished, practised, proficient, skilful, skilled, versed.

antonyms bungling, incompetent, inept.

n ace, dab hand, dabster, deacon, don, expert, genius, maestro, mahatma, master, old hand, pastmaster, wizard.

antonyms bungler, incompetent.

adequacy *n* adequateness, capability, commensurateness, competence, competency, efficacy, fairness, fitness, passability, requisiteness, satisfactoriness, serviceability, sufficiency, suitability, tolerability.

antonyms inadequacy, insufficiency.

adequate *adj* able, acceptable, capable, commensurate, competent, condign, efficacious, enough, fair, fit, passable, presentable, requisite, respectable, satisfactory, serviceable, sufficient, suitable, tolerable.

antonyms inadequate, insufficient.

adhere *v* abide by, accrete, agree, attach, cement, cleave, cleave to, cling, coalesce, cohere, combine, comply with, fasten, fix, follow, fulfil, glue, heed, hold, hold fast, join, keep, link, maintain, mind, obey, observe, paste, respect, stand by, stick, stick fast, support, unite.

adherent *n* admirer, advocate, aficionado, devotee, disciple, enthusiast, fan, follower, freak, hanger-on, henchman, nut, partisan, satellite, sectary, supporter, upholder, votary.

adhering *adj* adherent, clinging, coalescent, cohering, cohesive, holding, osculant, tenacious.

adhesion *n* adherence, adhesiveness, allegiance, attachment, bond, coherence, cohesion, constancy, devotion, faithfulness, fidelity, fulfilment, grip, heed, holding fast, loyalty, obedience, observation, respect, sticking, support, union.

adhesive *adj* adherent, adhering, attaching, clinging, cohesive, emplastic, gluey, glutinous, gummy, holding, mucilaginous, sticking, sticky, tacky, tenacious.

n cement, glue, gum, mountant, mucilage, paste, tape.

adieu *n* bon voyage, cheerio, conge, departure, farewell, goodbye, leave-taking, parting, valediction, valedictory.

adjacent *adj* abutting, adjoining, alongside, beside, bordering, close, conterminant, conterminate, conterminous, contiguous, juxtaposed, near, neighbouring, next, proximate, touching, vicinal.

adjoin *v* abut, add, affix, annex, append, approximate, attach, border, combine, communicate with, connect, couple, impinge, interconnect, join, juxtapose, link, meet, neighbour, touch, unite, verge.

adjoining *adj* abutting, adjacent, bordering, connecting, contiguous, impinging, interconnecting, joined, juxtaposed, near, neighbouring, next, next door, proximate, touching, verging, vicinal.

adjourn *v* continue, defer, delay, discontinue, interrupt, postpone, prorogue, put off, recess, stay, suspend.

antonym convene.

adjournment *n* break, deferment, deferral, delay, discontinuation, dissolution, interruption, pause, postponement, prorogation, putting off, recess, stay, suspension.

adjudicate *v* adjudge, arbitrate, decide, determine, judge, pronounce, ref, referee, settle, umpire.

adjudication *n* adjudgement, arbitration, conclusion, decision, determination, finding, judgement, pronouncement, reffing, ruling, settlement, verdict.

adjunct *n* accessory, addendum, addition, appanage, appendage, appendix, appurtenance, auxiliary, complement, extension, supplement.

adjure *v* appeal to, beg, beseech, charge, command, conjure, direct, enjoin, entreat, implore, importune, invoke, order, plead with, pray, request, supplicate.

adjust *v* acclimatise, accommodate, accustom, adapt, alter, arrange, balance, change, coapt, compose, concert, conform, convert, dispose, fine-tune, fit, fix, harmonise, jiggle, measure, modify, order, proportion, reconcile, rectify, redress, refashion, regulate, remodel, reshape, set, settle, shape, square, suit, temper, tune.

antonyms derange, disarrange, upset.

adjustable *adj* adaptable, alterable, flexible, malleable, modifiable, mouldable, movable, tractable.

antonyms fixed, inflexible.

adjustment *n* acclimatisation, accommodation, adaptation, alteration, arrangement, arranging, conforming, conversion, fitting, fixing, harmonisation, modification, naturalisation, ordering, orientation, reconciliation, rectification, redress, refashioning, regulation, remodelling, setting, settlement, settling in, shaping, tuning.

ad-lib *v* extemporise, improvise, invent, make up.

adj extemporaneous, extempore, extemporised, impromptu, improvised, made up, off-the-cuff, spontaneous, unpremeditated, unprepared, unrehearsed.

antonym prepared.

adv extemporaneously, extempore, impromptu, impulsively, off the cuff, off the top of one's head, spontaneously.

administer *v* adhibit, apply, assign, conduct, contribute, control, direct, disburse, dispense, dispose, distribute, dole out, execute, give, govern, head, impose, lead, manage, measure out, mete out, officiate, organise, oversee, perform, preside over, provide, regulate, rule, run, superintend, supervise, supply.

administration *n* adhibition, administering, application, conduct, control, direction, directorship, disbursement, dispensation, disposal, distribution, execution, executive, governing, governing body, government, leadership, management, ministry, organisation, overseeing, performance, provision, regime, regulation, rule, ruling, running, settlement, superintendence, supervision, supply, term of office.

administrative *adj* authoritative, directorial, executive, governmental, gubernatorial, legislative, management, managerial, organisational, regulatory, supervisory.

administrator *n* boss, controller, curator, custodian, director, factor, governor, guardian, leader, manager, organiser, overseer, ruler, superintendent, supervisor, trustee.

admirable *adj* choice, commendable, creditable, deserving, estimable, excellent, exquisite, fine, laudable, meritorious, praiseworthy, rare, respected, superior, valuable, wonderful, worthy.

antonym despicable.

admiration *n* adoration, affection, amazement, appreciation, approbation, approval, astonishment, awe, delight, esteem, fureur, idolism, pleasure, praise, regard, respect, reverence, surprise, veneration, wonder, wonderment, worship.

antonym contempt.

admire *v* adore, applaud, appreciate, approve, esteem, iconise, idolise, laud, praise, prize, respect, revere, value, venerate, worship.

antonym despise.

admirer *n* adherent, aficionado, beau, boyfriend, devotee, disciple, enthusiast, fan, follower, gallant, idolator, idoliser, lover, partisan, suitor, supporter, sweetheart, votary, wooer, worshipper.

antonyms critic, opponent.

admissible *adj* acceptable, allowable, allowed, equitable, justifiable, lawful, legitimate, licit, passable, permissible, permitted, tolerable, tolerated.

antonyms illegitimate, inadmissible.

admission *n* acceptance, access, acknowledgement, adhibition, admittance, admitting, affirmation, allowance, avowal, concession, confession, declaration, disclosure, divulgence, entrance, entree, entry, expose, granting, inclusion, ingress, initiation, introduction, owning, profession, revelation.

antonyms denial, exclusion.

admit *v* accept, acknowledge, adhibit, affirm, agree, allow, allow to enter, avow, concede, confess, declare, disclose, divulge, give access, grant, initiate, introduce, intromit, let, let in, permit, profess, receive, recognise, reveal, take in.

antonyms exclude, gainsay.

admittance *n* acceptance, access, admitting, allowing, entrance, entree, entry, ingress, letting in, passage, reception.

admixture *n* addition, amalgamation, blend, combination, commixture, fusion, intermixture, mingling, tincture, trace.

admonish *v* advise, berate, caution, censure, check, chide, counsel, enjoin, exhort, forewarn, rebuke, reprehend, reprimand, reproach, reprove, scold, upbraid, warn.

admonition *n* advice, berating, caution, censure, counsel, pi-jaw, rebuke, reprehension, reprimand, reproach, reproof, scolding, warning.

admonitory *adj* admonishing, advisory, cautionary, censorious, rebuking, reprimanding, reproachful, reproving, scolding, warning.

ado *n* agitation, bother, business, bustle, ceremony, commotion, confusion, delay, disturbance, excitement, ferment, flurry, fuss, hassle, hurly-burly, kerfuffle, labour, pother, romage, stir, to-do, trouble, tumult, turmoil.

antonyms calm, tranquillity.

adolescence *n* boyhood, boyishness, childishness, development, girlhood, girlishness, immaturity, juvenescence, juvenility, minority, puberty, puerility, teens, transition, youth, youthfulness.

antonym senescence.

adolescent *adj* boyish, girlish, growing, immature, juvenescent, juvenile, maturing, puerile, teenage, young, youthful.

n bobbysoxer, Halbstarker, halfling, juvenile, minor, teenager, youngster, youth.

Adonis *n* charmer, dish, Ganymede, god, golden boy, good-looker, he-man, idol, knockout, matinee idol.

adopt *v* accept, affect, appropriate, approve, assume, back, choose, embrace, endorse, espouse, follow, foster, maintain, ratify, sanction, select, support, take in, take on, take up.

antonyms disown, repudiate.

adoption *n* acceptance, affectation, approbation, appropriation, approval, assumption, cherishment, choice, embracement, embracing, endorsement, espousal, following, fosterage, fostering, maintenance, ratification, sanction, select, selection, support.

adorable *adj* appealing, attractive, bewitching, captivating, charming, darling, dear, delightful, enchanting, fetching, lovable, pleasing, precious, winning, winsome.

antonym hateful.

adoration *n* admiration, esteem, estimation, exaltation, glorification, honour, idolatry, idolisation, love, magnification, reverence, veneration, worship.

antonyms abhorrence, detestation.

adore *v* admire, cherish, dote on, esteem, exalt, glorify, honour, idolatrise, idolise, love, magnify, revere, reverence, venerate, worship.

antonyms abhor, hate.

adorn *v* adonise, apparel, array, beautify, bedeck, bedight, bedizen, begem, bejewel, bestick, crown, deck, decorate, dight, doll up, embellish, emblazon, enhance, enrich, furbish, garnish, gild, grace, impearl, miniate, ornament, tart up, trick out, trim.

adornment *n* accessory, beautification, bedizenment, decorating, decoration, embellishment, falbala, fallal, fallalery, fandangle, figgery, flounce, frill, frippery, furbelow, garnish, garnishry, garniture, gilding, ornament, ornamentation, ornateness, trappings, trimming.

adrift *adj* aimless, amiss, anchorless, astray, at sea, directionless, goalless, insecure, off course, purposeless, rootless, rudderless, unsettled, wrong.

antonyms anchored, stable.

adroit *adj* able, adept, apt, artful, clever, cunning, deft, dexterous, expert, habile, ingenious, masterful, neat, nimble, proficient, quick, resourceful, skilful, skilled, slick.

antonyms clumsy, inept, maladroit.

adroitness *n* ability, ableness, address, adeptness, aptness, artfulness, cleverness, cunning, deftness, dexterity, expertise, facility, finesse, ingeniousness, ingenuity, legerdemain, masterfulness, mastery, neatness, nimbleness, proficiency, quickness, resourcefulness, skilfulness, skill.

antonyms clumsiness, ineptitude.

adulation *n* blandishment, bootlicking, fawning, flattery, idolatory, idolisation, personality cult, sycophancy, worship.

antonym abuse.

adulatory *adj* blandishing, bootlicking, fawning, flattering, fulsome, grovelling, idolatrous, obsequious, praising, servile, slavish, sycophantic, unctuous, worshipping.

antonym unflattering.

adult *adj* developed, full-grown, fully grown, grown-up, mature, of age, ripe, ripened.

antonym immature.

adulterate *v* attenuate, bastardise, contaminate, corrupt, dash, debase, defile, depreciate, deteriorate, devalue, dilute, doctor, infect, load, pollute, taint, thin, vitiate, water down, weaken.

antonym refine.

adumbrate *v* augur, bedim, chart, conceal, darken, delineate, draft, eclipse, forecast, foreshadow, foretell, hint at, indicate, obfuscate, obscure, outline, overshadow, portend, predict, prefigure, presage, prognosticate, prophesy, silhouette, sketch, suggest, trace, veil.

advance *v* accelerate, adduce, allege, ameliorate, assist, benefit, bring forward, cite, elevate, expedite, facilitate, foster, furnish, further, go ahead, go forward, grow, hasten, improve, increase, lend, move on, multiply, offer, pay beforehand, present, press on, proceed, proffer, profit, progress, promote, prosper, provide, raise, send forward, speed, submit, suggest, supply, thrive, upgrade.

antonyms impede, retard, retreat.

n advancement, amelioration, betterment, breakthrough, credit, deposit, development, down payment, furtherance, gain, growth, headway, improvement, increase, loan, preferment, prepayment, profit, progress, promotion, retainer, rise, step.

antonym recession.

adj beforehand, early, foremost, forward, in front, leading, preliminary, prior.

advanced *adj* ahead, avant-garde, extreme, foremost, forward, forward-looking, higher, imaginative, late, leading, original, precocious, progressive.

antonyms backward, retarded.

advancement *n* advance, amelioration, betterment, development, forward movement, gain, growth, headway, improvement, maturation, onward movement, preferment, progress, promotion, rise.

antonyms demotion, retardation.

advances *n* addresses, approach, approaches, attentions, moves, overtures, proposals, proposition.

advantage *n* account, aid, ascendancy, asset, assistances, avail, benefit, blessing, boon, boot, convenience, dominance, edge, expediency, fruit, gain, good, help, hold, interest, lead, leverage, precedence, pre-eminence, profit, purchase, service, start, superiority, sway, upper hand, use, usefulness, utility, welfare.

antonyms disadvantage, hindrance.

advantageous *adj* beneficial, convenient, favourable, furthersome, gainful, helpful, opportune, profitable, propitious, remunerative, rewarding, superior, useful, valuable, worthwhile.

antonym disadvantageous.

advent *n* accession, appearance, approach, arrival, coming, dawn, entrance, inception, introduction, occurrence, onset, visitation.

adventitious *adj* accidental, casual, chance, contingent, extraneous, extrinsic, foreign, fortuitous, incidental, non-essential, serendipitous, supervenient, unexpected.

antonyms inherent, intrinsic.

adventure *n* chance, contingency, enterprise, experience, exploit, gest, hazard, incident, occurrence, risk, speculation, undertaking, venture.

adventurer *n* cowboy, daredevil, derring-doer, filibuster, fortune-hunter, freebooter, freelancer, gambler, hero, heroine, knight-errant, madcap, mercenary, opportunist, rogue, soldier of fortune, speculator, swashbuckler, traveller, venturer, voyager, wanderer.

adventuress *n* bloodsucker, gold-digger, harpy, man-eater, seductress, siren, temptress, vamp.

adventurous *adj* adventuresome, audacious, bold, dangerous, daredevil, daring, dauntless, doughty, enterprising, foolhardy, game, hazardous, headstrong, impetuous, intrepid, perilous, plucky, rash, reckless, risky, spunky, swashbuckling, temerarious, venturesome.

antonyms cautious, chary, prudent.

adversary *n* antagonist, assailant, attacker, competitor, contestant, enemy, foe, foeman, opponent, opposer, rival.

antonyms ally, supporter.

adverse *adj* antagonistic, conflicting, contrary, counter, counter-productive, detrimental, disadvantageous, hostile, hurtful, inauspicious, inexpedient, inimical, injurious, inopportune, negative, noxious, opposing, opposite, reluctant, repugnant, uncongenial, unfavourable, unfortunate, unfriendly, unlucky, unpropitious, untoward, unwilling.

antonyms advantageous, propitious.

adversity *n* affliction, ambs-ace, bad luck, calamity, catastrophe, contretemps, disaster, distress, hard times, hardship, ill-fortune, ill-luck, mischance, misery, misfortune, mishap, reverse, sorrow, suffering, trial, tribulation, trouble, woe, wretchedness.

antonym prosperity.

advertise *v* advise, announce, apprise, blazon, broadcast, bruit, declare, display, flaunt, herald, inform, make known, notify, plug, praise, proclaim, promote, promulgate, publicise, publish, puff, push, tout, trumpet.

advertisement *n* ad, advert, announcement, bill, blurb, circular, commercial, display, handbill, handout, hype, leaflet, notice, placard, plug, poster, promotion, propaganda, propagation, publicity, puff, puffery, trumpet-blowing.

advice *n* admonition, caution, communication, conseil, counsel, direction, do's and don'ts, guidance, help, information, injunction, instruction, intelligence, memorandum, notice, notification, opinion, recommendation, rede, suggestion, view, warning, wisdom, word.

advisable *adj* advantageous, appropriate, apt, beneficial, correct, desirable, expedient, fit, fitting, judicious, meet, politic, profitable, proper, prudent, recommended, seemly, sensible, sound, suggested, suitable, wise.

antonyms inadvisable, injudicious.

advise *v* acquaint, apprise, bethink, caution, commend, counsel, enjoin, forewarn, guide, inform, instruct, make known, notify, recommend, report, suggest, teach, tell, tutor, urge, warn.

adviser *n* admonitor, aide, authority, coach, confidant, consultant, counsel, counsellor, eminence grise, guide, helper, instructor, lawyer, mentor, monitor, preceptor, righthand man, solicitor, teacher, therapist, tutor.

advisory *adj* advising, consultative, consultatory, consulting, counselling, helping, hortatory, recommending.

advocacy *n* adoption, advancement, backing, campaigning, championing, championship, defence, encouragement, espousal, justification, patronage, pleading, promotion, promulgation, propagation, proposal, recommendation, spokesmanship, support, upholding, urging.

advocate *v* adopt, advise, argue for, campaign for, champion, countenance, defend, encourage, endorse, espouse, favour, justify, patronise, plead for, press for, promote, propose, recommend, subscribe to, support, uphold, urge.

antonyms deprecate, disparage, impugn.

n apologist, apostle, attorney, backer, barrister, campaigner, champion, counsel, counsellor, defender, interceder, intercessor, lawyer, mediator, paraclete, patron, pleader, promoter, proponent, proposer, solicitor, speaker, spokesman, supporter, upholder, vindicator.

antonyms critic, opponent.

aegis *n* advocacy, auspices, backing, championship, favour, guardianship, patronage, protection, shelter, sponsorship, support, wing.

aerial *adj* aeolian, aery, atmospheric, elevated, ethereal, incorporeal, insubstantial, lofty, unreal.

affability *n* accessibility, amiability, amicability, approachability, benevolence, benignity, civility, congeniality, conversableness, cordiality, courtesy, easiness, friendliness, geniality, good humour, good nature, graciousness, kindliness, mildness, obligingness, openness, pleasantness, sociability, suavity, urbanity, warmth.

antonyms coolness, reserve, reticence.

affable *adj* agreeable, amiable, amicable, approachable, benevolent, benign, civil, congenial, cordial, courteous, expansive, free, friendly, genial, good-humoured, good-natured, gracious, kindly, mild, obliging, open, pleasant, sociable, suave, urbane, warm.

antonyms cool, reserved, reticent, unfriendly.

affair *n* activity, adventure, amour, amourette, business, circumstance, concern, connection, episode, event, happening, incident, interest, intrigue, liaison, matter, occurrence, operation, organisation, party, proceeding, project, question, reception, relationship, responsibility, romance, subject, topic, transaction, undertaking.

affect[1] *v* act on, agitate, alter, apply to, attack, bear upon, change, concern, disturb, grieve, grip, impinge upon, impress, influence, interest, involve, melt, modify, move, overcome, penetrate, pertain to, perturb, prevail over, regard, relate to, seize, soften, stir, strike, sway, touch, transform, trouble, upset.

affect[2] *v* adopt, aspire to, assume, contrive, counterfeit, fake, feign, imitate, pretend, profess, put on, sham, simulate.

affectation *n* act, affectedness, appearance, artificiality, euphuism, façade, fakery, false display, imitation, insincerity, ladyism, mannerism, minanderie, pose, pretence, pretension, pretentiousness, sham, show, simulation, staginess, theatricality, theatricism, unnaturalness.

antonyms artlessness, ingenuousness.

affected[1] *adj* afflicted, agitated, altered, changed, concerned, damaged, distressed, gripped, hurt, impaired, impressed, influenced, injured, melted, moved, perturbed, smitten, stimulated, stirred, swayed, touched, troubled, upset.

affected[2] *adj* alembicated, artificial, assumed, bogus, chichi, conceited, contrived, counterfeit, debby, euphuistic, fake, feigned, fussy, greenery-yallery, hyperaesthesic, hyperaesthetic, insincere, lah-di-dah, literose, mannered, mincing, minikin, namby-pamby, niminy-piminy, phoney, pompous, precious, pretended, pretentious, put-on, sham, simulated, spurious, stiff, studied, unnatural.

antonyms genuine, natural.

affecting *adj* impressive, moving, pathetic, piteous, pitiable, pitiful, poignant, sad, saddening, stirring, touching, troubling.

affection *n* amity, attachment, care, desire, devotion, favour, feeling, fondness, friendliness, good will, inclination, kindness, liking, love, partiality, passion, penchant, predilection, predisposition, proclivity, propensity, regard, tenderness, warmth.

antonyms antipathy, dislike.

affectionate *adj* amiable, amorous, attached, caring, cordial, devoted, doting, fond, friendly, kind, loving, passionate, responsive, solicitous, tender, warm, warm-hearted.

antonyms cold, undemonstrative.

affiliate *v* ally, amalgamate, annex, associate, band together, combine, confederate, conjoin, connect, federate, incorporate, join, merge, syndicate, unite.

affiliation *n* alliance, amalgamation, association, coalition, combination, confederation, connection, federation, incorporation, joining, league, merger, merging, relationship, syndication, union.

affinity *n* alliance, analogy, attraction, closeness, compatibility, connection, correspondence, fondness, homogeneity, inclination, kinship, leaning, likeness, liking, partiality, predisposition, proclivity, propensity, rapport, relation, relationship, resemblance, similarity, similitude, sympathy.

antonym dissimilarity.

affirm *v* assert, asseverate, attest, aver, avouch, avow, certify, confirm, corroborate, declare, depose, endorse, maintain, pronounce, ratify, state, swear, testify, witness.

affirmation *n* affirmance, assertion, asseveration, attestation, averment, avouchment, avowal, certification, confirmation, corroboration, declaration, deposition, endorsement, oath, pronouncement, ratification, statement, testimony, witness.

affirmative *adj* affirmatory, agreeing, approving, assenting, assertory, asseverative, concurring, confirming, consenting, corroborative, emphatic, positive.

antonyms dissenting, negative.

affix *v* add, adjoin, annex, append, assign, attach, attribute, bind, connect, fasten, glue, join, paste, pin on, stick, subjoin, tack, tag.

antonym detach.

afflict *v* beset, burden, distress, grieve, harass, harm, harrow, hurt, oppress, pain, plague, rack, smite, strike, torment, torture, trouble, try, visit, wound, wring.

antonyms comfort, solace.

affliction *n* adversity, calamity, cross, curse, depression, disaster, disease, distress, grief, hardship, illness, misery, misfortune, ordeal, pain, plague, scourge, sickness, sorrow, suffering, torment, trial, tribulation, trouble, visitation, woe, wretchedness.

antonyms comfort, consolation, solace.

affluence *n* abundance, exuberance, fortune, opulence, plenty, profusion, property, prosperity, riches, substance, wealth, wealthiness.

antonym poverty.

affluent *adj* comfortable, flourishing, flush, loaded, moneyed, opulent, pecunious, prosperous, rich, wealthy, well-heeled, well-off, well-to-do.

antonyms impecunious, impoverished, poor.

afford *v* bear, bestow, cope with, engender, furnish, generate, give, grant, impart, manage, offer, produce, provide, render, spare, stand, supply, sustain, yield.

affray *n* brawl, brush, contest, disturbance, dogfight, Donnybrook, encounter, feud, fight, fisticuffs, fracas, fray, free-for-all, mêlee, quarrel, riot, row, scrap, scrimmage, scuffle, set-to, skirmish, squabble, tussle, wrangle.

affront *v* abuse, anger, annoy, displease, gall, incense, insult, irritate, nettle, offend, outrage, pique, provoke, slight, snub, vex.

antonyms appease, compliment.

n abuse, discourtesy, disrespect, facer, indignity, injury, insult, offence, outrage, provocation, rudeness, slap in the face, slight, slur, snub, vexation, wrong.

antonym compliment.

afoot *adv* about, abroad, afloat, agate, astir, brewing, circulating, current, going about, in preparation, in progress, in the air, in the wind, up.

afraid *adj* aghast, alarmed, anxious, apprehensive, cowardly, diffident, distrustful, faint-hearted, fearful, frightened, intimidated, nervous, regretful, reluctant, scared, sorry, suspicious, timid, timorous, tremulous, unhappy.

antonyms confident, unafraid.

afresh *adv* again, anew, da capo, de integro, de novo, newly, once again, once more, over again.

after *adv, prep* afterwards, as a result of, behind, below, following, in consequence of, later, post, subsequent to, subsequently, succeeding, thereafter.

antonym before.

aftermath *n* afterclap, after-effects, backwash, consequences, effects, end, fall-out, lattermath, outcome, repercussion, results, rowen, upshot, wake.

afternoon *n* mid-life, pip-emma, pm, post meridiem, siesta.

again *adv* afresh, also, anew, another time, au contraire, besides, bis, conversely, da capo, de integro, de novo, ditto, encore, furthermore, in addition, moreover, on the contrary, on the other hand, once more.

against *prep* abutting, across, adjacent to, athwart, close up to, confronting, contra, counter to, facing, fronting, hostile to, in contact with, in contrast to, in defiance of, in exchange for, in opposition to, in the face of, on, opposed to, opposing, opposite to, resisting, touching, versus.

antonyms for, pro.

age *n* (a)eon, agedness, anility, caducity, date, day, days, decline, decrepitude, dotage, duration, eld, elderliness, epoch, era, generation, lifetime, majority, maturity, old age, period, senescence, senility, seniority, span, the sere and yellow, time, years.

antonyms salad days, youth.

v decline, degenerate, deteriorate, grow old, mature, mellow, obsolesce, ripen, season.

aged *adj* advanced, age-old, ancient, antiquated, antique, decrepit, elderly, geriatric, grey, hoary, old, patriarchal, senescent, sere, superannuated, time-worn, venerable, worn-out.

antonyms young, youthful.

agency *n* action, activity, bureau, business, department, effect, effectuation, efficiency, finger, force, handling, influence, instrumentality, intercession, intervention, means, mechanism, mediation, medium, office, offices, operation, organisation, power, work, workings.

agenda *n* calendar, diary, list, menu, plan, programme, schedule, timetable.

agent *n* actor, agency, author, cause, channel, delegate, deputy, doer, emissary, envoy, executor, factor, force, functionary, go-between, instrument, intermediary, legate, means, middleman, mover, negotiator, operative, operator, organ, performer, power, practisant, rep, representative, substitute, surrogate, vehicle, vicar, worker.

ages *n* (a)eons, centuries, decades, donkey's years, years, yonks.

aggrandise *v* advance, amplify, augment, dignify, elevate, enhance, enlarge, ennoble, enrich, exaggerate, exalt, glamorise, glorify, increase, inflate, magnify, promote, upgrade, widen.

antonyms belittle, debase.

aggravate *v* annoy, exacerbate, exaggerate, exasperate, harass, hassle, heighten, incense, increase, inflame, intensify, irk, irritate, magnify, needle, nettle, peeve, pester, provoke, tease, vex, worsen.

antonyms alleviate, appease, mollify.

aggravation *n* annoyance, bore, drag, exacerbation, exacerbescence, exaggeration, exasperation, hassle, heightening, increase, inflammation, intensification, irksomeness, irritant, irritation, magnification, provocation, teasing, thorn in the flesh, vexation, worsening.

aggregate *n* accumulation, agglomeration, aggregation, amount, assemblage, body, bulk, collection, combination, entirety, generality, heap, herd, lump, mass, mixture, pile, sum, throng, total, totality, whole.

adj accumulated, added, assembled, collected, collective, combined, complete, composite, corporate, cumulative, mixed, total, united.

antonyms individual, particular.

v accumulate, add up, agglomerate, amass, amount to, assemble, cluster, collect, combine, conglomerate, heap, mix, pile, total.

aggregation *n* accumulation, agglomeration, amassment, asemblage, cluster, collection, combination, congeries, conglomeration, heap, mass, pile, stack.

aggression *n* aggressiveness, antagonism, assault, attack, bellicosity, belligerence, combativeness, destructiveness, encroachment, hostility, impingement, incursion, injury, intrusion, invasion, jingoism, militancy, offence, offensive, onslaught, provocation, pugnacity, raid.

aggressive *adj* argumentative, assertive, bare-knuckle, bellicose, belligerent, bold, butch, combative, contentious, destructive, disputatious, dynamic, energetic, enterprising, forceful, go-ahead, hostile, intrusive, invasive, jingoistic, militant, offensive, provocative, pugnacious, pushful, pushing, pushy, quarrelsome, scrappy, vigorous, zealous.

antonyms peaceable, submissive.

aggressor *n* assailant, assaulter, attacker, intruder, invader, offender, provoker.

antonym victim.

aggrieved *adj* afflicted, affronted, distressed, disturbed, harmed, hurt, ill-used, injured, insulted, maltreated, offended, pained, peeved, saddened, unhappy, woeful, wronged.

antonym pleased.

aghast *adj* afraid, amazed, appalled, astonished, astounded, awestruck, confounded, dismayed, frightened, horrified, horror-struck, shocked, startled, stunned, stupefied, terrified, thunder-struck.

agile *adj* active, acute, adroit, alert, brisk, clever, fleet, flexible, limber, lissome, lithe, lively, mobile, nimble, prompt, quick, quick-witted, sharp, sprightly, spry, supple, swift, withy.

antonyms clumsy, stiff, torpid.

agility *n* activity, acuteness, adroitness, alertness, briskness, cleverness, flexibility, lissomeness, litheness, liveliness, mobility, nimbleness, promptitude, promptness, quickness, quick-wittedness, sharpness, sprightliness, spryness, suppleness, swiftness.

antonyms sluggishness, stiffness, torpidity.

aging *adj* elderly, gerontic, obsolescent, senescent.

agitate *v* alarm, arouse, beat, churn, confuse, convulse, discompose, disconcert, disquiet, distract, disturb, excite, ferment, flurry, fluster, incite, inflame, perturb, rattle, rock, rouse, ruffle, shake, stimulate, stir, toss, trouble, unnerve, unsettle, upset, work up, worry.

antonyms calm, tranquillise.

agitated *adj* anxious, discomposed, distracted, dithery, feverish, flappable, flurried, flustered, in a lather, insecure, jumpy, nervous, perturbed, restive, restless, ruffled, tumultuous, twitchy, uneasy, unnerved, unsettled, upset, wrought-up.

antonyms calm, composed.

agitation *n* agitprop, alarm, anxiety, arousal, churning, clamour, commotion, confusion, controversy, convulsion, discomposure, disquiet, distraction, disturbance, doodah, ebullition, excitement, ferment, flurry, fluster, fomentation, hassle, incitement, inflammation, outcry, rocking, shake, shaking, solicitude, stimulation, stir, stirring, tail-spin, taking, tizz(y), tossing, trepidation, trouble, tumult, turbulence, turmoil, uneasiness, unrest, upset, welter, worry.

antonyms calm, tranquillity.

agitator *n* agent provocateur, bell-wether, demagogue, firebrand, fomenter, inciter, instigator, mob orator, rabble-rouser, revolutionary, soap-box orator, stirrer, troublemaker, tub-thumper.

agog *adj* avid, breathless, curious, desirous, eager, enthralled, enthusiastic, excited, expectant, impatient, in suspense, keen, on tenterhooks.

antonyms incurious, laid-back.

agonise *v* afflict, anguish, bleed, distress, excruciate, harrow, labour, pain, rack, strain, strive, struggle, suffer, toil, torment, torture, trouble, worry, wrestle, writhe.

agony *n* affliction, anguish, distress, misery, pain, pangs, paroxysm, spasm, suffering, throes, torment, torture, tribulation, woe, wretchedness.

agrarian *adj* agricultural, agronomic, farming, geoponic, georgic, praedial.

agree *v* accede, accord, acquiesce, admit, allow, answer, assent, chime, coincide, comply, concede, concord, concur, conform, consent, consort, contract, correspond, cotton, covenant, engage, fadge, fit, fix, get on, grant, harmonise, homologate, jibe, match, permit, promise, see eye to eye, settle, side with, square, suit, tally, yield.

antonyms conflict, disagree.

agreeable *adj* acceptable, acquiescent, amenable, amicable, appropriate, approving, attractive, befitting, compatible, complying, concurring, conformable, congenial, consenting, consistent, d'accord, delectable, delightful, enjoyable, fitting, gemütlich, gratifying, in accord, likeable, palatable, pleasant, pleasing, pleasurable, proper, responsive, satisfying, suitable, sympathetic, well-disposed, willing.

antonyms disagreeable, distasteful, incompatible, nasty.

agreement[1] *n* acceptance, accord, accordance, adherence, affinity, analogy, closing, compact, compatibility, complaisance, compliance, concert, concord, concordat, concurrence, conformity, congruence, congruity, consentience, consistency, consonance, consort, convention, correspondence, harmony, modus vivendi, preconcert, resemblance, respondence, similarity, suitableness, sympathy, unanimity, union, unison.

antonym disagreement.

agreement[2] *n* arrangement, bargain, compact, concordat, contract, covenant, deal, pact, settlement, treaty, understanding.

agricultural *adj* agrarian, agronomic, farming, geoponic, georgic, praedial.

agriculture *n* agribusiness, agronomics, agronomy, cultivation, culture, farming, geoponics, husbandry, tillage.

aground *adj, adv* ashore, beached, foundered, grounded, high and dry, marooned, on the rocks, stranded, stuck, wrecked.

antonym afloat.

ague *n* fever, fit, malaria, quaking, shivering, trembling, tremor.

ahead *adj, adv* advanced, along, at an advantage, at the head, before, earlier on, forwards, in advance, in front, in the forefront, in the lead, in the vanguard, leading, onwards, superior, to the fore, winning.

aid *v* abet, accommodate, adminiculate, assist, befriend, boost, ease, encourage, expedite, facilitate, favour, help, oblige, promote, prop, rally round, relieve, second, serve, subsidise, succour, support, sustain.

antonyms impede, obstruct.

n a leg up, adminicle, aidance, assistance, assistant, benefit, contribution, donation, encouragement, favour, help, helper, patronage, prop, relief, service, sponsorship, subsidy, subvention, succour, support, supporter.

antonyms impediment, obstruction.

aide *n* adjutant, adviser, advocate, aide de camp, assistant, attache, confidant, disciple, follower, galloper, henchman, right-hand man, supporter.

ail *v* afflict, annoy, be indisposed, bother, decline, distress, droop, fail, irritate, languish, pain, pine, sicken, trouble, upset, weaken, worry.

antonyms comfort, flourish.

ailing *adj* debilitated, diseased, feeble, frail, ill, indisposed, infirm, invalid, languishing, off-colour, out of sorts, peaky, poorly, sick, sickly, suffering, under the weather, unsound, unwell, weak, weakly.

antonyms flourishing, healthy.

ailment *n* affliction, complaint, disability, disease, disorder, illness, indisposition, infection, infirmity, malady, sickness, weakness.

aim *v* address, aspire, attempt, beam, design, direct, draw a bead, endeavour, essay, ettle, intend, level, mean, plan, point, propose, purpose, resolve, seek, set one's sights on, sight, strive, take aim, target, train, try, want, wish, zero in on.

n ambition, aspiration, course, desideratum, design, desire, direction, dream, end, goal, hope, intent, intention, mark, motive, object, objective, plan, purpose, scheme, target, telos, wish.

aimless *adj* chance, desultory, directionless, erratic, feckless, frivolous, goalless, haphazard, irresolute, pointless, purposeless, rambling, random, stray, undirected, unguided, unmotivated, unpredictable, vagrant, wayward.

antonyms determined, positive, purposeful.

air *n* ambience, ambient, appearance, aria, atmosphere, aura, bearing, blast, breath, breeze, character, demeanour, draught, effect, ether, feeling, flavour, heavens, impression, lay, look, manner, melody, mood, motif, oxygen, puff, quality, sky, song, strain, style, theme, tone, tune, waft, welkin, whiff, wind, zephyr.

v aerate, broadcast, circulate, communicate, declare, disclose, display, disseminate, divulge, exhibit, expose, express, freshen, give vent to, make known, make public, parade, proclaim, publicise, publish, reveal, tell, utter, vaunt, ventilate, voice.

airily *adv* animatedly, blithely, breezily, brightly, buoyantly, cheerfully, daintily, delicately, ethereally, flippantly, gaily, gracefully, happily, high-spiritedly, insouciantly, jauntily, light-heartedly, lightly, nonchalantly, unconcernedly.

antonyms concernedly, thoughtfully.

airless *adj* breathless, close, frowsty, frowsy, fusty, heavy, muggy, musty, oppressive, stale, stifling, stuffy, suffocating, sultry, unventilated.

antonyms airy, fresh.

airman *n* ace, aviator, erk, flyer, pilot.

airs *n* affectation, affectedness, arrogance, artificiality, haughtiness, hauteur, pomposity, posing, pretensions, pretentiousness, staginess, superciliousness, swank.

air-tight *adj* closed, impenetrable, impermeable, sealed, tight-fitting, wind-tight.

airy *adj* aerial, blithe, blowy, bodiless, breezy, buoyant, cheerful, cheery, debonair, delicate, disembodied, draughty, ethereal, fanciful, flimsy, fresh, frolicsome, gay, graceful, gusty, happy, high-spirited, illusory, imaginary, immaterial, incorporeal, insouciant, insubstantial, jaunty, light, light-hearted, lively, lofty, merry, nimble, nonchalant, offhand, open, roomy, spacious, spectral, sportive, sprightly, trifling, uncluttered, unreal, unsubstantial, vaporous, visionary, weightless, well-ventilated, windy.

antonyms close, heavy, oppressive, stuffy.

aisle *n* alleyway, ambulatory, corridor, deambulatory, division, gangway, lane, passage, passageway, path, walkway.

akin *adj* affiliated, agnate, alike, allied, analogous, cognate, comparable, congenial, connected, consanguineous, consonant, corresponding, kin, kindred, like, parallel, related, similar.

antonym alien.

alacrity *n* alertness, avidity, briskness, celerity, cheerfulness, dispatch, eagerness, enthusiasm, gaiety, liveliness, promptitude, promptness, quickness, readiness, speed, sprightliness, swiftness, willingness, zeal.

antonyms dilatoriness, slowness.

alarm *v* affright, agitate, daunt, dismay, distress, frighten, give (someone) a turn, panic, put the wind up (someone), scare, startle, terrify, terrorise, unnerve.

antonyms calm, reassure, soothe.

n alarm-bell, alert, anxiety, apprehension, bell, bleeper, consternation, danger signal, dismay, distress, distress signal, fear, fright, horror, larum, larum-bell, nervousness, panic, scare, siren, terror, tocsin, trepidation, unease, uneasiness, warning.

antonym composure.

alarming *adj* daunting, direful, dismaying, distressing, disturbing, dreadful, frightening, ominous, scaring, shocking, startling, terrifying, threatening, unnerving.

antonym reassuring.

alarmist *n* doomsman, doomwatcher, jitterbug, pessimist, scaremonger.

antonym optimist.

alas *interj* alack, alack-a-day, ewhow, good lack, waesucks, welladay, wel(l)away, woe.

albeit *conj* although, even if, even though, howbeit, notwithstanding that, though.

albumen *n* glair.

alchemy *n* hermetics, magic, sorcery, thaumaturgy, witchcraft, wizardry.

alcohol *n* bev(v)y, booze, firewater, hard stuff, hooch, John Barleycorn, (jungle) juice, liquor, medicine, moonshine, mountain dew, rotgut, spirits.

alcoholic *adj* ardent, brewed, distilled, fermented, hard, inebriant, inebriating, intoxicating, spirituous, strong, vinous.

n bibber, boozer, dipso, dipsomaniac, drunk, drunkard, hard drinker, inebriate, lush, piss artist, soak, sot, sponge, tippler, toper, tosspot, wino.

alcoholism *n* alcohol-addiction, crapulence, dipsomania, drunkenness, methomania, vinosity.

alcove *n* bay, booth, bower, carrel, compartment, corner, cubby-hole, cubicle, niche, nook, recess.

ale *n* beer, bitter, mild, morocco, nappy, swipes, wallop.

alert *adj* active, agile, attentive, brisk, careful, circumspect, gleg, heedful, lively, nimble, observant, on the ball, on the lookout, on the qui vive, perceptive, prepared, quick, ready, sharp-eyed, sharp-witted, spirited, sprightly, streetwise, vigilant, wary, watchful, wide-awake.

antonyms listless, slow.

n alarm, signal, siren, tocsin, warning.

v alarm, forewarn, inform, notify, signal, tip off, warn.

alertness *n* activeness, agility, attention, attentiveness, briskness, carefulness, circumspection, heedfulness, liveliness, nimbleness, perceptiveness, preparedness, promptitude, quickness, readiness, spiritedness, sprightliness, vigilance, wakefulness, wariness, watchfulness.

antonyms listlessness, slowness.

alias *n* allonym, anonym, assumed name, false name, nickname, nom de guerre, nom de plume, pen name, pseudonym, soubriquet, stage name.

adv alias dictus, also, also called, also known as, formerly, otherwise, otherwise called.

alibi *n* cover-up, defence, excuse, explanation, justification, plea, pretext, reason, story.

alien *adj* adverse, antagonistic, conflicting, contrary, estranged, exotic, extraneous, foreign, inappropriate, incompatible, incongruous, inimical, opposed, outlandish, remote, repugnant, separated, strange, unfamiliar.

antonym akin.

n emigrant, foreigner, immigrant, metic, newcomer, outlander, outsider, stranger.

antonym native.

alienate *v* antagonise, disaffect, divert, divorce, estrange, separate, set against, turn away, turn off, withdraw.

antonyms disarm, unite.

alienation *n* antagonisation, disaffection, disjunction, disunion, diversion, divorce, estrangement, indifference, remoteness, rupture, separation, severance, turning away, withdrawal.

antonym endearment.

alight[1] *v* come down, come to rest, debark, descend, detrain, disembark, disentrain, dismount, get down, get off, land, light, perch, settle, touch down.

antonyms ascend, board, rise.

alight[2] *adj* ablaze, afire, aflame, aglow, blazing, bright, brilliant, burning, fiery, flaming, flaring, ignited, illuminated, illumined, lighted, lit, lit up, on fire, radiant, shining.

antonym dark.

align *v* affiliate, agree, ally, arrange in line, associate, co-operate, co-ordinate, even, even up, join, line up, make parallel, order, range, regularise, regulate, side, straighten, sympathise.

alignment *n* adjustment, affiliation, agreement, alliance, arrangement, association, conformity, co-operation, co-ordination, evening, evening up, line, lining up, order, ranging, regularisation, regulating, regulation, sequence, straightening, sympathy, union.

alike *adj* akin, analogous, cognate, comparable, corresponding, duplicate, equal, equivalent, even, homologous, identical, parallel, resembling, similar, the same, uniform.

antonyms different, unlike.

adv analogously, correspondingly, equally, evenly, identically, in common, similarly, uniformly.

alive *adj* active, alert, animate, animated, awake, breathing, brisk, cheerful, eager, energetic, existent, existing, extant, functioning, having life, in existence, in force, life-like, live, lively, living, operative, quick, real, spirited, sprightly, spry, subsisting, vibrant, vigorous, vital, vivacious, zestful.

antonyms dead, lifeless.

alive with abounding in, bristling with, bustling with, buzzing with, crawling with, crowded with, infested with, lousy with, overflowing with, overrun by, stiff with, swarming with, teeming with, thronged with.

all *adj* complete, each, each and every, entire, every, every bit of, every one of, every single, full, greatest, gross, outright, perfect, the complete, the entire, the sum of, the total of, the totality of, the whole of, total, utter.

antonym none.

n aggregate, comprehensiveness, entirety, everything, sum, sum total, total, total amount, totality, universality, utmost, whole, whole amount.

adv altogether, completely, entirely, fully, holus-bolus, totally, utterly, wholesale, wholly.

all being well Deo volente, DV, God willing, if I'm spared, volente Deo.

all right *adj* acceptable, adequate, allowable, average, fair, hale, healthy, OK, passable, permissible, right as rain, safe, satisfactory, secure, sound, standard, unharmed, unhurt, unimpaired, uninjured, unobjectionable, well, whole.

antonyms unacceptable, uninjured.

adv acceptably, adequately, appropriately, OK, passably, reasonably, satisfactorily, suitably, unobjectionably, well enough.

antonyms unacceptably, unsatisfactorily.

all the time always, constantly, continually, continuously, ever, everlastingly, perpetually, unceasingly.

all thumbs butter-fingered, cack-handed, clumsy, ham-fisted, ham-handed, inept, maladroit, unhandy.

allay *v* allege, alleviate, appease, assuage, blunt, calm, check, compose, diminish, dull, ease, lessen, lull, mitigate, moderate, mollify, pacify, quell, quiet, reduce, relieve, slake, smooth, soften, soothe, subdue, tranquillise.

antonyms exacerbate, intensify.

allegation *n* accusation, affirmation, assertion, asseveration, attestation, averment, avowal, charge, claim, declaration, deposition, plea, profession, statement, testimony.

allege *v* adduce, advance, affirm, assert, asseverate, attest, aver, avow, charge, claim, contend, declare, depose, hold, insist, maintain, plead, profess, put forward, state.

alleged *adj* affirmed, asserted, averred, claimed, declared, described, designated, doubtful, dubious, inferred, ostensible, professed, purported, reputed, so-called, stated, supposed, suspect, suspicious.

allegiance *n* adherence, constancy, devotion, duty, faithfulness, fealty, fidelity, friendship, homage, loyalty, obedience, obligation, support.

antonyms disloyalty, enmity.

allegorical *adj* emblematic, figurative, parabolic, representative, significative, symbolic, symbolising, typical.

allegory *n* analogy, apologue, comparison, emblem, fable, metaphor, myth, parable, story, symbol, symbolism, tale.

allergic *adj* affected, antipathetic, averse, disinclined, dyspathetic, hostile, hypersensitive, loath, opposed, sensitised, sensitive, susceptible.

antonym tolerant.

allergy *n* antipathy, aversion, disinclination, dislike, dyspathy, hostility, hypersensitivity, loathing, opposition, sensitivity, susceptibility, vulnerability, weakness.

an.onyms affinity, tolerance.

alleviate *v* abate, allay, assuage, blunt, check, cushion, deaden, diminish, dull, ease, lessen, lighten, mitigate, moderate, modify, mollify, palliate, quell, quench, quiet, reduce, relieve, slacken, slake, smooth, soften, soothe, subdue, temper.

antonym aggravate.

alleviation *n* abatement, allegeance, assuagement, diminution, dulling, easing, lessening, lightening, mitigation, moderation, mollification, palliation, quelling, quenching, reduction, relief, slackening, slaking.

antonym aggravation.

alley *n* alleyway, back street, close, entry, gate, ginnel, lane, mall, passage, passageway, pathway, walk.

alliance *n* affiliation, affinity, agreement, association, bloc, bond, cartel, coalition, combination, compact, concordat, confederacy, confederation, conglomerate, connection, consociation, consortium, faction, federation, guild, league, marriage, pact, partnership, syndicate, treaty, union.

antonyms divorce, enmity, estrangement, hostility.

allied *adj* affiliated, agnate, amalgamated, associate, associated, bound, combined, confederate, congeric, connected, correlate(d), hand in glove, in cahoots, in league, joined, joint, kindred, leagued, linked, married, related, unified, united, wed.

antonym estranged.

allocate *v* allot, apportion, appropriate, assign, budget, designate, disperse, distribute, earmark, mete, ration, set aside, share out.

allocation *n* allotment, allowance, apportionment, appropriation, budget, grant, lot, measure, portion, quota, ration, share, stint.

allot *v* allocate, apportion, appropriate, assign, budget, designate, dispense, distribute, earmark, grant, mete, render, set aside, share out.

allotment *n* allocation, allowance, apportionment, appropriation, division, grant, lot, measure, partition, percentage, portion, quota, ration, share, stint.

all-out *adj* complete, determined, energetic, exhaustive, full, full-scale, intensive, maximum, no-holds-barred, optimum, powerful, resolute, supreme, thorough, thoroughgoing, total, undivided, unlimited, unremitting, unrestrained, unstinted, utmost, vigorous, wholesale.

antonyms half-hearted, perfunctory.

allow *v* accord, acknowledge, acquiesce, admeasure, admit, allocate, allot, apportion, approve, assign, authorise, bear, brook, concede, confess, deduct, endure, give, give leave, grant, let, own, permit, provide, put up with, remit, sanction, spare, stand, suffer, tolerate.

antonyms deny, forbid.

allow for arrange for, bear in mind, consider, foresee, include, keep in mind, keep in view, make allowances for, make concessions for, make provision for, plan for, provide for, take into account.

antonym discount.

allowable *adj* acceptable, admissible, all right, appropriate, approved, apt, legal(ised), legitimate, licit, permissible, sanctionable, sufferable, suitable, supportable, tolerable.

antonym unacceptable.

allowance *n* admission, allocation, allotment, amount, annuity, apportionment, batta, concession, deduction, discount, grant, lot, measure, pension, portion, quota, ration, rebate, reduction, remittance, sanction, share, stint, stipend, subsidy, sufferance, tolerance, weighting, X-factor.

alloy *n* admixture, amalgam, blend, coalescence, combination, composite, compound, fusion, hybrid, mix, mixture.

v admix, amalgamate, blend, combine, compound, debase, fuse, impair, mix, qualify, temper.

all-rounder *n* generalist, pancratist, Renaissance man.

antonym specialist.

allude *v* adumbrate, advert, cite, glance, hint, imply, infer, insinuate, intimate, mention, refer, remark, speak of, suggest, touch upon.

allure *v* attract, beguile, cajole, captivate, charm, coax, decoy, disarm, enchant, enrapture, entice, entrance, fascinate, interest, inveigle, lead on, lure, persuade, seduce, tempt, win over.

antonym repel.

n appeal, attraction, captivation, charm, enchantment, enticement, fascination, glamour, lure, magnetism, persuasion, seductiveness, temptation.

alluring *adj* agaçant(e), arousing, attractive, beguiling, bewitching, captivating, come-hither, enchanting, engaging, enticing, fascinating, fetching, intriguing, seductive, sensuous, sexy, tempting, voluptuous, winning.

antonyms repellant, unattractive.

allusion *n* citation, glance, hint, implication, innuendo, insinuation, intimation, mention, observation, quotation, reference, remark, suggestion.

ally *n* abettor, accessory, accomplice, associate, coadjutor, collaborator, colleague, confederate, confrere, consort, co-worker, friend, helper, helpmate, leaguer, partner, side-kick.

antonyms antagonist, enemy.

v affiliate, amalgamate, associate, band together, collaborate, combine, confederate, conjoin, connect, fraternise, join, join forces, league, marry, team up, unify, unite.

antonym estrange.

almanac *n* annual, calendar, ephemeris, register, year-book.

almighty *adj* absolute, all-powerful, awful, desperate, enormous, excessive, great, intense, invincible, loud, omnipotent, overpowering, overwhelming, plenipotent, severe, supreme, terrible, unlimited.

antonyms impotent, insignificant, weak.

almost *adv* about, all but, approaching, approximately, as good as, close to, just about, nearing, nearly, not far from, not quite, practically, towards, virtually, well-nigh.

alms *n* benefaction, beneficence, bounty, charity, donation, gift, largess(e), offerings, relief.

alone *adj, adv* abandoned, apart, by itself, by oneself, deserted, desolate, detached, discrete, forlorn, forsaken, incomparable, isolated, just, lonely, lonesome, matchless, mere, nonpareil, on one's own, on one's tod, only, peerless, separate, simply, single, single-handed, singular, sole, solitary, unaccompanied, unaided, unassisted, unattended, uncombined, unconnected, unequalled, unescorted, unique, unparalleled, unsurpassed.

aloof *adj* chilly, cold, cool, detached, distant, forbidding, formal, haughty, inaccessible, indifferent, offish, remote, reserved, reticent, stand-offish, supercilious, unapproachable, uncompanionable, unforthcoming, unfriendly, uninterested, unresponsive, unsociable, unsympathetic.

antonyms concerned, sociable.

aloofness *n* coolness, distance, indifference, offishness, remoteness, reservation, reserve, uncompanionability.

antonyms concern, sociability.

aloud *adv* audibly, clamorously, clangorously, clearly, distinctly, intelligibly, loudly, noisily, out loud, plainly, resoundingly, sonorously, vociferously.

antonym silently.

already *adv* at present, before now, beforehand, by now, by that time, by then, by this time, even now, heretofore, hitherto, just now, previously.

also *adv* additionally, along with, and, as well, as well as, besides, ditto, eke, further, furthermore, in addition, including, moreover, plus, therewithal, to boot, too.

alter *v* adapt, adjust, amend, bushel, castrate, change, convert, diversify, emend, metamorphose, modify, qualify, recast, reform, remodel, reshape, revise, shift, take liberties with, transform, transmute, transpose, turn, vary.

antonym fix.

alteration *n* adaptation, adjustment, amendment, castration, change, conversion, difference, diversification, emendation, interchanging, metamorphosis, modification, reciprocation, reformation, remodelling, reshaping, revision, rotation, shift, transfiguration, transformation, transmutation, transposition, variance, variation, vicissitude.

antonym fixity.

altercation *n* argument, bickering, clash, contention, controversy, debate, disagreement, discord, dispute, dissension, fracas, logomachy, quarrel, row, sparring, squabble, wrangle.

alternate *v* alter, change, fluctuate, follow one another, interchange, intersperse, oscillate, reciprocate, rotate, substitute, take turns, transpose, vary.

adj alternating, alternative, another, different, every other, every second, interchanging, reciprocal, reciprocating, reciprocative, rotating, second, substitute.

alternative *n* back-up, choice, option, other, preference, recourse, selection, substitute.

adj alternate, another, different, fall-back, fringe, other, second, substitute, unconventional, unorthodox.

although *conj* admitting that, albeit, conceding that, even if, even supposing, even though, granted that, howbeit, notwithstanding, though, while.

altitude *n* elevation, height, loftiness, stature, tallness.

antonym depth.

altogether *adv* absolutely, all in all, all told, as a whole, collectively, completely, entirely, fully, generally, holus-bolus, in all, in general, in sum, in toto, on the whole, perfectly, quite, thoroughly, totally, utterly, wholesale, wholly.

altruism *n* considerateness, disinterestedness, generosity, humanity, philanthropy, public spirit, self-abnegation, self-sacrifice, social conscience, unself, unselfishness.

antonym selfishness.

altruistic *adj* benevolent, charitable, considerate, disinterested, generous, humane, humanitarian, philanthropic, public-spirited, self-abnegating, self-sacrificing, unselfish.

always *adv* aye, consistently, constantly, continually, endlessly, eternally, ever, everlastingly, evermore, every time, forever, in perpetuum, invariably, perpetually, regularly, repeatedly, sempiternally, unceasingly, unfailingly, without exception.

antonym never.

amalgam *n* admixture, aggregate, alloy, amalgamation, blend, coalescence, combination, commixture, composite, compound, fusion, mixture, union.

amalgamate *v* alloy, ally, blend, coalesce, coalise, combine, commingle, compound, fuse, homogenise, incorporate, integrate, intermix, merge, mingle, synthesise, unify, unite.

antonym separate.

amalgamation *n* admixture, alliance, alloy, amalgam, amalgamating, blend, coalescence, coalition, combination, commingling, composite, compound, fusion, homogenisation, incorporation, integration, joining, merger, mingling, mixing, mixture, synthesis, unification, union.

amass *v* accumulate, agglomerate, agglutinate, aggregate, assemble, collect, compile, foregather, garner, gather, heap up, hoard, pile up, rake up, scrape together.

amateur *n* aficionado, buff, dabbler, dilettante, do-it-yourselfer, fancier, ham, layman, non-professional.

antonym professional.

amateurish *adj* amateur, clumsy, crude, dilettantish, hammy, incompetent, inept, inexpert, unaccomplished, unprofessional, unskilful, untrained.

antonyms professional, skilled.

amatory *adj* amatorial, amatorious, amorous, aphrodisiac, erogenous, erotic, erotogenous, lascivious, libidinous, love, passionate, romantic, sensual, sexual, sexy.

amaze *v* alarm, astonish, astound, bewilder, confound, daze, disconcert, dismay, dumbfound, electrify, flabbergast, floor, shock, stagger, startle, stun, stupefy, surprise, wow.

amazement *n* admiration, astonishment, bewilderment, confusion, dismay, incomprehension, marvel, perplexity, shock, stupefaction, surprise, wonder, wonderment.

ambassador *n* agent, apostle, consul, deputy, diplomat, elchi, embassador, emissary, envoy, legate, minister, nuncio, plenipotentiary, representative.

ambassadorial *adj* diplomatic, fetial, legatine, plenipotentiary, representative.

ambience *n* air, atmosphere, aura, character, climate, environment, feel, feeling, flavour, impression, milieu, mood, quality, setting, spirit, surroundings, tenor, tone, vibes, vibrations.

ambiguity *n* ambivalence, confusion, doubt, doubtfulness, dubiety, dubiousness, enigma, equivocacy, equivocality, equivocation, inconclusiveness, indefiniteness, indeterminateness, obscurity, puzzle, tergiversation, uncertainty, unclearness, vagueness, weasel word(s), woolliness.

antonym clarity.

ambiguous *adj* ambivalent, amphibolic, amphibological, amphibolous, confused, confusing, cryptic, Delphic, double-barrelled, double-meaning, doubtful, dubious, enigmatic, enigmatical, equivocal, inconclusive, indefinite, indeterminate, louche, multivocal, obscure, oracular, puzzling, uncertain, unclear, vague, woolly.

antonym clear.

ambit *n* circuit, compass, confines, environs, precincts, scope.

ambition *n* aim, aspiration, avidity, craving, design, desire, dream, drive, eagerness, end, enterprise, goal, hankering, hope, hunger, ideal, intent, longing, object, objective, purpose, push, striving, target, wish, yearning, zeal.

antonyms apathy, diffidence.

ambitious *adj* arduous, aspiring, assertive, avid, bold, challenging, demanding, desirous, difficult, driving, eager, elaborate, energetic, enterprising, enthusiastic, exacting, fervid, formidable, go-ahead, grandiose, hard, hopeful, impressive, industrious, intent, keen, pretentious, purposeful, pushy, severe, strenuous, striving, zealous.

antonym unassuming.

ambivalence *n* ambiguity, clash, conflict, confusion, contradiction, doubt, equivocation, fluctuation, hesitancy, inconsistency, indecision, instability, irresolution, opposition, uncertainty, vacillation, wavering.

antonym certainty.

ambivalent *adj* ambiguous, clashing, conflicting, confused, contradictory, debatable, doubtful, equivocal, fluctuating, hesitant, inconclusive, inconsistent, irresolute, mixed, opposed, uncertain, undecided, unresolved, unsettled, unsure, vacillating, warring, wavering.

antonym unequivocal.

amble *v* dawdle, drift, meander, mosey, perambulate, promenade, ramble, saunter, stroll, toddle, walk, wander.

antonyms march, stride.

ambush *n* ambuscade, concealment, cover, emboscata, hiding, hiding-place, retreat, shelter, snare, trap, waylaying.

v ambuscade, bushwhack, ensnare, entrap, surprise, trap, waylay.

ameliorate *v* advance, alleviate, amend, assuage, benefit, better, ease, elevate, emend, enhance, improve, meliorate, mend, mitigate, promote, raise, redress, reform, relieve, revise.

antonyms exacerbate, worsen.

amenable *adj* accountable, acquiescent, agreeable, answerable, biddable, chargeable, complaisant, conformable, docile, flexible, liable, open, persuadable, responsible, responsive, submissive, susceptible, tractable.

antonym intractable.

amend *v* adjust, alter, ameliorate, better, change, correct, emend, emendate, enhance, fix, improve, mend, modify, qualify, rectify, redress, reform, remedy, repair, revise.

antonyms impair, worsen.

amendment *n* addendum, addition, adjunct, adjustment, alteration, amelioration, betterment, change, clarification, correction, corrigendum, emendation, enhancement, improvement, mending, modification, qualification, rectification, redress, reform, remedy, repair, revision.

antonyms deterioration, impairment.

amends *n* atonement, compensation, expiation, indemnification, indemnity, mitigation, quittance, recompense, redress, reparation, requital, restitution, restoration, satisfaction.

amenity *n* advantage, attraction, beauty, charm, comfort, convenience, facility, pleasantness, refinement, service.

antonyms eyesore, inconvenience.

amiable *adj* accessible, affable, agreeable, approachable, attractive, benign, biddable, charming, cheerful, companionable, complaisant, congenial, conversable, couthie, delightful, engaging, friendly, gemütlich, genial, good-humoured, good-natured, good-tempered, kind, kindly, likable, lovable, obliging, pleasant, pleasing, sociable, sweet, winning, winsome.

antonyms hostile, unfriendly.

amicable *adj* amiable, brotherly, civil, civilised, cordial, courteous, easy, frank, fraternal, friendly, good-natured, harmonious, kind, kindly, neighbourly, open, peaceable, peaceful, polite, sociable, unreserved.

antonym hostile.

amid *conj* amidst, among, amongst, in the middle of, in the midst of, in the thick of, surrounded by.

amiss *adj* awry, defective, erroneous, fallacious, false, faulty, improper, inaccurate, inappropriate, incorrect, out of order, unsuitable, untoward, wonky, wrong.

adv ill, imperfect, imprecise, out of kilter.

antonyms right, well.

amity *n* accord, amicability, brotherhood, brotherliness, comity, comradeship, concord, cordiality, fellowship, fraternity, friendliness, friendship, goodwill, harmony, kindliness, kindness, peace, peacefulness, sympathy, tranquillity, understanding.

antonyms discord, hostility.

amnesty *n* absolution, condonation, dispensation, forgiveness, immunity, indulgence, lenience, mercy, oblivion, pardon, remission, reprieve.

amok *adv* amuck, berserk, crazy, in a frenzy, in a fury, insane, like a madman, mad, wild.

among *prep* amid, amidst, amongst, between, in the middle of, in the midst of, in the thick of, midst, mongst, surrounded by, together with, with.

amoral *adj* abandoned, free-living, intemperate, lax, loose, non-moral, uninhibited, unmoral, unrestrained.

antonym moral.

amorous *adj* affectionate, amatory, ardent, attached, doting, enamoured, erotic, fond, impassioned, in love, lovesick, loving, lustful, passionate, randy, tender, uxorious.

antonyms cold, indifferent.

amorphous *adj* chaotic, characterless, featureless, formless, inchoate, indeterminate, indistinct, irregular, nebulous, nondescript, shapeless, undefined, unformed, unshaped, unshapen, unstructured, vague.

antonyms definite, distinctive, shapely.

amount *n* addition, aggregate, bulk, entirety, expanse, extent, lot, magnitude, mass, measure, number, quantity, quantum, quota, sum, sum total, supply, total, volume, whole.

amount to add up to, aggregate, approximate to, be equivalent to, be tantamount to, become, come to, equal, grow, mean, purport, run to, total.

amour *n* affair, affaire de coeur, entanglement, intimacy, intrigue, liaison, love affair, relationship, romance.

ample *adj* abundant, big, bountiful, broad, capacious, commodious, considerable, copious, expansive, extensive, full, generous, goodly, great, handsome, large, lavish, liberal, munificent, plenteous, plentiful, plenty, profuse, rich, roomy, spacious, substantial, sufficient, unrestricted, voluminous, wide.

antonyms insufficient, meagre.

amplify *v* add to, augment, boost, broaden, bulk out, deepen, develop, dilate, elaborate, enhance, enlarge, expand, expatiate, extend, fill out, heighten, increase, intensify, lengthen, magnify, raise, strengthen, supplement, widen.

antonym reduce.

amplitude *n* abundance, ampleness, bigness, breadth, bulk, capaciousness, capacity, compass, completeness, copiousness, dimension, expanse, extent, fullness, greatness, hugeness, largeness, magnitude, mass, plenitude, plentifulness, plethora, profusion, range, reach, richness, scope, size, spaciousness, sweep, vastness, volume, width.

amply *adv* abundantly, bountifully, completely, copiously, extensively, fully, generously, greatly, handsomely, lavishly, liberally, munificently, plenteously, plentifully, profusely, richly, substantially, sufficiently, thoroughly, unstintingly, well.

antonym inadequately.

amputate *v* curtail, cut off, dissever, dock, excise, lop, remove, separate, sever, truncate.

amulet *n* abraxas, charm, fetish, juju, lucky charm, pentacle, periapt, phylactory, talisman, telesm.

amuse *v* absorb, beguile, charm, cheer, cheer up, delight, disport, divert, engross, enliven, entertain, enthral, gladden, interest, occupy, please, popjoy, recreate, regale, relax, slay, tickle.

antonym bore.

amusement *n* beguilement, delight, disportment, distraction, diversion, enjoyment, entertainment, fun, game, gladdening, hilarity, hobby, interest, joke, lark, laughter, merriment, mirth, pastime, pleasure, prank, recreation, regalement, sport.

antonyms bore, boredom.

amusing *adj* amusive, charming, cheerful, cheering, comical, delightful, diverting, droll, enjoyable, entertaining, facetious, funny, gladdening, hilarious, humorous, interesting, jocular, jolly, killing, laughable, lively, ludicrous, merry, pleasant, pleasing, rib-tickling, risible, sportive, witty.

antonym boring.

an eye for an eye justice, reciprocation, repayment, reprisal, requital, retaliation, retribution, revenge, tit for tat, vengeance.

anachronism *n* antique, archaism, back number, dinosaur, fogey, fossil, metachronism, parachronism, prochronism.

anaemic *adj* ashen, bloodless, chalky, characterless, colourless, dull, enervated, exsanguine, exsanguin(e)ous, feeble, frail, ineffectual, infirm, insipid, pale, pallid, pasty, peelie-wally, sallow, sickly, spiritless, wan, weak, whey-faced.

antonyms full-blooded, ruddy, sanguine.

anaesthetic *n* analgesic, anodyne, narcotic, opiate, pain-killer, palliative, sedative, soporific, stupefacient, stupefactive.

anaesthetise *v* benumb, deaden, desensitise, dope, dull, etherise, lull, mull, numb, stupefy.

analogous *adj* agreeing, akin, alike, comparable, correlative,, corresponding, equivalent, homologous, like, matching, parallel, reciprocal, related, resembling, similar.

antonym disparate.

analogy *n* agreement, comparison, correlation, correspondence, equivalence, homologue, homology, likeness, parallel, parallelism, relation, resemblance, semblance, similarity, similitude.

analyse *v* anatomise, assay, break down, consider, dissect, dissolve, divide, estimate, evaluate, examine, interpret, investigate, judge, reduce, resolve, review, scrutinise, separate, sift, study, test.

analysis *n* anatomisation, anatomy, assay, breakdown, dissection, dissolution, division, enquiry, estimation, evaluation, examination, exegesis, explanation, explication, exposition, interpretation, investigation, judgement, opinion, reasoning, reduction, resolution, review, scrutiny, separation, sifting, study, test.

analytic *adj* analytical, anatomical, critical, detailed, diagnostic, discrete, dissecting, enquiring, explanatory, expository, inquisitive, interpretative, interpretive, investigative, investigatory, logical, methodical, questioning, rational, searching, studious, systematic.

anarchic *adj* anarchical, anarchistic, chaotic, confused, disordered, disorganised, iconoclastic, lawless, libertarian, nihilist, rebellious, revolutionary, riotous, ungoverned.

antonyms orderly, submissive.

anarchist *n* anarch, apostate, iconoclast, insurgent, libertarian, nihilist, rebel, revolutionary, terrorist.

anarchy *n* anarchism, apostasy, bedlam, chaos, confusion, disorder, disorganisation, iconoclasm, insurrection, lawlessness, libertarianism, misgovernment, misrule, mutiny, nihilism, pandemonium, rebellion, revolution, riot, unrule.

antonyms control, order, rule.

anathema *n* abhorrence, abomination, aversion, ban, bane, bête noire, bugbear, condemnation, curse, damnation, denunciation, excommunication, execration, imprecation, malediction, object of loathing, pariah, proscription, taboo.

anatomise *v* analyse, break down, dissect, dissolve, divide, examine, pull apart, resolve, scrutinise, separate, study, vivisect.

anatomy *n* analysis, build, composition, constitution, construction, dissection, frame, framework, make-up, structure, vivisection, zootomy.

ancestor *n* antecedent, antecessor, forebear, forefather, forerunner, precursor, predecessor, primogenitor, progenitor, progenitress, progenitrix.

antonym descendant.

ancestral *adj* atavistic, avital, familial, genealogical, genetic, hereditary, lineal, parental.

ancestry *n* ancestors, antecedents, antecessors, blood, derivation, descent, extraction, family, forebears, forefathers, genealogy, heredity, heritage, house, line, lineage, origin, parentage, pedigree, progenitors, race, roots, stirps, stock.

anchor *n* grapnel, kedge, killick, mainstay, mud-hook, pillar of strength, prop, security, staff, support.

v affix, attach, fasten, fix, make fast, moor.

anchorage *n* bield, harbour, harbourage, haven, mooring, port, protection, refuge, sanctuary, shelter.

anchorite *n* anchoress, anchoret, ancress, ascetic, eremite, hermit, holy man, marabout, recluse, solitaire, solitarian, solitary, stylite.

ancient *adj* aged, age-old, antediluvian, antiquated, antique, archaic, bygone, demode, early, fossilised, hoary, immemorial, obsolete, old, olden, old-fashioned, original, outmoded, out-of-date, preadamic, prehistoric, primeval, primordial, pristine, superannuated, time-worn, venerable, world-old.

antonym modern.

ancillary *adj* accessory, additional, adjuvant, adminicular, auxiliary, contributory, extra, secondary, subordinate, subsidiary, supplementary.

androgynous *adj* bisexual, epicene, gynandrous, hermaphrodite, hermaphroditic.

anecdote *n* exemplum, fable, reminiscence, sketch, story, tale, yarn.

angel *n* archangel, backer, benefactor, cherub, darling, divine messenger, fairy godmother, guardian spirit, ideal, paragon, principality, saint, seraph, supporter, treasure.

antonyms devil, fiend.

angelic *adj* adorable, beatific, beautiful, celestial, cherubic, divine, entrancing, ethereal, exemplary, heavenly, holy, innocent, lovely, pious, pure, saintly, seraphic, unworldly, virtuous.

antonyms devilish, fiendish.

anger *n* annoyance, antagonism, bad blood, bile, bitterness, choler, dander, displeasure, dudgeon, exasperation, fury, gall, indignation, ire, irritability, irritation, monkey, outrage, passion, pique, rage, rancour, resentment, spleen, temper, vexation, wrath.

antonym forbearance.

v affront, aggravate, annoy, antagonise, bother, bug, displease, enrage, exasperate, fret, frustrate, gall, incense, infuriate, irk, irritate, madden, miff, needle, nettle, offend, outrage, pique, provoke, rile, ruffle, vex.

antonyms appease, calm, please.

angle *n* approach, aspect, bend, corner, crook, crotch, cusp, direction, edge, elbow, facet, flexure, hook, nook, outlook, perspective, point, point of view, position, side, slant, standpoint, turn, viewpoint.

angle for aim for, be after, be out for, contrive, fish for, have one's beady eye on, hunt, invite, scheme, seek, solicit.

angler *n* fisherman, piscator, piscatrix, rodman, rodsman, rodster.

angling *n* ars piscatoria, fishing, gentle craft.

angry *adj* aggravated, annoyed, antagonised, bitter, burned up, choked, choleric, chuffed, disgruntled, displeased, enraged, exasperated, furious, heated, hot, incensed, indignant, infuriated, irascible, irate, ireful, irked, irritable, irritated, mad, miffed, needled, nettled, outraged, passionate, piqued, provoked, raging, rancorous, ratty, red-headed, resentful, riled, shirty, splenetic, stomachful, tumultuous, uptight, waxy, wrathful, wroth.

antonyms calm, content.

angst *n* agony, angoisse, anguish, anxiety, apprehension, depression, dread, foreboding, future shock, mal du siècle, malaise, mid-life crisis, Weltschmerz, worry.

anguish *n* agony, angst, anxiety, desolation, distress, dole, dolour, grief, heartache, heartbreak, misery, pain, pang, rack, sorrow, suffering, torment, torture, tribulation, woe, wretchedness.

antonyms happiness, solace.

anguished *adj* afflicted, agonised, angst-ridden, distressed, dolorous, harrowed, miserable, racked, stricken, suffering, tormented, tortured, wretched.

angular *adj* bony, gauche, gaunt, gawky, lank, lanky, lean, rangy, rawboned, scrawny, skinny, spare, ungainly.

animal *n* barbarian, beast, brute, creature, critter, cur, hound, mammal, monster, pig, savage, swine.

adj animalic, bestial, bodily, brutish, carnal, faunal, feral, ferine, fleshly, gross, inhuman, instinctive, physical, piggish, savage, sensual, wild, zoic.

animate *v* activate, arouse, embolden, encourage, energise, enliven, excite, fire, galvanise, goad, impel, incite, inspire, inspirit, instigate, invest, invigorate, irradiate, kindle, move, quicken, reactivate, revive, revivify, rouse, spark, spur, stimulate, stir, suffuse, urge, vitalise, vivify.

antonyms dull, inhibit.

adj alive, breathing, conscious, live, living, sentient.

antonyms dull, spiritless.

animated *adj* active, airy, alive, ardent, brisk, buoyant, eager, ebullient, energetic, enthusiastic, excited, fervent, gay, glowing, impassioned, lively, passionate, quick, radiant, spirited, sprightly, vehement, vibrant, vigorous, vital, vivacious, vivid, zestful.

antonyms inert, sluggish.

animation *n* action, activity, ardour, briskness, buoyancy, ebullience, elation, energy, enthusiasm, excitement, exhilaration, fervour, gaiety, high spirits, life, liveliness, passion, pep, radiance, sparkle, spirit, sprightliness, verve, vibrancy, vigour, vitality, vivacity, zeal, zest, zing.

antonyms dullness, inertia.

animosity *n* acrimony, animus, antagonism, antipathy, bad blood, bitterness, enmity, feud, feuding, hate, hatred, hostility, ill-will, loathing, malevolence, malice, malignity, odium, rancour, resentment, spite.

antonym goodwill.

animus *n* acrimony, animosity, antagonism, antipathy, bad blood, bitterness, enmity, hate, hatred, hostility, ill-feeling, ill-will, impetus, intention, loathing, malevolence, malice, malignance, malignity, motive, odium, purpose, rancour, resentment, will.

antonym sympathy.

annals *n* accounts, archives, chronicles, history, journals, memoirs, memorials, records, registers, reports.

annex *v* acquire, add, adjoin, affix, append, appropriate, arrogate, attach, connect, conquer, expropriate, fasten, incorporate, join, occupy, purloin, seize, subjoin, tack, take over, unite, usurp.

n addendum, additament, addition, adjunct, appendix, attachment, supplement.

annexation *n* amalgamation, annexing, appropriation, arrogation, augmentation, combination, conquest, expropriation, occupation, seizure, takeover, usurpation.

annexe *n* addition, ell, expansion, extension, wing.

annihilate *v* abolish, assassinate, destroy, eliminate, eradicate, erase, exterminate, extinguish, extirpate, liquidate, murder, nullify, obliterate, raze, rub out, thrash, trounce, wipe out.

annihilation *n* abolition, assassination, defeat, destruction, elimination, eradication, erasure, extermination, extinction, extirpation, liquidation, nullification, obliteration.

annotate *v* comment, commentate, elucidate, explain, gloss, gloze, interpret, marginalise, note.

annotation *n* apparatus criticus, comment, commentary, elucidation, exegesis, explanation, explication, footnote, gloss, interpretation, marginalia, note, scholia, scholion, scholium.

announce *v* advertise, blazon, broadcast, declare, disclose, divulge, intimate, leak, make known, notify, preconise, proclaim, promulgate, propound, publicise, publish, report, reveal, state.

antonym suppress.

announcement *n* advertisement, broadcast, bulletin, communique, declaration, disclosure, dispatch, divulgation, divulgence, intimation, notification, proclamation, promulgation, publication, report, revelation, statement.

announcer *n* anchor man, broadcaster, commentator, commère, compère, crier, harbinger, herald, messenger, newscaster, news-reader, reporter.

annoy *v* aggravate, anger, badger, bore, bother, bug, chagrin, contrary, displease, disturb, exasperate, fash, gall, get, give the pigs, harass, harm, harry, hip, hump, incommode, irk, irritate, madden, miff, molest, needle, nettle, peeve, pester, pique, plague, provoke, rile, ruffle, tease, trouble, vex.

antonyms gratify, please.

annoyance *n* aggravation, anger, bind, bore, bother, desagrement, displeasure, disturbance, exasperation, fash, gêne, harassment, headache, irritant, irritation, nuisance, pain, pest, pique, plague, provocation, tease, trouble, vexation.

antonym pleasure.

annoyed *adj* bored, bugged, chagrined, displeased, exasperated, galled, harassed, hipped, irked, irritated, miffed, narked, peeved, piqued, provoked, shirty, vexed.

antonym pleased.

annoying *adj* aggravating, boring, bothersome, displeasing, disturbing, exasperating, fashious, galling, harassing, irksome, irritating, maddening, offensive, peeving, pesky, pesterous, pestful, pestiferous, pestilent, pestilential, plaguesome, plaguey, provoking, teasing, troublesome, vexatious.

antonyms pleasing, welcome.

annual *n* almanac, annal, ephemeris, year-book.

annul *v* abolish, abrogate, cancel, cashier, countermand, disannul, invalidate, negate, nullify, quash, recall, repeal, rescind, retract, reverse, revoke, suspend, void.

antonyms enact, restore.

annulment *n* abolition, abrogation, cancellation, cassation, countermanding, disannulment, invalidation, negation, nullification, quashing, recall, repeal, rescindment, rescission, retraction, reversal, revocation, suspension, voiding.

antonyms enactment, restoration.

anodyne *adj* analgesic, bland, blunting, calmative, deadening, desensitising, dulling, febrifugal, inoffensive, narcotic, numbing, pain-killing, pain-relieving, palliative, sedative.

antonym irritant.

n alleviative, analgesic, febrifuge, narcotic, pain-killer, pain-reliever, palliative, sedative.

antonym irritant.

anoint *v* anele, bless, consecrate, daub, dedicate, embrocate, grease, hallow, lard, lubricate, oil, rub, sanctify, smear.

anointing *n* aneling, blessing, consecration, dedication, embrocation, hallowing, sanctification, unction.

anomalous *adj* aberrant, abnormal, atypical, bizarre, deviant, eccentric, exceptional, freakish, incongruous, inconsistent, irregular, odd, peculiar, quirky, rare, singular, untypical, unusual.

antonyms normal, regular.

anomaly *n* aberration, abnormality, departure, deviant, deviation, divergence, eccentricity, exception, freak, incongruity, inconsistency, irregularity, misfit, oddity, peculiarity, rarity.

anonymous *adj* characterless, faceless, impersonal, incognito, innominate, nameless, nondescript, unacknowledged, unattested, unauthenticated, uncredited, unexceptional, unidentified, unknown, unnamed, unsigned, unspecified.

antonyms distinctive, identifiable, named.

anorak *n* blouson, golf-jacket, jerkin, lumber-jacket, parka, waterproof, windcheater, windjammer.

answer *n* acknowledgement, apology, comeback, counterbuff, countercharge, defence, explanation, outcome, plea, reaction, rebuttal, reciprocation, refutation, rejoinder, reply, report, resolution, response, retaliation, retort, return, riposte, solution, vindication.

v acknowledge, agree, balance, conform, correlate, correspond, do, echo, explain, fill, fit, fulfil, match up to, meet, pass, qualify, react, reciprocate, refute, rejoin, reply, resolve, respond, retaliate, retort, return, satisfy, serve, solve, succeed, suffice, suit, work.

answer back argue, cheek, contradict, disagree, dispute, rebut, retaliate, retort, riposte, talk back.

antonym acquiesce.

answerable[1] *adj* accountable, amenable, blameable, blameworthy, chargeable, liable, responsible, to blame.

answerable[2] *adj* defensible, deniable, disprovable, explicable, rebuttable, refutable, repudiable.

answering *adj* respondent, responsory.

ant *n* emmet, hymenopteran, pismire, termite.

antagonise *v* alienate, anger, annoy, disaffect, embitter, estrange, incense, insult, irritate, offend, provoke, repel.

antonym disarm.

antagonism *n* animosity, animus, antipathy, competition, conflict, contention, discord, dissension, friction, hostility, ill-feeling, ill-will, opposition, rivalry.

antonyms rapport, sympathy.

antagonist *n* adversary, competitor, contender, contestant, disputant, enemy, foe, opponent, opposer, rival.

antonyms ally, supporter.

antagonistic *adj* adverse, antipathetic, at variance, averse, bellicose, belligerent, conflicting, contentious, hostile, ill-disposed, incompatible, inimical, opposed, pugnacious, unfriendly.

antonyms friendly, sympathetic.

antecedents *n* ancestors, ancestry, antecessors, background, blood, descent, dossier, extraction, family, forebears, forefathers, genealogy, history, line, lineage, past, pedigree, prodromi, progenitors, record, stock.

antedate *v* antecede, anticipate, forego, forerun, go before, precede, predate.

antonym follow.

antediluvian *adj* anachronistic, ancient, antiquated, antique, archaic, bygone, demode, fossilised, obsolete, old-fashioned, out of the ark, out-of-date, passe, prehistoric, primal, primeval, primitive, primordial, superannuated.

antonyms up-to-date, with it.

anterior *adj* antecedent, earlier, foregoing, former, introductory, preceding, previous, prior, prodromal, prodromic.

antonym subsequent.

anthem *n* canticle, chant, chorale, hymn, introit, paean, psalm, song.

anthology *n* analects, choice, collection, compendium, compilation, digest, divan, florilegium, garland, miscellany, selection, spicilegium, treasury.

anticipate *v* antedate, apprehend, await, bank on, beat to it, count upon, earlierise, expect, forecast, foredate, foresee, forestall, foretaste, foretell, forethink, hope for, intercept, look for, look forward to, predict, pre-empt, prevent.

anticipation *n* apprehension, awaiting, expectancy, expectation, foresight, foretaste, forethought, forewarning, hope, preconception, premonition, prescience, presentiment, prodrome, prolepsis.

anticipatory *adj* anticipative, expectant, hopeful, intuitive, preparatory, proleptic, proleptical.

anticlimax *n* bathos, comedown, damp squib, disappointment, disenchantment, fiasco, let-down.

anticlockwise *adj* dextrorse, l(a)evorotatory.

antics *n* buffoonery, capers, clownery, clowning, didoes, doings, escapades, foolery, foolishness, frolics, larks, mischief, monkey tricks, playfulness, pranks, silliness, skylarking, stunts, tomfoolery, tricks, zanyism.

antidote *n* antitoxin, antivenin, corrective, counter-agent, countermeasure, cure, detoxicant, mithridate, neutraliser, preventive, remedy, specific, theriac, treacle.

antipathetic *adj* abhorrent, allergic, anathematical, antagonistic, antipathetical, averse, disgusting, distasteful, hateful, horrible, hostile, incompatible, inimical, invidious, loathsome, obnoxious, odious, offensive, repellent, repugnant, repulsive, revolting.

antonyms agreeable, harmonious, sympathetic.

antipathy *n* abhorrence, allergy, animosity, animus, antagonism, aversion, bad blood, contrariety, disgust, dislike, distaste, enmity, hate, hatred, hostility, ill-will, incompatibility, loathing, odium, opposition, rancour, repugnance, repulsion, resentment.

antonyms rapport, sympathy.

antipodes *n* underworld.

antiquary *n* antiquarian, archaeologist, archaist, bibliophile, collector, Dryasdust, palaeologist, virtuoso.

antiquated *adj* anachronistic, ancient, antediluvian, antique, archaic, dated, demode, elderly, fogeyish, fogram, fossilised, obsolete, old, old hat, old-fashioned, old-fogeyish, outdated, outmoded, out-of-date, outworn, passe, quaint, superannuated, unfashionable.

antonyms forward-looking, modern.

antique *adj* aged, ancient, antiquarian, archaic, elderly, obsolete, old, old-fashioned, outdated, quaint, superannuated, vintage.

n antiquity, bibelot, bygone, curio, curiosity, heirloom, knick-knack, museum-piece, object of virtu, period piece, rarity, relic.

antiquity *n* age, agedness, ancient times, ancientness, antique, distant past, e(i)ld, elderliness, fogramity, hoariness, old age, olden days, oldness, time immemorial, venerableness.

antonyms modernity, novelty.

antiseptic *adj* aseptic, bactericidal, clean, disinfectant, germ-free, germicidal, hygienic, medicated, pure, sanitary, sanitised, sterile, uncontaminated, unpolluted.

n bactericide, cleanser, decontaminant, disinfectant, germicide, purifier.

antisocial *adj* alienated, anarchic, antagonistic, asocial, belligerent, disorderly, disruptive, hostile, menacing, misanthropic, rebellious, reserved, retiring, unacceptable, unapproachable, uncommunicative, unfriendly, unsociable, withdrawn.

antonyms acceptable, sociable.

antithesis *n* antipode, contradiction, contradistinction, contraposition, contrariety, contrary, contrast, converse, inverse, inversion, opposite, opposite extreme, opposition, polarity, reversal, reverse.

antithetical *adj* antipodal, antipodean, antithetic, contradictory, contrary, contrasted, contrasting, converse, counter, inverse, opposed, opposite, polarised, poles apart, reverse.

anxiety *n* angst, anxiousness, apprehension, care, concern, craving, desire, disquiet, disquietude, distress, dread, dysthymia, eagerness, foreboding, fretfulness, impatience, keenness, misgiving, nervousness, presentiment, restlessness, solicitude, suspense, tension, torment, torture, unease, uneasiness, watchfulness, willingness, worriment, worry.

antonym composure.

anxious *adj* afraid, angst-ridden, apprehensive, avid, careful, concerned, desirous, disquieted, distressed, disturbed, eager, expectant, fearful, fretful, impatient, in suspense, intent, itching, keen, nervous, on tenterhooks, overwrought, restless, solicitous, taut, tense, tormented, tortured, troubled, uneasy, unquiet, watchful, worried, yearning.

antonym composed.

apace *adv* at full speed, at top speed, double-quick, expeditiously, fast, hastily, posthaste, quickly, rapidly, speedily, swiftly, without delay.

apart *adv* afar, alone, aloof, aside, asunder, away, by oneself, cut off, distant, distinct, divorced, excluded, in bits, in pieces, independent, independently, individually, into parts, isolated, on one's own, piecemeal, privately, separate, separated, separately, singly, to bits, to one side, to pieces.

apartment *n* accommodation, chambers, compartment, condominium, flat, living quarters, lodgings, maisonette, pad, penthouse, quarters, room, rooms, suite, tenement.

apathetic *adj* cold, cool, dispassionate, emotionless, impassive, indifferent, insensible, insentient, listless, numb, passive, phlegmatic, sluggish, stoic, torpid, unambitious, unconcerned, unemotional, unfeeling, uninterested, uninvolved, unmotivated, unmoved, unresponsive.

antonyms concerned, responsive.

apathy *n* accidie, acedia, coldness, coolness, emotionlessness, impassibility, impassivity, incuriousness, indifference, inertia, insensibility, lethargy, listlessness, passiveness, passivity, phlegm, sluggishness, torpor, unconcern, unfeelingness, uninterestedness, unresponsiveness.

antonyms concern, warmth.

ape *v* affect, caricature, copy, counterfeit, echo, imitate, mimic, mirror, mock, parody, parrot, take off.

n baboon, boor, brute, chimpanzee, gibbon, gorilla, jocko, monkey, oaf, orang-utan, pongid, pongo, savage.

aperture *n* breach, chink, cleft, crack, eye, eyelet, fissure, foramen, gap, hole, interstice, opening, orifice, passage, perforation, rent, rift, slit, slot, space, vent.

apex *n* acme, apogee, climax, consummation, crest, crown, crowning point, culmination, fastigium, height, high point, peak, pinnacle, point, summit, tip, top, vertex, zenith.

antonym nadir.

aphorism *n* adage, apothegm, axiom, dictum, epigram, gnome, maxim, mot, precept, proverb, saw, saying, sentence.

aphrodisiac *adj* amative, amatory, erogenous, erotic, erotogenous, venerous.

aplomb *n* assurance, audacity, balance, calmness, composure, confidence, coolness, equanimity, poise, sang-froid, savoir faire, self-assurance, self-confidence, self-possession.

antonym discomposure.

apocalyptic *adj* fatidic, ominous, oracular, portentous, prophetic, revelational, revelatory, signal, threatening, vatic.

apocryphal *adj* concocted, doubtful, dubious, equivocal, fabricated, fictitious, imaginary, legendary, mythical, phony, questionable, spurious, unauthenticated, uncanonical, unsubstantiated, unsupported, unverified.

antonym true.

apogee *n* acme, apex, climax, consummation, crest, crown, culmination, height, high point, meridian, peak, pinnacle, summit, tip, top, vertex, zenith.

antonyms nadir, perigee.

apologetic *adj* compunctious, conscience-stricken, contrite, excusatory, penitent, regretful, remorseful, repentant, rueful, sorry.

antonym defiant.

apologist *n* advocate, champion, defender, endorser, justifier, pleader, seconder, spokesman, supporter, upholder, vindicator.

antonym critic.

apology *n* acknowledgement, apologia, confession, defence, excuse, explanation, extenuation, justification, palliation, plea, semblance, substitute, travesty, vindication.

antonym defiance.

apophthegm *n* adage, aphorism, axiom, dictum, epigram, gnome, maxim, precept, proverb, saw, saying, sentence.

apostasy *n* defection, desertion, disloyalty, faithlessness, falseness, heresy, perfidy, rattery, ratting, recidivism, recreance, recreancy, renegation, renunciation, treachery, unfaithfulness.

antonyms loyalty, orthodoxy.

apostate *n* defector, deserter, heretic, recidivist, recreant, renegade, renegado, runagate, tergiversator, traitor, turncoat.

antonyms adherent, convert, loyalist.

adj disloyal, faithless, false, heretical, perfidious, recreant, renegate, traitorous, treacherous, unfaithful, unorthodox, untrue.

antonym faithful.

apostatise *v* backslide, defect, lapse, recant, renegue, renig, tergiversate, withdraw.

apostle *n* advocate, champion, crusader, evangelist, exponent, herald, messenger, missionary, pioneer, preacher, promoter, propagandist, propagator, proponent, proselytiser.

apotheosis *n* deification, elevation, exaltation, glorification, godding, idealisation, idolisation, immortalisation.

apotheosise *v* deify, elevate, exalt, glorify, god, idealise, idolise, immortalise.

appal *v* alarm, astound, daunt, disconcert, disgust, dishearten, dismay, frighten, harrow, horrify, intimidate, outrage, petrify, scare, shock, terrify, unnerve.

antonyms encourage, reassure.

appalling *adj* alarming, astounding, awful, daunting, dire, disheartening, dismaying, dreadful, fearful, frightening, frightful, ghastly, grim, harrowing, hideous, horrible, horrid, horrific, horrifying, intimidating, loathsome, petrifying, scaring, shocking, startling, terrible, terrifying, unnerving, wretched.

antonym reassuring.

apparatus *n* appliance, bureaucracy, contraption, device, equipment, framework, gadget, gear, gismo, hierarchy, implements, machine, machinery, materials, means, mechanism, network, organisation, outfit, set-up, structure, system, tackle, tools, utensils.

apparel *n* accoutrements, array, attire, clothes, clothing, costume, dress, equipment, garb, garments, garniture, gear, guise, habiliments, habit, outfit, raiment, rig-out, robes, suit, trappings, vestiture, vestments, wardrobe, weeds.

apparent *adj* clear, conspicuous, declared, discernible, distinct, evident, indubitable, manifest, marked, noticeable, obvious, on paper, open, ostensible, outward, overt, patent, perceptible, plain, seeming, specious, superficial, unmistakable, visible.

antonyms obscure, real.

apparently *adv* clearly, manifestly, obviously, ostensibly, outwardly, patently, plainly, seemingly, speciously, superficially.

apparition *n* chimera, eidolon, ghost, manifestation, materialisation, phantasm, phantom, presence, revenant, shade, spectre, spirit, spook, umbra, vision, visitant, visitation, wraith.

appeal[1] *n* adjuration, application, entreaty, imploration, invocation, orison, petition, plea, prayer, request, solicitation, suit, supplication.

v address, adjure, apply, ask, beg, beseech, call, call upon, entreat, implore, invoke, petition, plead, pray, refer, request, resort to, solicit, sue, supplicate.

appeal[2] *n* allure, attraction, attractiveness, beauty, charisma, charm, enchantment, fascination, interest, magnetism, winsomeness.

v allure, attract, charm, draw, engage, entice, fascinate, interest, invite, lure, please, tempt.

appear *v* act, arise, arrive, attend, be published, bob up, come into sight, come into view, come out, come to light, crop up, develop, emerge, enter, issue, leak out, look, loom, materialise, occur, perform, play, rise, seem, show, show up, surface, take part, transpire, turn out, turn up.

antonym disappear.

appearance *n* advent, air, appearing, arrival, aspect, bearing, brow, cast, character, coming, debut, demeanour, emergence, expression, façade, face, facies, favour, figure, form, front, guise, illusion, image, impression, introduction, look, looks, manner, mien, physiognomy, presence, pretence, seeming, semblance, show, the cut of one's jib.

antonyms disappearance, reality.

appease *v* allay, assuage, blunt, calm, compose, conciliate, diminish, ease, give a sop to, humour, lessen, lull, mitigate, mollify, pacify, placate, propitiate, quell, quench, quiet, reconcile, satisfy, soften, soothe, subdue, tranquillise.

antonym aggravate.

appeasement *n* acceding, accommodation, assuagement, compromise, concession, conciliation, humouring, lessening, mitigation, mollification, Munich, Munichism, pacification, placation, propitiation, quelling, quieting, satisfaction, softening, sop.

antonyms aggravation, resistance.

appellation *n* address, denomination, description, designation, epithet, label, monicker, name, nickname, sobriquet, style, term, title.

append *v* add, adjoin, affix, annex, attach, conjoin, fasten, join, subjoin, tack on.

appendage *n* accessory, addendum, addition, adjunct, affix, ancillary, annexe, appendix, appurtenance, attachment, auxiliary, excrescence, extremity, limb, member, projection, prosthesis, protuberance, supplement, tab, tag.

appendix *n* addendum, additament, addition, adjunct, appendage, codicil, epilogue, excursus, postscript, rider, supplement.

appertaining *adj* applicable, applying, belonging, characteristic, connected, germane, pertinent, related, relevant.

appetiser *n* antipasto, aperitif, bonne bouche, canape, cocktail, foretaste, hors d'oeuvre, preview, sample, taste, taster, titbit, whet.

appetising *adj* appealing, delicious, inviting, lip-smacking, moreish, mouthwatering, palatable, piquant, savoury, scrumptious, succulent, tasty, tempting, toothsome, yummy.

antonym disgusting.

appetite *n* appetence, appetency, craving, demand, desire, eagerness, hankering, hunger, inclination, keenness, liking, limosis, longing, orexis, passion, predilection, proclivity, propensity, relish, stomach, taste, willingness, yearning, zeal, zest.

antonym distaste.

applaud *v* acclaim, approve, cheer, clap, commend, compliment, congratulate, encourage, eulogise, extol, laud, ovate, praise.

antonyms censure, disparage.

applauding *adj* acclamatory, adulatory, approving, commendatory, complimentary, congratulatory, laudatory, plauditory, plausive.

antonym abusive.

applause *n* acclaim, acclamation, accolade, approbation, approval, cheering, cheers, commendation, congratulation, encomium, eulogies, eulogising, hand, laudation, ovation, plaudits, praise.

antonyms censure, disparagement.

appliance *n* apparatus, contraption, contrivance, device, gadget, gismo, implement, instrument, machine, mechanism, tool.

applicable *adj* apposite, appropriate, apropos, apt, befitting, fit, fitting, germane, legitimate, pertinent, proper, related, relevant, suitable, suited, useful, valid.

antonym inapplicable.

applicant *n* aspirant, candidate, claimant, competitor, contestant, inquirer, interviewee, petitioner, postulant, suitor.

application[1] *n* adhibition, appeal, appositeness, apposition, assiduity, attention, attentiveness, claim, commitment, dedication, diligence, effort, exercise, extension, function, germaneness, industry, inquiry, keenness, lesson, moral, perseverance, pertinence, petition, practice, purpose, reference, relevance, request, requisition, sedulity, sedulousness, solicitation, suit, use, value.

application[2] *n* balm, cream, dressing, emollient, lotion, medication, ointment, poultice, preparation, salve, unguent.

apply[1] *v* adhibit, administer, appose, assign, bring into play, bring to bear, direct, employ, engage, execute, exercise, implement, ply, practise, resort to, set, use, utilise, wield.

apply[2] *v* appertain, be relevant, fit, have force, pertain, refer, relate, suit.

apply[3] *v* anoint, cover with, lay on, paint, place, put on, rub, smear, spread on, use.

apply[4] *v* appeal, ask for, claim, indent for, inquire, petition, put in, request, requisition, solicit, sue.

apply[5] *v* address, bend, buckle down, commit, concentrate, dedicate, devote, direct, give, persevere, settle down, study, throw.

appoint *v* allot, arrange, assign, charge, choose, command, commission, constitute, co-opt, decide, decree, delegate, designate, destine, detail, determine, devote, direct, elect, engage, enjoin, equip, establish, fit out, fix, furnish, install, name, nominate, ordain, outfit, plenish, provide, select, set, settle, supply.

antonyms dismiss, reject.

appointed *adj* allotted, arranged, assigned, chosen, commanded, commissioned, co-opted, dative, decided, decreed, delegated, designated, determined, directed, elected, enjoined, equipped, established, fitted out, fixed, furnished, installed, invested, named, nominated, ordained, plenished, preordained, provided, selected, set, settled, supplied.

appointment *n* allotment, arrangement, assignation, assignment, choice, choosing, commissioning, consultation, date, delegation, election, engagement, installation, interview, job, meeting, naming, nomination, office, place, position, post, rendezvous, selection, session, situation, station, tryst.

appointments *n* accoutrements, appurtenances, equipage, fittings, fixtures, furnishings, furniture, gear, outfit, paraphernalia, plenishings, trappings.

apportion *v* accord, admeasure, allocate, allot, assign, award, deal, dispense, distribute, divide, dole out, grant, measure out, mete, morsel, portion out, ration, share.

apportionment *n* allocation, allotment, assignment, dealing, dispensation, dispensing, distribution, division, divvying up, doling, measuring, meting, partitioning, sharing.

apposite *adj* applicable, appropriate, apropos, apt, befitting, condign, felicitous, germane, in point, pertinent, proper, relevant, suitable, suited, to the point, to the purpose.

antonym inapposite.

appraisal *n* appreciation, assay, assaying, assessment, estimate, estimation, evaluation, examination, inspection, judgement, once-over, opinion, pricing, rating, reckoning, review, sizing-up, survey, valuation.

appraise *v* assay, assess, estimate, evaluate, examine, gauge, inspect, judge, price, rate, review, size up, survey, valuate, value.

appreciable *adj* apparent, ascertainable, clear-cut, considerable, definite, detectable, discernible, distinguishable, evident, marked, material, measurable, noticeable, obvious, perceivable, perceptible, pronounced, recognisable, significant, substantial, undeniable, visible.

antonyms imperceptible, negligible.

appreciate[1] *v* acknowledge, admire, be sensible of, be sensitive to, cherish, comprehend, dig, do justice to, enjoy, esteem, estimate, know, like, perceive, prize, realise, recognise, regard, relish, respect, savour, sympathise with, take kindly to, treasure, understand, value.

antonyms despise, overlook.

appreciate[2] *v* enhance, gain, grow, improve, increase, inflate, mount, rise, strengthen.

antonym depreciate.

appreciation[1] *n* acclamation, acknowledgement, admiration, appraisal, assessment, awareness, cognisance, comprehension, criticism, critique, enjoyment, esteem, estimation, gratefulness, gratitude, indebtedness, judgement, knowledge, liking, notice, obligation, perception, praise, realisation, recognition, regard, relish, respect, responsiveness, review, sensitivity, sympathy, thankfulness, thanks, tribute, understanding, valuation.

antonyms ingratitude, neglect.

appreciation[2] *n* climb, enhancement, gain, growth, improvement, increase, inflation, rise, the up-and-up.

antonym depreciation.

appreciative *adj* admiring, aware, beholden, cognisant, conscious, encouraging, enthusiastic, grateful, indebted, knowledgeable, mindful, obliged, perceptive, pleased, regardful, respectful, responsive, sensible, sensitive, supportive, sympathetic, thankful, understanding.

antonym ungrateful.

apprehend[1] *v* arrest, bust, capture, catch, collar, detain, get, grab, nab, nick, pinch, run in, seize, take.

apprehend[2] *v* appreciate, believe, comprehend, conceive, consider, discern, grasp, imagine, know, perceive, realise, recognise, see, twig, understand.

apprehension[1] *n* arrest, capture, catching, seizure, taking.

apprehension[2] *n* alarm, anxiety, apprehensiveness, awareness, belief, comprehension, concept, conception, concern, conjecture, discernment, disquiet, doubt, dread, fear, foreboding, grasp, idea, impression, intellect, intellection, intelligence, ken, knowledge, misgiving, mistrust, nervousness, notion, opinion, perception, premonition, presentiment, qualm, sentiment, suspicion, thought, understanding, unease, uneasiness, uptake, view, worry.

apprehensive *adj* afraid, alarmed, anxious, concerned, disquieted, distrustful, disturbed, doubtful, fearful, mistrustful, nervous, solicitous, suspicious, uneasy, worried.

antonym confident.

apprentice *n* beginner, cub, learner, neophyte, newcomer, novice, probationer, pupil, recruit, starter, student, trainee, tyro.

antonym expert.

apprise *v* acquaint, advise, brief, communicate, enlighten, inform, intimate, notify, tell, tip off, warn.

approach *v* advance, anear, appeal to, apply to, approximate, be like, begin, broach, catch up, come close, come near to, commence, compare with, draw near, embark on, gain on, introduce, make advances, make overtures, meet, mention, near, reach, resemble, set about, sound out, undertake.

n access, advance, advent, appeal, application, approximation, arrival, attitude, avenue, course, doorway, entrance, gesture, invitation, landfall, likeness, manner, means, method, mode, modus operandi, motion, nearing, offer, overture, passage, procedure, proposal, proposition, resemblance, road, semblance, style, system, technique, threshold, way.

approachable *adj* accessible, affable, agreeable, attainable, congenial, conversable, cordial, easy, friendly, informal, open, reachable, sociable.

antonym unapproachable.

approbation *n* acceptance, acclaim, acclamation, applause, approval, assent, commendation, congratulation, encouragement, endorsement, esteem, favour, kudos, laudation, praise, ratification, recognition, regard, sanction, support.

antonym disapprobation.

appropriate *adj* applicable, apposite, appurtenant, apropos, apt, becoming, befitting, belonging, condign, congruous, correct, felicitous, fit, fitting, germane, meet, merited, opportune, pertinent, proper, relevant, right, seasonable, seemly, spot-on, suitable, timely, to the point, well-chosen, well-suited, well-timed.

antonym inappropriate.

v allocate, allot, annex, apportion, arrogate, assign, assume, commandeer, confiscate, devote, earmark, embezzle, expropriate, filch, impound, impropriate, misappropriate, pilfer, pocket, possess oneself of, pre-empt, purloin, seize, set apart, steal, take, usurp.

appropriateness *n* applicability, appositeness, aptness, becomingness, condignness, congruousness, correctness, felicitousness, felicity, fitness, germaneness, justness, opportuneness, pertinence, properness, propriety, relevance, rightness, seemliness, suitability, timeliness.

appropriation *n* allocation, allotment, annexation, apportionment, arrogation, assignment, assumption, commandeering, confiscation, dispensation, earmarking, expropriation, impoundment, misappropriation, pre-emption, seizure, setting apart, usurpation.

approval *n* acclaim, acclamation, acquiescence, admiration, adoption, agreement, applause, appreciation, approbation, approof, assent, authorisation, blessing, certification, commendation, compliance, concurrence, confirmation, consent, countenance, endorsement, esteem, favour, go-ahead, good opinion, green light, honour, imprimatur, leave, licence, liking, mandate, OK, permission, plaudits, praise, ratification, recommendation, regard, respect, sanction, support, thumbs-up, validation.

antonym disapproval.

approve *v* accede to, accept, acclaim, admire, adopt, advocate, agree to, allow, applaud, appreciate, assent to, authorise, back, bless, commend, comply with, concur in, confirm, consent to, countenance, dig, endorse, esteem, favour, homologate, like, mandate, OK, pass, permit, praise, ratify, recommend, regard, respect, rubber-stamp, sanction, second, support, take kindly to, uphold, validate.

antonym disapprove.

approved *adj* acceptable, accepted, authorised, comme il faut, correct, favoured, official, permissible, permitted, preferred, proper, recognised, recommended, sanctioned.

antonym unorthodox.

approximate *adj* ballpark, close, comparable, conjectural, estimated, extrapolated, guessed, inexact, like, loose, near, relative, rough, similar, verging on.

antonym exact.

v approach, be tantamount to, border on, resemble, verge on.

approximately *adv* about, almost, around, circa, close to, coming up to, in round numbers, in the region of, in the vicinity of, just about, loosely, more or less, nearly, not far off, pushing, relatively, roughly, round about, well-nigh.

antonym exactly.

approximation *n* approach, conjecture, correspondence, estimate, estimation, extrapolation, guess, guesstimate, guesswork, likeness, proximity, resemblance, rough calculation, rough idea, semblance.

antonyms exactitude, precision.

appurtenance *n* accessory, accompaniment, addition, adjunct, annexe, appanage, appendage, appurtenant, attachment, auxiliary, concomitant, incidental, subordinate, subsidiary, supplement.

appurtenances *n* accessories, accompaniments, accoutrements, appendages, equipment, gear, impedimenta, kit, paraphernalia, trappings, traps.

apropos *adj* applicable, apposite, appropriate, apt, befitting, belonging, condign, correct, fit, fitting, germane, meet, opportune, pertinent, proper, related, relevant, right, seemly, suitable, timely, to the point.

antonym inappropriate.

adv appositely, appropriately, aptly, by the bye, by the way, en passant, in passing, incidentally, opportunely, pat, pertinently, properly, relevantly, suitably, to the point.

antonym inappropriately.

apropos of in connection with, in relation to, in respect of, on the subject of, re, regarding, respecting, with reference to, with regard to, with respect to.

apt *adj* accurate, adept, applicable, apposite, appropriate, apropos, astute, befitting, bright, clever, condign, correct, disposed, expert, fair, fit, fitting, germane, gifted, given, gleg, inclined, ingenious, intelligent, liable, likely, meet, pertinent, prompt, prone, proper, quick, ready, relevant, seasonable, seemly, sharp, skilful, smart, spot-on, suitable, talented, teachable, tending, timely.

antonym inapt.

aptitude *n* ability, aptness, bent, capability, capacity, cleverness, disposition, facility, faculty, flair, gift, inclination, intelligence, knack, leaning, penchant, predilection, proclivity, proficiency, proneness, propensity, quickness, talent, tendency.

antonym inaptitude.

aptness *n* ability, accuracy, applicability, appositeness, appropriateness, aptitude, becomingness, bent, capability, capacity, cleverness, condignness, congruousness, correctness, disposition, facility, faculty, felicitousness, felicity, fitness, fittingness, flair, germaneness, gift, inclination, intelligence, knack, leaning, liability, likelihood, likeliness, opportuneness, pertinence, predilection, proclivity, proficiency, proneness, propensity, properness, quickness, readiness, relevance, rightness, seemliness, suitability, talent, tendency, timeliness.

arbiter *n* adjudicator, arbiter elegantiarum, arbitrator, authority, controller, dictator, expert, intermediary, judge, master, mediator, negotiator, pundit, referee, ruler, umpire.

arbitrariness *n* absoluteness, capriciousness, despotism, dogmatism, fancifulness, high-handedness, imperiousness, inconsistency, irrationality, irresponsibility, peremptoriness, randomness, subjectivity, summariness, tyranny, unreasonableness, waywardness, whimsicality, wilfulness.

arbitrary *adj* absolute, autocratic, capricious, chance, despotic, dictatorial, discretionary, dogmatic, domineering, erratic, fanciful, high-handed, imperious, inconsistent, instinctive, magisterial, optional, overbearing, peremptory, personal, random, subjective, summary, tyrannical, tyrannous, unreasonable, unreasoned, unsupported, whimsical, wilful.

antonyms circumspect, rational, reasoned.

arbitrate *v* adjudge, adjudicate, decide, determine, judge, pass judgement, referee, settle, umpire.

arbitration *n* adjudication, arbitrament, decision, determination, intervention, judgement, mediation, negotiation, settlement.

arbitrator *n* adjudicator, arbiter, intermediary, judge, mediator, moderator, negotiator, referee, umpire.

arcade *n* cloister, colonnade, covered way, gallery, loggia, mall, peristyle, portico, precinct, stoa.

arcane *adj* abstruse, cabbalistic, cryptic, enigmatic, esoteric, hidden, mysterious, mystical, obscure, occult, profound, recondite, secret.

antonym commonplace.

arch[1] *n* arc, archway, bend, bow, concave, cupola, curvature, curve, dome, flexure, semicircle, span, vault.

v arc, bend, bow, camber, curve, embow, extend, vault.

arch[2] *adj* accomplished, chief, consummate, coy, egregious, espiègle, expert, finished, first, first-class, foremost, frolicsome, greatest, highest, knowing, leading, main, major, master, mischievous, pert, playful, pre-eminent, primary, principal, provocative, roguish, saucy, sly, top, waggish, wily.

archaic *adj* ancient, antediluvian, antiquated, antique, bygone, demode, fogram, obsolete, old, old hat, old-fashioned, outdated, outmoded, out-of-date, passe, primitive, quaint, superannuated, Wardour Street.

antonym modern.

archetype *n* classic, conception, exemplar, form, idea, ideal, model, original, paradigm, pattern, precursor, prototype, standard, type.

architect *n* artist, author, constructor, contriver, creator, designer, deviser, engineer, fabricator, fashioner, founder, instigator, inventor, maker, master builder, originator, planner, prime mover, shaper.

architecture *n* architectonics, arrangement, building, composition, construction, design, framework, make-up, planning, structure, style.

archive *n* library, muniment room, museum, record office, registry, repository.

archives *n* annals, chronicles, deeds, documents, ledgers, memorabilia, memorials, muniments, papers, records, registers, roll.

ardent *adj* amorous, avid, devoted, eager, enthusiastic, fervent, fervid, fierce, fiery, hot, hot-blooded, impassioned, intense, keen, lusty, passionate, perfervid, spirited, vehement, warm, zealous.

antonym dispassionate.

ardour *n* animation, avidity, devotion, eagerness, earnestness, empressement, enthusiasm, feeling, fervour, fire, heat, intensity, keenness, lust, passion, spirit, vehemence, warmth, zeal, zest.

antonyms coolness, indifference.

arduous *adj* backbreaking, burdensome, daunting, difficult, exhausting, fatiguing, formidable, gruelling, hard, harsh, herculean, laborious, onerous, punishing, rigorous, severe, strenuous, taxing, tiring, toilsome, tough, troublesome, trying, uphill, wearisome.

antonym easy.

area *n* arena, bailiwick, ball-park, breadth, canvas, compass, department, district, domain, environs, expanse, extent, field, locality, neighbourhood, part, patch, pidgin, portion, province, range, realm, region, scope, section, sector, size, sphere, stretch, terrain, territory, tract, width, zone.

arena *n* amphitheatre, area, battlefield, battleground, bowl, coliseum, field, ground, lists, park, ring, scene, stadium, stage.

argot *n* cant, dialect, idiom, jargon, lingo, parlance, patois, slang, terminology, usage, vernacular, vocabulary.

argue *v* altercate, argufy, assert, bicker, chop logic, claim, contend, convince, debate, demonstrate, denote, disagree, discuss, display, dispute, evidence, evince, exhibit, expostulate, fall out, fence, feud, fight, haggle, hold, imply, indicate, join issue, logicise, maintain, manifest, moot, persuade, plead, prevail upon, prove, quarrel, question, reason, remonstrate, show, squabble, suggest, talk into, wrangle.

argument *n* abstract, altercation, argumentation, assertion, barney, beef, bickering, case, claim, clash, contention, controversy, debate, defence, demonstration, dialectic, difference, disagreement, discussion, dispute, exposition, expostulation, feud, fight, gist, ground, lemma, logic, logomachy, outline, plea, pleading, plot, polemic, quarrel, questioning, quodlibet, reason, reasoning, remonstrance, remonstration, row, set-to, shouting-match, squabble, story, story line, subject, summary, synopsis, theme, thesis, wrangle.

argumentative *adj* belligerent, captious, combative, contentious, contrary, disputatious, disputative, dissentious, litigious, opinionated, perverse, polemical, quarrelsome, wranglesome.

antonym complaisant.

arid *adj* baked, barren, boring, colourless, desert, desiccated, dreary, droughty, dry, dull, empty, flat, infertile, jejune, lifeless, moistureless, monotonous, parched, spiritless, sterile, tedious, torrid, torrefied, uninspired, uninteresting, unproductive, vapid, waste, waterless.

antonyms fertile, lively.

aridity *n* aridness, barrenness, boredom, colourlessness, dreariness, dryness, dullness, emptiness, flatness, infertility, jejuneness, jejunity, lifelessness, monotony, sterility, tedium, vapidity, vapidness.

antonyms fertility, liveliness, productivity, variety.

aright *adv* accurately, aptly, correctly, de règle, deasil, duly, en règle, exactly, fitly, justly, properly, rightly, suitably, truly.

arise *v* appear, ascend, begin, climb, come to light, commence, crop up, derive, emanate, emerge, ensue, flow, follow, get up, go up, grow, happen, issue, lift, mount, occur, originate, proceed, result, rise, set in, soar, spring, stand up, start, stem, tower, wake up.

aristocracy *n* elite, gentility, gentry, haut monde, nobility, noblemen, noblesse, optimates, patricians, patriciate, peerage, quality, ruling class, top drawer, upper class, upper crust.

antonyms canaille, the plebs.

aristocrat *n* eupatrid, grand seigneur, grande dame, grandee, lady, lord, lordling, nob, noble, nobleman, noblewoman, optimate, patrician, peer, peeress, swell, toff.

antonym commoner.

aristocratic *adj* blue-blooded, courtly, dignified, elegant, elite, fine, gentle, gentlemanly, haughty, highborn, lordly, noble, patricianly, polished, refined, supercilious, thoroughbred, titled, upper-class, upper-crust, well-born, well-bred.

antonyms plebeian, vulgar.

arithmetic *n* algorism, algorithm, calculation, ciphering, computation, count, counting, mathematics, numeration, reckoning.

arm[1] *n* appendage, authority, bough, brachium, branch, channel, department, detachment, division, estuary, extension, firth, inlet, limb, offshoot, projection, section, sector, sound, strait, sway, tributary, upper limb.

arm[2] *v* accoutre, ammunition, array, brace, empanoply, equip, forearm, fortify, furnish, gird, issue with, munition, nuclearise, outfit, prepare, prime, protect, provide, reinforce, rig, steel, strengthen, supply.

armaments *n* ammunition, arms, artillery, cannon, guns, materiel, munitions, ordnance, weaponry, weapons.

armed *adj* accoutred, armoured, arrayed, braced, briefed, equipped, fitted out, forearmed, fortified, furnished, girded, guarded, prepared, primed, protected, provided, steeled, strengthened, thorny.

antonyms unarmed, unprepared.

armour *n* armature, carapace, chain-mail, garniture, iron-cladding, mail, shell, steel-plating.

armoured *adj* armour-plated, bomb-proof, bullet-proof, iron-clad, mail-clad, mailed, protected, steel-plated.

armoury *n* ammunition dump, arsenal, depot, garderobe, magazine, ordnance depot, repertoire, repository, stock, stock-in-trade, stockpile.

arms[1] *n* armaments, firearms, guns, instruments of war, ordnance, weaponry, weapons.

arms[2] *n* armorial bearings, blazonry, crest, escutcheon, hatchment, heraldry, insignia, scutcheon, shield.

army *n* armed force, array, arrière-ban, cohorts, fyrd, gang, horde, host, land forces, legions, military, militia, mob, multitude, pack, soldiers, soldiery, swarm, the junior service, throng, troops.

aroma *n* bouquet, fragrance, fumet(te), odour, perfume, redolence, savour, scent, smell.

aromatic *adj* balmy, fragrant, odoriferous, perfumed, pungent, redolent, savoury, spicy, sweet-smelling.

antonym acrid.

around *prep* about, approximately, circa, circling, circumambient, circumjacent, encircling, enclosing, encompassing, environing, more or less, on all sides of, on every side of, roughly, surrounding.

adv about, abroad, all over, at hand, close, close by, everywhere, here and there, in all directions, in the air, near, nearby, nigh, on all sides, to and fro.

arouse *v* agitate, animate, awaken, bestir, call forth, disentrance, enliven, evoke, excite, foment, foster, galvanise, goad, incite, inflame, instigate, kindle, move, prompt, provoke, quicken, rouse, sharpen, spark, spur, startle, stimulate, stir up, summon up, wake up, waken, warm, whet, whip up.

antonyms calm, lull, quieten.

arraign *v* accuse, attack, call to account, charge, denounce, impeach, impugn, incriminate, indict, prosecute.

arrange[1] *v* adjust, align, array, categorise, class, classify, collocate, concert, construct, contrive, co-ordinate, design, determine, devise, dispose, distribute, fettle, file, fix, form, format, group, lay out, marshal, methodise, order, organise, plan, position, prepare, project, range, rank, regulate, schedule, set out, settle, sift, sort, sort out, stage-manage, style, swing, systematise, tidy, trim.

arrange[2] *v* adapt, harmonise, instrument, orchestrate, score, set.

arrangement[1] *n* adjustment, agreement, alignment, array, Ausgleich, battery, classification, compact, compromise, construction, deal, design, display, disposition, form, grouping, layout, line-up, marshalling, method, modus vivendi, order, ordering, organisation, plan, planning, preconcert, preparation, provision, ranging, rank, schedule, scheme, settlement, set-up, spacing, structure, system, tabulation, taxis, terms.

arrangement[2] *n* adaptation, harmonisation, instrumentation, interpretation, orchestration, score, setting, version.

arrant *adj* absolute, atrocious, barefaced, blatant, brazen, complete, downright, egregious, extreme, flagrant, gross, incorrigible, infamous, monstrous, notorious, out-and-out, outright, rank, thorough, thoroughgoing, undisguised, unmitigated, unregenerate, utter, vile.

array *n* apparel, arrangement, assemblage, attire, battery, clothes, collection, display, disposition, dress, equipage, exhibition, exposition, finery, formation, garb, garments, line-up, marshalling, muster, order, parade, raiment, regalia, robes, show, supply.

v accoutre, adorn, align, apparel, arrange, assemble, attire, bedeck, bedizen, caparison, clothe, deck, decorate, display, dispose, draw up, dress, equip, exhibit, form up, garb, group, habilitate, line up, marshal, muster, order, outfit, parade, range, rig out, robe, show, supply, trick out, wrap.

arrest *v* absorb, apprehend, block, bust, capture, catch, check, collar, delay, detain, divert, end, engage, engross, fascinate, grip, halt, hinder, hold, impede, inhibit, interrupt, intrigue, lay, nab, nick, nip, obstruct, occupy, pinch, prevent, restrain, retard, run in, seize, slow, stall, stanch, stay, stem, stop, suppress.

n apprehension, blockage, bust, caption, capture, cessation, check, cop, delay, detention, end, halt, hindrance, inhibition, interruption, obstruction, prevention, restraint, seizure, stalling, stay, stoppage, suppression, suspension.

arresting *adj* amazing, conspicuous, engaging, extraordinary, impressive, notable, noteworthy, noticeable, outstanding, remarkable, striking, stunning, surprising.

antonyms inconspicuous, unremarkable.

arrival *n* accession, advent, appearance, approach, caller, comer, coming, debutant(e), entrance, entrant, happening, incomer, landfall, newcomer, occurrence, visitant, visitor.

antonym departure.

arrive *v* alight, appear, attain, befall, come, enter, fetch, get to the top, happen, land, make it, materialise, occur, reach, show, show up, succeed, turn up.

antonym depart.

arrogance *n* airs, conceit, conceitedness, condescension, contempt, contemptuousness, contumely, disdain, disdainfulness, haughtiness, hauteur, high-handedness, hubris, imperiousness, insolence, loftiness, lordliness, morgue, presumption, presumptuousness, pretension, pretentiousness, pride, scorn, scornfulness, superciliousness, superiority, uppishness.

antonym humility.

arrogant *adj* assuming, conceited, condescending, contemptuous, contumelious, disdainful, fastuous, haughty, high and mighty, high-handed, hubristic, imperious, insolent, lordly, on the high ropes, overbearing, overweening, presumptuous, proud, scornful, supercilious, superior, uppish.

antonym humble.

arrogate *v* appropriate, assume, commandeer, confiscate, demand, expropriate, misappropriate, possess oneself of, presume, seize, usurp.

arrow *n* bolt, dart, flight, indicator, pointer, shaft.

arsenal *n* ammunition dump, armoury, depot, magazine, ordnance depot, repository, stock, stockpile, store, storehouse, supply, warehouse.

arson *n* fire-raising, incendiarism, pyromania.

arsonist *n* fire-bug, fire-raiser, incendiary, pyromaniac.

art *n* address, adroitness, aptitude, artfulness, artifice, artistry, artwork, astuteness, contrivance, craft, craftiness, craftsmanship, cunning, deceit, dexterity, draughtsmanship, drawing, expertise, facility, finesse, guile, ingenuity, knack, knowledge, mastery, method, metier, painting, profession, sculpture, skill, slyness, subtlety, trade, trick, trickery, virtu, virtuosity, visuals, wiliness.

artful *adj* adept, adroit, canny, clever, crafty, cunning, deceitful, designing, devious, dexterous, fly, foxy, ingenious, masterly, politic, resourceful, ruse, scheming, sharp, shrewd, skilful, sly, smart, subtle, tricksy, tricky, vulpine, wily.

antonyms artless, ingenuous, naïve.

article *n* account, bit, clause, commodity, composition, constituent, count, detail, discourse, division, element, essay, feature, head, heading, item, matter, object, paper, paragraph, part, particular, piece, point, portion, report, review, section, story, thing, unit.

articulate[1] *adj* clear, coherent, comprehensible, distinct, eloquent, expressive, facile, fluent, intelligible, lucid, meaningful, understandable, vocal, well-spoken.

v breathe, elocute, enounce, enunciate, express, pronounce, say, speak, state, talk, utter, verbalise, vocalise, voice.

articulate[2] *v* attach, connect, couple, fasten, fit together, hinge, interlock, join, joint, link.

articulation[1] *n* delivery, diction, enunciation, expression, pronunciation, saying, speaking, talking, utterance, verbalisation, vocalisation, voicing.

articulation[2] *n* arthrosis, conjunction, connection, coupling, hinge, interlinking, interlock, joint, jointing, juncture, link.

artifice *n* adroitness, artfulness, chicanery, cleverness, contrivance, cozenage, craft, craftiness, cunning, deception, deftness, device, dodge, duplicity, expedient, facility, finesse, fraud, guile, hoax, invention, machination, manipulation, manoeuvre, ruse, scheme, shift, skill, slyness, stratagem, strategy, subterfuge, subtlety, tactic, trick, trickery, wile.

artificer *n* architect, artisan, builder, constructer, contriver, craftsman, creator, designer, deviser, fabricator, fashioner, framer, inventor, maker, mechanic, opificer, originator.

artificial *adj* affected, assumed, bogus, contrived, counterfeit, ersatz, factitious, fake, false, feigned, forced, hyped up, imitation, insincere, made-up, man-made, mannered, manufactured, meretricious, mock, non-natural, phoney, plastic, pretended, pseudo, sham, simulated, specious, spurious, stagey, synthetic, unnatural.

antonyms genuine, natural.

artillery *n* battery, cannon, cannonry, enginery, field-guns, field-pieces, gunnage, gunnery, guns, heavy metal, ordnance.

artisan *n* artificer, craftsman, expert, handicraftsman, journeyman, mechanic, operative, technician, workman.

artist *n* colourist, craftsman, draughtsman, expert, maestro, master, muralist, painter, portraitist, portrait-painter, sculptor, water-colourist.

artiste *n* actor, comedian, comedienne, comic, entertainer, moke, performer, player, trouper, variety artist, vaudevillian.

artistic *adj* aesthetic, beautiful, bohemian, creative, cultivated, cultured, decorative, elegant, exquisite, graceful, harmonious, imaginative, ornamental, refined, sensitive, skilled, stylish, talented, tasteful.

antonym inelegant.

artistry *n* accomplishment, art, brilliance, craft, craftsmanship, creativity, deftness, expertise, finesse, flair, genius, mastery, proficiency, sensibility, sensitivity, skill, style, talent, taste, touch, virtuosity, workmanship.

antonym ineptitude.

artless *adj* candid, childlike, direct, frank, genuine, guileless, honest, humble, ingenuous, innocent, naïf, naïve, naked, natural, open, plain, primitive, pure, simple, sincere, straightforward, true, trustful, trusting, unadorned, unaffected, uncontrived, undesigning, unpretentious, unsophisticated, unwary, unworldly.

antonym artful.

artlessness *n* candour, directness, frankness, genuineness, honesty, humbleness, humility, ingenuousness, innocence, naïvete, naïvety, naturalness, openness, purity, simplicity, sincerity, straightforwardness, trustfulness, unpretentiousness, unwariness, unworldliness.

antonym cunning.

as *conj, prep* because, being, considering that, for example, for instance, in that, in the character of, in the manner of, in the part of, in the role of, inasmuch as, like, seeing that, since, such as, that, to wit, what, when, which, while.

as a rule characteristically, customarily, generally, habitually, mainly, normally, ordinarily, regularly, typically, usually.

as for as regards, in connection with, in reference to, on the subject of, with reference to, with regard to, with relation to, with respect to.

as it were as it might be, in a manner of speaking, in a way, in some way, so to say, so to speak.

as long as assuming, on condition that, provided, supposing, with the provision that.

ascend *v* climb, float up, fly up, go up, lift off, mount, move up, rise, scale, slope upwards, soar, take off, tower.

antonym descend.

ascendancy *n* authority, command, control, dominance, domination, dominion, edge, hegemony, influence, leadership, lordship, mastery, power, predominance, pre-eminence, prestige, prevalence, reign, rule, sovereignty, superiority, supremacy, sway, upper hand.

antonyms decline, subordination.

ascendant *adj* ascending, authoritative, climbing, commanding, controlling, dominant, influential, levitating, lifting, mounting, powerful, predominant, pre-eminent, prevailing, rising, ruling, superior, supreme, upgoing, uphill, uppermost.

antonyms descending, subordinate.

ascension *n* arising, ascent, climb, levitation, lifting, mounting, raising, rise, rising.

antonym descent.

ascent *n* acclivity, advancement, anabasis, ascending, ascension, brae, clamber, clambering, climb, climbing, elevation, escalation, gradient, hill, incline, mounting, ramp, rise, rising, scaling, slope.

antonym descent.

ascertain *v* confirm, detect, determine, discover, establish, find out, fix, identify, learn, locate, make certain, settle, verify.

ascetic *n* abstainer, anchorite, celibate, flagellant, hermit, monk, nun, puritan, recluse, solitary, Spartan, stylite.

antonym voluptuary.

adj abstemious, abstinent, austere, celibate, continent, frugal, harsh, plain, puritanical, rigorous, self-controlled, self-denying, self-disciplined, severe, Spartan, stern, strict, temperate.

antonym voluptuous.

asceticism *n* abstemiousness, abstinence, ascesis, austerity, celibacy, continence, frugality, harshness, moderation, monasticism, plainness, puritanism, rigorousness, rigour, self-abnegation, self-control, self-denial, self-discipline, temperance.

antonym voluptuousness.

ascribe *v* accredit, arrogate, assign, attribute, chalk up to, charge, credit, impute, put down.

ashamed *adj* abashed, apologetic, bashful, blushing, chagrined, confused, conscience-stricken, crestfallen, discomfited, discomposed, distressed, embarrassed, guilty, hesitant, humbled, humiliated, modest, mortified, prudish, red in the face, redfaced, reluctant, remorseful, self-conscious, shamefaced, sheepish, shy, sorry, unwilling, verecund.

antonyms defiant, shameless.

ashen *adj* anaemic, ashy, blanched, bleached, colourless, ghastly, grey, leaden, livid, pale, pallid, pasty, wan, white.

antonym ruddy.

aside *adv* alone, apart, away, in isolation, in reserve, on one side, out of the way, privately, secretly, separately.

n departure, digression, excursion, excursus, interpolation, interposition, parenthesis, soliloquy, whisper.

asinine *adj* absurd, brainless, cretinous, daft, doltish, dunderheaded, fatuous, foolish, goofy, gormless, half-witted, idiotic, imbecile, imbecilic, inane, moronic, obstinate, potty, senseless, silly, stupid, witless.

antonyms intelligent, sensible.

ask *v* appeal, apply, beg, beseech, bid, catechise, claim, clamour, crave, demand, enquire, entreat, implore, importune, indent, interrogate, invite, order, petition, plead, pray, press, query, question, quiz, request, require, seek, solicit, sue, summon, supplicate.

askance *adv* contemptuously, disapprovingly, disdainfully, distrustfully, doubtfully, dubiously, indirectly, mistrustfully, obliquely, sceptically, scornfully, sideways, suspiciously.

askew *adv, adj* aglee, agley, aslant, asymmetric, awry, cock-eyed, crooked, crookedly, lopsided, oblique, off-centre, out of line, skew, skew-whiff, squint.

asleep *adj* benumbed, comatose, dead to the world, dormant, dormient, dozing, fast asleep, inactive, inert, napping, numb, reposing, sleeping, slumbering, snoozing, sound asleep, unconscious.

aspect *n* air, angle, appearance, attitude, bearing, condition, countenance, demeanour, direction, elevation, exposure, expression, face, facet, feature, look, manner, mien, outlook, physiognomy, point of view, position, prospect, scene, side, situation, standpoint, view, visage.

asperity *n* acerbity, acidity, acrimony, astringency, bitterness, causticity, churlishness, crabbedness, crossness, harshness, irascibility, irritability, peevishness, roughness, severity, sharpness, sourness.

antonym mildness.

aspersion *n* abuse, animadversion, calumny, censure, criticism, defamation, denigration, derogation, detraction, disparagement, mud-slinging, obloquy, reproach, slander, slur, smear, traducement, vilification, vituperation.

antonyms commendation, compliment.

asphyxiate *v* burke, choke, garrotte, smother, stifle, strangle, strangulate, suffocate, throttle.

aspirant *n* applicant, aspirer, candidate, competitor, contestant, hopeful, postulant, seeker, striver, suitor.

aspiration *n* aim, ambition, craving, desire, dream, eagerness, endeavour, goal, hankering, hope, ideal, intent, longing, object, objective, purpose, wish, yearning.

aspire *v* aim, crave, desire, dream, ettle, hanker, hope, intend, long, purpose, pursue, seek, wish, yearn.

aspiring *adj* ambitious, aspirant, eager, endeavouring, enterprising, hopeful, keen, longing, optimistic, striving, wishful, would-be.

ass[1] *n* blockhead, bonehead, cretin, dolt, dope, dunce, fool, half-wit, idiot, moron, nincompoop, ninny, nitwit, numskull, schmuck, simpleton, twerp, twit.

ass[2] *n* burro, cardophagus, cuddy, donkey, hinny, jackass, jenny, Jerusalem pony, moke, mule.

assail *v* abuse, assault, attack, belabour, berate, beset, bombard, charge, criticise, encounter, fall upon, impugn, invade, lay into, malign, maltreat, pelt, revile, set about, set upon, strike, vilify.

assailant *n* abuser, adversary, aggressor, assailer, assaulter, attacker, invader, opponent, reviler.

assassin *n* bravo, cut-throat, eliminator, executioner, hatchet man, hit-man, homicide, killer, liquidator, murderer, ninja, slayer, thug.

assassinate *v* dispatch, eliminate, hit, kill, liquidate, murder, rub out, slay.

assault *n* aggression, attack, blitz, charge, incursion, invasion, offensive, onset, onslaught, raid, storm, storming, strike.

v assail, attack, beset, charge, fall on, hit, invade, lay violent hands on, set upon, storm, strike.

assay *v* analyse, appraise, assess, estimate, evaluate, examine, inspect, investigate, prove, test, try, weigh.

n analysis, assaying, attempt, docimasy, endeavour, essay, examination, inspection, investigation, test, trial, try, valuation, venture.

assemblage *n* accumulation, aggregation, array, assembly, body, collection, company, congeries, conglomeration, crowd, flock, galaxy, gathering, group, mass, multitude, rally, throng.

assemble *v* accumulate, amass, build, collect, compose, congregate, construct, convene, convocate, convoke, erect, fabricate, flock, forgather, gather, group, join up, levy, make, manufacture, marshal, meet, mobilise, muster, muster (up), piece, rally, round up, set up, summon, together.

antonym disperse.

assembly *n* agora, assemblage, ball, body, building, collection, company, conclave, conference, congregation, congress, consistory, construction, convocation, council, crowd, diet, divan, ecclesia, erection, fabrication, fitting, flock, folkmoot, gathering, gemot, gorsedd, group, indaba, joining, kgotla, levy, manufacture, mass, meeting, moot, multitude, panegyry, rally, reception, setting up, soiree, synod, throng.

assent *v* accede, accept, acquiesce, agree, allow, approve, comply, concede, concur, consent, grant, permit, sanction, submit, subscribe, yield.

antonym disagree.

n acceptance, accession, accord, acquiescence, agreement, approval, capitulation, compliance, concession, concurrence, consent, permission, sanction, submission.

assert *v* advance, affirm, allege, asseverate, attest, aver, avouch, avow, claim, constate, contend, declare, defend, dogmatise, insist, lay down, maintain, predicate, press, profess, promote, pronounce, protest, state, stress, swear, testify to, thrust forward, uphold, vindicate.

antonym deny.

assertion *n* affirmance, affirmation, allegation, asservation, attestation, averment, avowal, claim, constatation, contention, declaration, dictum, gratis dictum, ipse dixit, predication, profession, pronouncement, statement, vindication, vouch, word.

antonym denial.

assertive *adj* aggressive, assuming, bold, bumptious, confident, decided, dogmatic, domineering, emphatic, firm, forceful, forward, insistent, opinionated, overbearing, presumptuous, pushy, self-assured, strong-willed.

antonym diffident.

assertiveness *n* aggressiveness, boldness, bumptiousness, decisiveness, dogmatism, forcefulness, forwardness, insistence, overbearingness, positiveness, presumption, presumptuousness, pushiness, self-assurance, self-confidence.

assess *v* affeer, appraise, compute, consider, demand, determine, estimate, evaluate, fix, gauge, impose, investigate, judge, levy, rate, review, size up, tax, value, weigh.

assessment *n* affeerment, appraisal, calculation, consideration, determination, estimate, estimation, evaluation, gauging, judgement, opinion, rating, review, taxation, valuation.

asset *n* advantage, aid, benefit, blessing, help, plus, resource, service, strength, virtue.

antonym liability.

assets *n* capital, estate, funds, goods, holdings, means, money, possessions, property, reserves, resources, securities, wealth, wherewithal.

asseverate *v* affirm, assert, attest, aver, avouch, avow, certify, declare, maintain, profess, pronounce, protest, state, swear, testify.

asseveration *n* affirmation, assertion, assurance, attestation, averment, avowal, declaration, deposition, predication, profession, pronouncement, protestation, statement, vow.

assiduity *n* application, assiduousness, attentiveness, conscientiousness, constancy, dedication, devotion, diligence, indefatigability, industriousness, industry, labour, perseverance, persistence, sedulity, sedulousness, steadiness, tirelessness.

antonym negligence.

assiduous *adj* attentive, conscientious, constant, dedicated, devoted, diligent, hard-working, indefatigable, industrious, persevering, persistent, sedulous, steady, studious, unflagging, untiring.

antonym negligent.

assign *v* accredit, adjudge, allocate, allot, apart, appoint, apportion, arrogate, ascribe, attribute, choose, consign, delegate, designate, determine, dispense, distribute, fix, give, grant, name, nominate, put down, select, set, specify, stipulate.

assignation *n* allocation, allotment, appointment, arrangement, date, engagement, meeting, rendezvous, tryst.

assignment *n* allocation, allotment, appointment, apportionment, ascription, attribution, charge, commission, consignment, delegation, designation, determination, dispensation, distribution, duty, errand, giving, grant, imposition, job, mission, nomination, position, post, responsibility, selection, specification, task.

assimilate *v* absorb, accept, acclimatise, accommodate, acculturate, accustom, adapt, adjust, blend, conform, digest, fit, homogenise, imbibe, incorporate, ingest, intermix, learn, merge, mingle, take in, tolerate.

antonym reject.

assimilation *n* absorption, acceptance, acclimatisation, accommodation, acculturation, adaptation, adjustment, conformity, homogenisation, incorporation, ingestion, learning, toleration.

antonym rejection.

assist *v* abet, accommodate, aid, back, benefit, bestead, boost, collaborate, co-operate, enable, expedite, facilitate, further, help, rally round, reinforce, relieve, second, serve, succour, support, sustain.

antonym thwart.

assistance *n* a leg up, abetment, accommodation, adjutancy, aid, backing, benefit, boost, collaboration, comfort, co-operation, furtherance, help, reinforcement, relief, succour, support, sustainment.

antonym hindrance.

assistant *n* abettor, accessory, accomplice, adjutant, aide, ally, ancillary, associate, auxiliary, backer, coadjutor, collaborator, colleague, confederate, co-operator, Girl Friday, helper, helpmate, henchman, Man Friday, partner, Person Friday, right-hand man, second, subordinate, subsidiary, supporter.

associate *v* accompany, affiliate, ally, amalgamate, combine, company, confederate, conjoin, connect, consort, correlate, couple, fraternise, hang around, hobnob, identify, join, league, link, mingle, mix, pair, relate, socialise, unite, yoke.

n affiliate, ally, assistant, bedfellow, coadjutor, collaborator, colleague, companion, compeer, comrade, confederate, confrère, co-worker, fellow, follower, friend, leaguer, mate, partner, peer, side-kick.

association *n* affiliation, alliance, analogy, band, blend, bloc, bond, cartel, clique, club, coalition, combination, combine, companionship, company, compound, comradeship, concomitance, confederacy, confederation, connection, consociation, consortium, conspiracy, co-operative, corporation, correlation, familiarity, federation, fellowship, fraternisation, fraternity, friendship, Gesellschaft, group, intimacy, joining, juxtaposition, league, linkage, mixture, organisation, pairing, partnership, relation, relations, relationship, resemblance, society, syndicate, syndication, tie, trust, union, Verein.

assorted *adj* different, differing, divergent, divers, diverse, diversified, heterogeneous, manifold, miscellaneous, mixed, motley, multifarious, multiform, several, sundry, varied, variegated, various.

assortment *n* arrangement, array, assemblage, categorisation, choice, classification, collection, disposition, distribution, diversity, farrago, grading, grouping, hotchpotch, jumble, medley, melange, miscellany, mishmash, mixture, olio, olla-podrida, pot-pourri, ranging, salad, salmagundi, selection, sift, sifting, sorting, variety.

assuage *v* allay, alleviate, appease, calm, dull, ease, lessen, lighten, lower, lull, mitigate, moderate, mollify, pacify, palliate, quench, quieten, reduce, relieve, satisfy, slake, soften, soothe, still, temper, tranquillise.

antonym exacerbate.

assume *v* accept, acquire, adopt, affect, appropriate, arrogate, believe, commandeer, counterfeit, deduce, don, embrace, expect, expropriate, fancy, feign, guess, imagine, infer, opine, postulate, pre-empt, premise, presume, presuppose, pretend to, put on, seize, sham, shoulder, simulate, strike, suppose, surmise, suspect, take, take for granted, take on, take over, take up, think, understand, undertake, usurp.

assumed *adj* accepted, adopted, affected, bogus, conjectural, counterfeit, expected, fake, false, feigned, fictitious, fiducial, hypothetical, made-up, phoney, presumed, presupposed, pretended, pseudonymous, seized, sham, simulated, specious, spurious, supposed, suppositional, surmised, usurped.

assuming *adj* arrogant, assertive, audacious, bold, brazen, bumptious, conceited, forward, impertinent, impudent, overconfident, presumptuous, pretentious, pushy, self-assertive, self-important, uppish.

antonym unassuming.

assumption *n* acceptance, acquisition, adoption, appropriation, arrogance, arrogation, audacity, belief, bumptiousness, conceit, conjecture, expectation, expropriation, fancy, guess, guesswork, hypothesis, impudence, inference, postulate, postulation, pre-emption, premise, premiss, presumption, presumptuousness, presupposition, pride, seizure, self-importance, supposition, surmise, suspicion, theory, understanding, undertaking, usurpation.

assurance *n* affirmation, aplomb, assertion, asseveration, assuredness, audacity, boldness, certainty, certitude, chutzpah, confidence, conviction, coolness, courage, declaration, firmness, gall, guarantee, nerve, oath, pledge, plerophory, poise, positiveness, profession, promise, protestation, security, self-confidence, self-reliance, sureness, vow, word.

antonym uncertainty.

assure *v* affirm, attest, boost, certify, clinch, comfort, confirm, convince, embolden, encourage, ensure, guarantee, hearten, persuade, pledge, promise, reassure, seal, secure, soothe, strengthen, swear, tell, vow, warrant.

assured *adj* assertive, audacious, belt-and-braces, bold, certain, clinched, cocksure, confident, confirmed, definite, ensured, fixed, guaranteed, indisputable, indubitable, irrefutable, overconfident, pert, poised, positive, secure, self-assured, self-confident, self-possessed, settled, sure, unquestionable.

antonym uncertain.

assuredly *adv* certainly, definitely, indisputably, indubitably, surely, truly, unquestionably.

astir *adj, adv* about, active, afoot, awake, circulating, in motion, in the air, roused, up.

astonish *v* amaze, astound, baffle, bewilder, confound, daze, dumbfound, electrify, flabbergast, floor, nonplus, shock, stagger, startle, stun, stupefy, surprise, wow.

astonished *adj* amazed, astounded, baffled, bewildered, bug-eyed, confounded, dazed, dumbfounded, electrified, flabbergasted, incredulous, staggered, startled, stunned, surprised, thunder-struck.

astonishing *adj* amazing, astounding, baffling, bewildering, breathtaking, dazzling, impressive, incredible, prodigious, staggering, startling, striking, stunning, stupefying, surprising.

astonishment *n* amazement, awe, bafflement, bewilderment, confusion, consternation, dismay, shock, stupefaction, surprise, wonder, wonderment.

astound *v* abash, amaze, astonish, baffle, bewilder, confound, daze, dumbfound, electrify, flabbergast, overwhelm, shake, shock, stagger, stun, stupefy, surprise, wow.

astounded *adj* abashed, amazed, baffled, bewildered, confounded, dazed, dumbfounded, electrified, flabbergasted, incredulous, overwhelmed, shaken, shocked, staggered, stunned, stupefied, wowed.

astounding *adj* amazing, astonishing, baffling, bewildering, breathtaking, electrifying, impressive, incredible, overwhelming, shocking, staggering, striking, stunning, stupefying, surprising.

astray *adv* adrift, amiss, awry, lost, off course, off the mark, off the rails, to the bad, wrong.

astringent *adj* acerb, acerbic, acid, astrictive, austere, biting, caustic, contractile, contractive, exacting, grim, hard, harsh, puckery, restringent, rigorous, scathing, severe, stern, strict, stringent, styptic, trenchant.

antonym bland.

astrology *n* astromancy, horoscopy, star-gazing.

astronomical *adj* astrophysical, celestial, cosmological, enormous, high, huge, Uranian.

astronomy *n* astrodynamics, astrography, astrophysics, cosmography, cosmology, star-gazing, uranography, uranology.

astute *adj* acute, adroit, artful, astucious, calculating, canny, clever, crafty, cunning, discerning, fly, foxy, intelligent, keen, knowing, penetrating, perceptive, percipient, perspicacious, politic, prudent, sagacious, sharp, shrewd, sly, subtle, wily, wise.

antonym stupid.

astuteness *n* acumen, acuteness, adroitness, artfulness, astucity, canniness, cleverness, craftiness, cunning, discernment, insight, intelligence, penetration, perceptiveness, percipience, perspicacity, sagacity, sharpness, shrewdness, slyness, subtlety, wiliness.

antonym stupidity.

asunder *adv* apart, in half, in pieces, in twain, in two, into pieces, to bits, to pieces.

asylum *n* bedlam, bughouse, cover, funny farm, harbour, haven, hospital, institution, loony-bin, madhouse, mental hospital, nuthouse, preserve, refuge, reserve, retreat, safety, sanctuary, shelter.

asymmetrical *adj* asymmetric, awry, crooked, disproportionate, disymmetric, gibbous, irregular, unbalanced, unequal, uneven, unsymmetrical.

antonym symmetrical.

asymmetry *n* disproportion, disymmetry, imbalance, inequality, irregularity, misproportion, unevenness, unsymmetry.

antonym symmetry.

at a loss baffled, bewildered, confounded, confused, helpless, nonplussed, perplexed, puzzled, resourceless, stuck, stumped.

at bay caught, cornered, trapped, up against it, with one's back to the wall.

at fault accountable, answerable, blamable, blameworthy, culpable, guilty, responsible.

at first sight on first acquaintance, on the surface, prima facie, superficially, to the outsider.

at hand approaching, at one's elbow, available, close, handy, immediate, imminent, impending, near, nearby, on tap, ready.

at home at ease, comfortable, contented, conversant, experienced, familiar, knowledgeable, proficient, relaxed, skilled, well-versed.

at large at liberty, footloose, free, independent, liberated, on the loose, on the run, roaming, unconfined, unconstrained.

at last at length, at long last, eventually, finally, in conclusion, in due course, in the end, in time, ultimately.

at leisure at ease, at liberty, disengaged, free, idle, off the hook, unbusy, unengaged.

at length at last, at long last, completely, eventually, exhaustively, finally, for ages, for hours, fully, in depth, in detail, in the end, in time, interminably, thoroughly, to the full, ultimately.

at liberty at large, at leisure, disengaged, footloose, free, idle, not confined, on the loose, unconstrained, unrestricted.

at odds at daggers drawn, at enmity, at loggerheads, at one another's throats, at outs, at variance, feuding, in conflict, in dispute, opposed, quarrelling.

at once at one go, at the same time, directly, ek dum, forthwith, immediately, in concert, in unison, incontinent, instantly, now, promptly, right away, simultaneously, straight away, straightway, this minute, together, unhesitatingly, without delay.

at one's wits' end at a loss, at the end of one's tether, baffled, bewildered, desperate, in despair, in dire straits, lost, resourceless, stuck, stumped.

at random accidentally, adventitiously, aimlessly, arbitrarily, casually, desultorily, fortuitously, haphazardly, indiscriminately, irregularly, purposelessly, randomly, unsystematically.

at rest asleep, at a standstill, calm, dead, idle, inactive, motionless, peaceful, resting, sleeping, still, stopped, tranquil, unmoving.

at sea adrift, astray, baffled, bewildered, confused, disoriented, insecure, lost, mystified, perplexed, puzzled, upset.

at the double at full speed, at once, briskly, immediately, in double-quick time, lickety-split, like lightning, posthaste, quickly, quick-sticks, without delay.

at work on the job.

atheism *n* disbelief, free-thinking, godlessness, heathenism, impiety, infidelity, irreligion, non-belief, paganism, rationalism, scepticism, unbelief, ungodliness.

atheist *n* disbeliever, free-thinker, heathen, infidel, irreligionist, non-believer, nullifidian, pagan, sceptic, unbeliever.

atheistic *adj* atheistical, disbelieving, free-thinking, heathen, impious, irreligious, irreverent, rationalistic, sceptical, unbelieving, ungodly, unreligious.

antonym religious.

athlete *n* agonist, competitor, contender, contestant, gymnast, jock, runner, sportsman, sportswoman.

athletic *adj* active, brawny, energetic, fit, husky, muscular, powerful, robust, sinewy, strapping, strong, sturdy, thewy, vigorous, well-knit, well-proportioned, wiry.

antonym puny.

athletics *n* agonistics, callisthenics, contests, events, exercises, games, gymnastics, races, sports, track events.

atmosphere *n* aerospace, aerosphere, air, ambience, aura, character, climate, environment, feel, feeling, flavour, heavens, milieu, mood, quality, sky, spirit, surroundings, tenor, tone, vibrations.

atmospheric *adj* aerial, climatic, epedaphic, meteorological.

atom *n* atomy, bit, crumb, grain, hint, iota, jot, mite, molecule, morsel, particle, scintilla, scrap, shred, smidgen, speck, spot, tittle, trace, whit.

atone *v* aby(e), compensate, expiate, make amends, make up for, offset, pay for, propitiate, recompense, reconcile, redeem, redress, remedy.

atonement *n* amends, compensation, expiation, indemnity, payment, penance, propitiation, recompense, redress, reparation, repayment, restitution, restoration, satisfaction.

atrocious *adj* abominable, barbaric, brutal, cruel, diabolical, execrable, fell, fiendish, flagitious, ghastly, grievous, heinous, hideous, horrible, horrifying, infamous, infernal, inhuman, monstrous, piacular, ruthless, savage, shocking, terrible, vicious, vile, villainous, wicked.

atrocity *n* abomination, atrociousness, barbarity, barbarousness, brutality, crime, cruelty, enormity, evil, flagitiousness, ghastliness, heinousness, hideousness, horror, infamy, inhumanity, monstrosity, monstrousness, outrage, ruthlessness, savagery, viciousness, vileness, villainy, wickedness.

atrophy *n* decay, decline, degeneration, deterioration, diminution, emaciation, marasmus, shrivelling, tabefaction, tabes, wasting, withering.
v decay, decline, degenerate, deteriorate, diminish, dwindle, emaciate, fade, shrink, shrivel, tabefy, waste, wither.

attach *v* add, adhere, adhibit, affix, annex, append, articulate, ascribe, assign, associate, attract, attribute, belong, bind, captivate, combine, connect, couple, fasten, fix, impute, join, link, place, put, relate to, secure, stick, tie, unite, weld.

antonyms detach, unfasten.

attached *adj* affectionate, affiliated, associated, connected, fond, loving.

attachment *n* accessory, accoutrement, adapter, addition, adhesion, adhibition, adjunct, affection, affinity, appendage, appurtenance, attraction, bond, codicil, cohesion, confiscation, connection, connector, coupling, devotion, esteem, extension, extra, fastener, fastening, fidelity, fitting, fixture, fondness, friendship, joint, junction, liking, link, love, loyalty, partiality, predilection, regard, seizure, supplement, tenderness, tie.

attack *n* abuse, access, aggression, assailment, assault, battery, blitz, bombardment, bout, broadside, censure, charge, convulsion, criticism, fit, foray, impugnment, incursion, inroad, invasion, invective, kamikaze, offensive, onset, onslaught, paroxysm, raid, rush, seizure, spasm, spell, strike, stroke.

v abuse, assail, assault, belabour, berate, blame, censure, charge, chastise, criticise, denounce, do over, fake, fall on, flay, have one's knife in, impugn, invade, inveigh against, lash, lay into, light into, make at, malign, mob, put the boot in, raid, rate, revile, rush, set about, set on, snipe, storm, strafe, strike, vilify, visit, wade into.

attacker *n* abuser, aggressor, assailant, assaulter, critic, invader, mugger, persecutor, raider, reviler, traducer.

antonyms defender, supporter.

attain *v* accomplish, achieve, acquire, arrive at, bag, compass, complete, earn, effect, fulfil, gain, get, grasp, net, obtain, procure, reach, realise, reap, secure, touch, win.

attainability *n* accessibility, availability, feasibility, obtainability, practicalness, procurability, realisability.

attainable *adj* accessible, achievable, available, feasible, manageable, obtainable, possible, potential, practicable, probable, procurable, reachable, realistic, within reach.

antonym unattainable.

attainment *n* ability, accomplishment, achievement, acquirement, acquisition, aptitude, art, capability, competence, completion, consummation, facility, feat, fulfilment, gift, mastery, procurement, proficiency, reaching, realisation, skill, success, talent.

attempt *n* assault, assay, attack, bash, bid, coup d'essai, crack, effort, endeavour, essay, experiment, go, move, push, shot, shy, stab, struggle, trial, try, undertaking, venture.

v aspire, endeavour, essay, experiment, have a bash, have a crack, have a go, have a shot, seek, strive, tackle, try, try one's hand at, try one's luck at, undertake, venture.

attend *v* accompany, appear, arise from, assist, be all ears, be present, care for, chaperon, companion, convoy, escort, follow, frequent, give ear, guard, hear, hearken, heed, help, lend an ear, listen, look after, mark, mind, minister to, note, notice, nurse, observe, pay attention, pay heed, pin back one's ears, regard, result from, serve, squire, succour, take care of, tend, usher, visit, wait upon, watch.

attend to concentrate on, control, cope with, deal with, direct, look after, manage, oversee, see to, supervise, take care of.

attendance *n* appearance, assistance, attending, audience, crowd, escortage, gate, house, ministration, presence, turn-out.

attendant *n* acolyte, aide, assistant, auxiliary, batman, bed captain, chaperon, companion, custodian, equerry, escort, famulus, flunkey, follower, ghillie, guard, guide, helper, jäger, Jeames, kavass, lackey, lady-help, lady-in-waiting, lady's-maid, livery-servant, marshal, menial, page, poursuivant, retainer, servant, steward, underling, usher, waiter.

adj accessory, accompanying, associated, attached, concomitant, consequent, incidental, related, resultant, subsequent.

attention *n* advertence, advertency, alertness, attentiveness, awareness, care, civility, concentration, concern, consciousness, consideration, contemplation, courtesy, deference, ear, gallantry, heed, heedfulness, intentness, mindfulness, ministration, notice, observation, politeness, recognition, regard, respect, service, thought, thoughtfulness, treatment, vigilance.

antonyms disregard, inattention.

attentive *adj* accommodating, advertent, alert, awake, careful, civil, concentrating, conscientious, considerate, courteous, deferential, devoted, gallant, gracious, heedful, intent, kind, mindful, obliging, observant, polite, regardant, studious, thoughtful, vigilant, watchful.

antonyms heedless, inattentive, inconsiderate.

attenuate *v* adulterate, debase, decrease, devaluate, dilute, diminish, draw out, elongate, enervate, enfeeble, extend, lengthen, rarefy, reduce, refine, sap, stretch out, taper, thin, thin out, water down, weaken.

antonyms expand, intensify, thicken.

attenuated *adj* adulterated, attenuate, debased, decreased, devalued, dilute, diluted, diminished, drawn out, elongated, enervated, enfeebled, extended, lengthened, rarefied, reduced, refined, sapped, slender, spun out, stretched out, tapering, thinned, watered down, weakened.

attest *v* adjure, affirm, assert, authenticate, aver, certify, confirm, corroborate, declare, demonstrate, depose, display, endorse, evidence, evince, exhibit, manifest, prove, ratify, seal, show, substantiate, swear, testify, verify, vouch, warrant, witness.

attestation *n* affirmation, asseveration, assurance, averment, avowal, certification, confirmation, corroboration, declaration, deposition, endorsement, evidence, evincement, testification, testimony, vouch, witness.

attire *n* accoutrements, apparel, array, clothes, clothing, costume, dress, finery, garb, garments, gear, get-up, habiliments, habit, outfit, raiment, rig-out, robes, togs, uniform, vestment, wear, weeds.

v accoutre, adorn, apparel, array, caparison, clothe, costume, deck out, dress, equip, garb, habilitate, outfit, prepare, rig out, robe, turn out.

attitude *n* affectation, air, Anschauung, approach, aspect, bearing, carriage, condition, demeanour, disposition, feeling, manner, mien, mood, opinion, outlook, perspective, point of view, pose, position, posture, stance, view, Weltanschauung.

attract *v* allure, appeal to, bewitch, captivate, charm, decoy, draw, enchant, engage, entice, fascinate, incline, induce, interest, inveigle, invite, lure, pull, seduce, tempt.

antonym repel.

attraction *n* allure, amenity, appeal, attractiveness, bait, captivation, charm, crowd-puller, draw, enchantment, entertainment, enticement, event, fascination, inducement, interest, invitation, lure, magnetism, pull, seduction, show, temptation.

antonym repulsion.

attractive *adj* agreeable, alluring, appealing, appetible, beautiful, beddable, captivating, catching, catchy, charming, comely, enchanting, engaging, enticing, epigamous, fair, fascinating, fetching, glamorous, good-looking, gorgeous, handsome, hunky, interesting, inviting, jolie laide, lovely, magnetic, nubile, personable, pleasant, pleasing, prepossessing, pretty, seductive, snazzy, stunning, taky, tempting, toothsome, voluptuous, winning, winsome.

antonyms repellent, unattractive.

attribute *v* accredit, apply, arrogate, ascribe, assign, blame, charge, credit, impute, put down, refer.

n affection, aspect, character, characteristic, facet, feature, idiosyncrasy, mark, note, peculiarity, point, property, quality, quirk, sign, symbol, trait, virtue.

attribution *n* accreditation, application, ascription, assignment, charge, crediting, imputation.

attrition *n* abrasion, attenuation, chafing, debilitation, detrition, erosion, fretting, friction, grinding, harassment, harrying, rubbing, scraping, weakening, wear, wearing away, wearing down.

attune *v* acclimatise, accustom, adapt, adjust, assimilate, co-ordinate, familiarise, harmonise, homologise, modulate, reconcile, regulate, set, tune.

atypical *adj* aberrant, abnormal, anomalous, deviant, divergent, eccentric, exceptional, extraordinary, freakish, untypical, unusual.

antonym typical.

au fait abreast of, acquainted, au courant, clued-up, conversant, hep, in the know, in the stream, in the swim, in touch, knowledgeable, on the ball, posted, up-to-date, well up, well-informed.

auburn *adj* chestnut, copper, henna, nutbrown, red, russet, rust, tawny, titian.

auction *n* cant, roup, sale, vendue.

audacious *adj* adventurous, assuming, assured, bold, brave, brazen, cheeky, courageous, dare-devil, daring, dauntless, death-defying, der-doing, disrespectful, enterprising, fearless, forward, impertinent, impudent, insolent, intrepid, pert, plucky, presumptuous, rash, reckless, risky, rude, shameless, unabashed, valiant, venturesome.

antonyms cautious, reserved, timid.

audacity *n* adventurousness, assurance, audaciousness, boldness, brass neck, bravery, brazenness, cheek, chutzpah, courage, daring, dauntlessness, defiance, derring-do, disrespectfulness, effrontery, enterprise, fearlessness, foolhardiness, forwardness, gall, guts, impertinence, impudence, insolence, intrepidity, nerve, pertness, presumption, rashness, recklessness, rudeness, shamelessness, valour, venturesomeness.

antonyms caution, reserve, timidity.

audible *adj* appreciable, clear, detectable, discernible, distinct, hearable, perceptible, recognisable.

antonym inaudible.

audience *n* assemblage, assembly, auditorium, congregation, crowd, devotees, fans, following, gallery, gathering, hearing, house, interview, listeners, market, meeting, onlookers, public, ratings, reception, regulars, spectators, turn-out, viewers.

audit *n* analysis, balancing, check, checking, examination, inspection, investigation, review, scrutiny, statement, verification.

v analyse, balance, check, examine, inspect, investigate, review, scrutinise, verify.

auditor *n* accountant, actuary, analyst, examiner, inspector, scrutator, scrutiniser.

augment *v* add to, amplify, boost, dilate, eke out, enhance, enlarge, expand, extend, grow, heighten, increase, inflate, intensify, magnify, multiply, raise, reinforce, strengthen, supplement, swell.

antonym decrease.

augur *n* auspex, divinator, diviner, haruspex, oracle, prognosticator, prophet, seer, soothsayer.

v auspicate, bespeak, betoken, bode, forebode, foreshadow, foretoken, harbinger, haruspicate, herald, import, portend, predict, prefigure, presage, promise, prophesy, signify.

augury *n* auspice, divination, foreboding, forerunner, forewarning, harbinger, haruspication, herald, omen, portent, precursor, prediction, presage, prodrome, prognostication, promise, prophecy, sign, soothsaying, token, warning.

august *adj* awful, dignified, exalted, glorious, grand, imposing, impressive, lofty, magnificent, majestic, monumental, noble, portentous, regal, revered, solemn, splendid, stately, venerable.

aura *n* air, ambience, aroma, atmosphere, effluvium, emanation, feel, feeling, hint, mood, nimbus, odour, quality, scent, suggestion, vibes, vibrations.

auspices *n* aegis, authority, backing, care, championship, charge, control, guidance, influence, patronage, protection, responsibility, sponsorship, superintendence, supervision, support, tutelage.

auspicious *adj* bright, cheerful, encouraging, favourable, felicitous, fortunate, happy, hopeful, lucky, opportune, optimistic, promising, propitious, prosperous, rosy, white.

antonyms inauspicious, ominous.

austere *adj* abstemious, abstinent, ascetic, astringent, bitter, bleak, chaste, cold, conservative, continent, Dantean, Dantesque, economical, exacting, forbidding, formal, grave, grim, hard, harsh, plain, puritanical, restrained, rigid, rigorous, self-denying, self-disciplined, serious, severe, simple, sober, solemn, sour, spare, Spartan, stark, stern, strict, stringent, unadorned, unembellished, unornamented, unrelenting.

antonyms elaborate, extravagant, genial.

austerity *n* abstemiousness, abstinence, asceticism, chasteness, chastity, coldness, continence, economy, formality, gravity, grimness, hardness, harshness, inflexibility, plainness, puritanism, reserve, restraint, rigidity, rigour, self-control, self-denial, self-discipline, seriousness, severity, simplicity, sobriety, solemnity, spareness, Spartanism, starkness, sternness, strictness.

antonyms elaborateness, extravagant, geniality.

authentic *adj* accurate, actual, authoritative, bona fide, certain, dependable, dinkum, factual, faithful, genuine, honest, kosher, legitimate, original, pure, real, reliable, simon-pure, true, true-to-life, trustworthy, valid. veracious, veritable.

antonyms counterfeit, inauthentic, spurious.

authenticate *v* accredit, attest, authorise, avouch, certify, confirm, corroborate, endorse, guarantee, validate, verify, vouch for, warrant.

authentication *n* accreditation, attestation, authorisation, certification, confirmation, corroboration, endorsement, guarantee, validation, verification, voucher, warrant.

authenticity *n* accuracy, actuality, authoritativeness, certainty, correctness, dependability, factualness, faithfulness, fidelity, genuineness, honesty, legitimacy, purity, reality, realness, reliability, trustworthiness, truth, truthfulness, validity, veracity, veritableness, verity.

antonyms invalidity, spuriousness.

author *n* architect, begetter, composer, creator, designer, fabricator, fashioner, father, forger, founder, framer, initiator, inventor, maker, mover, originator, paper-stainer, parent, pen, penman, penwoman, planner, prime mover, producer, volumist, writer.

authorisation *n* accreditation, approval, certification, credentials, go-ahead, green light, leave, licence, permission, permit, sanction, warrant.

authorise *v* accredit, allow, approve, commission, confirm, consent to, countenance, empower, enable, entitle, legalise, license, permit, ratify, sanction, validate, warrant.

authoritarian *adj* absolute, autocratic, despotic, dictatorial, disciplinarian, doctrinaire, dogmatic, domineering, harsh, heavy, imperious, inflexible, oppressive, repressive, rigid, severe, strict, tyrannical, unyielding.

antonym liberal.

n absolutist, autocrat, despot, dictator, disciplinarian, fascist, Hitler, tyrant.

authoritarianism *n* absolutism, autocracy, despotism, dictatorship, fascism, fascismo, Hildebrandism, Hitlerism, totalitarianism, tyranny.

antonyms laissez faire, liberalism.

authoritative *adj* accepted, accurate, approved, assured, authentic, authorised, cathedratic, commanding, confident, convincing, decisive, definitive, dependable, factual, faithful, learned, legitimate, magisterial, magistrial, masterly, official, reliable, sanctioned, scholarly, sound, sovereign, true, trustworthy, truthful, valid, veritable.

antonym unreliable.

authoritatively *adv* confidently, decisively, ex cathedra, legitimately, reliably, soundly.

authority[1] *n* administration, ascendancy, attestation, authorisation, avowal, charge, command, control, declaration, domination, dominion, evidence, force, government, imperium, influence, jurisdiction, justification, licence, management, might, officialdom, permission, permit, power, prerogative, profession, right, rule, sanction, sovereignty, statement, strength, supremacy, sway, testimony, textbook, warrant, weight, word.

authority[2] *n* arbiter, bible, connoisseur, expert, judge, master, professional, pundit, sage, scholar, specialist.

autocracy *n* absolutism, authoritarianism, despotism, dictatorship, fascism, Hitlerism, totalitarianism, tyranny.

antonym democracy.

autocrat *n* absolutist, authoritarian, Caesar, cham, despot, dictator, fascist, Hitler, panjandrum, totalitarian, tyrant.

autocratic *adj* absolute, all-powerful, authoritarian, despotic, dictatorial, dictatory, domineering, imperious, overbearing, totalitarian, tyrannical, tyrannous.

antonyms democratic, liberal.

automatic *adj* automated, certain, habitual, inescapable, inevitable, instinctive, involuntary, mechanical, mechanised, natural, necessary, perfunctory, push-button, reflex, robot, robot-like, routine, self-acting, self-activating, self-moving, self-propelling, self-regulating, spontaneous, unavoidable, unbidden, unconscious, unthinking, unwilled, vegetative.

automaton *n* Dalek, machine, mechanical man, robot.

autonomous *adj* autarkic, free, independent, self-determining, self-governing, sovereign, voluntary.

antonym subject.

autonomy *n* autarky, free will, freedom, home rule, independence, self-determination, self-government, self-rule, sovereignty.

antonyms compulsion, subjection.

auxiliary *adj* accessory, adjuvant, adminicular, aiding, ancillary, assistant, assisting, back-up, emergency, helping, reserve, secondary, subsidiary, substitute, supplementary, supporting, supportive.

n accessory, accomplice, adminicle, ally, ancillary, assistant, associate, companion, confederate, foederatus, helper, partner, reserve, subordinate, supporter.

avail *v* advance, advantage, aid, assist, benefit, boot, dow, exploit, help, make the most of, profit, serve, work.

n advantage, aid, assistance, benefit, boot, good, help, profit, purpose, service, use, value.

avail oneself of capitalise on, make use of, profit by, profit from, take advantage of, turn to account, use, utilise.

available *adj* accessible, at hand, attainable, convenient, disengaged, free, handy, obtainable, on hand, on tap, procurable, ready, to hand, vacant, within reach.

antonym unavailable.

avalanche *n* barrage, cascade, cataclysm, deluge, flood, inundation, landslide, landslip, laurine, torrent.

avant-garde *adj* advanced, enterprising, experimental, far-out, forward-looking, goey, innovative, innovatory, inventive, pioneering, progressive, unconventional, way-out.

antonyms conservative, dyed-in-the-wool.

avarice *n* acquisitiveness, cheese-paring, covetousness, cupidity, greed, greediness, meanness, miserliness, niggardliness, parsimoniousness, parsimony, penny-pinching, penuriousness, pleonexia, predatoriness, rapacity, stinginess, tight-fistedness.

antonym generosity.

avaricious *adj* acquisitive, cheese-paring, covetous, gare, grasping, greedy, gripple, mean, miserable, miserly, money-grubbing, niggardly, parsimonious, penny-pinching, penurious, pleonectic, predatory, rapacious, stingy, tight-fisted.

antonym generous.

avenge *v* punish, repay, requite, take revenge for, take vengeance for, vindicate.

avengement *n* punishment, repayment, reprisal, requital, retaliation, retribution, revenge, ultion, vengeance.

avenger *n* retributor, vindicator.

avenging *adj* retaliatory, retributive, vengeful, vindictive, wreakful.

avenue *n* access, alley, approach, boulevard, channel, course, drive, driveway, entrance, entree, entry, means, pass, passage, path, pathway, road, route, street, thoroughfare, vista, walk, way.

aver *v* affirm, allege, assert, asseverate, attest, avouch, avow, declare, insist, maintain, proclaim, profess, pronounce, protest, say, state, swear, testify, witness.

average *n* mean, mediocrity, medium, midpoint, norm, par, rule, run, standard.

antonyms exception, extreme.

adj common, commonplace, everyday, fair, general, indifferent, intermediate, mean, medial, median, mediocre, medium, middle, middling, moderate, normal, ordinary, passable, regular, run-of-the-mill, satisfactory, so-so, standard, tolerable, typical, undistinguished, unexceptional, unremarkable, usual.

antonyms exceptional, extreme.

averse *adj* antagonistic, antipathetic, disapproving, disinclined, hostile, ill-disposed, inimical, loath, opposed, reluctant, unfavourable, unwilling.

antonyms sympathetic, willing.

aversion *n* abhorrence, abomination, anathema, animosity, antagonism, antipathy, detestation, disapproval, disgust, disinclination, dislike, distaste, hate, hatred, horror, hostility, loathing, odium, opposition, phobia, phobism, reluctance, repugnance, repulsion, revulsion, unwillingness.

antonyms liking, sympathy.

avert *v* avoid, deflect, evade, fend off, forestall, frustrate, obviate, parry, preclude, prevent, stave off, turn, turn aside, turn away, ward off.

aviary *n* birdcage, birdhouse, volary.

aviation *n* aeronautics, flight, flying.

aviator *n* ace, aeronaut, airman, erk, flier, pilot.

avid *adj* acquisitive, ardent, avaricious, covetous, dedicated, devoted, eager, earnest, enthusiastic, fanatical, fervent, grasping, greedy, hungry, insatiable, intense, keen, passionate, rapacious, ravenous, thirsty, voracious, zealous.

antonym indifferent.

avidity *n* acquisitiveness, ardour, avarice, covetousness, craving, cupidity, desire, devotion, eagerness, enthusiasm, fervour, greed, greediness, hankering, hunger, insatiability, keenness, longing, rapacity, ravenousness, thirst, voracity, zeal.

antonym indifference.

avocation *n* business, calling, distraction, diversion, employment, hobby, interest, job, occupation, pastime, profession, pursuit, recreation, relaxation, sideline, trade, vocation, work.

avoid *v* abstain from, avert, balk, bypass, circumvent, dodge, duck, elude, escape, eschew, evade, evite, funk, get out of, obviate, prevent, refrain from, shirk, shun, side-step, steer clear of.

avoidable *adj* avertible, eludible, escapable, evadable, evitable, preventable, voidable.

antonym inevitable.

avoidance *n* abstention, abstinence, circumvention, dodge, dodging, eluding, elusion, escape, eschewal, evasion, evitation, prevention, refraining, shirking, shunning.

avow *v* acknowledge, admit, affirm, allege, assert, asseverate, attest, aver, confess, declare, maintain, own, proclaim, profess, recognise, state, swear, testify.

avowal *n* acknowledgment, admission, affirmation, allegation, assertion, asseveration, attestation, averment, confession, declaration, oath, owning, proclamation, profession, recognition, statement, swearing, testimony.

avowed *adj* acknowledged, admitted, confessed, declared, open, overt, professed, self-confessed, self-proclaimed, sworn.

avowedly *adv* admittedly, candidly, confessedly, ex professo, frankly, openly, overtly, professedly.

antonym secretly.

await *v* anticipate, attend, be in store for, expect, hope for, lie in wait, look for, look forward to, wait for.

awake *v* arouse, awaken, rouse, wake, wake up.

adj alert, alive, aroused, astir, attentive, awakened, aware, conscious, heedful, observant, sensitive, vigilant, wakeful, waking, watchful, wide-awake.

awaken *v* activate, alert, animate, arouse, awake, call forth, enliven, evoke, excite, fan, kindle, prompt, provoke, revive, rouse, stimulate, stir up, vivify, wake, waken.

antonyms lull, quell, quench.

awakening *n* activation, animating, arousal, awaking, birth, enlivening, evocation, kindling, prompting, provocation, revival, rousing, stimulation, vivification, wakening, waking.

award *v* accord, adjudge, allot, allow, apportion, assign, bestow, confer, determine, dispense, distribute, endow, gift, give, grant, present.

n adjudication, allotment, allowance, bestowal, conferment, conferral, decision, decoration, dispensation, endowment, gift, grant, judgement, order, presentation, prize, trophy.

aware *adj* acquainted, alive to, appreciative, apprised, attentive, au courant, cognisant, conscient, conscious, conversant, enlightened, familiar, heedful, hep, hip, informed, knowing, knowledgeable, mindful, observant, on the ball, on the qui vive, sensible, sensitive, sentient, sharp, shrewd.

antonyms insensitive, unaware.

awareness *n* acquaintance, appreciation, attention, cognisance, consciousness, enlightenment, familiarity, knowledge, observation, perception, realisation, recognition, sensibility, sensitivity, sentience, understanding.

antonyms insensitivity, unawareness.

awe *n* admiration, amazement, apprehension, astonishment, dread, fear, respect, reverence, terror, veneration, wonder, wonderment.

antonym contempt.

v amaze, astonish, cow, daunt, frighten, horrify, impress, intimidate, overwhelm, stun, terrify.

awe-inspiring *adj* amazing, astonishing, awesome, awful, breathtaking, daunting, fearsome, formidable, impressive, intimidating, magnificent, overwhelming, wonderful, wondrous.

antonyms contemptible, tame.

awesome *adj* alarming, amazing, astonishing, august, awe-inspiring, awful, breathtaking, daunting, dread, dreadful, fearful, fearsome, formidable, frightening, imposing, impressive, intimidating, magnificent, majestic, moving, overwhelming, redoubtable, solemn, stunning, stupefying, stupendous, terrible, terrifying, wonderful, wondrous.

awe-struck *adj* afraid, amazed, astonished, awed, awe-inspired, awe-stricken, cowed, daunted, dumbfounded, fearful, frightened, impressed, intimidated, speechless, struck dumb, stunned, terrified, wonder-struck.

awful *adj* abysmal, alarming, amazing, atrocious, august, awe-inspiring, awesome, blood-curdling, dire, dread, dreadful, eldritch, fearful, fearsome, frightful, ghastly, gruesome, harrowing, hideous, horrendous, horrible, horrific, horrifying, majestic, nasty, portentous, shocking, solemn, spine-chilling, terrible, tremendous, ugly, unpleasant.

awfully *adv* abysmally, badly, disgracefully, disputably, dreadfully, exceedingly, exceptionally, excessively, extremely, greatly, immensely, inadequately, quite, reprehensibly, shockingly, shoddily, terribly, unforgivably, unpleasantly, very, wickedly, woefully, wretchedly.

awkward *adj* annoying, bloody-minded, blundering, bungling, chancy, chuckle-headed, clownish, clumsy, coarse, compromising, cubbish, cumbersome, delicate, difficult, disobliging, embarrassed, embarrassing, exasperating, farouche, fiddly, gauche, gawky, graceless, ham-fisted, ham-handed, hazardous, ill at ease, inconvenient, inelegant, inept, inexpedient, inexpert, inopportune, intractable, intransigent, irritable, left-handed, maladroit, obstinate, painful, perplexing, perverse, prickly, risky, rude, spastic, sticky, stubborn, thorny, ticklish, touchy, troublesome, trying, uncomfortable, unco-operative, unco-ordinated, uncouth, ungainly, ungraceful, unhandy, unhelpful, unmanageable, unpleasant, unrefined, unskilful, untimely, untoward, unwieldy, vexatious, vexing.

antonyms amenable, convenient, elegant, graceful, straightforward.

awkwardness *n* bloody-mindedness, clumsiness, coarseness, cumbersomeness, delicacy, difficulty, discomfort, embarrassment, gaucheness, gaucherie, gawkihood, gracelessness, inconvenience, inelegance, ineptness, inexperience, intractability, intransigence, irritability, left-handedness, left-handiness, maladresse, maladroitness, obstinacy, painfulness, perilousness, perversity, prickliness, risk, riskiness, rudeness, stiffness, stubbornness, touchiness, troublesomeness, unco-operativeness, ungainliness, unhandiness, unhelpfulness, unmanageability, unpleasantness, untimeliness, unwieldiness.

antonyms amenability, convenience, elegance, grace, straightforwardness.

awning *n* baldachin, canopy, covering, sunshade, tarpaulin, velarium, wind-break.

awry *adv, adj* aglee, amiss, askew, asymmetrical, cock-eyed, crooked, misaligned, oblique, off-centre, out of kilter, skew-whiff, twisted, uneven, unevenly, wonky, wrong.

antonyms straight, symmetrical.

axe *v* cancel, chop, cleave, cut, cut down, discharge, discontinue, dismiss, eliminate, fell, fire, get rid of, hew, remove, sack, split, terminate, throw out, withdraw.

axiom *n* adage, aphorism, apophthegm, byword, dictum, fundamental, gnome, maxim, postulate, precept, principle, truism, truth.

axiomatic *adj* absolute, accepted, aphoristic, apodictic, apophthegmatic, assumed, certain, fundamental, given, gnomic, granted, indubitable, manifest, presupposed, proverbial, self-evident, understood, unquestioned.

axis *n* alliance, arbor, axle, bloc, centre-line, coalition, compact, entente, league, longitude, pact, pivot, plumb-line, shaft, spindle, vertical.

axle *n* arbor, axis, hinge, mandrel, pin, pivot, shaft, spindle.

B

babble *v* blab, burble, cackle, chatter, gabble, gibber, gurgle, jabber, mumble, murmur, mutter, prate, prattle, purl, twattle.

n burble, clamour, drivel, gabble, gibberish, lallation, lalling, murmur, purl, purling, twattle.

babbling *adj* burbling, cackling, chattering, drivelling, drooling, gabbling, gibbering, gurgling, incoherent, jabbering, long-tongued, murmuring, prattling, rambling, unco-ordinated, unintelligible.

babe *n* bab, baby, bairn, child, infant, nursling, papoose, suckling, wean, weanling, youngling.

babel *n* bedlam, chaos, clamour, commotion, confusion, din, disorder, hubbub, hullabaloo, pandemonium, tumult, turmoil, uproar.

antonyms calm, order.

baby *n* babe, bairn, child, infant, nursling, papoose, suckling, tiny, toddler, wean, weanling, youngling.

adj diminutive, dwarf, Lilliputian, little, midget, mini, miniature, minute, pygmy, small, small-scale, tiny, toy, wee.

v cocker, coddle, cosset, humour, indulge, mollycoddle, overindulge, pamper, pander to, pet, spoil, spoon-feed.

babyish *adj* baby, childish, foolish, immature, infantile, jejune, juvenile, naïve, namby-pamby, puerile, silly, sissy, soft, spoilt.

antonyms mature, precocious.

bacchanalian *adj* bacchaic, debauched, Dionysian, dissolute, drunken, frenzied, intemperate, licentious, maenadic, orgiastic, riotous, saturnalian, wanton.

back[1] *v* advocate, assist, boost, buttress, champion, countenance, countersign, encourage, endorse, favour, finance, sanction, second, side with, sponsor, subsidise, support, sustain, underwrite.

antonym discourage.

back up aid, assist, bolster, champion, confirm, corroborate, endorse, reinforce, second, substantiate, support.

antonym let down.

back[2] *n* backside, end, hind part, hindquarters, posterior, rear, reverse, stern, tail, tail end, tergum, verso.

adj end, hind, hindmost, posterior, rear, reverse, tail.

back[3] *v* backtrack, recede, recoil, regress, retire, retreat, reverse, withdraw.

back down accede, back-pedal, concede, give in, retreat, submit, surrender, withdraw, yield.

back out abandon, apostatise, bunk off, cancel, chicken out, give up, go back on, recant, renegue, resign, withdraw.

back[4] *adj* delayed, earlier, elapsed, former, outdated, overdue, past, previous, prior, superseded.

backbite *v* abuse, attack, calumniate, criticise, defame, denigrate, disparage, libel, malign, revile, slag, slander, traduce, vilify, vituperate.

antonym praise.

backbiting *n* abuse, aspersion, bitchiness, calumniation, calumny, cattiness, criticism, defamation, denigration, detraction, disparagement, gossip, malice, revilement, scandalmongering, slagging, slander, spite, spitefulness, vilification, vituperation.

antonym praise.

backbone *n* basis, bottle, character, core, courage, determination, firmness, foundation, grit, hardihood, mainstay, mettle, nerve, pluck, power, resolution, resolve, spine, stamina, staunchness, steadfastness, strength, support, tenacity, toughness, vertebral column, will.

antonyms spinelessness, weakness.

backbreaking *adj* arduous, crushing, exhausting, gruelling, hard, heavy, killing, laborious, punishing, strenuous, tiring, toilsome, wearing, wearisome.

antonym easy.

backer *n* advocate, benefactor, bottle-holder, champion, funder, patron, promoter, second, seconder, sponsor, subscriber, supporter, underwriter, well-wisher.

backfire *v* boomerang, come home to roost, fail, flop, miscarry, rebound, recoil, ricochet.

background *n* breeding, circumstances, credentials, culture, dossier, education, environment, experience, fond, grounding, history, milieu, preparation, record, surroundings, tradition, upbringing.

back-handed *adj* ambiguous, double-edged, doubtful, dubious, equivocal, ironic, oblique, sarcastic, sardonic, two-edged.

antonyms sincere, wholehearted.

backing *n* accompaniment, advocacy, aid, assistance, championing, championship, encouragement, endorsement, favour, funds, grant, helpers, moral support, patronage, sanction, seconding, sponsorship, subsidy, support.

backlash *n* backfire, boomerang, counterblast, kickback, reaction, recoil, repercussion, reprisal, resentment, response, retaliation.

backlog *n* accumulation, excess, hoard, leeway, mountain, reserve, reserves, resources, stock, supply.

backslide *v* apostatise, default, defect, fall from grace, lapse, regress, relapse, renegue, retrogress, revert, sin, slip, stray, weaken.

antonym persevere.

backslider *n* apostate, defaulter, defector, deserter, recidivist, recreant, renegade, reneguer, turncoat.

backsliding *n* apostasy, defaulting, defection, desertion, lapse, recidivism, recreancy, relapse, renegation.

backward *adj* bashful, behind, behindhand, diffident, dull, hesitant, hesitating, immature, late, reluctant, retarded, shy, slow, sluggish, stupid, subnormal, tardy, underdeveloped, unwilling, wavering.

antonyms forward, precocious.

backwoods *n* back of beyond, boondocks, bush, outback, sticks.

bacteria *n* bacilli, bugs, germs, listerias, microbes, micro-organisms, pathogens, schizomycetes, viruses.

bad *adj* adverse, ailing, base, blameworthy, conscience-stricken, contrite, corrupt, criminal, damaging, dangerous, decayed, defective, deficient, deleterious, delinquent, despondent, detrimental, disastrous, discouraged, discouraging, diseased, disobedient, distressed, distressing, evil, fallacious, faulty, gloomy, grave, grim, grotty, guilty, harmful, harsh, ill, illaudable, immoral, imperfect, inadequate, incorrect, inferior, injurious, mean, melancholy, mischievous, mouldy, naughty, no-good, noxious, off, offensive, onkus, painful, piacular, poor, putrid, rancid, regretful, remorseful, ropy, rotten, rueful, ruinous, sad, serious, severe, shoddy, sick, sinful, sombre, sorry, sour, spoilt, stormy, substandard, terrible, troubled, unfortunate, unhealthy, unpleasant, unruly, unsatisfactory, unwell, upset, vile, wicked, wrong.

bad blood acrimony, anger, animosity, antagonism, bad feeling, dislike, distrust, enmity, feud, hatred, hostility, malevolence, malice, nastiness, odium, rancour, resentment, upset, vendetta.

bad form bad style, barbarism, gaucherie, impropriety, indecorum, inelegance, infelicity, mauvais ton, solecism.

bad luck adversity, blow, deuce-ace, hard cheese, hard lines, hard luck, hoodoo, ill luck, mischance, misfortune, misluck, reverse, setback.

antonym luck.

bad manners boorishness, coarseness, discourtesy, disrespect, gaucherie, impoliteness, incivility, inconsideration, indelicacy, mismanners, unmannerliness.

antonym politeness.

bad taste coarseness, crudeness, grossness, indecency, indelicacy, mauvais goût, obscenity, offensiveness, poor taste, smuttiness, tactlessness, tastelessness, vulgarity.

antonyms delicacy, tastefulness.

bad time agony, going-over, grilling, mauvais moment, mauvais quart d'heure, nasty moment, suspense, third degree, torture.

badge *n* brand, cognisance, device, emblem, episemon, identification, insignia, logo, mark, sign, stamp, token, trademark.

badger *v* bait, bully, bullyrag, chivvy, goad, harass, harry, hassle, hound, importune, nag, pester, plague, torment.

badinage *n* banter, chaff, dicacity, drollery, give and take, humour, jocularity, mockery, persiflage, raillery, repartee, ribbing, teasing, waggery, word-play.

badly[1] *adv* carelessly, criminally, defectively, faultily, immorally, imperfectly, improperly, inadequately, incompetently, incorrectly, ineptly, negligently, poorly, shamefully, shoddily, unethically, unfairly, unfavourably, unfortunately, unsatisfactorily, unsuccessfully, wickedly, wrong, wrongly.

antonym mildly.

badly[2] *adv* acutely, bitterly, critically, crucially, deeply, desperately, exceedingly, extremely, gravely, greatly, intensely, painfully, seriously, severely.

antonym mildly.

bad-tempered *adj* cantankerous, captious, choleric, crabbed, cross, crotchety, dyspeptic, fractious, franzy, girnie, impatient, irascible, irritable, peevish, petulant, querulous, snappy, splenetic, stroppy, testy, vixenish, vixenly.

antonyms equable, genial.

baffle *v* amaze, astound, balk, bamboozle, bemuse, bewilder, check, confound, confuse, daze, defeat, disconcert, dumbfound, flabbergast, floor, flummox, foil, frustrate, hinder, mystify, nonplus, perplex, puzzle, stump, stun, stymie, thwart, upset.

antonyms enlighten, help.

baffling *adj* amazing, astounding, bemusing, confusing, extraordinary, frustrating, mysterious, perplexing, stupefying, surprising, thwarting, unfathomable.

antonyms enlightening, explanatory.

bag *v* acquire, appropriate, capture, catch, commandeer, corner, gain, get, grab, kill, land, obtain, reserve, shoot, take, trap.

n carrier, container, dorlach, Dorothy bag, dressing-case, Gladstone bag, grab-bag, grip, gripsack, handbag, haversack, hold-all, holder, pack, poke, reticule, rucksack, sack, satchel, satchet, scrip, shoulder-bag, tote-bag, valise.

baggage *n* accoutrements, bags, belongings, equipment, gear, impedimenta, luggage, paraphernalia, suit-cases, things, traps, viaticals.

baggy *adj* billowing, bulging, droopy, flaccid, floppy, ill-fitting, loose, oversize, pouchy, roomy, sagging, slack.

antonyms firm, tight.

bail *n* bond, guarantee, guaranty, pledge, security, surety, warranty.

bail out[1] aid, assist, finance, help, relieve, rescue.

bail out[2], bale outback out, cop out, escape, quit, retreat, withdraw.

bailiff *n* agent, beagle, constable, deputy, factor, huissier, magistrate, office, Philistine, sheriff.

bait *n* allurement, attraction, bribe, carrot, decoy, enticement, inducement, lure, temptation.

antonym disincentive.

v annoy, gall, goad, harass, hound, irk, irritate, needle, persecute, provoke, tease, torment.

balance *v* adjust, assess, calculate, compare, compute, consider, counteract, counterbalance, counterpoise, deliberate, equalise, equate, equilibrate, equipoise, equiponderate, estimate, evaluate, level, librate, match, neutralise, offset, parallel, poise, settle, square, stabilise, steady, tally, total, weigh.

antonyms overbalance, unbalance.

n composure, correspondence, difference, equality, equanimity, equilibrium, equipoise, equity, equivalence, evenness, parity, poise, remainder, residue, rest, self-possession, stability, stasis, steadiness, surplus, symmetry.

antonyms imbalance, instability.

balanced *adj* calm, equitable, even-handed, fair, impartial, just, self-possessed, sensible, unbiased, unprejudiced, well-rounded.

antonyms prejudiced, unbalanced.

balcony *n* gallery, gods, moucharaby, terrace, upper circle, veranda.

bald *adj* bald-headed, baldpated, bare, barren, bleak, depilated, direct, downright, exposed, forthright, glabrate, glabrous, hairless, naked, outright, peeled, plain, severe, simple, stark, straight, straightforward, treeless, unadorned, uncompromising, uncovered, undisguised, unvarnished.

antonyms adorned, hirsute.

balderdash *n* balls, bollocks, bullshit, bunk, bunkum, claptrap, drivel, gibberish, nonsense, poppycock, rot, rubbish, tommyrot, trash, tripe, twaddle.

baldness *n* alopecia, bald-headedness, bareness, calvities, calvousness, directness, glabrousness, hairlessness, psilosis, starkness.

antonym hirsuteness.

bale *n* bundle, fardel, pack, package, parcel, truss.

bale out *see* **bail out**.

baleful *adj* deadly, destructive, evil, fell, harmful, hurtful, injurious, malevolent, malignant, menacing, , mournful, noxious, ominous, pernicious, ruinous, sad, sinister, venomous, woeful.

antonyms auspicious, favourable.

balk, baulk *v* baffle, bar, boggle, check, counteract, defeat, demur, disconcert, dodge, evade, flinch, foil, forestall, frustrate, hesitate, hinder, jib, make difficulties, obstruct, prevent, recoil, refuse, resist, shirk, shrink, stall, thwart.

ball[1] *n* bauble, bobble, bullet, clew, conglomeration, drop, globe, globule, orb, pellet, pill, shot, slug, sphere, spheroid.

ball[2] *n* assembly, carnival, dance, dinner-dance, fandango, hop, masquerade, party, ridotto, rout, soirée.

ballad *n* carol, composition, ditty, folk-song, forebitter, lay, poem, shanty, song.

ballet *n* ballet-dancing, dancing, leg-business.

balloon *v* bag, belly, billow, blow up, bulge, dilate, distend, enlarge, expand, inflate, puff out, swell.

ballot *n* election, plebiscite, poll, polling, referendum, vote, voting.

ballyhoo *n* advertising, agitation, build-up, clamour, commotion, disturbance, excitement, fuss, hubbub, hue and cry, hullabaloo, hype, noise, promotion, propaganda, publicity, racket, tumult.

balm *n* anodyne, balsam, bromide, calmative, comfort, consolation, cream, curative, embrocation, emollient, lenitive, lotion, ointment, palliative, restorative, salve, sedative, solace, unguent.

antonyms irritant, vexation.

balmy[1] *adj* clement, gentle, mild, pleasant, soft, summery, temperate.

antonym inclement.

balmy[2] *adj* barmy, crazy, daft, dippy, dotty, foolish, idiotic, insane, loony, mad, nuts, nutty, odd, round the bend, silly, stupid.

antonyms rational, sane, sensible.

bamboozle *v* baffle, befool, befuddle, bemuse, cheat, con, confound, confuse, cozen, deceive, defraud, delude, dupe, fool, hoax, hoodwink, mystify, perplex, puzzle, stump, swindle, trick.

ban *v* anathematise, banish, bar, debar, disallow, exclude, forbid, interdict, ostracise, outlaw, prohibit, proscribe, restrict, suppress.

antonym permit.

n anathematisation, boycott, censorship, condemnation, curse, denunciation, embargo, interdiction, outlawry, prohibition, proscription, restriction, stoppage, suppression, taboo.

antonyms dispensation, permission.

banal *adj* boring, clichéd, cliché-ridden, commonplace, corny, empty, everyday, hackneyed, humdrum, jejune, old hat, ordinary, pedestrian, platitudinous, stale, stereotyped, stock, threadbare, tired, trite unimaginative, unoriginal, vapid.

antonym original.

banality *n* bromide, cliché, commonplace, dullness, platitude, prosaicism, triteness, triviality, truism, vapidity.

antonym originality.

band¹ *n* bandage, bandeau, belt, binding, bond, chain, cord, fascia, fasciole, fetter, fillet, ligature, manacle, ribbon, shackle, strap, strip, swath, tape, tie, vitta.

band² *n* association, body, clique, club, combo, company, coterie, crew, ensemble, flock, gang, group, herd, horde, orchestra, party, range, society, troop, waits.

v affiliate, ally, amalgamate, collaborate, consolidate, federate, gather, group, join, merge, unite.

antonyms disband, disperse.

bandage *n* compress, dressing, gauze, ligature, plaster, swaddle, swathe, tourniquet.

v bind, cover, dress, swaddle, swathe.

bandit *n* brigand, buccaneer, cowboy, dacoit, desperado, footpad, freebooter, gangster, gunman, highwayman, hijacker, marauder, outlaw, pirate, racketeer, robber, ruffian, thief.

banditry *n* brigandage, dacoitage, dacoity, freebooting, heist, hijacking, hold-up, latrociny, robbery, stickup, theft.

bandy¹ *v* barter, exchange, interchange, pass, reciprocate, swap, throw, toss, trade.

bandy² *adj* bandy-legged, bent, bowed, bow-legged, crooked, curved, valgous.

bane *n* adversity, affliction, annoyance, bête noire, blight, burden, calamity, curse, despair, destruction, disaster, distress, downfall, evil, irritation, misery, misfortune, nuisance, ordeal, pest, pestilence, plague, ruin, scourge, sorrow, torment, trial, trouble, vexation, woe.

antonym blessing.

baneful *adj* deadly, deleterious, destructive, disastrous, fell, harmful, hurtful, injurious, malevolent, noxious, pernicious, pestilential, ruinous, sinister, venomous.

antonym beneficent.

bang *n* blow, boom, box, bump, clang, clap, clash, collision, crash, cuff, detonation, explosion, hit, knock, noise, peal, pop, punch, report, shot, slam, smack, stroke, thud, thump, wallop, whack.

v bash, boom, bump, burst, clang, clatter, crash, detonate, drum, echo, explode, hammer, knock, peal, pound, pummel, rap, resound, slam, stamp, strike, thump, thunder.

adv directly, hard, headlong, noisily, plumb, precisely, right, slap, smack, straight, suddenly.

banish *v* ban, bar, blacklist, debar, deport, discard, dislodge, dismiss, dispel, eject, eliminate, eradicate, evict, exclude, excommunicate, exile, expatriate, expel, get rid of, ostracise, oust, outlaw, remove, shut out, transport.

antonyms recall, welcome.

banishment *n* deportation, eviction, exile, exilement, expatriation, expulsion, ostracisation, outlawry, proscription, transportation.

antonyms recall, return, welcome.

bank¹ *n* accumulation, cache, depository, fund, hoard, pool, repository, reserve, reservoir, savings, stock, stockpile, store, storehouse, treasury.

v accumulate, deposit, keep, save, stockpile, store.

antonym spend.

bank² *n* acclivity, banking, brink, bund, earthwork, edge, embankment, fail-dike, heap, margin, mass, mound, pile, rampart, ridge, rivage, shallow, shoal, shore, side, slope, tilt.

v accumulate, aggrade, amass, camber, cant, drift, heap, incline, mass, mound, pile, pitch, slant, slope, stack, tilt, tip.

bank³ *n* array, bench, echelon, file, group, line, rank, row, sequence, series, succession, tier, train.

bank-note *n* bill, flimsy, greenback, note, paper money, treasury note.

bankrupt *adj* beggared, broke, depleted, destitute, exhausted, failed, impecunious, impoverished, insolvent, lacking, penurious, ruined, spent.

antonyms solvent, wealthy.

n debtor, duck, dyvour, insolvent, pauper.

bankruptcy *n* beggary, disaster, dyvoury, exhaustion, failure, indebtedness, insolvency, lack, liquidation, penury, ruin, ruination.

antonyms solvency, wealth.

banner *n* banderol(e), bannerol, burgee, colours, ensign, fanion, flag, gonfalon, labarum, oriflamme, pennant, pennon, standard, streamer, vexillum.

banquet *n* binge, dinner, feast, meal, repast, revel, treat, wayzgoose.

banter *n* badinage, chaff, chaffing, cross-talk, derision, dicacity, jesting, joking, kidding, mockery, persiflage, pleasantry, quiz, raillery, repartee, ribbing, ridicule, word play.

baptise *v* admit, call, christen, cleanse, dub, enrol, immerse, initiate, introduce, name, purify, recruit, sprinkle, style, term, title.

baptism *n* beginning, chrism, christening, début, dedication, immersion, initiation, introduction, launch, launching, purification, sprinkling.

bar¹ *n* barricade, barrier, batten, check, cross-piece, deterrent, deterrment, hindrance, impediment, obstacle, obstruction, overslaugh, paling, pole, preventive, rail, railing, rod, shaft, stake, stanchion, stick, stop.

v ban, barricade, blackball, bolt, debar, exclude, fasten, forbid, hinder, latch, lock, obstruct, preclude, prevent, prohibit, restrain, secure.

bar² *n* bierkeller, boozer, canteen, counter, dive, doggery, dram-shop, estaminet, exchange, gin-palace, ginshop, groggery, grogshop, honky-tonk, howff, inn, joint, lounge, nineteenth hole, pub, public house, saloon, tavern, vaults, watering-hole.

bar³ *n* advocates, attorneys, barristers, bench, counsel, court, courtroom, dock, law court, tribunal.

bar⁴ *n* block, chunk, ingot, lump, nugget, slab, wedge.

barb *n* affront, arrow, barbule, bristle, cut, dig, fluke, gibe, home-thrust, home-truth, insult, point, prickle, prong, quill, rebuff, sarcasm, sneer, spicule, spike, spur, stab, thorn, thrust.

barbarian *n* ape, boor, brute, clod, hooligan, hottentot, hun, ignoramus, illiterate, lout, lowbrow, oaf, philistine, ruffian, savage, tramontane, vandal, vulgarian, yahoo.

adj boorish, brutish, coarse, crude, lowbrow, philistine, rough, tramontane, uncivilised, uncouth, uncultivated, uncultured, unsophisticated, vulgar.

barbaric *adj* barbarous, boorish, brutal, brutish, coarse, crude, cruel, ferocious, fierce, inhuman, primitive, rude, savage, uncivilised, uncouth, vulgar, wild.

antonyms civilised, humane.

barbarism *n* abuse, atrocity, barbarity, brutishness, coarseness, corruption, crudity, cruelty, enormity, misuse, outrage, savagery, solecism, vulgarism.

barbarity *n* barbarousness, boorishness, brutality, brutishness, cruelty, ferocity, inhumanity, rudeness, ruthlessness, savagery, viciousness, wildness.

antonyms civilisation, civility, humanity.

barbarous *adj* barbarian, barbaric, brutal, brutish, coarse, crude, cruel, ferocious, heartless, heathenish, ignorant, inhuman, monstrous, philistine, primitive, rough, rude, ruthless, savage, uncivilised, uncouth, uncultured, unlettered, unrefined, vicious, vulgar, wild.

antonyms civilised, cultured, educated.

barbed *adj* acerbic, acid, catty, caustic, critical, cutting, hooked, hostile, hurtful, jagged, nasty, pointed, prickly, pronged, snide, spiked, spiny, thorny, toothed, unkind.

bare *adj* austere, bald, barren, basic, blank, defoliate, defoliated, denudated, denuded, disfurnished, empty, essential, explicit, exposed, hard, lacking, literal, mean, naked, napless, nude, open, peeled, plain, poor, scanty, scarce, severe, sheer, shorn, simple, spare, stark, stripped, unadorned, unarmed, unclad, unclothed, uncovered, undisguised, undressed, unembellished, unforested, unfurnished, unprovided, unsheathed, untimbered, unvarnished, unwooded, vacant, void, wanting, woodless.

barefaced *adj* arrant, audacious, bald, blatant, bold, brash, brazen, flagrant, glaring, impudent, insolent, manifest, naked, obvious, open, palpable, patent, shameless, transparent, unabashed, unconcealed.

barefooted *adj* barefoot, discalced, shoeless, unshod.

antonym shod.

barely¹ *adv* almost, hardly, just, scarcely, sparingly, sparsely.

barely² *adv* explicitly, nakedly, openly, plainly.

bargain *n* agreement, arrangement, compact, contract, discount, giveaway, negotiation, pact, pledge, promise, reduction, snip, steal, stipulation, transaction, treaty, understanding.

v agree, barter, broke, buy, chaffer, contract, covenant, deal, dicker, haggle, higgle, negotiate, promise, sell, stipulate, trade, traffic, transact.

bargain for anticipate, consider, contemplate, expect, foresee, imagine, include, look for, plan for, reckon on.

bargaining *n* barter, bartering, dealing, dicker, haggling, higgling, horse-dealing, horse-trading, negotiation, trading, trafficking, wheeler-dealing.

barge¹ *v* bump, butt in, cannon, collide, elbow, encroach, gatecrash, hit, impinge, interfere, interrupt, intrude, muscle in, push, push in, shove.

barge² *n* birlinn, Bucentaur, canal boat, flatboat, house-boat, lighter, narrow-boat, transport.

bark *n* bawl, bay, growl, shout, snap, snarl, woof, yap, yell, yelp.

v advertise, bawl, bay, bluster, cough, growl, shout, snap, snarl, yap, yell, yelp.

barking *n* latration.

adj latrant.

barmy *adj* balmy, crazy, daft, dippy, dotty, foolish, idiotic, insane, loony, mad, nuts, nutty, odd, silly, stupid.

antonyms rational, sane, sensible.

baroque *adj* bizarre, bold, convoluted, elaborate, extravagant, exuberant, fanciful, fantastic, flamboyant, florid, grotesque, ornate, overdecorated, overwrought, rococo, vigorous, whimsical.

antonym plain.

barracks *n* accommodation, billet, camp, cantonment, caserne, encampment, garrison, guard-house, lodging, quarters.

barrage *n* assault, attack, battery, bombardment, broadside, burst, cannonade, deluge, fusillade, gunfire, hail, mass, onset, onslaught, plethora, profusion, rain, salvo, shelling, shower, storm, stream, torrent, volley.

barred *adj* banned, blackballed, disallowed, excluded, forbidden, outlawed, prohibited, proscribed, taboo.

antonym permissible.

barrel *n* butt, cade, cask, hogshead, keg, kilderkin, puncheon, rundlet, tierce, tun, water-butt, wood.

barren *adj* arid, boring, childless, desert, desolate, dry, dull, empty, flat, fruitless, infecund, infertile, jejune, lacklustre, pointless, profitless, stale, sterile, unbearing, unfruitful, uninformative, uninspiring, uninstructive, uninteresting, unproductive, unprolific, unrewarding, useless, vapid, waste.

antonyms fertile, productive, useful.

barricade *n* barrier, blockade, bulwark, fence, obstruction, palisade, protection, rampart, screen, stockade.

v bar, block, blockade, defend, fortify, obstruct, palisade, protect, screen.

barrier *n* bail, bar, barricade, blockade, boom, boundary, bulkhead, check, difficulty, ditch, drawback, fence, fortification, handicap, hindrance, hurdle, impediment, limitation, obstacle, obstruction, railing, rampart, restriction, stop, stumbling-block, transverse, wall.

barrow *n* hand-barrow, handcart, hurly, push-cart, wheelbarrow.

bartender *n* bar-keeper, barmaid, barman, publican, tapster.

barter *v* bargain, chaffer, deal, dicker, exchange, haggle, higgle, negotiate, niffer, sell, swap, trade, traffic, truck.

base[1] *n* basis, bed, bottom, camp, centre, core, essence, essential, foot, foundation, fundamental, groundwork, headquarters, heart, home, key, keystone, origin, pedestal, plinth, post, principal, rest, root, settlement, socle, source, stand, standard, starting-point, station, substrate, substructure, support, underpinning, understructure.

v build, construct, depend, derive, establish, found, ground, hinge, locate, station.

base[2] *adj* abject, contemptible, corrupt, counterfeit, depraved, disgraceful, disreputable, dog, evil, grovelling, humble, ignoble, ignominious, immoral, infamous, low, lowly, low-minded, low-thoughted, mean, menial, miserable, paltry, pitiful, poor, scandalous, servile, shameful, slavish, sordid, sorry, valueless, vile, villainous, vulgar, wicked, worthless, wretched.

base[3] *adj* adulterated, alloyed, artificial, bastard, counterfeit, debased, fake, forged, fraudulent, impure, inferior, pinchbeck, spurious.

base-born *adj* bastard, common, humble, illegitimate, low-born, low-bred, lowly, misborn, plebeian, proletarian, vulgar.

antonym highborn.

baseless *adj* gratuitous, groundless, unattested, unauthenticated, uncalled-for, unconfirmed, uncorroborated, unfounded, ungrounded, unjustifiable, unjustified, unsubstantiated, unsupported.

antonym justifiable.

baseness *n* contemptibility, degradation, depravation, depravity, despicability, ignominy, infamy, knavery, lowliness, meanness, misery, poverty, servility, slavishness, sordidness, sorriness, subservience, turpitude, vileness, villainy, worthlessness, wretchedness.

bash *v* belt, biff, break, crash, crush, ding, dunt, hit, punch, slosh, slug, smack, smash, sock, strike, swipe, wallop.

n attempt, crack, go, shot, stab, try, turn, whirl.

bashful *adj* abashed, backward, blushing, confused, coy, diffident, embarrassed, hesitant, inhibited, modest, nervous, reserved, reticent, retiring, self-conscious, self-effacing, shamefaced, sheepish, shrinking, shy, timid, timorous, unforthcoming, verecund.

antonym confident.

bashfulness *n* coyness, diffidence, embarrassment, hesitancy, inhibition, mauvaise honte, modesty, reserve, self-consciousness, shamefacedness, sheepishness, shyness, timidity, timorousness.

antonym confidence.

basic *adj* central, elementary, essential, fundamental, important, indispensable, inherent, intrinsic, key, necessary, primary, radical, root, underlying, vital.

antonyms inessential, peripheral.

basically *adv* à fond, at bottom, at heart, au fond, essentially, fundamentally, inherently, intrinsically, primarily, principally, radically.

basics *n* bedrock, brass tacks, core, essentials, facts, fundamentals, grass roots, necessaries, nitty-gritty, nuts and bolts, practicalities, principles, rock bottom, rudiments.

basin *n* aquamanile, bowl, cavity, crater, depression, dip, dish, hollow, porringer, sink.

basis *n* approach, base, bottom, core, essential, fond, footing, foundation, fundamental, ground, groundwork, heart, keynote, pedestal, premise, principle, support, thrust.

bask *v* apricate, delight in, enjoy, laze, lie, lounge, luxuriate, relax, relish, revel, savour, sunbathe, wallow.

basket *n* bassinet, corf, creel, dosser, frail, hamper, junket, pannier, pottle, punnet, skep, trug.

bass *adj* deep, deep-toned, grave, low, low-pitched, low-toned, resonant, sepulchral, sonorous.

bastard *n* by-blow, filius nullius, git, illegitimate, love child, love-child, lucky-piece, misfortune, mother-fucker, natural child, whoreson.

adj abnormal, adulterated, anomalous, artificial, base, baseborn, counterfeit, false, illegitimate, imperfect, impure, inferior, irregular, misbegotten, sham, spurious, synthetic.

antonyms genuine, legitimate.

bastardise *v* adulterate, cheapen, corrupt, debase, defile, degrade, demean, depreciate, devalue, distort, pervert, vitiate.

bastion *n* bulwark, citadel, defence, fastness, fortress, mainstay, pillar, prop, redoubt, rock, stronghold, support, tower of strength.

batch *n* amount, assemblage, assortment, bunch, collection, consignment, contingent, group, lot, pack, parcel, quantity, set.

bath *n* ablution, balneary, cleansing, douche, douse, hamman, Jacuzzi"trade", scrubbing, shower, soak, tub, wash.

v bathe, clean, douse, lave, shower, soak, tub, wash.

bathe *v* cleanse, cover, dook, dunk, encompass, flood, immerse, moisten, rinse, soak, steep, stew, suffuse, swim, wash, wet.

n dip, dook, rinse, soak, swim, wash.

bathetic *adj* anticlimactic, sublime to ridiculous.

bathos *n* anticlimax, comedown, let-down.

battalion *n* army, brigade, company, contingent, division, force, herd, horde, host, legion, mass, multitude, phalanx, platoon, regiment, squadron, throng.

batten *v* barricade, board up, clamp down, fasten, fix, nail down, secure, tighten.

batter *v* abuse, assault, bash, beat, belabour, bruise, buffet, crush, dash, deface, demolish, destroy, disfigure, distress, hurt, injure, lash, maltreat, mangle, manhandle, mar, maul, pelt, pound, pummel, ruin, shatter, smash, thrash, wallop.

battered *adj* abused, beaten, bruised, crumbling, crushed, damaged, dilapidated, ill-treated, injured, ramshackle, tumbledown, weather-beaten.

battery *n* artillery, assault, attack, barrage, beating, cannon, cannonry, emplacements, guns, mayhem, onslaught, progression, sequence, series, set, thrashing, violence.

battle *n* action, attack, campaign, clash, combat, conflict, contest, controversy, crusade, debate, disagreement, dispute, encounter, engagement, fight, fray, hostilities, row, skirmish, stour, strife, struggle, war, warfare.

v agitate, argue, campaign, clamour, combat, contend, contest, crusade, dispute, feud, fight, strive, struggle, war.

battle-axe *n* disciplinarian, harridan, martinet, Tartar, termagant, virago.

battle-cry *n* catchword, motto, slogan, war cry, war whoop, warsong, watchword.

batty *adj* barmy, bats, bonkers, cracked, crackers, crazy, daffy, daft, demented, dippy, dotty, eccentric, idiotic, insane, loony, lunatic, mad, nuts, nutty, odd, off one's rocker, peculiar, potty, queer, screwy, touched.

antonym sane.

bauble *n* bagatelle, flamfew, gewgaw, gimcrack, kickshaw, knick-knack, plaything, tinsel, toy, trifle, trinket.

baulk, balk *v* baffle, bar, boggle, check, counteract, defeat, demur, disconcert, dodge, evade, flinch, foil, forestall, frustrate, hesitate, hinder, jib, make difficulties, obstruct, prevent, recoil, refuse, resist, shirk, shrink, stall, thwart.

bawd *n* brothel-keeper, madam, panderess, pimp, procuress.

bawdy *adj* blue, coarse, dirty, erotic, gross, improper, indecent, indecorous, indelicate, lascivious, lecherous, lewd, libidinous, licentious, lustful, obscene, pornographic, prurient, ribald, risqué, rude, salacious, smutty, suggestive, vulgar.

antonyms chaste, clean.

bawl *v* bellow, blubber, call, caterwaul, clamour, cry, halloo, howl, roar, shout, sob, squall, vociferate, wail, waul, weep, yell.

bay[1] *n* arm, bight, cove, embayment, gulf, inlet, voe.

bay[2] *n* alcove, booth, carrel, compartment, cubicle, embrasure, niche, nook, opening, recess, stall.

bay[3] *v* bark, bawl, bell, bellow, cry, holler, howl, roar.

bayonet *v* impale, knife, pierce, spear, stab, stick.

bazaar *n* agora, alcaicería, alcázar, bring-and-buy, exchange, fair, fête, market, market-place, mart, sale.

be *v* abide, arise, befall, breathe, come about, come to pass, continue, develop, dwell, endure, exist, happen, inhabit, inhere, last, live, obtain, occur, persist, prevail, remain, reside, stand, stay, survive, take place.

beach *n* coast, foreshore, lido, littoral, machair, margin, plage, sand, sands, seaboard, seashore, seaside, shingle, shore, strand, water's edge.

beachcomber *n* Autolycus, forager, loafer, loiterer, scavenger, scrounger, wayfarer.

beacon *n* beam, bonfire, fanal, flare, lighthouse, pharos, rocket, sign, signal, watch-fire.

bead *n* blob, bubble, dot, drop, droplet, glob, globule, pearl, pellet, pill, spherule.

beak *n* bill, bow, mandibles, neb, nib, nose, nozzle, proboscis, projection, prow, ram, rostrum, snout, stem.

beaked *adj* curved, hooked, pointed, rostrate, rostrated, sharp.

beam *n* arbor, bar, boom, girder, gleam, glimmer, glint, glow, joist, plank, radiation, rafter, ray, shaft, spar, stanchion, stream, support, timber, transom.

v broadcast, effulge, emit, fulgurate, glare, glimmer, glitter, glow, grin, laugh, radiate, shine, smile, transmit.

beaming *adj* beautiful, bright, brilliant, cheerful, effulgent, flashing, gleaming, glistening, glittering, glowing, grinning, happy, joyful, lambent, radiant, refulgent, scintillating, shining, smiling, sparkling, sunny.

antonyms lowering, sullen.

bear[1] *v* abide, admit, allow, beget, bring, brook, carry, cherish, convey, endure, entertain, exhibit, hack, harbour, have, hold, maintain, move, permit, possess, put up with, shoulder, stomach, suffer, support, sustain, take, tolerate, tote, transport, undergo, uphold, weather, weigh upon.

bear down advance on, approach, attack, burden, close in, compress, converge on, encumber, near, oppress, press down, push, strain, weigh down.

bear in mind be cognisant of, be mindful of, beware, consider, heed, include, mind out for, note, remember.

bear on affect, appertain to, concern, connect with, involve, pertain to, refer to, relate to, touch on.

bear oneself acquit oneself, act, behave, comport oneself, demean oneself, deport oneself, perform.

bear out confirm, corroborate, demonstrate, endorse, justify, prove, substantiate, support, testify, uphold, vindicate.

bear up carry on, endure, keep one's pecker up, persevere, soldier on, suffer, withstand.

bear with be patient with, endure, forbear, make allowances for, put up with, suffer, tolerate.

bear witness attest, confirm, corroborate, demonstrate, depone, depose, evidence, evince, prove, show, testify, testify to, vouch for.

bear[2] *v* breed, bring forth, develop, drop, engender, generate, give birth to, give up, produce, propagate, yield.

bearable *adj* acceptable, endurable, livable(-with), manageable, sufferable, supportable, sustainable, tolerable.

beard *v* brave, challenge, confront, dare, defy, face, oppose.

n beaver, excrement, face fungus, goatee, imperial, moustache, mutton chops, sideburns, tuft, vandyke, whiskers.

bearded *adj* awned, bewhiskered, bristly, bushy, hairy, hirsute, shaggy, tufted, unshaven, whiskered.

antonyms beardless, clean-shaven, smooth.

bearer *n* beneficiary, carrier, consignee, conveyor, courier, holder, messenger, payee, porter, possessor, post, runner, servant.

bearing *n* air, application, aspect, attitude, behaviour, carriage, comportment, connection, course, demeanour, deportment, direction, import, manner, mien, pertinence, poise, posture, presence, reference, relation, relevance, significance.

bearings *n* aim, course, direction, inclination, location, orientation, position, situation, tack, track, way, whereabouts.

beast *n* animal, ape, barbarian, brute, creature, devil, fiend, monster, pig, sadist, savage, swine.

beastly *adj* barbarous, bestial, brutal, brutish, coarse, cruel, depraved, disagreeable, foul, inhuman, mean, monstrous, nasty, repulsive, rotten, sadistic, savage, sensual, swinish, terrible, unpleasant, vile.

beat[1] *v* bang, bash, baste, bastinade, bastinado, batter, belabour, bethump, bethwack, bless, bludgeon, bruise, buffet, cane, contuse, cudgel, curry, ding, drub, dunt, fashion, flog, forge, form, fustigate, hammer, hit, impinge, knobble, knock, knout, knubble, lam, lash, lay into, malleate, maul, mill, model, nubble, pelt, pound, punch, shape, slat, strap, strike, swipe, tan, thrash, thwack, trounce, vapulate, verberate, warm, welt, whale, wham, whip, work.

n blow, hit, lash, punch, shake, slap, strike, swing, thump.

adj exhausted, fatigued, jiggered, tired, wearied, worn out, zonked.

beat it go away, hop it, leave, scarper, scram, shoo, skedaddle, vamoose.

beat up assault, attack, batter, do over, duff over, duff up, fill in, hammer, knock about, knock around, thrash.

beat[2] *v* best, conquer, defeat, excel, hammer, outdo, outrun, outstrip, overcome, overwhelm, slaughter, subdue, surpass, trounce, vanquish.

beat[3] *v* flutter, palpitate, patter, pound, pulsate, pulse, quake, quiver, race, shake, throb, thump, tremble, vibrate.

n accent, cadence, flutter, measure, metre, palpitation, pulsation, pulse, rhyme, rhythm, stress, throb, time.

beat[4] *n* circuit, course, journey, path, round, rounds, route, territory, way.

beaten[1] *adj* baffled, cowed, defeated, disappointed, disheartened, frustrated, overcome, ruined, surpassed, thwarted, vanquished, worsted.

beaten[2] *adj* fashioned, forged, formed, hammered, malleated, shaped, stamped, worked.

beaten[3] *adj* blended, foamy, frothy, mixed, pounded, stirred, tenderised, whipped, whisked.

beatific *adj* angelic, blessed, blissful, divine, ecstatic, exalted, glorious, heavenly, joyful, rapturous, seraphic, serene, sublime.

beatify *v* bless, exalt, glorify, macarise, sanctify.

beating *n* belting, caning, chastisement, conquest, corporal punishment, defeat, downfall, dressing, drubbing, flogging, laldie, lamming, overthrow, rout, ruin, slapping, smacking, thrashing, vapulation, verberation, warming, whaling, whipping.

adj pounding, pulsatile, pulsating, pulsative, pulsatory, pulsing, racing, throbbing, thumping.

beatitude *n* beatification, blessedness, bliss, ecstasy, exaltation, felicity, happiness, holiness, joy, macarism, saintliness, sanctity.

beau *n* admirer, Adonis, boyfriend, cavalier, coxcomb, dandy, escort, fancy man, fiancé, fop, gallant, Jack-a-dandy, ladies' man, lover, popinjay, suitor, swain, sweetheart, swell.

beautician *n* beauty specialist, cosmetician, friseur, hairdresser, visagiste.

beautiful *adj* alluring, appealing, attractive, beau, beauteous, belle, charming, comely, delightful, exquisite, fair, fine, good-looking, gorgeous, graceful, handsome, lovely, pleasing, pulchritudinous, radiant, ravishing, stunning.

antonyms plain, ugly.

beautify *v* adorn, array, bedeck, bedizen, deck, decorate, embellish, enhance, garnish, gild, glamorise, grace, improve, ornament, tart up, titivate.

antonyms disfigure, spoil.

beauty[1] *n* allure, attractiveness, bloom, charm, comeliness, elegance, excellence, exquisitness, fairness, glamour, grace, handsomeness, loveliness, pleasure, pulchritude, seemliness, symmetry.

antonym ugliness.

beauty[2] *n* belle, charmer, corker, cracker, femme fatale, goddess, good-looker, knockout, lovely, siren, stunner, Venus.

antonym frump.

becalmed *adj* at a standstill, idle, motionless, still, stranded, stuck.

because *conj* as, by reason of, for, forasmuch, forwhy, in that, inasmuch as, on account of, owing to, since, thanks to.

beckon *v* allure, attract, bid, call, coax, decoy, draw, entice, gesticulate, gesture, invite, lure, motion, nod, pull, signal, summon, tempt, waft.

become *v* befit, behove, embellish, enhance, fit, flatter, grace, harmonise, ornament, set off, suit.

becoming *adj* appropriate, attractive, befitting, charming, comely, comme il faut, compatible, congruous, decent, decorous, enhancing, fit, fitting, flattering, graceful, maidenly, meet, neat, pretty, proper, seemly, suitable, tasteful, worthy.

antonym unbecoming.

bed[1] *n* bedstead, berth, bunk, cot, cote, couch, divan, kip, mattress, pallet, palliasse, sack, the downy.

bed[2] *n* base, border, bottom, channel, foundation, garden, groundwork, layer, matrix, patch, plot, row, stratus, strip, substratum, wadi, watercourse.

v base, embed, establish, fix, found, ground, implant, insert, plant, settle.

bedaub *v* begrime, besmear, blotch, daub, smear, smirch, soil, spatter, splash, stain.

bedclothes *n* bedding, bed-linen, blankets, counterpanes, coverlets, covers, downies, eiderdowns, pillows, quilts, sheets.

bedeck *v* adorn, array, beautify, bedight, bedizen, decorate, embellish, festoon, garnish, ornament, trick out, trim.

antonym strip.

bedevil *v* afflict, annoy, besiege, confound, distress, fret, frustrate, harass, irk, irritate, pester, plague, tease, torment, torture, trouble, vex, worry.

bedew *v* dampen, drench, imbue, moisten, shower, soak, spray, sprinkle, water, wet.

bedim *v* becloud, bedarken, befog, cloak, cloud, darken, dim, fog, obscure, overcast, shade, shadow, veil.

bedlam *n* anarchy, babel, chaos, clamour, commotion, confusion, furore, hubbub, hullabaloo, madhouse, noise, pandemonium, tumult, turmoil, uproar.

antonym calm.

bedraggled *adj* dirty, dishevelled, disordered, messy, muddied, muddy, scruffy, slovenly, sodden, soiled, stained, sullied, unkempt, untidy.

antonym tidy.

beef[1] *n* beefiness, brawn, bulk, flesh, fleshiness, heftiness, muscle, robustness, sinew, strength.

beef[2] *n* complaint, criticism, dispute, dissatisfaction, grievance, gripe, grouse, grumble, objection, protest.

v complain, criticise, gripe, grumble, moan, object.

antonym approve.

beefy *adj* brawny, bulky, burly, corpulent, fat, fleshy, heavy, hefty, hulking, muscular, plump, podgy, pudgy, rotund, stalwart, stocky, strapping, sturdy.

antonym slight.

beetle *v* dash, hurry, nip, run, rush, scamper, scoot, scurry, tear, zip.

beetling *adj* beetle, jutting, overhanging, pendent, poking, projecting, prominent, protruding.

befall *v* arrive, betide, chance, ensue, fall, follow, happen, materialise, occur, supervene, take place.

befitting *adj* appropriate, becoming, correct, decent, fit, fitting, meet, proper, right, seemly, suitable.

antonym unbecoming.

before *adv* ahead, earlier, formerly, in advance, in front, previously, sooner.

antonyms after, later.

prep ahead of, earlier than, in advance of, in anticipation of, in front of, in preparation for, previous to, prior to, sooner than.

conj in case, rather than.

beforehand *adv* already, before, earlier, in advance, preliminarily, previously, sooner.

befoul *v* bedung, begrime, besmirch, bespatter, defile, dirty, foul, muddy, pollute, soil, stain, sully, tarnish.

befriend *v* aid, assist, back, benefit, comfort, encourage, favour, help, patronise, stand by, succour, support, sustain, take a liking to, take under one's wing, uphold, welcome.

antonym neglect.

befuddle *v* baffle, bamboozle, befog, bewilder, confuse, daze, disorient, hocus, muddle, puzzle, stupefy.

befuddled *adj* baffled, bewildered, confused, dazed, fuddled, groggy, hazy, inebriated, intoxicated, muddled, woozy.

antonym lucid.

beg *v* beseech, cadge, crave, desire, entreat, fleech, implore, importune, petition, plead, pray, prog, request, require, schnorr, scrounge, shool, skelder, solicit, sponge on, supplicate, touch.

beg the question avoid, dodge, duck, equivocate, evade, hedge, shirk, shun, side-step, take for granted.

beget *v* breed, bring, cause, create, effect, engender, father, gender, generate, get, give rise to, occasion, procreate, produce, propagate, result in, sire, spawn.

beggar[1] *n* Abraham-man, bankrupt, beadsman, besognio, bluegown, cadger, canter, craver, down-and-out, gaberlunzie, lazzarone, mendicant, palliard, pauper, schnorrer, scrounger, sponger, starveling, supplicant, toe-rag, toe-ragger, tramp, vagrant.

beggar[2] *v* baffle, challenge, defy, exceed, surpass, transcend.

beggarly *adj* abject, contemptible, despicable, destitute, impoverished, inadequate, indigent, low, meagre, mean, miserly, needy, niggardly, paltry, pathetic, penurious, pitiful, poor, poverty-stricken, stingy, vile, wretched.

antonyms affluent, generous.

beggary *n* bankruptcy, destitution, indigence, mendicancy, need, neediness, pauperism, penury, poverty, vagrancy, want, wretchedness.
antonyms affluence, plenty.

begging *adj* beseeching, entreating, imploratory, imploring, longing, pleading, precative, precatory, wistful.
n cadging, entreaty, mendicancy, mendicity, petitioning, prayers, scrounging, soliciting, sponging, supplication.

begin *v* activate, actuate, appear, arise, commence, crop up, dawn, emerge, happen, inaugurate, initiate, instigate, institute, introduce, originate, prepare, set about, set in, spring, start.
antonyms end, finish.

beginner *n* abecedarian, alphabetarian, amateur, apprentice, cheechako, cub, fledgling, freshman, greenhorn, initiate, Johnny-raw, learner, neophyte, novice, recruit, rookie, rooky, starter, student, tenderfoot, tiro, trainee.
antonyms expert, old hand, veteran.

beginning *n* birth, commencement, embryo, establishment, fons et origo, fountainhead, germ, inauguration, inception, inchoation, initiation, introduction, onset, opening, origin, outset, preface, prelude, prime, rise, root, rudiments, seed, source, start, starting point.
antonyms end, finish.
adj early, elementary, inaugural, inauguratory, inceptive, inchoative, incipient, initial, introductory, nascent, primal, primary, primeval.

begrudge *v* covet, envy, grudge, mind, resent, stint.
antonym allow.

beguile *v* amuse, charm, cheat, cheer, cozen, deceive, delight, delude, distract, divert, dupe, engross, entertain, fool, hoodwink, mislead, occupy, pass, solace, trick, wile.

beguiling *adj* alluring, appealing, attractive, bewitching, captivating, charming, diverting, enchanting, entertaining, enticing, interesting, intriguing.
antonyms offensive, repulsive.

behalf *n* account, advantage, authority, benefit, defence, good, interest, name, part, profit, sake, side, support.

behave *v* acquit, act, bear, comport, conduct, demean, deport, function, operate, perform, react, respond, run, work.

behaviour *n* action, actions, bearing, carriage, comportment, conduct, dealings, demeanour, deportment, doings, functioning, habits, manner, manners, operation, performance, reaction, response, ways.

behead *v* decapitate, decollate, execute, guillotine, unhead.

behest *n* authority, bidding, charge, command, commandment, decree, dictate, direction, fiat, injunction, instruction, mandate, order, ordinance, precept, wish.

behind *prep* after, backing, causing, following, for, initiating, instigating, later than, responsible for, supporting.
adv after, afterwards, behindhand, en arrière, following, in arrears, in debt, in the wake of, next, overdue, subsequently.
n backside, bottom, butt, buttocks, derrière, posterior, prat, rear, rump, seat, sit-upon, tail.
behind one's back covertly, deceitfully, secretly, sneakily, sub rosa, surreptitiously, treacherously.
behind the times antiquated, dated, démodé, fogram, obsolete, old hat, old-fashioned, out of date, outdated, outmoded, passé, square.

behind-hand *adj* backward, dilatory, ill-provided, lag, late, remiss, slow, tardy.
antonym provident.

behold *v* consider, contemplate, descry, discern, espy, eye, look at, note, observe, perceive, regard, scan, survey, view, watch, witness.
interj ecce, lo, look, mark, observe, see, voici, voilà, watch.

beholden *adj* bound, grateful, indebted, obligated, obliged, owing, thankful.

behove *v* advance, be to one's advantage, befit, benefit, beseem, profit.

beige *adj* biscuit, buff, café au lait, camel, cinnamon, coffee, cream, ecru, fawn, greige, khaki, mushroom, neutral, oatmeal, sand, tan.

being[1] *n* actuality, animation, entity, essence, existence, haecceity, life, living, nature, quiddity, reality, soul, spirit, substance.

being[2] *n* animal, beast, body, creature, human being, individual, mortal, sentient, thing.

belabour *v* attack, bash, batter, beat, belt, berate, castigate, censure, chastise, criticise, flay, flog, lambast, lay into, thrash, whip.

belated *adj* behind-hand, delayed, late, overdue, retarded, tardy, unpunctual.
antonyms punctual, timely.

belch *v* burp, discharge, disgorge, emit, eruct, eructate, erupt, gush, hiccup, spew, vent.
n burp, eructation, eruption, hiccup.

beleaguered *adj* badgered, beset, besieged, bothered, harassed, hedged about, hedged in, persecuted, plagued, surrounded, vexed, worried.

belie *v* conceal, confute, contradict, deceive, deny, disguise, disprove, falsify, gainsay, mislead, misrepresent, negate, refute, repudiate, run counter to, understate.
antonym attest.

belief *n* assurance, confidence, conviction, credence, credit, credo, creed, doctrine, dogma, expectation, faith, feeling, ideology, impression, intuition, ism, judgement, notion, opinion, persuasion, presumption, principle, principles, reliance, sureness, surety, tenet, theory, trust, view.
antonym disbelief.

believable *adj* acceptable, authentic, authoritative, conceivable, credible, creditable, imaginable, likely, plausible, possible, probable, reliable, thinkable, trustworthy.
antonym unconvincing.

believe *v* accept, assume, be under the impression, conjecture, consider, count on, credit, deem, depend on, gather, guess, hold, imagine, judge, maintain, postulate, presume, reckon, rely on, speculate, suppose, swallow, swear by, think, trust, wear.

antonym disbelieve.

believer *n* adherent, catechumen, convert, devotee, disciple, follower, proselyte, supporter, upholder, votary, zealot.

antonyms apostate, sceptic, unbeliever.

belittle *v* decry, deprecate, depreciate, deride, derogate, detract, diminish, dismiss, disparage, downgrade, lessen, minimise, ridicule, run down, scorn, underestimate, underrate, undervalue, vilipend.

antonym exaggerate.

bellicose *adj* aggressive, antagonistic, argumentative, bare-knuckle, belligerent, combative, contentious, defiant, hawkish, hostile, jingoistic, militant, militaristic, provocative, pugnacious, quarrelsome, sabre-rattling, warlike, war-loving, warmongering.

antonym peacable.

belligerence *n* aggression, aggressiveness, animosity, antagonism, bellicosity, combativeness, contentiousness, pugnacity, quarrelsomeness, unfriendliness, violence.

antonym complaisance.

belligerent *adj* aggressive, antagonistic, argumentative, bellicose, bullying, combative, contentious, forceful, militant, pugnacious, quarrelsome, violent, warlike, warring.

antonym peaceable.

bellow *v* bell, call, clamour, cry, howl, roar, scream, shout, shriek, troat, yell.

belly *n* abdomen, bowels, bread-basket, corporation, gut, guts, insides, paunch, pot, sound-board, stomach, tummy, uterus, venter, vitals, womb.

v bag, balloon, billow, blow up, bulge, dilate, distend, expand, fill out, inflate, swell.

antonyms deflate, shrink.

belong *v* attach to, be connected with, be part of, be relevant to, be tied to, fit, go with, inhere, link up with, pertain to, relate to, tie up with.

belonging *n* acceptance, affinity, association, attachment, closeness, compatibility, fellow-feeling, fellowship, inclusion, kinship, link, linkage, loyalty, rapport, relationship.

antonym antipathy.

belonging to affiliated to, associated with, essential to, held by, included in, inherent in, intrinsic in, native to, owned by.

antonym alien to.

belongings *n* accoutrements, chattels, effects, gear, goods, impedimenta, paraphernalia, possessions, stuff, things, traps.

beloved *adj* admired, adored, cherished, darling, dear, dearest, favourite, loved, pet, precious, prized, revered, sweet, treasured.

n adored, darling, dear, dearest, favourite, inamorata, inamorato, lover, pet, precious, sweet, sweetheart.

below *adv* beneath, down, infra, lower, lower down, under, underneath.

prep inferior to, lesser than, 'neath, subject to, subordinate to, under, underneath, unworthy of.

below par below average, imperfect, inferior, lacking, not oneself, off, off-colour, off-form, poor, poorly, second-rate, substandard, under the weather, unfit, unhealthy, wanting.

below the belt cowardly, dirty, dishonest, foul, unfair, unjust, unscrupulous, unsporting, unsportsmanlike.

belt[1] *n* area, band, ceinture, cincture, cingulum, cummerbund, district, girdle, girth, layer, region, sash, strait, stretch, strip, swathe, tract, waistband, zone, zonule, zonulet.

v circle, encircle, girdle, ring, surround.

belt up be quiet, cut it out, leave it out, put a sock in, shut one's mouth, shut up, stow it.

belt[2] *v* bolt, career, charge, dash, hurry, race, rush, speed.

bemoan *v* bewail, deplore, grieve for, lament, mourn, regret, rue, sigh for, sorrow over, weep for.

antonym gloat.

bemuse *v* amaze, bewilder, confuse, daze, distract, muddle, overwhelm, perplex, pixillate, puzzle, stun.

antonyms enlighten, illuminate.

bemused *adj* absent-minded, befuddled, bewildered, confused, dazed, distracted, engrossed, fuddled, half-drunk, muddled, mused, perplexed, pixillated, stunned, stupefied, tipsy.

antonyms clear, clear-headed, lucid.

bench[1] *n* bleachers, board, counter, form, ledge, pew, seat, settle, stall, table, terrace, tier, work-bench, work-table.

bench[2] *n* court, courtroom, judge, judges, judicature, judiciary, magistrate, magistrates, tribunal.

benchmark *n* criterion, example, level, model, norm, reference, reference-point, standard, touchstone, yardstick.

bend *v* aim, bow, brace, buckle, compel, constrain, contort, couch, crankle, crimp, crouch, curve, deflect, direct, dispose, diverge, dog-leg, embow, fasten, flex, incline, incurvate, incurve, influence, lean, mould, nerve, persuade, shape, stoop, string, subdue, submit, sway, swerve, turn, twist, veer, warp, yield.

n angle, arc, bight, bought, bow, corner, crank, crook, curvature, curve, dog-leg, elbow, flexure, genu, hook, incurvation, incurvature, incurve, inflexure, loop, turn, twist, zigzag.

beneath *adv* below, lower, lower down, under, underneath.

prep below, inferior to, infra dig(nitatem), lower than, 'neath, subject to, subordinate to, unbefitting, under, underneath, unworthy of.

benediction *n* beatitude, Benedictus, benison, blessing, consecration, favour, grace, invocation, orison, prayer, thanksgiving.

antonyms anathema, curse, execration.

benefaction *n* aid, alms-giving, backing, beneficence, benevolence, bequest, boon, bounty, charity, contribution, donation, endowment, generosity, gift, grant, gratuity, help, legacy, liberality, munificence, offering, philanthropy, present, sponsorship, subsidy.

benefactor *n* angel, backer, contributor, donor, endower, friend, helper, patron, philanthropist, promoter, provider, sponsor, subscriber, subsidiser, supporter, well-wisher.

antonyms opponent, persecutor.

beneficence *n* aid, altruism, benefaction, benevolence, bestowal, bounty, charity, compassion, donation, generosity, gift, goodness, helpfulness, kindness, largess, largition, liberality, love, munificence, present, relief, succour, unselfishness, virtue.

antonym meanness.

beneficent *adj* altruistic, benevolent, benign, bounteous, bountiful, charitable, compassionate, generous, helpful, kind, liberal, munificent, unselfish.

antonym mean.

beneficial *adj* advantageous, benign, benignant, edifying, favourable, gainful, healthful, helpful, improving, nourishing, nutritious, profitable, restorative, rewarding, salubrious, salutary, serviceable, useful, valuable, wholesome.

antonym harmful.

beneficiary *n* assignee, devisee, donee, fructuary, heir, heiress, heritor, inheritor, legatee, payee, receiver, recipient, successor.

benefit *n* advantage, aid, asset, assistance, avail, betterment, blessing, boon, favour, gain, good, help, interest, plus, profit, service, use, weal, welfare.

antonym harm.

v advance, advantage, aid, ameliorate, amend, assist, avail, better, enhance, further, improve, profit, promote, serve.

antonyms harm, hinder, undermine.

benefits *n* advantages, bonuses, extras, freebies, loaves and fishes, perks, perquisites, pluses.

antonym disadvantages.

benevolence *n* altruism, benignity, bounty, charity, compassion, fellow-feeling, generosity, goodness, goodwill, humanity, kind-heartedness, kindliness, kindness, munificence, sympathy.

antonym meanness.

benevolent *adj* altruistic, beneficent, benign, bounteous, bountiful, caring, charitable, compassionate, considerate, generous, good-will, Grandisonian, humane, humanitarian, kind, kind-hearted, kindly, liberal, loving, philanthropic, solicitous, well-disposed.

antonym mean.

benign *adj* advantageous, amiable, auspicious, balmy, benefic, beneficent, beneficial, benevolent, complaisant, curable, curative, encouraging, favourable, friendly, generous, genial, gentle, good, gracious, harmless, healthful, kind, kindly, liberal, lucky, mild, obliging, propitious, refreshing, restorative, salubrious, salutary, sympathetic, temperate, warm, wholesome.

antonyms harmful, hostile, malign, malignant.

bent *adj* angled, arched, bowed, coudé, criminal, crooked, curved, dishonest, doubled, falcate, folded, homosexual, hunched, inbent, inflexed, retorted, retroverted, stolen, stooped, twisted, untrustworthy.

antonym straight.

n ability, aptitude, capacity, facility, faculty, flair, forte, gift, inclination, knack, leaning, penchant, preference, proclivity, propensity, talent, tendency.

bent on determined, disposed, fixed, heading for, inclined, insistent, resolved, set on.

benumbed *adj* anaesthetised, dazed, deadened, desensitised, dull, frozen, immobilised, insensible, insensitive, numb, numbed, paralysed, stunned, stupefied, unfeeling, unresponsive.

bequeath *v* assign, bestow, commit, demise, devise, endow, entrust, gift, give, grant, hand down, impart, pass on, settle, transmit, will.

bequest *n* bequeathal, bequeathment, bestowal, devisal, devise, donation, dower, endowment, estate, gift, heritage, inheritance, legacy, patrimony, settlement, trust.

berate *v* castigate, censure, chastise, chide, criticise, flyte, jump down the throat of, rail at, rate, rebuke, reprimand, reproach, reprove, revile, scold, tell off, upbraid, vituperate.

antonym praise.

bereave *v* afflict, deprive, despoil, dispossess, divest, orphan, rob, strip, widow.

bereavement *n* death, defiliation, deprivation, despoliation, dispossession, loss.

antonyms addition, increase.

bereft *adj* denuded, deprived, despoiled, destitute, devoid, lacking, minus, robbed, shorn, stripped, wanting.

berserk *adj* amok, crazy, demented, deranged, enraged, frantic, frenetic, frenzied, furious, insane, mad, maniacal, manic, rabid, raging, raving, uncontrollable, violent, wild.

antonyms calm, sane.

berth *n* anchorage, bed, billet, bunk, cot, dock, employment, hammock, harbour, harbourage, haven, job, landfall, pier, port, position, post, quay, shelter, sinecure, situation, slip, wharf.

v anchor, dock, drop anchor, land, moor, tie up.

antonym weigh anchor.

beseech *v* adjure, ask, beg, call on, conjure, crave, desire, entreat, implore, importune, obsecrate, petition, plead, pray, solicit, sue, supplicate.

beset *v* assail, attack, badger, bamboozle, bedevil, besiege, embarrass, encircle, enclose, encompass, entangle, environ, faze, harass, hassle, hem in, perplex, pester, plague, surround.

besetting *adj* compulsive, constant, dominant, habitual, harassing, inveterate, irresistible, obsessive, persistent, prevalent, recurring, troublesome, uncontrollable.

beside *prep* abreast of, abutting on, adjacent, bordering on, close to, near, neighbouring, next door to, next to, overlooking, upsides with.

beside oneself berserk, crazed, delirious, demented, deranged, distracted, distraught, frantic, frenetic, frenzied, furious, insane, mad, unbalanced, unhinged.

beside the point extraneous, immaterial, inapplicable, incidental, inconsequential, irrelevant, pointless, unimportant, unrelated.

antonym relevant.

besides *adv* additionally, also, as well, extra, further, furthermore, in addition, into the bargain, moreover, otherwise, to boot, too, withal.

prep apart from, in addition to, other than, over and above.

besiege *v* assail, badger, belay, beleaguer, beset, blockade, bother, confine, dun, encircle, encompass, environ, harass, harry, hound, importune, nag, pester, plague, surround, trouble.

besmirch *v* begrime, bespatter, daub, defame, defile, dirty, dishonour, muddy, slander, smear, soil, spatter, stain, sully, tarnish.

antonym enhance.

besotted *adj* befuddled, bewitched, confused, doting, drunk, foolish, hypnotised, inebriated, infatuated, intoxicated, muddled, obsessed, smitten, stupefied, witless.

antonyms disenchanted, indifferent, sober.

bespeak *v* attest, betoken, demonstrate, denote, display, evidence, evince, exhibit, forebode, foretell, imply, indicate, predict, proclaim, reveal, show, signify, suggest, testify to.

best *adj* advantageous, apt, correct, excellent, finest, first, first-class, first-rate, foremost, greatest, highest, incomparable, largest, leading, makeless, matchless, nonpareil, optimal, optimum, outstanding, perfect, pre-eminent, preferable, principal, right, superlative, supreme, transcendent, unequalled, unsurpassed.

antonym worst.

adv excellently, exceptionally, extremely, greatly, superlatively, surpassingly.

antonym worst.

n choice, cream, crème de la crème, élite, favourite, finest, first, flower, hardest, nonpareil, pick, prime, the tops, top, utmost.

antonym worst.

v beat, conquer, defeat, get the better of, have the laugh of, lick, outclass, outdo, outwit, surpass, thrash, trounce, vanquish, worst.

bestial *adj* animal, barbaric, barbarous, beastly, brutal, brutish, carnal, degraded, depraved, feral, gross, inhuman, savage, sensual, sordid, subhuman, swinish, vile.

antonyms civilised, humane.

bestir *v* activate, actuate, animate, arouse, awaken, energise, exert, galvanise, incite, motivate, rouse, stimulate.

antonyms calm, lull, quell.

bestow *v* accord, allot, apportion, award, bequeath, commit, confer, donate, dower, endow, entrust, give, grant, impart, lavish, lend, present, transmit, wreak.

antonym deprive.

bestowal *n* benefaction, bequeathal, bequeathment, conferring, distribution, donation, gift, giving, imparting, largition, presentation, transmission.

bestride *v* bestraddle, command, dominate, horse, overshadow, sit astride, stand astride, straddle.

bet *n* accumulator, ante, bid, flutter, gamble, hazard, pledge, risk, speculation, stake, venture, wager.

v ante, bid, chance, gamble, hazard, lay, pledge, punt, risk, speculate, stake, venture, wager.

bête noire abomination, anathema, aversion, bane, bogey, bugbear, curse, pet hate.

antonym favourite.

betide *v* bechance, befall, chance, develop, ensue, hap, happen, occur, overtake, supervene.

betimes *adv* early, expeditiously, punctually, seasonably, soon, speedily, timeously.

antonym late.

betoken *v* augur, bespeak, bode, declare, denote, evidence, forebode, foreshow, import, indicate, manifest, mark, portend, presage, prognosticate, promise, represent, signify, suggest.

betray *v* abandon, beguile, corrupt, deceive, delude, desert, disclose, discover, divulge, dob in, double-cross, dupe, ensnare, entrap, evince, expose, forsake, give away, grass, inform on, jilt, manifest, mislead, reveal, seduce, sell, sell down the river, sell out, shop, show, tell, turn Queen's (King's) evidence, undo.

antonyms defend, fulfil, protect.

betrayal *n* deception, disclosure, discovery, disloyalty, divulgence, double-dealing, duplicity, exposure, falseness, Judas-kiss, perfidy, rattery, ratting, revelation, sell-out, treachery, treason, trickery, unfaithfulness.

antonyms loyalty, protection.

betrayer *n* apostate, conspirator, , deceiver, double-crosser, grass, informer, renegade, supergrass, traitor.

antonyms protector, supporter.

betroth *v* affiance, contract, espouse, plight, plight one's troth, promise.

betrothal *n* engagement, espousal, fiançailles, handfast, plight, promise, troth, vow.

better *adj* bigger, cured, finer, fitter, greater, healthier, improving, larger, longer, on the mend, preferable, progressing, recovered, recovering, restored, stronger, superior, surpassing, worthier.

antonym worse.

v advance, ameliorate, amend, beat, cap, correct, enhance, exceed, excel, forward, further, go one further than, improve, improve on, increase, meliorate, mend, outdo, outstrip, overtake, overtop, promote, raise, rectify, redress, reform, strengthen, surpass, top, transcend.

antonyms deteriorate, worsen.

betterment *n* advancement, amelioration, edification, enhancement, furtherance, improvement, melioration.

antonyms deterioration, impairment.

betterness *n* advantage, ascendancy, meliority, preferability, superiority, transcendancy.

between *prep* amidst, among, amongst, betwixt, inter-, mid.

between ourselves entre nous, in confidence, in secret, privately, within these four walls.

bevel *n* angle, basil, bezel, bias, cant, chamfer, diagonal, mitre, oblique, slant, slope.

v bias, cant, chamfer, mitre, slant.

beverage *n* bevvy, draught, drink, libation, liquid, liquor, poison, potable, potation.

bevy *n* band, bunch, collection, company, crowd, flock, gaggle, gathering, group, pack, phalanx, throng, troupe.

bewail *v* bemoan, cry over, deplore, greet, grieve for, keen, lament, moan, mourn, regret, repent, rue, sigh over, sorrow over.

antonyms gloat, glory, vaunt.

beware *v* avoid, give a wide berth to, guard against, heed, look out, mind, shun, steer clear of, take heed, watch out.

antonym court.

interj fore, nix.

bewilder *v* baffle, bamboozle, befuddle, bemuse, buffalo, confound, confuse, daze, disconcert, disorient, fuddle, maze, muddle, mystify, perplex, puzzle, stupefy, tie in knots.

bewildered *adj* awed, baffled, bamboozled, bemused, confused, désorienté, disconcerted, disoriented, dizzy, giddy, muddled, mystified, nonplussed, perplexed, pixillated, pixy-led, puzzled, stunned, surprised, uncertain.

antonyms collected, unperturbed.

bewilderment *n* awe, confusion, daze, disconcertion, disorientation, mizmaze, mystification, perplexity, puzzledom, puzzlement, stupefaction, surprise, uncertainty.

antonyms composure, confidence.

bewitch *v* allure, attract, beguile, captivate, charm, elf-shoot, enchant, enrapture, ensorcell, entrance, fascinate, forspeak, hex, hoodoo, hypnotise, jinx, obsess, possess, spellbind, voodoo, witch.

bewitched *adj* charmed, elf-shot, enchanted, enthralled, entranced, fascinated, hexed, jinxed, mesmerised, obsessed, possessed, spellbound, transfixed, transformed.

antonym disenchanted.

bewitching *adj* beguiling, charming, enchanting, entrancing, fascinating, glamorous, hypnotic, intriguing, seductive, tantalising, witching.

antonym repellent.

beyond *prep* above, across, apart from, away from, before, further than, out of range, out of reach of, over, past, remote from, superior to, yonder.

beyond price inestimable, invaluable, irreplaceable, precious, priceless.

bias *n* angle, bent, bigotry, distortion, editorialisation, favouritism, inclination, intolerance, leaning, one-sidedness, parti pris, partiality, penchant, predilection, predisposition, prejudice, proclivity, proneness, propensity, slant, tendency, tendentiousness, turn, unfairness, viewiness.

antonyms fairness, impartiality.

v angle, distort, earwig, editorialise, influence, jaundice, load, load the dice, predispose, prejudice, slant, sway, twist, warp, weight.

biased *adj* angled, bigoted, blinkered, distorted, embittered, jaundiced, loaded, one-sided, partial, predisposed, prejudiced, slanted, swayed, tendentious, twisted, unfair, verkrampte, viewy, warped, weighted.

antonyms fair, impartial.

bibulous *adj* alcoholic, crapulous, dipsomaniac, drunken, inebriate, intemperate, sottish, thirsty, tipsy.

antonyms sober, temperate.

bicker *v* altercate, argue, clash, disagree, dispute, feud, fight, quarrel, row, scrap, spar, squabble, wrangle.

antonym agree.

bicycle *n* bike, boneshaker, cycle, dandy-horse, draisine, ordinary, penny-farthing, push-bike, racer, safety bicycle, tandem, two-wheeler, velocipede.

bid *v* ask, call, charge, command, desire, direct, enjoin, greet, instruct, invite, offer, proclaim, propose, request, require, say, solicit, summon, tell, wish.

n advance, amount, ante, attempt, crack, effort, endeavour, go, offer, price, proposal, proposition, submission, sum, tender, try, venture.

biddable *adj* acquiescent, agreeable, amenable, complaisant, co-operative, docile, obedient, responsive, teachable, tractable.

antonym recalcitrant.

bidding *n* behest, call, charge, command, demand, dictate, direction, injunction, instruction, invitation, order, request, requirement, summons.

big *adj* adult, altruistic, beefy, benevolent, boastful, bombastic, bulky, burly, buxom, colossal, considerable, corpulent, elder, elephantine, eminent, enormous, extensive, gargantuan, generous, gigantic, gracious, great, grown, grown-up, heroic, huge, hulking, immense, important, influential, large, leading, lofty, magnanimous, main, mammoth, man-sized, massive, mature, momentous, noble, paramount, plonking, ponderous, powerful, prime, principal, prodigious, prominent, serious, significant, sizable, skelping, spacious, stout, substantial, titanic, tolerant, unselfish, valuable, vast, voluminous, weighty.

antonyms little, small.

big shot big noise, bigwig, celebrity, dignitary, heavyweight, mogul, mugwump, nob, notability, notable, panjandrum, personage, somebody, VIP.

antonym nonentity.

bigamy *n* diandry.

bigot *n* chauvinist, dogmatist, fanatic, racist, religionist, sectarian, sexist, verkrampte, zealot.

antonyms humanitarian, liberal.

bigoted *adj* biased, blinkered, chauvinist, closed, dogmatic, illiberal, intolerant, narrow, narrow-minded, obstinate, opinionated, prejudiced, sectarian, twisted, verkrampte, warped.

antonyms broad-minded, enlightened, liberal.

bigotry *n* bias, chauvinism, discrimination, dogmatism, fanaticism, ignorance, illiberality, injustice, intolerance, jingoism, mindlessness, narrow-mindedness, prejudice, racialism, racism, religionism, sectarianism, sexism, unfairness.

bigwig *n* big gun, big noise, big shot, celebrity, dignitary, heavyweight, huzoor, mogul, mugwump, nabob, nob, notability, notable, panjandrum, personage, somebody, VIP.

antonym nobody.

bile *n* anger, bitterness, choler, gall, ill-humour, irascibility, irritability, peevishness, rancour, spleen, testiness.

bilingual *adj* diglot.

bilious *adj* choleric, crabby, cross, crotchety, grouchy, grumpy, irritable, liverish, nauseated, out of sorts, peevish, queasy, sick, sickly, testy.

bilk *v* balk, bamboozle, cheat, con, cozen, deceive, defraud, do, do out of, fleece, foil, rook, sting, swindle, thwart, trick.

bill[1] *n* account, advertisement, battels, broadsheet, broadside, bulletin, card, catalogue, charges, chit, circular, greenback, handbill, hand-out, inventory, invoice, leaflet, legislation, list, listing, measure, note, notice, placard, playbill, poster, programme, proposal, reckoning, roster, schedule, score, sheet, statement, syllabus, tab, tally.

v advertise, announce, charge, debit, invoice, list, post, reckon, record.

bill[2] *n* beak, mandible, neb, nib, rostrum.

billet *n* accommodation, barracks, berth, employment, housing, lodgement, lodging, occupation, post, quarterage, quarters.

v accommodate, berth, lodge, quarter, station.

billow *v* balloon, belly, expand, fill out, heave, puff out, roll, seethe, spread, surge, swell, undulate.

billowy *adj* billowing, heaving, rippling, rolling, surging, swelling, swirling, tossing, undulating, waving.

bind *v* astrict, astringe, attach, bandage, border, cinch, clamp, colligate, compel, complain, confine, constipate, constrain, cover, detain, dress, edge, encase, engage, fasten, finish, force, glue, hamper, harden, hinder, hitch, indenture, lash, necessitate, obligate, oblige, prescribe, require, restrain, restrict, rope, seal, secure, stick, strap, swathe, thirl, tie, trim, truss, wrap.

n bore, difficulty, dilemma, embarrassment, hole, impasse, nuisance, predicament, quandary.

binding *adj* compulsory, conclusive, imperative, indissoluble, irrevocable, mandatory, necessary, obligatory, permanent, requisite, strict, unalterable, unbreakable.

n bandage, border, covering, deligation, edging, stricture, syndesis, tape, trimming, wrapping.

binge *n* banquet, beano, bender, blind, bout, do, feast, fling, guzzle, jag, orgy, spree.

antonym fast.

biographical *adj* prosopographical.

biography *n* account, adventures, autobiography, biopic, curriculum vitae, exposé, fortunes, history, life, life story, memoir, memoirs, prosopography, recollections, record.

bird-like *adj* aquiline, avian, aviform, avine, hawk-like, ornithoid, volucrine.

birdwatcher *n* birder, twitcher.

birth *n* ancestry, background, beginning, birthright, blood, breeding, childbirth, delivery, derivation, descent, emergence, extraction, family, fell, genealogy, genesis, geniture, line, lineage, nativity, nobility, origin, parentage, parturition, pedigree, race, rise, source, stirps, stock, strain.

birthday *n* anniversary, day of birth, (dies) natalis, natalitium.

adj anniversary, genethliac, genethliacal, natal, natalitial.

birthmark *n* angioma, mole, mother's mark, motherspot, naevus, port wine stain.

birthplace *n* fount, incunabula, native country, native town, place of origin, provenance, roots, source.

biscuit *n* cake, cookie, cracker, hardtack, rusk, wafer.

bisect *v* bifurcate, cross, divide, fork, furcate, halve, intersect, separate, split.

bisexual *adj* androgynous, epicene, gynandromorphic, gynandromorphous, gynandrous, hermaphrodite, hermaphroditic, monoclinous.

antonyms heterosexual, homosexual.

bishop *n* abba, archbishop, diocesan, exarch, metropolitan, patriarch, prelate, primate, suffragan.

bit *n* atom, chip, crumb, fragment, grain, instant, iota, jiffy, jot, mammock, minute, mite, moment, morsel, part, period, piece, scrap, second, segment, sippet, slice, snippet, speck, spell, tick, time, tittle, while, whit.

bit by bit gradatim, gradually, insidiously, little by little, piecemeal, seriatim, step by step.

antonym wholesale.

bitch *n* back-biter, cat, doggess, fury, harridan, shrew, termagant, virago, vixen.

bitchy *adj* back-biting, catty, cruel, malicious, mean, nasty, poisonous, snide, spiteful, venomous, vicious, vindictive, vixenish, vixenly, waspish.

antonym kind.

bite *v* burn, champ, chew, clamp, corrode, crunch, crush, cut, gnaw, knap, masticate, nibble, nip, pierce, pinch, rend, seize, smart, snap, sting, tear, tingle, wound.

n edge, food, grip, kick, morsel, morsure, mouthful, nip, piece, pinch, piquancy, prick, punch, pungency, refreshment, smarting, snack, spice, sting, taste, wound.

bite the dust crumple, die, drop, drop dead, expire, fall, perish.

biting *adj* astringent, bitter, blighting, caustic, cold, cutting, cynical, freezing, harsh, hurtful, incisive, mordant, nipping, penetrating, piercing, raw, sarcastic, scathing, severe, sharp, stinging, tart, trenchant, withering.

antonyms bland, mild.

bitter *adj* acerb, acerbic, acid, acrid, acrimonious, astringent, begrudging, biting, calamitous, crabbed, cruel, cynical, dire, distressing, embittered, fierce, freezing, galling, grievous, harsh, hateful, heartbreaking, hostile, intense, ironic, jaundiced, merciless, morose, odious, painful, poignant, rancorous, raw, resentful, ruthless, sarcastic, savage, severe, sharp, sore, sour, stinging, sullen, tart, unsweetened, vexatious, vinegary, waspish.

antonyms contented, genial, sweet.

bitterness *n* acerbity, acidity, acrimoniousness, animosity, asperity, astringency, causticity, grudge, hostility, irony, mordancy, pique, rancour, resentment, sarcasm, sharpness, sourness, tartness, venom, virulence, wormwood.

antonyms contentment, geniality, sweetness.

bizarre *adj* abnormal, comical, curious, deviant, eccentric, extraordinary, extravagant, fantastic, freakish, grotesque, ludicrous, odd, off-beat, outlandish, outré, peculiar, Pythonesque, quaint, queer, ridiculous, strange, unusual, way-out, weird.

antonym normal.

bizarreness *n* bizarrerie, curiousness, eccentricity, freakishness, grotesqueness, grotesquerie, oddity, oddness, outlandishness, queerness, singularity, strangeness, weirdness.

antonym normality.

blab *v* blurt, disclose, divulge, gossip, leak, reveal, squeal, tattle, tell.

antonyms hide, hush up.

blabber *v* blather, blether, chatter, chinwag, earbash, gab, gabble, jabber, natter, prattle, whitter.

black *adj* angry, atrocious, bad, begrimed, coal-black, collied, dark, darksome, depressing, dingy, dirty, dismal, doleful, dusky, ebony. evil, filthy, funereal, furious, gloomy, grim, grimy, grubby, hopeless, horrible, hostile, inky, jet, jet-black, jetty, lugubrious, menacing, moonless, morel, mournful, murky, nefarious, ominous, overcast, pitchy, raven, resentful, sable, sad, sloe, soiled, sombre, sooty, stained, starless, Stygian, sullen, swarthy, threatening, thunderous, villainous, wicked.

v ban, bar, blacklist, boycott, taboo.

black eye keeker, mouse, shiner.

black magic black art, demonolatry, devil-worship, diabolism, hoodoo, necromancy, sorcery, voodoo, witchcraft, wizardry.

black out censor, collapse, conceal, cover up, darken, eclipse, extinguish, faint, flake out, gag, keel over, obfuscate, obliterate, pass out, shade, suppress, swoon, withhold.

black sheep disgrace, drop-out, ne'er-do-well, outcast, pariah, prodigal, reject, renegade, reprobate, wastrel.

antonym pride.

blackball *v* ban, bar, blacklist, debar, exclude, expel, ostracise, oust, pip, reject, repudiate, snub, veto.

blacken *v* befoul, begrime, besmirch, calumniate, cloud, colly, darken, decry, defame, defile, denigrate, detract, dishonour, malign, nigrify, revile, slander, smear, smirch, smudge, soil, stain, sully, taint, tarnish, traduce, vilify.

antonyms enhance, praise.

blackguard *n* bleeder, blighter, bounder, cur, devil, knave, miscreant, rascal, reprobate, rogue, rotter, scoundrel, stinker, swine, villain, wretch.

blackhead *n* comedo.

blackleg *n* fink, strike-breaker.

blacklist *v* ban, bar, blackball, boycott, debar, disallow, exclude, expel, ostracise, preclude, proscribe, reject, repudiate, snub, taboo, veto.

antonyms accept, allow.

blackmail *n* blood-sucking, chantage, exaction, extortion, hush money, intimidation, milking, pay-off, protection, ransom.

v bleed, bribe, coerce, compel, demand, force, hold to ransom, lean on, milk, put the black on, squeeze, threaten.

blackmailer *n* bloodsucker, extortioner, extortionist, highbinder, vampire.

blackness *n* darkness, duskiness, filthiness, gloom, griminess, inkiness, melanism, murkiness, nigrescence, nigritude, swarthiness, wickedness.

blackout *n* censorship, coma, concealment, cover-up, faint, oblivion, power cut, secrecy, suppression, swoon, syncope, unconsciousness.

bladder *n* aveole, bag, bursa, caecum, capsule, cell, cyst, pocket, pouch, receptacle, sac, saccule, theca, utricle, vesica, vesicle, vesicula.

blade *n* dagger, edge, knife, rapier, scalpel, sword, vane.

blamable *adj* accountable, answerable, at fault, blameworthy, culpable, guilty, liable, reprehensible, reproachable, reprovable, responsible, wrong.

blame *n* accountability, accusation, animadversion, castigation, censure, charge, complaint, condemnation, criticism, culpability, discommendation, fault, guilt, incrimination, liability, obloquy, onus, rap, recrimination, reprimand, reproach, reproof, responsibility, stick, stricture.

v accuse, admonish, censure, charge, chide, condemn, criticise, disapprove, discommend, dispraise, find fault with, rebuke, reprehend, reprimand, reproach, reprove, tax, upbraid.

antonym exonerate.

blameless *adj* above reproach, clean, clear, faultless, guiltless, immaculate, impeccable, inculpable, innocent, irreprehensible, irreproachable, irreprovable, perfect, sinless, stainless, unblamable, unblemished, unimpeachable, unspotted, unsullied, untarnished, upright, virtuous.

antonym guilty.

blameworthy *adj* censurable, culpable, discreditable, disreputable, flagitious, guilty, indefensible, inexcusable, reprehensible, reproachable, shameful, unworthy.

antonym blameless.

blanch *v* bleach, blench, drain, etiolate, fade, pale, wan, whiten.

antonyms blush, colour, redden.

bland *adv* affable, amiable, balmy, boring, calm, characterless, congenial, courteous, demulcent, dull, fair-spoken, flat, friendly, gentle, gracious, humdrum, hypo-allergenic, impassive, inscrutable, insipid, mild, mollifying, monotonous, nondescript, non-irritant, smooth, soft, soothing, suave, tasteless, tedious, temperate, unexciting, uninspiring, uninteresting, urbane, vapid, weak.

antonyms piquant, sharp.

blandishments *n* blarney, cajolery, coaxing, compliments, enticements, fawning, flattery, inducements, ingratiation, inveiglement, lip-salve, persuasiveness, soft soap, sweet talk, sycophancy, wheedling.

blank *adj* apathetic, bare, bewildered, clean, clear, confounded, confused, deadpan, disconcerted, dull, dumbfounded, empty, expressionless, featureless, glazed, hollow, immobile, impassive, inane, inscrutable, lifeless, muddled, nonplussed, plain, poker-faced, sheer, spotless, staring, uncomprehending, unfilled, unmarked, unrhymed, vacant, vacuous, vague, void, white.

n break, emptiness, gap, nothingness, space, tabula rasa, vacancy, vacuity, vacuum, void.

blanket *n* carpet, cloak, coat, coating, cover, covering, coverlet, envelope, film, housing, layer, mackinaw, manta, mantle, rug, sheet, wrapper, wrapping.

adj across-the-board, all-embracing, all-inclusive, comprehensive, inclusive, overall, sweeping, wide-ranging.

v cloak, cloud, coat, conceal, cover, deaden, eclipse, hide, mask, muffle, obscure, surround.

blankness *n* abstraction, bareness, emptiness, immobility, impassivity, inanity, incomprehension, indifference, inscrutability, obliviousness, vacancy, vacuity, void.

blare *v* blast, boom, clamour, clang, honk, hoot, peal, resound, ring, roar, scream, shriek, toot, trumpet.

blarney *n* blandishment, cajolery, coaxing, eloquence, flattery, persuasiveness, plausibility, soft soap, spiel, sweet talk, wheedling.

blasé *adj* apathetic, bored, dulled, glutted, indifferent, jaded, nonchalant, offhand, sated, satiated, surfeited, unconcerned, unexcited, unimpressed, unimpressible, uninspired, uninterested, unmoved, weary, world-weary.

antonyms enthusiastic, excited.

blaspheme *v* abuse, curse, damn, defile, desecrate, execrate, imprecate, profane, revile, swear.

blasphemous *adj* execrative, godless, hubristic, impious, imprecatory, irreligious, irreverent, profane, sacrilegious, ungodly.

blasphemy *n* curse, cursing, defilement, desecration, execration, expletive, hubris, impiety, impiousness, imprecation, irreverence, outrage, profanation, profaneness, profanity, sacrilege, swearing, violation.

blast[1] *n, v* blare, blow, boom, honk, hoot, peal, roar, scream, shriek, sound, wail.

blast[2] *n* bang, bluster, burst, clap, crack, crash, detonation, discharge, draught, eruption, explosion, flatus, gale, gust, hail, outburst, salvo, squall, storm, tempest, volley.

v assail, attack, blight, blow up, burst, castigate, demolish, destroy, explode, flay, kill, lash, ruin, shatter, shrivel, storm at, wither.

blasted *adj* blighted, desolated, destroyed, devastated, ravaged, ruined, scorched, shattered, wasted, withered.

blatant *adj* arrant, bald, barefaced, brazen, clamorous, conspicuous, egregious, flagrant, flaunting, glaring, harsh, loud, naked, noisy, obtrusive, obvious, ostentatious, outright, overt, prominent, pronounced, sheer, unmitigated.

blaze *n* blast, bonfire, brilliance, burst, conflagration, eruption, explosion, fire, flame, flames, flare, flare-up, flash, fury, glare, gleam, glitter, glow, light, outbreak, outburst, radiance, rush, storm.

v beam, burn, burst, erupt, explode, fire, flame, flare, flare up, flash, fume, glare, gleam, glow, seethe, shine.

blazon *v* announce, broadcast, bruit, celebrate, flaunt, flourish, proclaim, publicise, trumpet, vaunt.

antonyms deprecate, hush up.

bleach *v* blanch, decolorise, etiolate, fade, lighten, pale, peroxide, whiten.

bleak *adj* bare, barren, blae, blasted, cheerless, chilly, cold, colourless, comfortless, delightless, depressing, desolate, discouraging, disheartening, dismal, dreary, empty, exposed, gaunt, gloomy, grim, hopeless, joyless, leaden, loveless, open, raw, sombre, unsheltered, weather-beaten, windswept, windy.

antonyms cheerful, congenial.

bleary *adj* blurred, blurry, cloudy, dim, fogged, foggy, fuzzy, hazy, indistinct, misty, muddy, murky, obscured, rheumy, watery.

bleat *v* baa, bitch, blat, complain, growl, grumble, moan, whine, whinge.

bleed *v* blackmail, deplete, drain, exhaust, exploit, exsanguinate, extort, extract, extravasate, exude, fleece, flow, gush, haemorrhage, leech, milk, ooze, reduce, run, sap, seep, spurt, squeeze, suck dry, trickle, weep.

blemish *n* birthmark, blot, blotch, blur, botch, defect, deformity, disfigurement, disgrace, dishonour, fault, flaw, imperfection, mackle, macula, maculation, mark, naevus, smudge, speck, spot, stain, taint.

v besmirch, blot, blotch, blur, damage, deface, disfigure, flaw, impair, injure, maculate, mar, mark, smirch, smudge, spoil, spot, stain, sully, taint, tarnish.

blench *v* balk, boggle, cower, falter, flinch, hesitate, jib, quail, quake, quiver, recoil, shrink, shudder, shy, start, wince.

blend *v* amalgamate, coalesce, combine, complement, compound, contemper, fit, fuse, harmonise, intermix, meld, merge, mingle, mix, synthesise, unite.

antonym separate.

n alloy, amalgam, amalgamation, combination, composite, compound, concoction, fusion, interunion, meld, mix, mixture, synthesis, union.

bless *v* anoint, approve, bestow, consecrate, countenance, dedicate, endow, exalt, extol, favour, glorify, grace, hallow, magnify, ordain, praise, provide, sanctify, thank.

antonyms condemn, curse.

blessed *adj* adored, beatified, blissful, contented, divine, endowed, favoured, fortunate, glad, hallowed, happy, holy, joyful, joyous, lucky, prosperous, revered, sacred, sanctified, seely.

antonym cursed.

blessedness *n* beatitude, bliss, blissfulness, content, felicity, happiness, joy, sanctity, seel.

blessing *n* advantage, approbation, approval, authority, backing, benedicite, benediction, benefit, benison, boon, bounty, commendation, concurrence, consecration, consent, countenance, darshan, dedication, favour, gain, gift, godsend, grace, help, invocation, kiddush, kindness, leave, permission, profit, sanction, service, support, thanksgiving, windfall.

antonyms blight, condemnation, curse.

blether *n* blather, chatter, chatterbox, chatterer, chit-chat, claptrap, drivel, gibberish, gibble-gabble, gobbledegook, haverel, jabbering, loquacity, moonshine, nonsense, prattle, prattler, twaddle.

v blabber, chatter, gab, gabble, haver, jabber, prattle.

blight *n* affliction, bane, cancer, canker, check, contamination, corruption, curse, decay, depression, disease, evil, fungus, infestation, mildew, pest, pestilence, plague, pollution, rot, scourge, set-back, woe.

antonyms blessing, boon.

v annihilate, blast, crush, dash, destroy, disappoint, frustrate, injure, mar, ruin, shatter, shrivel, spoil, undermine, wither, wreck.

antonym bless.

blind *adj* amaurotic, beetle-eyed, blinkered, careless, closed, concealed, dark, dim, eyeless, hasty, heedless, hidden, ignorant, impetuous, inattentive, inconsiderate, indifferent, indiscriminate, injudicious, insensate, insensitive, irrational, mindless, neglectful, oblivious, obscured, obstructed, prejudiced, purblind, rash, reckless, sand-blind, senseless, sightless, stone-blind, thoughtless, unaware, uncontrollable, uncritical, undiscerning, unobservant, unobserving, unreasoning, unseeing, unsighted, unthinking, violent, visionless, wild.

antonyms aware, clear, sighted.

n camouflage, cloak, cover, cover-up, distraction, façade, feint, front, mask, masquerade, screen, smoke-screen.

blindfold *v* bamboozle, beguile, blind, deceive, delude, fool, hoodwink, mislead.

antonym enlighten.

blindly *adv* aimlessly, carelessly, confusedly, frantically, headlong, heedlessly, impetuously, impulsively, incautiously, inconsiderately, indiscriminately, madly, passionately, precipitately, purposelessly, recklessly, regardlessly, senselessly, thoughtlessly, wildly, wilfully.

antonym cautiously.

blindness *n* cecity, ignorance, indifference, insensitivity, narrow-mindedness, neglect, prejudice, prestriction, sightlessness, unawareness.

antonyms awareness, sight, sightedness.

blink *v* bat, condone, connive at, disregard, flash, flicker, flutter, gleam, glimmer, glimpse, ignore, nictate, nictitate, overlook, peer, pink, scintillate, shine, sparkle, squint, twinkle, wink.

bliss *n* beatitude, blessedness, blissfulness, ecstasy, euphoria, felicity, gladness, happiness, heaven, joy, nirvana, paradise, rapture, seel.

antonyms damnation, misery.

blissful *adj* beatific, delighted, ecstatic, elated, enchanted, enraptured, euphoric, happy, heavenly, joyful, joyous, rapturous.

antonym wretched.

blister *n* abscess, blain, bleb, boil, bubble, bulla, canker, carbuncle, cyst, furuncle, papilla, papula, papule, pimple, pompholyx, pustule, sore, swelling, ulcer, vesicle, vesicula, welt, wen.

blistering *adj* cruel, excoriating, hot, intense, sarcastic, savage, scathing, scorching, strenuous, vesicant, vesicatory, vicious, virulent, withering.

antonym mild.

blithe *adj* animated, buoyant, carefree, careless, casual, cheerful, cheery, debonair, gay, gladsome, happy, heedless, jaunty, light-hearted, lightsome, lively, merry, mirthful, nonchalant, sprightly, sunny, thoughtless, unconcerned, untroubled, vivacious.

antonym morose.

blizzard *n* snow-squall, snowstorm, squall, storm, tempest.

bloated *adj* blown up, bombastic, dilated, distended, dropsical, enlarged, expanded, inflated, oedematous, sated, swollen, tumescent, tumid, turgid.

antonyms shrivelled, shrunken, thin.

blob *n* ball, bead, bobble, bubble, dab, dew-drop, drop, droplet, glob, globule, gob, lump, mass, pearl, pellet, pill, spot.

bloc *n* alliance, axis, cabal, cartel, clique, coalition, combine, entente, faction, group, league, ring.

block *n* bar, barrier, blockage, brick, cake, chunk, cube, delay, hang-up, hindrance, hunk, impediment, ingot, jam, let, lump, mass, obstacle, obstruction, piece, resistance, square, stoppage, tranche.

v arrest, bar, check, choke, clog, close, dam up, deter, halt, hinder, impede, obstruct, obturate, oppilate, plug, scotch, stonewall, stop, stop up, thwart, trig.

blockade *n* barricade, barrier, beleaguerment, closure, encirclement, obstruction, restriction, siege, stoppage.

blockage *n* block, blocking, clot, embolism, hindrance, impediment, jam, log-jam, obstruction, occlusion, stoppage.

blockhead *n* bonehead, boodle, chump, dolt, dullard, dunce, fool, idiot, ignoramus, jobernowl, leather-head, loggerhead, log-head, noodle, numskull, pigsconce, pinhead, pot-head, thickhead, thickskin, thick-skull.

antonyms brain, genius.

bloke *n* bastard, bod, body, bugger, chap, character, cove, customer, fellow, individual, Johnny, oik, personage, punter.

blond, blonde *adj* bleached, fair, fair-haired, fair-skinned, flaxen, golden-haired, light-coloured, tow-headed.

blood *n* ancestry, anger, birth, bloodshed, consanguinity, descendants, descent, extraction, family, kindred, kinship, lineage, murder, relations, relationship, temper, temperament.

bloodcurdling *adj* appalling, chilling, dreadful, eldritch, fearful, frightening, hair-raising, horrendous, horrible, horrid, horrifying, scaring, spine-chilling, terrifying, weird.

bloodless *adj* anaemic, ashen, chalky, cold, colourless, drained, feeble, insipid, languid, lifeless, listless, pale, pallid, passionless, pasty, sallow, sickly, spiritless, torpid, unemotional, unfeeling, wan.

antonyms bloody, ruddy, vigorous.

bloodshed *n* bloodletting, butchery, carnage, gore, killing, massacre, murder, slaughter, slaying.

blood-sucker *n* blackmailer, extortioner, extortionist, leech, parasite, sponger.

bloodthirsty *adj* barbaric, barbarous, brutal, cruel, ferocious, inhuman, murderous, ruthless, sanguinary, savage, slaughterous, vicious, warlike.

bloody *adj* bleeding, bloodstained, blooming, brutal, cruel, ferocious, fierce, gaping, murderous, raw, sanguinary, sanguine, sanguineous, sanguinolent, savage.

bloom *n* beauty, blossom, blossoming, blow, blush, bud, efflorescence, florescence, flourishing, flower, flush, freshness, glaucescence, glow, health, heyday, lustre, perfection, prime, radiance, rosiness, vigour.

v blossom, blow, bud, burgeon, develop, flourish. grow, open, prosper, sprout, succeed, thrive, wax.

antonym wither.

blooming *adj* blossoming, bonny, florescent, flowering, healthful, healthy, rosy, ruddy.

antonym ailing.

blossom *n* bloom, bud, floret, flower, flowers.

v bloom, blow, burgeon, develop, effloresce, flourish, flower, grow, mature, progress, prosper, thrive.

antonym wither.

blot *n* blemish, blotch, defect, disgrace, fault, flaw, mackle, macula, mark, patch, smear, smudge, speck, splodge, spot, stain, taint.

v bespatter, blur, disfigure, disgrace, maculate, mar, mark, smudge, spoil, spot, stain, sully, taint, tarnish.

blot out cancel, darken, delete, destroy, eclipse, efface, erase, expunge, obliterate, obscure, shadow.

blotch *n* blemish, blot, mark, patch, pustule, smudge, splash, splodge, spot, stain.

blotchy *adj* blemished, macular, maculose, patchy, reddened, smeary, spotted, spotty, uneven.

blow[1] *v* bear, blare, blast, breathe, buffet, drive, exhale, fan, fling, flow, flutter, mouth, pant, pipe, play, puff, rush, sound, stream, sweep, toot, trumpet, vibrate, waft, whirl, whisk, wind.

n blast, draught, flurry, gale, gust, puff, squall, tempest, wind.

blow in(to) insufflate.

blow over cease, die down, disappear, dissipate, end, finish, fizzle out, pass, peter out, subside, vanish.

blow up balloon, belly out, bloat, dilate, distend, enlarge, exaggerate, expand, fill, fill out, heighten, inflate, magnify, overstate, puff up, pump up, swell.

blow[2] *n* affliction, bang, bash, bat, belt, biff, bombshell, bop, box, buff, buffet, calamity, catastrophe, clap, clip, clout, clump, comedown, concussion, counterbluff, devvel, disappointment, disaster, douse, fourpenny one, haymaker, jolt, knock, knuckle sandwich, misfortune, oner, paik, punch, rap, reverse, setback, shock, siserary, slap, slat, slosh, smack, sock, sockdologer, souse, stroke, swash, swat, swipe, thump, upset, wallop, wap, welt, whack, whang, winder.

blow up blast, blow one's top, bomb, burst, castigate, detonate, dynamite, erupt, explode, go off, go off the deep end, hit the roof, lose one's cool, lose one's rag, lose one's temper, rage, reprimand, rupture, scold, shatter.

blown *adj* breathless, effete, jaded, stale, tired, worthless.

blow-out *n* beanfeast, binge, blast, burst, carousal, detonation, eruption, escape, explosion, feast, fuse, leak, party, puncture, rupture, spree, tear.

blowy *adj* blustery, breezy, draughty, fresh, gusty, squally, stormy, windy.

blowzy *adj* bedraggled, dishevelled, draggle-tailed, flushed, frowzy, messy, ruddy, slatternly, slipshod, sloppy, slovenly, sluttish, tousled, ungroomed, unkempt, untidy.

antonyms neat, smart.

bludgeon *n* baton, club, cosh, cudgel, knobkerrie, life-preserver, night-stick, sap, shillelagh, truncheon.

v badger, batter, beat, browbeat, bulldoze, bully, club, coerce, cosh, cudgel, force, harass, hector, intimidate, sap, steam-roller, strike, terrorise, torment.

blue[1] *adj* aquamarine, azure, cerulean, cobalt, cyan, indigo, navy, sapphire, turquoise, ultramarine, watchet.

blue[2] *adj* black, bleak, dejected, depressed, despondent, dismal, dispirited, doleful, down in the dumps, downcast, down-hearted, fed up, gloomy, glum, low, melancholy, miserable, morose, sad, unhappy.

antonym cheerful.

blue[3] *adv* bawdy, coarse, dirty, improper, indecent, lewd, naughty, near the bone, near the knuckle, obscene, offensive, pornographic, risqué, smutty, vulgar.

antonym decent.

blue-pencil *v* bowdlerise, censor, clean up, correct, edit, expurgate, purge.

blueprint *n* archetype, design, draft, guide, model, outline, pattern, pilot, plan, project, prototype, sketch.

blues *n* blue devils, dejection, depression, despondency, doldrums, dumps, gloom, gloominess, glumness, melancholy, miseries, moodiness.

antonym euphoria.

blue-stocking *n* bas-bleu, femme savante, learned lady.

bluff[1] *n* bank, brow, cliff, crag, escarp, escarpment, foreland, headland, height, knoll, peak, precipice, promontory, ridge, scarp, slope.

adj affable, blunt, candid, direct, downright, frank, genial, good-natured, hearty, open, outspoken, plain-spoken, straightforward.

antonyms diplomatic, refined.

bluff[2] *v* bamboozle, blind, deceive, defraud, delude, fake, feign, grift, hoodwink, humbug, lie, mislead, pretend, sham.

n bluster, boast, braggadocio, bravado, deceit, deception, fake, fanfaronade, feint, fraud, grift, humbug, idle boast, lie, pretence, sham, show, subterfuge, trick.

blunder *n* bêtise, bevue, bish, bloomer, boner, boob, boo-boo, clanger, clinker, error, fault, faux pas, floater, fluff, gaffe, gaucherie, goof, howler, impropriety, inaccuracy, indiscretion, mistake, oversight, pratfall, slip, slip-up, solecism.

v blow it, botch, bumble, bungle, err, flounder, flub, fluff, fumble, goof, miscalculate, misjudge, mismanage, muff it, slip up, stumble.

blunderer *n* botcher, bungler, duffer, fool, goof, incompetent, josser.

blunt *adj* abrupt, bluff, brusque, candid, curt, direct, discourteous, downright, dull, dulled, edgeless, explicit, forthright, frank, honest, impolite, insensitive, obtuse, outspoken, plain-spoken, pointless, retuse, rounded, rude, straightforward, stubbed, stumpy, tactless, thick, trenchant, unceremonious, uncivil, unpolished, unsharpened.

antonyms sharp, tactful.

v abate, allay, alleviate, anaesthetise, bate, dampen, deaden, disedge, dull, hebetate, numb, obtund, palliate, rebate, retund, soften, stupefy, unedge, weaken.

antonyms intensify, sharpen.

bluntness *n* abruptness, brusqueness, candidness, dullness, forthrightness, frankness, hebetude, hebetudinarity, insensitivity, lack of ceremony, obtuseness, obtusity, tactlessness.

antonyms sharpness, tact.

blur *v* becloud, befog, blear, blemish, blot, blotch, cloud, darken, dim, fog, mask, obfuscate, obscure, scumble, smear, smutch, soften, spot, stain.

n blear, blot, blotch, cloudiness, confusion, dimness, fog, fuzziness, haze, indistinctness, muddle, obscurity, smear, smudge, spot, stain.

blurb *n* advertisement, commendation, copy, hype, puff, spiel.

blurred *adj* beclouded, bleary, blurry, clouded, confused, dim, faint, foggy, fuzzy, hazy, ill-defined, indistinct, misty, nebulous, unclear, vague.

antonym distinct.

blurt *v* babble, blab, cry, disclose, divulge, ejaculate, exclaim, gush, leak, let slip, let the cat out of the bag, reveal, spill, spill the beans, spout, utter.

antonym hush up.

blush *v* colour, crimson, flush, glow, mantle, redden.

antonym blanch.

n colour, erubescence, flush, glow, reddening, rosiness, ruddiness, suffusion.

blushing *adj* confused, discomfited, embarrassed, erubescent, flushed, glowing, red, rosy, rubescent, suffused.

antonyms composed, pale.

bluster *v* boast, brag, bully, domineer, fanfaronade, hector, rant, roar, rodomontade, roist, roister, storm, strut, swagger, swell, talk big, vapour, vaunt.

n bluff, boasting, bombast, braggadocio, bragging, bravado, crowing, fanfaronade, parade, racket, rodomontade, swagger, swaggering, vapour, vauntery.

blusterer *n* big mouth, big talker, boaster, braggart, fanfaron, rodomontader, roister, roisterer, show-off, swaggerer, swank, swashbuckler, swasher, vapourer, windbag.

blustery *adj* boisterous, gusty, noisy, squally, stormy, tempestuous, tumultuous, violent, wild, windy.

antonym calm.

board[1] *n* beam, clapboard, deal, lath, panel, plank, sheet, slab, slat, timber, two-by-four.

board[2] commons, food, grub, meals, provisions, rations, repasts, table, victuals.

v accommodate, bed, billet, feed, house, lodge, put up, quarter, room, table.

board[3] *n* advisers, chamber, commission, committee, conclave, council, directorate, directors, jury, panel, trustees.

board[4] *v* catch, embark, embus, emplane, enter, entrain, mount.

boarding-house *n* pension.

boast *v* be all mouth, blazon, blow, bluster, bounce, brag, claim, crow, exaggerate, exhibit, gasconade, possess, puff, rodomontade, show off, strut, swagger, talk big, trumpet, vaunt.

antonym deprecate.

n avowal, brag, claim, fanfaronade, gasconade, gem, joy, pride, rodomontade, swank, treasure, vaunt.

boaster *n* bangster, big mouth, big talker, blowhard, Bobadil, braggart, fanfaron, galah, gascon, gasconader, rodomontader, show-off, swaggerer, swank, vapourer, vaunter.

boastful *adj* blowhard, braggart, bragging, cocky, conceited, crowing, egotistical, proud, puffed-up, self-glorious, swaggering, swanky, swollen-headed, thrasonic, thrasonical, vain, vainglorious, vaunting, windy.

antonym modest.

boasting *n* bluster, bragging, conceit, fanfaronade, gasconade, gasconism, jactation, jactitation, ostentation, rodomontade, swagger, swank, vaingloriousness, vainglory, vauntery, vaunting, windiness.

antonym modesty.

boat *n* bateau, canoe, dahabiyah, dinghy, funny, gondola, ketch, punt, rowing-boat, speed-boat, water-craft.

boatman *n* ferryman, gondolier, oarsman, rower, sailor, voyageur, waterman, water-rat, wet bob, yachtsman.

bob *v* bounce, duck, hop, jerk, jolt, jounce, jump, leap, nod, oscillate, popple, quiver, shake, skip, spring, twitch, waggle, weave, wobble.

bob up appear, arise, arrive, crop up, emerge, materialise, pop up, rise, show up, spring up, surface.

bode *v* adumbrate, augur, betoken, forebode, foreshadow, foreshow, foretell, forewarn, import, indicate, intimate, omen, portend, predict, presage, prophesy, signify, threaten, warn.

bodily *adj* actual, carnal, concrete, corporal, corporeal, earthly, fleshly, incarnate, material, physical, real, somatic, substantial, tangible.

antonym spiritual.

adv altogether, as a whole, bag and baggage, collectively, completely, en masse, entirely, fully, in toto, totally, wholly.

antonym piecemeal.

body[1] *n* being, bod, build, bulk, cadaver, carcass, consistency, corpse, corpus, creature, density, essence, figure, firmness, form, frame, human, individual, mass, material, matter, mortal, opacity, person, physique, relics, remains, richness, shape, solidity, stiff, substance, substantiality, tabernacle, torso, trunk.

body[2] *n* association, band, bevy, bloc, cartel, collection, company, confederation, congress, corporation, crowd, group, horde, majority, mass, mob, multitude, society, syndicate, throng.

bodyguard *n* minder, praetorian, protector.

body-snatcher *n* desecrator, resurrectionist, resurrection-man.

boffin *n* backroom-boy, brain, designer, egghead, engineer, genius, headpiece, intellect, intellectual, inventor, mastermind, planner, scientist, thinker, wizard.

bog *n* fen, marsh, marshland, mire, morass, moss, muskeg, quag, quagmire, quicksands, slough, swamp, swampland, wetlands.

bog down delay, deluge, halt, hinder, impede, overwhelm, retard, sink, slow down, slow up, stall, stick.

boggle *v* blench, demur, dither, doubt, equivocate, falter, fight shy, flinch, funk, hang back, hesitate, hover, jib, jump, pause, recoil, shillyshally, shrink, shy, stagger, start, startle, vacillate, waver.

boggy *adj* fennish, fenny, marshy, miry, morassy, muddy, oozy, paludal, quaggy, soft, spongy, swampy, waterlogged.

antonym arid.

bogus *adj* artificial, counterfeit, dummy, ersatz, fake, false, forged, fraudulent, imitation, phoney, pinchbeck, pseudo, sham, spoof, spurious, unauthentic.

antonym genuine.

bogy, bogey *n* bête noire, bogeyman, boggart, bogle, bugaboo, bugbear, goblin, hobgoblin, imp, incubus, nightmare, spectre, spook.

bohemian *adj* alternative, artistic, arty, bizarre, eccentric, exotic, irregular, left-bank, nonconformist, offbeat, outré, unconventional, unorthodox, way-out.

antonyms bourgeois, conventional.

n beatnik, drop-out, hippie, iconoclast, nonconformist.

antonyms bourgeois, conformist.

boil[1] *v* agitate, brew, bubble, churn, decoct, effervesce, erupt, explode, fizz, foam, froth, fulminate, fume, gurgle, mantle, parboil, rage, rave, seethe, simmer, sizzle, spume, steam, stew, storm, wallop.

boil down abridge, abstract, concentrate, condense, decrease, digest, distil, epitomise, reduce, summarise, synopsise.

boil[2] *n* abscess, anthrax, blain, bleb, blister, carbuncle, furuncle, gathering, gumboil, inflammation, papule, parulis, pimple, pock, pustule, tumour, ulcer, whelk.

boiling *adj* angry, baking, blistering, bubbling, enraged, flaming, fuming, furious, gurgling, hot, incensed, indignant, infuriated, roasting, scorching, seething, torrid, turbulent.

boisterous *adj* blusterous, blustery, bouncy, clamorous, disorderly, exuberant, gusty, impetuous, loud, noisy, obstreperous, rackety, raging, rambunctious, riotous, roisting, rollicking, rough, rowdy, rumbustious, squally, tempestuous, termagant, tumultous, turbulent, unrestrained, unruly, uproarious, vociferous, wild.

antonyms calm, quiet, restrained.

bold *adj* adventurous, audacious, brash, brave, brazen, bright, cheeky, colourful, confident, conspicuous, courageous, daring, dauntless, enterprising, extrovert, eye-catching, fearless, flamboyant, flashy, forceful, forward, fresh, gallant, heroic, impudent, insolent, intrepid, jazzy, lively, loud, malapert, outgoing, pert, plucky, prominent, pronounced, saucy, shameless, showy, spirited, striking, strong, unabashed, unashamed, unbashful, valiant, valorous, venturesome, vivid.

antonyms diffident, restrained.

bolster *v* aid, assist, augment, boost, brace, buoy up, buttress, firm up, help, maintain, prop, reinforce, shore up, stay, stiffen, strengthen, supplement, support.

antonym undermine.

bolt *n* arrow, bar, bound, catch, dart, dash, elopement, escape, fastener, flight, flit, latch, lock, missile, peg, pin, projectile, rivet, rod, rush, shaft, sneck, sprint, thunderbolt.

v abscond, bar, bound, cram, dart, dash, devour, discharge, elope, escape, expel, fasten, fetter, flee, fly, gobble, gorge, gulp, guzzle, hurtle, jump, latch, leap, lock, run, rush, secure, spring, sprint, stuff, wolf.

bomb *n* A-bomb, bombshell, charge, egg, explosive, grenade, mine, missile, mortar-bomb, petrol bomb, projectile, rocket, shell, torpedo.

v attack, blow up, bombard, collapse, come a cropper, come to grief, destroy, fail, flop, misfire, shell, strafe, torpedo.

bombard *v* assail, assault, attack, barrage, batter, beset, besiege, blast, blitz, bomb, cannonade, dun, harass, hound, importune, pelt, pester, pound, shell, strafe.

bombardment *n* air-raid, assault, attack, barrage, blitz, bombing, cannonade, fire, flak, fusillade, salvo, shelling, strafe.

bombast *n* ampollosity, bluster, brag, braggadocio, euphuism, fustian, gasconade, Gongorism, grandiloquence, grandiosity, heroics, magniloquence, pomposity, portentiousness, pretentiousness, rant, rodomontade, verbosity, wordiness.

antonyms reserve, restraint.

bombastic *adj* bloated, declamatory, euphuistic, fustian, Gongoristic, grandiloquent, grandiose, high-flown, histrionic, inflated, magniloquent, pompous, turgid, verbose, windy, wordy.

bon viveur bon vivant, epicure, epicurean, gastronome, gourmet, hedonist, luxurist, pleasure-seeker, voluptuary.

antonym ascetic.

bona fide actual, authentic, genuine, honest, kosher, lawful, legal, legitimate, real, true, valid.

antonym bogus.

bond *n* affiliation, affinity, agreement, attachment, band, binding, chain, compact, connection, contract, copula, cord, covenant, fastening, fetter, ligament, ligature, link, manacle, nexus, obligation, pledge, promise, relation, shackle, tie, union, vinculum, word.

v bind, connect, fasten, fuse, glue, gum, paste, seal, unite.

bondage *n* captivity, confinement, durance, duress, enslavement, enthralment, imprisonment, incarceration, restraint, serfdom, servitude, slavery, subjection, subjugation, subservience, thraldom, vassalage, yoke.

antonyms freedom, independence.

bonfire *n* beacon, conflagration, feu de joie, pyre.

bonny *adj* attractive, beautiful, blithe, blooming, bouncing, buxom, cheerful, cheery, chubby, comely, fair, fine, gay, goodly, handsome, joyful, lovely, merry, pretty, shapely, sunny, sweet, wholesome, winsome.

antonym ill-favoured.

bonus *n* advantage, benefit, bounty, bribe, commission, dividend, douceur, extra, freebie, gift, gratuity, hand-out, honorarium, lagniappe, perk, perquisite, plus, premium, prize, profit, reward, tip.

antonyms disadvantage, disincentive, liability.

bony *adj* angular, drawn, emaciated, gangling, gaunt, gawky, knobbly, lanky, lean, osseous, rawboned, sclerous, scrawny, skinny, thin.

antonym plump.

boob *n* balls-up, bêtise, blunder, botch, clanger, error, fault, faux pas, gaffe, gaucherie, howler, inaccuracy, indiscretion, mistake, oversight, pratfall, slip, slip-up, solecism.

booby *n* blockhead, clod, clodpate, clodpoll, clot, dimwit, duffer, dunce, dunderhead, fool, goof, halfwit, idiot, muggins, nickumpoop, ni(n)compoop, ninny, palooka, prat, schmuck, simpleton.

antonym genius.

booby prize consolation prize, wooden spoon.

book *n* album, booklet, codex, companion, diary, hornbook, incunable, incunabulum, jotter, lectionary, manual, manuscript, notebook, pad, paperback, publication, roll, scroll, textbook, tome, tract, volume, work.

v arrange, arrest, bag, charter, engage, enter, insert, list, log, note, organise, post, procure, programme, record, register, reserve, schedule.

antonym cancel.

bookish *adj* academic, cultured, donnish, erudite, highbrow, intellectual, learned, lettered, literary, pedantic, scholarly, scholastic, studious, well-read.

antonyms lowbrow, unlettered.

boom[1] *v* bang, blare, blast, crash, explode, resound, reverberate, roar, roll, rumble, sound, thunder.

n bang, blast, burst, clang, clap, crash, explosion, reverberation, roar, rumble, thunder.

boom[2] *v* develop, escalate, expand, explode, flourish, gain, go from strength to strength, grow, increase, intensify, prosper, spurt, strengthen, succeed, swell, thrive.

antonyms collapse, fail.

n advance, boost, development, escalation, expansion, explosion, gain, growth, improvement, increase, jump, spurt, upsurge, upturn.

antonyms collapse, failure.

boon *n* advantage, benefaction, benefit, blessing, donation, favour, gift, godsend, grant, gratification, gratuity, kindness, petition, present, windfall.

antonyms blight, disadvantage.

boor *n* barbarian, brute, bumpkin, chuff, churl, clodhopper, goop, Goth, Grobian, hedgehog, hog, keelie, kerne, lout, oaf, peasant, philistine, rustic, vulgarian.

antonyms aesthete, charmer.

boorish *adj* awkward, barbaric, bearish, churlish, clodhopping, clownish, coarse, crude, goustrous, gross, gruff, ill-bred, jungli, kernish, loutish, lubberly, lumpen, oafish, rude, rustic, swailish, uncivilised, uncouth, uneducated, unrefined, vulgar.

antonyms cultured, polite, refined.

boorishness *n* awkwardness, barbarity, bluntness, coarseness, crudeness, gaucherie, Gothicism, grossièreté, grossness, hoggery, ignorance, impoliteness, loutishness, lubberliness, philistinism, roughness, rudeness, rudery, rusticity, uncouthness, vulgarity.

antonyms politeness, refinement.

boost *n* addition, advancement, ego-trip, encouragement, enhancement, expansion, fillip, heave, help, hoist, hype, improvement, increase, increment, jump, lift, praise, promotion, push, rise, supplement, thrust.

antonyms blow, setback.

v advance, advertise, aid, amplify, assist, augment, bolster, develop, elevate, encourage, enhance, enlarge, expand, foster, further, heave, heighten, hoist, improve, increase, inspire, jack up, lift, plug, praise, promote, push, raise, supplement, support, sustain, thrust.

antonyms hinder, undermine.

boot[1] *n* bootee, galosh, gumboot, jemima, Kletterschuh, larrigan, moon-boot, muckluck, overshoe, riding-boot, rubber, top-boot, wader, wellie, wellington.

v bounce, dismiss, eject, expel, fire, give the bum's rush, give the heave, kick, kick out, knock, oust, punt, sack, shove.

boot[2] *v* advantage, aid, avail, benefit, help, profit, serve.

booth *n* bay, carrel, cart, compartment, guichet, hut, kiosk, stall, stand, ticket-office.

bootless *adj* barren, fruitless, futile, ineffective, on a hiding to nothing, pointless, profitless, sterile, unavailing, unproductive, unsuccessful, useless, vain, worthless.

antonyms profitable, useful.

bootlicking *n* arse-licking, back-scratching, crawling, cringing, deference, faggery, fagging, fawning, flattery, grovelling, heepishness, ingratiation, lackeying, obsequiousness, servility, sycophancy, toadying.

booty *n* boodle, bunce, gains, haul, loot, pickings, pillage, plunder, spoil, spoils, swag, takings, winnings.

border *n* borderline, bound, boundary, bounds, brim, brink, circumference, confine, confines, demarcation, edge, fringe, frontier, hem, limit, limits, lip, list, march, margin, perimeter, periphery, rand, rim, screed, selvage, skirt, surround, trimming, valance, verge.

adj boundary, circumscriptive, dividing, frontier, limitary, limitrophe, marginal, perimeter, separating, side.

border on abut, adjoin, appear like, approach, approximate, communicate with, connect, contact, impinge, join, march, neighbour, resemble, touch, verge on.

bordered *adj* bounded, circumscribed, edged, fringed, hemmed, limbate, marginate, margined, rimmed, skirted, surrounded, trimmed.

borderline *adj* ambivalent, doubtful, iffy, indecisive, indefinite, indeterminate, marginal, problematic, uncertain.

antonyms certain, definite.

bore[1] *v* burrow, countermine, drill, gouge, mine, penetrate, perforate, pierce, sap, sink, thirl, thrill, tunnel, undermine.

bore[2] *v* annoy, bother, bug, fatigue, irk, irritate, jade, pester, tire, trouble, vex, weary, worry.

antonyms charm, interest.

n annoyance, bind, bother, drag, dullard, headache, nuisance, pain, pain in the neck, pest, schmo, terebrant, trial, turn-off, vexation, vieux jeu, yawn.

antonym pleasure.

bored *adj* brassed off, browned off, ennuied, ennuyé.

antonym interested.

boredom *n* acedia, apathy, doldrums, dullness, ennui, flatness, irksomeness, listlessness, monotony, sameness, tediousness, tedium, vapours, weariness, wearisomeness, world-weariness.

antonym interest.

boring *adj* commonplace, dead, draggy, dreary, dry, dull, ennuying, flat, ho-hum, humdrum, insipid, irksome, monotonous, repetitious, routine, stale, stupid, tedious, tiresome, tiring, trite, unamusing, undiverting, unedifying, uneventful, unexciting, unfunny, unimaginative, uninspired, uninteresting, unvaried, unwitty, vapid, wearisome.

antonyms interesting, original.

borrow *v* adopt, ape, appropriate, cadge, copy, crib, derive, draw, echo, filch, imitate, list, mimic, obtain, pilfer, pirate, plagiarise, scrounge, sponge, steal, take, use, usurp.

borrowing *n* adoption, appropriation, cadging, calque, copy, copying, crib, imitation, loan, loan-translation, loan-word, plagiarisation, scrounging, sponging.

bosom *n* breast, bust, centre, chest, circle, core, heart, midst, protection, sanctuary, shelter.

adj boon, cherished, close, confidential, dear, favourite, inseparable, intimate.

boss[1] *n* administrator, baron, captain, chief, director, employer, executive, foreman, gaffer, governor, head, leader, manager, master, overseer, owner, superintendent, supervisor, supremo.

v administrate, command, control, direct, employ, manage, oversee, run, superintend, supervise.

boss around browbeat, bulldoze, bully, dominate, domineer, dragoon, hector, oppress, order about, overbear, push around, tyrannise.

boss[2] *n* knob, knub, knubble, nub, nubble, omphalos, point, protuberance, stud, tip, umbo.

bossy *adj* arrogant, authoritarian, autocratic, demanding, despotic, dictatorial, domineering, exacting, hectoring, high-handed, imperious, insistent, lordly, oppressive, overbearing, tyrannical.

antonym unassertive.

botch *v* balls up, blunder, bungle, butcher, cobble, cock up, corpse, flub, fuck up, fudge, fumble, goof, louse up, mar, mend, mess, mismanage, muff, patch, ruin, screw up, spoil.

antonyms accomplish, succeed.

n balls-up, blunder, bungle, cock-up, failure, farce, hash, mess, miscarriage, muddle, shambles.

antonym success.

bother *v* alarm, annoy, bore, chivvy, concern, dismay, distress, disturb, dog, harass, harry, hassle, inconvenience, irk, irritate, molest, nag, pester, plague, pother, pudder, trouble, upset, vex, worry.

n aggravation, annoyance, bustle, consternation, difficulty, flurry, fuss, hassle, inconvenience, irritation, kerfuffle, molestation, nuisance, palaver, perplexity, pest, pother, problem, pudder, shtook, strain, trouble, vexation, worry.

bothersome *adj* aggravating, annoying, boring, distressing, exasperating, inconvenient, infuriating, irksome, irritating, laborious, tedious, tiresome, troublesome, vexatious, vexing, wearisome.

bottle *n* carafe, carboy, dead-man, decanter, demijohn, flacket, flacon, flagon, flask, jack, jar, phial, vial.

bottle up check, conceal, contain, curb, enclose, hide, hold in, inhibit, quell, restrain, restrict, suppress.

antonyms unbosom, unburden.

bottleneck *n* block, blockage, clogging, congestion, hindrance, hold-up, jam, obstacle, obstruction, snarl-up, traffic-jam.

bottom *n* arse, backside, base, basis, bed, behind, bum, butt, buttocks, core, depths, derrière, essence, floor, foot, foundation, fundament, fundus, ground, groundwork, heart, jacksie, nadir, origin, pedestal, plinth, posterior, principle, rear, rear end, root, rump, seat, sit-upon, socle, sole, source, substance, substratum, substructure, support, tail, underneath, underside, understratum.

bottom drawer hope chest.

bottomless *adj* abysmal, abyssal, boundless, deep, fathomless, immeasurable, inexhaustible, infinite, limitless, measureless, profound, unfathomable, unfathomed, unlimited, unplumbed.

antonym shallow.

bottomless pit Abaddon, abode of the damned, abysm, abyss, chasm, crevasse, fire and brimstone, Gehenna, gulf, Hades, Hell, hellfire, infernal regions, inferno, maw.

boulevard *n* avenue, mall, parade, promenade, prospect, row, street, terrace, thoroughfare.

bounce *v* bob, bound, bump, dap, dismiss, eject, jounce, jump, kick out, leap, oust, rebound, recoil, resile, ricochet, spring, stot, throw out.

n animation, bound, dap, dynamism, ebullience, elasticity, energy, exuberance, give, go, life, liveliness, pep, rebound, recoil, resilience, spring, springiness, vigour, vitality, vivacity, zip.

bouncing *adj* blooming, bonny, healthy, lively, robust, strong, thriving, vigorous.

bound[1] *adj* bandaged, beholden, cased, certain, chained, committed, compelled, constrained, destined, doomed, duty-bound, fastened, fated, fixed, forced, held, liable, manacled, obligated, obliged, pinioned, pledged, required, restricted, secured, sure, tied, tied up.

bound[2] *v* bob, bounce, caper, frisk, gallumph, gambol, hurdle, jump, leap, lope, loup, lunge, pounce, prance, skip, spring, vault.

n bob, bounce, caper, dance, frisk, gambado, gambol, jump, leap, lope, loup, lunge, pounce, prance, scamper, skip, spring, vault.

boundary *n* abuttal, barrier, border, borderline, bounds, bourne, brink, confines, demarcation, edge, extremity, fringe, frontier, junction, limes, limits, line, march, margin, mete, perimeter, termination, verge.

adj border, demarcation, frontier, limitary, limitrophe, perimeter.

bounded *adj* bordered, circumscribed, confined, controlled, defined, delimited, demarcated, edged, encircled, enclosed, encompassed, hemmed in, limit ed, restrained, restricted, surrounded, terminated.

bounder *n* blackguard, blighter, cad, cheat, cur, dastard, dirty dog, heel, knave, miscreant, oik, pig, rat, rip, rogue, rotter, swine.

boundless *adj* countless, endless, illimitable, immeasurable, immense, incalculable, indefatigable, inexhaustible, infinite, interminable, interminate, limitless, measureless, prodigious, unbounded, unconfined, unending, unflagging, unlimited, untold, vast.

antonym limited.

bounds *n* borders, boundaries, circumference, confines, edges, extremities, fringes, frontiers, limits, marches, margins, periphery, rim, verges.

bountiful *adj* abundant, ample, boundless, bounteous, copious, exuberant, generous, lavish, liberal, luxuriant, magnanimous, munificent, open-handed, overflowing, plenteous, plentiful, princely, profuse, prolific, ungrudging, unstinting.

antonyms meagre, mean, sparse.

bounty *n* allowance, almsgiving, annuity, assistance, beneficence, benevolence, bonus, charity, donation, generosity, gift, grace, grant, gratuity, kindness, largesse, liberality, philanthropy, premium, present, recompense, reward.

bouquet *n* anthology, aroma, boutonnière, bunch, buttonhole, corsage, florilegium, fragrance, garland, nosegay, odour, perfume, posy, redolence, savour, scent, smell, spray, wreath.

bourgeois *adj* Biedermeier, circumscribed, commonplace, conformist, conservative, conventional, dull, hide-bound, humdrum, kitsch, materialistic, middle-class, pedestrian, tawdry, traditional, trite, trivial, unadventurous, unimaginative, uninspired, unoriginal, vulgar.

antonyms bohemian, original, unconventional.

n conformist, petit bourgeois, philistine, plebeian, Pooter, stick-in-the-mud.

antonyms bohemian, nonconformist.

bout *n* battle, competition, contest, course, encounter, engagement, fight, fit, go, heat, match, period, round, run, session, set-to, spell, spree, stint, stretch, struggle, term, time, turn, venue.

bovine *adj* beefy, dense, dull, dumb, heavy, hulking, obtuse, slow, slow-witted, sluggish, stolid, stupid, thick.

antonym quick.

bow[1] *v* accept, acquiesce, bend, bob, capitulate, comply, concede, conquer, consent, crush, curtsey, defer, depress, droop, genuflect, give in, incline, kowtow, nod, overpower, stoop, subdue, subjugate, submit, surrender, vanquish, yield.

n acknowledgement, bending, bob, curtsey, genuflexion, inclination, kowtow, nod, obeisance, salaam, salutation.

bow out abandon, back out, bunk off, chicken out, defect, desert, give up, opt out, pull out, quit, resign, retire, stand down, step down, withdraw.

bow[2] *n* beak, head, prow, rostrum, stem.

bowdlerise *v* blue-pencil, censor, clean up, cut, edit, excise, expunge, expurgate, launder, modify, mutilate, purge, purify.

bowels *n* belly, centre, core, depths, entrails, guts, heart, hold, innards, inside, insides, interior, intestines, middle, viscera, vitals.

bower *n* alcove, arbour, bay, belvedere, boudoir, dwelling, gazebo, grot, grotto, hideaway, pleasance, recess, retreat, sanctuary, shelter, summer-house.

bowl[1] *n* basin, bicker, cruse, dish, pan, piggin, porringer, quaich, receptacle, sink, tureen, vessel.

bowl[2] *n* jack, wood.

v fling, hurl, pitch, revolve, roll, rotate, spin, throw, trundle, whirl.

bowl over amaze, astonish, astound, dumbfound, fell, flabbergast, floor, stagger, startle, stun, surprise, topple, unbalance.

bow-legs *n* bandiness, bandy legs, valgus.

bowler *n* billycock, bowler hat, hard hat, pot-hat.

box[1] *n* bijou, carton, case, casket, chest, coffer, coffin, coffret, consignment, container, coop, fund, pack, package, portmanteau, present, pyx, pyxis, receptacle, trunk.

v case, embox, encase, pack, package, wrap.

box in cage, circumscribe, confine, contain, coop up, cordon off, corner, enclose, hem in, imprison, restrict, surround, trap.

box[2] *v* buffet, butt, clout, cuff, fight, hit, punch, slap, sock, spar, strike, thwack, wallop, whack, wham, whang.

n blow, buffet, clout, cuff, punch, slap, stroke, thump, wallop, wham, whang.

boxing *n* fisticuffs, prize-fighting, pugilism, sparring, the noble art.

adj fistic, fistical, pugilistic.

boxing-match *n* bout, mill.

boy *n* callant, cub, dandiprat, fellow, gamin, gossoon, halfling, imp, junior, kid, lad, loon, loonie, man-child, nipper, puppy, schoolboy, spalpeen, stripling, urchin, whippersnapper, youngster, youth.

boycott *v* ban, bar, black, blackball, blacklist, cold-shoulder, disallow, embargo, exclude, ignore, ostracise, outlaw, prohibit, proscribe, refuse, reject, spurn.

antonyms encourage, support.

boyfriend *n* admirer, beau, date, fancy man, follower, lover, man, steady, suitor, swain, sweetheart, young man.

boyish *adj* adolescent, childish, gamine, immature, innocent, juvenile, puerile, tomboy, unfeminine, unmaidenly, young, youthful.

brace[1] *n* binder, bracer, bracket, buttress, cleat, corset, nogging, prop, reinforcement, shoring, stanchion, stay, strap, strut, support, truss.

v bandage, bind, bolster, buttress, fasten, fortify, prop, reinforce, shore (up), steady, strap, strengthen, support, tie, tighten.

brace[2] *n* couple, doubleton, duo, pair, twosome.

braces *n* gallowses, galluses, suspenders.

bracing *adj* brisk, crisp, energetic, energising, enlivening, exhilarating, fortifying, fresh, invigorating, refreshing, restorative, reviving, rousing, stimulating, strengthening, tonic, vigorous.

antonym debilitating.

brackish *adj* bitter, briny, saline, salt, saltish, salty.

antonym fresh.

brag *v* bluster, boast, crow, fanfaronade, rodomontade, swagger, talk big, trumpet, vapour, vaunt.

antonym deprecate.

braggart *n* bangster, big mouth, bluffer, blusterer, boaster, braggadocio, Brobadil, fanfaron, gascon, gasconader, rodomontader, show-off, swaggerer, swashbuckler, vapourer, whiffler.

bragging *n* bluster, boastfulness, boasting, bravado, exaggeration, fanfaronade, gasconade, jactation, jactitation, rodomontade, showing off, strutting, swagger, swank, talk, vauntery.

antonyms modesty, unobtrusiveness.

braid *v* entwine, interlace, intertwine, interweave, lace, plait, ravel, twine, twist, weave, wind.

antonyms undo, untwist.

brain[1] *n* boffin, egghead, expert, genius, highbrow, intellect, intellectual, mastermind, prodigy, pundit, sage, savant, scholar, wizard.

antonym simpleton.

brain[2] *n* cerebrum, grey matter, intellect, mind, sensorium, sensory.

brainless *adj* crazy, daft, foolish, half-witted, hen-witted, idiotic, incompetent, inept, mindless, senseless, stupid, thoughtless, unintelligent, witless.

antonyms sensible, shrewd, wise.

brains *n* capacity, common sense, grey matter, head, intellect, intelligence, mind, nous, reason, sagacity, savvy, sense, shrewdness, understanding, wit.

brain-teaser *n* conundrum, mind-bender, poser, problem, puzzle, riddle.

brainwash *v* alter, bludgeon, condition, grill, indoctrinate, persuade, pressure, pressurise, re-educate, verbal.

brainwashing *n* conditioning, double-think, grilling, indoctrination, menticide, mind-bending, persuasion, pressure, pressurisation, re-education, unlearning, verballing.

brainy *adj* bright, brilliant, clever, intellectual, intelligent, sapient, smart.

antonym dull.

brake *n* check, constraint, control, curb, drag, rein, restraint, restriction, retardment.

v check, decelerate, drag, halt, moderate, pull up, retard, slacken, slow, stop.

antonym accelerate.

branch *n* arm, bough, chapter, department, division, grain, limb, lodge, office, offshoot, part, prong, ramification, ramus, section, shoot, sprig, subdivision, subsection, whip, wing, witty.

branch out bifurcate, broaden out, develop, divaricate, diversify, enlarge, expand, extend, increase, move on, multiply, proliferate, ramify, vary.

brand *n* brand-name, class, emblem, grade, hallmark, kind, label, line, logo, make, mark, marker, marque, quality, sign, sort, species, stamp, symbol, trademark, type, variety.

v burn, censure, denounce, discredit, disgrace, label, mark, scar, stain, stamp, stigmatise, taint, type.

brandish *v* display, exhibit, flash, flaunt, flourish, parade, raise, shake, swing, wave, wield.

brand-new *adj* fire-new, fresh.

brash *adj* assuming, assured, audacious, bold, brazen, bumptious, cocky, foolhardy, forward, hasty, heedless, impertinent, impetuous, impudent, impulsive, incautious, indiscreet, insolent, precipitate, rash, reckless, rude, temerarious.

antonyms cautious, reserved, unobtrusive.

brass *n* assurance, audacity, brass neck, brazenness, cheek, effrontery, gall, impertinence, impudence, insolence, nerve, presumption, rudeness, self-assurance, temerity.

antonyms circumspection, timidity.

brassy *adj* blaring, blatant, bold, brash, brazen, cheap, dissonant, flamboyant, flashy, forward, garish, gaudy, grating, hard, harsh, jangling, jarring, jazzy, loud, loud-mouthed, meretricious, noisy, obtrusive, pert, piercing, raucous, saucy, showy, shrill, strident, tawdry, vulgar.

brat *n* cub, gamin, get, guttersnipe, jackanapes, kid, nipper, puppy, rascal, ruffian, toe-rag, urchin, varmint, whippersnapper, youngster.

bravado *n* bluster, boast, boastfulness, boasting, bombast, brag, braggadocio, bragging, fanfaronade, parade, pretence, rodomontade, show, showing off, swagger, swaggering, swank, swashbuckling, talk, vauntery, vaunting.

antonyms modesty, restraint.

brave *adj* audacious, bold, courageous, daring, dauntless, doughty, fearless, fine, gallant, game, glorious, hardy, heroic, indomitable, intrepid, plucky, resolute, resplendent, splendid, stalwart, stoic, stoical, stout-hearted, unafraid, undaunted, unflinching, valiant, valorous.

antonyms cowardly, timid.

v accost, bear, beard, challenge, confront, dare, defy, encounter, endure, face, face up to, stand up to, suffer, withstand.

antonyms capitulate, crumple.

bravely *adv* courageously, dauntlessly, fearlessly, gallantly, gamely, heroically, intrepidly, manfully, pluckily, resolutely, splendidly, stoically, unflinchingly, valiantly, womanfully.

antonym cravenly.

bravery *n* audacity, boldness, courage, daring, dauntlessness, doughtiness, fearlessness, fortitude, gallantry, grit, guts, hardihood, hardiness, heroism, indomitability, intrepidity, mettle, pluck, pluckiness, resoluteness, resolution, spirit, spunk, stalwartness, stoicism, stout-heartedness, valiance, valour.

antonyms cowardice, timidity.

bravura *n* animation, audacity, boldness, brilliance, brio, daring, dash, display, élan, energy, exhibitionism, extravagance, flamboyance, liveliness, ostentation, panache, pizzazz, punch, spirit, verve, vigour, virtuosity.

antonym restraint.

brawl *n* affray, altercation, argument, bagarre, battle, broil, bust-up, clash, disorder, dispute, dog-fight, Donnybrook, dust-up, fight, fracas, fray, free-for-all, mêlée, punch-up, quarrel, row, ruckus, rumpus, scrap, scuffle, squabble, tumult, uproar, wrangle.

v altercate, argue, argy-bargy, battle, dispute, fight, flyte, quarrel, row, scrap, scuffle, squabble, tussle, wrangle, wrestle.

brawn *n* beef, beefiness, brawniness, bulk, bulkiness, flesh, meat, might, muscle, muscles, muscularity, power, robustness, sinews, strength, thews.

brawny *adj* athletic, beefy, bovine, bulky, burly, fleshy, hardy, hefty, herculean, hulking, husky, lusty, massive, muscular, powerful, robust, sinewy, solid, stalwart, strapping, strong, sturdy, thewy, vigorous, well-built, well-knit.

antonyms frail, slight.

bray *v* blare, hoot, roar, screech, trumpet.

n bawl, bellow, blare, blast, cry, hoot, roar, screech, shout, shriek.

brazen *adj* assured, audacious, barefaced, blatant, bold, brash, brassy, defiant, flagrant, forward, immodest, impudent, insolent, malapert, pert, saucy, shameless, unabashed, unashamed.

antonym shamefaced.

breach *n* alienation, aperture, break, break-up, chasm, cleft, contravention, crack, crevice, difference, disaffection, disagreement, discontinuity, disobedience, disruption, dissension, dissociation, division, estrangement, fissure, gap, hole, infraction, infringement, lapse, offence, opening, parting, quarrel, rent, rift, rupture, schism, scission, scissure, secession, separation, severance, split, transgression, trespass, variance, violation.

bread *n* aliment, cash, diet, dough, fare, finance, food, funds, money, moolah, necessities, nourishment, nutriment, provisions, rooty, spondulicks, subsistence, sustenance, viands, victuals, wherewithal.

breadth *n* amplitude, area, beam, broadness, bulk, compass, comprehensiveness, dimension, expanse, extensiveness, extent, latitude, magnitude, measure, range, reach, scale, scope, size, space, span, spread, sweep, thickness, vastness, volume, wideness, width.

break *v* abandon, absorb, announce, appear, bankrupt, batter, beat, better, breach, burst, bust, contravene, cow, crack, crash, cripple, cushion, cut, dash, defeat, degrade, demolish, demoralise, destroy, diminish, discharge, disclose, discontinue, disintegrate, disobey, dispirit, disregard, divide, divulge, emerge, enervate, enfeeble, erupt, escape, exceed, excel, explode, flee, flout, fly, fract, fracture, fragment, go phut, happen, humiliate, impair, impart, incapacitate, inform, infract, infringe, interrupt, jigger, knacker, knap, lessen, moderate, modify, occur, outdo, outstrip, part, pause, proclaim, reduce, rend, rest, retard, reveal, ruin, separate, sever, shatter, shiver, smash, snap, soften, splinter, split, stave, stop, subdue, surpass, suspend, tame, tear, tell, transgress, undermine, undo, violate, weaken, worst.

n abruption, advantage, alienation, breach, breather, chance, cleft, crack, crevice, disaffection, discontinuity, dispute, disruption, divergence, division, estrangement, fissure, fortune, fracture, gap, gash, halt, hiatus, hole, interlude, intermission, interruption, interval, lapse, let-up, lull, opening, opportunity, pause, quarrel, recess, rent, respite, rest, rift, rupture, schism, separation, split, suspension, tear, time-out.

break away apostasise, depart, detach, escape, flee, fly, leave, part company, quit, renegue, revolt, run away, secede, separate, split.

break down analyse, anatomise, collapse, conk out, crack up, crush, demolish, dissect, fail, give way, go phut, seize up, stop.

break in burgle, encroach, impinge, interfere, interject, interpose, interrupt, intervene, intrude, invade, irrupt.

break off cease, desist, detach, disconnect, discontinue, dissever, divide, end, finish, halt, interrupt, part, pause, separate, sever, snap off, splinter, stop, suspend, terminate.

break out abscond, arise, begin, bolt, burst, commence, emerge, erupt, escape, flare up, flee, happen, occur, start.

break the ice begin, lead the way, oil the works, relax, set at ease, start the ball rolling, unbend.

break through achieve, emerge, gain ground, leap forward, make headway, pass, penetrate, progress, succeed.

break up adjourn, analyse, anatomise, demolish, destroy, disband, dismantle, disperse, disrupt, dissolve, divide, divorce, part, scatter, separate, sever, split, stop, suspend, terminate.

break with ditch, drop, finish with, jilt, part with, reject, renounce, repudiate, separate.

breakable *adj* brittle, crumbly, delicate, flimsy, fragile, frail, frangible, friable, insubstantial, murly.

antonyms durable, sturdy.

breakaway *adj* apostate, dissenting, heretical, rebel, renegade, schismatic, seceding, secessionist.

breakdown *n* analysis, cataclasm, categorisation, classification, collapse, disintegration, disruption, dissection, failure, interruption, itemisation, mishap, stoppage.

breakfast *n* dejeune, déjeuner, disjune, petit déjeuner.

break-in *n* burglary, housebreaking, intrusion, larceny, robbery, theft.

breakthrough *n* advance, development, discovery, find, finding, gain, headway, improvement, invention, leap, progress, step.

break-up *n* breakdown, crack-up, crumbling, disintegration, dispersal, dissolution, divorce, finish, parting, rift, separation, split, splitting, termination.

breakwater *n* dock, groyne, jetty, mole, pier, quay, wharf.

breast *n* bosom, bust, chest, front, heart, thorax.

breasts *n* boobs, bristols, bust, cans, dugs, knockers, paps, teats, tits.

breath *n* air, animation, aroma, breathing, breeze, energy, exhalation, existence, flatus, flutter, gasp, gulp, gust, hint, inhalation, life, murmur, odour, pant, pneuma, puff, respiration, sigh, smell, spirit, suggestion, suspicion, undertone, vapour, vitality, waft, wheeze, whiff, whisper.

breathe *v* articulate, exercise, exhale, expire, express, imbue, impart, infuse, inhale, inject, inspire, instil, live, murmur, pant, puff, respire, say, sigh, suspire, tire, transfuse, utter, voice, whisper.

breather *n* break, breathing-space, constitutional, halt, pause, recess, relaxation, respite, rest, walk.

breathless *adj* agog, anxious, avid, choking, eager, excited, exhausted, expectant, gasping, gulping, hushed, impatient, panting, peching, puffing, short-winded, spent, wheezing, wheezy, winded.

breathlessness *n* air-hunger, dyspnoea, gasping, panting, short-windedness, wheeziness.

breathtaking *adj* affecting, amazing, astonishing, awe-inspiring, awesome, exciting, impressive, magnificent, moving, overwhelming, stirring, stunning, thrilling.

breeches *n* galligaskins, knee-breeches, knee-cords, knickerbockers, knickers, moleskins, pantaloons, pants, plus-fours, trews, trousers.

breed *v* arouse, bear, beget, bring forth, bring up, cause, create, cultivate, develop, discipline, educate, engender, foster, generate, hatch, induce, instruct, make, multiply, nourish, nurture, occasion, originate, procreate, produce, propagate, raise, rear, reproduce, train.

n family, ilk, kind, line, lineage, pedigree, progeny, race, sort, species, stamp, stock, strain, type, variety.

breeding *n* ancestry, background, civility, courtesy, cultivation, culture, development, education, gentility, lineage, manners, nurture, polish, politeness, raising, rearing, refinement, reproduction, stock, strain, training, upbringing, urbanity.

antonym vulgarity.

breeding-ground *n* hotbed, nest, nursery, school, training ground.

breeze *n* air, breath, cat's-paw, draught, flurry, gale, gust, waft, whiff, wind, zephyr.

v flit, glide, hurry, sail, sally, sweep, trip, wander.

breezy *adj* airy, animated, blithe, blowing, blowy, blustery, bright, buoyant, carefree, careless, casual, cheerful, debonair, easy-going, exhilarating, fresh, gusty, informal, insouciant, jaunty, light, light-hearted, lively, nonchalant, sprightly, squally, sunny, untroubled, vivacious, windy.

antonyms calm, staid.

brevity *n* abruptness, briefness, brusqueness, conciseness, concision, crispness, curtness, economy, ephemerality, evanescence, fugacity, impermanence, incisiveness, laconicism, laconism, pithiness, shortness, succinctness, summariness, terseness, transience, transitoriness.

antonyms longevity, permanence, verbosity.

brew *v* boil, build up, concoct, contrive, cook, decoct, develop, devise, excite, ferment, foment, gather, hatch, infuse, mix, plan, plot, prepare, project, scheme, seethe, soak, steep, stew.

n beverage, blend, bouillon, brewage, broth, concoction, distillation, drink, fermentation, gruel, infusion, liquor, mixture, potion, preparation, stew.

bribable *adj* bent, buyable, corrupt, corruptible, purchasable, venal.

antonym incorruptible.

bribe *n* allurement, back-hander, baksheesh, boodle, dash, enticement, graft, grease, hush money, incentive, inducement, kickback, pay-off, payola, protection money, refresher, slush fund, sweetener.

v buy off, buy over, corrupt, reward, square, suborn.

bribery *n* corruption, graft, greasing, inducement, lubrication, palm-greasing, payola, protection, subornation.

bric-à-brac *n* antiques, baubles, bibelots, curios, curiosities, gewgaws, kickshaws, knick-knacks, ornaments, rattle-trap, trinkets, virtu.

brick *n* adobe, block, breeze block, brickbat, clanger, closer, faux pas, firebrick, fletton, gaffe, gaucherie, header, klinker, nogging, quoin, stretcher.

bridal *adj* conjugal, connubial, hymeneal, hymenean, marital, marriage, matrimonial, nuptial, sponsal, spousal, wedding.

bridge *n* arch, band, bond, causeway, connection, flyover, link, overpass, pontoon bridge, span, tie, viaduct, yoke.

v attach, bind, connect, couple, cross, fill, join, link, span, traverse, unite, yoke.

bridle *v* check, contain, control, curb, govern, master, moderate, rein in, repress, restrain, subdue.

brief *adj* abrupt, aphoristic, blunt, brusque, capsular, compendious, compressed, concise, crisp, cursory, curt, ephemeral, fast, fleeting, fugacious, fugitive, hasty, laconic, limited, momentary, passing, pithy, quick, sharp, short, short-lived, succinct, surly, swift, temporary, terse, thumbnail, transient, transitory.

antonyms long, long-lived, verbose.

n advice, argument, briefing, case, contention, data, defence, demonstration, directions, directive, dossier, instructions, mandate, orders, outline, précis, remit, summary.

v advise, direct, explain, fill in, gen up, guide, inform, instruct, prepare, prime.

briefing *n* advice, conference, directions, filling-in, gen, guidance, information, instruction, instructions, intimation, low-down, meeting, notification, orders, preamble, preparation, priming.

briefly *adv* abruptly, brusquely, concisely, cursorily, curtly, fleetingly, hastily, hurriedly, laconically, momentarily, precisely, quickly, shortly, summarily, temporarily, tersely.

antonyms fully, permanently.

brigade *n* band, body, company, contingent, corps, crew, force, group, guard, outfit, party, squad, team, troop, unit.

brigand *n* bandit, cateran, dacoit, desperado, footpad, freebooter, gangster, haiduk, heister, highwayman, klepht, marauder, outlaw, plunderer, robber, ruffian.

brigandage *n* banditry, brigandry, dacoitage, dacoity, freebootery, freebooting, gangsterism, heist, hold-up, robbery.

bright *adj* ablaze, acute, astute, auspicious, beaming, blazing, brainy, breezy, brilliant, burnished, cheerful, clear, clear-headed, clever, cloudless, dazzling, effulgent, encouraging, excellent, favourable, flashing, fulgent, gay, genial, glad, glaring, gleaming, glistening, glittering, glorious, glowing, golden, happy, hopeful, illuminated, illustrious, ingenious, intelligent, intense, inventive, jolly, joyful, joyous, keen, lambent, lamping, light-hearted, limpid, lively, lucent, lucid, luculent, luminous, lustrous, magnificent, merry, observant, optimistic, pellucid, perceptive, percipient, perspicacious, polished, prefulgent, promising, propitious, prosperous, quick, quick-witted, radiant, resplendent, rosy, scintillating, sharp, sheeny, shimmering, shining, smart, sparkling, splendid, sunny, translucent, transparent, twinkling, unclouded, undulled, untarnished, vivacious, vivid, wide-awake.

antonyms depressing, dull, stupid.

brighten *v* burnish, cheer up, clear up, encourage, enliven, flash, gladden, gleam, glow, hearten, illuminate, light up, lighten, perk up, polish, rub up, shine.

antonyms darken, dull, tarnish.

brightness *n* blaze, braininess, brains, breeziness, brilliance, brilliancy, cheer, cheerfulness, cleverness, effulgence, fulgency, fulgor, gladness, glare, glitter, glory, hopefulness, illumination, joy, liveliness, lucency, luminance, luminosity, lustre, magnificence, optimism, promise, propitiousness, radiance, refulgence, resplendence, sheen, sparkle, splendour, vivacity, vividness.

antonyms cheerlessness, darkness, dullness.

brilliance *n* animation, aptitude, blaze, braininess, bravura, brightness, brilliancy, cleverness, coruscation, dazzle, distinction, éclat, effulgence, excellence, fulgency, gaiety, genius, giftedness, glamour, glare, gleam, glitter, glory, gloss, gorgeousness, grandeur, greatness, illustriousness, intensity, inventiveness, lambency, lucency, luminosity, lustre, magnificence, pizzazz, radiance, refulgence, resplendence, scintillation, sheen, sparkle, splendour, talent, vivacity, vividness, wit.

brilliant *adj* ablaze, accomplished, adroit, animated, astute, blazing, brainy, bright, celebrated, clever, coruscating, dazzling, effulgent, eminent, exceptional, expert, famous, gemmy, gifted, glaring, glittering, glorious, glossy, illustrious, ingenious, intellectual, intelligent, intense, inventive, lambent, luminous, magnificent, masterly, outstanding, quick, refulgent, scintillating, shining, showy, skilful, sparkling, splendid, star, star-like, superb, talented, vivacious, vivid, witty.

antonyms dull, restrained, stupid, undistinguished.

brim *n* border, brink, circumference, edge, lip, marge, margin, perimeter, periphery, rim, skirt, verge.

bring *v* accompany, accustom, add, attract, bear, carry, cause, command, conduct, convey, convince, create, deliver, dispose, draw, earn, effect, engender, escort, fetch, force, gather, generate, get beget, gross, guide, induce, inflict, influence, introduce, lead, make, move, net, occasion, persuade, produce, prompt, return, sway, take, transfer, transport, usher, wreak, yield.

bring about accomplish, achieve, cause, compass, create, effect, effectuate, engender, engineer, fulfil, generate, manage, manipulate, manoeuvre, occasion, produce, realise.

bring down abase, break, debase, degrade, fell, floor, humble, lay low, level, lower, overthrow, overturn, reduce, ruin, shoot, topple, undermine.

bring forth afford, bear, beget, engender, furnish, generate, produce, provide, supply, yield.

bring home to convince, drive home, emphasise, impress upon, persuade, prove.

bring in accrue, earn, fetch, gross, introduce, net, produce, profit, realise, return, yield.

bring off accomplish, achieve, bring about, compass, discharge, execute, fulfil, perform, rescue.

bring on accelerate, advance, cause, expedite, generate, give rise to, induce, inspire, lead to, occasion, precipitate, prompt, provoke.

antonym inhibit.

bring out draw out, emphasise, enhance, highlight, introduce, issue, print, publish, utter.

bring to light dig up, disclose, discover, disinter, exhume, expose, reveal, show, uncover, unearth, unveil.

bring to nothing destroy, knock the bottom out of, mar, nullify, ruin, scupper, spoil, undermine, vitiate.

bring up advance, broach, disgorge, educate, form, foster, introduce, mention, nurture, propose, puke, raise, rear, regurgitate, submit, succeed, succour, support, teach, throw up, train, vomit.

brink *n* bank, border, boundary, brim, edge, extremity, fringe, limit, lip, marge, margin, point, rim, skirt, threshold, verge, waterside.

briny *adj* muriatic, salty.

brisk *adj* active, agile, alert, allegro, bracing, bright, brushy, bustling, busy, crank, crisp, effervescing, energetic, exhilarating, expeditious, fresh, galliard, invigorating, keen, lively, nimble, nippy, no-nonsense, prompt, quick, refreshing, sharp, snappy, speedy, spirited, sprightly, spry, stimulating, vigorous.

antonym sluggish.

briskly *adv* abruptly, actively, allegro, brightly, decisively, efficiently, energetically, expeditiously, incisively, nimbly, promptly, quickly, rapidly, readily, smartly, vigorously.

antonym sluggishly.

bristle *n* barb, hair, prickle, spine, stubble, thorn, vibrissa, whisker.

v bridle, draw oneself up, horripilate, prickle, react, rise, seethe, spit.

bristling *adj* abounding, crawling, horrent, horrid, horripilant, humming, incensed, indignant, seething, spitting, swarming, teeming.

bristly *adj* bearded, bewhiskered, bristling, hairy, hirsute, hispid, horrent, horripilant, prickly, rough, stubbly, thorny, unshaven, whiskered.

antonyms clean-shaven, smooth.

brittle *adj* anxious, breakable, crackly, crisp, crumbling, crumbly, curt, delicate, edgy, fragile, frail, frangible, friable, frush, irritable, nervous, nervy, shattery, shivery, short, spalted, tense.

antonyms durable, resilient, sturdy.

broach *v* crack open, introduce, launch into, mention, pierce, propose, puncture, raise, start, suggest, tap, uncork, utter.

broad *adj* all-embracing, ample, beamy, blue, capacious, catholic, coarse, comprehensive, eclectic, encyclopaedic, enlightened, expansive, extensive, far-reaching, general, generous, gross, improper, inclusive, indecent, indelicate, large, latitudinous, roomy, spacious, square, sweeping, tolerant, universal, unlimited, unrefined, vast, voluminous, vulgar, wide, wide-ranging, widespread.

antonym narrow.

broadcast *v* advertise, air, announce, beam, cable, circulate, disseminate, proclaim, promulgate, publicise, publish, radio, relay, report, show, spread, televise, transmit.

n programme, relay, show, telecast, transmission.

broaden *v* augment, branch out, develop, diversify, enlarge, enlighten, expand, extend, increase, open up, spread, stretch, supplement, swell, thicken, widen.

broad-minded *adj* catholic, cosmopolitan, dispassionate, enlightened, flexible, free-thinking, indulgent, liberal, open-minded, permissive, receptive, tolerant, unbiased, unprejudiced, verligte.

broadside *n* assault, attack, battering, blast, bombardment, brickbat, broadsheet, cannonade, counterblast, denunciation, diatribe, fulmination, harangue, invective, pamphlet, philippic.

brochure *n* advertisement, booklet, broadsheet, broadside, circular, folder, handbill, hand-out, leaflet, pamphlet.

broil *n* affray, altercation, argument, brawl, brouhaha, dispute, disturbance, fracas, fray, imbraglio, quarrel, scrimmage, scrum, stramash, strife, tumult, wrangle.

broke *adj* bankrupt, bust, destitute, impecunious, impoverished, insolvent, penniless, penurious, ruined, skint, stony-broke, strapped.

antonyms affluent, solvent.

broken *adj* bankrupt, beaten, betrayed, browbeaten, burst, crippled, crushed, defeated, defective, demolished, demoralised, destroyed, disconnected, discontinuous, dishonoured, disjointed, dismantled, dispersed, disregarded, disturbed, down, dud, duff, erratic, exhausted, faulty, feeble, forgotten, fracted, fractured, fragmentary, fragmented, halting, hesitating, humbled, ignored, imperfect, incoherent, incomplete, infirm, infringed, intermittent, interrupted, isolated, jiggered, kaput, knackered, oppressed, out of order, overpowered, prerupt, rent, retracted, routed, ruined, run-down, ruptured, separated, severed, shattered, shivered, spasmodic, spent, stammering, subdued, tamed, traduced, transgressed, uncertain, vanquished, variegated, weak.

broken-down *adj* collapsed, decayed, dilapidated, disintegrated, inoperative, kaput, out of order, ruined.

broken-hearted *adj* crestfallen, dejected, desolate, despairing, despondent, devastated, disappointed, disconsolate, grief-stricken, hard-hit, heartbroken, heart-sick, heartsore, inconsolable, miserable, mournful, prostrated, sorrowful, unhappy, wretched.

broker *n* agent, dealer, factor, handler, intermediary, middleman, negotiator, stockbroker.

bromide *n* anodyne, banality, cliché, commonplace, platitude, stereotype, truism.

bronze *adj* auburn, brazen, chestnut, copper, copper-coloured, reddish-brown, rust, tan, titian.

brooch *n* badge, breastpin, clasp, clip, pin, prop.

brood *v* agonise, cover, dwell on, fret, go over, hatch, incubate, meditate, mope, mull over, muse, ponder, rehearse, repine, ruminate.

n birth, chicks, children, clutch, family, get, hatch, issue, litter, nide, offspring, progeny, young.

brook[1] *n* beck, burn, channel, freshet, gill, inlet, mill, rill, rivulet, runnel, stream, streamlet, watercourse.

brook[2] *v* abide, accept, allow, bear, countenance, endure, permit, stand, stomach, submit to, suffer, support, swallow, thole, tolerate, withstand.

broom *n* besom, brush, sweeper, wisp.

brothel *n* bagnio, bawdy-house, bordello, cathouse, flash-house, house of ill fame, house of ill repute, kip, kip-shop, knocking-shop, red light, stews, vaulting-house, whorehouse.

brother *n* associate, blood-brother, brer, chum, colleague, companion, compeer, comrade, confrère, cousin, fellow, fellow-creature, friar, friend, kin, kinsman, mate, monk, pal, partner, relation, relative, religieux, religious, sibling.

brotherhood *n* affiliation, alliance, association, clan, clique, community, confederacy, confederation, confraternity, confrèrie, coterie, fraternity, guild, league, society, union.

brotherly *adj* affectionate, amicable, benevolent, caring, concerned, cordial, fraternal, friendly, kind, loving, neighbourly, philanthropic, supervisory, sympathetic.

antonyms callous, unbrotherly.

brow *n* appearance, aspect, bearing, brink, cliff, countenance, crown, edge, eyebrow, face, forehead, front, mien, peak, ridge, rim, summit, temples, tip, top, verge, visage.

browbeat *v* awe, batter, bludgeon, bulldoze, bully, coerce, cow, domineer, dragoon, hector, hound, intimidate, oppress, overbear, threaten, tyrannise.

antonym coax.

brown *adj* auburn, bay, brick, bronze, bronzed, browned, brunette, chestnut, chocolate, coffee, dark, donkey, dun, dusky, fuscous, ginger, hazel, mahogany, russet, rust, rusty, sunburnt, tan, tanned, tawny, titian, toasted, umber, vandyke brown.

brown study absence, absent-mindedness, absorption, abstraction, contemplation, meditation, musing, pensiveness, preoccupation, reflection, reverie, rumination.

browned off bored, bored stiff, brassed off, cheesed off, discontented, discouraged, disgruntled, disheartened, fed up, pissed off, weary.

antonyms fascinated, interested.

brownie *n* elf, fairy, goblin, hob, kobold, leprechaun, lob-lie-by-the-fire, lubber fiend, nix, nixie, pixie, Puck, Robin Goodfellow, sprite.

browse *v* crop, dip into, eat, feed, flick through, graze, leaf through, nibble, pasture, peruse, scan, skim, survey.

bruise *v* blacken, blemish, contund, contuse, crush, discolour, grieve, hurt, injure, insult, mar, mark, offend, pound, pulverise, stain, wound.

n blemish, contusion, discoloration, injury, mark, rainbow, shiner, swelling.

brunt *n* burden, force, impact, impetus, pressure, shock, strain, stress, thrust, violence, weight.

brush[1] *n* besom, broom, sweeper.

v buff, burnish, caress, clean, contact, flick, glance, graze, kiss, paint, polish, rub, scrape, shine, stroke, sweep, touch, wash.

brush aside belittle, dismiss, disregard, flout, ignore, override, pooh-pooh.

brush off cold-shoulder, discourage, disdain, dismiss, disown, disregard, ignore, rebuff, refuse, reject, repudiate, repulse, scorn, slight, snub, spurn.

antonyms cultivate, encourage.

brush up cram, freshen up, improve, read up, refresh, relearn, revise, study, swot.

brush[2] *n* brushwood, bushes, frith, ground cover, scrub, shrubs, thicket, undergrowth, underwood.

brush[3] *n* clash, conflict, confrontation, dust-up, encounter, fight, fracas, incident, run-in, scrap, set-to, skirmish, tussle.

brush-off *n* cold shoulder, discouragement, dismissal, go-by, rebuff, refusal, rejection, repudiation, repulse, slight, snub.

antonym encouragement.

brusque *adj* abrupt, blunt, curt, discourteous, gruff, hasty, impolite, sharp, short, surly, tactless, tart, terse, uncivil, undiplomatic.

antonyms courteous, tactful.

brutal *adj* animal, barbarous, bearish, beastly, bestial, bloodthirsty, boarish, brute, brutish, callous, carnal, coarse, crude, cruel, doggish, ferocious, gruff, harsh, heartless, impolite, inhuman, inhumane, insensitive, merciless, pitiless, remorseless, rough, rude, ruthless, savage, sensual, severe, uncivil, uncivilised, unfeeling, unmannerly, unsympathetic, vicious.

antonyms humane, kindly.

brutalise *v* decivilise, dehumanise, desensitise, harden, inure.

antonym civilise.

brutality *n* atrocity, barbarism, barbarity, bloodthirstiness, brutishness, callosity, callousness, coarseness, cruelty, ferocity, inhumanity, roughness, ruthlessness, savageness, savagery, viciousness.

antonyms gentleness, kindness.

brutally *adv* barbarically, barbarously, brutishly, callously, coarsely, cruelly, ferociously, fiercely, hard-heartedly, harshly, heartlessly, inhumanly, meanly, mercilessly, murderously, pitilessly, remorselessly, roughly, ruthlessly, savagely, unkindly, viciously.

antonyms gently, kindly.

brute *n* animal, barbarian, beast, bête, boor, creature, devil, fiend, lout, monster, ogre, sadist, savage, swine.

antonym gentleman.

adj bestial, bodily, carnal, coarse, depraved, fleshly, gross, instinctive, mindless, physical, senseless, sensual, unthinking.

antonym refined.

brutish *adj* barbarian, barbaric, barbarous, boorish, coarse, crass, crude, cruel, feral, ferine, gross, loutish, savage, stupid, subhuman, swinish, uncouth, vulgar.

antonym refined.

bubble[1] *n* ball, bead, bladder, blister, blob, drop, droplet, globule, vesicle.

v babble, boil, burble, effervesce, fizz, foam, froth, gurgle, murmur, percolate, purl, ripple, seethe, sparkle, trickle, trill, wallop.

bubble[2] *n* bagatelle, delusion, fantasy, fraud, illusion, sting, toy, trifle, vanity.

bubbles *n* effervescence, fizz, foam, froth, head, lather, spume, suds.

bubbly *adj* animated, bouncy, carbonated, curly, effervescent, elated, excited, fizzy, happy, lively, merry, sudsy.

antonym flat.

buccaneer *n* corsair, filibuster, freebooter, pirate, privateer, sea-robber, sea-rover, sea-wolf.

buck[1] *n* beau, blade, blood, coxcomb, dandy, fop, gallant, playboy, popinjay, spark, swell.

buck[2] *v* bound, cheer, dislodge, encourage, gladden, gratify, hearten, inspirit, jerk, jump, leap, please, prance, spring, start, throw, unseat, vault.

buck up brighten, cheer, cheer up, encourage, hearten, improve, inspirit, perk up, rally, stimulate, take heart.

antonym dishearten.

bucket *n* bail, barrel, basin, can, cask, kibble, pail, pan, pitcher, vessel.

buckle *n* bend, bulge, catch, clasp, clip, contortion, distortion, fastener, hasp, kink, twist, warp.

v bend, bulge, catch, cave in, clasp, close, collapse, connect, contort, crumple, distort, fasten, fold, hitch, hook, secure, twist, warp, wrinkle.

bucolic *adj* agrarian, agricultural, countrified, country, pastoral, rural, rustic.

antonyms industrial, urban.

bud *n* embryo, germ, knosp, shoot, sprig, sprout.

v burgeon, develop, grow, pullulate, shoot, sprout.

antonyms waste away, wither.

budding *adj* burgeoning, developing, embryonic, fledgling, flowering, germinal, growing, hopeful, incipient, intending, nascent, potential, promising.

antonym experienced.

budge *v* bend, change, convince, dislodge, give (way), inch, influence, move, persuade, propel, push, remove, roll, shift, slide, stir, sway, yield.

budget *n* allocation, allotment, allowance, cost, estimate, finances, fonds, funds, means, resources.

v allocate, apportion, cost, estimate, plan, ration.

buff[1] *adj* fawn, fulvid, fulvous, khaki, sandy, straw, tan, yellowish, yellowish-brown.

v brush, burnish, polish, polish up, rub, shine, smooth.

buff[2] *n* addict, admirer, aficionado, bug, cognoscente, connoisseur, devotee, enthusiast, expert, fan, fiend, freak.

buffer *n* bulwark, bumper, cushion, fender, intermediary, pad, pillow, safeguard, screen, shield, shock-absorber.

buffet[1] *n* café, cafeteria, counter, snack-bar, snack-counter.

buffet[2] *v* bang, batter, beat, box, bump, clobber, clout, cuff, flail, hit, jar, knock, pound, pummel, push, rap, shove, slap, strike, thump, wallop.

n bang, blow, box, bump, clout, cuff, jar, jolt, knock, push, rap, shove, slap, smack, thump, wallop.

buffoon *n* clown, comedian, comic, droll, fool, goliard, harlequin, jester, joker, merry-andrew, mountebank, scaramouch, Scoggin, tomfool, vice, wag, zany.

buffoonery *n* clowning, drollery, farce, harlequinade, jesting, nonsense, pantomime, silliness, tomfoolery, waggishness, zanyism.

bug *n* addict, admirer, bacterium, blemish, buff, catch, craze, defect, disease, enthusiast, error, fad, failing, fan, fault, fiend, flaw, freak, germ, gremlin, imperfection, infection, mania, micro-organism, obsession, rage, snarl-up, virus.

v annoy, badger, bother, disturb, get, harass, irk, irritate, needle, nettle, pester, plague, vex.

bugbear *n* anathema, bane, bęte noire, bloody-bones, bogey, bugaboo, devil, dread, fiend, horror, Mumbo-jumbo, nightmare, pet hate, poker, rawhead.

build *v* assemble, augment, base, begin, big, constitute, construct, develop, edify, enlarge, erect, escalate, establish, extend, fabricate, form, formulate, found, improve, inaugurate, increase, initiate, institute, intensify, knock together, make, originate, raise, strengthen.

antonyms destroy, knock down, lessen, weaken.

n body, figure, form, frame, physique, shape, size, structure.

build up advertise, amplify, assemble, boost, develop, enhance, expand, extend, fortify, heighten, hype, improve, increase, intensify, plug, promote, publicise, reinforce, strengthen.

antonyms lessen, weaken.

building *n* architecture, construction, domicile, dwelling, edifice, erection, fabric, fabrication, house, megastructure, pile, structure.

antonym destruction.

build-up *n* accretion, accumulation, ballyhoo, development, enlargement, escalation, expansion, gain, growth, heap, hype, increase, load, mass, plug, promotion, publicity, puff, stack, stockpile, store.

antonyms decrease, reduction.

built-in *adj* essential, fundamental, implicit, in-built, included, incorporated, inherent, inseparable, integral, intrinsic, necessary.

bulbous *adj* bellied, bellying, bloated, bulging, convex, distended, pulvinate(d), rounded, swelling, swollen.

bulge *n* belly, boost, bump, distension, hump, increase, intensification, lump, projection, protrusion, protuberance, rise, surge, swelling, upsurge.

v bag, belly, bulb, dilate, distend, enlarge, expand, hump, project, protrude, sag, strout, swell.

bulging *adj* bellied, bulbous, bunchy, convex, pulvinate, pulvinated, rounded, swelling, swollen.

bulk *n* amplitude, bigness, body, dimensions, extensity, extent, generality, immensity, largeness, magnitude, majority, mass, most, plurality, preponderance, size, substance, volume, weight.

bulky *adj* big, colossal, cumbersome, enormous, heavy, hefty, huge, hulking, immense, large, lumping, mammoth, massive, massy, ponderous, substantial, unmanageable, unwieldy, volumed, voluminous, weighty.

antonyms handy, insubstantial, small.

bulldoze *v* browbeat, buffalo, bully, clear, coerce, cow, demolish, drive, flatten, force, hector, intimidate, knock down, level, propel, push, push through, raze, shove, thrust.

bullet *n* ball, missile, pellet, plumb, projectile, shot, sinker, slug, weight.

bulletin *n* announcement, communication, communiqué, dispatch, dope, message, newsflash, notification, report, sitrep, statement.

bull's-eye *n* bull, centre, gold.

antonym miss.

bully *n* bouncer, browbeater, bucko, bully-boy, bully-rook, coercionist, Drawcansir, intimidator, killcrow, oppressor, persecutor, ruffian, termagant, tormentor, tough, tyrant.

v bluster, browbeat, bulldoze, bullyrag, coerce, cow, domineer, haze, hector, intimidate, oppress, overbear, persecute, push around, swagger, terrorise, tyrannise.

antonyms coax, persuade.

bulwark *n* bastion, buffer, buttress, defence, embankment, fortification, guard, mainstay, outwork, partition, rampart, redoubt, safeguard, security, support.

bumbling *adj* awkward, blundering, botching, bungling, clumsy, footling, foozling, incompetent, inefficient, inept, lumbering, maladroit, muddled, stumbling.

antonyms competent, efficient.

bump *v* bang, bounce, budge, collide (with), crash, dislodge, displace, hit, jar, jerk, jolt, jostle, jounce, knock, move, rattle, remove, shake, shift, slam, strike.

n bang, blow, bulge, collision, contusion, crash, hit, hump, impact, jar, jolt, knob, knock, knot, lump, node, nodule, protuberance, rap, shock, smash, swelling, thud, thump.

bump off assassinate, dispatch, do in, eliminate, kill, liquidate, murder, remove, rub out, top.

bumper *adj* abundant, bountiful, enormous, excellent, exceptional, great, huge, jumbo, large, massive, prodigal, spanking, teeming, unusual, whacking, whopping.

antonyms miserly, small.

bumpkin *n* boor, chaw-bacon, clodhopper, clown, corn-ball, hick, hillbilly, jake, looby, lout, lubbard, lubber, lummox, oaf, peasant, provincial, rustic, yokel.

antonym man of the world.

bumptious *adj* arrogant, boastful, brash, cocky, conceited, egotistic, forward, full of oneself, impudent, overbearing, over-confident, pompous, presumptuous, pushy, self-assertive, self-important, showy, swaggering, vainglorious, vaunting.

antonyms humble, modest.

bumpy *adj* bouncy, choppy, irregular, jarring, jerky, jolting, jolty, knobbly, knobby, lumpy, rough, rutted, uneven.

antonym smooth.

bunch *n* assortment, band, batch, bouquet, bundle, clump, cluster, collection, crew, crowd, fascicle, fascicule, flock, gang, gathering, group-knot, heap, lot, mass, mob, multitude, number, parcel, party, pile, quantity, sheaf, spray, stack, swarm, team, troop, tuft.

v assemble, bundle, cluster, collect, congregate, crowd, flock, group, herd, huddle, mass, pack.

antonyms scatter, spread out.

bunched *adj* clustered, concentrated, fascicled, fascicular, fasciculate(d), gathered, grouped.

antonyms scattered, spread out.

bundle *n* accumulation, assortment, bag, bale, batch, box, bunch, carton, collection, consignment, crate, dorlach, drum, fascicle, fascicule, group, heap, mass, Matilda, pack, package, packet, pallet, parcel, pile, quantity, roll, shock, shook, stack, stook, swag.

v bale, bind, fasten, pack, palletise, tie, truss, wrap.

bundled *adj* clustered, fascicled, fascicular, fasciculate(d), gathered, grouped, parcelled, tied.

antonyms loose, scattered.

bung *n* cork, dook, stopper.

bungle *v* blunder, bodge, boob, botch, bumble, cock up, duff, flub, footle, foozle, foul up, fuck up, fudge, goof, louse up, mar, mess up, miscalculate, mismanage, muff, mull, ruin, screw up, spoil.

n blunder, boob, boo-boo, botch-up, cock-up, foul-up, mull.

bungler *n* blunderer, botcher, butterfingers, duffer, footler, foozler, fumbler, incompetent, lubber, muddler, muff.

bungling *adj* awkward, blundering, botching, cack-handed, clumsy, footling, foozling, ham-fisted, ham-handed, incompetent, inept, maladroit, unskilful.

bunkum *n* balderdash, baloney, bilge, bosh, bunk, garbage, havers, hooey, horsefeathers, nonsense, piffle, poppycock, rot, rubbish, stuff and nonsense, tar(r)adiddle, tomfoolery, tommyrot, tosh, trash, tripe, twaddle.

antonym sense.

buoy *n* beacon, dolphin, float, marker, signal.

buoy up boost, cheer, encourage, hearten, lift, raise, support, sustain.

antonym depress.

buoyant *adj* afloat, animated, blithe, bouncy, breezy, bright, bullish, carefree, cheerful, debonair, floatable, floating, happy, jaunty, joyful, light, light-hearted, lively, peppy, rising, sprightly, sunny, weightless.

antonym depressed.

burble *n* babble, gurgle, lapping, murmur, purl, purling.

v babble, gurgle, lap, murmur, purl.

burden *n* affliction, anxiety, bear, care, cargo, clog, dead weight, encumbrance, grievance, load, millstone, obligation, obstruction, onus, responsibility, sorrow, strain, stress, trial, trouble, weight, worry.

v bother, encumber, handicap, lade, lie hard on, lie heavy on, load, oppress, overload, overwhelm, strain, tax, worry.

antonyms disburden, lighten, relieve.

burdensome *adj* crushing, difficult, distressing, exacting, heavy, irksome, onerous, oppressive, taxing, troublesome, trying, wearisome, weighty.

antonyms easy, light.

bureau *n* agency, branch, counter, department, desk, division, office, service.

bureaucracy *n* administration, city hall, civil service, directorate, government, ministry, officialdom, officialese, officials, red tape, regulations, the authorities, the system.

bureaucrat *n* administrator, apparatchik, bureaucratist, chinovnik, civil servant, functionary, mandarin, minister, office-holder, officer, official.

burglar *n* cat-burglar, cracksman, house-breaker, picklock, pilferer, robber, thief, yegg.

burglary *n* break-in, cat-burglary, house-breaking, larceny, pilferage, robbery, stealing, theft, thieving.

burial *n* burying, entombment, exequies, funeral, inhumation, interment, obsequies, sepulchre, sepulture.

burlesque *n* caricature, mickey-taking, mock, mockery, parody, ridicule, satire, send-up, spoof, take-off, travesty.

adj caricatural, comic, derisive, droll, farcical, hudibrastic, mocking, parodying, satirical.

antonym serious.

v ape, caricature, exaggerate, imitate, lampoon, mock, parody, ridicule, satirise, send up, spoof, take off, travesty.

burly *adj* athletic, beefy, big, brawny, bulky, heavy, hefty, hulking, husky, muscular, powerful, stocky, stout, strapping, strong, sturdy, thickset, well-built.

antonyms puny, slim, small, thin.

burn *v* bite, blaze, brand, calcine, cauterise, char, combust, conflagrate, consume, corrode, deflagrate, desire, expend, flame, flare, flash, flicker, fume, glow, hurt, ignite, incinerate, kindle, light, oxidise, pain, parch, scorch, seethe, shrivel, simmer, singe, smart, smoke, smoulder, sting, tingle, toast, use, wither, yearn.

burning *adj* acrid, acute, alight, ardent, biting, blazing, caustic, compelling, consuming, corrosive, critical, crucial, eager, earnest, essential, excessive, fervent, fiery, flaming, flashing, frantic, frenzied, gleaming, glowing, hot, illuminated, impassioned, important, intense, irritating, painful, passionate, piercing, pressing, prickling, pungent, reeking, scorching, significant, smarting, smouldering, stinging, tingling, urent, urgent, vehement, vital, zealous.

antonyms apathetic, cold, mild, unimportant.

burnish *v* brighten, buff, furbish, glaze, polish, polish up, rub, shine.

antonym tarnish.

n gloss, lustre, patina, polish, sheen, shine.

burrow *n* den, earth, hole, lair, retreat, set(t), shelter, tunnel, warren.

v delve, dig, earth, excavate, mine, tunnel, undermine.

burst *v* barge, blow up, break, crack, dehisce, disintegrate, erupt, explode, fragment, gush, puncture, run, rupture, rush, shatter, shiver, split, spout, tear.

n bang, blast, blasting, blow-out, blow-up, breach, break, crack, discharge, eruption, explosion, fit, gallop, gush, gust, outbreak, outburst, outpouring, rupture, rush, spate, split, spurt, surge, torrent.

adj broken, flat, kaput, punctured, rent, ruptured, split, torn.

burst-up *n* break, collapse, commotion, disruption, failure, separation.

bury *v* absorb, conceal, cover, embed, enclose, engage, engross, engulf, enshroud, entomb, hide, immerse, implant, inearth, inhume, inter, interest, lay to rest, occupy, secrete, sepulchre, shroud, sink, submerge.

antonyms disinter, uncover.

bus *n* charabanc, coach, jitney, mammy-wagon, omnibus.

bush *n* backwoods, brush, hedge, plant, scrub, scrubland, shrub, shrubbery, thicket, wilds, woodland.

bushy *adj* bosky, bristling, bristly, dasyphyllous, dumose, dumous, fluffy, fuzzy, luxuriant, rough, shaggy, spreading, stiff, thick, unruly, wiry.

antonyms neat, tidy, trim, well-kept.

busily *adv* actively, assiduously, briskly, diligently, earnestly, energetically, hard, industriously, intently, purposefully, speedily, strenuously.

business *n* affair, assignment, bargaining, calling, career, commerce, company, concern, corporation, craft, dealings, duty, employment, enterprise, establishment, firm, function, industry, issue, job, line, line of country, manufacturing, matter, merchandising, métier, occupation, organisation, palaver, point, problem, profession, pursuit, question, responsibility, selling, subject, task, topic, trade, trading, transaction(s), venture, vocation, work.

business-like *adj* correct, efficient, formal, impersonal, matter-of-fact, methodical, orderly, organised, practical, precise, professional, regular, routine, systematic, thorough, well-ordered.

antonyms disorganised, inefficient.

businessman *n* capitalist, employer, entrepreneur, executive, financier, homme d'affaires, industrialist, merchant, trader, tradesman, tycoon.

buskers *n* German-band, mariachi, street-entertainers, street-musicians.

bust *n* bosom, breast, carving, chest, head, statue, statuette, torso.

bustle *v* dash, flutter, fuss, hasten, hurry, rush, scamper, scramble, scurry, scuttle, stir, tear.

n activity, ado, agitation, commotion, excitement, flurry, fuss, haste, hurly-burly, hurry, palaver, pother, stir, to-do, toing and froing, tumult.

bustling *adj* active, astir, busy, buzzing, crowded, energetic, eventful, full, humming, lively, restless, rushing, stirring, swarming, teeming, thronged.

antonym quiet.

bust-up *n* brawl, disruption, disturbance, quarrel, separation.

busy *adj* active, assiduous, brisk, diligent, eident, employed, energetic, engaged, engrossed, exacting, full, fussy, hectic, industrious, inquisitive, interfering, lively, meddlesome, meddling, nosy, occupied, officious, persevering, prying, restless, slaving, stirabout, stirring, strenuous, tireless, tiring, troublesome, unleisured, versant, working.

antonyms idle, quiet.

v absorb, bother, concern, employ, engage, engross, immerse, interest, occupy.

busybody *n* eavesdropper, gossip, intriguer, intruder, meddler, nosey parker, pantopragmatic, prodnose, pry, scandalmonger, snoop, snooper, troublemaker.

butcher *n* destroyer, killcow, killer, murderer, slaughterer, slayer.

v assassinate, botch, carve, clean, cut, destroy, dress, exterminate, joint, kill, liquidate, massacre, mutilate, prepare, ruin, slaughter, slay, spoil, wreck.

butchery *n* blood-letting, bloodshed, carnage, killing, mass destruction, massacre, murder, slaughter.

butler *n* sommelier, wine-waiter.

butt[1] *n* base, end, foot, haft, handle, hilt, shaft, shank, stock, stub, tail, tip.

butt[2] *n* dupe, laughing-stock, mark, object, point, subject, target, victim.

butt[3] *v, n* buck, buffet, bump, bunt, hit, jab, knock, poke, prod, punch, push, ram, shove, thrust.

butt in cut in, interfere, interpose, interrupt, intrude, meddle.

butter up blarney, cajole, coax, flatter, soft-soap, wheedle.

buttocks *n* arse, backside, beam end, behind, bottom, breach, bum, derrière, doup, fanny, fud, haunches, hinder-end, hinderlin(g)s, hindquarters, hurdies, natch, nates, posterior, prat, rear, rump, seat.

button *n* bud, catch, clasp, fastening, frog, knob, pimple.

buttonhole *v* accost, bore, catch, detain, grab, importune, nab, pin, waylay.

buttress *n* abutment, brace, mainstay, pier, prop, reinforcement, shore, stanchion, stay, strut, support.

v bolster up, brace, hold up, prop up, reinforce, shore up, strengthen, support, sustain, uphold.

antonym weaken.

buxom *adj* ample, bosomy, busty, chesty, comely, debonair, hearty, jocund, jolly, lively, lusty, merry, plump, robust, voluptuous, well-rounded, winsome.

antonyms petite, slim, small.

buy *v* acquire, bribe, corrupt, fix, get, obtain, procure, purchase, square, suborn.

antonym sell.

n acquisition, bargain, deal, purchase.

buyer *n* emptor, purchaser, vendee.

antonyms seller, vendor.

buying *n* acquisition, emption, purchase.

buzz *n* bombilation, bombination, buzzing, drone, gossip, hearsay, hiss, hum, murmur, news, purr, report, ring, ringing, rumour, scandal, susurration, susurrus, whir(r), whisper, whizz.

v bombilate, bombinate, drone, hum, murmur, reverberate, ring, susurrate, whir(r), whisper, whizz.

by *prep* along, beside, near, next to, over, past, through, via.

adv aside, at hand, away, beyond, close, handy, near, past.

by all means absolutely, certainly, doubtlessly, of course, positively, surely.

by any means anyhow.

by chance perchance.

by degrees bit by bit, gently, gradually, imperceptibly, inch by inch, little by little, slowly, step by step.

antonyms all at one go, quickly, suddenly.

by far by a long chalk, by a long shot, easily, far and away, immeasurably, incomparably, much.

by fits and starts erratically, fitfully, intermittently, irregularly, now and again, on and off, spasmodically, sporadically, unsystematically.

antonyms constantly, continuously.

by force vi et armis.

by halves imperfectly, incompletely, scrappily, skimpily.

antonyms completely, totally.

by heart by rote, memoriter, off pat, parrot-fashion, pat, word for word.

by mistake in error, misapprehensively, mistakenly.

by no means in no way, not at all, not in the least, not the least bit, on no account.

by repute reputatively, reputedly, supposedly.

by the way en passant, in passing.

bygone *adj* ancient, antiquated, departed, erstwhile, forepast, forgotten, former, lost, olden, past, previous.

antonyms modern, recent.

n antique, grievance, oldie.

bypass *v* avoid, circumvent, ignore, neglect, outflank.

n detour, ring road.

by-product *n* after-effect, consequence, epiphenomenon, fall-out, repercussion, result, side-effect.

bystander *n* eye-witness, looker-on, observer, onlooker, passer-by, spectator, watcher, witness.

byword *n* adage, aphorism, apophthegm, catch-word, dictum, epithet, gnome, maxim, motto, precept, proverb, saw, saying, slogan.

C

cab *n* hackney carriage, minicab, taxi, taxicab, vettura.

cabal *n* caucus, clique, coalition, conclave, confederacy, conspiracy, coterie, faction, intrigue, junta, junto, league, machination, party, plot, plotters, scheme, set.

cabin *n* berth, bothy, chalet, compartment, cot, cot-house, cottage, crib, deck-house, hovel, hut, lodge, quarters, room, shack, shanty, shed.

cabin boy grummet.

cabinet *n* almirah, case, chiffonier, closet, commode, cupboard, dresser, escritoire, locker.

cabinetmaker *n* ebeniste.

cable *n* chain, cord, hawser, line, mooring, rope.

cabman *n* cabby, taxi-driver, vetturino.

cache *n* accumulation, fund, garner, hoard, repository, reserve, stockpile, store, storehouse, supply, treasure-store.

v bury, conceal, hide, secrete, stash, store, stow.

cackle *v,n* babble, chatter, chuckle, crow, gabble, gibber, giggle, jabber, laugh, prattle, snicker, snigger, titter.

cacophonous *adj* discordant, dissonant, grating, harsh, horrisonant, inharmonious, jarring, raucous, strident.

antonyms harmonious, pleasant.

cacophony *n* caterwauling, discord, disharmony, dissonance, horrisonance, stridency.

antonym harmony.

cad *n* blackguard, bounder, caitiff, churl, cur, dastard, heel, knave, oik, poltroon, rat, rotter, skunk, swine, worm.

antonym gentleman.

cadence *n* accent, beat, inflection, intonation, lilt, measure, metre, modulation, pattern, pulse, rate, rhythm, stress, swing, tempo, throb.

cadge *v* beg, bum, freeload, hitch, scrounge, sponge.

cadre *n* basis, core, framework, hierarchy, infrastructure, nucleus, official.

cafe *n* cafeteria, coffee bar, coffee shop, estaminet, greasy spoon, restaurant, snack bar, tea-room.

cage *v* confine, coop up, encage, fence in, immure, impound, imprison, incarcerate, lock up, mew, restrain, shut up.

antonyms free, let out.

n aviary, coop, corral, enclosure, pen, pound.

cag(e)y *adj* careful, chary, circumspect, discreet, guarded, non-committal, secretive, shrewd, wary, wily.

antonyms frank, indiscreet, open.

cajole *v* beguile, blandish, blarney, coax, decoy, dupe, entice, entrap, flatter, fleech, inveigle, lure, manoeuvre, mislead, seduce, soothe, sweet-talk, tempt, wheedle, whillywha(w), wile.

antonyms bully, force.

cajolery *n* beguilement, blandishments, blarney, coaxing, enticement, flattery, inducement(s), inveigling, persuasion, soft soap, sweet talk, wheedling.

antonyms bullying, force.

cake *v* bake, cement, coagulate, coat, condense, congeal, consolidate, cover, dry, encrust, harden, inspissate, ossify, solidify, thicken.

n block, jumbal, loaf, lump, madeleine, mass, slab.

calamitous *adj* cataclysmic, catastrophic, deadly, devastating, dire, disastrous, dreadful, fatal, ghastly, grievous, pernicious, ruinous, tragic, woeful.

antonyms fortunate, happy.

calamity *n* adversity, affliction, cataclysm, catastrophe, desolation, disaster, distress, downfall, misadventure, mischance, misfortune, mishap, reverse, ruin, scourge, tragedy, trial, tribulation, woe, wretchedness.

antonyms blessing, godsend.

calculate *v* aim, cipher, compute, consider, count, determine, enumerate, estimate, figure, gauge, intend, judge, plan, rate, reckon, value, weigh, work out.

calculated *adj* considered, deliberate, intended, intentional, planned, premeditated, purposed, purposeful, purposive, wilful.

antonyms unintended, unplanned.

calculating *adj* canny, cautious, contriving, crafty, cunning, designing, devious, Machiavellian, manipulative, politic, scheming, sharp, shrewd, sly.

antonyms artless, naïve, open.

calculation *n* answer, caution, ciphering, circumspection, computation, deliberation, estimate, estimation, figurework, figuring, forecast, foresight, forethought, judgement, planning, precaution, reckoning, result.

calibre *n* ability, bore, capacity, character, diameter, distinction, endowment, faculty, force, gauge, gifts, league, measure, merit, parts, quality, scope, size, stature, strength, talent, worth.

call *v* announce, appoint, arouse, assemble, awaken, bid, christen, collect, consider, contact, convene, convoke, cry, declare, decree, denominate, designate, dub, elect, entitle, estimate, gather, hail, halloo, invite, judge, label, muster, name, ordain, order, phone, proclaim, rally, regard, rouse, shout, style, summon, telephone, term, think, waken, yell.

n announcement, appeal, cause, claim, command, cry, demand, excuse, grounds, hail, invitation, justification, need, notice, occasion, order, plea, reason, request, right, ring, scream, shout, signal, summons, supplication, urge, visit, whoop, yell.

call for[1] demand, entail, involve, necessitate, need, occasion, require, suggest.

call for[2] collect, fetch, pick up, uplift.

call it a day finish, knock off, leave off, pack it in, pack up, shut up shop, stop, throw in the towel.

call off abandon, break off, cancel, desist, discontinue, drop, withdraw.

call on appeal, appeal to, ask, bid, call round, entreat, gam, go and see, invite, invoke, request, summon, supplicate, visit.

call the tune call the shots, command, dictate, give the orders, govern, lead, rule, rule the roost.

calling *n* business, career, employment, field, job, line, line of country, metier, mission, occupation, profession, province, pursuit, trade, vocation, work.

callous *adj* case-hardened, cold, hard-bitten, hard-boiled, hardened, hard-hearted, heartless, indifferent, indurated, insensate, insensible, insensitive, inured, obdurate, soulless, thick-skinned, uncaring, unfeeling, unresponsive, unsouled, unsusceptible, unsympathetic.

antonyms kind, sensitive, sympathetic.

callow *adj* fledgling, green, guileless, immature, inexperienced, jejune, juvenile, naïve, puerile, raw, unfledged, uninitiated, unsophisticated, untried.

antonym experienced.

calm *adj* balmy, collected, composed, cool, dispassionate, equable, halcyon, impassive, imperturbable, laid back, mild, pacific, passionless, peaceful, placid, quiet, relaxed, restful, sedate, self-collected, self-possessed, serene, smooth, still, stilly, tranquil, unapprehensive, unclouded, undisturbed, unemotional, uneventful, unexcitable, unexcited, unflappable, unflustered, unmoved, unperturbed, unruffled, untroubled, windless.

antonyms excitable, rough, stormy, wild, worried.

v compose, hush, mollify, pacify, placate, quieten, relax, soothe.

antonyms excite, irritate, worry.

n calmness, dispassion, hush, peace, peacefulness, quiet, repose, serenity, stillness.

antonyms restlessness, storminess.

calmness *n* ataraxia, ataraxy, calm, composure, cool, coolness, dispassion, equability, equanimity, hush, impassiveness, impassivity, imperturbability, motionless, peace, peacefulness, placidity, poise, quiet, repose, restfulness, sang-froid, self-possession, serenity, smoothness, stillness, tranquillity, unexcitableness, unflappableness.

antonyms excitability, restlessness, storminess.

calumniate *v* asperse, backbite, blacken, defame, denigrate, detract, disparage, lampoon, libel, malign, misrepresent, revile, slag, slander, stigmatise, traduce, vilify, vilipend.

calumny *n* abuse, aspersion, backbiting, calumniation, defamation, denigration, derogation, detraction, disparagement, insult, libel, lying, misrepresentation, obloquy, revilement, slagging, slander, smear, stigma, vilification, vituperation.

camaraderie *n* brotherhood, brotherliness, companionship, comradeship, esprit de corps, fellowship, fraternisation, good-fellowship, intimacy, togetherness.

camouflage *n* blind, cloak, concealment, cover, covering, deception, disguise, front, guise, mask, masquerade, screen, subterfuge.

v cloak, conceal, cover, disguise, hide, mask, obfuscate, obscure, screen, veil.

antonyms reveal, uncover.

camp[1] *adj* affected, artificial, campy, effeminate, exaggerated, homosexual, mannered, ostentatious, over the top, poncy, posturing, theatrical.

camp[2] *n* caucus, clique, crowd, faction, group, party, section, set, side.

campaign *n* attack, crusade, drive, excursion, expedition, jihad, movement, offensive, operation, promotion, push.

v advocate, attack, crusade, fight, promote, push.

camp-follower *n* hanger-on, henchman, lackey, lascar, leaguer-lady, leaguer-lass, toady.

can *n* canister, cannikin, container, jar, jerrycan, pail, receptacle, tin.

canal *n* waterway, zanja.

cancel *v* abolish, abort, abrogate, adeem, annul, compensate, counterbalance, countermand, delete, efface, eliminate, erase, expunge, neutralise, nullify, obliterate, offset, quash, redeem, repeal, repudiate, rescind, revoke, scrub, strike.

cancellation *n* abandoning, abandonment, abolition, ademption, annulment, deletion, elimination, neutralisation, nullifying, quashing, repeal, revocation.

cancer *n* blight, canker, carcinoma, corruption, evil, growth, malignancy, melanoma, pestilence, rot, sickness, tumour.

candelabrum *n* candlestick, menorah.

candid *adj* blunt, clear, fair, forthright, frank, free, guileless, ingenuous, just, open, outspoken, plain, shining, sincere, straightforward, truthful, unbiased, uncontrived, unequivocal, unposed, unprejudiced, upfront.

antonyms cagey, devious, evasive.

candidate *n* applicant, aspirant, claimant, competitor, contender, contestant, doctorand, entrant, nominee, possibility, pretendant, pretender, runner, solicitant, suitor.

candle *n* cerge, taper, wax-light.

candour *n* artlessness, directness, fairness, forthrightness, franchise, frankness, guilelessness, honesty, ingenuousness, naïvety, openness, outspokenness, plain-dealing, simplicity, sincerity, straightforwardness, truthfulness, unequivocalness.

antonyms cageyness, deviousness, evasiveness.

cane *n* ferula, ferule, Malacca-cane, Penang-lawyer, stick, walking-stick.

canker *n* bane, blight, boil, cancer, corrosion, corruption, infection, lesion, rot, scourge, sore, ulcer.

cannabis *n* benj, bhang, grass, hash, hashish, marijuana, pot.

cannibal *n* anthropophagite, man-eater.

cannibalism *n* anthropophagy, endophagy, exophagy.

canny *adj* acute, artful, astute, careful, cautious, circumspect, clever, comfortable, gentle, harmless, innocent, judicious, knowing, lucky, perspicacious, prudent, sagacious, sharp, shrewd, skilful, sly, subtle, wise, worldly-wise.

antonyms foolish, imprudent.

canon *n* catalogue, criterion, dictate, formula, list, precept, principle, regulation, roll, rule, standard, statute, yardstick.

canonical *adj* accepted, approved, authorised, authoritative, orthodox, recognised, regular, sanctioned.

antonym uncanonical.

canopy *n* awning, baldachin, covering, dais, shade, sunshade, tabernacle, tester, umbrella.

cant[1] *n* argot, humbug, hypocrisy, insincerity, jargon, lingo, pretentiousness, sanctimoniousness, slang, thieves' Latin, vernacular.

cant[2] *n* angle, bevel, incline, jerk, rise, slant, slope, tilt, toss.

cantankerous *adj* bad-tempered, captious, carnaptious, choleric, contrary, crabbed, crabby, cranky, crotchety, crusty, difficult, disagreeable, feisty, grouchy, grumpy, ill-humoured, ill-natured, irascible, irritable, peevish, perverse, piggish, quarrelsome, testy.

antonyms good-natured, pleasant.

canter *n* amble, dogtrot, jog, jog-trot, lope.

v amble, jog, lollop, lope, run.

canvass *v* agitate, analyse, ask for, campaign, debate, discuss, dispute, electioneer, examine, inspect, investigate, poll, scan, scrutinise, seek, sift, solicit, study.

n examination, investigation, poll, scrutiny, survey, tally.

canyon *n* box-canyon, cañon, coulée, gorge, gulch, gully, ravine.

cap *v* beat, better, complete, cover, crown, eclipse, exceed, excel, finish, outdo, outstrip, surpass, top, transcend.

n beret, biretta, bonnet, chapka, cowl, fez, hat, shako, skullcap, Tam o' Shanter, yarmulka.

capability *n* ability, capacity, competence, facility, faculty, means, potential, potentiality, power, proficiency, qualification, skill, talent.

capable *adj* able, accomplished, adept, adequate, apt, clever, competent, disposed, efficient, experienced, fitted, gifted, intelligent, liable, masterly, predisposed, proficient, qualified, skilful, suited, susceptible, talented.

antonyms incapable, incompetent, useless.

capacious *adj* ample, big, broad, comfortable, commodious, comprehensive, expansive, extensive, generous, huge, large, liberal, roomy, sizable, spacious, substantial, vast, voluminous, wide.

antonyms cramped, small.

capacity *n* ability, amplitude, appointment, aptitude, aptness, brains, calibre, capability, cleverness, compass, competence, competency, dimensions, efficiency, extent, facility, faculty, forte, function, genius, gift, intelligence, magnitude, office, position, post, power, province, range, readiness, role, room, scope, service, size, space, sphere, strength, volume.

cape[1] *n* chersonese, head, headland, ness, peninsula, point, promontory, tongue.

cape[2] *n* cloak, coat, cope, mantle, pelerine, pelisse, poncho, robe, shawl, wrap.

caper *v* bounce, bound, capriole, cavort, dance, frisk, frolic, gambol, hop, jump, leap, romp, skip, spring.

n affair, antic, business, capriole, dido, escapade, gambado, gambol, high jinks, hop, jape, jest, jump, lark, leap, mischief, prank, revel, sport, stunt.

capital[1] *adj* cardinal, central, chief, controlling, essential, excellent, fine, first, first-rate, foremost, great, important, leading, main, major, overruling, paramount, pre-eminent, primary, prime, principal, splendid, superb, upper-case.

antonyms minor, sad, unfortunate.

capital[2] *n* assets, cash, finance, finances, financing, fonds, funds, investment(s), means, money, principal, property, resources, stock, wealth, wherewithal.

capitulate *v* give in, relent, submit, succumb, surrender, throw in the towel/sponge, yield.

antonym fight on.

capitulation *n* accedence, relentment, submission, surrender, yielding.

caprice *n* boutade, changeableness, concetto, fad, fancy, fantasia, fantasy, fickleness, fitfulness, freak, humoresque, humour, impulse, inconstancy, notion, quirk, vagary, vapour, whim, whimsy.

capricious *adj* changeable, crotchety, erratic, fanciful, fickle, fitful, freakish, humorous, impulsive, inconstant, mercurial, odd, queer, quirky, uncertain, unpredictable, variable, wayward, whimsical.

antonyms sensible, steady.

capsize *v* invert, keel over, overturn, turn over, turn turtle, upset.

capsule *n* bolus, case, lozenge, module, pericarp, pill, pod, receptacle, sheath, shell, space-ship, tablet, troche, vessel.

captain *n* boss, chief, chieftain, commander, head, leader, master, officer, patron, pilot, skip, skipper.

captious *adj* acrimonious, cantankerous, carping, cavilling, censorious, crabbed, critical, cross, disparaging, exceptious, fault-finding, hypercritical, irritable, nagging, narky, nit-picking, peevish, testy, touchy.

antonyms amiable, good-natured, pleasant.

captivate *v* allure, attract, beguile, besot, bewitch, charm, dazzle, enamour, enchain, enchant, enrapture, enslave, ensnare, enthrall, entrance, fascinate, hypnotise, infatuate, lure, mesmerise, seduce, win.

antonyms appal, repel.

captivated *adj* beguiled, besotted, bewitched, crazy, enchanted, epris, infatuated.

captivating *adj* attractive, beautiful, beguiling, bewitching, catching, dazzling, enchanting.

antonyms ugly, unattractive.

captive *n* convict, detainee, hostage, internee, prisoner, slave.

adj caged, confined, enchained, enslaved, ensnared, imprisoned, incarcerated, restricted, secure, subjugated.

antonym free.

captivity *n* bondage, confinement, custody, detention, durance, duress, enchainment, enthralment, imprisonment, incarceration, internment, restraint, servitude, slavery, thraldom, vassalage.

antonym freedom.

capture *v* apprehend, arrest, bag, catch, collar, cop, feel someone's collar, lift, nab, secure, seize, snaffle, take.

n apprehension, arrest, catch, imprisonment, seizure, taking, trapping.

car *n* auto, autocar, automobile, banger, buggy, crate, drag, dragster, flivver, horseless carriage, hot rod, jalop(p)y, jalopy, machine, motor, motor-car, vehicle, vettura.

carafe *n* bottle, decanter, flagon, flask, jug, pitcher.

caravan *n* camel train, kafila.

carbuncle *n* anthrax, boil, inflammation, pimple, sore.

carcass *n* body, cadaver, corpse, framework, hulk, relics, remains, shell, skeleton, stiff.

card[1] *n* dial, domino, map, playing-card, programme.

card[2] *n* eccentric, person, wag.

cardinal *adj* capital, central, chief, essential, first, foremost, fundamental, greatest, highest, important, key, leading, main, paramount, pre-eminent, primary, prime, principal.

cardinal *n* red-hat.

cards *n* devil's (picture-)books.

care *n* affliction, anxiety, attention, burden, carefulness, caution, charge, circumspection, concern, consideration, control, custody, direction, disquiet, forethought, guardianship, hardship, heed, interest, keeping, leading-strings, management, meticulousness, ministration, pains, perplexity, pressure, protection, prudence, regard, responsibility, solicitude, stress, supervision, tribulation, trouble, vexation, vigilance, ward, watchfulness, woe, worry.

antonyms carelessness, inattention, thoughtlessness.

care for attend, delight in, desire, enjoy, foster, like, love, mind, nurse, prize, protect, take pleasure in, tend, want, watch over.

career *n* calling, course, employment, job, life-work, livelihood, occupation, passage, path, procedure, progress, pursuit, race, vocation, walk.

v bolt, dash, gallop, hurtle, race, run, rush, shoot, speed, tear.

carefree *adj* airy, blithe, breezy, buoyant, careless, cheerful, cheery, easy-going, happy, happy-go-lucky, insouciant, jaunty, laid-back, light-hearted, lightsome, radiant, sunny, untroubled, unworried.

antonyms anxious, worried.

careful *adj* accurate, alert, attentive, cautious, chary, circumspect, concerned, conscientious, discreet, fastidious, heedful, judicious, meticulous, mindful, painstaking, particular, precise, protective, prudent, punctilious, scrupulous, softly-softly, solicitous, thoughtful, thrifty, vigilant, wary, watchful.

antonyms careless, inattentive, thoughtless.

carefully *adv* cautiously, painstakingly, point-device, punctiliously, warily.

antonym carelessly.

careless *adj* absent-minded, casual, cursory, derelict, forgetful, heedless, hit-or-miss, inaccurate, incautious, inconsiderate, indiscreet, irresponsible, lackadaisical, messy, neglectful, negligent, nonchalant, offhand, perfunctory, regardless, remiss, slap-dash, slipshod, sloppy, thoughtless, uncaring, unconcerned, unguarded, unmindful, unstudied, untenty, unthinking.

antonyms accurate, careful, meticulous, thoughtful.

carelessness *n* absent-mindedness, heedlessness, inaccuracy, inattention, inconsiderateness, indiscretion, irresponsibility, messiness, neglect, negligence, omission, remissness, slackness, slipshodness, sloppiness, thoughtlessness.

antonyms accuracy, care, thoughtfulness.

caress *v* canoodle, cuddle, embrace, fondle, hug, kiss, lallygag (lollygag), nuzzle, paw, pet, rub, stroke, touch.

n cuddle, embrace, fondle, hug, kiss, pat, stroke.

caretaker *n* concierge, curator, custodian, dvornik, janitor, keeper, porter, superintendent, warden, watchman.

careworn *adj* exhausted, fatigued, gaunt, haggard, tired, weary, worn, worn-out.

antonyms lively, sprightly.

cargo *n* baggage, consignment, contents, freight, goods, haul, lading, load, merchandise, pay-load, shipment, tonnage, ware.

caricature *n* burlesque, cartoon, distortion, farce, lampoon, mimicry, parody, Pasquil, Pasquin, pasquinade, representation, satire, send-up, take-off, travesty.

v burlesque, distort, lampoon, mimic, mock, parody, pasquinade, ridicule, satirise, send up, take off.

carnage *n* blood-bath, bloodshed, butchery, havoc, holocaust, massacre, murder, shambles, slaughter.

carnal *adj* animal, bodily, corporeal, earthly, erotic, fleshly, human, impure, lascivious, lecherous, lewd, libidinous, licentious, lustful, mundane, natural, physical, profane, prurient, salacious, secular, sensual, sensuous, sexual, sublunary, temporal, unchaste, unregenerate, unspiritual, voluptuous, wanton, worldly.

antonyms chaste, pure, spiritual.

carnality *n* bestiality, brutishness, corporeality, fleshliness, lasciviousness, lechery, lust, lustfulness, prurience, salaciousness, sensuality, voluptuousness, worldliness.

antonyms chastity, purity, spirituality.

carnival *n* celebration, fair, Fasching, festival, fête, fiesta, gala, holiday, jamboree, jubilee, Mardi Gras, merrymaking, revelry, wassail, wassail-bout, wassailry.

carnivorous *adj* creophagous, meat-eating, zoophagous.

carol *n* canticle, canzonet, chorus, ditty, hymn, lay, noel, song, strain, wassail.

carouse *v* booze, drink, imbibe, quaff, revel, roister, wassail.

n beer-up, drinking-bout, party, wassail.

carousing *n* celebrating, drinking, mallemaroking, party, partying.

carp *v* cavil, censure, complain, criticise, hypercriticise, knock, nag, quibble, reproach, ultracrepidate.

antonym praise.

carpet *n* Axminster, kali, kilim, mat, rug, Wilton.

carping *adj* biting, bitter, captious, cavilling, critical, fault-finding, grouchy, hypercritical, nagging, nit-picking, picky, reproachful, Zoilean.

n censure, complaints, criticism, disparagement, knocking, reproofs, Zoilism.

antonyms compliments, praise.

carriage *n* air, bearing, behaviour, cab, carrying, coach, comportment, conduct, conveyance, conveying, delivery, demeanour, deportment, freight, gait, manner, mien, posture, presence, transport, transportation, vehicle, vettura, voiture, wagon, wagonette.

carrier *n* bearer, conveyor, delivery-man, messenger, porter, runner, transmitter, transporter, vector.

carry *v* accomplish, bear, bring, broadcast, capture, chair, communicate, conduct, convey, display, disseminate, drive, effect, fetch, gain, give, haul, hip, impel, influence, lift, lug, maintain, motivate, move, offer, publish, relay, release, secure, shoulder, spur, stand, stock, suffer, support, sustain, take, tote, transfer, transmit, transport, underpin, uphold, urge, win.

carry on administer, continue, endure, flirt, last, maintain, manage, misbehave, operate, perpetuate, persevere, persist, proceed, run.

carry out accomplish, achieve, bring off, discharge, do, effect, execute, fulfil, implement, perform, realise.

cart *n* barrow, buggy, chaise, curricle, float, gig, gurney, shay, trap, tray, truck, tumbrel, wagon, wain, wheel-barrow.

v bear, carry, convey, haul, hump, humph, jag, lug, move, tote, transport.

carton *n* box, case, container, pack, package, packet, parcel.

cartoon *n* animation, caricature, comic strip, drawing, fumetto, lampoon, parody, representation, sketch, take-off.

cartridge *n* canister, capsule, case, cassette, charge, container, cylinder, magazine, round, shell.

carve *v* chip, chisel, cut, divide, engrave, etch, fashion, form, grave, hack, hew, incise, indent, make, mould, sculp(t), sculpture, slash, slice, tool, whittle.

carving *n* bust, dendroglyph, incision, lithoglyph, petroglyph, sculpture, statue, statuette.

cascade *n* avalanche, cataract, deluge, falls, flood, force, fountain, outpouring, rush, shower, torrent, waterfall, water-works.

antonym trickle.

v descend, flood, gush, overflow, pitch, plunge, pour, rush, shower, spill, surge, tumble.

case[1] *n* box, cabinet, canister, capsule, carton, cartridge, casing, casket, chest, compact, container, cover, covering, crate, envelope, etui, folder, holder, integument, jacket, receptacle, sheath, shell, showcase, suit-case, tray, trunk, wrapper, wrapping.

v encase, enclose, skin.

case² *n* argument, circumstances, condition, context, contingency, dilemma, event, example, illustration, instance, occasion, occurrence, plight, point, position, predicament, situation, specimen, state, thesis.

v investigate, reconnoitre.

case³ *n* action, argument, cause, dispute, lawsuit, proceedings, process, suit, trial.

cash *n* bank-notes, bread, bullion, change, coin, coinage, currency, dough, funds, hard currency, hard money, money, notes, payment, readies, ready, ready money, resources, specie, wherewithal.

v encash, liquidate, realise.

cashier¹ *n* accountant, assistant, banker, bursar, check-out girl, clerk, purser, teller, treasurer.

cashier² *v* break, discard, discharge, dismiss, drum out, expel, sack, unfrock.

cask *n* barrel, barrico, butt, cade, firkin, hogshead, puncheon, tub, tun, vat, wood.

casket *n* box, case, chest, coffer, jewel-box, kist, pyxis.

casserole *n* pot-au-feu, stew-pan.

cast¹ *v* abandon, add, allot, appoint, assign, bestow, calculate, categorise, choose, chuck, compute, deposit, diffuse, distribute, drive, drop, emit, figure, fling, forecast, form, found, give, hurl, impel, launch, lob, model, mould, name, pick, pitch, project, radiate, reckon, reject, scatter, select, set, shape, shed, shy, sling, spread, throw, thrust, toss, total.

n air, appearance, complexion, demeanour, fling, form, lob, look, manner, mien, quality, semblance, shade, stamp, style, throw, thrust, tinge, tone, toss, turn.

cast down crush, deject, depress, desolate, discourage, dishearten, dispirit, sadden.

antonyms encourage, lift up.

cast² *n* actors, artistes, characters, company, dramatis personae, entertainers, performers, players, troupe.

caste *n* class, degree, estate, grade, lineage, order, position, race, rank, species, station, status, stratum.

castigate *v* beat, berate, cane, censure, chasten, chastise, chide, correct, discipline, flail, flay, flog, flyte, lash, rebuke, reprimand, scold, scourge, whip.

castle *n* casbah (kasba, kasbah), château, citadel, donjon, fastness, fortress, keep, mansion, motte and bailey, palace, peel, schloss, stronghold, tower.

castrate *v* emasculate, evirate, geld, neuter, unman, unsex.

casual *adj* accidental, apathetic, blase, chance, contingent, cursory, fortuitous, incidental, indifferent, informal, insouciant, irregular, lackadaisical, negligent, nonchalant, occasional, offhand, perfunctory, random, relaxed, serendipitous, stray, unceremonious, uncertain, unconcerned, unexpected, unforeseen, unintentional, unpremeditated.

antonyms deliberate, painstaking, planned.

casualty *n* death, injured, injury, loss, sufferer, victim, wounded.

casuistry *n* chicanery, equivocation, Jesuitism, Jesuitry, sophism, sophistry, speciousness.

cat *n* feline, gib, grimalkin, malkin, mawkin, mog, moggy, mouser, puss, pussy, tabby.

cataclysm *n* blow, calamity, catastrophe, collapse, convulsion, debacle (debâcle), devastation, disaster, upheaval.

catacomb *n* burial-vault, crypt, ossuary, tomb, vault.

catalogue *n* directory, gazetteer, index, inventory, list, litany, record, register, roll, roster, schedule, table.

v accession, alphabetise, classify, codify, file, index, inventory, list, record, register.

catapult *v* heave, hurl, hurtle, launch, pitch, plunge, propel, shoot, throw, toss.

cataract *n* cascade, deluge, downpour, falls, force, rapids, torrent, waterfall.

catastrophe *n* adversity, affliction, blow, calamity, cataclysm, conclusion, culmination, curtain, debacle (debâcle), denouement, devastation, disaster, end, failure, fiasco, finale, ill, mischance, misfortune, mishap, reverse, ruin, termination, tragedy, trial, trouble, upheaval, upshot, winding-up.

catcall *n* barracking, boo, gibe, hiss, jeer, raspberry, whistle.

v barrack, boo, deride, gibe, give (someone) the bird, hiss, jeer, whistle.

catch *v* apprehend, arrest, benet, bewitch, captivate, capture, charm, clutch, contract, cop, delight, detect, develop, discern, discover, enchant, enrapture, ensnare, entangle, entrap, expose, fascinate, feel, follow, grab, grasp, grip, hear, incur, nab, nail, perceive, recognise, seize, sense, snare, snatch, surprise, take, twig, unmask.

antonyms drop, free, miss.

n bolt, clasp, clip, detent, disadvantage, drawback, fastener, hasp, hitch, hook, latch, obstacle, parti, snag, sneck, snib, trap, trick.

catch sight of espy, glimpse, notice, recognise, spot, view.

catch up draw level with, gain on, make up leeway, overtake.

catching *adj* attractive, captivating, charming, communicable, contagious, enchanting, fascinating, fetching, infectious, infective, taking, transferable, transmissible, transmittable, winning, winsome.

antonyms boring, ugly, unattractive.

catchword *n* byword, catch-phrase, motto, parrot-cry, password, refrain, slogan, watchword.

catchy *adj* attractive, captivating, confusing, deceptive, haunting, memorable, popular.

antonyms boring, dull.

catechise *v* cross-examine, drill, examine, grill, instruct, interrogate, question, test.

catechumen *v* convert, disciple, initiate, learner, neophyte, novice, probationer, proselyte, pupil, tyro.

categorical *adj* absolute, clear, direct, downright, emphatic, explicit, express, positive, total, unambiguous, unconditional, unequivocal, unqualified, unquestionable, unreserved.

antonyms qualified, tentative, vague.

categorise *v* class, classify, grade, group, list, order, pigeonhole, rank, sort.

category *n* chapter, class, classification, department, division, grade, grouping, head, heading, list, order, rank, section, sort, type.

cater *v* furnish, humour, indulge, outfit, pander, provide, provision, purvey, supply, victual.

caterwaul *v* bawl, cry, howl, miaow, miaul, scream, screech, shriek, squall, wail, yowl.

catharsis *n* abreaction, abstersion, cleansing, epuration, lustration, purgation, purging, purification, purifying, release.

cathedral *n* dome, duomo, minster.

catholic *adj* all-embracing, all-inclusive, broad, broad-minded, charitable, comprehensive, eclectic, ecumenical, general, global, inclusive, liberal, tolerant, universal, whole, wide, wide-ranging, world-wide.

antonyms narrow, narrow-minded.

cattle *n* beasts, cows, kine, livestock, neat, nowt, stock.

catty *adj* back-biting, bitchy, ill-natured, malevolent, malicious, mean, rancorous, spiteful, venomous, vicious.

antonyms kind, pleasant.

caucus *n* assembly, clique, conclave, convention, gathering, get-together, meeting, parley, session, set.

causative *adj* factitive, factive, root.

cause *n* account, agency, agent, aim, attempt, basis, beginning, belief, causation, consideration, conviction, creator, end, enterprise, genesis, grounds, ideal, impulse, incentive, inducement, mainspring, maker, motivation, motive, movement, object, origin, originator, producer, purpose, reason, root, source, spring, stimulus, undertaking.

antonyms effect, result.

v begin, compel, create, effect, engender, gar, generate, give rise to, incite, induce, motivate, occasion, precipitate, produce, provoke, result in.

caustic *adj* acidulous, acrid, acrimonious, astringent, biting, bitter, burning, corroding, corrosive, cutting, escharotic, keen, mordant, pungent, sarcastic, scathing, severe, stinging, trenchant, virulent, waspish.

antonyms mild, soothing.

caution *n* admonition, advice, alertness, care, carefulness, circumspection, counsel, deliberation, discretion, forethought, heed, heedfulness, injunction, prudence, via trita, via tuta, vigilance, wariness, warning, watchfulness.

v admonish, advise, urge, warn.

cautious *adj* alert, cagey, careful, chary, circumspect, discreet, Fabian, guarded, heedful, judicious, prudent, scrupulous, softly-softly, tentative, unadventurous, vigilant, wary, watchful.

antonyms heedless, imprudent, incautious.

cautiousness *n* caginess, care, carefulness, caution, chariness, via trita, via tuta, wariness.

antonym heedlessness.

cavalcade *n* array, march-past, parade, procession, retinue, spectacle, train, troop.

cavalier *n* attendant, beau, blade, chevalier, equestrian, escort, gallant, gentleman, horseman, knight, partner, royalist.

adj arrogant, cavalierish, condescending, curt, disdainful, free-and-easy, gay, haughty, insolent, lofty, lordly, misproud, off-hand, scornful, supercilious, swaggering.

cave *n* antre, cavern, cavity, den, grotto, hollow, mattamore, pothole.

cave in collapse, fall, give way, slip, subside, yield.

caveat *n* admonition, alarm, caution, warning.

cavern *n* cave, cavity, den, grotto, hollow, pothole, vault.

cavernous *adj* concave, deep, deep-set, echoing, gaping, hollow, resonant, reverberant, sepulchral, sunken, yawning.

cavil *v* carp, censure, complain, hypercriticise, nit-pick, object, quibble.

n complaint, criticism, objection, quibble, quiddit, quiddity.

cavilling *adj* captious, carping, censorious, critical, fault-finding, hypercritical, nit-picking, quibbling, quidditative.

cavity *n* antrum, belly, caries, crater, dent, gap, hole, hollow, pit, pot-hole, sinus, vacuole, ventricle, well, womb.

cavort *v* caper, caracole, dance, frisk, frolic, gambol, hop, prance, romp, skip, sport.

cease *v* call a halt, call it a day, conclude, culminate, desist, die, discontinue, end, fail, finish, halt, pack in, poop out, refrain, stay, stop, terminate.

antonyms begin, start.

ceaseless *adj* constant, continual, continuous, endless, eternal, everlasting, incessant, indefatigable, interminable, never-ending, non-stop, perennial, perpetual, persistent, unending, unremitting, untiring.

antonyms irregular, occasional.

cede *v* abandon, abdicate, allow, concede, convey, give up, grant, relinquish, renounce, resign, surrender, transfer, yield.

celebrate *v* bless, commemorate, commend, emblazon, eulogise, exalt, extol, glorify, honour, keep, laud, live it up, observe, perform, praise, proclaim, publicise, rejoice, reverance, solemnise, toast, wassail, whoop it up.

celebrated *adj* acclaimed, big, distingue, distinguished, eminent, exalted, famed, famous, glorious, illustrious, lionised, notable, outstanding, popular, pre-eminent, prominent, renowned, revered, well-known.

antonyms obscure, unknown.

celebration *n* anniversary, carousal, commemoration, festival, festivity, gala, honouring, jollification, jubilee, junketing, merry-make, merrymaking, observance, orgy, party, performance, rave-up, rejoicings, remembrance, revelry, shindig, solemnisation.

celebrity *n* big name, big shot, bigwig, celeb, dignitary, distinction, eclat, eminence, fame, glory, honour, lion, luminary, name, notability, personage, personality, popularity, pre-eminence, prestige, prominence, renown, reputation, repute, star, stardom, superstar, VIP.

antonyms nobody, obscurity.

celerity *n* dispatch, expedition, fastness, fleetness, haste, promptness, quickness, rapidity, speed, swiftness, velocity.

antonyms sloth, slowness.

celestial *adj* angelic, astral, divine, elysian, empyrean, eternal, ethereal, godlike, heavenly, immortal, paradisaic(al), seraphic, spiritual, starry, sublime, supernatural, transcendental.

antonyms earthly, mundane.

celibacy *n* bachelorhood, chastity, continence, singleness, spinsterhood, virginity.

cell *n* caucus, cavity, chamber, compartment, coterie, cubicle, dungeon, group, little-ease, nucleus, peter, stall, unit.

cellar *n* basement, crypt, store-room, vault, wine-store.

cement *v* attach, bind, bond, cohere, combine, fix together, glue, gum, join, plaster, seal, solder, stick, unite, weld.

n adhesive, concrete, glue, gum, mortar, paste, plaster, sealant.

cemetery *n* boneyard, burial-ground, churchyard, God's acre, graveyard, necropolis.

censor *v* amend, blue-pencil, bowdlerise, cut, edit, expurgate.

censorious *adj* captious, carping, cavilling, condemnatory, critical, disapproving, disparaging, fault-finding, hypercritical, severe.

antonyms approving, complimentary, laudatory.

censure *n* admonishment, admonition, blame, castigation, condemnation, criticism, disapproval, obloquy, rebuke, remonstrance, reprehension, reprimand, reproach, reprobation, reproof, stricture, telling-off, vituperation.

antonyms approval, compliments, praise.

v abuse, admonish, animadvert, berate, blame, castigate, chide, condemn, criticise, decry, denounce, inveigh against, jump on, rebuke, reprehend, reprimand, reproach, reprobate, reprove, scold, slam, tell off, upbraid.

antonyms approve, compliment, praise.

central *adj* chief, essential, focal, fundamental, important, inner, interior, key, main, mean, median, mid, middle, pivotal, primary, principal, vital.

antonyms minor, peripheral.

centralise *v* amalgamate, compact, concentrate, condense, converge, gather together, incorporate, rationalise, streamline, unify.

antonym decentralise.

centre *n* bull's-eye, core, crux, focus, heart, hub, Mecca, mid, middle, mid-point, nave, nucleus, omphalos, pivot.

antonyms edge, outskirts, periphery.

v cluster, concentrate, converge, focus, gravitate, hinge, pivot, revolve.

centre-piece *n* cynosure, epergne, focus, highlight, ornament.

centrifugal *adj* diffusive, divergent, diverging, efferent, radial, radiating, scattering, spreading.

antonym centripetal.

centripetal *adj* afferent, clustering, concentrating, convergent, converging.

antonym centrifugal.

ceremonial *adj* dress, formal, liturgical, ritual, ritualistic, solemn, stately.

antonym informal.

n ceremony, formality, protocol, rite, ritual, solemnity.

ceremonious *adj* civil, courteous, courtly, deferential, dignified, exact, formal, grand, polite, pompous, precise, punctilious, ritual, solemn, starchy, stately, stiff.

antonyms informal, relaxed, unceremonious.

ceremony *n* celebration, ceremonial, commemoration, decorum, etiquette, event, form, formality, function, niceties, observance, parade, pomp, propriety, protocol, rite, ritual, service, show, solemnities.

certain *adj* ascertained, assured, banker, bound, conclusive, confident, constant, convinced, convincing, decided, definite, dependable, destined, determinate, established, express, fated, fixed, incontrovertible, individual, indubitable, ineluctable, inescapable, inevitable, inexorable, irrefutable, known, one, particular, plain, positive, precise, regular, reliable, resolved, satisfied, settled, some, special, specific, stable, steady, sure, true, trustworthy, undeniable, undoubted, unequivocal, unfailing, unmistakable, unquestionable, valid.

antonyms doubtful, hesitant, uncertain, unsure.

certainly *adv* doubtlessly, naturally, of course, without question.

certainty *n* assurance, authoritativeness, certitude, confidence, conviction, fact, faith, indubitableness, inevitability, nap, plerophoria, plerophory, positiveness, reality, sure thing, sureness, surety, trust, truth, validity.

antonyms doubt, hesitation, uncertainty.

certificate *n* attestation, authorisation, award, coupon, credentials, diploma, document, endorsement, guarantee, licence, pass, qualification, testimonial, validation, voucher, warrant.

certify *v* ascertain, assure, attest, authenticate, authorise, aver, avow, confirm, corroborate, declare, endorse, evidence, guarantee, notify, show, testify, validate, verify, vouch, witness.

certitude *n* assurance, certainty, confidence, conviction, plerophoria, plerophory.

antonym doubt.

cessation *n* abeyance, arrest, arresting, break, ceasing, desistance, discontinuance, discontinuation, discontinuing, end, ending, halt, halting, hiatus, intermission, interruption, interval, let-up, pause, recess, remission, respite, rest, standstill, stay, stoppage, stopping, suspension, termination.

antonym commencement.

cession *n* abandoning, abandonment, abnegation, capitulation, ceding, conceding, concession, conveyance, grant, relinquishing, relinquishment, renouncing, renunciation, surrender, yielding.

chafe *v* abrade, anger, annoy, enrage, exasperate, fret, fume, gall, get, grate, heat, incense, inflame, irritate, offend, provoke, rage, rasp, rub, scrape, scratch, vex, wear, worry.

chaff *n* badinage, banter, jesting, jokes, joking, persiflage, raillery, teasing.

v banter, chip, deride, jeer, laugh at, mock, pull (someone's) leg, rib, ridicule, scoff, taunt, tease.

chagrin *n* annoyance, discomfiture, discomposure, displeasure, disquiet, dissatisfaction, embarrassment, exasperation, fretfulness, humiliation, indignation, irritation, mortification, peevishness, spleen, vexation.

antonyms delight, pleasure.

v annoy, displease, disquiet, dissatisfy, embarrass, exasperate, humiliate, irk, irritate, mortify, peeve, vex.

chain *n* bond, catena, concatenation, coupling, fetter, fob, link, manacle, progression, restraint, sequence, series, set, shackle, string, succession, train, union, vinculum.

v bind, confine, enslave, fasten, fetter, gyve, handcuff, manacle, restrain, secure, shackle, tether, trammel.

antonyms free, release.

chairman *n* chair, chairperson, chairwoman, convenor, director, master of ceremonies, MC, president, presider, speaker, spokesman, toastmaster.

chalk up accumulate, achieve, ascribe, attain, attribute, charge, credit, enter, gain, log, mark, record, register, score, tally, win.

chalky *adj* ashen, calcareous, cretaceous, pale, pallid, powdery, wan, white.

challenge *v* accost, beard, brave, confront, dare, defy, demand, dispute, impugn, provoke, query, question, stimulate, summon, tax, test, throw down the gauntlet, try.

n confrontation, dare, defiance, gauntlet, hurdle, interrogation, obstacle, poser, provocation, question, test, trial, ultimatum.

chamber *n* apartment, assembly, bed-chamber, bedroom, boudoir, camera, cavity, closet, compartment, council, cubicle, enclosure, hall, legislature, parliament, room, vault.

chamberpot *n* jerry, po, pot, potty.

champion *n* backer, challenger, conqueror, defender, guardian, hero, kemper, kempery-man, nonpareil, paladin, Palmerin, patron, peer, promachos, protector, Roland, upholder, victor, vindicator, warrior, winner.

v advocate, back, defend, espouse, maintain, promote, stand up for, support, uphold.

chance *n* accident, act of God, coincidence, contingency, destiny, fate, fortuity, fortune, gamble, happenstance, hazard, jeopardy, liability, likelihood, luck, misfortune, occasion, odds, opening, opportunity, peril, possibility, probability, prospect, providence, risk, scope, speculation, time, uncertainty.

antonyms certainty, law, necessity.

v befall, gamble, happen, hazard, occur, risk, stake, transpire, try, venture, wager.

adj accidental, casual, contingent, fortuitous, inadvertent, incidental, random, serendipitous, unforeseeable, unforeseen, unintended, unintentional, unlooked-for.

antonyms certain, deliberate, intentional.

chancy *adj* dangerous, dicey, dodgy, fraught, hazardous, problematical, risky, speculative, tricky, uncertain.

antonyms safe, secure.

chandelier *n* corona, girandole, lustre.

change *v* alter, alternate, barter, convert, denature, displace, diversify, exchange, fluctuate, interchange, metamorphose, moderate, modify, mutate, reform, remodel, remove, reorganise, replace, restyle, shift, substitute, swap, take liberties with, trade, transfigure, transform, transmit, transmute, transpose, vacillate, vary, veer.

n alteration, break, chop, conversion, difference, diversion, exchange, innovation, interchange, metamorphosis, metanoia, modification, mutation, novelty, permutation, revolution, satisfaction, sea-change, shift, substitution, trade, transformation, transition, transmutation, transposition, upheaval, variation, variety, vicissitude.

change of heart metanoia.

changeable *adj* capricious, chameleon(ic), changeful, erratic, fickle, fitful, fluid, inconstant, irregular, kaleidoscopic, labile, mercurial, mobile, mutable, protean, shifting, uncertain, unpredictable, unreliable, unsettled, unstable, unsteady, vacillating, variable, vicissitudinous, volatile, wavering, windy.

antonyms constant, reliable, unchangeable.

changeling *n* elf-child, killcrop.

changing *adj* different, diverse, fluctuating, fluid, inconstant, kaleidoscopic, mobile, unstable, various, varying.

channel *n* approach, artery, avenue, canal, chamber, chamfer, communication, conduit, course, duct, euripus, fairway, fleet, flume, fluting, furrow, gat, groove, gullet, gut, gutter, level, main, means, medium, overflow, passage, path, route, sound, start, strait, trough, watercourse, waterway, way.

v conduct, convey, direct, force, furrow, guide, send, transmit.

chant *n* carol, chorus, mantra(m), melody, psalm, slogan, song, war-cry.

v cantillate, carol, chorus, croon, decantate, descant, intone, recite, sing.

chaos *n* anarchy, bedlam, confusion, disorder, disorganisation, entropy, lawlessness, mayhem, pandemonium, snafu, tohu bohu, tumult, unreason.

antonym order.

chaotic *adj* anarchic, confused, deranged, disordered, disorganised, lawless, purposeless, rampageous, riotous, shambolic, snafu, topsy-turvy, tumultous, tumultuary, uncontrolled.

antonyms organised, purposive.

chap *n* bloke, buffer, character, codger, cove, customer, fellow, guy, individual, Johnny, josser, oik, person, punter, shaver, sort, type.

chapel *n* bethel, Bethesda, Beulah, church, ebenezer, meeting-house, sacellum.

chaperon *n* companion, duenna, escort, gooseberry, gouvernante, governess.

v accompany, attend, escort, guard, matronise, protect, safeguard, shepherd, watch over.

chapter *n* assembly, branch, chapel, clause, division, episode, part, period, phase, section, stage, topic.

char *v* brown, burn, carbonise, cauterise, scorch, sear, singe.

character[1] *n* attributes, bent, calibre, cast, complexion, constitution, disposition, feature, honour, individuality, integrity, kidney, make-up, nature, peculiarity, personality, physiognomy, position, quality, rank, rectitude, reputation, stamp, status, strength, temper, temperament, type, uprightness.

character[2] *n* card, cove, customer, eccentric, fellow, guy, individual, oddball, oddity, original, part, person, persona, portrayal, role, sort, type.

character[3] *n* cipher, device, emblem, figure, hieroglyph, ideogram, ideograph, letter, logo, mark, rune, sign, symbol, type.

characterise *v* brand, distinguish, identify, indicate, inform, mark, represent, stamp, symptomise, typify.

characteristic *adj* discriminative, distinctive, distinguishing, idiosyncratic, individual, peculiar, representative, singular, special, specific, symbolic, symptomatic, typical, vintage.

antonyms uncharacteristic, untypical.

n attribute, faculty, feature, hallmark, idiosyncrasy, jizz, lineament, mannerism, mark, peculiarity, property, quality, symptom, thing, trait.

charade *n* fake, farce, mockery, pantomime, parody, pasquinade, pretence, travesty.

charge *v* accuse, adjuration, afflict, arraign, ask, assail, assault, attack, behest, bid, blame, burden, command, commit, count, demand, enjoin, entrust, exact, exhort, fill, impeach, incriminate, inculpate, indict, instil, instruct, involve, lade, load, onset, order, require, rush, storm, suffuse, tax, terms.

n accusation, allegation, amount, assault, attack, burden, care, command, concern, cost, custody, damage, demand, dictate, direction, duty, exhortation, expenditure, expense, imputation, indictment, injunction, instruction, mandate, office, onset, onslaught, order, outlay, payment, precept, price, rate, responsibility, rush, safekeeping, sortie, trust, ward.

charitable *adj* accommodating, beneficent, benevolent, benign, benignant, bountiful, broad-minded, clement, compassionate, considerate, eleemosynary, favourable, forgiving, generous, gracious, humane, indulgent, kind, kindly, lavish, lenient, liberal, magnanimous, mild, philanthropic, sympathetic, tolerant, understanding.

antonyms uncharitable, unforgiving.

charity *n* affection, agape, alms-giving, altruism, assistance, benefaction, beneficence, benevolence, benignity, benignness, bountifulness, bounty, clemency, compassion, endowment, fund, generosity, gift, goodness, hand-out, humanity, indulgence, love, philanthropy, relief, tender-heartedness.

charlatan *n* cheat, con man, fake, fraud, impostor, mountebank, phoney, pretender, quack, quacksalver, sham, swindler, trickster.

charm *v* allure, attract, becharm, beguile, bewitch, cajole, captivate, delight, enamour, enchant, enrapture, entrance, fascinate, mesmerise, please, win.

n abraxas, allure, allurement, amulet, appeal, attraction, attractiveness, desirability, enchantment, fascination, fetish, grisgris, idol, ju-ju, magic, magnetism, mascot, medicine, obeah, obi, phylactery, porte-bonheur, sorcery, spell, talisman, trinket, weird.

charming *adj* appealing, attractive, bewitching, captivating, delectable, delightful, engaging, eye-catching, fetching, honeyed, irresistible, lovely, pleasant, pleasing, seductive, sweet, winning, winsome.

antonyms ugly, unattractive.

chart *n* abac, alignment chart, blueprint, diagram, graph, map, nomograph, plan, table, tabulation.

v delineate, draft, draw, graph, map out, mark, outline, place, plot, shape, sketch.

charter *n* accreditation, authorisation, bond, concession, contract, deed, document, franchise, indenture, licence, permit, prerogative, privilege, right.

v authorise, commission, employ, engage, hire, lease, rent, sanction.

chary *adj* careful, cautious, circumspect, guarded, heedful, leery, prudent, reluctant, slow, suspicious, uneasy, unwilling, wary.

antonyms heedless, unwary.

chase *v* course, drive, expel, follow, hunt, hurry, pursue, rush, track.

n coursing, hunt, hunting, pursuit, race, run, rush, venery.

chasm *n* abysm, abyss, breach, canyon, cavity, cleft, crater, crevasse, fissure, gap, gorge, gulf, hiatus, hollow, opening, ravine, rent, rift, split, void.

chassis *n* anatomy, bodywork, bones, frame, framework, fuselage, skeleton, structure, substructure, undercarriage.

chaste *adj* austere, decent, decorous, elegant, immaculate, incorrupt, innocent, maidenly, modest, moral, neat, pure, refined, restrained, simple, unaffected, undefiled, unsullied, unvulgar, vestal, virginal, virginly, virtuous, wholesome.

antonyms indecorous, lewd.

chasten *v* admonish, afflict, castigate, chastise, correct, cow, curb, discipline, humble, humiliate, repress, reprove, soften, subdue, tame.

chastise *v* beat, berate, castigate, censure, correct, discipline, flog, flyte, lash, punish, reprove, scold, scourge, smack, spank, upbraid, whip.

chastity *n* abstinence, celibacy, continence, innocence, maidenhood, modesty, purity, restraint, self-restraint, temperateness, virginity, virtue.

antonym lechery.

chat *n* chatter, chinwag, confab, coze, crack, gossip, heart-to-heart, natter, rap, talk, tête-à-tête, visit.

v chatter, chew the fat, crack, gossip, jaw, natter, rabbit (on), talk, visit, yackety-yak.

chatter *n* babble, blather, blether, chat, chinwag, gab, gabnash, gossip, jabber, nashgab, natter, prate, prattle, prattlement, tattle, tongue-work, twaddle.

v babble, blather, blether, chat, clack, clatter, gab, gossip, jabber, natter, prate, prattle, prittle-prattle, talk like a pen-gun, tattle, twaddle, yackety-yak.

chatterer *n* big mouth, blabber, blatherskite, bletherskate, chatterbox, gabber, gabnash, gossip, loudmouth, nashgab, pie, prattlebox, windbag.

chattering *adj* blathering, blethering, clacking, long-tongued, prattling, tattling.

chatty *adj* colloquial, conversative, familiar, friendly, gossipy, informal, long-tongued, newsy, prattling, talkative.

antonym quiet.

chauvinist *adj* flag-flapping, jingoish, jingoistic, nationalistic, parochial.

cheap *adj* à bon marche, bargain, base, budget, common, contemptible, cut-price, despicable, dirt-cheap, dog-cheap, economical, economy, inexpensive, inferior, jitney, keen, knock-down, low, low-cost, low-priced, mean, paltry, poor, reasonable, reduced, sale, scurvy, second-rate, shoddy, sordid, tatty, tawdry, uncostly, vulgar, worthless.

antonyms costly, excellent, noble, superior.

cheapen *v* belittle, debase, degrade, demean, denigrate, depreciate, derogate, devalue, discredit, disparage, downgrade, lower, prostitute.

antonym enhance.

cheat *v* baffle, bam, bamboozle, beguile, bilk, check, chisel, chouse, cog, con, cozen, deceive, defeat, defraud, deprive, diddle, do, double-cross, dupe, finagle, fleece, fob, foil, fool, frustrate, fudge, grift, gudgeon, gull, gyp, hand (someone) a lemon, hoax, hocus, hoodwink, mislead, prevent, queer, rip off, screw, short-change, skin, smouch, swindle, thwart, touch, trick, trim, victimise.

n artifice, bilker, charlatan, cheater, chouse, cogger, con man, cozener, deceit, deceiver, deception, dodger, double-crosser, extortioner, fraud, grifter, impostor, imposture, knave, picaroon, rip-off, rogue, shark, sharp, sharper, short-changer, snap, swindle, swindler, trickery, trickster, welsher.

check[1] *v* compare, confirm, examine, give the once-over, inspect, investigate, monitor, note, probe, research, scrutinise, study, test, verify.

n audit, examination, inspection, investigation, research, scrutiny, tab, test.

check out examine, investigate, test.

check[2] *v* arrest, bar, blame, bridle, chide, control, curb, damp, delay, halt, hinder, impede, inhibit, limit, obstruct, pause, rebuke, repress, reprimand, reprove, restrain, retard, scold, stop, thwart.

n blow, constraint, control, curb, damp, damper, disappointment, frustration, hindrance, impediment, inhibition, limitation, obstruction, rejection, restraint, reverse, setback, stoppage.

check[3] *n* bill, counterfoil, token.

cheek[1] *n* audacity, brass, brass neck, brazenness, brazenry, disrespect, effrontery, gall, impertinence, impudence, insolence, lip, nerve, sauce, temerity.

cheek[2] *n* chap, face, gena, jowl.

cheeky *adj* audacious, disrespectful, forward, impertinent, impudent, insolent, insulting, lippy, malapert, pert, saucy.

antonyms polite, respectful.

cheer *v* acclaim, animate, applaud, brighten, clap, comfort, console, elate, elevate, encheer, encourage, enhearten, enliven, exhilarate, gladden, hail, hearten, hurrah, incite, inspirit, solace, uplift, warm.

antonyms boo, dishearten, jeer.

n acclamation, animation, applause, bravo, buoyancy, cheerfulness, comfort, gaiety, gladness, glee, hoorah, hopefulness, hurrah, joy, liveliness, merriment, merry-making, mirth, optimism, ovation, plaudits, solace.

cheerful *adj* animated, blithe, bobbish, bright, bucked, buoyant, canty, cheery, chipper, chirpy, chirrupy, contented, enlivening, enthusiastic, eupeptic, gay, gaysome, genial, glad, gladsome, happy, hearty, jaunty, jolly, jovial, joyful, joyous, light-hearted, lightsome, light-spirited, merry, optimistic, perky, pleasant, sparkling, sprightly, sunny, upbeat, winsome.

antonym sad.

cheerfulness *n* blitheness, buoyancy, cheeriness, exuberance, gaiety, geniality, gladness, happiness, jauntiness, joyfulness, joyousness, light-heartedness, sprightliness.

antonym sadness.

cheering *adj* auspicious, bright, comforting, encouraging, heartening, inspiring, promising, propitious, reassuring, stirring.

antonyms depressing, disheartening.

cheerless *adj* austere, barren, bleak, cold, comfortless, dank, dark, dejected, depressed, desolate, despondent, dingy, disconsolate, dismal, dolorous, drab, dreary, dull, forlorn, gloomy, grim, joyless, lonely, melancholy, miserable, mournful, sad, sombre, sorrowful, sullen, sunless, unhappy, uninviting, winterly, woebegone, woeful.

antonyms bright, cheerful.

cheers *interj* bottoms up, drink-hail, prosit, skoal, skol, slàinte.

cheery *adj* blithe, breezy, bright, carefree, cheerful, chipper, gay, good-humoured, happy, jovial, lightsome, light-spirited, lively, merry, pleasant, sparkling, sunny.

antonyms downcast, sad.

chemical *n* compound, element, substance, synthetic.

cherish *v* comfort, cosset, encourage, entertain, foster, harbour, make much of, nourish, nurse, nurture, prize, shelter, support, sustain, tender, treasure, value.

cherubic *adj* adorable, angelic, appealing, cute, heavenly, innocent, lovable, lovely, seraphic, sweet.

chest *n* ark, box, case, casket, coffer, crate, kist, strongbox, trunk.

chestnut *n* cliche, vieux jeu, war-horse.

chew *v* champ, crunch, gnaw, grind, manducate, masticate, munch.

chic *adj* à la mode, chichi, elegant, fashionable, modish, smart, stylish, trendy.

antonyms out-moded, unfashionable.

chicanery *n* artifice, cheating, chicane, deception, deviousness, dodge, double-dealing, duplicity, intrigue, jiggery-pokery, sharp practice, skulduggery, sophistry, stratagems, subterfuge, trickery, underhandedness, wiles, wire-pulling.

chick *n* baby, broad, chicken, girl, girlfriend, peeper.

chicken *n* chick, chook(ie), chuck(ie), fowl, hen, pullet.

chicken-feed *n* coppers, peanuts, pennies, pin money, pittance.

chide *v* admonish, berate, blame, censure, check, criticise, lecture, objurgate, rate, rebuke, reprehend, reprimand, reproach, reprove, scold, tell off, upbraid.

antonym praise.

chief *adj* capital, cardinal, central, especial, essential, foremost, grand, highest, key, leading, main, outstanding, paramount, predominant, pre-eminent, premier, prevailing, primal, primary, prime, principal, superior, supreme, uppermost, vital.

antonyms junior, minor, unimportant.

n boss, captain, chieftain, cock of the loft, commander, coryphaeus, director, duke, gaffer, governor, head, kaid, leader, lord, manager, master, paramount, paramount chief, principal, ringleader, ruler, superintendent, superior, supremo, suzerain.

chiefly *adv* especially, essentially, for the most part, generally, mainly, mostly, predominantly, primarily, principally, usually.

child *n* babe, baby, bairn, bambino, bantling, brat, chit, dandiprat, descendant, elf, get, git, gyte, infant, issue, juvenile, kid, kiddiewinkie, kiddywink, kinchin, littling, minor, nipper, nursling, offspring, papoose, pickaninny, progeny, shaver, sprog, suckling, toddler, tot, wean, youngling, youngster.

child prodigy wunderkind.

childbirth *n* accouchement, child-bearing, childbed, confinement, delivery, labour, lying-in, parturition, travail.

childhood *n* adolescence, babyhood, boyhood, girlhood, immaturity, infancy, minority, schooldays, youth.

childish *adj* boyish, foolish, frivolous, girlish, hypocoristic, hypocoristical, immature, infantile, juvenile, puerile, silly, simple, trifling, weak, young.

antonyms adult, sensible.

childlike *adj* artless, credulous, guileless, ingenuous, innocent, naïve, natural, simple, trustful, trusting.

children *n* line, offspring, progeny.

chill *adj* aloof, biting, bleak, chilly, cold, cool, depressing, distant, freezing, frigid, hostile, parky, raw, sharp, stony, unfriendly, unresponsive, unwelcoming, wintry.

antonyms friendly, warm.

v congeal, cool, dampen, depress, discourage, dishearten, dismay, freeze, frighten, refrigerate, terrify.

n bite, cold, coldness, coolness, coolth, crispness, frigidity, nip, rawness, sharpness.

chilly *adj* aloof, blowy, breezy, brisk, cold, cool, crisp, draughty, fresh, frigid, hostile, nippy, parky, penetrating, sharp, stony, unfriendly, unresponsive, unsympathetic, unwelcoming.

antonyms friendly, warm.

chime *v* clang, dong, jingle, mark, peal, ping. ring, sound, strike, tell, ting, tinkle, tintinnabulate, toll.

chimera *n* bogy, delusion, dream, fancy, fantasy, figment, hallucination, idle fancy, ignis fatuus, illusion, monster, monstrosity, snare, spectre, will-o'-the-wisp.

chimeric *adj* chimerical, delusive, fabulous, fanciful, fantastic, hallucinatory, illusive, illusory, imaginary, quixotic, unfounded, unreal, vain, visionary, whimsical, wild.

antonym real.

chimney *n* cleft, crevice, femerall, funnel, lum, shaft, vent.

chimpanzee *n* ape, jocko, pongo.

china *adj* ceramic, earthenware, porcelain, pottery, terracotta, wally.

chink[1] *n* aperture, cleft, crack, crevice, cut, fissure, flaw, gap, opening, rift, slot, space.

chink[2] *n* clink, ding, jangle, jingle, ping, ring, ting, tinkle.

chip *n* dent, flake, flaw, fragment, nick, notch, paring, scrap, scratch, shard, shaving, sliver, spall, wafer.

v chisel, damage, gash, nick, notch, spall, whittle.

chip in contribute, donate, interpose, interrupt, participate, pay, subscribe.

chiropodist *n* pedicurist.

chiropody *n* pedicure.

chirp *v, n* cheep, chirrup, peep, pipe, tweet, twitter, warble, whistle.

chirpy *adj* blithe, bright, cheerful, cheery, chipper, gay, happy, jaunty, merry, perky, sunny.

antonyms downcast, sad.

chivalrous *adj* bold, brave, chivalric, courageous, courteous, courtly, gallant, gentlemanly, Grandisonian, heroic, honourable, knightly, polite, true, valiant.

antonyms cowardly, ungallant.

chivalry *n* boldness, bravery, courage, courtesy, courtliness, gallantry, gentlemanliness, knight-errantry, knighthood, politeness.

chivvy *v* badger, harass, hassle, hound, importune, nag, pester, plague, pressure, prod, torment.

choice *n* alternative, choosing, decision, dilemma, discrimination, election, espousal, opting, option, pick, preference, say, selection, variety.

adj best, dainty, elect, elite, excellent, exclusive, exquisite, hand-picked, nice, plum, precious, prime, prize, rare, select, special, superior, uncommon, unusual, valuable.

antonym inferior.

choke *v* asphyxiate, bar, block, clog, close, congest, constrict, dam, gag, obstruct, occlude, overpower, reach, retch, smother, stifle, stop, strangle, suffocate, suppress, throttle.

choleric *adj* angry, bad-tempered, crabbed, crabby, crotchety, fiery, hasty, hot, hot-tempered, ill-tempered, irascible, irritable, petulant, quick-tempered, testy, touchy.

antonyms calm, placid.

choose *v* adopt, cull, designate, desire, elect, espouse, fix on, opt for, pick, plump for, predestine, prefer, see fit, select, settle on, single out, take, vote for, wish.

choosing *n* proairesis.

choosy *adj* discriminating, exacting, faddy, fastidious, fikish, fiky, finicky, fussy, particular, picky, selective.

antonym undemanding.

chop *v* cleave, cut, divide, fell, hack, hew, lop, sever, shear, slash, slice, truncate.

chop up cube, cut up, dice, divide, fragment, mince, slice (up).

choppy *adj* blustery, broken, rough, ruffled, squally, stormy, tempestuous, wavy, white.

antonym calm.

chore *n* burden, duty, errand, fag, job, stint, task, trouble.

chortle *v* cackle, chuckle, crow, guffaw, laugh, snigger.

chorus *n* burden, call, choir, choristers, ensemble, refrain, response, shout, singers, strain, vocalists.

chosen *adj* elect, elite, peculiar, predilect, predilected, selected.

christen *v* baptise, besprinkle, call, designate, dub, inaugurate, name, sprinkle, style, term, title, use.

Christmas *n* Noel (Nowell), Xmas, Yule, Yuletide.

chronic *adj* appalling, atrocious, awful, confirmed, deep-rooted, deep-seated, dreadful, habitual, incessant, incurable, ineradicable, ingrained, inveterate, persistent, terrible.

antonym temporary.

chronicle *n* account, annals, chanson de geste, diary, epic, gest(e), history, journal, narrative, record, register, saga, story.

v enter, list, narrate, record, recount, register, relate, report, tell, write down.

chronicler *n* annalist, chronographer, chronologer, diarist, historian, historiographer, narrator, recorder, reporter, scribe.

chronological *adj* consecutive, historical, ordered, progressive, sequential.

chubby *adj* buxom, flabby, fleshy, paunchy, plump, podgy, portly, rotund, round, stout, tubby.

antonyms skinny, slim.

chuck *v* cast, discard, fling, heave, hurl, jettison, pitch, reject, shy, sling, throw, toss.

chuckle *v* chortle, crow, exult, giggle, laugh, snigger, snort, titter.

chum *n* china, cobber, companion, comrade, crony, friend, mate, pal.

antonym enemy.

chummy *adj* affectionate, close, friendly, intimate, matey, pally, sociable, thick.

chunk *n* block, chuck, dod, dollop, hunk, lump, mass, piece, portion, slab, wad, wodge.

chunky *adj* beefy, blocky, brawny, dumpy, fat, square, stocky, stubby, thick, thickset.
antonym slim.

church *n* basilica, bethel, Bethesda, Beulah, cathedral, house of God, house of prayer, kirk, minster, preaching-house, steeple-house.
adj ecclesiastic, ecclesiastical, ecclesiological.

churl *n* boor, bumpkin, clodhopper, clown, curmudgeon, hill-billy, labourer, lout, oaf, peasant, rustic, yokel.

churlish *adj* boorish, brusque, crabbed, doggish, harsh, ill-tempered, impolite, loutish, morose, oafish, rude, sullen, surly, uncivil, unmannerly, unneighbourly, unsociable, vulgar.
antonyms polite, urbane.

churn *v* agitate, beat, boil, convulse, foam, froth, knot, seethe, swirl, toss, writhe.

chute *n* channel, funnel, gutter, incline, ramp, runway, shaft, slide, slope, trough.

cigarette *n* cancer-stick, cig, ciggy, coffin-nail, fag, gasper, joint, smoke, snout, whiff.

cinch *n* doddle, piece of cake, snip, stroll, walk-over.

cinema *n* big screen, filmhouse, flicks, movies, picture-house, picture-palace.

cipher *n* character, code, cryptograph, device, digit, figure, logo, mark, monogram, nil, nobody, nonentity, nothing, nought, number, numeral, symbol, yes-man, zero.

circle *n* area, assembly, band, bounds, circuit, circumference, class, clique, club, coil, company, compass, cordon, coterie, crowd, cycle, disc, domain, enclosure, fellowship, field, fraternity, globe, group, gyre, lap, loop, orb, orbit, perimeter, periphery, province, range, realm, region, revolution, ring, round, roundance, roundel, roundlet, rundle, scene, school, set, society, sphere, turn.
v belt, circumambulate, circumnavigate, circumscribe, coil, compass, curl, curve, encircle, enclose, encompass, envelop, gird, girdle, hem in, loop, pivot, revolve, ring, rotate, surround, tour, whirl.

circling *adj* eddying, vortical, wheeling, whirling.

circuit *n* ambit, area, boundary, bounds, circumference, compass, course, district, eyre, journey, lap, limit, orbit, perambulation, range, region, revolution, round, route, tour, track, tract.

circuitous *adj* ambagious, anfractuous, cagey, devious, indirect, labyrinthine, meandering, oblique, periphrastic, rambling, roundabout, tortuous, winding.
antonyms direct, straight.

circular *adj* annular, discoid(al), disc-shaped, hoop-shaped, ring-shaped, round.
n advert, announcement, handbill, leaflet, letter, notice, pamphlet.

circulate *v* broadcast, diffuse, disseminate, distribute, flow, go around, go the rounds, gyrate, issue, promulgate, propagate, publicise, publish, radiate, revolve, rotate, spread, spread abroad, swirl, whirl.

circulation *n* blood-flow, circling, currency, dissemination, distribution, flow, motion, rotation, spread, spreading, transmission.

circumference *n* border, boundary, bounds, circuit, edge, extremity, fringe, limits, margin, outline, perimeter, periphery, rim, verge.

circumlocution *n* diffuseness, discursiveness, euphemism, indirectness, periphrasis, prolixity, redundancy, roundaboutness, wordiness.

circumscribe *v* bound, confine, curtail, define, delimit, delineate, demarcate, encircle, enclose, encompass, environ, hem in, limit, pen in, restrain, restrict, surround, trim.

circumspect *adj* attentive, canny, careful, cautious, chary, deliberate, discreet, discriminating, guarded, heedful, judicious, leery, observant, politic, sagacious, sage, vigilant, wary, watchful.
antonyms unguarded, unwary.

circumspection *n* canniness, care, caution, chariness, deliberation, discretion, guardedness, prudence, wariness.

circumstance *n* accident, condition, contingency, detail, element, event, fact, factor, happening, happenstance, incident, item, occurrence, particular, position, respect, situation.

circumstances *n* conditions, galère, lifestyle, means, position, resources, situation, state, state of affairs, station, status, times.

circumstantial *adj* conjectural, contingent, detailed, evidential, exact, hearsay, incidental, indirect, inferential, minute, particular, presumptive, provisional, specific.
antonyms hard, inexact, vague.

circumvent *v* beguile, bypass, deceive, dupe, elude, ensnare, entrap, evade, get out of, get past, hoodwink, mislead, outflank, outgeneral, outwit, overreach, sidestep, steer clear of, thwart, trick.

circumvention *n* bypassing, chicanery, deceit, deception, dodge, duplicity, evasion, fraud, guile, imposition, imposture, thwarting, trickery, wiles.

cistern *n* basin, pool, reservoir, sink, tank, vat.

citadel *n* acropolis, bastion, castle, fortification, fortress, keep, stronghold, tower.

citation *n* award, commendation, cutting, excerpt, illustration, mention, passage, quotation, quote, reference, source.

cite *v* accite, adduce, advance, call, enumerate, evidence, extract, mention, name, quote, specify, subpoena, summon.

citizen *n* burgess, burgher, city-dweller, denizen, dweller, freeman, inhabitant, oppidan, ratepayer, resident, subject, townsman, urbanite.

city *n* conurbation, megalopolis, metropolis, municipality, town.

civic *adj* borough, city, communal, community, local, municipal, oppidan, public, urban.

civil *adj* accommodating, affable, civic, civilised, complaisant, courteous, courtly, domestic, home, interior, internal, internecine, lay, municipal, obliging, polished, polite, political, refined, secular, temporal, urbane, well-bred, well-mannered.
antonym uncivil.
civil servant bureaucrat, fonctionnaire.

civilisation *n* advancement, cultivation, culture, development, education, enlightenment, kultur, progress, refinement, sophistication, urbanity.
antonyms barbarity, primitiveness.

civilise *v* ameliorate, cultivate, educate, enlighten, humanise, improve, meliorate, perfect, polish, refine, sophisticate, tame.

civilised *adj* advanced, cultured, educated, enlightened, humane, polite, refined, sophisticated, tolerant, urbane.
antonyms barbarous, primitive.

civility *n* affability, amenity, amiability, attention, breeding, comity, complaisance, cordiality, courteousness, courtesy, graciousness, politeness, politesse, tact, urbanity.
antonyms rudeness, uncouthness.

claim *v* affirm, allege, arrogate, ask, assert, challenge, collect, demand, exact, hold, insist, maintain, need, profess, request, require, state, take, uphold.
n affirmation, allegation, application, assertion, call, demand, insistence, petition, pretension, privilege, protestation, request, requirement, right, title.

claimant *n* applicant, petitioner, pretendant, pretender, suppliant, supplicant.

clairvoyant *adj* extra-sensory, fey, oracular, prescient, prophetic, psychic, second-sighted, sibylline, telepathic, vatic, visionary.
n augur, diviner, fortune-teller, haruspex, oracle, prophet, prophetess, seer, sibyl, soothsayer, spaeman, spaer, spaewife, telepath, telepathist, visionary.

clamber *v* ascend, claw, climb, crawl, descend, scale, scrabble, scramble, shin.

clammy *adj* close, damp, dank, heavy, moist, muggy, pasty, slimy, sticky, sweating, sweaty, viscid.

clamorous *adj* blaring, deafening, insistent, lusty, noisy, riotous, tumultuous, uproarious, vehement, vociferant, vociferous.
antonym silent.

clamour *n* agitation, babel, blare, brouhaha, commotion, complaint, din, exclamation, hubbub, hue, hullabaloo, katzenjammer, noise, outcry, racket, shout, shouting, uproar, vociferation.
antonym silence.

clamp *n* brace, bracket, fastener, grip, press, vice.
v brace, clinch, fasten, fix, impose, secure.

clan *n* band, brotherhood, clique, confraternity, coterie, faction, family, fraternity, gens, group, house, phratry, race, sect, sept, set, society, sodality, tribe.

clandestine *adj* backroom, behind-door, cloak-and-dagger, closet, concealed, covert, fraudulent, furtive, hidden, private, secret, sly, sneaky, stealthy, subreptitious, surreptitious, underground, underhand, under-the-counter.
antonym open.

clandestinely *adv* covertly, furtively, on the q.t., on the quiet, quietly, secretly, surreptitiously.

clang *v* bong, chime, clank, clash, jangle, peal, resound, reverberate, ring, toll.
n bong, clank, clash, clatter, jangle, peal.

clannish *adj* cliqu(e)y, cliquish, close, exclusive, insular, narrow, parochial, sectarian, select, unfriendly.
antonyms friendly, open.

clap *v* acclaim, applaud, bang, cheer, pat, slap, smack, thrust, thwack, wallop, whack.

claptrap *n* affectation, balderdash, blarney, bombast, bunk, bunkum, codswallop, drivel, flannel, guff, hokum, hot air, humbug, nonsense, rodomontade, rubbish, tripe.

clarification *n* definition, elucidation, explanation, exposition, gloss, illumination, interpretation, simplification.
antonym obfuscation.

clarify *v* cleanse, define, elucidate, explain, gloss, illuminate, purify, refine, resolve, shed/throw light on, simplify.
antonym obscure.

clarity *n* clearness, comprehensibility, definition, explicitness, intelligibility, limpidity, lucidity, lucidness, obviousness, precision, simplicity, transparency, unambiguousness.
antonyms obscurity, vagueness.

clash *v* bang, clang, clank, clatter, conflict, crash, disagree, feud, fight, grapple, jangle, jar, quarrel, rattle, war, wrangle.
n brush, clank, clatter, collision, conflict, confrontation, disagreement, fight, jangle, jar, noise, show-down.

clasp *n* agraffe, brooch, buckle, catch, clip, embrace, fastener, fastening, grasp, grip, hasp, hold, hook, hug, pin, snap, tach(e).
v attach, clutch, concatenate, connect, embrace, enclasp, enfold, fasten, grapple, grasp, grip, hold, hug, press, seize, squeeze.

class[1] *n* calibre, caste, category, classification, collection, denomination, department, description, division, genre, genus, grade, group, grouping, ilk, kidney, kind, kingdom, league, order, phylum, quality, rank, section, set, sort, species, sphere, status, style, taxon, type, value.
v assort, brand, categorise, classify, codify, designate, grade, group, rank, rate.

class[2] *n* course, lecture, seminar, teach-in, tutorial.

classic *adj* abiding, ageless, archetypal, Augustan, best, characteristic, chaste, consummate, deathless, definitive, enduring, established, excellent, exemplary, finest, first-rate, ideal, immortal, lasting, master, masterly, model, paradigmatic, quintessential, refined, regular, restrained, standard, time-honoured, traditional, typical, undying, usual.

antonym second-rate.

n chef d'oeuvre, exemplar, masterpiece, masterwork, model, paradigm, pièce de resistance, prototype, standard.

classical *adj* attic, Attic, Augustan, chaste, elegant, established, excellent, grecian, Greek, harmonious, Hellenic, Latin, pure, refined, restrained, Roman, standard, symmetrical, traditional, well-proportioned.

classification *n* analysis, arrangement, cataloguing, categorisation, codification, digestion, grading, pigeon-holing, sorting, taxis, taxonomy.

classify *v* arrange, assort, catalogue, categorise, codify, digest, dispose, distribute, file, grade, pigeon-hole, rank, sort, systematise, tabulate.

classy *adj* elegant, exclusive, exquisite, fine, gorgeous, grand, high-class, posh, select, stylish, superior, swanky, up-market.

antonyms dowdy, plain, unstylish.

clause *n* article, chapter, condition, demand, heading, item, paragraph, part, passage, point, provision, proviso, section, specification, stipulation, subsection.

claw *n* griff(e), gripper, nail, nipper, pincer, pounce, talon, tentacle, unguis.

v dig, graze, lacerate, mangle, maul, rip, scrabble, scrape, scratch, tear.

clean *adj* antiseptic, chaste, clarified, complete, conclusive, decent, decisive, decontaminated, delicate, elegant, entire, exemplary, faultless, final, flawless, fresh, good, graceful, guiltless, honest, honourable, hygienic, immaculate, innocent, laundered, moral, natural, neat, perfect, pure, purified, respectable, sanitary, simple, spotless, sterile, sterilised, thorough, tidy, total, trim, unblemished, unadulterated, uncluttered, uncontaminated, undefiled, unimpaired, unpolluted, unsoiled, unspotted, unstained, unsullied, upright, virtuous, washed, whole.

antonyms dirty, indecent, polluted, unsterile.

v bath, cleanse, deodorise, deterge, disinfect, dust, launder, lave, mop, purge, purify, rinse, sanitise, scour, scrub, sponge, swab, sweep, vacuum, wash, wipe.

antonyms defile, dirty.

clean up sanitise, tidy, wash.

cleaner *n* char, charlady, charwoman, daily.

cleanse *v* absolve, absterge, catharise, clean, clear, deterge, detoxicate, detoxify, lustrate, porge, purge, purify, rinse, scavenge, scour, scrub, wash.

antonyms defile, dirty.

cleanser *n* abstergent, detergent, detersive, disinfectant, purifier, scourer, scouring-powder, soap, solvent.

cleansing *n* abstersion, detergence, detergency, detersion.

adj abstergent, abstersive, cathartic(al), detergent, detersive, purgative, purgatory.

clear *adj* apparent, audible, bright, certain, clean, cloudless, coherent, comprehensible, conspicuous, convinced, crystalline, decided, definite, diaphanous, disengaged, distinct, eidetic, empty, evident, explicit, express, fair, fine, free, glassy, guiltless, halcyon, hyaline, immaculate, incontrovertible, innocent, intelligible, light, limpid, lucid, luculent, luminous, manifest, obvious, open, palpable, patent, pellucid, perceptible, perspicuous, plain, positive, pronounced, pure, recognisable, resolved, satisfied, see-through, serene, sharp, shining, smooth, stainless, sunny, sure, translucent, transparent, unambiguous, unblemished, unclouded, undefiled, undimmed, undulled, unequivocal, unhampered, unhindered, unimpeded, unlimited, unmistakable, unobstructed, unquestionable, untarnished, untroubled, well-defined.

antonyms cloudy, fuzzy, guilty, vague.

v absolve, acquire, acquit, brighten, clarify, clean, cleanse, decode, decongest, deoppilate, disengage, disentangle, earn, emancipate, erase, excuse, exonerate, extricate, fix, free, gain, jump, justify, leap, liberate, lighten, loosen, make, miss, open, pass over, purify, reap, refine, rid, secure, strip, tidy, unblock, unclog, uncloud, unload, unpack, unscramble, vault, vindicate, wipe.

antonyms block, condemn, defile, dirty.

clear out beat it, clear off, decamp, depart, empty, exhaust, leave, retire, sort, throw out, withdraw.

clear up answer, clarify, elucidate, explain, fix, order, rearrange, remove, resolve, solve, sort, tidy, unravel.

clearance *n* allowance, authorisation, consent, endorsement, gap, go-ahead, headroom, leave, margin, OK, permission, riddance, sanction, space, the green light.

clear-cut *adj* clear, definite, distinct, explicit, plain, precise, specific, straightforward, unambiguous, unequivocal, well-defined.

antonyms ambiguous, vague.

clearing *n* dell, glade, hollow, opening, space.

adj deobstruent.

clearly *adv* distinctly, evidently, incontestably, incontrovertibly, manifestly, markedly, obviously, openly, plainly, undeniably, undoubtedly.

antonyms indistinctly, vaguely.

clearness *n* audibility, brightness, clarity, coherence, distinctness, explicitness, glassiness, intelligibility, limpidity, lucidity, lucidness, luminosity, transparency, transparentness, unambiguousness.

cleave[1] *v* adhere, attach, cling, cohere, hold, remain, stick, unite.

cleave[2] *v* chop, crack, dissever, disunite, divide, halve, hew, open, part, pierce, rend, rive, separate, sever, slice, split, sunder.

antonyms join, unite.

cleft *n* breach, break, chasm, chink, crack, cranny, crevice, fissure, fracture, gap, opening, rent, split.

adj cloven, divided, parted, rent, riven, ruptured, separated, split, sundered, torn.
antonym solid.

clemency *n* compassion, forebearance, forgiveness, generosity, humanity, indulgence, kindness, lenience, leniency, lenity, magnanimity, mercifulness, mercy, mildness, moderation, soft-heartedness, tenderness.
antonyms harshness, ruthlessness.

clement *adj* balmy, calm, compassionate, fair, fine, forbearing, forgiving, generous, gentle, humane, indulgent, kind, kind-hearted, lenient, magnanimous, merciful, mild, soft-hearted, temperate, tender.

antonyms harsh, ruthless.

clench *v* clasp, close, clutch, double, grasp, grip, grit, hold.

clergy *n* churchmen, clergymen, clerics, ecclesiastics, ministry, presbyterate, priesthood, the church, the cloth.

clergyman *n* chaplain, churchman, cleric, curate, deacon, dean, divine, father, levite, man of God, minister, padre, parson, pastor, presbyter, priest, rabbi, rector, reverend, sky-pilot, vicar.

clerical *adj* ecclesiastical, pastoral, priestly, sacerdotal.

clerk *n* account-keeper, assistant, copyist, official, pen-driver, pen-pusher, protocolist, quill-driver, quillman, receptionist, shop-assistant, writer.

clever *adj* able, adroit, apt, astute, brainy, bright, canny, capable, cunning, deep, dexterous, discerning, elegant, expert, gifted, gleg, good-natured, habile, ingenious, intelligent, inventive, keen, knowing, knowledgeable, quick, quick-witted, rational, resourceful, sagacious, sensible, shrewd, skilful, smart, talented, witty.

antonyms foolish, naïve, senseless.
clever dick smart Alec, smart-ass, smartypants, wiseling, witling, wit-monger.

cleverness *n* ability, adroitness, astuteness, brains, brightness, canniness, cunning, dexterity, flair, gift, gumption, ingenuity, intelligence, nous, quickness, resourcefulness, sagacity, sense, sharpness, shrewdness, smartness, smeddum, talent, wit.

antonyms foolishness, naïvety, senselessness.

cliche *n* banality, bromide, chestnut, penny-a-lineism, platitude, stereotype, tag, truism.

click *n, v* beat, clack, snap, snick, snip, tick.

client *n* applicant, buyer, consumer, customer, dependant, habitue, patient, patron, protege, shopper.

clientèle *n* business, clients, customers, following, market, patronage, patrons, regulars, trade.

cliff *n* bluff, crag, escarpment, face, overhang, precipice, rock-face, scar, scarp.

climactic *adj* climactical, critical, crucial, decisive, exciting, orgasmic, orgastic, paramount.

antonyms bathetic, trivial.

climate *n* ambience, atmosphere, clime, country, disposition, feeling, milieu, mood, region, setting, temper, temperature, tendency, trend, weather.

climax *n* acme, apogee, culmination, head, height, high point, highlight, orgasm, peak, summit, top, zenith.

antonyms bathos, low point, nadir.

climb *v* ascend, clamber, mount, rise, scale, shin up, soar, swarm (up), top.

climb down back down, clamber down, descend, dismount, eat crow, eat one's words, retract, retreat.

clinch *v* assure, bolt, cap, clamp, conclude, confirm, cuddle, decide, determine, embrace, fasten, fix, grasp, hug, nail, neck, rivet, seal, secure, settle, squeeze, verify.

cling *v* adhere, clasp, cleave, clutch, embrace, fasten, grasp, grip, hug, stick.

clinical *adj* analytic, business-like, cold, detached, disinterested, dispassionate, emotionless, impersonal, objective, scientific, unemotional.
antonyms biased, subjective.

clip[1] *v* crop, curtail, cut, dock, pare, poll, pollard, prune, shear, shorten, snip, trim.

clip[2] *v* box, clobber, clout, cuff, hit, knock, punch, skelp, slap, smack, sock, thump, wallop, whack.

n blow, box, clout, cuff, hit, knock, punch, skelp, slap, smack, sock, thump, wallop, whack.

clip[3] *n* gallop, lick, rate, speed.

clip[4] *v* attach, fasten, fix, hold, pin, staple.

clipping *n* citation, cutting, excerpt, extract, piece.

clique *n* bunch, circle, clan, coterie, crew, crowd, faction, gang, group, grouplet, mates, mob, pack, set.

cloak *n* blind, cape, coat, cover, front, mantle, mask, pretext, shield, wrap.

v camouflage, conceal, cover, disguise, hide, mask, obscure, screen, veil.

clodhopper *n* booby, boor, bumpkin, galoot, lout, lummox, lumpkin, oaf, ox, yokel.

clog *v* ball, block, burden, congest, dam up, gaum, hamper, hinder, impede, jam, obstruct, occlude, shackle, stop up, stuff.

antonym unblock.

n burden, dead-weight, drag, encumbrance, hindrance, impediment, obstruction.

cloistered *adj* cloistral, confined, enclosed, hermitic, insulated, protected, reclusive, restricted, secluded, sequestered, sheltered, shielded, withdrawn.
antonyms open, urbane.

close[1] *v* bar, block, cease, choke, clog, cloture, complete, conclude, confine, connect, cork, couple, culminate, discontinue, end, fill, finish, fuse, grapple, join, lock, mothball, obstruct, plug, seal, secure, shut, stop, terminate, unite, wind up.

n cadence, cessation, completion, conclusion, culmination, denouement, end, ending, finale, finish, junction, pause, stop, termination, wind-up.

close[2] *adj* accurate, adjacent, adjoining, airless, alert, approaching, approximative, assiduous, at hand, attached, attentive, careful, compact, concentrated, confidential, confined, congested, conscientious, cramped, cropped, crowded, dear, dense, detailed, devoted, dogged, earnest, exact, faithful, familiar, fixed, frowsty, fuggy, handy, hard by, heavy, hidden, humid, illiberal, imminent, impending, impenetrable, inseparable, intense, intent, intimate, jam-packed, keen, literal, loving, mean, mingy, minute, miserly, muggy, narrow, near, near-by, neighbouring, niggardly, nigh, oppressive, packed, painstaking, parsimonious, penurious, precise, private, reserved, reticent, retired, rigorous, searching, secluded, secret, secretive, short, solid, stale, stifling, stingy, strict, stuffy, suffocating, sweltering, taciturn, thick, thorough, tight, tight-fisted, uncommunicative, unforthcoming, ungenerous, unventilated.

antonyms careless, cool, far, unfriendly.

closed *adj* concluded, decided, ended, exclusive, fastened, finished, locked, over, resolved, restricted, sealed, settled, shut, terminated, wound-up.

antonyms open, unfastened, unsettled.

closure *n* cap, cessation, closing, cloture, conclusion, end, finish, guillotine, lid, plug, seal, stoppage, stopper, stricture, winding-up.

antonym opening.

clot[1] *n* clotting, coagulation, curdling, embolism, embolus, gob, grume, lump, mass, occlusion, thrombus.

v coagulate, coalesce, congeal, curdle, jell, thicken.

clot[2] *n* ass, buffoon, dolt, dope, dunderhead, fathead, fool, idiot, nincompoop, nit, nitwit, numbskull, twerp.

cloth *n* dish-cloth, duster, fabric, face-cloth, material, rag, stuff, textiles, tissue, towel.

clothe *v* accoutre, apparel, array, attire, bedizen, caparison, cover, deck, drape, dress, enclothe, endow, enwarp, equip, garb, habilitate, habit, invest, outfit, rig, robe, swathe, vest.

antonyms unclothe, undress.

clothes *n* apparel, attire, clobber, clothing, costume, dress, duds, ensemble, garb, garments, garmenture, gear, get-up, habiliments, habit(s), outfit, raiment, rig-out, threads, toggery, togs, vestiture, vestments, vesture, wardrobe, wear, weeds.

cloud *n* billow, crowd, darkness, flock, fog, gloom, haze, horde, host, mist, multitude, murk, nebula, nebulosity, obscurity, shower, swarm, throng, vapour, water-dog, weft, woolpack.

v becloud, confuse, darken, defame, dim, disorient, distort, dull, eclipse, impair, muddle, obfuscate, obscure, overcast, overshadow, shade, shadow, stain, veil.

antonym clear.

cloudiness *n* blurredness, dimness, haziness, murkiness, nebula, opacity.

antonym clearness.

cloudy *adj* blurred, blurry, confused, dark, dim, dismal, dull, emulsified, hazy, indistinct, leaden, lightless, lowering, muddy, murky, nebulous, nubilous, obscure, opaque, overcast, sombre, sullen, sunless.

antonyms clear, sunny.

clout *v* box, clobber, cuff, hit, skelp, slap, smack, sock, strike, thump, wallop, whack, wham.

n authority, cuff, influence, power, prestige, pull, skelp, slap, smack, sock, standing, thump, wallop, weight, whack.

cloven *adj* bisected, cleft, divided, split.

antonym solid.

clown *n* august(e), boor, buffoon, chuff, clodhopper, clout-shoe, comedian, dolt, fool, gracioso, harlequin, hob, jester, Joey, joker, joskin, merry-andrew, mountebank, peasant, pierrot, Pierrot, prankster, punchinello, swain, yahoo, yokel, zany.

clowning *n* buffoonery, jesting, joking, messing about, pantaloonery, pranks, skylarking.

clownish *adj* awkward, clumsy, comic, foolish, galumphing, hobbish, ill-bred, rough, rude, rustic, slapstick, uncivil, ungainly, vulgar, zany.

antonyms graceful, sophisticated.

cloy *v* choke, disgust, glut, gorge, nauseate, sate, satiate, sicken, surfeit, tire, weary.

antonyms please, whet.

cloying *adj* excessive, nauseating, oversweet, sickening, sickly.

club[1] *n* bat, bludgeon, cosh, cudgel, mace, mere, stick, truncheon, waddy.

v bash, baste, batter, beat, bludgeon, clobber, clout, cosh, hammer, hit, pummel, strike.

club[2] *n* association, bunch, circle, clique, combination, company, fraternity, group, guild, lodge, order, set, society, sodality, union.

clue *n* clavis, evidence, hint, idea, indication, inkling, intimation, lead, notion, pointer, sign, suggestion, suspicion, tip, tip-off, trace.

clump *n* bunch, bundle, cluster, mass, shock, thicket, tuffet, tuft.

v clomp, lumber, plod, stamp, stomp, stump, thud, thump, tramp, tread.

clumsiness *n* awkwardness, bungling, cack-handedness, gaucheness, indexterity, maladdress, maladroitness, unhandiness.

clumsy *adj* awkward, blundering, bumbling, bungling, cack-handed, chuckle, chuckle-headed, clumping, crude, gauche, gawky, ham-fisted, ham-handed, hammy, heavy, hulking, ill-made, inept, inexpert, looby, lubber, lubberly, lumbering, maladroit, ponderous, rough, shapeless, spastic, squab, unco-ordinated, uncouth, ungainly, ungraceful, unhandy, unskilful, unwieldy.

antonym graceful.

cluster *n* assemblage, batch, bunch, clump, collection, gathering, glomeration, group, knot, mass.

v assemble, bunch, collect, flock, gather, group.

clustered *adj* assembled, bunched, gathered, glomerate, grouped, massed.

clutch *v* catch, clasp, embrace, fasten, grab, grapple, grasp, grip, hang on to, seize, snatch.

clutches *n* claws, control, custody, dominion, embrace, grasp, grip, hands, keeping, mercy, possession, power, sway.

clutter *n* confusion, disarray, disorder, hotchpotch, jumble, litter, mess, muddle, untidiness.

v cover, encumber, fill, litter, scatter, strew.

coach[1] *n* grinder, instructor, repetiteur, teacher, trainer, tutor.

v cram, drill, instruct, prepare, teach, train, tutor.

coach[2] *n* bus, carriage, charabanc, landau, motor-bus, motor-coach, omnibus.

coagulate *v* clot, congeal, curdle, jell, solidify, thicken.

antonym melt.

coal *n* black diamonds.

coalesce *v* amalgamate, blend, cohere, combine, commingle, commix, consolidate, fuse, incorporate, integrate, merge, mix, unite.

coalition *n* affiliation, alliance, amalgam, amalgamation, association, bloc, coadunation, combination, compact, confederacy, confederation, conjunction, federation, fusion, integration, league, merger, union.

coal-scuttle *n* purdonium.

coarse *adj* barrack-room, bawdy, blowzy, boorish, brutish, coarse-grained, crude, earthly, foul-mouthed, homespun, immodest, impolite, improper, impure, indelicate, inelegant, loutish, mean, offensive, porterly, Rabelaisian, ribald, rough, rude, smutty, Sotadic, uncivil, unfinished, unpolished, unprocessed, unpurified, unrefined, vulgar.

antonyms fine, polite, refined, sophisticated.

coarsen *v* anaesthetise, blunt, deaden, desensitise, dull, harden, indurate, roughen.

antonyms civilise, sensitise.

coarseness *n* bawdiness, boorishness, crassitude, crudity, earthiness, grossièrete, indelicacy, offensiveness, ribaldry, roughness, smut, smuttiness, uncouthness, unevenness.

antonyms delicacy, politeness, sophistication.

coast *n* coastline, littoral, seaboard, seaside, shore.

v cruise, drift, free-wheel, glide, sail.

coat *n* Burberry, cloak, coating, covering, fleece, fur, hair, hide, layer, mac, mackinaw, mackintosh, mantle, overlay, pelt, raincoat, skin, wash, wool.

v apply, cover, plaster, smear, spread.

coated *adj* covered, furred, painted, proofed.

coating *n* blanket, coat, covering, dusting, film, finish, fur, glaze, lamination, layer, membrane, patina, pellicle, sheet, skin, varnish, veneer, wash.

coax *v* allure, beguile, cajole, decoy, entice, flatter, inveigle, persuade, soft-soap, sweet-talk, wheedle, whilly, whillywha(w), wile.

antonym force.

cobble *v* botch, bungle, knock up, mend, patch, put together, tinker.

cock *n* capon, chanticleer, rooster.

cock-eyed *adj* absurd, askew, asymmetrical, awry, crazy, crooked, daft, lop-sided, ludicrous, nonsensical, preposterous, skew-whiff, squint, tiddly, tipsy.

antonyms sensible, sober.

cocksure *adj* arrogant, brash, bumptious, cocky, hubristic, overconfident, presumptuous, self-confident.

antonym modest.

cocky *adj* arrogant, bouncy, brash, cocksure, conceited, egotistical, fresh, pert, swaggering, swollen-headed, vain.

cocoon *v* cover, cushion, envelop, insulate, pad, preserve, protect, sheathe, swaddle, swathe, wrap.

coddle *v* baby, cocker, cosset, humour, indulge, mollycoddle, nurse, pamper, pet, spoil.

code *n* canon, cipher, convention, cryptograph, custom, ethics, etiquette, manners, maxim, regulations, rules, system.

v encipher, encode.

coded *adj* cryptic, encrypted, hidden, secret.

codify *v* catalogue, classify, code, digest, organise, summarise, systematise, tabulate, write down.

coding *n* encryption.

coerce *v* bludgeon, browbeat, bulldoze, bully, compel, constrain, dragoon, drive, drum, force, intimidate, press-gang, pressurise.

antonyms coax, persuade.

coercion *n* browbeating, bullying, compulsion, constraint, direct action, duress, force, intimidation, pressure, threats.

antonym persuasion.

co-existent *adj* coetaneous, coeval, co-existing, concomitant, contemporaneous, contemporary, synchronous.

coffer *n* ark, case, casket, chest, kist, repository, strongbox, treasure, treasury.

cogency *n* conviction, force, persuasion, potency, power, strength.

antonym weakness.

cogent *adj* compelling, conclusive, convincing, effective, forceful, forcible, influential, irresistible, persuasive, potent, powerful, strong, unanswerable, urgent, weighty.

antonyms ineffective, unsound.

cogitate *v* cerebrate, consider, contemplate, deliberate, meditate, muse, ponder, reflect, ruminate, think.

cogitation *n* cerebration, consideration, contemplation, deliberation, meditation, reflection, rumination, thought.

cognate *adj* affiliated, agnate, akin, alike, allied, analogous, associated, connected, kindred, related, similar.

antonym unconnected.

cognisance *n* acknowledgement, apprehension, cognition, knowledge, notice, perception, percipience, recognition, regard.

antonym unawareness.

cognisant *adj* acquainted, aware, conscious, conversant, familiar, informed, knowledgeable, versed, witting.

antonym unaware.

cognition *n* apprehension, awareness, comprehension, discernment, insight, intelligence, perception, reasoning, understanding.

cohere *v* adhere, agree, bind, cling, coalesce, combine, consolidate, correspond, fuse, glue, hang together, harmonise, hold, square, stick, unite.

antonym separate.

coherence *n* agreement, comprehensibility, concordance, congruity, connection, consistency, consonance, correspondence, intelligibility, rationality, sense, union, unity.

antonym incoherence.

coherent *adj* articulate, comprehensible, consistent, intelligible, logical, lucid, meaningful, orderly, organised, rational, reasoned, sensible, systematic.

cohort *n* accomplice, assistant, associate, band, companion, company, comrade, contingent, crony, division, follower, henchman, legion, mate, myrmidon, partner, regiment, sidekick, squadron, supporter, toady, troop.

coil *v* convolute, curl, entwine, loop, snake, spiral, twine, twist, wind, wreathe, writhe.

n bight, convolution, curl, fank, loop, spiral, twist.

coin *v* conceive, create, devise, fabricate, forge, form, formulate, frame, introduce, invent, make up, mint, mould, originate, produce, think up.

n bit, cash, change, copper, jitney, loose change, lucky-piece, money, piece, silver, small change, specie.

coincide *v* accord, agree, co-exist, concur, correspond, harmonise, match, square, tally.

coincidence *n* accident, chance, concomitance, concurrence, conjunction, correlation, correspondence, eventuality, fluke, fortuity, luck, synchronism.

coincidental *adj* accident, casual, chance, coincident, concomitant, concurrent, fluky, fortuitous, lucky, simultaneous, synchronous, unintentional, unplanned.

antonyms deliberate, planned.

coitus *n* coition, congress, copulation, coupling, love-making, marriage-bed, mating, sexual intercourse, union.

cold *adj* agued, algid, aloof, apathetic, arctic, benumbed, biting, bitter, bleak, brumal, chill, chilled, chilly, cold-blooded, cool, dead, distant, freezing, frigid, frosty, frozen, gelid, glacial, icy, inclement, indifferent, inhospitable, lukewarm, numbed, parky, passionless, phlegmatic, raw, reserved, shivery, spiritless, stand-offish, stony, undemonstrative, unfeeling, unfriendly, unheated, unmoved, unresponsive, unsympathetic, wintry.

antonyms friendly, warm.

n catarrh, chill, chilliness, coldness, frigidity, frostiness, hypothermia, iciness, inclemency.

antonyms friendliness, warmth.

cold fish iceberg.

cold-blooded *adj* barbaric, barbarous, brutal, callous, cruel, dispassionate, fell, flinty, heartless, inhuman, merciless, obdurate, pitiless, ruthless, savage, steely, stony-hearted, uncompassionate, unemotional, unfeeling, unmoved.

antonyms compassionate, merciful.

cold-hearted *adj* callous, cold, detached, flinty, frigid, frozen, heartless, indifferent, inhuman, insensitive, stony-hearted, uncaring, uncompassionate, unfeeling, unkind, unsympathetic.

antonym warm-hearted.

collaborate *v* coact, collude, conspire, co-operate, co-produce, fraternise, participate, team up.

collaboration *n* alliance, association, coactivity, concert, co-operation, partnership, teamwork.

collaborator *n* assistant, associate, caballer, collaborationist, colleague, confederate, co-worker, fellow-traveller, partner, quisling, team-mate, traitor, turncoat.

collapse *v* crumple, fail, faint, fall, fold, founder, peg out, sink, subside.

n breakdown, cave-in, debacle (debâcle), detumescence, disintegration, downfall, efoulement, exhaustion, failure, faint, flop, subsidence.

collar *v* apprehend, appropriate, arrest, capture, catch, grab, nab, nick, seize.

n dog-collar, gorget, neckband, ring, ruff.

collate *v* adduce, analogise, arrange, collect, compare, compose, gather, sort.

collateral *n* assurance, deposit, funds, guarantee, pledge, security, surety.

adj concurrent, confirmatory, corroborative, indirect, parallel, related, supporting.

colleague *n* aide, aider, ally, assistant, associate, auxiliary, bedfellow, coadjutor, collaborator, companion, comrade, confederate, confrère, helper, partner, team-mate, workmate.

collect *v* accumulate, acquire, aggregate, amass, assemble, cluster, congregate, convene, converge, forgather, gather, gather together, heap, hoard, muster, obtain, raise, rally, save, secure, stockpile, uplift.

collected *adj* assembled, calm, composed, confident, cool, efficient, gathered, imperturbable, placid, poised, self-possessed, serene, together, unperturbed, unruffled.

antonyms disorganised, dithery, worried.

collection *n* accumulation, anthology, assemblage, assembly, assortment, caboodle, cluster, company, compilation, congeries, conglomerate, conglomeration, congregation, convocation, crowd, festschrift, gathering, group, harvesting, heap, hoard, ingathering, inning, jingbang, job-lot, mass, pile, set, spicilege, stockpile, store, whip-round.

collective *adj* aggregate, combined, common, composite, concerted, congregated, co-operative, corporate, cumulative, joint, shared, unified, united.

n aggregate, assemblage, corporation, gathering, group.

collision *n* accident, bump, clash, clashing, conflict, confrontation, crash, encounter, impact, opposition, pile-up, prang, rencontre, rencounter, skirmish, smash.

colloquial *adj* conversational, demotic, everyday, familiar, idiomatic, informal, non-technical, vernacular.

antonym formal.

collude *v* abet, cabal, coact, collaborate, complot, connive, conspire, contrive, intrigue, machinate, plot, scheme.

collusion *n* artifice, cahoots, coactivity, complicity, connivance, conspiracy, craft, deceit, fraudulent, intrigue.

colonise *v* people, pioneer, populate, settle.

colonist *n* colonial, coloniser, emigrant, frontiersman, homesteader, immigrant, oecist, oikist, pioneer, planter, settler.

colonnade *n* arcade, cloisters, columniation, peristyle, portico.

colony *n* dependency, dominion, outpost, possession, province, settlement, territory.

colossal *adj* Brobdingnagian, elephantine, enormous, gargantuan, gigantic, herculean, heroic, huge, immense, leviathan, mammoth, massive, monstrous, monumental, mountainous, prodigious, titanic, vast.

antonym tiny.

colour[1] *n* animation, appearance, bloom, blush, brilliance, chroma, colorant, coloration, complexion, disguise, dye, façade, flush, glow, guise, hue, liveliness, paint, pigment, pigmentation, plausibility, pretence, pretext, race, reason, rosiness, ruddiness, semblance, shade, timbre, tincture, tinge, tint, variety, vividness, wash, water-colour.

v blush, burn, colourwash, disguise, distort, dye, embroider, encolour, exaggerate, falsify, flush, misrepresent, paint, pervert, prejudice, redden, slant, stain, strain, taint, tinge, tint.

colour[2] *n* colours, ensign, flag, standard.

colour-blind *adj* dichromatic.

coloured *n* Asian, black, Hottentot, Negro.

adj Asian, black, brown-skinned, dark-skinned, Negro.

colourful *adj* bright, brilliant, distinctive, graphic, intense, interesting, jazzy, kaleidoscopic, lively, motley, multicoloured, parti-coloured, picturesque, psychedelic, rich, stimulating, unusual, variegated, vibrant, vivid.

antonyms colourless, drab, plain.

colourless *adj* achromatic, achromic, anaemic, ashen, bleached, characterless, drab, dreary, fade, faded, insipid, lacklustre, livid, neutral, pale, sickly, tame, transparent, uninteresting, unmemorable, vacuous, vapid, wan, washed out.

antonym colourful.

colours *n* banner, colour, emblem, ensign, flag, standard.

column *n* anta, cavalcade, file, line, list, obelisk, pilaster, pillar, post, procession, queue, rank, row, shaft, string, support, train, upright.

columnist *n* correspondent, critic, editor, journalist, reporter, reviewer, writer.

coma *n* catalepsy, drowsiness, hypnosis, insensibility, lethargy, oblivion, somnolence, sopor, stupor, torpor, trance, unconsciousness.

comatose *adj* cataleptic, drowsy, insensible, lethargic, sleepy, sluggish, somnolent, soporose, stupefied, torpid, unconscious.

antonym conscious.

comb *v* hackle, hunt, rake, ransack, rummage, scour, screen, search, sift, sweep.

n crest, hackle.

combat *n* action, battle, bout, clash, conflict, contest, duel, encounter, engagement, fight, hostilities, j(i)u-jitsu, judo, karate, kendo, kung fu, skirmish, struggle, war, warfare.

v battle, contend, contest, defy, engage, fight, oppose, resist, strive, struggle, withstand.

combatant *n* adversary, antagonist, belligerent, contender, enemy, fighter, opponent, serviceman, soldier, warrior.

adj active, battling, belligerent, combating, contending, fighting, opposing, warring.

combative *adj* aggressive, antagonistic, argumentative, bellicose, belligerent, contentious, militant, pugnacious, quarrelsome, truculent, warlike.

antonyms pacific, peaceful.

combination *n* alliance, amalgam, amalgamation, association, blend, cabal, cartel, coalescence, coalition, combine, composite, composition, compound, confederacy, confederation, conjunction, connection, consortium, conspiracy, federation, meld, merger, mix, mixture, syndicate, unification, union.

combine *v* amalgamate, associate, bind, blend, bond, coadunate, compound, conjoin, connect, cooperate, fuse, incorporate, integrate, join, link, marry, meld, merge, mix, peace, pool, synthesise, unify, unite.

antonym separate.

combustible *adj* excitable, explosive, flammable, incendiary, inflammable.

antonyms incombustible, non-flammable.

come *v* advance, appear, approach, arrive, attain, become, draw near, ejaculate, enter, happen, materialise, move, near, occur, originate, reach.

antonyms depart, go, leave.

come about arise, befall, come to pass, happen, occur, result, transpire.

come across bump into, chance upon, discover, encounter, find, happen on, meet, notice, unearth.

come along arise, arrive, develop, happen, improve, mend, progress, rally, recover, recuperate.

come apart break, crumble, disintegrate, fall to bits, separate, split, tear.

come between alienate, disunite, divide, estrange, interfere, meddle, part, separate, split up.

come by acquire, get, obtain, procure, secure.

antonyms give, lose.

come clean acknowledge, admit, confess, own, own up, reveal, spill the beans.

come down decline, degenerate, descend, deteriorate, fall, reduce, worsen.

come in appear, arrive, enter, finish, show up.

come on advance, appear, begin, develop, improve, proceed, progress, take place, thrive.

come out conclude, emerge, end, result, terminate.

come out with affirm, declare, disclose, divulge, own, say, state.

come round accede, acquiesce, allow, awake, awaken, concede, grant, mellow, recover, relent, revive, wake, waken, yield.

come through accomplish, achieve, endure, prevail, succeed, survive, triumph, withstand.

come to grief bomb, come unstuck, fail, miscarry.

antonyms succeed, triumph.

come to life revive, rouse.

antonym collapse.

come to light appear, come out, transpire, turn up.

come up with advance, create, discover, find, furnish, offer, present, produce, propose, provide, submit, suggest, think of, think out.

come-back *n* quip, rally, rebound, recovery, rejoinder, repartee, reply, response, resurgence, retaliation, retort, return, revival, riposte, triumph.

comedian *n* card, clown, comic, droll, funny man, gagster, humorist, jester, joker, jokesmith, laugh, wag, wit.

come-down *n* anticlimax, blow, decline, deflation, degradation, demotion, descent, disappointment, humiliation, let-down, reverse.

comedy *n* chaffing, clowning, drollery, facetiousness, farce, fun, hilarity, humour, jesting, joking, sitcom, slapstick, wisecracking, witticisms.

comely *adj* attractive, beautiful, becoming, blooming, bonny, buxom, callipygian, callipygous, decent, decorous, fair, fit, fitting, gainly, good-looking, graceful, handsome, lovely, pleasing, pretty, proper, pulchritudinous, seemly, suitable, wholesome, winsome.

come-uppance *n* chastening, deserts, dues, merit, punishment, rebuke, recompense, requital, retribution.

comfort *v* alleviate, assuage, cheer, console, ease, encheer, encourage, enliven, gladden, hearten, inspirit, invigorate, reassure, refresh, relieve, solace, soothe, strengthen.

n aid, alleviation, cheer, compensation, consolation, cosiness, ease, easy street, encouragement, enjoyment, help, luxury, opulence, relief, satisfaction, snugness, succour, support, well-being.

antonyms distress, torment.

comfortable *adj* adequate, affluent, agreeable, ample, canny, commodious, contented, convenient, cosy, delightful, easy, enjoyable, gemütlich, gratified, happy, homely, loose, loose-fitting, pleasant, prosperous, relaxed, relaxing, restful, roomy, serene, snug, well-off, well-to-do.

antonyms poor, uncomfortable.

comforting *adj* analeptic, cheering, consolatory, consoling, encouraging, heart-warming, inspiriting, reassuring, soothing.

antonym worrying.

comic *adj* amusing, comical, droll, facetious, farcical, funny, humorous, jocular, joking, light, rich, waggish, witty.

antonyms serious, tragic, unfunny.

n buffoon, clown, comedian, droll, funny, gagster, humorist, jester, joker, jokesmith, man, wag, wit.

comical *adj* absurd, amusing, comic, diverting, droll, entertaining, farcical, funny, hilarious, humorous, laughable, ludicrous, priceless, ridiculous, risible, side-splitting, silly, whimsical.

antonyms sad, unamusing.

coming *adj* approaching, aspiring, due, forthcoming, future, imminent, impending, near, next, nigh, promising, rising, up-and-coming.

n accession, advent, approach, arrival.

command *v* bid, charge, compel, control, demand, direct, dominate, enjoin, govern, head, lead, manage, order, reign over, require, rule, supervise, sway.

n authority, behest, bidding, charge, commandment, control, decree, dictation, diktat, direction, directive, domination, dominion, edict, fiat, government, grasp, injunction, instruction, management, mandate, mastery, order, power, precept, requirement, rule, supervision, sway, ukase, ultimatum.

commandeer *v* appropriate, confiscate, expropriate, hijack, requisition, seize, sequester, sequestrate, usurp.

commander *n* admiral, boss, captain, chief, commander-in-chief, commanding officer, director, general, head, imperator, leader, marshal, officer, ruler.

commanding *adj* advantageous, assertive, authoritative, autocratic, compelling, controlling, decisive, dominant, dominating, forceful, imposing, impressive, peremptory, superior.

commando *n* fedayee, Green Beret, soldier.

commemorate *v* celebrate, honour, immortalise, keep, memorialise, observe, remember, salute, solemnise.

commemoration *n* ceremony, honouring, observance, recordation, remembrance, tribute.

commemorative *adj* celebratory, dedicatory, in memoriam, memorial.

commence *v* begin, embark on, inaugurate, initiate, open, originate, start.

antonyms cease, finish.

commend *v* acclaim, applaud, approve, commit, compliment, confide, consign, deliver, entrust, eulogise, extol, praise, recommend, yield.

antonym criticise.

commendable *adj* admirable, creditable, deserving, estimable, excellent, exemplary, laudable, meritorious, noble, praiseworthy, worthy.

antonyms blameworthy, poor.

commendation *n* acclaim, acclamation, accolade, applause, approbation, approval, credit, encomium, encouragement, panegyric, praise, recommendation.

antonyms blame, criticism.

commensurate *adj* acceptable, adequate, appropriate, co-extensive, comparable, compatible, consistent, corresponding, due, equivalent, fitting, just, meet, proportionate, sufficient.

antonym inappropriate.

comment *v* animadvert, annotate, criticise, descant, elucidate, explain, gloss, interpose, interpret, mention, note, observe, opine, remark, say.

n animadversion, annotation, commentary, criticism, elucidation, explanation, exposition, footnote, illustration, marginal note, marginalia, note, observation, remark, statement.

commentary *n* analysis, critique, description, elucidation, exegesis, explanation, narration, notes, postil, review, treatise, voice-over.

commentator *n* annotator, commenter, critic, expositor, glossator, glosser, glossographer, interpreter, reporter, scholiast, sportscaster.

commerce *n* business, communication, dealing(s), exchange, intercourse, merchandising, relations, trade, traffic.

commercial *adj* business, exploited, marketable, materialistic, mercantile, mercenary, monetary, pecuniary, popular, profitable, profit-making, saleable, sales, sellable, trade, trading, venal.

commiseration *n* compassion, condolence, consolation, pity, sympathy.

commission *n* allowance, appointment, authority, board, brokerage, brok(er)age, charge, committee, compensation, cut, delegation, deputation, duty, employment, errand, fee, function, mandate, mission, percentage, rake-off, representative, task, trust, warrant.

v appoint, ask for, authorise, contract, delegate, depute, empower, engage, nominate, order, request, select, send.

commit *v* align, bind, commend, compromise, confide, confine, consign, deliver, deposit, do, enact, endanger, engage, entrust, execute, give, imprison, involve, obligate, perform, perpetrate, pledge.

commit oneself bind oneself, decide, promise, take the plunge, undertake.

commitment *n* adherence, assurance, dedication, devotion, duty, engagement, guarantee, involvement, liability, loyalty, obligation, pledge, promise, responsibility, tie, undertaking, vow, word.

committed *adj* active, card-carrying, engage, fervent, red-hot.

antonyms apathetic, uncommitted.

committee *n* advisory group, board, cabinet, commission, council, jury, panel, table, task force, think-tank, working party.

commodious *adj* ample, capacious, comfortable, expansive, extensive, large, loose, roomy, spacious.

antonym cramped.

commodities *n* goods, merchandise, output, produce, products, stock, things, wares.

common *adj* accepted, average, coarse, collective, commonplace, communal, conventional, customary, daily, everyday, familiar, flat, frequent, general, habitual, hackneyed, humdrum, inferior, low, mutual, obscure, ordinary, pedestrian, plain, plebby, plebeian, popular, prevailing, prevalent, public, regular, routine, run-of-the-mill, simple, social, stale, standard, stock, trite, tritical, undistinguished, unexceptional, universal, usual, vulgar, widespread, workaday.

antonyms noteworthy, uncommon.

common sense gumption, judgement, level-headedness, mother-wit, nous, practicality, prudence, soundness, wit.

commonly *adv* for the most part, generally, normally, usually, vulgo.

antonym rarely.

commonplace *adj* common, customary, everyday, humdrum, obvious, ordinary, pedestrian, quotidian, stale, threadbare, trite, uninteresting, widespread, worn out.

antonyms exceptional, rare.

n banality, cliche, platitude, truism.

common-sense *adj* astute, common-sensical, down-to-earth, hard-headed, judicious, level-headed, matter-of-fact, practical, pragmatical, realistic, reasonable, sane, savvy, sensible, shrewd, sound.

antonym foolish.

commotion *n* ado, agitation, ballyhoo, bobbery, brouhaha, burst-up, bustle, bust-up, carfuffle, disorder, disturbance, excitement, ferment, fracas, fraise, furore, fuss, hoo-ha, hubbub, hullabaloo, hurly-burly, perturbation, pother, pudder, racket, riot, rumpus, to-do, toss, tumult, turmoil, uproar.

communal *adj* collective, common, communistic, community, general, joint, public, shared.

antonyms personal, private.

commune *n* collective, colony, community, co-operative, encampment, fellowship, kibbutz, settlement.

v communicate, confer, converse, discourse, hold converse with, make contact with.

communicable *adj* catching, contagious, conveyable, impartible, infectious, infective, spreadable, transferable, transmittable.

communicate *v* acquaint, announce, bestow, connect, contact, convey, correspond, declare, diffuse, disclose, disseminate, divulge, fax, impart, inform, intimate, notify, proclaim, promulgate, publish, report, reveal, signify, spread, telex, transmit, unfold.

communication *n* announcement, bulletin, communique, connection, contact, conversation, converse, correspondence, disclosure, dispatch, dissemination, fax, information, intelligence, intercourse, intimation, message, news, promulgation, report, statement, telex, transmission, word.

communicative *adj* candid, chatty, conversable, conversational, expansive, extrovert, forthcoming, frank, free, friendly, informative, loquacious, open, outgoing, sociable, talkative, unreserved, voluble.

antonym reticent.

communion *n* accord, affinity, agreement, closeness, communing, concord, converse, empathy, Eucharist, fellow-feeling, fellowship, harmony, Holy Communion, housel, intercourse, Lord's Supper, Mass, participation, rapport, Sacrament, sympathy, togetherness, unity.

communique *n* announcement, bulletin, communication, dispatch, message, report, statement.

communism *n* Bolshevism, collectivism, Leninism, Marxism, socialism, sovietism, Stalinism, totalitarianism, Trotskyism.

communist *n* Bolshevik, collectivist, Leninist, Marxist, Red, socialist, soviet, Stalinist, totalitarian, Trot, Trotskyist, Trotskyite.

community *n* affinity, agreement, association, body politic, brotherhood, coincidence, colony, commonness, commonwealth, company, concurrence, confraternity, confrèrie, correspondence, district, fellowship, fraternity, identity, kibbutz, kindredness, likeness, locality, nest, people, populace, population, public, residents, sameness, similarity, society, state.

commute[1] *v* adjust, alter, curtail, decrease, lighten, mitigate, modify, reduce, remit, shorten, soften.

commute[2] *v* alternate, journey, strap-hang, travel.

commuter *n* exurbanite, strap-hanger, suburbanite, traveller.

antonym urbanite.

compact[1] *adj* brief, close, compendious, compressed, concise, condensed, dense, firm, impenetrable, solid, stocky, succinct, thick, well-knit.

antonyms diffuse, rambling, rangy.

v compress, condense, consolidate, cram, flatten, ram, squeeze, tamp.

compact[2] *n* agreement, alliance, arrangement, bargain, bond, concordat, contract, covenant, deal, entente, pact, settlement, treaty, understanding.

companion *n* accomplice, aide, ally, assistant, associate, attendant, attender, buddy, chaperon, cohort, colleague, compeer, complement, comrade, confederate, confidant, confidante, consort, counterpart, crony, duenna, escort, fellow, fere, follower, friend, intimate, mate, partner, satellite, shadow, squire, twin.

companionable *adj* affable, amiable, approachable, congenial, conversable, convivial, extrovert, familiar, friendly, genial, gregarious, informal, neighbourly, outgoing, sociable, sympathetic.

antonym unfriendly.

companionship *n* camaraderie, companionhood, company, comradeship, confraternity, consociation, conviviality, esprit de corps, fellowship, fraternity, friendship, rapport, support, sympathy, togetherness.

company[1] *n* assemblage, assembly, association, band, body, business, cartel, circle, collection, community, concern, concourse, consociation, consortium, convention, corporation, coterie, crew, crowd, ensemble, establishment, firm, fraternity, gathering, group, house, league, line, partnership, party, set, set-out, syndicate, throng, troop, troupe.

company[2] *n* attendance, callers, companionhood, companionship, fellowship, guests, party, presence, society, support, visitors.

comparable *adj* akin, alike, analogous, cognate, commensurate, correspondent, corresponding, equal, equivalent, kindred, parallel, proportionate, related, similar, tantamount.

antonym unlike.

compare *v* balance, collate, confront, contrast, correlate, emulate, equal, equate, juxtapose, liken, match, parallel, resemble, similise, vie, weigh.

comparison *n* analogy, collation, comparability, contrast, correlation, distinction, juxtaposition, likeness, parallel, parallelism, resemblance, similarity, similitude.

compartment *n* alcove, area, bay, berth, booth, box, carrel, carriage, category, cell, chamber, cubby-hole, cubicle, department, division, locker, niche, pigeon-hole, section, stall, subdivision.

compass *n* area, boundary, bounds, circle, circuit, circumference, diapason, enclosure, extent, field, gamut, girth, limit, range, reach, realm, round, scale, scope, space, sphere, stretch, zone.

v accomplish, achieve, beset, besiege, blockade, circumscribe, contrive, devise, effect, encircle, enclose, encompass, environ, manage, realise, surround.

compassion *n* charity, clemency, commiseration, concern, condolence, fellow-feeling, heart, humanity, kindness, loving-kindness, mercy, pity, ruth, sorrow, sympathy, tenderness, understanding, weltschmerz, yearning.

antonym indifference.

compassionate *adj* benevolent, caring, charitable, clement, humane, humanitarian, indulgent, kind-hearted, kindly, lenient, merciful, piteous, pitying, supportive, sympathetic, tender, tender-hearted, understanding, warm-hearted.

antonym indifferent.

compatibility *n* accord, affinity, agreement, amity, concord, congeniality, consistency, consonance, correspondence, empathy, fellowship, harmony, like-mindedness, rapport, reconcilability, sympathy, understanding, unity.

antonyms antagonism, antipathy, incompatibility.

compatible *adj* accordant, adaptable, agreeable, conformable, congenial, congruent, congruous, consistent, consonant, harmonious, kindred, like-minded, reconcilable, suitable, sympathetic.

antonyms antagonistic, antipathetic, incompatible.

compel *v* browbeat, bulldoze, bully, coact, coerce, constrain, dragoon, drive, enforce, exact, force, gar, hustle, impel, make, necessitate, obligate, oblige, press-gang, pressurise, strongarm, urge.

compelling *adj* binding, coercive, cogent, compulsive, conclusive, convincing, enchanting, enthralling, forceful, gripping, hypnotic, imperative, incontrovertible, irrefragable, irrefutable, irresistible, mesmeric, overriding, peremptory, persuasive, powerful, pressing, spellbinding, telling, unanswerable, unavoidable, unputdownable, urgent, weighty.

compendious *adj* abbreviated, abridged, brief, compact, comprehensive, concise, condensed, contracted, epitomised, short, shortened, succinct, summarised, summary, synoptic.

antonym enlarged.

compendium *n* abbreviation, abridgement, abstract, brief, companion, condensation, conspectus, digest, encapsulation, epitome, handbook, manual, precis, recapitulation, summary, synopsis, vade-mecum.

compensate *v* atone, balance, cancel, counteract, counterbalance, countervail, expiate, guerdon, indemnify, offset, recompense, recover, recuperate, redeem, redress, refund, reimburse, remunerate, repay, requite, restore, reward, satisfy.

compensation *n* amends, atonement, comfort, consolation, damages, guerdon, indemnification, indemnity, payment, quittance, recompense, redress, refund, reimbursement, remuneration, reparation, repayment, requital, restitution, restoration, return, reward, satisfaction, solatium.

compère *n* anchor-man, announcer, commère, emcee, host, link man, master of ceremonies, MC, presenter, ringmaster.

compete *v* battle, challenge, contend, contest, duel, emulate, fight, oppose, rival, strive, struggle, tussle, vie.

competence *n* ability, adequacy, appropriateness, aptitude, capability, capacity, competency, experience, expertise, facility, fitness, proficiency, skill, suitability, technique.

antonym incompetence.

competent *adj* able, adapted, adequate, appropriate, belonging, capable, clever, efficient, endowed, equal, fit, legitimate, masterly, pertinent, proficient, qualified, satisfactory, strong, sufficient, suitable, trained, well-qualified.

antonym incompetent.

competition *n* challenge, challengers, championship, combativeness, competitiveness, competitors, contention, contest, corrivalry, cup, emulation, event, field, match, opposition, quiz, race, rivalry, rivals, series, strife, struggle, tournament, tourney, trial.

competitive *adj* aggressive, ambitious, antagonistic, combative, contentious, cut-throat, emulative, emulous, keen, pushy, vying.

antonyms sluggish, unambitious.

competitiveness *n* aggression, aggressiveness, ambition, ambitiousness, antagonism, assertiveness, challenge, combativeness, contention, contentiousness, emulation, keenness, pugnacity, pushiness, rivalry, self-assertion.

antonyms backwardness, sluggishness.

competitor *n* adversary, agonist, antagonist, challenger, competition, contender, contestant, corrival, emulator, entrant, opponent, opposition, rival.

compilation *n* accumulation, amassment, anthology, arrangement, assemblage, assortment, collection, composition, florilegium, opus, selection, thesaurus, treasury, work.

compile *v* accumulate, amass, anthologise, arrange, assemble, collect, compose, cull, garner, gather, marshal, organise.

complacency *n* content, contentment, gloating, gratification, pleasure, pride, satisfaction, self-content, self-satisfaction, serenity, smugness, triumph.

antonyms diffidence, discontent.

complacent *adj* contented, gloating, gratified, pleased, proud, satisfied, self-assured, self-congratulatory, self-contented, self-righteous, self-satisfied, serene, smug, triumphant, unconcerned.

antonyms diffident, discontented.

complain *v* beef, belly-ache, bemoan, bewail, bind, bitch, bleat, carp, deplore, fuss, girn, grieve, gripe, groan, grouse, growl, grumble, kvetch, lament, moan, protest, squeal, whine, whinge.

complainer *n* belly-acher, bleater, fuss-pot, girner, grouser, grumbler, kvetch(er), moaner, nit-picker, protester, whiner, whinger, winger.

complaining *adj* bleating, cantankerous, captious, critical, fault-finding, fussy, hypercritical, moaning, nagging, nit-picking, peevish, protesting, querimonious, querulous, whingeing.

antonym contented.

complaint[1] *n* accusation, annoyance, beef, belly-ache, bitch, bleat, censure, charge, criticism, dissatisfaction, fault-finding, girn, gravamen, grievance, gripe, grouse, grumble, lament, moan, nit-picking, plaint, protest, querimony, remonstrance, squawk, stricture, wail, whinge, winge.

complaint[2] *n* affliction, ailment, disease, disorder, illness, indisposition, malady, malaise, sickness, trouble, upset.

complaisance *n* acquiescence, agreeableness, amenability, biddableness, compliance, conformability, deference, docility, obligingness.

antonyms obstinacy, perversity.

complaisant *adj* accommodating, agreeable, amenable, amiable, biddable, compliant, conciliatory, conformable, deferential, docile, douce, obedient, obliging, solicitous, tractable.

antonyms obstinate, perverse.

complement *n* aggregate, capacity, companion, completion, consummation, counterpart, entirety, fellow, quota, sum, supplement, total, totality, wholeness.

complementary *adj* companion, correlative, corresponding, dove-tailed, fellow, interdependent, interrelated, interrelating, interwoven, matched, reciprocal, reciprocative, reciprocatory.

complete *adj* absolute, accomplished, achieved, all, concluded, consummate, ended, entire, equipped, faultless, finished, full, intact, integral, integrate, out-and-out, perfect, plenary, root-and-branch, self-contained, thorough, thoroughgoing, thorough-paced, total, unabbreviated, unabridged, unbroken, uncut, undivided, unedited, unexpurgated, unimpaired, utter, whole, whole-hog.

antonyms imperfect, incomplete.

v accomplish, achieve, cap, clinch, close, conclude, consummate, crown, discharge, do, effect, end, execute, finalise, finish, fulfil, perfect, perform, realise, settle, terminate, wind up.

completely *adv* absolutely, altogether, diametrically, en bloc, en masse, entirely, every inch, from first to last, fully, heart and soul, in full, in toto, lock stock and barrel, perfectly, quite, root and branch, solidly, thoroughly, totally, utterly, wholly.

completion *n* accomplishment, achievement, attainment, close, conclusion, consummation, crowning, culmination, discharge, end, expiration, finalisation, finish, fruition, fulfilment, perfection, plenitude, realisation, settlement, telos, termination.

complex *adj* ambagious, Byzantine, circuitous, complicated, composite, compound, compounded, convoluted, Daedalian, devious, diverse, elaborate, heterogeneous, intricate, involved, knotty, labyrinthine, manifold, mingled, mixed, multifarious, multipartite, multiple, plexiform, polymerous, ramified, tangled, tortuous.

antonym simple.

n aggregate, composite, establishment, fixation, hang-up, idee fixe, institute, network, obsession, organisation, phobia, preoccupation, scheme, structure, syndrome, synthesis, system.

complexion *n* appearance, aspect, cast, character, colour, colouring, composition, countenance, disposition, guise, hue, kind, light, look, make-up, nature, pigmentation, rud, skin, stamp, temperament, type.

complexity *n* complication, convolution, deviousness, diversity, elaboration, entanglement, intricacy, involution, involvement, multifariousness, multiplicity, ramification, repercussion, tortuousness, variation, variety.

antonym simplicity.

compliance *n* acquiescence, agreement, assent, complaisance, concession, concurrence, conformability, conformity, consent, co-operation, deference, obedience, observance, passivity, submission, submissiveness, yielding.

antonyms defiance, disobedience.

compliant *adj* accommodating, acquiescent, agreeable, amenable, biddable, complaisant, conformable, deferential, docile, obedient, obliging, passive, submissive, tractable, yielding.

antonyms disobedient, intractable.

complicate *v* complexify, compound, confuse, elaborate, embroil, entangle, foul up, involve, mix up, muddle, tangle.

antonym simplify.

complicated *adj* ambivalent, baroque, Byzantine, complex, convoluted, devious, difficult, elaborate, entangled, Heath-Robinson, intricate, involved, labyrinthine, perplexing, problematic, puzzling, rigmarole, tangled, tortuous, troublesome.

antonyms easy, simple.

complication *n* aggravation, ambage, complexification, complexity, complicatedness, confusion, difficulty, drawback, elaboration, embarrassment, entanglement, factor, intricacy, mixture, obstacle, problem, ramification, repercussion, snag, web.

complicity *n* abetment, agreement, approval, collaboration, collusion, concurrence, connivance, involvement, knowledge.

antonyms ignorance, innocence.

compliment *n* accolade, admiration, bouquet, commendation, congratulations, courtesy, douceur, encomium, eulogy, favour, felicitation, flattery, honour, plaudit, praise, tribute.

antonyms criticism, insult.

v admire, applaud, commend, congratulate, eulogise, extol, felicitate, flatter, laud, praise, salute.

antonyms condemn, insult.

complimentary *adj* admiring, appreciative, approving, commendatory, congratulatory, courtesy, encomiastic, eulogistic, favourable, flattering, free, gratis, honorary, laudatory, panegyrical.

antonyms critical, insulting, unflattering.

compliments *n* best wishes, congratulations, devoirs, greetings, regards, remembrances, respects, salutation.

comply *v* accede, accommodate, accord, acquiesce, agree, assent, conform, consent, defer, discharge, fall in, follow, fulfil, obey, oblige, observe, perform, respect, satisfy, submit, yield.

antonyms disobey, resist.

component *n* bit, constituent, element, factor, ingredient, item, part, piece, spare part, unit.

comport *v* acquit, act, bear, behave, carry, conduct, demean, deport, perform.

compose *v* adjust, arrange, build, calm, collect, compound, comprise, constitute, construct, contrive, control, create, devise, fashion, form, frame, govern, imagine, indite, invent, make, meditate the muse, pacify, produce, quell, quiet, recollect, reconcile, regulate, resolve, settle, soothe, still, structure, tranquillise, write.

composed *adj* calm, collected, complacent, confident, cool, imperturbable, level-headed, placid, poised, relaxed, self-possessed, serene, together, tranquil, unflappable, unruffled, unworried.

antonym agitated.

composer *n* arranger, author, bard, creator, makar, maker, originator, poet, songsmith, songwriter, tunesmith, writer.

composite *adj* agglutinate, blended, combined, complex, compound, conglomerate, fused, mixed, patchwork, synthesised.

antonyms homogeneous, uniform.

n agglutination, alloy, amalgam, blend, combination, compound, conglomerate, fusion, mixture, pastiche, patchwork, synthesis.

composition *n* arrangement, balance, combination, compilation, compromise, concord, confection, configuration, congruity, consonance, constitution, creation, design, essay, exaration, exercise, form, formation, formulation, harmony, invention, lay-out, lucubration, make-up, making, mixture, opus, organisation, piece, placing, production, proportion, structure, study, symmetry, work, writing.

composure *n* aplomb, assurance, calm, calmness, confidence, cool, coolness, dignity, dispassion, ease, equanimity, impassivity, imperturbability, placidity, poise, sang-froid, savoir-faire, sedateness, self-assurance, self-possession, serenity, tranquillity.

antonym discomposure.

compound *v* aggravate, alloy, amalgamate, augment, blend, coalesce, combine, complicate, compose, concoct, exacerbate, fuse, heighten, increase, intensify, intermingle, magnify, mingle, mix, synthesise, unite, worsen.

n alloy, amalgam, amalgamation, blend, combination, composite, composition, confection, conglomerate, conglomeration, fusion, medley, mixture, synthesis.

adj complex, complicated, composite, conglomerate, intricate, mixed, multiple.

comprehend *v* appreciate, apprehend, assimilate, compass, comprise, conceive, cover, discern, embrace, encompass, fathom, grasp, include, know, penetrate, perceive, see, see daylight, tumble to, twig, understand.

antonym misunderstand.

comprehensible *adj* clear, coherent, conceivable, explicit, graspable, intelligible, knowable, lucid, plain, rational, simple, straightforward, understandable.

antonym incomprehensible.

comprehension *n* appreciation, apprehension, capacity, conception, discernment, grasp, intellection, intelligence, intension, judgement, knowledge, perception, realisation, sense, understanding.

antonym incomprehension.

comprehensive *adj* across-the-board, all-embracing, all-inclusive, blanket, broad, catholic, compendious, complete, encyclopedic, exhaustive, extensive, full, general, inclusive, omnibus, sweeping, thorough, wide.

antonyms incomplete, selective.

compress *v* abbreviate, astrict, astringe, compact, concentrate, condense, constrict, contract, cram, crowd, crush, flatten, impact, jam, precis, press, shorten, squash, squeeze, stuff, summarise, synopsise, telescope, wedge.

antonyms diffuse, expand, separate.

compressed *adj* abridged, coarctate, compact, compacted, compendious, concentrated, concise, condensed, consolidated, constricted, flattened, impacted, pressed, reduced, shortened, squashed, squeezed, synopsised.

compression *n* abbreviation, abridgement, astriction, concentration, condensation, consolidation, constriction, crushing, digest, impaction, pressure, reduction, squeezing, thlipsis.

antonyms enlargement, expansion.

comprise *v* comprehend, consist of, contain, cover, embody, embrace, encompass, include, incorporate, involve, subsume.

compromise[1] *v* adapt, adjust, agree, arbitrate, bargain, concede, make concessions, negotiate, retire, retreat, settle.

antonyms differ, quarrel.

n accommodation, accord, adjustment, agreement, bargain, concession, co-operation, settlement, trade-off, via media.

antonyms disagreement, intransigence.

compromise[2] *v* discredit, dishonour, embarrass, embroil, expose, hazard, imperil, implicate, involve, jeopardise, prejudice, undermine, weaken.

compulsion *n* coercion, constraint, demand, distress, drive, duress, exigency, force, impulse, necessity, need, obligation, obsession, preoccupation, pressure, pressurisation, urge, urgency.

antonyms freedom, liberty.

compulsive *adj* besetting, compelling, driving, hardened, hopeless, incorrigible, incurable, irredeemable, irresistible, obsessive, overmastering, overpowering, overwhelming, uncontrollable, unputdownable, urgent.

compulsory *adj* binding, de rigueur, forced, imperative, mandatory, obligatory, required, requisite, stipulated, stipulatory.

antonyms optional, voluntary.

compunction *n* contrition, hesitance, hesitation, misgiving, penitence, qualm, regret, reluctance, remorse, repentance, sorrow, unease, uneasiness.

antonyms callousness, defiance.

compute *v* assess, calculate, count, enumerate, estimate, evaluate, figure, measure, rate, reckon, sum, tally, total.

computer *n* adding machine, analogue computer, calculator, data processor, digital computer, mainframe, processor, word processor.

comrade *n* Achates, ally, associate, brother, buddy, bully-rook, butty, china, cobber, colleague, companion, compatriot, compeer, confederate, co-worker, crony, fellow, frater, friend, mate, pal, partner, sidekick.

con *v* bamboozle, beguile, bilk, bluff, bunko, cheat, cozen, deceive, defraud, double-cross, dupe, fiddle, grift, gull, hoax, hoodwink, humbug, inveigle, mislead, racket, rip off, rook, swindle, trick.

n bluff, deception, fraud, grift, kidology, scam, swindle, trick.

concatenation *n* chain, connection, course, interlinking, interlocking, linking, nexus, procession, progress, progression, sequence, series, string, succession, thread, trail, train.

concave *adj* cupped, depressed, emaciated, excavated, hollow, hollowed, incurved, indented, scooped, sunken.

antonym convex.

concavity *n* basin, bowl, cavity, depression, dimple, dint, dip, dish, fossa, fossula, fovea, foveola, foveole, hole, hollow, hollowness, indentation, invagination, pit, recess, sag, sink, umbilicus, vacuity.

antonyms convexity, mound, protuberance.

conceal *v* bury, camouflage, cloak, cover, disguise, dissemble, hide, keep dark, mask, obscure, screen, secrete, shelter, sink, smother, submerge, suppress, veil.

antonym reveal.

concealed *adj* clandestine, covered, covert, disguised, hidden, inconspicuous, masked, perdu(e), screened, secret, secreted, ulterior, unseen, veiled.

antonyms clear, plain.

concealment *n* ambush, camouflage, cloak, cover, disguise, hide-away, hideout, hiding, protection, screen, secrecy, shelter.

antonyms openness, revelation.

concede *v* accept, acknowledge, admit, allow, cede, confess, forfeit, grant, own, recognise, relinquish, sacrifice, surrender, yield.

antonyms deny, dispute.

conceit[1] *n* arrogance, assumption, cockiness, complacency, conceitedness, egotism, narcissism, pride, self-assumption, self-conceit, self-importance, self-love, self-pride, self-satisfaction, swagger, vainglory, vainness, vanity.

antonyms diffidence, modesty.

conceit[2] *n* belief, caprice, concetto, fancy, fantasy, freak, humour, idea, image, imagination, impulse, jeu d'esprit, judgement, notion, opinion, quip, quirk, thought, vagary, whim, whimsy, wit.

conceited *adj* arrogant, assuming, bigheaded, cocky, complacent, egotistical, highty-tighty, hoity-toity, immodest, narcissistic, overweening, self-important, self-satisfied, stuck-up, swell-headed, swollen-headed, toffee-nose(d), uppist, uppity, vain, vainglorious, windy.

antonyms diffident, modest.

conceivable *adj* believable, credible, imaginable, likely, possible, probable, supposable, tenable, thinkable.

antonym inconceivable.

conceive *v* appreciate, apprehend, believe, comprehend, contrive, create, design, develop, devise, envisage, fancy, form, formulate, germinate, grasp, ideate, imagine, invent, originate, produce, project, purpose, realise, suppose, think, understand, visualise.

concentrate *v* absorb, accumulate, attend, attract, centre, cluster, collect, condense, congregate, converge, crowd, draw, engross, focus, foregather, gather, huddle, intensify.

antonyms disperse, distract, separate.

n apozem, decoction, decocture, distillate, distillation, elixir, essence, extract, juice, quintessence.

concentrated *adj* all-out, compact, condensed, deep, dense, evaporated, hard, intense, intensive, reduced, rich, thickened, undiluted.

antonyms desultory, diffuse, diluted.

concentration *n* absorption, accumulation, agglomeration, aggregation, application, centralisation, centring, cluster, collection, combination, compression, conglomeration, consolidation, convergence, crowd, denseness, focusing, grouping, heed, horde, intensification, intensity, mass, single-mindedness.

antonyms dilution, dispersal, distraction.

concept *n* abstraction, conception, conceptualisation, construct, hyphothesis, idea, image, impression, invention, notion, pattern, picture, plan, theory, type, view, visualisation.

conception *n* appreciation, apprehension, beginning, birth, clue, comprehension, concept, design, envisagement, fertilisation, formation, germination, idea, image, impregnation, impression, inauguration, inception, initiation, inkling, insemination, invention, knowledge, launching, notion, origin, outset, perception, picture, plan, understanding, visualisation.

concern *v* affect, bother, disquiet, distress, disturb, interest, involve, pertain to, perturb, refer to, regard, relate to, touch, trouble, upset, worry.

n affair, anxiety, apprehension, attention, bearing, burden, business, care, charge, company, consideration, corporation, disquiet, disquietude, distress, enterprise, establishment, field, firm, heed, house, importance, interest, involvement, job, matter, mission, occupation, organisation, perturbation, reference, relation, relevance, responsibility, solicitude, stake, task, transaction, unease, uneasiness, worry.

antonym unconcern.

concerned *adj* active, anxious, apprehensive, attentive, bothered, caring, connected, disquieted, distressed, disturbed, exercised, implicated, interested, involved, perturbed, solicitous, troubled, uneasy, unhappy, upset, worried.

antonym unconcerned.

concerning *prep* about, anent, apropos of, as regards, germane to, in regard to, in the matter of, re, regarding, relating to, relevant to, respecting, touching, with reference to, with regard to.

concert[1] *n* accord, agreement, concord, concordance, consonance, diapason, harmony, unanimity, union, unison.

antonym disunity.

concert[2] *n* appearance, engagement, gig, performance, presentation, production, recital, rendering, rendition, show.

concerted *adj* collaborative, collective, combined, co-ordinated, joint, organised, planned, prearranged, shared, united.

antonyms disorganised, separate, unco-ordinated.

concert-hall *n* assembly room, auditorium, chamber, music hall, odeon, town hall.

concession *n* acknowledgement, adjustment, admission, allowance, assent, boon, compromise, exception, favour, grant, indulgence, permit, privilege, relaxation, sacrifice, surrender, yielding.

conciliate *v* appease, disarm, disembitter, mollify, pacify, placate, propitiate, satisfy, soften, soothe.

antonym antagonise.

conciliation *n* appeasement, indulgence, mollification, pacification, peace-making, placation, propitiation, reconciliation, satisfaction.

antonyms alienation, antagonisation.

conciliator *n* dove, intercessor, intermediary, mediator, negotiator, peace-maker, reconciler.

antonym trouble-maker.

conciliatory *adj* disarming, irenic, mollifying, pacific, pacificatory, peaceable, placatory, propitiative, propitiatory, reconciliatory.

antonym antagonistic.

concise *adj* abbreviated, abridged, aphoristic, brief, compact, compendious, compressed, condensed, epigrammatic, gnomic, laconic, pithy, short, succinct, summary, synoptic, terse, thumbnail.

antonyms diffuse, expansive.

conclave *n* assembly, cabal, cabinet, confabulation, conference, conspiracy, conventicle, council, meeting, parley, powwow, session.

conclude *v* accomplish, assume, cease, clinch, close, complete, consummate, culminate, decide, deduce, determine, effect, end, establish, finish, fix, gather, infer, judge, opine, reckon, resolve, settle, suppose, surmise, terminate.

concluding *adj* closing, epilogic, epilogistic, final, last, perorating, terminal, ultimate.

antonym introductory.

conclusion *n* answer, assumption, clincher, close, come-off, completion, consequence, consummation, conviction, culmination, decision, deduction, end, explicit, finale, fine, finis, finish, illation, inference, issue, judgement, opinion, outcome, resolution, result, settlement, solution, termination, upshot, verdict.

conclusive *adj* clear, clinching, convincing, decisive, definite, definitive, final, incontrovertible, irrefragable, irrefutable, manifest, ultimate, unanswerable, unappealable, unarguable, undeniable.

antonym inconclusive.

concoct *v* brew, contrive, decoct, design, develop, devise, digest, fabricate, form, formulate, hatch, invent, mature, plan, plot, prepare, project, refine.

concoction *n* blend, brew, combination, compound, contrivance, creation, decoction, fable, mixture, myth, potion, preparation, story.

concomitant *adj* accompanying, associative, attendant, co-existent, coincidental, collateral, complementary, concurrent, contemporaneous, conterminous, contributing, incidental, simultaneous, synchronous, syndromic.

antonyms accidental, unrelated.

n accompaniment, by-product, epiphenomenon, incidental, secondary, symptom.

concord *n* accord, agreement, amicability, amity, brotherliness, compact, concert, concordat, consensus, consonance, convention, diapason, entente, friendship, harmony, peace, protocol, rapport, treaty, unanimity, unison.

antonym discord.

concourse *n* assemblage, assembly, collection, confluence, convergence, crowd, crush, entrance, foyer, frequence, gathering, hall, lobby, lounge, meeting, multitude, piazza, plaza, press, swarm, throng.

concrete *adj* actual, calcified, compact, compressed, conglomerated, consolidated, definite, explicit, factual, firm, material, perceptible, petrified, physical, real, seeable, sensible, solid, solidified, specific, substantial, tactile, tangible, touchable, visible.

antonym abstract.

concubine *n* apple-squire, courtesan, hetaira, leman, lorette, lover, mistress, odalisque, paramour.

concupiscence *n* appetite, desire, horniness, lasciviousness, lechery, lewdness, libidinousness, libido, lickerishness, lubricity, lust, lustfulness, randiness, ruttishness.

concupiscent *adj* horny, lascivious, lecherous, lewd, libidinous, lickerish, lubricious, lustful, randy, ruttish.

concur *v* accede, accord, acquiesce, agree, approve, assent, coincide, combine, comply, consent, co-operate, harmonise, join, meet, unite.

antonym disagree.

concurrence *n* acquiescence, agreement, assent, association, co-existence, coincidence, common ground, community, concomitance, conjunction, consilience, contemporaneity, convergence, juxtaposition, simultaneity, synchrony, syndrome.

antonyms difference, disagreement.

concurrent *adj* co-existing, coincident, coinciding, concerted, concomitant, confluent, consilient, contemporaneous, convergent, converging, simultaneous, synchronous, syndromic, uniting.

condemn *v* ban, blame, castigate, censure, convict, damn, decry, denounce, disapprove, disparage, doom, pan, proscribe, reprehend, reproach, reprobate, reprove, revile, sentence, slam, slate, upbraid.

antonyms approve, praise.

condemnation *n* ban, blame, castigation, censure, conviction, damnation, denouncement, denunciation, disapproval, disparagement, judgement, proscription, reproach, reprobation, reproof, sentence, slating, stricture, thumbs-down.

antonyms approval, praise.

condemnatory *adj* accusatory, accusing, censorious, critical, damnatory, denunciatory, deprecatory, disapproving, discouraging, incriminating, proscriptive, reprobative, reprobatory, unfavourable.

antonyms approving, complimentary, indulgent, laudatory.

condensation *n* abridgement, compression, concentrate, concentration, condensate, consolidation, contraction, crystallisation, curtailment, decoction, deliquescence, digest, distillate, distillation, encapsulation, liquefaction, precipitate, precipitation, precis, reduction, synopsis.

condense *v* abbreviate, abridge, capsulise, coagulate, compact, compress, concentrate, contract, crystallise, curtail, decoct, distil, encapsulate, epitomise, evaporate, inspissate, precipitate, precis, reduce, shorten, solidify, summarise, synopsise, thicken.

antonyms dilute, expand.

condensed *adj* abbreviated, abridged, abstracted, capsular, clotted, coagulated, compact, compressed, concentrated, concise, contracted, crystallised, curtailed, distilled, epitomised, evaporated, precipitated, reduced, shortened, shrunken, summarised, thickened.

antonyms diluted, expanded.

condescend *v* bend, deign, patronise, see fit, stoop, submit, unbend, vouchsafe.

condescending *adj* de haut en bas, disdainful, gracious, haughty, imperious, lofty, lordly, patronising, snooty, stooping, supercilious, superior, unbending.

antonyms approachable, humble.

condescension *n* affability, airs, civility, courtesy, deference, disdain, favour, generosity, graciousness, haughtiness, loftiness, lordliness, superciliousness, superiority.

antonym humility.

condign *adj* adequate, apposite, appropriate, deserved, earned, fitting, just, meet, merited, suitable, well-earned, well-merited.

antonym unjust.

condition *n* ailment, arrangement, article, case, caste, circumstances, class, complaint, defect, demand, diathesis, disease, disorder, estate, fettle, fitness, grade, health, infirmity, kilter, level, liability, limitation, malady, modification, nick, obligation, order, plight, position, predicament, prerequisite, problem, provision, proviso, qualification, rank, requirement, requisite, restriction, rule, shape, situation, state, status, stipulation, stratum, terms, trim, understanding, weakness.

v accustom, adapt, adjust, attune, determine, educate, equip, groom, habituate, hone, indoctrinate, inure, limit, prepare, prime, ready, restrict, season, temper, train, tune.

conditional *adj* contingent, dependent, limited, provisional, qualified, relative, restricted, tied.

antonym unconditional.

conditioned *adj* acclimatised, accustomed, adapted, adjusted, attuned, familiarised, groomed, habituated, honed, indoctrinated, inured, prepared, primed, seasoned, tempered, trained, tuned, used.

conditioning *n* acculturation, adjustment, education, familiarisation, grooming, hardening, honing, indoctrination, inurement, preparation, priming, reorientation, seasoning, tempering, training, tuning.

conditions *n* atmosphere, background, circumstances, context, environment, habitat, medium, milieu, setting, situation, state, surroundings.

condolence *n* commiseration, compassion, condolences, consolation, pity, support, sympathy.

antonym congratulation.

condom *n* French letter, johnnie, johnny, protective, rubber, safe, scumbag, sheath.

condone *v* allow, brook, disregard, excuse, forgive, ignore, indulge, overlook, pardon, tolerate.

antonyms censure, disallow.

conducive *adj* advantageous, beneficial, contributive, contributory, encouraging, favourable, helpful, leading, productive, promotive, stimulative, tending.

antonyms adverse, unfavourable.

conduct *n* actions, administration, attitude, bearing, behaviour, carriage, comportment, control, co-ordination, demeanour, deportment, direction, discharge, escort, guidance, guide, leadership, management, manners, mien, orchestration, organisation, running, supervision, ways.

v accompany, acquit, act, administer, attend, bear, behave, carry, chair, comport, control, convey, demean, deport, direct, escort, govern, guide, handle, lead, manage, orchestrate, organise, pilot, regulate, run, solicit, steer, supervise, transact, usher.

conduit *n* canal, channel, chute, culvert, ditch, drain, duct, flume, gutter, lade, main, passage, pipe, rhine, tube, water-course, waterway.

confab *n* blether, chat, chinwag, conclave, confabulation, conference, conversation, discussion, gossip, jaw, natter, powwow, session, talk.

confabulate *v* blether, chat, clash, claver, confer, converse, discuss, gossip, natter, talk.

confederacy *n* alliance, Bund, cabal, coalition, compact, confederation, conspiracy, covenant, federation, junta, league, partnership, union.

confederate *adj* allied, associated, combined, federal, federated.

n abettor, accessory, accomplice, ally, assistant, associate, collaborator, colleague, conspirator, friend, leaguer, partner, practisant, supporter.

v ally, amalgamate, associate, bind, combine, federate, join, merge, unite, weld.

confer *v* accord, award, bestow, consult, converse, deliberate, discourse, discuss, give, grant, impart, lay heads together, lend, parley, powwow, present, talk, vouchsafe.

conference *n* colloquium, confab, confabulation, congress, consultation, convention, convocation, debate, diet, discussion, forum, indaba, meeting, moot, powwow, seminar, symposium, synod, teach-in.

confess *v* acknowledge, admit, affirm, agnise, allow, assert, attest, aver, betray, concede, confide, confirm, declare, disclose, divulge, evince, expose, grant, manifest, own, own up, profess, prove, recognise, reveal, show.

antonyms conceal, deny.

confession *n* acknowledgement, admission, affirmation, assertion, attestation, averment, avowal, confidences, confiteor, declaration, disclosure, divulgence, expose, exposure, profession, revelation, unbosoming, unburdening, verbal.

antonyms concealment, denial.

confidant *n* companion, confidante, crony, duenna, familiar, friend, inseparable, intimate, repository.

confide *v* admit, breathe, confess, disclose, divulge, impart, reveal, unburden, whisper.

antonyms hide, suppress.

confidence *n* aplomb, assurance, belief, boldness, calmness, communication, composure, confession, coolness, courage, credence, dependence, disclosure, divulgence, faith, firmness, morale, nerve, reliance, savoir-faire, secret, self-assurance, self-confidence, self-possession, self-reliance, trust.

antonyms diffidence, distrust.

confident *adj* assured, bold, certain, composed, convinced, cool, dauntless, fearless, persuaded, positive, sanguine, satisfied, secure, self-assured, self-confident, self-possessed, self-reliant, sure, unabashed, unbashful, unselfconscious.

antonyms diffident, sceptical.

confidential *adj* classified, close, closed, faithful, familiar, hush-hush, in camera, intimate, private, privy, secret, tête-à-tête, trusted, trustworthy, trusty.

antonyms common, public.

confidentially *adv* behind closed doors, between you me and the bed-post (lamp-post, gate-post), in camera, in confidence, in privacy, in private, in secret, on the quiet, personally, privately, under the rose, within these four walls.

antonym openly.

configuration *n* arrangement, cast, composition, conformation, contour, deployment, disposition, figure, form, Gestalt, outline, shape.

confine *v* bind, bound, cage, chamber, circumscribe, constrain, cramp, crib, emmew, enclose, immew, immure, imprison, incarcerate, inhibit, intern, keep, keep prisoner, limit, mew, repress, restrain, restrict, shackle, shut up, thirl, trammel.

antonym free.

confined *adj* circumscribed, enclosed, housebound, limited, pokey, poking, restricted.

antonyms free, unrestricted.

confinement *n* accouchement, birth, childbed, childbirth, constraint, custody, delivery, detention, down-lying, gander-month, gander-moon, house-arrest, imprisonment, incarceration, internment, labour, lying-in, parturition, time, travail.

antonym freedom.

confines *n* border, boundaries, bounds, circumference, edge, frontier, limits, perimeter, periphery, precincts.

confirm *v* approve, assure, attest, authenticate, back, buttress, clinch, corroborate, endorse, establish, evidence, fix, fortify, homologate, prove, ratify, reinforce, sanction, settle, strengthen, substantiate, support, validate, verify, witness to.

antonym deny.

confirmation *n* acceptance, agreement, approval, assent, attestation, authentication, backing, clincher, corroboration, endorsement, evidence, proof, ratification, sanction, substantiation, support, testimony, validation, verification, witness.

antonym denial.

confirmed *adj* authenticated, chronic, committed, corroborated, deep-dyed, dyed-in-the-wool, entrenched, established, habitual, hardened, incorrigible, incurable, ingrained, inured, inveterate, irredeemable, long-established, long-standing, proved, proven, rooted, seasoned, substantiated, unredeemed.

antonyms uncommitted, unconfirmed.

confiscate *v* appropriate, commandeer, distrain, escheat, expropriate, impound, remove, seize, sequester, sequestrate.

antonym restore.

confiscation *n* appropriation, distrainment, distraint, escheat, expropriation, forfeiture, impounding, seizure, sequestration, takeover.

antonym restoration.

conflagration *n* blaze, deflagration, fire, hellfire, holocaust, inferno, wildfire.

conflict *n* agony, ambivalence, antagonism, antipathy, Armageddon, battle, brawl, clash, collision, combat, confrontation, contention, contest, difference, disagreement, discord, dissension, encounter, engagement, feud, fight, fracas, friction, hostility, interference, opposition, quarrel, set-to, skirmish, strife, turmoil, unrest, variance, war, warfare.

antonyms agreement, concord.

v battle, clash, collide, combat, contend, contest, contradict, differ, disagree, fight, interfere, oppose, strive, struggle, war, wrangle.

antonym agree.

conflicting *adj* ambivalent, antagonistic, clashing, contradictory, contrary, discordant, inconsistent, opposed, opposing, opposite, paradoxical, turbulent, warring.

antonym compatible.

confluence *n* assemblage, assembly, concourse, concurrence, conflux, conjunction, convergence, crowd, disemboguement, host, junction, meeting, multitude, union, watersmeet.

conform *v* accommodate, accord, adapt, adjust, agree, assimilate, comply, correspond, follow, harmonise, match, obey, quadrate, square, suit, tally, yield.

antonym differ.

conformation *n* anatomy, arrangement, build, composition, configuration, form, framework, Gestalt, outline, shape, structure.

conformist *n* Babbitt, bourgeois, conventionalist, rubber-stamp, stick-in-the-mud, traditionalist, yes-man.

antonyms bohemian, nonconformist.

conformity *n* affinity, agreement, allegiance, Babbitry, compliance, congruity, consonance, conventionalism, conventionality, correspondence, Gleichschaltung, harmony, likeness, observance, orthodoxy, resemblance, similarity, traditionalism.

antonyms difference, nonconformity.

confound *v* abash, amaze, astonish, astound, baffle, bamboozle, bewilder, confuse, contradict, demolish, destroy, discombobulate, dismay, dumbfound, flabbergast, mystify, nonplus, overthrow, overwhelm, perplex, ruin, spif(f)licate, startle, stupefy, surprise, thwart, unshape, upset.

confounded *adj* arrant, astounded, baffled, bewildered, confused, consummate, cursed, discomfited, dismayed, dumbfounded, egregious, embarrassed, flabbergasted, frustrated, insufferable, mystified, nonplussed, notorious, outrageous, perplexed, rank, thwarted.

confront *v* accost, address, appose, beard, brave, challenge, defy, encounter, eyeball, face, front, oppose.

antonym evade.

confrontation *n* battle, collision, conflict, contest, crisis, disagreement, encounter, engagement, face-off, fight, quarrel, set-to, showdown.

confuse *v* abash, addle, baffle, befuddle, bemuse, bewilder, buffalo, burble, confound, darken, demoralise, disarrange, discomfit, discompose, disconcert, discountenance, disorder, disorient, disorientate, embarrass, embrangle, flummox, fluster, intermingle, involve, jumble, maze, mingle, mistake, mix up, mortify, muddle, mystify, nonplus, obscure, perplex, puzzle, rattle, shame, tangle, tie in knots, upset.

antonyms clarify, enlighten, reassure.

confused *adj* addle-brained, addle(d), addle-headed, addle-pated, baffled, bewildered, bushed, chaotic, dazed, desoriente, disarranged, discombobulated, disordered, disorderly, disorganised, disorientated, distracted, embarrassed, flummoxed, fuddled, higgledy-piggledy, jumbled, maffled, mistaken, misunderstood, muddled, muddle-headed, muzzy, nonplussed, perplexed, puzzled, puzzle-headed, streaked, topsy-turvy, tosticated, untidy, upset.

antonym clear.

confusing *adj* ambiguous, baffling, bewildering, complicated, contradictory, cryptic, difficult, inconclusive, inconsistent, involved, misleading, muddling, perplexing, puzzling, tortuous, unclear.

antonyms clear, definite.

confusion *n* abashment, Babel, balls-up, befuddlement, bemusement, bewilderment, bustle, chagrin, chaos, clutter, cock-up, combustion, commotion, demoralisation, disarrangement, discomfiture, disorder, disorganisation, disorientation, distraction, dudder, egarement, embarrassment, embroglio, embroilment, fluster, hotchpotch, hubble-bubble, hugger-mugger, imbroglio, jumble, mess, mix-up, muddle, mystification, overthrow, palaver, perdition, perplexity, perturbation, pie, puzzlement, shambles, shame, tangle, tizz(y), topsyturviness, topsyturvy, topsyturvydom, toss, turmoil, untidiness, upheaval, welter.

antonyms clarity, composure, order.

confute *v* annihilate, confound, controvert, disprove, give the lie to, impune, invalidate, nullify, oppugn, overthrow, overturn, rebut, refute, vitiate.

antonyms confirm, prove.

congeal *v* clot, coagulate, coalesce, concrete, condense, curdle, freeze, fuse, geal, gelatinate, gelatinise, harden, jell, jelly, pectise, set, solidify, stiffen, thicken.

antonyms dissolve, melt, separate.

congealment *n* clotting, coalescence, concretion, condensing, congelation, curdling, freezing, fusion, gelatination, gelatinisation, hardening, jelling, setting, solidification, stiffening, thickening.

antonyms liquefaction, melting, separation.

congenial *adj* agreeable, companionable, compatible, complaisant, cosy, delightful, favourable, friendly, gemütlich, genial, homely, kindly, kindred, like-minded, pleasant, pleasing, relaxing, suitable, sympathetic, well-suited.

antonym disagreeable.

congenital *adj* complete, connate, constitutional, hereditary, inborn, inbred, ingenerate, inherent, inherited, innate, inveterate, natural, thorough, utter.

congested *adj* blocked, clogged, crammed, engorged, full, jammed, overcharged, overcrowded, overfilled, overflowing, overfull, packed, saturated, stuffed, swollen, teeming.

antonym clear.

congestion *n* bottle-neck, clogging, engorgement, fullness, gridlock, jam, log-jam, mass, overcrowding, overfullness, snarl-up, surfeit, traffic-jam.

conglomerate *adj* agglutinated, amassed, clustered, coherent, composite, conglutinated, heterogeneous, massed.

v accumulate, agglomerate, agglutinate, aggregate, amass, assemble, clump, cohere, collect, congregate, foregather, gather, mass.

antonym separate.

n agglomerate, aggregate, composite, congeries, mass, multinational.

conglomeration *n* accumulation, agglomeration, agglutination, aggregation, assemblage, combination, composite, congeries, hotchpotch, mass, medley.

congratulate *v* compliment, felicitate, gratulate.

antonym commiserate.

congratulations *n* compliments, felicitations, good wishes, greetings.

antonyms commiserations, condolences.

congregate *v* accumulate, assemble, bunch, clump, cluster, collect, concentrate, conglomerate, convene, converge, convoke, crowd, flock, foregather, gather, mass, meet, muster, rally, rendezvous, throng.

antonyms dismiss, disperse.

congregation *n* assemblage, assembly, brethren, concourse, crowd, fellowship, flock, host, laity, multitude, parish, parishioners, throng.

congress *n* assembly, conclave, conference, convention, convocation, council, diet, forum, legislature, meeting, parliament, synod.

congruity *n* agreement, coincidence, compatibility, concinnity, concurrence, conformity, congruence, congruousness, consistency, correspondence, harmony, identity, match, parallelism.

antonym incongruity.

conical *adj* cone-shaped, conic, conoid, fastigiate(d), funnel-shaped, infundibular, infundibulate, infundibuliform, pointed, pyramidal, tapered, tapering.

conjectural *adj* academic, assumed, hypothetical, posited, postulated, speculative, supposed, suppositional, surmised, tentative, theoretical.

antonyms factual, real.

conjecture *v* assume, estimate, extrapolate, fancy, guess, hypothesise, imagine, infer, opine, reckon, speculate, suppose, surmise, suspect, theorise.

n assumption, conclusion, estimate, extrapolation, fancy, guess, guesstimate, guesswork, hypothesis, inference, notion, opinion, presumption, projection, speculation, supposition, surmise, theorising, theory.

conjugal *adv* bridal, connubial, epithalamic, hymeneal, marital, married, matrimonial, nuptial, spousal, wedded.

conjunction *n* amalgamation, association, coincidence, combination, concurrence, juxtaposition, syzygy, unification, union, unition.

conjuncture *n* combination, concomitance, concurrence, connection, crisis, crossroads, emergency, exigency, juncture, pass, predicament, simultaneity, stage.

conjure *v* adjure, beseech, bewitch, charm, compel, crave, enchant, entreat, fascinate, implore, importune, invoke, juggle, pray, raise, rouse, summon, supplicate.

conjure up awaken, contrive, create, evoke, excite, produce, recall, recollect.

conjuror, conjurer *n* illusionist, magician, miracle-worker, prestidigitator, prestigiator, sorcerer, thaumaturge, wizard.

conk out break down, collapse, fail, fall asleep.

connect *v* affix, ally, associate, cohere, combine, compaginate, concatenate, couple, enlink, fasten, join, link, relate, unite.

antonym disconnect.

connected *adj* affiliated, akin, allied, associate, associated, bracketed, combined, confederate, coupled, joined, linked, related, united.

antonyms disconnected, unconnected.

connection *n* acquaintance, affinity, alliance, ally, arthrosis, associate, association, attachment, bond, catenation, coherence, commerce, communication, compagination, conjunction, contact, context, correlation, correspondence, coupling, fastening, friend, hook-up, intercourse, interrelation, intimacy, junction, kin, kindred, kinsman, kith, link, marriage, reference, relation, relationship, relative, relevance, sponsor, tie, tie-in, union.

antonym disconnection.

connivance *n* abetment, abetting, collusion, complicity, condoning, consent, jobbery.

connive *v* cabal, coact, collude, complot, conspire, intrigue, plot, scheme.

connive at abet, aid, blink at, condone, disregard, let go, overlook, turn a blind eye to, wink at.

connoisseur *n* aficionado, appreciator, arbiter, authority, buff, cognoscente, devotee, expert, iconophilist, judge, savant, specialist, virtuoso.

connoisseurship *n* virtuosity.

connotation *n* association, colouring, hint, implication, nuance, overtone, significance, suggestion, undertone.

connote *v* betoken, hint at, imply, import, indicate, intimate, involve, purport, signify, suggest.

connubial *adj* conjugal, epithalamic, hymeneal, marital, married, matrimonial, nuptial, wedded.

conquer *v* acquire, annex, beat, best, checkmate, crush, defeat, discomfit, get the better of, humble, master, obtain, occupy, overcome, overpower, overrun, overthrow, prevail, quell, rout, seize, subdue, subjugate, succeed, surmount, triumph, vanquish, win, worst.

antonyms surrender, yield.

conqueror *n* champ, champion, conquistador, defeater, hero, lord, master, number one, subjugator, vanquisher, victor, winner.

conquest *n* acquisition, annexation, appropriation, captivation, coup, defeat, discomfiture, enchantment, enthralment, enticement, invasion, inveiglement, mastery, occupation, overthrow, rout, seduction, subjection, subjugation, takeover, triumph, vanquishment, victory.

conscience *n* ethics, morals, principles, scruples, standards.

conscience-stricken *adj* ashamed, compunctious, contrite, disturbed, guilt-ridden, guilty, penitent, regretful, remorseful, repentant, sorry, troubled.

antonyms unashamed, unrepentant.

conscientious *adj* careful, diligent, exact, faithful, hard-working, high-minded, high-principled, honest, honourable, incorruptible, just, meticulous, moral, painstaking, particular, punctilious, responsible, scrupulous, solicitous, straightforward, strict, thorough, upright.

antonyms careless, irresponsible.

conscious *adj* alert, alive, awake, aware, calculated, cognisant, deliberate, heedful, intentional, knowing, mindful, percipient, premeditated, rational, reasoning, reflective, regardful, responsible, responsive, self-conscious, sensible, sentient, studied, wilful, witting.

antonym unconscious.

consciousness *n* apprehension, awareness, intuition, knowledge, realisation, recognition, sensibility, sentience.

antonym unconciousness.

consecrate *v* beatify, dedicate, devote, exalt, hallow, ordain, revere, sanctify, venerate.

consecutive *adj* chronological, continuous, following, running, sequential, seriatim, succeeding, successive, unbroken, uninterrupted.

antonym discontinuous.

consensus *n* agreement, concord, concurrence, consent, consentience, harmony, unanimity, unity.

antonym disagreement.

consent *v* accede, acquiesce, admit, agree, allow, approve, assent, comply, concede, concur, grant, homologate, permit, yield.

antonyms oppose, refuse.

n accordance, acquiescence, agreement, approval, assent, compliance, concession, concurrence, consentience, go-ahead, green light, permission, sanction.

antonyms opposition, refusal.

consequence *n* account, concern, distinction, effect, eminence, end, event, fall-out, import, importance, interest, issue, moment, notability, note, outcome, portent, rank, repercussion, repute, result, side effect, significance, standing, status, upshot, value, weight.

antonym cause.

consequent *adj* ensuing, following, resultant, resulting, sequent, sequential, subsequent, successive.

consequential *adj* arrogant, bumptious, conceited, consequent, eventful, far-reaching, grave, important, impressive, indirect, inflated, momentous, noteworthy, pompous, pretentious, resultant, self-important, serious, significant, supercilious, vainglorious, weighty.

antonyms inconsequential, unimportant.

consequently *adv* accordingly, consequentially, ergo, hence, inferentially, necessarily, subsequently, therefore, thus.

conservation *n* custody, ecology, economy, guardianship, husbandry, keeping, maintenance, preservation, protection, safeguarding, safe-keeping, saving, upkeep.

antonyms destruction, neglect, waste.

conservatism *n* conservativeness, conventionalism, orthodoxy, traditionalism, via trita, via truta.

antonym radicalism.

conservative *adj* cautious, conventional, die-hard, establishmentarian, guarded, hidebound, middle-of-the-road, moderate, quiet, reactionary, right-wing, sober, Tory, traditional, unexaggerated, unprogressive, verkrampte.

antonyms left-wing, radical.

n diehard, moderate, moss-back, reactionary, right-winger, stick-in-the-mud, Tory, traditionalist.

antonyms left-winger, radical.

conservatory *n* academy, conservatoire, glasshouse, greenhouse, hothouse, institute.

conserve *v* guard, hoard, husband, keep, maintain, nurse, preserve, protect, save.

antonyms squander, use, waste.

consider *v* believe, bethink, cogitate, consult, contemplate, count, deem, deliberate, discuss, examine, judge, meditate, mull over, muse, perpend, ponder, rate, reflect, regard, remember, respect, revolve, ruminate, study, think, weigh.

antonym ignore.

considerable *adj* abundant, ample, appreciable, big, comfortable, distinguished, goodly, great, important, influential, large, lavish, marked, much, noteworthy, noticeable, plentiful, reasonable, renowned, significant, siz(e)able, substantial, tidy, tolerable, venerable.

antonyms insignificant, slight.

considerably *adv* abundantly, appreciably, greatly, markedly, much, noticeably, remarkably, significantly, substantially.

antonym slightly.

considerate *adj* attentive, charitable, circumspect, concerned, discreet, forbearing, gracious, kind, kindly, mindful, obliging, patient, solicitous, tactful, thoughtful, unselfish.

antonyms selfish, thoughtless.

consideration *n* analysis, attention, cogitation, concern, considerateness, contemplation, deliberation, discussion, examination, factor, fee, friendliness, issue, kindliness, kindness, meditation, payment, perquisite, point, recompense, reflection, regard, remuneration, respect, review, reward, rumination, scrutiny, solicitude, study, tact, thought, thoughtfulness, tip.

antonyms disdain, disregard.

consign *v* commit, convey, deliver, devote, entrust, hand over, relegate, seal, ship, sign, transfer, transmit.

consignment *n* assignment, batch, cargo, committal, delivery, dispatch, distribution, goods, load, relegation, sending, shipment, transmittal.

consist of amount to, comprise, contain, embody, embrace, include, incorporate, involve.

consist in inhere, lie, reside.

consistency *n* accordance, agreement, coherence, compactness, compatibility, concordance, congruity, constancy, correspondence, density, evenness, firmness, harmony, identity, regularity, sameness, steadfastness, steadiness, thickness, uniformity, viscosity.

antonym inconsistency.

consistent *adj* accordant, agreeing, coherent, compatible, congruous, consonant, constant, dependable, harmonious, logical, of a piece, persistent, regular, steady, unchanging, undeviating, unfailing, uniform.

antonyms erratic, inconsistent.

consolation *n* aid, alleviation, assuagement, cheer, comfort, ease, easement, encouragement, help, relief, solace, succour, support.

antonym discouragement.

console *v* assuage, calm, cheer, comfort, encourage, hearten, solace, soothe.

antonyms agitate, upset.

consolidate *v* affiliate, amalgamate, cement, combine, compact, condense, confederate, conjoin, federate, fortify, fuse, harden, join, reinforce, secure, solidify, stabilise, strengthen, thicken, unify, unite.

consolidation *n* affiliation, alliance, amalgamation, association, compression, condensation, confederation, federation, fortification, fusion, reinforcement, strengthening.

consonance *n* accord, agreement, compatibility, concord, conformity, congruence, congruity, consistency, correspondence, harmony, suitableness.

antonym dissonance.

consonant *adj* accordant, according, compatible, concordant, congruous, consistent, correspondent, harmonious, suitable.

antonym dissonant.

consort *n* associate, companion, fellow, helpmate, helpmeet, husband, partner, spouse, wife.

v accord, agree, associate, correspond, fraternise, harmonise, jibe, mingle, mix, square, tally.

conspectus *n* abstract, compendium, digest, epitome, outline, precis, report, resume, review, statement, summary, survey, syllabus, synopsis.

conspicuous *adj* apparent, blatant, clear, discernible, evident, flagrant, flashy, garish, glaring, kenspeck(le), manifest, noticeable, obvious, patent, perceptible, remarked, showy, visible.

antonym inconspicuous.

conspiracy *n* cabal, collusion, complot, confederacy, fix, frame-up, intrigue, league, machination, omerta, plot, scheme, treason.

conspirator *n* caballer, conspirer, highbinder, intriguer, plotter, practisant, schemer, traitor.

conspire *v* cabal, collude, combine, complot, concur, conduce, confederate, contribute, contrive, co-operate, devise, hatch, intrigue, machinate, manoeuvre, plot, scheme, tend, treason.

constancy *n* determination, devotion, faithfulness, fidelity, firmness, fixedness, loyalty, permanence, perseverance, regularity, resolution, stability, steadfastness, steadiness, tenacity, uniformity.

antonyms inconstancy, irregularity.

constant *adj* attached, ceaseless, changeless, continual, continuous, dependable, determined, devoted, dogged, endless, eternal, even, everlasting, faithful, firm, fixed, habitual, immutable, incessant, interminable, invariable, loyal, never-ending, non-stop, permanent, perpetual, persevering, persistent, regular, relentless, resolute, stable, staunch, steadfast, steady, sustained, tried-and-true, true, trustworthy, trusty, unalterable, unbroken, unchangeable, unfailing, unflagging, uniform, uninterrupted, unrelenting, unremitting, unshaken, unvarying, unwavering.

antonyms fickle, fitful, irregular, occasional, variable.

constantly *adv* always, continually, continuously, endlessly, everlastingly, incessantly, interminably, invariably, non-stop, perpetually, relentlessly, steadfastly, uniformly.

antonym occasionally.

consternation *n* alarm, amazement, anxiety, awe, bewilderment, confusion, dismay, disquietude, distress, dread, fear, fright, horror, panic, perturbation, shock, terror, trepidation.

antonym composure.

constituent *adj* basic, component, elemental, essential, inherent, integral, intrinsic.

n bit, component, element, essential, factor, ingredient, part, portion, principle, section, unit.

antonym whole.

constitute *v* appoint, authorise, commission, compose, comprise, create, delegate, depute, empower, enact, establish, fix, form, found, inaugurate, make, name, nominate, ordain.

constitution *n* build, character, composition, configuration, construction, disposition, establishment, form, formation, habit, health, make-up, nature, organisation, physique, structure, temper, temperament.

constitutional *adj* chartered, congenital, immanent, inborn, inherent, innate, intrinsic, organic, statutory, vested.

n airing, promenade, stroll, turn, walk.

constrain *v* bind, bulldoze, chain, check, coerce, compel, confine, constrict, curb, drive, force, impel, necessitate, oblige, pressure, pressurise, railroad, restrain, urge.

constrained *adj* embarrassed, forced, guarded, inhibited, reserved, reticent, stiff, subdued, uneasy, unnatural.

antonyms free, relaxed.

constraint *n* check, coaction, coercion, compulsion, curb, damper, deterrent, duress, force, hindrance, limitation, necessity, pressure, restraint, restriction.

constrict *v* choke, compact, compress, constringe, contract, cramp, inhibit, limit, narrow, pinch, restrict, shrink, squeeze, strangle, strangulate, tighten.

antonym expand.

constriction *n* blockage, compression, constraint, constringency, cramp, impediment, limitation, narrowing, pressure, reduction, restriction, squeezing, stenosis, stricture, tightening, tightness.

antonym expansion.

construct *v* assemble, build, compose, create, design, elevate, engineer, erect, establish, fabricate, fashion, form, formulate, found, frame, knock together, make, manufacture, model, organise, raise, shape.

antonyms demolish, destroy.

construction *n* assembly, building, composition, constitution, creation, edifice, erection, fabric, fabrication, figure, form, formation, model, organisation, shape, structure.

antonym destruction.

constructive *adj* advantageous, beneficial, helpful, positive, practical, productive, useful, valuable.

antonyms destructive, negative, unhelpful.

construe *v* analyse, decipher, deduce, explain, expound, infer, interpret, parse, read, render, take, translate.

consult *v* ask, commune, confer, consider, debate, deliberate, interrogate, parley, powwow, question, regard, respect.

consultant *n* adviser, authority, expert, specialist.

consultation *n* appointment, colloquy, conference, council, deliberation, dialogue, discussion, examination, hearing, interview, meeting, parley, session.

consumables *n* comestibles, eatables, fungibles.

consume *v* absorb, annihilate, decay, demolish, deplete, destroy, devastate, devour, discuss, dissipate, drain, eat, employ, engulf, envelop, exhaust, expend, gobble, guzzle, lessen, ravage, spend, squander, swallow, use (up), utilise, vanish, waste, wear out.

consumed *adj* absorbed, devoured, dominated, engrossed, monopolised, obsessed, preoccupied.

consumer *n* buyer, customer, end-user, purchaser, shopper, user.

consuming *adj* absorbing, compelling, devouring, dominating, engrossing, excruciating, gripping, immoderate, monopolising, overwhelming, tormenting.

consummate *v* accomplish, achieve, cap, compass, complete, conclude, crown, effectuate, end, finish, fulfil, perfect, perform, terminate.

adj absolute, accomplished, complete, conspicuous, distinguished, finished, matchless, perfect, polished, practised, skilled, superb, superior, supreme, total, transcendent, ultimate, unqualified, utter.

antonym imperfect.

consummation *n* achievement, actualisation, completion, culmination, end, fulfilment, perfection, realisation, termination.

consumption *n* consuming, decay, decline, decrease, depletion, destruction, diminution, dissipation, emaciation, exhaustion, expenditure, loss, phthisis, tabefaction, tabes, TB, tuberculosis, use, utilisation, waste.

contact *n* acquaintance, approximation, association, communication, connection, contiguity, contingence, impact, junction, juxtaposition, meeting, tangency, touch, union.

v approach, call, get hold of, notify, phone, reach, ring.

contagious *adj* catching, communicable, epidemic, epizootic, infectious, pestiferous, pestilential, spreading, transmissible, zymotic.

contain *v* accommodate, check, comprehend, comprise, control, curb, embody, embrace, enclose, entomb, hold, include, incorporate, involve, limit, repress, restrain, seat, stifle.

antonym exclude.

container *n* holder, hopper, receptacle, repository, vessel.

contaminate *v* adulterate, befoul, besmirch, corrupt, debase, defile, deprave, infect, pollute, soil, stain, sully, taint, tarnish, vitiate.

antonym purify.

contamination *n* adulteration, contagion, corruption, decay, defilement, desecration, filth, foulness, impurity, infection, poisoning, pollution, rottenness, taint, vitiation.

antonym purification.

contemplate *v* behold, cerebrate, consider, deliberate, design, envisage, examine, expect, eye, foresee, inspect, intend, mean, meditate, mull over, observe, plan, ponder, propose, reflect on, regard, ruminate, scrutinise, study, survey, view.

contemplation *n* cerebration, cogitation, consideration, deliberation, examination, inspection, meditation, musing, observation, pondering, reflection, reverie, rumination, scrutiny, survey, thought, viewing.

contemplative *adj* cerebral, intent, introspective, meditative, musing, pensive, rapt, reflective, ruminative, thoughtful.

antonyms impulsive, thoughtless.

contemporary *adj* à la mode, coetaneous, coeval, co-existent, co-existing, concurrent, contemporaneous, conterminous, coterminous, current, latest, modern, newfangled, present, present-day, recent, synchronous, ultra-modern, up-to-date, up-to-the-minute, with it.

antonyms preceding, succeeding.

contempt *n* condescension, contumely, derision, despite, detestation, disdain, disgrace, dishonour, disregard, disrespect, floccinaucinihilipilification, humiliation, loathing, mockery, neglect, scorn, shame, slight.

antonyms admiration, regard.

contemptible *adj* abject, base, cheap, degenerate, despicable, detestable, ignominious, loathsome, low, low-down, mean, paltry, pitiful, scurvy, shabby, shameful, vile, worthless, wretched.

antonyms admirable, honourable.

contemptuous *adj* arrogant, cavalier, condescending, contumacious, contumelious, cynical, derisive, disdainful, haughty, high and mighty, insolent, insulting, scornful, sneering, supercilious, tossy, withering.

antonyms humble, polite, respectful.

contemptuously *adv* arrogantly, de haut en bas, derisively, disdainfully, haughtily, insolently, pompously, scornfully, superciliously.

antonyms humbly, politely, respectfully.

contend *v* affirm, allege, argue, assert, aver, avow, clash, compete, contest, cope, debate, declare, dispute, emulate, grapple, hold, jostle, litigate, maintain, skirmish, strive, struggle, vie, wrestle.

content[1] *v* appease, delight, gladden, gratify, humour, indulge, mollify, pacify, placate, please, reconcile, satisfy, suffice.

antonym displease.

n comfort, contentment, delight, ease, gratification, happiness, peace, pleasure, satisfaction.

antonym discontent.

adj agreeable, comfortable, contented, fulfilled, pleased, satisfied, untroubled.

antonym dissatisfied.

content[2] *n* burden, capacity, essence, gist, ideas, load, matter, meaning, measure, significance, size, subject matter, substance, text, thoughts, volume.

contented *adj* cheerful, comfortable, complacent, content, glad, gratified, happy, placid, pleased, relaxed, satisfied, serene, thankful.

antonym discontented.

contention *n* affirmation, allegation, argument, assertion, asseveration, belief, claim, competition, contest, controversy, debate, declaration, discord, dispute, dissension, enmity, feuding, ground, hostility, idea, opinion, position, profession, rivalry, stand, strife, struggle, thesis, view, wrangling.

contentious *adj* antagonistic, argumentative, bickering, captious, cavilling, combative, controversial, cross, debat(e)able, disputatious, factious, hostile, litigious, peevish, perverse, pugnacious, quarrelsome, querulous, wrangling.

antonyms co-operative, peaceable, uncontroversial.

contentment *n* comfort, complacency, content, contentedness, ease, equanimity, fulfilment, gladness, gratification, happiness, peace, peacefulness, placidity, pleasure, repletion, satisfaction, serenity.

antonym dissatisfaction.

contents *n* chapters, constituents, divisions, elements, ingredients, items, load, parts, subjects, themes, topics.

contest *n* affray, altercation, battle, combat, competition, concours, conflict, controversy, debate, discord, dispute, encounter, fight, game, match, olympiad, set-to, shock, struggle, tournament, trial.

v argue against, challenge, compete, contend, debate, deny, dispute, doubt, fight, litigate, oppose, question, refute, strive, vie.

contestant *n* agonist, aspirant, candidate, competitor, contender, entrant, participant, player.

context *n* ambience, associations, background, circumstances, conditions, connection, frame of reference, framework, relation, situation.

contiguous *adj* abutting, adjacent, adjoining, beside, bordering, conjoining, conterminous, juxtaposed, juxtapositional, near, neighbouring, next, tangential, touching.

antonyms distort, separate.

continence *n* abstemiousness, abstinence, asceticism, celibacy, chastity, moderation, self-control, self-restraint, sobriety, temperance.

antonym incontinence.

continent *adj* abstemious, abstinent, ascetic, austere, celibate, chaste, pure, restrained, self-restrained, sober, virginal.

antonym incontinent.

contingency *n* accident, arbitrariness, chance, emergency, event, eventuality, fortuity, happening, incident, juncture, possibility, randomness, uncertainty.

contingent *n* batch, body, bunch, company, complement, deputation, detachment, group, mission, quota, section, set.

continual *adj* ceaseless, constant, continuous, endless, eternal, everlasting, frequent, incessant, interminable, oft-repeated, perpetual, recurrent, regular, repeated, repetitive, unbroken, unceasing, uninterrupted, unremitting.

antonyms intermittent, occasional, temporary.

continually *adv* always, ceaselessly, constantly, endlessly, eternally, everlastingly, forever, incessantly, interminably, non-stop, perpetually, persistently, repeatedly.

antonym occasionally.

continuance *n* continuation, duration, endurance, period, permanence, protraction, term.

continuation *n* addition, appendix, epilogue, extension, furtherance, maintenance, perpetuation, postscript, prolongation, resumption, sequel, supplement.

antonyms cessation, termination.

continue *v* abide, aby(e), adjourn, carry on, endure, extend, go on, last, lengthen, maintain, persevere, persist, proceed, project, prolong, pursue, reach, recommence, remain, rest, resume, stay, stick at, survive, sustain.

antonyms discontinue, stop.

continuing *adj* abiding, enduring, lasting, on-going, progressing, sustained.

continuity *n* cohesion, connection, extension, flow, interrelationship, linkage, progression, sequence, succession.

antonym discontinuity.

continuous *adj* connected, consecutive, constant, continued, extended, non-stop, prolonged, unbroken, unceasing, undivided, uninterrupted.

antonyms discontinuous, intermittent, sporadic.

contort *v* convolute, deform, disfigure, distort, gnarl, knot, misshape, squirm, twist, warp, wrench, wriggle, writhe.

contortionist *n* acrobat, gymnast, posture-maker, posture-master, tumbler.

contour *n* aspect, character, contorno, curve, figure, form, lines, outline, profile, relief, shape, silhouette.

contraband *adj* banned, black-market, bootleg, forbidden, hot, illegal, illicit, interdicted, prohibited, proscribed, smuggled, unlawful, verboten.

contract *v* abbreviate, abridge, acquire, agree, arrange, bargain, catch, clinch, close, compress, condense, confine, constrict, constringe, covenant, curtail, develop, dwindle, engage, epitomise, incur, lessen, narrow, negotiate, pledge, purse, reduce, shrink, shrivel, stipulate, tighten, wither, wrinkle.

antonyms enlarge, expand, lengthen.

n agreement, arrangement, bargain, bond, commission, commitment, compact, concordat, convention, covenant, deal, engagement, handfast, instrument, pact, settlement, stipulation, transaction, treaty, understanding.

contraction *n* abbreviation, astringency, compression, constriction, cramp, diminution, elision, narrowing, reduction, retrenchment, shortening, shrinkage, shrivelling, tensing, tightening.

antonyms expansion, growth.

contradict *v* belie, challenge, contravene, controvert, counter, counteract, deny, disaffirm, dispute, gainsay, impugn, negate, oppose.

antonyms agree, confirm, corroborate.

contradiction *n* conflict, confutation, contravention, denial, disaffirmance, disaffirmation, gainsay, Hibernicism, incongruity, inconsistency, negation, opposite.

antonyms agreement, confirmation, corroboration.

contradictory *adj* antagonistic, antithetical, conflicting, contrary, discrepant, dissident, double-mouthed, incompatible, inconsistent, irreconcilable, opposed, opposite, paradoxical, repugnant, unreconciled.

antonym consistent.

contraption *n* apparatus, contrivance, device, gadget, gizmo, mechanism, rig, thingumajig, widget.

contrary *adj* adverse, antagonistic, arsy-versy, awkward, balky, cantankerous, clashing, contradictory, counter, cross-grained, cussed, difficult, discordant, disobliging, froward, hostile, inconsistent, inimical, intractable, intractible, obstinate, opposed, opposite, paradoxical, perverse, stroppy, thrawn, unaccommodating, wayward, wilful.

antonyms like, obliging, similar.

n antithesis, converse, opposite, reverse.

contrast *n* comparison, contraposition, contrariety, counter-view, difference, differentiation, disparity, dissimilarity, distinction, divergence, foil, opposition, set-off.

antonym similarity.

v compare, differ, differentiate, discriminate, distinguish, oppose, set off.

contravene *v* break, contradict, counteract, cross, disobey, hinder, infract, infringe, interfere, oppose, refute, thwart, transgress, trespass, violate.

antonym uphold.

contretemps *n* accident, calamity, difficulty, hitch, misadventure, misfortune, mishap, mistake, predicament.

contribute *v* add, afford, bestow, conduce, dob in, donate, furnish, give, help, kick in, lead, provide, subscribe, supply, tend.

antonyms subtract, withhold.

contribution *n* addition, bestowal, donation, gift, grant, gratuity, handout, input, offering, subscription.

contributor *n* backer, benefactor, bestower, conferrer, correspondent, donor, freelance, freelancer, giver, journalist, patron, reporter, subscriber, supporter.

contrite *adj* chastened, conscience-stricken, guilt-ridden, humble, penitent, penitential, penitentiary, regretful, remorseful, repentant, sorrowful, sorry.

contrition *n* compunction, humiliation, penitence, remorse, repentance, sackcloth and ashes, self-reproach, sorrow.

contrivance *n* apparatus, appliance, artifice, contraption, design, device, dodge, equipment, excogitation, expedient, fabrication, formation, gadget, gear, implement, intrigue, invention, inventiveness, knack, machination, machine, measure, mechanism, plan, plot, project, ruse, scheme, stratagem, trick.

contrive *v* arrange, compass, concoct, construct, create, design, devise, effect, engineer, excogitate, fabricate, frame, improvise, invent, manage, manoeuvre, plan, plot, scheme, wangle.

contrived *adj* artificial, elaborate, false, forced, laboured, mannered, overdone, planned, recherche, strained, unnatural.

antonym natural.

control *v* boss, bridle, check, command, conduct, confine, constrain, contain, curb, determine, direct, dominate, govern, lead, limit, manage, manipulate, master, monitor, oversee, pilot, regiment, regulate, repress, restrain, rule, run, stage-manage, steer, subdue, superintend, supervise, suppress, verify.

n authority, brake, charge, check, clutches, command, curb, direction, dirigism(e), discipline, governance, government, guidance, jurisdiction, leading-strings, leash, limitation, management, mastery, oversight, regulation, rule, superintendence, supervision, supremacy.

controller *n* administrator, captain, compère, director, executive, executor, gerent, governor, gubernator, manager, marshal, navigator, pilot, ringmaster, ruler, steward.

controversial *adj* attacking, contentious, controvertible, debatable, disputable, disputed, doubtful, polemic, polemical, questionable.

controversy *n* altercation, argument, contention, debate, disagreement, discussion, dispute, dissension, polemic, quarrel, squabble, strife, war of words, wrangle, wrangling.

antonyms accord, agreement.

controvert *v* argue, challenge, contest, contradict, counter, debate, deny, disaffirm, discuss, dispute, gainsay, oppose, refute, wrangle.

contumacious *adj* haughty, headstrong, insubordinate, intractable, intransigent, mulish, obdurate, obstinate, perverse, pig-headed, rebellious, recalcitrant, refractory, stiff-necked, stubborn, wilful.

antonym obedient.

contumely *n* abuse, affront, arrogance, contempt, derision, disdain, humiliation, incivility, indignity, insolence, insult, invective, obloquy, opprobrium, rudeness, scorn, superciliousness.

contusion *n* bruise, bump, discolouration, injury, knock, lump, swelling.

conundrum *n* anagram, brain-teaser, enigma, poser, problem, puzzle, riddle.

convalescence *n* improvement, recovery, recuperation, rehabilitation, restoration.

convene *v* assemble, call, collect, congregate, convoke, gather, meet, muster, rally, summon.

convenience *n* accessibility, accommodation, advantage, amenity, appliance, appropriateness, availability, benefit, chance, comfort, ease, enjoyment, facility, fitness, handiness, help, leisure, opportuneness, opportunity, satisfaction, service, serviceability, suitability, timeliness, use, usefulness, utility.

convenient *adj* accessible, adapted, advantageable, appropriate, at hand, available, beneficial, commodious, fit, fitted, handy, helpful, labour-saving, nearby, opportune, seasonable, serviceable, suitable, suited, timely, useful, utile, well-timed.

antonyms awkward, inconvenient.

convention *n* agreement, assembly, bargain, code, compact, conclave, concordat, conference, congress, contract, convocation, council, custom, delegates, etiquette, formality, matter of form, meeting, pact, practice, propriety, protocol, representatives, stipulation, synod, tradition, treaty, understanding, usage.

conventional *adj* accepted, arbitrary, bourgeois, common, commonplace, copybook, correct, customary, decorous, expected, formal, formalist, habitual, hackneyed, hidebound, iconic, nomic, normal, ordinary, orthodox, pedestrian, prevailing, prevalent, proper, prosaic, regular, ritual, routine, run-of-the-mill, standard, stereotyped, straight, stylised, traditional, unoriginal, uptight, usual, wonted.

antonyms exotic, unconventional, unusual.

converge *v* approach, coincide, combine, concentrate, concur, focus, gather, join, meet, merge, mingle.

antonyms disperse, diverge.

convergence *n* approach, blending, coincidence, concentration, concurrence, confluence, conflux, conjunction, intersection, junction, meeting, merging, mingling, union.

antonym divergence.

conversant with acquainted with, apprised of, au fait with, experienced in, familiar with, informed about, knowledgeable about, practised in, proficient in, skilled in, versant with, versed in.

antonym ignorant of.

conversation *n* chat, chinwag, chitchat, colloquy, communication, communion, confab, confabulation, conference, converse, dialogue, discourse, discussion, exchange, gossip, intercourse, interlocution, powwow, talk, tête-à-tête.

conversational *adj* chatty, colloquial, communicative, confabulatory, informal, relaxed.

conversationalist *n* deipnosophist, table-philosopher.

converse[1] *v* chat, colloquise, commune, confabulate, confer, discourse, talk.

converse[2] *n* antithesis, contrary, counterpart, obverse, opposite, reverse.

adj antipodal, antipodean, contrary, counter, opposite, reverse, reversed, transposed.

conversion *n* adaptation, alteration, change, metamorphosis, metanoia, modification, permutation, proselytisation, rebirth, reconstruction, reformation, regeneration, remodelling, reorganisation, transfiguration, transformation, transmogrification, transmutation.

convert *v* adapt, alter, apply, appropriate, baptise, change, convince, interchange, metamorphose, modify, permute, proselytise, reform, regenerate, remodel, reorganise, restyle, revise, save, transform, transmogrify, transmute, transpose, turn.

n catechumen, disciple, neophyte, proselyte, vert.

convertible *adj* adaptable, adjustable, exchangeable, interchangeable, permutable.

convex *adj* bulging, gibbous, protuberant, rounded, tumid.

antonym concave.

convey *v* bear, bequeath, bring, carry, cede, communicate, conduct, deliver, demise, devolve, disclose, fetch, forward, grant, guide, impart, lease, move, relate, reveal, send, steal, support, tell, transfer, transmit, transport, waft, will.

conveyance *n* carriage, movement, shipment, transfer, transference, transmission, transport, transportation, tran(s)shipment, vehicle, wagonage.

convict *v* attaint, condemn, imprison, sentence.

n con, criminal, culprit, felon, forçat, jail-bird, lag, malefactor, prisoner.

conviction *n* assurance, belief, certainty, certitude, confidence, convincement, creed, earnestness, faith, fervour, firmness, opinion, persuasion, plerophory, principle, reliance, tenet, view.

convince *v* assure, confirm, persuade, reassure, satisfy, sway, win over.

convincing *adj* cogent, conclusive, credible, impressive, incontrovertible, likely, luculent, persuasive, plausible, powerful, probable, telling, verisimiliar.

antonyms dubious, improbable.

convivial *adj* back-slapping, cheerful, festive, friendly, fun-loving, gay, genial, hearty, hilarious, jolly, jovial, lively, merry, mirthful, sociable.

antonym taciturn.

conviviality *n* bonhomie, cheer, cordiality, festivity, gaiety, geniality, jollification, jollity, joviality, liveliness, merrymaking, mirth, sociability.

convocation *n* assemblage, assembly, conclave, concourse, congregation, congress, convention, council, diet, for(e)gathering, meeting, muster, synod.

convoke *v* assemble, collect, convene, gather, muster, rally, round up, summon.

convoluted *adj* complex, complicated, gyrose, involved, meandering, tangled, twisting, winding.

antonym straightforward.

convolution *n* coil, coiling, complexity, contortion, curlicue, gyrus, helix, intricacy, involution, loop, sinousness, sinuosity, spiral, tortuousness, twist, undulation, volution, whorl, winding.

convoy *n* attendance, attendant, escort, fleet, guard, protection, train.

convulsion *n* agitation, commotion, contortion, contraction, cramp, disturbance, eruption, fit, furore, outburst, paroxysm, seizure, shaking, spasm, throe, tremor, tumult, turbulence, upheaval.

convulsive *adj* churning, fitful, jerky, paroxysmal, spasmodic, spastic, sporadic, twitchy, violent.

cook *n* chef, chef de cuisine, confectioner, cuisinier, pastrycook.

v bake, boil, braise, broil, fry, grill, heat, prepare, roast, saute, simmer, steam, stew, toast.

cook up brew, concoct, contrive, devise, fabricate, improvise, invent, plan, plot, prepare, scheme.

cool *adj* aloof, apathetic, audacious, bold, brazen, calm, cheeky, chilled, chilling, chilly, coldish, collected, composed, cosmopolitan, degage, deliberate, dispassionate, distant, down-beat, elegant, frigid, impertinent, imperturbable, impudent, incurious, indifferent, laid-back, level-headed, lukewarm, nippy, offhand, placid, pleasant, presumptuous, quiet, refreshing, relaxed, reserved, satisfying, self-controlled, self-possessed, serene, shameless, sophisticated, stand-offish, together, uncommunicative, unconcerned, unemotional, unenthusiastic, unexcited, unfriendly, unheated, uninterested, unresponsive, unruffled, unwelcoming, urbane.

antonyms excited, friendly, hot, warm.

v abate, allay, assuage, calm, chill, dampen, defuse, fan, freeze, lessen, moderate, quiet, refrigerate, temper.

antonyms excite, heat, warm.

n calmness, collectedness, composure, control, poise, sangfroid, self-control, self-discipline, self-possession, temper.

cooling *n* air-conditioning, chilling, defervescence, defervescency, refrigeration, ventilation.

antonyms heating, warming.

adj freezing, refrigerant, refrigerative, refrigeratory.

antonym warming.

coop *n* box, cage, enclosure, hutch, mew, pen, pound.

v cage, confine, immure, impound, imprison, intern, pen.

co-operate *v* abet, aid, assist, collaborate, combine, concur, conduce, conspire, contribute, co-ordinate, help, play along, play ball.

co-operation *n* assistance, coaction, collaboration, concert, concurrence, give-and-take, helpfulness, participation, responsiveness, synergy, teamwork, unity.

co-operative *adj* accommodating, coactive, collective, combined, concerted, co-ordinated, helpful, joint, obliging, responsive, shared, supportive, synergetic, synergic, unified, united.

antonym unco-operative.

co-ordinate *v* codify, correlate, grade, graduate, harmonise, integrate, match, mesh, organise, relate, synchronise, systematise, tabulate.

adj coequal, correlative, correspondent, equal, equipotent, equivalent, parallel, reciprocal.

cop out abandon, desert, dodge, evade, quit, renege, renounce, revoke, shirk, skip, skive, withdraw.

cope *v* carry on, get by, make (a) shift, make do, manage, survive.

cope with contend with, deal with, dispatch, encounter, grapple with, handle, manage, struggle with, tangle with, tussle with, weather, wrestle with.

copious *adj* abundant, ample, bounteous, bountiful, extensive, exuberant, full, generous, great, huge, inexhaustible, lavish, liberal, luxuriant, overflowing, plenteous, plentiful, profuse, rich, superabundant.

antonyms meagre, scarce.

copiousness *n* abundance, amplitude, bountifulness, bounty, cornucopia, exuberance, fullness, lavishness, luxuriance, plenitude, plentifulness, plenty, prodigality, profusion, richness, superabundance.

antonym scarcity.

cop-out *n* alibi, dodge, evasion, fraud, pretence, pretext.

copulate *v* bonk, cover, enjoy, fuck, gender, horse, know, line, make love, mate, serve, tread.

copulation *n* carnal knowledge, coition, coitus, congress, coupling, covering, joining, love, lovemaking, mating, serving, sex, sexual intercourse, treading.

copy *n* apograph, archetype, autotype, borrowing, calque, carbon copy, counterfeit, crib, duplicate, ectype, engrossment, exemplar, facsimile, fax, flimsy, forgery, image, imitation, likeness, loan translation, loan-word, model, Ozalid®, pattern, photocopy, Photostat®, plagiarisation, print, replica, replication, representation, reproduction, tenor, tracing, transcript, transcription, Xerox®.

antonym original.

v ape, borrow, counterfeit, crib, duplicate, echo, emulate, engross, exemplify, extract, facsimile, follow, imitate, mimic, mirror, parrot, personate, photocopy, Photostat®, plagiarise, repeat, replicate, reproduce, simulate, transcribe, Xerox®.

coquettish *adj* amorous, arch, come-hither, coy, dallying, flighty, flirtatious, flirty, inviting, teasing, vampish.

cord *n* bond, connection, funicle, gimp, line, link, rope, strand, string, tie, twine.

cordial *adj* affable, affectionate, agreeable, cheerful, earnest, friendly, genial, heartfelt, hearty, invigorating, pleasant, restorative, sociable, stimulating, warm, warm-hearted, welcoming, whole-hearted.

antonyms aloof, cool, hostile.

cordiality *n* affability, affection, amiability, friendliness, geniality, goodwill, heartiness, sincerity, warmth, whole-heartedness.

antonyms coolness, hostility.

cordon *n* barrier, chain, fence, line, ring.

cordon off encircle, enclose, fence off, isolate, separate, surround.

core *n* centre, crux, essence, germ, gist, heart, kernel, nitty-gritty, nub, nucleus, pith.

antonyms exterior, perimeter, surface.

corner *n* angle, bend, cantle, cavity, cranny, crook, hide-away, hideout, hidey-hole, hole, joint, neuk, niche, nook, pickle, predicament, recess, retreat, spot.

corny *adj* banal, cliched, commonplace, dull, feeble, hackneyed, maudlin, mawkish, old-fashioned, platitudinous, sentimental, stale, stereotyped, trite.

antonyms new, original.

corollary *n* conclusion, consequence, deduction, fall-out, illation, induction, inference, result, upshot.

corporal *adj* anatomical, bodily, carnal, concrete, corporeal, fleshly, material, physical, somatic, tangible.

antonym spiritual.

corporate *adj* allied, amalgamated, collaborative, collective, combined, communal, concerted, joint, merged, pooled, shared, united.

corporation[1] *n* association, authorities, body, combine, conglomerate, council, society.

corporation[2] *n* beer belly, paunch, pod, pot, pot-belly, spare tyre.

corporeal *adj* actual, bodily, fleshly, human, hylic, material, mortal, physical, substantial, tangible.

antonym spiritual.

corps *n* band, body, brigade, company, contingent, crew, detachment, division, phalanx, regiment, squad, squadron, team, troop, unit.

corpse *n* body, cadaver, carcass, deader, remains, skeleton, stiff.

corpulence *n* adiposity, blubber, burliness, embonpoint, fatness, fleshiness, obesity, plumpness, portliness, rotundity, stoutness, tubbiness.

antonym thinness.

corpulent *adj* adipose, beefy, bulky, burly, fat, fattish, fleshy, large, lusty, obese, overweight, plump, poddy, podgy, portly, pot-bellied, pudgy, roly-poly, rotund, stout, tubby, well-padded.

antonym thin.

corpus *n* aggregation, body, collection, compilation, entirety, oeuvre, whole.

corral *n* coop, enclosure, fold, kraal, pound, stall, sty.

correct *v* adjust, admonish, amend, blue-pencil, chasten, chastise, chide, counterbalance, cure, debug, discipline, emend, emendate, improve, punish, rectify, redress, reform, regulate, remedy, reprimand, reprove, right.

adj acceptable, accurate, appropriate, comme il faut, diplomatic, equitable, exact, faultless, fitting, flawless, jake, just, OK, precise, proper, regular, right, seemly, standard, strict, true, well-formed, word-perfect.

antonyms inaccurate, incorrect, wrong.

correction *n* adjustment, admonition, alteration, amendment, castigation, chastisement, discipline, emendation, improvement, modification, punishment, rectification, reformation, reproof, righting.

corrective *adj* curative, disciplinary, emendatory, medicinal, palliative, penal, punitive, reformatory, rehabilitative, remedial, restorative, therapeutic.

correctly *adv* accurately, aright, faithfully, faultlessly, perfectly, precisely, properly, right, rightly.

antonyms incorrectly, wrongly.

correctness *n* accuracy, breeding, civility, decorum, exactitude, exactness, faithfulness, faultlessness, fidelity, perfection, preciseness, precision, propriety, regularity, seemliness, truth.

correlate *v* associate, compare, connect, co-ordinate, correspond, equate, interact, link, parallel, relate, tie in.

correlation *n* alternation, correspondence, equivalence, interaction, interchange, interdependence, interrelationship, link, reciprocity, relationship.

correspond *v* accord, agree, answer, coincide, communicate, complement, concur, conform, correlate, dovetail, fit, harmonise, match, square, tally, write.

correspondence *n* agreement, analogy, assonance, coincidence, communication, comparability, comparison, concurrence, conformity, congruity, correlation, equivalence, fitness, harmony, homology, homotypy, letters, mail, match, post, relation, resemblance, respondence, responding, similarity, writing.

antonyms divergence, incongruity.

correspondent *n* contributor, journalist, penpal, reporter, writer.

adj analogous, comparable, equivalent, like, matching, parallel, reciprocal, similar.

corresponding *adj* accordant, analogous, answering, collateral, complementary, correlative, correspondent, equivalent, homologous, homotypal, homotypic, identical, interrelated, matching, reciprocal, similar, synonymous.

corridor *n* aisle, ambulatory, foyer, hallway, lobby, passage, passageway, vestibule.

corroborate *v* authenticate, bear out, confirm, document, endorse, establish, prove, ratify, substantiate, support, sustain, underpin, validate.

antonym contradict.

corroborative *adj* confirmative, confirmatory, evidential, evidentiary, supportive, verificatory.

corrode *v* canker, consume, corrupt, crumble, deteriorate, disintegrate, eat away, erode, fret, impair, oxidise, rust, waste, wear away.

corrosive *adj* abrasive, acid, acrid, biting, caustic, consuming, corroding, cutting, incisive, mordant, sarcastic, trenchant, venomous, virulent, wasting, wearing.

corrugated *adj* channelled, creased, crinkled, fluted, furrowed, grooved, puckered, ribbed, ridged, rumpled, striate(d), wrinkled.

corrupt *adj* abandoned, adulterate(d), altered, bent, bribed, contaminated, crooked, debased, decayed, defiled, degenerate, demoralised, depraved, dishonest, dishonoured, dissolute, distorted, doctored, falsified, fraudulent, infected, polluted, profligate, putrescent, putrid, rotten, shady, tainted, unethical, unprincipled, unscrupulous, venal, vicious.

antonyms honest, trustworthy, upright.

v adulterate, barbarise, bribe, canker, contaminate, debase, debauch, defile, demoralise, deprave, doctor, empoison, entice, fix, infect, lure, pervert, putrefy, seduce, spoil, square, suborn, subvert, taint, vitiate.

antonym purify.

corruption *n* adulteration, baseness, bribery, bribing, crookedness, debasement, decadence, decay, defilement, degeneration, degradation, demoralisation, depravity, dishonesty, distortion, doctoring, evil, extortion, falsification, fiddling, foulness, fraud, fraudulence, fraudulency, graft, immorality, impurity, infection, iniquity, jobbery, leprosy, malversation, perversion, pollution, profiteering, profligacy, putrefaction, putrescence, rot, rottenness, shadiness, sinfulness, turpitude, ulcer, unscrupulousness, venality, vice, viciousness, virus, wickedness.

antonyms honesty, purification.

corset *n* belt, bodice, check, corselet, curb, curtailment, foundation garment, girdle, limit, limitation, panty girdle, restriction, stays.

cortège *n* cavalcade, column, entourage, parade, procession, retinue, suite, train.

cosmetic *adj* non-essential, superficial, surface.
antonym essential.

cosmetics *n* grease paint, make-up, maquillage, pancake.

cosmic *adj* boundless, grandiose, huge, illimitable, immense, infinite, limitless, measureless, universal, vast.

cosmopolitan *adj* catholic, international, sophisticated, universal, unprejudiced, urbane, well-travelled, worldly, worldy-wise.
antonyms insular, parochial, rustic.

cosmos *n* creation, galaxy, system, universe, world.

cosset *v* baby, cherish, coddle, cuddle, mollycoddle, pamper, pet.

cost *n* amount, charge, damage, deprivation, detriment, disbursement, expenditure, expense, figure, harm, hurt, injury, loss, outlay, payment, penalty, price, rate, sacrifice, worth.

costly *adj* catastrophic, damaging, dear, deleterious, disastrous, excessive, exorbitant, expensive, extortionate, gorgeous, harmful, highly-priced, lavish, loss-making, luxurious, opulent, precious, priceless, pricy, rich, ruinous, sacrificial, splendid, steep, sumptuous, valuable.
antonyms cheap, inexpensive.

costs *n* budget, expenses, oncosts, outgoings, overheads.

costume *n* apparel, attire, clothing, dress, ensemble, garb, get-up, livery, outfit, raiment, robes, uniform, vestment.

cosy *adj* comfortable, comfy, homelike, homely, intimate, secure, sheltered, snug, warm.
antonyms cold, uncomfortable.

coterie *n* camp, caucus, cenacle, circle, clique, galère, gang, group, outfit, set.

cottage *n* bothy, bungalow, but-and-ben, cabin, chalet, cot, hut, lodge, shack.

couch *v* bear, cradle, express, frame, phrase, support, utter, word.
n bed, chaise-longue, chesterfield, day-bed, divan, lounge, ottoman, settee, sofa.

cough *n* bark, hack, tussis.
v bark, hack, harrumph, hawk, hem, hoast.
cough up deliver, fork out, give, hand over, pay, pay out, shell out, surrender.

council *n* assembly, board, cabinet, chamber, committee, conclave, conference, congress, consistory, consult, convention, convocation, diet, divan, ministry, panchayat, panel, parliament, soviet, syndicate, synod, volost.

counsel *n* admonition, advice, advocate, attorney, barrister, caution, consideration, consultation, deliberation, direction, forethought, guidance, information, lawyer, plan, purpose, recommendation, solicitor, suggestion, warning.
v admonish, advise, advocate, caution, direct, exhort, guide, instruct, recommend, suggest, urge, warn.

counsellor *n* adviser, attorney, councillor, lawyer, representative, vizier, wazir.

count *v* add, ascribe, calculate, check, compute, consider, deem, enumerate, esteem, estimate, hold, impute, include, judge, list, matter, number, rate, reckon, regard, score, signify, tally, tell, think, tot up, total, weigh.
n addition, calculation, computation, enumeration, numbering, poll, reckoning, sum, tally, total.
count for nothing cut no ice, make no difference.
count on bank on, believe, depend on, expect, reckon on, rely on, trust.
count out exclude, include out.
antonym include.

countenance *n* acquiescence, aid, air, appearance, approval, aspect, assistance, backing, demeanour, endorsement, expression, face, favour, features, help, look, mien, physiognomy, sanction, support, visage.
v abet, acquiesce, agree to, aid, approve, back, brook, champion, condone, encourage, endorse, endure, help, sanction, support, tolerate.

counter[1] *adv* against, contrarily, contrariwise, conversely, in opposition.
adj adverse, against, antithetical, conflicting, contradictory, contrary, contrasting, obverse, opposed, opposing, opposite.
antonyms concurring, corroborating.
v answer, meet, offset, parry, resist, respond, retaliate, retort, return.

counter[2] *n* coin, disc, jet(t)on, marker, tiddlywink, token.

counteract *v* act against, annul, check, contravene, counterbalance, countervail, cross, defeat, foil, frustrate, hinder, invalidate, negate, neutralise, offset, oppose, resist, thwart, undo.
antonyms assist, support.

counterbalance *v* balance, compensate for, counterpoise, countervail, equalise, neutralise, offset.

counterfeit *v* copy, fabricate, fake, feign, forge, imitate, impersonate, phoney, pretend, sham, simulate.
adj bogus, Brummagem, copied, ersatz, faked, false, feigned, forged, fraudulent, imitation, phoney, postiche, pretend(ed), pseud, pseudo, sham, simular, simulated, simulate(d), spurious, supposititious.
antonym genuine.
n copy, fake, forgery, fraud, imitant, imitation, phantasm(a), phoney, reproduction, sham.

countermand *v* abrogate, annul, cancel, override, repeal, rescind, reverse, revoke.

counterpart *n* complement, copy, correlative, duplicate, equal, fellow, homologue, homotype, match, mate, opposite number, supplement, tally, twin, vis-à-vis.

countless *adj* endless, immeasurable, incalculable, infinite, innumerable, legion, limitless, measureless, multitudinous, myriad, numberless, uncounted, unnumbered, unsummed, untold.

antonym limited.

countrified *adj* agrestic, arcadian, bucolic, hick, homespun, idyllic, pastoral, provincial, rural, rustic.

antonyms oppidan, urban.

country *n* backwoods, boondocks, citizenry, citizens, clime, commonwealth, community, countryside, electors, farmland, fatherland, green belt, homeland, inhabitants, kingdom, land, motherland, nation, nationality, outback, outdoors, part, people, populace, provinces, public, realm, region, society, sovereign state, state, sticks, terrain, territory, voters.

adj agrarian, agrestic, arcadian, bucolic, georgic, landed, pastoral, provincial, rude, rural, rustic.

antonyms oppidan, urban.

countryman *n* bumpkin, compatriot, farmer, fellow countryman, hayseed, hind, husbandman, peasant, provincial, rustic, swain, yokel.

countryside *n* country, farmland, green belt, landscape, outback, outdoors, panorama, sticks.

county *n* airt, comitatus, district, province, region, shire.

coup *n* accomplishment, action, blow, coup d'etat, deed, exploit, feat, manoeuvre, masterstroke, putsch, revolution, stratagem, stroke, stunt, tour de force.

coup de grâce clincher, come-uppance, death-blow, kibosh, kill, quietus.

coup d'etat coup, overthrow, palace revolution, putsch, rebellion, revolt, revolution, takeover, uprising.

couple *n* brace, Darby and Joan, duo, dyad, pair, span, team, twain, twosome, yoke.

v accompany, buckle, clasp, conjoin, connect, copulate, fornicate, hitch, join, link, marry, pair, unite, wed, yoke.

coupon *n* billet, card, certificate, check, slip, ticket, token, voucher.

courage *n* boldness, bottle, bravery, daring, dauntlessness, fearlessness, firmness, fortitude, gallantry, grit, guts, hardihood, heroism, mettle, moxie, nerve, pluck, resolution, spirit, spunk, stomach, valour.

antonym cowardice.

courageous *adj* audacious, bold, brave, daring, dauntless, dreadless, fearless, gallant, gutsy, hardy, heroic, high-hearted, indomitable, intrepid, lion-hearted, plucky, resolute, stout-hearted, valiant, valorous.

antonym cowardly.

courier *n* bearer, carrier, emissary, envoy, estafette, guide, herald, legate, messenger, nuncio, pursuivant, representative, runner.

course *n* advance, advancement, channel, circuit, circus, classes, continuity, current, curriculum, development, diadrom, direction, duration, flight-path, flow, furtherance, hippodrome, lap, lapse, lectures, line, march, method, mode, movement, orbit, order, passage, passing, path, piste, plan, policy, procedure, programme, progress, progression, race, race-course, race-track, raik, regimen, road, round, route, schedule, sequence, series, studies, succession, sweep, syllabus, tack, term, time, track, trail, trajectory, unfolding, vector, voyage, way, wheel.

v chase, dash, flow, follow, gush, hunt, move, pour, pursue, race, run, scud, scurry, speed, stream, surge, tumble.

court *n* attendants, bailey, bar, bench, cloister, cortège, courtyard, durbar, entourage, hall, Hof, law-court, manor, palace, piazza, plaza, quad, quadrangle, retinue, square, suite, train, tribunal, yard.

v attract, chase, cultivate, date, flatter, incite, invite, lionise, pander to, prompt, provoke, pursue, seek, serenade, solicit, woo.

courteous *adj* affable, attentive, ceremonious, civil, considerate, courtly, debonair, elegant, gallant, gracious, mannerly, obliging, polished, polite, refined, respectful, urbane, well-bred, well-mannered.

antonyms discourteous, rude.

courtesan *n* call girl, Delilah, demi-mondaine, fille de joie, harlot, hetaira, kept woman, lorette, mistress, paramour, prostitute, scarlet woman, whore, woman of easy virtue, woman of the night, woman of the town.

courtesy *n* affability, attention, benevolence, breeding, civility, comity, consent, consideration, courteousness, courtliness, elegance, favour, gallantness, gallantry, generosity, gentilesse, graciousness, indulgence, kindness, manners, polish, politeness, urbanity.

antonyms discourtesy, rudeness.

courtier *n* attendant, chamberlain, follower, henchman, lady, lord, major-domo, noble, nobleman, page, pursuivant, squire, steward, sycophant, toady, train-bearer.

courtly *adj* affable, aristocratic, aulic, ceremonious, chivalric, chivalrous, civil, decorous, dignified, elegant, flattering, formal, gallant, high-bred, lordly, obliging, polished, polite, refined, stately.

antonyms inelegant, provincial, rough.

courtyard *n* area, cortile, enclosure, patio, peristyle, playground, quad, quadrangle, yard.

cove *n* anchorage, bay, bight, creek, estuary, fiord, firth, frith, harbour, inlet, sound.

covenant *n* arrangement, bargain, bond, commitment, compact, concordat, contract, convention, deed, engagement, pact, pledge, promise, stipulation, treaty, trust, undertaking.

v agree, bargain, contract, engage, pledge, promise, stipulate, undertake.

cover *v* balance, camouflage, canopy, clad, cloak, clothe, coat, compensate, comprehend, comprise, conceal, consider, contain, counterbalance, curtain, daub, defend, describe, detail, disguise, dress, eclipse, embody, embrace, encase, encompass, enshroud, envelop, examine, guard, hide, hood, house, include, incorporate, insure, invest, investigate, involve, layer, mantle, mask, narrate, obscure, offset, overlay, overspread, protect, recount, reinforce, relate, report, screen, secrete, shade, sheathe, shelter, shield, shroud, suffuse, survey, veil.

n bedspread, binding, camouflage, canopy, cap, case, cloak, clothing, coating, compensation, concealment, confederate, covering, cover-up, defence, disguise, dress, envelope, façade, front, guard, indemnity, insurance, jacket, lid, mask, payment, pretence, pretext, protection, refuge, reimbursement, sanctuary, screen, sheath, shelter, shield, smoke, spread, top, undergrowth, veil, woods, wrapper.

cover up coat, conceal, cover, dissemble, dissimulate, encrust, envelop, hide, hush up, plaster, repress, stonewall, suppress, swathe, whitewash.

antonym uncover.

coverage *n* analysis, assurance, description, insurance, protection, reportage, reporting, treatment.

covering *n* blanket, capping, casing, cloak, clothing, coating, cocoon, cope, cover, exoskeleton, housing, integument, layer, mask, masking, overlay, protection, sheath, shelter, tegmen, tegument, top, umbrella, wash, wrap, wrappage, wrapper, wrapping.

adj accompanying, descriptive, explanatory, introductory, masking, obscuring, protective.

covert *adj* clandestine, concealed, disguised, dissembled, hidden, private, secret, sneaky, stealthy, subreptitious, surreptitious, ulterior, under the table, underhand, unsuspected, veiled.

antonym open.

cover-up *n* complicity, concealment, conspiracy, dissemblance, dissimulation, front, pretence, smoke-screen, whitewash.

covet *v* after, begrudge, crave, desire, envy, fancy, hanker, long for, lust after, thirst for, want, yearn for, yen for.

antonym abjure.

covetous *adj* acquisitive, avaricious, close-fisted, envious, grasping, greedy, insatiable, jealous, mercenary, rapacious, thirsting, yearning.

antonyms generous, temperate.

covey *n* bevy, cluster, flight, flock, group, nide, nye, skein.

cow *v* awe, break, browbeat, bulldoze, bully, daunt, dishearten, dismay, domineer, frighten, intimidate, overawe, scare, subdue, terrorise, unnerve.

antonym encourage.

coward *n* caitiff, chicken, craven, dastard, faint-heart, funk, hilding, nithing, poltroon, recreant, renegade, scaredy-cat, skulker, sneak, viliaco, viliago, yellow-belly, yellow-dog.

antonym hero.

cowardice *n* faint-heartedness, fear, funk, gutlessness, pusillanimity, spinelessness.

antonyms courage, valour.

cowardly *adj* base, caitiff, chicken, chicken-hearted, chicken-livered, craven, dastard(ly), faint-hearted, fearful, gutless, hilding, lily-livered, nesh, nithing, pusillanimous, recreant, scared, shrinking, soft, spineless, timorous, unheroic, weak, weak-kneed, white-livered, yellow, yellow-bellied.

antonym courageous.

cowboy *n* bronco-buster, buckaroo, cattleman, cowhand, cowpoke, cowpuncher, drover, gaucho, herder, herdsman, rancher, ranchero, stockman, vaquero, waddy, wrangler.

cower *v* cringe, crouch, flinch, grovel, quail, ruck, shake, shiver, shrink, skulk, tremble.

coxcomb *n* beau, Beau Brummell, dandy, dude, exquisite, fop, Jack-a-dandy, jackanapes, macaroni, peacock, popinjay, princox, swell.

coy *adj* arch, backward, bashful, coquettish, demure, diffident, evasive, flirtatious, kittenish, maidenly, modest, prudish, reserved, retiring, self-effacing, shrinking, shy, skittish, timid, virginal.

antonyms forward, impudent, sober.

coyness *n* affectation, archness, bashfulness, coquettishness, demureness, diffidence, evasiveness, modesty, primness, prudery, prudishness, reserve, shyness, skittishness, timidity.

antonyms forwardness, impudence.

cozen *v* bamboozle, bilk, cheat, circumvent, con, deceive, diddle, double-cross, dupe, finagle, gull, hoodwink, inveigle, swindle, trick.

crabbed *adj* acid, acrid, acrimonious, awkward, bad-tempered, captious, churlish, crabby, cross, cross-grained, crotchety, cynical, difficult, fretful, grouchy, harsh, ill-humoured, ill-tempered, iracund, iracundulous, irascible, irritable, misanthropic, morose, perverse, petulant, prickly, snappish, snappy, sour, splenetic, surly, tart, testy, tough, trying.

antonyms calm, placid.

crack *v* break, buffet, burst, chap, chip, chop, cleave, clip, clout, collapse, crackle, crash, craze, cuff, decipher, detonate, explode, fathom, fracture, pop, ring, rive, slap, snap, solve, splinter, split, succumb, thump, wallop, whack, yield.

n attempt, blow, breach, break, buffet, burst, chap, chink, chip, clap, cleft, clip, clout, cranny, crash, craze, crevasse, crevice, cuff, dig, expert, explosion, fent, fissure, flaw, fracture, gag, gap, go, insult, interstice, jibe, joke, moment, opportunity, pop, quip, report, rift, slap, smack, snap, stab, thump, try, wallop, whack, wisecrack, witticism.

adj ace, choice, elite, excellent, first-class, first-rate, hand-picked, superior, top-notch.

crack down on act against, check, clamp down on, end, put a stop to, stop.

crack up break down, collapse, go crackers, go crazy, go to pieces.

crackdown *n* clampdown, crushing, end, repression, stop, suppression.

cracked *adj* bats, batty, broken, chipped, crackbrained, crackpot, crazed, crazy, daft, damaged, defective, deranged, eccentric, faulty, fissured, flawed, imperfect, insane, loony, nuts, nutty, rent, split, torn.

antonyms flawless, perfect, sane.

crackers *adj* cracked, crazy, daft, foolish, idiotic, loony, mad, nuts.

antonym sane.

crackle *v* crepitate, decrepitate, rustle.

n crepitation, crepitus, decrepitation, rustle.

crackpot *n* crackbrain, idiot, loony, nut, nutter.

cradle *n* bassinet, bed, beginning, berceau, birthplace, cot, crib, fount, fountain-head, holder, incunabula, origin, rest, source, spring, stand, well-spring.

v bear, couch, hold, lull, nestle, nurse, rock, support, tend.

craft *n* ability, aircraft, aptitude, art, artfulness, artifice, artistry, barque, boat, business, calling, cleverness, contrivance, craftiness, cunning, deceit, dexterity, duplicity, employment, expertise, expertness, guile, handicraft, handiwork, ingenuity, knack, know-how, line, occupation, plane, pursuit, ruse, scheme, ship, shrewdness, skill, spacecraft, spaceship, stratagem, subterfuge, subtlety, technique, trade, trickery, vessel, vocation, wiles, work, workmanship.

antonyms naïvety, openness.

craftiness *n* artfulness, astuteness, canniness, cunning, deceit, deviousness, double-dealing, duplicity, foxiness, guile, shrewdness, slyness, subtlety, trickiness, underhandedness, vulpinism, wiliness.

antonyms naïvety, openness.

craftsman *n* artificer, artisan, maker, master, opificer, smith, technician, wright.

craftsmanship *n* artistry, expertise, facture, mastery, technique, workmanship.

crafty *adj* artful, astute, calculating, canny, cunning, deceitful, designing, devious, duplicitous, foxy, fraudulent, guileful, insidious, knowing, machiavellian, scheming, sharp, shrewd, sly, subtle, tricksy, tricky, versute, vulpine, wily.

antonyms naïve, open.

crag *n* aiguille, bluff, cliff, peak, pinnacle, rock, tor(r).

craggy *adj* broken, brusque, cragged, jagged, jaggy, precipitous, rocky, rough, rugged, stony, surly, uneven.

antonyms pleasant, smooth.

cram *v* bag, compact, compress, con, crowd, crush, force, glut, gorge, gormandise, grind, guzzle, jam, mug up, overcrowd, overeat, overfeed, overfill, pack, press, ram, satiate, shove, squeeze, stodge, study, stuff, swot.

cramming *n* gavage, gluttony, gormandise, gourmandise, greed, packing, pressing, stuffing.

cramp[1] *v* check, circumscribe, clog, confine, constrain, encumber, frustrate, hamper, hamstring, handicap, hinder, impede, inhibit, obstruct, restrict, shackle, stymie, thwart, tie.

cramp[2] *n* ache, contraction, convulsion, crick, pain, pang, pins and needles, spasm, stiffness, stitch, twinge.

cramped *adj* awkward, circumscribed, confined, congested, crowded, incapacious, jam-packed, narrow, overcrowded, packed, restricted, riggling, squashed, squeezed, squeezy, tight, uncomfortable.

antonym spacious.

crane *n* block and tackle, davit, derrick, hoist, tackle, winch.

crank *n* eccentric, loony, madman, nutter.

cranky *adj* bizarre, capricious, crabbed, cross, crotchety, dotty, eccentric, erratic, Fifish, freakish, freaky, funny, idiosyncratic, irritable, odd, peculiar, prickly, queer, quirky, strange, surly, viewy, wacky.

antonyms normal, placid, sensible.

cranny *n* chink, cleavage, cleft, crack, crevice, fissure, gap, hole, interstice, nook, opening.

crash *n* accident, bang, bankruptcy, boom, bump, clang, clash, clatter, clattering, collapse, collision, debacle (debâcle), depression, din, downfall, failure, fragor, jar, jolt, pile-up, prang, racket, ruin, smash, smashing, smash-up, thud, thump, thunder, wreck.

v bang, break, bump, collapse, collide, dash, disintegrate, fail, fall, fold (up), fracture, fragment, go bust, go under, hurtle, lurch, overbalance, pitch, plunge, prang, shatter, shiver, smash, splinter, sprawl, topple.

adj concentrated, emergency, immediate, intensive, round-the-clock, telescoped, urgent.

crass *adj* asinine, blundering, boorish, bovine, coarse, dense, doltish, gross, indelicate, insensitive, lumpish, oafish, obtuse, stupid, tactless, unrefined, unsubtle, witless.

antonyms refined, sensitive.

crate *n* box, case, container, packing case, packing-box, tea-chest.

crave *v* ask, beg, beseech, desire, entreat, fancy, hanker after, hunger after, implore, long for, need, petition, pine for, require, seek, solicit, supplicate, thirst for, want, yearn for, yen for.

antonyms dislike, spurn.

craven *adj* caitiff, chicken-hearted, cowardly, dastardly, fearful, lily-livered, mean-spirited, nithing, pusillanimous, scared, spiritless, timorous, unheroic, weak, whey-faced, yellow.

antonym courageous.

n caitiff, coward, dastard, nithing, poltroon, recreant.

antonyms hero, renegade, yellow-belly.

craving *n* appetence, appetency, appetite, cacoethes, desire, hankering, hunger, longing, lust, thirst, urge, yearning, yen.

antonyms dislike, distaste.

craw *n* crop, gizzard, gullet, maw, oesophagous, throat.

crawl *v* creep, cringe, drag, eat crow, eat dirt, eat humble pie, fawn, grovel, inch, slither, swarm, teem, toady, truckle, wriggle, writhe.

craze *n* dernier cri, enthusiasm, fad, fashion, frenzy, infatuation, mania, mode, novelty, obsession, passion, preoccupation, rage, thing, trend, vogue.

v bewilder, confuse, dement, derange, distemper, distract, enrage, infatuate, inflame, madden, unbalance, unhinge.

crazed *adj* demented, maddened, maenadic, possessed.

antonym sane.

crazy *adj* absurd, ardent, bananas, barmy, bats, batty, berserk, bird-brained, bizarre, bonkers, cockeyed, cracked, crazed, cuckoo, daffy, daft, delirious, demented, deranged, derisory, devoted, dippy, eager, eccentric, enamoured, enthusiastic, fanatical, fantastic, fatuous, foolhardy, foolish, fruity, half-baked, hysterical, idiotic, ill-conceived, impracticable, imprudent, inane, inappropriate, infatuated, insane, irresponsible, ludicrous, lunatic, mad, maniacal, mental, nonsensical, nuts, nutty, odd, off one's rocker, outrageous, passionate, peculiar, pixil(l)ated, potty, preposterous, puerile, quixotic, ridiculous, scatty, senseless, short-sighted, silly, smitten, strange, touched, unbalanced, unhinged, unrealistic, unwise, unworkable, up the pole, wacky, weird, wild, zany, zealous.

antonyms sane, sensible.

creak *v* grate, grind, groan, rasp, scrape, scratch, screak, screech, squeak, squeal.

creaky *adj* creaking, grating, rasping, rusty, screaky, squeaking, squeaky, unoiled.

cream *n* best, cosmetic, crème de la crème, elite, emulsion, essence, flower, liniment, lotion, oil, ointment, paste, pick, prime, salve, the four hundred, unguent.

creamy *adj* buttery, cream-coloured, creamed, lush, milky, off-white, oily, rich, smooth, soft, velvety.

crease *v* corrugate, crimp, crinkle, crumple, fold, pucker, ridge, ruckle, rumple, wrinkle.

n bulge, corrugation, crumple, fold, groove, line, overlap, pucker, ridge, ruck, ruckle, rumple, tuck, wrinkle.

create *v* appoint, beget, cause, coin, compose, concoct, constitute, design, develop, devise, engender, establish, form, formulate, found, generate, hatch, initiate, install, institute, invent, invest, make, occasion, originate, produce, set up, sire, spawn.

antonym destroy.

creation *n* achievement, brainchild, chef d'oeuvre, concept, conception, concoction, constitution, cosmos, development, establishment, fathering, formation, foundation, generation, genesis, handiwork, inception, institution, invention, life, magnum opus, making, nature, origination, pièce de resistance, procreation, production, siring, universe, world.

antonym destruction.

creative *adj* adept, artistic, clever, fertile, gifted, imaginative, ingenious, inspired, inventive, original, productive, resourceful, stimulating, talented, visionary.

antonym unimaginative.

creativity *n* artistry, cleverness, fecundity, fertility, imagination, imaginativeness, ingenuity, inspiration, inventiveness, originality, resourcefulness, talent, vision.

antonym unimaginativeness.

creator *n* architect, auteur, author, begetter, demiurge, demiurgus, designer, father, framer, God, initiator, inventor, maker, originator.

creature *n* animal, beast, being, body, brute, character, critter, dependant, fellow, hanger-on, henchman, hireling, individual, instrument, lackey, man, minion, mortal, person, puppet, retainer, soul, toady, tool, wight, woman, wretch.

credence *n* belief, confidence, credit, dependence, faith, reliance, support, trust.

antonym distrust.

credentials *n* accreditation, attestation, authorisation, card, certificate, deed, diploma, docket, endorsement, letters of credence, licence, missive, passport, permit, recommendation, reference, testament, testimonial, title, voucher, warrant.

credibility *n* believableness, integrity, likeliness, plausibility, probability, reliability, tenability, trustworthiness.

antonym implausibility.

credible *adj* believable, conceivable, convincing, dependable, honest, imaginable, likely, persuasive, plausible, possible, probable, reasonable, reliable, sincere, supposable, tenable, thinkable, trustworthy, trusty.

antonyms implausible, unreliable.

credit *n* acclaim, acknowledgement, approval, belief, character, clout, commendation, confidence, credence, distinction, esteem, estimation, faith, fame, glory, honour, influence, kudos, merit, position, praise, prestige, recognition, regard, reliance, reputation, repute, standing, status, thanks, tribute, trust.

antonym discredit.

v accept, believe, buy, subscribe to, swallow, trust.

antonym disbelieve.

creditable *adj* admirable, commendable, deserving, estimable, excellent, exemplary, good, honourable, laudable, meritorious, praiseworthy, reputable, respectable, sterling, worthy.

antonyms blameworthy, shameful.

creditor *n* debtee. dun, lender.

credulity *n* credulousness, dupability, gullibility, naïvety, silliness, simplicity, stupidity.

antonym scepticism.

credulous *adj* dupable, green, gullible, naïve, trusting, uncritical, unsuspecting, unsuspicious, wide-eyed.

antonym sceptical.

creed *n* articles, belief, canon, catechism, confession, credo, doctrine, dogma, faith, persuasion, principles, tenets.

creek *n* bay, bight, brook, cove, fiord, firth, frith, inlet, rivulet, stream, streamlet, tributary, voe, watercourse.

creep *v* bootlick, cower, crawl, cringe, dawdle, drag, edge, fawn, grovel, inch, insinuate, kowtow, scrape, skulk, slink, slither, snail, sneak, squirm, steal, tiptoe, toady, truckle, worm, wriggle, writhe.

n bootlicker, Jack Nasty, jerk, sneak, sycophant, toady.

creeper *n* climber, liana, plant, rambler, runner, trailing vine.

creepy *adj* awful, direful, disturbing, eerie, frightening, ghoulish, gruesome, hair-raising, horrible, macabre, menacing, nightmarish, ominous, scary, sinister, spookish, spooky, terrifying, threatening, unearthly, unpleasant, weird.

antonyms normal, pleasant.

crescent-shaped *adj* bow-shaped, falcate(d), falciform, lunate(d), lunular, sickle-shaped.

crest *n* aigrette, apex, badge, caruncle, cockscomb, coma, comb, crown, device, emblem, head, height, insignia, mane, panache, peak, pinnacle, plume, ridge, summit, symbol, tassel, top, topknot, tuft.

crestfallen *adj* chopfallen, dejected, depressed, despondent, disappointed, disconsolate, discouraged, disheartened, dispirited, downcast, downhearted, woebegone.

antonym elated.

crevasse *n* abyss, bergschrund, chasm, cleavage, cleft, crack, fissure, gap.

crevice *n* chink, cleavage, cleft, crack, cranny, fissure, fracture, gap, hole, interstice, opening, rent, rift, slit, split.

crew *n* assemblage, band, bunch, company, complement, corps, crowd, galère, gang, hands, henchmen, herd, horde, lot, lower deck, mob, pack, party, posse, set, squad, swarm, team, troop.

crib *n* bassinet, bed, bin, borrowing, box, bunker, cot, cradle, key, manger, plagiarism, rack, stall, translation.

v borrow, cheat, copy, pinch, pirate, plagiarise, purloin, steal.

crick *n* convulsion, cramp, pain, spasm, stiffness, twinge.

v jar, rax, rick, sprain, twist, wrench.

crime *n* atrocity, corruption, delinquency, fault, felony, flagitiousness, guilt, illegality, iniquity, law-breaking, malefaction, malfeasance, misconduct, misdeed, misdemeanour, offence, outrage, sin, transgression, trespass, unrighteousness, vice, villainy, violation, wickedness, wrong, wrong-doing.

criminal *n* con, convict, crook, culprit, delinquent, evil-doer, felon, fraudsman, infractor, jail-bird, law-breaker, malefactor, offender, sinner, transgressor.

adj bent, corrupt, crooked, culpable, deplorable, felonious, flagitious, foolish, illegal, immoral, indictable,. iniquitous, lawless, malfeasant, nefarious, peccant, preposterous, ridiculous, scandalous, senseless, unlawful, unrighteous, vicious, villainous, wicked, wrong.

antonyms honest, upright.

cringe *v* bend, blench, bootlick, bow, cower, crawl, creep, crouch, dodge, duck, fawn, flinch, grovel, kneel, kowtow, quail, quiver, recoil, shrink, shy, sneak, start, stoop, submit, toady, tremble, truckle, wince.

crinkle *n* curl, fold, pucker, ruffle, rumple, rustle, scallop, twist, wave, wrinkle.

v crimp, crimple, crumple, curl, fold, pucker, ruffle, rumple, rustle, scallop, twist, wrinkle.

crinkly *adj* curly, fluted, frizzy, furrowed, gathered, kinky, puckered, ruffled, scalloped, wrinkled, wrinkly.

antonyms smooth, straight.

cripple *v* cramp, damage, debilitate, destroy, disable, enfeeble, halt, hamstring, impair, incapacitate, lame, maim, mutilate, paralyse, ruin, sabotage, spoil, vitiate, weaken.

crippled *adj* deformed, disabled, enfeebled, handicapped, incapacitated, invalid, lame, paralysed.

crisis *n* calamity, catastrophe, climacteric, climax, confrontation, conjuncture, crunch, crux, culmination, difficulty, dilemma, disaster, emergency, exigency, extremity, height, impasse, mess, pinch, plight, predicament, quandary, strait, trouble.

crisp *adj* bracing, brief, brisk, brittle, brusque, clear, crispy, crumbly, crunchy, decisive, firm, forthright, fresh, incisive, invigorating, neat, orderly, pithy, refreshing, short, smart, snappy, spruce, succinct, tart, terse, tidy, vigorous.

antonyms flabby, limp, vague.

criterion *n* bench-mark, canon, gauge, measure, norm, precedent, principle, proof, rule, shibboleth, standard, test, touchstone, yardstick.

critic *n* analyst, animadverter, arbiter, Aristarch, attacker, authority, carper, caviller, censor, censurer, commentator, connoisseur, detractor, expert, expositor, fault-finder, feuilletonist, judge, knocker, Momus, pundit, reviewer, reviler, ultracrepidarian, vilifier, Zoilist.

critical *adj* accurate, all-important, analytical, captious, carping, cavilling, censorious, climacteric, crucial, dangerous, deciding, decisive, derogatory, diagnostic, disapproving, discerning, discriminating, disparaging, fastidious, fault-finding, grave, hairy, high-priority, judgemental, judicious, momentous, nagging, niggling, nit-picking, penetrating, perceptive, perilous, pivotal, precarious, precise, pressing, psychological, risky, serious, sharp-tongued, ultracrepidarian, uncomplimentary, urgent, vital, Zoilean.

antonyms uncritical, unimportant.

criticise *v* analyse, animadvert, appraise, assess, badmouth, blame, carp, censure, condemn, crab, decry, disparage, evaluate, excoriate, judge, knock, pan, review, roast, scarify, slag, slam, slash, slate, snipe, ultracrepidate.

antonym praise.

criticism *n* analysis, animadversion, appraisal, appreciation, assessment, blame, brickbat, censure, comment, commentary, critique, disapproval, disparagement, elucidation, evaluation, fault-finding, flak, judgement, knocking, knocking-copy, notice, panning, review, slating, stick, stricture, ultracrepidation, vivisection, Zoilism.

antonym praise.

critique *n* analysis, appraisal, assessment, commentary, essay, evaluation, examination, review.

croak *v* caw, die, expire, gasp, grunt, kick the bucket, pass away, perish, snuff it, squawk, wheeze.

crockery *n* ceramics, china, dishes, earthenware, holloware, pottery, stoneware, whiteware.

croft *n* farm, pightle, plot, smallholding.

crone *n* bag, bat, beldam, gammer, grandam, grannam, hag, witch.

crony *n* accomplice, ally, associate, buddy, china, chum, colleague, companion, comrade, follower, friend, henchman, mate, pal, sidekick.

crook *n* cheat, criminal, knave, racketeer, robber, rogue, shark, shyster, swindler, thief, villain.

crooked[1] *adj* bent, corrupt, crafty, criminal, deceitful, discreditable, dishonest, dishonourable, dubious, fraudulent, illegal, knavish, nefarious, questionable, shady, shifty, treacherous, underhand, unethical, unlawful, unprincipled, unscrupulous.

antonym honest.

crooked[2] *adj* anfractuous, angled, askew, asymmetric, awry, bent, bowed, crank, cranky, crippled, crump, curved, deformed, deviating, disfigured, distorted, hooked, irregular, lopsided, meandering, misshapen, off-centre, skew-whiff, slanted, slanting, squint, tilted, tortuous, twisted, twisting, uneven, warped, winding, zigzag.

antonym straight.

crookedness *n* distortion, squintness, twistedness, warp.

antonym straightness.

crop[1] *n* fruits, gathering, growth, harvest, ingathering, produce, vintage, yield.

v browse, clip, collect, curtail, cut, garner, gather, graze, harvest, lop, mow, nibble, pare, pick, prune, reap, reduce, shear, shingle, shorten, snip, top, trim, yield.

crop up appear, arise, arrive, emerge, happen, occur.

crop[2] *n* craw, gizzard, gullet, maw, oesophagus, throat.

cross *adj* adverse, angry, annoyed, cantankerous, captious, churlish, contrary, cranky, crosswise, crotchety, crusty, disagreeable, displeased, fractious, fretful, grouchy, grumpy, hybrid, ill-humoured, ill-tempered, impatient, interchanged, intersecting, irascible, irritable, oblique, opposed, opposing, opposite, peeved, peevish, pettish, petulant, querulous, reciprocal, shirty, short, snappish, snappy, splenetic, sullen, surly, testy, transverse, unfavourable, vexed, waspish.

antonyms calm, placid, pleasant.

v annoy, bestride, blend, block, bridge, cancel, criss-cross, crossbreed, cross-fertilise, cross-pollinate, decussate, deny, foil, ford, frustrate, hinder, hybridise, impede, interbreed, intercross, interfere, intersect, intertwine, lace, meet, mix, mongrelise, obstruct, oppose, resist, span, thwart, traverse, zigzag.

n affliction, amalgam, blend, burden, combination, crossbreed, crossing, crossroads, crucifix, cur, grief, holy-rood, hybrid, hybridisation, intersection, load, misery, misfortune, mixture, mongrel, rood, trial, tribulation, trouble, woe, worry.

cross swords argue, dispute, fight, spar, take issue, wrangle.

cross-examine *v* catechise, give (someone) the third degree, grill, interrogate, pump, question, quiz.

crosspatch *n* bear, crank, crotcheteer, curmudgeon, grump, kill-joy, scold, shrew, sorehead, sourpuss.

cross-question *v* cross-examine, debrief, examine, grill.

crosswise *adv* across, aslant, athwart, awry, crisscross, crossways, diagonally, over, sideways, transversely.

crotchety *adj* awkward, bad-tempered, cantankerous, contrary, crabbed, crabby, cross, crusty, curmudgeonly, difficult, disagreeable, fractious, grumpy, iracund, iracundulous, irascible, irritable, obstreperous, peevish, prickly, surly, testy.

antonyms clam, placid, pleasant.

crouch *v* bend, bow, cower, cringe, duck, hunch, kneel, ruck, squat, stoop.

crow *v* bluster, boast, brag, exult, flourish, gloat, prate, rejoice, triumph, vaunt.

crowbar *n* gavelock, jemmy, jimmy.

crowd *n* army, assembly, attendance, audience, boodle, bunch, caboodle, circle, clique, company, concourse, flock, gate, group, herd, hoi polloi, horde, host, house, lot, many-headed beast/monster, mass, masses, mob, multitude, pack, people, populace, press, proletariat, public, rabble, riff-raff, set, spectators, squash, swarm, the many, throng, troupe.

v bundle, cluster, compress, congest, congregate, cram, elbow, flock, for(e)gather,

gather, huddle, jostle, mass, muster, pack, pile, press, push, shove, squeeze, stream, surge, swarm, throng.

crowded *adj* busy, congested, cramped, crushed, filled, full, huddled, jammed, jam-packed, mobbed, overflowing, packed, populous, swarming, teeming, thronged.

antonym empty.

crown *n* acme, apex, bays, chaplet, circlet, coronal, coronet, crest, diadem, distinction, forehead, garland, head, honour, kudos, laurel wreath, laurels, monarch, monarchy, pate, perfection, pinnacle, prize, royalty, ruler, skull, sovereign, sovereignty, summit, tiara, tip, top, trophy, ultimate, zenith.

v adorn, biff, box, cap, clout, complete, consummate, cuff, dignify, festoon, finish, fulfil, honour, instal, perfect, punch, reward, surmount, terminate, top.

crowned *adj* capped, incoronate(d), royal, ruling, sovereign, surmounted, topped, wreathed.

crowning *adj* climactic, consummate, culminating, final, paramount, perfect, sovereign, supreme, top, ultimate, unmatched, unsurpassed.

n coronation, incoronation, installation.

crucial *adj* central, critical, decisive, essential, important, key, momentous, pivotal, pressing, psychological, searching, testing, trying, urgent, vital.

antonym unimportant.

crucifix *n* cross, holy-rood, rood.

crucify *v* criticise, execute, harrow, lampoon, mock, pan, persecute, rack, ridicule, slam, torment, torture.

crude *adj* amateurish, blue, boorish, clumsy, coarse, crass, dirty, earthy, gross, half-baked, immature, inartistic, indecent, lewd, makeshift, natural, obscene, outline, primitive, raw, rough, rough-hewn, rude, rudimentary, sketchy, smutty, tactless, tasteless, uncouth, undeveloped, undigested, unfinished, unformed, unpolished, unprepared, unprocessed, unrefined, unsubtle, vulgar.

antonyms finished, polite, refined, tasteful.

crudity *n* bawdiness, brutalism, clumsiness, coarseness, crudeness, impropriety, indecency, indelicacy, lewdness, loudness, obscenity, offensiveness, primitiveness, roughness, rudeness, smuttiness, vulgarity.

antonyms polish, politeness, tastefulness.

cruel *adj* atrocious, barbarous, bitter, bloodthirsty, brutal, brutish, butcherly, callous, cold-blooded, cutting, depraved, excruciating, fell, ferocious, fierce, flinty, grim, hard, hard-hearted, harsh, heartless, heathenish, hellish, immane, implacable, inclement, inexorable, inhuman, inhumane, malevolent, marble-breasted, merciless, murderous, painful, pitiless, poignant, ravening, raw, relentless, remorseless, ruthless, sadistic, sanguinary, savage, severe, spiteful, stony-hearted, unfeeling, ungentle, unkind, unmerciful, unnatural, unrelenting, vengeful, vicious.

antonyms compassionate, kind, merciful.

cruelty *n* barbarity, bestiality, bloodthirstiness, brutality, brutishness, callousness, depravity, ferocity, fiendishness, hard-heartedness, harshness, heartlessness, immanity, inhumanity, mercilessness, murderousness, ruthlessness, sadism, savagery, severity, spite, spitefulness, tyranny, ungentleness, venom, viciousness.

antonyms compassion, kindness, mercy.

crumb *n* atom, bit, grain, iota, jot, mite, morsel, nirl, particle, scrap, shred, sliver, snippet, soupçon, speck.

crumble *v* break up, collapse, comminute, crumb, crush, decay, decompose, degenerate, deteriorate, disintegrate, fragment, granulate, grind, levigate, moulder, murl, perish, pound, powder, pulverise, triturate.

crumbly *adj* brittle, friable, murly, powdery, pulverulent, short.

crummy *adj* cheap, contemptible, grotty, half-baked, inferior, miserable, pathetic, poor, rotten, rubbishy, second-rate, shoddy, third-rate, trashy, useless, weak, worthless.

antonym excellent.

crumple *v* collapse, crease, crunkle, crush, fall, pucker, raffle, rumple, wrinkle.

crunch *v* champ, chomp, grind, masticate, munch, scranch.

n crisis, crux, emergency, pinch, test.

crusade *n* campaign, cause, drive, expedition, holy war, jihad, movement, push, undertaking.

crusader *n* advocate, campaigner, champion, enthusiast, fighter, missionary, reformer, zealot.

crush *v* abash, break, browbeat, bruise, chagrin, champ, comminute, compress, conquer, contuse, crease, crumble, crumple, crunch, embrace, enfold, extinguish, hug, humiliate, mash, mortify, overcome, overpower, overwhelm, pound, press, pulverise, quash, quell, rumple, shame, smash, squabash, squeeze, squelch, steam-roller, subdue, vanquish, wrinkle.

n check, crowd, huddle, jam.

crust *n* caking, coat, coating, concretion, covering, exterior, film, heel, impertinence, incrustation, layer, outside, rind, scab, shell, skin, surface.

crusty *adj* brittle, brusque, cantankerous, captious, choleric, crabbed, crabby, crisp, crispy, cross, curt, friable, grouchy, gruff, hard, ill-humoured, irritable, peevish, prickly, short, short-tempered, snappish, snappy, snarling, splenetic, surly, testy, touchy.

antonyms calm, pleasant, soft, soggy.

crux *n* core, essence, heart, nub, vexata quaestio, vexed question.

cry *v* advertise, announce, bark, bawl, beg, bellow, beseech, bewail, blubber, boo-hoo, broadcast, bruit, call, caterwaul, clamour, ejaculate, entreat, exclaim, greet, hail, halloo, hawk, holler, howl, implore, keen, lament, mewl, miaow, miaul, noise, plead, pray, proclaim, promulgate, pule, roar, scream, screech, shout, shriek, snivel, sob, squall, squeal, trumpet, vociferate, wail, weep, whimper, whine, whinge, whoop, yell, yowl.

n announcement, appeal, battle-cry, bawl(ing), bellow, blubber(ing), call, caterwaul, caterwaul(ing), ejaculation, entreaty, exclamation, greet, holler, hoot, howl, keening, lament, lamentation, miaow, miaul, outcry, petition, plaint, plea, prayer, proclamation, report, roar, rumour, scream, screech, shriek, slogan, snivel(ling), sob(bing), sorrowing, squall, squawk, squeal, supplication, utterance, wail(ing), watch-word, weep(ing), whoop, yell, yelp, yoo-hoo.

cry-baby *n* cissy, mardy, softy.

crypt *n* catacomb, mausoleum, tomb, undercroft, vault.

cryptic *adj* abstruse, ambiguous, apocryphal, arcane, bizarre, cabbalistic, dark, Delphic, enigmatic, equivocal, esoteric, hidden, mysterious, obscure, occult, oracular, perplexing, puzzling, recondite, secret, strange, vague, veiled.

antonyms clear, obvious, straightforward.

crystallise *v* appear, coalesce, emerge, form, harden, materialise, solidify.

cub *n* babe, beginner, fledgling, greenhorn, lad, learner, offspring, pup, puppy, recruit, tenderfoot, trainee, whelp, whippersnapper, young, youngster, youth.

antonym adult.

cubby-hole *n* compartment, den, hide-away, hole, niche, pigeonhole, priest hole, recess, slot, snug.

cube *n* cuboid, dice, die, hexahedron, solid.

cuddle *v* canoodle, clasp, cosset, dandle, doodle, embrace, fondle, hug, nestle, pet, smuggle, snuggle.

cuddly *adj* buxom, cosy, cuddlesome, curvaceous, huggable, lovable, plump, soft, warm.

cudgel *n* alpeen, bastinado, baton, bludgeon, club, cosh, plant, shillelagh, stick, truncheon.

v bang, baste, bastinado, batter, beat, bludgeon, cane, clobber, cosh, drub, maul, pound, pummel, thrash, thump, thwack.

cue *n* catchword, hint, feed-line, incentive, key, nod, prompt(ing), reminder, sign, signal, stimulus, suggestion.

cuff *v* bat, beat, belt, biff, box, buffet, clap, clobber, clout, knock, pummel, punch, slap, smack, smite, strike, thump, whack.

n belt, biff, blow, box, buffet, clout, knock, punch, rap, slap, smack, swat, thump, whack.

cull *v* amass, choose, collect, decimate, destroy, gather, glean, kill, pick, pick out, pluck, select, sift, thin, winnow.

culminate *v* climax, close, conclude, consummate, end (up), finish, peak, terminate.

antonyms begin, start.

culmination *n* acme, apex, apogee, climax, completion, conclusion, consummation, crown, finale, height, meridian, ne plus ultra, peak, perfection, pinnacle, summit, top, zenith.

antonyms beginning, start.

culpable *adj* answerable, blam(e)able, blameworthy, censurable, guilty, liable, offending, peccant, reprehensible, sinful, to blame, wrong.

antonyms blameless, innocent.

culprit *n* criminal, delinquent, evil-doer, felon, guilty party, law-breaker, malefactor, miscreant, offender, rascal, sinner, transgressor, wrong-doer.

cult *n* admiration, believers, body, clique, craze, denomination, devotion, faith, following, idolisation, party, religion, reverence, school, sect, veneration, worship.

cultivate *v* aid, ameliorate, better, cherish, civilise, court, develop, discipline, elevate, encourage, enrich, farm, fertilise, forward, foster, further, harvest, help, improve, patronise, plant, plough, polish, prepare, promote, pursue, refine, school, support, tend, till, train, work.

antonym neglect.

cultivation *n* advancement, advocacy, agronomy, breeding, civilisation, civility, culture, development, discernment, discrimination, education, encouragement, enhancement, enlightenment, farming, fostering, furtherance, gardening, gentility, help, husbandry, learning, letters, manners, nurture, patronage, planting, ploughing, polish, promotion, pursuit, refinement, schooling, study, support, taste, tillage, tilling, tilth, working.

cultural *adj* aesthetic, artistic, arty, broadening, civilising, developmental, edifying, educational, educative, elevating, enlightening, enriching, humane, humanising, liberal.

culture *n* accomplishment, aestheticism, agriculture, agronomy, art, breeding, civilisation, cultivation, customs, education, elevation, enlightenment, erudition, farming, gentility, husbandry, improvement, Kultur, lifestyle, mores, polish, politeness, refinement, society, taste, the arts, urbanity.

cultured *adj* accomplished, advanced, aesthetic, arty, civilised, educated, enlightened, erudite, genteel, highbrow, knowledgeable, polished, refined, scholarly, urbane, versed, well-bred, well-informed, well-read.

antonyms ignorant, uncultured.

culvert *n* channel, conduit, drain, duct, gutter, sewer, watercourse.

cumbersome *adj* awkward, bulky, burdensome, clumsy, cumbrous, embarrassing, heavy, hefty, incommodious, inconvenient, onerous, oppressive, ponderous, unmanageable, unwieldy, weighty.

antonyms convenient, manageable.

cumulative *adj* accumulative, additive, aggregate, collective, increasing.

cunning *adj* adroit, arch, artful, astute, canny, crafty, deep, deft, devious, dexterous, foxy, guileful, imaginative, ingenious, knowing, leery,

Machiavellian, ruse, sharp, shifty, shrewd, skilful, sneeky, subtle, tricky, vulpine, wily.

antonyms gullible, naïve.

n ability, adroitness, art, artfulness, artifice, astuteness, cleverness, craftiness, deceitfulness, deftness, deviousness, dexterity, finesse, foxiness, guile, ingenuity, policy, shrewdness, skill, slyness, subtlety, trickery, vulpinism, wiliness.

antonyms openness, simplicity.

cup *n* beaker, bidon, cannikin, cantharus, chalice, cupful, cylix, demitasse, dish, draught, drink, fingan, goblet, mazer, pokal, potion, tankard, tass, tazza, teacup, tig, trophy.

cupboard *n* almirah, ambry, armoire, cabinet, closet, locker, press.

cupidity *n* acquisitiveness, avarice, avidity, covetousness, eagerness, graspingness, greed, greediness, hankering, hunger, itching, longing, rapaciousness, rapacity, voracity, yearning.

cur *n* blackguard, canine, coward, dastard, good-for-nothing, heel, hound, mongrel, mutt, rat, rotter, scoundrel, stray, swine, villain, wretch.

curative *adj* alleviative, corrective, febrifugal, healing, healthful, health-giving, medicinal, remedial, restorative, salutary, therapeutic, tonic, vulnerary.

curb *v* bit, bridle, check, constrain, contain, control, hamper, hinder, hobble, impede, inhibit, moderate, muzzle, repress, restrain, restrict, retard, subdue, suppress.

antonyms encourage, foster, goad.

n brake, bridle, check, control, deterrent, hamper, hobble, limitation, rein, restraint.

curdle *v* clot, coagulate, condense, congeal, earn, ferment, sour, thicken, turn.

cure[1] *v* alleviate, correct, ease, heal, help, mend, rehabilitate, relieve, remedy, restore.

n alleviation, antidote, corrective, detoxicant, febrifuge, healing, medicine, panacea, panpharmacon, recovery, remedy, restorative, specific, treatment, vulnerary.

cure[2] *v* brine, dry, kipper, pickle, preserve, salt, smoke.

curio *n* antique, bibelot, bygone, curiosity, knick-knack, object of virtu, objet de vertu, trinket.

curiosity *n* bibelot, bygone, celebrity, curio, freak, inquisitiveness, interest, knick-knack, marvel, nosiness, novelty, object of virtu, objet d'art, objet de vertu, oddity, phenomenon, prying, rarity, sight, snooping, spectacle, trinket, wonder.

curiosities *n* exotica, novelties, virtu.

curious *adj* bizarre, enquiring, exotic, extraordinary, ferly, funny, inquisitive, interested, marvellous, meddling, mysterious, nosy, novel, odd, peculiar, peeping, peering, prying, puzzled, puzzling, quaint, queer, questioning, rare, searching, singular, snoopy, strange, unconventional, unexpected, unique, unorthodox, unusual, wonderful.

antonyms incurious, indifferent, normal, ordinary, uninterested.

curl *v* bend, coil, convolute, corkscrew, crimp, crimple, crinkle, crisp, curve, entwine, frizz, loop, meander, ripple, scroll, spiral, turn, twine, twirl, wind, wreathe, writhe.

antonym uncurl.

n coil, curlicue, kink, ringlet, spiral, swirl, tress, twist, whorl.

curly *adj* corkscrew, crimped, crimpy, crinkly, curled, curling, frizzy, fuzzy, kinky, spiralled, waved, wavy, whorled, winding.

antonym straight.

currency *n* acceptance, bills, circulation, coinage, coins, exposure, legal tender, money, notes, popularity, prevalence, publicity, reign, transmission, vogue.

current *adj* accepted, circulating, common, contemporary, customary, extant, fashionable, general, on-going, popular, present, present-day, prevailing, prevalent, reigning, rife, trendy, up-to-date, up-to-the-minute, widespread.

antonyms antiquated, old-fashioned.

n atmosphere, course, draught, drift, feeling, flow, inclination, jet, juice, mood, progression, river, stream, tendency, thermal, tide, trend, undercurrent.

curse *n* affliction, anathema, ban, bane, blasphemy, burden, calamity, cross, damn, denunciation, disaster, evil, excommunication, execration, expletive, imprecation, jinx, malediction, malison, misfortune, oath, obscenity, ordeal, plague, scourge, swearing, swear-word, torment, tribulation, trouble, vexation, woe.

antonyms advantage, blessing.

v accurse, afflict, anathematise, blaspheme, blight, blind, blow, burden, cuss, damn, destroy, doom, excommunicate, execrate, fulminate, imprecate, plague, scourge, swear, torment, trouble, vex.

antonym bless.

cursed *adj* abominable, accursed, bedevilled, bewitched, blessed, blighted, confounded, damnable, damned, destestable, devilish, doomed, excommunicate, execrable, fell, fey, fiendish, foredoomed, hateful, hexed, ill-fated, infamous, infernal, loathsome, odious, pernicious, pestilential, star-crossed, unholy, unsanctified, vile, villainous.

cursory *adj* brief, careless, casual, desultory, fleeting, hasty, hurried, offhand, passing, perfunctory, quick, rapid, slap-dash, slight, summary, superficial.

antonyms painstaking, thorough.

curt *adj* abrupt, blunt, brief, brusque, concise, gruff, laconic, offhand, pithy, rude, sharp, short, short-spoken, snappish, succinct, summary, tart, terse, unceremonious, uncivil, ungracious.

antonym voluble.

curtail *v* abbreviate, abridge, circumscribe, contract, cut, decrease, dock, lessen, lop, pare, prune, reduce, restrict, retrench, shorten, trim, truncate.

antonyms extend, lengthen, prolong.

curtailment *n* abbreviation, abridgement, contraction, cutback, cutting, docking, guillotine, pruning, restriction, retrenchment, truncation.

antonyms extension, lengthening, prolongation.

curtain *v* conceal, drape, hide, screen, shield, shroud, shutter, veil.

n arras, backdrop, drapery, hanging, portière, tab, tapestry, vitrage.

curtsy *n* bob, bow, genuflection, kowtow, salaam.

curvaceous *adj* bosomy, buxom, comely, curvy, Junoesque, shapely, voluptuous, well-proportioned, well-rounded, well-stacked.

curve *v* arc, arch, bend, bow, coil, decurve, hook, incurvate, incurve, inflect, spiral, swerve, turn, twist, wind.

n arc, bend, camber, curvature, half-moon, incurvation, incurvature, inflexure, loop, trajectory, turn.

curved *adj* arched, arc(k)ed, arcuate, bent, bowed, crooked, falcate, humped, inbent, incurvate, incurved, inflexed, rounded, serpentine, sinuous, sweeping, turned, twisted.

antonym straight.

cushion *n* bean-bag, bolster, buffer, hassock, headrest, pad, pillion, pillow, shock absorber, squab.

v allay, bolster, buttress, cradle, dampen, deaden, lessen, mitigate, muffle, pillow, protect, soften, stifle, support, suppress.

cushy *adj* comfortable, easy, jammy, plum, soft, undemanding.

antonyms demanding, tough.

custodian *n* caretaker, castellan, chatelaine, claviger, conservator, curator, guardian, keeper, overseer, protector, superintendent, warden, warder, watch-dog, watchman.

custody *n* aegis, arrest, auspices, care, charge, confinement, custodianship, detention, durance, duress, guardianship, holding, imprisonment, incarceration, keeping, observation, possession, preservation, protection, retention, safe-keeping, supervision, trusteeship, tutelage, ward, wardship, watch.

custom *n* consuetude, convention, customers, etiquette, fashion, form, formality, habit, habitualness, habitude, manner, mode, observance, observation, patronage, policy, practice, praxis, procedure, ritual, routine, rule, style, thew, trade, tradition, usage, use, way, wont.

customarily *adv* commonly, generally, habitually, normally, ordinarily, popularly, regularly, routinely, traditionally, usually.

antonyms occasionally, rarely.

customary *adj* accepted, accustomed, acknowledged, common, confirmed, conventional, established, everyday, familiar, fashionable, favourite, general, habitual, nomic, normal, ordinary, popular, prevailing, regular, routine, traditional, usual, wonted.

antonyms occasional, rare, unusual.

customer *n* buyer, client, consumer, habitue, patron, prospect, punter, purchaser, regular, shopper, vendee.

cut *v* abbreviate, abridge, avoid, bisect, carve, castrate, chip, chisel, chop, cleave, clip, cold-shoulder, condense, contract, crop, cross, curtail, decrease, delete, dissect, divide, dock, dod, edit, engrave, excise, fashion, fell, form, gash, gather, gride, grieve, hack, harvest, hew, hurt, ignore, incise, insult, interrupt, intersect, jump-cut, lacerate, lop, lower, mow, nick, notch, pain, pare, part, penetrate, pierce, precis, prune, rationalise, reap, reduce, saw, scissor, score, sculpt, sculpture, segment, sever, shape, share, shave, shorten, slash, slice, slight, slim, slit, sned, snub, split, spurn, sting, sunder, trim, truncate, whittle, wound.

n abscission, blow, chop, configuration, cutback, decrease, decrement, diminution, division, economy, fall, fashion, form, gash, graze, groove, incision, incisure, insection, kerf, kickback, laceration, look, lowering, mode, nick, percentage, piece, portion, race, rake-off, reduction, rent, rip, saving, section, shape, share, slash, slice, slit, snick, stroke, style, wound.

cut and dried automatic, fixed, organised, prearranged, predetermined, settled, sewn up.

cut back check, crop, curb, decrease, economise, lessen, lop, lower, prune, reduce, retrench, slash, trim.

cut down decrease, diminish, dispatch, fell, hew, kill, lessen, level, lop, lower, massacre, raze, reduce, slaughter, slay.

cut in interjaculate, interject, interpose, interrupt, intervene, intrude.

cut off abscind, block, disconnect, discontinue, disinherit, disown, end, excide, excise, exscind, halt, intercept, interclude, interrupt, intersect, isolate, obstruct, prescind, renounce, separate, sever, stop, suspend.

cut out cease, contrive, debar, delete, displace, eliminate, excise, exclude, exsect, extract, oust, remove, sever, shape, stop, supersede, supplant.

cut out for adapted, adequate, competent, designed, equipped, fitted, made, qualified, right, suitable, suited.

cut short abbreviate, abort, arrest, check, crop, curtail, dock, halt, interrupt, postpone, prune, reduce, stop, terminate.

antonym prolong.

cut up carve, chop, criticise, crucify, dice, divide, injure, knife, lacerate, mince, pan, ridicule, slash, slate, slice, vilify, wound.

cutback *n* cut, decrease, decrement, economy, lessening, reduction, retrenchment.

cut-price *adj* bargain, cheap, cut-rate, low-priced, reduced, sale.

cut-throat *n* assassin, bravo, butcher, executioner, hatchet man, hit-man, homicide, killer, liquidator, murderer, slayer, thug.

adj barbarous, bloodthirsty, bloody, brutal, competitive, cruel, dog-eat-dog, ferine, ferocious, fierce, homicidal, murderous, relentless, ruthless, savage, thuggish, unprincipled, vicious, violent.

cutting *adj* acid, acrimonious, barbed, biting, bitter, caustic, chill, hurtful, incisive, keen, malicious, mordant, numbing, penetrating, piercing, pointed, raw, sarcastic, sardonic, scathing, severe, sharp, stinging, trenchant, wounding.

n bit, cleavage, clipping, piece, scion, scission, slice.

cycle *n* aeon, age, circle, epoch, era, period, phase, revolution, rotation, round, sequence.

cyclist *n* velocipedean, velocipeder, velocipedestrian, velocipedian, velocipedist, wheeler.

cyclone *n* hurricane, monsoon, tempest, tornado, twister, typhoon, whirlwind.

cylinder *n* barrel, bobbin, column, drum, reel, spindle, spool, trunk.

cynic *n* doubter, killjoy, knocker, misanthrope, misanthropist, pessimist, sceptic, scoffer, spoilsport.

cynical *adj* contemptuous, derisive, distrustful, ironic, mephistophelian, mephistophilic, misanthropic(al), mocking, mordant, pessimistic, sarcastic, sardonic, sceptical, scoffing, scornful, sharp-tongued, sneering, streetwise.

cynicism *n* disbelief, distrust, doubt, misanthropy, pessimism, sarcasm, scepticism.

cyst *n* atheroma, bladder, bleb, blister, growth, sac, vesicle, wen.

D

dab[1] *v* blot, daub, pat, stipple, swab, tap, touch, wipe.

n bit, dollop, drop, fingerprint, fleck, flick, pat, peck, smear, smidgen, smudge, speck, spot, stroke, tap, touch, trace.

dab[2] ace, adept, dab hand, dabster, expert, pastmaster, wizard.

dabble *v* dally, dip, fiddle, guddle, moisten, paddle, potter, spatter, splash, sprinkle, tinker, toy, trifle, wet.

dabbler *n* amateur, dilettante, potterer, sciolist, tinkerer, trifler.

antonyms connoisseur, expert, professional.

daft *adj* absurd, asinine, berserk, besotted, crackers, crazy, daffy, delirious, demented, deranged, dop(e)y, doting, dotty, foolish, giddy, hysterical, idiotic, inane, infatuated, insane, lunatic, mad, mental, nuts, nutty, potty, scatty, screwy, silly, simple, stupid, touched, unhinged, witless.

antonyms bright, sane.

dagger *n* bayonet, dah, dirk, jambiya(h), kris, kukri, misericord(e), poniard, skean, skean-dhu, stiletto, whinger, whiniard, yatag(h)an.

daily *adj* circadian, common, commonplace, customary, day-to-day, diurnal, everyday, normal, ordinary, quotidian, regular, routine.

dainty *adj* charming, choice, choos(e)y, delectable, delicate, delicious, dinky, elegant, exquisite, fastidious, fine, finical, finicking, finicky, friand(e), fussy, genty, graceful, lickerish, liquorish, meticulous, mignon(ne), mincing, minikin, neat, nice, palatable, particular, petite, pretty, refined, savoury, scrupulous, tasty, tender, toothsome.

antonyms clumsy, gross.

n bonbon, bonne-bouche, delicacy, fancy, sweetmeat, titbit.

dale *n* bottom, clough, coomb, dell, dingle, ghyll, gill, glen, strath, vale, valley.

dally *v* canoodle, dawdle, delay, dilly-dally, fiddle-faddle, flirt, frivol, linger, loiter, play, procrastinate, sport, tamper, tarry, toy, trifle.

antonyms hasten, hurry.

dam *n* an(n)icut, barrage, barrier, blockage, embankment, hindrance, obstruction, wall.

v barricade, block, check, choke, confine, obstruct, restrict, stanch, staunch, stem.

damage *n* destruction, detriment, devastation, disprofit, harm, hurt, impairment, injury, loss, mischief, mutilation, scathe, suffering.

antonym repair.

v deface, harm, hurt, impair, incapacitate, injure, mar, mutilate, play havoc with, play hell with, ruin, spoil, tamper with, weaken, wreck.

antonyms fix, repair.

damages *n* amercement, compensation, fine, indemnity, reimbursement, reparation, satisfaction.

damaging *adj* deleterious, detrimental, disadvantageous, harmful, hurtful, injurious, pernicious, prejudicial, ruinous, unfavourable.

antonyms favourable, helpful.

dame *n* baroness, broad, dowager, female, lady, matron, noblewoman, peeress, woman.

damn *v* abuse, anathematise, blaspheme, blast, castigate, censure, condemn, criticise, curse, dang, darn, dash, denounce, denunciate, doom, excoriate, execrate, imprecate, pan, revile, sentence, slam, slate, swear.

antonym bless.

n brass farthing, darn, dash, hoot, iota, jot, monkey's, tinker's cuss, two hoots, whit.

damnable *adj* abominable, accursed, atrocious, culpable, cursed, despicable, detestable, execrable, hateful, horrible, iniquitous, offensive, sinful, wicked.

antonyms admirable, praiseworthy.

damnation *n* anathema, ban, condemnation, denunciation, doom, excommunication, malison, objurgation, perdition, proscription.

damned *adj* accursed, anathematised, condemned, confounded, danged, darned, dashed, despicable, detestable, deuced, doggone(d), doomed, dratted, effing, flipping, fucking, goddam(n), goddamned, hateful, infamous, infernal, loathsome, lost, reprobate, revolting, unhappy.

antonym blessed.

damning *adj* accusatorial, condemnatory, damnatory, dooming, implicative, incriminating, inculpatory.

damp *n* clamminess, dampness, dankness, dew, drizzle, fog, humidity, mist, moisture, mugginess, muzziness, vapour, wet.

antonym dryness.

adj clammy, dank, dewy, dripping, drizzly, humid, misty, moist, muggish, muggy, sodden, soggy, sopping, vaporous, vapourish, vapoury, wet.

antonyms arid, dry.

v allay, bedew, check, chill, cool, curb, dampen, dash, deaden, deject, depress, diminish, discourage, dispirit, dull, inhibit, moderate, moisten, restrain, stifle, wet.

antonym dry.

dampen *v* bedew, besprinkle, check, dash, deaden, decrease, depress, deter, diminish, dishearten, dismay, dull, lessen, moderate, moisten, muffle, reduce, restrain, smother, spray, stifle, wet.

antonyms dry, encourage.

dance *v* caper, frolic, gambol, hoof it, hop, jig, jive, juke, kantikoy, prance, rock, skip, spin, stomp, sway, swing, tread a measure, whirl.

n bal masque, bal pare, ball, hop, kantikoy, kick-up, knees-up, prom, shindig, social.

dancer *n* ballerina, ballet dancer, belly-dancer, coryphee, danseur, danseuse, hoofer, prima ballerina, tap-dancer.

dandy *n* Adonis, beau, blade, blood, buck, Corinthian, coxcomb, dapperling, dude, exquisite, fop, Jack-a-dandy, jay, macaroni, man-about-town, masher, muscadin, musk-cat, peacock, popinjay, swell, toff.

adj capital, dinky, excellent, fine, first-rate, great, splendid.

danger *n* endangerment, hazard, insecurity, jeopardy, liability, menace, peril, precariousness, risk, threat, trouble, venture, vulnerability.

antonyms safety, security.

dangerous *adj* alarming, breakneck, chancy, critical, daring, exposed, grave, hairy, harmful, hazardous, insecure, menacing, nasty, parlous, perilous, precarious, reckless, risky, serious, severe, threatening, tickly, treacherous, ugly, unsafe, vulnerable.

antonyms harmless, safe, secure.

dangle *v* droop, flap, flaunt, flourish, hang, lure, sway, swing, tantalise, tempt, trail, wave.

dangling *adj* disconnected, drooping, hanging, loose, pendulous, swaying, swinging, trailing.

dank *adj* chilly, clammy, damp, dewy, dripping, moist, rheumy, slimy, soggy.

antonym dry.

dapper *adj* active, brisk, chic, dainty, natty, neat, nimble, smart, spiffy, spruce, spry, stylish, trig, trim, well-dressed, well-groomed.

antonyms dishevelled, dowdy, scruffy, shabby, sloppy.

dappled *adj* bespeckled, brindled, checkered, dotted, flecked, freckled, mottled, piebald, pied, speckled, spotted, stippled, variegated.

dare *v* adventure, brave, challenge, defy, endanger, gamble, goad, have the gall, hazard, presume, provoke, risk, stake, taunt, venture.

n challenge, gauntlet, provocation, taunt.

daredevil *n* adventurer, desperado, exhibitionist, Hotspur, madcap, stuntman.

antonym coward.

adj adventurous, audacious, bold, daring, death-defying, fearless, madcap, rash, reckless.

antonyms cautious, prudent, timid.

daring *adj* adventurous, audacious, bold, brave, brazen, dauntless, fearless, game, impulsive, intrepid, plucky, rash, reckless, valiant, venturesome.

antonyms afraid, timid.

n audacity, boldness, bottle, bravery, bravura, courage, defiance, derring-do, fearlessness, gall, grit, guts, intrepidity, nerve, pluck, prowess, rashness, spirit, spunk, temerity.

antonyms cowardice, timidity.

dark *adj* abstruse, angry, aphotic, arcane, atrocious, benighted, black, bleak, brunette, caliginous, cheerless, cloudy, concealed, cryptic, damnable, darkling, dark-skinned, darksome, deep, dim, dingy, dismal, doleful, dour, drab, dusky, ebony, enigmatic, evil, forbidding, foul, frowning, gloomy, glowering, glum, grim, hellish, hidden, horrible, ignorant, indistinct, infamous, infernal, joyless, lightless, melanic, melanous, midnight, mirk, mirky, morbid, morose, mournful, murk, murky, mysterious, mystic, nefarious, obscure, occult, ominous, overcast, pitch-black, pitchy, puzzling, recondite, sable, satanic, scowling, secret, shadowy, shady, sinful, sinister, sombre, sulky, sullen, sunless, swarthy, tenebr(i)ous, threatening, uncultivated, unenlightened, unillumed, unilluminated, unlettered, unlit, vile, wicked.

antonyms bright, happy, light, lucid.

n concealment, darkness, dimness, dusk, evening, gloom, ignorance, mirk, mirkiness, murk, murkiness, night, nightfall, night-time, obscurity, secrecy, twilight, yin.

antonyms brightness, light.

darken *v* becloud, blacken, cloud, cloud over, darkle, deepen, deject, depress, dim, disilluminate, dispirit, dusken, eclipse, embrown, obscure, overshade, overshadow, sadden, shade, shadow.

antonyms brighten, lighten.

darkness *n* blackness, blindness, concealment, dark, dimness, dusk, duskiness, gloom, ignorance, mirk, mirkiness, murk, murkiness, mystery, nightfall, obscurity, privacy, secrecy, shade, shadiness, shadows, tenebr(os)ity.

antonyms brightness, daylight, lightness.

darling *n* acushla, apple of one's eye, asthore, beloved, blue-eyed boy, dear, dearest, fair-haired boy, favourite, jo(e), lady-love, love, lovey, machree, mavourneen, minikin, pet, poppet, sweetheart, true-love.

adj adored, beloved, cherished, dear, precious, treasured, white-headed.

dart *v* bound, cast, dartle, dash, flash, fling, flit, fly, hurl, launch, propel, race, run, rush, scoot, send, shoot, sling, spring, sprint, start, tear, throw, whistle, whiz.

n arrow, barb, bolt, flechette, flight, shaft.

dash[1] *v* abash, blight, break, cast, chagrin, confound, crash, dampen, destroy, ding, disappoint, discomfort, discourage, fling, foil, frustrate, hurl, ruin, shatter, shiver, slam, sling, smash, splinter, spoil, throw, thwart.

n bit, bravura, brio, da(u)d, drop, elan, flair, flavour, flourish, hint, little, panache, pinch, smack, soupçon, spirit, sprinkling, style, suggestion, tinge, touch, verve, vigour, vivacity.

dash[2] *v* be off like a shot, bolt, bound, dart, dartle, fly, haste(n), hurry, race, run, rush, speed, spring, sprint, tear.

n bolt, dart, race, run, rush, sprint, spurt.

dashing *adj* bold, dapper, daring, dazzling, debonair, doggy, elegant, exuberant, flamboyant, gallant, impressive, jaunty, lively, plucky, showy, smart, spirited, sporty, stylish, swashbuckling, swish.

antonym drab.

dastard *n* caitiff, coward, craven, cur, milksop, poltroon, worm.

dastardly *adj* base, caitiff, contemptible, cowardly, craven, despicable, faint-hearted, lily-livered, low, mean, niddering, pusillanimous, recreant, sneaking, sneaky, spiritless, timorous, underhand, vile.

antonyms heroic, noble.

data *n* details, documents, dope, facts, figures, info, information, input, materials, statistics.

date[1] *n* age, epoch, era, period, point, point in time, stage, time.

date[2] *n* appointment, assignation, engagement, escort, friend, meeting, partner, rendezvous, steady, tryst.

dated *adj* antiquated, archaic, demode, obsolescent, obsolete, old hat, old-fashioned, out, outdated, outmoded, out-of-date, passe, superseded, unfashionable.

antonyms fashionable, up-to-the-minute.

daub *v* begrime, besmear, blur, coat, cover, dedaub, deface, dirty, gaum, grime, paint, plaster, smear, smirch, smudge, spatter, splatter, stain, sully.

n blot, blotch, smear, splash, splodge, splotch, spot, stain.

daunt *v* alarm, appal, cow, deter, discourage, dishearten, dismay, dispirit, frighten, intimidate, overawe, put off, scare, shake, subdue, terrify, unnerve.

antonyms encourage, hearten.

daunted *adj* alarmed, cowed, demoralised, deterred, discouraged, disheartened, disillusioned, dismayed, dismayful, dispirited, downcast, frightened, hesitant, intimidated, overcome, put off, unnerved.

antonyms encouraged, heartened.

dauntless *adj* bold, brave, courageous, daring, doughty, fearless, gallant, game, heroic, indomitable, intrepid, lion-hearted, plucky, resolute, stout-hearted, undaunted, unflinching, valiant, valorous.

antonyms discouraged, disheartened.

dawdle *v* daidle, dally, delay, dilly-dally, fiddle, fritter, hang about, idle, lag, loaf, loiter, potter, shilly-shally, trail.

antonym hurry.

dawdler *n* laggard, lingerer, loafer, loiterer, shilly-shallier, slowcoach, snail, tortoise.

dawn *n* advent, aurora, beginning, birth, cock-crow(ing), dawning, daybreak, daylight, day-peep, dayspring, emergence, genesis, inception, morning, onset, origin, outset, peep of day, rise, start, sunrise, sun-up.

antonyms dusk, sundown, sunset.

v appear, begin, break, brighten, develop, emerge, gleam, glimmer, hit, initiate, lighten, occur, open, originate, register, rise, strike, unfold.

day *n* age, ascendancy, childhood, cycle, date, daylight, daytime, epoch, era, generation, height, heyday, period, prime, time, young days, youth, zenith.

antonym night.

day after day continually, endlessly, forever, monotonously, perpetually, persistently, regularly, relentlessly.

day by day daily, gradually, progressively, slowly but surely, steadily.

daybreak *n* break of day, cock-crow(ing), crack of dawn, dawn, day-peep, dayspring, first light, morning, peep of day, sunrise, sun-up.

antonyms sundown, sunset.

daydream *n* castles in Spain, castles in the air, dream, dwa(l)m, fantasy, figment, fond hope, imagining, musing, phantasm, pipe dream, reverie, star-gazing, vision, wish, wool-gathering.

v dream, fancy, fantasise, hallucinate, imagine, muse, stargaze.

daydreamer *n* fantasiser, rêveur, rêveuse, stargazer.

daze *v* amaze, astonish, astound, befog, benumb, bewilder, blind, confuse, dazzle, dumbfound, flabbergast, numb, paralyse, perplex, shock, stagger, startle, stun, stupefy, surprise.

n bewilderment, confusion, distraction, dwa(l)m, shock, stupor, trance.

dazed *adj* baffled, bemused, bewildered, confused, disorien(ta)ted, dizzy, dop(e)y, dumbstruck, flabbergasted, fuddled, groggy, light-headed, muddled, nonplussed, numbed, perplexed, punch-drunk, shocked, staggered, stunned, stupefied, totty, woozy.

dazzle *v* amaze, astonish, awe, bedazzle, blind, blur, confuse, daze, fascinate, hypnotise, impress, overawe, overpower, overwhelm, scintillate, sparkle, stupefy.

n brilliance, glitter, magnificence, razzle-dazzle, razzmatazz, scintillation, sparkle, splendour.

dazzling *adj* brilliant, foudroyant, glaring, glary, glittering, glorious, radiant, ravishing, scintillating, sensational, shining, sparkling, splendid, stunning, sublime, superb, virtuoso.

de facto *adv* actually, in effect, really.

adj actual, existing, real.

de jure legally, rightfully.

de luxe choice, costly, elegant, exclusive, expensive, grand, luxurious, opulent, palatial, plush, rich, select, special, splendid, sumptuous, superior.

de rigueur comme il faut, conventional, correct, decent, decorous, done, fitting, necessary, proper, required, right, the done thing.

de trop needless, redundant, supererogatory, superfluous, supernumerary, surplus, unnecessary, unneeded, unwanted, unwelcome.

dead[1] *adj* ad patres, apathetic, barren, boring, breathless, callous, cold, dead-and-alive, dead-beat, deceased, defunct, departed, dull, exhausted, extinct, flat, frigid, glassy, glazed, gone, inactive, inanimate, indifferent, inert, inoperative, insipid, late, lifeless, lukewarm, napoo, numb, obsolete, paralysed, perished, spent, spiritless, stagnant, stale, sterile, stiff, still, tasteless, tired, torpid, unemployed, uninteresting, unprofitable, unresponsive, useless, vapid, wooden, worn out.

antonyms active, alive, animated.

dead[2] *adj* absolute, complete, downright, entire, outright, perfect, thorough, total, unqualified, utter.

adv absolutely, completely, entirely, exactly, perfectly, quite, totally.

deaden *v* abate, allay, alleviate, anaesthetise, benumb, blunt, check, cushion, damp, dampen, desensitise, diminish, dull, hush, impair, lessen, muffle, mute, numb, obtund, paralyse, quieten, reduce, smother, stifle, suppress, weaken.

antonym enliven.

deadlock *n* halt, impasse, stalemate, standstill.

deadly *adj* accurate, ashen, baleful, baneful, boring, cruel, dangerous, death-dealing, deathful, deathlike, deathly, destructive, devastating, dull, effective, exact, fatal, feral, funest, ghastly, ghostly, grim, implacable, lethal, malignant, monotonous, mortal, noxious, pallid, pernicious, pestilent, poisonous, precise, ruthless, savage, sure, tedious, thanatoid, true, unerring, unfailing, uninteresting, unrelenting, venomous, wearisome, white.

antonyms harmless, healthy.

deadpan *adj* blank, dispassionate, empty, expressionless, impassive, inexpressive, inscrutable, poker-faced, straight-faced, unexpressive.

deaf *adj* hard of hearing, heedless, indifferent, oblivious, stone-deaf, unconcerned, unmindful, unmoved.

antonyms aware, conscious.

deafening *adj* booming, dinning, ear-piercing, ear-splitting, fortissimo, piercing, resounding, ringing, roaring, thunderous.

antonyms pianissimo, quiet.

deal *v* allot, apportion, assign, bargain, bestow, dispense, distribute, divide, dole out, give, mete out, negotiate, reward, sell, share, stock, trade, traffic, treat.

n agreement, amount, arrangement, bargain, buy, contract, degree, distribution, extent, hand, pact, portion, quantity, round, share, transaction, understanding.

deal with attend to, concern, consider, cope with, handle, manage, oversee, see to, treat.

dealer *n* chandler, chapman, marketer, merchandiser, merchant, monger, trader, tradesman, wholesaler.

dealings *n* business, commerce, intercourse, intertraffic, trade, traffic, transactions, truck.

dear *adj* beloved, cherished, close, costly, darling, esteemed, expensive, familiar, favourite, high-priced, intimate, loved, overpriced, precious, pric(e)y, prized, respected, treasured, valued.

antonyms cheap, hateful.

n angel, beloved, darling, dearie, deary, loved one, precious, treasure.

dearly *adv* affectionately, devotedly, extremely, fondly, greatly, lovingly, profoundly, tenderly.

dearth *n* absence, barrenness, deficiency, exiguousness, famine, inadequacy, insufficiency, lack, need, paucity, poverty, scantiness, scarcity, shortage, sparseness, sparsity, want.

antonyms abundance, excess.

death *n* annihilation, bane, bereavement, cessation, curtains, decease, demise, departure, destruction, dissolution, dormition, downfall, dying, end, eradication, exit, expiration, extermination, extinction, fatality, finish, grave, loss, obliteration, passing, quietus, release, ruin, ruination, undoing.

antonyms birth, life.

deathless *adj* eternal, everlasting, immortal, imperishable, incorruptible, never-ending, timeless, undying, unforgettable.

deathly *adj* ashen, cadaverous, deadly, deathlike, fatal, gaunt, ghastly, grim, haggard, intense, mortal, pale, pallid, terrible, wan.

debacle *n* cataclysm, catastrophe, collapse, defeat, devastation, disaster, downfall, farce, fiasco, havoc, overthrow, reversal, rout, ruin, ruination, stampede.

debar *v* bar, blackball, deny, eject, exclude, expel, hamper, hinder, obstruct, preclude, prevent, prohibit, restrain, segregate, shut out, stop.

antonym admit.

debase *v* abase, adulterate, allay, bastardise, cheapen, contaminate, corrupt, defile, degrade, demean, depreciate, devalue, diminish, disgrace, dishonour, embase, humble, humiliate, impair, lower, pollute, reduce, shame, taint, vitiate.

antonyms elevate, upgrade.

debased *adj* abandoned, adulterated, base, corrupt, debauched, degenerate, degraded, depraved, depreciated, devalued, diminished, fallen, impure, low, lowered, mixed, perverted, polluted, reduced, sordid, vile.

antonyms elevated, pure.

debasement *n* abasement, adulteration, baseness, contamination, corruption, degeneration, degradation, depravation, depreciation, devaluation, dishonour, perversion, pollution, reduction.

antonyms elevation, purification.

debatable *adj* arguable, borderline, contentious, contestable, controversial, controvertible, disputable, doubtful, dubious, moot, open to question, problematical, questionable, uncertain, undecided, unsettled.

antonyms certain, questionable.

debate *v* argue, cogitate, consider, contend, contest, controvert, deliberate, discuss, dispute, logicise, meditate on, mull over, ponder, question, reflect, revolve, ruminate, weigh, wrangle.

antonym agree.

n altercation, argument, cogitation, consideration, contention, controversy, deliberation, discussion, disputation, dispute, meditation, polemic, quodlibet, reflection.

antonym agreement.

debauch *v* corrupt, deflower, demoralise, deprave, over-indulge, pervert, pollute, ravish, ruin, seduce, subvert, violate, vitiate.

antonyms cleanse, purge, purify.

n bacchanalia, bender, bevvy, binge, booze-up, bout, fling, orgy, pub-crawl, saturnalia, spree, wet.

debauched *adj* abandoned, corrupt, corrupted, debased, degenerate, degraded, depraved, dissipated, dissolute, immoral, intemperate, lewd, licentious, perverted, profligate, raddled, rakehell, rakehelly, wanton.

antonyms decent, pure, virtuous.

debauchee *n* hell-bender, libertine, Lothario, playboy, profligate, rake, rake-hell, roue, sensualist, wanton.

debauchery *n* carousal, debauchedness, debauchment, depravity, dissipation, dissoluteness, excess, gluttony, immorality, incontinence, indulgence, intemperance, lewdness, licentiousness, lust, orgy, overindulgence, rakery, revel, riot, wantonness.

debilitate *v* devitalise, enervate, enfeeble, exhaust, impair, incapacitate, prostrate, relax, sap, undermine, unman, weaken, wear out.

antonyms energise, invigorate, strengthen.

debilitating *adj* enervating, enervative, enfeebling, exhausting, fatiguing, tiring, weakening.

antonyms invigorating, strengthening.

debility *n* asthenia, atonicity, atony, decrepitude, enervation, enfeeblement, exhaustion, faintness, feebleness, frailty, incapacity, infirmity, languor, malaise, sickliness, weakness.

antonyms strength, vigour.

debonair *adj* affable, breezy, buoyant, charming, cheerful, courteous, dashing, elegant, gay, jaunty, light-hearted, refined, smooth, sprightly, suave, urbane, well-bred.

debris *n* bits, brash, detritus, drift, dross, duff, eluvium, exuviae, fragments, litter, moraine, pieces, remains, rubbish, rubble, ruins, sweepings, trash, waste, wreck, wreckage.

debt *n* arrears, bill, claim, commitment, debit, due, duty, indebtedness, liability, obligation, score, sin.

antonyms asset, credit.

debtor *n* bankrupt, borrower, defaulter, insolvent, mortgagee, mortgagor.

antonym creditor.

debunk *v* deflate, disparage, explode, expose, lampoon, mock, puncture, ridicule, show up.

debut *n* appearance, beginning, bow, entrance, inauguration, initiation, introduction, launching, première, presentation.

decadence *n* corruption, debasement, decadency, decay, decline, degenerateness, degeneration, deterioration, dissipation, dissolution, fall, perversion, retrogression, symbolism.

antonyms flourishing, rise.

decadent *adj* corrupt, debased, debauched, decaying, declining, degenerate, degraded, depraved, dissolute, effete, fin-de-siècle, immoral, self-indulgent, symbolist.

antonym moral.

decamp *v* abscond, absquatulate, bolt, desert, do a bunk, escape, flee, flit, fly, guy, hightail it, levant, make off, mizzle, run away, scarper, skedaddle.

decapitate *v* behead, execute, guillotine, unhead.

decay *v* atrophy, canker, cavitate, corrode, crumble, decline, decompose, decompound, degenerate, deteriorate, disintegrate, dissolve, dote, dwindle, mortify, moulder, perish, putrefy, rot, shrivel, sink, spoil, wane, waste away, wear away, wither.

antonyms flourish, grow, ripen.

n atrophy, caries, collapse, consenescence, decadence, decline, decomposition, decrepitness, decrepitude, degeneracy, degeneration, deterioration, disintegration, dying, fading, failing, gangrene, labefactation, labefaction, mortification, perishing, putrefaction, putrescence, putridity, putridness, rot, rotting, wasting, withering.

decayed *adj* addled, bad, carious, carrion, corroded, decomposed, off, perished, putrefied, putrid, rank, rotten, spoiled, wasted, withered.

decaying *adj* crumbling, decrepit, deteriorating, disintegrating, doty, dricksie, druxy, gangrenous, perishing, putrescent, rotting.

decease *n* death, demise, departure, dissolution, dying, passing, release.

v cease, croak, die, expire, give up the ghost, kick the bucket, pass away, pass on, pass over, perish.

deceased *adj* dead, defunct, departed, expired, extinct, finished, former, gone, late, lifeless, lost.

n dead, decedent, departed.

deceit *n* abuse, artifice, blind, cheat, cheating, chicanery, con, cozenage, craftiness, cunning, deceitfulness, deception, dissimulation, double-dealing, duplicity, fake, feint, fraud, fraudulence, guile, hypocrisy, imposition, imposture, misrepresentation, phenakism, pretence, ruse, sham, shift, slyness, stratagem, subterfuge, swindle, treachery, trick, trickery, underhandedness, wile.

antonyms honesty, openness.

deceitful *adj* collusive, counterfeit, crafty, deceiving, deceptive, designing, dishonest, disingenuous, double-dealing, duplicitous, elusory, fallacious, false, fraudulent, guileful, hypocritical, illusory, insincere, knavish, prestigious, Punic, ruse, sneaky, treacherous, tricky, two-faced, underhand, untrustworthy.

antonyms honest, open, trustworthy.

deceive *v* abuse, bamboozle, befool, beguile, betray, camouflage, cheat, cog, con, cozen, delude, diddle, disappoint, dissemble, dissimulate, double-cross, dupe, ensnare, entrap, flam, fool, gag, gammon, gloze, gull, have on, hoax, hoodwink, impose upon, lead on, mislead, outwit, seel, swindle, take for a ride, take in, trick, two-time.

antonym enlighten.

deceiver *n* abuser, betrayer, charlatan, cheat, con man, cozener, crook, deluder, diddler, dissembler, dissimulator, double-dealer, fake, fraud, hypocrite, impostor, inveigler, mountebank, pretender, sharper, swindler, trickster.

decency *n* appropriateness, civility, correctness, courtesy, decorum, etiquette, fitness, good form, good manners, helpfulness, modesty, propriety, respectability, seemliness, thoughtfulness.

antonyms discourtesy, indecency.

decent *adj* acceptable, accommodating, adequate, ample, appropriate, average, becoming, befitting, chaste, comely, comme il faut, competent, courteous, decorous, delicate, fair, fit, fitting, friendly, generous, gracious, gradely, helpful, kind, modest, nice, obliging, passable, polite, presentable, proper, pure, reasonable, respectable, satisfactory, seemly, sufficient, suitable, thoughtful, tolerable.

antonyms disobliging, indecent, poor.

decentralisation *n* delegation, development, devolution.

antonym centralisation.

deception *n* artifice, bluff, cheat, conning, craftiness, cunning, deceitfulness, deceit, deceptiveness, decoy, defraudation, defraudment, dissembling, dissimulation, duplicity, false-pretences, feint, flim-flam, fraud, fraudulence, guile, gullery, hoax, hype, hypocrisy, illusion, imposition, imposture, insincerity, legerdemain, leg-pull, lie, ruse, sell, sham, snare, stratagem, subterfuge, take-in, treachery, trick, trickery, wile.

antonyms artlessness, openness.

deceptive *adj* ambiguous, catchy, delusive, delusory, dishonest, elusory, fake, fallacious, false, fraudulent, illusive, illusory, misleading, mock, specious, spurious, unreliable.

antonyms artless, genuine, open.

decide *v* adjudge, adjudicate, choose, conclude, decree, determine, dijudicate, elect, end, fix, judge, opt, purpose, reach a decision, resolve, settle.

decided *adj* absolute, assertive, categorical, certain, clear-cut, decisive, definite, deliberate, determined, distinct, emphatic, express, firm, forthright, indisputable, marked, noticeable, positive, pronounced, resolute, strong-willed, unambiguous, undeniable, undisputed, unequivocal, unfaltering, unhesitating, unmistakable, unquestionable.

antonyms indecisive, undecided.

decidedly *adv* absolutely, certainly, clearly, decisively, definitely, distinctly, downright, positively, quite, unequivocally, unmistakably, very.

decider *n* clincher, coup de grâce, determiner, floorer.

deciding *adj* chief, conclusive, critical, crucial, crunch, decisive, determining, final, influential, prime, principal, significant, supreme.

antonym insignificant.

decipher *v* construe, crack, decode, decrypt, deduce, explain, figure out, interpret, make out, read, solve, transliterate, uncipher, understand, unfold, unravel, unscramble.

antonym encode.

decipherment *n* decryption, interpretation, translation, transliteration, unscrambling.

antonym encoding.

decision *n* arbitrament, arbitration, arrêt, conclusion, decisiveness, determination, fetwa, finding, firmness, judgement, outcome, parti, purpose, purposefulness, resoluteness, resolution, resolve, result, ruling, settlement, verdict.

decisive *adj* absolute, conclusive, critical, crucial, crunch, decided, definite, definitive, determinate, determined, fateful, final, firm, forceful, forthright, incisive, influential, momentous, positive, resolute, significant, strong-minded, supreme, trenchant.

antonyms indecisive, insignificant.

deck *v* adorn, apparel, array, attire, beautify, bedeck, bedight, bedizen, betrim, clothe, decorate, doll up, dress, embellish, festoon, garland, grace, ornament, prettify, pretty up, primp, prink, rig out, smarten, titivate, tog out, tog up, trick out, trim.

declaim *v* bespout, harangue, hold forth, lecture, mouth, orate, perorate, preach, proclaim, rant, recite, rhetorise, speak, speechify, spiel, spout, tub-thump.

declamation *n* address, harangue, lecture, oration, rant, recitation, rhetoric, speech, speechifying, tirade.

declamatory *adj* bombastic, discursive, fustian, grandiloquent, grandiose, high-flown, inflated, magniloquent, oratorical, oro(ro)tund, overblown, pompous, rhetorical, stagy, stilted, theatrical, turgid.

declaration *n* acknowledgement, affirmation, announcement, assertion, asseveration, attestation, averment, avouchment, avowal, deposition, disclosure, edict, manifesto, notification, proclamation, profession, promulgation, pronouncement, pronunciamento, protestation, revelation, statement, testimony.

declare *v* affirm, announce, assert, attest, aver, avouch, avow, certify, claim, confess, confirm, convey, disclose, maintain, manifest, nuncupate, proclaim, profess, pronounce, reveal, show, state, swear, testify, validate, witness.

decline[1] *v* avoid, balk, decay, decrease, degenerate, deny, deteriorate, deviate, diminish, droop, dwindle, ebb, fade, fail, fall, fall off, flag, forgo, languish, lessen, pine, refuse, reject, shrink, sink, turn down, wane, weaken, worsen.

n abatement, consumption, decay, declension, decrepitude, degeneration, deterioration, deviation, diminution, downturn, dwindling, enfeeblement, failing, falling-off, lessening, paracme, phthisis, recession, senility, slump, tuberculosis, weakening, worsening.

decline[2] *v* descend, dip, sink, slant, slope.
n brae, declination, declivity, descent, deviation, dip, divergence, hill, incline, obliqueness, obliquity, slope.

declivity *n* brae, declination, decline, descent, incline, slant, slope.

antonym acclivity.

decode *v* decipher, decrypt, interpret, translate, transliterate, uncipher, unscramble.

antonym encode.

decomposable *adj* biodegradable, decompoundable, degradable, destructible.

decompose *v* analyse, atomise, break down, break up, crumble, decay, decompound, degrade, disintegrate, dissolve, distil, fall apart, fester, fractionate, putrefy, rot, separate, spoil.

antonyms combine, unite.

decomposition *n* atomisation, breakdown, corruption, decay, degradation, disintegration, dissolution, distillation, division, electrolysis, fractionation, hydrolysis, putrefaction, putrescence, putridity, rot.

antonyms combination, unification.

decor *n* colour-scheme, decoration, embellishments, furnishings, ornamentation, scenery.

decorate[1] *v* adorn, beautify, bedeck, colour, daiker, deck, do up, embellish, enrich, furbish, grace, impearl, miniate, ornament, paint, paper, prettify, renovate, tart up, trick out, trim, wallpaper.

decorate[2] *v* bemedal, cite, crown, garland, honour.

decorated *adj* baroque, elaborate, embellished, figured, garnished, ornate, rococo.

antonym plain.

decoration[1] *n* adornment, arabesque, bauble, beautification, curlicue, elaboration, embellishment, enrichment, falderal, flounce, flourish, frill, frou-frou, furbelow, garnish, ornament, ornamentation, pass(e)ment, passementerie, scroll, spangle, trimming, trinket.

decoration[2] *n* award, badge, colours, crown, emblem, garland, garter, laurel, laurel-wreath, medal, order, ribbon, star.

decorative *adj* adorning, arty-crafty, baroque, beautifying, embellishing, enhancing, fancy, non-functional, ornamental, ornate, pretty, rococo, superfluous.

antonyms plain, ugly.

decorous *adj* appropriate, becoming, befitting, comely, comme il faut, correct, courtly, decent, dignified, fit, maidenly, mannerly, modest, polite, proper, refined, sedate, seemly, staid, suitable, well-behaved.

antonym indecorous.

decorum *n* behaviour, breeding, courtliness, decency, deportment, dignity, etiquette, gentility, good manners, grace, gravity, modesty, politeness, politesse, propriety, protocol, punctilio, respectability, restraint, seemliness.

antonyms bad manners, indecorum.

decoy *n* attraction, bait, ensnarement, enticement, inducement, lure, pretence, roper(-in), shill, trap.

v allure, attract, bait, beguile, deceive, draw, ensnare, entice, entrap, inveigle, lead, lure, seduce, tempt.

decrease *v* abate, ablate, contract, curtail, cut down, decline, decrement, diminish, drop, dwindle, ease, fall off, lessen, lower, peter out, reduce, shrink, slacken, slim, subside, taper, wane.

antonym increase.

n abatement, ablation, contraction, cutback, decline, decrement, degression, diminution, downturn, dwindling, ebb, falling-off, lessening, loss, reduction, shrinkage, step-down, subsidence.

antonym increase.

decree *n* act, command, decretal, dictum, edict, enactment, firman, hatti-sherif, indiction, interlocution, interlocutor, law, mandate, order, ordinance, precept, proclamation, regulation, ruling, statute, ukase.

v command, decide, determine, dictate, enact, lay down, ordain, order, prescribe, proclaim, pronounce, rescript, rule.

decreed *adj* enacted, ordained, proclaimed, stated, writ, written.

decrepit *adj* aged, antiquated, battered, broken-backed, broken-down, crippled, debilitated, deteriorated, dilapidated, doddering, doddery, feeble, frail, incapacitated, infirm, ramshackle, rickety, run-down, superannuated, tumble-down, warby, wasted, weak, worn-out.

antonyms fit, well-cared-for, youthful.

decrepitude *n* debility, decay, degeneration, deterioration, dilapidation, disability, dotage, feebleness, incapacity, infirmity, invalidity, old age, senescence, senility, wasting, weakness.

antonyms good repair, youth.

decry *v* abuse, belittle, blame, censure, condemn, criticise, cry down, declaim against, denounce, depreciate, derogate, detract, devalue, discredit, disparage, inveigh against, rail against, run down, traduce, underestimate, underrate, undervalue.

antonyms praise, value.

dedicate *v* address, assign, bless, commit, consecrate, devote, give over to, hallow, inscribe, offer, pledge, present, sacrifice, sanctify, set apart, surrender.

dedicated *adj* committed, devoted, enthusiastic, given over to, purposeful, single-hearted, single-minded, sworn, whole-hearted, zealous.

antonyms apathetic, uncommitted.

dedication[1] *n* adherence, allegiance, attachment, commitment, devotedness, devotion, faithfulness, loyalty, self-sacrifice, single-mindedness, whole-heartedness.

antonym apathy.

dedication[2] *n* address, consecration, donation, hallowing, inscription, presentation, sanctification.

deduce *v* conclude, derive, draw, gather, glean, infer, reason, surmise, understand.

deducible *adj* a fortiori, a posteriori, derivable, inferable, traceable.

deduct *v* decrease by, knock off, reduce by, remove, subduct, subtract, take away, withdraw.

antonym add.

deduction[1] *n* assumption, conclusion, consectary, corollary, finding, inference, reasoning, result.

deduction[2] *n* abatement, allowance, decrease, diminution, discount, reduction, subduction, subtraction, withdrawal.

antonyms addition, increase.

deed[1] *n* achievement, act, action, exploit, fact, factum, feat, gest(e), performance, reality, truth.

deed[2] *n* contract, document, indenture, instrument, record, title, transaction.

deem *v* account, adjudge, believe, conceive, consider, esteem, estimate, hold, imagine, judge, reckon, regard, suppose, think.

deep *adj* absorbed, abstract, abstruse, abyssal, acute, arcane, artful, astute, bass, booming, bottomless, broad, canny, cryptic, cunning, dark, designing, devious, discerning, engrossed, esoteric, extreme, far, fathomless, full-toned, grave, great, hidden, immersed, inmost, inner, innermost, insidious, intense, knowing, learned, lost, low, low-pitched, mysterious, obscure, penetrating, preoccupied, profound, rapt, recondite, resonant, rich, sagacious, scheming, secret, shrewd, sonorous, strong, unfathomable, unfathomed, unplumbed, unsoundable, unsounded, vivid, wide, wise, yawning.

antonyms open, shallow.

n briny, drink, high seas, main, ocean, sea.

deepen *v* dredge, excavate, grow, hollow, increase, intensify, magnify, reinforce, scoop out, strengthen.

antonym fill in.

deeply *adv* acutely, affectingly, completely, distressingly, feelingly, gravely, intensely, mournfully, movingly, passionately, profoundly, sadly, seriously, severely, thoroughly, to the quick, very much.

antonym slightly.

deep-seated *adj* confirmed, deep, deep-rooted, entrenched, fixed, ineradicable, ingrained, inveterate, rooted, settled, subconscious, unconscious.

antonyms eradicable, temporary.

deer *n* buck, doe, hart, reindeer, roe, stag.

deface *v* blemish, damage, deform, destroy, disfeature, disfigure, impair, injure, mar, mutilate, obliterate, spoil, sully, tarnish, vandalise.

antonym repair.

defamation *n* aspersion, calumny, denigration, derogation, disparagement, innuendo, libel, mud-slinging, obloquy, opprobrium, scandal, slander, slur, smear, traducement, vilification.

antonym praise.

defamatory *adj* abusive, calumnious, contumelious, denigrating, derogatory, disparaging, injurious, insulting, libellous, pejorative, slanderous, vilifying, vituperative.

antonym complimentary.

defame *v* asperse, belie, besmirch, blacken, calumniate, cast aspersions on, cloud, denigrate, detract, discredit, disgrace, dishonour, disparage, infame, libel, malign, slander, smear, speak evil of, stigmatise, traduce, vilify, vituperate.

antonyms compliment, praise.

default *n* absence, defalcation, defect, deficiency, dereliction, failure, fault, lack, lapse, neglect, non-payment, omission, want.

v backslide, bilk, defraud, dodge, evade, fail, levant, neglect, rat, renegue, swindle, waddle, welsh.

defaulter *n* defalcator, defector, delinquent, duck, embezzler, levanter, non-payer, offender, peculator, welsher.

defeat *v* baffle, balk, beat, best, checkmate, clobber, confound, conquer, counteract, crush, disappoint, discomfit, down, foil, frustrate, get the better of, outbargain, overpower, overthrow, overwhelm, psych out, quell, repulse, rout, ruin, stump, subdue, subjugate, tank, thump, thwart, trounce, vanquish, vote down, whop.

n beating, conquest, debâcle, disappointment, discomfiture, failure, frustration, overthrow, rebuff, repulse, reverse, rout, setback, thwarting, trouncing, vanquishment, Waterloo.

defeated *adj* balked, beaten, bested, checkmated, confounded, conquered, crushed, licked, nonplussed, overcome, overpowered, overwhelmed, routed, thrashed, thwarted, trounced, vanquished, worsted.

antonyms conquering, triumphant.

defeatist *n* futilitarian, pessimist, prophet of doom, quitter.

antonym optimist.

adj cynical, despairing, despondent, fatalistic, gloomy, helpless, hopeless, pessimistic, resigned, resourceless.

antonym optimistic.

defecate *v* ease oneself, egest, empty, evacuate, excrete, pass a motion, poo, relieve oneself, shit, void (excrement).

defecation *n* dejection, egestion, elimination, evacuation, excrement, excretion, motion, movement, poo, shit, voiding.

defect *n* absence, blemish, bug, default, deficiency, error, failing, fault, flaw, frailty, hamartia, imperfection, inadequacy, lack, mistake, shortcoming, spot, taint, want, weakness.

v apostatise, break faith, desert, rebel, renegue, revolt, tergiversate.

defection *n* abandonment, apostasy, backsliding, defalcation, dereliction, desertion, rebellion, renegation, revolt.

defective *adj* abnormal, broken, deficient, faulty, flawed, imperfect, inadequate, incomplete, insufficient, kaput, out of order, retarded, scant, short, subnormal.

antonyms normal, operative.

defector *n* apostate, deserter, Grenzgänger, Judas, quisling, rat, recreant, renegade, runagate, tergiversator, turncoat.

defence[1] *n* aegis, armament, barricade, bastion, buckler, bulwark, buttress, cover, deterrence, fastness, fortification, guard, immunity, muniment, munition, protection, rampart, resistance, safeguard, security, shelter, shield.

antonym attack.

defence[2] *n* alibi, apologia, apology, argument, case, declaration, denial, excuse, exoneration, explanation, extenuation, justification, palliation, plea, pleading, rebuttal, testimony, vindication.

defenceless *adj* endangered, exposed, helpless, imperilled, naked, powerless, unarmed, undefended, unguarded, unprotected, unshielded, vulnerable, wide open.

antonym protected.

defend *v* assert, bulwark, champion, contest, cover, endorse, espouse, fortify, guard, justify, maintain, plead, preserve, protect, safeguard, screen, secure, shelter, shield, speak up for, stand by, stand up for, support, sustain, uphold, vindicate, watch over.

antonym attack.

defendant *n* accused, appellant, defender, litigant, offender, prisoner, respondent.

defender *n* advocate, bodyguard, champion, counsel, escort, guard, patron, promachos, protector, sponsor, supporter, vindicator.

antonym attacker.

defensible *adj* arguable, holdable, impregnable, justifiable, pardonable, permissible, plausible, safe, secure, tenable, unassailable, valid, vindicable.

antonyms indefensible, insecure.

defensive *adj* apologetic, aposematic, averting, cautious, defending, opposing, protective, safeguarding, self-justifying, wary, watchful, withstanding.

antonym bold.

defer[1] *v* adjourn, delay, hold over, postpone, procrastinate, prorogue, protract, put off, put on ice, shelve, suspend, waive.

defer[2] *v* accede, bow, capitulate, comply, give way, kowtow, respect, submit, yield.

deference *n* acquiescence, attention, capitulation, civility, complaisance, compliance, consideration, courtesy, esteem, homage, honour, morigeration, obedience, obeisance, obsequiousness, politeness, regard, respect, reverence, submission, submissiveness, thoughtfulness, veneration, yielding.

deferential *adj* civil, complaisant, considerate, courteous, dutiful, ingratiating, morigerous, obedient, obeisant, obsequious, polite, regardful, respectful, reverential, submissive.

antonyms arrogant, immodest.

deferment *n* adjournment, deferral, delay, moratorium, postponement, procrastination, putting off, stay, suspension.

defiance *n* challenge, confrontation, contempt, contumacy, disobedience, disregard, insolence, insubordination, obstinacy, opposition, provocation, rebelliousness, recalcitrance, spite.

antonyms acquiescence, submissiveness.

defiant *adj* aggressive, audacious, bold, challenging, contumacious, daring, disobedient, insolent, insubordinate, intransigent, mutinous, obstinate, provocative, rebellious, recalcitrant, refractory, truculent, unco-operative.

antonyms acquiescent, submissive.

deficiency *n* absence, dearth, defalcation, defect, deficit, demerit, failing, fault, flaw, frailty, imperfection, inadequacy, insufficiency, lack, paucity, scantiness, scarcity, shortage, shortcoming, want, wantage, weakness.

antonym superfluity.

deficient *adj* defectible, defective, exiguous, faulty, flawed, impaired, imperfect, inadequate, incomplete, inferior, insufficient, lacking, meagre, scanty, scarce, short, skimpy, unsatisfactory, wanting, weak.

antonyms excessive, superfluous.

deficit *n* arrears, defalcation, default, deficiency, lack, loss, shortage, shortfall.

antonym excess.

defile[1] *v* abuse, befoul, besmirch, contaminate, corrupt, debase, deflower, defoul, degrade, desecrate, dirty, disgrace, dishonour, inquinate, make foul, molest, pollute, profane, rape, ravish, seduce, smear, soil, stain, sully, taint, tarnish, violate, vitiate.

antonym cleanse.

defile[2] *n* gorge, gulch, gully, pass, passage, ravine.

defiled *adj* besmirched, desecrated, dishonoured, impure, maculate, polluted, profaned, ravished, spoilt, sullied, tainted, unclean.

antonyms clean, cleansed, pure.

definable *adj* ascertainable, definite, describable, determinable, explicable, perceptible, specific.

antonym indefinable.

define *v* bound, characterise, circumscribe, delimit, delimitate, delineate, demarcate.

describe, designate, detail, determine, explain, expound, interpret, limit, mark out, outline, specify, spell out.

definite *adj* assured, certain, clear, clear-cut, decided, determined, exact, explicit, express, fixed, guaranteed, marked, obvious, particular, positive, precise, settled, specific, substantive, sure.

antonyms indefinite, vague.

definitely *adv* absolutely, beyond doubt, categorically, certainly, clearly, decidedly, doubtless, doubtlessly, easily, finally, indeed, indubitably, obviously, plainly, positively, surely, undeniably, unequivocally, unmistakably, unquestionably, without doubt, without fail.

definition[1] *n* clarification, delimitation, delineation, demarcation, description, determination, elucidation, explanation, exposition, interpretation, outlining, settling.

definition[2] *n* clarity, clearness, contrast, distinctness, focus, precision, sharpness.

definitive *adj* absolute, authoritative, complete, conclusive, correct, decisive, exact, exhaustive, final, perfect, reliable, standard, ultimate.

antonym interim.

deflate[1] *v* chasten, collapse, contract, dash, debunk, disconcert, dispirit, empty, exhaust, flatten, humble, humiliate, mortify, press, puncture, put down, shrink, squash, squeeze, void.

antonym inflate.

deflate[2] *v* decrease, depreciate, depress, devalue, diminish, lessen, lower, reduce.

antonym increase.

deflect *v* avert, bend, deviate, diverge, glance off, ricochet, shy, sidetrack, slew, swerve, turn, turn aside, twist, veer, wind.

deflection *n* aberration, bend, bending, declination, deviation, divergence, drift, refraction, swerve, turning, veer.

deflower *v* assault, defile, deflorate, desecrate, despoil, force, harm, mar, molest, rape, ravish, ruin, seduce, spoil, violate.

deflowering *n* defloration, green gown, rape, ravishment, violation.

deform *v* corrupt, disfigure, distort, mangle, mar, pervert, ruin, spoil, twist, warp.

deformation *n* bend, curve, diastrophism, distortion, malformation, twist, warp.

deformed *adj* bent, blemished, buckled, contorted, corrupted, crippled, crooked, defaced, depraved, disfigured, distorted, gnarled, maimed, malformed, mangled, marred, misbegotten, misborn, miscreate(d), misshapen, mutilated, perverted, ruined, spoilt, twisted, warped.

deformity *n* abnormality, corruption, defect, depravity, disfigurement, distortion, dysmelia, irregularity, malformation, misfeature, misproportion, misshape, misshapenness, ugliness.

defraud *v* beguile, bilk, cheat, con, cozen, deceive, delude, diddle, do, dupe, embezzle, fleece, gull, gyp, outwit, rip off, rob, rock, sting, swindle, trick.

defray *v* clear, cover, discharge, foot, meet, pay, refund, repay, settle.

antonym incur.

defrayal *n* clearance, defrayment, discharge, payment, refund, settlement.

antonym incurrence.

deft *adj* able, adept, adroit, agile, clever, dexterous, expert, feat, habile, handy, neat, nifty, nimble, proficient, skilful.

antonym clumsy.

defunct *adj* dead, deceased, departed, expired, extinct, gone, inoperative, invalid, kaput, non-existent, obsolete, passe.

antonyms alive, live, operative.

defy *v* baffle, beard, beat, brave, challenge, confront, contemn, dare, defeat, despise, disregard, elude, face, flout, foil, frustrate, outdare, provoke, repel, repulse, resist, scorn, slight, spurn, thwart, withstand.

antonyms flinch, quail, yield.

degeneracy *n* corruption, debasement, decadence, decay, decline, decrease, degradation, depravation, depravity, deterioration, dissoluteness, effeteness, falling-off, immorality, inferiority, lapsing, meanness, poorness, turpitude.

antonyms morality, uprightness.

degenerate *adj* base, corrupt, debased, debauched, decadent, degenerated, degraded, depraved, deteriorated, dissolute, effete, fallen, immoral, low, mean, perverted.

antonyms upright, virtuous.

v age, decay, decline, decrease, deteriorate, fall off, lapse, regress, retrogress, rot, sink, slip, worsen.

antonym improve.

degeneration *n* debasement, decline, degeneracy, descent, deterioration, dissipation, dissolution, falling-off, lapse, lapsing, regression, retrogress, retrogression.

antonyms improvement, uprightness, virtue.

degradation *n* abasement, debasedness, debasement, decadence, decline, degeneracy, degeneration, demission, demotion, derogation, destitution, deterioration, discredit, disgrace, dishonour, downgrading, humiliation, ignominy, mortification, perversion, shame.

antonyms enhancement, virtue.

degrade *v* abase, adulterate, break, brutalise, cashier, cheapen, corrupt, debase, declass, demean, demote, depose, deprive, deteriorate. discredit, disennoble, disgrace, disgrade, dishonour, disrank, disrate, downgrade, embase, humble, humiliate, impair, injure, lower, pervert, shame, unfrock, ungown, vitiate, weaken.

antonyms enhance, improve.

degraded *adj* abandoned, abased, base, corrupt, debased, debauched, decadent, declasse, depraved, despicable, disgraced, disreputable, dissolute, low, mean, profligate, sordid, vicious, vile.

antonyms moral, upright.

degrading *adj* base, cheapening, contemptible, debasing, demeaning, disgraceful, dishonourable, humiliating, ignoble, infra dig, lowering, shameful, undignified, unworthy.

antonym enhancing.

degree *n* calibre, class, division, doctorate, extent, gradation, grade, intensity, interval, level, limit, mark, masterate, measure, notch, order, point, position, proportion, quality, quantity, range, rank, rate, ratio, run, scale, scope, severity, stage, standard, standing, station, status, step, unit.

dehydrate *v* desiccate, drain, dry out, dry up, effloresce, evaporate, exsiccate, parch.

deification *n* apotheosis, divinification, divinisation, elevation, ennoblement, exaltation, glorification, idolisation.

deify *v* apotheosise, divinify, divinise, elevate, ennoble, enthrone, exalt, extol, glorify, idealise, idolise, immortalise, venerate, worship.

deign *v* condescend, consent, demean oneself, lower oneself, stoop, vouchsafe.

deity *n* Allah, demigod, demigoddess, deva, divinity, god, goddess, godhead, godhood, idol, immortal, Jehovah, kami, power.

deject *v* cast down, crush, dampen, daunt, demoralise, depress, discourage, dishearten, dismay, dispirit, sadden.

dejected *adj* abattu, alamort, blue, cast down, crestfallen, depressed, despondent, disconsolate, disheartened, dismal, doleful, down, downcast, downhearted, gloomy, glum, jaw-fallen, low, low-spirited, melancholy, miserable, morose, sad, spiritless, woebegone, wretched.

antonyms bright, happy, high-spirited.

dejection *n* blues, depression, despair, despondency, disconsolateness, disconsolation, doldrums, downheartedness, dumps, gloom, gloominess, low spirits, melancholy, sadness, sorrow, unhappiness.

antonyms happiness, high spirits.

delay *v* arrest, bog down, check, dawdle, defer, detain, dilly-dally, drag, halt, hinder, hold back, hold over, hold up, impede, lag, linger, loiter, obstruct, play for time, postpone, procrastinate, prolong, protract, put off, retard, set back, shelve, stall, stave off, stop, suspend, table, tarry, temporise.

antonyms accelerate, expedite, hurry.

n ambage, check, cunctation, dawdling, deferment, detention, dilly-dallying, hindrance, hold-up, impediment, interruption, interval, lingering, loitering, obstruction, postponement, procrastination, setback, stay, stoppage, suspension, tarrying, wait.

antonyms hastening, hurry.

delaying *adj* cunctatious, cunctative, cunctatory, filibusterous, retardative, retardatory.

antonyms advancing, expediting.

delectable *adj* adorable, agreeable, ambrosial, ambrosian, appetising, charming, dainty, delicious, delightful, enjoyable, enticing, flavoursome, gratifying, inviting, luscious, lush, palatable, pleasant, pleasurable, satisfying, scrumptious, tasty, toothsome, yummy.

antonyms horrid, unpleasant.

delectation *n* amusement, comfort, contentment, delight, diversion, enjoyment, entertainment, gratification, happiness, pleasure, refreshment, relish, satisfaction.

antonym distaste.

delegate *n* agent, ambassador, commissioner, deputy, envoy, legate, messenger, nuncio, representative.

v accredit, appoint, assign, authorise, charge, commission, consign, depute, designate, devolve, empower, entrust, give, hand over, mandate, name, nominate, pass on, relegate, transfer.

delegated *adj* assigned, devolved, relegated, vicarate, vicarial, vicariate.

delegation *n* commission, contingent, deputation, embassy, legation, mission.

delete *v* blot out, blue-pencil, cancel, cross out, dele, edit, edit out, efface, erase, expunge, obliterate, remove, rub out, strike, strike out.

antonym add in.

deleterious *adj* bad, damaging, destructive, detrimental, harmful, hurtful, injurious, noxious, pernicious, prejudicial, ruinous.

antonyms enhancing, helpful.

deliberate *v* cogitate, consider, consult, debate, discuss, meditate, mull over, ponder, reflect, ruminate, think, weigh.

adj advised, calculated, careful, cautious, circumspect, conscious, considered, designed, heedful, intentional, measured, methodical, planned, ponderous, prearranged, premeditated, prudent, purposeful, slow, studied, thoughtful, unhurried, volitive, voulu, wary, wilful, willed, witting.

antonyms chance, unintentional.

deliberately *adv* by design, calculatingly, consciously, determinedly, emphatically, in cold blood, intentionally, knowingly, on purpose, pointedly, resolutely, wilfully, with malice aforethought, wittingly.

antonym unintentionally.

deliberation *n* calculation, canniness, care, carefulness, caution, circumspection, cogitation, conference, consideration, consultation, coolness, debate, discussion, forethought, meditation, prudence, purpose, reflection, rumination, speculation, study, thought, wariness.

delicacy *n* accuracy, bonne bouche, daintiness, dainty, discrimination, elegance, exquisiteness, fastidiousness, fineness, finesse, lightness, luxury, niceness, nicety, precision, purity, refinement, relish, savoury, sensibility, sensitiveness, sensitivity, subtlety, sweetmeat, tact, taste, titbit, treat.

antonyms indelicacy, tactlessness.

delicate *adj* accurate, ailing, careful, choice, considerate, critical, dainty, debilitated, deft, delicious, detailed, diaphanous, difficult, diplomatic, discreet, discriminating, eggshell, elegant, elfin, exquisite, faint, fastidious, fine, flimsy, fragile, frail, friand(e), gauzy, graceful, hazardous, kid-glove, minikin, minute, muted, nesh, pastel, precarious, precise, prudish, pure, refined, risky, savoury, scrupulous, sensible, sensitive, sickly, skilled, slender, slight, soft, softly-softly, squeamish, sticky, subdued, subtle, tactful, tender, ticklish, touchy, weak.

antonyms harsh, imprecise, strong.

delicious *adj* agreeable, ambrosial, ambrosian, appetising, charming, choice, dainty, delectable, delightful, enjoyable, entertaining, exquisite, flavoursome, goluptious, lip-smacking, luscious, mouthwatering, nectareous, palatable, pleasant, pleasing, savoury, scrummy, scrumptious, tasty, toothsome, yummy.

antonym unpleasant.

delight *n* bliss, ecstasy, enjoyment, felicity, gladness, gratification, happiness, heaven, joy, jubilation, pleasure, rapture, transport.

antonyms dismay, displeasure.

v amuse, charm, cheer, divert, enchant, gladden, gratify, please, ravish, rejoice, satisfy, thrill, tickle.

antonyms dismay, displease.

delight in appreciate, enjoy, gloat over, glory in, indulge in, like, love, relish, revel in, savour, take pride in.

delighted *adj* captivated, charmed, cock-a-hoop, ecstatic, elated, enchanted, gladdened, happy, joyous, jubilant, overjoyed, pleased, pleased as Punch, thrilled.

antonyms dismayed, displeased.

delightful *adj* agreeable, amusing, captivating, charming, congenial, delectable, delightsome, enchanting, engaging, enjoyable, entertaining, fascinating, fetching, gratifying, heavenly, pleasant, pleasing, pleasurable, rapturous, ravishing, scrummy, scrumptious, sweet, thrilling, wizard.

antonym horrible.

delimit *v* bound, define, demarcate, determine, establish, fix, mark.

delineate *v* characterise, chart, depict, describe, design, draw, figure, limn, outline, paint, picture, portray, render, represent, sketch, trace.

delineation *n* account, characterisation, chart, depiction, description, design, diagram, drawing, outline, picture, portrait, portrayal, representation, sketch, tracing.

delinquency *n* crime, criminality, fault, law-breaking, misbehaviour, misconduct, misdeed, misdemeanour, offence, wrong-doing.

delinquent *n* criminal, culprit, defaulter, hooligan, law-breaker, malefactor, miscreant, offender, rough, tough, wrong-doer, young offender.

adj careless, culpable, guilty, neglectful, negligent, remiss.

antonyms blameless, careful.

delirious *adj* bacchic, beside oneself, corybantic, crazy, demented, deranged, ecstatic, excited, frantic, frenzied, hysterical, incoherent, insane, light-headed, mad, maenadic, raving, unhinged, wild.

antonym sane.

delirium *n* derangement, ecstasy, fever, frenzy, fury, hallucination, hysteria, insanity, jimjams, lunacy, madness, passion, rage, raving.

deliver *v* acquit, administer, aim, announce, bear, bring, carry, cart, cede, commit, convey, deal, declare, direct, discharge, dispense, distribute, emancipate, feed, free, give, give forth, give up, grant, hand over, inflict, launch, liberate, loose, make over, pass, present, proclaim, pronounce, publish, ransom, read, redeem, release, relinquish, rescue, resign, save, strike, supply, surrender, throw, transfer, transport, turn over, utter, yield.

deliverance *n* emancipation, escape, extrication, liberation, ransom, redemption, release, rescue, salvation.

delivery[1] *n* consignment, conveyance, dispatch, distribution, shipment, surrender, transfer, transmission, transmittal, transport.

delivery[2] *n* articulation, elocution, enunciation, intonation, presentation, speech, utterance.

delivery[3] *n* accouchement, childbirth, confinement, labour, parturition, travail.

dell *n* dargle, dean, dimble, dingle, hollow, vale, valley.

delude *v* bamboozle, beguile, cheat, con, cozen, deceive, dupe, fool, gull, hoax, hoodwink, impose on, misguide, misinform, mislead, snow, take in, trick.

deluge *n* avalanche, barrage, cataclysm, downpour, flood, hail, inundation, rush, spate, torrent.

v bury, douse, drench, drown, engulf, flood, inundate, overload, overrun, overwhelm, soak, submerge, swamp.

delusion *n* deception, error, fallacy, fancy, fata Morgana, hallucination, illusion, mirage, misapprehension, misbelief, misconception, mistake, phantasm.

delve *v* burrow, dig into, examine, explore, investigate, poke, probe, ransack, research, root, rummage, search.

demagogue *n* agitator, Boanerges, firebrand, haranguer, mob-orator, orator, rabble-rouser, tub-thumper.

demand *v* ask, call for, challenge, claim, exact, expect, inquire, insist on, interrogate, involve, necessitate, need, order, question, request, require, take, want.

antonyms cede, supply.

n bidding, call, charge, claim, desire, inquiry, interrogation, necessity, need, order, question, request, requirement, requisition, want.

antonym supply.

demanding *adj* back-breaking, challenging, clamorous, difficult, exacting, exhausting, exigent, fatiguing, hard, imperious, importunate, insistent, nagging, pressing, taxing, tough, trying, urgent, wearing.

antonyms easy, easy-going, undemanding.

demarcate *v* define, delimit, determine, differentiate, distinguish, establish, fix, mark, mark out, separate.

demarcation *n* bound, boundary, bourn, confine, delimitation, differentiation, distinction, division, enclosure, limit, line, margin, pale, separation.

demean *v* abase, condescend, debase, degrade, deign, descend, humble, lower, stoop.

antonym enhance.

demeanour *n* air, bearing, behaviour, carriage, comportment, conduct, deportment, manner, mien, port.

demented *adj* crazed, crazy, deranged, distracted, distraught, dotty, foolish, frenzied, idiotic, insane, lunatic, mad, maenadic, maniacal, manic, non compos mentis, nutty, unbalanced, unhinged.

antonym sane.

demigod *n* demigoddess, kami, power, spirit.

demise[1] *n* collapse, death, decease, departure, dissolution, downfall, end, expiration, failure, fall, passing, ruin, termination.

demise[2] *n* alienation, conveyance, inheritance, transfer, transmission.

v bequeath, convey, grant, leave, transfer, will.

democracy *n* autonomy, commonwealth, populism, republic, self-government.

democratic *adj* autonomous, egalitarian, popular, populist, representative, republican, self-governing.

demolish *v* annihilate, bulldoze, consume, defeat, delapidate, destroy, devour, dismantle, down, eat, flatten, gobble, gulp, guzzle, knock down, level, overthrow, overturn, pull down, pulverize, raze, ruin, tear down, unbuild, undo, wreck.

antonym build up.

demolition *n* bulldozing, destruction, dismantling, levelling, razing, wrecking.

demon[1] *n* afrit, daemon, daimon, devil, evil spirit, fallen angel, fiend, genius, goblin, guardian spirit, incubus, monster, numen, rakshas, rakshasa, succubus, villain, warlock.

demon[2] *n* ace, addict, dab hand, fanatic, fiend, master, pastmaster, wizard.

demoniac *adj* crazed, d(a)emonic, demoniacal, devilish, diabolic, diabolical, fiendish, frantic, frenetic, frenzied, furious, hectic, hellish, infernal, mad, maniacal, manic, possessed, satanic.

demonstrable *adj* arguable, attestable, axiomatic, certain, clear, evident, evincible, incontrovertible, indubitable, irrefutable, obvious, palpable, positive, provable, self-evident, substantiable, undeniable, unmistakable, verifiable.

antonyms untestable, unverifiable.

demonstrate[1] *v* describe, display, establish, evidence, evince, exhibit, explain, expound, illustrate, indicate, manifest, prove, show, substantiate, teach, testify to.

demonstrate[2] *v* march, parade, picket, protest, rally, sit in.

demonstration[1] *n* affirmation, confirmation, deixis, description, display, evidence, exhibition, explanation, exposition, expression, illustration, manifestation, presentation, proof, substantiation, test, testimony, trial, validation.

demonstration[2] *v* demo, march, parade, picket, protest, rally, sit-in, work-in.

demonstrative *adj* affectionate, deictic, effusive, emotional, endeictic, evincive, expansive, explanatory, expository, expressive, illustrative, indicative, loving, open, symptomatic, unreserved, unrestrained.

antonyms cold, undemonstrative.

demoralisation *n* agitation, corruption, crushing, debasement, dejection, depravation, depression, despondency, devitalisation, discomfiture, enervation, lowering, panic, perturbation, perversion, trepidation, unmanning, vitiation, weakening.

antonym encouragement.

demoralise *v* corrupt, cripple, crush, daunt, debase, debauch, deject, deprave, depress, disconcert, discourage, dishearten, dispirit, enfeeble, lower, panic, pervert, rattle, sap, shake, undermine, unnerve, vitiate, weaken.

antonym encourage.

demoralised *adj* bad, base, broken, corrupt, crushed, degenerate, dejected, depraved, depressed, despondent, discouraged, disheartened, dispirited, dissolute, downcast, immoral, low, reprobate, sinful, subdued, unmanned, unnerved, weakened, wicked.

antonyms encouraged, heartened.

demote *v* declass, degrade, disrate, downgrade, reduce, relegate.

antonyms promote, upgrade.

demotic *adj* enchorial, enchoric, popular, vernacular, vulgar.

demur *v* balk, cavil, disagree, dispute, dissent, doubt, hesitate, object, pause, protest, refuse, take exception, waver.

n arrière pensee, compunction, demurral, demurrer, dissent, hesitation, misgiving, objection, protest, qualm, reservation, scruple.

demure *adj* coy, decorous, diffident, grave, maidenly, modest, priggish, prim, prissy, prudish, reserved, reticent, retiring, sedate, shy, sober, staid, strait-laced.

antonym forward.

den *n* cave, cavern, cloister, cubby-hole, earth, haunt, hide-away, hide-out. hole, lair, retreat, sanctuary, sanctum, set(t), shelter, study.

denial *n* abjuration, abnegation, contradiction, denegation, disaffirmance, disaffirmation, disavowal, disclaimer, dismissal, dissent, gainsay, negation, prohibition, rebuff, refusal, rejection, renunciation, repudiation, repulse, retraction, veto.

denigrate *v* abuse, assail, belittle, besmirch, blacken, calumniate, criticise, decry, defame, disparage, impugn, malign, revile, run down, slander, vilify, vilipend.

antonym praise.

denigration *n* aspersion, backbiting, decrial, defamation, derogation, detraction, disparagement, mud-slinging, obloquy, scandal, scurrility, slander, vilification.

antonym praise.

denizen *n* citizen, dweller, habitant, habitue, inhabitant, occupant, resident.

denominate *v* baptise, call, christen, designate, dub, entitle, name, phrase, style, term, title.

denomination *n* appellation, belief, body, category, class, classification, communion, creed, designation, grade, group, label, name, persuasion, religion, school, sect, size, style, taxon, term, title, unit, value.

denote *v* betoken, designate, express, imply, import, indicate, mark, mean, show, signify, stand for, symbolise, typify.

denouement *n* climax, close, conclusion, culmination, finale, finish, outcome, pay-off, resolution, solution, termination, upshot.

denounce *v* accuse, anathematise, arraign, assail, attack, brand, castigate, censure, condemn, declaim against, decry, denunciate, fulminate, hereticate, impugn, inveigh against, proscribe, revile, stigmatise, vilify, vilipend.

antonym praise.

dense *adj* blockish, close, close-knit, compact, compressed, condensed, crass, crowded, dull, heavy, impenetrable, jam-packed, obtuse, opaque, packed, slow, slow-witted, solid, stolid, stupid, substantial, thick, thickset, thick-witted.

antonyms clever, sparse.

denseness *n* crassness, density, dullness, obtuseness, slowness, stolidity, stupidity, thickness.

antonym acuteness.

density *n* body, bulk, closeness, compactness, consistency, crassitude, denseness, impenetrability, mass, solidity, solidness, spissitude, thickness, tightness.

antonym sparseness.

dent *n* bang, chip, concavity, crater, depression, dimple, dint, dip, dunt, hollow, impression, indentation, pit.

v depress, dint, gouge, indent, push in.

dentures *n* false teeth, wallies.

denude *v* bare, defoliate, deforest, divest, expose, strip, uncover.

antonym cover.

denunciation *n* accusation, assailment, castigation, censure, condemnation, criticism, decrial, decrying, denouncement, fulmination, incrimination, invective, obloquy, stigmatisation.

antonyms compliment, praise.

denunciatory *adj* accusatory, censorious, comminatory, condemnatory, decrying, execrative, fulminatory, incriminatory, recriminatory, reproachful.

antonym complimentary.

deny *v* abjure, begrudge, contradict, decline, disaffirm, disagree with, disallow, disavow, discard, disclaim, disown, disprove, forbid, gainsay, negative, oppose, rebuff, recant, refuse, refute, reject, renounce, repudiate, revoke, traverse, turn down, veto, withhold.

antonyms admit, allow.

deodorant *n* air-freshener, antiperspirant, deodoriser, disinfectant, fumigant, fumigator.

deodorise *v* aerate, disinfect, freshen, fumigate, purify, refresh, sweeten, ventilate.

depart *v* absent oneself, decamp, deviate, differ, digress, disappear, diverge, escape, exit, go, leave, levant, make off, migrate, mizzle, quit, remove, retire, retreat, set forth, stray, swerve, take one's leave, toddle, vanish, vary, veer, withdraw.

antonyms arrive, keep to.

departed *adj* dead, deceased, defunct, expired, late.

department *n* area, branch, bureau, district, division, domain, field, function, line, line of country, office, province, realm, region, responsibility, section, sector, speciality, sphere, station, subdivision, unit.

departure *n* abandonment, branching, branching out, change, decession, deviation, difference, digression, divergence, exit, exodus, going, innovation, leave-taking, leaving, lucky, novelty, removal, retirement, shift, variation, veering, withdrawal.

antonym arrival.

depend on anticipate, bank on, build upon, calculate on, count on, expect, hang on, hinge on, lean on, reckon on, rely upon, rest on, revolve around, trust in, turn to.

dependable *adj* certain, conscientious, faithful, gilt-edged, honest, reliable, responsible, steady, sure, trustworthy, trusty, unfailing.

antonyms undependable, unreliable.

dependant *n* child, client, galloglass, hanger-on, henchman, minion, minor, protege, relative, retainer, subordinate, vassal.

dependence *n* addiction, assurance, attachment, belief, confidence, craving, dependency, expectation, faith, helplessness, hope, need, reliance, subordination, subservience, trust, vassalage, vulnerability, weakness.

antonym independence.

dependent *adj* adjective, conditional, contingent, defenceless, depending, determined by, feudal, helpless, immature, liable to, relative, reliant, relying on, subject, subject to, subordinate, tributary, vulnerable, weak.

antonym independent.

depict *v* caricature, characterise, delineate, describe, detail, draw, illustrate, limn, narrate, outline, paint, picture, portray, render, reproduce, sculpt, sketch, trace.

depiction *n* caricature, delineation, description, drawing, illustration, image, likeness, outline, picture, portrayal, representation, sketch.

depilation *n* electrolysis, epilation, hair-removing.

deplete *v* attenuate, bankrupt, consume, decrease, drain, empty, evacuate, exhaust, expend, impoverish, lessen, reduce, use up.

depleted *adj* attenuated, consumed, decreased, depreciated, drained, emptied, exhausted, lessened, reduced, spent, wasted, weakened, worn out.

antonyms augmented, increased.

depletion *n* attenuation, consumption, decimation, decrease, deficiency, diminution, dwindling, exhaustion, expenditure, lessening, lowering, reduction, shrinkage.

antonyms increase, supply.

deplorable *adj* blameworthy, calamitous, dire, disastrous, disgraceful, dishonourable, disreputable, distressing, execrable, grievous, heartbreaking, lamentable, melancholy, miserable, opprobrious, pitiable, regrettable, reprehensible, sad, scandalous, shameful, unfortunate, wretched.

antonyms excellent, praiseworthy.

deplore *v* abhor, bemoan, bewail, censure, condemn, denounce, deprecate, grieve for, lament, mourn, regret, repent of, rue.

antonym praise.

deploy *v* arrange, darraign, dispose, distribute, embattle, extend, position, station, use, utilise.

depopulate *v* dispeople, empty, unpeople.

deport[1] *v* banish, exile, expatriate, expel, extradite, ostracise, oust.

deport[2] *v* acquit, act, bear, behave, carry, comport, conduct, hold, manage.

deportation *n* banishment, eviction, exile, expatriation, expulsion, extradition, ostracism, transportation.

deportment *n* air, appearance, aspect, bearing, behaviour, carriage, cast, comportment, conduct, demeanour, etiquette, manner, mien, pose, posture, stance.

depose *v* break, cashier, decrown, degrade, demote, dethrone, discrown, disestablish, dismiss, displace, downgrade, oust, topple, unking.

deposit[1] *v* drop, dump, lay, locate, park, place, precipitate, put, settle, sit.

n accumulation, alluvium, deposition, dregs, hypostasis, lees, precipitate, sediment, silt.

deposit[2] *v* amass, bank, consign, depone, entrust, file, hoard, lodge, reposit, save, store.

n bailment, down payment, instalment, money, part payment, pledge, retainer, security, stake, warranty.

deposition[1] *n* dethronement, dismissal, displacement, ousting, removal, toppling.

deposition[2] *n* affidavit, declaration, denunciation, evidence, information, statement, testimony.

depository *n* bond, depot, dump, godown, repository, store, storehouse, warehouse.

depot *n* arsenal, bond, depository, dump, garage, receiving-house, repository, station, storehouse, terminus, warehouse.

deprave *v* brutalise, contaminate, corrupt, debase, debauch, degrade, demoralise, infect, pervert, seduce, subvert, vitiate.

antonym improve.

depraved *adj* abandoned, base, corrupt, debased, debauched, degenerate, degraded, dissolute, evil, immoral, lewd, libertine, licentious, perverted, profligate, reprobate, shameless, sinful, vicious, vile, wicked.

antonym upright.

depravity *n* baseness, contamination, corruption, criminality, debasement, debauchery, degeneracy, degradation, depravation, depravedness, depravement, dissoluteness, evil, immorality, iniquity, lewdness, libertinage, licence, perversion, profligacy, reprobacy, sinfulness, turpitude, vice, viciousness, vileness, wickedness.

antonym uprightness.

deprecate *v* condemn, deplore, disapprove of, disparage, object to, protest at, reject.

antonyms approve, commend.

deprecation *n* condemnation, deploration, disapproval, dismissal, disparagement, protestation, rejection.

antonyms commendation, encouragement.

deprecatory *adj* apologetic, censorious, condemnatory, disapproving, dismissive, protesting, regretful, reproachful.

antonyms commendatory, encouraging.

depreciate *v* belittle, decrease, decry, deflate, denigrate, deride, derogate, detract, devaluate, devalue, disparage, downgrade, drop, fall, lessen, lower, minimise, misprise, reduce, ridicule, scorn, slump, traduce, underestimate, underrate, undervalue.

antonyms appreciate, overrate, praise.

depreciation *n* belittlement, deflation, depression, derogation, detraction, devaluation, disparagement, downgrading, drop, fall, misprising, misprision, pejoration, slump.

antonyms appreciation, exaggeration, praise.

depredation *n* denudation, desolation, despoiling, despoliation, destruction, devastation, harrying, laying waste, looting, marauding, pillage, plunder, raiding, ransacking, rapine, ravaging, ravin, robbery, spoliation, stripping, theft.

depress *v* burden, cheapen, chill, damp, daunt, debilitate, deject, depreciate, devaluate, devalue, devitalise, diminish, discourage, dishearten, dispirit, downgrade, drain, enervate, engloom, exhaust, flatten, hip, impair, lessen, level, lower, oppress, overburden, press, reduce, sadden, sap, squash, tire, undermine, upset, weaken, weary.

antonym cheer.

depressant *n* calmant, calmative, downer, relaxant, sedative, tranquilliser.

antonym stimulant.

depressed[1] *adj* a peg too low, accable, blue, cast down, crestfallen, debilitated, dejected, deprived, despondent, desponding, destitute, disadvantaged, discouraged, disheartened, dispirited, distressed, down, down-beat, downcast, downhearted, exanimate, fed up, glum, jaw-fallen, low, low-spirited, melancholy, miserable, Mondayish, moody, morose, needy, pessimistic, poor, sad, unhappy.

antonym cheerful.

depressed[2] *adj* concave, dented, dinted, dished, hollow, indented, invaginated, recessed, sunken.

antonyms convex, prominent, protuberant.

depressing *adj* black, bleak, cheerless, daunting, dejecting, discouraging, disheartening, dismal, dispiriting, distressing, dreary, gloomy, grey, heartbreaking, hopeless, lugubrious, melancholy, Mondayish, sad, saddening, sombre.

antonym encouraging.

depression[1] *n* blues, cafard, decline, dejection, demission, despair, despondency, doldrums, dolefulness, downheartedness, dullness, dumps, exanimation, gloominess, glumness, hard times, heart-heaviness, hopelessness, inactivity, low spirits, lowness, mal du siècle, megrims, melancholia, melancholy, panophobia, recession, sadness, slump, stagnation, vapours.

antonyms cheerfulness, prosperity.

depression[2] *n* basin, bowl, cavity, concavity, dent, dimple, dint, dip, dish, excavation, fossa, fossula, fovea, foveola, hollow, hollowness, impression, indentation, pit, sag, sink, umbilicus, valley.

antonyms convexity, prominence, protuberance.

deprivation *n* degradation, denial, denudation, deprival, despoliation, destitution, disadvantage, dispossession, distress, divestment, expropriation, hardship, need, privation, removal, want, withdrawal, withholding.

antonym bestowal.

deprive *v* amerce, bereave, denude, deny, despoil, dispossess, divest, expropriate, mulct, rob, starve, strip.

antonym bestow.

deprived *adj* benighted, bereft, denuded, depressed, destitute, disadvantaged, forlorn, impoverished, lacking, necessitous, needy, poor.

antonyms fortunate, prosperous.

depth *n* abstruseness, abysm, abyss, complexity, deepness, discernment, drop, exhaustiveness, extent, gulf, insight, intensity, measure, obscurity, penetration, pit, profoundness, profundity, reconditeness, richness, sagacity, shrewdness, strength, thoroughness, wisdom.

deputation *n* appointment, assignment, commission, delegates, delegation, deputies, deputing, designation, embassy, legation, mission, nomination, representatives.

depute *v* accredit, appoint, authorise, charge, commission, delegate, empower, entrust, mandate, nominate.

deputise *n* commission, delegate, depute, double, replace, represent, stand in for, substitute, understudy.

deputy *n* agent, alternate, ambassador, commis, commissary, commissioner, delegate, henchman, legate, lieutenant, nuncio, proxy, representative, second-in-command, substitute, suffragan, surrogate, vicar, vicegerent.

adj assistant, coadjutor, depute, subordinate, suffragan.

derange *v* confound, confuse, craze, dement, disarrange, disarray, discompose, disconcert, disorder, displace, disturb, drive crazy, madden, ruffle, unbalance, unhinge, unsettle, upset.

deranged *adj* aberrant, batty, berserk, brainsick, confused, crazed, crazy, delirious, demented, disarranged, disordered, distracted, distraught, disturbed, frantic, frenzied, insane, irrational, loony, lunatic, mad, maddened, nutty, unbalanced, unhinged.

antonyms calm, sane.

derangement *n* aberration, agitation, alienation, confusion, delirium, dementia, disarrangement, disarray, disorder, distraction, disturbance, frenzy, hallucination, insanity, irregularity, jumble, lunacy, madness, mania, muddle.

antonyms order, sanity.

derelict *adj* abandoned, deserted, desolate, dilapidated, discarded, forlorn, forsaken, neglected, ruined.

n dosser, down-and-out, drifter, hobo, outcast, toe-rag, tramp, vagrant, wastrel.

dereliction *n* abandonment, abdication, apostasy, betrayal, delinquency, desertion, evasion, failure, faithlessness, fault, forsaking, neglect, negligence, relinquishment, remissness, renegation, renunciation.

antonyms devotion, faithfulness, fulfilment.

deride *v* belittle, chiack, condemn, detract, disdain, disparage, flout, gibe, insult, jeer, knock, mock, pillory, pooh-pooh, rail at, ridicule, satirise, scoff, scorn, sneer, taunt, vilipend.

antonym praise.

derision *n* chiack, contempt, contumely, dicacity, disdain, disparagement, disrespect, insult, irrision, laughter, mockery, raillery, ridicule, satire, scoffing, scorn, sneering.

antonym praise.

derisive *adj* contemptuous, disdainful, disrespectful, irreverent, irrisory, jeering, mocking, scornful, taunting.

antonyms appreciative, flattering.

derisory *adj* absurd, contemptible, insulting, laughable, ludicrous, mockable, outrageous, paltry, preposterous, ridiculous, risible.

derivation *n* acquisition, ancestry, basis, beginning, deduction, descent, etymology, extraction, foundation, genealogy, inference, origin, root, source.

derivative *adj* acquired, borrowed, copied, cribbed, daughter, derived, hackneyed, imitative, inferred, obtained, plagiarised, plagiaristic, procured, regurgitated, rehashed, secondary, second-hand, transmitted, trite, unadventurous, uninventive, unoriginal.

n branch, by-product, derivation, descendant, development, formative, offshoot, outgrowth, product, refinement, spin-off.

derive *v* acquire, arise, borrow, collect, crib, deduce, descend, develop, draw, elicit, emanate, extract, flow, follow, gain, gather, get, glean, grow, infer, issue, lift, obtain, originate, proceed, procure, receive, spring, stem, trace.

derogate *v* belittle, decry, defame, denigrate, depreciate, detract, devalue, diminish, disparage, insult, lessen, misprise, slight, take away from.

antonyms add to, appreciate, praise.

derogatory *adj* aspersory, belittling, critical, damaging, defamatory, depreciative, destructive, detractive, detractory, disparaging, injurious, insulting, offensive, pejorative, slighting, snide, uncomplimentary, unfavourable, unflattering.

antonyms appreciative, favourable, flattering.

descend *v* alight, arrive, assail, assault, attack, condescend, degenerate, degringoler, deign, derive, deteriorate, develop, dip, dismount, drop, fall, gravitate, incline, invade, issue, leap, originate, plummet, plunge, pounce, proceed, raid, sink, slant, slope, spring, stem, stoop, subside, swoop, tumble.

descendants *n* children, epigones, epigoni, epigons, family, issue, line, lineage, offspring, posterity, progeny, race, scions, seed, sons and daughters, successors.

descent *n* ancestry, assault, attack, comedown, debasement, decadence, declination, decline, declivity, degradation, degringolade, deterioration, dip, drop, extraction, fall, family tree, foray, genealogy, heredity, incline, incursion, invasion, lineage, origin, parentage, plunge, pounce, raid, slant, slope, stoop, swoop.

antonyms ascent, improvement.

describe *v* characterise, define, delineate, depict, detail, draw, enlarge on, explain, express, illustrate, mark out, narrate, outline, portray, present, recount, relate, report, sketch, specify, tell, trace.

description *n* account, brand, breed, category, characterisation, class, delineation, depiction, detail, explanation, exposition, genre, genus, hypotyposis, ilk, kidney, kind, narration, narrative, order, outline, portrayal, presentation, report, representation, sketch, sort, species, specification, type, variety, word-painting, word-picture.

descriptive *adj* blow-by-blow, circumstantial, colourful, depictive, detailed, explanatory, expressive, graphic, illustrative, immediate, pictorial, picturesque, specific, vivid.

antonyms cursory, laconic.

descry *v* detect, discern, discover, distinguish, espy, glimpse, mark, notice, observe, perceive, recognise, see, sight, spot, spy.

desecrate *v* abuse, blaspheme, contaminate, debase, defile, despoil, dishallow, dishonour, insult, invade, pervert, pollute, profane, vandalise, violate.

desecration *n* blasphemy, debasement, defilement, dishonouring, impiety, insult, invasion, pollution, profanation, sacrilege, violation.

desert[1] *n* solitude, vacuum, vast, void, waste, wasteland, wilderness, wilds.

adj arid, bare, barren, desolate, droughty, dry, eremic, infertile, lonely, solitary, sterile, uncultivated, uninhabited, unproductive, untilled, waste, waterless, wild.

desert[2] *v* abandon, abscond, apostatise, backslide, betray, decamp, deceive, defect, forsake, give up, jilt, leave, leave in the lurch, maroon, quit, rat on, relinquish, renegue, renounce, resign, strand, tergiversate, vacate.

desert[3] *n* come-uppance, demerit, deserts, due, guerdon, meed, merit, payment, recompense, remuneration, requital, retribution, return, reward, right, virtue, worth.

deserted *adj* abandoned, benighted, bereft, betrayed, derelict, desolate, empty, forlorn, forsaken, friendless, godforsaken, isolated, left in the lurch, lonely, neglected, solitary, stranded, underpopulated, unfriended, unoccupied, unpopulous, vacant, vacated.

antonym populous.

deserter *n* absconder, apostate, backslider, betrayer, defector, delinquent, escapee, fugitive, rat, renegade, runaway, traitor, truant.

desertion *n* abandonment, absconding, apostasy, betrayal, defection, delinquency, departure, dereliction, escape, evasion, flight, forsaking, relinquishment, renegation, tergiversation, truancy.

deserve *v* ask for, earn, gain, incur, justify, merit, procure, rate, warrant, win.

deserved *adj* apposite, appropriate, apt, condign, due, earned, fair, fitting, just, justifiable, justified, legitimate, meet, merited, proper, right, rightful, suitable, warranted, well-earned.

antonyms gratuitous, undeserved.

deserving *adj* admirable, commendable, creditable, estimable, exemplary, laudable, meritorious, praiseworthy, righteous, worthy.

antonyms undeserving, unworthy.

desiccated *adj* arid, dead, dehydrated, drained, dried, dry, dry-as-dust, exsiccated, lifeless, parched, passionless, powdered, spiritless, sterile.

desiccation *n* aridity, dehydration, dryness, exsiccation, parching, sterility, xeransis.

desideratum *n* aim, aspiration, besoin, dream, essential, gap, goal, heart's desire, hope, ideal, lack, lacuna, need, object, objective, sine qua non, want, wish.

design *n* aim, arrangement, blueprint, composition, configuration, conformation, conspiracy, construction, contrivance, delineation, draft, drawing, end, enterprise, exemplar, figure, form, goal, guide, intent, intention, intrigue, logo, machination, manoeuvre, meaning, model, motif, object, objective, organisation, outline, pattern, plan, plot, project, prototype, purpose, schema, scheme, shape, sketch, structure, style, target, undertaking.

v aim, conceive, construct, contrive, create, delineate, describe, destine, develop, devise, draft, draw, draw up, fabricate, fashion, form, intend, invent, make, mean, model, originate, outline, plan, project, propose, purpose, scheme, shape, sketch, structure, tailor, trace.

designate *v* allot, appoint, assign, bill, call, characterise, choose, christen, code-name, deem, define, delegate, denominate, denote, depute, describe, docket, dub, earmark, entitle, indicate, label, name, nickname, nominate, select, show, specify, stipulate, style, term, ticket, title.

designation *n* appointment, category, characterisation, classification, code-name, definition, delegation, denomination, description, docket, epithet, indication, label, mark, name, nickname, nomination, selection, specification, title.

designedly *adv* calculatedly, consciously, deliberately, intentionally, knowingly, on purpose, premeditatedly, purposely, studiously, wilfully, willingly, with malice aforethought, wittingly.

antonyms innocently, unwittingly.

designer *n* architect, artificer, author, contriver, couturier, creator, deccie, deviser, fashioner, framer, inventor, maker, originator, stylist.

designing *adj* artful, conniving, conspiring, contriving, crafty, cunning, deceitful, devious, disingenuous, guileful, insidious, intriguing, Machiavellian, plotting, scheming, sharp, shrewd, sly, treacherous, tricky, underhand, unscrupulous, wily.

antonym artless.

desirability *n* advantage, advisability, attraction, attractiveness, beauty, benefit, merit, profit, seductiveness, usefulness, value, worth.

antonyms disadvantage, inadvisability, undesirability.

desirable *adj* adorable, advantageous, advisable, agreeable, alluring, appetible, appropriate, attractive, beneficial, captivating, covetable, eligible, enviable, expedient, fascinating, fetching, good, nubile, pleasing, plummy, preferable, profitable, seductive, sensible, sexy, tempting, worthwhile.

antonym undesirable.

desire *v* ask, aspire to, beg, covet, crave, desiderate, entreat, fancy, hanker after, hunger for, importune, lack, long for, need, petition, request, solicit, want, wish for, yearn for.

n appeal, appetence, appetency, appetite, ardour, aspiration, besoin, concupiscence, covetousness, craving, cupidity, desideration, entreaty, greed, hankering, hot pants, importunity, kama, kamadeva, lasciviousness, lechery, libido, longing, lust, lustfulness, month's mind, need, passion, petition, request, solicitation, supplication, velleity, want, wish, yearning, yen.

desired *adj* accurate, appropriate, correct, exact, expected, express, fitting, longed-for, looked-for, necessary, particular, proper, required, right, sought-after, wanted, wished-for.

antonyms undesired, unintentional.

desirous *adj* ambitious, anxious, appetent, aspiring, avid, burning, craving, cupidinous, eager, enthusiastic, hopeful, hoping, itching, keen, longing, ready, willing, wishing, yearning.

antonyms reluctant, unenthusiastic.

desist *v* abstain, break off, cease, come to a halt, discontinue, end, forbear, give over, give up, halt, leave off, pause, peter out, refrain, remit, stop, suspend.

antonyms continue, resume.

desk *n* bureau, davenport, ecritoire, lectern, prie-dieu, secretaire, writing-table.

desolate *adj* abandoned, arid, bare, barren, benighted, bereft, bleak, cheerless, comfortless, companionless, dejected, depopulated, depressed, depressing, desert, desolated, despondent, disconsolate, disheartened, dismal, dismayed, distressed, downcast, dreary, forlorn, forsaken, gloomy, god-forsaken, grieved, inconsolable, lonely, melancholy, miserable, ravaged, ruined, solitary, unfrequented, uninhabited, unpopulous, unsolaced, waste, wild, wretched.

antonym cheerful.

v denude, depopulate, despoil, destroy, devastate, lay waste, pillage, plunder, ravage, ruin, spoil, waste, wreck.

desolation *n* anguish, barrenness, bleakness, dejection, depopulation, desolateness, despair, desperation, despondency, destruction, devastation, disconsolateness, distress, emptiness, forlornness, gloom, gloominess, grief, havoc, isolation, loneliness, melancholy, misery, ravages, ruin, ruination, sadness, solitariness, solitude, sorrow, unhappiness, wildness, woe, wretchedness.

despair *v* capitulate, collapse, crumple, despond, give in, give up, lose heart, lose hope, quit, surrender.

antonym hope.

n anguish, dejection, depression, desperation, despond, despondency, emptiness, gloom, hopelessness, inconsolableness, melancholy, misery, ordeal, pain, resourcelessness, sorrow, trial, tribulation, wretchedness.

antonyms cheerfulness, resilience.

despairing *adj* anxious, broken-hearted, dejected, depressed, desolate, desperate, despondent, disconsolate, disheartened, distracted, distraught, downcast, frantic, grief-stricken, hopeless, inconsolable, melancholy, miserable, sorrowful, suicidal, wretched.

antonyms cheerful, resilient.

despatch *see* **dispatch**.

desperado *n* bandit, brigand, cateran, criminal, cut-throat, dacoit, gangster, gunman, heavy, hood, hoodlum, law-breaker, mugger, outlaw, ruffian, thug.

desperate *adj* grave, abandoned, acute, audacious, critical, dangerous, daring, despairing, despondent, determined, dire, do-or-die, drastic, extreme, foolhardy, forlorn, frantic, frenzied, furious, great, hasty, hazardous, headlong, headstrong, hopeless, impetuous, inconsolable, irremediable, irretrievable, madcap, precipitate, rash, reckless, risky, serious, severe, temerarious, urgent, violent, wild, wretched.

desperately *adv* appallingly, badly, critically, dangerously, distractedly, fearfully, frantically, frenziedly, frightfully, gravely, hopelessly, perilously, seriously, severely, shockingly.

desperation *n* agony, anguish, anxiety, defiance, despair, despondency, disconsolateness, distraction, distress, foolhardiness, franticness, frenzy, hastiness, heedlessness, hoplessness, madness, misery, pain, rashness, recklessness, sorrow, trouble, unhappiness, worry.

despicable *adj* abhorrent, abject, base, cheap, contemptible, degrading, detestable, disgraceful, disgusting, disreputable, hateful, ignoble, ignominious, infamous, low, mean, reprehensible, reprobate, scurvy, shameful, sordid, unprincipled, vile, worthless, wretched.

antonyms laudable, noble.

despise *v* abhor, condemn, deplore, deride, detest, disdain, dislike, disregard, ignore, loathe, misprise, revile, scorn, slight, spurn, undervalue, vilipend.

antonyms appreciate, prize.

despite *prep* against, defying, heedless of, in spite of, in the face of, in the teeth of, notwithstanding, regardless of, undeterred by.

despoil *v* bereave, denude, depredate, deprive, destroy, devastate, disgarnish, dispossess, divest, loot, maraud, pillage, plunder, ransack, ravage, rifle, rob, spoliate, strip, vandalise, wreck.

antonyms adorn, enrich.

despoliation *n* depredation, despoilment, destruction, devastation, havoc, looting, marauding, pillage, plunder, rapine, ravaging, ravin, ruin, spoliation, vandalism, wreckage.

antonyms adornment, enrichment.

despond *v* capitulate, despair, lose courage, lose heart, lose hope, mourn, quit, sorrow, surrender.

antonym hope.

despondency *n* broken-heartedness, dejection, depression, despair, desperation, disconsolateness, discouragement, dispiritedness, downheartedness, gloom, glumness, hopelessness, inconsolability, melancholia, melancholy, misery, sadness, sorrow, wretchedness.

antonyms cheerfulness, hopefulness.

despondent *adj* blue, broken-hearted, dejected, depressed, despairing, disconsolate, discouraged, disheartened, dispirited, doleful, down, downcast, downhearted, gloomy, glum, hopeless, inconsolable, low, low-spirited, melancholy, miserable, morose, mournful, overwhelmed, sad, sorrowful, woebegone, wretched.

antonyms cheerful, hopeful.

despot *n* absolutist, autocrat, boss, dictator, Hitler, monocrat, oppressor, tyrant.

antonyms democrat, egalitarian, liberal.

despotic *adj* absolute, absolutist, arbitrary, arrogant, authoritarian, autocratic, bossy, dictatorial, domineering, imperious, monocratic, oppressive, overbearing, peremptory, tyrannical.

antonyms democratic, egalitarian, liberal, tolerant.

despotism *n* absolutism, autarchy, autocracy, dictatorship, monarchism, monocracy, oppression, repression, totalitarianism, tyranny.

antonyms democracy, egalitarianism, liberalism, tolerance.

dessert *n* afters, doucet, pudding, sweet, sweet course.

destination *n* aim, ambition, aspiration, design, end, end in view, goal, harbour, haven, intention, journey's end, object, objective, port of call, purpose, station, stop, target, terminus.

destine *v* allot, appoint, assign, consecrate, decree, design, designate, devote, doom, earmark, fate, foredoom, head, intend, mark out, mean, ordain, predetermine, preordain, purpose, reserve.

destined *adj* assigned, booked, bound, certain, designed, directed, doomed, en route, fated, foreordained, headed, heading, ineluctable, inescapable, inevitable, intended, meant, ordained, predestined, predetermined, preordained, routed, scheduled, unavoidable.

destiny *n* cup, doom, fate, fortune, joss, karma, kismet, lot, Moira, portion, predestiny, weird.

destitute *adj* bankrupt, beggared, bereft, deficient, depleted, deprived, devoid of, distressed, down and out, impecunious, impoverished, indigent, innocent of, insolvent, lacking, necessitous, needy, penniless, penurious, poor, poverty-stricken, skint, strapped, wanting.

antonyms prosperous, wealthy.

destitution *n* bankruptcy, beggary, distress, impecuniousness, indigence, neediness, pauperdom, pauperism, pennilessness, penury, poverty, privation, starvation, straits, want.

antonyms prosperity, wealth.

destroy *v* annihilate, banjax, break, canker, crush, demolish, destruct, devastate, dismantle, dispatch, eliminate, eradicate, extinguish, extirpate, gut, kill, level, nullify, overthrow, ravage, raze, ruin, sabotage, scuttle, shatter, slay, slight, smash, stonker, thwart, torpedo, undermine, undo, unshape, vaporise, waste, wreck, zap.

antonym create.

destroyer *n* annihilator, demolisher, desolater, despoiler, iconoclast, Juggernaut, kiss of death, locust, Luddite, maelstrom, ransacker, ravager, vandal, wrecker.

antonym creator.

destruction *n* annihilation, bane, confutation, crushing, defeat, demolition, depopulation, desolation, devastation, downfall, elimination, end, eradication, estrepement, extermination, extinction, extirpation, havoc, liquidation, massacre, nullification, overthrow, ravagement, ruin, ruination, shattering, slaughter, undoing, wastage, wrack, wreckage.

antonym creation.

destructive *adj* adverse, antagonistic, baleful, baneful, calamitous, cataclysmic, catastrophic, contrary, damaging, deadly, deathful, deleterious, derogatory, detrimental, devastating, disastrous, discouraging, disparaging, disruptive, fatal, harmful, hostile, hurtful, injurious, invalidating, lethal, malignant, mischievous, negative, noxious, nullifying, pernicious, pestful, pestiferous, pestilent, pestilential, ruinous, slaughterous, subversive, undermining, vexatious, vicious.

antonyms creative, positive, productive.

desultory *adj* aimless, capricious, cursory, disconnected, discursive, disorderly, disorganised, erratic, fitful, haphazard, inconsistent, inconstant, inexact, irregular, loose, maundering, random, spasmodic, unco-ordinated, undirected, unmethodical, unsystematic.

antonyms concerted, methodical, systematic.

detach *v* abstract, alienate, cut off, deglutinate, disconnect, disengage, disentangle, disjoin, dissociate, disunite, divide, estrange, free, isolate, loosen, remove, segregate, separate, sever, uncouple, undo, unfasten, unfix, unhitch.

antonym attach.

detached *adj* aloof, disconnected, discrete, disinterested, disjoined, dispassionate, dissociated, divided, free, free-standing, impartial, impassive, impersonal, independent, loosened, neutral, objective, reserved, separate, severed, unattached, unbiased, uncommitted, unconcerned, unconnected, unimpassioned, uninvolved, unprejudiced.

antonyms concerned, connected, involved.

detachment[1] *n* aloofness, coolness, disconnection, disengagement, disinterestedness, disjoining, fairness, impartiality, impassivity, indifference, laissez-faire, neutrality, non-partisanship, objectivity, remoteness, separation, severance, severing, unconcern.

antonym concern.

detachment[2] *n* body, brigade, corps, detail, force, party, patrol, squad, task force, unit.

detail *n* aspect, attribute, complexity, complication, component, count, elaborateness, elaboration, element, fact, factor, feature, ingredient, intricacy, item, meticulousness, nicety, particular, particularity, point, refinement, respect, specific, specificity, technicality, thoroughness, triviality.

v allocate, appoint, assign, catalogue, charge, commission, delegate, delineate, depict, depute, describe, detach, enarrate, enumerate, individualise, itemise, list, narrate, overname, particularise, portray, recount, rehearse, relate, send, specify.

detailed *adj* blow-by-blow, circumstantial, complex, complicated, comprehensive, descriptive, elaborate, exact, exhaustive, fine, full, intricate, itemised, meticulous, minute, particular, particularised, refined, specific, thorough, unsparing.

antonyms brief, cursory, summary.

details *n* complexities, complications, ins and outs, intricacies, minutiae, niceties, particularities, particulars, specifics, trivia, trivialities.

detain *v* arrest, buttonhole, check, confine, delay, hinder, hold, hold up, impede, intern, keep, prevent, restrain, retard, slow, stay, stop.

antonym release.

detect *v* ascertain, catch, descry, discern, disclose, discover, distinguish, espy, expose, find, identify, note, notice, observe, perceive, recognise, reveal, scent, sight, spot, spy, track down, uncover, unmask.

detection *n* discernment, discovery, expose, exposure, identification, revelation, smelling out, sniffing out, tracking down, uncovering, unearthing, unmasking.

detective *n* busy, constable, cop, copper, dick, gumshoe, investigator, jack, private dick, private eye, private investigator, shamus, sleuth, sleuth-hound, tec, thief-catcher, thief-taker.

detention *n* confinement, constraint, custody, delay, detainment, duress, hindrance, holding back, imprisonment, incarceration, quarantine, restraint, withholding.

antonym release.

deter *v* caution, check, damp, daunt, debar, discourage, disincline, dissuade, frighten, hinder, inhibit, intimidate, prevent, prohibit, put off, repel, restrain, stop, turn off, warn.

antonym encourage.

detergent *n* abstergent, cleaner, cleanser, soap.

adj abstergent, abstersive, cleaning, cleansing, detersive.

deteriorate *v* backslide, crumble, decay, decline, decompose, degenerate, depreciate, disintegrate, ebb, fade, fail, fall off, go downhill, lapse, relapse, slide, slip, weaken, worsen.

antonym improve.

deterioration *n* atrophy, corrosion, debasement, decline, degeneration, degradation, degringolade, depreciation, descent, dilapidation, disintegration, downturn, drop, failing, fall, falling-off, lapse, pejoration, retrogression, slump, tabes, tabescence, vitiation, wastage, worsening.

antonym improvement.

determinate *adj* absolute, certain, clear-cut, conclusive, decided, decisive, defined, definite, definitive, delimited, determined, distinct, established, explicit, express, fixed, limited, positive, precise, quantified, settled, specific, specified.

antonym indeterminate.

determination *n* backbone, conclusion, constancy, conviction, decision, dedication, doggedness, drive, firmness, fortitude, indomitability, insistence, intention, judgement, obstinacy, perseverance, persistence, pertinacity, purpose, resoluteness, resolution, resolve, result, settlement, single-mindedness, solution, steadfastness, stubbornness, tenacity, verdict, will, will-power.

antonym irresolution.

determine *v* affect, arbitrate, ascertain, certify, check, choose, conclude, control, decide, detect, dictate, direct, discover, elect, end, establish, finish, fix, govern, guide, identify, impel, impose, incline, induce, influence, intend, lead, learn, modify, ordain, point, purpose, regulate, resolve, rule, settle, shape, terminate, undertake, verify.

determined *adj* backboned, bent, constant, convinced, decided, dogged, firm, fixed, indivertible, insistent, intent, obstinate, persevering, persistent, pertinacious, purposeful, resolute, set, single-minded, steadfast, strong-minded, strong-willed, stubborn, tenacious, tough-minded, undissuadable, unflinching, unhesitating, unwavering.

antonym irresolute.

deterrent *n* bar, barrier, check, curb, determent, difficulty, discouragement, disincentive, hindrance, impediment, obstacle, obstruction, repellent, restraint, turn-off.

antonym incentive.

detest *v* abhor, abominate, deplore, despise, dislike, execrate, hate, loathe, recoil from.

antonym adore.

detestable *adj* abhorred, abhorrent, abominable, accursed, despicable, disgusting, execrable, foul, hated, hateful, heinous, loathsome, nauseating, noisome, obnoxious, odious, offensive, pestiferous, pestilent, pestilential, repellent, repugnant, repulsive, revolting, rotten, shocking, sordid, swinish, vile, villainous.

antonyms admirable, adorable, pleasant.

detestation *n* abhorrence, abomination, anathema, animosity, animus, antipathy, aversion, despite, disgust, dislike, enmity, execration, hate, hatred, hostility, loathing, odium, repugnance, revulsion.

antonyms adoration, approval, love.

dethrone *v* depose, oust, topple, uncrown, unking, unseat, unthrone.

antonyms crown, enthrone.

detonate *v* blast, blow up, discharge, displode, explode, fulminate, ignite, kindle, set off, spark off.

detonation *n* bang, blast, blow-up, boom, burst, discharge, displosion, explosion, fulmination, igniting, ignition, report.

detour *n* bypass, bypath, byroad, byway, circumbendibus, deviation, digression, diversion, excursus.

detract *v* belittle, depreciate, derogate, devaluate, diminish, lessen, lower, negate, nullify, reduce, vilipend, vitiate.

antonyms add to, praise.

detraction *n* abuse, aspersion, belittlement, calumniation, calumny, defamation, denigration, depreciation, derogation, disparagement, innuendo, insinuation, misprision, misrepresentation, muck-raking, revilement, scandalmongering, scurrility, slander, traducement, vituperation.

antonyms appreciation, praise.

detractor *n* backbiter, belittler, defamer, denigrator, disparager, enemy, muck-raker, reviler, scandalmonger, slanderer, traducer, vilifier.

antonyms flatterer, supporter.

detriment *n* damage, disadvantage, disservice, evil, harm, hurt, ill, impairment, injury, loss, mischief, prejudice.

antonym advantage.

detrimental *adj* adverse, baleful, damaging, deleterious, destructive, disadvantageous, harmful, hurtful, inimical, injurious, mischievous, noxious, pernicious, prejudicial, unfavourable, untoward.

antonym advantageous.

detritus *n* debris, fragments, garbage, junk, litter, remains, rubbish, scum, waste, wreckage.

devaluation *n* decrease, deflation, devalorisation, lowering, reduction.

devalue *v* decrease, deflate, devalorise, devaluate, lower, reduce.

devastate *v* confound, demolish, depredate, desolate, despoil, destroy, discomfit, discompose, disconcert, floor, lay waste, level, maraud, nonplus, overwhelm, pillage, plunder, ransack, ravage, raze, ruin, sack, spoil, spoliate, waste, wreck.

devastation *n* annihilation, demolition, denudation, depredation, desolation, despoliation, destruction, havoc, pillage, plunder, ravages, ruin, ruination, spoliation, wrack, wreckage.

devastator *n* demolisher, desolater, despoiler, destroyer, devourer, locust, plunderer, ravager, spoliator, vandal, wrecker.

develop *v* acquire, advance, amplify, augment, begin, bloom, blossom, branch out, breed, broaden, commence, contract, cultivate, dilate, diversify, elaborate, engender, enlarge, ensue, establish, evolve, expand, flourish, follow, form, foster, generate, grow, happen, invent, make headway, mature, move on, originate, pick up, progress, promote, prosper, result, ripen, sprout, start, unfold.

development *n* advance, advancement, blooming, blossoming, change, circumstance, detail, elaboration, event, evolution, expansion, extension, furtherance, growth, happening, improvement, incident, increase, issue, maturation, maturity, occurrence, outcome, phenomenon, phylogenesis, phylogeny, progress, progression, promotion, refinement, result, ripening, situation, spread, unfolding, unravelling, upbuilding, upshot.

deviant *adj* aberrant, abnormal, anomalous, bent, bizarre, deviate, devious, divergent, freakish, freaky, heretical, heteromorphic, heteromorphous, heterotypic, irregular, kinky, perverse, perverted, queer, twisted, wayward.

antonym normal.

n deviate, freak, kook, misfit, oddball, pervert, queer, vert.

antonym straight.

deviate *v* aberrate, depart, differ, digress, divagate, diverge, drift, err, go astray, go off the rails, part, stray, swerve, turn, turn aside, vary, veer, wander, yaw.

deviation *n* aberrance, aberrancy, aberration, abnormality, alteration, ambage, anomaly, change, deflection, departure, detour, digression, discrepancy, disparity, divagation, divergence, driftage, eccentricity, fluctuation, freak, heteromorphism, heteromorphy, inconsistency, irregularity, kinkiness, quirk, shift, variance, variation, wandering.

antonym conformity.

device *n* apparatus, appliance, artifice, badge, blazon, colophon, contraption, contrivance, crest, design, dodge, emblem, episemon, expedient, figure, gadget, gambit, gimmick, gismo, implement, improvisation, insignia, instrument, invention, logo, machination, manoeuvre, motif, motto, plan, plot, ploy, project, ruse, scheme, shield, shift, stratagem, strategy, stunt, symbol, tactic, token, tool, trick, utensil, wile.

devil *n* Abaddon, Adversary, Apollyon, arch-fiend, bastard, beast, Beelzebub, Belial, bog(e)y-man, brute, bugger, cad, Clootie, creature, deil, demon, enthusiast, Evil One, fiend, goodman, Hornie, imp, incubus, jumpy, Lucifer, Mahoun(d), man of sin, Mephisto, Mephistopheles, monkey, monster, ogre, Old Harry, Old Nick, Old Scratch, Prince of Darkness, ragman, rascal, rogue, rotter, Satan, savage, scamp, scoundrel, shaitan, Slanderer, succubus, swine, terror, unfortunate, villain, wirricow, worricow, wretch.

devilish *adj* accursed, black-hearted, damnable, demoniac, demoniacal, diabolic, diabolical, execrable, fiendish, hellish, impious, infernal, iniquitous, mischievous, monstrous, nefarious, satanic, wicked.

devil-may-care *adj* careless, casual, cavalier, easy-going, flippant, frivolous, happy-go-lucky, heedless, insouciant, jaunty, lackadaisical, nonchalant, pococurante, reckless, swaggering, swashbuckling, unconcerned, unworried.

devilment *n* devilry, knavery, mischief, mischievousness, naughtiness, rascality, roguery, roguishness, sport, teasing.

devilry *n* black magic, chicanery, cruelty, devilment, deviltry, diablerie, diabolism, evil, jiggery-pokery, knavery, malevolence, malice, mischief, mischievousness, monkey-business, rascality, roguery, sorcery, trickiness, vice, viciousness, villainy, wickedness.

devious *adj* calculating, circuitous, confusing, crooked, cunning, deceitful, deviating, dishonest, disingenuous, double-dealing, erratic, evasive, excursive, indirect, insidious, insincere, misleading, rambling, roundabout, scheming, slippery, sly, subtle, surreptitious, tortuous, treacherous, tricky, underhand, wandering, wily, winding.

antonyms artless, candid, straightforward.

deviousness *n* cunning, deceit, dishonesty, disingenuity, evasion, evasiveness, indirectness, insincerity, slipperiness, slyness, subtlety, trickiness.

antonyms artlessness, openness.

devise *v* arrange, compass, compose, conceive, concoct, construct, contrive, design, excogitate, forge, form, formulate, frame, imagine, invent, plan, plot, prepare, project, scheme, shape.

devoid *adj* barren, bereft, deficient, denuded, destitute, empty, free, innocent, lacking, sans, vacant, void, wanting, without.

antonyms blessed, endowed.

devolution *n* decentralisation, delegation, dispersal, distribution, transference.

antonym centralisation.

devolve *v* alienate, be handed down, commission, consign, convey, delegate, deliver, depute, entrust, fall to, hand down, rest with, transfer.

devote *v* allocate, allot, apply, appropriate, assign, commit, consecrate, dedicate, enshrine, give, oneself, pledge, reserve, sacrifice, set apart, set aside, surrender.

devoted *adj* ardent, attentive, caring, committed, concerned, constant, dedicated, devout, faithful, fond, loving, loyal, staunch, steadfast, tireless, true, unremitting, unswerving.

antonyms inconstant, indifferent, negligent.

devotee *n* addict, adherent, admirer, aficionado, buff, devil, devot, disciple, enthusiast, fan, fanatic, fiend, follower, hound, merchant, supporter, votary, voteen, zealot.

antonyms adversary, sceptic.

devotion *n* adherence, adoration, affection, allegiance, ardour, assiduity, attachment, commitment, consecration, constancy, dedication, devoutness, earnestness, faith, faithfulness, fervour, fidelity, fondness, godliness, holiness, indefatigability, love, loyalty, partiality, passion, piety, prayer, regard, religiousness, reverence, sanctity, sedulousness, spirituality, steadfastness, support, worship, zeal.

antonyms inconstancy, negligence.

devotional *adj* devout, dutiful, holy, pietistic, pious, religious, reverential, sacred, solemn, spiritual.

devour *v* absorb, annihilate, bolt, consume, cram, destroy, dispatch, down, eat, engulf, feast on, feast one's eyes on, gluttonise, gobble, gorge, gormandise, gulp, guzzle, polish off, ravage, ravin, relish, revel in, spend, stuff, swallow, waste, wolf.

devourer *n* consumer, glutton, gobbler, gormandiser, gourmand, guzzler, locust, waster.

devout *adj* ardent, constant, deep, devoted, earnest, faithful, fervent, genuine, godly, heartfelt, holy, intense, orthodox, passionate, pious, prayerful, profound, pure, religious, reverent, saintly, serious, sincere, staunch, steadfast, unswerving, whole-hearted, zealous.

antonyms insincere, uncommitted.

devoutly *adv* deeply, faithfully, fervently, profoundly, sincerely, staunchly, steadfastly, whole-heartedly.

dewy *adj* blooming, innocent, roral, roric, rorid, roscid, starry-eyed, youthful.

dexterity *n* ability, address, adroitness, agility, aptitude, art, artistry, cleverness, cunning, deftness, effortlessness, expertise, expertness, facility, finesse, handiness, ingenuity, knack, legerdemain, mastery, neatness, nimbleness, proficiency, readiness, skilfulness, skill, smoothness, tact, touch.

antonyms clumsiness, ineptitude.

dexterous *adj* able, active, acute, adept, adroit, agile, apt, clever, cunning, deft, expert, facile, feat, habile, handy, ingenious, light-handed, masterly, neat, neat-handed, nifty, nimble, nimble-fingered, nippy, proficient, prompt, quick, skilful.

antonyms clumsy, inept.

diabolical *adj* damnable, devilish, diabolic, difficult, disastrous, dreadful, excruciating, fiendish, hellish, infernal, knavish, nasty, outrageous, shocking, tricky, unpleasant, vile, villainous, wicked.

diadem *n* circlet, coronet, crown, mitre, round, tiara.

diagnose *v* analyse, determine, distinguish, explain, identify, interpret, investigate, isolate, pinpoint, pronounce, recognise.

diagnosis *n* analysis, answer, conclusion, examination, explanation, identification, interpretation, investigation, isolation, opinion, pronouncement, scrutiny, verdict.

diagnostic *adj* analytical, demonstrative, distinctive, distinguishing, idiosyncratic, indicative, interpretative, interpretive, particular, peculiar, recognisable, symptomatic.

diagonal *adj* angled, cater-cornered, cornerways, crooked, cross, crossways, crosswise, oblique, slanting, slantwise, sloping.

diagonally *adv* aslant, at an angle, cornerwise, crosswise, obliquely, on the bias, on the cross, on the slant, slantwise.

diagram *n* abac, chart, drawing, figure, graph, illustration, lay-out, nomogram, outline, picture, plan, representation, schema, sketch, table.

diagrammatic *adj* diagrammatical, graphic, illustrative, representational, schematic, tabular.

antonyms imaginative, impressionistic.

dialect *n* accent, diction, Doric, idiom, jargon, language, lingo, localism, patois, pronunciation, provincialism, regionalism, speech, tongue, vernacular.

dialectic *adj* analytic, argumentative, deductive, dialectical, disceptatorial, inductive, logical, logistic, polemical, ratiocinative, ratiocinatory, rational, rationalistic.

n analysis, argumentation, casuistry, contention, debate, deduction, dialectics, disceptation, discussion, disputation, induction, logic, polemics, ratiocination, rationale, reasoning, sophistry.

dialogue *n* causerie, colloquy, communication, confabulation, conference, conversation, converse, debate, discourse, discussion, duologue, exchange, interchange, interlocution, lines, script, stichomythia, table talk, talk.

diametric *adj* antipodal, antithetical, contrary, contrasting, counter, diametral, diametrical, opposed, opposite.

diaphanous *adj* cobwebby, delicate, filmy, fine, gauzy, gossamer, gossamery, light, pellucid, see-through, sheer, thin, translucent, transparent, veily.

antonyms heavy, opaque, thick.

diarrhoea *n* dysentery, gippy tummy, holiday tummy, looseness, Montezuma's revenge, Spanish tummy, the runs, the trots.

antonym constipation.

diary *n* appointment book, chronicle, commonplace book, day-book, diurnal, engagement book, journal, journal intime, logbook, year-book.

diatribe *n* abuse, attack, castigation, criticism, denunciation, flyting, harangue, insult, invective, onslaught, philippic, reviling, stricture, tirade, upbraiding, vituperation.

antonyms bouquet, encomium, praise.

dice *n* astragals, bones, cubes, devil's bones, die, hazard.

dicey *adj* chancy, dangerous, difficult, dubious, hairy, iffy, problematic, risky, ticklish, tricky.

antonyms certain, easy.

dicky *adj* ailing, frail, infirm, queer, shaky, unreliable, unsound, unsteady, weak.

antonyms healthy, robust.

dictate *v* announce, command, decree, direct, enjoin, impose, instruct, ordain, order, prescribe, pronounce, rule, say, speak, transmit, utter.

n behest, bidding, code, command, decree, dictation, dictum, direction, edict, fiat, injunction, law, mandate, order, ordinance, precept, principle, requirement, rule, ruling, statute, ultimatum, word.

dictator *n* autarch, autocrat, Big Brother, boss, despot, Hitler, supremo, tyrant.

dictatorial *adj* absolute, almighty, arbitrary, autarchic, authoritarian, autocratic, bossy, despotic, dogmatic, domineering, imperious, magisterial, oppressive, overbearing, peremptory, repressive, totalitarian, tyrannical.

antonyms democratic, egalitarian, liberal, tolerant.

dictatorship *n* absolute rule, absolutism, autarchy, authoritarianism, autocracy, despotism, dictature, fascism, Hitlerism, totalitarianism, tyranny.

antonyms democracy, egalitarianism.

diction *n* articulation, delivery, elocution, enunciation, expression, fluency, idiom, inflection, intonation, language, phraseology, phrasing, pronunciation, speech, style, terminology, usage, vocabulary, wording.

dictionary *n* concordance, encyclopaedia, glossary, idioticon, lexicon, onomasticon, thesaurus, vocabulary, wordbook.

dictum *n* adage, axiom, command, decree, dictate, edict, fiat, gnome, maxim, order, precept, pronouncement, proverb, ruling, saw, saying, utterance.

didactic *adj* didascalic, educational, educative, homiletic, instructive, moral, moralising, pedagogic, pedantic, preceptive, prescriptive.

die *v* breathe one's last, croak, decay, decease, decline, depart, desire, disappear, dwindle, ebb, end, expire, fade, finish, fizzle out, gangrene, go over to the majority, go to one's (long) account, hunger, kick in, kick it, kick the bucket, languish, lapse, long for, pass, pass away, pass over, peg out, perish, peter out, pine for, pop off, run down, sink, slip the cable, snuff it, starve, stop, subside, succumb, suffer, vanish, wane, wilt, wither, yearn.

die-hard *n* blimp, Colonel Blimp, fanatic, fogey, hardliner, intransigent, reactionary, rightist, stick-in-the-mud, ultra-conservative, zealot.

adj blimpish, confirmed, dyed-in-the-wool, entrenched, hardcore, hardline, immovable, incorrigible, incurable, inflexible, intransigent, irreconcilable, obstinate, reactionary, rigid, stubborn, ultra-conservative, uncompromising, unyielding.

antonyms enlightened, flexible, progressive.

diet[1] *n* abstinence, aliment, board, comestibles, commons, dietary, edibles, fare, fast, food, foodstuffs, nourishment, nutriment, nutrition, provisions, rations, regime, regimen, subsistence, sustenance, viands, victuals.

v abstain, bant, fast, lose weight, reduce, slim, weight-watch.

diet[2] *n* assembly, chamber, congress, convention, convocation, council, divan, legislature, meeting, parliament, session, sitting, synod.

differ *v* argue, be at odds with, clash, conflict, contend, contradict, contrast, debate, demur, depart from, deviate, disagree, dispute, dissent, diverge, fall out, oppose, part company with, quarrel, take issue, vary.

antonyms agree, conform.

difference *n* alteration, argument, balance, change, clash, conflict, contention, contrariety, contrast, contretemps, controversy, debate, deviation, differentia, differentiation, difformity, disagreement, discordance, discrepancy, discreteness, disparateness, disparity, dispute, dissimilarity, distinction, distinctness, divergence, diversity, exception, idiosyncrasy, jizz, nuance, particularity, peculiarity, quarrel, remainder, rest, set-to, singularity, strife, tiff, unlikeness, variation, variety, wrangle.

antonyms agreement, conformity, uniformity.

different *adj* altered, anomalous, assorted, at odds, at variance, atypical, bizarre, changed, clashing, contrasting, deviating, discrepant, discrete, disparate, dissimilar, distinct, distinctive, divergent, divers, diverse, eccentric, extraordinary, inconsistent, individual, manifold, many, miscellaneous, multifarious, numerous, opposed, original, other, peculiar, rare, separate, several, singular, special, strange, sundry, unalike, uncommon, unconventional, unique, unlike, unusual, varied, various.

antonyms conventional, normal, same, similar, uniform.

differentiate *v* adapt, alter, change, contrast, convert, demarcate, discern, discriminate, distinguish, individualise, mark off, modify, nuance, particularise, separate, tell apart, transform.

antonyms assimilate, associate, confuse, link.

differentiation *n* contrast, demarcation, differentia, discrimination, distinction, distinguishing, individualisation, jizz, modification, particularisation, separation.

antonyms assimilation, association, confusion, connection.

difficult *adj* abstract, abstruse, arduous, Augean, awkward, baffling, burdensome, captious, complex, complicated, dark, delicate, demanding, difficile, disruptive, enigmatical, fastidious, formidable, fractious, fussy, Gordian, grim, hard, herculean, iffy, intractable, intricate, involved, knotty, laborious, obscure, obstinate, obstreperous, onerous, painful, perplexing, perverse, problematic, problematical, recalcitrant, refractory, rigid, steep, sticky, stiff, straitened, strenuous, stubborn, thorny, ticklish, tiresome, toilsome, tough, troublesome, trying, unamenable, unco-operative, unmanageable, uphill, wearisome.

antonyms easy, straightforward.

difficulty *n* a bad patch, arduousness, awkwardness, block, complication, dilemma, distress, embarrassment, fix, hang-up, hardship, hiccup, hindrance, hole, hurdle, impediment, jam, laboriousness, labour, mess, nineholes, objection, obstacle, opposition, pain, painfulness, perplexity, pickle, pinch, pitfall, plight, predicament, problem, protest, quandary, scruple, spot, strain, strait, straits, strenuousness, stumbling-block, trial, tribulation, trouble, vexata quaestio, vexed question.

antonyms advantage, ease.

diffidence *n* abashment, backwardness, bashfulness, constraint, doubt, fear, hesitancy, hesitation, humility, inhibition, insecurity, meekness, modesty, reluctance, reserve, self-consciousness, self-distrust, self-doubt, self-effacement, shamefacedness, shamefast, sheepishness, shyness, tentativeness, timidity, timidness, timorousness, unassertiveness.

antonym confidence.

diffident *adj* abashed, backward, bashful, constrained, distrustful, doubtful, hesitant, inhibited, insecure, meek, modest, reluctant, reserved, self-conscious, self-effacing, shamefaced, shamefast, sheepish, shrinking, shy, suspicious, tentative, timid, timorous, unadventurous, unassertive, unassuming, unobtrusive, unsure, withdrawn.

antonym confident.

diffuse *adj* ambagious, circuitous, circumlocutory, copious, diffused, digressive, disconnected, discursive, dispersed, long-winded, loose, maundering, meandering, prolix, rambling, scattered, unconcentrated, unco-ordinated, vague, verbose, waffling, wordy.

antonyms concentrated, succinct.

v circulate, dispense, disperse, disseminate, dissipate, distribute, propagate, scatter, spread, winnow.

antonyms concentrate, suppress.

dig[1] *v* burrow, delve, drive, excavate, go into, gouge, graft, grub, hoe, howk, investigate, jab, mine, penetrate, pierce, poke, probe, prod, punch, quarry, research, scoop, search, spit, thrust, till, tunnel.

n aspersion, barb, crack, cut, gibe, insinuation, insult, jab, jeer, poke, prod, punch, quip, sneer, taunt, thrust, wisecrack.

antonym compliment.

dig up discover, disinter, dredge, exhumate, exhume, expose, extricate, find, retrieve, track down, uncover, unearth.

antonyms bury, obscure.

dig[2] *v* adore, appreciate, be into, enjoy, fancy, follow, get a kick out of, get off on, go a bundle on, go for, go overboard about, groove, have the hots for, like, love, understand, warm to.

antonym hate.

digest *v* abridge, absorb, arrange, assimilate, classify, codify, compress, condense, consider, contemplate, dispose, dissolve, grasp, incorporate, ingest, macerate, master, meditate, methodise, ponder, process, reduce, shorten, stomach, study, summarise, systematise, tabulate, take in, understand.

n abbreviation, abridgement, abstract, compendium, compression, condensation, epitome, precis, reduction, resume, summary, synopsis.

digestion *n* absorption, assimilation, dyspepsia, eupepsia, ingestion, transformation.

dignified *adj* august, decorous, distinguished, exalted, formal, grave, honourable, imposing, impressive, lofty, lordly, majestic, noble, oro(ro)tund, reserved, solemn, stately, upright.

antonym undignified.

dignify *v* adorn, advance, aggrandise, apotheosise, distinguish, elevate, ennoble, exalt, glorify, honour, promote, raise.

antonyms degrade, demean.

dignitary *n* bigwig, celeb, celebrity, dignity, high-up, notability, notable, personage, pillar of society, VIP, worthy.

dignity *n* amour-propre, courtliness, decorum, elevation, eminence, excellence, glory, grandeur, gravitas, gravity, greatness, hauteur, honour, importance, loftiness, majesty, nobility, nobleness, pride, propriety, rank, respectability, self-esteem, self-importance, self-possession, self-regard, self-respect, solemnity, standing, stateliness, station, status.

digress *v* depart, deviate, divagate, diverge, drift, excurse, expatiate, go off at a tangent, ramble, stray, wander.

digression *n* apostrophe, aside, departure, detour, deviation, divagation, divergence, diversion, evagation, excursion, footnote, obiter dictum, parenthesis, straying, vagary, wandering.

dilapidated *adj* battered, broken-down, crumbling, decayed, decaying, decrepit, mouldering, neglected, ramshackle, rickety, ruined, ruinous, run-down, shabby, shaky, tumble-down, uncared-for, worn-out.

dilapidation *n* collapse, decay, demolition, destruction, deterioration, disintegration, disrepair, dissolution, downfall, ruin, ruination, waste.

dilate *v* amplify, broaden, descant, detail, develop, distend, dwell on, elaborate, enlarge, expand, expatiate, expound, extend, increase, puff out, spin out, stretch, swell, widen.

antonyms abbreviate, constrict, curtail.

dilated *adj* bloated, distended, enlarged, expanded, extended, inflated, outspread, swollen, tumescent, varicose.

antonyms contracted, shortened.

dilation *n* broadening, dilatation, distension, enlargement, expansion, extension, increase, spread, swelling, widening.

antonyms constriction, contraction.

dilatory *adj* backward, behind-hand, dallying, delaying, indolent, lackadaisical, laggard, lingering, loitering, procrastinating, slack, slothful, slow, sluggish, tardy, tarrying.

antonym diligent.

dilemma *n* bind, corner, difficulty, embarrassment, fix, jam, mess, perplexity, pickle, pinch, plight, predicament, problem, puzzle, quandary, spot, strait.

dilettante *n* aesthete, amateur, dabbler, sciolist, trifler.

diligence *n* activity, application, assiduity, assiduousness, attention, attentiveness, care, constancy, earnestness, heedfulness, industry, intentness, laboriousness, perseverance, pertinacity, sedulousness.

antonym laziness.

diligent *adj* active, assiduous, attentive, busy, careful, conscientious, constant, dogged, earnest, hard-working, indefatigable, industrious, laborious, painstaking, persevering, persistent, pertinacious, sedulous, studious, tireless.

antonyms dilatory, lazy.

dilly-dally *v* dally, dawdle, delay, dither, falter, hesitate, hover, linger, loiter, potter, procrastinate, shilly-shally, swither, tarry, trifle, vacillate, waver.

dilute *v* adulterate, allay, attenuate, cut, dash, decrease, diffuse, diminish, lessen, mitigate, reduce, temper, thin (out), water down, weaken.

antonym concentrate.

adj adulterated, attenuate(d), cut, diluted, thin, watered (down), waterish, weak.

antonym concentrated.

dim *adj* bleary, blurred, caliginous, cloudy, confused, dark, darkish, dense, depressing, dingy, discouraging, dull, dumb, dusky, faint, feeble, foggy, fuzzy, gloomy, grey, hazy, ill-defined, imperfect, indistinct, intangible, lack-lustre, misty, muted, obscure, obscured, obtuse, opaque, overcast, pale, remote, shadowy, slow, sombre, stupid, sullied, tarnished, tenebrious, thick, unclear, unfavourable, unilluminated, unpromising, vague, weak.

antonyms bright, distinct.

v becloud, bedim, blear, blur, cloud, darken, dull, fade, lower, obscure, tarnish.

antonyms brighten, illuminate.

dimension(s) *n* amplitude, bulk, capacity, extent, greatness, importance, largeness, magnitude, measure, range, scale, scope, size.

diminish *v* abate, bate, belittle, cheapen, contract, curtail, cut, deactivate, decline, decrease, de-emphasise, demean, depreciate, devalue, dwindle, ebb, fade, lessen, lower, minify, peter out, recede, reduce, retrench, shrink, shrivel, sink, slacken, subside, taper off, wane, weaken.

antonyms enhance, enlarge, increase.

diminishing *adj* abating, contracting, declining, decreasing, decrescent, dwindling, ebbing, fading, lessening, lowering, receding, reducing, shrinking, shrivelling, subsiding, waning.

antonyms growing, increasing.

diminution *n* abatement, contraction, curtailment, cut, cutback, deactivation, decay, decline, decrease, deduction, ebb, lessening, reduction, retrenchment, shortening, shrinkage, subsidence, weakening.

antonyms enlargement, increase.

diminutive *adj* bantam, dinky, Lilliputian, little, midget, mini, miniature, minute, petite, pint-size(d), pocket(-sized), pygmy, small, tiny, undersized, wee.

antonyms big, great, huge, large.

n hypocorisma, pet-name.

dimple *n* concavity, depression, dint, fovea, hollow, umbilicus.

dimwit *n* blockhead, bonehead, booby, dullard, dunce, dunderhead, ignoramus, nitwit, numskull, thick, thick-skull, twit.

din *n* babble, chirm, clamour, clangour, clash, clatter, commotion, crash, hubbub, hullabaloo, noise, outcry, pandemonium, racket, randan, row, shout, uproar.

antonyms calm, quiet.

dine *v* banquet, break bread, eat, feast, feed, lunch, sup.

dine on banquet, consume, dine off, eat, feast, feed, regale oneself.

dingy *adj* bedimmed, colourless, dark, dim, dirty, discoloured, drab, dreary, dull, dusky, faded, fuscous, gloomy, grimy, murky, obscure, run-down, seedy, shabby, soiled, sombre, tacky, worn.

antonyms bright, clean.

dining-room *n* dinette, frater, mess, refectory, triclinium.

dinky *adj* dainty, fine, mini, miniature, natty, neat, petite, small, trig, trim.

dinner *n* banquet, beanfeast, blow-out, collation, feast, meal, refection, repast, spread, supper, tea.

dint *n* blow, concavity, dent, depression, hollow, impression, indentation, stroke.

dip *v* bathe, decline, descend, disappear, dook, dop, douse, droop, drop, duck, dunk, fade, fall, immerse, ladle, lower, plunge, rinse, sag, scoop, set, sink, slope, slump, souse, spoon, subside, tilt.

n basin, bathe, concavity, concoction, decline, depression, dilution, dive, dook, douche, drenching, ducking, fall, hole, hollow, immersion, incline, infusion, lowering, mixture, plunge, preparation, sag, slip, slope, slump, soaking, solution, suspension, swim.

dip into browse, dabble, peruse, sample, skim, try.

diplomacy *n* artfulness, craft, delicacy, discretion, finesse, manoeuvring, savoir-faire, skill, statecraft, statesmanship, subtlety, tact, tactfulness.

diplomat *n* conciliator, go-between, mediator, moderator, negotiator, peacemaker, politician, tactician.

diplomatic *adj* discreet, judicious, polite, politic, prudent, sagacious, sensitive, subtle, tactful.

antonyms rude, tactless, thoughtless.

dire *adj* alarming, appalling, awful, calamitous, cataclysmic, catastrophic, critical, crucial, cruel, crying, desperate, disastrous, dismal, distressing, drastic, dreadful, exigent, extreme, fearful, gloomy, grave, grim, horrible, horrid, ominous, portentous, pressing, ruinous, terrible, urgent, woeful.

direct[1] *v* address, administer, advise, aim, bid, case, charge, command, conduct, control, dictate, dispose, enjoin, fix, focus, govern, guide, handle, indicate, instruct, intend, label, lead, level, mail, manage, mastermind, mean, order, oversee, point, regulate, route, rule, run, send, show, stage-manage, superintend, superscribe, supervise, train, turn.

direct[2] *adj* absolute, blunt, candid, categorical, downright, explicit, express, face-to-face, first-hand, frank, head-on, honest, immediate, man-to-man, matter-of-fact, non-stop, open, outright, outspoken, personal, plain, plain-spoken, point-blank, shortest, sincere, straight, straightforward, through, unambiguous, unbroken, undeviating, unequivocal, uninterrupted.

antonyms crooked, devious, indirect.

direction *n* address, administration, aim, approach, bearing, bent, bias, charge, command, control, course, current, drift, end, government, guidance, label, leadership, line, management, mark, order, orientation, oversight, path, proclivity, purpose, road, route, superintendence, superscription, supervision, tack, tendency, tenor, track, trend, way.

directions *n* briefing, guidance, guidelines, indication, instructions, orders, plan, recipe, recommendations, regulations.

directive *n* charge, command, decree, dictate, diktat, edict, fiat, imperative, injunction, instruction, mandate, notice, order, ordinance, regulation, ruling.

directly *adv* bluntly, candidly, dead, due, exactly, face-to-face, forthwith, frankly, honestly, immediately, instantaneously, instantly, openly, personally, plainly, point-blank, precisely, presently, promptly, pronto, quickly, right away, soon, speedily, straight, straightaway, straightforwardly, truthfully, unequivocally, unerringly, unswervingly.

antonym indirectly.

directness *n* bluffness, bluntness, candour, forthrightness, frankness, honesty, outspoken-ness, plain-speaking, sincerity, straightforwardness.

director *n* administrator, auteur, boss, chairman, chief, conductor, controller, corrector, executive, governor, head, leader, manager, monitor, organiser, principal, producer, supervisor.

dirge *n* coronach, dead-march, elegy, lament, monody, requiem, threnody.

dirt *n* clay, crud, dust, earth, excrement, filth, grime, impurity, indecency, loam, mire, muck, mud, obscenity, ordure, pornography, slime, smudge, smut, smutch, soil, sordor, stain, tarnish, vomit, yuck.

antonyms cleanliness, cleanness.

dirty *adj* angry, base, beggarly, begrimed, bitter, blue, clouded, contemptible, corrupt, cowardly, crooked, cruddy, dark, despicable, dishonest, dull, filthy, foul, fraudulent, grimy, grubby, grungy, ignominious, illegal, indecent, low, low-down, maculate, manky, mean, messy, miry, mucky, muddy, nasty, obscene, off-colour, piggish, polluted, pornographic, risque, salacious, scruffy, scurvy, shabby, sluttish, smutty, soiled, sordid, squalid, sullied, treacherous, unclean, unfair, unscrupulous, unsporting, unsterile, unswept, vile, vulgar, yucky.

antonyms clean, spotless.

v bedaub, begrime, besmear, besmirch, besmut, bespatter, blacken, defile, foul, mess up, muddy, pollute, smear, smirch, smudge, soil, soss, spoil, stain, sully.

antonyms clean, cleanse.

disability *n* affliction, ailment, complaint, crippledom, defect, disablement, disorder, disqualification, handicap, impairment, impotency, inability, incapacitation, incapacity, incompetency, infirmity, malady, unfitness, weakness.

disable *v* cripple, damage, debilitate, disenable, disqualify, enfeeble, hamstring, handicap, immobilise, impair, incapacitate, invalidate, lame, paralyse, prostrate, unfit, unman, weaken.

disabled *adj* bedridden, crippled, handicapped, hors de combat, immobilised, incapacitated, infirm, lame, maimed, mangled, mutilated, paralysed, weak, weakened, wrecked.

antonyms able, able-bodied.

disadvantage *n* burden, damage, debit, detriment, disamenity, disbenefit, disservice, drawback, flaw, fly in the ointment, handicap, hardship, harm, hindrance, hurt, impediment, inconvenience, injury, liability, loss, minus, nuisance, prejudice, privation, snag, trouble, unfavourableness, weakness.

antonyms advantage, benefit.

v hamper, handicap, hinder, inconvenience, wrong-foot.

antonyms aid, help.

disadvantaged *adj* deprived, handicapped, hindered, impeded, impoverished, struggling, underprivileged.

antonym privileged.

disadvantageous *adj* adverse, burdensome, damaging, deleterious, detrimental, harmful, hurtful, ill-timed, inauspicious, inconvenient, inexpedient, injurious, inopportune, prejudicial, unfavourable.

antonym advantageous.

disaffected *adj* alienated, antagonistic, antipathetic(al), discontented, disgruntled, disloyal, dissatisfied, estranged, hostile, mutinous, rebellious, seditious.

antonym contented.

disaffection *n* alienation, animosity, antagonism, antipathy, aversion, breach, coolness, disagreement, discontentment, discord, disharmony, dislike, disloyalty, dissatisfaction, estrangement, hostility, ill-will, repugnance, resentment, unfriendliness.

antonym contentment.

disagree *v* altercate, argue, bicker, bother, clash, conflict, contend, contest, contradict, counter, depart, deviate, differ, disaccord, discomfort, dissent, distress, diverge, fall out, hurt, nauseate, object, oppose, quarrel, run counter to, sicken, spat, squabble, take issue with, tiff, trouble, upset, vary, wrangle.

antonym agree.

disagreeable *adj* bad-tempered, brusque, churlish, contrary, cross, difficult, disgusting, dislik(e)able, disobliging, displeasing, distasteful, ill-natured, irritable, nasty, objectionable, obnoxious, offensive, peevish, repellent, repugnant, repulsive, rude, surly, unamiable, unappetising, unfriendly, ungracious, uninviting, unpalatable, unpleasant, unsavoury.

antonyms agreeable, friendly, pleasant.

disagreement *n* altercation, argument, clash, conflict, debate, difference, disaccord, discord, discrepancy, disparity, dispute, dissent, dissimilarity, dissimilitude, divergence, diversity, division, falling-out, incompatibility, incongruity, misunderstanding, quarrel, squabble, strife, tiff, unlikeness, variance, wrangle.

antonym agreement.

disallow *v* abjure, ban, cancel, chalk off, debar, disaffirm, disavow, disclaim, dismiss, disown, embargo, forbid, prohibit, proscribe, rebuff, refuse, reject, repudiate, veto.

antonyms allow, permit.

disallowed *adj* debarred, excepted, excluded, forbidden, impermissible, interdicted, prohibited, proscribed, rejected.

antonyms allowed, permissible.

disappear *v* cease, dematerialise, depart, dissolve, ebb, end, escape, evanesce, evaporate, expire, fade, flee, fly, go, pass, perish, recede, retire, scarper, vamoose, vanish, wane, withdraw.

antonym appear.

disappearance *n* dematerialisation, departure, desertion, disappearing, dispersal, dispersion, dissipation, eclipse, evanescence, evaporation, fading, flight, going, loss, melting, passing, vanishing.

antonym appearance.

disappoint *v* baffle, balk, chagrin, dash, deceive, defeat, delude, disconcert, disenchant, disgruntle, dishearten, disillusion, dismay, dissatisfy, fail, foil, frustrate, hamper, hinder, let down, miff, sadden, thwart, vex.

antonyms delight, please, satisfy.

disappointed *adj* balked, depressed, despondent, discontented, discouraged, disenchanted, disgruntled, disillusioned, dissatisfied, distressed, down-hearted, foiled, frustrated, let down, miffed, saddened, thwarted, upset.

antonyms delighted, pleased, satisfied.

disappointing *adj* anti-climactic, depressing, disagreeable, disconcerting, discouraging, inadequate, inferior, insufficient, pathetic, sad, sorry, unhappy, unsatisfactory, unworthy.

antonyms encouraging, pleasant, satisfactory.

disappointment[1] *n* bafflement, chagrin, discontent, discouragement, disenchantment, disillusionment, displeasure, dissatisfaction, distress, failure, frustration, mortification, regret.

antonyms delight, pleasure, satisfaction.

disappointment[2] *n* blow, calamity, comedown, disaster, drop, failure, fiasco, frost, lemon, let-down, misfortune, setback, swiz, swizzle.

antonyms boost, success.

disapprobation *n* blame, censure, condemnation, denunciation, disapproval, disfavour, dislike, displeasure, dissatisfaction, objection, reproach, reproof.

antonyms approbation, approval.

disapproval *n* censure, condemnation, criticism, denunciation, deprecation, disapprobation, disfavour, dislike, disparagement, displeasure, dissatisfaction, objection, reproach, thumbs-down.

antonyms approbation, approval, thumbs-up.

disapprove of blame, censure, condemn, denounce, deplore, deprecate, disallow, discountenance, dislike, disparage, object to, reject, spurn, take exception to.

antonym approve of.

disapproving *adj* censorious, condemnatory, critical, deprecatory, disapprobative, disapprobatory, disparaging, improbative, improbatory, reproachful.

disarm[1] *v* deactivate, demilitarise, demobilise, disable, disband, unarm, unweapon.

antonym arm.

disarm[2] appease, conciliate, modify, persuade, win over.

disarming *adj* charming, conciliatory, irresistible, likeable, mollifying, persuasive, winning.

disarrange *v* confuse, derange, disarray, discompose, dislocate, disorder, disorganise, disrank, disturb, jumble, muss(e), shuffle, unsettle, untidy.

antonym arrange.

disarray *n* chaos, clutter, confusion, discomposure, disharmony, dishevelment, dislocation, dismay, disorder, disorderliness, disorganisation, displacement, disunity, guddle, indiscipline, jumble, mess, muddle, shambles, tangle, unruliness, untidiness, upset.

antonyms array, order.

disaster *n* accident, act of God, blow, calamity, cataclysm, catastrophe, curtains, debacle, melt, misadventure, mischance, misfortune, mishap, reverse, ruin, ruination, stroke, tragedy, trouble.

antonyms success, triumph.

disastrous *adj* adverse, calamitous, cataclysmal, cataclysmic, catastrophic, destructive, detrimental, devastating, dire, dreadful, fatal, grievous, hapless, harmful, ill-fated, ill-starred, miserable, ruinous, terrible, tragic, unfortunate, unlucky.

antonyms successful, triumphant.

disband *v* break up, demobilise, dismiss, disperse, dissolve, part company, retire, scatter, separate.

antonyms assemble, band, combine.

disbelief *n* distrust, doubt, dubiety, incredulity, mistrust, rejection, scepticism, suspicion, unbelief.

antonym belief.

disbelieve *v* discount, discredit, miscredit, mistrust, reject, repudiate, suspect, unbelieve.

antonyms believe, trust.

disbeliever *n* agnostic, atheist, doubter, doubting Thomas, nullifidian, questioner, sceptic, scoffer, unbeliever.

antonym believer.

disbursement *n* disbursal, disposal, expenditure, outlay, payment, spending.

disc *n* circle, disk, diskette, face, plate, record, ring, roundel, roundlet, rundle.

discard *v* abandon, cashier, cast aside, dispense with, dispose of, ditch, drop, dump, jettison, leave off, reject, relinquish, remove, repudiate, scrap, shed.

antonyms adopt, embrace, espouse.

discern *v* ascertain, behold, descry, detect, determine, differentiate, discover, discriminate, distinguish, espy, judge, make out, notice, observe, perceive, recognise, see, wot.

discernible *adj* apparent, appreciable, clear, detectable, discoverable, distinct, distinguishable, manifest, noticeable, observable, obvious, patent, perceptible, plain, recognisable, sensible, visible.

antonym invisible.

discerning *adj* acute, astute, clear-sighted, critical, discriminating, eagle-eyed, eagle-sighted, ingenious, intelligent, judicious, knowing, penetrating, perceptive, percipient, perspicacious, piercing, sagacious, sensitive, sharp, shrewd, subtle, wise.

antonym obtuse.

discernment *n* acumen, acuteness, ascertainment, astuteness, awareness, clear-sightedness, cleverness, discrimination, ingenuity, insight, intelligence, judgement, keenness, penetration, perception, perceptiveness, percipience, perspicacity, sagacity, sharpness, understanding, wisdom.

discharge *v* absolve, accomplish, acquit, carry out, cashier, clear, detonate, disburden, discard, disembogue, dismiss, dispense, drum out, effectuate, egest, eject, emit, empty, excrete, execute, exonerate, expel, explode, exude, fire, free, fulfil, give off, gush, honour, leak, let off, liberate, meet, offload, ooze, oust, pardon, pay, perform, release, relieve, remove, sack, satisfy, set off, settle, shoot, unburden, unload, vent, void, volley.

antonyms employ, engage, hire.

n accomplishment, achievement, acquittal, acquittance, blast, burst, clearance, conge, defluxion, demobilisation, detonation, disburdening, discharging, dismissal, effluent, ejecta, ejectamenta, ejection, emission, emptying, excretion, execution, exoneration, explosion, firing, flight, flow, flux, fluxion, fulfilment, fusillade, gleet, glit, liberation, mittimus, observance, ooze, pardon, payment, performance, pus, quietus, quittance, release, remittance, report, salvo, satisfaction, secretion, seepage, settlement, shot, suppuration, the boot, the sack, unburdening, unloading, vent, voidance, voiding, volley, whiff.

disciple *n* acolyte, adherent, apostle, believer, catechumen, chela, convert, devotee, follower, learner, partisan, proselyte, pupil, student, supporter, votary.

disciplinarian *n* authoritarian, autocrat, despot, martinet, stickler, taskmaster, tyrant.

discipline *n* castigation, chastisement, conduct, control, correction, course, curriculum, drill, exercise, martinetism, method, orderliness, practice, punishment, regimen, regulation, restraint, self-control, speciality, strictness, subject, training.

antonyms carelessness, negligence.

v break in, castigate, chasten, chastise, check, control, correct, drill, educate, exercise, form, govern, habituate, instruct, inure, penalise, prepare, punish, regulate, reprimand, reprove, restrain, toughen, train.

disclaim *v* abandon, abjure, abnegate, decline, deny, disacknowledge, disaffirm, disallow, disavow, disown, forswear, reject, renounce, repudiate.

antonyms accept, acknowledge, claim.

disclaimer *n* abjuration, abnegation, contradiction, denial, disavowal, disownment, rejection, renunciation, repudiation, retraction.

disclose *v* broadcast, communicate, confess, discover, divulge, exhibit, expose, impart, lay, lay bare, leak, let slip, propale, publish, relate, reveal, show, tell, unbare, unbosom, unburden, uncover, unfold, unveil, utter.

antonyms conceal, hide.

disclosure *n* acknowledgement, admission, announcement, Apocalypse, broadcast, confession, declaration, discovery, divulgence, expose, exposure, leak, publication, revelation, uncovering.

discoloration *n* blemish, blot, blotch, dyschroa, ecchymosis, mark, patch, splotch, spot, stain.

discolour *v* disfigure, fade, mar, mark, rust, soil, stain, streak, tarnish, tinge, weather.

discomfit *v* abash, baffle, balk, beat, checkmate, confound, confuse, defeat, demoralise, discompose, disconcert, embarrass, faze, flurry, fluster, foil, frustrate, humble, humiliate, outwit, overcome, perplex, perturb, rattle, ruffle, thwart, trump, unsettle, vanquish, worry, worst.

discomfiture *n* abashment, beating, chagrin, confusion, defeat, demoralisation, disappointment, discomposure, embarrassment, failure, frustration, humiliation, overthrow, repulse, rout, ruin, shame, undoing, unease, vanquishment.

discomfort *n* ache, annoyance, disquiet, distress, hardship, hurt, inquietude, irritant, irritation, malaise, trouble, uneasiness, unpleasantness, unpleasantry, vexation.

antonyms comfort, ease.

discompose *v* agitate, annoy, bewilder, confuse, discomfit, disconcert, dishevel, displease, disturb, embarrass, faze, flurry, fluster, fret, irritate, perturb, rattle, ruffle, rumple, tousle, unsettle, upset, vex, worry.

antonym compose.

discomposure *n* agitation, anxiety, confusion, discomfiture, dislocation, disorder, disquiet, disquietude, distraction, disturbance, embarrassment, fluster, inquietude, malaise, nervousness, perturbation, uneasiness.

antonym composure.

disconcert *v* abash, agitate, baffle, balk, bewilder, confuse, discombobulate, discomfit, discompose, disturb, flurry, fluster, frustrate, hinder, nonplus, perplex, perturb, put someone's nose out of joint, rattle, ruffle, thwart, trouble, unbalance, undo, unsettle, upset, worry.

disconcerted *adj* annoyed, bewildered, confused, discombobulated, discomfited, distracted, disturbed, embarrassed, fazed, flurried, flustered, mixed-up, nonplussed, perturbed, rattled, ruffled, taken aback, thrown, troubled, unsettled, upset.

disconcerting *adj* alarming, awkward, baffling, bewildering, bothersome, confusing, discombobulating, dismaying, distracting, disturbing, embarrassing, off-putting, perplexing, upsetting.

disconnect *v* cut off, detach, disengage, divide, part, separate, sever, uncouple, ungear, unhitch, unhook, unlink, unplug, unyoke.

antonyms attach, connect, engage.

disconnected *adj* confused, disjointed, free, garbled, illogical, incoherent, irrational, jumbled, loose, rambling, unco-ordinated, unintelligible, wandering.

antonyms attached, coherent, connected.

disconsolate *adj* crushed, dejected, desolate, despairing, dispirited, forlorn, gloomy, grief-stricken, heartbroken, heavy-hearted, hopeless, inconsolable, melancholy, miserable, sad, unhappy, unsolaced, woeful, wretched.

antonyms cheerful, cheery.

discontent *n* discontentment, displeasure, disquiet, dissatisfaction, envy, fretfulness, impatience, regret, restlessness, uneasiness, unhappiness, unrest, vexation.

antonym content.

discontented *adj* brassed off, browned off, cheesed off, complaining, disaffected, disgruntled, displeased, dissatisfied, exasperated, fed up, fretful, impatient, miserable, scunnered, unhappy, vexed.

antonyms contented, happy, satisfied.

discontinue *v* abandon, break off, cancel, cease, drop, end, finish, halt, interrupt, pause, quit, stop, suspend, terminate.

antonym continue.

discontinuity *n* breach, disconnectedness, disconnection, disjointedness, disruption, disunion, incoherence, interruption, rupture.

antonym continuity.

discontinuous *adj* broken, disconnected, fitful, intermittent, interrupted, irregular, periodic, punctuated, spasmodic.

antonym continuous.

discord *n* cacophony, clashing, conflict, contention, difference, din, disagreement, discordance, disharmony, dispute, dissension, dissonance, disunity, division, friction, harshness, incompatibility, jangle, jarring, opposition, racket, rupture, split, strife, tumult, variance, wrangling.

antonyms agreement, concord, harmony.

discordant *adj* absonant, at odds, cacophonous, clashing, conflicting, contradictory, contrary, different, disagreeing, disharmonic, disharmonious, dissonant, grating, harsh, incompatible, incongruous, inconsistent, inharmonious, jangling, jarring, opposite, shrill, strident, unmelodious, untuneful.

antonyms concordant, harmonious.

discount[1] *v* disbelieve, disregard, gloss over, ignore, overlook.

discount[2] *n* abatement, allowance, concession, cut, deduction, mark-down, rebate, rebatement, reduction.

discountenance *v* abash, chagrin, confuse, discompose, disconcert, discourage, embarrass, humble, humiliate, shame.

antonyms countenance, support.

discourage *v* abash, awe, check, chill, cow, curb, damp, dampen, dash, daunt, deject, demoralise, deprecate, depress, deter, discountenance, disfavour, dishearten, dismay, dispirit, dissuade, frighten, hinder, inhibit, intimidate, overawe, prevent, put off, restrain, scare, unman, unnerve.

antonyms encourage, favour, hearten, inspire.

discouraged *adj* chopfallen, crestfallen, dashed, daunted, depressed, deterred, disheartened, dismayed, dispirited, downcast, glum, pessimistic.

antonyms encouraged, heartened.

discouragement *n* constraint, curb, damp, damper, dejection, depression, despair, despondency, deterrent, disappointment, discomfiture, disincentive, dismay, dismayedness, downheartedness, hindrance, hopelessness, impediment, obstacle, opposition, pessimism, rebuff, restraint, setback.

antonyms encouragement, incentive.

discouraging *adj* dampening, daunting, dehortatory, depressing, disappointing, disheartening, dispiriting, dissuasive, dissuasory, inauspicious, off-putting, unfavourable, unpropitious.

antonyms encouraging, heartening.

discourse *n* address, chat, communication, conversation, converse, descant, dialogue, discussion, disquisition, dissertation, essay, exercitation, homily, lecture, oration, sermon, speech, talk, treatise.

v confer, converse, debate, declaim, descant, dialogise, discuss, dissent, dissertate, expatiate, jaw, lecture, lucubrate, talk.

discourteous *adj* abrupt, bad-mannered, boorish, brusque, curt, disrespectful, ill-bred, ill-mannered, impolite, insolent, offhand, rude, slighting, unceremonious, uncivil, uncourteous, ungracious, unmannerly.

antonyms courteous, polite, respectful.

discourtesy *n* affront, bad manners, disrespectfulness, ill-breeding, impertinence, impoliteness, incivility, indecorousness, indecorum, insolence, insult, rebuff, rudeness, slight, snub, ungraciousness, unmannerliness.

antonyms courtesy, politeness.

discover *v* ascertain, conceive, contrive, descry, design, detect, determine, devise, dig up, discern, disclose, espy, find, invent, learn, light on, locate, notice, originate, perceive, pioneer, realise, recognise, reveal, see, spot, suss out, uncover, unearth.

antonyms conceal, hide.

discoverer *n* author, explorer, finder, founder, initiator, inventor, originator, pioneer.

discovery *n* ascertainment, breakthrough, coup, detection, disclosure, espial, eureka, exploration, find, finding, innovation, introduction, invention, locating, location, origination, revelation, uncovering.

antonym concealment.

discredit *v* blame, censure, challenge, defame, degrade, deny, disbelieve, discount, disgrace, dishonour, disparage, dispute, distrust, doubt, explode, mistrust, question, reproach, slander, slur, smear, vilify.

antonyms believe, credit.

n aspersion, blame, censure, disgrace, dishonour, disrepute, distrust, doubt, ignominy, ill-repute, imputation, mistrust, odium, opprobium, question, reproach, scandal, scepticism, shame, slur, smear, stigma, suspicion.

antonym credit.

discreditable *adj* blameworthy, degrading, disgraceful, dishonourable, humiliating, ignoble, ignominious, improper, infamous, reprehensible, scandalous, shameful, unbecoming, unprincipled, unworthy.

antonyms creditable, worthy.

discredited *adj* debunked, discarded, disgraced, dishonoured, exploded, exposed, outworn, refuted, rejected.

discreet *adj* careful, cautious, circumspect, considerate, delicate, diplomatic, discerning, guarded, judicious, politic, prudent, reserved, sagacious, sensible, softly-softly, tactful, wary.

antonyms careless, indiscreet, tactless.

discrepancy *n* conflict, contrariety, difference, disagreement, discordance, disparity, dissimilarity, dissonance, divergence, imparity, incongruity, inconsistency, inequality, variance, variation.

discrete *adj* detached, disconnected, discontinuous, disjoined, disjunct, distinct, individual, separate, unattached.

discretion *n* acumen, care, carefulness, caution, choice, circumspection, consideration, diplomacy, discernment, disposition, heedfulness, inclination, judgement, judiciousness, liking, maturity, mind, option, pleasure, predilection, preference, prudence, responsibility, sagacity, tact, volition, wariness, will, wisdom, wish.

antonym indiscretion.

discriminate[1] *v* assess, differentiate, discern, distinguish, evaluate, make a distinction, segregate, separate, sift, tell apart.

antonyms confound, confuse.

discriminate[2] (against) *v* be biased, be prejudiced, disfavour, victimise.

discriminating *adj* acute, astute, critical, cultivated, discerning, discriminant, fastidious, nasute, particular, perceptive, selective, sensitive, tasteful.

discrimination[1] *n* bias, bigotry, favouritism, inequity, intolerance, Jim Crow, prejudice, unfairness.

discrimination[2] *n* acumen, acuteness, discernment, insight, judgement, keenness, penetration, perception, percipience, refinement, sagacity, subtlety, taste.

discriminatory[1] *adj* biased, discriminative, favouring, inequitable, loaded, one-sided, partial, partisan, preferential, prejudiced, prejudicial, unfair, unjust, weighted.

antonyms fair, impartial, unbiased.

discriminatory[2] *adj* analytical, astute, differentiating, discerning, discriminating, perceptive, percipient, perspicacious.

discursive *adj* circuitous, desultory, diffuse, digressive, discursory, erratic, long-winded, loose, meandering, prolix, rambling, wide-ranging.

antonyms brief, short.

discuss *v* argue, confer, consider, consult, converse, debate, deliberate, examine, lay heads together, rap.

discussion *n* analysis, argument, colloquium, colloquy, confabulation, conference, conferencing, consideration, consultation, conversation, debate, deliberation, dialogue, discourse, examination, exchange, gabfest, moot, quodlibet, rap, review, scrutiny, seminar, symposium, talkfest, talk-in, teleconferencing.

disdain *v* belittle, contemn, deride, despise, disavow, disregard, misprise, pooh-pooh, rebuff, reject, scorn, slight, sneer at, spurn, undervalue.

antonyms admire, respect.

n arrogance, contempt, contumely, deprecation, derision, dislike, haughtiness, hauteur, imperiousness, indifference, scorn, sneering, snobbishness, superciliousness.

antonyms admiration, respect.

disdainful *adj* aloof, arrogant, contemptuous, derisive, haughty, hoity-toity, imperious, insolent, proud, scornful, sneering, supercilious, superior, uppish.

antonyms admiring, respectful.

disease *n* affection, affliction, ailment, blight, cancer, canker, complaint, condition, contagion, contamination, disorder, distemper, epidemic, epizootic, idiopathy, ill-health, illness, indisposition, infection, infirmity, lurgy, malady, malaise, murrain, pest, plague, sickness, upset.

antonym health.

diseased *adj* ailing, contaminated, distemperate, infected, poisoned, rotten, sick, sickly, tainted, unhealthy, unsound, unwell, unwholesome.

antonym healthy.

disembark *v* alight, arrive, debark, debus, deplane, detrain, disbark, land.

antonym embark.

disembodied *adj* bodiless, disbodied, discorporate, disfleshed, ghostly, immaterial, incorporeal, intangible, phantom, spectral, spiritual, unbodied.

disembowel *v* disbowel, draw, embowel, eviscerate, exenterate, gralloch, gut, paunch.

disenchanted *adj* blase, cynical, disappointed, disillusioned, fed up, indifferent, jaundiced, scunnered, soured, undeceived.

disenchantment *n* cynicism, disappointment, disillusion, disillusionment, revulsion, scunner.

disengage *v* detach, disconnect, disentangle, disentwine, disinvolve, disjoin, disunite, divide, ease, extricate, free, liberate, loosen, release, separate, undo, unloose, untie, untwine, withdraw.

antonyms attach, connect, engage.

disengaged *adj* disentangled, free(d), heart-free, heart-whole, inactive, liberated, loose, released, separate(d), unattached, unconnected, unhitched, unoccupied.

antonyms connected, joined, united.

disentangle *v* clarify, debarrass, detach, disconnect, disembarrass, disengage, disentwine, disinvolve, extricate, free, loose, ravel out, resolve, separate, sever, simplify, unfold, unravel, unsnarl, untangle, untwine, untwist.

antonym entangle.

disfavour *n* disapprobation, disapproval, discredit, disesteem, disgrace, disgust, dislike, displeasure, unpopularity.

antonym favour.

disfigure *v* blemish, damage, deface, deform, disfeature, distort, injure, maim, mar, mutilate, scar, spoil, uglify.

antonym adorn.

disfigured *adj* damaged, defaced, deformed, flawed, ruined, scarred, spoilt, ugly.

antonym adorned.

disfigurement *n* blemish, defacement, defect, deformity, disgrace, distortion, impairment, injury, mutilation, scar, spot, stain, uglification.

antonym adornment.

disgorge *v* belch, discharge, effuse, eject, empty, expel, regorge, regurgitate, relinquish, renounce, spew, spout, surrender, throw up, vomit.

disgrace *n* aspersion, attaint, baseness, blemish, blot, contempt, defamation, degradation, discredit, disesteem, disfavour, dishonour, disrepute, dog-house, ignominy, infamy, obloquy, odium, opprobium, reproach, scandal, shame, slur, stain, stigma.

antonyms esteem, honour, respect.

v abase, attaint, defame, degrade, discredit, disfavour, dishonour, disparage, humiliate, reproach, scandalise, shame, slur, stain, stigmatise, sully, taint.

antonyms honour, respect.

disgraced *adj* branded, degraded, discredited, dishonoured, humiliated, in the doghouse, stigmatised.

antonyms honoured, respected.

disgraceful *adj* appalling, blameworthy, contemptible, degrading, detestable, discreditable, dishonourable, disreputable, dreadful, ignominious, infamous, low, mean, opprobrious, scandalous, shameful, shocking, unworthy.

antonyms honourable, respectable.

disgruntled *adj* annoyed, brassed off, browned off, cheesed off, discontented, displeased, dissatisfied, grumpy, irritated, malcontent, peeved, peevish, petulant, put out, scunnered, sulky, sullen, testy, vexed.

antonyms pleased, satisfied.

disguise *v* camouflage, cloak, conceal, cover, deceive, dissemble, dissimulate, dress up, explain away, fake, falsify, fudge, hide, mask, misrepresent, screen, secrete, shroud, veil.

antonyms expose, reveal, uncover.

n camouflage, cloak, concealment, costume, cover, coverture, deception, dissimulation, façade, front, get-up, mask, masquerade, pretence, screen, semblance, travesty, trickery, veil, veneer, visor.

disguised *adj* camouflaged, cloaked, covert, fake, false, feigned, incognito, made up, masked, undercover, unrecognisable, visored.

disgust *v* displease, nauseate, offend, outrage, put off, repel, revolt, scandalise, scunner, sicken.

antonyms delight, gratify, tempt.

n abhorrence, abomination, antipathy, aversion, detestation, dislike, disrelish, distaste, hatefulness, hatred, loathing, nausea, odium, repugnance, repulsion, revulsion.

antonyms admiration, liking.

disgusted *adj* appalled, nauseated, offended, outraged, repelled, repulsed, scandalised, scunnered, sick (and tired), sickened.

antonyms attracted, delighted.

disgusting *adj* abominable, detestable, distasteful, foul, gross, hateful, loathsome, nasty, nauseating, nauseous, objectionable, obnoxious, obscene, odious, offensive, repellent, repugnant, revolting, shameless, sickening, sick-making, stinking, ugsome, unappetising, vile, vulgar.

antonyms attractive, delightful, pleasant.

dish[1] *n* bowl, fare, food, plate, platter, porringer, ramekin, recipe, salver, trencher.

dish out allocate, distribute, dole out, give out, hand out, hand round, inflict, mete out.

dish up dispense, ladle, prepare, present, produce, scoop, serve, spoon.

dish[2] *v* finish, ruin, spoil, torpedo, wreck.

disharmony *n* clash, conflict, disaccord, discord, discordance, dissonance, friction, incompatibility.

antonym harmony.

dishearten *v* cast down, crush, damp, dampen, dash, daunt, deject, depress, deter, discourage, dismay, dispirit, frighten, weary.

antonyms encourage, hearten.

disheartened *adj* crestfallen, crushed, daunted, dejected, depressed, disappointed, discouraged, dismayed, dispirited, downcast, downhearted, frightened, weary.

antonyms encouraged, heartened.

dishevelled *adj* bedraggled, blowsy, disarranged, disordered, frowsy, messy, mussy, ruffled, rumpled, slovenly, tousled, uncombed, unkempt, untidy.

antonyms neat, spruce, tidy.

dishonest *adj* bent, cheating, corrupt, crafty, crooked, deceitful, deceiving, deceptive, designing, disreputable, double-dealing, false, fraudulent, guileful, immoral, knavish, lying, mendacious, perfidious, shady, snide, swindling, treacherous, unethical, unfair, unprincipled, unscrupulous, untrustworthy, untruthful, wrongful.

antonyms fair, honest, scrupulous, trustworthy.

dishonesty *n* cheating, chicanery, corruption, craft, criminality, crookedness, deceit, duplicity, falsehood, falsity, fraud, fraudulence, graft, immorality, improbity, insincerity, mendacity, perfidy, stealing, treachery, trickery, unscrupulousness, wiliness.

antonyms honesty, truthfulness.

dishonour *v* abase, blacken, corrupt, debase, debauch, defame, defile, deflower, degrade, demean, discredit, disgrace, disparage, pollute, rape, ravish, seduce, shame, sully.

antonym honour.

n abasement, abuse, affront, aspersion, degradation, discourtesy, discredit, disfavour, disgrace, disrepute, ignominy, imputation, indignity, infamy, insult, obloquy, odium, offence, opprobrium, outrage, reproach, scandal, shame, slight, slur.

antonym honour.

dishonourable *adj* base, blackguardly, contemptible, corrupt, despicable, discreditable, disgraceful, disreputable, ignoble, ignominous, infamous, scandalous, shameful, shameless, treacherous, unethical, unprincipled, unscrupulous, untrustworthy, unworthy.

antonym honourable.

disillusioned *adj* disabused, disappointed, disenchanted, enlightened, indifferent, undeceived, unenthusiastic.

disincentive *n* barrier, constraint, damper, determent, deterrent, discouragement, dissuasion, hindrance, impediment, obstacle, repellent, restriction, turn-off.

antonyms encouragement, incentive.

disinclination *n* alienation, antipathy, averseness, aversion, demur, dislike, loathness, objection, opposition, reluctance, repugnance, resistance, unwillingness.

antonym inclination.

disinclined *adj* antipathetic, averse, hesitant, indisposed, loath, opposed, reluctant, resistant, undisposed, unenthusiastic, unwilling.

antonyms inclined, willing.

disinfect *v* clean, cleanse, decontaminate, deodorise, depurate, fumigate, purge, purify, sanitise, sterilise.

antonyms contaminate, infect.

disinfectant *n* antiseptic, decontaminative, depurant, germicide, sanitiser, steriliser.

disinfection *n* cleansing, decontamination, depuration, fumigation, purification, sanitisation, sterilisation.

disingenuous *adj* artful, cunning, deceitful, designing, devious, dishonest, duplicitous, guileful, insidious, insincere, shifty, two-faced, uncandid, wily.

antonyms artless, frank, ingenuous, naive.

disintegrate *v* break up, crumble, decompose, disunite, fall apart, moulder, rot, separate, shatter, splinter.

antonyms combine, merge, unite.

disinterest *n* candidness, detachment, disinterestedness, dispassionateness, equitableness, equity, fairness, impartiality, justice, neutrality, unbiasedness.

antonym interest.

disinterested *adj* candid, detached, dispassionate, equitable, even-handed, impartial, impersonal, neutral, open-minded, unbiased, uninvolved, unprejudiced, unselfish.

antonyms biased, concerned, interested, prejudiced.

disjoin *v* detach, disannex, disconnect, disengage, dismember, dissociate, disunite, divide, divorce, isolate, partition, segregate, separate, sever, split, uncouple.

antonyms connect, join.

disjoint *v* anatomise, disarrange, disarticulate, discompose, dislocate, dismember, disorder, displace, dissect, unjoint.

disjointed *adj* aimless, broken, confused, dearticulated, disarticulated, disconnected, dislocated, disordered, displaced, disunited, divided, fitful, incoherent, loose, rambling, separated, spasmodic, split, unconnected, unjointed.

antonym coherent.

dislike *n* animosity, animus, antagonism, antipathy, aversion, detestation, disapprobation, disapproval, disgust, disinclination, displeasure, disrelish, distaste, dyspathy, enmity, hatred, hostility, loathing, repugnance.

antonyms attachment, liking, predilection.

v abhor, abominate, despise, detest, disapprove, disfavour, disrelish, hate, keck, loathe, scorn, shun.

antonyms favour, like, prefer.

dislocate *v* derange, disarray, disarticulate, disconnect, disengage, disjoint, disorder, displace, disrupt, disturb, disunite, luxate, misplace, shift, unhinge.

dislocation *n* derangement, disarray, disarticulation, disconnection, disengagement, disorder, disorganisation, disruption, disturbance, luxation, misarrangement, misarray, misplacement, unhingement, unhinging.

antonym order.

dislodge *v* displace, disturb, eject, extricate, move, oust, remove, shift, uproot.

disloyal *adj* apostate, disaffected, faithless, false, perfidious, seditious, subversive, traitorous, treacherous, treasonable, two-faced, unfaithful, unleal, unpatriotic, untrustworthy, unwifely.

antonym loyal.

disloyalty *n* apostasy, betrayal, double-dealing, falseness, falsity, inconstancy, infidelity, lese-majesty, perfidiousness, perfidy, sedition, treachery, treason, unfaithfulness.

antonym loyalty.

dismal *adj* black, bleak, burdan, cheerless, dark, depressing, despondent, discouraging, doleful, dolorous, dowie, dreary, dreich, forlorn, funereal, ghostful, gloomy, gruesome, hopeless, incompetent, inept, lac(h)rymose, lonesome, long-faced, long-visaged, lowering, low-spirited, lugubrious, melancholy, poor, sad, sepulchral, sombre, sorrowful, stupid, thick, useless.

antonyms bright, cheerful.

dismantle *v* demolish, demount, disassemble, dismount, raze, strike, strip, unrig.

antonym assemble.

dismay *v* affright, alarm, appal, consternate, daunt, depress, disappoint, disconcert, discourage, dishearten, disillusion, dispirit, distress, frighten, horrify, paralyse, put off, scare, terrify, unnerve, unsettle.

antonym encourage.

n agitation, alarm, anxiety, apprehension, consternation, disappointment, distress, dread, fear, fright, funk, horror, panic, terror, trepidation, upset.

antonyms boldness, encouragement.

dismember *v* amputate, anatomise, disject, disjoint, dislimb, dislocate, dissect, divellicate, divide, mutilate, piecemeal, rend, sever.

antonyms assemble, join.

dismemberment *n* amputation, anatomisation, disjection, dislocation, dissection, division, mutilation.

antonyms assembly, joining, unifying.

dismiss *v* axe, banish, bounce, bowler-hat, cashier, chasse, chuck, disband, discharge, discount, dispel, disperse, disregard, dissolve, drop, fire, free, give (someone) the push, lay off, let go, oust, pooh-pooh, reject, release, relegate, remove, repudiate, sack, send packing, set aside, shelve, spurn.

antonyms accept, appoint.

dismissal *n* adjournment, cards, conge, dear John letter, discharge, dismission, end, expulsion, marching orders, mittimus, notice, release, removal, the boot, the bum's rush, the elbow, the mitten, the push, the sack, walking-orders, walking-papers, walking-ticket.

antonym appointment.

dismissive *adj* contemptuous, disdainful, dismissory, off-hand, scornful, sneering.

antonyms concerned, interested.

dismount *v* alight, descend, get down, light, unmount.

antonym mount.

disobedience *n* contrariness, contumacity, contumacy, indiscipline, infraction, insubordination, mutiny, non-observance, recalcitrance, revolt, unruliness, waywardness.

antonym obedience.

disobedient *adj* contrary, contumacious, defiant, disorderly, froward, insubordinate, intractable, mischievous, naughty, obstreperous, refractory, unruly, wayward, wilful.

antonym obedient.

disobey *v* contravene, defy, disregard, flout, ignore, infringe, overstep, rebel, resist, transgress, violate.

antonym obey.

disoblige *v* deny, disserve, refuse.

antonym oblige.

disobliging *adj* awkward, bloody-minded, cussed, disagreeable, discourteous, inaccommodating, rude, unaccommodating, uncivil, unco-operative, unhelpful.

antonym obliging.

disorder *n* affliction, ailment, brawl, chaos, clamour, clutter, commotion, complaint, confusion, derangement, disarray, disease, disorderliness, disorganisation, disturbance, fight, fracas, hubbub, hullabaloo, illness, indisposition, irregularity, jumble, malady, mess, misarrangement, misarray, misorder, misrule, muddle, muss(e), mussiness, quarrel, riot, rumpus, shambles, sickness, tumult, untidiness, uproar.

antonym order.

v clutter, confound, confuse, derange, disarrange, discompose, disorganise, disrank, disturb, jumble, mess up, misorder, mix up, muddle, scatter, unsettle, upset.

antonyms arrange, organise.

disordered *adj* confused, deranged, disarranged, dislocated, disorganised, displaced, higgledy-piggledy, indigest, jumbled, misplaced, muddle, mussy, onkus, out of kilter, turbid, untidy.

antonyms ordered, tidy.

disorderly *adj* chaotic, confused, disordinate, disorganised, disruptive, higgledy-piggledy, indiscriminate, irregular, jumbled, lawless, messy, obstreperous, rebellious, refractory, riotous, rowdy, shambolic, stormy, tumultuous, turbulent, undisciplined, ungovernable, unlawful, unmanageable, unruly, unsystematic, untidy.

antonyms tidy, well-behaved.

disorganisation *n* chaos, confusion, derangement, disarray, disjointedness, dislocation, disorder, disruption, incoherence, unconnectedness.

antonyms order, tidiness.

disorganise *v* break up, confuse, derange, destroy, disarrange, discompose, disorder, disrank, disrupt, disturb, jumble, muddle, play havoc with, play hell with, unsettle, upset.

antonym organise.

disorganised *adj* chaotic, confused, disordered, haphazard, jumbled, muddled, shambolic, shuffled, topsy-turvy, unmethodical, unorganised, unregulated, unsifted, unsorted, unstructured, unsystematic, unsystematised.

antonyms organised, tidy.

disorientate *v* confuse, dislocate, disorient, faze, feeze, mislead, muddle, perplex, puzzle, upset.

disorientated *adj* adrift, astray, at sea, bewildered, confused, disoriented, lost, mixed up, muddled, perplexed, puzzled, unbalanced, unsettled, upset.

disown *v* abandon, abnegate, cast off, deny, disacknowledge, disallow, disavow, disclaim, reject, renounce, repudiate, unget.

antonym accept.

disparage *v* belittle, criticise, decry, defame, degrade, denigrate, deprecate, depreciate, deride, derogate, detract from, discredit, disdain, dishonour, dismiss, disvalue, malign, minimise, ridicule, run down, scorn, slander, traduce, underestimate, underrate, undervalue, vilify, vilipend.

antonym praise.

disparagement *n* aspersion, belittlement, condemnation, contempt, contumely, criticism, debasement, decrial, decrying, degradation, denunciation, deprecation, depreciation, derision, derogation, detraction, discredit, disdain, ridicule, scorn, slander, underestimation, vilification.

antonym praise.

disparate *adj* contrary, contrasting, different, discordant, discrepant, dissimilar, distinct, diverse, unequal, unlike.

antonyms equal, similar.

disparity *n* contrast, difference, discrepancy, disproportion, dissimilarity, dissimilitude, distinction, gap, imbalance, imparity, incongruity, inequality, unevenness, unlikeness.

antonyms equality, similarity.

dispassionate *adj* calm, candid, collected, composed, cool, detached, disinterested, fair, impartial, impersonal, imperturbable, indifferent, moderate, neutral, objective, quiet, serene, sober, temperate, unbiased, unemotional, unexcitable, unexcited, uninvolved, unmoved, unprejudiced, unruffled.

antonyms biased, emotional.

dispatch[1], despatch *v* accelerate, conclude, discharge, dismiss, dispose of, expedite, finish, hasten, hurry, perform, quicken, settle.

antonym impede.

n alacrity, celerity, depêche, expedition, haste, precipitateness, promptitude, promptness, quickness, rapidity, speed, swiftness.

antonym slowness.

dispatch[2], despatch *v* consign, express, forward, remit, send, transmit.

n account, bulletin, communication, communique, document, instruction, item, letter, message, missive, news, piece, report, story.

dispatch[3], despatch *v* assassinate, bump off, execute, kill, murder, rub out, slaughter, slay, waste.

dispel *v* allay, banish, discuss, dismiss, disperse, dissipate, drive off, eliminate, expel, melt away, resolve, rout, scatter.

antonym give rise to.

dispensable *adj* disposable, expendable, inessential, needless, non-essential, replaceable, superfluous, unnecessary, useless.

antonym indispensable.

dispensation *n* administration, allotment, appointment, apportionment, award, bestowal, conferment, consignment, derogation, direction, disbursement, distribution, dole, economy, endowment, exception, exemption, immunity, indulgence, licence, management, part, permission, plan, portion, privilege, quota, regulation, relaxation, relief, remission, reprieve, scheme, share, stewardship, supplying, system.

dispensatory *adj* derogative, disobligatory, dispensative.

dispense *v* administer, allocate, allot, apply, apportion, assign, deal out, direct, disburse, discharge, distribute, dole out, enforce, except, excuse, execute, exempt, exonerate, implement, let off, measure, mete out, mix, operate, prepare, release, relieve, reprieve, share, supply, undertake.

dispense with abolish, cancel, dispose of, disregard, forgo, ignore, omit, pass over, relinquish, waive.

antonyms accept, use.

disperse *v* broadcast, circulate, diffuse, disappear, disband, dismiss, dispel, disseminate, dissipate, dissolve, distribute, drive off, evanesce, melt away, rout, scatter, separate, spread, strew, vanish.

antonym gather.

dispersion *n* broadcast, circulation, diaspora, diffusion, discussion, dispersal, dissemination, dissipation, distribution, galut(h), scattering, spread.

dispirit *v* damp, dampen, dash, deject, depress, deter, discourage, dishearten, put a damper on, sadden.

antonym encourage.

dispirited *adj* brassed off, browned off, cast down, crestfallen, dejected, depressed, despondent, discouraged, disheartened, down, downcast, fed up, gloomy, glum, low, morose, sad.

antonym encouraged.

displace *v* cashier, crowd out, depose, derange, disarrange, discard, discharge, dislocate, dislodge, dismiss, dispossess, disturb, eject, evict, fire, luxate, misplace, move, oust, remove, replace, sack, shift, succeed, supersede, supplant, transpose, unsettle.

displaced *adj* disarranged, ectopic, misplaced.

displacement *n* disarrangement, disturbance, ectopia, ectopy, heterotaxis, heterotopia, misplacement.

antonym order.

display *v* betray, blazon, boast, demonstrate, disclose, evidence, evince, exhibit, expand, expose, extend, flash, flaunt, flourish, manifest, model, parade, present, reveal, show, show off, showcase, splash, sport, unfold, unfurl, unveil, vaunt, wear.

antonym hide.

n array, demonstration, etalage, exhibition, exposition, exposure, flourish, manifestation, ostentation, pageant, parade, pomp, presentation, revelation, show, spectacle, splurge.

displease *v* aggravate, anger, annoy, disgust, dissatisfy, exasperate, gall, get, incense, infuriate, irk, irritate, nettle, offend, peeve, pique, provoke, put out, rile, upset, vex.

antonyms calm, please.

displeased *n* aggravated, angry, annoyed, chuffed, exasperated, furious, irritated, peeved, piqued, put out, upset.
antonym pleased.

displeasure *n* anger, annoyance, disapprobation, disapproval, discontent, disfavour, disgruntlement, dudgeon, huff, indignation, irritation, offence, pique, resentment, vexation, wrath.
antonyms gratification, pleasure.

disport *v* amuse, beguile, bound, caper, cavort, cheer, delight, divert, entertain, frisk, frolic, gambol, play, revel, romp, sport.

disposal *n* arrangement, array, assignment, authority, bequest, bestowal, clearance, conduct, consignment, control, conveyance, determination, direction, discarding, discretion, dispensation, disposition, distribution, dumping, ejection, gift, government, jettisoning, management, ordering, position, regulation, relinquishment, removal, responsibility, riddance, scrapping, settlement, transfer.
antonym provision.

dispose *v* actuate, adapt, adjust, align, arrange, array, bias, condition, determine, dispone, distribute, fix, group, incline, induce, influence, lay, lead, marshal, motivate, move, order, place, position, predispose, prompt, put, range, rank, regulate, set, settle, situate, stand, tempt.
dispose of bestow, deal with, decide, destroy, determine, discard, dump, end, get rid of, give, jettison, kibosh, make over, put the kibosh on, scrap, sell, settle, transfer, unload.
antonym provide.

disposed *adj* apt, given, inclined, liable, likely, minded, moved, predisposed, prone, ready, subject, willing.
antonym disinclined.

disposition *n* adjustment, arrangement, bent, bias, character, classification, constitution, control, direction, disposal, distribution, grain, grouping, habit, inclination, kidney, leaning, make-up, management, nature, ordering, organisation, placement, predisposition, proclivity, proneness, propensity, readiness, regulation, spirit, temper, temperament, tendency, velleity.

dispossess *v* deprive, dislodge, disseise, divest, eject, evict, expel, expropriate, oust, rob, strip, unhouse.
antonyms give, provide.

dispossession *n* dethronement, dethroning, disseisin, ejection, ejectment, eviction, expulsion, ousting.
antonym possession.

disproportion *n* asymmetry, discrepancy, disparity, imbalance, imparity, inadequacy, inequality, insufficiency, lopsidedness, unevenness.
antonyms balance, equality.

disproportionate *adj* excessive, inappropriate, incommensurate, inordinate, unbalanced, unequal, uneven, unreasonable.
antonyms appropriate, balanced.

disprove *v* answer, confute, contradict, controvert, discredit, explode, expose, invalidate, negate, rebut, refute.
antonym prove.

disputable *adj* arguable, controversial, debatable, doubtful, dubious, litigious, moot, questionable, uncertain.
antonym indisputable.

disputation *n* argumentation, controversy, debate, dispute, dissension, polemics, quodlibet.

disputatious *adj* argumentative, cantankerous, captious, cavilling, contentious, litigious, polemical, pugnacious, quarrelsome, wranglesome.

dispute *v* altercate, argue, brawl, challenge, clash, contend, contest, contradict, controvert, debate, deny, discuss, doubt, gainsay, impugn, litigate, moot, oppugn, quarrel, question, spar, squabble, traverse, wrangle.
antonym agree.
n altercation, argument, brawl, conflict, contention, controversy, debate, disagreement, discord, discussion, dissension, disturbance, feud, friction, quarrel, spar, squabble, strife, wrangle.
antonym agreement.

disputer *n* adversary, antagonist, arguer, contender, contestant, debater, discursist, discutant, opponent.

disqualified *adj* debarred, eliminated, ineligible.
antonyms accepted, eligible, qualified.

disqualify *v* debar, disable, disauthorise, disentitle, dishabilitate, disprivilege, incapacitate, invalidate, preclude, prohibit, rule out, unfit.
antonyms accept, allow.

disquiet *n* alarm, angst, anxiety, concern, disquietude, distress, disturbance, fear, foreboding, fretfulness, nervousness, restlessness, trouble, uneasiness, unrest, worry.
antonym calmness.
v agitate, annoy, bother, concern, discompose, distress, disturb, fret, harass, hassle, incommode, perturb, pester, plague, shake, trouble, unsettle, upset, vex, worry.
antonym calm.

disquieting *adj* annoying, bothersome, disconcerting, disquietful, disquietive, distressing, disturbing, irritating, perturbing, troubling, unnerving, unsettling, upsetting, vexing, worrying.
antonym calming.

disquisition *n* descant, discourse, dissertation, essay, exposition, monograph, paper, sermon, thesis, treatise.

disregard *v* brush aside, cold-shoulder, contemn, despise, discount, disdain, disobey, disparage, ignore, laugh off, make light of, neglect, overlook, pass over, pooh-pooh, slight, snub, turn a blind eye to.
antonyms note, pay attention to.
n brush-off, contempt, disdain, disesteem, disrespect, heedlessness, ignoring, inattention,

indifference, neglect, negligence, oversight, slight.

antonym attention.

disrepair *n* collapse, decay, deterioration, dilapidation, ruin, ruination, shabbiness, unrepair.

antonyms good repair, restoration.

disreputable *adj* base, contemptible, derogatory, discreditable, disgraceful, dishonourable, disorderly, disrespectable, ignominious, infamous, louche, low, mean, notorious, opprobrious, scandalous, seedy, shady, shameful, shocking, unprincipled.

antonyms decent, honourable.

disrepute *n* discredit, disesteem, disfavour, disgrace, dishonour, disreputation, ignominy, infamy, obloquy, shame.

antonyms esteem, honour.

disrespect *n* cheek, contempt, discourtesy, dishonour, disregard, impertinence, impoliteness, impudence, incivility, insolence, irreverence, misesteem, rudeness, unmannerliness.

antonym respect.

disrespectful *adj* bad-tempered, cheeky, contemptuous, discourteous, impertinent, impolite, impudent, insolent, insulting, irreverent, rude, uncivil, unmannerly.

antonym respectful.

disrobe *v* bare, denude, disapparel, divest, remove, shed, strip, take off, unclothe, uncover, undress.

antonyms cover, dress.

disrupt *v* agitate, break into, break up, confuse, derange, dislocate, disorder, disorganise, disturb, interrupt, intrude, obstruct, spoil, unsettle, upset.

disruption *n* burst-up, bust-up, cataclasm, confusion, disarray, disorder, disorderliness, dissembly, dissolution, disturbance, interference, interruption, stoppage, upheaval.

disruptive *adj* boisterous, disorderly, distracting, disturbing, obstreperous, troublesome, turbulent, undisciplined, unruly, unsettling, upsetting.

antonym well-behaved.

dissatisfaction *n* annoyance, chagrin, disappointment, discomfort, discontent, dislike, dismay, displeasure, distress, exasperation, frustration, irritation, non-fulfilment, regret, resentment, unfulfilment, unhappiness.

antonyms fulfilment, satisfaction.

dissatisfied *adj* chuffed, disappointed, discontented, disgruntled, displeased, fed up, frustrated, unfulfilled, unhappy, unsatisfied.

antonyms fulfilled, satisfied.

dissatisfy *v* annoy, disappoint, discontent, disgruntle, displease, exasperate, frustrate, irritate, put out, vex.

dissect *v* analyse, anatomise, break down, dismember, examine, explore, inspect, investigate, pore over, scrutinise, study.

dissection *n* analysis, anatomisation, anatomy, autopsy, breakdown, dismemberment, examination, inspection, investigation, necropsy, scrutiny, study.

dissemble *v* affect, camouflage, cloak, conceal, counterfeit, cover up, disguise, dissimulate, fake, falsify, feign, hide, mask, play possum, pretend, sham, simulate.

antonym admit.

dissembler *n* charlatan, con man, deceiver, dissimulator, fake, feigner, fraud, humbug, hypocrite, impostor, pretender, trickster, whited sepulchre.

disseminate *v* broadcast, circulate, diffuse, disperse, dissipate, distribute, evangelise, proclaim, promulgate, propagate, publicise, publish, scatter, sow, spread.

dissemination *n* broadcasting, circulation, diffusion, dispersion, distribution, evangelisation, evangelism, promulgation, propagation, publication, publishing, spread.

dissension *n* conflict, contention, difference, disagreement, discord, discordance, dispeace, dispute, dissent, friction, quarrel, strife, variance.

antonyms agreement, peace.

dissent *v* decline, differ, disagree, disconsent, object, protest, quibble, refuse.

antonyms agree, consent.

n difference, disagreement, discord, dissension, dissidence, nonconformity, objection, opposition, quibble, refusal, resistance.

antonym agreement.

dissenter *n* disputant, dissident, nonconformist, objector, protestant, protestor, recusant, schismatic, sectary.

dissentient *adj* conflicting, differing, disagreeing, dissenting, dissident, opposing, protesting, recusant.

antonym arguing.

dissertation *n* critique, discourse, disquisition, essay, exposition, monograph, paper, prolegomena, propaedeutic, thesis, treatise.

disservice *n* bad turn, disfavour, harm, injury, injustice, unkindness, wrong.

antonym favour.

dissever *v* cleave, disunite, divorce, part, rend, rift, rive, separate, sever, split, sunder.

dissidence *n* disagreement, discordance, dispute, dissent, feud, recusancy, rupture, schism, variance.

antonyms agreement, peace.

dissident *adj* differing, disagreeing, discordant, dissentient, dissenting, heterodox, nonconformist, recusant, schismatic.

antonyms acquiescent, agreeing.

n agitator, dissenter, protestor, rebel, recusant, refus(e)nik, schismatic.

antonym assenter.

dissimilar *adj* different, disparate, divergent, diverse, heterogeneous, incompatible, mismatched, unlike, unrelated, various.

antonyms compatible, similar.

dissimilarity *n* difference, discrepancy, disparity, dissimilitude, distinction, divergence, diversity, heterogeneity, incomparability, incompatibility, unlikeness, unrelatedness.
antonyms compatibility, similarity.

dissimulate *v* camouflage, cloak, conceal, disguise, dissemble, fake, feign, hide, mask, pretend.

dissimulation *n* act, affectation, concealment, deceit, deception, dissembling, double-dealing, duplicity, feigning, hypocrisy, play-acting, pretence, sham, wile.
antonym openness.

dissipate *v* burn up, consume, deplete, disappear, dispel, disperse, dissolve, evaporate, expend, fritter away, lavish, rig, scatter, spend, squander, vanish, wanton, waste.
antonym accumulate.

dissipated *adj* abandoned, consumed, debauched, destroyed, dissolute, exhausted, intemperate, profligate, rakehell, rakehelly, rakish, scattered, squandered, wasted.
antonyms conserved, virtuous.

dissipation *n* abandonment, debauchery, disappearance, disintegration, dispersion, dissemination, dissoluteness, dissolution, excess, extravagance, intemperance, prodigality, profligacy, rakery, rakishness, scattering, squandering, vanishing, wantonness, waste.
antonyms conservation, virtue.

dissociate *v* break off, detach, disband, disconnect, disrupt, distance, divorce, isolate, leave, quit, segregate, separate.
antonyms attach, share.

dissociation *n* break, detachment, disconnection, disengagement, dissevering, distancing, disunion, division, divorce, isolation, segregation, separation, severance, severing, split.
antonyms association, union.

dissolute *adj* abandoned, corrupt, debauched, degenerate, depraved, dissipated, immoral, lax, lewd, libertine, licentious, loose, profligate, rakehell, rakehelly, rakish, unrestrained, vicious, wanton, wide, wild.
antonym virtuous.

dissoluteness *n* abandon, corruption, debauchery, degeneracy, depravity, dissipation, immorality, lewdness, licence, licentiousness, profligacy, rakery, vice, wantonness.
antonym virtue.

dissolution *n* adjournment, break-up, conclusion, death, decay, decomposition, demise, destruction, disappearance, disbandment, discontinuation, disintegration, dismissal, dispersal, disruption, dissembly, division, divorce, end, ending, evaporation, extinction, finish, liquefaction, melting, overthrow, parting, resolution, ruin, separation, solution, suspension, termination.
antonym unification.

dissolve *v* break up, crumble, decompose, deliquesce, destroy, diffuse, disappear, discontinue, disintegrate, dismiss, disorganise, disperse, dissipate, disunite, divorce, dwindle, end, evanesce, evaporate, fade, flux, fuse, liquefy, loose, melt, overthrow, perish, ruin, separate, sever, soften, suspend, terminate, thaw, vanish, wind up.

dissonance *n* cacophony, difference, disagreement, discord, discordance, discrepancy, disharmony, disparity, dissension, harshness, incongruity, inconsistency, jangle, jarring, variance.
antonym harmony.

dissonant *adj* anomalous, cacophonous, different, differing, disagreeing, discordant, discrepant, disharmonious, dissentient, grating, harsh, incompatible, incongruous, inconsistent, inharmonious, irreconcilable, irregular, jangling, jarring, raucous, strident, tuneless, unmelodious.
antonyms compatible, harmonious.

dissuade *v* dehort, deter, discourage, disincline, divert, expostulate, put off, remonstrate, warn.
antonym persuade.

dissuasion *n* caution, dehortation, determent, deterrence, deterring, discouragement, expostulation, remonstrance, remonstration, setback.
antonym persuasion.

distance *n* absence, aloofness, coldness, coolness, extent, farness, frigidity, gap, interval, isolation, lapse, length, range, reach, remoteness, remove, reserve, restraint, separation, space, span, stand-offishness, stiffness, stretch, width.

distant *adj* abroad, afar, aloof, apart, ceremonious, cold, cool, disparate, dispersed, distinct, faint, far, faraway, far-flung, far-off, formal, haughty, indirect, indistinct, isolated, obscure, outlying, out-of-the-way, remote, removed, reserved, restrained, reticent, scattered, separate, slight, stand-offish, stiff, unapproachable, uncertain, unfriendly, withdrawn.
antonyms close, friendly.

distaste *n* abhorrence, antipathy, aversion, detestation, discontent, discontentment, disfavour, disgust, disinclination, dislike, displeasure, disrelish, dissatisfaction, horror, loathing, repugnance, revulsion.
antonym inclination.

distasteful *adj* abhorrent, aversive, disagreeable, displeasing, dissatisfying, loathsome, nasty, nauseous, objectionable, obnoxious, offensive, repugnant, repulsive, undesirable, uninviting, unpalatable, unpleasant, unsavoury.
antonym pleasing.

distend *v* balloon, bloat, bulge, dilate, enlarge, expand, fill out, increase, inflate, intumesce, puff, stretch, swell, widen.
antonym deflate.

distended *adj* astrut, bloated, dilated, emphysematous, enlarged, expanded, inflated, puffed-out, puffy, stretched, swollen, tumescent, varicose.
antonym deflated.

distension *n* dilatation, dilation, emphysema, enlargement, expansion, extension, inflation, intumescence, spread, swelling, tumescence.

distil *v* condense, drip, evaporate, extract, flow, purify, rectify, refine, sublimate, trickle, vaporise.

distinct *adj* apparent, clear, clear-cut, decided, definite, detached, different, discrete, dissimilar, evident, individual, lucid, manifest, marked, noticeable, obvious, palpable, patent, plain, recognisable, separate, several, sharp, unambiguous, unconnected, unmistakable, well-defined.

antonyms fuzzy, hazy, indistinct.

distinction[1] *n* characteristic, contradistinction, contrast, difference, differential, differentiation, diorism, discernment, discrimination, dissimilarity, distinctiveness, division, feature, individuality, mark, nuance, particularity, peculiarity, penetration, perception, quality, separation.

distinction[2] *n* account, celebrity, consequence, credit, eminence, excellence, fame, glory, greatness, honour, importance, merit, name, note, prestige, prominence, quality, rank, renown, reputation, repute, significance, superiority, worth.

antonym insignificance.

distinctive *adj* characteristic, different, discriminative, discriminatory, distinguishing, extraordinary, idiosyncratic, individual, inimitable, original, peculiar, singular, special, typical, uncommon, unique.

antonym common.

distinctness *n* clarity, clearness, difference, discreteness, disparateness, dissimilarity, dissociation, distinctiveness, individuality, lucidity, obviousness, plainness, sharpness, vividness.

antonyms fuzziness, haziness, indistinctness.

distinguish *v* ascertain, categorise, celebrate, characterise, classify, decide, determine, differentiate, dignify, discern, discriminate, honour, immortalise, individualise, judge, know, make out, mark, perceive, pick out, recognise, see, separate, signalise, tell, tell apart.

distinguishable *adj* appreciable, clear, conspicuous, discernible, evident, manifest, noticeable, observable, obvious, perceptible, plain, recognisable.

antonym indistinguishable.

distinguished *adj* acclaimed, celebrated, conspicuous, distingue, eminent, eximious, extraordinary, famed, famous, illustrious, marked, nameworthy, notable, noted, outstanding, renowned, signal, striking, well-known.

antonyms insignificant, ordinary.

distinguishing *adj* characteristic, different, differentiating, discriminative, discriminatory, distinctive, individual, individualistic, marked, peculiar, typical, unique.

distort *v* bend, bias, buckle, colour, contort, deform, disfigure, falsify, garble, miscolour, misrepresent, misshape, pervert, skew, slant, torture, twist, warp, wrench, wrest, wring.

distorted *adj* awry, biased, deformed, false, misshapen, skew, skewed, twisted, warped, wry.

antonym straight.

distortion *n* bend, bias, buckle, colouring, contortion, crookedness, deformity, falsification, malformation, misrepresentation, obliquity, perversion, skew, slant, twist, warp.

distract *v* agitate, amuse, beguile, bewilder, confound, confuse, derange, discompose, disconcert, disturb, divert, engross, entertain, faze, feeze, harass, madden, occupy, perplex, puzzle, sidetrack, torment, trouble.

distracted *adj* agitated, bemused, bewildered, confounded, confused, crazy, deranged, distraught, eperdu(e), flustered, frantic, frenzied, grief-stricken, harassed, hassled, insane, mad, maddened, overwrought, perplexed, puzzled, raving, troubled, wild, worked up, wrought up.

antonyms calm, untroubled.

distracting *adj* annoying, bewildering, confusing, disconcerting, disturbing, irritating, off-putting, perturbing.

distraction *n* aberration, abstraction, agitation, alienation, amusement, beguilement, bewilderment, commotion, confusion, delirium, derangement, desperation, discord, disorder, disturbance, diversion, divertissement, entertainment, frenzy, hallucination, harassment, incoherence, insanity, interference, interruption, mania, pastime, recreation.

distraught *adj* agitated, anxious, beside oneself, crazed, crazy, distracted, distressed, frantic, hysterical, mad, overwrought, raving, wild, worked up, wrought up.

antonyms calm, untroubled.

distress *n* adversity, affliction, agony, anguish, anxiety, calamity, depravation, desolation, destitution, difficulties, discomfort, grief, hardship, heartache, indigence, katzenjammer, misery, misfortune, need, pain, pauperism, poverty, privation, sadness, sorrow, strait(s), suffering, torment, torture, trial, trouble, woe, worry, wretchedness.

antonyms comfort, ease, security.

v afflict, agonise, bother, constrain, cut up, disturb, grieve, harass, harrow, pain, perplex, sadden, straiten, torment, trouble, upset, worry, wound.

antonyms assist, comfort.

distressed *adj* afflicted, agitated, anxious, cut up, destitute, distracted, distraught, indigent, needy, poor, poverty-stricken, saddened, straitened, tormented, troubled, upset, worried, wretched.

antonyms calm, untroubled.

distressing *adj* affecting, afflicting, afflictive, disquieting, distressful, disturbing, grievous, heart-breaking, hurtful, lamentable, nerve-racking, painful, perturbing, sad, trying, unnerving, upsetting, worrying.

antonyms assuaging, pleasant.

distribute *v* administer, allocate, allot, apportion, arrange, assign, assort, bestow, carve up, categorise, circulate, class, classify, convey, deal, deliver, diffuse, dish out, dispense, disperse, dispose, disseminate, divide, dole, file, give, group, hand out, mete, scatter, share, spread, strew.

antonyms collect, gather in.

distribution *n* allocation, allotment, apportionment, arrangement, assortment, bestowal, bestowing, circulation, classification, dealing, delivery, diffusion, dispensation, dispersal, dispersion, disposition, dissemination, division, dole, handling, largition, location, mailing, marketing, partition, placement, propagation, scattering, sharing, spreading, trading, transport, transportation.

antonyms collection, gathering.

district *n* area, canton, cantred, cantret, community, gau, hundred, locale, locality, neighbourhood, parish, precinct, quarter, region, sector, vicinity, ward.

distrust *v* disbelieve, discredit, doubt, misbelieve, miscredit, misdeem, mistrust, question, suspect.

antonym trust.

n disbelief, doubt, misfaith, misgiving, mistrust, qualm, question, scepticism, suspicion, untrust, wariness.

antonym trust.

distrustful *adj* chary, cynical, disbelieving, distrusting, doubtful, doubting, dubious, mistrustful, sceptical, suspicious, uneasy, untrustful, untrusting, wary.

antonyms trustful, unsuspecting.

disturb *v* affray, agitate, alarm, annoy, bother, concuss, confound, confuse, derange, disarrange, discompose, disorder, disorganise, disrupt, distract, distress, excite, fluster, harass, interrupt, muddle, perturb, pester, rouse, ruffle, shake, startle, trouble, unsettle, upset, worry.

antonyms calm, quiet, reassure.

disturbance *n* agitation, annoyance, bother, brawl, breeze, broil, burst-up, bust-up, commotion, confusion, derangement, disorder, distraction, fracas, fray, hindrance, hubbub, interruption, intrusion, katzenjammer, kick-up, misarrangement, molestation, muss(e), perturbation, riot, ruckus, ruction, shake-up, stour, stramash, tumult, turmoil, unrest, upheaval, uproar, upset, upturn.

antonyms peace, quiet.

disturbed *adj* agitated, anxious, apprehensive, bothered, concerned, confused, discomposed, disordered, disquieted, flustered, maladjusted, neurotic, troubled, unbalanced, uneasy, unrestful, upset, worried.

antonyms calm, sane.

disturbing *adj* agitating, alarming, disconcerting, discouraging, dismaying, disquieting, distressful, distressing, disturbant, disturbative, frightening, perturbing, startling, threatening, troubling, unsettling, upsetting, worrying.

antonym reassuring.

disunion *n* alienation, breach, detachment, disagreement, disconcert, disconnection, discord, disjunction, dissension, dissevering, dissidence, division, estrangement, feud, partition, rift, rupture, schism, separation, severance, split.

antonym unification.

disunite *v* alienate, detach, disband, disconnect, disengage, disjoin, disrupt, divide, estrange, part, segregate, separate, sever, split, sunder.

antonym unify.

disunity *n* alienation, breach, conflict, disagreement, discord, discordance, dissension, dissent, estrangement, rupture, schism, split, strife, variance.

antonym unity.

disuse *n* abandonment, decay, desuetude, discontinuance, disusage, idleness, neglect.

antonym use.

ditch *n* channel, drain, dyke, furrow, gully, ha-ha, level, moat, rhine, stank, trench, watercourse.

v abandon, discard, dispose of, drop, dump, jettison, scrap.

dither *v* faff about, falter, footer, haver, hesitate, oscillate, shilly-shally, swither, teeter, vacillate, waver.

antonym decide.

n bother, flap, fluster, flutter, indecision, panic, pother, stew, tizzy, twitter.

antonym decision.

diuretic *adj* emictory.

divan *n* chaise-longue, couch, lounger, ottoman, settee, sofa.

dive[1] *v* descend, dip, drop, duck, fall, jump, leap, nose-dive, pitch, plummet, plunge, rush, sound, submerge, swoop.

n dash, header, jump, leap, lunge, nose-dive, plunge, rush, spring, swoop.

dive[2] *n* den, honky-tonk, joint, lush-house.

diverge *v* bifurcate, branch, conflict, depart, deviate, differ, digress, disagree, dissent, divaricate, divide, fork, part, radiate, separate, split, spread, stray, vary, wander.

antonyms agree, come together, join.

divergence *n* branching-out, deflection, departure, deviation, difference, digression, disparity, divagation, parting, radiating, ramification, separation, variation.

antonym convergence.

divergent *adj* conflicting, deviating, different, differing, disagreeing, dissimilar, diverging, diverse, forking, parting, radial, radiating, separate, spreading, variant, varying.

antonym convergent.

divers *adj* different, manifold, many, miscellaneous, multifarious, numerous, several, some, sundry, varied, various.

diverse *adj* assorted, different, differing, discrete, disparate, dissimilar, distinct, divergent, diversified, heterogeneous, manifold, many, miscellaneous, multifarious, multiform, numerous, separate, several, some, sundry, unlike, varied, various, varying.

antonym identical.

diversify *v* alter, assort, branch out, change, expand, mix, spread out, variegate, vary.

diversion *n* alteration, amusement, beguilement, change, deflection, delight, departure, detour, deviation, digression, disportment, distraction, divertissement, enjoyment, entertainment, game, gratification, pastime, play, pleasure, recreation, relaxation, sport, variation.

diversionary *adj* distracting, divertive.

diversity *n* assortment, difference, dissimilarity, distinctiveness, divergence, diverseness, diversification, heterogeneity, medley, multifariousness, multiplicity, range, unlikeness, variance, variegation, variety.

antonyms sameness, similarity.

divert *v* amuse, avert, beguile, deflect, delight, detract, distract, entertain, gratify, hive off, recreate, redirect, regale, side-track, switch, tickle.

antonyms direct, irritate.

diverting *adj* amusing, beguiling, enjoyable, entertaining, fun, funny, humorous, pleasant, witty.

antonym irritating.

divest *v* denude, deprive, despoil, disinvest, dispossess, disrobe, disseise, doff, remove, strip, unclothe, undress.

antonym clothe.

divide *v* alienate, allocate, allot, apportion, arrange, bisect, break up, categorise, classify, cleave, cut, deal out, departmentalise, detach, disconnect, dispense, distribute, disunite, divvy, estrange, grade, group, part, partition, portion, segment, segregate, separate, sever, share, shear, sort, split, subdivide, sunder.

antonyms collect, gather, join.

divide out allocate, allot, apportion, dole out, measure out, morsel, parcel out, share, share out.

dividend *n* bonus, cut, divvy, extra, gain, gratuity, interest, lagniappe, plus, portion, share, surplus, whack.

divination *n* augury, clairvoyance, divining, dukkeripen, foretelling, fortune-telling, hariolation, -mancy, prediction, presage, prognostication, prophecy, second sight, soothsaying, taghairm.

divine *adj* angelic, beatific, beautiful, blissful, celestial, consecrated, exalted, excellent, glorious, godlike, heavenly, holy, marvellous, mystical, perfect, rapturous, religious, sacred, sanctified, spiritual, splendid, superhuman, superlative, supernatural, supreme, transcendent, transcendental, transmundane, wonderful.

n churchman, clergyman, cleric, ecclesiastic, minister, parson, pastor, prelate, priest, reverend.

v apprehend, conjecture, deduce, foretell, guess, hariolate, haruspicate, infer, intuit, perceive, prognosticate, suppose, surmise, suspect, understand.

diviner *n* astrologer, augur, divinator, dowser, haruspex, oracle, prophet, seer, sibyl, soothsayer, water-finder.

divinity *n* daemon, deity, deva, genius, god, goddess, godhead, godhood, godliness, godship, holiness, kami, sanctity, spirit.

divisible *adj* dividable, dividual, fractional, partible, separable, splittable.

division *n* allotment, apportionment, bisection, border, boundary, branch, breach, category, class, compartment, cutting, demarcation, department, detaching, dichotomy, disagreement, discord, distribution, disunion, divide, divider, dividing, estrangement, feud, group, head, part, partition, portion, rupture, schism, scission, section, sector, segment, separation, sept, sharing, side, split, splitting, stream, variance, wapentake, ward, watershed, wing.

antonyms agreement, multiplication, unification.

divisive *adj* alienating, discordant, disruptive, inharmonious.

antonyms harmonious, unifying.

divorce *n* annulment, breach, break, break-up, decree nisi, diffarreation, dissolution, disunion, rupture, separation, severance, split-up, talaq.

v annul, cancel, disconnect, dissever, dissociate, dissolve, disunite, divide, part, separate, sever, split up, sunder.

antonyms marry, unify.

divulge *v* betray, broadcast, communicate, confess, declare, disclose, evulgate, exhibit, expose, impart, leak, let slip, proclaim, promulgate, publish, reveal, spill, tell, uncover.

divvy *n* bit, cut, dividend, lagniappe, percentage, portion, quota, share, whack.

v apportion, cut, distribute, divide, parcel out, share, share out, split.

dizzy *adj* befuddled, bemused, bewildered, capricious, confused, dazed, dazzled, faint, fickle, flighty, foolish, frivolous, giddy, light-headed, lofty, muddled, reeling, scatter-brained, shaky, staggering, steep, swimming, vertiginous, wobbly, woozy.

do *v* accomplish, achieve, act, adapt, answer, arrange, behave, carry out, cause, cheat, complete, con, conclude, cover, cozen, create, deceive, decipher, decode, defraud, discharge, dupe, effect, end, execute, explore, fare, fix, fleece, give, hoax, implement, make, manage, organise, pass muster, perform, prepare, present, proceed, produce, put on, render, resolve, satisfy, serve, solve, suffice, suit, swindle, tour, transact, translate, transpose, travel, trick, undertake, visit, work, work out.

n affair, event, function, gathering, occasion, party.

do away with abolish, bump off, destroy, discard, discontinue, do in, eliminate, exterminate, get rid of, kill, liquidate, murder, remove, slay.

do for defeat, destroy, finish (off), kill, ruin, shatter, slay.

do in butcher, dispatch, eliminate, execute, exhaust, fag, fatigue, kill, knacker, liquidate, murder, rub out, shatter, slaughter, slay, tire, waste, wear out, weary.

do out of balk, bilk, cheat, con, deprive, diddle, fleece, rook, swindle, trick.

do's and don'ts code, customs, etiquette, instructions, niceties, p's and q's, punctilios, regulations, rules, standards.

do without abstain from, dispense with, forgo, give up, relinquish, waive.

docile *adj* amenable, biddable, complaisant, compliant, ductile, manageable, obedient, obliging, pliable, pliant, submissive, teachable, tractable, unmurmuring, unprotesting, unquestioning.

antonyms truculent, unco-operative.

docility *n* amenability, biddableness, complaisance, compliance, ductility, manageability, meekness, obedience, pliability, pliancy, submissiveness, tractability.

antonyms truculence, unco-operativeness.

dock[1] *n* boat-yard, harbour, marina, pier, quay, waterfront, wharf.

v anchor, berth, drop anchor, join up, land, link up, moor, put in, rendezvous, tie up, unite.

dock[2] *v* clip, crop, curtail, cut, decaudate, decrease, deduct, diminish, lessen, reduce, shorten, subtract, truncate, withhold.

docket *n* bill, certificate, chit, chitty, counterfoil, label, receipt, tab, tag, tally, ticket.

v catalogue, file, index, label, mark, register, tab, tag, ticket.

doctor *n* clinician, doctoress, doctress, general practitioner, GP, hakim, internist, leech, medic, medical officer, medical practitioner, medicaster, medico, physician, pill(s).

v adulterate, alter, botch, change, cobble, cook, cut, dilute, disguise, falsify, fix, fudge, hocus, load, medicate, mend, misrepresent, patch, pervert, repair, spike, tamper with, treat.

doctrinaire *adj* biased, doctrinarian, dogmatic, fanatical, hypothetical, ideological, impractical, inflexible, insistent, opinionated, pedantic, rigid, speculative, theoretical, unrealistic.

antonym flexible.

doctrine *n* belief, canon, concept, conviction, creed, dogma, ism, opinion, precept, principle, teaching, tenet.

document *n* certificate, chirograph, deed, form, instrument, paper, parchment, record, report.

v authenticate, back, certify, cite, corroborate, detail, enumerate, instance, list, particularise, prove, substantiate, support, validate, verify.

documentary *n* faction, feature, programme.

doddery *adj* aged, decrepit, doddering, doited, faltering, feeble, infirm, rambling, senile, shaky, shambling, tottery, trembly, unsteady, weak.

antonyms hale, youthful.

dodge *v* avoid, dart, deceive, duck, elude, equivocate, evade, fend off, fudge, hedge, parry, shift, shirk, shuffle, side-step, skive, swerve, swing the lead, trick.

n chicane, contrivance, device, fakery, feint, machination, manoeuvre, ploy, ruse, scheme, stratagem, subterfuge, trick, wheeze, wile.

dodger *n* evader, lead-swinger, shirker, skiver, slacker, slyboots, trickster.

dodgy *adj* chancy, dangerous, delicate, dicey, dicky, difficult, problematical, risky, ticklish, tricky, uncertain, unreliable, unsafe.

antonyms easy, safe.

doer *n* accomplisher, achiever, activist, bustler, dynamo, executer, go-getter, live wire, organiser, power-house, wheeler-dealer.

doff *v* discard, lift, raise, remove, shed, take off, throw off, tip, touch, undress.

antonym don.

dog *n* beast, bitch, blackguard, bowwow, canid, canine, cur, heel, hound, knave, mongrel, moppet, mutt, pooch, pup, puppy, scoundrel, tyke, villain, yapper, yapster.

v harry, haunt, hound, plague, pursue, shadow, tail, track, trail, trouble, worry.

dogged *adj* determined, firm, indefatigable, indomitable, obstinate, persevering, persistent, pertinacious, relentless, resolute, single-minded, staunch, steadfast, steady, stubborn, tenacious, unflagging, unshakable, unyielding.

antonym irresolute.

doggedness *n* determination, endurance, indomitablity, obstinacy, perseverance, persistence, pertinacity, relentlessness, resolution, single-mindedness, steadfastness, steadiness, stubbornness, tenaciousness, tenacity.

dogma *n* article, article of faith, belief, conviction, credendum, credo, creed, doctrine, opinion, precept, principle, teaching, tenet.

dogmatic *adj* affirmative, arbitrary, assertive, authoritative, canonical, categorical, dictatorial, didactic, doctrinaire, doctrinal, downright, emphatic, ex cathedra, high-dried, imperious, magisterial, obdurate, opinionated, oracular, overbearing, peremptory, pontific(al), positive.

dogmatism *n* arbitrariness, assertiveness, bigotry, dictatorialness, imperiousness, opinionatedness, peremptoriness, positiveness, presumption.

dogsbody *n* doormat, drudge, factotum, galley-slave, lackey, maid-of-all-work, man-of-all-work, menial, skivvy, slave.

doings *n* actions, activities, acts, adventures, affairs, concerns, dealings, deeds, events, exploits, goings-on, handiwork, happenings, proceedings, transactions.

doldrums *n* accidie, acedia, apathy, blues, boredom, depression, dullness, dumps, ennui, gloom, inertia, lassitude, listlessness, low-spiritedness, malaise, stagnation, tedium, torpor.

dole *n* allocation, allotment, allowance, alms, apportionment, benefit, dispensation, dispersal, distribution, division, donation, gift, grant, gratuity, issuance, modicum, parcel, pittance, portion, quota, share.

dole out administer, allocate, allot, apportion, assign, deal, dispense, distribute, divide, give, hand out, issue, mete, ration, share.

doleful *adj* blue, cheerless, depressing, dismal, distressing, dolorous, dreary, forlorn, funereal, gloomy, lugubrious, melancholy, mournful, painful, pathetic, pitiful, rueful, sad, sombre, sorrowful, woebegone, woeful, wretched.

antonym cheerful.

doll *n* dolly, figurine, kewpie doll, marionette, moppet, plaything, puppet, toy.

doll up deck out, dress up, preen, primp, prink, tart up, titivate, trick out.

dollar *n* buck, greenback, smacker, wheel.

dollop *n* ball, blob, bunch, clump, glob, gob, gobbet, lump.

dolorous *adj* anguished, distressing, doleful, grievous, harrowing, heart-rending, lugubrious, melancholy, miserable, mournful, painful, rueful, sad, sombre, sorrowful, woebegone, woeful, wretched.

antonym happy.

dolour *n* anguish, distress, grief, heartache, heartbreak, lamentation, misery, mourning, ruth, sadness, sorrow, suffering.

antonym beatitude.

dolt *n* ass, beetlebrain, beetlehead, besom-head, blockhead, bonehead, booby, boodle, bufflehead, bull-calf, calf, chump, clod, clodhopper, clodpate, clodpoll, clot, clunk, dimwit, dope, dullard, dunce, fool, galoot, half-wit, idiot, ignoramus, leatherhead, loggerhead, log-head, lurdan(e), lurden, mutt, mutton-head, nitwit, nutcase, palooka, sheep's-head, simpleton, turnip.

doltish *adj* boneheaded, brainless, clottish, daffy, dense, dimwitted, dopey, dumb, foolish, half-witted, idiotic, mindless, obtuse, silly, stupid, thick.

antonyms brainy, clever.

domain *n* area, authority, bailiwick, business, concern, demesne, department, discipline, dominion, empire, estate, field, jurisdiction, kingdom, lands, orbit, pidgin, policies, power, province, realm, region, scope, speciality, sphere, sway, territory.

domestic *adj* autochthonic, domal, domesticated, domiciliary, family, home, home-bred, home-loving, homely, house, household, house-trained, housewifely, indigenous, internal, native, pet, private, stay-at-home, tame, trained.

n au pair, char, charwoman, daily, daily help, help, maid, scullery maid, servant, slavey, woman.

domesticate *v* acclimatise, accustom, break, domesticise, familiarise, habituate, house-train, naturalise, tame, train.

domesticated *adj* broken (in), domestic, home-loving, homely, house-proud, housewifely, naturalised, tame, tamed.

antonyms feral, wild.

domesticity *n* domestic science, domestication, familism, home economics, homecraft, homemaking, housecraft, housekeeping, housewifery, housewifeship.

domicile *n* abode, dwelling, habitation, home, house, lodging(s), mansion, quarters, residence, residency, settlement.

dominance *n* ascendancy, authority, command, control, domination, government, hegemony, leadership, mastery, paramountcy, power, rule, supremacy, sway.

dominant *adj* ascendant, assertive, authoritative, besetting, chief, commanding, controlling, governing, influential, leading, main, outstanding, paramount, predominant, pre-eminent, presiding, prevailing, prevalent, primary, prime, principal, prominent, ruling, superior, supreme.

antonym subordinate.

dominate *v* bestride, control, direct, domineer, dwarf, eclipse, govern, have the whip hand, keep under one's thumb, lead, master, monopolise, outshine, overbear, overgang, overlook, overrule, overshadow, predominate, prevail, rule, tyrannise.

domination *n* ascendancy, authority, command, control, despotism, dictatorship, hegemony, influence, leadership, mastery, oppression, power, repression, rule, subjection, subordination, superiority, suppression, supremacy, sway, tyranny.

domineer *v* bluster, boss, browbeat, bully, command, hector, intimidate, jackboot, lord it over, menace, overbear, ride roughshod, rule, swagger, threaten, tyrannise.

domineering *adj* arrogant, authoritarian, autocratic, bossy, coercive, despotic, dictatorial, harsh, high-handed, imperious, iron-handed, magisterial, masterful, oppressive, overbearing, severe, tyrannical.

antonyms meek, obsequious, servile.

dominion *n* ascendancy, authority, colony, command, control, country, domain, domination, empire, government, hegemony, jurisdiction, kingdom, lordship, mastery, power, province, realm, region, rule, sovereignty, supremacy, sway, territory.

don *v* affect, assume, clothe oneself in, dress in, get into, put on.

antonym doff.

Don Juan *n* amoretto, amoroso, amourette, Casanova, gigolo, ladies' man, lady-killer, lover, muff, philander(er), romeo.

donate *v* bequeath, bestow, chip in, confer, contribute, cough up, fork out, gift, give, impart, present, proffer, subscribe.

donation *n* alms, benefaction, boon, conferment, contribution, gift, grant, gratuity, largess(e), offering, present, presentation, subscription.

done *adj* acceptable, accomplished, advised, agreed, completed, concluded, consummated, conventional, cooked, cooked to a turn, de rigueur, depleted, drained, ended, executed, exhausted, fatigued, finished, OK, over, perfected, proper, ready, realised, settled, spent, terminated, through, U, used up.

done for beaten, broken, dashed, defeated, destroyed, doomed, finished, foiled, for the high jump, lost, ruined, undone, vanquished, wrecked.

done in all in, bushed, dead, dead beat, dog-tired, exhausted, fagged, jiggered, knackered, pooped, worn to a frazzle, zonked.

donkey *n* ass, burro, cardophagus, cuddy, hinny, jackass, jennet, jenny, moke, mule.

donnish *adj* academic, bookish, erudite, formalistic, learned, pedagogic, pedantic, precise, scholarly, scholastic.

donor *n* benefactor, contributor, donator, fairy godmother, giver, granter, philanthropist, provider.

antonym beneficiary.

doom *n* Armageddon, catastrophe, condemnation, death, death-knell, decision, decree, destiny, destruction, Doomsday, downfall, fate, fortune, judgement, Judgement Day, karma, kismet, lot, portion, ruin, sentence, the Last Judgement, the last trump, verdict.

v condemn, consign, damn, decree, destine, foredoom, foreordain, judge, predestine, preordain, sentence, threaten.

doomed *adj* accursed, bedevilled, bewitched, condemned, cursed, fated, fey, hopeless, ill-fated, ill-omened, ill-starred, luckless, star-crossed.

door *n* doorstead, doorway, egress, entrance, entry, exit, ingress, opening, portal, vomitorium, vomitory.

doorkeeper *n* commissionaire, gate-keeper, huissier, janitor, jobsworth, ostiary, porter.

dope[1] *n* details, drugs, facts, gen, hallucinogen, info, information, low-down, narcotic, news, opiate, tip.

v anaesthetise, doctor, drug, inject, load, medicate, narcotise, sedate, stupefy.

dope[2] *n* blockhead, bonehead, clot, dimwit, dolt, dullard, dunce, fool, half-wit, idiot, simpleton.

dop(e)y *adj* dazed, dense, doltish, dozy, drowsy, drugged, dumb, foolish, groggy, hazy, idiotic, muzzy, senseless, silly, simple, slow, stupefied, stupid, thick, woozy.

antonyms alert, bright.

dormant *adj* asleep, comatose, fallow, hibernating, inactive, inert, inoperative, latent, latescent, quiescent, sleeping, sluggish, slumbering, suspended, torpid, undeveloped, unrealised.

antonym active.

dose *n* dosage, draught, drench, hit, measure, portion, potion, prescription, quantity, shot, slug.

v administer, dispense, drench, medicate, treat.

dot *n* atom, circle, dab, decimal point, dit, fleck, full stop, iota, jot, mark, mite, mote, pin-point, point, speck, spot.

v bespeckle, dab, dabble, fleck, punctuate, spot, sprinkle, stipple, stud.

dotage *n* anility, decrepitude, feebleness, imbecility, old age, second childhood, senility, weakness.

antonym youth.

dote on admire, adore, idolise, indulge, pamper, prize, spoil, treasure.

doting *adj* adoring, devoted, fond, foolish, indulgent, lovesick, soft.

dotty *adj* batty, crazy, eccentric, feeble-minded, loopy, peculiar, potty, touched, weird.

antonym sensible.

double *adj* bifarious, bifold, binate, coupled, diploid, doubled, dual, duple, duplex, duplicate, paired, twice, twin, twofold.

v duplicate, enlarge, fold, geminate, grow, increase, magnify, multiply, repeat.

n clone, copy, counterpart, dead ringer, dead spit, doppelgänger, duplicate, fellow, image, impersonator, lookalike, mate, replica, ringer, spitting image, twin.

double back backtrack, circle, dodge, evade, loop, retrace one's steps, return, reverse.

double entendre ambiguity, double meaning, innuendo, play on words, pun, suggestiveness, word-play.

double-cross *v* betray, cheat, con, cozen, defraud, hoodwink, mislead, swindle, trick, two-time.

double-dealer *n* betrayer, cheat, con man, cozener, deceiver, dissembler, double-crosser, fraud, hypocrite, Machiavellian, rogue, swindler, traitor, two-timer.

double-dealing *n* bad faith, betrayal, cheating, deceit, deception, dishonesty, duplicity, foul play, hypocrisy, Machiavellianism, mendacity, perfidy, treachery, trickery, two-timing.

adj cheating, crooked, deceitful, dishonest, duplicitous, fraudulent, hypocritical, lying, Machiavellian, perfidious, scheming, shifty, sneaky, swindling, treacherous, tricky, two-faced, two-timing, underhanded, unscrupulous, untrustworthy, wily.

doubly *adv* again, bis, twice, twofold.

doubt *v* be dubious, be uncertain, demur, discredit, distrust, dubitate, fear, fluctuate, hesitate, misgive, mistrust, query, question, scruple, suspect, vacillate, waver.

antonyms believe, trust.

n ambiguity, apprehension, arrière pensee, confusion, difficulty, dilemma, disquiet, distrust, dubiety, fear, hesitancy, hesitation, incredulity, indecision, irresolution, misgiving, mistrust, perplexity, problem, qualm, quandary, reservation, scepticism, suspense, suspicion, uncertainty, vacillation.

antonyms belief, certainty, confidence, trust.

doubter *n* agnostic, cynic, disbeliever, doubting Thomas, questioner, questionist, sceptic, scoffer, unbeliever.

antonym believer.

doubtful *adj* ambiguous, debatable, disreputable, distrustful, dubious, dubitable, equivocal, hazardous, hesitant, hesitating, iffy, inconclusive, indefinite, indeterminate, irresolute, litigious, obscure, perplexed, precarious, problematic, problematical, questionable, sceptical, shady, suspect, suspicious, tentative, uncertain, unclear, unconfirmed, unconvinced, undecided, unresolved, unsettled, unsure, vacillating, vague, wavering.

antonyms certain, definite.

doubtless *adv* apparently, assuredly, certainly, clearly, indisputably, most likely, of course, ostensibly, out of question, precisely, presumably, probably, questionless, seemingly, supposedly, surely, truly, undoubtedly, unquestionably, without doubt.

doughty *adj* able, bold, brave, courageous, daring, dauntless, fearless, gallant, game, hardy, heroic, intrepid, redoubtable, resolute, stout-hearted, strong, valiant, valorous.

antonyms cowardly, weak.

dour *adj* austere, dismal, dreary, forbidding, gloomy, grim, hard, humourless, inflexible, morose, obstinate, rigid, rigorous, severe, sour, Spartan, strict, sullen, uncompromising, unfriendly, unyielding.

antonyms bright, cheery, easy-going.

douse, dowse *v* blow out, dip, drench, duck, dunk, extinguish, immerge, immerse, plunge, put out, saturate, smother, snuff, soak, souse, steep, submerge.

dovetail *v* accord, agree, coincide, conform, correspond, fit, harmonise, interlock, join, link, match, mortise, splice, tailor, tally, tenon, unite.

dowdy *adj* dingy, drab, frowzy, frumpish, frumpy, ill-dressed, old-fashioned, scrubby, shabby, slovenly, tacky, tatty, unfashionable, unmodish, unsmart.

antonyms dressy, smart, spruce.

down[1] *n* bloom, floccus, floss, flue, fluff, fuzz, nap, pile, shag, thistledown, wool.

down[2] *v* drink, fell, floor, gulp, knock back, swallow, throw, topple, toss off.

down and out derelict, destitute, impoverished, on one's uppers, penniless, ruined.

down at heel dowdy, impoverished, out at elbows, run-down, seedy, shabby, slipshod, slovenly, slummy, worn.

down in the mouth blue, chopfallen, crestfallen, dejected, depressed, disheartened, dispirited, down, down in the dumps, downcast, in low spirits, in the doldrums, melancholy, sad, unhappy.

down the drain lost, out of the window, ruined, up the spout, wasted.

down with away with, exterminate, get rid of.

down-and-out *n* beggar, bum, derelict, dosser. loser, outcast, pauper, tramp, vagabond, vagrant.

downcast *adj* cheerless, chopfallen, crestfallen, daunted, dejected, depressed, despondent, disappointed, disconsolate, discouraged, disheartened, dismayed, dispirited, down, miserable, sad, unhappy.

antonyms cheerful, elated, happy.

downfall *n* breakdown, cloudburst, collapse, comedown, come-uppance, debacle, deluge, descent, destruction, disgrace, downpour, failure, fall, humiliation, overthrow, rainstorm, ruin, undoing, Waterloo.

downgrade *v* belittle, decry, degrade, demote, denigrate, detract from, disparage, humble, lower, reduce in rank, run down.

antonyms improve, upgrade.

downhearted *adj* blue, chopfallen, crestfallen, dejected, depressed, despondent, discouraged, disheartened, dismayed, dispirited, downcast, gloomy, glum, jaw-fallen, low-spirited, sad, sorrowful, unhappy.

antonyms cheerful, enthusiastic, happy.

downpour *n* cloudburst, deluge, downcome, flood, inundation, rainstorm, torrent, water-spout.

downright *adj* absolute, blatant, blunt, candid, categorical, clear, complete, explicit, forthright, frank, honest, open, out-and-out, outright, outspoken, plain, positive, simple, sincere, straightforward, thoroughgoing, total, undisguised, unequivocal, unqualified, utter, wholesale.

down-to-earth *adj* commonsense, commonsensical, hard-headed, matter-of-fact, mundane, no-nonsense, plain-spoken, practical, realistic, sane, sensible, unsentimental.

antonyms fantastic, impractical.

down-trodden *adj* abused, afflicted, distressed, exploited, helpless, oppressed, subjugated, subservient, trampled on, trampled underfoot, tyrannised, victimised.

downward *adj* declining, descending, downhill, sliding, slippery, slipping.

antonym upward.

downy *adj* eriophorous, feathery, fleecy, floccose, fluffy, lanuginose, lanuginous, nappy, plumate, plumulate, silky, soft, velvety, woolly.

dowry *n* dot, dower, endowment, faculty, gift, inheritance, legacy, portion, provision, share, talent, wedding-dower.

dowse *see* **douse**.

doze *v* catnap, dove, dover, drop off, drowse, kip, nap, nod, nod off, sleep, slumber, snooze, zizz.

n catnap, dogsleep, forty winks, kip, nap, shut-eye, siesta, snooze, zizz.

drab *adj* cheerless, colourless, dingy, dismal, dreary, dull, dun-coloured, flat, gloomy, grey, lack-lustre, mous(e)y, shabby, sombre, uninspired, vapid.

antonym bright.

draft[1] *v* compose, delineate, design, draw, draw up, formulate, outline, plan, sketch.

n abstract, delineation, ebauche, outline, plan, protocol, rough, sketch, version.

draft[2] *n* bill, cheque, order, postal order.

drag *v* crawl, creep, dawdle, draggle, draw, hale, harl, haul, inch, lag, linger, loiter, lug, pull, schlep, shamble, shuffle, straggle, sweep, tow, trail, tug, yank.

n annoyance, bore, bother, brake, drogue, nuisance, pain, pest, pill.

drag on, drag out draw out, extend, hang on, lengthen, persist, prolong, protract, spin out.

drag one's feet delay, obstruct, procrastinate, stall.

dragoon *v* browbeat, bully, coact, coerce, compel, constrain, drive, force, impel, intimidate, strong-arm.

drain *v* bleed, consume, deplete, discharge, dissipate, down, draw off, drink up, dry, effuse, empty, emulge, evacuate, exhaust, exude, finish, flow out, lade, leak, milk, ooze, quaff, remove, sap, seep, strain, swallow, tap, tax, trickle, use up, weary, withdraw.

antonym fill.

n channel, conduit, culvert, depletion, ditch, drag, duct, exhaustion, expenditure, grip, outlet, pipe, reduction, sap, sewer, sink, sough, stank, strain, trench, watercourse, withdrawal.

drainage *n* bilge, leaching, seepage, sewage, sewerage, waste.

dram *n* caulker, drop, glass, measure, nobbler, shot, slug, snifter, snort, tot.

drama *n* acting, crisis, dramatics, dramatisation, dramaturgy, excitement, histrionics, kabuki, kathakali, melodrama, play, scene, show, spectacle, stage-craft, theatre, theatricals, Thespian art, turmoil.

dramatic *adj* affecting, breathtaking, climactic, dramaturgic, dramaturgical, effective, electrifying, emotional, exciting, expressive, graphic, impressive, meaningful, melodramatic, moving, powerful, sensational, startling, striking, sudden, suspenseful, tense, theatrical, Thespian, thrilling, vivid.

antonyms normal, ordinary.

dramatise *v* act, exaggerate, overdo, overstate, play-act, put on, stage.

dramatist *n* comedian, dramaturge, dramaturgist, playwright, play-writer, screen-writer, scriptwriter, tragedian.

drape *v* adorn, array, cloak, cover, dangle, droop, drop, enrap, fold, hang, suspend, swathe, vest, wrap.

drapery *n* arras, backdrop, blind(s), covering(s), curtain(s), hanging(s), portière, tapestry, valance.

drastic *adj* desperate, dire, draconian, extreme, far-reaching, forceful, harsh, heroic, radical, severe, strong.

antonym mild.

draught *n* cup, current, dose, dragging, drawing, drench, drink, flow, haulage, influx, movement, portion, potation, puff, pulling, quantity, traction.

draw[1] *v* allure, attenuate, attract, borrow, breathe in, bring forth, choose, deduce, delineate, depict, derive, design, drag, drain, elicit, elongate, engage, entice, entrain, evoke, extend, extort, extract, get, haul, induce, infer, influence, inhale, inspire, invite, lengthen, make, map out, mark out, outline, paint, pencil, persuade, pick, portray, puff, pull, respire, select, sketch, stretch, suck, take, tow, trace, tug, unsheathe.

antonyms propel, push.

n appeal, attraction, bait, enticement, interest, lure, pull.

draw back recoil, resile, retract, retreat, shrink, start back, withdraw.

draw lots choose, decide, draw straws, pick, select, spin a coin, toss up.

draw on employ, exploit, extract, make use of, quarry, rely on, take from, use.

draw out drag out, elongate, extend, lengthen, prolong, prolongate, protract, spin out, stretch, string out.

antonym curtail.

draw the line lay down the law, object, put one's foot down, restrict, say no, set a limit.

draw up compose, draft, embattle, formulate, frame, halt, prepare, pull up, run in, stop, stop short, write out.

draw[2] *v* be equal, be even, be neck and neck, dead-heat, tie.

n dead-heat, deadlock, impasse, stalemate, tie.

drawback *n* block, defect, deficiency, desagrement, detriment, difficulty, disability, disadvantage, fault, flaw, fly in the ointment, handicap, hindrance, hitch, impediment, imperfection, nuisance, obstacle, pull-back, snag, stumbling, trouble.

antonym advantage.

drawing *n* cartoon, delineation, depiction, graphic, illustration, outline, picture, portrait, portrayal, representation, sketch, study.

drawl *v* dra(u)nt, drone, haw-haw, protract, twang.

drawn *adj* fatigued, fraught, haggard, harassed, harrowed, hassled, pinched, sapped, strained, stressed, taut, tense, tired, worn.

dread *v* cringe at, fear, flinch, quail, shrink from, shudder, shy, tremble.

n alarm, apprehension, aversion, awe, dismay, disquiet, fear, fright, funk, heebie-jeebies, horror, misgiving, terror, trepidation, worry.

antonyms confidence, security.

adj alarming, awe-inspiring, awful, dire, dreaded, dreadful, frightening, frightful, ghastly, grisly, gruesome, horrible, terrible, terrifying.

dreadful *adj* alarming, appalling, awful, dire, distressing, fearful, formidable, frightful, ghastly, grievous, grisly, gruesome, harrowing, hideous, horrendous, horrible, monstrous, shocking, terrible, tragic, tremendous.

antonym comforting.

dream *n* aisling, ambition, aspiration, beauty, castle in Spain, castle in the air, daydream, delight, delusion, design, desire, fantasy, goal, hallucination, hope, illusion, imagination, joy, marvel, notion, phantasm, pipe-dream, pleasure, reverie, speculation, trance, treasure, vagary, vision, wish.

v conjure, daydream, envisage, fancy, fantasise, hallucinate, imagine, muse, star-gaze, think, visualise.

dream up conceive, concoct, contrive, cook up, create, devise, hatch, imagine, invent, spin, think up.

dreamer *n* daydreamer, Don Quixote, fantasiser, fantasist, fantast, idealist, John o'dreams, Johnny-head-in-the-air, romancer, star-gazer, theoriser, utopian, visionary, Walter Mitty, wool-gatherer.

antonyms pragmatist, realist.

dreaminess *n* absent-mindedness, abstraction, dimness, dwam, ethereality, fancifulness, insubstantiality, kef, preoccupation, vagueness, whimsicality.

dreamlike *adj* chimerical, hallucinatory, illusory, insubstantial, phantasmagoric, phantasmagorical, phantom, surreal, trance-like, unreal, unsubstantial, visionary.

dreamy absent, abstracted, chimerical, daydreaming, dreamlike, fanciful, fantastic, faraway, gentle, imaginary, impractical, intangible, lulling, misty, musing, pensive, phantasmagoric, phantasmagorical, phantasmal, preoccupied, quixotic, romantic, shadowy, speculative, unreal, vague, visionary.

antonyms down-to-earth, realistic.

dreary *adj* bleak, boring, cheerless, colourless, comfortless, commonplace, depressing, dismal, doleful, downcast, drab, drear, dreich, dull, forlorn, gloomy, glum, gousty, humdrum, joyless, lifeless, lonely, lonesome, melancholy, monotonous, mournful, routine, sad, solitary, sombre, sorrowful, tedious, trite, uneventful, uninteresting, wearisome, wretched.

antonyms bright, interesting.

dredge *v* dig up, discover, drag up, draw up, expose, fish up, raise, rake up, scoop up, uncover, unearth.

dregs *n* canaille, deposit, draff, dross, excrement, faeces, fag-end, fecula, grounds, lags, lees, left-overs, mother, outcasts, rabble, residue, residuum, riff-raff, scourings, scum, sediment, tailings, trash, waste.

drench *v* douse, drouk, drown, duck, flood, imbrue, imbue, immerse, inundate, saturate, soak, souse, steep, wet.

dress *n* apparel, attire, caparison, clothes, clothing, costume, ensemble, frock, garb, garment, garments, gear, get-up, gown, guise, habiliments, habit, outfit, raiment, rig-out, robe, suit, togs, vestment.

v accoutre, adjust, adorn, align, apparel, arrange, array, attire, bandage, bedeck, bedizen, betrim, bind up, boun, busk, caparison, change, clothe, deck, decorate, dispose, don, drape, embellish, fit, furbish, garb, garnish, groom, habilitate, habit, ornament, plaster, prepare, put on, rig, robe, set, straighten, tend, treat, trim.

antonyms disrobe, strip, undress.

dress down berate, carpet, castigate, chide, flyte, haul over the coals, rebuke, reprimand, reprove, scold, tear off a strip, tell off, upbraid.

dress up adorn, beautify, dandify, deck, disguise, doll up, embellish, fig out, gild, improve, play-act, tart up, titivate, trick out.

dressing *n* bandage, compress, emplastron, emplastrum, ligature, pad, plaster, pledget, poultice, spica, tourniquet.

dressing-gown *n* housecoat, negligee, peignoir.

dressmaker *n* couturier, midinette, modiste, seamstress, sewing woman, tailor, tailoress.

dressy *adj* classy, elaborate, elegant, formal, natty, ornate, ritzy, smart, stylish, swanky, swish.

antonyms dowdy, scruffy.

dribble *v* drip, drivel, drool, drop, leak, ooze, run, saliva, seep, slaver, slobber, sprinkle, trickle.

n drip, droplet, gobbet, leak, seepage, sprinkling, trickle.

dried *adj* arid, dehydrated, desiccated, drained, exsiccated, mummified, parched, shrivelled, wilted, withered, wizened.

drift *v* accumulate, amass, coast, drive, float, freewheel, gather, meander, pile up, stray, waft, wander.

n accumulation, aim, bank, course, current, design, direction, dune, flow, gist, heap, implication, import, impulse, intention, mass, meaning, mound, movement, object, pile, purport, ridge, rush, scope, significance, sweep, tendency, tenor, thrust, trend.

drifter *n* beachcomber, hobo, intinerant, rolling stone, rover, swagman, tramp, vagabond, vagrant, wanderer.

drill[1] *v* coach, discipline, exercise, instruct, practise, rehearse, teach, train, tutor.

n coaching, discipline, exercise, instruction, practice, preparation, repetition, training, tuition.

drill[2] *v* bore, penetrate, perforate, pierce, puncture, transpierce.

n awl, bit, borer, gimlet.

drink *v* absorb, bib, booze, carouse, down, drain, dram, gulp, guzzle, hit the bottle, imbibe, indulge, knock back, liquefy, liquor up, partake of, quaff, revel, sip, suck, sup, swallow, swig, swill, tank up, tipple, tope, toss off, wassail, water.

n alcohol, ambrosia, beverage, bev(v)y, booze, deoch-an-doris, dose, dram, draught, glass, gulp, hooch, liquid, liquor, noggin, plonk, potion, refreshment, sensation, sip, slug, snifter, snort, spirits, stiffener, suck, swallow, swig, swizzle, taste, the bottle, tickler, tiff, tipple, toss, tot.

drink in absorb, assimilate, attend to, be absorbed by, ingest, soak up.

drink to pledge (the health of), salute, toast.

drinker *n* alcoholic, bibber, boozer, carouser, dipso, dipsomaniac, drunk, drunkard, guzzler, inebriate, lush, soak, sot, souse, sponge, tippler, toper, wino.

antonyms abstainer, teetotaller.

drip *v* dribble, drizzle, drop, exude, filter, plop, splash, sprinkle, trickle, weep.

n dribble, dripping, drop, leak, milk-sop, ninny, softy, stillicide, trickle, weakling, weed, wet.

drive *v* actuate, bear, coerce, compel, constrain, dash, dig, direct, force, goad, guide, hammer, handle, harass, herd, hurl, impel, manage, motivate, motor, oblige, operate, overburden, overwork, plunge, press, prod, propel, push, ram, ride, rush, send, sink, spur, stab, steer, task, tax, thrust, travel, urge.

n action, advance, ambition, appeal, campaign, crusade, determination, effort, energy, enterprise, excursion, get-up-and-go, hurl, initiative, jaunt, journey, motivation, outing, pressure, push, ride, run, spin, surge, trip, turn, vigour, vim, zip.

drive at aim, allude to, get at, imply, indicate, insinuate, intend, intimate, mean, refer to, signify, suggest.

drive up the wall annoy, dement, derange, drive round the bend, exasperate, infuriate, irritate, madden.

drivel *n* blathering, bunkum, eyewash, fosh, gibberish, gobbledegook, guff, gush, jive, mumbo-jumbo, nonsense, slush, stultiloquy, twaddle, waffle.

driver *n* cabbie, cabman, charioteer, chauffeur, coachman, Jehu, motorist, trucker, vetturino, voiturier, wag(g)oner.

driving *adj* compelling, dynamic, energetic, forceful, forthright, galvanic, heavy, sweeping, vigorous, violent.

drizzle *n* drow, mizzle, Scotch mist, serein.

v dribble, mizzle, rain, shower, spit, spot, spray, sprinkle.

droll *adj* amusing, clownish, comic, comical, diverting, eccentric, entertaining, farcical, funny, humorous, jocular, laughable, ludicrous, pawky, quaint, ridiculous, risible, waggish, whimsical, witty.

drollery *n* absurdity, archness, banter, buffoonery, comicality, farce, fun, humour, jocularity, pleasantry, waggery, waggishness, whimsicality, wit.

drone *v* bombilate, bombinate, buzz, chant, drawl, hum, intone, purr, thrum, vibrate, whirr.

n buzz, chant, hum, murmuring, purr, thrum, vibration, whirr, whirring.

drool *v* dote, dribble, drivel, enthuse, fondle, gloat, gush, rave, salivate, slaver, slobber, water at the mouth.

droop *v* bend, dangle, decline, despond, diminish, drop, fade, faint, fall down, falter, flag, hang (down) sag, languish, lose heart, sink, slouch, slump, stoop, wilt, wither.

antonyms rise, straighten.

drooping *adj* blue, dejected, disheartened, dispirited, doleful, downcast, droopy, flabby, flaccid, floppy, languid, languorous, lassitudinous, limp, pendulous, sagging, stooped, wilting.

antonyms stiff, straight.

drop *n* abyss, bead, bubble, chasm, cut, dab, dash, decline, declivity, decrease, descent, deterioration, downturn, drib, driblet, drip, droplet, fall, falling-off, glob, globule, globulet, goutte, gutta, lowering, mouthful, nip, pearl, pinch, plunge, precipice, reduction, shot, sip, slope, slump, spot, taste, tear, tot, trace, trickle.

v abandon, cease, chuck, decline, depress, descend, desert, diminish, discontinue, disown, dive, dribble, drip, droop, fall, forsake, give up, jilt, kick, leave, lower, plummet, plunge, quit, reject, relinquish, remit, renounce, repudiate, sink, stop, terminate, throw over, trickle, tumble.

antonyms mount, rise.

drop off catnap, decline, decrease, deliver, depreciate, diminish, doze, drowse, dwindle, fall off, have forty winks, leave, lessen, nod, nod off, set down, slacken, snooze.

antonym increase.

drop out abandon, back out, cry off, forsake, leave, quit, renegue, stop, withdraw.

drop-out *n* Bohemian, deviant, dissenter, dissentient, hippie, loner, malcontent, non-conformist, rebel, renegade.

droppings *n* dung, egesta, excrement, excreta, faeces, fumet, guano, manure, ordure, spraint, stools.

dross *n* crust, debris, dregs, impurity, lees, recrement, refuse, remains, rubbish, scoria, scum, trash, waste.

drought *n* aridity, dearth, deficiency, dehydration, desiccation, drouth, dryness, insufficiency, lack, need, parchedness, scarcity, shortage, want.

drove *n* collection, company, crowd, drift, flock, gathering, herd, horde, mob, multitude, press, swarm, throng.

drown *v* deaden, deluge, drench, engulf, extinguish, flood, go under, immerse, inundate, muffle, obliterate, overcome, overpower, overwhelm, silence, sink, stifle, submerge, swallow up, swamp, wipe out.

drowsiness *n* dopeyness, doziness, grogginess, lethargy, narcosis, oscitancy, sleepiness, sluggishness, somnolence, torpor.

drowsy *adj* comatose, dazed, dopey, dozy, dreamy, drugged, heavy, lethargic, lulling, nodding, restful, sleepy, somniculous, somnolent, soothing, soporific, tired, torpid.

antonyms alert, awake.

drubbing *n* beating, clobbering, defeat, flogging, hammering, licking, pounding, pummelling, thrashing, trouncing, walloping, whipping, whitewash.

drudge *n* afterguard, devil, dogsbody, factotum, galley-slave, hack, jackal, lackey, maid-of-all-work, man-of-all-work, menial, scullion, servant, skivvy, slave, toiler, worker.

v beaver, droil, grind, labour, moil, plod, plug away, slave, toil, work.

antonyms idle, laze.

drudgery *n* chore, collar-work, donkey-work, drudgism, fag, faggery, grind, hack-work, labor improbus, labour, skivvying, slavery, slog, sweat, sweated labour, toil.

drug *n* depressant, dope, kef, medicament, medication, medicine, Mickey, Mickey Finn, narcotic, opiate, physic, poison, potion, remedy, stimulant.

v anaesthetise, deaden, dope, dose, drench, knock out, load, medicate, numb, poison, stupefy, treat.

drug-addict *n* acid head, acidfreak, dope-fiend, head, hop-head, hype, junkie, tripper.

drugged *adj* comatose, doped, dopey, high, looped, spaced out, stoned, stupefied, tripping, turned on, zonked.

drum *v* beat, pulsate, rap, reverberate, tap, tattoo, throb, thrum.

drum into din into, drive home, hammer, harp on, instil, reiterate.

drum up attract, canvass, collect, gather, obtain, petition, round up, solicit.

drunk *adj* a peg too low, a sheet (three sheets) in the wind, bevvied, blind, blotto, bonkers, bottled, canned, cockeyed, corked, corny, drunken, fou, fuddled, half-seas-over, in liquor, inebriate, inebriated, intoxicated, legless, liquored, lit up, loaded, lushy, maggoty, maudlin, merry, moony, moppy, mops and brooms, mortal, muddled, nappy, obfuscated, paralytic, pickled, pie-eyed, pissed, pixil(l)ated, plastered, shickered, sloshed, smashed, soaked, sottish, soused, sow-drunk, sozzled, stewed, stoned, stotious, tanked up, temulent, tiddly, tight, tipsy, up the pole, well-oiled, wet.

antonym sober.

n boozer, drunkard, inebriate, lush, soak, sot, toper, wino.

drunkard *n* alcoholic, bacchant, carouser, dipsomaniac, drinker, drunk, lush, soak, sot, souse, sponge, tippler, toper, tosspot, wino.

drunken *adj* bacchanalian, bacchic, bibulous, boozing, boozy, crapulent, crapulous, debauched, Dionysiac, dissipated, drunk, inebriate, intoxicated, orgiastic, riotous, saturnalian, sodden, sottish, spongy, tippling, toping, under the influence.

antonym sober.

drunkenness *n* alcoholism, bibulousness, dipsomania, inebriety, insobriety, intemperance, intoxication, ivresse, methysis, sottishness, tipsiness.

antonym sobriety.

dry *adj* arid, barren, boring, cutting, cynical, deadpan, dehydrated, desiccated, dreary, dried up, droll, droughty, drouthy, dull, juiceless, keen, low-key, moistureless, monotonous, parched, pawky, plain, sapless, sarcastic, sec, secco, sharp, sly, tedious, thirsty, tiresome, torrid, uninteresting, waterless, withered, xeric.

antonyms interesting, sweet, wet.

v dehumidify, dehydrate, desiccate, drain, exsiccate, harden, mummify, parch, sear, shrivel, welt, wilt, wither, wizen.

antonyms soak, wet.

drying *n* dehumidification, dehydration, desiccation, exsiccation.

dryness *n* aridity, aridness, cynicality, dehydration, drought, drouth, pawkiness, sarcasm, thirst, thirstiness, xerosis.

antonym wetness.

dual *adj* binary, combined, coupled, double, duplex, duplicate, geminate, matched, paired, twin, twofold.

dub *v* bestow, call, christen, confer, denominate, designate, entitle, knight, label, name, nickname, style, tag, term.

dubiety *n* doubt, doubtfulness, dubiosity, dubiousness, equivocality, incertitude, indecision, misgiving, mistrust, qualm, scepticism, suspicion, uncertainty.

antonym certainty.

dubious *adj* ambiguous, debatable, doubtful, equivocal, fishy, hesitant, iffy, indefinite, indeterminate, obscure, problematical, questionable, sceptical, shady, speculative, suspect, suspicious, uncertain, unclear, unconvinced, undecided, undependable, unreliable, unsettled, unsure, untrustworthy, wavering.

antonyms certain, reliable, trustworthy.

duck[1] *v* avoid, bend, bob, bow, crouch, dodge, drop, escape, evade, lower, shirk, shun, sidestep, squat, stoop.

duck[2] *v* dip, dive, dook, douse, dunk, immerse, plunge, souse, submerge, wet.

duct *n* blood, canal, channel, conduit, fistula, funnel, passage, pipe, tube, vas, vessel.

ductile *adj* amenable, biddable, complaint, docile, extensible, flexible, malleable, manageable, manipul(at)able, plastic, pliable, pliant, tractable, yielding.

antonyms intractable, refractory.

dud *n* bum steer, failure, flop, lemon, stumer, wash-out.

adj broken, bust, duff, failed, inoperative, kaput, nugatory, valueless, worthless.

due *adj* adequate, ample, appropriate, becoming, bounden, deserved, enough, expected, fit, fitting, in arrears, just, justified, mature, merited, obligatory, outstanding, owed, owing, payable, plenty of, proper, requisite, returnable, right, rightful, scheduled, sufficient, suitable, unpaid, well-earned.

n birthright, come-uppance, deserts, merits, prerogative, privilege, right(s).

adv dead, direct, directly, exactly, precisely, straight.

duel *n* affair of honour, clash, competition, contest, duello, encounter, engagement, fight, monomachia, monomachy, rivalry, single combat, struggle.

v battle, clash, compete, contend, contest, fight, rival, struggle, vie.

dues *n* charge(s), contribution, fee, levy, subscription.

duffer *n* blunderer, bonehead, booby, bungler, clod, clot, dolt, galoot, lubber, lummox, muff, oaf.

dull *adj* apathetic, blank, blockish, blunt, blunted, Boeotian, boring, bovine, callous, cloudy, commonplace, corny, dead, dead-and-alive, dense, depressed, dim, dimwitted, dismal, doltish, dowie, drab, dreary, dry, dulled, edgeless, empty, faded, featureless, feeble, flat, gloomy, heavy, humdrum, inactive, indifferent, indistinct, insensible, insensitive, insipid, lack-lustre, leaden, lifeless, listless, monotonous, mopish, muffled, mumpish, murky, muted, opaque, opiate, opioid, overcast, passionless, pedestrian, plain, prosaic, run-of-the-mill, slack, sleepy, slow, sluggish, sombre, stodgy, stolid, stultifying, stupid, subdued, subfusc, sullen, sunless, tame, tedious, thick, tiresome, toneless, torpid, turbid, uneventful, unexciting, unfunny, ungifted, unidea'd, unimaginative, unintelligent, uninteresting, unlively, unresponsive, unsharpened, unsunny, unsympathetic, untalented, vacuous, vapid.

antonyms alert, bright, clear, exciting, sharp.

v allay, alleviate, assuage, blunt, cloud, dampen, darken, deject, depress, dim, discourage, disedge, dishearten, dispirit, fade, hebetate, lessen, mitigate, moderate, muffle, obscure, obtund, opiate, palliate, paralyse, rebate, relieve, sadden, soften, stain, stupefy, subdue, sully, tarnish.

antonyms brighten, sharpen, stimulate.

dullard *n* blockhead, bonehead, chump, clod, clot, dimwit, dolt, dope, dummy, dunce, dunderhead, flat tyre, idiot, ignoramus, imbecile, moron, nitwit, noodle, numskull, oaf, simpleton, vegetable.

antonym brain.

dullness *n* dreariness, dryness, emptiness, fadeur, flatness, hebetude, hebetudinosity, monotony, plainness, slowness, sluggishness, stolidity, stupidity, tedium, torpor, vacuity, vapidity.

antonyms brightness, clarity, excitement, interest, sharpness.

duly *adv* accordingly, appropriately, befittingly, condignly, correctly, decorously, deservedly, fitly, fittingly, properly, punctually, rightfully, suitably, sure enough.

dumb *adj* aphonic, aphonous, dense, dimwitted, dull, foolish, inarticulate, mum, mute, silent, soundless, speechless, stupid, thick, tongue-tied, unintelligent, voiceless, wordless.

antonym intelligent.

dum(b)founded *adj* amazed, astonished, astounded, bewildered, bowled over, breathless, confounded, confused, dumb, flabbergasted, floored, knocked sideways, nonplussed, overcome, overwhelmed, paralysed, speechless, staggered, startled, stunned, taken aback, thrown, thunderstruck.

dummy *n* blockhead, copy, counterfeit, dimwit, dolt, dullard, dunce, duplicate, figure, fool, form, imitation, lay-figure, manikin, mannequin, model, numskull, pacifier, sham, simpleton, substitute, teat.

adj artificial, bogus, dry, fake, false, imitation, mock, phoney, practice, sham, simulated, trial.

dump *v* deposit, discharge, dispose of, ditch, drop, empty out, get rid of, jettison, let fall, offload, park, scrap, throw away, throw down, tip, unload.

n coup, hole, hovel, joint, junk-yard, landhill, mess, midden, pigsty, rubbish-heap, rubbish-tip, shack, shanty, slum, tip.

dumpy *adj* chubby, chunky, fatling, homely, plump, podgy, pudgy, roly-poly, short, squab, squat, stout, stubby, tubby.

antonyms rangy, tall.

dun *v* beset, harass, harry, importune, pester, plague, press, urge.

dunce *n* ass, blockhead, bonehead, dimwit, dolt, donkey, duffer, dullard, dunderhead, goose, half-wit, ignoramus, loggerhead, log-head, loon, moron, nincompoop, numskull, simpleton.

antonyms brain, intellectual.

dung *n* excrement, faeces, fumet, guano, manure, ordure, spraint.

dungeon *n* cage, cell, donjon, lock-up, oubliette, pit, prison, vault.

dunghill *n* midden, middenstead, mixen, muck-heap, muck-midden.

dupe *n* cat's-paw, fall guy, flat, geck, gull, instrument, mug, pawn, pigeon, puppet, push-over, sap, simpleton, sitter, soft mark, stooge, sucker, tool, victim.

v bamboozle, beguile, cheat, con, cozen, deceive, defraud, delude, gammon, grift, gudgeon, gull, hoax, hoodwink, humbug, outwit, overreach, pigeon, rip off, swindle, trick.

duplicate *adj* corresponding, geminate, identical, matched, matching, twin, twofold.

n carbon copy, copy, facsimile, match, photocopy, Photostat®, replica, reproduction, Xerox®.

v clone, copy, ditto, double, echo, geminate, photocopy, Photostat®, repeat, replicate, reproduce, Xerox®.

duplication *n* clone, cloning, copy(ing), dittography, gemination, photocopy(ing), repetition, replication, reproduction.

duplicity *n* artifice, chicanery, deceit, deception, dishonesty, dissimulation, double-dealing, falsehood, fraud, guile, hypocrisy, mendacity, perfidy, treachery.

durability *n* constancy, durableness, endurance, imperishability, lastingness, longevity, permanence, persistence, stability, strength.

antonyms fragility, impermanence, weakness.

durable *adj* abiding, constant, dependable, enduring, fast, firm, fixed, hard-wearing, lasting, long-lasting, perdurable, permanent, persistent, reliable, resistant, sound, stable, strong, sturdy, substantial, tough, unfading.

antonyms fragile, impermanent, perishable, weak.

duration *n* continuance, continuation, extent, fullness, length, period, perpetuation, prolongation, span, spell, stretch, term-time.

antonym shortening.

duress *n* bullying, captivity, coaction, coercion, compulsion, confinement, constraint, force, hardship, imprisonment, incarceration, pressure, restraint, threat.

dusk *n* crepuscle, crepuscule, dark, darkness, evening, eventide, gloaming, gloom, murk, nightfall, obscurity, shade, shadowiness, sundown, sunset, twilight.

antonyms brightness, dawn.

duskiness *n* caliginosity, darkness, fuliginosity, murkiness, swarthiness.

antonyms brightness, lightness, whiteness.

dusky *adj* caliginous, cloudy, crepuscular, dark, dark-hued, darkish, dim, fuliginous, gloomy, murky, obscure, overcast, sable, shadowy, shady, sooty, subfusc, swarthy, tenebr(i)ous, twilight, twilit, umbrose, veiled.

antonyms bright, light, white.

dust *n* coom, dirt, earth, grime, grit, ground, particles, powder, soil.

v burnish, clean, cover, dredge, polish, powder, scatter, sift, spray, spread, sprinkle, wipe.

dustman *n* garbo, garbologist.

dust-storm *n* dust-devil, sand-storm.

dust-up *n* argument, argy-bargy, brawl, brush, commotion, conflict, disagreement, disturbance, encounter, fight, fracas, punch-up, quarrel, scrap, scuffle, set-to, shindig, skirmish, tussle.

dusty *adj* chalky, crumbly, dirty, filthy, friable, granular, grubby, powdery, pulverous, sandy, sooty, unswept.

antonyms clean, hard, polished, solid.

dutiful *adj* acquiescent, complaisant, compliant, conscientious, deferential, devoted, docile, duteous, filial, obedient, punctilious, regardful, respectful, reverential, submissive.

duty *n* allegiance, assignment, business, calling, charge, chore, customs, debt, deference, devoir, due, engagement, excise, function, impost, job, levy, loyalty, mission, obedience, obligation, office, onus, province, respect, responsibility, reverence, role, service, tariff, task, tax, toll, work.

dwarf *n* droich, durgan, elf, gnome, goblin, homuncle, homuncule, homunculus, hop-o'-my-thumb, Lilliputian, man(n)ikin, midget, pygmy, Tom Thumb.

adj baby, bonsai, diminutive, dwarfed, dwarfish, Lilliputian, mini, miniature, petite, pint-size(d), pocket, small, tiny, undersized.

antonym large.

v check, dim, diminish, dominate, lower, minimise, overshadow, retard, stunt.

dwarfish *adj* diminutive, durgy, pocket, pygmean, pygmy, small, stunted, undersized.

antonym large.

dwell *v* abide, bide, hang out, inhabit, live, lodge, people, populate, quarter, remain, reside, rest, settle, sojourn, stay, stop, tenant.

dwell on elaborate, emphasise, expatiate, harp on, harp on about, linger over, mull over.

antonym pass over.

dweller *n* denizen, inhabitant, occupant, occupier, resident.

dwelling *n* abode, domicile, dwelling-house, establishment, habitation, home, house, lodge, lodging, quarters, residence, tent, tepee, woning.

dwindle *v* abate, contract, decay, decline, decrease, die, die out, diminish, disappear, ebb, fade, fall, lessen, peter out, pine, shrink, shrivel, sink, subside, tail off, taper off, vanish, wane, waste away, weaken, wither.

antonym increase.

dye *n* colorant, colour, colouring, grain, pigment, stain, tinge, tint.

v colour, grain, imbue, pigment, stain, tincture, tinge, tint.

dyed-in-the-wool *adj* card-carrying, complete, confirmed, deep-rooted, die-hard, entrenched, established, fixed, hard-core, hardened, inflexible, inveterate, long-standing, settled, unchangeable, uncompromising, unshakable.

antonym superficial.

dying *adj* at death's door, declining, disappearing, ebbing, expiring, fading, failing, final, going, in articulo mortis, in extremis, moribund, mortal, not long for this world, obsolescent, passing, perishing, sinking, vanishing.

antonyms coming, reviving.

dynamic *adj* active, driving, electric, energetic, forceful, go-ahead, go-getting, high-powered, lively, powerful, self-starting, spirited, vigorous, vital, zippy.

antonyms apathetic, inactive, slow.

dynamism *n* drive, energy, enterprise, forcefulness, get-up-and-go, go, initiative, liveliness, pep, pizzazz, push, vigour, vim, zap, zip.

antonyms apathy, inactivity, slowness.

dynasty *n* ascendancy, authority, dominion, empire, government, house, regime, rule, sovereignty, succession, sway.

dyspeptic *adj* bad-tempered, crabbed, crabby, crotchety, gloomy, grouchy, indigested, peevish, short-tempered, snappish, testy, touchy.

E

each *adv* apiece, individually, per capita, per head, per person, respectively, separately, singly.

eager *adj* agog, anxious, ardent, athirst, avid, desirous, earnest, empressé, enthusiastic, fervent, fervid, fervorous, freck, greedy, gung-ho, hot, hungry, impatient, intent, keen, longing, perfervid, raring, unshrinking, vehement, yearning, zealous.

antonyms apathetic, unenthusiastic.

eagerly *adv* ardently, avidly, earnestly, enthusiastically, fain, fervently, greedily, intently, keenly, zealously.

antonyms apathetically, listlessly.

eagerness *n* ardour, avidity, earnestness, enthusiasm, fainness, fervency, fervidity, fervour, greediness, heartiness, hunger, impatience, impetuosity, intentness, keenness, longing, thirst, vehemence, yearning, zeal.

antonyms apathy, disinterest.

ear *n* ability, appreciation, attention, consideration, discrimination, hearing, heed, notice, perception, regard, sensitivity, skill, taste.

early *adj* advanced, forward, matutinal, matutine, prehistoric, premature, primeval, primitive, primordial, undeveloped, untimely, young.

adv ahead of time, beforehand, betimes, in advance, in good time, prematurely, too soon.

antonym late.

earmark *v* allocate, designate, keep back, label, put aside, reserve, set aside, tag.

earn *v* acquire, attain, bring in, collect, deserve, draw, gain, get, gross, make, merit, net, obtain, procure, rate, realise, reap, receive, warrant, win.

antonyms lose, spend.

earnest *adj* ardent, close, constant, determined, devoted, eager, enthusiastic, fervent, fervid, firm, fixed, grave, heartfelt, impassioned, intent, keen, passionate, purposeful, resolute, resolved, serious, sincere, solemn, stable, staid, steady, thoughtful, urgent, vehement, warm, zealous.

antonyms apathetic, flippant, unenthusiastic.

n assurance, deposit, determination, down payment, guarantee, pledge, promise, resolution, security, seriousness, sincerity, token, truth.

earnestly *adv* eagerly, ex animo, fervently, firmly, intently, keenly, resolutely, seriously, sincerely, warmly, zealously.

antonyms flippantly, listlessly.

earnestness *n* ardour, determination, devotion, eagerness, enthusiasm, fervency, fervour, gravity, intentness, keenness, passion, purposefulness, resolution, seriousness, sincerity, urgency, vehemence, warmth, zeal.

antonyms apathy, flippancy.

earnings *n* emoluments, gain, income, pay, proceeds, profits, receipts, remuneration, return, revenue, reward, salary, stipend, takings, wages.

antonyms expenses, outgoings.

earring *n* earbob, ear-drop.

earth[1] *n* Gaia, geosphere, globe, middle-earth, middle-world, Midgard, orb, planet, sphere, world.

earth[2] *n* clay, clod, dirt, ground, humus, land, loam, mould, sod, soil, topsoil.

earthenware *n* ceramics, crockery, crocks, pots, pottery.

adj ceramic, clay, fictile, figuline, terra-cotta, wally.

earthly *adj* base, carnal, conceivable, earthern, feasible, fleshly, gross, human, imaginable, likely, low, material, materialistic, mortal, mundane, physical, possible, practical, profane, secular, sensual, slight, slightest, sordid, sublunar, sublunary, tellurian, telluric, temporal, terrene, terrestrial, vile, worldly.

antonyms heavenly, spiritual.

earthquake *n* earth-tremor, quake, seism, shake, upheaval.

earthy *adj* bawdy, blue, coarse, crude, down-to-earth, homely, indecorous, lusty, natural, raunchy, ribald, robust, rough, simple, uninhibited, unrefined, unsophisticated, vulgar.

antonyms cultured, refined.

ease *n* affluence, aplomb, calmness, comfort, composure, content, contentment, deftness, dexterity, easiness, effortlessness, enjoyment, facileness, facility, flexibility, freedom, happiness, informality, insouciance, leisure, liberty, naturalness, nonchalance, peace, peace of mind, poise, quiet, quietude, readiness, relaxation, repose, rest, restfulness, serenity, simplicity, solace, tranquillity, unaffectedness, unconstraint, unreservedness.

antonyms difficulty, discomfort.

v abate, aid, allay, alleviate, appease, assist, assuage, calm, comfort, disburden, edge, expedite, facilitate, forward, further, guide, inch, lessen, lighten, manoeuvre, mitigate, moderate, mollify, pacify, palliate, quiet, relax, relent, relieve, simplify, slacken, slide, slip, smooth, solace, soothe, speed up, squeeze, steer, still, tranquillise.

antonyms hinder, retard, torment.

ease off abate, decrease, die away, die down, moderate, relent, slacken, subside, wane.

antonym increase.

easily[1] *adv* comfortably, effortlessly, facilely, readily, simply, smoothly, standing on one's head, with one arm tied behind one's back.

antonym laboriously.

easily[2] *adv* absolutely, by far, certainly, clearly, definitely, doubtlessly, far and away, indisputably, indubitably, plainly, probably, simply, surely, undeniably, undoubtedly, unequivocally, unquestionably, well.

easy *adj* a doddle, a piece of cake, a pushover, accommodating, affable, amenable, biddable, calm, carefree, casual, child's play, clear, comfortable, compliant, contented, cushy, docile, easeful, easy-going, effortless, facile, flexible, friendly, gentle, graceful, gracious, gullible, idiot-proof, indulgent, informal, leisurely, lenient, liberal, light, manageable, mild, moderate, natural, no bother, open, painless, peaceful, permissive, pleasant, pliant, quiet, relaxed, satisfied, serene, simple, smooth, soft, straightforward, submissive, suggestible, susceptible, temperate, tolerant, tractable, tranquil, trusting, unaffected, unburdensome, unceremonious, uncomplicated, unconstrained, undemanding, undisturbed, unexacting, unforced, unhurried, unlaboured, unoppressive, unpretentious, untroubled, unworried, user-friendly, well-to-do, yielding.

antonyms demanding, difficult, fast, impossible, intolerant.

easy-going *adj* amenable, calm, carefree, casual, complacent, downbeat, easy, easy-osy, even-tempered, flexible, happy-go-lucky, indulgent, insouciant, laid-back, lenient, liberal, mild, moderate, nonchalant, permissive, placid, relaxed, serene, tolerant, unconcerned, uncritical, undemanding, unhurried, unworried.

antonyms fussy, intolerant.

eat *v* banquet, break bread, chew, chop, consume, corrode, crumble, decay, devour, dine, dissolve, erode, feed, grub, ingest, knock back, manducate, munch, pig, rot, scoff, swallow, wear away.

eat one's words abjure, recant, rescind, retract, take back, unsay.

eatable *adj* comestible, digestible, edible, esculent, good, harmless, palatable, wholesome.

antonym unpalatable.

eatables *n* comestibles, food, grub, nosh, scoff.

eavesdrop *v* bug, earwig, listen in, monitor, overhear, snoop, spy, tap.

eavesdropper *n* listener, monitor, snoop, snooper, spy.

ebb *v* abate, decay, decline, decrease, degenerate, deteriorate, diminish, drop, dwindle, fade away, fall away, fall back, flag, flow back, go out, lessen, peter out, recede, reflow, retire, retreat, retrocede, shrink, sink, slacken, subside, wane, weaken, withdraw.

antonyms increase, rise.

n decay, decline, decrease, degeneration, deterioration, diminution, drop, dwindling, ebb tide, flagging, lessening, low tide, low water, reflow, refluence, reflux, regression, retreat, retrocession, shrinkage, sinking, slackening, subsidence, wane, waning, weakening, withdrawal.

antonyms flow, increase, rising.

ebony *adj* black, dark, jet, jet-black, jetty, sable, sooty.

ebullience *n* boiling, breeziness, brightness, bubbling, buoyancy, chirpiness, ebullition, effervescence, effusiveness, elation, enthusiasm, excitement, exhilaration, exuberance, ferment, fermentation, foaming, frothing, high spirits, seething, vivacity, zest.

antonyms apathy, dullness, lifelessness.

ebullient *adj* boiling, breezy, bright, bubbling, buoyant, chirpy, effervescent, effusive, elated, enthusiastic, excited, exhilarated, exuberant, foaming, frothing, frothy, gushing, irrepressible, seething, vivacious, zestful.

antonyms apathetic, dull, lifeless.

eccentric *adj* aberrant, abnormal, anomalous, bizarre, capricious, dotty, erratic, fey, freakish, fruity, idiosyncratic, irregular, nuts, nutty, odd, offbeat, outlandish, peculiar, queer, quirky, screwball, screwy, singular, spac(e)y, strange, uncommon, unconventional, way-out, weird, whimsical.

antonyms normal, sane.

n case, character, crank, freak, fruit-cake, nonconformist, nut, nutter, oddball, oddity, queer fish, screwball, weirdie, weirdo.

eccentricity *n* aberration, abnormality, anomaly, bizarreness, bizarrerie, caprice, capriciousness, foible, freakishness, idiosyncrasy, irregularity, nonconformity, oddity, outlandishness, peculiarity, queerness, quirk, singularity, strangeness, unconventionality, waywardness, weirdness, whimsicality.

antonyms normalcy, normality, ordinariness.

ecclesiastic *n* abbé, churchman, clergyman, cleric, divine, man of the cloth, minister, parson, priest.

ecclesiastic(al) *adj* church, churchly, churchy, clerical, divine, holy, pastoral, priestly, religious, spiritual, templar.

echelon *n* degree, grade, level, place, position, rank, status, step, tier.

echo *v* ape, copy, echoise, imitate, mimic, mirror, parallel, parrot, recall, reflect, reiterate, repeat, reproduce, resemble, resound, reverberate, ring, second.

n allusion, answer, copy, evocation, hint, image, imitation, intimation, memory, mirror image, parallel, reflection, reiteration, reminder, repetition, reproduction, reverberation, suggestion, sympathy, trace.

echoic *adj* imitative, onomatopoeic, onomatopoetic.

éclat *n* acclaim, acclamation, applause, approval, brilliance, celebrity, display, distinction, effect, fame, glory, lustre, ostentation, plaudits, pomp, renown, show, showmanship, splendour, success.

antonyms disapproval, dullness.

eclectic *adj* all-embracing, broad, catholic, comprehensive, dilettantish, diverse, diversified, general, heterogeneous, liberal, many-sided, multifarious, selective, varied, wide-ranging.

antonyms narrow, one-sided.

eclipse *v* blot out, cloud, darken, dim, dwarf, exceed, excel, extinguish, obscure, outdo, outshine, overshadow, shroud, surpass, transcend, veil.

n darkening, decline, deliquium, diminution, dimming, extinction, failure, fall, loss, obscuration, occultation, overshadowing, shading.

economic *adj* budgetary, business, cheap, commercial, cost-effective, economical, economy-size, fair, financial, fiscal, industrial, inexpensive, low, low-priced, mercantile, modest, monetary, money-making, pecuniary, productive, profitable, profit-making, reasonable, remunerative, solvent, trade, viable.

antonyms expensive, uneconomic.

economical *adj* careful, cheap, cost-effective, economic, economising, efficient, fair, frugal, inexpensive, labour-saving, low, low-priced, modest, prudent, reasonable, saving, scrimping, sparing, thrifty, time-saving.

antonyms expensive, uneconomical.

economics *n* plutology, plutonomy, political economy.

economise *v* cut back, cut corners, husband, retrench, save, scrimp, tighten one's belt.

antonym squander.

economy *n* frugality, frugalness, husbandry, parsimony, providence, prudence, restraint, retrenchment, saving, scrimping, sparingness, thrift, thriftiness.

antonym improvidence.

ecstasy *n* bliss, delight, ecstasis, elation, enthusiasm, euphoria, exaltation, fervour, frenzy, joy, rapture, ravishment, rhapsody, seventh heaven, sublimation, trance, transport.

antonym torment.

ecstatic *adj* blissful, delirious, elated, enraptured, enthusiastic, entranced, euphoric, exultant, fervent, frenzied, joyful, joyous, on cloud nine, over the moon, overjoyed, rapturous, rhapsodic, transported.

antonym downcast.

eddy *n* counter-current, counterflow, pirl, purl, swirl, vortex, well, whirlpool.

v swirl, whirl.

edge *n* acuteness, advantage, animation, arris, ascendancy, bezel, bite, border, bound, boundary, brim, brink, cantle, contour, dominance, effectiveness, force, fringe, incisiveness, interest, keenness, lead, limit, line, lip, margin, outline, perimeter, periphery, point, pungency, rim, sharpness, side, sting, superiority, threshold, upper hand, urgency, verge, zest.

v bind, border, creep, drib, ease, fringe, gravitate, hem, hone, inch, rim, shape, sharpen, sidle, steal, strop, trim, verge, whet, work, worm.

edgy *adj* anxious, ill at ease, irascible, irritable, keyed-up, nervous, on edge, prickly, restive, tense, testy, touchy.

antonym calm.

edible *adj* comestible, digestible, eatable, esculent, good, harmless, palatable, safe, wholesome.

antonym inedible.

edict *n* act, command, decree, dictate, dictum, enactment, fiat, injunction, law, mandate, manifesto, order, ordinance, proclamation, pronouncement, pronunciamento, regulation, rescript, ruling, statute, ukase.

edification *n* enlightenment, guidance, improvement, instruction, upbuilding.

edifice *n* building, construction, erection, structure.

edify *v* educate, elevate, enlighten, guide, improve, inform, instruct, nurture, school, teach, train, tutor.

edit *v* adapt, annotate, assemble, blue-pencil, bowdlerise, censor, check, compose, condense, correct, emend, polish, rearrange, redact, reorder, rephrase, revise, rewrite, select.

edition *n* copy, exemplar, impression, issue, number, printing, programme, version, volume.

educable *adj* instructible, teachable, trainable.

antonym ineducable.

educate *v* catechise, civilise, coach, cultivate, develop, discipline, drill, edify, exercise, improve, indoctrinate, inform, instruct, learn, mature, rear, school, teach, train, tutor.

educated *adj* civilised, coached, cultivated, cultured, enlightened, experienced, informed, instructed, knowledgeable, learned, lettered, literary, nurtured, polished, refined, schooled, sophisticated, taught, trained, tutored, well-bred.

antonyms uncultured, uneducated.

education *n* breeding, civilisation, coaching, cultivation, culture, development, discipline, drilling, edification, enlightenment, erudition, guidance, improvement, indoctrination, instruction, knowledge, nurture, scholarship, schooling, teaching, training, tuition, tutelage, tutoring.

educational *adj* cultural, didactic, edifying, educative, enlightening, improving, informative, instructive, scholastic.

antonym uninformative.

educative *adj* catechetic, catechismal, catechistic(al), didactic, edifying, educational, enlightening, improving, informative, instructive.

antonym uninformative.

educator *n* coach, dominie, edifier, educationalist, educationist, instructor, lecturer, pedagogue, schoolmaster, schoolmistress, schoolteacher, teacher, trainer, tutor.

eerie *adj* awesome, chilling, creepy, eldritch, fearful, frightening, ghastly, ghostly, mysterious, scary, spectral, spine-chilling, spooky, strange, uncanny, unearthly, unnatural, weird.

antonyms natural, ordinary.

efface *v* annihilate, blank out, blot out, blue-pencil, cancel, cross out, delete, destroy, dim, eliminate, eradicate, erase, excise, expunge, extirpate, humble, lower, obliterate, raze, remove, rub out, wipe out, withdraw.

effect *n* action, aftermath, clout, conclusion, consequence, drift, éclat, effectiveness, efficacy, efficiency, enforcement, essence, event, execution, fact, force, fruit, impact, implementation, import, impression, influence, issue, meaning, operation, outcome, power, purport, purpose, reality, result, sense, significance, strength, tenor, upshot, use, validity, vigour, weight, work.

v accomplish, achieve, actuate, cause, complete, consummate, create, effectuate, execute, fulfil, initiate, make, perform, produce, wreak.

effective *adj* able, active, adequate, capable, cogent, compelling, competent, convincing, current, effectual, efficacious, efficient, emphatic, energetic, forceful, forcible, implemental, impressive, moving, operative, perficient, persuasive, potent, powerful, productive, real, serviceable, striking, telling, useful.

antonyms ineffective, useless.

effectiveness *n* ability, capability, clout, cogency, effect, efficacy, efficiency, force, influence, potency, power, strength, success, use, validity, vigour, weight.

antonyms ineffectiveness, uselessness.

effects *n* belongings, chattels, gear, goods, movables, paraphernalia, possessions, property, things, trappings, traps.

effectual *adj* authoritative, binding, capable, effective, efficacious, efficient, forcible, influential, lawful, legal, licit, operative, perficient, potent, powerful, productive, serviceable, sound, successful, telling, useful, valid.

antonyms ineffective, useless.

effeminate *adj* delicate, epicene, feminine, pansy, poofy, sissy, soft, tender, unmanly, weak, womanish, womanlike, womanly.

antonym manly.

effervesce *v* boil, bubble, ferment, fizz, foam, froth, sparkle.

effervescence *n* animation, bubbles, bubbling, buoyancy, ebullience, ebulliency, enthusiasm, excitedness, excitement, exhilaration, exuberance, ferment, fermentation, fizz, foam, foaming, froth, frothing, gaiety, high spirits, liveliness, sparkle, vim, vitality, vivacity, zing, zip.

effervescent *adj* animated, bubbling, bubbly, buoyant, carbonated, ebullient, enthusiastic, excited, exhilarated, exuberant, fermenting, fizzing, fizzy, foaming, frothing, frothy, gay, irrepressible, lively, merry, sparkling, vital, vivacious, zingy.

antonyms apathetic, dull, flat.

effete *adj* barren, corrupt, debased, debilitated, decadent, decayed, decrepit, degenerate, dissipated, drained, enervated, enfeebled, exhausted, feeble, fruitless, incapable, ineffectual, infecund, infertile, overrefined, played out, spent, spoiled, sterile, tired out, unfruitful, unproductive, unprolific, used up, wasted, weak, worn out.

antonym vigorous.

efficacious *adj* active, adequate, capable, competent, effective, effectual, efficient, energetic, operative, potent, powerful, productive, serviceable, strong, successful, sufficient, useful.

antonyms ineffective, useless.

efficacy *n* ability, capability, competence, effect, effectiveness, efficaciousness, efficiency, energy, force, influence, potency, power, strength, success, use, virtue.

antonyms ineffectiveness, uselessness.

efficiency *n* ability, adeptness, capability, competence, competency, economy, effectiveness, efficacy, mastery, power, productivity, proficiency, readiness, skilfulness, skill.

antonym inefficiency.

efficient *adj* able, adept, businesslike, capable, competent, economic, effective, effectual, powerful, productive, proficient, ready, skilful, streamlined, well-conducted, well-ordered, well-organised, well-regulated, workmanlike.

antonym inefficient.

effigy *n* carving, dummy, figure, guy, icon, idol, image, likeness, mumbo-jumbo, picture, portrait, representation, statue.

effluent *n* discharge, effluence, effluvium, efflux, emanation, emission, exhalation, outflow, pollutant, pollution, sewage, waste.

effort *n* accomplishment, achievement, application, attempt, conatus, creation, deed, endeavour, energy, essay, exertion, feat, force, go, job, labour, molimen, nisus, pains, power, product, production, shot, stab, strain, stress, stretch, striving, struggle, toil, travail, trouble, try, work.

effortless *adj* easy, facile, painless, simple, smooth, uncomplicated, undemanding, unlaboured.

antonym difficult.

effrontery *n* arrogance, assurance, audacity, boldness, brashness, brass (neck), brazenness, cheek, cheekiness, disrespect, face, front, gall, impertinence, impudence, incivility, insolence, neck, nerve, presumption, rudeness, shamelessness, temerity.

effusion *n* address, discharge, effluence, efflux, emission, gush, outflow, outpouring, shedding, speech, stream, talk, utterance, voidance, word salad, writing.

effusive *adj* demonstrative, ebullient, enthusiastic, expansive, extravagant, exuberant, fulsome, gushing, gushy, lavish, overflowing, profuse, talkative, unreserved, unrestrained, voluble, wordy.

antonyms quiet, restrained.

egg on coax, encourage, exhort, goad, incite, prick, prod, prompt, push, spur, stimulate, urge, wheedle.

antonym discourage.

egghead *n* brain, Einstein, genius, headpiece, intellect, intellectual, scholar.

egoism *n* amour-propre, egocentricity, egomania, egotism, narcissism, self-absorption, self-centredness, self-importance, self-interest, selfishness, self-love, self-regard, self-seeking.

antonym altruism.

egoist *n* egomaniac, egotist, narcissist, self-seeker.

egoistic *adj* egocentric, egoistical, egomaniacal, egotistic, egotistical, narcissistic, self-absorbed, self-centred, self-important, self-involved, self-pleasing, self-seeking.

antonym altruistic.

egotism *n* bigheadedness, conceitedness, egocentricity, egoism, egomania, narcissism, self-admiration, self-centredness, self-conceit, self-esteem, self-importance, self-love, self-praise, self-pride, superiority, vainglory, vanity.

antonym humility.

egotist *n* bighead, boaster, braggadocio, braggart, egoist, egomaniac, swaggerer.

egotistic *adj* bigheaded, boasting, bragging, conceited, egocentric, egoistic, egoistical, egomaniacal, egotistical, narcissistic, opinionated, self-centred, self-important, superior, swollen-headed, vain, vainglorious.

antonym humble.

egregious *adj* arrant, flagrant, frabjous, glaring, grievous, gross, heinous, infamous, insufferable, intolerable, monstrous, notorious, outrageous, rank, scandalous, shocking.

antonym slight.

egress *n* emergence, escape, exit, exodus, issue, outlet, vent.

ejaculate[1] *v* discharge, eject, emit, spurt.

ejaculate[2] *v* blurt, call, cry, exclaim, scream, shout, utter, yell.

ejaculation[1] *n* discharge, ejection, emission, spurt.

ejaculation[2] *n* call, cry, exclamation, scream, shout, utterance, yell.

eject *v* banish, belch, boot out, bounce, deport, discharge, disgorge, dislodge, dismiss, dispossess, drive out, emit, evacuate, evict, exile, expel, fire, kick out, oust, remove, sack, spew, spout, throw out, turn out, unhouse, vomit.

ejection *n* banishment, defenestration, deportation, discharge, disgorgement, dislodgement, dismissal, dispossession, evacuation, eviction, exile, expulsion, firing, ouster, ousting, removal, sacking, spouting, the boot, the sack.

eke out add to, economise on, husband, increase, make (something) stretch, stretch, supplement.

elaborate *adj* careful, complex, complicated, daedal(ic), decorated, dedal(ian), detailed, exact, extravagant, fancy, fussy, Heath-Robinson, intricate, involved, laboured, minute, ornamental, ornate, ostentatious, painstaking, perfected, precise, showy, skilful, studied, thorough.

antonyms plain, simple.

v amplify, complicate, decorate, detail, develop, devise, embellish, enhance, enlarge, expand, expatiate, explain, flesh out, garnish, improve, ornament, polish, refine.

antonyms précis, simplify.

élan *n* animation, brio, dash, esprit, flair, flourish, impetuosity, liveliness, oomph, panache, pizzazz, spirit, style, verve, vigour, vivacity, zest.

antonyms apathy, lifelessness.

elapse *v* go by, lapse, pass, slip away.

elastic *adj* accommodating, adaptable, adjustable, bouncy, buoyant, complaisant, compliant, distensible, ductile, flexible, irrepressible, plastic, pliable, pliant, resilient, rubbery, springy, stretchable, stretchy, supple, tolerant, variable, yielding.

antonym rigid.

elasticity *n* adaptability, adjustability, bounce, buoyancy, complaisance, compliance, compliancy, compliantness, ductileness, ductility, flexibility, give, irrepressibility, plasticity, pliability, pliancy, resilience, rubberiness, springiness, stretch, stretchiness, suppleness, tolerance, variability.

antonym rigidity.

elated *adj* animated, blissful, cheered, delighted, ecstatic, euphoric, excited, exhilarated, exultant, gleeful, joyful, joyous, jubilant, on the high ropes, over the moon, overjoyed, pleased, proud, roused.

antonym downcast.

elation *n* bliss, delight, ecstasy, euphoria, exaltation, exhilaration, exultation, glee, high spirits, joy, joyfulness, joyousness, jubilation, rapture, transports of delight.

antonym depression.

elbow *v* bulldoze, bump, crowd, hustle, jostle, knock, nudge, plough, push, shoulder, shove.

elbow-room *n* freedom, latitude, Lebensraum, leeway, play, room, scope, space.

elder *adj* aîné(e), ancient, eigne, first-born, older, senior.

antonym younger.

n deacon, doyen, presbyter, senior.

elderly *adj* aged, aging, badgerly, hoary, old, senile.

antonyms young, youthful.

eldest *adj* first, first-begotten, first-born, oldest.

antonym youngest.

elect *v* adopt, appoint, choose, designate, determine, opt for, pick, prefer, select, vote.

adj choice, chosen, designate, designated, elite, hand-picked, picked, preferred, presumptive, prospective, select, selected, to be.

election *n* appointment, ballot-box, choice, choosing, decision, determination, judgement, preference, selection, vote, voting.

elector *n* constituent, selector, voter.

electric *adj* charged, dynamic, electrifying, exciting, rousing, stimulating, stirring, tense, thrilling.

antonyms tedious, unexciting.

electrify *v* amaze, animate, astonish, astound, excite, fire, galvanise, invigorate, jolt, rouse, shock, stagger, startle, stimulate, stir, stun, thrill.

antonym bore.

elegance *n* beauty, chic, concinnity, courtliness, dignity, discernment, distinction, exquisiteness, gentility, grace, gracefulness, grandeur, luxury, polish, politeness, propriety, refinement, style, sumptuousness, taste.

antonym inelegance.

elegant *adj* à la mode, appropriate, apt, artistic, beautiful, chic, choice, clever, comely, concinnous, courtly, cultivated, debonair, delicate, effective, exquisite, fashionable, fine, genteel, graceful, handsome, ingenious, luxurious, modish, neat, nice, polished, refined, simple, smart, smooth, stylish, sumptuous, tasteful.

antonym inelegant.

elegiac *adj* doleful, funereal, keening, lamenting, melancholy, mournful, nostalgic, plaintive, sad, threnetic, threnetical, threnodial, threnodic, valedictory.

antonym happy.

elegy *n* coronach, dirge, keen, lament, plaint, requiem, threnode, threnody.

element *n* basis, component, constituent, domain, environment, factor, feature, field, fragment, habitat, hint, ingredient, medium, member, milieu, part, piece, section, sphere, subdivision, trace, unit.

elementary *adj* basic, clear, easy, elemental, facile, fundamental, initial, introductory, original, plain, primary, principial, rudimentary, simple, straightforward, uncomplicated.

antonyms advanced, complex.

elements *n* basics, essentials, foundations, fundamentals, introduction, principia, principles, rudiments, weather.

elevate *v* advance, aggrandise, animate, augment, boost, brighten, buoy up, cheer, elate, exalt, excite, exhilarate, hearten, heighten, hoist, increase, intensify, lift, magnify, prefer, promote, raise, rouse, sublimate, swell, upgrade, uplift, upraise.

antonyms lessen, lower.

elevated *adj* animated, cheerful, cheery, dignified, elated, exalted, excited, exhilarated, grand, high, high-flown, high-minded, inflated, lofty, noble, overjoyed, raised, sublime, tipsy.

antonyms base, informal, lowly.

elevation *n* acclivity, advancement, aggrandisement, altitude, eminence, exaltation, exaltedness, grandeur, height, hill, hillock, loftiness, mountain, nobility, nobleness, preferment, promotion, rise, sublimation, sublimity, upgrading, uplift.

antonyms baseness, informality.

elfin *adj* arch, charming, delicate, elfish, elflike, elvish, frolicsome, impish, mischievous, petite, playful, puckish, small, sprightly.

elicit *v* cause, derive, draw out, educe, evoke, evolve, exact, extort, extract, fish, mole out, obtain, wrest, wring.

eligible *adj* acceptable, appropriate, available, desirable, fit, proper, qualified, suitable, suited, worthy.

antonym ineligible.

eliminate *v* annihilate, bump off, cut out, delete, dispense with, dispose of, disregard, do away with, drop, eject, eradicate, exclude, expel, expunge, exterminate, extinguish, get rid of, ignore, kill, knock out, liquidate, murder, omit, reject, remove, rub out, slay, stamp out, take out, terminate, waste.

antonym accept.

elite *n* aristocracy, best, cream, crème de la crème, elect, establishment, flower, gentry, high society, meritocracy, nobility, pick.

adj aristocratic, best, choice, crack, exclusive, first-class, noble, pick, selected, top, top-class, upper-class.

antonyms ordinary, run-of-the-mill.

elixir *n* concentrate, cure-all, daffy, essence, extract, mixture, nostrum, panacea, pith, potion, principle, quintessence, remedy, solution, syrup, tincture, treacle.

elliptical[1] *adj* egg-shaped, oval, oviform, ovoid(al).

elliptical[2] *adj* abstruse, ambiguous, concentrated, concise, condensed, cryptic, incomprehensible, laconic, obscure, recondite, terse, unfathomable.

antonym clear.

elocution *n* articulation, declamation, delivery, diction, enunciation, oratory, pronunciation, rhetoric, speech, speechmaking, utterance.

elongated *adj* extended, lengthened, long, prolonged, protracted, stretched.

elope *v* abscond, bolt, decamp, disappear, do a bunk, escape, leave, run away, run off, slip away, steal away.

eloquence *n* dick, expression, expressiveness, facundity, fluency, forcefulness, oratory, persuasiveness, rhetoric.

antonym inarticulateness.

eloquent *adj* articulate, Demosthenic, expressive, fluent, forceful, graceful, honeyed, meaningful, moving, persuasive, plausible, pregnant, revealing, silver-tongued, stirring, suggestive, telling, vivid, vocal, voluble, well-expressed.

antonyms inarticulate, tongue-tied.

elucidate *v* annotate, clarify, explain, explicate, expound, gloss, illuminate, illustrate, interpret, spell out, unfold.

antonyms confuse, obscure.

elucidation *n* annotation, clarification, comment, commentary, explanation, explication, exposition, foot-note, gloss, illumination, illustration, interpretation, marginalia.

elude *v* avoid, baffle, beat, circumvent, confound, dodge, duck, escape, evade, flee, foil, frustrate, outrun, puzzle, shirk, shun, stump, thwart.

elusive *adj* ambiguous, baffling, deceitful, deceptive, elusory, equivocal, evasive, fallacious, fleeting, fraudulent, fugitive, illusory, indefinable, intangible, misleading, puzzling, shifty, slippery, subtle, transient, transitory, tricky, unanalysable.

emaciated *adj* atrophied, attenuate, attenuated, cadaverous, gaunt, haggard, lank, lean, meagre, pinched, scrawny, skeletal, tabefied, tabescent, thin, wasted.

antonyms plump, well-fed.

emaciation *n* atrophy, attenuation, gauntness, haggardness, leanness, meagreness, scrawniness, tabefaction, tabes, tabescence, thinness.

antonym plumpness.

emanate *v* arise, come, derive, discharge, emerge, emit, exhale, flow, give off, give out, issue, originate, proceed, radiate, send out, spring, stem.

emanation *n* arising, derivation, discharge, ectoplasm, effluence, effluent, effluvium, efflux, effluxion, effusion, emergence, emission, exhalation, exoplasm, flow, generation, mephitis, origination, proceeding, procession, radiation.

emancipate *v* deliver, discharge, disencumber, disenthral, enfranchise, free, liberate, manumit, release, set free, unbind, unchain, unfetter, unshackle.

antonym enslave.

emancipation *n* deliverance, discharge, enfranchisement, freedom, liberation, liberty, manumission, release, unbinding, unchaining.

antonym enslavement.

emasculate *v* castrate, cripple, debilitate, enervate, geld, impoverish, neuter, soften, spay, weaken.

antonyms boost, vitalise.

embalm *v* cherish, consecrate, conserve, enshrine, immortalise, mummify, preserve, store, treasure.

embankment *n* bund, causeway, causey, defences, earthwork, levee, rampart.

embargo *n* ban, bar, barrier, blockage, check, hindrance, impediment, interdict, interdiction, prohibition, proscription, restraint, restriction, seizure, stoppage.

v ban, bar, block, check, embar, impede, interdict, prohibit, proscribe, restrict, seize, stop.

antonym allow.

embark *v* board ship, emplane, entrain, take ship.

antonym disembark.

embark on begin, broach, commence, engage, enter, initiate, launch, start, undertake.

antonym finish.

embarkation *n* boarding, entrainment.

antonym disembarkation.

embarrass *v* abash, chagrin, confuse, discomfit, discomfort, discompose, disconcert, discountenance, distress, fluster, mortify, shame, show up.

embarrassed *adj* abashed, constrained, discomfited, disconcerted, mortified, shamed, shown up, uncomfortable.

antonym unembarrassed.

embarrassing *adj* awkward, compromising, discomfiting, discomfortable, disconcerting, distressing, humiliating, mortifying, sensitive, shameful, shaming, touchy, tricky, uncomfortable.

embarrassment *n* awkwardness, bashfulness, bind, chagrin, confusion, constraint, difficulty, discomfiture, discomfort, discomposure, distress, excess, gêne, humiliation, mess, mortification, overabundance, pickle, predicament, scrape, self-consciousness, shame, superabundance, superfluity, surfeit, surplus.

embassy *n* consulate, delegation, deputation, embassade, embassage, legation, mission.

embed *v* fix, imbed, implant, insert, plant, root, set, sink.

embellish *v* adorn, beautify, bedeck, deck, decorate, dress up, elaborate, embroider, enhance, enrich, exaggerate, festoon, garnish, gild, grace, ornament, trim, varnish.

antonyms denude, simplify.

embellishment *n* adornment, decoration, elaboration, embroidery, enhancement, enrichment, exaggeration, fioritura, garnish, gilding, melisma, ornament, ornamentation, trimming, vignette.

embers *n* ashes, cinders.

embezzle *v* abstract, appropriate, defalcate, filch, misapply, misappropriate, misuse, peculate, pilfer, pinch, purloin, steal, sting.

embezzlement *n* abstraction, appropriation, defalcation, filching, fraud, larceny, misapplication, misappropriation, misuse, peculation, pilferage, pilfering, purloining, stealing, sting, theft, thieving.

embezzler *n* cheat, defalcator, fraud, peculator, thief.

embitter *v* acerbate, aggravate, alienate, anger, disaffect, disillusion, empoison, envenom, exacerbate, exasperate, poison, sour, worsen.

antonym pacify.

embittered *adj* bitter, disaffected, disillusioned, empoisoned, sour, soured.

antonym pacified.

emblazon *v* adorn, blazon, colour, decorate, depict, embellish, extol, glorify, illuminate, laud, ornament, paint, praise, proclaim, publicise, publish, trumpet.

emblem *n* badge, crest, device, figure, ichthys, image, insignia, mark, representation, sigil, sign, symbol, token, type.

emblematic *adj* emblematical, figurative, representative, representing, symbolic, symbolical.

embodiment *n* codification, collection, combination, comprehension, concentration, consolidation, example, exemplar, exemplification, expression, incarnation, inclusion, incorporation, integration, manifestation, organisation, personification, realisation, reification, representation, symbol, systematisation, type.

embody *v* codify, collect, combine, comprehend, comprise, concentrate, concretise, consolidate, contain, encarnalise, exemplify, express, incarnate, include, incorporate, integrate, manifest, organise, personify, realise, reify, represent, stand for, symbolise, systematise, typify.

embolden *v* animate, cheer, encourage, enhearten, fire, hearten, inflame, inspire, inspirit, invigorate, nerve, reassure, rouse, stimulate, stir, strengthen, vitalise.

antonym dishearten.

embrace *v* accept, canoodle, clasp, complect, comprehend, comprise, contain, cover, cuddle, dally, embody, embosom, encircle, enclose, encompass, enfold, enlace, espouse, grab, grasp, halse, hold, hug, inarm, include, incorporate, involve, neck, receive, seize, snog, squeeze, subsume, take up, welcome.

n abrazo, accolade, clasp, clinch, cuddle, hug, squeeze.

embrocation *n* cream, epithem, lotion, ointment, salve.

embroglio *see* **imbroglio**.

embroidery *n* fancywork, needle-point, needlework, sewing, tapestry, tatting.

embroil *v* confound, confuse, distract, disturb, encumber, enmesh, ensnare, entangle, implicate, incriminate, involve, mire, mix up, muddle, perplex, trouble.

embryo *n* beginning, embryon, germ, nucleus, root, rudiment.

embryonic *adj* beginning, early, germinal, immature, inchoate, incipient, primary, rudimentary, seminal, underdeveloped.

antonyms advanced, developed.

emend *v* alter, amend, correct, edit, improve, rectify, redact, revise, rewrite.

emendation *n* alteration, amendment, correction, corrigendum, editing, improvement, rectification, redaction, revision.

emerge *v* appear, arise, crop up, debouch, develop, eclose, emanate, issue, materialise, proceed, rise, surface, transpire, turn up.

antonyms disappear, fade.

emergence *n* advent, apparition, appearance, arrival, coming, dawn, development, disclosure, eclosion, emanation, emersion, issue, materialisation, rise.

antonyms decline, disappearance.

emergency *n* crisis, crunch, danger, difficulty, exigency, extremity, necessity, pass, pinch, plight, predicament, quandary, scrape, strait.

adj alternative, back-up, extra, fall-back, reserve, spare, substitute.

emergent *adj* budding, coming, developing, emerging, independent, rising.

antonyms declining, disappearing.

emetic *adj* emetical, vomitive, vomitory.

n vomit, vomitary, vomitive.

emigration *n* departure, exodus, journey, migration, removal.

eminence *n* celebrity, dignity, distinction, elevation, esteem, fame, greatness, height, hill, hillock, illustriousness, importance, knob, knoll, notability, note, peak, pre-eminence, prestige, prominence, rank, renown, reputation, repute, ridge, rise, summit, superiority.

eminent *adj* august, celebrated, conspicuous, distinguished, elevated, esteemed, exalted, famous, grand, great, high, high-ranking, illustrious, important, notable, noted, noteworthy, outstanding, paramount, pre-eminent, prestigious, prominent, renowned, reputable, respected, revered, signal, superior, well-known.

antonyms unimportant, unknown.

eminently *adv* conspicuously, exceedingly, exceptionally, extremely, greatly, highly, notably, outstandingly, par excellence, prominently, remarkably, signally, strikingly, surpassingly.

emissary *n* agent, ambassador, courier, delegate, deputy, envoy, herald, legate, messenger, nuncio, plenipotentiary, representative, scout, spy.

emission *n* diffusion, discharge, ejaculation, ejection, emanation, exhalation, exudation, issuance, issue, mephitis, radiation, release, shedding, transmission, utterance, vent, venting.

emit *v* diffuse, discharge, eject, emanate, exhale, exude, give off, give out, issue, radiate, shed, vent.

antonym absorb.

emollient *adj* assuaging, assuasive, balsamic, demulcent, lenitive, mitigative, mollifying, softening, soothing.

n balm, cream, lenitive, liniment, lotion, moisturiser, oil, ointment, poultice, salve, unguent.

emolument *n* allowance, benefit, compensation, earnings, fee, gain, hire, honorarium, pay, payment, profits, recompense, remuneration, return, reward, salary, stipend, wages.

emotion *n* affect, agitation, ardour, excitement, feeling, fervour, passion, perturbation, reaction, sensation, sentiment, vehemence, warmth.

emotional *adj* affecting, ardent, demonstrative, emotive, enthusiastic, excitable, exciting, feeling, fervent, fervid, fiery, heart-warming, heated, hot-blooded, impassioned, moved, moving, overcharged, passionate, pathetic, poignant, responsive, roused, sensitive, sentimental, stirred, stirring, susceptible, tear-jerking, temperamental, tempestuous, tender, thrilling, touching, volcanic, warm, zealous.

antonyms calm, cold, detached, emotionless, unemotional.

emotionless *adj* blank, cold, cold-blooded, cool, detached, distant, frigid, glacial, impassive, imperturbable, indifferent, phlegmatic, remote, toneless, undemonstrative, unemotional, unfeeling.

antonym emotional.

emotive *adj* affecting, ardent, controversial, delicate, emotional, enthusiastic, exciting, fervent, fervid, fiery, heart-warming, heated, impassioned, inflammatory, moving, passionate, pathetic, poignant, roused, sensitive, sentimental, stirred, stirring, tear-jerking, thrilling, touching, touchy, zealous.

emperor *n* imperator, kaiser, mikado, ruler, shogun, sovereign, tsar.

emphasis *n* accent, accentuation, attention, force, import, importance, impressiveness, insistence, intensity, mark, moment, positiveness, power, pre-eminence, priority, prominence, significance, strength, stress, underscoring, urgency, weight.

emphasise *v* accent, accentuate, dwell on, feature, highlight, insist on, intensify, play up, point up, press home, punctuate, spotlight, strengthen, stress, underline, underscore, weight.

antonyms depreciate, play down, understate.

emphatic *adj* absolute, categorical, certain, decided, definite, direct, distinct, earnest, energetic, forceful, forcible, graphic, important, impressive, insistent, marked, momentous, positive, powerful, pronounced, punctuated, resounding, significant, striking, strong, telling, trenchant, unequivocal, unmistakable, vigorous, vivid.

antonyms quiet, understated, unemphatic.

empire *n* authority, bailiwick, command, commonwealth, control, domain, dominion, government, imperium, jurisdiction, kingdom, power, realm, rule, sovereignty, supremacy, sway, territory.

empirical *adj* empiric, experiential, experimental, observed, practical, pragmatic.

antonyms conjectural, speculative, theoretical.

employ *v* apply, apprentice, bring to bear, commission, engage, enlist, exercise, exert, fill, hire, indent(ure), occupy, ply, retain, spend, take on, take up, use, utilise.

n employment, hire, pay, service.

employed *adj* active, busy, earning, engaged, hired, occupied, working.

antonym unemployed.

employee *n* hand, job-holder, member of staff, staffer, wage-earner, worker, workman.

employer *n* boss, business, company, establishment, firm, gaffer, organisation, outfit, owner, padrone, patron, proprietor, taskmaster, workmaster, workmistress.

employment *n* application, avocation, business, calling, craft, employ, engagement, enlistment, errand, exercise, exercitation, exertion, hire, job, line, métier, occupation, profession, pursuit, service, trade, use, utilisation, vocation, work.

antonym unemployment.

emporium *n* bazaar, establishment, market, mart, shop, store.

empower *v* accredit, allow, authorise, commission, delegate, enable, enfranchise, entitle, license, permit, qualify, sanction, warrant.

emptiness *n* absentness, aimlessness, banality, bareness, barrenness, blankness, cheapness, desertedness, desire, desolation, destitution, expressionlessness, frivolity, futility, hollowness, hunger, idleness, inanity, ineffectiveness, insincerity, insubstantiality, meaninglessness, purposelessness, ravening, senselessness, silliness, triviality, trivialness, unreality, unsatisfactoriness, vacancy, vacantness, vacuity, vacuousness, vacuum, vainness, valuelessness, vanity, void, waste, worthlessness.

antonym fullness.

empty *adj* absent, aimless, banal, bare, blank, bootless, cheap, clear, deserted, desolate, destitute, expressionless, famished, frivolous, fruitless, futile, hollow, hungry, idle, inane, ineffective, insincere, insubstantial, meaningless, purposeless, ravenous, senseless, silly, starving, superficial, trivial, unfed, unfilled, unfrequented, unfurnished, uninhabited, unintelligent, unoccupied, unreal, unsatisfactory, unsubstantial, untenanted, vacant, vacuous, vain, valueless, viduous, void, waste, worthless.

antonyms filled, full, replete.

v clear, consume, deplete, discharge, drain, dump, evacuate, exhaust, gut, lade, pour out, unburden, unload, vacate, void.

antonym fill.

empty-headed *adj* batty, brainless, dizzy, dotty, flighty, frivolous, giddy, hare-brained, inane, scatter-brained, scatty, silly, skittish, vacuous.

emulate *v* challenge, compete with, contend with, copy, echo, follow, imitate, match, mimic, rival, vie with.

emulation *n* challenge, competition, contention, contest, copying, echoing, envy, following, imitation, jealousy, matching, mimicry, rivalry, strife.

en masse all at once, all together, as a group, as a whole, as one, en bloc, ensemble, in a body, together, wholesale.

enable *v* accredit, allow, authorise, capacitate, commission, empower, endue, equip, facilitate, fit, license, permit, prepare, qualify, sanction, warrant.

antonyms inhibit, prevent.

enact *v* act (out), authorise, command, decree, depict, establish, impersonate, legislate, ordain, order, pass, perform, personate, play, portray, proclaim, ratify, represent, sanction.

antonym repeal.

enactment *n* acting, authorisation, command, commandment, decree, depiction, dictate, edict, impersonation, law, legislation, order, ordinance, performance, personation, play-acting, playing, portrayal, proclamation, ratification, regulation, representation, statute.

antonym repeal.

enamoured *adj* besotted, bewitched, captivated, charmed, enchanted, enraptured, entranced, fascinated, fond, infatuated, smitten, taken.

encampment *n* base, bivouac, camp, camping-ground, campsite, cantonment, duar, hutment, quarters, tents.

encapsulate *v* abridge, capture, compress, condense, digest, epitomise, exemplify, incapsulate, précis, represent, sum up, summarise, typify.

enchant *v* becharm, beguile, bewitch, captivate, charm, delight, enamour, enrapture, enravish, ensorcell, enthral, fascinate, hypnotise, mesmerise, spellbind.

antonyms bore, disenchant.

enchanter *n* conjurer, magician, magus, mesmerist, necromancer, reim-kennar, sorcerer, spellbinder, warlock, witch, wizard.

enchanting *adj* alluring, appealing, attractive, bewitching, captivating, charming, delightful, endearing, entrancing, fascinating, lovely, mesmerising, pleasant, ravishing, winsome, wonderful.

antonyms boring, repellent.

enchantment *n* allure, allurement, beguilement, bliss, charm, conjuration, delight, fascination, glamour, gramary(e), hypnotism, incantation, magic, mesmerism, necromancy, rapture, ravishment, sorcery, spell, transport, witchcraft, wizardry.

antonym disenchantment.

enchantress *n* charmer, Circe, conjurer, femme fatale, lamia, magician, necromancer, reim-kennar, seductress, siren, sorceress, spellbinder, vamp, witch.

encircle *v* begird, circle, circumscribe, compass, enclose, encompass, enfold, engird, engirdle, enlace, enring, envelop, environ, enwreathe, gird, girdle, hem in, ring, surround.

enclose *v* bound, circumscribe, compass, comprehend, confine, contain, cover, embale, embosom, embrace, encase, encircle, encompass, enlock, environ, fence, hedge, hem in, hold, inclose, include, incorporate, insert, pen, shut in, wall in, wrap.

enclosed *adj* bound, caged, cocooned, confined, contained, corralled, encased, encircled, encompassed, ensheathed, immured, imprisoned, included, sacculated, surrounded.

antonyms open, unenclosed.

enclosure *n* arena, bawn, boma, cloister, compound, corral, court, encasement, enceinte, fold, haining, hope, kraal, paddock, pen, pightle, pinfold, pound, ring, sept, seraglio, stockade, sty.

encompass *v* admit, begird, bring about, cause, circle, circumscribe, comprehend, comprise, contain, contrive, cover, devise, effect, embody, embrace, encircle, enclose, envelop, environ, girdle, hem in, hold, include, incorporate, involve, manage, ring, subsume, surround.

encounter *v* chance upon, clash with, combat, come upon, confront, contend, cross swords with, engage, experience, face, fight, grapple with, happen on, meet, rencontre, rencounter, run across, run into, strive, struggle.

n action, battle, brush, clash, collision, combat, conflict, confrontation, contest, dispute, engagement, fight, meeting, rencontre, rencounter, run-in, set-to, skirmish.

encourage *v* abet, advance, advocate, aid, animate, boost, buoy up, cheer, comfort, console, egg on, embolden, embrave, favour, forward, foster, further, hearten, help, incite, inspire, inspirit, promote, rally, reassure, rouse, second, spirit, spur, stimulate, strengthen, succour, support, urge.

antonyms depress, discourage, dissuade.

encouragement *n* advocacy, aid, boost, cheer, come-on, consolation, favour, help, hortation, incentive, incitement, inspiration, promotion, reassurance, stimulation, stimulus, succour, support, urging.

antonyms disapproval, discouragement.

encouraging *adj* auspicious, bright, cheerful, cheering, cohortative, comforting, heartening, hopeful, hortatory, incentive, proceleusmatic, promising, protreptic, reassuring, rosy, satisfactory, stimulating, uplifting.

antonym discouraging.

encroach *v* appropriate, arrogate, impinge, infringe, intrude, invade, make inroads, muscle in, obtrude, overstep, trench, trespass, usurp.

encroachment *n* appropriation, arrogation, impingement, incursion, infringement, inroad, intrusion, invasion, obtrusion, trespass, usurpation, violation.

encumber *v* burden, clog, cramp, cumber, embarrass, hamper, handicap, hinder, impede, incommode, inconvenience, lumber, obstruct, oppress, overload, retard, saddle, slow down, trammel, weigh down.

encumbrance *n* burden, clog, cumbrance, difficulty, drag, embarrassment, handicap, hindrance, impediment, inconvenience, liability, load, lumber, millstone, obstacle, obstruction, onus.

antonym aid.

encyclopaedic *adj* all-embracing, all-encompassing, all-inclusive, broad, compendious, complete, comprehensive, exhaustive, thorough, universal, vast, wide-ranging.

antonyms incomplete, narrow.

end *n* aim, annihilation, aspiration, attainment, bit, bound, boundary, butt, cessation, close, closure, completion, conclusion, consequence, consummation, culmination, curtain, death, demise, dénouement, design, destruction, dissolution, doom, downfall, drift, edge, ending, expiration, expiry, extent, extermination, extinction, extreme, extremity, finale, fine, finis, finish, fragment, goal, intent, intention, issue, left-over, limit, object, objective, outcome, part, pay-off, piece, point, portion, purpose, reason, remainder, remnant, resolution, responsibility, result, ruin, ruination, scrap, share, side, stop, stub, telos, termination, terminus, tip, upshot, wind-up.

antonyms beginning, opening, start.

v abate, abolish, annihilate, cease, close, complete, conclude, culminate, destroy, dissolve, expire, exterminate, extinguish, fetch up, finish, resolve, ruin, sopite, stop, terminate, wind up.

antonyms begin, start.

endanger *v* compromise, expose, hazard, imperil, jeopardise, risk, threaten.

antonyms protect, shelter, shield.

endearing *adj* adorable, attractive, captivating, charming, delightful, enchanting, engaging, lovable, sweet, winning, winsome.

endearment *n* affection, attachment, diminutive, fondness, hypocorisma, love, pet-name, sweet nothing.

endeavour *n* aim, attempt, conatus, crack, effort, enterprise, essay, go, nisus, shot, stab, trial, try, undertaking, venture.

v aim, aspire, attempt, essay, labour, strive, struggle, take pains, try, undertake, venture.

ending *n* catastrophe, cessation, climax, close, completion, conclusion, consummation, culmination, dénouement, desinence, end, epilogue, finale, finish, resolution, termination, wind-up.

antonyms beginning, start.

endless *adj* boundless, ceaseless, constant, continual, continuous, eternal, everlasting, immortal, incessant, infinite, interminable, interminate, limitless, measureless, monotonous, overlong, perpetual, Sisyphean, termless, unbounded, unbroken, undivided, undying, unending, uninterrupted, unlimited, whole.

endorse *v* adopt, advocate, affirm, approve, authorise, back, champion, confirm, countenance, countersign, favour, indorse, ratify, recommend, sanction, sign, subscribe to, superscribe, support, sustain, undersign, vouch for, warrant.

antonyms denounce, disapprove.

endorsement *n* advocacy, affirmation, approbation, approval, authorisation, backing, championship, commendation, comment, confirmation, corroboration, countersignature, favour, fiat, indorsement, OK, qualification, ratification, recommendation, sanction, seal of approval, signature, superscription, support, testimonial, warrant.

antonyms denouncement, disapproval.

endow *v* award, bequeath, bestow, confer, donate, dower, endue, enrich, favour, finance, fund, furnish, give, grant, invest, leave, make over, present, provide, settle on, supply, will.

antonym divest.

endowment *n* ability, aptitude, attribute, award, benefaction, bequest, bestowal, boon, capability, capacity, donation, dotation, dowry, faculty, flair, fund, genius, gift, grant, income, largesse, legacy, power, presentation, property, provision, qualification, quality, revenue, talent.

endurable *adj* bearable, sufferable, supportable, sustainable, tolerable.

antonyms intolerable, unbearable.

endurance *n* bearing, continuation, continuity, durability, fortitude, immutability, lastingness, longevity, patience, permanence, perseverance, persistence, pertinacity, resignation, resolution, stability, stamina, staying power, strength, submission, sufferance, sustainment, sustenance, tenacity, toleration.

endure *v* abear, abide, aby(e), allow, bear, brave, brook, continue, cope with, countenance, digest, dree, experience, go through, hold, last, live, perdure, permit, persist, prevail, put up with, remain, stand, stay, stick, stomach, submit to, suffer, support, survive, sustain, swallow, thole, tolerate, undergo, weather, withstand.

antonyms cease, end.

enduring *adj* abiding, continuing, durable, eternal, firm, immortal, imperishable, lasting, living, long(a)evous, long-lasting, perennial, permanent, persistent, persisting, prevailing, remaining, steadfast, steady, surviving, unfaltering, unwavering.

antonyms changeable, fleeting.

enemy *n* adversary, antagonist, competitor, foe, foeman, opponent, opposer, Philistine, rival, the opposition.

antonyms ally, friend.

energetic *adj* active, animated, brisk, dynamic, forceful, forcible, high-powered, indefatigable, lively, pithy, potent, powerful, spirited, strenuous, strong, throughgoing, tireless, vigorous, zippy.

antonyms idle, inactive, lazy, sluggish.

energise *v* activate, animate, electrify, enliven, galvanise, inspirit, invigorate, liven, motivate, pep up, quicken, stimulate, vitalise, vivify.

antonym daunt.

energy *n* activity, animation, ardour, brio, drive, efficiency, élan, exertion, fire, force, forcefulness, get-up-and-go, intensity, inworking, jism, juice, life, liveliness, pluck, power, spirit, stamina, steam, strength, strenuousness, verve, vigour, vim, vitality, vivacity, vroom, zeal, zest, zip.

antonyms inertia, lethargy, weakness.

enervate *v* debilitate, deplete, devitalise, enfeeble, exhaust, fatigue, incapacitate, paralyse, prostrate, sap, tire, unman, unnerve, weaken, wear out.

antonyms activate, energise.

enervated *adj* debilitated, depleted, devitalised, done in, effete, enervate, enfeebled, exhausted, fatigued, feeble, incapacitated, limp, paralysed, prostrate, prostrated, run-down, sapped, spent, tired, undermined, unmanned, unnerved, washed out, weak, weakened, worn out.

antonyms active, energetic.

enervation *n* debilitation, debility, depletion, effeteness, enfeeblement, exhaustedness, exhaustion, fatigue, feebleness, impotence, incapacity, infirmity, lassitude, paralysis, powerlessness, prostration, tiredness, unmanning, weakening, weakness.

enfeeble *v* debilitate, deplete, devitalise, diminish, enervate, exhaust, fatigue, geld, reduce, sap, undermine, unhinge, unnerve, weaken, wear out.

antonym strengthen.

enfold *v* clasp, embrace, encircle, enclose, encompass, envelop, enwrap, fold, hold, hug, shroud, swathe, wimple, wrap (up).

enforce *v* administer, apply, carry out, coact, coerce, compel, constrain, discharge, exact, execute, implement, impose, insist on, oblige, prosecute, reinforce, require, urge.

enforced *adj* binding, compelled, compulsory, constrained, dictated, imposed, involuntary, necessary, ordained, prescribed, required, unavoidable.

enforcement *n* administration, application, coaction, coercion, compulsion, constraint, execution, implementation, imposition, insistence, obligation, pressure, prosecution, requirement.

enfranchise *v* affranchise, emancipate, free, liberate, manumit, release.

antonym disenfranchise.

enfranchisement *n* affranchisement, emancipation, freedom, freeing, liberating, liberation, manumission, release, suffrage.

antonym disenfranchisement.

engage *v* absorb, activate, affiance, agree, allure, apply, appoint, arrest, assail, attach, attack, attract, bespeak, betroth, bind, book, busy, captivate, catch, charm, charter, combat, commission, commit, contract, covenant, draw, embark, employ, enamour, enchant, encounter, energise, engross, enlist, enrol, enter, fascinate, fit, fix, gain, grip, guarantee, hire, interact, interconnect, interlock, involve, join, lease, meet, mesh, obligate, oblige, occupy, operate, partake, participate, pledge, practise, prearrange, preoccupy, promise, rent, reserve, retain, secure, take on, tie up, undertake, vouch, vow, win.

antonyms discharge, disengage, dismiss.

engaged *adj* absorbed, affianced, betrothed, busy, committed, employed, engrossed, immersed, involved, occupied, pledged, preoccupied, promised, spoken for, tied up, unavailable.

engagement *n* action, affiance, appointment, arrangement, assurance, battle, betrothal, bond, combat, commission, commitment, compact, conflict, confrontation, contest, contract, date, employment, encounter, fight, gig, job, meeting, oath, obligation, pact, pledge, post, promise, situation, stint, subarr(h)ation, troth, undertaking, vow, word, work.

antonym disengagement.

engaging *adj* agreeable, appealing, attractive, beguiling, captivating, charming, enchanting, fascinating, fetching, lik(e)able, lovable, pleasant, pleasing, prepossessing, winning, winsome.

antonyms boring, loathsome.

engender *v* beget, breed, bring about, cause, create, encourage, excite, father, foment, generate, give rise to, hatch, incite, induce, instigate, lead to, make, nurture, occasion, precipitate, procreate, produce, propagate, provoke, sire, spawn.

engine *n* agency, agent, apparatus, appliance, contraption, contrivance, device, dynamo, implement, instrument, machine, means, mechanism, motor, tool, turbine, weapon.

engineer *n* architect, contriver, designer, deviser, driver, inventor, operator, originator, planner.

v cause, concoct, contrive, control, create, devise, effect, encompass, finagle, machinate, manage, manipulate, manoeuvre, mastermind, originate, plan, plot, scheme, wangle.

engrave *v* blaze, carve, chase, chisel, cut, embed, enchase, etch, fix, grave, impress, imprint, infix, ingrain, inscribe, lodge, mark, print.

engraved *adj* carved, chased, chiselled, cut, enchased, etched, graven, imprinted, incised, intagliated, marked, printed.

engraving *n* blaze, block, carving, chasing, chiselling, cutting, dendroglyph, dry-point, enchasing, etching, impression, inscribing, inscription, lithoglyph, mark, plate, print, woodcut.

engross *v* absorb, arrest, corner, engage, engulf, fixate, hold, immerse, involve, monopolise, occupy, preoccupy, rivet.

engrossed *adj* absorbed, captivated, caught up, enthralled, fascinated, fixated, gripped, immersed, intent, intrigued, lost, preoccupied, rapt, riveted, taken.

antonyms bored, disinterested.

engrossing *adj* absorbing, captivating, compelling, enthralling, fascinating, gripping, interesting, intriguing, riveting, suspenseful, taking, unputdownable.

antonym boring.

engulf *v* absorb, bury, consume, deluge, drown, encompass, engross, envelop, flood, immerse, ingulf, inundate, overrun, overwhelm, plunge, submerge, swallow up, swamp.

enhance *v* amplify, augment, boost, complement, deodorise, elevate, embellish, escalate, exalt, heighten, improve, increase, intensify, lift, magnify, raise, reinforce, strengthen, swell.

antonyms decrease, minimise.

enigma *n* brain-teaser, conundrum, mystery, poser, problem, puzzle, riddle.

enigmatic *adj* ambiguous, cryptic, Delphic, doubtful, enigmatical, equivocal, impenetrable, incomprehensible, indecipherable, inexplicable, inscrutable, mysterious, obscure, perplexing, puzzling, recondite, riddling, strange, uncertain, unfathomable, unintelligible.

antonyms simple, straightforward.

enjoin *v* advise, ban, bar, bid, call upon, charge, command, comply, counsel, demand, direct, disallow, forbid, instruct, interdict, obey, order, preclude, prescribe, prohibit, proscribe, require, restrain, urge, warn.

enjoy *v* appreciate, delight in, dig, experience, have, like, make a meal of, own, possess, rejoice in, relish, revel in, savour, take pleasure in, use.

antonyms abhor, detest.

enjoy oneself have a ball, have a good time, have fun, make merry, party.

enjoyable *adj* agreeable, amusing, delectable, delicious, delightful, entertaining, fun, good, gratifying, pleasant, pleasing, pleasurable, satisfying.

antonyms disagreeable, unpleasant.

enjoyment *n* advantage, amusement, benefit, comfort, delectation, delight, diversion, ease, entertainment, exercise, fun, gaiety, gladness, gratification, gusto, happiness, indulgence, jollity, joy, ownership, pleasure, possession, recreation, relish, satisfaction, use, zest.

antonyms displeasure, dissatisfaction.

enlarge *v* add to, amplify, augment, blow up, broaden, descant, develop, diffuse, dilate, distend, elaborate, elongate, expand, expatiate, extend, greaten, grow, heighten, increase, inflate, intumesce, jumboise, lengthen, magnify, multiply, stretch, swell, wax, widen.

antonyms decrease, diminish, shrink.

enlargement *n* ampliation, amplification, aneurysm, augmentation, blow-up, dilation, distension, emphysema, expansion, extension, growth, increase, increment, intumescence, magnification, oedema, protuberation, supplementation, swelling.

antonyms contraction, decrease.

enlighten *v* advise, apprise, civilise, counsel, edify, educate, illuminate, indoctrinate, inform, instruct, teach, undeceive.

antonyms confuse, puzzle.

enlightened *adj* aware, broad-minded, civilised, conversant, cultivated, educated, informed, knowledgeable, liberal, literate, open-minded, reasonable, refined, sophisticated, verligte, wise.

antonyms confused, ignorant.

enlightenment *n* awareness, broad-mindedness, civilisation, comprehension, cultivation, edification, education, erudition, information, insight, instruction, knowledge, learning, literacy, open-mindedness, refinement, sapience, sophistication, teaching, understanding, wisdom.

antonyms confusion, ignorance.

enlist *v* conscript, employ, engage, enrol, enter, gather, join (up), muster, obtain, procure, recruit, register, secure, sign up, volunteer.

enliven *v* animate, brighten, buoy up, cheer (up), excite, exhilarate, fire, gladden, hearten, inspire, inspirit, invigorate, juice up, kindle, liven (up), pep up, perk up, quicken, rouse, spark, stimulate, vitalise, vivify, wake up.

antonym subdue.

enmity *n* acrimony, animosity, animus, antagonism, antipathy, aversion, bad blood, bitterness, feud, hate, hatred, hostility, ill-will, invidiousness, malevolence, malice, malignity, rancour, spite, venom.

antonyms amity, friendship.

ennoble *v* aggrandise, dignify, elevate, enhance, exalt, gentle, glorify, honour, magnify, nobilitate, raise.

ennoblement *n* aggrandisement, dignification, elevation, exaltation, glorification, lionisation, magnification, nobilitation.

ennui *n* accidie, acedia, boredom, dissatisfaction, lassitude, listlessness, tedium, the doldrums.

enormity *n* abomination, atrociousness, atrocity, crime, depravity, disgrace, evil, evilness, flagitiousness, heinousness, horror, iniquity, monstrosity, monstrousness, nefariousness, outrage, outrageousness, turpitude, viciousness, vileness, villainy, wickedness.

antonyms triviality, unimportance.

enormous *adj* abominable, astronomic(al), atrocious, Brobdingnagian, colossal, cyclopean, depraved, disgraceful, evil, excessive, gargantuan, gigantic, gross, heinous, herculean, huge, hulking, immense, jumbo, leviathan, mammoth, massive, monstrous, mountainous, nefarious, odious, outrageous, prodigious, titanic, tremendous, vast, vasty, vicious, vile, villainous, wicked.

antonyms small, tiny.

enough *adj* abundant, adequate, ample, enow, plenty, sufficient.

n abundance, adequacy, plenitude, plenty, repletion, sufficiency.

adv abundantly, adequately, amply, aplenty, enow, fairly, moderately, passably, reasonably, satisfactorily, sufficiently, tolerably.

enquire, inquire *v* ask, examine, explore, inspect, investigate, probe, query, question, quiz, scrutinise, search, speir.

enquiry, inquiry *n* examination, exploration, inquest, inspection, investigation, probe, query, quest, question, research, scrutiny, search, study, survey.

enrage *v* acerbate, aggravate, anger, exasperate, incense, incite, inflame, infuriate, irritate, madden, make someone's hackles rise, provoke.

antonyms calm, placate, soothe.

enraged *adj* aggravated, angered, angry, exasperated, fizzing, fuming, furious, incensed, inflamed, infuriated, irate, irritated, livid, mad, raging, storming, wild.

antonym calm.

enrapture *v* beguile, bewitch, captivate, charm, delight, enchant, enravish, enthrall, entrance, fascinate, ravish, spellbind, thrill, transport.

enrich *v* adorn, aggrandise, ameliorate, augment, cultivate, decorate, develop, embellish, endow, enhance, fortify, grace, improve, ornament, prosper, refine, supplement.

antonym impoverish.

enrol *v* accept, admit, chronicle, empanel, engage, enlist, enregister, inscribe, join up, list, matriculate, note, record, recruit, register, sign on, sign up, take on.

antonyms leave, reject.

enrolment *n* acceptance, admission, empanelment, engagement, enlistment, matriculation, recruitment, register, registration.

ensconce *v* entrench, establish, install, locate, lodge, nestle, place, protect, put, screen, settle, shelter, shield.

ensemble *n* aggregate, assemblage, band, case, chorus, collection, company, corps de ballet, costume, entirety, get-up, group, outfit, rig-out, set, suit, sum, total, totality, troupe, whole.

enshrine *v* apotheosise, cherish, consecrate, dedicate, embalm, exalt, hallow, idolise, preserve, revere, sanctify, treasure.

enshroud *v* cloak, cloud, conceal, cover, enclose, enfold, envelop, enwrap, enwreathe, hide, obscure, pall, shroud, veil, wrap.

ensign *n* badge, banner, colours, flag, gonfalon, jack, oriflamme, pennant, pennon, standard, streamer.

enslave *v* bind, conquer, dominate, enchain, enthrall, overcome, subject, subjugate, yoke.

antonyms emancipate, free.

enslavement *n* bondage, captivity, dulosis, duress, enthralment, oppression, repression, serfdom, servitude, slavery, subjection, subjugation, thraldom, vassalage.

antonym emancipation.

ensnare *v* catch, embroil, enmesh, entangle, entrap, gin, illaqueate, net, snare, snarl, trap, trepan.

ensue *v* arise, attend, befall, derive, eventuate, flow, follow, happen, issue, proceed, result, stem, succeed, supervene, turn out, turn up.

antonym precede.

ensure *v* certify, clinch, confirm, effect, guarantee, guard, insure, protect, safeguard, secure, warrant.

entail *v* cause, demand, encompass, give rise to, impose, involve, lead to, necessitate, occasion, predetermine, require, result in.

entangle *v* ball, bewilder, catch, complicate, compromise, confuse, embroil, enlace, enmesh, ensnare, entoil, entrap, foul, implicate, involve, jumble, knot, mat, mix up, muddle, perplex, puzzle, ravel, snag, snare, snarl, tangle, trammel, trap, twist.

antonym disentangle.

entanglement *n* complication, confusion, difficulty, embarrassment, ensnarement, entoilment, entrapment, imbroglio, involvement, jumble, knot, liaison, mesh, mess, mix-up, muddle, predicament, snare, snarl-up, tangle, tie, toils, trap.

antonym disentanglement.

entente *n* agreement, arrangement, compact, deal, entente cordiale, friendship, pact, treaty, understanding.

enter *v* arrive, begin, board, commence, embark upon, enlist, enrol, inscribe, insert, introduce, join, list, log, note, offer, participate, participate in, penetrate, pierce, present, proffer, record, register, set about, set down, sign up, start, submit, take down, take up, tender.

antonyms delete, issue, leave.

enterprise *n* activity, adventure, adventurousness, alertness, audacity, boldness, business, company, concern, daring, dash, drive, eagerness, effort, emprise, endeavour, energy, enthusiasm, essay, establishment, firm, get-up-and-go, gumption, imagination, initiative, operation, plan, programme, project, push, readiness, resource, resourcefulness, spirit, undertaking, venture, vigour, zeal.

antonyms apathy, inertia.

enterprising *adj* active, adventurous, alert, ambitious, aspiring, audacious, bold, daring, dashing, eager, energetic, enthusiastic, go-ahead, goey, imaginative, intrepid, keen, pushful, ready, resourceful, self-reliant, spirited, stirring, up-and-coming, venturesome, vigorous, zealous.

antonyms lethargic, unadventurous.

entertain *v* accommodate, accourt, amuse, charm, cheer, cherish, conceive, consider, contemplate, countenance, delight, divert, fête, foster, harbour, hold, imagine, lodge, maintain, occupy, please, ponder, put up, recreate, regale, support, treat.

antonyms bore, reject.

entertainer *n* artiste, diseur, diseuse, performer, troubadour, trouper.

entertaining *adj* amusing, charming, cheering, delightful, diverting, droll, fun, funny, humorous, interesting, pleasant, pleasing, pleasurable, recreative, witty.

antonym boring.

entertainment *n* amusement, cheer, distraction, diversion, enjoyment, extravaganza, fun, pastime, play, pleasure, recreation, satisfaction, show, spectacle, sport, table, treat.

enthral(l) *v* beguile, captivate, charm, enchant, enrapture, enravish, entrance, fascinate, grip, hypnotise, intrigue, mesmerise, rivet, spellbind, thrill.

antonyms bore, weary.

enthralling *adj* beguiling, captivating, charming, compelling, compulsive, enchanting, entrancing, fascinating, gripping, hypnotising, intriguing, mesmeric, mesmerising, riveting, spellbinding, thrilling.

antonym boring.

enthuse *v* absorb, drool, ecstasise, effervesce, emote, excite, gush, impassion, inflame, involve, possess, wax lyrical.

enthusiasm *n* ardour, avidity, craze, devotion, eagerness, earnestness, empressement, entraînement, estro, excitement, fad, fervour, frenzy, hobby, hobby-horse, interest, keenness, mania, oomph, passion, rage, relish, spirit, vehemence, warmth, zeal, zest.

antonym apathy.

enthusiast *n* addict, admirer, aficionado, buff, bug, devotee, eager beaver, fan, fanatic, fiend, follower, freak, lover, supporter, whole-hogger, zealot.

antonym detractor.

enthusiastic *adj* ardent, avid, devoted, eager, earnest, ebullient, empressé, excited, exuberant, fervent, fervid, forceful, gung-ho, hearty, keen, keen as mustard, lively, passionate, spirited, unstinting, vehement, vigorous, warm, wholehearted, zealous.

antonyms apathetic, reluctant, unenthusiastic.

entice *v* allure, attract, beguile, blandish, cajole, coax, decoy, draw, induce, inveigle, lead on, lure, persuade, prevail on, seduce, sweet-talk, tempt, wheedle.

enticement *n* allurement, attraction, bait, beguilement, blandishments, cajolery, coaxing, come-on, decoy, inducement, inveiglement, lure, persuasion, seduction, sweet-talk, temptation.

entire *adj* absolute, all-in, complete, continuous, full, intact, integrated, outright, perfect, sound, thorough, total, unabridged, unbroken, uncut, undamaged, undiminished, undivided, unified, unmarked, unmarred, unmitigated, unreserved, unrestricted, whole.

antonyms impaired, incomplete, partial.

entirely *adv* absolutely, altogether, completely, every inch, exclusively, fully, hook line and sinker, in toto, lock stock and barrel, only, perfectly, solely, thoroughly, totally, unreservedly, utterly, wholly, without exception, without reservation.

antonym partially.

entirety *n* absoluteness, aggregate, completeness, fullness, sum, total, totality, unity, universality, whole, wholeness.

antonyms element, incompleteness, part.

entitle *v* accredit, allow, authorise, call, christen, denominate, designate, dub, empower, enable, enfranchise, label, license, name, permit, style, term, title, warrant.

entity *n* being, body, creature, essence, existence, haecceity, individual, individuum, object, organism, presence, quantity, quiddity, quintessence, substance, thing.

entombment *n* burial, inhumation, interment, inurnment, sepulture.

entourage *n* associates, attendants, claque, companions, company, cortège, coterie, court, escort, followers, following, retainers, retinue, staff, suite, train.

entrails *n* bowels, entera, gralloch, guts, harigal(d)s, ha(r)slet, innards, insides, intestines, offal, umbles, viscera.

entrance[1] *n* access, admission, admittance, appearance, arrival, atrium, avenue, beginning, commencement, debut, door, doorway, entrée, entry, gate, ingress, initiation, inlet, introduction, opening, outset, passage, portal, start.

antonyms departure, exit.

entrance[2] *v* bewitch, captivate, charm, delight, enchant, enrapture, enravish, enthrall, fascinate, gladden, hypnotise, magnetise, mesmerise, ravish, spellbind, transport.

antonyms bore, repel.

entrant *n* beginner, candidate, competitor, contender, contestant, convert, entry, initiate, neophyte, newcomer, novice, participant, player, probationer, tyro.

entrap *v* allure, beguile, capture, catch, decoy, embroil, enmesh, ensnare, entangle, entice, gin, implicate, inveigle, involve, lure, net, seduce, snare, trap, trepan, trick.

entreat *v* appeal to, ask, beg, beseech, conjure, crave, enjoin, exhort, flagitate, implore, importune, invoke, petition, plead with, pray, request, sue, supplicate.

entreaty *n* appeal, entreatment, exhortation, importunity, invocation, petition, plea, prayer, request, solicitation, suing, suit, supplication.

entrench *v* anchor, dig in, embed, encroach, ensconce, establish, fix, fortify, impinge, infix, infringe, ingrain, install, interlope, intrench, intrude, lodge, plant, root, seat, set, settle, trespass.

antonym dislodge.

entrenched *adj* deep-rooted, deep-seated, firm, fixed, implanted, inbred, indelible, ineradicable, ingrained, rooted, set, unshakable, well-established.

entrepreneur *n* businessman, businesswoman, contractor, financier, impresario, industrialist, magnate, tycoon, undertaker.

entrust *v* assign, authorise, charge, commend, commit, confide, consign, delegate, deliver, depute, invest, trust, turn over.

entry[1] *n* access, admission, admittance, appearance, avenue, door, doorway, entering, entrance, entrée, gate, ingress, initiation, inlet, introduction, opening, passage, passageway, portal, threshold.

antonym exit.

entry[2] *n* account, attempt, bulletin, candidate, competitor, contestant, effort, entrant, item, jotting, listing, memo, memorandum, minute, note, participant, player, record, registration, statement, submission.

entwine *v* braid, embrace, encircle, enlace, entwist, interlace, interlink, intertwine, interweave, intwine, knit, plait, splice, surround, thatch, twine, twist, weave, wind.

antonym unravel.

enumerate *v* calculate, cite, count, detail, itemise, list, mention, name, number, quote, recapitulate, recite, reckon, recount, rehearse, relate, specify, spell out, tell.

enunciate *v* articulate, broadcast, declare, enounce, proclaim, promulgate, pronounce, propound, publish, say, sound, speak, state, utter, vocalise, voice.

envelop *v* blanket, cloak, conceal, cover, embrace, encase, encircle, enclose, encompass, enfold, engulf, enshroud, enwrap, enwreathe, hide, obscure, sheathe, shroud, surround, swaddle, swathe, veil, wrap.

envelope *n* case, casing, coating, cover, covering, integument, jacket, sheath, shell, skin, theca, wrapper, wrapping.

enviable *adj* advantageous, blessed, covetable, desirable, excellent, favoured, fine, fortunate, good, lucky, privileged.

antonym unenviable.

envious *adj* begrudging, covetous, dissatisfied, green, green with envy, green-eyed, grudging, jaundiced, jealous, malcontent, malicious, resentful, spiteful.

environment *n* ambience, atmosphere, background, conditions, context, domain, element, entourage, habitat, locale, medium, milieu, scene, setting, situation, surroundings, territory.

environmentalist *n* conservationist, doomwatcher, ecofreak, econut, green.

environs *n* circumjacencies, district, locality, neighbourhood, outskirts, precincts, purlieus, suburbs, surround(ing)s, vicinage, vicinity.

envisage *v* anticipate, conceive of, conceptualise, contemplate, envision, fancy, foresee, ideate, image, imagine, picture, preconceive, predict, see, visualise.

envoy *n* agent, ambassador, courier, delegate, deputy, diplomat, elchi, emissary, intermediary, legate, messenger, minister, nuncio, plenipotentiary, representative.

envy *n* covetousness, cupidity, dissatisfaction, enviousness, grudge, hatred, ill-will, jealousy, malice, malignity, resentfulness, resentment, spite.

v begrudge, covet, crave, grudge, resent.

enwrap *v* encase, enclose, enfold, enshroud, envelop, enwind, enwreathe, parcel, sheathe, sheet, shroud, swaddle, swathe, wimple, wind.

ephemeral *adj* brief, evanescent, fleeting, flitting, fugacious, fugitive, fungous, impermanent, momentary, passing, short, short-lived, temporary, transient, transitory.

antonyms enduring, lasting, perpetual.

epic *adj* colossal, elevated, exalted, grand, grandiloquent, great, heroic, Homeric, huge, imposing, impressive, lofty, majestic, sublime, vast.

antonym ordinary.

epicure *n* arbiter elegantiae, bon vivant, bon viveur, connoisseur, epicurean, gastronome, glutton, gourmand, gourmet, hedonist, sensualist, sybarite, voluptuary.

epicurean *adj* gluttonous, gourmandising, hedonistic, libertine, luscious, lush, luxurious, self-indulgent, sensual, sybaritic, unrestrained, voluptuous.

n bon vivant, bon viveur, epicure, gastronome, gourmet, hedonist, sensualist, voluptuary.

epidemic *adj* epizootic, general, pandemic, prevailing, prevalent, rampant, rife, sweeping, wide-ranging, widespread.

n growth, outbreak, pandemic, plague, rash, spread, upsurge, wave.

epigram *n* aphorism, apophthegm, bon mot, gnome, quip, witticism.

epigrammatic *adj* aphoristic, apophthegmatic, concise, gnomic, laconic, piquant, pithy, pointed, pungent, sharp, short, succinct, terse, witty.

epilogue *n* afterword, coda, conclusion, exode, postscript.

antonyms foreword, preface, prologue.

episode *n* adventure, affaire, business, chapter, circumstance, event, experience, happening, incident, instalment, matter, occasion, occurrence, part, passage, scene, section.

episodic *adj* anecdotal, digressive, disconnected, disjointed, episod(i)al, intermittent, irregular, occasional, picaresque, spasmodic, sporadic.

epistle *n* communication, encyclical, letter, line, message, missive, note.

epithet *n* appellation, denomination, description, designation, epitheton, name, nickname, so(u)briquet, tag, title.

epitome *n* abbreviation, abridgement, abstract, archetype, compendium, compression, condensation, conspectus, contraction, digest, embodiment, essence, exemplar, personification, préis, quintessence, reduction, representation, résumé, summary, syllabus, synopsis, type.

epitomise *v* abbreviate, abridge, abstract, compress, condense, contract, curtail, cut, embody, encapsulate, exemplify, illustrate, incarnate, personify, précis, reduce, represent, shorten, summarise, symbolise, typify.

antonyms elaborate, expand.

epoch *n* age, date, epocha, era, period, time.

equable *adj* agreeable, calm, composed, consistent, constant, easy-going, even, even-tempered, imperturbable, level-headed, phlegmatic, placid, regular, serene, smooth, stable, steady, temperate, tranquil, unchanging, unexcitable, unflappable, uniform, unruffled, unvarying, unworrying.

antonyms excitable, variable.

equal *adj* able, adequate, alike, balanced, capable, commensurate, competent, corresponding, egalitarian, equable, equivalent, even, even-handed, evenly-balanced, evenly-matched, evenly-proportioned, fair, fifty-fifty, fit, identical, impartial, just, level-pegging, like, matched, proportionate, ready, regular, sufficient, suitable, symmetrical, tantamount, the same, unbiased, uniform, unvarying, up to.

antonyms different, inequitable, unequal.

n brother, coequal, compeer, counterpart, equivalent, fellow, match, mate, parallel, peer, rival, twin.

v balance, commeasure, correspond to, equalise, equate, even, level, match, parallel, rival, square with, tally with.

equalise *v* balance, compensate, draw level, equal, equate, even up, level, match, regularise, smooth, square, standardise.

equality *n* balance, coequality, correspondence, egalitarianism, equitability, equivalence, evenness, fairness, identity, likeness, par, parity, proportion, sameness, similarity, uniformity.

antonym inequality.

equanimity *n* aplomb, calm, calmness, composure, coolness, equability, equableness, imperturbability, level-headedness, peace, phlegm, placidity, poise, presence of mind, sang-froid, self-possession, serenity, steadiness, tranquillity.

antonyms alarm, anxiety, discomposure.

equate *v* agree, balance, compare, correspond to, correspond with, equalise, juxtapose, liken, match, offset, pair, parallel, square, tally.

equation *n* agreement, balancing, bracketing, comparison, correspondence, equalisation, equality, equating, equivalence, juxtaposition, likeness, match, pairing, parallel.

equestrian *n* cavalier, horseman, knight, postilion, rider.

equilibrium *n* balance, calm, calmness, collectedness, composure, cool, coolness, counterpoise, equanimity, equipoise, equiponderance, evenness, poise, rest, self-possession, serenity, stability, steadiness, symmetry.

antonym imbalance.

equip *v* accoutre, arm, array, attire, bedight, deck out, dight, dress, endow, fit out, fit up, furnish, habilitate, kit out, outfit, prepare, provide, rig, stock, supply.

equipage *n* accoutrements, apparatus, baggage, carriage, coach, equipment, gear, impedimenta, material, munitions, outfit, retinue, stores, suite, train, traps, turn-out.

equipment *n* accessories, accoutrements, apparatus, appurtenances, baggage, equipage, furnishings, furniture, gear, graith, impedimenta, implements, material, matériel, muniments, outfit, paraphernalia, rig-out, stuff, supplies, tackle, things, tools, traps.

equipoise *n* balance, ballast, counterbalance, counterpoise, counter-weight, equibalance, equilibrium, equiponderance, evenness, offset, poise, stability, steadiness, symmetry.

antonym imbalance.

equitable *adj* disinterested, dispassionate, due, ethical, even-handed, fair, fair-and-square, honest, impartial, just, legitimate, objective, proper, proportionate, reasonable, right, rightful, square, unbiased, unprejudiced.

antonyms inequitable, unfair.

equitably *adv* disinterestedly, dispassionately, even-handedly, ex aequo, fairly, fairly and squarely, honestly, impartially, justly, objectively, properly, reasonably, rightly.

antonym inequitably.

equity *n* disinterestedness, equality, equitableness, even-handedness, fair play, fair-mindedness, fairness, honesty, impartiality, integrity, justice, justness, objectivity, reasonableness, rectitude, righteousness, uprightness.

antonym inequity.

equivalence *n* agreement, alikeness, conformity, correspondence, equality, evenness, homology, identity, interchangeability, interchangeableness, likeness, match, parallel, parity, sameness, similarity, substitutability, synonymy.

antonyms dissimilarity, inequality, unlikeness.

equivalent *adj* alike, commensurate, comparable, convertible, correlative, correspondent, corresponding, equal, equipollent, equipotent, even, homologous, homotypal, homotypic, interchangeable, same, similar, substitutable, synonymous, tantamount, twin.

antonyms dissimilar, unlike.

n correlative, correspondent, counterpart, equal, homologue, homotype, match, opposite number, parallel, peer, twin.

equivocal *adj* ambiguous, ambivalent, casuistical, confusing, Delphic, doubtful, dubious, evasive, indefinite, indeterminate, misleading, oblique, obscure, oracular, questionable, suspicious, uncertain, vague.

antonyms clear, unequivocal.

equivocate *v* dodge, evade, fence, fudge, hedge, mislead, palter, parry, prevaricate, pussyfoot, quibble, shift, shuffle, sidestep, tergiversate, weasel.

equivocation *n* ambiguity, casuistry, confusion, double talk, doubtfulness, equivocacy, equivocality, equivocalness, equivoke, evasion, hedging, prevarication, quibbling, shifting, shuffling, sophistry, tergiversation, waffle, weasel-words.

antonym directness.

era *n* aeon, age, century, cycle, date, day, days, epoch, generation, period, stage, time.

eradicable *adj* destroyable, destructible, effaceable, eliminable, erasable, exterminable, extinguishable, extirpable, removable, washable.

antonyms ineradicable, permanent.

eradicate *v* abolish, annihilate, deracinate, destroy, efface, eliminate, erase, expunge, exterminate, extinguish, extirpate, get rid of, obliterate, rase, remove, root out, stamp out, suppress, unroot, uproot, weed out.

eradication *n* abolition, annihilation, deracination, destruction, effacement, elimination, erasure, expunction, extermination, extinction, extirpation, obliteration, removal, riddance, suppression.

erasable *adj* effaceable, eradicable, removable, washable.

antonyms ineradicable, permanent.

erase *v* blot out, cancel, cleanse, delete, efface, eliminate, eradicate, expunge, get rid of, obliterate, remove, rub out.

erasure *n* cancellation, cleansing, deletion, effacement, elimination, eradication, erasement, expunction, obliteration, rasure, razure, removal.

erect *adj* elevated, engorged, firm, hard, perpendicular, pricked, raised, rigid, standing, stiff, straight, taut, tense, tumescent, upright, upstanding, vertical.

antonyms limp, relaxed.

v assemble, build, constitute, construct, create, elevate, establish, fabricate, form, found, initiate, institute, lift, mount, organise, pitch, put up, raise, rear, set up.

erection *n* assembly, building, construction, creation, edifice, elevation, establishment, fabrication, manufacture, pile, raising, rigidity, stiffness, structure, tumescence.

ergo *adv* accordingly, consequently, for this reason, hence, in consequence, so, then, therefore, this being the case, thus.

erode *v* abrade, consume, corrade, corrode, denude, destroy, deteriorate, disintegrate, eat away, grind down, spoil, wear away, wear down.

eroded *adj* abraded, attrite, corraded, denuded, destroyed, disintegrated, eaten away, fragmented, ground down, undermined, worn away.

erosion *n* abrasion, attrition, consumption, corrasion, corrosion, denudation, destruction, deterioration, diminishment, disintegration, fragmentation, undermining.

erosive *adj* caustic, corrosive, denuding, destructive, disruptive, erodent, gnawing, nibbling, undermining.

erotic *adj* amatorial, amatorious, amatory, amorous, aphrodisiac, carnal, concupiscent, erogenic, erogenous, erotogenic, erotogenous, libidinous, lustful, page-three, rousing, seductive, sensual, sexy, stimulating, suggestive, titillating, venereal, voluptuous.

err *v* blunder, deviate, fail, go astray, lapse, misapprehend, misbehave, miscalculate, misjudge, mistake, misunderstand, offend, sin, slip up, stray, stumble, transgress, trespass, trip up, wander.

errand *n* assignment, charge, commission, duty, job, message, mission, task.

errant *adj* aberrant, deviant, erring, itinerant, journeying, loose, nomadic, offending, peccant, peripatetic, rambling, roaming, roving, sinful, sinning, stray, straying, vagrant, wandering, wayward, wrong.

erratic *adj* aberrant, abnormal, capricious, changeable, desultory, directionless, eccentric, fitful, fluctuating, inconsistent, inconstant, irregular, meandering, planetary, shifting, unpredictable, unreliable, unstable, variable, wandering, wayward.

antonyms consistent, reliable, stable, straight.

erring *adj* aberrant, backsliding, delinquent, disobedient, errant, faithless, guilty, peccant, sinful, sinning, straying, wandering, wayward.

erroneous *adj* amiss, fallacious, false, faulty, flawed, illogical, inaccurate, incorrect, inexact, invalid, mistaken, specious, spurious, unfounded, unsound, untrue, wrong.

antonym correct.

error *n* barbarism, bêtise, bish, bloomer, blunder, boner, boob, corrigendum, delinquency, delusion, deviation, erratum, fallacy, fault, faux pas, flaw, gaucherie, howler, ignorance, ignoratio elenchi, illusion, inaccuracy, inexactitude, lapse, lapsus calami, lapsus linguae, lapsus memoriae, literal, malapropism, misapprehension, miscalculation, misconception, miscopy, miscorrection, misdeed, misprint, mistake, misunderstanding, mumpsimus, offence, omission, oversight, overslip, sin, slip, slip-up, solecism, transgression, trespass, wrong, wrongdoing.

erstwhile *adj* bygone, ex, former, late, old, once, one-time, past, previous, quondam, sometime, umwhile, whilom.

erudite *adj* academic, cultivated, cultured, educated, highbrow, knowledgeable, learned, lettered, literate, profound, recondite, scholarly, scholastic, well-educated, well-read, wise.

antonym unlettered.

erudition *n* culture, data, education, facts, knowledge, knowledgeableness, learnedness, learning, letters, lore, profoundness, profundity, reconditeness, scholarliness, scholarship, wisdom.

erupt *v* belch, break, break out, burst, discharge, eruct, eructate, explode, flare, gush, rift, spew, spout, vent, vomit.

eruption *n* discharge, ejection, emphysis, empyesis, eructation, explosion, inflammation, outbreak, outburst, rash, sally, venting.

escalate *v* accelerate, amplify, ascend, climb, enlarge, expand, extend, grow, heighten, increase, intensify, magnify, mount, raise, rise, spiral, step up.

antonym diminish.

escalator *n* elevator, lift, moving staircase.

escapable *adj* avertible, avoidable, eludible, evadable, evitable.

antonym inevitable.

escapade *n* adventure, antic, caper, doing, escapado, exploit, fling, fredaine, gest, lark, prank, romp, scrape, spree, stunt, trick.

escape *v* abscond, avoid, baffle, bolt, break free, break loose, break off, break out, circumvent, decamp, discharge, do a bunk, dodge, drain, duck, elude, emanate, evade, flee, flit, flow, fly, foil, get away, gush, issue, leak, ooze, pass, pour forth, scape, scarper, seep, shake off, shun, skedaddle, skip, slip, slip away, spurt, take it on the run, take to one's heels, trickle, vamoose.

n abscondence, avoidance, bolt, break, break-out, circumvention, decampment, discharge, distraction, diversion, drain, effluence, effluent, efflux, effluxion, elusion, emanation, emission, escapism, evasion, flight, flit, getaway, gush, jail-break, leak, leakage, meuse, out, outflow, outlet, outpour, pastime, recreation, relaxation, relief, safety-valve, seepage, spurt, vent.

escape route bolthole, egress, escape road, exit, loophole, meuse, out, outlet, secret passage, slip road, vent.

escapee *n* absconder, defector, deserter, fugitive, jail-breaker, runaway.

escapist *n* daydreamer, dreamer, fantasiser, non-realist, ostrich, Walter Mitty, wishful thinker.

antonym realist.

eschew *v* abandon, abjure, abstain from, avoid, disdain, forgo, forswear, give up, keep clear of, refrain from, renounce, repudiate, shun, spurn, swear off.

antonym embrace.

escort *n* aide, attendant, beau, bodyguard, chaperon, cicisbeo, companion, company, convoy, cortège, entourage, gigolo, guard, guardian, guide, partner, pilot, procession, protection, protector, retinue, safeguard, squire, suite, train.

v accompany, chaperon, chum, company, conduct, convoy, guard, guide, lead, partner, protect, shepherd, squire, usher.

esoteric *adj* abstruse, acroamatic, acroamatical, arcane, cabbalistic, confidential, cryptic, hermetic, hidden, inner, inscrutable, inside, mysterious, mystic, mystical, obscure, occult, private, recondite, secret.

antonyms familiar, popular.

especial *adj* chief, conspicuous, distinguished, eminent, exceptional, exclusive, express, extraordinary, individual, marked, notable, noteworthy, outstanding, particular, peculiar, personal, pre-eminent, principal, private, proper, remarkable, signal, singular, special, specific, striking, uncommon, unique, unusual.

especially *adv* chiefly, conspicuously, eminently, exceedingly, exceptionally, exclusively, expressly, extraordinarily, mainly, markedly, notably, noticeably, outstandingly, particularly, passing, peculiarly, pre-eminently, principally, remarkably, signally, singularly, specially, specifically, strikingly, supremely, uncommonly, uniquely, unusually, very.

espionage *n* counter-intelligence, infiltration, intelligence, investigation, probing, reconnaissance, spying, surveillance, undercover operations.

espousal *n* adoption, advocacy, affiance, alliance, backing, betrothal, betrothing, bridal, championing, championship, defence, embracing, engagement, espousing, maintenance, marriage, matrimony, nuptials, plighting, spousal, support, wedding.

espouse *v* adopt, advocate, affiance, back, befriend, betroth, champion, choose, defend, embrace, maintain, marry, opt for, patronise, support, take to wife, take up, wed.

espy *v* behold, descry, detect, discern, discover, distinguish, glimpse, make out, notice, observe, perceive, see, sight, spot, spy.

essay[1] *n* article, assignment, commentary, composition, critique, discourse, disquisition, dissertation, essayette, leader, paper, piece, review, thesis, tract, treatise.

essay[2] *n* attempt, bash, bid, crack, effort, endeavour, exertion, experiment, go, shot, stab, struggle, test, trial, try, undertaking, venture, whack, whirl.

v attempt, endeavour, go for, have a bash, have a crack, have a go, have a stab, strain, strive, struggle, tackle, take on, test, try, undertake.

essence *n* alma, attar, attributes, being, centre, character, characteristics, concentrate, core, crux, decoction, decocture, distillate, elixir, ens, entity, esse, extract, fragrance, haecceity, heart, hypostasis, inscape, kernel, life, lifeblood, marrow, meaning, nature, perfume, pith, principle, properties, qualities, quality, quiddit, quiddity, quintessence, scent, significance, soul, spirit, spirits, substance, tincture, virtuality, whatness.

essential[1] *adj* absolute, basic, cardinal, characteristic, complete, constituent, constitutional, constitutive, crucial, definitive, elemental, elementary, formal, fundamental, ideal, important, indispensable, inherent, innate, intrinsic, key, main, must, necessary, needed, perfect, principal, quintessential, required, requisite, typical, vital.

antonym inessential.

n basic, fundamental, must, necessary, necessity, prerequisite, principle, qualification, quality, requirement, requisite, rudiment, sine qua non.

antonym inessential.

essential[2] *adj* concentrated, decocted, distilled, ethereal, extracted, pure, purified, rectified, refined, volatile.

establish *v* affirm, attest to, authenticate, authorise, base, certify, confirm, constitute, corroborate, create, decree, demonstrate, enact, ensconce, entrench, fix, form, found, ground, implant, inaugurate, install, institute, introduce, invent, lodge, ordain, organise, plant, prove, radicate, ratify, root, sanction, seat, secure, set up, settle, show, start, station, substantiate, validate, verify.

established *adj* accepted, attested, confirmed, conventional, ensconced, entrenched, experienced, fixed, proved, proven, radicate, radicated, respected, routed, secure, settled, stated, steadfast, traditional.

antonyms impermanent, unreliable.

establishment *n* abode, building, business, company, concern, construction, corporation, creation, domicile, dwelling, edifice, enactment, enterprise, erection, factory, firm, formation, foundation, founding, hacienda, home, house, household, implantation, inauguration, inception, installation, institute, institution, introduction, invention, office, ordination, organisation, outfit, plant, quarters, radication, residence, ruling class, set-up, structure, system, the powers that be, the system.

estate *n* area, assets, barony, belongings, caste, class, condition, demesne, domain, effects, estancia, fortune, goods, grade, hacienda, holdings, lands, latifundium, lot, manor, order, period, place, position, possessions, property, quality, ranch, rank, situation, standing, state, station, status, wealth.

esteem *v* account, adjudge, admire, believe, calculate, cherish, consider, count, deem, estimate, hold, honour, include, judge, like, love, prize, rate, reckon, regard, regard highly, respect, revere, reverence, think, treasure, value, venerate, view.

n account, admiration, consideration, count, credit, estimation, good opinion, honour, judgement, love, reckoning, regard, respect, reverence, veneration.

esteemed *adj* admirable, admired, distinguished, excellent, highly-regarded, honourable, honoured, prized, reputable, respectable, respected, revered, treasured, valued, venerated, well-respected, well-thought-of, worthy.

estimable *adj* admirable, commendable, considerable, distinguished, egregious, esteemed, excellent, good, honourable, laudable, meritorious, notable, noteworthy, praiseworthy, reputable, respectable, respected, valuable, valued, worthy.

antonyms despicable, insignificant.

estimate *v* appraise, approximate, assess, believe, calculate, compute, conjecture, consider, count, evaluate, gauge, guess, judge, number, opine, rank, rate, reckon, surmise, think, value.

n appraisal, appraisement, approximation, assessment, belief, computation, conceit, conception, conjecture, estimation, evaluation, guess, guesstimate, judgement, opinion, reckoning, surmise, valuation.

estimation *n* account, admiration, appraisal, appreciation, assessment, belief, calculation, computation, conception, consideration, credit, esteem, estimate, evaluation, good opinion, honour, judgement, opinion, rating, reckoning, regard, respect, reverence, veneration, view.

estrange *v* alienate, antagonise, disaffect, disunite, divide, drive a wedge between, drive apart, part, put a barrier between, separate, set at variance, sever, sunder, withdraw, withhold.

antonyms ally, attract, bind, unite.

estrangement *n* alienation, antagonisation, antipathy, breach, break-up, disaffection, dissociation, disunity, division, hostility, parting, separation, severance, split, sunderance, sundering, unfriendliness, withdrawal, withholding.

estuary *n* arm, creek, firth, fjord, inlet, mouth, sea-loch, wash, wick.

et cetera and so forth, and so on, and the like, and the rest, &c, et ainsi de suite, et al, et alia, et alii, et hoc genus omne, et sequentia, et sic de ceteris, et sic de similibus, etc, kai ta leipomena, kai ta loipa, ktl, und so weiter, usw.

etch *v* bite, burn, carve, corrode, cut, dig, engrave, furrow, grave, groove, hatch, impress, imprint, incise, ingrain, inscribe, stamp.

etching *n* carving, cut, engraving, impression, imprint, print, sketch.

eternal *adj* abiding, aeonian, ceaseless, changeless, constant, deathless, durable, endless, enduring, eterne, everlasting, eviternal, illimitable, immortal, immutable, imperishable, incessant, indestructible, infinite, interminable, lasting, limitless, never-ending, perennial, permanent, perpetual, sempiternal, timeless, unbegotten, unceasing, unchanging, undying, unending, unextinguishable, unremitting.

antonyms changeable, ephemeral, temporary.

eternally *adv* ceaselessly, constantly, endlessly, everlastingly, immutably, incessantly, indestructibly, interminably, lastingly, never-endingly, perennially, permanently, perpetually, unendingly.

antonyms briefly, temporarily.

eternity *n* aeon, afterlife, age, ages, changelessness, endlessness, everlasting, everlastingness, eviternity, Ewigkeit, heaven, hereafter, illimitability, immortality, immutability, imperishability, incorruptibility, incorruption, infinitude, infinity, next world, paradise, perpetuity, sempiternity, timelessness, world to come.

ethereal *adj* aerial, airy, celestial, dainty, delicate, diaphanous, elemental, empyreal, empyrean, essential, etheric, etherical, exquisite, fairy, fine, gossamer, heavenly, impalpable, insubstantial, intangible, light, rarefied, rectified, refined, spiritual, subtle, tenuous, unearthly, unworldly.

antonyms earthly, solid.

ethical *adj* commendable, conscientious, correct, decent, fair, fitting, good, honest, honourable, just, meet, moral, noble, principled, proper, right, righteous, seemly, upright, virtuous.

antonym unethical.

ethics *n* code, conscience, deontics, deontology, equity, mind philosophy, moral ethology, moral philosophy, moral values, morality, principles, probity, propriety, rule, rules, seemliness, standards.

ethnic *adj* aboriginal, ancestral, autochthonous, cultural, folk, gentilic, historic, indigenous, national, native, racial, traditional, traditive, tribal.

ethos *n* attitude, beliefs, character, code, disposition, ethic, geist, manners, moeurs, morality, principles, rationale, spirit, standards, tenor.

etiquette *n* ceremony, civility, code, convention, conventionalities, correctness, courtesy, customs, decency, decorum, formalities, manners, politeness, politesse, propriety, protocol, rules, seemliness, usage, use.

etymology *n* derivation, descent, lexicology, linguistics, origin, pedigree, philology, semantics, source, word history, word-lore.

eulogise *v* acclaim, adulate, applaud, approve, belaud, celebrate, commend, compliment, congratulate, cry up, exalt, extol, flatter, glorify, honour, laud, magnify, panegyrise, praise.

antonym condemn.

eulogistic *adj* adulatory, approbatory, commendatory, complimentary, encomiastic, epaenetic, favourable, flattering, laudatory, panegyrical.

antonym unfavourable.

eulogy *n* acclaim, acclamation, accolade, applause, commendation, compliment, encomium, exaltation, glorification, laud, laudation, laudatory, paean, panegyric, plaudit, praise, tribute.

antonym condemnation.

euphemism *n* evasion, fig-leaf, genteelism, hypocorism, hypocorisma, polite term, politeness, substitution, understatement.

euphonious *adj* canorous, clear, consonant, dulcet, dulcifluous, dulciloquent, euphonic, harmonious, honeyed, mellifluent, mellifluous, mellow, melodic, melodious, musical, silvery, soft, sugared, sweet, sweet-sounding, sweet-toned, symphonious, tunable, tuneful.

antonym cacophonous.

euphony *n* consonance, dulciloquy, euphoniousness, harmoniousness, harmony, mellifluousness, mellowness, melodiousness, melody, music, musicality, tunefulness.

antonym cacophony.

euphoria *n* bliss, buoyancy, cheerfulness, cloud nine, ecstasy, elation, enthusiasm, euphory, exaltation, exhilaration, exultation, glee, high, high spirits, intoxication, joy, joyousness, jubilation, rapture, transport.

antonym depression.

euphoric *adj* blissful, buoyant, cheerful, ecstatic, elated, enraptured, enthusiastic, exhilarated, exultant, exulted, gleeful, happy, high, intoxicated, joyful, joyous, jubilant, rapturous.

antonym depressed.

euthanasia *n* euthanasy, mercy killing, quietus.

evacuate[1] *v* abandon, clear, clear out, decamp, depart, desert, forsake, leave, quit, relinquish, remove, retire from, vacate, withdraw.

evacuate[2] *v* defecate, discharge, eject, eliminate, empty, excrete, expel, purge, void.

evacuation[1] *n* abandonment, clearance, departure, desertion, exodus, quitting, relinquishment, removal, retiral, retreat, vacation, withdrawal.

evacuation[2] *n* catharsis, defecation, discharge, ejection, elimination, emptying, excretion, expulsion, purgation, purging, urination, voidance.

evade *v* avert, avoid, balk, blink, chicken out of, circumvent, cop out, decline, dodge, duck, elude, equivocate, escape, fence, fend off, fudge, give the runaround, hedge, parry, prevaricate, quibble, scrimshank, shirk, shun, sidestep, skive, steer clear of, temporise.

antonym face.

evaluate *v* appraise, assay, assess, calculate, compute, estimate, gauge, judge, rank, rate, reckon, size up, value, weigh.

evaluation *n* appraisal, assessment, calculation, computation, estimate, estimation, judgement, opinion, rating, reckoning, valuation.

evanescence *n* brevity, briefness, ephemerality, ephemeralness, fleetingness, fugaciousness, fugacity, fugitiveness, impermanence, inconstancy, instability, momentariness, temporariness, transience, transitoriness.

antonym permanence.

evanescent *adj* brief, changing, disappearing, ephemeral, fading, fleeting, fugacious, fugitive, impermanent, insubstantial, momentary, passing, perishable, short-lived, temporary, transient, transitory, unstable, vanishing.

antonym permanent.

evangelical *adj* campaigning, crusading, evangelistic, missionary, propagandising, propagandist, proselytising, zealous.

evangelise *v* baptise, campaign, convert, crusade, gospelise, missionarise, missionise, preach, propagandise, proselytise.

evaporate *v* condense, dehydrate, dematerialise, desiccate, disappear, dispel, disperse, dissipate, dissolve, distil, dry, evanesce, exhale, fade, melt (away), vanish, vaporise, vapour.

evaporation *n* condensation, dehydration, dematerialisation, desiccation, disappearance, dispelling, dispersal, dissipation, dissolution, distillation, drying, evanescence, fading, melting, vanishing, vaporisation, water-smoke.

evasion *n* artifice, avoidance, casuistry, circumvention, cop-out, cunning, dodge, elusion, equivocation, escape, euphemism, evasiveness, excuse, fudging, obfuscation, obliqueness, pretext, prevarication, put-off, ruse, shift, shirking, shuffling, sophism, sophistry, subterfuge, trickery, weasel-words.

antonyms directness, frankness.

evasive *adj* ambiguous, cag(e)y, casuistic, casuistical, cunning, deceitful, deceptive, devious, disingenuous, dissembling, elusive, elusory, equivocating, indirect, misleading, oblique, prevaricating, secretive, shifty, shuffling, slippery, sophistical, tricky, unforthcoming, vacillating.

antonyms direct, frank.

eve *n* brink, edge, evening, moment, point, threshold, verge, vigil.

even *adj* abreast, alongside, balanced, calm, coequal, commensurate, comparable, complanate, composed, constant, cool, disinterested, dispassionate, drawn, equable, equal, equalised, equanimous, equitable, even-tempered, fair, fair and square, fifty-fifty, flat, fluent, flush, horizontal, identical, impartial, impassive, imperturbable, just, level, level-pegging, like, matching, metrical, monotonous, neck and neck, on a par, parallel, peaceful, placid, plane, plumb, proportionate, quits, regular, rhythmical, serene, side by side, similar, smooth, square, stable, steady, straight, symmetrical, tied, tranquil, true, unbiased, unbroken, undisturbed, unexcitable, unexcited, uniform, uninterrupted, unprejudiced, unruffled, unvarying, unwavering, well-balanced.

antonyms unequal, uneven.

adv all the more, also, although, as well, at all, directly, exactly, hardly, including, just, much, scarcely, so much as, still, yet.

v align, balance, equal, equalise, flatten, flush, level, match, regularise, regulate, smooth, square, stabilise, steady, straighten.

even so all the same, despite that, however, however that may be, in spite of that, natheless, nevertheless, nonetheless, notwithstanding that, still, yet.

even-handed *adj* balanced, disinterested, dispassionate, equitable, fair, fair and square, impartial, just, neutral, non-discriminatory, reasonable, square, unbiased, unprejudiced, without fear or favour.

antonym inequitable.

evening *n* crepuscule, dusk, eve, even, eventide, forenight, gloaming, Hesper, Hesperus, nightfall, sundown, sunset, twilight, vesper.

adj crepuscular, twilight, vesperal, vespertinal, vespertine.

evenness *n* alikeness, balance, calmness, commensurateness, comparability, composure, constancy, coolness, equability, equableness, equality, equanimity, flatness, fluency, identicalness, impassivity, imperturbability, levelness, monotony, peacableness, placidity, proportion, regularity, rhythmicality, serenity, similarity, smoothness, stability, steadiness, straightness, symmetry, tranquillity, trueness, uniformity.

antonyms inequality, unevenness.

event *n* adventure, affair, bout, business, case, circumstance, competition, conclusion, consequence, contest, effect, end, engagement, episode, eventuality, experience, fact, game, happening, incident, issue, match, matter, milestone, occasion, occurrence, outcome, possibility, result, termination, tournament, upshot.

even-tempered *adj* calm, composed, cool, cool-headed, equable, equanimous, impassive, imperturbable, level-headed, peaceable, peaceful, placid, serene, stable, steady, tranquil, unexcitable, unfussed, unruffled.

antonym excitable.

eventful *adj* active, busy, consequential, critical, crucial, decisive, epochal, exciting, fateful, full, historic, important, interesting, lively, memorable, momentous, notable, noteworthy, portentous, remarkable, significant, unforgettable.

antonyms dull, ordinary, uneventful.

eventual *adj* concluding, consequent, ensuing, final, future, impending, last, later, overall, planned, projected, prospective, resulting, subsequent, ultimate.

eventuality *n* case, chance, circumstance, contingency, crisis, emergency, event, happening, happenstance, likelihood, mishap, outcome, possibility, probability.

eventually *adv* after all, at last, at length, finally, in one's own good time, sooner or later, subsequently, ultimately.

ever *adv* always, at all, at all times, at any time, ceaselessly, constantly, continually, endlessly, eternally, everlastingly, evermore, for ever, in any case, in any circumstances, incessantly, on any account, perpetually, unceasingly, unendingly.

everlasting *adj* abiding, boring, ceaseless, changeless, constant, continual, continuous, deathless, durable, endless, enduring, eternal, immarcescible, immortal, imperishable, incessant, indestructible, infinite, interminable, lasting, monotonous, never-ending, perdurable, permanent, perpetual, relentless, tedious, timeless, unceasing, unchanging, undying, unfading, uninterrupted, unremitting.

antonyms temporary, transient.

evermore *adv* always, eternally, ever, ever after, for aye, for ever, for ever and a day, for ever and ever, henceforth, hereafter, in perpetuum, in saecula saeculorum, till doomsday, to the end of time, unceasingly.

evert *v* evaginate, turn inside out, turn out.

everted *adj* evaginated, extrorse, turned inside out.

everybody *n* all and sundry, each one, everyone, one and all, the whole world, tout le monde.

everyday *adj* accustomed, banal, boring, circadian, common, common-or-garden, commonplace, conventional, customary, daily, diurnal, dull, familiar, frequent, habitual, informal, monotonous, mundane, normal, ordinary, plain, prosaic, quotidian, regular, routine, run-of-the-mill, simple, stock, unexceptional, unimaginative, usual, wonted, workaday.

antonyms exceptional, special.

everyone *n* all and sundry, each one, every man-jack, every mother's son, everybody, one and all, the whole jingbang, the whole world, tout le monde.

everything *n* all, lock stock and barrel, the aggregate, the entirety, the lot, the sum, the total, the whole caboodle, the whole lot, the whole shoot, the whole shooting-match.

everywhere *adv* all along the line, all around, all over, far and near, far and wide, high and low, left right and centre, omnipresent, passim, ubique, ubiquitous.

evict *v* boot out, cast out, chuck out, defenestrate, dislodge, dispossess, disseise, eject, expel, expropriate, give the bum's rush, kick out, oust, put out, remove, show the door, turf out.

eviction *n* clearance, defenestration, dislodgement, dispossession, disseisin, ejection, expropriation, expulsion, ouster, removal, the bum's rush.

evidence *n* affirmation, attestation, betrayal, confirmation, corroboration, data, declaration, demonstration, deposition, documentation, grounds, hint, indication, manifestation, mark, pledge, proof, sign, substantiation, suggestion, testimony, token, voucher, witness.

v affirm, attest, betray, confirm, demonstrate, denote, display, establish, evince, exhibit, indicate, manifest, prove, reveal, show, signify, testify to, witness.

evident *adj* apparent, clear, clear-cut, confessed, conspicuous, detectable, discernible, distinct, incontestable, incontrovertible, indisputable, manifest, noticeable, obvious, ostensible, palpable, patent, perceptible, plain, tangible, undeniable, unmistakable, visible.

antonym uncertain.

evidently *adv* apparently, clearly, distinctly, doubtless, doubtlessly, incontestably, incontrovertibly, indisputably, indubitably, irrefragably, manifestly, obviously, ostensibly, outwardly, patently, plainly, seemingly, undoubtedly, unmistakably, unquestionably.

evil *adj* adverse, bad, baleful, baneful, base, blackguardly, black-hearted, calamitous, catastrophic, corrupt, cruel, deadly, deleterious, depraved, destructive, detrimental, devilish, dire, disastrous, facinorous, flagitious, foul, ghastly, grim, harmful, heinous, hurtful, immoral, inauspicious, inimical, iniquitous, injurious, knavish, malefactory, malefic, maleficent, malevolent, malicious, malignant, mephitic, mischievous, miscreant, nefarious, nefast, nocuous, noisome, noxious, offensive, painful, perfidious, pernicious, pestiferous, pestilential, poisonous, putrid, reprobate, ruinous, sinful, sorrowful, ugly, unfortunate, unlucky, unpleasant, unspeakable, vicious, vile, villainous, wicked, woeful, wrong.

n adversity, affliction, amiss, badness, bane, baseness, blow, calamity, catastrophe, corruption, curse, demonry, depravity, disaster, distress, facinorousness, flagitiousness, foulness, harm, heinousness, hurt, hydra, ill, immorality, impiety, improbity, iniquity, injury, knavery, maleficence, malignity, mischief, misery, misfortune, pain, perfidy, ruin, sin, sinfulness, sorrow, suffering, turpitude, ulcer, vice, viciousness, villainy, wickedness, woe, wrong, wrong-doing.

evil eye blight, cantrip, charm, curse, hoodoo, jettatura, jinx, malocchio, spell, voodoo.

evil spirit bogey, bogle, cacodaemon, demon, devil, fiend, ghost, goblin, gremlin, hobgoblin, imp, incubus, jumby, kelpie, kobold, nicker, nightmare, nix, nixie, succubus, troll.

evil-doer *n* blackguard, caitiff, criminal, delinquent, knave, malefactor, malfeasant, miscreant, offender, reprobate, rogue, scamp, scapegrace, scoundrel, sinner, villain, wrong-doer.

evince *v* attest, bespeak, betoken, betray, confess, declare, demonstrate, display, establish, evidence, exhibit, express, indicate, manifest, reveal, show, signify.

antonyms conceal, suppress.

eviscerate *v* disembowel, draw, exenterate, gralloch, gut.

evisceration *n* disembowelment, drawing, exenteration, gralloching, gutting.

evocation *n* activation, actuation, arousal, echo, eduction, elicitation, excitation, kindling, recall, stimulation, stirring, suggestion, summoning-up.

evoke *v* activate, actuate, arouse, awaken, call, call forth, call up, conjure up, educe, elicit, excite, induce, invoke, produce, provoke, raise, recall, rekindle, stimulate, stir, summon, summon up.

antonyms quell, suppress.

evolution *n* convolution, Darwinism, derivation, descent, development, evolvement, expansion, growth, gyration, increase, maturation, progress, progression, ripening, unfolding, unrolling.

evolve *v* derive, descend, develop, disclose, elaborate, emerge, enlarge, expand, grow, increase, mature, progress, result, unravel.

exacerbate *v* aggravate, deepen, embitter, enrage, envenom, exaggerate, exasperate, excite, heighten, increase, inflame, infuriate, intensify, irritate, provoke, sharpen, vex, worsen.

antonym soothe.

exact *adj* accurate, blow-by-blow, careful, close, correct, definite, detailed, explicit, express, factual, faithful, faultless, finical, finicky, flawless, identical, letter-perfect, literal, methodical, meticulous, nice, orderly, painstaking, particular, perfectionist, perjink, precise, punctilious, right, rigorous, scrupulous, severe, specific, square, strict, true, unambiguous, unequivocal, unerring, veracious, very, word-perfect.

antonym inexact.

v bleed, claim, command, compel, demand, extort, extract, force, impose, insist on, milk, require, requisition, squeeze, wrest, wring.

exactable *adj* demandable, exigible, imposable, requirable.

exacting *adj* arduous, demanding, difficult, exig(e)ant, exigent, hard, harsh, imperious, laborious, oppressive, painstaking, rigid, rigorous, severe, stern, strict, stringent, taxing, toilsome, tough, trying, tyrannical, unsparing, uphill.

antonyms easy, tolerant.

exaction *n* blackmail, bleeding, compulsion, contribution, demand, extortion, imposition, milking, rapacity, requirement, requisition, tribute.

exactitude *n* accuracy, authenticity, care, carefulness, clarity, conscientiousness, correctness, detail, exactness, faithfulness, faultlessness, fidelity, meticulousness, nicety, orderliness, painstakingness, perfectionism, preciseness, precision, promptitude, promptness, punctilio, punctuality, regularity, rigorousness, rigour, scrupulosity, scrupulousness, strictness, thoroughness, truth, veracity.

antonyms carelessness, inaccuracy.

exactly *adv* absolutely, accurately, bang, carefully, correctly, dead, definitely, explicitly, expressly, faithfully, faultlessly, just, literally, literatim, methodically, particularly, plumb, precisely, punctiliously, quite, rigorously, scrupulously, severely, specifically, strictly, to the letter, truly, truthfully, unambiguously, unequivocally, unerringly, veraciously, verbatim.

interj absolutely, agreed, certainly, indeed, just so, of course, precisely, quite, right, true.

exactness *n* accuracy, authenticity, carefulness, correctness, detail, exactitude, faithfulness, faultlessness, fidelity, meticulousness, nicety, orderliness, painstakingness, perfectionism, preciseness, precision, promptitude, punctilio, regularity, rigorousness, rigour, scrupulousness, strictness, truth, veracity, verity.

antonyms carelessness, inaccuracy.

exaggerate *v* amplify, bounce, caricature, distend, embellish, embroider, emphasise, enlarge, exalt, hyperbolise, inflate, magnify, overdo, overdraw, overemphasise, overestimate, oversell, overstate, pile it on.

antonyms belittle, understate.

exaggerated *adj* amplified, bloated, bombastic, burlesqued, caricatured, embellished, euphuistic, exalted, excessive, extravagant, hyperbolic, hyperbolical, inflated, overblown, overcharged, overdone, overestimated, overstated, pretentious, tall, turgid.

antonym understated.

exaggeration *n* amplification, burlesque, caricature, embellishment, emphasis, enlargement, exaltation, excess, extravagance, hyperbole, inflation, magnification, overemphasis, overestimation, overstatement, parody, pretension, pretentiousness, stretcher.

antonyms meiosis, understatement.

exalt *v* acclaim, advance, aggrandise, animate, apotheosise, applaud, arouse, bless, crown, deify, delight, dignify, elate, electrify, elevate, enliven, ennoble, enthrone, excite, exhilarate, extol, fire, glorify, heighten, honour, idolise, inspire, inspirit, laud, magnify, praise, promote, raise, revere, reverence, stimulate, sublimise, thrill, upgrade, uplift, venerate, worship.

antonym debase.

exaltation *n* acclaim, acclamation, adoration, adulation, advancement, aggrandisement, animation, apotheosis, applause, blessing, bliss, canonisation, deification, delight, dignification, dignity, ecstasy, elation, elevation, eminence, ennoblement, enthusiasm, excitement, exhilaration, extolment, exultation, glorification, glory, grandeur, homage, honour, idealisation, idolisation, inspiration, joy, joyfulness, joyousness, jubilation, laudation, lionisation, loftiness, magnification, panegyric, plaudits, praise, prestige, promotion, rapture, reverence, rise, stimulation, transport, tribute, upgrading, uplift, veneration, worship.

antonym debasement.

exalted *adj* animated, august, blissful, dignified, ecstatic, elate, elated, elevated, eminent, enhanced, enlivened, enthusiastic, exaggerated, excessive, excited, exhilarated, exultant, glorified, glorious, grand, happy, high, high-minded, high-ranking, honoured, ideal, idealised, in high spirits, in seventh heaven, inflated, inspired, inspirited, intellectual, joyful, joyous, jubilant, lofty, lordly, noble, overblown, prestigious, pretentious, princely, rapturous, stately, stimulated, sublime, superior, transcendent, transported, uplifted, uplifting.

antonym debased.

examination *n* analysis, appraisal, assay, audit, catechism, check, check-up, critique, cross-examination, cross-questioning, docimasy, exam, exploration, inquiry, inquisition, inspection, interrogation, investigation, observation, once-over, perusal, probe, questioning, quiz, research, review, scan, scrutinisation, scrutiny, search, sift, study, survey, test, trial, visitation, viva.

examine *v* analyse, appraise, assay, audit, case, catechise, check (out), consider, cross-examine, cross-question, explore, eyeball, grill, inquire, inspect, interrogate, investigate, jerque, peruse, ponder, pore over, probe, question, quiz, review, scan, scrutinise, sift, study, survey, sus out, test, vet, visit, weigh.

examinee *n* applicant, candidate, competitor, contestant, entrant, examinant, examinate, interviewee.

examiner *n* adjudicator, analyst, arbiter, assayer, assessor, auditor, censor, critic, examinant, examinator, inspector, interlocutor, interviewer, judge, marker, questioner, reader, reviewer, scrutator, scrutineer, scrutiniser, tester.

example *n* admonition, archetype, case, case in point, caution, citation, ensample, exemplar, exemplification, exemplum, ideal, illustration, instance, lesson, mirror, model, occurrence, paradigm, paragon, parallel, pattern, praxis, precedent, prototype, sample, specimen, standard, type, warning.

exasperate *v* aggravate, anger, annoy, bug, enrage, exacerbate, excite, exulcerate, gall, get, get in someone's hair, get on someone's nerves, get on someone's wick, get to, goad, incense, inflame, infuriate, irk, irritate, madden, needle, nettle, peeve, pique, plague, provoke, rankle, rile, rouse, vex.

antonyms calm, soothe.

exasperated *adj* aggravated, angered, angry, annoyed, at the end of one's tether, bored, bugged, fed up, galled, goaded, incensed, indignant, infuriated, irked, irritated, maddened, needled, nettled, peeved, piqued, provoked, riled, vexed.

exasperating *adj* aggravating, annoying, boring, bothersome, disagreeable, galling, infuriating, irksome, irritating, maddening, pernicious, pesky, pestiferous, pestilential, provoking, troublesome, vexatious, vexing.

exasperation *n* aggravation, anger, annoyance, arousal, discontent, disgust, displeasure, dissatisfaction, enragement, exacerbation, exulceration, fury, gall, indignation, inflammation, ire, irritation, passion, pique, provocation, rage, resentment, vexation, wrath.

antonym calmness.

excavate *v* burrow, cut, delve, dig, dig out, dig up, disinter, drive, exhume, gouge, hollow, mine, quarry, sap, scoop, stope, trench, tunnel, uncover, undermine, unearth.

excavation *n* burrow, cavity, cut, cutting, delf, dig, diggings, ditch, dugout, hole, hollow, mine, pit, quarry, sap, sapping, shaft, souterrain, stope, trench, trough, undermining.

exceed *v* beat, better, cap, contravene, eclipse, excel, outdistance, outdo, outreach, outrival, outrun, outshine, outstrip, overdo, overstep, overtake, pass, surmount, surpass, take liberties with, top, transcend, transgress.

exceeding *adj* amazing, astonishing, enormous, exceptional, excessive, extraordinary, great, huge, outstanding, pre-eminent, superior, superlative, surpassing, transcendent, unequalled, unprecedented, unusual, vast.

exceedingly *adv* amazingly, astonishingly, enormously, especially, exceeding, exceptionally, excessively, extraordinarily, extremely, greatly, highly, hugely, inordinately, passing, superlatively, surpassingly, unprecedentedly, unusually, vastly, very.

excel *v* beat, better, cap, eclipse, exceed, outclass, outdo, outperform, outrank, outrival, outshine, outstrip, overshadow, pass, predominate, shine, stand out, surmount, surpass, top, transcend, trump.

excellence *n* distinction, eminence, fineness, goodness, greatness, merit, perfection, pre-eminence, purity, quality, superiority, supremacy, transcendence, virtue, water, worth.

antonym inferiority.

excellent *adj* A1, admirable, beaut, bonzer, boshta, bosker, boss, brave, bully, capital, champion, choice, commendable, copacetic, corking, crack, cracking, dilly, distinguished, estimable, exemplary, eximious, exquisite, fine, first-class, first-rate, good, great, hot stuff, laudable, meritorious, nonpareil, notable, noted, noteworthy, outstanding, peerless, prime, remarkable, ripping, select, splendid, sterling, stunning, superb, supereminent, superior, superlative, surpassing, tipping, tiptop, top-flight, top-notch, topping, unequalled, unexceptionable, up to dick, way-out, wonderful, worthy.

antonym inferior.

except *prep* apart from, bar, barring, besides, but, except for, excepting, excluding, exclusive of, leaving out, less, minus, not counting, omitting, other than, save, saving.

v ban, bar, debar, disallow, eliminate, exclude, leave out, omit, pass over, reject, rule out.

exception *n* abnormality, anomaly, curiosity, debarment, departure, deviation, disallowment, eccentricity, excepting, exclusion, exemption, freak, inconsistency, irregularity, oddity, omission, peculiarity, prodigy, quirk, rarity, rejection, special case.

exceptional *adj* aberrant, abnormal, anomalous, atypical, curious, deviant, eccentric, excellent, extraordinary, freakish, inconsistent, irregular, marvellous, notable, noteworthy, odd, outstanding, peculiar, phenomenal, prodigious, quirky, rare, remarkable, singular, special, strange, superior, superlative, uncommon, unconventional, unequalled, unexpected, unusual.

antonyms mediocre, unexceptional.

exceptionally *adv* amazingly, especially, excellently, extraordinarily, marvellously, notably, outstandingly, peculiarly, phenomenally, prodigiously, remarkably, singularly, specially, splendidly, superlatively, uncommonly, unusually, wonderfully.

excerpt *n* citation, extract, fragment, gobbet, part, passage, pericope, portion, quotation, quote, scrap, section, selection.

v borrow, cite, crib, cull, extract, lift, mine, quarry, quote, select.

excess *n* debauchery, diarrhoea, dissipation, dissoluteness, excesses, exorbitance, extravagance, glut, gluttony, immoderateness, immoderation, intemperance, left-over, libertinism, licentiousness, nimiety, overabundance, overdose, overflow, overflush, overindulgence, overkill, overload, plethora, prodigality, remainder, superabundance, superfluity, surfeit, surplus, unrestraint.

antonym dearth.

adj additional, extra, left-over, redundant, remaining, residual, spare, superfluous, supernumerary, surplus.

excessive *adj* disproportionate, exaggerated, exorbitant, extravagant, extreme, fanatical, immoderate, inordinate, intemperate, needless, nimious, overdone, overmuch, prodigal, profligate, steep, stiff, supererogatory, superfluous, unasked-for, uncalled-for, unconscionable, undue, unnecessary, unneeded, unreasonable.

antonym insufficient.

excessively *adv* disproportionately, exaggeratedly, exorbitantly, extravagantly, extremely, fanatically, immoderately, inordinately, intemperately, needlessly, overly, overmuch, prodigally, superfluously, unconscionably, unduly, unnecessarily, unreasonably.

antonym insufficiently.

exchange *v* bandy, bargain, barter, change, commute, convert, interchange, reciprocate, replace, substitute, swap, switch, toss about, trade, truck.

n bargain, barter, bourse, brush, chat, commerce, conversation, converse, conversion, dealing, interchange, intercourse, market, quid pro quo, reciprocity, replacement, substitution, swap, switch, tit for tat, trade, traffic, truck.

excise[1] *n* customs, duty, impost, levy, surcharge, tariff, tax, toll, VAT.

excise[2] *v* bowdlerise, cut, cut out, delete, destroy, eradicate, erase, expunge, expurgate, exterminate, extirpate, extract, remove, rescind.

excision *n* bowdlerisation, deletion, destruction, eradication, expunction, expurgation, extermination, extirpation, removal.

excitable *adj* edgy, emotional, explosive, feisty, fiery, hasty, highly-strung, high-strung, hot-headed, hot-tempered, inflammable, irascible, mercurial, nervous, nervy, passionate, quick-tempered, restive, restless, sensitive, susceptible, temperamental, unstable, violent, volatile.

antonyms calm, impassive.

excite *v* activate, actuate, aerate, affect, agitate, animate, arouse, awaken, discompose, disturb, elate, electrify, elicit, engender, evoke, fire, foment, galvanise, generate, ignite, impress, incite, induce, inflame, initiate, inspire, instigate, kindle, motivate, move, provoke, quicken, rouse, stimulate, stir up, suscitate, sway, thrill, titillate, touch, turn on, upset, waken, warm, whet.

antonyms bore, quell.

excited *adj* aflame, agitated, animated, aroused, awakened, breathless, corybantic, discomposed, disturbed, eager, elated, enthused, enthusiastic, feverish, flurried, flustered, fluttered, frantic, frenzied, high, impassioned, moved, nervous, overwrought, restive, restless, roused, ruffled, stimulated, stirred, thrilled, titillated, upset, wild, worked up, wrought-up.

antonyms apathetic, bored.

excitement *n* action, activity, ado, adventure, agitation, animation, brouhaha, clamour, commotion, deliriousness, delirium, discomposure, eagerness, elation, enthusiasm, excitation, ferment, fever, flurry, furore, fuss, heat, hubbub, hue and cry, hurly-burly, kerfuffle, kicks, passion, perturbation, restlessness, stimulation, stimulus, tew, thrill, titillation, tumult, unrest, urge.

antonyms apathy, calm.

exciting *adj* cliff-hanging, electrifying, encouraging, enthralling, exhilarating, impressive, inspiring, intoxicating, moving, nail-biting, promising, provocative, rousing, sensational, stimulating, stirring, striking, suspenseful, swashbuckling, thrilling, titillating.

antonyms boring, unexciting.

exclaim *v* blurt, call, cry, declare, ejaculate, interject, proclaim, shout, utter, vociferate.

exclamation *n* call, cry, ecphonesis, ejaculation, expletive, interjection, outcry, shout, utterance, vociferation.

exclamatory *adj* dramatic, ejaculatory, exclamative, interjaculatory, interjectional, interjectionary, interjectural, melodramatic, sensationalist.

exclude *v* anathematise, ban, bar, blackball, blacklist, bounce, boycott, debar, disallow, eject, eliminate, embargo, evict, except, excommunicate, expel, forbid, ignore, include out, interclude, interdict, keep out, leave out, omit, ostracise, oust, preclude, prohibit, proscribe, refuse, reject, remove, repudiate, rule out, shut out, veto.

antonyms admit, allow, include.

exclusion *n* ban, bar, boycott, debarment, disfellowship, ejection, elimination, embargo, eviction, exception, expulsion, forbiddal, forbiddance, interdict, non-admission, omission, ostracisation, preclusion, prohibition, proscription, refusal, rejection, removal, repudiation, veto.

antonyms admittance, allowance, inclusion.

exclusive *adj* absolute, arrogant, chic, choice, clannish, classy, cliquey, cliquish, closed, complete, confined, discriminative, elegant, entire, esoteric, exclusory, fashionable, full, limited, luxurious, monopolistic, narrow, only, peculiar, posh, private, restricted, restrictive, select, selective, selfish, single, snobbish, sole, total, undivided, unique, unshared, whole.

exclusive of barring, debarring, except, except for, excepting, excluding, omitting, ruling out.

antonym inclusive of.

excommunicate *v* anathematise, ban, banish, bar, blacklist, debar, denounce, disfellowship, eject, exclude, execrate, expel, outlaw, proscribe, remove, repudiate, unchurch.

excrescence *n* appendage, bump, excrement, growth, intumescence, knob, lump, misgrowth, outgrowth, process, projection, prominence, protrusion, protuberance, swelling, tumour, wart.

excrete *v* crap, defecate, discharge, egest, eject, eliminate, evacuate, expel, exude, secrete, shit, urinate, void.

excretion *n* crap, defecation, discharge, droppings, dung, eccrisis, egesta, ejection, elimination, evacuation, excrement, excreta, expulsion, exudation, ordure, perspiration, rejectamenta, shit(e), skat, stool, sudation, urination, voidance.

excretory *adj* defecatory, egestive, emunctory, excremental, excrementitial, excrementitious, exudative, faecal, perspiratory, sudatory, urinary, urinative.

excruciating *adj* acute, agonising, atrocious, bitter, burning, exquisite, extreme, harrowing, insufferable, intense, intolerable, painful, piercing, racking, savage, searing, severe, sharp, tormenting, torturing, torturous, unbearable, unendurable.

exculpate *v* absolve, acquit, clear, deliver, discharge, disculpate, excuse, exonerate, forgive, free, justify, let off, pardon, release, vindicate.

antonyms blame, condemn.

exculpation *n* absolution, acquittal, clearance, discharge, excuse, exoneration, expurgation, freedom, justification, pardon, release, vindication.

antonym condemnation.

excursion *n* airing, breather, day trip, detour, deviation, digression, divagation, ecbole, episode, excursus, expedition, jaunt, journey, outing, ramble, ride, sashay, tour, trip, walk, wandering, wayzgoose.

excusable *adj* allowable, defensible explainable, explicable, forgivable, ignorable, justifiable, minor, pardonable, permissible, slight, understandable, venial, vindicable, warrantable.

antonym blameworthy.

excuse *v* absolve, acquit, apologise for, condone, defend, discharge, exculpate, exempt, exonerate, explain, extenuate, forgive, free, ignore, indulge, justify, let off, liberate, mitigate, overlook, palliate, pardon, release, relieve, sanction, spare, tolerate, vindicate, warrant, wink at.

n alibi, apology, cop-out, defence, disguise, evasion, exculpation, exoneration, expedient, explanation, extenuation, grounds, justification, makeshift, mitigation, mockery, palliation, parody, plea, pretence, pretext, put-off, reason, semblance, shift, substitute, subterfuge, travesty, vindication.

ex-directory *adj* unlisted.

execrable *adj* abhorrent, abominable, accursed, appalling, atrocious, damnable, deplorable, despicable, detestable, disgusting, foul, hateful, heinous, horrible, loathsome, nauseous, obnoxious, odious, offensive, repulsive, revolting, shocking, sickening, vile.

antonyms admirable, esteemable.

execrate *v* abhor, abominate, anathematise, blast, condemn, curse, damn, denounce, denunciate, deplore, despise, detest, excoriate, fulminate, hate, imprecate, inveigh against, loathe, revile, vilify.

antonyms commend, praise.

execration *n* abhorrence, abomination, anathema, condemnation, contempt, curse, damnation, detestation, excoriation, fulmination, hate, hatred, imprecation, invective, loathing, malediction, odium, revilement, vilification, vituperation.

antonyms commendation, praise.

execute[1] *v* behead, burn, crucify, decapitate, decollate, electrocute, guillotine, hang, kill, liquidate, put to death, shoot.

execute[2] *v* accomplish, achieve, administer, complete, consummate, deliver, discharge, dispatch, do, effect, effectuate, enact, enforce, expedite, finish, fulfil, implement, perform, prosecute, realise, render, seal, serve, sign, validate.

execution[1] *n* auto-da-fé, beheading, burning, capital punishment, crucifixion, death, death penalty, decapitation, decollation, electrocution, firing squad, fusillation, guillotining, hanging, killing, shooting.

execution[2] *n* accomplishment, achievement, administration, completion, consummation, delivery, discharge, dispatch, effect, effectuation, enactment, enforcement, exercitation, implementation, manner, mode, operation, performance, prosecution, realisation, rendering, rendition, style, technique, warrant, writ.

executioner *n* assassin, exterminator, hangman, headsman, hit man, killer, liquidator, murderer, slayer.

executive *n* administration, administrator, controller, director, directorate, directors, government, hierarchy, leadership, management, manager, official, organiser.

adj administrative, controlling, decision-making, directing, directorial, governing, gubernatorial, guiding, leading, managerial, organisational, organising, regulating, supervisory.

exemplar *n* archetype, copy, criterion, embodiment, epitome, example, exemplification, ideal, illustration, instance, model, paradigm, paragon, pattern, prototype, specimen, standard, type, yardstick.

exemplary *adj* admirable, admonitory, cautionary, commendable, correct, estimable, excellent, faultless, flawless, good, honourable, ideal, laudable, meritorious, model, monitory, perfect, praiseworthy, punctilious, sterling, unerring, unexceptionable, warning, worthy.

antonyms imperfect, unworthy.

exemplify *v* demonstrate, depict, display, embody, ensample, epitomise, evidence, example, exhibit, illustrate, instance, manifest, represent, show, typify.

exempt *v* absolve, discharge, dismiss, except, excuse, exonerate, free, let off, liberate, make an exception of, release, relieve, spare.

adj absolved, clear, discharged, excepted, excluded, excused, favoured, free, immune, liberated, released, spared.

antonym liable.

exemption *n* absolution, discharge, dispensation, exception, exclusion, exoneration, freedom, immunity, indulgence, overslaugh, privilege, release.

antonym liability.

exercise *v* afflict, agitate, annoy, apply, burden, discharge, discipline, distress, disturb, drill, employ, enjoy, exert, habituate, inure, occupy, operate, pain, perturb, practise, preoccupy, train, trouble, try, upset, use, utilise, vex, wield, work out, worry.

n accomplishment, action, activity, aerobics, application, assignment, daily dozen, discharge, discipline, drill, drilling, effort, employment, enjoyment, exercitation, exertion, fulfilment, implementation, krieg(s)spiel, labour, lesson, operation, physical jerks, practice, problem, schooling, school-work, task, toil, training, use, utilisation, war-game, work, work-out.

exert *v* apply, bring to bear, employ, exercise, expend, use, utilise, wield.

exert oneself apply oneself, concentrate, endeavour, labour, strain, strive, struggle, sweat, take pains, toil, work.

exertion *n* action, application, assiduity, attempt, diligence, effort, employment, endeavour, exercise, industry, labour, operation, pains, perseverance, sedulousness, strain, stretch, struggle, toil, travail, trial, use, utilisation, work.

antonyms idleness, rest.

exhalation *n* air, aura, breath, discharge, ectoplasm, effluvium, efflux, emanation, emission, evaporation, exhaust, expiration, flow, fog, fume, fumes, mist, respiration, smoke, steam, vapour, vapours.

antonym inhalation.

exhale *v* breathe (out), discharge, eject, emanate, emit, evaporate, expel, expire, give off, issue, respire, steam.

antonym inhale.

exhaust *v* bankrupt, beggar, bugger, consume, cripple, debilitate, deplete, disable, dissipate, drain, dry, empty, enervate, enfeeble, expend, fatigue, finish, impoverish, overtax, overtire, overwork, prostrate, run through, sap, spend, squander, strain, tax, tire (out), use up, void, waste, weaken, wear out, weary.

antonym refresh.

n discharge, eduction, effluvium, emanation, emission, exhalation, fumes.

exhausted *adj* all in, bare, beat, buggered, burned out, clapped-out, consumed, crippled, dead, dead tired, dead-beat, debilitated, depleted, disabled, dissipated, dog-tired, done, done in, drained, dry, effete, empty, enervated, enfeebled, expended, fatigued, finished, fogged out, forjeskit, forswunk, gone, jaded, jiggered, knackered, out for the count, outspent, pooped, prostrated, sapped, spent, squandered, tired out, used up, void, washed-out, washed-up, wasted, weak, weary, whacked, worn out, zonked.

antonyms conserved, fresh, vigorous.

exhausting *adj* arduous, backbreaking, crippling, debilitating, difficult, draining, enervating, fatiguing, formidable, gruelling, hard, knackering, laborious, punishing, sapping, severe, strenuous, taxing, testing, tiring, vigorous.

antonym refreshing.

exhaustion *n* consumption, debilitation, depletion, effeteness, emptying, enervation, fatigue, feebleness, inanition, jet-lag, lassitude, prostration, tiredness, weariness.

antonym freshness.

exhaustive *adj* all-embracing, all-inclusive, all-out, complete, comprehensive, definitive, detailed, encyclopaedic, expansive, extensive, far-reaching, full, full-scale, in-depth, intensive, sweeping, thorough, thoroughgoing, total.

antonym incomplete.

exhibit *v* air, demonstrate, disclose, display, evidence, evince, expose, express, flaunt, indicate, manifest, offer, parade, present, reveal, show, showcase, sport.

antonym hide.

n display, exhibition, illustration, model, show.

exhibition *n* airing, array, demonstration, display, exhibit, expo, exposition, fair, manifestation, panopticon, performance, presentation, representation, show, showcase, showing, spectacle.

exhibitionist *n* extrovert, flasher, pervert, self-advertiser, show-off.

exhilarate *v* animate, cheer, delight, elate, energise, enhearten, enliven, exalt, excite, gladden, hearten, inspirit, invigorate, lift, stimulate, thrill, vitalise.

antonyms bore, discourage.

exhilarating *adj* breathtaking, cheering, enlivening, euphoriant, exalting, exciting, exhilarant, exhilarative, exhilaratory, gladdening, heartsome, invigorating, mind-blowing, stimulating, thrilling, vitalising.

antonyms boring, discouraging.

exhilaration *n* animation, ardour, cheerfulness, dash, delight, élan, elation, exaltation, excitement, gaiety, gladness, glee, gleefulness, gusto, high spirits, hilarity, joy, joyfulness, liveliness, mirth, sprightliness, vivacity, zeal.

antonyms boredom, discouragement.

exhort *v* admonish, advise, beseech, bid, call upon, caution, counsel, encourage, enjoin, entreat, goad, implore, incite, inflame, inspire, instigate, persuade, press, spur, urge, warn.

exhortation *n* admonition, advice, allocution, beseeching, bidding, caution, counsel, encouragement, enjoinder, entreaty, goading, incitement, lecture, paraenesis, persuasion, protreptic, sermon, urging, warning.

exhortative *adj* begging, beseeching, imploring, paraenetic(al), persuasive, protreptic, protreptical.

exhume *v* dig up, disentomb, disinhume, disinter, excavate, unbury, unearth.

antonym bury.

exigency *n* acuteness, bind, constraint, crisis, criticalness, crunch, demand, difficulty, distress, emergency, exigence, extremity, fix, hardship, imperativeness, jam, juncture, necessity, need, needfulness, pass, pickle, pinch, plight, predicament, pressure, quandary, requirement, scrape, stew, strait, stress, urgency.

exigent *adj* acute, arduous, constraining, critical, crucial, demanding, difficult, exacting, exhausting, hard, harsh, imperative, importunate, insistent, necessary, needful, pressing, rigorous, severe, stiff, strict, stringent, taxing, tough, urgent.

antonym mild.

exile *n* banishment, deportation, deportee, émigré, exilement, expatriate, expatriation, expulsion, galut(h), ostracism, outcast, proscription, refugee, separation.

v banish, deport, drive out, expatriate, expel, ostracise, oust, proscribe.

exist *v* abide, be, be available, be extant, breathe, continue, endure, happen, have one's being, last, live, obtain, occur, prevail, remain, stand, subsist, survive.

existence *n* actuality, animation, being, breath, continuance, continuation, creation, creature, duration, endurance, entity, esse, haecceity, inbeing, life, reality, subsistence, survival, the world, thing.

antonym non-existence.

existent *adj* abiding, actual, around, current, enduring, existing, extant, living, obtaining, present, prevailing, real, remaining, standing, surviving.

antonym non-existent.

exit *n* adieu, aperture, congé, departure, door, doorway, egress, evacuation, exodus, farewell, gate, going, leave-taking, outlet, retirement, retreat, vent, way out, withdrawal.

antonym entrance.

v arrive, depart, enter, issue, leave, retire, retreat, take one's leave, withdraw.

exodus *n* departure, evacuation, exit, flight, hegira, leaving, long march, migration, retirement, retreat, withdrawal.

exonerate *v* absolve, acquit, clear, discharge, disculpate, dismiss, except, exculpate, excuse, exempt, free, justify, let off, liberate, pardon, release, relieve, vindicate.

antonym incriminate.

exoneration *n* absolution, acquittal, amnesty, deliverance, discharge, dismissal, exception, exculpation, exemption, freeing, immunity, indemnity, justification, liberation, pardon, release, relief, vindication.

antonym incrimination.

exorbitance *n* excess, excessiveness, extravagance, immoderateness, immoderation, inordinateness, monstrousness, nimiety, preposterousness, unreasonableness.

antonyms fairness, reasonableness.

exorbitant *adj* enormous, excessive, extortionate, extravagant, extreme, immoderate, inordinate, monstrous, outrageous, preposterous, unconscionable, undue, unreasonable, unwarranted.

antonyms fair, reasonable.

exorcise *v* adjure, cast out, drive out, expel, exsufflate, purify.

exorcism *n* adjuration, deliverance, expulsion, exsufflation, purification.

exotic *adj* alien, bizarre, colourful, curious, different, external, extraneous, extraordinary, extrinsic, fascinating, foreign, foreign-looking, glamorous, imported, introduced, mysterious, naturalised, outlandish, outré, peculiar, recherché, strange, striking, unfamiliar, unusual.

antonym ordinary.

expand *v* amplify, augment, bloat, blow up, branch out, broaden, develop, diffuse, dilate, dispread, distend, diversify, elaborate, embellish, enlarge, expatiate, expound, extend, fatten, fill out, flesh out, grow, heighten, increase, inflate, lengthen, magnify, multiply, open, outspread, prolong, protract, snowball, spread, stretch, swell, thicken, unfold, unfurl, unravel, unroll, wax, widen.

antonyms contract, précis.

expanded *adj* bloated, blown out, blown up, dilated, distended, enlarged, increased, inflated, puffed out, swollen.

expanse *n* area, breadth, extent, field, plain, range, space, stretch, sweep, tract, vast, vastness.

expansible *adj* distensible, distensile, expansile, inflatable.

expansion *n* amplification, augmentation, development, diffusion, dilatation, dilation, distension, diversification, enlargement, expanse, extension, growth, increase, inflation, magnification, multiplication, spread, swelling, unfolding, unfurling.

antonym contraction.

expansive *adj* affable, all-embracing, broad, communicative, comprehensive, dilating, distending, easy, effusive, elastic, expanding, expatiative, expatiatory, extendable, extensive, far-reaching, free, friendly, garrulous, genial, inclusive, loquacious, open, outgoing, sociable, stretching, stretchy, swelling, talkative, thorough, unreserved, voluminous, warm, wide, wide-ranging, widespread.

antonyms cold, reserved.

expatiate *v* amplify, descant, develop, dilate, dwell on, elaborate, embellish, enlarge, expound.

expatriate *n* displaced person, emigrant, émigré, exile, ex-pat, refugee.

v banish, deport, exile, expel, ostracise, oust, proscribe.

adj banished, emigrant, émigré, exiled.

expect *v* anticipate, assume, await, bank on, bargain for, believe, calculate, conjecture, contemplate, count on, demand, envisage, forecast, foresee, hope for, imagine, insist on, look for, look forward to, predict, presume, project, reckon, rely on, require, suppose, surmise, think, trust, want, wish.

expectancy *n* anticipation, assumption, belief, conjecture, curiosity, eagerness, expectation, hope, likelihood, outlook, prediction, presumption, probability, prospect, supposition, surmise, suspense, waiting.

expectant *adj* agog, anticipating, anxious, apprehensive, awaiting, curious, eager, enceinte, expecting, gravid, hopeful, in suspense, pregnant, ready, watchful.

expectantly *adv* eagerly, expectingly, hopefully, in anticipation, optimistically.

expectation *n* anticipation, apprehension, assumption, assurance, belief, calculation, chance, confidence, conjecture, demand, eagerness, expectancy, fear, forecast, hope, insistence, likelihood, optimism, outlook, possibility, prediction, presumption, probability, projection, promise, prospect, reliance, requirement, supposition, surmise, suspense, trust, want, wish.

expected *adj* anticipated, awaited, en l'aire, hoped-for, longed-for, predicted, promised.

antonym unexpected.

expecting *adj* enceinte, expectant, gravid, in the club, in the family way, pregnant, with child.

expedience *n* advantage, advantageousness, advisability, appropriateness, aptness, benefit, convenience, desirability, effectiveness, expediency, fitness, gainfulness, helpfulness, judiciousness, meetness, practicality, pragmatism, profitability, profitableness, properness, propriety, prudence, suitability, usefulness, utilitarianism, utility.

expedient *adj* advantageous, advisable, appropriate, beneficial, convenient, desirable, effective, fit, helpful, judicious, meet, opportune, politic, practical, pragmatic, profitable, proper, prudent, serviceable, suitable, useful, utilitarian, worthwhile.

antonym inexpedient.

n contrivance, device, dodge, makeshift, manoeuvre, means, measure, method, resort, resource, ruse, scheme, shift, stop-gap, stratagem, substitute.

expedite *v* accelerate, advance, aid, assist, dispatch, facilitate, forward, further, hasten, hurry, precipitate, press, promote, quicken, rush, speed.

antonym delay.

expedition[1] *n* company, crusade, enterprise, excursion, exploration, explorers, hike, journey, mission, pilgrimage, quest, raid, ramble, safari, sail, team, tour, travellers, trek, trip, undertaking, voyage, voyagers.

expedition[2] *n* alacrity, briskness, celerity, dispatch, expeditiousness, haste, hurry, immediacy, promptness, quickness, rapidity, readiness, speed, swiftness.

antonym delay.

expeditious *adj* active, alert, brisk, diligent, efficient, fast, hasty, immediate, instant, meteoric, prompt, quick, rapid, ready, speedy, swift.

antonym slow.

expel *v* ban, banish, bar, belch, blackball, cast out, disbar, discharge, dislodge, dismiss, drive out, drum out, egest, eject, evict, exclude, exile, expatriate, hoof out, oust, proscribe, remove, send packing, spew, throw out, turf out.

antonym admit.

expend *v* consume, disburse, dissipate, employ, exhaust, fork out, pay, shell out, spend, use, use up.

antonym save.

expendable *adj* dispensable, disposable, inessential, non-essential, replaceable, unimportant, unnecessary.

antonyms indispensable, necessary.

expenditure *n* application, charge, consumption, cost, disbursement, expense, outgo, outgoings, outlay, output, payment, spending.

antonyms profit, savings.

expense *n* charge, consumption, cost, damage, disbursement, expenditure, loss, outlay, output, payment, sacrifice, spending, toll, use.

expenses *n* costs, incidentals, outgoings, outlay, overheads.

expensive *adj* costly, dear, excessive, exorbitant, extortionate, extravagant, high-priced, inordinate, lavish, overpriced, rich, steep, stiff.

antonyms cheap, inexpensive.

experience *n* adventure, affair, assay, contact, doing, encounter, episode, event, evidence, exposure, familiarity, happening, incident, involvement, know-how, knowledge, observation, occurrence, ordeal, participation, practice, proof, taste, test, training, trial, understanding.

antonym inexperience.

v apprehend, behold, empathise, encounter, endure, face, feel, have, know, meet, observe, perceive, sample, sense, suffer, sustain, taste, try, undergo.

experienced *adj* accomplished, adept, capable, competent, expert, familiar, knowing, knowledgeable, master, mature, practised, professional, qualified, schooled, seasoned, skilful, sophisticated, streetwise, tested, trained, travailed, travelled, tried, veteran, well-versed, wise, worldly, worldly-wise.

antonym inexperienced.

experiment *n* assay, attempt, ballon d'essai, examination, experimentation, heurism, investigation, procedure, proof, research, test, trial, trial and error, trial run, venture.

v assay, examine, investigate, research, sample, test, try, verify.

experimental *adj* empiric(al), exploratory, heuristic, peirastic, pilot, preliminary, probationary, provisional, speculative, tentative, test, trial, trial-and-error.

expert *n* ace, adept, authority, boffin, connoisseur, dab hand, dabster, deacon, dean, maestro, master, pastmaster, pro, professional, specialist, virtuoso, wizard.

adj able, adept, adroit, apt, clever, crack, deft, dexterous, experienced, facile, handy, knowledgeable, master, masterly, practised, professional, proficient, qualified, skilful, skilled, trained, virtuoso.

antonym novice.

expertise *n* ableness, adroitness, aptness, cleverness, command, deftness, dexterity, expertness, facility, judgement, knack, know-how, knowledge, masterliness, mastery, proficiency, skilfulness, skill, virtuosity.

antonym inexpertness.

expertness *n* ableness, adroitness, aptness, command, deftness, dexterity, expertise, facility, finesse, judgement, know-how, knowledge, masterliness, mastery, proficiency, savoir-faire, skilfulness, skill.

antonym inexpertness.

expiation *n* amends, atonement, penance, ransom, redemption, redress, shrift.

expiatory *adj* atoning, piacular, purgative, purgatory, redemptive.

expire *v* cease, close, conclude, decease, depart, die, discontinue, emit, end, exhale, finish, lapse, perish, run out, stop, terminate.

antonyms begin, continue.

expiry *n* cease, cessation, close, conclusion, death, decease, demise, departure, end, expiration, finis, finish, termination.

antonyms beginning, continuation.

explain *v* account for, clarify, clear up, construe, decipher, decode, define, demonstrate, describe, disclose, elucidate, enucleate, excuse, explicate, expound, gloss, gloze, illustrate, interpret, justify, resolve, simplify, solve, spell out, teach, translate, unfold, unravel, untangle.

antonyms obfuscate, obscure.

explanation *n* account, answer, cause, clarification, definition, demonstration, description, éclaircissement, elucidation, enucleation, excuse, exegesis, explication, exposition, gloss, illustration, interpretation, justification, legend, meaning, mitigation, motive, reason, resolution, sense, significance, solution, vindication, voice-over.

explanatory *adj* demonstrative, descriptive, elucidative, elucidatory, exegetic, exegetical, explicative, expositive, expository, illuminative, illustrational, illustrative, illustratory, interpretive, justifying.

explicable *adj* accountable, definable, determinable, explainable, exponible, intelligible, interpretable, justifiable, resolvable, solvable, understandable.

explicate *v* clarify, construct, develop, devise, elucidate, evolve, explain, expound, formulate, interpret, set forth, unfold, unravel, untangle, work out.

antonyms confuse, obscure.

explicit *adj* absolute, accurate, categorical, certain, clear, declared, definite, detailed, direct, distinct, exact, express, frank, open, outspoken, patent, plain, positive, precise, specific, stated, straightforward, unambiguous, unequivocal, unqualified, unreserved.

antonyms inexplicit, vague.

explode *v* belie, blow up, burst, debunk, detonate, discharge, discredit, disprove, erupt, give the lie to, go off, invalidate, rebut, refute, repudiate, set off, shatter, shiver.

antonym prove.

exploit *n* accomplishment, achievement, adventure, attainment, deed, feat, gest(e), stunt.

v abuse, bleed, capitalise on, cash in on, fleece, impose on, make capital out of, manipulate, milk, misuse, profit by, rip off, skin, soak, take advantage of, turn to account, use, utilise.

exploitation *n* abuse, imposition, manipulation, misuse, rip-off, sexploitation, speciesism.

exploration *n* analysis, examination, expedition, inquiry, inquisition, inspection, investigation, probe, reconnaissance, research, safari, scrutiny, search, study, survey, tour, travel, trip, voyage.

exploratory *adj* analytic(al), experimental, fact-finding, investigative, pilot, probing, searching, tentative, trial, wildcat.

explore *v* analyse, case, examine, inspect, investigate, probe, prospect, reconnoitre, research, scout, scrutinise, search, survey, tour, travel, traverse.

explosion *n* bang, blast, burst, clap, crack, debunking, detonation, discharge, discrediting, eruption, fit, outbreak, outburst, paroxysm, refutation, report.

explosive *adj* charged, dangerous, fiery, hazardous, overwrought, perilous, stormy, tense, touchy, ugly, unstable, vehement, violent, volatile, volcanic.

antonym calm.

n cordite, dynamite, gelignite, gun-powder, jelly, lyddite, melinite, nitroglycerine, TNT.

exponent *n* advocate, backer, champion, commentator, defender, demonstrator, elucidator, example, executant, exegetist, exemplar, expositor, expounder, illustration, illustrator, indication, interpreter, model, performer, player, presenter, promoter, propagandist, proponent, representative, sample, specimen, spokesman, spokeswoman, supporter, type, upholder.

expose *v* air, betray, bring to light, denounce, detect, disclose, display, divulge, endanger, exhibit, hazard, imperil, jeopardise, manifest, present, reveal, risk, show, uncover, unearth, unmask, unveil, wash one's dirty linen in public.

antonym cover.

expose to acquaint with, bring into contact with, familiarise with, introduce to, lay open to, subject to.

antonym protect.

exposé *n* account, article, disclosure, divulgence, expose, exposure, revelation, uncovering.

exposed *adj* bare, exhibited, laid bare, liable, on display, on show, on view, open, prey to, revealed, shown, susceptible, unconcealed, uncovered, unprotected, unsheltered, unveiled, vulnerable.

antonyms covered, sheltered.

exposition *n* account, commentary, critique, demonstration, description, discourse, display, elucidation, exegesis, exhibition, explanation, explication, expo, fair, illustration, interpretation, monograph, paper, presentation, show, study, thesis.

expository *adj* declaratory, descriptive, elucidative, exegetic, explanatory, explicative, explicatory, hermeneutic, illustrative, interpretative, interpretive.

expostulate *v* argue, dissuade, plead, protest, reason, remonstrate.

exposure *n* acquaintance, airing, aspect, betrayal, cold, contact, conversance, conversancy, danger, denunciation, detection, disclosure, discovery, display, divulgence, divulging, exhibition, experience, exposé, familiarity, frontage, hazard, introduction, jeopardy, knowledge, lack of shelter, location, manifestation, outlook, position, presentation, publicity, revelation, risk, setting, showing, uncovering, unmasking, unveiling, view, vulnerability.

expound *v* describe, elucidate, explain, explicate, illustrate, interpet, preach, sermonise, set forth, spell out, unfold.

express *v* articulate, assert, asseverate, bespeak, communicate, conceive, convey, couch, declare, denote, depict, designate, disclose, divulge, embody, enunciate, evince, exhibit, extract, force out, formulate, formulise, indicate, intimate, manifest, phrase, pronounce, put, put across, represent. reveal, say, show, signify, speak, stand for, state, symbolise, tell, testify, utter, verbalise, voice, word.

adj accurate, categorical, certain, clear, clear-cut, definite, direct, distinct, especial, exact, explicit, fast, high-speed, manifest, non-stop, outright, particular, plain, pointed, precise, quick, rapid, singular, special, speedy, stated, swift, unambiguous, unqualified.

antonym vague.

expression *n* air, announcement, appearance, aspect, assertion, asseveration, communication, countenance, declaration, delivery, demonstration, diction, embodiment, emphasis, enunciation, execution, exhibition, face, idiom, indication, intonation, language, locution, look, manifestation, mention, mien, phrase, phraseology, phrasing, pronouncement, reflex, remark, representation, set phrase, show, sign, speaking, speech, statement, style, symbol, term, token, turn of phrase, utterance, verbalisation, verbalism, voicing, word, wording.

expressionless *adj* blank, dead-pan, dull, empty, glassy, impassive, inscrutable, poker-faced, straight-faced, vacuous, wooden.

antonym expressive.

expressive *adj* allusive, demonstrative, eloquent, emphatic, energetic, forcible, indicative, informative, lively, meaningful, mobile, moving, poignant, pointed, pregnant, representative, revealing, significant, striking, strong, suggestive, sympathetic, telling, thoughtful, vivid.

antonyms expressionless, poker-faced.

expressly *adv* absolutely, categorically, clearly, decidedly, definitely, distinctly, especially, exactly, explicitly, intentionally, manifestly, on purpose, outright, particularly, plainly, pointedly, positively, precisely, purposely, specially, specifically, unambiguously, unequivocally.

expropriate *v* annex, appropriate, arrogate, assume, commandeer, confiscate, dispossess, disseise, impound, requisition, seize, sequester, take, unhouse.

expulsion *n* banishment, debarment, disbarment, discharge, dislodgement, dislodging, dismissal, ejection, ejectment, eviction, exclusion, exile, expatriation, extrusion, proscription, removal.

expunge *v* abolish, annihilate, annul, blot out, cancel, delete, destroy, efface, eradicate, erase, exterminate, extinguish, extirpate, obliterate, raze, remove, uncreate, unmake, wipe out.

expurgate *v* blue-pencil, bowdlerise, censor, clean up, cut, emend, purge, purify, sanitise.

exquisite *adj* acute, admirable, alembicated, appreciative, attractive, beautiful, charming, choice, comely, consummate, cultivated, dainty, delicate, delicious, discerning, discriminating, elegant, excellent, excruciating, fastidious, fine, flawless, impeccable, incomparable, intense, keen, lovely, matchless, meticulous, outstanding, peerless, perfect, piercing, pleasing, poignant, polished, precious, rare, refined, select, selective, sensitive, sharp, splendid, striking, superb, superlative, too-too.

antonyms flawed, imperfect, poor, ugly.

extant *adj* alive, existent, existing, in existence, living, remaining, subsistent, subsisting, surviving.

antonyms dead, extinct, non-existent.

extemporary *adj* ad-lib, expedient, extemporaneous, extempore, free, impromptu, improvisatory, improvised, jazz, made-up, makeshift, offhand, off-the-cuff, on-the-spot, spontaneous, temporary, unplanned, unpremeditated, unprepared, unrehearsed.

antonym planned.

extemporise *v* ad-lib, autoschediaze, improvise, make up, play by ear.

extend *v* advance, amplify, attain, augment, bestow, broaden, confer, continue, develop, dilate, drag out, draw out, elongate, enhance, enlarge, expand, give, grant, hold out, impart, increase, last, lengthen, offer, present, proffer, prolong, protract, pull out, reach, spin out, spread, stretch, supplement, take, uncoil, unfold, unfurl, unroll, widen, yield.

antonym shorten.

extension *n* accretion, addendum, addition, adjunct, amplification, annexe, appendage, appendix, augmentation, branch, broadening, continuation, delay, development, dilatation, distension, el, elongation, enhancement, enlargement, expansion, extent, increase, lengthening, postponement, prolongation, protraction, spread, stretching, supplement, widening, wing.

extensive *adj* all-inclusive, broad, capacious, commodious, comprehensive, expanded, expansive, extended, far-flung, far-reaching, general, great, huge, large, large-scale, lengthy, long, pervasive, prevalent, protracted, roomy, spacious, sweeping, thorough, thoroughgoing, universal, unrestricted, vast, voluminous, wholesale, wide, widespread.

antonyms narrow, restricted.

extent *n* amount, amplitude, area, bounds, breadth, bulk, compass, degree, dimension(s), duration, expanse, expansion, length, magnitude, measure, play, proportions, quantity, range, reach, scope, size, sphere, spread, stretch, sweep, term, time, volume, width.

extenuate *v* decrease, diminish, excuse, lessen, minimise, mitigate, moderate, modify, palliate, qualify, reduce, soften, temper, weaken.

extenuating *adj* exculpatory, extenuative, extenuatory, justifying, mitigating, moderating, palliative, qualifying.

exterior *n* appearance, aspect, coating, covering, externals, façade, face, finish, outside, shell, skin, superficies, surface.

antonym interior.

adj alien, exotic, external, extraneous, extrinsic, foreign, outer, outermost, outside, outward, peripheral, superficial, surface, surrounding.

antonym interior.

exterminate *v* abolish, annihilate, deracinate, destroy, eliminate, eradicate, extirpate, massacre, wipe out.

extermination *n* annihilation, deracination, destruction, elimination, eradication, extirpation, genocide, massacre.

external *adj* alien, apparent, exoteric, exotic, exterior, extern, externe, extramural, extraneous, extrinsic, foreign, independent, outer, outermost, outside, outward, superficial, surface, visible.

antonym internal.

extinct *adj* abolished, dead, defunct, doused, ended, exterminated, extinguished, gone, inactive, lost, obsolete, out, quenched, terminated, vanished, void.

antonyms extant, living.

extinction *n* abolition, annihilation, death, destruction, eradication, excision, extermination, extinguishment, extirpation, obliteration, oblivion, quietus.

extinguish *v* abolish, annihilate, destroy, douse, dout, eliminate, end, eradicate, erase, expunge, exterminate, extirpate, kill, obscure, put out, quench, remove, slake, smother, snuff out, stifle, suppress.

extirpate *v* abolish, annihilate, cut out, deracinate, destroy, eliminate, eradicate, erase, expunge, exterminate, extinguish, remove, root out, uproot, wipe out.

extol *v* acclaim, applaud, celebrate, commend, cry up, eulogise, exalt, glorify, laud, magnify, panegyrise, praise, puff.

antonyms blame, denigrate.

extort *v* blackmail, bleed, bully, coerce, exact, extract, force, milk, squeeze, wrest, wring.

extortion *n* blackmail, coercion, compulsion, demand, exaction, exorbitance, expensiveness, force, milking, oppression, overcharging, rapacity.

extortionate *adj* blood-sucking, exacting, excessive, exorbitant, extorsive, extortive, extravagant, grasping, hard, harsh, immoderate, inflated, inordinate, oppressive, outrageous, preposterous, rapacious, rigorous, severe, sky-high, unreasonable, usurious.

antonym reasonable.

extra *adj* accessory, added, additional, ancillary, auxiliary, excess, extraneous, for good measure, fresh, further, gash, inessential, leftover, more, needless, new, other, redundant, reserve, spare, supererogatory, superfluous, supernumerary, supplemental, supplementary, surplus, unnecessary, unneeded, unused.

antonym integral.

n accessory, addendum, addition, adjunct, affix, appendage, appurtenance, attachment, bonus, complement, extension, lagniappe, plus(s)age, supernumerary, supplement.

adv especially, exceptionally, extraordinarily, extremely, particularly, remarkably, uncommonly, unusually.

extract *v* abstract, choose, cite, cull, decoct, deduce, derive, develop, distil, draw, draw out, educe, elicit, enucleate, evoke, evolve, evulse, exact, express, extirpate, gather, get, glean, obtain, quote, reap, remove, select, uproot, withdraw, wrest, wring.

antonym insert.

n abstract, apozem, citation, clip, clipping, concentrate, cutting, decoction, decocture, distillate, distillation, essence, excerpt, juice, passage, quotation, selection.

extraction *n* ancestry, birth, blood, derivation, descent, distillation, drawing, educt, enucleation, extirpation, family, lineage, origin, parentage, pedigree, pulling, race, removal, separation, stock, withdrawal.

antonym insertion.

extraneous *adj* accidental, additional, adventitious, alien, exotic, exterior, external, extra, extrinsic, foreign, immaterial, impertinent, inadmissible, inapplicable, inapposite, inappropriate, inapt, incidental, inessential, irrelevant, needless, non-essential, peripheral, redundant, strange, superfluous, supplementary, tangential, unconnected, unessential, unnecessary, unneeded, unrelated.

antonym integral.

extraordinary *adj* amazing, bizarre, curious, exceptional, fantastic, marvellous, notable, noteworthy, odd, outstanding, particular, peculiar, phenomenal, rare, remarkable, significant, singular, special, strange, striking, surprising, uncommon, uncontemplated, unfamiliar, unheard-of, unimaginable, unique, unprecedented, unusual, unwonted, weird, wonderful.

antonyms commonplace, ordinary.

extravagance *n* absurdity, dissipation, exaggeration, excess, exorbitance, folly, hyperbole, immoderation, improvidence, lavishness, outrageousness, overspending, preposterousness, prodigality, profligacy, profusion, recklessness, squandering, unreasonableness, unrestraint, unthrift, unthriftiness, waste, wastefulness, wildness.

antonyms moderation, thrift.

extravagant *adj* absurd, costly, exaggerated, excessive, exorbitant, expensive, extortionate, fanciful, fancy, fantastic, flamboyant, flashy, foolish, garish, gaudy, grandiose, hyperbolic, hyperbolical, immoderate, improvident, imprudent, inordinate, lavish, ornate, ostentatious, outrageous, outré, overpriced, preposterous, pretentious, prodigal, profligate, reckless, showy, spendthrift, steep, thriftless, unreasonable, unrestrained, unthrifty, wasteful, wild.

antonyms moderate, thrifty.

extravaganza *n* display, féerie, pageant, show, spectacle, spectacular.

extravert *see* **extrovert**.

extreme *adj* acute, deep-dyed, dire, double-dyed, downright, Draconian, drastic, egregious, exaggerated, exceptional, excessive, exquisite, extraordinary, extravagant, fanatical, faraway, far-off, farthest, final, great, greatest, harsh, high, highest, immoderate, inordinate, intemperate, intense, last, maximum, out-and-out, outermost, outrageous, radical, red-hot, remarkable, remotest, rigid, severe, sheer, stern, strict, supreme, terminal, ultimate, ultra, unbending, uncommon, uncompromising, unconventional, unreasonable, unusual, utmost, utter, uttermost, worst, zealous.

antonyms mild, moderate.

n acme, apex, apogee, boundary, climax, consummation, depth, edge, end, excess, extremity, height, limit, maximum, minimum, nadir, peak, pinnacle, pole, termination, top, ultimate, utmost, zenith.

extremely *adv* acutely, awfully, exceedingly, exceptionally, excessively, extraordinarily, greatly, highly, inordinately, intensely, markedly, mortal, passing, quite, severely, terribly, too, too-too, ultra, uncommonly, unusually, utterly, very.

extremism *n* fanaticism, radicalism, terrorism, ultraism, zeal, zealotism, zealotry.

antonym moderation.

extremist *n* die-hard, fanatic, militant, radical, terrorist, ultra, ultraconservative, zealot.

antonym moderate.

extremity *n* acme, acuteness, adversity, apex, apogee, border, bound, boundary, brim, brink, climax, consummation, crisis, crunch, depth, disaster, edge, emergency, end, excess, exigency, extreme, foot, frontier, hand, hardship, height, limit, margin, maximum, minimum, nadir, peak, pinnacle, plight, pole, rim, setback, terminal, termination, terminus, tip, top, trouble, ultimate, utmost, verge, zenith.

extricate *v* clear, deliver, disembarrass, disembrangle, disembroil, disengage, disentangle, disintricate, free, liberate, release, relieve, remove, rescue, withdraw.

antonym involve.

extrinsic *adj* accidental, alien, exotic, exterior, external, extraneous, foreign, imported, inessential, non-essential, outside, superficial.

antonym essential.

extroversion *n* amiability, amicability, extraversion, exuberance, friendliness, heartiness, sociability, viscerotonia.

extrovert *adj* amiable, amicable, extravert, exuberant, friendly, hail-fellow-well-met, hearty, outgoing, social, viscerotonic.

antonym introvert.

n joiner, life and soul of the party, mixer, socialiser.

antonyms introvert, loner.

exuberance *n* abundance, animation, buoyancy, cheerfulness, copiousness, eagerness, ebullience, effervescence, effusiveness, energy, enthusiasm, exaggeration, excessiveness, excitement, exhilaration, fulsomeness, high spirits, lavishness, life, liveliness, lushness, luxuriance, pizzazz, plenitude, prodigality, profusion, rankness, richness, spirit, sprightliness, superabundance, superfluity, vigour, vitality, vivacity, zest.

antonyms apathy, lifelessness, scantiness.

exuberant *adj* abundant, animated, baroque, buoyant, cheerful, copious, eager, ebullient, effervescent, effusive, elated, energetic, enthusiastic, exaggerated, excessive, excited, exhilarated, fulsome, high-spirited, lavish, lively, lush, luxuriant, overdone, overflowing, plenteous, plentiful, prodigal, profuse, rambunctious, rank, rich, sparkling, spirited, sprightly, superabundant, superfluous, teeming, vigorous, vivacious, zestful.

antonyms apathetic, lifeless, scant.

exude *v* bleed, discharge, display, emanate, emit, excrete, exhibit, flow out, issue, leak, manifest, ooze, perspire, radiate, secrete, seep, show, sweat, trickle, weep, well.

exult *v* boast, brag, celebrate, crow, delight, gloat, glory, jubilate, rejoice, relish, revel, taunt, triumph.

exultant *adj* cock-a-hoop, delighted, elated, exulting, gleeful, joyful, joyous, jubilant, over the moon, overjoyed, rejoicing, revelling, transporting, triumphant.

antonym depressed.

exultation *n* boasting, bragging, celebration, crowing, delight, elation, glee, gloating, glory, glorying, joy, joyfulness, joyousness, jubilation, merriness, paean, rejoicing, revelling, transport, triumph.

antonym depression.

eye *n* appreciation, belief, discernment, discrimination, eyeball, glim, judgement, keeker, mind, opinion, optic, orb, peeper, perception, recognition, taste, viewpoint.

v contemplate, examine, eye up, gaze at, glance at, inspect, leer at, look at, make eyes at, observe, ogle, peruse, regard, scan, scrutinise, stare at, study, survey, view, watch.

eye-catching *adj* arresting, attractive, beautiful, captivating, gorgeous, imposing, impressive, showy, spectacular, striking, stunning.

antonyms plain, unattractive.

eyeful *n* beauty, dazzler, knockout, show, sight, sight for sore eyes, spectacle, stunner, view, vision.

eyeglasses *n* glasses, lorgnette, lorgnon, monocle, pince-nez, specs, spectacles.

eyesight *n* observation, perception, sight, view, vision.

eyesore *n* atrocity, blemish, blight, blot, disfigurement, disgrace, dissight, horror, mess, monstrosity, sight, ugliness.

eye-witness *n* beholder, bystander, looker-on, observer, onlooker, passer-by, spectator, viewer, watcher, witness.

F

fable *n* allegory, apologue, fabliau, fabrication, fairy story, falsehood, fantasy, fib, fiction, figment, invention, legend, lie, Märchen, myth, narrative, old wives' tale, parable, romance, saga, story, tale, tall story, untruth, yarn.

fabled *adj* fabulous, famed, famous, feigned, fictional, legendary, mythical, renowned, storied.
antonym unknown.

fabric *n* cloth, constitution, construction, foundations, framework, infrastructure, make-up, material, organisation, structure, stuff, textile, texture, web.

fabricate *v* assemble, build, coin, concoct, construct, create, devise, erect, fake, falsify, fashion, feign, forge, form, frame, invent, make, manufacture, shape, trump up.

fabrication *n* assemblage, assembly, building, cock-and-bull story, concoction, construction, erection, fable, fairy story, fake, falsehood, fiction, figment, forgery, frame-up, invention, lie, manufacture, myth, production, story, untruth.
antonym truth.

fabulous *adj* amazing, apocryphal, astounding, breathtaking, fabled, false, fantastic, feigned, fictitious, imaginary, immense, inconceivable, incredible, invented, legendary, marvellous, mythical, phenomenal, renowned, spectacular, superb, unbelievable, unreal, wonderful.
antonyms moderate, real, small.

façade *n* appearance, cloak, cover, disguise, exterior, face, front, frontage, guise, mask, pretence, semblance, show, veil, veneer.

face *n* air, appearance, aspect, assurance, audacity, authority, boatrace, boldness, brass neck, cheek, confidence, countenance, cover, dial, dignity, disguise, display, effrontery, expression, exterior, façade, facet, favour, features, front, frown, gall, grimace, honour, image, impudence, kisser, lineaments, look, mask, metope, moue, mug, nerve, outside, phiz, phizog, physiognomy, pout, prestige, presumption, pretence, reputation, sauce, scowl, self-respect, semblance, show, side, smirk, snoot, standing, status, surface, visage.

v clad, coat, confront, cope with, cover, deal with, defy, dress, encounter, experience, finish, front, give on to, level, line, meet, oppose, overlay, overlook, sheathe, surface, tackle, veneer.

face to face à deux, confronting, eye to eye, eyeball to eyeball, in confrontation, opposite, tête-à-tête, vis-à-vis.

face up to accept, acknowledge, come to terms with, confront, cope with, deal with, meet head-on, recognise, square up to, stand up to.

face-lift *n* cosmetic surgery, plastic surgery, redecoration, renovation, restoration, rhytidectomy.

facet *n* angle, aspect, characteristic, face, feature, part, phase, plane, point, side, slant, surface.

facetious *adj* amusing, comical, droll, facete, flippant, frivolous, funny, humorous, jesting, jocose, jocular, merry, playful, pleasant, tongue-in-cheek, unserious, waggish, witty.
antonym serious.

facile *adj* adept, adroit, complaisant, cursory, dexterous, easy, effortless, fluent, glib, hasty, light, plausible, proficient, quick, ready, shallow, simple, skilful, slick, smooth, superficial, uncomplicated, yielding.
antonyms clumsy, implausible, profound.

facilitate *v* assist, ease, expedite, forward, further, grease, help, promote, speed up.

facilities *n* amenity, appliance, convenience, equipment, means, mod cons, opportunity, prerequisites, resource.

facility *n* ability, adeptness, adroitness, bent, dexterity, ease, efficiency, effortlessness, expertness, fluency, gift, knack, proficiency, quickness, readiness, skilfulness, skill, smoothness, talent, turn.

facing *n* cladding, coating, façade, false front, overlay, reinforcement, revetment, skin, surface, trimming, veneer.

facsimile *n* carbon, carbon copy, copy, duplicate, image, mimeograph, photocopy, Photostat®, print, replica, repro, reproduction, transcript, Xerox®.

fact *n* act, actuality, certainty, circumstance, datum, deed, detail, event, fait accompli, feature, gospel, happening, incident, item, occurrence, particular, point, reality, specific, truth.

faction[1] *n* band, bloc, cabal, cadre, camp, caucus, clique, coalition, combination, confederacy, contingent, coterie, crowd, division, gang, ginger group, group, grouplet, junta, lobby, minority, party, pressure group, ring, section, sector, set, splinter group, splinter party, troop.

faction[2] *n* conflict, disagreement, discord, disharmony, dissension, disunity, division, divisiveness, fighting, friction, infighting, quarrelling, rebellion, sedition, strife, tumult, turbulence.

antonyms agreement, peace.

factious *adj* conflicting, contentious, disputatious, dissident, divisive, insurrectionary, litigious, malcontent, mutinous, partisan, quarrelling, quarrelsome, rebellious, refractory, rival, sectarian, seditious, troublemaking, tumultuous, turbulent, warring.

antonyms calm, co-operative.

factitious *adj* affected, artificial, assumed, contrived, counterfeit, engineered, fabricated, fake, false, imitation, insincere, made-up, manufactured, mock, phoney, pinchbeck, put-on, sham, simulated, spurious, supposititious, synthetic, unnatural, unreal.

antonym genuine.

factor *n* agent, aspect, cause, circumstance, component, consideration, deputy, determinant, element, estate manager, influence, item, joker, middleman, parameter, part, point, reeve, steward, thing, unknown quantity.

factors *n* considerations, details, pros and cons.

factory *n* hacienda, manufactory, mill, plant, shop, shop-floor, works.

factotum *n* do-all, famulus, handyman, jack-of-all-trades, Johnnie a'thing, maid-of-all-work, Man (or Girl) Friday, odd-jobman, orra man.

facts *n* data, details, gen, info, information, story, the low-down, the score.

factual *adj* accurate, authentic, circumstantial, close, correct, credible, detailed, exact, faithful, genuine, literal, objective, precise, real, straight, sure, true, unadorned, unbiased, veritable.

antonym false.

faculties *n* capabilities, functions, intelligence, powers, reason, senses, wits.

faculty[1] *n* academics, department, discipline, lecturers, profession, school, staff.

faculty[2] *n* ability, adroitness, aptitude, bent, brain-power, capability, capacity, cleverness, dexterity, facility, gift, knack, power, propensity, readiness, skill, talent, turn.

faculty[3] *n* authorisation, authority, licence, prerogative, privilege, right.

fad *n* affectation, craze, crotchet, cult, fancy, fashion, mania, mode, rage, trend, vogue, whim.

fade *v* blanch, bleach, blench, decline, die, dim, diminish, disappear, discolour, disperse, dissolve, droop, dull, dwindle, ebb, etiolate, evanesce, fail, fall, flag, languish, pale, perish, shrivel, vanish, wane, wilt, wither, yellow.

faded *adj* bleached, dim, discoloured, dull, etiolated, indistinct, lustreless, pale, passé, past one's best, washed-out.

antonym bright.

faeces *n* dregs, droppings, dung, excrement, excreta, ordure, scat, sediment, stools.

fag *n* bind, bore, bother, chore, drag, inconvenience, irritation, nuisance, pest.

fagged *adj* all in, beat, exhausted, fatigued, jaded, jiggered, knackered, on one's last legs, wasted, weary, worn out, zonked.

antonym refreshed.

fail *v* abandon, cease, come to grief, conk out, crack up, crash, cut out, decline, desert, die, disappoint, droop, dwindle, fade, fall, flop, flub, flunk, fold, forget, forsake, founder, fudge, give out, give up, go bankrupt, go bust, go to the wall, go under, gutter, languish, lay an egg, let down, miscarry, misfire, miss, miss one's trip, neglect, omit, peter out, plough, sink, smash, underachieve, underperform, wane, weaken.

antonyms gain, improve, prosper, succeed.

failing *n* blemish, blind spot, decay, decline, defect, deficiency, deterioration, drawback, error, failure, fault, flaw, foible, frailty, hamartia, imperfection, lapse, miscarriage, misfortune, peccadillo, shortcoming, weakness.

antonyms advantage, strength.

adj collapsing, decaying, declining, deteriorating, drooping, dwindling, dying, flagging, languishing, moribund, waning, weak, weakening.

antonyms thriving, vigorous.

prep in default of, in the absence of, lacking, wanting, without.

failure *n* abortion, also-ran, bankruptcy, breakdown, bummer, collapse, crash, cropper, damp squib, dead duck, decay, decline, default, defeat, deficiency, dereliction, deterioration, disappointment, downfall, dud, failing, fiasco, flivver, flop, folding, frost, frustration, goner, incompetent, insolvency, loser, loss, melt, miscarriage, neglect, negligence, no-hoper, non-performance, omission, remissness, ruin, shortcoming, slip-up, stoppage, turkey, unsuccess, wash-out, wreck.

antonym success.

faint *adj* bleached, delicate, dim, distant, dizzy, drooping, dull, enervated, exhausted, faded, faltering, fatigued, feeble, feint, giddy, hazy, hushed, ill-defined, indistinct, languid, lethargic, light, light-headed, low, muffled, muted, muzzy, remote, slight, soft, subdued, thin, unenthusiastic, vague, vertiginous, weak, whispered, woozy.

antonyms clear, strong.

v black out, collapse, droop, drop, flag, flake out, keel over, pass out, swoon.

n blackout, collapse, deliquium, swoon, syncope, unconsciousness.

faint-hearted *adj* diffident, faint-heart, half-hearted, hen-hearted, irresolute, lily-livered, spiritless, timid, timorous, weak.

antonym courageous.

fair[1] *adj* adequate, all right, average, beauteous, beautiful, bonny, bright, clean, clear, clement, cloudless, comely, decent, disinterested, dispassionate, dry, equal, equitable, even-handed, favourable, fine, handsome, honest, honourable, impartial, just, lawful, legitimate, lovely, mediocre, middling, moderate, not bad, objective, OK, on the level, passable, pretty, proper, reasonable, respectable, satisfactory, so-so, square, sunny, sunshiny, tolerable, trustworthy, unbiased, unclouded, unprejudiced, upright, well-favoured.

antonyms cloudy, inclement, poor, unfair.

fair[2] *adj* blond(e), fair-haired, fair-headed, flaxen, light, tow-headed.

antonym dark.

fair[3] *n* bang, bazaar, carnival, expo, exposition, festival, fête, gaff, gala, kermis, market, show.

fairly *adv* absolutely, adequately, deservedly, equitably, ex aequo, fully, honestly, impartially, justly, moderately, objectively, plainly, positively, pretty, properly, quite, rather, really, reasonably, somewhat, tolerably, unbiasedly, veritably.

antonym unfairly.

fairness *n* decency, disinterestedness, equitableness, equity, impartiality, justice, legitimacy, legitimateness, rightfulness, rightness, unbiasedness, uprightness.

antonym unfairness.

fairy *n* brownie, buggane, elf, fay, fée, hob, hobgoblin, leprechaun, Mab, peri, pisky, pixie, Robin Goodfellow, rusalka, sprite.

fairy tale cock-and-bull story, fabrication, fairy story, fantasy, fiction, folk-tale, invention, lie, Märchen, Munch(h)ausen, myth, romance, tall story, untruth.

fairyland *n* féerie, never-never-land, toyland.

faith *n* allegiance, assurance, belief, church, communion, confidence, constancy, conviction, credence, credit, creed, denomination, dependence, dogma, faithfulness, fealty, fidelity, honesty, honour, loyalty, persuasion, pledge, promise, reliance, religion, sincerity, trust, truth, truthfulness, uberrima fides, vow, word, word of honour.

antonyms mistrust, treachery, unfaithfulness.

faithful *adj* accurate, attached, card-carrying, close, constant, convinced, dependable, devoted, exact, just, leal, loyal, precise, reliable, soothfast, soothful, staunch, steadfast, strict, true, true-blue, true-hearted, trusty, truthful, unswerving, unwavering.

antonyms disloyal, inaccurate, treacherous.

n adherents, believers, brethren, communicants, congregation, followers, supporters.

faithfulness *n* accuracy, adherence, closeness, constancy, dependability, devotion, exactness, fealty, fidelity, justice, loyalty, scrupulousness, staunchness, strictness, trustworthiness, truth.

antonyms disloyalty, inaccuracy, treachery.

faithless *adj* adulterous, delusive, disloyal, doubting, false, false-hearted, fickle, inconstant, perfidious, punic, recreant, traitorous, treacherous, unbelieving, unfaithful, unreliable, untrue, untrustworthy, untruthful.

antonyms believing, faithful.

faithlessness *n* adultery, apostasy, betrayal, disloyalty, fickleness, inconstancy, infidelity, perfidy, treachery, unfaithfulness.

antonyms belief, faithfulness.

fake *v* affect, assume, copy, counterfeit, fabricate, feign, forge, phon(e)y, pretend, put on, sham, simulate.

n charlatan, copy, forgery, fraud, hoax, imitant, imitation, impostor, mountebank, phon(e)y, reproduction, sham, simulation.

adj affected, artificial, assumed, bastard, bogus, counterfeit, ersatz, false, forged, hyped up, imitation, mock, phon(e)y, pinchbeck, pretended, pseudo, reproduction, sham, simulated, spurious.

antonym genuine.

fall *v* abate, backslide, become, befall, capitulate, cascade, chance, collapse, come about, come to pass, crash, decline, decrease, depreciate, descend, die, diminish, dive, drop, drop down, dwindle, ebb, err, fall away, fall off, fall out, flag, give in, give up, give way, go a purler, go astray, go down, happen, incline, keel over, lapse, lessen, measure one's length, meet one's end, nose-dive, occur, offend, perish, pitch, plummet, plunge, push, resign, settle, sin, sink, slope, slump, souse, stumble, subside, succumb, surrender, take place, topple, transgress, trespass, trip, trip over, tumble, yield, yield to temptation.

antonym rise.

n capitulation, collapse, cropper, cut, death, decline, declivity, decrease, defeat, degradation, descent, destruction, diminution, dip, dive, downfall, downgrade, drop, dwindling, failure, incline, lapse, lessening, lowering, nose-dive, overthrow, plummet, plunge, pusher, reduction, resignation, ruin, sin, slant, slip, slope, slump, souse, spill, surrender, transgression, tumble, voluntary.

antonym rise.

fall apart break, crumble, decay, decompose, disband, disintegrate, disperse, dissolve, rot, shatter.

fall asleep doze off, drop off, nod off.

fall back on have recourse to, look to, resort to, turn to, use.

fall for accept, be taken in by, swallow.

fall guy dupe, patsy, scapegoat, victim.

fall in cave in, collapse, come down, crumble, give way, sink.

fall in with accept, acquiesce, agree with, assent, come across, comply, concur with, co-operate with, go along with, meet, support.

fall off decelerate, decline, decrease, deteriorate, drop, slacken, slow, slump, wane, worsen.

fall on assail, assault, attack, descend on, lay into, pounce on, snatch.

fall out[1] altercate, argue, bicker, clash, differ, disagree, fight, quarrel, squabble.

antonym agree.

fall out[2] befall, chance, happen, occur, result, take place.

fall through collapse, come to nothing, fail, fizzle out, founder, miscarry.

antonym succeed.

fall to apply oneself, begin, commence, get stuck in, set about, start.

fallacious *adj* casuistical, deceptive, delusive, delusory, erroneous, false, fictitious, illogical, illusory, incorrect, misleading, mistaken, sophistic, sophistical, spurious, untrue, wrong.

antonyms correct, true.

fallacy *n* casuistry, deceit, deception, deceptiveness, delusion, error, falsehood, faultiness, flaw, illusion, inconsistency, misapprehension, misconception, mistake, sophism, sophistry, untruth.

antonym truth.

fallible *adj* errant, erring, frail, human, ignorant, imperfect, mortal, uncertain, weak.

antonym infallible.

fallow *adj* dormant, idle, inactive, inert, resting, uncultivated, undeveloped, unplanted, unsown, untilled, unused.

false *adj* artificial, bastard, bogus, concocted, counterfeit, deceitful, deceiving, deceptive, delusive, dishonest, dishonourable, disloyal, double-dealing, double-faced, duplicitous, erroneous, ersatz, faithless, fake, fallacious, false-hearted, faulty, feigned, fictitious, forged, fraudulent, hypocritical, illusive, imitation, improper, inaccurate, incorrect, inexact, invalid, lying, mendacious, misleading, mistaken, mock, perfidious, postiche, pretended, pseud, pseudo, sham, simulated, spurious, synthetic, treacherous, treasonable, trumped-up, truthless, two-faced, unfaithful, unfounded, unreal, unreliable, unsound, untrue, untrustworthy, untruthful, wrong.

antonyms honest, reliable, true.

falsehood *n* deceit, deception, dishonesty, dissimulation, fable, fabrication, fib, fiction, inexactitude, inveracity, lie, mendacity, misstatement, perjury, prevarication, pseudery, story, unfact, untruth, untruthfulness.

antonyms truth, truthfulness.

falsification *n* adulteration, alteration, change, deceit, dissimulation, distortion, forgery, misrepresentation, perversion, tampering.

falsify *v* adulterate, alter, belie, cook, counterfeit, distort, doctor, fake, forge, garble, misrepresent, misstate, pervert, sophisticate, take liberties with, tamper with.

falter *v* break, fail, flag, flinch, halt, hem and haw, hesitate, shake, stammer, stumble, stutter, totter, tremble, vacillate, waver.

faltering *adj* broken, failing, flagging, hesitant, irresolute, stammering, stumbling, tentative, timid, uncertain, unsteady, weak.

antonyms firm, strong.

fame *n* celebrity, credit, eminence, esteem, glory, honour, illustriousness, kudos, name, prominence, renown, reputation, repute, stardom.

famed *adj* acclaimed, celebrated, famous, noted, recognised, renowned, well-known, widely-known.

antonym unknown.

familiar *adj* abreast, accustomed, acquainted, amicable, au courant, au fait, aware, bold, chummy, close, common, common-or-garden, confidential, conscious, conventional, conversant, cordial, customary, disrespectful, domestic, easy, everyday, forward, free, free-and-easy, frequent, friendly, household, impudent, informal, intimate, intrusive, knowledgeable, mundane, near, open, ordinary, overfree, presuming, presumptuous, private, recognisable, relaxed, repeated, routine, stock, unceremonious, unconstrained, unreserved, versed, well-known.

antonyms formal, reserved, unfamiliar, unversed.

familiarise *v* acclimatise, accustom, brief, coach, habituate, instruct, inure, prime, school, season, train.

familiarity *n* acquaintance, acquaintanceship, awareness, boldness, cheek, closeness, conversance, disrespect, ease, experience, fellowship, forwardness, freedom, friendliness, grasp, impertinence, impudence, informality, intimacy, liberties, liberty, licence, naturalness, openness, presumption, sociability, unceremoniousness, understanding.

antonyms formality, reservation, unfamiliarity.

family *n* ancestors, ancestry, birth, blood, brood, children, clan, class, classification, descendants, descent, dynasty, extraction, folk, forebears, forefathers, genealogy, genre, group, house, household, issue, kin, kind, kindred, kinsmen, kith and kin, line, lineage, ménage, network, offspring, parentage, pedigree, people, progeny, quiverful, race, relations, relatives, sept, stemma, stirps, strain, subdivision, system, tribe.

family tree ancestry, extraction, genealogy, line, lineage, pedigree, stemma, stirps.

famine *n* dearth, destitution, hunger, scarcity, starvation, want.

antonym plenty.

famished *adj* famishing, hungry, ravening, ravenous, starved, starving, voracious.

antonym sated.

famous *adj* acclaimed, celebrated, conspicuous, distinguished, eminent, excellent, famed, far-famed, glorious, great, honoured, illustrious, legendary, lionised, notable, noted, prominent, remarkable, renowned, signal, well-known.

antonym unknown.

fan[1] *v* aggravate, agitate, air-condition, air-cool, arouse, blow, cool, enkindle, excite, impassion, increase, provoke, refresh, rouse, stimulate, stir up, ventilate, whip up, winnow, work up.

n air-conditioner, blower, extractor fan, flabellum, propeller, punkah, vane, ventilator.

fan[2] *n* adherent, admirer, aficionado, buff, devotee, enthusiast, fiend, follower, freak, groupie, lover, rooter, supporter, zealot.

fanatic *n* activist, addict, bigot, demoniac, devotee, energumen, enthusiast, extremist, fiend, freak, militant, visionary, zealot.

fanatical *adj* bigoted, burning, demoniac, demoniacal, enthusiastic, extreme, fervent, fervid, frenzied, immoderate, mad, obsessive, overenthusiastic, passionate, rabid, visionary, wild, zealous.

antonyms moderate, unenthusiastic.

fanaticism *n* bigotry, dedication, devotion, enthusiasm, extremism, fervidness, fervour, immoderacy, immoderateness, immoderation, infatuation, madness, monomania, obsessiveness, overenthusiasm, single-mindedness, zeal, zealotism, zealotry.

antonym moderation.

fanciful *adj* airy-fairy, capricious, chimeric(al), curious, extravagant, fabulous, fairy-tale, fantastic, ideal, imaginary, imaginative, metaphysical, mythical, poetic, romantic, unreal, vaporous, visionary, whimsical, wild.

antonym ordinary.

fancy *v* be attracted to, believe, conceive, conjecture, crave, desire, dream of, favour, go for, guess, hanker after, have an eye for, imagine, infer, like, long for, lust after, picture, prefer, reckon, relish, suppose, surmise, take a liking to, take to, think, think likely, whim, wish for, yearn for, yen for.

antonym dislike.

n caprice, chim(a)era, conception, daydream, delusion, desire, dream, fantasy, fondness, hankering, humour, idea, image, imagination, impression, impulse, inclination, liking, nightmare, notion, partiality, penchant, phantasm, predilection, preference, relish, thought, urge, vapour, velleity, vision, whim.

antonyms dislike, fact, reality.

adj baroque, capricious, chimerical, decorated, decorative, delusive, elaborate, elegant, embellished, extravagant, fanciful, fantastic, far-fetched, illusory, ornamented, ornate, rococo, whimsical.

antonym plain.

fanfare *n* fanfarade, fanfaronade, flourish, trump, trumpet call, tucket.

fang *n* prong, tang, tooth, tusk, venom-tooth.

fantasise *v* build castles in the air, daydream, dream, hallucinate, imagine, invent, live in a dream, romance.

fantastic *adj* absurd, ambitious, capricious, chimerical, comical, eccentric, enormous, excellent, exotic, extravagant, extreme, fanciful, fantasque, far-fetched, first-rate, freakish, grandiose, great, grotesque, illusory, imaginative, implausible, incredible, irrational, ludicrous, mad, marvellous, odd, out of this world, outlandish, outré, overwhelming, peculiar, phantasmagorical, preposterous, Pythonesque, quaint, queer, ridiculous, rococo, sensational, severe, strange, superb, tremendous, unlikely, unreal, unrealistic, visionary, weird, whimsical, wild, wonderful.

antonyms ordinary, plain, poor.

fantasy *n* apparition, caprice, creativity, daydream, delusion, dream, dreamery, fancy, fantasia, fantasque, flight of fancy, hallucination, illusion, imagination, invention, mirage, nightmare, originality, phantasy, pipe-dream, reverie, vision, whims(e)y.

antonym reality.

far *adv* a good way, a long way, afar, considerably, decidedly, deep, extremely, greatly, incomparably, miles, much.

antonym near.

adj distal, distant, faraway, far-flung, far-off, far-removed, further, god-forsaken, long, opposite, other, outlying, out-of-the-way, remote, removed.

antonyms close, nearby.

far and wide all about, broadly, everywhere, extensively, far and near, widely, worldwide.

faraway *adj* absent, absent-minded, abstracted, distant, dreamy, far, far-flung, far-off, lost, outlying, remote.

antonyms alert, nearby.

farce *n* absurdity, buffoonery, burlesque, comedy, commedia dell'arte, exode, joke, lazzo, low comedy, mockery, nonsense, parody, ridiculousness, satire, sham, slapstick, travesty.

farcical *adj* absurd, amusing, comic, derisory, diverting, droll, facetious, funny, laughable, ludicrous, nonsensical, preposterous, ridiculous, risible, silly, slapstick, stupid.

antonym sensible.

fare[1] *n* charge, cost, fee, passage, passenger, pick-up, price, traveller.

fare[2] *n* board, commons, diet, eatables, food, meals, menu, provisions, rations, sustenance, table, victuals.

fare[3] *v* be, do, get along, get on, go, go on, happen, make out, manage, proceed, prosper, turn out.

farewell *n* adieu, departure, good-bye, leave-taking, parting, send-off, valediction.

antonym hello.

adj final, parting, valedictory.

interj aloha, bye-bye, cheers, ciao, good-bye.

far-fetched *adj* crazy, doubtful, dubious, fantastic, forced, implausible, improbable, incredible, preposterous, strained, unbelievable, unconvincing, unlikely, unnatural, unrealistic.

antonym plausible.

farm *n* acreage, acres, bowery, croft, farmstead, grange, holding, homestead, kolkhoz, land, mains, plantation, ranch, smallholding, station.

v cultivate, operate, plant, till, work the land.

farmer *n* agriculturist, agronomist, countryman, crofter, gebur, husbandman, smallholder, yeoman.

farming *n* agriculture, agronomy, crofting, husbandry.

farrago *n* dog's breakfast, gallimaufry, hash, hotchpotch, jumble, medley, mélange, miscellany, mishmash, mixture, pot-pourri, salmagundi.

far-reaching *adj* broad, consequential, extensive, important, momentous, pervasive, significant, sweeping, widespread.

antonym insignificant.

far-sighted *adj* acute, canny, cautious, circumspect, discerning, far-seeing, judicious, politic, prescient, provident, prudent, sage, shrewd, wise.

antonyms imprudent, unwise.

fascinate *v* absorb, allure, beguile, bewitch, captivate, charm, delight, enchant, engross, enrapture, enravish, enthrall, entrance, hypnotise, infatuate, intrigue, mesmerise, rivet, spellbind, transfix.

antonym bore.

fascinated *adj* absorbed, beguiled, bewitched, captivated, charmed, engrossed, enthralled, entranced, hooked, hypnotised, infatuated, mesmerised, smitten, spellbound.

antonyms bored, uninterested.

fascinating *adj* alluring, bewitching, captivating, charming, compelling, delightful, enchanting, engaging, engrossing, enticing, gripping, interesting, intriguing, irresistible, mesmerising, ravishing, riveting, seductive, witching.

antonyms boring, uninteresting.

fascination *n* allure, attraction, charm, enchantment, glamour, interest, lure, magic, magnetism, pull, sorcery, spell, witchery.

antonym boredom.

fascism *n* absolutism, authoritarianism, autocracy, dictatorship, Hitlerism, totalitarianism.

fascist *n* absolutist, authoritarian, autocrat, Blackshirt, Hitlerist, Hitlerite, totalitarian.

adj absolutist, authoritarian, autocratic, fascistic, Hitlerist, Hitlerite, totalitarian.

fashion *n* appearance, attitude, beau monde, configuration, convention, craze, cult, custom, cut, demeanour, dernier cri, description, fad, figure, form, guise, haut ton, haute couture, high society, jet set, kind, latest, line, look, make, manner, method, mode, model, mould, pattern, rage, shape, sort, style, trend, type, usage, vogue, way.

v accommodate, adapt, adjust, alter, construct, contrive, create, design, fit, forge, form, make, manufacture, mould, shape, suit, tailor, work.

fashionable *adj* à la mode, alamode, all the rage, chic, chichi, contemporary, cult, current, customary, funky, genteel, in, in vogue, latest, modern, modish, mondain, popular, prevailing, smart, snazzy, stylish, swagger, tippy, ton(e)y, ton(n)ish, trendsetting, trendy, up-to-date, up-to-the-minute, usual, with it.

antonym unfashionable.

fast[1] *adj* accelerated, brisk, fleet, flying, hasty, hurried, mercurial, nippy, quick, rapid, spanking, speedy, swift, winged.

antonym slow.

adv apace, hastily, hell for leather, hurriedly, like a flash, like a shot, posthaste, presto, quickly, rapidly, speedily, swiftly, ventre à terre.

antonym slowly.

fast[2] *adj* close, constant, fastened, firm, fixed, fortified, immovable, impregnable, lasting, loyal, permanent, secure, sound, staunch, steadfast, tight, unflinching, unwavering.

antonyms impermanent, loose.

adv close, deeply, firmly, fixedly, near, rigidly, securely, soundly, sound(ly), tightly, unflinchingly.

antonym loosely.

fast[3] *adj* dissipated, dissolute, extravagant, immoral, intemperate, licentious, loose, profligate, promiscuous, rakehell, rakehelly, rakish, reckless, self-indulgent, wanton, whorish, wild.

antonyms chaste, moral.

fast[4] *v* abstain, bant, diet, go hungry, starve.

n abstinence, diet, fasting, starvation, xerophagy.

antonyms gluttony, self-indulgence.

fasten *v* affix, aim, anchor, attach, belay, bend, bind, bolt, chain, clamp, concentrate, connect, direct, fix, focus, grip, infibulate, join, lace, link, lock, nail, rivet, seal, secure, spar, tie, unite.

antonym unfasten.

fasten together interdigitate, interlink, interlock, join, link, unite.

antonyms unfasten, untie.

fastened *adj* anchored, attached, bolted, chained, clamped, closed, fixed, joined, knotted, linked, locked, lockfast, nailed, sealed, secured, shut, tied.

fastening *n* bond, catch, clasp, clip, copula, fastness, hasp, holder, hook, latch, latchet, link, lock, nexus, tach(e), tie, vinculum.

fastidious *adj* choosy, critical, dainty, difficult, discriminating, finical, finicky, fussy, hypercritical, meticulous, overnice, particular, pernickety, picky, precise, punctilious, squeamish.

antonym undemanding.

fasting *n* abstinence, banting, dieting, reducing, self-denial, slimming, starvation, xerophagy.

antonyms gluttony, self-indulgence.

fat *adj* abdominous, adipose, affluent, beefy, blowzy, corpulent, cushy, elephantine, fatling, fatty, fertile, fleshed, fleshy, flourishing, fozy, fruitful, greasy, gross, heavy, jammy, lucrative, lush, obese, oily, oleaginous, overweight, paunchy, pinguid, plump, poddy, podgy, portly, pot-bellied, productive, profitable, prosperous, pudgy, remunerative, rich, roly-poly, rotund, round, solid, squab, stout, suety, thriving, tubbish, tubby, well-upholstered.

antonyms thin, unproductive.

n adipose tissue, blubber, brown fat, cellulite, corpulence, degras, embonpoint, fatness, flab, obesity, overweight, paunch, pot (belly), speck.

fatal *adj* baleful, baneful, calamitous, catastrophic, deadly, destructive, disastrous, final, incurable, killing, lethal, malignant, mortal, mortiferous, mortific, pernicious, ruinous, terminal, vital.

antonym harmless.

fatality *n* casualty, deadliness, death, disaster, lethalness, loss, mortality, unavoidability.

fate *n* chance, cup, death, destiny, destruction, divine will, doom, downfall, end, fortune, future, horoscope, issue, joss, karma, kismet, lot, Moira, nemesis, outcome, portion, predestination, predestiny, providence, ruin, stars, upshot, weird.

fated *adj* destined, doomed, foreordained, ineluctable, inescapable, inevitable, predestined, pre-elected, preordained, sure, unavoidable, written.

antonym avoidable.

fateful *adj* critical, crucial, deadly, decisive, destructive, disastrous, fatal, important, lethal, momentous, ominous, portentous, ruinous, significant.

antonym unimportant.

Fates *n* Fatal Sisters, Moirai, Norns, Parcae, Providence, Three Sisters, Weird Sisters.

fathead *n* ass, booby, dimwit, dolt, dope, dumbcluck, dumbo, dunderhead, fool, goose, idiot, imbecile, jackass, nincompoop, nitwit, numskull, twerp, twit.

father *n* abbé, ancestor, architect, author, begetter, confessor, creator, curé, dad, daddy, elder, forebear, forefather, founder, generant, genitor, governor, inventor, leader, maker, old boy, old man, originator, pa, padre, papa, pappy, parent, pastor, pater, paterfamilias, patriarch, patron, pop, poppa, pops, predecessor, priest, prime mover, procreator, progenitor, senator, sire.

v beget, conceive, create, dream up, engender, establish, found, get, institute, invent, originate, procreate, produce, sire.

fatherland *n* home, homeland, mother-country, motherland, native land, old country.

fatherly *adj* affectionate, avuncular, benevolent, benign, forbearing, indulgent, kind, kindly, paternal, patriarchal, protective, supportive, tender.

antonyms cold, harsh, unkind.

fathom *v* comprehend, deduce, divine, estimate, gauge, get to the bottom of, grasp, interpret, measure, penetrate, plumb, plummet, probe, see, sound, understand, work out.

fatigue *v* do in, drain, exhaust, fag, jade, knacker, overtire, shatter, tire, weaken, wear out, weary, whack.

antonym refresh.

n debility, decay, degeneration, ennui, failure, heaviness, languor, lethargy, listlessness, overtiredness, tiredness.

antonyms energy, freshness.

fatigued *adj* all in, beat, bushed, dead-beat, exhausted, fagged, jaded, jiggered, knackered, overtired, tired, tired out, wasted, weary, whacked, zonked.

antonym refreshed.

fatness *n* bulk, bulkiness, corpulence, embonpoint, flab, flesh, fleshiness, girth, grossness, heaviness, obesity, overweight, podginess, portliness, rotundity, size, stoutness, tubbiness, weight.

fatten *v* bloat, broaden, build up, coarsen, cram, distend, expand, feed, feed up, fertilise, nourish, overfeed, pinguefy, spread, stuff, swell, thicken, thrive.

fatty *adj* adipose, fat, greasy, oily, oleaginous, suet(t)y.

n fatso, fustilugs, gor-belly, heavyweight, horse-godmother, podge, pudding, pudge, roly-poly.

fatuity *n* absurdity, asininity, brainlessness, daftness, denseness, fatuousness, folly, foolishness, idiocy, imbecility, inanity, insanity, ludicrousness, lunacy, mindlessness, stupidity.

antonym sense.

fatuous *adj* absurd, asinine, brainless, daft, dense, dull, fatuitous, foolish, idiotic, imbecile, inane, ludicrous, lunatic, mindless, moony, moronic, puerile, silly, stupid, vacuous, weak-minded, witless.

antonym sensible.

fault *n* accountability, blemish, blunder, boner, boob, booboo, culpability, defect, deficiency, delict, delinquency, demerit, disdemeanour, dislocation, drawback, error, failing, flaw, frailty, goof, hamartia, imperfection, inaccuracy, indiscretion, infirmity, lack, lapse, liability, misconduct, misdeed, mistake, negligence, offence, omission, oversight, peccadillo, responsibility, shortcoming, sin, slip, slip-up, snag, solecism, transgression, trespass, weakness, wrong.

antonyms advantage, strength.

v blame, call to account, censure, criticise, find fault with, impugn, pick a hole in someone's coat, pick at, pick holes in.

antonym praise.

fault-finder *n* carper, caviller, grumbler, hair-splitter, hypercritic, kvetch(er), nagger, niggler, nit-picker, pettifogger, ultracrepidarian.

fault-finding *n* carping, cavilling, finger-pointing, grumbling, hair-splitting, hypercriticism, kvetching, nagging, niggling, nit-picking, ultracrepidation.

antonym praise.

adj captious, carping, cavilling, censorious, critical, grumbling, hypercritical, nagging, pettifogging, querulous, ultracrepidarian.

antonym complimentary.

faultless *adj* accurate, blameless, classic, correct, exemplary, faithful, flawless, foolproof, guiltless, immaculate, impeccable, innocent, irreproachable, model, perfect, pure, sinless, spotless, stainless, unblemished, unspotted, unsullied, untainted, word-perfect.

antonym imperfect.

faulty *adj* bad, blemished, broken, casuistic, damaged, defective, erroneous, fallacious, flawed, illogical, impaired, imperfect, imprecise, inaccurate, incorrect, invalid, malfunctioning, out of order, specious, unsound, weak, wrong.

faux pas blunder, boner, boob, booboo, clanger, gaffe, gaucherie, goof, impropriety, indiscretion, solecism.

favour *n* acceptance, approbation, approval, backing, badge, benefit, bias, boon, championship, courtesy, decoration, esteem, favouritism, friendliness, gift, good turn, goodwill, grace, indulgence, keepsake, kindness, knot, love-token, memento, obligement, partiality, patronage, present, regard, rosette, service, smile, souvenir, support, token.

antonym disfavour.

v abet, accommodate, advance, advocate, aid, approve, assist, back, befriend, champion, choose, commend, countenance, ease, encourage, esteem, extenuate, facilitate, fancy, have in one's good books, help, indulge, like, oblige, opt for, pamper, patronise, prefer, promote, resemble, spare, spoil, succour, support, take after, take kindly to, value.

antonyms disfavour, hinder, thwart.

favourable *adj* advantageous, affirmative, agreeable, amicable, appropriate, approving, auspicious, beneficial, benign, convenient, encouraging, enthusiastic, fair, Favonian, fit, friendly, good, helpful, hopeful, kind, opportune, positive, promising, propitious, reassuring, roseate, suitable, sympathetic, timely, understanding, welcoming, well-disposed, well-minded, white.

antonym unfavourable.

favourably *adv* advantageously, agreeably, approvingly, auspiciously, benignly, conveniently, enthusiastically, fortunately, genially, graciously, helpfully, opportunely, profitably, propitiously, sympathetically, well.

antonym unfavourably.

favoured *adj* advantaged, blessed, chosen, elite, favourite, lucky, pet, predilect, predilected, preferred, privileged, recommended, selected.

favourite *adj* best-loved, choice, dearest, esteemed, favoured, pet, preferred.

antonyms hated, unfavourite.

n beloved, blue-eyed boy, choice, darling, dear, form horse, idol, pet, pick, preference, teacher's pet, the apple of one's eye, whitehead, whiteheaded boy.

antonym pet hate.

favouritism *n* bias, biasedness, injustice, jobs for the boys, nepotism, old school tie, one-sidedness, partiality, partisanship, preference, preferential treatment.

antonym impartiality.

fawn[1] *v* bootlick, bow and scrape, court, crawl, creep, cringe, curry favour, dance attendance, flatter, grovel, ingratiate oneself, kneel, kowtow, pay court, smarm, toady, truckle.

fawn[2] *adj* beige, buff, khaki, sand-coloured, sandy.

fawning *adj* abject, bootlicking, crawling, cringing, deferential, flattering, grovelling, knee-crooking, obsequious, servile, slavish, sycophantic, toad-eating, toadying, toadyish, unctuous.

antonyms cold, proud.

fear *n* agitation, alarm, anxiety, apprehension, apprehensiveness, awe, bogey, bugbear, concern, consternation, cravenness, danger, dismay, disquietude, distress, doubt, dread, foreboding(s), fright, funk, heart-quake, horror, likelihood, misgiving(s), nightmare, panic, phobia, phobism, qualms, reverence, risk, solicitude, spectre, suspicion, terror, timidity, tremors, trepidation, unease, uneasiness, veneration, wonder, worry.

antonyms courage, fortitude.

v anticipate, apprehend, dread, expect, foresee, respect, reverence, shudder at, suspect, take fright, tremble, venerate, worry.

fear for tremble for, worry about.

fearful[1] *adj* afraid, alarmed, anxious, apprehensive, diffident, faint-hearted, feared, frightened, hesitant, intimidated, jittery, jumpy, nervous, nervy, panicky, pusillanimous, scared, shrinking, tense, timid, timorous, uneasy.

antonym courageous.

fearful[2] *adj* appalling, atrocious, awful, dire, distressing, dreadful, fearsome, ferly, frightful, ghastly, grievous, grim, gruesome, hair-raising, hideous, horrendous, horrible, horrific, monstrous, shocking, terrible, unspeakable.

antonym delightful.

fearless *adj* aweless, bold, brave, confident, courageous, daring, dauntless, doughty, gallant, game, gutsy, heroic, impavid, indomitable, intrepid, lion-hearted, plucky, unabashed, unafraid, unapprehensive, unblenching, unblinking, undaunted, unflinching, valiant, valorous.

antonyms afraid, timid.

fearlessness *n* boldness, bravery, confidence, courage, dauntlessness, guts, indomitability, intrepidity, intrepidness, lion-heartedness, nerve, pluck, pluckiness, prowess, valour.

antonyms fear, timidness.

fearsome *adj* alarming, appalling, awe-inspiring, awesome, awful, daunting, dismaying, formidable, frightening, frightful, hair-raising, horrendous, horrible, horrific, horrifying, menacing, terrible, unco, unnerving.

antonym delightful.

feasible *adj* achievable, attainable, likely, possible, practicable, practical, realisable, reasonable, viable, workable.

antonym impossible.

feast *n* banquet, barbecue, beanfeast, beano, binge, blow-out, carousal, carouse, celebration, delight, dinner, enjoyment, entertainment, epulation, festival, fête, gala day, gaudy, gratification, holiday, holy day, jollification, junket, pig, pleasure, potlatch, repast, revels, saint's day, spread, treat.

v delight, eat one's fill, entertain, gladden, gorge, gormandise, gratify, indulge, overindulge, regale, rejoice, stuff, stuff one's face, thrill, treat, wine and dine.

feat *n* accomplishment, achievement, act, attainment, deed, exploit, gest(e), performance.

feather *n* aigrette, egret, penna, pinion, plume, plumula, plumule, quill.

feathery *adj* downy, feathered, featherlike, fluffy, pennaceous, penniform, plumate, plumed, plumose, plumy, wispy.

feature *n* article, aspect, attraction, attribute, character, characteristic, column, comment, draw, facet, factor, hallmark, highlight, innovation, item, lineament, mark, peculiarity, piece, point, property, quality, report, special, speciality, specialty, story, trait.

v accentuate, emphasise, headline, highlight, play up, present, promote, push, recommend, show, spotlight, star.

features *n* countenance, face, lineaments, looks, mug, phiz, phizog, physiognomy.

febrile *adj* burning, delirious, febrific, fevered, feverish, fiery, flushed, hot, inflamed, pyretic.

feckless *adj* aimless, étourdi(e), feeble, futile, gormless, hopeless, incompetent, ineffectual, irresponsible, shiftless, useless, weak, worthless.

antonyms efficient, sensible.

fecund *adj* feracious, fertile, fructiferous, fructuous, fruitful, productive, prolific, teeming.
antonym infertile.

fecundity *n* feracity, fertility, fructiferousness, fruitfulness, productiveness.
antonym infertility.

fed up annoyed, blue, bored, brassed off, browned off, cheesed off, depressed, discontented, dismal, dissatisfied, down, gloomy, glum, scunnered, sick and tired, tired, weary.
antonym contented.

federate *v* amalgamate, associate, combine, confederate, integrate, join together, league, syndicate, unify, unite.
antonyms disunite, separate.

federation *n* alliance, amalgamation, association, Bund, coalition, combination, confederacy, confederation, copartnership, copartnery, entente, federacy, league, syndicate, union.

fee *n* account, bill, charge, compensation, emolument, hire, honorarium, pay, payment, recompense, remuneration, retainer, reward, terms, toll.

feeble *adj* debilitated, delicate, doddering, effete, enervated, enfeebled, exhausted, failing, faint, flat, flimsy, forceless, frail, fushionless, inadequate, incompetent, indecisive, ineffective, ineffectual, inefficient, inform, insignificant, insufficient, lame, languid, paltry, poor, powerless, puny, shilpit, sickly, silly, slight, tame, thin, unconvincing, vacillating, weak, weakened, weakly.
antonyms strong, worthy.

feeble-minded *adj* addle-pated, cretinised, cretinoid, cretinous, deficient, dim-witted, dull, dumb, half-witted, idiotic, imbecilic, irresolute, lacking, moronic, retarded, simple, slow on the uptake, slow-witted, soft in the head, stupid, two bricks short of a load, vacant, weak-minded.
antonyms bright, intelligent.

feebleness *n* debility, delicacy, effeteness, enervation, etiolation, exhaustion, faintness, flimsiness, forcelessness, foziness, frailness, frailty, inadequacy, incapacity, incompetence, indecisiveness, ineffectualness, infirmity, insignificance, insufficiency, lameness, languor, lassitude, sickliness, weakness.
antonyms strength, weariness.

feed *v* augment, bolster, cater for, dine, eat, encourage, fare, foster, fuel, graze, grub, nourish, nurture, pasture, provide for, provision, strengthen, subsist, supply, sustain, victual.
n banquet, feast, fodder, food, forage, meal, nosh, pasturage, pasture, provender, repast, silage, spread, tuck-in, victuals.
feed in inject, input, key in, supply.
feed on consume, devour, eat, exist on, live on, partake of.

feel *v* appear, believe, caress, consider, deem, empathise, endure, enjoy, experience, explore, finger, fondle, fumble, go through, grope, handle, have, have a hunch, hold, intuit, judge, know, manipulate, maul, notice, observe, paw, perceive, reckon, resemble, seem, sense, sound, stroke, suffer, take to heart, test, think, touch, try, undergo.
n bent, feeling, finish, gift, impression, knack, quality, sense, surface, texture, touch, vibes.
feel for be sorry for, bleed for, commiserate (with), compassionate, condole, empathise with, pity, sympathise with.
feel like desire, fancy, want.

feeler *n* advance, antenna, approach, ballon d'essai, horn, overture, probe, tentacle, trawl, trial balloon.

feeling *n* (a)esthesia, (a)esthesis, affection, air, ambience, appreciation, apprehension, ardour, atmosphere, aura, compassion, concern, consciousness, emotion, empathy, Empfindung, feel, fervour, fondness, heat, hunch, idea, impression, inclination, inkling, instinct, intensity, mood, notion, opinion, passion, perception, pity, point of view, presentiment, quality, sensation, sense, sensibility, sensitivity, sentiment, sentimentality, suspicion, sympathy, touch, understanding, vibes, vibrations, view, warmth.

feelings *n* affections, ego, emotions, passions, self-esteem, sensitivities, susceptibilities.

feign *v* act, affect, assume, counterfeit, devise, dissemble, dissimulate, fabricate, fake, forge, imitate, invent, make a show of, pretend, put on, sham, simulate.

feigned *adj* affected, artificial, assumed, counterfeit, fabricated, fake, false, imitation, insincere, personated, pretend, pretended, pseudo, sham, simulated, spurious.
antonyms genuine, sincere.

feint *n* artifice, blind, bluff, deception, distraction, dodge, dummy, expedient, gambit, manoeuvre, mock-assault, play, pretence, ruse, stratagem, subterfuge, wile.

felicitous *adj* apposite, appropriate, apropos, apt, delightful, fitting, happy, inspired, neat, opportune, pat, propitious, prosperous, suitable, timely, well-chosen, well-timed, well-turned.
antonyms inappropriate, inept.

felicity *n* applicability, appropriateness, aptness, becomingness, blessedness, blessing, bliss, blissfulness, delectation, delight, ecstasy, effectiveness, eloquence, grace, happiness, joy, propriety, suitability, suitableness.
antonyms inappropriateness, ineptitude, sadness.

feline *adj* catlike, graceful, leonine, seductive, sensual, sinuous, sleek, slinky, smooth, stealthy.

fell[1] *v* cut down, demolish, flatten, floor, hew down, lay level, level, prostrate, raze, strike down.

fell[2] *adj* baneful, barbarous, bloody, cruel, deadly, destructive, fatal, ferocious, fierce, grim, implacable, inhuman, maleficent, malevolent, malicious, malign, malignant, merciless, mortal, nefarious, noxious, pernicious, pestilential, pitiless, relentless, ruinous, ruthless, sanguinary, savage, vicious.
antonyms benign, gentle, kind.

fellow[1] *n* bloke, boy, buffer, bugger, cat, chal, chap, character, codger, cove, cuss, customer, dandiprat, dog, fucker, gadgie, gink, guy, hangdog, individual, Johnny, joker, josser, kipper, man, person, punter.

fellow[2] *n* associate, brother, colleague, companion, compeer, comrade, counterpart, co-worker, double, equal, fellow-member, friend, like, match, mate, member, partner, peer, twin.
adj associate, associated, co-, like, related, similar.

fellow-feeling *n* commiseration, compassion, empathy, sympathy, understanding.

fellowship *n* amity, association, brotherhood, camaraderie, club, communion, companionability, companionableness, companionship, endowment, familiarity, fraternisation, fraternity, guild, intercourse, intimacy, kindliness, league, order, sisterhood, sociability, society, sodality.

female *adj* distaff, feminal, feminine, petticoat, womanish, womanly, yin.
antonym male.

femaleness *n* feminality, femineity, feminility, feminineness, femininity, feminity.
antonym maleness.

feminine *adj* delicate, effeminate, effete, gentle, girlish, graceful, ladylike, modest, petticoat, sissy, soft, tender, unmanly, unmasculine, weak, womanish, womanly.
antonym masculine.

femininity *n* delicacy, effeminacy, effeteness, feminineness, gentleness, girlishness, muliebrity, sissiness, softness, unmanliness, womanhood, womanishness, womanliness, Yin.
antonym masculinity.

feminism *n* female emancipation, women's emancipation, women's liberation, women's movement, women's rights.

femme fatale charmer, enchantress, seductress, siren, temptress, vamp.

fen *n* bog, marsh, morass, moss, quag, quagmire, slough, swamp.

fence[1] *n* barricade, barrier, defence, guard, hedge, paling, palisade, railings, rampart, sepiment, sept, shield, stockade, wall, windbreak.
v bound, circumscribe, confine, coop, defend, encircle, enclose, fortify, guard, hedge, pen, protect, restrict, secure, separate, surround.

fence[2] *v* beat about the bush, cavil, digladiate, dodge, equivocate, evade, hedge, parry, prevaricate, pussyfoot, quibble, shift, stonewall, tergiversate.

fencing[1] *n* iaido, kendo, swordplay, swordsmanship.

fencing[2] *n* beating about the bush, double talk, equivocation, evasiveness, hedging, parrying, prevarication, pussyfooting, quibbling, stonewalling, tergiversation, weasel-words.

fend for look after, maintain, provide for, shift for, support, sustain.

fend off avert, beat off, defend, deflect, hold at bay, keep off, parry, repel, repulse, resist, shut out, stave off, ward off.

feral *adj* bestial, brutal, brutish, fell, ferae naturae, ferine, ferocious, fierce, savage, unbroken, uncultivated, undomesticated, untamed, vicious, wild.
antonym tame.

ferment *v* agitate, boil, brew, bubble, concoct, effervesce, excite, fester, foam, foment, froth, heat, incite, inflame, leaven, provoke, rise, rouse, seethe, smoulder, stir up, work, work up.
n agitation, brouhaha, commotion, disruption, excitement, fever, frenzy, furore, glow, heat, hubbub, imbroglio, stew, stir, tumult, turbulence, turmoil, unrest, uproar, yeast, zymosis.
antonym calm.

ferocious *adj* barbaric, barbarous, bloodthirsty, bloody, brutal, brutish, catamountain, cruel, fearsome, feral, fiendish, fierce, homicidal, inhuman, merciless, murderous, pitiless, predatory, rapacious, ravening, relentless, ruthless, sadistic, sanguinary, savage, truculent, vicious, violent, wild.
antonyms gentle, mild.

ferocity *n* barbarity, bloodthirstiness, brutality, cruelty, ferity, ferociousness, fiendishness, fierceness, inhumanity, murderousness, rapacity, ruthlessness, sadism, savageness, savagery, truculence, viciousness, wildness.
antonyms gentleness, mildness.

ferret out dig up, disclose, discover, disinter, drive out, elicit, extract, find, hunt down, nose out, root out, run to earth, smell out, sniff out, sus out, trace, track down, unearth, worm out.

ferry *v* carry, chauffeur, convey, drive, move, remove, run, shift, ship, shuttle, taxi, transport.

fertile *adj* abundant, fat, fecund, feracious, flowering, fructiferous, fructuous, frugiferous, fruit-bearing, fruitful, generative, lush, luxuriant, plenteous, plentiful, potent, productive, prolific, rich, teeming, uberous, virile, yielding.
antonyms arid, barren.

fertilisation *n* dressing, dunging, enrichment, fecundation, implantation, impregnation, insemination, manuring, mulching, pollination, procreation, propagation, top-dressing.

fertilise *v* compost, dress, dung, enrich, fecundate, feed, fructify, impregnate, inseminate, manure, mulch, pollinate, top-dress.

fertiliser *n* compost, dressing, dung, guano, manure, marl, plant-food.

fertility *n* abundance, fatness, fecundity, feracity, fruitfulness, lushness, luxuriance, plenteousness, potency, productiveness, prolificity, prolificness, richness, uberty, virility.
antonyms aridity, barrenness.

fervent *adj* animated, ardent, devout, eager, earnest, emotional, empressé, energetic, enthusiastic, excited, fervid, fiery, full-blooded, heartfelt, impassioned, intense, passionate, perfervid, spirited, vehement, vigorous, warm, whole-hearted, zealous.

fervour *n* animation, ardour, eagerness, earnestness, empressment, energy, enthusiasm, excitement, fervency, fervidity, fervidness, hwyl, intensity, passion, spirit, unction, unctuousness, vehemence, verve, vigour, warmth, zeal.

antonym apathy.

fester *v* chafe, decay, discharge, gall, gather, irk, maturate, putrefy, rankle, smoulder, suppurate, ulcerate.

antonyms dissipate, heal.

festering *n* discharging, galling, gathering, infected, inflamed, mattering, mattery, maturating, poisonous, purulent, pussy, putrescent, rankling, septic, smouldering, suppurating, ulcerated, venomous, virulent.

festival *n* anniversary, carnival, celebration, commemoration, eisteddfod, entertainment, feast, festa, festivities, fête, field day, fiesta, gala, holiday, holy day, jubilee, junketing, merry-make, merrymaking, merry-night, mod, potlatch, puja, saint's day, treat.

festive *adj* carnival, celebratory, cheery, Christmassy, convivial, cordial, en fête, festal, festivous, gala, gay, gleeful, happy, hearty, holiday, jolly, jovial, joyful, joyous, jubilant, merry, mirthful, rollicking, sportive, uproarious.

antonyms gloomy, sober, sombre.

festivities *n* bacchanalia, banqueting, carousal, celebration, entertainment, feasting, festival, fun and games, glorification, jollification, jollities, junketings, party, rejoicings, revelries, revels.

festivity *n* amusement, conviviality, enjoyment, feasting, festal, fun, gaiety, jollification, jollity, joviality, joyfulness, junketing, merriment, merrymaking, mirth, pleasure, revelry, sport, wassail.

festoon *n* chaplet, decoration, garbe, garland, lei, swag, swathe, wreathe.

v adorn, array, bedeck, bedizen, beribbon, deck, decorate, drape, garland, garnish, hang, swathe, wreath.

fetch *v* be good for, bring, bring in, carry, conduct, convey, deliver, draw, earn, elicit, escort, evoke, get, go for, lead, make, obtain, produce, realise, retrieve, sell for, transport, uplift, utter, yield.

fetch up arrive, come, come to a halt, end up, finish, finish up, halt, land, reach, stop, turn up.

fetching *adj* alluring, attractive, beguiling, captivating, charming, cute, disarming, enchanting, enticing, fascinating, pretty, sweet, taking, winning, winsome.

antonym repellent.

fête *n* bazaar, carnival, fair, festival, gala, garden party, sale of work.

v banquet, bring out the red carpet for, entertain, honour, lionise, make much of, regale, treat, welcome, wine and dine.

fetid *adj* corrupt, disgusting, filthy, foul, malodorous, mephitic, nauseating, noisome, noxious, odorous, offensive, rancid, rank, reeking, sickly, smelly, stinking.

antonym fragrant.

fetish *n* amulet, charm, cult object, fixation, idée fixe, idol, image, ju-ju, mania, obsession, periapt, phylactery, talisman, thing, totem.

fetter *v* bind, chain, confine, curb, encumber, entrammel, gyve, hamper, hamshackle, hamstring, hobble, manacle, pinion, restrain, restrict, shackle, tie (up), trammel, truss.

antonym free.

fetters *n* bilboes, bondage, bonds, bracelets, captivity, chains, check, constraint, curb, gyve, gyves, hampers, hamshackle, handcuffs, hindrance, hobble, hopple, inhibition, irons, manacles, obstruction, restraint, shackles, trammel.

feud *n* animosity, antagonism, argument, bad blood, bickering, bitterness, conflict, contention, disagreement, discord, dispute, dissension, enmity, estrangement, faction, feuding, grudge, hostility, ill will, quarrel, rivalry, row, strife, variance, vendetta.

antonyms agreement, peace.

v altercate, argue, be at odds, bicker, brawl, clash, contend, dispute, duel, fight, quarrel, row, squabble, war, wrangle.

antonym agree.

fever *n* agitation, calenture, delirium, ecstasy, excitement, febricity, febricula, febricule, ferment, fervour, feverishness, flush, frenzy, heat, intensity, passion, pyrexia, restlessness, temperature, turmoil, unrest.

fevered *adj* burning, febrile, feverish, feverous, fever-ridden, fiery, flushed, hectic, hot, pyretic, pyrexial, pyrexic.

antonym cool.

feverish *adj* agitated, anxious, burning, distracted, eager, excited, fanatical, febrile, fevered, feverous, flurried, flushed, flustered, frantic, frenetic, frenzied, hasty, hectic, hot, hurried, impatient, inflamed, nervous, obsessive, overwrought, pyretic, restless.

antonyms calm, cool.

feverishness *n* agitation, bustle, commotion, distraction, excitement, febricity, febrility, ferment, fever, flurry, flush, franticness, frenzy, fuss, haste, hurry, kerfuffle, pother, pyrexia, restlessness, stir, turmoil.

antonyms calmness, coolness.

few *adj* few and far between, hard to come by, in short supply, inadequate, inconsiderable, infrequent, insufficient, meagre, negligible, rare, scant, scanty, scarce, scattered, sparse, sporadic, thin, uncommon.

pron a couple, handful, not many, oddments, one or two, scarcely any, scattering, small number, small quantity, some, sprinkling.

fewness *n* dearth, inadequacy, infrequency, insufficiency, lack, negligibility, paucity, rareness, rarity, scantiness, scarceness, scarcity, sparseness, thinness, uncommonness, want.

antonyms abundance, glut.

fiancé(e) *n* betrothed, bridegroom-to-be, bride-to-be, husband-to-be, intended, wife-to-be.

fiasco *n* bummer, calamity, catastrophe, collapse, cropper, damp squib, debacle, disaster, failure, flivver, flop, mess, non-success, rout, ruin, turkey, unsuccess, wash-out.

antonym success.

fiat *n* authorisation, command, decree, dictate, dictum, diktat, directive, edict, injunction, mandate, OK, order, ordinance, permission, precept, prescript, proclamation, sanction, ukase, warrant.

fib *n* concoction, evasion, falsehood, fantasy, fiction, invention, lie, misrepresentation, prevarication, story, tale, untruth, white lie, whopper, yarn.

v dissemble, evade, fabricate, falsify, fantasise, invent, lie, prevaricate, sidestep.

fibre *n* backbone, bast, calibre, character, courage, determination, essence, fibril, filament, filasse, funicle, grit, guts, nature, nerve, pile, pluck, quality, resolution, sinew, spirit, stamina, staple, strand, strength, substance, temperament, tenacity, tendril, texture, thread, toughness.

fibrous *adj* fibred, fibriform, fibrillar, fibrillary, fibrillate, fibrillose, fibrillous, fibroid, filamentous, filiform, filose, funicular, funiculate, penicillate, sinewy, stringy, tendinous, thread-like, wiry.

fickle *adj* capricious, chameleon(ic), changeable, disloyal, dizzy, erratic, faithless, fitful, flighty, fluctuating, inconstant, irresolute, mercurial, mutable, quicksilver, treacherous, unfaithful, unpredictable, unreliable, unstable, unsteady, vacillating, variable, volage, volageous, volatile, wind-changing.

antonym constant.

fickleness *n* capriciousness, changeability, changeableness, disloyalty, faithlessness, fitfulness, flightiness, inconstancy, mutability, treachery, unfaithfulness, unpredictability, unreliability, unsteadiness, volatility.

antonym constancy.

fiction *n* canard, cock-and-bull story, concoction, fable, fabrication, falsehood, fancy, fantasy, feuilleton, fib, figment, imagination, improvisation, invention, legend, lie, myth, novel, parable, romance, story, story-telling, tale, tall story, untruth, whopper, yarn.

antonym truth.

fictional *adj* fabulous, imaginary, invented, legendary, made-up, mythical, non-existent, unreal.

antonyms real, true.

fictitious *adj* aprocryphal, artificial, assumed, bogus, counterfeit, fabricated, false, fanciful, feigned, fictive, fraudulent, imaginary, imagined, improvised, invented, made-up, make-believe, mythical, non-existent, spurious, supposed, suppositional, supposititious, unreal, untrue.

antonyms genuine, real.

fiddle[1] *v* cheat, cook, cook the books, diddle, fidget, finagle, finger, fix, gerrymander, graft, interfere, juggle, manoeuvre, mess around, play, racketeer, swindle, tamper, tinker, toy, trifle, wangle.

n chicanery, con, fix, fraud, graft, monkey-business, racket, rip-off, sharp practice, swindle, trickery, wangle.

fiddle[2] *n* viol, viola, viola da braccio, viola da spalla, viola d'amore, violin.

fiddling *adj* footling, futile, insignificant, negligible, paltry, pettifogging, petty, trifling, trivial.

antonyms important, significant.

fidelity *n* accuracy, adherence, allegiance, authenticity, closeness, constancy, correspondence, dedication, dependability, devotedness, devotion, dutifulness, exactitude, exactness, faith, faithfulness, fealty, incorruptibility, integrity, lealty, loyalty, preciseness, precision, reliability, scrupulousness, staunchness, steadfastness, true-heartedness, trustworthiness.

antonyms inaccuracy, inconstancy, treachery.

fidget *v* bustle, chafe, fiddle, fidge, fike, fret, jerk, jiggle, jitter, jump, mess about, play around, squirm, toy, twitch, worry.

n agitation, anxiety, creeps, discomposure, edginess, fidgetiness, fidgets, heebie-jeebies, jimjams, jitteriness, jitters, jumpiness, nerves, nerviness, nervousness, restlessness, shakes, twitchiness, unease, uneasiness, willies.

fidgety *adj* agitated, frisky, impatient, jerky, jittery, jumpy, nervous, nervy, on edge, restive, restless, skittish, twitchy, uneasy.

antonym still.

field[1] *n* arena, battlefield, battleground, glebe, grassland, green, greensward, lawn, lay, lea, mead, meadow, padang, paddock, pasture, pitch, playing-field, theatre.

field[2] *n* applicants, candidates, competition, competitors, contenders, contestants, entrants, opponents, opposition, possibilities, runners.

field[3] *n* area, bailiwick, ball park, bounds, confines, department, discipline, domain, environment, forte, limits, line, métier, period, pidgin, province, purview, range, scope, speciality, specialty, territory.

field[4] *v* answer, catch, cope with, deal with, deflect, handle, parry, pick up, receive, retrieve, return, stop.

fiend *n* addict, aficionado, barbarian, beast, brute, degenerate, demon, devil, devotee, enthusiast, evil spirit, fanatic, freak, ghoul, goblin, hellhound, hobgoblin, incubus, lamia, maniac, monster, nut, ogre, Satan, savage, succubus.

fiendish *adj* accursed, atrocious, baleful, black-hearted, cruel, damnable, demoniac, devilish, diabolic, diabolical, hellish, impious, implacable, infernal, inhuman, malefic, maleficent, malevolent, malicious, malign, malignant, Mephistophelean, Mephistophelic, mischievous, monstrous, nefarious, satanic, savage, ungodly, unspeakable, vicious, vile, wicked.

fierce *adj* baleful, barbarous, blustery, boisterous, brutal, cruel, cut-throat, dangerous, fearsome, fell, feral, ferocious, fiery, frightening, furious, grim, howling, intense, keen, menacing, merciless, murderous, passionate, powerful, raging, relentless, savage, stern, stormy, strong, tempestuous, threatening, truculent, tumultuous, uncontrollable, unrelenting, untamed, vicious, violent, wild.

antonyms calm, gentle, kind.

fiercely *adv* ardently, bitterly, fanatically, ferociously, furiously, implacably, intensely, keenly, menacingly, mercilessly, murderously, passionately, relentlessly, savagely, sternly, tempestuously, tigerishly, tooth and nail, viciously, violently, wildly, zealously.

antonyms gently, kindly.

fierceness *n* ardour, avidity, bitterness, bluster, destructiveness, fanaticism, fearsomeness, ferocity, fervidness, fervour, fieriness, intensity, keenness, mercilessness, passion, relentlessness, roughness, ruthlessness, savageness, savagery, sternness, storminess, strength, tempestuousness, turbulence, viciousness, violence, wildness, zeal.

antonyms gentleness, kindness.

fiery *adj* ablaze, afire, aflame, aglow, ardent, blazing, burning, choleric, excitable, febrile, fervent, fervid, fevered, feverish, fierce, flaming, flushed, glowing, heated, hot, hot-headed, impatient, impetuous, impulsive, inflamed, irascible, irritable, passionate, peppery, perfervid, precipitate, red-hot, sultry, torrid, truculent, violent, volcanic.

antonyms cold, impassive.

fight *v* altercate, argue, assault, battle, bear arms against, bicker, box, brawl, clash, close, combat, conduct, conflict, contend, contest, cross swords, defy, dispute, do battle, engage, exchange blows, fence, feud, grapple, joust, lock horns, measure strength, measure swords, mell, mix it, oppose, prosecute, quarrel, resist, scrap, scuffle, skirmish, spar, squabble, stand up to, strive, struggle, take the field, tilt, tussle, wage, wage war, war, withstand, wrangle, wrestle.

n action, affray, altercation, argument, barney, battle, belligerence, bicker, bout, brawl, brush, clash, combat, conflict, contest, courage, dispute, dissension, dogfight, duel, encounter, engagement, fisticuffs, fracas, fray, free-for-all, gameness, hostilities, joust, luctation, mêlée, mettle, militancy, monomachy, passage of arms, pluck, pugnacity, quarrel, rammy, resilience, resistance, riot, row, ruck, rumble, scrap, scuffle, set-to, skirmish, spirit, strength, struggle, tenacity, tussle, war.

fight back[1] defend oneself, give as good as one gets, put up a fight, reply, resist, retaliate, retort.

fight back[2] bottle up, contain, control, curb, hold back, hold in check, repress, resist, restrain, suppress.

fight off beat off, hold off, keep at bay, put to flight, rebuff, repel, repress, repulse, resist, rout, stave off, ward off.

fight shy of avoid, disdain, eschew, give a wide berth, keep at arm's length, shun, spurn, steer clear of.

fighter *n* adventurer, antagonist, battler, belligerent, boxer, brave, bruiser, champion, combatant, contender, contestant, disputant, fighting man, filibuster, free lance, gladiator, man-at-arms, mercenary, militant, prize-fighter, pugilist, soldier, soldier of fortune, swordsman, trouper, warrior, wrestler.

fighting *adj* aggressive, argumentative, bellicose, belligerent, combative, contentious, disputatious, fierce, hawkish, martial, militant, militaristic, pugnacious, quarrelsome, sabre-rattling, truculent, warfaring, warlike.

n battle, bloodshed, boxing, brawling, clash, combat, conflict, encounter, engagement, fisticuffs, fray, handicuffs, hostilities, mêlée, quarrelling, scuffle, scuffling, struggle, war, warfare, wrangling, wrestling.

figment *n* concoction, creation, deception, delusion, fable, fabrication, falsehood, fancy, fiction, illusion, improvisation, invention, mare's nest, production, work.

figurative *adj* allegorical, analogous, descriptive, embellished, emblematic, emblematical, fanciful, florid, flowery, metaphorical, ornate, parabolic, pictorial, picturesque, poetical, representative, symbolic, symbolical, tropical, typical.

antonym literal.

figure *n* amount, body, build, celebrity, character, chassis, cipher, configuration, conformation, cost, depiction, design, device, diagram, digit, dignitary, drawing, embellishment, emblem, form, frame, illustration, image, leader, motif, notability, notable, number, numeral, outline, pattern, personage, personality, physique, presence, price, proportions, representation, shadow, shape, sign, silhouette, sketch, somebody, sum, symbol, torso, total, trope, value.

v act, add, appear, believe, calculate, compute, count, estimate, feature, guess, judge, opine, reckon, sum, surmise, tally, think, tot up, work out.

figure of speech conceit, concetto, figure, image, imagery, rhetorical device, trope, turn of phrase.

figure out calculate, comprehend, compute, decipher, excogitate, explain, fathom, make out, puzzle out, reason out, reckon, resolve, see, understand, work out.

figured *adj* adorned, decorated, embellished, marked, ornamented, patterned, printed, sprigged, variegated.

antonym plain.

figurehead *n* bust, carving, cipher, dummy, front man, image, leader, man of straw, mouthpiece, name, nominal head, nonentity, puppet, straw man, titular head, token.

filament *n* cilium, fibre, fibril, file, funicle, hair, pile, staple, strand, string, thread, whisker, wire.

filch *v* abstract, borrow, crib, drib, embezzle, fake, finger, half-inch, lift, misappropriate, nick, palm, peculate, pilfer, pinch, plagiarise, prig, purloin, rip off, snaffle, snitch, steal, swipe, take, thieve.

file[1] *v* abrade, burnish, furbish, grate, hone, pare, plane, polish, rasp, refine, rub (down), sand, scour, scrape, shape, shave, smooth, trim, whet.

file[2] *n* binder, cabinet, case, date, documents, dossier, folder, information, portfolio, record.

v capture, document, enter, memorise, pigeonhole, process, record, register, slot in, store.

file[3] *n* column, cortège, line, list, procession, queue, row, stream, string, trail, train.

v defile, march, parade, stream, trail, troop.

filial *adj* affectionate, daughterly, devoted, dutiful, fond, loving, loyal, respectful, sonlike, sonly.

antonyms disloyal, unfilial.

filibuster[1] *n* delay, hindrance, impediment, obstruction, peroration, postponement, procrastination, speechifying.

v delay, hinder, impede, obstruct, perorate, prevent, procrastinate, put off, speechify.

antonym expedite.

filibuster[2] *n* adventurer, buccaneer, corsair, free lance, freebooter, pirate, rover, sea rat, sea-robber, sea-rover, soldier of fortune.

filigree *n* fret-work, interlace, lace, lacework, lattice, lattice-work, scrollwork, tracery, wirework.

fill *v* assign, block, bung, charge, clog, close, congest, cork, cram, crowd, discharge, drench, engage, englut, engorge, execute, fulfil, furnish, glut, gorge, hold, imbue, impregnate, inflate, load, occupy, officiate, overspread, pack, perform, permeate, pervade, plug, replenish, sate, satiate, satisfy, saturate, seal, soak, stock, stop, stuff, suffuse, supply, surfeit, swell, take up.

antonyms clear, empty.

n abundance, ample, enough, plenty, sufficiency, sufficient.

fill in acquaint, act for, advise, answer, apprise, brief, bring up to date, complete, deputise, fill out, inform, put wise, replace, represent, stand in, sub, substitute, understudy.

filling *n* contents, filler, grouting, infill, infilling, innards, inside, insides, nogging, padding, rubble, stuffing, wadding.

adj ample, big, bulky, generous, heavy, large, nutritious, satisfying, solid, square, substantial, sustaining, tidy.

antonym insubstantial.

fillip *n* boost, flick, goad, impetus, incentive, prod, push, shove, spice, spur, stimulus, zest.

antonym damper.

film[1] *n* bloom, blur, cloud, coat, coating, covering, dusting, gauze, glaze, haze, haziness, integument, layer, membrane, mist, opacity, pellicle, screen, scum, sheet, skin, tissue, veil, web, weft.

v blear, blur, cloud, dull, glaze, haze, mist, screen, veil.

film[2] *n* documentary, epic, feature film, flick, horse-opera, motion picture, movie, oldie, picture, short, spaghetti western, video, western.

v photograph, shoot, take, video, videotape.

filmy *adj* cobwebby, delicate, diaphanous, fine, flimsy, floaty, fragile, gauzy, gossamer, gossamery, insubstantial, light, see-through, sheer, shimmering, thin, translucent, transparent.

antonym opaque.

filter *v* clarify, dribble, escape, exude, filtrate, leach, leak, ooze, penetrate, percolate, purify, refine, screen, seep, sieve, sift, strain, transpire, transude, trickle, well.

n colander, gauze, membrane, mesh, riddle, sieve, sifter, strainer.

filth *n* bilge, carrion, coarseness, colluvies, contamination, coprolalia, coprophilia, corruption, crud, defilement, dirt, dirty-mindedness, dung, excrement, excreta, faeces,, faex, filthiness, foulness, garbage, grime, grossness, gunge, impurity, indecency, muck, nastiness, obscenity, ordure, pollution, pornography, putrefaction, putrescence, refuse, scatology, sewage, slime, sludge, smut, smuttiness, soil, sordes, sordidness, squalor, sullage, uncleanness, vileness, vulgarity.

antonyms cleanliness, decency, purity.

filthy *adj* Augean, base, bawdy, begrimed, black, blackened, blue, coarse, contemptible, coprolaliac, coprophilous, corrupt, depraved, despicable, dirty, dirty-minded, faecal, feculent, foul, foul-mouthed, grimy, gross, grubby, impure, indecent, lavatorial, lewd, licentious, low, mean, miry, mucky, muddy, nasty, nasty-minded, obscene, offensive, polluted, pornographic, putrid, scatological, scurrilous, slimy, smoky, smutty, sooty, sordid, squalid, suggestive, swinish, unclean, unwashed, vicious, vile, vulgar.

antonyms clean, decent, inoffensive, pure.

final *adj* absolute, clinching, closing, concluding, conclusive, conclusory, decided, decisive, definite, definitive, desinent, desinential, determinate, dying, eleventh-hour, end, eventual, finished, incontrovertible, irrefragable, irrefutable, irrevocable, last, last-minute, latest, settled, terminal, terminating, ultimate, undeniable.

finale *n* climax, close, conclusion, crescendo, crowning glory, culmination, curtain, dénouement, epilogue, final curtain, finis, last act, supreme moment.

finalise *v* agree, clinch, complete, conclude, decide, dispose of, finish, get signed and sealed, get taped, resolve, round off, seal, settle, sew up, tie up, work out, wrap up.

finality *n* certitude, conclusiveness, conviction, decidedness, decisiveness, definiteness, firmness, inevitability, inevitableness, irreversibility, irrevocability, resolution, ultimacy, unavoidability.

finally *adv* absolutely, at last, at length, completely, conclusively, convincingly, decisively, definitely, eventually, for ever, for good, for good and all, in conclusion, in the end, inescapably, inexorably, irreversibly, irrevocably, lastly, once and for all, permanently, ultimately.

finance *n* accounting, accounts, banking, business, commerce, economics, investment, money, money management, stock market, trade.

v back, bail out, bankroll, capitalise, float, fund, guarantee, habilitate, pay for, set up, subsidise, support, underwrite.

finances *n* affairs, assets, bank account, bread, budget, capital, cash, coffers, dibs, fisc, funds, income, liquidity, money, moolah, purse, resources, revenue, spondulicks, wealth, wherewithal.

financial *adj* budgetary, chrematistic, commercial, economic, fiscal, monetary, money, pecuniary.

financier *n* banker, broker, cambist, financialist, gnome, investor, money-maker, speculator, stockbroker.

find *v* achieve, acquire, ascertain, attain, bring, catch, chance on, come across, consider, contribute, cough up, descry, detect, discover, earn, encounter, espy, experience, expose, ferret out, furnish, gain, get, hit on, judge, learn, light on, locate, meet, note, notice, observe, obtain, perceive, procure, provide, reach, realise, recognise, recover, rediscover, regain, remark, repossess, retrieve, spot, stumble on, supply, think, track down, turn up, uncover, unearth, win.

n acquisition, asset, bargain, catch, coup, discovery, good buy, unconsidered trifle.

find fault bitch, carp, cavil, censure, complain, criticise, depreciate, disparage, gripe, hypercriticise, kvetch, nag, niggle, nitpick, pick holes, pull to pieces, quarrel with, quibble, reprove, take to task, ultracrepidate.

antonym praise.

find out ascertain, catch, detect, dig up, disclose, discover, establish, expiscate, expose, learn, note, observe, perceive, realise, reveal, rumble, show up, speir, sus out, tumble to, uncover, unmask.

finding *n* award, breakthrough, conclusion, decision, decree, discovery, evidence, find, judgement, pronouncement, recommendation, verdict.

fine[1] *adj* abstruse, acceptable, acute, admirable, agreeable, all right, attractive, balmy, beau, beaut, beautiful, bonny, brave, braw, bright, brilliant, choice, clear, clement, cloudless, convenient, critical, cutting, dainty, dandy, delicate, diaphanous, discriminating, dry, elegant, elusive, excellent, exceptional, expensive, exquisite, fair, fastidious, fine-drawn, first-class, first-rate, flimsy, four-square, fragile, gauzy, good, good-looking, goodly, gorgeous, gossamer, great, hair-splitting, handsome, honed, hunky, hunky-dory, impressive, intelligent, jake, keen, light, lovely, magnificent, masterly, minute, nice, OK, ornate, outstanding, pleasant, polished, powdery, precise, pure, quick, rare, refined, robust, satisfactory, select, sensitive, sharp, sheer, showy, skilful, skilled, slender, small, smart, solid, splendid, sterling, strong, sturdy, stylish, sublime, subtle, suitable, sunny, superior, supreme, tasteful, tenuous, thin, tickety-boo, unalloyed, virtuoso, well-favoured, wiredrawn.

fine[2] *v* amerce, mulct, penalise, punish, sting.

n amercement, amerciament, damages, forfeit, forfeiture, mulct, penalty, punishment.

finery *n* bedizenment, decorations, frills and furbelows, frippery, gaud, gaudery, gauds, gear, gewgaws, glad rags, jewellery, ornaments, showiness, splendour, Sunday best, trappings.

finesse *n* address, adeptness, adroitness, artfulness, artifice, cleverness, craft, deftness, delicacy, diplomacy, discretion, elegance, expertise, gracefulness, know-how, neatness, polish, quickness, refinement, savoir-faire, skill, sophistication, subtlety, tact.

v bluff, evade, manipulate, manoeuvre, trick.

finger *v* caress, feel, fiddle with, fondle, handle, manipulate, maul, meddle with, palpate, paw, play about with, stroke, touch, toy with.

n claw, digit, digital, index, phalanges, talon.

finical *adj* choosy, dainty, dandified, dandyish, fastidious, finicky, foppish, fussy, natty, neat, nice, nipperty-tipperty, particular, pernickety, precise.

finicky *adj* choosy, critical, dainty, delicate, difficult, fastidious, finical, finicking, fussy, hypercritical, meticulous, nice, nit-picking, overnice, particular, pernickety, scrupulous, squeamish, tricky.

antonyms easy, easy-going.

finish *v* accomplish, achieve, annihilate, best, buff, burnish, cease, close, coat, complete, conclude, consume, consummate, culminate, deal with, defeat, destroy, devour, discharge, dispatch, dispose of, do, drain, drink, eat, elaborate, empty, encompass, end, execute, exhaust, expend, exterminate, face, finalise, fulfil, get rid of, gild, hone, kill, lacquer, overcome, overpower, overthrow, perfect, polish, put an end to, put the last hand to, refine, round off, rout, ruin, settle, smooth, smooth off, sophisticate, spend, stain, stop, terminate, texture, use (up), veneer, wax, wind up, worst, zap.

n annihilation, appearance, bankruptcy, burnish, cessation, close, closing, completion, conclusion, coup de grâce, culmination, cultivation, culture, curtain, curtains, death, defeat, dénouement, elaboration, end, end of the road, ending, finale, gloss, grain, liquidation, lustre, patina, perfection, polish, refinement, ruin, shine, smoothness, sophistication, surface, termination, texture, wind-up.

finished *adj* accomplished, bankrupt, clapped-out, classic, consummate, cultivated, defeated, done, done for, doomed, drained, elegant, empty, exhausted, expert, faultless, flawless, impeccable, jiggered, lost, masterly, napoo, overpast, perfected, played out, polished, professional, proficient, refined, ruined, skilled, smooth, sophisticated, spent, through, undone, urbane, virtuoso, washed up, wrecked, zonked.

antonyms coarse, crude, unfinished.

finite *adj* bounded, calculable, circumscribed, compassable, definable, delimited, demarcated, fixed, limited, measurable, restricted, terminable.

antonym infinite.

fire *n* animation, ardour, bale-fire, barrage, blaze, bombardment, bonfire, brio, broadside, burning, cannonade, combustion, conflagration, dash, eagerness, earnestness, élan, enthusiasm, excitement, feeling, fervency, fervidity, fervidness, fervour, feu de joie, fierceness, flak, flames, force, fusillade, hail, heat, impetuosity, inferno, intensity, life, light, lustre, passion, radiance, salvo, scintillation, shelling, sniping, sparkle, spirit, splendour, verve, vigour, virtuosity, vivacity, volley, warmth, zeal.

v activate, animate, arouse, boot out, cashier, depose, detonate, discharge, dismiss, eject, electrify, enkindle, enliven, excite, explode, galvanise, give marching orders, give the bum's rush, hurl, ignite, impassion, incite, inflame, inspire, inspirit, kindle, launch, let off, light, loose, put a match to, quicken, rouse, sack, send off, set alight, set fire to, set off, set on fire, shell, shoot, show the door, stimulate, stir, touch off, trigger off, whet.

firearm *n* automatic, gun, handgun, musket, musketoon, muzzle-loader, muzzler, pistol, revolver, rifle, shooter, shooting-iron, shotgun, weapon.

fireworks *n* devils, explosions, feux d'artifice, firecrackers, gerbes, hysterics, illuminations, maroon, pyrotechnics, rage, rockets, rows, sparks, storm, temper, trouble, uproar.

firm[1] *adj* abiding, adamant, anchored, balanced, braced, cast-iron, cemented, changeless, committed, compact, compressed, concentrated, congealed, constant, convinced, crisp, definite, dense, dependable, determined, dogged, durable, embedded, enduring, established, fast, fastened, fixed, grounded, hard, hardened, immovable, impregnable, indurate, inelastic, inflexible, iron-hearted, jelled, jellified, motionless, obdurate, reliable, resolute, resolved, rigid, robust, secure, secured, set, settled, solid, solidified, stable, stationary, staunch, steadfast, steady, stiff, strict, strong, sturdy, substantial, sure, taut, tight, true, unalterable, unassailable, unbending, unchanging, undeviating, unfaltering, unflinching, unmoved, unmoving, unshakable, unshakeable, unshaken, unshifting, unswerving, unwavering, unyielding, well-knit.

antonyms infirm, soft, unsound.

firm[2] *n* association, business, company, concern, conglomerate, corporation, enterprise, establishment, house, institution, organisation, outfit, partnership, set-up, syndicate.

firmly *adv* compactly, decisively, definitely, determinedly, doggedly, enduringly, four-square, immovably, inflexibly, motionlessly, resolutely, robustly, securely, solidly, squarely, stably, staunchly, steadfastly, steadily, strictly, strongly, sturdily, surely, tightly, unalterably, unchangeably, unflinchingly, unshakeably, unwaveringly.

antonyms hesitantly, uncertainly, unsoundly.

firmness *n* changelessness, compactness, constancy, conviction, density, dependability, determination, doggedness, durability, fixedness, fixity, hardness, immovability, impregnability, indomitability, inelasticity, inflexibility, obduracy, reliability, resistance, resolution, resolve, rigidity, solidity, soundness, stability, staunchness, steadfastness, steadiness, stiffness, strength, strength of will, strictness, sureness, tautness, tension, tightness, will, will-power.

antonyms infirmity, uncertainty, unsoundness.

first *adj* basic, cardinal, chief, earliest, eldest, elementary, embryonic, foremost, fundamental, head, highest, initial, introductory, key, leading, maiden, main, oldest, opening, original, paramount, predominant, pre-eminent, premier, primal, primary, prime, primeval, primitive, primordial, principal, prior, pristine, rudimentary, ruling, senior, sovereign, uppermost.

adv at the outset, before all else, beforehand, early on, firstly, in preference, in the beginning, initially, originally, primarily, rather, sooner, to begin with, to start with.

first name baptismal name, Christian name, font name, forename, given name.

first-born *adj* aîné(e), eigne, elder, eldest, older, primogenit, senior.

first-fruits *n* annates, primitiae, tribute.

firsthand *adj* direct, immediate, personal, straight from the horse's mouth.

antonyms hearsay, indirect.

first-rate *adj* A1, admirable, crack, élite, excellent, exceptional, exclusive, fine, first-class, jake, leading, matchless, nonpareil, outstanding, peerless, prime, second-to-none, splendid, superb, superior, superlative, tiptop, top, top-flight, top-notch, tops.

antonym inferior.

fiscal *adj* budgetary, bursal, economic, financial, monetary, money, pecuniary, treasury.

fish *v* angle, cast, delve, elicit, hint, hunt, invite, seek, solicit, trawl, troll.

n aquatic, chap, drip, fellow.

fish out come up with, dredge up, extract, extricate, find, haul up, produce.

fish out of water freak, horse marine, maverick, misfit, nonconformist, rogue, square peg in a round hole.

antonym conformist.

fisherman *n* angler, fisher, peter-man, piscator, piscatorian, rod-fisher, rodman, rodsman, rodster.

fishing *n* angling, fishery, halieutics, piscary, trawling, trolling.

adj halieutic, piscatorial, piscatory.

fishy *adj* doubtful, dubious, fish-like, funny, glassy, implausible, improbable, irregular, odd, piscatorial, piscatory, pisciform, piscine, queer, questionable, rummy, shady, suspect, suspicious, unlikely, vacant.

antonyms honest, legitimate.

fissile *adj* cleavable, divisible, easily split, fissionable, fissive, flaky, scissile, separable, severable.

fission *n* breaking, cleavage, division, parting, rending, rupture, schism, scission, severance, splitting.

fissure *n* breach, break, chasm, chink, cleavage, cleft, crack, cranny, crevasse, crevice, fault, foramen, fracture, gap, gash, grike, hole, interstice, opening, rent, rift, rupture, scissure, slit, split, sulcus, vein.

fist *n* duke, mitt, nieve, paw, pud, puddy.

fit[1] *adj* able, able-bodied, adapted, adequate, apposite, appropriate, apt, becoming, blooming, capable, commensurate, competent, condign, convenient, correct, deserving, due, eligible, equipped, expedient, fit as a fiddle, fitted, fitting, hale, hale and hearty, healthy, in fine fettle, in good form, in good nick, in good shape, in good trim, in the pink, meet, prepared, proper, qualified, ready, right, robust, satisfactory, seemly, sound, strapping, strong, sturdy, suitable, suited, trained, trim, well, well-suited, worthy.

antonym unfit.

v accommodate, accord, adapt, adjust, agree, alter, arrange, assimilate, belong, change, concur, conform, correspond, dispose, dovetail, fashion, fay, figure, follow, gee, go, harmonise, interlock, join, match, meet, modify, place, position, reconcile, shape, suit, tally.

fit out accommodate, accoutre, arm, caparison, equip, kit out, outfit, prepare, provide, rig out, supply.

fit[2] *n* access, attack, bout, burst, caprice, convulsion, eruption, exies, explosion, fancy, humour, mood, outbreak, outburst, paroxysm, seizure, spasm, spell, storm, surge, whim.

fitful *adj* broken, desultory, disturbed, erratic, fluctuating, haphazard, intermittent, irregular, occasional, spasmodic, sporadic, uneven, unstable, unsteady, variable.

antonyms regular, steady.

fitfully *adv* desultorily, erratically, haphazardly, in fits and starts, in snatches, intermittently, interruptedly, irregularly, off and on, spasmodically, sporadically, unevenly, unsteadily.

antonyms regularly, steadily.

fitness *n* adaptation, adequacy, applicability, appropriateness, aptness, competence, condition, eligibility, haleness, health, healthiness, pertinence, preparedness, propriety, qualifications, readiness, robustness, seemliness, strength, suitability, vigour.

antonym unfitness.

fitted *adj* accoutred, adapted, appointed, armed, booted and spurred, built-in, caparisoned, equipped, fit, furnished, kitted, outfitted, permanent, prepared, provided, qualified, rigged out, right, suitable, supplied, tailor-made.

antonym unfitted.

fitting *adj* apposite, appropriate, apt, becoming, comme il faut, condign, correct, decent, decorous, deserved, desirable, harmonious, meet, merited, proper, right, seasonable, seemly, suitable.

antonym unsuitable.

n accessory, attachment, component, connection, fitment, fixture, part, piece, unit.

fittings *n* accessories, accoutrements, appointments, appurtenances, conveniences, equipment, extras, fitments, fixtures, furnishings, furniture, plenishing, trimmings.

fivefold *adj* pentaploid, quintuple, quintuplicate.

fix[1] *v* adjust, agree on, anchor, appoint, arrange, arrive at, attach, bind, cement, conclude, confirm, congeal, connect, consolidate, correct, couple, decide, define, determine, direct, embed, establish, fasten, fiddle, finalise, firm, focus, freeze, glue, harden, implant, inculcate, influence, install, irradicate, limit, link, locate, make, manipulate, manoeuvre, mend, nail, name, ordain, pin, place, plant, point, position, prearrange, preordain, produce, regulate, repair, resolve, restore, rigidify, rigidise, rivet, root, seal, seat, secure, see to, set, settle, solidify, sort, sort out, specify, stabilise, stick, stiffen, straighten, swing, thicken, tidy, tie.

n corner, difficulty, dilemma, embarrassment, hole, jam, mess, muddle, nineholes, pickle, plight, predicament, quagmire, quandary, scrape, spot.

fix up accommodate, agree on, arrange (for), bring about, equip, fix, furnish, lay on, organise, plan, produce, provide, settle, sort out, supply.

fix[2] *n* dose, hit, injection, jag, score, shot, slug.

fixation *n* complex, compulsion, fetish, hang-up, idée fixe, infatuation, mania, monomania, obsession, preoccupation, thing.

fixed *adj* agreed, anchored, arranged, attached, decided, definite, determinate, entrenched, established, fast, fiddled, fiducial, firm, framed, immovable, inflexible, ingrained, intent, invariable, lasting, level, manipulated, packed, permanent, planned, put-up, radicate, resolute, resolved, rigged, rigid, rooted, secure, set, settled, standing, steadfast, steady, sure, unalterable, unbending, unblinking, unchanging, undeviating, unflinching, unvarying, unwavering, unyielding.

antonyms alterable, variable.

fixity *n* determination, doggedness, fixedness, intentness, perseverance, persistence, resoluteness, resolve, stability, steadiness, strength, tenacity.

fizz *v* bubble, effervesce, fizzle, froth, fume, hiss, sizzle, sparkle, spit, sputter.

fizzle out abort, collapse, come to nothing, die away, die down, disappear, dissipate, evaporate, fail, fall through, fold, peter out, stop, subside, taper off.

fizzy *adj* aerated, bubbling, bubbly, carbonated, effervescent, frothy, gassy, sparkling.

flabbergasted *adj* amazed, astonished, astounded, bowled over, confounded, dazed, disconcerted, dumbfounded, nonplussed, overcome, overwhelmed, speechless, staggered, stunned, stupefied.

flabbiness *n* bloat, bloatedness, embonpoint, fat, flab, flaccidity, flesh, fleshiness, heaviness, laxness, limpness, looseness, overweight, pendulousness, plumpness, slackness.

antonyms firmness, leanness, strength.

flabby *adj* baggy, drooping, effete, enervated, feckless, feeble, flaccid, fleshy, floppy, fushionless, hanging, impotent, ineffective, ineffectual, inert, lax, limp, loose, nerveless, pendulous, plump, sagging, slack, sloppy, spineless, toneless, unfit, weak, yielding.

antonyms firm, lean, strong.

flaccid *adj* clammy, drooping, flabby, floppy, hypotonic, inert, lax, limp, loose, nerveless, relaxed, sagging, slack, soft, toneless, weak.

antonym firm.

flaccidity *n* clamminess, droopiness, flabbiness, floppiness, limpness, looseness, nervelessness, slackness, softness, tonelessness.

antonym firmness.

flag[1] *v* abate, decline, degenerate, deteriorate, die, diminish, droop, dwindle, ebb, fade, fail, faint, fall (off), falter, flop, languish, lessen, peter out, sag, sink, slow, slump, subside, succumb, taper off, tire, wane, weaken, weary, wilt.

antonym revive.

flag[2] *n* banderole, banner, burgee, colours, ensign, fanion, gonfalon, jack, Jolly Roger, labarum, oriflamme, pennant, pennon, pen(n)oncel(le), standard, streamer, vane.

v docket, hail, indicate, label, mark, motion, note, salute, signal, tab, tag, warn, wave.

flagellation *n* beating, castigation, chastisement, flaying, flogging, lashing, scourging, thrashing, vapulation, verberation, whaling, whipping.

flagging *adj* declining, decreasing, deteriorating, diminishing, drooping, dwindling, ebbing, fading, failing, faltering, lessening, sagging, sinking, slowing, subsiding, tiring, waning, weakening, wilting.

antonyms returning, reviving.

flagrant *adj* arrant, atrocious, audacious, barefaced, blatant, bold, brazen, conspicuous, crying, egregious, enormous, flagitious, flaunting, glaring, heinous, immodest, infamous, notorious, open, ostentatious, outrageous, overt, rank, scandalous, shameless, unashamed, undisguised.

antonyms covert, secret.

flail *v* beat, scutch, swinge, thrash, thresh, whip.

flair *n* ability, accomplishment, acumen, aptitude, chic, dash, discernment, elegance, facility, faculty, feel, genius, gift, knack, mastery, nose, panache, skill, style, stylishness, talent, taste.

antonym ineptitude.

flak *n* abuse, animadversions, aspersions, bad press, brickbats, censure, complaints, condemnation, criticism, disapprobation, disapproval, disparagement, fault-finding, hostility, invective, opposition, stick, strictures.

flake *n* chip, disc, flaught, floccule, flocculus, lamina, layer, paring, peeling, scale, shaving, sliver, squama, wafer.

v blister, chip, delaminate, desquamate, exfoliate, peel, scale.

flaky *adj* desquamative, desquamatory, dry, exfoliative, furfuraceous, laminar, layered, scabrous, scaly, scurfy.

flamboyance *n* brilliance, colour, dash, élan, extravagance, glamour, ostentation, panache, pizzazz, showiness, style, theatricality.

antonyms diffidence, restraint.

flamboyant *adj* baroque, brilliant, colourful, dashing, dazzling, elaborate, exciting, extravagant, flashy, florid, gaudy, glamorous, jaunty, ornate, ostentatious, rich, showy, striking, stylish, swashbuckling, theatrical.

antonyms modest, restrained.

flame *v* beam, blaze, burn, flare, flash, glare, glow, radiate, shine.

n affection, ardour, beau, blaze, brightness, enthusiasm, fervency, fervour, fire, flake, flammule, heart-throb, intensity, keenness, light, lover, passion, radiance, sweetheart, warmth, zeal.

flaming *adj* ablaze, afire, alight, angry, ardent, aroused, blazing, brilliant, burning, fervid, fiery, frenzied, glowing, hot, impassioned, intense, raging, red, red-hot, scintillating, smouldering, vehement, vivid.

flammable *adj* combustible, combustive, deflagrable, ignitable, inflammable.

antonyms fire-resistant, flameproof, incombustible, non-flammable, non-inflammable.

flange *n* flanch, flare, lip, rim, skirt, splay.

flank *n* edge, flitch, ham, haunch, hip, loin, quarter, side, thigh, wing.

v accompany, border, bound, confine, edge, fringe, line, screen, skirt, wall.

flap[1] *v* agitate, beat, dither, flacker, flaff, flaffer, flail, flutter, fuss, panic, shake, swing, swish, thrash, thresh, vibrate, wag, wave.

n agitation, commotion, dither, fluster, flutter, fuss, kerfuffle, pother, state, stew, sweat, tizzy, twitter.

flap[2] *n* aileron, apron, cover, fly, fold, lapel, lappet, lug, overlap, skirt, slat, tab, tag, tail.

flare *v* blaze, burn (up), burst, dazzle, erupt, explode, flame, flash, flicker, flutter, fulgurate, glare, waver.

n bell-bottom, blaze, broadening, burst, dazzle, flame, flanch, flange, flash, flicker, glare, gore, splay, widening.

flare out broaden, flanch, flaunch, splay, spread out, widen.

flare up blaze, blow one's top, erupt, explode, fly off the handle, lose one's cool.

flash *v* blaze, bolt, brandish, coruscate, dart, dash, display, exhibit, expose, flare, flaunt, flicker, flourish, fly, fulgurate, fulminate, glare, gleam, glint, glisten, glitter, light, race, scintillate, shimmer, shoot, show, sparkle, speed, sprint, streak, sweep, twinkle, whistle.

n blaze, bluette, burst, coruscation, dazzle, demonstration, display, flare, flaught, flicker, fulguration, gleam, hint, instant, jiff, jiffy, manifestation, moment, outburst, ray, scintillation, second, shaft, shake, shimmer, show, sign, spark, sparkle, split second, streak, touch, trice, twinkle, twinkling.

flashing *adj* coruscant, coruscating, dancing, flaring, flickering, fulgid, fulgurant, fulgurous, glittering, lambent, scintillating, sparkling, twinkling.

antonym steady.

flashy *adj* bold, brassy, cheap, flamboyant, flash, garish, gaudy, glamorous, glittery, glitzy, jazzy, loud, meretricious, obtrusive, ostentatious, raffish, rakish, ritzy, showy, snazzy, tacky, tasteless, tawdry, tig(e)rish, tinselly, vulgar.

antonyms plain, simple, tasteful.

flask *n* carafe, flacket, lekythos, matrass, pocket-pistol.

flat[1] *adj* even, horizontal, lamellar, lamelliform, level, levelled, low, outstretched, planar, plane, prone, prostrate, reclining, recumbent, smooth. spread-eagled, supine, unbroken, uniform.

n lowland, marsh, morass, moss, mud flat, plain, shallow, shoal, strand, swamp.

flat out all out, at full speed, at full tilt, at top speed, double-quick, for all one is worth, hell for leather, posthaste.

flat[2] *adj* bored, boring, burst, collapsed, dead, deflated, depressed, dull, empty, flavourless, insipid, jejune, lacklustre, lifeless, monotonous, pointless, prosaic, punctured, spiritless, stale, tedious, uninteresting, unpalatable, vapid, watery, weak.

flat[3] *adj* absolute, categorical, direct, downright, explicit, final, fixed, out-and-out, peremptory, plain, point-blank, positive, straight, total, uncompromising, unconditional, unequivocal, unqualified.

antonym equivocal.

adv absolutely, categorically, completely, entirely, exactly, point-blank, precisely, totally, utterly.

flat[4] *n* apartment, bed-sit, bed-sitter, maison(n)ette, pad, penthouse, pied-à-terre, rooms, tenement.

flatly *adv* absolutely, categorically, completely, peremptorily, point-blank, positively, uncompromisingly, unconditionally, unhesitatingly.

flatness *n* boredom, dullness, emptiness, evenness, horizontality, insipidity, languor, levelness, monotony, smoothness, staleness, tastelessness, tedium, uniformity, vapidity.

flatten *v* compress, crush, demolish, even out, fell, floor, iron out, knock down, level, overwhelm, planish, plaster, prostrate, raze, roll, slight, smooth, squash, subdue, trample.

flatter *v* adulate, become, beslobber, blandish, blarney, butter up, cajole, claw, collogue, compliment, court, enhance, eulogise, fawn, flannel, fleech, gloze, humour, inveigle, laud, play up to, praise, sawder, set off, show to advantage, soap, soft-soap, soothe, suit, sweet-talk, sycophantise, wheedle.

antonym criticise.

flatterer *n* adulator, back-scratcher, bootlicker, earwig, encomiast, eulogiser, fawner, flunkey, groveller, incenser, lackey, sycophant, toady.

antonyms critic, opponent.

flattering *adj* adulatory, becoming, complimentary, effective, effusive, enhancing, favourable, fawning, fulsome, gnathonic, gratifying, honeyed, honey-tongued, ingratiating, kind, laudatory, obsequious, servile, smooth-spoken, smooth-tongued, sugared, sugary, sycophantic, unctuous.

antonyms candid, uncompromising, unflattering.

flattery *n* adulation, backscratching, blandishment, blarney, bootlicking, butter, cajolement, cajolery, eulogy, fawning, flannel, flapdoodle, fleechment, fulsomeness, ingratiation, obsequiousness, servility, soap, soft sawder, soft soap, sugar, sweet talk, sycophancy, sycophantism, taffy, toadyism, unctuousness.

antonym criticism.

flatulence *n* borborygmus, eructation, flatulency, flatus, gas, gassiness, pomposity, prolixity, turgidity, ventosity, wind, windiness.

flatulent *v* gassy, pompous, prolix, swollen, turgid, ventose, windy.

flaunt *v* air, boast, brandish, dangle, display, disport, exhibit, flash, flourish, parade, show off, sport, vaunt, wield.

flavour *n* aroma, aspect, character, essence, extract, feel, feeling, flavouring, hint, odour, piquancy, property, quality, relish, sapidity, savour, savouriness, seasoning, smack, soupçon, stamp, style, suggestion, tang, taste, tastiness, tinge, tone, touch, zest, zing.

v contaminate, ginger up, imbue, infuse, lace, leaven, season, spice, taint.

flavourful *adj* delicious, flavorous, flavoursome, high-tasted, palatable, sapid, savoury, tasty, toothsome.

antonyms insipid, tasteless.

flavouring *n* essence, extract, seasoning, spirit, tincture, zest.

flaw *n* blemish, breach, break, cleft, crack, craze, crevice, defect, disfigurement, failing, fallacy, fault, fissure, fracture, hamartia, imperfection, lapse, macula, mark, mistake, rent, rift, shortcoming, slip, speck, split, spot, tear, weakness, wreath.

flawed *adj* blemished, broken, chipped, cracked, damaged, defective, disfigured, erroneous, faulty, imperfect, marked, marred, spoilt, unsound, vicious, vitiated.

antonyms flawless, perfect.

flawless *adj* faultless, immaculate, impeccable, intact, irreproachable, perfect, sound, spotless, stainless, unblemished, unbroken, undamaged, unsullied, whole.

antonyms flawed, imperfect.

flay *v* castigate, excoriate, execrate, flench, flog, lambast, pull to pieces, revile, scourge, skin, skin alive, tear a strip off, upbraid.

flea-ridden *adj* crawling, decrepit, dingy, flea-bitten, fly-blown, frowsty, grotty, grubby, infested, insalubrious, lousy, mangy, mean, moth-eaten, mucky, pediculous, run-down, scabby, scruffy, scurfy, sleazy, slummy, sordid, squalid, tatty, unhealthy, unhygienic.

antonym salubrious.

fleck *v* bespeckle, besprinkle, dapple, dot, dust, freak, mark, mottle, speckle, spinkle, spot, stipple, streak, variegate.

n dot, freak, macula, mark, point, speck, speckle, spot, streak.

fledgling *n* apprentice, beginner, chick, greenhorn, learner, neophyte, nestling, newcomer, novice, novitiate, recruit, rookie, tenderfoot, trainee, tyro.

flee *v* abscond, avoid, beat a hasty retreat, bolt, bunk (off), cut and run, decamp, depart, escape, fly, get away, leave, make off, make oneself scarce, scarper, scram, shun, skedaddle, split, take flight, take it on the lam, take off, take to one's heels, vamoose, vanish, withdraw.

antonyms stand, stay.

fleece *v* bilk, bleed, cheat, clip, con, defraud, diddle, mulct, overcharge, plunder, rifle, rip off, rob, rook, shear, skin, soak, squeeze, steal, sting, swindle.

fleecy *adj* downy, eriophorous, floccose, flocculate, fluffy, hairy, lanuginose, nappy, pilose, shaggy, soft, velvety, woolly.

antonyms bald, smooth.

fleet[1] *n* argosy, armada, escadrille, flota, flotilla, navy, squadron, task force.

fleet[2] *adj* expeditious, fast, flying, light-footed, mercurial, meteoric, nimble, quick, rapid, speedy, swift, velocipede, winged.

antonym slow.

fleeting *adj* brief, disappearing, ephemeral, evanescent, flitting, flying, fugacious, fugitive, impermanent, momentary, passing, short, short-lived, temporary, transient, transitory, vanishing.

antonym lasting.

fleetness *n* celerity, dispatch, expedition, expeditiousness, light-footedness, nimbleness, quickness, rapidity, speed, speediness, swiftness, velocity.

antonym sluggishness.

flesh *n* animality, beef, blood, body, brawn, carnality, corporeality, dead-meat, family, fat, fatness, flesh and blood, food, human nature, kin, kindred, kinsfolk, kith and kin, matter, meat, physicality, pulp, relations, relatives, sensuality, substance, tissue.

fleshiness *n* adiposity, chubbiness, corpulence, embonpoint, flabbiness, heaviness, obesity, plumpness, portliness, stoutness, tubbiness.

fleshly *adj* animal, bestial, bodily, brutish, carnal, corporal, corporeal, earthly, earthy, erotic, human, lustful, material, mundane, physical, secular, sensual, terrestrial, wordly.

antonym spiritual.

fleshy *adj* ample, beefy, brawny, carneous, carnose, chubby, chunky, corpulent, fat, flabby, hefty, meaty, obese, overweight, paunchy, plump, podgy, portly, rotund, stout, tubby, well-padded.

antonym thin.

flex *v* angle, bend, bow, contract, crook, curve, double up, ply, tighten.

antonyms extend, straighten.

flexibility *n* adaptability, adjustability, agreeability, amenability, bendability, complaisance, elasticity, flexion, give, pliability, pliancy, resilience, spring, springiness, suppleness, tensility.

antonym inflexibility.

flexible *adj* accommodating, adaptable, adjustable, agreeable, amenable, bendable, biddable, complaisant, compliant, discretionary, docile, double-jointed, ductile, elastic, flexile, gentle, limber, lissome, lithe, loose-limbed, manageable, mobile, mouldable, open, plastic, pliable, pliant, responsive, springy, stretchy, supple, tensile, tractable, variable, whippy, willowy, withy, yielding.

antonym inflexible.

flibbertigibbet *n* backfisch, bird-brain, butterfly, featherbrain, fizgig, flapper, giddy goat, madcap, rattle-brain, rattle-head, rattle-pate, scatterbrain, tearaway.

flick *v* bat, click, dab, fillip, flap, flicker, flip, flirt, hit, jab, peck, rap, strike, tap, touch, whip.

n click, fillip, flap, flip, flutter, jab, peck, rap, tap, touch.

flick through flip, glance, riffle, scan, skim, skip, thumb.

flicker *v* coruscate, flare, flash, flutter, glimmer, gutter, quiver, scintillate, shimmer, sparkle, twinkle, vibrate, waver.

n atom, breath, coruscation, drop, flare, flash, gleam, glimmer, glint, indication, inkling, iota, scintillation, spark, trace, vestige.

flickering *n* coruscant, coruscating, guttering, lambent, sparkling, twinkling, unsteady.

flight[1] *n* aeronautics, air transport, air travel, aviation, cloud, echelon, escadrille, flip, flock, flying, formation, journey, mounting, soaring, squadron, swarm, trip, unit, volitation, voyage, wing, winging.

flight[2] *n* breakaway, departure, escape, exit, exodus, fleeing, getaway, guy, hegira, retreat, running away.

flightiness *n* capriciousness, changeability, dizziness, fickleness, flippancy, frivolity, giddiness, inconstancy, irresponsibility, levity, lightness, mercurialness, volatility, wildness.

antonym steadiness.

flighty *adj* bird-brained, bird-witted, bubble-headed, capricious, changeable, dizzy, fickle, frivolous, giddy, hare-brained, impetuous, impulsive, inconstant, irresponsible, light-headed, mercurial, rattle-brained, rattle-headed, rattle-pated, scatterbrained, silly, skittish, thoughtless, unbalanced, unstable, unsteady, volage, volageous, volatile, whisky-frisky, wild.

antonym steady.

flimsy *adj* cardboard, chiffon, cobwebby, delicate, diaphanous, ethereal, feeble, fragile, frail, frivolous, gauzy, gimcrack, gossamer, implausible, inadequate, insubstantial, light, makeshift, meagre, poor, rickety, shaky, shallow, sheer, slight, superficial, thin, transparent, trivial, unconvincing, unsatisfactory, unsubstantial, vaporous, weak.

antonym sturdy.

flinch *v* baulk, blench, cower, cringe, draw back, duck, flee, quail, quake, recoil, retreat, shake, shirk, shiver, shrink, shudder, shy away, start, swerve, tremble, wince, withdraw.

fling *v* bung, cant, cast, catapult, chuck, heave, hurl, jerk, let fly, lob, pitch, precipitate, propel, send, shoot, shy, sling, slug, souse, throw, toss.

n attempt, bash, binge, cast, crack, gamble, go, heave, indulgence, lob, pitch, shot, spree, stab, throw, toss, trial, try, turn, venture, whirl.

flip *v* cast, fillip, flap, flick, jerk, pitch, snap, spin, throw, toss, turn, twirl, twist.

n bob, fillip, flap, flick, jerk, toss, turn, twirl, twist.

flippancy *n* cheek, cheekiness, disrespect, disrespectfulness, frivolity, glibness, impertinence, irreverence, levity, persiflage, pertness, sauciness, superficiality.

antonym earnestness.

flippant *adj* brash, cheeky, cocky, disrespectful, flip, frivolous, glib, impertinent, impudent, irreverent, malapert, nonchalant, offhand, pert, pococurante, rude, saucy, superficial, unserious.

antonym earnest.

flirt *v* chat up, coquet, dally, ogle, philander, tease.

n chippy, coquet(te), gillet, gillflirt, heart-breaker, hussy, philanderer, tease, trifler, wanton.

flirt with consider, dabble in, entertain, make up to, play with, toy with, trifle with, try.

flirtation *n* affair, amorousness, amour, chatting up, coquetry, dalliance, dallying, intrigue, philandering, sport, teasing, toying, trifling.

flirtatious *adj* amorous, arch, come-hither, come-on, coquettish, coy, flirty, loose, promiscuous, provocative, sportive, teasing, wanton.

flit *v* beat, bob, dance, dart, elapse, flash, fleet, flutter, fly, pass, skim, slip, speed, volitate, whisk, wing.

flitting *adj* bobbing, dancing, darting, ephemeral, fleet, fleeting, flittering, fluttering, skimming, volitant.

float *v* bob, drift, glide, hang, hover, initiate, launch, poise, promote, ride, sail, set up, slide, swim, waft.

antonym sink.

floating *adj* afloat, bobbing, buoyant, buoyed up, fluctuating, free, migratory, movable, ocean-going, sailing, swimming, unattached, uncommitted, unfixed, unsinkable, unsubmerged, variable, wandering, water-borne.

flock *v* bunch, cluster, collect, congregate, converge, crowd, gather, gravitate, group, herd, huddle, mass, swarm, throng, troop.

n assembly, bevy, collection, colony, company, congregation, convoy, crowd, drove, flight, gaggle, gathering, group, herd, horde, host, mass, multitude, pack, shoal, skein, swarm, throng.

flog *v* beat, birch, breech, chastise, drive, drub, flagellate, flay, hide, knout, k(o)urbash, larrup, lash, overexert, overtax, overwork, punish, push, scourge, strain, swish, tat, tax, thrash, trounce, vapulate, verberate, welt, whack, whale, whang, whip, whop.

flogging *n* beating, caning, drubbing, flagellation, flaying, hiding, horsewhipping, lashing, scourging, thrashing, trouncing, vapulation, verberation, whaling, whipping, whopping.

flood *v* bog down, brim, choke, deluge, drench, drown, engulf, fill, flow, glut, gush, immerse, inundate, overflow, oversupply, overwhelm, pour, rush, saturate, soak, submerge, surge, swamp, swarm, sweep.

n abundance, alluvion, bore, cataclysm, debacle, deluge, diluvion, diluvium, downpour, eagre, flash flood, flow, freshet, glut, inundation, multitude, outpouring, overflow, plethora, profusion, rush, spate, stream, superfluity, tide, torrent.

antonyms dearth, drought, trickle.

floor *n* base, basis, deck, étage, landing, level, stage, storey, tier.

v baffle, beat, bewilder, confound, conquer, defeat, discomfit, disconcert, down, dumbfound, frustrate, nonplus, overthrow, overwhelm, perplex, prostrate, puzzle, stump, stun, throw, trounce, worst.

flop *v* bomb, close, collapse, dangle, droop, drop, fail, fall, fall flat, flap, flump, fold, founder, hang, misfire, plump, sag, slump, topple, tumble.

n balls-up, cock-up, debacle, disaster, failure, fiasco, loser, no go, non-starter, turkey, wash-out.

floppy *adj* baggy, dangling, droopy, flabby, flaccid, flapping, flappy, flopping, hanging, limp, loose, pendulous, sagging, soft.

antonym firm.

flora *n* botany, herbage, plantage, plant-life, plants, vegetable kingdom, vegetation.

florid *adj* baroque, blowzy, bombastic, busy, coloratura, elaborate, embellished, euphuistic, figurative, flamboyant, flourishy, flowery, flushed, fussy, grandiloquent, high-coloured, high-falutin(g), high-flown, melismatic, ornate, overelaborate, purple, raddled, red, rococo, rubicund, ruddy.

antonyms pale, plain.

flotsam *n* debris, detritus, jetsam, junk, oddments, scum, sweepings, waveson, wreckage.

flounce *v* bob, bounce, fling, jerk, spring, stamp, storm, throw, toss, twist.

n falbala, frill, fringe, furbelow, ruffle, trimming, valance.

flounder *v* blunder, bungle, falter, flail, fumble, grope, muddle, plunge, stagger, struggle, stumble, thrash, toss, tumble, wallop, wallow, welter.

flourish[1] *v* advance, bloom, blossom, boom, burgeon, develop, do well, flower, get on, grow, increase, mushroom, progress, prosper, succeed, thrive, wax.

antonyms fail, languish.

flourish[2] *v* brandish, display, flaunt, flutter, parade, shake, sweep, swing, swish, twirl, vaunt, wag, wave, wield.

n arabesque, brandishing, ceremony, curlicue, dash, decoration, display, élan, embellishment, fanfare, ornament, ornamentation, panache, parade, paraph, pizzazz, plume, shaking, show, sweep, twirling, wave.

flourishing *adj* blooming, booming, burgeoning, developing, going strong, in the pink, lush, luxuriant, mushrooming, progressing, prospering, rampant, rank, riotous, successful, thriving.

antonyms failing, languishing.

flout *v* affront, contemn, defy, deride, disregard, insult, jeer at, mock, outrage, reject, ridicule, scoff at, scorn, scout, spurn, taunt.

antonym respect.

flow *v* arise, bubble, cascade, circulate, course, deluge, derive, distil, drift, emanate, emerge, flood, glide, gush, inundate, issue, move, originate, overflow, pour, proceed, purl, result, ripple, roll, run, rush, slide, slip, spew, spill, spring, spurt, squirt, stream, surge, sweep, swirl, teem, well, whirl.

n abundance, cascade, course, current, deluge, drift, effluence, efflux, effusion, emanation, flood, flowage, flux, fluxion, gush, outflow, outpouring, plenty, plethora, spate, spurt, stream, succession, tide, train, wash.

flower *n* best, bloom, blossom, choice, cream, crème de la crème, efflorescence, élite, fleuret, fleuron, floret, floscule, floweret, freshness, height, pick, prime, vigour.

v blossom, blow, burgeon, dehisce, effloresce, flourish, mature, open, unfold.

flowering *adj* blooming, bloomy, blossoming, efflorescent, florescent.

n anthesis, blooming, blossoming, burgeoning, development, florescence, flourishing, flowerage, maturing.

flowery *adj* affected, baroque, elaborate, embellished, euphuistic, fancy, figurative, floral, floriated, florid, fulsome, high-flown, ornate, overelaborate, overwrought, rhetorical, Wardour Street.

antonym plain.

flowing *adj* abounding, brimming, cantabile, cascading, continuous, cursive, easy, facile, falling, flooded, fluent, full, gushing, overrun, prolific, rich, rolling, rushing, smooth, streaming, surging, sweeping, teeming, unbroken, uninterrupted, voluble.

antonyms hesitant, interrupted.

fluctuate *v* alter, alternate, change, ebb and flow, float, hesitate, oscillate, pendulate, rise and fall, seesaw, shift, shuffle, sway, swing, undulate, vacillate, vary, veer, waver.

fluctuating *adj* capricious, changeable, fickle, fluctuant, irresolute, mutable, oscillating, oscillatory, rising and falling, swaying, swinging, unstable, unsteady, vacillant, vacillating, vacillatory, variable, wavering.

antonym stable.

fluctuation *n* alternation, ambivalence, capriciousness, change, ficklessness, inconstancy, instability, irresolution, oscillation, shift, swing, unsteadiness, vacillation, variability, variableness, variation, wavering.

fluency *n* articulateness, assurance, command, control, ease, eloquence, facility, facundity, glibness, readiness, slickness, smoothness, volubility.

antonym incoherence.

fluent *adj* articulate, easy, effortless, eloquent, facile, flowing, fluid, glib, mellifluous, natural, ready, smooth, smooth-talking, voluble, well-versed.

antonym tongue-tied.

fluff *n* down, dust, dustball, floccus, flosh, floss, flue, fug, fuzz, lint, nap, oose, pile.

v balls up, botch, bungle, cock up, fumble, mess up, muddle, muff, screw up, spoil.

antonym bring off.

fluffy *adj* downy, eriophorous, feathery, fleecy, floccose, flocculate, flossy, fuzzy, gossamer, hairy, lanuginose, lanuginous, nappy, oozy, shaggy, silky, soft, velvety, woolly.

antonym smooth.

fluid *adj* adaptable, adjustable, aqueous, changeable, diffluent, easy, elegant, feline, flexible, floating, flowing, fluctuating, fluent, fluidal, fluidic, graceful, inconstant, indefinite, liquefied, liquid, melted, mercurial, mobile, molten, mutable, protean, running, runny, shifting, sinuous, smooth, unstable, watery.

antonyms solid, stable.

n humour, juice, liquid, liquor, sanies, sap, solution.

fluke *n* accident, blessing, break, chance, coincidence, fortuity, freak, lucky break, quirk, serendipity, stroke, windfall.

fluky *adj* accidental, chance, chancy, coincidental, fortuitous, fortunate, freakish, incalculable, lucky, serendipitous, uncertain.

flummox *v* baffle, bamboozle, befuddle, bewilder, confound, confuse, defeat, fox, mystify, nonplus, perplex, puzzle, stump, stymie.

flummoxed *adj* at a loss, at sea, baffled, befuddled, bewildered, confounded, confused, foxed, mystified, nonplussed, perplexed, puzzled, stumped, stymied.

flunkey *n* assistant, boot-licker, creature, cringer, drudge, footman, hanger-on, healer, lackey, manservant, menial, minion, slave, toady, tool, underling, valet, yes-man.

flurry *n* ado, agitation, burst, bustle, commotion, disturbance, excitement, ferment, flap, flaw, fluster, flutter, furore, fuss, gust, hubbub, hurry, kerfuffle, outbreak, pother, spell, spurt, squall, stir, to-do, tumult, upset, whirl.

v abash, agitate, bewilder, bother, bustle, confuse, disconcert, discountenance, disturb, fluster, flutter, fuss, hassle, hurry, hustle, perturb, rattle, ruffle, unsettle, upset.

flush[1] *v* blush, burn, colour, crimson, flame, glow, go red, mantle, redden, rouge, suffuse.

antonym pale.

n bloom, blush, colour, freshness, glow, redness, rosiness, rud, vigour.

flush[2] *v* cleanse, douche, drench, eject, empty, evacuate, expel, hose, rinse, swab, syringe, wash.

adj abundant, affluent, full, generous, in funds, lavish, liberal, moneyed, overflowing, prodigal, prosperous, rich, rolling, wealthy, well-heeled, well-off, well-supplied, well-to-do.

flush[3] *adj* even, flat, level, plane, smooth, square, true.

flush[4] *v* discover, disturb, drive out, force out, rouse, run to earth, start, uncover.

flushed *adj* ablaze, aflame, aglow, animated, aroused, blowzy, blushing, burning, crimson, elated, embarrassed, enthused, excited, exhilarated, exultant, febrile, feverish, glowing, hectic, high, hot, inspired, intoxicated, red, rosy, rubicund, ruddy, sanguine, scarlet, thrilled.

antonym pale.

fluster *v* abash, agitate, bother, bustle, confound, confuse, discombobulate, disconcert, discountenance, disturb, embarrass, excite, faze, flurry, hassle, heat, hurry, perturb, pother, pudder, rattle, ruffle, unnerve, unsettle, upset.

antonym calm.

n agitation, bustle, commotion, discomposure, distraction, disturbance, dither, embarrassment, faze, flap, flurry, flutter, furore, kerfuffle, perturbation, ruffle, state, tizzy, turmoil.

antonym calm.

fluted *adj* chamfered, channelled, corrugated, furrowed, gouged, grooved, ribbed, ridged, rutted, valleculate.

flutter *v* agitate, bat, beat, dance, discompose, flap, flichter, flicker, flit, flitter, fluctuate, hover, palpitate, quiver, ripple, ruffle, shiver, toss, tremble, vibrate, volitate, wave, waver.

n agitation, commotion, confusion, discomposure, dither, excitement, flurry, fluster, nervousness, palpitation, perturbation, quiver, quivering, shiver, shudder, state, tremble, tremor, tumult, twitching, upset, vibration, volitation.

fluttering *adj* beating, dancing, flapping, flickering, flitting, hovering, palpitating, quivering, tossing, trembling, volitant, waving.

flux *n* alteration, change, chaos, development, flow, fluctuation, fluidity, instability, modification, motion, movement, mutability, mutation, stir, transition, unrest.

antonym stability.

fly[1] *v* abscond, aviate, avoid, bolt, career, clear out, dart, dash, decamp, disappear, display, elapse, escape, flap, flee, flit, float, flutter, get away, glide, hare, hasten, hasten away, hedge-hop, hightail it, hoist, hover, hurry, light out, mount, operate, pass, pilot, race, raise, retreat, roll by, run, run for it, rush, sail, scamper, scarper, scoot, shoot, show, shun, skim, soar, speed, sprint, take flight, take off, take to one's heels, take wing, tear, vamoose, volitate, wave, whisk, whiz, wing, zoom.

fly at assail, assault, attack, fall upon, go for, have at, light into, pitch into, rush at.

fly in the face of affront, defy, disobey, flout, insult, oppose.

fly[2] *adj* alert, artful, astute, canny, careful, cunning, knowing, nobody's fool, on the ball, prudent, sagacious, sharp, shrewd, smart, wide-awake.

fly-by-night *adj* brief, cowboy, discreditable, disreputable, dubious, ephemeral, here today - gone tomorrow, impermanent, irresponsible, questionable, shady, short-lived, undependable, unreliable, untrustworthy.

antonym reliable.

flying *adj* airborne, brief, express, fast, flapping, fleet, fleeting, floating, fluttering, fugacious, fugitive, gliding, hasty, hovering, hurried, mercurial, mobile, rapid, rushed, short-lived, soaring, speedy, streaming, transitory, vanishing, volant, volatic, volitant, volitational, volitorial, waving, wind-borne, winged, winging.

foam *n* barm, bubbles, effervescence, foaminess, froth, frothiness, head, lather, scum, spume, spumescence, suds, surf.

v boil, bubble, effervesce, fizz, froth, lather, spume.

foamy *adj* barmy, bubbly, foaming, frothy, lathery, spumescent, spumous, spumy, sudsy.

fob off appease, deceive, dump, foist, get rid of, give a sop to, impose, inflict, palm off, pass off, placate, put off, stall, unload.

focus *n* axis, centre, centre of attraction, core, crux, cynosure, focal point, headquarters, heart, hinge, hub, kernel, linchpin, nucleus, pivot, target.

v aim, centre, concentrate, concentre, converge, direct, fix, focalise, home in, join, meet, rivet, spotlight, zero in, zoom in.

fodder *n* browsing, feed, food, foodstuff, forage, fuel, nourishment, pabulum, provand, provend, provender, proviant, rations, silage.

foe *n* adversary, antagonist, enemy, foeman, ill-wisher, opponent, rival.

antonym friend.

fog *n* bewilderment, blanket, blindness, brume, confusion, daze, gloom, haze, London particular, miasma, mist, muddle, murk, murkiness, obscurity, pea-souper, perplexity, puzzlement, smog, stupor, trance, vagueness.

v becloud, bedim, befuddle, bewilder, blanket, blind, cloud, confuse, darken, daze, dim, dull, mist, muddle, obfuscate, obscure, perplex, shroud, steam up, stupefy.

fog(e)y *n* anachronism, antique, archaism, dodo, eccentric, fossil, fuddy-duddy, moss-back, mumpsimus, oddity, period piece, relic, square, stick-in-the-mud.

foggy *adj* beclouded, befuddled, bewildered, blurred, blurry, brumous, clouded, cloudy, confused, dark, dazed, dim, grey, hazy, indistinct, misty, muddled, muggish, muggy, murky, muzzy, nebulous, obscure, shadowy, smoggy, stupefied, stupid, unclear, vague, vaporous.

antonym clear.

foible *n* crotchet, defect, eccentricity, failing, fault, habit, idiosyncrasy, imperfection, infirmity, oddity, oddness, peculiarity, quirk, shortcoming, strangeness, weakness.

foil[1] *v* baffle, balk, check, checkmate, circumvent, counter, defeat, disappoint, elude, frustrate, nullify, obstruct, outsmart, outwit, spike (someone's) guns, stop, stump, thwart.

antonym abet.

foil[2] *n* antithesis, background, balance, complement, contrast, relief, setting.

foist *v* fob off, force, get rid of, impose, insert, insinuate, interpolate, introduce, palm off, pass off, thrust, unload, wish on.

fold *v* bend, clasp, close, collapse, crash, crease, crimp, crumple, dog-ear, double, embrace, enclose, enfold, entwine, envelop, fail, fake, gather, go bust, hug, intertwine, overlap, pleat, ply, shut down, tuck, wrap, wrap up.

n bend, corrugation, crease, crimp, duplicature, furrow, knife-edge, layer, overlap, pleat, ply, turn, wimple, wrinkle.

folder *n* binder, envelope, file, folio, holder, portfolio.

foliage *n* foliation, foliature, frondescence, greenery, leafage, verdure, vernation.

folk *n* clan, family, kin, kindred, kinfolk, kinsmen, nation, people, race, society, tribe.

adj ancestral, ethnic, indigenous, national, native, traditional, tribal.

folklore *n* fables, folk-tales, legends, lore, mythology, myths, superstitions, tales, tradition.

follow *v* accompany, accord, act according to, appreciate, arise, attend, catch, catch on, chase, come after, come next, comply, comprehend, conform, cultivate, dangle, develop, dog, emanate, ensue, escort, fathom, get, get the picture, grasp, haunt, heed, hound, hunt, imitate, keep abreast of, live up to, mind, note, obey, observe, pursue, realise, regard, result, second, see, shadow, stag, stalk, succeed, supersede, supervene, supplant, support, tag along, tail, track, trail, twig, understand, watch.

antonyms desert, precede.

follow through complete, conclude, consummate, continue, finish, fulfil, implement, pursue, see through.

follow up check out, consolidate, continue, investigate, pursue, reinforce, substantiate.

follower *n* acolyte, adherent, admirer, aficionado, Anthony, apostle, attendant, backer, believer, buff, cohort, companion, convert, devotee, disciple, emulator, fan, fancier, freak, galloglass, habitué, hanger-on, heeler, helper, henchman, imitator, lackey, minion, partisan, poodle-dog, poursuivant, pupil, representative, retainer, running dog, servitor, sidekick, supporter, tantony, votary, worshipper.

antonyms leader, opponent.

following *adj* coming, consecutive, consequent, consequential, ensuing, later, next, resulting, sequent, subsequent, succeeding, successive.

n audience, backing, circle, claque, clientèle, coterie, entourage, fans, followers, patronage, public, retinue, suite, support, supporters, train.

folly[1] *n* absurdity, craziness, daftness, fatuity, foolishness, idiocy, illogicality, imbecility, imprudence, indiscretion, insanity, irrationality, irresponsibility, lunacy, madness, moonraking, moria, nonsense, preposterousness, rashness, recklessness, senselessness, silliness, stupidity, unreason, unwisdom.

antonym prudence.

folly[2] *n* belvedere, gazebo, monument, tower, whim.

foment *v* activate, agitate, arouse, brew, encourage, excite, foster, goad, incite, instigate, kindle, promote, prompt, provoke, quicken, raise, rouse, spur, stimulate, stir up, whip up, work up.

antonym quell.

fomenter *n* abettor, agitator, demagogue, firebrand, incendiary, inciter, instigator, mob-orator, rabble-rouser, troublemaker, tub-thumper.

fond *adj* absurd, adoring, affectionate, amorous, caring, credulous, deluded, devoted, doting, empty, foolish, indiscreet, indulgent, loving, naive, over-optimistic, sanguine, tender, uxorious, vain, warm.

antonyms hostile, realistic.

fond of addicted to, attached to, enamoured of, hooked on, keen on, partial to, predisposed towards, stuck on, sweet on.

fondle *v* caress, cocker, coddle, cuddle, dandle, lallygag, pat, pet, smuggle, stroke.

fondly *adv* absurdly, adoringly, affectionately, credulously, dearly, foolishly, indulgently, lovingly, naïvely, over-optimistically, sanguinely, stupidly, tenderly, vainly.

fondness *n* affection, attachment, devotion, engouement, enthusiasm, fancy, inclination, kindness, leaning, liking, love, partiality, penchant, predilection, preference, soft spot, susceptibility, taste, tenderness, weakness.

antonym aversion.

food *n* aliment, ambrosia, board, bread, cheer, chow, comestibles, commons, cooking, cuisine, diet, eatables, eats, edibles, fare, feed, fodder, foodstuffs, forage, grub, larder, meat, menu, nosh, nourishment, nouriture, nutriment, nutrition, pabulum, pap, prog, provand, provend, provender, proviant, provisions, rations, refreshment, scoff, scran, stores, subsistence, sustenance, table, tack, tommy, tuck, tucker, viands, victuals, vittles, vivers.

fool *n* ass, bécasse, berk, besom-head, bête, bird-brain, blockhead, bonehead, boodle, buffethead, buffoon, burk, butt, capocchia, Charlie, chump, clodpate, clot, clown, cluck, comic, coxcomb, cuckoo, daftie, daw, dawcock, dimwit, dizzard, Dogberry, dolt, dope, dottle, droll, drongo, dumb-bell, dumb-cluck, dumbo, dunce, dunderhead, dunderpate, dupe, easy mark, fall guy, fathead, fon, galah, gaupus, git, goon, goop, goose, greenhorn, gudgeon, gull, halfwit, harlequin, idiot, ignoramus, illiterate, imbecile, jackass, Jack-fool, jerk, jester, jobernowl, josh, joskin, leather-head, loggerhead, log-head, loon, madhaun, merry-andrew, mooncalf, moron, motley, mug, nerd, nig-nog, nincompoop, ninny, nit, nitwit, nong, noodle, numskull, nurd, pierrot, pillock, pot-head, prat, prick, punchinello, sap, saphead, sawney, schlep, schmo, schmuck, silly, silly-billy, simpleton, soft, soft-head, softie, softy, stooge, stupe, stupid, sucker, thicko, tomfool, Tom-noddy, turnip, twerp, twit, wally, want-wit, wimp, witling, wooden-head, yap, zany, zombie.

v act dido, act the fool, act up, bamboozle, be silly, beguile, bluff, cavort, cheat, clown, con, cozen, cut capers, daff, deceive, delude, diddle, dupe, feign, fiddle, fon, frolic, gull, have on, hoax, hoodwink, horse around, jest, joke, kid, lark, meddle, mess, mess about, mislead, monkey, play, play the fool, play the goat, play up, pretend, put one over on, string, string along, swindle, take in, tamper, tease, toy, trick, trifle.

fool about dawdle, idle, kill time, lark, lark about, mess about, play about, trifle.

foolery *n* antics, buffoonery, capers, carry-on, childishness, clowning, desipience, dido, drollery, espièglerie, farce, folly, fooling, high jinks, horseplay, larks, mischief, monkey tricks, nonsense, practical jokes, pranks, shenanigans, silliness, tomfoolery, waggery, zanyism.

foolhardy *adj* adventurous, bold, dare-devil, hot-headed, ill-advised, ill-considered, impetuous, imprudent, incautious, irresponsible, madcap, precipitate, rash, reckless, temerarious, unheeding, unwary, venturesome, venturous.

antonym cautious.

fooling *n* bluffing, buffoonery, clownishness, desipience, drollery, farce, jesting, joking, kidding.

kidology, mockery, nonsense, pretence, shamming, skylarking, teasing, tricks, trifling, waggery, zanyism.

foolish *adj* absurd, brainless, cockle-brained, crazy, daft, desipient, dilly, doited, doltish, dotish, dottled, dunderheaded, étourdi(e), fatuous, glaikit, gudgeon, half-baked, half-witted, hare-brained, idiotic, idle-headed, ill-advised, illaudable, ill-considered, ill-judged, imbecile, imbecilic, imprudent, incautious, indiscreet, inept, injudicious, insipient, lean-witted, ludicrous, mad, moronic, nonsensical, potty, ridiculous, senseless, short-sighted, silly, simple, simple-minded, sottish, stupid, tomfool, unintelligent, unreasonable, unwise, weak, wet, witless.
antonym wise.

foolishly *adv* absurdly, fatuously, fondly, idiotically, ill-advisedly, imprudently, incautiously, indiscreetly, ineptly, injudiciously, mistakenly, ridiculously, senselessly, short-sightedly, stupidly, unwisely.
antonym wisely.

foolishness *n* absurdity, bunk, bunkum, claptrap, étourderie, folly, foolery, imprudence, inanity, incaution, incautiousness, indiscretion, ineptitude, insipience, irresponsibility, malarkey, niaiserie, nonsense, rubbish, silliness, stupidity, unreason, unwisdom, weakness.
antonyms prudence, wisdom.

foolproof *adj* certain, fail-safe, guaranteed, idiot-proof, infallible, never-failing, safe, sure-fire, unassailable, unbreakable.
antonym unreliable.

footing *n* base, basis, condition, conditions, establishment, foot-hold, foundation, grade, ground, groundwork, installation, position, purchase, rank, relations, relationship, settlement, standing, state, status, terms.

footnotes *n* annotations, apparatus criticus, commentary, marginalia, notes, scholia.

footprint *n* footmark, spoor, trace, track, trail, vestige.

footstep *n* footfall, plod, step, tramp, tread, trudge.

fop *n* beau, coxcomb, dandy, dude, exquisite, Jack-a-dandy, Jessie, macaroni, muscadin, musk-cat, pansy, peacock, petit maître, popinjay, spark, swell.

foppish *adj* affected, coxcombical, dainty, dandiacal, dandified, dandyish, dapper, dressy, finical, la-di-da, natty, overdressed, preening, prinking, spruce, vain.
antonym unkempt.

for dear life desperately, energetically, for all one is worth, intensely, strenuously, urgently, vigorously, with might and main.

for example eg, exempli gratia, par exemple, zum Beispiel.

for fun facetiously, for kicks, for thrills, in jest, jokingly, light-heartedly, mischievously, playfully, roguishly, sportively, teasingly, tongue in cheek.

for good finally, for ever, irreparably, irreversibly, irrevocably, once and for all, permanently, sine die.

for good measure as a bonus, as an extra, besides, gratis, in addition, into the bargain, to boot.

for love for nothing, for pleasure, free of charge, freely, gratis, voluntarily.

for love or money by any means, ever, for anything, on any condition, under any circumstances.

for the most part chiefly, commonly, generally, in the main, largely, mainly, mostly, on the whole, principally, usually.

for the present for a while, for now, for the moment, for the nonce, for the time being, in the interim, in the meantime, pro tem, pro tempore, provisionally, temporarily.

for the time being for now, for the moment, for the nonce, for the present, in the meantime, meantime, meanwhile, pro tem, pro tempore, temporarily.

forage *n* étape, feed, fodder, food, foodstuffs, pabulum, pasturage, provender.
v cast about, explore, hunt, plunder, prog, raid, ransack, rummage, scavenge, scour, scrounge, search, seek.

foray *n* depredation, descent, excursion, incursion, inroad, invasion, irruption, offensive, raid, razzia, reconnaissance, sally, sortie, spreagh, swoop.

forbear *v* abstain, avoid, cease, decline, desist, eschew, hesitate, hold, hold back, keep from, omit, pause, refrain, restrain oneself, stay, stop, withhold.

forbearance *n* abstinence, avoidance, clemency, endurance, indulgence, leniency, lenity, longanimity, long-suffering, mildness, moderation, patience, refraining, resignation, restraint, self-control, sufferance, temperance, tolerance, toleration.
antonym intolerance.

forbearing *adj* clement, easy, forbearant, forgiving, indulgent, lenient, longanimous, long-suffering, merciful, mild, moderate, patient, restrained, self-controlled, tolerant.
antonyms intolerant, merciless.

forbid *v* ban, block, contraindicate, debar, deny, disallow, exclude, hinder, inhibit, interdict, outlaw, preclude, prevent, prohibit, proscribe, refuse, rule out, veto.
antonym allow.

forbidden *adj* banned, barred, debarred, disallowed, interdit, out of bounds, outlawed, prohibited, proscribed, taboo, verboten, vetoed.

forbidding *adj* abhorrent, awesome, daunting, formidable, frightening, gaunt, grim, hostile, inhospitable, menacing, off-putting, ominous, repellent, repulsive, sinister, stern, threatening, unapproachable, unfriendly.
antonyms approachable, congenial.

force[1] *n* aggression, arm-twisting, beef, big stick, bite, coercion, cogency, compulsion, constraint, drive, duress, dynamism, effect, effectiveness, efficacy, emphasis, energy, enforcement, fierceness, foison, forcefulness, fushion, impact, impetus, impulse, incentive, influence, intensity, jism, life, mailed fist, might, momentum, motivation, muscle, persistence, persuasiveness, potency, power, pressure, punch, shock, steam, stimulus, strength, stress, validity, vehemence, vigour, violence, vis, vitality, weight.

v bulldoze, coerce, compel, constrain, drag, drive, exact, extort, impel, impose, lean on, make, necessitate, obligate, oblige, press, press-gang, pressure, pressurise, prise, propel, push, strong-arm, thrust, urge, wrench, wrest, wring.

force[2] *n* army, battalion, body, corps, detachment, detail, division, effective, enomoty, host, legion, patrol, phalanx, regiment, squad, squadron, troop, unit, Wehrmacht.

forced *adj* affected, artificial, compulsory, contrived, enforced, false, feigned, insincere, involuntary, laboured, mandatory, obligatory, stiff, stilted, strained, synthetic, unnatural, unspontaneous, wooden.

antonyms spontaneous, voluntary.

forceful *adj* cogent, compelling, convincing, domineering, drastic, dynamic, effective, emphatic, energetic, persuasive, pithy, potent, powerful, strong, telling, urgent, vigorous, weighty.

antonym feeble.

forcible *adj* active, aggressive, coercive, cogent, compelling, compulsory, drastic, effective, efficient, energetic, forceful, impressive, mighty, pithy, potent, powerful, strong, telling, urgent, vehement, violent, weighty.

antonym feeble.

forcibly *adv* against one's will, by main force, compulsorily, emphatically, obligatorily, under compulsion, under duress, vehemently, vigorously, violently, willy-nilly.

ford *n* causeway, crossing, drift.

forebear *n* ancestor, antecedent, antecessor, father, forefather, forerunner, predecessor, primogenitor, progenitor.

antonym descendant.

forebode *v* augur, betoken, foreshadow, foreshow, foretell, foretoken, forewarn, import, indicate, omen, portend, predict, presage, prognosticate, promise, signify, warn.

foreboding *n* anticipation, anxiety, apprehension, apprehensiveness, augury, boding, chill, dread, fear, foreshadowing, foretoken, hoodoo, intuition, misgiving, omen, portent, prediction, prefigurement, premonition, presage, presentiment, prodrome, prodromus, prognostication, sign, token, warning, worry.

forecast *v* augur, bode, calculate, conjecture, divine, estimate, expect, foresee, foretell, plan, predict, prognosticate, prophesy.

n augury, conjecture, foresight, forethought, guess, guesstimate, outlook, planning, prediction, prognosis, prognostication, projection, prophecy.

forefather *n* ancestor, antecedent, antecessor, father, forebear, forerunner, predecessor, primogenitor, primogenitrix, procreator, progenitor, progenitress, progenitrix.

antonym descendant.

forefront *n* avant-garde, centre, firing line, fore, foreground, front, front line, lead, prominence, spearhead, van, vanguard.

antonym rear.

forego *see* **forgo**.

foregoing *adj* above, aforementioned, antecedent, anterior, earlier, former, preceding, previous, prior, prodromal, prodromic.

foregone *adj* anticipated, cut-and-dried, foreseen, inevitable, open and shut, predetermined, predictable.

antonym unpredictable.

foreground *n* centre, fore, forefront, front, limelight, prominence.

antonym background.

forehead *n* brow, front, metope, temples.

foreign *adj* adventitious, adventive, alien, borrowed, distant, exotic, external, extraneous, extrinsic, fremd, imported, incongruous, irrelevant, outlandish, outside, overseas, remote, strange, tramontane, unassimilable, uncharacteristic, unfamiliar, unknown, unnative, unrelated.

antonym native.

foreigner *n* alien. Ausländer, barbarian, dago, étranger, étrangère, immigrant, incomer, metic, newcomer, outlander, stranger, uitlander, wog, wop.

antonym native.

foreknowledge *n* clairvoyance, foresight, forewarning, precognition, premonition, prescience, prevision, prognostication, second sight.

foreman *n* charge-hand, charge-man, gaffer, ganger, gangsman, overman, overseer, oversman, steward, straw boss, supervisor.

foremost *adj* cardinal, central, chief, first, front, headmost, highest, inaugural, initial, leading, main, paramount, pre-eminent, primary, prime, principal, salient, supreme, uppermost.

foreordain *v* appoint, destine, doom, fate, foredoom, ordain, prearrange, predestine, predetermine, preordain.

foreordained *adj* appointed, foredoomed, prearranged, predestined, predetermined, predevote, preordained.

forerunner *n* ancestor, announcer, antecedent, antecessor, envoy, forebear, foregoer, foretoken, harbinger, herald, indication, omen, portent, precursor, predecessor, premonition, prodrome, prodromus, progenitor, prognostic, prototype, sign, token, vaunt-courier.

antonyms aftermath, result.

foresee *v* anticipate, augur, divine, envisage, expect, forebode, forecast, foreknow, foretell, predict, previse, prognosticate, prophesy, vaticinate.

foreshadow *v* adumbrate, anticipate, augur, betoken, bode, forebode, forepoint, foreshow, foresignify, foretoken, imply, import, indicate, omen, portend, predict, prefigure, presage, promise, prophesy, signal.

foresight *n* anticipation, care, caution, circumspection, far-sightedness, forethought, perspicacity, precaution, preparedness, prescience, prevision, providence, provision, prudence, readiness, vision.

antonym improvidence.

forest *n* greenwood, monte, plantation, urman, wood, woodland.

forestall *v* anticipate, avert, balk, circumvent, frustrate, head off, hinder, intercept, obstruct, obviate, parry, preclude, pre-empt, prevent, thwart, ward off.

antonyms encourage, facilitate.

forester *n* gamekeeper, woodman, woodsman, woodward.

forestry *n* afforestation, arboriculture, dendrology, forestation, silviculture, woodcraft, woodmanship.

foretaste *n* example, foretoken, forewarning, indication, pregustation, prelibation, prelude, preview, sample, specimen, trailer, warning, whiff.

foretell *v* adumbrate, augur, bode, forebode, forecast, foresay, foreshadow, foreshow, forespeak, forewarn, portend, predict, presage, presignify, prognosticate, prophesy, signify, soothsay, vaticinate.

forethought *n* anticipation, circumspection, far-sightedness, foresight, precaution, preparation, providence, provision, prudence.

antonym improvidence.

foretold *adj* forecast, foreshown, forespoken, predicted, prophesied, written.

antonym unforeseen.

forever *adv* always, ceaselessly, constantly, continually, endlessly, eternally, everlastingly, evermore, for all time, for good and all, for keeps, in perpetuity, in saecula saeculorum, incessantly, interminably, permanently, perpetually, persistently, till the cows come home, till the end of time, unremittingly, world without end.

forewarn *v* admonish, advise, alert, apprise, caution, dissuade, previse, tip off.

foreword *n* exordium, introduction, preamble, preface, preliminary, proem, prolegomenon, prologue.

antonyms epilogue, postscript.

forfeit *n* amercement, damages, escheat, fine, forfeiture, loss, mulct, penalisation, penalty, surrender.

v abandon, forgo, give up, lose, relinquish, renounce, sacrifice, surrender.

forfeiture *n* attainder, confiscation, déchéance, escheat, forgoing, giving up, loss, relinquishment, sacrifice, sequestration, surrender.

forge[1] *v* beat out, cast, coin, construct, contrive, copy, counterfeit, create, devise, fabricate, fake, falsify, fashion, feign, form, frame, hammer out, imitate, invent, make, mould, shape, simulate, work.

forge[2] *v* advance, gain ground, improve, make great strides, make headway, press on, proceed, progress, push on.

forger *n* coiner, contriver, counterfeiter, creator, deviser, fabricator, faker, falsifier, framer, truqueur.

forgery *n* coining, counterfeit, counterfeiting, dud, fake, falsification, fraud, fraudulence, imitation, phoney, sham, stumer.

antonym original.

forget *v* consign to oblivion, discount, dismiss, disregard, fail, ignore, lose sight of, misremember, neglect, omit, overlook, think no more of, unlearn.

antonym remember.

forgetful *adj* absent-minded, amnesiac, amnesic, careless, dreamy, heedless, inattentive, lax, neglectful, negligent, oblivious, unmindful, unretentive.

antonyms attentive, heedful.

forgetfulness *n* absent-mindedness, abstraction, amnesia, carelessness, dreaminess, heedlessness, inattention, lapse, laxness, Lethe, oblivion, obliviousness, obliviscence, wool-gathering.

antonyms attentiveness, heedfulness.

forgivable *adj* excusable, innocent, minor, pardonable, petty, slight, trifling, venial.

antonym unforgivable.

forgive *v* absolve, acquit, condone, exculpate, excuse, exonerate, let off, overlook, pardon, remit, shrive.

antonym censure.

forgiveness *n* absolution, acquittal, amnesty, condonation, exculpation, exoneration, mercy, pardon, remission, shrift, shriving.

antonyms blame, censure.

forgiving *adj* clement, compassionate, forbearing, humane, indulgent, lenient, magnanimous, merciful, mild, remissive, soft-hearted, sparing, tolerant.

antonym censorious.

forgo, forego *v* abandon, abjure, abstain from, cede, do without, eschew, forfeit, give up, pass up, refrain from, relinquish, renounce, resign, sacrifice, surrender, waive, yield.

antonyms claim, indulge in, insist on.

forgotten *adj* blotted out, buried, bygone, disregarded, ignored, irrecoverable, irretrievable, lost, neglected, obliterated, omitted, out of mind, overlooked, past, past recall, past recollection, unrecalled, unremembered, unretrieved.

antonym remembered.

fork *v* bifurcate, branch, branch off, divaricate, diverge, divide, part, ramify, separate, split.

n bifurcation, branching, divarication, divergence, division, furcation, intersection, junction, ramification, separation, split.

forked *adj* bifurcate, branched, branching, cloven, divaricated, divided, forficate, furcal, furcate, furcular, pronged, ramified, split, tined, zigzag.

forlorn *adj* abandoned, abject, bereft, cheerless, comfortless, deserted, desolate, desperate, destitute, disconsolate, forgotten, forsaken, friendless, helpless, homeless, hopeless, lonely, lost, miserable, pathetic, piteous, pitiable, pitiful, unhappy, woebegone, woeful, wretched.

antonym hopeful.

form *v* accumulate, acquire, appear, arrange, assemble, bring up, build, combine, compose, comprise, concoct, constitute, construct, contract, contrive, create, crystallise, cultivate, design, develop, devise, discipline, dispose, draw up, educate, establish, evolve, fabricate, fashion, forge, formulate, found, frame, group, grow, hatch, instruct, invent, make, make up, manufacture, materialise, model, mould, organise, pattern, plan, produce, put together, rear, rise, school, serve as, settle, shape, take shape, teach, train.

n anatomy, appearance, application, arrangement, behaviour, being, body, build, cast, ceremony, character, class, condition, conduct, configuration, construction, convention, custom, cut, description, design, document, etiquette, fashion, fettle, figure, fitness, formality, format, formation, frame, framework, genre, Gestalt, grade, guise, harmony, health, kind, manifestation, manner, manners, matrix, method, mode, model, mould, nature, nick, order, orderliness, organisation, outline, paper, pattern, person, physique, plan, practice, procedure, proportion, protocol, questionnaire, rank, ritual, rule, schedule, semblance, shape, sheet, silhouette, sort, species, spirits, stamp, structure, style, symmetry, system, trim, type, variety, way.

formal *adj* academic, aloof, approved, ceremonial, ceremonious, conventional, correct, exact, explicit, express, fixed, full-dress, impersonal, lawful, legal, methodical, nominal, official, perfunctory, precise, prescribed, prim, punctilious, recognised, regular, reserved, rigid, ritualistic, set, solemn, starch, starched, starchy, stiff, stiff-necked, stilted, strict, unbending.

antonym informal.

formality *n* ceremoniousness, ceremony, convenance, convention, conventionality, correctness, custom, decorum, etiquette, form, formalism, gesture, matter of form, politeness, politesse, procedure, propriety, protocol, punctilio, red tape, rite, ritual.

antonym informality.

format *n* appearance, arrangement, configuration, construction, dimensions, form, lay-out, look, make-up, pattern, plan, shape, structure, style, type.

formation *n* accumulation, appearance, arrangement, compilation, composition, configuration, constitution, construction, creation, crystallisation, design, development, disposition, emergence, establishment, evolution, fabrication, figure, format, forming, generation, genesis, grouping, manufacture, organisation, pattern, production, rank, shaping, structure.

formative *adj* controlling, determinative, determining, developmental, dominant, guiding, impressionable, influential, malleable, mouldable, moulding, pliant, sensitive, shaping, susceptible.

antonym destructive.

former *adj* above, aforementioned, aforesaid, ancient, antecedent, anterior, bygone, departed, earlier, erstwhile, ex-, first mentioned, foregoing, late, long ago, of yore, old, old-time, one-time, past, preceding, pre-existent, previous, prior, pristine, quondam, sometime, umwhile, whilom.

antonyms current, future, later, present, prospective, subsequent.

formerly *adv* already, at one time, before, earlier, erstwhile, heretofore, hitherto, lately, once, previously, umwhile, while-ere, whilom.

antonyms currently, later, now, presently, subsequently.

formidable *adj* alarming, appalling, arduous, awesome, challenging, colossal, dangerous, daunting, difficult, dismaying, dreadful, enormous, fearful, frightening, frightful, great, horrible, huge, impressive, indomitable, intimidating, leviathan, mammoth, menacing, mighty, onerous, overwhelming, powerful, puissant, redoubtable, shocking, staggering, terrific, terrifying, threatening, toilsome, tremendous.

antonyms easy, genial.

formless *adj* amorphous, chaotic, confused, disorganised, inchoate, incoherent, indefinite, indeterminate, indigest, nebulous, shapeless, unformed, unshaped, vague.

antonyms definite, orderly.

formula *n* blueprint, code, form, formulary, method, modus operandi, password, precept, prescription, principle, procedure, recipe, rite, ritual, rubric, rule, rule of thumb, way, wording.

formulate *v* block out, codify, create, define, detail, develop, devise, evolve, express, form, frame, invent, originate, particularise, plan, specify, systematise, work out.

forsake *v* abandon, abdicate, cast off, desert, discard, disown, forgo, forswear, give up, jettison, jilt, leave, leave in the lurch, quit, reject, relinquish, renounce, repudiate, surrender, throw over, turn one's back on, vacate, yield.

antonyms resume, revert to.

forsaken *adj* abandoned, cast off, deserted, desolate, destitute, discarded, disowned, forlorn, friendless, ignored, isolated, jilted, left in the lurch, lonely, lorn, lovelorn, marooned, outcast, rejected, shunned, solitary.

forswear *v* abandon, abjure, burn one's faggot, deny, disavow, disclaim, disown, drop, forgo, forsake, give up, lie, perjure oneself, recant, reject, renegue, renounce, repudiate, retract, swear off.

antonym revert to.

fort *n* acropolis, blockhouse, camp, castle, citadel, fastness, fortification, fortress, garrison, hill-fort, rath, redoubt, station, stronghold, tower.

forte *n* aptitude, bent, gift, long suit, métier, skill, speciality, strength, strong point, talent.

antonyms inadequacy, weak point.

forthcoming[1] *adj* accessible, approaching, at hand, available, coming, expected, future, imminent, impending, obtainable, projected, prospective, ready.

forthcoming[2] *adj* chatty, communicative, conversational, expansive, frank, free, informative, loquacious, open, sociable, talkative, unreserved.

antonyms bygone, distant, lacking, reserved.

forthright *adj* above-board, blunt, bold, candid, direct, four-square, frank, open, outspoken, plain-speaking, plain-spoken, straightforward, straight-from-the-shoulder, trenchant, unequivocal.

antonyms devious, tactful.

forthwith *adv* at once, directly, eftsoons, immediately, incontinent, instanter, instantly, posthaste, pronto, quickly, right away, straightaway, tout de suite, without delay.

fortification *n* abatis, bastion, bulwark, buttressing, castle, citadel, defence, earthwork, embattlement, entrenchment, fastness, fort, fortress, keep, munition, outwork, protection, rampart, redoubt, reinforcement, stockade, strengthening, stronghold.

fortify *v* boost, brace, bulwark, buttress, cheer, confirm, embattle, embolden, encourage, entrench, garrison, hearten, invigorate, lace, load, mix, munify, protect, reassure, reinforce, secure, shore up, spike, steel, stiffen, strengthen, support, sustain.

antonyms dilute, weaken.

fortitude *n* backbone, bottle, braveness, bravery, courage, dauntlessness, determination, endurance, fearlessness, firmness, grit, guts, hardihood, indomitability, intrepidity, long-suffering, patience, perseverance, pluck, resoluteness, resolution, staying power, stout-heartedness, strength, strength of mind, valour.

antonyms cowardice, weakness.

fortress *n* alcázar, burg, castle, citadel, fastness, fortification, kasbah, stronghold.

fortuitous *adj* accidental, adventitious, arbitrary, casual, chance, coincidental, contingent, felicitous, fluky, fortunate, happy, incidental, lucky, providential, random, serendipitous, unexpected, unforeseen, unintentional, unplanned.

antonym intentional.

fortunate *adj* advantageous, auspicious, blessed, bright, convenient, encouraging, favourable, favoured, felicitous, fortuitous, golden, happy, helpful, lucky, opportune, profitable, promising, propitious, prosperous, providential, rosy, serendipitous, successful, timely, well-off, well-timed.

antonym unfortunate.

fortunately *adv* happily, luckily, providentially.

antonym unfortunately.

fortune[1] *n* affluence, assets, bomb, bundle, estate, income, king's ransom, means, mint, opulence, packet, pile, possessions, property, prosperity, riches, treasure, wealth.

fortune[2] *n* accident, adventures, chance, circumstances, contingency, cup, destiny, doom, expectation, experience, fate, fortuity, hap, happenstance, hazard, history, kismet, life, lot, luck, portion, providence, star, success, weird.

fortune-telling *n* augury, chiromancy, crystal-gazing, divination, dukkeripen, palmistry, prediction, prognostication, prophecy, second sight.

forward[1] *adj* advance, advanced, early, enterprising, first, fore, foremost, forward-looking, front, go-ahead, head, leading, onward, precocious, premature, progressive, well-advanced, well-developed.

antonym retrograde.

adv ahead, en avant, forth, forwards, into view, on, onward, out, outward, to light, to the fore, to the surface.

antonym backward.

v accelerate, advance, aid, assist, back, dispatch, encourage, expedite, facilitate, favour, foster, freight, further, hasten, help, hurry, post, promote, route, send, send on, ship, speed, support, transmit.

antonyms impede, obstruct.

forward[2] *adj* assertive, assuming, audacious, bare-faced, bold, brash, brass-necked, brazen, brazen-faced, cheeky, confident, familiar, fresh, impertinent, impudent, malapert, officious, overweening, pert, presuming, presumptuous, pushy.

antonym diffident.

forward-looking *adj* avant-garde, dynamic, enlightened, enterprising, far-sighted, go-ahead, goey, go-getting, innovative, liberal, modern, progressive, reforming.

antonyms conservative, retrograde.

forwardness *n* assurance, audacity, boldness, brashness, brazenness, cheek, cheekiness, impertinence, impudence, malapertness, overconfidence, pertness, presumption, presumptuousness.

antonyms reserve, retiring.

fossilised *adj* anachronistic, antediluvian, antiquated, archaic, archaistic, dead, démodé, extinct, exuvial, inflexible, obsolete, old-fashioned, old-fog(e)yish, ossified, out of date, outmoded, passé, petrified, prehistoric, stony, superannuated.

antonym up-to-date.

foster *v* accommodate, bring up, care for, cherish, cultivate, encourage, entertain, feed, foment, harbour, make much of, nourish, nurse, nurture, promote, raise, rear, stimulate, support, sustain, take care of.

antonyms discourage, neglect.

foul *adj* abhorrent, abominable, abusive, bad, base, blasphemous, blue, blustery, choked, coarse, contaminated, crooked, despicable, detestable, dirty, disagreeable, disfigured, disgraceful, disgusting, dishonest, dishonourable, entangled, fetid, filthy, foggy, foul-mouthed, fraudulent, gross, hateful, heinous, impure, indecent, inequitable, infamous, iniquitous, lewd, loathsome, low, malodorous, mephitic, murky, nasty, nauseating, nefarious, noisome, notorious, obscene, offensive, polluted, profane, putrid, rainy, rank, repulsive, revolting, rotten, rough, scandalous, scatological, scurrilous, shady, shameful, smutty, squalid, stinking, stormy, sullied, tainted, unclean, underhand, unfair, unfavourable, unjust, unsportsmanlike, untidy, vicious, vile, virose, vulgar, wet, wicked, wild.

antonyms clean, fair, pure, worthy.

v befoul, begrime, besmear, besmirch, block, catch, choke, clog, contaminate, defile, dirty, ensnare, entangle, foul up, jam, pollute, smear, snarl, soil, stain, sully, taint, twist.

antonyms clean, clear, disentangle.

foul play chicanery, corruption, crime, deception, dirty work, double-dealing, duplicity, fraud, funny business, jiggery-pokery, perfidy, roguery, sharp practice, skulduggery, treachery, villainy.

antonyms fair play, justice.

foul-mouthed *adj* abusive, blasphemous, coarse, foul-spoken, obscene, offensive, profane.

found *v* base, bottom, build, constitute, construct, create, endow, erect, establish, fix, ground, inaugurate, initiate, institute, organise, originate, plant, raise, rest, root, set up, settle, start, sustain.

foundation *n* base, basis, bedrock, bottom, endowment, establishment, fond, footing, ground, groundwork, inauguration, institution, organisation, setting up, settlement, substance, substratum, substructure, underpinning.

founder[1] *n* architect, author, beginner, benefactor, builder, constructor, designer, endower, establisher, father, framer, generator, initiator, institutor, inventor, maker, organiser, originator, patriarch.

founder[2] *v* abort, break down, collapse, come to grief, come to nothing, fail, fall, fall through, go lame, lurch, miscarry, misfire, sink, sprawl, stagger, stick, stumble, submerge, subside, trip.

foundling *n* enfant trouvé, orphan, outcast, stray, urchin, waif.

fountain *n* fons et origo, font, fount, fountain-head, gerbe, inspiration, jet, origin, reservoir, source, spout, spray, spring, waterworks, well, well-head, well-spring.

fourfold *adj* quadruple, quadruplex, quadruplicate, tetraploid.

four-square *adv* firmly, frankly, honestly, resolutely, squarely.

adj firm, forthright, frank, honest, immovable, resolute, solid, steady, strong, unyielding.

antonyms uncertain, wavering.

fox *n* cunning devil, Lowrie, Lowrie-tod, reynard, sly one, slyboots, tod, Tod-Lowrie.

foxy *adj* artful, astute, canny, crafty, cunning, devious, fly, guileful, knowing, sharp, shrewd, sly, tricky, vulpine, wily.

antonyms naïve, open.

foyer *n* antechamber, anteroom, entrance hall, hall, lobby, reception, vestibule.

fracas *n* affray, aggro, bagarre, barney, brawl, disturbance, Donnybrook, fight, free-for-all, mêlée, quarrel, riot, row, ruckus, ruction, rumpus, scrimmage, scuffle, shindy, trouble, uproar.

fractious *adj* awkward, captious, choleric, crabbed, crabby, cross, crotchety, fretful, froward, grouchy, irritable, peevish, pettish, petulant, quarrelsome, querulous, recalcitrant, refractory, testy, touchy, unruly.

antonyms complaisant, placid.

fracture *n* breach, break, cleft, crack, fissure, gap, opening, rent, rift, rupture, schism, scission, split.

v break, crack, rupture, splinter, split.

antonym join.

fragile *adj* breakable, brittle, dainty, delicate, feeble, fine, flimsy, frail, frangible, infirm, insubstantial, shattery, slight, weak.

antonyms durable, robust, tough.

fragility *n* breakableness, brittleness, delicacy, feebleness, frailty, frangibility, infirmity, weakness.

antonyms durability, robustness, strength.

fragment *n* bit, cantlet, chip, flinder, fraction, frazzle, fritter, morceau, morsel, ort, part, particle, piece, portion, remnant, scrap, shard, shatter, sheave, shiver, shred, sliver.

v break, break up, come apart, come to pieces, crumble, disintegrate, disunite, divide, fractionalise, fritter, shatter, shiver, splinter, split, split up.

antonyms hold together, join.

fragmentary *adj* bitty, broken, disconnected, discrete, disjointed, fractionary, incoherent, incomplete, partial, piecemeal, scattered, scrappy, separate, sketchy, unsystematic.

antonym complete.

fragrance *n* aroma, balm, balminess, bouquet, fragrancy, odour, perfume, redolence, scent, smell.

fragrant *adj* aromatic, balmy, balsamy, odoriferous, odorous, perfumed, redolent, suaveolent, sweet, sweet-scented, sweet-smelling.

antonyms smelly, unscented.

frail *adj* breakable, brittle, decrepit, delicate, feeble, flimsy, fragile, frangible, infirm, insubstantial, puny, slight, tender, unchaste, unsound, vulnerable, weak.

antonyms firm, robust, strong, tough.

frailty *n* blemish, defect, deficiency, failing, fallibility, fault, feebleness, flaw, foible, frailness, imperfection, infirmity, peccability, peccadillo, peccancy, puniness, shortcoming, susceptibility, unchasteness, unchastity, vice, weakness.

antonyms firmness, robustness, strength, toughness.

frame *v* assemble, block out, build, case, compose, conceive, concoct, constitute, construct, contrive, cook up, devise, draft, draw up, enclose, enframe, fabricate, fashion, forge, form, formulate, hatch, institute, invent, make, manufacture, map out, model, mould, mount, plan, put together, redact, set up, shape, sketch, surround, trap, victimise.

n anatomy, body, bodyshell, bodywork, build, carcass, casing, chassis, construction, fabric, flake, form, framework, monture, morphology, mount, mounting, physique, scaffolding, scheme, setting, shell, skeleton, structure, system.

frame of mind attitude, disposition, fettle, humour, mood, morale, outlook, spirit, state, temper, vein.

frame-up *n* fabrication, fit-up, fix, put-up job, trap, trumped-up charge.

framework *n* bare bones, core, fabric, foundation, frame, gantry, groundwork, plan, schema, shell, skeleton, structure.

franchise *n* authorisation, charter, concession, exemption, freedom, immunity, liberty, prerogative, privilege, right, suffrage, vote.

frank *adj* artless, blunt, candid, direct, downright, forthright, four-square, free, honest, ingenuous, open, outright, outspoken, plain, plain-spoken, simple-hearted, sincere, straight, straightforward, transparent, truthful, unconcealed, undisguised, unreserved, unrestricted.

antonyms evasive, insincere.

frankly *adv* bluntly, candidly, directly, freely, honestly, in truth, openly, plainly, straight, to be frank, to be honest, unreservedly, without reserve.

antonyms evasively, insincerely.

frankness *n* bluntness, candour, forthrightness, franchise, glasnost, ingenuousness, openness, outspokenness, plain speaking, truthfulness, unreserve.

frantic *adj* berserk, beside oneself, desperate, distracted, distraught, fraught, frenetic, frenzied, furious, hairless, hectic, mad, overwrought, raging, raving, wild.

antonym calm.

fraternise *v* affiliate, associate, concur, consort, cooperate, forgather, hobnob, mingle, mix, socialise, sympathise, unite.

antonyms ignore, shun.

fraternity *n* association, brotherhood, camaraderie, circle, clan, club, companionship, company, comradeship, confraternity, confrèrie, fellowship, fratry, guild, kinship, league, set, society, sodality, union.

fraud[1] *n* artifice, cheat, chicane, chicanery, craft, deceit, deception, double-dealing, duplicity, fake, forgery, guile, hoax, humbug, imposture, sham, sharp practice, spuriousness, swindling, swiz, swizzle, take-in, treachery, trickery.

fraud[2] *n* bluffer, charlatan, cheat, counterfeit, double-dealer, hoaxer, impostor, malingerer, mountebank, phoney, pretender, pseud, quack, swindler.

fraudulent *adj* bogus, counterfeit, crafty, criminal, crooked, deceitful, deceptive, dishonest, double-dealing, duplicitous, false, knavish, phoney, sham, specious, spurious, swindling, treacherous.

antonyms genuine, honest.

fraught *adj* abounding, accompanied, agitated, anxious, attended, bristling, charged, difficult, distracted, distressed, distressing, emotive, filled, full, heavy, hotching, laden, replete, stuffed, tense, tricky, troublesome, trying, uptight, worrisome.

antonyms calm, untroublesome.

fray *n* affray, bagarre, barney, battle, brawl, broil, clash, combat, conflict, disturbance, Donnybrook, dust-up, fight, free-for-all, mêlée, quarrel, rammy, riot, row, ruckus, ruction, rumble, rumpus, scuffle, set-to, shindy.

frayed *adj* edgy, frazzled, on edge, ragged, shreddy, tattered, threadbare, worn.

antonyms calm, tidy.

freak[1] *n* aberration, abnormality, abortion, anomaly, caprice, crotchet, fad, fancy, folly, grotesque, humour, irregularity, lusus naturae, malformation, misgrowth, monster, monstrosity, mutant, oddity, queer fish, quirk, rara avis, sport, teratism, turn, twist, vagary, weirdie, weirdo, whim, whimsy.

adj aberrant, abnormal, atypical, bizarre, capricious, erratic, exceptional, fluky, fortuitous, odd, queer, surprise, unaccountable, unexpected, unforeseen, unparalleled, unpredictable, unpredicted, unusual.

antonyms common, expected.

freak[2] *n* addict, aficionado, buff, devotee, enthusiast, fan, fanatic, fiend, monomaniac, nut, votary.

freakish *adj* aberrant, abnormal, arbitrary, bizarre, capricious, changeable, erratic, fanciful, fantastic, fitful, freakful, freaky, grotesque, malformed, monstrous, odd, outlandish, outré, preternatural, strange, teratoid, unconventional, unpredictable, unusual, vagarious, vagarish, wayward, weird, whimsical.

antonym ordinary.

freckle *n* ephelis, fernitickle, heatspot, lentigo.

free *adj* able, allowed, at large, at leisure, at liberty, autarchic, autonomous, available, bounteous, bountiful, buckshee, casual, charitable, clear, complimentary, cost-free, dégagé, democratic, désoevré, disengaged, eager, easy, emancipated, empty, extra, familiar, footloose, forward, frank, free and easy, free of charge, generous, gratis, hospitable, idle, independent, informal, laid-back, lavish, lax, leisured, liberal, liberated, loose, munificent, natural, off the hook, on the house, on the loose, open, open-handed, permitted, prodigal, relaxed, self-governing, self-ruling, solute, sovereign, spare, spontaneous, unattached, unbidden, unbowed, unceremonious, uncommitted, unconstrained, unemployed, unencumbered, unengaged, unfettered, unforced, unhampered, unhindered, unimpeded, uninhabited, uninhibited, unobstructed, unoccupied, unpaid, unpent, unpreoccupied, unregimented, unregulated, unrestrained, unrestricted, unsparing, unstinting, untrammelled, unused, vacant, willing, without charge.

antonyms attached, confined, costly, formal, mean, niggardly, restricted, tied.

adv abundantly, copiously, for free, for love, for nothing, freely, gratis, idly, loosely, without charge.

antonym meanly.

v absolve, affranchise, clear, debarrass, declassify, decolonise, decontrol, deliver, disburden, discage, discharge, disembarrass, disembrangle, disenchain, disengage, disenslave, disentangle, disenthral, disimprison, disprison, emancipate, exempt, extricate, let go, liberate, loose, manumit, ransom, release, relieve, rescue, rid, set free, turn loose, unbind, unburden, uncage, unchain, undo, unfetter, unhand, unleash, unlock, unloose, unmanacle, unmew, unpen, unshackle, unstick, untether, untie, unyoke.

antonyms confine, enslave, imprison.

free hand authority, carte-blanche, discretion, freedom, latitude, liberty, permission, power, scope.

free of devoid of, exempt from, immune to, innocent of, lacking, not liable to, safe from, sans, unaffected by, unencumbered by, untouched by, without.

freebooter *n* bandit, brigand, buccaneer, cateran, filibuster, highwayman, looter, marauder, moss-trooper, pillager, pirate, plunderer, raider, reiver, robber, rover.

freedom *n* abandon, ability, affranchisement, autonomy, boldness, brazenness, candour, carte-blanche, deliverance, directness, discretion, disrespect, ease, elbow-room, emancipation, exemption, facility, familiarity, flexibility, forwardness, frankness, free rein, home rule, immunity, impertinence, impunity, independence, informality, ingenuousness, lack of restraint or reserve, latitude, laxity, leeway, liberty, Liberty Hall, licence, manumission, openness, opportunity, overfamiliarity, play, power, presumption, privilege, range, release, scope, self-government, uhuru, unconstraint.

antonyms confinement, reserve, restriction.

freely *adv* abundantly, amply, bountifully, candidly, cleanly, copiously, easily, extravagantly, frankly, generously, lavishly, liberally, loosely, of one's own accord, open-handedly, openly, plainly, readily, smoothly, spontaneously, sponte sua, unchallenged, unreservedly, unstintingly, voluntarily, willingly.

antonyms evasively, meanly, roughly, under duress.

free-thinker *n* agnostic, deist, doubter, esprit fort, infidel, rationalist, sceptic, unbeliever.

free-will *n* autarky, autonomy, election, freedom, independence, liberty, self-determination, self-sufficiency, spontaneity, volition.

freeze *v* benumb, chill, congeal, enfreeze, fix, glaciate, harden, hold, ice, ice over, inhibit, peg, rigidify, shelve, solidify, stiffen, stop, suspend.

n abeyance, discontinuation, embargo, freeze-up, frost, halt, interruption, moratorium, postponement, shut-down, standstill, stay, stoppage, suspension.

freezing *adj* arctic, biting, bitter, brumous, chill, chilled, chilly, cutting, frigorific, frosty, gelid, glacial, icy, numbing, penetrating, polar, raw, Siberian, wintry.

antonyms hot, warm.

freight *n* bulk, burden, cargo, carriage, charge, consignment, contents, conveyance, fee, goods, haul, lading, load, merchandise, pay-load, shipment, tonnage, transportation.

frenetic *adj* demented, distraught, excited, fanatical, frantic, frenzical, frenzied, hyperactive, insane, mad, maniacal, obsessive, overwrought, phrenetic, unbalanced, wild.

antonyms calm, placid.

frenzied *adj* agitated, convulsive, distracted, distraught, excited, feverish, frantic, frenetic, frenzical, furious, hysterical, mad, maniacal, must, musty, rabid, uncontrolled, wild.

antonyms calm, placid.

frenzy *n* aberration, agitation, bout, burst, convulsion, delirium, derangement, distraction, fit, fury, hysteria, insanity, lunacy, madness, mania, must, oestrus, outburst, paroxysm, passion, rage, seizure, spasm, transport, turmoil.

antonyms calm, placidness.

frequency *n* constancy, frequence, frequentness, oftenness, periodicity, prevalence, recurrence, repetition.

antonym infrequency.

frequent[1] *adj* common, commonplace, constant, continual, customary, everyday, familiar, habitual, incessant, numerous, persistent, recurrent, recurring, regular, reiterated, repeated, usual.

antonym infrequent.

frequent[2] *v* associate with, attend, crowd, hang about, hang out at, haunt, haunt about, patronise, resort, visit.

frequenter *n* client, customer, denizen, habitué, haunter, patron, regular.

frequently *adv* commonly, continually, customarily, habitually, many a time, many times, much, oft, often, oftentimes, over and over, persistently, repeatedly.

antonyms infrequently, seldom.

fresh *adj* added, additional, alert, artless, auxiliary, blooming, bold, bouncing, bracing, brazen, bright, brisk, callow, cheeky, chipper, clean, clear, cool, crisp, crude, dewy, different, disrespectful, energetic, extra, fair, familiar, flip, florid, forward, further, glowing, green, hardy, healthy, impudent, inexperienced, innovative, insolent, inventive, invigorated, invigorating, keen, latest, lively, malapert, modern, modernistic, more, natural, new, new-fangled, novel, original, other, pert, presumptuous, pure, raw, recent, refreshed, refreshing, renewed, rested, restored, revived, rosy, ruddy, saucy, span, spanking, sparkling, spick, sprightly, spry, stiff, supplementary, sweet, unblown, unconventional, uncultivated, undimmed, unhackneyed, unjaded, unjaundiced, unpolluted, unsoured, unspoilt, untrained, untried, unusual, unwarped, unwearied, up-to-date, verdant, vernal, vigorous, virescent, vital, vivid, warm, wholesome, young, youthful.

antonyms experienced, faded, old hat, polite, stale, tired.

freshen *v* air, enliven, liven, purify, refresh, reinvigorate, restore, resuscitate, revitalise, spruce up, tart up, titivate, ventilate, vernalise.

antonym tire.

freshman *n* bajan, bejant, first-year, fresher, pennal, sophomore, underclassman.

freshness *n* bloom, brightness, cleanness, clearness, dewiness, fraîcheur, glow, newness, novelty, originality, shine, sparkle, vigour, virescence, wholesomeness.

antonyms staleness, tiredness.

fret *v* abrade, agitate, agonise, annoy, bother, brood, chafe, chagrin, corrode, distress, disturb, eat into, erode, fray, gall, goad, grieve, harass, irk, irritate, nag, nettle, peeve, pique, provoke, rankle, repine, rile, ripple, rub, ruffle, torment, trouble, vex, wear, wear away, worry.

antonym calm.

fretful *adj* cantankerous, captious, complaining, cross, crotchety, edgy, fractious, irritable, peevish, petulant, querulous, short-tempered, snappish, snappy, splenetic, testy, thrawn, touchy, uneasy.

antonym calm.

friable *adj* brittle, crisp, crumbly, murly, powdery, pulverisable.

antonyms clayey, solid.

friar *n* mendicant, monk, religieux, religionary, religioner, religious.

friction *n* abrasion, animosity, antagonism, attrition, bad blood, bad feeling, bickering, chafing, conflict, contention, disagreement, discontent, discord, disharmony, dispute, dissension, erosion, fretting, grating, hostility, ill-feeling, incompatibility, irritation, limation, opposition, quarrelling, rasping, resentment, resistance, rivalry, rubbing, scraping, wearing away, wrangling, xerotripsis.

friend *n* Achates, adherent, advocate, ally, alter ego, associate, backer, benefactor, boon companion, bosom friend, buddy, china, chum, cobber, companion, comrade, confidant, crony, familiar, gossip, intimate, mate, paisano, pal, partisan, partner, patron, playmate, side-kick, soul mate, supporter, well-wisher.

antonym enemy.

friendless *adj* abandoned, alienated, alone, deserted, estranged, forlorn, forsaken, isolated, lonely, lonely-heart, lonesome, ostracised, shunned, solitary, unattached, unbefriended, unbeloved, unfriended, unloved.

friendliness *n* affability, amiability, approachability, companionability, congeniality, conviviality, Gemütlichkeit, geniality, kindliness, matyness, neighbourliness, sociability, warmth.

antonyms coldness, unsociableness.

friendly *adj* affable, affectionate, amiable, amicable, approachable, attached, attentive, auspicious, beneficial, benevolent, benign, chummy, close, clubby, companionable, comradely, conciliatory, confiding, convivial, cordial, familiar, Favonian, favourable, fond, fraternal, gemütlich, genial, good, helpful, intimate, kind, kindly, maty, neighbourly, outgoing, palsy-walsy, peaceable, propitious, receptive, sociable, sympathetic, thick, welcoming, well-disposed.

antonyms cold, unsociable.

friendship *n* affection, affinity, alliance, amity, attachment, benevolence, closeness, concord, familiarity, fellowship, fondness, friendliness, goodwill, harmony, intimacy, love, neighbourliness, rapport, regard.

antonym enmity.

fright *n* alarm, apprehension, consternation, dismay, dread, eyesore, fear, fleg, funk, horror, mess, monstrosity, panic, quaking, scare, scarecrow, shock, sight, spectacle, sweat, terror, the shivers, trepidation.

frighten *v* affray, affright, affrighten, alarm, appal, cow, daunt, dismay, fleg, intimidate, petrify, scare, scare stiff, shock, spook, startle, terrify, terrorise, unman, unnerve.

antonyms calm, reassure.

frightened *adj* affrighted, affrightened, afraid, alarmed, cowed, dismayed, frightsome, frozen, panicky, petrified, scared, scared stiff, startled, terrified, terrorised, terror-stricken, unnerved, windy.

antonyms calm, courageous.

frightening *adj* alarming, appalling, bloodcurdling, daunting, dismaying, dreadful, fearful, fearsome, hair-raising, horrifying, intimidating, menacing, scary, shocking, spine-chilling, spooky, terrifying, traumatic, unnerving.

antonym reassuring.

frightful *adj* alarming, appalling, awful, dire, disagreeable, dread, dreadful, fearful, fearsome, frightsome, ghastly, great, grim, grisly, gruesome, harrowing, hideous, horrendous, horrible, horrid, insufferable, macabre, petrifying, shocking, terrible, terrific, terrifying, traumatic, unnerving, unpleasant, unspeakable.

antonyms agreeable, pleasant.

frigid *adj* aloof, arctic, austere, brumous, chill, chilly, cold, cold-hearted, cool, forbidding, formal, frore, frost-bound, frosty, frozen, gelid, glacial, icy, lifeless, passionless, passive, repellent, rigid, stand-offish, stiff, unanimated, unapproachable, unbending, unfeeling, unloving, unresponsive, wintry.

antonyms responsive, warm.

frigidity *n* aloofness, austerity, chill, chilliness, cold-heartedness, coldness, frostiness, iciness, impassivity, lifelessness, passivity, stiffness, unapproachability, unresponsiveness, wintriness.

antonyms responsiveness, warmth.

frill *n* flounce, furbelow, gathering, orphrey, purfle, ruche, ruching, ruff, ruffle, trimming, tuck, valance.

frills *n* accessories, additions, affectation, decoration, embellishment, extras, fanciness, fandangles, finery, frilliness, frippery, froth, frothery, frou-frous, gewgaws, mannerisms, nonsense, ornamentation, ostentation, superfluities, tomfoolery, trimmings.

frilly *adj* fancy, flouncy, frothy, lacy, ornate, overornate, ruched, ruffled.

antonyms plain, unadorned.

fringe *n* borderline, edge, fimbriation, frisette, limits, march, marches, margin, outskirts, perimeter, periphery.

adj alternative, unconventional, unofficial, unorthodox.

v border, edge, enclose, fimbriate, skirt, surround, trim.

fringed *adj* bordered, edged, fimbriated, fringy, tasselled, tasselly, trimmed.

frippery *n* adornments, baubles, decorations, fanciness, fandangles, finery, flashiness, foppery, frilliness, frills, froth, frothery, fussiness, gaudiness, gewgaws, glad rags, knick-knacks, meretriciousness, nonsense, ornaments, ostentation, pretentiousness, showiness, tawdriness, trifles, trinkets, trivia, triviality.

antonym plainness.

frisk[1] *v* bounce, caper, cavort, curvet, dance, frolic, gambol, hop, jump, leap, pirouette, play, prance, rollick, romp, skip, sport, trip.

frisk[2] *v* check, inspect, search, shake down.

frisky *adj* bouncy, buckish, coltish, frolicsome, gamesome, high-spirited, kittenish, lively, playful, rollicking, romping, skittish, spirited, sportive.

antonym quiet.

fritter *v* blow, dissipate, idle, misspend, run through, squander, waste.

frivolity *n* childishness, flightiness, flippancy, flummery, folly, frivolousness, froth, fun, gaiety, giddiness, jest, levity, light-heartedness, lightness, nonsense, puerility, shallowness, silliness, skittishness, superficiality, trifling, triviality.

antonym seriousness.

frivolous *adj* bubble-headed, childish, dizzy, empty-headed, extravagant, facetious, flighty, flip, flippant, foolish, giddy, idle, ill-considered, impractical, jocular, juvenile, light, light-minded, petty, pointless, puerile, shallow, silly, skittish, superficial, trifling, trivial, unimportant, unserious, vacuous, vain.

antonym serious.

frizzy *adj* corrugated, crimped, crisp, curled, curly, frizzed, wiry.

antonym straight.

frolic *v* caper, cavort, cut capers, frisk, gambol, gammock, lark, make merry, play, rollick, romp, skylark, sport, wanton.

n amusement, antic, drollery, escapade, fun, gaiety, gambado, gambol, game, gammock, gilravage, high jinks, lark, merriment, prank, razzle-dazzle, revel, rig, romp, skylarking, sport, spree.

frolicsome *adj* coltish, espiègle, frisky, gamesome, gay, kittenish, kitteny, lively, merry, playful, rollicking, sportive, sprightly, wanton.

antonym quiet.

from hand to mouth dangerously, from day to day, improvidently, in poverty, insecurely, necessitously, on the breadline, precariously, uncertainly.

from time to time at times, every now and then, every so often, intermittently, now and then, occasionally, on occasion, once in a while, sometimes, spasmodically, sporadically.

antonym constantly.

front *n* air, anterior, appearance, aspect, bearing, beginning, blind, countenance, cover, cover-up, demeanour, disguise, expression, exterior, façade, face, facing, fore, forefront, foreground, forepart, front line, frontage, head, lead, manner, mask, metope, mien, obverse, pretence, pretext, show, top, van, vanguard.

antonym back.

adj anterior, anticous, first, fore, foremost, head, lead, leading.

antonyms back, last, least, posterior.

v confront, face, look over, meet, oppose, overlook.

frontier *n* borderland, borderline, bound, boundary, bourn(e), confines, edge, limit, march, marches, perimeter, verge.

adj backwoods, limitrophe, outlying, pioneering.

frost *n* coldness, disappointment, failure, freeze, freeze-up, hoar-frost, rime.

frosty *adj* chilly, cold, discouraging, frigid, frozen, hoar, ice-capped, icicled, icy, off-putting, rimy, stand-offish, stiff, unfriendly, unwelcoming, wintry.

antonym warm.

froth *n* bubbles, effervescence, foam, frivolity, frothery, head, lather, scum, spume, suds, triviality.

v bubble, effervesce, ferment, fizz, foam, lather.

frothy *adj* barmy, bubbling, bubbly, empty, foaming, foamy, frilly, frivolous, insubstantial, light, slight, spumescent, spumous, spumy, sudsy, trifling, trivial, trumpery, vain.

antonym flat.

frown *v* glare, glower, grimace, lower, scowl.

n dirty look, glare, glower, grimace, moue, scowl.

frown on deprecate, disapprove of, discountenance, discourage, dislike, look askance at, object to, take a dim view of.

antonym approve of.

frowzy *adj* blowzed, blowzy, dirty, dishevelled, draggle-tailed, frumpish, frumpy, messy, slatternly, sloppy, slovenly, sluttish, ungroomed, unkempt, untidy, unwashed.

antonym well-groomed.

frozen *adj* arctic, chilled, fixed, frigid, frore, frosted, icebound, ice-cold, ice-covered, icy, in abeyance, numb, pegged, petrified, rigid, rooted, shelved, solidified, stiff, stock-still, stopped, suspended, turned to stone.

antonym warm.

frugal *adj* abstemious, careful, cheese-paring, economical, meagre, niggardly, parsimonious, penny-wise, provident, prudent, saving, sparing, Spartan, thrifty, ungenerous.

antonym wasteful.

frugality *n* carefulness, conservation, economising, economy, frugalness, good management, husbandry, providence, prudence, thrift, thriftiness.

antonym wastefulness.

fruit *n* advantage, benefit, consequence, crop, effect, fruitage, fruitery, harvest, outcome, produce, product, profit, result, return, reward, yield.

fruitful *adj* abundant, advantageous, beneficial, copious, effective, fecund, feracious, fertile, flush, fructiferous, fructuous, gainful, plenteous, plentiful, productive, profitable, profuse, prolific, rewarding, rich, spawning, successful, teeming, uberous, useful, well-spent, worthwhile.

antonyms barren, fruitless.

fruitfulness *n* fecundity, feracity, fertility, productiveness, profitability, uberty, usefulness.

antonym fruitlessness.

fruition *n* accomplishment, actualisation, attainment, completion, consummation, enjoyment, fulfilment, materialisation, maturation, maturity, perfection, realisation, ripeness, success.

antonym failure.

fruitless *adj* abortive, barren, bootless, futile, hopeless, idle, ineffectual, pointless, profitless, unavailing, unfruitful, unproductive, unprofitable, unsuccessful, useless, vain.

antonyms fruitful, successful.

fruity *adj* bawdy, blue, full, indecent, indelicate, juicy, mellow, racy, resonant, rich, ripe, risqué, salacious, saucy, sexy, smutty, spicy, suggestive, titillating, vulgar.

antonyms decent, light.

frump *n* dowd, dowdy, draggle-tail, fright, Judy, mopsy, scarecrow, slattern, sloven, slut.

frumpish badly-dressed, blowzed, blowzy, dated, dingy, dowdy, drab, dreary, frumpy, ill-dressed, out of date.

antonyms chic, well-groomed.

frustrate *v* baffle, balk, block, bugger, check, circumvent, confront, counter, countermine, crab, defeat, depress, disappoint, discourage, dishearten, foil, forestall, inhibit, neutralise, nullify, scotch, spike, stymie, thwart.

antonyms fulfil, further, promote.

frustrated *adj* disappointed, discontented, discouraged, disheartened, embittered, foiled, irked, resentful, scunnered, thwarted.

antonym fulfilled.

frustration *n* annoyance, balking, circumvention, contravention, curbing, disappointment, dissatisfaction, failure, foiling, irritation, non-fulfilment, non-success, obstruction, resentment, thwarting, vexation.

antonyms fulfilment, furthering, promoting.

fuddled *adj* bemused, confused, drunk, groggy, hazy, inebriated, intoxicated, muddled, mused, muzzy, sozzled, stupefied, tipsy, woozy.

antonyms clear, sober.

fuddy-duddy *n* back number, carper, conservative, dodo, fogey, fossil, museum piece, old fog(e)y, square, stick-in-the-mud, stuffed shirt.

adj carping, censorious, old-fashioned, old-fog(e)yish, prim, stick-in-the-mud, stuffy.

antonym up-to-date.

fudge *v* avoid, cook, dodge, equivocate, evade, fake, falsify, fiddle, fix, hedge, misrepresent, shuffle, stall.

fuel *n* ammunition, eilding, encouragement, fodder, food, incitement, material, means, nourishment, provocation.

v charge, encourage, fan, feed, fire, incite, inflame, nourish, stoke up, sustain.

antonyms damp down, discourage.

fug *n* fetidity, fetidness, fetor, frowst, frowstiness, fustiness, reek, staleness, stink, stuffiness.

antonym airiness.

fuggy *adj* airless, close, fetid, foul, frowsty, fusty, noisome, noxious, stale, stuffy, suffocating, unventilated.

antonym airy.

fugitive *n* deserter, escapee, refugee, runagate, runaway.

adj brief, elusive, ephemeral, evanescent, fleeing, fleeting, flitting, flying, fugacious, intangible, momentary, passing, short, short-lived, temporary, transient, transitory, unstable.

antonym permanent.

fulfil *v* accomplish, achieve, answer, carry out, complete, comply with, conclude, conform to, consummate, discharge, effect, effectuate, execute, fill, finish, implement, keep, meet, obey, observe, perfect, perform, realise, satisfy.

antonyms break, defect, fail, frustrate.

fulfilment *n* accomplishment, achievement, attainment, bringing about, carrying out, completion, consummation, crowning, discharge, discharging, effecting, effectuation, end, implementation, observance, perfection, performance, realisation, success.

antonyms failure, frustration.

full *adj* abundant, adequate, all-inclusive, ample, baggy, brimful, brimming, broad, buxom, capacious, chock-a-block, chock-full, clear, complete, comprehensive, copious, crammed, crowded, curvaceous, deep, detailed, distinct, entire, exhaustive, extensive, filled, generous, gorged, intact, jammed, large, loaded, loud, maximum, occupied, orotund, packed, plenary, plenteous, plentiful, plump, replete, resonant, rich, rounded, sated, satiated, satisfied, saturated, stocked, sufficient, taken, thorough, unabbreviated, unabridged, uncut, unedited, unexpurgated, voluminous, voluptuous.

antonyms empty, incomplete.

full-blooded *adj* gutsy, hearty, lusty, mettlesome, red-blooded, thoroughbred, vigorous, virile, whole-hearted.

full-grown *adj* adult, developed, full-aged, full-blown, full-scale, grown-up, marriageable, mature, nubile, of age, ripe.

antonyms undeveloped, young.

fullness *n* abundance, adequateness, ampleness, broadness, clearness, completeness, comprehensiveness, copiousness, curvaceousness, dilation, distension, enlargement, entirety, extensiveness, fill, glut, loudness, orotundity, plenitude, plenty, pleroma, profusion, repletion, resonance, richness, roundness, satiety, saturation, strength, sufficiency, swelling, totality, tumescence, vastness, voluptuousness, wealth. wholeness.

antonyms emptiness, incompleteness.

full-scale *adj* all-encompassing, all-out, comprehensive, exhaustive, extensive, full-dress, in-depth, intensive, major, proper, sweeping, thorough, thoroughgoing, wide-ranging.

antonym partial.

fully *adv* absolutely, abundantly, adequately, altogether, amply, completely, comprehensively, enough, entirely, every inch, from first to last, heart and soul, in all respects, intimately, perfectly, plentifully, positively, quite, satisfactorily, sufficiently, thoroughly, totally, utterly, wholly, without reserve.

antonym partly.

fully-fledged *adj* experienced, full-blown, full-fledged, graduate, mature, professional, proficient, qualified, senior, trained.

antonym inexperienced.

fulminate *v* animadvert, criticise, curse, denounce, detonate, fume, inveigh, protest, rage, rail, thunder, vilipend, vituperate.

antonym praise.

fulmination *n* condemnation, denunciation, detonation, diatribe, invective, obloquy, philippic, reprobation, thundering, tirade.

antonym praise.

fulsome *adj* adulatory, cloying, effusive, excessive, extravagant, fawning, gross, immoderate, ingratiating, inordinate, insincere, nauseating, nauseous, offensive, overdone, rank, saccharine, sickening, smarmy, sycophantic, unctuous.

antonym sincere.

fumble *v* botch, bumble, bungle, faff, flail, flounder, fluff, footer, grope, misfield, mishandle, mismanage, muff, mumble, paw, scrabble, spoil.

fume *v* boil, chafe, fizz, get steamed up, give off, rage, rant, rave, reek, seethe, smoke, smoulder, storm.

fumes *n* effluvium, exhalation, exhaust, gas, haze, mephitis, miasma, pollution, reek, smog, smoke, stench, vapour.

fumigate *v* cleanse, deodorise, disinfect, purify, sanitise, sterilise.

fuming *adj* angry, boiling, enraged, fizzing, incensed, raging, roused, seething, spitting, steamed up.

antonym calm.

fun *n* amusement, buffoonery, cheer, clowning, distraction, diversion, enjoyment, entertainment, foolery, frolic, gaiety, game, gammock, high jinks, horseplay, jesting, jocularity, joking, jollification, jollity, joy, junketing, merriment, merrymaking, mirth, nonsense, play, playfulness, pleasure, recreation, romp, skylarking, sport, teasing, tomfoolery, treat, waggery, whoopee.

function¹ *n* activity, business, capacity, charge, concern, duty, employment, exercise, faculty, job, mission, occupation, office, operation, part, post, province, purpose, raison d'être, responsibility, role, situation, task.

v act, be in running order, behave, do duty, functionate, go, officiate, operate, perform, run, serve, work.

function² *n* affair, dinner, do, gathering, junket, luncheon, party, reception, shindig.

functional *adj* hard-wearing, operational, operative, plain, practical, serviceable, useful, utilitarian, utility, working.

antonyms effective, inoperative, ornate, useless.

functionary *n* bureaucrat, dignitary, employee, office-bearer, office-holder, officer, official.

functionless *adj* aimless, decorative, futile, hollow, idle, inactive, inert, irrelevant, needless, otiose, pointless, redundant, superfluous, useless.

antonym useful.

fund *n* cache, capital, endowment, foundation, hoard, kitty, mine, pool, repository, reserve, reservoir, source, stack, stock, store, storehouse, supply, treasury, vein, well.

v back, capitalise, endow, finance, float, promote, stake, subsidise, support, underwrite.

fundamental *adj* axiomatic, basal, basic, basilar, cardinal, central, constitutional, crucial, elementary, essential, first, important, indispensable, integral, intrinsic, key, keynote, necessary, organic, primal, primary, prime, principal, rudimentary, underlying, vital.

antonym advanced.

n axiom, basic, cornerstone, essential, first principle, keystone, law, principle, rudiment, rule, sine qua non.

fundamentally *adv* à fond, at bottom, at heart, au fond, basically, essentially, intrinsically, primarily, radically.

fundamentals *n* basics, brass tacks, business, nitty-gritty, practicalities.

funds *n* backing, bread, capital, cash, dough, finance, hard cash, money, moola(h), pelf, ready money, resources, savings, spondulicks, the ready, the wherewithal.

funeral *n* burial, inhumation, interment, obit, obsequies.

funereal *adj* dark, deathlike, depressing, dirgelike, dismal, dreary, exequial, feral, funebral, funebrial, gloomy, grave, lamenting, lugubrious, mournful, sad, sepulchral, solemn, sombre, woeful.

antonyms happy, lively.

funk *v* balk at, blench, chicken out of, cop out, dodge, duck out of, flinch from, recoil from, shirk from.

funnel *v* channel, conduct, convey, direct, filter, move, pass, pour, siphon, transfer.

funny *adj* a card, a caution, a scream, absurd, amusing, comic, comical, curious, diverting, droll, dubious, entertaining, facetious, farcical, funny ha-ha, funny peculiar, hilarious, humorous, jocose, jocular, jolly, killing, laughable, ludicrous, mirth-provoking, mysterious, odd, peculiar, perplexing, puzzling, queer, remarkable, rib-tickling, rich, ridiculous, riotous, risible, side-splitting, silly, slapstick, strange, suspicious, unusual, waggish, weird, witty.

antonyms sad, solemn, unamusing, unfunny.

fur *n* coat, down, fell, fleece, flix, flue, hide, pelage, pelt, skin, wool.

Furies *n* Dirae, Erinyes, Eumenides, Furiae, Semnai.

furious *adj* acharné, agitated, angry, boiling, boisterous, enraged, fierce, fizzing, frantic, frenzied, fuming, furibund, impetuous, incensed, infuriated, intense, livid, mad, maddened, maenadic, raging, savage, stormy, tempestuous, tumultuous, turbulent, up in arms, vehement, violent, waxy, wild, wrathful, wroth.

antonyms calm, pleased.

furnish *v* afford, appoint, bedight, bestow, decorate, endow, equip, fit out, fit up, give, grant, offer, outfit, present, provide, provision, reveal, rig, stake, stock, store, suit, supply.

antonym divest.

furniture *n* appliances, appointments, appurtenances, chattels, effects, equipment, fittings, furnishing, goods, household goods, movables, plenishing, possessions, things.

furore *n* commotion, craze, disturbance, enthusiasm, excitement, flap, frenzy, fury, fuss, hullabaloo, mania, outburst, outcry, rage, stir, to-do, tumult, uproar.

antonym calm.

furrow *n* chamfer, channel, corrugation, crease, crow's-foot, flute, fluting, groove, hollow, line, rut, seam, trench, vallecula, wrinkle.

v corrugate, crease, draw together, flute, knit, seam, wrinkle.

furrowed *adj* channelled, corrugated, exarate, fluted, gouged, grooved, ribbed, ridged, rutted, seamed, vallecular, valleculate, wrinkled.

further *adj* additional, distant, extra, far, fresh, more, new, opposite, other, supplementary.

v accelerate, advance, aid, assist, champion, contribute to, ease, encourage, expedite, facilitate, forward, foster, hasten, help, patronise, plug, promote, push, speed, succour.

antonyms frustrate, stop.

furtherance *n* advancement, advancing, advocacy, backing, boosting, carrying-out, championship, promoting, promotion, prosecution, pursuit.

furthermore *adv* additionally, also, as well, besides, further, in addition, into the bargain, likewise, moreover, not to mention, to boot, too, what's more.

furthest *adj* extreme, farthest, furthermost, most distant, outermost, outmost, remotest, ultimate, uttermost.

antonym nearest.

furtive *adj* back-door, backstairs, clandestine, cloaked, conspiratorial, covert, hidden, secret, secretive, skulking, slinking, sly, sneaking, sneaky, stealthy, surreptitious, underhand.

antonym open.

fury[1] *n* anger, desperation, ferocity, fierceness, force, frenzy, impetuosity, intensity, ire, madness, passion, power, rage, savagery, severity, tempestuousness, turbulence, vehemence, violence, wax, wrath.

antonym calm.

fury[2] *n* bacchante, hag, harridan, hell-cat, shrew, spitfire, termagant, virago, vixen.

fuse *v* agglutinate, amalgamate, ankylose, blend, coalesce, combine, commingle, federate, integrate, intermingle, intermix, join, meld, melt, merge, smelt, solder, unite, weld.

fusillade *n* barrage, broadside, burst, discharge, fire, hail, mitraille, outburst, salvo, volley.

fusion *n* alloy, amalgam, amalgamation, blend, blending, coalescence, commingling, commixture, federation, integration, liquefaction, liquefying, melting, merger, merging, mixture, smelting, synthesis, union, uniting, welding.

fuss *n* ado, agitation, bother, brouhaha, bustle, coil, commotion, confusion, difficulty, display, doodah, excitement, fantigue, fash, fidget, fikery, flap, flurry, fluster, flutter, furore, hassle, hoo-ha, hurry, kerfuffle, objection, palaver, pother, pudder, row, squabble, stew, stir, to-do, trouble, unrest, upset, worry.

antonym calm.

v bustle, chafe, complain, emote, fash, fidget, flap, fret, fume, niggle, pother, pudder, take pains, worry.

fussiness *n* busy-ness, choosiness, daintiness, elaborateness, faddiness, faddishness, fastidiousness, finicality, finicalness, meticulousness, niceness, niggling, particularity, perfectionism, pernicketiness.

antonym unfastidiousness.

fuss-pot *n* fantod, fidget, fuss-budget, hypercritic, nit-picker, old woman, perfectionist, worrier.

fussy *adj* busy, chichi, choosy, cluttered, dainty, difficult, discriminating, exacting, faddish, faddy, fastidious, finical, finicking, finicky, finikin, hard to please, niggling, nipperty-tipperty, nit-picking, old womanish, old-maidish, overdecorated, overelaborate, overparticular, particular, pernickety, picky, squeamish.

antonyms plain, uncritical, undemanding.

fustiness *n* airlessness, closeness, dampness, frowst, frowstiness, fug, fust, mouldiness, mustiness, staleness, stuffiness.

antonym airiness.

fusty *adj* airless, antediluvian, antiquated, archaic, close, damp, dank, frowsty, fuggy, ill-smelling, malodorous, mildewed, mildewy, mouldering, mouldy, musty, old-fashioned, old-fog(e)yish, outdated, out-of-date, passé, rank, stale, stuffy, unventilated.

antonyms airy, chic, up-to-date.

futile *adj* abortive, barren, bootless, empty, forlorn, fruitless, hollow, idle, ineffectual, nugatory, otiose, pointless, profitless, Sisyphean, sterile, trifling, trivial, unavailing, unimportant, unproductive, unprofitable, unsuccessful, useless, vain, valueless, worthless.

antonyms fruitful, profitable.

futility *n* aimlessness, bootlessness, emptiness, fruitlessness, hollowness, idleness, ineffectiveness, otioseness, pointlessness, triviality, unimportance, uselessness, vanity.

antonyms fruitfulness, profitability.

future *n* expectation, futurition, futurity, hereafter, outlook, prospects.

antonym past.

adj approaching, coming, designate, destined, eventual, expected, fated, forthcoming, impending, in the offing, later, prospective, rising, subsequent, to be, to come, ultimate, unborn.

antonym past.

fuzz *n* down, fibre, flock, floss, flue, fluff, fug, hair, lint, nap, ooze, pile.

fuzzy *adj* bleary, blurred, blurry, distanceless, distorted, downy, faint, fluffy, frizzy, hazy, ill-defined, indistinct, linty, muffled, napped, shadowy, unclear, unfocused, vague, woolly.

antonyms base, distinct.

G

gab *v* babble, blabber, blather, blether, buzz, chatter, drivel, gossip, jabber, jaw, prattle, talk, tattle, yabber, yak, yatter.

n blab, blarney, blethering, blethers, chat, chatter, chitchat, conversation, drivel, gossip, loquacity, palaver, prattle, prattling, small talk, tête-à-tête, tittle-tattle, tongue-wagging, yabber, yackety-yak, yak, yatter.

gabble *v* babble, blab, blabber, blether, cackle, chatter, gaggle, gibber, gush, jabber, prattle, rattle, splutter, spout, sputter, yabber, yatter.

n babble, blabber, blethering, cackling, chatter, drivel, gibberish, jargon, nonsense, prattle, twaddle, waffle, yabber, yatter.

gad about dot about, gallivant, ramble, range, roam, rove, run around, stray, traipse, wander.

gadabout *n* gallivanter, pleasure-seeker, rambler, rover, runabout, stravaiger, wanderer.

gadget *n* appliance, contraption, contrivance, device, doodad, gimmick, gismo, gizmo, invention, jiggumbob, jigjam, jigmaree, novelty, thing, thingumajig, tool, widget.

gaffe *n* bloomer, blunder, boner, boob, boo-boo, brick, clanger, faux pas, gaucherie, goof, howler, indiscretion, mistake, slip, solecism.

gaffer *n* boss, foreman, ganger, manager, overman, overseer, superintendent, supervisor.

gag[1] *v* choke, choke up, curb, disgorge, gasp, heave, muffle, muzzle, puke, quiet, retch, silence, spew, stifle, still, stop up, suppress, throttle, throw up, vomit.

gag[2] *n* funny, hoax, jest, joke, one-liner, pun, quip, wisecrack, witticism.

gaiety *n* animation, blitheness, blithesomeness, brightness, brilliance, celebration, cheerfulness, colour, colourfulness, conviviality, effervescence, elation, exhilaration, festivity, fun, galliardise, gaudiness, glee, glitter, good humour, high spirits, hilarity, joie de vivre, jollification, jollity, joviality, joyousness, light-heartedness, liveliness, merriment, merrymaking, mirth, revelry, revels, show, showiness, sparkle, sprightliness, vivacity.

antonyms drabness, dreariness, sadness.

gaily *adv* blithely, brightly, brilliantly, cheerfully, colourfully, fancily, flamboyantly, flashily, gaudily, gleefully, happily, joyfully, joyously, light-heartedly, merrily, showily.

antonyms dully, sadly.

gain *v* achieve, acquire, advance, arrive at, attain, avail, bag, bring in, capture, clear, collect, come to, earn, enlist, gather, get, get to, glean, harvest, impetrate, improve, increase, make, net, obtain, pick up, procure, produce, profit, progress, reach, realise, reap, secure, win, win over, yield.

antonym lose.

n accretion, achievement, acquisition, advance, advancement, advantage, attainment, benefit, bunce, dividend, earnings, emolument, growth, headway, improvement, income, increase, increment, lucre, proceeds, produce, profit, progress, pudding, return, rise, winnings, yield.

antonyms loss, losses.

gain on approach, catch up, catch up with, close with, come up with, encroach on, leave behind, level with, narrow the gap, outdistance, overtake, widen the gap.

gain time delay, drag one's feet, procrastinate, stall, temporise.

gainful *adj* advantageous, beneficial, feracious, fructuous, fruitful, lucrative, moneymaking, paying, productive, profitable, remunerative, rewarding, useful, worthwhile.

antonym useless.

gains *n* booty, bunce, earnings, fruits, gainings, loaves and fishes, pickings, prize, proceeds, profits, revenue, takings, velvet, winnings.

antonym losses.

gainsay *v* contradict, contravene, controvert, deny, disaffirm, disagree with, dispute, nay-say.

antonym agree.

gait *n* bearing, carriage, manner, pace, step, stride, tread, walk.

gala *n* carnival, celebration, festival, festivity, fête, glorification, jamboree, jubilee, Mardi Gras, pageant, party, procession.

gale *n* blast, burst, cyclone, eruption, explosion, fit, howl, hurricane, outbreak, outburst, peal, ripsnorter, shout, shriek, squall, storm, tempest, tornado, typhoon.

gall[1] *n* acrimony, animosity, animus, antipathy, assurance, bad blood, bile, bitterness, brass, brass neck, brazenness, cheek, effrontery, enmity, hostility, impertinence, impudence, insolence, malevolence, malice, malignity, neck, nerve, presumption, presumptuousness, rancour, sauciness, sourness, spite, spleen, venom, virulence.

antonyms friendliness, modesty, reserve.

gall² *v* abrade, aggravate, annoy, bark, bother, chafe, exasperate, excoriate, fret, get, get to, graze, harass, hurt, irk, irritate, nag, nettle, peeve, pester, plague, provoke, rankle, rile, rub raw, ruffle, scrape, skin, vex.

gallant *adj* attentive, august, bold, brave, chivalrous, courageous, courteous, courtly, daring, dashing, dauntless, dignified, doughty, elegant, fearless, game, gentlemanly, glorious, gracious, grand, heroic, high-spirited, honourable, imposing, indomitable, intrepid, lion-hearted, lofty, magnanimous, magnificent, manful, manly, mettlesome, noble, plucky, polite, splendid, stately, valiant, valorous.

antonyms cowardly, craven, ungentlemanly.

n admirer, adventurer, beau, blade, boyfriend, buck, cavalier, champion, cicisbeo, dandy, daredevil, escort, fop, hero, knight, ladies' man, lady-killer, lover, paramour, suitor, wooer.

gallantry *n* attention, attentiveness, audacity, boldness, bravery, chivalry, courage, courageousness, courteousness, courtesy, courtliness, daring, dauntlessness, derring-do, elegance, fearlessness, gentlemanliness, graciousness, heroism, intrepidity, manliness, mettle, nerve, nobility, pluck, politeness, politesse, prowess, spirit, valiance, valour.

antonyms cowardice, ungentlemanliness.

gallery *n* arcade, art-gallery, balcony, circle, gods, grandstand, loggia, museum, passage, pawn, spectators, walk.

galley *n* bireme, long-ship, lymphad, quadrireme, quinquereme, trireme.

galling *adj* aggravating, annoying, bitter, bothersome, exasperating, harassing, humiliating, infuriating, irksome, irritating, nettling, plaguing, provoking, rankling, vexatious, vexing.

antonym pleasing.

gallivant *v* dot about, gad about, ramble, range, roam, rove, run around, stravaig, stray, traipse, travel, wander.

gallop *v* bolt, career, dart, dash, fly, gal(l)umph, hasten, hie, hurry, lope, race, run, rush, scud, shoot, speed, sprint, tear, zoom.

gallows *n* dule-tree, hempen caudle, nubbing-cleat, scaffold, the rope.

galore *adv* aplenty, everywhere, heaps of, in abundance, in numbers, in profusion, lots of, millions of, stacks of, to spare, tons of.

antonym scarce.

galvanise *v* animate, arouse, awaken, electrify, excite, fire, inspire, invigorate, jolt, move, prod, provoke, quicken, shock, spur, startle, stimulate, stir, thrill, vitalise, wake.

antonym retard.

gambit *n* artifice, device, manoeuvre, move, ploy, stratagem, trick, wile.

gamble *v* back, bet, chance, gaff, game, have a flutter, hazard, play, punt, risk, speculate, stake, stick one's neck out, take a chance, try one's luck, venture, wager.

n bet, chance, flutter, leap in the dark, lottery, punt, risk, speculation, uncertainty, venture, wager.

gambler *n* better, gaffer, gamester, punter, throwster, wagerer.

gambol *v* bounce, bound, caper, cavort, curvet, cut a caper, frisk, frolic, hop, jump, prance, rollick, skip.

n antic, bound, caper, frisk, frolic, gambado, hop, jump, prance, skip, spring.

game¹ *n* adventure, amusement, business, competition, contest, design, device, distraction, diversion, enterprise, entertainment, event, frolic, fun, jest, joke, lark, line, main, match, meeting, merriment, merry-making, occupation, pastime, plan, play, plot, ploy, proceeding, recreation, romp, round, scheme, sport, stratagem, strategy, tactic, tournament, trick, undertaking.

game² *n* animals, bag, flesh, game-birds, meat, prey, quarry, spoils.

game³ *adj* bold, brave, courageous, dauntless, desirous, disposed, dogged, eager, fearless, gallant, gamy, heroic, inclined, interested, intrepid, persevering, persistent, plucky, prepared, ready, resolute, spirited, spunky, unflinching, valiant, valorous, willing.

antonyms cowardly, unwilling.

game⁴ *adj* bad, crippled, deformed, disabled, gammy, gouty, hobbling, incapacitated, injured, lame, maimed.

gamekeeper *n* keeper, venerer, verderer, warden.

gamut *n* area, catalogue, compass, field, gamme, range, scale, scope, series, spectrum, sweep.

gang *n* band, circle, clique, club, coffle, company, core, coterie, crew, crowd, group, herd, horde, lot, mob, pack, party, ring, set, shift, squad, team, troupe.

gangling *adj* angular, awkward, bony, gangly, gauche, gawky, lanky, loose-jointed, rangy, raw-boned, skinny, spindly, tall, ungainly.

gangster *n* bandit, brigand, crook, desperado, heavy, hood, hoodlum, mobster, racketeer, robber, rough, ruffian, thug, tough.

gaol *see* **jail**.

gap *n* blank, breach, break, chink, cleft, crack, cranny, crevice, diastema, difference, disagreement, discontinuity, disparateness, disparity, divergence, divide, hiatus, hole, inconsistency, interlude, intermission, interruption, interspace, interstice, interval, lacuna, lull, opening, pause, recess, rent, rift, space, vacuity, void.

gape *v* crack, dehisce, gawk, gawp, goggle, open, split, stare, wonder, yawn.

gaping *adj* broad, cavernous, dehiscent, fatiscent, great, hiant, open, ringent, vast, wide, yawning.

antonym tiny.

garage *n* lock-up, petrol station, service station.

garb *n* accoutrements, apparel, appearance, array, aspect, attire, clothes, clothing, costume, covering, cut, dress, fashion, garment, gear, guise, habiliment, habit, look, mode, outfit, raiment, robes, style, uniform, vestments, wear.

v apparel, array, attire, clothe, cover, dress, habilitate, rig out, robe.

garbage *n* bits and pieces, debris, detritus, dross, filth, gash, junk, litter, muck, odds and ends, offal, refuse, rubbish, scourings, scraps, slops, sweepings, swill, trash, waste.

garble *v* confuse, corrupt, distort, doctor, edit, falsify, jumble, misinterpret, misquote, misreport, misrepresent, misstate, mistranslate, mix up, muddle, mutilate, pervert, slant, tamper with, twist.

antonym decipher.

garden *n* backyard, garth, orchard, park, plot, yard.

gargantuan *adj* big, Brobdingnag(ian), colossal, elephantine, enormous, giant, gigantic, huge, immense, large, leviathan, mammoth, massive, monstrous, monumental, mountainous, prodigious, titanic, towering, tremendous, vast.

antonym small.

gargoyle *n* grotesque, spout.

garish *adj* brassy, brummagem, cheap, criant, flash, flashy, flaunting, flaunty, gaudy, glaring, glittering, glitzy, loud, meretricious, raffish, showy, tasteless, tawdry, vulgar.

antonyms modest, plain, quiet.

garland *n* bays, chaplet, coronal, crown, festoon, honours, laurels, lei, stemma, swag, wreath.

v adorn, crown, deck, engarland, festoon, wreathe.

garments *n* apparel, array, attire, clothes, clothing, costume, dress, duds, garb, gear, get-up, habiliment, habit, outfit, raiment, robes, togs, uniform, vestments, wear.

garner *v* accumulate, amass, assemble, collect, cull, deposit, gather, hoard, husband, lay up, put by, reserve, save, stockpile, store, stow away, treasure.

antonym dissipate.

garnish *v* adorn, beautify, bedeck, deck, decorate, embellish, enhance, furnish, grace, ornament, set off, trim.

antonym divest.

n adornment, decoration, embellishment, enhancement, garnishment, garnishry, garniture, ornament, ornamentation, relish, trim, trimming.

garrison *n* armed force, barracks, base, camp, casern(e), command, detachment, encampment, fort, fortification, fortress, post, station, stronghold, troops, unit, zareba.

v assign, defend, furnish, guard, man, mount, occupy, place, position, post, protect, station.

garrulity *n* babble, babbling, chatter, chattering, chattiness, diffuseness, effusiveness, gabbiness, garrulousness, gassing, gift of the gab, glibness, long-windedness, loquaciousness, loquacity, prating, prattle, prolixity, prosiness, talkativeness, verbosity, volubility, windiness, wordiness.

antonyms taciturnity, terseness.

garrulous *adj* babbling, chattering, chatty, diffuse, effusive, gabby, gassy, glib, gossiping, gushing, long-winded, loquacious, mouthy, prating, prattling, prolix, prosy, talkative, verbose, voluble, windy, wordy, yabbering.

antonyms taciturn, terse.

gash *v* cleave, cut, gouge, incise, lacerate, nick, notch, rend, score, slash, slit, split, tear, wound.

n cleft, cut, gouge, incision, laceration, nick, notch, rent, score, slash, slit, split, tear, wound.

gasp *v* blow, breathe, choke, ejaculate, gulp, pant, puff, utter.

n blow, breath, ejaculation, exclamation, gulp, pant, puff.

gate *n* barrier, door, doorway, entrance, exit, gateway, opening, passage, port, portal, portcullis, wicket.

gather *v* accumulate, amass, assemble, assume, build, clasp, collect, conclude, congregate, convene, crop, cull, deduce, deepen, draw, embrace, enfold, enlarge, expand, flock, fold, foregather, garner, glean, group, grow, harvest, heap, hear, heighten, hoard, hold, hug, increase, infer, intensify, learn, make, marshal, mass, muster, pick, pile up, pleat, pluck, pucker, rake up, reap, rise, round up, ruche, ruffle, select, shirr, stockpile, surmise, swell, thicken, tuck, understand, wax.

antonyms dissipate, scatter.

gathering *n* accumulation, acquisition, aggregate, assemblage, assembly, collection, company, concentration, conclave, concourse, congregation, congress, convention, convocation, crowd, fest, flock, gain, galère, get-together, group, heap, hoard, jamboree, kgotla, knot, mass, meeting, moot, muster, omnium-gatherum, party, pile, procurement, rally, round-up, rout, stock, stockpile, throng, turn-out.

antonym scattering.

gauche *adj* awkward, clumsy, farouche, gawky, graceless, ignorant, ill-bred, ill-mannered, inelegant, inept, insensitive, maladroit, tactless, uncultured, ungainly, ungraceful, unpolished, unsophisticated.

antonym graceful.

gaucherie *n* awkwardness, bad taste, bloomer, blunder, boner, boob, brick, clanger, clumsiness, faux pas, gaffe, gaucheness, goof, gracelessness, ignorance, ill-breeding, indiscretion, inelegance, ineptness, insensitivity, maladroitness, mistake, slip, solecism, tactlessness.

antonym elegance.

gaudy *adj* bright, brilliant, brummagem, chintzy, flash, flashy, florid, garish, gay, glaring, glitzy, loud, meretricious, ostentatious, raffish, showy, tasteless, tawdry, tinsel(ly), vulgar.

antonyms drab, plain, quiet.

gauge[1] *v* adjudge, adjust, appraise, ascertain, assess, calculate, check, compute, count, determine, estimate, evaluate, figure, guess, judge, measure, rate, reckon, value, weigh.

n basis, criterion, example, exemplar, guide, guideline, indicator, measure, meter, micrometer, model, pattern, rule, sample, standard, test, touchstone, yardstick.

gauge[2] *n* bore, calibre, capacity, degree, depth, extent, height, magnitude, measure, scope, size, span, thickness, width.

gaunt *adj* angular, attenuated, bare, bleak, bony, cadaverous, desolate, dismal, dreary, emaciated, forbidding, forlorn, grim, haggard, hagged, harsh, hollow-eyed, lank, lean, meagre, pinched, rawboned, scraggy, scrawny, skeletal, skinny, spare, thin, wasted.

antonyms hale, plump.

gauzy *adj* delicate, diaphanous, filmy, flimsy, gossamer, insubstantial, light, see-through, sheer, thin, transparent, unsubstantial.

antonyms heavy, thick.

gawk *v* gape, gaup, gaze, goggle, look, ogle, stare.

gawky *adj* awkward, clownish, clumsy, gangling, gauche, loutish, lumbering, lumpish, maladroit, oafish, uncouth, ungainly, ungraceful.

antonym graceful.

gay[1] *adj* animated, blithe, boon, bright, brilliant, carefree, cavalier, cheerful, colourful, convivial, debonair, festive, flamboyant, flashy, fresh, frivolous, frolicsome, fun-loving, gamesome, garish, gaudy, glad, gleeful, happy, hilarious, insouciant, jolly, jovial, joyful, joyous, lifesome, light-hearted, lightsome, lively, merry, playful, pleasure-seeking, rakish, riant, rich, rollicking, rorty, showy, sparkish, sparkling, sportive, sunny, tit(t)upy, vivacious, vivid, waggish.

antonyms gloomy, sad.

gay[2] *adj* bent, dikey, homosexual, lesbian, queer.

antonyms heterosexual, straight.

n dike, homo, homosexual, lesbian, poof, queer, sapphist.

antonym heterosexual.

gaze *v* contemplate, gape, gaup, gawp, look, ogle, regard, stare, view, watch.

n gaup, gawp, look, stare.

gazebo *n* belvedere, hut, pavilion, shelter, summer-house.

gazette *n* despatch, journal, magazine, newspaper, news-sheet, notice, organ, paper, periodical.

gear *n* accessories, accoutrements, affair, apparatus, apparel, armour, array, attire, baggage, belongings, business, clothes, clothing, cog, costume, doings, dress, effects, equipment, garb, garments, gearing, get-up, habit, harness, instruments, kit, luggage, machinery, matter, mechanism, outfit, paraphernalia, possessions, rigging, rig-out, stuff, supplies, tackle, things, togs, tools, trappings, traps, wear, works.

v adapt, adjust, equip, fit, harness, rig, suit, tailor.

gears *n* cams, cam-wheels, cogs, cogwheels, engrenage, gear-wheels, mechanism, workings, works.

gelatinous *adj* congealed, gluey, glutinous, gooey, gummy, jellied, jellified, jelly, jellyform, jelly-like, mucilaginous, rubbery, sticky, viscid, viscous.

gem *n* angel, bijou, brick, flower, honey, jewel, masterpiece, pearl, pick, pièce de résistance, precious stone, prize, stone, treasure.

gen *n* background, data, details, facts, info, information, low-down.

genealogy *n* ancestry, background, blood-line, derivation, descent, extraction, family, family tree, line, lineage, pedigree, progeniture, stemma, stirps, stock, strain.

general *adj* accepted, accustomed, across-the-board, all-inclusive, approximate, blanket, broad, catholic, collective, common, comprehensive, conventional, customary, ecumenic, ecumenical, encyclop(a)edic, everyday, extensive, generic, habitual, ill-defined, imprecise, inaccurate, indefinite, indiscriminate, inexact, loose, miscellaneous, normal, ordinary, panoramic, popular, prevailing, prevalent, public, regular, sweeping, total, typical, universal, unspecific, usual, vague, widespread.

antonyms limited, novel, particular.

n chief, c-in-c, commander, commander in chief, generalissimo, hetman, leader, marshal, officer.

generality *n* approximateness, breadth, catholicity, commonness, comprehensiveness, ecumenicity, extensiveness, generalisation, impreciseness, indefiniteness, inexactness, looseness, miscellaneity, popularity, prevalence, sweeping statement, universality, vagueness.

antonyms detail, exactness, particular, uncommonness.

generally *adv* approximately, as a rule, broadly, by and large, characteristically, chiefly, commonly, conventionally, customarily, extensively, for the most part, habitually, in the main, largely, mainly, mostly, normally, on average, on the whole, ordinarily, popularly, predominantly, principally, publicly, regularly, typically, universally, usually, widely.

antonym rarely.

generate *v* beget, breed, bring about, cause, create, engender, father, form, gender, give rise to, initiate, make, originate, procreate, produce, propagate, spawn, whip up.

antonym prevent.

generation *n* age, age group, begetting, breed, breeding, creation, crop, day, days, engendering, engenderment, engend(r)ure, epoch, era, formation, generating, genesis, geniture, origination, period, procreation, production, progeniture, propagation, reproduction, time, times.

generic *adj* all-inclusive, blanket, collective, common, comprehensive, general, inclusive, sweeping, universal, wide.

antonym particular.

generosity *n* beneficence, benevolence, big-heartedness, bounteousness, bounty, charity, goodness, high-mindedness, kindness, large-heartedness, liberality, magnanimity, munificence, nobleness, open-handedness, soft-heartedness, unselfishness, unsparingness.

antonyms meanness, selfishness.

generous *adj* abundant, ample, beneficent, benevolent, big-hearted, bounteous, bountiful, charitable, copious, disinterested, free, full, good, high-minded, hospitable, kind, large-hearted, large-minded, lavish, liberal, lofty, magnanimous, munificent, noble, open-handed, overflowing, plentiful, princely, rich, soft-boiled, soft-hearted, ungrudging, unreproachful, unresentful, unselfish, unsparing, unstinted, unstinting.

antonyms mean, selfish.

genesis *n* beginning, birth, commencement, creation, dawn, engendering, formation, foundation, founding, generation, inception, initiation, origin, outset, propagation, root, source, start.

antonym end.

genial *adj* affable, agreeable, amiable, cheerful, cheery, congenial, convivial, cordial, easy-going, expansive, friendly, glad, good-natured, happy, hearty, jolly, jovial, joyous, kind, kindly, merry, pleasant, sunny, sunshiny, warm, warm-hearted.

antonym cold.

geniality *n* affability, agreeableness, amiability, cheerfulness, cheeriness, congenialness, conviviality, cordiality, friendliness, gladness, good nature, happiness, heartiness, jollity, joviality, kindliness, kindness, mirth, openness, pleasantness, sunniness, warm-heartedness, warmth.

antonym coldness.

genie *n* demon, (d)jinni, fairy, jann, jinnee, spirit.

genitals *n* fanny, genitalia, private parts, privates, pudenda, pudendum, pussy, quim, yoni.

genius[1] *n* adept, brain, expert, intellect, maestro, master, master-hand, mastermind, pastmaster, virtuoso.

genius[2] *n* ability, aptitude, bent, brightness, brilliance, capacity, endowment, faculty, flair, gift, inclination, intellect, knack, propensity, talent, turn.

genius[3] *n* daemon, double, genie, ka, spirit.

genocide *n* ethnocide, extermination, massacre, slaughter.

genre *n* brand, category, character, class, fashion, genus, group, kind, race, school, sort, species, strain, style, type, variety.

genteel *adj* aristocratic, civil, courteous, courtly, cultivated, cultured, elegant, fashionable, formal, gentlemanly, graceful, ladylike, mannerly, polished, polite, refined, respectable, stylish, urbane, well-bred, well-mannered.

antonyms crude, rough, unpolished.

Gentile *n* goy.

gentility *n* aristocracy, blue blood, breeding, civility, courtesy, courtliness, cultivation, culture, decorum, elegance, elite, etiquette, formality, gentilesse, gentle birth, gentlefolk, gentrice, gentry, good family, high birth, mannerliness, manners, nobility, nobles, polish, politeness, propriety, rank, refinement, respectability, upper class, urbanity.

antonyms crudeness, discourteousness, roughness.

gentle *adj* amiable, aristocratic, balmy, benign, biddable, bland, broken, calm, canny, clement, compassionate, courteous, cultured, docile, easy, elegant, genteel, gentlemanlike, gentlemanly, gradual, high-born, humane, imperceptible, kind, kindly, ladylike, lamb-like, lenient, light, low, maidenly, manageable, meek, merciful, mild, moderate, muted, noble, pacific, peaceful, placid, polished, polite, quiet, refined, serene, slight, slow, smooth, soft, soothing, sweet, sweet-tempered, tame, temperate, tender, tractable, tranquil, untroubled, upper-class, well-born, well-bred.

antonyms crude, rough, unkind, unpolished.

gentleman *n* duniewassal, gemman, gent, gentilhomme, hidalgo, sahib, Sen^•or, Signor(e), sir.

gentlemanly *adj* civil, civilised, courteous, cultivated, gallant, genteel, gentlemanlike, gentlewomanly, honourable, mannerly, noble, obliging, polished, polite, refined, reputable, suave, urbane, well-bred, well-mannered.

antonyms impolite, rough.

gentry *n* aristocracy, elite, gens de condition, gentility, gentlefolk, nobility, nobles, quality, squirearchy, upper class.

genuine *adj* actual, artless, authentic, bona fide, candid, earnest, frank, heartfelt, honest, kosher, legitimate, natural, original, pukka, pure, real, simon-pure, sincere, sound, sterling, sure-enough, true, unadulterate(d), unaffected, unalloyed, unfeigned, unsophisticated, veritable.

antonyms artificial, insincere.

genus *n* breed, category, class, division, genre, group, kind, order, race, set, sort, species, taxon, type.

geography *n* chorography, layout, lie.

geology *n* geognosy, geogony, geotectonics.

germ *n* bacterium, beginning, bud, bug, cause, egg, embryo, microbe, micro-organism, nucleus, origin, ovule, ovum, root, rudiment, seed, source, spark, spore, sprout, virus, zyme.

germane *adj* akin, allied, applicable, apposite, appropriate, apropos, apt, cognate, connected, fitting, kin, kindred, material, pertinent, proper, related, relevant, suitable.

antonym irrelevant.

germinal *adj* developing, embryonic, preliminary, rudimentary, seminal, undeveloped.

germinate *v* bud, develop, generate, grow, originate, pullulate, root, shoot, sprout, swell, vegetate.

gestation *n* conception, development, drafting, evolution, incubation, maturation, planning, pregnancy, ripening.

gesticulate *v* gesture, indicate, motion, point, sign, signal, wave.

gesticulation *n* ch(e)ironomy, motion, sign, signal, wave.

gesture *n* act, action, gesticulation, indication, motion, sign, signal, wave.

v gesticulate, indicate, motion, point, sign, signal, wave.

get *v* achieve, acquire, affect, annoy, arouse, arrange, arrest, arrive, attain, baffle, bag, become, bother, bring, bug, capture, catch, coax, collar, come, come by, come down with, communicate with, comprehend, confound, contact, contract, contrive, convince, earn, excite, fathom, fetch, fix, follow, gain, glean, grab, grow, hear, impetrate, impress, induce, influence, inherit, irk, irritate, make, make it, manage, move, mystify, net, nonplus, notice, obtain, perceive, perplex, persuade, pick up, pique, prevail upon, procure, puzzle, reach, realise, reap, receive, secure, see, seize, stimulate, stir, stump, succeed, sway, take, touch, trap, turn, twig, understand, upset, vex, wangle, wax, wheedle, win.

antonyms lose, misunderstand, pacify.

get a move on get cracking, get going, go to it, hurry (up), jump to it, make haste, shake a leg, speed up, step on it.

antonym slow down.

get across bring home to, communicate, convey, cross, ford, impart, negotiate, put over, transmit, traverse.

get ahead advance, flourish, get there, go places, make good, make it, progress, prosper, succeed, thrive.

antonyms fail, fall behind.

get along cope, develop, fare, get by, get on, harmonise, hit it off, make (a) shift, make out, manage, progress, shift, survive.

antonym argue.

get at acquire, annoy, attack, attain, blame, bribe, buy off, carp, corrupt, criticise, find fault with, hint, imply, influence, intend, irritate, make fun of, mean, mock, nag, pervert, pick on, poke fun at, suborn, suggest, tamper with, taunt.

antonym praise.

get away break out, decamp, depart, disappear, escape, flee, get out, leave, run away.

get back get even, get one's own back (on), recoup, recover, regain, repossess, retaliate, retrieve, return, revenge oneself (on), revert, revisit.

get by contrive, cope, exist, fare, get along, make both ends meet, manage, negotiate, pass muster, shift, subsist, survive.

get down alight, depress, descend, disembark, dishearten, dismount, dispirit, lower, sadden.

antonyms board, encourage.

get even even the score, get one's own back, pay back, reciprocate, repay, requite, revenge oneself, settle the score.

get in alight, appear, arrive, collect, come, embark, enter, gather in, include, infiltrate, insert, interpose, land, mount, penetrate, take.

antonym get out.

get off alight, depart, descend, detach, disembark, dismount, doff, escape, exit, learn, leave, remove, shed, swot up.

antonyms arrive, board, put on.

get on advance, agree, ascend, board, climb, concur, cope, embark, fare, get along, harmonise, hit it off, make out, manage, mount, proceed, progress, prosper, succeed.

antonyms alight, argue.

get out alight, break out, clear out, decamp, deliver, escape, evacuate, extricate oneself, flee, flit, free oneself, leave, produce, publish, quit, scarper, vacate, withdraw.

antonym board.

get out of avoid, dodge, escape, evade, shirk, skive.

get over communicate, convey, cross, defeat, explain, ford, get the better of, impart, master, overcome, pass, put across, recover from, shake off, surmount, survive, traverse.

get ready arrange, fix up, get psyched up, gird one's loins, inspan, prepare, psych oneself up, ready, rehearse, set out.

get rid of dispense with, dispose of, do away with, dump, eject, eliminate, expel, jettison, remove, rid oneself of, shake off, unload.

antonyms accumulate, acquire.

get round bypass, cajole, circumvent, coax, convert, edge, evade, outmanoeuvre, persuade, prevail upon, skirt, talk over, talk round, wheedle.

get the better of beat, best, defeat, outdo, outfox, outsmart, outwit, surpass, worst.

get the hang of absorb, comprehend, grasp, understand.

get the message catch on, comprehend, get it, get the point, see, take the hint, twig, understand.

antonym misunderstand.

get there advance, arrive, go places, make good, make it, prosper, succeed.

get together accumulate, assemble, collaborate, collect, congregate, convene, converge, gather, join, meet, muster, rally, unite.

get under one's skin annoy, get, get to, infuriate, irk, irritate, needle, nettle.

antonym pacify.

get up arise, arrange, ascend, climb, fix up, increase, learn, memorise, mount, organise, rise, scale, stand.

getaway *n* break, break-out, decampment, escape, flight, start.

get-together *n* do, function, gabfest, gathering, party, reception, social, soirée.

gewgaw *n* bagatelle, bauble, bijou, gaud, gimcrack, kickshaw(s), knick-knack, novelty, plaything, toy, trifle, trinket.

ghastly *adj* ashen, cadaverous, deathlike, deathly, dreadful, frightful, ghostly, grim, grisly, gruesome, hideous, horrendous, horrible, horrid, livid, loathsome, lurid, pale, pallid, repellent, shocking, spectral, terrible, terrifying, wan.

antonym delightful.

ghost *n* apparition, astral body, duppy, eidolon, fetch, glimmer, gytrash, hint, jumby, larva, lemur, manes, phantasm, phantom, possibility, revenant, semblance, shade, shadow, simulacrum, soul, spectre, spirit, spook, suggestion, trace, umbra, visitant, white-lady.

ghostly *adj* chthonian, eerie, eldritch, faint, ghostlike, illusory, insubstantial, phantasmal, phantom, spectral, spooky, supernatural, uncanny, unearthly, weird, wraith-like.

ghoulish *adj* grisly, gruesome, macabre, morbid, revolting, sick, unhealthy, unwholesome.

giant *n* behemoth, colossus, Goliath, Hercules, jotun, leviathan, monster, Patagonian, titan.

adj Atlantean, Babylonian, Brobdingnag(ian), colossal, cyclopean, elephantine, enormous, gargantuan, gigantean, gigantesque, gigantic, huge, immense, jumble, king-size, large, leviathan, mammoth, monstrous, Patagonian, prodigious, rounceval, titanic, vast.

gibber *v* babble, blab, blabber, blather, cackle, cant, chatter, claptrap, gabble, jabber, prattle.

gibberish *n* abracadabra, babble, balderdash, blather, drivel, gabble, gobbledegook, jabber, jabberwock(y), jargon, mumbo-jumbo, nonsense, prattle, slipslop, twaddle, yammer.

antonym sense.

gibe *see* **jibe**.

giddiness *n* dizziness, faintness, light-headedness, nausea, vertigo, wobbliness, wooziness.

giddy *adj* capricious, careless, changeable, changeful, dizzy, dizzying, erratic, faint, fickle, flighty, frivolous, heedless, impulsive, inconstant, irresolute, irresponsible, light-headed, reckless, reeling, scatterbrained, scatty, silly, thoughtless, unbalanced, unstable, unsteady, vacillating, vertiginous, volage, volageous, volatile, wild.

antonyms sensible, sober.

gift *n* ability, aptitude, attribute, benefaction, benificence, bent, bequest, bonus, boon, bounty, cadeau, capability, capacity, contribution, cumshaw, deodate, dolly, donary, donation, donative, douceur, earnest, endowment, faculty, flair, foy, freebie, genius, grant, gratuity, knack, largess(e), legacy, manna, offering, potlatch, power, present, sop, talent, turn, xenium.

gifted *adj* able, accomplished, ace, adroit, bright, brilliant, capable, clever, expert, ingenious, intelligent, masterly, skilful, skilled, talented.

antonym dull.

gigantic *adj* Atlantean, Babylonian, Brobdingnag(ian), colossal, cyclopean, elephantine, enormous, gargantuan, giant, herculean, huge, immense, leviathan, mammoth, monstrous, Patagonian, prodigious, rounceval, stupendous, titanic, tremendous, vast.

antonym small.

giggle *v* chortle, chuckle, laugh, snigger, tee-hee, titter.

n chortle, chuckle, fou rire, laugh, snigger, tee-hee, titter.

gild *v* adorn, array, beautify, bedeck, brighten, coat, deck, dress up, embellish, embroider, enhance, enrich, festoon, garnish, grace, ornament, paint, trim.

gilded *adj* gilt, gold, golden, inaurate.

gimcrack *adj* cheap, rubbishy, shoddy, tawdry, trashy, trumpery.

antonyms solid, well-made.

gimmick *n* angle, attraction, contrivance, device, dodge, gadget, gambit, gizmo, manoeuvre, ploy, scheme, stratagem, stunt, trick.

gin *n* mother's ruin (mothers' ruin).

gingerly *adv* carefully, cautiously, charily, circumspectly, daintily, delicately, fastidiously, gently, hesitantly, reluctantly, squeamishly, suspiciously, timidly, warily.

antonyms carelessly, roughly.

gipsy *see* **gypsy**.

gird *v* belt, bind, blockade, brace, encircle, enclose, encompass, enfold, engird, environ, enzone, fortify, girdle, hem in, pen, prepare, ready, ring, steel, surround.

girdle *n* band, belt, ceinture, cestus, cincture, cingulum, corset, cummerbund, fillet, sash, waistband, zona, zone, zonule.

v bind, bound, encirle, enclose, encompass, engird, environ, enzone, gird, gird round, go round, hem, ring, surround.

girl *n* backfisch, bird, chick, chicken, chit, colleen, damsel, daughter, demoiselle, filly, fizgig, flapper, flibbertigibbet, floosie, fluff, fräulein, gal, giglet, girl-friend, gouge, grisette, judy, lass, lassie, maid, maiden, miss, moppet, peach, piece, popsy(-wopsy), quean, quine, sheila, sweetheart, wench.

girth *n* band, belly-band, bulk, circumference, measure, saddle-band, size, strap.

gist *n* core, direction, drift, essence, force, idea, import, marrow, matter, meaning, nub, pith, point, quintessence, sense, significance, substance.

give *v* accord, administer, admit, allow, announce, award, bend, bestow, break, cause, cede, collapse, commit, communicate, concede, confer, consign, contribute, deliver, demonstrate, devote, display, do, donate, emit, engender, entrust, evidence, fall, furnish, grant, hand, hand over, impart, indicate, issue, lead, lend, make, make over, manifest, notify, occasion, offer, pay, perform, permit, present, produce, proffer, pronounce, provide, publish, recede, relinquish, render, retire, set forth, show, sink, state, supply, surrender, transmit, utter, vouchsafe, yield.

antonyms hold out, take, withstand.

give away betray, disclose, divulge, expose, grass, inform on, leak, let out, let slip, rat, reveal, uncover.

give in capitulate, collapse, comply, concede, crack, give way, quit, submit, surrender, yield.

antonym hold out.

give off discharge, emit, exhale, exude, outpour, pour out, produce, release, send out, throw out, vent.

give on to lead to, open on to, overlook.

give out announce, broadcast, communicate, discharge, disseminate, emit, exhale, exude, give off, impart, notify, outpour, pour out, produce, publish, release, send out, transmit, utter, vent.

antonym take in.

give rise to breed, bring about, bring on, cause, effect, engender, generate, produce, provoke, result in.

give up abandon, capitulate, cease, cede, cut out, desist, despair, forswear, hand over, leave off, quit, relinquish, renounce, resign, stop, surrender, throw in the towel, throw up the sponge, waive.

antonym hold out.

give way accede, acquiesce, back down, bend, break (down), cave in, cede, collapse, concede, crack, crumple, fall, give ground, give place, sink, submit, subside, withdraw, yield.

antonyms hold out, withstand.

give-and-take *n* adaptability, compliance, flexibility, giff-gaff, good-will, willingness.

given *adj* addicted, admitted, agreed, apt, bestowed, disposed, granted, inclined, liable, likely, prone, specified.

glacial *adj* antagonistic, arctic, biting, bitter, brumous, chill, chilly, cold, freezing, frigid, frore, frosty, frozen, gelid, hostile, icy, inimical, piercing, polar, raw, Siberian, stiff, unfriendly, wintry.

antonym warm.

glad *adj* animated, blithe, blithesome, bright, cheerful, cheering, cheery, chuffed, contented, delighted, delightful, felicitous, gay, gleeful, gratified, gratifying, happy, jocund, jovial, joyful, joyous, merry, over the moon, overjoyed, pleasant, pleased, pleasing, willing.

antonym sad.

gladden *v* brighten, cheer, delight, elate, enliven, exhilarate, gratify, hearten, please, rejoice.

antonym sadden.

gladly *adv* blithely, blithesomely, cheerfully, fain, freely, gaily, gleefully, happily, jovially, joyfully, joyously, merrily, readily, willingly, with good grace, with pleasure.

antonyms sadly, unwillingly.

gladness *n* animation, blitheness, blithesomeness, brightness, cheerfulness, delight, felicity, gaiety, glee, happiness, high spirits, hilarity, jollity, joy, joyousness, mirth, pleasure.

antonym sadness.

glamorous *adj* alluring, attractive, beautiful, bewitching, captivating, charming, classy, dazzling, elegant, enchanting, entrancing, exciting, exotic, fascinating, glittering, glossy, gorgeous, lovely, prestigious, smart.

antonyms boring, drab, plain.

glamour *n* allure, appeal, attraction, beauty, bewitchment, charm, enchantment, fascination, magic, magnetism, prestige, ravishment, witchery.

glance[1] *v* browse, dip, flip, gaze, glimpse, leaf, look, peek, peep, riffle, scan, skim, thumb, touch on, view.

n allusion, coup d'oeil, dekko, gander, glimpse, look, mention, once over, peek, peep, reference, squint, view.

glance[2] *v* bounce, brush, cannon, carom, coruscate, flash, gleam, glimmer, glint, glisten, glister, glitter, graze, rebound, reflect, ricochet, shimmer, shine, skim, twinkle.

glare *v* blaze, coruscate, dazzle, flame, flare, frown, glower, look daggers, lower, scowl, shine.

n black look, blaze, brilliance, dazzle, dirty look, flame, flare, flashiness, floridness, frown, gaudiness, glow, glower, light, look, loudness, lower, scowl, showiness, stare, tawdriness.

glaring *adj* audacious, blatant, blazing, bright, conspicuous, dazzling, dreadful, egregious, flagrant, flashy, florid, garish, glowing, gross, horrendous, loud, manifest, obvious, open, outrageous, outstanding, overt, patent, rank, terrible, unconcealed, visible.

antonyms dull, hidden, minor.

glass *n* beaker, crystal, goblet, lens, looking-glass, magnifying glass, pane, pocket-lens, roemer, rummer, schooner, tumbler, vitrics, window.

glass case display cabinet, vitrine, vivarium, Wardian case.

glassiness *n* vitreosity, vitreousness.

glassware *n* crystal, glass, vitrics.

glassy *adj* blank, clear, cold, dazed, dull, empty, expressionless, fixed, glasslike, glazed, glazy, glossy, hyaline, icy, lifeless, shiny, slick, slippery, smooth, transparent, vacant, vitreous, vitriform.

glaze *v* burnish, coat, crystallise, enamel, furbish, gloss, lacquer, polish, varnish.

n coat, enamel, finish, gloss, lacquer, lustre, patina, polish, shine, varnish.

gleam *n* beam, brightness, brilliance, coruscation, flash, flicker, glimmer, glint, gloss, glow, hint, inkling, lustre, ray, sheen, shimmer, sparkle, splendour, suggestion, trace.

v coruscate, flare, flash, glance, glimmer, glint, glisten, glister, glitter, glow, scintillate, shimmer, shine, sparkle.

gleaming *adj* ablaze, bright, brilliant, burnished, glistening, glowing, lustrous, polished, shining.

antonym dull.

glean *v* accumulate, amass, collect, cull, find out, garner, gather, harvest, learn, pick (up), reap, select.

glee *n* cheerfulness, delight, elation, exhilaration, exuberance, exultation, fun, gaiety, gladness, gratification, hilarity, jocularity, jollity, joviality, joy, joyfulness, joyousness, liveliness, merriment, mirth, pleasure, sprightliness, triumph, verve.

gleeful *adj* beside oneself, cheerful, cock-a-hoop, delighted, elated, exuberant, exultant, gay, gleesome, gratified, happy, jovial, joyful, joyous, jubilant, merry, mirthful, over the moon, overjoyed, pleased, triumphant.

antonym sad.

glib *adj* artful, easy, facile, fast-talking, fluent, garrulous, insincere, logodaedalic, plausible, quick, ready, slick, slippery, smooth, smooth-spoken, smooth-tongued, suave, talkative, voluble.

antonyms implausible, tongue-tied.

glibness *n* logodaedaly, patter, plausibility, slickness, smoothness, suaveness, suavity.

glide *v* coast, drift, float, flow, fly, glissade, roll, run, sail, skate, skim, slide, slip, soar, volplane.

glimmer *v* blink, flicker, gleam, glint, glisten, glitter, glow, shimmer, shine, sparkle, twinkle.

n blink, flicker, gleam, glimmering, glint, glow, grain, hint, inkling, ray, shimmer, sparkle, suggestion, trace, twinkle.

glimpse *n* glance, gliff, glim, glisk, look, peek, peep, sight, sighting, squint.

v descry, espy, sight, spot, spy, view.

glint *v* flash, gleam, glimmer, glitter, reflect, shine, sparkle, twinkle.

n flash, gleam, glimmer, glimmering, glitter, shine, sparkle, twinkle, twinkling.

glisten *v* coruscate, flash, glance, glare, gleam, glimmer, glint, glister, glitter, scintillate, shimmer, shine, sparkle, twinkle.

glitter *v* coruscate, flare, flash, glare, gleam, glimmer, glint, glisten, scintillate, shimmer, shine, spangle, sparkle, twinkle.

n beam, brightness, brilliance, clinquant, display, flash, gaudiness, glamour, glare, gleam, lustre, pageantry, radiance, scintillation, sheen, shimmer, shine, show, showiness, sparkle, splendour, tinsel.

gloat *v* crow, exult, eye, glory, ogle, rejoice, relish, revel in, rub it in, triumph, vaunt.

global *adj* all-encompassing, all-inclusive, all-out, comprehensive, encylopaedic, exhaustive, general, globular, international, pandemic, planetary, spherical, thorough, total, unbounded, universal, unlimited, world, world-wide.

antonyms limited, parochial.

globe *n* ball, earth, orb, planet, round, roundure, sphere, world.

globular *adj* globate, globated, globoid, globous, globulous, orbicular, round, spherical, spheroid.

globule *n* bead, bubble, drop, droplet, globulet, particle, pearl, pellet, vesicle, vesicula.

gloom *n* blackness, blues, cloud, cloudiness, damp, dark, darkness, dejection, depression, desolation, despair, despondency, dimness, downheartedness, dullness, dusk, duskiness, gloominess, glumness, low spirits, melancholy, misery, murk, murkiness, obscurity, sadness, shade, shadow, sorrow, twilight, unhappiness, woe.

antonym brightness.

gloominess *n* cheerlessness, darkness, dejection, depression, despondency, dreariness, dullness, gloom, glumness, melancholy, mirkiness, misery, moroseness, mumps, murkiness, pessimism.

antonym brightness.

gloomy *adj* bad, black, blue, chapfallen, cheerless, comfortless, crepuscular, crestfallen, dark, darksome, dejected, delightless, depressing, despondent, dim, disheartening, dismal, dispirited, dispiriting, down, down in the dumps, down in the mouth, downbeat, downcast, downhearted, dreary, dreich, dull, dusky, gloomful, glum, joyless, long-faced, long-visaged, low-spirited, melancholy, mirk(y), miserable, moody, morose, murk(y), obscure, overcast, pessimistic, sad, saddening, saturnine, sepulchral, shadowy, sombre, Stygian, sullen, tenebrous.

antonym bright.

glorification *n* doxology, exaltation, glorifying, idolising, magnification, panegyric, praise, praising, romanticising.

antonyms blame, vilification.

glorify *v* adore, adorn, aggrandise, apotheosise, augment, beatify, bless, canonise, celebrate, deify, dignify, elevate, enhance, ennoble, enshrine, eulogise, exalt, extol, honour, hymn, idolise, illuminate, immortalise, laud, lift up, magnify, panegyrise, praise, raise, revere, sanctify, venerate, worship.

antonyms denounce, vilify.

glorious *adj* beautiful, bright, brilliant, celebrated, dazzling, delightful, distinguished, divine, drunk, effulgent, elated, elevated, eminent, enjoyable, excellent, famed, famous, fine, gorgeous, grand, great, heavenly, honoured, illustrious, intoxicated, magnificent, majestic, marvellous, noble, noted, pleasurable, radiant, renowned, resplendent, shining, splendid, sublime, superb, tipsy, triumphant, wonderful.

antonyms dreadful, inglorious, plain, unknown.

glory *n* adoration, beauty, benediction, blessing, brightness, brilliance, celebrity, dignity, distinction, effulgence, eminence, exaltation, fame, gloire, gloria, gorgeousness, grandeur, gratitude, greatness, heaven, homage, honour, illustriousness, immortality, kudos, laudation, lustre, magnificence, majesty, nobility, pageantry, pomp, praise, prestige, radiance, renown, resplendence, richness, splendour, sublimity, thanksgiving, triumph, veneration, worship.

antonyms blame, restraint.

v boast, crow, delight, exult, gloat, pride oneself, rejoice, relish, revel, triumph.

gloss[1] *n* appearance, brightness, brilliance, burnish, façade, front, gleam, lustre, mask, polish, semblance, sheen, shine, show, surface, varnish, veneer, window-dressing.

gloss over camouflage, conceal, disguise, double-glaze, explain away, gild, glaze over, hide, mask, smooth over, veil, whitewash.

gloss[2] *n* annotation, comment, commentary, elucidation, explanation, footnote, interpretation, note, postillation, scholion, scholium, translation.

v annotate, comment, construe, elucidate, explain, interpret, postil, postillate, translate.

glossary *n* dictionary, idioticon, lexicon, phrase-book, vocabulary, word-book, word-list.

glossy *adj* bright, brilliant, burnished, enamelled, glacé, glassy, glazed, lustrous, polished, sheeny, shining, shiny, silken, silky, sleek, smooth.

antonym mat(t).

glow *n* ardour, bloom, blush, brightness, brilliance, burning, earnestness, effulgence, enthusiasm, excitement, fervour, flush, gleam, glimmer, gusto, impetuosity, incandescence, intensity, lambency, light, luminosity, passion, phosphorescence, radiance, reddening, redness, rosiness, splendour, vehemence, vividness, warmth.

v blush, brighten, burn, colour, fill, flush, gleam, glimmer, glowing, radiate, redden, shine, smoulder, thrill, tingle.

glower *v* frown, glare, look daggers, lower, scowl.

n black look, dirty look, frown, glare, look, lower, scowl, stare.

glowing *adj* adulatory, aglow, beaming, bright, complimentary, ecstatic, enthusiastic, eulogistic, flaming, florid, flushed, gleamy, lambent, laudatory, luminous, panegyrical, rave, red, rhapsodic, rich, ruddy, suffused, vibrant, vivid, warm.

antonyms dull, restrained.

glue *n* adhesive, cement, fish-glue, gum, isinglass, mucilage, paste, size.

v affix, agglutinate, cement, fix, gum, paste, seal, stick.

gluey *adj* adhesive, glutinous, gummy, sticky, viscid, viscous.

glum *adj* chapfallen, churlish, crabbed, crestfallen, dejected, doleful, down, gloomy, glumpish, glumpy, gruff, grumpy, ill-humoured, low, moody, morose, pessimistic, saturnine, sour, sulky, sullen, surly.

antonyms ecstatic, happy.

glut *n* excess, overabundance, oversupply, pleroma, plethora, saturation, superabundance, superfluity, surfeit, surplus.

antonyms lack, scarcity.

v choke, clog, cram, deluge, englut, fill, flesh, flood, gorge, inundate, overfeed, overload, oversupply, sate, satiate, saturate, stuff.

glutinous *adj* adhesive, cohesive, emplastic, gluey, gummy, mucilaginous, ropy, sticky, viscid, viscous.

glutton *n* cormorant, free-liver, gannet, gobbler, gorger, gormandiser, gourmand, guzzler, hog, omnivore, pig, trencherman, vulture, whale.

antonym ascetic.

gluttonous *adj* edacious, esurient, gluttonish, gormandising, greedy, gutsy, hoggish, insatiable, omnivorous, piggish, rapacious, ravenous, ventripotent, voracious.

antonyms abstemious, ascetic.

gluttony *n* edacity, esurience, gormandising, go(u)rmandise, go(u)rmandism, greed, greediness, gulosity, insatiability, omnivorousness, piggishness, rapaciousness, rapacity, voraciousness, voracity.

antonyms abstinence, asceticism.

gnarled *adj* contorted, distorted, gnarly, gnarred, knarred, knotted, knotty, knurled, leathery, rough, rugged, twisted, weather-beaten, wrinkled.

gnaw *v* bite, chew, consume, devour, distress, eat, erode, fret, harry, haunt, munch, nag, nibble, niggle, plague, prey, trouble, wear, worry.

go *v* accord, advance, agree, avail, beat it, blend, chime, complement, concur, conduce, connect, contribute, correspond, decamp, decease, depart, develop, die, disappear, elapse, eventuate, expire, extend, fare, fit, flow, function, gee, happen, harmonise, incline, jib, journey, lapse, lead, lead to, leave, levant, make for, match, mosey, move, naff off, nip, operate, pass, pass away, perform, perish, proceed, progress, rate, reach, repair, result, retreat, roll, run, sally, scram, serve, shift, shove off, slip, sod off, span, spread, stretch, suit, take one's leave, tend, travel, trot, vanish, wag, walk, wend, withdraw, work.

n animation, attempt, bid, crack, drive, dynamism, effort, energy, essay, force, get-up-and-go, life, oomph, pep, shot, spirit, stab, try, turn, verve, vigour, vim, vitality, vivacity, whack, whirl, zest.

go about address, approach, begin, circulate, get abroad, journey, set about, tackle, travel, undertake, wander.

go ahead advance, begin, continue, march on, move, proceed, progress.

go at argue, attack, blame, criticise, impugn, set about, turn on.

go away bugger off, decamp, depart, disappear, eff off, exit, fuck off, get lost, hop it, imshi, leave, piss off, recede, retreat, scat, scram, vanish, withdraw.

go back backslide, desert, forsake, renege, repudiate, retract, retreat, return, revert.

go by adopt, elapse, flow, follow, heed, observe, pass, proceed, trust.

go down collapse, decline, decrease, degenerate, deteriorate, drop, fail, fall, founder, go under, lose, set, sink, submerge, submit, succumb.

go far advance, blaze a trail, do well, progress, succeed.

go for admire, assail, assault, attack, be into, choose, clutch at, dig, enjoy, fall on, favour, fetch, hold with, like, lunge at, obtain, prefer, reach, seek, set about.

go ill with destroy, endanger, harm, imperil, injure, jeopardise, put at hazard, put at risk, ruin.

go in for adopt, embrace, engage in, enter, enter for, espouse, follow, participate in, practise, pursue, take part in, take up, undertake.

go into analyse, begin, check out, consider, delve into, develop, discuss, dissect, enquire into, enter, examine, investigate, make a study of, participate in, probe, pursue, review, scrutinise, study, sus out, undertake.

go mad go bonkers, go crazy, go nuts, take leave of one's senses.

go missing be nowhere to be found, disappear, get lost, scarper, vamoose, vanish.

go off abscond, blow up, decamp, depart, deteriorate, detonate, dislike, explode, fire, happen, leave, occur, part, proceed, quit, rot, turn, vamoose, vanish.

go on behave, blether, chatter, continue, endure, happen, last, last out, occur, persist, prattle, proceed, ramble on, stay, waffle, witter.

go out depart, die out, exit, expire, fade out, leave, obsolesce.

go over detail, examine, inspect, list, overname, peruse, read, recall, recapitulate, rehearse, reiterate, review, revise, scan, skim, study.

go through bear, brave, check, consume, endure, examine, exhaust, experience, explore, face, hunt, investigate, look, rehearse, search, squander, suffer, tolerate, undergo, use, withstand.

go to bed bed down, go to sleep, hit the hay, hit the sack, kip, kip down, retire, turn in.

go together accord, agree, chime, fit, gee, harmonise, jibe, match.

go to pieces break down, capitulate, collapse, crack up, crumble, crumple, disintegrate, fall apart, lose control, lose one's head.

go to seed decay, decline, degenerate, deteriorate, go downhill, go to pot, go to waste, underachieve.

go to the dogs be ruined, degenerate, deteriorate, fail, go down the drain, go to pot, go to rack and ruin.

go under close down, collapse, default, die, drown, fail, fold, founder, go down, sink, submerge, succumb.

go with accompany, agree, blend, chime, complement, concur, correspond, court, date, fit, gee, go steady, harmonise, jibe, match, suit.

go wrong boob, break, break down, come to grief, come to nothing, come ungummed, come unstuck, conk out, cut out, err, fail, fall through, flop, go astray, go off the rails, go on the blink, go phut, lapse, malfunction, miscarry, misfire, sin, slip up.

goad *n* fillip, impetus, incentive, incitement, irritation, jab, motivation, poke, pressure, prod, push, spur, stimulation, stimulus, thrust, urge.

v annoy, arouse, badger, bullyrag, chivvy, drive, egg on, exasperate, exhort, harass, hassle, hector, hound, impel, incite, infuriate, instigate, irritate, lash, madden, nag, needle, persecute, prick, prod, prompt, propel, push, spur, stimulate, sting, urge, vex, worry.

go-ahead *n* agreement, assent, authorisation, clearance, consent, fiat, green light, leave, OK, permission, sanction.

antonyms ban, embargo, moratorium, veto.

adj ambitious, avant-garde, enterprising, goey, go-getting, pioneering, progressive, up-and-coming.

antonyms sluggish, unenterprising.

goal *n* aim, ambition, aspiration, bourn(e), design, destination, destiny, end, grail, intention, limit, mark, object, objective, purpose, target.

goat-like *adj* capriform, caprine, concupiscent, foolish, giddy, goatish, hircine, horny, lascivious, libidinous, lustful, randy, silly.

gobble *v* bolt, consume, cram, devour, gorge, gulp, guttle, guzzle, hog, put away, shovel, slabber, stuff, swallow, wire into, wolf.

go-between *n* agent, broker, contact, dealer, factor, informer, intermediary, internuncio, liaison, mediator, medium, messenger, middleman, ombudsman, pander, pimp, procuress.

goblet *n* balloon glass, brandy-glass, chalice, drinking-cup, hanap, Paris goblet, quaich, rummer, tass, wine-glass.

goblin *n* barghest, bogey, bogle, brownie, bugbear, demon, esprit follet, fiend, gremlin, hobgoblin, imp, kelpie, kobold, lubber fiend, nis, nix, nixie, pooka, red-cap, red-cowl, spirit, sprite.

God, god *n* Allah, avatar, Brahma, deity, divinity, genius, Godhead, Holy One, idol, Jah, Jehovah, joss, Jove, kami, lar, Lord, Lord God, monad, Mumbo-jumbo, numen, penates, power, Providence, spirit, the Almighty, the Creator, tutelar, tutelary, Yahweh, Zeus.

god-forsaken *adj* abandoned, backward, benighted, bleak, deserted, desolate, dismal, dreary, forlorn, gloomy, isolated, lonely, miserable, neglected, remote, unfrequented, wretched.

antonym congenial.

godless *adj* atheistic, depraved, evil, heathen, impious, irreligious, irreverent, nullifidian, pagan, profane, sacrilegious, ungodly, unholy, unprincipled, unrighteous, wicked.

antonyms godly, pious.

godlike *adj* celestial, deiform, divine, exalted, heavenly, saintly, sublime, superhuman, theomorphic, transcendent.

godly *adj* blameless, devout, god-fearing, good, holy, innocent, pious, pure, religious, righteous, saintly, virtuous.

antonyms godless, impious.

godsend *n* blessing, boon, fluke, lucky break, manna, miracle, stroke of luck, windfall.

antonyms blow, bolt from the blue, bombshell, setback.

going-over *n* analysis, beating, buffeting, castigation, chastisement, check, check-up, chiding, doing, dressing-down, drubbing, examination, inspection, investigation, lecture, probe, rebuke, reprimand, review, row, scolding, scrutiny, study, survey, thrashing, thumping, treatment, trouncing, whipping.

golden *adj* advantageous, aureate, auric, auspicious, best, blissful, blond(e), bright, brilliant, delightful, excellent, fair, favourable, favoured, flaxen, flourishing, glorious, happy, inaurate, invaluable, joyful, lustrous, opportune, precious, priceless, promising, propitious, prosperous, resplendent, rich, rosy, shining, successful, timely, valuable, xanthous, yellow.

goldmine *n* dripping roast, Golconda, gold-dust, golden goose, widow's cruse.

gone *adj* absent, astray, away, broken, bygone, closed, concluded, consumed, dead, deceased, defunct, departed, disappeared, done, elapsed, ended, extinct, finished, kaput, lacking, lost, missed, missing, over, over and done with, past, pregnant, spent, used, vanished, wanting.

goo *n* crud, glaur, grease, grime, gunge, gunk, matter, mire, muck, mud, ooze, scum, slime, sludge, slush, stickiness.

good *adj* able, acceptable, accomplished, adept, adequate, admirable, adroit, advantageous, agreeable, altruistic, amiable, ample, appropriate, approved, approving, auspicious, authentic, balmy, beneficent, beneficial, benevolent, benign, bona fide, bonzer, boshta, bosker, bright, brotherly, budgeree, buoyant, calm, capable, capital, charitable, cheerful, choice, clear, clever, cloudless, commendable, competent, complete, congenial, considerate, convenient, convivial, correct, decorous, dependable, deserving, dexterous, dutiful, eatable, efficient, enjoyable, entire, estimable, ethical, excellent, exemplary, expert, extensive, fair, favourable, fine, first-class, first-rate, fit, fitting, friendly, full, genuine, gracious, gratifying, great, happy, healthy, helpful, honest, honourable, humane, kind, kindly, large, legitimate, long, loyal, mannerly, merciful, meritorious, mild, moral, nice, noble, nourishing, nutritious, obedient, obliging, opportune, orderly, pious, pleasant, pleasing, pleasurable, polite, positive, praiseworthy, precious, presentable, professional, proficient, profitable, proper, propitious, rattling, real, reliable, right, righteous, safe, salubrious, salutary, satisfactory, satisfying, seemly, serviceable, sizeable, skilful, skilled, solid, sound, special, splendid, substantial, sufficient, suitable, sunny, super, superior, sustaining, talented, tested, thorough, tranquil, true, trustworthy, uncorrupted, untainted, upright, useful, valid, valuable, virtuous, well-behaved, well-disposed, well-mannered, whole, wholesome, worthwhile, worthy.

n advantage, avail, behalf, behoof, benefit, boon, convenience, excellence, gain, goodness, interest, merit, morality, probity, profit, rectitude, right, righteousness, service, uprightness, use, usefulness, virtue, weal, welfare, well-being, worth, worthiness.

good health *interj* à votre santé, cheers, Gesundheit, kia-ora, prosit, salud, salute, your health.

n haleness, hardiness, health, healthiness, heartiness, lustiness, robustness, soundness, strength, vigour, vitality.

antonyms ill health, invalidism.

good-bye *n, interj* adieu, adiós, arrivederci, au revoir, auf Wiedersehen, chin-chin, ciao, farewell, leave-taking, parting, valediction, valedictory.

good-for-nothing *n* black sheep, bum, drone, idler, layabout, lazy-bones, loafer, lorel, losel, mauvais sujet, ne'er-do-well, profligate, rapscallion, reprobate, scapegrace, vaurien, waster, wastrel.

antonyms achiever, success, winner.

adj do-nothing, feckless, idle, indolent, irresponsible, lorel, losel, no-good, profligate, reprobate, slothful, useless, worthless.

antonyms conscientious, successful.

good-humoured *adj* affable, amiable, approachable, blithe, cheerful, congenial, expansive, genial, good-tempered, happy, jocund, jovial, pleasant.

antonym ill-humoured.

good-looking *adj* attractive, beautiful, bonny, comely, easy on the eye, fair, handsome, personable, presentable, pretty, well-favoured, well-looking, well-proportioned, well-set-up.

antonyms ill-favoured, plain, ugly.

good-luck charm amulet, periapt, phylactery, porte-bonheur, talisman.

antonym evil eye.

goodly *adj* ample, considerable, good, large, significant, sizeable, substantial, sufficient, tidy.

antonym inadequate.

good-natured *adj* agreeable, amenable, approachable, benevolent, broad-minded, friendly, gentle, good-hearted, helpful, kind, kind-hearted, kindly, neighbourly, open-minded, sympathetic, tolerant, warm-hearted.

antonym ill-natured.

goodness *n* advantage, altruism, beneficence, benefit, benevolence, condescension, excellence, fairness, friendliness, generosity, goodwill, graciousness, honesty, honour, humaneness, humanity, integrity, justness, kindliness, kindness, mercy, merit, morality, nourishment, nutrition, piety, probity, quality, rectitude, righteousness, salubriousness, superiority, unselfishness, uprightness, value, virtue, wholesomeness, worth.

antonyms badness, inferiority, wickedness.

goods *n* appurtenances, bags and baggage, belongings, chattels, commodities, effects, furnishings, furniture, gear, merchandise, movables, paraphernalia, plenishing, possessions, property, stock, stuff, traps, vendibles, wares.

goodwill *n* altruism, amity, benevolence, compassion, earnestness, favour, friendliness, friendship, generosity, heartiness, kindliness, loving-kindness, sincerity, sympathy, zeal.

antonym ill-will.

goody-goody *adj* pious, priggish, sanctimonious, self-righteous, ultra-virtuous, unctuous.

gooey *adj* clarty, gluey, glutinous, gummy, gungy, maudlin, mawkish, mucilaginous, sentimental, slushy, soft, sticky, syrupy, tacky, thick, viscid, viscous.

gooseberry *n* goosegob, goosegog, groser, groset, third person.

gooseflesh *n* creeps, duck bumps, formication, goose bumps, goose-pimples, grue, heebie-jeebies, horripilation, horrors, shivers, shudders.

gore[1] *n* blood, bloodiness, bloodshed, butchery, carnage, cruor, grume, slaughter.

gore[2] *v* impale, penetrate, pierce, rend, spear, spit, stab, stick, transfix, wound.

n flare, gair, godet, gusset.

gorge[1] *n* abyss, barranca, canyon, chasm, cleft, clough, defile, fissure, gap, gulch, gully, pass, ravine.

gorge[2] *v* bolt, cram, devour, feed, fill, fill one's face, glut, gluttonise, gobble, gormandise, gulp, guzzle, hog, make a pig of oneself, overeat, ravin, sate, satiate, stuff, surfeit, swallow, wolf.

antonym abstain.

gorgeous *adj* attractive, beautiful, bright, brilliant, dazzling, delightful, elegant, enjoyable, exquisite, fine, flamboyant, glamorous, glittering, glorious, good, good-looking, grand, lovely, luxuriant, luxurious, magnificent, opulent, pleasing, ravishing, resplendent, rich, showy, splendid, splendiferous, stunning, sumptuous, superb.

antonyms dull, plain, seedy.

gory *adj* blood-soaked, bloodstained, bloodthirsty, bloody, brutal, ensanguined, murderous, sanguinary, sanguineous, sanguinolent, savage.

gospel *n* certainty, credo, creed, doctrine, evangel, fact, kerygma, message, news, revelation, teaching, testament, tidings, truth, verity.

gossamer *adj* airy, cobwebby, delicate, diaphanous, fine, flimsy, gauzy, insubstantial, light, sheer, shimmering, silky, thin, translucent, transparent.

antonyms heavy, opaque, thick.

gossip[1] *n* blether, bush telegraph, causerie, chinwag, chitchat, clash, clash-ma-clavers, clish-clash, clishmaclaver, gup, hearsay, idle talk, jaw, newsmongering, prattle, report, rumour, scandal, schmooze, small talk, tittle-tattle, yackety-yak.

gossip[2] *n* babbler, blatherskite, blether, bletherskate, busybody, chatterbox, chatterer, gossip-monger, newsmonger, nosy parker, prattler, quidnunc, rumourer, scandalmonger, tabby, talebearer, tattler, telltale, whisperer.

v blather, blether, bruit, chat, clash, gabble, jaw, prattle, rumour, tattle, tell tales, whisper.

gouge *v* chisel, claw, cut, dig, extract, force, gash, grave, groove, hack, hollow, incise, scoop, score, scratch, slash.

n cut, furrow, gash, groove, hack, hollow, incision, notch, scoop, score, scratch, slash, trench.

gourmand *n* cormorant, free-liver, gannet, glutton, gorger, gormandiser, guzzler, hog, omnivore, pig, trencherman, whale.

antonym ascetic.

gourmet *n* arbiter elegantiae, arbiter elegantiarum, bon vivant, bon viveur, connoisseur, dainty eater, epicure, epicurean, gastronome, gastronomer, gastrosoph, gastrosopher.

antonym omnivore.

govern *v* administer, allay, bridle, check, command, conduct, contain, control, curb, decide, determine, direct, discipline, guide, influence, inhibit, lead, manage, master, order, oversee, pilot, preside, quell, regulate, reign, restrain, rule, steer, subdue, superintend, supervise, sway, tame, underlie.

governess *n* companion, duenna, gouvernante, guide, instructress, mentor, teacher, tutoress, tutress.

governing *adj* commanding, dominant, dominative, guiding, leading, overriding, predominant, prevailing, reigning, ruling, supreme, transcendent, uppermost.

government *n* administration, authority, charge, command, conduct, control, direction, domination, dominion, Establishment, executive, governance, guidance, kingcraft, law, management, ministry, polity, powers-that-be, raj, régime, regimen, regulation, restraint, rule, sovereignty, state, statecraft, superintendence, supervision, surveillance, sway.

governor *n* adelantado, administrator, alcalde, alderman, boss, chief, commander, commissioner, comptroller, controller, corrector, director, executive, gubernator, hakim, head, leader, manager, naik, overseer, ruler, superintendent, supervisor, vali.

gown *n* costume, creation, dress, dressing-gown, frock, garb, garment, habit, kirtle, négligé, robe.

grab *v* affect, annex, appropriate, bag, capture, catch, catch hold of, clutch, collar, commandeer, grasp, grip, impress, latch on to, nab, pluck, ramp, rap, seize, snap up, snatch, strike, usurp.

grace[1] *n* attractiveness, beauty, benefaction, beneficence, benevolence, benignity, benison, breeding, charity, charm, clemency, comeliness, compassion, compassionateness, consideration, courtesy, cultivation, decency, decorum, deftness, ease, elegance, eloquence, etiquette, favour, finesse, fluency, forgiveness, generosity, goodness, goodwill, gracefulness, graciousness, indulgence, kindliness, kindness, leniency, lenity, love, loveliness, mannerliness, manners, mercifulness, mercy, merit, pardon, pleasantness, poise, polish, propriety, quarter, refinement, reprieve, shapeliness, tact, tastefulness, unction, virtue.

v adorn, beautify, bedeck, deck, decorate, dignify, distinguish, dress, elevate, embellish, enhance, enrich, favour, garnish, glorify, honour, ornament, prettify, set off, trim.

antonyms deface, detract from, spoil.

grace[2] *n* benediction, benedictus, blessing, consecration, prayer, thanks, thanksgiving.

graceful *adj* agile, balletic, beautiful, becoming, charming, comely, deft, easy, elegant, facile, feat, feline, fine, flowing, fluid, gainly, genty, gracile, lightsome, natural, pleasing, pliant, slender, smooth, suave, supple, tasteful, willowish, willowy.

antonym graceless.

graceless *adj* awkward, barbarous, boorish, brazen, clumsy, coarse, crude, forced, gauche, gawky, ill-mannered, improper, incorrigible, indecorous, inelegant, inept, loutish, reprobate, rough, rude, shameless, uncouth, ungainly, ungraceful, unmannerly, unsophisticated, untutored, vulgar.

antonym graceful.

gracious *adj* accommodating, affable, affluent, amenable, amiable, beneficent, benevolent, benign, benignant, charitable, chivalrous, civil, compassionate, complaisant, condescending, considerate, cordial, courteous, courtly, elegant, friendly, grand, hospitable, indulgent, kind, kindly, lenient, loving, luxurious, merciful, mild, obliging, pleasant, pleasing, polite, refined, sweet, well-mannered.

antonym ungracious.

gradation *n* ablaut, arrangement, array, classification, degree, depth, grade, grading, grouping, level, mark, measurement, notch, ordering, place, point, position, progress, progression, rank, sequence, series, shading, sorting, stage, step, succession.

grade *n* acclivity, bank, brand, category, class, condition, dan, declivity, degree, downgrade, echelon, gradation, gradient, group, hill, incline, level, mark, notch, order, place, position, quality, rank, rise, rung, size, slope, stage, station, step, upgrade.

v arrange, blend, brand, categorise, class, classify, docket, evaluate, group, label, mark, order, pigeonhole, range, rank, rate, shade, size, sort, type, value.

gradient *n* acclivity, bank, decline, declivity, downgrade, grade, hill, incline, rise, slope, upgrade.

gradual *adj* cautious, continuous, deliberate, even, gentle, graduated, leisurely, measured, moderate, piecemeal, progressive, regular, slow, steady, step-by-step, successive, unhurried.

antonyms precipitate, sudden.

gradually *adv* bit by bit, by degrees, cautiously, drop by drop, evenly, gently, gingerly, imperceptibly, in penny numbers, inch by inch, inchmeal, little by little, moderately, piece by piece, piecemeal, progressively, slowly, steadily, step by step, unhurriedly.

graduate[1] *v* arrange, calibrate, classify, grade, group, make the grade, mark off, measure out, order, pass, proportion, qualify, range, rank, regulate, sort.

graduate[2] *n* alumna, alumnus, bachelor, diplomate, diplômé, diplômée, doctor, fellow, graduand, licentiate, literate, master, member.

graft *n* bud, engraft, engraftation, engraftment, heteroplasty, imp, implant, implantation, insert, scion, shoot, splice, sprout, transplant.

v engraft, implant, insert, join, splice, transplant.

grain *n* atom, bit, cereals, corn, crumb, doit, fibre, fragment, granule, grist, grits, iota, jot, kernel, marking, mite, modicum, molecule, morsel, mote, nap, ounce, panic, particle, pattern, piece, scintilla, scrap, scruple, seed, smidgeon, spark, speck, surface, suspicion, texture, trace, weave, whit.

grammarian *n* grammaticaster, grammatist, linguist, linguistician, philologist, Priscianist.

grand *adj* A1, admirable, affluent, ambitious, august, chief, condescending, dignified, elevated, eminent, exalted, excellent, fine, first-class, first-rate, glorious, gracious, grandiose, great, haughty, head, highest, illustrious, imperious, imposing, impressive, large, leading, lofty, lordly, luxurious, magnificent, main, majestic, marvellous, monumental, noble, opulent, ostentatious, outstanding, palatial, patronising, pompous, pre-eminent, pretentious, princely, principal, regal, senior, smashing, splendid, stately, striking, sublime, sumptuous, super, superb, supreme, wonderful.

grandeur *n* augustness, dignity, graciousness, gravitas, greatness, hauteur, imperiousness, importance, loftiness, magnificence, majesty, morgue, nobility, pomp, splendour, state, stateliness, sublimity.

antonyms humbleness, lowliness, simplicity.

grandfather *n* gaffer, goodsire, grandad, grand(d)addy, grandpa, grandsire, granfer, gutcher.

grandiloquence *n* affectation, bombast, euphuism, fustian, Gongorism, magniloquence, orotundity, pomposity, pretentiousness, rhetoric, turgidity.

antonyms plainness, restraint, simplicity.

grandiloquent *adj* bombastic, euphuistic, flowery, fustian, Gongoristic, grandiloquous, high-flown, high-sounding, inflated, magniloquent, orotund, pompous, pretentious, rhetorical, swollen, turgid.

antonyms plain, restrained, simple.

grandiose *adj* affected, ambitious, bombastic, euphuistic, extravagant, flamboyant, grand, high-flown, imposing, impressive, lofty, magnificent, majestic, monumental, ostentatious, pompous, ponderous, pretentious, showy, stately, Wagnerian, weighty.

antonym unpretentious.

grandmother *n* gammer, gran, grandma, grandmama, granny.

grant *v* accede to, accord, acknowledge, admit, agree to, allocate, allot, allow, apportion, assign, award, bestow, cede, concede, confer, consent to, convey, deign, dispense, donate, give, impart, permit, present, provide, transfer, transmit, vouchsafe, yield.

antonyms deny, refuse.

n accord, admission, allocation, allotment, allowance, annuity, award, benefaction, bequest, boon, bounty, bursary, concession, donation, endowment, gift, honorarium, present, scholarship, subsidy, subvention.

granular *adj* crumbly, grainy, granulase, granulated, granulous, gravelly, gritty, murly, rough, sabulose, sabulous, sandy.

granule *n* atom, bead, crumb, fragment, grain, iota, jot, molecule, particle, pellet, scrap, seed, speck.

graph *n* chart, diagram, grid, histogram, table.

graphic *adj* blow-by-blow, clear, cogent, delineated, delineative, descriptive, detailed, diagrammatic, drawn, explicit, expressive, forcible, illustrative, lively, lucid, pictorial, picturesque, representational, seen, specific, striking, telling, visible, visual, vivid.

antonyms impressionistic, vague.

grapple *v* attack, battle, catch, clash, clasp, clinch, close, clutch, combat, come to grips, confront, contend, cope, deal with, encounter, engage, face, fasten, fight, grab, grasp, grip, gripe, hold, hug, lay hold, make fast, seize, snatch, struggle, tackle, tussle, wrestle.

antonyms avoid, evade.

grasp *v* catch, catch on, clasp, clinch, clutch, comprehend, follow, get, grab, grapple, grip, gripe, hold, lay hold of, realise, savvy, see, seize, snatch, twig, understand.

n acquaintance, apprehension, awareness, capacity, clasp, clutches, compass, competence, comprehension, control, conversance, conversancy, embrace, expertness, extent, familiarity, grip, hold, holt, intimacy, ken, knowledge, mastery, perception, possession, power, range, reach, realisation, scope, sway, sweep, tenure, understanding.

grasping *adj* acquisitive, avaricious, close-fisted, covetous, greedy, mean, mercenary, miserly, niggardly, parsimonious, penny-pinching, rapacious, selfish, stingy, tight-fisted, usurious.

antonym generous.

grass *n* fog, foggage, grama, grassland, green, greensward, hay, herbage, lawn, pasturage, pasture, sward, turf, verdure.

grasshopper *n* cicada, cigale, cricket, grig, katydid, locust.

grassland *n* downs, lay, lea, ley, llano, meadow, meadowland, pampas, pasture, prairie, savanna, steppe, sward, veldt.

grate *v* aggravate, annoy, chafe, comminute, creak, exasperate, fret, gall, get on one's nerves, granulate, gride, grind, irk, irritate, jar, mince, nettle, peeve, pulverise, rankle, rasp, rub, scrape, scratch, set one's teeth on edge, shred, triturate, vex.

grateful *adj* appreciative, aware, beholden, indebted, mindful, obligated, obliged, sensible, thankful.

antonym ungrateful.

gratification *n* contentment, delight, elation, enjoyment, fruition, fulfilment, glee, indulgence, joy, jubilation, kicks, pleasure, recompense, relish, reward, satisfaction, thrill, triumph.

antonym frustration.

gratify *v* appease, cater to, content, delight, favour, fulfil, gladden, humour, indulge, pander to, please, pleasure, recompense, requite, satisfy, thrill.

antonyms frustrate, thwart.

grating[1] *adj* annoying, cacophonous, disagreeable, discordant, displeasing, grinding, harsh, horrisonant, irksome, irritating, jarring, rasping, raucous, scraping, squeaky, strident, unharmonious, unmelodious, unpleasant, vexatious.

antonyms harmonious, pleasing.

grating[2] *n* grid, grill, grille, hack, heck, lattice, lattice-work, treillage, treille, trellis, trelliswork.

gratitude *n* acknowledgement, appreciation, awareness, gratefulness, indebtedness, mindfulness, obligation, recognition, thankfulness, thanks.

antonym ingratitude.

gratuitous *adj* assumed, baseless, buckshee, causeless, complimentary, free, gratis, groundless, irrelevant, needless, spontaneous, superfluous, unasked-for, uncalled-for, undeserved, unearned, unfounded, unjustified, unmerited, unnecessary, unpaid, unprovoked, unrewarded, unsolicited, unwarranted, voluntary, wanton.

antonyms justified, reasonable.

gratuity *n* baksheesh, beer-money, benefaction, bonus, boon, bounty, dash, donation, donative, douceur, drink-money, gift, lagniappe, largess, perquisite, pourboire, present, recompense, reward, tip, Trinkgeld.

grave[1] *n* barrow, burial-place, burying-place, cairn, cist, crypt, long home, mausoleum, pit, sepulchre, tomb, vault.

grave[2] *adj* acute, Catonian, critical, crucial, dangerous, depressing, dignified, disquieting, dour, dull, earnest, exigent, gloomy, grim, grim-faced, hazardous, heavy, important, leaden, long-faced, momentous, muted, perilous, ponderous, preoccupied, pressing, quiet, reserved, restrained, sad, sage, saturnine, sedate, serious, severe, significant, sober, solemn, sombre, staid, subdued, thoughtful, threatening, unsmiling, urgent, vital, weighty.

antonyms cheerful, light, slight, trivial.

gravel *n* chesil, grail, hogging, shingle.

gravelly *adj* ginny, glareous, grainy, granular, grating, gritty, gruff, guttural, harsh, hoarse, pebbly, sabulose, sabulous, shingly, throaty.

antonyms clear, fine, powdery.

graveyard *n* boneyard, burial-ground, burial-place, burying-place, cemetery, churchyard, God's acre, Golgotha, necropolis.

gravitate *v* descend, drop, fall, head for, incline, lean, move, precipitate, settle, sink, tend.

gravity *n* acuteness, consequence, demureness, dignity, earnestness, exigency, gloom, gravitas, grimness, hazardousness, importance, magnitude, moment, momentousness, perilousness, ponderousness, reserve, restraint, sedateness, seriousness, severity, significance, sobriety, solemnity, sombreness, thoughtfulness, urgency, weightiness.

antonyms gaiety, levity, triviality.

graze[1] *v* batten, browse, crop, feed, fodder, pasture.

graze[2] *v* abrade, bark, brush, chafe, gride, rub, scart, score, scotch, scrape, scratch, shave, skim, skin, touch.

n abrasion, score, scrape, scratch.

grease *n* dope, dripping, fat, gunge, lard, oil, ointment, sebum, tallow, unction, unguent, wax.

greasy *adj* fatty, fawning, glib, grovelling, ingratiating, lardy, oily, oleaginous, sebaceous, slick, slimy, slippery, smarmy, smeary, smooth, sycophantic, tallowy, toadying, unctuous, waxy.

great *adj* able, ace, active, adept, admirable, adroit, august, big, bulky, capital, celebrated, chief, colossal, consequential, considerable, crack, critical, crucial, decided, devoted, dignified, distinguished, eminent, enormous, enthusiastic, exalted, excellent, excessive, expert, extended, extensive, extravagant, extreme, fab, fabulous, famed, famous, fantastic, fine, finished, first-rate, generous, gigantic, glorious, good, grand, grave, great-hearted, grievous, heavy, heroic, high, high-minded, huge, idealistic, illustrious, immense, important, impressive, inordinate, invaluable, jake, keen, large, leading, lengthy, lofty, long, magnanimous, main, major, mammoth, manifold, marked, marvellous, massive, masterly, momentous, multitudinous, munificent, noble, nonpareil, notable, noteworthy, noticeable, outstanding, paramount, ponderous, precious, pre-eminent, priceless, primary, princely, principal, prodigious, proficient, prolific, prolonged, prominent, pronounced, protracted, remarkable, renowned, senior, serious, significant, skilful, skilled, strong, stupendous, sublime, superb, superior, superlative, swingeing, talented, terrific, tremendous, valuable, vast, virtuoso, voluminous, weighty, wonderful, zealous.

antonyms insignificant, pusillanimous, small, unimportant.

greatly *adv* abundantly, considerably, enormously, exceedingly, extremely, highly, hugely, immensely, impressively, markedly, mightily, much, notably, noticeably, powerfully, remarkably, significantly, substantially, tremendously, vastly.

greatness *n* amplitude, bulk, celebrity, dignity, distinction, eminence, excellence, fame, force, generosity, genius, glory, grandeur, gravity, great-heartednes, heaviness, heroism, high-mindedness, hugeness, idealism, illustriousness, immensity, import, importance, intensity, largeness, length, loftiness, lustre, magnanimity, magnitude, majesty, mass, moment, momentousness, nobility, nobleness, note, potency, power, prodigiousness, renown, seriousness, significance, size, stateliness, strength, sublimity, superbness, urgency, vastness, weight.

antonyms insignificance, pettiness, pusillanimity, smallness.

greed *n* acquisitiveness, anxiety, avidity, covetousness, craving, cupidity, desire, eagerness, edacity, esurience, esuriency, gluttony, gormandising, gormandism, gourmandise, greediness, gulosity, hunger, insatiability, insatiableness, itchy palm, land-hunger, longing, pleonexia, plutolatry, rapacity, ravenousness, selfishness, voraciousness, voracity.

antonym abstemiousness.

greedy *adj* acquisitive, anxious, avaricious, avid, covetous, craving, curious, desirous, eager, edacious, esurient, gare, gluttonish, gluttonous, gormandising, grasping, gripple, gutsy, hoggery, hoggish, hungry, impatient, insatiable, itchy-palmed, land-grabbing, money-grubbing, piggish, pleonectic, rapacious, ravenous, selfish, ventripotent, voracious.

antonym abstemious.

green *adj* blooming, budding, callow, covetous, credulous, emerald, envious, flourishing, fresh, glaucous, grassy, grudging, gullible, ignorant, ill, immature, inexperienced, inexpert, ingenuous, innocent, jealous, leafy, naive, nauseous, new, pale, pliable, raw, recent, resentful, sick, starry-eyed, supple, tender, unhealthy, unpractised, unripe, unseasoned, unsophisticated, untrained, untried, unversed, verdant, verdurous, vert, virescent, virid, viridescent, vitreous, wan, wet behind the ears, young.

n common, grass, greensward, lawn, sward, turf.

greenery *n* foliage, greenness, greenth, vegetation, verdancy, verdure, virescence, viridescence, viridity.

greenhorn *n* apprentice, beginner, catechumen, fledgling, ignoramus, ingénué, initiate, Johnnie raw, learner, naïf, neophyte, newcomer, novice, novitiate, recruit, rookie, simpleton, tenderfoot, tyro.

antonyms old hand, veteran.

greenhouse *n* conservatory, glasshouse, hothouse, nursery, pavilion, vinery.

greet *v* accost, acknowledge, address, compliment, hail, hallo, halloo, meet, receive, salute, wave to, welcome.

antonym ignore.

greeting *n* abrazo, accost, acknowledgement, address, aloha, hail, kiss of peace, reception, salaam, salutation, salute, salve, the time of day, welcome.

greetings *n* best wishes, civilities, compliments, devoirs, formalities, good wishes, love, regards, respects, salutations.

gregarious *adj* affable, chummy, companionable, convivial, cordial, extrovert, friendly, outgoing, pally, sociable, social, warm.

antonym unsociable.

grey *adj* aged, ancient, anonymous, ashen, bloodless, characterless, cheerless, cloudy, colourless, dark, depressing, dim, dismal, drab, dreary, dull, elderly, experienced, glaucous, gloomy, grège, greige, griseous, grizzle, grizzled, hoar, hoary, indistinct, leaden, liard, livid, mature, murksome, murky, neutral, old, overcast, pale, pallid, sunless, uncertain, unclear, unidentifiable, venerable, wan.

grid *n* graticule, grating, gridison, grill, grille, lattice.

grief *n* ache, affliction, agony, anguish, bereavement, blow, burden, dejection, desiderium, desolation, distress, dole, grievance, heartache, heartbreak, lamentation, misery, mournfulness, mourning, pain, regret, remorse, sadness, sorrow, suffering, tragedy, trial, tribulation, trouble, woe.

antonym happiness.

grief-stricken *adj* afflicted, agonised, broken, broken-hearted, crushed, desolate, despairing, devastated, disconsolate, distracted, grieving, heartbroken, inconsolable, mourning, overcome, overwhelmed, sad, sorrowful, sorrowing, stricken, unhappy, woebegone, wretched.

antonym overjoyed.

grievance *n* affliction, beef, bitch, charge, complaint, damage, distress, gravamen, grief, gripe, grouse, hardship, injury, injustice, moan, peeve, resentment, sorrow, trial, tribulation, trouble, unhappiness, wrong.

grieve *v* ache, afflict, agonise, bemoan, bewail, complain, crush, cut to the quick, deplore, distress, disturb, eat one's heart out, harrow, hurt, injure, lament, mourn, pain, regret, rue, sadden, sorrow, suffer, upset, wail, weep, wound.

grieved *adj* abashed, affronted, ashamed, desolated, displeased, distressed, horrified, hurt, injured, offended, pained, sad, saddened, shocked, sorry, upset, wounded.

grievous *adj* appalling, atrocious, burdensome, calamitous, damaging, deplorable, devastating, distressing, dreadful, flagrant, glaring, grave, harmful, heart-rending, heavy, heinous, hurtful, injurious, intolerable, lamentable, monstrous, mournful, offensive, oppressive, outrageous, overwhelming, painful, pitiful, plightful, severe, shameful, shocking, sorrowful, tragic, unbearable, wounding.

grievously *adv* appallingly, badly, deplorably, dernly, desperately, distressingly, dreadfully, gravely, heinously, lamentably, monstrously, outrageously, painfully, seriously, severely, shamefully, shockingly, unforgivably.

grim *adj* adamant, cruel, doom-laden, dour, fearsome, ferocious, fierce, forbidding, formidable, frightening, frightful, ghastly, grisly, gruesome, harsh, hideous, horrible, horrid, implacable, merciless, morose, relentless, repellent, resolute, ruthless, severe, shocking, sinister, stern, sullen, surly, terrible, unpleasant, unrelenting, unwelcome, unyielding.

antonyms benign, congenial, pleasant.

grimace *n* face, fit of the face, frown, moue, mouth, pout, scowl, smirk, sneer, wry face.

v fleer, frown, girn, make a face, mop, mop and mow, mouth, mow, mug, pout, scowl, smirk, sneer.

grime *n* dirt, filth, muck, smut, soot, squalor.

grimy *adj* begrimed, besmeared, besmirched, contaminated, dirty, filthy, foul, grubby, murky, reechy, smudgy, smutty, soiled, sooty, squalid.

antonyms clean, pure.

grind *v* abrade, beaver, bray, comminute, crush, drudge, file, gnash, granulate, grate, grit, kibble, labour, levigate, lucubrate, mill, polish, pound, powder, pulverise, sand, scrape, sharpen, slave, smooth, sweat, swot, toil, triturate, whet.

n chore, drudgery, exertion, grindstone, labour, round, routine, slavery, sweat, task, toil.

grind down afflict, crush, harass, harry, hound, oppress, persecute, plague, trouble, tyrannise.

grip *n* acquaintance, clasp, clutches, comprehension, control, domination, embrace, grasp, handclasp, hold, influence, keeping, mastery, perception, possession, power, purchase, sway, tenure, understanding.

v absorb, catch, clasp, clutch, compel, divert, engross, enthrall, entrance, fascinate, grasp, hold, involve, latch on to, mesmerise, rivet, seize, spellbind, thrill, vice.

gripe *v* beef, bellyache, bitch, carp, complain, groan, grouch, grouse, grumble, moan, nag, whine, whinge.

n ache, aching, affliction, beef, bitch, colic, collywobbles, complaint, cramps, distress, grievance, griping, groan, grouch, grouse, grumble, moan, objection, pain, pang, pinching, spasm, stomach-ache, twinge.

gripping *adj* absorbing, compelling, compulsive, diverting, engrossing, enthralling, entrancing, exciting, fascinating, riveting, spellbinding, suspenseful, thrilling, unputdownable.

grisly *adj* abominable, appalling, awful, dreadful, eldritch, frightful, ghastly, grim, gruesome, hair-raising, hideous, horrible, horrid, macabre, shocking, sickening, terrible, terrifying, weird.

antonym delightful.

grit[1] *n* chesil, dust, grail, gravel, hogging, pebbles, sand, shingle, swarf.

v clench, gnash, grate, grind, lock.

grit[2] backbone, bottle, bravery, courage, determination, doggedness, foison, fortitude, fushion, gameness, guts, hardihood, mettle, nerve, perseverance, pluck, resolution, spine, spirit, spunk, stamina, staying power, tenacity, toughness.

gritty *adj* abrasive, brave, courageous, determined, dogged, dusty, game, grainy, granular, gravelly, hardy, mettlesome, pebbly, plucky, resolute, rough, sabulose, sabulous, sandy, shingly, spirited, spunky, steadfast, tenacious, tough.

antonyms fine, smooth, spineless.

grizzle *v* cry, fret, girn, mewl, pule, sniffle, snivel, snuffle, whimper, whine, whinge.

grizzled *adj* canescent, grey, grey-haired, grey-headed, greying, griseous, grizzly, hoar, hoary, pepper-and-salt.

groan *n* complaint, cry, moan, objection, outcry, protest, sigh, wail.

antonym cheer.

v complain, cry, lament, moan, object, protest, sigh, wail.

antonym cheer.

grocer *n* dealer, épicier, greengrocer, Italian warehouseman, purveyor, spicer, storekeeper, supplier, victualler.

groggy *adj* befuddled, confused, dazed, dizzy, dopey, faint, fuddled, knocked-up, muzzy, punch-drunk, reeling, shaky, stunned, stupefied, unsteady, weak, wobbly, woozy.

antonym lucid.

groom *v* brush, clean, coach, curry, dress, drill, educate, neaten, nurture, preen, prepare, prime, primp, prink, ready, school, smarten, spruce up, tart up, tend, tidy, titivate, train, turn out, tutor.

groove *n* canal, cannelure, chamfer, channel, chase, cut, cutting, flute, furrow, gutter, hollow, indentation, kerf, rabbet, rebate, rigol, rut, score, scrobe, sulcus, trench, vallecula.

antonym ridge.

grooved *adj* chamfered, channelled, exarate, fluted, furrowed, rabbeted, rutted, scored, scrobiculate, sulcal, sulcate.

antonym ridged.

grope *v* cast about, feel, feel about, feel up, finger, fish, flounder, fumble, goose, grabble, probe, scrabble, search.

gross[1] *adj* apparent, arrant, bawdy, bestial, big, blatant, blue, boorish, broad, brutish, bulky, callous, coarse, colossal, corpulent, crass, crude, cumbersome, dense, downright, dull, earthy, egregious, fat, flagrant, foul, glaring, great, grievous, heavy, heinous, huge, hulking, ignorant, immense, imperceptive, improper, impure, indecent, indelicate, insensitive, large, lewd, low, lumpish, manifest, massive, obese, obscene, obtuse, obvious, offensive, outrageous, outright, overweight, plain, rank, ribald, rude, sensual, serious, shameful, shameless, sheer, shocking, slow, sluggish, smutty, tasteless, thick, uncivil, uncouth, uncultured, undiscriminating, undisguised, unfeeling, unmitigated, unseemly, unsophisticated, unwieldy, utter, vulgar.

antonyms delicate, fine, seemly, slight.

gross[2] *n* aggregate, bulk, entirety, sum, total, totality, whole.

adj aggregate, all-inclusive, complete, entire, inclusive, total, whole.

v accumulate, aggregate, bring, earn, make, rake in, take, total.

grossness *n* bawdiness, bestiality, bigness, blatancy, brutishness, bulkiness, coarseness, corpulence, crassness, crudity, earthiness, egregiousness, fatness, flagrancy, foulness, greatness, grievousness, grossièreté, heaviness, hugeness, ignorance, immensity, impurity, incivility, indecency, indelicacy, insensitivity, licentiousness, lumpishness, obesity, obscenity, obtuseness, obviousness, offensiveness, rankness, ribaldry, rudeness, sensuality, seriousness, shamefulness, shamelessness, sluggishness, smut, smuttiness, tastelessness, thickness, uncouthness, unseemliness, unwieldiness, vulgarity.

antonyms delicacy, fineness, seemliness, slightness.

grotesque *adj* absurd, antic, bizarre, deformed, distorted, extravagant, fanciful, fantastic, freakish, gruesome, hideous, incongruous, laughable, ludicrous, macabre, malformed, misshapen, monstrous, odd, outlandish, preposterous, ridiculous, rococo, strange, ugly, unnatural, unsightly, weird.

n bizarrerie, extravaganza, fantastic figure, gargoyle, gobbo, grotesquerie, manikin.

grotto *n* catacomb, cave, cavern, chamber, dene-hole, grot, souterrain, subterranean (chamber), subterrene, underground chamber.

grouch *v* beef, bellyache, bitch, carp, complain, find fault, gripe, grouse, grumble, moan, whine, whinge.

antonym acquiesce.

n belly-acher, churl, complainer, complaint, crab, crosspatch, crotcheteer, curmudgeon, fault-finder, grievance, gripe, grouse, grouser, grumble, grumbler, malcontent, moan, moaner, murmer, murmurer, mutterer, objection, whiner, whinge, whinger.

grouchy *adj* bad-tempered, cantankerous, captious, churlish, complaining, cross, crotchety, discontented, dissatisfied, grumbling, grumpy, ill-tempered, irascible, irritable, mutinous, peevish, petulant, querulous, sulky, surly, testy, truculent.

antonym contented.

ground *n* arena, background, ball-park, bottom, clay, clod, deck, dirt, dry land, dust, earth, field, foundation, land, loam, mould, park, pitch, sod, soil, solum, stadium, surface, terra firma, terrain, turf.

v acquaint with, base, build up, coach, drill, establish, familiarise with, fix, found, inform, initiate, instruct, introduce, prepare, set, settle, teach, train, tutor.

groundless *adj* absurd, baseless, chimerical, empty, false, gratuitous, idle, illusory, imaginary, irrational, unauthorised, uncalled-for, unfounded, unjustified, unproven, unprovoked, unreasonable, unsubstantiated, unsupported, unwarranted.

antonyms justified, reasonable.

grounds[1] *n* acres, area, country, district, domain, estate, fields, gardens, habitat, holding, land, park, property, realm, surroundings, terrain, territory, tract.

grounds[2] *n* account, argument, base, basis, call, cause, excuse, factor, foundation, inducement, justification, motive, occasion, premise, pretext, principle, rationale, reason, score, vindication.

grounds[3] *n* deposit, dregs, grouts, lees, precipitate, precipitation, sediment, settlings.

groundwork *n* base, basis, cornerstone, essentials, footing, foundation, fundamentals, homework, preliminaries, preparation, research, spadework, underpinnings.

group *n* accumulation, aggregation, assemblage, association, band, batch, bracket, bunch, category, caucus, circle, class, classification, classis, clique, clump, cluster, clutch, cohort, collection, collective, combination, company, conclave, conglomeration, congregation, constellation, core, coterie, covey, crowd, detachment, faction, formation, front, galère, gang, gathering, Gemeinschaft, genus, grouping, knot, lot, nexus, organisation, pack, parti, party, pop-group, set, shower, species, squad, squadron, team, troop.

v arrange, assemble, associate, assort, band, bracket, categorise, class, classify, cluster, collect, congregate, consort, deploy, dispose, fraternise, gather, get together, link, marshal, mass, order, organise, range, sort.

grouse *v* beef, belly-ache, bitch, carp, complain, find fault, fret, fuss, gripe, grouch, grumble, moan, mutter, whine, whinge.

antonym acquiesce.

n belly-ache, complaint, grievance, gripe, grouch, grumble, moan, murmur, mutter, objection, peeve, whine, whinge.

grove *n* arbour, avenue, bosk, bosket, brake, coppice, copse, covert, hurst, plantation, spinney, thicket, wood, woodland.

grovel *v* abase oneself, backscratch, bootlick, cower, crawl, creep, cringe, crouch, defer, demean oneself, fawn, flatter, kowtow, sneak, sycophantise, toady.

grovelling *adj* backscratching, bootlicking, fawning, flattering, ingratiating, obsequious, sycophantic, wormy.

antonyms outspoken, straightforward.

grow *v* advance, arise, augment, become, branch out, breed, broaden, burgeon, cultivate, develop, diversify, enlarge, evolve, expand, extend, farm, flourish, flower, germinate, get, heighten, improve, increase, issue, mature, multiply, nurture, originate, produce, progress, proliferate, propagate, prosper, raise, ripen, rise, shoot, spread, spring, sprout, stem, stretch, succeed, swell, thicken, thrive, turn, vegetate, wax, widen.

antonyms decrease, fail, halt.

growing *adj* accrescent, blossoming, broadening, burgeoning, crescent, crescive, deepening, developing, elongating, enlarging, escalating, expanding, extending, flourishing, heightening, increasing, increscent, intumescent, lengthening, maturing, mounting, multiplying, proliferating, rising, spreading, swelling, thickening, thriving, tumescent, waxing, widening.

antonyms decreasing, failing, stagnant, static, waning.

growl *v* gnar, gnarl, gnarr, knar, snap, snarl, yap.

grown-up *adj* adult, full-grown, fully-fledged, fully-grown, mature, of age.

antonyms childish, immature.

n adult, gentleman, lady, man, woman.

antonym child.

growth *n* accrescence, accretion, advance, advancement, aggrandisement, augmentation, auxesis, broadening, change, crop, cultivation, development, diversification, enlargement, evolution, excrement, excrescence, expansion, extension, flowering, gall, germination, growing, heightening, improvement, increase, intumescence, lump, maturation, multiplication, outgrowth, produce, production, progress, proliferation, prosperity, protuberance, ripening, rise, shooting, sprouting, stretching, success, swelling, thickening, transformation, tumour, vegetation, waxing, widening.

antonyms decrease, failure, stagnation, stoppage.

grub[1] *v* burrow, delve, dig, explore, ferret, forage, grout, hunt, investigate, nose, probe, pull up, root, rootle, rummage, scour, uproot.

n caterpillar, chrysalis, larva, maggot, nymph, pupa, worm.

grub[2] *n* chow, commons, eats, edibles, fodder, food, nosh, provisions, rations, scoff, sustenance, victuals.

grubby *adj* crummy, dirty, filthy, fly-blown, frowzy, grimy, manky, mean, messy, mucky, scruffy, seedy, shabby, slovenly, smutty, soiled, sordid, squalid, unkempt, untidy, unwashed.

antonyms clean, smart.

grudge *n* animosity, animus, antagonism, antipathy, aversion, bitterness, dislike, enmity, envy, grievance, hard feelings, hate, ill-will, jealousy, malevolence, malice, pique, rancour, resentment, spite.

antonyms favour, regard.

v begrudge, covet, dislike, envy, mind, niggard, object to, regret, repine, resent, stint, take exception to.

antonyms applaud, approve.

grudging *adj* cautious, guarded, half-hearted, hesitant, reluctant, secret, unenthusiastic, unwilling.

gruelling *adj* arduous, backbreaking, brutal, crushing, demanding, difficult, exhausting, fatiguing, fierce, grinding, hard, hard-going, harsh, laborious, punishing, severe, stern, stiff, strenuous, taxing, tiring, tough, trying, uphill, wearing, wearying.

antonym easy.

gruesome *adj* abominable, awful, chilling, eldritch, fearful, fearsome, ghastly, grim, grisly, grooly, hideous, horrible, horrid, horrific, horrifying, loathsome, macabre, monstrous, repellent, repugnant, repulsive, shocking, sick, spine-chilling, terrible, weird.

antonyms charming, congenial.

gruff *adj* abrupt, bad-tempered, bearish, blunt, brusque, churlish, crabbed, croaking, crusty, curt, discourteous, gravelly, grouchy, grumpy, guttural, harsh, hoarse, husky, ill-humoured, ill-natured, impolite, low, rasping, rough, rude, sour, sullen, surly, throaty, uncivil, ungracious, unmannerly.

antonyms clear, courteous, sweet.

grumble *v* beef, bellyache, bitch, bleat, carp, chunter, complain, croak, find fault, gripe, grouch, grouse, growl, gurgle, moan, murmur, mutter, nark, repine, roar, rumble, whine.

antonym acquiesce.

n beef, bitch, bleat, complaint, grievance, gripe, grouch, grouse, growl, gurgle, moan, murmur, muttering, objection, roar, rumble, whinge.

grumpy *adj* bad-tempered, cantankerous, churlish, crabbed, cross, crotchety, discontented, grouchy, grumbling, ill-tempered, irritable, mutinous, peevish, petulant, querulous, sulky, sullen, surly, testy, truculent.

antonyms civil, contented.

guarantee *n* assurance, attestation, bond, certainty, collateral, covenant, earnest, endorsement, guaranty, insurance, oath, pledge, promise, security, surety, testimonial, undertaking, voucher, warranty, word, word of honour.

v answer for, assure, avouch, certify, ensure, insure, maintain, make certain, make sure of, pledge, promise, protect, secure, swear, underwrite, vouch for, warrant.

guarantor *n* angel, backer, bailsman, bondsman, covenanter, guarantee, referee, sponsor, supporter, surety, underwriter, voucher, warrantor.

guard *v* be on the qui vive, be on the watch, beware, conserve, cover, defend, escort, keep, look out, mind, oversee, patrol, police, preserve, protect, safeguard, save, screen, secure, sentinel, shelter, shield, supervise, tend, ward, watch.

n attention, backstop, barrier, buffer, bulwark, bumper, care, caution, convoy, custodian, defence, defender, escort, guarantee, heed, lookout, minder, pad, patrol, picket, precaution, protection, protector, rampart, safeguard, screen, security, sentinel, sentry, shield, vigilance, wall, warder, wariness, watch, watchfulness, watchman.

guarded *adj* cagey, careful, cautious, circumspect, discreet, disingenuous, non-committal, prudent, reserved, restrained, reticent, secretive, suspicious, uncommunicative, unforthcoming, wary, watchful.

antonyms frank, whole-hearted.

guardian *n* attendant, carer, champion, conservator, curator, custodian, defender, depositary, depository, escort, fiduciary, guard, keeper, minder, preserver, protector, trustee, warden, warder.

guardianship *n* aegis, attendance, care, companionship, curatorship, custodianship, custody, defence, escort, guard, guidance, hands, keeping, patronage, protection, safekeeping, trust, trusteeship, wardenry, wardenship, wardship.

guerrilla *n* bushwhacker, franc-tireur, freedom-fighter, guerrillero, haiduck, irregular, maquisard, partisan, resistance fighter, sniper.

guess *v* assume, believe, conjecture, dare say, deem, divine, estimate, fancy, fathom, feel, guesstimate, hazard, hypothesise, imagine, intuit, judge, opine, penetrate, predict, reckon, solve, speculate, suppose, surmise, suspect, think, work out.

n assumption, belief, conjecture, fancy, feeling, guesstimate, hypothesis, intuition, judgement, notion, opinion, prediction, reckoning, shot (in the dark), speculation, supposition, surmise, suspicion, theory.

guesswork *n* assumption, conjecture, estimation, intuition, presumption, presupposition, reckoning, speculation, supposition, surmise, suspicion, theory.

guest *n* boarder, caller, company, freeloader, habitué, lodger, parasite, regular, roomer, visitant, visitor.

guest-house *n* boarding-house, hospice, hospitium, hostel, hostelry, hotel, inn, pension, rooming-house, xenodochium.

guidance *n* advice, aegis, auspices, clues, conduct, control, counsel, counselling, direction, government, guidelines, help, illumination, indications, instruction, leadership, management, pointers, recommendation, regulation, steering, teaching.

guide *v* accompany, advise, attend, command, conduct, control, convoy, counsel, direct, educate, escort, govern, handle, head, influence, instruct, lead, manage, manoeuvre, oversee, pilot, point, regulate, rule, shape, shepherd, steer, superintend, supervise, sway, teach, train, usher, vector.

n ABC, adviser, attendant, beacon, catalogue, chaperon, cicerone, clue, companion, conductor, controller, counsellor, courier, criterion, director, directory, dragoman, escort, example, exemplar, guide-book, guideline, handbook, ideal, index, indication, informant, inspiration, instructions, key, landmark, leader, lodestar, manual, mark, marker, master, mentor, model, monitor, paradigm, pilot, pointer, praxis, sign, signal, signpost, standard, steersman, teacher, template, usher, vade-mecum.

guiding *adj* advisory, consultant, consultative, consultatory, consulting, controlling, counselling, directorial, directory, formative, governing, influential, instructional, instructive, managing, monitoring, piloting, shepherding, steering, supervisory, tutorial.

guild *n* association, brotherhood, chapel, club, company, corporation, fellowship, fraternity, incorporation, league, lodge, order, organisation, society, union.

guile *n* art, artfulness, artifice, cleverness, craft, craftiness, cunning, deceit, deception, deviousness, disingenuity, duplicity, gamesmanship, knavery, ruse, slyness, treachery, trickery, trickiness, wiliness.

antonyms artlessness, guilelessness.

guileful *adj* artful, clever, crafty, cunning, deceitful, devious, disingenuous, duplicitous, foxy, sly, sneaky, treacherous, tricky, underhand, wily.

antonyms artless, guileless.

guileless *adj* artless, candid, direct, frank, genuine, honest, ingenuous, innocent, naïve, natural, open, simple, sincere, straightforward, transparent, trusting, truthful, unreserved, unsophisticated, unworldly.

antonyms artful, guileful.

guilt *n* blamability, blame, blameworthiness, compunction, conscience, contrition, criminality, culpability, delinquency, disgrace, dishonour, guiltiness, guilty conscience, infamy, iniquity, mens rea, regret, remorse, responsibility, self-condemnation, self-reproach, self-reproof, shame, sinfulness, stigma, wickedness, wrong.

antonyms innocence, shamelessness.

guiltless *adj* blameless, clean, clear, immaculate, impeccable, inculpable, innocent, irreproachable, pure, sinless, spotless, unimpeachable, unspotted, unsullied, untainted, untarnished.

antonyms guilty, tainted.

guilty *adj* ashamed, blamable, blameworthy, compunctious, conscience-stricken, contrite, convicted, criminal, culpable, delinquent, errant, erring, evil, felonious, guilt-ridden, hangdog, illicit, iniquitous, nefarious, nocent, offending, penitent, regretful, remorseful, repentant, reprehensible, responsible, rueful, shamefaced, sheepish, sinful, sorry, wicked, wrong.

antonyms guiltless, innocent.

guise *n* air, appearance, aspect, behaviour, custom, demeanour, disguise, dress, façade, face, fashion, features, form, front, likeness, manner, mask, mode, pretence, semblance, shape, show.

gulf *n* abyss, basin, bay, bight, breach, chasm, cleft, gap, gorge, opening, rent, rift, separation, split, void, whirlpool.

gull *n* maw, mew, seagull, sea-mew.

gullet *n* craw, crop, maw, oesophagus, the Red Lane, throat, weasand.

gullibility *n* credulity, glaikitness, innocence, naïvety, simplicity, trustfulness, verdancy.

antonym astuteness.

gullible *adj* born yesterday, credulous, foolish, glaikit, green, innocent, naïve, trusting, unsuspecting, verdant.

antonym astute.

gully *n* channel, ditch, donga, geo, gio, gulch, gutter, ravine, watercourse.

gulp *v* bolt, choke, devour, gasp, gobble, gollop, gormandise, guzzle, knock back, quaff, stifle, stuff, swallow, swig, swill, toss off, wolf.

antonyms nibble, sip.

n draught, mouthful, slug, swallow, swig.

gum *n* adhesive, cement, glue, goo, mucilage, paste, resin, sap.

v affix, block, cement, clog, fix, glue, paste, seal, stick.

gumboil *n* abscess, parulis, swelling.

gummy *adj* adhesive, gluey, gooey, sticky, tacky, viscid, viscous.

gumption *n* ability, acumen, acuteness, astuteness, cleverness, common sense, discernment, enterprise, horse sense, initiative, mother wit, nous, resourcefulness, sagacity, savvy, shrewdness, smeddum, spirit, wit(s).

antonym foolishness.

gun *n* equaliser, gat, heater, peacemaker, persuader, piece, pistol, shooter, shooting-iron, tool.

gunman *n* assassin, bandit, bravo, desperado, gangster, gunsel, gunslinger, hatchet man, hit man, killer, mobster, murderer, shootist, sniper, terrorist, thug.

gurgle *v* babble, bubble, burble, crow, guggle, lap, murmur, plash, purl, ripple, splash.

n babble, guggle, murmur, purl, ripple.

guru *n* authority, instructor, leader, luminary, maharishi, master, mentor, pundit, sage, Svengali, swami, teacher, tutor.

gush *v* babble, blather, burst, cascade, chatter, drivel, effuse, enthuse, flood, flow, fountain, jabber, jet, pour, run, rush, spout, spurt, stream, yatter.

n babble, burst, cascade, chatter, ebullition, effusion, eruption, exuberance, flood, flow, jet, outburst, outflow, rush, spout, spurt, stream, tide, torrent.

gushing *adj* cloying, effusive, emotional, excessive, fulsome, gushy, mawkish, over-enthusiastic, saccharine, sentimental, sickly.

antonyms restrained, sincere.

gust *n* blast, blow, breeze, burst, flaught, flaw, flurry, gale, puff, rush, squall, williwaw.

v blast, blow, bluster, breeze, puff, squall.

gusto *n* appetite, appreciation, brio, delight, élan, enjoyment, enthusiasm, exhilaration, exuberance, fervour, liking, pleasure, relish, savour, verve, zeal, zest.

antonyms apathy, distaste.

gusty *adj* blowy, blustering, blustery, breezy, gustful, squally, stormy, tempestuous, windy.

antonym calm.

gut *v* clean, clean out, despoil, disembowel, draw, dress, empty, eviscerate, exenterate, gill, pillage, plunder, ransack, ravage, rifle, sack, strip.

adj basic, deep-seated, emotional, heartfelt, innate, instinctive, intuitive, involuntary, natural, spontaneous, strong, unthinking, visceral.

gutless *adj* abject, chicken, chicken-hearted, chicken-livered, cowardly, craven, faint-hearted, feeble, irresolute, lily-livered, spineless, submissive, timid, weak.

antonym courageous.

guts *n* audacity, backbone, belly, boldness, bottle, bowels, courage, daring, endurance, entrails, forcefulness, grit, hardihood, innards, insides, intestines, inwards, mettle, nerve, paunch, pluck, spirit, spunk, stamina, staying power, stomach, tenacity, toughness, viscera.

antonym spinelessness.

gutsy *adj* bold, brave, courageous, determined, gallant, game, indomitable, lusty, mettlesome, passionate, plucky, resolute, spirited, staunch.

antonyms quiet, timid.

gutter *n* channel, conduit, ditch, drain, duct, grip, kennel, pipe, rigol(l), sluice, trench, trough, tube.

guttersnipe *n* gamin, mudlark, ragamuffin, street Arab, tatterdemalion, urchin, waif.

guttural *adj* deep, grating, gravelly, gruff, harsh, hoarse, husky, low, rasping, rough, thick, throaty.
antonym dulcet.

guy *n* bloke, buffer, cat, chap, codger, cove, customer, fellow, individual, josser, lad, man, oik, person, punter, youth.

guzzle *v* bolt, carouse, cram, devour, gobble, gormandise, stuff, wolf.

gypsy *n* Bohemian, diddicoy, faw, gipsy, gitana, gitano, nomad, rambler, roamer, Romany, rover, tink, tinker, traveller, tsigane, tzigany, vagabond, vagrant, wanderer, Zigeuner, Zincalo, Zingaro.

gyrate *v* circle, gyre, pirouette, revolve, rotate, spin, spiral, twirl, whirl.

gyrating *adj* gyral, gyrant, revolving, rotating, spinning, twirling, whirling.

gyration *n* convolution, pirouette, revolution, rotation, spin, spinning, spiral, twirl, vertigo, whirl, whirling.

H

habit[1] *n* accustomedness, addiction, assuetude, bent, constitution, convention, custom, dependence, diathesis, disposition, fixation, frame of mind, habitude, inclination, make-up, manner, mannerism, mode, mores, nature, obsession, practice, proclivity, propensity, quirk, routine, rule, second nature, tendency, usage, vice, way, weakness, wont.

habit[2] *n* apparel, attire, clothes, clothing, dress, garb, garment, habiliment.

habitat *n* abode, domain, element, environment, home, locality, surroundings, terrain, territory.

habitation *n* abode, cottage, domicile, dwelling, dwelling-place, home, house, hut, inhabitance, inhabitancy, inhabitation, living quarters, lodging, mansion, occupancy, occupation, quarters, residence, tenancy.

habitual *adj* accustomed, chronic, common, confirmed, constant, customary, established, familiar, fixed, frequent, hardened, ingrained, inveterate, natural, normal, ordinary, persistent, recurrent, regular, routine, standard, traditional, usual, wonted.

antonym occasional.

habituate *v* acclimatise, accustom, break in, condition, discipline, familiarise, harden, inure, school, season, tame, train.

habitué *n* denizen, frequenter, patron, regular, regular customer.

hack[1] *v* bark, chop, cough, cut, gash, haggle, hew, kick, lacerate, mangle, mutilate, notch, rasp, slash.

n bark, chop, cough, cut, gash, notch, rasp, slash.

hack[2] *adj* banal, hackneyed, mediocre, pedestrian, poor, stereotyped, tired, undistinguished, uninspired, unoriginal.

n crock, drudge, horse, jade, journalist, nag, paper-stainer, penny-a-liner, scribbler, slave.

hackneyed *adj* banal, clichéd, common, commonplace, corny, hack, hand-me-down, overworked, pedestrian, percoct, played-out, run-of-the-mill, second-hand, stale, stereotyped, stock, threadbare, time-worn, tired, trite, unoriginal, worn-out.

antonyms arresting, new.

hack-work *n* drudgery, pot-boiler.

haemorrhoids *n* emerods, piles.

hag *n* battle-axe, beldame, crone, fury, harpy, harridan, ogress, shrew, termagant, virago, vixen, witch.

haggard *adj* cadaverous, careworn, drawn, emaciated, gaunt, ghastly, hagged, hollow-eyed, pinched, shrunken, thin, wan, wasted, wrinkled.

antonym hale.

haggle *v* bargain, barter, bicker, cavil, chaffer, dicker, dispute, higgle, palter, quarrel, squabble, wrangle.

hail[1] *n* barrage, bombardment, rain, shower, storm, torrent, volley.

v assail, barrage, batter, bombard, pelt, rain, shower, storm, volley.

hail[2] *v* acclaim, accost, acknowledge, address, applaud, call, cheer, exalt, flag down, glorify, greet, halloo, honour, salute, shout, signal to, wave, welcome.

n call, cry, halloo, holla, shout.

hair *n* locks, mane, mop, shock, tresses, vibrissa, villus.

hair removal depilation, electrolysis, epilation.

hair-do *n* coiffure, cut, haircut, hairstyle, perm, set, style.

hairdresser *n* barber, coiffeur, coiffeuse, friseur, hair-stylist, stylist.

hairless *adj* bald, bald-headed, beardless, clean-shaven, depilated, desperate, frantic, glabrate, glabrous, shorn, tonsured.

antonym hairy.

hairpiece *n* postiche, wig.

hair-raising *adj* alarming, bloodcurdling, breathtaking, creepy, eerie, exciting, frightening, ghastly, ghostly, horrifying, petrifying, scary, shocking, spine-chilling, startling, terrifying, thrilling.

antonym calming.

hair's-breadth *n* fraction, hair, inch, jot, whisker.

antonym mile.

hair-splitting *adj* captious, carping, cavilling, fault-finding, fine, finicky, nice, niggling, nit-picking, overnice, over-refined, pettifogging, quibbling, subtle, word-splitting.

antonym unfussy.

hairy *adj* bearded, bewhiskered, bushy, crinigerous, crinite, crinose, dangerous, dicey, difficult, fleecy, furry, hazardous, hirsute, hispid, lanuginose, lanuginous, perilous, pilose, pilous, risky, scaring, shaggy, stubbly, tricky, villose, villous, woolly.

antonyms bald, clean-shaven.

halcyon *adj* balmy, calm, carefree, flourishing, gentle, golden, happy, mild, pacific, peaceful, placid, prosperous, quiet, serene, still, tranquil, undisturbed.

antonym stormy.

hale *adj* able-bodied, athletic, blooming, fit, flourishing, healthy, hearty, in fine fettle, in the pink, robust, sound, strong, vigorous, well, youthful.

antonym ill.

half *n* bisection, division, fifty per cent, fraction, half-back, half-share, hemisphere, portion, section, segment, term.

adj divided, fractional, halved, incomplete, limited, moderate, part, partial, semi-.

antonym whole.

adv barely, imperfectly, in part, inadequately, incompletely, partially, partly, slightly.

antonym completely.

half-baked *adj* brainless, crazy, foolish, harebrained, ill-conceived, ill-judged, impractical, senseless, short-sighted, silly, stupid, unplanned.

antonym sensible.

half-breed, half-caste *n* griff(e), mestee, mestiza, mestizo, metif, métis, métisse, miscegen, miscegene, miscegine, mongrel, mulatta, mulatto, mulattress, mustee, quadroon, quarter-blood, quarteroon, quintroon, zambo.

half-hearted *adj* apathetic, cool, indifferent, lackadaisical, lacklustre, listless, lukewarm, neutral, passive, perfunctory, uninterested.

antonym enthusiastic.

halfway *adv* barely, imperfectly, in the middle, incompletely, midway, moderately, nearly, partially, partly, rather, slightly.

antonym completely.

adj central, equidistant, incomplete, intermediate, mid, middle, midway, partial, part-way.

antonym complete.

half-wit *n* cretin, dimwit, dolt, dullard, dunce, dunderhead, fool, gaupus, idiot, imbecile, moron, nitwit, nut, simpleton, underwit, witling.

antonym brain.

half-witted *adj* addle-brained, barmy, batty, crazy, cretinous, dull, dull-witted, feeble-minded, foolish, idiotic, moronic, nuts, nutty, silly, simple, simple-minded, stupid, two bricks short of a load.

antonym clever.

hall *n* assembly-room, auditorium, aula, basilica, chamber, concert-hall, concourse, corridor, entrance-hall, entry, foyer, hallway, lobby, salon, saloon, vestibule.

hallmark *n* authentication, badge, brand-name, device, emblem, endorsement, indication, mark, seal, sign, stamp, symbol, trademark.

hallo! *see* **hello**.

hallowed *adj* age-old, beatified, blessed, consecrated, dedicated, established, holy, honoured, inviolable, revered, sacred, sacrosanct, sanctified.

hallucinate *v* aberrate, daydream, envision, fantasise, freak out, imagine, trip.

hallucination *n* aberration, apparition, delusion, dream, fantasy, figment, illusion, mirage, phantasmagoria, pink elephants, vision.

halo *n* aura, aureola, aureole, corona, gloria, gloriole, glory, halation, nimbus, radiance.

halt *v* arrest, block, break off, call it a day, cease, check, curb, desist, draw up, end, impede, obstruct, pack it in, quit, rest, stem, stop, terminate, wait.

antonyms assist, continue, start.

n arrest, break, close, end, étape, impasse, interruption, pause, stand, standstill, stop, stoppage, termination, way point.

antonyms continuation, start.

halting *adj* awkward, broken, faltering, hesitant, imperfect, laboured, stammering, stumbling, stuttering, uncertain.

antonym fluent.

halve *v* bisect, cut down, divide, go Dutch, lessen, reduce, share, split.

halved *adj* bisected, dimidiate, divided, split.

hammer *v* bang, beat, clobber, defeat, din, dolly, drive, drive home, drub, drum, form, grind, hit, impress upon, instruct, knock, make, malleate, pan, repeat, shape, slate, thrash, trounce, worst.

n beetle, gavel, madge, mall, mallet, maul, monkey.

hammer out accomplish, bring about, complete, contrive, excogitate, fashion, finish, negotiate, produce, settle, sort out, thrash out.

hamper *v* bind, cramp, cumber, curb, curtail, distort, embarrass, encumber, entangle, fetter, frustrate, hamshackle, hamstring, handicap, hinder, hobble, hold up, impede, interfere with, obstruct, pinch, prevent, restrain, restrict, shackle, slow down, tangle, thwart, trammel.

antonyms aid, expedite.

hamstrung *adj* balked, crippled, disabled, foiled, frustrated, handicapped, helpless, hors de combat, incapacitated, paralysed, stymied.

hand[1] *n* ability, agency, aid, applause, art, artistry, assistance, calligraphy, cheirography, clap, daddle, direction, fist, flipper, handwriting, help, influence, mitt, ovation, palm, part, participation, paw, penmanship, pud, puddy, script, share, skill, support.

v aid, assist, conduct, convey, deliver, give, guide, help, lead, offer, pass, present, provide, transmit, yield.

hand down bequeath, give, grant, pass on, transfer, will.

hand in glove allied, in cahoots, in collusion, in league, intimate.

hand out deal out, disburse, dish out, dispense, disseminate, distribute, give out, mete, share out.

hand over deliver, donate, fork out, present, release, relinquish, surrender, turn over, yield.

antonym retain.

hand[2] *n* artificer, artisan, craftsman, employee, farm-hand, hired man, hireling, labourer, operative, orra man, redneck, worker, workman.

handbook *n* Baedeker, book of words, companion, guide, guidebook, instruction book, manual, vade-mecum.

handcuff *v* fasten, fetter, manacle, secure, shackle, tie.

handcuffs *n* bracelets, cuffs, darbies, fetters, manacles, mittens, shackles, wristlets.

handful *n* few, scattering, smattering, sprinkling, wheen.

antonym lot.

handicap *n* barrier, block, defect, disability, disadvantage, drawback, encumbrance, hindrance, impairment, impediment, impost, limitation, millstone, obstacle, odds, penalty, restriction, shortcoming, stumbling-block.

antonyms assistance, benefit.

v burden, disadvantage, encumber, hamper, hamstring, hinder, impede, limit, restrict, retard.

antonyms assist, further.

handicraft *n* art, artisanship, craft, craftsmanship, handiwork, skill, workmanship.

handiness *n* accessibility, adroitness, aptitude, availability, cleverness, closeness, convenience, deftness, dexterity, efficiency, expertise, knack, practicality, proficiency, proximity, skill, usefulness, workability.

antonym clumsiness.

handiwork *n* achievement, artefact, craft, creation, design, doing, handicraft, handwork, invention, product, production, result, work.

handkerchief *n* fogle, handkercher, hanky, monteith, mouchoir, nose-rag, romal, rumal, sudary, wipe.

handle *n* ear, grip, haft, handfast, handgrip, heft, helve, hilt, knob, lug, stock, wythe.

v administer, carry, conduct, control, cope with, deal in, deal with, direct, discourse, discuss, feel, finger, fondle, grasp, guide, hold, manage, manipulate, manoeuvre, market, maul, operate, paw, pick up, poke, sell, steer, stock, supervise, touch, trade, traffic in, treat, use, wield.

handling *n* administration, approach, conduct, direction, discussion, management, manipulation, operation, running, transaction, treatment.

hand-out[1] *n* alms, charity, dole, freebie, issue, largess(e), share, share-out.

hand-out[2] *n* bulletin, circular, free sample, leaflet, literature, press release, statement.

hand-picked *adj* choice, chosen, elect, elite, picked, recherché, screened, select, selected.

hands *n* authority, care, charge, command, control, custody, disposal, guardianship, guidance, jurisdiction, keeping, possession, power, supervision, tutelage.

hands down easily, effortlessly, in a canter, with ease.

antonym with difficulty.

handsome *adj* abundant, admirable, ample, attractive, beau, becoming, bountiful, braw, comely, considerable, elegant, feat(e)ous, featuous, featurely, fine, generous, good-looking, graceful, gracious, large, liberal, magnanimous, majestic, personable, plentiful, seemly, sizeable, stately, well-favoured, well-looking, well-proportioned, well-set-up.

antonyms mean, stingy, ugly.

handsomely *adv* abundantly, amply, bountifully, generously, lavishly, liberally, magnanimously, munificently, plentifully, richly, unsparingly, unstintingly.

antonym stingily.

handwriting *n* cacography, calligraphy, cheirography, fist, hand, longhand, penmanship, scrawl, script.

handy *adj* accessible, adept, adroit, at hand, available, clever, close, convenient, deft, dexterous, expert, helpful, manageable, near, nearby, neat, nimble, practical, proficient, ready, serviceable, skilful, skilled, useful.

antonyms clumsy, inconvenient, unwieldy.

handyman *n* DIYer, factotum, famulus, hobjobber, Jack-of-all-trades, man-of-the-world, odd-jobman, orra man.

hang *v* adhere, attach, bow, cling, cover, dangle, deck, decorate, depend, drape, drift, droop, drop, execute, fasten, fix, float, furnish, gibbet, hold, hover, incline, lean, loll, lower, remain, rest, sag, stick, string up, suspend, supercollate, swing, trail, weep.

hang about/around associate with, dally, frequent, haunt, linger, loiter, resort, roam, tarry, waste time.

hang back demur, hesitate, hold back, recoil, shy away.

hang fire delay, hang back, hold back, hold on, procrastinate, stall, stick, stop, vacillate, wait.

antonym press on.

hang on carry on, cling, clutch, continue, depend on, endure, grasp, grip, hang fire, hang in there, hinge, hold fast, hold on, hold out, hold the line, persevere, persist, remain, rest, stop, turn on, wait.

antonym give up.

hang over impend, loom, menace, threaten.

hangdog *adj* abject, browbeaten, cowed, cringing, defeated, downcast, furtive, guilty, miserable, shamefaced, sneaking, wretched.

antonym bold.

hanger-on *n* camp follower, dependant, follower, freeloader, lackey, leech, minion, parasite, sponger, sycophant, toad-eater, toady.

hanging[1] *adj* dangling, drooping, flapping, flopping, floppy, loose, pendent, pendulous, pensile, suspended, swinging, unattached, undecided, unresolved, unsettled, unsupported.

hanging[2] *n* dossal, dossel, drape, drapery, drop, drop-scene, frontal.

hangman *n* Jack Ketch.

hang-out *n* den, dive, haunt, home, howf(f), joint, local, resort, watering-hole.

hangover *n* after-effects, crapulence, katzenjammer.

hang-up *n* block, difficulty, idée fixe, inhibition, mental block, obsession, preoccupation, problem, thing.

hank *n* coil, fank, length, loop, piece, roll, skein.

hanker for/after covet, crave, desire, hunger for, itch for, long for, lust after, pine for, thirst for, want, wish, yearn for, yen for.

antonym dislike.

hankering *n* craving, desire, hunger, itch, longing, pining, thirst, urge, wish, yearning, yen.

antonym dislike.

hanky-panky *n* cheating, chicanery, deception, devilry, dishonesty, funny business, jiggery-pokery, knavery, machinations, mischief, monkey business, nonsense, shenanigans, subterfuge, trickery, tricks.

antonym openness.

haphazard *adj* accidental, aimless, arbitrary, careless, casual, chance, disorderly, disorganised, flukey, hit-or-miss, indiscriminate, promiscuous, random, slapdash, slipshod, unmethodical, unsystematic.

antonyms deliberate, planned.

hapless *adj* cursed, ill-fated, ill-starred, jinxed, luckless, miserable, star-crossed, unfortunate, unhappy, unlucky, wretched.

antonym lucky.

happen *v* appear, arise, befall, chance, come about, crop up, develop, ensue, eventuate, fall out, follow, materialise, occur, result, supervene, take place, transpire, turn out.

happen on chance on, come on, discover, find, hit on, light on, stumble on.

happening *n* accident, adventure, affair, case, chance, circumstance, episode, event, experience, incident, occasion, occurrence, phenomenon, proceeding, scene.

happily *adv* agreeably, appropriately, aptly, auspiciously, blithely, by chance, cheerfully, contentedly, delightedly, enthusiastically, favourably, felicitously, fittingly, fortunately, freely, gaily, gladly, gleefully, gracefully, heartily, joyfully, joyously, luckily, merrily, opportunely, perhaps, propitiously, providentially, seasonably, successfully, willingly.

antonym unhappily.

happiness *n* beatitude, blessedness, bliss, cheer, cheerfulness, cheeriness, chirpiness, contentment, delight, ecstasy, elation, enjoyment, exuberance, felicity, gaiety, gladness, high spirits, joy, joyfulness, jubilation, light-heartedness, merriment, pleasure, satisfaction, well-being.

antonym unhappiness.

happy *adj* advantageous, appropriate, apt, auspicious, befitting, blessed, blest, blissful, blithe, chance, cheerful, content, contented, convenient, delighted, ecstatic, elated, enviable, favourable, felicitous, fit, fitting, fortunate, glad, gratified, gruntled, idyllic, jolly, joyful, joyous, jubilant, lucky, merry, opportune, over the moon, overjoyed, pleased, promising, propitious, satisfactory, Saturnian, seasonable, starry-eyed, successful, sunny, thrilled, timely, well-timed.

antonym unhappy.

happy medium aurea mediocritas, golden mean, juste milieu.

antonym excess.

happy-go-lucky *adj* blithe, carefree, casual, cheerful, devil-may-care, easy-going, heedless, improvident, insouciant, irresponsible, light-hearted, nonchalant, reckless, unconcerned, untroubled, unworried.

antonyms anxious, wary.

harangue *n* address, declamation, diatribe, discourse, exhortation, homily, lecture, oration, paternoster, peroration, philippic, sermon, speech, spiel, tirade.

v address, declaim, descant, exhort, hold forth, lecture, monolog(u)ise, orate, perorate, preach, rant, rhetorise, sermonise, spout.

harass *v* annoy, badger, bait, beleaguer, bother, chivvy, distress, disturb, exasperate, exhaust, fatigue, harry, hassle, hound, perplex, persecute, pester, plague, tease, tire, torment, trash, trouble, vex, wear out, weary, worry.

antonym assist.

harassed *adj* careworn, distraught, distressed, harried, hassled, hounded, pestered, plagued, pressured, pressurised, strained, stressed, tormented, troubled, vexed, worried.

antonym carefree.

harassment *n* aggravation, annoyance, badgering, bedevilment, bother, distress, hassle, irritation, molest, molestation, nuisance, persecution, pestering, pressuring, torment, trouble, vexation.

antonym assistance.

harbinger *n* avant-courier, forerunner, foretoken, herald, indication, messenger, omen, portent, precursor, presage, sign, warning.

harbour *n* anchorage, asylum, covert, destination, haven, marina, port, refuge, roadstead, sanctuary, sanctum, security, shelter.

v believe, cherish, cling to, conceal, entertain, foster, hide, hold, imagine, lodge, maintain, nurse, nurture, protect, retain, secrete, shelter, shield.

hard *adj* acrimonious, actual, adamantine, alcoholic, angry, antagonistic, arduous, backbreaking, baffling, bare, bitter, burdensome, calamitous, callous, cast-iron, cold, compact, complex, complicated, cruel, crusty, dark, definite, dense, difficult, disagreeable, disastrous, distressing, driving, exacting, exhausting, fatiguing, fierce, firm, flinty, forceful, formidable, grievous, grim, habit-forming, hard-hearted, harsh, heavy, Herculean, hostile, impenetrable, implacable, indisputable, inflexible, intolerable, intricate, involved, irony, knotty, laborious, marbly, obdurate, painful, perplexing, pitiless, plain, powerful, puzzling, rancorous, resentful, rigid, rigorous, ruthless, sclerous, severe, shrewd, solid, stern, stiff, stony, strenuous, strict, strong, stubborn, tangled, thorny, toilsome, tough, undeniable, unfathomable, unfeeling, ungentle, unjust, unkind, unpleasant, unrelenting, unsparing, unsympathetic, unvarnished, unyielding, uphill, verified, violent, wearying.

antonyms harmless, kind, mild, non-alcoholic, pleasant, pleasing, soft, yielding.

adv agonisingly, assiduously, badly, bitterly, close, completely, determinedly, diligently, distressingly, doggedly, earnestly, energetically, fiercely, forcefully, forcibly, fully, hardly, harshly, heavily, industriously, intensely, intently, keenly, laboriously, near, painfully, persistently, powerfully, rancorously, reluctantly, resentfully, roughly, severely, sharply, slowly, sorely, steadily, strenuously, strongly, uneasily, untiringly, vigorously, violently, with difficulty.

antonyms gently, mildly, moderately, unenthusiastically.

hard and fast binding, fixed, immutable, incontrovertible, inflexible, invariable, rigid, set, strict, stringent, unalterable, unchangeable, unchanging.

antonym flexible.

hard up bankrupt, broke, bust, cleaned out, destitute, impecunious, impoverished, in the red, penniless, penurious, poor, short, skint, strapped for cash.

antonym rich.

hard-bitten *adj* callous, case-hardened, cynical, down-to-earth, hard-boiled, hard-headed, hard-nosed, matter-of-fact, practical, realistic, ruthless, shrewd, tough, unsentimental.

antonym callow.

hard-core *adj* blatant, dedicated, die-hard, dyed-in-the-wool, explicit, extreme, intransigent, obstinate, rigid, staunch, steadfast.

antonym moderate.

harden *v* accustom, anneal, bake, brace, brutalise, buttress, cake, case-harden, concrete, fortify, freeze, gird, habituate, indurate, inure, nerve, reinforce, sclerose, season, set, solidify, steel, stiffen, strengthen, toughen, train.

antonym soften.

hardened *adj* accustomed, chronic, fixed, habitual, habituated, incorrigible, inured, inveterate, irredeemable, obdurate, reprobate, seasoned, set, shameless, toughened, unfeeling.

antonyms callow, soft.

hardening *n* annealing, clotting, coagulation, congealing, sclerosis, setting, solidifying, vulcanisation.

hard-headed *adj* astute, clear-thinking, cool, hard-boiled, level-headed, practical, pragmatic, realistic, sensible, shrewd, tough, unsentimental.

antonym unrealistic.

hard-hearted *adj* callous, cold, cruel, hard, heartless, indifferent, inhuman, insensitive, intolerant, iron-hearted, marble-breasted, marble-hearted, merciless, pitiless, stony, uncaring, uncompassionate, unfeeling, unkind, unsympathetic.

antonyms kind, merciful.

hard-hitting *adj* condemnatory, critical, forceful, no-holds-barred, strongly-worded, tough, unsparing, vigorous.

antonym mild.

hardihood *n* assurance, audacity, backbone, boldness, bottle, bravery, courage, daring, determination, effrontery, firmness, foolhardiness, grit, guts, hardiness, impertinence, impetuousness, intrepidity, mettle, nerve, pluck, prowess, rashness, recklessness, resolution, spirit, spunk, strength, temerity.

antonyms sense, timidity.

hardiness *n* boldness, courage, fortitude, hardihood, intrepidity, resilience, resolution, robustness, ruggedness, sturdiness, toughness, valour.

antonym timidity.

hardline *adj* definite, extreme, immoderate, inflexible, intransigent, militant, tough, uncompromising, undeviating, unyielding.

antonym moderate.

hardly *adv* barely, by no means, faintly, harshly, infrequently, just, no way, not at all, not quite, only, only just, roughly, scarcely, severely, with difficulty.

antonyms easily, very.

hardness *n* coldness, difficulty, firmness, harshness, inhumanity, insensitivity, laboriousness, pitilessness, rigidity, severity, solidity, steel, sternness, toughness.

antonyms ease, mildness, softness.

hard-pressed *adj* hard-pushed, harassed, harried, pushed, under pressure, up against it, with one's back to the wall.

antonym untroubled.

hardship *n* adversity, affliction, austerity, burden, calamity, destitution, difficulty, fatigue, grievance, labour, misery, misfortune, need, oppression, persecution, privation, strait, suffering, toil, torment, trial, tribulation, trouble, want.

antonym ease.

hard-wearing *adj* durable, resilient, rugged, stout, strong, sturdy, tough.

antonym delicate.

hard-working *adj* assiduous, busy, conscientious, diligent, energetic, indefatigable, industrious, sedulous, workaholic, zealous.

antonym lazy.

hardy *adj* audacious, bold, brave, brazen, courageous, daring, firm, fit, foolhardy, hale, headstrong, healthy, hearty, heroic, impudent, intrepid, lusty, manly, plucky, rash, reckless, resolute, robust, rugged, sound, spartan, stalwart, stout, stout-hearted, strong, sturdy, tough, valiant, valorous, vigorous.

antonyms unhealthy, weak.

hare-brained *adj* asinine, careless, daft, empty-headed, flighty, foolish, giddy, half-baked, harum-scarum, headlong, heedless, inane, mindless, rash, reckless, scatter-brained, scatty, unstable, unsteady, wild.

antonym sensible.

harem *n* gynaeceum, seraglio, serai(l), women's quarters, zenana.

hark *v* attend, give ear, hear, hearken, listen, mark, note, notice, pay attention, pay heed.

hark back go back, recall, recollect, regress, remember, revert.

harlot *n* call-girl, fallen woman, hussy, loon, loose fish, loose woman, lorette, Paphian, pro, prostitute, scrubber, street-walker, strumpet, tart, tramp, whore.

harm *n* abuse, damage, detriment, disservice, evil, hurt, ill, immorality, impairment, iniquity, injury, loss, mischief, misfortune, scathe, sin, sinfulness, vice, wickedness, wrong.

antonyms benefit, service.

v abuse, blemish, damage, hurt, ill-treat, ill-use, impair, injure, maltreat, mar, molest, ruin, scathe, spoil, wound.

antonyms benefit, improve.

harmful *adj* baleful, baneful, damaging, deleterious, destructive, detrimental, disadvantageous, evil, hurtful, injurious, noxious, pernicious, pestful, pestiferous, pestilent, scatheful.

antonym harmless.

harmless *adj* gentle, innocent, innocuous, innoxious, inoffensive, non-toxic, safe, scatheless, unharmed, uninjured, unobjectionable, unscathed.

antonym harmful.

harmonious *adj* according, agreeable, amicable, compatible, concinnous, concordant, congenial, congruous, consonant, consonous, co-ordinated, cordial, correspondent, dulcet, euharmonic, euphonic, euphonious, eurhythmic, friendly, harmonic, harmonising, matching, mellifluous, melodious, musical, sweet-sounding, sympathetic, symphonious, tuneful.

antonym inharmonious.

harmonise *v* accommodate, accord, adapt, agree, arrange, attune, blend, chime, cohere, compose, co-ordinate, correspond, jibe, match, reconcile, suit, tally, tone.

antonym clash.

harmony *n* accord, agreement, amicability, amity, balance, chime, compatibility, concinnity, concord, conformity, congruity, consensus, consistency, consonance, co-operation, co-ordination, correspondence, correspondency, diapason, euphony, eurhythmy, fitness, friendship, goodwill, like-mindedness, melodiousness, melody, parallelism, peace, rapport, suitability, symmetry, sympathy, tune, tunefulness, unanimity, understanding, unity.

antonym discord.

harness *n* equipment, gear, reins, straps, tack, tackle, trappings.

v apply, channel, control, couple, employ, exploit, make use of, mobilise, saddle, turn to account, use, utilise, yoke.

harp on (about) dwell on, labour, press, reiterate, renew, repeat.

harpoon *n* arrow, barb, dart, grains, spear, trident.

harpy *n* gold-digger, harriden, man-eater, vamp, vampire.

harridan *n* battle-axe, dragon, fury, gorgon, harpy, hell-cat, nag, scold, shrew, tartar, termagant, virago, vixen, witch, Xanthippe.

harried *adj* agitated, anxious, beset, bothered, distressed, hag-ridden, harassed, hard-pressed, hassled, plagued, pressured, pressurised, ravaged, tormented, troubled, worried.

antonym untroubled.

harrow *v* agonise, daunt, dismay, distress, harass, lacerate, perturb, rack, rend, tear, torment, torture, vex, wound, wring.

antonyms assuage, hearten.

harrowing *adj* agonising, alarming, chilling, distressing, disturbing, excruciating, frightening, heart-rending, lacerant, nerve-racking, racking, soaring, terrifying, tormenting, traumatic.

antonyms calming, heartening.

harry *v* annoy, badger, bedevil, chivvy, depredate, despoil, devastate, disturb, fret, harass, hassle, maraud, molest, persecute, pester, pillage, plague, plunder, raid, ravage, rob, sack, tease, torment, trouble, vex, worry.

antonyms aid, calm.

harsh *adj* abrasive, abusive, austere, bitter, bleak, brutal, coarse, comfortless, croaking, crude, cruel, discordant, dissonant, dour, Draconian, glaring, grating, grim, guttural, hard, jarring, pitiless, punitive, rasping, raucous, relentless, rough, ruthless, scabrous, severe, sharp, Spartan, stark, stern, strident, stringent, unfeeling, ungentle, unkind, unmelodious, unpleasant, unrelenting.

antonyms mild, smooth, soft.

harshness *n* abrasiveness, acerbity, acrimony, asperity, austerity, bitterness, brutality, churlishness, coarseness, crudity, hardness, ill-temper, rigour, roughness, severity, sourness, starkness, sternness, strictness.

antonyms mildness, softness.

harum-scarum *adj* careless, erratic, flighty, giddy, haphazard, hare-brained, hasty, ill-considered, impetuous, imprudent, irresponsible, precipitate, rash, reckless, scatter-brained, scatty, wild.

antonym sensible.

harvest *n* collection, consequence, crop, effect, fruition, harvesting, harvest-time, hockey, ingathering, inning, produce, product, reaping, result, return, vendage, yield.

v accumulate, acquire, amass, collect, garner, gather, mow, pick, pluck, reap.

hash[1] *n* botch, confusion, cow's arse, fuck-up, hotchpotch, jumble, mess, mishmash, mix-up, muddle, shambles.

hash[2] *n* goulash, hotpot, lob's course, lobscouse, stew.

hash[3] *see* **hashish**.

hashish *n* bhang, cannabis, charas, churrus, dope, ganja, grass, hash, hemp, marijuana, pot.

hassle *n* altercation, argument, bickering, bother, difficulty, disagreement, dispute, fight, inconvenience, nuisance, problem, quarrel, squabble, struggle, trial, trouble, tussle, upset, wrangle.

antonyms agreement, peace.

v annoy, badger, bother, bug, chivvy, harass, harry, hound, pester.

antonyms assist, calm.

haste *n* alacrity, briskness, bustle, celerity, dispatch, expedition, fleetness, hastiness, hurry, hustle, impetuosity, nimbleness, precipitance, precipitancy, precipitateness, precipitation, promptitude, quickness, rapidity, rapidness, rashness, recklessness, rush, speed, swiftness, urgency, velocity.

antonyms care, deliberation, slowness.

hasten *v* accelerate, advance, bolt, dash, dispatch, expedite, fly, gallop, goad, haste, have it on one's toes, hightail it, hurry, make haste, precipitate, press, quicken, race, run, rush, scurry, scuttle, speed, speed up, sprint, step on it, step up, tear, trot, urge.

antonym dawdle.

hastily *adv* apace, chop-chop, double-quick, fast, heedlessly, hurriedly, impetuously, impulsively, posthaste, precipitately, promptly, quickly, rapidly, rashly, recklessly, speedily, straightaway.

antonyms carefully, deliberately, slowly.

hasty *adj* brief, brisk, brusque, cursory, eager, excited, expeditious, fast, fiery, fleet, fleeting, foolhardy, headlong, heedless, hot-headed, hot-tempered, hurried, impatient, impetuous, impulsive, indiscreet, irascible, irritable, passing, passionate, perfunctory, precipitant, precipitate, prompt, quick-tempered, rapid, rash, reckless, rushed, short, snappy, speedy, subitaneous, superficial, swift, thoughtless, urgent.

antonyms careful, deliberate, placid, slow.

hat *n* beret, biretta, boater, bonnet, bowler, cap, lid, night-cap, poke-bonnet, skull-cap, sombrero, sou'wester, titfer, top-hat, trilby, yarmulka.

hatch *v* breed, brood, conceive, concoct, contrive, cook up, design, develop, devise, dream up, incubate, originate, plan, plot, project, scheme, think up.

hate *v* abhor, abominate, despise, detest, dislike, execrate, loathe, spite.

antonym like.

n abhorrence, abomination, animosity, animus, antagonism, antipathy, averseness, aversion, detestation, dislike, enmity, execration, hatred, hostility, loathing, odium, odium theologicum.

antonym like.

hateful *adj* abhorrent, abominable, damnable, despicable, detestable, disgusting, execrable, forbidding, foul, hateworthy, heinous, horrible, loathsome, obnoxious, odious, offensive, repellent, repugnant, repulsive, revolting, vile.

antonym pleasing.

hatred *n* abomination, animosity, animus, antagonism, antipathy, aversion, despite, detestation, dislike, enmity, execration, hate, ill-will, misandry, misanthropy, odium, repugnance, revulsion.

antonym like.

haughtiness *n* airs, aloofness, arrogance, conceit, contempt, contemptuousness, disdain, hauteur, insolence, loftiness, pomposity, pride, snobbishness, snootiness, superciliousness.

antonyms friendliness, humility.

haughty *adj* arrogant, assuming, cavalier, conceited, contemptuous, disdainful, fastuous, high, high and mighty, highty-tighty, hoity-toity, imperious, lofty, overweening, proud, scornful, snobbish, snooty, stiff-necked, stomachful, stuck-up, supercilious, superior, uppish.

antonyms friendly, humble.

haul *v* bouse, carry, cart, convey, drag, draw, hale, heave, hump, lug, move, pull, tow, trail, transport, trice, tug.

n booty, bunce, catch, drag, find, gain, harvest, heave, loot, pull, spoils, swag, takings, tug, yield.

haunches *n* buttocks, huckles, hucks, hunkers, nates, thighs.

haunt *v* beset, frequent, obsess, plague, possess, prey on, recur, repair, resort, torment, trouble, visit, walk.

n den, gathering-place, hangout, howf(f), meeting place, rendezvous, resort, stamping ground.

haunted *adj* cursed, eerie, ghostly, hag-ridden, jinxed, obsessed, plagued, possessed, preoccupied, spooky, tormented, troubled, worried.

haunting *adj* disturbing, eerie, evocative, indelible, memorable, nostalgic, persistent, poignant, recurrent, recurring, unforgettable.

antonym unmemorable.

have *v* accept, acquire, allow, bear, beget, cheat, comprehend, comprise, consider, contain, deceive, deliver, dupe, embody, endure, enjoy, entertain, experience, feel, fool, gain, get, give birth to, hold, include, keep, obtain, occupy, outwit, own, permit, possess, procure, produce, put up with, receive, retain, secure, suffer, sustain, swindle, take, tolerate, trick, undergo.

have done with be through with, cease, desist, finish with, give up, stop, throw over, wash one's hands of.

have to be compelled, be forced, be obliged, be required, have got to, must, ought, should.

haven *n* anchorage, asylum, harbour, hithe, port, refuge, retreat, roads, roadstead, sanctuary, sanctum, shelter.

havoc *n* carnage, chaos, confusion, damage, depopulation, desolation, despoliation, destruction, devastation, disorder, disruption, mayhem, rack and ruin, ravages, ruin, shambles, slaughter, waste, wreck.

hawk[1] *v* bark, cry, market, offer, peddle, sell, tout, vend.

hawk[2] *n* buzzard, falcon, goshawk, haggard, t(i)ercel, warmonger.

hawker *n* barrow-boy, cheap-jack, colporteur, coster, costermonger, crier, huckster, pedlar, vendor.

haywire *adj* amiss, chaotic, confused, crazy, disarranged, disordered, disorganised, erratic, kaput, mad, shambolic, tangled, topsy-turvy, wild.

antonyms correct, in order.

hazard *n* accident, chance, coincidence, danger, death-trap, endangerment, fluke, imperilment, jeopardy, luck, mischance, misfortune, mishap, peril, risk, threat.

antonym safety.

v advance, attempt, chance, conjecture, dare, endanger, expose, gamble, imperil, jeopardise, offer, presume, proffer, risk, speculate, stake, submit, suggest, suppose, threaten, venture, volunteer.

hazardous *adj* chancy, dangerous, dicey, difficult, fraught, hairy, haphazard, insecure, perilous, precarious, risky, thorny, ticklish, uncertain, unpredictable, unsafe.

antonyms safe, secure.

haze *n* cloud, dimness, film, fog, mist, nebulosity, obscurity, smog, smokiness, steam, unclearness, vapour.

hazy *adj* blurry, clouded, cloudy, dim, distanceless, dull, faint, foggy, fuzzy, ill-defined, indefinite, indistinct, loose, milky, misty, muddled, muzzy, nebulous, obscure, overcast, smoky, uncertain, unclear, vague, veiled.

antonyms clear, definite.

head *n* ability, apex, aptitude, bean, beginning, bonce, boss, brain, brains, branch, capacity, cape, captain, caput, category, chief, chieftain, chump, class, climax, commander, commencement, conclusion, conk, cop, cranium, crest, crisis, crown, culmination, department, director, division, end, faculty, flair, fore, forefront, foreland, front, godfather, head teacher, heading, headland, headmaster, headmistress, height, intellect, intelligence, knowledge box, leader, loaf, manager, master, mastermind, mentality, mind, nab, napper, nob, noddle, nut, origin, pate, peak, pitch, point, principal, promontory, rise, sconce, section, skull, source, start, subject, summit, superintendent, supervisor, talent, tête, thought, tip, top, topic, topknot, turning-point, understanding, upperworks, van, vanguard, vertex.

antonyms foot, subordinate, tail.

adj arch, chief, dominant, first, foremost, front, highest, leading, main, pre-eminent, premier, prime, principal, supreme, top, topmost.

v aim, cap, command, control, crown, direct, govern, guide, lead, make a beeline, make for, manage, oversee, point, precede, rule, run, steer, superintend, supervise, top, turn.

head for aim for, direct towards, gravitate towards, make for, point to, steer for, turn for, zero in on.

head off avert, deflect, distract, divert, fend off, forestall, intercept, interpose, intervene, parry, prevent, stop, ward off.

head over heels completely, intensely, recklessly, thoroughly, uncontrollably, utterly, whole-heartedly, wildly.

headache *n* bane, bother, cephalalgia, hassle, hemicrania, inconvenience, migraine, neuralgia, nuisance, problem, trouble, vexation, worry.

heading *n* caption, category, class, descriptor, division, headline, lemma, name, rubric, section, superscription, title.

headland *n* bill, bluff, cape, cliff, foreland, head, morro, mull, naze, point, promontory.

headlong *adj* breakneck, dangerous, hasty, head-first, head-foremost, head-on, hell-for-leather, impetuous, impulsive, inconsiderate, precipitate, reckless, thoughtless.

adv hastily, head first, head foremost, head-on, heedlessly, hell for leather, helter-skelter, hurriedly, lickety-split, pell-mell, precipitately, rashly, thoughtlessly, wildly.

head-man *n* captain, chief, leader, muqaddam, ruler, sachem.

headquarters *n* base camp, head office, high command, HQ, nerve centre, praetorium.

headstrong *adj* bull-headed, contrary, foolhardy, fractious, froward, heedless, imprudent, impulsive, intractable, mulish, obstinate, perverse, pig-headed, rash, reckless, self-willed, stubborn, ungovernable, unruly, wilful.

antonyms biddable, docile, obedient.

headway *n* advance, improvement, inroad(s), progress, progression, way.

heady *adj* exciting, exhilarating, hasty, impetuous, impulsive, inconsiderate, inebriant, intoxicating, overpowering, potent, precipitate, rash, reckless, spirituous, stimulating, strong, thoughtless, thrilling.

heal *v* alleviate, ameliorate, balsam, compose, conciliate, cure, harmonise, mend, patch up, physic, reconcile, regenerate, remedy, restore, salve, settle, soothe, treat.

healing *adj* analeptic, assuaging, comforting, curative, emollient, epulotic, gentle, lenitive, medicinal, mild, mitigative, palliative, remedial, restorative, restoring, sanative, sanatory, soothing, styptic, therapeutic, vulnerary.

health *n* condition, constitution, fettle, fitness, form, good condition, haleness, heal, healthiness, robustness, salubrity, shape, soundness, state, strength, tone, vigour, weal, welfare, well-being.

antonyms disease, infirmity.

healthy *adj* active, beneficial, blooming, bracing, fine, fit, flourishing, good, hale (and hearty), hardy, healthful, health-giving, hearty, hygienic, in fine feather, in fine fettle, in fine form, in good condition, in good shape, in the pink, invigorating, nourishing, nutritious, physically fit, robust, salubrious, salutary, salutiferous, sound, strong, sturdy, vigorous, well, wholesome.

antonyms diseased, ill, infirm, sick, unhealthy.

heap *n* accumulation, acervation, aggregation, bing, clamp, cock, collection, cumulus, hoard, lot, mass, mound, mountain, pile, ruck, stack, stockpile, store.

v accumulate, amass, assign, augment, bank, bestow, build, burden, collect, confer, gather, hoard, increase, lavish, load, mound, pile, shower, stack, stockpile, store.

heaps *n* a lot, abundance, great deal, lashings, load(s), lots, mass, millions, mint, ocean(s), oodles, plenty, pot(s), quantities, scores, stack(s), tons.

hear *v* acknowledge, ascertain, attend, catch, discover, eavesdrop, examine, find, gather, hark, hearken, heed, investigate, judge, learn, listen, overhear, pick up, try, understand.

hearing *n* audience, audition, auditory, auditory range, ear, ear-shot, inquest, inquiry, inquisition, interview, investigation, perception, range, reach, review, sound, trial.

hearsay *n* bruit, buzz, gossip, grapevine, on-dit, report, rumour, talk, talk of the town, tittle-tattle, word of mouth.

heart *n* affection, benevolence, boldness, bravery, centre, character, compassion, concern, core, courage, crux, disposition, emotion, essence, feeling, fortitude, guts, hub, humanity, inclination, kernel, love, marrow, mettle, middle, mind, nature, nerve, nerve centre, nub, nucleus, pith, pity, pluck, purpose, quintessence, resolution, root, sentiment, soul, spirit, spunk, sympathy, temperament, tenderness, ticker, understanding, will.

heart and soul absolutely, completely, devotedly, eagerly, entirely, gladly, heartily, unreservedly, whole-heartedly.

heartache *n* affliction, agony, anguish, bitterness, dejection, despair, despondency, distress, grief, heartbreak, heart-sickness, pain, remorse, sorrow, suffering, torment, torture.

heartbreak *n* agony, anguish, dejection, desolation, despair, grief, misery, pain, sorrow, suffering.

antonyms elation, joy, relief.

heartbreaking *adj* agonising, bitter, desolating, disappointing, distressing, grievous, harrowing, heart-rending, pitiful, poignant, sad, tragic.

antonyms heartening, heartwarming, joyful.

heartbroken *adj* broken-hearted, crestfallen, crushed, dejected, desolate, despondent, disappointed, disconsolate, disheartened, dispirited, down, downcast, grieved, heart-sick, miserable, woebegone.

antonyms delighted, elated.

hearten *v* animate, assure, buck up, buoy up, cheer, comfort, console, embolden, encourage, gladden, incite, inspire, inspirit, pep up, reassure, revivify, rouse, stimulate.

antonym dishearten.

heart-felt *adj* ardent, cordial, deep, devoted, devout, earnest, fervent, genuine, hearty, honest, impassioned, infelt, profound, sincere, unfeigned, warm, whole-hearted.

antonyms false, insincere.

heartily *adv* absolutely, completely, cordially, deeply, eagerly, earnestly, enthusiastically, feelingly, genuinely, gladly, profoundly, resolutely, sincerely, thoroughly, totally, unfeignedly, very, vigorously, warmly, zealously.

heartless *adj* brutal, callous, cold, cold-blooded, cold-hearted, cruel, hard, hard-hearted, harsh, inhuman, merciless, pitiless, stern, uncaring, unfeeling, unkind.

antonyms considerate, kind, merciful, sympathetic.

heart-rending *adj* affecting, distressing, harrowing, heartbreaking, moving, pathetic, piteous, pitiful, poignant, sad, tear-jerking, tragic.

heart-throb *n* dreamboat, matinée idol, pin-up, star.

heartwarming *adj* affecting, cheering, encouraging, gladsome, gratifying, heartening, moving, pleasing, rewarding, satisfying, touching, warming.

antonym heart-breaking.

hearty *adj* active, affable, ample, ardent, cordial, doughty, eager, earnest, ebullient, effusive, energetic, enthusiastic, exuberant, filling, friendly, generous, genial, genuine, hale, hardy, healthy, heartfelt, honest, jovial, nourishing, real, robust, sincere, sizeable, solid, sound, square, stalwart, strong, substantial, true, unfeigned, unreserved, vigorous, warm, well, whole-hearted.

antonyms cold, emotionless.

heat *n* agitation, ardour, calefaction, earnestness, excitement, fervour, fever, fieriness, fury, hotness, impetuosity, incandescence, intensity, passion, sizzle, sultriness, swelter, torridity, vehemence, violence, warmness, warmth, zeal.

antonyms cold(ness), coolness.

v animate, calefy, chafe, excite, flush, glow, impassion, inflame, inspirit, reheat, rouse, stimulate, stir, toast, warm up.

antonyms chill, cool.

heated *adj* acrimonious, angry, bitter, excited, fierce, fiery, frenzied, furious, impassioned, intense, passionate, perfervid, raging, stormy, tempestuous, vehement, violent.

antonym dispassionate.

heathen *n* barbarian, gentile, idolator, idolatress, infidel, nations, nullifidian, pagan, philistine, savage, unbeliever.

antonym believer.

adj barbaric, gentile, godless, heathenish, idolatrous, infidel, irreligious, nullifidian, pagan, philistine, savage, uncivilised, unenlightened.

antonyms Christian, godly.

heave *v* billow, breathe, cast, chuck, dilate, drag, elevate, exhale, expand, fling, gag, groan, haul, heft, hitch, hoist, hurl, let fly, lever, lift, palpitate, pant, pitch, puff, pull, raise, retch, rise, send, sigh, sling, sob, spew, surge, suspire, swell, throb, throw, throw up, toss, tug, vomit, yomp.

heaven *n* bliss, ecstasy, Elysian fields, Elysium, empyrean, enchantment, ether, felicity, fiddler's green, firmament, happiness, happy hunting-ground(s), hereafter, Land of the Leal, next world, nirvana, paradise, rapture, sky, Swarga, transport, utopia, Valhalla, welkin, Zion.

antonym hell.

heavenly *adj* alluring, ambrosial, angelic, beatific, beautiful, blessed, blest, blissful, celestial, delightful, divine, empyrean, entrancing, exquisite, extra-terrestrial, glorious, godlike, holy, immortal, lovely, paradisaic(al), paradisal, paradisean, paradisial, paradisian, paradisic, rapturous, ravishing, seraphic, sublime, superhuman, supernal, supernatural, Uranian, wonderful.

antonym hellish.

heavens *n* ether, firmament, sky, the blue, the wild blue yonder, welkin.

heavily *adv* awkwardly, closely, clumsily, compactly, completely, considerably, copiously, decisively, deep, deeply, dejectedly, densely, dully, excessively, fast, frequently, gloomily, hard, heftily, laboriously, painfully, ponderously, profoundly, roundly, sluggishly, solidly, sound, soundly, thick, thickly, thoroughly, to excess, utterly, weightily, woodenly.

antonym lightly.

heaviness *n* arduousness, burdensomeness, deadness, dejection, depression, despondency, drowsiness, dullness, gloom, gloominess, glumness, gravity, grievousness, heftiness, languor, lassitude, melancholy, numbness, onerousness, oppression, oppressiveness, ponderousness, sadness, seriousness, severity, sleepiness, sluggishness, somnolence, torpor, weight, weightiness.

antonyms lightness, liveliness.

heavy *adj* abundant, apathetic, boisterous, bulky, burdened, burdensome, clumpy, complex, considerable, copious, crestfallen, deep, dejected, depressed, despondent, difficult, disconsolate, downcast, drowsy, dull, encumbered, excessive, gloomy, grave, grieving, grievous, hard, harsh, hefty, inactive, indolent, inert, intolerable, laborious, laden, large, leaden, listless, loaded, lumping, lumpish, massive, melancholy, onerous, oppressed, oppressive, ponderous, portly, profound, profuse, rough, sad, serious, severe, slow, sluggish, solemn, sorrowful, squabbish, stodgy, stormy, stupid, tedious, tempestuous, torpid, turbulent, vexatious, violent, wearisome, weighted, weighty, wild, wooden.

antonyms airy, insignificant, light.

heavy-handed *adj* autocratic, awkward, bungling, clumsy, domineering, graceless, ham-fisted, ham-handed, harsh, inconsiderate, inept, inexpert, insensitive, maladroit, oppressive, overbearing, tactless, thoughtless, unsubtle.

heavy-hearted *adj* crushed, depressed, despondent, discouraged, disheartened, downcast, downhearted, forlorn, glum, heart-sick, heart-sore, melancholy, miserable, morose, mournful, sad, sorrowful.

antonym light-hearted.

heckle *v* bait, barrack, catcall, disrupt, gibe, interrupt, jeer, pester, shout down, taunt.

hectic *adj* animated, boisterous, chaotic, excited, fast, fevered, feverish, flurrying, flustering, frantic, frenetic, frenzied, furious, heated, rapid, riotous, rumbustious, tumultuous, turbulent, wild.

antonym leisurely.

hector *v* badger, bluster, boast, browbeat, bully, bullyrag, chivvy, harass, huff, intimidate, menace, nag, provoke, roister, threaten, worry.

hedge *n* barrier, boundary, compensation, counterbalance, dike, dyke, guard, hedgerow, insurance, protection, quickset, screen, wind-break.

v block, circumscribe, confine, cover, dodge, duck, equivocate, fortify, guard, hem in, hinder, insure, obstruct, protect, quibble, restrict, safeguard, shield, sidestep, stall, temporise, waffle.

hedonism *n* dolce vita, epicureanism, epicurism, gratification, luxuriousness, pleasure-seeking, self-indulgence, sensualism, sensuality, sybaritism, voluptuousness.

antonym asceticism.

hedonist *n* bon vivant, epicure, epicurean, pleasure-seeker, sensualist, swinger, sybarite, voluptuary.

antonym ascetic.

hedonistic *adj* epicurean, luxurious, pleasure-seeking, self-indulgent, swinging, sybaritic, voluptuous.

antonyms ascetic, austere.

heed *n* animadversion, attention, care, caution, consideration, ear, heedfulness, mind, note, notice, reck, regard, respect, thought, watchfulness.

antonyms inattention, indifference, unconcern.

v animadvert, attend, consider, follow, listen, mark, mind, note, obey, observe, regard, take notice of.

antonyms disregrad, ignore.

heedful *adj* attentive, careful, cautious, chary, circumspect, mindful, observant, prudent, regardful, vigilant, wary, watchful.

antonym heedless.

heedless *adj* careless, étourdi(e), foolhardy, imprudent, inattentive, incautious, incurious, inobservant, neglectful, negligent, oblivious, precipitate, rash, reckless, thoughtless, uncaring, unconcerned, unheedful, unheedy, unmindful, unobservant, unthinking.

antonym heedful.

heel *n* blackguard, bounder, cad, crust, end, hallux, hock, remainder, rotter, rump, scoundrel, spur, stub, stump, swine.

hefty *adj* ample, awkward, beefy, big, brawny, bulky, burly, colossal, cumbersome, forceful, heavy, hulking, husky, large, massive, muscular, ponderous, powerful, robust, solid, strapping, strong, substantial, thumping, tremendous, unwieldy, vigorous, weighty.

antonyms slight, small.

height *n* acme, altitude, apex, apogee, ceiling, celsitude, climax, crest, crown, culmination, degree, dignity, elevation, eminence, exaltation, extremity, grandeur, highness, hill, limit, loftiness, maximum, mountain, ne plus ultra, peak, pinnacle, prominence, stature, summit, tallness, top, ultimate, utmost, uttermost, vertex, zenith.

antonym depth.

heighten *v* add to, aggrandise, aggravate, amplify, augment, elevate, enhance, ennoble, exalt, greaten, improve, increase, intensify, magnify, raise, sharpen, strengthen, uplift.

antonyms decrease, diminish.

heinous *adj* abhorrent, abominable, atrocious, awful, evil, execrable, facinorous, flagrant, grave, hateful, hideous, immitigable, infamous, iniquitous, monstrous, nefarious, odious, outrageous, revolting, shocking, unspeakable, vicious, villainous.

heir *n* beneficiary, co-heir, heiress, heritor, inheritor, inheritress, inheritrix, parcener, scion, successor.

hell *n* Abaddon, abyss, Acheron, affliction, agony, anguish, Erebus, Gehenna, Hades, hellfire, infernal regions, inferno, lower regions, Malebolge, martyrdom, misery, nether world, nightmare, ordeal, suffering, Tartarus, Tophet, torment, trial, underworld, wretchedness.

antonym heaven.

hell-bent *adj* bent, determined, dogged, fixed, inflexible, intent, intransigent, obdurate, resolved, set, settled, tenacious, unhesitating, unwavering.

hellish *adj* abominable, accursed, atrocious, barbarous, cruel, damnable, damned, demoniacal, detestable, devilish, diabolical, execrable, fiendish, infernal, inhuman, monstrous, nefarious, Stygian, sulphurous, vicious, wicked.

antonym heavenly.

helm *n* command, control, direction, driving seat, leadership, reins, rudder, rule, saddle, tiller, wheel.

hello *interj* chin-chin, ciao, hail, hi, hiya, how-do-you-do, howdy, salve, what cheer, wotcher.

antonym good-bye.

help[1] *v* abet, abstain, aid, alleviate, ameliorate, assist, avoid, back, befriend, bestead, control, co-operate, cure, ease, eschew, facilitate, forbear, heal, hinder, improve, keep from, lend a hand, mitigate, prevent, promote, rally round, refrain from, relieve, remedy, resist, restore, save, second, serve, shun, stand by, succour, support, withstand.

antonym hinder.

n adjuvant, advice, aid, aidance, assistance, avail, benefit, co-operation, guidance, leg up, service, support, use, utility.

antonym hindrance.

help[2] *n* assistant, daily, employee, hand, helper, worker.

helper *n* abettor, adjutant, aide, aider, ally, assistant, attendant, auxiliary, coadjutor, collaborator, colleague, deputy, girl Friday, helpmate, man Friday, mate, PA, partner, person Friday, right-hand man, Samaritan, second, subsidiary, supporter.

helpful *adj* accommodating, adjuvant, advantageous, beneficent, beneficial, benevolent, caring, considerate, constructive, co-operative, favourable, fortunate, friendly, furthersome, kind, neighbourly, practical, productive, profitable, serviceable, supportive, sympathetic, timely, useful.

antonyms futile, useless, worthless.

helping *n* amount, dollop, piece, plateful, portion, ration, serving, share.

helpless *adj* abandoned, adynamic, aidless, debilitated, defenceless, dependent, destitute, disabled, exposed, feeble, forlorn, friendless, impotent, incapable, incompetent, infirm, paralysed, powerless, unfit, unprotected, vulnerable, weak.

antonyms competent, enterprising, independent, resourceful, strong.

helpmate *n* assistant, associate, better half, companion, consort, helper, helpmeet, husband, other half, partner, spouse, support, wife.

helter-skelter *adv* carelessly, confusedly, hastily, headlong, hurriedly, impulsively, pell-mell, rashly, recklessly, wildly.

adj anyhow, confused, disordered, disorganised, haphazard, higgledy-piggledy, hit-or-miss, jumbled, muddled, random, topsy-turvy, unsystematic.

hem *n* border, edge, fringe, margin, skirt, trimming.

v beset, border, circumscribe, confine, edge, enclose, engird, environ, fimbriate, gird, hedge, restrict, skirt, surround.

hence *adv* accordingly, ergo, therefore, thus.

henceforth *adv* hence, henceforward, hereafter, hereinafter.

henchman *n* aide, associate, attendant, bodyguard, cohort, crony, follower, gallo(w)glass, heavy, heeler, house-carl, jackal, led captain, minder, minion, myrmidon, right-hand man, running dog, satellite, sidekick, subordinate, supporter.

henpeck *v* badger, browbeat, bully, carp, cavil, chide, chivvy, criticise, domineer, find fault, harass, hector, intimidate, nag, niggle, pester, scold, torment.

henpecked *adj* browbeaten, bullied, cringing, dominated, intimidated, meek, subject, subjugated, timid.

antonym dominant.

herald *n* courier, crier, forerunner, harbinger, indication, messenger, omen, precursor, sign, signal, token, vaunt-courier.

v advertise, announce, broadcast, forebode, foretoken, harbinger, indicate, pave the way, portend, precede, presage, proclaim, prognosticate, promise, publicise, publish, show, trumpet, usher in.

heraldry *n* arms, badge, blazonry, crest, emblazonry, emblem, ensign, (e)scutcheon, hatchment, insignia, pageantry, regalia.

herculean *adj* arduous, athletic, brawny, colossal, daunting, demanding, difficult, enormous, exacting, exhausting, formidable, gigantic, great, gruelling, hard, heavy, huge, husky, laborious, large, mammoth, massive, mighty, muscular, onerous, powerful, prodigious, rugged, sinewy, stalwart, strapping, strenuous, strong, sturdy, titanic, toilsome, tough, tremendous.

herd *n* assemblage, canaille, collection, cowherd, crowd, crush, drove, flock, herdboy, herdsman, horde, mass, mob, multitude, populace, press, rabble, riff-raff, shepherd, swarm, the hoi polloi, the masses, the plebs, throng, vulgus.

v assemble, associate, collect, congregate, drive, flock, force, gather, goad, guard, guide, huddle, lead, muster, protect, rally, shepherd, spur, watch.

herdsman *n* cowherd, cowman, drover, grazier, stockman, vaquero, wrangler.

here and there from pillar to post, hither and thither, passim, sporadically, to and fro.

hereafter *adv* eventually, hence, henceforth, henceforward, in future, later.

n after-life, Elysian fields, happy hunting-ground, heaven, life after death, next world.

hereditary *adj* ancestral, bequeathed, congenital, family, genetic, handed down, inborn, inbred, inheritable, inherited, patrimonial, traditional, transmissible, transmittable, transmitted, willed.

heresy *n* apostasy, dissidence, error, free-thinking, heterodoxy, iconoclasm, impiety, revisionism, schism, unorthodoxy.

antonym orthodoxy.

heretic *n* apostate, dissenter, dissident, free-thinker, nonconformist, renegade, revisionist, schismatic, sectarian, separatist.

antonym conformist.

heretical *adj* free-thinking, heterodox, iconoclastic, idolatrous, impious, infidel, irreverent, rationalistic, revisionist, schismatic.

antonyms conformist, conventional, orthodox.

heritage *n* bequest, birthright, deserts, due, endowment, estate, history, inheritance, legacy, lot, past, patrimony, portion, record, share, tradition.

hermetic *adj* airtight, hermetical, sealed, shut, watertight.

hermit *n* anchoret, anchorite, ascetic, eremite, monk, recluse, solitaire, solitarian, solitary, stylite.

hero *n* celebrity, champion, conqueror, exemplar, goody, heart-throb, idol, male lead, paragon, protagonist, star, superstar, victor.

heroic *adj* bold, brave, classic, classical, courageous, daring, dauntless, doughty, elevated, epic, exaggerated, extravagant, fearless, gallant, game, grand, grandiose, gritty, high-flown, Homeric, inflated, intrepid, legendary, lion-hearted, mythological, spunky, stout-hearted, undaunted, valiant, valorous.

antonyms cowardly, pusillanimous, timid.

heroin *n* horse, shit, smack.

heroine *n* celebrity, female lead, goddess, ideal, idol, protagonist, star, superstar.

heroism *n* boldness, bravery, courage, courageousness, daring, derring-do, fearlessness, fortitude, gallantry, gameness, grit, intrepidity, prowess, spirit, valour.

antonyms cowardice, pusillaniminity, timidity.

hero-worship *n* admiration, adoration, adulation, deification, idealisation, idolisation, veneration.

hesitancy *n* demur, disinclination, doubt, doubtfulness, dubiousness, dubitance, dubitation, indecision, irresolution, misgiving, qualm, reluctance, reservation, swithering, uncertainty, unwillingness, wavering.

antonyms certainty, willingness.

hesitant *adj* diffident, dilatory, doubtful, half-hearted, halting, hesitating, hesitative, hesitatory, irresolute, reluctant, sceptical, shy, swithering, timid, uncertain, unsure, vacillating, wavering.

antonyms resolute, staunch.

hesitate *v* balk, be reluctant, be uncertain, be unwilling, boggle, delay, demur, dither, doubt, dubitate, falter, fumble, halt, haver, pause, scruple, shillyshally, shrink from, stammer, stumble, stutter, swither, think twice, vacillate, wait, waver.

hesitation *n* delay, demurral, doubt, dubiety, faltering, fumbling, hesitancy, indecision, irresolution, misdoubt, misgiving(s), qualm(s), reluctance, scruple(s), second thought(s), stammering, stumbling, stuttering, swithering, uncertainty, unwillingness, vacillation.

antonyms alacrity, assurance, eagerness.

heterodox *adj* dissident, free-thinking, heretical, iconoclastic, revisionist, schismatic, unorthodox, unsound.

antonym orthodox.

heterogeneous *adj* assorted, catholic, contrary, contrasted, different, discrepant, disparate, dissimilar, divergent, diverse, diversified, incongruous, miscellaneous, mixed, motley, multiform, opposed, polymorphic, unlike, unrelated, varied.

antonym homogeneous.

hew *v* axe, carve, chop, cut, fashion, fell, form, hack, lop, make, model, sculpt, sculpture, sever, shape, smooth, split.

heyday *n* bloom, boom time, florescence, floruit, flower, flowering, golden age, pink, prime, salad days, vigour.

hiatus *n* aperture, blank, breach, break, chasm, discontinuance, discontinuity, gap, interruption, interval, lacuna, lapse, opening, rift, space, void.

hidden *adj* abstruse, cabbalistic(al), clandestine, close, concealed, covered, covert, cryptic, dark, de(a)rn, delitescent, doggo, hermetic, hermetical, latent, mysterious, mystic, mystical, obscure, occult, recondite, secret, shrouded, ulterior, unapparent, unseen, veiled.

antonyms open, showing.

hide[1] *v* abscond, bury, cache, camouflage, cloak, conceal, cover, disguise, earth, eclipse, ensconce, feal, go to ground, go underground, hole up, keep dark, lie low, mask, obscure, occult, screen, secrete, shadow, shelter, shroud, stash, suppress, take cover, tappice, veil, withhold.

antonyms display, reveal, show.

hide[2] *n* deacon, fell, flaught, nebris, pelt, skin.

hide-away *n* cloister, haven, hideout, hiding-place, nest, refuge, retreat, sanctuary.

hidebound *adj* conventional, entrenched, narrow, narrow-minded, rigid, set, set in one's ways, strait-laced, ultra-conservative, unprogressive.

antonyms liberal, unconventional.

hideous *adj* abominable, appalling, awful, detestable, disgusting, dreadful, frightful, gash, gashful, gashly, ghastly, grim, grisly, grotesque, gruesome, horrendous, horrible, horrid, loathsome, macabre, monstrous, odious, repulsive, revolting, shocking, sickening, terrible, terrifying, ugly, ugsome, unsightly.

antonym beautiful.

hideout *n* den, hide-away, hiding-place, hole, lair, retreat, shelter.

hiding[1] *n* beating, caning, drubbing, flogging, hammering, larruping, lathering, leathering, licking, spanking, tanning, thrashing, walloping, whaling, whipping.

hiding[2] *n* camouflage, concealment, de(a)rn, disguise, screening, secretion, veiling.

hiding-place *n* den, haven, hide-away, hideout, hole, lair, lurking-place, mew, priest hole, refuge, retreat, sanctuary, starting-hole, stash.

hierarchy *n* echelons, grading, peck(ing) order, ranking, scale, strata.

higgledy-piggledy *adv* any old how, anyhow, confusedly, haphazardly, helter-skelter, indiscriminately, pell-mell, topsy-turvy.

adj confused, disorderly, disorganised, haphazard, indiscriminate, jumbled, muddled, topsy-turvy.

high *adj* acute, altissimo, alto, arch, arrogant, boastful, boisterous, bouncy, bragging, capital, cheerful, chief, consequential, costly, dear, delirious, despotic, distinguished, domineering, elated, elevated, eminent, euphoric, exalted, excessive, excited, exhilarated, exorbitant, expensive, extraordinary, extravagant, extreme, exuberant, freaked out, gamy, grand, grave, great, haughty, high-pitched, important, inebriated, influential, intensified, intoxicated, joyful, lavish, leading, light-hearted, lofty, lordly, luxurious, merry, mountain(s)-high, niffy, orthian, ostentatious, overbearing, penetrating, piercing, piping, pongy, powerful, prominent, proud, rich, ruling, serious, sharp, shrill, significant, soaring, soprano, spaced out, steep, stiff, stoned, strident, strong, superior, tainted, tall, towering, treble, tripping, tumultuous, turbulent, tyrannical, vainglorious, whiffy.

antonyms deep, low, lowly, short.

n apex, apogee, delirium, ecstasy, euphoria, height, intoxication, level, peak, record, summit, top, trip, zenith.

antonyms low, nadir.

high and dry abandoned, bereft, destitute, helpless, marooned, stranded.

high and mighty arrogant, cavalier, conceited, disdainful, haughty, imperious, overbearing, overweening, self-important, snobbish, stuck-up, superior.

high society aristocracy, beautiful people, crème de la crème, éite, gentry, grand monde, haut monde, jet set, nobility, upper crust.

antonym hoi polloi.

high spirits boisterousness, bounce, buoyancy, exhilaration, exuberance, good cheer, hilarity, joie de vivre, liveliness, sparkle, vivacity.

high-born *adj* aristocratic, blue-blooded, gentle, noble, patrician, pedigreed, thoroughbred, well-born, well-connected.

highbrow *n* aesthete, boffin, Brahmin, brain, egghead, intellectual, long-hair, mandarin, mastermind, savant, scholar.

adj bookish, brainy, cultivated, cultured, deep, intellectual, long-haired, serious, sophisticated.

antonym lowbrow.

high-class *adj* A1, choice, classy, de luxe, elite, exclusive, first-rate, high-quality, posh, quality, select, superior, tiptop, top-flight, tops, U, upper-class.

antonyms mediocre, ordinary.

highest *adj* apical, apogaeic, peak, record, top, topmost, upmost, uppermost, zenithal.

antonyms bottom(most), lowest.

high-falutin(g) *adj* affected, big, bombastic, florid, grandiose, high-flown, high-sounding, la(h)-di-da(h), lofty, magniloquent, pompous, pretentious, supercilious, swanky.

high-flown *adj* elaborate, elevated, exaggerated, extravagant, florid, grandiose, high-falutin(g), inflated, la(h)-di-da(h), lofty, magniloquent, overblown, pretentious, turgid.

high-handed *adj* arbitrary, autocratic, bossy, despotic, dictatorial, discourteous, disdainful, domineering, imperious, inconsiderate, oppressive, overbearing, peremptory, self-willed, tyrannical, wilful.

highlight *n* best, climax, cream, feature, focal point, focus, high point, high spot, peak, zenith.

v accent, accentuate, emphasise, feature, focus on, illuminate, play up, point up, set off, show up, spotlight, stress, underline.

highly *adv* appreciatively, approvingly, considerably, decidedly, eminently, enthusiastically, exceptionally, extraordinarily, extremely, favourably, greatly, immensely, supremely, tremendously, vastly, very, warmly, well.

highly-strung *adj* edgy, excitable, irascible, irritable, jittery, nervous, nervy, neurotic, restless, sensitive, skittish, stressed, taut, temperamental, tense.

antonyms calm, relaxed.

high-minded *adj* elevated, ethical, fair, good, honourable, idealistic, lofty, magnanimous, moral, noble, principled, pure, righteous, scrupulous, upright, virtuous, worthy.

antonyms immoral, unscrupulous.

high-powered *adj* aggressive, driving, dynamic, effective, energetic, enterprising, forceful, go-ahead, go-getting, industrious, vigorous.

high-priced *adj* costly, dear, excessive, exorbitant, expensive, extortionate, high, pricy, steep, stiff, unreasonable.

antonym cheap.

high-quality *adj* blue-chip, choice, classy, de luxe, gilt-edged, quality, select, superior, tiptop, top-class.

high-sounding *adj* affected, artificial, bombastic, extravagant, flamboyant, florid, grandiloquent, grandiose, high-flown, magniloquent, orotund, ostentatious, overblown, pompous, ponderous, pretentious, stilted, strained.

high-spirited *adj* animated, boisterous, bold, bouncy, daring, dashing, ebullient, effervescent, energetic, exuberant, frolicsome, lively, mettlesome, peppy, sparkling, spirited, spunky, vibrant, vital, vivacious.

antonyms downcast, glum.

highwayman *n* bandit, bandolero, footpad, knight of the road, land-pirate, rank-rider, robber.

hijack *v* commandeer, expropriate, kidnap, seize, skyjack, snatch, steal.

hike *v* back-pack, footslog, hoof it, leg it, plod, ramble, tramp, treck, trudge, walk.

n march, plod, ramble, tramp, trek, trudge, walk.

hilarious *adj* amusing, comical, convivial, entertaining, funny, gay, happy, humorous, hysterical, jolly, jovial, joyful, joyous, killing, merry, mirthful, noisy, rollicking, side-splitting, uproarious.

antonyms grave, serious.

hilarity *n* amusement, boisterousness, cheerfulness, conviviality, entertainment, exhilaration, exuberance, frivolity, gaiety, glee, high spirits, jollification, jollity, joviality, joyousness, laughter, levity, merriment, mirth, uproariousness.

antonyms gravity, seriousness.

hill *n* acclivity, berg, brae, butte, climb, dod, down, drift, elevation, eminence, fell, gradient, heap, height, hillock, hilltop, how, hummock, incline, knoll, knowe, kop, koppie, law, mamelon, mesa, mound, mount, pike, pile, prominence, rise, slope, stack, tor.

hillock *n* barrow, dune, hummock, knap, knoll, knowe, monticulus, mote, motte, mound, tump.

hilt *n* grip, haft, handgrip, handle, heft, helve.

hind *adj* after, back, caudal, hinder, posterior, rear, tail.

antonym fore.

hinder *v* arrest, check, counteract, debar, delay, deter, embar, encumber, forelay, frustrate, hamper, hamstring, handicap, hold back, hold up, impede, interrupt, obstruct, oppose, prevent, retard, slow down, stop, stymie, thwart, trammel.

antonyms aid, assist, help.

hindmost *adj* concluding, endmost, final, furthest, lag, last, rearmost, remotest, tail, terminal, trailing, ultimate.

antonym foremost.

hindrance *n* bar, barrier, check, demurrage, deterrent, difficulty, drag, drawback, encumbrance, handicap, hitch, impediment, interruption, limitation, obstacle, obstruction, pull-back, remora, restraint, restriction, snag, stoppage, stumbling-block, trammel.

antonyms aid, assistance, help.

hinge *v* be contingent, centre, depend, hang, pivot, rest, revolve around, turn.

n articulation, condition, foundation, garnet, joint, premise, principle.

hint *n* advice, allusion, breath, clue, dash, help, implication, indication, inkling, innuendo, insinuation, intimation, mention, pointer, reminder, scintilla, sign, signal, soupçon, speck, subindication, suggestion, suspicion, taste, tinge, tip, tip-off, touch, trace, undertone, whiff, whisper, wrinkle.

v allude, imply, indicate, inkle, innuendo, insinuate, intimate, mention, prompt, subindicate, suggest, tip off.

hinterland *n* back-blocks, back-country, backveld, hinderland, interior.

hip *n* buttocks, croup, haunch, hindquarters, huck, huckle, loin, pelvis, posterior, rump.

hippy *n* beatnik, bohemian, drop-out, flower child, hippie.

hire *v* appoint, book, charter, commission, employ, engage, lease, let, rent, reserve, retain, sign up, take on.

antonyms dismiss, fire.

n charge, cost, fare, fee, price, rent, rental, toll.

hire-purchase *n* easy terms, never-never.

hirsute *adj* bearded, bewhiskered, bristly, crinigerous, crinite, crinose, hairy, hispid, shaggy, unshaven.

antonyms bald, hairless.

hiss *n* boo, buzz, catcall, contempt, derision, hissing, hoot, jeer, mockery, raspberry, sibilance, sibilation, whistle.

v boo, catcall, condemn, damn, decry, deride, hoot, jeer, mock, rasp, revile, ridicule, shrill, sibilate, siffle, wheeze, whirr, whiss, whistle, whiz.

historic *adj* celebrated, consequential, epoch-making, extraordinary, famed, famous, momentous, notable, outstanding, red-letter, remarkable, renowned, significant.

historical *adj* actual, archival, attested, authentic, documented, factual, real, traditional, verifiable.

history *n* account, annals, antecedents, antiquity, autobiography, biography, chronicle, chronology, days of old, days of yore, genealogy, memoirs, narration, narrative, olden days, recapitulation, recital, record, relation, saga, story, tale, the past.

histrionic *adj* affected, artificial, bogus, dramatic, forced, ham, insincere, melodramatic, ranting, sensational, theatrical, unnatural.

histrionics *n* dramatics, overacting, performance, ranting and raving, scene, staginess, tantrums, temperament, theatricality.

hit *v* accomplish, achieve, affect, arrive at, attain, bang, bash, batter, bean, beat, belt, bump, clip, clobber, clock, clonk, clout, collide with, crown, cuff, damage, devastate, flog, frap, fustigate, gain, impinge on, influence, knock, lob, move, overwhelm, prop, punch, reach, secure, slap, slog, slosh, slug, smack, smash, smite, sock, strike, swat, thump, touch, volley, wallop, whack, wham, whap, w(h)op, wipe.

n blow, bump, clash, clout, collision, cuff, impact, knock, rap, sell-out, sensation, shot, slap, slog, slosh, smack, smash, sock, stroke, success, swipe, triumph, venue, wallop, winner.

hit back recalcitrate, reciprocate, retaliate.

hit on arrive at, chance on, contrive, discover, guess, invent, light on, realise, stumble on.

hit out assail, attack, castigate, condemn, criticise, denounce, inveigh, lash, lay about one, rail.

hitch *v* attach, connect, couple, fasten, harness, heave, hike (up), hitch-hike, hoi(c)k, hoist, jerk, join, pull, tether, thumb a lift, tie, tug, unite, yank, yoke.

antonyms unfasten, unhitch.

n catch, check, delay, difficulty, drawback, hiccup, hindrance, hold-up, impediment, mishap, problem, snag, stick, stoppage, trouble.

hitherto *adv* beforehand, heretofore, previously, so far, thus far, till now, until now, up to now.

hit-or-miss *adj* aimless, apathetic, casual, cursory, disorganised, haphazard, indiscriminate, lackadaisical, perfunctory, random, undirected, uneven.

hoard *n* accumulation, cache, fund, heap, mass, pile, profusion, reserve, reservoir, stockpile, store, supply, treasure-trove.

v accumulate, amass, cache, coffer, collect, deposit, garner, gather, hive, husband, lay up, put by, reposit, save, stash away, stockpile, store, treasure.

antonyms spend, squander, use.

hoarder *n* collector, gatherer, magpie, miser, niggard, squirrel.

hoarse *adj* croaky, discordant, grating, gravelly, growling, gruff, guttural, harsh, husky, rasping, raspy, raucous, rough, throaty.

antonyms clear, smooth.

hoary *adj* aged, ancient, antiquated, antique, canescent, frosty, grey, grey-haired, grizzled, hoar, old, senescent, silvery, venerable, white, white-haired.

hoax *n* bam, cheat, cod, con, deception, fast one, fraud, grift, hum, huntiegowk, hunt-the-gowk, imposture, joke, josh, leg-pull, practical joke, prank, put-on, quiz, ruse, spoof, string, swindle, trick.

v bam, bamboozle, befool, bluff, cod, con, deceive, delude, dupe, fool, gammon, gull, have on, hoodwink, hornswoggle, hum, lead on, pull someone's leg, spoof, string, stuff, swindle, take for a ride, trick.

hoaxer *n* bamboozler, grifter, hoodwinker, humbug, joker, mystifier, practical joker, prankster, quiz, quizzer, spoofer, trickster.

hobble *v* clog, dodder, falter, fasten, fetter, halt, hamshackle, hamstring, hirple, limp, restrict, shackle, shamble, shuffle, stagger, stumble, tie, totter.

hobby *n* avocation, diversion, pastime, pursuit, recreation, relaxation, sideline.

hobgoblin *n* apparition, bog(e)y, bugaboo, bugbear, buggan(e), buggin, goblin, hob, imp, spectre, spirit, sprite.

hobnob *v* associate, consort, fraternise, hang about, keep company, mingle, mix, pal around, socialise.

hocus-pocus *n* abracadabra, artifice, cant, cheat, chicanery, conjuring, deceit, deception, delusion, finesse, gibberish, gobbledegook, hoax, humbug, imposture, jargon, jugglery, legerdemain, mumbo-jumbo, nonsense, prestidigitation, rigmarole, sleight of hand, swindle, trickery, trompe-l'oeil.

hogwash *n* balderdash, bilge, bunk, bunkum, claptrap, drivel, eyewash, hooey, nonsense, piffle, rot, rubbish, tar(r)adiddle, tosh, trash, tripe, twaddle.

hoi polloi *n* admass, canaille, citizenry, commonalty, riff-raff, the common people, the great unwashed, the herd, the masses, the plebs, the populace, the proles, the proletariat, the rabble, the third estate.

antonyms aristocracy, élite, nobility.

hoist *v* elevate, erect, heave, jack up, lift, raise, rear, uplift, upraise.

n crane, davit, elevator, jack, lift, tackle, winch.

hoity-toity *adj* arrogant, conceited, disdainful, haughty, high and mighty, lofty, overweening, pompous, proud, scornful, snobbish, snooty, stuck-up, supercilious, toffee-nosed, uppish, uppity.

hold *v* accommodate, account, adhere, apply, arrest, assemble, assume, be in force, be the case, bear, believe, bond, brace, call, carry, carry on, celebrate, check, clasp, cleave, clinch, cling, clip, clutch, comprise, conduct, confine, consider, contain, continue, convene, cradle, curb, deem, delay, detain, embrace, endure, enfold, entertain, esteem, exist, grasp, grip, have, hold good, imprison, judge, keep, last, maintain, occupy, operate, own, persevere, persist, possess, preside over, presume, prop, reckon, regard, remain, remain true, remain valid, resist, restrain, retain, run, seat, shoulder, solemnise, stand up, stay, stick, stop, summon, support, suspend, sustain, take, think, view, wear.

n anchorage, asendancy, authority, clasp, clout, clutch, control, dominance, dominion, foothold, footing, grasp, grip, holt, influence, leverage, mastery, prop, pull, purchase, stay, support, sway, vantage.

hold back check, control, curb, desist, forbear, inhibit, refuse, repress, restrain, retain, stifle, suppress, withhold.

antonym release.

hold forth declaim, descant, discourse, go on, harangue, lecture, orate, preach, sermonise, speak, speechify, spiel, spout.

hold off avoid, defer, delay, fend off, keep off, postpone, put off, rebuff, refrain, repel, repulse, stave off, wait.

hold out continue, endure, extend, give, hang on, last, offer, persevere, persist, porrect, present, proffer, stand fast.

hold over adjourn, defer, delay, postpone, put off, shelve, suspend.

hold up brace, delay, detain, display, endure, exhibit, hinder, impede, last, lift, present, raise, retard, show, slow, stop, survive, sustain, waylay, wear.

hold water bear scrutiny, convince, make sense, pass the test, ring true, wash, work.

hold with accept, agree to, approve of, countenance, go along with, subscribe to, support.

holder *n* bearer, case, container, cover, cradle, custodian, housing, incumbent, keeper, occupant, owner, possessor, proprietor, purchaser. receptacle, rest, sheath, stand.

holdings *n* assets, bonds, estate, investments, land, possessions, property, real estate, resources, securities, shares, stocks.

hold-up[1] *n* bottle-neck, delay, difficulty, gridlock, hitch, obstruction, setback, snag, stoppage, (traffic) jam, trouble, wait.

hold-up[2] *n* heist, robbery, stick-up.

hole *n* aperture, breach, break, burrow, cave, cavern, cavity, chamber, covert, crack, defect, den, depression, dilemma, dimple, discrepancy, dive, dump, earth, error, excavation, eyelet, fallacy, fault, fissure, fix, flaw, foramen, fovea, gap, hollow, hovel, imbroglio, inconsistency, jam, joint, lair, loophole, mess, nest, opening, orifice, outlet, perforation, pit, pocket, pore, predicament, puncture, quandary, rent, retreat, scoop, scrape, shaft, shelter, slum, split, spot, tangle, tear, tight spot, vent, ventage.

hole-and-corner *adj* back-door, backstairs, back-stairs, clandestine, covert, furtive, hugger-mugger, hush-hush, secret, secretive, sneaky, stealthy, surreptitious, underhand, under-the-counter.

antonyms open, public.

holiday *n* anniversary, break, celebration, exeat, feast, festival, festivity, fête, furlough, gala, hols, leave, recess, respite, rest, sabbatical, saint's day, time off, vacation.

holier-than-thou *adj* complacent, goody-goody, pietistic(al), pious, priggish, religiose, sanctimonious, self-approving, self-righteous, self-satisfied, smug, unctuous.

antonyms humble, meek.

holiness *n* blessedness, devoutness, divinity, evangelicism, godliness, halidom, pietism, piety, priggishness, purity, religiosity, religiousness, righteousness, sacredness, saintliness, sanctimoniousness, sanctity, self-righteousness, spirituality, unctuosity, unctuousness, virtuousness.

antonyms impiety, wickedness.

holler *n, v* bawl, bellow, call, cheer, clamour, cry, hail, halloo, hollo, howl, hurrah, huzzah, roar, shout, shriek, whoop, yell, yelp, yowl.

hollow *adj* artificial, cavernous, concave, coreless, cynical, deaf, deceitful, deceptive, deep, deep-set, depressed, dished, dull, empty, expressionless, faithless, false, famished, flat, fleeting, flimsy, fruitless, futile, gaunt, glenoid(al), hungry, hypocritical, indented, insincere, lantern-jawed, low, meaningless, muffled, muted, pointless, Pyrrhic, ravenous, reverberant, rumbling, sepulchral, specious, starved, sunken, toneless, treacherous, unavailing, unfilled, unreal, unreliable, unsound, useless, vacant, vain, void, weak, worthless.

n basin, bottom, bowl, cave, cavern, cavity, channel, concave, concavity, coomb, crater, cup, dale, dell, den, dent, depression, dimple, dingle, dint, dish, druse, excavation, fossa, fossula, fovea, foveola, foveole, geode, gilgie, glen, gnamma hole, groove, hole, hope, how(e), indentation, invagination, pit, trough, umbilicus, vacuity, valley, vlei, well, womb.

v burrow, channel, dent, dig, dint, dish, excavate, furrow, gouge, groove, indent, pit, scoop.

holocaust *n* annihilation, carnage, conflagration, destruction, devastation, extermination, extinction, flames, genocide, hecatomb, immolation, inferno, mass murder, massacre, pogrom, sacrifice, slaughter.

holy *adj* blessed, consecrated, dedicated, devout, divine, evangelical, evangelistic, faithful, god-fearing, godly, good, hallowed, perfect, pietistic, pious, pure, religiose, religious, righteous, sacred, sacrosanct, saintly, sanctified, sanctimonious, spiritual, sublime, unctuous, venerable, venerated, virtuous.

antonyms impious, unsanctified, wicked.

homage *n* acknowledgement, admiration, adoration, adulation, allegiance, awe, deference, devotion, duty, esteem, faithfulness, fealty, fidelity, honour, loyalty, obeisance, praise, recognition, regard, respect, reverence, service, tribute, veneration, worship.

home *n* abode, almshouse, asylum, birthplace, blighty, clinic, domicile, dwelling, dwelling-place, element, environment, family, fireside, habitat, habitation, haunt, hearth, home ground, home town, homestead, hospice, hospital, house, household, institution, native heath, nest, nursing-home, old people's home, pad, pied-à-terre, range, residence, roof, sanatorium, stamping-ground, territory.

adj candid, central, direct, domestic, domiciliary, familiar, family, household, incisive, inland, internal, intimate, local, national, native, penetrating, plain, pointed, unanswerable, uncomfortable, wounding.

homeland *n* fatherland, mother country, motherland, native country, native heath, native land, native soil.

homeless *adj* abandoned, destitute, disinherited, displaced, dispossessed, down-and-out, exiled, forlorn, forsaken, houseless, itinerant, outcast, unsettled, vagabond, wandering.

n derelicts, dossers, down-and-outs, nomads, squatters, tramps, travellers, vagrants.

homely *adj* comfortable, comfy, congenial, cosy, domestic, easy, everyday, familiar, folksy, friendly, gemütlich, homelike, homespun, hom(e)y, informal, intimate, modest, natural, ordinary, plain, relaxed, simple, snug, unaffected, unassuming, unpretentious, unsophisticated, welcoming.

antonyms formal, unfamiliar.

Homeric *adj* epic, grand, heroic, imposing, impressive, Virgilian.

homesickness *n* Heimweh, mal du pays, nostalgia, nostomania.

antonym wanderlust.

homespun *adj* amateurish, artless, coarse, crude, folksy, homely, home-made, inelegant, plain, rough, rude, rustic, unpolished, unrefined, unsophisticated.

antonym sophisticated.

homicidal *adj* blood-thirsty, deadly, death-dealing, lethal, maniacal, mortal, murderous, sanguinary, violent.

homicide *n* assassin, assassination, bloodshed, cut-throat, killer, killing, liquidator, manslaughter, murder, murderer, slayer, slaying.

homily *n* address, discourse, harangue, heart-to-heart, lecture, postil, preachment, sermon, spiel, talk.

homogeneity *n* agreement, akinness, analogousness, comparability, consistency, consonancy, correspondence, identicalness, likeness, oneness, resemblance, sameness, similarity, similitude, uniformity.

antonyms difference, disagreement.

homogeneous *adj* akin, alike, analogous, cognate, comparable, consistent, consonant, harmonious, identical, indiscrete, kindred, of a piece, similar, uniform, unvarying.

antonym different.

homologous *adj* analogous, comparable, correspondent, corresponding, equivalent, like, matching, parallel, related, similar.

antonyms different, dissimilar.

homosexual *n* catamite, dike, dyke, fag, fairy, fruit, Ganymede, gunsel, homophile, invert, les, lesbian, lez, Nancy, paederast, poof, pooftah, poove, puff, punk, queen, queer, rent-boy, sapphist, tribade, urning.

antonyms heterosexual, straight.

adj bent, camp, dikey, dykey, fruity, gay, homoerotic, lesbian, paederastic, poofy, poovy, queer, sapphic.

antonyms heterosexual, straight.

homosexuality *n* gayness, homoeroticism, homoerotism, homosexualism, paederasty, poovery, queerdom, sapphism, tribadism, tribady.

antonym heterosexuality.

hone *v* edge, file, grind, point, polish, rasp, sharpen, strop, whet.

honest *adj* above-board, authentic, bona fide, candid, chaste, conscientious, decent, direct, equitable, ethical, fair, fair and square, forthright, four-square, frank, genuine, high-minded, honourable, humble, impartial, ingenuous, jake, just, law-abiding, legitimate, modest, objective, on the level, open, outright, outspoken, plain, plain-hearted, proper, real, reliable, reputable, respectable, scrupulous, seemly, simple, sincere, soothfast, square, straight, straightforward, true, trustworthy, trusty, truthful, undisguised, unequivocal, unfeigned, unreserved, upright, veracious, virtuous, well-gotten, well-won, white.

antonyms covert, devious, dishonest, dishonourable.

honestly *adv* by fair means, candidly, cleanly, conscientiously, directly, dispassionately, equitably, ethically, fairly, frankly, honourably, in all sincerity, in good faith, justly, lawfully, legally, legitimately, objectively, on the level, openly, outright, plainly, really, scrupulously, sincerely, straight, straight out, truly, truthfully, undisguisedly, unreservedly, uprightly, verily.

antonyms dishonestly, dishonourably.

honesty *n* artlessness, bluntness, candour, equity, even-handedness, explicitness, fairness, faithfulness, fidelity, frankness, genuineness, honour, incorruptibility, integrity, justness, morality, objectivity, openness, outspokenness, plain-heartedness, plainness, plain-speaking, probity, rectitude, reputability, scrupulousness, sincerity, sooth, squareness, straightforwardness, straightness, trustworthiness, truthfulness, unreserve, uprightness, veracity, verity, virtue.

antonyms deviousness, dishonesty.

honorary *adj* complimentary, ex officio, formal, honorific, honoris causa, in name only, nominal, titular, unofficial, unpaid, virtute officii.

antonyms gainful, paid, salaried, waged.

honour *n* acclaim, accolade, acknowledgement, admiration, adoration, chastity, commendation, compliment, credit, decency, deference, dignity, distinction, duty, elevation, esteem, fairness, favour, good name, goodness, homage, honesty, honorificabilitudinity, honourableness, innocence, integrity, kudos, laudation, laurels, loyalty, modesty, morality, pleasure, praise, principles, privilege, probity, purity, rank, recognition, rectitude, regard, renown, reputation, repute, respect, reverence, righteousness, self-respect, tribute, trust, trustworthiness, uprightness, veneration, virginity, virtue, worship.

antonyms disgrace, dishonour, obloquy.

v accept, acclaim, acknowledge, admire, adore, applaud, appreciate, carry out, cash, celebrate, clear, commemorate, commend, compliment, credit, crown, decorate, dignify, discharge, esteem, exalt, execute, fulfil, glorify, hallow, homage, keep, laud, laureate, lionise, observe, pass, pay, pay homage, perform, praise, prize, remember, respect, revere, reverence, take, value, venerate, worship.

antonyms betray, debase, disgrace, dishonour.

honourable *adj* creditable, distinguished, eminent, equitable, estimable, ethical, fair, great, high-minded, honest, illustrious, irreproachable, just, meritorious, moral, noble, prestigious, principled, proper, renowned, reputable, respectable, respected, right, righteous, sincere, straight, true, trustworthy, trusty, unexceptionable, upright, upstanding, venerable, virtuous, worthful, worthy.

antonyms dishonest, dishonourable, unworthy.

honours *n* awards, crowns, decorations, dignities, distinctions, laurels, prizes, rewards, titles, trophies.

antonyms aspersions, indignities.

hood *n* capeline, capuche, cowl, domino.

hoodwink *v* bamboozle, befool, blear, cheat, con, cozen, deceive, delude, dupe, fool, gammon, gull, gyp, have on, hoax, impose, mislead, rook, seel, swindle, take in, trick.

hoof *n* cloot, cloven hoof, foot, trotter, ungula.

hoofed *adj* cloven-footed, cloven-hoofed, ungulate, unguligrade.

hook *n* agraffe, barb, catch, clasp, fastener, fluke, hamulus, hasp, holder, link, lock, peg, sickle, snag, snare, springe, trap, uncus.

v bag, catch, clasp, collar, enmesh, ensnare, entangle, entrap, fasten, fix, grab, hasp, hitch, nab, secure, snare, trap.

hooked *adj* addicted, adunc, aquiline, barbed, beaked, beaky, bent, curled, curved, devoted, enamoured, falcate, hamate, hamose, hamous, hamular, hamulate, obsessed, sickle-shaped, uncate, unciform, uncinate.

hooligan *n* apache, bovver boy, delinquent, droog, hood, hoodlum, lout, mobster, ned, rough, roughneck, rowdy, ruffian, thug, tityre-tu, tough, toughie, vandal, yob, yobbo.

hoop *n* annulus, bail, band, circlet, gird, girdle, loop, ring, round, wheel.

hoot *n* beep, boo, call, card, catcall, caution, cry, hiss, howl, jeer, laugh, raspberry, scream, shout, shriek, toot, whistle, whoop, yell.

v beep, boo, catcall, condemn, cry, decry, deride, explode, hiss, howl down, jeer, ridicule, scream, shout, shriek, toot, ululate, whistle, whoop, yell, yell at.

hop *v* bound, caper, dance, fly, frisk, hitch, hobble, jump, leap, limp, nip, prance, skip, spring, vault.

n ball, barn-dance, bounce, bound, crossing, dance, flight, jump, leap, skip, social, spring, step, trip, vault.

hope *n* ambition, anticipation, aspiration, assumption, assurance, belief, confidence, conviction, desire, dream, expectancy, expectation, faith, hopefulness, longing, optimism, promise, prospect, wish.

antonyms apathy, despair, pessimism.

v anticipate, aspire, assume, await, believe, contemplate, desire, expect, foresee, long, reckon on, rely, trust, wish.

antonym despair.

hopeful *adj* assured, auspicious, bright, bullish, buoyant, cheerful, confident, encouraging, expectant, favourable, heartening, optimistic, promising, propitious, reassuring, rosy, sanguine.

antonyms despairing, discouraging, pessimistic.

n great white hope, white hope, wunderkind.

hopefully *adv* all being well, bullishly, conceivably, confidently, deo volente, eagerly, expectantly, expectedly, feasibly, optimistically, probably, sanguinely, with a bit of luck.

hopeless *adj* defeatist, dejected, demoralised, despairing, desperate, despondent, disconsolate, downhearted, foolish, forlorn, futile, helpless, impossible, impracticable, inadequate, incompetent, incorrigible, incurable, ineffectual, irredeemable, irremediable, irreparable, irreversible, lost, madcap, no-win, past cure, pessimistic, pointless, poor, reckless, unachievable, unattainable, useless, vain, woebegone, worthless, wretched.

antonyms curable, hopeful, optimistic.

horde *n* band, bevy, concourse, crew, crowd, drove, flock, gang, herd, host, mob, multitude, pack, press, swarm, throng, troop.

horizon *n* compass, ken, perspective, prospect, purview, range, realm, scope, skyline, sphere, stretch, verge, vista.

hornless *adj* muley, polled.

horny[1] *adj* callous, ceratoid, corneous, corny.

horny[2] *adj* ardent, concupiscent, lascivious, lecherous, libidinous, lickerish, lubricious, lustful, priapic, randy, ruttish.

antonyms cold, frigid.

horrible *adj* abhorrent, abominable, appalling, atrocious, awful, beastly, bloodcurdling, cruel, disagreeable, dreadful, fearful, fearsome, frightful, ghastly, grim, grisly, gruesome, heinous, hideous, horrid, horrific, loathsome, macabre, nasty, repulsive, revolting, shameful, shocking, terrible, terrifying, unkind, unpleasant, weird.

antonyms agreeable, pleasant.

horrid *adj* abominable, alarming, appalling, awful, beastly, bloodcurdling, cruel, despicable, disagreeable, disgusting, dreadful, formidable, frightening, hair-raising, harrowing, hateful, hideous, horrible, horrific, mean, nasty, odious, offensive, repulsive, revolting, shocking, terrible, terrifying, unkind, unpleasant.

antonyms agreeable, lovely, pleasant.

horrific *adj* appalling, awful, dreadful, frightening, frightful, ghastly, grim, grisly, hair-raising, harrowing, horrendous, horrifying, scaring, shocking, spine-chilling, terrifying.

horrify *v* abash, affright, alarm, appal, disgust, dismay, frighten, harrow, intimidate, outrage, petrify, scandalise, scare, shock, sicken, startle, terrify, unnerve.

antonyms delight, gratify, please.

horror *n* abhorrence, abomination, alarm, antipathy, apprehension, aversion, awe, awfulness, consternation, detestation, disgust, dismay, dread, fear, fright, frightfulness, ghastliness, gooseflesh, goose-pimples, grimness, hatred, hideousness, horripilation, loathing, outrage, panic, repugnance, revulsion, shock, terror.

horror-struck *adj* aghast, appalled, frightened, horrified, horror-stricken, petrified, shocked, stunned.

antonyms delighted, pleased.

horse *n* bayard, bronc(h)o, brumby, caple, cayuse, charger, cob, crock, cuddy, destrier, dobbin, garran, gee-gee, hack, hackney, hobbler, hobby, horseflesh, hoss, jade, jennet, mare, mount, mustang, nag, pad, palfrey, pony, stallion, steed, tit, waler, war-horse, warragal.

horse sense brains, common sense, gumption, head, judgement, mother wit, native intelligence, nous, practicality, sense.

antonym stupidity.

horse-cloth *n* caparison, horse-blanket, housing, manta, trap, trappings.

horseman *n* broncobuster, buckaroo, cavalier, cavalryman, cowboy, dragoon, equestrian, gaucho, horse-soldier, hussar, jockey, rider.

horsemanship *n* equestrianism, equitation, haute école, manège.

horseplay *n* buffoonery, capers, clowning, desipience, fooling, fooling around, fun and games, high jinks, pranks, romping, rough-and-tumble, rough-housing, rough-stuff, rumpus, skylarking.

horse-trainer *n* breaker, broncobuster, cowboy, handler, hippodamist, horse-breaker, horse-tamer, trainer.

hortatory *adj* didactic, edifying, encouraging, exhortative, exhortatory, heartening, homiletic, hortative, incitative, inspiriting, instructive, pep, practical, preceptive, stimulating.

horticulture *n* arboriculture, cultivation, floriculture, gardening.

hospitable *adj* accessible, amenable, amicable, approachable, bountiful, congenial, convivial, cordial, couthie, friendly, gemütlich, generous, genial, gracious, kind, liberal, liv(e)able, open-minded, receptive, responsive, sociable, tolerant, welcoming.

antonyms hostile, inhospitable.

hospital *n* clinic, lazaret, lazaretto, leprosarium, leproserie, leprosery, sanatorium.

hospitality *n* cheer, congeniality, conviviality, cordiality, friendliness, generosity, graciousness, open-handedness, philoxenia, sociability, warmth, welcome.

antonyms hostility, inhospitality.

host[1] *n* anchor-man, announcer, compère, emcee, entertainer, innkeeper, landlord, link man, master of ceremonies, MC, presenter, proprietor, visitee.

v compère, introduce, present.

host[2] *n* army, array, band, company, drove, horde, legion, multitude, myriad, pack, swarm, throng.

hostel *n* boarding-house, dormitory, doss-house, flophouse, Gasthaus, Gasthof, guest-house, hospice, hospital, hospitium, hostelry, hotel, inn, residence, xenodochium, youth hostel.

hostile *adj* adverse, alien, antagonistic, anti, antipathetic, bellicose, belligerent, contrary, ill-disposed, inhospitable, inimical, malevolent, opposed, opposite, oppugnant, rancorous, unfriendly, ungenial, unkind, unpropitious, unsympathetic, unwelcoming, warlike.

antonyms friendly, sympathetic.

hostilities *n* battle, bloodshed, conflict, encounter, fighting, state of war, strife, war, warfare.

hostility *n* abhorrence, animosity, animus, antagonism, antipathy, aversion, breach, detestation, disaffection, dislike, enmity, estrangement, hate, hatred, ill-will, malevolence, malice, opposition, resentment, unfriendliness.

antonyms friendliness, sympathy.

hot *adj* acrid, animated, approved, ardent, biting, blistering, boiling, burning, candent, clever, close, dangerous, eager, excellent, excited, exciting, favoured, febrile, fervent, fervid, fevered, feverish, fierce, fiery, flaming, fresh, heated, hotheaded, impetuous, impulsive, in demand, in vogue, incandescent, inflamed, intense, irascible, latest, lustful, near, new, passionate, peppery, perfervid, piping, piquant, popular, pungent, quick, raging, recent, risky, roasting, scalding, scorching, searing, sensual, sharp, sizzling, skilful, sought-after, spicy, steaming, stormy, strong, sultry, sweltering, torrid, touchy, tropical, vehement, violent, voluptuous, warm, zealous.

antonyms calm, cold, mild, moderate.

hot air balderdash, blather, blether, bluster, bombast, bosh, bullshit, bunk, bunkum, cant, claptrap, emptiness, flatulence, foam, froth, gas, guff, jejuneness, nonsense, rant, vapour, verbiage, wind, words.

antonym wisdom.

hotbed *n* breeding-ground, cradle, den, forcing-house, hive, nest, nidus, nursery, school, seedbed.

hot-blooded *adj* ardent, bold, eager, excitable, fervent, fiery, heated, high-spirited, homothermous, impetuous, impulsive, lustful, lusty, passionate, perfervid, precipitate, rash, sensual, spirited, temperamental, warm-blooded, wild.

antonyms cool, dispassionate.

hotchpotch *n* collection, commixture, confusion, congeries, conglomeration, farrago, gallimaufry, hash, jumble, medley, mélange, mess, miscellany, mishmash, mix, mixture, olio, olla-podrida, omnium gatherum, pot-pourri.

hotel *n* auberge, boarding-house, doss-house, flophouse, Gasthaus, Gasthof, guest-house, hostelry, hydro, hydropathic, inn, motel, pension, pub, public house, tavern.

hotfoot *adv* at top speed, hastily, helter-skelter, hurriedly, in haste, pell-mell, posthaste, quickly, rapidly, speedily, without delay.

antonyms dilatorily, slowly.

hothead *n* daredevil, desperado, hotspur, madcap, madman, tearaway, terror.

hotheaded *adj* daredevil, fiery, foolhardy, hasty, headstrong, hot-tempered, impetuous, impulsive, intemperate, madcap, over-eager, precipitate, quick-tempered, rash, reckless, unruly, volatile.

antonyms calm, cool.

hothouse *n* conservatory, glasshouse, greenhouse, nursery, plant-house, vinery.

hot-tempered *adj* choleric, explosive, fiery, hasty, irascible, irritable, petulant, quick-tempered, short-tempered, testy, violent, volcanic, wrathy.

antonyms calm, cool, imperturbable.

hound *v* badger, chase, chivvy, drive, dun, goad, harass, harry, hunt (down), impel, importune, persecute, pester, prod, provoke, pursue.

house *n* abode, ancestry, biggin, blood, building, business, clan, company, concern, domicile, dwelling, dynasty, edifice, establishment, family, family tree, firm, gens, habitation, home, homestead, hostelry, hotel, household, inn, kindred, line, lineage, lodgings, maison, maison(n)ette, ménage, organisation, outfit, parliament, partnership, pied-à-terre, public house, race, residence, roof, stem, tavern, tribe.

v accommodate, bed, billet, board, contain, cover, domicile, domiciliate, harbour, hold, keep, lodge, place, protect, put up, quarter, sheathe, shelter, store, take in.

household *n* establishment, family, family circle, home, house, ménage, set-up.

adj common, domestic, domiciliary, established, everyday, familiar, family, home, ordinary, plain, well-known.

householder *n* franklin, freeholder, goodman, head of the household, home-owner, housefather, landlord, occupant, occupier, owner, property owner, proprietor, resident, tenant.

housekeeper *n* châtelaine, concièrge, gouvernante, home economist, housewife, lady-help.

houseman *n* house-physician, house-surgeon, intern(e), resident.

house-trained *adj* domesticated, house-broken, tame, tamed, well-mannered.

antonym unsocial.

housewife *n* consort, hausfrau, home economist, homemaker, housekeeper, hussif, mate.

housing *n* accommodation, case, casing, container, cover, covering, dwellings, enclosure, habitation, holder, homes, houses, living quarters, matrix, protection, roof, sheath, shelter.

hovel *n* bothy, but-and-ben, cabin, cot, croft, cruve, den, doghole, dump, hole, hut, hutch, shack, shanty, shed.

hover *v* alternate, dally, dither, drift, falter, flap, float, fluctuate, flutter, fly, hang, hang about, hesitate, impend, linger, loom, menace, oscillate, pause, poise, seesaw, threaten, vacillate, waver.

however *conj* anyhow, but, even so, howbeit, in spite of that, natheless, nevertheless, nonetheless, notwithstanding, still, though, yet.

howl *n* bay, bellow, clamour, cry, groan, holler, hoot, outcry, roar, scream, shriek, ululation, wail, yell, yelp, yowl.

v bellow, cry, holler, hoot, lament, quest, roar, scream, shout, shriek, ululate, wail, waul, weep, yawl, yell, yelp.

howler *n* bêtise, bloomer, blunder, boner, bull, clanger, error, gaffe, malapropism, mistake, solecism.

hub *n* axis, centre, core, focal point, focus, heart, linchpin, middle, nave, nerve centre, pivot.

hubbub *n* ado, agitation, babel, bedlam, brouhaha, chaos, clamour, coil, confusion, din, disorder, disturbance, hue and cry, hullabaloo, hurly-burly, kerfuffle, noise, palaver, pandemonium, racket, riot, rowdedow, rowdydow, ruckus, ruction, rumpus, tumult, turbulence, uproar, upset.

antonym calm.

huckster *n* barker, chapman, dealer, haggler, hawker, packman, pedlar, pitcher, salesman, tinker, vendor.

huddle *n* clump, clutch, conclave, confab, conference, confusion, crowd, discussion, disorder, heap, jumble, knot, mass, meeting, mess, muddle.

v cluster, conglomerate, congregate, converge, crouch, crowd, cuddle, curl up, flock, gather, gravitate, hunch, nestle, press, ruck, snuggle, throng.

antonym disperse.

hue *n* aspect, cast, character, colour, complexion, dye, light, nuance, shade, tincture, tinge, tint, tone.

hue and cry ado, brouhaha, chase, clamour, furore, howls, hullabaloo, humdudgeon, outcry, pursuit, ruction, rumpus, uproar.

huff *n* anger, bad mood, mood, passion, pet, pique, sulks, tiff.

huffy *adj* angry, crabbed, cross, crotchety, crusty, disgruntled, grumpy, hoity-toity, huffish, irritable, miffed, miffy, moody, moping, morose, offended, peevish, pettish, petulant, querulous, resentful, shirty, short, snappy, sulky, surly, testy, touchy, waspish.

antonyms cheery, happy.

hug *v* cherish, clasp, cling to, cuddle, embrace, enclose, enfold, follow, grip, hold, lock, nurse, retain, skirt, squeeze.

n clasp, clinch, cuddle, embrace, squeeze.

huge *adj* Babylonian, Brobdingnagian, bulky, colossal, Cyclopean, enormous, extensive, gargantuan, giant, gigantean, gigantesque, gigantic, great, gross, immense, jumbo, large, leviathan, mammoth, massive, monumental, mountainous, Patagonian, prodigious, rounceval, stupendous, swingeing, thundering, titanic, tremendous, unwieldy, vast, walloping, whacking.

antonyms dainty, tiny.

hugeness *n* bulkiness, enormousness, extensiveness, gigantism, greatness, grossness, immensity, largeness, massiveness, over-development, overgrowth, prodigiousness, size, stupendousness, tremendousness, unwieldiness, vastness.

antonyms daintiness, smallness.

hulk *n* clod, derelict, frame, hull, lout, lubber, lump, oaf, ox, shell, shipwreck, wreck.

hulking *adj* awkward, bulky, cloddish, clodhopping, clumsy, cumbersome, galumphing, gross, hulky, loutish, lubberly, lumbering, lumpish, massive, oafish, overgrown, ponderous, ungainly, unwieldy.

antonyms delicate, small.

hull[1] *n* body, casing, covering, frame, framework, hulk, skeleton, structure.

hull[2] *n* capsule, epicarp, husk, legume, peel, pod, rind, shell, shuck, skin, theca.

v husk, pare, peel, shell, shuck, skin, strip, trim.

hullabaloo *n* agitation, babel, bedlam, brouhaha, chaos, clamour, commotion, confusion, din, disturbance, furore, fuss, hubbub, hue and cry, hurly-burly, kerfuffle, noise, outcry, pandemonium, panic, racket, ruckus, ruction, rumpus, to-do, tumult, turmoil, uproar.

hum *v* bombilate, bombinate, bum, bustle, buzz, croon, drone, lilt, move, mumble, murmur, pulsate, pulse, purr, sing, stir, susurrate, throb, thrum, vibrate, whirr, zoom.

n bombilation, bombination, bustle, busyness, buzz, drone, mumble, murmur, noise, pulsation, pulse, purr, purring, singing, stir, susurration, susurrus, throb, thrum, vibration, whirr.

human *adj* anthropoid, approachable, compassionate, considerate, fallible, fleshly, forgivable, hominoid, humane, kind, kindly, man-like, mortal, natural, reasonable, susceptible, understandable, understanding, vulnerable.

antonym inhuman.

n body, child, creature, hominid, homo sapiens, human being, individual, living soul, man, mortal, person, soul, wight, woman.

humane *adj* beneficent, benevolent, benign, charitable, civilising, clement, compassionate, forbearing, forgiving, gentle, good, good-natured, human, humanising, kind, kind-hearted, kindly, lenient, loving, magnanimous, merciful, mild, sympathetic, tender, understanding.

antonym inhumane.

humanise *v* break, civilise, cultivate, domesticate, edify, educate, enlighten, improve, mellow, polish, reclaim, refine, soften, tame, temper.

antonym brutalise.

humanitarian *adj* altruistic, beneficent, benevolent, charitable, compassionate, humane, philanthropic, philanthropical, public-spirited.

n altruist, benefactor, do-gooder, Good Samaritan, philanthrope, philanthropist.

antonyms egoist, self-seeker.

humanitarianism *n* beneficence, benevolence, charitableness, charity, compassionateness, do-goodery, generosity, goodwill, humanism, loving-kindness, philanthropy.

antonyms egoism, self-seeking.

humanity *n* altruism, benevolence, benignity, brotherly love, charity, compassion, everyman, fellow-feeling, flesh, generosity, gentleness, goodwill, Homo sapiens, human nature, human race, humankind, humaneness, kind-heartedness, kindness, loving-kindness, man, mandom, mankind, men, mercy, mortality, people, philanthropy, sympathy, tenderness, tolerance, understanding.

antonym inhumanity.

humble *adj* common, commonplace, courteous, deferential, demiss, docile, homespun, humdrum, insignificant, low, low-born, lowly, mean, meek, modest, obedient, obliging, obscure, obsequious, ordinary, plebeian, polite, poor, respectful, self-effacing, servile, simple, submissive, subservient, supplicatory, unassertive, unassuming, undistinguished, unimportant, unostentatious, unpretending, unpretentious.

antonyms assertive, important, pretentious, proud.

v abase, abash, break, bring down, bring low, chagrin, chasten, confound, crush, debase, deflate, degrade, demean, discomfit, discredit, disgrace, humiliate, lower, mortify, reduce, shame, sink, subdue, take down a peg.

antonyms exalt, raise.

humbleness *n* abjectness, courtesy, deference, fawning, grovelling, heepishness, insignificance, lowliness, meanness, meekness, modestness, modesty, obscurity, obsequiousness, ordinariness, politeness, respectfulness, servility, simplicity, slavishness, smarminess, submissiveness, subservience, unimportance, unpretentiousness.

antonyms assertiveness, pride.

humbly *adv* deferentially, diffidently, docilely, heepishly, meekly, modestly, obsequiously, respectfully, servilely, simply, submissively, subserviently, unassumingly, unpretentiously.

antonyms confidently, defiantly.

humbug *n* baloney, berley, blague, bluff, bounce, bullshit, bunk, bunkum, burley, cant, charlatan, charlatanry, cheat, claptrap, con, con man, deceit, deception, dodge, eyewash, faker, feint, fraud, fudge, gaff, gammon, hoax, hollowness, hype, hypocrisy, imposition, impostor, imposture, mountebank, nonsense, phoney, pretence, pseud, quack, quackery, rubbish, ruse, sham, shenanigans, swindle, swindler, trick, trickery, trickster, wile.

v bamboozle, befool, beguile, cajole, cheat, cozen, deceive, delude, dupe, fool, gammon, gull, hoax, hoodwink, impose, mislead, swindle, trick.

humdrum *adj* boring, commonplace, dreary, droning, dull, everyday, humble, monotonous, mundane, ordinary, prosy, repetitious, routine, tedious, tiresome, uneventful, uninteresting, unvaried, wearisome.

antonyms exceptional, unusual.

humid *adj* clammy, damp, dank, moist, muggy, soggy, steamy, sticky, sultry, vaporous, watery, wet.

antonym dry.

humidity *n* clamminess, damp, dampness, dankness, dew, humidness, moistness, moisture, mugginess, sogginess, steaminess, vaporosity, vaporousness, wetness.

antonym dryness.

humiliate *v* abase, abash, bring low, chagrin, chasten, confound, crush, debase, deflate, degrade, discomfit, discredit, disgrace, embarrass, humble, mortify, shame, subdue, undignify.

antonyms boost, dignify, exalt, vindicate.

humiliating *adj* chastening, crushing, deflating, degrading, discomfiting, disgraceful, disgracing, embarrassing, humbling, humiliant, humiliative, humiliatory, ignominious, inglorious, mortifying, shaming, snubbing.

antonyms gratifying, triumphant.

humiliation *n* abasement, affront, chagrin, condescension, deflation, degradation, discomfiture, discrediting, disgrace, dishonour, embarrassment, humbling, ignominy, indignity, mortification, put-down, rebuff, resignation, shame, snub.

antonyms gratification, triumph.

humility *n* deference, diffidence, humbleness, lowliness, meekness, modesty, obedience, resignation, self-abasement, servility, submissiveness, unassertiveness, unpretentiousness.

antonym pride.

hummock *n* barrow, elevation, hillock, hump, knoll, mound, prominence.

humorist *n* buffoon, clown, comedian, comédienne, comic, droll, eccentric, entertainer, funny man, jester, joker, parodist, satirist, wag, wisecracker, wit, zany.

humorous *adj* absurd, amusing, comic, comical, entertaining, facetious, farcical, funny, hilarious, humoristic, jocose, jocular, laughable, ludicrous, merry, playful, pleasant, Rabelaisian, satirical, side-splitting, waggish, whimsical, wisecracking, witty, zany.

antonym humourless.

humour *n* amusement, badinage, banter, bent, bias, caprice, choler, comedy, conceit, disposition, drollery, facetiousness, fancy, farce, frame of mind, fun, funniness, gags, jesting, jests, jocoseness, jocosity, jocularity, jokes, joking, ludicrousness, melancholy, mood, phlegm, pleasantries, propensity, quirk, raillery, repartee, spirits, temper, temperament, vagary, vein, whim, wisecracks, wit, witticisms, wittiness.

v accommodate, appease, coax, comply with, cosset, favour, flatter, go along with, gratify, indulge, mollify, pamper, spoil.

antonym thwart.

humourless *adj* austere, boring, crass, dour. dry, dull, glum, heavy-going, inflated, mirthless, morose, obtuse, po, po-faced, self-important, tedious, thick, thick-skinned, unamused, unamusing, unfunny, unwitty.

antonyms humorous, witty.

hump *n* bulge, bump, excrescence, hunch, knob, lump, mound, projection, prominence, protrusion, protuberance, swelling.

v arch, carry, curve, heave, hoist, hunch, lift, lug, shoulder, yomp

humpback *n* crookback, gibbosity, gibbus, gobbo, hunchback, kyphosis, Quasimodo, torticollis, wry-neck.

hump-backed *adj* crookbacked, crooked, deformed, gibbous, humped, hunchbacked, hunched, kyphotic, misshapen, stooped.

antonyms straight, upright.

humped *adj* arched, bent, crooked, curved, gibbous, hunched.

antonyms flat, straight.

hunch *n* feeling, guess, guesswork, idea, impression, inkling, intuition, premonition, presentiment, suspicion.

v arch, bend, crouch, curl up, curve, draw in, huddle, hump, shrug, squat, stoop, tense.

hunger *n* appetence, appetency, appetite, craving, desire, emptiness, esurience, esuriency, famine, greediness, hungriness, itch, lust, rapacity, ravenousness, starvation, voracity, yearning, yen, yird-hunger.

antonyms appeasement, satisfaction.

v ache, crave, desire, hanker, itch, long, lust, pine, starve, thirst, want, wish, yearn.

hungry *adj* aching, appetitive, athirst, avid, bulimic, covetous, craving, desirous, eager, empty, esurient, famished, famishing, greedy, hollow, hungerful, keen, lean, longing, peckish, ravenous, sharp-set, starved, starving, underfed, undernourished, voracious, yearning.

antonyms replete, satisfied.

hunk *n* block, chunk, clod, dod, dollop, gobbet, lump, mass, piece, slab, wedge, wodge.

hunt *v* chase, chevy, course, dog, ferret, forage, gun for, hound, investigate, look for, pursue, rummage, scour, search, seek, stalk, track, trail.

n battue, chase, chevy, hue and cry, hunting, investigation, pursuit, quest, search, venation.

hunted *adj* angst-ridden, careworn, desperate, distraught, gaunt, haggard, hag-ridden, harassed, harried, henpecked, persecuted, stricken, terror-stricken, tormented, worn, worried.

antonym serene.

hunting *adj* cynegetic, venatic, venatical, venatorial.

huntsman *n* chaser, chasseur, hunter, jaeger, jäger, montero, venator, venerer, woodman, woodsman.

hurdle *n* barricade, barrier, complication, difficulty, fence, handicap, hedge, hindrance, impediment, jump, obstacle, obstruction, problem, snag, stumbling-block, wall.

hurl *v* cast, catapult, chuck, dash, fire, fling, heave, launch, let fly, pitch, project, propel, send, shy, sling, throw, toss.

hurly-burly *n* agitation, bedlam, brouhaha, bustle, chaos, commotion, confusion, disorder, distraction, frenzy, furore, hassle, hubbub, hustle, storm and stress, Sturm und Drang, tumult, turbulence, turmoil, upheaval.

hurricane *n* baguio, cordonazo, cyclone, gale, squall, storm, tempest, tornado, twister, typhoon, whirlwind, willy-willy.

hurried *adj* breakneck, brief, careless, cursory, hasty, headlong, hectic, passing, perfunctory, precipitate, quick, rushed, shallow, short, slapdash, speedy, superficial, swift, unthorough.

antonym leisurely.

hurry *v* accelerate, belt, bustle, dash, dispatch, expedite, festinate, fly, get a move on, goad, hasten, hightail it, hump, hustle, jump to it, look lively, move, pike, quicken, rush, scoot, scurry, scutter, scuttle, shake a leg, shift, speed up, step on it, step on the gas, urge.

antonyms dally, delay.

n bustle, celerity, commotion, dispatch, expedition, flurry, haste, precipitance, precipitancy, precipitation, promptitude, quickness, rush, scurry, speed, sweat, urgency.

antonyms calm, leisureliness.

hurt *v* abuse, ache, afflict, aggrieve, annoy, bruise, burn, damage, disable, distress, grieve, harm, impair, injure, maim, maltreat, mar, pain, sadden, smart, spoil, sting, throb, tingle, torture, upset, wound.

n abuse, bruise, damage, detriment, disadvantage, discomfort, distress, harm, injury, lesion, loss, mischief, pain, pang, scathe, sore, soreness, suffering, wound, wrong.

adj aggrieved, annoyed, bruised, crushed, cut, damaged, displeased, grazed, harmed, huffed, injured, maimed, miffed, offended, pained, piqued, rueful, sad, saddened, scarred, scraped, scratched, wounded.

hurtful *adj* catty, cruel, cutting, damaging, derogatory, destructive, detrimental. disadvantageous, distressing, harmful, humiliating, injurious, malefactory, malefic, maleficent, malicious, malificious, malignant, mean, mischievous, nasty, nocuous, pernicious, pestful, pestiferous, pestilent(ial), pointed, prejudicial, scathing, spiteful, unkind, upsetting, vicious, wounding.

antonyms helpful, kind.

hurtle *v* bowl, charge, chase, crash, dash, fly, plunge, race, rattle, rush, scoot, scramble, shoot, speed, spin, spurt, tear.

husband[1] *v* budget, conserve, economise, eke out, hoard, ration, save, save up, store, use sparingly.

antonyms squander, waste.

husband[2] *n* Benedick, consort, goodman, hubby, man, married man, mate, old man, spouse.

husbandry *n* agriculture, agronomics, agronomy, conservation, cultivation, economy, farming, frugality, good housekeeping, land management, management, thrift, thriftiness, tillage.

antonym wastefulness.

hush *v* calm, compose, mollify, mute, muzzle, quieten, settle, shush, silence, soothe, still.

antonyms disturb, rouse.

n calm, calmness, peace, peacefulness, quiet, quietness, repose, serenity, silence, still, stillness, tranquillity.

antonyms clamour, uproar.

interj belt up, euphemeite, favete linguis, hold your tongue, leave it out, not another word, pipe down, quiet, say no more, shush, shut up, ssh, stow it, unberufen, wheesht, whisht.

hush up conceal, cover up, gag, keep dark, muzzle, smother, soft-pedal, squash, stifle, suppress.

antonym publicise.

hush-hush *adj* classified, confidential, hushy, restricted, secret, top-secret, under wraps, unpublished.

antonyms open, public.

husk *n* bark, bract, bran, case, chaff, covering, glume, hull, pod, rind, shell, shuck, tegmen.

huskiness *n* croakiness, dryness, gruffness, gutturalness, harshness, hoarseness, roughness, throatiness.

antonym clarity.

husky[1] *adj* croaking, croaky, gruff, guttural, harsh, hoarse, low, rasping, raucous, rough, roupy, throaty.

husky[2] *adj* beefy, brawny, burly, hefty, muscular, powerful, rugged, stocky, strapping, strong, sturdy, thickset, tough.

hussy *n* baggage, broad, floozy, jade, minx, piece, scrubber, slut, strumpet, tart, temptress, tramp, trollop, vamp, wanton, wench.

hustle *v* bustle, crowd, elbow, force, frog-march, haste, hasten, hurry, impel, jog, jostle, pressgang, pressure, push, rush, shove, thrust.

hut *n* booth, bothan, bothy, cabin, caboose, crib, den, hogan, hovel, kraal, lean-to, shack, shanty, shebang, shed, shelter, shiel, shieling, tilt.

hybrid *n* amalgam, combination, composite, compound, conglomerate, cross, crossbreed, half-blood, half-breed, heterogeny, mixture, mongrel, mule, pastiche.

adj bastard, combined, composite, compound, cross, heterogeneous, hybridous, hyphenated, mixed, mongrel, mule, patchwork.

antonyms pure, pure-bred.

hybridity *n* bastardisation, compositeness, cross-breeding, crossing, heterogeneity, hybridism, interbreeding, pastiche.

antonym purity.

hygiene *n* asepsis, cleanliness, disinfection, hygienics, purity, salubriousness, salubrity, salutariness, sanitariness, sanitation, sterility, wholesomeness.

antonyms filth, insanitariness.

hygienic *adj* aseptic, clean, cleanly, disinfected, germ-free, healthy, pure, salubrious, salutary, sanitary, sterile, wholesome.

antonym unhygenic.

hymn *n* anthem, bhajan, cantata, canticle, canticum, carol, chant, choral(e), dithyramb, doxology, introit, mantra(m), motet, offertory, om, paean, paraphrase, psalm, song of praise.

hype *n* advertisement, advertising, ballyhoo, build-up, deception, fuss, kidology, plugging, publicity, puffery, puffing, racket, razzmatazz, trumpet-blowing.

hyperbole *n* enlargement, exaggeration, excess, extravagance, magnification, overkill, overplay, overstatement.

antonyms meiosis, understatement.

hypercritical *adj* captious, carping, cavilling, censorious, exceptious, fault-finding, finicky, fussy, hair-splitting, niggling, nit-picking, over-particular, pedantic, pernickety, quibbling, strict, ultracrepidarian, Zoilean.

antonyms tolerant, uncritical.

hypnotic *adj* compelling, dazzling, fascinating, irresistible, magnetic, mesmeric, mesmerising, narcotic, opiate, sleep-inducing, somniferous, soothing, soporific, spellbinding.

hypnotise *v* bewitch, captivate, dazzle, entrance, fascinate, magnetise, mesmerise, spellbind, stupefy.

hypnotism *n* animal magnetism, hypnosis, hypnotherapy, mesmerism, suggestion.

hypochondria *n* hypochondrianism, hypochondriasis, neurosis, valetudinarianism.

hypochondriac *n* hypochondriast, valetudinarian.

adj hypochondriacal, neurotic, valetudinarian.

hypocrisy *n* cant, deceit, deceitfulness, deception, dissembling, double-talk, duplicity, falsity, imposture, insincerity, lip-service, pharisaicalness, pharisaism, phariseeism, phoneyness, pietism, pretence, quackery, sanctimoniousness, self-righteousness speciousness, Tartuffism, two-facedness.

antonyms humility, sincerity.

hypocrite *n* canter, charlatan, deceiver, dissembler, fraud, Holy Willie, impostor, mountebank, Pharisee, phon(e)y, pretender, pseud, pseudo, Tartuffe, whited sepulchre.

hypocritical *adj* canting, deceitful, deceptive, dissembling, double-faced, duplicitous, false, fraudulent, hollow, insincere, Pecksniffian, pharisaic(al), phoney, pietistic, sanctimonious, self-pious, self-righteous, specious, spurious, Tartuffian, Tartuffish, two-faced.

antonyms genuine, humble, sincere.

hypothesis *n* assumption, conjecture, guess, postulate, postulatum, premise, premiss, presumption, proposition, starting-point, supposition, theory, thesis.

hypothetical *adj* academic, assumed, conjectural, imaginary, postulated, proposed, putative, speculative, supposed, suppositional, theoretical.

antonyms actual, real.

hysteria *n* agitation, frenzy, hysterics, hysteromania, instability, madness, neurosis, panic, psychoneurosis, unreason.

antonyms calm, composure, reason.

hysterical *adj* berserk, comical, crazed, distracted, distraught, falling about, farcical, frantic, frenzied, hairless, hilarious, mad, neurotic, overwrought, priceless, psychoneurotic, psychosomatic, raving, side-splitting, uncontrollable, uproarious.

antonyms calm, composed.

hysterics *n* drama, dramatics, emotionalism, emotionality, histrionics, melodrama, (screaming) habdabs.

ice *n* chill, chilliness, coldness, distance, formality, frazil, frigidity, frost, frostiness, ice-cream, iciness, icing, reserve, rime, stiffness, verglas.

v freeze, frost, glaciate, glaze.

ice-cold *adj* algid, arctic, biting, bitter, chilled to the bone, freezing, frigid, frozen, frozen to the marrow, gelid, glacial, icy, icy cold, raw, refrigerated.

iced *adj* frappé(e), frosted, glazed.

icon *n* figure, idol, ikon, image, portrait, portrayal, representation, symbol.

iconoclasm *n* criticism, demythologisation, denunciation, disabusing, dissent, dissidence, heresy, irreverence, opposition, questioning, radicalism, scepticism, subversion, unbelief, undeceiving.

antonyms credulity, trustfulness.

iconoclast *n* critic, denouncer, denunciator, dissenter, dissident, heretic, idoloclast, image-breaker, opponent, questioner, radical, rebel, sceptic, unbeliever.

antonyms believer, devotee.

iconclastic *adj* critical, denunciatory, dissentient, dissident, heretical, impious, innovative, irreverent, questioning, radical, rebellious, sceptical, subversive.

antonyms trustful, uncritical, unquestioning.

icy *adj* algid, aloof, arctic, biting, bitter, chill, chilling, chilly, cold, distant, forbidding, formal, freezing, frigid, frore, frost-bound, frosty, frozen over, gelid, glacial, glassy, hoar, hostile, ice-cold, indifferent, raw, reserved, rimy, slippery, slippy, steely, stiff, stony, unfriendly.

idea *n* abstraction, aim, approximation, archetype, belief, clue, conceit, concept, conception, conceptualisation, conclusion, conjecture, construct, conviction, design, doctrine, end, essence, estimate, fancy, form, guess, guesstimate, hint, hypothesis, idée fixe, image, import, impression, inkling, intention, interpretation, intimation, judgement, meaning, monomania, notion, object, opinion, pattern, perception, plan, purpose, reason, recept, recommendation, scheme, sense, significance, solution, suggestion, surmise, suspicion, teaching, theory, thought, type, understanding, view, viewpoint, vision.

ideal *n* archetype, criterion, dreamboat, epitome, example, exemplar, image, last word, model, ne plus ultra, nonpareil, paradigm, paragon, pattern, perfection, pink of perfection, principle, prototype, standard, type.

adj abstract, archetypal, best, classic, complete, conceptual, consummate, fanciful, highest, hypothetical, imaginary, impractical, model, optimal, optimum, perfect, quintessential, supreme, theoretical, transcendent, transcendental, unattainable, unreal, Utopian, visionary.

idealisation *n* apotheosis, ennoblement, exaltation, glorification, romanticisation, romanticising, worship.

idealise *v* apotheosise, deify, ennoble, exalt, glorify, romanticise, utopianise, worship.

antonyms caricature, travesty.

idealism *n* impracticality, perfectionism, romanticism, utopianism, utopism.

antonyms pragmatism, realism.

idealist *n* dreamer, perfectionist, romantic, romanticist, utopian, utopianiser, utopiast, utopist, visionary.

antonyms pragmatist, realist.

idealistic *adj* impracticable, impractical, optimistic, perfectionist, quixotic, romantic, starry-eyed, unrealistic, utopian, visionary.

antonyms pragmatic, realistic.

idée fixe complex, fixation, fixed idea, hang-up, leitmotiv, monomania, obsession.

identical *adj* alike, clonal, coincident, corresponding, duplicate, equal, equivalent, identic, indistinguishable, interchangeable, like, matching, monozygotic, same, self-same, synonymous, twin.

antonym different.

identifiable *adj* ascertainable, detectable, discernible, distinguishable, known, noticeable, perceptible, recognisable, unmistakable.

antonyms indefinable, unfamiliar, unidentifiable, unknown.

identification *n* association, cataloguing, classifying, connection, credentials, detection, diagnosis, documents, empathy, fellow-feeling, ID, involvement, labelling, naming, papers, pinpointing, rapport, recognition, relating, relationship, sympathy.

identify *v* catalogue, classify, detect, diagnose, distinguish, finger, know, label, make out, name, pick out, pinpoint, place, recognise, single out, specify, spot, tag.

identify with ally with, associate with, connect with, empathise with, equate with, feel for, relate to, respond to.

identity *n* accord, coincidence, correspondence, empathy, existence, haecceity, individuality, oneness, particularity, personality, quiddity, rapport, sameness, self, selfhood, singularity, unanimity, uniqueness, unity.

ideologist *n* ideologue, theorist, thinker, visionary.

ideology *n* belief(s), convictions, creed, doctrine(s), dogma, ethic, faith, ideas, metaphysics, philosophy, principles, speculation, tenets, Weltanschauung, world view.

idiocy *n* amentia, asininity, cretinism, dementia, fatuity, fatuousness, folly, foolishness, imbecility, inanity, insanity, irrationality, lunacy, mental deficiency, senselessness, silliness, stupidity, tomfoolery.

antonyms sanity, wisdom.

idiom *n* colloquialism, expression, idiolect, idiotism, jargon, language, locution, parlance, phrase, regionalism, set phrase, style, talk, turn of phrase, usage, vernacular.

idiomatic *adj* colloquial, correct, dialectal, dialectical, grammatical, idiolectal, idiolectic, native, vernacular.

antonym unidiomatic.

idiosyncrasy *n* characteristic, eccentricity, feature, freak, habit, kink, mannerism, oddity, oddness, peculiarity, quirk, singularity, trait.

idiosyncratic *adj* characteristic, distinctive, eccentric, individual, individualistic, inimitable, odd, peculiar, quirky, typical.

antonyms common, general.

idiot *n* ament, ass, bampot, blockhead, booby, crazy, cretin, cuckoo, dimwit, dolt, dumbbell, dummy, dunderhead, fat-head, featherbrain, fool, golem, half-wit, imbecile, klutz, knuckle-head, mental defective, mooncalf, moron, natural, nidget, nig-nog, nincompoop, nitwit, nong, noodle, omadhaun, pillock, saphead, schlep, schmo, schmuck, simpleton, thick, thickhead, thicko.

idiotic *adj* asinine, crazy, cretinous, daft, dumb, fat-headed, fatuous, foolhardy, foolish, hair-brained, half-witted, harebrained, idiotical, imbecile, imbecilic, inane, insane, knuckle-headed, loony, lunatic, moronic, nutty, screwy, senseless, simple, stupid, tomfool, unintelligent.

antonyms sane, sensible.

idle *adj* abortive, bootless, dead, dormant, dronish, empty, foolish, frivolous, fruitless, futile, good-for-nothing, groundless, inactive, indolent, ineffective, ineffectual, inoperative, jobless, lackadaisical, lazy, mothballed, nugatory, of no avail, otiose, pointless, purposeless, redundant, shiftless, slothful, sluggish, stationary, superficial, torpid, trivial, unavailing, unbusy, unemployed, unproductive, unsuccessful, unused, useless, vain, work-shy, worthless.

antonyms active, effective, purposeful.

v coast, dally, dawdle, drift, fool, fritter, kill time, lallygag, laze, lie up, loiter, lounge, potter, rest on one's laurels, shirk, skive, slack, take it easy, tick over, vegetate, waste, while.

antonyms act, work.

idleness *n* dolce far niente, ease, flânerie, idlesse, inaction, inactivity, indolence, inertia, inoccupation, laziness, lazing, leisure, loafing, pottering, shiftlessness, skiving, sloth, slothfulness, sluggishness, torpor, unemployment, vegetating.

antonyms activity, employment.

idler *n* clock-watcher, dawdler, dodger, do-naught, donnat, donnot, do-nothing, do-nought, drone, fainéant, flâneur, good-for-nothing, laggard, layabout, lazybones, loafer, lotus-eater, lounger, malingerer, shirker, skiver, slacker, sloth, slouch, sluggard, waster, wastrel.

idling *adj* dawdling, drifting, ligging, loafing, pottering, resting, resting on one's oars, shirking, skiving, taking it easy, ticking over.

idol *n* beloved, darling, deity, favourite, fetish, god, graven image, hero, icon, image, joss, ju-ju, mammet, Mumbo-jumbo, pet, pin-up, superstar.

idolater *n* admirer, adorer, devotee, iconolater, idolatress, idolist, idol-worshipper, votary, worshipper.

idolatrous *adj* adoring, adulatory, idolising, idol-worshipping, reverential, uncritical, worshipful.

idolatry *n* adoration, adulation, deification, exaltation, glorification, hero-worship, iconolatry, idolising, idolism, mammetry, whoredom.

antonym vilification.

idolise *v* admire, adore, apotheosise, deify, dote on, exalt, glorify, hero-worship, iconise, lionise, love, revere, reverence, venerate, worship.

antonym vilify.

idyllic *adj* arcadian, charming, delightful, halcyon, happy, heavenly, idealised, innocent, pastoral, peaceful, picturesque, rustic, unspoiled.

antonym disagreeable.

ignite *v* burn, catch fire, combust, conflagrate, fire, flare up, inflame, kindle, light, set alight, set fire to, spark off, touch off.

antonym quench.

ignoble *adj* abject, base, base-born, caddish, common, contemptible, cowardly, craven, dastardly, degenerate, degraded, despicable, disgraceful, dishonourable, heinous, humble, infamous, low, low-born, lowly, mean, petty, plebeian, shabby, shameless, unworthy, vile, vulgar, worthless, wretched.

antonyms honourable, noble.

ignominious *adj* abject, crushing, degrading, despicable, discreditable, disgraceful, dishonourable, disreputable, humiliating, indecorous, inglorious, mortifying, scandalous, shameful, sorry, undignified.

antonyms honourable, triumphant.

ignominy *n* contempt, degradation, discredit, disgrace, dishonour, disrepute, humiliation, indignity, infamy, mortification, obloquy, odium, opprobrium, reproach, scandal, shame, stigma.

antonyms credit, honour.

ignoramus *n* ass, blockhead, bonehead, booby, dolt, donkey, duffer, dullard, dunce, fool, ignaro, illiterate, know-nothing, lowbrow, num(b)skull, simpleton.

antonyms high-brow, intellectual, scholar.

ignorance *n* benightedness, blindness, crassness, denseness, greenness, illiteracy, illiterateness, inexperience, innocence, naïvety, nescience, oblivion, unawareness, unconsciousness, unfamiliarity.

antonyms knowledge, wisdom.

ignorant *adj* as thick as two short planks, benighted, blind, bookless, clueless, crass, dense, green, gross, half-baked, idealess, ill-informed, illiterate, ill-versed, inexperienced, innocent, innumerate, insensitive, know-nothing, naïve, nescient, oblivious, pig-ignorant, stupid, thick, unacquainted, unaware, unconscious, uncultivated, uneducated, unenlightened, unidea'd, uninformed, uninitiated, uninstructed, unknowing, unlearned, unlettered, unread, unscholarly, unschooled, untaught, untrained, untutored, unwitting.

antonyms knowlegeable, wise.

ignore *v* blink, cold-shoulder, cut, disregard, neglect, omit, overlook, pass over, pay no attention to, pidgeon-hole, reject, send to Coventry, set aside, shut one's eyes to, slight, take no notice of, turn a blind eye to, turn a deaf ear to, turn one's back on.

antonym note.

ilk *n* brand, breed, cast cut, character, class, description, kidney, kind, make, sort, stamp, style, type, variety.

ill[1] *adj* ailing, dicky, diseased, frail, funny, indisposed, infirm, laid up, not up to snuff, off-colour, on the sick list, out of sorts, peelie-wally, poorly, queasy, queer, seedy, sick, under the weather, unhealthy, unwell, valetudinarian.

antonym well.

n affliction, ailment, complaint, disease, disorder, illness, indisposition, infection, infirmity, malady, malaise, sickness.

ill[2] *adj* acrimonious, adverse, antagonistic, bad, cantankerous, cross, damaging, deleterious, detrimental, difficult, disturbing, evil, foul, harmful, harsh, hateful, hostile, hurtful, inauspicious, incorrect, inimical, iniquitous, injurious, malevolent, malicious, ominous, reprehensible, ruinous, sinister, sullen, surly, threatening, unfavourable, unfortunate, unfriendly, unhealthy, unkind, unlucky, unpromising, unpropitious, unwholesome, vile, wicked, wrong.

antonyms beneficial, fortunate, good, kind.

n abuse, affliction, badness, cruelty, damage, depravity, destruction, evil, harm, hurt, ill-usage, injury, malice, mischief, misery, misfortune, pain, sorrow, suffering, trial, tribulation, trouble, unpleasantness, wickedness, woe.

antonym benefit.

adv amiss, badly, by no means, hard, hardly, inauspiciously, insufficiently, poorly, scantily, scarcely, unfavourably, unluckily, wrongfully.

antonym well.

ill at ease anxious, awkward, disquieted, disturbed, edgy, embarrassed, fidgety, hesitant, like a cat on hot bricks, nervous, on edge, on tenterhooks, restless, self-conscious, strange, tense, uncomfortable, uneasy, unrelaxed, unsettled, unsure, worried.

antonym at ease.

ill-advised *adj* daft, foolhardy, foolish, hasty, hazardous, ill-considered, ill-judged, impolitic, imprudent, inappropriate, incautious, indiscreet, injudicious, misguided, overhasty, rash, reckless, short-sighted, thoughtless, unseemly, unwise, wrong-headed.

antonym sensible.

ill-assorted *adj* discordant, incompatible, incongruous, inharmonious, misallied, mismatched, uncongenial, unsuited.

antonym harmonious.

ill-bred *adj* bad-mannered, boorish, churlish, coarse, crass, crude, discourteous, ill-mannered, impolite, indelicate, non-U, rude, uncivil, uncivilised, uncouth, ungallant, ungentlemanly, ungracious, unladylike, unmannerly, unrefined, vulgar.

antonym urbane.

ill-considered *adj* careless, follish, hasty, heedless, ill-advised, ill-judged, improvident, imprudent, injudicious, overhasty, precipitate, rash, unwise.

antonym sensible.

ill-defined *adj* blurred, blurry, dim, fuzzy, hazy, imprecise, indefinite, indistinct, nebulous, shadowy, unclear, vague, woolly.

antonym clear.

ill-disposed *adj* against, antagonistic, anti, antipathetic, averse, hostile, inimical, opposed, unco-operative, unfriendly, unsympathetic, unwelcoming.

antonym well-disposed.

illegal *adj* actionable, backyard, banned, black-market, contraband, criminal, felonious, forbidden, illicit, outlawed, pirate, prohibited, proscribed, unauthorised, unconstitutional, under-the-counter, unlawful, unlicensed, wrongful, wrongous.

antonym legal.

illegality *n* crime, criminality, felony, illegitimacy, illicitness, lawlessness, unconstitutionality, unlawfulness, wrong, wrongfulness, wrongness.

antonym legality.

illegible *adj* crabbed, faint, hieroglyphic, indecipherable, indistinct, obscure, scrawled, undecipherable, unreadable.

antonym legible.

illegitimacy *n* bar-sinister, bastardism, bastardy, baton-sinister, illegality, illicitness, irregularity, unconstitutionality, unlawfulness.

antonym legitimacy.

illegitimate *adj* bastard, born on the wrong side of the blanket, born out of wedlock, fatherless, illegal, illicit, illogical, improper, incorrect, invalid, misbegotten, natural, spurious, unauthorised, unconstitutional, unfathered, unjustifiable, unjustified, unlawful, unsanctioned, unsound, unwarrantable, unwarranted.

antonym legitimate.

ill-fated *adj* blighted, doomed, forlorn, hapless, ill-omened, ill-starred, infaust, luckless, star-crossed, unfortunate, unhappy, unlucky.

antonym lucky.

ill-favoured *adj* hideous, homely, plain, repulsive, ugly, unattractive, unlovely, unprepossessing, unsightly.

antonym beautiful.

ill-feeling *n* animosity, animus, antagonism, bad blood, bitterness, disgruntlement, dissatisfaction, dudgeon, enmity, frustration, grudge, hard-feelings, hostility, ill-will, odium, offence, rancour, resentment, sourness, spite.

antonyms friendship, goodwill.

ill-humour *n* acrimony, choler, crabbiness, crassness, disagreeableness, dishumour, distemper, grumpiness, irascibility, moroseness, petulance, spleen, sulkiness, the dods.

antonym amiability.

ill-humoured *adj* acrimonious, bad-tempered, cantankerous, crabbed, crabby, cross, cross-grained, disagreeable, grumpy, huffy, impatient, irascible, irritable, moody, morose, peevish, petulant, sharp, snappish, snappy, sulky, sullen, tart, testy, waspish.

antonym amiable.

illiberal *adj* bigoted, close-fisted, hidebound, intolerant, mean, miserly, narrow-minded, niggardly, parsimonious, petty, prejudiced, reactionary, small-minded, sordid, stingy, tight, tightfisted, uncharitable, ungenerous, verkrampte.

antonym liberal.

illiberality *n* bigotry, intolerance, meanness, miserliness, narrow-mindedness, narrowness, niggardliness, parsimony, pettiness, prejudice, small-mindedness, stinginess.

antonym liberality.

illicit *adj* black, black-market, bootleg, clandestine, contraband, criminal, felonious, forbidden, furtive, guilty, illegal, illegitimate, ill-gotten, immoral, improper, inadmissible, prohibited, unauthorised, unlawful, unlicensed, unsanctioned, wrong.

antonyms legal, licit.

illiterate *adj* analphabetic, benighted, ignorant, uncultured, uneducated, unlettered, untaught, untutored.

antonym literate.

ill-judged *adj* daft, foolhardy, foolish, hasty, ill-advised, ill-considered, impolitic, imprudent, incautious, indiscreet, injudicious, misguided, overhasty, rash, reckless, short-sighted, unwise, wrong-headed.

antonym sensible.

ill-mannered *adj* badly-behaved, boorish, churlish, coarse, crude, discourteous, ill-behaved, ill-bred, impolite, insensitive, insolent, loutish, rude, uncivil, uncouth, ungallant, unmannerly.

antonym polite.

ill-natured *adj* bad-tempered, churlish, crabbed, cross, cross-grained, disagreeable, disobliging, malevolent, malicious, malignant, mean, nasty, perverse, petulant, spiteful, sulky, sullen, surly, unfriendly, unkind, unpleasant, vicious, vindictive.

antonym good-natured.

illness *n* affliction, ailment, attack, complaint, disability, disease, disorder, distemper, dyscrasia, idiopathy, ill-being, ill-health, indisposition, infirmity, lurgy, malady, malaise, sickness.

antonym health.

illogical *adj* absurd, fallacious, faulty, Fifish, illegitimate, inconclusive, inconsistent, incorrect, invalid, Irish, irrational, meaningless, senseless, sophistical, specious, spurious, unreasonable, unscientific, unsound.

antonym logical.

illogicality *n* absurdity, fallaciousness, fallacy, inconsistency, invalidity, Irishness, irrationality, senselessness, speciousness, unreason, unsoundness.

antonym logicality.

ill-omened *adj* doomed, ill-fated, inauspicious, infaust, star-crossed, unfortunate, unhappy, unlucky.

antonym fortunate.

ill-tempered *adj* bad-tempered, choleric, cross, curt, grumpy, ill-humoured, ill-natured, impatient, irascible, irritable, sharp, spiteful, testy, tetchy, touchy, vicious, vixenish, vixenly.

antonym good-tempered.

ill-timed *adj* awkward, crass, inappropriate, inconvenient, inept, inopportune, tactless, unseasonable, untimely, unwelcome, wrong-timed.

antonym well-timed.

ill-treat *v* abuse, damage, harass, harm, harry, ill-use, injure, maltreat, manhandle, mishandle, mistreat, misuse, neglect, oppress, wrong.

antonym care for.

ill-treatment *n* abuse, damage, harm, ill-use, injury, maltreatment, manhandling, mishandling, mistreatment, misuse, neglect.

antonym care.

illuminate *v* adorn, beacon, brighten, clarify, clear up, decorate, edify, elucidate, enlighten, explain, illumine, illustrate, instruct, irradiate, light, light up, limn, miniate, ornament.

antonyms darken, deface, divest.

illuminating *adj* edifying, enlightening, explanatory, helpful, informative, instructive, revealing, revelatory.

antonym unhelpful.

illumination *n* adornment, awareness, beam, brightening, brightness, clarification, decoration, edification, enlightenment, insight, inspiration, instruction, light, lighting, lights, limning, miniation, ornamentation, perception, radiance, ray, revelation, splendour, understanding.

antonym darkness.

illusion *n* apparition, chimera, daydream, deception, delusion, error, fallacy, fancy, fantasy, figment, hallucination, ignis fatuus, maya, mirage, misapprehension, misconception, phantasm, semblance, will-o'-the-wisp.

antonym reality.

illusory *adj* apparent, Barmecidal, beguiling, chimerical, deceitful, deceptive, deluding, delusive, fallacious, false, hallucinatory, illusive, misleading, mistaken, seeming, sham, unreal, unsubstantial, untrue, vain.

antonym real.

illustrate *v* adorn, clarify, decorate, demonstrate, depict, draw, elucidate, emphasise, exemplify, exhibit, explain, illuminate, instance, interpret, miniate, ornament, picture, show, sketch.

illustrated *adj* decorated, embellished, illuminated, miniated, pictorial.

illustration *n* adornment, analogy, case, case in point, clarification, decoration, delineation, demonstration, drawing, elucidation, example, exemplification, explanation, figure, graphic, half-tone, instance, interpretation, photograph, picture, plate, representation, sketch, specimen.

illustrative *adj* delineative, descriptive, diagrammatic, explanatory, explicatory, expository, graphic, illustrational, illustratory, interpretive, pictorial, representative, sample, specimen, typical.

illustrious *adj* brilliant, celebrated, distinguished, eminent, exalted, excellent, famed, famous, glorious, great, magnificent, noble, notable, noted, outstanding, prominent, remarkable, renowned, resplendent, signal, splendid.

antonyms inglorious, shameful.

ill-will *n* acrimony, animosity, animus, antagonism, antipathy, aversion, bad blood, dislike, enmity, envy, grudge, hard feelings, hatred, hostility, malevolence, malice, odium, rancour, resentment, spite, unfriendliness, venom.

antonyms friendship, good-will.

image *n* appearance, conceit, concept, conception, counterpart, dead ringer, Doppelgänger, double, effigies, effigy, eidolon, eikon, facsimile, figure, icon, idea, idol, impression, likeness, perception, picture, portrait, reflection, replica, representation, semblance, similitude, simulacrum, spit, spitting image, statue, trope.

imaginable *adj* believable, comprehensible, conceivable, credible, likely, plausible, possible, predictable, supposable, thinkable, visualisable.

antonym unimaginable.

imaginary *adj* assumed, Barmecidal, chimerical, dreamlike, fancied, fanciful, fictional, fictitious, hallucinatory, hypothetical, ideal, illusive, illusory, imagined, insubstantial, invented, legendary, made-up, mythological, non-existent, phantasmal, shadowy, supposed, unreal, unsubstantial, visionary.

antonym real.

imagination *n* chimera, conception, creativity, enterprise, fancy, idea, ideality, illusion, image, imaginativeness, ingenuity, innovativeness, innovatoriness, insight, inspiration, invention, inventiveness, notion, originality, resourcefulness, supposition, unreality, vision, wit, wittiness.

antonyms reality, unimaginativeness.

imaginative *adj* clever, creative, dreamy, enterprising, fanciful, fantastic, fertile, ingenious, innovative, inspired, inventive, original, poetical, resourceful, visionary, vivid.

antonym unimaginative.

imagine *v* apprehend, assume, believe, conceive, conceptualise, conjecture, conjure up, create, deduce, deem, devise, dream up, envisage, envision, fancy, fantasise, frame, gather, guess, ideate, infer, invent, judge, picture, plan, project, realise, scheme, suppose, surmise, suspect, take it, think, think of, think up, visualise.

imbalance *n* bias, disparity, disproportion, imparity, inequality, lopsidedness, partiality, top-heaviness, unequalness, unevenness, unfairness.

antonym parity.

imbecile *n* ament, blockhead, bungler, clown, cretin, dolt, dotard, fool, half-wit, idiot, moron, thickhead.

adj anile, asinine, doltish, fatuous, feeble-minded, foolish, idiotic, imbecilic, inane, ludicrous, moronic, senile, simple, stupid, thick, witless.

antonyms intelligent, sensible.

imbecility *n* amentia, anility, asininity, childishness, cretinism, fatuity, foolishness, idiocy, inanity, incompetency, senility, stupidity.

antonyms intelligence, sense.

imbibe *v* absorb, acquire, assimilate, consume, drink, drink in, gain, gather, gulp, ingest, knock back, lap up, quaff, receive, sink, sip, soak in, soak up, swallow, swig, take in.

imbroglio, embroglio *n* confusion, difficulty, dilemma, embroilment, entanglement, involvement, mess, muddle, quandary, scrape, tangle.

imbue *v* bathe, colour, dye, fill, impregnate, inculcate, infuse, ingrain, instil, moisten, permeate, pervade, saturate, stain, steep, suffuse, tinge, tint.

imitate *v* affect, ape, burlesque, caricature, clone, copy, copy-cat, counterfeit, do, duplicate, echo, emulate, follow, follow suit, forge, impersonate, mimic, mirror, mock, monkey, parody, parrot, personate, repeat, reproduce, send up, simulate, spoof, take off, travesty.

imitation *n* apery, aping, copy, counterfeit, counterfeiting, duplication, echoing, echopraxia, echopraxis, fake, forgery, impersonation, impression, likeness, me-tooism, mimesis, mimicry, mockery, parody, reflection, replica, reproduction, resemblance, sham, simulation, substitution, take-off, travesty.

adj artificial, dummy, ersatz, man-made, mock, phoney, pinchbeck, pseudo, repro, reproduction, sham, simulated, synthetic.

antonym genuine.

imitative *adj* apish, copied, copycat, copying, derivative, echoic, me-too, mimetic, mimicking, mock, onomatopoeic, parodistic, parrot-like, plagiarised, pseudo, put-on, second-hand, simulated, unoriginal.

imitator *n* ape, aper, copier, copy-cat, echo, epigone, follower, impersonator, impressionist, me-tooer, mimic, parodist, parrot.

immaculate *adj* blameless, clean, faultless, flawless, guiltless, impeccable, incorrupt, innocent, neat, perfect, pure, scrupulous, sinless, spick-and-span, spotless, spruce, stainless, trim, unblemished, uncontaminated, undefiled, unexceptionable, unpolluted, unsullied, untainted, untarnished, virtuous.

antonyms contaminated, spoiled.

immaterial *adj* airy, disembodied, ethereal, extraneous, ghostly, impertinent, inapposite, inconsequential, inconsiderable, incorporeal, inessential, insignificant, insubstantial, irrelevant, metaphysical, minor, spiritual, trifling, trivial, unimportant, unnecessary, unsubstantial.

antonyms important, material, solid.

immature *adj* adolescent, babyish, callow, childish, crude, green, immatured, imperfect, inexperienced, infantile, jejune, juvenile, premature, puerile, raw, under-age, undeveloped, unfinished, unfledged, unformed, unripe, unseasonable, untimely, young.

antonym mature.

immaturity *n* babyishness, callowness, childishness, crudeness, crudity, greenness, immatureness, imperfection, inexperience, juvenility, prematureness, prematurity, puerility, rawness, unpreparedness, unripeness.

antonym maturity.

immeasurable *adj* bottomless, boundless, endless, illimitable, immense, immensurable, incalculable, inestimable, inexhaustible, infinite, limitless, measureless, unbounded, unfathomable, unlimited, unmeasureable, vast.

antonym limited.

immediacy *n* directness, imminence, instancy, instantaneity, promptness, simultaneity, spontaneity, swiftness.

antonym remoteness.

immediate *adj* actual, adjacent, close, contiguous, current, direct, existing, extant, instant, instantaneous, near, nearest, neighbouring, next, on hand, present, pressing, primary, prompt, proximate, recent, unhesitating, up-to-date, urgent.

antonym distant.

immediately *adv* at once, closely, directly, ek dum, forthwith, incontinent, instantly, lickety-split, nearly, now, off the top of one's head, on the instant, posthaste, promptly, pronto, right away, soonest, straight away, straight off, straight way, tout de suite, unhesitatingly, without delay.

antonyms eventually, never.

immemorial *adj* age-old, ancestral, ancient, archaic, fixed, hoary, long-standing, time-honoured, traditional.

antonym recent.

immense *adj* Brobdingnag(ian), colossal, cyclopean, elephantine, enormous, extensive, giant, gigantic, great, herculean, huge, illimitable, immeasurable, infinite, interminable, jumbo, large, limitless, mammoth, massive, monstrous, monumental, prodigious, rounceval, stupendous, Titanesque, titanic, tremendous, vast.

antonym minute.

immensity *n* bulk, enormousness, expanse, extent, greatness, hugeness, infinity, magnitude, massiveness, scope, size, sweep, vastness.

antonym minuteness.

immerse *v* bathe, demerge, demerse, dip, douse, duck, dunk, plunge, sink, submerge, submerse.

immersed *adj* absorbed, buried, busy, consumed, deep, engrossed, involved, occupied, preoccupied, rapt, sunk, taken up, wrapped up.

immersion *n* absorption, baptism, bathe, concentration, demersion, dip, dipping, dousing, ducking, dunking, involvement, plunging, preoccupation, submersion.

immigrant *n* incomer, newcomer. settler, wetback.

antonym emigrant.

immigrate *v* come in, migrate, move in, remove, resettle, settle.

antonym emigrate.

imminence *n* approach, immediacy, impendency, instancy, menace, propinquity, threat.

antonym remoteness.

imminent *adj* afoot, approaching, at hand, brewing, close, coming, forthcoming, gathering, impending, in the air, in the offing, looming, menacing, near, nigh, overhanging, threatening.

antonym far-off.

immobile *adj* at a standstill, at rest, cataplectic, expressionless, fixed, frozen, immobilised, immotile, immovable, motionless, rigid, riveted, rooted, solid, stable, static, stationary, stiff, still, stock-still, stolid, unexpressive, unmoving.

antonyms mobile, moving.

immobilise *v* cripple, disable, fix, freeze, halt, paralyse, stop, transfix.

antonym mobilise.

immobility *n* disability, firmness, fixedness, fixity, immovability, inertness, motionlessness, stability, steadiness, stillness.

antonym mobility.

immoderate *adj* distemperate, egregious, enormous, exaggerated, excessive, exorbitant, extravagant, extreme, hubristic, inordinate, intemperate, over the top, profligate, steep, uncalled-for, unconscionable, uncontrolled, undue, unjustified, unreasonable, unrestrained, unwarranted, wanton.

antonym moderate.

immoderately *adv* exaggeratedly, excessively, exorbitantly, extravagantly, extremely, inordinately, unduly, unjustifiably, unreasonably, unrestrainedly, wantonly, without measure.

antonym moderately.

immoderation *n* excess, exorbitance, extravagance, immoderateness, intemperance, overindulgence, prodigality, unreason, unrestraint.

antonym moderation.

immodest *adj* bawdy, bold, brass-necked, brazen, coarse, depraved, forward, fresh, gross, immoral, improper, impudent, impure, indecent, indecorous, indelicate, lewd, obscene, pushy, revealing, risqué, shameless, titillating, unblushing, unchaste, unmaidenly.

antonym modest.

immodesty *n* audacity, bawdiness, boldness, brass, coarseness, forwardness, gall, impudence, impurity, indecorousness, indecorum, indelicacy, lewdness, obscenity, shamelessness, temerity.

antonym modesty.

immoral *adj* abandoned, bad, corrupt, debauched, degenerate, depraved, dishonest, dissolute, evil, foul, impure, indecent, iniquitous, lecherous, lewd, licentious, nefarious, obscene, pornographic, profligate, reprobate, sinful, unchaste, unethical, unprincipled, unrighteous, unscrupulous, vicious, vile, wanton, wicked, wrong.

antonym moral.

immorality *n* badness, corruption, debauchery, depravity, dissoluteness, evil, iniquity, libertinage, licence, licentiousness, profligacy, sin, turpitude, vice, wickedness, wrong.

antonym morality.

immortal *adj* abiding, ambrosial, constant, deathless, endless, enduring, eternal, everlasting, imperishable, incorruptible, indestructable, lasting, perennial, perpetual, sempiternal, timeless, undying, unfading, unforgettable.

antonym mortal.

n deity, divinity, genius, god, goddess, great, hero, Olympian.

immortalise *v* apotheosise, celebrate, commemorate, deify, enshrine, eternalise, eternise, exalt, glorify, hallow, memorialise, perpetuate, solemnise.

immortality *n* athanasy, celebrity, deathlessness, deification, endlessness, eternity, everlasting life, fame, glorification, gloriousness, glory, greatness, incorruptibility, indestructibility, perpetuity, renown, timelessness.

antonym mortality.

immovable *adj* adamant, constant, determined, entrenched, fast, firm, fixed, immutable, impassive, inflexible, jammed, marble-constant, moveless, obdurate, obstinate, resolute, rooted, secure, set, stable, stationary, steadfast, stony, stuck, unbudgeable, unchangeable, unimpressionable, unmovable, unshakable, unshaken, unwavering, unyielding.

antonym movable.

immune *adj* clear, exempt, free, insusceptible, insusceptive, invulnerable, proof, protected, resistant, safe, unaffected, unsusceptible.

antonym susceptible.

immunisation *n* injection, inoculation, jab, jag, protection, vaccination.

immunise *v* inject, inoculate, protect, safeguard, vaccinate.

immunity *n* amnesty, charter, exemption, exoneration, franchise, freedom, immunisation, indemnity, insusceptibility, invulnerability, liberty, licence, mithridatism, prerogative, privilege, protection, release, resistance, right.

antonym susceptibility.

immure *v* cage, cloister, confine, enclose, enwall, imprison, incarcerate, jail, shut up, wall in.

antonym free.

immutability *n* changelessness, constancy, durability, fixedness, immutableness, invariability, permanence, stability, unalterableness, unchangeableness.

antonym mutability.

immutable *adj* abiding, changeless, constant, enduring, fixed, inflexible, invariable, lasting, permanent, perpetual, sacrosanct, solid, stable, steadfast, unalterable, unchangeable.

antonym mutable.

imp *n* brat, demon, devil, flibbertigibbet, gamin, minx, prankster, rascal, rogue, scamp, sprite, trickster, urchin.

impact *n* aftermath, bang, blow, brunt, bump, burden, collision, concussion, consequences, contact, crash, effect, force, impression, influence, jolt, knock, knock-on effect, meaning, power, repercussions, shock, significance, smash, stroke, thrust, thump, weight.

v clash, collide, crash, crush, fix, hit, press together, strike, wedge.

impair *v* blunt, craze, damage, debilitate, decrease, deteriorate, devalue, diminish, enervate, enfeeble, harm, hinder, injure, lessen, mar, reduce, spoil, undermine, vitiate, weaken, worsen.

antonym enhance.

impaired *adj* damaged, defective, faulty, flawed, imperfect, poor, unsound, vicious, vitiated.

antonym enhanced.

impairment *n* damage, deterioration, disablement, dysfunction, fault, flaw, harm, hurt, injury, reduction, ruin, vitiation.

antonym enhancement.

impale *v* ga(u)nch, lance, perforate, pierce, puncture, run through, skewer, spear, spike, spit, stick, transfix.

impalpable *adj* airy, delicate, disembodied, elusive, fine, imperceptible, inapprehensible, incorporeal, indistinct, insubstantial, intangible, shadowy, tenuous, thin, unsubstantial.

antonym palpable.

impalpably *adv* imperceptibly, insensibly, intangibly, slightly.

antonym perceptibly.

imparity *n* bias, disparity, disproportion, imbalance, inequality, inequity, partiality, unequalness, unevenness, unfairness.

antonym parity.

impart *v* accord, afford, bestow, communicate, confer, contribute, convey, disclose, discover, divulge, give, grant, hand over, lend, make known, offer, pass on, relate, reveal, tell, yield.

impartial *adj* crossbench, detached, disinterested, dispassionate, equal, equitable, even-handed, fair, just, neutral, non-discriminating, non-partisan, objective, open-minded, umcommitted, unbiased, unprejudiced.

antonym biased.

impartiality *n* detachment, disinterest, disinterestedness, dispassion, equality, equity, even-handedness, fairness, neutrality, non-partisanship, objectivity, open-mindedness, unbiasedness.

antonym bias.

impassable *adj* blocked, closed, impenetrable, invious, obstructed, pathless, trackless, unnavigable, unpassable.

antonym passable.

impasse *n* blind alley, cul-de-sac, dead end, deadlock, halt, nonplus, stalemate, stand-off, standstill.

impassioned *adj* animated, ardent, blazing, enthusiastic, excited, fervent, fervid, fiery, furious, glowing, heated, inflamed, inspired, intense, passionate, rousing, spirited, stirring, vehement, vigorous, violent, vivid, warm.

antonyms apathetic, mild.

impassive *adj* aloof, apathetic, blockish, callous, calm, composed, cool, dispassionate, emotionless, expressionless, immobile, impassible, imperturbable, indifferent, inscrutable, insensible, insusceptible, laid back, phlegmatic, poker-faced, reserved, serene, stoical, stolid, unconcerned, unemotional, unexcitable, unfeeling, unimpressible, unmoved, unruffled.

antonyms moved, responsive, warm.

impassivity *n* aloofness, calmness, composure, coolness, dispassion, impassibility, impassiveness, imperturbability, indifference, inscrutability, insensibility, phlegm, sang-froid, stoicism, stolidity.

antonyms compassion, responsiveness, warmth.

impatience *n* agitation, anxiety, avidity, avidness, eagerness, edginess, haste, hastiness, heat, impetuosity, intolerance, irritability, irritableness, nervousness, rashness, restiveness, restlessness, shortness, snappishness, testiness, uneasiness, vehemence.

antonym patience.

impatient *adj* abrupt, brusque, chafing, champing at the bit, curt, demanding, eager, edgy, fretful, hasty, headlong, hot-tempered, impetuous, intolerant, irritable, precipitate, quick-tempered, restless, snappy, testy, vehement, violent.

antonym patient.

impeach *v* accuse, arraign, blame, cast doubt on, censure, challenge, charge, denounce, disparage, grass on, impugn, indict, peach on, question, tax.

impeachment *n* accusation, arraignment, charge, disparagement, indictment.

impeccable *adj* blameless, exact, exquisite, flawless, immaculate, incorrupt, innocent, irreproachable, perfect, precise, pure, scrupulous, sinless, squeaky-clean, stainless, unblemished, unerring, unimpeachable.

antonym flawed.

impecunious *adj* broke, cleaned out, destitute, impoverished, indigent, insolvent, penniless, penurious, poor, poverty-stricken, skint, stony.

antonym rich.

impede *v* bar, block, brake, check, clog, curb, delay, disrupt, hamper, hinder, hobble, hold up, let, obstruct, restrain, retard, slow, stop, thwart, trammel.

antonym aid.

impediment *n* bar, barrier, block, burr, check, clog, curb, defect, difficulty, encumbrance, hindrance, let, log, obstacle, obstruction, snag, stammer, stumbling-block, stutter.

antonym aid.

impel *v* actuate, chivvy, compel, constrain, drive, excite, force, goad, incite, induce, influence, inspire, instigate, motivate, move, oblige, poke, power, prod, prompt, propel, push, spur, stimulate, urge.

antonym dissuade.

impending *adj* approaching, brewing, close, collecting, coming, forthcoming, gathering, hovering, imminent, in store, looming, menacing, near, nearing, threatening.

antonym remote.

impenetrable *adj* arcane, baffling, cabbalistic, cryptic, dark, dense, enigmatic(al), fathomless, hermetic, hidden, impassable, impermeable, impervious, incomprehensible, indiscernible, inexplicable, inscrutable, inviolable, mysterious, obscure, solid, thick, unfathomable, unintelligible, unpiercable.

antonyms imtelligible, penetrable.

impenitence *n* defiance, hard-heartedness, impenitency, incorrigibility, obduracy, recidivism, stubbornness.

antonym penitence.

impenitent *adj* defiant, hardened, incorrigible, obdurate, recidivisitic, remorseless, unabashed, unashamed, uncontrite, unreformed, unregenerate, unremorseful, unrepentant.

antonym penitent.

imperative *adj* authoritative, autocratic, bossy, commanding, compulsory, crucial, dictatorial, domineering, essential, exigent, high-handed, imperious, indispensable, insistent, lordly, magisterial, obligatory, peremptory, pressing, tyrannical, tyrannous, urgent, vital.

antonyms humble, optional.

imperceptible *adj* faint, fine, gradual, impalpable, inapparent, inappreciable, inaudible, inconsensequential, indiscernible, indistinguishable, infinitesimal, insensible, invisible, microscopic, minute, shadowy, slight, small, subtle, tiny, undetectable, unnoticeable.

antonym perceptible.

imperceptibly *adv* inappreciably, indiscernibly, insensibly, invisibly, little by little, slowly, subtly, unnoticeably, unobtrusively, unseen.

antonym perceptibly.

imperceptive *adj* crass, dim, dull, impercipient, insensitive, obtuse, superficial, unappreciative, unaware, undiscerning, unobservant, unseeing.

antonym perceptive.

imperfect *adj* abortive, broken, damaged, defective, deficient, faulty, flawed, impaired, incomplete, inexact, limited, partial, patchy, rudimentary, unfinished, unideal.

antonym perfect.

imperfection *n* blemish, blot, blotch, crack, defect, deficiency, dent, failing, fallibility, fault, flaw, foible, frailty, glitch, inadequacy, incompleteness, insufficiency, peccadillo, shortcoming, stain, taint, weakness.

antonyms asset, perfection.

imperial *adj* august, exalted, grand, great, imperatorial, imperious, kingly, lofty, magnificent, majestic, noble, princely, queenly, regal, royal, sovereign, superior, supreme.

imperialism *n* acquisitiveness, adventurism, colonialism, empire-building, expansionism.

imperil *v* compromise, endanger, expose, hazard, jeopardise, risk, threaten.

imperious *adj* arrogant, authoritarian, autocratic, bossy, commanding, demanding, despotic, dictatorial, domineering, exacting, haughty, high-and-mighty, high-handed, imperative, lordly, magisterial, overbearing, overweening, peremptory, tyrannical, tyrannous.

antonym humble.

imperishable *adj* abiding, deathless, enduring, eternal, everlasting, immortal, incorruptible, indestructible, inextinguishable, perennial, permanent, perpetual, undying, unfading, unforgettable.

antonym perishable.

impermanent *adj* brief, elusive, ephemeral, evanescent, fleeting, fly-by-night, flying, fugacious, fugitive, inconstant, momentary, mortal, passing, perishable, short-lived, temporary, transient, transitory, unfixed, unsettled, unstable.

antonym permanent.

impermeable *adj* damp-proof, hermetic, impassable, impenetrable, impervious, non-porous, proof, resistant, waterproof, water-repellent, water-resistant.

antonym permeable.

impersonal *adj* aloof, bureaucratic, businesslike, cold, detached, dispassionate, faceless, formal, frosty, glassy, inhuman, neutral, official, remote, unfriendly, unsympathetic.

antonym friendly.

impersonate *v* act, ape, caricature, do, imitate, masquerade as, mimic, mock, parody, personate, pose as, take off.

impersonation *n* apery, aping, burlesque, caricature, imitation, impression, mimicry, parody, take-off.

impertinence *n* assurance, audacity, backchat, boldness, brass, brazenness, cheek, discourtesy, disrespect, effrontery, forwardness, impoliteness, impudence, incivility, insolence, malapertness, nerve, pertness, politeness, presumption, rudeness, sauce, sauciness.

impertinent *adj* bold, brattish, brazen, bumptious, cheeky, discourteous, disrespectful, forward, fresh, ill-mannered, impolite, impudent, insolent, interfering, malapert, pert, presumptuous, rude, saucy, uncivil, unmannerly.

antonym polite.

imperturbability *n* calmness, complacency, composure, coolness, equanimity, self-possession, tranquility.

antonyms jitteriness, touchiness.

imperturbable *adj* calm, collected, complacent, composed, cool, equanimous, impassible, optimistic, sanguine, sedate, self-possessed, stoical, tranquil, unexcitable, unflappable.

antonyms jittery, touchy.

impervious *adj* closed, damp-proof, hermetic, immune, impassable, impenetrable, impermeable, imperviable, invulnerable, resistant, sealed, unaffected, unmoved, unreceptive, unswayable, untouched.

antonyms pervious, responsive.

impetuosity *n* dash, élan, haste, hastiness, impetuousness, impulsiveness, precipitancy, precipitateness, rashness, vehemence, violence.

antonym circumspection.

impetuous *adj* ardent, bull-headed, eager, furious, hasty, headlong, impassioned, impulsive, overhasty, passionate, precipitate, rash, spontaneous, tearaway, unplanned, unpremeditated, unreflecting, unrestrained, unthinking.

antonym circumspect.

impetuously *adv* impulsively, passionately, precipitately, rashly, recklessly, spontaneously, unthinkingly, vehemently.

antonym circumspectly.

impetus *n* drive, energy, force, goad, impulse, impulsion, incentive, momentum, motivation, motive, power, push, spur, stimulus.

impiety *n* blasphemy, godlessness, hubris, iniquity, irreligion, irreverence, profaneness, profanity, sacrilege, sacrilegiousness, sinfulness, ungodliness, unholiness, unrighteousness, wickedness.
antonym piety.

impinge *v* affect, clash, collide, dash, encroach, enter, hit, influence, infringe, intrude, invade, obtrude, strike, touch, touch on, trespass, violate.

impious *adj* blasphemous, godless, hubristic, iniquitous, irreligious, irreverent, profane, sacrilegious, sinful, ungodly, unholy, unrighteous, wicked.
antonym pious.

impish *adj* arch, devilish, elfin, frolicsome, gamin, mischievous, naughty, pranksome, puckish, rascally, roguish, sportive, tricksome, tricksy, waggish, wanton, wicked.

impishness *n* archness, devilry, deviltry, gaminerie, mischief, naughtiness, puckishness, roguery, roguishness, sportiveness, waggishness, wickedness.

implacability *n* implacableness, inexorability, inflexibility, instransigence, intractability, irreconcilability, mercilessness, pitilessness, rancorousness, relentlessness, remorselessness, ruthlessness, unforgivingness, vengefulness.
antonym placability.

implacable *adj* cruel, immovable, inappeasable, inexorable, inflexible, intractable, intransigent, irreconcilable, merciless, pitiless, rancorous, relentless, remorseless, ruthless, unappeasable, unbending, uncompromising, unforgiving, unrelenting, unyielding.
antonym placable.

implant *v* embed, fix, graft, inculcate, infix, infuse, ingraft, inoculate, inseminate, insert, inset, instil, place, plant, root, sow.

implausible *adj* dubious, far-fetched, flimsy, improbable, incredible, suspect, thin, transparent, unbelievable, unconvincing, unlikely, unplausible, unreasonable, weak.
antonym plausible.

implement *n* agent, apparatus, appliance, device, gadget, gimmick, gismo, instrument, tool, utensil.
v accomplish, bring about, carry out, complete, discharge, do, effect, enforce, execute, fulfil, perfect, perform, realise.

implementation *n* accomplishment, carrying out, completion, discharge, effecting, enforcement, execution, fulfilling, fulfilment, performance, performing, realisation.

implicate *v* associate, compromise, connect, embroil, entangle, include, incriminate, inculpate, involve, throw suspicion on.
antonyms absolve, exonerate.

implicated *adj* associated, compromised, embroiled, entangled, incriminated, inculpated, involved, suspected.
antonym exonerated.

implication *n* association, assumption, conclusion, connection, entanglement, hint, incrimination, inference, innuendo, insinuation, involvement, meaning, overtone, presupposition, ramification, repercusssion, significance, signification, suggestion, undertone.

implicit *adj* absolute, constant, contained, entire, firm, fixed, full, implied, inherent, latent, presupposed, steadfast, tacit, total, undeclared, understood, unhesitating, unqualified, unquestioning, unreserved, unshakable, unshaken, unspoken, wholehearted.
antonym explicit.

implicitly *adv* absolutely, by implication, completely, firmly, unconditionally, unhesitatingly, unquestioningly, unreservedly, utterly.
antonym explicitly.

implied *adj* assumed, hinted, implicit, indirect, inherent, insinuated, suggested, tacit, undeclared, understood, unexpressed, unspoken, unstated.
antonym stated.

implore *v* ask, beg, beseech, crave, entreat, importune, plead, pray, solicit, supplicate, wheedle.

imply *v* betoken, connote, denote, entail, evidence, hint, import, indicate, insinuate, intimate, involve, mean, point to, presuppose, require, signify, suggest.
antonym state.

impolite *adj* abrupt, bad-mannered, boorish, churlish, clumsy, coarse, cross, discourteous, disrespectful, gauche, ill-bred, ill-mannered, indecorous, indelicate, inept, insolent, loutish, rough, rude, uncivil, uncourteous, ungallant, ungentlemanly, ungracious, unladylike, unmannerly, unrefined.
antonym polite.

impoliteness *n* abruptness, bad manners, boorishness, churlishness, clumsiness, coarseness, crassness, discourtesy, disrespect, gaucherie, incivility, indelicacy, ineptitude, insolence, rudeness, unmannerliness.
antonym politeness.

impolitic *adj* daft, foolish, ill-advised, ill-judged, imprudent, indiscreet, inexpedient, injudicious, maladroit, misguided, rash, undiplomatic, unwise.
antonym politic.

import *n* bearing, consequence, drift, essence, gist, implication, importance, intention, magnitude, meaning, message, moment, nub, purport, sense, significance, substance, thrust, weight.
v betoken, bring in, imply, indicate, introduce, mean, purport, signify.

importance *n* concern, concernment, consequence, consideration, distinction, eminence, esteem, gravitas, import, influence, interest, mark, moment, momentousness, pith, pre-eminence, prestige, prominence, significance, signification, standing, status, substance, usefulness, value, weight, worth.
antonym unimportance.

important *adj* basic, earthshaking, earthshattering, eminent, essential, far-reaching, foremost, grave, heavy, high-level, high-ranking, influential, key, keynote, large, leading, material, meaningful, momentous, notable, noteworthy, on the map, outstanding, powerful, pre-eminent, primary, prominent, relevant, salient, seminal, serious, signal, significant, substantial, urgent, valuable, valued, weighty.

antonym unimportant.

importunate *adj* impatient, insistent, persistent, pertinacious, pressing, tenacious, urgent, wheedlesome, wheedling, whilly, whillywha(w).

importune *v* badger, beset, besiege, cajole, dun, earwig, entreat, flagitate, harass, hound, pester, plague, plead with, press, solicit, urge.

importunity *n* cajolery, entreaties, harassment, insistence, persistence, solicitation, urgency, urging.

impose[1] *v* appoint, burden, charge (with), decree, dictate, encumber, enforce, enjoin, establish, exact, fix, impone, inflict, institute, introduce, lay, levy, ordain, place, prescribe, promulgate, put, saddle, set.

impose[2] *v* butt in, encroach, foist, force oneself, gate crash, horn in, impone, interpose, intrude, obtrude, presume, take liberties, trespass.

impose on abuse, deceive, exploit, fool, hoodwink, mislead, play on, take advantage of, trick, use.

imposing *adj* august, commanding, dignified, distinguished, effective, grand, grandiose, impressive, majestic, ortund, pompous, stately, striking.

antonyms modest, unimposing.

imposition[1] *n* application, decree, exaction, infliction, introduction, levying, promulgation.

imposition[2] *n* burden, charge, cheek, constraint, deception, duty, encroachment, intrusion, levy, liberty, lines, presumption, punishment, task, tax.

impossibility *n* hopelessness, impracticability, inability, inconceivability, unattainableness, unobtainableness, untenability, unviability.

antonym possibility.

impossible *adj* absurd, hopeless, impracticable, inadmissible, inconceivable, insoluble, intolerable, ludicrous, outrageous, preposterous, unacceptable, unachievable, unattainable, ungovernable, unobtainable, unreasonable, untenable, unthinkable, unviable, unworkable.

antonym possible.

impostor *n* charlatan, cheat, con man, deceiver, faitor, fake, fraud, grifter, hypocrite, impersonator, mountebank, phoney, pretender, quack, rogue, sham, swindler, trickster.

imposture *n* artifice, cheat, con, con trick, counterfeit, deception, fraud, grift, hoax, impersonation, quackery, swindle, trick.

impotence *n* disability, enervation, feebleness, frailty, helplessness, impuissance, inability, inadequacy, incapacity, incompetence, ineffectiveness, inefficacy, inefficiency, infirmity, ligature, paralysis, powerlessness, resourcelessness, uselessness, weakness.

antonym strength.

impotent *adj* disabled, enervated, feeble, frail, helpless, impuissant, inadequate, incapable, incapacitated, incompetent, ineffective, infirm, paralysed, powerless, resourceless, unable, unmanned, weak.

antonyms potent, strong.

impoverish *v* bankrupt, beggar, break, denude, depauperate, deplete, diminish, drain, exhaust, pauperise, reduce, ruin, weaken.

antonym enrich.

impoverished *adj* arid, bankrupt, barren, decayed, denuded, depauperate(d), depleted, destitute, distressed, drained, empty, exhausted, impecunious, in reduced circumstances, indigent, jejune, necessitous, needy, on the rocks, penurious, poor, poorly off, reduced, skint, spent, straitened.

antonym rich.

impracticability *n* futility, hopelessness, impossibility, impracticality, infeasibility, unsuitableness, unviability, unworkability, uselessness.

antonym practicability.

impracticable *adj* awkward, doctrinaire, impossible, impractical, inapplicable, inconvenient, infeasible, unachievable, unattainable, unfeasible, unpractical, unserviceable, unsuitable, unworkable, useless, visionary.

antonym practicable.

impractical *adj* academic, idealistic, impossible, impracticable, inoperable, ivory-tower, non-viable, romantic, starry-eyed, unbusinesslike, unrealistic, unserviceable, unworkable, visionary, wild.

antonym practical.

impracticality *n* hopelessness, idealism, impossibility, infeasibility, romanticism, unworkability, unworkableness.

antonym practicality.

imprecation *n* abuse, anathema, blasphemy, curse, denunciation, execration, malediction, profanity, vilification, vituperation.

imprecise *adj* ambiguous, careless, equivocal, estimated, fluctuating, hazy, ill-defined, inaccurate, indefinite, indeterminate, inexact, inexplicit, loose, rough, sloppy, unprecise, unscholarly, unscientific, vague, woolly.

antonym precise.

impregnable *adj* fast, fortified, immovable, impenetrable, impugnable, indestructible, invincible, invulnerable, secure, solid, strong, unassailable, unbeatable, unconquerable.

antonym vulnerable.

impregnate *v* fecundate, fertilise, fill, fructify, imbrue, imbue, infuse, inseminate, knock up, percolate, permeate, pervade, saturate, soak, steep, suffuse.

impregnation *n* fecundation, fertilisation, fertilising, fructification, fructifying, imbruement, imbruing, imbuing, insemination, saturation.

impress *v* affect, emboss, emphasise, engrave, excite, fix, grab, imprint, inculcate, indent, influence, inspire, instil, make one's mark, mark, move, namedrop, print, slay, stamp, stand out, stir, strike, sway, touch, wow.

impressed *adj* affected, épris, excited, grabbed, imprinted, indented, influenced, marked, moved, stamped, stirred, struck, taken, touched, turned on.

antonym unimpressed.

impression[1] *n* awareness, belief, concept, consciousness, conviction, effect, fancy, feeling, hunch, idea, impact, influence, memory, notion, opinion, reaction, recollection, sense, suspicion, sway.

impression[2] *n* dent, edition, engram, engramma, hollow, impress, imprint, imprinting, incuse, indentation, issue, mark, niello, outline, pressure, printing, stamp, stamping.

impression[3] *n* apery, aping, burlesque, imitation, impersonation, parody, send-up, take-off.

impressionability *n* greenness, impressibility, ingenuousness, naïvety, receptiveness, receptivity, sensitivity, suggestibility, susceptibility, vulnerability.

impressionable *adj* gullible, impressible, ingenuous, naïve, open, receptive, responsive, sensitive, suggestible, susceptible, vulnerable.

impressive *adj* affecting, effective, exciting, forcible, foudroyant, frappant, imposing, moving, powerful, stirring, striking, touching.

antonym unimpressive.

imprint *n* badge, brand mark, impression, indentation, logo, mark, print, sign, stamp.

v brand, engrave, etch, fix, impress, mark, print, stamp.

imprison *v* cage, confine, constrain, detain, encage, enchain, immure, incarcerate, intern, jail, lock up, put away, quod, send down.

antonym free.

imprisoned *adj* bars, behind, caged, captive, confined, doing bird, doing time, immured, incarcerated, jailed, locked up, put away, sent down.

antonym free.

imprisonment *n* bird, confinement, custody, detention, durance, duress(e), enchainment, incarceration, internment, porridge, quod.

antonym freedom.

improbability *n* doubt, doubtfulness, dubiety, dubiousness, far-fetchedness, implausibility, uncertainty, unlikelihood, unlikeliness.

antonym probability.

improbable *adj* doubtful, dubious, fanciful, far-fetched, implausible, preposterous, questionable, tall, unbelievable, uncertain, unconvincing, unlikely, weak.

antonym probable.

impromptu *adj* ad-lib, autoschediastic, extemporaneous, extempore, extemporised, improvised, off the cuff, off-hand, offhand, spontaneous, unpremeditated, unprepared, unrehearsed, unscripted, unstudied.

antonyms planned, rehearsed.

adv ad lib, extempore, off the cuff, off the top of one's head, on the spur of the moment, spontaneously.

n autoschediasm, extemporisation, improvisation, voluntary.

improper *adj* abnormal, erroneous, false, illegitimate, ill-timed, impolite, inaccurate, inadmissible, inapplicable, inapposite, inappropriate, inapt, incongruous, incorrect, indecent, indecorous, indelicate, infelicitous, inopportune, irregular, malapropos, off-colour, out of place, risqué, smutty, suggestive, unbecoming, uncalled-for, unfit, unfitting, unmaidenly, unparliamentary, unprintable, unquotable, unrepeatable, unseasonable, unseemly, unsuitable, unsuited, untoward, unwarranted, vulgar, wrong.

antonym proper.

impropriety *n* bad taste, blunder, faux pas, gaffe, gaucherie, immodesty, incongruity, indecency, indecorousness, indecorum, lapse, mistake, slip, solecism, unseemliness, unsuitability, vulgarity.

antonym propriety.

improve *v* advance, ameliorate, amend, augment, better, correct, culture, deodorise, develop, embourgeoise, enhance, gentrify, help, increase, look up, meliorate, mend, mend one's ways, perk up, pick up, polish, progress, rally, recover, rectify, recuperate, reform, rise, touch up, turn over a new leaf, turn the corner, up, upgrade.

antonyms decline, diminish.

improvement *n* advance, advancement, amelioration, amendment, augmentation, bettering, betterment, correction, development, embourgeoisement, enhancement, furtherance, gain, gentrification, increase, melioration, progress, rally, recovery, rectification, reformation, rise, upswing.

antonyms decline, retrogression.

improvidence *n* carelessness, extravagance, fecklessness, heedlessness, imprudence, Micawberism, negligence, prodigality, profligacy, thriftlessness, wastefulness.

antonym thrift.

improvident *adj* careless, feckless, heedless, imprudent, Micawberish, negligent, prodigal, profligate, reckless, shiftless, spendthrift, thoughtless, thriftless, underprepared, uneconomical, unprepared, unthrifty, wasteful.

antonym thrifty.

improving *adj* convalescing, edifying, educational, instructive, meliorative, on the mend, recuperating, uplifting.

antonyms harmful, unedifying.

improvisation *n* ad hocery, ad-lib, ad-libbing, autoschediasm, expedient, extemporising, impromptu, invention, makeshift, spontaneity, vamp.

improvise *v* ad-lib, autoschediaze, coin, concoct, contrive, devise, extemporise, improvisate, invent, make do, noodle, play it by ear, throw together, vamp.

improvised *adj* ad-lib, extemporaneous, extempore, extemporised, improvisational, improvisatory, makeshift, off-the-cuff, spontaneous, unprepared, unrehearsed.

antonym rehearsed.

imprudence *n* carelessness, folly, foolhardiness, foolishness, haste, hastiness, heedlessness, improvidence, inadvisability, incaution, incautiousness, inconsiderateness, indiscretion, irresponsibility, rashness, recklessness, short-sightedness, temerity.

antonym prudence.

imprudent *adj* careless, foolhardy, foolish, hasty, heedless, ill-advised, ill-considered, ill-judged, impolitic, improvident, incautious, inconsiderate, indiscreet, injudicious, irresponsible, overhasty, rash, reckless, short-sighted, temerarious, unthinking, unwise.

antonym prudent.

impudence *n* assurance, audacity, backchat, boldness, brass neck, brazenness, cheek, chutzpah, effrontery, face, impertinence, impudicity, insolence, lip, malapertness, neck, nerve, pertness, presumption, presumptuousness, rudeness, sauciness, shamelessness.

antonym politeness.

impudent *adj* audacious, bold, bold-faced, brazen, brazen-faced, cheeky, cocky, forward, fresh, immodest, impertinent, insolent, malapert, pert, presumptuous, rude, saucy, shameless.

antonym polite.

impugn *v* assail, attack, call in question, challenge, criticise, dispute, oppose, question, resist, revile, traduce, vilify, vilipend, vituperate.

antonym praise.

impulse *n* caprice, catalyst, conatus, desire, drive, feeling, force, impetus, incitement, inclination, influence, instinct, momentum, motive, movement, notion, passion, pressure, push, resolve, stimulus, surge, thrust, urge, whim, wish.

impulsive *adj* hasty, headlong, impetuous, instinctive, intuitive, passionate, precipitant, precipitate, quick, rash, reckless, spontaneous, unconsidered, unpredictable, unpremeditated.

antonym cautious.

impulsiveness *n* haste, hastiness, impetuosity, impetuousness, precipitateness, precipitation, rashness, recklessness.

antonym caution.

impunity *n* amnesty, dispensation, excusal, exemption, freedom, immunity, liberty, licence, permission, security.

antonym liability.

impure *adj* admixed, adulterated, alloyed, carnal, coarse, contaminated, corrupt, debased, defiled, dirty, feculent, filthy, foul, gross, immodest, immoral, indecent, indelicate, infected, lascivious, lewd, licentious, lustful, mixed, obscene, polluted, prurient, salacious, smutty, sullied, tainted, turbid, unchaste, unclean, unrefined, unwholesome, vicious, vitiated.

antonyms chaste, pure.

impurity *n* admixture, adulteration, befoulment, carnality, coarseness, contaminant, contamination, corruption, defilement, dirt, dirtiness, dross, feculence, filth, foreign body, foreign matter, foulness, grime, grossness, immodesty, immorality, indecency, infection, lasciviousness, lewdness, licentiousness, mark, mixture, obscenity, pollutant, pollution, prurience, salaciousness, scum, smuttiness, spot, stain, taint, turbidity, turbidness, unchastity, uncleanness, vulgarity.

antonyms chasteness, purity.

imputable *adj* ascribable, attributable, blameable, chargeable, referable, traceable.

imputation *n* accusation, arrogation, ascription, aspersion, attribution, blame, censure, charge, insinuation, reproach, slander, slur, suggestion.

impute *v* accredit, ascribe, assign, attribute, charge, credit, put down to, refer.

in a state agitated, anxious, distressed, disturbed, flustered, hassled, het up, in a stew, in a tizzy, panic-stricken, ruffled, steamed up, troubled, upset, worked up, worried.

antonym calm.

in a word briefly, concisely, in a nutshell, in short, succinctly, to be brief, to put it briefly, to sum up.

antonym at length.

in abeyance dormant, hanging fire, on ice, pending, shelved, suspended.

in addition additionally, also, as well, besides, further, furthermore, into the bargain, moreover, over and above, to boot, too, withal.

in advance ahead, beforehand, earlier, in front, in the forefront, in the lead, in the van, previously, sooner.

antonyms behind, later.

in ambush embusqué, lying in wait.

in camera behind closed doors, hugger-mugger, in private, in secret, privately, secretly, sub rosa, under the rose.

antonym openly.

in confidence in private, privately, secretly, sub rosa, under the rose.

in conflict at daggers drawn, at loggerheads, at odds, at variance, at war, disagreeing, disunited, in disagreement, opposed.

antonyms at peace, in agreement.

in crowds gregatim, in droves, in flocks, in force, in herds, in hordes, in large numbers, in strength, in troops.

antonym in penny numbers.

in depth comprehensively, exhaustively, extensively, in detail, intensively, thoroughly.

antonyms broadly, superficially.

in detail comprehensively, exhaustively, in depth, in particular, inside out, item by item, particularly, point by point, thoroughly.

antonyms broadly, superficially.

in difficulties in a hole, in dire straights, in the shit, up shit creek, up the creek, up the pole.

in effect actually, effectively, essentially, for practical purposes, in actuality, in fact, in reality, in the end, in truth, really, to all intents and purposes, virtually, when all is said and done.

in fact actually, en effet, in point of fact, in reality, in truth, indeed, really, truly.

in favour of all for, backing, for, on the side of, pro, supporting, to the advantage of.

antonym against.

in force binding, current, effective, gregatim, in crowds, in droves, in flocks, in hordes, in large numbers, in operation, in strength, on the statute book, operative, valid, working.

antonym inoperative.

in French Gallice.

in front ahead, before, first, in advance, in the van, leading, preceding, to the fore.

antonym behind.

in full completely, entirely, in its entirety, in total, in toto, unabridged, uncut, wholly.

antonyms partially, partly.

in German Germanice.

in good part cheerfully, cordially, good-naturedly, laughingly, well.

antonyms angrily, touchily.

in Greek Graece.

in gross en bloc, en masse, in aggregate, in bulk, in toto, wholesale.

antonym retail.

in hiding concealed, doggo, hidden, latitant.

in keeping appropriate, befitting, fit, fitting, harmonious, in harmony, of a piece, suitable.

antonym inappropriate.

in kind in like manner, similarly, tit for tat.

in Latin Latine.

in league allied, collaborating, conniving, conspiring, hand in glove, in cahoots, in collusion.

antonym at odds.

in love besotted, charmed, doting, enamoured, enraptured, hooked, infatuated, smitten.

in motion afoot, functioning, going, in progress, moving, on the go, operational, running, sailing, travelling, under way.

antonym stationary.

in my opinion for my money, me judice.

in order acceptable, all right, allowed, appropriate, arranged, called for, correct, done, fitting, in sequence, neat, OK, orderly, permitted, right, shipshape, suitable, tidy.

antonyms disallowed, out of order.

in order to intending to, so that, to, with a view to, with the intention of, with the purpose of.

in part a little, in some measure, part way, partially, partly, slightly, somewhat, to a certain extent, to some degree.

antonym wholly.

in particular distinctly, especially, exactly, expressly, in detail, particularly, specifically.

in passing accidentally, by the by(e), by the way, en passant, incidentally.

in penny numbers in dribs and drabs, in ones and twos.

antonyms in crowds, in force.

in person as large as life, bodily, in propria persona, personally.

in pieces broken, burst, damaged, disintegrated, in bits, in smithereens, kaput, piecemeal, ruined, shattered, smashed.

in place of as a replacement for, as a substitute for, as an alternative to, in exchange for, in lieu of, instead of.

in principle en principe, ideally, in essence, in theory, theoretically.

in private behind closed doors, hugger-mugger, in camera, in confidence, in secret, privately, secretly, sub rosa, under the rose.

antonym openly.

in progress going on, happening, occurring, proceeding, under way.

in proportion pro rata.

in public coram populo, for all to see, in full view, in open view, in the open, openly, publicly.

antonyms in camera, in secret.

in return en revanche.

in secret hugger-mugger, in confidence, in gremio, in pectore, in petto, inly, inwardly, on the q.t., on the quiet, sub rosa, under the rose.

antonym openly.

in spite of despite, notwithstanding.

in the interest(s) of for the sake of, on behalf of, on the part of, to the advantage of, to the benefit of.

in the light of bearing/keeping in mind, because of, considering, in view of, taking into account.

in the making budding, coming, developing, emergent, growing, nascent, potential, up and coming.

in the middle of among, busy with, during, engaged in, in the midst of, in the process of, occupied with, surrounded by, while.

in the midst of among, during, in the middle of, in the thick of, surrounded by.

in the money affluent, flush, loaded, opulent, prosperous, rich, rolling in it, wealthy, well-heeled, well-off, well-to-do.

antonym poor.

in the mood disposed, in the right frame of mind, inclined, interested, keen, minded, of a mind, willing.

in the offing at hand, close at hand, coming up, imminent, in sight, on the horizon, on the way.

antonym far off.

in the red bankrupt, in arrears, in debt, insolvent, on the rocks, overdrawn.

antonym in credit.

in the right justified, right.

antonym in the wrong.

in the wrong at fault, blameworthy, guilty, in error, mistaken, to blame.

antonym in the right.

in toto as a whole, completely, entirely, in its entirety, in total, totally, unabridged, uncut, wholly.

in two minds dithering, hesitant, hesitating, shilly-shallying, swithering, uncertain, undecided, unsure, vacillating, wavering.

antonym certain.

in vain bootlessly, fruitlessly, ineffectually, to no avail, unsuccessfully, uselessly, vainly.

antonym successfully.

inability *n* disability, disqualification, handicap, impotence, inadequacy, incapability, incapacity, incompetence, ineptitude, ineptness, powerlessness, weakness.

antonym ability.

inaccessible *adj* impassible, isolated, remote, solitary, unapproachable, unattainable, uncom(e)atable, unfrequented, unget-at-able, unreachable.

antonym accessible.

inaccuracy *n* blunder, boob, carelessness, corrigendum, defect, erratum, erroneousness, error, fault, faultiness, howler, imprecision, incorrectness, inexactness, looseness, miscalculation, mistake, slip, unreliability.

antonym accuracy.

inaccurate *adj* careless, defective, discrepant, erroneous, faulty, imprecise, in error, incorrect, inexact, loose, mistaken, out, unfaithful, unreliable, unrepresentative, unsound, wide of the mark, wild, wrong.

antonym accurate.

inaccurately *adv* carelessly, clumsily, imprecisely, inexactly, loosely, unfaithfully, unreliably, wildly.

antonym accurately.

inaction *n* dormancy, idleness, immobility, inactivity, inertia, rest, stagnation, stasis, torpidity, torpor.

antonym activeness.

inactivate *v* cripple, disable, immobilise, knock the bottom out of, mothball, paralyse, scupper, stabilise, stop.

antonym activate.

inactive *adj* abeyant, dormant, dull, idle, immobile, indolent, inert, inoperative, jobless, kicking one's heels, latent, lazy, lethargic, low-key, mothballed, out of service, out of work, passive, quiet, sedentary, sleepy, slothful, slow, sluggish, somnolent, stagnant, stagnating, torpid, unemployed, unoccupied, unused.

antonym active.

inactivity *n* abeyance, abeyancy, dilatoriness, dolce far niente, dormancy, dullness, heaviness, hibernation, idleness, immobility, inaction, indolence, inertia, inertness, languor, lassitude, laziness, lethargy, passivity, quiescence, sloth, sluggishness, stagnation, stasis, torpor, unemployment, vegetation.

antonym activeness.

inadequacy *n* dearth, defect, defectiveness, deficiency, failing, faultiness, imperfection, inability, inadequateness, inaptness, incapacity, incompetence, incompetency, incompleteness, ineffectiveness, ineffectuality, ineffectualness, inefficacy, inefficiency, insufficiency, lack, meagreness, paucity, poverty, scantiness, shortage, shortcoming, skimpiness, unfitness, unsuitableness, want, weakness.

antonym adequacy.

inadequate *adj* defective, deficient, faulty, imperfect, inapt, incapable, incommensurate, incompetent, incomplete, ineffective, ineffectual, inefficacious, inefficient, insubstantial, insufficient, leaving a little/a lot/much to be desired, meagre, niggardly, scanty, short, sketchy, skimpy, sparse, unequal, unfitted, unqualified, wanting.

antonym adequate.

inadequately *adv* badly, carelessly, imperfectly, insufficiently, meagrely, poorly, scantily, sketchily, skimpily, sparsely, thinly.

antonym adequately.

inadmissible *adj* disallowed, immaterial, improper, inappropriate, incompetent, irrelevant, prohibited, unacceptable, unallowable, unqualified.

antonym admissible.

inadvertence *n* blunder, boob, boo-boo, carelessness, clanger, error, heedlessness, inadvertency, inattention, inconsideration, inobservance, mistake, neglect, negligence, oversight, remissness, thoughtlessness.

antonym care.

inadvertent *adj* accidental, careless, chance, heedless, inattentive, negligent, thoughtless, unguarded, unheeding, unintended, unintentional, unplanned, unpremeditated, unthinking, unwitting.

antonym deliberate.

inadvertently *adv* accidentally, by accident, by mistake, carelessly, heedlessly, involuntarily, mistakenly, negligently, remissly, thoughtlessly, unguardedly, unintentionally, unthinkingly, unwittingly.

antonym deliberately.

inadvisable *adj* daft, foolish, ill-advised, ill-judged, impolitic, imprudent, incautious, indiscreet, inexpedient, injudicious, misguided, unwise.

antonym advisable.

inalienable *adj* absolute, entailed, imprescriptible, indefeasible, infrangible, inherent, inviolable, non-negotiable, non-transferable, permanent, sacrosanct, unassailable, unremovable, untransferable.

antonym impermanent.

inane *adj* asinine, daft, drippy, empty, fatuous, foolish, frivolous, futile, idiotic, imbecilic, mindless, nutty, puerile, senseless, silly, stupid, trifling, unintelligent, vacuous, vain, vapid, worthless.

antonym sensible.

inanimate *adj* abiotic, dead, defunct, dormant, dull, exanimate, extinct, heavy, inactive, inert, inorganic, insensate, insentient, leaden, lifeless, listless, slow, spiritless, stagnant, torpid.

antonyms alive, animate, lively, living.

inanity *n* asininity, bêtise, daftness, drippiness, emptiness, fatuity, folly, foolishness, frivolity, imbecility, puerility, senselessness, silliness, vacuity, vapidity, waffle.

antonym sense.

inapplicable *adj* inapposite, inappropriate, inapt, inconsequent, irrelevant, unrelated, unsuitable, unsuited.

antonym applicable.

inappropriate *adj* disproportionate, ill-fitted, ill-suited, ill-timed, improper, incongruous, infelicitous, malapropos, out of place, tactless, tasteless, unbecoming, unbefitting, unfit, unfitting, unseemly, unsuitable, untimely.

antonym appropriate.

inappropriately *adv* malapropos, tactlessly, tastelessly.

antonym appropriately.

inapt *adj* awkward, clumsy, crass, dull, gauche, ill-fitted, ill-suited, ill-timed, inapposite, inappropriate, incompetent, inept, inexpert, infelicitous, inopportune, maladroit, slow, stupid, tactless, unapt, unfortunate, unhappy, unsuitable, unsuited.

antonym apt.

inaptitude *n* awkwardness, clumsiness, crassness, inaptness, incompetence, inopportuneness, maladroitness, tactlessness, unfitness, unreadiness, unsuitableness.

antonym aptitude.

inarticulacy *n* inarticulateness, incoherence, mumbling, speechlessness, tongue-tiedness, unintelligibility.

antonym articulacy.

inarticulate *adj* blurred, dumb, dysarthric, dysphasic, dyspraxic, faltering, halting, hesitant, incoherent, incomprehensible, indistinct, muffled, mumbled, mute, silent, speechless, tongue-tied, unclear, unintelligible, unspoken, unuttered, unvoiced, voiceless, wordless.

antonym articulate.

inattention *n* absence of mind, absent-mindedness, carelessness, daydreaming, disregard, dwam, forgetfulness, heedlessness, inadvertence, inattentiveness, neglect, preoccupation, wool-gathering.

antonym attentiveness.

inattentive *adj* absent-minded, careless, deaf, distracted, distrait, dreaming, dreamy, heedless, inadvertent, neglectful, negligent, preoccupied, regardless, remiss, unheeding, unmindful, unobservant, vague.

antonym attentive.

inaudible *adj* faint, imperceptible, indistinct, low, muffled, mumbled, mumbling, muted, noiseless, out of earshot, silent.

antonym audible.

inaugural *adj* consecratory, dedicatory, exordial, first, initial, introductory, launching, maiden, opening.

inaugurate *v* begin, christen, commence, commission, consecrate, dedicate, enthrone, han(d)sel, induct, initiate, install, instate, institute, introduce, invest, kick off, launch, open, ordain, originate, set up, start, start off, usher in.

inauguration *n* consecration, enthronement, han(d)sel, induction, initiation, installation, installing, institution, investiture, launch, launching, opening, setting up.

inauspicious *adj* bad, black, discouraging, ill-boding, ill-omened, ominous, threatening, unfavourable, unfortunate, unlucky, unpromising, unpropitious, untoward.

antonym auspicious.

inborn *adj* congenital, connate, hereditary, inbred, ingenerate, ingrained, inherent, inherited, innate, instinctive, intuitive, native, natural.

antonym learned.

inbred *adj* connate, constitutional, ingenerate, ingrained, inherent, innate, native, natural.

antonym learned.

inbreeding *n* endogamy, homogamy.

incalculable *adj* boundless, countless, enormous, immense, incomputable, inestimable, infinite, innumerable, limitless, measureless, numberless, uncountable, unforeseeable, unlimited, unmeasureable, unpredictable, untold, vast.

antonym limited.

incantation *n* abracadabra, chant, charm, conjuration, formula, hex, invocation, mantra(m), om, rune, spell.

incapable *adj* disqualified, drunk, feeble, helpless, impotent, inadequate, incompetent, ineffective, ineffectual, inept, insufficient, powerless, tipsy, unable, unfit, unfitted, unqualified, weak.

antonyms capable, sober.

incapacitate *v* cripple, disable, disqualify, hamstring, immobilise, lay up, paralyse, prostrate, put out of action, scupper, unfit.

antonyms facilitate, set up.

incapacitated *adj* disqualified, drunk, hamstrung, immobilised, indisposed, laid up, out of action, prostrate, scuppered, tipsy, unfit, unwell.

antonym operative.

incapacity *n* disability, disqualification, feebleness, impotence, inability, inadequacy, incapability, incompetency, ineffectiveness, powerlessness, unfitness, weakness.

antonym capability.

incapsulate *see* encapsulate.

incarcerate *v* cage, commit, confine, coop up, detain, encage, gaol, immure, impound, imprison, intern, jail, lock up, put away, restrain, restrict, send down, wall in.

antonym free.

incarceration *n* bondage, captivity, confinement, custody, detention, imprisonment, internment, jail, restraint, restriction.

antonym freedom.

incarnate *adj* embodied, made flesh, personified, typified.

incarnation *n* avatar, embodiment, exemplification, impersonation, manifestation, personification, type.

incautious *adj* careless, hasty, heedless, ill-advised, ill-judged, improvident, imprudent, impulsive, inconsiderate, indiscreet, injudicious, negligent, overhasty, precipitate, rash, reckless, thoughtless, unchary, unguarded, unthinking, unwary, wareless.

antonym cautious.

incendiary[1] *n* arsonist, firebug, fire-raiser, pétroleur, pétroleuse, pyromaniac.

incendiary[2] *n* agitator, demagogue, firebrand, insurgent, rabble-rouser, revolutionary.

adj dissentious, inciting, inflammatory, proceleusmatic, protreptic, provocative, rabble-rousing, seditious, subversive.

antonym calming.

incense[1] *n* adulation, aroma, balm, bouquet, fragrance, homage, joss-stick, perfume, scent, worship.

incense[2] *v* anger, enrage, exasperate, excite, inflame, infuriate, irritate, madden, make one see red, make one's blood boil, make one's hackles rise, provoke, raise one's hackles, rile.

antonym calm.

incensed *adj* angry, enraged, exasperated, fuming, furibund, furious, in a paddy, indignant, infuriated, irate, ireful, mad, maddened, on the warpath, steamed up, up in arms, waxy, wrathful.

antonym calm.

incentive *n* bait, carrot, cause, consideration, encouragement, enticement, impetus, impulse, inducement, lure, motivation, motive, reason, reward, spur, stimulant, stimulus.

antonym disincentive.

inception *n* beginning, birth, commencement, dawn, inauguration, initiation, installation, kick-off, origin, outset, rise, start.

antonym end.

incessant *adj* ceaseless, constant, continual, continuous, endless, eternal, everlasting, interminable, never-ending, non-stop, perpetual, persistent, relentless, unbroken, unceasing, unending, unrelenting, unremitting, weariless.

antonym intermittent.

incidence *n* amount, commonness, degree, extent, frequency, occurrence, prevalence, range, rate.

incident *n* adventure, affair(e), brush, circumstance, clash, commotion, confrontation, contretemps, disturbance, episode, event, fight, happening, mishap, occasion, occurrence, scene, skirmish.

incidental *adj* accidental, accompanying, ancillary, attendant, casual, chance, concomitant, contingent, contributory, fortuitous, incident, inconsequential, inessential, irrelevant, minor, non-essential, occasional, odd, random, related, secondary, subordinate, subsidiary.

antonym essential.

incidentally *adv* accidentally, by chance, by the by(e), by the way, casually, digressively, en passant, fortuitously, in passing, parenthetically.

incidentals *n* contingencies, epiphenomena, extras, odds and ends.

antonym essentials.

incinerate *v* burn, char, cremate, reduce to ashes.

incipient *adj* beginning, commencing, developing, embryonic, inceptive, inchoate, nascent, originating, rudimentary, starting.

antonym developed.

incise *v* carve, chisel, cut, cut into, engrave, etch, gash.

incised *adj* carved, cut, engraved, intagliated.

incision *n* cut, discission, gash, incisure, insection, notch, opening, slash, slit.

incisive *adj* acid, acute, astucious, astute, biting, caustic, cutting, keen, mordant, penetrating, perceptive, perspicacious, piercing, sarcastic, sardonic, satirical, severe, sharp, tart, trenchant.

antonym woolly.

incisiveness *n* acidity, astucity, astuteness, keenness, penetration, perspicacity, pungency, sarcasm, sharpness, tartness, trenchancy.

antonym woolliness.

incite *v* abet, animate, drive, egg on, encourage, excite, foment, goad, impel, inflame, instigate, prompt, provoke, put up to, rouse, set on, solicit, spur, stimulate, stir up, urge, whip up.

antonym restrain.

incitement *n* abetment, agitation, encouragement, goad, hortation, impetus, impulse, inducement, instigation, motivation, motive, prompting, provocation, spur, stimulus.

antonyms check, discouragement.

inciting *adj* exciting, incendiary, inflammatory, proceleusmatic, protreptic, protreptical, provocative, rabble-rousing.

antonym calming.

incivility *n* bad manners, boorishness, coarseness, discourteousness, discourtesy, disrespect, ill-breeding, impoliteness, inurbanity, roughness, rudeness, unmannerliness, vulgarity.

antonym civility.

inclemency *n* bitterness, boisterousness, callousness, cruelty, harshness, mercilessness, pitilessness, rawness, rigour, roughness, severity, storminess, tyranny, unfeelingness, ungeniality.

antonym clemency.

inclement *adj* bitter, boisterous, callous, cruel, draconian, foul, harsh, intemperate, merciless, pitiless, rigorous, rough, severe, stormy, tempestuous, tyrannical, unfeeling, ungenial, unmerciful.

antonym clement.

inclination[1] *n* affection, aptitude, bent, bias, clinamen, desire, disposition, fancy, fondness, ingenium, leaning, liking, month's mind, partiality, penchant, predilection, predisposition, prejudice, proclivity, proneness, propensity, stomach, taste, tendency, turn, turn of mind, velleity, wish.

antonym disinclination.

inclination[2] *n* angle, bend, bending, bow, bowing, clinamen, deviation, gradient, incline, leaning, nod, pitch, slant, slope, tilt.

incline[1] *v* affect, bias, dispose, influence, nod, persuade, predispose, prejudice, stoop, sway.

incline[2] *v* bend, bevel, bow, cant, deviate, diverge, lean, slant, slope, tend, tilt, tip, veer.

n acclivity, ascent, brae, declivity, descent, dip, grade, gradient, hill, ramp, rise, slope.

inclined *adj* apt, bent, disposed, given, liable, likely, minded, oblique, of a mind, predisposed, prone, sloping, tilted, willing.

antonym flat.

inclose *see* enclose.

include *v* add, allow for, comprehend, comprise, connote, contain, cover, embody, embrace, enclose, encompass, incorporate, involve, number among, rope in, subsume, take in, take into account.

antonyms exclude, ignore.

inclusion *n* addition, incorporation, insertion, involvement.

antonym exclusion.

inclusive *adj* across-the-board, all in, all-embracing, blanket, catch-all, compendious, comprehensive, full, general, overall, sweeping, umbrella.

antonyms exclusive, narrow.

incognito *adj* disguised, in disguise, masked, unknown, unrecognisable, unrecognised, veiled.

antonyms openly, undisguised.

incoherence *n* confusion, disconnectedness, disjointedness, illogicality, inarticulateness, inconsistency, unintelligibility, wildness.

antonym coherence.

incoherent *adj* confused, disconnected, disjointed, dislocated, disordered, inarticulate, inconsequent, inconsistent, jumbled, loose, muddled, rambling, stammering, stuttering, unconnected, unco-ordinated, unintelligible, unjointed, wandering, wild.

antonym coherent.

incombustible *adj* fireproof, fire-resistant, flameproof, flame-resistant, non-flammable, non-inflammable.

antonym combustible.

income *n* earnings, gains, interest, means, pay, proceeds, profits, receipts, returns, revenue, salary, takings, wages, yield.

antonym expenses.

incoming *adj* accruing, approaching, arriving, coming, ensuing, entering, homeward, landing, new, next, returning, succeeding.

antonym outgoing.

incommensurate *adj* disproportionate, excessive, extravagant, extreme, inadequate, inequitable, inordinate, insufficient, unequal.

antonym appropriate.

incommunicable *adj* indescribable, ineffable, inexpressible, unimpartable, unspeakable, unutterable.

antonym expressible.

incomparable *adj* brilliant, inimitable, matchless, paramount, peerless, superb, superlative, supreme, transcendent, unequalled, unmatched, unparalleled, unrivalled.

antonyms poor, run-of-the-mill.

incomparably *adv* brilliantly, by far, eminently, far and away, immeasurably, superbly, superlatively.

antonyms poorly, slightly.

incompatibility *n* antagonism, clash, conflict, difference, discrepancy, disparateness, disparity, incongruity, inconsistency, irreconcilability, mismatch, uncongeniality.

antonym compatibility.

incompatible *adj* antagonistic, antipathetic, clashing, conflicting, contradictory, discordant, discrepant, disparate, ill-assorted, incongruous, inconsistent, inconsonant, inharmonious, irreconcilable, mismatched, uncongenial, unsuitable, unsuited.

antonym compatible.

incompetence *n* bungling, inability, inadequacy, incapability, incapacity, incompetency, ineffectiveness, ineffectuality, ineffectualness, inefficiency, ineptitude, ineptness, insufficiency, stupidity, unfitness, uselessness.

antonym competence.

incompetent *adj* bungling, floundering, incapable, incapacitated, ineffective, ineffectual, inept, inexpert, insufficient, stupid, unable, unfit, unfitted, unskilful, useless.

antonym competent.

incomplete *adj* broken, defective, deficient, fragmentary, imperfect, incondite, inexhaustive, insufficient, lacking, part, partial, short, unaccomplished, undeveloped, undone, unexecuted, unfinished, wanting.

antonym complete.

incomprehensible *adj* above one's head, all Greek, arcane, baffling, beyond one's comprehension, beyond one's grasp, double-Dutch, enigmatic, impenetrable, inapprehensible, inconceivable, inscrutable, mysterious, obscure, opaque, perplexing, puzzling, unfathomable, unimaginable, unintelligible, unthinkable.

antonym comprehensible.

inconceivable *adj* implausible, incogitable, incredible, mind-boggling, out of the question, staggering, unbelievable, unheard-of, unimaginable, unknowable, unthinkable.

antonym conceivable.

inconclusive *adj* ambiguous, indecisive, indeterminate, open, uncertain, unconvincing, undecided, unsatisfying, unsettled, vague.

antonym conclusive.

incongruity *n* conflict, discrepancy, disparity, dissociability, dissociableness, inappropriateness, inaptness, incompatibility, inconcinnity, inconsistency, inharmoniousness, unsuitability.

antonyms consistency, harmoniousness.

incongruous *adj* absurd, conflicting, contradictory, contrary, disconsonant, discordant, dissociable, extraneous, improper, inappropriate, inapt, incoherent, incompatible, inconcinnous, inconsistent, out of keeping, out of place, unbecoming, unsuitable, unsuited.

antonyms consistent, harmonious.

inconsequential *adj* illogical, immaterial, inconsequent, inconsiderable, insignificant, minor, negligible, paltry, petty, trifling, trivial, unimportant.

antonym important.

inconsiderable *adj* exiguous, inconsequential, insignificant, light, minor, negligible, petty, piddling, piffling, slight, small, small-time, trifling, trivial, unimportant, unnoticeable.

antonym considerable.

inconsiderate *adj* careless, imprudent, indelicate, insensitive, intolerant, rash, rude, self-centred, selfish, tactless, thoughtless, unconcerned, ungracious, unkind, unthinking.

antonym considerate.

inconsiderateness *n* carelessness, étourderie, indelicacy, insensitivity, rudeness, selfishness, tactlessness, thoughtlessness, unconcern, unkindness.

antonym considerateness.

inconsistency *n* changeableness, contrariety, disagreement, discrepancy, disparity, divergence, fickleness, incompatibility, incongruity, inconsonance, inconstancy, instability, paradox, unpredictability, unreliability, unsteadiness, variance.

antonym consistency.

inconsistent *adj* at odds, at variance, capricious, changeable, conflicting, contradictory, contrary, discordant, discrepant, erratic, fickle, incoherent, incompatible, incongruous, inconstant, irreconcilable, irregular, unpredictable, unstable, unsteady, variable, varying.

antonym constant.

inconsistently *adv* contradictorily, differently, eccentrically, erratically, illogically, inequably, randomly, unequally, unfairly, unpredictably, variably.

antonym consistently.

inconsolable *adj* brokenhearted, desolate, desolated, despairing, devastated, disconsolate, heartbroken, wretched.

antonym consolable.

inconspicuous *adj* camouflaged, hidden, insignificant, low-key, modest, muted, ordinary, plain, quiet, retiring, unassuming, unnoticeable, unobtrusive, unostentatious.

antonym conspicuous.

inconstant *adj* capricious, chameleon(ic), changeable, changeful, erratic, fickle, fluctuating, inconsistent, irresolute, mercurial, moonish, mutable, uncertain, undependable, unreliable, unsettled, unstable, unsteady, vacillating, variable, varying, volatile, wavering, wayward.

antonym constant.

incontestable *adj* certain, clear, evident, incontrovertible, indisputable, indubitable, irrefutable, obvious, self-evident, sure, undeniable, unquestionable.

antonym uncertain.

incontinence *n* enuresis.

incontinent *adj* debauched, dissipated, dissolute, enuretic, lascivious, lecherous, lewd, licentious, loose, lustful, profligate, promiscuous, unbridled, unchaste, unchecked, uncontrollable, uncontrolled, ungovernable, ungoverned, unrestrained, wanton.

antonym continent.

incontrovertible *adj* certain, clear, established, evident, incontestable, indisputable, indubitable, irrefutable, positive, self-evident, sure, undeniable, unquestionable, unshakable.

antonym uncertain.

inconvenience *n* annoyance, awkwardness, bother, cumbersomeness, difficulty, disadvantage, disruption, disturbance, disutility, drawback, fuss, hindrance, nuisance, trouble, uneasiness, unhandiness, unsuitableness, untimeliness, unwieldiness, upset, vexation.

antonym convenience.

v bother, disaccommodate, discommode, disrupt, disturb, irk, put out, put to trouble, trouble, upset.

antonym convenience.

inconvenient *adj* annoying, awkward, bothersome, cumbersome, difficult, disadvantageous, disturbing, embarrassing, inopportune, tiresome, troublesome, unhandy, unmanageable, unseasonable, unsocial, unsuitable, untimely, untoward, unwieldy, vexatious.

antonym convenient.

incorporate *v* absorb, amalgamate, assimilate, blend, coalesce, combine, consolidate, embody, fuse, incarnate, include, integrate, merge, mix, subsume, unite.

antonyms separate, split off.

incorporation *n* absorption, amalgamation, assimilation, association, blend, coalescence, company, federation, fusion, inclusion, integration, merger, society, unification, unifying.

antonyms separation, splitting off.

incorporeal *adj* bodiless, ethereal, ghostly, illusory, intangible, phantasmal, phantasmic, spectral, spiritual, unfleshy, unreal.

antonym real.

incorrect *adj* erroneous, false, faulty, flawed, illegitimate, imprecise, improper, inaccurate, inappropriate, inexact, mistaken, out, specious, ungrammatical, unidiomatic, unsuitable, untrue, wrong.

antonym correct.

incorrectness *n* erroneousness, error, fallacy, falseness, faultiness, illegitimacy, impreciseness, imprecision, impropriety, inaccuracy, inexactness, speciousness, ungrammaticalness, unsoundness, unsuitability, wrongness.

antonym correctness.

incorrigible *adj* hardened, hopeless, impenitent, incurable, indocile, intractable, inveterate, irreclaimable, irredeemable, irreformable, unreformable, unreformed, unteachable.

antonym reformable.

incorruptibility *n* honesty, honour, integrity, justness, nobility, probity, uprightness, virtue.

antonym corruptibility.

incorruptible *adj* everlasting, honest, honourable, imperishable, incorrupt, just, straight, trustworthy, unbribable, undecaying, upright.

antonym corruptible.

increase *v* add to, advance, aggrandise, amplify, augment, boost, build up, develop, dilate, eke, eke out, enhance, enlarge, escalate, expand, extend, greaten, grow, heighten, inflate, intensify, magnify, mount, multiply, proliferate, prolong, pullulate, raise, snowball, soar, spread, step up, strengthen, swell, wax.

antonym decrease.

n accrescence, addition, augment, augmentation, auxesis, boost, development, enlargement, escalation, expansion, extension, gain, growth, increment, intensification, proliferation, rise, step-up, surge, upsurge, upsurgence, upturn.

antonym decrease.

increasing *adj* accrescent, addititious, advancing, broadening, crescent, crescive, developing, expanding, growing, intensifying, mounting, rising, rocketing, sprouting, waxing, widening.

antonym decreasing.

incredible *adj* absurd, amazing, astonishing, astounding, extraordinary, fabulous, far-fetched, great, implausible, impossible, improbable, inconceivable, inspired, marvellous, preposterous, prodigious, superb, superhuman, unbelievable, unimaginable, unthinkable, wonderful.

antonyms believable, run-of-the-mill.

incredulity *n* disbelief, distrust, doubt, doubting, incredulousness, scepticism, unbelief.

antonym credulity.

incredulous *adj* disbelieving, distrustful, doubtful, doubting, dubious, mistrustful, sceptical, suspicious, unbelieving, uncertain, unconvinced.

antonym credulous.

increment *n* accretion, accrual, accrument, addendum, addition, advancement, augmentation, enlargement, expansion, extension, gain, growth, increase, step up, supplement.

antonym decrease.

incriminate *v* accuse, arraign, blame, charge, criminate, impeach, implicate, inculpate, indict, involve, point the finger at, recriminate, stigmatise.

antonym exonerate.

incubator *n* eccaleobion, hatchery.

incubus *n* affliction, angst, burden, cacod(a)emon, cross, demon, devil, dread, ephialtes, evil spirit, fear, fiend, load, nightmare, oppression, pressure, sorrow, spirit, stress, succubus, trial, worry.

inculcate *v* drill into, drum into, engrain, hammer into, implant, impress, indoctrinate, infuse, instil, teach.

inculpate *v* accuse, blame, censure, charge, connect, criminate, drag into, impeach, implicate, incriminate, involve, recriminate.

antonym exonerate.

incumbent *adj* binding, compulsory, mandatory, necessary, obligatory, prescribed, up to.

incur *v* arouse, bring upon, contract, draw, earn, expose oneself to, gain, induce, meet with, provoke, run up, suffer.

incurable *adj* dyed-in-the-wool, fatal, hopeless, immedicable, incorrigible, inoperable, inveterate, irrecoverable, irremediable, recidivistic, remediless, terminal, unmedicinable, untreatable.
antonym curable.

incurious *adj* apathetic, careless, inattentive, indifferent, unconcerned, uncurious, unenquiring, uninquiring, uninquisitive, uninterested, unreflective.
antonym curious.

incursion *n* attack, foray, infiltration, inroads, invasion, irruption, penetration, raid.

indebted *adj* beholden, grateful, in debt, obligated, obliged, thankful.

indecency *n* bawdiness, coarseness, crudity, foulness, grossness, immodesty, impropriety, impurity, indecorum, indelicacy, lewdness, licentiousness, obscenity, outrageousness, pornography, Rabelaisianism, smut, smuttiness, unseemliness, vileness, vulgarity.
antonyms decency, modesty.

indecent *adj* blue, coarse, crude, dirty, filthy, foul, gross, immodest, improper, impure, indecorous, indelicate, lewd, licentious, near the knuckle, offensive, outrageous, pornographic, Rabelaisian, salacious, scatological, smutty, tasteless, unbecoming, uncomely, unseemly, vile, vulgar.
antonyms decent, modest.

indecipherable *adj* crabbed, cramped, illegible, indistinct, indistinguishable, tiny, unclear, unintelligible, unreadable.
antonym readable.

indecision *n* ambivalence, doubt, hesitancy, hesitation, indecisiveness, irresoluteness, irresolution, shilly-shallying, swither, uncertainty, vacillation, wavering.
antonym decisiveness.

indecisive *adj* doubtful, faltering, hesitating, hung, in two minds, inconclusive, indefinite, indeterminate, irresolute, pussyfooting, swithering, tentative, uncertain, unclear, undecided, undetermined, unsure, vacillating, wavering.
antonym decisive.

indecorous *adj* boorish, churlish, coarse, crude, ill-bred, immodest, impolite, improper, indecent, rough, rude, tasteless, uncivil, uncouth, undignified, unmannerly, unseemly, untoward, vulgar.
antonym decorous.

indeed *adv* actually, certainly, doubtlessly, forsooth, positively, really, strictly, to be sure, truly, undeniably, undoubtedly, verily, veritably.

indefatigable *adj* assiduous, diligent, dogged, inexhaustible, patient, persevering, pertinacious, relentless, sedulous, tireless, undying, unfailing, unflagging, unremitting, unresting, untireable, untiring, unweariable, unwearied, unwearying.
antonyms flagging, slothful.

indefensible *adj* faulty, inexcusable, insupportable, unforgivable, unjustifiable, unjustified, unpardonable, untenable, unwarrantable, wrong.
antonym defensible.

indefinable *adj* dim, hazy, impalpable, indescribable, indistinct, inexpressible, nameless, obscure, subtle, unclear, unrealised, vague.
antonym definable.

indefinite *adj* ambiguous, confused, doubtful, equivocal, evasive, general, ill-defined, imprecise, indeterminate, indistinct, inexact, loose, obscure, uncertain, unclear, undecided, undefined, undetermined, unfixed, unfocus(s)ed, unformed, unformulated, unknown, unlimited, unresolved, unsettled, vague.
antonyms clear, limited.

indefinitely *adv* ad infinitum, continually, endlessly, eternally, for ever, for life, sine die, time without end, world without end.

indelible *adj* enduring, indestructible, ineffaceable, ineradicable, inerasable, inexpungible, inextirpable, ingrained, lasting, permanent, unerasable.
antonyms erasable, impermanent.

indelicacy *n* bad taste, coarseness, crudity, grossness, immodesty, impropriety, indecency, obscenity, offensiveness, rudeness, smuttiness, suggestiveness, tastelessness, underniceness, vulgarity.
antonym delicacy.

indelicate *adj* blue, coarse, crude, embarrassing, gross, immodest, improper, indecent, indecorous, low, obscene, off-colour, offensive, risqué, rude, suggestive, tasteless, unbecoming, unmaidenly, unseemly, untoward, vulgar, warm.
antonym delicate.

indemnify *v* compensate, endorse, exempt, free, guarantee, insure, pay, protect, reimburse, remunerate, repair, repay, requite, satisfy, secure, underwrite.

indemnity *n* amnesty, compensation, excusal, exemption, guarantee, immunity, impunity, insurance, privilege, protection, redress, reimbursement, remuneration, reparation, requital, restitution, satisfaction, security.

indent[1] *v* cut, dent, dint, mark, nick, notch, pink, scallop, serrate.

indent[2] *v* ask for, demand, order, request, requisition.

indentation *n* bash, cut, dent, depression, dimple, dint, dip, hollow, jag, nick, notch, pit.

indented *adj* dancetté, dented, impressed, notched, zigzag.

independence *n* affranchisement, autarchy, autarky, autonomy, decolonisation, freedom, home rule, individualism, liberty, manumission, self-determination, self-government, self-reliance, self-rule, self-sufficiency, separation, sovereignty, uhuru, unconventionality.
antonyms conventionality, dependence.

independent *adj* absolute, autarchical, autocephalous, autogenous, autonomous, bold, crossbench, decontrolled, free, individualistic, liberated, non-aligned, one's own man, self-contained, self-determining, self-governing, self-reliant, self-sufficient, self-supporting, separate, separated, sovereign, unaided, unbiased, unconnected, unconstrained, uncontrolled, unconventional, unrelated, upon one's legs.

antonyms conventional, dependent, timid.

independently *adv* alone, autonomously, by oneself, individually, on one's own, on one's tod, separately, solo, unaided.

antonym together.

indescribable *adj* incommunicable, indefinable, ineffable, inexpressible, phraseless, unutterable.

antonym describable.

indestructible *adj* abiding, durable, enduring, eternal, everlasting, immortal, imperishable, incorruptible, indissoluble, infrangible, lasting, permanent, unbreakable, unfading.

antonyms breakable, mortal.

indeterminacy *n* impreciseness, inconclusiveness, indefiniteness, inexactness, open-endedness, uncertainty, vagueness.

antonym definiteness.

indeterminate *adj* imprecise, inconclusive, indefinite, inexact, open-ended, uncertain, undecided, undefined, undetermined, unfixed, unspecified, unstated, unstipulated, vague.

antonyms exact, limited.

index *n* clue, guide, hand, indication, indicator, mark, needle, pointer, sign, symptom, table, token.

indicate *v* add up to, bespeak, betoken, denote, designate, display, evince, express, imply, manifest, mark, point out, point to, read, record, register, reveal, show, signify, specify, suggest, telegraph, tip.

indicated *adj* advisable, called-for, desirable, necessary, needed, recommended, required, suggested.

indication *n* clue, endeixis, evidence, explanation, forewarning, hint, index, inkling, intimation, manifestation, mark, note, omen, portent, prognostic, sign, signal, signpost, suggestion, symptom, warning.

indicative *adj* denotative, exhibitive, indicatory, indicial, significant, suggestive, symptomatic.

indicator *n* display, gauge, gnomon, guide, index, mark, marker, meter, pointer, sign, signal, signpost, symbol, winker.

indict *v* accuse, arraign, charge, criminate, impeach, incriminate, prosecute, recriminate, summon, summons, tax.

antonym exonerate.

indictment *n* accusation, allegation, charge, crimination, impeachment, incrimination, prosecution, recrimination, summons.

antonym exoneration.

indifference *n* aloofness, apathy, callousness, coldness, coolness, detachment, disinterestedness, dispassion, disregard, equity, heedlessness, impartiality, inattention, insignificance, irrelevance, latitudinarianism, negligence, neutrality, objectivity, pococurant(e)ism, stoicalness, unconcern, unimportance.

antonyms bias, interest.

indifferent *adj* aloof, apathetic, average, callous, careless, cold, cool, detached, disinterested, dispassionate, distant, equitable, fair, heedless, immaterial, impartial, impervious, inattentive, incurious, insignificant, jack easy, mediocre, middling, moderate, neutral, non-aligned, objective, ordinary, passable, perfunctory, pococurante, regardless, so-so, unbiased, uncaring, unconcerned, undistinguished, unenquiring, unenthusiastic, unexcited, unimportant, unimpressed, uninspired, uninterested, uninvolved, unmoved, unprejudiced, unresponsive, unsympathetic.

antonyms biased, interested.

indigence *n* deprivation, destitution, distress, necessity, need, penury, poverty, privation, want.

antonym affluence.

indigenous *adj* aboriginal, autochthonous, home-grown, indigene, local, native, original.

antonym foreign.

indigent *adj* destitute, impecunious, impoverished, in forma pauperis, in want, necessitous, needy, penniless, penurious, poor, poverty-stricken, straitened.

antonym affluent.

indigestion *n* cardialgia, dyspepsia, dyspepsy, heartburn, water-brash.

indignant *adj* angry, annoyed, disgruntled, exasperated, fuming, furibund, furious, heated, huffy, in a paddy, in a wax, incensed, irate, livid, mad, marked, miffed, peeved, provoked, resentful, riled, scornful, sore, waxy, wrathful, wroth.

antonym pleased.

indignation *n* anger, exasperation, fury, ire, pique, rage, resentment, scorn, umbrage, wax, wrath.

antonym pleasure.

indignity *n* abuse, affront, contempt, contumely, disgrace, dishonour, disrespect, humiliation, incivility, injury, insult, obloquy, opprobrium, outrage, reproach, slight, snub.

antonym honour.

indirect *adj* ancillary, backhanded, circuitous, circumlocutory, collateral, contingent, crooked, devious, incidental, meandering, mediate, oblique, periphrastic, rambling, roundabout, secondary, slanted, subsidiary, tortuous, unintended, wandering, winding, zigzag.

antonym direct.

indirectly *adv* circumlocutorily, deviously, hintingly, obliquely, periphrastically, roundaboutedly, roundaboutly, second-hand.

antonym directly.

indiscernible *adj* hidden, impalpable, imperceptible, indistinct, indistinguishable, invisible, minuscule, minute, tiny, unapparent, undiscernible.

antonym clear.

indiscreet *adj* careless, foolish, hasty, heedless, ill-advised, ill-considered, ill-judged, impolitic, imprudent, incautious, injudicious, naïve, rash, reckless, tactless, temerarious, temerous, undiplomatic, unthinking, unwise.

antonym discreet.

indiscretion *n* boob, brick, error, faux pas, folly, foolishness, gaffe, imprudence, mistake, rashness, recklessness, slip, slip of the tongue, tactlessness, temerarity.

antonym discretion.

indiscriminate *adj* aimless, careless, chaotic, confused, desultory, general, haphazard, higgledy-piggledy, hit or miss, indiscriminating, indiscriminative, jumbled, mingled, miscellaneous, mixed, mongrel, motley, promiscuous, random, sweeping, uncritical, undifferentiated, undiscriminating, undistinguishable, unmethodical, unparticular, unselective, unsystematic, wholesale.

antonyms deliberate, selective.

indiscriminately *adv* carelessly, haphazardly, in the mass, randomly, unsystematically, wholesale, without fear or favour.

antonyms deliberately, selectively.

indispensable *adj* basic, crucial, essential, imperative, key, necessary, needed, needful, required, requisite, vital.

antonym unnecessary.

indisposed[1] *adj* ailing, ill, laid up, poorly, sick, sickly, under the weather, unwell.

antonym well.

indisposed[2] *adj* averse, disinclined, loath, not of a mind (to), not willing, reluctant, unwilling.

antonym inclined.

indisposition[1] *n* ailment, illness, sickness.

antonym health.

indisposition[2] *n* aversion, disinclination, dislike, distaste, hesitancy, reluctance, unwillingness.

antonym inclination.

indisputable *adj* absolute, certain, evident, incontestable, incontrovertible, indubitable, irrebuttable, irrefragable, irrefutable, positive, sure, unanswerable, unassailable, undeniable, unquestionable.

antonym doubtful.

indissoluble *adj* abiding, binding, enduring, eternal, fixed, imperishable, incorruptible, indestructible, inseparable, inviolable, lasting, permanent, sempiternal, solid, unbreakable.

antonym impermanent.

indistinct *adj* ambiguous, bleary, blurred, confused, dim, distant, doubtful, faint, fuzzy, hazy, ill-defined, indefinite, indeterminate, indiscernible, indistinguishable, misty, muffled, mumbled, obscure, shadowy, slurred, unclear, undefined, unintelligible, vague.

antonym distinct.

indistinguishable *adj* alike, identical, interchangeable, same, tantamount, twin.

antonyms distinguishable, unalike.

individual *n* being, bloke, body, chap, character, creature, fellow, individuum, mortal, party, person, personage, punter, soul.

adj characteristic, discrete, distinct, distinctive, exclusive, identical, idiosyncratic, own, particular, peculiar, personal, personalised, proper, respective, separate, several, single, singular, special, specific, unique.

individualism *n* anarchism, egocentricity, egoism, free-thinking, free-thought, independence, libertarianism, originality, self-direction, self-interest, self-reliance.

antonym conventionality.

individualist *n* anarchist, free-thinker, independent, libertarian, lone wolf, loner, maverick, nonconformist, original.

antonym conventionalist.

individualistic *adj* anarchistic, characteristic, distinctive, egocentric, egoistic, iconoclastic, idiosyncratic, independent, individual, libertarian, non-conformist, original, particular, self-reliant, special, typical, unconventional, unique.

antonym conventionalistic.

individuality *n* character, discreteness, distinction, distinctiveness, haecceity, originality, peculiarity, personality, separateness, singularity, unicity, uniqueness.

antonym sameness.

individually *adv* independently, particularly, separately, seriatim et privatim, severally, singly.

antonym together.

indivisible *adj* impartible, indiscerptible, inseparable, undividable.

antonym divisible.

indoctrinate *v* brainwash, catechise, drill, ground, imbue, initiate, instruct, school, teach, train.

indoctrination *n* brainwashing, catechesis, catechetics, inculcation, instruction, schooling, training.

indolence *n* do-nothingism, fainéance, heaviness, idleness, inactivity, inertia, inertness, languidness, languor, laziness, lethargy, shirking, slacking, sloth, sluggishness, torpidity, torpidness, torpitude, torpor.

antonyms activeness, enthusiasm, industriousness.

indolent *adj* fainéant, idle, inactive, inert, lackadaisical, languid, lazy, lethargic, listless, lumpish, slack, slothful, slow, sluggard, sluggish, torpid.

antonyms active, enthusiastic, industrious.

indomitable *adj* bold, intrepid, invincible, resolute, staunch, steadfast, unbeatable.

unconquerable, undaunted, unflinching, untameable, unyielding.

antonyms compliant, timid.

indoor *adj* inside, umbratile, umbratilous.

antonym outdoor.

indubitable *adj* certain, evident, incontestable, incontrovertible, indisputable, irrebuttable, irrefragable, irrefutable, obvious, sure, unanswerable, unarguable, undeniable, undoubtable, undoubted, unquestionable, veritable.

antonym arguable.

induce *v* actuate, bring about, cause, convince, draw, effect, encourage, engender, generate, get, give rise to, impel, incite, influence, instigate, lead to, move, occasion, persuade, press, prevail upon, produce, prompt, talk into.

inducement *n* attraction, bait, carrot, cause, come-on, consideration, encouragement, impulse, incentive, incitement, influence, lure, motive, reason, reward, spur, stimulus.

antonym disincentive.

induct *v* consecrate, enthrone, inaugurate, initiate, install, introduce, invest, ordain, swear in.

induction *n* conclusion, consecration, deduction, enthronement, generalisation, inauguration, inference, initiation, installation, institution, introduction, investiture, ordination.

indulge *v* baby, cocker, coddle, cosset, favour, foster, give in to, go along with, gratify, humour, mollycoddle, pamper, pander to, pet, regale, satiate, satisfy, spoil, treat (oneself), yield to.

indulge in give free rein to, give oneself up to, give way to, luxuriate in, revel in, wallow in.

indulgence *n* appeasement, courtesy, excess, extravagance, favour, forbearance, good will, gratification, immoderateness, immoderation, intemperance, intemperateness, kindness, leniency, luxury, pampering, partiality, patience, permissiveness, privilege, prodigality, profligacy, profligateness, satiation, satisfaction, self-gratification, self-indulgence, spoiling, tolerance, treat, understanding.

antonyms moderation, strictness.

indulgent *adj* complaisant, compliant, easy-going, favourable, fond, forbearing, gentle, gratifying, intemperate, kind, kindly, lenient, liberal, mild, permissive, prodigal, self-indulgent, tender, tolerant, understanding.

antonyms moderate, strict.

industrialist *n* baron, boss, capitalist, captain of industry, financier, magnate, manufacturer, mill-owner, producer, tycoon.

industrious *adj* active, assiduous, busy, conscientious, deedy, diligent, energetic, hard-working, laborious, persevering, persistent, productive, purposeful, sedulous, steady, tireless, zealous.

antonym indolent.

industriously *adv* assiduously, conscientiously, diligently, doggedly, hard, perseveringly, sedulously, steadily, with one's nose to the grindstone.

antonym indolently.

industry *n* activity, application, assiduity, business, commerce, determination, diligence, effort, labour, manufacturing, perseverance, persistence, production, tirelessness, toil, trade, vigour, zeal.

antonym indolence.

inebriate *v* addle, animate, arouse, carry away, excite, exhilarate, fire, fuddle, intoxicate, stimulate, stupefy.

antonyms dampen, sober up.

inebriated *adj* befuddled, blind drunk, blotto, drunk, glorious, half seas over, half-cut, half-drunk, in one's cups, incapable, inebriate, intoxicated, legless, merry, paralytic, pie-eyed, plastered, sloshed, smashed, sozzled, stoned, stotious, three sheets in the wind, tight, tipsy, tired and emotional, under the influence.

antonym sober.

inebriation *n* drunkenness, inebriety, insobriety, intemperance, intoxication, sottishness, tipsiness.

antonym sobriety.

inedible *adj* deadly, harmful, inesculent, injurious, noxious, poisonous, uneatable.

antonym edible.

ineducable *adj* incorrigible, indocile, unteachable.

antonym educable.

ineffable *adj* incommunicable, indescribable, inexpressible, unimpartible, unspeakable, unutterable.

antonym describable.

ineffective, ineffectual *adj* abortive, barren, bootless, emasculate, feeble, fruitless, futile, idle, impotent, inadequate, incompetent, ineffective, ineffectual, inefficacious, inefficient, inept, lame, powerless, unavailing, unproductive, useless, vain, void, weak, worthless.

antonyms effective, effectual.

inefficacy *n* futility, inadequacy, ineffectiveness, ineffectuality, ineffectualness, unproductiveness, uselessness.

antonym efficacy.

inefficiency *n* carelessness, disorganisation, incompetence, muddle, negligence, slackness, sloppiness, waste, wastefulness.

antonym efficiency.

inefficient *adj* incompetent, inept, inexpert, money-wasting, negligent, slipshod, sloppy, time-wasting, unworkmanlike, wasteful.

antonym efficient.

inelegant *adj* awkward, barbarous, clumsy, coarse, crass, crude, gauche, graceless, indelicate, laboured, rough, uncourtly, uncouth, uncultivated, ungainly, ungraceful, unpolished, unrefined, unsophisticated.

antonym elegant.

ineligible *adj* disqualified, improper, inappropriate, incompetent, objectionable, unacceptable, undesirable, unequipped, unfit, unfitted, unqualified, unsuitable, unworthy.

antonym eligible.

inept *adj* absurd, awkward, bungling, cack-handed, clumsy, fatuous, futile, gauche, improper, inappropriate, inapt, incompetent, inexpert, infelicitous, irrelevant, maladroit, malapropos, meaningless, ridiculous, unfit, unhandy, unskilful, unworkmanlike.

antonyms adroit, apt.

ineptitude *n* absurdity, clumsiness, crassness, fatuity, futility, gaucheness, gaucherie, inappropriateness, incapacity, incompetence, ineptness, inexpertness, irrelevance, pointlessness, stupidity, unfitness, unhandiness, uselessness.

antonyms aptitude, skill.

inequality *n* bias, difference, disparity, disproportion, dissimilarity, diversity, imparity, inadequacy, irregularity, preferentiality, prejudice, unequalness, unevenness.

antonym equality.

inequitable *adj* biased, discriminatory, one-sided, partial, partisan, preferential, prejudiced, unequal, unfair, unjust, wrongful.

antonym equitable.

inequity *n* abuse, bias, discrimination, injustice, maltreatment, mistreatment, one-sidedness, partiality, prejudice, unfairness, unjustness.

antonym equity.

inert *adj* apathetic, dead, dormant, dull, idle, immobile, inactive, inanimate, indolent, insensible, lazy, leaden, lifeless, motionless, nerveless, numb, passive, quiescent, senseless, slack, sleepy, slothful, sluggish, somnolent, static, still, torpid, unmoving, unreacting, unresponsive.

antonyms alive, animated.

inertia *n* accedia, accidie, apathy, deadness, drowsiness, dullness, idleness, immobility, inactivity, indolence, insensibility, languor, lassitude, laziness, lethargy, listlessness, nervelessness, numbness, passivity, sleepiness, sloth, sluggishness, somnolence, stillness, stupor, torpor, unresponsiveness.

antonyms activity, liveliness.

inescapable *adj* certain, destined, fated, ineluctable, inevitable, inexorable, irrevocable, sure, unalterable, unavoidable, unpreventable.

antonym escapable.

inessential *adj* accidental, dispensable, expendable, extraneous, extrinsic, irrelevant, needless, non-essential, optional, redundant, secondary, spare, superfluous, surplus, unasked-for, uncalled-for, unessential, unimportant, unnecessary.

antonym essential.

n accessory, appendage, expendable, extra, extravagance, luxury, non-essential, superfluity, trimming.

antonym essential.

inestimable *adj* immeasurable, immense, incalculable, incomputable, infinite, invaluable, measureless, precious, priceless, prodigious, uncountable, unfathomable, unlimited, untold, vast.

antonym insignificant.

inevitable *adj* assured, automatic, certain, compulsory, decreed, destined, fated, fixed, ineluctable, inescapable, inexorable, irrevocable, mandatory, necessary, obligatory, ordained, settled, sure, unalterable, unavertable, unavoidable, unpreventable, unshunnable.

antonyms alterable, avoidable, uncertain.

inevitably *adv* automatically, certainly, incontestably, ineluctably, inescapably, necessarily, of necessity, perforce, surely, unavoidably.

inexact *adj* erroneous, fuzzy, imprecise, inaccurate, incorrect, indefinite, indeterminate, indistinct, lax, loose, muddled, woolly.

antonym exact.

inexactitude *n* blunder, error, impreciseness, imprecision, inaccuracy, incorrectness, indefiniteness, inexactness, laxness, looseness, misalculation, mistake, woolliness.

antonym exactitude.

inexcusable *adj* blameworthy, indefensible, inexpiable, intolerable, outrageous, reprehensible, shameful, unacceptable, unforgivable, unjustifiable, unpardonable, unwarrantable.

antonyms excusable, venial.

inexhaustible *adj* abundant, bottomless, boundless, copious, endless, exhaustless, illimitable, indefatigable, infinite, lavish, limitless, measureless, never-ending, never-failing, tireless, unbounded, undaunted, unfailing, unflagging, unlimited, untiring, unwearied, unwearying.

antonym limited.

inexorable *adj* adamant, cruel, hard, harsh, immovable, implacable, ineluctable, inescapable, inflexible, intransigent, irreconcilable, irresistible, irrevocable, merciless, obdurate, pitiless, relentless, remorseless, severe, unalterable, unappeasable, unavertable, unbending, uncompromising, unrelenting, unyielding.

antonyms flexible, lenient, yielding.

inexorably *adv* implacably, ineluctably, inescapably, irresistibly, irrevocably, mercilessly, pitilessly, relentlessly, remorselessly, resistlessly.

inexpedient *adj* detrimental, disadvantageous, foolish, ill-advised, ill-chosen, ill-judged, impolitic, impractical, imprudent, inadvisable, inappropriate, indiscreet, injudicious, misguided, senseless, unadvisable, undesirable, undiplomatic, unfavourable, unsuitable, unwise, wrong.

antonym expedient.

inexpensive *adj* bargain, bon marché, budget, cheap, economical, low-cost, low-priced, modest, reasonable, uncostly.

antonym expensive.

inexperience *n* callowness, greenness, ignorance, inexpertness, innocence, naïvety, nescience, newness, rawness, strangeness, unexpertness, unfamiliarity, unsophistication, verdancy.

antonym experience.

inexperienced *adj* amateur, callow, fresh, green, immature, inexpert, innocent, nescient, new, raw, unaccustomed, unacquainted, unbearded, unfamiliar, unpractical, unpractised, unschooled, unseasoned, unskilled, unsophisticated, untrained, untravelled, untried, unused, unversed, verdant.

antonym experienced.

inexpert *adj* amateurish, awkward, blundering, bungling, clumsy, hammy, incompetent, inept, maladroit, unhandy, unpractised, unprofessional, unskilful, unskilled, untaught, untrained, untutored, unworkmanlike.

antonym expert.

inexplicable *adj* baffling, enigmatic, impenetrable, incomprehensible, incredible, inscrutable, insoluble, intractable, miraculous, mysterious, mystifying, puzzling, strange, unaccountable, unexplainable, unfathomable, unintelligible, unsolvable.

antonym explicable.

inexplicably *adv* bafflingly, incomprehensibly, incredibly, miraculously, mysteriously, mystifyingly, puzzlingly, strangely, unaccountably, unexplainably.

antonym explicably.

inexpressible *adj* incommunicable, indefinable, indescribable, ineffable, nameless, undescribable, unsayable, unspeakable, untellable, unutterable.

inexpressive *adj* bland, blank, dead-pan, emotionless, empty, expressionless, immobile, impassive, inanimate, inscrutable, lifeless, poker-faced, stolid, stony, unexpressive, vacant.

antonym expressive.

inextinguishable *adj* deathless, enduring, eternal, everlasting, immortal, imperishable, indestructible, irrepressible, lasting, unconquerable, undying, unquellable, unquenchable, unsuppressible.

antonyms impermanent, perishable.

inextricably *adv* indissolubly, indistinguishably, inseparably, intricately, irresolubly, irretrievably, irreversibly.

infallibility *n* accuracy, dependability, faultlessness, impeccability, inerrancy, inevitability, irrefutability, irreproachability, omniscience, perfection, reliability, safety, supremacy, sureness, trustworthiness, unerringness.

antonym fallibility.

infallible *adj* accurate, certain, dependable, fail-safe, faultless, foolproof, impeccable, inerrable, inerrant, irreproachable, omniscient, perfect, reliable, sound, sure, sure-fire, trustworthy, unbeatable, unerring, unfailing, unfaltering, unfaulty, unimpeachable.

antonym fallible.

infamous *adj* abhorrent, abominable, atrocious, base, dastardly, despicable, detestable, discreditable, disgraceful, dishonourable, disreputable, egregious, execrable, facinorous, flagitious, hateful, heinous, ignoble, ignominious, ill-famed, iniquitous, knavish, loathsome, monstrous, nefarious, notorious, odious, opprobrious, outrageous, scandalous, scurvy, shameful, shocking, vile, villainous, wicked.

antonym glorious.

infamy *n* atrocity, baseness, crime, dastardliness, depravity, discredit, disgrace, dishonour, disrepute, enormity, ignominy, improbity, notoriety, obloquy, odium, opprobrium, outrageousness, scandal, shame, stain, stigma, turpitude, villainy, wickedness.

antonym glory.

infancy *n* babyhood, beginnings, birth, childhood, commencement, cradle, dawn, embryonic stage, emergence, genesis, inception, origins, outset, start, youth.

antonym adulthood.

infant *n* babe, babe in arms, baby, bairn, bambino, child, neonate, nipper, nurseling, papoose, suckling, tiny, toddler, tot, wean, weanling, youngling.

antonym adult.

adj baby, childish, dawning, developing, early, emergent, growing, immature, inchoate, incipient, initial, juvenile, nascent, newborn, rudimentary, unfledged, unformed, young, youthful.

antonym adult.

infantile *adj* adolescent, babyish, childish, immature, juvenile, puerile, tender, undeveloped, young, youthful.

antonyms adult, mature.

infatuated *adj* befooled, beguiled, besotted, bewitched, captivated, crazy, deluded, enamoured, enraptured, fascinated, fixated, hypnotised, intoxicated, mad, mesmerised, obsessed, possessed, ravished, smitten, spellbound.

antonyms disenchanted, indifferent.

infatuation *n* besottedness, crush, dotage, engouement, fascination, fixation, folly, fondness, intoxication, madness, mania, obsession, passion, possession.

antonyms disenchantment, indifference.

infect *v* affect, blight, canker, contaminate, corrupt, defile, enthuse, influence, inject, inspire, pervert, poison, pollute, taint, touch, vitiate.

infection *n* contagion, contamination, corruption, defilement, disease, epidemic, illness, inflammation, influence, miasma, pestilence, poison, pollution, sepsis, septicity, taint, virus.

infectious *adj* catching, communicable, contagious, contaminating, corrupting, deadly, defiling, epidemic, infective, miasmic, miasmous, pestilential, poisoning, poisonous, polluting, spreading, transmissible, transmittable, venemous, virulent, vitiating.

infelicitous *adj* gauche, ill-timed, inappropriate, inopportune, maladroit, tactless, unapt, unfortunate, unhappy, unsuitable, untimely.

antonym felicitous.

infelicity *n* despair, gaucheness, inappositeness, inappropriateness, inaptness, incongruity, inopportuneness, misery, misfortune, sadness, sorrow, tactlessness, unfortunateness, unhappiness, unsuitability, untimeliness, woe, wretchedness, wrongness.

antonyms aptness, felicity, happiness.

infer *v* assume, conclude, conjecture, construe, deduce, derive, extract, extrapolate, gather, presume, surmise, understand.

inference *n* assumption, conclusion, conjecture, consequence, construction, corollary, deduction, extrapolation, illation, interpretation, presumption, reading, surmise.

inferior *adj* bad, crummy, dog, grotty, humble, imperfect, indifferent, junior, lesser, low, lower, low-grade, mean, mediocre, menial, minor, one-horse, paravail, poor, poorer, provant, schlock, secondary, second-class, second-rate, shoddy, slipshod, slovenly, subordinate, subsidiary, substandard, under, underneath, undistinguished, unsatisfactory, unworthy, worse.

antonym superior.

n junior, menial, minion, subordinate, underling, understrapper, vassal.

antonym superior.

inferiority *n* badness, baseness, deficiency, humbleness, imperfection, inadequacy, insignificance, lowliness, meanness, mediocrity, shoddiness, slovenliness, subordination, subservience, unimportance, unworthiness, worthlessness.

antonym superiority.

infernal *adj* accursed, Acherontic, chthonian, chthonic, damnable, damned, demonic, devilish, diabolical, fiendish, Hadean, hellish, malevolent, malicious, Mephistophelian, Plutonian, satanic, Stygian, Tartarean, underworld.

antonym heavenly.

infertile *adj* acarpous, arid, barren, dried-up, effete, infecund, infructuous, non-productive, parched, sterile, unbearing, unfruitful, unproductive.

antonym fertile.

infertility *n* aridity, aridness, barrenness, effeteness, infecundity, sterility, unfruitfulness, unproductiveness.

antonym fertility.

infest *v* beset, flood, infiltrate, invade, overrun, overspread, penetrate, permeate, pervade, ravage, swarm, throng.

infested *adj* alive, beset, bristling, crawling, infiltrated, lousy, overrun, overspread, permeated, pervaded, plagued, ravaged, ridden, swarming, teeming, vermined, verminy.

infidel *n* atheist, disbeliever, free-thinker, giaour, heathen, heretic, iconoclast, irreligionist, nullifidian, pagan, sceptic, unbeliever.

antonym believer.

infidelity *n* adultery, apostasy, bad faith, betrayal, cheating, disbelief, disloyalty, duplicity, faithlessness, false-heartedness, falseness, iconoclasm, irreligion, perfidy, recreancy, renegation, scepticism, traitorhood, traitorousness, treachery, unbelief, unfaithfulness.

antonym fidelity.

infiltrate *v* creep into, filter, infilter, insinuate, interpenetrate, intrude, penetrate, percolate, permeate, pervade, sift.

infiltration *n* entr(y)ism, insinuation, interpenetration, intrusion, penetration, percolation, permeation, pervasion.

infiltrator *n* entr(y)ist, insinuator, intruder, penetrator, seditionary, spy, subversive, subverter.

infinite *adj* absolute, bottomless, boundless, countless, enormous, eternal, everlasting, fathomless, illimitable, immeasurable, immense, incomputable, inestimable, inexhaustible, interminable, limitless, measureless, never-ending, numberless, perpetual, stupendous, total, unbounded, uncountable, uncounted, unfathomable, untold, vast, wide.

antonym finite.

infinitesimal *adj* atomic, exiguous, imperceptible, inappreciable, inconsiderable, insignificant, microscopic, minuscule, minute, negligible, paltry, teeny, tiny, unnoticeable, wee.

antonyms significant, substantial.

infinity *n* boundlessness, countlessness, endlessness, eternity, everlasting, everlastingness, for ever, illimitibleness, immeasurableness, immensity, inexhaustibility, infinitude, interminableness, limitlessness, perpetuity, vastness.

antonyms finiteness, limitation.

infirm *adj* ailing, crippled, debilitated, decrepit, dicky, doddering, doddery, enfeebled, failing, faltering, feeble, fickle, frail, hesitant, indecisive, insecure, irresolute, lame, poorly, sickly, unreliable, wavering, weak, wobbly.

antonyms healthy, strong.

infirmity *n* ailment, complaint, debility, decrepitude, defect, deficiency, dickiness, disease, disorder, failing, fault, feebleness, foible, frailty, ill health, illness, imperfection, instability, malady, sickliness, sickness, vulnerability, weakness.

antonyms health, strength.

inflame *v* aggravate, agitate, anger, arouse, dynamise, embitter, enkindle, enrage, exacerbate, exasperate, excite, fan, fire, foment, fuel, galvanise, heat, ignite, impassion, incense, increase, infatuate, infuriate, intensify, intoxicate, kindle, madden, provoke, ravish, rile, rouse, stimulate, worsen.

antonyms cool, quench.

inflamed *adj* angry, chafing, enraged, erythematous, excited, festering, fevered, heated, hot, impassioned, incensed, infected, poisoned, red, septic, sore, swollen.

inflammable *adj* burnable, choleric, combustible, deflagrable, flammable, incendiary, irascible, piceous, pyrophorous, short-tempered, volatile.

antonyms flame-proof, incombustible, non-flammable, non-inflammable.

inflammation *n* abscess, burning, empyema, erythema, heat, infection, painfulness, rash, redness, sepsis, septicity, sore, soreness, tenderness.

inflammatory *adj* anarchic, demagogic, explosive, fiery, incendiary, incitative, inflaming, instigative, insurgent, intemperate, provocative, rabble-rousing, rabid, riotous, seditious.

antonyms calming, pacific.

inflate *v* aerate, aggrandise, amplify, balloon, bloat, blow out, blow up, bombast, boost, dilate, distend, enlarge, escalate, exaggerate, expand, increase, puff out, puff up, pump up, swell, tumefy.

antonym deflate.

inflated *adj* ballooned, bloated, blown up, bombastic, dilated, distended, euphuistic, exaggerated, flatulent, grandiloquent, magniloquent, ostentatious, overblown, pompous, puffed out, swollen, tumefied, tumid, turgid.

antonym deflated.

inflation *n* aggrandisement, ballooning, bloating, dilation, distension, enhancement, enlargement, escalation, expansion, extension, hyperinflation, increase, intensification, rise, spread, swelling, tumefaction.

antonym deflation.

inflexibility *n* fixity, hardness, immovability, immutability, immutableness, inelasticity, intractability, intransigence, obduracy, obstinacy, rigidity, steeliness, stiffness, stringency, stubbornness, unsuppleness.

antonym flexibility.

inflexible *adj* adamant, dyed-in-the-wool, entrenched, fast, firm, fixed, hard, hardened, immovable, immutable, implacable, inelastic, inexorable, intractable, intransigent, iron, non-flexible, obdurate, obstinate, relentless, resolute, rigid, rigorous, set, steadfast, steely, stiff, strict, stringent, stubborn, taut, unaccommodating, unadaptable, unbending, unchangeable, uncompromising, unpliable, unpliant, unsupple, unyielding.

antonym flexible.

inflict *v* administer, afflict, apply, burden, deal, deliver, enforce, exact, force, impose, lay, levy, mete, perpetrate, visit, wreak.

infliction *n* administration, affliction, burden, castigation, chastisement, exaction, imposition, nemesis, penalty, perpetration, punishment, retribution, trouble, visitation, worry, wreaking.

influence *n* agency, ascendancy, authority, bias, charisma, clout, connections, control, credit, direction, domination, drag, effect, éminence grise, good offices, guidance, hold, importance, leverage, magnetism, mastery, power, pressure, prestige, pull, reach, rule, scope, spell, standing, strength, string-pulling, sway, teaching, training, weight, wire-pulling.

v affect, alter, arouse, bias, change, control, direct, dispose, dominate, edge, guide, head, impel, impress, incite, incline, induce, instigate, manipulate, manoeuvre, modify, motivate, move, persuade, point, predispose, prompt, pull, pull wires, rouse, strings, sway, teach, train, weigh with.

influential *adj* ascendant, authoritative, charismatic, cogent, compelling, controlling, dominant, dominating, effective, efficacious, forcible, guiding, important, instrumental, leading, momentous, moving, persuasive, potent, powerful, significant, strong, telling, weighty, well-placed.

antonym ineffectual.

influenza *n* dog's disease, flu, grip, grippe.

influx *n* access, accession, arrival, consignment, convergence, flood, flow, incursion, inflow, inrush, instreaming, inundation, invasion, rush.

inform[1] *v* acquaint, advise, apprise, brief, clue up, communicate, conscientise, enlighten, fill in, illuminate, impart, instruct, intimate, leak, notify, teach, tell, tip off, wise up.

inform on accuse, betray, blab, blow the whistle, clype, denounce, denunciate, dob (in), grass, incriminate, inculpate, nark, peach, rat, sing, snitch, squeal, tell on, whistle.

inform[2] *v* animate, characterise, endue, fill, illuminate, imbue, inspire, invest, irradiate, light up, permeate, suffuse, typify.

informal *adj* approachable, casual, colloquial, congenial, cosy, easy, familiar, free, homely, irregular, natural, relaxed, relaxing, simple, unbuttoned, unceremonious, unconstrained, unofficial, unorthodox, unpretentious, unsolemn.

antonym formal.

informality *n* approachability, casualness, congeniality, cosiness, ease, familiarity, freedom, homeliness, irregularity, naturalness, relaxation, simplicity, unceremoniousness, unpretentiousness.

antonym formality.

informally *adj* casually, colloquially, confidentially, cosily, easily, en famille, familiarly, freely, on the quiet, privately, simply, unceremoniously, unofficially.

antonym formally.

information *n* advices, blurb, briefing, bulletin, bumf, clues, communiqué, conscientisation, data, databank, database, dope, dossier, enlightenment, facts, gen, illumination, info, input, instruction, intelligence, knowledge, low-down, message, news, notice, report, tidings, word.

informative *adj* chatty, communicative, constructive, edifying, educational, enlightening, forthcoming, gossipy, illuminating, informatory, instructive, newsy, revealing, revelatory, useful, valuable.

antonym uninformative.

informed *adj* abreast, acquainted, apprised, au courant, au fait, authoritative, briefed, clued up, conversant, enlightened, erudite, expert, familiar, filled in, genned up, hep, in the know, knowledgeable, learned, posted, primed, scholarly, trained, up to date, versed, well-informed, well-read, well-researched.

antonyms ignorant, unaware.

informer *n* betrayer, canary, denouncer, denunciator, fink, fiz(z)gig, grass, Judas, nark, singer, sneak, snitch(er), snout, squeak, squealer, stool pigeon, stoolie, supergrass, whistle-blower.

infrequent *adj* exceptional, intermittent, occasional, rare, scanty, sparse, spasmodic, sporadic, uncommon, unusual.

antonym frequent.

infringe *v* break, contravene, defy, disobey, encroach, flout, ignore, infract, intrude, invade, overstep, transgress, trespass, violate.

infringement *n* breach, contravention, defiance, encroachment, evasion, infraction, intrusion, invasion, non-compliance, non-observance, transgression, trespass, violation.

infuriate *v* anger, antagonise, bug, enrage, exasperate, incense, irritate, madden, provoke, put someone's back up, rile, rouse, vex.

antonyms calm, mollify.

infuriated *adj* agitated, angry, beside oneself, enraged, exasperated, flaming, furious, heated, incensed, irate, irritated, maddened, provoked, roused, vexed, violent, wild.

antonyms calm, gratified, pleased.

infuriating *adj* aggravating, annoying, exasperating, frustrating, galling, intolerable, irritating, maddening, mortifying, pesky, pestiferous, pestilential, provoking, thwarting, unbearable, vexatious.

antonyms agreeable, pleasing.

infuse *v* breathe into, brew, draw, imbue, impart to, implant, inculcate, inject, inspire, instil, introduce, leach, macerate, saturate, soak, steep.

infusion *n* brew, implantation, inculcation, infusing, instillation, leachate, maceration, soaking, steeping.

ingenious *adj* adroit, bright, brilliant, clever, crafty, creative, cunning, daedal, Daedalian, daedalic, dedalian, deft, dexterous, fertile, Gordian, Heath-Robinson, imaginative, innovative, intricate, inventive, masterly, original, pretty, ready, resourceful, shrewd, skilful, sly, subtle.

antonyms clumsy, unimaginative.

ingenuity *n* adroitness, cleverness, cunning, deftness, faculty, flair, genius, gift, ingeniousness, innovativeness, invention, inventiveness, knack, originality, resourcefulness, sharpness, shrewdness, skill, slyness, turn.

antonyms clumsiness, dullness.

ingenuous *adj* artless, candid, childlike, frank, guileless, honest, innocent, naïf, naïve, open, plain, simple, sincere, trustful, trusting, unreserved, unsophisticated, unstudied.

antonyms artful, sly.

ingenuousness *n* artlessness, candour, frankness, guilelessness, innocence, naïvety, openness, trustfulness, unreserve, unsophisticatedness.

antonyms artfulness, slyness, subterfuge.

inglorious *adj* discreditable, disgraceful, dishonourable, disreputable, humiliating, ignoble, ignominious, infamous, mortifying, obscure, shameful, unheroic, unhonoured, unknown, unsuccessful, unsung.

antonym glorious.

ingrain *v* dye, embed, engrain, entrench, fix, imbue, implant, impress, imprint, infix, instil, root.

ingrained *adj* constitutional, deep-rooted, deep-seated, entrenched, fixed, fundamental, hereditary, immovable, inborn, inbred, inbuilt, indelible, ineradicable, infixed, inherent, intrinsic, inveterate, permanent, rooted.

antonym superficial.

ingratiate *v* blandish, crawl, curry, favour, fawn, flatter, get in with, grovel, insinuate, suck up, toady, worm.

ingratiating *adj* bland, bootlicking, crawling, fawning, flattering, obsequious, servile, smooth-tongued, suave, sycophantic, time-serving, toadying, unctuous, whilly, whillywha(w).

ingratitude *n* thanklessness, unappreciativeness, ungraciousness, ungratefulness.

antonym gratitude.

ingredient *n* component, constituent, element, factor, part.

inhabit *v* abide, bide, dwell, habit, live, lodge, make one's home, occupy, people, populate, possess, reside, settle, settle in, stay, take up one's abode, tenant.

inhabitant *n* aborigine, autochthon, burgher, citizen, denizen, dweller, habitant, indigene, indweller, inmate, lodger, native, occupant, occupier, resident, residentiary, resider, settler, tenant.

inhabited *adj* colonised, developed, held, lived-in, occupied, overrun, peopled, populated, possessed, settled, tenanted.

antonym uninhabited.

inhalation *n* breath, breathing, inhaling, inspiration, respiration, spiration, suction, toke.

inhale *v* breathe in, draw, draw in, inbreathe, inspire, respire, suck in, toke, whiff.

inharmonious *adj* antipathetic, atonal, cacophonous, clashing, conficting, discordant, dissonant, grating, harsh, horrisonant, incompatible, inconsonant, jangling, jarring, raucous, strident, tuneless, unharmonious, unmelodious, unmusical, untuneful.

antonym harmonious.

inherent *adj* basic, characteristic, congenital, connate, essential, fundamental, hereditary, immanent, inborn, inbred, inbuilt, ingrained, inherited, innate, instinctive, intrinsic, inwrought, native, natural.

inherit *v* accede to, assume, be bequeathed, be left, come in for, come into, fall heir to, receive, succeed to.

inheritance *n* accession, bequest, birthright, descent, heredity, heritage, heritament, legacy, patrimony, succession.

inheritor *n* beneficiary, co-heir, co-heiress, coheritor, devisee, heir, heiress, heritor, heritrix, inheritress, inheritrix, legatee, recipient, reversionary, successor.

inhibit *v* arrest, bar, bridle, check, constrain, cramp, curb, debar, discourage, forbid, frustrate, hinder, hold, impede, interfere with, obstruct, prevent, prohibit, repress, restrain, stanch, stem, stop, suppress, thwart.

inhibited *adj* bashful, constrained, diffident, frustrated, guarded, repressed, reserved, reticent, self-conscious, shamefaced, shy, strained, subdued, tense, uptight, withdrawn.

antonym uninhibited.

inhibition *n* bar, check, constraint, embargo, hang-up, hindrance, impediment, interdict, interference, obstacle, obstruction, prohibition, repression, reserve, restraint, restriction, reticence, self-consciousness, shyness, suppression.

antonym freedom.

inhospitable *adj* antisocial, bare, barren, bleak, cold, cool, desolate, forbidding, hostile, inimical, intolerant, sterile, unaccommodating, uncivil, uncongenial, unfavourable, unfriendly, ungenerous, uninhabitable, unkind, unneighbourly, unreceptive, unsociable, unwelcoming, xenophobic.

antonyms favourable, hospitable.

inhospitality *n* coldness, coolness, hostility, incivility, inimicality, intolerance, uncongeniality, unfriendliness, unkindness, unneighbourliness, unreceptiveness, unsociability, xenophobia.

antonym hospitality.

inhuman *adj* animal, barbaric, barbarous, bestial, brutal, brutish, callous, cold-blooded, cruel, diabolical, fiendish, heartless, inhumane, insensate, merciless, pitiless, remorseless, ruthless, savage, sublime, unfeeling, vicious.

antonym human.

inhumane *adj* brutal, callous, cold-hearted, cruel, heartless, indurate, inhuman, insensitive, pitiless, uncaring, uncompassionate, unfeeling, unkind, unsympathetic.

antonym humane.

inhumanity *n* atrocity, barbarism, barbarity, brutality, brutishness, callousness, cold-bloodedness, cold-heartedness, cruelty, hard-heartedness, heartlessness, pitilessness, ruthlessness, sadism, unkindness, viciousness.

antonym humanity.

inimical *adj* adverse, antagonistic, antipathetic, contrary, destructive, disaffected, harmful, hostile, hurtful, ill-disposed, inhospitable, injurious, intolerant, noxious, opposed, oppugnant, pernicious, repugnant, unfavourable, unfriendly, unwelcoming.

antonyms favourable, friendly, sympathetic.

inimitable *adj* consummate, distinctive, exceptional, incomparable, matchless, nonpareil, peerless, sublime, superlative, supreme, unequalled, unexampled, unique, unmatched, unparalleled, unrivalled, unsurpassable, unsurpassed.

iniquitous *adj* abominable, accursed, atrocious, awful, base, criminal, dreadful, evil, facinorous, flagitious, heinous, immoral, infamous, nefarious, nefast, reprehensible, reprobate, sinful, unjust, unrighteous, vicious, wicked.

antonym virtuous.

iniquity *n* abomination, baseness, crime, enormity, evil, evil-doing, heinousness, impiety, infamy, injustice, misdeed, offence, sin, sinfulness, ungodliness, unrighteousness, vice, viciousness, wickedness, wrong, wrong-doing.

antonym virtue.

initial *adj* beginning, commencing, early, embryonic, first, formative, inaugural, inauguratory, inceptive, inchoate, incipient, infant, introductory, opening, original, primary.

antonym final.

initially *adv* at first, at the beginning, at the outset, at the start, first, first of all, firstly, in the beginning, introductorily, originally, prefatorily, to begin with, to start with.

antonym finally.

initiate *v* activate, actuate, begin, cause, coach, commence, inaugurate, indoctrinate, induce, induct, instate, institute, instruct, introduce, invest, launch, open, originate, prompt, start, stimulate, teach, train.

n authority, beginner, catechumen, cognoscente, connoisseur, convert, entrant, epopt, expert, insider, learner, member, newcomer, novice, novitiate, probationer, proselyte, recruit, sage, savant, tenderfoot, tiro.

initiation *n* admission, commencement, début, enrolment, entrance, entry, inauguration, inception, induction, installation, instatement, instruction, introduction, investiture, reception, rite of passage.

initiative *n* advantage, ambition, drive, dynamism, energy, enterprise, forcefulness, get-up-and-go, goeyness, innovativeness, inventiveness, lead, move, originality, prompting, push, recommendation, resource, resourcefulness, suggestion.

inject *v* add, bring, fix, hit, infuse, inoculate, insert, instil, interject, introduce, jab, mainline, pop, shoot, shoot up, skin-pop, vaccinate.

injection *n* dose, fix, hit, infusion, inoculation, insertion, interjection, introduction, jab, mainlining, popping, shot, skin-popping, vaccination, vaccine.

injudicious *adj* foolish, hasty, ill-advised, ill-judged, ill-timed, impolitic, imprudent, inadvisable, incautious, inconsiderate, indiscreet, inexpedient, misguided, rash, stupid, unthinking, unwise, wrong-headed.

antonym judicious.

injunction *n* admonition, behest, command, dictate, direction, directive, enjoinment, exhortation, instruction, interdict, mandate, order, precept, ruling.

injure *v* abuse, aggrieve, blemish, blight, break, cripple, damage, deface, disable, disfigure, disserve, harm, hurt, ill-treat, impair, maim, maltreat, mar, ruin, scathe, spoil, tarnish, undermine, vandalise, vitiate, weaken, wound, wrong.

injured *adj* abused, aggrieved, blemished, broken, cut to the quick, defamed, disabled, disgruntled, displeased, grieved, hurt, ill-treated, insulted, lamed, long-suffering, maligned, maltreated, misused, offended, pained, put out, stung, tarnished, undermined, unhappy, upset, vilified, weakened, wounded, wronged.

injurious *adj* adverse, bad, baneful, calumnious, corrupting, damaging, deleterious, destructive, detrimental, disadvantageous, harmful, hurtful, iniquitous, insulting, libellous, mischievous, noxious, pernicious, prejudicial, ruinous, slanderous, unconducive, unhealthy, unjust, wrongful.

antonyms beneficial, favourable.

injury *n* abuse, annoyance, damage, damnification, detriment, disservice, evil, grievance, harm, hurt, ill, impairment, injustice, insult, lesion, loss, mischief, noyance, prejudice, ruin, scathe, trauma, vexation, wound, wrong.

injustice *n* bias, discrimination, disparity, favouritism, imposition, inequality, inequitableness, inequity, iniquity, one-sidedness, oppression, partiality, partisanship, prejudice, unevenness, unfairness, unjustness, unlawfulness, unreason, wrong.

antonym justice.

inkling *n* allusion, clue, conception, earthly, faintest, foggiest, glimmering, hint, idea, indication, intimation, notion, pointer, sign, suggestion, suspicion, umbrage, whisper.

inlaid *adj* damascened, empaestic, enchased, set, studded, tessellated.

inland *adj* central, domestic, inner, interior, internal, up-country.

inlay *n* damascene, emblema, tessellation.

inlet *n* bay, bight, cove, creek, entrance, fjord, fleet, hope, ingress, opening, passage, wick.

inmost *adj* basic, buried, central, closest, dearest, deep, deepest, esoteric, essential, hidden, innermost, intimate, personal, private, secret.

inn *n* albergo, alehouse, auberge, caravanserai, hostelry, hotel, howff, khan, local, public, public house, roadhouse, saloon, serai, tavern.

innards *n* entera, entrails, gralloch, guts, insides, interior, intestines, inwards, mechanism, organs, umbles, viscera, vitals, works.

innate *adj* basic, congenital, connate, constitutional, essential, fundamental, immanent, inborn, inbred, ingenerate, ingrained, inherent, inherited, instinctive, intrinsic, intuitive, native, natural.

inner *adj* central, concealed, emotional, esoteric, essential, hidden, inly, inside, interior, internal, intimate, inward, mental, middle, personal, private, psychical, psychological, secret, spiritual.

antonyms outer, patent.

innkeeper *n* aubergiste, boniface, host, hostess, hotelier, hotel-keeper, innholder, landlady, landlord, mine host, padrone, publican, restaurateur.

innocence *n* artlessness, blamelessness, chastity, credulousness, freshness, greenness, guilelessness, guiltlessness, gullibility, harmlessness, honesty, ignorance, incorruptibility, incorruption, inexperience, ingenuousness, innocuity, innocuousness, inoffensiveness, irreproachability, naïvety, naturalness, nescience, probity, purity, righteousness, simplicity, sinlessness, stainlessness, trustfulness, unawareness, unfamiliarity, unimpeachability, unsophistication, unworldliness, virginity, virtue.

antonyms experience, guilt, knowledge.

innocent *adj* Arcadian, artless, benign, bereft of, blameless, canny, chaste, childlike, clear, credulous, dewy-eyed, faultless, frank, free of, fresh, green, guileless, guiltless, gullible, harmless, honest, immaculate, impeccable, incorrupt, ingenuous, innocuous, inoffensive, intact, irreproachable, naïve, natural, nescient, open, pristine, pure, righteous, simple, sinless, spotless, stainless, trustful, trusting, unblemished, uncontaminated, unimpeachable, unobjectionable, unoffending, unsullied, unsuspicious, untainted, untouched, unworldly, verdant, virginal, well-intentioned, well-meaning, well-meant.

antonyms experienced, guilty, knowing.

n babe, babe in arms, beginner, child, greenhorn, infant, ingénu, ingénue, neophyte, tenderfoot.

antonyms connoisseur, expert.

innocently *adv* artlessly, blamelessly, credulously, harmlessly, ingenuously, innocuously, inoffensively, like a lamb to the slaughter, simply, trustfully, trustingly, unoffendingly, unsuspiciously.

innocuous *adj* bland, harmless, hypo-allergenic, innocent, innoxious, inoffensive, non-irritant, safe, unimpeachable, unobjectionable.

antonym harmful.

innovation *n* alteration, change, departure, introduction, modernisation, modernism, neologism, neoterism, newness, novation, novelty, progress, reform, variation.

innovative *adj* adventurous, bold, daring, enterprising, fresh, go-ahead, goey, groundbreaking, imaginative, inventive, modernising, new, on the move, original, progressive, reforming, resourceful, revolutionary.

antonyms conservative, unimaginative.

innuendo *n* aspersion, hint, implication, imputation, insinuation, intimation, overtone, slant, slur, suggestion, whisper.

innumerable *adj* countless, incalculable, incomputable, infinite, many, multitudinous, myriad, numberless, numerous, uncountable, uncounted, unnumbered, untold.

inoculate *v* immunise, inject, jag, protect, safeguard, vaccinate.

inoculation *n* immunisation, injection, jag, protection, shot, vaccination.

inoffensive *adj* gentle, harmless, humble, innocent, innocuous, innoxious, mild, mousy, non-provocative, peaceable, quiet, retiring, unassertive, unobjectionable, unobtrusive, unoffending.

antonyms malicious, offensive.

inoperable *adj* impracticable, impractical, intractable, irremovable, non-viable, unrealistic, unworkable.

antonyms operable, practicable.

inoperative *adj* broken, broken-down, defective, hors de combat, idle, ineffective, ineffectual, inefficacious, invalid, non-active, non-functioning, nugatory, out of action, out of commission, out of order, out of service, unserviceable, unused, unworkable, useless.

antonym operative.

inopportune *adj* clumsy, ill-chosen, ill-timed, inappropriate, inauspicious, inconvenient, infelicitous, malapropos, mistimed, tactless, unfortunate, unpropitious, unseasonable, unsuitable, untimely, wrong-timed.

antonym opportune.

inordinate *adj* disproportionate, excessive, exorbitant, extravagant, hubristic, immoderate, intemperate, overweening, preposterous, prohibitive, unconscionable, undue, unreasonable, unrestrained, unwarranted.

antonyms moderate, reasonable.

input *v* capture, code, feed in, insert, key in, process, store.

inquietude *n* agitation, anxiety, apprehension, discomposure, disquiet, disquietude, jumpiness, nervousness, perturbation, restlessness, solicitude, unease, uneasiness, worry.

antonym composure.

inquire *v* ask, catechise, delve, enquire, examine, explore, inspect, interrogate, investigate, look into, probe, query, quest, question, reconnoitre, scout, scrutinise, search, speir.

inquirer *n* explorer, interrogator, investigator, querist, quester, questioner, researcher, searcher, seeker, student.

inquiring *adj* analytical, curious, doubtful, eager, inquisitive, interested, interrogatory, investigative, investigatory, nosy, outward-looking, probing, prying, questing, questioning, sceptical, searching, wondering, zetetic.

antonym incurious.

inquiry *n* enquiry, examination, exploration, inquest, interrogation, investigation, perquisition, post-mortem, probe, query, question, research, scrutiny, search, study, survey, witch-hunt, zetetic.

inquisition *n* catechism, cross-examination, cross-questioning, examination, grilling, inquest, inquiry, interrogation, investigation, questioning, quizzing, third degree, witch-hunt.

inquisitive *adj* curious, eager, inquiring, intrusive, investigative, meddlesome, nosy, peeping, peering, probing, prying, questing, questioning, snooping, snoopy.

antonym incurious.

inroad *n* advance, encroachment, foray, impingement, incursion, intrusion, invasion, irruption, onslaught, raid, sally, sortie, trespass.

insane *adj* barmy, batty, bizarre, bonkers, brainsick, cracked, crackers, crazed, cuckoo, daft, delirious, demented, deranged, distracted, disturbed, fatuous, foolish, idiotic, impractical, irrational, irresponsible, loony, loopy, lunatic, mad, manic, mental, mentally ill, non compos mentis, nuts, nutty, preposterous, psychotic, queer, schizoid, schizophrenic, screwy, senseless, stupid, touched, unbalanced, unhinged.

antonym sane.

insanitary *adj* contaminated, dirty, disease-ridden, feculent, filthy, foul, impure, infected, infested, insalubrious, insalutary, noisome, noxious, polluted, unclean, unhealthful, unhealthy, unhygienic, unsanitary.

antonym sanitary.

insanity *n* aberration, alienation, amentia, brainsickness, brainstorm, craziness, delirium, dementia, derangement, folly, frenzy, infatuation, irresponsibility, lunacy, madness, mania, mental illness, neurosis, preposterousness, psychoneurosis, psychosis, senselessness, stupidity.

antonym sanity.

insatiable *adj* esurient, gluttonous, greedy, immoderate, incontrollable, inordinate, insatiate, intemperate, persistent, quenchless, rapacious, ravenous, unappeasable, uncurbable, unquenchable, unsatisfiable, voracious.

antonym moderate.

inscribe[1] *v* carve, cut, engrave, etch, grave, impress, imprint, incise, stamp.

inscribe[2] *v* address, autograph, dedicate, enlist, enrol, enter, record, register, sign, write.

inscription *n* autograph, caption, dedication, engraving, epigraph, epitaph, label, legend, lettering, saying, signature, words.

inscrutable *adj* baffling, blank, cryptic, dead-pan, deep, enigmatic, esoteric, expressionless, hidden, impassive, impenetrable, incomprehensible, inexplicable, mysterious, poker-faced, sphinx-like, undiscoverable, unexplainable, unfathomable, unintelligible, unknowable, unsearchable.

antonyms clear, comprehensible, expressive.

insecure *adj* afraid, anxious, apprehensive, dangerous, defenceless, diffident, exposed, expugnable, flimsy, frail, hazardous, insubstantial, jerry-built, loose, nervous, perilous, precarious, pregnable, rickety, rocky, shaky, shoogly, uncertain, unconfident, uneasy, unguarded, unprotected, unsafe, unshielded, unsound, unstable, unsteady, unsure, vulnerable, weak, wobbly, worried.

antonyms confident, safe, secure.

insecurity *n* anxiety, apprehension, danger, defencelessness, diffidence, dubiety, fear, flimsiness, frailness, hazard, instability, nervousness, peril, precariousness, ricketiness, risk, shakiness, uncertainty, uneasiness, unsafeness, unsafety, unsteadiness, unsureness, vulnerability, weakness, worry.

antonyms confidence, safety, security.

insensibility *n* apathy, blindness, callousness, coma, crassness, deafness, dullness, indifference, inertness, insensitivity, lethargy, nervelessness, numbness, oblivion, thoughtlessness, torpor, unawareness, unconsciousness.

antonyms consciousness, sensibilty.

insensible[1] *adj* anaesthetised, apathetic, blind, callous, cataleptic, cold, deaf, dull, hard-hearted, impassive, impercipient, impervious, indifferent, inert, insensate, marble, nerveless, numb, numbed, oblivious, senseless, stupid, torpid, unaffected, unaware, unconscious, unfeeling, unmindful, unmoved, unnoticing, unobservant, unresponsive, unsusceptible, untouched.

antonyms conscious, sensible.

insensible[2] *adj* imperceivable, imperceptible, inappreciable, minuscule, minute, negligible, tiny, unnoticeable.

antonym appreciable.

insensitive *adj* blunted, callous, crass, dead, hardened, immune, impenetrable, imperceptive, impercipient, impervious, indifferent, insusceptible, obtuse, pachydermatous, proof, resistant, tactless, thick-skinned, tough, unaffected, uncaring, unconcerned, unfeeling, unimpressionable, unmoved, unreactive, unresponsive, unsensitive, unsusceptible.

antonym sensitive.

insensitivity *n* bluntness, callousness, crassness, hard-headedness, hypalgesia, hypalgia, impenetrability, imperceptiveness, impercipience, imperviousness, indifference, obtuseness, tactlessness, unconcern, unresponsiveness.

antonym sensitivity.

inseparable *adj* bosom, close, conjoined, devoted, impartible, inalienable, indiscerptible, indissociable, indissoluble, individuate, indivisible, inextricable, inseverable, intimate, undividable.

antonym separable.

insert *v* embed, engraft, enter, immit, implant, infix, inset, intercalate, interject, interlaminate, interlard, interleave, interline, interpolate, interpose, introduce, intromit, let in, place, pop in, put, put in, set, stick in.

n ad, advertisement, empiecement, enclosure, engraftment, godet, graft, gusset, implant, insertion, inset, notice.

insertion *n* addition, entry, implant, inclusion, insert, inset, intercalation, interpolation, introduction, intromission, intrusion, supplement.

inside *n* content, contents, interior.

adv indoors, inly, internally, inwardly, privately, secretly, within.

adj classified, confidential, esoteric, exclusive, hush-hush, inner, innermost, interior, internal, intramural, inward, private, restricted, secret.

insides *n* belly, bowels, entera, entrails, gut, guts, innards, organs, stomach, viscera, vitals.

insidious *adj* artful, crafty, crooked, cunning, deceitful, deceptive, designing, devious, disingenuous, duplicitous, furtive, guileful, intriguing, Machiavellian, slick, sly, smooth, sneaking, stealthy, subtle, surreptitious, treacherous, tricky, wily.

insight *n* acumen, acuteness, apprehension, awareness, comprehension, discernment, grasp, ingenuity, intelligence, intuition, intuitiveness, judgement, knowledge, observation, penetration, perception, percipience, perspicacity, sensitivity, shrewdness, understanding, vision, wisdom.

insightful *adj* acute, astute, discerning, intelligent, knowledgeable, observant, penetrating, perceptive, percipient, perspicacious, prudent, sagacious, sage, shrewd, understanding, wise.

antonym superficial.

insignia *n* badge, brand, crest, decoration, emblem, ensign, hallmarks, mark, regalia, signs, symbol, trademark.

insignificance *n* immateriality, inconsequence, inconsequentiality, insubstantiality, irrelevance, meaninglessness, meanness, negligibility, nugatoriness, paltriness, pettiness, tininess, triviality, unimportance, worthlessness.

antonym significance.

insignificant *adj* dinky, flimsy, humble, immaterial, inappreciable, inconsequential, inconsiderable, insubstantial, irrelevant, meagre, meaningless, Mickey Mouse, minor, negligible, nondescript, nonessential, nugatory, paltry, petty, piddling, scanty, scrub, tiny, trifling, trivial, unimportant, unsubstantial.

antonym significant.

insincere *adj* artificial, canting, deceitful, deceptive, devious, dishonest, disingenuous, dissembling, dissimulating, double-dealing, duplicitous, evasive, faithless, false, hollow, hypocritical, lip-deep, lying, mendacious, perfidious, phoney, pretended, synthetic, two-faced, unfaithful, ungenuine, untrue, untruthful.

antonym sincere.

insincerity *n* artificiality, cant, deceitfulness, deviousness, dishonesty, disingenuousness, dissembling, dissimulation, duplicity, evasiveness, faithlessness, falseness, falsity, hollowness, hypocrisy, lip service, mendacity, perfidy, phoniness, pretence, untruthfulness.

antonym sincerity.

insinuate *v* allude, get at, hint, imply, indicate, innuendo, intimate, suggest.

insinuate oneself curry favour, get in with, ingratiate, sidle, work, worm, wriggle.

insinuation *n* allusion, aspersion, hint, implication, infiltration, ingratiating, innuendo, intimation, introduction, slant, slur, suggestion.

insipid *adj* anaemic, banal, bland, characterless, colourless, dilute, drab, dry, dull, fade, flat, flavourless, insulse, jejune, lash, lifeless, limp, missish, missy, monotonous, pointless, prosaic, prosy, savourless, spiritless, stale, tame, tasteless, trite, unappetising, unimaginative, uninteresting, unsavoury, vapid, watery, weak, wearish, weedy, wishy-washy.

antonyms appetising, piquant, punchy, tasty.

insipidity *n* anaemicness, banality, blandness, characterlessness, colournessness, diluteness, drabness, dryness, dullness, fadeur, flatness, jejuneness, jejunity, lifelessness, limpness, monotony, prosiness, spiritlessness, staleness, tameness, tastelessness, triteness, vapidity, wateriness, weakness, weediness.

antonyms character, liveliness, piquancy, punch, tastiness.

insist *v* assert, asseverate, aver, claim, contend, demand, dwell on, emphasise, harp on, hold, maintain, persist, reiterate, repeat, request, require, stand firm, stress, swear, urge, vow.

insistence *n* advice, assertion, averment, certainty, contention, demand, determination, emphasis, encouragement, entreaty, exhortation, firmness, importunity, instance, persistence, persuasion, pressing, reiteration, solicitations, stress, urgency, urging.

insistent *adj* demanding, dogged, emphatic, exigent, forceful, importunate, incessant, peremptory, persevering, persistent, pressing, relentless, tenacious, unrelenting, unremitting, urgent.

insobriety *n* crapulence, drunkenness, inebriation, inebriety, intemperance, intoxication, tipsiness.

antonym sobriety.

insolence *n* abuse, arrogance, assurance, audacity, backchat, boldness, cheek, cheekiness, chutzpah, contemptuousness, contumely, defiance, disrespect, effrontery, forwardness, gall, gum, hubris, impertinence, impudence, incivility, insubordination, lip, malapertness, offensiveness, pertness, presumption, presumptuousness, rudeness, sauce, sauciness.

antonyms politeness, respect.

insolent *adj* abusive, arrogant, bold, brazen, cheeky, contemptuous, contumelious, defiant, disrespectful, forward, fresh, hubristic, impertinent, impudent, insubordinate, insulting, malapert, pert, presumptuous, rude, saucy, uncivil.

antonyms polite, respectful.

insoluble *adj* baffling, impenetrable, indecipherable, inexplicable, inextricable, intractable, mysterious, mystifying, obscure, perplexing, unaccountable, unexplainable, unfathomable, unsolvable.

antonym explicable.

insolvency *n* bankruptcy, default, failure, liquidation, ruin.

antonym solvency.

insolvent *adj* bankrupt, broke, bust, defaulting, destitute, failed, flat broke, in queer street, on the rocks, ruined.

antonym solvent.

insomnia *n* insomnolence, restlessness, sleeplessness, wakefulness.

antonym sleep.

insouciance *n* airiness, breeziness, carefreeness, ease, flippancy, heedlessness, indifference, jauntiness, light-heartedness, nonchalance, pococurantism, unconcern.

antonyms anxiety, care.

insouciant *adj* airy, breezy, buoyant, carefree, casual, easy-going, flippant, gay, happy-go-lucky, heedless, indifferent, jaunty, light-hearted, nonchalant, pococurante, sunny, unconcerned, untroubled, unworried.

antonyms anxious, careworn.

inspect *v* audit, check, examine, give the once-over, investigate, look over, oversee, peruse, reconnoitre, scan, scrutinise, search, study, superintend, supervise, survey, vet, visit.

inspection *n* audit, autopsy, check, check-up, examination, investigation, once-over, post-mortem, reconnaissance, review, scan, scrutiny, search, superintendence, supervision, surveillance, survey, vidimus, visitation.

inspector *n* censor, checker, conner, controller, critic, examiner, investigator, overseer, reviewer, scrutineer, scrutiniser, superintendent, supervisor, surveyor, tester, viewer.

inspiration *n* afflation, afflatus, Aganippe, arousal, awakening, brainstorm, brain-wave, creativity, elevation, encouragement, enthusiasm, estro, exaltation, genius, Hippocrene, hwyl, illumination, influence, insight, muse, Muse, revelation, spur, stimulation, stimulus, Svengali, taghairm.

inspire *v* activate, animate, arouse, encourage, enkindle, enliven, enthuse, excite, fill, galvanise, hearten, imbue, influence, infuse, inhale, inspirit, instil, motivate, produce, quicken, spark off, spur, stimulate, stir, trigger.

inspired *adj* afflated, aroused, brilliant, dazzling, elated, enthralling, enthused, enthusiastic, exalted, exciting, exhilarated, fired, galvanised, impressive, invigorated, memorable, outstanding, possessed, reanimated, stimulated, superlative, thrilled, thrilling, uplifted, wonderful.

antonyms dull, uninspired.

inspiring *adj* affecting, emboldening, encouraging, exciting, exhilarating, heartening, inspiriting, invigorating, moving, rousing, stimulating, stirring, uplifting.

antonyms dull, uninspiring.

inspirit *v* animate, cheer, embolden, encourage, enliven, exhilarate, fire, galvanise, gladden, hearten, incite, inspire, invigorate, move, nerve, quicken, refresh, reinvigorate, rouse, stimulate.

instability *n* capriciousness, changeableness, fickleness, fitfulness, flimsiness, fluctuation, fluidity, frailty, imbalance, impermanence, inconstancy, insecurity, insolidity, irresolution, lability, mutability, oscillation, precariousness, restlessness, shakiness, transience, uncertainty, undependableness, unpredictability, unreliability, unsafeness, unsoundness, unsteadiness, vacillation, variability, volatility, wavering, weakness.

antonym stability.

instal(l) *v* consecrate, ensconce, establish, fix, inaugurate, induct, instate, institute, introduce, invest, lay, locate, lodge, ordain, place, plant, position, put, set, set up, settle, site, situate, station.

installation *n* base, consecration, equipment, establishment, fitting, inauguration, induction, instalment, instatement, investiture, location, machinery, ordination, placing, plant, positioning, post, siting, station, system.

instalment *n* chapter, consignment, delivery, division, episode, fascicule, heft, part, portion, repayment, section.

instance[1] *n* case, case in point, citation, example, illustration, occasion, occurrence, precedent, sample, situation, time.

v adduce, cite, mention, name, point to, quote, refer to, specify.

instance[2] *n* advice, application, behest, demand, entreaty, exhortation, importunity, impulse, incitement, initiative, insistence, instigation, pressure, prompting, request, solicitation, urging.

instant *n* flash, jiffy, juncture, minute, mo, moment, occasion, point, second, shake, split second, tick, time, trice, twinkling, two shakes.

adj convenience, direct, fast, immediate, instantaneous, on-the-spot, precooked, prompt, quick, rapid, ready-mixed, split-second, unhesitating, urgent.

instantaneous *adj* direct, immediate, instant, on-the-spot, prompt, rapid, unhesitating.

antonym eventual.

instantaneously *adv* at once, directly, forthwith, immediately, instantly, on the spot, promptly, rapidly, straight away, there and then, unhesitatingly.

antonym eventually.

instantly *adv* at once, directly, ek dum, forthwith, immediately, instantaneously, now, on the spot, pronto, quick-sticks, right away, straight away, there and then, tout de suite, without delay.

antonym eventually.

instead *adv* alternatively, as a substitute, as an alternative, in lieu, in preference, preferably, rather.

instead of as proxy for, in default of, in lieu of, in place of, in preference to, on behalf of, rather than.

instigate *v* actuate, cause, encourage, excite, foment, generate, impel, incite, influence, initiate, inspire, kindle, move, persuade, prompt, provoke, rouse, set on, spur, start, stimulate, stir up, urge, whip up.

instigation *n* behest, bidding, encouragement, incentive, incitement, initiative, insistence, instance, prompting, urging.

instigator *n* agent provocateur, agitator, firebrand, fomenter, goad, incendiary, inciter, leader, mischief-maker, motivator, prime mover, provoker, ringleader, spur, troublemaker.

instil *v* din into, engender, engraft, imbue, implant, impress, inculcate, infix, infuse, inject, insinuate, introduce.

instinct *n* ability, aptitude, faculty, feel, feeling, flair, gift, gut feeling, gut reaction, id, impulse, intuition, knack, nose, predisposition, proclivity, sixth sense, talent, tendency, urge.

instinctive *adj* automatic, gut, immediate, impulsive, inborn, inherent, innate, instinctual, intuitional, intuitive, involuntary, mechanical, native, natural, reflex, spontaneous, unlearned, unpremeditated, unthinking, visceral.

antonyms conscious, deliberate, voluntary.

instinctively *adv* automatically, intuitively, involuntarily, mechanically, naturally, spontaneously, unthinkingly, without thinking.

antonyms consciously, deliberately, voluntarily.

institute[1] *v* appoint, begin, commence, constitute, create, enact, establish, fix, found, inaugurate, induct, initiate, install, introduce, invest, launch, open, ordain, organise, originate, pioneer, set up, settle, start.

antonyms abolish, cancel, discontinue.

institute[2] *n* custom, decree, doctrine, dogma, edict, firman, indiction, irade, law, maxim, precedent, precept, principle, regulation, rescript, rule, tenet, ukase.

institute[3] *n* academy, association, college, conservatory, foundation, guild, institution, organisation, poly, polytechnic, school, seminary, society.

institution[1] *n* constitution, creation, enactment, establishment, formation, foundation, founding, inception, initiation, installation, introduction, investiture, organisation, protectory.

institution[2] *n* convention, custom, fixture, law, practice, ritual, rule, tradition, usage.

institution[3] *n* academy, college, concern, corporation, establishment, foundation, hospital, institute, organisation, school, seminary, society, university.

institutional *adj* accepted, bureaucratic, cheerless, clinical, cold, conventional, customary, drab, dreary, dull, established, establishment, forbidding, formal, impersonal, institutionary, monotonous, orthodox, regimented, ritualistic, routine, set, societal, uniform, unwelcoming.

antonyms individualistic, unconventional.

instruct *v* acquaint, advise, apprise, bid, brief, catechise, charge, coach, command, counsel, direct, discipline, drill, educate, enjoin, enlighten, ground, guide, inform, mandate, notify, order, school, teach, tell, train, tutor.

instruction *n* apprenticeship, briefing, catechesis, catechising, coaching, command, direction, directive, discipline, drilling, education, enlightenment, grounding, guidance, information, injunction, lesson(s), mandate, order, preparation, ruling, schooling, teaching, training, tuition, tutelage.

instructions *n* advice, book of words, commands, directions, guidance, handbook, information, key, legend, orders, recommendations, rules.

instructive *adj* cautionary, didactic, edificatory, edifying, educational, educative, educatory, enlightening, helpful, illuminating, improving, inculcative, informative, instructional, revealing, useful.

antonym unenlightening.

instructor *n* adviser, catechiser, catechist, coach, demonstrator, edifier, Egeria, exponent, guide, guru, instructress, maharishi, master, mentor, mistress, pedagogue, preceptor, schoolmaster, schoolmistress, teacher, trainer, tutor.

instrument *n* agency, agent, apparatus, appliance, cat's-paw, channel, contraption, contrivance, device, doodad, dupe, factor, force, gadget, implement, means, mechanism, medium, organ, pawn, puppet, tool, utensil, vehicle, way, widget.

instrumental *adj* active, assisting, auxiliary, conducive, contributive, contributory, helpful, helping, implemental, influential, involved, subsidiary, useful.

antonyms obstructive, unhelpful.

insubordinate *adj* contumacious, defiant, disobedient, disorderly, fractious, impertinent, impudent, insurgent, mutinous, rebellious, recalcitrant, refractory, riotous, rude, seditious, turbulent, undisciplined, ungovernable, unruly.

antonyms docile, obedient.

insubordination *n* defiance, disobedience, impertinence, impudence, indiscipline, insurrection, mutinousness, mutiny, rebellion, recalcitrance, revolt, riotousness, rudeness, sedition, ungovernability.

antonyms docility, obedience.

insubstantial *adj* chimerical, ephemeral, false, fanciful, feeble, flimsy, frail, idle, illusory, imaginary, immaterial, incorporeal, moonshine, poor, slight, tenuous, thin, unreal, vaporous, weak, windy, yeasty.

antonyms real, strong.

insufferable *adj* detestable, dreadful, hateful, impossible, insupportable, intolerable, loathesome, outrageous, unbearable, unendurable, unliv(e)able, unspeakable.

antonyms pleasant, tolerable.

insufficiency *n* dearth, deficiency, inadequacy, inadequateness, lack, need, paucity, poverty, scantiness, scarcity, shortage, sparsity, want.

antonyms excess, sufficiency.

insufficient *adj* deficient, inadequate, incapable, incommensurate, lacking, scanty, scarce, short, sparse, wanting.

antonyms excessive, sufficient.

insular *adj* blinkered, circumscribed, closed, contracted, cut off, detached, illiberal, inward-looking, isolated, limited, narrow, narrow-minded, parish-pump, parochial, petty, prejudiced, provincial, xenophobic.

antonym cosmopolitan.

insularity *n* isolation, narrow-mindedness, parochiality, parochialness, prejudice, xenophobia.

antonyms open-mindedness, openness.

insulate *v* cocoon, cushion, cut off, isolate, protect, quarantine, separate off, sequester, shield.

insulation *n* cushioning, deadening, deafening, padding, protection, stuffing.

insult *v* abuse, affront, call names, fling/throw mud at, give offence to, injure, libel, miscall, offend, outrage, revile, slag, slander, slight, snub, vilify, vilipend.

antonyms compliment, honour.

n abuse, affront, aspersion, contumely, indignity, insolence, libel, offence, outrage, rudeness, slander, slap in the face, slight, snub.

antonyms compliment, honour.

insulting *adj* abusive, affronting, contemptuous, degrading, disparaging, insolent, libellous, offensive, rude, scurrilous, slanderous, slighting.

antonyms complimentary, respectful.

insuperable *adj* formidable, impassable, insurmountable, invincible, overwhelming, unconquerable.

antonym surmountable.

insupportable *adj* detestable, dreadful, hateful, indefensible, insufferable, intenable, intolerable, invalid, loathesome, unbearable, unendurable, unjustifiable, untenable.

antonym bearable.

insuppressible *adj* energetic, go-getting, incorrigible, irrepressible, lively, obstreperous, uncontrollable, ungovernable, unruly, unstoppable, unsubduable.

antonym suppressible.

insurance *n* assurance, cover, coverage, guarantee, indemnification, indemnity, policy, premium, protection, provision, safeguard, security, warranty.

insure *v* assure, cover, guarantee, indemnify, protect, underwrite, warrant.

insurer *n* assurer, underwriter.

insurgent *n* insurrectionist, mutineer, partisan, rebel, resister, revolter, revoluntionist, revolutionary, rioter.

adj disobedient, insubordinate, insurrectionary, mutinous, partisan, rebellious, revolting, revolutionary, riotous, seditious.

insurmountable *adj* hopeless, impassable, impossible, insuperable, invincible, overwhelming, unclimable, unconquerable, unscalable, unsurmountable.

antonym surmountable.

insurrection *n* coup, inqilab, insurgence, insurgency, mutiny, putsch, rebellion, revolt, revolution, riot, rising, sedition, uprising.

intact *adj* all in one piece, complete, entire, inviolate, perfect, scatheless, sound, together, unbroken, undamaged, undefiled, unharmed, unhurt, unimpaired, uninjured, unscathed, untouched, unviolated, virgin, whole.

antonyms broken, damaged, harmed.

intaglio *n* diaglyph.

intangible *adj* airy, bodiless, dim, elusive, ethereal, evanescent, impalpable, imperceptible, incorporeal, indefinite, insubstantial, invisible, shadowy, unreal, unsubstantial, vague.

antonyms real, tangible.

integral *adj* basic, complete, component, constituent, elemental, entire, essential, full, fundamental, indispensable, intact, intrinsic, necessary, requisite, undivided, unitary, whole.

antonyms accessory, partial.

integrate *v* accommodate, amalgamate, assimilate, blend, coalesce, combine, commingle, desegregate, fuse, harmonise, incorporate, intermix, join, knit, merge, mesh, mix, unite.

antonym separate.

integrated *adj* cohesive, concordant, connected, desegregated, harmonious, interrelated, part and parcel, unified, unsegregated, unseparated.

antonym unintegrated.

integration *n* amalgamation, assimilation, blending, combining, commingling, desegregation, fusing, harmony, incorporation, mixing, unification.

antonym separation.

integrity *n* candour, coherence, cohesion, completeness, entireness, goodness, honesty, honour, incorruptibility, principle, probity, purity, rectitude, righteousness, soundness, unity, uprightness, virtue, wholeness.

antonyms dishonesty, incompleteness, unreliability.

intellect *n* brain, brain power, brains, egghead, genius, highbrow, intellectual, intelligence, judgement, mind, nous, reason, sense, thinker, understanding.

antonym dunce.

intellectual *adj* bookish, cerebral, deep-browed, discursive, highbrow, intelligent, mental, noetic, rational, scholarly, studious, thoughtful.

antonym low-brow.

n academic, egghead, headpiece, highbrow, mastermind, thinker.

antonym low-brow.

intelligence *n* acuity, acumen, advice, alertness, aptitude, brain power, brains, brightness, capacity, cleverness, comprehension, data, discernment, disclosure, facts, findings, gen, grey matter, information, intellect, intellectuality, knowledge, low-down, mind, news, notice, notification, nous, penetration, perception, quickness, reason, report, rumour, tidings, tip-off, understanding, word.

antonym foolishness.

intelligent *adj* acute, alert, apt, brainy, bright, clever, deep-browed, discerning, enlightened, instructed, knowing, penetrating, perspicacious, quick, quick-witted, rational, razor-sharp, sharp, smart, thinking, well-informed.

antonyms foolish, unintelligent.

intelligentsia *n* academics, brains, eggheads, eggmass, highbrows, illuminati, intellectuals, literati.

intelligibility *n* clarity, clearness, comprehensibility, comprehensibleness, distinctness, explicitness, lucidity, lucidness, plainness, precision, simplicity.

antonym unintelligibility.

intelligible *adj* clear, comprehensible, decipherable, distinct, fathomable, lucid, open, penetrable, plain, understandable.

antonym unintelligible.

intemperance *n* crapulence, drunkenness, excess, extravagance, immoderation, inebriation, insobriety, intoxication, licence, overindulgence, self-indulgence, unrestraint.

antonym temperance.

intemperate *adj* drunken, excessive, extravagant, extreme, immoderate, incontinent, inordinate, intoxicated, irrestrainable, licentious, over the top, passionate, prodigal, profligate, self-indulgent, severe, tempestuous, unbridled, uncontrollable, ungovernable, unrestrained, violent, wild.

antonym temperate.

intend *v* aim, consign, contemplate, design, destine, determine, earmark, have a mind, mark out, mean, meditate, plan, project, propose, purpose, scheme, set apart.

intended *adj* betrothed, deliberate, designate, designated, destined, future, intentional, planned, proposed, prospective.

antonym accidental.

n betrothed, fiancé, fiancée, husband-to-be, wife-to-be.

intense *adj* acute, agonising, ardent, burning, close, concentrated, consuming, eager, earnest, energetic, fanatical, fervent, fervid, fierce, forceful, forcible, great, harsh, heightened, impassioned, intensive, keen, passionate, powerful, profound, severe, strained, strong, vehement.

antonyms apathetic, mild.

intensely *adv* ardently, deeply, extremely, fervently, fiercely, greatly, passionately, profoundly, strongly, very.

antonym mildly.

intensification *n* acceleration, building-up, build-up, deepening, escalation, exacerbescence, heightening, increase, worsening.

antonym lessening.

intensify *v* add to, aggravate, boost, concentrate, deepen, emphasise, enhance, escalate, exacerbate, fire, fuel, heighten, hot up, increase, magnify, quicken, redouble, reinforce, sharpen, step up, strengthen, whet, whip up.

antonyms damp down, die down.

intensity *n* accent, ardour, concentration, depth, earnestness, emotion, energy, excess, extremity, fanaticism, fervency, fervour, fierceness, fire, force, intenseness, keenness, passion, potency, power, severity, strain, strength, tension, vehemence, vigour, voltage.

intensive *adj* all-out, comprehensive, concentrated, demanding, detailed, exhaustive, in detail, in-depth, thorough, thoroughgoing.

antonym superficial.

intent *adj* absorbed, alert, attentive, bent, committed, concentrated, concentrating, determined, eager, earnest, engrossed, fixed, hell-bent, industrious, intense, mindful, occupied, piercing, preoccupied, rapt, resolute, resolved, set, steadfast, steady, watchful, wrapped up.

antonyms absent-minded, distracted.

n aim, design, end, goal, intention, meaning, object, objective, plan, purpose.

intention *n* aim, concept, design, end, end in view, goal, idea, intent, meaning, object, objective, plan, point, purpose, scope, target, view.

intentional *adj* calculated, deliberate, designed, intended, meant, planned, prearranged, preconcerted, premeditated, purposed, studied, wilful.

antonym accidental.

intentionally *adv* by design, deliberately, designedly, meaningly, on purpose, wilfully, with malice aforethought.

antonym accidentally.

intently *adv* attentively, carefully, closely, fixedly, hard, keenly, searchingly, staringly, steadily, watchfully.

antonym absent-mindedly.

inter *v* bury, entomb, inhume, inurn, lay to rest, sepulchre.

antonym exhume.

interbreed *v* cross, cross-breed, hybridise, miscegenate.

interbreeding *n* cross-breeding, crossing, hybridisation, miscegenation.

intercede *v* advocate, arbitrate, interpose, intervene, mediate, plead, speak.

intercept *v* arrest, block, catch, check, cut off, deflect, delay, frustrate, head off, impede, interrupt, obstruct, retard, seize, stop, take, thwart.

intercession *n* advocacy, agency, beseeching, entreaty, good offices, intervention, mediation, plea, pleading, prayer, solicitation, supplication.

interchange *n* alternation, crossfire, exchange, interplay, intersection, junction, reciprocation, trading.

interchangeable *adj* commutable, equal, equivalent, exchangeable, identical, reciprocal, similar, standard, synonymous, the same, transposable.

antonym different.

intercourse[1] *n* association, commerce, communication, communion, congress, connection, contact, conversation, converse, correspondence, dealings, intercommunication, traffic, truck.

intercourse[2] *n* carnal knowledge, coition, coitus, copulation, embraces, greens, intimacy, love-making, sex, sexual relations, venery.

interdict *v* ban, bar, debar, disallow, forbid, outlaw, preclude, prevent, prohibit, proscribe, rule out, veto.

antonym allow.

n ban, disallowance, injunction, interdiction, prohibition, proscription, taboo, veto.

antonym permission.

interest *n* activity, advantage, affair, affection, attention, attentiveness, attraction, authority, bag, benefit, business, care, claim, commitment, concern, consequence, curiosity, diversion, finger, gain, good, hobby, importance, influence, investment, involvement, line of country, matter, moment, note, notice, participation, pastime, portion, preoccupation, profit, pursuit, regard, relaxation, relevance, right, share, significance, stake, study, suspicion, sympathy, weight.

antonyms boredom, irrelevance.

v affect, amuse, attract, concern, divert, engage, engross, fascinate, intrigue, involve, move, touch, warm.

antonym bore.

interested *adj* affected, attentive, attracted, biased, concerned, curious, drawn, engrossed, fascinated, implicated, intent, involved, keen, partisan, predisposed, prejudiced, responsive, simulated.

antonyms apathetic, indifferent, unaffected.

interesting *adj* absorbing, amusing, amusive, appealing, attractive, compelling, curious, engaging, engrossing, entertaining, gripping, intriguing, provocative, stimulating, thought-provoking, unusual, viewable, visitable.

antonym boring.

interfere *v* block, butt in, clash, collide, conflict, cramp, frustrate, hamper, handicap, hinder, impede, inhibit, interlope, intermeddle, interpose, intervene, intrude, meddle, obstruct, poke one's nose in, stick one's oar in, tamper, trammel

antonyms assist, forbear.

interference *n* clashing, collision, conflict, do-goodery, do-goodism, impedance, intervention, intrusion, meddlesomeness, meddling, mush, obstruction, opposition, paternalism, prying, shash, statics, white noise.
antonyms assistance, forbearance.

interim *adj* acting, caretaker, improvised, intervening, makeshift, permanent, pro tem, provisional, stand-in, stop-gap, temporary.
n interregnum, interval, meantime, meanwhile.

interior *adj* central, domestic, hidden, home, inland, inly, inner, inside, internal, intimate, inward, mental, pectoral, personal, private, remote, secret, spiritual, up-country.
antonyms exterior, external.
n bowels, centre, core, heart, heartland, hinterland, inside, up-country.

interject *v* call, cry, exclaim, interjaculate, interpolate, interpose, interrupt, introduce, shout.

interjection *n* call, cry, ejaculation, exclamation, interpolation, interposition, shout.

interlace *v* braid, cross, enlace, entwine, interlock, intermix, intersperse, intertwine, interweave, interwreathe, knit, plait, reticulate, twine.

interlink *v* clasp together, interconnect, intergrow, interlock, intertwine, interweave, knit, link, link together, lock together, mesh.
antonym separate.

interlock *v* interdigitate, intertwine, lock together.

interloper *n* gate-crasher, intruder, trespasser, uninvited guest.

interlude *n* break, breathing-space, breathing-time, breathing-while, delay, episode, halt, hiatus, intermission, interval, pause, respite, rest, spell, stop, stoppage, wait.

intermarriage *n* miscegenation.

intermediary *n* agent, broker, entrepreneur, go-between, in-between, internuncio, mediator, middleman, ombudsman, ombudswoman.

intermediate *adj* halfway, in-between, intermediary, interposed, intervening, mean, medial, median, mid, middle, midway, transitional.
antonym extreme.

interment *n* burial, burying, funeral, inhumation, obsequies, obsequy, sepulture.
antonym exhumation.

interminable *adj* boundless, ceaseless, dragging, endless, everlasting, immeasurable, infinite, limitless, long, long-drawn-out, long-winded, never-ending, perpetual, prolix, protracted, unbounded, unlimited, wearisome.
antonym limited.

intermingle *v* amalgamate, blend, combine, commingle, commix, fuse, interlace, intermix, interweave, merge, mix, mix together, mix up.
antonym separate.

intermission *n* break, breather, breathing-space, breathing-while, cessation, entr'acte, interlude, interruption, interval, let-up, lull, pause, recess, remission, respite, rest, stop, stoppage, suspense, suspension.

intermittent *adj* broken, discontinuous, fitful, irregular, occasional, periodic, periodical, punctuated, recurrent, recurring, remittent, spasmodic, sporadic, stop-go.
antonym continuous.

intern *v* confine, detain, hold, imprison, jail.
antonym free.

internal *adj* domestic, in-house, inner, inside, interior, intimate, inward, private, subjective.
antonym external.

international *adj* cosmopolitan, general, global, intercontinental, interterritorial, universal, worldwide.
antonym parochial.

internecine *adj* bloody, civil, deadly, destructive, exterminating, exterminatory, family, fatal, internal, internecive, mortal, murderous, ruinous.

interplay *n* exchange, give-and-take, interaction, interchange, meshing, reciprocation, reciprocity.

interpolate *v* add, insert, intercalate, interjaculate, interject, introduce.

interpolation *n* addition, aside, insert, insertion, intercalation, interjaculation, interjection, introduction.

interpose *v* come between, insert, intercede, interfere, interjaculate, interject, interrupt, intervene, introduce, intrude, mediate, offer, place between, step in, thrust in.
antonym forbear.

interpret *v* adapt, clarify, construe, decipher, decode, define, elucidate, explain, explicate, expound, paraphrase, read, render, solve, take, throw light on, translate, understand, unfold.

interpretation *n* anagoge, anagogy, analysis, clarification, construction, diagnosis, elucidation, exegesis, explanation, explication, exposition, meaning, performance, portrayal, reading, rendering, rendition, sense, signification, translation, understanding, version.

interpretative *adj* clarificatory, exegetic, explanatory, explicatory, expository, hermeneutic, interpretive.

interpreter *n* annotator, commentator, dobhash, dragoman, elucidator, exegete, exegetist, exponent, expositor, hermeneutist, interpretress, linguister, munshi, scholiast, translator, truchman, ulema.

interrogate *v* ask, catechise, cross-examine, cross-question, debrief, enquire, examine, give (someone) the third degree, grill, inquire, investigate, pump, question, quiz.

interrogation *n* catachesis, cross-examination, cross-questioning, enquiry, examination, grilling, inquiry, inquisition, probing, questioning, third degree.

interrogative *adj* catechetical, curious, erotetic, inquiring, inquisitional, inquisitive, inquisitorial, interrogatory, questioning, quizzical.

interrupt *v* barge in, break, break in, break off, butt in, check, cut, cut off, cut short, delay, disconnect, discontinue, disjoin, disturb, disunite, divide, heckle, hinder, hold up, interfere, interjaculate, interject, intrude, obstruct, punctuate, separate, sever, stay, stop, suspend.

antonym forbear.

interrupted *adj* broken, cut off, disconnected, discontinuous, disturbed, incomplete, intermittent, uneven, unfinished.

antonyms complete, continuous.

interruption *n* break, cessation, Derby dog, disconnection, discontinuance, disruption, dissolution, disturbance, disuniting, division, halt, hiatus, hindrance, hitch, impediment, intrusion, obstacle, obstruction, pause, separation, severance, stop, stoppage, suspension.

intersect *v* bisect, criss-cross, cross, cut, cut across, decussate, divide, divide up, meet.

intersection *n* bisection, crossing, crossroads, decussation, division, interchange, junction.

intersperse *v* diversify, dot, interlard, intermix, pepper, scatter, sprinkle.

intertwine *v* braid, convolute, cross, entwine, interlace, intertangle, intertwist, interweave, interwreathe, inweave, link, reticulate, twist.

interval *n* break, delay, distance, entr'acte, gap, hiatus, in-between, interim, interlude, intermission, interspace, interstice, meantime, meanwhile, opening, pause, period, playtime, rest, season, space, spell, term, time, wait.

intervene *v* arbitrate, befall, ensue, happen, intercede, interfere, interpose oneself, interrupt, intrude, involve, mediate, occur, step in, succeed, supervene, take a hand.

intervening *adj* between, interjacent, interposing, intervenient, mediate.

intervention *n* agency, intercession, interference, interposition, intervening, intrusion, mediation.

interview *n* audience, conference, consultation, dialogue, enquiry, evaluation, inquisition, meeting, oral, oral examination, press conference, talk, viva.

v examine, interrogate, question, viva.

interviewer *n* examiner, inquisitor, inquisitress, interlocutor, interrogant, interrogator, investigator, questioner, reporter.

interweave *v* blend, braid, criss-cross, cross, interlace, intertangle, intertwine, intertwist, interwork, interwreathe, reticulate, splice.

interweaving *n* interramification, intertangling, intertwining, intertwisting.

interwoven *adj* blended, connected, entwined, inmixed, interconnected, interlaced, interlocked, intermingled, intertangled, intertwisted, interworked, interwreathed, interwrought, knit.

intestinal *adj* abdominal, coeliac, duodenal, ileac, internal, stomachic, visceral.

intestines *n* bowels, chitterlings, entrails, guts, innards, insides, offal, umbles, viscera, vitals.

intimacy *n* brotherliness, closeness, coition, coitus, confidence, confidentiality, copulating, copulation, familiarity, fornication, fraternisation, friendship, intercourse, sexual intercourse, sisterliness, understanding.

intimate[1] *v* allude, announce, communicate, declare, hint, impart, imply, indicate, insinuate, state, suggest, tell.

intimate[2] *adj* as thick as thieves, bosom, cherished, close, confidential, cosy, dear, deep, deep-seated, detailed, exhaustive, friendly, gremial, informal, innermost, internal, near, palsy-walsy, penetrating, personal, private, privy, profound, secret, warm.

antonyms cold, distant, unfriendly.

n Achates, associate, bosom buddy, buddy, china, chum, comrade, confidant, confidante, crony, familiar, friend, mate, mucker, pal, repository.

antonym stranger.

intimately *adv* affectionately, closely, confidentially, confidingly, exhaustively, familiarly, fully, in detail, inside out, personally, tenderly, thoroughly, warmly.

antonyms coldly, distantly.

intimation *n* allusion, announcement, communication, declaration, hint, indication, inkling, insinuation, notice, reminder, statement, suggestion, warning.

intimidate *v* alarm, appal, browbeat, bulldoze, bully, coerce, cow, daunt, dishearten, dismay, dispirit, frighten, lean on, overawe, psych out, put the frighteners on, scare, subdue, terrify, terrorise, threaten.

antonym persuade.

intimidation *n* arm-twisting, browbeating, bullying, coercion, fear, menaces, pressure, terror, terrorisation, terrorising, threats.

antonym persuasion.

intolerable *adj* beyond the pale, excruciating, impossible, insufferable, insupportable, painful, unbearable, unendurable.

antonym tolerable.

intolerance *n* bigotry, chauvinism, discrimination, dogmatism, fanaticism, illiberality, impatience, jingoism, narrow-mindedness, narrowness, opinionativeness, prejudice, racialism, racism, xenophobia.

antonym tolerance.

intolerant *adj* bigoted, chauvinistic, dictatorial, dogmatic, fanatical, illiberal, impatient, narrow, narrow-minded, opinionated, opinionative, opinioned, persecuting, prejudiced, racialist, racist, small-minded, uncharitable.

antonym tolerant.

intonation *n* accentuation, cadence, chant, incantation, inflection, mantra(m), modulation, tone.

intone *v* chant, croon, declaim, intonate, monotone, pronounce, recite, sing, utter.

intoxicate *n* addle, befuddle, elate, excite, exhilarate, fuddle, inebriate, inflame, stimulate, stupefy.

antonym sober.

intoxicated *adj* blotto, canned, cut, disguised in liquor, dizzy, drunk, drunken, ebriate, ebriated, ebriose, elated, enraptured, euphoric, excited, exhilarated, fuddled, glorious, half seas over, high, in one's cups, incapable, inebriate, inebriated, infatuated, legless, lit up, looped, pickled, pissed, pixil(l)ated, plastered, sent, sloshed, smashed, sozzled, stewed, stiff, stimulated, stoned, stotious, three sheets in the wind, tight, tipsy, under the influence, up the pole, zonked.

antonym sober.

intoxicating *adj* alcoholic, dizzy, euphoric, exciting, exhilarating, heady, inebriant, intoxicant, spirituous, stimulating, strong, thrilling.

antonym sobering.

intoxication *n* delirium, drunkenness, ebriety, ebriosity, elation, euphoria, exaltation, excitement, exhilaration, inebriation, inebriety, infatuation, insobriety, tipsiness.

antonym sobriety.

intractability *n* awkwardness, cantankerousness, contrariness, incorrigibility, indiscipline, indocility, mulishness, obduracy, obstinacy, perverseness, perversity, pig-headedness, stubbornness, unamenability, unco-operativeness, ungovernability, waywardness.

antonym amenability.

intractable *adj* awkward, bull-headed, cantankerous, contrary, difficult, fractious, haggard, headstrong, incurable, insoluble, intransigent, obdurate, obstinate, perverse, pig-headed, refractory, self-willed, stubborn, unamenable, unbending, unco-operative, undisciplined, ungovernable, unmanageable, unruly, unyielding, wayward, wild, wilful.

antonym amenable.

intransigent *adj* hardline, immovable, intractable, irreconcilable, obdurate, obstinate, stubborn, tenacious, tough, unamenable, unbending, unbudgeable, uncompromising, unpersuadable, unyielding, uppity.

antonym amenable.

intrepid *adj* audacious, bold, brave, courageous, daring, dashing, dauntless, doughty, fearless, gallant, game, gutsy, heroic, lion-hearted, nerveless, plucky, resolute, stalwart, stout-hearted, unafraid, undashed, undaunted, unflinching, valiant, valorous.

antonyms cowardly, timid.

intrepidness *n* audacity, boldness, bravery, courage, daring, dauntlessness, doughtiness, fearlessness, fortitude, gallantry, guts, heroism, intrepidity, lion-heartedness, nerve, pluck, prowess, spirit, stout-heartedness, undauntedness, valour.

antonyms cowardice, timidity.

intricacy *n* complexedness, complexity, complexness, complication, convolutions, elaborateness, entanglement, intricateness, involution, involvement, knottiness, obscurity.

antonym simplicity.

intricate *adj* Byzantine, complex, complicated, convoluted, daedal(e), Daedalian, daedalic, dedal, dedalian, difficult, elaborate, entangled, fancy, Gordian, involved, knotty, labyrinthine, perplexing, rococo, sophisticated, tangled, tortuous.

antonym simple.

intrigue[1] *v* attract, charm, fascinate, interest, puzzle, rivet, tantalise, tickle one's fancy, titillate.

antonym bore.

intrigue[2] *n* affair, amour, brigue, cabal, chicanery, collusion, conspiracy, double-dealing, intimacy, knavery, liaison, machination, machination(s), manipulation, manoeuvre, plot, romance, ruse, scheme, sharp practice, stratagem, string-pulling, trickery, wheeler-dealing, wile, wire-pulling.

v connive, conspire, machinate, manoeuvre, plot, scheme.

intriguer *n* conniver, intrigant(e), Machiavellian, machinator, plotter, schemer, wangler, wheeler-dealer, wire-puller.

intriguing *adj* beguiling, compelling, diverting, exciting, fascinating, interesting, puzzling, tantalising, titillating.

antonyms boring, uninteresting.

intrinsic *adj* basic, basically, built-in, central, congenital, constitutional, constitutionally, elemental, essential, essentially, fundamental, fundamentally, genuine, inborn, inbred, inherent, intrinsically, inward, native, natural, underlying.

antonym extrinsic.

introduce *v* acquaint, add, advance, air, announce, begin, bring in, bring up, broach, commence, conduct, establish, familiarise, found, inaugurate, initiate, inject, insert, institute, interpolate, interpose, launch, lead in, lead into, moot, offer, open, organise, pioneer, preface, present, propose, put forward, put in, recommend, set forth, start, submit, suggest, throw in, ventilate.

antonym take away.

introduction *n* addition, baptism, commencement, debut, establishment, exordium, foreword, inauguration, induction, initiation, insertion, institution, interpolation, intro, launch, lead-in, opening, overture, pioneering, preamble, preface, preliminaries, prelude, presentation, prodrome, prodromus, proem, prolegomena, prolegomenon, prologue, prooemion, prooemium.

antonym withdrawal.

introductory *adj* early, elementary, exordial, first, inaugural, initial, initiatory, opening, precursory, prefatory, preliminary, preparatory, proemial, prolegomenary, prolegomenous, prolusory, starting.

introspection *n* brooding, heart-searching, introversion, self-analysis, self-examination, self-observation, soul-searching.

introspective *adj* brooding, contemplative, introverted, inward-looking, meditative, pensive, ruminative, subjective, thoughtful.

antonym outward-looking.

introverted *adj* indrawn, intervertive, introspective, introversive, inward-looking, self-centred, self-contained, withdrawn.

antonym extroverted.

intrude *v* aggress, butt in, encroach, infringe, interfere, interrupt, meddle, obtrude, trespass, violate.

antonyms stand back, withdraw.

intruder *n* burglar, Derby dog, gate-crasher, infiltrator, interloper, invader, prowler, raider, snooper, trespasser.

intrusion *n* aggression, encroachment, incursion, infringement, ingression, interference, interruption, invasion, trespass, violation.

antonym withdrawal.

intrusive *adj* disturbing, forward, impertinent, importunate, interfering, invasive, meddlesome, nosy, obtrusive, officious, presumptuous, pushy, uncalled-for, unwanted, unwelcome.

antonyms unintrusive, welcome.

intuition *n* discernment, feeling, gut feeling, hunch, insight, instinct, perception, presentiment, sixth sense.

antonym reasoning.

intuitive *adj* innate, instinctive, instinctual, involuntary, spontaneous, unreflecting, untaught.

antonym reasoned.

inundate *v* bury, deluge, drown, engulf, fill, flood, glut, immerse, overflow, overrun, overwhelm, submerge, swamp.

inundation *n* deluge, deluvion, deluvium, flood, glut, overflow, tidal wave, torrent.

antonym trickle.

inure *v* accustom, desensitise, familiarise, flesh, habituate, harden, strengthen, temper, toughen, train.

invade *v* assail, assault, attack, burst in, come upon, descend upon, encroach, enter, fall upon, infest, infringe, irrupt, occupy, overrun, overspread, penetrate, pervade, raid, rush into, seize, swarm over, violate.

antonym withdraw.

invader *n* aggressor, attacker, intruder, raider, trespasser.

invalid[1] *adj* ailing, bedridden, disabled, feeble, frail, ill, infirm, invalidish, poorly, sick, sickly, valetudinarian, valetudinary, weak.

antonym healthy.

n case, convalescent, patient, sufferer, valetudinarian, valetudinary.

invalid[2] *adj* baseless, fallacious, false, ill-founded, illogical, incorrect, inoperative, irrational, nugatory, null, null and void, unfounded, unscientific, unsound, untrue, void, worthless.

antonym valid.

invalidate *v* abrogate, annul, cancel, nullify, overrule, overthrow, quash, rescind, undermine, undo, vitiate, weaken.

antonym validate.

invalidity *n* fallaciousness, fallacy, falsity, illogicality, inconsistency, incorrectness, invalidness, irrationality, sophism, speciousness, unsoundness, voidness.

invaluable *adj* costly, exquisite, inestimable, precious, priceless, valuable.

antonym worthless.

invariable *adj* changeless, consistent, constant, fixed, immutable, inflexible, permanent, regular, rigid, set, static, unalterable, unchangeable, unchanging, unfailing, uniform, unvarying, unwavering.

antonym variable.

invariably *adv* always, consistently, customarily, habitually, inevitably, perpetually, regularly, unfailingly, without exception, without fail.

antonym variably.

invasion *n* aggression, assault, attack, breach, encroachment, foray, incursion, infiltration, infraction, infringement, inroad, intrusion, irruption, offensive, onslaught, raid, seizure, usurpation, violation.

antonym withdrawal.

invective *n* abuse, berating, billingsgate, castigation, censure, contumely, denunciation, diatribe, flyting, obloquy, philippic, philippic(s), reproach, revilement, sarcasm, scolding, tirade, tongue-lashing, vilification, vituperation.

antonym praise.

inveigh *v* berate, blame, castigate, censure, condemn, denounce, expostulate, flite, fulminate, lambast, rail, recriminate, reproach, scold, sound off, tongue-lash, upbraid, vituperate.

antonym praise.

inveigle *v* allure, bamboozle, beguile, cajole, coax, con, decoy, ensnare, entice, entrap, lead on, lure, manipulate, manoeuvre, persuade, seduce, sweet-talk, wheedle, wile.

antonym force.

invent *v* coin, conceive, concoct, contrive, cook up, create, design, devise, discover, dream up, fabricate, formulate, frame, imagine, improvise, make up, originate, think up, trump up.

invention *n* brainchild, coinage, contraption, contrivance, contrivement, creation, creativeness, creativity, deceit, design, development, device, discovery, excogitation, fabrication, fake, falsehood, fantasy, fib, fiction, figment of (someone's) imagination, forgery, gadget, genius, imagination, ingenuity, inspiration, inventiveness, inveracity, lie, originality, prevarication, resourcefulness, sham, story, tall story, untruth, yarn.

antonym truth.

inventive *adj* creative, daedal(e), Daedalian, daedalic, dedal, excogitative, fertile, gifted, imaginative, ingenious, innovative, inspired, original, resourceful.

antonym uninventive.

inventor *n* architect, author, builder, coiner, creator, designer, father, framer, inventress, maker, originator.

inventory *n* account, catalogue, equipment, file, list, listing, record, register, roll, roster, schedule, stock.

inverse *adj* contrary, converse, inverted, opposite, reverse, reversed, transposed, upside down.

inversion *n* antipode, antithesis, contraposition, contrariety, contrary, hysteron-proteron, opposite, reversal, transposal, transposition.

invert *v* capsize, introvert, inverse, overturn, reverse, transpose, turn turtle, turn upside down, upset, upturn.

antonym right.

invest *v* adopt, advance, authorise, charge, consecrate, devote, empower, endow, endue, enthrone, establish, inaugurate, induct, install, lay out, license, ordain, provide, put in, sanction, sink, spend, supply, vest.

antonym divest.

investigate *v* consider, enquire into, examine, explore, go into, inspect, look into, probe, scrutinise, search, see how the land lies, sift, study, suss out.

investigation *n* analysis, enquiry, examination, exploration, fact finding, hearing, inquest, inquiry, inspection, probe, research, review, scrutiny, search, study, survey, witch-hunt, zetetic.

investigative *adj* fact-finding, heuristic, inspecting, investigating, research, researching, zetetic.

investigator *n* detective, dick, enquirer, examiner, gumshoe, inquisitor, private detective, private eye, researcher, shamus, sleuth, sleuth-hound.

investiture *n* admission, coronation, enthronement, inauguration, induction, installation, instatement, investing, investment, ordination.

investment *n* ante, asset, besieging, blockade, contribution, investing, investiture, siege, speculation, stake, transaction, venture.

inveterate *adj* chronic, confirmed, deep-dyed, deep-rooted, deep-seated, diehard, dyed-in-the-wool, entrenched, established, habitual, hard-core, hardened, incorrigible, incurable, ineradicable, ingrained, irreformable, long-standing, obstinate.

antonym impermanent.

invidious *adj* discriminating, discriminatory, hateful, objectionable, obnoxious, odious, offensive, repugnant, slighting, undesirable.

antonym desirable.

invigorate *v* animate, brace, buck up, energise, enliven, exhilarate, fortify, freshen, galvanise, harden, inspirit, liven up, nerve, pep up, perk up, quicken, refresh, rejuvenate, revitalise, stimulate, strengthen, vitalise, vivify.

antonyms dishearten, weary.

invigorating *adj* bracing, energising, exhilarating, fresh, generous, healthful, inspiriting, refreshing, rejuvenating, rejuvenative, restorative, salubrious, stimulating, tonic, uplifting, vivifying.

antonyms disheartening, wearying.

invincible *adj* impenetrable, impregnable, indestructible, indomitable, inseparable, insuperable, invulnerable, irreducible, unassailable, unbeatable, unconquerable, unreducible, unsurmountable, unyielding.

antonym beatable.

inviolability *n* holiness, inalienability, inviolableness, inviolacy, invulnerability, sacredness, sacrosanctness, sanctity.

antonym violability.

inviolable *adj* hallowed, holy, inalienable, intemerate, sacred, sacrosanct, unalterable.

antonym violable.

inviolate *adj* entire, intact, pure, sacred, stainless, unbroken, undefiled, undisturbed, unhurt, uninjured, unpolluted, unprofaned, unstained, unsullied, untouched, virgin, whole.

antonym sullied.

invisible *adj* concealed, disguised, hidden, imperceptible, inappreciable, inconspicuous, indetectable, indiscernible, infinitesimal, microscopic, out of sight, unperceivable, unseeable, unseen.

antonym visible.

invitation *n* allurement, asking, begging, bidding, call, challenge, come-on, coquetry, enticement, exhortation, glad eye, incitement, inducement, invite, overture, provocation, request, solicitation, summons, supplication, temptation.

invite *v* allure, ask, ask for, attract, beckon, beg, bid, bring on, call, court, draw, encourage, entice, lead, provoke, request, seek, solicit, summon, tempt, welcome.

antonyms force, order.

inviting *adj* alluring, appealing, appetising, attractive, beguiling, captivating, delightful, engaging, enticing, fascinating, intriguing, magnetic, mouthwatering, pleasing, seductive, tantalising, tempting, warm, welcoming, winning.

antonym uninviting.

invocation *n* appeal, beseeching, conjuration, entreaty, epiclasis, imploration, petition, prayer, supplication.

invoke *v* adjure, appeal to, apply, base on, beg, beseech, call upon, conjure, conjure up, entreat, implement, implore, initiate, petition, pray, put into effect, refer to, resort to, solicit, supplicate, use.

involuntary *adj* automatic, blind, compulsory, conditioned, forced, instinctive, instinctual, obligatory, reflex, reluctant, spontaneous, unconscious, uncontrolled, unintentional, unthinking, unwilled, unwilling, vegetative.

antonym voluntary.

involve *v* absorb, affect, associate, bind, commit, comprehend, comprise, compromise, concern, connect, contain, cover, draw in, embrace, engage, engross, entail, grip, hold, implicate, imply, include, incorporate, incriminate, inculpate, mean, mix up, necessitate, number among, preoccupy, presuppose, require, rivet, take in, touch.

involved *adj* anfractuous, caught up/in, complex, complicated, concerned, confusing, convoluted, difficult, elaborate, implicated, in on, intricate, knotty, labyrinthine, mixed up in/with, occupied, participating, sophisticated, tangled, tortuous.

antonyms simple, uninvolved.

involvement *n* association, commitment, complexity, complication, concern, connection, dedication, difficulty, embarrassment, entanglement, imbroglio, implication, interest, intricacy, participation, problem, ramification, responsibility.

invulnerability *n* impenetrability, inviolability, safety, security, strength, unassailability.

antonym vulnerability.

invulnerable *adj* impenetrable, indestructible, insusceptible, invincible, proof against, safe, secure, unassailable, unwoundable.

antonym vulnerable.

inward *adj* confidential, entering, hidden, inbound, incoming, inflowing, ingoing, inly, inmost, inner, innermost, inpouring, inside, interior, internal, penetrating, personal, private, privy, secret.

antonyms external, outward.

inwardly *adv* at heart, deep down, in gremio, in pectore, in petto, inly, inside, privately, secretly, to oneself, within.

antonyms externally, outwardly.

iota *n* atom, bit, drop, grain, hint, jot, mite, particle, scintilla, scrap, smidgeon, soupçon, speck, tittle, trace, whit.

IOU *n* debenture.

irascibility *n* asperity, bad temper, cantankerousness, choler, crabbiness, crossness, edginess, fieriness, ill-temper, impatience, irritability, irritation, petulance, shortness, snappishness, testiness, touchiness.

antonym placidness.

irascible *adj* bad-tempered, cantankerous, choleric, crabbed, crabby, cross, hasty, hot-tempered, ill-natured, ill-tempered, iracund, iracundulous, irritable, narky, peppery, petulant, prickly, quick-tempered, short-tempered, testy, touchy, volcanic.

antonym placid.

irate *adj* angered, angry, annoyed, enraged, exasperated, fuming, furibund, furious, gusty, in a paddy, incensed, indignant, infuriated, ireful, irritated, livid, mad, piqued, provoked, riled, up in arms, waxy, worked up, wrathful, wroth.

antonym calm.

ire *n* anger, annoyance, choler, displeasure, exasperation, fury, indignation, passion, rage, wax, wrath.

antonym calmness.

iridescence *n* glittering, iridisation, opalescence, reflet, shimmering.

iridescent *adj* glittering, iridial, iridian, irisated, irised, nacreous, opalescent, opaline, pearly, polychromatic, prismatic, rainbow, rainbow-coloured, rainbow-like, shimmering, shot.

iris *n* flag, fleur-de-lis, gladdon.

Irish *adj* green, Hibernian, Milesian.

irk *v* aggravate, annoy, bug, disgust, distress, gall, get, get to, irritate, miff, nettle, peeve, provoke, put out, rile, rub up the wrong way, ruffle, vex, weary.

antonym please.

irksome *adj* aggravating, annoying, boring, bothersome, burdensome, disagreeable, exasperating, infuriating, irritating, tedious, tiresome, troublesome, trying, vexatious, vexing, wearisome.

antonym pleasing.

iron *adj* adamant, cruel, fast-binding, fixed, grating, hard, harsh, heavy, immovable, implacable, indomitable, inflexible, insensitive, obdurate, rigid, robust, steel, steely, strong, tough, unbending, unyielding.

antonyms pliable, weak.

v flatten, press, smooth, uncrease.

n flatiron, goose.

iron out clear up, deal with, eliminate, eradicate, erase, expedite, fix, get rid of, harmonise, put right, reconcile, resolve, settle, smooth over, solve, sort out, straighten out.

ironic *adj* contemptuous, derisive, incongruous, ironical, irrisory, mocking, paradoxical, sarcastic, sardonic, satirical, scoffing, scornful, sneering, wry.

irons *n* bilboes, bonds, chains, fetters, gyves, manacles, shackles, trammels.

irony *n* asteism, contrariness, incongruity, irrision, mockery, paradox, sarcasm, satire.

irradiate *v* brighten, enlighten, expose, illume, illuminate, illumine, light up, lighten, radiate, shine on.

irrational *adj* aberrant, absurd, alogical, brainless, crazy, demented, foolish, illogical, injudicious, insane, mindless, muddle-headed, nonsensical, preposterous, raving, senseless, silly, unreasonable, unreasoning, unsound, unstable, unthinking, unwise, wild.

antonym rational.

irrationality *n* absurdity, brainlessness, illogicality, insanity, lunacy, madness, preposterousness, senselessness, unreason, unreasonableness, unsoundness.

antonym rationality.

irreconcilable *adj* clashing, conflicting, hardline, implacable, incompatible, incongruous, inconsistent, inexorable, inflexible, intransigent, opposed, unappeasable, uncompromising, unreconcilable.

antonym reconcilable.

irrecoverable *adj* irreclaimable, irredeemable, irremediable, irreparable, irretrievable, lost, unrecoverable, unsalvageable, unsavable.

antonym recoverable.

irrefutable *adj* apod(e)ictic, certain, impregnable, incontestable, incontrovertible, indisputable, indubitable, invincible, irrebuttable, irrefragable, irresistible, sure, unanswerable, unassailable, undeniable, ungainsayable, unquestionable.

antonym refutable.

irregular *adj* abnormal, anomalistic(al), anomalous, asymmetrical, broken, bumpy, capricious, craggy, crooked, difform, disconnected, disorderly, eccentric, erratic, exceptional, extraordinary, extravagant, fitful, fluctuating, fragmentary, haphazard, holey, immoderate, improper, inappropriate, incondite, inordinate, intermittent, jagged, lop-sided, lumpy, occasional, odd, patchy, peculiar, pitted, queer, quirky, ragged, random, rough, serrated, shifting, snatchy, spasmodic, sporadic, uncertain, unconventional, unequal, uneven, unofficial, unorthodox, unprocedural, unpunctual, unsteady, unsuitable, unsymmetrical, unsystematic, unusual, variable, wavering.

antonyms conventional, regular, smooth.

irregularity *n* aberration, abnormality, anomaly, asymmetry, breach, bumpiness, confusion, crookedness, desultoriness, deviation, difformity, disorderliness, disorganisation, eccentricity, freak, haphazardness, heterodoxy, jaggedness, lop-sidedness, lumpiness, malfunction, malpractice, oddity, patchiness, peculiarity, raggedness, randomness, roughness, singularity, uncertainty, unconventionality, unevenness, unorthodoxy, unpunctuality, unsteadiness.

antonyms conventionality, regularity, smoothness.

irregularly *adv* anyhow, by fits and starts, disconnectedly, eccentrically, erratically, fitfully, haphazardly, intermittently, jerkily, now and again, occasionally, off and on, spasmodically, unevenly, unmethodically.

antonym regularly.

irrelevance *n* inappositeness, inappropriateness, inaptness, inconsequence, irrelevancy, unimportance.

antonym relevance.

irrelevant *adj* alien, extraneous, foreign, immaterial, impertinent, inapplicable, inapposite, inappropriate, inapt, inconsequent, inessential, peripheral, tangential, unapt, unconnected, unnecessary, unrelated.

antonym relevant.

irreligious *adj* agnostic, atheistic, blasphemous, free-thinking, godless, heathen, heathenish, iconoclastic, impious, irreverent, nullifidian, pagan, profane, rationalistic, sacrilegious, sceptical, sinful, unbelieving, undevout, ungodly, unholy, unreligious, unrighteous, wicked.

antonyms pious, religious.

irremediable *adj* deadly, fatal, final, hopeless, incorrigible, incurable, inoperable, irrecoverable, irredeemable, irreparable, irretrievable, irreversible, mortal, remediless, terminal, unmedicinable.

antonym remediable.

irremovable *adj* durable, fast, fixed, immovable, indestructible, ineradicable, ingrained, inoperable, obdurate, obstinate, permanent, persistent, rooted, set, stuck.

antonym removable.

irreparable *adj* incurable, irreclaimable, irrecoverable, irremediable, irretrievable, irreversible, unrepairable.

antonyms recoverable, remediable.

irreplaceable *adj* essential, indispensable, inimitable, invaluable, matchless, peerless, priceless, sublime, unique, unmatched, vital.

antonym replaceable.

irrepressible *adj* boisterous, bubbling over, buoyant, ebullient, effervescent, inextinguishable, insuppressible, resilient, uncontainable, uncontrollable, ungovernable, uninhibited, unmanageable, unquenchable, unrestrainable, unstoppable.

antonyms depressed, depressive, despondent, resistible.

irreproachable *adj* blameless, faultless, guiltless, immaculate, impeccable, inculpable, innocent, irreprehensible, irreprovable, perfect, pure, reproachless, stainless, taintless, unblemished, unimpeachable.

antonyms blameworthy, culpable.

irresistible *adj* alluring, beckoning, beguiling, charming, compelling, enchanting, fascinating, imperative, ineluctable, inescapable, inevitable, inexorable, overmastering, overpowering, overwhelming, potent, pressing, ravishing, resistless, seductive, tempting, unavoidable, uncontrollable, urgent.

antonyms avoidable, resistible.

irresolute *adj* dithering, doubtful, faint-hearted, fickle, fluctuating, half-hearted, hesitant, hesitating, indecisive, infirm, shifting, shilly-shallying, swithering, tentative, undecided, undetermined, unsettled, unstable, unsteady, vacillating, variable, wavering, weak.

antonym resolute.

irresolution *n* dithering, faint-heartedness, fluctuation, half-heartedness, hesitancy, hesitation, inconsistency, inconstancy, indecisiveness, infirmity, infirmness, shifting, shilly-shally, shilly-shallying, tentativeness, uncertainty, unsteadiness, vacillation, wavering.

antonym resolution.

irresponsible *adj* carefree, careless, feather-brained, feckless, flibbertigibbit, flighty, foot-loose, giddy, harebrained, harum-scarum, heedless, ill-considered, immature, light-hearted, madcap, negligent, rash, reckless, scatter-brained, shiftless, thoughtless, undependable, unreliable, untrustworthy, wild.

antonym responsible.

irretrievable *adj* damned, hopeless, irrecoverable, irredeemable, irremediable, irreparable, irreversible, irrevocable, lost, unrecallable, unrecoverable, unsalvageable.

antonyms recoverable, reversible.

irreverence *n* blasphemy, cheek, cheekiness, derision, discourtesy, disrespect, disrespectfulness, flippancy, godlessness, iconoclasm, impertinence, impiety, impudence, levity, mockery, profanity, sauce.

antonym reverence.

irreverent *adj* blasphemous, cheeky, contemptuous, derisive, discourteous, disrespectful, flip, flippant, godless, iconoclastic, impertinent, impious, impudent, mocking, profane, rude, sacrilegious, saucy, tongue-in-cheek.

antonym reverent.

irreversible *adj* final, hopeless, immedicable, incurable, inoperable, irremediable, irreparable, irretrievable, irrevocable, lasting, lost, permanent, remediless, unalterable, unmedicinable.

antonyms curable, remediable, reversible.

irrevocable *adj* changeless, fated, fixed, hopeless, immutable, inexorable, invariable, irremediable, irrepealable, irretrievable, irreversible, predestined, predetermined, settled, unalterable, unchangeable.

antonyms alterable, flexible, mutable, reversible.

irrigate *v* dampen, flood, humect, humify, inundate, moisten, water, wet.

irritability *n* edge, edginess, erethism, fractiousness, fretfulness, hypersensitivity, ill-humour, ill-temper, impatience, irascibility, peevishness, petulance, prickliness, testiness, tetchiness, touchiness.

antonyms bonhomie, cheerfulness, complacence, good humour.

irritable *adj* bad-tempered, cantankerous, captious, choleric, crabbed, crabby, cross, crotchety, crusty, edgy, feisty, fractious, fretful, hasty, hypersensitive, ill-humoured, ill-tempered, impatient, irascible, narky, nettlesome, peevish, petulant, prickly, querulous, short, short-tempered, snappish, snappy, snarling, sore, tense, testy, te(t)chy, thin-skinned, touchy.

antonyms cheerful, complacent.

irritant *n* annoyance, bore, bother, goad, menace, nuisance, pain, pest, pin-prick, plague, provocation, rankle, tease, thorn in the flesh, trouble, vexation.

antonyms pleasure, sop, sweetness.

irritate *v* acerbate, aggravate, anger, annoy, bedevil, bother, bug, chafe, emboil, enrage, exacerbate, exasperate, faze, fret, get on one's nerves, get to, give the pip, gravel, grig, harass, incense, inflame, infuriate, intensify, irk, needle, nettle, offend, pain, peeve, pester, pique, provoke, put out, rankle, rile, rouse, rub, ruffle, vex.

antonyms gratify, mollify, placate, please.

irritated *adj* angry, annoyed, bothered, cross, discomposed, displeased, edgy, exasperated, fazed, flappable, flustered, harassed, impatient, irked, irritable, nettled, peeved, piqued, put out, ratty, riled, roused, ruffled, uptight, vexed.

antonyms composed, gratified, pleased.

irritating *adj* abrasive, aggravating, annoying, bothersome, displeasing, disturbing, galling, infuriating, irksome, maddening, nagging, pesky, pesterous, pestful, pestiferous, pestilent, pestilential, plaguey, provoking, thorny, troublesome, trying, upsetting, urticant, vexatious, vexing, worrisome.

antonyms pleasant, pleasing.

irritation *n* aggravation, anger, annoyance, crossness, displeasure, dissatisfaction, exasperation, fury, goad, impatience, indignation, irritability, irritant, itch, nuisance, pain, pain in the neck, pest, pin-prick, provocation, rankle, resentment, shortness, snappiness, tease, testiness, vexation, wrath.

antonyms pleasure, satisfaction.

island *n* ait, atoll, cay, eyot, holm, inch, isle, islet, key.

isolate *v* abstract, cut off, detach, disconnect, divorce, exclude, identify, insulate, keep apart, ostracise, pinpoint, quarantine, remove, seclude, segregate, separate, sequester, set apart.

antonyms assimilate, incorporate.

isolated *adj* abnormal, anomalous, atypical, backwoods, deserted, detached, dissociated, eremitic, exceptional, freak, godforsaken, hermitical, hidden, incommunicado, insular, lonely, monastic, outlying, out-of-the-way, random, reclusive, remote, retired, secluded, single, solitary, special, sporadic, unfrequented, unique, unrelated, untrodden, untypical, unusual, unvisited.

antonyms populous, typical.

isolation *n* aloofness, detachment, disconnection, dissociation, exile, insularity, insulation, lazaretto, loneliness, quarantine, reclusion, remoteness, retirement, seclusion, segregation, self-sufficiency, separation, solitariness, solitude, withdrawal.

issue[1] *n* affair, argument, concern, controversy, crux, debate, matter, point, problem, question, subject, topic.

issue[2] *n* announcement, broadcast, circulation, copy, delivery, dispersal, dissemination, distribution, edition, emanation, flow, granting, handout, impression, instalment, issuance, issuing, number, printing, promulgation, propagation, publication, release, supply, supplying, vent.

v announce, broadcast, circulate, deal out, deliver, distribute, emit, give out, mint, produce, promulgate, publicise, publish, put out, release, supply.

issue[3] *n* conclusion, consequence, culmination, dénouement, effect, end, finale, outcome, pay-off, product, result, termination, upshot.

v arise, burst forth, debouch, emanate, emerge, flow, leak, originate, proceed, rise, spring, stem.

issue[4] *n* brood, children, descendants, heirs, offspring, progeny, scions, seed, young.

itch *v* crawl, prickle, tickle, tingle, yuke.

n cacoethes, craving, desire, eagerness, formication, hankering, hunger, irritation, itchiness, keenness, longing, lust, passion, prickling, scabies, tingling, yearning, yen.

itching *adj* aching, avid, burning, dying, eager, greedy, hankering, impatient, inquisitive, itch, longing, raring, spoiling.

itchy *adj* avaricious, eager, edgy, fidgety, greedy, impatient, restive, restless, roving, unsettled, yuky.

item *n* account, article, aspect, bulletin, component, consideration, detail, element, entry, factor, feature, ingredient, matter, minute, note, notice, object, paragraph, particular, piece, point, report, thing.

itemise *v* count, detail, document, enumerate, instance, inventory, list, mention, number, overname, particularise, record, specify, tabulate.

itinerancy *n* drifting, nomadism, peregrination, roaming, rootlessness, roving, travelling, vagabondism, vagrancy, wandering, wanderlust, wayfaring.

itinerant *adj* ambulatory, drifting, journeying, migratory, nomadic, peregrinatory, peripatetic, rambling, roaming, rootless, roving, travelling, vagabond, vagrant, wandering, wayfaring.

antonyms settled, stationary.

n diddicoy, dusty-foot, gypsy, hobo, nomad, perigrinator, peripatetic, piepowder, pilgrim, Romany, tinker, toe-rag, tramp, traveller, vagabond, vagrant, wanderer, wayfarer.

itinerary *n* circuit, course, journey, line, plan, programme, route, schedule, tour.

J

jab *v* dig, elbow, jag, lunge, nudge, poke, prod, punch, push, shove, stab, tap, thrust.

jabber *v* babble, blather, blether, chatter, drivel, gab, gabble, gash, jaw, mumble, prate, rabbit, ramble, tattle, witter, yap.

jacket *n* blouson, case, casing, coat, cover, covering, envelope, folder, jerkin, jupon, mackinaw, sheath, shell, skin, wrap, wrapper, wrapping.

jackpot *n* award, big time, bonanza, kitty, pool, pot, prize, reward, stakes, winnings.

jade *n* baggage, broad, draggle-tail, floosie, harridan, hussy, nag, shrew, slattern, slut, strumpet, tart, trollop, vixen, wench.

jaded *adj* blunted, bored, cloyed, disjaskit, dulled, effete, exhausted, fagged, fatigued, played-out, satiated, spent, surfeited, tired, tired out, weary.

antonyms fresh, refreshed.

jag *n* barb, denticle, dentil, notch, point, projection, protrusion, snag, spur, tooth.

jagged *adj* barbed, broken, craggy, denticulate, hackly, indented, irregular, notched, pointed, ragged, ridged, rough, saw-edged, serrate, serrated, snagged, snaggy, spiked, spiky, toothed, uneven.

antonym smooth.

jail, gaol *n* borstal, bridewell, brig, calaboose, can, cells, choky, clink, cooler, coop, custody, guardhouse, hoos(e)gow, house of correction, inside, jailhouse, jankers, jug, lock-up, nick, pen, penitentiary, pokey, porridge, prison, quod, reformatory, slammer, stir, tollbooth.

v confine, detain, immure, impound, imprison, incarcerate, intern, lock up, quod, send down.

jailer, gaoler *n* captor, guard, keeper, prison officer, screw, turnkey, warden, warder.

jam[1] *v* block, clog, compact, confine, congest, cram, crowd, crush, force, obstruct, pack, press, ram, sandwich, squash, squeeze, stall, stick, stuff, throng, thrust, vice, wedge.

n bottle-neck, concourse, crowd, crush, gridlock, herd, horde, mass, mob, multitude, pack, press, swarm, throng, traffic jam.

jam[2] *n* bind, contretemps, difficulty, dilemma, fix, hitch, hole, hot water, imbroglio, impasse, pickle, plight, predicament, quandary, scrape, spot, straits, tangle, tight corner, trouble.

jam[3] *n* confiture, confyt, conserve, jelly, marmalade, preserve, spread.

jamboree *n* carnival, carouse, celebration, convention, festival, festivity, fête, field day, frolic, gathering, get-together, jubilee, junket, merriment, party, potlatch, rally, revelry, shindig, spree.

jangle *v* chime, clank, clash, clatter, jar, jingle, rattle, upset, vibrate.

n cacophony, clang, clangour, clash, din, dissonance, jar, racket, rattle, reverberation, stridence, stridency, stridor.

antonyms euphony, harmony.

janitor *n* caretaker, concierge, custodian, doorkeeper, doorman, janitress, janitrix, ostiary, porter.

jar[1] *n* amphora, aquamanile, bellarmine, can, carafe, container, crock, cruet, cruse, ewer, flagon, jug, kang, mug, olla, pitcher, pot, receptacle, stamnos, stoup, urn, vase, vessel.

jar[2] *v* agitate, annoy, clash, convulse, disagree, discompose, disturb, grate, grind, interfere, irk, irritate, jangle, jolt, nettle, offend, quarrel, rasp, rattle, rock, shake, upset, vibrate.

n clash, disagreement, discord, dissonance, grating, irritation, jangle, jolt, quarrel, rasping, wrangling.

jargon *n* argot, balderdash, baragouin, bunkum, cant, computerese, criminalese, dialect, diplomatese, double-Dutch, drivel, gabble, gibberish, gobbledegook, gobbledygook, Greek, idiom, jive, lingo, mumbo-jumbo, nonsense, palaver, parlance, patois, rigmarole, slang, tongue, twaddle, vernacular.

jarring *adj* cacophonous, discordant, dissonant, disturbing, grating, horrisonant, irritating, jangling, jolting, rasping, strident, upsetting.

jaundiced *adj* biased, bitter, cynical, disbelieving, distorted, distrustful, envious, hostile, jaded, jealous, misanthropic, partial, pessimistic, preconceived, prejudiced, resentful, sceptical, suspicious.

antonyms fresh, naïve, optimistic.

jaunty *adj* airy, breezy, buoyant, carefree, cheeky, chipper, dapper, debonair, gay, high-spirited, insouciant, lively, perky, self-confident, showy, smart, sparkish, sprightly, spruce, trim.

antonyms anxious, depressed, dowdy, seedy.

jaw[1] *n* chops, dewlap, flews, jaws, mandible, masticator, maw, maxilla, mouth, muzzle, proboscis, trap.

jaw² *v* abuse, babble, censure, chat, chatter, criticise, gab, gabble, gossip, lecture, prate, revile, scold, talk.

n chat, chinwag, conversation, discussion, gab, gossip, natter, talk.

jazz *n* bebop, blues, boogie, boogie-woogie, crap, Dixieland, guff, hard rock, heavy metal, lies, New Wave, ragtime, rhythm, rock, spiel, swing, talk.

jazzy *adj* animated, avant-garde, bold, fancy, flashy, gaudy, goey, lively, smart, snazzy, spirited, stylish, swinging, vivacious, wild, zestful.

antonyms conservative, prosaic, square.

jealous *adj* anxious, apprehensive, attentive, careful, covetous, desirous, emulous, envious, green, green-eyed, grudging, guarded, heedful, invidious, mistrustful, possessive, proprietorial, protective, resentful, rival, solicitous, suspicious, vigilant, wary, watchful, zealous.

jealousy *n* covetousness, distrust, emulation, envy, grudge, heart-burning, ill-will, mistrust, possessiveness, resentment, spite, suspicion, vigilance, watchfulness, zelotypia.

jeer *v* banter, barrack, chaff, contemn, deride, explode, fleer, flout, flyte, gibe, heckle, hector, knock, mock, rail, razz, ridicule, scoff, sneer, taunt, twit.

n abuse, aspersion, catcall, chaff, derision, dig, fleer, flyte, flyting, gibe, hiss, hoot, mockery, raillery, raspberry, ridicule, scoff, sneer, taunt, thrust.

jejune *adj* arid, banal, barren, callow, childish, colourless, dry, dull, empty, foolish, immature, impoverished, inane, insipid, juvenile, meagre, naïve, pointless, prosaic, puerile, senseless, silly, simple, spiritless, trite, uninteresting, unoriginal, unsophisticated, vapid, wishy-washy.

antonyms mature, meaningful.

jell, gel *v* coagulate, congeal, crystallise, finalise, form, gee, gel, gelatinate, gelatinise, harden, jelly, materialise, set, solidify, take form, take shape, thicken.

antonym disintegrate.

jeopardise *v* chance, endanger, expose, gamble, hazard, imperil, jeopard, menace, risk, stake, threaten, venture.

antonyms protect, safeguard.

jeopardy *n* danger, endangerment, exposure, hazard, imperilment, insecurity, liability, peril, plight, precariousness, risk, venture, vulnerability.

antonyms safety, security.

jerk¹ *n* bounce, jog, jolt, lurch, pluck, pull, shrug, throw, thrust, tug, tweak, twitch, wrench, yank.

v bounce, flirt, jigger, jog, jolt, jounce, lurch, peck, pluck, pull, shrug, throw, thrust, tug, tweak, twitch, wrench, yank.

jerk² *n* bum, clod, clot, clown, creep, dimwit, dolt, dope, fool, halfwit, idiot, klutz, ninny, prick, schlep, schmo, schmuck, twit.

jerky *adj* bouncy, bumpy, convulsive, disconnected, fitful, incoherent, jolting, jumpy, rough, shaky, spasmodic, tremulous, twitchy, uncontrolled, unco-ordinated.

antonym smooth.

jerry-built *adj* cheap, cheapjack, defective, faulty, flimsy, insubstantial, ramshackle, rickety, shoddy, slipshod, unsubstantial.

antonyms firm, stable, substantial.

jersey *n* guernsey, jumper, lammy, pullover, sweater, sweat-shirt, woolly.

jest *n* banter, bon mot, clowning, cod, crack, desipience, foolery, fooling, fun, gag, hoax, jape, jeu d'esprit, joke, josh, kidding, leg-pull, pleasantry, prank, quip, sally, sport, trick, trifling, waggery, wisecrack, witticism.

v banter, chaff, clown, deride, fool, gibe, jeer, joke, josh, kid, mock, quip, scoff, tease, trifle.

jester *n* buffoon, clown, comedian, comic, droll, fool, goliard, harlequin, humorist, joculator, joker, juggler, merry-andrew, merryman, motley, mummer, pantaloon, patch, prankster, quipster, wag, wit, zany.

jet¹ *n* atomiser, flow, fountain, gush, issue, nose, nozzle, rose, rush, spout, spray, sprayer, spring, sprinkler, spurt, squirt, stream, surge.

jet² *adj* atramentous, black, coal-black, ebon, ebony, inky, jetty, pitch-black, pitchy, raven, sable, sloe, sooty.

jetsam *n* jetsom, jetson, lagan, waif, wreckage.

jettison *v* abandon, chuck, discard, ditch, dump, eject, expel, heave, offload, scrap, unload.

antonyms load, take on.

jetty *n* breakwater, dock, groyne, jutty, mole, pier, quay, wharf.

jewel *n* bijou, brilliant, charm, find, flower, gaud, gem, gemstone, humdinger, locket, masterpiece, ornament, paragon, pearl, precious stone, pride, prize, rarity, rock, sparkler, stone, treasure, wonder.

jewellery *n* bijouterie, bijoux, finery, gauds, gemmery, gems, jewels, ornaments, regalia, treasure, trinkets.

Jezebel *n* Delilah, femme fatale, harlot, hussy, jade, man-eater, scarlet woman, seductress, temptress, vamp, wanton, whore, witch.

jib *v* back off, balk, recoil, refuse, retreat, shrink, stall, stop short.

jibe, gibe *v* deride, fleer, flout, jeer, mock, rail, ridicule, scoff, scorn, sneer, taunt, twit.

n barb, crack, derision, dig, fleer, fling, jeer, mockery, poke, quip, raillery, ridicule, sarcasm, scoff, slant, sneer, taunt, thrust.

jiffy *n* flash, instant, minute, moment, no time, sec, second, split second, tick, trice, twinkling, two shakes, two ticks, whiff.

antonym age.

jig *v* bob, bobble, bounce, caper, hop, jerk, jiggle, jounce, jump, prance, shake, skip, twitch, wiggle, wobble.

jigger *v* balls up, botch up, break, bugger up, destroy, kibosh, louse up, make a pig's ear of, queer, ruin, scupper, spoil, undermine, vitiate, wreck.

jiggery-pokery *n* chicanery, deceit, deception, dishonesty, fraud, funny business, hanky-panky, monkey-business, subterfuge, trickery.

jiggle *v* agitate, bounce, fidget, jerk, jig, jog, joggle, shake, shift, shimmy, twitch, waggle, wiggle, wobble.

jilt *v* abandon, betray, brush off, chuck, deceive, desert, discard, ditch, drop, forsake, reject, repudiate, spurn, throw over.

antonym cleave to.

jingle[1] *v* chime, chink, clatter, clink, jangle, rattle, ring, tink, tinkle, tintinnabulate.

n clang, clangour, clink, rattle, reverberation, ringing, tink, tinkle, tintinnabulation.

jingle[2] *n* chant, chime, chorus, couplet, ditty, doggerel, limerick, melody, poem, rhyme, song, tune, verse.

jingoism *n* chauvinism, flag-waving, imperialism, insularity, nationalism, parochialism, patriotism, xenophobia.

jinx *n* black magic, charm, curse, evil eye, gremlin, hex, hoodoo, jettatura, Jonah, plague, spell, voodoo.

v bedevil, bewitch, curse, doom, hex, hoodoo, plague.

jitters *n* anxiety, fidgets, habdabs, heebie-jeebies, jimjams, nerves, nervousness, tenseness, the creeps, the shakes, the shivers, the willies.

jittery *adj* agitated, anxious, edgy, fidgety, flustered, jumpy, nervous, panicky, perturbed, quaking, quivering, shaky, shivery, trembling, uneasy.

antonyms calm, composed, confident.

job *n* activity, affair, allotment, assignment, batch, business, calling, capacity, career, charge, chore, commission, concern, consignment, contract, contribution, craft, duty, employment, enterprise, errand, function, livelihood, lot, message, métier, mission, occupation, office, output, part, piece, place, portion, position, post, proceeding, product, profession, project, province, pursuit, responsibility, role, share, situation, stint, task, trade, undertaking, venture, vocation, work.

jobless *adj* idle, inactive, laid off, on the dole, out of work, unemployed, unoccupied, unused, workless.

antonym employed.

jockey *v* cajole, coax, ease, edge, engineer, finagle, induce, inveigle, manage, manipulate, manoeuvre, negotiate, wheedle.

jocose *adj* blithe, comical, droll, facetious, funny, humorous, jesting, jocular, jocund, jovial, joyous, lepid, merry, mirthful, mischievous, playful, pleasant, sportive, teasing, waggish, witty.

antonym morose.

jocular *adj* amusing, arch, blithe, comical, desipient, droll, entertaining, facetious, frolicsome, funny, humorous, jesting, jocose, jocund, joking, jolly, jovial, merry, playful, roguish, sportive, teasing, waggish, whimsical, witty.

antonym serious.

jocularity *n* absurdity, comicality, desipience, drollery, facetiousness, fooling, gaiety, hilarity, humour, jesting, jocoseness, jocosity, jolliness, joviality, laughter, merriment, playfulness, pleasantry, roguishness, sport, sportiveness, teasing, waggery, waggishness, whimsicality, whimsy, wit.

jog[1] *v* activate, arouse, bounce, jar, jerk, joggle, jolt, jostle, jounce, nudge, poke, prod, prompt, push, remind, rock, shake, shove, stimulate, stir.

n jerk, jiggle, jolt, nudge, poke, prod, push, reminder, shake, shove.

jog[2] *v, n* bump, canter, dogtrot, jogtrot, lope, lumber, pad, run, trot.

joie de vivre blitheness, bounce, buoyancy, cheerfulness, ebullience, enjoyment, enthusiasm, gaiety, get-up-and-go, gusto, joy, joyfulness, merriment, mirth, pleasure, relish, zest.

antonym depression.

join *v* abut, accompany, accrete, add, adhere, adjoin, affiliate, alligate, amalgamate, annex, append, associate, attach, border, border on, butt, cement, coincide, combine, compaginate, conglutinate, conjoin, conjugate, connect, couple, dock, enlist, enrol, enter, fasten, knit, link, march with, marry, meet, merge, reach, sign up, splice, team, tie, touch, unite, verge on, yoke.

antonyms leave, separate.

join in chip in, contribute, co-operate, help, lend a hand, muck in, partake, participate, pitch in.

join up enlist, enroll, enter, sign up, take the king's shilling.

joint[1] *n* articulation, commissure, connection, geniculation, gimmel, ginglymus, gomphosis, hinge, intersection, junction, juncture, knot, nexus, node, seam, union.

adj adjunct, amalgamated, collective, combined, communal, concerted, consolidated, co-operative, co-ordinated, joined, mutual, shared, united.

v articulate, carve, connect, couple, cut up, dismember, dissect, divide, fasten, fit, geniculate, join, segment, sever, sunder, unite.

joint[2] *n* dance-hall, dive, haunt, honky-tonk, jerry-shop, night-club, place, pub.

joint[3] *n* reefer, roach, stick.

jointed *adj* articulate, geniculate(d), gimmelled.

joke *n* buffoon, butt, clown, conceit, concetto, frolic, fun, funny, gag, guy, hoot, jape, jest, jeu d'esprit, lark, laughing-stock, play, pun, quip, quirk, sally, simpleton, sport, target, whimsy, wisecrack, witticism, yarn, yell.

v banter, chaff, clown, deride, fool, frolic, gambol, jest, kid, laugh, mock, quip, ridicule, spoof, taunt, tease, wisecrack.

joke-book *n* jest-book, Joe Miller.

joker *n* buffoon, card, character, clown, comedian, comic, droll, humorist, jester, joculator, jokesmith, kidder, prankster, sport, trickster, wag, wit.

jollification *n* beanfeast, beano, celebration, frolic, jollity, junket, knees-up, merriment, merry-making, party, rave-up, shindig, spree, thrash.

antonym lamentation.

jolly *adj* blithe, blithesome, buxom, carefree, cheerful, cheery, convivial, exuberant, festive, frisky, frolicsome, funny, gay, gladsome, happy, hearty, hilarious, jaunty, jocund, jovial, joyful, joyous, jubilant, merry, mirthful, playful, sportive, sprightly, sunny.

antonym sad.

jolt *v* astonish, bounce, bump, discompose, disconcert, dismay, disturb, jar, jerk, jog, jostle, jounce, knock, nonplus, perturb, push, shake, shock, shove, stagger, startle, stun, surprise, upset.

n blow, bolt from the blue, bombshell, bump, hit, impact, jar, jerk, jog, jump, lurch, quiver, reversal, setback, shake, shock, start, surprise, thunderbolt.

jostle *v* bump, butt, crowd, elbow, force, hustle, jog, joggle, jolt, press, push, rough up, scramble, shake, shoulder, shove, squeeze, throng, thrust.

jot *n* ace, atom, bit, detail, fraction, gleam, glimmer, grain, hint, iota, mite, morsel, particle, scintilla, scrap, smidgen, speck, tittle, trace, trifle, whit.

jot down enter, list, note, record, register, scribble, take down, write down.

journal *n* book, chronicle, commonplace, daily, daybook, diary, ephemeris, gazette, log, magazine, monthly, newspaper, organ, paper, periodical, publication, record, register, review, tabloid, waste-book, weekly.

journalism *n* copy-writing, correspondence, feature-writing, Fleet Street, fourth estate, gossip-writing, Grub Street, news, press, reportage, reporting, writing.

journalist *n* broadcaster, chronicler, columnist, commentator, contributor, correspondent, diarist, feature-writer, hack, hackette, hatchet man, journo, newshound, newsman, newspaperman, news-writer, periodicalist, pressman, reporter, scribe, stringer, sub, subeditor.

journey *n* career, course, excursion, expedition, eyre, hadj, itinerary, jaunt, odyssey, outing, passage, peregrination, pilgrimage, progress, raik, ramble, route, safari, tour, travel, trek, trip, voyage, wanderings.

v fare, fly, gallivant, go, jaunt, peregrinate, proceed, ramble, range, roam, rove, safari, tour, tramp, travel, traverse, trek, voyage, wander, wend.

journeyer *n* hadji, peregrinator, pilgrim, rambler, tourist, traveller, trekker, tripper, viator, voyager, wanderer, wayfarer.

joust *n* contest, encounter, engagement, pas d'armes, skirmish, tilt, tournament, tourney, trial.

jovial *adj* affable, airy, animated, blithe, buoyant, cheery, convivial, cordial, ebullient, expansive, Falstaffian, gay, glad, happy, hilarious, jaunty, jocose, jocund, jolly, jubilant, merry, mirthful.

antonyms morose, sad, saturnine.

joviality *n* affability, buoyancy, cheerfulness, cheeriness, ebullience, fun, gaiety, gladness, glee, happiness, hilarity, jollity, merriment, mirth.

antonyms moroseness, sadness.

joy *n* blessedness, bliss, charm, delight, ecstasy, elation, exaltation, exultation, felicity, festivity, gaiety, gem, gladness, gladsomeness, glee, gratification, happiness, hilarity, jewel, joyance, joyfulness, joyousness, pleasure, pride, prize, rapture, ravishment, satisfaction, seel, transport, treasure, treat, triumph, wonder.

antonyms mourning, sorrow.

joyful *adj* blithe, blithesome, delighted, ecstatic, elated, enraptured, glad, gladsome, gratified, happy, jocund, jolly, jovial, jubilant, light-hearted, merry, pleased, rapturous, satisfied, seely, transported, triumphant.

antonyms mournful, sorrowful.

joyless *adj* bleak, cheerless, dejected, depressed, despondent, discouraged, discouraging, dismal, dispirited, doleful, dour, downcast, dreary, forlorn, gloomy, glum, grim, miserable, sad, sombre, sunless, unhappy.

antonym joyful.

joyous *adj* cheerful, ecstatic, festal, festive, frabjous, glad, gladsome, gleeful, happy, joyful, jubilant, merry, rapturous.

antonym sad.

jubilant *adj* celebratory, delighted, elated, enraptured, euphoric, excited, exuberant, exultant, flushed, glad, gratified, joyous, over the moon, overjoyed, rejoicing, thrilled, triumphal, triumphant.

antonyms defeated, depressed.

jubilation *n* celebration, ecstasy, elation, euphoria, excitement, exultation, festivity, jamboree, jollification, joy, jubilee, triumph.

antonyms depression, lamentation.

jubilee *n* anniversary, carnival, celebration, commemoration, festival, festivity, fête, gala, holiday.

Judas *n* betrayer, deceiver, quisling, renegade, tergiversator, traitor, turncoat.

judge *n* adjudicator, alcalde, arbiter, arbiter elegantiae, arbitrator, arbitratrix, assessor, authority, beak, connoisseur, critic, Daniel, deemster, dempster, doomster, elegantiarum, evaluator, expert, hakim, justice, justiciar, justiciary, Law Lord, magistrate, mediator, moderator, pundit, referee, umpire, virtuoso, wig.

v adjudge, adjudicate, appraise, appreciate, arbitrate, ascertain, assess, conclude, condemn, consider, criticise, decern, decide, decree, determine, dijudicate, discern, distinguish, doom, esteem, estimate, evaluate, examine, find, gauge, mediate, opine, rate, reckon, referee, review, rule, sentence, sit, try, umpire, value.

judgement *n* acumen, appraisal, arbitration, arrêt, assessment, assize, award, belief, common sense, conclusion, conviction, damnation, decision, decree, decreet, deduction, determination, diagnosis, discernment, discretion, discrimination, doom, enlightenment, estimate, expertise, fate, fetwa, finding, intelligence, mediation, misfortune, opinion, order, penetration, perceptiveness, percipience, perspicacity, prudence, punishment, result, retribution, ruling, sagacity, sense, sentence, shrewdness, taste, understanding, valuation, verdict, view, virtuosity, wisdom.

judicial *adj* critical, decretory, discriminating, distinguished, forensic, impartial, judiciary, juridical, legal, magisterial, magistral, official.

judicious *adj* acute, astute, canny, careful, cautious, circumspect, considered, diplomatic, discerning, discreet, discriminating, enlightened, expedient, informed, percipient, perspicacious, politic, prescient, prudent, rational, reasonable, sagacious, sage, sane, sapient, sensible, shrewd, skilful, sober, sound, thoughtful, wary, well-advised, well-judged, well-judging, wise.

antonym injudicious.

jug *n* amphora, aquamanile, bellarmine, blackjack, carafe, churn, container, crock, ewer, flagon, jar, pitcher, stoup, urn, vessel.

juggle *v* alter, change, cook, disguise, doctor, fake, falsify, fix, hocus-pocus, manipulate, manoeuvre, misrepresent, modify, rig, tamper with.

juice *n* essence, extract, fluid, latex, liquid, liquor, nectar, sap, secretion, serum, succus.

juicy *adj* colourful, gamy, interesting, lactiferous, lush, moist, naughty, provocative, racy, risqué, salacious, sappy, scatological, sensational, serous, spicy, succose, succous, succulent, suggestive, vivid, watery.

antonym dry.

jumble *v* confuse, disarrange, disarray, disorder, disorganise, mingle-mangle, mix, mix up, muddle, shuffle, tangle, tumble, wuzzle.

antonym order.

n agglomeration, chaos, clutter, collection, confusion, congeries, conglomeration, disarrangement, disarray, disorder, farrago, gallimaufry, hotch-potch, medley, mess, mingle-mangle, miscellany, mishmash, mixture, mix-up, muddle, olio, olla-podrida, pastiche, pot-pourri, raffle, salad.

jumbled *adj* chaotic, confused, disarrayed, disordered, disorganised, mingle-mangle, miscellaneous, mixed-up, muddled, shuffled, tangled, tumbled, unsorted, untidy.

antonym orderly.

jump[1] *v* bounce, bound, caper, clear, dance, frisk, frolic, gambol, hop, hurdle, jig, leap, pounce, prance, skip, spring, vault.

n bounce, bound, capriole, curvet, dance, frisk, frolic, gambado, hop, jeté, leap, pounce, prance, saltation, skip, spring, vault.

jump[2] *v* avoid, bypass, digress, disregard, evade, ignore, leave out, miss, omit, overshoot, pass over, skip, switch.

n breach, break, gap, hiatus, interruption, interval, lacuna, lapse, omission, saltation, saltus, switch.

jump[3] *v* advance, appreciate, ascend, boost, escalate, gain, hike, increase, mount, rise, spiral, surge.

n advance, ascent, augmentation, boost, escalation, increase, increment, mounting, rise, upsurge, upturn.

jump[4] *v* flinch, jerk, jump out of one's skin, leap in the air, quail, recoil, resile, shrink, start, wince.

n jar, jerk, jolt, lurch, quiver, shiver, shock, spasm, start, swerve, twitch, wrench.

jump[5] *n* barricade, barrier, fence, gate, hedge, hurdle, impediment, obstacle, pons asinorum, rail.

jump at accept, agree to, fall for, grab, pounce on, seize, snatch, swallow, swoop on.

antonym recoil.

jump on berate, blame, castigate, censure, chide, criticise, fly at, flyte, rate, rebuke, reprimand, reproach, reprove, revile, scold, tick off, upbraid.

jumper *n* guernsey, jersey, lammy, pullover, sweater, sweat-shirt, woolly.

jumping *adj* desultory, disconnected, incoherent, jumpy, salient, saltatorial, saltatorious, saltatory, saltigrade, unco-ordinated.

jumpy *adj* agitated, anxious, apprehensive, discomposed, edgy, fidgety, jittery, nervous, nervy, restive, restless, shaky, tense, tremulous, uneasy.

antonyms calm, composed.

junction *n* abutment, combination, confluence, conjunction, connection, coupling, disemboguement, intersection, interstice, join, joining, joint, juncture, linking, meeting-point, nexus, seam, union.

juncture *n* bond, conjunction, connection, convergence, crisis, crux, emergency, intersection, join, joining, junction, link, minute, moment, nexus, occasion, period, point, predicament, seam, stage, time, union, weld.

junior *adj* inferior, lesser, lower, minor, puisne, secondary, subordinate, subsidiary, younger.

antonym senior.

junk *n* clutter, debris, detritus, dregs, garbage, litter, oddments, refuse, rejectamenta, rubbish, rummage, scrap, trash, waste, wreckage.

junta *n* cabal, camarilla, cartel, clique, combination, conclave, confederacy, convocation, coterie, council, crew, faction, gang, league, oligarchy, party, ring, set.

jurisdiction *n* area, authority, bailiwick, bounds, cognisance, command, control, domination, dominion, field, influence, judicature, orbit, power, prerogative, province, range, reach, rule, scope, sovereignty, sphere, sway, verge, zone.

jury *n* jurors, jurymen, jurywomen, panel, tales, talesmen, veniremen.

just *adj* accurate, apposite, appropriate, apt, blameless, condign, conscientious, correct, decent, deserved, disinterested, due, equitable, even-handed, exact, fair, fair-minded, faithful, fitting, four-square, good, honest, honourable, impartial, impeccable, irreproachable, justified, lawful, legitimate, merited, normal, precise, proper, pure, reasonable, regular, right, righteous, rightful, sound, suitable, true, unbiased, unimpeachable, unprejudiced, upright, virtuous, well-deserved.

antonym unjust.

justice[1] *n* amends, appositeness, appropriateness, compensation, correction, dharma, equitableness, equity, fairness, honesty, impartiality, integrity, justifiableness, justness, law, legality, legitimacy, nemesis, penalty, propriety, reasonableness, recompense, rectitude, redress, reparation, requital, right, rightfulness, rightness, satisfaction.

antonym injustice.

justice[2] *n* beak, JP, judge, Justice of the Peace, justiciar, magistrate.

justifiable *adj* acceptable, allowable, defensible, excusable, explainable, explicable, fit, forgivable, justified, lawful, legitimate, licit, maintainable, pardonable, proper, reasonable, right, sound, tenable, understandable, valid, vindicable, warrantable, warranted, well-founded.

antonyms culpable, illicit, unjustifiable.

justification *n* absolution, apology, approval, authorisation, basis, defence, exculpation, excuse, exoneration, explanation, extenuation, foundation, grounds, mitigation, palliation, plea, rationalisation, reason, substance, vindication, warrant.

justify *v* absolve, acquit, condone, confirm, defend, establish, exculpate, excuse, exonerate, explain, forgive, legalise, legitimise, maintain, pardon, substantiate, support, sustain, uphold, validate, vindicate, warrant.

justly *adv* accurately, condignly, conscientiously, correctly, duly, equally, equitably, even-handedly, fairly, honestly, impartially, lawfully, legitimately, objectively, properly, rightfully, rightly.

antonym unjustly.

jut *v* beetle, bulge, extend, impend, overhang, poke, project, protrude, stick out.

antonym recede.

juvenile *n* adolescent, boy, child, girl, halfling, infant, kid, minor, young person, youngster, youth.

antonym adult.

adj adolescent, babyish, boyish, callow, childish, girlish, immature, impressionable, inexperienced, infantile, jejune, puerile, tender, undeveloped, unsophisticated, young, youthful.

antonym mature.

juxtaposition *n* adjacency, closeness, contact, contiguity, immediacy, nearness, propinquity, proximity, vicinity.

antonyms dissociation, separation.

K

kaleidoscopic *adj* changeable, ever-changing, fluctuating, fluid, manifold, many-coloured, many-splendoured, mobile, motley, multicoloured, multifarious, poikilitic, polychromatic, polychrome, variegated.

antonyms dull, monochrome, monotonous.

kaput *adj* broken, conked out, dead, defunct, destroyed, extinct, fini, finished, phut, ruined, smashed, undone, wrecked.

keel over black out, capsize, collapse, crumple, drop, faint, fall, founder, go out like a light, overturn, pass out, stagger, swoon, topple over, upset.

keen *adj* acid, acute, anxious, ardent, argute, assiduous, astute, avid, biting, brilliant, canny, caustic, clever, cutting, devoted, diligent, discerning, discriminating, eager, earnest, ebullient, edged, enthusiastic, fervid, fierce, fond, forthright, gleg, impassioned, incisive, industrious, intense, intent, mordant, penetrating, perceptive, perfervid, perspicacious, piercing, pointed, pungent, quick, razorlike, sagacious, sapient, sardonic, satirical, scathing, sedulous, sensitive, sharp, shrewd, shrill, tart, trenchant, wise, zealous.

antonyms apathetic, blunt, dull.

keenness *n* acerbity, anxiety, ardour, assiduity, astuteness, avidity, avidness, canniness, cleverness, diligence, discernment, eagerness, earnestness, ebullience, enthusiasm, fervour, forthrightness, harshness, impatience, incisiveness, industriousness, industry, insight, intensity, intentness, mordancy, passion, penetration, perfervidity, pungency, rigour, sagacity, sapience, sedulity, sensitivity, severity, sharpness, shrewdness, sternness, trenchancy, virulence, wisdom, zeal, zest.

antonyms apathy, bluntness, dullness.

keep[1] *v* accumulate, amass, carry, collect, conserve, control, deal in, deposit, furnish, garner, hang on to, heap, hold, hold on to, maintain, pile, place, possess, preserve, retain, stack, stock, store.

keep an eye on guard, keep tabs on, keep under surveillance, look after, look to, monitor, observe, regard, scrutinise, supervise, survey, watch.

keep at be steadfast, beaver away at, carry on, complete, continue, drudge, endure, finish, grind, labour, last, maintain, persevere, persist, plug away at, remain, slave, slog at, stay, stick at, toil.

antonyms abandon, neglect.

keep on carry on, continue, endure, hold on, keep at it, last, maintain, persevere, persist, prolong, remain, retain, soldier on, stay, stay the course.

keep on at badger, chivvy, dun, go on at, harass, harry, importune, nag, pester, plague, pursue.

keep one's distance avoid, be aloof, give a wide berth, keep at arm's length, keep oneself to oneself, shun, withdraw.

keep secret conceal, dissemble, hide, keep back, keep dark, keep under one's hat, keep under wraps, suppress, wash one's dirty linen at home.

antonym reveal.

keep track of follow, grasp, keep up with, monitor, oversee, plot, record, trace, track, understand, watch.

keep up be on a par with, compete, contend, continue, emulate, equal, keep pace, maintain, match, pace, persevere, preserve, rival, support, sustain, vie.

keep[2] *v* be responsible for, board, care for, defend, feed, foster, guard, have charge of, have custody of, look after, maintain, manage, mind, nourish, nurture, operate, protect, provide for, provision, safeguard, shelter, shield, subsidise, support, sustain, tend, victual, watch, watch over.

n board, food, livelihood, living, maintenance, means, nourishment, nurture, subsistence, support, upkeep.

keep[3] *v* arrest, block, check, constrain, control, curb, delay, detain, deter, hamper, hamstring, hinder, hold, hold back, hold up, impede, inhibit, interfere with, keep back, limit, obstruct, prevent, restrain, retard, shackle, stall, trammel, withhold.

keep back censor, check, conceal, constrain, control, curb, delay, hide, hold back, hush up, impede, limit, prohibit, quell, ration, reserve, restrain, restrict, retain, retard, stifle, stop, suppress, withhold.

keep in bottle up, conceal, confine, control, detain, hide, inhibit, keep back, quell, restrain, retain, stifle, stop up, suppress.

antonyms declare, release.

keep[4] *v* adhere to, celebrate, commemorate, comply with, fulfil, hold, honour, keep faith with, keep up, maintain, obey, observe, perform, perpetuate, recognise, respect, ritualise, solemnise.

keep[5] *n* castle, citadel, donjon, dungeon, fastness, fort, fortress, motte, peel-house, peel-tower, stronghold, tower.

keeper *n* attendant, caretaker, conservator, conservatrix, curator, custodian, defender, gaoler, governor, guard, guardian, inspector, jailer, mahout, nab, overseer, steward, superintendent, supervisor, surveyor, warden, warder.

keeping *n* accord, accordance, aegis, agreement, auspices, balance, care, charge, compliance, conformity, congruity, consistency, correspondence, cure, custody, guardianship, harmony, keep, maintenance, obedience, observance, patronage, possession, proportion, protection, safe-keeping, supervision, surveillance, trust, tutelage, ward.

keepsake *n* emblem, favour, memento, pledge, relic, remembrance, reminder, souvenir, token.

keg *n* barrel, butt, cask, drum, firkin, hogshead, puncheon, round, rundlet, tierce, tun, vat.

ken *n* acquaintance, appreciation, awareness, cognisance, compass, comprehension, field, grasp, knowledge, notice, perception, range, reach, realisation, scope, sight, understanding, view, vision.

kerchief *n* babushka, bandana, cravat, fichu, headscarf, headsquare, kaffiyeh, madras, neck-cloth, neckerchief, scarf, shawl, square, sudary, veronica.

kernel *n* core, essence, germ, gist, grain, heart, marrow, nitty-gritty, nub, pith, seed, substance.

key *n* answer, clavis, clue, code, crib, cue, digital, explanation, glossary, guide, index, indicator, interpretation, lead, means, pointer, secret, sign, solution, table, translation.

adj basic, cardinal, central, chief, core, crucial, decisive, essential, fundamental, hinge, important, leading, main, major, pivotal, principal, salient.

key in capture, input, load, process, store.

keynote *n* accent, centre, core, emphasis, essence, flavour, flavour of the month, gist, heart, kernel, leitmotiv, marrow, motif, pith, stress, substance, theme.

keystone *n* base, basis, core, cornerstone, crux, foundation, fundamental, ground, linchpin, mainspring, motive, principle, quoin, root, source, spring.

kick *v* abandon, boot, break, desist from, drop, foot, give up, leave off, leave out, punt, quit, spurn, stop, toe.

n bite, buzz, dash, élan, enjoyment, excitement, feeling, force, fun, gratification, gusto, intensity, panache, pep, pizzazz, pleasure, power, punch, pungency, relish, snap, sparkle, stimulation, strength, tang, thrill, verve, vitality, zest, zing, zip.

kick off begin, break the ice, commence, get under way, inaugurate, initiate, introduce, open, open the proceedings, set the ball rolling, start.

kick out chuck out, defenestrate, discharge, dismiss, eject, evict, expel, get rid of, give the bum's rush, oust, reject, remove, sack, throw out, toss out.

kick-off *n* beginning, bully-off, commencement, face-off, inception, introduction, opening, outset, start, word go.

kid[1] *n* babe, baby, bairn, bambino, boy, child, dandiprat, girl, halfling, infant, juvenile, kiddy, lad, nipper, shaver, stripling, teenager, tot, wean, whippersnapper, youngster, youth.

kid[2] *v* bamboozle, befool, beguile, con, cozen, delude, dupe, fool, gull, have on, hoax, hoodwink, humbug, jest, joke, josh, mock, pretend, pull someone's leg, put one over on, rag, ridicule, tease, trick.

kidnap *v* abduct, capture, hijack, rape, remove, seize, skyjack, snatch, steal.

kidnapped *adj* abducted, enlevé, hijacked, rapt, seized, stolen.

kidnapping *n* abduction, child-stealing, enlevement, kidnap, plagium, rape, seizure.

kill *v* abolish, annihilate, assassinate, beguile, bump off, butcher, cancel, cease, deaden, defeat, destroy, dispatch, do away with, do in, do to death, eliminate, eradicate, execute, exterminate, extinguish, extirpate, fill, finish off, halt, kibosh, knock off, knock on the head, liquidate, mar, martyr, massacre, murder, napoo, neutralise, nip in the bud, nullify, obliterate, occupy, pass, pip, put to death, quash, quell, rub out, ruin, scotch, slaughter, slay, smite, smother, spoil, stifle, still, stonker, stop, suppress, top, veto, vitiate, while away, zap.

n climax, conclusion, coup de grâce, death, death-blow, dénouement, dispatch, end, finish, mop-up, shoot-out.

killer *n* assassin, butcher, cut-throat, destroyer, executioner, exterminator, fratricide, gunman, hatchet man, hit-man, homicide, infanticide, liquidator, matricide, murderer, parricide, patricide, regicide, ripper, shootist, slaughterer, slayer, sororicide, triggerman, uxoricide.

killing[1] *n* assassination, bloodshed, carnage, elimination, ethnocide, execution, extermination, fatality, fratricide, homicide, infanticide, liquidation, mactation, manslaughter, massacre, matricide, murder, parricide, patricide, pogrom, regicide, slaughter, slaying, sororicide, thuggee, uxoricide.

adj deadly, death-dealing, deathly, debilitating, enervating, exhausting, fatal, fatiguing, final, lethal, lethiferous, mortal, mortiferous, murderous, prostrating, punishing, tiring, vital.

killing[2] *n* big hit, bomb, bonanza, bunce, clean-up, coup, fortune, gain, hit, lucky break, profit, success, windfall, winner.

killing[3] *adj* absurd, amusing, comical, funny, hilarious, ludicrous, side-splitting, uproarious.

killjoy *n* complainer, cynic, dampener, damper, grouch, misery, moaner, pessimist, prophet of doom, sceptic, spoil-sport, trouble-mirth, Weary Willie, wet blanket, whiner.

antonyms enthusiast, optimist, sport.

kin *n* affines, affinity, blood, clan, connection, connections, consanguinity, cousins, extraction, family, flesh and blood, kindred, kinsfolk, kinship, kinsmen, kith, lineage, people, relations, relationship, relatives, stock, tribe.

adj affine, akin, allied, close, cognate, congener, connected, consanguine, consanguineous, interconnected, kindred, linked, near, related, similar, twin.

kind[1] *n* brand, breed, category, character, class, description, essence, family, genus, habit, ilk, kidney, manner, mould, nature, persuasion, race, set, sort, species, stamp, style, temperament, type, variety.

kind[2] *adj* accommodating, affectionate, altruistic, amiable, amicable, avuncular, beneficent, benevolent, benign, benignant, bonhomous, boon, bounteous, bountiful, brotherly, charitable, clement, compassionate, congenial, considerate, cordial, courteous, diplomatic, fatherly, friendly, generous, gentle, giving, good, gracious, hospitable, humane, indulgent, kind-hearted, kindly, lenient, loving, mild, motherly, neighbourly, obliging, philanthropic, propitious, sisterly, soft-boiled, soft-hearted, sweet, sympathetic, tactful, tender-hearted, thoughtful, understanding.

antonyms cruel, inconsiderate, unhelpful.

kind-hearted *adj* altruistic, amicable, benign, big-hearted, compassionate, considerate, generous, good-hearted, good-natured, gracious, helpful, humane, humanitarian, kind, kindly, obliging, philanthropic, sympathetic, tender-hearted, warm, warm-hearted.

antonym ill-natured.

kindle *v* activate, actuate, agitate, animate, arouse, awaken, deflagrate, enkindle, exasperate, excite, fan, fire, foment, ignite, incite, induce, inflame, initiate, inspire, inspirit, light, provoke, rouse, set alight, sharpen, stimulate, stir, thrill.

kindliness *n* amiability, beneficence, benevolence, benignity, charity, compassion, friendliness, generosity, kindness, loving-kindness, sympathy, warmth.

antonyms cruelty, meanness, unkindness.

kindly *adj* benefic, beneficent, beneficial, benevolent, benign, charitable, comforting, compassionate, cordial, favourable, generous, genial, gentle, giving, good-natured, good-willy, hearty, helpful, indulgent, kind, mild, patient, pleasant, polite, sympathetic, tender, warm.

adv agreeably, charitably, comfortingly, considerately, cordially, generously, gently, graciously, indulgently, patiently, politely, tenderly, thoughtfully.

antonyms cruel, inconsiderate, uncharitable, unpleasant.

kindness *n* affection, aid, aloha, altruism, amiability, assistance, benefaction, beneficence, benevolence, benignity, bonhomie, bounty, charity, chivalry, clemency, compassion, cordiality, courtesy, favour, forbearance, friendliness, gallantry, generosity, gentilesse, gentleness, good will, goodness, grace, help, hospitality, humaneness, humanity, indulgence, kindliness, liberality, loving-kindness, magnanimity, mildness, munificence, obligingness, patience, philanthropy, service, tenderness, tolerance, understanding.

antonyms cruelty, illiberality, inhumanity.

kindred *n* affines, affinity, clan, connections, consanguinity, family, flesh, folk, kin, kinsfolk, kinship, kinsmen, lineage, people, relations, relationship, relatives.

adj affiliated, affine, akin, allied, cognate, common, congenial, connected, corresponding, kin, like, matching, related, similar.

king *n* boss, chief, chieftain, doyen, emperor, kingpin, leading light, luminary, majesty, monarch, overlord, paramount, patriarch, potentate, prince, royalet, ruler, sovereign, supremo, suzerain.

kingdom *n* area, commonwealth, country, division, domain, dominion, dynasty, empire, field, land, monarchy, nation, palatinate, principality, province, realm, reign, royalty, sovereignty, sphere, state, territory, tract.

kingly *adj* august, basilical, glorious, grand, grandiose, imperial, imperious, imposing, lordly, majestic, monarchical, noble, regal, royal, sovereign, splendid, stately, sublime, supreme.

kink[1] *n* bend, coil, complication, corkscrew, crick, crimp, defect, dent, difficulty, entanglement, flaw, hitch, imperfection, indentation, knot, loop, tangle, twist, wrinkle.

v bend, coil, crimp, curl, tangle, twist, wrinkle.

kink[2] *n* caprice, crotchet, eccentricity, fetish, foible, freak, idiosyncracy, idiosyncrasy, oddity, quirk, singularity, vagary, whim.

kinky[1] *adj* coiled, crimped, crumpled, curled, curly, frizzy, tangled, twisted, wrinkled.

kinky[2] *adj* bizarre, capricious, crotchety, degenerate, depraved, deviant, eccentric, freakish, idiosyncratic, licentious, odd, outlandish, peculiar, perverted, queer, quirky, strange, unconventional, unnatural, warped, weird, whimsical.

kinsfolk *n* affines, clan, connections, cousins, family, kin, kindred, kinsmen, relations, relatives.

kinship *n* affinity, alliance, association, bearing, community, conformity, connection, consanguinity, correspondence, kin, relation, relationship, similarity.

kinsman *n* affine, cousin, relation, relative.

kiosk *n* bookstall, booth, box, cabin, counter, hut, news-stand, stall, stand.

kismet *n* destiny, doom, fate, fortune, joss, karma, lot, portion, predestiny, providence, weird.

kiss[1] *v* buss, canoodle, neck, osculate, peck, salute, smooch, snog.

n buss, osculation, peck, plonker, salute, smack, smacker, snog.

kiss[2] *v* brush, caress, fan, glance, graze, lick, scrape, touch.

kit *n* accoutrements, apparatus, appurtenances, baggage, effects, equipage, equipment, gear, impedimenta, implements, instruments, luggage, matériel, muniments, outfit, paraphernalia, provisions, rig, rig-out, set, supplies, tackle, tools, trappings, traps, utensils.

kit out accoutre, arm, deck out, dight, dress, equip, fit out, fix up, furnish, habilitate, outfit, prepare, supply.

kittenish *adj* arch, coquettish, coy, cute, flirtatious, frisky, frolicsome, playful, sportive.

antonym staid.

knack *n* ability, adroitness, aptitude, bent, capacity, dexterity, expertise, expertness, facility, faculty, flair, forte, genius, gift, handiness, hang, ingenuity, propensity, quickness, skilfulness, skill, talent, trick, trick of the trade, turn.

knapsack *n* backpack, bag, dufflebag, haversack, musette, pack, rucksack, tuckerbag.

knave *n* bastard, blackguard, blighter, bounder, cheat, dastard, drôle, fripon, rapscallion, rascal, reprobate, rogue, rotter, scallywag, scamp, scapegrace, scoundrel, stinker, swindler, swine, varlet, villain.

knavery *n* chicanery, corruption, deceit, deception, devilry, dishonesty, double-dealing, duplicity, fraud, friponnerie, hanky-panky, imposture, knavishness, mischief, monkey-business, rascality, roguery, ropery, trickery, villainy.

knavish *adj* contemptible, corrupt, damnable, dastardly, deceitful, deceptive, devilish, dishonest, dishonourable, fiendish, fraudulent, furciferous, lying, mischievous, rascally, reprobate, roguish, scoundrelly, unprincipled, unscrupulous, villainous, wicked.

antonyms honest, honourable, scrupulous.

knead *v* form, knuckle, manipulate, massage, mould, ply, press, rub, shape, squeeze, work.

kneel *v* fall to one's knees, genuflect.

knell *n* chime, knoll, peel, ringing, sound, tintinnabulation, toll.

knickers *n* bloomers, breeks, briefs, Directoire knickers, drawers, knickerbockers, panties, pants, smalls, underwear.

knick-knack *n* bagatelle, bauble, bibelot, bric-à-brac, gadget, gaud, gewgaw, gimcrack, gismo, jimjam, kickshaw, object of virtu, plaything, pretty, pretty-pretty, quip, rattle-trap, toy, trifle, trinket, whigmaleerie, whim-wham.

knife *n* blade, carver, chakra, chiv, cutter, dagger, dah, flick-knife, jack-knife, machete, parang, pen-knife, pocket-knife, skean, skene, skene-dhu, skene-occle, switchblade, whittle.

v cut, impale, lacerate, pierce, rip, slash, stab, wound.

knight *n* cavalier, champion, chevalier, free-lance, gallant, horseman, kemper, kempery-man, knight-at-arms, knight-errant, man-at-arms, preux chevalier, ritter, soldier, warrior.

knightly *adj* bold, chivalrous, courageous, courtly, dauntless, gallant, gracious, heroic, honourable, intrepid, noble, soldierly, valiant, valorous.

antonyms cowardly, ignoble, ungallant.

knit *v* ally, bind, connect, crease, crotchet, fasten, furrow, heal, interlace, intertwine, join, knot, link, loop, mend, secure, tie, unite, weave, wrinkle.

knob *n* boll, boss, bump, caput, door-handle, knot, knub, knurl, lump, nub, projection, protrusion, protuberance, snib, stud, swell, swelling, tuber, tumour, umbo.

knock[1] *v* buffet, clap, cuff, ding, hit, knobble, (k)nubble, punch, rap, slap, smack, smite, strike, thump, thwack.

n blow, box, chap, clip, clout, con, cuff, hammering, rap, slap, smack, thump.

knock about[1] associate, go around, loaf, ramble, range, roam, rove, saunter, traipse, travel, wander.

knock about[2] abuse, bash, batter, beat up, biff, bruise, buffet, damage, hit, hurt, maltreat, manhandle, maul, mistreat.

knock down batter, clout, demolish, destroy, fell, floor, level, pound, prop, raze, smash, wallop, wreck.

knock off[1] cease, clock off, clock out, complete, conclude, finish, pack (it) in, stop, terminate.

knock off[2] deduct, filch, nick, pilfer, pinch, purloin, rob, steal, take away, thieve.

knock off[3] assassinate, bump off, do away with, do in, kill, liquidate, murder, rub out, slay, waste.

knock up achieve, build, construct, erect, make.

antonym demolish.

knock[2] *v* abuse, belittle, carp, cavil, censure, condemn, criticise, deprecate, disparage, find fault, lambaste, run down, slam, vilify, vilipend.

n blame, censure, condemnation, criticism, defeat, failure, rebuff, rejection, reversal, setback, stricture.

antonyms boost, praise.

knockout *n* bestseller, coup de grâce, hit, kayo, KO, sensation, smash, smash-hit, stunner, success, triumph, winner.

antonyms flop, loser.

knoll *n* barrow, hill, hillock, hummock, knowe, koppie, mound.

knot *v* bind, entangle, entwine, knit, loop, secure, tangle, tether, tie, weave.

n aggregation, bond, bow, braid, bunch, burl, clump, cluster, collection, connection, gnar, gnarl, heap, hitch, joint, knag, knar, knarl, ligature, loop, mass, pile, rosette, tie, tuft.

knotty *adj* anfractuous, baffling, bumpy, Byzantine, complex, complicated, difficult, gnarled, hard, intricate, knobby, knotted, mystifying, nodose, nodous, nodular, perplexing, problematical, puzzling, rough, rugged, thorny, tricky, troublesome.

know *v* apprehend, comprehend, discern, distinguish, experience, fathom, identify, intuit, ken, learn, make out, notice, perceive, realise, recognise, see, tell, undergo, understand, wist.

know-all *n* Besserwisser, clever-clogs, smart Alec, smarty-pants.

know-how *n* ability, adroitness, aptitude, capability, dexterity, experience, expertise, faculty, flair, gumption, ingenuity, knack, knowledge, proficiency, savoir-faire, savvy, skill, talent.

knowing *adj* acute, astute, aware, clever, competent, conscious, cunning, discerning, downy, eloquent, experienced, expert, expressive, gnostic, gnostical, hep, intelligent, meaningful, perceptive, qualified, sagacious, shrewd, significant, skilful, well-informed.

antonyms ignorant, obtuse.

knowingly *adv* consciously, deliberately, designedly, intentionally, on purpose, purposely, studiedly, wilfully, wittingly.

knowledge *n* ability, acquaintance, acquaintanceship, apprehension, book-learning, booklore, cognisance, cognition, comprehension, consciousness, cum-savvy, discernment, education, enlightenment, erudition, familiarity, gnosis, grasp, information, instruction, intelligence, intimacy, judgement, know-how, learning, multiscience, notice, pansophy, recognition, scholarship, schooling, science, tuition, understanding, wisdom.

antonym ignorance.

knowledgeable *adj* acquainted, au courant, au fait, aware, book-learned, bright, cognisant, conscious, conversant, educated, erudite, experienced, familiar, in the know, intelligent, learned, lettered, scholarly, well-informed.

antonym ignorant.

known *adj* acknowledged, admitted, avowed, celebrated, commonplace, confessed, familiar, famous, manifest, noted, obvious, patent, plain, published, recognised, well-known.

knuckle under accede, acquiesce, capitulate, defer, give in, give way, submit, succumb, surrender, truckle, yield.

kowtow *v* bow, court, cringe, defer, fawn, flatter, genuflect, grovel, kneel, pander, suck up, toady, truckle.

kudos *n* acclaim, applause, distinction, esteem, fame, glory, honour, laudation, laurels, plaudits, praise, prestige, regard, renown, repute.

L

label *n* badge, brand, categorisation, characterisation, classification, company, description, docket, epithet, mark, marker, sticker, tag, tally, ticket, trademark.

v brand, call, categorise, characterise, class, classify, define, describe, designate, docket, dub, identify, mark, name, stamp, tag.

laborious *adj* arduous, assiduous, backbreaking, burdensome, difficult, diligent, fatiguing, forced, hard, hard-working, heavy, herculean, indefatigable, industrious, laboured, onerous, operose, painstaking, persevering, ponderous, sedulous, strained, strenuous, tireless, tiresome, toilsome, tough, unflagging, uphill, wearing, wearisome.

antonyms easy, effortless, relaxing, simple.

labour[1] *n* chore, donkey-work, drudgery, effort, employees, exertion, grind, hands, industry, job, labor improbus, labourers, moil, pains, painstaking, slog, sweat, task, toil, undertaking, work, workers, workforce, workmen.

antonyms ease, leisure, relaxation, rest.

v drudge, endeavour, grind, heave, moil, pitch, plod, roll, slave, strive, struggle, suffer, sweat, toil, toss, travail, work.

antonyms idle, laze, loaf, lounge.

labour[2] *n* birth, childbirth, contractions, delivery, labour pains, pains, parturition, throes, travail.

v dwell on, elaborate, overdo, overemphasise, overstress, strain.

laboured *adj* affected, awkward, complicated, contrived, difficult, forced, heavy, overdone, overwrought, ponderous, stiff, stilted, strained, studied, unnatural.

antonyms easy, natural.

labourer *n* drudge, farm-hand, hand, hireling, hobbler, hobo, hodman, hunky, husbandman, land-girl, manual worker, navvy, redneck, worker, working man, workman.

labyrinth *n* circumvolution, coil, complexity, complication, convolution, entanglement, Gordian knot, intricacy, jungle, maze, perplexity, puzzle, riddle, tangle, windings.

labyrinthine *adj* Byzantine, complex, confused, convoluted, Daedalian, dedalian, faveolate, Gordian, intricate, involved, knotty, mazy, mizmaze, perplexing, puzzling, tangled, tortuous, winding.

antonyms simple, straightforward.

lace[1] *n* crochet, dentelle, filigree, mesh-work, netting, open-work, orris, tatting.

lace[2] *n* babiche, bootlace, cord, lanyard, shoelace, string, thong, tie.

v attach, bind, close, do up, fasten, intertwine, interweave, interwork, string, thread, tie.

lace[3] *v* add to, fortify, intermix, mix in, spike.

lacerate *v* afflict, claw, cut, distress, gash, ga(u)nch, harrow, jag, lancinate, maim, mangle, rend, rip, slash, tear, torment, torture, wound.

laceration *n* cut, gash, injury, lancination, maim, mutilation, rent, rip, slash, tear, wound.

lachrymose *adj* crying, dolorous, lugubrious, mournful, sad, sobbing, tearful, teary, weeping, weepy, woeful.

antonyms happy, laughing.

lack *n* absence, dearth, deficiency, deprivation, destitution, emptiness, insufficiency, need, privation, scantiness, scarcity, shortage, shortcoming, shortness, vacancy, void, want.

antonyms abundance, profusion.

v miss, need, require, want.

lackadaisical *adj* abstracted, apathetic, dreamy, dronish, dull, enervated, fainéant, half-hearted, idle, indifferent, indolent, inert, languid, languorous, lazy, lethargic, limp, listless, spiritless, supine.

antonyms active, dynamic, energetic, vigorous.

lackey *n* attendant, creature, fawner, flatterer, flunky, footman, gofer, hanger-on, instrument, manservant, menial, minion, parasite, pawn, servitor, sycophant, toady, tool, valet, yes-man.

lacking *adj* defective, deficient, flawed, impaired, inadequate, minus, missing, needing, sans, short of, wanting, without.

lacklustre *adj* boring, dim, drab, dry, dull, flat, leaden, lifeless, lustreless, mundane, muted, prosaic, sombre, spiritless, unimaginative, uninspired, vapid.

antonyms brilliant, polished.

laconic *adj* brief, close-mouthed, compact, concise, crisp, curt, pithy, sententious, short, succinct, taciturn, terse.

antonyms garrulous, verbose, wordy.

lacuna *n* blank, break, cavity, gap, hiatus, omission, space, void.

lad *n* boy, bucko, callant, chap, fellow, guy, halfling, juvenile, kid, laddie, nipper, schoolboy, shaver, stripling, youngster, youth.

laden *adj* burdened, charged, chock-a-block, chock-full, encumbered, fraught, full, hampered, jammed, loaded, oppressed, packed, stuffed, taxed, weighed down, weighted.

antonym empty.

la-di-da *adj* affected, conceited, foppish, high-falutin(g), mannered, mincing, over-refined, posh, precious, pretentious, put-on, snobbish, snooty, stuck-up, toffee-nosed, too-too.

ladies' man Casanova, Don Juan, gigolo, lady-killer, libertine, muff, poodle-faker, womaniser.

ladle *v* bail, dip, dish, lade, scoop, shovel, spoon.

ladle out disburse, dish out, distribute, dole out, hand out.

lady *n* begum, dame, damsel, don(n)a, Frau, gentlewoman, hidalga, madam(e), matron, memsahib, milady, noblewoman, Sen^•ora, signora, woman.

lady-killer *n* Casanova, Don Juan, heartbreaker, ladies' man, libertine, Lothario, philanderer, rake, roué, stud, wolf, womaniser.

ladylike *adj* courtly, cultured, decorous, elegant, genteel, matronly, modest, polite, proper, queenly, refined, respectable, well-bred.

lag *v* dawdle, delay, hang back, idle, linger, loiter, mosey, saunter, shuffle, straggle, tarry, trail.

antonym lead.

laggard *n* dawdler, idler, lingerer, loafer, loiterer, lounger, saunterer, slowcoach, slowpoke, slug-a-bed, sluggard, snail, straggler.

antonyms dynamo, go-getter, livewire.

lagoon *n* bayou, bog, fen, haff, lake, marsh, pond, pool, shallows, shoal, swamp.

laid up bedridden, disabled, hors de combat, housebound, ill, immobilised, incapacitated, injured, on the sick list, out of action, sick.

laid-back *adj* at ease, calm, casual, cool, easy-going, free and easy, passionless, relaxed, unflappable, unhurried, untroubled, unworried.

antonyms tense, uptight.

lair *n* burrow, den, earth, form, hideout, hole, nest, refuge, retreat, roost, sanctuary, stronghold.

lake *n* lagoon, loch, lochan, lough, mere, reservoir, tarn.

lam *v* batter, beat, clout, hit, knock, lambaste, leather, pelt, pound, pummel, strike, thrash, thump.

lambast *v* beat, berate, bludgeon, castigate, censure, cudgel, drub, flay, flog, leather, rebuke, reprimand, roast, scold, strike, thrash, upbraid, whip.

lambent *adj* brilliant, dancing, flickering, fluttering, gleaming, glistening, glowing, incandescent, licking, light, luminous, lustrous, radiant, refulgent, shimmering, sparkling, touching, twinkling.

lame *adj* crippled, defective, disabled, disappointing, feeble, flimsy, game, half-baked, halt, handicapped, hobbling, inadequate, insufficient, limping, poor, thin, unconvincing, unsatisfactory, weak.

v cripple, damage, disable, hamstring, hobble, hurt, incapacitate, injure, maim, wing.

lament *v* bemoan, bewail, beweep, complain, deplore, grieve, keen, mourn, regret, sorrow, wail, weep, yammer.

antonyms celebrate, rejoice.

n complaint, coronach, dirge, dumka, elegy, jeremiad, keening, lamentation, moan, moaning, monody, plaint, requiem, threnody, ululation, wail, wailing.

lamentable *adj* deplorable, disappointing, distressing, funest, grievous, inadequate, insufficient, low, meagre, mean, miserable, mournful, pitiful, poor, regrettable, sorrowful, tragic, unfortunate, unsatisfactory, woeful, wretched.

lamentation *n* deploration, dirge, grief, grieving, jeremiad, keen, keening, lament, moan, mourning, plaint, sobbing, sorrow, ululation, wailing, weeping.

antonyms celebration, rejoicing.

laminate *v* coat, cover, exfoliate, face, flake, foliate, layer, plate, separate, split, stratify, veneer.

lamp *n* beacon, flare, floodlight, lampad, lantern, light, limelight, searchlight, torch, veilleuse.

lampoon *n* burlesque, caricature, mickey-take, parody, Pasquil, Pasquin, pasquinade, satire, send-up, skit, spoof, squib, take-off.

v burlesque, caricature, make fun of, mock, parody, Pasquil, Pasquin, pasquinade, ridicule, satirise, send up, spoof, squib, take off, take the mickey out of.

lampooner *n* caricaturist, parodist, pasquilant, pasquiler, pasquinader, satirist.

land[1] *n* country, countryside, dirt, district, earth, estate, farmland, fatherland, ground, grounds, loam, motherland, nation, property, province, real estate, realty, region, soil, terra firma, territory, tract.

v alight, arrive, berth, bring, carry, cause, come to rest, debark, deposit, disembark, dock, drop, end up, plant, touch down, turn up, wind up.

land[2] *v* achieve, acquire, capture, gain, get, net, obtain, secure, win.

landlord *n* freeholder, host, hotelier, hotel-keeper, innkeeper, lessor, letter, owner, proprietor, publican.

antonym tenant.

landmark *n* beacon, boundary, cairn, feature, milestone, monument, signpost, turning-point, watershed.

lands *n* acreage, acres, demesne, estate(s), grounds, manor, policies, spread.

landscape *n* aspect, countryside, outlook, panorama, prospect, scene, scenery, view, vista.

landslide *n* avalanche, earthfall, éboulement, landslip, lauwine, rock-fall.

adj decisive, emphatic, overwhelming, runaway.

lane *n* alley(way), avenue, boreen, byroad, byway, channel, driveway, footpath, footway, gut, loan, passage(way), path(way), towpath, vennel, way, wynd.

language *n* argot, cant, conversation, dialect, diction, discourse, expression, idiolect, idiom, interchange, jargon, langue, lingo, lingua franca, parlance, parole, patois, phraseology, phrasing, speech, style, talk, terminology, tongue, utterance, vernacular, vocabulary, wording.

languid *adj* debilitated, drooping, dull, enervated, faint, feeble, heavy, inactive, indifferent, inert, lackadaisical, languorous, lazy, lethargic, limp, listless, pining, sickly, slow, sluggish, spiritless, torpid, unenthusiastic, uninterested, weak, weary.

antonyms alert, lively, vivacious.

languish *v* brood, decline, desire, despond, droop, fade, fail, faint, flag, grieve, hanker, hunger, long, mope, pine, repine, rot, sicken, sigh, sink, sorrow, suffer, sulk, want, waste, waste away, weaken, wilt, wither, yearn.

antonym flourish.

languishing *adj* brooding, declining, deteriorating, dreamy, drooping, droopy, fading, failing, flagging, longing, lovelorn, lovesick, melancholic, moping, nostalgic, pensive, pining, sickening, sinking, soulful, sulking, tender, wasting away, weak, weakening, wilting, wistful, withering, woebegone, yearning.

antonyms flourishing, thriving.

languor *n* apathy, asthenia, calm, debility, dreaminess, drowsiness, enervation, ennui, faintness, fatigue, feebleness, frailty, heaviness, hush, indolence, inertia, lassitude, laziness, lethargy, listlessness, lull, oppressiveness, relaxation, silence, sleepiness, sloth, stillness, torpor, weakness, weariness.

antonyms alacrity, gusto.

lank *adj* attenuated, drooping, dull, emaciated, flabby, flaccid, gaunt, lanky, lean, lifeless, limp, long, lustreless, rawboned, scraggy, scrawny, skinny, slender, slim, spare, straggling, thin.

antonym burly.

lanky *adj* angular, bony, gangling, gangly, gaunt, loose-jointed, rangy, rawboned, scraggy, scrawny, spare, tall, thin, twiggy, weedy.

antonyms short, squat.

lap[1] *v* drink, lick, sip, sup, tongue.

lap[2] *v* gurgle, plash, purl, ripple, slap, slosh, splash, swish, wash.

lap[3] *n* ambit, circle, circuit, course, distance, loop, orbit, round, tour.

v cover, encase, enfold, envelop, fold, surround, swaddle, swathe, turn, twist, wrap.

lapse *n* aberration, backsliding, break, caducity, decline, descent, deterioration, drop, error, failing, fall, fault, gap, indiscretion, intermission, interruption, interval, lull, mistake, negligence, omission, oversight, passage, pause, relapse, slip.

v backslide, decline, degenerate, deteriorate, drop, end, expire, fail, fall, run out, sink, slide, slip, stop, terminate, worsen.

lapsed *adj* discontinued, ended, expired, finished, invalid, obsolete, out of date, outdated, outworn, run out, unrenewed.

larceny *n* burglary, expropriation, heist, misappropriation, pilfering, piracy, purloining, robbery, stealing, theft.

large *adj* abundant, ample, big, broad, bulky, capacious, colossal, comprehensive, considerable, copious, decuman, enormous, extensive, full, generous, giant, gigantic, goodly, grand, grandiose, great, huge, immense, jumbo, king-sized, liberal, mammoth, man-sized, massive, monumental, outsize, Patagonian, plentiful, plonking, roomy, sizeable, spacious, spanking, substantial, sweeping, swingeing, tidy, vast, wide.

antonyms diminutive, little, slight, small, tiny.

largely *adv* abundantly, by and large, chiefly, considerably, extensively, generally, greatly, highly, mainly, mostly, predominantly, primarily, principally, widely.

largeness *n* bigness, breadth, broadness, bulk, bulkiness, dimension, enormity, enormousness, expanse, extent, greatness, heaviness, heftiness, height, immensity, magnitude, mass, massiveness, measure, mightiness, obesity, prodigiousness, size, vastness, wideness, width.

antonym smallness.

large-scale *adj* broad, country-wide, epic, expansive, extensive, far-reaching, global, nation-wide, sweeping, vast, wholesale, wide, wide-ranging.

antonym minor.

largess(e) *n* aid, allowance, alms, benefaction, bequest, bounty, charity, donation, endowment, generosity, gift, grant, handout, liberality, munificence, open-handedness, philanthropy, present.

antonym meanness.

lark *n* antic, caper, escapade, fling, fredaine, frolic, fun, gambol, game, gammock, guy, jape, mischief, prank, revel, rollick, romp, skylark, spree.

v caper, cavort, frolic, gambol, gammock, play, rollick, romp, skylark, sport.

lascivious *adj* bawdy, blue, coarse, crude, dirty, horny, indecent, lecherous, lewd, libidinous, licentious, lustful, obscene, offensive, Paphian, pornographic, prurient, randy, ribald, salacious, scurrilous, sensual, smutty, suggestive, tentiginous, unchaste, voluptuous, vulgar, wanton.

lash[1] *n* blow, cat, cat-o'-nine-tails, hit, quirt, stripe, stroke, swipe, whip.

v attack, beat, belabour, berate, birch, buffet, castigate, censure, chastise, criticise, dash, drum, flagellate, flay, flog, hammer, hit, horsewhip, knock, lace, lam, lambast, lampoon, larrup, pound, ridicule, satirise, scold, scourge, smack, strike, tear into, thrash, upbraid, welt, whip.

lash[2] *v* affix, bind, fasten, join, make fast, rope, secure, strap, tether, tie.

lass *n* bird, chick, colleen, damsel, girl, lassie, maid, maiden, miss, quean, quine, schoolgirl.

lassitude *n* apathy, drowsiness, dullness, enervation, ennui, exhaustion, fatigue, heaviness, languor, lethargy, listlessness, oscitancy, prostration, sluggishness, tiredness, torpor, weariness.

antonyms energy, vigour.

last[1] *adj* aftermost, closing, concluding, conclusive, definitive, extreme, final, furthest, hindmost, latest, rearmost, remotest, terminal, ultimate, utmost.

antonyms first, initial.

adv after, behind, finally, ultimately.

antonyms first, firstly.

n close, completion, conclusion, curtain, end, ending, finale, finish, termination.

antonyms beginning, start.

last word[1] final decision, final say, ultimatum.

last word[2] best, cream, crème de la crème, dernier cri, latest, ne plus ultra, perfection, pick, quintessence, rage, ultimate, vogue.

last[2] *v* abide, carry on, continue, endure, hold on, hold out, keep (on), perdure, persist, remain, stand up, stay, survive, wear.

last-ditch *adj* all-out, desperate, eleventh-hour, final, frantic, heroic, last-gasp, straining, struggling.

lasting *adj* abiding, continuing, deep-rooted, durable, enduring, immutable, indelible, indestructible, lifelong, long-standing, long-term, perennial, permanent, perpetual, sempiternal, unceasing, unchanging, undying, unending.

antonyms ephemeral, fleeting, short-lived.

lastly *adv* finally, in conclusion, in fine, in the end, to sum up, ultimately.

antonym firstly.

latch *n* bar, bolt, catch, fastening, hasp, hook, lock, sneck.

latch on to apprehend, attach oneself to, comprehend, twig, understand.

late[1] *adj* behind, behind-hand, belated, delayed, dilatory, last-minute, overdue, slow, tardy, unpunctual.

antonyms early, punctual.

adv behind-hand, belatedly, dilatorily, formerly, recently, slowly, tardily, unpunctually.

antonyms early, punctually.

late[2] *adj* dead, deceased, defunct, departed, ex-, former, old, past, preceding, previous.

lately *adv* formerly, heretofore, latterly, recently.

lateness *n* belatedness, delay, dilatoriness, retardation, tardiness, unpunctuality.

antonym earliness.

latent *adj* concealed, delitescent, dormant, hidden, inherent, invisible, lurking, potential, quiescent, secret, underlying, undeveloped, unexpressed, unrealised, unseen, veiled.

antonyms active, live, patent.

later *adv* after, afterwards, next, sequentially, subsequently, successively, thereafter.

antonym earlier.

lateral *adj* edgeways, flanking, marginal, oblique, side, sideward, sideways.

antonym central.

latest *adj* current, fashionable, in, modern, newest, now, ultimate, up-to-date, up-to-the-minute, with it.

antonym earliest.

lather[1] *n* bubbles, foam, froth, shampoo, soap, soap-suds, suds.

v foam, froth, shampoo, soap, whip up.

lather[2] *n* agitation, dither, fever, flap, fluster, flutter, fuss, pother, state, stew, sweat, tizzy, twitter.

lather[3] *v* beat, cane, drub, flog, lambast, lash, leather, strike, thrash, whip.

latitude *n* breadth, clearance, compass, elbow-room, extent, field, freedom, indulgence, laxity, leeway, liberty, licence, play, range, reach, room, scope, space, span, spread, sweep, width.

latrine *n* bog, head, jakes, outhouse, privy, rear, toilet.

latter *adj* closing, concluding, ensuing, last, last-mentioned, later, latest, modern, recent, second, succeeding, successive.

antonym former.

latterly *adv* hitherto, lately, of late, recently.

antonym formerly.

lattice *n* espalier, fret-work, grate, grating, grid, grille, lattice-work, mesh, network, open-work, reticulation, tracery, trellis, web.

laud *v* acclaim, applaud, approve, celebrate, extol, glorify, hail, honour, magnify, praise.

antonyms blame, condemn, curse, damn.

laudable *adj* admirable, commendable, creditable, estimable, excellent, exemplary, meritorious, of note, praiseworthy, sterling, worthy.

antonyms damnable, execrable.

laudation *n* acclaim, acclamation, accolade, adulation, blessing, celebrity, commendation, devotion, encomion, encomium, eulogy, extolment, glorification, glory, homage, kudos, paean, panegyric, praise, reverence, tribute, veneration.

antonyms condemnation, criticism.

laudatory *adj* acclamatory, adulatory, approbatory, approving, celebratory, commendatory, complimentary, encomiastic(al), epaenetic, eulogistic, glorifying, panegyrical.

antonym damning.

laugh *v* cachinnate, chortle, chuckle, crease up, fall about, giggle, guffaw, snicker, snigger, split one's sides, te(e)hee, titter, yok.

antonym cry.

n belly-laugh, card, case, caution, chortle, chuckle, clown, comedian, comic, cure, entertainer, giggle, guffaw, hoot, humorist, joke, lark, scream, snicker, snigger, te(e)hee, titter, wag, wit, yok.

laugh at belittle, deride, jeer, lampoon, make fun of, mock, ridicule, scoff at, scorn, take the mickey out of, taunt.

laugh off belittle, brush aside, dismiss, disregard, ignore, make little of, minimise, pooh-pooh, shrug off.

laughable *adj* absurd, amusing, comical, derisive, derisory, diverting, droll, farcical, funny, gelastic, hilarious, humorous, laughworthy, ludicrous, mirthful, mockable, nonsensical, preposterous, ridiculous, risible.

antonyms impressive, serious, solemn.

laughing *adj* cackling, cheerful, cheery, chortling, chuckling, giggling, gleeful, guffawing, happy, jocund, jolly, jovial, merry, mirthful, riant, rident, snickering, sniggering, tittering.

laughing-stock *n* Aunt Sally, butt, derision, fair game, figure of fun, pointing-stock, target, victim.

laughter *n* amusement, asbestos gelos, cachinnation, chortling, chuckling, convulsions, fou rire, giggling, glee, guffawing, hilarity, Homeric laughter, horselaugh, laughing, merriment, mirth, tittering.

launch *v* begin, cast, commence, discharge, dispatch, embark on, establish, fire, float, found, inaugurate, initiate, instigate, introduce, open, project, propel, send off, set in motion, start, throw.

lavatory *n* bathroom, bog, can, cloakroom, cludge, cludgie, comfort station, convenience, dike, draught-house, dunnakin, dunny, dyke, earth-closet, garderobe, Gents, George, head(s), jakes, john, Ladies, latrine, lav, loo, office, powder-room, privy, public convenience, smallest room, toilet, urinal, washroom, water-closet, WC.

lavish *adj* abundant, bountiful, copious, effusive, exaggerated, excessive, extravagant, exuberant, free, generous, gorgeous, immoderate, improvident, intemperate, liberal, lush, luxuriant, munificent, open-handed, opulent, plentiful, princely, prodigal, profuse, prolific, sumptuous, thriftless, unlimited, unreasonable, unrestrained, unstinting, wasteful, wild.

antonyms economical, frugal, parsimonious, scanty, sparing, thrifty.

v bestow, deluge, dissipate, expend, heap, pour, shower, spend, squander, waste.

law *n* act, axiom, brocard, canon, charter, code, command, commandment, constitution, consuetudinary, covenant, criterion, decree, dharma, edict, enactment, formula, institute, jurisprudence, order, ordinance, precept, principle, regulation, rule, standard, statute.

antonym chance.

law-abiding *adj* compliant, decent, dutiful, good, honest, honourable, lawful, obedient, orderly, peaceable, peaceful, upright.

antonym lawless.

law-breaker *n* convict, criminal, crook, culprit, delinquent, felon, infractor, miscreant, offender, outlaw, sinner, transgressor, trespasser, wrong-doer.

lawful *adj* allowable, authorised, constitutional, hal(l)al, kosher, legal, legalised, legitimate, licit, permissible, proper, rightful, valid, warranted.

antonyms illegal, illicit, lawless, unlawful.

lawless *adj* anarchic(al), chaotic, disorderly, felonious, insubordinate, insurgent, mutinous, rebellious, reckless, riotous, ruleless, seditious, unbridled, ungoverned, unrestrained, unruly, wild.

antonym lawful.

lawlessness *n* anarchy, chaos, disorder, insurgency, mobocracy, mob-rule, ochlocracy, piracy, racketeering, rent-a-mob.

antonym order.

lawsuit *n* action, argument, case, cause, contest, dispute, litigation, proceedings, process, prosecution, suit, trial.

lawyer *n* advocate, attorney, barrister, counsel, counsellor, green-bag, jurisconsult, law-agent, lawmonger, legist, solicitor.

lax *adj* broad, careless, casual, derelict, easy-going, flabby, flaccid, general, imprecise, inaccurate, indefinite, inexact, lenient, loose, neglectful, negligent, overindulgent, remiss, shapeless, slack, slipshod, soft, vague, wide, wide-open, yielding.

antonyms rigid, strict, stringent.

laxative *n* aperient, cathartic, eccoprotic, loosener, purgative, purge, salts.

adj aperient, cathartic, eccoprotic, lenitive, purgative.

laxness *n* carelessness, freedom, heedlessness, imprecision, indifference, indulgence, laissez-faire, latitude, latitudinarianism, laxism, laxity, leniency, looseness, neglect, negligence, nonchalance, permissiveness, slackness, sloppiness, slovenliness, softness, tolerance.

antonyms severity, strictness.

lay[1] *v* advance, allay, alleviate, allocate, allot, appease, apply, arrange, ascribe, assess, assign, assuage, attribute, bet, burden, calm, charge, concoct, contrive, deposit, design, devise, dispose, encumber, establish, gamble, hatch, hazard, impose, impute, leave, locate, lodge, offer, organise, place, plan, plant, plot, posit, position, prepare, present, put, quiet, relieve, risk, saddle, set, set down, set out, settle, soothe, spread, stake, still, submit, suppress, tax, wager, work out.

lay aside abandon, cast aside, discard, dismiss, pigeon-hole, postpone, put aside, put off, reject, shelve, store.

lay bare disclose, divulge, exhibit, exhume, explain, expose, reveal, show, uncover, unveil.

lay down affirm, assert, assume, couch, discard, drop, establish, formulate, give, give up, ordain, postulate, prescribe, relinquish, state, stipulate, surrender, yield.

lay down the law crack down, dictate, dogmatise, emphasise, pontificate, read the riot act, rule the roost.

lay hands on acquire, assault, attack, beat up, bless, clasp, clutch, confirm, consecrate, discover, find, get, get hold of, grab, grasp, grip, lay hold of, lay into, ordain, seize, set on, unearth.

lay in accumulate, amass, build up, collect, gather, glean, hoard, stock up, stockpile, store (up).

lay into assail, attack, belabour, berate, chastise, lambast, let fly at, pitch into, set about, slam, tear into, turn on.

lay it on butter up, exaggerate, flatter, overdo it, overpraise, soft-soap, sweet-talk.

lay off axe, cease, desist, discharge, dismiss, drop, give it a rest, give over, give up, leave alone, leave off, let go, let up, make redundant, oust, pay off, quit, stop, withhold.

lay on contribute, furnish, give, provide, set up, supply.

lay out arrange, demolish, design, disburse, display, exhibit, expend, fell, flatten, fork out, give, invest, knock out, pay, plan, set out, shell out, spend, spread out.

lay up accumulate, amass, garner, hive, hoard, hospitalise, incapacitate, keep, preserve, put away, salt away, save, squirrel away, store up, treasure.

lay waste depredate, desolate, despoil, destroy, devastate, pillage, rape, ravage, raze, ruin, sack, spoil, vandalise.

lay[2] *adj* amateur, inexpert, laic, laical, non-professional, non-specialist, secular.

lay[3] *n* ballad, canzone(t), lyric, madrigal, ode, poem, roundelay, song.

layabout *n* beachcomber, good-for-nothing, idler, laggard, loafer, lounger, ne'er-do-well, shirker, skiver, slug-a-bed, waster.

layer *n* bed, blanket, coat, coating, cover, covering, film, folium, lame, lamella, lamina, mantle, plate, ply, row, seam, sheet, stratum, table, thickness, tier, touch.

layman *n* amateur, layperson, outsider, parishioner.

lay-off *n* discharge, dismissal, redundancy, unemployment.

layout *n* arrangement, blueprint, design, draft, formation, geography, map, outline, plan, sketch.

laze *v* idle, lie around, loaf, loll, lounge, sit around.

laziness *n* dilatoriness, faineance, fainéancy, idleness, inactivity, indolence, otiosity, pococurant(e)ism, slackness, sloth, slothfulness, slowness, sluggishness, tardiness.

antonym industriousness.

lazy *adj* dormant, drowsy, idle, inactive, indolent, inert, languid, languorous, lethargic, otiose, remiss, shiftless, slack, sleepy, slobby, slothful, slow, slow-moving, sluggish, somnolent, torpid, work-shy.

antonyms active, diligent, energetic, industrious.

lazy-bones *n* hallion, idler, laggard, loafer, lounger, shirker, skiver, sleepy-head, slouch, slug-a-bed, sluggard.

leach *v* drain, extract, filter, filtrate, lixiviate, osmose, percolate, seep, strain.

lead *v* antecede, cause, command, conduct, direct, dispose, draw, escort, exceed, excel, experience, govern, guide, have, head, incline, induce, influence, live, manage, outdo, outstrip, pass, persuade, pilot, precede, preside over, prevail, prompt, spend, steer, supervise, surpass, transcend, undergo, usher.

antonym follow.

n advance, advantage, clue, direction, edge, example, first place, guidance, guide, hint, indication, leadership, margin, model, precedence, primacy, principal, priority, protagonist, starring role, start, suggestion, supremacy, tip, title role, trace, van, vanguard.

adj chief, first, foremost, head, leading, main, premier, primary, prime, principal, star.

lead off begin, commence, get going, inaugurate, initiate, kick off, open, start, start off, start out, start the ball rolling.

lead on beguile, deceive, draw on, entice, hoax, inveigle, lure, persuade, seduce, string along, tempt, trick.

lead to bring about, bring on, cause, conduce, contribute to, produce, result in, tend towards.

lead up to approach, intimate, introduce, make advances, make overtures, overture, pave the way, prepare (the way) for.

leaden *adj* ashen, burdensome, crushing, cumbersome, dingy, dismal, dreary, dull, gloomy, grey, greyish, heavy, humdrum, inert, laboured, lacklustre, languid, lead, lifeless, listless, lowering, lustreless, onerous, oppressive, overcast, plodding, sluggish, sombre, spiritless, stiff, stilted, wooden.

leader *n* bell-wether, boss, captain, chief, chieftain, commander, conductor, coryphaeus, counsellor, director, doyen, figurehead, flagship, guide, head, mahatma, principal, ringleader, ruler, skipper, superior, supremo.

antonym follower.

leadership *n* administration, authority, command, control, direction, directorship, domination, guidance, hegemony, influence, initiative, management, pre-eminence, premiership, running, superintendency, supremacy, sway.

leading *adj* chief, dominant, first, foremost, governing, greatest, highest, main, number one, outstanding, paramount, pre-eminent, primary, principal, ruling, superior, supreme.

antonym subordinate.

leaf *n* blade, bract, calyx, cotyledon, flag, folio, foliole, frond, needle, pad, page, sepal, sheet.

v browse, flip, glance, riffle, skim, thumb (through).

leaflet *n* advert, bill, booklet, brochure, circular, handbill, handout, pamphlet.

leafy *adj* bosky, dasyphyllous, foliose, frondescent, frondose, green, leafed, leaved, shaded, shady, verdant, wooded, woody.

league *n* alliance, association, band, Bund, cartel, category, class, coalition, combination, combine, compact, confederacy, confederation, consortium, federation, fellowship, fraternity, group, guild, level, partnership, sorority, syndicate, union.

v ally, amalgamate, associate, band, collaborate, combine, confederate, consort, join forces, unite.

leak *n* aperture, chink, crack, crevice, disclosure, divulgence, drip, fissure, hole, leakage, leaking, oozing, opening, percolation, perforation, puncture, seepage

v discharge, disclose, divulge, drip, escape, exude, give away, let slip, let the cat out of the bag, make known, make public, make water, ooze, pass, pass on, percolate, reveal, seep, spill, spill the beans, tell, trickle, weep.

leaky *adj* cracked, holey, leaking, perforated, permeable, porous, punctured, split, waterlogged.

lean[1] *v* bend, confide, count on, depend, favour, incline, list, prefer, prop, recline, rely, repose, rest, slant, slope, tend, tilt, tip, trust.

lean[2] *adj* angular, bare, barren, bony, emaciated, gaunt, inadequate, infertile, lank, meagre, pitiful, poor, rangy, scanty, scragged, scraggy, scrawny, skinny, slender, slim, slink(y), spare, sparse, thin, unfruitful, unproductive, wiry.

antonyms fat, fleshy.

lean on force, persuade, pressurise, put pressure on.

leaning *n* aptitude, bent, bias, disposition, inclination, liking, partiality, penchant, predilection, proclivity, proneness, propensity, susceptibility, taste, tendency, velleity.

leap *v* advance, bounce, bound, caper, capriole, cavort, clear, curvet, escalate, frisk, gambol, hasten, hop, hurry, increase, jump, jump (over), reach, rocket, rush, salto, skip, soar, spring, surge, vault.

antonyms drop, fall, sink.

n bound, caper, capriole, curvet, escalation, frisk, hop, increase, jump, rise, sally, salto, skip, spring, surge, upsurge, upswing, vault, volt(e).

learn *v* acquire, ascertain, assimilate, attain, cognise, con, detect, determine, discern, discover, find out, gather, get off pat, grasp, hear, imbibe, learn by heart, master, memorise, pick up, see, understand.

learned *adj* academic, adept, blue, cultured, erudite, experienced, expert, highbrow, intellectual, lettered, literate, proficient, sage, scholarly, skilled, versed, well-informed, well-read, wise.

antonyms ignorant, illiterate, uneducated.

learner *n* abecedarian, alphabetarian, apprentice, beginner, catechumen, cheechako, disciple, neophyte, novice, pupil, scholar, student, tenderfoot, trainee, tyro.

learning *n* acquirements, attainments, culture, edification, education, enlightenment, erudition, information, knowledge, letters, literature, lore, research, scholarship, schoolcraft, schooling, study, tuition, wisdom.

lease *v* charter, farm out, hire, let, loan, rent, sublet.

leash *n* check, control, curb, discipline, hold, lead, lyam, rein, restraint, tether.

least *adj* fewest, last, lowest, meanest, merest, minimum, minutest, poorest, slightest, smallest, tiniest.

antonym most.

leathery *adj* coriaceous, corious, durable, hard, hardened, leathern, rough, rugged, tough, wrinkled.

leave[1] *v* abandon, allot, assign, bequeath, cause, cease, cede, commit, consign, decamp, depart, deposit, desert, desist, disappear, do a bunk, drop, entrust, exit, flit, forget, forsake, generate, give over, give up, go, go away, hand down, leave behind, levant, move, produce, pull out, quit, refer, refrain, relinquish, renounce, retire, set out, stop, surrender, take off, transmit, will, withdraw.

antonym arrive.

leave off abstain, break off, cease, desist, discontinue, end, give over, halt, knock off, lay off, quit, refrain, stop, terminate.

leave out bar, cast aside, count out, cut (out), disregard, eliminate, except, exclude, ignore, neglect, omit, overlook, pass over, reject.

leave[2] *n* allowance, authorisation, concession, consent, dispensation, exeat, freedom, furlough, holiday, indulgence, liberty, permission, sabbatical, sanction, time off, vacation.

antonyms refusal, rejection.

leaven *v* elevate, expand, ferment, imbue, inspire, lighten, permeate, pervade, quicken, raise, stimulate, suffuse, work.

leavings *n* bits, detritus, dregs, dross, fragments, left-overs, orts, pieces, refuse, remains, remnants, residue, scraps, spoil, sweepings, waste.

lecher *n* adulterer, Casanova, debauchee, Don Juan, fornicator, goat, letch, lewdsby, lewdster, libertine, libidinist, profligate, rake, roué, satyr, seducer, sensualist, wanton, whoremonger, wolf, womaniser.

lecherous *adj* carnal, concupiscent, goatish, lascivious, lewd, libidinous, licentious, lickerish, liquorish, lubricous, lustful, prurient, randy, raunchy, salacious, unchaste, wanton, womanising.

lechery *n* carnality, concupiscence, debauchery, goatishness, lasciviousness, lecherousness, leching, lewdness, libertinism, libidinousness, licentiousness, lubricity, lust, lustfulness, profligacy, prurience, rakishness, randiness, raunchiness, salaciousness, sensuality, wantonness, womanising.

lecture *n* address, castigation, censure, chiding, discourse, disquisition, dressing-down, going-over, harangue, instruction, lesson, prelection, rebuke, reprimand, reproof, scolding, speech, talk, talking-to, telling-off, wigging.

v address, admonish, berate, carpet, castigate, censure, chide, discourse, expound, harangue, hold forth, jawbone, lucubrate, prelect, rate, reprimand, reprove, scold, speak, talk, teach, tell off.

lecturer *n* declaimer, expounder, haranguer, lector, orator, pedagogue, preacher, prelector, sermoniser, speaker, speechifier, speech-maker, talker, teacher, tutor.

ledge *n* berm, mantle, projection, ridge, shelf, shelve, sill, step.

leech *n* bloodsucker, freeloader, hanger-on, parasite, sponger, sycophant, usurer.

leer *v* eye, fleer, gloat, goggle, grin, ogle, smirk, squint, stare, wink.

n grin, ogle, smirk, squint, stare, wink.

leery *adj* careful, cautious, chary, distrustful, doubting, dubious, guarded, sceptical, shy, suspicious, uncertain, unsure, wary.

lees *n* deposit, draff, dregs, grounds, precipitate, refuse, residue, sediment, settlings.

leeway *n* elbow-room, latitude, play, room, scope, space.

left *adj* communist, left-hand, leftist, left-wing, liberal, port, progressive, radical, red, sinistral, socialist.

antonym right.

left-handed *adj* ambiguous, awkward, dubious, equivocal, gauche, sinistral, southpaw, unlucky.

antonym right-handed.

left-overs *n* dregs, fag-end, leavings, oddments, odds and ends, orts, refuse, remainder, remains, remnants, residue, scraps, surplus, sweepings.

leg *n* brace, gam, lap, limb, member, part, pin, portion, prop, section, segment, shank, stage, stretch, stump, support, upright.

legacy *n* bequest, birthright, devise, endowment, estate, gift, heirloom, hereditament, heritage, heritance, inheritance, patrimony.

legal *adj* above-board, allowable, allowed, authorised, constitutional, forensic, judicial, juridical, lawful, legalised, legitimate, licit, permissible, proper, rightful, sanctioned, valid, warrantable.

antonym illegal.

legalise *v* allow, approve, authorise, decriminalise, legitimate, legitimise, license, permit, sanction, validate, warrant.

legality *n* admissibleness, constitutionality, lawfulness, legitimacy, permissibility, rightfulness, validity.

antonym illegality.

legate *n* ambassador, delegate, depute, deputy, emissary, envoy, exarch, messenger, nuncio.

legatee *n* beneficiary, co-heir(ess), devisee, heir, inheritor, inheritrix, recipient.

legation *n* commission, consulate, delegation, deputation, embassy, ministry, mission, representation.

legend *n* caption, celebrity, cipher, code, device, fable, fiction, folk-tale, household name, inscription, key, luminary, marvel, motto, myth, narrative, phenomenon, prodigy, saga, spectacle, story, tale, tradition, wonder.

legendary *adj* apocryphal, celebrated, fabled, fabulous, famed, famous, fanciful, fictional, fictitious, illustrious, immortal, mythical, renowned, romantic, storied, story-book, traditional, unhistoric(al), well-known.

legerdemain *n* artfulness, artifice, chicanery, contrivance, craftiness, cunning, deception, feint, hocus-pocus, manipulation, manoeuvring, prestidigitation, sleight of hand, subterfuge, thaumaturgics, trickery.

legible *adj* clear, decipherable, discernible, distinct, intelligible, neat, readable.

antonym illegible.

legion *n* army, battalion, brigade, cohort, company, division, drove, force, horde, host, mass, multitude, myriad, number, regiment, swarm, throng, troop.

adj countless, illimitable, innumerable, multitudinous, myriad, numberless, numerous.

legislate *v* authorise, codify, constitute, constitutionalise, enact, establish, ordain, prescribe.

legislation *n* act, authorisation, bill, charter, codification, constitutionalisation, enactment, law, law-making, measure, prescription, regulation, ruling, statute.

legislative *adj* congressional, judicial, juridical, jurisdictional, jurisdictive, law-giving, law-making, ordaining, parliamentary, senatorial.

legislator *n* law-giver, law-maker, nomothete, parliamentarian.

legislature *n* assembly, chamber, congress, diet, governing body, house, parliament, senate.

legitimate *adj* acknowledged, admissible, authentic, authorised, correct, genuine, just, justifiable, kosher, lawful, legal, legit, licit, logical, proper, real, reasonable, rightful, sanctioned, sensible, statutory, true, true-born, valid, warranted, well-founded.

antonym illegitimate.

v authorise, charter, entitle, legalise, legitimise, license, permit, sanction.

legitimise *v* authorise, charter, entitle, legalise, legitimate, license, permit, sanction.

leisure *n* breather, ease, freedom, holiday, let-up, liberty, opportunity, pause, quiet, recreation, relaxation, respite, rest, retirement, spare time, time off, vacation.

antonyms toil, work.

leisurely *adj* carefree, comfortable, deliberate, easy, gentle, indolent, laid-back, lazy, lingering, loose, relaxed, restful, slow, tranquil, unhasty, unhurried.

antonyms hectic, hurried, rushed.

lend *v* add, advance, afford, bestow, confer, contribute, furnish, give, grant, impart, lease, loan, present, provide, supply.

antonym borrow.

lend a hand aid, assist, do one's bit, give a helping hand, help, help out, pitch in.

lend an ear give ear, hearken, heed, listen, pay attention, take notice.

length *n* distance, duration, elongation, extensiveness, extent, lengthiness, longitude, measure, operoseness, operosity, period, piece, portion, prolixity, protractedness, reach, section, segment, space, span, stretch, tediousness, term.

lengthen *v* continue, draw out, eke, eke out, elongate, expand, extend, increase, pad out, prolong, prolongate, protract, spin out, stretch.

antonym shorten.

lengthwise *adv* endlong, endways, endwise, horizontally, lengthways, longitudinally, vertically.

lengthy *adj* diffuse, drawn-out, extended, interminable, lengthened, long, long-drawn-out, long-winded, loquacious, marathon, overlong, prolix, prolonged, protracted, rambling, tedious, verbose, voluble.

antonym short.

leniency *n* clemency, compassion, forbearance, gentleness, indulgence, lenience, lenity, mercy, mildness, moderation, permissiveness, soft-heartedness, softness, tenderness, tolerance.

antonym severity.

lenient *adj* clement, compassionate, easy-going, forbearing, forgiving, gentle, indulgent, kind, merciful, mild, soft, soft-hearted, sparing, tender, tolerant.

antonym severe.

lenitive *adj* alleviating, alleviative, assuaging, calmative, calming, easing, mitigating, mitigative, mollifying, palliative, relieving, soothing.

antonym irritant.

lens *n* eye, eyeglass, eye-piece, glass, loupe, magnifying-glass, monocle, ocular.

leper *n* lazar, outcast, pariah, undesirable, untouchable.

lesbian *n* butch, dike, gay, homophile, homosexual, les, lez(z), lezzy, sapphist, tribade.

adj butch, dikey, gay, homosexual, lesbic, sapphic, tribadic.

lesion *n* abrasion, bruise, contusion, cut, gash, hurt, impairment, injury, scrape, scratch, sore, trauma, wound.

lessen *v* abate, abridge, bate, contract, curtail, deaden, decrease, de-escalate, degrade, die down, diminish, dwindle, ease, erode, fail, flag, impair, lighten, lower, minimise, moderate, narrow, reduce, shrink, slack, slow down, weaken.

antonym increase.

lessening *n* abatement, bating, contraction, curtailment, deadening, decline, decrease, de-escalation, diminution, dwindling, ebbing, erosion, failure, flagging, let-up, minimisation, moderation, petering out, reduction, shrinkage, slackening, waning, weakening.

antonym increase.

lesser *adj* inferior, lower, minor, secondary, slighter, smaller, subordinate.

antonym greater.

lesson *n* admonition, assignment, censure, chiding, class, coaching, deterrent, drill, example, exemplar, exercise, homework, instruction, lection, lecture, message, model, moral, pericope, period, practice, precept, punishment, reading, rebuke, recitation, reprimand, reproof, schooling, scolding, task, teaching, tutorial, tutoring, warning.

let[1] *v* agree to, allow, authorise, cause, charter, consent to, empower, enable, entitle, give leave, give permission, give the go-ahead, give the green light, grant, hire, lease, make, OK, permit, rent, sanction, tolerate.

antonym forbid.

let down abandon, betray, desert, disappoint, disenchant, disillusion, dissatisfy, fail, fall short.

antonym satisfy.

let go free, liberate, manumit, release, set free, unhand.

antonyms catch, imprison.

let in accept, admit, include, incorporate, receive, take in, welcome.

antonym bar.

let off absolve, acquit, detonate, discharge, dispense, emit, excuse, exempt, exonerate, explode, exude, fire, forgive, give off, ignore, leak, pardon, release, spare.

antonym punish.

let on act, admit, counterfeit, disclose, dissemble, dissimulate, divulge, feign, give away, leak, let out, make believe, make known, make out, pretend, profess, reveal, say, simulate.

antonym keep mum.

let out betray, discharge, disclose, emit, free, give, give vent to, leak, let fall, let go, let slip, liberate, make known, produce, release, reveal, utter.

antonym keep in.

let up abate, cease, decrease, diminish, ease, ease up, end, halt, moderate, slacken, stop, subside.

antonym continue.

let slip blab, blurt out, come out with, disclose, divulge, give away, leak, let out, let the cat out of the bag, reveal.

antonym keep mum.

let[2] *n* check, constraint, hindrance, impediment, interference, obstacle, obstruction, prohibition, restraint, restriction.

antonym assistance.

let-down *n* anticlimax, betrayal, blow, desertion, disappointment, disillusionment, frustration, lemon, set-back, wash-out.

antonym satisfaction.

lethal *adj* baleful, dangerous, deadly, deathful, deathly, destructive, devastating, fatal, lethiferous, mortal, mortiferous, murderous, noxious, pernicious, poisonous, virulent.

antonym harmless.

lethargic *adj* apathetic, comatose, debilitated, drowsy, dull, enervated, heavy, hebetant, hebetated, hebetudinous, inactive, indifferent, inert, languid, lazy, listless, sleepy, slothful, slow, sluggish, somnolent, stupefied, torpid.

antonym lively.

lethargy *n* apathy, drowsiness, dullness, hebetation, hebetude, hebetudinosity, inaction, indifference, inertia, languor, lassitude, listlessness, sleepiness, sloth, slowness, sluggishness, stupor, torpidity, torpor.

antonym liveliness.

letter[1] *n* acknowledgement, answer, billet, chit, communication, da(w)k, dispatch, encyclical, epistle, epistolet, line, message, missive, note, reply.

letter[2] *n* character, grapheme, lexigram, logogram, logograph, sign, symbol.

lettered *adj* accomplished, cultivated, cultured, educated, erudite, highbrow, informed, knowledgeable, learned, literary, literate, scholarly, studied, versed, well-educated, well-read.

antonym ignorant.

letters *n* academia, belles-lettres, books, culture, erudition, humanities, learning, literature, scholarship, writing.

let-up *n* abatement, break, breather, cessation, interval, lessening, lull, pause, recess, remission, respite, slackening.

antonym continuation.

level[1] *adj* abreast, aligned, balanced, calm, champaign, commensurate, comparable, consistent, equable, equal, equivalent, even, even-tempered, flat, flush, horizontal, neck and neck, on a par, plain, proportionate, smooth, stable, steady, uniform.

antonyms behind, uneven, unstable.

v aim, beam, bulldoze, couch, demolish, destroy, devastate, direct, equalise, even out, flatten, flush, focus, knock down, lay low, plane, point, pull down, raze, smooth, tear down, train, wreck.

n altitude, bed, class, degree, echelon, elevation, floor, grade, height, horizontal, layer, plain, plane, position, rank, stage, standard, standing, status, storey, stratum, zone.

level[2] *v* admit, avow, come clean, confess, divulge, open up, tell.

antonym prevaricate.

level-headed *adj* balanced, calm, collected, commonsensical, composed, cool, dependable, even-tempered, reasonable, sane, self-possessed, sensible, steady, together, unflappable.

lever *n* bar, crowbar, handle, jemmy, joy-stick.

v dislodge, force, heave, jemmy, move, prise, pry, purchase, raise, shift.

leverage *n* advantage, ascendancy, authority, clout. force, influence, pull, purchase, rank, strength, weight.

leviathan *n* behemoth, colossus, giant, hulk, mammoth, monster, sea-monster, Titan, whale.

levity *n* buoyancy, facetiousness, fickleness, flightiness, flippancy, frivolity, giddiness, irreverence, light-heartedness, silliness, skittishness, triviality, whifflery.

antonyms seriousness. sobriety.

levy *v* assemble, call, call up, charge, collect, conscript, demand. exact, gather, impose, mobilise, muster, press, raise. summon, tax.

n assessment, collection, contribution, duty, exaction, excise, fee, gathering, imposition, impost, subscription, tariff, tax, toll.

lewd *adj* bawdy, blue, Cyprian, dirty, harlot, impure, indecent, lascivious, libidinous, licentious, loose, lubric, lubrical, lubricious, lubricous, lustful, obscene, pornographic, profligate, salacious, smutty, unchaste, vile, vulgar, wanton. wicked.

antonyms chaste, polite.

lewdness *n* bawdiness, carnality, crudity, debauchery, depravity, impurity, indecency, lasciviousness, lechery, licentiousness, lubricity, lustfulness, obscenity, pornography, priapism, profligacy, randiness, salaciousness, smut, smuttiness, unchastity, vulgarity, wantonness.

antonyms chasteness, politeness.

lexicographer *n* dictionary-writer, glossarist, lexiconist, vocabulist.

lexicon *n* dictionary, encyclopaedia, glossary, phrase-book, vocabulary, word-book, word-list.

liability *n* accountability, albatross, answerability, arrears, burden, culpability, debit, debt, disadvantage, drag, drawback, duty, encumbrance, handicap, hindrance, impediment, inconvenience, indebtedness, likeliness, millstone, minus, nuisance, obligation, onus, responsibility.

antonyms asset(s), unaccountability.

liable *adj* accountable, amenable, answerable, apt, bound, chargeable, disposed, exposed, inclined, likely, obligated, open, predisposed, prone, responsible, subject, susceptible, tending, vulnerable.

antonyms unaccountable, unlikely.

liaison *n* affair, amour, communication, conjunction, connection, contact, entanglement, interchange, intermediary, intrigue, link. love affair, romance, union.

liar *n* Ananias, bouncer, deceiver, fabricator, falsifier, fibber, perjurer, prevaricator, storyteller.

libel *n* aspersion, calumny, defamation, denigration, obloquy, slander, slur, smear, vilification, vituperation.

antonym praise.

v blacken, calumniate, defame, derogate, malign, revile, slander, slur, smear, traduce, vilify, vilipend, vituperate.

antonym praise.

libellous *adj* aspersive, aspersory, calumniatory, calumnious, defamatory, defaming, derogatory, false, injurious. malicious, maligning, scurrilous, slanderous, traducing, untrue, vilifying, vituperative.

antonyms laudative, praising.

liberal *adj* abundant, advanced, altruistic. ample, beneficent, bounteous, bountiful, broad, broad-minded, catholic, charitable. copious, enlightened, flexible, free, free-handed, general, generous, handsome, high-minded, humanistic, humanitarian, indulgent, inexact, kind, large-hearted, latitudinarian, lavish, lenient, libertarian, loose, magnanimous, munificent, open-handed. open-hearted, permissive, plentiful, profuse, progressive, radical, reformist, rich, tolerant, unbiased, unbigoted, unprejudiced. unstinting, verligte, Whig, Whiggish.

antonyms conservative, illiberal, mean, narrow-minded.

liberalism *n* free-thinking, humanitarianism, latitudinarianism, libertarianism, progressivism, radicalism, Whiggery, Whiggism.

antonyms conservatism, narrow-mindedness.

liberality *n* altruism, beneficence, benevolence, bounty, breadth, broad-mindedness, candour, catholicity, charity, free-handedness, generosity, impartiality, kindness, large-heartedness, largess(e), latitude, liberalism, libertarianism, magnanimity, munificence, open-handedness, open-mindedness, permissiveness, philanthropy, progressivism, tolerance, toleration.

antonyms illiberality, meanness.

liberate *v* affranchise, deliver, discharge, disenthral, emancipate, free, let go, let loose, let out, manumit, ransom, redeem, release, rescue, set free, uncage, unchain, unfetter, unpen, unshackle.

antonyms enslave, imprison, restrict.

liberating *adj* eleutherian, emancipatory, freeing, redeeming.

antonym restricting.

liberation *n* deliverance, emancipation, enfranchisement, freedom, freeing, liberating, liberty, manumission, ransoming, redemption, release, uncaging, unchaining, unfettering, unpenning, unshackling.

antonyms enslavement, imprisonment, restriction.

liberator *n* deliverer, emancipator, freer, manumitter, ransomer, redeemer, rescuer, saviour.

antonyms enslaver, jailer.

libertarian *n* anarchist, free-thinker, libertine.

adj anarchistic.

liberties *n* audacity, disrespect, familiarity, forwardness, impertinence, impropriety, impudence, insolence, misuse, overfamiliarity, presumption, presumptuousness.

antonyms politeness, respect.

libertine *n* debauchee, gay deceiver, lecher, loose fish, loose-liver, lovelace, profligate, rake, reprobate, roué, seducer, sensualist, voluptuary, womaniser.

liberty *n* authorisation, autonomy, carte-blanche, dispensation, emancipation, exemption, franchise, free rein, freedom, immunity, independence, latitude, leave, liberation, licence, permission, prerogative, privilege, release, right, sanction, self-determination, sovereignty.

antonyms imprisonment, restriction, slavery.

libidinous *adj* carnal, concupiscent, cupidinous, debauched, impure, incontinent, lascivious, lecherous, lewd, lickerish, loose, lustful, prurient, randy, ruttish, salacious, sensual, unchaste, wanton, wicked.

antonyms modest, temperate.

library *n* Athenaeum, bibliotheca, genizah, reading-room, reference-room, stack, study.

libretto *n* book, lines, lyrics, script, text, words.

licence[1] *n* authorisation, authority, carte blanche, certificate, charter, dispensation, entitlement, exemption, freedom, immunity, imprimatur, independence, indult, latitude, leave, liberty, permission, permit, privilege, right, self-determination, warrant.

antonyms banning, dependence, restriction.

licence[2] *n* abandon, amorality, anarchy, debauchery, disorder, dissipation, dissoluteness, excess, immoderation, impropriety, indulgence, intemperance, irresponsibility, lawlessness, laxity, profligacy, unruliness.

antonyms decorum, temperance.

license *v* accredit, allow, authorise, certificate, certify, commission, empower, entitle, permit, sanction, warrant.

antonym ban.

licentious *adj* abandoned, cupidinous, debauched, disorderly, dissolute, immoral, impure, lascivious, lax, lewd, libertine, libidinous, lickerish, lubric, lubrical, lubricious, lubricous, lustful, profligate, promiscuous, sensual, uncontrollable, uncontrolled, uncurbed, unruly, wanton.

licentiousness *n* abandon, cupidinousness, debauchery, dissipation, dissoluteness, lechery, lewdness, libertinism, libidinousness, lubriciousness, lubricity, lust, lustfulness, priapism, profligacy, promiscuity, prurience, salaciousness, salacity, wantonness.

antonyms modesty, temperance.

lick[1] *v* brush, dart, flick, lap, play over, smear, taste, tongue, touch, wash.

n bit, brush, dab, hint, little, sample, smidgeon, speck, spot, stroke, taste, touch.

lick one's lips anticipate, drool over, enjoy, relish, savour.

lick[2] *v* beat, best, defeat, excel, flog, outdo, outstrip, overcome, rout, skelp, slap, smack, spank, strike, surpass, thrash, top, trounce, vanquish, wallop.

lick[3] *n* clip, gallop, pace, rate, speed.

licking *n* beating, defeat, drubbing, flogging, hiding, skelping, smacking, spanking, tanning, thrashing, trouncing, whipping.

lie[1] *v* dissimulate, equivocate, fabricate, falsify, fib, forswear oneself, invent, misrepresent, perjure, prevaricate.

n bam, bounce, caulker, cram, crammer, cretism, deceit, fabrication, falsehood, falsification, falsity, fib, fiction, flam, invention, inveracity, mendacity, plumper, prevarication, stretcher, tar(r)adiddle, untruth, whacker, white lie, whopper.

antonym truth.

lie[2] *v* be, belong, couch, dwell, exist, extend, inhere, laze, loll, lounge, recline, remain, repose, rest, slump, sprawl, stretch out.

lie low go to earth, hide, hide away, hide out, hole up, keep a low profile, lie doggo, lurk, skulk, take cover.

lie in wait for ambuscade, ambush, forelay, skulk, waylay.

life *n* activity, animation, autobiography, behaviour, being, biography, breath, brio, career, conduct, confessions, continuance, course, creatures, duration, élan vital, energy, entity, essence, existence, fauna, flora and fauna, get-up-and-go, go, growth, heart, high spirits, history, life story, life-blood, life-style, lifetime, liveliness, memoirs, oomph, organisms, sentience, soul, span, sparkle, spirit, story, the world, this mortal coil, time, verve, viability, vigour, vita, vital flame, vital spark, vitality, vivacity, way of life, wildlife, zest.

lifeless *adj* abiotic, apathetic, bare, barren, cold, colourless, comatose, dead, deceased, defunct, desert, dull, empty, extinct, flat, heavy, hollow, inanimate, inert, insensate, insensible, insipid, lacklustre, lethargic, listless, nerveless, out cold, out for the count, passive, pointless, slow, sluggish, spent, spiritless, static, sterile, stiff, torpid, unconscious, uninhabited, unproductive, waste, wooden.

antonyms alive, lively.

lifelike *adj* authentic, exact, expressive, faithful, graphic, natural, photographic, pictorial, picturesque, real, realistic, true, true-to-life, undistorted, vivid.

antonyms inexact, unnatural.

lifelong *adj* abiding, constant, deep-rooted, deep-seated, enduring, entrenched, inveterate, lasting, lifetime, long-lasting, long-standing, perennial, permanent, persistent.

antonyms impermanent, temporary.

lifetime *n* career, course, day(s), existence, floruit, life, life span, period, span, time.

lift[1] *v* advance, ameliorate, annul, appropriate, arrest, ascend, boost, buoy up, cancel, climb, collar, copy, countermand, crib, dignify, disappear, disperse, dissipate, draw up, elevate, end, enhance, exalt, half-inch, heft, hoist, improve, mount, nab, nick, pick up, pilfer, pinch, pirate, plagiarise, pocket, promote, purloin, raise, rear, relax, remove, rescind, revoke, rise, steal, stop, take, terminate, thieve, up, upgrade, uplift, upraise, vanish.

antonyms drop, fall, impose, lower.

n boost, encouragement, fillip, pick-me-up, reassurance, shot in the arm, spur, uplift.

antonym discouragement.

lift[2] *n* drive, hitch, ride, run, transport.

lift[3] *n* elevator, escalator, hoist, paternoster.

ligature *n* band, bandage, binding, bond, connection, cord, ligament, link, rope, strap, string, thong, tie, tourniquet.

light[1] *n* beacon, blaze, brightness, brilliance, bulb, candle, cockcrow, dawn, day, daybreak, daylight, daytime, effulgence, flame, flare, flash, glare, gleam, glim, glint, glow, illumination, incandescence, lambency, lamp, lampad, lantern, lighter, lighthouse, luminescence, luminosity, lustre, match, morn, morning, phosphorescence, radiance, ray, refulgence, scintillation, shine, sparkle, star, sunrise, sunshine, taper, torch, window, Yang.

antonym darkness.

v animate, beacon, brighten, cheer, fire, floodlight, ignite, illuminate, illumine, inflame, irradiate, kindle, light up, lighten, put on, set alight, set fire to, switch on, turn on.

antonyms darken, extinguish.

adj bleached, blond, bright, brilliant, faded, faint, fair, glowing, illuminated, lightful, lightsome, lucent, luminous, lustrous, pale, pastel, shining, sunny, well-lit.

antonym dark.

light[2] *n* angle, approach, aspect, attitude, awareness, clue, comprehension, context, elucidation, enlightenment, example, exemplar, explanation, hint, illustration, information, insight, interpretation, knowledge, model, paragon, point of view, slant, understanding, viewpoint.

light[3] *adj* agile, airy, amusing, animated, blithe, buoyant, carefree, cheerful, cheery, crumbly, delicate, delirious, digestible, diverting, dizzy, easy, effortless, entertaining, facile, faint, fickle, flimsy, friable, frivolous, frugal, funny, gay, gentle, giddy, graceful, humorous, idle, imponderous, inconsequential, inconsiderable, indistinct, insignificant, insubstantial, light-footed, light-headed, light-hearted, lightweight, lithe, lively, loose, manageable, merry, mild, minute, moderate, modest, nimble, pleasing, porous, portable, reeling, restricted, sandy, scanty, simple, slight, small, soft, spongy, sprightly, sunny, superficial, thin, tiny, trifling, trivial, unchaste, undemanding, underweight, unexacting, unheeding, unsteady, unsubstantial, untaxing, volatile, wanton, weak, witty, worthless.

antonyms clumsy, harsh, heavy, important, sad, severe, sober, solid, stiff.

light on chance on, come across, discover, encounter, find, happen upon, hit on, spot, stumble on.

lighten[1] *v* beacon, brighten, illume, illuminate, illumine, light up, shine.

antonym darken.

lighten[2] *v* alleviate, ameliorate, assuage, brighten, buoy up, cheer, disburden, disencumber, ease, elate, encourage, facilitate, gladden, hearten, inspire, inspirit, lessen, lift, mitigate, perk up, reduce, relieve, revive, unload, uplift.

antonyms burden, depress, oppress.

light-fingered *adj* crafty, crooked, dishonest, furtive, pilfering, shifty, sly, thieving, thievish.

antonym honest.

light-footed *adj* active, agile, buoyant, feat, graceful, lightsome, lithe, nimble, sprightly, spry, swift, tripping, winged.

antonyms clumsy, slow.

light-giving *adj* luciferous, luminant, luminiferous, luminous.

light-headed *adj* bird-brained, delirious, dizzy, faint, feather-brained, fickle, flighty, flippant, foolish, frivolous, giddy, hazy, inane, shallow, silly, superficial, thoughtless, trifling, unsteady, vacuous, vertiginous, woozy.

antonym sober.

light-hearted *adj* blithe, blithesome, bright, carefree, cheerful, effervescent, elated, frolicsome, gay, glad, gleeful, happy-go-lucky, insouciant, jocund, jolly, jovial, joyful, joyous, light-spirited, merry, perky, playful, sunny, untroubled, upbeat.

antonym sad.

lighthouse *n* fanal, pharos.

lightly *adv* airily, breezily, carelessly, delicately, easily, effortlessly, facilely, faintly, flippantly, frivolously, gaily, gently, gingerly, heedlessly, indifferently, moderately, readily, simply, slightingly, slightly, softly, sparingly, sparsely, thinly, thoughtlessly, timidly, wantonly.

antonyms heavily, soberly.

lightness *n* agility, airiness, animation, blitheness, buoyancy, cheerfulness, cheeriness, crumbliness, delicacy, delicateness, facileness, faintness, fickleness, flimsiness, frivolity, gaiety, grace, idleness, inconsequentiality, indistinctness, insignificance, legerity, levity, light-heartedness, litheness, liveliness, mildness, minuteness, moderation, nimbleness, porosity, porousness, sandiness, scantiness, slightness, triviality, wantonness.

antonyms clumsiness, harshness, heaviness, importance, sadness, severity, sobriety, solidness, stiffness.

lightning *n* thunderbolt, thunder-dart, wildfire.

lightweight *adj* inconsequential, insignificant, negligible, nugatory, paltry, petty, slight, trifling, trivial, unimportant, worthless.

antonyms important, major.

like[1] *adj* akin, alike, allied, analogous, approximating, cognate, corresponding, equivalent, homologous, identical, parallel, related, relating, resembling, same, similar.

antonym unlike.

n counterpart, equal, fellow, match, opposite number, parallel, peer, twin.

prep in the same manner as, on the lines of, similar to.

like[2] *v* admire, adore, appreciate, approve, care to, cherish, choose, choose to, delight in, desire, dig, enjoy, esteem, fancy, feel inclined, go a bundle on, go for, hold dear, love, prefer, prize, relish, revel in, select, take a shine to, take kindly to, take to, want, wish.

antonym dislike.

n cup of tea, favourite, liking, love, partiality, penchant, predilection, preference.

antonym dislike.

likeable *adj* agreeable, amiable, appealing, attractive, charming, congenial, engaging, friendly, genial, loveable, nice, pleasant, pleasing, sympathetic, winning, winsome.

antonym disagreeable.

likelihood *n* chance, liability, likeliness, possibility, probability, prospect, reasonableness, verisimilitude.

antonym unlikeliness.

likely *adj* acceptable, agreeable, anticipated, appropriate, apt, befitting, believable, bright, credible, disposed, expected, fair, favourite, feasible, fit, foreseeable, hopeful, inclined, liable, odds-on, on the cards, plausible, pleasing, possible, predictable, probable, promising, prone, proper, qualified, reasonable, suitable, tending, up-and-coming, verisimilar.

antonyms unlikely, unsuitable.

adv doubtlessly, in all probability, like as not, like enough, no doubt, odds on, presumably, probably, very like.

like-minded *adj* agreeing, compatible, harmonious, in accord, in agreement, in harmony, in rapport, of one mind, of the same mind, unanimous.

antonym disagreeing.

liken *v* associate, compare, equate, juxtapose, link, match, parallel, relate, set beside.

likeness *n* affinity, appearance, copy, correspondence, counterpart, delineation, depiction, effigies, effigy, facsimile, form, guise, image, model, photograph, picture, portrait, replica, representation, reproduction, resemblance, semblance, similarity, similitude, simulacrum, study.

antonym unlikeness.

likewise *adv* also, besides, by the same token, eke, further, furthermore, in addition, moreover, similarly, too.

antonym contrariwise.

liking *n* affection, affinity, appreciation, attraction, bent, bias, desire, favour, fondness, inclination, love, partiality, penchant, predilection, preference, proneness, propensity, satisfaction, soft spot, stomach, taste, tendency, weakness.

antonym dislike.

lilt *n* air, beat, cadence, measure, rhythm, song, sway, swing.

lily-white *adj* chaste, incorrupt, innocent, irreproachable, milk-white, pure, spotless, uncorrupt, uncorrupted, unsullied, untainted, untarnished, virgin, virtuous.

antonym corrupt.

limb *n* appendage, arm, bough, branch, extension, extremity, fork, leg, member, offshoot, part, projection, ramus, spur, wing.

limber *adj* agile, elastic, flexible, flexile, graceful, lissom, lithe, loose-jointed, loose-limbed, plastic, pliable, pliant, supple.

antonym stiff.

limber up exercise, loosen up, prepare, warm up, work out.

antonym stiffen up.

limelight *n* attention, big time, celebrity, fame, prominence, public notice, publicity, recognition, renown, stardom, the public eye, the spotlight.

limit *n* bitter end, border, bound, boundary, bourne(e), brim, brink, ceiling, check, compass, confines, curb, cut-off point, deadline, edge, end, extent, frontier, limitation, maximum, mete, obstruction, outrance, perimeter, periphery, precinct, restraint, restriction, rim, saturation point, termination, terminus, terminus a quo, terminus ad quem, threshold, ultimate, utmost, verge.

v bound, check, circumscribe, condition, confine, constrain, curb, delimit, delimitate, demarcate, fix, hem in, hinder, ration, restrain, restrict, specify.

antonyms extend, free.

limitation *n* block, check, condition, constraint, control, curb, definitude, delimitation, demarcation, disadvantage, drawback, impediment, obstruction, qualification reservation, restraint, restriction, snag.

antonyms asset, extension, furtherance.

limited *adj* borné, bounded, checked, circumscribed, confined, constrained, controlled, cramped, curbed, defined, determinate, diminished, finite, fixed, hampered, hemmed in, inadequate, insufficient, minimal, narrow, reduced, restricted, short, unsatisfactory.

antonym limitless.

limitless *adj* boundless, countless, endless, illimitable, illimited, immeasurable, immense, immensurable, incalculable, inexhaustible, infinite, measureless, never-ending, numberless, unbounded, undefined, unending, unlimited, untold, vast.

antonym limited.

limp[1] *v* dot, falter, halt, hamble, hirple, hitch, hobble, hop, shamble, shuffle.

n claudication, hitch, hobble, lameness.

limp[2] *adj* debilitated, drooping, enervated, exhausted, flabby, flaccid, flexible, flexile, floppy, hypotonic, lax, lethargic, limber, loose, pliable, pooped, relaxed, slack, soft, spent, tired, toneless, weak, worn out.

antonym strong.

limpid *adj* bright, clear, comprehensible, crystal-clear, crystalline, glassy, hyaline, intelligible, lucid, pellucid, pure, still, translucent, transparent, unruffled, untroubled.

antonyms muddy, ripply, turbid, unintelligible.

line[1] *n* band, bar, border, borderline, boundary, cable, chain, channel, column, configuration, contour, cord, crease, crocodile, crow's foot, dash, demarcation, disposition, edge, features, figure, filament, file, firing line, formation, front, front line, frontier, furrow, groove, limit, mark, outline, position, procession, profile, queue, rank, rope, row, rule, score, scratch, sequence, series, silhouette, stipe, strand, streak, string, stroke, tail, thread, trail, trenches, underline, wire, wrinkle.

v border, bound, crease, cut, draw, edge, fringe, furrow, hatch, inscribe, mark, rank, rim, rule, score, skirt, verge.

line up align, arrange, array, assemble, dispose, engage, fall in, form ranks, hire, lay on, marshal, obtain, order, organise, prepare, procure, produce, queue up, range, regiment, secure, straighten.

line[2] *n* activity, approach, area, avenue, axis, belief, business, calling, course, course of action, department, direction, employment, field, forte, ideology, interest, job, line of country, method, occupation, path, policy, position, practice, procedure, profession, province, pursuit, route, scheme, specialisation, specialism, speciality, specialty, system, track, trade, trajectory, vocation.

line[3] *n* ancestry, breed, family, lineage, pedigree, race, stirps, stock, strain, succession.

line[4] *n* card, clue, hint, indication, information, lead, letter, memo, memorandum, message, note, postcard, report, word.

line[5] *v* ceil, cover, encase, face, fill, reinforce, strengthen, stuff.

lineage *n* ancestors, ancestry, birth, breed, descendants, descent, extraction, family, forebears, forefathers, genealogy, heredity, house, line, offspring, pedigree, progeny, race, stirp(s), stock, succession.

lineaments *n* appearance, aspect, configuration, countenance, face, features, lines, outline(s), physiognomy, traits, visage.

lined *adj* feint, furrowed, lineate(d), lineolate, ruled, wizened, worn, wrinkled.

antonyms smooth, unlined.

linen *n* bed-linen, napery, sheets, table-linen, white goods.

lines[1] *n* appearance, configuration, contour, convention, cut, example, model, outline, pattern, plan, principle, procedure, shape, style.

lines[2] *n* book, libretto, part, script, text, words.

lines[3] *n* cross-hatching, hatching, shading.

line-up *n* arrangement, array, bill, cast, queue, row, selection, team.

linger *v* abide, continue, dally, dawdle, delay, dilly-dally, endure, hang around, hang on, hold out, idle, lag, last out, loiter, persist, procrastinate, remain, stay, stop, survive, tarry, wait.

antonyms leave, rush.

lingerie *n* frillies, inexpressibles, linen, smalls, underclothes, underclothing, undergarments, underlinen, underset, unmentionables.

lingering *adj* dragging, long-drawn-out, persistent, prolonged, protracted, remaining, slow.

antonym quick.

lingo *n* argot, cant, dialect, idiom, jargon, language, parlance, patois, patter, speech, talk, terminology, tongue, vernacular, vocabulary.

linguist *n* linguistic scientist, linguistician, verbalist, vocabularian.

liniment *n* balm, balsam, cream, embrocation, emollient, lotion, ointment, salve, unguent, wash.

lining *n* backing, encasement, inlay, interfacing, interlining, padding, stiffening.

link *n* association, attachment, bond, communication, component, connection, constituent, division, element, joint, knot, liaison, member, part, piece, relationship, tie, tie-up, union.

v associate, attach, bind, bracket, catenate, concatenate, connect, couple, fasten, identify, join, relate, tie, unite, yoke.

antonyms separate, unfasten.

link up ally, amalgamate, connect, dock, hook up, join, join forces, merge, team up, unify.

antonym separate.

link-up *n* alliance, amalgamation, association, connection, merger, tie-in, union.

antonym separation.

lion-hearted *adj* bold, brave, courageous, daring, dauntless, dreadless, gallant, heroic, intrepid, resolute, stalwart, stout-hearted, valiant, valorous.

antonym cowardly.

lionise *v* acclaim, adulate, aggrandise, celebrate, eulogise, exalt, fête, glorify, hero-worship, honour, idolise, magnify, praise, sing the praises of.

antonym vilify.

lion-like *adj* leonine, lion-hearted, lionly.

lip[1] *n* border, brim, brink, edge, margin, rim, verge.

lip[2] *n* backchat, cheek, effrontery, impertinence, impudence, insolence, rudeness, sauce.

antonym politeness.

liquefaction *n* deliquescence, dissolution, dissolving, fusion, liquefying, melting, thawing.

antonym solidification.

liquefy *v* deliquesce, dissolve, fluidise, flux, fuse, liquesce, liquidise, melt, run, smelt, thaw.

antonym solidify.

liquid *n* drink, fluid, juice, liquor, lotion, potation, sap, solution.

adj aqueous, clear, convertible, dulcet, flowing, fluid, limpid, liquefied, mellifluent, mellifluous, melted, molten, negotiable, running, runny, serous, shining, smooth, soft, sweet, thawed, translucent, transparent, watery, wet.

antonyms harsh, solid.

liquidate *v* abolish, annihilate, annul, assassinate, bump off, cancel, cash, clear, destroy, discharge, dispatch, dissolve, do away with, do in, eliminate, exterminate, finish off, honour, kill, massacre, murder, pay, pay off, realise, remove, rub out, sell off, sell up, settle, silence, square, terminate, wipe out.

liquor[1] *n* aguardiente, alcohol, booze, drink, fire-water, grog, hard stuff, hooch, intoxicant, juice, jungle juice, potation, rotgut, spirits, strong drink, tape.

liquor[2] *n* broth, essence, extract, gravy, infusion, juice, liquid, stock.

lissom(e) *adj* agile, flexible, graceful, light, limber, lithe, lithesome, loose-jointed, loose-limbed, nimble, pliable, pliant, supple, willowy.

antonym stiff.

list[1] *n* catalogue, directory, enumeration, file, index, inventory, invoice, leet, listing, litany, matricula, record, register, roll, schedule, series, syllabus, table, tabulation, tally.

v alphabeticise, bill, book, catalogue, enrol, enter, enumerate, file, index, itemise, note, record, register, schedule, set down, tabulate, write down.

list[2] *v* cant, careen, heel, heel over, incline, lean, slope, tilt, tip.

n cant, leaning, slant, slope, tilt.

listen *v* attend, get a load of, give ear, give heed to, hang on (someone's) words, hang on (someone's) lips, hark, hear, hearken, heed, keep one's ears open, lend an ear, mind, obey, observe, pay attention, pin back one's ears, prick up one's ears, take notice.

listless *adj* apathetic, bored, depressed, enervated, ennuyed, heavy, impassive, inattentive, indifferent, indolent, inert, languid, languishing, lethargic, lifeless, limp, lymphatic, mopish, sluggish, spiritless, supine, torpid, uninterested, vacant.

antonym lively.

listlessness *n* accidie, acedia, apathy, enervation, ennui, inattention, indifference, indolence, languidness, languor, lethargy, lifelessness, sloth, sluggishness, spiritlessness, supineness, torpidity, torpor.

antonym liveliness.

litany *n* account, catalogue, enumeration, invocation, list, narration, narrative, petition, prayer, recital, recitation, refrain, repetition, supplication, tale.

literacy *n* ability, articulacy, articulateness, cultivation, culture, education, erudition, intelligence, knowledge, learning, proficiency, scholarship.

antonym illiteracy.

literal *adj* accurate, actual, boring, close, colourless, down-to-earth, dull, exact, factual, faithful, genuine, matter-of-fact, plain, prosaic, prosy, real, simple, strict, true, unexaggerated, unimaginative, uninspired, unvarnished, verbatim, word-for-word.

antonym loose.

literally *adv* actually, closely, exactly, faithfully, literatim, plainly, precisely, really, simply, strictly, to the letter, truly, verbatim, word for word.

antonym loosely.

literary *adj* bookish, cultivated, cultured, erudite, formal, learned, lettered, literate, refined, scholarly, well-read.

antonym illiterate.

literature *n* belles-lettres, blurb, brochure(s), bumf, circular(s), hand-out(s), information, leaflet(s), letters, lore, pamphlet(s), paper(s), writings.

lithe *adj* double-jointed, flexible, flexile, limber, lissom(e), lithesome, loose-jointed, loose-limbed, pliable, pliant, supple.

antonym stiff.

litigant *n* claimant, complainant, contender, contestant, disputant, litigator, party, plaintiff.

litigation *n* action, case, contention, lawsuit, process, prosecution, suit.

litigious *adj* argumentative, belligerent, contentious, disputable, disputatious, quarrelsome.

antonym easy-going.

litter[1] *n* clutter, confusion, debris, detritus, disarray, disorder, fragments, jumble, mess, muck, refuse, rubbish, scatter, scoria, shreds, untidiness, wastage.

v bestrew, clutter, derange, disarrange, disorder, mess up, scatter, strew.

antonym tidy.

litter[2] *n* brood, family, offspring, progeny, quiverful, young.

litter[3] *n* couch, palanquin, stretcher.

little *adj* babyish, base, brief, cheap, diminutive, dwarf, elfin, fleeting, hasty, immature, inconsiderable, infant, infinitesimal, insignificant, insufficient, junior, Lilliputian, meagre, mean, microscopic, miniature, minor, minute, negligible, paltry, passing, petite, petty, piccaninny, pint-size(d), pygmy, scant, short, short-lived, skimpy, slender, small, sparse, tiny, transient, trifling, trivial, undeveloped, unimportant, wee, young.

antonyms important, large, long.

adv barely, hardly, infrequently, rarely, scarcely, seldom.

antonyms frequently, greatly.

n bit, dab, dash, drib, fragment, hint, modicum, particle, pinch, snippet, speck, spot, taste, touch, trace, trifle.

antonym lot.

little by little bit by bit, by degrees, gradually, imperceptibly, in penny numbers, piecemeal, progressively, slowly, step by step.

antonyms all at one go, quickly.

liturgical *adj* ceremonial, eucharistic, formal, hieratic, ritual, sacerdotal, sacramental, solemn.

antonym secular.

liturgy *n* celebration, ceremony, form, formula, office, rite, ritual, sacrament, service, usage, worship.

live[1] *v* abide, breathe, continue, draw breath, dwell, earn a living, endure, exist, fare, feed, get along, hang out, inhabit, last, lead, lodge, make ends meet, pass, persist, prevail, remain, reside, settle, stay, subsist, survive.

antonyms cease, die.

live it up celebrate, go on the spree, have a ball, make merry, make whoopee, paint the town red, revel.

live[2] *adj* active, alert, alight, alive, animate, blazing, breathing, brisk, burning, connected, controversial, current, dynamic, earnest, energetic, existent, glowing, hot, ignited, lively, living, pertinent, pressing, prevalent, relevant, sentient, smouldering, topical, unsettled, vigorous, vital, vivid, wide-awake.

antonyms apathetic, dead, out.

liveable *adj* acceptable, adequate, bearable, comfortable, endurable, habitable, inhabitable, possible, satisfactory, sufferable, supportable, tolerable, worthwhile.

antonyms unbearable, uninhabitable.

liveable with bearable, companionable, compatible, congenial, gemütlich, harmonious, passable, sociable, tolerable.

antonyms impossible, unbearable.

livelihood *n* employment, income, job, living, maintenance, means, occupation, subsistence, support, sustenance, work.

liveliness *n* activity, animation, boisterousness, brio, briskness, dynamism, energy, entrain, gaiety, nowness, quickness, smartness, spirit, sprightliness, vitality, vivacity.

antonyms apathy, inactivity.

livelong complete, enduring, entire, full, long, protracted, whole.

antonym partial.

lively *adj* active, agile, alert, animated, astir, blithe, blithesome, breezy, bright, brisk, buckish, bustling, busy, buxom, buzzing, canty, cheerful, chipper, chirpy, colourful, crowded, energetic, eventful, exciting, forceful, frisky, frolicsome, galliard, gay, invigorating, keen, lifesome, lightsome, merry, mouvementé, moving, nimble, perky, quick, racy, refreshing, skittish, sparkling, spirited, sprightly, spry, stimulating, stirring, swinging, tit(t)upy, vigorous, vivacious, vivid, zippy.

antonyms apathetic, inactive, moribund.

liven up animate, brighten, buck up, energise, enliven, hot up, invigorate, pep up, perk up, put life into, rouse, stir, stir up, vitalise, vivify.

antonyms deaden, dishearten.

liverish *adj* crabbed, crabby, crotchety, crusty, disagreeable, grumpy, ill-humoured, irascible, irritable, peevish, snappy, splenetic, testy, tetchy.

antonyms calm, easy-going.

livery *n* apparel, attire, clothes, clothing, costume, dress, garb, habit, raiment, regalia, suit, uniform, vestments.

live-wire ball of fire, cricket, dynamo, go-getter, grig, hustler, life and soul of the party, self-starter.

antonym wet blanket.

livid[1] *adj* angry, beside oneself, boiling, enraged, exasperated, fuming, furibund, furious, incensed, indignant, infuriated, irate, ireful, mad, outraged, waxy.

antonym calm.

livid[2] *adj* angry, ashen, black-and-blue, blanched, bloodless, bruised, contused, discoloured, doughy, greyish, leaden, pale, pallid, pasty, purple, wan, waxen, waxy.

antonyms healthy, rosy.

living *adj* active, alive, animated, breathing, existing, live, lively, strong, vigorous, vital.

antonyms dead, sluggish.

n being, benefice, existence, income, job, life, livelihood, maintenance, occupation, profession, property, subsistence, support, sustenance, way of life, work.

load *n* affliction, albatross, bale, burden, cargo, consignment, encumbrance, freight, goods, lading, millstone, onus, oppression, pressure, shipment, trouble, weight, worry.

v adulterate, burden, charge, cram, doctor, drug, encumber, fill, fortify, freight, hamper, heap, lade, oppress, overburden, pack, pile, prime, saddle with, stack, stuff, trouble, weigh down, weight, worry.

loaded *adj* affluent, artful, biased, burdened, charged, distorted, drugged, drunk, fixed, flush, freighted, full, high, inebriated, insidious, intoxicated, laden, manipulative, moneyed, prejudicial, primed, rich, rolling, tight, tipsy, tricky, under the influence, wealthy, weighted, well-heeled, well-off, well-to-do.

antonyms poor, sober, straightforward, unloaded.

loads *n* a million, dozens, heaps, hordes, hundreds, lots, millions, scores, thousands, tons.

loaf[1] *n* block, cake, cube, lump, mass, slab.

loaf[2] *v* idle, laze, lie around, loiter, loll, lounge around, mooch, moon, stand about, take it easy.

antonym toil.

loaf[3] *n* brains, chump, common sense, gumption, head, noddle, nous, sense, smeddum.

loafer *n* beachcomber, bludger, bum, bummer, burn, corner-boy, do-nothing, drone, idler, layabout, lazybones, lounge-lizard, lounger, ne'er-do-well, shirker, skiver, sluggard, time-waster, wastrel.

antonym worker.

loan *n* accommodation, advance, allowance, calque, credit, lend-lease, loan translation, loan-word, mortgage, touch.

v accommodate, advance, allow, credit, lend, let out, oblige.

antonym borrow.

lo(a)th *adj* against, averse, backward, counter, disinclined, grudging, hesitant, indisposed, opposed, reluctant, resisting, unwilling.

antonym willing.

loathe *v* abhor, abominate, despise, detest, dislike, execrate, hate, keck.

antonym like.

loathing *n* abhorrence, abomination, antipathy, aversion, detestation, disgust, dislike, execration, hatred, horror, nausea, odium, repugnance, repulsion, revulsion.

antonym liking.

loathsome *adj* abhorrent, abominable, detestable, disgusting, execrable, hateful, horrible, loathful, nasty, nauseating, obnoxious, odious, offensive, repellent, repugnant, repulsive, revolting, vile.

antonym likeable.

lob *v* chuck, fling, heave, launch, lift, loft, pitch, shy, throw, toss.

lobby[1] *v* call for, campaign for, demand, influence, persuade, press for, pressure, promote, pull strings, push for, solicit, urge.

n ginger group, pressure group.

lobby[2] *n* anteroom, corridor, entrance hall, foyer, hall, hallway, passage, passageway, porch, vestibule, waiting-room.

local *adj* community, confined, district, limited, narrow, neighbourhood, parish, parochial, provincial, pump, regional, restricted, small-town, vernacular, vicinal.

antonym far-away.

n denizen, inhabitant, native, resident, yokel.

antonym incomer.

locale *n* area, locality, location, locus, place, position, scene, setting, site, spot, venue, zone.

localise *v* ascribe, assign, circumscribe, concentrate, confine, contain, delimit, delimitate, limit, narrow down, pin-point, restrain, restrict, specify, zero in on.

locality *n* area, district, locale, location, neck of the woods, neighbourhood, place, position, region, scene, setting, site, spot, vicinity, zone.

locate *v* detect, discover, establish, find, fix, identify, lay one's hands on, pin-point, place, put, run to earth, seat, set, settle, situate, track down, unearth.

location *n* bearings, locale, locus, place, point, position, site, situation, spot, ubiety, venue, whereabouts.

lock[1] *n* bolt, clasp, fastening, padlock, sneck.

v bolt, clasp, clench, close, clutch, disengage, embrace, encircle, enclose, engage, entangle, entwine, fasten, grapple, grasp, hug, join, latch, link, mesh, press, seal, secure, shut, sneck, unite, unlock.

lock out ban, bar, debar, exclude, keep out, ostracise, refuse admittance to, shut out.

lock together interdigitate, interlock.

lock up cage, close up, confine, detain, enclose, imprison, incarcerate, jail, pen, secure, shut, shut in, shut up.

antonym free.

lock[2] *n* curl, plait, ringlet, strand, tress, tuft.

lock-up *n* brig, can, cell, clink, cooler, gaol, garage, hoos(e)gow, jail, jug, pen, penitentiary, prison, quod, tolbooth.

locomotion *n* action, ambulation, headway, motion, movement, moving, progress, progression, travel, travelling.

locution *n* accent, articulation, cliché, collocation, diction, expression, idiom, inflection, intonation, phrase, phrasing, style, term, turn of phrase, wording.

lodge *n* abode, assemblage, association, branch, cabin, chalet, chapter, club, cot, cot-house, cottage, den, gang-hut, gatehouse, group, haunt, house, hunting-lodge, hut, lair, meeting-place, retreat, shelter, society.

v accommodate, billet, board, deposit, dig, entertain, file, get stuck, harbour, imbed, implant, lay, place, put, put on record, put up, quarter, register, room, set, shelter, sojourn, stay, stick, stop, submit.

lodger *n* boarder, guest, inmate, paying guest, renter, resident, roomer, tenant.

lodgings *n* abode, accommodation, apartments, billet, boarding, digs, dwelling, gite, habitation, pad, quarters, residence, rooms, shelter.

lofty *adj* arrogant, condescending, dignified, disdainful, distinguished, elevated, esteemed, exalted, grand, haughty, high, high and mighty, illustrious, imperial, imposing, lordly, majestic, noble, patronising, proud, raised, renowned, sky-high, snooty, soaring, stately, sublime, supercilious, superior, tall, toffee-nosed, towering.

antonyms humble, low(ly), modest.

log[1] *n* billet, block, bole, chunk, loggat, stump, timber, trunk.

log[2] *n* account, chart, daybook, diary, journal, listing, logbook, record, tally.

v book, chart, note, record, register, report, tally, write down, write in, write up.

logic *n* argumentation, deduction, dialectic(s), ratiocination, rationale, rationality, reason, reasoning, sense.

logical *adj* clear, cogent, coherent, consistent, deducible, elenctic, judicious, necessary, obvious, pertinent, plausible, rational, reasonable, relevant, sensible, sound, valid, well-founded, well-grounded, well-organised, wise.

antonyms illogical, irrational.

logistics *n* co-ordination, engineering, management, masterminding, orchestration, organisation, planning, plans, strategy.

loins *n* genitalia, manliness, potency, power, reins, strength, virility.

loiter *v* dally, dawdle, delay, dilly-dally, hang about, idle, lag, lallygag, linger, loaf, loll, lollygag, mooch, mouch, saunter, skulk, stroll.

loll *v* dangle, depend, droop, drop, flap, flop, hang, lean, loaf, lounge, recline, relax, sag, slouch, slump, sprawl.

lone *adj* deserted, isolated, lonesome, one, only, separate, separated, single, sole, solitary, unaccompanied, unattached, unattended.

antonym accompanied.

loneliness *n* aloneness, desolation, forlornness, friendlessness, isolation, lonesomeness, seclusion, solitariness, solitude.

lonely *adj* abandoned, alone, apart, companionless, destitute, estranged, forlorn, forsaken, friendless, isolated, lonely-heart, lonesome, outcast, out-of-the-way, remote, secluded, sequestered, solitary, unfrequented, uninhabited, untrodden.

loner *n* hermit, individualist, lone wolf, maverick, outsider, pariah, recluse, solitary, solitudinarian.

lonesome *adj* cheerless, companionless, deserted, desolate, dreary, forlorn, friendless, gloomy, isolated, lone, lonely, solitary.

long *adj* dragging, elongated, expanded, expansive, extended, extensive, far-reaching, interminable, late, lengthy, lingering, long-drawn-out, marathon, prolonged, protracted, slow, spread out, stretched, sustained, tardy.

antonyms abbreviated, brief, fleeting, short.

long for covet, crave, desire, dream of, hanker for, hunger after, itch for, lust after, pine, thirst for, want, wish, yearn for, yen for.

long-drawn-out *adj* interminable, lengthy, long-drawn, long-winded, marathon, overextended, overlong, prolix, prolonged, protracted, spun out, tedious.

antonyms brief, curtailed.

longing *n* ambition, aspiration, coveting, craving, desire, hankering, hungering, itch, thirst, urge, wish, yearning, yen.

adj anxious, appetence, appetency, ardent, avid, craving, desiderium, desirous, eager, hungry, languishing, pining, wishful, wistful, yearning.

long-lasting *adj* abiding, continuing, enduring, entrenched, established, evergreen, imperishable, lifelong, long-lived, long-standing, perdurable, permanent, prolonged, protracted, unchanging, unfading.

antonyms ephemeral, short-lived, transient.

long-lived *adj* durable, enduring, lasting, longevous, long-lasting, long-standing, macrobian, macrobiotic.

antonyms brief, ephemeral, short-lived.

long-standing *adj* abiding, enduring, established, fixed, hallowed, long-established, long-lasting, long-lived, time-honoured, traditional.

long-suffering *adj* easy-going, forbearant, forbearing, forgiving, patient, placid, resigned, stoical, tolerant, uncomplaining.

long-winded *adj* circumlocutory, diffuse, discursive, garrulous, lengthy, long-drawn-out, overlong, prolix, prolonged, rambling, repetitious, tedious, verbose, voluble, wordy.

antonyms brief, compact, curt, terse.

long-windedness *n* diffuseness, discursiveness, garrulity, lengthiness, longueur, macrology, prolixity, repetitiousness, tediousness, verbosity, volubility, wordiness.

antonyms brevity, curtness.

look *v* appear, behold, consider, contemplate, display, evidence, examine, exhibit, eye, gape, gawk, gawp, gaze, get a load of, glance, goggle, inspect, observe, ogle, peep, regard, rubberneck, scan, scrutinise, see, seem, show, stare, study, survey, take a butcher's, take a gander, take a shufti, view, watch.

n air, appearance, aspect, bearing, butcher's, cast, complexion, countenance, decko, demeanour, effect, examination, expression, eyeful, eye-glance, face, fashion, gander, gaze, glance, glimpse, guise, inspection, look-see, manner, mien, observation, once-over, peek, review, semblance, shufti, sight, squint, survey, view.

look after attend to, care for, chaperon, guard, keep an eye on, mind, nurse, protect, supervise, take care of, take charge of, tend, watch.

antonym neglect.

look down on contemn, despise, disdain, hold in contempt, look down one's nose at, misprise, pooh-pooh, scorn, sneer at, spurn, turn one's nose up at.

antonyms approve, esteem.

look for forage for, hunt, hunt for, hunt out, quest, search for, seek.

look forward to anticipate, await, count on, envisage, envision, expect, hope for, long for, look for, wait for.

look into check out, delve into, enquire about, examine, explore, fathom, follow up, go into, inspect, investigate, look over, plumb, probe, research, scrutinise, study.

look like resemble, take after.

look out be careful, be on the qui vive, beware, keep an eye out, keep one's eyes peeled, keep one's eyes skinned, pay attention, watch out.

look out on face, front, front on, give on (to), overlook.

look over cast an eye over, check, examine, flick through, give a once-over, inspect, look through, monitor, peruse, scan, view.

look to/for anticipate, await, count on, expect, hope for, reckon on, rely on.

look up[1] call on, drop by, drop in on, find, hunt for, look in on, pay a visit to, research, search for, seek out, stop by, track down, visit.

look up[2] ameliorate, come on, get better, improve, meliorate, perk up, pick up, progress, shape up.

look up to admire, esteem, have a high opinion of, honour, respect, revere.

look-alike *n* clone, dead ringer, doppel-gänger, double, living image, replica, ringer, spit, spit and image, spitting image, twin.

look-out *n* affair, beacon, business, citadel, concern, funeral, guard, post, problem, readiness, sentinal, sentry, tower, vedette, vigil, watch, watchman, watch-tower, weather-eye, worry.

loom *v* appear, bulk, dominate, emerge, hang over, hover, impend, materialise, menace, mount, overhang, overshadow, overtop, rise, soar, take shape, threaten, tower.

loop *n* arc, bend, circle, coil, convolution, curl, curve, eyelet, hoop, kink, loophole, noose, ring, spiral, turn, twirl, twist, whorl.

v bend, braid, circle, coil, connect, curl, curve round, encircle, fold, gird, join, knot, roll, spiral, turn, twist.

loophole *n* aperture, avoidance, escape, evasion, excuse, get-out, let-out, opening, plea, pretence, pretext, slot, subterfuge.

loose[1] *adj* baggy, crank, diffuse, disconnected, disordered, easy, floating, free, hanging, ill-defined, imprecise, inaccurate, indefinite, indistinct, inexact, insecure, loosened, movable, rambling, random, relaxed, released, shaky, slack, slackened, sloppy, solute, unattached, unbound, unconfined, unfastened, unfettered, unrestricted, unsecured, untied, vague, wobbly.

antonyms close, compact, precise, strict, taut, tense, tight.

v absolve, detach, disconnect, disengage, ease, free, let go, liberate, loosen, release, set free, slacken, unbind, unbrace, unclasp, uncouple, undo, unfasten, unhand, unleash, unlock, unloose, unmew, unmoor, unpen, untie.

antonyms bind, fasten, fix, secure.

loose[2] *adj* abandoned, careless, debauched, disreputable, dissipated, dissolute, fast, heedless, immoral, imprudent, lax, lewd, libertine, licentious, negligent, profligate, promiscuous, rash, thoughtless, unchaste, unmindful, wanton.

antonyms strict, stringent, tight.

loosen *v* deliver, detach, free, let go, let out, liberate, release, separate, set free, slacken, unbind, undo, unfasten, unloose, unloosen, unstick, untie.

antonym tighten.

loosen up ease up, go easy, lessen, let up, mitigate, moderate, relax, soften, unbend, weaken.

loot *n* boodle, booty, cache, goods, haul, plunder, prize, riches, spoils, swag.

v burglarise, despoil, maraud, pillage, plunder, raid, ransack, ravage, rifle, rob, sack.

lop *v* abscind, chop, clip, crop, curtail, cut, detach, detruncate, dock, hack, prune, sever, shorten, trim, truncate.

lope *v* bound, canter, gallop, lollop, run, spring, stride.

lop-sided *adj* askew, asymmetrical, awry, cockeyed, crooked, disproportionate, ill-balanced, off balance, one-sided, out of true, squint, tilting, unbalanced, unequal, uneven, warped.

antonyms balanced, straight, symmetrical.

loquacious *adj* babbling, blathering, chattering, chatty, conversative, gabby, garrulous, gassy, gossipy, multiloquent, multiloquous, talkative, voluble, wordy.

antonyms pauciloquent, succinct, taciturn, terse.

loquacity *n* chattiness, effusiveness, garrulity, gassiness, multiloquence, multiloquy, talkativeness, volubility.

antonyms succinctness, taciturnity, terseness.

lord *n* baron, commander, count, daimio, duke, earl, governor, Herr, king, leader, liege, liege-lord, master, monarch, noble, nobleman, overlord, peer, potentate, prince, ruler, seigneur, seignior, sovereign, superior, suzerain, viscount.

lord it over act big, boss around, domineer, oppress, order around, pull rank, put on airs, repress, swagger, tyrannise.

lordly *adj* aristocratic, arrogant, authoritarian, condescending, despotic, dictatorial, dignified, disdainful, domineering, exalted, gracious, grand, haughty, high and mighty, high-handed, hoity-toity, imperial, imperious, lofty, majestic, masterful, noble, overbearing, patronising, princely, proud, regal, stately, stuck-up, supercilious, swanky, toffee-nosed, tyrannical.

antonyms humble, low(ly), mean.

lore *n* beliefs, doctrine, erudition, experience, know-how, knowledge, learning, letters, mythus, saws, sayings, scholarship, schooling, teaching, traditions, wisdom.

lorry *n* camion, double-bottom, drag, drawbar outfit, float, juggernaut, pick-up, truck.

lose *v* capitulate, come a cropper, come to grief, consume, default, deplete, displace, dissipate, dodge, drain, drop, duck, elude, escape, evade, exhaust, expend, fail, fall short, forfeit, forget, get the worst of, give (someone) the slip, lap, lavish, leave behind, lose out on, misfile, mislay, misplace, miss, misspend, outdistance, outrun, outstrip, overtake, pass, pass up, shake off, slip away, squander, stray from, suffer defeat, take a licking, throw off, use up, wander from, waste, yield.

antonyms gain, make, win.

loser *n* also-ran, bum, bum steer, bummer, dud, failure, flop, lemon, no-hoper, runner-up, sucker, underdog, wash-out.

antonym winner.

loss *n* bereavement, cost, damage, debit, debt, defeat, deficiency, deficit, depletion, deprivation, destruction, detriment, disadvantage, disappearance, failure, forfeiture, harm, hurt, impairment, injury, losing, losings, misfortune, privation, ruin, shrinkage, squandering, waste, write-off.

antonyms benefit, gain.

losses *n* casualties, dead, death toll, disprofit, fatalities, missing, wounded.

lost *adj* abandoned, abolished, absent, absorbed, abstracted, adrift, annihilated, astray, baffled, bewildered, confused, consumed, corrupt, damned, demolished, depraved, destroyed, devastated, disappeared, disoriented, dissipated, dissolute, distracted, dreamy, engrossed, entranced, eradicated, exterminated, fallen, forfeited, frittered away, irreclaimable, licentious, misapplied, misdirected, mislaid, misplaced, missed, missing, misspent, misused, mystified, obliterated, off-course, off-track, perished, perplexed, preoccupied, profligate, puzzled, rapt, ruined, spellbound, squandered, strayed, unrecallable, unrecapturable, unrecoverable, untraceable, vanished, wanton, wasted, wayward, wiped out, wrecked.

antonym found.

lot *n* accident, allowance, assortment, batch, chance, collection, consignment, crowd, cut, destiny, doom, fate, fortune, group, hazard, jing-bang, parcel, part, percentage, piece, plight, portion, quantity, quota, ration, set, share, weird.

loth *see* **loath**.

lotion *n* balm, cream, embrocation, fomentation, liniment, salve, solution.

lots *n* a great deal, abundance, oodles, scade, tons.

lottery *n* chance, draw, gamble, hazard, raffle, risk, sweepstake, tombola, toss-up, uncertainty, venture.

loud *adj* blaring, blatant, boisterous, booming, brash, brassy, brazen, clamorous, coarse, crass, crude, deafening, ear-piercing, ear-splitting, flamboyant, flashy, garish, gaudy, glaring, high-sounding, loud-mouthed, lurid, noisy, offensive, ostentatious, piercing, raucous, resounding, rowdy, showy, sonorous, stentorian, streperous, strepitant, strident, strong, tasteless, tawdry, thundering, tumultuous, turbulent, vehement, vocal, vociferous, vulgar.

antonyms low, quiet, soft.

loudly *adv* clamorously, deafeningly, fortissimo, lustily, noisily, resoundingly, shrilly, streperously, strepitantly, stridently, strongly, uproariously, vehemently, vigorously, vocally, vociferously.

antonyms quietly, softly.

loudmouth *n* big mouth, blusterer, boaster, Bobadil, brag, braggadocio, braggart, Drawcansir, gasbag, swaggerer, windbag.

loud-voiced *adj* full-throated, leather-lunged, penetrating, piercing, roaring, sonorous, stentorian.

antonyms quiet, soft.

lounge *v* dawdle, idle, kill time, laze, lie about, lie back, loaf, loiter, loll, potter, recline, relax, slump, sprawl, take it easy, waste time.

n day-room, drawing-room, parlour, sitting-room.

lour, lower *v* be brewing, blacken, cloud over, darken, frown, give a dirty look, glare, glower, impend, look daggers, loom, menace, scowl, threaten.

louring, lowering *adj* black, brooding, browning, clouded, cloudy, dark, darkening, forbidding, foreboding, gloomy, glowering, grey, grim, heavy, impending, menacing, minatory, ominous, overcast, scowling, sullen, surly, threatening.

lousy *adj* awful, bad, base, contemptible, crap, despicable, dirty, hateful, inferior, lice-infested, lice-ridden, low, mean, miserable, no good, pedicular, pediculous, poor, rotten, second-rate, shoddy, slovenly, terrible, trashy, vicious, vile.

antonyms excellent, superb.

lout *n* bear, booby, boor, bull-calf, bumpkin, calf, chuckle-head, churl, clod, dolt, gawk, hallion, hick, hob, hobbledehoy, jake, lager lout, lob, lubber, lummox, oaf, swad, yahoo, yob, yobbo.

loutish *adj* bearish, boorish, bungling, churlish, clodhopping, coarse, doltish, gawky, gross, ill-bred, ill-mannered, lubberly, lumpen, lumpish, oafish, rough, stolid, swinish, uncouth, unmannerly, yobbish.

lovable *adj* adorable, amiable, attractive, captivating, charming, cuddly, delightful, enchanting, endearing, engaging, fetching, likable, lovely, pleasing, sweet, taking, winning, winsome.

antonym hateful.

love *v* adore, adulate, appreciate, cherish, delight in, desire, dote on, enjoy, fancy, hold dear, idolise, like, prize, relish, savour, take pleasure in, think the world of, treasure, want, worship.

antonyms detest, hate, loathe.

n adoration, adulation, affection, agape, aloha, amity, amorosity, amorousness, ardour, attachment, delight, devotion, enjoyment, fondness, friendship, inclination, infatuation, liking, partiality, passion, rapture, regard, relish, soft spot, taste, tenderness, warmth, weakness.

antonyms detestation, hate, loathing.

love-affair *n* affair, amour, grande passion, intrigue, liaison, love, mania, passion, relationship, romance.

loveless *adj* cold, cold-hearted, disliked, forsaken, friendless, frigid, hard, heartless, icy, insensitive, lovelorn, passionless, unappreciated, uncherished, unfeeling, unfriendly, unloved, unloving, unresponsive, unvalued.

antonym passionate.

lovely *adj* admirable, adorable, agreeable, amiable, attractive, beautiful, captivating, charming, comely, delightful, enchanting, engaging, enjoyable, exquisite, graceful, gratifying, handsome, idyllic, nice, pleasant, pleasing, pretty, sweet, taking, winning.

antonyms hideous, ugly, unlovely.

love-making *n* amation, carnal knowledge, coition, coitus, congress, copulation, courtship, dalliance, foreplay, gallantry, intercourse, intimacy, mating, sexual intercourse, sexual relations, sexual union, venery.

lover *n* admirer, amoretto, amorist, amoroso, beau, beloved, bidie-in, bon ami, boyfriend, Casanova, fancy man, fancy woman, fiancé(e), flame, gigolo, girlfriend, inamorata, inamorato, mistress, paramour, philanderer, suitor, swain, sweetheart.

lovesick *adj* desiring, infatuated, languishing, longing, lovelorn, mashed, pining, yearning.

loving *adj* affectionate, amative, amatorial, amatorian, amatorious, amorous, ardent, cordial, dear, demonstrative, devoted, doting, fond, friendly, kind, passionate, solicitous, tender, warm, warm-hearted.

low[1] *adj* abject, base, base-born, blue, brassed off, browned off, cheap, coarse, common, contemptible, crude, dastardly, debilitated, deep, deficient, degraded, dejected, depleted, depraved, depressed, despicable, despondent, disgraceful, disheartened, dishonourable, disreputable, down, down in the dumps, downcast, dying, economical, exhausted, fed up, feeble, forlorn, frail, gloomy, glum, gross, humble, hushed, ignoble, ill, ill-bred, inadequate, inexpensive, inferior, insignificant, little, low-born, low-grade, lowly, low-lying, meagre, mean, mediocre, meek, menial, miserable, moderate, modest, morose, muffled, muted, nasty, obscene, obscure, paltry, plain, plebeian, poor, prostrate, puny, quiet, reasonable, reduced, rough, rude, sad, scant, scurvy, second-rate, servile, shallow, shoddy, short, simple, sinking, small, soft, sordid, sparse, squat, stricken, stunted, subdued, substandard, sunken, trifling, unbecoming, undignified, unhappy, unpretentious, unrefined, unworthy, vile, vulgar, weak, whispered, worthless.

antonyms elevated, high, lofty, noble.

low point all-time low, low-watermark, nadir, perigee.

low[2] *v* bellow, moo.

low-born *adj* mean-born, plebeian, unexalted.

lowbrow *adj* crude, ignorant, rude, uncultivated, uncultured, uneducated, unlearned, unlettered, unrefined, unscholarly.

antonym highbrow.

low-down *n* dope, gen, info, information, inside story, intelligence, news.

lower[1] *adj* inferior, insignificant, junior, lesser, low-level, lowly, minor, secondary, second-class, smaller, subordinate, subservient, under, unimportant.

v abase, abate, belittle, condescend, couch, curtail, cut, debase, decrease, degrade, deign, demean, demolish, depress, devalue, diminish, discredit, disgrace, downgrade, drop, fall, humble, humiliate, lessen, let down, minimise, moderate, prune, raze, reduce, sink, slash, soften, stoop, submerge, take down, tone down.

antonyms elevate, increase, raise, rise.

lower[2] *see* **lour**.

lowering *see* **louring**.

low-grade *adj* bad, cheap-jack, inferior, poor, second-class, second-rate, substandard, third-rate.

antonyms good, quality.

low-key *adj* downbeat, low-pitched, muffled, muted, quiet, restrained, slight, soft, subdued, understated.

lowly *adj* average, common, docile, dutiful, homespun, humble, ignoble, inferior, low-born, mean, mean-born, meek, mild, modest, obscure, ordinary, plain, plebeian, poor, proletarian, simple, submissive, subordinate, unassuming, unexalted, unpretentious.

antonyms lofty, noble.

low-minded *adj* coarse, crude, depraved, dirty, disgusting, filthy, foul, gross, immoral, indecent, obscene, rude, scurril(e), smutty, uncouth, vulgar.

antonym high-minded.

low-spirited *adj* apathetic, blue, brassed off, browned off, dejected, depressed, despondent, down, down in the dumps, down-hearted, fed up, gloomy, glum, heavy-hearted, low, miserable, moody, pissed off, sad, unhappy.

antonyms cheerful, high-spirited.

loyal *adj* attached, constant, dependable, devoted, dutiful, faithful, honest, leal, patriotic, sincere, staunch, steadfast, true, true-blue, true-hearted, trustworthy, trusty, unswerving, unwavering.

antonyms disloyal, traitorous.

loyalty *n* allegiance, constancy, dependability, devotion, faithfulness, fealty, fidelity, honesty, lealty, patriotism, reliability, sincerity, staunchness, steadfastness, true-heartedness, trueness, trustiness, trustworthiness.

antonyms disloyalty, treachery.

lozenge *n* cough-drop, jujube, pastille, tablet, troche, trochiscus, trochisk.

lubberly *adj* awkward, blundering, bungling, churlish, clodhopping, clownish, clumsy, coarse, crude, dense, doltish, gawky, heavy-handed, loutish, lumbering, lumpen, lumpish, oafish, obtuse, uncouth, ungainly.

lubricate *v* grease, lard, oil, smear, wax.

lucid *adj* beaming, bright, brilliant, clear, clear-cut, clear-headed, compos mentis, comprehensible, crystalline, diaphanous, distinct, effulgent, evident, explicit, glassy, gleaming, intelligible, limpid, luminous, obvious, pellucid, perspicuous, plain, pure, radiant, rational, reasonable, resplendent, sane, sensible, shining, sober, sound, translucent, transparent.

antonyms dark, murky, unclear.

luck *n* accident, blessing, break, chance, destiny, fate, fluke, fortuity, fortune, godsend, good fortune, hap, happenstance, hazard, jam, joss, prosperity, serendipity, stroke, success, windfall.

antonym misfortune.

luckily *adv* feliciter, fortuitously, fortunately, haply, happily, opportunely, propitiously, providentially.

antonym unfortunately.

luckless *adj* calamitous, catastrophic, cursed, disastrous, doomed, fey, hapless, hopeless, ill-fated, ill-starred, jinxed, star-crossed, unfortunate, unhappy, unlucky, unpropitious, unsuccessful.

antonym lucky.

lucky *adj* advantageous, adventitious, auspicious, blessed, canny, charmed, favoured, fluk(e)y, fortuitous, fortunate, jammy, opportune, propitious, prosperous, providential, serendipitous, successful, timely.

antonyms luckless, unlucky.

lucky dip bran tub, grab-bag.

lucrative *adj* advantageous, fecund, fertile, fruitful, gainful, paying, productive, profitable, remunerative, well-paid.

antonym unprofitable.

lucre *n* gain(s), mammon, money, moolah, pelf, profit, riches, spoils, velvet, wealth.

ludicrous *adj* absurd, amusing, burlesque, comic, comical, crazy, drôle, droll, farcical, funny, incongruous, laughable, nonsensical, odd, outlandish, preposterous, ridiculous, risible, silly, zany.

lug *v* carry, drag, haul, heave, hump, humph, pull, tote, tow, yank.

luggage *n* baggage, bags, cases, gear, impedimenta, paraphernalia, suitcases, things, traps, trunks.

lugubrious *adj* dismal, doleful, dreary, funereal, gloomy, glum, melancholy, morose, mournful, sad, sepulchral, serious, sombre, sorrowful, Wertherian, woebegone, woeful.
antonyms cheerful, jovial, merry.

lukewarm *adj* apathetic, cold, cool, half-hearted, indifferent, laodicean, Laodicean, lew, phlegmatic, tepid, unconcerned, unenthusiastic, uninterested, unresponsive, warm.

lull *v* abate, allay, calm, cease, compose, decrease, diminish, dwindle, ease off, hush, let up, lullaby, moderate, pacify, quell, quiet, quieten down, sedate, slacken, soothe, still, subdue, subside, tranquillise, wane.
antonym agitate.
n calm, calmness, hush, let-up, pause, peace, quiet, respite, silence, stillness, tranquillity.
antonym agitation.

lullaby *n* berceuse, cradle-song, Wiegenlied.

lumber[1] *n* bits and pieces, clutter, jumble, junk, odds and ends, refuse, rubbish, trash, trumpery.
v burden, charge, encumber, hamper, impose, land, load, saddle.

lumber[2] *v* clump, galumph, plod, shamble, shuffle, stump, trudge, trundle, waddle.

lumbering *adj* awkward, blundering, bovine, bumbling, clumsy, elephantine, heavy, heavy-footed, hulking, lubberly, lumpish, massive, overgrown, ponderous, ungainly, unwieldy.
antonyms agile, nimble.

luminary *n* celeb, celebrity, dignitary, leader, leading light, lion, notable, personage, star, superstar, VIP, worthy.

luminescent *adj* bright, dayglow, effulgent, fluorescent, glowing, luciferous, luminous, phosphorescent, radiant, shining.

luminous *adj* bright, brilliant, dayglow, glowing, illuminated, lighted, lit, lucent, luminescent, luminiferous, lustrous, radiant, resplendent, shining, vivid.

lump[1] *n* ball, bulge, bump, bunch, cake, chuck, chump, chunk, clod, cluster, cyst, dab, daud, dod, gob, gobbet, group, growth, hunch, hunk, (k)nub, (k)nubble, lob, mass, nugget, piece, protrusion, protuberance, spot, swelling, tuber, tumescence, tumour, wedge, wen, wodge.
v coalesce, collect, combine, consolidate, group, mass, unite.

lump[2] *v* bear (with), brook, endure, put up with, stand, stomach, suffer, swallow, take, thole, tolerate.

lumpish *adj* awkward, boorish, bovine, bungling, clumsy, doltish, dull-witted, elephantine, gawky, heavy, lethargic, lumbering, oafish, obtuse, stolid, stupid, ungainly.

lumpy *adj* bumpy, bunched, cloggy, clotted, curdled, grainy, granular, knobbly, nodose, nodous, nodular, nodulose, nodulous.
antonyms even, smooth.

lunacy *n* aberration, absurdity, craziness, dementia, derangement, folly, foolhardiness, foolishness, idiocy, imbecility, insanity, madness, mania, moon-madness, moonraking, psychosis, senselessness, stupidity, tomfoolery.
antonym sanity.

lunatic *n* bug, loony, madman, maniac, nut, nutcase, nutter, psychopath.
adj barmy, bonkers, crazy, daft, demented, deranged, insane, irrational, mad, maniacal, moon-stricken, moon-struck, nuts, psychotic, unhinged.
antonyms sane, sensible.

lunch *n* dejeune, déjeuner, luncheon, nooning, nuncheon, tiffin.

lunge *v* bound, charge, cut, dash, dive, fall upon, grab (at), hit (at), jab, leap, pitch into, plunge, poke, pounce, set upon, stab, strike (at), thrust.
n charge, cut, jab, pass, pounce, spring, stab, swing, swipe, thrust, venue.

lurch *v* heave, lean, list, pitch, reel, rock, roll, stagger, stumble, sway, tilt, totter, wallow, weave, welter.

lure *v* allure, attract, beckon, decoy, draw, ensnare, entice, inveigle, invite, lead on, seduce, tempt, trepan.
n allurement, attraction, bait, carrot, come-on, decoy, enticement, inducement, magnet, siren, song, temptation, train.

lurid *adj* ashen, bloody, disgusting, exaggerated, fiery, flaming, ghastly, glaring, glowering, gory, graphic, grim, grisly, gruesome, intense, livid, loud, macabre, melodramatic, pale, pallid, revolting, sallow, sanguine, savage, sensational, shocking, startling, unrestrained, violent, vivid, wan.

lurk *v* crouch, hide, hide out, lie in wait, lie low, prowl, skulk, slink, sneak, snook, snoop.

luscious *adj* appetising, delectable, delicious, honeyed, juicy, luxuriant, luxurious, mouth-watering, palatable, rich, savoury, scrumptious, succulent, sweet, tasty, toothsome, yummy.
antonym austere.

lush *adj* abundant, dense, elaborate, extravagant, flourishing, grand, green, juicy, lavish, luxuriant, luxurious, opulent, ornate, overgrown, palatial, plush, prolific, rank, ripe, ritzy, succulent, sumptuous, superabundant, teeming, tender, verdant.

lust *n* appetence, appetency, appetite, avidity, carnality, concupiscence, covetousness, craving, cupidity, desire, greed, Kama, Kamadeva, lasciviousness, lech, lechery, lewdness, libido, licentiousness, longing, passion, prurience, randiness, salaciousness, sensuality, thirst, wantonness.

lust after crave, desire, have hot-pants for, have the hots for, hunger for, need, slaver over, thirst for, want, yearn for, yen for.

lustful *adj* carnal, concupiscent, craving, goatish, hankering, horny, lascivious, lecherous, lewd, libidinous, licentious, passionate, prurient, randy, raunchy, ruttish, sensual, unchaste, venerous, wanton.

lustily *adv* forcefully, hard, loudly, powerfully, robustly, stoutly, strongly, vigorously, with all one's might, with might and main.

antonym weakly.

lustiness *n* energy, haleness, hardihood, hardiness, health, healthiness, power, robustness, stoutness, strength, sturdiness, toughness, vigour, virility.

lustre *n* brightness, brilliance, burnish, dazzle, distinction, effulgence, fame, gleam, glint, glitter, glory, gloss, glow, gorm, honour, illustriousness, lambency, luminousness, prestige, radiance, renown, resplendence, sheen, shimmer, shine, sparkle, water.

lustrous *adj* bright, burnished, dazzling, gleaming, glistening, glittering, glossy, glowing, lambent, luminous, radiant, shimmering, shining, shiny, sparkling.

antonyms dull, lacklustre, matt.

lusty *adj* blooming, brawny, energetic, gutsy, hale, healthy, hearty, in fine fettle, muscular, powerful, red-blooded, robust, rugged, stalwart, stout, strapping, strong, sturdy, vigorous, virile.

antonyms effete, weak.

luxuriance *n* abundance, copiousness, denseness, excess, exuberance, fecundity, fertility, lavishness, lushness, profusion, rankness, richness, sumptuousness.

luxuriant *adj* abundant, ample, baroque, copious, dense, elaborate, excessive, extravagant, exuberant, fancy, fecund, fertile, festooned, flamboyant, florid, flowery, lavish, lush, opulent, ornate, overflowing, plenteous, plentiful, prodigal, productive, profuse, prolific, rank, rich, riotous, rococo, sumptuous, superabundant, teeming, thriving.

antonyms barren, infertile.

luxuriate *v* abound, bask, bloom, burgeon, delight, enjoy, flourish, grow, have a ball, indulge, live high off the hog, live the life of Riley, prosper, relish, revel, thrive, wallow, wanton.

luxurious *adj* comfortable, costly, deluxe, epicurean, expensive, hedonistic, lavish, magnificent, opulent, pampered, plush, plushy, rich, ritzy, self-indulgent, sensual, splendid, sumptuous, sybaritic, voluptuous, well-appointed.

antonyms ascetic, austere, economical, frugal, scant(y), spartan.

luxury *n* affluence, bliss, comfort, delight, dolce vita, enjoyment, extra, extravagance, flesh-pots, flesh-pottery, frill, gratification, hedonism, indulgence, milk and honey, non-essential, opulence, pleasure, richness, satisfactiion, splendour, sumptuousness, treat, voluptuousness, well-being.

antonym essential.

lying *adj* accumbent, deceitful, decumbent, dishonest, dissembling, double-dealing, duplicitous, false, guileful, mendacious, perfidious, treacherous, two-faced, untruthful.

antonyms honest, truthful.

n deceit, dishonesty, dissimulation, double-dealing, duplicity, fabrication, falsity, fibbing, guile, mendacity, perjury, prevarication, pseudology, untruthfulness.

antonyms honesty, truthfulness.

lyrical *adj* carried away, ecstatic, effusive, emotional, enthusiastic, expressive, impassioned, inspired, musical, passionate, poetic, rapturous, rhapsodic.

lyrics *n* book, libretto, text, words.

M

macabre *adj* cadaverous, deathlike, deathly, dreadful, eerie, frightening, frightful, ghastly, ghostly, ghoulish, grim, grisly, gruesome, hideous, horrible, horrid, morbid, sick, weird.

macerate *v* blend, liquefy, mash, pulp, soak, soften, steep.

Machiavellian *adj* amoral, artful, astute, calculating, crafty, cunning, cynical, deceitful, designing, double-dealing, foxy, guileful, intriguing, opportunist, perfidious, scheming, shrewd, sly, underhand, unscrupulous, wily.

machinate *v* conspire, contrive, design, devise, engineer, finagle, hatch, intrigue, invent, manoeuvre, plan, plot, scheme, work.

machination *n* artifice, cabal, conspiracy, design, device, dodge, finagling, intrigue, manoeuvre, plot, ploy, ruse, scheme, shenanigans, stratagem, trick.

machine *n* agency, agent, apparatus, appliance, automaton, contraption, contrivance, device, engine, gadget, gizmo, instrument, machinery, mechanism, organisation, party, puppet, robot, set-up, structure, system, tool, zombi(e).

machine-gun *n* Bren (gun), gatling-gun, mitrailleur, mitrailleuse, pompom, tommy-gun.

machinery *n* agency, apparatus, channels, enginery, equipment, gear, instruments, kit, machine, mechanism, organisation, procedure, structure, system, tackle, tools, works.

mad *adj* abandoned, aberrant, absurd, agitated, angry, ardent, avid, bananas, barmy, bats, batty, berserk, boisterous, bonkers, crackers, crazed, crazy, cuckoo, daft, delirious, demented, deranged, devoted, distracted, dotty, ebullient, enamoured, energetic, enraged, enthusiastic, exasperated, excited, fanatical, fond, foolhardy, foolish, frantic, frenetic, frenzied, fuming, furious, gay, gyte, have bats in the belfry, hooked, impassioned, imprudent, in a paddy, incensed, infatuated, infuriated, insane, irate, irrational, irritated, keen, livid, loony, loopy, ludicrous, lunatic, madcap, mental, moon-stricken, moon-struck, non compos mentis, nonsensical, nuts, nutty, off one's chump, off one's head, off one's nut, off one's rocker, off one's trolley, out of one's mind, possessed, preposterous, psychotic, rabid, raging, raving, resentful, riotous, round the bend, round the twist, screwball, screwy, senseless, unbalanced, uncontrolled, unhinged, unreasonable, unrestrained, unsafe, unsound, unstable, up the pole, waxy, wild, wrathful, zealous.
antonyms lucid, rational, sane.

madcap *adj* bird-brained, crazy, flighty, foolhardy, hare-brained, heedless, hot-headed, ill-advised, imprudent, impulsive, lively, rash, reckless, silly, thoughtless, wild.

madden *v* annoy, craze, dement, dementate, derange, enrage, exasperate, incense, inflame, infuriate, irritate, provoke, unhinge, upset, vex.
antonyms calm, pacify, please.

made-up *adj* fabricated, fairy-tale, false, fictional, imaginary, invented, make-believe, mythical, specious, trumped-up, unreal, untrue.

madhouse *n* asylum, Babel, bedlam, chaos, disarray, disorder, funny farm, loony bin, nut-house, pandemonium, snake-pit, turmoil, uproar.

madly *adv* absurdly, crazily, deliriously, dementedly, desperately, devotedly, distractedly, energetically, exceedingly, excessively, excitedly, extremely, fanatically, foolishly, frantically, frenziedly, furiously, hastily, hurriedly, hysterically, insanely, intensely, irrationally, like mad, ludicrously, nonsensically, passionately, quickly, rabidly, rapidly, recklessly, senselessly, speedily, to distraction, unreasonably, violently, wildly.

madman *n* bedlamite, détraqué, furioso, loony, lunatic, madling, maniac, mattoid, mental case, nut, nutcase, nutter, psycho, psychopath, psychotic, schizo, screwball.

madness *n* abandon, aberration, absurdity, agitation, anger, ardour, craze, craziness, daftness, delusion, dementia, demoniacism, demonomania, derangement, distraction, enthusiasm, exasperation, excitement, fanaticism, folie, folly, fondness, foolhardiness, foolishness, frenzy, furore, fury, infatuation, insanity, intoxication, ire, keenness, lunacy, lycanthropy, mania, monomania, moon-madness, moonraking, nonsense, passion, preposterousness, psychopathy, psychosis, rage, raving, riot, unrestraint, uproar, wildness, wrath, zeal.
antonym sanity.

maelstrom *n* bedlam, chaos, Charybdis, confusion, disorder, mess, pandemonium, tumult, turmoil, uproar, vortex, whirlpool.

maestro *n* expert, genius, master, prodigy, virtuoso, wizard.

magazine[1] *n* fanzine, journal, monthly, pamphlet, paper, periodical, quarterly, weekly.

magazine[2] *n* ammunition dump, arsenal, depot, ordnance, powder-room, store, storehouse.

magic *n* allurement, black art, charm, conjuring, conjury, diablerie, enchantment, fascination, glamour, goety, gramary(e), hocus-pocus, hoodoo, illusion, jiggery-pokery, jugglery, legerdemain, magnetism, medicine, necromancy, occultism, prestidigitation, sleight of hand, sorcery, sortilege, spell, thaumaturgics, thaumaturgism, thaumaturgy, theurgy, trickery, voodoo, witchcraft, wizardry, wonder-work.

adj bewitching, charismatic, charming, enchanting, entrancing, fascinating, goetic, hermetic, magical, magnetic, marvellous, miraculous, mirific, mirifical, sorcerous, spellbinding, spellful.

magician *n* archimage, conjurer, conjuror, enchanter, enchantress, genius, illusionist, maestro, mage, Magian, magus, marvel, miracle-worker, necromancer, prestidigitator, prestigiator, sorcerer, spellbinder, thaumaturge, theurgist, virtuoso, warlock, witch, witch-doctor, wizard, wonder-monger, wonder-worker.

magisterial *adj* arrogant, assertive, authoritarian, authoritative, bossy, commanding, despotic, dictatorial, domineering, high-handed, imperious, lordly, masterful, overbearing, peremptory.

magistrate *n* aedile, bailiff, bail(l)ie, beak, JP, judge, jurat, justice, justice of the peace, mittimus, queer cuffin, stipendiary, tribune.

magnanimity *n* beneficence, big-heartedness, bountifulness, charitableness, charity, generosity, high-mindedness, largess(e), liberality, munificence, nobility, open-handedness, selflessness, unselfishness.

antonym meanness.

magnanimous *adj* altruistic, beneficent, big, big-hearted, bountiful, charitable, free, generous, great-hearted, handsome, high-minded, kind, kindly, large-hearted, large-minded, liberal, munificent, noble, open-handed, philanthropic, selfless, ungrudging, unselfish, unstinting.

antonyms mean, paltry, petty.

magnate *n* aristocrat, baron, bashaw, big cheese, big noise, big shot, big wheel, bigwig, captain of industry, chief, fat cat, grandee, leader, magnifico, merchant, mogul, nabob, noble, notable, personage, plutocrat, prince, tycoon, VIP.

magnet *n* appeal, attraction, bait, draw, enticement, lodestone, lure, solenoid.

antonym repellent.

magnetic *adj* absorbing, alluring, attractive, captivating, charismatic, charming, enchanting, engrossing, entrancing, fascinating, gripping, hypnotic, irresistible, mesmerising, seductive.

antonyms repellent, repugnant, repulsive.

magnetism *n* allure, appeal, attraction, attractiveness, charisma, charm, draw, drawing power, enchantment, fascination, grip, hypnotism, lure, magic, mesmerism, power, pull, seductiveness, spell.

magnification *n* aggrandisement, amplification, augmentation, blow-up, boost, build-up, deepening, dilation, enhancement, enlargement, exaggeration, expansion, extolment, heightening, increase, inflation, intensification, lionisation.

antonyms diminution, reduction.

magnificence *n* brilliance, glory, gorgeousness, grandeur, grandiosity, impressiveness, luxuriousness, luxury, majesty, nobility, opulence, pomp, resplendence, splendour, stateliness, sublimity, sumptuousness.

antonyms modesty, plainness, simplicity.

magnificent *adj* august, brilliant, elegant, elevated, exalted, excellent, fine, glorious, gorgeous, grand, grandiose, imposing, impressive, lavish, luxurious, majestic, noble, opulent, outstanding, plush, posh, princely, regal, resplendent, rich, ritzy, splendid, stately, sublime, sumptuous, superb, superior, transcendent.

antonyms humble, modest, plain, simple.

magnify *v* aggrandise, aggravate, amplify, augment, blow up, boost, build up, deepen, dilate, dramatise, enhance, enlarge, exaggerate, expand, greaten, heighten, increase, inflate, intensify, lionise, overdo, overemphasise, overestimate, overplay, overrate, overstate, praise.

antonyms belittle, play down.

magniloquence *n* bombast, euphuism, fustian, grandiloquence, loftiness, orotundity, pomposity, pretentiousness, rhetoric, turgidity.

antonyms simplicity, straightforwardness.

magniloquent *adj* bombastic, declamatory, elevated, euphuistic, exalted, fustian, grandiloquent, high-flown, high-sounding, lofty, orotund, overblown, pompous, pretentious, rhetorical, sonorous, stilted, turgid.

antonyms simple, straightforward.

magnitude *n* amount, amplitude, bigness, brightness, bulk, capacity, consequence, dimensions, eminence, enormousness, expanse, extent, grandeur, greatness, hugeness, immensity, importance, intensity, largeness, mark, mass, measure, moment, note, proportions, quantity, significance, size, space, strength, vastness, volume, weight.

antonym smallness.

magnum opus Almagest, chef d'oeuvre, masterpiece, master-work, pièce de résistance.

maid *n* abigail, bonne, damsel, dresser, femme de chambre, fille de chambre, gentlewoman, girl, handmaiden, housemaid, lady's maid, lass, lassie, maiden, maid-of-all-work, maid-servant, miss, nymph, servant, serving-maid, soubrette, tirewoman, tiring-woman, virgin, waitress, wench.

maiden *n* damozel, damsel, demoiselle, girl, lass, lassie, maid, may, miss, nymph, virgin, wench.

adj chaste, female, first, fresh, inaugural, initial, initiatory, intact, introductory, new, pure, unbroached, uncaptured, undefiled, unmarried, unpolluted, untapped, untried, unused, unwed, virgin, virginal.

antonyms defiled, deflowered, unchaste.

maidenly *adj* becoming, chaste, decent, decorous, demure, gentle, girlish, modest, proper, pure, reserved, seemly, undefiled, vestal, virginal, virtuous.

antonym immodest.

mail *n* correspondence, da(w)k, delivery, letters, packages, parcels, post.

v air-mail, dispatch, forward, post, send.

maim *v* cripple, disable, hack, haggle, hamstring, hurt, impair, incapacitate, injure, lame, mangle, mar, mutilate, savage, wound.

antonyms heal, repair.

main[1] *adj* absolute, brute, capital, cardinal, central, chief, critical, crucial, direct, downright, entire, essential, extensive, first, foremost, general, great, head, leading, mere, necessary, outstanding, paramount, particular, predominant, pre-eminent, premier, primary, prime, principal, pure, sheer, special, staple, supreme, undisguised, utmost, utter, vital.

antonyms minor, unimportant.

n effort, foison, force, might, potency, power, puissance, strength, vigour.

antonym weakness.

main[2] *n* cable, channel, conduit, duct, line, pipe.

mainly *adv* above all, as a rule, chiefly, especially, for the most part, generally, in general, in the main, largely, mostly, on the whole, overall, predominantly, primarily, principally, substantially, usually.

mainspring *n* cause, driving force, fountainhead, generator, impulse, incentive, inspiration, motivation, motive, origin, prime mover, source, wellspring.

mainstay *n* anchor, backbone, bulwark, buttress, linchpin, pillar, prop, support.

mainstream *adj* accepted, average, conventional, established, general, normal, orthodox, received, regular, standard.

antonyms heterodox, peripheral.

maintain *v* advocate, affirm, allege, argue, assert, asseverate, aver, avouch, avow, back, care for, carry on, champion, claim, conserve, contend, continue, declare, defend, fight for, finance, hold, insist, justify, keep, keep up, look after, make good, nurture, observe, perpetuate, plead for, practise, preserve, profess, prolong, provide, retain, stand by, state, supply, support, sustain, take care of, uphold, vindicate.

antonyms deny, neglect, oppose.

maintenance *n* aliment, alimony, allowance, care, conservation, continuance, continuation, defence, food, keep, keeping, livelihood, living, nurture, perpetuation, preservation, prolongation, protection, provision, repairs, retainment, subsistence, supply, support, sustainment, sustenance, sustention, upkeep.

antonym neglect.

majestic *adj* august, awesome, dignified, distinguished, elevated, exalted, grand, grandiose, imperial, imperious, imposing, impressive, kingly, lofty, magisterial, magnificent, monumental, noble, pompous, princely, queenly, regal, royal, splendid, stately, sublime, superb.

antonyms unimportant, unimpressive.

majesty *n* augustness, awesomeness, dignity, exaltedness, glory, grandeur, impressiveness, kingliness, loftiness, magnificence, majesticness, nobility, pomp, queenliness, regalness, resplendence, royalty, splendour, state, stateliness, sublimity.

antonyms unimportance, unimpressiveness.

major *adj* better, bigger, chief, critical, crucial, elder, grave, great, greater, higher, important, key, keynote, larger, leading, main, most, notable, older, outstanding, pre-eminent, radical, senior, serious, significant, superior, supreme, uppermost, vital, weighty.

antonym minor.

majority *n* adulthood, bulk, manhood, mass, maturity, plurality, preponderance, seniority, superiority, the many, womanhood, years of discretion.

antonyms childhood, minority.

make *v* accomplish, acquire, act, add up to, amount to, appoint, arrive at, assemble, assign, attain, beget, bring about, build, calculate, carry out, catch, cause, clear, coerce, compel, compose, conclude, constitute, constrain, construct, contract, contribute, convert, create, designate, do, dragoon, draw up, drive, earn, effect, elect, embody, enact, engage in, engender, establish, estimate, execute, fabricate, fashion, fix, flow, force, forge, form, frame, gain, gar, gauge, generate, get, give rise to, impel, induce, install, invest, judge, lead to, manufacture, meet, mould, net, nominate, oblige, obtain, occasion, ordain, originate, pass, perform, practise, press, pressurise, prevail upon, proceed, produce, prosecute, put together, reach, reckon, render, require, secure, shape, smith(y), suppose, synthesise, take in, tend, think, turn, win.

antonyms dismantle, lose, persuade.

n brand, build, character, composition, constitution, construction, cut, designation, disposition, form, formation, humour, kind, make-up, manner, manufacture, mark, model, nature, shape, sort, stamp, structure, style, temper, temperament, texture, type, variety.

make believe act, dream, enact, fantasise, feign, imagine, play, play-act, pretend.

make do cope, get along, get by, improvise, make out, manage, muddle through, scrape by, survive.

make eyes at flirt, give (someone) the come-on, leer at, make sheep's eyes at, ogle.

make for aim for, conduce to, contribute to, facilitate, favour, forward, further, head for, promote.

make fun of deride, lampoon, laugh at, make sport of, mock, parody, poke fun at, queer, quiz, rag, rib, ridicule, roast, rot, satirise, scoff at, send up, sneer at, take off, taunt.

antonym praise.

make inroads into consume, eat away, eat into, eat up, encroach upon, get on with, make progress with, progress with.

antonym add to.

make it arrive, come through, get on, prosper, pull through, reach, succeed, survive.

antonym fail.

make love canoodle, copulate, cuddle, embrace, enjoy, fuck, gender, go to bed, neck, pet, romance, screw, smooch.

make merry carouse, celebrate, feast, frolic, junket, make whoopee, paint the town red, revel, whoop it up.

make no difference be six and half a dozen, count for nothing, cut no ice.

make off abscond, beat a hasty retreat, bolt, clear off, cut and run, decamp, depart, flee, fly, have it on one's toes, leave, make away, run away, run for it, run off, take to one's heels.

make off with abduct, appropriate, carry off, filch, kidnap, knock off, nab, nick, pilfer, pinch, purloin, run away, run off with, steal, swipe, walk off with.

antonym bring.

make one's mark get on, make good, make it, make the big-time, prosper, succeed.

antonym fail.

make out assert, claim, complete, comprehend, decipher, demonstrate, describe, descry, detect, discern, discover, distinguish, draw up, espy, fare, fathom, fill in, fill out, follow, get on, grasp, imply, infer, inscribe, let on, make as if, manage, perceive, pretend, prosper, prove, realise, recognise, represent, see, show, succeed, survive, thrive, understand, work out, write, write out.

antonym fail.

make sense of apprehend, comprehend, fathom, figure out, grasp, make head or tail of, make much of, make out, understand.

make tracks beat it, dash, dash off, depart, disappear, go, hit the road, hurry, leave, make off, scram, set out, split, take off.

make up[1] arrange, coin, collect, complement, complete, compose, comprise, concoct, constitute, construct, cook up, create, devise, dream up, fabricate, feign, fill, form, formulate, frame, hatch, invent, meet, originate, parcel, put together, repair, supplement, supply, trump up, write.

make up[2] bury the hatchet, call it quits, come to terms, forgive and forget, make peace, mend one's fences, settle, settle differences, shake hands.

make up for atone for, balance, compensate, expiate, make amends for, offset, recompense, redeem, redress, requite.

make up one's mind choose, decide, determine, resolve, settle.

antonym waver.

make up to butter up, chat up, court, curry favour with, fawn on, flirt with, make overtures to, toady to, woo.

make-believe *n* charade, dream, fantasy, imagination, play-acting, pretence, role-play, unreality.

antonym reality.

adj dream, fantasised, fantasy, feigned, imaginary, imagined, made-up, mock, pretend, pretended, sham, simulated, unreal.

antonym real.

maker *n* architect, author, builder, constructor, contriver, creator, director, fabricator, framer, manufacturer, producer.

antonym dismantler.

makeshift *adj* band-aid, cutcha, expedient, haywire, improvised, kacha, make-do, provisional, rough and ready, stop-gap, substitute, temporary.

antonyms finished, permanent.

n band-aid, expedient, fig-leaf, shift, stop-gap, substitute.

make-up[1] *n* cosmetics, fard, fucus, greasepaint, maquillage, paint, powder, war paint, white-face.

make-up[2] *n* arrangement, assembly, build, cast, character, complexion, composition, configuration, constitution, construction, disposition, figure, form, format, formation, make, nature, organisation, stamp, structure, style, temper, temperament.

making *n* assembly, building, composition, construction, creation, fabrication, forging, manufacture, modelling, moulding, production.

antonym dismantling.

makings *n* beginnings, capability, capacity, earnings, income, ingredients, materials, possibilities, potential, potentiality, proceeds, profits, promise, qualities, returns, revenue, takings.

maladjusted *adj* alienated, confused, disturbed, estranged, hung-up, muddled, neurotic, unstable.

antonym well-adjusted.

maladministration *n* blundering, bungling, corruption, dishonesty, incompetence, inefficiency, malfeasance, malpractice, malversation, misconduct, misfeasance, misgovernment, mismanagement, misrule, stupidity.

maladroit *adj* awkward, bungling, cack-handed, clumsy, gauche, graceless, ham-fisted, ill-timed, inconsiderate, inelegant, inept, inexpert, insensitive, tactless, thoughtless, undiplomatic, unhandy, unskilful, untoward.

antonyms adroit, tactful.

malady *n* affliction, ailment, breakdown, complaint, disease, disorder, illness, indisposition, infirmity, malaise, sickness.

antonym health.

malaise *n* angst, anguish, anxiety, depression, discomfort, disquiet, distemper, doldrums, enervation, future shock, illness, indisposition, lassitude, melancholy, sickness, unease, uneasiness, weakness.

antonyms happiness, well-being.

malapropos *adj* ill-timed, inapposite, inappropriate, inapt, inopportune, misapplied, tactless, uncalled-for, unseemly, unsuitable, untimely.

antonyms appropriate, tactful.

adv inappositely, inappropriately, inaptly, inopportunely, tactlessly, unseasonably, unsuitably.

antonyms appropriately, tactfully.

malapropism *n* Dogberryism, misapplication, misuse.

malcontent *adj* belly-aching, disaffected, discontented, disgruntled, dissatisfied, dissentious, factious, ill-disposed, morose, rebellious, resentful, restive, unhappy, unsatisfied.

antonym contented.

n agitator, belly-acher, complainer, grouch, grouser, grumbler, mischief-maker, moaner, rebel, troublemaker.

male *adj* bull, cock, dog, manlike, manly, masculine, virile.

antonym female.

n boy, bull, cock, daddy, dog, father, man.

antonym female.

malediction *n* anathema, anathematisation, curse, damnation, damning, denunciation, execration, imprecation, malison.

antonyms blessing, praise.

malefactor *n* convict, criminal, crook, culprit, delinquent, evil-doer, felon, law-breaker, miscreant, misfeasor, offender, outlaw, transgressor, villain, wrong-doer.

maleficent *adj* baleful, deleterious, destructive, detrimental, evil, harmful, hurtful, injurious, malefactory, malefic, maleficial, malign, malignant, noxious, pernicious.

antonyms beneficent, harmless.

malevolence *n* bitterness, hate, hatred, hostility, ill-will, malice, maliciousness, malignance, malignancy, malignity, rancour, spite, spitefulness, vengefulness, venom, viciousness, vindictiveness.

antonym benevolence.

malevolent *adj* baleful, bitter, despiteful, evil-minded, hostile, ill-natured, malicious, malign, malignant, pernicious, rancorous, spiteful, vengeful, venomous, vicious, vindictive.

antonym benevolent.

malformation *n* crookedness, deformity, distortion, irregularity, misshape, misshapenness, warp, warpedness, warping.

malformed *adj* abnormal, bent, contorted, crooked, deformed, distorted, imperfect, irregular, misshapen, twisted, warped.

antonym perfect.

malfunction *n* breakdown, defect, failure, fault, flaw, glitch, impairment.

v break down, fail, go wrong, misbehave.

malice *n* animosity, animus, bad blood, bitterness, despite, enmity, hate, hatred, ill-will, malevolence, maliciousness, malignity, rancour, spite, spitefulness, spleen, vengefulness, venom, viciousness, vindictiveness.

antonym kindness.

malicious *adj* baleful, bitchy, bitter, catty, despiteful, evil-minded, hateful, ill-natured, injurious, malevolent, malignant, mischievous, pernicious, rancorous, resentful, sham, spiteful, vengeful, venomous, vicious.

antonyms kind, thoughtful.

malign *adj* bad, baleful, baneful, deleterious, destructive, evil, harmful, hostile, hurtful, injurious, malevolent, malignant, noxious, pernicious, venomous, vicious, wicked.

antonym benign.

v abuse, badmouth, blacken the name of, calumniate, defame, denigrate, derogate, disparage, harm, injure, libel, revile, run down, slander, smear, traduce, vilify, vilipend.

antonym praise.

malignant *adj* baleful, bitter, cancerous, cankered, dangerous, deadly, destructive, devilish, evil, fatal, harmful, hostile, hurtful, inimical, injurious, irremediable, malevolent, malicious, malign, pernicious, spiteful, uncontrollable, venomous, vicious, viperish, viperous, virulent.

antonyms harmless, kind.

malignity *n* animosity, animus, bad blood, balefulness, bitterness, deadliness, destructiveness, gall, harmfulness, hate, hatred, hostility, hurtfulness, ill-will, malevolence, malice, maliciousness, perniciousness, rancour, spite, vengefulness, venom, viciousness, vindictiveness, virulence, wickedness.

antonyms harmlessness, kindness.

malinger *v* dodge, loaf, shirk, skive, slack, swing the lead.

antonym toil.

malingerer *n* dodger, lead-swinger, loafer, shirker, skiver, slacker.

antonym toiler.

malleable *adj* adaptable, biddable, compliant, ductile, governable, impressionable, manageable, plastic, pliable, pliant, soft, tractable, tractile, workable.

antonyms intractable, unworkable.

malnutrition *n* anorexia (nervosa), hunger, inanition, starvation, undernourishment.

antonym nourishment.

malodorous *adj* evil-smelling, f(o)etid, foul-smelling, mephitic, miasmal, miasmatic, miasmatous, miasmic, miasmous, nauseating, niffy, noisome, offensive, putrid, rank, reeking, smelly, stinking.

antonym sweet-smelling.

malpractice *n* abuse, dereliction, malversation, misbehaviour, misconduct, misdeed, mismanagement, negligence, offence, transgression.

maltreat *v* abuse, bully, damage, harm, hurt, ill-treat, injure, mistreat, misuse, mousle.

antonym care for.

maltreatment *n* abuse, bullying, harm, ill-treatment, ill-usage, ill-use, injury, mistreatment, misuse.

antonym care.

mammoth *adj* Brobdingnag, Brobdingnagian, colossal, enormous, formidable, gargantuan, giant, gigantic, herculean, huge, immense, leviathan, massive, mighty, monumental, mountainous, prodigious, rounceval, stupendous, titanic, vast.

antonym small.

man[1] *n* adult, attendant, beau, bloke, body, boyfriend, cat, chap, chiel, employee, fellow, follower, gentleman, guy, hand, hireling, hombre, human, human being, husband, individual, lover, male, manservant, partner, person, retainer, servant, soldier, spouse, subject, subordinate, valet, vassal, worker, workman.

v crew, fill, garrison, occupy, operate, people, staff, take charge of.

man in the street homme moyen sensuel, John Doe, Tom Dick or Harry.

man of fashion bean, buck, dandy, homme du monde, swell toff.

man of straw Jack-straw, nobody, straw man.

man[2] *n* Homo sapiens, human race, humanity, humankind, humans, mankind, mortals, people.

manacle *v* bind, chain, check, clap in irons, confine, constrain, curb, fetter, gyve, hamper, hamstring, handcuff, inhibit, put in chains, restrain, shackle, trammel.

antonym unshackle.

manacles *n* bonds, bracelets, chains, fetters, gyves, handcuffs, irons, shackles.

manage *v* accomplish, administer, arrange, bring about, bring off, carry on, command, concert, conduct, contrive, control, cope, cope with, deal with, direct, dominate, effect, engineer, fare, get along, get by, get on, govern, guide, handle, influence, make do, make out, manipulate, muddle through, operate, oversee, pilot, ply, preside over, rule, run, shift, solicit, stage-manage, steer, succeed, superintend, supervise, survive, train, use, wield.

antonym fail.

manageable *adj* amenable, biddable, compliant, controllable, convenient, docile, easy, governable, handy, submissive, tamable, tractable, wieldable, wieldy.

antonym unmanageable.

management *n* administration, board, bosses, care, charge, command, conduct, control, direction, directorate, directors, employers, executive, executives, governance, government, governors, guidance, handling, managers, manipulation, operation, oversight, rule, running, stewardry, superintendence, supervision, supervisors.

manager *n* administrator, boss, comptroller, conductor, controller, director, executive, factor, gaffer, governor, head, impresario, organiser, overseer, proprietor, steward, superintendent, supervisor.

mandate *n* authorisation, authority, bidding, charge, command, commission, decree, dedimus, directive, edict, fiat, firman, injunction, instruction, irade, order, precept, rescript, right, sanction, ukase, warrant.

mandatory *adj* binding, compulsory, imperative, necessary, obligatory, required, requisite.

antonym optional.

manful *adj* bold, brave, courageous, daring, determined, gallant, hardy, heroic, indomitable, intrepid, lion-hearted, manly, noble, noble-minded, powerful, resolute, stalwart, stout, stout-hearted, strong, unflinching, valiant, vigorous.

antonyms half-hearted, timid.

manfully *adv* boldly, bravely, courageously, desperately, determinedly, gallantly, hard, heroically, intrepidly, nobly, pluckily, powerfully, resolutely, stalwartly, steadfastly, stoutly, strongly, unflinchingly, valiantly, vigorously.

antonyms half-heartedly, timidly.

mangle *v* butcher, crush, cut, deform, destroy, disfigure, distort, hack, haggle, lacerate, maim, mar, maul, mutilate, rend, ruin, spoil, tear, twist, wreck.

mangy *adj* dirty, grotty, mean, moth-eaten, ratty, scabby, scruffy, seedy, shabby, shoddy, squalid, tatty.

antonyms clean, neat, spruce.

manhandle *v* carry, haul, heave, hump, knock about, lift, maltreat, manoeuvre, maul, mishandle, mistreat, misuse, paw, pull, push, rough up, shove, tug.

manhood *n* adulthood, bravery, courage, determination, firmness, fortitude, hardihood, machismo, manfulness, manliness, masculinity, maturity, mettle, resolution, spirit, strength, valour, virility.

antonym timidness.

mania *n* aberration, cacoethes, compulsion, craving, craze, craziness, delirium, dementia, derangement, desire, disorder, enthusiasm, fad, fetish, fixation, frenzy, infatuation, insanity, itch, lunacy, madness, obsession, partiality, passion, preoccupation, rage, thing.

maniac *n* détraqué(e), enthusiast, fan, fanatic, fiend, freak, fruit-cake, loony, lunatic, madman, madwoman, nutcase, nutter, psycho, psychopath.

manic *adj* berserk, crazed, crazy, demented, deranged, frenzied, insane, lunatic, mad, maniacal, psychotic, raving, screwy, unbalanced, unhinged, wild.

antonym sane.

manifest *adj* apparent, clear, conspicuous, distinct, evident, glaring, noticeable, obvious, open, palpable, patent, plain, unconcealed, undeniable, unmistakable, visible.

antonym unclear.

v demonstrate, display, establish, evidence, evince, exhibit, expose, illustrate, prove, reveal, set forth, show.

antonym hide.

manifestation *n* appearance, demonstration, disclosure, display, exhibition, exposure, expression, indication, instance, mark, mass-meeting, materialisation, procession, reflex, revelation, show, sign, sit-in, symptom, token.

manifesto *n* declaration, platform, policies, policy, pronunciamento.

manifold *adj* abundant, assorted, copious, diverse, diversified, kaleidoscopic, many, multifarious, multifold, multiple, multiplex, multiplied, multitudinous, numerous, varied, various.

antonym simple.

manipulate *v* conduct, control, cook, direct, employ, engineer, gerrymander, guide, handle, influence, juggle with, manoeuvre, negotiate, operate, ply, shuffle, steer, use, wield, work.

mankind *n* Everyman, fellow-men, Homo sapiens, human race, humanity, humankind, man, mandom, mortality, people.

manliness *n* boldness, bravery, courage, fearlessness, firmness, hardihood, heroism, independence, intrepidity, machismo, manfulness, manhood, masculinity, mettle, resolution, stalwartness, stout-heartedness, valour, vigour, virility.

antonyms timidity, unmanliness.

manly *adj* bold, brave, courageous, daring, dauntless, fearless, gallant, hardy, heroic, macho, male, manful, masculine, muscular, noble, powerful, resolute, robust, stalwart, stout-hearted, strapping, strong, sturdy, valiant, valorous, vigorous, virile.

antonyms timid, unmanly.

man-made *adj* artificial, ersatz, imitation, manufactured, simulated, synthetic.

antonym natural.

manner *n* address, air, appearance, approach, aspect, bearing, behaviour, brand, breed, category, character, comportment, conduct, custom, demeanour, deportment, description, fashion, form, genre, habit, kind, line, look, means, method, mien, mode, nature, practice, presence, procedure, process, routine, sort, style, tack, tenor, tone, type, usage, variety, way, wise, wont.

mannered *adj* affected, artificial, euphuistic, posed, precious, pretentious, pseudo, put-on, stilted.

antonym natural.

mannerism *n* characteristic, feature, foible, habit, idiosyncrasy, peculiarity, quirk, stiltedness, trait, trick.

mannerly *adj* civil, civilised, courteous, decorous, deferential, formal, genteel, gentlemanly, gracious, ladylike, polished, polite, refined, respectful, well-behaved, well-bred, well-mannered.

antonym unmannerly.

manners *n* bearing, behaviour, breeding, carriage, ceremony, comportment, conduct, courtesy, decorum, demeanour, deportment, etiquette, formalities, mores, polish, politeness, politesse, proprieties, protocol, p's and q's, refinement, social graces.

antonyms impoliteness, indecorousness.

mannish *adj* butch, hoydenish, masculine, tomboyish, unfeminine, unladylike, unwomanly, viraginian, viraginous, viragoish, virilescent.

antonym womanish.

mannishness *n* butchness, hoydenism, masculinity, unfemininity, unladylikeness, unwomanliness, virilescence, virilism.

antonym womanishness.

manoeuvre *n* action, artifice, device, dodge, exercise, gambit, intrigue, machination, move, movement, operation, plan, plot, ploy, ruse, scheme, stratagem, subterfuge, tactic, trick.

v contrive, deploy, devise, direct, drive, engineer, exercise, guide, handle, intrigue, jockey, machinate, manage, manipulate, move, navigate, negotiate, pilot, plan, plot, pull strings, scheme, steer, wangle.

man-of-all-work *n* factotum, famulus, handyman, hobjobber, odd-jobman, orra man, servant.

manor *n* barony, big house, château, hall, Hof, schloss, seat, vill.

manse *n* glebe-house, vicarage.

manservant *n* butler, gentleman's gentleman, retainer, valet, valet-de-chambre.

mansion *n* abode, big house, castle, château, dwelling, habitation, hall, home, house, manor, manor-house, residence, schloss, seat, villa.

mantle *n* blanket, canopy, cape, cloak, cloud, cover, covering, curtain, envelope, hood, mantlet, pall, pelerine, pelisse, screen, shawl, shroud, veil, wrap.

manual[1] *n* bible, book of words, companion, enchi(e)ridion, guide, guide-book, handbook, instructions, primer, vade-mecum.

manual[2] *adj* hand, hand-operated, human, physical.

manufacture *v* assemble, build, churn out, compose, concoct, construct, cook up, create, devise, fabricate, forge, form, hatch, invent, make, make up, mass-produce, mould, process, produce, shape, think up, trump up, turn out.

n assembly, construction, creation, fabrication, facture, formation, making, mass-production, production.

manufacturer *n* builder, constructor, creator, fabricant, fabricator, factory-owner, industrialist, maker, mill-owner, producer.

manure *n* compost, droppings, dung, fertiliser, guano, muck, ordure.

manuscript *n* autograph, deed, document, handwriting, holograph, palimpsest, parchment, scroll, text, vellum.

many *adj* abundant, copious, countless, divers, frequent, innumerable, manifold, multifarious, multifold, multitudinous, myriad, n, numerous, profuse, sundry, umpteen, umpty, varied, various.

antonym few.

map *n* atlas, chart, graph, mappemond, plan, plot, street plan.

mar *v* blemish, blight, blot, damage, deface, detract from, disfigure, foul up, harm, hurt, impair, injure, maim, mangle, mutilate, pollute, ruin, scar, spoil, stain, sully, taint, tarnish, temper, vitiate, wreck.

antonym enhance.

maraud *v* depredate, despoil, forage, foray, harry, loot, pillage, plunder, raid, ransack, ravage, reive, sack, spoliate.

marauder *n* bandit, brigand, buccaneer, cateran, corsair, depredator, freebooter, moss-trooper, outlaw, pillager, pirate, plunderer, raider, ravager, reiver, robber, spoliater.

march *v* countermarch, file, flounce, goose-step, pace, parade, slog, stalk, stride, strut, stump, tramp, tread, walk.

n advance, career, demo, demonstration, development, evolution, footslog, gait, hike, pace, parade, passage, procession, progress, progression, step, stride, tramp, trek, walk.

margin *n* allowance, border, bound, boundary, brim, brink, compass, confine, edge, extra, latitude, leeway, limit, marge, perimeter, periphery, play, rand, rim, room, scope, side, skirt, space, surplus, verge.

antonyms centre, core.

marginal *adj* bordering, borderline, doubtful, infinitesimal, insignificant, low, minimal, minor, negligible, peripheral, slight, small.

antonyms central, core.

marijuana *n* bhang, cannabis, charas (churrus), dope, ganja, grass, greens, hash, hashish, hemp, kif, mary jane, pot, tea, weed.

marina *n* dock, harbour, mooring, port, yacht station.

marine *adj* maritime, nautical, naval, ocean-going, oceanic, pelagic, salt-water, sea, seafaring, sea-going, thalassian, thalassic.

n galoot, leather-neck, sailor.

mariner *n* bluejacket, deckhand, hand, Jack Tar, matelot, matlo(w), navigator, sailor, salt, sea-dog, seafarer, seaman, tar.

marital *adj* conjugal, connubial, hymeneal, hymenean, married, matrimonial, nuptial, sponsal, spousal, wedded.

maritime *adj* coastal, littoral, marine, nautical, naval, oceanic, pelagic, sea, seafaring, seaside, thalassian, thalassic.

mark *n* aim, badge, blaze, blemish, blot, blotch, brand, bruise, character, characteristic, consequence, criterion, dent, device, dignity, distinction, earmark, emblem, eminence, end, evidence, fame, feature, fingermark, footmark, footprint, goal, hallmark, importance, impression, incision, index, indication, influence, label, level, line, lineament, marque, measure, nick, norm, notability, note, noteworthiness, notice, object, objective, pock, prestige, print, proof, purpose, quality, regard, scar, scratch, seal, sign, smudge, splotch, spot, stain, stamp, standard, standing, streak, symbol, symptom, target, token, trace, track, trail, vestige, yardstick.

v appraise, assess, attend, betoken, blemish, blot, blotch, brand, bruise, characterise, colour-code, correct, denote, dent, distinguish, evaluate, evince, exemplify, grade, hearken, heed, identify, illustrate, impress, imprint, label, list, listen, mind, nick, note, notice, observe, print, regard, remark, scar, scratch, show, smudge, splotch, stain, stamp, streak, take to heart, traumatise, watch.

marked *adj* apparent, clear, considerable, conspicuous, decided, distinct, doomed, emphatic, evident, glaring, indicated, manifest, notable, noted, noticeable, obvious, outstanding, patent, prominent, pronounced, remarkable, salient, signal, striking, strong, suspected, watched.

antonyms slight, unnoticeable.

market *n* bazaar, demand, fair, market-place, mart, need, outlet, shop, souk.

v hawk, peddle, retail, sell, vend.

antonym buy.

marketable *adj* in demand, merchantable, salable, sellable, sought after, vendible, wanted.

antonym unsalable.

marksman *n* bersagliere, crack shot, dead shot, sharpshooter, shootist, sniper.

maroon *v* abandon, cast away, desert, isolate, leave, put ashore, strand.

antonym rescue.

marriage *n* alliance, amalgamation, association, confederation, coupling, espousal, link, match, matrimony, matronage, matronhood, merger, nuptials, spousage, spousals, union, wedding, wedlock.

antonym divorce.

married *adj* conjugal, connubial, hitched, husbandly, joined, marital, matrimonial, nuptial, spliced, spousal, united, wed, wedded, wifely, wived, yoked.

antonyms divorced, single.

marrow *n* core, cream, essence, gist, heart, kernel, nub, pith, quick, quintessence, soul, spirit, stuff, substance.

marry *v* ally, bond, espouse, get hitched, get spliced, join, jump the broomstick, knit, link, match, merge, splice, tie, tie the knot, unify, unite, wed, wive, yoke.

antonyms divorce, separate.

marsh *n* bayou, bog, carr, fen, maremma, marshland, morass, moss, muskeg, quagmire, slough, slump, soak, swale, swamp, wetland.

marshal *v* align, arrange, array, assemble, collect, conduct, convoy, deploy, dispose, draw up, escort, gather, group, guide, lead, line up, muster, order, organise, rank, shepherd, take, usher.

marshy *adj* boggy, fennish, fenny, miry, paludal, paludinal, paludine, paludinous, quaggy, slumpy, spongy, swampy, waterlogged, wet.

antonym solid.

martial *adj* bellicose, belligerent, brave, combative, heroic, militant, military, soldierly, warlike.

antonym pacific.

martinet *n* disciplinarian, formalist, slave-driver, stickler, tyrant.

martyrdom *n* agony, anguish, death, excruciation, ordeal, persecution, suffering, torment, torture, witness.

marvel *n* genius, miracle, non(e)such, phenomenon, portent, prodigy, sensation, spectacle, whiz, wonder.

v gape, gaze, goggle, wonder.

marvellous *adj* amazing, astonishing, astounding, beyond belief, breathtaking, épatant, excellent, extraordinary, fabulous, fantastic, glorious, great, hell of a, implausible, improbable, incredible, magnificent, miraculous, mirific(al), phenom, phenomenal, prodigious, remarkable, sensational, singular, smashing, spectacular, splendid, stupendous, super, superb, surprising, terrific, unbelievable, unlikely, wonderful, wondrous.

antonyms ordinary, plausible, run-of-the-mill.

masculine *adj* bold, brave, butch, gallant, hardy, macho, male, manlike, manly, mannish, muscular, powerful, red-blooded, resolute, robust, stout-hearted, strapping, strong, tomboyish, vigorous, virile.

antonym feminine.

masculinity *n* butchness, hoydenism, maleness, manhood, manliness, mannishness, potency, sexuality, tomboyishness, unladylikeness, unwomanliness, virileness, virilescence, virilism, virility, Yang.

antonym femininity.

mash *v* beat, champ, comminute, crush, grind, pound, pulverise, pummel, smash, triturate.

mask *n* blind, camouflage, cloak, concealment, cover, cover-up, disguise, domino, façade, false face, front, guise, pretence, screen, semblance, show, veil, veneer, visard-mask, visor, vizard.

v camouflage, cloak, conceal, cover, disguise, hide, obscure, screen, shield, veil.

antonym uncover.

masked *adj* camouflaged, cloaked, concealed, covered, disguised, screened, shielded, shrouded, visored, vizarded.

antonyms uncovered, unshielded.

masquerade *n* cloak, costume, costume ball, counterfeit, cover, cover-up, deception, disguise, dissimulation, domino, fancy dress party, front, guise, imposture, mask, masked ball, masque, mummery, pose, pretence, put-on, revel, screen, subterfuge.

v disguise, dissemble, dissimulate, impersonate, mask, pass oneself off, play, pose, pretend, profess.

mass[1] *n* accumulation, aggregate, aggregation, assemblage, band, batch, block, body, bulk, bunch, chunk, collection, combination, concretion, congeries, conglomeration, crowd, dimension, entirety, extensity, group, heap, horde, host, hunk, lion's share, load, lot, lump, magnitude, majority, mob, number, piece, pile, preponderance, quantity, size, stack, sum, sum total, throng, totality, troop, welter, whole.

adj across-the-board, blanket, comprehensive, extensive, general, indiscriminate, large-scale, pandemic, popular, sweeping, wholesale, widespread.

antonym limited.

v assemble, cluster, collect, congregate, crowd, for(e)gather, gather, muster, rally.

antonym separate.

mass[2] *n* communion, eucharist, holy communion, housel, Lord's Supper, Lord's Table, nagmaal.

massacre *n* annihilation, blood bath, butchery, carnage, decimation, extermination, holocaust, killing, murder, slaughter.

v annihilate, butcher, decimate, exterminate, kill, mow down, murder, slaughter, slay, wipe out.

massage *n* effleurage, kneading, malaxage, malaxation, manipulation, petrissage, rubbing, rub-down, shiatsu.

v knead, manipulate, rub, rub down.

mass-book *n* breviary, missal, prayer-book, service-book.

massive *adj* big, bulky, colossal, cyclopean, enormous, extensive, gargantuan, gigantic, great, heavy, hefty, huge, hulking, immense, imposing, impressive, jumbo, mammoth, monster, monstrous, monumental, ponderous, rounceval, solid, substantial, titanic, vast, weighty, whacking, whopping.

antonyms slight, small.

master *n* ace, adept, baas, boss, bwana, captain, chief, commander, controller, dab hand, deacon, director, doyen, employer, expert, genius, governor, guide, guru, head, Herr, instructor, lord, maestro, manager, overlord, overseer, owner, past master, pedagogue, preceptor, principal, pro, ruler, schoolmaster, skipper, superintendent, swami, teacher, tutor, virtuoso, wizard.

antonyms amateur, learner, pupil, servant, slave.

adj ace, adept, chief, controlling, crack, expert, foremost, grand, great, leading, main, masterly, predominant, prime, principal, proficient, skilful, skilled.

antonyms copy, subordinate, unskilled.

v acquire, bridle, check, command, conquer, control, curb, defeat, direct, dominate, get the hang of, govern, grasp, learn, manage, overcome, quash, quell, regulate, rule, subdue, subjugate, suppress, tame, triumph over, vanquish.

master race Herrenvolk.

masterful *adj* adept, adroit, arrogant, authoritative, autocratic, bossy, clever, consummate, crack, deft, despotic, dexterous, dictatorial, domineering, excellent, expert, exquisite, fine, finished, first-rate, high-handed, imperious, magisterial, masterly, overbearing, overweening, peremptory, powerful, professional, self-willed, skilful, skilled, superior, superlative, supreme, tyrannical.

antonyms clumsy, humble, unskilful.

masterly *adj* adept, adroit, clever, consummate, crack, dexterous, excellent, expert, exquisite, fine, finished, first-rate, magistral, masterful, skilful, skilled, superb, superior, superlative, supreme.

antonyms clumsy, poor, unskilled.

mastermind *v* conceive, design, devise, direct, dream up, forge, frame, hatch, manage, organise, originate, plan.

n architect, authority, brain(s), creator, director, engineer, genius, intellect, manager, organiser, originator, planner, prime mover, virtuoso.

masterpiece *n* chef d'oeuvre, classic, jewel, magnum opus, master-work, museum-piece, pièce de résistance, tour de force.

mastery *n* ability, acquirement, advantage, ascendancy, attainment, authority, cleverness, command, comprehension, conquest, control, conversancy, deftness, dexterity, domination, dominion, expertise, familiarity, finesse, grasp, know-how, knowledge, pre-eminence, proficiency, prowess, rule, skill, superiority, supremacy, sway, triumph, understanding, upper hand, victory, virtuosity, whip-hand.

antonyms clumsiness, unfamiliarity.

masticate *v* champ, chew, crunch, eat, knead, manducate, munch, ruminate.

masturbate *v* frig, jerk off, play with oneself, toss (it) off, wank.

masturbation *n* auto-eroticism, frig, frigging, frottage, onanism, self-abuse, self-stimulation, tribadism, tribady, wanking.

mat *n* carpet, doormat, drugget, felt, rug, underfelt, underlay.

match[1] *n* bout, competition, contest, game, main, test, trial, venue.

v compete, contend, oppose, pit against, rival, vie.

match[2] *n* affiliation, alliance, combination, companion, complement, copy, counterpart, couple, dead ringer, double, duet, duplicate, equal, equivalent, fellow, like, look-alike, marriage, mate, pair, pairing, parallel, partnership, peer, replica, ringer, rival, spit, spitting image, tally, twin, union.

v accompany, accord, adapt, agree, ally, blend, combine, compare, co-ordinate, correspond, couple, emulate, equal, fit, gee, go together, go with, harmonise, join, link, marry, mate, measure up to, pair, relate, rival, suit, tally, team, tone with, unite, yoke.

antonyms clash, separate.

match[3] *n* Congreve-match, fuse, fusee, light, lucifer, lucifer-match, safety match, spill, taper, vesta, vesuvian.

matching *adj* analogous, comparable, co-ordinating, corresponding, double, duplicate, equal, equivalent, homochromous, identical, like, parallel, pared, same, similar, toning, twin.

antonyms clashing, different.

matchless *adj* consummate, excellent, exquisite, incomparable, inimitable, nonpareil, peerless, perfect, superlative, supreme, unequalled, unique, unmatched, unparalleled, unrivalled, unsurpassed.

antonyms commonplace, poor.

mate *n* assistant, associate, better half, buddy, china, chum, colleague, companion, compeer, comrade, confidant(e), co-worker, crony, double, fellow, fellow-worker, fere, friend, gossip, helper, helpmate, helpmeet, husband, match, pal, partner, repository, side-kick, spouse, subordinate, twin, wife.

v breed, copulate, couple, join, marry, match, pair, wed, yoke.

material *n* body, cloth, constituents, data, element, evidence, fabric, facts, information, literature, matter, notes, stuff, substance, textile, work.

adj applicable, apposite, apropos, bodily, central, concrete, consequential, corporeal, essential, fleshly, germane, grave, gross, hylic, important, indispensable, key, meaningful, momentous, non-spiritual, palpable, pertinent, physical, relevant, serious, significant, substantial, tangible, vital, weighty, worldly.

antonyms ethereal, immaterial.

materialise *v* appear, arise, happen, occur, take shape, turn up.

antonym disappear.

materialism *n* hylicism, hylism, mammon, mammonism, money-grubbing.

materialist *n* hylicist, hylist, mammonite, money-grubber, mug-hunter, pot-hunter.

materialistic *adj* banausic, Kensington, mammonist, mammonistic, mercenary, money-grubbing.

antonym spiritual.

materially *adv* basically, considerably, essentially, fundamentally, gravely, greatly, much, palpably, physically, seriously, significantly, substantially, tangibly.

antonym insignificantly.

maternal *adj* loving, matronal, motherly, protective.

antonym paternal.

mating *n* breeding, coition, copulating, copulation, coupling, fusing, jointing, matching, pangamy, service, sexual intercourse, tupping, twinning, uniting.

matrimonial *adj* conjugal, connubial, marital, marriage, married, nuptial, sponsal, spousal, wedded, wedding.

matrimony *n* espousals, marriage, nuptials, sponsalia, spousage, spousal, wedlock.

matron *n* dame, dowager, matriarch.

matted *adj* knotted, tangled, tangly, tousled, uncombed.

antonyms tidy, untangled.

matter[1] *n* affair, amount, argument, body, business, complication, concern, consequence, context, difficulty, distress, episode, event, hyle, import, importance, incident, issue, material, moment, note, occurrence, problem, proceeding, purport, quantity, question, sense, significance, situation, stuff, subject, substance, sum, text, thesis, thing, topic, transaction, trouble, upset, weight, worry.

antonym insignificance.

v count, make a difference, mean something, signify.

matter[2] *n* discharge, purulence, pus, secretion, suppuration.

v discharge, secrete.

matter-of-fact *adj* deadpan, direct, down-to-earth, dry, dull, emotionless, flat, lifeless, literal, mundane, plain, prosaic, sober, unembellished, unimaginative, unsentimental, unvarnished.

antonym emotional.

mattress *n* futon, pallet, palliasse.

mature *adj* adult, complete, due, fit, full-blown, full-grown, fully fledged, grown, grown-up, matured, mellow, nubile, perfect, perfected, prepared, ready, ripe, ripened, seasoned, well-thought-out.

antonym immature.

v accrue, age, bloom, come of age, develop, fall due, grow up, maturate, mellow, perfect, ripen, season.

maturity *n* adulthood, completion, experience, fullness, majority, manhood, maturation, matureness, nubility, perfection, readiness, ripeness, wisdom, womanhood.

antonym immaturity.

maudlin *adj* drunk, emotional, fuddled, half-drunk, icky, lachrymose, mawkish, mushy, sentimental, sickly, slushy, soppy, tearful, tipsy, weepy.

antonym matter-of-fact.

maul *v* abuse, batter, beat, beat up, claw, ill-treat, knock about, lacerate, maltreat, mangle, manhandle, molest, paw, pummel, rough up, thrash.

maunder *v* babble, blather, blether, chatter, drivel, gabble, grumble, mutter, prattle, rabbit, ramble, witter.

maw *n* abyss, chasm, craw, crop, gulf, gullet, jaws, mouth, stomach, throat.

mawkish *adj* disgusting, emotional, feeble, flat, foul, gushy, icky, insipid, jejune, loathsome, maudlin, mushy, nauseous, offensive, schmaltzy, sentimental, sickly, slushy, soppy, squeamish, stale, vapid.

antonyms matter-of-fact, pleasant.

maxim *n* adage, aphorism, apophthegm, axiom, byword, epigram, gnome, mot, motto, precept, proverb, rule, saw, saying, sentence.

maximum *adj* biggest, greatest, highest, largest, maximal, most, paramount, supreme, topmost, utmost.

antonym minimum.

n apogee, ceiling, crest, extremity, height, most, ne plus ultra, peak, pinnacle, summit, top (point), upper limit, utmost, zenith.

antonym mimimum.

maybe *adv* haply, happen, mayhap, peradventure, perchance, perhaps, possibly.

antonym definitely.

maze *n* confusion, convolutions, imbroglio, intricacy, labyrinth, meander, mesh, mizmaze, puzzle, snarl, tangle, web.

meadow *n* field, haugh, holm, inch, lea, ley, mead, pasture.

meagre *adj* barren, bony, deficient, emaciated, exiguous, gaunt, hungry, inadequate, infertile, insubstantial, lank, lean, little, negligible, paltry, penurious, poor, puny, scanty, scraggy, scrawny, scrimpy, short, skimpy, skinny, slender, slight, small, spare, sparse, starved, thin, underfed, unfruitful, unproductive, weak.

antonyms fertile, substantial.

meal[1] *n* banquet, barbecue, beanfeast, beano, blow-out, breakfast, brunch, chota-hazri, collation, déjeuner, déjeuner à la fourchette, dinner, feast, lunch, luncheon, nosh, nosh-up, petit déjeuner, picnic, repast, scoff, snack, spread, supper, tea, tiffin(g), tuck-in.

meal[2] *n* farina, flour, grits, oatmeal, powder.

mealy-mouthed *adj* equivocal, euphemistic, flattering, glib, hestitant, indirect, mincing, overdelicate, over-squeamish, plausible, prim, reticent, smooth-tongued.

mean[1] *adj* abject, bad-tempered, base, base-born, beggarly, callous, cheese-paring, churlish, close, close-fisted, close-handed, common, contemptible, degraded, despicable, disagreeable, disgraceful, dishonourable, down-at-heel, excellent, fast-handed, good, great, hard-hearted, hostile, humble, ignoble, illiberal, inconsiderable, inferior, insignificant, low, low-born, lowly, malicious, malignant, mean-spirited, menial, mercenary, mingy, miserable, miserly, modest, narrow-minded, nasty, near, niggardly, obscure, one-horse, ordinary, paltry, parsimonious, penny-pinching, penurious, petty, plebeian, poor, proletarian, pusillanimous, rude, run-down, scrub, scurvy, seedy, selfish, servile, shabby, shameful, skilful, slink, small-minded, snippy, sordid, sour, squalid, stingy, tawdry, tight, tight-fisted, undistinguished, unfriendly, ungenerous, ungiving, unhandsome, unpleasant, vicious, vile, vulgar, wretched.

antonyms generous, kind, noble, superior.

mean[2] *v* adumbrate, aim, aspire, augur, betoken, cause, connote, contemplate, convey, denote, design, desire, destine, drive at, engender, entail, express, fate, fit, foreshadow, foretell, get at, give rise to, herald, hint, imply, indicate, insinuate, intend, involve, lead to, make, match, necessitate, omen, plan, portend, predestine, preordain, presage, produce, promise, propose, purport, purpose, represent, result in, say, set out, signify, spell, stand for, suggest, suit, symbolise, want, wish.

mean[3] *adj* average, half-way, intermediate, medial, median, medium, middle, middling, moderate, normal, standard.

antonym extreme.

n aurea mediocritas, average, balance, compromise, golden mean, happy medium, median, middle, middle course, middle way, mid-point, norm, via media.

antonym extreme.

meander *v* amble, curve, ramble, snake, stravaig, stray, stroll, turn, twist, wander, wind, zigzag.

meandering *adj* circuitous, convoluted, indirect, meandrous, roundabout, serpentine, sinuous, snaking, tortuous, twisting, wandering, winding.

antonym straight.

meaning *n* aim, connotation, construction, denotation, design, drift, end, explanation, force, gist, goal, idea, implication, import, intention, interpretation, matter, message, object, plan, point, purport, purpose, sense, significance, signification, substance, thrust, trend, upshot, validity, value, worth.

meaningful *adj* eloquent, expressive, important, material, meaningful, pointed, pregnant, purposeful, relevant, serious, significant, speaking, suggestive, useful, valid, warning, worthwhile.

meaningless *adj* absurd, aimless, empty, expressionless, futile, hollow, inane, inconsequential, insignificant, insubstantial, nonsense, nonsensical, nugatory, pointless, purposeless, senseless, trifling, trivial, unmeaning, useless, vain, valueless, worthless.

antonym meaningful.

meanness *n* abjectness, baseness, beggarliness, churlishness, close-fistedness, close-handedness, contemptibleness, degradation, despicableness, disagreeableness, disgracefulness, dishonourableness, humbleness, illiberality, insignificance, lowliness, malice, maliciousness, malignity, mean-spiritedness, minginess, miserliness, narrow-mindedness, nastiness, niggardliness, obscurity, paltriness, parsimony, penuriousness, pettiness, poorness, pusillanimity, rudeness, scurviness, seediness, selfishness, servility, shabbiness, shamefulness, sordidness, sourness, squalor, stinginess, tawdriness, tight-fistedness, unfriendliness, unpleasantness, viciousness, vileness, wretchedness.

antonyms generosity, kindness, nobility, superiority.

means *n* ability, affluence, agency, avenue, capacity, capital, channel, course, estate, expedient, fortune, funds, income, instrument, machinery, measure, medium, method, mode, money, process, property, resources, riches, substance, way, wealth, wherewithal.

meantime, meanwhile *advs* at the same time, concurrently, en attendant, for now, for the moment, in the interim, in the interval, in the meantime, in the meanwhile, simultaneously.

measly *adj* beggarly, contemptible, meagre, mean, mingy, miserable, miserly, niggardly, paltry, pathetic, petty, piddling, pitiful, poor, puny, scanty, skimpy, stingy, trivial, ungenerous.

measurable *adj* appreciable, assessable, computable, determinable, fathomable, gaugeable, material, mensurable, perceptible, quantifiable, quantitative, significant.

antonym measureless.

measure *n* act, action, allotment, allowance, amount, amplitude, beat, bill, bounds, cadence, capacity, control, course, criterion, deed, degree, démarche, enactment, example, expedient, extent, foot, gauge, jigger, law, limit, limitation, magnitude, manoeuvre, means, method, metre, model, moderation, norm, portion, procedure, proceeding, proportion, quantity, quota, range, ration, reach, resolution, restraint, rhythm, rule, scale, scope, share, size, standard, statute, step, system, test, touchstone, verse, yardstick.

v admeasure, appraise, assess, calculate, calibrate, choose, compute, determine, estimate, evaluate, fathom, gauge, judge, mark out, measure off, measure out, plumb, quantify, rate, size, sound, step, survey, value, weigh.

measure off circumscribe, delimit, demarcate, determine, fix, lay down, lay off, limit, mark out, measure (out), pace out.

measure out allot, apportion, assign, deal out, dispense, distribute, divide, dole out, hand out, issue, measure (off), mete out, parcel out, pour out, proportion, share out.

measure up do, fill the bill, make the grade, pass muster, shape up, suffice.

measure up to compare with, equal, match, meet, rival, touch.

measured *adj* calculated, considered, constant, deliberate, dignified, even, exact, gauged, grave, leisurely, metronomic, modulated, planned, precise, predetermined, premeditated, quantified, reasoned, regular, regulated, sedate, slow, sober, solemn, standard, stately, steady, studied, unhurried, uniform, verified, well-thought-out.

measureless *adj* bottomless, boundless, endless, immeasurable, immense, incalculable, inestimable, infinite, innumerable, limitless, unbounded, vast.

antonym measurable.

measurement *n* amount, amplitude, appraisal, appreciation, area, assessment, calculation, calibration, capacity, computation, depth, dimension, estimation, evaluation, extent, gauging, height, judgement, length, magnitude, mensuration, metage, size, survey, valuation, volume, weight, width.

meat[1] *n* aliment, charqui, cheer, chow, comestibles, eats, fare, flesh, food, grub, jerk, nourishment, nutriment, provender, provisions, rations, subsistence, sustenance, viands, victuals.

meat[2] *n* core, crux, essence, fundamentals, gist, heart, kernel, marrow, nub, nucleus, pith, point, substance.

meaty *adj* beefy, brawny, burly, fleshy, hearty, heavy, husky, interesting, matterful, meaningful, muscular, nourishing, pithy, profound, rich, significant, solid, strapping, sturdy, substantial.

mechanic *n* artificer, engineer, fitter, machinist, mechanician, operative, operator, opificer, repairman, technician.

mechanical *adj* automated, automatic, cold, cursory, dead, dull, emotionless, habitual, impersonal, instinctive, involuntary, lack-lustre, lifeless, machine-driven, machine-like, matter-of-fact, perfunctory, routine, spiritless, unanimated, unconscious, unfeeling, unthinking.

mechanism *n* action, agency, apparatus, appliance, components, contrivance, device, execution, functioning, gadgetry, gears, innards, instrument, machine, machinery, means, medium, method, motor, operation, performance, procedure, process, structure, system, technique, tool, workings, works.

medal *n* award, decoration, gong, honour, medalet, medallion, prize, reward, trophy.

meddle *v* interfere, interlope, interpose, intervene, intrude, mell, pry, put one's oar in, tamper.

meddlesome *adj* interfering, intruding, intrusive, meddling, mischievous, officious, prying, ultracrepidarian.

medi(a)eval *adj* antediluvian, antiquated, antique, archaic, old-fashioned, old-world, outmoded, primitive, unenlightened.

mediate *v* arbitrate, conciliate, incubate, intercede, interpose, intervene, moderate, negotiate, reconcile, referee, resolve, settle, step in, umpire.

mediation *n* arbitration, conciliation, good offices, intercession, interposition, intervention, negotiation, parley, reconciliation.

mediator *n* advocate, arbiter, arbitrator, go-between, honest broker, interceder, intermediary, interventor, judge, middleman, moderator, negotiator, ombudsman, ombudswoman, peacemaker, referee, umpire.

medical *adj* Hippocratic, iatric(al), medicinal.

medical practitioner allopath, consultant, doc, doctor, feldsher, GP, healer, homeopath, intern, medico, MO, physician, sawbones, surgeon.

medicinal *adj* adjuvant, analeptic, curative, healing, homeopathic, medical, medicamental, medicamentary, remedial, restorative, roborant, sanatory, therapeutic.

medicine[1] *n* cure, diapente, diatessaron, drug, electuary, elixir, febrifuge, Galenical, materia medica, medicament, medication, nostrum, panacea, physic, remedy, specific, tincture, vermifuge.

medicine[2] *n* acupuncture, allopathy, homeopathy, leech-craft, surgery, therapeutics.

medicine-man *n* angek(k)ok, mystery-man, shaman, witch-doctor.

mediocre *adj* amateurish, average, commonplace, indifferent, inferior, insignificant, mean, medium, middling, ordinary, passable, pedestrian, run-of-the-mill, second-rate, so-so, undistinguished, unexceptional, uninspired.

antonyms excellent, exceptional, extraordinary.

mediocrity *n* amateurishness, cipher, indifference, inferiority, insignificance, lightweight, nobody, nonentity, ordinariness, poorness, second-rater, unimportance.

meditate *v* be in a brown study, cerebrate, cogitate, consider, contemplate, deliberate, devise, excogitate, intend, mull over, muse, plan, ponder, purpose, reflect, ruminate, scheme, speculate, study, think, think over.

meditation *n* brown study, cerebration, cogitation, concentration, contemplation, excogitation, musing, pondering, reflection, reverie, ruminating, rumination, speculation, study, thought.

meditative *adj* cogitative, contemplative, deliberative, museful, pensive, reflective, ruminant, ruminative, studious, thoughtful.

medium[1] *adj* average, fair, intermediate, mean, medial, median, mediocre, middle, middling, midway, standard.

n aurea mediocritas, average, centre, compromise, golden mean, happy medium, mean, middle, middle ground, midpoint, via media, way.

medium[2] *n* agency, avenue, base, channel, excipient, form, instrument, instrumentality, means, mode, organ, vehicle, way.

medium[3] *n* clairvoyant, psychic, spiritist, spiritualist.

medium[4] *n* ambience, atmosphere, circumstances, conditions, element, environment, habitat, influences, milieu, setting, surroundings.

medley *n* assortment, collection, confusion, conglomeration, farrago, galimatias, gallimaufry, hodge-podge, hotchpotch, jumble, macaroni, macédoine, mélange, mingle-mangle, miscellany, mishmash, mixture, olio, olla-podrida, omnium-gatherum, pastiche, patchwork, pot-pourri, quodlibet, salmagundi.

meek *adj* acquiescent, compliant, deferential, docile, forbearing, gentle, humble, long-suffering, mild, modest, patient, peaceful, resigned, slavish, soft, spineless, spiritless, subdued, submissive, tame, timid, unambitious, unassuming, unpretentious, unresisting, weak, yielding.

antonyms arrogant, rebellious.

meekness *n* acquiescence, compliance, deference, docility, forbearance, gentleness, humbleness, humility, long-suffering, lowliness, mildness, modesty, patience, peacefulness, resignation, self-abasement, self-disparagement, self-effacement, softness, spinelessness, spiritlessness, submission, submissiveness, tameness, timidity, weakness.

antonym arrogance.

meet *v* abut, adjoin, answer, assemble, bear, bump into, chance on, collect, come across, come together, comply, confront, congregate, connect, contact, convene, converge, cross, discharge, encounter, endure, equal, experience, face, find, forgather, fulfil, gather, go through, gratify, handle, happen on, intersect, join, link up, match, measure up to, muster, perform, rally, rencontre, rencounter, run across, run into, satisfy, suffer, touch, undergo, unite.

meeting *n* abutment, assembly, assignation, audience, company, conclave, concourse, conference, confluence, confrontation, congregation, conjunction, consult, conventicle, convention, convergence, convocation, crossing, encounter, engagement, forum, gathering, gemot, get-together, gorsedd, indaba, intersection, introduction, junction, meet, moot, rally, rencontre, rencounter, rendezvous, reunion, session, synod, tryst, union, watersmeet.

meeting-point *n* confluence, convergence, convergency, crossroads, interface, intersection, junction, watersmeet.

megalomania *n* conceitedness, delusions of grandeur, folie de grandeur, overestimation, self-importance.

melancholy *adj* blue, dejected, depressed, despondent, disconsolate, dismal, dispirited, doleful, down, down in the dumps, down in the mouth, downcast, down-hearted, gloomy, glum, heavy-hearted, hipped, joyless, low, low-spirited, lugubrious, melancholic, miserable, moody, mournful, pensieroso, pensive, sad, sombre, sorrowful, splenific, unhappy, woebegone, woeful.

antonyms cheerful, gay, happy, joyful.

n blues, dejection, depression, despondency, dole, dolour, gloom, gloominess, glumness, low spirits, pensiveness, sadness, sorrow, unhappiness, woe.

antonym exhilaration.

mélange *n* assortment, confusion, farrago, galimatias, gallimaufry, hash, hodge-podge, hotch-potch, jumble, medley, mingle-mangle, miscellany, mishmash, mix, mixed bag, mixture, olio, omnium-gatherum, pastiche, potpourri, salmagundi.

mêlée *n* affray, battle royal, brawl, broil, dogfight, donnybrook, fight, fracas, fray, free-for-all, ruckus, ruction, rumpus, scrimmage, scrum, scuffle, set-to, stramash, tussle.

mellifluous *adj* canorous, dulcet, euphonious, honeyed, mellow, silvery, smooth, soft, soothing, sweet, sweet-sounding, tuneful.

antonyms discordant, grating, harsh.

mellow *adj* cheerful, cordial, delicate, dulcet, elevated, expansive, full, full-flavoured, genial, happy, jolly, jovial, juicy, mature, mellifluous, melodious, merry, perfect, placid, relaxed, rich, ripe, rounded, serene, smooth, soft, sweet, tipsy, tranquil, well-matured.

antonyms immature, unripe.

v improve, mature, perfect, ripen, season, soften, sweeten, temper.

melodious *adj* arioso, canorous, concordant, dulcet, euphonious, harmonious, melodic, musical, silvery, sonorous, sweet-sounding, tuneful.

antonyms discordant, grating, harsh.

melodramatic *adj* blood-and-thunder, exaggerated, hammy, histrionic, overdone, overdramatic, overemotional, overwrought, sensational, stagy, theatrical.

melody *n* air, aria, arietta, arriette, euphony, harmony, melisma, melodiousness, music, musicality, refrain, song, strain, theme, tune, tunefulness.

melt *v* deliquesce, diffuse, disarm, dissolve, flux, fuse, liquate, liquefy, mollify, relax, soften, thaw, touch, uncongeal, unfreeze.

antonyms freeze, harden, solidify.

melt away dematerialise, disappear, disperse, dissolve, evanesce, evaporate, fade, vanish.

member *n* appendage, arm, associate, component, constituent, element, extremity, fellow, initiate, leg, limb, organ, part, portion, representative.

membership *n* adherence, allegiance, associates, body, enrolment, fellows, fellowship, members, participation.

membrane *n* diaphragm, fell, film, hymen, integument, partition, septum, skin, tissue, veil, velum.

memento *n* keepsake, memorial, record, relic, remembrance, reminder, souvenir, token, trophy.

memoir *n* account, biography, essay, journal, life, monograph, narrative, record, register, report.

memoirs *n* annals, autobiography, chronicles, confessions, diary, experiences, journals, life, life story, memories, personalia, recollections, records, reminiscences, transactions.

memorable *adj* catchy, celebrated, distinguished, extraordinary, famous, historic, illustrious, important, impressive, marvellous, momentous, notable, noteworthy, outstanding, remarkable, signal, significant, striking, unforgettable.

antonym forgettable.

memorial *n* cairn, cromlech, dolmen, martyry, mausoleum, memento, menhir, monument, plaque, record, remembrance, souvenir, stone.

adj celebratory, commemorative, monumental.

memorise *v* con, learn, learn by heart, learn by rote, learn off, mug up, swot up.

antonym forget.

memory *n* bank, celebrity, commemoration, database, fame, glory, honour, memorial, name, recall, recollection, remembrance, reminiscence, renown, reputation, repute, retention, store.

antonym forgetfulness.

menace *v* alarm, browbeat, bully, comminate, cow, frighten, impend, intimidate, loom, lour (lower), terrorise, threaten.

n annoyance, commination, danger, hazard, intimidation, jeopardy, nuisance, peril, pest, plague, scare, terror, threat, troublemaker, warning.

menacing *adj* alarming, Damoclean, dangerous, frightening, impending, intimidating, intimidatory, looming, louring (lowering), minacious, minatory, ominous, portentous, threatening.

mend *v* ameliorate, amend, better, bushel, cobble, convalesce, correct, cure, darn, emend, fix, heal, improve, patch, recover, rectify, recuperate, refit, reform, remedy, renew, renovate, repair, restore, retouch, revise, solder.

antonyms break, destroy, deteriorate.

n clout, darn, patch, repair, stitch.

mendacious *adj* deceitful, deceptive, dishonest, duplicitous, fallacious, false, fraudulent, insincere, inveracious, lying, perfidious, perjured, untrue, untruthful, unveracious.

antonyms honest, truthful.

mendacity *n* deceit, deceitfulness, dishonesty, distortion, duplicity, falsehood, falsification, fraudulence, insincerity, inveracity, lie, lying, mendaciousness, misrepresentation, perfidy, perjury, untruth, untruthfulness, unveracity.

antonyms honesty, truthfulness.

mendicant *adj* begging, cadging, petitionary, scrounging, supplicant.

n almsman, beachcomber, beggar, bum, cadger, hobo, moocher, panhandler, pauper, scrounger, tramp, vagabond, vagrant.

menial *adj* abject, attending, base, boring, degrading, demeaning, dull, fawning, grovelling, helping, humble, humdrum, ignoble, ignominious, low, lowly, mean, obsequious, routine, servile, slavish, sorry, subservient, sycophantic, unskilled, vile.

n attendant, creature, dog's-body, domestic, drudge, eta, flunky, labourer, lackey, peon, serf, servant, skivvy, slave, underling.

menstruation *n* catamenia, courses, flow, menorrhoea, menses, monthlies, period, the curse, the usual.

mensuration *n* assessment, calculation, calibration, computation, estimation, evaluation, measurement, measuring, metage, survey, surveying, valuation.

mental[1] *adj* abstract, cerebral, cognitive, conceptual, ideational, ideative, intellectual, noetic, rational, theoretical.

antonym physical.

mental[2] *adj* crazy, deranged, disturbed, insane, loony, loopy, lunatic, mad, psychiatric, psychotic, unbalanced, unstable.

antonyms balanced, sane.

mentality *n* attitude, brains, capacity, character, comprehension, disposition, endowment, faculty, frame of mind, intellect, IQ, make-up, mind, outlook, personality, psychology, rationality, understanding, wit.

mentally *adv* emotionally, intellectually, inwardly, psychologically, rationally, subjectively, temperamentally.

mention *v* acknowledge, adduce, advise, allude to, apprise, bring up, broach, cite, communicate, declare, disclose, divulge, hint at, impart, intimate, make known, name, point out, recount, refer to, report, reveal, speak of, state, tell, touch on.

n acknowledgement, allusion, announcement, citation, indication, notification, observation, recognition, reference, remark, tribute.

mentioned *adj* above-mentioned, aforesaid, cited, fore-cited, forementioned, forenamed, forequoted, foresaid, quoted, reported, stated.

mentor *n* adviser, coach, counsellor, guide, guru, instructor, pedagogue, swami, teacher, tutor.

menu *n* bill of fare, card, carte du jour, list, tariff.

mercantile *adj* commercial, marketable, merchantable, sal(e)able, trade, trading.

mercenary *adj* acquisitive, avaricious, bought, covetous, grasping, greedy, hack, hired, mammonish, mammonistic, materialistic, meretricious, money-grubbing, paid, sordid, venal.

n condottiere, free companion, free-lance, hireling, landsknecht, lansquenet, merc, soldier of fortune.

merchandise *n* cargo, commodities, freight, goods, produce, products, shipment, staples, stock, stock in trade, truck, vendibles, wares.

v carry, deal in, distribute, market, peddle, retail, sell, supply, trade, traffic in, vend.

merchant *n* broker, dealer, jobber, négociant, retailer, salesman, seller, shopkeeper, trader, tradesman, trafficker, vendor, wholesaler.

merciful *adj* beneficent, benignant, clement, compassionate, condolent, forbearing, forgiving, generous, gracious, humane, humanitarian, kind, lenient, liberal, mild, pitying, soft, sparing, sympathetic, tender-hearted.

antonyms cruel, merciless.

merciless *adj* barbarous, callous, cruel, hard, hard-hearted, harsh, heartless, implacable, inexorable, inhuman, inhumane, pitiless, relentless, remorseless, ruthless, severe, unappeasable, unforgiving, unmerciful, unpitying, unsparing.

antonym merciful.

mercurial *adj* active, capricious, changeable, erratic, fickle, flighty, gay, impetuous, impulsive, inconstant, irrepressible, light-hearted, lively, mobile, spirited, sprightly, temperamental, unpredictable, unstable, variable, volatile.

antonym saturnine.

mercy *n* benevolence, blessing, boon, charity, clemency, compassion, favour, forbearance, forgiveness, godsend, grace, humanitarianism, kindness, leniency, pity, quarter, relief.

antonyms cruelty, revenge.

mere *adj* absolute, bare, common, complete, entire, paltry, petty, plain, pure, pure and simple, sheer, simple, stark, unadulterated, unmitigated, unmixed, utter, very.

merge *v* amalgamate, blend, coalesce, combine, commingle, confederate, consolidate, converge, fuse, incorporate, intermix, join, liquesce, meet, meld, melt into, mingle, mix, unite.

merger *n* amalgamation, coalescence, coalition, combination, confederation, consolidation, fusion, incorporation, union.

merit *n* advantage, asset, claim, credit, desert, due, excellence, good, goodness, integrity, justification, quality, right, strong point, talent, value, virtue, worth, worthiness.

antonyms demerit, fault.

v deserve, earn, incur, justify, rate, warrant.

merited *adj* appropriate, condign, deserved, due, earned, entitled, fitting, just, justified, rightful, warranted, worthy.

antonyms inappropriate, unjustified.

meritorious *adj* admirable, commendable, creditable, deserving, estimable, excellent, exemplary, good, honourable, laudable, praiseworthy, right, righteous, virtuous, worthful, worthy.

antonym unworthy.

merriment *n* amusement, conviviality, elation, exhilaration, festivity, frolic, fun, gaiety, glee, hilarity, jocosity, jocularity, jocundity, jollity, joviality, laughter, levity, liveliness, merry-making, mirth, revelry, sport, waggery.

antonyms gloom, gravity, sadness, seriousness.

merry *adj* amusing, blithe, blithesome, boon, carefree, cheerful, chirpy, comic, comical, convivial, crank, elevated, facetious, festive, frolicsome, fun-loving, funny, gay, glad, gleeful, happy, heartsome, hilarious, humorous, jocular, jocund, jolly, joyful, joyous, light-hearted, mellow, mirthful, rollicking, rorty, saturnalian, sportful, sportive, squiffy, tiddly, tipsy, vivacious.

antonyms gloomy, glum, grave, melancholy, serious, sober, sombre.

merry-go-round *n* carousel, joy-wheel, roundabout, whirligig.

merrymaking *n* carousal, carouse, carousing, celebration, conviviality, festivity, fun, gaiety, gil(l)ravage, jollification, mafficking, mallemaroking, merriment, mollie, party, rejoicings, revel, revelry.

mesh *n* entanglement, lattice, net, netting, network, plexus, reticulation, snare, tangle, toils, tracery, trap, web.

v catch, combine, come together, connect, co-ordinate, dovetail, engage, enmesh, entangle, fit, harmonise, inmesh, interlock, knit.

mesmerise *v* benumb, captivate, enthral, entrance, fascinate, grip, hypnotise, magnetise, spellbind, stupefy.

mess *n* bollocks, botch, chaos, clutter, cock-up, confusion, difficulty, dilemma, dirtiness, disarray, disorder, disorganisation, fix, guddle, hash, imbroglio, jam, jumble, litter, mishmash, mix-up, muddle, muss(e), perplexity, pickle, plight, predicament, shambles, shemozzle, soss, stew, turmoil, untidiness, yuck.

antonyms order, tidiness.

v befoul, besmirch, clutter, dirty, disarrange, disarray, dishevel, foul, litter, muss(e), pollute, tousle.

antonyms order, tidy.

mess about amuse oneself, arse about, dabble, fiddle, footle, interfere, meddle, mess around, mess on, muck about, play, play about, play around, potter, tamper, tinker, toy, trifle.

mess up botch, bungle, disrupt, jumble, make a hash of, muck up, muddle, spoil, tangle.

mess with fiddle with, interfere, meddle with, play with, tamper with, tangle with, tinker with.

message *n* bulletin, cable, commission, communication, communiqué, dépêche, dispatch, errand, fax, idea, import, intimation, job, letter, meaning, memorandum, mission, missive, moral, note, notice, point, purport, send, task, Telemessage®, telex, theme, tidings, word.

messenger *n* agent, ambassador, bearer, carrier, courier, delivery boy, emissary, envoy, errand-boy, go-between, harbinger, herald, in-between, internuncio, mercury, nuncio, runner, send, vaunt-courier.

messy *adj* chaotic, cluttered, confused, dirty, dishevelled, disordered, disorganised, grubby, grungy, littered, muddled, shambolic, sloppy, slovenly, unkempt, untidy, yucky.

antonyms neat, ordered, tidy.

metamorphose *v* alter, change, convert, modify, mutate, remake, remodel, reshape, transfigure, transform, translate, transmogrify, transmute, transubstantiate.

metamorphosis *n* alteration, change, change-over, conversion, modification, mutation, rebirth, transfiguration, transformation, translation, transmogrification, transmutation, transubstantiation.

metaphor *n* allegory, analogy, apologue, emblem, figure of speech, image, symbol, trope.

metaphorical *adj* allegorical, emblematic, emblematical, figurative, Pickwickian, symbolic, tropical.

metaphysical *adj* abstract, abstruse, basic, deep, esoteric, essential, eternal, fundamental, general, high-flown, ideal, immaterial, impalpable, incorporeal, insubstantial, intangible, intellectual, oversubtle, philosophical, profound, recondite, speculative, spiritual, subjective, supernatural, theoretical, transcendental, universal, unreal, unsubstantial.

mete out administer, allot, apportion, assign, deal out, dispense, distribute, divide out, dole out, hand out, measure out, parcel out, portion, ration out, share out.

meteor *n* aerolite, aerolith, bolide, comet, fire-ball, meteorite, meteoroid, shooting-star.

meteoric *adj* brief, brilliant, dazzling, fast, instantaneous, momentary, overnight, rapid, spectacular, speedy, sudden, swift.

meteorologist *n* climatologist, met-man, weatherman, weather-prophet.

method *n* approach, arrangement, course, design, fashion, form, manner, mode, modus operandi, order, orderliness, organisation, pattern, plan, planning, practice, procedure, process, programme, purpose, regularity, routine, rule, scheme, structure, style, system, technique, way.

methodical *adj* business-like, deliberate, disciplined, efficient, meticulous, neat, ordered, orderly, organised, painstaking, planned, precise, punctilious, regular, scrupulous, structured, systematic, tidy.

antonyms confused, desultory, irregular.

meticulous *adj* accurate, detailed, exact, fastidious, fussy, microscopic, nice, painstaking, particular, perfectionist, precise, punctilious, scrupulous, strict, thorough.

antonyms careless, slapdash.

métier *n* calling, craft, field, forte, line, occupation, profession, pursuit, speciality, specialty, sphere, trade, vocation.

metropolis *n* capital, city, megalopolis.

mettle *n* ardour, boldness, bottle, bravery, calibre, character, courage, daring, disposition, fire, fortitude, gallantry, gameness, ginger, grit, guts, hardihood, heart, indomitability, kidney, life, make-up, nature, nerve, pith, pluck, quality, resolution, resolve, spirit, spunk, stamp, temper, temperament, valour, vigour.

mew *v* caterwaul, meow, mewl, miaow, miaul, pule, whine.

mewl *v* blubber, cry, girn, grizzle, pule, snivel, whimper, whine, whinge.

miasma *n* effluvium, fetor, mephitis, odour, pollution, reek, smell, stench, stink.

miasmal *adj* fetid, foul, insalubrious, malodorous, mephitic, miasm(at)ic, miasm(at)ous, noisome, noxious, polluted, putrid, reeking, smelly, stinking, unwholesome.

microbe *n* bacillus, bacterium, bug, germ, micro-organism, pathogen, virus.

microscopic *adj* imperceptible, indiscernible, infinitesimal, invisible, minuscule, minute, negligible, tiny.

antonyms huge, vast.

midday *n* lunchtime, noon, noonday, noontide, twelve.

middle *adj* central, halfway, inner, inside, intermediate, intervening, mean, medial, median, mediate, medium, mid, middle-bracket.

n aurea mediocritas, centre, focus, golden mean, halfway mark, halfway point, happy medium, heart, inside, mean, middle way, midpoint, midriff, midsection, midst, thick, via media, waist.

antonyms beginning, border, edge, end, extreme.

middle-class *adj* bourgeois, conventional, preppy, suburban.

middleman *n* broker, distributor, entrepreneur, fixer, go-between, intermediary, negotiator, retailer.

middling *adj* adequate, average, fair, indifferent, mean, median, mediocre, medium, moderate, modest, OK, ordinary, passable, run-of-the-mill, so-so, tolerable, unexceptional, unremarkable.

midget *n* dwarf, gnome, homuncule, homunculus, manikin, minikin, minnow, pygmy, shrimp, Tom Thumb.

antonym giant.

adj dwarf, Lilliputian, little, miniature, pocket, pocket-sized, pygmy, small, teeny, tiny.

antonym giant.

midst *n* bosom, centre, core, depths, epicentre, heart, hub, interior, middle, mid-point, thick.

midway *adv* betwixt and between, halfway, in the middle, partially.

mien *n* air, appearance, aspect, aura, bearing, carriage, complexion, countenance, demeanour, deportment, look, manner, presence, semblance.

miffed *adj* aggrieved, annoyed, chagrined, disgruntled, displeased, hurt, in a huff, irked, irritated, narked, nettled, offended, piqued, put out, resentful, upset, vexed.

antonyms chuffed, delighted, pleased.

might *n* ability, capability, capacity, clout, efficacy, efficiency, energy, force, heftiness, muscularity, potency, power, powerfulness, prowess, puissance, strength, sway, valour, vigour.

mightily *adv* decidedly, energetically, exceedingly, extremely, forcefully, greatly, highly, hugely, intensely, lustily, manfully, much, powerfully, strenuously, strongly, very, very much, vigorously.

mighty *adj* bulky, colossal, doughty, enormous, forceful, gigantic, grand, great, hardy, hefty, huge, immense, indomitable, large, lusty, manful, massive, monumental, muscular, potent, powerful, prodigious, puissant, robust, stalwart, stout, strapping, strenuous, strong, stupendous, sturdy, titanic, towering, tremendous, vast, vigorous.

antonyms frail, weak.

migrant *n* drifter, emigrant, globe-trotter, gypsy, immigrant, itinerant, land-louper, nomad, rover, tinker, transient, traveller, vagrant, wanderer.

adj drifting, globe-trotting, gypsy, immigrant, itinerant, migratory, nomadic, roving, shifting, transient, travelling, vagrant, wandering.

migrate *v* drift, emigrate, journey, move, roam, rove, shift, transhume, travel, trek, voyage, wander.

migration *n* diaspora, emigration, journey, movement, roving, shift, transhumance, travel, trek, Völkerwanderung, voyage, wandering.

migratory *adj* gipsy, itinerant, migrant, nomadic, peripatetic, roving, shifting, transient, transitory, travelling, vagrant, wandering.

mild *adj* amiable, balmy, bland, calm, clement, compassionate, docile, easy, easy-going, equable, forbearing, forgiving, gentle, indulgent, kind, lenient, meek, mellow, merciful, moderate, pacific, passive, peaceable, placid, pleasant, serene, smooth, soft, temperate, tender, tranquil, warm.

antonyms fierce, harsh, stormy, strong, violent.

mildewy *adj* fetid, fusty, mucedinous, mucid, musty, rotten.

mildness *n* blandness, calmness, clemency, docility, forbearance, gentleness, indulgence, kindness, leniency, lenity, meekness, mellowness, moderation, passivity, placidity, smoothness, softness, temperateness, tenderness, tractability, tranquillity, warmth.

antonyms ferocity, harshness, strength, violence.

mil(e)ometer *n* hodometer, perambulator, tachograph, waywiser.

milieu *n* arena, background, element, environment, locale, location, medium, scene, setting, sphere, surroundings.

militant *adj* active, aggressive, assertive, belligerent, combating, combative, contending, embattled, fighting, hawkish, pugnacious, vigorous, warring.

n activist, aggressor, belligerent, combatant, fighter, partisan, struggler, warrior.

military *adj* armed, martial, service, soldier-like, soldierly, warlike.

n armed forces, army, forces, services, soldiers, soldiery.

militate against contend, count against, counter, counteract, oppose, resist, tell against, weigh against.

militate for advance, aid, back, further, help, promote, speak for.

militia *n* fencibles, minutemen, National Guard, reserve, reservists, Territorial Army, train-band, yeomanry.

milk *v* bleed, drain, draw off, emulge, exploit, express, extract, impose on, press, pump, siphon, squeeze, tap, use, wring.

milk-and-water *adj* bland, feeble, innocuous, insipid, jejune, tasteless, vapid, weak, wishy-washy.

milksop *n* chinless wonder, coward, milquetoast, Miss Nancy, molly, mollycoddle, namby-pamby, pansy, sissy, weakling.

milky *adj* alabaster, albescent, chalky, clouded, cloudy, milk-white, opaque, white, whitish.

mill[1] *n* ball-mill, crusher, grinder, quern.

v comminute, crush, granulate, grate, grind, pound, powder, press, pulverise, roll.

mill[2] *n* factory, foundry, plant, shop, works.

mill[3] *v* crowd, scurry, seethe, swarm, throng, wander.

millstone *n* affliction, burden, drag, encumbrance, grindstone, load, quernstone, weight.

mime *n* dumb show, gesture, mimicry, mummery, pantomime.

v act out, gesture, impersonate, mimic, represent, signal, simulate.

mimic *v* ape, caricature, echo, imitate, impersonate, look like, mirror, parody, parrot, personate, resemble, simulate, take off.

n caricaturist, copy, copy-cat, imitator, impersonator, impressionist, parodist, parrot.

adj echoic, fake, imitation, imitative, make-believe, mimetic, mock, pseudo, sham, simulated.

mimicry *n* apery, burlesque, caricature, copying, imitating, imitation, impersonation, impression, mimesis, mimicking, mockery, parody, parrotry, take-off.

mince[1] *v* chop, crumble, cut, dice, grind, hash.

n hachis, hash.

mince[2] *v* diminish, euphemise, extenuate, hold back, moderate, palliate, play down, soften, spare, suppress, tone down, weaken.

mince[3] *v* attitudinise, ponce, pose, posture, simper.

mincing *adj* affected, coxcombic(al), dainty, effeminate, foppish, lah-di-dah, minikin, nice, niminy-piminy, poncy, precious, pretentious, ripperty-tipperty, sissy.

mind[1] *n* attention, attitude, belief, bent, brains, concentration, desire, disposition, fancy, feeling, genius, grey matter, head, imagination, inclination, inner, intellect, intellectual, intelligence, intention, judgement, leaning, marbles, memory, mentality, notion, opinion, outlook, point of view, psyche, purpose, rationality, reason, recollection, remembrance, sanity, sense, senses, sensorium, sensory, sentiment, spirit, tendency, thinker, thinking, thoughts, understanding, urge, view, will, wish, wits.

mind's eye contemplation, head, imagination, memory, mind, recollection, remembrance.

mind[2] *v* care, demur, disapprove, dislike, object, resent, take offence.

mind[3] *v* adhere to, attend, attend to, be careful, be on one's guard, comply with, ensure, follow, guard, have charge of, heed, keep an eye on, listen to, look after, make certain, mark, note, notice, obey, observe, pay attention, pay heed to, regard, respect, take care, take care of, take heed, tend, watch.

mind out be careful, be on one's guard, beware, keep one's eyes open, look out, pay attention, take care, watch, watch out.

mindful *adj* alert, alive (to), attentive, aware, careful, chary, cognisant, compliant, conscious, heedful, obedient, regardful, remindful, respectful, sensible, thoughtful, wary, watchful.

antonyms heedless, inattentive, mindless.

mindless *adj* asinine, automatic, brainless, brutish, careless, foolish, forgetful, gratuitous, heedless, idiotic, illogical, imbecilic, inattentive, irrational, mechanical, moronic, neglectful, negligent, oblivious, obtuse, stupid, thoughtless, unintelligent, unmindful, unreasoning, unthinking, witless.

antonyms intelligent, mindful, thoughtful.

mine[1] *n* abundance, coalfield, colliery, deposit, excavation, fund, hoard, lode, pit, reserve, sap, shaft, source, stock, store, supply, treasury, trench, tunnel, vein, wealth, wheal.

v delve, dig for, dig up, excavate, extract, hew, quarry, remove, sap, subvert, tunnel, undermine, unearth, weaken.

mine[2] *n* bomb, depth charge, egg, explosive, land-mine.

miner *n* coal-miner, collier, pitman.

mingle *v* alloy, associate, blend, circulate, coalesce, combine, commingle, compound, hobnob, intermingle, intermix, interweave, join, marry, mell, merge, mix, rub shoulders, socialise, unite.

miniature *adj* baby, diminutive, dwarf, Lilliputian, little, midget, mini, minuscule, minute, pint-size(d), pocket, pocket-sized, pygmy, reduced, scaled-down, small, tiny, toy, wee.

antonym giant.

minimal *adj* least, littlest, minimum, minuscule, minute, nominal, slightest, smallest, token.

minimise *v* abbreviate, attenuate, belittle, curtail, decrease, decry, dedramatise, de-emphasise, deprecate, depreciate, diminish, discount, disparage, make light of, make little of, play down, prune, reduce, shrink, underestimate, underrate.
antonym maximise.

minimum *n* bottom, least, lowest point, nadir, slightest.
antonym maximum.
adj least, littlest, lowest, minimal, slightest, smallest, tiniest, weeniest, weest.
antonym maximum.

minion *n* arse-licker, backscratcher, bootlicker, creature, darling, dependant, favourite, flatterer, flunky, follower, hanger-on, heeler, henchman, hireling, lackey, lickspittle, myrmidon, parasite, pet, sycophant, toady, underling, yes-man.

minister *n* administrator, agent, aide, ambassador, assistant, churchman, clergyman, cleric, delegate, diplomat, divine, ecclesiastic, envoy, executive, Levite, office-holder, official, parson, pastor, plenipotentiary, preacher, priest, servant, subordinate, underling, vicar, vizier.
v accommodate, administer, attend, cater to, nurse, pander to, serve, take care of, tend.

ministration *n* aid, assistance, care, favour, help, patronage, relief, service, succour, supervision, support.

ministry[1] *n* administration, bureau, cabinet, council, department, office.

ministry[2] *n* holy orders, the church, the priesthood.

minor *adj* inconsequential, inconsiderable, inferior, insignificant, junior, lesser, light, negligible, paltry, petty, piddling, secondary, second-class, slight, small, smaller, subordinate, trifling, trivial, unclassified, unimportant, younger.
antonym major.

minstrel *n* bard, joculator, jongleur, musician, rhymer, rimer, singer, troubadour.

mint *v* cast, coin, construct, devise, fabricate, fashion, forge, invent, make, make up, manufacture, monetise, produce, punch, stamp, strike.
adj brand-new, excellent, first-class, fresh, immaculate, perfect, unblemished, undamaged, untarnished.
n bomb, bundle, fortune, heap, million, packet, pile, stack.

minuscule *adj* diminutive, fine, infinitesimal, itsy-bitsy, Lilliputian, little, microscopic, miniature, minute, teensy-weensy, teeny, tiny.
antonyms gigantic, huge.

minute[1] *n* flash, instant, jiff, jiffy, mo, moment, sec, second, shake, tick, trice.

minute[2] *adj* close, critical, detailed, diminutive, exact, exhaustive, fine, inconsiderable, infinitesimal, itsy-bitsy, Lilliputian, little, meticulous, microscopic, miniature, minim, minuscule, negligible, painstaking, paltry, petty, picayune, piddling, precise, punctilious, puny, slender, slight, small, tiny, trifling, trivial, unimportant.
antonyms gigantic, huge, immense.

minutely *adv* closely, critically, exactly, exhaustively, in detail, meticulously, painstakingly, precisely, scrupulously, systematically, with a fine-tooth comb.

minutes *n* details, memorandum, notes, proceedings, record(s), tapes, transactions, transcript.

minutiae *n* details, niceties, particulars, subtleties, trifles, trivialities.

minx *n* baggage, coquette, flirt, harpy, harridan, hoyden, hussy, jade, tomboy, wanton.

miracle *n* deus ex machina, marvel, miraculum, phenomenon, prodigy, thaumaturgy, wonder, wonder-work.

miraculous *adj* amazing, astonishing, astounding, extraordinary, incredible, inexplicable, magical, marvellous, otherworldly, phenomenal, preternatural, prodigious, stupendous, superhuman, supernatural, thaumaturgic, unaccountable, unbelievable, wonderful, wondrous.
antonyms natural, normal.

mirage *n* fata Morgana, hallucination, illusion, optical illusion, phantasm.

mire *n* bog, difficulties, dirt, fen, glaur, marsh, morass, muck, mud, ooze, quag, quagmire, slime, swamp, trouble.

mirror *n* copy, double, glass, hand-glass, image, keeking-glass, likeness, looking-glass, pocket-glass, reflection, reflector, replica, representation, speculum, spit and image, spitting image, twin.
v copy, depict, echo, emulate, follow, imitate, mimic, reflect, represent, show.

mirth *n* amusement, cheerfulness, festivity, frolic, fun, gaiety, gladness, glee, hilarity, jocosity, jocularity, jocundity, jollity, joviality, joyousness, laughter, levity, merriment, merrymaking, pleasure, rejoicing, revelry, sport.
antonyms gloom, glumness, melancholy.

mirthful *adj* amused, amusing, blithe, cheerful, cheery, festive, frolicsome, funny, gay, glad, gladsome, happy, hilarious, jocose, jocund, jolly, jovial, laughable, laughing, light-hearted, merry, playful, sportive, uproarious, vivacious.
antonyms gloomy, glum, melancholy, mirthless.

miry *adj* boggy, dirty, fenny, glaury, marshy, mucky, muddy, oozy, slimy, swampy.

misadventure *n* accident, calamity, cataclysm, catastrophe, debacle, disaster, failure, ill fortune, ill luck, mischance, misfortune, mishap, reverse, setback, tragedy.

misanthropic *adj* antisocial, cynical, egoistic, inhumane, malevolent, surly, unfriendly, unsociable, unsympathetic.
antonym philanthropic.

misanthropy *n* antisociality, cynicism, egoism, inhumanity, malevolence, unsociableness.
antonym philanthropy.

misapply *v* abuse, exploit, misappropriate, misemploy, misuse, pervert.

misapprehend *v* get the wrong idea, miscomprehend, misconceive, misconstrue, misinterpret, misknow, misread, mistake, misunderstand.

antonym apprehend.

misapprehension *n* delusion, error, fallacy, misacceptation, misconception, misconstruction, misinterpretation, misreading, mistake, misunderstanding.

antonym apprehension.

misappropriate *v* abuse, defalcate, embezzle, misapply, misspend, misuse, peculate, pervert, pocket, steal, swindle.

misappropriation *n* defalcation, embezzlement, misapplication, misuse, peculation, pocketing, stealing, theft.

misbegotten *adj* abortive, dishonest, disreputable, hare-brained, ill-advised, ill-conceived, ill-gotten, illicit, monstrous, poorly thought-out, purloined, shady, stolen, unlawful.

misbehave *v* act up, carry on, get up to mischief, kick over the traces, mess about, muck about, offend, transgress, trespass.

antonym behave.

misbehaviour *n* disobedience, impropriety, incivility, indiscipline, insubordination, mayhem, misconduct, misdeeds, misdemeanour, monkey business, naughtiness, rudeness, shenanigans.

misbelief *n* delusion, error, fallacy, heresy, heterodoxy, miscreance, unorthodoxy.

miscalculate *v* blunder, boob, err, get wrong, misjudge, overestimate, overrate, overvalue, slip up, underestimate, underrate, undervalue.

miscarriage *n* abortion, botch, breakdown, casualty, disappointment, error, failure, misadventure, mischance, misfire, mishap, mismanagement, perversion, thwarting, undoing.

antonym success.

miscarry *v* abort, bite the dust, come to grief, come to nothing, fail, fall through, flounder, gang agley, misfire, warp.

antonym succeed.

miscellaneous *adj* assorted, confused, diverse, diversified, farraginous, heterogeneous, indiscriminate, jumbled, manifold, many, mingled, mixed, motley, multifarious, multiform, omnifarious, promiscuous, sundry, varied, various.

miscellany *n* anthology, assortment, collection, diversity, farrago, gallimaufry, hash, hotch-potch, jumble, medley, mélange, mixed bag, mixture, olla-podrida, omnium-gatherum, pot-pourri, salmagundi, variety.

mischance *n* accident, bad break, blow, calamity, contretemps, disaster, ill-chance, ill-fortune, ill-luck, infelicity, misadventure, misfortune, mishap, tragedy.

mischief[1] *n* bane, damage, detriment, devilment, deviltry, diablerie, disruption, evil, harm, hurt, impishness, injury, misbehaviour, misfortune, monkey business, naughtiness, pranks, roguery, roguishness, shenanigans, trouble, waggery, waywardness.

mischief[2] *n* devil, imp, monkey, nuisance, pest, rapscallion, rascal, rascallion, rogue, scallywag, scamp, tyke, villain.

antonym angel.

mischievous *adj* arch, bad, damaging, deleterious, destructive, detrimental, elfish, elvan, elvish, evil, exasperating, frolicsome, harmful, hurtful, impish, injurious, malicious, malignant, naughty, pernicious, playful, puckish, rascally, roguish, sinful, spiteful, sportive, teasing, tricksy, troublesome, vexatious, vicious, wayward, wicked.

antonyms good, well-behaved.

misconceive *v* misapprehend, misconstrue, misinterpret, misjudge, misread, mistake, misunderstand.

misconception *n* delusion, error, fallacy, misapprehension, misconstruction, misreading, misunderstanding, the wrong end of the stick.

misconduct *n* delinquency, dereliction, hanky-panky, immorality, impropriety, malfeasance, malpractice, malversation, misbehaviour, misdemeanour, misfeasance, mismanagement, naughtiness, rudeness, transgression, wrong-doing.

misconstruction *n* delusion, misapprehension, misinterpretation, misreading, mistake, misunderstanding.

misconstrue *v* misapprehend, misconceive, misinterpret, misjudge, misread, misreckon, mistake, mistranslate, misunderstand, take the wrong way.

miscreant *n* blackguard, caitiff, criminal, dastard, evil-doer, knave, malefactor, mischief-maker, profligate, rascal, reprobate, rogue, scallywag, scamp, scapegrace, scoundrel, sinner, trouble-maker, vagabond, varlet, villain, wretch, wrong-doer.

antonym worthy.

misdeed *n* crime, delict, delinquency, error, fault, felony, malefice, misconduct, misdemeanour, offence, peccadillo, sin, transgression, trespass, villainy, wrong.

misdemeanour *n* delict, fault, indiscretion, infringement, lapse, malfeasance, misbehaviour, misconduct, misdeed, offence, peccadillo, transgression, trespass.

miser *n* cheapskate, curmudgeon, hunks, mammonist, meanie, money-grubber, muck-worm, niggard, penny-pincher, pinchfist, pinchgut, pinchpenny, save-all, screw, Scrooge, skinflint, snudge, tightwad.

antonym spendthrift.

miserable *adj* abject, agelastic, anguished, bad, broken-hearted, caitiff, cheerless, contemptible, crestfallen, crushed, dejected, deplorable, depressed, depressive, desolate, despicable, despondent, destitute, detestable, disconsolate, disgraceful, dismal, distressed, doleful, dolorous, down, downcast, dreary, forlorn, gloomy, glum, grief-stricken, hapless, heartbroken, ignominious, impoverished, indigent, joyless, lachrymose, lamentable, low, luckless, lugubrious, meagre, mean, melancholic, melancholy, miz, mournful, needy, niggardly, paltry, pathetic, penniless, piteous, pitiable, pitiful, poor, sad, scanty, scurvy, shabby, shameful, sordid, sorrowful, sorrowing, sorry, squalid, star-crossed, stricken, tearful, unhappy, vile, woebegone, worthless, wretched.

antonyms cheerful, comfortable, generous, honourable, noble.

miserliness *n* avarice, cheese-paring, churlishness, close-fistedness, covetousness, frugality, meanness, minginess, misery, nearness, niggardliness, parsimony, penny-pinching, penuriousness, stinginess, thrift, thriftiness, tight-fistedness.

antonyms generosity, lavishness, prodigality.

miserly *adj* avaricious, beggarly, cheese-paring, close, close-fisted, close-handed, covetous, curmudgeonly, gare, grasping, grudging, illiberal, mean, mercenary, mingy, money-grubbing, near, niggardly, parsimonious, penny-pinching, penurious, sordid, sparing, stingy, thrifty, tight-fisted, ungenerous.

antonyms generous, lavish, prodigal, spendthrift.

misery[1] *n* abjectness, adversity, affliction, agony, anguish, bale, bane, bitter pill, blow, burden, calamity, catastrophe, cross, curse, depression, desolation, despair, destitution, disaster, discomfort, distress, dole, dolour, extremity, gloom, grief, hardship, heartache, heartbreak, humiliation, indigence, living death, load, melancholia, melancholy, misfortune, miz, mortification, need, oppression, ordeal, penury, poverty, privation, prostration, sadness, sordidness, sorrow, squalor, suffering, torment, torture, trial, tribulation, trouble, unhappiness, want, woe, wretchedness.

misery[2] *n* agelast, grouch, Jeremiah, Job's comforter, killjoy, moaner, moper, pessimist, prophet of doom, ray of sunshine, sourpuss, spoil-sport, Weary Willie, wet blanket, whiner, whinger.

antonym sport.

misfire *v* abort, bomb, come a cropper, come to grief, fail, fall flat, fall short, fall through, fizzle out, flop, founder, go phut, go wrong, miscarry.

antonym succeed.

misfit *n* drop-out, eccentric, fish out of water, horse marine, individualist, lone wolf, loner, maverick, nonconformist, odd man out, oddball, rogue, square peg in a round hole, weirdo.

antonym conformist.

misfortune *n* accident, adversity, affliction, bad luck, blow, buffet, calamity, catastrophe, disaster, failure, grief, hardship, harm, ill-luck, infelicity, infortune, loss, misadventure, mischance, misery, mishap, reverse, setback, sorrow, tragedy, trial, tribulation, trouble, woe.

antonyms luck, success.

misgiving *n* anxiety, apprehension, backward glance, compunction, distrust, doubt, dubiety, fear, hesitation, misdoubt, niggle, presentiment, qualm, reservation, scruple, second thoughts, suspicion, uncertainty, unease, worry.

antonym confidence.

misguided *adj* deluded, erroneous, foolish, ill-advised, ill-considered, ill-judged, imprudent, incautious, injudicious, misconceived, misled, misplaced, mistaken, rash, unreasonable, unsuitable, unwarranted, unwise.

antonym sensible.

mishandle *v* balls up, bollocks, botch, bungle, fumble, make a balls of, make a hash of, make a mess of, make a pig's ear of, mess up, misguggle, misjudge, mismanage, mousle, muff, screw up.

antonyms cope, manage.

mishap *n* accident, adversity, balls-up, calamity, contretemps, disaster, hiccup, ill-fortune, ill-luck, misadventure, mischance, misfortune, misventure, setback.

mishmash *n* conglomeration, farrago, gallimaufry, hash, hotchpotch, jumble, medley, mess, muddle, olio, olla-podrida, pastiche, pot-pourri, salad, salmagundi.

misinform *v* bluff, deceive, give a bum steer, hoodwink, lead up the garden path, misdirect, misguide, mislead, mistell, mizzle, snow, take for a ride.

misinformation *n* baloney, bluff, bum steer, disinformation, dope, eyewash, guff, hype, lies, misdirection, misleading, nonsense.

misinterpret *v* distort, garble, get the wrong end of the stick, misappreciate, misapprehend, misconceive, misconstruct, misconstrue, misjudge, misread, misrepresent, mistake, misunderstand, pervert, warp, wrest.

misjudge *v* miscalculate, miscount, misestimate, misinterpret, misprise, mistake, overestimate, overrate, underestimate, underrate, undervalue.

mislay *v* lose, lose sight of, misplace, miss.

mislead *v* beguile, bluff, deceive, delude, fool, give a bum steer, hoodwink, lead up the garden path, misadvise, misdirect, misguide, misinform, mizzle, pull the wool over someone's eyes, snow, take for a ride, take in.

misleading *adj* ambiguous, biased, casuistical, confusing, deceitful, deceptive, delusive, delusory, disingenuous, distorted, equivocatory, evasive, fallacious, false, falsidical, loaded, mendacious, sophistical, specious, spurious, tricky, unreliable.

antonyms authentic, authoritative, informative, plain, unequivocal.

mismanage *v* balls up, bollocks, botch, bungle, fluff, foul up, louse up, make a hash of, make a mess of, maladminister, mangle, mar, mess up, misconduct, misdirect, misgovern, mishandle, misjudge, misrule, misspend, muff, screw up, squander, waste.

mismatched *adj* antipathetic, clashing, discordant, disparate, ill-assorted, incompatible, incongruous, irregular, misallied, mismated, unmatching, unreconcilable, unsuited.

antonyms compatible, matching.

misogynist *n* anti-feminist, male chauvinist, male supremacist, misogamist, sexist, woman-hater.

antonym feminist.

misplace *v* lose, misapply, misassign, misfile, mislay, miss.

misprint *n* corrigendum, erratum, error, literal, mistake, transposition, typo.

misprise *v* belittle, depreciate, disparage, hold cheap, look down on, mistake, misunderstand, slight, underestimate, underrate, undervalue.

antonyms appreciate, understand.

misquote *v* distort, falsify, garble, misremember, misreport, misrepresent, misstate, muddle, pervert, twist.

misrepresent *v* belie, bend, disguise, distort, exaggerate, falsify, garble, load, minimise, miscolour, misconstrue, misinterpret, misquote, misstate, pervert, slant, twist.

misrule *n* anarchy, chaos, confusion, disorder, disorganisation, indiscipline, lawlessness, maladministration, misgovernment, mismanagement, riot, tumult, turbulence, turmoil, unreason.

miss[1] *v* avoid, bypass, circumvent, err, escape, evade, fail, forego, jump, lack, leave out, let go, let slip, lose, miscarry, mistake, obviate, omit, overlook, pass over, pass up, sidestep, skip, slip, trip.

n blunder, error, failure, fault, fiasco, flop, lack, lacuna, loss, mistake, need, omission, oversight, want.

miss out bypass, dispense with, disregard, ignore, jump, leave out, omit, pass over, skip.

miss[2] *v* grieve for, lack, lament, long for, mourn, need, pine for, regret, sorrow for, want, wish, yearn for.

miss[3] *n* backfisch, child, damsel, demoiselle, flapper, Fraülein, girl, girly, Jungfrau, junior miss, kid, lass, lassie, mademoiselle, maid, maiden, missy, Ms, nymphet, schoolgirl, spinster, teenager, young thing.

missal *n* breviary, euchologion, formulary, mass-book, office-book, prayer-book, service-book, Triodion.

misshapen *adj* contorted, crippled, crooked, deformed, distorted, grotesque, ill-made, ill-proportioned, malformed, monstrous, thrawn, twisted, ugly, ungainly, unshapely, unsightly, warped, wry.

antonyms regular, shapely.

missile *n* arrow, ball, bomb, dart, flying bomb, grenade, projectile, rocket, shaft, shell, shot, torpedo, V-bomb, weapon.

missing *adj* absent, astray, disappeared, gone, lacking, lost, minus, misgone, mislaid, misplaced, strayed, unaccounted-for, wanting.

antonyms found, present.

mission *n* aim, assignment, business, calling, campaign, charge, commission, crusade, delegation, deputation, duty, embassy, errand, goal, job, legation, mandate, ministry, object, office, operation, purpose, pursuit, quest, raison d'être, remit, task, task force, trust, undertaking, vocation, work.

missionary *n* ambassador, apostle, campaigner, champion, crusader, emissary, envoy, evangelist, exponent, gospeller, preacher, promoter, propagandist, proselytiser, teacher.

missish *adj* affected, arch, bossy, coy, demanding, flighty, giggly, girlish, hoity-toity, impossible, indulged, obstinate, self-willed, sentimental, silly, spoilt, squeamish, wilful.

missive *n* bulletin, communication, communiqué, dispatch, epistle, letter, line, memo, memorandum, message, note, report.

misspent *adj* dissipated, frittered away, idle, idled away, misapplied, misused, prodigal, profitless, squandered, thrown away, unprofitable, wasted.

antonym profitable.

misstate *v* distort, falsify, garble, misquote, misrelate, misremember, misreport, misrepresent, mistell, pervert, twist.

mist *n* brume, cloud, condensation, dew, dimness, drizzle, exhalation, film, fog, haar, haze, mizzle, roke, smir, smog, spray, steam, vapour, veil, water-smoke.

v becloud, bedim, befog, blur, cloud, dim, film, fog, glaze, obscure, steam up, veil.

antonym clear.

mistake *n* aberration, bêtise, bevue, bish, bloomer, blunder, boner, boob, boo-boo, clanger, clinker, corrigendum, erratum, error, fallacy, false move, fault, faux pas, floater, folly, gaffe, gaucherie, goof, howler, inaccuracy, indiscretion, inexactitude, lapse, lapsus, lapsus calami, lapsus linguae, lapsus memoriae, literal, malapropism, misapprehension, miscalculation, misconception, misjudgement, misprint, misprision, mispronunciation, misreading, misspelling, misunderstanding, mumpsimus, oversight, scape, slip, slip-up, solecism, stumer, tactlessness, trespass.

v blunder, confound, confuse, err, get the wrong end of the stick, goof, misapprehend, miscalculate, misconceive, misconstrue, misinterpret, misjudge, misobserve, misprise, misrate, misread, misreckon, misunderstand, slip up.

mistaken *adj* deceived, deluded, erroneous, fallacious, false, faulty, ill-judged, inaccurate, inappropriate, inauthentic, incorrect, inexact, misguided, misinformed, misinstructed, mislead, misprised, off base, off beam, unfair, unfounded, unjust, unsound, untrue, wide of the mark, wrong.

antonyms correct, justified.

mistakenly *adv* by mistake, erroneously, fallaciously, falsely, inaccurately, inappropriately, incorrectly, misguidedly, unfairly, unjustly, wrongly.

antonyms appropriately, correctly, fairly, justly.

mistimed *adj* ill-timed, inconvenient, infelicitous, inopportune, malapropos, tactless, unfortunate, unseasonable, unsynchronised, untimely.

antonym opportune.

mistreat *v* abuse, batter, brutalise, bully, harm, hurt, ill-treat, ill-use, injure, knock about, maltreat, manhandle, maul, mishandle, misuse, molest, rough up.

antonym pamper.

mistreatment *n* abuse, battering, brutalisation, bullying, cruelty, harm, ill-treatment, ill-usage, ill-use, injury, maltreatment, manhandling, mauling, mishandling, misuse, molestation, unkindness.

antonyms cosseting, pampering.

mistress *n* amante, canary-bird, châtelaine, concubine, courtesan, demi-mondaine, doxy, fancy woman, girlfriend, hetaira, inamorata, kept woman, lady, lady-love, lover, odalisque, owner, paramour, popsy, proprietress, teacher, woman.

mistrust *n* apprehension, caution, chariness, distrust, doubt, dubiety, fear, hesitancy, misdoubt, misgiving, reservations, scepticism, suspicion, uncertainty, wariness.

antonym trust.

v be wary of, beware, disbelieve, distrust, doubt, fear, fight shy of, look askance at, misdoubt, mislippen, question, suspect.

antonym trust.

mistrustful *adj* apprehensive, cautious, chary, cynical, distrustful, doubtful, dubious, fearful, hesitant, leery, sceptical, shy, suspicious, uncertain, wary.

antonym trustful.

misty *adj* blear, bleared, bleary, blurred, blurry, cloudy, dark, dim, faint, foggy, fuzzy, gauzy, hazy, indistinct, mistful, murky, muzzy, nebulous, obscure, opaque, roky, smoky, translucent, unclear, vague, veiled.

antonyms bright, clear.

misunderstand *v* get the wrong end of the stick, get wrong, misapprehend, miscomprehend, misconceive, misconstrue, misesteem, mishear, misinterpret, misjudge, misknow, misprise, misread, miss the point, mistake, take up wrong(ly).

antonyms grasp, understand.

misunderstanding *n* argument, breach, clash, conflict, difference, difficulty, disagreement, discord, disharmony, dispute, dissension, error, malentendu, misacceptation, misapprehension, misconception, misconstruction, misinterpretation, misjudgement, misknowledge, misprision, misreading, mistake, mix-up, quarrel, rift, rupture, squabble, variance.

antonyms agreement, reconciliation.

misunderstood *adj* ill-judged, misappreciated, misconstrued, misheard, misinterpreted, misjudged, misprised, misread, misrepresented, mistaken, unappreciated, unrecognised.

misuse *n* abusage, abuse, barbarism, catachresis, corruption, desecration, dissipation, distortion, exploitation, harm, ill-treatment, ill-usage, injury, malappropriation, malapropism, maltreatment, manhandling, misapplication, misappropriation, misemployment, mistreatment, misusage, perversion, profanation, prostitution, solecism, squandering, wastage, waste.

v abuse, brutalise, corrupt, desecrate, dissipate, distort, exploit, harm, ill-treat, ill-use, injure, malappropriate, maltreat, manhandle, maul, misapply, misappropriate, misemploy, mistreat, molest, overload, overtax, pervert, profane, prostitute, squander, strain, waste, wrong.

mite *n* atom, grain, iota, jot, modicum, morsel, ounce, scrap, smidgen, spark, trace, whit.

mitigate *v* abate, allay, alleviate, appease, assuage, attemper, blunt, calm, check, decrease, diminish, dull, ease, extenuate, lenify, lessen, lighten, moderate, modify, mollify, pacify, palliate, placate, quiet, reduce, remit, slake, soften, soothe, still, subdue, temper, tone down, weaken.

antonyms aggravate, exacerbate, increase.

mitigating *adj* exculpatory, extenuating, extenuative, justificatory, justifying, lenitive, mitigative, mitigatory, modifying, palliating, palliative, qualifying, vindicating.

mitigation *n* abatement, allaying, alleviation, appeasement, assuagement, decrease, diminution, easement, extenuation, lessening, moderation, mollification, palliation, qualification, reduction, relief, remission, tempering.

antonyms aggravation, exacerbation, increase.

mix *v* allay, alloy, amalgamate, associate, blend, coalesce, combine, commingle, commix, compound, consort, contemper, cross, dash, fold in, fraternise, fuse, hobnob, homogenise, immingle, incorporate, intermingle, intermix, interweave, join, jumble, mell, merge, mingle, shuffle, socialise, synthesise, unite.

antonym separate.

n alloy, amalgam, assortment, blend, combination, composite, compound, conglomerate, fusion, medley, mishmash, mixture, pastiche, synthesis.

mix in admix, blend, immingle, immix, incorporate, infiltrate, infuse, inject, interject, interlard, intermingle, interpolate, intersperse, introduce, merge.

antonyms extract, isolate.

mix up bewilder, blend, combine, complicate, confound, confuse, disturb, embroil, entangle, fluster, garble, implicate, involve, jumble, mix, muddle, perplex, puzzle, scramble, snarl up, upset.

mixed *adj* alloyed, amalgamated, ambivalent, assorted, blended, combined, composite, compound, cosmopolitan, crossbred, diverse, diversified, ecumenical, equivocal, fused, heterogeneous, hybrid, incorporated, indecisive, integrated, interbred, interdenominational, international, joint, linsey-woolsey, mingled, miscegenate, miscellaneous, mongrel, mongrelly, motley, polyglot, promiscuous, uncertain, united, unsegregated, varied.

mixed up bewildered, chaotic, complicated, confused, désorienté, disordered, disoriented, distracted, distraught, disturbed, maladjusted, mingle-mangle, muddled, perplexed, puzzled, upset.

mixer[1] *n* busybody, disrupter, interferer, makebate, meddler, mischief-maker, stirrer, subversive, trouble-maker.

antonym peacemaker.

mixer[2] *n* everybody's friend, extrovert, joiner, life and soul of the party, socialiser.

antonyms introvert, loner, recluse.

mixing *n* amalgamation, association, blending, coalescence, combination, fraternisation, fusion, hybridisation, interbreeding, intercourse, interflow, intermingling, minglement, miscegenation, socialising, synthesis, union.

antonym separation.

mixture *n* admixture, alloy, amalgam, amalgamation, association, assortment, blend, brew, coalescence, combination, combine, composite, compost, compound, concoction, conglomeration, cross, fusion, galimatias, gallimaufry, half-breed, hotchpotch, hybrid, jumble, macédoine, medley, mélange, miscegen, miscegenation, miscellany, mix, mixed bag, mongrel, olio, olla-podrida, omnium-gatherum, pastiche, pot-pourri, salad, salmagundi, synthesis, union, variety.

mix-up *n* balls-up, chaos, complication, confusion, disorder, fankle, foul-up, jumble, mess, mistake, misunderstanding, muddle, nonsense, snafu, snarl-up, tangle.

moan *n* beef, belly-ache, bitch, complaint, gripe, groan, grouch, grouse, grumble, howl, keen, lament, lamentation, sigh, snivel, sob, sough, ululation, wail, whimper, whine, whinge.

v beef, belly-ache, bemoan, bewail, bitch, carp, complain, deplore, grieve, gripe, groan, grouch, grouse, grumble, howl, keen, lament, mourn, sigh, snivel, sob, sough, ululate, wail, weep, whimper, whine, whinge, wuther.

antonym rejoice.

mob *n* assemblage, bevy, body, canaille, class, collection, common herd, commonalty, company, crew, crowd, drove, faex populi, flock, galère, gang, gathering, great unwashed, group, herd, hoi polloi, horde, host, jingbang, lot, many-headed beast, many-headed monster, mass, masses, mobile, multitude, pack, plebs, populace, press, rabble, rent-a-crowd, rent-a-mob, riff-raff, rout, scum, set, swarm, throng, tribe, troop, vulgus.

v besiege, charge, cram, crowd, crowd round, descend on, fill, jam, jostle, overrun, pack, pester, set upon, surround, swarm round.

antonym shun.

mobile *adj* active, agile, ambulatory, animated, changeable, changing, energetic, ever-changing, expressive, flexible, fluid, itinerant, lively, locomobile, locomotive, mercurial, migrant, motile, movable, moving, nimble, peripatetic, portable, roaming, roving, supple, travelling, vagile, vivacious, wandering.

antonym immobile.

mobilise *v* activate, animate, assemble, call up, enlist, galvanise, levy, marshal, muster, organise, prepare, rally, ready, shift, stir, summon.

mobility *n* agility, animation, expressiveness, flexibility, locomobility, locomotion, locomotivity, motility, motion, motivity, movability, movableness, portability, suppleness, vagility, vivacity.

antonyms immobility, inflexibility, rigidity.

mob-rule *n* lynch-law, mobocracy, ochlocracy, Reign of Terror.

mock *v* ape, baffle, befool, burlesque, caricature, chaff, cheat, counterfeit, debunk, deceive, defeat, defy, delude, deride, disappoint, disparage, dupe, elude, explode, fleer, flout, foil, fool, frustrate, guy, imitate, insult, jeer, lampoon, laugh at, laugh in (someone's) face, laugh to scorn, make fun of, make sport of, mimic, parody, parrot, poke fun at, queer, quiz, ridicule, satirise, scoff, scorn, send up, sneer, take the mickey, taunt, tease, thwart, travesty, twit.

antonyms flatter, praise.

adj artificial, bogus, counterfeit, dummy, ersatz, fake, faked, false, feigned, forged, fraudulent, imitation, phoney, pinchbeck, pretended, pseudo, sham, simulated, spurious, synthetic.

mocker *n* derider, detractor, fleerer, flouter, iconoclast, jeerer, lampooner, lampoonist, pasquinader, reviler, ridiculer, satirist, scoffer, scorner, sneerer, tease, tormentor, vilifier.

antonyms flatterer, supporter.

mockery *n* apology, burlesque, caricature, contempt, contumely, deception, derision, disappointment, disdain, disrespect, farce, fleer, gibes, iconoclasm, imitation, insults, invective, irrision, jeering, joke, lampoon, lampoonery, let-down, mickey-taking, mimesis, mimicry, misrepresentation, parody, pasquinade, pretence, quiz, ridicule, sarcasm, satire, scoffing, scorn, send-up, sham, spoof, take-off, travesty, wisecracks.

mocking *adj* contemptuous, contumelious, cynical, derisive, derisory, disdainful, disrespectful, iconoclastic, impudent, insulting, irreverent, irrisory, sarcastic, sardonic, satiric, satirical, scoffing, scornful, snide, taunting.

antonym laudatory.

mode *n* approach, condition, convention, course, craze, custom, dernier cri, fad, fashion, form, latest thing, look, manner, method, plan, practice, procedure, process, quality, rage, rule, state, style, system, technique, trend, vein, vogue, way.

model *n* archetype, configuration, copy, criterion, design, draft, dummy, embodiment, epitome, example, exemplar, facsimile, form, gauge, ideal, image, imitation, kind, loadstar, manikin, mannequin, maquette, mark, miniature, mock-up, mode, mould, original, paradigm, paragon, pattern, personification, plan, poser, praxis, prototype, replica, representation, sitter, sketch, standard, style, subject, template, touchstone, type, variety, version, yardstick.

adj archetypal, complete, consummate, dummy, exemplary, facsimile, ideal, illustrative, imitation, miniature, par excellence, paradigmatic, perfect, prototypal, prototypical, representative, standard, typical.

v base, carve, cast, create, design, display, fashion, form, make, mould, pattern, plan, sculpt, shape, show off, sport, wear, work.

moderate *adj* abstemious, average, calm, centrist, continent, controlled, cool, deliberate, disciplined, equable, fair, fairish, frugal, gentle, indifferent, judicious, limited, mediocre, medium, middle-of-the-road, middling, mild, modest, non-extreme, ordinary, passable, peaceable, quiet, rational, reasonable, restrained, sensible, sober, soft-shell(ed), so-so, steady, temperate, unexceptional, well-regulated.

v abate, allay, alleviate, appease, assuage, attemper, blunt, calm, chasten, check, control, curb, cushion, decrease, diminish, dwindle, ease, lenify, lessen, mitigate, modify, modulate, pacify, palliate, play down, quiet, regulate, repress, restrain, slake, soften, soft-pedal, subdue, subside, tame, temper, tone down.

moderately *adv* fairly, frugally, gently, in moderation, modestly, passably, pretty, quite, rather, reasonably, slightly, soberly, somewhat, sparingly, to a certain degree, to a certain extent, to some extent, tolerably, unpretentiously, within limits, within measure, within reason.

antonym immoderately.

moderation *n* abatement, abstemiousness, alleviation, aurea mediocritas, calmness, caution, centrism, chastity, composure, continence, control, coolness, decrease, diminution, discipline, discretion, easing, equanimity, extenuation, fairness, golden mean, judiciousness, justice, justness, let-up, mildness, mitigation, moderateness, modification, modulation, palliation, reasonableness, reduction, restraint, self-control, sobriety, temperance, via media.

antonyms increase, intemperance.

modern *adj* advanced, avant-garde, contemporary, current, emancipated, fashionable, fresh, go-ahead, goey, innovative, inventive, jazzy, late, latest, mod, modernistic, modish, neoteric, new, newfangled, novel, present, present-day, progressive, recent, stylish, trendy, twentieth-century, up-to-date, up-to-the-minute, with-it.

antonyms antiquated, old.

modernise *v* do up, improve, modify, neoterise, progress, redesign, reform, refresh, refurbish, regenerate, rejuvenate, remake, remodel, renew, renovate, revamp, streamline, tart up, transform, update.

antonym regress.

modernity *n* contemporaneity, currency, fashionableness, freshness, goeyness, innovation, innovativeness, newness, novelty, nowness, originality, recentness.

antonyms antiquatedness, antiquity.

modest *adj* bashful, blushing, chaste, chastened, coy, demure, diffident, discreet, fair, humble, limited, maidenly, meek, middling, moderate, ordinary, proper, quiet, reserved, reticent, retiring, seemly, self-conscious, self-effacing, shamefaced, shy, simple, small, timid, unassuming, unexceptional, unpresuming, unpresumptuous, unpretending, unpretentious, verecund.

antonyms conceited, immodest, pretentious, vain.

modesty *n* aidos, bashfulness, coyness, decency, demureness, diffidence, discreetness, humbleness, humility, meekness, propriety, quietness, reserve, reticence, seemliness, self-effacement, shamefacedness, shamefastness, shyness, simplicity, timidity, unobtrusiveness, unpretentiousness.

antonyms conceit, immodesty, vanity.

modicum *n* atom, bit, crumb, dash, drop, fragment, grain, hint, inch, iota, little, mite, ounce, particle, pinch, scrap, shred, speck, suggestion, tinge, touch, trace.

modification *n* adjustment, alteration, change, limitation, moderation, modulation, mutation, qualification, refinement, reformation, restriction, revision, tempering, variation.

modify *v* abate, adapt, adjust, allay, alter, attemper, change, convert, improve, lessen, limit, lower, moderate, modulate, qualify, recast, redesign, redo, reduce, refashion, reform, remodel, reorganise, reshape, restrain, restrict, revise, rework, soften, temper, tone down, transform, vary.

modish *adj* à la mode, all the rage, avant-garde, chic, contemporary, current, fashionable, goey, hip, in, jazzy, latest, mod, modern, modernistic, now, smart, stylish, trendy, up-to-the-minute, vogue, voguish, with-it.

antonyms dowdy, old-fashioned.

modulate *v* adjust, alter, attune, balance, harmonise, inflect, lower, moderate, regulate, soften, tone, tune, vary.

antonyms increase, raise.

modulation *n* accent, adjustment, alteration, inflection, inflexion, intonation, moderation, regulation, shade, shift, tone, tuning, variation.

modus operandi manner, method, operation, plan, practice, praxis, procedure, process, rule, rule of thumb, system, technique, way.

mogul *n* baron, bashaw, big cheese, big gun, big noise, big pot, big shot, big wheel, bigwig, grandee, magnate, magnifico, Mr Big, nabob, notable, panjandrum, personage, potentate, supremo, top dog, tycoon, VIP.

antonym nobody.

moist *adj* clammy, damp, dampish, dampy, dank, dewy, dripping, drizzly, humid, marshy, muggy, rainy, soggy, swampy, tearful, vaporous, watery, wet, wettish.

antonyms arid, dry.

moisten *v* bedew, damp, dampen, embrocate, humect, humectate, humidify, humify, imbue, irrigate, lick, madefy, moistify, moisturise, slake, soak, water, wet.

antonym dry.

moistening *n* dampening, damping, humectation, humidification, humification, irrigation, moisturisation, soaking, watering, wetting.

antonym drying.

adj dampening, damping, humectant, humective, moisturising.

antonym drying.

moisture *n* damp, dampness, dankness, dew, humidity, humour, liquid, mugginess, perspiration, sweat, tears, vapour, water, wateriness, wet, wetness.

antonym dryness.

mole[1] *n* barrier, breakwater, dike, dyke, embankment, groyne, jetty, jutty, pier.

mole[2] *n* moudiewart, mouldwarp.

mole[3] *n* agent, double agent, infiltrator, secret agent, spy.

molest *v* abuse, accost, afflict, annoy, assail, attack, badger, beset, bother, bug, disturb, faze, harass, harm, harry, hassle, hector, hound, hurt, ill-treat, injure, irritate, maltreat, manhandle, mistreat, persecute, pester, plague, tease, torment, trouble, upset, vex, worry.

mollify *v* abate, allay, appease, assuage, blunt, calm, compose, conciliate, cushion, ease, lessen, lull, mellow, mitigate, moderate, modify, pacify, placate, propitiate, quell, quiet, relax, relieve, soften, soothe, sweeten, temper.

antonyms aggravate, anger.

mollycoddle *v* baby, coddle, cosset, indulge, mother, overprotect, pamper, pander to, pet, ruin, spoil, spoon-feed.

antonyms ill-treat, neglect.

moment[1] *n* breathing-while, flash, hour, instant, jiff, jiffy, juncture, less than no time, minute, mo, point, second, shake, split second, stage, tick, time, trice, twink, twinkling.

moment[2] *n* concern, consequence, gravity, import, importance, note interest, seriousness, significance, substance, value, weight, weightiness, worth.

antonym insignificance.

momentarily *adv* briefly, fleetingly, for a moment, for a second, for an instant, temporarily.

momentary *adj* brief, elusive, ephemeral, evanescent, fleeting, flying, fugitive, hasty, momentaneous, passing, quick, short, short-lived, temporary, transient, transitory.

antonyms lasting, permanent.

momentous *adj* apocalyptic, consequential, critical, crucial, decisive, earth-shaking, epoch-making, eventful, fateful, grave, historic, important, major, pivotal, serious, significant, tremendous, vital, weighty.

antonym insignificant.

momentum *n* drive, energy, force, impact, impetus, impulse, incentive, power, propulsion, push, speed, stimulus, strength, thrust, urge, velocity.

monarch *n* despot, dynast, emperor, empress, king, potentate, prince, princess, queen, ruler, sovereign, tyrant.

monarchy *n* absolutism, autocracy, despotism, empire, kingdom, kinghood, kingship, majesty, monocracy, princedom, princehood, principality, principate, realm, royalism, rule, sovereignty, tyranny.

monastery *n* abbey, ashram, béguinage, Charterhouse, Chartreuse, cloister, coenobium, convent, fratery, fratry, friary, gompa, house, lamasery, nunnery, priory, vihara, wat.

monastic *adj* anchoritic, ascetic, austere, celibate, cloistered, cloistral, coenobitic, contemplative, conventual, eremital, eremitic, hermitical, monachal, monasterial, monastical, monkish, recluse, reclusive, secluded, sequestered, withdrawn.

antonyms gregarious, materialistic, worldly.

monasticism *n* anchoritsm, asceticism, austerity, coenobitism, eremitism, monachism, monkery, monkhood, recluseness, reclusion, seclusion.

monetary *adj* budgetary, bursal, capital, cash, economic, financial, fiscal, money, pecuniary.

money *n* akkas, akkers, baksheesh, banco, banknotes, bankroll, boodle, brass, bread, capital, cash, chips, coin, currency, dibbs, dibs, dough, dumps, fat, filthy lucre, fonds, funds, gelt, gold, gravy, greens, hard cash, hard money, legal tender, lolly, loot, mazuma, mint-sauce, money of account, moolah, oof, pelf, readies, ready money, rhino, riches, scrip, shekels, siller, silver, specie, spondulix (spondulicks), stumpy, sugar, the needful, the ready, the wherewithal, tin, wealth.

money-box *n* cash-box, chest, coffer, penny-pig, pig, piggy-bank, safe.

moneyed, monied *adj* affluent, comfortable, flush, loaded, opulent, prosperous, rich, rolling, stinking, warm, wealthy, well-heeled, well-off, well-to-do.

antonym impoverished.

money-grubber *n* mammonist, mammonite, muck-worm, quaestuary.

money-grubbing *adj* acquisitive, grasping, mammonish, mammonistic, mercenary, miserly, quaestuary.

mongrel *n* bigener, cross, crossbreed, half-breed, hybrid, lurcher, mule, mutt, yellow-dog.

adj bastard, crossbred, half-breed, hybrid, ill-defined, mixed, mongrelly, nondescript.

antonyms pedigree, pure-bred.

monitor *n* adviser, detector, guide, invigilator, overseer, prefect, recorder, scanner, screen, supervisor, watchdog.

v check, detect, follow, keep an eye on, keep track of, keep under surveillance, note, observe, oversee, plot, record, scan, supervise, survey, trace, track, watch.

monk *n* beghard, béguin, brother, cloisterer, coenobite, contemplative, conventual, frate, frater, friar, gyrovague, hermit, mendicant, monastic, religieux, religionary, religioner, religious.

monkey[1] *n* ape, primate, simian.

monkey[2] *n* ass, butt, devil, dupe, fool, imp, jackanapes, laughing-stock, mug, rapscallion, rascal, rogue, scallywag, scamp.

v fiddle, fidget, fool, interfere, meddle, mess, play, potter, tamper, tinker, trifle.

monkey business carry-on, chicanery, clowning, dishonesty, foolery, hanky-panky, jiggery-pokery, jugglery, legerdemain, mischief, monkey tricks, pranks, shenanigans, skulduggery, sleight-of-hand, tomfoolery, trickery.

antonyms honesty, probity.

monochrome *adj* black-and-white, monochroic, monochromatic, monotone, monotonous, sepia, unicolor, unicolorate, unicolorous, unicolour, unicoloured.

antonym kaleidoscopic.

monocle *n* eyeglass, glass, quiz, quizzing-glass.

monogamous *adj* monandrous, monogamic, monogynous.

antonyms bigamous, polygamous.

monogamy *n* monandry, monogyny.

antonyms bigamy, polygamy.

monolingual *adj* monoglot, unilingual.

antonym polyglot.

monolith *n* megalith, menhir, sarsen, shaft, standing stone.

monolithic *adj* colossal, faceless, giant, gigantic, huge, immobile, immovable, inflexible, intractable, massive, monumental, rigid, solid, undifferentiated, unvaried, vast.

monologue *n* harangue, homily, lecture, oration, sermon, soliloquy, speech, spiel.

antonyms conversation, dialogue, discussion.

monomania *n* bee in one's bonnet, fanaticism, fetish, fixation, hobby-horse, idée fixe, mania, neurosis, obsession, ruling passion, thing.

monopolise *v* appropriate, control, corner, dominate, engross, hog, occupy, preoccupy, take over, take up, tie up.

antonym share.

monopoly *n* ascendancy, control, corner, domination, exclusive right, monopsony, sole right.

monotheism *n* henotheism, unitarianism.

antonym polytheism.

monotonous *adj* boring, colourless, droning, dull, flat, humdrum, monochrome, plodding, prosaic, repetitious, repetitive, routine, samey, soul-destroying, tedious, tiresome, toneless, unchanging, uneventful, uniform, uninflected, unvaried, unvarying, wearisome.

antonyms colourful, lively, varied.

monotony *n* boredom, colourlessness, dullness, flatness, humdrumness, monotonousness, prosaicness, repetitiousness, repetitiveness, routine, routineness, sameness, tediousness, tedium, tiresomeness, uneventfulness, uniformity, wearisomeness.

antonyms colour, liveliness.

monster *n* abortion, barbarian, basilisk, beast, behemoth, bogeyman, brute, centaur, chimera, cockatrice, colossus, Cyclops, demon, devil, fiend, freak, giant, Gorgon, harpy, hellhound, hippocampus, hippogriff, Hydra, jabberwock, kraken, lamia, leviathan, lindworm, mammoth, manticore, Medusa, Minotaur, miscreation, monstrosity, mutant, ogre, ogress, prodigy, rye-wolf, savage, Sphinx, teratism, titan, villain, windigo, wivern.

adj Brobdingnagian, colossal, cyclopean, enormous, gargantuan, giant, gigantic, huge, immense, jumbo, mammoth, massive, monstrous, prodigious, rounceval, stupendous, titanic, tremendous, vast.

antonym minute.

monstrosity *n* abnormality, abortion, atrocity, dreadfulness, enormity, evil, eyesore, freak, frightfulness, heinousness, hellishness, hideousness, horror, loathsomeness, miscreation, monster, mutant, obscenity, ogre, prodigy, teras, teratism.

monstrous *adj* abhorrent, abnormal, atrocious, colossal, criminal, cruel, cyclopean, deformed, devilish, diabolical, disgraceful, dreadful, egregious, elephantine, enormous, evil, fiendish, foul, freakish, frightful, gargantuan, giant, gigantic, great, grotesque, gruesome, heinous, hellish, hideous, horrendous, horrible, horrific, horrifying, huge, hulking, immense, infamous, inhuman, intolerable, loathsome, malformed, mammoth, massive, miscreated, misshapen, monster, obscene, odious, outrageous, prodigious, rounceval, satanic, scandalous, shocking, stupendous, teratoid, terrible, titanic, towering, tremendous, unnatural, vast, vicious, villainous, wicked.

monthly *adj* mensal, menstrual, mensual.

monument *n* ancient monument, antiquity, barrow, cairn, cenotaph, commemoration, cross, dolmen, evidence, gravestone, headstone, marker, martyry, mausoleum, memento, memorial, obelisk, pillar, prehistoric monument, record, relic, remembrance, reminder, shaft, shrine, statue, testament, token, tombstone, tumulus, witness.

monumental *adj* abiding, awe-inspiring, awesome, catastrophic, classic, colossal, commemorative, conspicuous, cyclopean, durable, egregious, enduring, enormous, epoch-making, funerary, gigantic, great, historic, horrible, huge, immense, immortal, important, imposing, impressive, indefensible, lasting, magnificent, majestic, massive, memorable, memorial, monolithic, notable, outstanding, overwhelming, prodigious, significant, staggering, statuary, stupendous, terrible, tremendous, vast, whopping.

antonyms insignificant, unimportant.

mood *n* blues, caprice, depression, disposition, doldrums, dumps, fit, frame of mind, grumps, humour, melancholy, pique, spirit, state of mind, sulk, temper, tenor, the sulks, vein, whim.

moody *adj* angry, atrabilious, broody, cantankerous, capricious, cast-down, changeable, choleric, crabbed, crabby, cranky, cross, crotchety, crusty, dejected, depressive, dismal, doleful, dour, downcast, erratic, faddish, fickle, fitful, flighty, gloomy, glum, huffish, huffy, ill-humoured, impulsive, inconstant, introspective, introvert, irascible, irritable, lugubrious, melancholy, mercurial, miserable, mopy, morose, peevish, pensive, petulant, piqued, sad, saturnine, short-tempered, splenetic, sulky, sullen, temperamental, testy, touchy, unpredictable, unsociable, unstable, unsteady, volatile, waspish.

antonyms cheerful, equable.

moon[1] *v* brood, daydream, dream, fantasise, idle, languish, loaf, mooch, mope, pine, potter.

moon[2] *n* crescent, Cynthia, demilune, Diana, full moon, half-moon, lune, lunule, meniscus, Paddy's lantern, Phoebe, Selene.

moon-like *adj* crescent, crescentic, lunar, lunate, lunular, meniscoid, moon-shaped, moony, selenic.

moonshine[1] *n* baloney, blather, blether, bosh, bullshit, bunk, bunkum, claptrap, crap, eyewash, gas, guff, havers, hogwash, hot air, nonsense, piffle, rot, rubbish, stuff, tarradiddle, tommyrot, tosh, tripe, twaddle.

antonym sense.

moonshine[2] *n* bootleg, hoo(t)ch, pot(h)een.

moor[1] *v* anchor, berth, bind, dock, drop anchor, fasten, fix, hitch, lash, secure, tie up.

antonym loose.

moor[2] *n* brae, downs, fell, heath, moorland, muir, upland, wold.

moot *v* advance, argue, bring up, broach, debate, discuss, introduce, pose, propose, propound, put forward, submit, suggest, ventilate.

adj academic, arguable, contestable, controversial, crucial, debatable, disputable, disputed, doubtful, insoluble, knotty, open, open to debate, problematic, questionable, undecided, undetermined, unresolvable, unresolved, unsettled, vexed.

moot point controversial issue, crux, difficulty, knot, poser, problem, question mark, stumbling-block, vexata quaestio, vexed question.

mop *n* head of hair, mane, mass, mat, shock, sponge, squeegee, swab, tangle, thatch.

v absorb, clean, soak, sponge, swab, wash, wipe.

mop up absorb, account for, clean up, eliminate, finish off, neutralise, round up, secure, soak up, sponge, swab, take care of, tidy up, wash, wipe.

mope *v* agonise, boody, brood, despair, despond, droop, fret, grieve, idle, languish, mooch, moon, pine, sulk.

n depressive, grouch, grump, introvert, killjoy, melancholiac, melancholic, misery, moaner, moper, mopus, pessimist, Weary Willie.

moral *adj* blameless, chaste, clean-living, decent, equitable, ethical, good, high-minded, honest, honourable, incorruptible, innocent, just, meritorious, moralistic, noble, principled, proper, pure, responsible, right, righteous, square, straight, temperate, upright, upstanding, virtuous.

antonym immoral.

n adage, aphorism, apophthegm, dictum, epigram, gnome, import, lesson, maxim, meaning, message, motto, point, precept, proverb, saw, saying, significance, teaching.

morale *n* confidence, esprit de corps, heart, mettle, mood, resolve, self-esteem, spirit, spirits, state of mind, temper.

moralise *v* discourse, edify, ethicise, lecture, pontificate, pontify, preach, sermonise.

morality *n* chastity, conduct, decency, deontology, equity, ethicality, ethicalness, ethics, ethos, goodness, habits, honesty, ideals, integrity, justice, manners, morals, mores, philosophy, principle, principles, probity, propriety, rationale, rectitude, righteousness, standards, tightness, uprightness, virtue.

antonym immorality.

morals *n* behaviour, conduct, deontics, deontology, equity, ethics, ethos, habits, ideals, integrity, manners, morality, mores, principles, probity, propriety, rectitude, scruples, standards.

morass *n* bog, can of worms, chaos, clutter, confusion, fen, flow, jam, jumble, marsh, marshland, mess, mire, mix-up, moss, muddle, quag, quagmire, quicksand, slough, swamp, tangle.

moratorium *n* ban, delay, embargo, freeze, halt, postponement, respite, standstill, stay, stoppage, suspension.

antonyms go-ahead, green light.

morbid *adj* ailing, brooding, corrupt, deadly, diseased, dreadful, ghastly, ghoulish, gloomy, grim, grisly, gruesome, hideous, horrid, hypochondriacal, infected, lugubrious, macabre, malignant, melancholy, neurotic, pathological, peccant, pessimistic, putrid, sick, sickly, sombre, unhealthy, unsalubrious, unsound, unwholesome, vicious, Wertherian.

mordant *adj* acerbic, acid, acidic, acidulous, acrimonious, astringent, biting, bitter, caustic, corrosive, cutting, edged, harsh, incisive, mordacious, pungent, sarcastic, scathing, sharp, stinging, trenchant, venomous, vicious, waspish, wounding.

antonyms gentle, sparing.

more *adj* added, additional, alternative, extra, fresh, further, increased, new, other, renewed, repeated, spare, supplementary.

adv again, better, further, longer.

moreover *adv* additionally, also, as well, besides, further, furthermore, in addition, into the bargain, likewise, may I add, more, more to the point, to boot, too, what is more, withal.

morgue *n* deadhouse, mortuary.

moribund *adj* at a standstill, caducous, collapsing, comatose, crumbling, dead and alive, declining, doomed, dwindling, dying, ebbing, fading, failing, in extremis, obsolescent, on one's last legs, on the way out, senile, stagnant, stagnating, waning, wasting away, weak, with one foot in the grave.

antonyms alive, flourishing, lively, nascent.

morning *n* ack emma, am, break of day, cock-crow, dawn, daybreak, daylight, dayspring, first thing, foreday, forenoon, morn, sunrise, sun-up.

adj antemeridian, auroral, aurorean, dawn, forenoon, matinal, matutinal, matutive.

moron *n* ass, blockhead, bonehead, clot, cretin, daftie, dimwit, dolt, dope, dumbbell, dummy, dunce, dunderhead, fool, halfwit, idiot, imbecile, klutz, mental defective, mooncalf, muttonhead, natural, nong, numbskull, schmo, schmuck, simpleton, thickhead, vegetable, zombie.

moronic *adj* asinine, brainless, cretinous, daft, defective, dimwitted, doltish, dopey, foolish, gormless, halfwitted, idiotic, imbecilic, lacking, mindless, retarded, simple, simple-minded, stupid, subnormal, thick, unintelligent.

morose *adj* blue, cheerless, churlish, crabbed, crabby, cross, crusty, depressed, dour, down, gloomy, glum, grim, grouchy, gruff, grum, huffy, humourless, ill-humoured, ill-natured, ill-tempered, low, melancholy, misanthropic, moody, mournful, perverse, pessimistic, saturnine, sour, stern, sulky, sullen, surly, taciturn, testy, unsociable.

antonyms cheerful, communicative.

morsel *n* atom, bit, bite, bonne-bouche, crumb, fraction, fragment, grain, modicum, morceau, mouthful, nibble, part, piece, scrap, segment, slice, smidgen, snack, soupçon, taste, titbit.

mortal *adj* agonising, awful, bodily, corporeal, deadly, deathful, dire, earthly, enormous, ephemeral, extreme, fatal, fleshly, grave, great, human, impermanent, implacable, intense, irreconcilable, lethal, lethiferous, mortiferous, passing, perishable, relentless, remorseless, severe, sublunary, sworn, temporal, terrible, transient, unrelenting, worldly.

antonym immortal.

n being, body, creature, earthling, human, human being, individual, man, person, sublunar, sublunary, woman.

antonyms god, immortal.

mortality *n* bloodshed, caducity, carnage, corruptibility, death, destruction, ephemerality, fatality, humanity, humans, impermanence, killing, mankind, mortals, perishability, temporality, transience, transitoriness.

antonym immortality.

mortgage *v* dip, pawn, pledge, put in hock.

n bond, debenture, lien, loan, pledge, security, wadset.

mortification *n* abasement, annoyance, ascesis, asceticism, chagrin, chastening, confounding, conquering, control, corruption, defeat, denial, discipline, discomfiture, dissatisfaction, embarrassment, festering, gangrene, humiliation, ignominy, loss of face, necrosis, overthrow, punishment, putrescence, shame, subjugation, vexation.

mortified *adj* abashed, affronted, annoyed, ashamed, chagrined, chastened, confounded, crushed, dead, decayed, deflated, discomfited, displeased, embarrassed, gangrenous, humbled, humiliated, necrotic, put out, put to shame, putrefied, putrid, rotted, rotten, shamed, vexed.

antonyms elated, jubilant.

mortify *v* abase, abash, affront, annoy, chagrin, chasten, confound, conquer, control, corrupt, crush, deflate, deny, die, disappoint, discipline, discomfit, embarrass, fester, gangrene, humble, humiliate, macerate, necrose, put to shame, putrefy, shame, subdue, vex.

mortifying *adj* chastening, crushing, discomfiting, embarrassing, humbling, humiliating, ignominious, overwhelming, punishing, salutary, shaming, thwarting.

mortuary *n* deadhouse, funeral parlour, morgue.

mostly *adv* as a rule, characteristically, chiefly, commonly, customarily, feckly, for the most part, generally, largely, mainly, normally, on the whole, particularly, predominantly, primarily, principally, typically, usually.

mote *n* atom, grain, iota, jot, mite, particle, speck, spot, trace.

moth-eaten *adj* ancient, antiquated, archaic, dated, decayed, decrepit, dilapidated, mangy, moribund, mothed, mouldy, musty, obsolete, old-fashioned, outdated, outworn, ragged, seedy, shabby, stale, tattered, threadbare, worn-out.

antonyms fresh, new.

mother *n* dam, generatrix, genetrix, ma, mam, mama, mamma, mammy, mater, materfamilias, mom, momma, mommy, mum, mummy, old lady, old woman.

v baby, bear, care for, cherish, cosset, foster, fuss over, indulge, nurse, nurture, overprotect, pamper, produce, protect, raise, rear, spoil, tend.

antonym neglect.

motherly *adj* affectionate, caring, comforting, fond, gentle, indulgent, kind, kindly, loving, maternal, protective, solicitous, tender, warm.

antonyms indifferent, neglectful, uncaring.

motif *n* concept, decoration, design, device, figure, form, idea, leitmotiv, logo, notion, ornament, pattern, shape, strain, subject, theme.

motion *n* action, change, dynamics, flow, flux, gesticulation, gesture, inclination, kinesics, kinetics, locomotion, mechanics, mobility, motility, move, movement, nod, passage, passing, progress, proposal, proposition, recommendation, sign, signal, submission, suggestion, transit, travel, wave.

v beckon, direct, gesticulate, gesture, nod, sign, signal, usher, wave.

motionless *adj* at a standstill, at rest, calm, fixed, frozen, halted, immobile, inanimate, inert, lifeless, moveless, paralysed, resting, rigid, stagnant, standing, static, stationary, still, stock-still, transfixed, unmoved, unmoving.

antonym active.

motivate *v* actuate, arouse, bring, cause, draw, drive, encourage, impel, incite, induce, inspire, inspirit, instigate, kindle, lead, move, persuade, prompt, propel, provoke, push, spur, stimulate, stir, trigger, urge.

antonyms deter, prevent.

motivation *n* ambition, desire, drive, hunger, impulse, incentive, incitement, inducement, inspiration, instigation, interest, momentum, motive, persuasion, provocation, push, reason, spur, stimulus, urge, wish.

antonyms discouragement, prevention.

motive *n* cause, consideration, design, desire, encouragement, ground(s), impulse, incentive, incitement, inducement, influence, inspiration, intention, mainspring, motivation, object, occasion, purpose, rationale, reason, spur, stimulus, thinking, urge.

antonyms deterrent, discouragement, disincentive.

adj activating, actuating, agential, driving, impelling, initiating, motivating, moving, operative, prompting, propellent.

antonyms deterrent, inhibitory, preventive.

motley *adj* assorted, chequered, disparate, dissimilar, diverse, diversified, haphazard, heterogeneous, ill-assorted, kaleidoscopic, mingled, miscellaneous, mixed, multicoloured, particoloured, patchwork, polychromatic, polychrome, polychromous, promiscuous, rainbow, unlike, varied, variegated.

antonyms homogeneous, monochrome, uniform.

mottled *adj* blotchy, brindled, chequered, dappled, flecked, freaked, freckled, jaspé, marbled, piebald, pied, poikilitic, skewbald, speckled, spotted, stippled, streaked, tabby, variegated, veined, watered.

antonyms monochrome, plain, uniform.

motto *n* adage, apophthegm, byword, catchword, cry, dictum, epigraph, formula, gnome, golden rule, ichthys, maxim, precept, proverb, rule, saw, saying, sentence, slogan, watchword.

mould[1] *n* arrangement, brand, build, calibre, cast, character, configuration, construction, cut, design, die, fashion, form, format, frame, framework, ilk, kidney, kind, line, make, matrix, model, moulage, nature, pattern, quality, shape, sort, stamp, structure, style, template, type.

v affect, carve, cast, construct, control, create, design, direct, fashion, fit, forge, form, hew, influence, make, model, sculpt, sculpture, shape, stamp, work.

mould[2] *n* black, black spot, blight, fungus, mildew, mouldiness, must, mustiness, rust.

mould[3] *n* clods, dirt, dust, earth, ground, humus, loam, soil.

moulder *v* corrupt, crumble, decay, decompose, disintegrate, humify, perish, rot, turn to dust, waste.

mouldy *adj* bad, blighted, corrupt, decaying, fusty, mildewed, mucedinous, mucid, muggish, muggy, musty, putrid, rotten, rotting, spoiled, stale, vinewed.

antonyms fresh, wholesome.

mound *n* agger, bank, barrow, bing, bulwark, drift, dune, earthwork, elevation, embankment, heap, hill, hillock, hummock, knoll, mote, motte, pile, rampart, rick, ridge, rise, stack, tuffet, tumulus, tussock, yardang.

mount *v* accumulate, arise, ascend, bestride, build, clamber up, climb, climb on, climb up on, copulate, cover, deliver, display, emplace, enchase, escalade, escalate, exhibit, fit, frame, get astride, get on, get up, get up on, go up, grow, horse, increase, install, intensify, jump on, launch, lift, multiply, pile up, place, position, prepare, produce, put in place, put on, ready, ride, rise, rocket, scale, set, set in motion, set off, set up, soar, stage, straddle, swell, tower, tread.

n backing, base, fixture, foil, frame, horse, monture, mounting, pedestal, podium, setting, stand, steed, support.

mountain *n* abundance, alp, backlog, ben, berg, elevation, eminence, fell, heap, height, mass, massif, mound, mount, Munro, peak, pile, reserve, stack, ton.

mountainous *adj* alpine, daunting, enormous, formidable, gigantic, great, gross, high, highland, hilly, huge, hulking, immense, mammoth, mighty, monumental, ponderous, prodigious, rocky, rugged, soaring, steep, towering, unwieldy, upland.

antonyms easy, flat, small.

mountebank *n* charlatan, cheat, con man, confidence, fake, fraud, huckster, impostor, phoney, pretender, pseud, quack, quacksalver, rogue, spieler, swindler, trickster.

mourn *v* bemoan, bewail, beweep, deplore, grieve, keen, lament, miss, regret, rue, sorrow, wail, weep.

antonyms bless, rejoice.

mourner *n* bereaved, griever, keener, mute, sorrower.

mournful *adj* afflicting, broken-hearted, calamitous, cast-down, cheerless, chopfallen, dearnful, dejected, deplorable, depressed, desolate, disconsolate, dismal, distressing, doleful, dolorous, downcast, funereal, gloomy, grief-stricken, grieving, grievous, heartbroken, heavy, heavy-hearted, joyless, lachrymose, lamentable, long-faced, long-visaged, lugubrious, melancholy, miserable, painful, piteous, plaintive, plangent, rueful, sad, sombre, sorrowful, stricken, tragic, unhappy, woeful, woesome.

antonyms cheerful, joyful.

mourning *n* bereavement, black, desolation, grief, grieving, keening, lamentation, sackcloth and ashes, sadness, sorrow, wailing, weeds, weeping, widow's weeds, woe.

antonym rejoicing.

mouse-like *adj* cowering, diffident, diminutive, mous(e)y, murine, shy, timid, timorous.

mous(e)y *adj* brownish, characterless, colourless, diffident, drab, dull, indeterminate, ineffectual, mouse-like, plain, quiet, self-effacing, shy, timid, timorous, unassertive, unforthcoming, uninteresting, withdrawn.

antonyms assertive, bright, extrovert, irrepressible.

moustache *n* excrement, face fungus, handlebar moustache, mustachio, mustachios, toothbrush moustache, walrus, whiskers.

mouth[1] *n* aperture, cake-hole, cavity, chops, crevice, débouché, debouchment, debouchure, disemboguement, door, embouchure, entrance, estuary, gateway, gob, inlet, jaws, kisser, lips, mandibles, maw, moue, opening, orifice, outlet, portal, potato-trap, pout, proboscis, rattle-trap, scowl, threshold, trap, vent.

v articulate, declaim, elegise, enunciate, form, pronounce, shape, spout, utter, whisper.

mouth[2] *n* backchat, boasting, braggadocio, bragging, cheek, effrontery, gas, hot air, impudence, insolence, lip, rudeness, sauce.

mouthful *n* bit, bite, bonne bouche, drop, forkful, gob, gobbet, gulp, morsel, sample, sip, slug, spoonful, sup, swallow, taste, titbit.

mouthpiece *n* agent, delegate, fugleman, journal, organ, propagandist, representative, spokesman, spokeswoman.

movable *adj* adjustable, alterable, changeable, detachable, flexible, mobile, portable, portative, transferable, transportable.

antonyms fixed, immovable.

movables *n* belongings, chattels, effects, furniture, gear, goods, impedimenta, plenishings, possessions, property, stuff, things, traps.

move *v* activate, actuate, adjust, advance, advise, advocate, affect, agitate, budge, carry, cause, change, cover the ground, decamp, depart, disturb, drift, drive, ease, edge, excite, flit, get, give rise to, go, go away, gravitate, impel, impress, incite, induce, influence, inspire, instigate, jiggle, lead, leave, locomote, make strides, march, migrate, motivate, move house, operate, persuade, proceed, progress, prompt, propel, propose, pull, push, put forward, quit, recommend, relocate, remove, rouse, run, set going, shift, shove, start, stimulate, stir, submit, suggest, switch, take, touch, transfer, transport, transpose, turn, urge, walk.

n act, action, deed, démarche, dodge, draught, flit, flitting, go, manoeuvre, measure, migration, motion, movement, ploy, relocation, removal, ruse, shift, step, stratagem, stroke, tack, tactic, transfer, turn.

movement *n* act, action, activity, advance, agitation, beat, cadence, campaign, change, crusade, current, development, displacement, division, drift, drive, evolution, exercise, faction, flow, front, gesture, ground swell, group, grouping, innards, machinery, manoeuvre, measure, mechanism, metre, motion, move, moving, operation, organisation, pace, part, party, passage, progress, progression, rhythm, section, shift, steps, stir, stirring, swing, tempo, tendency, transfer, trend, workings, works.

movie *n* feature, film, flick, motion picture, picture, silent, talkie, video.

movies *n* cinema, film, films, flicks, pictures, silver screen.

moving *adj* affecting, ambulant, ambulatory, arousing, dynamic, emotional, emotive, exciting, impelling, impressive, inspirational, inspiring, locomobile, mobile, motile, motivating, movable, pathetic, persuasive, poignant, portable, propelling, running, stimulating, stimulative, stirring, touching, unfixed.

antonyms fixed, stationary, unemotional.

mow *v* clip, crop, cut, scythe, shear, trim.

mow down butcher, cut down, cut to pieces, decimate, massacre, shoot down, slaughter.

much *adv* considerably, copiously, decidedly, exceedingly, frequently, greatly, often.

adj a lot of, abundant, ample, considerable, copious, great, plenteous, plenty of, siz(e)able, substantial.

n heaps, lashings, loads, lots, oodles, plenty, scads.

antonym little.

muck *n* dirt, droppings, dung, faeces, filth, gunge, gunk, manure, mire, mud, ooze, ordure, scum, sewage, slime, sludge.

muck up botch, bungle, make a mess of, make a muck of, mar, mess up, muff, ruin, screw up, spoil, waste.

mucky *adj* begrimed, bespattered, dirty, filthy, grimy, messy, miry, mud-caked, muddy, oozy, soiled, sticky.

antonym clean.

mucous *adj* gelatinous, glutinous, gummy, mucilaginous, slimy, snotty, viscid, viscous.

mud *n* adobe, clabber, clay, dirt, fango, glaur, mire, ooze, silt, slab, sleech, slob, sludge, slush.

muddle *v* befuddle, bewilder, confound, confuse, daze, disarrange, disorder, disorganise, disorient(ate), fuddle, fuzzle, jumble, make a mess of, mess, mix up, mull, perplex, scramble, spoil, stupefy, tangle.

n bollocks, chaos, clutter, cock-up, confusion, daze, disarray, disorder, disorganisation, fankle, guddle, jumble, mess, mix-up, mull, perplexity, pie, plight, predicament, puddle, snarl-up, tangle.

muddle through cope, get along, get by, make it, manage, muddle along, scrape by.

muddled *adj* at sea, befuddled, bewildered, chaotic, confused, dazed, disarrayed, disordered, disorganised, disorient(at)ed, higgledy-piggledy, incoherent, jumbled, loose, messy, mixed-up, muddle-headed, perplexed, puzzle-headed, scrambled, stupefied, tangled, unclear, vague, woolly.

muddy *adj* bespattered, blurred, boggy, clarty, cloudy, confused, dingy, dirty, dredgy, drumly, dull, foul, fuzzy, glaury, grimy, grouty, hazy, impure, indistinct, marshy, miry, mucky, mud-caked, muddled, opaque, quaggy, slabby, sleechy, sloppy, soiled, swampy, turbid, unclear, vague, woolly.

antonyms clean, clear.

v bedash, bedaub, begrime, bespatter, cloud, dirty, smear, smirch, soil.

antonym clean.

muff *v* botch, bungle, fluff, mess up, mishit, mismanage, miss, spoil.

muffle *v* cloak, conceal, cover, damp down, dampen, deaden, disguise, dull, envelop, gag, hood, hush, mask, mute, muzzle, quieten, shroud, silence, soften, stifle, suppress, swaddle, swathe, wrap up.

antonym amplify.

mug[1] *n* beaker, cup, flagon, jug, pot, stoup, tankard, toby jug.

mug[2] *n* chump, fool, gull, innocent, mark, muggins, sap, saphead, simpleton, soft touch, sucker.

mug[3] *n* clock, countenance, dial, face, features, mush, phiz(og), puss, visage.

mug up bone up, con, cram, get up, study, swot.

mug[4] *v* attack, bash, batter, beat up, garrotte, jump (on), mill, rob, roll, set upon, steal from, waylay.

muggy *adj* clammy, close, damp, humid, moist, oppressive, sticky, stuffy, sudorific, sultry, sweltering.

antonym dry.

mulish *adj* bull-headed, cross-grained, defiant, difficult, headstrong, inflexible, intractable, intransigent, obstinate, perverse, pig-headed, recalcitrant, refractory, rigid, self-willed, stiff-necked, stubborn, unreasonable, wilful, wrong-headed.

mull *v* chew, con, consider, contemplate, deliberate, examine, meditate, muse on, ponder, reflect on, review, ruminate, study, think about, think over, weigh up.

multifarious *adj* different, diverse, diversified, legion, manifold, many, miscellaneous, multiform, multiple, multiplex, multitudinous, numerous, sundry, varied, variegated.

multiple *adj* collective, manifold, many, multifarious, multiplex, multitudinous, numerous, several, sundry, various.

multiplicity *n* abundance, array, diversity, heaps, host, loads, lot, lots, manifoldness, mass, multeity, myriad, number, numerousness, oodles, piles, profusion, scores, stacks, tons, variety.

multiply *v* accumulate, augment, boost, breed, build up, expand, extend, increase, intensify, proliferate, propagate, reproduce, spread.

antonyms decrease, lessen.

multitude *n* army, assemblage, assembly, collection, commonalty, concourse, congregation, crowd, herd, hive, hoi polloi, horde, host, legion, lot, lots, mass, mob, myriad, people, populace, proletariat, public, rabble, sea, swarm, throng.

antonyms handful, scattering.

multitudinous *adj* abounding, abundant, considerable, copious, countless, great, infinite, innumerable, legion, manifold, many, myriad, numerous, profuse, swarming, teeming, umpteen.

mum *adj* close-lipped, close-mouthed, dumb, mute, quiet, reticent, secretive, silent, tight-lipped, uncommunicative, unforthcoming.

mumbo-jumbo *n* abracadabra, cant, chant, charm, claptrap, conjuration, double talk, gibberish, gobbledegook, hocus-pocus, humbug, incantation, jargon, magic, mummery, nonsense, rigmarole, rite, ritual, spell, superstition.

munch *v* champ, chew, chomp, crunch, eat, masticate, scrunch.

mundane *adj* banal, commonplace, day-to-day, earthly, everyday, fleshly, human, humdrum, material, mortal, ordinary, prosaic, routine, secular, subastral, sublunar(y), temporal, terrestrial, workaday, worldly.

antonyms cosmic, extraordinary, supernatural.

municipal *adj* borough, burgh(al), city, civic, community, public, town, urban.

municipality *n* borough, burgh, city, département, department, district, precinct, town, township.

munificence *n* beneficence, benevolence, bounteousness, bounty, generosity, generousness, hospitality, largess(e), liberality, magnanimousness, open-handedness, philanthropy.

antonym meanness.

munificent *adj* beneficent, benevolent, big-hearted, bounteous, bountiful, free-handed, generous, hospitable, lavish, liberal, magnanimous, open-handed, philanthropical, princely, rich, unstinting.

antonym mean.

murder *n* agony, assassination, bloodshed, butchery, carnage, danger, deicide, difficulty, filicide, fractricide, hell, homicide, infanticide, killing, manslaughter, massacre, misery, ordeal, parricide, patricide, slaying, trial, trouble.

v abuse, assassinate, bump off, burke, butcher, destroy, dispatch, do in, drub, eliminate, hammer, hit, kill, mangle, mar, massacre, misuse, rub out, ruin, slaughter, slay, spoil, thrash, waste.

murderer *n* assassin, butcher, cut-throat, filicide, hit-man, homicide, killer, matricide, parricide, patricide, slaughterer, slayer.

murderous *adj* ardous, barbarous, bloodthirsty, bloody, brutal, cruel, cut-throat, dangerous, deadly, death-dealing, destructive, devastating, difficult, exhausting, fatal, fell, ferocious, harrowing, hellish, internecine, killing, lethal, sanguinary, sapping, savage, slaughterous, strenuous, unpleasant, withering.

murky *adj* cloudy, dark, dim, dismal, dreary, dull, dusky, enigmatic, foggy, gloomy, grey, misty, mysterious, obscure, overcast, veiled.

antonyms bright, clear.

murmur *n* babble, brool, burble, buzz, buzzing, complaint, croon, drone, grumble, humming, moan, mumble, muttering, purl, purling, purr, rumble, susurrus, undertone, whisper, whispering.

v babble, burble, burr, buzz, drone, gurgle, hum, mumble, mutter, purl, purr, rumble.

murmuring *adj* buzzing, droning, mumbling, murmurous, muttering, purring, rumbling, whispering.

n buzz(ing), drone, mumble, mumbling, murmuration, muttering, purr(ing), rumble, rumbling, susurrus, whisper(ing).

muscle *n* brawn, clout, depressor, force, forcefulness, levator, might, potency, power, sinew, stamina, strength, sturdiness, tendon, thew, weight.

muscle in butt in, elbow one's way in, force one's way in, impose oneself, jostle, push in, shove, strongarm.

muscular *adj* athletic, beefy, brawny, hefty, husky, lusty, powerful, powerfully-built, robust, sinewy, stalwart, strapping, strong, sturdy, vigorous, well-knit, wiry.

antonyms delicate, feeble, flabby, puny, weak.

muse *v* brood, chew, cogitate, consider, contemplate, diliberate, dream, meditate, mull over, ponder, reflect, review, ruminate, speculate, think, think over, weigh.

mush *n* corn, dough, hogwash, mash, mawkishness, pap, paste, pulp, schmaltz, sentimentality, slush, swill.

mushroom *v* boom, burgeon, expand, flourish, grow, increase, luxuriate, proliferate, shoot up, spread, spring up, sprout.

n champignon, chanterelle, fungus, morel, pixy-stool, puffball, toadstool.

mushy *adj* doughy, maudlin, mawkish, pappy, pulpous, pulpy, saccharine, schmaltzy, sentimental, sloppy, slushy, soft, squashy, squelchy, squidgy, sugary, syrupy, weepy, wet.

musical *adj* canorous, dulcet, euphonious, Euterpean, harmonious, lilting, lyrical, melodic, melodious, sweet-sounding, tuneful.

antonym unmusical.

musician *n* accompanist, bard, composer, conductor, instrumentalist, minstrel, performer, player, singer, vocalist.

musing *n* absent-mindedness, abstraction, brown study, cerebration, cogitation, contemplation, daydreaming, dreaming, introspection, meditation, ponderment, reflection, reverie, rumination, thinking, wool-gathering.

must *n* basic, duty, essential, fundamental, imperative, necessity, obligation, prerequisite, provision, requirement, requisite, sine qua non, stipulation.

muster *v* assemble, call together, call up, collect, come together, congregate, convene, convoke, enrol, gather, group, marshal, mass, meet, mobilise, rally, round up, summon, throng.

n assemblage, assembly, collection, concourse, congregation, convention, convocation, gathering, mass, meeting, mobilisation, rally, round-up, throng.

musty *adj* airless, ancient, antediluvian, antiquated, banal, clichéd, dank, decayed, dull, foughty, frowsty, fusty, hackneyed, hoary, mildewed, mildewy, moth-eaten, mouldy, mucedinous, mucid, obsolete, old, old-fashioned, smelly, stale, stuffy, threadbare, trite, vinewed, worn-out.

mutability *n* alterability, changeableness, interchangeability, permutability, variability, variation.

mutable *adj* adaptable, alterable, changeable, changing, fickle, flexible, inconsistent, inconstant, interchangeable, irresolute, permutable, uncertain, undependable, unreliable, unsettled, unstable, unsteady, vacillating, variable, volatile, wavering.

antonyms constant, invariable, permanent.

mutation *n* alteration, anomaly, change, deviant, deviation, evolution, metamorphosis, modification, mutant, transfiguration, transformation, variation, vicissitude.

mute *adj* aphonic, dumb, mum, noiseless, silent, speechless, unexpressed, unpronounced, unspeaking, unspoken, voiceless, wordless.

antonyms articulate, vocal, voluble.

v dampen, deaden, lower, moderate, muffle, silence, soften, soft-pedal, subdue, tone down.

muted *adj* dampened, dull, faint, low-key, muffled, quiet, soft, stifled, suppressed.

mutilate *v* adulterate, amputate, bowdlerise, butcher, censor, cut, cut to pieces, cut up, damage, detruncate, disable, disfigure, dismember, distort, expurgate, hack, hamble, injure, lacerate, lame, maim, mangle, mar, spoil.

mutilation *n* amputation, bowdlerisation, damage, detruncation, disfigurement, dismembering, maiming.

mutinous *adj* bolshie, bolshy, contumacious, disobedient, insubordinate, insurgent, rebellious, recusant, refractory, revolutionary, riotous, seditious, subversive, turbulent, ungovernable, unmanageable, unruly.

antonyms compliant, dutiful, obedient.

mutiny *n* defiance, disobedience, insubordination, insurrection, putsch, rebellion, resistance, revolt, revolution, riot, rising, strike, uprising.

v disobey, protest, rebel, resist, revolt, rise up, strike.

mutt *n* cur, dog, dolt, drongo, dunderhead, fool, idiot, ignoramus, imbecile, mongrel, moron, nong, sap, saphead, thickhead.

mutter *v* chunter, complain, grouch, grouse, grumble, mumble, murmur, mussitate, rumble.

mutual *adj* common, communal, complementary, exchanged, interchangeable, interchanged, joint, reciprocal, reciprocated, requited, returned, shared.

muzzle *n* bit, curb, gag, guard, jaws, mouth, nose, snaffle, snout.

v censor, choke, curb, gag, mute, restrain, silence, stifle, suppress.

muzzy *adj* addled, befuddled, bewildered, blurred, confused, dazed, hazy, muddled, mused, tipsy.

antonym clear.

myopic *adj* half-blind, near-sighted, short-sighted.

antonym far-sighted.

myriad *adj* boundless, countless, immeasurable, incalculable, innumerable, limitless, multitudinous, untold.

n army, flood, horde, host, millions, mountain, multitude, scores, sea, swarm, thousands, throng.

mysterious *adj* abstruse, arcane, baffling, concealed, covert, cryptic, curious, dark, enigmatic, furtive, hidden, impenetrable, incomprehensible, inexplicable, inscrutable, insoluble, mystical, mystifying, obscure, perplexing, puzzling, recondite, secret, secretive, strange, uncanny, unfathomable, unsearchable, veiled, weird.

antonyms comprehensible, frank, straightforward.

mystery *n* arcanum, conundrum, enigma, problem, puzzle, question, riddle, secrecy, secret.

mystical *adj* abstruse, arcane, cab(b)alistic(al), cryptic, enigmatical, esoteric, hidden, inscrutable, metaphysical, mysterious, mystic, occult, otherworldly, paranormal, preternatural, supernatural, transcendental.

mystify *v* baffle, bamboozle, beat, bewilder, confound, confuse, escape, metagrabolise, metagrobolise, perplex, puzzle, stump.

mystique *n* appeal, awe, charisma, charm, fascination, glamour, magic, spell.

myth *n* allegory, delusion, fable, fairy tale, fancy, fantasy, fiction, figment, illusion, legend, old wives' tale, parable, saga, story, superstition, tradition, untruism.

mythical *adj* fabled, fabricated, fabulous, fairy-tale, fanciful, fantasy, fictitious, imaginary, invented, legendary, made-up, make-believe, mythological, non-existent, pretended, unhistoric(al), unreal.

antonyms actual, historical, real, true.

mythological *adj* fabulous, folkloric, legendary, mythic, mythical, traditional.

mythology *n* folklore, folk-tales, legend, lore, myths, mythus, tales, tradition(s).

N

nab *v* apprehend, arrest, capture, catch, collar, grab, nail, nick, seize, snatch.

nabob *n* bigwig, billionaire, celebrity, Croesus, financier, luminary, magnate, millionaire, multimillionaire, panjandrum, personage, tycoon, VIP.

nadir *n* all-time low, bottom, depths, low point, lowest point, low-watermark, minimum, rock bottom, zero.

antonyms acme, apex, peak, zenith.

nag[1] *v* annoy, badger, berate, chivvy, goad, harass, harry, henpeck, irritate, kvetch, pain, pester, plague, scold, torment, upbraid, vex.

n harpy, harridan, kvetch(er), scold, shrew, tartar, termagant, virago.

nag[2] *n* hack, horse, jade, keffel, plug, rip, Rosinante.

nagging *adj* continuous, critical, distressing, irritating, painful, persistent, scolding, shrewish, tormenting, upsetting, worrying.

nail *v* apprehend, attach, beat, capture, catch, clinch, collar, fasten, fix, hammer, join, nab, nick, pin, secure, seize, tack.

n brad, hobnail, peg, pin, rivet, screw, skewer, spike, staple, tack, tacket.

naïve *adj* artless, callow, candid, childlike, confiding, credulous, dewy-eyed, facile, frank, green, guileless, gullible, ingenuous, innocent, jejune, natural, open, simple, simplistic, small-town, trusting, unaffected, uncritical, unpretentious, unsophisticated, unsuspecting, unsuspicious, unworldly, verdant, wide-eyed.

antonyms experienced, sophisticated.

naïvety *n* artlessness, callowness, candour, credulity, experience, frankness, guilelessness, gullibility, inexperience, ingenuousness, innocence, naturalness, openness, simplicity, sophistication.

naked *adj* adamic, bare, blatant, defenceless, denuded, disrobed, divested, evident, exposed, helpless, in puris naturalibus, in the altogether, in the buff, insecure, manifest, mother-naked, nude, open, overt, patent, plain, simple, skyclad, stark, starkers, stark-naked, stripped, unadorned, unarmed, unclothed, unconcealed, uncovered, undisguised, undraped, undressed, unexaggerated, unguarded, unmistakable, unprotected, unqualified, unvarnished, vulnerable.

antonyms clothed, concealed, covered.

nakedness *n* baldness, bareness, nudity, openness, plainness, simplicity, starkness, the altogether, the buff, undress.

namby-pamby *adj* anaemic, colourless, feeble, insipid, mawkish, pretty-pretty, prim, prissy, sentimental, spineless, vapid, weak, weedy, wet, white-shoe, wishy-washy.

name *n* acronym, agname, agnomen, appellation, character, cognomen, compellation, compellative, credit, denomination, designation, distinction, eminence, epithet, esteem, fame, handle, honour, moni(c)ker, nickname, note, praise, renown, reputation, repute, sobriquet, stage name, term, title, to-name.

v appoint, baptise, bename, betitle, call, choose, christen, cite, classify, cognominate, commission, denominate, designate, dub, entitle, identify, label, mention, nominate, select, specify, style, term, title.

named *adj* appointed, baptised, called, chosen, christened, cited, classified, commissioned, denominated, designated, dit, dubbed, entitled, identified, known as, labelled, mentioned, nominated, onymous, picked, selected, singled out, specified, styled, termed.

antonym nameless.

nameless *adj* abominable, anonymous, dreadful, fearsome, horrendous, horrible, incognito, indescribable, ineffable, inexpressible, innominate, obscure, terrible, undesignated, undistinguished, unheard-of, unknown, unmentionable, unnamed, unspeakable, unsung, untitled, unutterable.

antonym named.

namely *adv* ie, specifically, that is, that is to say, to wit, videlicet, viz.

nap[1] *v* catnap, doze, drop off, drowse, kip, nod, nod off, rest, sleep, snooze, zizz.

n catnap, forty winks, kip, rest, shuteye, siesta, sleep, zizz.

nap[2] *n* down, downiness, fibre, fuzz, grain, pile, shag, weave.

nappy *n* diaper, doily, hipping, napkin, serviette, towel.

narcissistic *adj* conceited, egocentric, egomaniacal, ego(t)istic, self-centred, self-loving, vain.

narcotic *n* anaesthetic, analgesic, anodyne, drug, hop, kef, opiate, pain-killer, sedative, tranquilliser.

adj analgesic, calming, dulling, hypnotic, Lethean, numbing, pain-killing, sedative, somniferous, somnific, soporific, stupefacient, stupefactive, stupefying.

nark *v* annoy, bother, bug, exasperate, gall, get, irk, irritate, miff, nettle, peeve, pip, pique, provoke, rile.

narrate *v* chronicle, describe, detail, recite, recount, rehearse, relate, repeat, report, set forth, state, tell, unfold.

narration *n* description, enarration, explanation, reading, recital, recountal, rehearsal, relation, story-telling, telling, voice-over.

narrative *n* account, chronicle, detail, history, parable, report, statement, story, tale.

narrator *n* annalist, author, bard, chronicler, commentator, raconteur, reciter, relater, relator, reporter, story-teller, writer.

narrow *adj* attenuated, avaricious, biased, bigoted, circumscribed, close, confined, constricted, contracted, cramped, dogmatic, exclusive, fine, illiberal, incapacious, intolerant, limited, meagre, mean, mercenary, narrow-minded, near, niggardly, partial, pinched, prejudiced, reactionary, restricted, scanty, select, short-head, simplistic, slender, slim, small-minded, spare, straitened, tapering, thin, tight, ungenerous.

antonyms broad, liberal, tolerant, wide.

v circumscribe, constrict, constringe, diminish, limit, reduce, simplify, straiten, tighten.

antonyms broaden, increase, loosen, widen.

narrowing *n* attenuation, compression, constipation, constriction, contraction, curtailment, emaciation, reduction, stenosis, tapering, thinning.

antonyms broadening, widening.

narrowly *adv* barely, by a hair's breadth, by a whisker, carefully, closely, just, only just, painstakingly, precisely, scarcely, scrutinisingly, strictly.

narrow-minded *adj* biased, bigoted, blinkered, borné, conservative, hidebound, illiberal, insular, intolerant, mean, opinionated, parochial, petty, prejudiced, provincial, reactionary, short-sighted, small-minded, strait-laced.

antonym broad-minded.

narrowness *n* attentuation, closeness, constriction, crowdedness, exclusiveness, insularity, limitation, meagreness, narrow-mindedness, nearness, parochialism, restrictedness, slenderness, thinness, tightness.

antonyms breadth, width.

nascent *adj* advancing, budding, developing, embryonic, evolving, growing, incipient, naissant, rising, young.

antonym dying.

nastiness *n* defilement, dirtiness, disagreeableness, filth, filthiness, foulness, impurity, indecency, licentiousness, malice, meanness, obscenity, offensiveness, pollution, porn, pornography, ribaldry, smuttiness, spitefulness, squalor, uncleanliness, unpleasantness, unsavouriness, waspishness.

nasty *adj* abusive, annoying, bad, bad-tempered, base, beastly, critical, dangerous, despicable, dirty, disagreeable, disgusting, distasteful, filthy, foul, gross, horrible, impure, indecent, lascivious, lewd, licentious, loathsome, low-down, malicious, malodorous, mean, mephitic, nauseating, noisome, objectionable, obnoxious, obscene, odious, offensive, painful, polluted, pornographic, repellent, repugnant, ribald, serious, severe, sickening, smutty, spiteful, unappetising, unpleasant, unsavoury, vicious, vile, waspish.

antonyms agreeable, clean, decent, pleasant.

nation *n* citizenry, commonwealth, community, country, people, population, race, realm, society, state, tribe.

national *adj* civil, countrywide, domestic, general, governmental, internal, nationwide, public, social, state, widespread.

n citizen, indigene, inhabitant, native, resident, subject.

nationalism *n* allegiance, chauvinism, ethnocentricity, fealty, jingoism, loyalty, nationality, patriotism, xenophobia, xenophoby.

nationalistic *adj* chauvinistic, ethnocentrist, jingoistic, loyal, patriotic, xenophobic.

nationality *n* birth, clan, ethnic group, nation, race, tribe.

native *adj* aboriginal, autochthonous, built-in, congenital, domestic, endemic, genuine, hereditary, home, home-born, home-bred, home-grown, home-made, inborn, inbred, indigene, indigenous, ingrained, inherent, inherited, innate, instinctive, intrinsic, inveterate, local, mother, natal, natural, original, real, vernacular.

n aborigine, autochthon, citizen, countryman, dweller, indigene, inhabitant, national, resident.

antonyms foreigner, outsider, stranger.

nativity *n* birth, childbirth, delivery, parturition.

natter *v* blather, blether, chatter, confab, confabulate, gab, gabble, gossip, jabber, jaw, prate, prattle, talk.

n blather, blether, chat, chinwag, chitchat, confab, confabulation, conversation, gab, gabble, gabfest, gossip, jabber, jaw, palaver, prattle, talk.

natty *adj* chic, dapper, elegant, fashionable, neat, ritzy, smart, snazzy, spruce, stylish, swanky, trim.

natural *adj* artless, candid, characteristic, common, congenital, constitutional, essential, everyday, frank, genuine, inborn, indigenous, ingenuous, inherent, innate, instinctive, intuitive, legitimate, logical, natal, native, normal, open, ordinary, organic, plain, pure, real, regular, simple, spontaneous, typical, unaffected, unbleached, unforced, unlaboured, unlearned, unmixed, unpolished, unpretentious, unrefined, unsophisticated, unstudied, untaught, usual, whole.

antonyms abnormal, affected, alien, artificial, pretended, unnatural.

naturalise *v* acclimate, acclimatise, acculturate, accustom, adapt, adopt, domesticate, endenizen, enfranchise, familiarise, habituate.

naturalistic *adj* graphic, lifelike, natural, photographic, realistic, real-life, representational, true-to-life.

naturally *adj* absolutely, artlessly, as a matter of course, candidly, certainly, customarily, frankly, genuinely, informally, normally, of course, plainly, simply, spontaneously, typically, unaffectedly, unpretentiously.

naturalness *n* artlessness, candidness, frankness, genuineness, informality, ingenuousness, openness, plainness, pureness, purity, realism, simpleness, simplicity, spontaneity, spontaneousness, unaffectedness, unpretentiousness, wholeness.

nature[1] *n* attributes, category, character, complexion, constitution, cosmos, creation, description, disposition, earth, environment, essence, features, humour, inbeing, inscape, kind, make-up, mood, outlook, quality, sort, species, style, temper, temperament, traits, type, universe, variety, world.

nature[2] *n* country, countryside, landscape, natural history, scenery.

naught *n* nil, nothing, nothingness, nought, zero, zilch.

naughty *adj* annoying, bad, bawdy, blue, disobedient, exasperating, fractious, impish, improper, lewd, misbehaved, mischievous, obscene, off-colour, perverse, playful, refractory, remiss, reprehensible, ribald, risqué, roguish, sinful, smutty, teasing, vulgar, wayward, wicked, worthless.

antonyms good, polite, well-behaved.

nausea *n* abhorrence, aversion, biliousness, disgust, loathing, motion sickness, qualm(s), queasiness, repugnance, retching, revulsion, sickness, squeamishness, vomiting.

nauseate *v* disgust, horrify, offend, repel, repulse, revolt, sicken, turn one's stomach.

nauseating *adj* abhorrent, detestable, disgusting, distasteful, fulsome, loathsome, nauseous, offensive, repugnant, repulsive, revolting, sickening.

nautical *adj* boating, marine, maritime, naval, oceanic, sailing, seafaring, sea-going, yachting.

naval *adj* marine, maritime, nautical, sea.

navel *n* belly-button, centre, hub, middle, omphalos, tummy-button, umbilicus.

navigate *v* con, cross, cruise, direct, drive, guide, handle, helm, journey, manoeuvre, pilot, plan, plot, sail, skipper, steer, voyage.

navigation *n* aviation, cruising, helmsmanship, pilotage, sailing, seamanship, steering, voyaging.

navigator *n* helmsman, mariner, pilot, seaman.

navvy *n* digger, ganger, labourer, worker, workman.

navy *n* argosy, armada, fleet, flota, flotilla, navarchy, ships, warships.

near *adj* accessible, adjacent, adjoining, akin, allied, alongside, approaching, at close quarters, attached, beside, bordering, close, connected, contiguous, dear, familiar, forthcoming, handy, imminent, impending, in the offing, intimate, looming, near-at-hand, nearby, neighbouring, next, nigh, on the cards, proximal, related, touching.

antonyms distant, far, remote.

near thing close shave, narrow escape, nasty moment, near miss.

nearby *adj* accessible, adjacent, adjoining, convenient, handy, near, neighbouring.

antonym faraway.

adv at close quarters, close at hand, near, not far away, within reach.

nearly *adv* about, all but, almost, approaching, approximately, as good as, closely, just about, not quite, practically, pretty much, pretty well, roughly, virtually, well-nigh.

nearness *n* accessibility, availability, chumminess, closeness, contiguity, dearness, familiarity, handiness, immediacy, imminence, intimacy, juxtaposition, propinquity, proximity, vicinity.

neat *adj* accurate, adept, adroit, agile, apt, clean-cut, clever, dainty, deft, dexterous, dinky, efficient, effortless, elegant, expert, fastidious, genty, graceful, handy, methodical, nice, nimble, orderly, practised, precise, pure, shipshape, skilful, smart, spick-and-span, spruce, straight, stylish, systematic, tiddley, tidy, trig, trim, uncluttered, undiluted, unmixed, well-judged.

antonyms disordered, disorderly, messy, untidy.

neaten *v* arrange, clean up, groom, put to rights, smarten, straighten, tidy, trim.

neatly *adv* accurately, adeptly, adroitly, agilely, aptly, cleverly, daintily, deftly, dexterously, efficiently, effortlessly, elegantly, expertly, fastidiously, featly, gracefully, handily, methodically, nicely, nimbly, precisely, skilfully, smartly, sprucely, stylishly, systematically, tidily.

antonyms inelegantly, inexpertly, unskilfully, untidily.

neatness *n* accuracy, adeptness, adroitness, agility, aptness, cleverness, daintiness, deftness, dexterity, disorderliness, efficiency, elegance, expertness, fastidiousness, grace, gracefulness, handiness, inelegance, methodicalness, niceness, nicety, nimbleness, orderliness, preciseness, precision, skilfulness, skill, smartness, spruceness, straightness, style, stylishness, tidiness, trimness, untidyness.

nebulous *adj* ambiguous, amorphous, cloudy, confused, dim, fuzzy, hazy, imprecise, indefinite, indeterminate, indistinct, misty, murky, obscure, shadowy, shapeless, uncertain, unclear, unformed, unspecific, vague.

antonym clear.

necessarily *adv* accordingly, automatically, axiomatically, by definition, certainly, compulsorily, consequently, incontrovertibly, ineluctably, inescapably, inevitably, inexorably, naturally, nolens volens, of course, of necessity, perforce, therefore, thus, willy-nilly.

necessary *adj* certain, compulsory, de rigueur, essential, fated, imperative, indispensable, ineluctable, inescapable, inevitable, inexorable, mandatory, must, needed, needful, obligatory, required, requisite, unavoidable, vital.

antonyms inessential, unimportant, unnecessary.

necessitate *v* call for, coerce, compel, constrain, demand, entail, force, impel, involve, oblige, require.

necessities *n* essentials, exigencies, fundamentals, indispensables, needs, requirements.

necessity *n* ananke, compulsion, demand, desideratum, destiny, destitution, essential, exigency, extremity, fate, fundamental, indigence, indispensability, inevitability, inexorableness, necessary, need, needfulness, obligation, penury, poverty, prerequisite, privation, requirement, requisite, sine qua non, want.

neck *n* halse, nape, scrag, scruff.

necklace *n* carcanet, chain, choker, gorget, lavallière, locket, negligée, pendant, rivière, torc, torque.

necromancy *n* black art, black magic, conjuration, demonology, divination, enchantment, hoodoo, magic, sorcery, thaumaturgy, voodoo, witchcraft, witchery, wizardry.

need *v* call for, crave, demand, lack, miss, necessitate, require, want.

n besoin, demand, deprivation, desideratum, destitution, distress, egence, egency, emergency, essential, exigency, extremity, impecuniousness, inadequacy, indigence, insufficiency, lack, longing, necessity, neediness, obligation, paucity, penury, poverty, privation, requirement, requisite, shortage, urgency, want, wish.

antonym sufficiency.

needed *adj* called for, compulsory, desired, essential, lacking, necessary, obligatory, required, requisite, wanted.

antonyms unnecessary, unneeded.

needful *adj* essential, indispensable, necessary, needed, needy, required, requisite, stipulated, vital.

antonyms excess, needless, superfluous.

needle *v* aggravate, annoy, bait, goad, harass, irk, irritate, nag, nettle, pester, prick, prod, provoke, rile, ruffle, spur, sting, taunt, torment.

needless *adj* causeless, dispensable, excessive, expendable, gratuitous, groundless, inessential, non-essential, pointless, purposeless, redundant, superfluous, uncalled-for, unessential, unnecessary, unwanted, useless.

antonyms necessary, needful.

needy *adj* deprived, destitute, disadvantaged, impecunious, impoverished, indigent, penniless, penurious, poor, poverty-stricken, underprivileged.

antonyms affluent, wealthy, well-off.

ne'er-do-well *n* black sheep, good-for-nothing, idler, layabout, loafer, scapegallows, vaurien, waster, wastrel.

nefarious *adj* abominable, atrocious, base, criminal, depraved, detestable, dreadful, evil, execrable, foul, heinous, horrible, infamous, infernal, iniquitous, monstrous, odious, opprobrious, satanic, shameful, sinful, unholy, vicious, vile, villainous, wicked.

antonym exemplary.

negate *v* abrogate, annul, cancel, contradict, countermand, deny, disallow, disprove, gainsay, invalidate, neutralise, nullify, oppose, quash, refute, repeal, rescind, retract, reverse, revoke, void, wipe out.

antonym affirm.

negation *n* antithesis, cancellation, contradiction, contrary, converse, counterpart, denial, disavowal, disclaimer, inverse, neutralisation, nullification, opposite, rejection, renunciation, repeal, reverse, veto.

antonym affirmation.

negative *adj* annulling, antagonistic, apathetic, below zero, colourless, contradictory, contrary, counteractive, cynical, denying, dissenting, gloomy, invalidating, jaundiced, neutralising, nullifying, opposing, pessimistic, refusing, rejecting, unco-operative, unenthusiastic, uninterested, unwilling, weak.

antonyms optimistic, positive.

n contradiction, denial, opposite, refusal.

neglect *v* contemn, disdain, disprovide, disregard, forget, ignore, leave alone, let slide, omit, overlook, pass by, pigeon-hole, rebuff, scorn, shirk, skimp, slight, spurn.

antonyms cherish, nurture, treasure.

n carelessness, default, dereliction, disdain, disregard, disrespect, failure, forgetfulness, heedlessness, inattention, indifference, laches, laxity, laxness, neglectfulness, negligence, oversight, slackness, slight, slovenliness, unconcern.

neglected *adj* abandoned, derelict, disregarded, overgrown, unappreciated, uncared-for, uncultivated, underestimated, undervalued, unhusbanded, unmaintained, untended, untilled, unweeded.

antonyms cherished, treasured.

neglectful *adj* careless, disregardful, forgetful, heedless, inattentive, indifferent, lax, negligent, oblivious, remiss, thoughtless, uncaring, unmindful.

antonyms attentive, careful.

negligence *n* carelessness, default, dereliction, disregard, failure, forgetfulness, heedlessness, inadvertence, inattention, inattentiveness, indifference, laxity, laxness, neglect, neglectfulness, omission, oversight, remissness, shortcoming, slackness, slight, stupidity, thoughtlessness.

antonyms attentiveness, care, regard.

negligent *adj* careless, cursory, disregardful, forgetful, inattentive, indifferent, lax, neglectful, nonchalant, offhand, regardless, remiss, slack, thoughtless, uncareful, uncaring, unmindful, unthinking.

antonyms attentive, careful, heedful, scrupulous.

negligible *adj* imperceptible, inconsequential, insignificant, minor, minute, neglectable, nugatory, petty, small, trifling, trivial, unimportant.

antonym significant.

negotiate *v* adjudicate, arbitrate, arrange, bargain, broke, clear, conciliate, confer, consult, contract, cross, deal, debate, discuss, get past, handle, manage, mediate, parley, pass, settle, surmount, transact, traverse, treat, work out.

negotiation *n* arbitration, bargaining, debate, diplomacy, discussion, mediation, transaction, wheeler-dealing.

negotiator *n* adjudicator, ambassador, arbitrator, broker, delegate, diplomat, go-between, intermediary, mediator, moderator.

neigh *v* bray, hinny, whinny.

neighbourhood *n* community, confines, district, environs, locale, locality, precincts, proximity, purlieus, quarter, region, surroundings, vicinage, vicinity.

neighbouring *adj* abutting, adjacent, adjoining, bordering, connecting, contiguous, near, nearby, nearest, next, surrounding, vicinal.

antonyms distant, faraway, remote.

neighbourly *adj* amiable, chummy, civil, companionable, considerate, friendly, genial, helpful, hospitable, kind, obliging, sociable, social, solicitous, well-disposed.

nemesis *n* destiny, destruction, fate, punishment, retribution, vengeance.

nerve *n* audacity, boldness, bottle, brass, bravery, brazenness, cheek, chutzpah, coolness, courage, daring, determination, effrontery, endurance, energy, fearlessness, firmness, force, fortitude, gall, gameness, grit, guts, hardihood, impertinence, impudence, insolence, intrepidity, mettle, might, pluck, resolution, sauce, spirit, spunk, steadfastness, temerity, vigour, will.

antonyms cowardice, weakness.

v bolster, brace, embolden, encourage, fortify, hearten, invigorate, steel, strengthen.

antonym unnerve.

nerveless *adj* afraid, cowardly, debilitated, enervated, feeble, flabby, inert, nervous, slack, spineless, timid, unnerved, weak.

antonyms bold, grave, strong.

nerve-racking *adj* annoying, difficult, disquieting, distressing, frightening, harassing, harrowing, maddening, stressful, tense, trying, worrisome, worrying.

nerves *n* anxiety, fretfulness, (h)abdabs, heebie-jeebies, nervousness, strain, stress, tension, worry.

nervous *adj* agitated, anxious, apprehensive, edgy, excitable, fearful, fidgety, flustered, hesitant, highly-strung, high-strung, hysterical, jittery, jumpy, nervy, neurotic, on edge, shaky, tense, timid, timorous, twitchy, uneasy, uptight, weak, windy, worried.

antonyms bold, calm, confident, cool, relaxed.

nervousness *n* agitation, anxiety, disquiet, excitability, fluster, (h)abdabs, heebie-jeebies, perturbation, tension, timidity, touchiness, tremulousness, vapours, willies, worry.

antonyms calmness, coolness.

nervy *adj* agitated, anxious, excitable, fidgety, jittery, jumpy, nervous, on edge, restless, tense, unquiet.

antonyms calm, relaxed.

nest *n* breeding-ground, burrow, den, drey, earth, form, formicary, haunt, hideaway, hotbed, nid(e), nidus, refuge, resort, retreat.

nest-egg *n* bottom drawer, cache, deposit, fund(s), reserve(s), savings, store.

nestle *v* cuddle, curl up, ensconce, huddle, nuzzle, snuggle.

nestling *adj* baby, chick, fledgling, suckling, weanling.

net[1] *n* drag, drag-net, drift, drift-net, drop-net, lattice, mesh, netting, network, open-work, reticulum, tracery, web.

v apprehend, bag, benet, capture, catch, enmesh, ensnare, entangle, nab, trap.

net[2] *adj* after tax, clear, final, lowest, nett.

v accumulate, bring in, clear, earn, gain, make, obtain, realise, reap, receive, secure.

nether *adj* basal, below, beneath, bottom, inferior, infernal, lower, Plutonian, Stygian, under, underground.

nettle *v* annoy, chafe, discountenance, exasperate, fret, goad, harass, incense, irritate, needle, pique, provoke, ruffle, sting, tease, vex.

nettled *adj* aggrieved, angry, annoyed, chafed, cross, exasperated, galled, goaded, harassed, huffy, incensed, irritable, irritated, miffed, needled, peeved, peevish, piqued, provoked, riled, ruffled, stung, vexed.

network *n* arrangement, channels, circuitry, complex, convolution, grid, grill, interconnections, labyrinth, maze, mesh, meshwork, net, nexus, organisation, plexus, rete, reticulation, structure, system, tracks, web.

neurosis *n* abnormality, affliction, derangement, deviation, disturbance, instability, maladjustment, obsession, phobia.

neurotic *adj* abnormal, anxious, compulsive, deviant, disordered, distraught, disturbed, maladjusted, manic, morbid, nervous, obsessive, overwrought, unhealthy, unstable, wearisome.

antonyms normal, stable.

neuter *v* caponise, castrate, doctor, dress, emasculate, fix, geld, spay.

neutral *adj* colourless, disinterested, dispassionate, dull, even-handed, expressionless, impartial, indeterminate, indifferent, indistinct, indistinguishable, intermediate, non-aligned, non-committal, nondescript, non-partisan, unbia(s)sed, uncommitted, undecided, undefined, uninvolved, unprejudiced.

antonyms biased, prejudiced.

neutralise *v* cancel, counteract, counterbalance, counterpoise, frustrate, invalidate, negate, nullify, offset, undo.

neutrality *n* detachment, disinterest, disinterestedness, impartiality, impartialness, non-alignment, non-intervention, non-involvement, unbiasedness.

never *adv* at no time, Greek calends, not at all, not on your life, not on your Nellie, on no account, under no circumstances, when pigs fly.

antonym always.

never-ending *adj* boundless, ceaseless, constant, continual, continuous, eternal, everlasting, incessant, interminable, non-stop, permanent, perpetual, persistent, relentless, Sisyphean, unbroken, unceasing, unchanging, uninterrupted, unremitting.

antonyms fleeting, transitory.

nevertheless *adv* anyhow, anyway, but, even so, however, nonetheless, notwithstanding, regardless, still, yet.

new *adj* added, advanced, altered, changed, contemporary, current, different, extra, fresh, improved, latest, modern, modernised, modernistic, modish, more, newborn, newfangled, novel, original, recent, redesigned, renewed, restored, supplementary, topical, trendy, ultra-modern, unfamiliar, unknown, unused, unusual, up-to-date, up-to-the-minute, virgin.

antonyms hackneyed, old, outdated, out-of-date, usual.

newcomer *n* alien, arrival, arriviste, beginner, colonist, foreigner, immigrant, incomer, Johnny-come-lately, novice, outsider, parvenu, settler, stranger.

newfangled *adj* contemporary, fashionable, futuristic, gimmicky, modern, modernistic, new, novel, recent, trendy.

antonym old-fashioned.

newly *adv* afresh, anew, freshly, just, lately, latterly, recently.

newness *n* freshness, innovation, novelty, oddity, originality, recency, strangeness, unfamiliarity, uniqueness, unusualness.

antonyms oldness, ordinariness.

news *n* account, advice, bulletin, communiqué, disclosure, dispatch, exposé, gen, gossip, hearsay, information, intelligence, latest, leak, release, report, revelation, rumour, scandal, statement, story, tidings, update, word.

newspaper *n* blat(t), daily, gazette, journal, organ, paper, periodical, publication, rag, sheet, tabloid.

newsworthy *adj* arresting, important, interesting, notable, noteworthy, remarkable, reportable, significant, stimulating, unusual.

next *adj* adjacent, adjoining, closest, consequent, ensuing, following, later, nearest, neighbouring, sequent, sequential, subsequent, succeeding.

antonyms preceding, previous.

adv afterwards, later, subsequently, then, thereafter.

nibble *n* bit, bite, crumb, morsel, peck, piece, snack, soupçon, taste, titbit.

v bite, eat, gnaw, knap, knapple, munch, nip, nosh, peck, pickle.

nice *adj* accurate, agreeable, amiable, attractive, careful, charming, commendable, courteous, critical, cultured, dainty, delicate, delightful, discriminating, exact, exacting, fastidious, fine, finical, friendly, genteel, good, kind, lik(e)able, meticulous, neat, particular, pleasant, pleasurable, polite, precise, prepossessing, punctilious, purist, refined, respectable, rigorous, scrupulous, strict, subtle, tidy, trim, virtuous, well-bred, well-mannered.

antonyms careless, disagreeable, haphazard, nasty, unpleasant.

nicely *adv* acceptably, accurately, agreeable, amiably, attractively, carefully, charmingly, commendably, courteously, critically, daintily, delicately, delightfully, discriminatingly, elegantly, exactingly, exactly, fastidiously, finely, genteelly, kindly, lik(e)ably, meticulously, neatly, pleasantly, pleasingly, pleasurably, politely, precisely, prepossessingly, respectably, rigorously, scrupulously, strictly, subtly, tidily, trimly, virtuously, well.

antonyms carelessly, disagreeably, haphazardly, nastily, unpleasantly.

niceness *n* accuracy, agreeableness, amiability, attractiveness, care, carefulness, charm, courtesy, daintiness, delicacy, delightfulness, discrimination, exactitude, exactness, fastidiousness, fineness, friendliness, gentility, goodness, kindness, lik(e)ableness, meticulousness, neatness, pleasantness, pleasurableness, politeness, preciseness, precision, punctilio, punctiliousness, purism, refinement, respectability, rigorousness, rigour, scrupulosity, scrupulousness, strictness, subtleness, subtlety, tidiness, trimness, virtue.

antonyms carelessness, disagreeableness, haphazardness, nastiness, unpleasantness.

nicety *n* accuracy, daintiness, delicacy, discrimination, distinction, exactness, fastidiousness, finesse, finicality, meticulousness, minuteness, nuance, precision, punctilio, quiddit(y), refinement, subtlety.

niche[1] *n* alcove, corner, cubby, cubby-hole, hollow, nook, opening, recess.

niche[2] *n* calling, métier, pigeon-hole, place, position, slot, vocation.

nick[1] *n* chip, cut, damage, dent, indent, indentation, mark, notch, scar, score, scratch, snick.

v chip, cut, damage, dent, indent, mark, notch, scar, score, scratch, snick.

nick[2] *v* finger, knap, knock off, lag, pilfer, pinch, snitch, steal.

nickname *n* cognomen, diminutive, epithet, familiarity, label, moni(c)ker, pet name, sobriquet.

nifty *adj* adroit, agile, apt, chic, clever, deft, enjoyable, excellent, neat, nippy, pleasing, quick, sharp, smart, spruce, stylish.

niggardliness *n* avarice, avariciousness, beggarliness, cheese-paring, closeness, covetousness, frugality, grudgingness, inadequacy, insufficiency, meagreness, meanness, mercenariness, miserableness, miserliness, nearness, paltriness, parsimony, penuriousness, scantiness, skimpiness, smallness, sordidness, sparingness, stinginess, thrift, tight-fistedness, ungenerousness, wretchedness.

antonyms bountifulness, generosity.

niggardly *adj* avaricious, beggarly, cheese-paring, close, covetous, frugal, grudging, hard-fisted, inadequate, insufficient, meagre, mean, mercenary, miserable, miserly, near, paltry, parsimonious, penurious, scanty, skimpy, small, sordid, sparing, stinging, stingy, tight-fisted, ungenerous, ungiving, wretched.

antonyms bountiful, generous.

night *n* dark, darkmans, darkness, dead of night, hours of darkness, night-time.

antonyms day, daytime.

nightclub *n* cabaret, club, disco, discotheque, nightspot, niterie, nitery, watering-hole.

nightfall *n* crepuscule, dusk, eve, evening, eventide, gloaming, moonrise, sundown, sunset, twilight, vespers.

antonyms dawn, sunrise.

nightmare *n* bad dream, ephialtes, hallucination, horror, incubus, ordeal, succubus, torment, trial, tribulation.

nightmarish *adj* agonising, alarming, creepy, disturbing, dreadful, fell, frightening, harrowing, horrible, horrific, scaring, terrifying, unreal.

nihilism *n* abnegation, agnosticism, anarchy, atheism, cynicism, denial, disbelief, disorder, emptiness, lawlessness, negation, negativism, non-existence, nothingness, nullity, oblivion, pessimism, rejection, renunciation, repudiation, scepticism, terrorism.

nihilist *n* agitator, agnostic, anarchist, antinomian, atheist, cynic, disbeliever, extremist, negationist, negativist, pessimist, revolutionary, sceptic, terrorist.

nil *n* duck, goose-egg, love, naught, nihil, none, nothing, zero.

nimble *adj* active, agile, alert, brisk, deft, dexterous, light-foot(ed), lissom(e), lively, nippy, proficient, prompt, quick, quick-witted, ready, smart, sprightly, spry, swift, volant.

antonyms awkward, clumsy.

nimbleness *n* adroitness, agility, alacrity, alertness, deftness, dexterity, finesse, grace, legerity, lightness, niftiness, nippiness, skill, smartness, sprightliness, spryness.

nimbly *adv* actively, acutely, agilely, alertly, briskly, deftly, dexterously, easily, fast, featly, fleetly, proficiently, promptly, quickly, quick-wittedly, readily, sharply, smartly, snappily, speedily, spryly, swiftly.

antonyms awkwardly, clumsily.

nincompoop *n* blockhead, dimwit, dolt, dunce, fool, idiot, ignoramus, ninny, nitwit, noodle, numskull, sap, saphead, simpleton.

nip[1] *v* bite, catch, check, clip, compress, grip, nibble, pinch, snag, snap, sneap, snip, squeeze, tweak, twitch.

nip[2] *n* dram, draught, drop, finger, mouthful, peg, portion, shot, sip, slug, snifter, soupçon, sup, swallow, taste.

nipple *n* breast, dug, mamilla, pap, teat, tit, titty, udder.

nippy[1] *adj* astringent, biting, chilly, nipping, pungent, sharp, stinging.

nippy[2] *adj* active, agile, fast, nimble, quick, speedy, sprightly, spry.

antonym slow.

nirvana *n* bliss, ecstasy, exaltation, joy, paradise, peace, serenity, tranquillity.

nit-picking *adj* captious, carping, cavilling, finicky, fussy, hair-splitting, hypercritical, pedantic, pettifogging, quibbling.

nitwit *n* dimwit, drongo, dummy, fool, half-wit, nincompoop, ninny, numskull, simpleton.

no doubt admittedly, assuredly, certainly, doubtless, doubtlessly, presumably, probably, surely, unquestionably.

nob *n* aristocrat, big shot, bigwig, fat cat, nabob, personage, toff, VIP.

nobble *v* bribe, disable, filch, get at, grab, hamper, handicap, incapacitate, influence, injure, intimidate, knock off, nick, outwit, pilfer, pinch, purloin, snitch, steal, swipe, take, weaken.

nobility *n* aristocracy, dignity, élite, eminence, excellence, generosity, gentry, grandeur, greatness, high society, honour, illustriousness, incorruptibility, integrity, loftiness, lords, magnanimity, magnificence, majesty, nobleness, nobles, patricians, peerage, stateliness, sublimity, superiority, uprightness, virtue, worthiness.

antonyms baseness, proletariat.

noble *n* aristocrat, baron, gentilhomme, grand seigneur, lord, nobleman, patrician, peer.

antonyms pleb, prole.

adj aristocratic, august, blue-blooded, dignified, distinguished, elevated, eminent, excellent, generous, gentle, grand, great, high-born, honourable, honoured, imposing, impressive, lofty, lordly, magnanimous, magnificent, majestic, patrician, splendid, stately, titled, upright, virtuous, worthy.

antonyms base, ignoble, low-born.

nobody *n* also-ran, cipher, lightweight, man of straw, menial, minnow, nonentity, no-one, nothing, Walter Mitty.

antonym somebody.

nod *v* acknowledge, agree, assent, beckon, bob, bow, concur, dip, doze, droop, drowse, duck, gesture, indicate, nap, salute, sign, signal, sleep, slip up, slump.

n acknowledgement, beck, cue, gesture, greeting, indication, salute, sign, signal.

node *n* bud, bump, burl, caruncle, growth, knob, knot, lump, nodule, process, protuberance, swelling.

noise *n* babble, ballyhoo, blare, brattle, chirm, clamour, clash, clatter, coil, commotion, cry, din, fracas, hubbub, outcry, pandemonium, racket, row, sound, talk, tumult, uproar.

antonyms quiet, silence.

v advertise, announce, bruit, circulate, gossip, publicise, repeat, report, rumour.

noiseless *adj* hushed, inaudible, mous(e)y, mute, muted, quiet, silent, soundless, still.

antonyms loud, noisy.

noisome *adj* bad, baneful, deleterious, disgusting, fetid, foul, fulsome, harmful, hurtful, injurious, malodorous, mephitic, mischievous, noxious, offensive, pernicious, pestiferous, pestilential, poisonous, putrid, reeking, smelly, stinking, unhealthy, unwholesome.

antonyms balmy, pleasant, wholesome.

noisy *adj* boisterous, cacophonous, chattering, clamorous, clangorous, deafening, ear-piercing, ear-splitting, horrisonant, loud, obstreperous, piercing, plangent, rackety, riotous, strepitant, strident, tumultuous, turbulent, uproarious, vocal, vociferous.

antonyms peaceful, quiet, silent.

nom de plume alias, allonym, assumed name, nom de guerre, pen name, pseudonym.

nomad *n* drifter, itinerant, migrant, rambler, roamer, rover, traveller, vagabond, vagrant, wanderer.

nomadic *adj* drifting, gypsy, itinerant, migrant, migratory, peregrinating, peripatetic, roaming, roving, travelling, unsettled, vagrant, wandering.

nomenclature *n* classification, codification, locution, naming, phraseology, taxonomy, terminology, vocabulary.

nominal *adj* fainéant, figurehead, formal, inconsiderable, insignificant, minimal, ostensible, pretended, professed, puppet, purported, self-styled, small, so-called, soi-disant, supposed, symbolic, theoretical, titular, token, trifling, trivial.

antonyms actual, genuine, real, true.

nominate *v* appoint, assign, choose, commission, designate, elect, elevate, empower, mention, name, present, propose, put up, recommend, select, submit, suggest, term.

nomination *n* appointment, choice, designation, election, proposal, recommendation, selection, submission, suggestion.

nominee *n* appointee, assignee, candidate, contestant, entrant, protégé, runner.

non compos mentis crazy, deranged, insane, mentally ill, of unsound mind, unbalanced, unhinged.

antonyms sane, stable.

non-aligned *adj* impartial, independent, neutral, uncommitted, undecided.

nonchalance *n* aplomb, calm, composure, cool, equanimity, imperturbability, indifference, insouciance, pococurant(e)ism, sang-froid, self-possession, unconcern.

antonyms anxiousness, worriedness.

nonchalant *adj* airy, apathetic, blasé, calm, careless, casual, collected, cool, detached, dispassionate, impassive, indifferent, insouciant, offhand, pococurante, unconcerned, unemotional, unperturbed.

antonyms anxious, careful, concerned, worried.

non-committal *adj* ambiguous, careful, cautious, circumspect, cunctatious, cunctative, cunctatory, discreet, equivocal, evasive, guarded, indefinite, neutral, politic, reserved, tactful, temporising, tentative, unrevealing, vague, wary.

nonconformist *n* deviant, dissenter, dissentient, eccentric, heretic, iconoclast, individualist, maverick, oddball, protester, radical, rebel, seceder, secessionist.

antonym conformist.

nonconformity *n* deviation, dissent, eccentricity, heresy, heterodoxy, secession, unconventionality.

antonym conformity.

nondescript *adj* commonplace, dull, featureless, indeterminate, mousy, ordinary, plain, unclassified, undistinctive, undistinguished, unexceptional, uninspiring, uninteresting, unmemorable, unremarkable, vague.

none *pron* nil, nobody, no-one, not any, not one, zero, zilch.

nonentity *n* cipher, dandiprat, drip, drongo, earthworm, gnatling, lightweight, mediocrity, nobody.

non-essential *adj* dispensable, excessive, expendable, extraneous, extrinsic(al), inessential, peripheral, superfluous, supplementary, unimportant, unnecessary.

antonym essential.

none-the-less *adv* even so, howbeit, however, natheless, nevertheless, notwithstanding, yet.

non-existence *n* illusiveness, insubtantiality, unbeing, unreality.

antonym existence.

non-existent *adj* chimerical, fancied, fictional, hallucinatory, hypothetical, illusory, imaginary, imagined, immaterial, incorporeal, insubstantial, legendary, missing, mythical, null, unreal.

antonyms actual, existing, real.

non-flammable *adj* fire-proof, fire-resistant, flame-resistant, incombustible, uninflammable.

antonyms flammable, inflammable.

non-partisan *adj* detached, dispassionate, even-handed, impartial, independent, neutral, objective, unbiased, unprejudiced.

antonym partisan.

nonplus *v* astonish, astound, baffle, bewilder, confound, confuse, discomfit, disconcert, discountenance, dismay, dumbfound, embarrass, flabbergast, flummox, mystify, perplex, puzzle, stump, stun, take aback.

nonsense *n* absurdity, balderdash, balls, baloney, bilge, blah, blather, blethers, bollocks, bombast, bosh, bull, bullshit, bunk, bunkum, claptrap, cobblers, codswallop, crap, double-Dutch, drivel, fadaise, faddle, fandangle, fatuity, fiddle-de-dee, fiddle-faddle, fiddlesticks, flapdoodle, folly, foolishness, fudge, gaff, galimatias, gammon, gas and gaiters, gibberish, gobbledygook, havers, hogwash, hooey, inanity, jabberwock(y), jest, ludicrousness, moonshine, no-meaning, piffle, pulp, ridiculousness, rot, rubbish, senselessness, silliness, squish, squit, stuff, stultiloquence, stupidity, tar(r)adiddle, tommy-rot, tosh, trash, twaddle, twattle, unreason, waffle.

antonym sense.

nonsensical *adj* absurd, crazy, daft, fatuous, foolish, inane, incomprehensible, irrational, ludicrous, meaningless, ridiculous, senseless, silly.

antonyms logical, sensible.

non-stop *adj* ceaseless, constant, continuous, direct, endless, incessant, interminable, never-ending, on-going, relentless, round-the-clock, steady, unbroken, unceasing, unending, unfaltering, uninterrupted, unrelenting, unremitting.

antonyms intermittent, occasional.

adv ceaselessly, constantly, continuously, directly, endlessly, incessantly, interminably, relentlessly, round-the-clock, steadily, unbrokenly, unceasingly, unendingly, unfalteringly, uninterruptedly, unrelentingly, unremittingly.

antonyms imtermittently, occasionally.

non-violent *adj* dov(e)ish, irenic, pacifist, passive, peaceable, peaceful.

antonym violent.

nook *n* alcove, cavity, corner, cranny, crevice, cubby-hole, hide-out, ingle-nook, nest, niche, opening, recess, retreat, shelter.

norm *n* average, bench-mark, canon, criterion, mean, measure, model, pattern, reference, rule, standard, type, yardstick.

normal *adj* accustomed, acknowledged, average, common, common-or-garden, conventional, habitual, mainstream, natural, ordinary, par for the course, popular, rational, reasonable, regular, routine, run-of-the-mill, sane, standard, straight, typical, usual, well-adjusted.

antonyms abnormal, irregular, odd, peculiar.

normality *n* accustomedness, adjustment, balance, commonness, conventionality, naturalness, ordinariness, popularity, rationality, reason, regularity, routine, routineness, sanity, typicality, usualness.

antonyms abnormality, irregularity, oddity, peculiarity.

normally *adv* as a rule, characteristically, commonly, habitually, ordinarily, regularly, straight, typically, usually.

antonym abnormally.

northern *adj* Arctic, boreal, hyperborean, north, northerly, polar, septentrional.

antonym southern.

nose *n* beak, bill, boko, conk, hooter, neb, proboscis, schnozzle, snitch, snout.

v detect, inquire, interface, intrude, meddle, nudge, nuzzle, pry, push, scent, search, shove, smell, sniff, snoop.

nose-dive *n* dive, drop, header, plummet, plunge, purler.

v dive, drop, plummet, plunge, submerge.

nosegay *n* bouquet, boutonniėe, corsage, posy, spray.

nos(e)y *adj* curious, eavesdropping, inquisitive, interfering, intermeddling, intrusive, meddlesome, officious, prying, snooping.

nostalgia *n* Heimweh, homesickness, longing, mal du pays, pining, regret, regretfulness, remembrance, reminiscence, wistfulness, yearning.

nostalgic *adj* emotional, homesick, longing, maudlin, regretful, romantic, sentimental, wistful.

nosy *see* **nosey**.

not bad all right, average, fair, fair to middling, moderate, OK, passable, reasonable, respectable, satisfactory, so-so, tolerable.

notability *n* celebrity, dignitary, distinction, eminence, esteem, fame, luminary, magnate, notable, personage, renown, somebody, VIP, worthy.

antonym nonentity.

notable *adj* celebrated, conspicuous, distinguished, eminent, evident, extraordinary, famous, impressive, manifest, marked, memorable, noteworthy, noticeable, notorious, outstanding, overt, pre-eminent, pronounced, rare, remarkable, renowned, signal, striking, uncommon, unusual, well-known.

antonyms commonplace, ordinary, usual.

n celebrity, dignitary, luminary, notability, personage, somebody, VIP, worthy.

antonyms nobody, nonentity.

notably *adv* conspicuously, distinctly, eminently, especially, impressively, markedly, noticeably, outstandingly, particularly, remarkably, signally, strikingly, uncommonly.

notation *n* alphabet, characters, code, noting, record, script, shorthand, signs, symbols, system.

notch *n* cleft, cut, degree, grade, incision, indentation, insection, kerf, level, mark, nick, score, sinus, snip, step.

v cut, gimp, indent, mark, nick, raffle, scallop, score, scratch.

notch up achieve, gain, make, record, register, score.

notched *adj* crenellate(d), emarginate, eroded, erose, jagged, jaggy, pinked, serrate(d), serrulate(d).

note *n* annotation, apostil(le), billet, celebrity, character, comment, communication, consequence, distinction, eminence, epistle, epistolet, fame, gloss, heed, indication, jotting, letter, line, mark, memo, memorandum, message, minute, notice, observation, prestige, record, regard, remark, reminder, renown, reputation, signal, symbol, token.

v denote, designate, detect, enter, indicate, mark, mention, notice, observe, perceive, record, register, remark, see, witness.

noted *adj* acclaimed, celebrated, conspicuous, distinguished, eminent, famous, great, illustrious, notable, notorious, prominent, recognised, renowned, respected, well-known.

notes *n* draft, impressions, jottings, outline, record, report, sketch, synopsis.

noteworthy *adj* exceptional, extraordinary, important, notable, on the map, outstanding, remarkable, significant, unusual, visitable.

antonyms commonplace, ordinary, unexceptional, usual.

nothing *n* bagatelle, cipher, damn all, emptiness, nada, naught, nix, nobody, nonentity, non-existence, nothingness, nought, nullity, sweet Fanny Adams, (sweet) fuck all, trifle, void, zero.

antonyms everything, something.

nothingness *n* nada, nihilism, nihility, non-existence, nullity, oblivion, vacuum.

notice *v* descry, detect, discern, distinguish, espy, heed, mark, mind, note, observe, perceive, remark, see, spot.

antonyms ignore, overlook.

n advertisement, advice, affiche, announcement, attention, bill, civility, cognisance, comment, communication, consideration, criticism, heed, instruction, intelligence, intimation, news, note, notification, observation, order, poster, regard, respect, review, sign, warning.

noticeable *adj* appreciable, clear, conspicuous, distinct, dramatic, evident, manifest, measurable, observable, obvious, perceptible, plain, significant, striking, unmistakable.

antonyms hidden, insignificant, obscure.

notification *n* advice, alert, announcement, declaration, disclosure, information, intelligence, message, notice, publication, revelation, statement, telling, warning.

notify *v* acquaint, advise, alert, announce, apprise, declare, disclose, inform, publish, reveal, tell, warn.

notion *n* apprehension, belief, caprice, conceit, concept, conception, concetto, construct, desire, fancy, idea, image, impression, impulse, inclination, inkling, judgement, knowledge, opinion, sentiment, understanding, view, whim, wish.

notional *adj* abstract, classificatory, conceptual, fanciful, hypothetical, ideational, imaginary, speculative, thematic, theoretical, unfounded, unreal, visionary.

antonym real.

notoriety *n* disfame, dishonour, disrepute, esclandre, infamy, obloquy, opprobrium, scandal.

notorious *adj* arrant, blatant, dishonourable, disreputable, egregious, flagrant, glaring, infamous, obvious, open, opprobrious, overt, patent, scandalous, undisputed.

notoriously *adv* arrantly, blatantly, dishonourably, disreputably, egregiously, flagrantly, glaringly, infamously, notably, obviously, openly, opprobriously, overtly, particularly, patently, scandalously, spectacularly, undisputedly.

notwithstanding *adv* although, despite, howbeit, however, natheless, nevertheless, nonetheless, though, withal, yet.

nought *n* naught, nil, nix, nothing, nothingness, zero, zilch.

nourish *v* attend, cherish, comfort, cultivate, encourage, feed, foster, furnish, harbour, maintain, nurse, nurture, promote, supply, support, sustain, tend.

nourishing *adj* alimentative, beneficial, good, healthful, health-giving, nutritious, nutritive, substantial, wholesome.

nourishment *n* aliment, diet, food, goodness, nutriment, nutrition, pabulum, provender, sustenance, viands, victuals.

novel *adj* different, fresh, imaginative, innovative, new, original, rare, singular, strange, surprising, uncommon, unconventional, unfamiliar, unusual.

antonyms familiar, ordinary.

n fiction, narrative, romance, saga, story, tale, yarn.

novelty *n* bagatelle, bauble, curiosity, freshness, gadget, gewgaw, gimcrack, gimmick, innovation, knick-knack, memento, neoterism, newness, oddity, originality, peculiarity, souvenir, strangeness, surprise, trifle, trinket, unfamiliarity, uniqueness.

novice *n* amateur, apprentice, beginner, catechumen, convert, cub, griffin, Johnny-raw, learner, neophyte, newcomer, novitiate, probationer, proselyte, pupil, tiro.

antonyms doyen, expert, professional.

now *adv* at once, at present, directly, ek dum, immediately, instanter, instantly, next, nowadays, presently, promptly, straightaway, these days.

now and then at times, desultorily, from time to time, infrequently, intermittently, now and again, occasionally, on and off, on occasion, once in a while, periodically, sometimes, spasmodically, sporadically.

nowadays *adv* any more, as things are, at the moment, now, these days, today.

noxious *adj* baneful, corrupting, deadly, deleterious, destructive, detrimental, foul, harmful, hurtful, injurious, insalubrious, mephitic(al), morbiferous, morbific, noisome, pernicious, pestilential, poisonous, unhealthy, unwholesome.

antonyms innocuous, wholesome.

nuance *n* degree, distinction, gradation, hint, nicety, overtone, refinement, shade, soupçon, subtlety, suggestion, suspicion, tinge, touch, trace.

nub *n* centre, core, crux, essence, gist, heart, kernel, nitty-gritty, nucleus, pith, point.

nubile *adj* marriageable, ripe, sexy, voluptuous.

nucleus *n* basis, centre, core, crux, focus, heart, heartlet, kernel, nub, pivot.

nude *adj* au naturel, bare, disrobed, exposed, in one's birthday suit, in puris naturalibus, in the altogether, in the buff, naked, starkers, stark-naked, stripped, unattired, unclad, unclothed, uncovered, undraped, undressed, without a stitch.

antonyms clothed, covered, dressed.

nudge *v, n* bump, dig, jog, poke, prod, prompt, push, shove, touch.

nudity *n* bareness, deshabille, dishabille, nakedness, nudism, undress.

nugatory *adj* bootless, futile, inadequate, inconsequential, ineffectual, inoperative, insignificant, invalid, null and void, trifling, trivial, unavailing, useless, vain, valueless, worthless.

antonyms important, significant.

nugget *n* chunk, clump, hunk, lump, mass, piece, wodge.

nuisance *n* annoyance, bore, bother, desagrement, drag, drawback, inconvenience, infliction, irritation, offence, pain, pest, plague, problem, trouble, vexation.

null *adj* characterless, immaterial, incorporeal, ineffectual, inoperative, invalid, non-existent, powerless, useless, vain, valueless, void, worthless.

antonym valid.

nullify *v* abate, abolish, abrogate, annul, cancel, counteract, countervail, invalidate, negate, neutralise, quash, repeal, rescind, revoke, undermine, veto, vitiate, void.

antonym validate.

nullity *n* characterlessness, immateriality, incorporeality, ineffectualness, invalidity, non-existence, powerlessness, uselessness, voidness, worthlessness.

antonym validity.

numb *adj* benumbed, dead, deadened, frozen, immobilised, insensate, insensible, insensitive, paralysed, stunned, stupefied, torpid, unfeeling.

antonym sensitive.

v anaesthetise, benumb, deaden, dull, freeze, immobilise, obtund, paralyse, stun, stupefy.

antonym sensitise.

number[1] *n* aggregate, amount, character, collection, company, count, crowd, digit, figure, folio, horde, index, integer, many, multitude, numeral, quantity, several, sum, throng, total, unit.

v account, add, apportion, calculate, compute, count, enumerate, include, inventory, reckon, tell, total.

number[2] *n* copy, edition, impression, imprint, issue, printing, volume.

numberless *adj* countless, endless, infinite, innumerable, multitudinous, myriad, uncounted, unnumbered, unsummed, untold.

numbness *n* anaesthetisation, deadness, dullness, insensateness, insensibility, insensitivity, paralysis, stupefaction, torpor, unfeelingness.

antonym sensitivity.

numeral *n* character, cipher, digit, figure, folio, integer, number.

numerous *adj* abundant, copious, divers, many, multitudinous, myriad, plentiful, profuse, several, sundry.

antonyms few, scanty.

numerousness *n* abundance, copiousness, manifoldness, multiety, multiplicity, multitudinousness, plentifulness, plurality, profusion.

antonyms scantiness, scarcity.

numskull *n* blockhead, bonehead, buffoon, clot, dimwit, dolt, dope, drongo, dullard, dummy, dunce, dunderhead, fathead, fool, sap, saphead, simpleton, thickhead, twit.

nun *n* abbess, anchoress, ancress, bride of Christ, canoness, mother superior, prioress, sister, vestal, vowess.

nunnery *n* abbey, cloister, convent, priory.

nuptial *adj* bridal, conjugal, connubial, epithalamial, epithalamic, hymeneal, marital, matrimonial, wedded, wedding.

nuptials *n* bridal, espousal, marriage, matrimony, spousals, wedding.

nurse *v* breast-feed, care for, cherish, cultivate, encourage, feed, foster, harbour, keep, nourish, nurture, preserve, promote, succour, suckle, support, sustain, tend, treat, wet-nurse.

n amah, district-nurse, home-nurse, mammy, nanny, nursemaid, sister of mercy, wet nurse.

nurture *n* care, cultivation, development, diet, discipline, education, food, instruction, nourishment, rearing, training, upbringing.

v bring up, care for, cultivate, develop, discipline, educate, feed, instruct, nourish, nurse, rear, school, support, sustain, tend, train.

nut[1] *n* kernel, pip, seed, stone.

nut[2] *n* brain, crackpot, crank, eccentric, head, head-banger, loony, lunatic, madman, maniac, mind, nutcase, nutter, psychopath, reason, senses.

nutriment *n* aliment, diet, food, foodstuff, nourishment, nutrition, pabulum, provender, subsistence, support, sustenance.

nutrition *n* eutrophy, food, nourishment, nutriment, sustenance.

nutritious *adj* alimental, alimentative, beneficial, good, healthful, health-giving, invigorating, nourishing, nutritive, strengthening, substantial, wholesome.

antonyms bad, unwholesome.

nuts *adj* bananas, batty, crazy, demented, deranged, eccentric, insane, irrational, loony, loopy, mad, nutty, psychopathic, unbalanced, unhinged.

antonym sane.

nuts and bolts basics, bits and pieces, components, details, essentials, fundamentals, nitty-gritty, practicalities.

nuzzle *v* burrow, cuddle, fondle, nestle, nudge, pet, snuggle.

nymph *n* damsel, dryad, girl, hamadryad, houri, lass, maid, maiden, naiad, oread, sprite, sylph, undine.

O

oaf *n* baboon, blockhead, bonehead, booby, brute, clod, dolt, dullard, dummy, dunce, fool, galoot, gawk, goon, gorilla, half-wit, hick, hobbledehoy, hulk, idiot, imbecile, lout, lummox, moron, nincompoop, oik, sap, schlemiel, schlep, simpleton, yob.

oafish *adj* blockish, Boeotian, boneheaded, boorish, bovine, brutish, crass, dense, dim, dimwitted, doltish, dull, dumb, heavy, loutish, lubberly, lumbering, moronic, obtuse, schleppy, stupid, thick.

oasis *n* enclave, haven, island, refuge, resting-place, retreat, sanctuary, sanctum, watering-hole.

oath *n* affirmation, assurance, avowal, blasphemy, bond, curse, cuss, expletive, imprecation, malediction, pledge, plight, profanity, promise, swear-word, vow, word, word of honour.

obdurate *adj* adamant, callous, dogged, firm, fixed, flinty, hard, hard-hearted, harsh, immovable, implacable, inexorable, inflexible, intransigent, iron, mulish, obstinate, perverse, pig-headed, relentless, stiff-necked, stony, stubborn, unbending, unfeeling, unrelenting, unshakable, unyielding.

antonyms submissive, tender.

obedience *n* accordance, acquiescence, agreement, allegiance, amenableness, compliance, conformability, deference, docility, dutifulness, duty, observance, passivity, respect, reverence, submission, submissiveness, subservience, tractability.

antonym disobedience.

obedient *adj* acquiescent, amenable, biddable, compliant, deferential, docile, duteous, dutiful, law-abiding, observant, passive, regardful, respectful, sequacious, submissive, subservient, tractable, unquestioning, unresisting, well-trained, yielding.

antonyms disobedient, rebellious, refractory, unruly, wilful.

obeisance *n* bow, congé, curts(e)y, deference, genuflection, homage, kowtow, respect, reverence, salaam, salutation, salute.

obese *adj* bulky, corpulent, Falstaffian, fat, fleshy, gross, heavy, outsize, overweight, paunchy, plump, podgy, ponderous, portly, pursy, roly-poly, rotund, stout, tubby.

antonyms skinny, slender, thin.

obesity *n* bulk, chubbiness, corpulence, embonpoint, fatness, fleshiness, grossness, middle-age(d) spread, overweight, portliness, stoutness, tubbiness.

antonyms skinniness, slenderness, thinness.

obey *v* abide by, act upon, adhere to, be ruled by, bow to, carry out, comply, conform, defer (to), discharge, embrace, execute, follow, fulfil, give in, give way, heed, implement, keep, knuckle under, mind, observe, perform, respond, serve, submit, surrender, take orders from, toe the line, yield.

antonym disobey.

object[1] *n* aim, article, body, butt, design, end, entity, fact, focus, goal, idea, intent, intention, item, motive, objective, phenomenon, point, purpose, raison d'être, reality, reason, recipient, target, thing, victim, visible.

object[2] *v* argue, complain, demur, dissent, expostulate, oppose, protest, rebut, refuse, repudiate, take exception.

antonyms accede, acquiesce, agree, assent.

objection *n* cavil, censure, challenge, complaint, counter-argument, demur, doubt, exception, niggle, opposition, protest, remonstrance, scruple.

antonyms agreement, assent.

objectionable *adj* abhorrent, antisocial, deplorable, despicable, detestable, disagreeable, dislik(e)able, displeasing, distasteful, exceptionable, indecorous, insufferable, intolerable, loathsome, noxious, obnoxious, offensive, regrettable, repugnant, unacceptable, undesirable, unpleasant, unseemly.

antonyms acceptable, pleasant, welcome.

objective *adj* calm, detached, disinterested, dispassionate, equitable, even-handed, fair, impartial, impersonal, judicial, just, open-minded, sensible, sober, unbiased, uncoloured, unemotional, unimpassioned, uninvolved, unprejudiced.

antonyms biased, subjective.

n aim, ambition, aspiration, design, destination, end, goal, intention, mark, object, prize, purpose, target.

objectivity *n* detachment, disinterest, disinterestedness, dispassion, equitableness, even-handedness, impartiality, impersonality, open mind, open-mindedness.

antonyms bias, subjectivity.

obligation *n* accountability, accountableness, agreement, bond, burden, charge, commitment, compulsion, contract, debt, duty, engagement, indebtedness, liability, must, obstriction, onus, promise, requirement, responsibility, stipulation, trust, understanding.

antonyms choice, discretion.

obligatory *adj* binding, bounden, coercive, compulsory, de rigueur, enforced, essential, imperative, mandatory, necessary, required, requisite, statutory, unavoidable.

antonym optional.

oblige *v* accommodate, assist, benefit, bind, coerce, compel, constrain, do a favour, favour, force, gratify, help, impel, indulge, make, necessitate, obligate, please, require, serve.

obliged *adj* appreciative, beholden, bound, compelled, constrained, forced, grateful, gratified, in debt (to), indebted, obligated, required, thankful, under an obligation, under compulsion.

obliging *adj* accommodating, agreeable, aidful, amiable, civil, complaisant, considerate, co-operative, courteous, eager, friendly, good-natured, helpful, kind, polite, willing.

antonyms inconsiderate, unhelpful, unkind.

oblique *adj* angled, aslant, at an angle, back-handed, circuitous, circumlocutory, evasive, inclined, indirect, roundabout, sidelong, skew, slanted, slanting, sloped, sloping, tilted, transverse.

obliquely *adv* askance, askant, aslant, aslope, at an angle, circuitously, diagonally, evasively, in a roundabout way, indirectly, not in so many words, slantwise.

obliterate *v* annihilate, blot out, cancel, delete, destroy, efface, eradicate, erase, expunge, extirpate, rub out, vaporise, wipe out.

obliteration *n* annihilation, blotting out, deletion, effacement, elimination, eradication, erasure, expunction, extirpation, rasure.

oblivion *n* abeyance, blackness, coma, darkness, disregard, eclipse, extinction, forgetfulness, insensibility, Lethe, limbo, neglect, nothingness, obliviousness, obscurity, stupor, unawareness, unconsciousness, void.

antonyms awareness, consciousness.

oblivious *adj* blind, careless, comatose, deaf, disregardful, forgetful, heedless, ignorant, inattentive, insensible, neglectful, negligent, nescient, regardless, unaware, unconcerned, unconscious, unmindful, unobservant.

antonyms aware, conscious.

obloquy *n* abuse, animadversion, aspersion, attack, bad press, blame, calumny, censure, contumely, criticism, defamation, detraction, discredit, disfavour, disgrace, dishonour, humiliation, ignominy, infamy, invective, odium, opprobrium, reproach, shame, slander, stigma, vilification.

obnoxious *adj* abhorrent, abominable, detestable, disagreeable, disgusting, dislik(e)able, foul, fulsome, hateful, horrid, insufferable, loathsome, nasty, nauseating, nauseous, noisome, objectionable, odious, offensive, repellent, reprehensible, repugnant, repulsive, revolting, sickening, unpleasant.

antonyms agreeable, lik(e)able, pleasant.

obscene *adj* atrocious, barrack-room, bawdy, blue, coarse, dirty, disgusting, evil, Fescennine, filthy, foul, gross, heinous, immodest, immoral, improper, impure, indecent, lewd, licentious, loathsome, loose, offensive, outrageous, pornographic, prurient, Rabelaisian, ribald, salacious, scabrous, scurrilous, shameless, shocking, sickening, smutty, suggestive, unchaste, unwholesome, vile, wicked.

antonyms clean, decent, decorous.

obscenity *n* abomination, affront, atrocity, bawdiness, blight, blueness, coarseness, dirtiness, evil, expletive, facetiae, filthiness, foulness, four-letter word, grossness, immodesty, impropriety, impurity, indecency, indelicacy, lewdness, licentiousness, offence, outrage, pornography, profanity, prurience, salacity, scurrility, smut, smuttiness, suggestiveness, swear-word, vileness, vulgarism.

obscure *adj* abstruse, ambiguous, arcane, blurred, caliginous, clear as mud, clouded, cloudy, concealed, confusing, cryptic, deep, Delphic, dim, doubtful, dusky, enigmatic, esoteric, faint, gloomy, hazy, hermetic, hidden, humble, incomprehensible, inconspicuous, indefinite, indistinct, inglorious, intricate, involved, little-known, lowly, minor, misty, murky, mysterious, nameless, obfuscated, occult, opaque, oracular, out-of-the-way, recondite, remote, riddling, shadowy, shady, sombre, tenebr(i)ous, tenebrose, twilight, unclear, undistinguished, unheard-of, unhonoured, unimportant, unknown, unlit, unnoted, unobvious, unrenowned, unseen, unsung, vague, veiled.

antonyms clear, definite, explicit, famous, lucid.

v bedim, befog, block out, blur, cloak, cloud, conceal, cover, darken, dim, disguise, dull, eclipse, hide, mask, muddy, obfuscate, overshadow, screen, shade, shadow, shroud, veil.

antonyms clarify, illuminate.

obscurity *n* abstruseness, ambiguity, complexity, darkness, dimness, dusk, duskiness, fogginess, gloom, haze, haziness, impenetrability, incomprehensibility, inconspicuousness, indistinctness, ingloriousness, insignificance, intricacy, lowliness, mirk, mirkiness, murk, murkiness, mysticism, namelessness, reconditeness, shadowiness, shadows, unimportance, vagueness.

antonyms clarity, fame, lucidity.

obsequious *adj* abject, cringing, deferential, dough-faced, fawning, flattering, grovelling, ingratiating, knee-crooking, menial, oily, servile, slavish, slimy, smarmy, submissive, subservient, sycophantic, toadying, unctuous.

antonym assertive.

observable *adj* apparent, appreciable, clear, detectable, discernible, evident, measurable, noticeable, obvious, open, patent, perceivable, perceptible, recognisable, significant, visible.

observance *n* adherence, attention, celebration, ceremonial, ceremony, compliance, custom, discharge, fashion, form, formality, fulfilment, heeding, honouring, notice, obedience, observation, orthodoxy, performance, practice, rite, ritual, service, tradition.

observant *adj* alert, attentive, eagle-eyed, eagle-sighted, falcon-eyed, heedful, mindful, perceptive, percipient, quick, sharp-eyed, vigilant, watchful, wide-awake.

antonyms inattentive, unobservant.

observation *n* annotation, attention, cognition, comment, consideration, discernment, examination, experience, finding, information, inspection, knowledge, monitoring, note, notice, obiter dictum, opinion, perception, pronouncement, reading, reflection, remark, review, scrutiny, study, surveillance, thought, utterance, watching.

observe *v* abide by, adhere to, animadvert, celebrate, commemorate, comment, comply, conform to, contemplate, declare, detect, discern, discover, espy, follow, fulfil, heed, honour, keep, keep an eye on, keep tabs on, mention, mind, monitor, note, notice, obey, opine, perceive, perform, regard, remark, remember, respect, say, scrutinise, see, solemnise, spot, state, study, surveille, survey, view, watch, witness.

antonyms break, miss, overlook, violate.

observer *n* beholder, bystander, commentator, discerner, eyewitness, looker-on, noter, onlooker, spectator, spotter, viewer, watcher, witness.

obsess *v* bedevil, consume, dominate, engross, grip, haunt, hold, monopolise, nag, plague, possess, preoccupy, prey on, rule, torment.

obsessed *adj* bedevilled, beset, dominated, gripped, hag-ridden, haunted, hounded, hung up on, immersed in, in the grip of, infatuated, plagued, preoccupied.

antonyms detached, indifferent, unconcerned.

obsession *n* bee in one's bonnet, complex, enthusiasm, fetish, fixation, hang-up, idée fixe, infatuation, mania, monomania, phobia, preoccupation, ruling passion, thing, zelotypia.

obsessive *adj* besetting, compulsive, consuming, fixed, gripping, haunting, maddening, nagging, tormenting, unforgettable.

obsolescent *adj* ag(e)ing, declining, disappearing, dying out, fading, moribund, on the decline, on the wane, on the way out, past its prime, waning.

obsolete *adj* anachronistic, ancient, antediluvian, antiquated, antique, archaic, bygone, dated, dead, démodé, discarded, disused, extinct, fogram, horse-and-buggy, musty, old, old hat, old-fashioned, out, out of date, outmoded, outworn, passé, superannuated.

antonyms contemporary, current, modern, new, up-to-date.

obstacle *n* bar, barrier, boyg, catch, check, chicane, difficulty, drawback, hindrance, hitch, hurdle, impediment, interference, interruption, obstruction, pons asinorum, remora, snag, stop, stumbling-block, stumbling-stone.

antonyms advantage, help.

obstinacy *n* doggedness, firmness, frowardness, inflexibility, intransigence, mulishness, obduracy, perseverance, persistence, pertinacity, perversity, pig-headedness, resoluteness, stubbornness, tenacity, wilfulness, wrong-headedness.

antonyms co-operativeness, flexibility, submissiveness.

obstinate *adj* bullet-headed, bull-headed, bullish, camelish, contumacious, determined, dogged, firm, headstrong, immovable, inflexible, intractable, intransigent, mulish, obdurate, opinionated, persistent, pertinacious, perverse, pervicacious, pig-headed, recalcitrant, refractory, restive, rusty, self-willed, steadfast, stomachful, strong-minded, stubborn, sturdy, tenacious, unadvisable, unyielding, uppity, wilful, wrong-headed.

antonyms co-operative, flexible, pliant, submissive.

obstreperous *adj* boisterous, clamorous, disorderly, intractable, loud, noisy, out of hand, rackety, rambunctious, rampaging, raucous, refractory, restive, riotous, rip-roaring, roistering, roisterous, rough, rowdy, stroppy, tempestuous, tumultous, turbulent, uncontrolled, undisciplined, unmanageable, unruly, uproarious, vociferous, wild.

antonyms calm, disciplined, quiet.

obstruct *v* arrest, bar, barricade, block, check, choke, clog, crab, cumber, curb, cut off, frustrate, hamper, hamstring, hide, hinder, hold up, impede, inhibit, interfere with, interrupt, mask, obscure, occlude, prevent, restrict, retard, shield, shut off, slow down, stall, stonewall, stop, stuff, thwart, trammel.

antonym help.

obstruction *n* bar, barricade, barrier, blockage, check, difficulty, filibuster, hindrance, impediment, snag, stop, stoppage, trammel, traverse.

antonym help.

obstructive *adj* awkward, blocking, delaying, difficult, hindering, inhibiting, restrictive, stalling, unaccommodating, unco-operative, unhelpful.

antonym helpful.

obtain[1] *v* achieve, acquire, attain, come by, compass, earn, gain, get, impetrate, procure, secure.

obtain[2] *v* be in force, be prevalent, be the case, exist, hold, prevail, reign, rule, stand.

obtainable *adj* accessible, achievable, at hand, attainable, available, on call, on tap, procurable, ready, realisable, to be had.

antonym unobtainable.

obtrusive *adj* blatant, forward, importunate, interfering, intrusive, manifest, meddling, nosy, noticeable, obvious, officious, prominent, protruding, protuberant, prying, pushy.

antonym unobtrusive.

obtuse *adj* blunt, boneheaded, crass, dense, dopey, dull, dull-witted, dumb, imperceptive, impercipient, inattentive, insensitive, retarded, rounded, slow, stolid, stupid, thick, thick-skinned, uncomprehending, unintelligent.

antonyms bright, sharp.

obviate *v* anticipate, avert, counter, counteract, divert, forestall, preclude, prevent, remove.

obvious *adj* apparent, clear, conspicuous, discernible, distinct, evident, glaring, indisputable, manifest, noticeable, open, open-and-shut, overt, palpable, patent, perceptible, plain, prominent, pronounced, recognisable, self-evident, self-explanatory, straightforward, transparent, unconcealed, undeniable, undisguised, unmistakable, unsubtle, visible.

antonyms obscure, unclear.

obviously *adv* certainly, clearly, distinctly, evidently, manifestly, of course, palpably, patently, plainly, undeniably, unmistakably, unquestionably, visibly, without doubt.

occasion *n* affair, call, case, cause, celebration, chance, convenience, event, excuse, experience, ground(s), incident, inducement, influence, instance, justification, moment, motive, occurrence, opening, opportunity, prompting, provocation, reason, time.

v bring about, bring on, cause, create, effect, elicit, engender, evoke, generate, give rise to, induce, influence, inspire, lead to, make, originate, persuade, produce, prompt, provoke.

occasional *adj* casual, desultory, fitful, incidental, infrequent, intermittent, irregular, odd, periodic, rare, scattered, sporadic, uncommon.

antonym frequent.

occasionally *adv* at intervals, at times, every so often, from time to time, infrequently, irregularly, now and again, now and then, off and on, on and off, on occasion, once in a while, periodically, sometimes, sporadically.

antonym frequently.

occult *adj* abstruse, arcane, cabbalistic, concealed, esoteric, faint, hidden, impenetrable, invisible, magical, mysterious, mystic, mystical, mystifying, obscure, preternatural, recondite, secret, supernatural, unknown, unrevealed, veiled.

v conceal, cover (up), enshroud, hide, mask, obscure, screen, shroud, veil.

antonym reveal.

occultism *n* black magic, diabolism, magic, mysticism, sorcery, spiritualism, supernaturalism, the black arts, witchcraft.

occupancy *n* domiciliation, habitation, holding, inhabitancy, occupation, ownership, possession, residence, tenancy, tenure, term, use.

occupant *n* addressee, denizen, holder, householder, incumbent, indweller, inhabitant, inmate, lessee, occupier, resident, squatter, tenant, user.

occupation[1] *n* absorption, activity, business, calling, craft, employment, job, line, post, profession, pursuit, trade, vocation, walk of life, work.

occupation[2] *n* billet, conquest, control, habitation, holding, invasion, occupancy, possession, residence, seizure, subjugation, takeover, tenancy, tenure, use.

occupied *adj* absorbed, busy, employed, engaged, engrossed, full, hard at it, in use, inhabited, lived-in, peopled, settled, taken, tenanted, tied up, unavailable, working.

antonym unoccupied.

occupy *v* absorb, amuse, beguile, busy, capture, conquer, cover, divert, dwell in, employ, engage, engross, ensconce oneself in, entertain, establish oneself in, fill, garrison, hold, immerse, inhabit, interest, invade, involve, keep, keep busy, live in, monopolise, overrun, own, permeate, pervade, possess, preoccupy, reside in, seize, stay in, take over, take possession of, take up, tenant, tie up, use, utilise.

occur *v* appear, arise, be found, be met with, be present, befall, betide, chance, come about, come off, come to pass, crop up, develop, eventuate, exist, happen, intervene, manifest itself, materialise, obtain, result, show itself, take place, transpire, turn up.

occur to come to mind, come to one, cross one's mind, dawn on, enter one's head, present itself, spring to mind, strike one, suggest itself.

occurrence *n* action, adventure, affair, appearance, case, circumstance, development, episode, event, existence, happening, incident, instance, manifestation, materialisation, proceeding, transaction.

ocean *n* briny, main, profound, sea, the deep, the drink.

odd[1] *adj* abnormal, atypical, bizarre, curious, deviant, different, eccentric, exceptional, extraordinary, fantastic, freak, freakish, freaky, funky, funny, irregular, kinky, outlandish, peculiar, quaint, queer, rare, remarkable, singular, strange, uncanny, uncommon, unconventional, unexplained, unusual, weird, whimsical.

antonym normal.

odd[2] *adj* auxiliary, casual, fragmentary, ill-matched, incidental, irregular, left-over, lone, miscellaneous, occasional, periodic, random, remaining, seasonal, single, solitary, spare, sundry, surplus, uneven, unmatched, unpaired, varied, various.

oddity *n* abnormality, anomaly, bizarreness, card, character, crank, curiosity, eccentricity, extraordinariness, freak, freakishness, idiosyncrasy, incongruity, irregularity, kink, maverick, misfit, oddball, oddness, outlandishness, peculiarity, phenomenon, queerness, quirk, quizziness, rara avis, rarity, screwball, singularity, strangeness, unconventionality, unnaturalness, weirdie, weirdo.

oddment *n* bit, end, fragment, leftover, offcut, patch, remnant, scrap, shred, sliver, snippet.

odds *n* advantage, allowance, ascendancy, balance, chances, difference, discrepancy, disparity, dissimilarity, distinction, edge, lead, likelihood, probability, superiority.

odds and ends bits, bits and pieces, debris, flotsam and jetsam, junk, leavings, litter, oddments, odds and sods, remnants, rubbish, scraps, tatt.

odious *adj* abhorrent, abominable, annoying, detestable, disgusting, execrable, foul, hateful, heinous, horrible, horrid, insufferable, loathsome, obnoxious, offensive, repellent, repugnant, repulsive, revolting, unpleasant, vile.

antonym pleasant.

odium *n* abhorrence, animosity, antipathy, censure, condemnation, contempt, detestation, disapprobation, disapproval, discredit, disfavour, disgrace, dishonour, dislike, disrepute, execration, hatred, infamy, obloquy, opprobrium, reprobation, shame.

odorous *adj* aromatic, balmy, fragrant, odoriferous, perfumed, pungent, redolent, scented, sweet-smelling.

antonym odourless.

odour *n* air, aroma, atmosphere, aura, bouquet, breath, emanation, essence, exhalation, flavour, fragrance, perfume, quality, redolence, scent, smell, spirit, stench, stink.

odyssey *n* journey, travels, wandering.

of course certainly, definitely, doubtlessly, indubitably, naturally, no doubt, obviously, undoubtedly.

off *adj* abnormal, absent, bad, below par, cancelled, decomposed, disappointing, disheartening, displeasing, finished, gone, high, inoperative, mouldy, poor, postponed, quiet, rancid, rotten, slack, sour, substandard, turned, unavailable, unsatisfactory, wrong.

adv apart, aside, at a distance, away, elsewhere, out.

off and on fitfully, from time to time, intermittently, now and again, now and then, occasionally, on and off, once in a while, periodically, sometimes, sporadically.

off guard napping, unprepared, unready, unwary, with one's defences down, with one's pants down.

off the cuff ad lib, extempore, impromptu, improvised, offhand, spontaneous, spontaneously, unofficially, unprepared, unrehearsed, unscripted.

off the hook acquitted, cleared, exonerated, in the clear, scot free, vindicated.

off the record confidential, confidentially, private, privately, sub rosa, unofficial, unofficially.

antonym officially.

off-colour *adj* faded, ill, indecent, indisposed, off form, out of sorts, pasty-faced, peaky, peelie-wally, poorly, queasy, sick, under the weather, unwell.

off-duty *adj* at leisure, at liberty, free, not at work, off, off work, on holiday.

offence *n* affront, anger, annoyance, crime, delict, delinquency, displeasure, fault, hard feelings, harm, huff, hurt, indignation, indignity, infraction, infringement, injury, injustice, insult, ire, lapse, misdeed, misdemeanour, needle, outrage, peccadillo, pique, put-down, resentment, sin, slight, snub, transgression, trespass, umbrage, violation, wrath, wrong, wrong-doing.

offend *v* affront, annoy, disgruntle, disgust, displease, fret, gall, hip, hurt, insult, irritate, miff, nauseate, outrage, pain, pique, provoke, repel, repulse, rile, sicken, slight, snub, transgress, turn off, upset, vex, violate, wound, wrong.

antonym please.

offended *adj* affronted, disgruntled, disgusted, displeased, huffy, in a huff, miffed, outraged, pained, piqued, put out, resentful, smarting, stung, upset, wounded.

antonym pleased.

offender *n* criminal, culprit, delinquent, guilty party, law-breaker, malefactor, miscreant, misfeasor, sinner, transgressor, wrong-doer.

offensive *adj* abominable, abusive, aggressive, annoying, attacking, detestable, disagreeable, discourteous, disgusting, displeasing, disrespectful, embarrassing, grisly, impertinent, insolent, insulting, intolerable, invading, irritating, loathsome, nasty, nauseating, noisome, objectionable, obnoxious, odious, rank, repellent, repugnant, revolting, rude, sickening, uncivil, unmannerly, unpalatable, unpleasant, unsavoury, vile.

antonyms defensive, pleasing.

n attack, drive, onslaught, push, raid, sortie, thrust.

offer *v* advance, afford, bid, extend, furnish, give, hold out, make available, move, present, proffer, propose, propound, provide, put forth, put forward, show, submit, suggest, tender, volunteer.

n approach, attempt, bid, endeavour, essay, overture, presentation, proposal, proposition, submission, suggestion, tender.

offering *n* contribution, donation, gift, oblation, present, sacrifice, subscription, xenium.

offhand *adj* abrupt, aloof, brusque, careless, casual, cavalier, curt, glib, informal, offhanded, perfunctory, take-it-or-leave-it, unappreciative, uncaring, unceremonious, unconcerned, uninterested.

antonyms calculated, planned.

adv at once, extempore, immediately, off the cuff, off the top of one's head, straightaway.

office *n* appointment, bath, business, capacity, charge, commission, duty, employment, function, obligation, occupation, place, post, responsibility, role, room, service, situation, station, trust, work.

officer *n* administrator, agent, appointee, bureaucrat, dignitary, executive, functionary, office-holder, official, public servant, representative.

offices *n* advocacy, aegis, aid, auspices, backing, back-up, favour, help, intercession, intermediation, intervention, mediation, patronage, recommendation, referral, support, word.

official *adj* accredited, approved, authentic, authenticated, authorised, authoritative, bona fide, certified, ex cathedra, formal, legitimate, licensed, proper, sanctioned.

antonym unofficial.

n agent, bureaucrat, executive, fonctionnaire, functionary, gauleiter, hakim, intendant, jack-in-office, mandarin, office-bearer, officer, representative.

officiate *v* adjudicate, chair, conduct, emcee, manage, oversee, preside, referee, serve, superintend, umpire.

officious *adj* bustling, dictatorial, forward, impertinent, inquisitive, interfering, intermeddling, intrusive, meddlesome, meddling, mischievous, obtrusive, opinionated, over-zealous, pragmatical, pushy, self-important.

offish *adj* aloof, cool, haughty, standoffish, stuck-up, unsociable.

antonyms friendly, sociable.

off-key *adj* discordant, dissonant, inappropriate, indecent, inharmonious, jarring, out of keeping, out of tune, unsuitable.

offload *v* deposit, disburden, discharge, drop, dump, get rid of, jettison, shift, transfer, unburden, unload, unship.

off-putting *adj* daunting, demoralising, discomfiting, disconcerting, discouraging, disheartening, dismaying, dispiriting, disturbing, formidable, frustrating, intimidating, unnerving, unsettling, upsetting.

offset *v* balance out, cancel out, compare, compensate for, counteract, counterbalance, counterpoise, countervail, juxtapose, make up for, neutralise.

n balance, compensation, counterbalance, counterweight, equipoise, equivalent, redress.

offshoot *n* adjunct, appendage, arm, branch, by-product, development, embranchment, limb, outgrowth, spin-off, sprout, spur.

offspring *n* brood, child, children, creation, descendant, descendants, family, fry, heir, heirs, issue, kids, litter, progeny, quiverful, result, scion, seed, spawn, successor, successors, young.

antonym parent(s).

often *adv* again and again, frequently, generally, habitually, many a time, much, oft, over and over, regularly, repeatedly, time after time, time and again.

antonym seldom.

ogle *v* eye, eye up, leer, look, make eyes at, stare.

ogre *n* bogey, bogeyman, bogle, boyg, bugaboo, bugbear, demon, devil, giant, humgruffi(a)n, monster, spectre.

oik *n* bloke, bounder, cad, chap, ignoramus, twerp.

oil *v* anoint, embrocate, grease, lubricate.

n balm, cream, grease, liniment, lotion, lubricant, ointment, oleum, salve, unguent.

oily *adj* fatty, flattering, fulsome, glib, greasy, hypocritical, obsequious, oiled, oleaginous, plausible, sebaceous, servile, slippery, smarmy, smeary, smooth, swimming, unctuous.

ointment *n* balm, balsam, cerate, cream, demulcent, embrocation, emollient, liniment, lotion, salve, unction, unguent.

okay *adj* acceptable, accurate, adequate, all right, approved, convenient, correct, fair, fine, good, in order, not bad, OK, passable, permitted, reasonable, right as rain, satisfactory, tolerable.

n agreement, approbation, approval, assent, authorisation, consent, endorsement, go-ahead, green light, OK, permission, sanction, say-so, seal of approval, support.

v accredit, agree to, approve, authorise, consent to, endorse, give the go-ahead to, give the green light to, OK, pass, rubber-stamp, sanction, validate.

interj agreed, all right, fine, OK, right, very good, very well, yes.

old *adj* aboriginal, aged, age-old, ancient, antediluvian, antiquated, antique, archaic, bygone, cast-off, crumbling, dated, decayed, decrepit, done, earlier, early, elderly, erstwhile, ex-, experienced, familiar, former, grey, grey-haired, grizzled, hackneyed, hardened, hoary, immemorial, long-established, long-standing, mature, obsolete, of old, of yore, Ogygian, olden, old-fashioned, one-time, original, out of date, outdated, outmoded, over the hill, passé, patriarchal, practised, preadamic(al), prehistoric, previous, prim(a)eval, primitive, primordial, pristine, quondam, remote, senescent, senile, skilled, stale, superannuated, time-honoured, time-worn, traditional, unfashionable, unoriginal, venerable, versed, veteran, vintage, worn-out.

antonym young.

old age advancing years, age, agedness, Anno Domini, dotage, e(i)ld, second childhood, senescence, senility, twilight of one's life.

antonym youth.

old man boss, elder, elder statesman, employer, father, gaffer, geezer, grandfather, grey, greybeard, hoarhead, husband, OAP, old codger, old stager, oldster, old-timer, patriarch, senior citizen, white-beard, wrinkly.

old woman bag, complainer, crone, fag(g)ot, fuss-pot, gammer, grandam, grannam, granny, grouch, grumbler, hag, mother, old dear, wet, wife, wimp, wrinkly.

old-fashioned *adj* ancient, antiquated, archaic, arriéré, behind the times, corny, dated, dead, démodé, fog(e)yish, fusty, horse-and-buggy, musty, neanderthal, obsolescent, obsolete, old hat, old-fog(e)yish, old-time, out of date, outdated, outmoded, passé, past, quill-pen, retro, rinky-dink, square, superannuated, unfashionable.

antonyms contemporary, modern, up-to-date.

old-world *adj* archaic, ceremonious, chivalrous, conservative, courtly, formal, gallant, old-fashioned, picturesque, quaint, traditional.

Olympian *adj* elevated, exalted, glorious, godlike, Jovian, lofty, majestic, rarefied, splendid, sublime.

omen *n* augury, auspice, boding, foreboding, foretoken, freit, indication, portent, premonition, presage, prognostic, prognostication, sign, straw in the wind, warning, writing on the wall.

ominous *adj* baleful, bodeful, dark, fateful, inauspicious, menacing, minatory, portentous, premonitory, presageful, sinister, threatening, unpromising, unpropitious.

antonym auspicious.

omission *n* avoidance, bowdlerisation, default, ellipsis, exclusion, failure, forgetfulness, gap, lack, neglect, oversight.

antonyms addition, inclusion.

omit *v* disregard, drop, edit out, eliminate, exclude, fail, forget, give something a miss, leave out, leave undone, let slide, miss out, neglect, overlook, pass over, pretermit, skip.

antonyms add, include.

omnibus *adj* all-embracing, compendious, comprehensive, encyclop(a)edic, inclusive, wide-ranging.

antonym selective.

omnipotence *n* divine right, invincibility, mastery, plenipotence, sovereignty, supremacy.

antonym impotence.

omnipotent *adj* all-powerful, almighty, plenipotent, supreme.

antonym impotent.

omnipresent *adj* pervasive, ubiquitary, ubiquitous, universal.

omniscient *adj* all-knowing, all-seeing, pansophic.

on and off discontinuously, fitfully, from time to time, intermittently, now and again, now and then, off and on, on occasion, periodically, sometimes, spasmodically, sporadically.

on duty at work, busy, engaged, working.

antonym off.

on edge apprehensive, eager, edgy, excited, fidgety, ill at ease, impatient, irascible, irritable, keyed up, nervous, on tenterhooks, tense, touchy, uptight.

antonym relaxed.

on fire ablaze, aflame, alight, ardent, blazing, burning, eager, enthusiastic, excited, fiery, fired, flaming, ignited, in flames, inspired, kindled, passionate.

on guard alert, cautious, chary, circumspect, excubant, on the alert, on the lookout, on the qui vive, prepared, ready, vigilant, wary, watchful, wide awake.

on one's last legs at death's door, dying, exhausted, fading fast, failing, moribund, with one foot in the grave, worn out.

on one's own alone, by oneself, independently, isolated, off one's own bat, on one's tod, singly, unaccompanied, unaided, unassisted.

on purpose deliberately, designedly, intentionally, knowingly, premeditatedly, purposely, wilfully, wittingly.

antonym accidentally.

on the ball alert, attentive, aware, in touch, informed, on one's toes, quick, wide awake.

on the dot exactly, on time, precisely, promptly, punctually, spot on, to the minute.

on the fence between two stools, dithering, irresolute, shilly-shallying, uncertain, uncommitted, undecided, unsure, vacillating.

on the increase accelerating, escalating, expanding, growing, increasing, multiplying, proliferating, rising, spreading.

antonym on the wane.

on the level above board, candid, fair, frank, genuine, honest, open, sincere, square, straight, straightforward, up front.

on the mend convalescent, convalescing, healing, improving, recovering, recuperating, reviving.

on the move active, advancing, astir, moving, on the go, progressing, stirring, succeeding.

on the rampage amok, berserk, frenzied, in a frenzy, rampageous(ly), rampant(ly), riotous(ly), violent(ly), wild(ly).

on the scrap-heap discarded, ditched, dumped, forgotten, jettisoned, redundant, rejected, written off.

on the sly clandestinely, covertly, furtively, on the q.t., privately, secretly, surreptitiously, underhandedly.

antonym openly.

on the spur of the moment capriciously, impetuously, impromptu, impulsively, on impulse, on the spot, thoughtlessly, unpremeditatedly, unthinkingly.

on the wane declining, degenerating, deteriorating, dropping, dwindling, ebbing, fading, lessening, moribund, obsolescent, on its last legs, on the decline, on the way out, subsiding, tapering off, weakening, withering.

antonym on the increase.

on the whole all in all, all things considered, as a rule, by and large, for the most part, generally, generally speaking, in general, in the main, mostly, predominantly.

on thin ice at risk, in jeopardy, insecure, open to attack, precarious, unsafe, vulnerable.

on top of the world ecstatic, elated, exhilarated, exultant, happy, on cloud nine, over the moon, overjoyed, thrilled.

once *adv* at one time, formerly, heretofore, in the old days, in the past, in times gone by, in times past, long ago, once upon a time, previously.

once (and) for all conclusively, decisively, definitively, finally, for good, for the last time, permanently, positively.

once in a blue moon hardly ever, infrequently, rarely, seldom.

oncoming *adj* advancing, approaching, forthcoming, gathering, imminent, impending, looming, onrushing, upcoming.

one *adj* alike, compatible, complete, entire, equal, harmonious, identical, like-minded, united, whole.

oneness *n* completeness, consistency, distinctness, identicalness, identity, individuality, sameness, singleness, unicity, unity, wholeness.

onerous *adj* backbreaking, burdensome, crushing, demanding, difficult, exacting, exhausting, exigent, formidable, grave, hard, heavy, herculean, laborious, oppressive, responsible, taxing, troublesome, weighty.

antonyms easy, light.

one-sided *adj* asymmetrical, biased, coloured, discriminatory, inequitable, lopsided, partial, partisan, prejudiced, unequal, unfair, unilateral, unjust.

antonym impartial.

one-time *adj* erstwhile, ex-, former, late, previous, quondam, sometime, umquhile, whilom.

ongoing *adj* advancing, continuing, continuous, current, developing, evolving, extant, growing, in progress, lasting, progressing, successful, unfinished, unfolding.

onlooker *n* bystander, eye-witness, looker-on, observer, rubber-neck, spectator, viewer, watcher, witness.

only *adv* at most, barely, exclusively, just, merely, purely, simply, solely.

adj exclusive, individual, lone, single, sole, solitary, unique.

onrush *n* career, cascade, charge, flood, flow, onset, onslaught, push, rush, stampede, stream, surge.

onset *n* assault, attack, beginning, charge, commencement, inception, kick-off, onrush, onslaught, outbreak, outset, start.

antonyms end, finish.

onslaught *n* assault, attack, barrage, blitz, bombardment, charge, offensive, onrush, onset.

onus *n* burden, duty, encumbrance, liability, load, obligation, responsibility, task.

onward(s) *adv* ahead, beyond, forth, forward, frontward(s), in front, on.

antonym backward(s).

oodles *n* abundance, bags, heaps, lashings, loads, lots, masses, oodlins, tons.

antonym scarcity.

oomph *n* animation, bounce, energy, enthusiasm, exuberance, get-up-and-go, pep, pizzazz, sex-appeal, sparkle, vigour, vitality, vivacity, zing.

ooze *v* bleed, discharge, drain, dribble, drip, drop, emit, escape, exude, filter, leach, leak, osmose, overflow with, percolate, seep, strain, sweat, transude, weep.

n alluvium, deposit, mire, muck, mud, sediment, silt, slime, sludge.

oozy *adj* dewy, dripping, miry, moist, mucky, muddy, slimy, sloppy, sludgy, sweaty, uliginous, weeping.

opacity *n* cloudiness, density, dullness, filminess, impermeability, milkiness, murkiness, obfuscation, obscurity, opaqueness, unclearness.

antonym transparency.

opaque *adj* abstruse, baffling, clouded, cloudy, cryptic, difficult, dim, dull, enigmatic, filmy, fuliginous, hazy, impenetrable, incomprehensible, inexplicable, lustreless, muddied, muddy, murky, obfuscated, obscure, turbid, unclear, unfathomable, unintelligible.

antonym transparent.

open *adj* above-board, accessible, agape, airy, ajar, apparent, arguable, artless, available, avowed, bare, barefaced, blatant, bounteous, bountiful, candid, champaign, clear, conspicuous, debatable, disinterested, downright, evident, expanded, exposed, extended, extensive, fair, filigree, flagrant, frank, free, fretted, gaping, general, generous, guileless, holey, honest, honeycombed, impartial, ingenuous, innocent, lacy, liberal, lidless, loose, manifest, moot, munificent, natural, navigable, noticeable, objective, obvious, overt, passable, plain, porous, public, receptive, revealed, rolling, sincere, spacious, spongy, spread out, sweeping, transparent, unbarred, unbiased, unclosed, uncluttered, uncommitted, unconcealed, unconditional, uncovered, uncrowded, undecided, undefended, undisguised, unenclosed, unengaged, unfastened, unfenced, unfolded, unfortified, unfurled, unlidded, unlocked, unobstructed, unoccupied, unprejudiced, unprotected, unqualified, unreserved, unresolved, unrestricted, unroofed, unsealed, unsettled, unsheltered, unwalled, upfront, vacant, visible, wide, wide-open, yawning.

antonyms closed, shut.

v begin, clear, come apart, commence, crack, disclose, divulge, exhibit, explain, expose, inaugurate, initiate, launch, lay bare, ope, pour out, rupture, separate, set in motion, show, split, spread (out), start, throw wide, unbar, unbare, unblock, unclose, uncork, uncover, undo, unfasten, unfold, unfurl, unlatch, unlid, unlock, unroll, unseal, unshutter.

antonyms close, shut.

open to accessible, disposed, exposed, liable, susceptible, vulnerable.

open-air *adj* alfresco, hypaethral, outdoor, plein-air.

antonym indoor.

open-and-shut *adj* obvious, simple, straightforward.

open-handed *adj* bountiful, eleemosynary, free, generous, large-hearted, lavish, liberal, munificent, unstinting.

antonym tight-fisted.

opening *n* adit, aperture, beginning, birth, breach, break, chance, chasm, chink, cleft, commencement, crack, dawn, fissure, fistula, foramen, gap, hole, inauguration, inception, initiation, interstice, kick-off, launch, launching, occasion, onset, opportunity, orifice, ostiole, outset, perforation, place, rent, rupture, slot, space, split, start, vacancy, vent, vista.

antonyms closing, closure.

adj beginning, commencing, early, first, inaugural, inauguratory, inceptive, initial, initiatory, introductory, maiden, primary.

antonym closing.

openly *adv* blatantly, brazenly, candidly, face to face, flagrantly, forthrightly, frankly, glaringly, in full view, in public, overtly, plainly, publicly, shamelessly, unabashedly, unashamedly, unhesitatingly, unreservedly, wantonly.

antonyms secretly, slyly.

open-minded *adj* broad, broad-minded, catholic, dispassionate, enlightened, free, impartial, latidutinarian, liberal, objective, reasonable, receptive, tolerant, unbiased, unprejudiced.

antonyms bigoted, intolerant, prejudiced.

open-mouthed *adj* amazed, astounded, clamorous, dumbfounded, edacious, expectant, flabbergasted, greedy, spellbound, thunderstruck, voracious.

operate *v* act, function, go, handle, manage, manoeuvre, perform, run, serve, use, utilise, work.

operation *n* action, activity, affair, agency, assault, business, campaign, course, deal, effect, effort, employment, enterprise, exercise, force, influence, instrumentality, manipulation, manoeuvre, motion, movement, performance, procedure, proceeding, process, surgery, transaction, undertaking, use, utilisation, working.

operational *adj* functional, going, in service, in working order, on duty, operative, prepared, ready, usable, viable, workable, working.

antonym out of order.

operative *adj* active, crucial, current, effective, efficient, engaged, functional, functioning, important, in action, in force, in operation, indicative, influential, key, operational, relevant, serviceable, significant, standing, workable.

antonym inoperative.

n artisan, employee, hand, labourer, machinist, mechanic, operator, worker.

operator *n* administrator, conductor, contractor, dealer, director, driver, handler, machinator, machinist, manager, manipulator, mechanic, mover, operant, operative, practitioner, punter, shyster, speculator, technician, trader, wheeler-dealer, worker.

opiate *n* anodyne, bromide, depressant, downer, drug, narcotic, nepenthe, pacifier, sedative, soporific, stupefacient, tranquilliser.

opine *v* believe, conceive, conclude, conjecture, declare, guess, judge, presume, say, suggest, suppose, surmise, suspect, think, venture, volunteer.

opinion *n* assessment, belief, conception, conjecture, conventional wisdom, doxy, estimation, feeling, idea, idée reçue, impression, judgement, mind, notion, perception, persuasion, point of view, sentiment, stance, tenet, theory, view, voice, vox pop, vox populi.

opinionated *adj* adamant, biased, bigoted, bull-headed, cocksure, dictatorial, doctrinaire, dogmatic, high-dried, inflexible, obdurate, obstinate, overbearing, partisan, pig-headed, prejudiced, self-assertive, single-minded, stubborn, uncompromising, wilful.

antonym open-minded.

opponent *n* adversary, antagonist, challenger, competitor, contestant, disputant, dissentient, dissident, enemy, foe, objector, opposer, opposition, rival.

antonyms ally, proponent.

opportune *adj* advantageous, appropriate, apt, auspicious, convenient, favourable, felicitous, fit, fitting, fortunate, good, happy, lucky, pertinent, proper, propitious, seasonable, suitable, timely, well-timed.

antonym inopportune.

opportunism *n* adventurism, expediency, exploitation, Machiavellianism, making hay while the sun shines, pragmatism, realism, Realpolitik, taking advantage, trimming, unscrupulousness.

opportunity *n* break, chance, convenience, hour, moment, occasion, opening, scope, shot, time, turn.

oppose *v* bar, beard, breast, check, combat, compare, confront, contradict, contrary, contrast, contravene, controvert, counter, counterattack, counterbalance, defy, face, fight, fly in the face of, gainsay, hinder, obstruct, pit against, play off, prevent, recalcitrate, resist, stand up to, take a stand against, take issue with, thwart, withstand.

antonyms favour, support.

opposed *adj* against, agin, antagonistic, anti, antipathetic, antithetical, clashing, conflicting, contrary, contrasted, dissentient, hostile, in opposition, incompatible, inimical, opposing, opposite.

antonym in favour.

opposing *adj* antagonistic, antipathetic, clashing, combatant, conflicting, contentious, contrary, disputatious, enemy, hostile, incompatible, irreconcilable, opposed, opposite, oppugnant, rival, warring.

opposite *adj* adverse, antagonistic, antipodal, antipodean, antithetical, conflicting, contradictory, contrary, contrasted, corresponding, different, differing, diverse, facing, fronting, hostile, inconsistent, inimical, irreconcilable, opposed, reverse, unlike.

antonym same.

n antipode(s), antipole, antithesis, contradiction, contrary, converse, inverse, reverse.

antonym same.

opposition *n* antagonism, antagonist, clash, colluctation, competition, contraposition, contrariety, counteraction, counter-stand, counter-time, counter-view, disapproval, foe, hostility, obstruction, obstructiveness, opponent, other side, polarity, prevention, resistance, rival, syzygy, unfriendliness.

antonyms co-operation, support.

oppress *v* abuse, afflict, burden, crush, depress, dispirit, harass, harry, lie hard on, lie heavy on, maltreat, overpower, overwhelm, persecute, sadden, subdue, subjugate, suppress, torment, trample, tyrannise, vex, weigh heavy.

oppressed *adj* abused, browbeaten, burdened, disadvantaged, downtrodden, enslaved, harassed, henpecked, maltreated, misused, persecuted, prostrate, slave, subject, subjugated, troubled, tyrannised, underprivileged.

antonym free.

oppression *n* abuse, brutality, calamity, cruelty, hardship, harshness, injury, injustice, jackboot, liberticide, maltreatment, misery, persecution, severity, subjection, suffering, tyranny.

oppressive *adj* airless, brutal, burdensome, close, cruel, despotic, grinding, harsh, heavy, inhuman, intolerable, muggy, onerous, overbearing, overpowering, overwhelming, repressive, severe, stifling, stuffy, suffocating, sultry, torrid, tyrannical, unendurable, unjust.

antonym gentle.

oppressor *n* autocrat, bully, coercionist, despot, dictator, harrier, intimidator, liberticide, persecutor, scourge, slave-driver, taskmaster, tormentor, tyrant.

opprobrious *adj* abusive, calumniatory, calumnious, contemptuous, contumelious, damaging, defamatory, derogatory, dyslogistic, insolent, insulting, invective, offensive, scandalous, scurrilous, vitriolic, vituperative.

opprobrium *n* calumny, censure, contumely, debasement, degradation, discredit, disfavour, disgrace, dishonour, disrepute, ignominy, infamy, obloquy, odium, reproach, scurrility, shame, slur, stigma.

opt *v* choose, decide (on), elect, go for, plump for, prefer, select, single out.

optimistic *adj* assured, bright, bullish, buoyant, cheerful, confident, encouraged, expectant, heartened, hopeful, idealistic, Panglossian, Panglossic, pollyann(a)ish, positive, sanguine, upbeat, Utopian.

antonym pessimistic.

optimum *adj* A1, best, choicest, highest, ideal, optimal, peak, perfect, superlative, top.

antonym worst.

n best, peak, zenith.

option *n* alternative, choice, election, possibility, preference, selection.

optional *adj* discretionary, elective, extra, open, possible, unforced, voluntary.

antonym compulsory.

opulence *n* abundance, affluence, copiousness, cornucopia, easy street, fortune, fullness, lavishness, luxuriance, luxury, plenty, pleroma, profusion, prosperity, riches, richness, sumptuousness, superabundance, wealth.

antonyms penury, poverty.

opulent *adj* abundant, affluent, copious, lavish, luxuriant, luxurious, moneyed, plentiful, profuse, prolific, prosperous, rich, sumptuous, superabundant, wealthy, well-heeled, well-off, well-to-do.

antonyms penurious, poor.

opus *n* brainchild, composition, creation, lucubration, oeuvre, piece, production, work.

oracle *n* adviser, answer, augur, augury, authority, divination, guru, high priest, mastermind, mentor, prediction, prognostication, prophecy, prophet, pundit, python, revelation, sage, seer, sibyl, soothsayer, vision, wizard.

oracular *adj* ambiguous, arcane, auspicious, authoritative, cryptic, Delphic, dictatorial, dogmatic, equivocal, grave, haruspical, mantic, mysterious, obscure, ominous, portentous, positive, predictive, prescient, prognostic, prophetic, pythonic, sage, sibylline, significant, two-edged, vatic, vaticinal, venerable, wise.

oral *adj* acroamatic(al), spoken, unwritten, verbal, vocal.

antonym written.

orate *v* declaim, discourse, harangue, hold forth, pontificate, sermonise, speak, speechify, talk.

oration *n* address, declamation, discourse, éloge, harangue, homily, lecture, sermon, speech, spiel.

orator *n* declaimer, demagogue, lecturer, phrasemaker, phraseman, phrasemonger, phraser, public speaker, rhetorician, speaker, spellbinder, spieler.

oratorical *adj* bombastic, Ciceronian, declamatory, Demosthenic, elocutionary, eloquent, grandiloquent, high-flown, magniloquent, rhetorical, silver-tongued, smooth-tongued, sonorous.

oratory *n* declamation, diction, elocution, eloquence, grandiloquence, public speaking, rhetoric, speech, speechifying, speech-making.

orb *n* ball, circle, globe, globule, mound, ring, round, sphere, spherule.

orbit *n* ambit, circle, circumgyration, circumvolution, compass, course, cycle, domain, ellipse, influence, path, range, reach, revolution, rotation, scope, sphere, sphere of influence, sweep, track, trajectory.

v circle, circumnavigate, circumvolve, encircle, revolve.

orchestrate *v* arrange, compose, concert, co-ordinate, fix, integrate, organise, prepare, present, score, stage-manage.

ordain *v* anoint, appoint, call, consecrate, decree, destine, dictate, elect, enact, enjoin, fate, fix, foredoom, foreordain, frock, instruct, intend, invest, lay down, legislate, nominate, order, predestine, predetermine, prescribe, pronounce, require, rule, set, will.

ordeal *n* affliction, agony, anguish, nightmare, pain, persecution, suffering, test, torture, trial, tribulation(s), trouble(s).

order[1] *n* application, arrangement, array, behest, booking, calm, categorisation, chit, classification, codification, command, commission, control, cosmos, decree, dictate, diktat, direction, directive, discipline, disposal, disposition, eutaxy, grouping, harmony, injunction, instruction, law, law and order, layout, line, line-up, mandate, method, neatness, ordering, orderliness, ordinance, organisation, pattern, peace, placement, plan, precept, progression, propriety, quiet, regularity, regulation, request, requisition, reservation, rule, sequence, series, stipulation, structure, succession, symmetry, system, tidiness, tranquillity.

antonym disorder.

v adjure, adjust, align, arrange, authorise, bid, book, catalogue, charge, class, classify, command, conduct, control, decree, direct, dispose, enact, engage, enjoin, group, instruct, lay out, manage, marshal, neaten, ordain, organise, prescribe, put to rights, regulate, request, require, reserve, sort out, systematise, tabulate, tidy.

antonym disorder.

order[2] *n* association, breed, brotherhood, cast, caste, class, community, company, degree, family, fraternity, genre, genus, grade, guild, hierarchy, ilk, kind, league, lodge, organisation, pecking order, phylum, position, rank, sect, sisterhood, society, sodality, sort, species, status, subclass, tribe, type, union.

orderly *adj* businesslike, controlled, cosmic, decorous, disciplined, in order, law-abiding, methodical, neat, non-violent, peaceable, quiet, regular, restrained, ruly, scientific, shipshape, systematic, systematised, tidy, trim, well-behaved, well-organised, well-regulated.

antonym disorderly.

ordinance *n* canon, ceremony, command, decree, dictum, directive, edict, enactment, fiat, injunction, institution, law, observance, order, practice, precept, prescript, regulation, rite, ritual, rule, ruling, sacrament, statute, usage.

ordinarily *adv* as a rule, commonly, conventionally, customarily, familiarly, generally, habitually, in general, normally, usually.

ordinary *adj* accustomed, average, common, common-or-garden, commonplace, conventional, customary, established, everyday, fair, familiar, habitual, homespun, household, humble, humdrum, inconsequential, indifferent, inferior, mean, mediocre, modest, normal, pedestrian, plain, prevailing, prosaic, quotidian, regular, routine, run-of-the-mill, settled, simple, standard, stock, typical, undistinguished, unexceptional, unmemorable, unpretentious, unremarkable, usual, wonted, workaday.

antonyms extraordinary, special, unusual.

ordnance *n* arms, artillery, big guns, cannon, guns, matériel, missil(e)ry, munitions, weapons.

ordure *n* dirt, dung, excrement, filth.

organ *n* agency, channel, device, element, forum, harmonium, hurdy-gurdy, implement, instrument, journal, kist of whistles, means, medium, member, mouthpiece, newspaper, paper, part, periodical, process, publication, structure, tool, unit, vehicle, viscus, voice.

organic *adj* anatomical, animate, biological, biotic, constitutional, formal, fundamental, inherent, innate, integral, integrated, live, living, methodical, natural, ordered, organised, structural, structured, systematic, systematised.

organisation *n* arrangement, assembling, assembly, association, body, business, chemistry, combine, company, composition, concern, confederation, configuration, conformation, consortium, constitution, construction, co-ordination, corporation, design, disposal, federation, firm, format, formation, formulation, framework, group, grouping, institution, league, make-up, management, method, methodology, organism, outfit, pattern, plan, planning, regulation, running, standardisation, structure, structuring, syndicate, system, unity, whole.

antonym disorganisation.

organise *v* arrange, catalogue, classify, codify, constitute, construct, co-ordinate, dispose, establish, form, frame, group, marshal, pigeonhole, regiment, run, see to, set up, shape, structure, systematise, tabulate.

antonym disorganise.

organised *adj* arranged, neat, orderly, planned.

antonym disorganised.

organism *n* animal, being, body, cell, creature, entity, living thing, structure.

orgy *n* bacchanal, bacchanalia, binge, bout, carousal, debauch, excess, indulgence, love-in, overindulgence, revel, revelry, saturnalia, splurge, spree, surfeit.

orient *v* acclimatise, accommodate, adapt, adjust, align, familiarise, get one's bearings, habituate, orientate.

orientation *n* acclimatisation, adaptation, adjustment, assimilation, attunement, bearings, collimation, co-ordination, direction, familiarisation, introduction, location, position, sense of direction, settling in.

orifice *n* aperture, cleft, hole, inlet, mouth, opening, perforation, pore, rent, slit, vent.

origin *n* ancestry, base, basis, beginning, beginnings, birth, cause, commencement, creation, dawning, derivation, descent, emergence, etymology, etymon, extraction, family, fons et origo, font, foundation, fountain, fountain-head, genesis, heritage, inauguration, inception, incunabula, launch, lineage, occasion, origination, outset, parentage, paternity, pedigree, provenance, root, roots, source, spring, start, stirps, stock, well-spring.

antonyms end, termination.

original *adj* aboriginal, archetypal, authentic, autochthonous, commencing, creative, earliest, early, embryonic, fertile, first, first-hand, fresh, genuine, imaginative, infant, ingenious, initial, innovative, innovatory, introductory, inventive, master, new, novel, opening, primal, primary, primigenial, primitical, primitive, primordial, pristine, prototypical, resourceful, rudimentary, seminal, starting, unborrowed, unconventional, unhackneyed, unprecedented, unusual.

antonym unoriginal.

n archetype, case, character, cure, eccentric, master, model, nonconformist, oddity, paradigm, pattern, prototype, queer fish, standard, type, weirdo.

originality *n* boldness, cleverness, creative spirit, creativeness, creativity, daring, eccentricity, freshness, imagination, imaginativeness, individuality, ingenuity, innovation, innovativeness, inventiveness, newness, novelty, resourcefulness, singularity, unconventionality, unorthodoxy.

originally *adv* at first, at the outset, at the start, by birth, by derivation, first, in origin, in the beginning, initially.

originate *v* arise, be born, begin, come, commence, conceive, create, derive, develop, discover, emanate, emerge, establish, evolve, flow, form, formulate, generate, give birth to, inaugurate, initiate, institute, introduce, invent, issue, launch, pioneer, proceed, produce, result, rise, set up, spring, start, stem.

antonyms end, terminate.

originator *n* architect, author, creator, designer, father, founder, generator, innovator, inventor, mother, pioneer, prime mover, the brains.

ornament *n* accessory, adornment, bauble, decoration, doodah, embellishment, fallal, fandangle, figgery, flower, frill, furbelow, garnish, gaud, honour, jewel, leading light, pride, treasure, trimming, trinket.

v adorn, beautify, bedizen, bespangle, brighten, caparison, deck, decorate, dress up, embellish, festoon, garnish, gild, grace, prettify, prink, trim.

ornamental *adj* attractive, beautifying, decorative, embellishing, flashy, for show, grandiose, showy.

ornamentation *n* adornment, decoration, elaboration, embellishment, embroidery, fallalery, frills, garniture, ornateness.

ornate *adj* arabesque, aureate, baroque, beautiful, bedecked, busy, convoluted, decorated, elaborate, elegant, fancy, florid, flowery, fussy, ornamented, rococo, sumptuous.

antonyms austere, plain.

oro(ro)tund *adj* dignified, imposing, magniloquent, pompous, pretentious.

orthodox *adj* accepted, approved, conformist, conventional, correct, customary, doctrinal, established, kosher, official, received, sound, traditional, true, usual, well-established.

antonym unorthodox.

orthodoxy *n* authenticity, authoritativeness, authority, conformism, conformity, conventionality, devotion, devoutness, faithfulness, inflexibility, properness, received wisdom, soundness, traditionalism, trueness.

oscillate *v* fluctuate, librate, seesaw, sway, swing, vacillate, vary, vibrate, waver, wigwag, yo-yo.

oscillation *n* fluctuation, instability, seesawing, shilly-shallying, swing, swinging, vacillation, variation, wavering.

ossified *adj* bony, fixed, fossilised, frozen, hardened, indurate(d), inflexible, petrified, rigid, rigidified, solid, stiff.

ostensible *adj* alleged, apparent, avowed, exhibited, manifest, outward, plausible, presumed, pretended, professed, purported, put-on, seeming, so-called, specious, superficial, supposed.

ostensibly *adv* apparently, professedly, purportedly, reputedly, seemingly, supposedly.

ostentation *n* affectation, boasting, display, exhibitionism, flamboyance, flashiness, flaunting, flourish, foppery, pageantry, parade, pomp, pretension, pretentiousness, show, showiness, showing off, swank, tinsel, trappings, vaunting, window-dressing.

antonym unpretentiousness.

ostentatious *adj* aggressive, boastful, conspicuous, extravagant, fastuous, flamboyant, flash, flashy, garish, gaudy, loud, obtrusive, pretentious, self-advertising, showy, splashy, swanking, swanky, vain, vulgar.

antonyms quiet, restrained.

ostracise *v* avoid, banish, bar, black, blackball, blacklist, boycott, cast out, cold-shoulder, cut, debar, disfellowship, exclude, excommunicate, exile, expatriate, expel, reject, segregate, send to Coventry, shun, snub.

antonyms accept, receive, reinstate, welcome.

ostracism *n* avoidance, banishment, boycott, cold-shouldering, disfellowship, exclusion, excommunication, exile, expulsion, isolation, proscription, rejection.

antonyms acceptance, reinstatement, welcome.

other *adj* added, additional, alternative, auxiliary, contrasting, different, differing, dissimilar, distinct, diverse, extra, fresh, further, more, new, remaining, separate, spare, supplementary, unrelated.

otherworldly *adj* absent-minded, bemused, dreamy, ethereal, fey, preoccupied, rapt.

antonyms mundane, solid, substantial, worldly.

ounce *n* atom, crumb, drop, grain, iota, jot, modicum, morsel, particle, scrap, shred, speck, spot, trace, whit.

oust *v* depose, disinherit, dislodge, displace, dispossess, drive out, eject, evict, expel, overthrow, replace, supplant, throw out, topple, turn out, unseat, upstage.

antonyms ensconce, install, reinstate, settle.

out[1] *adj* abroad, absent, away, disclosed, elsewhere, evident, exposed, gone, manifest, not at home, outside, public, revealed.

out of bounds banned, barred, disallowed, forbidden, off-limits, prohibited, taboo.

out of date antiquated, archaic, behind the times, dated, fogram, horse-and-buggy, moribund, obsolete, old, old hat, old-fashioned, outmoded, passé.

antonyms fashionable, modern, new.

out of doors alfresco, en plein air, out, outdoors, outside.

antonym indoors.

out of focus blurred, blurry, fuzzy, hazy, ill-defined, indistinct, muzzy.

antonyms clear, sharp.

out of order broken, broken down, burst, conked out, gone phut, haywire, in disrepair, inoperative, kaput, non-functional, on the blink, out of commission.

antonym serviceable.

out of place disarranged, in disorder, inappropriate, malapropos, tactless, topsy-turvy, unbecoming, unfitting, unseemly, unsuitable.

antonyms appropriate, apropos.

out of sorts below par, depressed, down in the dumps, down in the mouth, fed up, gloomy, ill, moody, mops and brooms, off-colour, peelie-wally, poorly, sick, under the weather.

antonyms cheerful, well.

out of the blue all of a sudden, suddenly, unexpectedly.

out of the wood(s) home and dry, in the clear, on dry land, out of danger, out of difficulty, safe, safe and sound, secure.

antonyms insecure, vulnerable.

out of this world excellent, fabulous, fantastic, great, incredible, indescribable, marvellous, phenomenal, remarkable, superb, unbelievable, wonderful.

antonyms mundane, ordinary.

out of work idle, jobless, laid off, on the dole, redundant, unemployed, workless.

antonyms busy, employed, occupied.

out[2] *adj* antiquated, banned, blacked, dated, dead, démodé, disallowed, ended, excluded, exhausted, expired, extinguished, finished, forbidden, impossible, not on, old hat, old-fashioned, out of date, passé, square, taboo, unacceptable, unfashionable, used up.

antonyms acceptable, fashionable, in.

out-and-out *adj* absolute, arrant, complete, consummate, downright, dyed-in-the-wool, inveterate, outright, perfect, thoroughgoing, total, uncompromising, unmitigated, unqualified, utter, whole-hog.

outbreak *n* burst, ebullition, epidemic, eruption, excrescence, explosion, flare-up, flash, outburst, pompholyx, rash, spasm, upsurge.

outburst *n* access, attack, boutade, discharge, eruption, explosion, fit, fit of temper, flare-up, gale, gush, outbreak, outpouring, paroxysm, seizure, spasm, storm, surge, volley.

outcast *n* abject, castaway, derelict, exile, leper, outsider, pariah, persona non grata, refugee, reject, reprobate, unperson, untouchable, vagabond, wretch.

antonyms favourite, idol.

outclass *v* beat, eclipse, excel over, leave standing, outdistance, outdo, outrank, outrival, outshine, outstrip, overshadow, put in the shade, surpass, top, transcend.

outcome *n* after-effect, aftermath, conclusion, consequence, effect, end, end result, harvest, issue, pay-off, result, sequel, upshot.

outcry *n* clamour, commotion, complaint, cry, exclamation, flap, howl, hue and cry, hullaballoo, noise, outburst, protest, row, scream, screech, uproar, vociferation, yell.

outdated *adj* antediluvian, antiquated, antique, archaic, behind the times, dated, démodé, fogram, obsolescent, obsolete, old-fashioned, out of date, out of style, outmoded, passé, square, unfashionable, unmodish.

antonyms fashionable, modern, modish.

outdistance *v* leave behind, leave standing, outpace, outrun, outstrip, overhaul, overtake, pass, pull ahead of, shake off, surpass.

outdo *v* beat, best, eclipse, excel over, get the better of, outclass, outdistance, outfox, out-Herod, outmanoeuvre, outshine, outsmart, outstrip, outwit, overcome, surpass, top, transcend.

outdoor *adj* alfresco, extraforaneous, open-air, out-of-door(s), outside.

antonym indoor.

outer *adj* distal, distant, exterior, external, further, outlying, outside, outward, peripheral, remote, superficial, surface.

antonyms central, inner, mesial, proximal.

outface *v* beard, brave, brazen out, confront, defy, outstare, stare down.

antonyms capitulate, succumb.

outfit[1] *n* accoutrements, clothes, costume, ensemble, equipage, equipment, garb, gear, get-up, kit, paraphernalia, rig, rig-out, set-out, suit, togs, trappings, turn-out.

v accoutre, apparel, appoint, attire, equip, fit out, fit up, furnish, kit out, provision, stock, supply, turn out.

outfit[2] *n* business, clan, clique, company, corps, coterie, crew, firm, galère, gang, group, organisation, set, set-out, set-up, squad, team, unit.

outfitter *n* clothier, costumer, costumier, couturier, couturière, dressmaker, haberdasher, modiste, sartor, tailor.

outflow *n* debouchment, discharge, disemboguement, drainage, ebb, effluence, effluent, effluvium, efflux, effluxion, effusion, emanation, emergence, gush, jet, outfall, outpouring, rush, spout.

outflowing *adj* debouching, discharging, effluent, emanant, gushing, leaking, rushing, spurting.

outgoing *adj* affable, approachable, chatty, communicative, cordial, demonstrative, departing, easy, ex-, expansive, extrovert, former, friendly, genial, gregarious, informal, last, open, past, retiring, sociable, sympathetic, unreserved, warm, withdrawing.

antonyms incoming, introvert, new, unsociable.

outgoings *n* costs, disbursal, disbursement, expenditure, expenses, outlay, overheads, spending.

antonym income.

outgrowth *n* consequence, effect, emanation, excrescence, offshoot, product, protuberance, shoot, sprout, swelling.

outing *n* excursion, expedition, jaunt, picnic, pleasure trip, ramble, spin, trip, wayzgoose.

outlandish *adj* alien, barbarous, bizarre, eccentric, exotic, extraordinary, fantastic, foreign, grotesque, odd, outré, preposterous, queer, strange, unheard-of, weird.

antonyms familiar, ordinary.

outlandishness *n* bizarreness, eccentricity, exoticness, grotesqueness, oddness, peregrinity, queerness, strangeness, weirdness.

antonyms commonplaceness, familiarity.

outlast *v* come through, outlive, outstay, ride, survive, weather.

outlaw *n* bandit, brigand, bushranger, cateran, dacoit, desperado, freebooter, fugitive, highwayman, klepht, marauder, outcast, outsider, pariah, proscript, robber.

v ban, banish, bar, condemn, debar, decitizenise, disallow, embargo, exclude, excommunicate, forbid, illegalise, illegitimate, interdict, prohibit, proscribe, waive.

antonyms allow, legalise.

outlawed *adj* banished, banned, condemned, disallowed, embargoed, excommunicated, hors la loi, proscribed.

outlay *n* cost, disbursal, disbursement, expenditure, expenses, investment, outgoings, payment, price.

antonym income.

outlet *n* avenue, channel, débouché, debouchment, duct, egress, emissary, exit, femerall, market, opening, orifice, outfall, release, safety valve, vent, way out.

antonyms entry, inlet.

outline *n* bare facts, configuration, contorno, contour, croquis, delineation, draft, drawing, figure, form, frame, framework, lay-out, lineament(s), plan, profile, recapitulation, résumé, rough, run-down, scenario, schema, shape, silhouette, skeleton, sketch, summary, synopsis, thumbnail sketch, tracing.

v adumbrate, delineate, draft, plan, recapitulate, rough out, sketch, summarise, trace.

outlive *v* come through, live through, outlast, survive, weather.

antonym predecease.

outlook *n* angle, aspect, attitude, expectations, forecast, frame of mind, future, look-out, panorama, perspective, point of view, prognosis, prospect, scene, slant, standpoint, vantage-point, view, viewpoint, views, vista.

outlying *adj* distant, far-away, far-flung, far-off, forane, further, outer, outlandish, peripheral, provincial, remote.

antonyms central, inner.

outmanoeuvre *v* beat, circumvent, get the better of, outdo, outflank, outfox, outgeneral, outsmart, outthink, outwit, put the dead wood on.

outmoded *adj* anachronistic, antediluvian, antiquated, antique, archaic, behind the times, bygone, dated, démodé, fogram, fossilised, horse-and-buggy, obsolescent, obsolete, olden, old-fashioned, old-fogeyish, out of date, outworn, passé, square, superannuated, superseded, unfashionable, unmodish, unusable.

antonyms fashionable, fresh, modern, modish, new.

out-of-the-way *adj* abnormal, abstruse, curious, distant, exceptional, extraordinary, far-away, far-flung, far-off, inaccessible, isolated, little-known, lonely, obscure, odd, outlandish, outlying, peculiar, remote, secluded, strange, uncommon, unfamiliar, unfrequented, unget-at-able, unusual.

outpace *v* beat, outdistance, outdo, outrun, outstrip, overhaul, overtake, pass, surpass.

outpouring *n* cascade, debouchment, débouchure, deluge, disemboguement, effluence, efflux, effusion, emanation, flow, flux, logorrhoea, outflow, spate, spurt, stream, torrent, word salad.

output *n* achievement, manufacture, outturn, print-out, product, production, productivity, read-out, yield.

antonyms input, outlay.

outrage *n* hurt, abuse, affront, anger, atrocity, barbarism, crime, desecration, disgrace, enormity, evil, fury, grand guignol, horror, indignation, indignity, inhumanity, injury, insult, offence, profanation, rape, ravishing, resentment, scandal, shock, violation, violence, wrath.

v abuse, affront, astound, defile, desecrate, disgust, épater le bourgeois, incense, infuriate, injure, insult, madden, make someone's blood boil, maltreat, offend, rape, ravage, ravish, repel, scandalise, shock, violate.

outrageous *adj* abominable, atrocious, barbaric, beastly, disgraceful, egregious, excessive, exorbitant, extortionate, extravagant, flagrant, godless, heinous, horrible, immoderate, infamous, inhuman, iniquitous, inordinate, monstrous, nefarious, offensive, preposterous, scandalous, shocking, steep, turbulent, unconscionable, ungodly, unholy, unreasonable, unspeakable, villainous, violent, wicked.

antonyms acceptable, irreproachable.

outrider *n* advance guard, attendant, bodyguard, escort, guard, harbinger, herald, precursor, scout, squire, vanguard.

outright *adj* absolute, arrant, categorical, complete, consummate, definite, direct, downright, flat, out-and-out, perfect, point-blank, pure, straightforward, thorough, thoroughgoing, total, uncompromising, unconditional, undeniable, unequivocal, unmitigated, unqualified, utter, wholesale.

antonyms ambiguous, indefinite, provisional.

adv absolutely, at once, cleanly, completely, directly, explicitly, immediately, instantaneously, instantly, on the spot, openly, positively, straight away, straightaway, straightforwardly, there and then, thoroughly, unhesitatingly, without restraint.

outrun *v* beat, exceed, excel, leave behind, lose, outdistance, outdo, outpace, outstrip, overhaul, overtake, pass, shake off, surpass.

outset *n* beginning, commencement, early days, forthgoing, inauguration, inception, kick-off, opening, start.

antonyms conclusion, end, finish.

outshine *v* beat, best, dwarf, eclipse, excel, outclass, outdo, outrank, outstrip, overshadow, put in the shade, surpass, top, transcend, upstage.

outside[1] *adj* exterior, external, extraforaneous, extramural, extraneous, extreme, outdoor, outer, outermost, outward, superficial, surface.

antonym inside.

n cover, exterior, façade, face, front, skin, superficies, surface, topside.

antonym inside.

prep furth, outwith, without.

outside[2] *adj* distant, faint, infinitesimal, marginal, minute, negligible, remote, slight, slim, small, unlikely.

antonyms likely, real, substantial.

outsider *n* alien, foreigner, immigrant, incomer, interloper, intruder, layman, misfit, newcomer, non-member, non-resident, observer, odd man out, outcast, outlander, outlier, settler, stranger.

antonyms inhabitant, insider, local, member, native, resident, specialist.

outskirts *n* borders, boundary, edge, environs, faubourgs, fringes, margin, periphery, purlieus, suburbia, suburbs, vicinity.

antonyms centre, city-centre.

outsmart *v* beat, best, deceive, dupe, get the better of, outfox, outmanoeuvre, outperform, out-think, outwit, trick.

outspoken *adj* abrupt, blunt, candid, direct, explicit, forthright, frank, free, open, plain-spoken, pointed, Rabelaisian, rude, sharp, trenchant, unceremonious, unequivocal, unreserved.

antonyms diplomatic, tactful.

outspread *adj* expanded, extended, fanned out, flared, open, opened, outstretched, spread out, stretched, unfolded, unfurled, wide, wide-open.

outstanding[1] *adj* ace, arresting, celebrated, conspicuous, distinguished, egregious, eminent, excellent, exceptional, extraordinary, eye-catching, great, important, impressive, marked, memorable, notable, noteworthy, pre-eminent, prominent, prosilient, remarkable, salient, signal, singular, special, striking, superior, superlative, surpassing.

antonyms ordinary, unexceptional.

outstanding[2] *adj* due, left, ongoing, open, over, owing, payable, pending, remaining, uncollected, undone, unpaid, unresolved, unsettled.

outstrip *v* beat, best, better, eclipse, exceed, excel, gain on, leave behind, leave standing, outclass, outdistance, outdo, outpace, outperform, outrun, outshine, overhaul, overtake, pass, surpass, top, transcend.

outward *adj* alleged, apparent, avowed, evident, exterior, external, noticeable, observable, obvious, ostensible, outer, outside, professed, public, superficial, supposed, surface, visible.

antonyms inner, private.

outwardly *adv* apparently, at first sight, evidently, externally, in appearance, officially, on the surface, ostensibly, seemingly, superficially, supposedly, to all appearances, to the eye.

antonyms internally, inwardly, privately.

outweigh *v* cancel out, compensate for, eclipse, make up for, outbalance, overcome, override, overrule, predominate, preponderate, prevail over, take precedence over, tip the scales in favour of, transcend.

outwit *v* beat, best, better, cheat, circumvent, deceive, defraud, dupe, get the better of, gull, make a monkey of, outfox, outmanoeuvre, outsmart, outthink, swindle, trick.

outworn *adj* abandoned, antiquated, clichéd, defunct, discredited, disused, exhausted, fogeyish, fogram, hackneyed, horse-and-buggy, moth-eaten, obsolete, out of date, outdated, outmoded, overused, rejected, stale, superannuated, threadbare, tired, trite, worn-out.

antonyms fresh, new.

oval *adj* egg-shaped, ellipsoidal, elliptical, lens-shaped, lenticular, lentiform, lentoid, obovate, obovoid, ovate, oviform, ovoid, ovoidal, vulviform.

ovation *n* acclaim, acclamation, applause, bravos, cheering, cheers, clapping, éclat, laudation, plaudits, praises, tribute.

antonyms abuse, boos, catcalls, mockery.

over[1] *adj* accomplished, bygone, closed, completed, concluded, done with, ended, finished, forgotten, gone, in the past, past, settled, up.

over[2] *prep* above, exceeding, in charge of, in command of, in excess of, more than, on, on top of, superior to, upon.

adv above, aloft, beyond, extra, in addition, in excess, left, on high, overhead, remaining, superfluous, surplus, unclaimed, unused, unwanted.

over and above added to, along with, as well as, besides, in addition to, let alone, not to mention, on top of, plus, together with.

over and over (again) ad infinitum, ad nauseam, again and again, continually, endlessly, frequently, often, repeatedly, seventy times seven, time and (time) again.

over the top a bit much, excessive, histrionic, immoderate, inordinate, overdone, too much, uncalled-for.

overabundance *n* embarras de choix, embarras de richesse, excess, glut, oversupply, plethora, profusion, superabundance, superfluity, surfeit, surplus, too much of a good thing.

antonyms dearth, lack.

overact *v* emote, exaggerate, ham, ham up, overdo, overplay.

antonyms underact, underplay.

overall *adj* all-embracing, all-inclusive, all-over, blanket, broad, complete, comprehensive, general, global, inclusive, total, umbrella.

antonyms narrow, short-term.

adv by and large, generally speaking, in general, in the long term, on the whole.

overalls *n* boiler-suit, coverall, dungarees, work-wear.

overawe *v* abash, alarm, awe, browbeat, cow, daunt, disconcert, dismay, frighten, intimidate, petrify, scare, terrify, unnerve.

antonym reassure.

overbalance *v* capsize, fall over, keel over, lose (one's) balance, lose one's footing, overset, overturn, slip, tip over, topple over, trip, tumble, turn turtle, upset.

overbearing *adj* arrogant, autocratic, bossy, cavalier, despotic, dictatorial, dogmatic, domineering, haughty, high and mighty, high-handed, imperious, lordly, magisterial, officious, oppressive, overweening, peremptory, pompous, supercilious, superior, tyrannical.

antonyms modest, unassertive, unassuming.

overcast *adj* black, clouded, clouded over, cloudy, dark, darkened, dismal, dreary, dull, grey, hazy, leaden, lowering, murky, sombre, sunless, threatening.

antonyms bright, clear, sunny.

overcharge *v* cheat, diddle, do, extort, fleece, mulct, rip off, rook, short-change, sting, surcharge.

antonym undercharge.

overcome *v* beat, best, better, conquer, crush, defeat, expugn, lick, master, overpower, overthrow, overwhelm, prevail, rise above, subdue, subjugate, surmount, survive, triumph over, vanquish, weather, worst.

adj affected, beaten, bowled over, broken, defeated, exhausted, overpowered, overwhelmed, speechless, swept off one's feet.

over-confident *adj* arrogant, brash, cocksure, cocky, foolhardy, hubristic, incautious, over-optimistic, overweening, presumptuous, rash, sanguine, temerarious, uppish.

antonyms cautious, diffident.

overcritical *adj* captious, carping, cavilling, fault-finding, hair-splitting, hard to please, hypercritical, nit-picking, over-nice, overparticular, pedantic, pernickety, purist, ultracrepidarian, Zoilean.

antonyms easygoing, tolerant, uncritical.

overcrowded *adj* chock-a-block, chock-full, choked, congested, crammed full, hotching, jam-packed, overloaded, overpopulated, packed, packed out, seething, swarming.

antonyms deserted, empty.

overdo *v* do to death, exaggerate, gild the lily, go to extremes, go too far, labour, lay it on thick, overact, overexert, overindulge, overplay, overreach, overstate, overtax, overuse, overwork.

antonyms neglect, underuse.

overdone *adj* burnt, burnt to a cinder, charred, dried up, effusive, exaggerated, excessive, fulsome, histrionic, immoderate, inordinate, over the top, overcooked, overelaborate, overplayed, overstated, percoct, preposterous, spoiled, supererogatory, undue, unnecessary.

antonyms raw, underdone, underplayed, understated.

overdue *adj* behind schedule, behindhand, belated, delayed, late, owing, slow, tardy, unpunctual.

antonym early.

overeat *v* binge, eat like a horse, gluttonise, gorge, gormandise, guzzle, make a pig of oneself, overindulge, pack away, stuff, stuff oneself.

antonyms abstain, starve.

overeating *n* bingeing, bulimia, gluttony, gormandise, gormandism, gourmandise, gourmandism, guzzling, hyperphagia, overindulgence.

antonyms abstemiousness, abstention.

overemphasise *v* belabour, exaggerate, labour, overdramatise, overstress.

antonyms belittle, minimise, underplay, understate.

overexert oneself break a leg, burn the candle at both ends, drive oneself too hard, fatigue, knock oneself out, overdo it, overstrain oneself, overtax oneself, overtire oneself, overwork, push oneself too hard, strain oneself, wear oneself out, work oneself to death.

antonyms idle, laze.

overflow *v* brim over, bubble over, cover, deluge, discharge, drown, flood, inundate, pour over, shower, soak, spill, spray, submerge, surge, swamp, well over.

n flood, inundation, overabundance, overspill, spill, superfluity, surplus.

overflowing *adj* abounding, bountiful, brimful, copious, inundant, plenteous, plentiful, profuse, rife, superabundant, swarming, teeming, thronged.

antonyms lacking, scarce.

overgrowth *n* escalation, hypertrophy, overabundance, overdevelopment, superabundance.

antonyms decline, failure, shrinkage, wasting.

overhang *v* beetle, bulge, extend, impend, jut, loom, menace, project, protrude, stick out, threaten.

overhanging *adj* beetling, jutting, pensile, projecting, protruding.

overhaul[1] *v* check, do up, examine, fix, inspect, mend, recondition, re-examine, repair, restore, service, survey.

n check, check-up, examination, going-over, inspection, reconditioning, repair, restoration, service.

overhaul[2] *v* gain on, outpace, outstrip, overtake, pass, pull ahead of.

overhead *adv* above, aloft, on high, up above, upward.

antonyms below, underfoot.

adj aerial, elevated, overhanging, roof, upper.

antonyms floor, ground, underground.

overheads *n* burden, expenses, oncost, operating costs, outgoings, running costs.

antonyms income, profit.

overheated *adj* agitated, excited, fiery, flaming, impassioned, inflamed, overexcited, overwrought, passionate, roused.

antonyms calm, cool, dispassionate, impassive.

overheating *n* heatstroke, hyperpyrexia, hyperthermia, sunstroke.

antonyms chill, hypothermia.

overindulge *v* binge, booze, debauch, gluttonise, gorge, gormandise, guzzle.

antonym abstain.

overindulgence *n* binge, debauch, excess, immoderation, intemperance, overeating, surfeit.

antonyms abstemiousness, abstention.

overjoyed *adj* delighted, delirious, ecstatic, elated, enraptured, euphoric, in raptures, joyful, jubilant, on cloud nine, over the moon, rapturous, thrilled, tickled pink, transported.

antonyms disappointed, sad.

overlap *v* coincide, cover, flap over, imbricate, overlay, overlie, shingle.

overlapping *adj* coinciding, covering, imbricated, layered, limbous, overlying, shingled.

overload *v* burden, encumber, oppress, overburden, overcharge, overtax, saddle, strain, surcharge, tax, weigh down.

overlook[1] *v* condone, disregard, excuse, forget, forgive, ignore, let pass, let ride, miss, neglect, omit, pardon, pass, pass over, skip, slight, turn a blind eye to, wink at.

antonyms animadvert, note, notice, penalise, record, remember.

overlook[2] *v* command a view of, face, front on to, give upon, look on to.

overlooked *adj* unconsidered, unheeded, unhonoured, unnoted, unprized, unregarded, unremarked, unvalued.

antonyms appreciated, prized, sought-after, valued.

overly *adv* exceedingly, excessively, immoderately, inordinately, over, too, unduly, unreasonably.

antonyms inadequately, insufficiently.

over-nice *adj* finical, nit-picking, overfastidious, over-meticulous, overparticular, overprecise, overscrupulous, oversensitive, oversubtle, pernickety, rose-water.

antonyms casual, uncritical.

overpower *v* beat, best, conquer, crush, defeat, floor, immobilise, master, overcome, overthrow, overwhelm, quell, subdue, subjugate, vanquish.

overpowering *adj* compelling, convincing, extreme, forceful, insuppressible, invincible, irrefutable, irrepressible, irresistible, nauseating, oppressive, overwhelming, powerful, sickening, strong, suffocating, telling, unbearable, uncontrollable.

overrate *v* blow up, magnify, make too much of, overestimate, overpraise, overprize, oversell, overvalue.

antonym underrate.

override *v* abrogate, annul, cancel, countermand, disregard, ignore, nullify, outweigh, overrule, quash, rescind, reverse, ride roughshod over, set aside, supersede, trample, upset, vanquish.

overriding *adj* cardinal, compelling, determining, dominant, essential, final, first, major, number one, overruling, paramount, pivotal, predominant, prevailing, primary, prime, prior, ruling, supreme, ultimate.

antonyms insignificant, unimportant.

overrule *v* abrogate, annul, cancel, countermand, disallow, invalidate, outvote, override, overturn, recall, repeal, rescind, reverse, revoke, set aside, veto, vote down.

antonyms allow, approve.

overrun[1] *v* choke, infest, inundate, invade, occupy, overflow, overgrow, overspread, overwhelm, permeate, ravage, run riot, spread over, surge over, swamp, swarm over.

antonyms desert, evacuate.

overrun[2] *v* exceed, overdo, overshoot, overstep.

overseas *adj* exotic, foreign, outland, outlandish, ultramarine.

antonyms domestic, home.

adv abroad, in/to foreign climes, in/to foreign parts.

n foreign climes, foreign parts, outland, outremer.

antonym home.

overseer *n* boss, chief, foreman, forewoman, gaffer, headman, manager, master, super, superintendent, superior, supervisor, surveyor, workmaster, workmistress.

overshadow *v* adumbrate, becloud, bedim, blight, cloud, darken, dim, dominate, dwarf, eclipse, excel, mar, obfuscate, obscure, outshine, outweigh, protect, put in the shade, rise above, ruin, shelter, spoil, surpass, tower above, veil.

oversight[1] *n* administration, care, charge, control, custody, direction, guidance, handling, inspection, keeping, management, responsibility, superintendence, supervision, surveillance.

oversight[2] *n* blunder, boob, carelessness, delinquency, error, fault, inattention, lapse, laxity, mistake, neglect, omission, slip, slip-up.

overt *adj* apparent, avowed, evident, manifest, observable, obvious, open, patent, plain, professed, public, unconcealed, undisguised, visible.

antonyms covert, secret.

overtake *v* befall, catch up with, come upon, draw level with, engulf, happen, hit, outdistance, outdo, outstrip, overhaul, pass, pull ahead of, strike.

overthrow *v* abolish, beat, bring down, conquer, crush, defeat, demolish, depose, destroy, dethrone, displace, knock down, level, master, oust, overcome, overpower, overturn, overwhelm, raze, ruin, subdue, subjugate, subvert, topple, unseat, upset, vanquish.

antonyms install, reinstate.

n bouleversement, confounding, defeat, deposition, destruction, dethronement, discomfiture, disestablishment, displacement, dispossession, downfall, end, fall, humiliation, labefactation, labefaction, ousting, prostration, rout, ruin, subjugation, subversion, suppression, undoing, unseating.

overtone *n* association, connotation, feeling, flavour, hint, implication, innuendo, intimation, nuance, sense, slant, something, suggestion, undercurrent.

overture *n* advance, approach, introduction, invitation, motion, move, offer, opening, (opening) gambit, opening move, prelude, proposal, proposition, signal, suggestion, tender.

overturn *v* abolish, abrogate, annul, capsize, countermand, depose, destroy, invalidate, keel over, knock down, knock over, overbalance, overset, overthrow, quash, repeal, rescind, reverse, set aside, spill, tip over, topple, tumble, unseat, upend, upset, upturn.

overused *adj* bromidic, clichéd, commonplace, hackneyed, platitudinous, played out, stale, stereotyped, threadbare, tired, trite, unoriginal, worn.

antonyms fresh, original.

overweening *adj* arrogant, cavalier, cocksure, cocky, conceited, egotistical, excessive, extravagant, haughty, high-handed, hubristic, immoderate, inflated, insolent, lordly, opinionated, overblown, pompous, presumptuous, proud, self-confident, supercilious, swollen, uppish, vain, vainglorious.

antonyms diffident, unassuming.

overweight *adj* ample, bulky, buxom, chubby, chunky, corpulent, fat, flabby, fleshy, gross, heavy, hefty, huge, massive, obese, outsize, plump, podgy, portly, pot-bellied, stout, tubby, well-padded, well-upholstered.

antonyms emaciated, skinny, thin, underweight.

overwhelm *v* bowl over, bury, confuse, crush, cut to pieces, defeat, deluge, destroy, devastate, engulf, floor, inundate, knock for six, massacre, overcome, overpower, overrun, prostrate, rout, snow under, stagger, submerge, swamp.

overwhelming *adj* breathtaking, crushing, devastating, foudroyant, insuppressible, invincible, irrepressible, irresistible, overpowering, shattering, stunning, towering, uncontrollable, vast.

antonyms insignificant, negligible, resistible.

overwork *v* burden, burn the midnight oil, exhaust, exploit, fatigue, oppress, overburden, overload, overstrain, overtax, overuse, prostrate, strain, sweat, tax, wear out, weary, work one's fingers to the bone.

overwrought *adj* agitated, beside oneself, distracted, emotional, excited, frantic, keyed up, on edge, overcharged, overexcited, overheated, overworked, stirred, strung up, tense, uptight, worked up, wound up.

antonyms calm, cool, impassive.

owing *adj* due, in arrears, outstanding, overdue, owed, payable, unpaid, unsettled.

owing to as a result of, because of, imputable to, on account of, thanks to.

own[1] *adj* idiosyncratic, individual, inimitable, particular, personal, private.

own[2] *v* acknowledge, admit, agree, allow, avow, concede, confess, disclose, enjoy, grant, have, hold, keep, possess, recognise, retain.

own up admit, come clean, confess, make a clean breast of it, spill the beans, tell the truth.

owner *n* franklin, freeholder, holder, laird, landlady, landlord, lord, master, mistress, possessor, proprietor, proprietress, proprietrix.

ownership *n* dominion, freehold, possession, proprietary rights, proprietorship, right of possession, title.

ox *n* bison, buffalo, bullock, clod, dolt, gaur, g(a)yal, lout, oaf, steer.

P

pace *n* celerity, clip, gait, lick, measure, momentum, motion, movement, progress, quickness, rapidity, rate, speed, step, stride, tempo, time, tread, velocity, walk.

v count, determine, march, mark out, measure, pad, patrol, pound, step, stride, tramp, tread, walk.

pacific *adj* appeasing, calm, complaisant, conciliatory, diplomatic, dovelike, dovish, eirenic, equable, friendly, gentle, halcyon, irenic, mild, nonbelligerent, nonviolent, pacificatory, pacifist, peaceable, peaceful, peace-loving, peacemaking, placatory, placid, propitiatory, quiet, serene, smooth, still, tranquil, unruffled.

antonyms aggressive, belligerent, contentious, pugnacious.

pacifism *n* non-violence, pacificism, passive resistance, satyagraha.

pacifist *n* conchie, conscientious objector, dove, pacificist, passive resister, peace-lover, peacemonger, peacenik, satyagrahi.

antonyms hawk, warmonger.

pacify *v* allay, ameliorate, appease, assuage, calm, chasten, compose, conciliate, crush, humour, lull, moderate, mollify, placate, propitiate, put down, quell, quiet, repress, silence, smooth down, soften, soothe, still, subdue, tame, tranquillise.

antonyms aggravate, anger.

pack *n* assemblage, back-pack, bale, band, boodle, bunch, bundle, burden, collection, company, crew, crowd, deck, drove, fardel, flock, galère, gang, group, haversack, herd, kit, kitbag, knapsack, load, lot, Matilda, mob, outfit, package, packet, parcel, rucksack, set, troop, truss.

v batch, bundle, burden, charge, compact, compress, cram, crowd, empocket, fill, jam, load, mob, package, packet, press, ram, steeve, store, stow, stuff, tamp, throng, thrust, wedge.

package *n* agreement, amalgamation, arrangement, bale, box, carton, combination, consignment, container, deal, entity, kit, pack, packet, parcel, proposal, proposition, unit, whole.

v batch, box, pack, pack up, packet, parcel, parcel up, wrap, wrap up.

packed *adj* brimful, brim-full, chock-a-block, chock-full, congested, cram-full, crammed, crowded, filled, full, hotching, jammed, jam-packed, overflowing, overloaded, seething, swarming.

antonyms deserted, empty.

packet[1] *n* bag, carton, case, container, pack, package, packing, parcel, poke, wrapper, wrapping.

packet[2] *n* a bob or two, bomb, bundle, fortune, king's ransom, lot, lots, mint, pile, pot, pots, pretty penny, small fortune, tidy sum.

pack-horse *n* beast of burden, led horse, pack-animal, sumpter, sumpter-horse.

pact *n* agreement, alliance, arrangement, bargain, bond, cartel, compact, concord, concordat, contract, convention, covenant, deal, entente, league, protocol, treaty, understanding.

antonyms breach, disagreement, quarrel.

pad[1] *n* block, buffer, cushion, jotter, notepad, pillow, protection, pulvillus, pulvinar, stiffening, stuffing, tablet, wad, writing-pad.

v cushion, fill, line, pack, protect, shape, stuff, wrap.

pad out amplify, augment, bombast, eke, elaborate, expand, fill out, flesh out, inflate, lengthen, protract, spin out, stretch.

pad[2] *n* foot, footprint, paw, print, sole.

pad[3] *n* apartment, flat, hang-out, home, penthouse, place, quarters, room, rooms.

pad[4] *v* lope, move, run, step, tiptoe, tramp, tread, trudge, walk.

padding *n* bombast, circumlocution, filling, hot air, packing, perissology, prolixity, stuffing, verbiage, verbosity, wadding, waffle, wordiness.

paddle[1] *n* oar, scull, sweep.

v oar, ply, propel, pull, row, scull, steer.

paddle[2] *v* dabble, plash, slop, splash, stir, trail, wade.

paddy *n* bate, fit of temper, fury, paddywhack, passion, pet, rage, taking, tantrum, temper, tiff, wax.

paean *n* anthem, dithyramb, doxology, encomium, eulogy, hymn, ovation, panegyric, psalm.

antonyms denunciation, satire.

pagan *n* atheist, Gentile, heathen, idolater, infidel, nullifidian, polytheist, unbeliever.

antonym believer.

adj atheistic, Gentile, godless, heathen, heathenish, idolatrous, infidel, irreligious, nullifidian, polytheistic.

page[1] *n* chapter, episode, epoch, era, event, folio, incident, leaf, period, phase, point, recto, sheet, side, stage, time, verso.

page² *n* attendant, bell-boy, bellhop, boy, buttons, cupbearer, footboy, footman, page-boy, servant, squire.

v announce, bid, call, call out, preconise, seek, send for, summon.

pageant *n* display, extravaganza, masque, parade, play, procession, representation, ritual, scene, show, spectacle, tableau, tableau vivant.

pageantry *n* ceremony, display, drama, extravagance, glamour, glitter, grandeur, magnificence, melodrama, ostentation, parade, pomp, show, showiness, spectacle, splash, splendour, state, theatricality.

pail *n* bail, bucket, churn, piggin, tub.

pain *n* ache, affliction, aggravation, agony, anguish, annoyance, bitterness, bore, bother, burden, cramp, discomfort, distress, dole, dolour, drag, grief, gyp, headache, heartache, heartbreak, hurt, irritation, lancination, misery, nuisance, pang, pest, smart, soreness, spasm, suffering, tenderness, throb, throe, torment, torture, tribulation, trouble, twinge, vexation, woe, wretchedness.

v afflict, aggrieve, agonise, annoy, chagrin, cut to the quick, disappont, disquiet, distress, exasperate, gall, grieve, harass, hurt, irritate, nettle, rile, sadden, torment, torture, vex, worry, wound, wring.

antonyms gratify, please.

pained *adj* aggrieved, chagrined, cut to the quick, cut up, disappointed, distressed, galled, grieved, hurt, injured, miffed, nettled, offended, reproachful, saddened, stung, upset, wounded.

antonyms gratified, pleased.

painful *adj* aching, achy, afflictive, agonising, arduous, difficult, disagreeable, distasteful, distressing, doloriferous, dolorific, excruciating, grievous, hard, harrowing, laborious, lancinating, saddening, severe, smarting, sore, tedious, tender, troublesome, trying, unpleasant, vexatious.

antonyms easy, painless.

painfully *adv* alarmingly, clearly, deplorably, distressingly, dreadfully, excessively, markedly, pitiably, pitifully, sadly, unfortunately, woefully, wretchedly.

painkiller *n* alleviative, anaesthetic, analgesic, anodyne, drug, lenitive, palliative, paregoric, remedy, sedative.

antonym irritant.

painless *adj* downhill, easy, effortless, fast, pain-free, plain sailing, quick, simple, trouble-free, undemanding.

antonyms difficult, painful.

pains *n* assiduity, assiduousness, birth-pangs, bother, care, contractions, diligence, effort, industry, labour, sedulity, sedulousness, throes, trouble.

painstaking *adj* assiduous, careful, conscientious, dedicated, devoted, diligent, earnest, exacting, hardworking, industrious, meticulous, perfectionist, persevering, punctilious, scrupulous, sedulous, strenuous, thorough, thoroughgoing.

antonyms careless, negligent.

paint *n* colour, colouring, cosmetics, distemper, dye, emulsion, enamel, glaze, greasepaint, lacquer, lake, make-up, maquillage, oils, pigment, primer, stain, tint, undercoat, warpaint, wash, water-colour, whitewash.

v apply, coat, colour, cover, daub, decorate, delineate, depict, describe, distemper, evoke, glaze, lacquer, limn, picture, portray, recount, render, represent.

painter *n* artist, colourist, dauber, delineator, depicter, limner, miniaturist, muralist, oil-painter, water-colourist.

painting *n* aquarelle, camaieu, daubery, depiction, fresco, illustration, kakemono, landscape, miniature, mural, oil, oil-painting, picture, portrait, portraiture, portrayal, representation, scene, seascape, still life, tablature, water-colour.

pair *n* brace, combination, couple, doublet, doubleton, duad, duo, dyad, match, span, twins, two of a kind, twosome, yoke.

v bracket, couple, join, link, marry, match, match up, mate, pair off, put together, splice, team, twin, wed, yoke.

antonyms dissever, sever.

paired *adj* associated, bracketed, coupled, didymous, double, in twos, joined, linked, matched, mated, twinned, yoked.

antonym single.

pal *n* amigo, buddy, china, chum, companion, comrade, confidant(e), crony, friend, gossip, intimate, mate, partner, side-kick, soul mate.

antonym enemy.

palace *n* alcázar, basilica, château, dome, palazzo, schloss.

antonym hovel.

palatable *adj* acceptable, agreeable, appetising, attractive, enjoyable, fair, pleasant, sapid, satisfactory, savoury, tasty, toothsome.

antonyms unacceptable, unpleasant.

palate *n* appetite, appreciation, enjoyment, gout, gusto, heart, liking, relish, stomach, taste, zest.

palatial *adj* de luxe, grand, grandiose, illustrious, imposing, luxurious, magnificent, majestic, opulent, plush, posh, regal, spacious, splendid, stately, sumptuous, swanky.

antonyms cramped, poky.

palaver *n* activity, babble, blather, blether, business, bustle, carry-on, chatter, colloquy, confab, conference, confusion, discussion, fuss, fuss about nothing, get-together, hubbub, natter, parley, performance, pow-wow, prattle, procedure, rigmarole, session, song and dance, to-do, tongue-wagging, yak.

v blab, blather, blether, chatter, confab, confer, discuss, gabble, jabber, jaw, natter, parley, powwow, prattle, tattle, yak.

pale *adj* anaemic, ashen, ashy, bleached, bloodless, chalky, colourless, dim, etiolated, faded, faint, feeble, inadequate, light, lily-livered, pallid, pasty, poor, sallow, thin, wan, washed-out, waxy, weak, whey-faced, white, white-livered, whitish.

antonym ruddy.

v blanch, decrease, dim, diminish, dull, etiolate, fade, lessen, whiten.

antonyms blush, colour.

palisade *n* barricade, bulwark, defence, enclosure, fence, fortification, paling, palisado, stockade.

pall[1] *n* check, cloud, cold water, damp, damper, dismay, gloom, mantle, melancholy, shadow, shroud, sindon, veil.

pall[2] *v* bore, cloy, glut, jade, lose savour, satiate, sicken, surfeit, tire, weary.

palliate *v* abate, allay, alleviate, assuage, cloak, conceal, cover, diminish, ease, excuse, extenuate, lenify, lessen, lighten, minimise, mitigate, moderate, mollify, relieve, soften, soothe, temper.

palliative *adj* alleviative, anodyne, assuasive, calmative, calming, demulcent, lenitive, mitigative, mitigatory, mollifying, paregoric, sedative, soothing.

antonym irritant.

n analgesic, anodyne, calmative, demulcent, lenitive, painkiller, paregoric, sedative, tranquilliser.

pallid *adj* anaemic, ashen, ashy, bloodless, cadaverous, colourless, doughy, etiolated, insipid, lifeless, livid, pale, pasty, pasty-faced, peelie-wally, sallow, spiritless, sterile, tame, tired, uninspired, vapid, wan, waxen, waxy, whey-faced, whitish.

antonyms high-complexioned, ruddy, vigorous.

pallor *n* bloodlessness, chalkiness, etiolation, paleness, pallidness, sallowness, wanness, whiteness.

antonym ruddiness.

pally *adj* affectionate, chummy, close, familiar, friendly, intimate, palsy, palsy-walsy, thick.

antonym unfriendly.

palm *n* hand, mitt, paw, vola.

v appropriate, conceal, grab, half-inch, nick, sneak, snitch.

palm off fob off, foist, foist off, impose, offload, pass off, thrust, unload.

palmistry *n* chirognomy, chiromancy, fortune-telling, palm reading.

palmy *adj* carefree, flourishing, fortunate, glorious, golden, halcyon, happy, joyous, luxurious, prosperous, salad, thriving, triumphant.

palpable *adj* apparent, blatant, clear, concrete, conspicuous, evident, manifest, material, obvious, open, overt, patent, plain, real, solid, substantial, tangible, touchable, unmistakable, visible.

antonyms elusive, impalpable, imperceptible, intangible.

palpitate *v* beat, flutter, pitapat, pit-pat, pitter-patter, pittypat, pound, pulsate, pulse, quiver, shiver, throb, thump, tremble, vibrate.

palsied *adj* agued, arthritic, atonic, crippled, debilitated, disabled, helpless, paralysed, paralytic, rheumatic, sclerotic, shaking, shaky, shivering, spastic, trembling, tremulous.

paltry *adj* base, beggarly, contemptible, derisory, despicable, inconsiderable, insignificant, jitney, low, meagre, mean, minor, miserable, negligible, pettifogging, petty, picayunish, piddling, piffling, pimping, pitiful, poor, puny, rubbishy, slight, small, sorry, tinpot, trifling, trivial, two-bit, twopenny-halfpenny, unimportant, worthless, wretched.

antonyms significant, substantial.

pamper *v* baby, cocker, coddle, cosset, fondle, gratify, humour, indulge, mollycoddle, mother, overindulge, pet, spoil.

antonyms ill-treat, neglect.

pampered *adj* coddled, cosseted, high-fed, indulged, mollycoddled, overfed, petted, spoilt.

antonyms abused, neglected.

pamphlet *n* booklet, broadside, brochure, chapbook, folder, leaflet, tract, tractate, treatise.

pan[1] *n* casserole, container, fryer, marmite, pancheon, pot, saucepan, skillet, spider, stewpot, vessel, wok.

v censure, criticise, flay, hammer, knock, pick to pieces, pull to pieces, roast, rubbish, slam, slate.

antonym praise.

pan out be exhausted, come to an end, culminate, eventuate, happen, result, turn out, work out, yield.

pan[2] *v* circle, follow, move, scan, sweep, swing, track, traverse, turn.

panacea *n* catholicon, cure-all, diacatholicon, elixir, nostrum, panpharmacon, theriac, treacle.

panache *n* brio, dash, élan, enthusiasm, flair, flamboyance, flourish, grand manner, ostentation, pizzazz, spirit, style, swagger, theatricality, verve, vigour, zest.

pandemonium *n* babel, bedlam, chaos, clamour, commotion, confusion, din, disorder, Donnybrook, frenzy, hubbub, hue and cry, hullaballoo, racket, ruckus, ruction, rumpus, to-do, tumult, turbulence, turmoil, uproar.

antonyms calm, order, peace.

pander *v* cater to, furnish, gratify, indulge, pamper, please, provide, purvey, satisfy.

n bawd, go-between, mack, pimp, ponce, procurer, procuress, white-slaver, whoremaster, whoremonger.

panegyric *n* accolade, citation, commendation, encomium, eulogium, eulogy, homage, paean, praise, tribute.

antonym censure.

adj commendatory, complimentary, encomiastic, eulogistic, favourable, flattering, glowing, laudatory, panegyrical, praiseful, praising.

antonyms censorious, damning.

panel *n* compartment, rectangle, strip, table.

panelling *n* dado, panel-work, wainscot, wainscot(t)ing.

pang *n* ache, agony, anguish, crick, discomfort, distress, gripe, pain, prick, spasm, stab, sting, stitch, throe, twinge, twitch, wrench.

panic *n* agitation, alarm, consternation, dismay, fear, fright, hassle, horror, hysteria, scare, terror, tizzy, to-do.

antonyms assurance, confidence.

v alarm, get one's knickers in a twist, go to pieces, lose one's cool, lose one's nerve, overreact, put the wind up, scare, startle, terrify, unnerve.

antonyms reassure, relax.

panic-stricken *adj* affrighted, aghast, agitated, alarmed, appalled, fearful, frenzied, frightened, horrified, horror-stricken, hysterical, in a cold sweat, panicky, perturbed, petrified, scared, scared stiff, startled, stunned, stupefied, terrified, terror-stricken, unnerved.

antonyms confident, laid-back, relaxed.

panoply *n* armour, array, attire, dress, equipment, garb, gear, get-up, insignia, raiment, regalia, show, trappings, turn-out.

panorama *n* bird's-eye view, overview, perspective, prospect, scene, scenery, spectacle, survey, view, vision, vista.

panoramic *adj* bird's-eye, comprehensive, extensive, far-reaching, gazy, general, inclusive, overall, panned, scenic, sweeping, universal, wide, widespread.

antonym limited.

pansy *n* fag, faggot, homo, homosexual, Jessie, milksop, Miss Nancy, molly, mollycoddle, namby-pamby, poof, poofter, queen, queer.

pant *v* ache, blow, breathe, covet, crave, desire, flaff, gasp, hanker, heave, huff, hunger, long, palpitate, pine, puff, sigh, thirst, throb, want, wheeze, yearn, yen.

n gasp, huff, puff, throb, wheeze.

panting *adj* anxious, breathless, eager, gasping, impatient, out of breath, puffed, puffed out, puffing, short-winded, winded.

pantomime *n* charade, dumb-show, galantry show, panto.

pants *n* briefs, drawers, knickers, panties, shorts, slacks, trews, trousers, trunks, underpants, undershorts, Y-fronts.

paper *n* analysis, archive, article, assignment, authorisation, certificate, composition, credential, critique, daily, deed, diary, dissertation, document, dossier, essay, examination, file, gazette, instrument, journal, letter, monograph, news, newspaper, notepaper, organ, rag, record, report, script, stationery, study, thesis, treatise.

papery *adj* delicate, flimsy, fragile, frail, insubstantial, light, lightweight, paper-thin, thin, translucent.

papism *n* papery, papistry, Roman Catholicism.

papist *n* Catholic, Fenian, papisher, Roman Catholic.

adj Catholic, Fenian, papish, popish, Roman Catholic.

par *n* accordance, average, balance, correspondence, equal footing, equality, equilibrium, equivalence, level, mean, median, norm, parity, similarity, standard, usual.

parable *n* allegory, apologue, exemplum, fable, homily, lesson, story.

parade *n* array, cavalcade, ceremony, column, corso, display, exhibition, flaunting, march, motorcade, ostentation, pageant, panache, pizzazz, pomp, procession, promenade, review, show, spectacle, train, vaunting.

v air, brandish, defile, display, exhibit, flaunt, make a show of, march, peacock, process, show, show off, strut, swagger, vaunt.

paradigm *n* archetype, example, exemplar, framework, ideal, model, original, pattern, prototype.

paradise *n* bliss, City of God, delight, Eden, Elysian fields, Elysium, felicity, garden of delights, Garden of Eden, heaven, heavenly kingdom, Land o' the Leal, Olympus, Promised Land, seventh heaven, utopia, Valhalla, Zion.

antonyms Hades, hell.

paradox *n* absurdity, ambiguity, anomaly, contradiction, enigma, equivocation, incongruity, inconsistency, mystery, oddity, puzzle, riddle.

paradoxical *adj* absurd, ambiguous, baffling, conflicting, confounding, contradictory, enigmatic, equivocal, Gilbertian, illogical, impossible, improbable, incongruous, inconsistent, puzzling, self-contradictory.

paragon *n* apotheosis, archetype, crème de la crème, criterion, cynosure, epitome, exemplar, ideal, jewel, masterpiece, model, non(e)such, nonpareil, paradigm, pattern, prototype, quintessence, standard, the bee's knees.

paragraph *n* clause, item, notice, part, passage, portion, section, subdivision, subsection.

parallel *adj* akin, aligned, alongside, analogous, co-extensive, collateral, connate, correspondent, corresponding, equidistant, homologous, like, matching, resembling, similar, uniform.

antonyms divergent, separate.

n analogue, analogy, comparison, corollary, correlation, correspondence, counterpart, duplicate, equal, equivalent, homologue, likeness, match, parallelism, resemblance, similarity, twin.

v agree, compare, conform, correlate, correspond, duplicate, emulate, equal, match.

antonyms diverge, separate.

paralyse *v* anaesthetise, arrest, benumb, clamp down on, cripple, debilitate, disable, freeze, halt, immobilise, incapacitate, lame, numb, obtund, petrify, stun, stupefy, torpefy, transfix.

paralysis *n* arrest, break-down, halt, hemiplegia, immobility, monoplegia, palsy, paraplegia, paresis, quadriplegia, shut-down, stagnation, standstill, stoppage, torpor.

paralytic[1] *adj* crippled, disabled, hemiplegic, immobile, immobilised, incapacitated, lame, monoplegic, numb, palsied, paralysed, quadriplegic.

paralytic² *adj* canned, drunk, inebriated, intoxicated, legless, pie-eyed, pissed, plastered, sloshed, smashed, stewed, stoned, stotious, three sheets in the wind.

antonym (stone-cold) sober.

parameter *n* boundary, constant, criterion, framework, guideline, indication, limit, limitation, restriction, specification, variable.

paramount *adj* capital, cardinal, chief, dominant, eminent, first, foremost, highest, main, outstanding, predominant, pre-eminent, premier, primary, prime, principal, superior, supreme, topmost, top-rank.

antonyms inferior, last, lowest.

paramour *n* beau, concubine, courtesan, doxy, fancy man, fancy woman, hetaira, inamorata, kept woman, lover, mistress, woman.

paranoia *n* delusions, megalomania, monomania, obsession, psychosis.

parapet *n* barbican, bartisan, bastion, battlement, bulwark, fortification, rampart.

paraphernalia *n* accessories, accoutrements, apparatus, appurtenances, baggage, belongings, bits and pieces, clobber, clutter, effects, equipage, equipment, gear, impedimenta, material, odds and ends, stuff, tackle, things, trappings, traps.

paraphrase *n* farse, gloss, interpretation, recapitulation, rehash, rendering, rendition, rephrasing, restatement, rewording, translation, version.

v farse, gloss, interpret, recapitulate, rehash, render, rephrase, restate, reword, translate.

parasite *n* bloodsucker, cadger, endophyte, endozoon, entozoon, epiphyte, epizoan, epizoon, free-loader, hanger-on, leech, lick-trencher, scrounger, sponge, sponger, sucker.

parasitic *adj* biogenous, bloodsucking, cadging, epizoan, epizoic, free-loading, leechlike, parasitical, scrounging, sponging.

parcel *n* band, batch, bunch, bundle, carton, collection, company, crew, crowd, da(w)k, gang, group, lot, pack, package, packet, plot, portion, property, quantity, set, tract.

v bundle, collect, pack, package, tie up, wrap.

parcel out allocate, allot, apportion, carve up, deal out, dispense, disperse, distribute, divide, dole out, mete out, portion out, separate, share out.

parch *v* blister, burn, dehydrate, desiccate, dry up, exsiccate, roast, scorch, sear, shrivel, wither.

parched *adj* arid, dehydrated, dried up, drouthy, dry, scorched, shrivelled, thirsty, waterless, withered.

parchment *n* certificate, charter, diploma, document, palimpsest, scroll, vellum.

pardon *v* absolve, acquit, amnesty, condone, emancipate, exculpate, excuse, exonerate, forgive, free, let off, liberate, overlook, release, remit, reprieve, respite, vindicate.

n absolution, acquittal, allowance, amnesty, compassion, condonation, discharge, excuse, exoneration, forgiveness, grace, humanity, indulgence, mercy, release, remission, reprieval, reprieve.

pardonable *adj* allowable, condonable, dispensable, excusable, forgivable, justifiable, minor, permissible, remissible, understandable, venial, warrantable.

antonym inexcusable.

pare *v* clip, crop, cut, cut back, decrease, diminish, dock, flaught, float, lop, peel, prune, reduce, retrench, shave, shear, skin, skive, trim.

parent *n* architect, author, begetter, cause, creator, father, forerunner, generant, genetrix, genitor, guardian, mother, origin, originator, procreator, progenitor, progenitress, progenitrix, prototype, root, sire, source.

parentage *n* affiliation, ancestry, birth, derivation, descent, extraction, family, filiation, line, lineage, origin, paternity, pedigree, race, source, stirps, stock.

parenthetic *adj* adventitious, bracketed, elucidative, explanatory, extraneous, extrinsic, in parenthesis, incidental, inserted, interposed, intervening, parenthetical, qualifying.

antonyms basic, original.

pariah *n* black sheep, castaway, exile, Ishmael, leper, outcast, outlaw, undesirable, unperson, untouchable.

paring *n* clipping, cutting, flake, flaught, fragment, peel, peeling, rind, shaving, shred, skin, slice, sliver, snippet.

parish *n* brethren, church, churchgoers, community, congregation, district, flock, fold, parishioners, vicariate.

parity *n* affinity, agreement, analogy, conformity, congruence, congruity, consistency, consonance, correspondence, equality, equivalence, likeness, par, parallelism, resemblance, sameness, semblance, similarity, similitude, uniformity, unity.

park¹ *n* estate, garden, grounds, paddock, parkland, pleasance, pleasure garden, reserve, woodland.

park² *v* deposit, dump, leave, position, station.

parlance *n* argot, cant, diction, idiom, jargon, language, lingo, phraseology, speech, talk, tongue.

parley *n* colloquy, confab, conference, council, deliberation, dialogue, discussion, get-together, meeting, negotiation, palaver, powwow, talk(s), tête-à-tête.

v confabulate, confer, consult, deliberate, discuss, get together, negotiate, palaver, powwow, speak, talk.

parliament *n* assembly, conclave, congress, convocation, council, Dail, diet, house, legislature, senate, talking-shop, Tynwald.

parliamentary *adj* congressional, deliberative, governmental, law-making, legislative, legislatorial, senatorial.

parlour *n* drawing-room, living-room, lounge, sitting-room.

parochial *adj* blinkered, confined, incestuous, insular, inward-looking, limited, narrow, narrow-minded, parish-pump, petty, provincial, restricted, small-minded.

parochialism *n* insularity, narrow-mindedness, pettiness, provincialism.

parody *n* burlesque, caricature, imitation, lampoon, mimicry, pasquinade, satire, send-up, skit, spoof, take-off.

v burlesque, caricature, lampoon, mimic, pasquinade, satirise, send up, spoof, take off, travesty.

paroxysm *n* attack, convulsion, eruption, explosion, fit, flare-up, outbreak, outburst, seizure, spasm, tantrum.

parrot *n* ape, copy-cat, imitator, mimic, phraser, repeater.

v ape, copy, echo, imitate, mimic, rehearse, reiterate, repeat.

parrot-fashion *adv* automatically, by rote, mechanically, mindlessly, unthinkingly.

parry *v* avert, avoid, block, circumvent, deflect, divert, dodge, duck, evade, fence, fend off, field, forestall, obviate, rebuff, repel, repulse, shun, sidestep, stave off, ward off.

parsimonious *adj* cheese-paring, close, close-fisted, close-handed, frugal, grasping, mean, mingy, miserable, miserly, money-grubbing, niggardly, penny-pinching, penny-wise, penurious, saving, scrimpy, sparing, stingy, stinting, tight-fisted.

antonyms generous, liberal, open-handed.

parsimony *n* frugality, meanness, minginess, niggardliness, penny-pinching, stinginess, tight-fistedness.

antonyms generosity, liberality.

parson *n* churchman, clergyman, cleric, divine, ecclesiastic, incumbent, Jack-priest, man of God, mar-text, minister, padre, pastor, preacher, priest, rector, reverend, vicar.

part *n* airt, area, behalf, bit, branch, business, capacity, cause, character, charge, clause, complement, component, concern, constituent, department, district, division, duty, element, faction, factor, fraction, fragment, function, heft, ingredient, interest, involvement, limb, lines, lot, member, module, neck of the woods, neighbourhood, office, organ, particle, partwork, party, piece, place, portion, quarter, region, responsibility, role, scrap, section, sector, segment, share, side, slice, task, territory, tip of the iceberg, unit, vicinity, work.

v break, break up, cleave, come apart, depart, detach, disband, disconnect, disjoin, dismantle, disperse, disunite, divide, go, go away, leave, part company, quit, rend, scatter, separate, sever, split, split up, sunder, take leave, tear, withdraw.

part with abandon, cede, discard, forgo, give up, jettison, let go of, relinquish, renounce, sacrifice, surrender, yield.

partake *v* be involved, engage, enter, participate, share, take part.

partake of consume, drink, eat, evince, evoke, have, manifest, receive, share, show, suggest, take.

partial[1] *adj* fragmentary, imperfect, incomplete, inexhaustive, limited, part, uncompleted, unfinished.

antonyms complete, exhaustive, total.

partial[2] *adj* affected, biased, coloured, discriminatory, ex parte, influenced, interested, one-sided, partisan, predisposed, prejudiced, tendentious, unfair, unjust.

antonyms disinterested, fair, unbiased.

partial to crazy about, daft about, fond of, keen on, mad about, taken with.

partiality *n* affinity, bias, discrimination, favouritism, fondness, inclination, liking, love, partisanship, penchant, predilection, predisposition, preference, prejudice, proclivity, propensity, soft spot, taste, weakness.

antonyms dislike, justice.

partially *adv* fractionally, in part, incompletely, partly, somewhat.

participant *n* associate, contributor, co-operator, helper, member, partaker, participator, party, shareholder, worker.

participate *v* be involved, co-operate, engage, enter, join, muck in, partake, perform, share, take part.

participation *n* a piece of the action, assistance, contribution, co-operation, involvement, mucking in, partaking, partnership, sharing.

particle *n* atom, atom(y), bit, corn, crumb, drop, electron, grain, iota, jot, kaon, mite, molecule, morsel, mote, neutrino, neutron, piece, pion, proton, scrap, shred, sliver, smidgen, speck, tittle, whit.

parti-coloured *adj* motley, piebald, polychromatic, polychromic, variegated, versicoloured.

antonyms monochromatic, plain.

particular[1] *adj* blow-by-blow, circumstantial, detailed, distinct, especial, exact, exceptional, express, itemised, marked, minute, notable, noteworthy, painstaking, peculiar, precise, remarkable, selective, several, singular, special, specific, thorough, uncommon, unique, unusual, very.

antonym general.

n circumstance, detail, fact, feature, item, point, specific, specification.

particular[2] *adj* choosy, critical, dainty, demanding, discriminating, exacting, fastidious, finical, finicky, fussy, meticulous, nice, overnice, perjink, pernickety, picky.

antonym casual.

particularise *v* detail, enumerate, individualise, individuate, itemise, specify, stipulate.

particularity *n* accuracy, carefulness, characteristic, choosiness, circumstance, detail, distinctiveness, fact, fastidiousness, feature, fussiness, idiosyncrasy, individuality, instance, item, mannerism, meticulousness, peculiarity, point, precision, property, quirk, singularity, thoroughness, trait, uniqueness.

particularly *adv* decidedly, distinctly, especially, exceptionally, explicitly, expressly, extraordinarily, in particular, markedly, notably, noticeably, outstandingly, peculiarly, remarkably, singularly, specifically, surprisingly, uncommonly, unusually.

parting *n* adieu, breaking, departure, detachment, disjunction, disunion, divergence, division, farewell, going, goodbye, leave-taking, partition, rift, rupture, separation, severance, split, valediction.

antonyms convergence, meeting.

adj closing, concluding, deathbed, departing, dying, farewell, final, last, stirrup, valedictory.

antonyms arriving, first.

partisan *n* adherent, backer, champion, devotee, disciple, factionary, factionist, follower, guerrilla, irregular, party-man, stalwart, supporter, upholder, votary.

adj biased, discriminatory, factional, guerrilla, interested, irregular, one-sided, partial, predisposed, prejudiced, resistance, sectarian, tendentious, underground.

partisanship *n* bias, factionalism, fanaticism, partiality, partyism, sectarianism.

partition[1] *n* allocation, allotment, apportionment, distribution, dividing, division, part, portion, rationing out, section, segregation, separation, severance, share, splitting.

v allocate, allot, apportion, assign, divide, parcel out, portion, section, segment, separate, share, split up, subdivide.

partition[2] *n* barrier, diaphragm, dissepiment, divider, hallan, membrane, room-divider, screen, septum, traverse, wall.

v bar, divide, fence off, screen, separate, wall off.

partly *adv* halfway, in part, incompletely, moderately, partially, relatively, slightly, somewhat, to a certain degree, to a certain extent, up to a point.

antonyms completely, in toto, totally.

partner *n* accomplice, ally, associate, bedfellow, butty, collaborator, colleague, companion, comrade, confederate, consort, co-partner, gigolo, helper, helpmate, helpmeet, husband, mate, participant, side-kick, spouse, team-mate, wife.

partnership *n* affiliation, alliance, association, brotherhood, combination, combine, companionship, company, conglomerate, connection, co-operation, co-operative, co-partnership, corporation, fellowship, firm, fraternity, house, interest, participation, sharing, society, syndicate, union.

parts *n* ability, accomplishments, attributes, calibre, capabilities, endowments, expertise, faculties, genius, gifts, intellect, intelligence, skill, talents.

party[1] *n* assembly, at-home, bash, beanfeast, beano, ceilidh, celebration, do, drag, drum, entertainment, -fest, festivity, function, gathering, get-together, hooley, hoot(e)nanny, housewarming, hurricane, jollification, knees-up, rave-up, reception, rout, shindig, social, soirée, thrash.

party[2] *n* alliance, association, band, body, bunch, cabal, caucus, clique, coalition, combination, company, confederacy, contingent, contractor, coterie, crew, defendant, detachment, faction, gang, gathering, group, grouping, individual, junto, league, litigant, participant, person, plaintiff, set, side, squad, team, unit.

parvenu *n* arriviste, climber, new rich, nouveau riche, pretender, upstart, vulgarian.

adj nouveau riche, upstart, vulgarian.

pass[1] *v* accept, adopt, answer, approve, authorise, beat, befall, beguile, blow over, cease, come up, come up to scratch, convey, declare, decree, defecate, delate, deliver, depart, develop, devote, die, die away, disappear, discharge, disregard, dissolve, do, dwindle, ebb, elapse, eliminate, employ, empty, enact, end, establish, evacuate, evaporate, exceed, excel, exchange, excrete, expel, experience, expire, express, fade, fall out, fill, flow, get through, give, go, go beyond, go by, go past, graduate, hand, happen, ignore, impersonate, lapse, leave, legislate, melt away, miss, move, neglect, occupy, occur, omit, ordain, outdistance, outdo, outstrip, overlook, overtake, pass muster, proceed, pronounce, qualify, ratify, roll, run, sanction, send, serve as, skip, spend, succeed, suffer, suffice, suit, surmount, surpass, take place, terminate, throw, transcend, transfer, transmit, undergo, utter, validate, vanish, void, waft, wane, while away.

pass[2] *n* advances, approach, authorisation, chit, condition, feint, identification, jab, juncture, laissez-passer, licence, lunge, overture, passport, permission, permit, pinch, play, plight, predicament, proposition, push, safe-conduct, situation, stage, state, state of affairs, straits, suggestion, swing, thrust, ticket, warrant.

pass away croak, decease, die, expire, give up the ghost, kick the bucket, pass on, pass over, peg out, snuff it.

pass by disregard, forget, ignore, leave, miss, neglect, omit, overlook, pass over, pretermit.

pass muster be adequate, be up to scratch, fill the bill, make the grade, measure up, qualify.

pass off come to an end, counterfeit, die away, disappear, dismiss, disregard, emit, evaporate, fade out, fake, feign, give off, go off, happen, ignore, occur, palm off, pass by, send forth, take place, turn out, utter, vanish, vaporise, wink at.

pass out[1] black out, die, drop, faint, flake out, keel over, lose consciousness, swoon.

pass out[2] deal out, dispense, distribute, dole out, give out, hand out, share out.

pass over ignore, neglect, omit, overlook, pretermit.

pass[3] *n* canyon, col, defile, gap, gha(u)t, gorge, halse, nek, ravine.

passable *adj* acceptable, adequate, admissible, all right, allowable, average, clear, fair, mediocre, middling, moderate, navigable, OK, open, ordinary, presentable, so-so, tolerable, traversable, unblocked, unexceptional, unobstructed.

passably *adv* after a fashion, fairly, moderately, rather, reasonably, relatively, somewhat, tolerably.

passage *n* acceptance, access, adit, advance, allowance, authorisation, avenue, change, channel, citation, clause, close, communication, conduit, conversion, corridor, course, crossing, deambulatory, doorway, drift, dromos, duct, enactment, entrance, entrance hall, establishment, excerpt, exit, extract, fistula, flow, freedom, gallery, gut, hall, hallway, journey, lane, legalisation, legislation, lobby, motion, movement, opening, orifice, paragraph, part, passageway, passing, path, permission, piece, portion, progress, progression, quotation, ratification, reading, right, road, route, safe-conduct, section, sentence, spiracle, text, thorough, thoroughfare, tour, transit, transition, trek, trip, vent, verse, vestibule, visa, vista, voyage, warrant, way.

passageway *n* aisle, alley, corridor, entrance, exit, hall, hallway, lane, lobby, passage, pend, vennel, wynd.

passé *adj* antiquated, dated, démodé, obsolete, old hat, old-fashioned, out, outdated, outmoded, out-of-date, outworn, past one's best, unfashionable.

antonyms fashionable, in.

passenger *n* commuter, fare, hitch-hiker, pillionist, pillion-rider, rider, traveller.

passer-by *n* bystander, looker-on, onlooker, spectator, witness.

passing *adj* brief, casual, cursory, ephemeral, evanescent, fleeting, fly-by-night, fugitive, glancing, hasty, impermanent, momentary, quick, shallow, shirt, short, short-lived, slight, superficial, temporary, transient, transitory.

antonyms long-lasting, permanent.

n death, decease, demise, end, expiration, finish, loss, quietus, termination.

passion *n* adoration, affection, anger, animation, ardour, attachment, avidity, bug, chafe, concupiscence, craving, craze, dander, desire, eagerness, emotion, enthusiasm, excitement, fancy, fascination, feeling, fervency, fervour, fire, fit, flare-up, fondness, frenzy, fury, heat, idol, indignation, infatuation, intensity, ire, itch, joy, keenness, love, lust, mania, monomania, obsession, outburst, paroxysm, rage, rapture, resentment, spirit, storm, transport, vehemence, verve, vivacity, warmth, wax, wrath, zeal, zest.

antonyms calm, coolness, self-possession.

passionate *adj* amorous, animated, ardent, aroused, choleric, desirous, eager, emotional, enthusiastic, erotic, excitable, excited, fervent, fervid, fierce, fiery, frenzied, heartfelt, heated, hot, hot-headed, hot-tempered, impassioned, impetuous, impulsive, incensed, inflamed, inspirited, intense, irascible, irate, irritable, loving, lustful, peppery, quick-tempered, sensual, sexy, stormy, strong, sultry, tempestuous, torrid, vehement, violent, wanton, warm, wild, zealous.

antonyms frigid, laid-back, phlegmatic.

passionless *adj* apathetic, callous, calm, cold, cold-blooded, cold-hearted, detached, dispassionate, emotionless, frigid, frosty, icy, impartial, impassive, inappetent, indifferent, insensible, neutral, restrained, uncaring, unemotional, unfeeling, uninvolved, unloving, unresponsive, withdrawn.

antonyms caring, sensitive, sympathetic.

passive *adj* acquiescent, compliant, docile, enduring, impassive, inactive, indifferent, indolent, inert, lifeless, long-suffering, non-participating, non-violent, patient, quiescent, receptive, resigned, submissive, supine, unaffected, unassertive, uninvolved, unresisting.

antonyms active, involved, lively.

passive resistance non-violence, satyagraha, vis inertiae.

passport *n* authorisation, laissez-passer, pass, permit, visa.

password *n* countersign, open sesame, parole, shibboleth, signal, watchword.

past *adj* accomplished, ancient, bygone, completed, defunct, done, early, elapsed, ended, erstwhile, extinct, finished, foregone, forgotten, former, gone, gone by, late, long-ago, no more, olden, over, over and done with, preceding, previous, prior, quondam, recent, spent, vanished.

n antiquity, auld lang syne, background, days of yore, dossier, experience, former times, good old days, history, life, old times, olden days, track record, yesteryear.

past one's best not what one was, over the hill, passé.

paste *n* adhesive, cement, dope, dough, glue, gum, mastic, mucilage, pastry, putty.

v beat, cement, fasten, fix, glue, gum, hammer, stick, thrash, thump, whitewash.

pastel *adj* delicate, faint, gentle, light, muted, pale, soft, soft-hued, subdued.

n chalk, crayon, drawing, pastille, sketch, vignette, wood.

pastiche *n* blend, composition, farrago, gallimaufry, hotchpotch, medley, mélange, miscellany, mixture, motley, olla-podrida, patchwork, pot-pourri.

pastille *n* confection, cough drop, cough sweet, jujube, lozenge, pastel, sweet, tablet, troche.

pastime *n* activity, amusement, avocation, distraction, diversion, divertisement, entertainment, game, hobby, play, recreation, relaxation, sport, Zeitvertreib.

antonyms business, employment, occupation, vocation, work.

pastmaster *n* ace, adept, artist, dab hand, expert, old hand, proficient, virtuoso, wizard.

antonym incompetent.

pastor *n* canon, churchman, clergyman, cleric, divine, ecclesiastic, minister, parson, prebendary, priest, rector, vicar.

pastoral *adj* agrarian, Arcadian, bucolic, clerical, countrified, country, ecclesiastical, georgic, idyllic, ministerial, priestly, rural, rustic, simple.

antonyms oppidan, urban.

pasture *n* alp, eddish, grass, grassland, grazing, herbage, lay, lea, ley, machair, mead, meadow, pasturage, pasture-land, raik, shieling.

pasty *adj* anaemic, doughy, gluey, glutinous, mucilaginous, pale, pallid, pasty-faced, peelie-wally, sallow, sickly, starchy, sticky, unhealthy, viscous, wan, waxy, whey-faced.

antonyms healthy, rubicund.

pat *v* caress, clap, dab, fondle, pet, rub, slap, stroke, tap, touch.

n cake, caress, clap, dab, lump, piece, portion, slap, stroke, tap, touch.

adv exactly, faultlessly, flawlessly, fluently, glibly, just right, off pat, opportunely, perfectly, plumb, precisely, relevantly, seasonably.

antonyms imprecisely, wrongly.

adj apposite, appropriate, apropos, apt, automatic, easy, facile, felicitous, fitting, glib, happy, neat, pertinent, ready, relevant, right, simplistic, slick, smooth, spot-on, suitable, to the point, well-chosen.

antonyms irrelevant, unsuitable.

patch *n* area, bit, clout, ground, land, lot, parcel, piece, plot, scrap, shred, spot, stretch, tract.

v botch, cover, fix, mend, reinforce, repair, sew up, stitch, vamp.

patchwork *n* confusion, farrago, gallimaufry, hash, hotchpotch, jumble, medley, mishmash, mixture, pastiche.

patchy *adj* bitty, erratic, fitful, incongruous, inconsistent, inharmonious, irregular, maculate, random, sketchy, spotty, uneven, variable, varying.

antonyms consistent, even, regular, uniform.

patent *adj* apparent, blatant, clear, clear-cut, conspicuous, downright, evident, explicit, flagrant, glaring, indisputable, manifest, obvious, open, ostensible, overt, palpable, transparent, unconcealed, unequivocal, unmistakable.

antonyms hidden, opaque.

n certificate, copyright, invention, licence, privilege, registered trademark.

paternal *adj* benevolent, concerned, fatherlike, fatherly, indulgent, patrilineal, patrimonial, patroclinic, patroclinous, protective, solicitous, vigilant.

paternity *n* authorship, descent, extraction, family, fatherhood, fathership, lineage, origination, parentage.

path *n* avenue, course, direction, footpath, footway, gate, pad, passage, pathway, procedure, ridgeway, road, route, towpath, track, trail, walk, walkway, way.

pathetic *adj* affecting, contemptible, crummy, deplorable, dismal-looking, distressing, feeble, heartbreaking, heart-rending, inadequate, lamentable, meagre, melting, miserable, moving, paltry, petty, piteous, pitiable, pitiful, plaintive, poignant, poor, puny, rubbishy, sad, sorry, tender, touching, trashy, uninteresting, useless, woebegone, woeful, worthless.

antonyms admirable, cheerful.

pathos *n* inadequacy, misery, pitiableness, pitifulness, plaintiveness, poignancy, sadness.

patience *n* calmness, composure, constancy, cool, diligence, endurance, equanimity, forbearance, fortitude, long-suffering, perseverance, persistence, resignation, restraint, self-control, serenity, stoicism, submission, sufferance, tolerable, toleration.

antonyms impatience, intolerance.

patient[1] *adj* accommodating, calm, composed, enduring, even-tempered, forbearing, forgiving, indulgent, lenient, long-suffering, mild, persevering, persistent, philosophical, quiet, resigned, restrained, self-controlled, self-possessed, serene, stoical, submissive, tolerant, uncomplaining, understanding, untiring.

antonyms impatient, intolerant.

patient[2] *n* case, client, invalid, sufferer.

patois *n* argot, cant, dialect, jargon, lingo, lingua franca, patter, slang, vernacular.

patriarch *n* elder, father, founder, grand old man, grandfather, greybeard, paterfamilias, sire.

patrician *n* aristocrat, gentleman, grandee, noble, nobleman, peer.

antonyms commoner, pleb.

adj aristocratic, blue-blooded, gentle, high-born, high-class, lordly, noble, thoroughbred, well-born.

antonyms common, humble.

patrimony *n* bequest, birthright, estate, heritage, inheritance, legacy, portion, revenue, share.

patriot *n* chauvinist, flag-waver, jingo, jingoist, loyalist, nationalist.

patriotic *adj* chauvinistic, flag-waving, jingoish, jingoistic, loyal, nationalistic.

patriotism *n* chauvinism, flag-waving, jingoism, loyalty, nationalism.

patrol *n* defence, garrison, guard, guarding, policing, protecting, roundvigilance, sentinel, surveillance, watch, watching, watchman.

v cruise, go the rounds, guard, inspect, perambulate, police, range, tour.

patron *n* advocate, backer, benefactor, buyer, champion, client, customer, defender, fautor, frequenter, friend, guardian, habitué, helper, Maecenas, partisan, philanthropist, protector, regular, shopper, sponsor, subscriber, supporter, sympathiser.

patronage *n* aegis, aid, assistance, backing, benefaction, business, championship, clientèle, commerce, custom, encouragement, help, participation, promotion, sponsorship, subscription, support, sustenance, trade, trading, traffic.

patronise *v* assist, back, befriend, encourage, foster, frequent, fund, habituate, help, humour, maintain, promote, shop at, sponsor, support, talk down to.

patronising *adj* condescending, contemptuous, disdaining, gracious, haughty, high-handed, imperious, lofty, overbearing, snobbish, stooping, supercilious, superior, toffee-nosed.

antonym humble.

patter[1] *v* beat, pat, pelt, pitapat, pit-pat, pitter-patter, pittypat, rat-a-rat, scurry, scuttle, skip, spatter, tap, tiptoe, trip.

n pattering, pitapat, pit-pat, pitter-patter, pittypat, tapping.

patter[2] *n* argot, cant, chatter, gabble, glib talk, jabber, jargon, line, lingo, monologue, patois, pitch, prattle, slang, spiel, vernacular, yak.

pattern *n* archetype, arrangement, criterion, cynosure, decoration, delineation, design, device, diagram, examplar, example, figuration, figure, Gestalt, guide, instructions, kind, method, model, motif, norm, order, orderliness, original, ornament, ornamentation, paradigm, paragon, plan, prototype, sample, sequence, shape, sort, specimen, standard, stencil, style, system, template, type, variety.

v copy, decorate, design, emulate, follow, form, imitate, match, model, mould, order, shape, stencil, style, trim.

patterned *adj* decorated, figured, moiré, ornamented, printed, stamped, watered.

paucity *n* dearth, deficiency, exiguousness, fewness, insufficiency, lack, meagreness, paltriness, poverty, rarity, scantiness, scarcity, shortage, slenderness, slightness, smallness, sparseness, sparsity, want.

antonym abundance.

paunch *n* abdomen, beer-belly, beer-gut, belly, bread-basket, corporation, pot, pot-belly.

paunchy *adj* adipose, corpulent, fat, podgy, portly, pot-bellied, pudgy, rotund, tubby.

pauper *n* bankrupt, beggar, church-mouse, down-and-out, have-not, indigent, insolvent, mendicant.

pause *v* break, cease, cut, delay, desist, discontinue, halt, hesitate, interrupt, rest, take a break, take a breather, take five, wait, waver.

n abatement, break, breather, caesura, cessation, delay, discontinuance, dwell, gap, halt, hesitation, interlude, intermission, interruption, interval, let-up, lull, respite, rest, slackening, stay, stoppage, suspension, wait.

pave *v* asphalt, concrete, cover, flag, floor, macadamise, revet, slab, surface, tar, tile.

pavement *n* bed, causeway, floor, footway, pavé, sidewalk.

paw *v* grab, manhandle, maul, mishandle, molest.

n foot, forepaw, hand, pad, pud, puddy.

pawn[1] *n* cat's-paw, creature, dupe, instrument, plaything, puppet, stooge, tool, toy.

pawn[2] *v* deposit, dip, gage, hazard, hock, impawn, impignorate, lay in lavender, mortgage, pledge, pop, stake, wager.

n hostage, security.

pawnbroker *n* gombeen-man, lender, money-lender, uncle, usurer.

pawnshop *n* leaving-shop, mont-de-piété, monte de pietà, pop-shop.

pay *v* ante, benefit, bestow, bring in, clear, compensate, cough up, disburse, discharge, extend, foot, get even with, give, grant, honour, indemnify, liquidate, meet, offer, pay out, present, produce, proffer, profit, punish, reciprocate, recompense, reimburse, remit, remunerate, render, repay, requite, return, reward, serve, settle, square, square up, yield.

n allowance, compensation, consideration, earnings, emoluments, fee, hire, honorarium, income, payment, recompense, reimbursement, remuneration, reward, salary, stipend, takings, wages.

pay back avenge, chasten, get even with, get one's own back, punish, reciprocate, recompense, refund, reimburse, repay, retaliate, return, settle up, settle with, square.

pay for answer for, atone, compensate, face the music, get one's deserts, make amends, suffer.

pay off clear, discharge, dismiss, fire, lay off, liquidate, sack, satisfy, settle, square, succeed, work.

pay out cough up, disburse, dish out, expend, fork out, hand over, lay out, render, shell out, spend.

payable *adj* due, in arrears, mature, obligatory, outstanding, owed, owing, receivable, unpaid.

payment *n* advance, alimony, ante, consideration, defrayal, deposit, discharge, fee, hire, instalment, outlay, paying, portion, premium, remittance, remuneration, reward, settlement, sub, wage.

pay-off *n* climax, clincher, conclusion, consequence, crunch, culmination, day of reckoning, dénouement, judgement, moment of truth, outcome, punch-line, reimbursement, result, retribution, reward, settlement, upshot.

peace *n* accord, agreement, amity, armistice, calm, calmness, cease-fire, composure, conciliation, concord, contentment, frith, harmony, hush, pacification, pax, peacefulness, placidity, quiet, quietude, relaxation, repose, rest, serenity, silence, stillness, tranquillity, treaty, truce.

antonyms disagreement, disturbance, war.

peace studies irenology.

peaceable *adj* amiable, amicable, compatible, conciliatory, douce, dovish, easy-going, friendly, gentle, inoffensive, mild, non-belligerent, pacific, peaceful, peace-loving, placid, unwarlike.

antonyms belligerent, offensive.

peaceful *adj* amicable, at peace, becalmed, calm, conciliatory, friendly, gentle, halcyon, harmonious, irenic (eirenic), non-violent, pacific, peaceable, peace-loving, placatory, placid, quiet, restful, serene, still, tranquil, unagitated, undisturbed, unruffled, untroubled, unwarlike.

antonyms disturbed, noisy, troubled.

peacemaker *n* appeaser, arbitrator, conciliator, interceder, intercessor, mediator, mediatress, mediatrix, pacifier, peacemonger.

peacemaking *adj* appeasing, conciliatory, irenic(al), mediating, mediative, mediatorial, mediatory, pacific.

peace-pipe *n* calumet, pipe of peace.

peak *n* acme, aiguille, apex, apogee, brow, climax, crest, crown, culmination, cuspid, high noon, high point, maximum, ne plus ultra, pinnacle, point, summit, tip, top, visor, zenith.

antonyms nadir, trough.

v climax, come to a head, culminate, spire, tower.

peaky *adj* drooping, emaciated, ill, off-colour, pale, peelie-wally, pinched, poorly, shilpit, sick, sickly, under the weather, unwell, wan, washed-out, wilting.

antonyms healthy, in the pink.

peal *n* blast, carillon, chime, clamour, clang, clangour, clap, clash, crash, resounding, reverberation, ring, ringing, roar, rumble, sound, tintinnabulation.

v chime, clash, crack, crash, resonate, resound, reverberate, ring, roar, roll, rumble, sound, tintinnabulate, toll, vibrate.

peanut *n* goober, ground-nut, monkey-nut.

peanuts *n* chickenfeed, pennies, pittance.

peasant *n* boor, bumpkin, churl, countryman, fellah, hind, jungli, kulak, lout, moujik, mujik, muzhik, oaf, oik, provincial, rustic, swain, yokel.

antonym sophisticate.

pebble *n* agate, chip, gallet, stone.

peccadillo *n* boob, delinquency, error, fault, indiscretion, infraction, lapse, misdeed, misdemeanour, slip, slip-up.

peck *n* criticism, food, jab, kiss, strike.

v eat, jab, kiss, nibble.

peculiar[1] *adj* abnormal, bizarre, curious, eccentric, exceptional, extraordinary, far-out, freakish, funky, funny, odd, offbeat, outlandish, out-of-the-way, quaint, queer, singular, strange, uncommon, unconventional, unusual, way-out, weird.

antonyms normal, ordinary.

peculiar[2] *adj* appropriate, characteristic, discriminative, distinct, distinctive, distinguishing, endemic, idiosyncratic, individual, local, particular, personal, private, quintessential, restricted, special, specific, unique.

antonyms general, uncharacteristic.

peculiarity *n* abnormality, attribute, bizarreness, characteristic, distinctiveness, eccentricity, exception, feature, foible, freakishness, idiosyncrasy, kink, mannerism, mark, oddity, particularity, property, quality, queerness, quirk, singularity, speciality, trait, whimsicality.

pecuniary *adj* commercial, financial, fiscal, monetary, nummary, nummulary.

pedagogue *n* dogmatist, dominie, don, educationalist, educationist, educator, instructor, master, mistress, pedant, preceptor, schoolmaster, schoolmistress, teacher.

pedagogy *n* instruction, pedagogics, teaching, training, tuition, tutelage.

pedant *n* casuist, doctrinaire, dogmatist, Dryasdust, gerund-grinder, grammaticaster, grammatist, hair-splitter, literalist, mandarin, nit-picker, pedagogue, pettifogger, precisian, quibbler, scholastic, vocabularian.

pedantic *adj* abstruse, academic, bookish, cavilling, didactic, donnish, erudite, finical, formal, fussy, hair-splitting, learned, nit-picking, particular, pedagogic, perfectionist, pompous, precise, punctilious, scholastic, schoolmasterly, sententious, stilted.

antonyms casual, imprecise, informal.

pedantry *n* bookishness, cavilling, finicality, hair-splitting, pedagogism, pedagoguery, pedagoguishness, pedantism, pomposity, punctiliousness, quibbling, stuffiness.

peddle *v* dilly-dally, flog, hawk, huckster, idle, loiter, market, piddle, push, retail, sell, tout, trade, trifle, vend.

pedestal *n* base, dado, foot, foundation, mounting, pier, platform, plinth, podium, socle, stand, support, understructure.

pedestrian *n* footslogger, foot-traveller, voetganger, walker.

adj banal, boring, commonplace, dull, flat, humdrum, indifferent, mediocre, mundane, ordinary, plodding, prosaic, run-of-the-mill, stodgy, tolerable, unimaginative, uninspired, uninteresting.

antonyms bright, brilliant, exciting, imaginative.

pedigree *n* ancestry, blood, breed, derivation, descent, dynasty, extraction, family, family tree, genealogy, heritage, line, lineage, parentage, race, stemma, stirps, stock, succession.

pedigreed *adj* aristocratic, full-blooded, pedigree, pure-bred, thoroughbred.

pedlar *n* boxwallah, chapman, cheap-jack, colporteur, gutter-man, gutter-merchant, hawker, huckster, seller, street-trader, vendor, walker, yagger.

peek *v* glance, keek, look, peep, peer, spy.

n blink, dekko, gander, glance, glimpse, keek, look, look-see, peep, shufti.

peel *v* decorticate, denude, desquamate, flake (off), pare, scale, skin, strip (off), undress.

n epicarp, exocarp, integument, peeling, rind, skin, zest.

peep *v* blink, emerge, glimpse, issue, keek, peek, peer.

n blink, dekko, gander, glim, glimpse, keek, look, look-see, peek, shufti.

peephole *n* aperture, chink, cleft, crack, crevice, fissure, hole, interstice, keyhole, opening, pinhole, slit, spy-hole.

peer[1] *v* appear, blink, emerge, examine, gaze, inspect, peep, scan, scrutinise, snoop, spy, squint.

peer[2] *n* aristocrat, baron, count, duke, earl, lord, marquess, marquis, noble, nobleman, thane, viscount.

peer[3] *n* compeer, counterpart, equal, equipollent, equivalent, fellow, like, match.

peerage *n* aristocracy, lords and ladies, nobility, patriciate, top drawer, upper crust.

peeress *n* baroness, countess, dame, duchess, lady, marchioness, noblewoman, viscountess.

peerless *adj* beyond compare, excellent, incomparable, matchless, nonpareil, outstanding, paramount, second to none, superlative, supreme, unbeatable, unequalled, unexcelled, unique, unmatched, unparalleled, unrivalled, unsurpassed.

peeved *adj* annoyed, exasperated, galled, irked, irritated, miffed, narked, nettled, pipped, piqued, put out, riled, sore, upset, vexed.

peevish *adj* acrimonious, cantankerous, captious, childish, churlish, crabbed, cross, crotchety, crusty, dorty, fractious, frampold, franzy, fretful, grumpy, hipped, ill-natured, ill-tempered, irritable, miffy, perverse, pettish, petulant, querulous, ratty, short-tempered, snappy, splenetic, sulky, sullen, surly, testy, touchy, waspish.

antonym good-tempered.

peevishness *n* acrimony, captiousness, ill-temper, irritability, perversity, pet, petulance, pique, protervity, querulousness, testiness.

peg *v* attach, control, fasten, fix, freeze, insert, join, limit, mark, pierce, score, secure, set, stabilise.

n dowel, hook, knob, marker, pin, post, stake, thole(-pin), toggle.

peg away apply oneself, beaver away, hang in, keep at it, persevere, persist, plod along, plug away, stick at it, work away.

pejorative *adj* bad, belittling, condemnatory, damning, debasing, deprecatory, depreciatory, derogatory, detractive, detractory, disparaging, negative, slighting, uncomplimentary, unflattering, unpleasant.

antonyms complimentary, laudatory.

pell-mell *adv* feverishly, full tilt, hastily, heedlessly, helter-skelter, hurriedly, hurry-scurry, impetuously, posthaste, precipitously, rashly, recklessly.

adj chaotic, confused, disordered, disorganised, haphazard, indiscriminate, scrambled, tumultuous.

pelt[1] *v* assail, batter, beat, belabour, belt, bombard, bucket, career, cast, charge, dash, hit, hurl, hurry, pepper, pour, pummel, rain cats and dogs, rush, shoot, shower, sling, speed, strafe, strike, tear, teem, thrash, throw, wallop, whiz.

pelt[2] *n* coat, fell, fleece, fur, hide, skin.

pen[1] *v* author, compose, draft, jot down, scribble, write.

pen name alias, allonym, nom de plume, pseudonym.

pen[2] *n* cage, coop, crib, cru(i)ve, enclosure, fold, hutch, stall, sty.

v cage, confine, coop, corral, crib, enclose, fence, hedge, hem in, hurdle, mew (up), shut up.

penal servitude bird, lag, porridge, stretch, time.

penalise *v* amerce, correct, disadvantage, discipline, handicap, mulct, punish.

antonym reward.

penalty *n* amende, amercement, disadvantage, fine, forfeit, forfeiture, handicap, mulct, price, punishment, retribution.

antonym reward.

penance *n* atonement, mortification, penalty, placation, propitiation, punishment, reparation, sackcloth and ashes.

penchant *n* affinity, bent, bias, disposition, fondness, inclination, leaning, liking, partiality, predilection, predisposition, preference, proclivity, proneness, propensity, soft spot, taste, tendency, turn.

antonym dislike.

pendant *n* drop, lavaliere, locket, medallion, necklace.

pendent *adj* dangling, drooping, hanging, nutant, pendulous, pensile, suspended, swinging.

pending *adj* awaiting, forthcoming, hanging, imminent, impending, in the balance, in the offing, on the back burner, undecided, undetermined, unfinished, unsettled.

antonyms finished, settled.

pendulous *adj* dangling, drooping, droopy, hanging, pendent, sagging, suspended, swaying, swinging.

penetrable *adj* accessible, clear, comprehensible, explicable, fathomable, intelligible, open, passable, permeable, pervious, porous, understandable.

antonym impenetrable.

penetrate *v* affect, bore, come across, come home, comprehend, decipher, diffuse, discern, enter, fathom, get through to, get to the bottom of, grasp, impress, infiltrate, perforate, permeate, pervade, pierce, prick, probe, seep, sink, stab, strike, suffuse, touch, understand, unravel.

penetrating *adj* acute, astute, biting, carrying, critical, discerning, discriminating, harsh, incisive, intelligent, intrusive, keen, observant, penetrative, perceptive, percipient, perspicacious, pervasive, piercing, profound, pungent, quick, sagacious, searching, sharp, sharp-witted, shrewd, shrill, stinging, strong.

antonyms gentle, obtuse, soft.

penetration *n* acumen, acuteness, astuteness, discernment, entrance, entry, incision, inroad, insight, interpenetration, invasion, keenness, perception, perforation, perspicacity, piercing, puncturing, sharpness, shrewdness, wit.

peninsula *n* cape, chersonese, doab, mull, point, tongue.

penis *n* cock, dick, John Thomas, knob, membrum virile, pecker, phallus, pizzle, prick, rod, shaft, tool, winkle.

penitence *n* compunction, contrition, regret, regretfulness, remorse, repentance, rue, self-reproach, shame, sorrow.

penitent *adj* abject, apologetic, atoning, conscience-stricken, contrite, humble, in sackcloth and ashes, regretful, remorseful, repentant, rueful, sorrowful, sorry.

antonym unrepentant.

penniless *adj* bankrupt, broke, bust(ed), cleaned out, destitute, flat broke, impecunious, impoverished, indigent, moneyless, necessitous, needy, obolary, on one's uppers, on the rocks, penurious, poor, poverty-stricken, ruined, skint, stoney-broke, strapped.

antonyms rich, wealthy.

pennon *n* banderol(e), banner, burgee, ensign, gonfalon, jack, oriflamme, pencel, pencil, pennant, pensel, streamer.

penny-pincher *n* meany, miser, niggard, pinchfist, pinchgut, pinchpenny, screw, Scrooge, skinflint.

penny-pinching *adj* cheeseparing, close, frugal, mean, mingy, miserly, near, niggardly, parsimonious, scrimping, stingy, tight-fisted, ungenerous.

antonyms generous, open-handed.

pension *n* allowance, annuity, benefit, maintenance, stipend, superannuation.

pensive *adj* absent-minded, absorbed, cogitative, contemplative, dreamy, grave, meditative, melancholy, musing, preoccupied, reflective, ruminative, serious, sober, solemn, thoughtful, wistful.

pent-up *adj* bottled-up, bridled, checked, constrained, curbed, inhibited, repressed, restrained, smothered, stifled, suppressed.

penurious *adj* beggarly, bust(ed), cheeseparing, close, close-fisted, deficient, destitute, flat broke, frugal, grudging, impecunious, impoverished, inadequate, indigent, meagre, mean, miserable, miserly, near, needy, niggardly, obolary, paltry, parsimonious, penniless, poor, poverty-stricken, scanty, skimping, stingy, tight-fisted, ungenerous.

antonyms generous, wealthy.

penury *n* beggary, dearth, deficiency, destitution, indigence, lack, mendicancy, mendicity, need, paucity, pauperism, poverty, privation, scantiness, scarcity, shortage, sparseness, straitened circumstances, straits, want.

antonym prosperity.

people *n* citizens, clan, commonalty, community, crowd, demos, family, folk, general public, gens, grass roots, hoi polloi, human beings, humanity, humans, inhabitants, mankind, many-headed beast, many-headed monster, masses, mob, mortals, multitude, nation, persons, plebs, populace, population, public, punters, rabble, race, rank and file, the herd, the million, tribe.

v colonise, inhabit, occupy, populate, settle, tenant.

pep *n* animation, energy, exuberance, get-up-and-go, gusto, high spirits, life, liveliness, pizzazz, spirit, verve, vigour, vim, vitality, vivacity, zip.

pep up animate, energise, enliven, excite, exhilarate, inspire, invigorate, jazz up, quicken, stimulate, vitalise, vivify.

peppery *adj* astringent, biting, caustic, choleric, fiery, grumpy, hot, hot-tempered, incisive, irascible, irritable, nippy, piquant, pungent, quick-tempered, sarcastic, sharp, snappish, spicy, stinging, testy, touchy, trenchant, waspish.

perceive *v* appreciate, apprehend, be aware of, behold, catch, comprehend, conclude, deduce, descry, discern, discover, distinguish, espy, feel, gather, get, grasp, intuit, know, learn, make out, note, observe, realise, recognise, remark, see, sense, spot, understand.

perceptible *adj* apparent, appreciable, clear, conspicuous, detectable, discernible, distinct, distinguishable, evident, noticeable, observable, obvious, palpable, perceivable, recognisable, salient, tangible, visible.

antonym imperceptible.

perception *n* Anschauung, apprehension, awareness, conception, consciousness, discernment, feeling, grasp, idea, impression, insight, intellection, notion, observation, recognition, sensation, sense, taste, understanding, uptake.

perceptive *adj* able to see through a millstone, acute, alert, astute, aware, discerning, insightful, observant, penetrating, percipient, perspicacious, quick, responsive, sagacious, sapient, sensitive, sharp.

antonym unobservant.

perch *v* alight, balance, drop, land, light, rest, roost, settle, sit on.

percipience *n* acuity, acuteness, alertness, astuteness, awareness, discernment, insight, intuition, judgement, penetration, perception, perspicacity, sagacity, sensitivity, understanding.

percipient *adj* alert, alive, astute, aware, discerning, discriminating, intelligent, judicious, knowing, penetrating, perceptive, perspicacious, quick-witted, sharp, wide-awake.

antonyms obtuse, unaware.

percolate *v* drain, drip, exude, filter, filtrate, leach, leak, ooze, osmose, penetrate, permeate, pervade, seep, strain, transfuse.

perdition *n* condemnation, damnation, destruction, doom, downfall, hell, hellfire, ruin, ruination.

peregrination *n* excursion, expedition, exploration, globe-trotting, journey, odyssey, roaming, roving, tour, travel, travelling, trek, trekking, trip, voyage, wandering, wayfaring.

peremptory *adj* abrupt, absolute, arbitrary, assertive, authoritative, autocratic, binding, bossy, categorical, commanding, compelling, curt, decisive, dictatorial, dogmatic, domineering, final, high-handed, imperative, imperious, incontrovertible, intolerant, irrefutable, obligatory, overbearing, summary, undeniable.

perennial *adj* abiding, ceaseless, chronic, constant, continual, continuing, deathless, enduring, eternal, evergreen, everlasting, immortal, imperishable, incessant, inveterate, lasting, lifelong, never-ending, never-failing, permanent, perpetual, persistent, recurrent, sempiternal, unceasing, unchanging, undying, unfailing, uninterrupted.

perfect *adj* absolute, accomplished, accurate, adept, blameless, close, complete, completed, consummate, copybook, correct, entire, exact, excellent, experienced, expert, faithful, faultless, finished, flawless, full, ideal, immaculate, impeccable, irreproachable, masterly, model, polished, practised, precise, pure, right, sheer, skilful, skilled, splendid, spotless, spot-on, strict, sublime, superb, superlative, supreme, true, unadulterated, unalloyed, unblemished, unerring, unimpeachable, unmarred, unmitigated, untarnished, utter, whole.

antonyms flawed, imperfect.

v accomplish, achieve, carry out, complete, consummate, effect, elaborate, finish, fulfil, perfectionate, perform, realise, refine.

perfection *n* accomplishment, achievement, acme, completeness, completion, consummation, crown, evolution, exactness, excellence, exquisiteness, flawlessness, fulfilment, ideal, integrity, maturity, nonpareil, paragon, perfectness, pinnacle, precision, purity, realisation, sublimity, superiority, wholeness.

antonyms flaw, imperfection.

perfectionist *n* formalist, idealist, precisian, precisionist, purist, stickler.

perfectly *adv* absolutely, admirably, altogether, completely, consummately, entirely, exquisitely, faultlessly, flawlessly, fully, ideally, impeccably, incomparably, irreproachably, quite, superbly, superlatively, supremely, thoroughly, to perfection, totally, unimpeachably, utterly, wholly, wonderfully.

antonyms imperfectly, partially.

perfidious *adj* corrupt, deceitful, dishonest, disloyal, double-dealing, double-faced, duplicitous, faithless, false, Machiavellian, Punic, recreant, traitorous, treacherous, treasonous, two-faced, unfaithful, untrustworthy.

antonyms faithful, honest, loyal.

perfidy *n* betrayal, deceit, disloyalty, double-dealing, duplicity, faithlessness, falsity, infidelity, perfidiousness, Punic faith, traitorousness, treachery, treason.

antonyms faithfulness, honesty, loyalty.

perforate *v* bore, drill, hole, honeycomb, penetrate, pierce, prick, punch, puncture, stab.

perforated *adj* bored, drilled, ethmoid, fenestrate(d), fenestrial, foraminous, holed, pierced, porous, punched, punctured.

perforation *n* bore, cut, dotted line, fenestration, hole, prick, puncture, slit, space.

perforce *adv* inevitably, necessarily, of necessity, unavoidably, willy-nilly.

perform *v* accomplish, achieve, act, appear as, bring about, bring off, carry out, complete, depict, discharge, do, effect, enact, execute, fulfil, function, functionate, manage, observe, play, present, produce, pull off, put on, render, represent, satisfy, stage, transact, work.

performance *n* accomplishment, account, achievement, act, acting, action, appearance, behaviour, bother, business, carrying out, carry-on, completion, conduct, consummation, discharge, efficiency, execution, exhibition, exploit, feat, fulfilment, functioning, fuss, gig, implementation, interpretation, melodrama, operation, play, portrayal, practice, presentation, production, rendition, representation, rigmarole, running, show, to-do, work, working.

performer *n* actor, actress, artiste, moke, mummer, play-actor, player, Thespian, trouper.

perfume *n* aroma, attar, balm, balminess, bouquet, cologne, essence, fragrance, incense, odour, redolence, scent, smell, sweetness, toilet water.

perfunctory *adj* automatic, brief, careless, cursory, heedless, hurried, inattentive, indifferent, mechanical, negligent, offhand, routine, sketchy, slipshod, slovenly, stereotyped, superficial, wooden.

antonym cordial.

perhaps *adv* conceivably, feasibly, happen, maybe, mayhap, peradventure, perchance, possibly, you never know.

peril *n* danger, exposure, hazard, imperilment, insecurity, jeopardy, menace, pitfall, risk, threat, uncertainty, vulnerability.

antonyms safety, security.

perilous *adj* chancy, dangerous, desperate, dicey, difficult, dire, exposed, hairy, hazardous, menacing, parlous, precarious, risky, threatening, unsafe, unsure, vulnerable.

antonyms safe, secure.

perimeter *n* ambit, border, borderline, boundary, bounds, circumference, confines, edge, fringe, frontier, limit, margin, periphery.

antonyms centre, heart, middle.

period[1] *n* aeon, age, course, cycle, date, days, end, epoch, era, generation, interval, season, space, span, spell, stage, stint, stop, stretch, term, time, turn, while, years.

period[2] *n* menses, menstrual flow, menstruation, monthlies, the curse.

periodic *adj* cyclic, cyclical, desultory, etesian, infrequent, intermittent, occasional, periodical, recurrent, regular, repeated, seasonal, spasmodic, sporadic.

periodical *n* gazette, journal, magazine, monthly, organ, paper, publication, quarterly, review, serial, weekly.

peripatetic *adj* ambulant, ambulatory, itinerant, journeying, migrant, mobile, nomadic, roaming, roving, travelling, vagabond, vagrant, wandering.

antonym fixed.

peripheral *adj* borderline, exterior, external, incidental, inessential, irrelevant, marginal, minor, outer, outermost, outlying, outside, perimetric, secondary, superficial, surface, tangential, unimportant, unnecessary.

antonyms central, crucial.

periphery *n* ambit, border, boundary, brim, brink, circuit, circumference, edge, fringe, hem, margin, outskirts, perimeter, rim, skirt, verge.

antonyms centre, nub.

perish *v* collapse, croak, crumble, decay, decline, decompose, decrease, die, disappear, disintegrate, end, expire, fall, moulder, pass away, rot, vanish, waste, wither.

perishable *adj* biodegradable, corruptible, decomposable, destructible, fast-decaying, fast-deteriorating, short-lived, unstable.

perjury *n* false oath, false statement, false swearing, false witness, falsification, forswearing, mendacity.

perk *n* benefit, bonus, bunce, dividend, extra, freebie, fringe benefit, perquisite, plus.

perk up brighten, buck up, cheer up, improve, liven up, look up, pep up, rally, recover, recuperate, revive, take heart, upturn.

perky *adj* animated, bouncy, bright, bubbly, buoyant, cheerful, cheery, effervescent, gay, jaunty, lively, peppy, spirited, sprightly, sunny, vivacious.

antonyms cheerless, dull, gloomy.

permanence *n* constancy, continuance, continuity, deathlessness, dependability, durability, duration, endurance, finality, fixedness, fixity, immortality, imperishability, indestructibility, lastingness, longevity, perdurability, permanency, perpetuity, stability, survival.

antonym impermanence.

permanent *adj* abiding, constant, durable, enduring, everlasting, fixed, immutable, imperishable, indestructible, ineffaceable, ineradicable, inerasable, invariable, lasting, long-lasting, perennial, perpetual, persistent, stable, standing, steadfast, unchanging, unfading.

antonyms ephemeral, fleeting, temporary.

permanently *adv* always, ceaselessly, constantly, continually, endlessly, eternally, ever more, everlastingly, for keeps, forever, once and for all, umremittingly, unendingly.

antonym temporarily.

permeable *adj* absorbent, absorptive, passable, penetrable, pervious, porous, spongeous, spongy.

antonyms impermeable, watertight.

permeate *v* charge, fill, filter through, imbue, impenetrate, impregnate, infiltrate, interfuse, interpenetrate, pass through, penetrate, percolate, pervade, saturate, seep through, soak through.

permissible *adj* acceptable, admissible, all right, allowable, allowed, authorised, kosher, lawful, leal, legit, legitimate, licit, OK, permitted, proper, sanctioned.

antonym prohibited.

permission *n* allowance, approval, assent, authorisation, consent, dispensation, freedom, go-ahead, green light, imprimatur, indult, leave, liberty, licence, permit, sanction, sufferance.

antonym prohibition.

permissive *adj* acquiescent, complaisant, easy-going, forbearing, free, indulgent, latitudinarian, lax, lenient, liberal, open-minded, overindulgent, tolerant.

antonym strict.

permit *v* admit, agree, allow, authorise, consent, empower, enable, endorse, endure, give leave, grant, let, warrant.

antonym prohibit.

n authorisation, carnet, liberty, licence, pass, passport, permission, sanction, visa, warrant.

antonym prohibition.

permutation *n* alteration, change, commutation, shift, transformation, transmutation, transposition, transubstantiation.

pernicious *adj* bad, baleful, baneful, damaging, dangerous, deadly, deleterious, destructive, detrimental, evil, fatal, harmful, hurtful, injurious, maleficent, malevolent, malicious, malign, malignant, noisome, noxious, offensive, pestilent, poisonous, ruinous, toxic, unhealthy, unwholesome, venomous, wicked.

antonym innocuous.

pernickety *adj* careful, carping, detailed, exacting, fastidious, fiddly, fikish, fiky, fine, finical, finicky, fussy, hair-splitting, nice, nit-picking, over-precise, painstaking, particular, punctilious, tricky.

peroration *n* closing remarks, conclusion, recapitulation, recapping, reiteration, summary, summing-up.

perpendicular *adj* plumb, precipitous, sheer, straight, upright, vertical.

antonym horizontal.

perpetrate *v* carry out, commit, do, effect, enact, execute, inflict, perform, practise, wreak.

perpetual *adj* abiding, ceaseless, constant, continual, continuous, deathless, endless, enduring, eternal, everlasting, immortal, incessant, infinite, interminable, lasting, never-ending, never-failing, perennial, permanent, persistent, recurrent, repeated, sempiternal, unceasing, unchanging, undying, unending, unfailing, unflagging, uninterrupted, unremitting, unvarying.

antonyms ephemeral, intermittent, transient.

perpetuate *v* commemorate, continue, eternalise, immortalise, keep alive, keep up, maintain, preserve, protract, sustain.

perplex *v* baffle, befuddle, beset, bewilder, complicate, confound, confuse, dumbfound, embrangle, encumber, entangle, gravel, hobble, involve, jumble, mix up, muddle, mystify, nonplus, pother, pudder, puzzle, stump, tangle, thicken, throw.

perplexed *adj* at a loss, baffled, bamboozled, bewildered, confounded, disconcerted, fuddled, muddled, mystified, puzzled, worried.

perplexing *adj* amazing, baffling, bewildering, complex, complicated, confusing, difficult, distractive, enigmatic, hard, inexplicable, intricate, involved, knotty, labyrinthine, mysterious, mystifying, paradoxical, puzzling, strange, taxing, thorny, unaccountable, vexatious, weird.

antonyms easy, simple.

perplexity *n* bafflement, bewilderment, complexity, confusion, difficulty, dilemma, enigma, incomprehension, intricacy, involvement, labyrinth, mystery, mystification, nonplus, obfuscation, obscuration, obscurity, paradox, puzzle, puzzlement, snarl, stupefaction.

perquisite *n* ap(p)anage, baksheesh, benefit, bonus, dividend, extra, fringe benefit, gratuity, perk, plus, tip.

persecute *v* afflict, annoy, badger, bait, bother, castigate, crucify, distress, dragoon, harass, haze, hound, hunt, ill-treat, injure, maltreat, martyr, molest, oppress, pester, pursue, tease, torment, torture, tyrannise, vex, victimise, worry.

antonyms accommodate, humour, indulge, pamper.

persecution *n* abuse, baiting, bashing, castigation, discrimination, maltreatment, molestation, oppression, punishment, subjugation, suppression, torture, tyranny.

perseverance *n* abidance, assiduity, constancy, dedication, determination, diligence, doggedness, endurance, indefatigability, persistence, pertinacity, purposefulness, resolution, sedulity, stamina, steadfastness, tenacity.

persevere *v* adhere, carry on, continue, endure, go on, hang on, hold fast, hold on, keep going, persist, plug away, pursue, remain, soldier on, stand firm, stick at.

antonyms desist, discontinue, give up, stop.

persist *v* abide, carry on, continue, endure, insist, keep at it, last, linger, perdure, persevere, remain, stand fast, stand firm.

antonyms desist, stop.

persistence *n* assiduity, assiduousness, constancy, determination, diligence, doggedness, endurance, grit, indefatigableness, perseverance, pertinacity, pluck, resolution, sedulity, stamina, steadfastness, tenacity, tirelessness.

persistent *adj* assiduous, constant, continual, continuous, determined, dogged, endless, enduring, fixed, hydra-headed, immovable, incessant, indefatigable, indomitable, interminable, never-ending, obdurate, obstinate, perpetual, persevering, pertinacious, relentless, repeated, resolute, steadfast, steady, stubborn, tenacious, tireless, unflagging, unrelenting, unremitting, zealous.

person *n* being, bod, body, cat, chal, character, codger, cookie, customer, human, human being, individual, individuum, living soul, party, soul, specimen, type, wight.

persona *n* character, façade, face, front, image, mask, part, personality, public face, role.

personable *adj* affable, agreeable, amiable, attractive, charming, good-looking, handsome, lik(e)able, nice, outgoing, pleasant, pleasing, presentable, warm, winning.

antonyms disagreeable, unattractive.

personage *n* big shot, celebrity, dignitary, headliner, luminary, name, notable, personality, public figure, somebody, VIP, worthy.

personal *adj* bodily, corporal, corporeal, derogatory, disparaging, exclusive, exterior, idiosyncratic, individual, inimitable, insulting, intimate, material, nasty, offensive, own, particular, peculiar, pejorative, physical, private, privy, slighting, special, tête-à-tête.

antonyms general, public, universal.

personality *n* attraction, attractiveness, celebrity, character, charisma, charm, disposition, dynamism, humour, identity, individuality, lik(e)ableness, magnetism, make-up, nature, notable, personage, pleasantness, psyche, selfhood, selfness, star, temper, temperament, traits.

personally *adv* alone, idiosyncratically, independently, individually, privately, solely, specially, subjectively.

personification *n* delineation, embodiment, image, incarnation, likeness, manifestation, portrayal, recreation, representation, semblance.

personify *v* embody, epitomise, exemplify, express, hypostatise, image, incarnate, mirror, personise, represent, symbolise, typify.

personnel *n* crew, employees, helpers, human resources, liveware, manpower, members, people, staff, workers, workforce.

perspective *n* angle, aspect, attitude, context, objectivity, outlook, overview, panorama, proportion, prospect, relation, scene, slant, view, vista.

perspicacious *adj* acute, alert, astute, aware, clear-eyed, clear-sighted, clever, discerning, far-sighted, keen, observant, penetrating, perceptive, percipient, sagacious, sharp, sharp-witted, shrewd.

antonyms obtuse, unobservant.

perspicacity *n* acuity, acumen, acuteness, brains, cleverness, discernment, discrimination, insight, keenness, penetration, perceptiveness, percipience, perspicaciousness, perspicuity, sagaciousness, sagacity, sharpness, shrewdness, wit.

perspicuity *n* clarity, clearness, comprehensibility, comprehensibleness, distinctness, explicitness, intelligibility, limpidity, limpidness, lucidity, penetrability, plainness, precision, straightforwardness, transparency.

perspicuous *adj* apparent, clear, comprehensible, crystal-clear, distinct, explicit, intelligible, limpid, lucid, manifest, obvious, plain, self-evident, straightforward, transparent, unambiguous, understandable.

perspiration *n* dew, diaphoresis, exudation, hidrosis, moisture, sudor, sweat, wetness.

perspire *v* drip, exude, glow, secrete, sudate, sweat, swelter.

persuadable *adj* acquiescent, agreeable, amenable, compliant, flexible, impressionable, malleable, persuasible, pliable, receptive, susceptive.

antonyms firm, inflexible, stubborn.

persuade *v* actuate, advise, allure, bring round, cajole, coax, convert, convince, counsel, entice, fast-talk, impel, incite, induce, influence, inveigle, lead on, lean on, prevail upon, prompt, satisfy, sway, sweet-talk, talk into, urge, win over.

antonyms discourage, dissuade.

persuasion *n* belief, blandishment, cajolery, camp, certitude, cogency, come-on, conversion, conviction, credo, creed, cult, denomination, enticement, exhortation, faction, faith, force, inducement, influence, inveiglement, opinion, party, persuasiveness, potency, power, pull, school (of thought), sect, side, suasion, sweet talk, tenet, views, wheedling.

persuasive *adj* cogent, compelling, convincing, credible, effective, eloquent, forceful, honeyed, impelling, impressive, inducing, influential, logical, moving, persuasory, plausible, potent, sound, telling, touching, valid, weighty, whilly, whillywha(w), winning.

pert *adj* bold, brash, brisk, cheeky, daring, dicacious, flip, flippant, forward, fresh, gay, impertinent, impudent, insolent, jaunty, lively, nimble, perky, presumptuous, saucy, smart, spirited, sprightly, tossy.

antonyms coy, shy.

pertain *v* appertain, apply, be appropriate, be part of, be relevant, bear on, befit, belong, come under, concern, refer, regard, relate.

pertinacious *adj* determined, dogged, headstrong, inflexible, intractable, mulish, obdurate, obstinate, persevering, persistent, perverse, purposeful, relentless, resolute, self-willed, strong-willed, stubborn, tenacious, uncompromising, unyielding, wilful.

pertinent *adj* ad rem, admissible, analogous, applicable, apposite, appropriate, apropos, apt, befitting, fit, fitting, germane, material, pat, proper, relevant, suitable, to the point, to the purpose.

antonyms inappropriate, irrelevant, unsuitable.

pertness *n* audacity, boldness, brashness, brass, brazenness, bumptiousness, cheek, cheekiness, chutzpah, cockiness, didacity, effrontery, forwardness, freshness, impertinence, impudence, insolence, presumption, rudeness, sauciness.

perturb *v* aerate, agitate, alarm, bother, confuse, disarrange, discompose, disconcert, discountenance, disorder, disquiet, disturb, faze, feeze, fluster, muddle, ruffle, trouble, unsettle, upset, vex, worry.

antonyms compose, reassure.

perturbed *adj* agitated, alarmed, anxious, discomposed, disconcerted, disturbed, dithery, fearful, flappable, flurried, flustered, nervous, restless, shaken, troubled, uncomfortable, uneasy, unsettled, upset, worried.

antonym unperturbed.

perusal *n* browse, check, examination, inspection, look, read, run-through, scrutiny, study.

peruse *v* browse, check, examine, inspect, look through, pore over, read, scan, scrutinise, study, vet.

pervade *v* affect, charge, diffuse, extend, fill, imbue, infuse, osmose, overspread, penetrate, percolate, permeate, saturate, suffuse.

pervasive *adj* common, diffuse, extensive, general, immanent, inescapable, omnipresent, permeating, pervading, prevalent, rife, ubiquitous, universal, widespread.

perverse *adj* abnormal, balky, camstairy, cantankerous, churlish, contradictory, contrary, contumacious, crabbed, cross, cross-grained, cussed, delinquent, depraved, deviant, disobedient, dogged, fractious, froward, headstrong, ill-natured, ill-tempered, improper, incorrect, intractable, intransigent, miscreant, mulish, obdurate, obstinate, peevish, petulant, pig-headed, rebellious, recalcitrant, refractory, spiteful, stroppy, stubborn, surly, thrawn, thwart, troublesome, unhealthy, unmanageable, unreasonable, unyielding, uppity, wayward, wilful, wrong-headed, wry.

antonyms normal, reasonable.

perversion *n* aberration, abnormality, anomaly, corruption, debauchery, depravity, deviance, deviancy, deviation, distortion, falsification, immorality, kink, kinkiness, misapplication, misinterpretation, misrepresentation, misuse, paraphilia, twisting, unnaturalness, vice, vitiation, wickedness.

perversity *n* contradictoriness, contrariness, contumacy, cussedness, frowardness, gee, intransigence, obduracy, protervity, refractoriness, waywardness, wrong-headedness.

pervert *v* abuse, bend, corrupt, debase, debauch, degrade, deprave, distort, divert, falsify, garble, lead astray, misapply, misconstrue, misinterpret, misrepresent, misuse, subvert, twist, vitiate, warp, wrest.

n debauchee, degenerate, deviant, paraphiliac, vert, weirdo.

perverted *adj* aberrant, abnormal, corrupt, debased, debauched, depraved, deviant, distorted, evil, freakish, immoral, impaired, kinky, misguided, queer, sick, twisted, unhealthy, unnatural, vicious, vitiated, warped, wicked.

pessimism *n* cynicism, dejection, depression, despair, despondency, distrust, doomwatch, gloom, gloominess, glumness, hopelessness, melancholy, Weltschmerz.

antonym optimism.

pessimist *n* Cassandra, cynic, defeatist, dismal Jimmy, doom-merchant, doomster, doomwatcher, gloom and doom merchant, killjoy, melancholic, wet blanket, worrier.

antonym optimist.

pessimistic *adj* bleak, cynical, dark, defeatist, dejected, depressed, despairing, despondent, dismal, distrustful, downhearted, fatalistic, gloomy, glum, hopeless, melancholy, misanthropic, morose, resigned, sad, worried.

antonym optimistic.

pest *n* annoyance, bane, blight, bore, bother, bug, canker, curse, irritation, nuisance, pain (in the neck), scourge, thorn in one's flesh, trial, vexation.

pester *v* annoy, badger, bedevil, bother, bug, chivvy, disturb, dog, drive round the bend, drive up the wall, fret, get at, harass, harry, hassle, hector, hound, irk, nag, pick on, plague, ride, torment, worry.

pestilent *adj* annoying, bothersome, catching, communicable, contagious, contaminated, corrupting, deleterious, destructive, detrimental, diseased, disease-ridden, evil, galling, harmful, infected, infectious, injurious, irksome, irritating, morbiferous, morbific, pernicious, plague-ridden, plagu(e)y, ruinous, tainted, tiresome, vexing, vicious.

pestilential *adj* annoying, catching, contagious, contaminated, dangerous, deadly, deleterious, destructive, detrimental, disease-ridden, evil, foul, harmful, hazardous, infectious, injurious, malignant, morbiferous, morbific, noxious, pernicious, pesky, pestiferous, poisonous, ruinous, troublesome, venomous.

pet *n* darling, dautie, dilling, doll, duck, ewe-lamb, favourite, idol, jewel, treasure, whitehead.

adj cherished, dearest, favoured, favourite, particular, preferred, special.

v baby, canoodle, caress, coddle, cosset, cuddle, daut, dote on, fondle, indulge, kiss, mollycoddle, neck, pamper, pat, smooch, snog, spoil, stroke.

peter out cease, dissolve, dwindle, ebb, evaporate, fade, fail, stop, taper off, wane.

petite *adj* bijou, dainty, delicate, dinky, elfin, little, slight, small.

antonyms big, large.

petition *n* address, appeal, application, boon, entreaty, imploration, invocation, plea, prayer, request, rogation, round robin, solicitation, suit, supplication.

v appeal, ask, beg, beseech, bid, call upon, crave, entreat, implore, memorialise, plead, pray, press, solicit, sue, supplicate, urge.

pet-name *n* diminutive, endearment, hypocorisma, nickname.

petrified *adj* aghast, appalled, benumbed, dazed, dumbfounded, fossilised, frozen, horrified, horror-stricken, numb, ossified, scared stiff, shocked, speechless, stunned, stupefied, terrified, terror-stricken.

petrify *v* amaze, appal, astonish, astound, benumb, calcify, confound, dumbfound, fossilise, gorgonise, harden, horrify, immobilise, numb, paralyse, set, solidify, stun, stupefy, terrify, transfix, turn to stone.

petticoat *n* crinoline, farthingale, half-slip, jupon, kirtle, slip, underskirt.

pettifogging *adj* captious, casuistic, cavilling, circumlocutary, equivocating, hair-splitting, mean, niggling, nit-picking, over-refined, paltry, petty, quibbling, sophistical, sophisticated, subtle.

pettish *adj* cross, fractious, fretful, grumpy, huffy, ill-humoured, irritable, peevish, petulant, querulous, snappish, splenetic, sulky, tetchy, thin-skinned, touchy, waspish.

petty *adj* cheap, contemptible, grudging, inconsiderable, inessential, inferior, insignificant, junior, lesser, little, lower, mean, measly, minor, negligible, one-horse, paltry, picayune, picayunish, piddling, pimping, poking, poky, secondary, shabby, slight, small, small-minded, small-town, spiteful, stingy, subordinate, trifling, trivial, ungenerous, unimportant.

antonyms generous, important, large-hearted, significant, vital.

petulance *n* bad temper, crabbedness, crabbiness, ill-humour, ill-temper, irritability, peevishness, pettishness, pique, procacity, querulousness, spleen, sulkiness, sullenness, waspishness.

petulant *adj* bad-tempered, captious, cavilling, crabbed, cross, crusty, fretful, ill-humoured, impatient, irascible, irritable, moody, peevish, perverse, pettish, procacious, querulous, snappish, sour, sulky, sullen, ungracious, waspish.

phantom *n* apparition, chimera, eidolon, figment (of the imagination), ghost, hallucination, illusion, manes, phantasm(a), revenant, shade, simulacrum, spectre, spirit, spook, vision, wraith.

pharisaical *adj* canting, formal, goody-goody, holier-than-thou, hypocritical, insincere, moralising, pharisaic, pietistic, preachy, sanctimonious, self-righteous, Tartuf(f)ian, Tartuf(f)ish.

pharisee *n* canter, dissembler, dissimulator, fraud, Holy Willie, humbug, hypocrite, phoney, pietist, Tartuf(f)e, whited sepulchre.

phase *n* aspect, chapter, condition, development, juncture, period, point, position, season, spell, stage, state, step, time.

phase out close, deactivate, dispose of, ease off, eliminate, get rid of, remove, replace, run down, taper off, terminate, wind down, withdraw.

phenomenal *adj* amazing, exceptional, extraordinary, fantastic, marvellous, miraculous, outstanding, prodigious, remarkable, sensational, singular, stupendous, uncommon, unique, unparalleled, unusual, wondrous.

phenomenon *n* appearance, circumstance, curiosity, episode, event, fact, happening, incident, marvel, miracle, occurrence, prodigy, rarity, sensation, sight, spectacle, wonder.

philanderer *n* Casanova, dallier, Don Juan, flirt, gallant, gay deceiver, ladies' man, lady-killer, libertine, Lothario, playboy, stud, trifler, venerean, wencher, wolf, womaniser.

philanthropic *adj* alms-giving, altruistic, beneficent, benevolent, benignant, bounteous, bountiful, charitable, eleemosynary, gracious, humane, humanitarian, kind, kind-hearted, kindly, munificent, public-spirited.

antonym misanthropic.

philanthropist *n* alms-giver, altruist, angel, benefactor, contributor, donor, giver, good fairy, humanitarian, patron.

antonyms misanthrope, misanthropist.

philanthropy *n* agape, alms-giving, altruism, beneficence, benevolence, benignity, bounty, brotherly love, charitableness, charity, generosity, humanitarianism, kind-heartedness, liberality, munificence, open-handedness, patronage, public-spiritedness, unselfishness.

Philistine *n* Babbit, barbarian, Boeotian, boor, bourgeois, Goth, ignoramus, lout, lowbrow, vulgarian, yahoo.

antonym aesthete.

adj Boeotian, boorish, bourgeois, crass, ignorant, lowbrow, tasteless, uncultivated, uncultured, uneducated, unlettered, unread, unrefined.

philosopher *n* deipnosophist, dialectician, epistemologist, logician, metaphysician, sage, theorist, thinker, vocabularian.

philosophical *adj* abstract, analytical, calm, collected, composed, cool, dispassionate, equanimous, erudite, impassive, imperturbable, learned, logical, metaphysical, patient, philosophic, rational, resigned, sagacious, serene, stoical, theoretical, thoughtful, tranquil, unruffled, wise.

philosophy *n* aesthetics, attitude, beliefs, convictions, doctrine, epistemology, ideology, knowledge, logic, metaphysics, principle, rationale, rationalism, reason, reasoning, tenets, thinking, thought, values, viewpoint, Weltanschauung, wisdom, world-view.

phlegmatic *adj* apathetic, bovine, cold, dull, frigid, heavy, impassive, imperturbable, indifferent, lethargic, listless, lymphatic, matter-of-fact, nonchalant, placid, sluggish, stoical, stolid, unconcerned, undemonstrative, unemotional.

antonyms demonstrative, passionate.

phobia *n* anxiety, aversion, detestation, dislike, distaste, dread, fear, hang-up, hatred, horror, loathing, neurosis, obsession, phobism, repulsion, revulsion, terror, thing.

antonyms liking, love.

phoney *adj* affected, assumed, bogus, counterfeit, fake, false, forged, imitation, pseudo, put-on, quack, quacksalving, sham, spurious, trick.

antonyms real, true.

n counterfeit, fake, faker, forgery, fraud, humbug, imposter, mountebank, pretender, pseud, quack, sham.

phosphorescent *adj* bright, glowing, luminescent, luminous, noctilucent, noctilucous, radiant, refulgent.

photograph *n* ambrotype, angiogram, daguerreotype, ferrotype, image, likeness, photo, picture, print, shot, slide, snap, snapshot, transparency.

v film, record, shoot, snap, take, video.

photographic *adj* accurate, cinematic, detailed, exact, faithful, filmic, graphic, lifelike, minute, natural, naturalistic, pictorial, precise, realistic, representational, retentive, visual, vivid.

phrase *n* construction, expression, idiom, locution, mention, motto, remark, saying, tag, utterance.

v couch, express, formulate, frame, present, pronounce, put, say, style, term, utter, voice, word.

phraseology *n* argot, cant, diction, expression, idiom, language, parlance, patois, phrase, phrasing, speech, style, syntax, wording.

physical *adj* actual, bodily, carnal, concrete, corporal, corporeal, earthly, fleshly, incarnate, material, mortal, natural, palpable, real, sensible, solid, somatic, substantial, tangible, visible.

antonyms mental, spiritual.

physician *n* doc, doctor, doctor of medicine, general practitioner, GP, hakim, healer, houseman, intern, leech, MD, medic, medical practitioner, medico, registrar, specialist.

physiognomy *n* clock, countenance, dial, face, features, look, mug, phiz, phizog, visage, visnomy.

physique *n* body, build, chassis, constitution, figure, form, frame, make-up, shape, structure.

pick *v* break into, break open, choose, collect, crack, cull, cut, decide on, elect, embrace, espouse, fix upon, foment, gather, harvest, incite, instigate, opt for, pluck, prise, provoke, pull, screen, select, settle on, sift out, single out, start.

antonym reject.

n best, brightest and best, choice, choicest, choosing, cream, crème de la crème, decision, elect, élite, flower, option, preference, pride, prize, selection, tops.

pick at nibble, peck, play with, toy with.

pick off detach, drill, hit, kill, plug, remove, shoot, strike.

pick on badger, bait, blame, bully, carp at, cavil at, criticise, find fault with, get at, nag, needle, quibble with, tease, torment.

pick out choose, cull, differentiate, discriminate, distinguish, hand-pick, notice, perceive, recognise, select, separate, single out, tell apart.

pick up acquire, apprehend, arrest, bust, buy, call for, collar, collect, come across, fetch, find, gain, gain ground, garner, gather, grasp, happen on, hoist, improve, learn, lift, master, mend, nab, nick, obtain, perk up, pinch, pull in, purchase, raise, rally, recover, recuperate, run in, score, snap up, uplift.

picket *n* demonstrator, dissenter, guard, look-out, outpost, pale, paling, palisade, patrol, peg, picketer, post, protester, scout, sentinel, sentry, spotter, stake, stanchion, upright, vedette, watchman.

v blockade, boycott, corral, demonstrate, enclose, fence, hedge in, palisade, pen in, protest.

pickings *n* booty, bunce, earnings, gravy, loot, plunder, proceeds, profits, returns, rewards, spoils, take, yield.

pickle *n* bind, crisis, difficulty, dilemma, exigency, fix, hot water, jam, pinch, predicament, quandary, scrape, spot, straits, tight spot.

v conserve, cure, marinade, preserve, steep.

pick-me-up *n* boost, cordial, fillip, refreshment, restorative, roborant, shot in the arm, stimulant, tonic.

pick-pocket *n* dip, diver, file, pick-purse, snatcher, wire.

picnic[1] *n* excursion, fête champêtre, outdoor meal, outing, wayzgoose.

picnic[2] *n* child's play, cinch, doddle, piece of cake, pushover, sinecure, snap, walkover.

pictorial *adj* diagrammatic, expressive, graphic, illustrated, picturesque, representational, scenic, schematic, striking, vivid.

picture *n* account, archetype, carbon copy, copy, dead ringer, delineation, depiction, description, double, drawing, duplicate, effigy, embodiment, engraving, epitome, essence, film, flick, graphic, illustration, image, impression, kakemono, likeness, living image, lookalike, motion picture, movie, painting, personification, photograph, portrait, portrayal, print, re-creation, replica, report, representation, ringer, scene, similitude, sketch, spit, spitting image, tablature, table, twin, vraisemblance.

v conceive of, delineate, depict, describe, draw, envisage, envision, illustrate, image, imagine, paint, photograph, portray, render, represent, see, show, sketch, visualise.

picturesque *adj* attractive, beautiful, charming, colourful, descriptive, graphic, pretty, quaint, scenic, striking, vivid.

piebald *adj* brindled, dappled, flecked, mottled, pied, pinto, skewbald, speckled, spotted.

piece *n* allotment, article, bit, case, chunk, component, composition, constituent, creation, division, element, example, fraction, fragment, instance, item, length, mammock, morsel, mouthful, objet d'art, occurrence, offcut, part, piecemeal, portion, production, quantity, sample, scrap, section, segment, share, shred, slice, snippet, specimen, stroke, study, work, work of art.

piece together assemble, attach, compose, fit, fix, join, mend, patch, repair, restore, unite.

pièce de résistance *n* chef-d'oeuvre, jewel, magnum opus, masterpiece, masterwork, prize, showpiece.

piecemeal *adv* at intervals, bit by bit, by degrees, fitfully, in dribs and drabs, in penny numbers, intermittently, little by little, parcel-wise, partially, slowly.

antonyms completely, entirely, wholly.

adj discrete, fragmentary, intermittent, interrupted, partial, patchy, scattered, unsystematic.

antonyms complete, entire, whole, wholesale.

pied *adj* brindle(d), dappled, flecked, irregular, motley, mottled, multicoloured, particoloured, piebald, skewbald, spotted, streaked, varicoloured, variegated.

pier *n* buttress, column, jetty, jutty, landing-place, pile, piling, pillar, post, promenade, quay, support, upright, wharf.

pierce *v* affect, barb, bore, comprehend, discern, discover, drift, drill, enter, excite, fathom, grasp, gride, hurt, impale, lancinate, move, pain, penetrate, perforate, pink, prick, probe, prog, puncture, realise, rouse, run through, see, spike, stab, stick into, sting, stir, strike, thrill, thrust, touch, transfix, transpierce, understand, wound.

pierced *adj* impaled, perforated, pertusate, pertuse(d), punctured, stung.

piercing *adj* acute, agonising, alert, algid, arctic, aware, biting, bitter, cold, ear-piercing, ear-splitting, excruciating, exquisite, fierce, freezing, frore, frosty, gelid, high-pitched, intense, keen, loud, nipping, nippy, numbing, painful, penetrating, perceptive, perspicacious, powerful, probing, quick-witted, racking, raw, searching, severe, sharp, shattering, shooting, shrewd, shrill, Siberian, stabbing, wintry.

piety *n* devotion, devoutness, dutifulness, duty, faith, godliness, grace, holiness, piousness, religion, religiosity, reverence, saintliness, sanctity, veneration.

antonym impiety.

piffle *n* balderdash, balls, bullshit, bunk, bunkum, codswallop, drivel, guff, hooey, nonsense, poppycock, rot, rubbish, tarradiddle, tommy-rot, tosh, trash, tripe, twaddle.

pig *n* animal, beast, boar, boor, brute, glutton, gormandiser, go(u)rmand, greedy guts, grunter, guzzler, hog, piggy, piglet, porker, shoat, slob, sloven, sow, swine.

pigeonhole *n* box, category, class, classification, compartment, cubbyhole, cubicle, locker, niche, place, section, slot.

v alphabetise, catalogue, characterise, classify, codify, compartmentalise, defer, file, label, postpone, put off, shelve, slot, sort, typecast.

pig-headed *adj* bull-headed, contrary, cross-grained, dense, froward, inflexible, intractable, intransigent, mulish, obstinate, perverse, self-willed, stiff-necked, stubborn, stupid, unyielding, wilful, wrong-headed.

antonyms flexible, tractable.

pigment *n* colour, colo(u)rant, colouring, colouring matter, dye, dyestuff, hue, paint, stain, tempera, tincture, tint.

pile[1] *n* accumulation, assemblage, assortment, bing, bomb, building, cock, collection, edifice, erection, fortune, heap, hoard, mass, mint, money, mound, mountain, mow, packet, pot, stack, stockpile, structure, wealth.

v accumulate, amass, assemble, build up, charge, climb, collect, crowd, crush, flock, flood, gather, heap, hoard, jam, load up, mass, pack, rush, stack, store, stream.

pile[2] *n* bar, beam, column, foundation, pier, piling, pill, post, rib, stanchion, support, upright.

pile[3] *n* down, fur, fuzz, fuzziness, hair, nap, plush, shag.

piles[1] *n* a great deal, a lot, loads, millions, oceans, oodles, quantities, stacks.

piles[2] *n* haemorrhoids.

pilfer *v* appropriate, embezzle, filch, finger, help oneself to, knock off, lift, mooch, nick, peculate, pickle, pinch, purloin, rifle, rob, steal, thieve.

pilgrim *n* crusader, hadji, palmer, peregrine, traveller, wanderer, wayfarer.

pilgrimage *n* crusade, excursion, expedition, hadj, journey, mission, odyssey, peregrination, tour, trip.

pill *n* ball, bolus, capsule, contraceptive, globule, pellet, pilule, tablet.

pillage *v* depredate, despoil, freeboot, loot, maraud, plunder, raid, ransack, ravage, raze, reive, rifle, rob, sack, spoil, spoliate, strip, vandalise.

n booty, depredation, devastation, harrying, loot, marauding, plunder, rapine, robbery, sack, seizure, spoils, spoliation.

pillar *n* balluster, bastion, cippus, column, leader, leading light, mainstay, mast, pier, pilaster, piling, post, prop, rock, shaft, stanchion, support, supporter, tower of strength, upholder, upright, worthy.

pillory *v* brand, cast a slur on, denounce, hold up to shame, lash, mock, pour scorn on, ridicule, show up, stigmatise.

pilot *n* airman, aviator, captain, conductor, coxswain, director, flier, guide, helmsman, hobbler, hoveller, leader, lodesman, navigator, steersman.

v boss, conduct, control, direct, drive, fly, guide, handle, lead, manage, navigate, operate, run, shepherd, steer.

adj experimental, model, test, trial.

pimp *n* bawd, fancy man, fleshmonger, go-between, mack, pander, panderer, procurer, white-slaver, whoremaster, whoremonger.

pimple *n* black-head, boil, papula, papule, plook, pustule, quat, spot, swelling, whelk, zit.

pin *v* affix, attach, fasten, fix, hold down, hold fast, immobilise, join, nail, pinion, press, restrain, secure, tack.

n bolt, breastpin, brooch, clip, fastener, nail, peg, rivet, screw, spike, spindle, stick pin, tack, tie-pin.

pin down bind, compel, confine, constrain, designate, determine, fix, force hold, hold down, home in on, identify, immobilise, locate, make, nail, nail down, name, pinpoint, press, pressurise, specify, tie down, zero in on.

pincers *n* forceps, forfex, tweezers.

pinch *v* afflict, apprehend, arrest, bust, chafe, check, collar, compress, confine, cramp, crush, distress, do, economise, filch, grasp, hurt, knap, knock off, lay, lift, nab, nick, nip, oppress, pain, pick up, pilfer, press, prig, pull in, purloin, rob, run in, scrimp, skimp, snaffle, snatch, sneap, snitch, spare, squeeze, steal, stint, swipe, tweak.

n bit, crisis, dash, difficulty, emergency, exigency, hardship, jam, jot, mite, necessity, nip, oppression, pass, pickle, plight, predicament, pressure, soupçon, speck, squeeze, strait, stress, taste, tweak.

pinched *adj* careworn, drawn, gaunt, haggard, narrowed, peaky, starved, straightened, thin, worn.

pine *v* ache, covet, crave, decay, decline, desire, droop, dwindle, dwine, fade, flag, hanker, hunger, languish, long, peak, sicken, sigh, sink, thirst, waste, weaken, wilt, wish, wither, yearn, yen.

pinion *v* bind, chain, confine, fasten, fetter, hobble, immobilise, manacle, pin down, shackle, tie, truss.

pink[1] *n* acme, best, extreme, flower, height, peak, perfection, summit, tiptop, top.

adj flushed, reddish, rose, roseate, rosy, salmon.

pink[2] *v* crenellate, incise, notch, perforate, prick, punch, scallop, score, serrate.

pinnacle *n* acme, apex, apogee, cap, cone, crest, crown, eminence, height, needle, obelisk, peak, pyramid, spire, steeple, summit, top, turret, vertex, zenith.

pin-point *v* define, distinguish, home in on, identify, locate, place, spot, zero in on.

pint-size *adj* diminutive, dwarf, little, midget, miniature, pocket, pocket-sized, small, tiny, wee.

antonyms giant, huge.

pioneer *n* coloniser, colonist, developer, explorer, founder, founding father, frontiersman, innovator, leader, settler, trail-blazer, voortrekker, way-maker.

v blaze a trail, create, develop, discover, establish, found, initiate, instigate, institute, invent, launch, lead, open up, originate, prepare, start.

pious *adj* dedicated, devoted, devout, God-fearing, godly, good, goody-goody, holier-than-thou, holy, hypocritical, moral, pietistic, religiose, religious, reverent, righteous, saintly, sanctimonious, self-righteous, spiritual, unctuous, virtuous.

antonym impious.

pipe *n* briar, clay, conduit, conveyor, duct, fife, fistula, flue, hookah, horn, hose, kalian, line, main, meerschaum, overflow, passage, pipeline, tooter, tube, whistle.

v carry, channel, cheep, chirp, conduct, convey, funnel, peep, play, sing, siphon, sound, supply, tootle, transmit, trill, tweet, twitter, warble, whistle.

pipe-dream *n* castle in Spain, castle in the air, chimera, daydream, delusion, dream, fantasy, mirage, notion, reverie, romance, vagary.

pipeline *n* channel, conduit, conveyor, duct, line, passage, pipe, tube.

pipsqueak *n* creep, hobbledehoy, nobody, nonentity, nothing, oik, squirt, twerp, upstart, whippersnapper.

antonym somebody.

piquancy *n* bite, colour, edge, excitement, flavour, ginger, interest, juice, kick, pep, pepperiness, pizzazz, punch, pungency, raciness, relish, sharpness, spice, spiciness, spirit, tang, vigour, vitality, zest, zip.

piquant *adj* biting, interesting, lively, peppery, poignant, provocative, pungent, racy, salty, savoury, scintillating, sharp, sparkling, spicy, spirited, stimulating, stinging, tangy, tart, zesty.

antonyms banal, jejune.

pique *n* annoyance, displeasure, grudge, huff, irritation, miff, offence, pet, resentment, umbrage, vexation.

v affront, annoy, arouse, displease, excite, gall, galvanise, get, goad, incense, irk, irritate, kindle, miff, mortify, nettle, offend, peeve, provoke, put out, rile, rouse, spur, stimulate, sting, stir, vex, whet, wound.

piracy *n* bootlegging, buccaneering, freebooting, hijacking, infringement, plagiarism, rapine, robbery, stealing, theft.

pirate *n* buccaneer, corsair, filibuster, freebooter, infringer, marauder, marque, picaroon, plagiariser, plagiarist, raider, rover, sallee-man, sea-rat, sea-robber, sea-rover, sea-wolf, water-rat.

v appropriate, borrow, copy, crib, lift, nick, pinch, plagiarise, poach, reproduce, steal.

pirouette *n* gyration, pivot, spin, turn, twirl, whirl.

v gyrate, pivot, spin, turn, twirl, whirl.

pistol *n* dag, derringer, gat, gun, hand-gun, iron, Luger, piece, revolver, rod, sidearm, six-shooter.

pit *n* abyss, alveole, alveolus, cavity, chasm, coal-mine, crater, dent, depression, dimple, excavation, gulf, hole, hollow, indentation, mine, oubliette, pock-mark, pothole, trench, variole.

pit against match, oppose, set against.

pitch *v* bung, cast, chuck, dive, drop, erect, fall headlong, fix, fling, flounder, heave, hurl, launch, lob, locate, lurch, peck, place, plant, plunge, raise, roll, set up, settle, sling, stagger, station, throw, topple, toss, tumble, wallow, welter.

n angle, cant, degree, dip, gradient, ground, harmonic, height, incline, level, line, modulation, park, patter, playing-field, point, sales talk, slope, sound, spiel, sports field, steepness, summit, tilt, timbre, tone.

pitch-dark *adj* black, dark, inky, jet-black, pitch-black, pitchy, Stygian, unilluminated, unlit.

pitcher *n* bottle, can, container, crock, ewer, jack, jar, jug, urn, vessel.

piteous *adj* affecting, deplorable, distressing, doleful, doloriferous, dolorific, grievous, heartbreaking, heart-rending, lamentable, miserable, mournful, moving, pathetic, pitiable, pitiful, plaintive, poignant, sad, sorrowful, touching, woeful, wretched.

pitfall *n* catch, danger, difficulty, downfall, drawback, hazard, peril, pit, snag, snare, stumbling-block, trap.

pith *n* consequence, core, crux, depth, essence, force, gist, gravamen, heart, import, importance, kernel, marrow, matter, meat, moment, nub, point, power, quintessence, salient point, significance, strength, substance, value, weight.

pithy *adj* aphoristic, apo(ph)thegmatic(al), brief, cogent, compact, concise, epigrammatic, expressive, forceful, laconic, matterful, meaningful, pointed, short, succinct, telling, terse, trenchant.

antonyms prolix, verbose, wordy.

pitiable *adj* contemptible, distressed, distressful, distressing, doleful, grievous, lamentable, miserable, mournful, pathetic, piteous, poor, sad, sorry, woeful, woesome, wretched.

pitiful *adj* abject, base, beggarly, contemptible, deplorable, despicable, distressing, grievous, heartbreaking, heart-rending, hopeless, inadequate, insignificant, lamentable, low, mean, miserable, paltry, pathetic, piteous, pitiable, ruthful, sad, scurvy, shabby, sorry, vile, woeful, worthless, wretched.

pitiless *adj* brutal, callous, cold-blooded, cold-hearted, cruel, flinty, hard-hearted, harsh, heartless, implacable, inexorable, inhuman, merciless, obdurate, relentless, ruthless, uncaring, unfeeling, unmerciful, unpitying, unsympathetic.

antonyms compassionate, gentle, kind, merciful.

pittance *n* chicken-feed, crumb, drop (in the ocean), mite, modicum, peanuts, trifle.

pitted *adj* blemished, dented, dinted, gouged, holey, indented, lacunose, marked, nicked, notched, pock-marked, pocky, potholed, punctuate, punctuated, riddled, rough, rutty, scarred, scratched.

pity *n* charity, clemency, commiseration, compassion, condolence, crime, crying shame, fellow-feeling, forbearance, kindness, mercy, misfortune, regret, ruth, shame, sin, sympathy, tenderness, understanding.

antonyms cruelty, disdain, scorn.

v absolve, bleed for, commiserate with, condole with, feel for, forgive, grieve for, pardon, reprieve, sympathise with, weep for.

pivot *n* axis, axle, centre, focal point, fulcrum, heart, hinge, hub, kingpin, linchpin, spindle, swivel.

v depend, hang, hinge, lie, rely, revolve, rotate, spin, swing, swivel, turn, twirl.

pivotal *adj* axial, central, climactic, critical, crucial, decisive, determining, focal, vital.

pixie *n* brownie, elf, fairy, goblin, leprechaun, pisky, sprite.

placard *n* advertisement, affiche, bill, poster, public notice, sandwich-board, sticker.

placate *v* appease, assuage, calm, conciliate, humour, lull, mollify, pacify, propitiate, quiet, satisfy, soothe, win over.

antonyms anger, enrage, incense, infuriate.

placatory *adj* appeasing, conciliatory, pacificatory, peace-making, propitiative, propitiatory.

place *n* abode, accommodation, affair, apartment, appointment, area, berth, billet, charge, city, concern, district, domicile, duty, dwelling, employment, flat, function, grade, home, house, job, locale, locality, location, locus, manor, mansion, neighbourhood, pad, point, position, post, prerogative, property, quarter, rank, region, residence, responsibility, right, role, room, seat, site, situation, space, spot, station, status, stead, town, venue, vicinity, village, whereabouts.

v allocate, appoint, arrange, assign, associate, bung, charge, class, classify, commission, deposit, dispose, dump, entrust, establish, fix, give, grade, group, identify, install, know, lay, locate, order, plant, position, put, put one's finger on, rank, recognise, remember, rest, set, settle, situate, sort, stand, station, stick.

placement *n* appointment, arrangement, assignment, classification, deployment, disposition, distribution, emplacement, employment, engagement, installation, locating, location, ordering, positioning, ranking, stationing.

placid *adj* calm, collected, composed, cool, equable, even, even-tempered, gentle, halcyon, imperturbable, level-headed, mild, peaceful, quiet, reposeful, restful, self-possessed, serene, still, tranquil, undisturbed, unexcitable, unmoved, unruffled, untroubled.

antonyms agitated, jumpy.

plagiarise *v* appropriate, borrow, counterfeit, crib, infringe, lift, pirate, reproduce, steal, thieve.

plagiarism *n* appropriation, borrowing, copying, counterfeiting, cribbing, infringement, lifting, piracy, reproduction, theft.

plagiarist *n* Autolycus, copier, imitator, pirate, robber, thief.

plague *n* affliction, aggravation, annoyance, bane, blight, bother, calamity, cancer, contagion, curse, death, disease, epidemic, evil, infection, irritant, nuisance, pain, pandemic, pest, pestilence, problem, scourge, thorn in the flesh, torment, trial, vexation, visitation.

v afflict, annoy, badger, bedevil, bother, distress, disturb, fret, harass, harry, hassle, haunt, hound, molest, pain, persecute, pester, tease, torment, torture, trouble, vex.

plain *adj* apparent, artless, austere, bare, basic, blunt, candid, clear, clinical, common, commonplace, comprehensible, direct, discreet, distinct, downright, even, everyday, evident, flat, forthright, frank, frugal, guileless, home-bred, homely, homespun, honest, ill-favoured, ingenuous, legible, level, lowly, lucid, manifest, modest, muted, obvious, open, ordinary, outspoken, patent, penny-plain, plane, pure, restrained, self-coloured, severe, simple, sincere, smooth, Spartan, stark, straightforward, transparent, ugly, unadorned, unaffected, unambiguous, unattractive, unbeautiful, understandable, undistinguished, unelaborate, unembellished, unfigured, unhandsome, unlovely, unmistakable, unobstructed, unornamented, unpatterned, unprepossessing, unpretentious, untrimmed, unvarnished, visible, whole-coloured, workaday.

antonyms abstruse, attractive, elaborate, exaggerated, ostentatious, rich, striking, unclear.

n flat, grassland, llano, lowland, maidan, plateau, prairie, steppe, tableland, vega, veld(t).

plain-spoken *adj* blunt, candid, direct, downright, explicit, forthright, frank, honest, open, outright, outspoken, straightforward, truthful, unequivocal.

plaintive *adj* disconsolate, dismal, doleful, dolorous, grief-stricken, grievous, heart-rending, melancholy, mournful, pathetic, piteous, pitiful, rueful, sad, sorrowful, wistful, woebegone, woeful.

plan *n* blueprint, chart, contrivance, delineation, design, device, diagram, drawing, idea, illustration, layout, map, method, plot, procedure, programme, project, proposal, proposition, representation, scenario, schedule, scheme, sketch, strategy, suggestion, system.

v aim, arrange, complot, concoct, conspire, contemplate, contrive, design, devise, draft, envisage, foreplan, foresee, formulate, frame, intend, invent, mean, organise, outline, plot, prepare, propose, purpose, represent, scheme.

plane[1] *n* class, condition, degree, echelon, footing, level, position, rank, rung, stage, stratum.

adj even, flat, flush, horizontal, level, plain, planar, regular, smooth, uniform.

plane[2] *n* aeroplane, aircraft, airliner, bomber, fighter, glider, jet, jumbo, jumbo jet, sea-plane, swing-wing, VTOL.

v fly, glide, sail, skate, skim, volplane, wing.

plangent *adj* clangorous, deep, loud, mournful, plaintive, resonant, resounding, reverberating, ringing, sonorous, vibrant.

plant[1] *n* bush, flower, herb, shrub, vegetable, weed, wort.

v bury, establish, fix, found, imbed, implant, inlay, insert, inset, institute, lodge, put in the ground, root, scatter, seed, set, set out, settle, sow, transplant.

plant[2] *n* apparatus, equipment, factory, foundry, gear, machinery, mill, shop, works, workshop, yard.

plaque *n* badge, brooch, cartouche, medal, medallion, panel, plaquette, plate, shield, slab, tablet.

plaster *n* bandage, cataplasm, dressing, gypsum, mortar, plaster of Paris, sticking-plaster, stucco.

v bedaub, besmear, coat, cover, daub, overlay, parge, parget, smear, spread, teer.

plastic *adj* compliant, docile, ductile, fictile, flexible, impressionable, malleable, manageable, mouldable, pliable, pliant, receptive, responsive, soft, supple, tractable.

antonyms inflexible, rigid.

plasticity *n* flexibility, malleability, pliability, pliableness, pliancy, softness, suppleness, tractability.

antonyms inflexibility, rigidity.

plate *n* ashet, charger, course, dish, helping, illustration, lame, lamella, lath, layer, lithograph, palette, panel, platter, portion, print, scale, serving, sheet, slab, trencher.

v anodise, coat, cover, electroplate, face, galvanise, gild, laminate, nickel, overlay, platinise, silver, tin, veneer, zinc, zinc(k)ify.

plateau *n* grade, highland, level, mesa, plane, stability, stage, table, tableland, upland.

platform *n* dais, estrade, gantry, manifesto, objective(s), party line, podium, policy, principle, programme, rostrum, stage, stand, tenet(s).

platitude *n* banality, bromide, chestnut, cliché, commonplace, inanity, stereotype, truism.

platitudinous *adj* banal, clichéd, commonplace, corny, dull, flat, hack, hackneyed, overworked, set, stale, stereotyped, stock, tired, trite, truistic, vapid, well-worn.

platonic *adj* ideal, idealistic, incorporeal, intellectual, non-physical, spiritual, transcendent.

platoon *n* battery, company, group, outfit, patrol, squad, squadron, team.

platter *n* ashet, charger, dish, meat-plate, plate, salver, tray, trencher.

plaudits *n* acclaim, acclamation, accolade, applause, approbation, approval, clapping, commendation, congratulations, hand, hurrahs, kudos, ovation, praise, standing ovation.

plausible *adj* believable, colourable, conceivable, convincing, credible, facile, fair-spoken, glib, likely, persuasive, possible, probable, reasonable, smooth, smooth-talking, smooth-tongued, specious, tenable, voluble.

antonyms implausible, improbable, unlikely.

play *v* act, bet, caper, challenge, chance, compete, contend, execute, fiddle, fidget, flirt, fool around, frisk, frolic, gamble, gambol, hazard, impersonate, interfere, lilt, participate, perform, personate, portray, punt, represent, revel, risk, rival, romp, speculate, sport, string along, take, take on, take part, take the part of, trifle, vie with, wager.

antonym work.

n action, activity, amusement, caper, comedy, diversion, doodle, drama, elbowroom, employment, entertainment, exercise, farce, foolery, frolic, fun, function, gambling, gambol, game, gaming, give, humour, jest, joking, lark, latitude, leeway, margin, masque, motion, movement, operation, pastime, performance, piece, prank, range, recreation, romp, room, scope, show, space, sport, sweep, swing, teasing, tragedy, transaction, working.

play around dally, flirt, fool, mess around, philander, trifle, womanise.

play ball collaborate, co-operate, go along, play along, reciprocate, respond, show willing.

play by ear ad-lib, extemporise, improvisate, improvise.

play down gloss over, make light of, make little of, minimise, soft-pedal, underplay, underrate, undervalue.

play for time delay, drag one's feet, filibuster, hang fire, hesitate, procrastinate, stall, temporise.

play havoc with confuse, demolish, destroy, devastate, disorganise, disrupt, mess up, ruin, wreck.

play on abuse, capitalise on, exploit, milk, misuse, profit by, take advantage of, trade on, turn to account, utilise.

play the fool act the (giddy) goat, clown around, fool around, horse around, mess about, mess on, monkey around, skylark.

play the game acquiesce, conform, keep in step, play by the rules, play fair, toe the line, yield.

play up accentuate, begin, bother, emphasise, exaggerate, fool, highlight, hurt, magnify, make a fool of, malfunction, overemphasise, pain, spotlight, start, stress, strike up, trouble.

play up to blandish, bootlick, butter up, fawn, flatter, ingratiate oneself, soft-soap, suck up to, toady.

playboy *n* debauchee, ladies' man, lady-killer, libertine, man about town, philanderer, rake, roué, socialite, womaniser.

player *n* actor, actress, artist(e), bandsman, competitor, contestant, cricketer, entertainer, footballer, instrumentalist, musician, participant, performer, sportsman, sportswoman, Thespian, trouper.

playful *adj* arch, cheerful, coltish, coquettish, coy, espiègle, flirtatious, frisky, frolicsome, gamesome, gay, good-natured, humorous, impish, jesting, jokey, joking, joyous, kittenish, kitteny, larkish, larky, lively, ludic, merry, mischievous, puckish, reasing, roguish, rollicking, spirited, sportive, sprightly, tongue-in-cheek, toyish, toysome, vivacious, waggish.

antonyms serious, stern.

playmate *n* buddy, chum, companion, comrade, friend, marrow, neighbour, pal, playfellow.

plaything *n* amusement, bauble, game, gewgaw, gimcrack, pastime, puppet, toy, trifle, trinket.

playwright *n* dramatist, dramaturge, dramaturgist, screen-writer, scriptwriter.

plea *n* action, allegation, apology, appeal, begging, cause, claim, defence, entreaty, excuse, explanation, extenuation, imploration, intercession, invocation, justification, overture, petition, placit(um), prayer, pretext, request, suit, supplication, vindication.

plead *v* adduce, allege, appeal, argue, ask, assert, beg, beseech, crave, entreat, implore, importune, maintain, moot, petition, put forward, request, solicit, supplicate.

pleasant *adj* acceptable, affable, agreeable, amene, amiable, amusing, charming, cheerful, cheery, congenial, cool, delectable, delightful, delightsome, engaging, enjoyable, fine, friendly, genial, good-humoured, gratifying, likeable, listenable, lovely, nice, pleasing, pleasurable, refreshing, satisfying, sunshiny, toothsome, welcome, winsome.

antonyms distasteful, nasty, repugnant, unpleasant.

pleasantry *n* badinage, banter, bon mot, jest, joke, persiflage, quip, sally, witticism.

please *v* amuse, captivate, charm, cheer, choose, content, delight, desire, enchant, entertain, gladden, go for, gratify, humour, indulge, like, opt, prefer, rejoice, satisfy, see fit, suit, think fit, tickle, tickle pink, want, will, wish.

antonyms anger, annoy, displease.

pleased *adj* chuffed, contented, delighted, elated, euphoric, glad, gratified, gruntled, happy, in high spirits, over the moon, satisfied, thrilled, tickled, tickled pink.

antonyms annoyed, displeased.

pleasing *adj* acceptable, agreeable, amiable, amusing, attractive, charming, congenial, delightful, engaging, enjoyable, entertaining, good, gratifying, likable, nice, pleasurable, polite, satisfying, welcome, winning.

antonym unpleasant.

pleasurable *adj* agreeable, amusing, congenial, delightful, diverting, enjoyable, entertaining, fun, good, gratifying, groovy, lovely, nice, pleasant, welcome.

antonyms bad, disagreeable.

pleasure *n* amusement, bliss, choice, comfort, command, complacency, contentment, delectation, delight, desire, diversion, ease, enjoyment, gladness, gratification, happiness, inclination, joy, mind, option, preference, purpose, recreation, satisfaction, solace, will, wish.

antonyms displeasure, pain, sorrow, trouble.

pleat *v* crease, crimp, flute, fold, gather, goffer, plait, pucker, shirr, tuck.

plebeian *adj* base, coarse, common, ignoble, low, low-born, lower-class, mean, non-U, peasant, proletarian, uncultivated, unrefined, vulgar, working-class.

antonyms aristocratic, noble, patrician.

n common man, commoner, man in the street, peasant, pleb, prole, proletarian, roturier, worker.

antonyms aristocrat, noble, patrician.

plebiscite *n* ballot, poll, referendum, straw poll, vote.

pledge *n* assurance, bail, bond, collateral, covenant, deposit, earnest, gage, guarantee, health, oath, pawn, promise, security, surety, toast, undertaking, vow, wadset(t), warrant, word, word of honour.

v bind, contract, drink to, engage, ensure, gage, guarantee, mortgage, plight, promise, secure, swear, toast, undertake, vouch, vow.

plenary *adj* absolute, complete, entire, full, general, integral, open, sweeping, thorough, unconditional, unlimited, unqualified, unrestricted, whole.

plenipotentiary *n* ambassador, dignitary, emissary, envoy, legate, minister, nuncio, plenipo.

plenitude *n* abundance, amplitude, bounty, completeness, copiousness, cornucopia, entireness, excess, fullness, plenteousness, plentifulness, plenty, plethora, profusion, repletion, wealth.

antonym scarcity.

plenteous *adj* abounding, abundant, ample, bounteous, bountiful, bumper, copious, fertile, fruitful, generous, inexhaustible, infinite, lavish, liberal, luxuriant, overflowing, plentiful, productive, profuse, prolific.

antonym scarce.

plentiful *adj* abounding, abundant, ample, bounteous, bountiful, bumper, complete, copious, fertile, fruitful, generous, inexhaustible, infinite, lavish, liberal, luxuriant, overflowing, plenteous, productive, profuse, prolific.

antonyms rare, scanty, scarce.

plenty *n* abundance, affluence, copiousness, enough, fertility, fruitfulness, fund, heap(s), lots, luxury, mass, masses, milk and honey, mine, mountain(s), oodles, opulence, pile(s), plenitude, plenteousness, plentifulness, plethora, profusion, prosperity, quantities, quantity, stack(s), store, sufficiency, volume, wealth.

antonyms lack, need, scarcity, want.

plethora *n* excess, glut, overabundance, overful(l)ness, profusion, superabundance, superfluity, surfeit, surplus.

pliability *n* adaptability, amenability, bendability, compliance, docility, ductility, elasticity, flexibility, impressionableness, malleability, mobility, plasticity, pliancy, suggestibility, susceptibility, tractableness.

antonyms inflexibilty, rigidity.

pliable *adj* accommodating, adaptable, bendable, bendy, compliant, docile, ductile, flexible, impressionable, influenceable, limber, lithe, malleable, manageable, persuadable, plastic, pliant, receptive, responsive, suggestible, supple, susceptible, tractable, yielding.

antonyms inflexible, rigid.

pliant *adj* adaptable, bendable, bendy, biddable, compliant, ductile, easily led, flexible, impressionable, influenceable, lithe, manageable, persuadable, plastic, pliable, supple, susceptible, tractable, whippy, yielding.

antonyms inflexible, intractable.

plight[1] *n* case, circumstances, condition, difficulty, dilemma, extremity, galère, hole, jam, perplexity, pickle, predicament, quandary, scrape, situation, spot, state, straits, trouble.

plight[2] *n* affiance, contract, covenant, engage, guarantee, pledge, promise, propose, swear, vouch, vow.

plod *v* clump, drag, drudge, grind, grub, labour, lumber, moil, peg, persevere, plough through, plug, slog, soldier on, stomp, sweat, toil, tramp, tread, trudge.

plodder *n* drudge, dullard, mug, sap, slogger, toiler.

antonym high-flier.

plot[1] *n* action, cabal, conspiracy, covin, design, intrigue, machination(s), narrative, outline, plan, scenario, scheme, story, story line, stratagem, subject, theme, thread.

v brew, cabal, calculate, chart, collude, compass, compute, conceive, concoct, conspire, contrive, cook up, design, devise, draft, draw, frame, hatch, imagine, intrigue, lay, locate, machinate, manoeuvre, map, mark, outline, plan, project, scheme.

plot[2] *n* allotment, area, erf, green, ground, lot, parcel, patch, tract.

plotter *n* caballer, conspirator, intriguer, Machiavellian, machinator, schemer, strategist.

plough *v* break, cultivate, dig, furrow, ridge, spade, till.

ploy *n* artifice, contrivance, device, dodge, gambit, game, manoeuvre, move, ruse, scheme, strategem, subterfuge, tactic, trick, wile.

pluck[1] *n* backbone, boldness, bottle, bravery, courage, determination, fortitude, gameness, grit, guts, hardihood, heart, intrepidity, mettle, nerve, resolution, spirit, spunk, tenacity.

pluck[2] *v* catch, clutch, collect, depilate, deplume, displume, draw, evulse, gather, harvest, jerk, pick, plunk, pull, pull off, pull out, snatch, strum, thrum, tug, twang, tweak, unplume, yank.

plucky *adj* bold, brave, courageous, daring, doughty, game, gamy, gritty, gutsy, hardy, heroic, intrepid, mettlesome, spirited, spunky, tenacious, unflinching, valiant.

antonyms feeble, weak.

plug *n* advert, advertisement, bung, cake, chew, cork, dook, dossil, dottle, good word, hype, mention, pigtail, publicity, puff, push, quid, spigot, spile, stopper, stopple, studdle, tamp(i)on, twist, wad.

v advertise, block, build up, bung, choke, close, cork, cover, drudge, fill, grind, hype, labour, mention, pack, peg away, plod, promote, publicise, puff, push, seal, slog, stop, stop up, stopper, stopple, stuff, tamp, toil.

plum *n* bonus, cushy number, find, pick, prize, sinecure, treasure.

adj best, choice, cushy, first-class, prize.

plumb *n* lead, plumb bob, plummet, sinker, weight.

adv bang, dead, exactly, perpendicularly, precisely, slap, spot-on, square, up and down, vertically.

v delve, explore, fathom, gauge, investigate, mark, measure, penetrate, probe, search, sound, unravel.

plume *n* aigrette, crest, feather, pappus, pinion, quill, tuft.

plume oneself on boast about, congratulate oneself, exult in, pat oneself on the back, pique oneself, preen oneself, pride oneself.

plummet *v* crash, descend, dive, drop, fall, hurtle, nose-dive, plunge, stoop, swoop, tumble.

antonym soar.

plump[1] *adj* beefy, burly, buxom, chopping, chubby, corpulent, dumpy, embonpoint, endomorphic, fat, fleshy, full, matronly, obese, podgy, portly, roly-poly, rotund, round, stout, tubby, well-upholstered.

antonyms skinny, thin.

plump[2] *v* collapse, descend, drop, dump, fall, flop, sink, slump.

adv abruptly, directly, straight.

plump for back, choose, favour, opt for, select, side with, support.

plumpness *n* chubbiness, corpulence, embonpoint, fatness, fleshiness, obesity, podginess, portliness, pudginess, rotundity, stoutness, tubbiness.

antonyms skinniness, thinness.

plunder *v* depredate, despoil, devastate, loot, pillage, raid, ransack, ravage, reive, rifle, rob, sack, spoil, spoliate, steal, strip.

n booty, despoilment, ill-gotten gains, loot, pickings, pillage, prey, prize, rapine, spoils, swag.

plunge *v* career, cast, charge, dash, demerge, demerse, descend, dip, dive, dive-bomb, dook, douse, drop, fall, go down, hurtle, immerse, jump, lurch, nose-dive, pitch, plummet, rush, sink, submerge, swoop, tear, throw, tumble.

n collapse, descent, dive, dook, drop, fall, immersion, jump, submersion, swoop, tumble.

plurality *n* bulk, diversity, galaxy, majority, mass, most, multiplicity, multitudinousness, numerousness, preponderance, profusion, variety.

plus *n* advantage, asset, benefit, bonus, credit, extra, gain, good point, perk, surplus.

antonym minus.

plush *adj* affluent, costly, de luxe, lavish, luxurious, luxury, opulent, palatial, rich, ritzy, sumptuous.

plutocrat *n* billionaire, capitalist, Croesus, Dives, fat cat, magnate, millionaire, moneybags, multimillionaire, rich man, tycoon.

ply[1] *v* assail, beseige, beset, bombard, carry on, employ, exercise, feed, follow, furnish, handle, harass, importune, manipulate, practise, press, provide, pursue, supply, swing, urge, utilise, wield, work at.

ply[2] *n* bend, fold, layer, leaf, sheet, strand, thickness.

poach *v* appropriate, encroach, infringe, intrude, pilfer, plunder, rob, steal, trespass.

pocket *n* bag, compartment, envelope, hollow, pouch, receptacle, reticule, sack.

adj abridged, compact, concise, dwarf, little, mini, miniature, pint-size(d), portable, potted, small.

v appropriate, filch, help oneself to, impocket, lift, nick, pilfer, pinch, purloin, snaffle, steal, take.

pockmark *n* blemish, pit, pock, pockpit, scar.

pod *n* case, hull, husk, legume, shell, shuck.

podgy *adj* chubby, chunky, corpulent, dumpy, fat, fleshy, paunchy, plump, roly-poly, rotund, squat, stout, stubby, stumpy, tubby.

antonym skinny.

podium *n* dais, platform, rostrum, stage, stand.

poem *n* acrostic, ballad(e), dit(t), ditty, eclogue, elegy, epicede, epicedium, epinicion, epithalamion, epithalamium, epopee, fabliau, genethliac(on), idyll, jingle, lay, limerick, lipogram, lyric, madrigal, monody, ode, palinode, rhyme, song, sonnet, verse, verselet, verset, versicle.

poet *n* bard, griot, iambist, iambographer, idyllist, lyricist, makar, maker, Meistersinger, metrician, metricist, minnesinger, minstrel, monodist, odist, Parnassian, poetaster, poeticule, rhymer, rhymester, rhymist, rimer, skald, verse-man, verse-monger, verser, verse-smith, versificator, versifier, verslibrist.

poetic *adj* artistic, elegiac, flowing, graceful, lyric, lyrical, metrical, moving, rhythmical.

antonym prosaic.

poetry *n* free verse, gay science, iambics, lyrics, macaronics, muse, Parnassus, pennill, poems, poesy, rhyme, rhyming, vers libre, verse, versing.

poignancy *n* bitterness, emotion, emotionalism, evocativeness, feeling, intensity, keenness, painfulness, pathos, piquancy, piteousness, plaintiveness, pungency, sadness, sentiment, sharpness, tenderness.

poignant *adj* acrid, acute, affecting, agonising, biting, bitter, caustic, distressing, heartbreaking, heart-rending, intense, keen, moving, painful, pathetic, penetrating, piercing, piquant, pointed, pungent, sad, sarcastic, severe, sharp, stinging, tender, touching, upsetting.

point[1] *n* aim, aspect, attribute, burden, characteristic, circumstance, condition, core, crux, degree, design, detail, dot, drift, end, essence, extent, facet, feature, full stop, gist, goal, import, instance, instant, intent, intention, item, juncture, location, mark, marrow, matter, meaning, moment, motive, nicety, nub, object, objective, particular, peculiarity, period, pith, place, position, property, proposition, purpose, quality, question, reason, respect, score, side, site, speck, spot, stage, station, stop, subject, tally, text, theme, thrust, time, trait, unit, use, usefulness, utility.

v aim, denote, designate, direct, draw attention to, hint, indicate, level, show, signal, signify, suggest, train.

point of view angle, approach, attitude, belief, judgement, opinion, orientation, outlook, perspective, position, slant, stance, standpoint, view, viewpoint.

point out allude to, bring up, call attention to, identify, indicate, mention, remind, reveal, show, specify.

point up accentuate, emphasise, headline, spotlight, stress, underline, underscore.

point[2] *n* apex, bill, cacumen, cape, end, fastigium, foreland, head, headland, neb, ness, nib, promontory, prong, spike, spur, summit, tang, tine, tip, top.

point-blank *adj* abrupt, blunt, categorical, direct, downright, explicit, express, forthright, plain, plain-spoken, straightforward, unreserved.

adv bluntly, brusquely, candidly, directly, explicitly, forthrightly, frankly, openly, plainly, straight, straightforwardly, unequivocally.

pointed *adj* accurate, acicular, aciform, aculeate(d), acuminate, acute, barbed, biting, cuspidate, cutting, edged, fastigiate(d), incisive, keen, lanceolate(d), lancet, lanciform, mucronate, penetrating, pertinent, sharp, telling, trenchant.

pointer *n* advice, caution, fingerpost, guide, hand, hint, indication, indicator, information, needle, recommendation, suggestion, tip, warning.

pointless *adj* absurd, aimless, bootless, fruitless, futile, inane, ineffectual, irrelevant, meaningless, nonsensical, profitless, senseless, silly, stupid, unavailing, unbeneficial, unproductive, unprofitable, useless, vague, vain, worthless.

antonyms meaningful, profitable.

poise *n* aplomb, assurance, calmness, collectedness, composure, cool, coolness, dignity, elegance, equanimity, equilibrium, grace, presence, presence of mind, sangfroid, savoir-faire, self-possession, serenity.

v balance, float, hang, hold, hover, librate, position, support, suspend.

poised *adj* calm, collected, composed, cool, dignified, expectant, graceful, nonchalant, prepared, ready, self-confident, self-possessed, serene, suave, unruffled, urbane, waiting.

poison *n* aconite, aconitum, bane, blight, cancer, canker, contagion, contamination, corruption, malignancy, miasma, toxin, venom, virus.

v adulterate, contaminate, corrupt, defile, deprave, empoison, envenom, infect, kill, murder, pervert, pollute, subvert, taint, undermine, vitiate, warp.

poisonous *adj* aconitic, baleful, baneful, corruptive, deadly, evil, fatal, lethal, malicious, mephitic, mortal, muscarinic, noxious, pernicious, pestiferous, pestilential, toxic, venomous, vicious, virose, virous, virulent.

poke *v* butt, butt in, dig, elbow, hit, interfere, intrude, jab, meddle, nose, nudge, peek, prod, prog, pry, punch, push, shove, snoop, stab, stick, tamper, thrust.

n butt, dig, dunt, jab, nudge, prod, punch, shove, thrust.

poke fun at chaff, guy, jeer, make fun of, mock, parody, prog, rag, rib, ridicule, send up, spoof, take the mickey, tease.

poky *adj* confined, cramped, crowded, incommodious, narrow, small, tight, tiny.

antonym spacious.

polarity *n* ambivalence, contradiction, contrariety, dichotomy, duality, oppositeness, opposition, paradox.

pole[1] *n* bar, lug, mast, post, rod, shaft, spar, staff, stake, standard, stang, stick.

pole[2] *n* antipode, extremity, limit, terminus, (ultima) Thule.

poles apart at opposite extremes, incompatible, irreconcilable, like chalk and cheese, like night and day, worlds apart.

polemic *n* argument, controversy, debate, dispute.

adj argumentative, contentious, controversial, disputatious, eristic(al), polemical.

polemicist *n* arguer, contender, controversialist, debater, disputant, disputer, logomachist, polemist.

polemics *n* argument, argumentation, contention, controversy, debate, disputation, dispute, logomachy.

police *n* boys in blue, constabulary, fuzz, gendarmerie, law, myrmidons of the law, (the) Old Bill.

v check, control, defend, guard, keep a check on, keep guard over, keep in order, keep the peace, monitor, observe, oversee, patrol, protect, regulate, stand guard over, supervise, watch.

policeman *n* beetle-crusher, bluebottle, bobby, bogey, bull, catchpole, constable, cop, copper, crusher, flatfoot, flic, fuzz, garda, gendarme, gumshoe, hammer(-beak), headborough, mountie, officer, peeler, pig, rozzer, sepoy, slop.

policy *n* action, approach, code, course, custom, discretion, good sense, guideline, line, plan, position, practice, procedure, programme, protocol, prudence, rule, sagacity, scheme, shrewdness, stance, stratagem, theory, wisdom.

polish *v* brighten, brush up, buff, burnish, clean, correct, cultivate, emend, emery, enhance, file, finish, furbish, improve, lustre, perfect, planish, refine, rub, rub up, shine, shine up, slick, slicken, smooth, touch up, wax.

antonyms dull, tarnish.

n breeding, brightness, brilliance, class, cultivation, elegance, eutrapelia, expertise, finesse, finish, glaze, gloss, grace, lustre, perfectionism, politesse, proficiency, refinement, savoir-faire, sheen, smoothness, sophistication, sparkle, style, suavity, urbanity, varnish, veneer, wax.

antonyms clumsiness, dullness, gaucherie.

polish off bolt, bump off, consume, devour, dispose of, down, eat, eliminate, finish, gobble, kill, liquidate, murder, put away, rub out, shift, stuff, wolf.

polished *adj* accomplished, adept, bright, burnished, civilised, courtly, cultivated, educated, elegant, expert, faultless, fine, finished, flawless, furbished, genteel, glassy, gleaming, glossy, graceful, gracious, impeccable, lustrous, masterly, outstanding, perfected, polite, professional, refined, sheeny, shining, skilful, slippery, smooth, sophisticated, suave, superlative, urbane, well-bred.

antonyms clumsy, dull, gauche, inexpert, tarnished.

polite *adj* affable, attentive, civil, civilised, complaisant, considerate, cordial, courteous, courtly, cultured, deferential, diplomatic, discreet, elegant, genteel, gentlemanly, gracious, Grandisonian, ladylike, mannerly, obliging, polished, refined, respectful, tactful, thoughtful, urbane, well-behaved, well-bred, well-mannered.

antonyms impolite, uncultivated.

politeness *n* attention, civility, complaisance, considerateness, cordiality, courtesy, courtliness, cultivation, culture, deference, diplomacy, discretion, elegance, gentilesse, gentility, gentlemanliness, grace, graciousness, mannerliness, manners, polish, refinement, respect, respectfulness, tact, thoughtfulness.

antonym impoliteness.

politic *adj* advantageous, advisable, artful, astute, canny, crafty, cunning, designing, diplomatic, discreet, expedient, ingenious, intriguing, judicious, Machiavellian, opportune, prudent, sagacious, sage, scheming, sensible, shrewd, sly, subtle, tactful, unscrupulous, wise.

antonym impolitic.

politician *n* agitator, legislator, Machiavellian, machinator, manipulator, Member of Parliament, MP, opportunist, politicaster, politico, statesman, statist, stirrer, tactician, wheeler-dealer.

politics *n* affairs of state, civics, diplomacy, government, ideology, Machiavellianism, Machiavellism, machination, Machtpolitik, manipulation, political science, polity, power-politics, Realpolitik, statecraft, statesmanship, Weltpolitik, wheeler-dealing.

poll[1] *n* ballot, canvass, census, count, figures, kite-flying, plebiscite, returns, sampling, straw-poll, survey, tally, vote, voting.

poll[2] *v* clip, dishorn, dod, pollard, shear, trim.

pollute *v* adulterate, befoul, besmirch, canker, contaminate, corrupt, debase, debauch, defile, deprave, desecrate, dirty, dishonour, foul, infect, mar, poison, profane, soil, spoil, stain, sully, taint, violate, vitiate.

pollution *n* adulteration, befouling, contamination, corruption, defilement, desecration, dirtying, foulness, impurity, infection, profanation, soilure, stain, taint, uncleanness, violation, vitiation.

antonyms purification, purity.

polychromatic *adj* kaleidoscopic, many-coloured, many-hued, motley, mottled, multicoloured, parti-coloured, poikilitic, polychrome, rainbow, varicoloured, variegated.

antonyms monochromatic, monochrome.

polyglot *adj* cosmopolitan, international, multilingual, multiracial, polyglottal, polyglottic.

antonym monoglot.

n linguist, multilinguist.

polymath *n* all-rounder, know-all, mine of information, oracle, pansophist, polyhistor, Renaissance man, walking encyclopaedia.

antonym ignoramus.

pomp *n* ceremonial, ceremoniousness, ceremony, display, éclat, flourish, formality, grandeur, grandiosity, magnificence, ostentation, pageant, pageantry, parade, pomposity, ritual, show, solemnity, splendour, state, vainglory.

antonyms austerity, simplicity.

pomposity *n* affectation, airs, arrogance, bombast, euphuism, fustian, grandiloquence, grandiosity, loftiness, magniloquence, oro(ro)tundity, pompousness, pontificating, portentousness, preachiness, presumption, pretension, pretentiousness, ranting, rhetoric, self-importance, stuffiness, turgidity, vainglory, vanity.

antonyms economy, simplicity.

pompous *adj* affected, aldermanlike, aldermanly, arrogant, bloated, bombastic, budge, chesty, euphuistic, flatulent, fustian, grandiloquent, grandiose, high-flown, imperious, inflated, magisterial, magniloquent, oro(ro)tund, ostentatious, overbearing, overblown, pontifical, portentous, pretentious, prosy, ranting, self-important, stilted, stuffy, supercilious, turgid, vainglorious, windy.

antonyms economical, modest, simple, unaffected, unassuming.

ponder *v* analyse, brood, cerebrate, cogitate, contemplate, consider, deliberate, examine, excogitate, give thought to, incubate, meditate, mull over, muse, ponderate, puzzle over, ratiocinate, reason, reflect, ruminate over, study, think, volve, weigh.

ponderous *adj* awkward, bulky, clumsy, cumbersome, cumbrous, dreary, dull, elephantine, graceless, heavy, heavy-footed, heavy-handed, hefty, huge, humourless, laborious, laboured, lifeless, long-winded, lumbering, massive, pedantic, pedestrian, plodding, portentous, prolix, slow-moving, stilted, stodgy, stolid, tedious, unwieldy, verbose, weighty.

antonyms delicate, light, simple.

ponderousness *n* gravitas, heaviness, humourlessness, laboriousness, seriousness, stodginess, stolidity, tedium, unwieldiness, weightiness.

antonyms delicacy, lightness, subtlety.

poniard *n* bodkin, dagger, dirk, misericord, skene, stiletto, stylet.

pontifical *adj* apostolic, bloated, condescending, didactic, dogmatic, ecclesiastical, homiletical, imperious, magisterial, overbearing, papal, pompous, portentous, preachy, prelatic, pretentious, self-important, sermonising.

antonyms reticent, unassuming.

pontificate *v* declaim, dogmatise, expertise, expound, harangue, hold forth, lay down the law, lecture, moralise, perorate, pontify, preach, pronounce, sermonise, sound off.

pooh-pooh *v* belittle, brush aside, deride, disdain, dismiss, disparage, disregard, make little of, minimise, play down, reject, ridicule, scoff, scorn, slight, sneer, sniff at, spurn, turn up one's nose at.

antonyms consider, exaggerate, magnify, regard.

pool[1] *n* dub, lake, lasher, leisure pool, linn, mere, pond, puddle, splash, stank, swimming bath, swimming pool, tarn, water-hole, watering-hole.

pool[2] *n* accumulation, bank, cartel, collective, combine, consortium, funds, group, jackpot, kitty, pot, purse, reserve, ring, stakes, syndicate, team, trust.

v amalgamate, chip in, combine, contribute, dob in, merge, muck in, put together, share.

poor[1] *adj* badly off, bankrupt, beggared, beggarly, broke, deficient, destitute, distressed, embarrassed, exiguous, hard up, impecunious, impoverished, in reduced circumstances, inadequate, indigent, insufficient, lacking, meagre, miserable, moneyless, necessitious, needy, niggardly, obolary, on one's beam-ends, on one's uppers, on the rocks, pauperised, penniless, penurious, pinched, pitiable, poverty-stricken, reduced, scanty, skimpy, skint, slight, sparse, stony-broke, straitened, without means, without the wherewithal.

antonyms affluent, opulent, rich, wealthy.

poor[2] *adj* bad, bare, barren, below par, depleted, exhausted, faulty, feeble, fruitless, grotty, humble, imperfect, impoverished, inferior, infertile, insignificant, jejune, low-grade, lowly, mean, mediocre, modest, paltry, pathetic, pitiful, plain, ropy, rotten, rubbishy, second-rate, shabby, shoddy, sorry, spiritless, sterile, substandard, third-rate, trivial, unfruitful, unimpressive, unproductive, unsatisfactory, valueless, weak, worthless.

antonym superior.

poor[3] *adj* accursed, cursed, forlorn, hapless, ill-fated, luckless, miserable, pathetic, pitiable, star-crossed, unfortunate, unhappy, unlucky, wretched.

antonym lucky.

poorly *adv* badly, crudely, faultily, feebly, inadequately, incompetently, inexpertly, inferiorly, insufficiently, meanly, rottenly, shabbily, shoddily, unjustly, unsatisfactorily, unsuccessfully.

antonym well.

adj ailing, below par, dicky, frail, groggy, ill, indisposed, off colour, out of sorts, rotten, seedy, shaky, sick, sickly, under the weather, unhealthy, unwell.

antonyms healthy, robust, well.

pop *v* appear, bang, bulge, burst, call, come, crack, drop, drop in, explode, go, go bang, go off, go phut, insert, jump, nip, protrude, push, put, report, shove, slide, slip, snap, spring, step, stick, thrust, tuck, visit.

n bang, burst, crack, explosion, noise, report, snap.

pope *n* Bishop of Rome, His Holiness, Holy Father, papa, pontiff, sovereign pontiff, Vicar of Christ.

popinjay *n* beau, buck, coxcomb, dandy, dude, exquisite, fop, fopling, jackanapes, macaroni, pansy, peacock, princox, spark, swell, toff.

antonyms he-man, macho.

poppycock *n* babble, balderdash, balls, baloney, bullshit, bunk, bunkum, drivel, eyewash, gibberish, gobbledegook, guff, hooey, nonsense, rot, rubbish, tommyrot, tosh, trash, twaddle.

antonym sense.

populace *n* canaille, common herd, commonalty, crowd, general public, hoi polloi, inhabitants, masses, mob, multitude, people, plebs, proletariat, public, punters, rabble, rank and file, throng, vulgus.

antonyms aristocracy, élite, nobility.

popular *adj* accepted, approved, celebrated, common, conventional, current, democratic, demotic, famous, fashionable, favoured, favourite, fêted, general, hip, household, idolised, in, in demand, in favour, liked, lionised, modish, overpopular, overused, prevailing, prevalent, public, sought-after, standard, stock, trite, ubiquitous, universal, vernacular, voguey, voguish, vulgar, well-liked, widespread.

antonyms exclusive, unpopular, unusual.

popularise *v* debase, democratise, disseminate, familiarise, give currency to, propagate, simplify, spread, universalise, vulgarise.

antonym discredit.

popularity *n* acceptance, acclaim, adoration, adulation, approbation, approval, celebrity, currency, esteem, fame, favour, glory, idolisation, kudos, lionisation, mass appeal, recognition, regard, renown, reputation, repute, vogue, worship.

antonym unpopularity.

popularly *adv* commonly, conventionally, customarily, generally, in the vernacular, ordinarily, regularly, traditionally, universally, usually, vernacularly, vulgarly, widely.

populate *v* colonise, establish oneself in, habit, inhabit, live in, occupy, overrun, people, put down roots in, settle, tenant.

population *n* citizenry, citizens, community, denizens, folk, inhabitants, natives, occupants, people, populace, residents, society.

populous *n* crawling, crowded, frequented, overpeopled, overpopulated, packed, populated, swarming, teeming, thickly populated, thronged.

antonyms deserted, unfrequented.

pore *v* brood, con, contemplate, devour, dwell on, examine, go over, peruse, ponder, read, scan, scrutinise, study.

pornographic *adj* bawdy, blue, coarse, dirty, filthy, girlie, gross, indecent, lewd, nudie, obscene, off-colour, offensive, porn, porno, prurient, risqué, salacious, smutty.

antonyms innocent, inoffensive.

pornography *n* bawdiness, dirt, erotica, facetiae, filth, grossness, indecency, obscenity, porn, porno, sexploitation, smut.

porous *adj* absorbent, absorptive, cellular, foraminous, foveate, honeycombed, penetrable, permeable, pervious, pitted, sponge-like, spongy.

antonyms impermeable, impervious.

port *n* anchorage, harbour, harbourage, haven, hithe, roads, roadstead, seaport.

portable *adj* carriageable, compact, convenient, handy, light, lightweight, manageable, movable, portatile, portative, transportable.

antonyms fixed, immovable.

portend *v* adumbrate, announce, augur, bespeak, betoken, bode, forebode, forecast, foreshadow, foretell, foretoken, forewarn, harbinger, herald, indicate, omen, point to, predict, presage, prognosticate, promise, signify, threaten, warn of.

portent *n* augury, foreboding, forecast, forerunner, foreshadowing, forewarning, harbinger, indication, omen, precursor, prefiguration, premonition, presage, presentiment, prodrome, prognostic, prognostication, sign, signification, threat, warning.

portentous *adj* alarming, amazing, astounding, awe-inspiring, bloated, charged, consequential, crucial, earth-shaking, epoch-making, extraordinary, fateful, heavy, important, menacing, minatory, miraculous, momentous, ominous, phenomenal, pompous, ponderous, pontifical, pregnant, prodigious, remarkable, significant, sinister, solemn, threatening.

antonyms insignificant, unimportant, unimpressive.

porter[1] *n* baggage attendant, baggage man, bearer, caddie, carrier.

porter[2] *n* caretaker, commissionaire, concierge, door-keeper, doorman, doors-man, dvornik, gatekeeper, huissier, janitor, porteress, portress.

portion *n* allocation, allotment, allowance, assignment, bit, cup, destiny, division, fate, fortune, fraction, fragment, helping, kismet, lot, luck, measure, meed, moiety, morsel, parcel, part, piece, quantity, quota, rake-off, ration, scrap, section, segment, serving, share, slice, something, tranche, whack.

v allocate, allot, apportion, assign, carve up, deal, distribute, divide, divvy up, dole, parcel, partion, partition, share out, slice up.

portliness *n* ampleness, beefiness, chubbiness, corpulence, dumpiness, embonpoint, fleshiness, fullness, heaviness, obesity, paunchiness, plumpness, rotundity, roundness, stoutness, tubbiness.

portly *adj* ample, beefy, bulky, chubby, corpulent, dumpy, embonpoint, fat, fleshy, full, gaucie, heavy, large, obese, overweight, paunchy, plump, rotund, round, stout, tubby.

antonyms slight, slim.

portrait *n* account, caricature, characterisation, depiction, description, icon, image, likeness, miniature, mug shot, painting, photograph, picture, portraiture, portrayal, profile, representation, sketch, thumbnail, vignette.

portray *v* act, capture, characterise, delineate, depict, describe, draw, emblazon, encapsulate, evoke, figure, illustrate, impersonate, limn, paint, personate, personify, picture, play, present, render, represent, sketch, suggest.

portrayal *n* characterisation, delineation, depiction, description, evocation, hypotyposis, impersonation, interpretation, performance, picture, presentation, rendering, representation, sketch.

pose *v* advance, affect, arrange, assert, attitudinise, claim, feign, impersonate, masquerade, model, pass oneself off, place, posit, position, posture, present, pretend, profess to be, propound, put, put forward, put on an act, set, sham, sit, state, strike an attitude, submit.

n act, affectation, air, attitude, bearing, con, façade, front, mark, masquerade, mien, position, posture, pretence, role, sham, stance, take-in.

poser[1] *n* brain-teaser, chinese puzzle, conundrum, enigma, mystery, problem, puzzle, question, riddle, vexed question.

poser[2] *n* attitudiniser, poseur, poseuse, posturer, posturist.

poseur *n* attitudiniser, charlatan, con, exhibitionist, impostor, masquerader, mountebank, phoney, poser, poseuse, posturer, posturist, pseud, quack.

posh *adj* classy, de-luxe, elegant, exclusive, fashionable, grand, high-class, lavish, luxurious, luxury, opulent, plummy, ritzy, select, smart, stylish, sumptuous, swanky, swell, swish, up-market, upper-class.

antonyms cheap, inferior.

posit *v* advance, assert, assume, pose, postulate, predicate, presume, propound, put forward, state, submit.

position *n* angle, area, arrangement, attitude, bearings, belief, berth, billet, capacity, character, circumstances, condition, deployment, disposition, duty, employment, function, grade, importance, job, level, locale, locality, location, niche, occupation, office, opinion, outlook, pass, perspective, pinch, place, placement, placing, plight, point, point of view, pose, positioning, post, posture, predicament, prestige, rank, reference, reputation, role, set, setting, site, situation, slant, slot, spot, stance, stand, standing, standpoint, state, station, stature, status, ubiety, view, viewpoint, whereabouts.

v arrange, array, deploy, dispose, fix, lay out, locate, place, pose, put, range, set, settle, stand, stick.

positive *adj* absolute, actual, affirmative, arrant, assertive, assured, authoritative, beneficial, categorical, certain, clear, clear-cut, cocksure, complete, conclusive, concrete, confident, constructive, consummate, convinced, decided, decisive, definite, direct, dogmatic, downright, effective, efficacious, emphatic, explicit, express, firm, forceful, forward-looking, helpful, hopeful, incontestable, incontrovertible, indisputable, irrefragable, irrefutable, open-and-shut, opinionated, optimistic, out-and-out, peremptory, perfect, practical, productive, progressive, promising, rank, real, realistic, resolute, secure, self-evident, sheer, stubborn, sure, thorough, thoroughgoing, uncompromising, undeniable, unequivocal, unmistakable, unmitigated, unquestioning, useful, utter.

antonyms indecisive, indefinite, negative, uncertain.

positively *adv* absolutely, assuredly, authoritatively, categorically, certainly, conclusively, constructively, decisively, definitely, dogmatically, emphatically, expressly, finally, firmly, incontestably, incontrovertibly, indisputably, surely, uncompromisingly, undeniably, unequivocally, unmistakably, unquestionably.

possess *v* acquire, be endowed with, control, dominate, enjoy, have, hold, obtain, occupy, own, possess oneself of, seize, take, take over, take possession of.

possessed *adj* bedevilled, berserk, besotted, bewitched, consumed, crazed, cursed, demented, dominated, enchanted, entêté, frenzied, hag-ridden, haunted, infatuated, maddened, mesmerised, obsessed, raving.

possession *n* colony, control, custody, dependency, dominion, enjoyment, fruition, hold, mandate, occupancy, occupation, ownership, proprietorship, protectorate, province, tenure, territory, title.

possessions *n* assets, belongings, chattels, effects, estate, goods, goods and chattels, junk, meum et tuum, movables, paraphernalia, property, riches, stuff, things, traps, wealth, worldly wealth.

possessive *adj* acquisitive, clinging, covetous, dominating, domineering, grasping, jealous, overprotective, proprietorial, selfish.

antonyms generous, sharing, unassertive.

possibilities *n* advantages, capabilities, expectations, potential, potentiality, promise, prospects, talent.

antonyms disadvantages, liabilities.

possibility *n* achievability, chance, conceivability, feasibility, hazard, hope, liability, likelihood, odds, plausibility, potentiality, practicability, probability, prospect, realisability, risk, workableness.

antonym impossibility.

possible *adj* accomplishable, achievable, alternative, attainable, available, conceivable, credible, doable, feasible, hopeful, hypothetical, imaginable, likely, on, potential, practicable, probable, promising, realisable, tenable, viable, workable.

antonym impossible.

possibly *adv* at all, by any chance, by any means, Deo volente, DV, God willing, haply, happen, hopefully, in any way, maybe, mayhap, peradventure, perchance, perhaps, very like(ly).

post[1] *n* baluster, banister, column, leg, newel, pale, palisade, picket, pier, pillar, pin, pole, shaft, stake, stanchion, standard, stock, strut, support, upright.

v advertise, affix, announce, denounce, display, make known, placard, preconise, proclaim, promulgate, publicise, publish, report, stick up.

post[2] *n* appointment, assignment, beat, berth, billet, employment, incumbency, job, office, place, position, situation, station, vacancy.

v appoint, assign, establish, locate, move, place, position, put, second, send, shift, situate, station, transfer.

post[3] *n* collection, delivery, dispatch, mail, postal service, uplifting.

v acquaint, advise, apprise, brief, dispatch, fill in on, inform, keep posted, mail, notify, report to, send, transmit.

poster *n* advertisement, affiche, announcement, bill, handbill, notice, placard, sign, sticker.

posterior *adj* after, back, behind, dorsal, ensuing, following, hind, hinder, later, latter, posticous, rear, rearward, subsequent, succeeding.

antonyms anterior, front, previous.

n backside, behind, bottom, bum, buttocks, haunches, hinder end, hindquarters, rear, rump, seat, tail.

posterity *n* children, descendants, epigons, family, future, heirs, issue, offspring, progeny, scions, seed, successors.

antonyms ancestors, antiquity, forebears, past.

posthaste *adv* at once, directly, double-quick, ek dum, full tilt, hastily, immediately, promptly, pronto, quickly, speedily, straightaway, swiftly, with all speed.

antonyms eventually, gradually, slowly.

postman *n* letter-carrier, mail-carrier, post, postie.

postmortem *n* analysis, autopsy, dissection, examination, necropsy, review.

postpone *v* adjourn, defer, delay, freeze, hold over, pigeonhole, prorogue, put back, put off, put on ice, shelve, suspend, table, waive.

antonyms advance, forward.

postponed *adj* adjourned, deferred, frozen, in abeyance, on ice, pigeonholed, shelved, suspended.

antonym advanced.

postponement *n* adjournment, deferment, deferral, delay, freeze, moratorium, prorogation, put-off, respite, stay, suspension.

postscript *n* addendum, addition, afterthought, afterword, appendix, codicil, epilogue, PS, supplement.

antonyms introduction, prologue.

postulate *v* advance, assume, hypothesise, lay down, posit, predicate, presuppose, propose, stipulate, suppose, take for granted, theorise.

posture *n* attitude, bearing, carriage, decubitus, disposition, mien, port, pose, position, set, stance.

v affect, attitudinise, ponce, pose, put on airs, show off, strike attitudes, strut.

posy *n* bouquet, boutonniere, buttonhole, corsage, inscription, motto, nosegay, spray, verse, verselet.

pot *n* basin, beaker, bowl, coffee-pot, crock, crucible, cruse, cupel, flask, gallipot, jar, marmite, pan, pig, pipkin, planter, receptacle, samovar, teapot, test, urn, vase, vessel.

potato *n* murphy, pratie, praty, spud, tater, tattie.

pot-bellied *adj* bloated, corpulent, distended, fat, gor-bellied, obese, overweight, paunchy, portly, tubby.

pot-belly *n* beer belly, belly, corporation, gor-belly, gut, paunch, pot, spare tyre.

potency *n* authority, capacity, cogency, control, effectiveness, efficaciousness, efficacy, energy, force, headiness, influence, kick, might, muscle, persuasiveness, potential, power, puissance, punch, strength, sway, vigour.

antonyms impotence, weakness.

potent *adj* authoritative, cogent, commanding, compelling, convincing, dominant, dynamic, effective, efficacious, eloquent, forceful, formidable, heady, impressive, influential, intoxicating, mighty, moving, persuasive, powerful, puissant, pungent, strong, telling, vigorous, weighty.

antonyms impotent, weak.

potentate *n* chief, chieftain, despot, dictator, dynast, emperor, empress, head of state, king, leader, mogul, monarch, overlord, prince, queen, ruler, sovereign, tyrant.

potential *adj* budding, concealed, conceivable, dormant, embryonic, future, hidden, imaginable, in embryo, in posse, inherent, latent, likely, possible, probable, promising, prospective, undeveloped, unrealised.

n ability, aptitude, capability, capacity, flair, possibility, potentiality, power, talent, the makings, what it takes, wherewithal.

potentiality *n* ability, aptitude, capability, capacity, likelihood, possibilities, potential, promise, prospect, virtuality.

potion *n* beverage, brew, concoction, cup, dose, draught, drink, electuary, elixir, medicine, mixture, philtre, potation, tonic, treacle.

pot-pourri *n* collection, combination, gallimaufry, hotchpotch, jumble, medley, mélange, miscellany, mixture, motley, olio, olla-podrida, pastiche, patchwork, salad, salmagundi.

potter *v* dabble, da(c)ker, dodder, fettle, fiddle, fidget, footle, fribble, frig, fritter, mess about, mooch, moon, tinker.

pottery *n* ceramics, china, China-ware, crockery, delf, earthenware, pig, porcelain, stoneware, terra cotta, ware.

adj ceramic, china, clay, earthenware, fictile, figuline, porcelain, stoneware, wally.

potty *adj* bananas, barmy, bonkers, crackers, crazy, daft, demented, dippy, dotty, eccentric, foolish, footling, insignificant, nuts, nutty, petty, piddling, silly, soft, touched, trifling, trivial.

pouch *n* bag, container, marsupium, pocket, poke, purse, reticule, sac, sack, sporran, wallet.

pounce *v* ambush, attack, dash at, dive on, drop, fall upon, grab, jump, leap at, lunge at, snatch, spring, strike, swoop.

n assault, attack, bound, dive, grab, jump, leap, lunge, spring, swoop.

pound[1] *v* bang, bash, baste, batter, beat, belabour, bray, bruise, clobber, clomp, clump, comminute, crush, drum, hammer, levigate, march, palpitate, pelt, powder, pulsate, pulse, pulverise, pummel, smash, stomp, strike, strum, thrash, throb, thrum, thud, thump, thunder, tramp, triturate.

pound[2] *n* compound, corral, enclosure, fank, fold, pen, yard.

pour *v* bucket, cascade, course, crowd, decant, effuse, emit, exude, flow, gush, rain, rain cats and dogs, run, rush, sheet, spew, spill, spout, stream, swarm, teem, throng, tumble.

pour out debouch, decant, discharge, disembogue, disgorge, embogue, emit, issue, lave, spew forth.

pout *v* glower, grimace, lower, mope, pull a face, scowl, sulk.

antonyms grin, smile.

n glower, grimace, long face, moue, scowl.

antonyms grin, smile.

poverty *n* aridity, bareness, barrenness, beggary, dearth, deficiency, depletion, destitution, distress, exhaustion, hardship, ill-being, impoverishment, inadequacy, indigence, infertility, insolvency, insufficiency, jejuneness, lack, meagreness, necessitousness, necessity, need, paucity, pauperism, pennilessness, penury, poorness, poortith, privation, proletarianism, scarcity, shortage, sterility, thinness, unfruitfulness, want.

antonyms affluence, fertility, fruitfulness, riches, richness.

poverty-stricken *adj* bankrupt, beggared, broke, destitute, distressed, impecunious, impoverished, indigent, necessitous, needy, obolary, on one's beam-ends, on one's uppers, penniless, penurious, poor, skint, stony, stony-broke, strapped.

antonyms affluent, rich.

powder *n* bran, dust, pounce, pulvil, pulville, pulvil(l)io, talc, triturate.

v bray, comminute, cover, crush, dredge, dust, granulate, grind, levigate, pestle, pound, pulverise, scatter, sprinkle, strew, triturate.

powdery *adj* chalky, crumbling, crumbly, dry, dusty, fine, friable, grainy, granular, levigate, loose, powder, pulverised, pulverous, pulverulent, sandy.

power *n* ability, ascendancy, autarchy, authorisation, authority, brawn, capability, capacity, clout, clutches, command, competence, competency, control, dominance, domination, dominion, efficience, energy, faculty, force, forcefulness, heavy metal, hegemony, imperium, influence, intensity, juice, kami, licence, mana, mastery, might, muscle, omnipotence, plenipotence, potency, potential, prerogative, privilege, right, rule, sovereignty, strength, supremacy, sway, teeth, vigour, virtue, vis, voltage, vroom, warrant, weight.

powerful *adj* ascendant, authoritative, cogent, commanding, compelling, controlling, convincing, dominant, effective, effectual, energetic, forceful, forcible, impressive, influential, leading, masterful, mighty, muscular, omnipotent, persuasive, plutocratic, potent, pre-eminent, prepotent, prevailing, puissant, robust, souped-up, sovereign, stalwart, strapping, strong, sturdy, supreme, telling, vigorous, weighty, winning.

antonyms impotent, ineffective, weak.

powerfully *adv* cogently, convincingly, forcefully, forcibly, hard, impressively, mightily, persuasively, potently, strongly, tellingly, vigorously, with might and main.

powerless *adj* adynamic, debilitated, defenceless, dependent, disabled, effete, feeble, frail, helpless, impotent, incapable, incapacitated, ineffective, ineffectual, inefficacious, inerm, infirm, nerveless, paralysed, prostrate, subject, tied, unarmed, vulnerable, weak, weak-headed.

antonyms commanding, potent, powerful.

practicability *n* feasibility, handiness, operability, possibility, practicality, use, usefulness, utility, value, viability, workability, workableness.

antonym impracticability.

practicable *adj* accomplishable, achievable, attainable, compassable, doable, effectible, feasible, negotiable, passable, performable, possible, viable, workable.

antonym impracticable.

practical *adj* accomplished, active, applicative, applied, businesslike, commonsense, commonsensical, down-to-earth, efficient, empirical, everyday, expedient, experienced, experimental, factual, feasible, functional, hands-on, hard-headed, hard-nosed, material, matter-of-fact, mundane, nuts-and-bolts, ordinary, practicable, practive, pragmatic, proficient, qualified, realistic, seasoned, sensible, serviceable, skilled, sound, trained, unsentimental, useful, utilitarian, workable, workaday, working.

antonym impractical.

practicality *n* basics, common sense, experience, feasibility, nitty-gritty, nuts and bolts, practicability, practicalities, practicalness, practice, pragmatism, realism, sense, serviceability, soundness, usefulness, utility, workability.

practically[1] *adv* actually, all but, almost, essentially, fundamentally, in effect, in practice, in principle, just about, nearly, not quite, pretty nearly, pretty well, very nearly, virtually, well-nigh.

practically[2] *adv* clearly, from a commonsense angle, matter-of-factly, rationally, realistically, reasonably, sensibly, unsentimentally.

practice *n* action, application, business, career, clientèle, convention, custom, discipline, drill, dry run, dummy run, effect, exercise, experience, habit, ism, method, mode, modus operandi, operation, patronage, performance, policy, practic, practicalities, practicum, praxis, preparation, procedure, profession, rehearsal, repetition, routine, rule, run-through, study, system, tradition, training, usage, use, vocation, way, wont, work, work-out.

practise *v* apply, carry out, discipline, do, drill, enact, engage in, execute, exercise, follow, implement, live up to, observe, perfect, perform, ply, prepare, pursue, put into practice, rehearse, repeat, run through, study, train, undertake, warm up.

practised *adj* able, accomplished, consummate, experienced, expert, finished, highly-developed, knowing, knowledgeable, perfected, proficient, qualified, refined, seasoned, skilled, trained, versed, veteran, well-trained.

antonyms inexpert, unpractised.

pragmatic *adj* businesslike, efficient, factual, hard-headed, opportunistic, practical, realistic, sensible, unidealistic, unsentimental, utilitarian.

antonyms idealistic, romantic, unrealistic.

pragmatism *n* ad hocery, hard-headedness, humanism, opportunism, practicalism, practicality, realism, unidealism, utilitarianism.

antonyms idealism, romanticism.

pragmatist *n* humanist, opportunist, practicalist, realist, utilitarian.

antonyms idealist, romantic.

praise *n* acclaim, acclamation, accolade, acknowledgement, adoration, adulation, applause, approbation, approval, bouquet, cheering, commend, commendation, compliment, compliments, congratulation, devotion, encomium, eulogium, eulogy, extolment, flattery, glory, homage, honour, kudos, laud, laudation, ovation, panegyric, plaudit, puff, rave, recognition, salvoes, testimonial, thanks, thanksgiving, tribute, worship.

antonyms criticism, revilement.

v acclaim, acknowledge, admire, adore, applaud, approve, belaud, bless, celebrate, cheer, compliment, congratulate, cry up, eulogise, exalt, extol, flatter, give thanks to, glorify, hail, honour, laud, magnify, panegyrise, pay tribute to, promote, puff, rave over, recognise, tout, wax lyrical, worship.

antonyms criticise, revile.

praiseworthy *adj* admirable, commendable, creditable, deserving, estimable, excellent, exemplary, fine, honourable, laudable, meritorious, reputable, sterling, worthy.

antonyms discreditable, dishonourable, ignoble.

praising adj, adulatory, approbatory, approving, commendatory, complimentary, congratulatory, encomiastic, eulogistic, favourable, flattering, laudative, laudatory, panegyric, plauditory, promotional, recommendatory, worshipful.

antonyms condemnatory, critical.

prance *v* bound, caper, capriole, caracole, cavort, curvet, dance, frisk, frolic, gambol, jump, leap, parade, prank, prankle, romp, show off, skip, spring, stalk, strut, swagger, swank, vault.

prank *n* antic, caper, dido, escapade, fredaine, frolic, galliardise, guy, jape, joke, lark, piece of mischief, practical joke, rig, spree, stunt, trick, vagary.

prate *v* babble, blather, bleat, blether, boast, brag, burble, chatter, drivel, gab, gas, haver, jabber, jaw, maunder, palaver, prattle, ramble, witter, yak.

prattle *v* babble, blather, blether, chat, chatter, clack, clash, drivel, gabble, gossip, jabber, patter, rattle, twitter, witter.

n bavardage, bletheration, blethers, chat, chatter, clack, clash, claver, drivel, foolishness, gab, gabnash, gibberish, gossip, gup, haverings, havers, hot air, jaw, maundering, nashgab, nonsense, prating, talk, tattle.

prattler *n* babbler, blabbermouth, blatherskite, blether, bletherskate, chatterbox, chatterer, gabbler, gabnash, gossip, loudmouth, magpie, nashgab, pie, prater, prattlebox, rattle-brain, talker, tatler, tattler, windbag.

antonym clam.

pray *v* adjure, ask, beg, beseech, call on, crave, entreat, implore, importune, invoke, obsecrate, petition, plead, press, request, solicit, sue, supplicate, urge.

prayer *n* appeal, collect, communion, devotion, entreaty, invocation, kyrie, kyrie eleison, litany, orison, paternoster, petition, plea, request, solicitation, suffrage, suit, supplication.

prayer-book *n* breviary, euchologion, euchologue, euchology, ma(c)hzor, missal, ordinal, siddur.

preach *v* address, admonish, advocate, ethicise, evangelise, exhort, harangue, lecture, moralise, orate, pontificate, pontify, preachify, prose, sermonise, urge.

preacher *n* canter, clergyman, devil-dodger, evangelist, homilist, mar-text, minister, missionary, moraliser, parson, pontificater, predicant, pulpite(e)r, ranter, revivalist, sermoniser.

preachiness *n* cant, didacticism, dogmatism, moralising, pharisaism, pietism, pomposity, portentousness, preachment, pulpitry, religiosity, sanctimoniousness, sanctimony, self-righteousness, sermonising.

preaching *n* doctrine, dogma, evangel, evangelism, exhortation, gospel, homiletics, homilies, instruction, kerygma, message, pontificating, precepts, sermonising, sermons, teaching.

preachy *adj* canting, didactic, dogmatic, edifying, exhortatory, holier-than-thou, homiletic, hortatory, moralising, pharisaic, pietistic, pontifical, pontificating, preceptive, religiose, sanctimonious, self-righteous, sermonising.

preamble *n* exordium, foreword, introduction, lead-in, overture, preface, preliminaries, prelude, preparation, proem, prolegomenon, prologue.

antonyms epilogue, postscript.

precarious *adj* chancy, dangerous, delicate, dicey, dodgy, doubtful, dubious, hairy, hazardous, iffy, insecure, parlous, periculous, perilous, problematic, risky, shaky, slippery, ticklish, tricky, uncertain, unpredictable, unreliable, unsafe, unsettled, unstable, unsteady, unsure, vulnerable.

antonyms certain, safe, secure.

precaution *n* anticipation, backstop, buffer, care, caution, circumspection, foresight, forethought, insurance, preparation, prophylaxis, protection, providence, provision, prudence, safeguard, safety measure, security, surety, wariness.

precautionary *adj* anticipatory, cautious, foresighted, foresightful, judicious, preliminary, preparatory, preventive, prophylactic, protective, provident, provisional, prudent, safety, self-protective.

precede *v* antecede, antedate, anticipate, come first, forerun, front, go before, head, herald, introduce, lead, preface, prefix, prelude, premise, prevene, take precedence.

antonym follow.

precedence *n* antecedence, first place, lead, pre-eminence, preference, pride of place, primacy, priority, rank, seniority, superiority, supremacy.

precedent *n* antecedent, authority, citation, criterion, example, exemplar, guideline, instance, judgement, model, paradigm, past instance, pattern, prototype, ruling, standard, yardstick.

preceding *adj* above, aforementioned, aforesaid, antecedent, anterior, earlier, foregoing, former, past, precedent, precursive, previous, prior, supra.

antonyms following, later.

precept *n* axiom, behest, bidding, byword, canon, charge, command, commandment, convention, decree, dictum, direction, directive, guideline, injunction, institute, instruction, law, mandate, maxim, motto, order, ordinance, principle, regulation, rubric, rule, saying, sentence, statute.

precinct *n* area, banlieue, bound, boundary, confine, district, division, enclosure, limit, peribolos, quarter, section, sector, zone.

precincts *n* area, borders, bounds, confines, district, environs, limits, locality, milieu, neighbourhood, purlieus, region, surrounds, vicinity.

preciosity *n* affectation, alembication, artificiality, chichi, floweriness, Marivaudage, over-refinement, tweeness.

precious *adj* adored, affected, artificial, arty-farty, beloved, cherished, chichi, choice, costly, darling, dear, dearest, expensive, exquisite, fastidious, favourite, fine, flowery, greenery-yallery, idolised, inestimable, invaluable, irreplaceable, loved, namby-pamby, overnice, over-refined, priceless, prized, rare, recherché, treasured, twee, valuable, valued.

precipice *n* bluff, brink, cliff, cliff face, crag, drop, escarp, escarpment, height, krantz, scarp, steep.

precipitate *v* accelerate, advance, bring on, cast, cause, chuck, discharge, drive, expedite, fling, further, hasten, hurl, hurry, induce, launch, occasion, pitch, press, project, quicken, speed, throw, trigger.

adj abrupt, breakneck, brief, frantic, Gadarene, hasty, headlong, heedless, hot-headed, hurried, impatient, impetuous, impulsive, incautious, indiscreet, madcap, pell-mell, plunging, precipitous, quick, quixotic, rapid, rash, reckless, rushing, sudden, swift, unannounced, unexpected, violent.

antonym cautious.

precipitous *adj* abrupt, dizzy, giddy, high, perpendicular, sheer, steep, vertiginous.

antonyms gradual, sloping.

précis *n* abbreviation, abridgement, abstract, aperçu, compendium, condensation, conspectus, contraction, digest, encapsulation, epitome, outline, résumé, run-down, sketch, summary, synopsis, table.

v abbreviate, abridge, abstract, compress, condense, contract, digest, encapsulate, epitomise, outline, shorten, sum up, summarise, synopsise.

antonyms amplify, expand.

precise *adj* absolute, accurate, actual, authentic, blow-by-blow, buckram, careful, ceremonious, clear-cut, correct, definite, delimitative, determinate, distinct, exact, explicit, express, expressis verbis, factual, faithful, fastidious, finical, finicky, fixed, formal, identical, literal, meticulous, minute, nice, particular, prim, punctilious, puritanical, rigid, scrupulous, specific, strict, succinct, unequivocal, verbatim, word-for-word.

antonym imprecise.

precisely *adv* absolutely, accurately, bang, blow by blow, correctly, dead, distinctly, exactly, expressis verbis, just, just so, literally, minutely, plumb, slap, smack, square, squarely, strictly, verbatim, word for word.

precision *n* accuracy, care, correctness, definiteness, detail, exactitude, exactness, explicitness, expressness, faithfulness, fastidiousness, fidelity, meticulousness, minuteness, neatness, niceness, nicety, particularity, preciseness, punctilio, punctiliousness, rigour, scrupulosity, specificity.

antonym imprecision.

preclude *v* avoid, check, debar, eliminate, exclude, forestall, hinder, inhibit, obviate, prevent, prohibit, restrain, rule out, stop.

antonyms incur, involve.

precocious *adj* advanced, ahead, bright, clever, developed, fast, forward, gifted, mature, precocial, premature, quick, smart.

antonym backward.

preconceive *v* anticipate, assume, conceive, conceptualise, envisage, ideate, imagine, picture, presume, presuppose, project, visualise.

preconception *n* anticipation, assumption, bias, conjecture, notion, predisposition, prejudice, prenotion, prepossession, presumption, presupposition.

precondition *n* essential, must, necessity, need, prerequisite, proviso, requirement, requisite, sine qua non, stipulation.

precursor *n* antecedent, forebear, forerunner, harbinger, herald, indication, messenger, originator, pathfinder, pioneer, predecessor, prodrome, prodromus, sign, trail-blazer, usher, vanguard, warning, way-maker.

antonyms after-effect, aftermath.

precursory *adj* antecedent, anterior, introductory, preambulatory, preceding, precursive, prefatory, preliminary, preludial, prelusive, premonitory, preparatory, prevenient, previous, prior, prodromal, warning.

antonyms following, resulting, subsequent.

predatory *adj* acquisitive, avaricious, carnivorous, covetous, despoiling, greedy, hunting, lupine, marauding, pillaging, plundering, predacious, predative, preying, rapacious, raptatorial, raptorial, ravaging, ravening, thieving, voracious, vulturine, vulturous, wolfish.

predecessor *n* ancestor, antecedent, antecessor, forebear, forefather, forerunner, precursor, progenitor.

antonyms descendant, successor.

predestination *n* ananke, destiny, doom, election, fate, foreordainment, foreordination, karma, lot, necessity, portion, predestiny, predetermination, preordainment, preordination, weird.

predestine *v* destine, doom, fate, foredoom, foreordain, intend, mean, predestinate, predetermine, pre-elect, preordain.

predetermined *adj* agreed, cut and dried, decided beforehand, deliberate, fixed, foregone, foreordained, prearranged, preordained, preplanned, set, set up, settled.

predicament *n* can of worms, corner, crisis, dilemma, embarrassment, emergency, fix, galère, hole, hot water, impasse, jam, kettle of fish, mess, pickle, pinch, plight, quandary, scrape, situation, spot, state, trouble.

predicate *v* affirm, assert, aver, avouch, avow, base, build, contend, declare, establish, found, ground, maintain, posit, postulate, premise, proclaim, rest, state.

predict *v* augur, auspicate, divine, forebode, forecast, foresay, foresee, foreshow, forespeak, foretell, portend, presage, prognosticate, project, prophesy, second-guess, soothsay, vaticinate.

predictable *adj* anticipated, calculable, certain, dependable, determinate, expected, finite, foregone, foreseeable, foreseen, imaginable, likely, presumable, probable, reliable, sure.

antonym unpredictable.

prediction *n* augury, auspication, divination, forecast, fortune-telling, prognosis, prognostication, prophecy, second sight, soothsaying, vaticination.

predictive *adj* augural, diagnostic, divinatory, foretelling, prognostic, prophetic.

predilection *n* affection, affinity, bent, bias, enthusiasm, fancy, fondness, inclination, leaning, liking, love, partiality, penchant, predisposition, preference, proclivity, proneness, propensity, soft spot, taste, tendency, weakness.

antonyms antipathy, disinclination.

predispose *v* affect, bias, dispose, head, incline, induce, influence, lead, lean, make, make liable, prejudice, prepare, prime, prompt, sway.

predisposed *adj* agreeable, amenable, biased, disposed, favourable, inclined, liable, minded, not unwilling, nothing loth, prejudiced, prepared, prone, ready, subject, susceptible, well-disposed, willing.

predisposition *n* bent, bias, disposition, inclination, leaning, liability, likelihood, mind, penchant, potentiality, predilection, preference, prejudice, proclivity, proneness, propensity, susceptibility, tendency, vulnerability, willingness.

predominance *n* ascendancy, control, dominance, dominion, edge, hegemony, hold, influence, leadership, mastery, numbers, paramountcy, power, prepollence, prepollency, preponderance, prepotence, prepotency, prevalence, superiority, supremacy, sway, upper hand, weight.

antonyms ineffectiveness, weakness.

predominant *adj* ascendant, capital, chief, controlling, dominant, forceful, important, influential, leading, main, paramount, potent, powerful, prepollent, preponderant, prepotent, prevailing, prevalent, primary, prime, principal, prominent, ruling, sovereign, strong, superior, supreme.

antonyms ineffective, lesser, minor, weak.

predominate *v* dominate, obtain, outnumber, outweigh, override, overrule, overshadow, preponderate, prevail, reign, rule, tell, transcend.

pre-eminence *n* distinction, excellence, fame, incomparability, matchlessness, paramountcy, peerlessness, predominance, prestige, prominence, renown, repute, superiority, supremacy, transcendence.

pre-eminent *adj* chief, consummate, distinguished, excellent, exceptional, facile princeps, foremost, incomparable, inimitable, leading, matchless, nonpareil, outstanding, paramount, passing, peerless, predominant, prominent, renowned, superior, superlative, supreme, surpassing, transcendent, unequalled, unmatched, unrivalled, unsurpassed.

antonyms undistinguished, unknown.

pre-eminently *adv* conspicuously, eminently, emphatically, especially, exceptionally, exclusively, incomparably, inimitably, matchlessly, notably, par excellence, particularly, peerlessly, signally, singularly, strikingly, superlatively, supremely, surpassingly.

pre-empt *v* acquire, anticipate, appropriate, arrogate, assume, bag, forestall, secure, seize, usurp.

preen *v* adorn, array, beautify, clean, deck, do up, doll up, dress up, fig out, groom, plume, prank, prettify, primp, prink, slick, spruce up, tart up, titivate, trick out, trim.

preen (oneself) bask, congratulate, exult, gloat, pique, plume, pride.

preface *n* exordium, foreword, intro, introduction, preamble, preliminaries, prelims, prelude, proem, prolegomena, prolegomenon, prologue, prooemion, prooemium.

antonyms afterthought, epilogue, postscript.

v begin, introduce, launch, lead up to, open, precede, prefix, prelude, premise, start.

antonyms append, complete, finish.

prefatory *adj* antecedent, exordial, explanatory, introductory, opening, preambulatory, precursory, prefatorial, preliminary, preludial, prelusive, prelusory, preparatory, proemial, prolegomenal.

antonyms closing, final.

prefect *n* administrator, monitor, praefect, praeposter, prepositor, supervisor.

prefer[1] *v* adopt, advocate, back, be partial to, choose, desire, elect, endorse, fancy, favour, go for, incline towards, like better, opt for, pick, plump for, recommend, select, single out, support, want, wish, would rather, would sooner.

antonym reject.

prefer[2] *v* bring, file, lodge, place, present, press.

prefer[3] *v* advance, aggrandise, dignify, elevate, exalt, promote, raise, upgrade.

antonym demote.

preferable *adj* advantageous, advisable, best, better, choice, chosen, desirable, eligible, expedient, favoured, nicer, preferred, stronger, superior, worthier.

antonyms ineligible, inferior, undesirable.

preferably *adv* first, for choice, for preference, rather, sooner.

preference[1] *n* choice, desire, election, fancy, favourite, first choice, inclination, liking, option, partiality, pick, predilection, selection, wish.

preference[2] *n* advantage, favour, favouritism, precedence, preferential treatment, priority, special consideration, special treatment.

preferential *adj* advantageous, better, biased, favourable, favoured, partial, partisan, prior, privileged, special, superior.

antonym equal.

preferment *n* advancement, aggrandisement, betterment, dignity, elevation, exaltation, furtherance, improvement, promotion, rise, step up, upgrading.

antonym demotion.

preferred *adj* approved, authorised, choice, chosen, desired, favoured, predilect, recommended, sanctioned, selected.

antonyms rejected, undesirable.

pregnancy *n* child-bearing, conception, family way, fertilisation, gestation, gravidity, impregnation.

pregnant[1] *adj* big, big-bellied, enceinte, expectant, expecting, gravid, impregnated, in an interesting condition, in the club, in the family way, in the pudding club, parturient, preggers, teeming, with child.

pregnant[2] *adj* charged, eloquent, expressive, full, heavy, loaded, meaning, meaningful, ominous, pithy, pointed, significant, suggestive, telling, weighty.

antonym jejune.

prehistoric *adj* ancient, antediluvian, antiquated, archaic, earliest, early, fogram, hoary, obsolete, Ogygian, old, outmoded, out-of-date, primeval, primitive, primordial.

antonym modern.

prejudge *v* anticipate, assume, forejudge, judge prematurely, predetermine, prejudicate, presume, presuppose.

prejudice[1] *n* bias, bigotry, chauvinism, discrimination, injustice, intolerance, narrow-mindedness, partiality, partisanship, preconception, prejudgement, racism, sexism, unfairness, viewiness, warp.

antonyms fairness, tolerance.

v bias, colour, condition, distort, incline, indoctrinate, influence, jaundice, load, poison, predispose, prepossess, slant, sway, warp, weight.

prejudice[2] *n* damage, detriment, disadvantage, harm, hurt, impairment, injury, loss, mischief, ruin, vitiation, wreck.

antonyms advantage, benefit.

v damage, harm, hinder, hurt, impair, injure, mar, ruin, spoil, undermine, vitiate, wreck.

antonyms advance, benefit, help.

prejudiced *adj* biased, bigoted, chauvinist, conditioned, discriminatory, distorted, ex parte, illiberal, influenced, intolerant, jaundiced, loaded, narrow-minded, one-sided, opinionated, partial, partisan, prepossessed, racist, sexist, subjective, unenlightened, unfair, verkrampte, viewy, warped, weighted.

antonyms fair, tolerant.

prejudicial *adj* counter-productive, damaging, deleterious, detrimental, disadvantageous, harmful, hostile, hurtful, inimical, injurious, mischievous, noxious, pernicious, ruinous, undermining, unfavourable.

antonyms advantageous, beneficial.

preliminaries *n* basics, beginning, first round, formalities, foundations, groundwork, initiation, introduction, opening, preamble, preface, prelims, prelude, preparation, proem, prolegomena, rudiments, start.

preliminary *adj* earliest, early, embryonic, exordial, experimental, exploratory, first, inaugural, initial, initiative, initiatory, introductory, opening, pilot, precursory, prefatory, prelusive, preparatory, primary, prior, qualifying, test, trial.

antonyms closing, final.

prelude *n* beginning, commencement, curtain-raiser, exordium, foreword, introduction, intro, opener, overture, praeludium, preamble, precursor, preface, preliminary, preludio, prelusion, preparation, prodrome, proem, prolegomenon, prologue, prooemion, prooemium, start, taster, verset, Vorspiel.

antonyms aftermath, epilogue, postscript.

premature *adj* abortive, early, embryonic, forward, green, half-formed, hasty, ill-considered, ill-timed, immature, imperfect, impulsive, incomplete, inopportune, overhasty, precipitate, precocious, preterm, previous, rash, raw, undeveloped, unfledged, unripe, unseasonable, untimely.

antonyms late, tardy.

premeditated *adj* aforethought, calculated, cold-blooded, conscious, considered, contrived, deliberate, intended, intentional, planned, plotted, prearranged, predetermined, prepense, preplanned, studied, wilful.

antonyms spontaneous, unpremeditated.

premeditation *n* deliberateness, deliberation, design, determination, forethought, intention, malice aforethought, planning, plotting, prearrangement, predetermination, purpose, scheming.

antonyms impulse, spontaneity.

premier *n* chancellor, chief minister, first minister, head of government, prime minister, secretary of state.

adj arch, cardinal, chief, earliest, first, foremost, head, highest, initial, leading, main, original, paramount, pre-eminent, primary, prime, principal, supreme, top.

premiere *n* début, first night, opening, opening night.

premise *v* assert, assume, hypothesise, lay down, posit, postulate, predicate, presuppose, state, stipulate, take as true.

n argument, assertion, assumption, ground, hypothesis, postulate, postulation, predication, premiss, presupposition, proposition, statement, stipulation, supposition, thesis.

premises *n* building, establishment, estate, grounds, office, place, property, site.

premonition *n* anxiety, apprehension, fear, feeling, foreboding, forewarning, hunch, idea, intuition, misgiving, niggle, omen, portent, presage, presentiment, sign, suspicion, unease, uneasiness, warning, worry.

preoccupation *n* absence of mind, absent-mindedness, absorption, abstraction, brown study, concern, daydreaming, distraction, engrossment, enthusiasm, fixation, hang-up, hobby-horse, idée fixe, immersion, inattention, inattentiveness, musing, oblivion, obliviousness, obsession, pensiveness, raptness, reverie, wool-gathering.

preoccupied *adj* absent-minded, absorbed, abstracted, daydreaming, distracted, distrait, engrossed, entêté, faraway, fixated, heedless, immersed, intent, oblivious, obsessed, pensive, rapt, taken up, unaware, visited, wrapped up.

preordain *v* destine, doom, fate, foreordain, prearrange, predestine, predetermine.

preparation[1] *n* alertness, anticipation, arrangement, assignment, basics, development, expectation, foresight, foundation, groundwork, homework, imposition, lesson, measure, plan, precaution, preliminaries, prep, preparedness, provision, readiness, revision, rudiments, safeguard, schoolwork, study, task.

preparation[2] *n* application, composition, compound, concoction, lotion, medicine, mixture, potion, tincture.

preparatory *adj* basic, elementary, exordial, fundamental, initial, introductory, opening, prefatory, preliminary, preparative, primary, proemial, rudimentary.

preparatory to before, in advance of, in anticipation of, in expectation of, previous to, prior to.

prepare *v* accoutre, adapt, adjust, anticipate, arrange, assemble, boun, brace, brief, busk, coach, compose, concoct, confect, construct, contrive, develop, devise, dispose, do one's homework, draft, draw up, dress, equip, fashion, fettle, fit, fit out, fix up, forearm, form, format, fortify, furnish, get up, gird, groom, instruct, limber up, make, make ready, outfit, plan, practise, predispose, prime, produce, provide, psych up, ready, rehearse, rig out, steel, strengthen, supply, train, trim, warm up.

prepare oneself brace oneself, fortify oneself, get psyched up, gird oneself, limber up, psych oneself up, ready oneself, steel oneself.

prepared *adj* able, arranged, briefed, disposed, expectant, fit, forearmed, inclined, minded, planned, predisposed, primed, psyched up, ready, set, waiting, well-rehearsed, willing, word-perfect.

antonyms unprepared, unready.

preparedness *n* alertness, anticipation, expectancy, fitness, order, preparation, readiness.

antonym unreadiness.

preponderance *n* ascendancy, bulk, dominance, domination, dominion, extensiveness, force, lion's share, majority, mass, power, predominance, prevalence, superiority, supremacy, sway, weight.

preponderant *adj* ascendant, controlling, dominant, extensive, foremost, greater, important, larger, overriding, overruling, paramount, predominant, prevailing, prevalent, significant, superior.

preponderate *v* dominate, outnumber, override, overrule, predominate, prevail, rule, tell, turn the balance, turn the scale, weigh with.

prepossessing *adj* alluring, amiable, appealing, attractive, beautiful, bewitching, captivating, charming, delightful, disarming, enchanting, engaging, fair, fascinating, fetching, good-looking, handsome, inviting, likable, lovable, magnetic, pleasing, striking, taking, winning, winsome.

antonyms unattractive, unprepossessing.

prepossession *n* absorption, bias, engrossment, inclination, leaning, liking, partiality, predilection, predisposition, prejudice, preoccupation.

preposterous *adj* absurd, asinine, bizarre, crazy, derisory, excessive, exorbitant, extravagant, extreme, fatuous, foolish, imbecile, impossible, inane, incredible, insane, intolerable, irrational, laughable, ludicrous, monstrous, nonsensical, outrageous, ridiculous, risible, senseless, shocking, unbelievable, unconscionable, unreasonable, unthinkable.

antonym reasonable.

prerequisite *adj* basic, essential, fundamental, imperative, indispensable, mandatory, necessary, needed, needful, obligatory, required, requisite, vital.

antonym unnecessary.

n condition, essential, imperative, must, necessity, precondition, provision, proviso, qualification, requirement, requisite, sine qua non.

antonym extra.

prerogative *n* advantage, authority, birthright, carte blanche, choice, claim, droit, due, exemption, immunity, liberty, licence, perquisite, privilege, right, sanction, title.

presage *v* adumbrate, augur, betoken, bode, divine, feel, forebode, forecast, forefeel, foreknow, forepoint, foresee, foreshadow, foretell, forethink, foretoken, forewarn, intuit, omen, point to, portend, predict, previse, prognosticate, prophesy, sense, signify, soothsay, vaticinate, warn.

n apprehension, augury, auspice, bad vibes, bodement, boding, feeling, foreboding, forecast, forewarning, harbinger, intimation, intuition, misgiving, omen, portent, prediction, premonition, presentiment, prodrome, prodromus, prognostic, prognostication, prophecy, sign, warning.

prescience *n* clairvoyance, far-sightedness, foreknowledge, foresight, precognition, prevision, prophecy, propheticness, second sight.

prescient *adj* clairvoyant, discerning, divinatory, divining, far-seeing, far-sighted, foreknowing, foresighted, mantic, perceptive, previsional, prophetic, psychic.

antonym imperceptive.

prescribe *v* appoint, assign, command, decree, define, dictate, direct, enjoin, fix, impose, lay down, limit, ordain, order, require, rule, set, set bounds to, specify, stipulate.

prescribed *adj* assigned, decreed, formulary, laid down, ordained, set, specified, stipulated.

prescription *n* direction, drug, formula, instruction, medicine, mixture, preparation, recipe, remedy, treatment.

prescriptive *adj* authoritarian, customary, dictatorial, didactic, dogmatic, legislating, preceptive, prescribing, rigid.

presence *n* air, apparition, appearance, aspect, attendance, aura, bearing, carriage, closeness, companionship, company, comportment, demeanour, ease, existence, ghost, habitation, inhabitance, manifestation, mien, nearness, neighbourhood, occupancy, personality, poise, propinquity, proximity, residence, revenant, self-assurance, shade, spectre, spirit, statuesqueness, vicinity.

antonym absence.

presence of mind alertness, aplomb, calmness, composure, cool, coolness, gumption, imperturbability, level-headedness, nous, quickness, sang-froid, self-assurance, self-command, self-possession, wits.

antonyms agitation, confusion.

present[1] *adj* at hand, attending, available, contemporary, current, existent, extant, here, immediate, instant, near, ready, there, to hand.

antonyms absent, out-of-date, past.

present[2] *v* acquaint with, adduce, advance, award, bestow, confer, declare, demonstrate, display, donate, entrust, exhibit, expound, extend, furnish, give, grant, hand over, hold out, introduce, mount, offer, porrect, pose, produce, proffer, put on, raise, recount, relate, show, stage, state, submit, suggest, tender.

antonym take.

n benefaction, boon, bounty, cadeau, compliment, donation, endowment, favour, gift, grant, gratuity, largess, nuzzer, offering, pressie, prezzie, refresher.

presentable *adj* acceptable, becoming, clean, decent, neat, passable, proper, respectable, satisfactory, suitable, tidy, tolerable.

antonyms unpresentable, untidy.

presentation *n* appearance, arrangement, award, bestowal, conferral, delivery, demonstration, display, donation, exhibition, exposition, giving, introduction, investiture, offering, pageant, performance, production, rendition, representation, show, staging, submission.

present-day *adj* contemporary, current, existing, fashionable, hodiernal, living, modern, present, up-to-date.

antonyms future, past.

presenter *n* anchorman, compère, frontman, host, master of ceremonies, MC.

presentiment *n* anticipation, apprehension, bad vibes, expectation, fear, feeling, forebodement, foreboding, forecast, forethought, hunch, intuition, misgiving, premonition, presage.

presently *adv* anon, before long, by and by, directly, immediately, in a minute, shortly, soon.

preservation *n* conservation, defence, keeping, maintenance, perpetuation, protection, retention, safeguarding, safekeeping, safety, salvation, security, storage, support, upholding, upkeep.

antonyms destruction, ruination.

preserve *v* care for, confect, conserve, continue, defend, embalm, entreasure, guard, keep, maintain, perpetuate, protect, retain, safeguard, save, secure, shelter, shield, store, sustain, uphold.

antonyms destroy, ruin.

n area, confection, confiture, conserve, domain, field, game park, game reserve, jam, jelly, konfyt, marmalade, pigeon, realm, reservation, reserve, safari park, sanctuary, specialism, speciality, specialty, sphere, thing.

preside *v* administer, chair, conduct, control, direct, govern, head, lead, manage, officiate, run, supervise.

press[1] *v* adpress, afflict, appress, assail, beg, beset, besiege, calendar, clasp, cluster, compel, compress, condense, constrain, crowd, crush, demand, depress, disquiet, dun, embrace, encircle, enfold, enforce, enjoin, entreat, exhort, finish, flatten, flock, force, force down, gather, harass, hasten, herd, hug, hurry, implore, importune, insist on, iron, jam, mangle, mash, mill, petition, plague, plead, pressurise, push, reduce, rush, seethe, smooth, squeeze, steam, stuff, sue, supplicate, surge, swarm, throng, torment, trouble, urge, vex, worry.

antonyms expand, hang back, lighten, relieve.

n bunch, bustle, crowd, crush, demand, flock, hassle, herd, horde, host, hurry, mob, multitude, pack, pressure, push, strain, stress, swarm, throng, urgency.

press[2] *n* columnists, correspondents, Fleet Street, fourth estate, hacks, journalism, journalists, news media, newsmen, newspapers, paparazzi, papers, photographers, pressmen, reporters, writers.

pressed *adj* browbeaten, bullied, coerced, constrained, forced, harassed, hurried, pressured, pressurised, pushed, rushed, short.

antonyms unhurried, well-off.

pressing *adj* burning, constraining, crowding, crucial, essential, exigent, high-priority, imperative, important, importunate, serious, thronging, urgent, vital.

antonyms trivial, unimportant.

pressure *n* adversity, affliction, burden, coercion, compressing, compression, compulsion, constraint, crushing, demands, difficulty, distress, exigency, force, hassle, heat, heaviness, hurry, influence, load, obligation, power, powerplay, press, pression, squeezing, strain, stress, sway, urgency, weight.

v browbeat, bulldoze, bully, coerce, compel, constrain, dragoon, drive, force, impel, induce, lean on, oblige, persuade, press, pressurise, squeeze.

pressurise *v* browbeat, bulldoze, bully, coerce, compel, constrain, dragoon, drive, force, impel, induce, lean on, oblige, persuade, press, pressure, squeeze.

prestige *n* authority, cachet, celebrity, clout, credit, distinction, eminence, esteem, fame, honour, importance, influence, kudos, pull, regard, renown, reputation, standing, stature, status, weight.

antonyms humbleness, unimportance.

prestigious *adj* blue-chip, celebrated, eminent, esteemed, exalted, great, illustrious, important, imposing, impressive, influential, prominent, renowned, reputable, respected, up-market.

antonyms humble, modest.

presumably *adv* apparently, as like as not, doubtless, doubtlessly, in all likelihood, in all probability, most likely, no doubt, probably, seemingly.

presume *v* assume, bank on, believe, conjecture, count on, dare, depend on, go so far, have the audacity, hypothesise, hypothetise, infer, make bold, make so bold, posit, postulate, presuppose, rely on, suppose, surmise, take for granted, take it, take the liberty, think, trust, undertake, venture.

presumption[1] *n* assurance, audacity, boldness, brass, brass neck, cheek, effrontery, forwardness, gall, impudence, insolence, neck, nerve, presumptuousness, temerity.

antonyms humility, politeness.

presumption[2] *n* anticipation, assumption, basis, belief, chance, conjecture, grounds, guess, hypothesis, likelihood, opinion, plausibility, premiss, presupposition, probability, reason, supposition, surmise.

presumptive *adj* assumed, believable, believed, conceivable, credible, designate, expected, hypothetical, inferred, likely, plausible, possible, probable, prospective, reasonable, supposed, understood.

antonyms known, unlikely.

presumptuous *adj* arrogant, audacious, big-headed, bold, conceited, foolhardy, forward, impertinent, impudent, insolent, over-confident, over-familiar, overweening, presuming, pushy, rash, uppish.

antonym modest.

presuppose *v* accept, assume, consider, imply, posit, postulate, premise, presume, suppose, take for granted.

presupposition *n* assumption, belief, hypothesis, preconception, premise, premiss, presumption, supposition, theory.

pretence *n* acting, affectation, aim, allegation, appearance, artifice, blague, bounce, charade, claim, cloak, colour, cover, deceit, deception, display, excuse, fabrication, façade, faking, falsehood, feigning, garb, guise, humbug, invention, make-believe, mask, masquerade, posing, posturing, pretentiousness, pretext, profession, pseudery, purpose, ruse, semblance, sham, show, simulation, subterfuge, trickery, veil, veneer, wile.

antonyms honesty, openness, reason.

pretend *v* act, affect, alge, allege, aspire, assume, claim, counterfeit, dissemble, dissimulate, fake, falsify, feign, go through the motions, imagine, impersonate, make believe, pass oneself off, profess, purport, put on, sham, simulate, suppose.

pretended *adj* alleged, avowed, bogus, counterfeit, fake, false, feigned, fictitious, imaginary, ostensible, phoney, pretend, professed, pseudo, purported, sham, so-called, specious, spurious, supposed, supposititious.

antonym real.

pretender *n* aspirant, claimant, claimer, pretendant.

pretension *n* affection, airs, aspiration, assertion, assumption, claim, conceit, demand, hypocrisy, ostentation, pomposity, pretence, pretentiousness, pretext, profession, self-importance, show, showiness, snobbery, snobbishness, vainglory, vanity.

antonyms humility, modesty, simplicity, straightforwardness.

pretentious *adj* affected, ambitious, assuming, bombastic, chichi, conceited, euphemistic, exaggerated, extravagant, flaunting, grandiloquent, grandiose, highfalutin, high-flown, high-sounding, hollow, inflated, magniloquent, mannered, oro(ro)tund, ostentatious, overambitious, overassuming, pompous, pseud, pseudish, pseudo, showy, snobbish, specious, uppish, vainglorious.

antonyms humble, modest, simple, straightforward.

pretentiousness *n* attitudinising, flamboyance, floridness, floweriness, ostentation, posing, posturing, pretension, pseudery, show, theatricality.

antonyms humbleness, modesty, simplicity, straightforwardness.

pretext *n* appearance, cloak, cover, device, excuse, guise, mask, ploy, pretence, rationale, ruse, semblance, show, simulation, umbrage, veil.

prettify *v* adorn, beautify, bedeck, deck, deck out, decorate, do up, doll up, embellish, garnish, gild, ornament, primp, prink up, smarten up, tart up, titivate, trick out, trim.

antonyms mar, uglify.

pretty *adj* appealing, attractive, beautiful, bijou, bonny, charming, comely, cute, dainty, delicate, elegant, fair, fine, good-looking, graceful, lovely, neat, nice, personable, pleasing, sightly, tasteful, trim.

antonyms tasteless, ugly.

adv fairly, moderately, passably, quite, rather, reasonably, somewhat, tolerably.

prevail *v* abound, obtain, overcome, overrule, predominate, preponderate, reign, rule, succeed, triumph, win.

antonym lose.

prevail upon bring round, convince, dispose, dissuade, incline, induce, influence, persuade, prompt, sway, talk into, talk out of, talk round, win over.

prevailing *adj* common, controlling, current, customary, dominant, established, fashionable, general, in style, in vogue, influential, main, mainstream, operative, ordinary, popular, predominating, preponderating, prepotent, prevalent, principal, ruling, set, usual, widespread.

antonyms minor, uncommon.

prevalence *n* acceptance, ascendancy, commonness, currency, frequency, hold, mastery, omnipresence, pervasiveness, popularity, predominance, preponderance, primacy, profusion, regularity, rule, sway, ubiquity, universality.

antonym uncommonness.

prevalent *adj* accepted, ascendant, common, commonplace, compelling, current, customary, dominant, epidemic, established, everyday, extensive, frequent, general, governing, habitual, popular, powerful, predominant, prevailing, rampant, regnant, rife, successful, superior, ubiquitous, universal, usual, victorious, widespread.

antonyms subordinate, uncommon.

prevaricate *v* cavil, deceive, dodge, equivocate, evade, fib, hedge, lie, palter, quibble, shift, shuffle, temporise, tergiversate.

prevarication *n* cavil, cavillation, cavilling, deceit, deception, equivocation, evasion, falsehood, falsification, fibbing, fib(s), half-truth, lie, misrepresentation, pretence, quibbling, tergiversation, untruth.

prevaricator *n* Ananias, casuist, caviller, deceiver, dissembler, dodger, equivocator, evader, fibber, hypocrite, liar, pettifogger, quibbler, sophist.

prevent *v* anticipate, avert, avoid, balk, bar, block, check, counteract, debar, defend against, foil, forestall, frustrate, hamper, head off, hinder, impede, inhibit, intercept, obstruct, obviate, preclude, restrain, stave off, stop, stymie, thwart, ward off.

antonyms cause, foster, help.

prevention *n* anticipation, avoidance, bar, check, deterrence, elimination, forestalling, forethought, frustration, hindrance, impediment, interruption, obstacle, obstruction, obviation, precaution, preclusion, prophylaxis, safeguard, stoppage, thwarting.

antonyms causing, fostering, help.

preventive *adj* counteractive, deterrent, hampering, hindering, impeding, inhibitory, obstructive, precautionary, prevenient, preventative, prophylactic, protective, shielding.

antonyms causative, fostering.

n block, condom, deterrent, hindrance, impediment, neutraliser, obstacle, obstruction, prevention, prophylactic, protection, protective, remedy, safeguard, shield.

antonyms cause, encouragement, incitement.

previous *adj* antecedent, anterior, arranged, earlier, erstwhile, ex-, foregoing, former, one-time, past, preceding, precipitate, premature, prior, quondam, sometime, umwhile, untimely, whilom.

antonyms later, timely.

previously *adv* before, beforehand, earlier, formerly, heretofore, hitherto, once.

antonym later.

prey *n* booty, dupe, fall guy, game, kill, mark, mug, plunder, quarry, target, victim.

prey on blackmail, bleed, bully, burden, devour, distress, eat, eat away, exploit, feed on, gnaw at, haunt, hunt, intimidate, live off, moth-eat, oppress, seize, take advantage of, terrorise, trouble, victimise, waste, weigh down, weigh heavily, worry.

price *n* amount, assessment, bill, bounty, charge, consequences, cost, damage, estimate, expenditure, expense, fee, figure, levy, odds, outlay, payment, penalty, rate, reward, sacrifice, sum, toll, valuation, value, worth.

v assess, cost, estimate, evaluate, offer, put, rate, valorise, value.

priceless[1] *adj* beyond price, cherished, costly, dear, expensive, incalculable, incomparable, inestimable, invaluable, irreplaceable, precious, prized, rare, rich, treasured, without price.

antonyms cheap, run-of-the-mill.

priceless[2] *adj* a hoot, a scream, absurd, amusing, comic, droll, funny, hilarious, killing, rib-tickling, ridiculous, riotous, risible, side-splitting.

price-list *n* catalogue, menu, price(s)-current.

pric(e)y *adj* costly, dear, excessive, exorbitant, expensive, extortionate, high-priced, over the odds, steep.

antonym cheap.

prick *v* bite, bore, itch, jab, jag, pain, perforate, pierce, pink, point, prickle, prog, punch, puncture, raise, rise, smart, stab, sting, thorn, tingle, touch, trouble.

n jag, pang, perforation, pinhole, prickle, prog, puncture, smart, spasm, sting, twinge, wound.

prickle *n* acantha, barb, formication, needle, point, smart, spike, spine, spur, thorn, tickle, tingle, tingling.

v itch, jab, nick, nip, prick, smart, sting, tingle.

prickly *adj* acanaceous, aculeate(d), barbed, brambly, bristly, cantankerous, complicated, crawling, difficult, echinate, edgy, fractious, grumpy, intricate, involved, irritable, itchy, jaggy, knotty, peevish, pettish, petulant, pricking, prickling, scratchy, sharp, short-tempered, smarting, spiny, stinging, tetchy, thorny, ticklish, tingling, touchy, tricky, troublesome, trying, waspish.

antonyms easy-going, simple, smooth.

pricy *see* **pric(e)y**.

pride *n* amour-propre, arrogance, best, big-headedness, boast, choice, conceit, cream, delight, dignity, egotism, élite, flower, gem, glory, gratification, haughtiness, hauteur, high spirits, honour, hubris, jewel, joy, loftiness, magnificence, mettle, morgue, ostentation, pick, pleasure, presumption, pretension, pretensiousness, pride and joy, prize, satisfaction, self-esteem, self-importance, self-love, self-respect, smugness, snobbery, splendour, superciliousness, treasure, vainglory, vanity.

antonym humility.

pride (oneself on) boast, brag, congratulate oneself, crow, exult, flatter oneself, glory, pat oneself on the back, pique, plume, preen, revel, take pride, vaunt.

antonyms belittle, humble.

priest *n* abbé, churchman, clergyman, cleric, curate, divine, ecclesiast, ecclesiastic, father, father confessor, flamen, holy man, Jack-priest, lama, Levite, Magus, man of God, man of the cloth, mar-text, masspriest, minister, padre, priestling, vicar.

priestess *n* abbess, beguine, canoness, clergy-woman, deaconess, mambo, nun, prioress, religious, sister, vestal.

priestly *adj* Aaronic(al), canonical, clerical, ecclesiastical, flaminical, hieratic, pastoral, priestlike, sacerdotal.

prig *n* goody-goody, holy Joe, Holy Willie, Mrs Grundy, old maid, precisian, prude, puritan.

priggish *adj* goody-goody, holier-than-thou, narrow-minded, pedantic, prim, prudish, pudibund, puritanical, self-righteous, self-satisfied, smug, starchy, stiff, stuffy.

antonyms broad-minded, informal.

prim *adj* demure, fastidious, formal, fussy, governessy, old-maidish, old-maidist, particular, perjink, po-faced, precise, priggish, prissy, proper, prudish, pudibund, puritanical, school-marmish, sedate, starchy, stiff, strait-laced.

antonyms broad-minded, informal.

primacy *n* ascendancy, command, dominance, dominion, leadership, paramoun(t)cy, pre-eminence, seniority, sovereignty, superiority, supremacy.

antonym inferiority.

primal *adj* central, chief, earliest, first, fundamental, greatest, highest, initial, main, major, original, paramount, primary, prime, primeval, primitive, primordial, principal, pristine.

antonyms later, minor.

primarily *adv* at first, basically, chiefly, especially, essentially, fundamentally, generally, initially, mainly, mostly, originally, principally.

antonym secondarily.

primary *adj* aboriginal, basic, beginning, best, capital, cardinal, chief, dominant, earliest, elemental, elementary, essential, first, first-formed, first-made, fundamental, greatest, highest, initial, introductory, leading, main, original, paramount, primal, prime, primeval, primigenial, primitial, primitive, primordial, principal, pristine, radical, rudimentary, simple, top, ultimate, underlying.

antonym secondary.

prime[1] *adj* basic, best, capital, chief, choice, earliest, excellent, first-class, first-rate, fundamental, highest, leading, main, original, predominant, pre-eminent, primary, principal, quality, ruling, select, selected, senior, superior, top, underlying.

antonyms minor, secondary, second-rate.

n beginning, flowering, height, heyday, maturity, morning, opening, peak, perfection, spring, springtide, springtime, start, zenith.

prime[2] *v* brief, charge, clue up, coach, cram, fill, fill in, gen up, groom, inform, notify, post up, prepare, train.

primer *n* Donat, introduction, manual, prodrome, prodromus, text-book.

primeval *adj* ancient, earliest, early, first, Ogygian, old, original, prehistoric, primal, primitial, primitive, primordial, pristine.

antonyms developed, later, modern.

primitive *adj* aboriginal, barbarian, barbaric, childlike, crude, earliest, early, elementary, first, naïve, neanderthal, original, primal, primary, primeval, primordial, pristine, rough, rude, rudimentary, savage, simple, uncivilised, uncultivated, undeveloped, unrefined, unsophisticated, untrained, untutored.

antonyms advanced, civilised, developed.

primordial *adj* basic, earliest, elemental, first, first-formed, first-made, fundamental, original, prehistoric, primal, primeval, primigenial, primitial, primitive, pristine, radical.

antonyms developed, later, modern.

prince *n* lord, mogul, monarch, nabob, nawab, potentate, ruler, sovereign.

princely *adj* august, bounteous, bountiful, dignified, generous, gracious, grand, imperial, imposing, lavish, liberal, lofty, magnanimous, magnificent, majestic, munificent, noble, open-handed, regal, rich, royal, sovereign, stately, sumptuous.

antonyms humble, mean.

principal[1] *adj* capital, cardinal, chief, controlling, decuman, dominant, essential, first, foremost, highest, key, leading, main, paramount, pre-eminent, primary, prime, strongest, truncal.

antonyms least, lesser, minor.

n boss, chief, dean, director, first violin, head, head teacher, headmaster, headmistress, lead, leader, master, prima ballerina, prima donna, rector, star, superintendent.

principal[2] *n* assets, capital, capital funds, money.

principality *n* princedom, principate.

principally *adv* above all, chiefly, especially, mainly, mostly, particularly, predominantly, primarily.

principle *n* assumption, attitude, axiom, belief, canon, code, conscience, credo, criterion, dictum, doctrine, dogma, duty, element, ethic, formula, fundamental, golden rule, honour, institute, integrity, law, maxim, moral, morality, morals, opinion, precept, principium, probity, proposition, rectitude, rule, scruples, standard, tenet, truth, uprightness, verity.

antonyms corruption, wickedness.

principled *adj* clear, clear-cut, conscientious, correct, decent, ethical, high-minded, honourable, just, logical, moral, rational, reasoned, righteous, right-minded, scrupulous, sensible, thought-out, upright, virtuous.

antonym unprincipled.

print *v* engrave, impress, imprint, issue, mark, produce, publish, put to bed, reproduce, run off, stamp, write.

n book, characters, copy, dab, engraving, face, fingerprint, font, fount, impression, lettering, letters, magazine, mould, newspaper, newsprint, periodical, photo, photograph, picture, publication, reproduction, stamp, type, typeface, typescript.

prior *adj* aforementioned, antecedent, anterior, earlier, foregoing, former, preceding, pre-existent, previous.

antonym later.

prior to before, earlier than, preceding, preparatory to, previous to.

antonym after.

priority *n* precedence, pre-eminence, preference, prerogative, privilege, rank, right of way, seniority, superiority, supremacy, the lead.

antonyms inferiority, subordinateness.

priory *n* abbey, béguinage, cloister, convent, monastery, nunnery, religious house.

prise *see* **prize**.

prison *n* bagnio, bastille, borstal(l), bridewell, brig, cage, calaboose, can, cell, chok(e)y, clink, confinement, cooler, coop, dungeon, gaol, glasshouse, gulag, hoos(e)gow, house of correction, imprisonment, jail, jug, lock-up, panopticon, penal institution, penitentiary, pokey, porridge, prison-house, prison-ship, quod, slammer, slink, stalag, stir, tank, tol(l)booth.

prisoner *n* canary-bird, captive, collegian, con, convict, detainee, détenu(e), forçat, hostage, inmate, internee, jail-bird, lag.

prissy *adj* effeminate, fastidious, finicky, fussy, old-maidish, overnice, po-faced, precious, prim, prim and proper, prudish, pudibund, school-marmish, squeamish, starchy, strait-laced.

antonyms broad-minded, informal.

pristine *adj* earliest, first, former, initial, original, primal, primary, primeval, primigenial, primitial, primitive, primordial, uncorrupted, undefiled, unspoiled, unsullied, untouched, virgin.

antonyms developed, later, spoiled.

privacy *n* clandestineness, concealment, confidentiality, isolation, privateness, quietness, quietude, retirement, retreat, seclusion, secrecy, separateness, sequestration, solitude.

antonym publicness.

private *adj* clandestine, closet, concealed, confidential, exclusive, home-felt, hush-hush, in camera, independent, individual, inside, intimate, intraparietal, inward, isolated, off the record, own, particular, personal, privy, reserved, retired, secluded, secret, separate, sequestrated, solitary, special, unofficial, withdrawn.

antonyms open, public.

n enlisted man, private soldier, squaddy, swad, swaddy, tommy, Tommy Atkins.

private detective pinkerton, private eye, private investigator, shamus.

private parts fanny, genitalia, genitals, privates, pudenda, pussy, quim.

privateer *n* buccaneer, corsair, freebooter, marque, pirate, sea-robber, sea-wolf.

privation *n* affliction, austerity, destitution, distress, hardship, indigence, lack, loss, misery, necessary, need, neediness, penury, poverty, suffering, want.

antonyms affluence, wealth.

privatise *v* denationalise.

antonym nationalise.

privilege *n* advantage, benefit, birthright, claim, concession, droit, due, entitlement, franchise, freedom, immunity, liberty, licence, prerogative, right, sanction, title.

antonym disadvantage.

privileged *adj* advantaged, allowed, authorised, élite, empowered, entitled, exempt(ed), favoured, free, granted, honoured, indulged, licensed, permitted, powerful, ruling, sanctioned, special, vested.

antonyms disadvantaged, under-privileged.

privy *n* bog, cloaca, closet, cludge, earth-closet, head, John, latrine, lavatory, loo, reredorter, toilet, water-closet.

adj confidential, hidden, hush-hush, intimate, off the record, personal, private, secret, top secret.

antonym public.

privy to apprised of, aware of, cognisant of, in on, in the know, informed about, wise to.

antonym unaware.

prize[1] *n* accolade, aim, ambition, award, conquest, desire, gain, goal, haul, honour, hope, jackpot, premium, purse, reward, stake(s), trophy, windfall, winnings.

adj award-winning, best, champion, excellent, first-rate, outstanding, top, top-notch, winning.

antonym second-rate.

v appreciate, cherish, esteem, hold dear, revere, reverence, set store by, treasure, value.

antonyms despise, undervalue.

prize[2] *n* booty, capture, loot, pickings, pillage, plunder, spoils, trophy.

prize[3], prise¢prize, prise" *v* force, jemmy, lever, pry, winkle.

prize-winner *n* champ, champion, cup-winner, dux, medallist, prize-man, winner.

probability *n* assumption, chance, chances, expectation, liability, likelihood, likeliness, odds, presumption, prospect.

antonym improbability.

probable *adj* apparent, credible, feasible, likely, odds-on, on the cards, plausible, possible, presumed, reasonable, seeming, verisimilar.

antonym improbable.

probably *adv* as likely as not, doubtless, happen, in all likelihood, in all probability, likely, maybe, most likely, perhaps, possibly, presumably.

antonym improbably.

probation *n* apprenticeship, examination, initiation, noviciate, proof, test, testing, trial, trial period.

probe *v* examine, explore, go into, investigate, look into, pierce, poke, prod, query, scrutinise, search, sift, sound, test, verify.

n bore, detection, drill, examination, exploration, inquest, inquiry, investigation, research, scrutiny, study, test.

probity *n* equity, fairness, fidelity, goodness, honesty, honour, honourableness, integrity, justice, morality, rectitude, righteousness, sincerity, trustworthiness, truthfulness, uprightness, virtue, worth.

antonym improbity.

problem *n* boyg, brain-teaser, complication, conundrum, difficulty, dilemma, disagreement, dispute, doubt. enigma, no laughing matter, poser, predicament, puzzle, quandary, question, riddle, trouble, vexata quaestio, vexed question.

adj delinquent, difficult, intractable, perverse, refractory, uncontrollable, unmanageable, unruly.

antonyms manageable, well-behaved.

problematic *adj* chancy, debatable, doubtful, dubious, enigmatic, moot, problematical, puzzling, questionable, tricky, uncertain, unestablished, unsettled, unsure.

antonym certain.

procedure *n* action, conduct, course, custom, form, formula, method, modus operandi, move, operation, performance, plan of action, policy, practice, process, routine, scheme, step, strategy, system, transaction.

proceed *v* advance, arise, carry on, come, continue, derive, emanate, ensue, flow, follow, go ahead, issue, move on, originate, press on, progress, result, set in motion, spring, start, stem.

antonyms retreat, stop.

proceedings *n* account, action, affair, affairs, annals, archives, business, course of action, dealings, deeds, doings, event(s), matters, measures, minutes, moves, procedure, process, records, report, steps, transactions, undertaking.

proceeds *n* earnings, emoluments, gain, income, motser, motza, produce, products, profit, receipts, returns, revenue, takings, yield.

antonyms losses, outlay.

process[1] *n* action, advance, case, course, course of action, development, evolution, formation, growth, manner, means, measure, method, mode, movement, operation, performance, practice, procedure, proceeding, progress, progression, stage, step, suit, system, transaction, trial, unfolding.

v alter, convert, deal with, digitise, dispose of, fulfil, handle, prepare, refine, transform, treat.

process[2] *n* node, nodosity, nodule, projection, prominence, protuberance, protusion.

processing *n* conversion, datamation, handling, preparation, refinement.

procession *n* cavalcade, column, concatenation, cortege, course, cycle, file, march, motorcade, parade, run, sequence, series, skimmington, string, succession, train.

proclaim *v* advertise, affirm, announce, annunciate, blaze, blazon, circulate, declare, enounce, enunciate, give out, herald, indicate, make known, preconise, profess, promulgate, publish, show, testify, trumpet.

proclamation *n* announcement, annunciation, ban, declaration, decree, edict, firman, hatti-sherif, indiction, interlocution, irade, manifesto, notice, notification, proclaim, promulgation, pronouncement, pronunciamento, publication, ukase.

proclivity *n* bent, bias, disposition, facility, inclination, leaning, liability, liableness, penchant, predilection, predisposition, proneness, propensity, tendency, weakness.

antonym disinclination.

procrastinate *v* adjourn, dally, defer, delay, dilly-dally, drag one's feet, gain time, penelopise, play for time, postpone, prolong, protract, put off, retard, stall, temporise.

antonyms advance, proceed.

procrastination *n* dallying, deferral, delaying, dilly-dallying, foot-dragging, stalling, temporising.

procreate *v* beget, breed, conceive, engender, father, generate, mother, produce, propagate, reproduce, sire, spawn.

procure *v* acquire, appropriate, bag, buy, come by, earn, effect, find, gain, get, induce, lay hands on, obtain, pander, pick up, pimp, purchase, secure, win.

antonym lose.

procurer *n* bawd, madam, pander, panderer, pimp, procuress, white-slaver, whoremonger.

prod *v* dig, drive, egg on, elbow, goad, impel, incite, jab, motivate, move, nudge, poke, prick, prog, prompt, propel, push, rouse, shove, spur, stimulate, urge.

n boost, cue, dig, elbow, jab, nudge, poke, prog, prompt, push, reminder, shove, signal, stimulus.

prodigal *adj* bounteous, bountiful, copious, excessive, extravagant, exuberant, immoderate, improvident, intemperate, lavish, luxuriant, profligate, profuse, reckless, spendthrift, squandering, sumptuous, superabundant, teeming, unsparing, unthrift, unthrifty, wanton, wasteful.

antonyms modest, parsimonious, thrifty.

n big spender, profligate, spendall, spendthrift, squanderer, waster, wastrel.

prodigality *n* abandon, abundance, amplitude, bounteousness, bounty, copiousness, dissipation, excess, extravagance, exuberance, immoderation, intemperance, lavishness, luxuriance, plenteousness, plenty, profligacy, profusion, recklessness, richness, squandering, sumptuousness, unthrift, unthriftiness, wantonness, waste, wastefulness.

antonyms modesty, parsimony, thrift.

prodigious *adj* abnormal, amazing, astounding, colossal, enormous, exceptional, extraordinary, fabulous, fantastic, flabbergasting, giant, gigantic, huge, immeasurable, immense, impressive, inordinate, mammoth, marvellous, massive, miraculous, monstrous, monumental, phenomenal, remarkable, spectacular, staggering, startling, striking, stupendous, tremendous, unusual, vast, wonderful.

antonyms commonplace, small, unremarkable.

prodigy *n* abnormality, child genius, curiosity, freak, genius, grotesque, marvel, matermind, miracle, monster, monstrosity, mutation, phenomenon, rara avis, rarity, sensation, spectacle, talent, whiz, whiz kid, wizard, wonder, wonder child, wonder-work, wunderkind.

produce[1] *v* advance, afford, bear, beget, breed, bring forth, cause, compose, construct, create, deliver, demonstrate, develop, direct, effect, engender, exhibit, fabricate, factify, factuate, furnish, generate, give, give rise to, invent, make, manufacture, mount, occasion, offer, originate, present, provoke, put forward, put on, render, result in, show, stage, supply, throw, yield.

antonyms consume, result from.

n crop, harvest, product, yield.

produce[2] *v* continue, elongate, extend, lengthen, prolong, protract.

producer *n* director, farmer, grower, impresario, maker, manager, manufacturer, presenter, régisseur.

product *n* artefact, commodity, concoction, consequence, creation, effect, facture, fruit, goods, invention, issue, legacy, merchandise, offshoot, offspring, outcome, output, produce, production, result, returns, spin-off, upshot, work, yield.

antonym cause.

production *n* assembly, construction, creation, direction, fabrication, facture, formation, fructification, making, management, manufacture, manufacturing, origination, preparation, presentation, producing, staging.

antonym consumption.

productive *adj* advantageous, beneficial, constructive, creative, dynamic, effective, energetic, fecund, fertile, fructiferous, fructuous, fruitful, gainful, generative, gratifying, inventive, plentiful, producing, profitable, prolific, rewarding, rich, teeming, uberous, useful, valuable, vigorous, voluminous, worthwhile.

antonyms fruitless, unproductive.

productivity *n* abundance, output, production, productiveness, uberty, work-rate, yield.

antonym unproductiveness.

profane *adj* abusive, blasphemous, coarse, crude, disrespectful, filthy, forbidden, foul, godless, heathen, idolatrous, impious, impure, irreligious, irreverent, lay, obscene, pagan, sacrilegious, secular, sinful, temporal, terefa(h), unclean, unconsecrated, ungodly, unhallowed, unholy, uninitiated, unsanctified, vulgar, wicked, worldly.

antonyms initiated, permitted, religious, sacred.

v abuse, contaminate, debase, defile, degrade, desecrate, misemploy, misuse, pervert, pollute, prostitute, violate, vitiate.

antonym revere.

profanity *n* abuse, blasphemy, curse, cursing, execration, expletive, four-letter word, impiety, imprecation, inquination, irreverence, malediction, obscenity, profaneness, sacrilege, swearing, swear-word.

antonyms politeness, reverence.

profess *v* acknowledge, admit, affirm, allege, announce, assert, asseverate, aver, avow, certify, claim, confess, confirm, declare, enunciate, fake, feign, maintain, make out, own, pretend, proclaim, propose, propound, purport, sham, state, vouch.

professed *adj* acknowledged, avowed, certified, confirmed, declared, ostensible, pretended, proclaimed, purported, self-acknowledged, self-confessed, self-styled, so-called, soi-disant, supposed, would-be.

profession *n* acknowledgement, affirmation, assertion, attestation, avowal, business, calling, career, claim, confession, declaration, employment, job, line (of work), manifesto, métier, occupation, office, position, sphere, statement, testimony, vocation, vow, walk of life.

professional *adj* adept, competent, crack, efficient, experienced, expert, finished, masterly, polished, practised, proficient, qualified, skilled, slick, trained, virtuose, virtuosic, well-skilled.

antonyms amateur, unprofessional.

n adept, authority, dab hand, expert, maestro, master, pastmaster, pro, proficient, specialist, virtuoso, wizard.

proffer *v* advance, extend, hand, hold out, offer, present, propose, propound, submit, suggest, tender, volunteer.

proficiency *n* ability, accomplishment, aptitude, competence, conversancy, dexterity, expertise, expertness, facility, finesse, knack, know-how, mastery, skilfulness, skill, talent, virtuosity.

antonyms clumsiness, incompetence.

proficient *adj* able, accomplished, adept, apt, capable, clever, competent, conversant, efficient, experienced, expert, gifted, masterly, qualified, skilful, skilled, talented, trained, versed, virtuose, virtuosic.

antonyms clumsy, incompetent.

profile *n* analysis, biography, biopic, characterisation, chart, contour, diagram, drawing, examination, figure, form, graph, outline, portrait, review, shape, side view, silhouette, sketch, study, survey, table, thumbnail sketch, vignette.

profit *n* a fast buck, advancement, advantage, avail, benefit, boot, bottom line, bunce, earnings, emoluments, fruit, gain, gelt, good, graft, gravy, grist, interest, melon, percentage, proceeds, receipts, return, revenue, surplus, takings, use, value, velvet, winnings, yield.

antonym loss.

v advance, advantage, aid, avail, benefit, better, boot, contribute, gain, help, improve, line one's pockets, promote, serve, stand in good stead.

antonyms harm, hinder.

profit by/from capitalise on, cash in on, exploit, learn from, put to good use, reap the benefit of, take advantage of, turn to account, turn to advantage, use, utilise.

antonym lose by.

profitable *adj* advantageable, advantageous, beneficial, commercial, cost-effective, emolumental, emolumentary, fruitful, gainful, lucrative, money-making, paying, plummy, productive, remunerative, rewarding, serviceable, useful, utile, valuable, worthwhile.

antonym unprofitable.

profiteer *n* exploiter, extortioner, extortionist, racketeer.

v exploit, extort, fleece, make a fast buck, make a quick killing, overcharge, racketeer.

profiteering *n* exploitation, extortion, Rachmanism, racketeering.

profitless *adj* bootless, fruitless, futile, gainless, idle, ineffective, ineffectual, pointless, thankless, unavailing, unproductive, unprofitable, unremunerative, useless, vain, worthless.

antonym profitable.

profligacy *n* abandon, corruption, debauchery, degeneracy, depravity, dissipation, dissoluteness, excess, extravagance, immorality, improvidence, lavishness, laxity, libertinism, licentiousness, prodigality, promiscuity, recklessness, squandering, unrestraint, unthrift, unthriftiness, wantonness, waste, wastefulness.

antonyms morality, parsimony, thrift, uprightness.

profligate *adj* abandoned, corrupt, Cyprian, debauched, degenerate, depraved, dissipated, dissolute, extravagant, immoderate, immoral, improvident, iniquitous, libertine, licentious, loose, prodigal, promiscuous, reckless, shameless, spendthrift, squandering, unprincipled, vicious, vitiated, wanton, wasteful, whorish, wicked, wild.

antonyms moral, parsimonious, thrifty, upright.

n debauchee, degenerate, libertine, prodigal, racketeer, rake, reprobate, roué, spendthrift, squanderer, waster, wastrel.

profound *adj* abject, absolute, abstruse, abysmal, acute, awful, bottomless, cavernous, complete, consummate, deep, deep-seated, discerning, erudite, exhaustive, extensive, extreme, far-reaching, fathomless, great, heartfelt, heart-rending, hearty, intense, keen, learned, penetrating, philosophical, pronounced, recondite, sagacious, sage, serious, sincere, skilled, subtle, thoroughgoing, thoughtful, total, utter, weighty, wise, yawning.

antonyms mild, shallow, slight.

profoundly *adv* abjectly, acutely, awfully, deeply, dreadfully, extremely, greatly, heartily, intensely, keenly, seriously, sincerely, thoroughly.

antonym slightly.

profundity *n* abstruseness, acuity, acumen, depth, erudition, extremity, insight, intelligence, intensity, learning, penetration, perceptiveness, perspecuity, perspicacity, profoundness, sagacity, seriousness, severity, strength, wisdom.

antonym shallowness.

profuse *adj* abundant, ample, bountiful, copious, excessive, extravagant, exuberant, fulsome, generous, immoderate, large-handed, lavish, liberal, luxuriant, open-handed, over the top, overflowing, plentiful, prodigal, prolific, teeming, unstinting.

antonyms sparing, sparse.

profusion *n* abundance, bounty, copiousness, cornucopia, excess, extravagance, exuberance, glut, lavishness, luxuriance, multitude, plenitude, pleroma, plethora, prodigality, quantity, riot, superabundance, superfluity, surplus, wealth.

antonyms sparingness, sparsity.

progenitor *n* ancestor, antecedent, begetter, father, forebear, forefather, forerunner, founder, instigator, mother, originator, parent, precursor, predecessor, primogenitor, procreator, source.

progeny *n* breed, children, descendants, family, issue, lineage, offspring, posterity, quiverful, race, scions, seed, stock, young.

prognosis *n* diagnosis, expectation, forecast, outlook, prediction, prognostication, projection, prospect, speculation, surmise.

prognosticate *v* augur, betoken, divine, forebore, forecast, foreshadow, foretell, harbinger, herald, indicate, portend, predict, presage, prophesy, soothsay.

prognostication *n* expectation, forecast, horoscope, prediction, prognosis, projection, prophecy, speculation, surmise.

programme *n* agenda, broadcast, curriculum, design, line-up, list, listing, order of events, order of the day, performance, plan, plan of action, presentation, procedure, production, project, schedule, scheme, show, syllabus, transmission.

v arrange, bill, book, brainwash, design, engage, formulate, itemise, lay on, line up, list, map out, plan, prearrange, schedule, work out.

progress *n* advance, advancement, amelioration, betterment, breakthrough, circuit, continuation, course, development, gain, growth, headway, improvement, increase, journey, movement, passage, procession, progression, promotion, step forward, way.

antonyms decline, deterioration.

v advance, ameliorate, better, blossom, come on, continue, develop, forge ahead, gain, gather momentum, grow, improve, increase, make headway, make strides, mature, proceed, prosper, travel.

antonyms decline, deteriorate.

progression *n* advance, advancement, chain, concatenation, course, cycle, furtherance, gain, headway, order, progress, sequence, series, string, succession.

antonyms decline, deterioration.

progressive *adj* accelerating, advanced, advancing, avant-garde, continuing, continuous, developing, dynamic, enlightened, enterprising, escalating, forward-looking, go-ahead, growing, increasing, intensifying, liberal, modern, ongoing, radical, reactionary, reformist, regressive, revolutionary, up-and-coming.

prohibit *v* ban, bar, constrain, debar, disallow, forbid, hamper, hinder, impede, interdict, obstruct, outlaw, preclude, prevent, proscribe, restrict, rule out, stop, veto.

antonym permit.

prohibited *adj* banned, barred, disallowed, embargoed, forbidden, interdicted, off-limits, proscribed, taboo, verboten, vetoed.

antonym permitted.

prohibition *n* ban, bar, constraint, disallowance, embargo, exclusion, forbiddal, forbiddance, injunction, interdict, interdiction, negation, obstruction, prevention, proscription, restruction, veto.

antonym permission.

prohibitionist *n* abolitionist, dry, pussyfoot, teetotaller.

prohibitive *adj* excessive, exorbitant, extortionate, forbidding, impossible, preposterous, prohibiting, prohibitory, proscriptive, repressive, restraining, restrictive, sky-high, steep, suppressive.

antonyms encouraging, reasonable.

project *n* activity, assignment, conception, design, enterprise, idea, job, occupation, plan, programme, proposal, purpose, scheme, task, undertaking, venture, work.

v beetle, bulge, calculate, cast, contemplate, contrive, design, devise, discharge, draft, estimate, exsert, extend, extrapolate, extrude, fling, forecast, frame, gauge, hurl, jut, launch, map out, outline, overhang, plan, predetermine, predict, propel, prophesy, propose, protrude, purpose, reckon, scheme, shoot, stand out, stick out, throw, transmit.

projectile *n* ball, bullet, grenade, missile, mortar-bomb, rocket, shell, shot.

projecting *adj* beetling, exsertile, extrusive, extrusory, overhanging, protrudent, protruding, protrusive.

projection *n* blueprint, bulge, calculation, computation, diagram, eaves, estimate, estimation, extrapolation, forecast, jut, jutty, ledge, map, nab, outjet, outjut, outline, overhang, plan, prediction, process, prominence, protrusion, protuberance, reckoning, representation, ridge, shelf, sill.

proletariat *n* canaille, common people, commonalty, commoners, great unwashed, herd, hoi polloi, lower classes, masses, mob, plebs, proles, rabble, working class.

proliferate *v* breed, burgeon, escalate, expand, exuberate, increase, multiply, mushroom, run riot, snowball.

antonym dwindle.

proliferation *n* build-up, concentration, duplication, escalation, expansion, extension, increase, intensification, multiplication, mushrooming, snowballing, spread.

antonym decrease.

prolific *adj* abounding, abundant, bountiful, copious, fecund, fertile, fertilising, fruitful, generative, luxuriant, productive, profuse, rank, reproductive, rich, teeming, voluminous.

antonyms infertile, scarce.

prolix *adj* diffuse, digressive, discursive, lengthy, long, long-winded, prolonged, prosy, protracted, rambling, tedious, tiresome, verbose, windy, wordy.

antonym succinct.

prolixity *n* boringness, circuity, diffuseness, discursiveness, long-windedness, macrology, maundering, pleonasm, prosiness, rambling, tediousness, verbiage, verboseness, verbosity, wandering, windiness, wordiness.

antonym succinctness.

prologue *n* exordium, foreword, introduction, preamble, preface, preliminary, prelude, proem, prolegomena, prooemion, prooemium.

prolong *v* continue, delay, drag out, draw out, extend, lengthen, lengthen out, perpetuate, produce, protract, spin out, stretch.

antonym shorten.

promenade[1] *n* boulevard, esplanade, front, parade, prom, sea-front, terrace, walkway.

promenade[2] *n* airing, breather, constitutional, saunter, stroll, turn, walk, walkabout.

v flaunt, mosey, parade, perambulate, sally forth, saunter, stroll, strut, swagger, walk.

prominence[1] *n* bulge, bump, cliff, crag, crest, elevation, headland, height, hummock, hump, jutting, lump, mound, pinnacle, process, projection, prominency, promontory, protrusion, protuberance, rise, spur, swelling.

prominence[2] *n* celebrity, conspicuousness, distinction, eminence, fame, greatness, importance, markedness, name, notability, outstandingness, precedence, pre-eminence, prestige, rank, reputation, salience, specialness, standing, top billing, visibility, weight.

antonyms inconspicuousness, unimportance.

prominent *adj* beetling, bulging, celebrated, chief, conspicuous, distinguished, eminent, eye-catching, famous, foremost, high-profile, important, jutting, leading, main, noted, noticeable, obtrusive, obvious, outstanding, popular, pre-eminent, projecting, pronounced, protruding, protrusive, protuberant, remarkale, renowned, respected, salient, standing out, striking, top, unmistakable, weighty, well-known.

antonyms inconspicuous, unimportant.

promiscuity *n* abandon, amorality, debauchery, depravity, dissipation, immorality, laxity, laxness, lechery, libertinism, licentiousness, looseness, permissiveness, profligacy, promiscuousness, protervity, wantonness, whoredom, whoring, whorishness.

antonym chastity.

promiscuous *adj* abandoned, accidental, careless, casual, chaotic, confused, debauched, disordered, dissipated, dissolute, diverse, fast, haphazard, heterogeneous, ill-assorted, immoral, indiscriminate, intermingled, intermixed, jumbled, libertine, licentious, loose, mingled, miscellaneous, mixed, motley, of easy virtue, profligate, random, unbridled, unchaste, uncontrolled, undiscriminating, unselective, wanton, whoremasterly, whorish, wild.

antonyms chaste, controlled, selective.

promise *v* assure, augur, bespeak, betoken, bid fair, contract, denote, engage, guarantee, hint at, indicate, look like, pledge, plight, predict, presage, prophesy, stipulate, suggest, swear, take an oath, undertake, vouch, vow, warrant.

n ability, aptitude, assurance, bond, capability, capacity, commitment, compact, covenant, engagement, flair, guarantee, oath, pledge, pollicitation, potential, talent, undertaking, vow, word, word of honour.

promised land land of milk and honey, paradise, Shangri-la, Zion.

promising *adj* able, auspicious, bright, encouraging, favourable, gifted, good, hopeful, likely, propitious, reassuring, rising, rosy, talented, up-and-coming.

antonym unpromising.

promontory *n* cape, foreland, head, headland, hoe, mull, nab, naze, ness, peninsula, point, projection, ridge, spur.

promote *v* advance, advertise, advocate, aggrandise, aid, assist, back, blazon, boost, champion, contribute to, develop, dignify, elevate, encourage, endorse, espouse, exalt, forward, foster, further, help, honour, hype, kick upstairs, nurture, plug, popularise, prefer, publicise, puff, push, raise, recommend, sell, sponsor, stimulate, support, trumpet, upgrade, urge.

antonyms demote, disparage, obstruct.

promotion *n* advancement, advertising, advocacy, aggrandisement, backing, ballyhoo, boosting, campaign, cultivation, development, elevation, encouragement, ennoblement, espousal, exaltation, fanfare, furtherance, honour, hype, plugging, preferment, promo, propaganda, publicity, puffery, pushing, rise, support, trumpeting, upgrading.

antonyms demotion, disparagement, obstruction.

prompt[1] *adj* alert, brisk, eager, early, efficient, expeditious, immediate, instant, instantaneous, on time, punctual, quick, rapid, ready, responsive, smart, speedy, swift, timely, timeous, unhesitating, willing.

antonym slow.

adv exactly, on the dot, promptly, punctually, sharp, to the minute.

prompt[2] *v* advise, assist, call forth, cause, cue, elicit, evoke, give rise to, impel, incite, induce, inspire, instigate, motivate, move, occasion, prod, produce, provoke, remind, result in, spur, stimulate, urge.

antonym dissuade.

n cue, help, hint, instigation, jog, jolt, prod, reminder, spur, stimulus.

prompting *n* admonition, advice, assistance, encouragement, hint, incitement, influence, jogging, persuasion, pressing, pressure, prodding, protreptic, pushing, reminder, reminding, suggestion, urging.

antonym dissuasion.

promptly *adv* directly, ek dum, forthwith, immediately, instantly, on time, posthaste, pronto, punctually, quickly, speedily, swiftly, unhesitatingly.

promptness *n* alacrity, alertness, briskness, dispatch, eagerness, expedition, haste, promptitude, punctuality, quickness, readiness, speed, swiftness, willingness.

antonym tardiness.

promulgate *v* advertise, announce, broadcast, circulate, communicate, declare, decree, disseminate, issue, notify, preconise, proclaim, promote, publicise, publish, spread.

promulgation *n* announcement, communication, declaration, dissemination, issuance, proclamation, promulgating, publication, publicising.

prone[1] *adj* apt, bent, disposed, given, inclined, liable, likely, predisposed, propense, subject, susceptible, tending, vulnerable.

antonym unlikely.

prone[2] *adj* face down, flat, full-length, horizontal, procumbent, prostrate, recumbent, stretched.

antonym upright.

proneness *n* aptness, bent, bias, disposition, inclination, leaning, liability, penchant, proclivity, propensity, susceptibility, tendency, weakness.

antonym dislike.

prong *n* fork, grain, point, projection, spike, spur, tine, tip.

pronounce *v* accent, affirm, announce, articulate, assert, breathe, declaim, declare, decree, deliver, enunciate, judge, proclaim, say, sound, speak, stress, utter, vocalise, voice.

pronounceable *adj* articulable, enunciable, expressible, sayable, speakable, utterable, vocable.

antonym unpronounceable.

pronounced *adj* broad, clear, conspicuous, decided, definite, distinct, evident, marked, noticeable, obvious, positive, striking, strong, unmistakable.

antonyms unnoticeable, vague.

pronouncement *n* announcement, assertion, declaration, decree, dictum, edict, ipse dixit, ipsissima verba, judgement, manifesto, notification, proclamation, promulgation, pronunciamento, statement.

pronunciation *n* accent, accentuation, articulation, diction, elocution, enunciation, inflection, intonation, modulation, speech, stress.

proof *n* assay, attestation, authentication, certification, confirmation, corroboration, demonstration, documentation, evidence, examination, experiment, ordeal, scrutiny, substantiation, test, testimony, trial, verification, voucher.

adj impenetrable, impervious, proofed, rainproof, repellent, resistant, strong, tight, treated, waterproof, weatherproof, windproof.

antonyms permeable, untreated.

prop *v* bolster, buttress, lean, maintain, rest, set, shore, stand, stay, strut, support, sustain, truss, underpin, uphold.

n brace, buttress, mainstay, stanchion, stay, strut, studdle, support, truss.

propaganda *n* advertising, agitprop, ballyhoo, brainwashing, hype, promotion, publicity, puffery, puffs.

propagandist *n* advocate, canvasser, evangelist, indoctrinator, pamphleteer, plugger, promoter, proponent, proselytiser, publicist.

propagate *v* beget, breed, broadcast, circulate, diffuse, disseminate, engender, generate, increase, multiply, proclaim, procreate, produce, proliferate, promote, promulgate, provine, publicise, publish, reproduce, spawn, spread, transmit.

propagation *n* breeding, circulation, communication, diffusion, dissemination, distribution, generation, increase, issuance, multiplication, procreation, proliferation, promotion, promulgation, reproduction, spawning, spread, spreading, transmission.

propel *v* drive, force, impel, launch, push, send, shoot, shove, start, thrust, waft.

antonyms slow, stop.

propensity *n* aptness, bent, bias, disposition, foible, inclination, leaning, liability, penchant, predisposition, proclivity, proneness, readiness, susceptibility, tendency, weakness.

antonym disinclination.

proper *adj* accepted, accurate, appropriate, apt, becoming, befitting, characteristic, conventional, correct, decent, decorous, established, exact, fit, fitting, formal, genteel, gentlemanly, gradely, graithly, individual, kosher, ladylike, legitimate, mannerly, meet, orthodox, own, particular, peculiar, perjink, personal, polite, precise, prim, prissy, punctilious, refined, respectable, respective, right, sedate, seemly, special, specific, suitable, suited, well-becoming, well-beseeming.

antonyms common, general, improper.

property[1] *n* acres, assets, belongings, building(s), capital, chattels, effects, estate, freehold, goods, holding, holdings, house(s), land, means, meum et tuum, possessions, real estate, realty, resources, riches, title, wealth.

property[2] *n* ability, affection, attribute, characteristic, feature, hallmark, idiosyncrasy, mark, peculiarity, quality, trait, virtue.

prophecy *n* augury, divination, forecast, foretelling, hariolation, prediction, prognosis, prognostication, revelation, second-sight, soothsaying, taghairm, vaticination.

prophesy *v* augur, divine, forecast, foresee, foretell, forewarn, hariolate, predict, presage, prognosticate, soothsay, vaticinate.

prophet *n* augur, Cassandra, clairvoyant, divinator, diviner, forecaster, foreteller, Nostradamus, oracle, prognosticator, prophesier, seer, sibyl, soothsayer, tipster, vaticinator.

prophet of doom Cassandra, doomwatcher, Jeremiah, pessimist.

prophetic *adj* augural, divinatory, fatidical, fey, foreshadowing, mantic, oracular, predictive, presaging, prescient, prognostic, sibylline, vatic, vaticidal.

antonym unprophetic.

propinquity *n* adjacency, affiliation, affinity, blood, closeness, connection, consanguinity, contiguity, kindredness, kindredship, kinship, nearness, neighbourhood, proximity, relation, relationship, tie, vicinity.

antonym remoteness.

propitiate *v* appease, conciliate, mollify, pacify, placate, reconcile, satisfy, soothe.

antonyms anger, provoke.

propitiation *n* appeasement, conciliation, mollification, pacification, pacifying, peacemaking, placation, reconciliation.

antonyms angering, provocation.

propitiatory *adj* appeasing, assuaging, conciliatory, mollifying, pacificatory, pacifying, peacemaking, placative, placatory, propitiative, reconciliatory, soothing.

antonym provocative.

propitious *adj* advantageous, auspicious, beneficial, benevolent, benign, bright, encouraging, favourable, fortunate, friendly, gracious, happy, kindly, lucky, opportune, promising, prosperous, reassuring, rosy, timely, well-disposed.

antonym inauspicious.

proponent *n* advocate, apologist, backer, champion, defender, enthusiast, exponent, friend, partisan, patron, proposer, propounder, subscriber, supporter, upholder, vindicator.

antonym opponent.

proportion *n* agreement, amount, balance, congruity, correspondence, cut, distribution, division, eurhythmy, fraction, harmony, measure, part, percentage, quota, ratio, relationship, segment, share, symmetry.

antonyms disproportion, imbalance.

proportional *adj* balanced, commensurate, comparable, compatible, consistent, correspondent, corresponding, equitable, even, fair, just, logistical, proportionate.

antonyms disproportionate, unjust.

proportionally *adv* commensurately, comparably, correspondingly, evenly, pro rata, proportionately.

antonym disproportionately.

proportions *n* amplitude, breadth, bulk, capacity, dimensions, expanse, extent, magnitude, measurements, range, scope, size, volume.

proposal *n* bid, design, draft, manifesto, motion, offer, outline, overture, plan, platform, presentation, proffer, programme, project, proposition, recommendation, scheme, sketch, suggestion, suit, tender, terms.

propose *v* advance, aim, bring up, design, enunciate, have in mind, intend, introduce, invite, lay before, mean, move, name, nominate, pay suit, plan, pop the question, present, proffer, propound, purpose, put forward, put up, recommend, scheme, submit, suggest, table, tender.

antonyms oppose, withdraw.

proposition *n* manifesto, motion, plan, programme, project, proposal, recommendation, scheme, suggestion, tender.
v accost, solicit.

propound *v* advance, advocate, contend, enunciate, lay down, move, postulate, present, propose, put forward, set forth, submit, suggest.
antonym oppose.

proprietor *n* châtelaine, deed holder, freeholder, landlady, landlord, landowner, owner, patron, patronne, possessor, proprietary, proprietress, proprietrix, title-holder.

propriety *n* appropriateness, aptness, becomingness, breeding, correctness, courtesy, decency, decorum, delicacy, etiquette, fitness, gentlemanliness, manners, modesty, politeness, protocol, punctilio, rectitude, refinement, respectability, rightness, seemliness, suitableness.

antonym impropriety.

proprieties *n* civilities, conventions, decencies, decorum, etiquette, niceties, protocol, p's and q's, social graces.
antonym boorishness.

propulsion *n* drive, impetus, impulse, impulsion, momentum, power, pressure, push, thrust.

prosaic *adj* banal, boring, bromidic, commonplace, dry, dull, everyday, flat, hackneyed, humdrum, matter-of-fact, mundane, ordinary, pedestrian, routine, stale, tame, trite, unimaginative, uninspired, uninspiring, unpoetical, vapid, workaday.

antonyms imaginative, interesting.

proscribe *v* attant, ban, banish, bar, black, blackball, boycott, censure, condemn, damn, denounce, deport, doom, embargo, exclude, excommunicate, exile, expatriate, expel, forbid, interdict, ostracise, outlaw, prohibit, reject.

antonyms admit, allow.

proscription *n* attander, ban, banishment, bar, barring, boycott, censure, condemnation, damning, denunciation, deportation, ejection, embargo, eviction, exclusion, excommunication, exile, expatriation, expulsion, interdict, ostracism, outlawry, prohibition, rejection.

antonyms admission, allowing.

prosecute *v* arraign, bring suit against, bring to trial, carry on, conduct, continue, direct, discharge, engage in, execute, follow through, indict, litigate, manage, perform, persevere, persist, practise, prefer charges, pursue, put on trial, see through, sue, summon, take to court, try, work at.

antonym desist.

proselytise *v* bring into the fold, bring to God, convert, evangelise, make converts, persuade, propagandise, spread the gospel, win over.

prospect *n* calculation, chance, contemplation, expectation, future, hope, landscape, likelihood, odds, opening, outlook, panorama, perspective, plan, possibility, presumption, probability, promise, proposition, scene, sight, spectacle, thought, view, vision, vista.

antonym unlikelihood.

v explore, fossick, nose, quest, search, seek, survey.

prospective *adj* anticipated, approaching, awaited, coming, designate, designated, destined, eventual, expected, forthcoming, future, imminent, intended, likely, possible, potential, soon-to-be, to come, -to-be.

antonyms agreed, current.

prospectus *n* account, announcement, catalogue, conspectus, list, manifesto, outline, pamphlet, plan, platform, programme, scheme, syllabus, synopsis.

prosper *v* advance, bloom, boom, burgeon, fare well, flourish, flower, get on, grow rich, make good, progress, succeed, thrive, turn out well.

antonym fail.

prosperity *n* affluence, boom, ease, fortune, good fortune, luxury, plenty, prosperousness, riches, success, the good life, weal, wealth, well-being.
antonym poverty.

prosperous *adj* affluent, blooming, booming, burgeoning, flourishing, fortunate, in the money, lucky, moneyed, opulent, palmy, profitable, rich, successful, thriving, wealthy, well-heeled, well-off, well-to-do.

antonym poor.

prostitute *n* bawd, brass, broad, call-girl, cocotte, courtesan, dolly-mop, drab, fallen woman, fille de joie, fille des rues, floosie, grande cocotte, harlot, hooker, hustler, loon, loose woman, loose-fish, lorette, moll, Paphian, pro, punk, rent-boy, street-walker, strumpet, tart, trollop, trull, vizard-mask, wench, white slave, whore, woman of the town, working girl.

v cheapen, debase, degrade, demean, devalue, misapply, misuse, pervert, profane.

prostitution *n* harlotry, meretriciousness, street-walking, the game, the oldest profession, vice, whoredom, whoring.

prostrate *adj* abject, brought to one's knees, crushed, defenceless, dejected, depressed, desolate, disarmed, done, drained, exhausted, fagged, fallen, flat, helpless, horizontal, impotent, inconsolable, knackered, kowtowing, overcome, overwhelmed, paralysed, pooped, powerless, procumbent, prone, reduced, shattered, spent, worn out.

antonyms elated, erect, hale, happy, strong, triumphant.

v crush, depress, disarm, drain, exhaust, fag out, fatigue, knacker, lay low, overcome, overthrow, overturn, overwhelm, paralyse, poop, reduce, ruin, sap, shatter, tire, wear out, weary.

antonyms elate, exalt, strengthen.

prostrate oneself abase oneself, bend the knee, bow down, cringe, grovel, kneel, kowtow, submit.
antonym exalt oneself.

prostration *n* abasement, bow, collapse, dejection, depression, desolation, despair, despondency, exhaustion, genuflection, grief, helplessness, kneeling, kowtow, obeisance, paralysis, slough of despond, submission, weakness, weariness.

antonyms elation, exaltation, happiness, triumph.

protagonist *n* advocate, champion, chief character, exponent, hero, heroine, lead, leader, mainstay, prime mover, principal, proponent, standard-bearer, supporter.

protean *adj* amoebic, changeable, ever-changing, inconstant, many-sided, mercurial, multiform, mutable, polymorphic, polymorphous, variable, volatile.

antonyms stable, unchanging.

protect *v* care for, chaperon, convoy, cover, cover up for, defend, escort, guard, harbour, keep, look after, preserve, safeguard, save, screen, secure, shelter, shield, stand guard over, support, watch over.

antonyms attack, threaten.

protection *n* aegis, armour, backstop, barrier, buffer, bulwark, care, charge, cover, custody, defence, guard, guardianship, guarding, preservation, protecting, refuge, safeguard, safekeeping, safety, screen, security, shelter, shield, umbrella, wardship.

antonyms attack, threat.

protective *adj* careful, conservationist, covering, custodial, defensive, fatherly, insulating, jealous, maternal, motherly, paternal, possessive, safeguarding, sheltering, shielding, tutelary, vigilant, warm, watchful.

antonyms aggressive, threatening.

protector *n* advocate, benefactor, bodyguard, champion, counsel, defender, father-figure, guard, guardian, patron, protectress, protectrix, safeguard.

antonyms attacker, threat.

protégé(e) *n* blue-eyed boy, charge, dependant, discovery, pupil, student, ward, white-headed boy.

antonym guardian.

protest *n* complaint, declaration, demur, demurral, dharna, disapproval, dissent, formal complaint, objection, obtestation, outcry, protestation, remonstrance.

antonym acceptance.

v affirm, argue, assert, asseverate, attest, avow, complain, contend, cry out, declare, demonstrate, demur, disagree, disapprove, expostulate, insist, maintain, object, obtest, oppose, profess, remonstrate, squawk, take exception, testify, vow.

antonym accept.

protestation *n* affirmation, asseveration, assurance, avowal, complaint, declaration, disagreement, dissent, expostulation, oath, objection, outcry, pledge, profession, protest, remonstrance, remonstration, statement, vow.

protester *n* agitator, demonstrator, dissenter, dissident, rebel, remonstrant, remonstrator.

protocol *n* conventions, courtesies, customs, decorum, etiquette, formalities, good form, manners, politesse, procedure, propriety, p's and q's.

antonym boorishness.

prototype *n* archetype, example, exemplar, mock-up, model, original, paradigm, pattern, precedent, standard, type.

protract *v* continue, draw out, extend, keep going, lengthen, prolong, spin out, stretch out, sustain.

antonym shorten.

protracted *adj* dragged out, drawn-out, extended, interminable, lengthy, long, long-drawn-out, overlong, prolix, prolonged, wearisome, wordy.

antonym shortened.

protrude *v* bulge, come through, exsert, extend, extrude, jut out, obtrude, point, pop, project, protuberate, stand out, start, stick out, strout.

protruding *adj* astrut, exsertive, extrusive, extrusory, jutting, prominent, protrudent, protrusive, protuberant, proud.

antonyms flat, flush.

protrusion *n* bulge, bump, jut, lump, outgrowth, process, projection, protuberance, swelling.

protuberance *n* apophysis, bulb, bulge, bump, excrescence, knob, lump, mamelon, mamilla, outgrowth, process, projection, prominence, protrusion, swelling, tuber, tubercle, tumour, umbo, venter, wart, welt.

protuberant *adj* astrut, beetling, bulbous, bulging, bunched, exsertive, extrusive, extrusory, gibbous, jutting, popping, prominent, protrudent, protruding, protrusive, proud, swelling, swollen.

antonym flat.

proud *adj* appreciative, arrogant, august, boastful, conceited, content, contented, dickty, disdainful, distinguished, egotistical, eminent, exalted, glad, glorious, grand, gratified, gratifying, great, haughty, high and mighty, honoured, illustrious, imperious, imposing, lofty, lordly, magnificent, majestic, memorable, misproud, noble, orgulous, overbearing, overweening, pleased, pleasing, presumptuous, prideful, projecting, raised, red-letter, rewarding, satisfied, satisfying, self-important, self-respecting, snobbish, snobby, snooty, splendid, stately, stuck-up, supercilious, toffee-nosed, vain.

antonym humble.

provable *adj* attestable, confirmable, corroborable, demonstrable, establishable, evincible, testable, verifiable.

antonym unprovable.

prove *v* analyse, ascertain, assay, attest, authenticate, bear out, check, confirm, corroborate, demonstrate, determine, document, establish, evidence, evince, examine, experience, experiment, justify, show, substantiate, suffer, test, try, turn out, verify.

antonyms discredit, disprove, falsify.

proven *adj* accepted, attested, authentic, certified, checked, confirmed, corroborated, definite, dependable, established, proved, reliable, tested, tried, trustworthy, undoubted, valid, verified.

antonym unproven.

provenance *n* birthplace, derivation, origin, provenience, source.

provender *n* comestibles, eatables, eats, edibles, fare, feed, fodder, food, foodstuffs, forage, groceries, grub, nosh, provand, proviant, provisions, rations, supplies, sustenance, victuals.

proverb *n* adage, aphorism, apophthegm, bromide, byword, dictum, gnome, maxim, precept, saw, saying.

proverbial *adj* accepted, acknowledged, apophthegmatic, archetypal, axiomatic, bromidic, conventional, current, customary, famed, famous, legendary, notorious, self-evident, time-honoured, traditional, typical, unquestioned, well-known.

provide *v* accommodate, add, afford, anticipate, arrange for, bring, cater, contribute, determine, equip, forearm, furnish, give, impart, lay down, lend, outfit, plan for, prepare for, present, produce, provision, render, require, serve, specify, state, stipulate, stock up, suit, supply, take measures, take precautions, yield.

antonyms remove, take.

provide for dower, endow, fend, keep, maintain, support, sustain.

antonyms ignore, neglect.

providence *n* care, caution, destiny, discretion, divine intervention, far-sightedness, fate, foresight, forethought, fortune, God's will, karma, kismet, perspicacity, predestination, predetermination, presence of mind, prudence.

antonym improvidence.

provident *adj* canny, careful, cautious, discreet, economical, equipped, far-seeing, far-sighted, frugal, imaginative, long-sighted, prudent, sagacious, shrewd, thrifty, vigilant, wary, well-prepared, wise.

antonym improvident.

providential *adj* convenient, fortuitous, fortunate, happy, heaven-sent, lucky, opportune, timely, welcome.

antonym untimely.

provider *n* angel, benefactor, breadwinner, donor, earner, funder, giver, mainstay, source, supplier, supporter, wage-earner.

providing *conj* as long as, contingent upon, given, on condition, on the assumption, on the understanding, provided, subject to, with the proviso.

province *n* area, bailiwick, business, capacity, charge, colony, concern, county, department, dependency, district, division, domain, duty, employment, field, function, line, orbit, part, pigeon, post, region, responsibility, role, section, sphere, territory, tract, zone.

provincial *adj* bucolic, country, home-grown, homespun, insular, inward-looking, limited, local, mofussil, narrow, narrow-minded, parish-pump, parochial, rural, rustic, small-minded, small-town, uninformed, unsophisticated.

antonyms sophisticated, urban.

provincialism *n* insularity, localism, narrow-mindedness, parochialism, provinciality, regionalism, sectionalism.

antonym sophistication.

provision *n* accoutrement, agreement, arrangement, catering, clause, condition, demand, equipping, fitting out, furnishing, plan, prearrangement, precaution, preparation, prerequisite, providing, proviso, purveyance, purveying, requirement, specification, stipulation, supplying, term, victualling.

antonyms neglect, removal.

provisional *adj* conditional, contingent, interim, limited, pro tem, provisory, qualified, stop-gap, temporary, tentative, transitional.

antonyms definite, fixed, permanent.

provisionally *adv* for the time being, interim, meanwhile, pro tem, pro tempore.

provisions *n* comestibles, eatables, eats, edibles, fare, food, foodstuff, groceries, grub, piece, prog, provand, provender, proviant, rations, stores, supplies, sustenance, viands, viaticum, victuallage, victuals, vittles.

proviso *n* clause, condition, limitation, provision, qualification, requirement, reservation, restriction, rider, small print, stipulation.

provisory *adj* conditional, interim, provisional, qualified, temporary, tentative.

antonyms definite, fixed, permanent.

provocation *n* affront, aggravation, annoyance, casus belli, cause, challenge, dare, grievance, grounds, incitement, indignity, inducement, injury, instigation, insult, justification, motivation, motive, offence, reason, red rag, stimulus, taunt, vexation.

provocative *adj* abusive, aggravating, alluring, annoying, arousing, challenging, disturbing, erotic, exciting, galling, goading, incensing, insulting, inviting, offensive, outrageous, provocatory, provoking, seductive, sexy, stimulating, suggestive, tantalising, tempting.

antonyms pacificatory, unprovocative.

provoke *v* affront, aggravate, anger, annoy, cause, chafe, elicit, enrage, evoke, exasperate, excite, fire, gall, generate, give rise to, incense, incite, induce, inflame, infuriate, inspire, instigate, insult, irk, irritate, kindle, madden, motivate, move, occasion, offend, pique, precipitate, produce, promote, prompt, put out, rile, rouse, stimulate, stir, vex.

antonyms pacify, please, result.

provoking *adj* aggravating, annoying, exasperating, galling, infuriating, irking, irksome, irritating, maddening, obstructive, offensive, pesky, pestiferous, tiresome, vexatious, vexing.

antonyms pacificatory, pleasing.

prow *n* bow(s), cut-water, fore, forepart, front, head, nose, prore, stem.

antonym stern.

prowess *n* ability, accomplishment, adeptness, adroitness, aptitude, attainment, bravery, command, daring, dauntlessness, dexterity, doughtiness, excellence, expertise, expertness, facility, genius, heroism, mastery, skill, talent, valour.

antonyms clumsiness, mediocrity.

prowl *v* creep, cruise, hunt, lurk, nose, patrol, range, roam, rove, scavenge, search, skulk, slink, sneak, snook, stalk, steal.

proximity *n* adjacency, closeness, contiguity, juxtaposition, nearness, neighbourhood, propinquity, proximation, vicinity.

antonym remoteness.

proxy *n* agent, attorney, delegate, deputy, factor, locum, representative, stand-in, substitute, surrogate.

prude *n* Mrs Grundy, old maid, prig, puritan, school-marm, Victorian.

prudence *n* canniness, care, caution, circumspection, common sense, discretion, economy, far-sightedness, foresight, forethought, frugality, good sense, heedfulness, husbandry, judgement, judiciousness, planning, policy, precaution, preparedness, providence, sagacity, saving, thrift, vigilance, wariness, wisdom.

antonym imprudence.

prudent *adj* canny, careful, cautious, circumspect, discerning, discreet, economical, far-sighted, frugal, judicious, politic, provident, sagacious, sage, sensible, shrewd, sparing, thrifty, vigilant, wary, well-advised, wise, wise-hearted.

antonym imprudent.

prudish *adj* demure, narrow-minded, old-maidish, overmodest, overnice, po-faced, priggish, prim, prissy, proper, pudibund, puritanical, school-marmish, squeamish, starchy, strait-laced, stuffy, ultra-virtuous, Victorian.

antonyms easy-going, lax.

prudishness *n* Grundyism, old-maidishness, overmodesty, priggishness, primness, prissiness, prudery, pudibundity, puritanism, squeamishness, starchiness, strictness, stuffiness.

antonym laxness.

prune *v* clip, cut, dehorn, dock, lop, pare, reduce, shape, shorten, snip, trim.

prurient *adj* concupiscent, cupidinous, desirous, dirty, erotic, indecent, itching, lascivious, lecherous, lewd, libidinous, lickerish, lustful, obscene, pornographic, salacious, smutty, voyeuristic.

antonym decent.

pry *v* delve, dig, ferret, interfere, intrude, meddle, nose, peep, peer, poke, poke one's nose in, snoop.

antonym mind one's own business.

prying *adj* curious, inquisitive, interfering, intrusive, meddlesome, meddling, nosy, peering, peery, snooping, snoopy, spying.

antonym uninquisitive.

psalm *n* canticle, chant, hymn, paean, paraphrase, song.

pseud *n* fraud, humbug, phoney, poser, poseur, trendy.

pseudo *adj* artificial, bogus, counterfeit, ersatz, fake, false, imitation, mock, phoney, pretended, pseud, quasi-, sham, spurious, ungenuine.

antonym genuine.

pseudonym *n* alias, allonym, anonym, assumed name, false name, incognito, monicker, nom de guerre, nom de plume, pen name, stage name.

psyche *n* anima, awareness, consciousness, individuality, intellect, intelligence, mind, personality, pneuma, self, soul, spirit, subconscious, understanding.

psychiatrist *n* analyst, headshrinker, psychoanalyser, psychoanalyst, psychologist, psychotherapist, shrink, therapist, trick-cyclist.

psychic *adj* clairvoyant, cognitive, extra-sensory, intellectual, mental, mystic, mystical, occult, preternatural, psychogenic, psychological, spiritual, spiritualistic, supernatural, telekinetic, telepathic.

psychological *adj* affective, cerebral, cognitive, emotional, imaginary, intellectual, irrational, mental, psychosomatic, subconscious, subjective, unconscious, unreal.

psychology *n* brains, craft, craftiness, cunning, psychiatry, psychics, slyness, subtlety, wiliness.

psychopath *n* lunatic, madman, maniac, psycho, psychotic, sociopath.

psychotic *adj* certifiable, demented, deranged, insane, lunatic, mad, mental, psychopathic, unbalanced.

antonym sane.

puberty *n* adolescence, juvenescence, maturity, nubility, pubescence, teens, youth.

antonyms childhood, immaturity.

public *adj* accessible, acknowledged, circulating, civic, civil, common, communal, community, exposed, general, high-profile, important, known, national, notorious, obvious, open, overt, patent, plain, popular, prominent, published, recognised, respected, social, state, universal, unrestricted, well-known, widespread.

antonym private.

n audience, buyers, citizens, clientèle, commonalty, community, country, electorate, everyone, followers, following, masses, multitude, nation, patrons, people, populace, population, punters, society, supporters, voters.

public house alehouse, bar, bierkeller, bodega, boozer, brasserie, cantina, dram-shop, hostelry, inn, jerry-shop, local, lush-house, pot-house, pot-shop, pub, roadhouse, tap-house, tavern, tippling-house, vaults.

publican *n* barman, inn-keeper, mine host, padrone, taverner.

publication *n* advertisement, airing, announcement, appearance, book, booklet, broadcasting, brochure, declaration, disclosure, dissemination, divulgation, handbill, issue, leaflet, magazine, newspaper, notification, pamphlet, periodical, proclamation, promulgation, publishing, publishment, reporting, vent.

publicise *v* advertise, blaze, blazon, broadcast, hype, plug, promote, puff, push, spotlight, spread about, write off.

antonym keep secret.

publicity *n* advertising, attention, ballyhoo, boost, build-up, hype, plug, press, promotion, public notice, puff, puffery, réclame, splash.

antonym secrecy.

public-spirited *adj* altruistic, charitable, community-minded, conscientious, generous, humanitarian, philanthropic, unselfish.

antonym selfish.

publish *v* advertise, announce, bring out, broadcast, circulate, communicate, declare, diffuse, disclose, distribute, divulgate, divulge, evulgate, issue, leak, part, print, proclaim, produce, promulgate, publicise, reveal, spread, vent.

antonym keep secret.

pucker *v* compress, contract, crease, crinkle, crumple, furrow, gather, purse, ruck, ruckle, ruffle, screw up, shirr, shrivel, tighten, wrinkle.

n crease, crinkle, crumple, fold, ruck, ruckle, shirr, wrinkle.

puckered *adj* creased, gathered, pursy, rucked, ruckled, wrinkled.

antonym smooth.

puckish *adj* frolicsome, impish, mischievous, naughty, pawky, playful, roguish, sly, sportive, teasing, waggish, whimsical.

antonym solemn.

pudding *n* afters, dessert, dumpling, pud, sweet.

puddle *n* dub, plash, plashet, pool, slop, sop, soss.

pudenda *n* fanny, genitalia, genitals, private parts, privates, pussy, quim.

puerile *adj* babyish, childish, foolish, immature, inane, infantile, irresponsible, jejune, juvenile, naïve, petty, ridiculous, silly, trifling, trivial, weak.

antonym mature.

puff *n* advertisement, blast, breath, commendation, drag, draught, emanation, flurry, gust, mention, plug, pull, smoke, waft, whiff.

v bloat, blow, breathe, dilate, distend, drag, draw, exhale, expand, gasp, gulp, hype, inflate, inhale, pant, plug, praise, promote, publicise, pull, push, smoke, suck, swell, waft, wheeze, whiff, whiffle.

puffed *adj* breathless, done in, exhausted, gasping, out of breath, panting, winded.

antonym vigorous.

puffed up arrogant, big-headed, full of oneself, high and mighty, prideful, proud, swollen-headed, too big for one's boots.

antonym modest.

puffy *adj* bloated, distended, enlarged, inflamed, inflated, oedematous, puffed up, pursy, swollen.

antonym flat.

pugilism *n* boxing, fighting, fistiana, prize-fighting, the fancy, the noble art, the noble science, the prize-ring, the ring.

pugilist *n* boxer, bruiser, fighter, prize-fighter, pug, pugil.

pugnacious *adj* aggressive, antagonistic, argumentative, bare-knuckle, bellicose, belligerent, choleric, combative, contentious, disputatious, hostile, hot-tempered, irascible, petulant, quarrelsome.

antonym easy-going.

puke *v* disgorge, heave, posset, regurgitate, retch, spew, throw up, vomit.

pull *v* attract, cull, dislocate, drag, draw, draw out, entice, extract, gather, haul, jerk, lure, magnetise, pick, pluck, remove, rend, rip, schlep, sprain, strain, stretch, take out, tear, tow, track, trail, tug, tweak, uproot, weed, whang, wrench, yank.

antonyms deter, push, repel.

n advantage, allurement, attraction, clout, drag, drawing power, effort, exertion, force, forcefulness, influence, inhalation, jerk, leverage, lure, magnetism, muscle, power, puff, seduction, tug, twitch, weight, yank.

antonyms deterring, push, repelling.

pull a face frown, glower, grimace, knit one's brows, lower, pout, scowl, sulk.

pull a fast one on cheat, con, deceive, defraud, grift, hoodwink, put one over on, sting, swindle, take for a ride, trick.

pull apart attack, carp at, criticise, dismember, divellicate, find fault, flay, knock, lay into, pan, part, pick holes in, pull to pieces, run down, separate, slam, slate, sunder.

antonym praise.

pull down bulldoze, demolish, destroy, dismantle, knock down, raze, remove.

antonym put up.

pull in arrest, arrive, attract, bring in, bust, clear, collar, come in, draw, draw in, draw up, earn, gain, gross, make, nab, nail, net, park, pinch, pocket, reach, run in, stop, take home.

antonyms lose, pull away, repel.

pull off accomplish, achieve, bring off, carry out, manage, succeed, swing.

antonym fail.

pull out abandon, depart, draw out, evacuate, evulse, leave, quit, retreat, withdraw.

antonym join.

pull someone's leg chaff, deceive, fool, make fun of, tease, trick.

pull the wool over someone's eyes bamboozle, con, deceive, delude, dupe, fool, hoodwink, lead up the garden path, pull a fast one on, put one over on, snow, take in, trick.

pull through rally, recover, recuperate, survive, weather.

antonym fail.

pull together collaborate, co-operate, team up, work together.

antonym fight.

pull up admonish, brake, carpet, castigate, draw in, draw up, halt, lift, raise, rebuke, reprimand, reprove, stop, take to task, tell off, tick off, uproot.

pulp *n* flesh, marrow, mash, mush, pap, paste, pomace, soft part, triturate.

v crush, liquidise, mash, pulverise, squash.

pulpit *n* dais, lectern, platform, rostrum, soap-box, wood.

pulpy *adj* fleshy, mushy, pappy, sloppy, soft, squashy, succulent.

antonym hard.

pulsate *v* beat, drum, hammer, oscillate, palpitate, pound, pulse, quiver, throb, thud, thump, tick, vibrate.

pulsating *adj* oscillating, palpitating, pulsatile, pulsative, pulsatory, pulsing, vibratile, vibrating, vibrative.

pulsation *n* ictus, oscillation, palpitation, vibration, vibratiuncle.

pulse *n* beat, beating, drumming, oscillation, pulsation, rhythm, stroke, throb, throbbing, thudding, vibration.

v beat, drum, pulsate, throb, thud, tick, vibrate.

pulverise *v* annihilate, bray, comminute, crush, defeat, demolish, destroy, flatten, granulate, grind, hammer, levigate, mill, pestle, pound, smash, triturate, vanquish, wreck.

pummel *v* bang, batter, beat, fib, hammer, knead, knock, nevel, pound, punch, strike, thump.

pump *v* catechise, cross-examine, debrief, drive, force, grill, inject, interrogate, pour, probe, push, question, quiz, send, supply.

pump out bail out, drain, draw off, empty, force out, siphon.

pump up blow up, dilate, distend, inflate, puff up.

pun *n* clinch, double entendre, equivoke, jeu de mots, paronomasia, paronomasy, play on words, quip, witticism.

punch[1] *v* bash, biff, bop, box, clout, fib, hit, plug, pummel, slam, slug, smash, sock, strike, wallop.

n bash, biff, bite, blow, bop, clout, drive, effectiveness, force, forcefulness, hit, impact, jab, knock, knuckle sandwich, lander, muzzler, panache, pizzazz, plug, point, sock, thump, verve, vigour, wallop.

antonym feebleness.

punch[2] *v* bore, cut, drill, perforate, pierce, pink, prick, puncture, stamp.

punch-drunk *adj* befuddled, confused, dazed, dizzy, groggy, punchy, reeling, slap-happy, staggering, stupefied, unsteady, woozy.

punch-up *n* argument, brawl, ding-dong, Donnybrook, dust-up, fight, free-for-all, row, ruckus, scrap, set-to, shindy, stand-up fight.

punchy *adj* aggressive, dynamic, effective, forceful, incisive, lively, powerful, spirited, vigorous, zappy.

antonyms feeble, weak.

punctilio *n* ceremony, convention, delicacy, distinction, exactitude, exactness, fine point, finickiness, formality, meticulousness, nicety, particular, particularity, preciseness, precision, punctiliousness, refinement, scrupulousness, strictness.

antonyms boorishness, informality.

punctilious *adj* careful, ceremonious, conscientious, exact, finicky, formal, formalist, fussy, meticulous, nice, overnice, particular, precise, proper, scrupulous, strict.

antonyms boorish, easy-going, informal.

punctual *adj* early, exact, in good time, on the dot, on time, precise, prompt, punctilious, strict, timely, up to time.

antonym unpunctual.

punctuality *n* promptitude, promptness, readiness, regularity, strictness.

antonym unpunctuality.

punctually *adv* on the dot, on time, precisely, prompt, promptly, sharp.

antonym unpunctually.

punctuate *v* accentuate, break, emphasise, interject, interrupt, intersperse, pepper, point, sprinkle.

puncture *n* break, cut, fissure, flat, flat tyre, hole, leak, nick, opening, perforation, rupture, slit.

v bore, cut, deflate, discourage, disillusion, flatten, humble, nick, penetrate, perforate, pierce, prick, rupture, take down a peg or two.

pundit *n* authority, buff, deipnosophist, expert, guru, maestro, master, teacher.

pungent *adj* acid, acrid, acrimonious, acute, aromatic, barbed, biting, bitter, caustic, cutting, fell, hot, incisive, keen, mordant, painful, penetrating, peppery, piercing, piquant, poignant, pointed, sarcastic, scathing, seasoned, sharp, sour, spicy, stinging, stringent, strong, tangy, tart, telling, trenchant.

antonyms feeble, mild, tasteless.

punish *v* abuse, amerce, batter, beat, castigate, chasten, chastise, correct, crucify, discipline, flog, give a lesson to, give someone laldie, harm, hurt, injure, keelhaul, knee-cap, lash, maltreat, manhandle, masthead, misuse, oppress, penalise, rough up, scour, scourge, sort, strafe, trounce.

punishable *adj* blameworthy, chargeable, convictable, criminal, culpable, indictable, unlawful.

punishing *adj* arduous, backbreaking, burdensome, demanding, exhausting, fatiguing, grinding, gruelling, hard, strenuous, taxing, tiring, wearing.

antonym easy.

punishment *n* abuse, beating, chastening, chastisement, come-uppance, correction, damnation, deserts, discipline, jankers, knee-capping, laldie, maltreatment, manhandling, medicine, pain, pay-off, penalty, penance, punition, retribution, sanction, toco, torture, victimisation.

punitive *adj* penal, punitory, retaliative, retaliatory, retributive, revengeful, vindictive.

punter *n* backer, better, bloke, buffer, chap, client, cove, customer, fellow, gambler, guy, individual, josser, oik, person, shaver.

puny *adj* diminutive, dwarfish, feeble, frail, inconsequential, inferior, insignificant, little, meagre, minor, paltry, petty, piddling, pimping, reckling, runted, runtish, runty, sickly, stunted, tiny, trifling, trivial, underfed, undersized, undeveloped, weak, weakly, worthless.

antonyms important, large, strong.

pupil *n* beginner, catechumen, disciple, learner, neophyte, novice, protégé, scholar, schoolboy, schoolgirl, student, tiro, tutee.

antonym teacher.

puppet *n* cat's-paw, creature, doll, dupe, figurehead, gull, instrument, marionette, mouthpiece, pawn, quisling, stooge, tool.

puppet-show *n* bunraku, fantoccini, Punch and Judy show, puppet-play, puppetry.

puppy *n* braggart, cub, jackanapes, popinjay, pup, shaver, whelp, whippersnapper.

purchase *v* achieve, acquire, attain, buy, earn, gain, invest in, obtain, pay for, procure, ransom, realise, secure, win.

antonym sell.

n acquisition, advantage, asset, buy, edge, emption, foothold, footing, gain, grasp, grip, hold, influence, investment, lever, leverage, possession, property, ransoming, support, toehold.

antonym sale.

purchaser *n* buyer, chap, chapman, client, consumer, customer, emptor, hirer, shopper, vendee.

pure *adj* absolute, abstract, academic, antiseptic, authentic, blameless, chaste, clean, clear, disinfected, flawless, genuine, germ-free, guileless, high-minded, honest, hygienic, immaculate, innocent, intemerate, maidenly, modest, natural, neat, pasteurised, perfect, philosophical, real, refined, sanitary, Saturnian, sheer, simple, sincere, snow-white, speculative, spiritous, spotless, stainless, sterile, sterilised, straight, taintless, theoretical, thorough, true, unadulterate, unadulterated, unalloyed, unblemished, uncontaminated, uncorrupted, undefiled, unmingled, unmitigated, unmixed, unpolluted, unqualified, unsoiled, unspoilt, unspotted, unstained, unsullied, untainted, untarnished, upright, utter, virgin, virginal, virginly, virtuous, wholesome.

antonyms adulterated, applied, defiled, immoral, impure, polluted, tainted.

pure-bred *adj* blooded, full-blooded, pedigree, pedigreed, pure-blood, pure-blooded, thoroughbred.

antonyms cross-bred, hybrid, mixed, mongrel.

purely *adv* absolutely, completely, entirely, exclusively, just, merely, only, plainly, sheerly, simply, solely, thoroughly, totally, utterly, wholly.

purgation *n* abstersion, catharsis, cleansing, clearing, depuration, evacuation, exculpation, exoneration, justification, purge, purging, purification, riddance, ridding, vindication.

purgative *n* abstersive, aperient, cathartic, clyster, depurative, diacatholicon, eccoprotic, emetic, enema, evacuant, laxative, purge.

adj abstersive, aperient, cathartic, cathartical, cleansing, depurative, eccoprotic, evacuant, laxative, purging.

purge *v* absolve, absterge, catharise, clean out, cleanse, clear, dismiss, eject, eradicate, exonerate, expel, expiate, exterminate, extract, forgive, get rid of, kill, liquidate, oust, pardon, purify, remove, rid, root out, scour, wash, wipe out.

n aperient, catharsis, cathartic, clyster, depurative, ejection, elimination, emetic, enema, eradication, expulsion, extermination, laxative, liquidation, purgative, removal, witch hunt.

purification *n* absolution, beneficiation, catharsis, clarification, cleaning, cleansing, decontamination, deodorisation, depuration, desalination, disinfection, epuration, filtration, fumigation, furbishing, lustration, lustre, lustrum, mundification, purgation, redemption, refinement, sanctification, sanitisation.

antonyms contamination, defilement, pollution.

purify *v* absolve, beneficiate, catharise, chasten, clarify, clean, cleanse, decontaminate, deodorise, depurate, desalinate, disinfect, epurate, filter, fumigate, furbish, lustrate, mundify, redeem, refine, sanctify, sanitise, shrive, sublimise, wash.

antonyms contaminate, defile, pollute.

purifying *adj* cathartic, cleansing, depurative, lustral, mundificative, purgative, purging, purificatory, refining.

antonyms contaminating, defiling, polluting.

purism *n* Atticism, austerity, classicism, fastidiousness, formalism, fussiness, orthodoxy, over-precision, pedantry, restraint, strictness.

antonyms liberality, open-mindedness, tolerance.

purist *n* Atticist, classicist, formalist, grammaticaster, grammatist, mandarin, nit-picker, pedant, precisian, precisianist, precisionist, quibbler, stickler, vocabularian.

antonym liberal.

adj austere, captious, fastidious, finicky, fussy, hypercritical, nit-picking, over-exact, over-fastidious, over-meticulous, over-particular, over-precise, pedantic, puristic, quibbling, strict, uncompromising.

antonyms liberal, open-minded, tolerant.

puritan *n* bluenose, disciplinarian, fanatic, kill-joy, moralist, pietist, prude, rigorist, spoil-sport, zealot.

antonyms hedonist, libertarian.

adj ascetic, austere, disciplinarian, hard-line, hide-bound, intolerant, moralistic, narrow, narrow-minded, prim, prudish, puritanical, self-disciplined, severe, stern, strait-laced, strict, uncompromising.

antonyms broad-minded, hedonistic, indulgent, liberal.

puritanical *adj* abstemious, abstinent, ascetic, austere, bigoted, disapproving, disciplinarian, fanatical, narrow, narrow-minded, prim, proper, prudish, puritan, rigid, severe, stern, stiff, strait-laced, strict, stuffy, uncompromising, zealous.

antonyms broad-minded, hedonistic, indulgent, liberal.

puritanism *n* abstemiousness, abstinence, asceticism, austerity, bigotry, fanaticism, narrow-mindedness, narrowness, priggishness, primness, propriety, prudishness, rigidity, rigorousness, self-denial, self-discipline, severity, sternness, stiffness, strictness, uncompromisingness, zealotry.

antonyms broad-mindedness, hedonism, indulgence, liberality.

purity *n* blamelessness, chasteness, chastity, clarity, classicism, cleanliness, clearness, decency, faultlessness, fineness, genuineness, immaculateness, incorruption, innocence, integrity, morality, piety, pureness, rectitude, refinement, sanctity, simplicity, sincerity, spotlessness, stainlessness, truth, unspottedness, untaintedness, uprightness, virginity, virtue, virtuousness, wholesomeness.

antonyms immorality, impurity.

purlieus *n* banlieue, borders, bounds, confines, environs, fringes, limits, neighbourhood, outskirts, perimeter, periphery, precincts, suburbs, vicinity.

purloin *v* abstract, appropriate, filch, finger, half-inch, lift, nick, nobble, palm, pilfer, pinch, pocket, prig, remove, rob, snaffle, snitch, steal, swipe, take, thieve.

purport *v* allege, argue, assert, betoken, claim, convey, declare, denote, express, give out, imply, import, indicate, intend, maintain, mean, portend, pose as, pretend, proclaim, profess, seem, show, signify, suggest.

n bearing, direction, drift, gist, idea, implication, import, meaning, point, significance, spirit, substance, tendency, tenor, theme, thrust.

purpose *n* advantage, aim, ambition, aspiration, assiduity, avail, benefit, constancy, contemplation, decision, dedication, design, determination, devotion, drive, effect, end, firmness, function, gain, goal, good, hope, idea, ideal, intention, motive, object, objective, outcome, persistence, pertinacity, plan, point, principle, profit, project, rationale, reason, resolution, resolve, result, return, scheme, service, single-mindedness, steadfastness, target, telos, tenacity, use, usefulness, utility, view, vision, will, wish, zeal.

v aim, aspire, contemplate, decide, design, desire, determine, ettle, intend, mean, meditate, plan, propose, resolve.

purposeful *adj* assiduous, decided, deliberate, determined, firm, fixed, hormic, motivated, persevering, persistent, pertinacious, positive, purposive, resolute, resolved, sedulous, settled, single-minded, steadfast, strong-willed, teleological, tenacious, unfaltering, unswerving.

antonym purposeless.

purposeless *adj* aimless, empty, goalless, gratuitous, motiveless, needless, nonsensical, objectless, pointless, senseless, thoughtless, unasked-for, uncalled-for, unnecessary, useless, vacuous, vain, wanton.

antonym purposeful.

purposely *adv* by design, calculatedly, consciously, deliberately, designedly, expressly, intentionally, knowingly, on purpose, premeditatedly, specifically, wilfully, with malice aforethought.

antonyms impulsively, spontaneously, unpremeditatedly.

purse *n* award, burse, coffers, exchequer, finances, fisc, funds, means, money, money-bag, monkey-bag, pocket-book, porte-monnaie, pouch, prize, resources, reward, sporran, treasury, wallet, wealth.

v close, compress, contract, draw together, pucker, tighten, wrinkle.

pursuance *n* accomplishment, achievement, completion, discharge, effecting, effectuation, execution, following, fulfilment, performance, prosecution, pursuing.

pursue *v* accompany, adhere to, aim at, aim for, aspire to, attend, bedevil, beset, besiege, carry on, chase, check out, conduct, continue, course, court, cultivate, desire, dog, engage in, follow, follow up, go for, gun for, harass, harry, haunt, hold to, hound, hunt, inquire into, investigate, keep on, maintain, perform, persecute, persevere in, persist in, plague, ply, practise, proceed, prosecute, purpose, seek, set one's cap at, shadow, stalk, strive for, tackle, tail, track, trail, try for, wage, woo.

antonyms eschew, shun.

pursuit[1] *n* chase, chevy, hounding, hue and cry, hunt, hunting, inquiry, investigation, quest, search, seeking, stalking, tracking, trail, trailing.

pursuit[2] *n* activity, craft, hobby, interest, line, occupation, parergon, pastime, pleasure, side-line, speciality, vocation.

purvey *v* cater, communicate, deal in, disseminate, furnish, pass on, propagate, provide, provision, publicise, publish, put about, retail, sell, spread, stock, supply, trade in, transmit, victual.

purveyor *n* communicator, dealer, disseminator, propagater, provider, provisor, retailer, stockist, supplier, trader, transmitter, victualler.

push *v* advance, advertise, boost, browbeat, bulldoze, bully, coerce, constrain, depress, dragoon, drive, edge, egg on, elbow, encourage, expedite, force, hurry, hype, incite, influence, inveigle, jockey, jog, joggle, jostle, manhandle, manoeuvre, oblige, peddle, persuade, plug, poke, press, prod, promote, propagandise, propel, publicise, puff, ram, shoulder, shove, speed, spur, squeeze, thrust, urge, wedge, whang.

n advance, ambition, assault, attack, bunt, butt, charge, determination, discharge, dismissal, drive, dynamism, effort, energy, enterprise, go, impetus, impulse, initiative, jolt, knock, notice, nudge, offensive, one's books, one's cards, one's marching orders, onset, onslaught, poke, pressure, prod, shove, the axe, the boot, the bum's rush, the chop, the sack, thrust, vigour, vim, vitality, zip.

push off depart, go away, leave, make a move, make tracks, move, push along, shift, shove off.

pushed *adj* harassed, hard-pressed, hard-up, harried, hurried, in difficulties, pinched, pressed, rushed, short of, strapped, stretched, under pressure.

pushing *adj* aggressive, ambitious, assertive, bold, brash, bumptious, determined, driving, dynamic, enterprising, forceful, forward, go-ahead, high-powered, impertinent, intrusive, presumptuous, purposeful, pushful, pushy, resourceful, self-assertive, thrusting.

antonyms conservative, diffident, unassertive, unassuming, unenterprising.

push-over *n* child's play, cinch, doddle, dupe, easy mark, fall guy, gull, mug, picnic, piece of cake, sinecure, sitting duck, sitting target, soft mark, soft touch, stooge, sucker, walk-over.

antonyms challenge, labour.

pushy *adj* aggressive, ambitious, arrogant, assertive, assuming, bold, bossy, brash, bumptious, forceful, forward, loud, obtrusive, offensive, officious, over-confident, presumptuous, pushing, self-assertive.

antonyms quiet, restrained, unassertive, unassuming.

pusillanimity *n* cowardliness, cravenness, faint-heartedness, fearfulness, feebleness, gutlessness, poltroonery, recreancy, spinelessness, timidity, timorousness, weakness, yellow-streak.

pusillanimous *adj* caitiff, chicken, chicken-hearted, cowardly, craven, faint-hearted, fearful, feeble, gutless, lily-livered, mean-spirited, poltroon, recreant, scared, spineless, timid, timorous, unassertive, unenterprising, weak, weak-kneed, yellow.

antonyms ambitious, courageous, forceful, strong.

pussyfoot *v* beat about the bush, creep, equivocate, hedge, mess about, pad, prevaricate, prowl, sidestep, slink, steal, tergiversate, tiptoe.

pustule *n* abscess, blister, boil, bulla, carbuncle, eruption, fester, furuncle, gathering, impostume, papilla, papule, pimple, pock, ulcer, whelk, whitlow.

put *v* advance, apply, assign, bring, bring forward, cast, commit, condemn, consign, constrain, couch, deploy, deposit, dispose, drive, employ, enjoin, establish, express, fit, fix, fling, force, formulate, forward, frame, heave, hurl, impel, impose, induce, inflict, land, lay, levy, lob, make, oblige, offer, park, phrase, pitch, place, plonk, pose, position, post, present, propose, push, render, require, rest, send, set, set down, settle, situate, state, station, subject, submit, suggest, tender, throw, thrust, toss, utter, voice, word, write.

put across bring home to, communicate, convey, explain, express, get through to, put over, spell out.

put an end to abolish, annihilate, annul, cancel, check, destroy, discontinue, jugulate, kibosh, knock on the head, nullify, put a stop to, put paid to, put the kibosh on, put the lid on, put the mockers on, stem, stop, terminate.

put aside[1] cache, deposit, hoard, keep, lay by, put by, reserve, retain, salt away, save, set aside, stash, stockpile, store, stow.

put aside[2] abandon, bury, discard, discount, dispense with, disregard, forget, ignore, set aside.

put away certify, commit, consume, divorce, eat, imprison, institutionalise, kill, put aside, remove, renounce, replace, repudiate, return, save, shift, store, tidy, wolf.

put back delay, postpone, replace, repulse, reschedule, return.

put down[1] enter, inscribe, log, note, record, register, report, state, transcribe, write down.

put down[2] abash, condemn, crush, defeat, deflate, degrade, destroy, dismiss, disparage, humble, humiliate, kill, mortify, put to sleep, quash, quell, reject, repress, shame, silence, slight, snub, suppress, take down a peg, topple.

put down[3] ascribe, assign, attribute, impute.

put forward advance, introduce, move, nominate, offer, present, press, proffer, propose, recommend, submit, suggest, table, tender.

put in enter, input, insert, key in.

put off abash, confuse, daunt, defer, delay, demoralise, deter, discomfit, disconcert, discourage, dishearten, dismay, dispirit, dissuade, distress, divert, nonplus, perturb, postpone, put out, rattle, reschedule, throw, unnerve, unsettle.

antonym encourage.

put on add, affect, affix, apply, assume, attach, back, bet, deceive, do, don, dress, fake, feign, gain, impose, increase by, lay, make believe, mislead, mount, place, present, pretend, produce, sham, show, simulate, stage, stake, wager.

put one's finger on discover, find out, hit the nail on the head, hit upon, identify, indicate, isolate, locate, pin down, pinpoint, place, recall, remember.

put out affront, anger, announce, annoy, bother, broadcast, circulate, confound, discomfit, discommode, discompose, disconcert, discountenance, dislocate, dismiss, disturb, douse, embarrass, exasperate, exert, expel, extinguish, give out, harass, hurt, impose on, incommode, inconvenience, irk, irritate, issue, nettle, offend, perturb, produce, provoke, publish, quench, release, smother, trouble, upset, vex.

put the wind up agitate, alarm, daunt, discourage, frighten, panic, perturb, scare, sound the alarm, startle, unnerve.

antonym reassure.

put through accomplish, achieve, bring off, conclude, effect, execute, finalise, manage.

put to death execute, exterminate, kill, liquidate, martyr.

put to shame disgrace, eclipse, humble, humiliate, outclass, outdo, outstrip, shame, show up, surpass.

put up accommodate, advance, assemble, board, build, construct, entertain, erect, fabricate, float, give, house, invest, lodge, nominate, offer, pay, pledge, present, propose, provide, put forward, quarter, raise, recommend, shelter, submit, supply.

put up to abet, encourage, goad, incite, instigate, prompt, urge.

antonyms discourage, dissuade.

put up with abide, allow, bear, brook, endure, lump, stand, stand for, stomach, suffer, swallow, take, take lying down, thole, tolerate.

antonyms object to, protest against, reject.

put upon exploit, impose on, inconvenience, take a loan of, use.

put wise alert, apprise, clue in, fill in, inform, intimate to, make wise to, notify, put in the picture, tell, tip off, warn, wise up.

putative *adj* alleged, assumed, conjectural, hypothetical, imputed, presumed, presumptive, reported, reputative, reputed, supposed, suppositional, supposititious.

put-down *n* affront, dig, disparagement, gibe, humiliation, insult, rebuff, sarcasm, slap in the face, slight, sneer, snub.

put-off *n* constraint, curb, damper, deterrent, discouragement, disincentive, hindrance, obstacle, restraint.

antonyms encouragement, incentive.

putrefy *v* addle, corrupt, decay, decompose, deteriorate, fester, foost, gangrene, go bad, mortify, mould, necrose, perish, rot, spoil, stink, taint.

putrescent *adj* decaying, decomposing, festering, mephitic, perishing, putrefying, rotting, stinking.

putrid *adj* addle, addled, bad, contaminated, corrupt, decayed, decomposed, fetid, foosty, foul, gangrenous, mephitic, mouldy, necrosed, noisome, off, putrefied, rancid, rank, reeking, rotten, rotting, sphacelate(d), spoiled, stinking, tainted.

antonyms fresh, wholesome.

put-upon *adj* abused, beset, exploited, harassed, harried, henpecked, ill-used, imposed on, inconvenienced, overworked, persecuted.

puzzle[1] *v* baffle, bamboozle, beat, bewilder, confound, confuse, fickle, floor, flummox, gravel, metagrobolise, mystify, nonplus, perplex, pother, pudder, stump, worry.

n acrostic, anagram, brain-teaser, confusion, conundrum, crossword, difficulty, dilemma, enigma, jigsaw, knot, koan, logogram, logograph, logogriph, maze, mind-bender, mystery, paradox, poser, problem, quandary, question, rebus, riddle, Sphinx, tickler.

puzzle[2] *v* brood, cogitate, consider, deliberate, figure, meditate, mull over, muse, ponder, rack one's brains, ratiocinate, reason, ruminate, study, think, wonder, worry.

puzzle out clear up, crack, decipher, decode, excogitate, figure out, metagrobolise, reason out, resolve, see, solve, sort out, think out, unravel, unriddle, untangle, work out.

puzzled *adj* at a loss, at sea, baffled, bamboozled, beaten, bemused, bewildered, confounded, confused, disorientated, doubtful, flummoxed, in a haze, lost, mixed up, mizzled, mystified, nonplussed, perplexed, stuck, stumped, stymied, uncertain.

antonyms certain, clear.

puzzlement *n* astonishment, bafflement, bamboozlement, bewilderment, confusion, disorientation, doubt, doubtfulness, incertitude, mystification, perplexity, surprise, uncertainty, wonder.

antonyms certainty, clarity, lucidity.

puzzling *adj* abstruse, ambiguous, baffling, bewildering, bizarre, cabalistic, circuitous, confusing, cryptic, curious, enigmatic, equivocal, impenetrable, inexplicable, intricate, involved, knotty, labyrinthine, mind-bending, mind-boggling, misleading, mysterious, mystical, mystifying, peculiar, perplexing, queer, riddling, Sphynx-like, strange, tangled, tortuous, unaccountable, unclear, unfathomable.

pygmy *n* dwarf, fingerling, half-pint, homunculus, hop-o'-my-thumb, Lilliputian, manikin, midget, runt, shrimp, thumbling, Tom Thumb.

antonym giant.

adj baby, diminutive, dwarf, dwarfish, elfin, half-pint, Lilliputian, midget, miniature, minuscule, minute, pint-sized, pocket, pygmaean, small, stunted, tiny, toy, undersized, wee.

antonym gigantic.

pyromaniac *n* arsonist, firebug, fire-raiser, incendiary, pétroleur, pétroleuse.

Q

quack *n* charlatan, cowboy, empiric, fake, fraud, humbug, impostor, masquerader, medicaster, mountebank, phoney, pretender, pseud, quacksalver, sham, spieler, swindler, trickster, witch-doctor.

adj bogus, counterfeit, fake, false, fraudulent, phoney, pretended, sham, so-called, spurious, supposed, unqualified.

antonym genuine.

quackery *n* charlatanism, charlatanry, empiricism, fraud, fraudulence, humbug, imposture, mountebankery, mountebankism, phoniness, sham.

quaff *v* booze, carouse, down, drain, drink, gulp, guzzle, imbibe, knock back, swallow, swig, swill, tipple, tope, toss off.

n bevvy, cup, dram, draught, drink, jorum, slug, snifter, swig.

quagmire *n* bog, everglade, fen, marsh, mire, morass, moss, mudflat, quag, quicksand, slough, swamp.

quail *v* back away, blanch, blench, cower, droop, faint, falter, flinch, quake, recoil, shake, shrink, shudder, shy away, tremble, wince.

quaint *adj* absurd, antiquated, antique, bizarre, charming, curious, droll, eccentric, fanciful, fantastic, freaky, funky, Heath-Robinson, ingenious, odd, old-fashioned, old-time, old-world, peculiar, picturesque, queer, rum, singular, strange, unconventional, unusual, weird, whimsical.

quake *v* convulse, heave, jolt, move, pulsate, quail, quiver, rock, shake, shiver, shudder, sway, throb, totter, tremble, vibrate, waver, wobble.

qualification[1] *n* ability, accomplishment, adequacy, aptitude, attribute, capability, capacity, certification, competence, eligibility, fitness, skill, suitability, suitableness, training.

qualification[2] *n* adaptation, adjustment, allowance, caveat, condition, criterion, exception, exemption, limitation, modification, objection, provision, proviso, reservation, restriction, stipulation.

qualified[1] *adj* able, accomplished, adept, adequate, capable, certificated, certified, competent, efficient, eligible, equipped, experienced, expert, fit, habilitated, knowledgeable, licensed, practised, proficient, skilful, talented, trained.

antonym unqualified.

qualified[2] *adj* bounded, cautious, circumscribed, conditional, confined, contingent, equivocal, guarded, limitative, limited, modificatory, modified, provisional, qualificatory, reserved, restricted.

qualify[1] *v* authorise, capacitate, certificate, empower, endow, equip, fit, graduate, habilitate, permit, prepare, sanction, shape, train.

antonym unfit.

qualify[2] *v* abate, adapt, adjust, alleviate, assuage, categorise, characterise, circumscribe, classify, define, delimit, describe, designate, diminish, distinguish, ease, lessen, limit, mitigate, moderate, modify, modulate, reduce, regulate, restrain, restrict, soften, temper, vary, weaken.

quality *n* aspect, attribute, calibre, character, characteristic, class, complexion, condition, constitution, deal, description, distinction, essence, excellence, feature, fineness, grade, kidney, kind, make, mark, merit, nature, peculiarity, position, pre-eminence, property, rank, refinement, sort, standing, status, superiority, talent, timbre, tone, trait, value, water, worth.

qualm *n* anxiety, apprehension, compunction, disquiet, doubt, fear, hesitation, misgiving, pang, presentiment, regret, reluctance, remorse, scruple, twinge, uncertainty, unease, uneasiness, worry.

quandary *n* bewilderment, confusion, corner, difficulty, dilemma, doubt, embarrassment, entanglement, fix, hole, imbroglio, impasse, jam, kettle of fish, mess, perplexity, plight, predicament, problem, puzzle, uncertainty.

quantity *n* aggregate, allotment, amount, breadth, bulk, capacity, content, dosage, expanse, extent, greatness, length, lot, magnitude, mass, measure, number, part, portion, proportion, quantum, quota, share, size, spread, strength, sum, total, volume, weight.

quarantine *n* detention, isolation, lazaret, lazaretto, segregation.

quarrel *n* affray, altercation, argument, barney, beef, bicker, brattle, brawl, breach, breeze, broil, clash, commotion, conflict, contention, controversy, coolness, debate, difference, disagreement, discord, disputation, dispute, dissension, dissidence, disturbance, dust-up, estrangement, feud, fight, fracas, fratch, fray, misunderstanding, row, rupture, schism, scrap, shouting match, slanging match, spat, split, squabble, strife, tiff, tumult, vendetta, wrangle.

antonyms agreement, harmony.

v altercate, argue, be at loggerheads, be at variance, bicker, brawl, carp, cavil, clash, contend, differ, disagree, dispute, dissent, fall out, fight, find fault, object, pick holes, question, row, spar, spat, squabble, take exception, tiff, vitilitigate, wrangle.

antonym agree.

quarrelling *n* altercation, argumentation, argy-bargying, bickering, contention, discord, disharmony, disputation, dissension, feuding, rowing, strife, variance, vitilitigation, wrangling.

antonyms concord, harmony.

adj at loggerheads, at odds, at variance, bickering, contending, discordant, dissentient, feuding, fighting, rowing, scrapping, squabbling, waring, wrangling.

antonyms amicable, friendly.

quarrelsome *adj* altercative, antagonistic, argumentative, bellicose, belligerent, cantankerous, captious, choleric, combative, contentious, contrary, cross, disputatious, fractious, ill-tempered, irascible, irritable, peevish, perverse, petulant, pugnacious, querulous, stroppy, testy, truculent, turbulent, wranglesome.

antonyms peaceable, placid.

quarry *n* game, goal, kill, object, objective, prey, prize, target, victim.

quarter[1] *n* area, direction, district, division, locality, location, neighbourhood, part, place, point, position, province, quartier, region, section, sector, side, spot, station, territory, vicinity, zone.

quarter[2] *n* clemency, compassion, favour, forgiveness, grace, indulgence, leniency, mercy, pardon, pity.

quarter[3] *n* fardel, forpit, fourth, quartern, term.

v decussate, divide in four, quadrisect.

quarter[4] *v* accommodate, bed, billet, board, house, install, lodge, place, post, put up, shelter, station.

quarters *n* abode, accommodation, apartment, barracks, billet, cantonment, caserne, chambers, digs, domicile, dwelling, habitation, lodging, lodgings, post, quarterage, residence, rooms, station.

quash *v* annul, cancel, crush, declare null and void, defeat, disannul, disenact, invalidate, nullify, overrule, overthrow, quell, repress, rescind, reverse, revoke, set aside, squash, subdue, suppress, void.

antonyms confirm, justify, reinstate, vindicate.

quaver *v* break, crack, flicker, flutter, oscillate, pulsate, quake, quiver, shake, shudder, tremble, trill, twitter, vibrate, warble.

n break, quaveriness, quiver, shake, sob, throb, tremble, trembling, tremolo, tremor, trill, vibration, vibrato, warble.

quay *n* dock, harbour, jetty, levee, pier, wharf.

queasy *adj* bilious, dizzy, faint, giddy, green, groggy, ill, indisposed, nauseated, off-colour, qualmish, qualmy, queer, sick, sickened, squeamish, unwell.

queen *n* beauty, belle, consort, diva, doyenne, empress, goddess, grande dame, idol, maharani, mistress, monarch, nonpareil, prima donna, princess, rani, ruler, sovereign, star, sultana, tsarina, Venus.

queenly *adj* dignified, gracious, grand, imperial, imperious, majestic, noble, regal, royal, sovereign, stately.

antonym undignified.

queer *adj* aberrant, abnormal, absurd, anomalous, atypical, bizarre, cranky, crazy, curious, daft, demented, deranged, deviant, disquieting, dizzy, doubtful, droll, dubious, eccentric, eerie, eldritch, erratic, exceptional, extraordinary, faint, fanciful, fantastic, fey, fishy, freakish, funny, giddy, grotesque, homosexual, idiosyncratic, ill, irrational, irregular, light-headed, mad, mysterious, odd, offbeat, outlandish, outré, peculiar, preternatural, puzzling, quaint, queasy, questionable, reeling, remarkable, rum, screwy, shady, shifty, singular, strange, suspect, suspicious, touched, unaccountable, unbalanced, uncanny, uncommon, unconventional, uneasy, unhinged, unnatural, unorthodox, unusual, unwell, unwonted, weird.

antonyms common, ordinary, straightforward, unexceptional, usual.

v botch, cheat, endanger, foil, frustrate, harm, impair, imperil, injure, jeopardise, mar, ruin, spoil, stymie, thwart, upset, wreck.

queerness *n* aberrance, abnormality, absurdity, anomalousness, atypicalness, bizarreness, crankiness, craziness, curiousness, deviance, drollness, dubiety, dubiousness, eccentricity, eeriness, fishiness, grotesqueness, idiosyncrasy, individuality, irrationality, irregularity, light-headedness, madness, mysteriousness, mystery, oddity, oddness, outlandishness, peculiarity, puzzle, quaintness, shadiness, shiftiness, singularity, strangeness, suspiciousness, uncanniness, uncommonness, unconventionality, unnaturalness, unorthodoxy, unusualness, unwontedness.

quell *v* allay, alleviate, appease, assuage, blunt, calm, compose, conquer, crush, deaden, defeat, dull, extinguish, hush, mitigate, moderate, mollify, overcome, overpower, pacify, put down, quash, quench, quiet, reduce, silence, soothe, squash, stifle, subdue, subjugate, suppress, vanquish.

quench *v* allay, appease, check, cool, crush, damp down, destroy, douse, end, extinguish, overcome, put out, quash, quell, sate, satisfy, silence, slake, smother, snuff out, stifle, suppress.

querulous *adj* cantankerous, captious, carping, cavilling, censorious, complaining, crabbed, critical, cross, cross-grained, crusty, discontented, dissatisfied, exacting, fault-finding, fretful, fussy, grouchy, grumbling, hypercritical, intolerant, irascible, irritable, peevish, perverse, petulant, plaintive, quarrelsome, querimonious, sour, testy, thrawn, waspish, whingeing, whining.

antonyms contented, equable, placid, uncomplaining.

querulousness *n* cantankerousness, captiousness, censoriousness, crabbedness, criticalness, crossness, crustiness, discontent, discontentedness, dissatisfaction, fault-finding, fretfulness, fussiness, grouchiness, intolerance, irrascibility, irritability, peevishness, perversity, petulance, querimony, sourness, testiness, waspishness.

antonyms contentedness, equableness, placidity.

query *v* ask, be sceptical of, call in question, challenge, disbelieve, dispute, distrust, doubt, enquire, misdoubt, mistrust, quarrel with, question, suspect.

antonym accept.

n demand, doubt, hesitation, inquiry, misdoubt, misgiving, objection, problem, quaere, question, quibble, reservation, scepticism, suspicion, uncertainty.

quest *n* adventure, crusade, enterprise, expedition, exploration, hunt, inquiry, investigation, journey, mission, pilgrimage, pursuit, search, undertaking, venture, voyage.

question *v* ask, be sceptical of, catechise, challenge, controvert, cross-examine, debrief, disbelieve, dispute, distrust, doubt, enquire, examine, grill, impugn, interpellate, interrogate, interview, investigate, misdoubt, mistrust, oppose, probe, pump, quarrel with, query, quiz, suspect.

n argument, confusion, contention, controversy, debate, difficulty, dispute, doubt, dubiety, erotema, erotesis, examination, inquiry, interpellation, interrogation, investigation, issue, misdoubt, misgiving, motion, point, problem, proposal, proposition, quaere, query, quibble, scepsis, subject, theme, topic, uncertainty.

questionable *adj* arguable, borderline, controversial, debatable, disputable, doubtful, dubious, dubitable, equivocal, fishy, iffy, impugnable, moot, problematical, queer, shady, suspect, suspicious, uncertain, undetermined, unproven, unreliable, unsettled, vexed.

antonyms certain, indisputable, straightforward.

questioner *n* agnostic, catechiser, catechist, disbeliever, doubter, examiner, inquirer, inquisitor, interlocutor, interrogator, interviewer, investigator, sceptic.

questionnaire *n* answer-sheet, catechism, form, questionary, quiz, test.

queue *n* file, line, line-up, order, procession, sequence, series, string, succession, tail, tail-back, train.

quibble *v* carp, cavil, chop logic, equivocate, pettifog, prevaricate, shift, split hairs.

n carriwitchet, casuistry, cavil, complaint, criticism, equivocation, equivoke, evasion, niggle, objection, pettifoggery, prevarication, query, quiddit, quiddity, quillet, quip, quirk, sophism, subterfuge.

quibbler *n* casuist, caviller, chop-logic, criticaster, equivocator, hair-splitter, logic-chopper, niggler, nit-picker, pettifogger, sophist.

quibbling *adj* ambiguous, captious, carping, casuistic, cavilling, critical, equivocating, evasive, hair-splitting, logic-chopping, niggling, nit-picking, overnice, pettifogging, quidditative, sophistical.

quick *adj* able, active, acute, adept, adroit, agile, alert, animated, apt, astute, awake, brief, bright, brisk, clever, cursory, deft, dexterous, discerning, energetic, expeditious, express, fast, fleet, flying, hasty, headlong, hurried, immediate, instant, instantaneous, intelligent, keen, lively, nifty, nimble, nippy, penetrating, perceptive, perfunctory, precipitate, prompt, quick-witted, rapid, ready, receptive, responsive, sharp, shrewd, skilful, smart, snappy, speedy, spirited, sprightly, spry, sudden, summary, swift, unhesitating, vivacious, wide-awake, winged.

antonyms dull, slow.

quicken *v* accelerate, activate, advance, animate, arouse, dispatch, energise, enliven, excite, expedite, galvanise, hasten, hurry, impel, incite, inspire, invigorate, kindle, precipitate, reactivate, refresh, reinvigorate, resuscitate, revitalise, revive, revivify, rouse, sharpen, speed, stimulate, strengthen, vitalise, vivify.

antonyms dull, retard.

quickly *adv* abruptly, at a rate of knots, at the double, before you can say Jack Robinson, briskly, by leaps and bounds, cursorily, ek dum, expeditiously, express, fast, hastily, hell for leather, hotfoot, hurriedly, immediately, instantaneously, instantly, lickety-split, like a bat out of hell, perfunctorily, posthaste, promptly, pronto, quick, rapidly, readily, soon, speedily, swiftly, unhesitatingly.

antonyms slowly, tardily, thoroughly.

quickness *n* acuteness, agility, alertness, aptness, astuteness, briskness, deftness, dexterity, expedition, hastiness, immediacy, instantaneousness, intelligence, keenness, liveliness, nimbleness, penetration, precipitation, promptitude, promptness, quick-wittedness, rapidity, readiness, receptiveness, sharpness, shrewdness, speed, speediness, suddenness, summariness, swiftness, turn of speed.

antonyms dullness, slowness, tardiness.

quick-tempered *adj* choleric, excitable, explosive, fiery, hot-tempered, impatient, impulsive, irascible, irritable, petulant, quarrelsome, shrewish, snappy, splenetic, temperamental, testy, touchy, volcanic, waspish.

antonyms cool, dispassionate.

quick-witted *adj* acute, alert, astute, bright, clever, crafty, ingenious, intelligent, keen, nimble-witted, penetrating, perceptive, ready-witted, resourceful, sharp, shrewd, smart, wide-awake, witty.

antonyms dull, slow, stupid.

quiescent *adj* asleep, calm, dormant, in abeyance, inactive, inert, latent, motionless, passive, peaceful, placid, quiet, reposeful, resting, serene, silent, sleeping, smooth, still, tranquil, undisturbed, untroubled.

antonym active.

quiet *adj* calm, composed, conservative, contemplative, contented, docile, dumb, even-tempered, gentle, hushed, inaudible, isolated, lonely, low, low-pitched, meek, mild, modest, motionless, noiseless, pacific, passive, peaceable, peaceful, placid, plain, private, removed, reserved, restful, restrained, retired, retiring, secluded, secret, sedate, self-contained, sequestered, serene, shtoom, shy, silent, simple, smooth, sober, soft, soundless, still, stilly, subdued, taciturn, thoughtful, tranquil, uncommunicative, unconversable, undisturbed, uneventful, unexcitable, unexciting, unforthcoming, unfrequented, uninterrupted, unobtrusive, untroubled.

antonyms busy, noisy, obtrusive.

n calm, calmness, ease, hush, lull, peace, quiescence, quietness, quietude, repose, rest, serenity, silence, stillness, tranquillity.

antonyms bustle, disturbance, noise.

quieten *v* abate, allay, alleviate, appease, assuage, blunt, calm, compose, deaden, diminish, dull, hush, lull, mitigate, mollify, muffle, mute, pacify, palliate, quell, quiet, reduce, silence, smooth, sober, soothe, stifle, still, stop, subdue, tranquillise.

antonyms aggravate, discompose, disturb, exacerbate.

quietly *adv* calmly, composedly, confidentially, contentedly, demurely, diffidently, dispassionately, docilely, gently, humbly, inaudibly, meekly, mildly, modestly, mutely, noiselessly, obediently, patiently, peacefully, placidly, privately, secretly, serenely, silently, softly, soundlessly, surreptitiously, tranquilly, undemonstratively, unobtrusively, unostentatiously, unpretentiously.

antonyms noisily, obtrusively.

quietness *n* calm, calmness, composure, dullness, hush, inactivity, inertia, lull, peace, placidity, quiescence, quiet, quietude, repose, serenity, silence, still, stillness, tranquillity, uneventfulness.

antonyms activity, bustle, commotion, disturbance, noise, racket.

quietus *n* acquittance, coup de grâce, death, death-blow, death-stroke, decease, demise, discharge, dispatch, end, extinction, finishing stroke, quittance, silencing.

quilt *n* bed quilt, bedcover, bedspread, comforter, counterpane, coverlet, Downie®, duvet, eiderdown, Federbett.

quintessence *n* core, distillation, embodiment, essence, exemplar, extract, gist, heart, kernel, marrow, pattern, pith, quiddity, soul, spirit, sum and substance.

quintessential *adj* archetypical, complete, consummate, definitive, entire, essential, ideal, perfect, prototypical, ultimate.

quip *n* bon mot, carriwitchet, crack, epigram, gag, gibe, jest, jeu d'esprit, joke, mot, one-liner, pleasantry, quirk, retort, riposte, sally, wisecrack, witticism.

v gag, gibe, jest, joke, quirk, retort, riposte, wisecrack.

quirk *n* aberration, caprice, characteristic, curiosity, eccentricity, fancy, fetish, foible, freak, habit, idiosyncrasy, kink, mannerism, oddity, oddness, peculiarity, singularity, trait, turn, twist, vagary, warp, whim.

quisling *n* betrayer, collaborationist, collaborator, fifth columnist, Judas, puppet, renegade, traitor, turncoat.

quit *v* abandon, abdicate, apostatise, cease, conclude, decamp, depart, desert, disappear, discontinue, drop, end, exit, forsake, give up, go, halt, leave, relinquish, renege, renounce, repudiate, resign, retire, stop, surrender, suspend, vamoose, vanish, withdraw.

quit of clear of, discharged from, done with, finished with, free of, released from, rid of.

quite *adv* absolutely, comparatively, completely, entirely, exactly, fairly, fully, moderately, perfectly, precisely, rather, relatively, somewhat, totally, utterly, wholly.

quits *adj* equal, even, level, square.

quitter *n* apostate, defector, delinquent, deserter, rat, recreant, renegade, shirker, skiver.

quiver *v* agitate, bicker, convulse, flichter, flicker, flutter, oscillate, palpitate, pulsate, quake, quaver, shake, shiver, shudder, tremble, vibrate, wobble.

n convulsion, flicker, flutter, oscillation, palpitation, pulsation, shake, shiver, shudder, spasm, throb, tic, tremble, tremor, vibration, wobble.

quixotic *adj* chivalrous, extravagant, fanciful, fantastical, idealistic, impetuous, impracticable, impulsive, romantic, starry-eyed, unrealistic, unworldly, Utopian, visionary.

antonyms hard-headed, practical, realistic.

quiz *n* catechism, examination, investigation, questioning, questionnaire, test.

v ask, catechise, cross-examine, cross-question, debrief, examine, grill, interrogate, investigate, pump, question.

quizzical *adj* amused, arch, bantering, curious, humorous, inquiring, mocking, questioning, sardonic, satirical, sceptical, teasing, waggish, whimsical.

quizzicality *n* archness, humorousness, humour, mockery, satiricalness, scepticism, teasing, waggishness, whimsicality.

quota *n* allocation, allowance, assignment, cut, part, percentage, portion, proportion, quotum, ration, share, slice, whack.

quotation[1] *n* citation, crib, cutting, excerpt, extract, gobbet, locus classicus, passage, piece, quote, reference, remnant.

quotation[2] *n* charge, cost, estimate, figure, price, quote, rate, tender.

quote *v* adduce, attest, cite, detail, echo, Hansardise, instance, name, parrot, recall, recite, recollect, refer to, repeat, reproduce, retell.

quoted *adj* above-mentioned, cited, fore-cited, forementioned, instanced, referred to, reported, reproduced, stated.

quotidian *adj* common, commonplace, customary, daily, day-to-day, diurnal, everyday, habitual, normal, ordinary, recurrent, regular, repeated, routine, workaday.

R

rabbit *n* bunny, bunny rabbit, cony, cottontail, daman, dassie, hyrax.

rabble *n* canaille, clamjamphrie, colluvies, commonalty, commoners, crowd, doggery, dregs, faex populi, galère, herd, hoi polloi, horde, masses, mob, peasantry, plebs, populace, proles, proletariat, raffle, raggle-taggle, rag-tag (and bobtail), rascality, riffraff, scum, swarm, tagrag, throng, trash.

antonyms aristocracy, elite, nobility.

rabble-rouser *n* agitator, demagogue, firebrand, fomenter, incendiary, mischief-maker, mob-orator, ringleader, troublemaker, tub-thumper.

Rabelaisian *adj* barrack-room, bawdy, blue, broad, coarse, earthy, extravagant, exuberant, gross, indecent, lewd, lusty, racy, ribald, risqué, robust, salacious, satirical, scabrous, uninhibited, unrestrained, vulgar.

rabid *adj* berserk, bigoted, crazed, extreme, fanatical, fervent, frantic, frenzied, furious, hydrophobic, hysterical, infuriated, intemperate, intolerant, irrational, mad, maniacal, narrow-minded, obsessive, overzealous, raging, unreasoning, violent, wild, zealous.

rabies *n* hydrophobia, rabidity, rabidness.

race[1] *n* chase, competition, contention, contest, corso, dash, derby, foot-race, kermesse, marathon, pursuit, quest, rat race, regatta, rivalry, scramble, sprint, steeplechase.

v career, compete, contest, dart, dash, fly, gallop, hare, hasten, hurry, run, rush, speed, sprint, tear, zoom.

race[2] *n* ancestry, blood, breed, clan, descent, family, folk, house, issue, kin, kindred, line, lineage, nation, offspring, people, progeny, seed, stirps, stock, strain, tribe, type.

race-course *n* circuit, circus, course, dromos, flaptrack, hippodrome, race-track, route, speedway, track, turf.

racial *adj* ancestral, avital, ethnic, ethnological, folk, genealogical, genetic, inherited, national, tribal.

raciness *n* animation, bawdiness, boisterousness, breeziness, buoyancy, doubtfulness, dubiousness, dynamism, ebullience, energy, exhilaration, freshness, gaminess, indecency, indelicacy, jauntiness, lewdness, naughtiness, piquancy, pungency, relish, ribaldry, richness, salaciousness, sharpness, smuttiness, spiciness, suggestiveness, tanginess, tastiness, zest, zestfulness.

rack[1] *n* frame, framework, gantry, gondola, hack, shelf, stand, structure.

rack[2] *n* affliction, agony, anguish, distress, misery, pain, pangs, persecution, suffering, torment, torture.

v afflict, agonise, convulse, crucify, distress, excruciate, harass, harrow, lacerate, oppress, pain, shake, strain, stress, stretch, tear, torment, torture, wrench, wrest, wring.

racket[1] *n* babel, ballyhoo, clamour, clangour, commotion, din, disturbance, fuss, hubbub, hullabaloo, hurly-burly, kerfuffle, noise, outcry, pandemonium, row, shouting, tumult, uproar.

racket[2] *n* business, con, deception, dodge, fiddle, fraud, game, scheme, swindle, trick.

racy *adj* animated, bawdy, blue, boisterous, breezy, broad, buoyant, distinctive, doubtful, dubious, dynamic, ebullient, energetic, entertaining, enthusiastic, exciting, exhilarating, gamy, heady, immodest, indecent, indelicate, jaunty, lewd, lively, naughty, piquant, pungent, Rabelaisian, ribald, rich, risqué, salacious, sharp, smutty, sparkling, spicy, spirited, stimulating, strong, suggestive, tangy, tasty, vigorous, zestful.

antonyms dull, ponderous.

radiance *n* brightness, brilliance, delight, effulgence, gaiety, glare, gleam, glitter, glow, happiness, incandescence, joy, lambency, light, luminosity, lustre, pleasure, rapture, refulgence, resplendence, shine, splendour, warmth.

radiant *adj* aglow, alight, beaming, beamish, beamy, beatific, blissful, bright, brilliant, delighted, ecstatic, effulgent, gleaming, glittering, glorious, glowing, happy, illuminated, incandescent, joyful, joyous, lambent, luminous, lustrous, profulgent, rapturous, refulgent, resplendent, shining, sparkling, splendid, sunny.

antonym dull.

radiate *v* branch, diffuse, disseminate, divaricate, diverge, emanate, emit, eradiate, gleam, glitter, issue, pour, scatter, shed, shine, spread, spread out.

radiation *n* emanation, emission, insolation, rays.

radical *adj* basic, complete, comprehensive, constitutional, deep-seated, entire, essential, excessive, extreme, extremist, fanatical, far-reaching, fundamental, inherent, innate, intrinsic, native, natural, organic, primary, profound, revolutionary, rooted, severe, sweeping, thorough, thoroughgoing, total, violent.

antonym superficial.

n extremist, fanatic, jacobin, left-winger, militant, reformer, reformist, revolutionary.

raffish *adj* bohemian, careless, casual, cheap, coarse, dashing, devil-may-care, disreputable, dissipated, dissolute, flamboyant, flashy, garish, gaudy, gross, improper, jaunty, loud, meretricious, rakish, showy, sporty, tasteless, tawdry, trashy, uncouth, vulgar.

antonyms decorous, proper, sedate, staid.

raffle *n* draw, lottery, sweep, sweepstake, tombola.

rag *v* badger, bait, bullyrag, chaff, chiack, haze, jeer, mock, rib, ridicule, taunt, tease, torment, twit.

ragamuffin *n* dandiprat, gamin, guttersnipe, mudlark, scarecrow, street arab, tatterdemalion, urchin, waif.

ragbag *n* assemblage, confusion, hotchpotch, jumble, medley, miscellany, mixture, olio, olla podrida, omnium-gatherum, pastiche, pot-pourri, salad.

rage *n* agitation, anger, bate, chafe, conniption, craze, dernier cri, enthusiasm, fad, fashion, frenzy, fury, ire, madness, mania, obsession, paddy, passion, style, tantrum, vehemence, violence, vogue, wrath.

v chafe, explode, fret, fulminate, fume, inveigh, ramp, rampage, rant, rave, seethe, storm, surge, thunder.

ragged *adj* broken, deckled, desultory, disorganised, down-at-heel, duddie, erratic, fragmented, frayed, irregular, jagged, moth-eaten, notched, patchy, raguly, rent, ripped, rough, rugged, scraggy, serrated, shabby, shaggy, tattered, tattery, tatty, threadbare, torn, uneven, unfinished, unkempt, worn-out.

raging *adj* enraged, fizzing, frenzied, fulminating, fuming, furibund, furious, incensed, infuriated, irate, ireful, mad, rabid, rampageous, raving, seething, wrathful.

rags *n* clouts, duddery, duds, raggedness, remnants, shreds, tats, tatters.

raid *n* attack, break-in, bust, descent, foray, incursion, inroad, invasion, irruption, onset, onslaught, razzia, sally, seizure, sortie, strike, swoop.

v attack, bust, descend on, do, forage, foray, invade, loot, maraud, pillage, plunder, ransack, reive, rifle, rush, sack.

raider *n* attacker, brigand, cateran, depredator, despoiler, forager, freebooter, invader, looter, marauder, pirate, plunderer, ransacker, reiver, robber, rustler, sacker, thief.

rail *v* abuse, arraign, attack, castigate, censure, criticise, decry, denounce, fulminate, inveigh, jeer, mock, revile, ridicule, scoff, upbraid, vituperate, vociferate.

railing *n* balustrade, barrier, fence, paling, parapet, rail, rails.

raillery *n* badinage, banter, chaff, chiacking, diatribe, dicacity, invective, irony, jeering, jesting, joke, joking, kidding, mockery, persiflage, pleasantry, ragging, repartee, ribbing, ridicule, satire, sport, teasing.

railway *n* line, metro, permanent way, railroad, rails, subway, track, tramway, tube, underground.

rain *n* cloudburst, deluge, downpour, drizzle, fall, flood, hail, mizzle, precipitation, raindrops, rainfall, rains, serein, shower, spate, squall, stream, torrent, volley.

v bestow, bucket, deluge, deposit, drizzle, drop, expend, fall, heap, lavish, mizzle, pour, shower, spit, sprinkle, teem.

rainbow *n* arc, iris, prism, spectrum.

adj iridescent, irisated, irised, kaleidoscopic, nacreous, opalescent, prismatic, rainbow-like, shot, spectral, variegated.

antonym monochrome.

rainy *adj* damp, dripping, drizzly, hyetal, mizzly, pluviose, pluvious, showery, wet.

antonym dry.

raise *v* abandon, activate, advance, aggrade, aggrandise, aggravate, amplify, arouse, assemble, augment, awaken, boost, breed, broach, build, cause, collect, construct, create, cultivate, develop, discontinue, elate, elevate, emboss, embourgeoise, end, engender, enhance, enlarge, erect, escalate, evoke, exaggerate, exalt, excite, foment, form, foster, gather, gentrify, get, grow, heave, heighten, hoist, incite, increase, inflate, instigate, intensify, introduce, kindle, levy, lift, loft, magnify, mass, mobilise, moot, motivate, muster, nurture, obtain, occasion, originate, pose, prefer, produce, promote, propagate, provoke, rally, rear, recruit, reinforce, relinquish, remove, sky, start, strengthen, sublime, suggest, terminate, up, upgrade, uplift.

antonyms debase, decrease, degrade, dismiss, lower, reduce, suppress.

raised *adj* applied, appliqué, cameo, embossed, relief, rilievo.

antonyms engraved, incised, intaglio.

raising *n* abandonment, advancement, aggradation, ascension, assumption, breeding, construction, development, elation, elevation, enhancement, erection, exaltation, fostering, increase, intensification, levitation, lifting, mobilisation, nurture, preferment, promotion, rearing, recruitment, rise, rising, upgrading, upping.

rake[1] *v* accumulate, amass, bombard, collect, comb, drag, enfilade, examine, gather, graze, harrow, haul in, hoe, hunt, make, pepper, ransack, remove, scan, scour, scrape, scratch, scrutinise, search, strafe, sweep.

rake[2] *n* blood, debauchee, degenerate, dissolute, hedonist, lecher, libertine, loose-liver, playboy, pleasure-seeker, prodigal, profligate, rakehell, roué, sensualist, spendthrift, swinger, voluptuary.

antonyms ascetic, puritan.

rakish *adj* abandoned, breezy, dapper, dashing, debauched, debonair, degenerate, depraved, devil-may-care, dissipated, dissolute, flamboyant, flashy, immoral, jaunty, lecherous, libertine, licentious, loose, natty, prodigal, profligate, raffish, sharp, sinful, smart, snazzy, sporty, stylish, wanton.

rally[1] *v* assemble, bunch, cheer, cluster, collect, congregate, convene, embolden, encourage, gather, hearten, improve, marshal, mass, mobilise, muster, organise, pick up, rally round, reassemble, recover, recuperate, re-form, regroup, reorganise, revive, round up, summon, unite.

n assembly, comeback, concourse, conference, congregation, convention, convocation, gathering, improvement, jamboree, meeting, recovery, recuperation, regrouping, renewal, reorganisation, resurgence, reunion, revival, stand.

rally[2] *v* chaff, mock, rag, rib, ridicule, send up, taunt, tease, twit.

ram *v* beat, butt, cram, crash, crowd, dash, drive, drum, force, hammer, hit, impact, jam, pack, pound, pun, slam, smash, strike, stuff, tamp, thrust.

ramble *v* amble, babble, chatter, digress, divagate, dodder, drift, expatiate, maunder, meander, perambulate, peregrinate, range, roam, rove, saunter, snake, straggle, stravaig, stray, stroll, traipse, walk, wander, wind, zigzag.

n divagation, excursion, hike, perambulation, peregrination, roaming, roving, saunter, stroll, tour, traipse, trip, walk.

rambler *n* drifter, globe-trotter, hiker, peregrinator, roamer, rover, stroller, walker, wanderer, wayfarer.

rambling *adj* circuitous, desultory, diffuse, digressive, disconnected, discursive, disjointed, excursive, incoherent, irregular, long-drawn-out, long-winded, periphrastic, prolix, sprawling, spreading, straggling, trailing, wordy.

antonym direct.

ramification *n* branch, complication, consequence, development, dichotomy, divarication, division, excrescence, extension, fork, offshoot, outgrowth, ramulus, ramus, result, sequel, subdivision, upshot.

ramp *n* grade, gradient, incline, rise, slope.

rampage *v* rage, rant, rave, run amuck, run riot, run wild, rush, storm, tear.

n destruction, frenzy, furore, fury, rage, storm, tempest, tumult, uproar, violence.

rampant *adj* aggressive, dominant, epidemic, erect, excessive, exuberant, fierce, flagrant, luxuriant, outrageous, prevalent, prodigal, profuse, raging, rampaging, rank, rearing, rife, riotous, standing, unbridled, unchecked, uncontrollable, uncontrolled, ungovernable, unrestrained, upright, vehement, violent, wanton, widespread, wild.

rampart *n* barricade, bastion, breastwork, bulwark, defence, earthwork, embankment, fence, fort, fortification, guard, parapet, security, stronghold, vallum, wall.

ramshackle *adj* broken-down, crumbling, decrepit, derelict, dilapidated, flimsy, haywire, jerry-built, rickety, shaky, tottering, tumbledown, unsafe, unsteady.

antonyms solid, stable.

ranch *n* estancia, estate, farm, hacienda, plantation, station.

rancid *adj* bad, fetid, foul, frowsty, fusty, musty, off, putrid, rank, reasty, rotten, sour, stale, strong-smelling, tainted.

antonym sweet.

rancorous *adj* acrimonious, bitter, hostile, implacable, malevolent, malignant, resentful, spiteful, splenetic, vengeful, venomous, vindictive, virulent.

rancour *n* acrimony, animosity, animus, antipathy, bitterness, enmity, grudge, hate, hatred, hostility, ill-feeling, ill-will, malevolence, malice, malignity, resentfulness, resentment, spite, spleen, venom, vindictiveness.

random *adj* accidental, adventitious, aimless, arbitrary, casual, chance, desultory, fortuitous, haphazard, incidental, indiscriminate, purposeless, scattershot, spot, stray, unfocused, unplanned, unpremeditated.

antonyms deliberate, systematic.

randy *adj* amorous, aroused, concupiscent, goatish, horny, hot, lascivious, lecherous, lustful, raunchy, satyric, sexy, turned-on.

range *n* amplitude, area, assortment, band, bounds, chain, class, collection, compass, confines, diapason, distance, domain, extent, field, file, gamme, gamut, kind, latitude, limits, line, lot, orbit, order, palette, parameters, province, purview, radius, raik, rank, reach, row, scale, scope, selection, sequence, series, sort, span, spectrum, sphere, string, sweep, tessitura, tier, variety.

v aim, align, arrange, array, bracket, catalogue, categorise, class, classify, cruise, direct, dispose, explore, extend, file, fluctuate, go, grade, group, level, order, pigeonhole, point, raik, ramble, rank, reach, roam, rove, run, straggle, stravaig, stray, stretch, stroll, sweep, train, traverse, wander.

rangy *adj* gangling, lanky, leggy, long-legged, rawboned, skinny, weedy.

antonyms compact, dumpy.

rank[1] *n* caste, class, classification, column, condition, degree, dignity, division, echelon, estate, état, file, formation, grade, group, level, line, nobility, order, position, quality, range, row, series, sort, standing, station, status, stratum, tier, type.

v align, arrange, array, class, classify, dispose, grade, locate, marshal, order, organise, place, position, range, sort.

rank[2] *adj* absolute, abundant, abusive, arrant, atrocious, bad, blatant, coarse, complete, crass, dense, disagreeable, disgusting, downright, egregious, excessive, extravagant, exuberant, fetid, filthy, flagrant, flourishing, foul, fusty, gamy, glaring, gross, indecent, lush, luxuriant, mephitic, musty, nasty, noisome, noxious, obscene, off, offensive, out-and-out, outrageous, productive, profuse, pungent, putrid, rampant, rancid, repulsive, revolting, scurrilous, sheer, shocking, stale, stinking, strong-smelling, thorough, thoroughgoing, total, undisguised, unmitigated, utter, vigorous, vulgar.

antonyms sparse, sweet.

rankle *v* anger, annoy, chafe, embitter, fester, gall, irk, irritate, nettle, peeve, rile.

ransack *v* comb, depredate, despoil, explore, gut, loot, maraud, pillage, plunder, raid, rake, ravage, rifle, rummage, sack, scour, search, strip.

ransom *n* deliverance, liberation, money, payment, pay-off, price, redemption, release, rescue.

v buy out, deliver, extricate, liberate, redeem, release, rescue.

rant *v* bellow, bluster, cry, declaim, mouth it, rave, roar, shout, slang-whang, spout, tub-thump, vociferate, yell.

n bluster, bombast, declamation, diatribe, fanfaronade, harangue, philippic, rhetoric, storm, tirade, tub-thumping, vociferation.

rap *v* bark, castigate, censure, chat, confabulate, converse, crack, criticise, discourse, flirt, hit, knock, pan, reprimand, scold, strike, talk, tap.

n blame, blow, castigation, censure, chat, chiding, clout, colloquy, confabulation, conversation, crack, dialogue, discourse, discussion, knock, punishment, rebuke, reprimand, responsibility, sentence, talk, tap.

rapacious *adj* avaricious, esurient, extortionate, grasping, greedy, insatiable, marauding, plundering, predatory, preying, ravening, ravenous, usurious, voracious, vulturine, vulturish, vulturous, wolfish, wolvish.

rapacity *n* avarice, avidity, cupidity, esurience, esuriency, graspingness, greed, greediness, insatiableness, predatoriness, rapaciousness, ravenousness, shark's manners, usury, voraciousness, voracity, wolfishness.

rape *n* abuse, defilement, deflowering, depredation, desecration, despoilment, despoliation, maltreatment, outrage, perversion, pillage, plundering, rapine, ravaging, ravishment, sack, spoliation, violation.

v assault, despoil, loot, pillage, plunder, ransack, ravish, sack, spoliate, stuprate, violate.

rapid *adj* brisk, expeditious, express, fast, fleet, flying, hasty, headlong, hurried, precipitate, prompt, quick, speedy, swift, tantivy.

antonyms leisurely, slow, sluggish.

rapidity *n* alacrity, briskness, celerity, dispatch, expedition, expeditiousness, fleetness, haste, hurry, precipitateness, promptitude, promptness, quickness, rush, speed, speediness, swiftness, velocity.

antonym slowness.

rapidly *adv* briskly, expeditiously, fast, hastily, hurriedly, lickety-split, precipitately, promptly, quickly, speedily, swiftly.

antonym slowly.

rapids *n* dalles, white water, wild water.

rapine *n* depredation, despoilment, despoliation, looting, marauding, pillage, plunder, ransacking, rape, ravaging, robbery, sack, sacking, seizure, spoliation, theft.

rapport *n* affinity, bond, compatibility, empathy, harmony, link, relationship, sympathy, understanding.

rapprochement *n* agreement, détente, harmonisation, reconcilement, reconciliation, reunion, softening.

rapscallion *n* blackguard, cad, cur, disgrace, good-for-nothing, knave, ne'er-do-well, rascal, reprobate, rogue, scallywag, scamp, scoundrel, wastrel, wretch.

rapt *adj* absorbed, beatific, bewitched, captivated, charmed, delighted, ecstatic, enchanted, engrossed, enraptured, enthralled, entranced, fascinated, gripped, held, intent, preoccupied, rapturous, ravished, spellbound, transported.

rapture *n* beatitude, bliss, delectation, delight, ecstasy, enthusiasm, entrancement, euphoria, exaltation, felicity, happiness, joy, ravishment, rhapsody, spell, transport.

rapturous *adj* blissful, delighted, ecstatic, enthusiastic, entranced, euphoric, exalted, happy, joyful, joyous, overjoyed, ravished, rhapsodic, transported.

rare *adj* admirable, choice, curious, excellent, exceptional, exquisite, extreme, few, fine, great, incomparable, infrequent, invaluable, peerless, precious, priceless, recherché, rich, scarce, singular, sparse, sporadic, strange, superb, superlative, uncommon, unusual.

antonyms abundant, common, usual.

rarefied *adj* clannish, cliquish, elevated, esoteric, exalted, exclusive, high, lofty, noble, occult, private, refined, select, spiritual, sublime.

rarely *adv* atypically, exceptionally, extraordinarily, finely, hardly, infrequently, little, notably, remarkably, seldom, singularly, uncommonly, unusually.

antonyms frequently, often.

raring *adj* agog, athirst, avid, desperate, eager, enthusiastic, impatient, itching, keen, longing, ready, willing, yearning.

rarity *n* choiceness, curio, curiosity, excellence, exquisiteness, find, fineness, gem, incomparability, incomparableness, infrequency, object of virtu, one-off, pearl, peerlessness, preciousness, pricelessness, quality, richness, scarcity, shortage, singularity, sparseness, strangeness, treasure, uncommonness, unusualness, value, worth.

antonyms commonness, commonplace.

rascal *n* blackguard, caitiff, cullion, devil, disgrace, good-for-nothing, hellion, hempy, imp, knave, loon, lorel, losel, miscreant, ne'er-do-well, rake, ra(p)scallion, reprobate, rogue, scallywag, scamp, scoundrel, skeesicks, spalpeen, toe-rag, toe-ragger, varmint, villain, wastrel, wretch.

rascally *adj* bad, base, crooked, dishonest, disreputable, evil, furciferous, good-for-nothing, knavish, low, mean, reprobate, scoundrelly, unscrupulous, vicious, villainous, wicked.

rash[1] *adj* adventurous, audacious, brash, careless, foolhardy, harebrained, harum-scarum, hasty, headlong, headstrong, heedless, helter-skelter, hot-headed, ill-advised, ill-considered, impetuous, imprudent, impulsive, incautious, indiscreet, injudicious, insipient, madcap, precipitant, precipitate, premature, reckless, slap-dash, temerarious, temerous, thoughtless, unguarded, unthinking, unwary, venturesome.

antonyms calculating, careful, considered, wary.

rash[2] *n* epidemic, eruption, exanthem(a), flood, hives, nettlerash, outbreak, plague, pompholyx, series, spate, succession, urticaria, wave.

rashness *n* adventurousness, audacity, brashness, carelessness, foolhardiness, hastiness, heedlessness, incaution, incautiousness, indiscretion, precipitance, precipitation, precipitency, recklessness, temerity, thoughtlessness.

antonyms carefuleness, cautiousness.

rasp *n* croak, grating, grinding, harshness, hoarseness, scrape, scratch.

v abrade, croak, excoriate, file, grate, grind, irk, irritate, jar, rub, sand, scour, scrape.

rasping *adj* creaking, croaking, croaky, grating, gravelly, gruff, harsh, hoarse, husky, jarring, raspy, raucous, rough, scratchy, stridulant.

rat *n* cad, ratfink, renegade, swine, turncoat.

rate[1] *n* basis, charge, class, classification, cost, degree, dues, duty, fee, figure, gait, grade, hire, measure, pace, percentage, position, price, proportion, quality, rank, rating, ratio, reckoning, relation, scale, speed, standard, status, tariff, tax, tempo, time, toll, value, velocity, worth.

v adjudge, admire, appraise, assess, class, classify, consider, count, deserve, esteem, estimate, evaluate, figure, grade, judge, measure, measure up, merit, perform, rank, reckon, regard, respect, value, weigh.

rate[2] *v* admonish, berate, blame, castigate, censure, chide, criticise, lecture, rebuke, reprimand, reprove, roast, scold, tongue-lash, upbraid.

rather *adv* a bit, fairly, instead, kinda, kind of, moderately, noticeably, preferably, pretty, quite, relatively, significantly, slightly, somewhat, sooner, sort of, very.

ratify *v* affirm, approve, authenticate, authorise, bind, certify, confirm, corroborate, endorse, establish, homologate, legalise, recognise, sanction, sign, uphold, validate.

antonyms reject, repudiate.

rating[1] *n* class, classification, degree, designation, estimate, evaluation, grade, grading, order, placing, position, rank, rate, sort, sorting, standing, status.

rating[2] *n* castigation, chiding, dressing-down, lecture, rebuke, reprimand, reproof, roasting, row, scolding, telling-off, ticking-off, tongue-lashing, upbraiding, wigging.

ratio *n* arrangement, balance, correlation, correspondence, equation, fraction, percentage, proportion, quotient, rate, relation, relationship.

ration *n* allocation, allotment, allowance, amount, dole, helping, measure, part, portion, provision, quota, share.

v allocate, allot, apportion, budget, conserve, control, deal, dispense, distribute, dole, issue, limit, mete, restrict, save, supply.

rational *adj* balanced, cerebral, cognitive, compos mentis, dianoetic, enlightened, intelligent, judicious, logical, lucid, normal, ratiocinative, realistic, reasonable, reasoning, sagacious, sane, sensible, sound, thinking, well-founded, well-grounded, wise.

antonyms crazy, illogical, irrational.

rationale *n* excuse, exposition, grounds, logic, motivation, philosophy, pretext, principle, raison d'être, reasons, theory.

rationalise *v* elucidate, excuse, extenuate, justify, reason out, reorganise, resolve, streamline, trim, vindicate.

rations *n* commons, étape, food, prog, provender, provisions, stores, supplies.

rattle *v* bang, bounce, bump, clank, clatter, clitter, crepitate, discomfit, discompose, disconcert, discountenance, disturb, faze, frighten, jangle, jiggle, jolt, jounce, perturb, scare, shake, upset, vibrate.

rattle off anote, enumerate, itemise, list, recite, reel off, rehearse, repeat, run through.

rattle on blether, cackle, chatter, gab, gabble, gibber, jabber, prate, prattle, rabbit on, witter, ya(c)k.

ratty *adj* angry, annoyed, crabbed, cross, impatient, irritable, peeved, short, short-tempered, snappy, testy, touchy.

antonyms calm, patient.

raucous *adj* grating, harsh, hoarse, husky, loud, noisy, rasping, rough, rusty, strident.

ravage *v* demolish, depredate, desolate, despoil, destroy, devastate, gut, lay waste, loot, pillage, plunder, ransack, raze, ruin, sack, shatter, spoil, wreck.

n damage, defilement, demolition, depredation, desecration, desolation, destruction, devastation, havoc, pillage, plunder, rapine, ruin, ruination, spoliation, waste, wreckage.

ravaged *adj* battle-torn, desolate, destroyed, devastated, ransacked, shattered, spoilt, war-torn, war-wasted, war-worn, wrecked.

antonym unspoilt.

rave *v* babble, declaim, fulminate, fume, harangue, rage, ramble, rant, roar, splutter, storm, thunder.

adj ecstatic, enthusiastic, excellent, fantastic, favourable, laudatory, wonderful.

ravenous *adj* avaricious, covetous, devouring, esurient, famished, ferocious, gluttonous, grasping, greedy, insatiable, insatiate, predatory, rapacious, ravening, starved, starving, voracious, wolfish, wolvish.

rave-up *n* bash, blow-out, carousal, celebration, debauch, do, orgy, party, shindig, thrash, wing-ding.

ravine *n* arroyo, canyon, chine, clough, defile, flume, gap, gorge, grike, gulch, gully, khor, khud, kloof, linn, lin(n), pass.

raving *adj* berserk, bonkers, crazed, crazy, delirious, frantic, frenzied, furious, hysterical, insane, irrational, mad, manic, rabid, raging, wild.

ravish *v* abuse, captivate, charm, deflorate, deflower, delight, enchant, enrapture, entrance, fascinate, outrage, overjoy, rape, spellbind, transport, violate.

ravishing *adj* alluring, beautiful, bewitching, charming, dazzling, delightful, enchanting, entrancing, gorgeous, lovely, radiant, seductive, stunning.

raw *adj* abraded, bare, basic, biting, bitter, bleak, bloody, blunt, brutal, callow, candid, chafed, chill, chilly, coarse, cold, crude, damp, frank, freezing, fresh, grazed, green, harsh, ignorant, immature, inexperienced, naked, natural, new, open, organic, piercing, plain, realistic, rough, scraped, scratched, sensitive, skinned, sore, tender, unadorned, uncooked, undisciplined, undisguised, undressed, unfinished, unpleasant, unpractised, unprepared, unprocessed, unrefined, unripe, unseasoned, unskilled, untrained, untreated, untried, unvarnished, verdant, wet.

antonyms cooked, experienced, refined.

ray *n* bar, beam, flash, flicker, gleam, glimmer, glint, hint, indication, scintilla, shaft, spark, stream, trace.

raze *v* bulldoze, delete, demolish, destroy, dismantle, efface, erase, expunge, extinguish, extirpate, flatten, level, obliterate, remove, ruin.

re *prep* about, anent, apropos, concerning, regarding, respecting, touching, with reference to, with regard to.

reach *v* amount to, arrive at, attain, contact, drop, fall, get to, grasp, hand, land at, make, move, pass, rise, sink, stretch, strike, touch.

n ambit, capacity, command, compass, distance, extension, extent, grasp, influence, jurisdiction, latitude, mastery, power, purview, range, scope, spread, stretch, sweep.

react *v* acknowledge, act, answer, behave, emote, function, operate, proceed, reply, respond, work.

reaction *n* acknowledgement, answer, antiperistasis, backwash, compensation, conservatism, counteraction, counterbalance, counterbuff, counterpoise, counter-revolution, feedback, obscurantism, recoil, reply, response, swing-back.

reactionary *adj* blimpish, conservative, counter-revolutionary, obscurantist, obstructive, reactionist, rightist.

antonyms progressive, radical, revolutionary.

n Colonel Blimp, conservative, counter-revolutionary, die-hard, obscurantist, obstructionist, reactionist, rightist, right-winger.

antonyms progressive, radical, revolutionary.

read *v* announce, comprehend, con, construe, decipher, declaim, deliver, discover, display, indicate, interpret, peruse, pore over, recite, record, refer to, register, scan, see, show, speak, study, understand, utter.

readable *adj* clear, compelling, comprehensible, compulsive, decipherable, enjoyable, entertaining, enthralling, gripping, intelligible, interesting, legible, plain, pleasant, understandable, unputdownable.

antonyms illegible, unreadable.

readily *adv* cheerfully, eagerly, easily, effortlessly, fain, freely, gladly, lief, promptly, quickly, smoothly, speedily, unhesitatingly, voluntarily, willingly.

readiness *n* adroitness, alacrity, aptitude, aptness, dexterity, eagerness, ease, facility, fitness, gameness, handiness, inclination, keenness, maturity, preparation, preparedness, promptitude, promptness, quickness, rapidity, ripeness, skill, willingness.

reading *n* book-learning, conception, construction, edification, education, emendation, erudition, examination, grasp, homily, impression, inspection, interpretation, knowledge, learning, lecture, lesson, performance, pericope, perusal, recital, rendering, rendition, review, scholarship, scrutiny, sermon, study, treatment, understanding, version.

ready *adj* à la main, about, accessible, acute, ad manum, adroit, agreeable, alert, apt, arranged, astute, available, bright, clever, close, completed, convenient, deft, dexterous, disposed, eager, expert, facile, fit, game, glad, handy, happy, inclined, intelligent, keen, liable, likely, minded, near, on call, on tap, organised, overflowing, perceptive, predisposed, prepared, present, primed, prompt, prone, quick, quick-witted, rapid, resourceful, ripe, set, sharp, skilful, smart, willing.

antonyms unprepared, unready.

v alert, arrange, equip, order, organise, prepare, prime, set.

real *adj* absolute, actual, authentic, bona fide, certain, dinkum, dinky-di(e), essential, existent, factual, genuine, heartfelt, honest, intrinsic, legitimate, positive, right, rightful, simon-pure, sincere, substantial, substantive, sure-enough, tangible, thingy, true, unaffected, unfeigned, valid, veritable.

antonyms imaginary, unreal.

realisation *n* accomplishment, achievement, actualisation, appreciation, apprehension, awareness, cognisance, completion, comprehension, conception, concretisation, consciousness, consummation, effectuation, fulfilment, grasp, imagination, perception, recognition, understanding.

realise *v* accomplish, achieve, acquire, actualise, appreciate, apprehend, catch on, clear, complete, comprehend, conceive, concretise, consummate, do, earn, effect, effectuate, fulfil, gain, get, grasp, imagine, implement, make, net, obtain, perform, produce, recognise, reify, take in, twig, understand.

realism *n* actuality, practicality, pragmatism, rationality, saneness, sanity, sensibleness.

realistic *adj* authentic, businesslike, clear-eyed, clear-sighted, common-sense, detached, down-to-earth, faithful, genuine, graphic, hard-headed, level-headed, lifelike, matter-of-fact, natural, naturalistic, objective, practical, pragmatic, rational, real, real-life, representational, sensible, sober, true, truthful, unromantic, unsentimental.

antonyms fanciful, impractical, irrational, unrealistic.

reality *n* actuality, authenticity, certainty, corporeality, fact, factuality, genuineness, materiality, nitty-gritty, palpability, realism, tangibility, truth, validity, verisimilitude, verity.

really *adv* absolutely, actually, assuredly, categorically, certainly, essentially, genuinely, indeed, intrinsically, positively, surely, truly, undoubtedly, verily.

realm *n* area, bailiwick, branch, country, department, domain, dominion, empire, field, jurisdiction, kingdom, land, monarchy, orbit, principality, province, region, sphere, state, territory, world, zone.

reap *v* acquire, collect, crop, cut, derive, gain, garner, gather, get, harvest, mow, obtain, realise, secure, win.

rear[1] *n* back, backside, bottom, buttocks, croup, end, hindquarters, posterior, rearguard, rump, stern, tail.

antonym front.

adj aft, after, back, following, hind, hindmost, last.

antonym front.

rear[2] *v* breed, build, construct, cultivate, educate, elevate, erect, fabricate, foster, grow, hoist, lift, loom, nurse, nurture, parent, raise, rise, soar, tower, train.

rearrange *v* adjust, alter, rejig, rejigger, reorder, reposition, shift, vary.

reason *n* aim, apologia, apology, apprehension, argument, basis, bounds, brains, case, cause, common sense, comprehension, consideration, defence, design, end, excuse, explanation, exposition, goal, ground, grounds, gumption, impetus, incentive, inducement, intellect, intention, judgement, justification, limits, logic, mentality, mind, moderation, motive, nous, object, occasion, propriety, purpose, ratiocination, rationale, rationality, reasonableness, reasoning, sanity, sense, sensibleness, soundness, target, understanding, vindication, warrant, wisdom.

v conclude, deduce, infer, intellectualise, ratiocinate, resolve, solve, syllogise, think, work out.

reason with argue, debate, dispute, dissuade, expostulate, make representations, move, persuade, protest, remonstrate, talk, urge.

reasonable *adj* acceptable, advisable, arguable, average, believable, credible, equitable, fair, fit, honest, inexpensive, intelligent, judicious, just, justifiable, logical, moderate, modest, OK, passable, plausible, possible, practical, proper, rational, reasoned, right, sane, satisfactory, sensible, sober, sound, tenable, tolerable, viable, well-advised, well-thought-out, wise.

antonyms crazy, extravagant, irrational, outrageous, unreasonable.

reasoned *adj* clear, judicious, logical, methodical, rational, sensible, sound, systematic, well-thought-out.

antonyms illogical, unsystematic.

reasoning *n* analysis, argument, case, cogitation, deduction, explication, exposition, hypothesis, interpretation, logic, proof, ratiocination, reason, supposition, thinking, thought.

reassure *v* bolster, brace, comfort, encourage, hearten, inspirit, nerve, rally.

rebate *n* allowance, bonus, deduction, discount, reduction, refund, repayment.

rebel *v* defy, disobey, dissent, flinch, kick over the traces, mutiny, recoil, resist, revolt, rise up, run riot, shrink.

n apostate, dissenter, heretic, insurgent, insurrectionary, Jacobin, malcontent, mutineer, nonconformist, revolutionary, revolutionist, schismatic, secessionist.

adj insubordinate, insurgent, insurrectionary, malcontent(ed), mutinous, rebellious, revolutionary.

rebellion *n* apostasy, defiance, disobedience, dissent, heresy, inqilab, insubordination, insurgence, insurgency, insurrection, intifada, Jacquerie, mutiny, nonconformity, resistance, revolt, revolution, rising, schism, sedition, uprising.

rebellious *adj* contumacious, defiant, difficult, disaffected, disloyal, disobedient, disorderly, incorrigible, insubordinate, insurgent, insurrectionary, intractable, malcontent(ed), mutinous, obstinate, rebel, recalcitrant, refractory, resistant, revolutionary, seditious, turbulent, ungovernable, unmanageable, unruly.

antonyms obedient, submissive.

rebirth *n* reactivation, reanimation, regeneration, reincarnation, rejuvenation, renaissance, renascence, renewal, restoration, resurgence, resurrection, revitalisation, revival.

rebound *v* backfire, boomerang, bounce, misfire, recoil, redound, resile, resound, return, ricochet.

n back-wash, bounce, reflection, repercussion, return, reverberation, ricochet.

rebuff *v* cold-shoulder, cut, decline, deny, discourage, put someone's nose out of joint, refuse, reject, repulse, resist, slight, snub, spurn, turn down.

n brush-off, check, cold shoulder, defeat, denial, discouragement, flea in one's ear, noser, opposition, refusal, rejection, repulse, rubber, set-down, slight, snub.

rebuild *v* haussmannise, reassemble, reconstruct, re-edify, refashion, remake, remodel, renovate, restore.

antonyms demolish, destroy.

rebuke *v* admonish, berate, blame, carpet, castigate, censure, chide, countercheck, jobe, keelhaul, lecture, lesson, rate, reprehend, reprimand, reproach, reprove, scold, slap down, tell off, tick off, trim, trounce, upbraid.

antonyms compliment, praise.

n admonition, blame, castigation, censure, countercheck, dressing-down, lecture, reprimand, reproach, reproof, reproval, row, slap, telling-off, ticking-off, tongue-lashing, wigging.
antonyms compliment, praise.

rebut *v* confute, defeat, discredit, disprove, explode, give the lie to, invalidate, negate, overturn, quash, refute.

rebuttal *n* confutation, defeat, disproof, invalidation, negation, overthrow, refutation.

recalcitrant *adj* contrary, contumacious, defiant, disobedient, insubordinate, intractable, obstinate, refractory, renitent, stubborn, uncontrollable, unco-operative, ungovernable, unmanageable, unruly, unsubmissive, unwilling, wayward, wilful.
antonym amenable.

recall *v* abjure, annul, cancel, cast one's mind back, countermand, evoke, mind, nullify, place, recognise, recollect, remember, repeal, rescind, retract, revoke, withdraw.
n abrogation, annulment, cancellation, memory, nullification, recision, recollection, remembrance, repeal, rescission, retraction, revocation, withdrawal.

recant *v* abjure, abrogate, apostatise, deny, disavow, disclaim, disown, forswear, recall, renounce, repudiate, rescind, retract, revoke, unsay, withdraw.

recantation *n* abjuration, apostasy, denial, disavowal, disclaimer, disownment, renunciation, repudiation, retractation, retraction, revocation, revoke, withdrawal.

recapitulate *v* give a resumé, recap, recount, reiterate, repeat, restate, review, sum up, summarise.

recede *v* abate, decline, decrease, diminish, dwindle, ebb, fade, lessen, regress, retire, retreat, retrogress, return, shrink, sink, slacken, subside, wane, withdraw.
antonyms advance, proceed.

receipt *n* acceptance, acknowledgement, counterfoil, delivery, receiving, reception, recipience, slip, stub, ticket, voucher.

receipts *n* gains, gate, income, proceeds, profits, return, take, takings.

receive *v* accept, accommodate, acquire, admit, apprehend, bear, collect, derive, encounter, entertain, experience, gather, get, greet, hear, meet, obtain, perceive, pick up, react to, respond to, suffer, sustain, take, undergo, welcome.
antonyms donate, give.

receiver *n* beneficiary, donee, Fagin, fence, handset, radio, recipient, tuner, wireless.
antonym donor.

recent *adj* contemporary, current, fresh, late, latter, latter-day, modern, neoteric(al), new, novel, present-day, up-to-date, young.
antonyms dated, old, out-of-date.

recently *adv* currently, freshly, lately, latterly, newly.

receptacle *n* container, holder, pantechnicon, repository, reservatory, vessel.

reception *n* acceptance, acknowledgement, admission, do, durbar, entertainment, function, greeting, levee, party, reaction, receipt, receiving, recipience, recognition, response, shindig, soirée, treatment, welcome.

receptive *adj* accessible, alert, amenable, approachable, bright, favourable, friendly, hospitable, interested, open, open-minded, perceptive, responsive, sensitive, suggestible, susceptible, sympathetic, welcoming.

recess *n* alcove, apse, apsidiole, bay, break, cavity, cessation, closure, corner, depression, embrasure, holiday, hollow, indentation, intermission, interval, loculus, niche, nook, oriel, respite, rest, vacation.

recesses *n* bowels, depths, heart, innards, interior, penetralia, reaches, retreats.

recession *n* decline, depression, downturn, slump, stagflation.
antonyms boom, upturn.

recherché *adj* abstruse, arcane, choice, esoteric, exotic, far-fetched, rare, refined, select.
antonym commonplace.

recipe *n* directions, formula, ingredients, instructions, method, prescription, procedure, process, programme, receipt, system, technique.

recipient *n* assignee, beneficiary, donee, grantee, legatee, receiver, suscipient.
antonyms donor, giver.

reciprocal *adj* alternate, complementary, correlative, corresponding, equivalent, give-and-take, interchangeable, interdependent, mutual, reciprocative, reciprocatory, shared.

reciprocate *v* alternate, barter, correspond, equal, exchange, interchange, match, reply, requite, respond, return, swap, trade.

recital *n* account, convert, description, detailing, enumeration, interpretation, narration, narrative, performance, reading, recapitulation, recitation, rehearsal, relation, rendering, rendition, repetition, statement, story, tale, telling.

recitation *n* lecture, narration, party piece, passage, performance, piece, reading, recital, rendering, rendition, telling.

recite *v* articulate, declaim, deliver, describe, detail, enumerate, itemise, narrate, orate, perform, recapitulate, recount, rehearse, relate, repeat, speak, tell.

reckless *adj* careless, daredevil, devil-may-care, foolhardy, harebrained, hasty, headlong, heedless, ill-advised, imprudent, inattentive, incautious, indiscreet, irresponsible, madcap, mindless, negligent, precipitate, rantipole, rash, regardless, tearaway, thoughtless, wild.
antonyms calculating, careful, cautious.

recklessness *n* carelessness, foolhardiness, gallowsness, heedlessness, imprudence, inattention, incaution, irresponsibleness, irresposibility, madness, mindlessness, motorway madness, negligence, rashness, thoughtlessness.
antonym carefulness.

reckon *v* account, add up, adjudge, appraise, assess, assume, believe, calculate, compute, conjecture, consider, count, deem, enumerate, esteem, estimate, evaluate, expect, fancy, gauge, guess, hold, imagine, judge, number, opine, rate, regard, suppose, surmise, tally, think, total.

reckon on bank, calculate, count, depend, figure on, hope for, rely, trust in.

reckon with anticipate, bargain for, consider, cope with, deal with, expect, face, foresee, handle, plan for, take into account, treat.

reckoning *n* account, adding, addition, bill, calculation, charge, computation, count, counting, doom, due, enumeration, estimate, judgement, retribution, score, settlement, summation, working.

reclaim *v* impolder, recapture, recover, redeem, reform, regain, regenerate, reinstate, rescue, restore, retrieve, salvage.

recline *v* couch, lean, lie, loll, lounge, repose, rest, sprawl, stretch out.

recluse *n* anchoress, anchoret, anchorite, ancress, ascetic, eremite, hermit, monk, solitaire, solitarian, solitary, stylite.

reclusive *adj* anchoretic(al), anchoritic(al), ascetic, cloistered, eremitic, hermitical, isolated, monastic, recluse, retiring, secluded, sequestered, solitary, withdrawn.

recognise *v* accept, acknowledge, admit, allow, appreciate, approve, avow, concede, confess, grant, greet, honour, identify, know, notice, own, perceive, place, realise, recall, recollect, remember, respect, salute, see, spot, understand, wot.

recognition *n* acceptance, acknowledgement, admission, allowance, appreciation, approval, avowal, awareness, cognisance, confession, detection, discovery, enlightenment, gratitude, greeting, honour, identification, notice, perception, realisation, recall, recollection, remembrance, respect, salute, understanding.

recoil *v* backfire, boomerang, falter, flinch, kick, misfire, quail, react, rebound, redound, resile, shrink.

n backlash, kick, reaction, rebound, redound(ing), repercussion.

recollect *v* call up, cast one's mind back, mind, place, recall, remember, reminisce.

recollection *n* image, impression, memory, recall, remembrance, reminiscence, souvenir.

recommend *v* advance, advise, advocate, approve, commend, counsel, endorse, enjoin, exhort, plug, praise, propose, puff, suggest, urge, vouch for.

antonyms disapprove, veto.

recommendation *n* advice, advocacy, approbation, approval, blessing, commendation, counsel, endorsement, plug, praise, proposal, puff, reference, sanction, suggestion, testimonial, urging.

antonyms disapproval, veto.

recompense *v* compensate, guerdon, indemnify, pay, redress, reimburse, remunerate, repay, requite, reward, satisfy.

n amends, compensation, damages, emolument, guerdon, indemnification, indemnity, pay, payment, remuneration, reparation, repayment, requital, restitution, return, reward, satisfaction, wages.

reconcile *v* accept, accommodate, accord, adjust, appease, compose, conciliate, harmonise, pacify, placate, propitiate, rectify, resign, resolve, reunite, settle, square, submit, yield.

antonym estrange.

reconciliation *n* accommodation, adjustment, agreement, appeasement, bridge-building, compromise, conciliation, détente, harmony, pacification, propitiation, rapprochement, reconcilement, rectification, reunion, settlement, understanding.

antonyms estrangement, separation.

recondite *adj* abstruse, arcane, cabbalistic, complicated, concealed, dark, deep, difficult, esoteric, hidden, intricate, involved, mysterious, mystical, obscure, occult, profound, secret.

antonyms simple, straightforward.

recondition *v* fix, overhaul, refurbish, remodel, renew, renovate, repair, restore, revamp, sort.

reconnaissance *n* examination, exploration, inspection, investigation, observation, patrol, probe, recce, reconnoitring, scan, scouting, scrutiny, survey.

reconnoitre *v* case, examine, explore, inspect, investigate, observe, patrol, probe, recce, scan, scout, scrutinise, spy out, survey.

reconsider *v* modify, reassess, re-examine, rethink, review, revise, think better of, think over, think twice.

reconstruct *v* reassemble, rebuild, recreate, re-establish, refashion, reform, reformulate, regenerate, remake, remodel, renovate, reorganise, restore.

record *n* account, album, annals, archives, background, career, chronicle, curriculum vitae, diary, disc, document, documentation, dossier, entry, EP, evidence, file, form, forty-five, gramophone record, history, journal, log, LP, memoir, memorandum, memorial, minute, noctuary, performance, platter, recording, register, release, remembrance, report, single, talky, testimony, trace, tracing, track record, witness.

v annalise, chalk up, chronicle, contain, cut, diarise, document, enregister, enrol, enter, indicate, inscribe, log, minute, note, preserve, read, register, report, say, score, show, tape, tape-record, transcribe, video, video-tape, wax.

recorder *n* annalist, archivist, chronicler, chronographer, chronologer, clerk, diarist, historian, registrar, score-keeper, scorer, scribe, stenographer.

recording *n* cut, disc, gramophone record, performance, record, recordation, release, tape, video.

recount *v* communicate, delineate, depict, describe, detail, enumerate, narrate, portray, recite, rehearse, relate, repeat, report, tell.

recoup *v* compensate, indemnify, make good, recover, redeem, refund, regain, reimburse, remunerate, repay, requite, retrieve, satisfy.

recourse *n* access, alternative, appeal, choice, expedient, option, refuge, remedy, resort.

recover *v* convalesce, heal, improve, mend, pick up, pull through, rally, recapture, reclaim, recoup, recuperate, redeem, regain, repair, replevy, repossess, restore, retake, retrieve, revive.

antonyms forfeit, lose, worsen.

recovery *n* amelioration, betterment, convalescence, healing, improvement, mending, rally, recapture, reclamation, recoupment, recuperation, redemption, rehabilitation, repair, repossession, restoration, retrieval, revival, upturn.

antonyms forfeit, loss, worsening.

recreation *n* amusement, distraction, diversion, enjoyment, entertainment, exercise, fun, games, hobby, leisure activity, pastime, play, pleasure, refreshment, relaxation, relief, sport.

recrimination *n* accusation, bickering, counter-attack, counterblast, countercharge, name-calling, quarrel, retaliation, retort, squabbling.

recruit *v* augment, draft, engage, enlist, enrol, gather, headhunt, impress, levy, mobilise, muster, obtain, procure, proselytise, raise, refresh, reinforce, renew, replenish, restore, strengthen, supply, trawl.

n apprentice, beginner, conscript, convert, draftee, greenhorn, helper, initiate, learner, neophyte, nig-nog, novice, proselyte, rookie, trainee, tyro, yob.

rectify *v* adjust, amend, correct, distil, emend, fix, improve, mend, purify, redress, refine, reform, remedy, repair, right, separate, square, straighten.

rectitude *n* accuracy, correctness, decency, equity, exactness, goodness, honesty, honour, incorruptibility, integrity, irreproachability, justice, morality, precision, principle, probity, righteousness, rightness, scrupulousness, sinlessness, soundness, unimpeachability, uprightness, verity, virtue.

recumbent *adj* flat, horizontal, leaning, lounging, lying, prone, prostrate, reclining, resting, sprawling, supine.

antonyms erect, upright.

recuperate *v* convalesce, get better, improve, mend, pick up, rally, recoup, recover, regain, revive.

antonym worsen.

recur *v* persist, reappear, repeat, return.

recurrent *adj* continued, cyclical, frequent, habitual, haunting, periodic, recurring, regular, repeated, repetitive.

recycle *v* reclaim, reconstitute, reprocess, reuse, salvage, save.

red *adj* bay, bloodshot, bloodstained, bloody, blooming, blushing, cardinal, carmine, carroty, cherry, chestnut, coral, crimson, damask, embarrassed, ensanguined, flame-coloured, flaming, florid, flushed, foxy, glowing, gory, gules, healthy, horseflesh, incarnadine, inflamed, Judas-coloured, lateritious, maroon, pink, reddish, rose, roseate, rosy, rubicund, rubied, rubineous, rubious, ruby, ruby-red, ruddy, sandy, sanguine, scarlet, shamefaced, suffused, titian, vermeil, vermilion, wine.

red-blooded *adj* hearty, lively, lusty, manly, robust, strong, vigorous, virile, vital.

redden *v* blush, colour, crimson, flush, rubefy, suffuse.

reddish *adj* bloodshot, ginger, pink, rosy, rubicund, ruddy, rufescent, rufous, russet, sandy.

redeem *v* absolve, acquit, atone for, cash (in), change, compensate for, defray, deliver, discharge, emancipate, exchange, extricate, free, fulfil, keep, liberate, make good, make up for, meet, offset, outweigh, perform, ransom, reclaim, recoup, recover, recuperate, redress, regain, rehabilitate, reinstate, repossess, repurchase, rescue, retrieve, salvage, satisfy, save, trade in.

redemption *n* amends, atonement, compensation, deliverance, discharge, emancipation, exchange, expiation, fulfilment, liberation, performance, ransom, reclamation, recovery, rehabilitation, reinstatement, release, reparation, repossession, repurchase, rescue, retrieval, salvation, trade-in.

redolent *adj* aromatic, evocative, fragrant, odorous, perfumed, remindful, reminiscent, scented, suggestive, sweet-smelling.

redoubtable *adj* courageous, doughty, dreadful, fearful, fearsome, formidable, heroic, mighty, powerful, resolute, strong, terrible, valiant.

redound *v* accrue, conduce, contribute, effect, ensue, rebound, recoil, reflect, resile, result, tend.

redress *v* adjust, amend, balance, correct, ease, expiate, mend, recompense, rectify, reform, regulate, relieve, remedy, repair, square.

n aid, amends, assistance, atonement, compensation, correction, cure, ease, expiation, help, indemnification, justice, payment, quittance, recompense, rectification, relief, remedy, reparation, requital, restitution, satisfaction.

antonyms boost, fatten, increase.

reduce *v* abate, abridge, bankrupt, break, cheapen, conquer, contract, curtail, cut, debase, decimate, decrease, degrade, demote, deoxidate, deoxidise, depress, diet, dilute, diminish, discount, downgrade, drive, force, humble, humiliate, impair, impoverish, lessen, lower, master, moderate, overpower, pauperise, rebate, ruin, scant, shorten, slake, slash, slenderise, slim, subdue, trim, truncate, vanquish, weaken.

antonyms boost, fatten, increase, upgrade.

reduction *n* abbreviation, abridgement, abstraction, alleviation, attenuation, compression, condensation, constriction, contraction, curtailment, cut, cutback, decline, decrease, deduction, degradation, demotion, deoxidation, deoxidisation, deposal, depreciation, devaluation, diminution, discount, drop, easing, ellipsis, limitation, loss, miniature, mitigation, moderation, modification, muffling, muting, narrowing, rebate, rebatement, refund, restriction, shortening, shrinkage, slackening, softening, subtraction, summarisation, summary, syncope.

antonyms enlargement, improvement, increase.

redundancy *n* battology, excess, pleonasm, prolixity, repetition, superfluity, surplus, tautology, uselessness, verbosity, wordiness.

redundant *adj* de trop, diffuse, excessive, extra, inessential, inordinate, padded, periphrastic, pleonastical, prolix, repetitious, supererogatory, superfluous, supernumerary, surplus, tautological, unemployed, unnecessary, unneeded, unwanted, verbose, wordy.

antonyms concise, essential, necessary.

reef *n* cay, key, ridge, sand-bank, sand-bar.

reek *v* exhale, fume, hum, pong, smell, smoke, stink.

n effluvium, exhalation, fetor, fume(s), malodour, mephitis, odour, pong, smell, smoke, stench, stink, vapour.

reel *v* gyrate, lurch, pitch, revolve, rock, roll, spin, stagger, stumble, sway, swim, swirl, totter, twirl, waver, wheel, whirl, wobble.

refer *v* accredit, adduce, advert, allude, apply, ascribe, assign, attribute, belong, cite, commit, concern, consign, consult, credit, deliver, direct, go, guide, hint, impute, invoke, look up, mention, pertain, point, recommend, relate, send, speak of, submit, touch on, transfer, turn to.

referee *n* adjudicator, arbiter, arbitrator, arbitratrix, arbitress, judge, ref, umpire.

v adjudicate, arbitrate, judge, ref, umpire.

reference *n* allusion, applicability, bearing, certification, character, citation, concern, connection, consideration, credentials, endorsement, illustration, instance, mention, note, quotation, recommendation, regard, relation, remark, respect, testimonial.

refine *v* chasten, civilise, clarify, cultivate, distil, elevate, exalt, filter, hone, improve, perfect, polish, process, purify, rarefy, spiritualise, sublimise, subtilise, temper.

refined *adj* Attic, Augustan, civil, civilised, clarified, clean, courtly, cultivated, cultured, delicate, discerning, discriminating, distilled, elegant, exact, fastidious, filtered, fine, genteel, gentlemanly, gracious, ladylike, nice, polished, polite, precise, processed, punctilious, pure, purified, sensitive, sophisticated, sublime, subtle, urbane, well-bred, well-mannered.

antonyms brutish, coarse, earthy, rude, vulgar.

refinement *n* breeding, chastity, civilisation, civility, clarification, cleansing, courtesy, courtliness, cultivation, culture, delicacy, discrimination, distillation, elegance, fastidiousness, filtering, fineness, finesse, finish, gentility, grace, graciousness, manners, nicety, nuance, polish, politeness, politesse, precision, processing, purification, rarefaction, rectification, sophistication, style, subtlety, taste, urbanity.

antonyms coarseness, earthiness, vulgarity.

reflect *v* bespeak, cogitate, communicate, consider, contemplate, deliberate, demonstrate, display, echo, evince, exhibit, express, imitate, indicate, manifest, meditate, mirror, mull (over), muse, ponder, reproduce, return, reveal, ruminate, show, think, wonder.

reflection *n* aspersion, censure, cerebration, cogitation, consideration, contemplation, counterpart, criticism, deliberation, derogation, echo, idea, image, impression, imputation, meditation, musing, observation, opinion, pondering, reflex, reproach, rumination, slur, study, thinking, thought, view.

reflective *adj* absorbed, cogitating, contemplative, deliberative, dreamy, meditative, pensive, pondering, reasoning, ruminative, thoughtful.

reform *v* ameliorate, amend, better, correct, emend, improve, mend, purge, rebuild, reclaim, reconstitute, reconstruct, rectify, regenerate, rehabilitate, remodel, renovate, reorganise, repair, restore, revamp, revolutionise.

n amelioration, amendment, betterment, correction, improvement, purge, rectification, rehabilitation, renovation, shake-out.

reformer *n* do-gooder, revolutionary, whistle-blower.

refractory *adj* balky, cantankerous, contentious, contumacious, difficult, disobedient, disputatious, headstrong, intractable, mulish, obstinate, perverse, recalcitrant, resistant, restive, stubborn, uncontrollable, unco-operative, unmanageable, unruly, wilful.

antonyms co-operative, malleable, obedient.

refrain[1] *v* abstain, avoid, cease, desist, eschew, forbear, leave off, quit, renounce, stop, swear off.

refrain[2] *n* burden, chorus, epistrophe, falderal, melody, song, tune, undersong, wheel.

refresh *v* brace, cheer, cool, energise, enliven, freshen, inspirit, jog, prod, prompt, reanimate, reinvigorate, rejuvenate, renew, renovate, repair, replenish, restore, revitalise, revive, revivify, stimulate.

antonyms exhaust, tire.

refreshing *adj* bracing, cooling, different, energising, fresh, inspiriting, invigorating, new, novel, original, refrigerant, restorative, revivifying, stimulating, thirst-quenching.

antonyms exhausting, tiring.

refreshment *n* enlivenment, freshening, reanimation, reinvigoration, renewal, renovation, repair, restoration, revitalisation, revival, stimulation.

refreshments *n* aliment, drinks, food, provisions, snacks, sustenance, titbits.

refrigerate *v* chill, congeal, cool, freeze.

antonyms heat, warm.

refuge *n* asylum, bolthole, funk-hole, harbour, haven, hide-away, hideout, holt, protection, resort, retreat, sanctuary, security, shelter.

refugee *n* absconder, deserter, displaced person, émigré, escapee, exile, fugitive, runaway.

refulgent *adj* beaming, bright, brilliant, gleaming, glistening, glittering, irradiant, lambent, lustrous, radiant, resplendent, shining.

refund *v* rebate, reimburse, repay, restore, return.

n rebate, reimbursement, repayment, return.

refurbish *v* mend, overhaul, recondition, re-equip, refit, remodel, renovate, repair, restore, revamp.

refusal *n* choice, consideration, defiance, denial, incompliance, nay-say, negation, no, opportunity, option, rebuff, rejection, repudiation.

antonym acceptance.

refuse[1] *v* decline, deny, nay-say, reject, repel, repudiate, spurn, withhold.

antonyms accept, allow.

refuse[2] *n* chaff, dregs, dross, excrementa, garbage, hogwash, husks, junk, lag(s), landfill, leavings, lees, left-overs, litter, mullock, offscourings, rejectamenta, riddlings, rubbish, scum, sediment, slops, sordes, sullage, sweepings, tailings, trash, waste, wastrel.

refutation *n* confutation, disproof, elenchus, negation, overthrow, rebuttal.

refute *v* confute, counter, discredit, disprove, give the lie to, negate, overthrow, rebut, silence.

regain *v* reattain, recapture, reclaim, recoup, recover, redeem, re-establish, repossess, retake, retrieve, return to.

regal *adj* kingly, magnificent, majestic, monarch(i)al, monarchic(al), noble, princely, proud, queenly, royal, sovereign, stately.

regale *v* amuse, captivate, delight, divert, entertain, fascinate, feast, gratify, ply, refresh, serve.

regard *v* account, adjudge, attend, behold, believe, concern, consider, deem, esteem, estimate, eye, heed, hold, imagine, interest, judge, mark, mind, note, notice, observe, pertain to, rate, relate to, remark, respect, scrutinise, see, suppose, think, treat, value, view, watch.

antonyms despise, disregard.

n account, advertence, advertency, affection, aspect, attachment, attention, bearing, care, concern, connection, consideration, deference, detail, esteem, feature, gaze, glance, heed, honour, item, look, love, matter, mind, note, notice, particular, point, reference, relation, relevance, reputation, repute, respect, scrutiny, stare, store, sympathy, thought.

antonyms contempt, disapproval, disregard.

regardful *adj* attentive, aware, cany, careful, circumspect, considerate, dutiful, heedful, mindful, observant, respectful, thoughtful, watchful.

antonyms heedless, inattentive, regardless, unobservant.

regarding *prep* about, apropos, as regards, as to, concerning, in re, in respect of, in the matter of, on the subject of, re, respecting, touching, with reference to, with regard to.

regardless *adj* disregarding, heedless, inattentive, inconsiderate, indifferent, neglectful, negligent, nonchalant, rash, reckless, remiss, uncaring, unconcerned, unmindful.

antonyms attentive, heedful, regardful.

adv anyhow, anyway, come what may, despite everything, in any case, nevertheless, no matter what, nonetheless, willy-nilly.

regards *n* compliments, devoirs, greetings, respects, salutations.

regenerate *v* change, inspirit, invigorate, reawaken, reconstitute, reconstruct, re-establish, refresh, reinvigorate, rejuvenate, renew, renovate, reproduce, restore, revive, revivify, uplift.

regeneration *n* homomorphosis, reconstitution, reconstruction, re-establishment, reinvigoration, rejuvenation, renewal, renovation, reproduction, restoration.

regime *n* administration, command, control, establishment, government, leadership, management, reign, rule, system.

regiment *n* band, battery, body, brigade, cohort, company, crew, gang, group, platoon, squadron.

regimented *adj* controlled, co-ordinated, disciplined, methodical, ordered, organised, regulated, severe, standardised, stern, strict, systematic.

antonyms disorganised, free, lax, loose.

region *n* area, clime, country, district, division, domain, expanse, field, land, locality, neighbourhood, part, place, province, quarter, range, realm, scope, section, sector, sphere, terrain, terrene, territory, tract, vicinity, world, zone.

regional *adj* district, local, localised, parochial, provincial, sectional, zonal.

register *n* almanac, annals, archives, catalogue, chronicle, diary, file, ledger, list, log, matricula, memorandum, notitia, record, roll, roster, schedule.

v bespeak, betray, catalogue, chronicle, display, enlist, enrol, enter, exhibit, express, indicate, inscribe, list, log, manifest, mark, note, read, record, reflect, reveal, say, score, show, sign on.

registrar *n* administrator, annalist, archivist, cataloguer, chronicler, clerk, greffier, protocolist, recorder, secretary.

regress *v* backslide, degenerate, deteriorate, ebb, lapse, recede, relapse, retreat, retrocede, retrogress, return, revert, wane.

antonym progress.

regret *v* bemoan, bewail, deplore, grieve, lament, miss, mourn, repent, rue, sorrow.

n bitterness, compunction, contrition, disappointment, grief, lamentation, penitence, remorse, repentance, ruefulness, self-reproach, shame, sorrow.

regretful *adj* apologetic, ashamed, conscience-stricken, contrite, disappointed, mournful, penitent, remorseful, repentant, rueful, sad, sorrowful, sorry.

antonyms impenitent, unashamed.

regrettable *adj* deplorable, disappointing, distressing, ill-advised, lamentable, pitiable, sad, shameful, sorry, unfortunate, unhappy, unlucky, woeful, wrong.

antonyms fortunate, happy.

regular *adj* approved, balanced, bona fide, classic, common, commonplace, consistent, constant, consuetudinary, conventional, correct, customary, daily, dependable, efficient, established, even, everyday, fixed, flat, formal, habitual, level, methodical, normal, official, ordered, orderly, ordinary, orthodox, periodic, prevailing, proper, rhythmic, routine, sanctioned, set, smooth, standard, standardised, stated, steady, straight, symmetrical, systematic, time-honoured, traditional, typical, uniform, unvarying, usual.

antonyms irregular, sporadic, unconventional.

regulate *v* adjust, administer, arrange, balance, conduct, control, direct, fit, govern, guide, handle, manage, moderate, modulate, monitor, order, organise, oversee, regiment, rule, run, settle, square, superintend, supervise, systematise, tune.

regulation *n* adjustment, administration, arrangement, commandment, control, decree, dictate, direction, edict, governance, government, law, management, modulation, order, ordinance, precept, prodecure, regimentation, requirement, rule, statute, supervision, tuning.

adj accepted, customary, mandatory, normal, official, prescribed, required, standard, stock, usual.

regurgitate *v* disgorge, puke, regorge, spew, throw up, vomit.

rehabilitate *v* adjust, clear, convert, mend, normalise, rebuild, recondition, reconstitute, reconstruct, redeem, redintegrate, re-establish, reform, reinstate, reintegrate, reinvigorate, renew, renovate, restore, save.

rehash *n* rearrangement, rejig, rejigging, reshuffle, restatement, reworking, rewrite.

v alter, change, rearrange, refashion, rejig, rejigger, reshuffle, restate, rework, rewrite.

rehearsal *n* account, catalogue, description, drill, dry-run, enumeration, list, narration, practice, preparation, reading, recital, recounting, relation, run-through, telling.

rehearse *v* act, delineate, depict, describe, detail, drill, enumerate, list, narrate, practise, prepare, ready, recite, recount, relate, repeat, review, run through, spell out, study, tell, train, trot out.

reign *n* ascendancy, command, control, dominion, empire, hegemony, influence, monarchy, power, rule, sovereignty, supremacy, sway.

v administer, authority, command, govern, influence, kingship, obtain, predominate, prevail, rule.

reimburse *v* compensate, indemnify, recompense, refund, remunerate, repay, requite, restore, return, square up.

rein *n* brake, bridle, check, check-rein, control, curb, harness, hold, overcheck, restraint, restriction.

v arrest, bridle, check, control, curb, halt, hold, hold back, limit, restrain, restrict, stop.

reincarnation *n* metempsychosis, palingenesis, rebirth, transmigration.

reinforce *v* augment, bolster, buttress, emphasise, fortify, harden, increase, prop, recruit, steel, stiffen, strengthen, stress, supplement, support, toughen, underline.

antonyms undermine, weaken.

reinforcement *n* addition, amplification, augmentation, brace, buttress, emphasis, enlargement, fortification, hardening, increase, prop, shore, stay, strengthening, supplement, support.

reinforcements *n* auxiliaries, back-up, reserves, support.

reinstate *v* reappoint, recall, re-establish, rehabilitate, reinstall, replace, restore, return.

reiterate *v* ding, iterate, recapitulate, repeat, resay, restate, retell.

reject *v* athetise, condemn, decline, deny, despise, disallow, discard, eliminate, exclude, explode, jettison, jilt, pip, rebuff, refuse, renounce, repel, reprobate, repudiate, repulse, scrap, spike, spurn, veto.

antonyms accept, select.

n cast-off, discard, failure, second.

rejection *n* athetesis, brush-off, dear John letter, denial, dismissal, elimination, exclusion, rebuff, refusal, renunciation, repudiation, veto.

antonyms acceptance, selection.

rejoice *v* celebrate, delight, exult, glory, joy, jubilate, maffick, revel, triumph.

rejoicing *n* celebration, cheer, delight, elation, exultation, festivity, gaiety, gladness, happiness, joy, jubilation, mafficking, mallemaroking, merrymaking, revelry, triumph.

rejoin *v* answer, quip, repartee, reply, respond, retort, riposte.

rejoinder *n* answer, come-back, counter, countercharge, counter-claim, quip, repartee, reply, response, retort, riposte.

rejuvenate *v* reanimate, recharge, refresh, regenerate, reinvigorate, rekindle, renew, restore, revitalise, revivify.

relapse *v* backslide, degenerate, deteriorate, fade, fail, lapse, regress, retrogress, revert, sicken, sink, weaken, worsen.

n backsliding, deterioration, hypostrophe, lapse, recidivism, recurrence, regression, retrogression, reversion, setback, weakening, worsening.

relate *v* ally, appertain, apply, associate, chronicle, concern, connect, co-ordinate, correlate, couple, describe, detail, empathise, feel for, identify with, impart, join, link, narrate, pertain, present, recite, recount, refer, rehearse, report, sympathise, tell, understand.

related *adj* accompanying, affiliated, affine(d), agnate, akin, allied, associated, cognate, concomitant, connected, consanguine, consanguineous, correlated, interconnected, joint, kin, kindred, linked.

antonyms different, unconnected, unrelated.

relation *n* account, affiliation, affine, affinity, agnate, agnation, application, bearing, bond, comparison, connection, consanguinity, correlation, description, german, interdependence, kin, kindred, kinship, kinsman, kinswoman, link, narration, narrative, pertinence, propinquity, recital, recountal, reference, regard, relationship, relative, report, sib, similarity, story, tale, tie-in.

relations *n* affairs, associations, clan, communications, connections, contact, dealings, doings, family, interaction, intercourse, kin, kindred, kinsmen, liaison, meetings, rapport, relationship, relatives, terms, tribe, truck.

relationship *n* affaire, association, bond, communications, conjunction, connection, contract, correlation, dealings, exchange, intercourse, kinship, liaison, link, parallel, proportion, rapport, ratio, similarity, tie-up.

relative *adj* allied, applicable, apposite, appropriate, appurtenant, apropos, associated, comparative, connected, contingent, correlative, corresponding, dependent, germane, interrelated, pertinent, proportionate, reciprocal, related, relevant, respective.

n cognate, connection, german, kinsman, kinswoman, relation, sib.

relatively *adv* comparatively, fairly, quite, rather, somewhat.

relax *v* abate, diminish, disinhibit, ease, ebb, lessen, loosen, lower, mitigate, moderate, reduce, relieve, remit, rest, slacken, soften, tranquillise, unbend, unclench, unwind, weaken.

antonyms intensify, tighten.

relaxation *n* abatement, amusement, délassement, détente, diminution, disinhibition, distraction, easing, emollition, enjoyment, entertainment, fun, leisure, lessening, let-up, moderation, pleasure, recreation, reduction, refreshment, rest, slackening, weakening.

antonyms intensification, tension.

relaxed *adj* calm, carefree, casual, collected, composed, cool, downbeat, easy-going, even-tempered, happy-go-lucky, informal, insouciant, laid-back, mellow, mild, nonchalant, placid, serene, together, tranquil, unhurried.

antonyms edgy, nervous, stiff, tense, uptight.

relay *n* broadcast, communication, dispatch, message, programme, relief, shift, transmission, turn.

v broadcast, carry, communicate, rebroadcast, send, spread, supply, transmit.

release *v* absolve, acquit, break, circulate, declassify, decontrol, deliver, discage, discharge, disengage, disenthral, disimprison, disinhibit, disoblige, dispense, disprison, disseminate, distribute, drop, emancipate, exempt, excuse, exonerate, extricate, free, furlough, issue, launch, liberate, loose, manumit, present, publish, unbind, uncage, unchain, undo, unfasten, unfetter, unhand, unleash, unloose, unmew, unpen, unshackle, untie, unveil.

antonyms check, detain.

n absolution, acquittal, acquittance, announcement, deliverance, delivery, discharge, disimprisonment, disinhibition, dispensation, emancipation, exemption, exoneration, freedom, issue, let-off, liberation, liberty, manumission, offering, proclamation, publication, quittance, relief.

antonym detention.

relegate *v* assign, banish, consign, delegate, demote, deport, dispatch, downgrade, eject, entrust, exile, expatriate, expel, refer, transfer.

antonym promote.

relent *v* acquiesce, capitulate, drop, ease, fall, forbear, give in, melt, relax, slacken, slow, soften, unbend, weaken, yield.

relentless *adj* cruel, fierce, grim, hard, harsh, implacable, incessant, inexorable, inflexible, merciless, non-stop, persistent, pitiless, punishing, remorseless, ruthless, stern, sustained, unabated, unbroken, uncompromising, undeviating, unfaltering, unflagging, unforgiving, unrelenting, unrelieved, unremitting, unstoppable, unyielding.

antonyms submissive, yielding.

relevant *adj* ad rem, admissible, applicable, apposite, appropriate, appurtenant, apt, congruous, fitting, germane, material, pertinent, proper, related, relative, significant, suitable, suited.

antonym irrelevant.

reliable *adj* banker, certain, constant, copper-bottomed, dependable, faithful, honest, predictable, regular, responsible, safe, solid, sound, stable, staunch, sure, true, trustworthy, trusty, unfailing, upright, white.

antonyms doubtful, suspect, unreliable, untrustworthy.

reliance *n* assurance, belief, confidence, credence, credit, dependence, faith, trust.

relic *n* fragment, keepsake, memento, potsherd, remembrance, remnant, scrap, souvenir, survival, token, trace, vestige.

relief *n* abatement, aid, alleviation, assistance, assuagement, balm, break, breather, comfort, cure, deliverance, diversion, ease, easement, help, let-up, load off one's mind, mitigation, palliation, refreshment, relaxation, release, remedy, remission, respite, rest, solace, succour, support, sustenance.

relieve *v* abate, aid, alleviate, appease, assist, assuage, break, brighten, calm, comfort, console, cure, deliver, diminish, discharge, disembarrass, disencumber, dull, ease, exempt, free, help, interrupt, lighten, mitigate, mollify, palliate, relax, release, salve, slacken, soften, solace, soothe, spell, stand in for, substitute for, succour, support, sustain, take over from, take the place of, unburden, vary.

antonyms aggravate, intensify.

religious *adj* church-going, conscientious, devotional, devout, divine, doctrinal, exact, faithful, fastidious, God-fearing, godly, holy, meticulous, pious, punctilious, pure, reverent, righteous, rigid, rigorous, sacred, scriptural, scrupulous, sectarian, spiritual, strict, theological, unerring, unswerving.

antonyms irreligious, lax, ungodly.

relinquish *n* abandon, abdicate, cede, desert, discard, drop, forgo, forsake, hand over, leave, quit, release, renounce, repudiate, resign, surrender, vacate, waive, yield.

antonyms keep, retain.

relish *v* appreciate, degust, enjoy, fancy, lap up, like, prefer, revel in, savour, taste.

n appetiser, appetite, appreciation, condiment, enjoyment, fancy, flavour, fondness, gout, gusto, liking, love, partiality, penchant, piquancy, predilection, sauce, savour, seasoning, smack, spice, stomach, tang, taste, trace, zest.

reluctance *n* aversion, backwardness, disinclination, dislike, distaste, hesitancy, indisposition, loathing, recalcitrance, repugnance, unwillingness.

antonyms eagerness, willingness.

reluctant *adj* averse, backward, disinclined, grudging, hesitant, indisposed, loath, loathful, loth, recalcitrant, renitent, slow, squeamish, unenthusiastic, unwilling.

antonyms eager, willing.

rely *v* bank, bet, count, depend, lean, reckon, swear by, trust.

remain *v* abide, bide, cling, continue, delay, dwell, endure, last, linger, persist, prevail, rest, sojourn, stand, stay, survive, tarry, wait.

antonyms depart, go, leave.

remainder *n* balance, dregs, excess, leavings, remanent, remanet, remnant, residuum, rest, surplus, trace, vestige(s).

remaining *adj* abiding, extant, lasting, left, lingering, outstanding, persisting, residual, surviving, unfinished, unspent, unused.

remains *n* ashes, balance, body, cadaver, carcass, corpse, crumbs, debris, detritus, dregs, fragments, leavings, left-overs, oddments, pieces, relics, reliquiae, remainder, remnants, residue, rest, scraps, traces, vestiges.

remark *v* animadvert, comment, declare, espy, heed, mark, mention, note, notice, observe, perceive, reflect, regard, say, see, state.

n acknowledgement, assertion, attention, comment, consideration, declaration, heed, mention, notice, observation, opinion, recognition, reflection, regard, say, statement, thought, utterance, word.

remarkable *adj* amazing, conspicuous, distinguished, exceptional, extraordinary, famous, impressive, miraculous, notable, noteworthy, odd, outstanding, phenomenal, pre-eminent, prominent, rare, signal, singular, strange, striking, surprising, unco, uncommon, unusual, wonderful.

antonyms average, commonplace, ordinary.

remedy *n* antidote, corrective, counteractive, countermeasure, cure, magistery, medicament, medicine, nostrum, panacea, physic, prescript, redress, relief, restorative, simillimum, solution, specific, therapy, treatment.

v alleviate, ameliorate, assuage, control, correct, counteract, cure, ease, fix, heal, help, mitigate, palliate, put right, rectify, redress, reform, relieve, repair, restore, solve, soothe, treat.

remember *v* commemorate, place, recall, recognise, recollect, reminisce, retain, summon up, think back.

antonym forget.

remembrance *n* anamnesis, commemoration, keepsake, memento, memorial, memory, mind, monument, recall, recognition, recollection, recordation, regard, relic, remembrancer, reminder, reminiscence, retrospect, souvenir, testimonial, thought, token.

remind *v* bring to mind, call to mind, call up, cue, hint, jog one's memory, prompt, put in mind, refresh one's memory.

reminder *n* aide-mémoire, cue, hint, memo, memorandum, nudge, prompt(ing), suggestion.

reminisce *v* hark back, look back, recall, recollect, remember, retrospect, review, think back.

reminiscence *n* anecdote, memoir, memory, personalia, recall, recollection, reflection, remembrance, retrospection, review.

reminiscent *adj* evocative, nostalgic, redolent, remindful, similar, suggestive.

remiss *adj* careless, culpable, delinquent, derelict, dilatory, fainéant, forgetful, heedless, inattentive, indifferent, lackadaisical, lax, neglectful, negligent, regardless, slack, slipshod, sloppy, slothful, slow, tardy, thoughtless, unmindful.

antonyms careful, scrupulous.

remission *n* abatement, abeyance, absolution, acquittal, alleviation, amelioration, amnesty, decrease, diminution, discharge, ebb, excuse, exemption, exoneration, forgiveness, indulgence, lessening, let-up, lull, moderation, pardon, reduction, relaxation, release, relinquishment, reprieve, respite, slackening, suspension.

remit *v* abate, alleviate, cancel, decrease, defer, delay, desist, desist from, diminish, dispatch, dwindle, forbear, forward, halt, mail, mitigate, moderate, post, postpone, put back, reduce, relax, repeal, rescind, send, send back, shelve, sink, slacken, soften, stop, suspend, transfer, transmit, wane, weaken.

n authorisation, brief, guidelines, instructions, orders, responsibility, scope, terms of reference.

remittance *n* allowance, consideration, dispatch, fee, payment, sending.

remnant *n* balance, bit, end, fent, fragment, hangover, left-overs, piece, remainder, remains, remane(n)t, residue, residuum, rest, rump, scrap, shred, survival, trace, vestige.

remonstrance *n* complaint, exception, expostulation, grievance, objection, petition, protest, protestation, reprimand, reproof.

remonstrate *v* argue, challenge, complain, dispute, dissent, expostulate, gripe, object, protest.

remorse *n* anguish, bad conscience, compassion, compunction, contrition, grief, guilt, penitence, pity, regret, repentance, ruefulness, ruth, self-reproach, shame, sorrow.

remorseful *adj* apologetic, ashamed, chastened, compunctious, conscience-stricken, contrite, guilt-ridden, guilty, penitent, regretful, repentant, rueful, sad, sorrowful, sorry.

antonyms impenitent, remorseless.

remorseless *adj* callous, cruel, hard, hard-hearted, harsh, implacable, inexorable, inhumane, merciless, pitiless, relentless, ruthless, savage, stern, undeviating, unforgiving, unmerciful, unrelenting, unremitting, unstoppable.

antonyms remorseful, sorry.

remote *adj* abstracted, alien, aloof, backwoods, cold, detached, distant, doubtful, dubious, extraneous, extrinsic, faint, far, faraway, far-off, foreign, god-forsaken, immaterial, implausible, inaccessible, inconsiderable, indifferent, introspective, introverted, irrelevant, isolated, lonely, meagre, negligible, outlying, out-of-the-way, outside, poor, removed, reserved, secluded, slender, slight, slim, small, standoffish, unconnected, uninterested, uninvolved, unlikely, unrelated, withdrawn.

antonyms adjacent, close, nearby, significant.

removal *n* ablation, abstraction, demigration, departure, dislodgement, dismissal, displacement, dispossession, ejection, elimination, eradication, erasure, expulsion, expunction, extraction, flitting, metastasis, move, purge, purging, relocation, riddance, stripping, subtraction, transfer, uprooting, withdrawal.

remove *v* ablate, abolish, abstract, amove, amputate, assassinate, delete, depart, depose, detach, dethrone, discharge, dislodge, dismiss, displace, doff, efface, eject, eliminate, erase, execute, expunge, extract, flit, flit (move house), guy, kill, liquidate, move, murder, oust, purge, quit, relegate, relocate, shave, shear, shed, shift, sideline, strike, subduct, transfer, transmigrate, transport, unseat, vacate, withdraw.

remunerate *v* compensate, fee, guerdon, indemnify, pay, recompense, redress, reimburse, repay, requite, reward.

remuneration *n* compensation, earnings, emolument, fee, guerdon, income, indemnity, pay, payment, profit, recompense, reimbursement, remittance, reparation, repayment, retainer, return, reward, salary, stipend, wages.

remunerative *adj* fruitful, gainful, lucrative, moneymaking, paying, profitable, rewarding, rich, worthwhile.

renaissance *n* awakening, new birth, new dawn, reappearance, reawakening, rebirth, recrudescence, re-emergence, regeneration, rejuvenation, renascence, renewal, restoration, resurgence, resurrection, revival.

renascent *adj* born-again, reanimated, reawakened, reborn, redivivus, re-emergent, renewed, resurgent, resurrected, revived.

rend *v* afflict, anguish, break, burst, cleave, crack, dissever, distress, disturb, disunite, divide, fracture, hurt, lacerate, pain, pierce, pull, rip, rive, rupture, separate, sever, shatter, smash, splinter, split, stab, sunder, tear, torment, wound, wrench, wring.

render *v* act, cede, clarify, construe, contribute, deliver, depict, display, do, evince, exchange, exhibit, explain, furnish, give, give back, give up, hand over, interpret, leave, make, make up, manifest, melt, pay, perform, play, portray, present, provide, put, relinquish, repay, represent, reproduce, restate, restore, return, show, show forth, submit, supply, surrender, swap, tender, trade, transcribe, translate, yield.

rendezvous *n* appointment, assignation, date, engagement, haunt, meeting, meeting-place, resort, tryst, trysting-place, venue.

v assemble, collect, convene, converge, gather, meet, muster, rally.

rendition *n* arrangement, construction, delivery, depiction, execution, explanation, interpretation, metaphrase, metaphrasis, performance, portrayal, presentation, reading, rendering, transcription, translation, version.

renegade *n* apostate, backslider, betrayer, defector, deserter, dissident, mutineer, outlaw, rebel, recreant, renegado, renegate, runaway, tergiversator, traitor, turncoat.

antonyms adherent, disciple, follower.

adj apostate, backsliding, disloyal, dissident, mutinous, outlaw, perfidious, rebel, rebellious, recreant, runaway, traitorous, unfaithful.

renegue *v* apostatise, cross the floor, default, renege, renig, repudiate, welsh.

renew *v* continue, extend, mend, modernise, overhaul, prolong, reaffirm, recommence, recreate, re-establish, refashion, refit, refresh, refurbish, regenerate, rejuvenate, remodel, renovate, reopen, repair, repeat, replace, replenish, restate, restock, restore, resume, revitalise, transform.

renewal *n* instauration, kiss of life, recommencement, reconditioning, reconstitution, reconstruction, recreation, recruit, recruital, refurbishment, reinvigoration, reiteration, rejuvenation, renovation, repair, replenishment, resumption, resurrection, resuscitation, revitalisation, revivification.

renounce *v* abandon, abdicate, abjure, abnegate, decline, deny, discard, disclaim, disown, disprofess, eschew, forgo, forsake, forswear, put away, quit, recant, reject, relinquish, repudiate, resign, spurn.

renovate *v* do up, furbish, improve, modernise, overhaul, recondition, reconstitute, recreate, refit, reform, refurbish, rehabilitate, remodel, renew, repair, restore, revamp.

renovation *n* face-lift, improvement, modernisation, reconditioning, refit, refurbishment, renewal, repair, restoration.

renown *n* acclaim, celebrity, distinction, eminence, fame, glory, honour, illustriousness, kudos, lustre, mark, note, reputation, repute, stardom.

antonyms anonymity, obscurity.

renowned *adj* acclaimed, celebrated, distinguished, eminent, esteemed, famed, famous, illustrious, notable, noted, pre-eminent, supereminent, well-known.

antonyms anonymous, obscure, unknown.

rent[1] *n* fee, gale, hire, lease, payment, rental, tariff.

v charter, farm out, hire, lease, let, sublet, take.

rent[2] *n* breach, break, chink, cleavage, crack, dissension, disunion, division, flaw, gash, hole, opening, perforation, rift, rip, rupture, schism, slash, slit, split, tear.

renunciation *n* abandonment, abdication, abjuration, abnegation, abstention, denial, disavowal, disclaimer, eschewal, forgoing, forswearing, recantation, rejection, relinquishment, repudiation, resignation, spurning, surrender, waiver.

repair[1] *v* debug, fix, heal, mend, patch up, recover, rectify, redress, renew, renovate, restore, retrieve, square.

n adjustment, condition, darn, fettle, form, improvement, mend, nick, overhaul, patch, restoration, shape, state.

repair[2] *v* go, wend one's way, move, remove, resort, retire, turn, withdraw.

reparable *adj* corrigible, curable, recoverable, rectifiable, remediable, restorable, retrievable, salvageable, savable.

antonym irreparable.

reparation *n* amends, atonement, compensation, damages, indemnity, propitiation, recompense, redress, renewal, repair, requital, restitution, satisfaction, solatium.

repartee *n* badinage, banter, jesting, persiflage, pleasantry, raillery, riposte, sally, waggery, wit, witticism, wittiness, wordplay.

repast *n* collation, feed, food, meal, nourishment, refection, snack, spread, victuals.

repay *v* avenge, compensate, get even with, make restitution, reciprocate, recompense, refund, reimburse, remunerate, requite, restore, retaliate, return, revenge, reward, settle the score, square.

repayment *n* amends, avengement, compensation, rebate, reciprocation, recompense, redress, refund, reimbursement, remuneration, reparation, requital, restitution, retaliation, retribution, revenge, reward, ultion, vengeance.

repeal *v* abolish, abrogate, annul, cancel, countermand, invalidate, nullify, quash, recall, rescind, reverse, revoke, set aside, void, withdraw.

antonyms enact, establish.

n abolition, abrogation, annulment, cancellation, invalidation, nullification, quashing, rescinding, rescindment, rescission, reversal, revocation, withdrawal.

antonyms enactment, establishment.

repeat *v* duplicate, echo, iterate, quote, rebroadcast, recapitulate, recite, re-do, rehearse, reiterate, relate, renew, replay, reproduce, rerun, reshow, restate, retell.

n duplicate, echo, rebroadcast, recapitulation, reiteration, repetition, replay, reproduction, rerun, reshowing.

repeatedly *adv* again and again, frequently, often, oftentimes, ofttimes, over and over, recurrently, time after time, time and (time) again.

repel *v* check, confront, decline, disadvantage, disgust, fight, hold off, nauseate, offend, oppose, parry, rebuff, refuse, reject, repulse, resist, revolt, sicken, ward off.

antonym attract.

repellent *adj* abhorrent, abominable, discouraging, disgusting, distasteful, hateful, horrid, loathsome, nauseating, noxious, obnoxious, odious, offensive, off-putting, rebarbative, repugnant, repulsive, revolting, sickening.

antonym attractive.

repent *n* atone, bewail, deplore, lament, regret, relent, rue, sorrow.

repentance *n* compunction, contrition, grief, guilt, metanoia, penitence, regret, remorse, self-reproach, sorriness, sorrow.

repentant *adj* apologetic, ashamed, chastened, compunctious, contrite, penitent, regretful, remorseful, rueful, sorry.

antonym unrepentant.

repercussion *n* aftermath, backlash, backwash, consequence, echo, rebound, recoil, result, reverberation, side effect.

repertory *n* collection, list, range, repertoire, repository, reserve, reservoir, stock, store, supply.

repetition *n* anaphora, dittography, duplication, echo, echolalia, epanalepsis, epanaphora, iteration, reappearance, recapitulation, recital, recurrence, redundancy, rehearsal, reiteration, relation, renewal, repeat, repetitiousness, replication, restatement, return, tautology.

repetitious *adj* battological, long-winded, pleonastic(al), prolix, redundant, tautological, tedious, verbose, windy, wordy.

repetitive *adj* boring, dull, interminable, mechanical, monotonous, recurrent, samey, tedious, unchanging, unvaried.

rephrase *v* paraphrase, recast, reword, rewrite.

repine *v* beef, brood, complain, fret, grieve, grouse, grumble, lament, languish, moan, mope, murmur, sulk.

replace *v* deputise, follow, make good, oust, re-establish, reinstate, restore, substitute, succeed, supersede, supplant, supply.

replacement *n* double, fill-in, proxy, replacer, stand-in, substitute, succedaneum, successor, surrogate, understudy.

replenish *v* fill, furnish, provide, recharge, recruit, refill, reload, renew, replace, restock, restore, stock, supply, top up.

replete *adj* abounding, brimful, brimming, charged, chock-a-block, chock-full, crammed, filled, full, full up, glutted, gorged, jammed, jam-packed, sated, satiated, stuffed, teeming, well-provided, well-stocked.

repletion *n* completeness, fullness, glut, overfullness, plethora, satiation, satiety, superabundance, superfluity.

replica *n* clone, copy, duplicate, facsimile, imitation, model, reproduction.

replicate *v* ape, clone, copy, duplicate, follow, mimic, recreate, reduplicate, repeat, reproduce.

reply *v* acknowledge, answer, counter, echo, react, reciprocate, rejoin, repartee, respond, retaliate, retort, return, riposte.

n acknowledgement, answer, comeback, counter, echo, reaction, reciprocation, rejoinder, repartee, response, retaliation, retort, return, riposte.

report *n* account, announcement, article, bang, blast, boom, bruit, character, communication, communiqué, crack, crash, declaration, description, detail, detonation, discharge, dispatch, esteem, explosion, fame, gossip, hearsay, information, message, narrative, news, noise, note, paper, piece, procès-verbal, recital, record, regard, relation, reputation, repute, reverberation, rumour, sound, statement, story, summary, tale, talk, tidings, version, word, write-up.

v air, announce, appear, arrive, broadcast, bruit, circulate, come, communicate, cover, declare, describe, detail, document, mention, narrate, note, notify, proclaim, publish, recite, record, recount, relate, relay, state, tell.

reporter *n* announcer, correspondent, hack, Jenkins, journalist, leg-man, leg-woman, newscaster, newshound, newspaperman, newspaperwoman, pressman, stringer, writer.

repose[1] *n* aplomb, calm, calmness, composure, dignity, ease, equanimity, inactivity, peace, poise, quiet, quietness, quietude, relaxation, respite, rest, restfulness, self-possession, serenity, sleep, slumber, stillness, tranquillity.

antonyms activity, strain, stress.

v laze, recline, relax, rest, sleep, slumber.

repose[2] *v* confide, deposit, entrust, invest, lodge, place, put, set, store.

repository *n* archive, depository, depot, emporium, magazine, promptuary, receptacle, repertory, store, storehouse, treasury, vault, warehouse.

reprehensible *adj* bad, blamable, blameworthy, censurable, condemnable, culpable, delinquent, discreditable, disgraceful, errant, erring, ignoble, objectionable, opprobrious, remiss, shameful, unworthy.

antonyms creditable, good, praiseworthy.

represent *v* act, appear as, be, betoken, delineate, denote, depict, depicture, describe, designate, embody, enact, epitomise, equal, evoke, exemplify, exhibit, express, illustrate, mean, outline, perform, personify, picture, portray, produce, render, reproduce, show, sketch, stage, symbolise, typify.

representation *n* account, argument, bust, committee, delegates, delegation, delineation, depiction, description, embassy, exhibition, explanation, exposition, expostulation, icon, idol, illustration, image, likeness, model, narration, narrative, performance, petition, picture, play, portrait, portrayal, production, relation, remonstrance, resemblance, show, sight, sketch, spectacle, statue.

representative *n* agent, archetype, commissioner, councillor, delegate, depute, deputy, embodiment, epitome, exemplar, member, MP, personification, proxy, rep, representant, salesman, spokesman, spokesperson, spokeswoman, traveller, type.

adj archetypal, characteristic, chosen, delegated, elected, elective, emblematic, evocative, exemplary, illustrative, normal, symbolic, typical, usual.

antonyms atypical, unrepresentative.

repress *v* bottle up, chasten, check, control, crush, curb, hamper, hinder, impede, inhibit, master, muffle, overcome, overpower, quash, quell, reprime, restrain, silence, smother, stifle, subdue, subjugate, suppress, swallow.

repression *n* authoritarianism, censorship, coercion, constraint, control, denial, despotism, domination, gagging, inhibition, restraint, subjugation, suffocation, suppression, tyranny.

repressive *adj* absolute, authoritarian, autocratic, coercive, despotic, dictatorial, harsh, iron-handed, oppressive, severe, tough, tyrannical.

reprieve *v* abate, allay, alleviate, mitigate, palliate, pardon, redeem, relieve, rescue, respite.

n abatement, abeyance, alleviation, amnesty, deferment, let-up, mitigation, palliation, pardon, postponement, redemption, relief, remission, rescue, respite, suspension.

reprimand *n* admonition, blame, bollocking, castigation, censure, dressing-down, jawbation, jobation, lecture, rebuke, reprehension, reproach, reproof, row, schooling, talking-to, telling-off, ticking-off, tongue-lashing, wigging.

v admonish, bawl out, blame, bollock, bounce, castigate, censure, check, chide, jobe, keelhaul, lecture, lesson, rebuke, reprehend, reproach, reprove, scold, slate, tongue-lash, upbraid.

reprisal *n* counter-stroke, recaption, requital, retaliation, retribution, revenge, ultion, vengeance.

reproach *v* abuse, blame, censure, chide, condemn, criticise, defame, discredit, disparage, dispraise, rebuke, reprehend, reprimand, reprove, scold, upbraid.

n abuse, blame, blemish, censure, condemnation, contempt, disapproval, discredit, disgrace, dishonour, disrepute, ignominy, indignity, nayword, obloquy, odium, opprobrium, reproof, scorn, shame, slight, slut, stain, stigma, upbraiding.

reproachful *adj* abusive, admonitory, aggrieved, castigatory, censorious, condemnatory, contemptuous, critical, disappointed, disapproving, fault-finding, opprobrious, reproving, scolding, upbraiding.

antonym complimentary.

reprobate *adj* abandoned, bad, base, condemnatory, corrupt, damned, degenerate, depraved, dissolute, hardened, immoral, incorrigible, profligate, reprobative, reprobatory, shameless, sinful, unprincipled, vile, wicked.

antonym upright.

n blackguard, degenerate, evildoer, knave, miscreant, ne'er-do-well, outcast, pariah, profligate, rake, rakehell, rascal, rogue, roué, scamp, scoundrel, sinner, villain, wastrel, wretch, wrongdoer.

reproduce *v* ape, breed, copy, duplicate, echo, emulate, facsimile, generate, imitate, match, mirror, multiply, parallel, parrot, print, procreate, proliferate, propagate, recreate, regurgitate, repeat, replicate, represent, simulate, spawn, transcribe.

reproduction *n* amphimixis, breeding, copy, duplicate, ectype, facsimile, fructuation, gamogenesis, generation, imitation, increase, multiplication, picture, print, procreation, proliferation, propagation, replica.

antonym original.

reproductive *adj* generative, genital, procreative, progenitive, propagative, sex, sexual.

reproof *n* admonition, blame, castigation, censure, chiding, condemnation, criticism, dressing-down, rebuke, reprehension, reprimand, reproach, reproval, reproving, scolding, ticking-off, tongue-lashing, upbraiding.

antonym praise.

reprove *v* abuse, admonish, berate, blame, censure, check, chide, condemn, rap, rate, rebuke, reprehend, reprimand, scold, upbraid.

antonym praise.

repudiate *v* abandon, abjure, cast off, deny, desert, disaffirm, disavow, discard, disclaim, disown, disprofess, divorce, forsake, reject, renounce, rescind, retract, reverse, revoke.

antonyms admit, own.

repudiation *n* abjuration, denial, disaffirmance, disaffirmation, disavowal, disclaimer, disowning, recantation, rejection, renouncement, renunciation, retraction.

antonym acceptance.

repugnance *n* abhorrence, abhorring, antipathy, aversion, disgust, dislike, disrelish, distaste, hatred, inconsistency, loathing, reluctance, repugnancy, repulsion, revulsion.

antonyms liking, pleasure.

repugnant *adj* abhorrent, abominable, adverse, antagonistic, antipathetic, averse, contradictory, disgusting, distasteful, foul, hateful, horrid, hostile, incompatible, inconsistent, inimical, loathsome, nauseating, objectionable, obnoxious, odious, offensive, opposed, repellent, revolting, sickening, unacceptable, vile.

antonyms acceptable, consistent, pleasant.

repulse *v* beat off, check, defeat, disdain, disregard, drive back, rebuff, refuse, reject, repel, snub, spurn.

n check, defeat, disappointment, failure, rebuff, refusal, rejection, repudiation, reverse, snub, spurning.

antonyms acceptance, success.

repulsion *n* abhorrence, aversion, detestation, disgust, disrelish, distaste, hatred, loathing, repellence, repellency, repugnance, revulsion.

antonym liking.

repulsive *adj* abhorrent, abominable, cold, disagreeable, disgusting, distasteful, forbidding, foul, hateful, hideous, horrid, ill-faced, loathsome, nauseating, objectionable, obnoxious, odious, offensive, repellent, reserved, revolting, sickening, ugly, unpleasant, vile.

antonyms friendly, pleasant.

reputable *adj* creditable, dependable, estimable, excellent, good, honourable, honoured, irreproachable, legitimate, principled, reliable, respectable, trustworthy, unimpeachable, upright, worthy.

antonyms disreputable, infamous.

reputation *n* bad name, character, credit, distinction, esteem, estimation, fame, good name, honour, infamy, name, opinion, renown, repute, standing, stature.

repute *n* celebrity, distinction, esteem, estimation, fame, good name, name, renown, reputation, standing, stature.

antonym infamy.

reputed *adj* accounted, alleged, believed, considered, deemed, estimated, held, ostensible, putative, reckoned, regarded, reputative, rumoured, said, seeming, supposed, thought.

antonym actual.

reputedly *adv* allegedly, apparently, ostensibly, reputatively, seemingly, supposedly.

antonym actually.

request *v* ask, ask for, beg, beseech, demand, desire, entreat, impetrate, importune, petition, pray, requisition, seek, solicit, supplicate.

n appeal, application, asking, begging, call, demand, desire, entreaty, impetration, petition, prayer, representation, requisition, solicitation, suit, supplication.

require *v* ask, beg, beseech, bid, command, compel, constrain, crave, demand, desire, direct, enjoin, exact, force, instruct, involve, lack, make, miss, necessitate, need, oblige, order, request, take, want, wish.

required *adj* compulsory, demanded, essential, mandatory, necessary, needed, obligatory, prescribed, recommended, requisite, set, stipulated, unavoidable, vital.

antonyms inessential, optional.

requirement *n* demand, desideratum, essential, lack, must, necessity, need, precondition, prerequisite, provision, proviso, qualification, requisite, sine qua non, specification, stipulation, term, want.

antonym inessential.

requisite *adj* essential, imperative, indispensable, mandatory, necessary, needed, needful, obligatory, prerequisite, required, vital.

antonyms inessential, optional.

n condition, desiderative, desideratum, essential, must, necessity, need, precondition, prerequisite, requirement, sine qua non.

antonym inessential.

requisition *v* appropriate, commandeer, confiscate, demand, occupy, put in for, request, seize, take.

n application, appropriation, call, commandeering, demand, occupation, order, request, seizure, summons, takeover, use.

requital *n* amends, compensation, indemnification, indemnity, payment, pay-off, quittance, recompense, redress, reparation, repayment, restitution, satisfaction.

requite *v* avenge, compensate, pay, reciprocate, recompense, redress, reimburse, remunerate, repay, respond, retaliate, return, reward, satisfy.

rescind *v* abrogate, annul, cancel, countermand, invalidate, negate, nullify, overturn, quash, recall, repeal, retract, reverse, revoke, void.

antonym enforce.

rescission *n* abrogation, annulment, cancellation, invalidation, negation, nullification, recall, repeal, rescindment, retraction, reversal, revocation, voidance.

antonym enforcement.

rescue *v* deliver, extricate, free, liberate, ransom, recover, redeem, release, salvage, save.

antonym capture.

n deliverance, delivery, extrication, liberation, recovery, redemption, release, relief, salvage, salvation, saving.

antonym capture.

research *n* analysis, delving, examination, experimentation, exploration, fact-finding, groundwork, inquiry, investigation, probe, quest, scrutiny, search, study.

v analyse, examine, experiment, explore, ferret, investigate, probe, scrutinise, search, study.

researcher *n* analyst, boffin, field worker, inquirer, inspector, investigator, student.

resemblance *n* affinity, analogy, assonance, closeness, comparability, comparison, conformity, correspondence, counterpart, facsimile, image, kinship, likeness, parallel, parity, sameness, semblance, similarity, similitude.

antonym dissimilarity.

resemble *v* approach, duplicate, echo, favour, mirror, parallel, take after.

antonym differ from.

resent *v* begrudge, chafe at, dislike, grudge, grumble at, object to, take amiss, take exception to, take offence at, take the huff, take umbrage at.

antonyms accept, like.

resentful *adj* aggrieved, angry, bitter, embittered, exasperated, grudging, huffish, huffy, hurt, incensed, indignant, irate, ireful, jealous, miffed, offended, peeved, piqued, put out, resentive, revengeful, stomachful, unforgiving, wounded.

antonym contented.

resentment *n* anger, animosity, bitterness, disaffection, discontentment, displeasure, fury, grudge, huff, hurt, ill-feeling, ill-will, indignation, ire, irritation, malice, pique, rage, rancour, umbrage, vexation, vindictiveness, wrath.

antonym contentment.

reservation[1] *n* arrière pensée, condition, demur, doubt, hesitancy, hesitation, inhibition, proviso, qualification, restraint, scepticism, scruple, second thought, stipulation.

reservation[2] enclave, homeland, park, preserve, reserve, sanctuary, territory, tract.

reserve[1] *v* bespeak, book, conserve, defer, delay, engage, hoard, hold, husband, keep, postpone, prearrange, preserve, retain, save, secure, set apart, spare, stockpile, store, withhold.

antonym use up.

n backlog, cache, capital, fund, hoard, park, preserve, reservation, reservoir, sanctuary, savings, stock, stockpile, store, substitute, supply, tract.

reserve[2] aloofness, constraint, coolness, formality, limitation, modesty, reluctance, reservation, restraint, restriction, reticence, secretiveness, shyness, silence, taciturnity.

antonyms friendliness, informality.

adj additional, alternate, auxiliary, extra, secondary, spare, substitute.

reserved[1] *adj* booked, bound, designated, destined, earmarked, engaged, fated, held, intended, kept, meant, predestined, restricted, retained, set aside, spoken for, taken.

antonym unreserved.

reserved[2] aloof, cautious, close-mouthed, cold, cool, demure, formal, modest, prim, restrained, reticent, retiring, secretive, shy, silent, stand-offish, taciturn, unapproachable, unclub(b)able, uncommunicative, uncompanionable, unconversable, undemonstrative, unforthcoming, unresponsive, unsociable.

antonyms friendly, informal.

reservoir *n* accumulation, basin, container, fund, holder, lake, pond, pool, receptacle, repository, reservatory, reserves, source, stock, stockpile, store, supply, tank.

reshuffle *n* change, interchange, realignment, rearrangement, redistribution, regrouping, reorganisation, restructuring, revision, shake-up, upheaval.

v change, interchange, realign, rearrange, redistribute, regroup, reorganise, restructure, revise, shake up, shift, shuffle.

reside *v* abide, consist, dwell, exist, inhabit, inhere, lie, live, lodge, remain, settle, sit, sojourn, stay.

residence *n* abode, country-house, country-seat, domicile, dwelling, habitation, hall, home, house, household, lodging, manor, mansion, occupancy, occupation, pad, palace, place, quarters, seat, sojourn, stay, tenancy, villa.

resident *n* citizen, commorant, denizen, habitant, indweller, inhabitant, local, lodger, occupant, tenant.

antonym non-resident.

adj dwelling, en poste, gremial, inhabiting, living, local, neighbourhood, permanent, settled.

antonym non-resident.

residential *adj* commuter, exurban, suburban.

residential area commuter belt, dormitory town, exurbia, suburbia, suburbs.

residual *adj* left-over, net(t), reliquary, remaining, residuary, residuous, unconsumed, unused, vestigial.

antonym core.

residue *n* balance, difference, dregs, excess, extra, left-overs, overflow, overplus, remainder, remains, remnant, residuum, rest, surplus.

antonym core.

resign *v* abandon, abdicate, cede, forgo, forsake, leave, quit, relinquish, renounce, sacrifice, stand down, surrender, vacate, waive, yield.

antonyms join, maintain.

resign oneself accede, accept, acquiesce, bow, comply, reconcile, submit, yield.

antonym resist.

resignation *n* abandonment, abdication, acceptance, acquiescence, compliance, defeatism, demission, departure, endurance, forbearing, fortitude, leaving, non-resistance, notice, passivity, patience, relinquishment, renunciation, retirement, submission, sufferance, surrender.

antonym resistance.

resigned *adj* acquiescent, compliant, defeatist, long-suffering, patient, stoical, subdued, submissive, unprotesting, unresisting.

antonym resisting.

resilience *n* adaptability, bounce, buoyancy, elasticity, flexibility, give, hardiness, plasticity, pliability, recoil, spring, springiness, strength, suppleness, toughness, unshockability.

antonyms inflexibility, rigidity.

resilient *adj* adaptable, bouncy, buoyant, elastic, flexible, hardy, irrepressible, plastic, pliable, springy, strong, supple, tough, unshockable.

antonyms downcast, rigid.

resist *v* avoid, battle, check, combat, confront, counteract, countervail, curb, defy, dispute, fight back, forbear, forgo, hinder, oppose, recalcitrate, refuse, repel, thwart, weather, withstand.

antonyms accept, submit.

resistance *n* antiperistasis, battle, combat, contention, counteraction, counter-stand, counter-time, defiance, fight, fighting, hindrance, impedance, impediment, intransigence, Maquis, obstruction, opposition, partisans, refusal, resistant, resistors, struggle, underground.

antonyms acceptance, submission.

resistant *adj* antagonistic, combative, defiant, dissident, hard, hostile, impervious, insusceptible, intractible, intransigent, opposed, recalcitrant, renitent, resistive, stiff, strong, tough, unsusceptible, unwilling, unyielding.

antonyms compliant, yielding.

resolute *adj* bold, constant, determined, dogged, firm, fixed, indissuadable, indivertible, inflexible, obstinate, persevering, purposeful, relentless, set, staunch, steadfast, stout, strong-minded, strong-willed, stubborn, sturdy, tenacious, unbending, undaunted, unflinching, unshakable, unshaken, unwavering.

antonym irresolute.

resolution *n* aim, answer, boldness, constancy, courage, decision, declaration, dedication, dénouement, determination, devotion, doggedness, earnestness, end, energy, finding, firmness, fortitude, intent, intention, judgement, motion, obstinacy, outcome, perseverance, pertinacity, purpose, relentlessness, resoluteness, resolve, settlement, sincerity, solution, solving, staunchness, steadfastness, stubbornness, tenacity, unravelling, verdict, will power, zeal.

antonym indecision.

resolve *v* agree, alter, analyse, anatomise, answer, banish, break up, change, clear, conclude, convert, crack, decide, design, determine, disentangle, disintegrate, dispel, dissect, dissipate, dissolve, elucidate, explain, fathom, fix, intend, liquefy, melt, metamorphose, purpose, reduce, relax, remove, separate, settle, solve, transform, transmute, undertake, unravel.

antonyms blend, waver.

n boldness, conclusion, conviction, courage, decision, design, determination, earnestness, firmness, intention, objective, project, purpose, resoluteness, resolution, sense of purpose, steadfastness, undertaking, will power.

antonym indecision.

resonant *adj* booming, canorous, echoing, full, plummy, resounding, reverberant, reverberating, rich, ringing, sonorous, vibrant.

antonym faint.

resort *v* frequent, go, haunt, hie, repair, visit.

antonym avoid.

n alternative, chance, course, expedient, haunt, health resort, hope, howf(f), possibility, recourse, reference, refuge, retreat, spa, spot, watering-place.

resort to employ, exercise, go so far as to, lower oneself to, stoop to, use, utilise.

resound *v* boom, echo, re-echo, resonate, reverberate, ring, sound, thunder.

resounding *adj* booming, conclusive, crushing, decisive, echoing, full, plangent, powerful, reboant, resonant, reverberating, rich, ringing, sonorous, sounding, thorough, vibrant, vocal.

antonyms faint, slight.

resource *n* ability, appliance, cache, capability, cleverness, contrivance, course, device, expedient, hoard, ingenuity, initiative, inventiveness, means, quick-wittedness, reserve, resort, resourcefulness, shift, source, stockpile, supply, talent.

antonym unimaginativeness.

resourceful *adj* able, bright, capable, clever, creative, fertile, imaginative, ingenious, innovative, inventive, originative, quick-witted, sharp, slick, talented.

resourceless *adj* feckless, feeble, fushionless, helpless, hopeless, inadequate, shiftless, useless.

antonym unimaginative.

resources *n* assets, capital, fisc, funds, holdings, materials, means, money, pelf, property, purse, reserves, riches, supplies, wealth, wherewithal.

respect *n* admiration, appreciation, approbation, aspect, bearing, characteristic, connection, consideration, deference, detail, esteem, estimation, facet, feature, homage, honour, matter, particular, point, recognition, reference, regard, relation, reverence, sense, veneration, way.

antonym disrespect.

v admire, appreciate, attend, esteem, follow, heed, honour, notice, obey, observe, pay homage to, recognise, regard, revere, reverence, value, venerate.

antonym scorn.

respectable *adj* admirable, ample, appreciable, clean-living, considerable, decent, decorous, dignified, estimable, fair, good, goodly, honest, honourable, large, passable, presentable, proper, reasonable, reputable, respected, seemly, sizable, substantial, tidy, tolerable, upright, venerable, well-to-do, worthy.

antonyms disreputable, miserly, unseemly.

respectful *adj* civil, courteous, courtly, deferential, dutiful, filial, gracious, humble, mannerly, obedient, polite, regardful, reverent, reverential, self-effacing, solicitous, submissive, subservient, well-mannered.

antonym disrespectful.

respecting *prep* about, concerning, considering, in respect of, regarding, with regard to, with respect to.

respective *adj* corresponding, individual, own, particular, personal, relevant, separate, several, special, specific, various.

respects *n* compliments, devoirs, duty, greetings, regards, salutations.

respite *n* adjournment, break, breather, cessation, delay, gap, halt, hiatus, intermission, interruption, interval, let-up, lull, moratorium, pause, postponement, recess, relaxation, relief, remission, reprieve, rest, stay, suspension.

resplendent *adj* beaming, bright, brilliant, dazzling, effulgent, fulgent, gleaming, glittering, glorious, irradiant, luminous, lustrous, radiant, refulgent, shining, splendid, splendiferous.

antonym dull.

respond *v* acknowledge, answer, answer back, come back, counter, react, reciprocate, rejoin, reply, retort, return.

response *n* acknowledgement, answer, comeback, counterblast, feedback, reaction, rejoinder, reply, respond, retort, return, riposte.

antonym query.

responsibility *n* accountability, amenability, answerability, authority, blame, burden, care, charge, conscientiousness, culpability, dependability, duty, fault, guilt, importance, level-headedness, liability, maturity, obligation, onus, power, rationality, reliability, sense, sensibleness, soberness, stability, trust, trustworthiness.

antonym irresponsibility.

responsible *adj* accountable, adult, amenable, answerable, authoritative, bound, chargeable, conscientious, culpable, decision-making, dependable, duty-bound, ethical, executive, guilty, high, important, level-headed, liable, mature, public-spirited, rational, reliable, right, sensible, sober, sound, stable, steady, subject, trustworthy.

antonym irresponsible.

responsive *adj* alive, awake, aware, forthcoming, impressionable, open, perceptive, reactive, receptive, respondent, responsorial, sensitive, sharp, susceptible, sympathetic.

antonym unresponsive.

rest[1] *n* base, break, breather, breathing-space, breathing-time, breathing-while, calm, cessation, cradle, doze, halt, haven, holder, holiday, idleness, inactivity, interlude, intermission, interval, leisure, lie-down, lie-in, lodging, lull, motionlessness, nap, pause, prop, refreshment, refuge, relaxation, relief, repose, retreat, shelf, shelter, shut-eye, siesta, sleep, slumber, snooze, somnolence, spell, stand, standstill, stillness, stop, support, tranquillity, trestle, vacation.

antonyms action, activity, restlessness.

v alight, base, cease, continue, depend, desist, discontinue, doze, found, halt, hang, hinge, idle, keep, land, lay, laze, lean, lie, lie back, lie down, lie in, perch, prop, recline, relax, rely, remain, repose, reside, settle, sit, sleep, slumber, snooze, spell, stand, stay, stop, turn.

antonyms change, continue, work.

rest[2] *n* balance, core, excess, left-overs, majority, others, remainder, remains, remnants, residue, residuum, rump, surplus.

restaurant *n* automat, bistro, brasserie, buffet, café, cafeteria, diner, dining-car, dining-room, eatery, eating-house, grill-room, grub-shop, porter-house, snack bar, steak-house.

restful *adj* calm, calming, comfortable, easeful, languid, pacific, peaceful, placid, quiet, relaxed, relaxing, serene, sleepy, soothing, tranquil, tranquillising, undisturbed, unhurried.

antonyms disturbed, disturbing.

restitution *n* amends, compensation, damages, indemnification, indemnity, recompense, redress, refund, reimbursement, remuneration, reparation, repayment, requital, restoration, restoring, return, satisfaction.

restive *adj* agitated, edgy, fidgety, fractious, fretful, impatient, jittery, jumpy, nervous, obstinate, recalcitrant, refractory, restless, uneasy, unquiet, unruly.

antonyms calm, relaxed.

restless *adj* active, agitated, anxious, bustling, changeable, disturbed, edgy, fidgety, fitful, footloose, fretful, hurried, inconstant, irresolute, jumpy, moving, nervous, nomadic, restive, roving, shifting, sleepless, transient, troubled, turbulent, uneasy, unquiet, unresting, unruly, unsettled, unstable, unsteady, wandering, worried.

antonyms calm, relaxed.

restlessness *n* activity, agitation, anxiety, bustle, disquiet, disturbance, edginess, fitfulness, fretfulness, heebie-jeebies, hurry, hurry-scurry, inconstancy, inquietude, insomnia, instability, jitters, jumpiness, movement, nervousness, restiveness, transience, turbulence, turmoil, uneasiness, unrest, unsettledness, wanderlust, worriedness.

antonyms calmness, relaxation.

restoration *n* instauration, kiss of life, reconstruction, recovery, recruit, recruital, re-establishment, refreshment, refurbishing, rehabilitation, reinstallation, reinstatement, rejuvenation, renewal, renovation, repair, replacement, restitution, return, revitalisation, revival.

antonyms damage, removal, weakening.

restore *v* fix, mend, reanimate, rebuild, recondition, reconstitute, reconstruct, recover, recruit, redintegrate, re-enforce, re-establish, refresh, refurbish, rehabilitate, reimpose, reinstate, reintroduce, rejuvenate, renew, renovate, repair, replace, retouch, return, revitalise, revive, revivify, strengthen.

antonyms damage, remove, weaken.

restrain *v* arrest, bind, bit, bridle, chain, check, cohibit, confine, constrain, control, curb, curtail, debar, detain, fetter, govern, hamper, hamshackle, handicap, harness, hinder, hold, imprison, inhibit, jail, keep, limit, manacle, muzzle, pinion, prevent, repress, restrict, stay, subdue, suppress, tie.

antonyms encourage, liberate.

restrained *adj* calm, controlled, discreet, low-key, mild, moderate, muted, quiet, reasonable, reticent, self-controlled, soft, steady, subdued, tasteful, temperate, undemonstrative, understated, unemphatic, unobtrusive.

antonym unrestrained.

restraint *n* arrest, ban, bondage, bonds, bridle, captivity, chains, check, coercion, cohibition, command, compulsion, confinement, confines, constraint, control, cramp, curb, curtailment, dam, detention, embargo, fetters, grip, hindrance, hold, imprisonment, inhibition, interdict, lid, limit, limitation, manacles, moderation, pinions, prevention, rein, restriction, self-control, self-discipline, self-possession, self-restraint, stint, straitjacket, suppression, taboo, tie.

antonym freedom.

restrict *v* astrict, bound, circumscribe, condition, confine, constrain, contain, cramp, demarcate, hamper, handicap, impede, inhibit, limit, regulate, restrain, restringe, scant, thirl, tie.

antonyms broaden, encourage, free.

restriction *n* check, condition, confinement, constraint, containment, control, curb, demarcation, handicap, inhibition, limitation, regulation, restraint, rule, squeeze, stint, stipulation.

antonyms broadening, encouragement, freedom.

result *n* conclusion, consequence, decision, development, effect, end, end-product, event, fruit, issue, outcome, produce, reaction, sequel, termination, upshot.

antonyms beginning, cause.

v appear, arise, culminate, derive, develop, emanate, emerge, end, ensue, eventuate, finish, flow, follow, happen, issue, proceed, spring, stem, terminate.

antonyms begin, cause.

resume *v* continue, pick up, proceed, recommence, reinstitute, reopen, restart, take up.

antonym cease.

résumé *n* abstract, digest, epitome, overview, précis, recapitulation, review, run-down, summary, synopsis.

resumption *n* continuation, epanalepsis, re-establishment, renewal, reopening, restart, resurgence.

antonym cessation.

resurgence *n* rebirth, recrudescence, re-emergence, renaissance, renascence, resumption, resurrection, return, revival, revivification, risorgimento.

antonym decrease.

resurrect *v* come to life, disinter, reintroduce, renew, restore, revive.

antonyms bury, kill off, quash.

resurrection *n* comeback, reactivation, reappearance, rebirth, renaissance, renascence, renewal, restoration, resurgence, resuscitation, return, revival, revivification.

antonyms burying, killing off, quashing.

resuscitate *v* quicken, reanimate, reinvigorate, renew, rescue, restore, resurrect, revitalise, revive, revivify, save.

resuscitated *adj* redintegrate(d), redivivus, restored, resurrected, revived.

retain *v* absorb, commission, contain, detail, employ, engage, grasp, grip, hire, hold, hold back, keep, keep in mind, keep up, maintain, memorise, pay, preserve, recall, recollect, remember, reserve, restrain, save.

antonyms release, spend.

retainer[1] *n* attendant, dependant, domestic, flunky, footman, galloglass, lackey, menial, servant, supporter, valet, vassal.

retainer[2] *n* advance, deposit, fee, retaining fee.

retaliate *v* fight back, get back at, get even with, get one's own back, give as good as one gets, hit back, reciprocate, repay in kind, return like for like, revenge oneself, strike back, take revenge.

antonyms accept, submit.

retaliation *n* a taste of one's own medicine, counterblow, counterstroke, reciprocation, repayment, reprisal, requital, retort, retortion, retribution, revenge, tit for tat, vengeance.

antonyms acceptance, submission.

retard *v* arrest, brake, check, clog, decelerate, defer, delay, detain, encumber, handicap, hinder, impede, keep back, obstruct, slow, stall.

antonym advance.

retardation *n* deficiency, delay, dullness, hindering, hindrance, impeding, incapability, incapacity, lag, mental handicap, obstruction, retardment, slowing, slowness.

antonym advancement.

retch *v* disgorge, gag, heave, puke, reach, regurgitate, spew, throw up, vomit.

retching *n* gagging, nausea, puking, reaching, vomiting, vomiturition.

reticence *n* muteness, quietness, reserve, restraint, secretiveness, silence, taciturnity, uncommunicativeness, unforthcomingness.

antonyms communicativeness, forwardness, frankness.

reticent *adj* boutonné, close-lipped, close-mouthed, mum, mute, quiet, reserved, restrained, secretive, silent, taciturn, tight-lipped, uncommunicative, unforthcoming, unspeaking.

antonyms communicative, forward, frank.

retinue *n* aides, attendants, cortège, entourage, escort, followers, following, personnel, servants, staff, suite, train.

retiral *n* abdication, decumbiture, departure, exit, flight, resignation, retirement, retreat, withdrawal.

antonym advance.

retire *v* decamp, depart, draw back, ebb, exit, leave, recede, remove, retreat, withdraw.

antonyms enter, join.

retired *adj* emeritus, ex-, former, past.

retirement *n* loneliness, obscurity, privacy, retiral, retreat, seclusion, solitude, withdrawal.

antonyms company, limelight.

retiring *adj* bashful, coy, demure, diffident, humble, meek, modest, mousy, quiet, reclusive, reserved, reticent, self-effacing, shamefaced, shrinking, shy, timid, timorous, unassertive, unassuming.

antonyms assertive, forward.

retort *v* answer, counter, rejoin, repartee, reply, respond, retaliate, return, riposte.

n answer, backword, come-back, quip, rejoinder, repartee, reply, response, riposte, sally.

retract *v* abjure, cancel, deny, disavow, disclaim, disown, recall, recant, renounce, repeal, repudiate, rescind, reverse, revoke, unsay, unspeak, withdraw.

antonym maintain.

retreat *v* depart, ebb, leave, quit, recede, recoil, retire, shrink, turn tail, withdraw.

antonym advance.

n asylum, den, departure, ebb, evacuation, flight, funk-hole, growlery, haunt, haven, hibernacle, hibernaculum, hideaway, privacy, refuge, resort, retirement, sanctuary, seclusion, shelter, withdrawal.

antonyms advance, company, limelight.

retrench *v* curtail, cut, decrease, diminish, economise, husband, lessen, limit, pare, prune, reduce, save, slim down, trim.

antonym increase.

retrenchment *n* contraction, cost-cutting, curtailment, cut, cutback, economy, pruning, reduction, run-down, shrinkage.

antonym increase.

retribution *n* compensation, justice, Nemesis, payment, punishment, reckoning, recompense, redress, repayment, reprisal, requital, retaliation, revenge, reward, satisfaction, talion, vengeance.

retrieve *v* fetch, make good, recall, recapture, recoup, recover, redeem, regain, repair, repossess, rescue, restore, return, salvage, save.

antonym lose.

retrograde *adj* backward, declining, degenerative, denigrating, deteriorating, downward, inverse, negative, regressive, relapsing, retreating, retrogressive, reverse, reverting, waning, worsening.

antonym progressive.

retrogress *v* backslide, decline, degenerate, deteriorate, drop, ebb, fall, recede, regress, relapse, retire, retreat, retrograde, return, revert, sink, wane, withdraw, worsen.

antonym progress.

retrogression *n* decline, deterioration, drop, ebb, fall, recidivism, regress, relapse, retrogradation, return, worsening.

antonyms increase, progress.

retrospect *n* afterthought, contemplation, hindsight, recollection, re-examination, reference, regard, remembrance, reminiscence, review, survey.

antonym prospect.

retrospective *adj* backward-looking, retroactive, retro-operative.

return *v* announce, answer, choose, communicate, convey, deliver, earn, elect, make, net, pick, reappear, rebound, reciprocate, recoil, recompense, recur, redound, re-establish, refund, reimburse, reinstate, rejoin, remit, render, repair, repay, replace, reply, report, requite, respond, restore, retort, retreat, revert, send, submit, transmit, volley, yield.

antonyms leave, take.

n account, advantage, answer, benefit, comeback, compensation, form, gain, home-coming, income, interest, list, proceeds, profit, quip, reappearance, rebound, reciprocation, recoil, recompense, recrudescence, recurrence, redound, re-establishment, reimbursement, reinstatement, rejoinder, reparation, repayment, replacement, reply, report, requital, response, restoration, retaliation, retort, retreat, revenue, reversion, reward, riposte, sally, statement, summary, takings, yield.

antonyms disappearance, expense, loss, payment.

re-use *v* reconstitute, recycle.

revamp *v* do up, overhaul, rebuild, recast, recondition, reconstruct, refit, refurbish, rehabilitate, renovate, repair, restore, revise.

reveal *v* announce, bare, betray, broadcast, communicate, disbosom, disclose, dismask, display, divulge, exhibit, expose, impart, leak, lift the lid off, manifest, open, proclaim, publish, show, spill a bibful, tell, unbare, unbosom, uncover, unearth, unfold, unmask, unshadow, unveil.

antonym hide.

revel *v* carouse, celebrate, live it up, make merry, paint the town red, push the boat out, raise the roof, roist, roister, whoop it up.

n bacchanal, carousal, carouse, celebration, comus, debauch, festivity, gala, jollification, merry-make, merrymaking, party, saturnalia, spree.

revel in bask, crow, delight, gloat, glory, indulge, joy, lap up, luxuriate, rejoice, relish, savour, take pleasure, thrive on, wallow.

antonym dislike.

revelation *n* announcement, apocalypse, betrayal, broadcasting, communication, disclosure, discovery, display, exhibition, exposé, exposition, exposure, giveaway, leak, manifestation, news, proclamation, publication, telling, uncovering, unearthing, unveiling.

reveller *n* bacchanal, bacchant, carouser, celebrator, merrymaker, party-goer, pleasure-seeker, roister, roisterer, royster, roysterer, wassailer.

revelry *n* carousal, carouse, celebration, debauch, debauchery, festivity, fun, jollification, jollity, merrymaking, party, revel-rout, riot, roistering, saturnalia, spree, wassail, wassailing, wassailry.

antonym sobriety.

revenge *n* a dose/taste of one's own medicine, ravanche, reprisal, requital, retaliation, retribution, revengement, satisfaction, ultion, vengeance, vindictiveness.

v avenge, even the score, get one's own back, get satisfaction, repay, requite, retaliate, vindicate.

revengeful *adj* bitter, implacable, malevolent, malicious, malignant, merciless, pitiless, resentful, spiteful, unforgiving, unmerciful, vengeful, vindictive, wreakful.

antonym forgiving.

revenue *n* gain, income, interest, proceeds, profits, receipts, returns, rewards, take, takings, yield.

antonym expenditure.

reverberate *v* echo, rebound, recoil, re-echo, reflect, resound, ring, vibrate.

reverberation *n* echo, rebound, recoil, re-echoing, reflection, resonance, resounding, ringing, vibration, wave.

reverberations *n* consequences, effects, repercussions, results, ripples, shock wave.

revere *v* adore, defer to, exalt, honour, pay homage to, respect, reverence, venerate, worship.

antonyms despise, scorn.

reverence *n* admiration, adoration, awe, deference, devotion, dulia, esteem, genuflection, homage, honour, hyperdulia, latria, puja, respect, veneration, worship.

antonym scorn.

v acknowledge, admire, adore, honour, respect, revere, venerate, worship.

antonyms despise, scorn.

reverent *adj* adoring, awed, decorous, deferential, devout, dutiful, humble, loving, meek, pious, respectful, reverential, solemn, submissive.

antonym irreverent.

reverie *n* absent-mindedness, abstraction, brown study, daydream, daydreaming, dreamery, inattention, musing, preoccupation, trance, woolgathering.

reversal *n* abrogation, annulment, cancellation, countermanding, defeat, delay, difficulty, disaster, enantiodromia, misfortune, mishap, nullification, problem, repeal, rescinding, rescission, reverse, revocation, set-back, turnabout, turnaround, turnround, upset, U-turn, volte-face.

antonyms advancement, progress.

reverse *v* alter, annul, back, backtrack, cancel, change, countermand, hark back, invalidate, invert, negate, overrule, overset, overthrow, overturn, quash, repeal, rescind, retract, retreat, revert, revoke, transpose, undo, up-end, upset.

antonym enforce.

n adversity, affliction, antithesis, back, blow, check, contradiction, contrary, converse, defeat, disappointment, failure, hardship, inverse, misadventure, misfortune, mishap, opposite, rear, repulse, reversal, setback, trial, underside, verso, vicissitude, woman.

adj backward, contrary, converse, inverse, inverted, opposite, verso.

revert *v* backslide, lapse, recur, regress, relapse, resume, retrogress, return, reverse.

antonym progress.

review *v* assess, criticise, discuss, evaluate, examine, inspect, judge, reassess, recall, recapitulate, recollect, reconsider, re-evaluate, re-examine, rehearse, remember, rethink, revise, scrutinise, study, weigh.

n analysis, assessment, commentary, criticism, critique, evaluation, examination, journal, judgement, magazine, notice, periodical, reassessment, recapitulation, recension, reconsideration, re-evaluation, re-examination, report, rethink, retrospect, revision, scrutiny, study, survey.

reviewer *n* arbiter, commentator, connoisseur, critic, essayist, judge, observer.

revile *v* abuse, blackguard, calumniate, defame, denigrate, libel, malign, miscall, reproach, scorn, slander, smear, traduce, vilify, vilipend, vituperate.

antonym praise.

revise *v* alter, amend, change, correct, edit, emend, memorise, modify, recast, recense, reconsider, reconstruct, redo, re-examine, reread, revamp, review, rewrite, study, swot up, update.

revision *n* alteration, amendment, change, correction, editing, emendation, homework, memorising, modification, recast, recasting, recension, reconstruction, re-examination, rereading, review, rewriting, rifacimento, studying, swotting, updating.

revitalise *v* reactivate, reanimate, refresh, rejuvenate, renew, restore, resurrect, revive, revivify.

antonyms dampen, suppress.

revival *n* awakening, quickening, reactivation, reanimation, reawakening, rebirth, recrudescence, renaissance, renascence, renewal, restoration, resurgence, resurrection, resuscitation, revitalisation, revivification, risorgimento.

antonym suppression.

revive *v* animate, awaken, cheer, comfort, invigorate, quicken, rally, reactivate, reanimate, recover, refresh, rekindle, renew, renovate, restore, resuscitate, revitalise, revivify, rouse.

antonyms suppress, weary.

revivify *v* inspirit, invigorate, reactivate, reanimate, refresh, renew, restore, resuscitate, revive.

antonyms dampen, depress.

reviving *adj* bracing, enheartening, exhilarating, invigorating, reanimating, refreshening, regenerating, reinvigorating, revivescent, revivifying, reviviscent, stimulating, tonic.

antonyms disheartening, exhausting.

revocation *n* abolition, annulment, cancellation, countermanding, nullification, quashing, repeal, repealing, repudiation, rescinding, rescission, retractation, retraction, reversal, revoking, withdrawal.

antonym enforcement.

revoke *v* abolish, abrogate, annul, cancel, countermand, disclaim, dissolve, invalidate, negate, nullify, quash, recall, recant, renounce, repeal, repudiate, rescind, retract, reverse, withdraw.

antonym enforce.

revolt[1] *n* breakaway, defection, inqilab, insurgency, insurrection, Jacquerie, mutiny, putsch, rebellion, revolution, rising, secession, sedition, uprising.

v defect, mutiny, rebel, resist, riot, rise.

antonym submit.

revolt[2] *v* disgust, nauseate, offend, outrage, repel, repulse, scandalise, shock, sicken.

antonym please.

revolting *adj* abhorrent, abominable, appalling, disgusting, distasteful, fetid, foul, horrible, horrid, loathsome, nasty, nauseating, nauseous, noisome, obnoxious, obscene, offensive, repellent, repugnant, repulsive, shocking, sickening, sickly.

antonym pleasant.

revolution *n* cataclysm, change, circle, circuit, coup, coup d'état, cycle, gyration, innovation, inqilab, insurgency, Jacquerie, lap, metamorphosis, metanoia, mutiny, orbit, putsch, rebellion, reformation, revolt, rising, rotation, round, shift, spin, transformation, turn, upheaval, uprising, volution, wheel, whirl.

revolutionary *n* anarchist, insurgent, insurrectionary, insurrectionist, Jacobin, mutineer, rebel, revolutionist, Trot, Trotskyite.

adj anarchistic, avant-garde, different, drastic, experimental, extremist, fundamental, innovative, insurgent, insurrectionary, mutinous, new, novel, progressive, radical, rebel, seditious, subversive, thoroughgoing.

antonyms commonplace, establishment.

revolve *v* circle, circumgyrate, circumvolve, gyrate, orbit, rotate, spin, turn, wheel, whirl.

revolver *n* air-gun, firearm, gun, hand-gun, heater, peace-maker, piece, pistol, rod, shooter, six-shooter.

revolving *adj* gyral, gyrating, gyratory, rotating, spinning, turning, whirling.

antonym stationary.

revulsion *n* abhorrence, abomination, aversion, detestation, disgust, dislike, distaste, hatred, loathing, recoil, repugnance, repulsion.

antonym pleasure.

reward *n* benefit, bonus, bounty, come-up(p)ance, compensation, desert, gain, guerdon, honour, meed, merit, payment, pay-off, premium, prize, profit, punishment, recompense, remuneration, repayment, requital, retribution, return, wages.

antonym punishment.

v compensate, guerdon, honour, pay, recompense, remunerate, repay, requite.

antonym punish.

rewarding *adj* advantageous, beneficial, edifying, enriching, fruitful, fulfilling, gainful, gratifying, pleasing, productive, profitable, remunerative, rewardful, satisfying, valuable, worthwhile.

antonym unrewarding.

rewording *n* metaphrase, metaphrasis, paraphrase, rephrasing, revision.

rewrite *v* correct, edit, emend, recast, redraft, revise, reword, rework.

rhetoric *n* bombast, declamation, eloquence, fustian, grandiloquence, hyperbole, magniloquence, oratory, pomposity, rant, verbosity, wordiness.

rhetorical *adj* artificial, bombastic, declamatory, false, flamboyant, flashy, florid, flowery, grandiloquent, high-flown, high-sounding, hyperbolic, inflated, insincere, linguistic, magniloquent, oratorical, over-decorated, pompous, pretentious, rhetoric, showy, silver-tongued, stylistic, verbal, verbose, windy.

antonym simple.

rhyme *n* chime, ditty, doggerel, jingle, limerick, ode, poem, poesie, poetry, song, verse.

rhythm *n* accent, beat, cadence, cadency, eurhythmy, flow, lilt, measure, metre, movement, pattern, periodicity, pulse, rhythmicity, swing, tempo, time.

rhythmic *adj* cadenced, flowing, harmonious, lilting, melodious, metric, metrical, musical, periodic, pulsating, rhythmical, throbbing.

antonym unrhythmical.

rib *n* band, bar, bone, costa, moulding, purlin(e), ribbing, ridge, shaft, support, vein, wale.

ribald *adj* base, bawdy, blue, broad, coarse, derisive, earthy, filthy, foul-mouthed, gross, indecent, irrisory, jeering, licentious, low, mean, mocking, naughty, obscene, off-colour, Rabelaisian, racy, risqué, rude, scurrilous, smutty, vulgar.

antonym polite.

ribaldry *n* baseness, bawdiness, billingsgate, coarseness, derision, earthiness, filth, grossness, indecency, irrision, jeering, licentiousness, lowness, mockery, naughtiness, obscenity, raciness, rudeness, scurrility, smut, smuttiness, vulgarity.

ribbon *n* band, cord, fillet, hair-band, head-band, jag, sash, shred, strip, taenia, tatter.

rich *adj* abounding, abundant, affluent, ample, bright, copious, costly, creamy, deep, delicious, dulcet, elaborate, elegant, expensive, exquisite, exuberant, fatty, fecund, fertile, fine, flavoursome, flush, fruitful. full, full-bodied, full-flavoured, full-toned, gay, gorgeous, heavy, highly-flavoured, humorous, in the money, intense, juicy, laughable, lavish, loaded, ludicrous, luscious, lush, luxurious, mellifluous, mellow, moneyed, opulent, palatial, pecunious, plenteous, plentiful, plutocratic, precious, priceless, productive, prolific, propertied, property, prosperous, resonant, ridiculous, risible, rolling, savoury, side-splitting, spicy, splendid, strong, succulent, sumptuous, superb, sweet, tasty, uberous, valuable, vibrant, vivid, warm, wealthy, well-heeled, well-off, well-provided, well-stocked, well-supplied, well-to-do.

antonyms harsh, miserly, plain, poor, simple, tasteless, thin, unfertile.

riches *n* a long purse, abundance, affluence, assets, fortune, gold, mint, money, opulence, pelf, plenty, property, resources, richness, substance, treasure, uberty, wealth.

antonym poverty.

richly *adv* amply, appropriately, condignly, elaborately, elegantly, expensively, exquisitely, fully, gorgeously, lavishly, luxuriously, opulently, palatially, properly, splendidly, suitably, sumptuously, thoroughly, well.

antonyms poorly, scantily.

rickety *adj* broken, broken-down, decrepit, derelict, dilapidated, feeble, flimsy, frail, imperfect, infirm, insecure, jerry-built, precarious, ramshackle, shaky, shoogly, tottering, tottery, unsound, unstable, unsteady, weak, wobbly.

antonyms stable, strong.

rid *v* clear, deliver, disabuse, disburden, disembarrass, disencumber, expel, free, purge, relieve, unburden.

antonym burden.

riddance *n* clearance, deliverance, disposal, ejection, elimination, expulsion, extermination, freedom, purgation, release, relief, removal.

antonym burdening.

riddle[1] *n* brain-teaser, charade, conundrum, enigma, logogram, logograph, logogriph, mystery, poser, problem, puzzle, rebus.

riddle[2] *v* boult, corrupt, damage, fill, filter, impair, infest, invade, mar, pepper, perforate, permeate, pervade, pierce, puncture, screen, sieve, sift, spoil, strain, winnow.

n boulter, sieve, strainer.

ride *v* control, dominate, enslave, float, grip, handle, haunt, hurl, journey, manage, move, oppress, progress, sit, survive, travel, weather.

n drive, hurl, jaunt, journey, lift, outing, spin, trip, whirl.

ridge *n* arête, band, costa, crinkle, drum, drumlin, escarpment, eskar, hill, hog's back, hummock, lump, reef, ripple, saddle, wale, weal, welt, yardang, zastruga.

ridicule *n* banter, chaff, derision, gibe, irony, irrision, jeering, jeers, laughter, mockery, raillery, sarcasm, satire, scorn, sneers, taunting.

antonym praise.

v banter, burlesque, caricature, cartoon, chaff, crucify, deride, humiliate, jeer, josh, lampoon, mock, parody, pillory, pooh-pooh, queer, quiz, rib, satirise, scoff, send up, sneer at, take the mickey out of, taunt.

antonym praise.

ridiculous *adj* absurd, comical, contemptible, damfool, derisory, farcical, foolish, funny, hilarious, incredible, laughable, laughworthy, ludicrous, nonsensical, outrageous, preposterous, risible, silly, stupid, unbelievable.

antonym sensible.

riding-school *n* manège, school of equitation.

rife *adj* abounding, abundant, common, commonplace, current, epidemic, frequent, general, plentiful, prevailing, prevalent, raging, rampant, teeming, ubiquitous, universal, widespread.

antonym scarce.

riff-raff *n* canaille, hoi polloi, mob, rabble, raffle, raggle-taggle, rag-tag, rag-tag and bobtail, rascality, rent-a-mob, scum, undesirables.

rifle[1] *v* burgle, despoil, gut, loot, maraud, pillage, plunder, ransack, rob, rummage, sack, strip.

rifle[2] *n* air-gun, bundook, carbine, firearm, firelock, flintlock, fusil, gun, musket, shotgun.

rift *n* alienation, beach, breach, break, chink, cleavage, cleft, crack, cranny, crevice, difference, disaffection, disagreement, dissure, division, estrangement, fault, flaw, fracture, gap, opening, quarrel, schism, separation, space, split.

antonym unity.

rig[1] *v* accoutre, equip, fit up, furnish, kit out, outfit, provision, supply.

n accoutrements, apparatus, ensemble, equipage, equipment, fitments, fittings, fixtures, gear, machinery, outfit, tackle.

rig out accoutre, array, attire, caparison, clothe, costume, dress, dress up, equip, fit, fit out, fit up, furnish, kit out, outfit.

rig up arrange, assemble, build, construct, erect, fit up, fix up, improvise, knock up.

antonym dismantle.

rig[2] *v* arrange, cook, doctor, engineer, fake, falsify, fiddle, fix, gerrymander, juggle, manipulate, tamper with, trump up.

right *adj* absolute, accurate, admissible, advantageous, appropriate, authentic, balanced, becoming, characteristic, comme il faut, complete, compos mentis, conservative, correct, deserved, desirable, dexter, dextral, direct, done, due, equitable, ethical, exact, factual, fair, favourable, fine, fit, fitting, genuine, good, healthy, honest, honourable, ideal, just, lawful, lucid, moral, normal, opportune, out-and-out, perpendicular, precise, proper, propitious, rational, reactionary, real, reasonable, righteous, rightful, rightist, rightward, right-wing, sane, satisfactory, seemly, sound, spot-on, straight, suitable, thorough, thoroughgoing, Tory, true, unerring, unimpaired, upright, utter, valid, veracious, veritable, virtuous, well.

antonyms left, left-wing, mad, unfit, wrong.

adv absolutely, accurately, advantageously, altogether, appropriate, aptly, aright, bang, befittingly, beneficially, completely, correctly, directly, entirely, ethically, exactly, factually, fairly, favourably, fittingly, fortunately, genuinely, honestly, honourably, immediately, instantly, justly, morally, perfectly, precisely, promptly, properly, quickly, quite, righteously, rightward(s), satisfactorily, slap-bang, squarely, straight, straightaway, suitably, thoroughly, totally, truly, utterly, virtuously, well, wholly.

antonyms incorrectly, left, unfairly, wrongly.

n authority, business, claim, droit, due, equity, freedom, good, goodness, honour, integrity, interest, justice, lawfulness, legality, liberty, licence, morality, permission, power, prerogative, privilege, propriety, reason, rectitude, righteousness, rightfulness, rightness, title, truth, uprightness, virtue.

antonyms depravity, wrong.

v avenge, correct, fix, rectify, redress, repair, righten, settle, stand up, straighten, vindicate.

right away at once, chop-chop, directly, forthwith, immediately, instantly, now, promptly, right off, straight off, straightaway, straightway, this instant, tout de suite, without delay, without hesitation.

antonym eventually.

righteous *adj* blameless, equitable, ethical, fair, God-fearing, good, guiltless, honest, honourable, incorrupt, just, law-abiding, moral, pure, rectitudinous, saintly, sinless, upright, virtuous.

antonym unrighteous.

n Holy Willies, just, Pharisees, saints, unco guid, well-doers.

antonym unrighteous.

righteousness *n* blamelessness, dharma, equity, ethicalness, faithfulness, goodness, honesty, honour, integrity, justice, morality, probity, purity, rectitude, uprightness, virtue.

antonym unrighteousness.

rightful *adj* authorised, bona fide, correct, de jure, due, just, lawful, legal, legitimate, licit, prescribed, proper, real, suitable, true, valid.

antonyms incorrect, unlawful.

rightfully *adv* correctly, de jure, justifiably, justly, lawfully, legally, legitimately, properly, rightly.

antonyms incorrectly, unjustifiably.

right-handed *adj* dext(e)rous.

antonym left-handed.

right-handedness *n* dexterity, dextrality.

antonym left-handedness.

rigid *adj* adamant, austere, cast-iron, exact, fixe harsh, inflexible, intransigent, invariable, rigorou set, severe, starch(y), stern, stiff, stony, stric stringent, tense, unalterable, unbendin uncompromising, undeviating, unrelentin unyielding.

antonym flexible.

rigmarole *n* balderdash, bother, carry-o gibberish, hassle, jargon, nonsense, palave performance, red tape, riddle-me-ree, to-d trash, twaddle.

rigorous *adj* accurate, austere, challengin conscientious, demanding, exact, exactin extreme, firm, hard, harsh, inclement, inflexibl inhospitable, meticulous, nice, painstakin precise, punctilious, Rhadamanthine, rigi scrupulous, severe, spartan, stern, stric stringent, thorough, tough, unsparing.

antonyms lenient, mild.

rigour *n* accuracy, asperity, austerit conscientiousness, exactitude, exactnes firmness, hardness, hardship, harshnes inflexibility, meticulousness, ordeal, precisenes precision, privation, punctiliousness, rigidit rigorism, rigourousness, sternness, strictnes stringency, suffering, thoroughness, trial.

antonyms leniency, mildness.

rig-out *n* apparel, clobber, clothing, costum dress, ensemble, garb, gear, get-up, habit, liver outfit, raiment, rig, togs, uniform.

rile *v* anger, annoy, bug, exasperate, gall, get, ir irritate, miff, nark, nettle, peeve, pique, provok put out, upset, vex.

antonym soothe.

rim *n* border, brim, brink, circumference, edge, li margin, skirt, verge.

antonym centre.

rind *n* crust, epicarp, husk, integument, pee skin, zest.

ring[1] *n* annulation, annulet, annulus, aren association, band, cabal, cartel, cell, circl circuit, circus, clique, collar, collet, combin coterie, crew, enclosure, gang, group, gyre, hal hoop, knot, loop, mob, organisation, rink, roun rundle, syndicate.

v circumscribe, encircle, enclose, encompas gash, gird, girdle, mark, score, surround.

ring[2] *v* bell, buzz, call, chime, clang, clink, pea phone, resonate, resound, reverberate, soun tang, telephone, ting, tinkle, tintinnabulate, toll.

n buzz, call, chime, clang, clink, knell, pea phone-call, tang, ting, tinkle, tintinnabulation.

ringleader *n* bell-wether, brains, chief, fuglema leader, spokesman.

rinse *v* bathe, clean, cleanse, dip, sluice, splas swill, synd, wash, wet.

n bath, dip, dye, splash, tint, wash, wetting.

riot *n* anarchy, bagarre, boisterousness, carous commotion, confusion, debauchery, disord display, disturbance, Donnybrook, émeut excess, extravaganza, festivity, flourish, fra frolic, high, insurrection, jinks, jollificatio lawlessness, merry-make, merrymaking, quarrel, revelry, riotousness, riotry, romp, rookery, rout, row, ruction, ruffle, shindig, shindy, show, splash, strife, tumult, turbulence, turmoil, uproar.

antonyms calm, order.

v carouse, frolic, rampage, rebel, revel, revolt, rise up, roister, romp, run riot, run wild.

riotous *adj* anarchic, boisterous, disorderly, insubordinate, insurrectionary, lawless, loud, luxurious, mutinous, noisy, orgiastic, rambunctious, rampageous, rebellious, refractory, roisterous, rollicking, rowdy, saturnalian, side-splitting, tumultuous, ungovernable, unrestrained, unruly, uproarious, violent, wanton, wild.

antonyms orderly, restrained.

rip *v* burst, claw, cut, gash, hack, lacerate, rend, rupture, score, separate, slash, slit, split, tear.

n cleavage, cut, gash, hole, laceration, rent, rupture, slash, slit, split, tear.

rip off cheat, con, defraud, diddle, do, dupe, exploit, filch, fleece, lift, mulct, overcharge, pilfer, pinch, rob, rogue, steal, sting, swindle, swipe, thieve, trick.

ripe *adj* accomplished, auspicious, complete, developed, favourable, finished, grown, ideal, mature, mellow, opportune, perfect, prepared, promising, propitious, ready, right, ripened, seasoned, suitable, timely.

antonyms inopportune, untimely.

ripen *v* age, burgeon, develop, mature, mellow, prepare, season.

rip-off *n* cheat, con, con trick, daylight robbery, diddle, exploitation, fraud, robbery, sting, swindle, theft.

riposte *n* answer, come-back, quip, rejoinder, repartee, reply, response, retort, return, sally.

v answer, quip, reciprocate, rejoin, reply, respond, retort, return.

ripple *n* babble, burble, disturbance, eddy, gurgle, lapping, pirl, purl, ripplet, undulation, wave, wimple.

rise *v* advance, appear, arise, ascend, buoy, climb, crop up, emanate, emerge, enlarge, eventuate, flow, get up, grow, happen, improve, increase, intensify, issue, kite, levitate, lift, mount, mutiny, occur, originate, progress, prosper, rebel, resist, revolt, slope, slope up, soar, spring, spring up, stand up, surface, swell, tower, volume, wax.

antonyms descend, fall.

n acclivity, advance, advancement, aggrandisement, ascent, climb, elevation, hillock, improvement, incline, increase, increment, origin, progress, promotion, raise, rising, upsurge, upswing, upturn, upward turn.

antonyms descent, fall.

risible *adj* absurd, amusing, comic, comical, droll, farcical, funny, hilarious, humorous, laughable, ludicrous, rib-tickling, ridiculous, side-splitting.

antonyms serious, unfunny.

rising *n* émeute, insurrection, revolt, revolution, riot, uprising.

adj advancing, approaching, ascending, assurgent, emerging, growing, increasing, intensifying, mounting, soaring, swelling.

antonym decreasing.

risk *n* adventure, chance, danger, gamble, hazard, jeopardy, peril, possibility, speculation, uncertainty, venture.

antonyms certainty, safety.

v adventure, chance, dare, endanger, gamble, hazard, imperil, jeopardise, speculate, venture.

risky *adj* chancy, dangerous, dicey, dodgy, fraught, hazardous, iffy, perilous, precarious, riskful, touch-and-go, tricky, uncertain, unsafe.

antonym safe.

risqué *adj* bawdy, blue, coarse, crude, daring, earthy, immodest, improper, indecent, indecorous, indelicate, naughty, near the knuckle, off colour, Rabelaisian, racy, ribald, suggestive.

antonym decent.

rite *n* act, ceremonial, ceremony, custom, form, formality, liturgy, mystery, observance, office, ordinance, practice, procedure, ritual, sacrament, service, solemnity, usage, worship.

ritual *n* ceremonial, ceremony, communion, convention, custom, form, formality, habit, liturgy, mystery, observance, ordinance, practice, prescription, procedure, rite, routine, sacrament, service, solemnity, tradition, usage, wont.

adj ceremonial, ceremonious, conventional, customary, formal, formulary, habitual, prescribed, procedural, routine, stereotyped.

antonyms informal, unusual.

rival *n* adversary, antagonist, challenger, collateral, compeer, competitor, contender, contestant, corrival, emulator, equal, equivalent, fellow, match, opponent, peer, rivaless.

antonyms associate, colleague, co-worker.

adj competing, competitive, conflicting, corrival, emulating, emulous, opposed, opposing.

antonyms associate, co-operating.

v compete, contend, emulate, equal, match, oppose, rivalise, vie with.

antonym co-operate.

rivalry *n* antagonism, competition, competitiveness, conflict, contention, contest, duel, emulation, opposition, rivality, rivalship, struggle, vying.

antonym co-operation.

river *n* beck, burn, creek, ea, flood, flow, gush, riverway, rush, spate, stream, surge, tributary, waterway.

adj fluvial, riverain, riverine.

river-bank *n* rivage.

river-mouth *n* broads, delta, estuary, firth, frith, ostium.

riveting *adj* absorbing, arresting, captivating, engrossing, enthralling, fascinating, gripping, hypnotic, magnetic, spellbinding.

antonym boring.

road *n* Autobahn, autopista, autoroute, autostrada, avenue, boulevard, camino real, carriageway, clearway, course, crescent, direction, drift, drive, driveway, freeway, highway, lane, motorway, path, pathway, roadway, route, street, thoroughfare, track, way.

roam *v* drift, meander, peregrinate, prowl, ramble, range, rove, squander, stravaig, stray, stroll, travel, walk, wander.

antonym stay.

roar *v* bawl, bay, bell, bellow, blare, clamour, crash, cry, guffaw, hoot, howl, rumble, shout, thunder, vociferate, wuther, yell.

antonym whisper.

n bellow, belly-laugh, blare, clamour, crash, cry, guffaw, hoot, howl, outcry, rumble, shout, thunder, yell.

antonym whisper.

rob *v* bereave, blag, bunko, cheat, con, defraud, deprive, despoil, dispossess, do, flake, flimp, gyp, heist, hold up, loot, mill, pillage, plunder, raid, ramp, ransack, reive, rifle, rip off, roll, sack, sting, strip, swindle, thieve.

antonyms give, provide.

robber *n* bandit, brigand, burglar, cateran, cheat, con man, dacoit, fraud, highwayman, hijacker, klepht, ladrone, land-pirate, latron, looter, motor-bandit, pirate, plunderer, raider, reiver, stealer, swindler, thief, vulture.

robbery *n* blag, burglary, dacoitage, dacoity, depredation, embezzlement, filching, fraud, heist, high toby, hold-up, larceny, low toby, pillage, plunder, purse-snatching, purse-taking, raid, rapine, rip-off, spoliation, stealing, stick-up, swindle, theft, thievery.

robe *n* bathrobe, costume, dressing-gown, gown, habit, housecoat, peignoir, vestment, wrap, wrapper.

v apparel, attire, clothe, drape, dress, garb, vest.

robot *n* android, automaton, Dalek, golem, machine, zombie.

robust *adj* able-bodied, athletic, boisterous, brawny, coarse, down-to-earth, earthy, fit, hale, hard-headed, hardy, healthy, hearty, husky, indecorous, lusty, muscular, over-hearty, powerful, practical, pragmatic, raw, realistic, robustious, roisterous, rollicking, rough, rude, rugged, sensible, sinewy, sound, staunch, sthenic, stout, straightforward, strapping, strong, sturdy, thick-set, tough, unsubtle, vigorous, well.

antonyms mealy-mouthed, unhealthy, unrealistic, weak.

rock[1] *n* anchor, boulder, bulwark, cornerstone, danger, foundation, hazard, logan, log(g)an-stone, mainstay, obstacle, pebble, problem, protection, stone, support.

rock[2] *v* astonish, astound, daze, dumbfound, jar, lurch, pitch, reel, roll, shake, shock, stagger, stun, surprise, sway, swing, tilt, tip, toss, wobble.

rocky[1] *adj* craggy, flinty, hard, pebbly, rocklike, rough, rugged, stony.

antonyms smooth, soft.

rocky[2] *adj* dizzy, doubtful, drunk, ill, inebriated, intoxicated, rickety, shaky, sick, sickly, staggering, tipsy, tottering, uncertain, undependable, unpleasant, unreliable, unsatisfactory, unstable, unsteady, unwell, weak, wobbly, wonky.

antonyms dependable, steady, well.

rod *n* bar, baton, birch, cane, dowel, ferula, ferule, mace, pole, sceptre, shaft, spoke, staff, stick, strut, switch, verge, wand.

rogue *n* blackguard, charlatan, cheat, con man, crook, deceiver, devil, fraud, Greek, knave, miscreant, mountebank, nasty piece/bit of work, ne'er-do-well, picaroon, rapscallion, rascal, reprobate, saltimbanco, scamp, scapegallows, scoundrel, sharper, swindler, vagrant, villain, wag.

antonym saint.

roguish *adj* arch, bantering, cheeky, confounded, coquettish, criminal, crooked, deceitful, deceiving, dishonest, espiègle, fraudulent, frolicsome, hempy, impish, knavish, mischievous, playful, puckish, raffish, rascally, roguing, shady, sportive, swindling, unprincipled, unscrupulous, villainous, waggish.

antonyms honest, serious.

roguishly *adv* archly, cheekily, coquettishly, en badinant, impishly, mischievously, playfully.

antonym seriously.

roguishness *n* archness, badinage, bantering, cheekiness, coquettishness, deceitfulness, dishonesty, espièglerie, fraud, impishness, mischief, mischievousness, playfulness, roguery, tricks, unscrupulousness, villainy, waggishness.

antonym seriousness.

roister *v* bluster, boast, brag, carouse, celebrate, frolic, make merry, paint the town red, revel, roist, rollick, romp, strut, swagger, whoop it up.

roisterer *n* blusterer, boaster, braggart, carouser, ranter, reveller, roister, swaggerer.

roisterous *adj* boisterous, clamorous, disorderly, exuberant, loud, noisy, obstreperous, roisting, rowdy, uproarious, wild.

antonyms orderly, restrained.

role *n* capacity, character, duty, function, impersonation, job, job of work, part, portrayal, position, post, representation, task.

roll *v* billow, bind, boom, coil, curl, drum, echo, elapse, enfold, entwine, envelop, even, flatten, flow, furl, grumble, gyrate, level, lumber, lurch, pass, peel, pivot, press, reel, resound, reverberate, revolve, roar, rock, rotate, rumble, run, smooth, spin, spread, stagger, swagger, swathe, sway, swing, swivel, thunder, toss, trill, trindle, trundle, tumble, turn, twirl, twist, undulate, volume, waddle, wallow, wander, welter, wheel, whirl, wind, wrap.

n annals, ball, bobbin, boom, catalogue, census, chronicle, cycle, cylinder, directory, drumming, growl, grumble, gyration, index, inventory, list, notitia, record, reel, register, resonance, reverberation, revolution, roar, roller, roster, rotation, rumble, run, schedule, scroll, spin, spool, table, thunder, turn, twirl, undulation, volume, wheel, whirl.

roll up arrive, assemble, cluster, congregate, convene, forgather, gather.

antonyms leave, scatter.

rollicking *adj* boisterous, carefree, cavorting, devil-may-care, exuberant, frisky, frolicsome, hearty, jaunty, jovial, joyous, lively, merry, playful, rip-roaring, roisterous, roisting, romping, spirited, sportive, sprightly, swashbuckling.

antonyms restrained, serious.

rolling *adj* heaving, rippling, surging, undulant, undulating, waving.

antonym flat.

roly-poly *adj* buxom, chubby, fat, overweight, plump, podgy, pudgy, roll-about, rotund, roundabout, rounded, tubby.

antonym slim.

romance *n* absurdity, adventure, affair(e), amour, attachment, charm, colour, exaggeration, excitement, fabrication, fairy tale, falsehood, fantasy, fascination, fiction, gest(e), glamour, idyll, intrigue, invention, legend, liaison, lie, love affair, love story, melodrama, mystery, novel, passion, relationship, sentiment, story, tale, tear-jerker.

v exaggerate, fantasise, lie, overstate.

romantic *adj* amorous, charming, chimerical, colourful, dreamy, exaggerated, exciting, exotic, extravagant, fabulous, fairy-tale, fanciful, fantastic, fascinating, fictitious, fond, glamorous, high-flown, idealistic, idyllic, imaginary, imaginative, impractical, improbable, legendary, lovey-dovey, loving, made-up, mushy, mysterious, passionate, picturesque, quixotic, romantical, sentimental, sloppy, soppy, starry-eyed, tender, unrealistic, utopian, visionary, whimsical, wild.

antonyms humdrum, practical, real, sober, unromantic.

n Don Quixote, dreamer, idealist, romancer, sentimentalist, utopian, visionary.

antonym realist.

Romeo *n* Casanova, Don Juan, gigolo, ladies' man, lady-killer, Lothario, lover.

romp *v* caper, cavort, frisk, frolic, gambol, revel, rig, roister, rollick, skip, sport.

n caper, frolic, lark, rig, spree.

rook *v* bilk, cheat, clip, con, defraud, diddle, do, fleece, mulct, overcharge, rip off, soak, sting, swindle.

room *n* allowance, apartment, area, capacity, chamber, chance, compartment, compass, elbow-room, expanse, extent, house-room, latitude, leeway, margin, occasion, office, opportunity, play, range, salon, saloon, scope, space, territory, volume.

roomy *adj* ample, broad, capacious, commodious, extensive, generous, large, sizable, spacious, voluminous, wide.

antonym cramped.

root[1] *n* base, basis, beginnings, bottom, cause, core, crux, derivation, essence, foundation, fountainhead, fundamental, germ, heart, mainspring, more, nub, nucleus, occasion, origin, radicle, radix, rhizome, root-cause, rootlet, seat, seed, source, starting point, stem, tuber.

v anchor, embed, entrench, establish, fasten, fix, ground, implant, moor, set, sink, stick.

root and branch completely, entirely, finally, radically, thoroughly, totally, utterly, wholly.

antonyms not at all, slightly.

root[2] *v* burrow, delve, dig, ferret, forage, grout, hunt, nose, poke, pry, rootle, rummage.

root out abolish, clear away, destroy, dig out, discover, efface, eliminate, eradicate, erase, exterminate, extirpate, produce, remove, root up, turn up, uncover, unearth, uproot.

antonyms cover, establish.

rooted *adj* confirmed, deep, deeply, deep-seated, entrenched, established, felt, firm, fixed, ingrained, radical, rigid, root-fast.

antonyms superficial, temporary.

roots *n* background, beginning(s), birthplace, cradle, family, heritage, home, origins.

rope *n* cable, cord, fake, hawser, lariat lasso, line, marline, strand, warp, widdy.

v bind, catch, fasten, hitch, lash, lasso, moor, pinion, tether, tie.

rope in embroil, engage, enlist, inveigle, involve, lure, persuade.

antonym keep out.

ropy *adj* below par, deficient, inadequate, indifferent, inferior, off colour, poorly, rough, sketchy, stringy, substandard, unwell.

antonyms good, well.

roster *n* bead-roll, list, listing, register, roll, rota, schedule, table.

rostrum *n* dais, hustings, platform, podium, stage.

rosy *adj* auspicious, blooming, blushing, bright, cheerful, encouraging, favourable, fresh, glowing, healthy-looking, hopeful, optimistic, pink, promising, reassuring, red, reddish, rose, roseate, rose-coloured, rose-hued, roselike, rose-pink, rose-red, rose-scented, rosy-fingered, rubicund, ruddy, sunny.

antonyms depressed, depressing, sad.

rot *v* corrode, corrupt, crumble, decay, decline, decompose, degenerate, deteriorate, disintegrate, fester, go bad, languish, moulder, perish, putrefy, ret, spoil, taint.

n balderdash, blight, bosh, bunk, bunkum, canker, claptrap, codswallop, collapse, corrosion, corruption, decay, decomposition, deterioration, disintegration, drivel, flapdoodle, guff, hogwash, moonshine, mould, nonsense, poppycock, putrefaction, putrescence, rubbish, tommyrot, tosh, twaddle.

rotary *adj* gyrating, gyratory, revolving, rotating, rotational, rotatory, spinning, turning, whirling.

antonym fixed.

rotate *v* alternate, gyrate, interchange, pirouette, pivot, reel, revolve, spell, spin, switch, swivel, turn, twiddle, wheel.

rotation *n* alternation, cycle, gyration, interchanging, orbit, pirouette, reel, revolution, sequence, spin, spinning, succession, switching, turn, turning, volution, wheel.

rotten *adj* addle(d), bad, base, below par, bent, contemptible, corroded, corrupt, crooked, crumbling, crummy, decayed, decaying, deceitful, decomposed, decomposing, degenerate, deplorable, despicable, dirty, disagreeable, disappointing, dishonest, dishonourable, disintegrating, disloyal, faithless, festering, fetid, filthy, foul, grotty, ill-considered, ill-thought-out, immoral, inadequate, inferior, lousy, low-grade, manky, mean, mercenary, mouldering, mouldy, nasty, off colour, perfidious, perished, poor, poorly, punk, putid, putrescent, putrid, rank, regrettable, ropy, rough, scurrilous, sick, sorry, sour, stinking, substandard, tainted, treacherous, unacceptable, unfortunate, unlucky, unpleasant, unsatisfactory, unsound, untrustworthy, unwell, venal, vicious, vile, wicked.

antonyms good, honest, practical, sensible, well.

rotter *n* bastard, blackguard, blighter, bounder, cad, cur, dastard, fink, louse, rat, scoundrel, stinker, swine.

antonym saint.

rotund *adj* bulbous, chubby, corpulent, fat, fleshy, full, globular, grandiloquent, heavy, magniloquent, obese, orbed, orbicular, orby, oro(ro)tund, plump, podgy, portly, resonant, rich, roly-poly, rotundate, round, rounded, sonorous, spheral, spheric, spherical, spherular, sphery, stout, tubby.

antonyms flat, gaunt, slim.

roué *n* debauchee, lecher, libertine, profligate, rake, rakehell, sensualist, wanton.

rough *adj* agitated, amorphous, approximate, arduous, austere, basic, bearish, bluff, blunt, boisterous, bristly, broken, brusque, bumpy, bushy, cacophonous, choppy, churlish, coarse, craggy, crude, cruel, cursory, curt, discordant, discourteous, dishevelled, disordered, drastic, estimated, extreme, foggy, formless, fuzzy, general, grating, gruff, hairy, hard, harsh, hasty, hazy, husky, ill, ill-bred, ill-mannered, imperfect, impolite, imprecise, inclement, incomplete, inconsiderate, indelicate, inexact, inharmonious, irregular, jagged, jarring, loutish, nasty, off colour, poorly, quick, rasping, raspy, raucous, raw, rocky, ropy, rotten, rough-and-ready, rowdy, rude, rudimentary, rugged, rusty, scabrous, severe, shaggy, shapeless, sharp, sick, sketchy, spartan, squally, stony, stormy, tangled, tempestuous, tough, tousled, tousy, turbulent, unceremonious, uncivil, uncomfortable, uncouth, uncultured, uncut, undressed, uneven, unfeeling, unfinished, ungracious, unjust, unmannerly, unmusical, unpleasant, unpolished, unprocessed, unrefined, unshaven, unshorn, untutored, unwell, unwrought, upset, vague, violent, wild.

antonyms accurate, calm, harmonious, mild, polite, smooth, well.

n bruiser, bully, corner-boy, draft, hooligan, keelie, mock-up, model, outline, roughneck, rowdy, ruffian, sketch, thug, tough, yob, yobbo.

rough up bash, batter, beat up, do, knock about, maltreat, manhandle, mistreat, mug, thrash.

rough-and-ready *adj* adequate, approximate, crude, impoverished, makeshift, provisional, sketchy, stop-gap, unpolished, unrefined.

antonyms exact, refined.

rough-and-tumble *n* affray, bagarre, barney, brawl, Donnybrook, dust-up, fight, fracas, mêlée, punch-up, rookery, rout, ruction, ruffle, rumpus, scrap, scuffle, shindy, struggle.

roughen *v* abrade, asperate, coarsen, granulate, graze, harshen, rough, scuff.

antonym smooth.

roughneck *n* apache, bruiser, bully boy, corner-boy, hooligan, keelie, lout, Mohock, myrmidon, rough, rowdy, ruffian, thug, toe-rag, toe-ragger, tough.

round *adj* ample, annular, ball-shaped, blunt, bowed, bulbous, candid, circular, complete, curved, curvilinear, cylindrical, direct, discoid, disc-shaped, entire, fleshy, frank, full, full-fleshed, globular, mellifluous, orbed, orbicular, orby, orotund, outspoken, plain, plump, resonant, rich, ring-shaped, roly-poly, rotund, rotundate, rounded, solid, sonorous, spheral, spheric, spherical, spherular, sphery, straightforward, unbroken, undivided, unmodified, whole.

antonyms evasive, niggardly, partial, thin.

n ambit, ball, band, beat, bout, bullet, cartridge, circle, circuit, compass, course, cycle, disc, discharge, division, globe, lap, level, orb, period, ring, routine, schedule, sequence, series, session, shell, shot, sphere, spheroid, spherule, stage, succession, tour, turn.

v bypass, circle, circumnavigate, encircle, flank, sail round, skirt, turn.

round off cap, close, complete, conclude, crown, end, finish, finish off, settle.

antonym begin.

round on abuse, assail, attack, bite (someone's) head off, retaliate, snap at, turn on.

round the bend barmy, batty, bonkers, crazy, cuckoo, daft, dotty, eccentric, insane, mad, nuts, nutty, off one's rocker, screwy.

antonym sane.

round up assemble, collect, drive, gather, gather in, group, herd, marshal, muster, rally.

antonym disperse.

roundabout *adj* ambagious, circuitous, circumlocutory, devious, discursive, evasive, indirect, meandering, oblique, periphrastic, tortuous, twisting, winding.

antonyms direct, straight, straightforward.

roundly *adv* bluntly, completely, fiercely, forcefully, frankly, intensely, openly, outspokenly, rigorously, severely, sharply, thoroughly, vehemently, violently.

antonym mildly.

round-up *n* assembly, collation, collection, gathering, herding, marshalling, muster, overview, précis, rally, summary, survey.

antonym dispersal.

rouse *v* agitate, anger, animate, arouse, awaken, bestir, call, disturb, enkindle, excite, exhilarating, firk, flush, galvanise, incite, inflame, instigate, move, provoke, rise, start, startle, stimulate, stir, suscitate, unbed, wake, whip up.

antonym calm.

rousing *adj* brisk, electrifying, excitant, excitative, excitatory, exciting, exhilarating, hypnopompic, inflammatory, inspiring, lively, moving, spirited, stimulating, stirring, vigorous.

antonym calming.

rout *n* beating, brawl, clamour, crowd, debacle, defeat, disturbance, Donnybrook, drubbing, flight, fracas, fuss, herd, hiding, licking, mob, overthrow, pack, rabble, riot, rookery, ruffle, ruin, shambles, stampede, thrashing.

antonyms calm, win.

v beat, best, chase, conquer, crush, defeat, destroy, discomfit, dispel, drub, fleme, fley, hammer, lick, overthrow, scatter, thrash, worst.

route *n* avenue, beat, circuit, course, direction, flightpath, itinerary, journey, passage, path, road, round, run, way.

v convey, direct, dispatch, forward, send.

routine *n* act, bit, custom, formula, grind, groove, heigh, jog-trot, line, method, order, pattern, performance, piece, practice, procedure, programme, spiel, usage, way, wont.

adj banal, boring, clichéd, conventional, customary, day-by-day, dull, everyday, familiar, habitual, hackneyed, humdrum, mundane, normal, ordinary, predictable, run-of-the-mill, standard, tedious, tiresome, typical, unimaginative, uninspired, unoriginal, usual, wonted, workaday.

antonyms exciting, unusual.

rove *v* cruise, drift, gallivant, meander, ramble, range, roam, stravaig, stray, stroll, traipse, waltz Matilda, wander.

antonym stay.

rover *n* drifter, gadabout, gypsy, itinerant, nomad, rambler, ranger, stravaiger, transient, traveller, vagrant, wanderer.

antonym stay-at-home.

row[1] *n* bank, colonnade, column, file, line, queue, range, rank, sequence, series, string, tier.

row[2] *n* altercation, brawl, castigation, commotion, controversy, dispute, disturbance, Donnybrook, dressing-down, falling-out, fracas, fray, fuss, lecture, noise, quarrel, racket, rammy, reprimand, reproof, rhubarb, rollicking, rookery, rout, ruckus, ruction, ruffle, rumpus, scrap, shemozzle, shindig, shindy, slanging match, squabble, talking-to, telling-off, ticking-off, tiff, tongue-lashing, trouble, tumult, uproar.

antonym calm.

v argue, argufy, brawl, dispute, fight, scrap, squabble, wrangle.

rowdy *adj* boisterous, disorderly, loud, loutish, noisy, obstreperous, roisterous, roisting, rorty, rough, rumbustious, stroppy, unruly, uproarious, wild.

antonyms quiet, restrained.

n brawler, corner-boy, hoodlum, hooligan, keelie, lout, rough, ruffian, tearaway, tough, yahoo, yob, yobbo.

royal *adj* august, basilical, grand, imperial, impressive, kinglike, kingly, magnificent, majestic, monarchical, princely, queenlike, queenly, regal, sovereign, splendid, stately, superb, superior.

rub *v* abrade, apply, caress, chafe, clean, embrocate, fray, grate, knead, malax, malaxate, massage, polish, put, scour, scrape, shine, smear, smooth, spread, stroke, wipe.

n caress, catch, difficulty, drawback, hindrance, hitch, impediment, kneading, malaxage, malaxation, massage, obstacle, polish, problem, shine, snag, stroke, trouble, wipe.

rub out assassinate, cancel, delete, efface, erase, expunge, kill, murder, obliterate, remove.

rub up the wrong way anger, annoy, bug, get, get one's goat, get to, get under one's skin, irk, irritate, needle, niggle, peeve, vex.

antonym calm.

rubbish *n* balderdash, balls, baloney, bosh, bunkum, clamjamphrie, claptrap, cobblers, codswallop, crap, dead-wood, debris, draff, dreck, drivel, dross, flotsam and jetsam, garbage, gibberish, gobbledegook, guff, havers, hogwash, junk, kibosh, kitsch, landfill, leavings, litter, lumber, moonshine, mullock, nonsense, offal, offscourings, offscum, piffle, poppycock, raffle, refuse, riddlings, rot, scoria, scrap, stuff, sullage, sweepings, tommyrot, tosh, trash, trashery, truck, trumpery, twaddle, vomit, waste.

antonym sense.

rubbish-dump *n* kitchen-midden, landfill, laystall, tip.

rubbishy *adj* brummagem, cheap, draffish, draffy, gimcrack, grotty, paltry, petty, shoddy, tatty, tawdry, third-rate, throw-away, trashy, twopenny-halfpenny, valueless, worthless.

antonym classy.

ruction *n* altercation, brawl, commotion, dispute, disturbance, Donnybrook, fracas, fuss, quarrel, racket, rookery, rout, row, ruffle, rumpus, scrap, storm, to-do, trouble, uproar.

antonym calm.

ruddy *adj* blooming, blushing, crimson, flammulated, florid, flushed, fresh, glowing, healthy, pink, red, reddish, roseate, rose-hued, rose-pink, rosy, rosy-cheeked, rubicund, rubineous, rubious, ruby, sanguine, scarlet, sunburnt.

antonyms pale, unhealthy.

rude *adj* abrupt, abusive, artless, barbarous, blunt, boorish, brusque, brutish, cheeky, churlish, coarse, crude, curt, discourteous, disrespectful, graceless, gross, harsh, ignorant, illiterate, ill-mannered, impertinent, impolite, impudent, inartistic, inconsiderate, inelegant, insolent, insulting, loutish, low, makeshift, oafish, obscene, offhand, peremptory, primitive, raw, rough, savage, scurrilous, sharp, short, simple, startling, sudden, uncivil, uncivilised, uncouth, uncultured, uneducated, ungracious, unmannerly, unpleasant, unpolished, unrefined, untutored, violent, vulgar.

antonyms graceful, polished, polite, smooth.

rudeness *n* abruptness, abuse, abusiveness, bad manners, barbarism, bluntness, boorishness, brusqueness, cheek, churlishness, curtness, discourtesy, disrespect, grossièreté, ill-manners, impertinence, impoliteness, impudence, incivility, insolence, oafishness, sharpness, uncouthness, vulgarity.

antonym politeness.

rudimentary *adj* abecedarian, basic, early, elementary, embryonic, fundamental, germinal, immature, inchoate, initial, introductory, primary, primitive, primordial, undeveloped, vestigial.

antonyms advanced, developed.

rudiments *n* ABC, basics, beginnings, elements, essentials, foundation, fundamentals, germin, principia, principles, prolegomena.

rue *v* bemoan, bewail, beweep, deplore, grieve, lament, mourn, regret, repent.

antonym rejoice.

rueful *adj* conscience-stricken, contrite, dismal, doleful, grievous, long-visaged, lugubrious, melancholy, mournful, penitent, pitiable, pitiful, plaintive, regretful, remorseful, repentant, sad, self-reproachful, sorrowful, sorry, woebegone, woeful.

antonym glad.

ruffian *n* apache, bruiser, brute, bully, bully-boy, corner-boy, cut-throat, hoodlum, hooligan, keelie, lout, miscreant, Mohock, myrmidon, plug-ugly, rascal, rogue, rough, roughneck, rowdy, scoundrel, thug, toe-rag, toe-ragger, tough, villain, yob, yobbo.

ruffle *v* agitate, annoy, confuse, derange, disarrange, discompose, disconcert, dishevel, disorder, disquiet, disturb, fluster, harass, irritate, mess up, muss up, muss(e), nettle, peeve, perturb, rattle, rumple, stir, torment, tousle, trouble, unsettle, upset, vex, worry, wrinkle.

antonym smooth.

rugged *adj* arduous, austere, barbarous, beefy, blunt, brawny, broken, bumpy, burly, churlish, crabbed, craggy, crude, demanding, difficult, dour, exacting, graceless, gruff, hale, hard, hard-featured, hardy, harsh, husky, irregular, jagged, laborious, muscular, ragged, rigorous, robust, rocky, rough, rude, severe, sour, stark, stern, strenuous, strong, sturdy, surly, taxing, tough, trying, uncompromising, uncouth, uncultured, uneven, unpolished, unrefined, vigorous, weather-beaten, weathered, worn.

antonyms easy, refined, smooth.

ruin *n* bankruptcy, bouleversement, breakdown, collapse, crash, damage, decay, defeat, destitution, destruction, devastation, disintegration, disrepair, dissolution, downfall, failure, fall, havoc, heap, insolvency, nemesis, overthrow, ruination, subversion, undoing, Waterloo, wreck, wreckage.

antonyms development, reconstruction.

v banjax, bankrupt, botch, break, crush, damage, defeat, demolish, destroy, devastate, disfigure, impoverish, injure, jigger, mangle, mar, mess up, overthrow, overturn, overwhelm, pauperise, raze, scupper, scuttle, shatter, smash, spoil, unmake, unshape, wreck.

antonyms develop, restore.

ruinous *adj* baleful, baneful, broken-down, calamitous, cataclysmic, catastrophic, crippling, deadly, decrepit, deleterious, derelict, destructive, devastating, dilapidated, dire, disastrous, extravagant, fatal, immoderate, injurious, murderous, noxious, pernicious, ramshackle, ruined, shattering, wasteful, withering.

antonym beneficial.

ruins *n* chaos, debris, devastation, havoc, shambles.

rule *n* administration, ascendancy, authority, axiom, canon, command, condition, control, convention, course, criterion, custom, decree, direction, domination, dominion, empire, form, formula, governance, government, guide, guideline, habit, influence, institute, jurisdiction, law, leadership, mastery, maxim, method, order, ordinance, policy, power, practice, precept, prescript, principle, procedure, raj, regime, regulation, reign, routine, ruling, standard, supremacy, sway, tenet, way, wont.

v adjudge, adjudicate, administer, command, control, decide, decree, determine, direct, dominate, establish, find, govern, guide, judge, lead, manage, obtain, predominate, preponderate, prevail, pronounce, regulate, reign, resolve, settle.

rule out ban, debar, disallow, dismiss, eliminate, exclude, forbid, obviate, preclude, prevent, prohibit, proscribe, reject.

ruler *n* commander, controller, emperor, empress, gerent, governor, gubernator, head of state, imperator, king, leader, lord, monarch, potentate, prince, princess, queen, sovereign, suzerain.

antonym subject.

ruling *n* adjudication, decision, decree, finding, firman, hatti-sherif, indiction, interlocution, irade, judgement, pronouncement, resolution, ukase, verdict.

adj boss, chief, commanding, controlling, dominant, governing, leading, main, predominant, pre-eminent, preponderant, prevailing, prevalent, principal, regnant, reigning, supreme, upper.

rum *adj* abnormal, bizarre, curious, freakish, funny, funny-peculiar, odd, peculiar, queer, singular, strange, suspect, suspicious, unusual, weird.

rumbustious *adj* boisterous, clamorous, disorderly, exuberant, loud, noisy, obstreperous, refractory, robust, roisterous, roisting, rorty, rough, rowdy, unmanageable, unruly, uproarious, wayward, wild, wilful.

antonyms quiet, restrained, sensible.

ruminate *v* brood, chew over, chew the cud, cogitate, consider, contemplate, deliberate, meditate, mull over, muse, ponder, reflect, revolve, think.

rummage *v* delve, examine, explore, hunt, poke around, ransack, root, rootle, rout, search.

rumour *n* breeze, bruit, bush telegraph, buzz, canard, fame, furphy, gossip, grapevine, hearsay, kite, news, on-dit, report, story, talk, tidings, underbreath, whisper, word.

v bruit, circulate, gossip, publish, put about, report, say, tell, whisper.

rump *n* backside, bottom, bum, buttocks, croup, dock, haunch, hindquarters, nache, posterior, rear, seat.

rumple *v* crease, crinkle, crumple, crush, derange, dishevel, disorder, muss up, muss(e), pucker, ruffle, scrunch, tousle, wrinkle.

antonym smooth.

rumpus *n* bagarre, barney, brouhaha, commotion, confusion, disruption, disturbance, Donnybrook, fracas, furore, fuss, kerfuffle, noise, rhubarb, rookery, rout, row, ruction, shemozzle, shindig, shindy, tumult, uproar.

antonym calm.

run *v* abscond, administer, bear, beat it, bleed, bolt, boss, career, carry, cascade, challenge, circulate, clear out, climb, compete, conduct, contend, continue, control, convey, co-ordinate, course, creep, dart, dash, decamp, depart, direct, discharge, display, dissolve, drive to, escape, extend, feature, flee, flow, function, fuse, gallop, glide, go, gush, hare, hasten, head, hie, hotfoot, hurry, issue, jog, ladder, last, lead, leak, lie, liquefy, lope, manage, manoeuvre, mastermind, melt, mix, move, operate, oversee, own, pass, perform, ply, pour, print, proceed, propel, publish, race, range, reach, regulate, roll, rush, scamper, scarper, scramble, scud, scurry, skedaddle, skim, slide, speed, spill, spout, spread, sprint, stand, stream, stretch, superintend, supervise, tear, tick, trail, transport, unravel, work.

antonyms stay, stop.

n application, category, chain, class, coop, course, current, cycle, dash, demand, direction, drift, drive, enclosure, excursion, flow, gallop, jaunt, jog, journey, joy, kind, ladder, lift, motion, movement, order, outing, passage, path, pen, period, pressure, progress, race, ride, rip, round, rush, season, sequence, series, snag, sort, spell, spin, sprint, spurt, streak, stream, stretch, string, tear, tendency, tenor, tide, trend, trip, type, variety, way.

run after chase, follow, pursue, stalk, tail.

antonym flee.

run away abscond, beat it, bolt, clear out, decamp, elope, escape, flee, scarper, scoot, scram, skedaddle, take it on the lam.

antonym stay.

run down belittle, capture, criticise, curtail, cut, debilitate, decrease, decry, defame, denigrate, disparage, drop, exhaust, hit, knock, knock over, reduce, revile, run over, strike, tire, trim, vilify, weaken.

antonyms increase, miss, praise.

run for it bolt, do a bunk, escape, flee, fly, have it on one's toes, make off, retreat, scarper, scram, skedaddle.

antonym stay.

run in apprehend, arrest, bust, collar, feel (someone's) collar, jail, lift, nab, nick, pick up, pinch.

run into bash, encounter, hit, meet, ram, strike.

antonym miss.

run off abscond, bleed, bolt, decamp, drain, duplicate, elope, escape, have it on one's toes, make off, print, produce, scarper, siphon, skedaddle, tap.

antonym stay.

run out cease, close, dry up, end, expire, fail, finish, terminate.

run over hit, knock down, overflow, rehearse, reiterate, review, run down, spill, strike, survey.

run riot cut loose, go on the rampage, kick over the traces, rampage, sow one's wild oats, spread.

run through blow, check, dissipate, examine, exhaust, fritter away, pierce, practise, read, rehearse, review, spit, squander, stab, stick, survey, transfix, waste.

run together amalgamate, blend, coalesce, combine, commingle, fuse, intermingle, intermix, join, merge, mingle, mix, unite.

antonym separate.

runaway *n* absconder, deserter, escapee, escaper, fleer, fugitive, refugee, truant.

adj escaped, fleeing, fugitive, loose, uncontrolled, wild.

rundown *n* briefing, cut, decrease, drop, lessening, outline, précis, recap, reduction, résumé, review, run-through, sketch, summary, synopsis.

run-down *adj* broken-down, debilitated, decrepit, dilapidated, dingy, drained, enervated, exhausted, fatigued, grotty, peaky, ramshackle, scabby, seedy, shabby, tumble-down, unhealthy, weak, weary, worn-out.

antonym well-kept.

run-in *n* altercation, argument, brush, confrontation, contretemps, difference of opinion, dispute, dust-up, encounter, fight, quarrel, set-to, skirmish, tussle, wrangle.

runner[1] *n* athlete, competitor, courier, harrier, jogger, messenger, miler, participant, sprinter.

runner[2] *n* flagellum, offshoot, sarmentum, shoot, sprig, sprout, stem, stolon, tendril.

running *adj* consecutive, constant, continuous, current, flowing, incessant, moving, perpetual, streaming, successive, together, unbroken, unceasing, uninterrupted.

antonyms broken, ceased, occasional.

n administration, charge, competition, conduct, contention, contest, control, co-ordination, direction, functioning, going, leadership, maintenance, management, operation, organisation, pace, performance, regulation, superintendency, supervision, working.

runny *adj* dilute, diluted, flowing, fluid, liquefied, liquid, melted, molten, watery.

antonym solid.

run-of-the-mill *adj* average, common, commonplace, everyday, fair, mediocre, middling, modest, ordinary, passable, routine, tolerable, undistinguished, unexceptional, unexciting, unimaginative, unimpressive, unremarkable.

antonym exceptional.

rupture *n* altercation, breach, break, breaking, burst, bust-up, cleavage, cleft, contention, crack, disagreement, disruption, dissolution, estrangement, falling-out, feud, fissure, fracture, hernia, hostility, quarrel, rent, rift, schism, split, splitting, tear.

v break, burst, cleave, crack, disrupt, dissever, divide, fracture, puncture, rend, separate, sever, split, sunder, tear.

rural *adj* agrarian, agrestic, agricultural, Arcadian, bucolic, countrified, country, forane, mofussil, pastoral, pr(a)edical, rustic, sylvan, yokelish.

antonym urban.

ruse *n* artifice, blind, deception, device, dodge, hoax, imposture, manoeuvre, ploy, sham, stall, stratagem, subterfuge, trick, wile.

rush *v* accelerate, attack, bolt, capture, career, charge, dart, dash, dispatch, expedite, fly, hasten, hightail it, hotfoot, hurry, hustle, overcome, press, push, quicken, race, run, scour, scramble, scurry, shoot, speed, speed up, sprint, stampede, storm, tear, wallop, w(h)oosh.

n assault, charge, dash, dispatch, expedition, flow, haste, hurry, onslaught, push, race, scramble, speed, stampede, storm, streak, surge, swiftness, tantivy, tear, urgency.

adj brisk, careless, cursory, emergency, expeditious, fast, hasty, hurried, prompt, quick, rapid, superficial, swift, urgent.

rush about rampage.

rust *n* blight, corrosion, fungus, mildew, mould, must, oxidation, patina, rot, stain, verdigris.

v atrophy, corrode, corrupt, decay, decline, degenerate, deteriorate, oxidise, rot, stagnate, tarnish.

rust-coloured *adj* auburn, chestnut, copper, coppery, ginger, gingery, red, reddish, reddish-brown, russet, rusty, sandy, tawny, titian.

rustic *adj* agrarian, agrestic, Arcadian, artless, awkward, boorish, bucolic, churlish, cloddish, clodhopping, clownish, clumsy, coarse, countrified, country, crude, georgic, graceless, hick, hodden, homely, homespun, loutish, lumpish, maladroit, oafish, pastoral, plain, provincial, rough, rude, rural, silvatic, silvestrian, simple, sylvan, unaffected, uncouth, uncultured, unmannerly, unpolished, unrefined, unsophisticated, yokelish.

antonyms cultivated, polished, sophisticated, urban, urbane.

n boor, bumpkin, carl, chaw-bacon, chuff, churl, clod, clodhopper, clown, Corydon, country cousin, countryman, countrywoman, hayseed, hick, hillbilly, hind, hob, Hobinoll, Hodge, kern, oaf, peasant, provincial, swain, yokel.

antonyms dandy, man-about-town, sophisticate.

rustle *v* crackle, crepitate, susurrate, swish, whisper, whoosh.

n crackle, crepitation, crepitus, crinkling, rustling, susurration, susurrus, swish, whisper, whispering, whoosh.

rusty *adj* aeruginous, ancient, antiquated, antique, corroded, creaking, creaky, croaking, croaky, dated, deficient, discoloured, dull, encrusted, fogram, hoarse, impaired, old-fashioned, outmoded, oxidised, passé, patinated, raucous, rough, rust-covered, rusted, sluggish, stagnated, stale, stiff, tarnished, time-worn, unpractised, weak.

rut *n* channel, ditch, furrow, gouge, groove, gutter, habit, indentation, pattern, pothole, routine, score, sulcus, system, track, trough, vallecula, wheelmark.

v channel, cut, furrow, gouge, groove, hole, indent, mark, score.

ruthless *adj* adamant, adamantine, barbarous, brutal, callous, cruel, cut-throat, dog-eat-dog, ferocious, fierce, hard, hard-hearted, harsh, heartless, implacable, inexorable, inhuman, merciless, pitiless, relentless, remorseless, savage, severe, stern, stony, unfeeling, unmerciful, unpitying, unrelenting.

antonyms compassionate, merciful.

S

sable *adj* black, coal-black, dark, dusky, ebon, ebony, inky, jet, jetty, midnight, pitch-black, pitch-dark, pitchy, reven, sombre.

sabotage *v* cripple, damage, destroy, disable, disrupt, incapacitate, mar, nullify, ratten, scupper, subvert, thwart, undermine, vandalise, vitiate, wreck.

n damage, destruction, disablement, disruption, impairment, marring, rattening, subversion, treachery, treason, undermining, vandalism, vitiation, wrecking.

sac *n* bag, bladder, bursa, capsule, cyst, follicle, pocket, pod, pouch, saccule, theca, vesica, vesicle, vesicula.

saccharine *adj* cloying, honeyed, maudlin, mawkish, nauseating, oversweet, schmaltzy, sentimental, sickly, sickly-sweet, sloppy, soppy, sugary, syrupy, treacly.

antonyms bitter, tart.

sack[1] *v* axe, discharge, dismiss, fire, lay off, make redundant.

n discharge, dismissal, notice, one's books, one's cards, one's marching orders, the axe, the boot, the bum's rush, the chop, the elbow, the push.

sack[2] *v* demolish, depredate, desecrate, despoil, destroy, devastate, lay waste, level, loot, maraud, pillage, plunder, raid, rape, ravage, raze, rifle, rob, ruin, spoil, strip, waste.

n depredation, desecration, despoliation, destruction, devastation, levelling, looting, marauding, pillage, plunder, plundering, rape, rapine, ravage, razing, ruin, waste.

sacred *adj* blessed, consecrated, dedicated, devotional, divine, ecclesiastical, godly, hallowed, heavenly, holy, inviolable, inviolate, invulnerable, priestly, protected, religious, revered, sacrosanct, saintly, sanctified, secure, solemn, venerable, venerated.

antonyms mundane, profane, temporal.

sacredness *n* divinity, godliness, holiness, inviolability, invulnerability, sacrosanctity, saintliness, sanctity, solemnity.

antonyms profaneness, worldliness.

sacrifice *v* abandon, forego, forfeit, immolate, let go, lose, offer, relinquish, renounce, slaughter, surrender.

n corban, destruction, hecatomb, holocaust, host, immolation, loss, mactation, oblation, offering, renunciation, surrender, victim, votive offering.

sacrificial *adj* atoning, expiatory, oblatory, piacular, propitiatory, reparative, votive.

sacrilege *n* blasphemy, defilement, desecration, disrespect, heresy, impiety, impiousness, irreverence, mockery, outrage, profanation, profaneness, profanity, violation.

antonyms piety, respect, reverence.

sacrilegious *adj* blasphemous, desecrating, disrespectful, godless, heretical, impious, irreligious, irreverent, profanatory, profane, ungodly, unholy.

antonyms pious, respectful, reverent.

sacrosanct *adj* hallowed, impregnable, inviolable, inviolate, sacred, sanctified, untouchable.

sad *adj* bad, blue, calamitous, cheerless, chopfallen, crestfallen, crushed, dark, dejected, deplorable, depressed, depressing, desolated, despondent, disastrous, disconsolate, dismal, dispirited, distressed, distressing, doleful, dolesome, doloriferous, dolorific, doughy, dour, dowie, downcast, down-hearted, drear, dreary, gloomy, glum, grave, grief-stricken, grieved, grieving, grievous, heart-rending, heavy, heavy-hearted, jaw-fallen, joyless, lachrymose, lamentable, long-faced, low, low-spirited, lugubrious, melancholy, miserable, mournful, moving, painful, pathetic, pensive, piteous, pitiable, pitiful, poignant, regrettable, serious, shabby, sober, sober-minded, sombre, sorrowful, sorry, sportless, stiff, tearful, touching, tragic, triste, uncheerful, unfortunate, unhappy, unsatisfactory, upsetting, wan, wistful, woebegone, woeful, wretched.

antonyms cheerful, fortunate, happy, lucky.

sadden *v* aggrieve, dash, deject, depress, desolate, discourage, dishearten, dispirit, distress, grieve, hurt, oppress, upset.

antonyms cheer, delight, gratify, please.

saddle *v* burden, charge, encumber, impose, land, load, lumber, task, tax.

n demipique, pack-saddle, pigskin, pillion, seat.

sadism *n* barbarity, bestiality, brutality, callousness, cruelty, heartlessness, inhumanity, malevolence, ruthlessness, sado-masochism, savagery, spite, unnaturalness, viciousness.

sadistic *adj* barbarous, bestial, brutal, cruel, heartless, inhuman, malevolent, perverted, ruthless, savage, spiteful, unnatural, vicious.

sadness *n* bleakness, cheerlessness, darkness, dejection, depression, desolation, despondency, disconsolateness, dismalness, distress, dole, dolefulness, dolour, gloominess, glumness, gravity, grief, joylessness, low spirits, lugubriousness, melancholy, misery, misfortune, mournfulness, pain, pathos, poignancy, regret, sombreness, sorrow, sorrowfulness, tearfulness, tragedy, unhappiness, wanness, wistfulness, woe, wretchedness.

antonyms cheerfulness, delight, happiness.

safe *adj* alive and well, all right, cautious, certain, circumspect, conservative, dependable, discreet, foolproof, guarded, hale, harmless, immune, impregnable, innocuous, intact, invulnerable, non-poisonous, non-toxic, OK, out of harm's way, protected, proven, prudent, pure, realistic, reliable, scatheless, secure, sound, sure, tame, tested, tried, trustworthy, unadventurous, uncontaminated, undamaged, unfailing, unharmed, unhurt, uninjured, unscathed, wholesome.

antonyms exposed, harmful, unsafe, vulnerable.

n cash-box, chest, coffer, deposit box, peter, repository, strongbox, vault.

safe-conduct *n* authorisation, convoy, laissez-passer, licence, pass, passport, permit, safeguard, warrant.

safeguard *v* assure, defend, guard, insure, preserve, protect, screen, secure, shelter, shield.

antonyms endanger, jeopardise.

n armour, assurance, bulwark, convoy, cover, defence, escort, guarantee, guard, insurance, long-stop, Palladium, precaution, preventive, protection, security, shield, surety.

safekeeping *n* aegis, care, charge, custody, guard, guardianship, keeping, lock and key, protection, supervision, surveillance, trust, tutelage, vigilance, ward, wardship, watch.

safety *n* assurance, cover, deliverance, dependability, harmlessness, immunity, impregnability, invulnerability, protection, refuge, reliability, safeguard, salvation, sanctuary, security, shelter, sureness, via trita, via tuta.

antonyms danger, jeopardy.

adj fail-safe, precautionary, preventative, protective.

sag *v* bag, decline, dip, drag, droop, drop, dwindle, fail, fall, flag, give, give way, hang, settle, sink, slide, slip, slump, wane, weaken, wilt.

antonyms bulge, rise.

n decline, depression, dip, downturn, drop, dwindling, fall, low, low point, reduction, slide, slip, slump.

antonyms peak, rise.

saga *n* adventure, chronicle, epic, epopee, epopeia, epos, history, narrative, romance, roman-fleuve, soap opera, story, tale, yarn.

sagacious *adj* able, acute, apt, astute, canny, cute, discerning, downy, far-sighted, fly, insightful, intelligent, judicious, knowing, long-headed, long-sighted, penetrating, perceptive, percipient, perspicacious, quick, sage, sapient, sharp, shrewd, smart, wary, wide-awake, wily, wise.

antonyms foolish, obtuse, short-sighted.

sagacity *n* acumen, acuteness, astuteness, canniness, discernment, foresight, insight, judgement, judiciousness, knowingness, penetration, percipience, perspicacity, prudence, sapience, sense, sharpness, shrewdness, understanding, wariness, wiliness, wisdom.

antonyms folly, foolishness, obtuseness.

sage *adj* astute, canny, discerning, intelligent, judicious, knowing, knowledgeable, learned, perspicacious, politic, prudent, sagacious, sapient, sensible, wise.

antonym foolish.

n acharya, authority, elder, expert, guru, hakam, maharishi, mahatma, master, Nestor, oracle, philosopher, pundit, rishi, savant, Solomon, Solon, teacher, wise man.

antonym ignoramus.

sail *v* captain, cruise, drift, embark, float, fly, glide, navigate, pilot, plane, put to sea, scud, shoot, skim, skipper, soar, steer, sweep, take ship, voyage, waft, weigh anchor, wing.

sail into assault, attack, belabour, lambaste, lay into, let fly, set about, tear into, turn on.

sailor *n* AB, able seaman, able-bodied seaman, galiongee, gob, hearty, Jack Tar, lascar, leatherneck, limey, marine, mariner, matelot, matlow, navigator, rating, salt, sea dog, sea-dog, seafarer, seaman, tar, tarpaulin, tarry-breeks, water-rat.

saintliness *n* asceticism, blessedness, chastity, devoutness, faith, godliness, goodness, holiness, morality, piety, purity, righteousness, sanctity, self-denial, selflessness, self-sacrifice, spirituality, spotlessness, unselfishness, uprightness, virtue.

antonyms godlessness, unholiness, wickedness.

saintly *adj* angelic, beatific, blameless, blessed, blest, celestial, devout, god-fearing, godly, holy, immaculate, innocent, pious, pure, religious, righteous, sainted, saintlike, seraphic, sinless, spotless, stainless, upright, virtuous, worthy.

antonyms godless, unholy, unrighteous, wicked.

sake *n* account, advantage, aim, behalf, benefit, cause, consideration, end, gain, good, interest, motive, object, objective, principle, profit, purpose, reason, regard, respect, score, welfare, wellbeing.

salacious *adj* bawdy, blue, carnal, coarse, concupiscent, erotic, horny, improper, indecent, lascivious, lecherous, lewd, libidinous, lickerish, lubricious, lustful, obscene, pornographic, prurient, randy, raunchy, ribald, ruttish, scurrilous, smutty, steamy, wanton.

antonyms clean, decent, proper.

salaried *adj* emolumental, emolumentary, paid, remunerated, stipendiary, waged.

antonyms honorary, unpaid, voluntary.

salary *n* earnings, emolument, honorarium, income, pay, remuneration, screw, stipend, wage, wages.

sale *n* auction, deal, disposal, marketing, sell, selling, trade, traffic, transaction, vending, vendition, vendue.

saleable *adj* desirable, marketable, merchantable, sought-after, vendible.

antonyms unmarketable, unsaleable.

salesperson *n* bagman, clerk, counter-jumper, counter-skipper, sales assistant, salesclerk, salesgirl, saleslady, salesman, saleswoman, shop assistant, shop-boy, shopgirl, shop-keeper, vendeuse.

salient *adj* arresting, chief, conspicuous, important, jutting, main, marked, noticeable, obvious, outstanding, principal, projecting, prominent, pronounced, protruding, remarkable, signal, significant, striking.

sallow *adj* anaemic, bilious, colourless, pale, pallid, pasty, sickly, unhealthy, wan, yellowish.

antonyms rosy, sanguine.

sally[1] *v* breeze, charge, erupt, foray, issue, mosey, promenade, rush, saunter, sortie, stroll, surge, venture.

antonym retreat.

n assault, dash, drive, escapade, excursion, foray, frolic, incursion, jaunt, offensive, raid, rush, sortie, surge, thrust, trip, venture.

antonyms retire, retreat.

sally[2] *n* bon mot, crack, jest, jeu d'esprit, joke, quip, retort, riposte, wisecrack, witticism.

salt *n* acuteness, Attic salt, Attic wit, bite, dryness, flavour, liveliness, merum sal, pawkiness, piquancy, punch, pungency, relish, sarcasm, savour, seasoning, sharpness, smack, taste, trenchancy, vigour, wit, zest, zip.

adj brackish, briny, saline, salted, saltish, salty.

antonym fresh.

salt away accumulate, amass, bank, cache, collect, hide, hoard, save, stash, stockpile, store up.

antonyms spend, squander.

salty *adj* brackish, briny, colourful, dry, humorous, keen, lively, pawky, piquant, pungent, racy, saline, salsuginous, salt, salted, saltish, spicy, tangy, tart, witty, wry, zestful.

salubrious *adj* beneficial, bracing, healthful, health-giving, healthy, hygienic, invigorating, refreshing, restorative, salutary, sanitary, wholesome.

antonyms insalubrious, unwholesome.

salutary *adj* advantageous, beneficial, good, healthful, healthy, helpful, much-needed, practical, profitable, salubrious, seasonable, timely, useful, valuable, wholesome.

salutation *n* address, greeting, homage, obeisance, respects, reverence, salaam, salute, welcome.

salute *v* accost, acknowledge, address, bow, greet, hail, honour, kiss, knuckle, nod, recognise, salaam, wave, welcome.

n acknowledgement, address, bow, gesture, greeting, hail, handclap, handshake, hello, kiss, nod, obeisance, recognition, reverence, salaam, salutation, salve, salvo, tribute, wave.

salvage *v* conserve, glean, preserve, reclaim, recover, recuperate, redeem, repair, rescue, restore, retrieve, salve, save.

antonyms abandon, lose, waste.

salvation *n* deliverance, escape, liberation, lifeline, preservation, reclamation, redemption, rescue, restoration, retrieval, safety, saving, soteriology.

antonyms damnation, loss.

salve *n* application, balm, cream, dressing, embrocation, emollient, liniment, lotion, lubricant, medication, ointment, preparation, unguent.

same *adj* aforementioned, aforesaid, alike, analogous, changeless, comparable, consistent, corresponding, duplicate, equal, equivalent, homologous, identical, indistinguishable, interchangeable, invariable, matching, mutual, reciprocal, selfsame, similar, substitutable, synonymous, twin, unaltered, unchanged, undiminished, unfailing, uniform, unvarying, very.

antonyms changeable, different, incompatible, inconsistent, variable.

n ditto, the above-mentioned, the above-named, the aforementioned, the aforesaid.

sameness *n* changelessness, consistency, deja vu, duplication, identicalness, identity, indistinguishability, invariability, likeness, monotony, oneness, predictability, repetition, resemblance, similarity, standardisation, tedium, uniformity.

antonyms difference, variety.

sample *n* cross section, demonstration, ensample, example, exemplification, foretaste, free sample, freebie, illustration, indication, instance, model, pattern, representative, sign, specimen, swatch.

v experience, inspect, investigate, pree, sip, taste, test, try.

adj demonstration, illustrative, pilot, representative, specimen, test, trial.

sanctify *v* anoint, bless, cleanse, consecrate, dedicate, divinify, divinise, exalt, hallow, make holy, purify, sanction.

antonyms defile, degrade, desecrate.

sanctimonious *adj* canting, false, goody-goody, holier-than-thou, holy, hypocritical, moralising, pharisaical, pi, pietistic, pious, preaching, priggish, righteous, self-righteous, self-satisfied, smug, superior, Tartuffian, Tartuffish, unctuous.

antonym humble.

sanctimoniousness *n* cant, canting, complacency, holiness, humbug, hypocrisy, moralising, pharisaism, pietism, preachiness, priggishness, righteousness, self-righteousness, self-satisfaction, smugness, Tartuffism, unctuousness.

antonym humility.

sanction *n* accreditation, agreement, allowance, approbation, approval, authorisation, authority, backing, cachet, confirmation, countenance, endorsement, go-ahead, green light, imprimatur, licence, OK, permission, ratification, seal, support.

antonyms disapproval, veto.

v accredit, allow, approve, authorise, back, confirm, countenance, countersign, endorse, fiat, license, permit, ratify, support, underwrite, warrant.

antonyms disallow, disapprove, veto.

sanctions *n* ban, boycott, embargo, interdict, penalty, prohibition, proscription, restrictions.

sanctity *n* devotion, godliness, goodness, grace, holiness, inviolability, piety, purity, religiousness, righteousness, sacredness, sacrosanctity, saintliness, saintship, sanctitude, solemnity, spirituality, venerableness.

antonyms godlessness, impurity, secularity, unholiness, worldliness.

sanctuary *n* adytum, altar, ark, asylum, chancel, church, delubrum, frith, grith, harbourage, haven, holy of holies, naos, presbytery, protection, refuge, retreat, sacrarium, sanctum, sanctum sanctorum, seclusion, shelter, shrine, tabernacle, temple.

sanctum *n* cubby-hole, den, growlery, hideaway, holy of holies, refuge, retreat, sanctuary, sanctum sanctorum, shrine, snug, snuggery, study.

sand *n* arena, beach, gravel, grit, sands, shore, strand.

sand-bank *n* bar, cay, dune, hurst, key, reef, sand-bar, sand-hill, yardang.

sandy *adj* arenaceous, auburn, coppery, ginger, gingerous, gingery, gritty, psammitic, red, reddish, reddish-yellow, rusty, tawny, titian, xanthous, yellow, yellowish, yellowy.

sane *adj* all there, balanced, compos mentis, dependable, judicious, level-headed, lucid, moderate, normal, rational, reasonable, reliable, right-minded, sensible, sober, sound, stable.

sang-froid *n* aplomb, assurance, calmness, composure, cool, cool-headedness, coolness, dispassion, equanimity, imperturbability, indifference, nerve, nonchalance, phlegm, poise, self-control, self-possession, unflappability.

antonyms discomposure, excitability, hysteria, panic.

sanguinary *adj* bloodied, bloodthirsty, bloody, brutal, cruel, fell, gory, grim, merciless, murderous, pitiless, ruthless, savage.

sanguine[1] *adj* animated, ardent, assured, buoyant, cheerful, confident, expectant, hopeful, lively, optimistic, over-confident, over-optimistic, Panglossian, roseate, spirited, unabashed, unappalled, unbowed.

antonyms cynical, depressive, gloomy, melancholy, pessimistic, realistic.

sanguine[2] *adj* florid, flushed, fresh, fresh-complexioned, pink, red, rosy, rubicund, ruddy.

antonyms pale, sallow.

sanitary *adj* aseptic, clean, disinfected, germ-free, healthy, hygienic, pure, salubrious, uncontaminated, unpolluted, wholesome.

antonyms insanitary, unwholesome.

sanity *n* balance of mind, common sense, dependability, judiciousness, level-headedness, lucidity, normality, rationality, reason, reasonableness, reliability, saneness, sense, soundness, stability.

antonyms foolishness, insanity.

sap *v* bleed, deplete, devitalise, diminish, drain, enervate, exhaust, impair, reduce, rob, undermine, weaken.

antonyms build up, increase, strengthen.

sarcasm *n* acidity, bitterness, contempt, cynicism, derision, diatribe, invective, irony, mockery, mordancy, satire, scorn, sneering, venom, vitriol.

sarcastic *adj* acerbic, acid, acrimonious, biting, caustic, contemptuous, cutting, cynical, derisive, disparaging, incisive, ironical, mocking, mordant, sardonic, sarky, satirical, scathing, sharp, sharp-tongued, sneering, taunting, withering.

sardonic *adj* biting, bitter, cynical, derisive, dry, heartless, ironical, jeering, malevolent, malicious, malignant, mocking, mordant, quizzical, sarcastic, satirical, scornful, sneering, wry.

sash *n* baldric, belt, cincture, cummerbund, girdle, surcingle, vitta, waistband, zone.

Satan *n* Abaddon, Apollyon, Beelzebub, Belial, Clootie, Cloots, Hornie, Lucifer, Mephistopheles, Old Nick, Prince of Darkness, The Adversary, The Devil, The Enemy, The Evil One, The Tempter.

satanic *adj* accursed, black, demoniac, demoniacal, demonic, devilish, diabolic, diabolical, evil, fell, fiendish, hellish, infernal, inhuman, iniquitous, malevolent, malignant, Mephistophelian, satanical, wicked.

antonyms benevolent, benign, divine, godlike, godly, heavenly, holy.

sate *v* cloy, fill, glut, gorge, gratify, overfill, satiate, satisfy, saturate, sicken, slake, surfeit, weary.

antonyms deprive, dissatisfy, starve.

satellite *n* adherent, aide, attendant, dependant, disciple, follower, hanger-on, lackey, minion, moon, moonlet, parasite, puppet, retainer, sidekick, sputnik, subordinate, sycophant, tributary, vassal, votary.

satiate *v* cloy, engorge, glut, gorge, jade, nauseate, overfeed, overfill, sate, satisfy, slake, stuff, surfeit.

antonyms deprive, dissatisfy, underfeed.

satiety *n* fullness, gratification, over-fullness, overindulgence, repleteness, repletion, satiation, satisfaction, saturation, surfeit.

satire *n* burlesque, caricature, diatribe, invective, irony, lampoon, parody, Pasquil, Pasquin, pasquinade, raillery, ridicule, sarcasm, send-up, skit, spoof, squib, takeoff, travesty, wit.

satirical *adj* biting, bitter, burlesque, caustic, cutting, cynical, derisive, Hudibrastic, iambic, incisive, ironical, irreverent, mocking, mordant, pungent, sarcastic, sardonic, satiric, taunting.

satirise *v* abuse, burlesque, caricature, censure, criticise, deride, lampoon, make fun of, make sport of, mock, parody, Pasquil, Pasquin, pasquinade, pillory, ridicule, send up, squib, take off, travesty.

antonyms acclaim, celebrate, honour.

satirist *n* caricaturist, cartoonist, lampooner, lampoonist, mocker, parodist, pasquilant, pasquiler, pasquinader, ridiculer.

satisfaction *n* achievement, amends, appeasing, assuaging, atonement, comfort, compensation, complacency, content, contentedness, contentment, conviction, damages, ease, enjoyment, fulfilment, fullness, gratification, guerdon, happiness, indemnification, justice, payment, pleasure, pride, quittance, recompense, redress, reimbursement, remuneration, reparation, repleteness, repletion, requital, resolution, restitution, reward, satiety, self-satisfaction, sense of achievement, settlement, vindication, well-being.

antonyms discontent, displeasure, dissatisfaction, frustration.

satisfactory *adj* acceptable, adequate, all right, average, competent, fair, fit, OK, passable, proper, sufficient, suitable, tickety-boo, up to the mark.

antonyms inadequate, unacceptable, unsatisfactory.

satisfied *adj* appeased, complacent, content, contented, convinced, full, happy, mollified, pacified, persuaded, pleased, positive, reassured, replete, sated, satiated, self-satisfied, smug, sure.

antonyms dissatisfied, hungry, unconvinced.

satisfy *v* answer, appease, assuage, assure, atone, compensate, content, convince, delight, discharge, do, fill, fulfil, glut, gratify, guerdon, indemnify, indulge, meet, mollify, pacify, pay, persuade, placate, please, qualify, quench, quiet, reassure, recompense, reimburse, remunerate, replete, requite, reward, sate, satiate, serve, settle, slake, square up, suffice, surfeit.

antonyms disappoint, dissatisfy, fail, frustrate, thwart.

satisfying *adj* cheering, convincing, cool, filling, fulfilling, gratifying, persuasive, pleasing, pleasurable, satisfactory.

antonyms dissatisfying, frustrating, thwarting, unsatisfactory.

saturate *v* douse, drench, drouk, imbue, impregnate, infuse, permeate, ret, soak, souse, steep, suffuse, waterlog.

saturated *adj* drenched, dripping, droukit, imbued, impregnated, permeated, soaked, soaking, sodden, soggy, sopping, soused, steeped, suffused, waterlogged, wringing.

saturnine *adj* austere, dismal, dour, dull, gloomy, glum, grave, heavy, melancholy, mirthless, moody, morose, phlegmatic, severe, sombre, stern, taciturn, uncommunicative, withdrawn.

antonyms cheerful, jovial.

satyr *n* faun, goat, lecher, Pan, philanderer, womaniser, wood-house, woodwose.

sauce *n* archness, assurance, audacity, backchat, brass, brazenness, cheek, cheekiness, disrespect, disrespectfulness, flippancy, freshness, impertinence, impudence, insolence, irreverence, lip, malapertness, nerve, pertness, presumption, presumptuousness, rudeness, sass, sauciness.

antonyms politeness, respectfulness.

saucy *adj* arch, audacious, cheeky, dashing, disdainful, disrespectful, flip, flippant, forward, fresh, gay, impertinent, impudent, insolent, irreverent, jaunty, lippy, malapert, natty, perky, pert, presumptuous, provocative, rakish, rude, sassy, sporty.

antonyms polite, respectful.

saunter *v* amble, dacker, dally, dander, daunder, dawdle, linger, loiter, meander, mooch, mosey, perambulate, promenade, ramble, roam, rove, sally forth, stravaig, stroll, wander.

n airing, amble, breather, constitutional, outing, perambulation, promenade, ramble, sally, stroll, turn, walk.

savage *adj* barbarous, beastly, bestial, blistering, bloodthirsty, bloody, brutal, brutish, catamountain, cruel, devilish, diabolical, dog-eat-dog, fell, feral, ferocious, fierce, harsh, immane, inhuman, merciless, murderous, pitiless, primitive, ravening, rough, rude, rugged, ruthless, sadistic, sanguinary, uncivilised, uncultivated, undomesticated, uneducated, unenlightened, unsparing, untamed, untaught, vicious, wild.

antonyms benign, civilised, humane.

n aboriginal, aborigine, ape, autochthon, barbarian, bear, beast, boor, brute, fiend, heathen, illiterate, indigene, lout, monster, native, oaf, philistine, primitive, roughneck, yahoo, yobbo.

v attack, claw, hammer, lacerate, mangle, maul, pan, scarify, tear.

savagery *n* barbarity, bestiality, bloodthirstiness, brutality, brutishness, cruelty, ferity, ferocity, fierceness, inhumanity, mercilessness, murderousness, pitilessness, primitiveness, roughness, ruthlessness, sadism, viciousness, wildness.

antonyms civilisation, civility, humanity.

savant *n* authority, guru, intellectual, man of letters, master, mastermind, philosopher, pundit, rishi, sage, savante, scholar.

antonyms amateur, duffer, ignoramus.

save *v* cache, collect, conserve, cut back, deliver, economise, free, gather, guard, hinder, hoard, hold, husband, keep, lay up, liberate, obviate, preserve, prevent, protect, put aside, put by, reclaim, recover, redeem, rescue, reserve, retain, retrench, safeguard, salt away, salvage, screen, shield, spare, squirrel, stash, store.

antonyms discard, spend, squander, waste.

saving *adj* careful, compensatory, economical, extenuating, frugal, mitigating, qualifying, redeeming, soterial, sparing, thrifty.

n bargain, conservation, cut, discount, economy, preservation, reclamation, redemption, reduction, rescue, retrenchment, salvage, salvation.

antonyms expense, loss, waste.

savings *n* capital, fund, nest egg, reserve fund, reserves, resources, store.

saviour *n* champion, defender, emancipator, guardian, knight-errant, liberator, messiah, preserver, protector, rescuer, salvation.

antonyms destroyer, enemy.

savoir-faire *n* ability, accomplishment, address, assurance, capability, confidence, diplomacy, discretion, expertise, finesse, know-how, poise, tact, urbanity.

antonyms awkwardness, clumsiness, incompetence, inexperience.

savour *n* excitement, fascination, flavour, interest, piquancy, relish, salt, sapor, smack, smell, spice, tang, taste, zest.

v appreciate, dwell on, enjoy, gloat over, like, luxuriate in, partake, rehearse, relish, revel in.

antonyms shrink from, wince at.

savoury *adj* agreeable, appetising, aromatic, dainty, decent, delectable, delicious, edifying, full-flavoured, gamy, good, gusty, honest, luscious, mouthwatering, palatable, piquant, reputable, respectable, rich, salubrious, scrumptious, spicy, tangy, tasty, toothsome, wholesome.

antonyms insipid, tasteless, unappetising.

n appetiser, bonne bouche, canape, hors d'oeuvre.

saw *n* adage, aphorism, apophthegm, axiom, byword, commonplace, dictum, epigram, gnome, maxim, mot, proverb, saying.

say *v* add, affirm, allege, announce, answer, assert, assume, bruit, claim, comment, communicate, conjecture, convey, declare, deliver, disclose, divulge, do, enunciate, estimate, express, guess, imagine, imply, intimate, judge, maintain, mention, opine, orate, perform, presume, pronounce, read, recite, reckon, rehearse, rejoin, remark, render, repeat, reply, report, respond, retort, reveal, rumour, signify, speak, state, suggest, surmise, tell, utter, voice.

n authority, chance, clout, crack, go, influence, power, sway, turn, voice, vote, weight, word.

saying *n* adage, aphorism, apophthegm, axiom, byword, dictum, gnome, maxim, mot, motto, precept, proverb, remnant, saw, slogan.

sayings *n* analects, bon mots, dicta, gems, logia, mots, obiter dicta, quotations, quotes, remarks, remnants, tags, words of wisdom.

say-so *n* affirmation, agreement, approval, assertion, asseveration, assurance, authorisation, authority, backing, consent, dictum, guarantee, OK, permission, ratification, sanction, word.

scald *v* blister, burn, sear.

scale[1] *n* calibration, compass, continuum, degree, degrees, extent, gamut, gradation, grading, graduation, hierarchy, ladder, measure, order, progression, proportion, range, ranking, ratio, reach, register, scope, sequence, series, spectrum, spread, steps.

v adjust, level, move, proportion, prorate, regulate, shift.

scale[2] *n* crust, encrustation, film, flake, furfur, lamella, lamina, layer, plate, scutellum, shield, squama, squamella, squamula, squamule.

v clean, desquamate, exfoliate, flake, peel, scrape.

scale[3] *v* ascend, clamber, climb, escalade, mount, scramble, shin up, surmount, swarm.

scaliness *n* dandruff, flakiness, furfur, scabrousness, scurfiness, squamosity.

scaly *adj* branny, desquamative, desquamatory, flaky, furfuraceous, furfurous, lepidote, leprose, leprous, scabby, scabrous, scurfy, squamose, squamous, squamulose.

scamp *n* blighter, caitiff, devil, fripon, imp, knave, lorel, losel, mischief-maker, monkey, prankster, rascal, rogue, ruffian, scallywag, scapegrace, toe-rag, tyke, whippersnapper, wretch.

scamper *v* chevy, dart, dash, fly, frisk, frolic, gambol, hasten, hurry, pelt, romp, run, rush, scoot, scurry, scuttle, skedaddle, sprint.

scan *v* check, con, examine, glance through, investigate, pan, pan over, scrutinise, search, skim, survey, sweep.

n check, examination, investigation, probe, review, screening, scrutiny, search, survey.

scandal *n* abuse, aspersion, backbiting, calumniation, calumny, crime, defamation, detraction, dirt, discredit, disgrace, dishonour, embarrassment, enormity, evil, furore, gossip, gossiping, ignominy, infamy, muck-raking, obloquy, odium, offence, opprobrium, outcry, outrage, reproach, rumours, shame, sin, slander, stigma, talk, tattle, traducement, uproar, Watergate, wrongdoing.

scandalise *v* affront, appal, astound, disgust, dismay, horrify, nauseate, offend, outrage, repel, revolt, shock, sicken.

scandalmonger *n* busybody, calumniator, defamer, gossip, gossip-monger, muck-raker, quidnunc, scandal-bearer, tabby, tabby-cat, tale-bearer, tattle, tattler, traducer.

scandalous *adj* abominable, atrocious, calumnious, defamatory, disgraceful, disreputable, evil, exorbitant, extortionate, gamy, gossiping, immoderate, improper, infamous, libellous, monstrous, odious, opprobrious, outrageous, scurrilous, shameful, shocking, slanderous, unseemly, unspeakable, untrue.

scant *adj* bare, deficient, hardly any, inadequate, insufficient, limited, little, little or no, minimal, sparse.

antonyms adequate, ample, sufficient.

scanty *adj* bare, beggarly, deficient, exiguous, inadequate, insubstantial, insufficient, light, meagre, narrow, parsimonious, poor, restricted, scant, scrimp, scrimpy, short, shy, skimped, skimpy, slender, sparing, sparse, thin.

antonyms ample, plentiful, substantial.

scapegoat *n* fall guy, patsy, victim, whipping-boy.

scapegrace *n* blighter, good-for-nothing, imp, ne'er-do-well, rapscallion, rascal, reprobate, rogue, scallywag, scamp, toe-rag.

scar *n* blemish, cicatrix, injury, lesion, mark, proud flesh, scar tissue, scarring, stigma, trauma, ulosis, wound.

v brand, cicatrise, damage, disfigure, mark, stigmatise, traumatise.

scarce *adj* deficient, few, infrequent, insufficient, lacking, rare, scanty, sparse, thin on the ground, uncommon, unusual, wanting.

antonyms common, copious, plentiful.

scarcely *adv* barely, hardly, just and no more, not readily, not willingly, only just, scarce.

scarcity *n* dearth, deficiency, infrequency, insufficiency, lack, niggardliness, paucity, poverty, rareness, rarity, scantiness, shortage, sparseness, uncommonness, want.

antonyms abundance, enough, glut, plenty, sufficiency.

scare *v* affright, alarm, appal, daunt, dismay, frighten, gally, intimidate, panic, shock, startle, terrify, terrorise, unnerve.

antonym reassure.

n agitation, alarm, alarm and despondency, alert, consternation, dismay, fright, hysteria, panic, shock, start, terror.

antonym reassurance.

scarecrow *n* craw-bogle, craw-deil, crowboggart, crow-keeper, fright, gally-bagger, gally-crow, mess, sight, tatterdemalion.

scared *adj* affrighted, affrightened, agitated, anxious, appalled, dismayed, fearful, frightened, nervous, panicky, panic-stricken, petrified, shaken, startled, terrified, worried.

antonyms confident, reassured.

scaremonger *n* alarmist, Cassandra, doom and gloom merchant, doomsman, doomwatcher, jitterbug, pessimist, prophet of doom.

scarf *n* babushka, boa, cravat, fichu, headscarf, headsquare, kerchief, muffler, neckerchief, necktie, shawl, stole, tawdry-lace.

scarper *v* abscond, absquatulate, beat it, bolt, bunk off, clear off, decamp, depart, disappear, do a bunk, escape, flee, flit, go, hightail it, run away, run for it, scram, skedaddle, vamoose, vanish.

scary *adj* alarming, anxious, bloodcurdling, chilling, creepy, disturbing, eldritch, frightening, hair-raising, hairy, horrendous, horrible, horrifying, intimidating, shocking, spine-chilling, spooky, terrifying, unnerving, upsetting, worrying.

scathing *adj* acid, biting, bitter, brutal, caustic, critical, cutting, excoriating, harsh, lacerating, mordant, sarcastic, savage, scornful, searing, trenchant, unsparing, virulent, vitriolic, withering, wounding.

antonym complimentary.

scatter *v* bestrew, break up, broadcast, diffuse, disband, disintegrate, disject, dispel, disperse, disseminate, dissipate, disunite, divide, fling, flurr, litter, propagate, separate, shower, sow, spatter, splutter, spread, sprinkle, squander, strew.

antonyms collect, concentrate.

scatter-brained *adj* bird-brained, careless, dizzy, empty-headed, feather-brained, flighty, forgetful, frivolous, giddy, inattentive, irresponsible, madcap, scatty, silly, slap-happy, thoughtless, undependable, unreliable.

antonyms careful, efficient, sensible, sober.

scattering *n* break-up, diaspora, diffusion, disgregation, disjection, dispersal, dispersion, dissemination, dissipation, dissolution, few, fistful, handful, propagation, scatter, separation, smatter, smattering, sprinkling.

antonyms abundance, mass.

adj disintegrative, dispersive, disseminative, dissipative, divisive.

antonym unifying.

scavenger *n* Autolycus, cleaner, dustman, forager, garbage collector, raker, rummager, scavager, scrounger, street orderly, street-cleaner, sweeper.

scenario *n* outline, plan, plot, projection, resume, rundown, scheme, sequence, situation, skeleton, sketch, story line, summary, synopsis.

scene *n* act, area, arena, backdrop, background, business, carry-on, chapter, circumstances, commotion, confrontation, display, disturbance, division, drama, environment, episode, exhibition, focus, fuss, incident, landscape, locale, locality, location, melodrama, milieu, mise en scène, outburst, pageant, panorama, part, performance, picture, place, position, prospect, representation, row, set, setting, show, sight, site, situation, spectacle, spot, stage, tableau, tantrum, to-do, upset, view, vista, whereabouts, world.

scenery *n* backdrop, background, decor, flats, landscape, mise en scène, outlook, panorama, set, setting, sight, surroundings, terrain, tormentors, view, vista.

scenic *adj* awe-inspiring, beautiful, breathtaking, grand, impressive, magnificent, panoramic, picturesque, pretty, spectacular, striking, stupendous.

antonyms dreary, dull, unspectacular.

scent *n* aroma, bouquet, fragrance, fumet, odour, perfume, redolence, smell, spoor, trace, track, trail, waft, whiff.

antonym stink.

v detect, discern, nose, nose out, perceive, recognise, sense, smell, sniff, sniff out.

scented *adj* aromatic, fragrant, odoriferous, perfumed, redolent, sweet-smelling.

antonyms malodorous, noisome, stinking.

sceptic *n* agnostic, atheist, cynic, disbeliever, doubter, doubting Thomas, nullifidian, Pyrrhonist, questioner, questionist, rationalist, scoffer, unbeliever.

antonym believer.

sceptical *adj* cynical, disbelieving, distrustful, doubtful, doubting, dubious, hesitating, incredulous, mistrustful, pessimistic, questioning, quizzical, scoffing, suspicious, unbelieving, unconvinced, unpersuaded, untrustful.

antonyms convinced, naïve, trusting.

scepticism *n* agnosticism, atheism, cynicism, disbelief, distrust, doubt, incredulity, pessimism, Pyrrhonism, rationalism, suspicion, unbelief, Voltairianism, Voltairism.

antonyms belief, faith, naïvety.

schedule *n* agenda, calendar, catalogue, diary, form, inventory, itinerary, list, plan, programme, scheme, scroll, table, timetable.

v appoint, arrange, book, list, organise, plan, programme, slot, table, time.

schematic *adj* diagrammatic, diagrammatical, graphic, illustrative, representational, simplified, simplistic, symbolic.

scheme *n* arrangement, blueprint, chart, codification, configuration, conformation, conspiracy, contrivance, dart, design, device, diagram, disposition, dodge, draft, game, idea, intrigue, lay-out, machinations, manoeuvre, method, outline, pattern, plan, plot, ploy, procedure, programme, project, proposal, proposition, racket, ruse, schedule, schema, shape, shift, stratagem, strategy, subterfuge, suggestion, system, tactics, theory.

v collude, conspire, contrive, design, devise, frame, imagine, intrigue, machinate, manipulate, manoeuvre, mastermind, plan, plot, project, pull strings, pull wires, work out.

schemer *n* conniver, deceiver, eminence grise, fox, intriguer, Machiavelli, Machiavellian, machinator, mastermind, plotter, politician, wangler, wheeler-dealer, wire-puller.

scheming *adj* artful, calculating, conniving, crafty, cunning, deceitful, designing, devious, duplicitous, foxy, insidious, Machiavellian, slippery, sly, tricky, underhand, unscrupulous, wily.

antonyms artless, honest, open, transparent.

schism *n* breach, break, cleavage, discord, disunion, division, estrangement, faction, quarrel, rift, rupture, sect, separation, severance, splinter group, splintering, split, sunderance.

scholar *n* academe, academic, authority, bookman, bookworm, egghead, intellectual, man of letters, maulvi, pupil, savant, scholastic, schoolboy, schoolchild, schoolgirl, schoolman, student.

antonyms dullard, dunce, ignoramus, illiterate, philistine.

scholarly *adj* academic, analytical, bookish, clerk-like, clerkly, conscientious, critical, erudite, intellectual, knowledgeable, learned, lettered, scholastic, scientific, studious, well-read, wissenschaftlich.

antonyms illiterate, unscholarly.

scholarship[1] *n* attainments, book-learning, education, erudition, insight, knowledge, learnedness, learning, lore, scholarliness, wisdom, Wissenschaft.

scholarship[2] *n* award, bursary, endowment, exhibition, fellowship, grant.

scholastic *adj* academic, analytical, bookish, learned, lettered, literary, pedagogic, pedantic, precise, scholarly, subtle.

school *n* academy, adherents, alma mater, circle, class, clique, college, creed, denomination, department, devotees, disciples, discipline, doctrine, dogma, externat, faction, faculty, faith, followers, following, group, gymnasium, institute, institution, lycee, outlook, pedagoguery, persuasion, pupils, sect, seminary, set, students, teaching, view, votaries.

v coach, discipline, drill, educate, habituate, harden, indoctrinate, instruct, inure, prepare, prime, train, tutor, verse.

schooling *n* book-learning, booklore, coaching, drill, education, grounding, guidance, inculcation, indoctrination, instruction, preparation, schoolcraft, teaching, training, tuition.

schoolteacher *n* dominie, educator, instructor, master, mistress, pedagogue, school-dame, school-ma'am, schoolmarm, schoolmaster, schoolmistress, teacher, usher.

science *n* art, discipline, knowledge, ology, proficiency, skill, specialisation, technique, technology, Wissenschaft.

scientific *adj* accurate, analytical, controlled, exact, mathematical, methodical, precise, scholarly, systematic, thorough, wissenschaftlich.

scintillate *v* blaze, coruscate, flash, gleam, glint, glisten, glitter, shine, spark, sparkle, twinkle, wink.

scintillating *adj* animated, blazing, blinding, bright, brilliant, coruscant, coruscating, dazzling, ebullient, exciting, flashing, glittering, lively, shining, sparkling, stimulating, vivacious, winking, witty.

antonym dull.

scion *n* branch, child, descendant, graft, heir, imp, offshoot, offspring, shoot, slip, sprig, sprout, successor, twig.

scoff[1] *v* belittle, deride, despise, fleer, flout, geck, gibe, jeer, knock, mock, poke fun, pooh-pooh, rail, revile, rib, ridicule, scorn, sneer, taunt, twit.

antonyms compliment, flatter, praise.

scoff[2] *v* bolt, consume, cram, devour, fill one's face, gobble, gulp, guzzle, pig, put away, shift, wolf.

antonym abstain.

n chow, comestibles, commons, eatables, eats, edibles, fare, feed, fodder, food, grub, meal, nosh, nosh-up, provisions, rations, scran, tuck, victuals.

scoffing *adj* cynical, fiendish, Mephistophelian, sarcastic.

scold *v* admonish, bawl out, berate, blame, castigate, censure, chide, find fault with, flyte, jaw, jawbone, lecture, nag, rate, rebuke, remonstrate, reprimand, reproach, reprove, rollick, take to task, tell off, tick off, upbraid, vituperate, wig.

antonyms commend, praise.

n battle-axe, beldam, fishwife, Fury, harridan, nag, shrew, termagant, virago, vixen, Xanthippe.

scolding *n* a piece of one's mind, castigation, dirdum, dressing-down, earful, flyting, jaw, jawbation, jawing, jobation, lecture, rebuke, reprimand, reproof, rollicking, row, siserary, talking-to, telling-off, throughgoing, ticking-off, tongue-lashing, upbraiding, wigging.

antonym commendation.

scoop[1] *n* backhoe, bail, bailer, bucket, dipper, lade, ladle, spoon.

v bail, dig, dip, empty, excavate, gather, gouge, hollow, ladle, lift, pick up, remove, scrape, shovel, sweep.

scoop[2] *n* coup, exclusive, expose, inside story, latest, low-down, revelation, sensation.

scoot *v* beat it, bolt, bowl, career, dart, dash, hurry, run, scamper, scarper, scud, scurry, scuttle, shoot, skedaddle, sprint, tootle, vamoose, zip.

scope *n* ambit, application, area, breadth, capacity, compass, competence, confines, coverage, elbow-room, extent, freedom, latitude, liberty, opportunity, orbit, outlook, purview, range, reach, remit, room, space, span, sphere, terms of reference, tessitura.

scorch *v* blacken, blister, burn, char, parch, roast, scald, sear, shrivel, singe, sizzle, torrefy, wither.

scorched *adj* arid, baked, blackened, blistered, burnt, charred, cracked, parched, sear, seared, shrivelled, torrid, withered.

scorching *adj* baking, blistering, boiling, broiling, burning, fiery, flaming, parching, red-hot, roasting, scalding, searing, sizzling, sweltering, torrid, tropical, withering.

score *n* a bone to pick, account, amount, basis, bill, cause, charge, debt, due, gash, grade, gravamen, grievance, ground, grounds, grudge, injury, injustice, line, mark, notch, obligation, outcome, points, reason, reckoning, record, result, scratch, sum total, tab, tally, total, wrong.

v achieve, adapt, amass, arrange, attain, be one up, benefit, chalk up, count, cut, deface, earn, engrave, furrow, gain, gouge, grave, graze, groove, hatch, have the advantage, have the edge, impress, incise, indent, knock up, make, make a hit, mark, nick, notch, notch up, orchestrate, profit, realise, record, register, scrape, scratch, set, slash, tally, total, win.

score out cancel, cross out, delete, efface, erase, expunge, obliterate, remove, strike out.

antonyms reinstate, restore.

scores *n* crowds, droves, hosts, hundreds, legions, lots, masses, millions, multitudes, myriads, shoals, swarms.

scorn *n* contempt, contemptuousness, contumely, derision, despite, disdain, disgust, dismissiveness, disparagement, geck, mockery, sarcasm, scornfulness, slight, sneer.

antonyms admiration, respect.

v contemn, deride, despise, disdain, dismiss, flout, hold in contempt, laugh at, laugh in the face of, look down on, misprise, pooh-pooh, refuse, reject, scoff at, slight, sneer at, spurn.

antonyms admire, respect.

scornful *adj* arrogant, contemptuous, contumelious, defiant, derisive, disdainful, dismissive, disparaging, haughty, insulting, jeering, mocking, sarcastic, sardonic, scathing, scoffing, slighting, sneering, supercilious, withering.

antonyms admiring, complimentary, respectful.

scornfully *adv* arrogantly, contemptuously, derisively, disdainfully, dismissively, disparagingly, haughtily, scathingly, slightingly, sneeringly, superciliously, witheringly.

antonyms admiringly, respectfully.

scot-free *adj* clear, ininjured, safe, scatheless, undamaged, unharmed, unhurt, unpunished, unrebuked, unreprimanded, unreproached, unscathed, without a scratch.

scoundrel *n* blackguard, blighter, bounder, caitiff, cheat, cur, dastard, good-for-nothing, heel, hound, knave, louse, miscreant, ne'er-do-well, picaroon, rascal, rat, reprobate, rogue, rotter, ruffian, scab, scallywag, scamp, scapegrace, stinker, swine, vagabond, villain.

scour[1] *v* abrade, buff, burnish, clean, cleanse, flush, furbish, polish, purge, rub, scrape, scrub, wash, whiten.

scour[2] *v* beat, comb, drag, forage, go over, hunt, rake, ransack, search, turn upside-down.

scourge *n* affliction, bane, cat, cat-o'-nine-tails, curse, evil, flagellum, infliction, knout, lash, menace, misfortune, penalty, pest, pestilence, plague, punishment, strap, switch, terror, thong, torment, visitation, whip.

antonyms benefit, blessing, boon, godsend.

v afflict, beat, belt, cane, castigate, chastise, curse, devastate, discipline, excoriate, flagellate, flail, flog, harass, horsewhip, lambast, lash, lather, leather, plague, punish, tan, terrorise, thrash, torment, trounce, verberate, visit, wallop, whale, whip.

scout *v* case, check out, do a recce, explore, hunt, investigate, look, observe, pickeer, probe, reconnoitre, search, seek, snoop, spy, spy out, survey, track, watch.

n emissary, escort, lookout, outrider, pickeerer, precursor, reconnoitrer, spy, vanguard.

scowl *v* frown, glare, glower, grimace, lower.

n frown, glare, glower, grimace, moue.

antonyms beam, grin, smile.

scrabble *v* clamber, claw, dig, grope, grub, paw, root, scramble, scrape, scratch.

scraggy *adj* angular, bony, emaciated, gangling, gaunt, lank, lanky, lean, meagre, rawboned, scranny, scrawny, skinny, spare, undernourished, wasted.

antonyms plump, rounded, sleek.

scram *v* beat it, bolt, clear off, clear out, depart, disappear, do a bunk, flee, get lost, go away, leave, quit, scarper, scoot, shove off, skedaddle, take to one's heels, vamoose.

scramble *v* clamber, climb, contend, crawl, hasten, jostle, jumble, push, run, rush, scale, scrabble, shuffle, sprawl, strive, struggle, swarm, vie.

n climb, commotion, competition, confusion, contention, free-for-all, hustle, mêlee, muddle, race, rat race, rivalry, rush, strife, struggle, trek, trial, tussle.

scrap[1] *n* atom, bit, bite, crumb, fraction, fragment, grain, iota, junk, mite, modicum, morsel, mouthful, part, particle, piece, portion, remnant, shard, shred, sliver, snap, snatch, snippet, trace, vestige, waste, whit.

v abandon, axe, break up, cancel, chuck, demolish, discard, ditch, drop, jettison, junk, shed, throw out, write off.

antonyms reinstate, restore, resume.

scrap[2] *n* argument, bagarre, barney, battle, brawl, disagreement, dispute, dust-up, fight, quarrel, row, ruckus, ruction, rumpus, scuffle, set-to, shindy, squabble, tiff, wrangle.

antonyms agreement, peace.

v argue, argufy, bicker, clash, fall out, fight, spat, squabble, wrangle.

antonym agree.

scrape *v* abrade, bark, claw, clean, erase, file, grate, graze, grind, pinch, rasp, remove, rub, save, scour, scrabble, scratch, screech, scrimp, scuff, skimp, skin, squeak, stint.

n abrasion, difficulty, dilemma, distress, fix, graze, mess, pickle, plight, predicament, pretty kettle of fish, rub, scratch, scuff, shave, spot, trouble.

scrappy *adj* bitty, disjointed, fragmentary, incomplete, perfunctory, piecemeal, sketchy, slapdash, slipshod, superficial.

antonyms complete, finished.

scraps *n* bits, leavings, leftovers, remains, scrapings.

scratch *v* annul, cancel, claw, curry, cut, damage, delete, eliminate, erase, etch, grate, graze, incise, lacerate, mark, race, retire, rub, scarify, score, scrab, scrabble, scrape, withdraw.

n blemish, claw mark, gash, graze, laceration, mark, race, scrape, streak.

adj haphazard, impromptu, improvised, rough, rough-and-ready, unrehearsed.

antonym polished.

scrawl *n* cacography, scrabble, scratch, scribble, squiggle, writing.

scrawny *adj* angular, bony, emaciated, gaunt, lanky, lean, rawboned, scraggy, skeletal, skinny, thin, underfed, under-nourished.

antonym plump.

scream[1] *v* bawl, clash, cry, holler, jar, roar, screak, screech, shriek, shrill, squeal, wail, yell, yelp, yowl.

n howl, outcry, roar, screak, screech, shriek, squeal, wail, yell, yelp, yowl.

antonym whisper.

scream[2] *n* card, caution, character, comedian, comic, cure, hoot, joker, laugh, riot, sensation, wit.

antonym bore.

screech *v* cry, screak, scream, shriek, squawk, squeal, ululate, yelp.

antonym whisper.

screen *v* cloak, conceal, cover, cull, defend, evaluate, examine, filter, gauge, grade, guard, hide, mask, process, protect, riddle, safeguard, scan, shade, shelter, shield, shroud, sieve, sift, sort, veil, vet.

antonyms broadcast, present, show, uncover.

n abat-jour, awning, canopy, cloak, concealment, cover, divider, guard, hallan, hedge, hoarding, mantle, mesh, net, partition, shade, shelter, shield, shroud.

screw *v* adjust, bleed, cheat, coerce, compress, constrain, contort, contract, crumple, distort, extort, extract, fasten, force, oppress, pressurise, pucker, squeeze, tighten, turn, twist, wind, wrest, wring, wrinkle.

screw up botch, bungle, close, contort, contract, crumple, disrupt, distort, knot, louse up, make a hash of, mess up, mishandle, mismanage, pucker, queer, spoil, tighten, wrinkle.

antonyms manage, unscrew.

screwy *adj* batty, cracked, crackers, crazy, daft, dotty, eccentric, mad, nutty, odd, queer, round the bend, round the twist, weird.

antonym sane.

scribble *v* dash off, doodle, jot, pen, scratch, scrawl, write.

scribbler *n* hack, ink-slinger, paper-stainer, pen-driver, penny-a-liner, pen-pusher, pot-boiler, quill-driver, quillman, writer.

scribe *n* amanuensis, clerk, copyist, hierographer, notary, penman, scrivener, secretary, tabellion, writer.

scrimmage *n* affray, bovver, brawl, disturbance, dust-up, fight, fray, free-for-all, mêlee, riot, row, scrap, scuffle, set-to, shindy, skirmish, squabble, stramash, struggle.

antonym calmness.

scrimp *v* curtail, economise, limit, pinch, reduce, restrict, save, scrape, shorten, skimp, stint.

antonym spend.

script *n* book, calligraphy, cheirography, copy, hand, handwriting, letters, libretto, lines, longhand, manuscript, penmanship, text, words, writing.

scripture *n* Analects, Bhagavad Gita, Granth, Holy Bible, Holy Scripture, Holy Writ, Koran, New Testament, Old Testament, Pentateuch, shaster, shastra, sutra(s), the Bible, the Good Book, the Gospels, the Scriptures, the Word, the Word of God, Tripitaka, Upanishad(s), Veda(s), Zend-Avesta.

scroll *n* inventory, list, parchment, roll, volume, volute.

Scrooge *n* cheapskate, meanie, miser, money-grubber, niggard, penny-pincher, skinflint, tightwad.

antonym spendthrift.

scrounge *v* beg, bludge, bum, cadge, freeload, purloin, sponge, wheedle.

scrounger *n* bludger, bum, cadger, freeloader, parasite, scunge, sponger.

scrub *v* abandon, abolish, cancel, clean, cleanse, delete, discontinue, ditch, drop, forget, give up, rub, scour.

scruff *n* draggle-tail, ragamuffin, ragbag, scarecrow, sloven, slut, tatterdemalion, tramp.

scruffy *adj* disreputable, dog-eared, draggletailed, frowzy, grotty, ill-groomed, mangy, messy, ragged, run-down, scrubby, seedy, shabby, slatternly, slovenly, sluttish, squalid, tattered, ungroomed, unkempt, untidy.

antonyms tidy, well-dressed.

scrumptious *adj* appetising, delectable, delicious, delightful, exquisite, luscious, magnificent, moreish, mouth-watering, succulent, yummy.

antonym unappetising.

scrunch *v* champ, chew, crumple, crunch, crush, grate, grind, mash, squash.

scruple *v* balk at, demur at, falter, hesitate, object to, recoil from, shrink from, stick at, vacillate, waver.

n caution, compunction, difficulty, doubt, hesitation, misgiving, pang, perplexity, qualm, reluctance, squeamishness, uneasiness.

scrupulous *adj* careful, conscientious, conscionable, exact, fastidious, honourable, meticulous, minute, moral, nice, painstaking, precise, principled, punctilious, rigorous, squeaky-clean, strict, upright.

antonym careless.

scrutinise *v* analyse, dissect, examine, explore, give a once-over, inspect, investigate, peruse, probe, scan, search, sift, study.

scrutiny *n* analysis, docimasy, examination, exploration, inquiry, inspection, investigation, once-over, perusal, search, sifting, study.

scud *v* blow, dart, fly, hasten, race, sail, shoot, skim, speed.

scuff *v* abrade, brush, drag, graze, rub, scratch, shuffle, skin.

scuffle *v* clash, contend, fight, grapple, hocus, jostle, struggle, tussle.

n affray, bagarre, barney, brawl, commotion, disturbance, dog-fight, fight, fray, ruck, ruckus, ruction, rumpus, scrap, set-to, tussle.

sculpt *v* carve, chisel, cut, fashion, form, hew, model, mould, represent, sculp, sculpture, shape.

scum *n* algae, canaille, crust, dregs, dross, film, froth, impurities, offscourings, offscum, pellicle, rabble, rag-tag and bobtail, riff-raff, rubbish, scruff, spume, sullage, trash, vomit.

scupper *v* defeat, demolish, destroy, disable, overthrow, overwhelm, put a spanner in the works, ruin, torpedo, wreck.

antonyms advance, promote.

scurf *n* dandruff, flakiness, furfur, scabrousness, scaliness.

scurfy *adj* furfuraceous, furfurous, lepidote, leprose, leprous, scaberulous, scabrid, scabrous, scaly.

scurrility *n* abuse, abusiveness, billingsgate, coarseness, grossness, indecency, invective, nastiness, obloquy, obscenity, offensiveness, rudeness, scurrilousness, vituperation, vulgarity.

antonym politeness.

scurrilous *adj* abusive, coarse, defamatory, Fescennial, foul, foul-mouthed, gross, indecent, insulting, low, nasty, obscene, offensive, Rabelaisian, ribald, rude, salacious, scabrous, scandalous, slanderous, vituperative, vulgar.

antonym polite.

scurry *v* dart, dash, fly, hurry, race, scamper, scoot, scud, scuttle, skedaddle, skelter, skim, sprint, trot, whisk.

antonym stroll.

n flurry, hustle and bustle, scampering, whirl.

antonym calm.

scurvy *adj* abject, bad, base, caddish, contemptible, despicable, dirty, dishonourable, ignoble, low, low-down, mean, pitiful, rotten, scabby, shabby, sorry, vile, worthless.

antonyms good, honourable.

scuttle *v* bustle, hare, hasten, hurry, run, rush, scamper, scoot, scramble, scud, scurry, scutter, trot.

antonym stroll.

sea *n* abundance, briny, deep, ditch, drink, expanse, main, mass, multitude, ocean, oggin, plethora, profound, profusion, waves.

adj aquatic, marine, maritime, naval, ocean, ocean-going, oceanic, pelagic, salt, saltwater, sea-going.

antonyms air, land.

seafaring *adj* marine, maritime, nautical, naval, oceanic, sailing.

antonym land.

seal *v* assure, attest, authenticate, bung, clinch, close, conclude, confirm, consummate, cork, enclose, establish, fasten, finalise, plug, ratify, secure, settle, shake hands on, shut, stamp, stop, stopper, validate, waterproof.

antonym unseal.

n assurance, attestation, authentication, bulla, confirmation, imprimatur, insignia, notification, ratification, sigil, signet, stamp.

seal off block up, close off, cut off, fence off, isolate, quarantine, segregate, shut off.

antonym open up.

sealed *adj* closed, corked, hermetic, plugged, shut.

antonym unsealed.

seam *n* closure, crack, furrow, joint, layer, line, lode, ridge, scar, stratum, suture, vein, wrinkle.

seaman *n* AB, deck-hand, hand, Jack tar, lascar, matelot, matlo(w), sailor, seacunny, sea-dog, seafarer, steersman, tar.

seamy *adj* corrupt, dark, degraded, disagreeable, disreputable, low, nasty, rough, sleazy, sordid, squalid, unpleasant, unwholesome.
antonyms pleasant, respectable.

sear *v* blight, brand, brown, burn, cauterise, desiccate, dry up, harden, scorch, seal, shrivel, sizzle, wilt, wither.

search *v* check, comb, examine, explore, ferret, forage, frisk, inquire, inspect, investigate, jerque, look, probe, pry, quest, ransack, rifle, rummage, scour, scrutinise, sift, test.
n examination, exploration, going-over, hunt, inquiry, inspection, investigation, perquisition, perscrutation, pursuit, quest, researches, rummage, scrutiny, zetetic.

searching *adj* close, intent, keen, minute, penetrating, piercing, probing, quizzical, severe, sharp, thorough, zetetic.
antonyms superficial, vague.

seasickness *n* mal de mer, nausea, queasiness.

season *n* division, interval, period, span, spell, term, time.
v acclimatise, accustom, anneal, colour, condiment, condition, discipline, enliven, flavour, habituate, harden, imbue, inure, lace, leaven, mature, mitigate, moderate, prepare, qualify, salt, spice, temper, toughen, train.

seasonable *adj* appropriate, convenient, fit, opportune, providential, suitable, timely, timeous, welcome, well-timed.
antonym unseasonable.

seasoned *adj* acclimatised, battle-scarred, experienced, hardened, long-serving, mature, old, practised, time-served, veteran, weathered, well-versed.
antonym novice.

seasoning *n* condiment, dressing, flavouring, pepper, relish, salt, sauce, spice.

seat *n* abode, axis, base, bed, bench, bottom, capital, cause, centre, chair, constituency, cradle, footing, foundation, ground, groundwork, headquarters, heart, house, hub, incumbency, location, mansion, membership, pew, place, residence, seat-stick, sedes, settle, shooting-stick, site, situation, source, stall, station, stool, throne.
v accommodate, assign, contain, deposit, fit, fix, hold, install, locate, place, set, settle, sit, slot, take.

seating *n* accommodation, chairs, gradin(e), places, room, seats.

seaweed *n* arame, gulf-weed, kelp, laver, laverbread, sargasso, sea-moss, sea-tang, sea-tangle, sea-ware, sea-wrack, varec(h), wrack.

secede *v* apostatise, disaffiliate, leave, quit, resign, retire, separate, split off, withdraw.
antonyms join, unite with.

secession *n* apostasy, break, defection, disaffiliation, schism, schismatics, seceders, seceding, split, withdrawal.
antonyms amalgamation, unification.

secluded *adj* claustral, cloistered, cloistral, cut off, isolated, lonely, out-of-the-way, private, reclusive, remote, retired, sequestered, sheltered, solitary, umbratile, umbratilous, unfrequented.
antonyms busy, public.

seclusion *n* concealment, hiding, isolation, privacy, purdah, recluseness, remoteness, retirement, retreat, shelter, solitude.

second[1] *adj* additional, alternate, alternative, double, duplicate, extra, following, further, inferior, lesser, lower, next, other, repeated, reproduction, secondary, subordinate, subsequent, succeeding, supplementary, supporting, twin.
n assistant, backer, helper, supporter.
v advance, agree with, aid, approve, assist, back, encourage, endorse, forward, further, help, promote, support.
second coming parousia.

second[2] *n* instant, jiff, jiffy, minute, mo, moment, sec, tick, trice, twinkling.

secondary *adj* alternate, auxiliary, back-up, consequential, contingent, derivative, derived, extra, indirect, inferior, lesser, lower, minor, relief, reserve, resultant, resulting, second, second-hand, second-rate, spare, subordinate, subsidiary, supporting, unimportant.
antonym primary.

second-class *adj* declasse(e), indifferent, inferior, mediocre, second-best, second-rate, undistinguished, uninspired, uninspiring.

second-hand *adj* borrowed, derivative, hand-me-down, old, plagiarised, used, vicarious, worn.
antonym new.

second-rate *adj* cheap, cheap and nasty, grotty, inferior, low-grade, mediocre, poor, rubbishy, shoddy, substandard, tacky, tawdry, undistinguished, uninspired, uninspiring.
antonym first-rate.

secrecy *n* clandestineness, concealment, confidence, confidentiality, covertness, furtiveness, hugger-mugger, mystery, privacy, retirement, seclusion, secretiveness, silence, solitude, stealth, stealthiness, surreptitiousness.
antonym openness.

secret *adj* abstruse, arcane, back-door, backstairs, cabbalistic(al), camouflaged, clandestine, classified, cloak-and-dagger, close, closet, concealed, conspiratorial, covered, covert, cryptic, deep, discreet, disguised, esoteric, furtive, hidden, hole-and-corner, hush-hush, inly, mysterious, occult, out-of-the-way, private, privy, recondite, reticent, retired, secluded, secretive, sensitive, shrouded, sly, stealthy, tête-à-tête, undercover, underground, underhand, under-the-counter, undisclosed, unfrequented, unknown, unpublished, unrevealed, unseen.
antonyms open, public.
n arcanum, code, confidence, enigma, formula, key, mystery, recipe.

secretary *n* assistant, clerk, famulus, girl Friday, PA, person Friday, personal assistant, stenographer, typist.

secrete[1] *v* appropriate, bury, cache, conceal, cover, disguise, harbour, hide, screen, secure, shroud, stash away, stow, veil.

antonym reveal.

secrete[2] *v* emanate, emit, extravasate, extrude, exude, osmose, secern, separate.

secretion *n* discharge, emission, excretion, extravasation, exudation, osmosis, secernment.

secretive *adj* cagey, close, close-lipped, close-mouthed, cryptic, deep, enigmatic, quiet, reserved, reticent, tight-lipped, uncommunicative, unforthcoming, withdrawn.

antonyms communicative, open.

secretly *adv* clandestinely, confidentially, covertly, furtively, in camera, in confidence, in private, in secret, on the q.t., on the quiet, on the sly, privately, privily, quietly, stealthily, surreptitiously, unobserved.

antonym openly.

sect *n* camp, denomination, division, faction, group, party, school, splinter group, subdivision, wing.

sectarian *adj* bigoted, clannish, cliquish, doctrinaire, dogmatic, exclusive, factional, fanatic, fanatical, insular, limited, narrow, narrow-minded, parochial, partisan, rigid, ultra.

antonyms broad-minded, cosmopolitan, non-sectarian.

n adherent, bigot, disciple, dogmatist, extremist, fanatic, fractionalist, partisan, zealot.

section *n* area, article, component, cross section, department, district, division, fraction, fractionlet, fragment, instalment, part, passage, piece, portion, region, sample, sector, segment, slice, subdivision, wing, zone.

antonym whole.

sectional *adj* class, divided, exclusive, factional, local, localised, partial, racial, regional, sectarian, separate, separatist.

antonyms general, universal.

sector *n* area, category, district, division, part, quarter, region, section, stratum, subdivision, zone.

antonym whole.

secular *adj* civil, laic, laical, lay, non-religious, profane, state, temporal, worldly.

antonym religious.

secularise *v* deconsecrate.

secure *adj* absolute, assured, certain, conclusive, confident, definite, dependable, easy, fast, fastened, firm, fixed, fortified, immovable, immune, impregnable, on velvet, over-confident, protected, reassured, reliable, safe, sheltered, shielded, solid, stable, steadfast, steady, sure, tight, unassailable, undamaged, unharmed, well-founded.

antonyms insecure, uncertain.

v acquire, assure, attach, batten down, bolt, chain, ensure, fasten, fix, gain, get, get hold of, guarantee, insure, land, lash, lock, lock up, moor, nail, obtain, padlock, procure, rivet, seize.

antonyms lose, unfasten.

security *n* assurance, asylum, care, certainty, collateral, confidence, conviction, cover, custody, defence, gage, guarantee, guards, hostage, immunity, insurance, pawn, pledge, positiveness, precautions, preservation, protection, refuge, reliance, retreat, safeguards, safe-keeping, safety, sanctuary, sureness, surety, surveillance, warranty.

antonym insecurity.

sedate *adj* calm, collected, composed, cool, decorous, deliberate, demure, dignified, douce, earnest, grave, imperturbable, middle-aged, placed, proper, quiet, seemly, serene, serious, slow-moving, sober, solemn, staid, tranquil, unflappable, unruffled.

antonyms flippant, hasty, undignified.

sedative *adj* allaying, anodyne, calmative, calming, depressant, lenitive, relaxing, soothing, soporific, tranquillising.

antonym rousing.

n anodyne, calmative, downer, narcotic, opiate, quietive, sleeping-pill, tranquilliser.

sedentary *adj* desk, desk-bound, inactive, motionless, seated, sedent, sitting, stationary, still, torpid, unmoving.

antonym active.

sediment *n* deposit, draff, dregs, faeces, fecula, grounds, lees, precipitate, residium, settlings, warp.

sedition *n* agitation, disloyalty, rabble-rousing, ruckus, rumpus, subversion, treason, tumult.

antonyms calm, loyalty.

seditious *adj* disloyal, dissident, insubordinate, mutinous, rebellious, refractory, revolutionary, subversive, traitorous.

antonyms calm, loyal.

seduce *v* allure, attract, beguile, betray, bewitch, corrupt, debauch, deceive, decoy, deflower, deprave, dishonour, ensnare, entice, inveigle, lure, mislead, ruin, tempt.

seducer *n* cad, Casanova, charmer, deceiver, Don Juan, flirt, gay deceiver, goat, libertine, Lothario, philanderer, wolf, womaniser.

seduction *n* allure, allurement, come-on, corruption, defloration, enticement, lure, ruin, seducement, snare, temptation.

seductive *adj* alluring, attractive, beguiling, bewitching, captivating, come-hither, come-on, enticing, flirtatious, honeyed, inviting, irresistible, page-three, provocative, ravishing, seducing, sexy, siren, specious, tempting.

antonym unattractive.

seductress *n* Circe, femme fatale, Lorelei, siren, temptress, vamp.

sedulous *adj* assiduous, busy, conscientious, constant, determined, diligent, industrious, laborious, painstaking, persevering, persistent, resolved, tireless, unflagging, unremitting, untiring.

antonym half-hearted.

see *v* accompany, anticipate, appreciate, ascertain, attend, behold, comprehend, consider, consult, court, date, decide, deem, deliberate, descry, determine, discern, discover, distinguish, divine, encounter, ensure, envisage, escort, espy, experience, fathom, feel, follow, foresee, foretell, get, glimpse, grasp, guarantee, heed, identify, imagine, interview, investigate, judge, know, lead, learn, look, make out, mark, meet, mind, note, notice, observe, perceive, picture, realise, receive, recognise, reflect, regard, show, sight, spot, take, understand, usher, view, visit, visualise, walk, witness.

see eye to eye accord, agree, coincide, concur, get along, get on, harmonise, jibe, speak the same language, subscribe.

antonym disagree.

see red blow one's top, blow up, boil, go mad, go off one's head, lose one's rag, lose one's temper.

see to arrange, attend to, deal with, do, fix, look after, manage, organise, repair, sort out, take care of, take charge of.

seed *n* beginning, children, descendants, egg, embryo, germ, grain, heirs, inkling, issue, kernel, nucleus, offspring, ovule, ovum, pip, progeny, quiverful, race, scions, semen, source, spawn, sperm, spore, start, successors, suspicion.

antonym ancestors.

seedy *adj* ailing, crummy, decaying, dilapidated, faded, grotty, grubby, ill, mangy, manky, off-colour, old, peelie-wally, poorly, run-down, scruffy, shabby, sickly, sleazy, slovenly, squalid, tatty, unkempt, unwell, worn.

antonyms posh, well.

seek *v* aim, ask, aspire to, attempt, beg, busk, desire, endeavour, entreat, essay, follow, hunt, inquire, invite, petition, pursue, request, solicit, strive, try, want.

seeker *n* chela, disciple, inquirer, novice, searcher, student, zetetic.

seem *v* appear, look, look like, pretend, sound like.

seeming *adj* apparent, appearing, illusory, ostensible, outward, pseudo, quasi-, specious, surface.

antonym real.

seemingly *adv* allegedly, apparently, as far as one can see, on the face of it, on the surface, ostensibly, outwardly, superficially.

antonym really.

seemly *adj* appropriate, attractive, becoming, befitting, comely, comme il faut, decent, decorous, fit, fitting, handsome, maidenly, meet, nice, proper, suitable, suited.

antonym unseemly.

seep *v* exude, leak, ooze, osmose, percolate, permeate, soak, trickle, weep, well.

seepage *n* exudation, leak, leakage, oozing, osmosis, percolation.

seer *n* augur, prophet, sibyl, soothsayer, spaeman, spaewife.

seesaw *v* alternate, fluctuate, oscillate, pitch, swing, teeter.

n pendulum, wild mare.

seethe *v* boil, bubble, churn, ferment, fizz, foam, foam at the mouth, froth, fume, hotch, marinate, rage, rise, saturate, simmer, smoulder, soak, souse, steep, storm, surge, swarm, swell, teem.

see-through *adj* diaphanous, filmy, flimsy, gauzy, gossamer(y), sheer, translucent, transparent.

antonym opaque.

segment *n* articulation, bit, compartment, division, part, piece, portion, section, slice, wedge.

antonym whole.

v anatomise, cut up, divide, halve, separate, slice, split.

segregate *v* cut off, discriminate against, dissociate, isolate, quarantine, separate, set apart.

antonym unite.

segregation *n* apartheid, discrimination, isolation, quarantine, separation.

antonym unification.

seize *v* abduct, annex, apprehend, appropriate, arrest, capture, catch, claw, clutch, cly, collar, commander, confiscate, crimp, distrain, distress, fasten, fix, for(e)hent, get, grab, grasp, grip, hijack, impound, nab, prehend, smug, snatch, take.

antonym let go.

seizure *n* abduction, annexation, apprehension, arrest, attachment, attack, capture, commandeering, confiscation, convulsion, distraint, distress, fit, grabbing, paroxysm, spasm, taking.

antonym liberation.

seldom *adv* infrequently, occasionally, rarely, scarcely.

antonym often.

select *v* choose, cull, pick, prefer, single out.

adj choice, elite, excellent, exclusive, first-class, first-rate, hand-picked, limited, picked, posh, preferable, prime, privileged, rare, selected, special, superior, top, top-notch.

antonyms general, second-rate.

selection *n* anthology, assortment, choice, choosing, collection, line-up, medley, miscellany, option, palette, pick, potpourri, preference, range, variety.

selective *adj* careful, discerning, discriminating, discriminatory, eclectic, elitist, particular.

antonym unselective.

self *n* ego, egoity, I, identity, person, personality, soul.

self-assertive *adj* aggressive, authoritarian, bossy, commanding, dictatorial, domineering, forceful, heavy-handed, high-handed, overbearing, overweening, peremptory, pushing, pushy.

antonym compliant.

self-assurance *n* assurance, cockiness, cocksureness, confidence, overconfidence, positiveness, self-confidence, self-possession.

antonyms humility, unsureness.

self-assured *adj* assured, cocksure, cocky, confident, overconfident, self-collected, self-possessed, sure of oneself.

antonyms humble, unsure.

self-centred *adj* egotistic(al), narcissistic, self-absorbed, self-interested, selfish, self-seeking, self-serving.

antonym altruistic.

self-confidence *n* aplomb, assurance, confidence, nerve, poise, self-assurance, self-possession, self-reliance.

antonyms humility, unsureness.

self-confident *adj* assured, confident, fearless, poised, secure, self-assured, self-collected, self-possessed, self-reliant.

antonyms humble, unsure.

self-conscious *adj* affected, awkward, bashful, coy, diffident, embarrassed, ill at ease, insecure, nervous, retiring, self-effacing, shamefaced, sheepish, shrinking, uncomfortable.

antonyms natural, unaffected.

self-control *n* calmness, composure, cool, coolness, discipline, encraty, restraint, self-command, self-discipline, self-government, self-mastery, self-restraint, temperance, will-power.

self-denial *n* abstemiousness, asceticism, moderation, renunciation, self-abandonment, self-abnegation, selflessness, self-renunciation, self-sacrifice, temperance, unselfishness.

antonym self-indulgence.

self-esteem *n* amour-propre, dignity, pride, self-assurance, self-confidence, self-pride, self-regard, self-respect.

antonym humility.

self-evident *adj* axiomatic, clear, incontrovertible, inescapable, manifest, obvious, undeniable, unquestionable.

self-glorification *n* egotheism, egotism, self-admiration, self-advertisement, self-aggrandisement, self-exaltation.

antonym humility.

self-government *n* autarchy, autonomy, democracy, home rule, independence, self-sovereignty.

antonym subjection.

self-importance *n* arrogance, big-headedness, bumptiousness, cockiness, conceit, conceitedness, pomposity, pompousness, pushiness, self-consequence, self-opinion, vanity.

antonym humility.

self-important *adj* arrogant, big-headed, bumptious, cocky, conceited, consequential, overbearing, pompous, pushy, self-consequent, strutting, swaggering, swollen-headed, vain.

antonym humble.

self-indulgence *n* dissipation, dissoluteness, excess, extravagance, high living, incontinence, intemperance, profligacy, self-gratification, sensualism.

antonym self-denial.

self-indulgent *adj* dissipated, dissolute, extravagant, intemperate, profligate, sensualistic.

antonym abstemious.

self-interest *n* self, selfishness, self-love, self-regard, self-serving.

antonym selflessness.

selfish *adj* egoistic, egoistical, egotistic, egotistical, greedy, mean, mercenary, narrow, self-centred, self-interested, self-seeking, self-serving.

antonym unselfish.

selfishness *n* egoism, egotism, greed, meanness, self-centredness, self-interest, self-love, self-regard, self-seeking, self-serving.

antonym selflessness.

selfless *adj* altruistic, generous, magnanimous, self-denying, self-forgetful, self-sacrificing, ungrudging, unselfish.

antonym selfish.

self-possessed *adj* calm, collected, composed, confident, cool, poised, self-assured, self-collected, together, unruffled.

antonym worried.

self-possession *n* aplomb, calmness, composure, confidence, cool, coolness, poise, sang-froid, self-command, self-confidence, unflappability.

antonym worry.

self-propelling *adj* automobile, locomobile, self-moving.

self-reliance *n* autarky, independence, self-sufficiency, self-support, self-sustainment, self-sustenance, self-sustentation.

antonym dependence.

self-reliant *adj* autarkic(al), independent, self-sufficient, self-supporting, self-sustaining.

antonym dependent.

self-respect *n* amour-propre, dignity, pride, self-assurance, self-confidence, self-esteem, self-pride, self-regard.

antonym self-doubt.

self-restraint *n* abstemiousness, encraty, forbearance, moderation, patience, self-command, self-control, self-denial, self-discipline, self-government, temperance, will-power.

antonym licence.

self-righteous *adj* complacent, goody-goody, holier-than-thou, hypocritical, pharisaical, pi, pietistic(al), pious, priggish, sanctimonious, self-satisfied, smug, superior, Tartuffian, Tartuffish.

antonym understanding.

self-righteousness *n* goodiness, goody-goodiness, pharisaicalness, pharisaism, piousness, priggishness, sanctimoniousness.

antonyms humility, understanding.

self-sacrifice *n* altruism, generosity, self-abandonment, self-abnegation, self-denial, selflessness, self-renunciation.

antonym selfishness.

self-satisfaction *n* complacency, contentment, pride, self-appreciation, self-approbation, self-approval, smugness.

antonym humility.

self-satisfied *adj* complacent, puffed up, self-approving, self-congratulatory, self-righteous, smug.

antonym humble.

self-seeking *adj* acquisitive, calculating, careerist, fortune-hunting, gold-digging, mercenary, on the make, opportunistic, self-endeared, self-interested, selfish, self-loving, self-serving.

antonym altruistic.

self-styled *adj* professed, pseudo, self-appointed, so-called, soi-disant, would-be.

self-supporting *adj* autarkic(al), self-financing, self-reliant, self-sufficient, self-sustaining.

antonym dependent.

self-willed *adj* bloody-minded, cussed, headstrong, intractable, obstinate, opinionated, pig-headed, refractory, self-opinionated, self-opinionative, stiff-necked, stubborn, ungovernable, wilful.

antonym complaisant.

sell *v* barter, cheat, convince, deal in, exchange, handle, hawk, impose on, market, merchandise, peddle, persuade, promote, retail, sell out, stock, surrender, trade, trade in, traffic in, trick, vend.

antonym buy.

sell out betray, double-cross, fail, fink on, rat on, sell down the river, stab in the back.

antonym back.

seller *n* agent, dealer, merchant, rep, representative, retailer, salesgirl, saleslady, salesman, saleswoman, shopkeeper, storekeeper, tradesman, traveller, vendor.

antonym buyer.

selling *n* dealing, marketing, merchandising, merchanting, promotion, salesmanship, trading, traffic, transactions, vendition.

antonym buying.

semblance *n* air, apparition, appearance, aspect, bearing, façade, figure, form, front, guise, image, likeness, mask, mien, pretence, resemblance, show, similarity, veneer.

semen *n* jism, seed, spawn, sperm, spunk.

semicircle *n* half-round, hemicycle.

seminal *adj* creative, formative, imaginative, important, influential, innovative, major, original, productive, seminary.

antonym derivative.

seminary *n* academy, college, institute, institution, school, training-college.

send *v* broadcast, cast, charm, communicate, consign, convey, delight, deliver, direct, discharge, dispatch, electrify, emit, enrapture, enthrall, excite, exude, fire, fling, forward, grant, hurl, intoxicate, move, please, propel, radiate, ravish, remit, shoot, stir, thrill, titillate, transmit.

send for call for, call out, command, order, request, summon.

antonym dismiss.

send up burlesque, imitate, lampoon, mickey-take, mimic, mock, parody, satirise, spook, take off, take the mickey out of.

send-off *n* departure, farewell, going-away, leave-taking, start, valediction.

antonym arrival.

send-up *n* imitation, mickey-take, mockery, parody, satire, skit, spoof, take-off.

senile *adj* anile, decrepit, doddering, doited, doting, failing, imbecile, senescent.

senility *n* anility, caducity, decrepitude, dotage, eld, infirmity, paracme, second childhood, senescence, senile dementia.

senior *adj* aîne(e), doyen(ne), elder, first, higher, high-ranking, major, older, superior.

antonym junior.

seniority *n* eldership, precedence, priority, rank, standing, superiority.

antonym juniority.

sensation *n* agitation, awareness, commotion, consciousness, emotion, Empfindung, excitement, feeling, furore, hit, impression, perception, scandal, sense, stir, surprise, thrill, tingle, vibes, vibrations, wow.

sensational *adj* amazing, astounding, blood-and-thunder, breathtaking, dramatic, electrifying, excellent, exceptional, exciting, fabulous, gamy, hair-raising, horrifying, impressive, lurid, marvellous, melodramatic, mind-blowing, revealing, scandalous, sensationalistic, shocking, smashing, spectacular, staggering, startling, superb, thrilling.

antonym run-of-the-mill.

sense *n* advantage, appreciation, atmosphere, aura, awareness, brains, clear-headedness, cleverness, consciousness, definition, denotation, direction, discernment, discrimination, drift, faculty, feel, feeling, gist, good, gumption, implication, import, impression, intelligence, interpretation, intuition, judgement, logic, marbles, meaning, message, mother wit, nous, nuance, opinion, perception, point, premonition, presentiment, purport, purpose, quickness, reason, reasonableness, sagacity, sanity, savvy, sensation, sensibility, sentiment, sharpness, significance, signification, smeddum, substance, tact, understanding, use, value, wisdom, wit(s), worth.

antonym foolishness.

v appreciate, comprehend, detect, divine, feel, grasp, notice, observe, perceive, realise, suspect, understand.

senseless *adj* absurd, anaesthetised, asinine, crazy, daft, deadened, dotty, fatuous, foolish, halfwitted, idiotic, illogical, imbecilic, inane, incongruous, inconsistent, insensate, insensible, irrational, ludicrous, mad, meaningless, mindless, moronic, nonsensical, numb, numbed, out, out for the count, pointless, ridiculous, silly, simple, stunned, stupid, unconscious, unfeeling, unintelligent, unreasonable, unwise.

antonym sensible.

sensibilities *n* emotions, feelings, sensitivities, sentiments, susceptibilities.

sensibility *n* appreciation, awareness, delicacy, discernment, insight, intuition, perceptiveness, responsiveness, sensitiveness, sensitivity, susceptibility, taste.

antonym insensibility.

sensible *adj* appreciable, canny, considerable, delicate, discernable, discreet, discriminating, down-to-earth, far-sighted, intelligent, judicious, level-headed, matter-of-fact, noticeable, palpable, perceptible, practical, prudent, rational, realistic, reasonable, right-thinking, sagacious, sage, sane, senseful, shrewd, significant, sober, solid, sound, tangible, visible, well-advised, well-thought-out, wise.

antonyms imperceptible, senseless.

sensible of acquainted with, alive to, aware of, cognisant of, conscious of, convinced of, mindful of, observant of, sensitive to, understanding.

antonym unaware of.

sensitive *adj* acute, controversial, delicate, fine, hyper(a)esthesic, hyper(a)esthetic, hyperconscious, impressionable, irritable, keen, nociceptive, perceptive, precise, reactive, responsive, secret, sensitised, sentient, susceptible, temperamental, tender, thin-skinned, touchy, umbrageous.

antonym insensitive.

sensitivity *n* delicacy, hyper(a)esthesia, hyperconsciousness, reactiveness, reactivity, receptiveness, responsiveness, sensitiveness, susceptibility.

antonym insensitivity.

sensual *adj* animal, bodily, carnal, epicurean, erotic, fleshly, lascivious, lecherous, lewd, libidinous, licentious, lustful, luxurious, pandemian, physical, randy, raunchy, self-indulgent, sexual, sexy, voluptuous, worldly.

antonyms ascetic, Puritan.

sensualist *n* bon vivant, bon viveur, debauchee, epicure, Epicurean, gourmand, gourmet, hedonist, libertine, profligate, roue, sybarite, voluptuary.

antonyms ascetic, Puritan.

sensuality *n* animal magnetism, animalism, carnality, debauchery, eroticism, gourmandise, lasciviousness, lecherousness, lewdness, libertinism, libidinousness, licentiousness, lustfulness, profligacy, prurience, salaciousness, sexiness, voluptuousness.

antonyms asceticism, Puritanism.

sensuous *adj* epicurean, gratifying, hedonistic, lush, luxurious, pleasurable, rich, sensory, sumptuous, sybaritic, voluptuous.

antonyms ascetic, plain, simple.

sentence *n* aphorism, apophthegm, condemnation, decision, decree, doom, gnome, judgement, maxim, opinion, order, pronouncement, ruling, saying, verdict.

v condemn, doom, judge, pass judgement on, penalise, pronounce judgement on.

sententious *adj* aphoristic, axiomatic, brief, canting, compact, concise, epigrammatic, gnomic, laconic, moralising, moralistic, pithy, pointed, pompous, ponderous, preachy, sanctimonious, short, succinct, terse.

antonyms humble, prolix.

sentient *adj* aware, conscious, live, living, reactive, responsive, sensitive.

antonym insentient.

sentiment *n* attitude, belief, emotion, emotionalism, feeling, idea, judgement, mawkishness, maxim, opinion, persuasion, romanticism, saying, sensibility, sentimentalism, sentimentality, slush, soft-heartedness, tenderness, thought, view.

antonyms hard-heartedness, straightforwardness.

sentimental *adj* corny, dewy-eyed, drippy, emotional, gushing, gushy, gutbucket, impressionable, lovey-dovey, maudlin, mawkish, mushy, nostalgic, pathetic, romantic, rose-water, schmaltzy, simpering, sloppy, slushy, soft-hearted, tearful, tear-jerking, tender, too-too, touching, treacly, weepy, wertherian.

antonym unsentimental.

sentimentality *n* bathos, corniness, emotionalism, gush, mawkishness, mush, nostalgia, pulp, romanticism, schmaltz, sentimentalism, sloppiness, slush, tenderness.

sentry *n* guard, look-out, picket, sentinel, vedette, watch, watchman.

separable *adj* detachable, discerptible, distinguishable, divisible, partible, scissile, severable.

antonym inseperable.

separate *v* abstract, bifurcate, decouple, deglutinate, demerge, departmentalise, detach, disaffiliate, disally, discerp, disconnect, disentangle, disjoin, dislink, dispart, dissever, distance, disunite, divaricate, diverge, divide, divorce, eloi(g)n, estrange, exfoliate, isolate, part, part company, prescind, remove, secede, secern, seclude, segregate, sever, shear, split, split up, sunder, uncouple, winnow, withdraw.

antonyms join, unite.

adj alone, apart, autonomous, detached, disconnected, discrete, disjointed, disjunct, disparate, distinct, divided, divorced, independent, individual, isolated, particular, several, single, solitary, sundry, unattached, unconnected.

antonyms attached, together.

separated *adj* apart, disassociated, disconnected, disunited, divided, isolated, parted, segregated, separate, split up, sundered.

antonyms attached, together.

separately *adv* alone, apart, discretely, discriminately, divisim, independently, individually, personally, severally, singly.

antonym together.

separating *adj* discretive, disjunctive, divellent, dividing, divisive, divulsive, intervening, isolating, partitioning, segregating.

antonym unifying.

separation *n* break, break-up, demerger, detachment, diaeresis, dialysis, diaspora, diastasis, discerption, disconnection, disengagement, disgregation, disjunction, disjuncture, disseverance, disseveration, disseverment, dissociation, disunion, division, divorce, estrangement, farewell, gap, leave-taking, parting, rift, segregation, severance, solution, split, split-up.

antonyms togetherness, unification.

septic *adj* festering, infected, poisoned, purulent, putrefactive, putrefying, putrid, pyogenic, pyoid, suppurating.

sepulchral *adj* cheerless, deep, dismal, funereal, gloomy, grave, hollow, lugubrious, melancholy, morbid, mournful, reverberating, sad, sepultural, sepulchrous, sombre, sonorous, woeful.

antonym cheerful.

sepulchre *n* grave, mausoleum, tomb, vault.

sequel *n* conclusion, consequence, continuation, development, end, follow-up, issue, outcome, pay-off, prequel, result, upshot.

sequence *n* arrangement, chain, consequence, course, cycle, order, procession, progression, series, set, succession, track, train.

sequestered *adj* backveld, cloistered, isolated, lonely, outback, out-of-the-way, private, quiet, remote, retired, secluded, unfrequented.

antonyms busy, frequented, public.

seraphic *adj* angelic, beatific, blissful, celestial, divine, heavenly, holy, innocent, pure, saintly, seraphical, sublime.

antonym demonic.

serene *adj* calm, composed, cool, halcyon, imperturbable, peaceful, placid, tranquil, unclouded, undisturbed, unflappable, unruffled, untroubled.

antonym troubled.

serenity *n* calm, calmness, composure, cool, peace, peacefulness, placidity, quietness, quietude, stillness, tranquillity, unflappability.

antonyms anxiety, disruption.

serf *n* bondmaid, bondservant, bond-slave, bon(d)sman, bond(s)-woman, helot, servant, slave, thrall, villein.

antonym master.

series *n* arrangement, catena, chain, concatenation, consecution, course, cycle, enfilade, line, order, progression, run, scale, sequence, set, string, succession, train.

serious *adj* acute, alarming, critical, crucial, dangerous, deep, deliberate, determined, difficult, earnest, far-reaching, fateful, genuine, grave, grim, heavy, honest, humourless, important, long-faced, momentous, pensive, pressing, resolute, resolved, sedate, severe, significant, sincere, sober, solemn, staid, stern, thoughtful, unsmiling, urgent, weighty, worrying.

antonyms facetious, light, slight, smiling, trivial.

seriously *adv* acutely, badly, critically, dangerously, distressingly, earnestly, gravely, grieviously, joking apart, severely, sincerely, solemnly, sorely, thoughtfully.

antonyms casually, slightly.

seriousness *n* danger, earnestness, gravitas, gravity, humourless, importance, moment, sedateness, significance, sobriety, solemnity, staidness, sternness, urgency, weight.

antonyms casualness, slightness, triviality.

sermon *n* address, dressing-down, exhortation, harangue, homily, lecture, preachment, talking-to.

sermonise *v* preach, preachify.

sermonising *n* pi-jaw, preachifying, preachment, pulpitry.

serpentine *adj* coiling, crooked, meandering, serpentiform, sinuous, snakelike, snaking, snaky, tortuous, twisting, winding.

antonym straight.

serrated *adj* notched, sawlike, saw-toothed, serrate, serratulate, serriform, serrulate(d), toothed.

antonym smooth.

serried *adj* close, close-set, compact, crowded, dense, massed.

antonym scattered.

servant *n* aia, amah, ancillary, attendant, ayah, bearer, boy, daily, day, day-woman, domestic, drudge, esne, flunkey, footman, galopin, garçon, gentleman's gentleman, gossoon, gyp, haiduk, handmaid, handmaiden, help, helper, hind, hireling, Jeeves, khidmutgar, kitchen-maid, knave, lackey, lady's maid, livery-servant, maid, maid of all work, maître d'hôtel, major-domo, man, manservant, menial, ministrant, retainer, scout, seneschal, servitor, skivvy, slave, slavey, steward, valet, vassal, woman.

antonyms master, mistress.

serve *v* act, aid, answer, arrange, assist, attend, avail, complete, content, dance attendance, deal, deliver, discharge, distribute, do, fulfil, further, handle, help, minister to, oblige, observe, officiate, pass, perform, present, provide, satisfy, succour, suffice, suit, supply, undergo, wait on, work for.

service *n* advantage, assistance, avail, availability, benefit, business, ceremony, check, disposal, duty, employ, employment, expediting, function, help, labour, maintenance, ministrations, observance, office, overhaul, performance, rite, servicing, set, supply, use, usefulness, utility, work, worship.

v check, maintain, overhaul, recondition, repair, tune.

serviceable *adj* advantageous, beneficial, convenient, dependable, durable, efficient, functional, hard-wearing, helpful, operative, plain, practical, profitable, simple, strong, tough, unadorned, usable, useful, utilitarian.

antonym unserviceable.

servile *adj* abject, base, bootlicking, controlled, craven, cringing, fawning, grovelling, humble, low, mean, menial, obsequious, slavish, subject, submissive, subservient, sycophantic, toadying, toadyish, unctuous.

antonyms aggressive, bold.

servility *n* abjection, abjectness, arse-licking, baseness, bootlicking, fawning, grovelling, meanness, obsequiousness, self-abasement, slavishness, submissiveness, subservience, sycophancy, toad-eating, toadyism, unctuousness.

antonyms aggressiveness, boldness.

servitude *n* bondage, bonds, chains, enslavement, obedience, serfdom, slavery, subjugation, thraldom, thrall, vassalage, villeinage.

antonym freedom.

session *n* assembly, conference, discussion, get-together, go, hearing, meeting, period, semester, sitting, term, year.

set[1] *v* adjust, aim, allocate, allot, apply, appoint, arrange, assign, cake, conclude, condense, congeal, co-ordinate, crystallise, decline, decree, deposit, designate, determine, dip, direct, disappear, embed, establish, fasten, fix, fix up, gelatinise, harden, impose, install, jell, lay, locate, lodge, mount, name, ordain, park, place, plant, plonk, plump, position, prepare, prescribe, propound, put, rectify, regulate, resolve, rest, schedule, seat, settle, sink, situate, solidify, specify, spread, stake, station, stick, stiffen, subside, synchronise, thicken, turn, vanish.

n attitude, bearing, carriage, fit, hang, inclination, mise-en-scène, position, posture, scene, scenery, setting, turn.

adj agreed, appointed, arranged, artificial, conventional, customary, decided, definite, deliberate, entrenched, established, firm, fixed, formal, hackneyed, immovable, inflexible, intentional, prearranged, predetermined, prescribed, regular, rehearsed, rigid, routine, scheduled, settled, standard, stereotyped, stock, strict, stubborn, traditional, unspontaneous, usual.

antonyms free, movable, spontaneous, undecided.

set about assail, assault, attack, bash, beat up, begin, belabour, lambaste, mug, start, tackle, wade into.

set against alienate, balance, compare, contrast, disunite, divide, estrange, juxtapose, mix, oppose, weigh.

set apart choose, elect, peculiarise, put aside, separate.

set aside abrogate, annul, cancel, discard, dismiss, keep, keep back, lay aside, nullify, overrule, overturn, put aside, quash, reject, repudiate, reserve, reverse, save, select, separate.

set back delay, hamper, hinder, hold up, impede, interrupt, retard, slow.

set eyes on behold, clap eyes on, come across, come upon, encounter, lay eyes on, meet, meet with, notice, observe, see.

set free decontrol, deliver, disembarrass, disentangle, disimprison, disprison, emancipate, extricate, free, liberate, loose, manumit, ransom, release, rescue, rid, save, unpen.

antonyms confine, enslave.

set off depart, detonate, display, embark, enhance, explode, ignite, leave, light, make tracks, present, sally forth, show off, touch off, trigger off.

set on assail, assault, attack, beat up, fall upon, fly at, go for, incite, instigate, lay into, mug, pitch into, sail into, set about, set upon, turn on, urge.

set out arrange, array, begin, describe, detail, display, dispose, elaborate, elucidate, embark, exhibit, explain, lay out, make a move, make tracks, present, sally forth, set off, start, start out.

set up arrange, assemble, back, begin, boost, build, cheer, compose, construct, create, elate, elevate, erect, establish, finance, form, found, gratify, inaugurate, initiate, install, institute, introduce, organise, prearrange, prepare, promote, raise, revivify, start, strengthen, subsidise.

set[2] *n* apparatus, assemblage, assortment, band, batch, circle, class, clique, collection, company, compendium, coterie, covey, crew, crowd, faction, gang, group, kit, outfit, sect, sequence, series.

setback *n* blow, check, defeat, delay, disappointment, hiccup, hitch, hold-up, knock-back, misfortune, problem, rebuff, relapse, reverse, snag, throw-back, upset.

antonyms advance, advantage, boost, help.

setting *n* adjustment, age, backcloth, backdrop, background, context, environment, frame, locale, location, milieu, mise en scène, mounting, period, perspective, position, scene, scenery, set, site, surround, surroundings.

setting-up *n* creation, establishment, foundation, founding, inauguration, inception, institution, introduction, start.

antonyms abolition, termination.

settle *v* adjust, agree, alight, appoint, arrange, bed, calm, choose, clear, colonise, compact, complete, compose, conclude, confirm, decide, decree, descend, determine, discharge, dispose, dower, drop, dwell, endow, establish, fall, fix, found, hush, inhabit, land, light, liquidate, live, lower, lull, occupy, ordain, order, pacify, pay, people, pioneer, plant, plump, populate, quell, quiet, quieten, quit, reassure, reconcile, relax, relieve, reside, resolve, sedate, sink, soothe, square, square up, subside, tranquillise.

settlement[1] *n* accommodation, adjustment, agreement, allowance, arrangement, Ausgleich, clearance, clearing, completion, conclusion, confirmation, decision, defrayal, diktat, discharge, disposition, establishment, income, liquidation, payment, resolution, satisfaction, termination.

settlement[2] *n* colonisation, colony, community, encampment, hamlet, immigration, kibbutz, nahal, occupation, outpost, peopling, plantation, population.

settlement[3] *n* compacting, drop, fall, sinkage, subsidence.

settler *n* coloniser, colonist, frontiersman, immigrant, incomer, kibbutznik, newcomer, pioneer, planter, squatter.

antonym native.

set-to *n* altercation, argument, argy-bargy, barney, brush, conflict, contest, disagreement, dust-up, exchange, fight, fracas, quarrel, row, scrap, spat, squabble, wrangle.

set-up *n* arrangement, business, circumstances, conditions, menage, organisation, regime, structure, system.

sever *v* alienate, bisect, cleave, cut, detach, disconnect, disjoin, dissever, dissociate, dissolve, dissunder, disunite, divide, estrange, part, rend, separate, split, sunder, terminate.

antonyms join, unite.

several *adj* assorted, different, discrete, disparate, distinct, divers, diverse, individual, many, particular, respective, separate, single, some, some few, specific, sundry, various.

severally *adv* discretely, individually, particularly, respectively, separately, seriatim, specifically.

antonyms simultaneously, together.

severe *adj* acute, arduous, ascetic, astringent, austere, biting, bitter, Catonian, caustic, chaste, classic, classical, cold, critical, cruel, cutting, dangerous, demanding, difficult, disapproving, distressing, dour, Draconian, Draconic, Dracontic, eager, exacting, extreme, fierce, flinty, forbidding, functional, grave, grim, grinding, hard, harsh, inclement, inexorable, intense, iron-handed, oppressive, pitiless, plain, punishing, relentless, restrained, Rhadamanthine, rigid, rigorous, satirical, scathing, serious, shrewd, simple, sober, Spartan, stern, strait-laced, strict, stringent, taxing, tight-lipped, tough, trying, unadorned, unbending, unembellished, ungentle, unrelenting, unsmiling, unsparing, unsympathetic, violent.

antonyms compassionate, kind, lenient, mild, sympathetic.

severely *adv* acutely, austerely, badly, bitterly, coldly, critically, dangerously, disapprovingly, dourly, extremely, gravely, grimly, hard, harshly, rigorously, sharply, sorely, sternly, strictly, unsympathetically.

severity *n* acuteness, asceticism, austerity, coldness, gravity, hardness, harshness, plainness, rigour, seriousness, severeness, sharpness, sternness, stringency, strictness, toughness, ungentleness.

antonyms compassion, kindness, leniency, mildness.

sex *n* coition, coitus, congress, copulation, desire, fornication, gender, intercourse, intimacy, libido, lovemaking, nookie, poontang, reproduction, screw, sexual intercourse, sexual relations, sexuality, union, venery.

sex appeal allure, desirability, glamour, it, magnetism, nubility, oomph, seductiveness, sensuality, sex attraction, sexiness, voluptuousness.

sexless *adj* asexual, neuter, parthenogenetic, undersexed, unfeminine, unmasculine, unsexed, unsexual.

sexpot *n* enchantress, houri, Lolita, nymphet, seductress, sex goddess, sex-bomb, siren.

sexton *n* caretaker, fossor, grave-digger, grave-maker, sacristan, verger.

sexual *adj* carnal, coital, erotic, gamic, genital, intimate, procreative, reproductive, sensual, sex, sex-related, venereal.

antonym asexual.

sexual intercourse bonk, carnal knowledge, coition, coitus, commerce, congress, consummation, copulation, coupling, fuck, fucking, greens, mating, nookie, penetration, poontang, pussy, screw, screwing, sex, shag, shagging, tail, union.

sexuality *n* carnality, desire, eroticism, lust, sensuality, sexiness, sexual instincts, sexual urge, virility, voluptuousness.

sexy *adj* arousing, beddable, come-hither, cuddly, curvaceous, epigamic, erotic, flirtatious, inviting, kissable, naughty, nubile, pornographic, provocative, provoking, seductive, sensual, sensuous, slinky, suggestive, titillating, virile, voluptuous.

antonym sexless.

shabby *adj* cheap, contemptible, dastardly, despicable, dilapidated, dingy, dirty, dishonourable, disreputable, dog-eared, down-at-heel, faded, frayed, ignoble, low, low-down, low-life, low-lived, mangy, mean, moth-eaten, neglected, paltry, poking, poky, poor, ragged, raunchy, rotten, run-down, scruffy, seedy, shameful, shoddy, tacky, tattered, tatty, threadbare, ungentlemanly, unworthy, worn, worn-out.

antonyms honourable, smart.

shack *n* bothy, but and ben, cabin, dump, hole, hovel, hut, hutch, lean-to, shanty, shed, shiel, shieling.

shackle *n* bond, bracelets, chain, darbies, fetter, gyve, hamper, handcuff, hobble, iron, leg-iron, manacle, rope, shackles, tether, trammel.

v bind, chain, constrain, embarrass, encumber, fetter, gyve, hamper, hamstring, handcuff, handicap, hobble, hogtie, impede, inhibit, limit, manacle, obstruct, pinion, restrain, restrict, secure, tether, thwart, tie, trammel.

shade *n* amount, apparition, blind, canopy, colour, coolness, cover, covering, curtain, darkness, dash, degree, difference, dimness, dusk, eidolon, ghost, gloaming, gloom, gloominess, gradation, hint, hue, manes, murk, nuance, obscurity, phantasm, phantom, screen, semblance, semi-darkness, shadiness, shadow, shadows, shelter, shield, shroud, spectre, spirit, stain, suggestion, suspicion, tinge, tint, tone, trace, twilight, umbra, umbrage, variation, variety, veil, wraith.

v cloud, conceal, cover, darken, dim, hide, inumbrate, mute, obscure, overshadow, protect, screen, shadow, shield, shroud, veil.

shadow *n* affliction, blight, caliginosity, cloud, companion, cover, darkness, detective, dimness, dusk, ghost, gloaming, gloom, hint, image, inseparable, obscurity, pal, phantom, protection, remnant, representation, sadness, shade, shelter, sidekick, sleuth, spectre, spirit, suggestion, suspicion, tenebrity, tenebrosity, trace, umbrage, vestige.

v darken, dog, follow, obscure, overhang, overshadow, screen, shade, shield, stalk, tail, tail-up, trail, watch.

shadowy *adj* caliginous, crepuscular, dark, dim, dreamlike, dusky, faint, ghostly, gloomy, half-remembered, hazy, illusory, imaginary, impalpable, indistinct, intangible, murky, nebulous, obscure, shaded, shady, spectral, tenebrious, tenebrose, tenebrous, umbratile, umbratilous, undefined, unreal, unsubstantial, vague, wraithlike.

shady[1] *adj* bosky, bowery, caliginous, cool, dark, dim, leafy, shaded, shadowy, tenebrous, umbrageous, umbratile, umbratilous, umbriferous, umbrose, umbrous.

antonyms bright, sunlit, sunny.

shady[2] *adj* crooked, discreditable, dishonest, disreputable, dubious, fishy, louche, questionable, shifty, slippery, suspect, suspicious, underhand, unethical, unscrupulous, untrustworthy.

antonyms honest, trustworthy.

shaft *n* arbor, arrow, barb, beam, cut, dart, gibe, gleam, haft, handle, missile, pole, ray, rod, shank, stem, stick, sting, streak, thrust, upright, well, winze.

shaggy *adj* crinose, hairy, hirsute, long-haired, nappy, rough, tousled, tousy, unkempt, unshorn.

antonyms bald, shorn.

shake *n* agitation, convulsion, disturbance, instant, jar, jerk, jiffy, jolt, jounce, moment, no time, pulsation, quaking, second, shiver, shock, shudder, tick, trembling, tremor, trice, twitch, vellication, vibration.

v agitate, brandish, bump, churn, concuss, convulse, didder, discompose, distress, disturb, flourish, fluctuate, frighten, heave, impair, intimidate, jar, joggle, jolt, jounce, move, oscillate, quake, quiver, rattle, rock, rouse, shimmy, shiver, shock, shog, shoggle, shudder, split, stir, succuss, sway, totter, tremble, twitch, undermine, unnerve, unsettle, upset, vellicate, vibrate, wag, waggle, wave, waver, weaken, wobble.

shake a leg get a move on, get cracking, hurry, look lively, step on it, stir one's stumps.

shake off dislodge, elude, get rid of, give the slip, leave behind, lose, outdistance, outpace, outstrip.

shake-up *n* disturbance, rearrangement, reorganisation, reshuffle, upheaval.

shaky *adj* dubious, faltering, inexpert, insecure, precarious, questionable, quivery, rickety, rocky, shoogly, suspect, tottering, tottery, uncertain, undependable, unreliable, unsound, unstable, unsteady, unsupported, untrustworthy, weak, wobbly.

antonyms firm, strong.

shallow *adj* empty, flimsy, foolish, frivolous, idle, ignorant, meaningless, puerile, simple, skin-deep, slight, superficial, surface, trivial, unanalytical, unintelligent, unscholarly.

antonyms analytical, deep.

sham *n* charlatan, counterfeit, feint, forgery, fraud, gold-brick, hoax, humbug, imitation, impostor, imposture, mountebank, phoney, pretence, pretender, pseud, stumer.

adj artificial, bogus, Brummagem, counterfeit, ersatz, faked, false, feigned, imitation, mock, pasteboard, phoney, pinchbeck, pretended, pseud, pseudo, put-on, simulated, snide, spurious, synthetic.

antonym genuine.

v affect, counterfeit, fake, feign, malinger, pretend, put on, simulate.

shaman *n* angekkok, magician, medicine-man, pawaw, powwow, sorcerer, witch-doctor.

shambles *n* anarchy, bedlam, chaos, confusion, disarray, disorder, disorganisation, havoc, madhouse, mess, muddle, pigsty, wreck.

shambling *adj* awkward, clumsy, disjointed, loose, lumbering, lurching, shuffling, unco-ordinated, ungainly, unsteady.

antonyms agile, neat, nimble, spry.

shame *n* aidos, bashfulness, blot, chagrin, compunction, contempt, degradation, derision, discredit, disgrace, dishonour, disrepute, embarrassment, humiliation, ignominy, infamy, mortification, obloquy, odium, opprobrium, reproach, scandal, shamefacedness, stain, stigma.

antonyms distinction, honour, pride.

v abash, blot, confound, debase, defile, degrade, discomfit, disconcert, discredit, disgrace, dishonour, embarrass, humble, humiliate, mortify, put to shame, reproach, ridicule, show up, smear, stain, sully, taint.

interj fi donc, fie, fie upon you, for shame, fy, shame on you.

shamefaced *adj* abashed, apologetic, ashamed, bashful, blushing, chagrined, conscience-stricken, contrite, diffident, discomfited, embarrassed, hesitant, humiliated, modest, mortified, pudibund, red-faced, remorseful, shamefast, sheepish, shrinking, shy, timid, uncomfortable.

antonyms proud, unashamed.

shameful *adj*. abominable, atrocious, base, contemptible, dastardly, degrading, discreditable, disgraceful, dishonourable, embarrassing, humiliating, ignominious, indecent, infamous, low, mean, mortifying, outrageous, reprehensible, scandalous, shaming, unbecoming, unworthy, vile, wicked.

antonyms creditable, honourable.

shameless *adj* abandoned, abashless, audacious, barefaced, blatant, brash, brazen, corrupt, defiant, depraved, dissolute, flagrant, hardened, immodest, improper, impudent, incorrigible, indecent, insolent, ithyphallic, profligate, reprobate, unabashed, unashamed, unblushing, unprincipled, unscrupulous, wanton.

antonyms ashamed, contrite, shamefaced.

shanty *n* bothy, cabin, hovel, hut, hutch, lean-to, shack, shed.

shape *n* apparition, appearance, aspect, build, condition, configuration, conformation, contours, cut, dimensions, fettle, figure, form, format, frame, Gestalt, guise, health, kilter, likeness, lines, make, model, mould, outline, pattern, physique, profile, semblance, silhouette, state, template, trim.

v accommodate, adapt, brute, construct, create, define, develop, devise, embody, fashion, forge, form, frame, girdle, guide, make, model, modify, mould, plan, prepare, produce, redact, regulate, remodel.

shapeless *adj* amorphous, asymmetrical, battered, characterless, dumpy, embryonic, formless, inchoate, indeterminate, indigest, irregular, misshapen, nebulous, undeveloped, unformed, unshapely, unstructured.

antonym shapely.

shapely *adj* comely, curvaceous, elegant, featous, gainly, graceful, neat, pretty, trim, voluptuous, well-formed, well-proportioned, well-set-up, well-turned.

antonym shapeless.

share *v* allot, apportion, assign, chip in, distribute, divide, divvy, divvy up, go Dutch, go fifty-fifty, go halves, muck in, partake, participate, split, whack.

n a piece of the action, allotment, allowance, contribution, cut, dividend, division, divvy, due, finger, lot, part, portion, proportion, quota, ration, snap, snip, stint, whack.

share out allot, apportion, assign, distribute, divide up, give out, parcel out, prorate.

antonym monopolise.

shark *n* chiseller, crook, extortioner, fleecer, parasite, politician, sharper, slicker, sponger, swindler, wheeler-dealer.

sharp *adj* abrupt, acerbic, acicular, acid, acidulous, acrid, acrimonious, acute, alert, apt, artful, astute, barbed, biting, bitter, bright, burning, canny, caustic, chic, chiselled, classy, clear, clear-cut, clever, crafty, crisp, cunning, cutting, discerning, dishonest, distinct, dressy, eager, edged, excruciating, extreme, fashionable, fierce, fit, fly, harsh, honed, hot, hurtful, incisive, intense, jagged, keen, knife-edged, knifelike, knowing, long-headed, marked, natty, nimble-witted, noticing, observant, painful, penetrating, peracute, perceptive, piercing, piquant, pointed, pungent, quick, quick-witted, rapid, razor-sharp, ready, sarcastic, sardonic, saw-edged, scathing, serrated, severe, sharpened, shooting, shrewd, sly, smart, snappy, snazzy, sour, spiky, stabbing, stinging, stylish, subtle, sudden, tart, trenchant, trendy, unblurred, undulled, unscrupulous, vinegary, violent, vitriolic, waspish, wily.

antonyms blunt, dull, mild, obtuse, slow, stupid.

adv abruptly, exactly, on the dot, out of the blue, precisely, promptly, punctually, suddenly, unexpectedly.

sharpen *v* acuminate, de-blur, edge, file, grind, hone, strop, taper, whet.

antonym blunt.

sharpness *n* acuity, acuteness, astuteness, discernment, eagerness, fierceness, incisiveness, intensity, keenness, observation, penetration, perceptiveness, pungency, quickness, severity, shrewdness, whet.

antonyms dullness, sloth.

sharp-sighted *adj* eagle-eyed, gimlet-eyed, hawk-eyed, keen-sighted, lyncean, lynx-eyed, noticing, observant, perceptive.

antonyms short-sighted, unobservant.

shatter *v* blast, blight, break, burst, crack, crush, demolish, destroy, devastate, disable, disshiver, dumbfound, exhaust, explode, impair, implode, overturn, overwhelm, pulverise, ruin, shiver, smash, smithereen, split, stun, torpedo, undermine, upset, wreck.

shattered *adj* all in, crushed, dead beat, devastated, dog-tired, done in, exhausted, jiggered, knackered, overwhelmed, undermined, weary, worn out, zonked.

shattering *adj* crushing, damaging, devastating, foudroyant, overwhelming, paralysing, severe, stunning.

shave *v* barber, brush, crop, fleece, graze, pare, plane, plunder, scrape, shear, tonsure, touch, trim.

sheaf *n* armful, bunch, bundle, dorlach, gait, garbe, truss.

sheath *n* armour, carapace, case, casing, coat, coating, condom, covering, envelope, French letter, protective layer, rubber, safe, shell, sleeve, vagina, vaginula.

shed[1] *v* afford, cast, cast off, diffuse, discard, drop, emit, exuviate, give, moult, pour, radiate, scatter, shower, slough, spill, throw.

shed light on clarify, clear up, effuse, elucidate, exfoliate, explain, illuminate, simplify.

shed[2] *n* barn, hut, lean-to, lock-up, outhouse, shack.

shedding *n* casting, diffusion, discarding, ecdysis, effusion, emission, exfoliation, exuviation, moulting, radiation, scattering, sloughing.

sheen *n* brightness, brilliance, burnish, gleam, gloss, lustre, patina, polish, shimmer, shine, shininess.

antonyms dullness, tarnish.

sheep *n* bell-wether, eanling, ewe, jumbuck, lamb, ram, tup, wether, yow.

sheepish *adj* abashed, ashamed, chagrined, chastened, embarrassed, foolish, mortified, self-conscious, shamefaced, silly, uncomfortable.

antonym unabashed.

sheer[1] *adj* abrupt, absolute, arrant, complete, downright, mere, out-and-out, perpendicular, precipitous, pure, rank, steep, thorough, thoroughgoing, total, unadulterated, unalloyed, unmingled, unmitigated, unqualified, utter, vertical.

sheer[2] diaphanous, fine, flimsy, gauzy, gossamer, pellucid, see-through, thin, translucent, transparent.

antonyms heavy, thick.

sheet *n* blanket, broadsheet, broadside, circular, coat, covering, expanse, film, flyer, folio, handbill, handout, lamina, layer, leaf, leaflet, membrane, nappe, news-sheet, overlay, pane, panel, piece, plate, shroud, skin, slab, stratum, surface, veneer.

shelf *n* bank, bar, bench, bracket, ledge, mantel, mantelpiece, platform, projection, reef, sandbank, sand-bar, shoal, step, terrace.

shell *n* carapace, case, casing, chassis, covering, crust, dop, frame, framework, hull, husk, nacelle, pod, rind, shuck, skeleton, structure.

v attack, barrage, batter, blitz, bomb, bombard, cannonade, hull, husk, shuck, strafe, strike.

shell out ante, contribute, cough up, disburse, donate, expend, fork out, give, lay out, pay out, subscribe.

shelter *v* accommodate, cover, defend, ensconce, guard, harbour, hide, protect, put up, safeguard, screen, shade, shadow, shield, shroud, skug.

antonym expose.

n accommodation, aegis, asylum, bield, bunker, cover, covert, coverture, defence, dugout, funk-hole, guard, gunyah, harbourage, haven, lean-to, lee, lodging, protection, refuge, retreat, roof, safety, sanctuary, sconce, screen, screening, security, shade, shadow, shiel, umbrage, umbrella.

antonym exposure.

sheltered *adj* cloistered, conventual, cosy, hermitic, isolated, lee, protected, quiet, reclusive, retired, screened, secluded, shaded, shielded, snug, unworldly, warm, withdrawn.

antonym exposed.

shelve *v* defer, dismiss, freeze, halt, mothball, pigeonhole, postpone, put aside, put in abeyance, put off, put on ice, suspend, table.

antonyms expedite, implement.

shepherd *n* guardian, herd, herdboy, herd-groom, herdsman, protector, shepherd boy, shepherdess, shepherdling.

v conduct, convoy, escort, guide, herd, lead, marshal, steer, usher.

shield *n* aegis, ancile, buckler, bulwark, cover, defence, escutcheon, guard, pelta, protection, rampart, safeguard, screen, scutum, shelter, targe, ward.

v cover, defend, guard, protect, safeguard, screen, shade, shadow, shelter.

antonym expose.

shift *v* adjust, alter, budge, change, dislodge, displace, fluctuate, manoeuvre, move, quit, rearrange, relocate, remove, reposition, rid, scoff, swallow, swerve, switch, transfer, transpose, vary, veer, wolf.

n alteration, artifice, change, contrivance, craft, device, displacement, dodge, equivocation, evasion, expedient, fluctuation, manoeuvre, modification, move, permutation, rearrangement, removal, resource, ruse, shifting, sleight, stratagem, subterfuge, switch, transfer, trick, veering, wile.

shiftless *adj* aimless, directionless, feckless, goalless, good-for-nothing, idle, incompetent, indolent, ineffectual, inefficient, inept, irresponsible, lackadaisical, lazy, resourceless, slothful, unambitious, unenterprising.

antonyms ambitious, aspiring, eager, enterprising.

shifty *adj* contriving, crafty, deceitful, devious, dishonest, disingenuous, dubious, duplicitous, evasive, fly-by-night, furtive, scheming, shady, slippery, tricky, underhand, unprincipled, untrustworthy, wily.

antonyms honest, open.

shilly-shally *v* dilly-dally, dither, falter, fluctuate, haver, hem and haw, hesitate, mess about, prevaricate, seesaw, shuffle, swither, teeter, vacillate, waver.

shimmer *v* coruscate, gleam, glisten, glitter, phosphoresce, scintillate, twinkle.

n coruscation, gleam, glimmer, glitter, glow, incandescence, iridescence, lustre, phosphorescence.

shimmering *adj* aventurine, gleaming, glistening, glittering, glowing, incandescent, iridescent, luminous, lustrous, shining, shiny.

antonyms dull, matt.

shin *v* ascend, clamber, climb, mount, scale, scramble, shoot, soar, swarm.

shine *v* beam, brush, buff, burnish, coruscate, effulge, excel, flash, glare, gleam, glimmer, glisten, glitter, glow, lustre, polish, radiate, resplend, scintillate, shimmer, sparkle, stand out, star, twinkle.

n brightness, burnish, effulgence, glare, glaze, gleam, gloss, glow, lambency, light, luminosity, lustre, patina, polish, radiance, sheen, shimmer, sparkle.

shininess *n* brightness, burnish, effulgence, gleam, glitter, glossiness, lustre, polish, sheen, shine.

antonym dullness.

shining *adj* beaming, bright, brilliant, celebrated, conspicuous, distinguished, effulgent, eminent, fulgent, gleaming, glistening, glittering, glorious, glowing, illustrious, lamping, leading, lucent, luminous, nitid, outstanding, profulgent, radiant, resplendent, rutilant, shimmering, sparkling, splendid, twinkling.

shiny *adj* agleam, aglow, bright, burnished, gleaming, glistening, glossy, lustrous, nitid, polished, satiny, sheeny, shimmery, sleek.

antonyms dark, dull.

ship *n* argosy, bark, barque, boat, ferry, galleon, galley, liner, prore, prow, steamer, tanker, trawler, vessel, yacht.

shipshape *adj* businesslike, neat, orderly, seamanlike, spick-and-span, spruce, tidy, trig, trim, well-organised, well-planned, well-regulated.

antonyms disorderly, untidy.

shirk *v* avoid, bludge, dodge, duck, duck out of, evade, funk, shun, sidestep, skive, skrimshank, slack, swing the lead.

shirker *n* absentee, bludger, clock-watcher, dodger, embusque, idler, layabout, loafer, malingerer, quitter, shirk, skiver, skrimshanker, slacker.

shiver *v* palpitate, quake, quiver, shake, shudder, tremble, vibrate.

n flutter, frisson, grue, quiver, shudder, start, thrill, tremble, trembling, tremor, twitch, vibration.

shivery *adj* chilled, chilly, cold, fluttery, nervous, quaking, quivery, shaking, shuddery, trembly.

shoal *n* assemblage, flock, horde, mass, mob, multitude, swarm, throng.

shock *v* agitate, appal, astound, confound, disgust, dismay, disquiet, horrify, jar, jolt, nauseate, numb, offend, outrage, paralyse, revolt, scandalise, shake, sicken, stagger, startle, stun, stupefy, traumatise, unnerve, unsettle.

antonyms delight, gratify, please, reassure.

n blow, bombshell, breakdown, clash, collapse, collision, concussion, consternation, dismay, distress, disturbance, encounter, fright, impact, jarring, jolt, perturbation, prostration, stupefaction, stupor, succussion, thunderbolt, trauma, turn, upset.

antonyms delight, pleasure.

shocking *adj* abhorrent, abominable, appalling, astounding, atrocious, deplorable, detestable, disgraceful, disgusting, disquieting, distressing, dreadful, execrable, foul, frightful, ghastly, hideous, horrible, horrific, horrifying, insufferable, intolerable, loathsome, monstrous, nauseating, nefandous, odious, offensive, outrageous, repugnant, repulsive, revolting, scandalous, sickening, stupefying, unbearable, unspeakable.

antonyms acceptable, delightful, pleasant, satisfactory.

shoddy *adj* cheap, cheap-jack, flimsy, gimcrack, inferior, junky, poor, rubbishy, second-rate, slipshod, tacky, tatty, tawdry, trashy, trumpery.

antonyms fine, well-made.

shoemaker *n* bootmaker, cobbler, cordiner, cordwainer, snab, snob, souter.

shoemaking *n* bootmaking, cobblery, cobbling, gentle craft.

shoot[1] *v* bag, blast, bolt, charge, dart, dash discharge, dump, emit, enfilade, film, fire, flash flung, gun down, hit, hurl, hurtle, kill, launch open fire, photograph, pick off, plug, precipitate project, propel, race, rake, rush, scoot, speed spring, sprint, streak, take, tear, whisk, whiz, zap

shoot[2] *n* branch, bud, germen, offshoot, scion slip, sprig, sprout, tendron, twig.

v bolt, bud, burgeon, detonate, germinate, grow shoot up, sprout, stretch, tower.

shop *n* boutique, chain, dolly-shop, emporium hypermarket, hypermart, market, mart megastore, store, superette, supermarket workshop.

shopping precinct arcade, complex, mall, market plaza.

shore[1] *n* beach, coast, foreshore, lakeside, littoral, margin, offing, promenade, rivage, sands, seaboard, sea-front, seashore, strand, waterfront water's edge, waterside.

shore[2] *v* brace, buttress, hold, prop, reinforce, shore up, stay, strengthen, support, underpin.

shorn *adj* bald, beardless, crew-cut, cropped, deprived, nott, polled, shaved, shaven, stripped.

short *adj* abbreviated, abridged, abrupt, blunt, brief, brittle, brusque, compendious, compressed concise, crisp, crumbly, crusty, curt, curtailed. deficient, diminutive, direct, discourteous, dumpy, ephemeral, evanescent, fleeting, friable, gruff, impolite, inadequate, insufficient, lacking, laconic. limited, little, low, meagre, momentary, murly, offhand, passing, petite, pithy, poor, precised, sawn-off, scant, scanty, scarce, sententious, sharp, shortened, short-handed, short-lived. short-term, slender, slim, small, snappish, snappy, sparse, squat, straight, succinct, summarised, summary, tart, terse, tight, tiny transitory, uncivil, understaffed, unplentiful wanting, wee.

antonyms adequate, ample, expansive, large, lasting, long, long-lived, polite, tall.

short of apart from, deficient in, except, lacking, less than, low on, missing, other than, pushed for short on, wanting.

shortage *n* absence, dearth, deficiency, deficit, failure, inadequacy, insufficiency, lack, leanness, meagreness, paucity, poverty, scantiness scarcity, shortfall, sparseness, want, wantage.

antonyms abundance, sufficiency.

shortcoming *n* defect, drawback, faible, failing, fault, flaw, foible, frailty, imperfection inadequacy, weakness.

shorten *v* abbreviate, abridge, crop, curtail, cut, decrease, diminish, dock, foreshorten, lessen, lop, precis, prune, reduce, take up, telescope trim, truncate.

antonyms amplify, enlarge, lengthen.

shortened *adj* abbreviated, abbreviatory, abridged, abstracted, compendious, condensed, summarised.

antonym amplified.

shorthand *n* brachygraphy, phonography, stenography, tachygraphy.

antonym longhand.

short-lived *adj* brief, caducous, ephemeral, evanescent, fleeting, fugacious, impermanent, momentary, passing, short, temporary, transient, transitory.

antonyms abiding, enduring, lasting, long-lived.

shortly *adv* abruptly, anon, briefly, concisely, curtly, directly, laconically, presently, sharply, soon, succinctly, tartly, tersely.

short-sighted *adj* careless, hasty, ill-advised, ill-considered, impolitic, impractical, improvident, imprudent, injudicious, myopic, near-sighted, unimaginative, unthinking.

antonyms far-sighted, hypermetropic, long-sighted.

short-tempered *adj* choleric, crusty, fiery, hot-tempered, impatient, irascible, irritable, peppery, quick-tempered, ratty, testy, touchy.

antonyms calm, patient, placid.

short-winded *adj* breathless, gasping, panting, peching, puffing, pursy.

shot[1] *n* attempt, ball, bash, blast, bullet, cannon-ball, chance, conjecture, contribution, crack, discharge, dram, effort, endeavour, essay, go, guess, injection, lead, lob, marksman, opportunity, pellet, projectile, range, reach, shooter, shy, slug, spell, stab, stroke, surmise, throw, try, turn.

shot in the arm boost, encouragement, fillip, fresh talent, impetus, lift, stimulus, uplift.

shot in the dark blind guess, conjecture, guess, guesswork, speculation.

shot[2] *adj* iridescent, moire, mottled, variegated, watered.

shoulder *v* accept, assume, barge, bear, carry, elbow, jostle, press, push, shove, sustain, take on, thrust.

shout *n* bay, bellow, belt, call, cheer, cry, roar, scream, shriek, yell.

v bawl, bay, bellow, call, cheer, cry, holler, roar, scream, shriek, yell.

shove *v* barge, crowd, drive, elbow, force, impel, jostle, press, propel, push, shoulder, thrust.

shove off beat it, clear off, clear out, depart, do a bunk, get lost, leave, push off, put out, scarper, scram, skedaddle, vamoose.

shovel *n* backhoe, bail, bucket, scoop, spade.

v convey, dredge, heap, ladle, load, move, scoop, shift, spade, spoon, toss.

show *v* accompany, accord, assert, attend, attest, bestow, betray, clarify, conduct, confer, demonstrate, disclose, display, divulge, elucidate, escort, evidence, evince, exemplify, exhibit, explain, grant, guide, illustrate, indicate, instruct, lead, manifest, offer, present, prove, register, reveal, teach, usher, witness.

n affectation, air, appearance, array, dash, demonstration, display, eclat, elan, entertainment, exhibition, exhibitionism, expo, exposition, extravaganza, façade, fair, feerie, flamboyance, gig, illusion, indication, likeness, manifestation, ostentation, pageant, pageantry, panache, parade, performance, pizzazz, plausibility, pose, presentation, pretence, pretext, production, profession, razzle-dazzle, representation, semblance, sight, sign, spectacle, swagger, view.

show off advertise, boast, brag, brandish, demonstrate, display, enhance, exhibit, flaunt, grandstand, parade, peacock, set off, strut, swagger, swank.

show up appear, arrive, come, disgrace, embarrass, expose, highlight, humiliate, lay bare, let down, mortify, pinpoint, reveal, shame, show, stand out, turn up, unmask.

show-down *n* clash, climax, confrontation, crisis, culmination, denouement, expose, face-off.

shower[1] *n* barrage, deluge, douche, down-come, drift, fusillade, hail, plethora, precipitation, rain, spout, stream, torrent, volley.

v deluge, douche, douse, heap, inundate, lavish, load, overwhelm, pour, rain, sparge, spray, sprinkle.

shower[2] *n* crew, galère, gang, mob, rabble.

showiness *n* flamboyance, flashiness, glitter, glitz, ostentation, pizzazz, razzle-dazzle, razzmatazz, swank.

antonym restraint.

showing *n* account, appearance, display, evidence, exhibition, impression, past performance, performance, presentation, record, representation, show, staging, statement, track record.

adj demonstrative, descriptive, elucidative, endeictic, explanatory, explicatory, illustrative, indicative, representative, revelatory, significant, symbolic.

showing-off *n* boasting, braggadocio, bragging, egotism, exhibitionism, hokum, peacockery, self-advertisement, swagger, swank, vainglory.

antonym modesty.

showman *n* entertainer, impresario, performer, publicist, ring-master, self-advertiser, show-off.

show-off *n* boaster, braggadocio, braggart, egotist, exhibitionist, peacock, self-advertiser, swaggerer, swanker, vaunter.

showy *adj* epideictic, euphuistic, exotic, flamboyant, flash, flashy, florid, flossy, garish, gaudy, glitzy, loud, ostentatious, pompous, pretentious, sparkish, specious, splashy, swanking, swanky, tawdry, tinselly.

antonyms quiet, restrained.

shred *n* atom, bit, fragment, grain, iota, jot, mammock, mite, piece, rag, ribbon, scrap, sliver, snippet, tatter, trace, whit, wisp.

shrew *n* bitch, dragon, Fury, harridan, henpecker, nag, scold, spitfire, termagant, virago, vixen, Xanthippe.

shrewd *adj* acute, arch, argute, artful, astucious, astute, calculated, calculating, callid, canny, clever, crafty, cunning, discerning, discriminating, downy, far-seeing, far-sighted, fly, gnostic, intelligent, judicious, keen, knowing, long-headed, observant, perceptive, perspicacious, sagacious, sharp, sly, smart, well-advised, wily.

antonyms naïve, obtuse, unwise.

shrewdly *adv* artfully, astutely, cannily, cleverly, craftily, far-sightedly, judiciously, knowingly, perceptively, perspicaciously, sagaciously, wisely.

shrewdness *n* acumen, acuteness, astucity, astuteness, callidity, canniness, discernment, grasp, intelligence, judgement, penetration, perceptiveness, perspicacity, sagacity, sharpness, smartness, wisdom.

antonyms foolishness, naïvety, obtuseness.

shrewish *adj* bad-tempered, captious, complaining, discontented, fault-finding, henpecking, ill-humoured, ill-natured, ill-tempered, nagging, peevish, petulant, quarrelsome, querulous, scolding, sharp-tongued, vixenish.

antonyms affectionate, peaceable, placid, supportive.

shriek *v* bellow, caterwaul, cry, holler, howl, scream, screech, shout, squeal, wail, yell.

n bellow, caterwaul, cry, howl, scream, screech, shout, squeal, wail.

shrill *adj* acute, argute, carrying, ear-piercing, ear-splitting, high, high-pitched, penetrating, piercing, piping, screaming, screeching, screechy, sharp, strident, treble.

antonyms gentle, low, soft.

shrine *n* chapel, dagoba, darga, delubrum, dome, fane, martyry, sanctuary, stupa, tabernacle, temple, tope, vimana.

shrink *v* back away, balk, contract, cower, cringe, decrease, deflate, diminish, dwindle, flinch, lessen, narrow, quail, recoil, retire, shorten, shrivel, shun, shy away, wince, withdraw, wither, wrinkle.

antonyms embrace, expand, stretch, warm to.

shrivel *v* burn, dehydrate, desiccate, dwindle, frizzle, gizzen, parch, pucker, scorch, sear, shrink, wilt, wither, wizen, wrinkle.

shrivelled *adj* desiccated, dried up, dry, emaciated, gizzen, puckered, sere, shrunken, withered, wizened, wrinkled, writhled.

shroud *v* blanket, cloak, conceal, cover, enshroud, envelop, enwrap, hide, screen, sheet, swathe, veil, wrap.

antonyms expose, uncover.

n cerecloth, cerement, cloud, covering, grave-clothes, mantle, pall, screen, sindon, veil, winding-sheet.

shrouded *adj* blanketed, cloaked, clouded, concealed, covered, enshrouded, enveloped, hidden, swathed, veiled, wrapped.

antonyms exposed, uncovered.

shrunken *adj* cadaverous, contracted, emaciated, gaunt, reduced, shrivelled, shrunk.

antonyms full, generous, rounded, sleek.

shudder *v* convulse, heave, quake, quiver, shake, shiver, tremble.

n convulsion, frisson, grue, horror, quiver, spasm, trembling, tremor.

shuffle[1] *v* drag, hobble, limp, scrape, scuff, scuffle, shamble.

shuffle[2] chop and change, confuse, disarrange, disorder, intermix, jumble, mix, rearrange, reorganise, shift, shift around, switch around.

shun *v* avoid, cold-shoulder, elude, eschew, evade, ignore, ostracise, shy away from, spurn, steer clear of.

antonyms accept, embrace.

shut *v* bar, bolt, cage, close, fasten, latch, lock, seal, secure, slam, spar.

antonym open.

shut down cease, close, discontinue, halt, inactivate, shut up, stop, suspend, switch off, terminate.

shut in box in, circumscribe, confine, enclose, hedge round, hem in, imprison, incarcerate.

shut off cut off, isolate, remove, seclude, segregate, separate, sequester.

shut out banish, bar, conceal, cover, debar, exclude, hide, lock out, mask, muffle, ostracise, screen, veil.

shut up cage, clam up, confine, coop up, gag, gaol, hold one's tongue, hush up, immure, imprison, incarcerate, intern, jail, muzzle, pipe down, silence.

shutter *n* abat-jour, jalousie, louvre, screen.

shuttle *v* alternate, commute, go to and fro, ply, seesaw, shunt, shuttlecock, travel.

shy *adj* backward, bashful, cautious, chary, coy, diffident, distrustful, farouche, hesitant, inhibited, modest, mousy, nervous, reserved, reticent, retiring, self-conscious, self-effacing, shrinking, suspicious, timid, unassertive, wary.

antonyms bold, confident.

v back away, balk, buck, flinch, quail, rear, recoil, shrink, start, swerve, wince.

shyness *n* bashfulness, constraint, coyness, diffidence, hesitancy, inhibition, modesty, mousiness, nervousness, reticence, self-consciousness, timidity, timidness, timorousness.

antonyms boldness, confidence.

sibling *n* brother, german, sib, sister, twin.

sibyl *n* oracle, prophetess, Pythia, pythoness, seer, seeress, sorceress, wise woman.

sick *adj* ailing, black, blase, bored, diseased, disgusted, displeased, dog-sick, fed up, feeble, ghoulish, glutted, ill, indisposed, jaded, laid up, morbid, mortified, nauseated, pining, poorly, puking, qualmish, queasy, sated, satiated, sickly, tired, under the weather, unwell, vomiting, weak, weary.

antonyms healthy, well.

sicken *v* disgust, nauseate, put off, repel, revolt, scunner, turn off.

antonyms attract, delight.

sickening *adj* disgusting, distasteful, foul, loathsome, mephitic, offensive, putrid, repulsive, revolting, vile.

antonyms attractive, delightful, pleasing.

sickly *adj* ailing, bilious, bloodless, cloying, delicate, faint, feeble, frail, icky, indisposed, infirm, lacklustre, languid, mawkish, nauseating, pallid, peaked, peaky, peelie-wally, pimping, pining, puly, revolting, saccharine, sweet, syrupy, treacly, unhealthy, wan, weak, weakly.

antonyms robust, sturdy.

sickness *n* affliction, ailment, bug, complaint, derangement, disease, disorder, dwam, ill-health, illness, indisposition, infirmity, insanity, malady, nausea, pestilence, qualmishness, queasiness, vomiting.

antonym health.

side *n* airs, angle, arrogance, aspect, bank, border, boundary, brim, brink, camp, cause, department, direction, division, edge, elevation, face, facet, faction, flank, flitch, fringe, gang, hand, insolence, light, limit, margin, opinion, ostentation, page, part, party, perimeter, periphery, position, pretentiousness, quarter, region, rim, sect, sector, slant, stand, standpoint, surface, team, twist, verge, view, viewpoint.

adj flanking, incidental, indirect, irrelevant, lateral, lesser, marginal, minor, oblique, roundabout, secondary, subordinate, subsidiary.

side with agree with, befriend, favour, second, support, team up with, vote for.

sidelong *adj* covert, indirect, oblique, sideward, sideways.

antonyms direct, overt.

sidestep *v* avoid, bypass, circumvent, dodge, duck, elude, evade, find a way round, shirk, skip, skirt.

antonym tackle.

sidetrack *v* deflect, distract, divert, head off.

sideways *adv* askance, crabwise, edgeways, edgewise, laterally, obliquely, sidelong, sidewards.

adj oblique, side, sidelong, sideward, slanted.

sidle *v* creep, edge, inch, ingratiate, insinuate, slink, sneak, steal, wriggle.

siesta *n* catnap, doze, forty winks, nap, relaxation, repose, rest, sleep, snooze.

sieve *v* boult, remove, riddle, separate, sift, strain.

n boulter, colander, riddle, screen, sifter, strainer.

sift *v* analyse, boult, discuss, examine, fathom, filter, investigate, pan, part, probe, review, riddle, screen, scrutinise, separate, sieve, sort, sprinkle, temse, winnow.

n analysis, colation, examination, filtering, filtration, review, screening, separation, sort, sorting, straining.

sigh *n* moan, sough, suspiration, wuther.

v breathe, complain, grieve, lament, moan, sorrow, sough, suspire, wuther.

sigh for grieve, lament, languish, long, mourn, pine, weep, yearn.

sight *n* appearance, apprehension, decko, display, estimation, exhibition, eye, eyes, eye-shot, eyeshot, eyesight, eyesore, field of vision, fright, gander, glance, glimpse, judgement, ken, look, mess, monstrosity, observation, opinion, pageant, perception, range, scene, seeing, show, spectacle, view, viewing, visibility, vision, vista.

v behold, discern, distinguish, glimpse, observe, perceive, see, spot.

sights *n* amenities, beauties, curiosities, features, marvels, Sehenswürdigkeiten, splendours, videnda, wonders.

sightseer *n* excursionist, holidaymaker, rubber-neck, tourist, tripper, visitor.

sign *n* augury, auspice, badge, beck, betrayal, board, character, cipher, clue, device, emblem, ensign, evidence, figure, foreboding, forewarning, gesture, giveaway, grammalogue, hierogram, hint, indication, indicium, insignia, intimation, lexigram, logo, logogram, logograph, manifestation, mark, marker, miracle, note, notice, omen, placard, pointer, portent, presage, proof, reminder, representation, rune, signal, signature, signification, signpost, spoor, suggestion, symbol, symptom, token, trace, trademark, vestige, warning.

v autograph, beckon, endorse, gesticulate, gesture, indicate, initial, inscribe, motion, signal, subscribe, wave.

sign over consign, convey, deliver, entrust, make over, surrender, transfer, turn over.

sign up appoint, contract, employ, engage, enlist, enrol, hire, join, join up, recruit, register, sign on, take on, volunteer.

signal *n* alarm, alert, beacon, beck, cue, flare, flash, gesture, go-ahead, griffin, impulse, indication, indicator, light, mark, OK, password, rocket, sign, tip-off, token, transmitter, waft, warning, watchword.

adj conspicuous, distinguished, eminent, exceptional, extraordinary, famous, glorious, impressive, memorable, momentous, notable, noteworthy, outstanding, remarkable, significant, striking.

v beckon, communicate, gesticulate, gesture, indicate, motion, nod, sign, telegraph, waft, wave.

signature *n* autograph, endorsement, initials, inscription, mark, sign.

significance *n* consequence, consideration, force, implication, implications, import, importance, impressiveness, interest, matter, meaning, message, moment, point, purport, relevance, sense, signification, solemnity, weight.

antonym unimportance.

significant *adj* critical, denoting, eloquent, expressing, expressive, important, indicative, knowing, material, meaning, meaningful, momentous, noteworthy, ominous, pregnant, senseful, serious, solemn, suggestive, symbolic, symptomatic, vital, weighty.

antonyms meaningless, unimportant.

significantly *adj* appreciably, considerably, critically, crucially, eloquently, knowingly, materially, meaningfully, meaningly, noticeably, perceptibly, suggestively, vitally.

signify *v* announce, augur, betoken, carry weight, communicate, connote, convey, count, denote, evidence, exhibit, express, imply, indicate, intimate, matter, mean, omen, portend, presage, proclaim, represent, show, stand for, suggest, symbolise, transmit.

signpost *n* clue, fingerpost, guidepost, hand-post, pointer, sign, way-post.

silence *n* calm, dumbness, hush, lull, muteness, noiselessness, obmutescence, peace, quiescence, quiet, quietness, reserve, reticence, secretiveness, speechlessness, stillness, taciturnity, uncommunicativeness.

v deaden, dumbfound, extinguish, gag, muffle, muzzle, quell, quiet, quieten, stifle, still, strike dumb, subdue, suppress.

silent *adj* aphonic, aphonous, dumb, hushed, idle, implicit, inaudible, inoperative, mum, mute, muted, noiseless, quiet, reticent, shtoom, soundless, speechless, still, stilly, tacit, taciturn, tongue-tied, uncommunicative, understood, unexpressed, unforthcoming, unpronounced, unsounded, unspeaking, unspoken, voiceless, wordless.

antonyms loud, noisy, talkative.

silently *adv* dumbly, ex tacito, inaudibly, mutely, noiselessly, quietly, soundlessly, speechlessly, tacitly, unheard, wordlessly.

silhouette *n* configuration, delineation, form, outline, profile, shadow-figure, shadowgraph, shape.

silky *adj* fine, satiny, silken, sleek, smooth, soft, velvety.

silly *adj* absurd, addled, asinine, benumbed, bird-brained, brainless, childish, cuckoo, daft, dazed, dopey, drippy, fatuous, feather-brained, flighty, foolhardy, foolish, frivolous, gaga, giddy, groggy, hen-witted, idiotic, illogical, immature, imprudent, inane, inappropriate, inept, irrational, irresponsible, meaningless, mindless, muzzy, pointless, preposterous, puerile, ridiculous, scatter-brained, senseless, spoony, stunned, stupefied, stupid, unwise, witless.

antonyms collected, mature, sane, sensible, wise.

n clot, dope, duffer, goose, half-wit, ignoramus, ninny, silly-billy, simpleton, twit, wally.

silt *n* alluvium, deposit, mud, ooze, residue, sediment, sludge.

silt up block, choke, clog, congest, dam.

silvan *adj* arboreous, bosky, forestal, forested, forestine, leafy, tree-covered, wooded, woodland.

antonym treeless.

similar *adj* alike, analogous, close, comparable, compatible, congruous, corresponding, homogeneous, homogenous, homologous, related, resembling, self-like, uniform.

antonym different.

similarity *n* affinity, agreement, analogy, closeness, coincidence, comparability, compatibility, concordance, congruence, correspondence, equivalence, homogeneity, likeness, relation, resemblance, sameness, similitude, uniformity.

antonym difference.

similarly *adv* by analogy, by the same token, correspondingly, likewise, uniformly.

simmer *v* boil, burn, fizz, fume, rage, seethe, smart, smoulder.

simmer down calm down, collect oneself, contain oneself, control oneself, cool down, cool off, recollect oneself, settle down, take it easy.

simpering *adj* affected, arch, coy, giggling, missish, schoolgirlish, self-conscious, silly.

simple *adj* artless, bald, basic, brainless, childlike, classic, classical, clean, clear, credulous, dense, direct, dumb, easy, elementary, feeble, feeble-minded, foolish, frank, green, guileless, half-witted, homely, honest, humble, idiot-proof, inelaborate, ingenuous, innocent, inornate, intelligible, lowly, lucid, manageable, modest, moronic, naïf, naive, naïve, naked, natural, obtuse, one-fold, plain, pure, rustic, Saturnian, shallow, silly, sincere, single, slow, Spartan, stark, straightforward, stupid, thick, unadorned, unaffected, unalloyed, unblended, uncluttered, uncombined, uncomplicated, undeniable, understandable, undisguised, undivided, unelaborate, unembellished, unfussy, uninvolved, unlearned, unmixed, unornate, unpretentious, unschooled, unskilled, unsophisticated, unsuspecting, unvarnished, user-friendly.

antonyms artful, clever, complicated, difficult, fancy, intricate.

simple-minded *adj* addle-brained, artless, backward, brainless, cretinous, dim-witted, dopey, feeble-minded, foolish, goofy, idiot, idiotic, imbecile, moronic, natural, retarded, simple, stupid, unsophisticated.

antonyms bright, clever.

simpleton *n* Abderite, blockhead, booby, daftie, dizzard, dolt, dope, dullard, dunce, dupe, flat, flathead, fool, gaby, gander, gomeril, goon, goop, goose, goose-cap, goosy, Gothamist, Gothamite, green goose, greenhorn, gump, gunsel, idiot, imbecile, jackass, Johnny, juggins, maffling, moron, nincompoop, ninny, ninny-hammer, numskull, soft-head, spoon, stupid, twerp.

antonym brain.

simplicity *n* artlessness, baldness, candour, clarity, classicism, clearness, directness, ease, easiness, elementariness, guilelessness, innocence, intelligibility, modesty, naïvete, naïvety, naturalness, obviousness, openness, plainness, purity, restraint, simpleness, sincerity, straightforwardness, uncomplicatedness.

antonyms difficulty, guile, intricacy, sophistication.

simplify *v* abridge, decipher, disentangle, facilitate, prune, reduce, streamline.

antonyms complicate, elaborate.

simplistic *adj* naïve, oversimplified, schematic, shallow, simple, superficial, sweeping, unanalytical.

antonyms analytical, detailed.

simply *adv* absolutely, altogether, artlessly, baldly, clearly, completely, directly, easily, intelligibly, just, merely, modestly, naturally, obviously, only, plainly, purely, quite, really, simpliciter, sincerely, solely, straightforwardly, totally, unaffectedly, undeniably, unpretentiously, unquestionably, unreservedly, utterly, wholly.

simulate *v* act, affect, assume, counterfeit, duplicate, echo, fabricate, fake, feign, imitate, mimic, parrot, pretend, put on, reflect, reproduce, sham.

simulated *adj* artificial, assumed, bogus, fake, feigned, imitation, inauthentic, insincere, make-believe, man-made, mock, phoney, pinchbeck, pretended, pseudo, put-on, sham, spurious, substitute, synthetic, ungenuine.

antonyms genuine, real.

simultaneous *adj* accompanying, coincident, coinciding, concomitant, concurrent, contemporaneous, parallel, synchronic, synchronous.

antonyms asynchronous, separate.

sin *n* crime, damnation, debt, error, evil, fault, guilt, hamartia, impiety, iniquity, lapse, misdeed, offence, sinfulness, transgression, trespass, ungodliness, unrighteousness, wickedness, wrong, wrongdoing.

v err, fall, fall from grace, go astray, lapse, misbehave, offend, stray, transgress, trespass.

sincere *adj* artless, bona fide, candid, deep-felt, earnest, frank, genuine, guileless, heartfelt, heart-whole, honest, natural, open, plain-hearted, plain-spoken, pure, real, serious, simple, simple-hearted, single-hearted, soulful, straightforward, true, true-hearted, truthful, unadulterated, unaffected, unfeigned, unmixed, wholehearted.

antonym insincere.

sincerely *adv* earnestly, genuinely, honestly, in earnest, really, seriously, simply, truly, truthfully, unaffectedly, wholeheartedly.

sincerity *n* artlessness, bona fides, candour, earnestness, frankness, genuineness, good faith, guilelessness, honesty, plain-heartedness, probity, seriousness, straightforwardness, truth, truthfulness, wholeheartedness.

antonym insincerity.

sinecure *n* cinch, cushy job, doddle, gravy train, money for jam, picnic, plum job, soft option.

sinewy *adj* athletic, brawny, lusty, muscular, powerful, robust, stringy, strong, sturdy, tendinous, vigorous, wiry.

sinful *adj* bad, corrupt, criminal, depraved, erring, fallen, guilty, immoral, impious, iniquitous, irreligious, peccable, peccant, ungodly, unholy, unrighteous, unvirtuous, wicked, wrongful.

antonyms righteous, sinless.

sinfulness *n* corruption, depravity, guilt, immorality, impiety, iniquity, peccability, peccancy, sin, transgression, ungodliness, unrighteousness, wickedness.

antonym righteousness.

sing *v* betray, bizz, blow the whistle, cantillate, carol, caterwaul, chant, chirp, croon, finger, fink, grass, hum, inform, intone, lilt, melodise, peach, pipe, purr, quaver, rat, render, serenade, spill the beans, squeal, talk, trill, vocalise, warble, whine, whistle, yodel.

sing out bawl, bellow, call, cooee, cry, halloo, holler, shout, yell.

singe *v* blacken, burn, cauterise, char, scorch, sear.

singer *n* balladeer, balladist, bard, cantabank, cantatrice, cantor, caroller, chanteuse, choirboy, choirgirl, choirman, chorister, crooner, diva, griot, jongleur, Meistersinger, minstrel, precentor, prima donna, psalmodist, songster, troubadour, vocalist.

single *adj* celibate, distinct, exclusive, free, individual, lone, man-to-man, one, one-fold, one-to-one, only, particular, separate, simple, sincere, single-minded, singular, sole, solitary, unattached, unblended, unbroken, uncombined, uncompounded, undivided, unique, unmarried, unmixed, unshared, unwed, wholehearted.

single out choose, cull, distinguish, hand-pick, highlight, isolate, pick, pinpoint, select, separate, set apart.

single-handed *adj, adv* alone, independently, solo, unaccompanied, unaided, unassisted.

single-minded *adj* dedicated, determined, dogged, fixed, hell-bent, monomaniacal, resolute, steadfast, stubborn, tireless, undeviating, unswerving, unwavering.

singular *adj* atypical, conspicuous, curious, eccentric, eminent, exceptional, extraordinary, individual, noteworthy, odd, out-of-the-way, outstanding, peculiar, pre-eminent, private, prodigious, proper, puzzling, queer, rare, remarkable, separate, single, sole, strange, uncommon, unique, unparalleled, unusual.

antonyms normal, usual.

singularity *n* abnormality, curiousness, eccentricity, extraordinariness, idiosyncrasy, irregularity, oddity, oddness, oneness, particularity, peculiarity, queerness, quirk, strangeness, twist, unicity, uniqueness.

antonym normality.

singularly *adv* bizarrely, conspicuously, especially, exceptionally, extraordinarily, notably, outstandingly, particularly, prodigiously, remarkably, signally, surprisingly, uncommonly, unusually.

sinister *adj* dire, disquieting, evil, inauspicious, injurious, left, louche, malevolent, malign, malignant, menacing, ominous, threatening, underhand, unlucky.

antonyms harmless, innocent.

sink *v* abandon, abate, abolish, bore, collapse, conceal, decay, decline, decrease, defeat, degenerate, degrade, delapse, descend, destroy, dig, diminish, dip, disappear, drill, drive, droop, drop, drown, dwindle, ebb, engulf, excavate, fade, fail, fall, finish, flag, founder, invest, lapse, lay, lessen, lower, merge, overwhelm, pay, penetrate, plummet, plunge, relapse, retrogress, ruin, sag, scupper, slip, slope, slump, stoop, submerge, subside, succumb, suppress, weaken, worsen.

antonyms float, rise, uplift.

sinless *adj* faultless, guiltless, immaculate, impeccable, innocent, pure, unblemished, uncorrupted, undefiled, unspotted, unsullied, virtuous.

antonym sinful.

sinner *n* backslider, evil-doer, malefactor, miscreant, offender, reprobate, transgressor, trespasser, wrong-doer.

sinuous *adj* coiling, crooked, curved, curvy, lithe, mazy, meandering, serpentine, slinky, supple, tortuous, undulating, winding.

antonym straight.

sip *v* delibate, sample, sup, taste.

n drop, mouthful, spoonful, swallow, taste, thimbleful.

siren *n* charmer, Circe, femme fatale, houri, Lorelei, seductress, temptress, vamp, witch.

sissy *n* baby, coward, milksop, mollycoddle, mummy's boy, namby-pamby, pansy, softy, weakling, wet.

adj cowardly, effeminate, feeble, namby-pamby, pansy, sissified, soft, unmanly, weak, wet.

sit *v* accommodate, assemble, befit, brood, contain, convene, deliberate, hold, meet, officiate, perch, pose, preside, reside, rest, seat, settle.

site *n* ground, location, lot, place, plot, position, setting, spot, station.

v dispose, install, locate, place, position, set, situate, station.

sitting *n* assembly, consultation, get-together, hearing, meeting, period, seat, session, spell.

situation *n* ball-game, berth, case, circumstances, condition, employment, galère, job, kettle of fish, lie of the land, locale, locality, location, office, place, plight, position, post, predicament, rank, scenario, seat, setting, set-up, site, sphere, spot, state, state of affairs, station, status.

sizable *adj* biggish, considerable, decent, decent-sized, goodly, large, largish, respectable, significant, substantial, tidy.

antonym small.

size *n* amount, amplitude, bigness, bulk, dimensions, extent, greatness, height, hugeness, immensity, largeness, magnitude, mass, measurement(s), proportions, range, vastness, volume.

size up appraise, assess, evaluate, gauge, measure.

sizzle *v* crackle, frizzle, fry, hiss, scorch, sear, spit, sputter.

skedaddle *v* abscond, beat it, bolt, decamp, disappear, do a bunk, flee, hop it, run away, scarper, scoot, scram, split, vamoose.

skeletal *adj* cadaverous, drawn, emaciated, fleshless, gaunt, haggard, hollow-cheeked, shrunken, skin-and-bone, wasted.

skeleton *n* bare bones, draft, endoskeleton, frame, framework, outline, sketch, structure.

sketch *v* block out, delineate, depict, draft, draw, outline, paint, pencil, plot, portray, represent, rough out.

n croquis, delineation, design, draft, drawing, ebauche, esquisse, outline, plan, scenario, skeleton, vignette.

sketchily *adv* cursorily, hastily, imperfectly, inadequately, incompletely, patchily, perfunctorily, roughly, vaguely.

antonym fully.

sketchy *adj* bitty, crude, cursory, imperfect, inadequate, incomplete, insufficient, outline, perfunctory, rough, scrappy, skimpy, slight, superficial, unfinished, vague.

antonym full.

skilful *adj* able, accomplished, adept, adroit, apt, canny, clever, competent, dexterous, experienced, expert, handy, masterly, nimble-fingered, practised, professional, proficient, quick, ready, skilled, tactical, trained.

antonyms awkward, clumsy, inept.

skill *n* ability, accomplishment, adroitness, aptitude, art, cleverness, competence, dexterity, experience, expertise, expertness, facility, finesse, handiness, ingenuity, intelligence, knack, proficiency, quickness, readiness, savoir-faire, savvy, skilfulness, talent, technique, touch.

skilled *adj* able, accomplished, crack, experienced, expert, masterly, practised, professional, proficient, schooled, skilful, trained.

antonym unskilled.

skim *v* brush, coast, cream, dart, despumate, float, fly, glide, plane, sail, scan, separate, skip, soar.

skimp *v* conserve, cut corners, economise, pinch, scamp, scant, scrimp, stint, withhold.

skimpy *adj* beggarly, exiguous, inadequate, insufficient, meagre, measly, miserly, niggardly, scanty, short, sketchy, sparse, thin, tight.

antonym generous.

skin *n* casing, coating, crust, deacon, epidermis, fell, film, hide, husk, integument, membrane, mouton, outside, peel, pellicle, pelt, rind, tegument.

v abrade, bark, excoriate, flay, fleece, graze, peel, scrape, strip.

skin-deep *adj* artificial, empty, external, meaningless, outward, shallow, superficial, surface.

skinflint *n* cheese-parer, meanie, miser, niggard, penny-pincher, Scrooge, tightwad.

skinny *adj* attenuate(d), emaciated, lean, scragged, scraggy, skeletal, skin-and-bone, thin, twiggy, underfed, undernourished, weedy.

antonym fat.

skip *v* bob, bounce, caper, cavort, cut, dance, eschew, flisk, flit, frisk, gambol, hop, miss, omit, overleap, play truant, prance, trip.

skirmish *n* affair, affray, battle, brush, clash, combat, conflict, contest, dust-up, encounter, engagement, fracas, incident, scrap, scrimmage, set-to, spat, tussle, velitation.

v clash, collide, pickeer, scrap, tussle.

skirt *v* avoid, border, bypass, circle, circumambulate, circumnavigate, circumvent, detour, edge, evade, flank, steer clear of.

skit *n* burlesque, caricature, parody, satire, sketch, spoof, take-off, travesty, turn.

skittish *adj* coltish, excitable, fickle, fidgety, frivolous, highly-strung, jumpy, kittenish, kitteny, lively, nervous, playful, restive.

skittles *n* kettle-pins, kittle-pins, ninepins, pins, tenpins.

skive *v* dodge, dodge the column, idle, malinger, shirk, skrimshank, skulk, slack, swing the lead.

skiver *n* dodger, do-nothing, idler, loafer, malingerer, scrimshanker, shirker, slacker.

skulduggery *n* chicanery, double-dealing, duplicity, fraudulence, jiggery-pokery, machinations, shenanigan(s), swindling, trickery, underhandedness, unscrupulousness.

skulk *v* creep, lie in wait, loiter, lurk, pad, prowl, pussyfoot, slink, sneak.

sky *n* air, ambient, atmosphere, azure, blue, empyrean, firmament, heavens, vault of heaven, welkin.

slab *n* briquette, chunk, hunk, lump, piece, planch, portion, slice, wedge, wodge.

slack *adj* baggy, crank, dull, easy, easy-going, flaccid, flexible, idle, inactive, inattentive, lax, lazy, limp, loose, neglectful, negligent, permissive, quiet, relaxed, remiss, slow, slow-moving, sluggish, tardy.

antonyms busy, diligent, quick, rigid, stiff, taut.

n excess, give, inactivity, leeway, looseness, play, relaxation, room.

v dodge, idle, malinger, neglect, relax, shirk, skive, slacken.

slacken off abate, decrease, diminish, fail, flag, lessen, loosen, moderate, reduce, relax, release, slow, slow down, tire.

antonyms increase, quicken, tighten.

slacker *n* clock-watcher, dawdler, dodger, do-nothing, embusque, faineant, good-for-nothing, idler, layabout, loafer, malingerer, passenger, shirk(er), skiver, skrimshanker.

slag *v* abuse, berate, criticise, deride, insult, lambaste, malign, mock, slam, slang, slate.

slake *v* abate, allay, assuage, deaden, extinguish, gratify, mitigate, moderate, moisten, quench, reduce, sate, satiate, satisfy, slacken, subside.

slam *v* attack, bang, castigate, clap, crash, criticise, damn, dash, excoriate, fling, hurl, lambaste, pan, pillory, slate, smash, swap, swop, throw, thump, vilify.

slander *n* aspersion, backbiting, calumniation, calumny, defamation, detraction, libel, misrepresentation, muck-raking, obloquy, scandal, smear, traducement, traduction.

v asperse, backbite, calumniate, decry, defame, detract, disparage, libel, malign, muck-rake, scandalise, slur, smear, traduce, vilify, vilipend.

antonyms glorify, praise.

slanderous *adj* abusive, aspersive, aspersory, calumnious, damaging, defamatory, libellous, malicious.

slang *v* abuse, berate, castigate, excoriate, insult, lambaste, malign, revile, scold, slag, vilify, vituperate.

antonym praise.

slanging match altercation, argument, argy-bargy, barney, dispute, quarrel, row, set-to, shouting match, spat.

slant *v* angle, bend, bevel, bias, cant, colour, distort, incline, lean, list, shelve, skew, slope, tilt, twist, warp, weight.

n angle, attitude, bias, camber, declination, diagonal, emphasis, gradient, incline, leaning, obliquity, pitch, prejudice, rake, ramp, slope, tilt, viewpoint.

slanting *adj* angled, askew, aslant, asymmetrical, bent, canted, cater-cornered, diagonal, inclined, oblique, sideways, skew-whiff, slanted, slantwise, sloping, tilted, tilting.

antonym level.

slap *n* bang, blow, clap, clout, cuff, paddy-whack, skelp, smack, spank, wallop, whack.

v bang, clap, clout, cuff, daub, hit, plaster, plonk, skelp, spank, spread, strike, whack.

adv bang, dead, directly, exactly, plumb, precisely, right, slap-bang, smack.

slap down berate, keelhaul, rebuke, reprimand, restrain, squash, upbraid.

slap in the face affront, blow, humiliation, indignity, insult, put-down, rebuff, rebuke, rejection, repulse, snub.

slap-dash *adj* careless, clumsy, disorderly, haphazard, hasty, hurried, last-minute, messy, negligent, offhand, perfunctory, rash, slipshod, sloppy, slovenly, thoughtless, thrown-together, untidy.

antonyms careful, orderly.

slap-happy *adj* boisterous, casual, dazed, giddy, haphazard, happy-go-lucky, hit-or-miss, irresponsible, nonchalant, punch-drunk, reckless, reeling, slap-dash, woozy.

slapstick *n* buffoonery, comedy, farce, horseplay, knockabout, tomfoolery.

slap-up *adj* elaborate, excellent, first-class, first-rate, lavish, luxurious, magnificent, princely, splendid, sumptuous, superb, superlative.

slash *v* criticise, cut, drop, gash, hack, lacerate, lash, lower, reduce, rend, rip, score, slit.

n cut, gash, incision, laceration, lash, rent, rip, slit.

slashing *adj* aggressive, biting, brutal, ferocious, harsh, savage, searing, unsparing, vicious.

slate *v* abuse, berate, blame, castigate, censure, criticise, lambaste, pan, rebuke, reprimand, roast, scold, slag, slam, slang.

antonym praise.

slatternly *adj* bedraggled, dirty, dowdy, draggle-tailed, frowzy, frumpish, frumpy, slipshod, sloppy, slovenly, sluttish, unclean, unkempt, untidy.

slaughter *n* battue, blood-bath, bloodshed, butchery, carnage, extermination, holocaust, killing, liquidation, massacre, murder, schechita(h), shochet, slaying.

v butcher, crush, defeat, destroy, exterminate, halal, hammer, kill, liquidate, massacre, murder, overwhelm, rout, scupper, slay, thrash, trounce, vanquish.

slave *n* abject, bondservant, bond-slave, bond(s)man, bond(s)woman, captive, drudge, esne, helot, Mameluke, scullion, serf, servant, skivvy, slavey, thrall, vassal, villein.

v drudge, grind, labour, skivvy, slog, struggle, sweat, toil.

slaver *v* dribble, drivel, drool, salivate, slabber, slobber.

slavery *n* bondage, captivity, duress(e), enslavement, impressment, serfdom, servitude, subjugation, thraldom, thrall, vassalage, yoke.

antonym freedom.

slavish *adj* abject, base, conventional, cringing, despicable, fawning, grovelling, imitative, laborious, literal, low, mean, menial, obsequious, servile, strict, submissive, sycophantic, unimaginative, uninspired, unoriginal.

antonyms independent, original.

slay *v* amuse, annihilate, assassinate, butcher, destroy, dispatch, eliminate, execute, exterminate, impress, kill, massacre, murder, rub out, slaughter, wow.

slaying *n* annihilation, assassination, butchery, destruction, dispatch, elimination, extermination, killing, mactation, massacre, murder, shambles, slaughter.

sleazy *adj* crummy, disreputable, low, run-down, seedy, sordid, squalid, tacky.

sleek *adj* glossy, insinuating, lustrous, plausible, shiny, smooth, smug, well-fed, well-groomed.

sleep *v* catnap, doss (down), doze, drop off, drowse, hibernate, nod off, repose, rest, slumber, snooze, snore, zizz.

n coma, dormancy, doss, doze, forty winks, hibernation, nap, repose, rest, shut-eye, siesta, slumber(s), snooze, sopor, zizz.

sleepiness *n* doziness, drowsiness, heaviness, lethargy, oscitancy, somnolence, torpor.

antonyms alertness, wakefulness.

sleeping *adj* asleep, becalmed, daydreaming, dormant, dormient, hibernating, idle, inactive, inattentive, off guard, passive, slumbering, unaware.

antonyms alert, awake.

sleepless *adj* alert, disturbed, insomniac, insomnious, restless, unsleeping, vigilant, wakeful, watchful, wide-awake.

sleeplessness *n* insomnia, insomnolence, wakefulness.

sleep-walker *n* noctambulist, somnambulist.

sleep-walking *n* noctambulation, noctambulism, somnambulation, somnambulism.

sleepy *adj* drowsy, dull, heavy, hypnotic, inactive, lethargic, quiet, slow, sluggish, slumb(e)rous, slumbersome, slumbery, somnolent, soporific, soporose, soporous, torpid.

antonyms alert, awake, restless, wakeful.

sleight of hand adroitness, artifice, dexterity, legerdemain, magic, manipulation, prestidigitation, skill, trickery.

slender *adj* acicular, faint, feeble, flimsy, fragile, gracile, inadequate, inconsiderable, insufficient, lean, little, meagre, narrow, poor, remote, scanty, slight, slim, small, spare, svelte, sylph-like, tenuous, thin, thready, wasp-waisted, weak, willowish, willowy.

antonyms considerable, fat, thick.

sleuth *n* bloodhound, detective, dick, gumshoe, private eye, private investigator, shadow, tail, tracker.

slice *n* cut, frustum, helping, piece, portion, rasher, section, segment, share, sheave, shive, slab, sliver, tranche, wafer, wedge, whack, whang.

v carve, chop, cut, divide, segment, sever, sliver, whittle.

slick *adj* adroit, deft, dexterous, glib, meretricious, plausible, polished, professional, sharp, skilful, sleek, smooth, sophistical, specious, trim.

antonyms amateurish, clumsy, coarse.

slide *v* coast, glide, glissade, lapse, skate, skim, slidder, slip, slither, toboggan, veer.

slight *adj* delicate, feeble, flimsy, fragile, gracile, inconsiderable, insignificant, insubstantial, meagre, minor, modest, negligible, paltry, scanty, slender, slim, small, spare, superficial, trifling, trivial, unimportant, weak.

antonyms considerable, large, major, significant.

v affront, cold-shoulder, cut, despise, disdain, disparage, disrespect, ignore, insult, neglect, scorn, snub.

antonyms compliment, flatter.

n affront, contempt, discourtesy, disdain, disregard, disrespect, inattention, indifference, insult, neglect, rebuff, rudeness, slur, snub.

slighting *adj* abusive, belittling, defamatory, derogatory, disdainful, disparaging, disrespectful, insulting, offensive, scornful, slanderous, supercilious, uncomplimentary.

antonym complimentary.

slim *adj* ectomorphic, faint, gracile, lean, narrow, poor, remote, slender, slight, svelte, sylph-like, thin, trim.

antonyms chubby, fat, strong.

v bant, diet, lose weight, reduce, slenderise.

slime *n* bitumen, cludge, filth, gleet, glit, goo, gunk, mess, muck, mucus, mud, ooze.

slimy *adj* clammy, creeping, disgusting, glutinous, grovelling, miry, mucous, muddy, obsequious, oily, oozy, servile, smarmy, soapy, sycophantic, toadying, uliginous, unctuous, viscous.

sling *v* cast, catapult, chuck, dangle, fling, hang, heave, hurl, lob, pitch, shy, suspend, swing, throw, toss.

n band, bandage, catapult, loop, parbuckle, selvagee, strap, support.

slink *v* creep, prowl, pussyfoot, scunge, sidle, skulk, slip, sneak, steal.

slinky *adj* clinging, close-fitting, feline, figure-hugging, lean, sinuous, skin-tight, sleek.

slip[1] *v* blunder, boob, conceal, creep, disappear, discharge, dislocate, elude, err, escape, fall, get away, glide, hide, lapse, loose, miscalculate, misjudge, mistake, skate, skid, slidder, slide, slink, slither, sneak, steal, trip.

n bloomer, blunder, boob, error, failure, fault, imprudence, indiscretion, lapsus, lapsus calami, lapsus linguae, lapsus memoriae, mistake, omission, oversight, slip-up.

slip[2] *n* certificate, coupon, cutting, offshoot, pass, piece, runner, scion, shoot, sliver, sprig, sprout, strip.

slipper *n* flip-flop, loafer, moccasin, mule, pabouche, pantable, pantof(f)le, panton, pantoufle, pump, sandal.

slippery *adj* crafty, cunning, devious, dishonest, duplicitous, evasive, false, foxy, glassy, greasy, icy, lubric(al), lubric(i)ous, perilous, shifty, skiddy, sliddery, slippy, smooth, sneaky, treacherous, tricky, two-faced, unpredictable, unreliable, unsafe, unstable, unsteady, untrustworthy.

slippy *adj* elusive, evasive, greasy, icy, lubric(i)ous, smooth, uncertain, unstable.

slipshod *adj* careless, casual, loose, negligent, slap-dash, sloppy, slovenly, unsystematic, untidy.

antonyms careful, fastidious, neat, tidy.

slit *v* cut, gash, knife, lance, pierce, rip, slash, slice, split.

n cut, fent, fissure, gash, incision, opening, rent, split, tear, vent.

adj cut, pertusate, pertuse(d), rent, split, torn.

slither *v* glide, skitter, slidder, slide, slink, slip, snake, undulate.

sliver *n* chip, flake, fragment, paring, shaving, shiver, shred, slip, splinter.

slob *n* boor, brute, churl, lout, oaf, philistine, sloven, yahoo, yob.

slobber *v* dribble, drivel, drool, salivate, slabber, slaver, splutter, water at the mouth.

slog *v* bash, belt, hit, labour, persevere, plod, plough through, slave, slosh, slug, smite, sock, strike, thump, toil, tramp, trek, trudge, wallop, work.

n effort, exertion, grind, hike, labour, struggle, tramp, trek, trudge.

slogan *n* battle-cry, catch-phrase, catchword, chant, jingle, motto, rallying-cry, war cry, watchword.

slop *v* overflow, slobber, slosh, spatter, spill, splash, splatter, wash away.

slope *v* batter, delve, fall, incline, lean, pitch, rise, slant, tilt, verge, weather.

n bajada, brae, cant, declination, declivity, descent, downgrade, escarp, glacis, gradient, inclination, incline, ramp, rise, scarp, slant, tilt, versant.

sloping *adj* acclivitous, acclivous, bevelled, canting, declivitous, declivous, inclined, inclining, leaning, oblique, slanting.

antonym level.

sloppy *adj* amateurish, banal, careless, clumsy, gushing, hit-or-miss, inattentive, mawkish, messy, mushy, schmaltzy, sentimental, slipshod, slovenly, sludgy, slushy, soppy, splashy, trite, unkempt, untidy, watery, weak, wet.

antonyms careful, exact, precise.

slosh *v* bash, biff, flounder, hit, plash, pour, punch, shower, slap, slog, slop, slug, sock, splash, spray, strike, swash, swipe, thump, thwack, wade, wallop.

slot *n* aperture, channel, gap, groove, hole, niche, opening, place, position, slit, space, time, vacancy.

v adjust, assign, fit, insert, pigeonhole, place, position.

sloth *n* accidie, acedia, faineance, idleness, inactivity, indolence, inertia, laziness, listlessness, slackness, slothfulness, sluggishness, torpor.

antonyms diligence, industriousness, sedulity.

slothful *adj* do-nothing, faineant, idle, inactive, indolent, inert, lazy, listless, skiving, slack, sluggish, torpid, workshy.

antonyms diligent, industrious, sedulous.

slouch *v* droop, hunch, loll, shamble, shuffle, slump, stoop.

slouching *adj* careless, disorderly, heedless, loose, negligent, shambling, shuffling, slack, slap-dash, slatternly, slipshod, sloppy, unkempt, untidy.

slow *adj* adagio, backward, behind, behindhand, boring, bovine, conservative, creeping, dawdling, dead, dead-and-alive, delayed, deliberate, dense, dilatory, dim, dull, dull-witted, dumb, easy, gradual, inactive, lackadaisical, laggard, lagging, late, lazy, leaden, leisurely, lingering, loitering, long-drawn-out, measured, obtuse, one-horse, pedetentous, plodding, ponderous, prolonged, protracted, quiet, retarded, slack, sleepy, slow-moving, slow-witted, sluggardly, sluggish, stagnant, stupid, tame, tardy, tedious, thick, time-consuming, uneventful, unhasty, unhurried, uninteresting, unproductive, unprogressive, unpunctual, unresponsive, wearisome.

antonyms active, fast, quick, rapid, swift.

v brake, check, curb, decelerate, delay, detain, draw rein, handicap, hold up, lag, relax, restrict, retard.

slow to averse, disinclined, hesitant, indisposed, loath, reluctant, unwilling.

slowly *adv* adagio, gradually, inchmeal, larghetto, largo, lazily, leisurely, lento, ploddingly, ponderously, sluggishly, steadily, unhurriedly.

antonym quickly.

sludge *n* dregs, gunge, gunk, mire, muck, mud, ooze, residue, sediment, silt, slag, slime, slop, slush, swill.

sluggish *adj* dull, heavy, inactive, indolent, inert, lethargic, lifeless, listless, lurdan, lymphatic, phlegmatic, slothful, slow, slow-moving, torpid, unresponsive.

antonyms brisk, dynamic, eager, quick, vigorous.

sluggishness *n* apathy, drowsiness, dullness, faineance, heaviness, indolence, inertia, languor, lassitude, lethargy, listlessness, slothfulness, slowness, somnolence, stagnation, torpor.

antonyms dynamism, eagerness, quickness.

sluice *v* cleanse, drain, drench, flush, irrigate, slosh, swill, wash.

slumber *v* doze, drowse, nap, repose, rest, sleep, snooze.

slummy *adj* decayed, dirty, overcrowded, ramshackle, run-down, seedy, sleazy, sordid, squalid, wretched.

slump *v* bend, collapse, crash, decline, deteriorate, droop, drop, fall, hunch, loll, plummet, plunge, sag, sink, slip, slouch, worsen.

n collapse, crash, decline, depreciation, depression, downturn, drop, failure, fall, falling-off, low, recession, reverse, stagnation, trough, worsening.

antonym boom.

slur *n* affront, aspersion, blot, brand, calumny, discredit, disgrace, innuendo, insinuation, insult, reproach, slander, slight, smear, stain, stigma.

slut *n* dolly-map, drab, d(r)aggle-tail, dratchell, jade, slattern, sloven, trollop.

sly *adj* arch, artful, astute, canny, clever, conniving, covert, crafty, cunning, devious, foxy, furtive, guileful, impish, insidious, knowing, mischievous, peery, roguish, scheming, secret, secretive, shifty, sleeky, stealthy, subtle, surreptitious, underhand, vulpine, wily.

antonyms frank, honest, open, straightforward.

smack *v* box, clap, cuff, hit, pandy, pat, skelp, slap, sock, spank, strike, tap, thwack, whack.

n blow, box, crack, cuff, hit, pandy, pat, skelp, slap, sock, spank, strike, tap, thwack, whack.

adv directly, exactly, plumb, point-blank, precisely, right, slap, slap-bang, squarely, straight.

smack one's lips anticipate, delight in, drool over, enjoy, relish, savour.

small *adj* bantam, base, dilute, diminutive, dwarf(ish), grudging, humble, illiberal, immature, inadequate, incapacious, inconsiderable, insignificant, insufficient, itsy-bitsy, lesser, limited, little, meagre, mean, mignon(ne), mini, miniature, minor, minuscule, minute, modest, narrow, negligible, paltry, petite, petty, pigmean, pint-size(d), pocket, pocket-sized, puny, pygmaean, pygmean, scanty, selfish, slight, small-scale, tichy, tiddl(e)y, tiny, trifling, trivial, undersized, unimportant, unpretentious, wee, young.

antonyms big, huge, large.

small-minded *adj* bigoted, envious, grudging, hidebound, insular, intolerant, mean, narrow-minded, parochial, petty, rigid, ungenerous.

antonyms broad-minded, liberal, tolerant.

small-time *adj* inconsequential, insignificant, minor, no-account, petty, piddling, unimportant.

antonyms important, major.

smarminess *n* obsequiousness, oiliness, servility, suavity, sycophancy, toadying, unctuosity, unctuousness.

smarmy *adj* bootlicking, crawling, fawning, fulsome, greasy, ingratiating, obsequious, oily, servile, smooth, soapy, suave, sycophantic, toadying, unctuous.

smart[1] *adj* acute, adept, agile, apt, astute, bright, brisk, canny, chic, clever, cracking, dandy, effective, elegant, fashionable, fine, impertinent, ingenious, intelligent, jaunty, keen, lively, modish, natty, neat, nimble, nimble-witted, nobby, pert, pointed, quick, quick-witted, rattling, ready, ready-witted, saucy, sharp, shrewd, smart-alecky, snappy, spanking, spirited, spruce, stylish, swagger, swish, tippy, trim, vigorous, vivacious, well-appointed, witty.

antonyms dowdy, dumb, slow, stupid, unfashionable, untidy.

smart Alec(k) Besserwisser, clever clogs, clever dick, know-all, smart-arse, smartyboots, smartypants, wise guy, wiseacre.

smart[2] *v* burn, hurt, nip, pain, sting, throb, tingle, twinge.

adj hard, keen, nipping, nippy, painful, piercing, resounding, sharp, stinging.

n nip, pain, pang, smarting, soreness, sting, twinge.

smarten *v* beautify, clean, groom, neaten, polish, primp, prink, spruce up, tidy.

smash *v* break, collide, crash, crush, defeat, demolish, destroy, disintegrate, lay waste, overthrow, prang, pulverise, ruin, shatter, shiver, squabash, wreck.

n accident, collapse, collision, crash, defeat, destruction, disaster, downfall, failure, pile-up, prang, ruin, shattering, smash-up.

smashing *adj* braw, excellent, exhilarating, fab, fabulous, fantastic, first-class, first-rate, great, magnificent, marvellous, sensational, stupendous, super, superb, superlative, terrific, tremendous, wonderful.

smattering *n* basics, bit, dash, elements, modicum, rudiments, smatter, soupçon, sprinkling.

smear *v* asperse, bedaub, bedim, besmirch, blacken, blur, calumniate, coat, cover, dab, daub, dirty, drag (someone's) name through the mud, gaum, malign, patch, plaster, rub on, slubber, smarm, smudge, soil, spread over, stain, sully, tarnish, traduce, vilify.

n blot, blotch, calumny, daub, defamation, gaum, libel, mudslinging, slander, smudge, splodge, streak, vilification, whispering campaign.

smell *n* aroma, bouquet, fetor, fragrance, fumet(te), funk, malodour, mephitis, nose, odour, perfume, pong, redolence, scent, sniff, stench, stink, whiff.

v be malodorous, hum, inhale, nose, pong, reek, scent, sniff, snuff, stink, stink to high heaven, whiff.

smelly *adj* bad, evil-smelling, fetid, foul, foul-smelling, frowsty, funky, graveolent, high, malodorous, mephitic, noisome, off, pongy, putrid, reeking, stinking, strong, strong-smelling, whiffy.

smirk *n* grin, leer, simper, sneer, snigger.

smitten *adj* afflicted, beguiled, beset, bewitched, bowled over, burdened, captivated, charmed, enamoured, infatuated, plagued, struck, troubled.

smoke *n* exhaust, film, fog, fume, funk, gas, mist, reek, roke, smog, vapour.

v cure, dry, fume, fumigate, reek, roke, smoulder, vent.

smoky *adj* begrimed, black, caliginous, grey, grimy, hazy, murky, reechy, reeky, roky, sooty, thick.

smooth *adj* agreeable, bland, calm, classy, easy, effortless, elegant, equable, even, facile, fair-spoken, flat, flowing, fluent, flush, frictionless, glassy, glib, glossy, hairless, horizontal, ingratiating, level, levigate, mellow, mild, mirror-like, peaceful, persuasive, plain, plane, pleasant, polished, regular, rhythmic, serene, shiny, silken, silky, sleek, slick, slippery, smarmy, smug, soft, soothing, steady, suave, tranquil, unbroken, unctuous, undisturbed, uneventful, uniform, uninterrupted, unpuckered, unruffled, unrumpled, untroubled, unwrinkled, urbane, velvety, well-ordered.

antonyms coarse, harsh, irregular, rough, unsteady.

v allay, alleviate, appease, assuage, calm, dub, ease, emery, extenuate, facilitate, flatten, iron, level, levigate, mitigate, mollify, palliate, plane, polish, press, slicken, soften, unknit, unwrinkle.

antonym roughen.

smoothly *adv* calmly, easily, effortlessly, equably, evenly, fluently, ingratiatingly, legato, mildly, peacefully, pleasantly, serenely, slickly, soothingly, steadily, suavely, tranquilly.

smoothness *n* calmness, ease, efficiency, effortlessness, evenness, facility, felicity, finish, flow, fluency, glassiness, glibness, levelness, lubricity, oiliness, placidity, polish, regularity, rhythm, serenity, silkiness, sleekness, slickness, smarminess, softness, stillness, suavity, unbrokenness, urbanity, velvetiness.

antonyms coarseness, harshness, roughness.

smooth-talking *adj* bland, facile, glib, logodaedalic, persuasive, plausible, slick, smooth, suave.

smother *v* choke, cocoon, conceal, cover, envelop, extinguish, heap, hide, inundate, muffle, overlie, overwhelm, repress, shower, shroud, snuff, stifle, strangle, suffocate, suppress, surround.

smoulder *v* boil, burn, fester, fume, rage, seethe, simmer, smoke.

smudge *v* blacken, blur, daub, dirty, mark, smear, smirch, soil, spot, stain.

n blemish, blot, blur, smear, smut, smutch, spot, stain.

smug *adj* cocksure, complacent, conceited, holier-than-thou, priggish, self-opinionated, self-righteous, self-satisfied, superior, unctuous.

antonym modest.

smuggler *n* bootlegger, contrabandist, courier, moonshiner, mule, rum-runner, runner, wrecker.

smutty *adj* bawdy, blue, coarse, crude, dirty, filthy, gross, improper, indecent, indelicate, lewd, obscene, off colour, pornographic, prurient, racy, raunchy, ribald, risque, salacious, suggestive, vulgar.

antonyms clean, decent.

snack *n* bite, break, elevens, elevenses, nacket, nibble, nocket, quick-lunch, refreshment(s), rere-supper, running-banquet, titbit, zakuska.

snag *n* bug, catch, complication, difficulty, disadvantage, drawback, hitch, inconvenience, obstacle, problem, snub, stick, stumbling block.

v catch, hole, ladder, rip, tear.

snap *v* bark, bite, break, catch, chop, click, crack, crackle, crepitate, flash, grip, growl, knap, nip, pop, retort, seize, separate, snarl, snatch.

n bite, break, crack, crackle, energy, fillip, flick, get-up-and-go, go, grabe, liveliness, nip, pizazz, pop, vigour, zip.

adj abrupt, immediate, instant, offhand, on-the-spot, sudden, unexpected, unpremeditated.

snap up grab, grasp, nab, pick up, pluck, pounce on, seize, snatch.

snappy *adj* brusque, chic, crabbed, cross, dapper, edgy, fashionable, hasty, ill-natured, irritable, modish, natty, quick-tempered, smart, snappish, stylish, tart, testy, touchy, trendy, up-to-the-minute, waspish.

snare *v* catch, ensnare, entrap, illaqueate, net, seize, springe, trap, trepan, wire.

n catch, cobweb, gin, lime, lime-twig, net, noose, pitfall, springe, springle, toils, trap, wire.

snarl[1] *v* complain, gnarl, gnar(r), growl, grumble, knar.

snarl[2] *v* complicate, confuse, embroil, enmesh, entangle, entwine, jam, knot, muddle, ravel, tangle.

snarl-up *n* confusion, entanglement, jumble, mess, mix-up, muddle, tangle, traffic jam.

snatch *v* clutch, gain, grab, grasp, grip, kidnap, nab, pluck, pull, ramp, rap, rescue, seize, spirit, take, win, wrench, wrest.

n bit, fraction, fragment, part, piece, section, segment, smattering, snippet, spell.

snazzy *adj* attractive, dashing, fashionable, flamboyant, flashy, jazzy, raffish, ritzy, showy, smart, snappy, sophisticated, sporty, stylish, swinging, with-it.

antonyms drab, unfashionable.

sneak *v* cower, cringe, grass on, inform on, lurk, pad, peach, sidle, skulk, slink, slip, smuggle, spirit, steal, tell tales.

n informer, snake in the grass, sneaker, telltale.

adj clandestine, covert, furtive, quick, secret, stealthy, surprise, surreptitious.

sneaking *adj* contemptible, dim, furtive, half-formed, hidden, intuitive, mean, nagging, niggling, persistent, private, secret, sly, sneaky, suppressed, surreptitious, two-faced, uncomfortable, underhand, unexpressed, unvoiced, worrying.

sneaky *adj* base, contemptible, cowardly, deceitful, devious, dishonest, disingenuous, double-dealing, furtive, guileful, low, low-down, malicious, mean, nasty, shady, shifty, slippery, sly, snide, unethical, unreliable, unscrupulous, untrustworthy.

antonyms honest, open.

sneer *v* deride, disdain, fleer, gibe, jeer, laugh, look down on, mock, ridicule, scoff, scorn, sniff at, snigger.

n derision, disdain, fleer, gibe, jeer, mockery, ridicule, scorn, smirk, snidery, snigger.

sneezing *adj* errhine, sternutatory.

snide *adj* base, cynical, derogatory, dishonest, disparaging, hurtful, ill-natured, insinuating, malicious, mean, nasty, sarcastic, scornful, sneering, spiteful, unkind.

sniff *v* breathe, inhale, nose, smell, snuff, snuffle, vent.

sniffy *adj* condescending, contemptuous, disdainful, haughty, scoffing, sneering, supercilious, superior.

snigger *v, n* giggle, laugh, sneer, snicker, snort, titter.

snip *v* clip, crop, cut, nick, notch, prune, shave, slit, trim.

n bargain, bit, clipping, fragment, giveaway, piece, scrap, shred, slit, snippet.

snippet *n* fragment, part, particle, piece, portion, scrap, section, segment, shred, snatch.

snivelling *adj* blubbering, crying, girning, grizzling, mewling, moaning, sniffling, snuffling, weeping, whimpering, whingeing, whining.

snobbery *n* airs, arrogance, condescension, loftiness, lorliness, pretension, pride, side, snobbishness, snootiness, uppishness.

snobbish *adj* arrogant, condescending, dickty, high and mighty, high-hat, hoity-toity, lofty, lordly, patronising, pretentious, snooty, stuck-up, superior, toffee-nosed, uppish, uppity, upstage.

snoop *v* interfere, prodnose, pry, sneak, spy.

snooper *n* busybody, meddler, nosy parker, Paul Pry, prodnose, pry, snoop, spy.

snooze *v* catnap, doze, drowse, kip, nap, nod off, sleep.

n catnap, doze, forty winks, kip, nap, shut-eye, siesta, sleep.

snout *n* muzzle, neb, proboscis, schnozzle, snitch, trunk.

snub *v* check, cold-shoulder, cut, humble, humiliate, mortify, rebuff, rebuke, shame, slight, sneap, squash, squelch, wither.

n affront, brush-off, check, humiliation, insult, put-down, rebuff, rebuke, slap in the face, sneap.

snug *adj* close, close-fitting, comfortable, comfy, compact, cosy, homely, intimate, neat, sheltered, trim, warm.

snuggle *v* cuddle, embrace, hug, nestle, nuzzle.

so far hitherto, thus far, till now, to date.

soak *v* bathe, damp, drench, imbue, immerse, infuse, interfuse, marinate, moisten, penetrate, permeate, saturate, sog, souse, steep, wet.

soaking *adj* drenched, dripping, drookit, saturated, soaked, sodden, sopping, streaming, waterlogged, wringing.

antonym dry.

soar *v* ascend, climb, escalate, fly, mount, plane, rise, rocket, tower, wing.

antonym plummet.

sob *v* bawl, blubber, boohoo, cry, greet, howl, mewl, moan, shed tears, snivel, weep.

sober *adj* abstemious, abstinent, calm, clear-headed, cold, composed, cool, dark, dispassionate, douce, drab, grave, level-headed, lucid, moderate, peaceful, plain, practical, quiet, rational, realistic, reasonable, restrained, sedate, serene, serious, severe, solemn, sombre, sound, staid, steady, subdued, temperate, unexcited, unruffled.

antonyms drunk, excited, frivolous, gay, intemperate, irrational.

sobriety *n* abstemiousness, abstinence, calmness, composure, continence, coolness, gravity, level-headedness, moderation, reasonableness, restraint, sedateness, self-restraint, seriousness, soberness, solemnity, staidness, steadiness, temperance.

antonyms drunkenness, excitement, frivolity.

so-called *adj* alleged, nominal, ostensible, pretended, professed, self-styled, soi-disant, supposed.

sociability *n* affability, chumminess, companionability, congeniality, conviviality, cordiality, friendliness, gregariousness, neighbourliness.

sociable *adj* accessible, affable, approachable, chummy, companionable, conversable, convivial, cordial, familiar, friendly, genial, gregarious, neighbourly, outgoing, social, viscerotonic, warm.

antonyms unfriendly, unsociable, withdrawn.

social *adj* collective, common, communal, community, companionable, friendly, general, gregarious, group, neighbourly, organised, public, sociable, societal.

n ceilidh, do, gathering, get-together, hoolly, hoot(e)nanny, party.

socialise *v* entertain, fraternise, get together, go out, hang out, mix, party.

socialism *n* communism, leftism, Leninism, Marxism, Stalinism, Trotskyism, welfarism.

socialist *adj* commie, communist, leftie, leftist, left-wing, pink, red, Trot, Trotskyist, Trotskyite.

n commie, communist, leftie, leftist, left-winger, parlour pink, pink(o), red, Trot, Trotskyist, Trotskyite, welfarist.

society *n* association, beau monde, brotherhood, camaraderie, circle, civilisation, club, companionship, company, corporation, culture, elite, fellowship, fraternity, fratry, friendship, gentry, Gesellschaft, group, guild, haut monde, humanity, institute, league, mankind, organisation, people, population, sisterhood, the nobs, the public, the smart set, the swells, the toffs, the top drawer, the world, union, upper classes, upper crust, Verein.

sodden *adj* boggy, drenched, drookit, marshy, miry, saturated, soaked, soggy, sopping, waterlogged, wet.

antonym dry.

soft *adj* balmy, bendable, bland, caressing, comfortable, compassionate, cottony, creamy, crumby, cushioned, cushiony, cushy, daft, delicate, diffuse, diffused, dim, dimmed, doughy, downy, ductile, dulcet, easy, easy-going, effeminate, elastic, faint, feathery, feeble-minded, flabby, flaccid, fleecy, flexible, flowing, fluid, foolish, furry, gelatinous, gentle, impressible, indulgent, kind, lash, lax, lenient, liberal, light, limp, low, malleable, mellifluous, mellow, melodious, mild, mouldable, murmured, muted, namby-pamby, non-alcoholic, overindulgent, pale, pampered, pastel, permissive, pitying, plastic, pleasant, pleasing, pliable, pulpy, quaggy, quiet, restful, sensitive, sentimental, shaded, silky, silly, simple, smooth, soothing, soppy, spineless, spongy, squashy, subdued, supple, swampy, sweet, sympathetic, temperate, tender, tender-hearted, undemanding, understated, unprotected, velvety, weak, whispered, yielding.

antonyms hard, harsh, heavy, loud, rigid, rough, severe, strict.

soft spot fondness, liking, partiality, penchant, weakness.

soften *v* abate, allay, alleviate, anneal, appease, assuage, calm, cushion, digest, diminish, ease, emolliate, intenerate, lessen, lighten, lower, macerate, malax, malaxate, melt, mitigate, moderate, modify, mollify, muffle, palliate, quell, relax, soothe, still, subdue, temper.

soften up conciliate, disarm, melt, persuade, soft-soap, weaken, win over.

soft-hearted *adj* benevolent, charitable, clement, compassionate, generous, indulgent, kind, merciful, sentimental, sympathetic, tender, tender-hearted, warm-hearted.

antonym hard-hearted.

soft-pedal *v* de-emphasise, go easy, moderate, play down, subdue, tone down.

antonyms emphasise, play up.

soggy *adj* boggy, dripping, heavy, moist, mushy, pulpy, saturated, soaked, sodden, sopping, soppy, spiritless, spongy, waterlogged.

soil[1] *n* clay, country, dirt, dust, earth, glebe, ground, humus, land, loam, region, terra firma.

soil[2] *v* bedaggle, bedraggle, befoul, begrime, besmirch, besmut, defile, dirty, foul, maculate, muddy, pollute, smear, spatter, spot, stain, sully, tarnish.

soiled *adj* dirty, grimy, maculate, manky, polluted, spotted, stained, sullied, tarnished.

antonyms clean, immaculate.

sojourn *n* peregrination, rest, stay, stop, stopover, visit.

v abide, dwell, lodge, reside, rest, stay, stop, tabernacle, tarry.

solace *n* alleviation, assuagement, comfort, consolation, relief, succour, support.

v allay, alleviate, comfort, console, mitigate, soften, soothe, succour, support.

soldier *n* buff-coat, buff-jerkin, fighter, gallo(w)glass, galoot, ghazi, GI, guardee, guardsman, hoplite, Ironside, jackman, jäger, janissary, jawan, kern(e), lancer, landsknecht, lansquenet, leather-neck, Mameluke, man-at-arms, marine, poilu, redcoat, rifleman, sepoy, serviceman, soldado, squaddy, swad(dy), sweat, Tommy, trooper, warrior.

sole *adj* alone, exclusive, individual, one, only, single, singular, solitary, unique.

antonyms multiple, shared.

solecism *n* absurdity, anacoluthon, blunder, boo-boo, cacology, faux pas, gaffe, gaucherie, impropriety, incongruity, indecorum, lapse, mistake.

solely *adv* alone, completely, entirely, exclusively, merely, only, single-handedly, singly, uniquely.

solemn *adj* august, awed, awe-inspiring, ceremonial, ceremonious, devotional, dignified, earnest, formal, glum, grand, grave, hallowed, holy, imposing, impressive, majestic, momentous, pompous, portentous, religious, reverential, ritual, sacred, sanctified, sedate, serious, sober, sombre, staid, stately, thoughtful, venerable.

antonyms frivolous, gay, light-hearted.

solemnise *v* celebrate, commemorate, dignify, honour, keep, observe.

solemnities *n* celebration, ceremonial, ceremony, formalities, observance, proceedings, rite, ritual.

solemnity *n* dignity, earnestness, grandeur, gravity, impressiveness, momentousness, portentousness, sacredness, sanctity, seriousness, stateliness.

antonym frivolity.

solicit *v* ask, beg, beseech, canvass, crave, entreat, implore, importune, petition, pray, seek, sue, supplicate, tout.

solicitor *n* advocate, attorney, barrister, DA, law-agent, lawmonger, lawyer, notary (public), QC, silk.

solicitous *adj* anxious, apprehensive, ardent, attentive, careful, caring, concerned, eager, earnest, fearful, troubled, uneasy, worried, zealous.

solicitude *n* anxiety, attentiveness, care, concern, considerateness, consideration, disquiet, regard, uneasiness, worry.

solid *adj* agreed, compact, complete, concrete, constant, continuous, cubic(al), decent, dense, dependable, estimable, firm, genuine, good, hard, law-abiding, level-headed, massed, pure, real, reliable, sensible, serious, sober, sound, square, stable, stocky, strong, sturdy, substantial, trusty, unalloyed, unanimous, unbroken, undivided, uninterrupted, united, unmixed, unshakeable, unvaried, upright, upstanding, wealthy, weighty, worthy.

antonyms broken, insubstantial, liquid.

solidarity *n* accord, camaraderie, cohesion, concord(ance), consensus, consentaneity, esprit de corps, harmony, like-mindedness, soundness, stability, team spirit, unanimity, unification, unity.

antonyms discord, division, schism.

solidify *v* cake, clot, coagulate, cohere, congeal, harden, jell, jellify, set.

antonyms dissolve, liquefy, soften.

solitary *adj* alone, cloistered, companionless, de(a)rnful, desolate, friendless, hermitical, hidden, isolated, lone, lonely, lonesome, out-of-the-way, reclusive, remote, retired, secluded, separate, sequestered, single, sole, unfrequented, unsociable, unsocial, untrodden, unvisited.

antonyms accompanied, gregarious.

solitude *n* aloneness, desert, emptiness, isolation, loneliness, privacy, reclusiveness, retirement, seclusion, waste, wasteland, wilderness.

antonym companionship.

solution *n* answer, blend, clarification, compound, decipherment, denouement, disconnection, dissolution, elucidation, emulsion, explanation, explication, key, liquefaction, melting, mix, mixture, resolution, result, solvent, solving, suspension, unfolding, unravelling.

solve *v* answer, clarify, crack, decipher, disentangle, dissolve, elucidate, explain, expound, interpret, resolve, settle, unbind, unfold, unravel, work out.

sombre *adj* dark, dim, dismal, doleful, drab, dull, dusky, funereal, gloomy, grave, joyless, lugubrious, melancholy, mournful, obscure, sad, sepulchral, shadowy, shady, sober, sombrous, subfusc.

antonyms bright, cheerful, happy.

somebody *n* big noise, big shot, big wheel, bigwig, celebrity, dignitary, heavyweight, household name, luminary, magnate, mogul, nabob, name, notable, panjandrum, personage, quidam, star, superstar, VIP.

antonym nobody.

someday *adv* eventually, one day, sometime, ultimately.

antonym never.

somehow *adv* by fair means or foul, by hook or by crook, come hell or high water, come what may, one way or another.

sometimes *adv* at times, from time to time, now and again, now and then, occasionally, off and on, once in a while, otherwhiles.

antonyms always, never.

somnolent *adj* comatose, dozy, drowsy, half-awake, heavy-eyed, oscitant, sleepy, soporific, torpid.

son *n* boy, descendant, disciple, inhabitant, lad(die), native, offspring.

song *n* air, anthem, ballad, barcarol(l)e, canticle, cantilena, canto, canzone, canzonet, carol, chanson, chansonette, chant, chorus, ditty, elegy, epicede, epicedium, epinicion, epithalamion, epithalamium, fit, folk-song, hymn, lay, lied, lilt, lullaby, lyric, madrigal, melody, number, ode, paean, poem, psalm, shanty, strain, tune, volkslied, war-song, wassail.

song and dance ado, commotion, flap, furore, fuss, hoo-ha, kerfuffle, performance, pother, shindig, shindy, squall, stir, tizzy, to-do, tumult, variety, vaudeville.

songster *n* balladeer, chanteuse, chorister, crooner, minstrel, singer, troubadour, vocalist, warbler.

sonorous *adj* full, full-mouthed, full-throated, full-voiced, grandiloquent, high-flown, high-sounding, loud, oro(ro)tund, plangent, resonant, resounding, rich, ringing, rounded, sounding.

soon *adv* anon, betimes, in a minute, in a short time, in the near future, presently, shortly.

soothe *v* allay, alleviate, appease, assuage, calm, coax, comfort, compose, ease, hush, lull, mitigate, mollify, pacify, quiet, relieve, salve, settle, soften, still, tranquillise.

antonyms annoy, irritate, vex.

soothing *adj* anetic, assuasive, balmy, balsamic, calming, demulcent, easeful, emollient, lenitive, palliative, relaxing, restful.

antonyms annoying, irritating, vexing.

soothsayer *n* augur, Chaldee, diviner, foreteller, haruspex, prophet, seer, sibyl.

sophisticated *adj* advanced, blase, citified, complex, complicated, cosmopolitan, couth, cultivated, cultured, delicate, elaborate, highly-developed, intricate, jet-set, mondain, multifaceted, refined, seasoned, subtle, urbane, worldly, worldly-wise, world-weary.

antonyms artless, naïve, simple, unsophisticated.

sophistication *n* culture, elegance, experience, finesse, poise, savoir-faire, savoir-vivre, urbanity, worldliness.

antonyms naïvety, simplicity.

sophistry *n* casuistry, elenchus, fallacy, paralogism, quibble, sophism.

soporific *adj* dormitive, hypnagogic, hypnic, hypnogenetic, hypnogenic, hypnogenous, hypnotic, poppied, sedative, sleep-inducing, sleepy, somniferous, somnolent, tranquillising.

antonyms invigorating, stimulating.

n anaesthetic, hypnic, hypnotic, narcotic, opiate, sedative, tranquilliser.

antonym stimulant.

soppy *adj* cloying, corny, daft, drippy, gushy, lovey-dovey, mawkish, mushy, pathetic, schmaltzy, sentimental, silly, slushy, soft, weepy.

sorcerer *n* angek(k)ok, enchanter, mage, Magian, magician, magus, necromancer, reim-kennar, sorceress, voodoo, warlock, witch, wizard.

sorcery *n* black art, black magic, charm, diablerie, divination, enchantment, hoodoo, incantation, magic, necromancy, pishogue, spell, voodoo, warlockry, witchcraft, witchery, witching, wizardry.

sordid *adj* avaricious, base, corrupt, covetous, debauched, degenerate, degraded, despicable, dingy, dirty, disreputable, filthy, foul, grasping, low, mean, mercenary, miserly, niggardly, rapacious, seamy, seedy, selfish, self-seeking, shabby, shameful, sleazy, slovenly, slummy, squalid, tawdry, unclean, ungenerous, venal, vicious, vile, wretched.

sore *adj* acute, afflicted, aggrieved, angry, annoyed, annoying, burning, chafed, critical, desperate, dire, distressing, extreme, grieved, grievous, harrowing, hurt, inflamed, irked, irritable, irritated, pained, painful, peeved, pressing, raw, reddened, resentful, sensitive, severe, sharp, smarting, stung, tender, touchy, troublesome, upset, urgent, vexed.

n abscess, boil, canker, carbuncle, chafe, gathering, inflammation, swelling, ulcer, wound.

sorrow *n* affliction, anguish, blow, distress, dole, grief, hardship, heartache, heartbreak, lamentation, misery, misfortune, mourning, regret, ruth, sadness, trial, tribulation, trouble, unhappiness, woe, worry.

antonyms happiness, joy.

v agonise, bemoan, bewail, beweep, grieve, lament, moan, mourn, pine, weep.

antonym rejoice.

sorrowful *adj* affecting, afflicted, dejected, depressed, disconsolate, distressing, doleful, grievous, heartbroken, heart-rending, heavy-hearted, lamentable, lugubrious, melancholy, miserable, mournful, painful, piteous, rueful, ruthful, sad, sorry, tearful, unhappy, wae, woebegone, woeful, wretched.

antonyms happy, joyful.

sorry *adj* abject, apologetic, base, commiserative, compassionate, conscience-stricken, contrite, deplorable, disconsolate, dismal, distressed, distressing, grieved, guilt-ridden, mean, melancholy, miserable, mournful, moved, paltry, pathetic, penitent, piteous, pitiable, pitiful, pitying, poor, regretful, remorseful, repentant, ruthful, sad, self-reproachful, shabby, shamefaced, sorrowful, sympathetic, unhappy, unworthy, vile, wretched.

antonym glad.

sort *n* alphasort, brand, breed, category, character, class, denomination, description, family, genre, genus, group, ilk, kidney, kind, make, nature, order, quality, race, species, stamp, style, type, variety.

v alphasort, arrange, assort, catalogue, categorise, choose, class, classify, distribute, divide, file, grade, group, neaten, order, rank, screen, select, separate, systematise, tidy.

sort out clarify, clear up, divide, organise, resolve, segregate, select, separate, sift, tidy up.

so-so *adj* adequate, average, fair, fair to middling, indifferent, middling, moderate, neutral, not bad, OK, ordinary, passable, respectable, run-of-the-mill, tolerable, undistinguished, unexceptional.

soul *n* alma, animation, ardour, being, body, courage, creature, element, embodiment, energy, essence, feeling, fervour, force, incarnation, individual, inner man, inspiration, inspirer, intellect, leader, life, man, mind, mortal, nobility, person, personification, pneuma, psyche, quintessence, reason, spirit, type, vital force, vitality, vivacity, woman.

soulful *adj* eloquent, emotional, expressive, heartfelt, meaningful, mournful, moving, profound, sensitive.

soulless *adj* callous, cold, cruel, dead, ignoble, inhuman, lifeless, mean, mean-spirited, mechanical, soul-destroying, spiritless, unfeeling, uninteresting, unkind, unsympathetic.

sound[1] *n* description, din, earshot, hearing, idea, implication, impression, look, noise, range, report, resonance, reverberation, tenor, tone, utterance, voice.

v announce, appear, articulate, chime, declare, echo, enunciate, express, knell, look, peal, pronounce, resonate, resound, reverberate, ring, seem, signal, toll, utter, voice.

sound[2] *adj* complete, copper-bottomed, correct, deep, entire, established, fair, fere, firm, fit, hale, healthy, hearty, intact, just, level-headed, logical, orthodox, peaceful, perfect, proper, proven, prudent, rational, reasonable, recognised, reliable, reputable, responsible, right, right-thinking, robust, safe, secure, sensible, solid, solvent, stable, sturdy, substantial, thorough, tried-and-true, true, trustworthy, unbroken, undamaged, undisturbed, unhurt, unimpaired, uninjured, untroubled, valid, vigorous, wakeless, well-founded, well-grounded, whole, wise.

antonyms shaky, unfit, unreliable, unsound.

sound[3] *v* examine, fathom, inspect, investigate, measure, plumb, probe, test.

sound out ask, canvass, examine, probe, pump, question.

sound[4] *n* channel, estuary, firth, fjord, inlet, passage, strait, voe.

soup *n* bisque, broth, chowder, consomme, julienne, potage.

sour *adj* acerb(ic), acetic, acid, acidulated, acrid, acrimonious, bad, bitter, churlish, crabbed, curdled, cynical, disagreeable, discontented, embittered, fermented, grouchy, grudging, ill-natured, ill-tempered, inharmonious, jaundiced, off, peevish, pungent, rancid, rank, sharp, tart, turned, ungenerous, unpleasant, unsavoury, unsuccessful, unsweet, unwholesome, vinegarish, vinegary, waspish.

antonyms good-natured, sweet.

v alienate, curdle, disenchant, embitter, envenom, exacerbate, exasperate, spoil.

source *n* author, authority, begetter, beginning, cause, commencement, derivation, fons et origo, fountain-head, informant, klondike, milch-cow, mine, origin, originator, primordium, quarry, rise, spring, water-head, well-head, ylem.

sourpuss *n* crosspatch, grouse, grumbler, grump, killjoy, kvetch, misery, shrew, whiner, whinger.

souse *v* douse, drench, dunk, immerse, marinate, pickle, plunge, soak, steep.

souvenir *n* fairing, gift, keepsake, memento, memory, relic, remembrance(r), reminder, token.

sovereign *n* autarch, chief, dynast, emperor, empress, kaiser, king, monarch, potentate, prince, queen, ruler, shah, tsar.

adj absolute, august, chief, dominant, effectual, efficacious, efficient, excellent, imperial, kingly, majestic, monarch(ic)al, paramount, predominant, principal, queenly, regal, royal, ruling, supreme, unlimited.

sovereignty *n* ascendancy, domination, imperium, kingship, primacy, raj, regality, supremacy, suzerainty, sway.

sow *v* broadcast, disseminate, drill, implant, inseminate, lodge, plant, scatter, seed, spread, strew.

space *n* accommodation, amplitude, berth, blank, capacity, chasm, diastema, distance, duration, elbow-room, expanse, extension, extent, gap, house-room, interval, lacuna, leeway, margin, omission, period, place, play, room, scope, seat, spaciousness, span, time, volume.

spacious *adj* ample, big, broad, capacious, comfortable, commodious, expansive, extensive, huge, large, roomy, sizable, uncrowded, vast, wide.

antonyms confined, cramped, narrow, small.

spadework *n* donkey-work, drudgery, foundation, groundwork, labour, preparation.

span *n* amount, compass, distance, duration, extent, length, period, reach, scope, spell, spread, stretch, term.

v arch, bridge, cover, cross, encompass, extend, link, overarch, traverse, vault.

spank *v* belt, cane, cuff, leather, slap, slipper, smack, tan, wallop, whack.

spanking *adj* brand-new, brisk, energetic, fast, fine, gleaming, invigorating, lively, quick, smart, snappy, speedy, swift, vigorous.

antonym slow.

spar *v* argue, bicker, contend, contest, dispute, fall out, scrap, skirmish, spat, squabble, tiff, wrangle, wrestle.

spare *adj* additional, economical, emergency, extra, free, frugal, gash, gaunt, lank, lean, leftover, meagre, modest, odd, over, remaining, scanty, slender, slight, slim, sparing, superfluous, supernumerary, surplus, unoccupied, unused, unwanted, wiry.

antonyms corpulent, necessary, profuse.

v afford, allow, bestow, give quarter, grant, leave, let off, pardon, part with, refrain from, release, relinquish.

sparing *adj* careful, chary, cost-conscious, economical, frugal, lenten, prudent, saving, thrifty.

antonyms lavish, liberal, unsparing.

spark *n* atom, flake, flare, flash, flaught, flicker, gleam, glint, hint, jot, scintilla, scintillation, scrap, spit, trace, vestige.

v animate, cause, excite, inspire, kindle, occasion, precipitate, provoke, set off, start, stimulate, stir, trigger.

sparkle *v* beam, bubble, coruscate, dance, effervesce, emicate, fizz, fizzle, flash, gleam, glint, glisten, glister, glitter, glow, scintillate, shimmer, shine, spark, twinkle, wink.

n animation, brilliance, coruscation, dash, dazzle, effervescence, elan, emication, flash, flicker, gaiety, gleam, glint, glitter, life, panache, pizzazz, radiance, scintillation, spark, spirit, twinkle, vim, vitality, vivacity, wit, zip.

sparkling *adj* animated, bubbly, carbonated, coruscating, effervescent, emicant, fizzy, flashing, frizzante, gleaming, glistening, glittering, scintillating, twinkling, witty.

antonyms dull, flat.

sparse *adj* infrequent, meagre, scanty, scarce, scattered, sporadic.

antonyms dense, lush, thick.

spartan *adj* abstemious, abstinent, ascetic, austere, bleak, disciplined, extreme, frugal, hardy, joyless, plain, rigorous, self-denying, severe, stern, strict, stringent, temperate, unflinching.

spasm *n* access, burst, contraction, convulsion, eruption, fit, frenzy, jerk, outburst, paroxysm, seizure, throe, twitch.

spasmodic *adj* convulsive, erratic, fitful, intermittent, irregular, jerky, occasional, paroxysmal, sporadic.

antonyms continuous, uninterrupted.

spate *n* deluge, epidemic, flood, flow, outpouring, rush, torrent.

spatter *v* bedaub, bespatter, bespot, besprinkle, bestrew, daub, dirty, scatter, soil, speckle, splash, splodge, spray, sprinkle.

speak *v* address, advert to, allude to, argue, articulate, breathe, comment on, communicate, converse, deal with, declaim, declare, discourse, discuss, enunciate, express, harangue, lecture, mention, plead, pronounce, refer to, say, speechify, spiel, state, talk, tell, utter, voice.

speak to accost, address, admonish, apostrophise, bring to book, dress down, lecture, rebuke, reprimand, scold, tell off, tick off, upbraid, warn.

speaker *n* lecturer, mouthpiece, orator, prolocutor, speechifier, speech-maker, spieler, spokesman, spokesperson, spokeswoman.

spearhead *v* front, head, initiate, launch, lead, pioneer.

special *adj* appropriate, certain, characteristic, chief, choice, detailed, distinctive, distinguished, especial, exceptional, exclusive, extraordinary, festive, gala, important, individual, intimate, main, major, memorable, momentous, particular, peculiar, precise, primary, red-letter, select, significant, specialised, specific, uncommon, unique, unusual.

antonyms common, normal, ordinary, usual.

specialist *n* adept, authority, connoisseur, consultant, expert, master, professional, proficient.

speciality *n* bag, forte, metier, pièce de resistance, scene, special, specialty, strength.

species *n* breed, category, class, collection, denomination, description, genus, group, kind, sort, type, variety.

specific *adj* characteristic, clear-cut, definite, delimitative, distinguishing, especial, exact, explicit, express, limited, particular, peculiar, precise, special, unambiguous, unequivocal.

antonyms general, vague.

specification *n* condition, description, detail, enumeration, item, itemisation, listing, particular, qualification, requirement, stipulation.

specify *v* cite, define, delineate, describe, designate, detail, enumerate, indicate, individualise, itemise, list, mention, name, particularise, spell out, stipulate.

specimen *n* copy, embodiment, ensample, example, exemplar, exemplification, exhibit, illustration, individual, instance, model, paradigm, pattern, person, proof, representative, sample, type.

specious *adj* casuistic, deceptive, fallacious, false, misleading, pageant, plausible, sophistic, sophistical, unsound, untrue.

antonym valid.

speck *n* atom, bit, blemish, blot, defect, dot, fault, flaw, fleck, grain, iota, jot, macula, mark, mite, modicum, mote, particle, shred, speckle, spot, stain, tittle, trace, whit.

speckled *adj* brinded, brindle(d), dappled, dotted, flecked, fleckered, freckled, lentiginous, mottled, spotted, spotty, sprinkled, stippled.

spectacle *n* curiosity, display, event, exhibition, extravaganza, marvel, pageant, parade, performance, phenomenon, scene, show, sight, wonder.

spectacles *n* cheaters, eyeglasses, glasses, goggles, lorgnette, lorgnon, opera-glasses, pince-nez, specs.

spectacular *adj* amazing, breathtaking, daring, dazzling, dramatic, eye-catching, fabulous, fantastic, grand, impressive, magnificent, marked, remarkable, sensational, splendid, staggering, striking, stunning.

antonyms ordinary, unspectacular.

n display, extravaganza, pageant, show, spectacle.

spectator *n* beholder, bystander, eye-witness, looker-on, observer, onlooker, passer-by, viewer, watcher, witness.

antonyms contestant, participant, player.

spectral *adj* disembodied, eerie, ghostly, incorporeal, insubstantial, phantasmal, phantom, shadowy, spooky, supernatural, uncanny, unearthly, weird.

spectre *n* apparition, ghost, larva, lemur, phantom(a), presence, revenant, shade, shadow, spirit, vision, wraith.

speculate *v* cogitate, conjecture, consider, contemplate, deliberate, gamble, guess, hazard, hypothesise, meditate, muse, reflect, risk, scheme, suppose, surmise, theorise, venture, wonder.

speculation *n* conjecture, consideration, contemplation, deliberation, flight of fancy, gamble, gambling, guess, guesswork, hazard, hypothesis, ideology, land-jobbing, opinion, risk, supposition, surmise, theory.

speculative *adj* abstract, academic, chancy, conjectural, dicey, hazardous, hypothetical, iffish, iffy, notional, projected, risky, suppositional, tentative, theoretical, uncertain, unpredictable.

speech *n* address, articulation, colloquy, communication, conversation, dialect, dialogue, diction, discourse, discussion, disquisition, enunciation, harangue, homily, idiom, intercourse, jargon, language, lecture, lingo, oration, parlance, parole, peroration, say, spiel, talk, tongue, utterance, voice, winged words.

speechless *adj* aghast, amazed, astounded, dazed, dumb, dumbfounded, dumbstruck, inarticulate, mum, mute, obmutescent, shocked, silent, thunderstruck, tongue-tied, wordless.

speed *n* acceleration, celerity, dispatch, expedition, fleetness, haste, hurry, lick, momentum, pace, precipitation, quickness, rapidity, rush, swiftness, tempo, velocity.

v advance, aid, assist, belt, bomb, boost, bowl along, career, dispatch, expedite, facilitate, flash, fleet, further, gallop, hasten, help, highball, hurry, impel, lick, press on, promote, put one's foot down, quicken, race, rush, sprint, step on it, step on the gas, step on the juice, tear, urge, vroom, zap, zoom.

antonyms delay, hamper, restrain, slow.

speedily *adv* fast, hastily, hurriedly, posthaste, promptly, quickly, rapidly, swiftly, ventre à terre.

antonym slowly.

speedy *adj* clipping, expeditious, express, fast, fleet, hasty, headlong, hurried, immediate, nimble, precipitate, prompt, quick, rapid, summary, swift, winged, zappy.

antonyms dilatory, slow, tardy.

spell[1] *n* bout, course, innings, interval, patch, period, season, stint, stretch, term, time, turn.

spell[2] *n* abracadabra, allure, bewitchment, charm, conjuration, enchantment, exorcism, fascination, glamour, hex, incantation, jettatura, love-charm, magic, open sesame, paternoster, philtre, rune, sorcery, trance, weird, witchery.

spell[3] *v* augur, herald, imply, indicate, mean, portend, presage, promise, signal, signify, suggest.

spell out clarify, elucidate, emphasise, explain, specify.

spellbound *adj* bemused, bewitched, captivated, charmed, enchanted, enthralled, entranced, fascinated, gripped, hooked, mesmerised, possessed, rapt, transfixed, transported.

spend *v* apply, bestow, blow, blue, concentrate, consume, cough up, deplete, devote, disburse, dispense, dissipate, drain, employ, empty, exhaust, expend, fill, fork out, fritter, invest, lavish, lay out, occupy, pass, pay out, shed, shell out, splash out, squander, use, use up, waste.

antonyms hoard, save.

spendthrift *n* big spender, prodigal, profligate, spendall, spender, squanderer, unthrift, waster, wastrel.

antonyms hoarder, miser, saver.

adj extravagant, improvident, prodigal, profligate, thriftless, wasteful.

spent *adj* all in, burnt out, bushed, consumed, dead beat, debilitated, dog-tired, done in, drained, exhausted, expended, fagged (out), finished, gone, jiggered, knackered, played out, prostrate, shattered, tired out, used up, weakened, wearied, weary, whacked, worn out, zonked.

spew *v* belch, disgorge, posset, puke, regurgitate, retch, spit out, throw up, vomit.

sphere *n* ball, capacity, circle, compass, department, domain, employment, field, function, globe, globule, milieu, orb, province, range, rank, realm, scope, spheroid, spherule, station, stratum, territory.

spherical *adj* globate, globed, globe-shaped, globoid, globose, globular, orbicular, rotund, round.

spice *n* colour, excitement, flavouring, gusto, kick, life, pep, piquancy, relish, savour, seasoning, tang, zap, zest, zip.

spick and span clean, immaculate, neat, polished, scrubbed, shipshape, spotless, spruce, tidy, trim, well-kept.

antonyms dirty, untidy.

spicy *adj* aromatic, flavoursome, fragrant, hot, improper, indecorous, indelicate, off-colour, piquant, pointed, pungent, racy, ribald, risque, savoury, scandalous, seasoned, sensational, showy, suggestive, tangy, titillating, unseemly.

antonym bland.

spiel *v* harangue, hold forth, lecture, orate, recite, sermonise, speechify, spout.

n harangue, oration, patter, pitch, recital, sales patter, sermon, speech.

spike *n* barb, nail, point, prong, spine, spire, tine.

v block, foil, frustrate, impale, reject, spear, spit, stick, thwart.

spill *v* discharge, disgorge, overflow, overturn, scatter, shed, slop, slosh, upset.

n accident, cropper, fall, overturn, tumble, upset.

spill the beans blab, blow the gaff, give the game away, grass, inform, let the cat out of the bag, rat, split, squeal, tattle.

spin *v* birl, concoct, develop, gyrate, gyre, hurtle, invent, narrate, pirouette, purl, recount, reel, relate, revolve, rotate, spirt, swim, swirl, tell, turn, twirl, twist, unfold, wheel, whirl.

n agitation, commotion, drive, flap, gyration, hurl, panic, pirouette, revolution, ride, roll, run, state, tizzy, turn, twist, whirl.

spin out amplify, delay, extend, lengthen, maintain, pad out, prolong, prolongate, protract, sustain.

spindle *n* arbor, axis, axle, fusee, pivot.

spindly *adj* attenuate(d), gangling, gangly, lanky, leggy, skeletal, skinny, spidery, spindle-shanked, thin, twiggy, weedy.

antonyms stocky, thickset.

spine *n* backbone, barb, needle, quill, rachis, ray, spicule, spiculum, spike, spur, vertebrae, vertebral column.

spine-chilling *adj* bloodcurdling, eerie, frightening, hair-raising, horrifying, scary, spine-tingling, spooky, terrifying.

spineless *adj* cowardly, faint-hearted, feeble, gutless, inadequate, ineffective, irresolute, lily-livered, soft, spiritless, squeamish, submissive, vacillating, weak, weak-kneed, weak-willed, wet, wishy-washy, yellow.

antonyms brave, strong.

spiny *adj* acanthaceous, acanthous, briery, prickly, spicular, spiculate, spiniferous, spinigerous, spinose, spinous, thistly, thorny.

spiral *adj* circular, cochlear, cochleate, coiled, corkscrew, gyral, gyroidal, helical, scrolled, spiraliform, voluted, volutoid, whorled, winding.

n coil, convolution, corkscrew, curlicue, gyre, helix, screw, volute, volution, whorl.

spire *n* cone, flèche, peak, pinnacle, point, shoot, spike, sprout, stalk, steeple, summit, tip, top.

spirit *n* air, animation, apparition, ardour, Ariel, atmosphere, attitude, backbone, bravura, breath, brio, character, complexion, courage, daemon, dauntlessness, deva, disposition, div, djinni, earnestness, energy, enterprise, enthusiasm, entrain, Erdgeist, esprit follet, essence, familiar, faun, feeling, feelings, fire, foison, force, gameness, geist, genie, genius, genius loci, ghost, ghoul, gist, grit, guts, humour, intent, intention, jinnee, jinni, ka, kobold, life, liveliness, manito(u), marid, meaning, mettle, mood, morale, motivation, outlook, phantom, pneuma, psyche, purport, purpose, python, quality, resolution, resolve, revenant, sense, shade, shadow, soul, sparkle, spectre, spook, sprite, spunk, stout-heartedness, substance, sylph, temper, temperament, tenor, tone, verve, vigour, vision, vivacity, warmth, water-horse, water-nymph, water-rixie, water-sprite, Weltgeist, wili, will, will power, Zeitgeist, zest.

v abduct, abstract, capture, carry, convey, kidnap, purloin, remove, seize, snaffle, steal, whisk.

spirited *adj* active, animated, ardent, bold, courageous, energetic, game, gamy, high-spirited, lively, mettlesome, plucky, sparkling, sprightly, spunky, stomachful, vigorous, vivacious.

antonyms lazy, spiritless, timid.

spiritless *adj* anaemic, apathetic, dejected, depressed, despondent, dispirited, droopy, dull, lacklustre, languid, lifeless, listless, low, melancholic, melancholy, mopy, torpid, unenthusiastic, unmoved, wishy-washy.

antonym spirited.

spirits *n* alcohol, fire-water, hooch, liquor, moonshine, strong drink, strong liquor, the hard stuff.

spiritual *adj* aery, devotional, divine, ecclesiastical, ethereal, ghostly, holy, immaterial, incorporeal, otherwordly, pneumatic, pure, religious, sacred, unfleshly, unworldly.

antonyms material, physical.

spit *v* discharge, drizzle, eject, expectorate, hawk, hiss, spew, splutter, sputter.

n dribble, drool, expectoration, phlegm, saliva, slaver, spittle, sputum.

spite *n* animosity, bitchiness, despite, gall, grudge, hate, hatred, ill-nature, malevolence, malice, malignity, pique, rancour, spitefulness, spleen, venom, viciousness.

antonyms affection, goodwill.

v annoy, discomfit, gall, harm, hurt, injure, irk, irritate, needle, nettle, offend, peeve, pique, provoke, put out, vex.

spiteful *adj* barbed, bitchy, catty, cruel, ill-disposed, ill-natured, malevolent, malicious, malignant, nasty, rancorous, snide, splenetic, vengeful, venomous, vindictive, waspish.

antonyms affectionate, charitable.

spitting image clone, dead ringer, dead spit, double, likeness, lookalike, picture, replica, ringer, spit, twin.

splash *v* bathe, batter, bespatter, blazon, break, broadcast, buffet, dabble, dash, flaunt, flouse, floush, headline, paddle, plash, plaster, plop, plunge, publicise, shower, slop, slosh, smack, spatter, splodge, spray, spread, sprinkle, squirt, strew, strike, surge, tout, trumpet, wade, wallow, wash, wet.

n burst, dash, display, effect, excitement, impact, ostentation, patch, publicity, sensation, spattering, splatter, splodge, splurge, stir, touch.

splash out invest in, lash out, push the boat out, spend, splurge.

spleen *n* acrimony, anger, animosity, animus, bad temper, bile, biliousness, bitterness, gall, hatred, hostility, ill-humour, ill-will, malevolence, malice, malignity, peevishness, petulance, pique, rancour, resentment, spite, spitefulness, venom, vindictiveness, wrath.

splendid *adj* admirable, beaming, bright, brilliant, costly, dazzling, excellent, exceptional, fantastic, fine, first-class, glittering, glorious, glowing, gorgeous, grand, great, heroic, illustrious, imposing, impressive, lavish, lustrous, luxurious, magnificent, marvellous, ornate, outstanding, phenom, pontific(al), radiant, rare, refulgent, remarkable, renowned, resplendent, rich, splendiferous, splend(o)rous, sterling, sublime, sumptuous, superb, supreme, tiptop, top-hole, top-notch, topping, wonderful.

antonyms drab, ordinary, run-of-the-mill.

splendour *n* brightness, brilliance, ceremony, dazzle, display, effulgence, fulgo(u)r, glory, gorgeousness, grandeur, lustre, magnificence, majesty, pomp, radiance, refulgence, renown, resplendence, richness, show, solemnity, spectacle, stateliness, sumptuousness.

splenetic *adj* acid, atrabilious, bilious, bitchy, choleric, churlish, crabbed, crabby, cross, envenomed, fretful, irascible, irritable, morose, peevish, petulant, rancorous, sour, spiteful, sullen, testy, touchy.

splice *v* bind, braid, entwine, graft, interlace, interlink, intertwine, intertwist, interweave, join, knit, marry, mesh, plait, tie, unite, wed, yoke.

splinter *n* chip, flake, flinder, fragment, needle, paring, shaving, sliver, spall, spalt, spicule, stob.

v disintegrate, fracture, fragment, shatter, shiver, smash, spalt, split.

split *v* allocate, allot, apportion, betray, bifurcate, branch, break, burst, cleave, crack, delaminate, disband, distribute, disunite, divaricate, diverge, divide, divulge, fork, gape, grass, halve, inform on, open, parcel out, part, partition, peach, rend, rip, separate, share out, skive, slash, slice up, slit, sliver, snap, spell, splinter, squeal.

n breach, break, break-up, cleft, crack, damage, dichotomy, difference, discord, disruption, dissension, disunion, divergence, division, estrangement, fissure, gap, partition, race, rent, rift, rip, rupture, schism, scissure, separation, slash, slit, tear.

adj ambivalent, bisected, broken, cleft, cloven, cracked, divided, dual, fractured, ruptured, twofold.

split hairs cavil, find fault, nit-pick, over-refine, pettifog, quibble.

split up break up, disband, dissolve, divorce, part, part company, separate.

spoil *v* addle, baby, blemish, bugger, butcher, cocker, coddle, cosset, curdle, damage, debase, decay, decompose, deface, despoil, destroy, deteriorate, disfigure, go bad, go off, harm, impair, indulge, injure, jigger, louse up, mar, mildew, mollycoddle, pamper, plunder, putrefy, queer, rot, ruin, screw, spoon-feed, turn, upset, wreck.

spoils *n* acquisitions, boodle, booty, gain, haul, loot, pickings, pillage, plunder, prey, prizes, rapine, spoliation, swag, winnings.

spoil-sport *n* damper, dog in the manger, killjoy, mar-sport, meddler, misery, party-pooper, wet blanket, wowser.

spoken *adj* declared, expressed, oral, phonetic, said, stated, told, unwritten, uttered, verbal, viva voce, voiced.

antonyms unspoken, written.

sponge *v* cadge, freeload, mooch, scrounge, shool.

sponger *n* bloodsucker, cadge, cadger, freeloader, hanger-on, leech, moocher, parasite, scrounger, smell-feast.

spongy *adj* absorbent, bibulous, cushioned, cushiony, elastic, fozy, light, porous, springy.

sponsor *n* angel, backer, godparent, guarantor, patron, promoter, surety, underwriter.

v back, finance, fund, guarantee, patronise, promote, subsidise, underwrite.

spontaneous *adj* extempore, free, impromptu, impulsive, instinctive, natural, ultroneous, unbidden, uncompelled, unconstrained, unforced, unhesitating, unlaboured, unpremeditated, unprompted, unstudied, untaught, voluntary, willing.

antonyms forced, planned, studied.

spontaneously *adv* ex mero motu, ex proprio motu, extempore, freely, impromptu, impulsively, instinctively, of one's own accord, off the cuff, on impulse, unprompted, voluntarily, willingly.

spoof *n* bluff, burlesque, caricature, con, deception, fake, game, hoax, joke, lampoon, leg-pull, mockery, parody, prank, satire, send-up, take-off, travesty, trick.

spooky *adj* chilling, creepy, eerie, eldritch, frightening, ghostly, hair-raising, mysterious, scary, spine-chilling, supernatural, uncanny, unearthly, weird.

spoonerism *n* marrowsky, transposition.

spoon-feed *v* baby, cosset, featherbed, indulge, mollycoddle, pamper, spoil.

sporadic *adj* erratic, infrequent, intermittent, irregular, isolated, occasional, random, scattered, spasmodic, uneven.

antonyms frequent, regular.

sport *n* activity, amusement, badinage, banter, brick, buffoon, butt, dalliance, derision, diversion, entertainment, exercise, fair game, frolic, fun, game, jest, joking, kidding, laughing-stock, merriment, mirth, mockery, pastime, play, plaything, raillery, recreation, ridicule, sportsman, teasing.

v caper, dally, display, disport, exhibit, flirt, frolic, gambol, philander, play, romp, show off, toy, trifle, wear.

sporting *adj* considerate, fair, gentlemanly, sportsmanlike.

antonyms unfair, ungentlemanly, unsporting.

sportive *adj* coltish, frisky, frolicsome, gamesome, gay, jaunty, joyous, kittenish, lively, merry, playful, prankish, rollicking, skittish, sprightly.

sporty *adj* athletic, casual, energetic, flamboyant, flashy, gay, hearty, informal, jaunty, jazzy, loud, natty, outdoor, raffish, rakish, showy, snazzy, stylish, trendy.

spot *n* bit, blemish, blot, blotch, daub, difficulty, discoloration, flaw, little, locality, location, macula, maculation, macule, mark, mess, morsel, pimple, place, plight, plook, point, position, predicament, pustule, quandary, scene, site, situation, smudge, speck, splash, stain, stigma, taint, trouble.

v besmirch, blot, descry, detect, dirty, discern, dot, espy, fleck, identify, maculate, mark, mottle, observe, recognise, see, sight, soil, spatter, speckle, splodge, splotch, stain, sully, taint, tarnish.

spotless *adj* blameless, chaste, faultless, flawless, gleaming, immaculate, innocent, irreproachable, pure, shining, snowy, spick and span, unblemished, unimpeachable, unstained, unsullied, untarnished, virgin, virginal, white.

antonyms dirty, impure, spotted.

spotlight *v* accentuate, emphasise, feature, focus on, highlight, illuminate, point up, throw into relief.

n attention, emphasis, fame, interest, limelight, notoriety, public eye.

spotted *adj* brinded, brindle(d), dappled, dotted, flecked, fleckered, guttate(d), macled, macular, maculate, maculose, mottled, parded, pied, polka-dot, specked, speckled.

antonym spotless.

spotty *adj* blotchy, pimpled, pimply, plooky, speckled, spotted.

spouse *n* better half, companion, consort, fere, helpmate, husband, mate, partner, wife.

spout *v* declaim, discharge, emit, erupt, expatiate, gush, jet, orate, pontificate, rabbit on, ramble (on), rant, sermonise, shoot, speechify, spiel, spray, spurt, squirt, stream, surge.

n chute, fistula, fountain, gargoyle, geyser, jet, nozzle, outlet, rose, spray.

sprawl *v* flop, loll, lounge, ramble, recline, repose, slouch, slump, spread, straggle, trail.

spray[1] *v* atomise, diffuse, douse, drench, scatter, shower, sprinkle, wet.

n aerosol, atomiser, drizzle, droplets, foam, froth, mist, moisture, spindrift, spoondrift, sprinkler.

spray[2] *n* bough, branch, corsage, garland, shoot, sprig, wreath.

spread *v* advertise, arrange, array, blazon, bloat, broadcast, broaden, bruit, cast, circulate, couch, cover, diffuse, dilate, dispread, disseminate, distribute, divulgate, divulge, effuse, escalate, expand, extend, fan out, furnish, lay, metastasise, multiply, mushroom, open, overlay, prepare, proclaim, proliferate, promulgate, propagate, publicise, publish, radiate, scatter, set, shed, sprawl, stretch, strew, swell, transmit, unfold, unfurl, unroll, widen.

antonyms close, compress, contain, fold.

n advance, advancement, array, banquet, blow-out, compass, cover, development, diffusion, dispersion, dissemination, divulgation, divulgence, escalation, expanse, expansion, extent, feast, increase, period, proliferation, ranch, reach, repast, span, spreading, stretch, suffusion, sweep, term, transmission.

spree *n* bacchanalia, bender, binge, blind, bum, carouse, debauch, fling, jag, jamboree, junketing, orgy, randan, razzle-dazzle, revel, splurge, tear.

sprightly *adj* active, agile, airy, alert, animated, blithe, brisk, cheerful, energetic, frolicsome, gamesome, gay, hearty, jaunty, joyous, lively, nimble, perky, playful, spirited, sportive, spry, vivacious.

antonym inactive.

spring[1] *v* appear, arise, bounce, bound, burgeon, come, dance, derive, descend, develop, emanate, emerge, grow, hop, issue, jump, leap, mushroom, originate, proceed, rebound, recoil, shoot up, sprout, start, stem, vault.

n bounce, bounciness, bound, buck, buoyancy, elasticity, flexibility, gambado, give, hop, jump, leap, rebound, recoil, resilience, saltation, springiness, vault.

spring[2] *n* beginning, cause, eye, fountain-head, origin, root, source, well, well-spring.

springy *adj* bouncy, buoyant, elastic, flexible, resilient, rubbery, spongy, stretchy.

antonyms rigid, stiff.

sprinkle *v* asperge, diversify, dot, dredge, dust, pepper, powder, scatter, seed, shower, sparge, spatter, spray, strew.

sprinkling *n* admixture, dash, dusting, few, handful, scatter, scattering, smattering, sprinkle, touch, trace.

sprint *v* belt, dart, dash, gallop, hare, hotfoot, race, run, scamper, shoot, tear, whiz.

sprite *n* apparition, brownie, dryad, elf, fairy, goblin, imp, kelpie, leprechaun, naiad, nymph, pixie, pouke, puck, spirit, sylph.

sprout *v* bud, develop, germinate, grow, pullulate, push, shoot, spring, vegetate.

spruce *adj* dainty, dapper, elegant, natty, neat, sleek, slick, smart, smirk, trig, trim, well-groomed, well-turned-out.

antonyms dishevelled, untidy.

spruce up groom, neaten, preen, primp, smarten up, tidy, titivate.

spry *adj* active, agile, alert, brisk, energetic, nimble, nippy, peppy, quick, ready, sprightly, supple.

antonyms doddering, inactive, lethargic.

spunk *n* backbone, bottle, chutzpah, courage, gameness, grit, guts, heart, mettle, nerve, pluck, resolution, spirit, toughness.

antonym funk.

spur *v* animate, drive, goad, impel, incite, poke, press prick, prod, prompt, propel, stimulate, urge.

antonym curb.

n fillip, goad, impetus, impulse, incentive, incitement, inducement, motive, prick, rowel, stimulus.

antonym curb.

spurious *adj* adulterate, adulterine, apocryphal, artificial, bastard, bogus, contrived, counterfeit, deceitful, dog, fake, false, feigned, forged, illegitimate, imitation, mock, phoney, pretended, pseudish, pseudo, sham, simulated, specious, suppositious, unauthentic.

antonyms authentic, genuine, real.

spurn *v* cold-shoulder, contemn, cut, despise, disdain, disregard, rebuff, reject, repulse, scorn, slight, snub, turn down.

antonym embrace.

spurt *v* burst, effuse, erupt, gush, jet, shoot, spew, squirt, surge.

n access, burst, effusion, fit, rush, spate, surge.

spy *n* beagle, double agent, fifth columnist, foreign agent, mole, scout, secret agent, secret service man, snooper, spook, undercover agent.

v descry, discover, espy, glimpse, notice, observe, spot.

squabble *v* argue, bicker, brawl, clash, dispute, fall out, fight, quarrel, row, scrap, spat, tiff, wrangle.

n argument, barney, clash, disagreement, dispute, fight, rhubarb, row, scrap, set-to, spat, tiff.

squad *n* band, brigade, company, crew, force, gang, group, outfit, team, troop.

squalid *adj* broken-down, decayed, dingy, dirty, disgusting, fetid, filthy, foul, low, nasty, neglected, poverty-stricken, repulsive, run-down, seedy, sleazy, slovenly, slummy, sordid, uncared-for, unclean, unkempt.

antonyms clean, pleasant.

squall *n* blow, drow, gale, gust, hurricane, storm, tempest, williwaw, wind-storm.

squally *adj* blowy, blustery, gusty, rough, stormy, tempestuous, turbulent, wild, windy.

squalor *n* decay, dinginess, filth, foulness, meanness, neglect, sleaziness, squalidness, wretchedness.

squander *v* blow, blue, consume, dissipate, expend, fritter away, lavish, misspend, misuse, scatter, spend, splurge, throw away, waste.

square *v* accommodate, accord, adapt, adjust, agree, align, appease, balance, bribe, conform, correspond, corrupt, discharge, fit, fix, harmonise, level, liquidate, match, quit, reconcile, regulate, rig, satisfy, settle, suborn, suit, tailor, tally, true.

adj above-board, bourgeois, broad, complete, conservative, conventional, decent, equitable, ethical, even, exact, fair, fitting, full, genuine, honest, just, old-fashioned, on the level, opposed, orthodox, quadrate, right-angled, satisfying, solid, straight, straightforward, strait-laced, stuffy, suitable, thick-set, traditional, true, unequivocal, unhip, upright.

n antediluvian, conformer, conformist, conservative, conventionalist, die-hard, fuddy-duddy, (old) fogy, stick-in-the-mud, traditionalist.

squash *v* annihilate, compress, crowd, crush, distort, flatten, humiliate, mash, pound, press, pulp, quash, quell, silence, smash, snub, squelch, stamp, suppress, trample.

antonyms elongate, stretch.

squashy *adj* mushy, pappy, pulpy, soft, spongy, squelchy, squishy, yielding.

antonym firm.

squat *adj* chunky, dumpy, fubby, short, squabby, stocky, stubby, stumpy, thickset.

antonyms lanky, slender.

v absquatulate, bend, camp out, crouch, hunch, hunker, ruck, settle, stoop.

squawk *v* cackle, complain, crow, cry, grouse, hoot, protest, screech, shriek, squeal, yelp.

squeak *v* chirk, peep, pipe, shrill, squeal, whine, yelp.

squeal *n* scream, screech, shriek, ululation, wail, yell, yelp, yowl.

v betray, blab, complain, grass, inform on, moan, peach, protest, rat on, scream, screech, shout, shriek, shrill, snitch, squawk, ululate, wail, yelp.

squeamish *adj* coy, delicate, fastidious, finicky, nauseous, particular, prissy, prudish, punctilious, qualmish, queasy, queer, reluctant, scrupulous, sick, sickish, strait-laced.

squeeze *v* bleed, chirt, clasp, clutch, compress, cram, crowd, crush, cuddle, embrace, enfold, extort, force, grip, hug, jam, jostle, lean on, milk, nip, oppress, pack, pinch, press, pressurise, ram, scrounge, squash, strain, stuff, thrust, wedge, wrest, wring.

n clasp, congestion, crowd, crush, embrace, grasp, handclasp, hold, hug, jam, press, pressure, restriction, squash.

squint *adj* askew, aslant, awry, cockeyed, crooked, indirect, oblique, off-centre, skew-whiff, strabismic.

antonym straight.

squire *v* accompany, attend, conduct, escort.

squirm *v* agonise, fidget, flounder, move, shift, squiggle, twist, wiggle, wriggle, writhe.

squirt *v* chirt, discharge, ejaculate, eject, emit, expel, jet, shoot, spout, spurt.

n chirt, jet, spray, spurt.

stab *v* bayonet, cut, dirk, gore, injure, jab, knife, pierce, pink, puncture, spear, stick, thrust, transfix, wound.

n ache, attempt, endeavour, essay, gash, incision, jab, pang, pink, prick, puncture, rent, thrust, try, twinge, venture, wound.

stab in the back betray, deceive, double-cross, inform on, let down, sell out, slander.

stabbing *adj* acute, lancinating, piercing, shooting, stinging.

stability *n* constancy, durability, firmness, fixity, permanence, solidity, soundness, steadfastness, steadiness, strength, sturdiness.

antonyms insecurity, instability, unsteadiness, weakness.

stable *adj* abiding, constant, deep-rooted, durable, enduring, established, fast, firm, fixed, immutable, invariable, lasting, permanent, reliable, secure, self-balanced, sound, static, steadfast, steady, strong, sturdy, sure, unalterable, unchangeable, unwavering, well-founded.

antonyms shaky, unstable, weak, wobbly.

stack *n* accumulation, clamp, cock, heap, hoard, load, mass, mound, mountain, pile, ruck, stockpile.

v accumulate, amass, assemble, gather, load, pile, save, stockpile, store.

staff *n* caduceus, cane, crew, employees, lecturers, lituus, officers, organisation, personnel, pole, prop, rod, stave, teachers, team, wand, workers, workforce.

stage *n* division, floor, juncture, lap, leg, length, level, period, phase, point, shelf, step, storey, subdivision, tier.

v arrange, do, engineer, give, mount, orchestrate, organise, perform, present, produce, put on, stage-manage.

stagger *v* alternate, amaze, astonish, astound, confound, daddle, daidle, dumbfound, falter, flabbergast, hesitate, lurch, nonplus, overlap, overwhelm, reel, shake, shock, step, stun, stupefy, surprise, sway, teeter, titubate, totter, vacillate, waver, wobble, zigzag.

stagnant *adj* becalmed, brackish, lethargic, motionless, sluggish, stale, standing, still, torpid.

stagnate *v* decay, decline, degenerate, deteriorate, fester, idle, languish, rot, rust, vegetate.

staid *adj* calm, composed, decorous, demure, grave, quiet, sedate, self-restrained, serious, sober, sober-blooded, solemn, steady, Victorian.

antonyms debonair, frivolous, jaunty, sportive.

stain *v* bedye, besmirch, blacken, blemish, blot, colour, contaminate, corrupt, defile, deprave, dirty, discolour, disgrace, distain, dye, imbue, mark, smutch, soil, spot, sully, taint, tarnish, tinge.

n blemish, blot, discoloration, disgrace, dishonour, dye, infamy, reproach, shame, slur, smirch, smutch, soil, splodge, spot, stigma, tint.

stake[1] *n* loggat, pale, paling, picket, pile, pole, post, spike, standard, stang, stave, stick.

v brace, fasten, pierce, prop, secure, support, tether, tie, tie up.

stake out define, delimit, demarcate, keep an eye on, mark out, outline, reserve, stake off, survey, watch.

stake[2] *n* ante, bet, chance, claim, concern, hazard, interest, investment, involvement, peril, pledge, prize, risk, share, venture, wager.

v ante, bet, chance, gage, gamble, hazard, imperil, jeopardise, pledge, risk, venture, wager.

stale *adj* antiquated, banal, cliche'd, cliche-ridden, common, commonplace, decayed, drab, dry, effete, faded, fetid, flat, fozy, fusty, hackneyed, hard, insipid, musty, old, old hat, overused, platitudinous, repetitious, sour, stagnant, stereotyped, tainted, tasteless, threadbare, trite, unoriginal, vapid, worn-out.

antonym fresh.

stalemate *n* deadlock, draw, halt, impasse, standstill, stop, tie, zugzwang.

antonym progress.

stalk[1] *v* approach, follow, haunt, hunt, march, pace, pursue, shadow, stride, strut, tail, track.

stalk[2] *n* bole, branch, kex, shoot, spire, stem, sterigma, trunk.

stall[1] *v* delay, equivocate, hedge, obstruct, penelopise, play for time, prevaricate, stonewall, temporise.

antonym advance.

stall[2] *n* bay, bench, booth, compartment, cowshed, pew, seat, stable, table.

stalwart *adj* athletic, beefy, brawny, daring, dependable, determined, hefty, husky, indomitable, intrepid, lusty, manly, muscular, redoubtable, resolute, robust, rugged, sinewy, staunch, stout, strapping, strong, sturdy, valiant, vigorous.

antonyms timid, weak.

stamina *n* energy, fibre, force, grit, indefatigability, lustiness, power, resilience, resistence, staying power, strength, vigour.

antonym weakness.

stammer *v* falter, gibber, hesitate, splutter, stumble, stutter.

stamp *v* beat, brand, bray, categorise, characterise, crush, engrave, exhibit, fix, identify, impress, imprint, inscribe, label, mark, mint, mould, pound, print, pronounce, reveal, strike, trample.

n attestation, authorisation, brand, breed, cast, character, cut, description, earmark, evidence, fashion, form, hallmark, impression, imprint, incuse, kind, mark, mould, sign, signature, sort, stomp, type.

stamp out crush, destroy, eliminate, end, eradicate, extinguish, extirpate, kill, quell, quench, scotch, suppress.

antonym encourage.

stampede *n* charge, dash, debacle, flight, rout, rush, scattering, sprint.

v charge, dash, flee, fly, gallop, hightail it, hot-foot it, run, rush, scurry, shoot, sprint, tear.

antonyms walk, wander.

stance *n* angle, attitude, bearing, carriage, deportment, point of view, position, posture, stand, standpoint, station, viewpoint.

stanch *v* arrest, block, check, dam, halt, plug, stay, stem, stop.

antonyms increase, promote.

stand *v* abide, allow, bear, belong, brook, continue, cost, countenance, demur, endure, erect, exist, experience, halt, handle, hold, mount, obtain, pause, place, position, prevail, put, rank, remain, rest, rise, scruple, set, stay, stomach, stop, suffer, support, sustain, take, thole, tolerate, undergo, wear, weather, withstand.

antonym advance.

n attitude, base, booth, bracket, cradle, dais, determination, erection, frame, grandstand, halt, holder, loss, opinion, place, platform, position, rack, rank, resistance, rest, stage, staging, stall, stance, standpoint, standstill, stay, stop, stop-over, stoppage, support, table, tub, vat, witness-box.

antonym progress.

stand by adhere to, back, befriend, champion, defend, hold to, reiterate, repeat, speak for, stick up for, support, uphold.

antonym let down.

stand down abdicate, cede, give away, give up, quit, resign, step down, withdraw.

antonyms ascend, join.

stand for bear, betoken, brook, champion, countenance, denote, embody, endure, epitomise, exemplify, indicate, mean, personify, represent, signify, suffer, symbolise, tolerate, typify, wear.

stand in for cover for, deputise for, hold the fort for, replace, substitute for, understudy.

stand out bulk large, catch the eye, jut out, project, stare one in the face, stick out, stick out a mile, stick out like a sore thumb.

stand up cohere, hold up, hold water, stand, wash.

stand up for champion, defend, fight for, side with, speak for, speak up for, stick up for, support, uphold.

antonym attack.

stand up to brave, confront, defy, endure, face, front, oppose, resist, withstand.

antonym give in to.

standard[1] *n* average, bench-mark, canon, criterion, example, exempler, gauge, grade, guide, guideline, level, measure, model, norm, norma, pattern, principle, requirement, rule, sample, specification, touchstone, type, yardstick.

adj accepted, approved, authoritative, average, basic, classic, customary, definitive, established, mainstream, normal, official, orthodox, popular, prevailing, recognised, regular, set, staple, stock, typical, usual.

antonyms abnormal, irregular, unusual.

standard[2] *n* banner, colours, ensign, flag, gonfalon, gonfanon, labarum, pennant, pennon, rallying-point, streamer, vexillum.

standard-bearer *n* cornet, ensign, gonfalonier, standard, vexillary.

standardise *v* assimilate, equalise, institutionalise, mass-produce, normalise, regiment, stereotype.

antonym differentiate.

standards *n* ethics, ideals, morals, principles.

standing *n* condition, continuance, credit, duration, eminence, estimation, existence, experience, footing, position, prestige, rank, reputation, repute, seniority, station, status.

adj erect, fixed, lasting, on one's feet, permanent, perpendicular, perpetual, rampant, regular, repeated, up-ended, upright, vertical.

antonyms horizontal, lying.

standing-stone *n* megalith, menhir, monolith.

stand-offish *adj* aloof, cold, distant, haughty, remote, reserved, unapproachable, uncommunicative, unsociable, untalkative.

antonym friendly.

standpoint *n* angle, point of view, position, post, stance, station, vantage-point, viewpoint, Weltanschauung.

standstill *n* arrest, cessation, dead-finish, deadlock, halt, hold-up, impasse, lapse, log-jam, lull, moratorium, pause, reprieve, respite, rest, stalemate, stay, stop, stoppage, termination.

antonym progress.

staple *adj* basic, chief, essential, fundamental, key, leading, main, major, predominant, primary, principle.

antonym minor.

star[1] *n* asterisk, asteroid, comet, etoile, meteor, meteorite, nova, planet, pulsar, quasar, red dwarf, red giant, satellite, shooting-star, starlet, sun, supernova, white dwarf.

star[2] *n* celebrity, draw, idol, lead, leading, leading lady, leading man, luminary, main attraction, name, starlet, vedette.

adj brilliant, celebrated, illustrious, leading, major, paramount, pre-eminent, principal, prominent, talented, well-known.

antonym minor.

starchy *adj* ceremonious, conventional, formal, prim, punctilious, stiff, strait-laced, stuffy.

antonym informal.

stare *v* gape, gawk, gawp, gaze, glare, goggle, look, watch.

n fish-eye, gaze, glare, glower, leer, look, ogle, scowl.

stark *adj* absolute, arrant, austere, bald, bare, barren, bleak, blunt, cold, consummate, depressing, desolate, downright, drear, dreary, entire, flagrant, forsaken, grim, harsh, out-and-out, palpable, patent, plain, pure, severe, sheer, simple, solitary, stern, stiff, strong, unadorned, unalloyed, unmitigated, unyielding, utter.

antonyms mild, slight.

adv absolutely, altogether, clean, completely, entirely, quite, stoutly, totally, utterly, wholly.

antonyms mildly, slightly.

stark-naked *adj* in one's birthday suit, in the altogether, in the buff, in the nude, in the raw, naked, nude, stark, starkers, stripped, unclad, undressed.

antonym clothed.

start *v* activate, appear, arise, begin, blench, break away, commence, create, dart, depart, engender, establish, father, flinch, found, inaugurate, initiate, instigate, institute, introduce, issue, jerk, jump, kick off, launch, leave, open, originate, pioneer, recoil, sally forth, set off, set out, set up, shoot, shy, spring forward, twitch.

antonyms finish, stop.

n advantage, backing, beginning, birth, break, chance, commencement, convulsion, dawn, edge, fit, foundation, inauguration, inception, initiation, introduction, jar, jump, kick-off, lead, onset, opening, opportunity, outburst, outset, spasm, sponsorship, spurt, twitch.

antonyms finish, stop.

startle *v* affray, agitate, alarm, amaze, astonish, astound, electrify, flush, frighten, scare, shock, spook, start, surprise.

antonym calm.

startling *adj* alarming, astonishing, astounding, dramatic, electric, electrifying, extraordinary, shocking, staggering, sudden, surprising, unexpected, unforeseen.

antonyms boring, calming, ordinary.

starvation *n* famishment, hunger, inanition, malnutrition, underfeeding, undernourishment.

antonym plenty.

starve *v* clem, deny, deprive, die, diet, fast, hunger, perish, refuse.

antonym provide.

starving *adj* famished, hungering, hungry, ravenous, sharp-set, starved, underfed, undernourished.

antonym fed.

stash *v* cache, closet, conceal, hide, hoard, lay up, salt away, save up, secrete, stockpile, stow.

antonyms bring out, uncover.

state[1] *v* affirm, articulate, assert, asseverate, aver, declare, enumerate, explain, expound, express, formalise, formulate, formulise, present, propound, put, report, say, specify, voice.

n attitude, bother, case, category, ceremony, circumstances, condition, dignity, display, flap, glory, grandeur, humour, majesty, mode, mood, panic, pass, phase, plight, pomp, position, pother, predicament, shape, situation, spirits, splendour, stage, station, style, tizzy.

antonym calmness.

state of affairs case, circumstances, condition, crisis, galère, juncture, kettle of fish, lie of the land, plight, position, predicament, situation.

state[2] *n* body politic, commonwealth, country, federation, government, kingdom, land, leviathan, nation, republic, territory.

adj ceremonial, ceremonious, formal, governmental, magnificent, national, official, pompous, public, solemn.

stately *adj* august, ceremonious, deliberate, dignified, elegant, grand, imperial, imposing, impressive, Junoesque, kingly, lofty, majestic, measured, noble, pompous, princely, queenly, regal, royal, solemn.

antonyms informal, unimpressive.

statement *n* account, announcement, bulletin, communication, communique, constatation, declaration, explanation, factoid, ipse dixit, ipsissima verba, proclamation, recital, relation, report, testimony, utterance, verbal.

statesman *n* diplomat, Elder Statesman, GOM, homme d'etat, politician.

static *adj* changeless, constant, fixed, immobile, inert, motionless, resting, stable, stagnant, stationary, still, unmoving, unvarying.

antonyms active, dynamic, moving.

station *n* appointment, base, business, calling, depot, employment, grade, habitat, headquarters, location, occupation, office, place, position, post, rank, seat, situation, sphere, stance, standing, standing-place, status, stopping-place.

v appoint, assign, establish, fix, garrison, install, locate, post, send, set.

stationary *adj* fixed, inert, moored, motionless, parked, resting, settled, standing, static, stock-still, unmoving.

antonym moving.

statue *n* acrolith, bronze, bust, carving, caryatid, effigy, figure, figurine, head, idol, statuette, xoanon.

statuesque *adj* dignified, imposing, majestic, regal, stately, statuary.

antonym small.

stature *n* consequence, eminence, importance, prestige, prominence, rank, size, standing, weight.

antonym unimportance.

status *n* character, condition, consequence, degree, distinction, eminence, grade, importance, position, prestige, rank, standing, state, weight.

antonym unimportance.

statute *n* act, decree, edict, enactment, firman, hatti-sherif, indiction, interlocution, irade, law, ordinance, regulation, rescript, rule, ukase.

staunch[1] *adj* constant, dependable, faithful, firm, hearty, loyal, reliable, resolute, sound, steadfast, stout, strong, sure, true, true-blue, trustworthy, trusty, watertight, yeomanly, zealous.

antonyms unreliable, wavering, weak.

staunch[2] *same as* **stanch**.

stave off avert, delay, evade, fend off, foil, hold off, keep at bay, keep back, parry, ward off.

antonyms cause, encourage.

stay[1] *v* abide, adjourn, allay, arrest, check, continue, curb, defer, delay, detain, discontinue, dwell, endure, halt, hinder, hold, hold out, hover, impede, last, linger, live, lodge, loiter, obstruct, pause, prevent, prorogue, remain, reside, restrain, settle, sojourn, stand, stop, suspend, tarry, visit, wait.

antonyms advance, leave.

n continuance, deferment, delay, halt, holiday, pause, postponement, remission, reprieve, sojourn, stop, stopover, stopping, suspension, visit.

stay[2] *n* brace, buttress, prop, reinforcement, shoring, stanchion, support.

v buttress, prop, prop up, shore up, support, sustain.

steadfast *adj* constant, dedicated, dependable, established, faithful, fast, firm, fixed, intent, loyal, perseverant, persevering, reliable, resolute, single-minded, stable, staunch, steady, unfaltering, unflinching, unswerving, unwavering.

antonyms unreliable, wavering, weak.

steady *adj* balanced, calm, ceaseless, confirmed, consistent, constant, continuous, dependable, equable, even, faithful, firm, fixed, habitual, immovable, imperturbable, incessant, industrious, level-headed, non-stop, persistent, regular, reliable, rhythmic, safe, sedate, sensible, serene, serious-minded, settled, sober, stable, staid, steadfast, substantial, unbroken, unchangeable, unfaltering, unfluctuating, unhasting, unhasty, unhurried, uniform, uninterrupted, unremitting, unswerving, unvarying, unwavering.

antonyms unsteady, wavering.

v balance, brace, firm, fix, secure, stabilise, support.

steal *v* appropriate, bone, cly, convey, creep, embezzle, filch, flit, half-inch, heist, knap, knock off, lag, lift, mill, misappropriate, nab, nick, peculate, pilfer, pinch, pirate, plagiarise, poach, purloin, relieve someone of, rip off, shoplift, slink, slip, smouch, smug, snaffle, snatch, sneak, snitch, swipe, take, thieve, tiptoe.

antonym return.

stealing *n* embezzlement, larcency, misappropriation, peculation, pilferage, pilfering, plagiarism, rip-off, robbery, shoplifting, theft, thievery, thieving.

stealth *n* covertness, furtiveness, secrecy, slyness, sneakiness, stealthiness, surreptitiousness, unobtrusiveness.

antonym openness.

stealthy *adj* cat-like, clandestine, covert, furtive, quiet, secret, secretive, skulking, sly, sneaking, sneaky, surreptitious, underhand.

antonym open.

steam *n* condensation, dampness, fumes, haze, mist, moisture, roke, vapour.

steamboat *n* packet, packet-boat, packet-ship, paddle-boat, paddle-steamer, puffer, steamer, steam-packet, steamship, steam-tug, steam-vessel, steam-yacht, vaporetto.

steamy *adj* close, damp, gaseous, hazy, humid, misty, muggy, roky, steaming, stewy, sticky, sultry, sweaty, sweltering, vaporiform, vaporous, vapourish, vapoury.

steed *n* charger, hack, horse, jade, mount, nag, Rosinante.

steel *v* brace, fortify, harden, nerve, toughen.

antonym weaken.

steep[1] *adj* abrupt, bluff, excessive, exorbitant, extortionate, extreme, headlong, high, overpriced, precipitious, sheer, stiff, uncalled-for, unreasonable.

antonyms gentle, moderate.

steep[2] *v* brine, damp, drench, fill, imbrue, imbue, immerse, infuse, macerate, marinate, moisten, permeate, pervade, pickle, saturate, seethe, soak, souse, submerge, suffuse.

steer *v* con, conduct, control, direct, govern, guide, pilot.

steer clear of avoid, bypass, circumvent, dodge, escape, eschew, evade, shun, skirt.

antonym seek.

stem[1] *n* axis, branch, family, house, line, lineage, peduncle, race, shoot, stalk, stock, trunk.

stem from arise from, come from, derive from, develop from, emanate from, flow from, issue from, originate in, spring from.

antonym give rise to.

stem[2] *v* check, contain, curb, dam, oppose, resist, restrain, stanch, stay, stop, tamp.

antonyms encourage, increase.

stench *n* mephitis, odour, pong, reek, stink, whiff.

step *n* act, action, advance, advancement, deed, degree, demarche, doorstep, expedient, footfall, footprint, footstep, gait, halfpace, impression, level, manoeuvre, means, measure, move, pace, phase, point, print, procedure, proceeding, process, progression, rank, remove, round, rung, stage, stair, stride, trace, track, tread, walk.

v move, pace, stalk, stamp, tread, walk.

step by step gradatim, gradually, slowly.

step down abdicate, bow out, leave, quit, resign, retire, stand down, withdraw.

antonyms ascend, join.

step up accelerate, augment, boost, build up, escalate, increase, intensify, raise, speed up, up.

antonym decrease.

stereotype *n* convention, formula, mould, pattern.

v categorise, conventionalise, dub, mass-produce, pigeonhole, standardise, typecast.

antonym differentiate.

stereotyped *adj* banal, cliche'd, cliche-ridden, conventional, corny, hackneyed, mass-produced, overused, platitudinous, stale, standard, standardised, stock, threadbare, tired, trite, unoriginal.

antonyms different, unconventional.

sterile *adj* abortive, acarpous, antiseptic, aseptic, bare, barren, disinfected, dry, empty, fruitless, germ-free, infecund, pointless, sterilised, unfruitful, unimaginative, unproductive, unprofitable, unprolific.

antonyms fruitful, septic.

sterilise *v* clean, cleanse, disinfect, fumigate, purify.

antonyms contaminate, infect.

sterility *n* asepsis, atocia, barrenness, cleanness, fruitlessness, futility, impotence, ineffectiveness, inefficacy, pointlessness, purity, unfecundity, unfruitfulness, uselessness.

antonyms fertility, fruitfulness.

sterling *adj* authentic, excellent, first-class, genuine, great, pure, real, sound, standard, substantial, superlative, true, worthy.

antonyms false, poor.

stern *adj* austere, authoritarian, bitter, cruel, flinty, forbidding, frowning, grim, hard, harsh, inflexible, relentless, rigid, rigorous, serious, severe, stark, steely, strict, unrelenting, unsmiling, unsparing, unyielding.

antonym mild.

stew *v* agonise, boil, braise, fret, fricassee, fuss, jug, perspire, seethe, simmer, sweat, swelter, worry.

n agitation, bother, bouillabaisse, chowder, daube, fluster, fret, fuss, goulash, hash, lobscouse, pot-au-feu, pother, ragout, tizzy, worry.

steward *n* chamberlain, dewan, factor, grieve, homme d'affaires, maître d'hôtel, major-domo, manciple, marshal.

stick[1] *v* abid, adhere, affix, attach, bind, bond, bulge, catch, cement, cleave, cling, clog, deposit, dig, drop, endure, extend, fasten, fix, fuse, glue, gore, hold, insert, install, jab, jam, join, jut, lay, linger, lodge, obtrude, paste, penetrate, persist, pierce, pin, place, plant, plonk, poke, position, prod, project, protrude, puncture, put, put up with, remain, set, show, snag, spear, stab, stand, stay, stomach, stop, store, stuff, take, thole, thrust, tolerate, transfix, weld.

antonym unstick.

stick at[1] continue, hang on in, keep at, persevere in, persist, plug away at.

antonym give up.

stick at[2] balk, demur, doubt, draw the line at, hesitate, pause, recoil, scruple, shrink from, stop at.

stick to adhere to, cleave to, honour, keep to, persevere in, stand by.

antonyms give up, quit.

stick up for champion, defend, speak for, speak up for, stand up for, support, take the part or side of, uphold.

antonym attack.

stick[2] *n* baton, bavin, birch, bludgeon, branch, cane, lathi, lug, pole, quarterstaff, rod, sceptre, staff, stake, stave, switch, twig, waddy, wand, whip, withy.

stick[3] *n* abuse, blame, criticism, flak, hostility, punishment, reproof.

antonym praise.

stickiness *n* adhesiveness, gaum, glueyness, glutinousness, goo, gooeyness, gumminess, syrupiness, tack, tackiness, viscidity.

stick-in-the-mud *adj* antediluvian, antiquated, conservative, fogram, fogyish, fossilised, outmoded, unadventurous, Victorian.

antonyms adventurous, modern.

n conservative, fog(e)y, fogram, fogramite, fossil.

stickler *n* fanatic, fusspot, maniac, martinet, nut, pedant, perfectionist, precisianist, purist.

sticky *adj* adhesive, awkward, claggy, clammy, clinging, clingy, cloggy, close, dauby, delicate, difficult, discomforting, embarrassing, gluey, glutinous, gooey, gummy, hairy, humid, muggy, nasty, oppressive, painful, smeary, sultry, sweltering, syrupy, tacky, tenacious, thorny, tricky, unpleasant, viscid, viscous.

antonyms cool, dry, easy.

stiff *adj* arduous, arthritic, artificial, austere, awkward, brisk, brittle, buckram, budge, ceremonious, chilly, clumsy, cold, constrained, creaky, crude, cruel, difficult, drastic, exacting, excessive, extreme, fatiguing, firm, forced, formal, formidable, fresh, graceless, great, hard, hardened, harsh, heavy, inelastic, inelegant, inexorable, inflexible, jerky, laborious, laboured, mannered, oppressive, pertinaceous, pitiless, pokerish, pompous, powerful, priggish, prim, punctilious, resistant, rheumaticky, rigid, rigorous, severe, sharp, solid, solidified, stand-offish, starch(y), stark, stilted, strict, stringent, strong, stubborn, taut, tense, tight, toilsome, tough, trying, unbending, uneasy, ungainly, ungraceful, unnatural, unrelaxed, unsupple, unyielding, uphill, vigorous, wooden.

antonyms flexible, graceful, informal, mild.

stiffen *v* ankylose, brace, coagulate, congeal, crystallise, harden, jell, reinforce, rigidify, rigidise, set, solidify, starch, tauten, tense, thicken.

stiff-necked *adj* arrogant, contumacious, haughty, obstinate, opinionated, proud, stubborn, uncompromising.

antonyms flexible, humble.

stifle *v* asphyxiate, check, choke, curb, dampen, extinguish, hush, muffle, prevent, repress, restrain, silence, smother, stop, strangle, suffocate, suppress.

antonym encourage.

stigma *n* blemish, blot, brand, disgrace, dishonour, imputation, mark, reproach, shame, slur, smirch, spot, stain.

antonym credit.

stigmatise *v* brand, condemn, denounce, discredit, fame, label, mark, pillory, vilify, vilipend.

antonym praise.

still *adj* calm, hushed, inert, lifeless, motionless, noiseless, pacific, peaceful, placid, quiet, restful, serene, silent, smooth, stagnant, stationary, stilly, tranquil, undisturbed, unruffled, unstirring.

antonyms agitated, busy, disturbed, noisy.

v allay, alleviate, appease, calm, hold back, hush, lull, pacify, quiet, quieten, restrain, settle, silence, smooth, soothe, subdue, tranquillise.

antonyms agitate, stir up.

n hush, peace, peacefulness, quiet, quietness, silence, stillness, tranquillity.

antonyms agitation, disturbance, noise.

adv but, even so, even then, however, nevertheless, nonetheless, notwithstanding, yet.

stilted *adj* artificial, bombastic, constrained, forced, grandiloquent, high-flown, high-sounding, inflated, laboured, mannered, pedantic, pompous, pretentious, stiff, unnatural, wooden.

antonyms flowing, fluent.

stimulant *n* analeptic, bracer, excitant, hype, incitant, oestrus, pep pill, pick-me-up, restorative, reviver, tonic, upper, whetstone.

antonym depressant.

stimulate *v* animate, arouse, dynamise, encourage, fan, fire, foment, get psyched up, goad, hop up, hype up, impel, incite, inflame, instigate, jog, prompt, provoke, psych oneself up, quicken, rouse, spur, titillate, urge, whet.

antonym discourage.

stimulating *adj* excitant, excitative, excitatory, exciting, exhilarating, galvanic, inspiring, intriguing, provocative, provoking, rousing, stirring, thought-provoking.

antonyms boring, depressing, uninspiring.

stimulus *n* carrot, encouragement, fillip, ginger, goad, incentive, incitement, inducement, prick, provocation, spur.

antonym discouragement.

sting *v* anger, burn, cheat, con, defraud, do, fleece, gall, hurt, incense, inflame, infuriate, nettle, overcharge, pain, pique, provoke, rile, rip off, smart, swindle, tingle, urticate, wound.

antonym soothe.

n agony, anguish, bite, bitterness, distress, goad, incentive, incitement, nip, prick, pungency, smarting, spur, stimulus, tingle, torment, torture, woe.

stinging *adj* aculeate(d), burning, nippy, smarting, tingling, urent, urticant.

antonyms mild, soothing.

stingy *adj* avaricious, cheeseparing, close-fisted, covetous, illiberal, inadequate, insufficient, meagre, mean, measly, mingy, miserly, near, niggardly, parsimonious, penny-pinching, penurious, save-all, scanty, scrimping, small, tightfisted, ungenerous, ungiving.

antonym generous.

stink *v* niff, pong, reek, whiff.

n brouhaha, commotion, disturbance, fetor, foulness, fuss, hubbub, malodour, mephitis, niff, odour, pong, row, rumpus, scandal, stench, stir, to-do, uproar, upset, whiff.

stinker *n* affliction, beast, bounder, cad, creep, cur, dastard, difficulty, fink, heel, horror, impediment, plight, poser, predicament, problem, rat, rotter, scab, scoundrel, shocker, sod, swine.

stinking *adj* boozed, canned, contemptible, disgusting, drunk, fetid, foul-smelling, graveolent, grotty, ill-smelling, intoxicated, low, low-down, malodorous, mean, mephitic, noisome, pissed, plastered, pongy, reeking, rotten, smashed, smelly, sozzled, stenchy, stewed, stoned, unpleasant, vile, whiffy, wretched.

antonyms good, pleasant, sober.

stint *n* assignment, bit, period, quota, share, shift, spell, stretch, term, time, tour, trick, turn.

v begrudge, economise, pinch, save, scrimp, skimp on, withhold.

stipulate *v* agree, contract, covenant, engage, guarantee, insist upon, lay down, pledge, postulate, promise, provide, require, settle, specify.

antonym imply.

stipulation *n* agreement, clause, condition, contract, engagement, precondition, prerequisite, provision, proviso, qualification, requirement, restriction, settlement, sine qua non, small print, specification, term.

antonym implication.

stir *v* affect, agitate, beat, bestir, budge, disturb, electrify, emove, excite, fire, flutter, hasten, inspire, look lively, mix, move, quiver, rustle, shake, shake a leg, thrill, touch, tremble.

antonyms bore, calm, stay.

n activity, ado, agitation, bustle, commotion, disorder, disturbance, excitement, ferment, flurry, fuss, hustle and bustle, movement, to-do, toing and froing, tumult, uproar.

antonym calm.

stir up animate, arouse, awaken, excite, incite, inflame, instigate, jog, kindle, mix, prompt, provoke, quicken, raise, spur, stimulate, urge.

antonyms calm, discourage.

stirring *adj* animating, dramatic, emotive, exciting, exhilarating, heady, impassioned, inspiring, intoxicating, lively, martial, moving, rousing, spirited, stimulating, thrilling.

antonyms calming, uninspiring.

stock *n* ancestry, array, assets, assortment, background, beasts, block, breed, cache, capital, cattle, choice, commodities, descent, equipment, estimation, extraction, family, flocks, forebears, fund, funds, goods, handle, herds, hoard, horses, house, inventory, investment, kindred, line, lineage, livestock, log, merchandise, parentage, pedigree, post, property, race, range, repertoire, repute, reserve, reservoir, selection, sheep, source, stem, stockpile, store, strain, stump, supply, trunk, type, variety, wares.

adj banal, basic, bromidic, cliche'd, commonplace, conventional, customary, formal, hackneyed, ordinary, overused, regular, routine, run-of-the-mill, set, standard, staple, stereotyped, traditional, trite, usual, worn-out.

antonym original.

v deal in, handle, keep, sell, supply, trade in.

stock up accumulate, amass, equip, fill, furnish, gather, hoard, lay in, pile up, provision, replenish, save, store (up), supply.

stocky *adj* blocky, chunky, dumpy, mesomorphic, short, solid, stubby, stumpy, sturdy, thickset.

antonyms skinny, tall.

stodgy *adj* boring, dull, filling, formal, fuddy-duddy, heavy, laboured, leaden, solemn, spiritless, staid, starchy, stuffy, substantial, tedious, turgid, unenterprising, unexciting, unimaginative, uninspired.

antonyms exciting, informal, light.

stoical *adj* calm, cool, dispassionate, impassive, imperturbable, indifferent, long-suffering, patient, philosophic(al), phlegmatic, resigned, stoic, stolid.

antonyms anxious, depressed, furious, irascible.

stoicism *n* acceptance, ataraxia, ataraxy, calmness, dispassion, fatalism, forbearance, fortitude, impassivity, imperturbability, indifference, long-suffering, patience, resignation, stolidity.

antonyms anxiety, depression, fury.

stolid *adj* apathetic, beefy, blockish, bovine, doltish, dull, heavy, impassive, lumpish, obtuse, po, po-faced, slow, stoic(al), stupid, unemotional, wooden.

antonyms interested, lively.

stomach *n* abdomen, appetite, belly, bread-basket, craw, desire, gizzard, gut, inclination, inner man, inside(s), king's-hood, little Mary, maw, mind, paunch, pot, potbelly, relish, spare tyre, taste, tummy.

v abide, bear, endure, submit to, suffer, swallow, take, thole, tolerate.

stone *n* boulder, cobble, concretion, endocarp, flagstone, gem, gemstone, gravestone, headstone, jewel, kernel, lapis, pebble, pip, pit, rock, seed, set(t), slab, tombstone.

stone circle henge, peristalith.

stony *adj* adamant, blank, callous, chilly, expressionless, frigid, hard, heartless, hostile, icy, indifferent, inexorable, lapideous, lapilliform, lithoid(al), merciless, obdurate, pitiless, steely, stonelike, unfeeling, unforgiving, unresponsive.

antonyms forgiving, friendly, soft-hearted.

stooge *n* butt, cat's paw, dupe, fall guy, foil, henchman, lackey, patsy, pawn, puppet.

stoop *v* bend, bow, couch, crouch, descend, duck, hunch, incline, kneel, lean, squat.

n droop, inclination, round-shoulderedness, sag, slouch, slump.

stoop to condescend, deign, descend, go so far as, go so low as, lower oneself, resort, sink, vouchsafe.

stop *v* arrest, bar, block, break, cease, check, close, conclude, desist, discontinue, embar, end, finish, forestall, frustrate, halt, hinder, impede, intercept, intermit, interrupt, knock off, leave off, lodge, obstruct, pack (it) in, pack in, pack up, pause, plug, poop out, prevent, quit, refrain, repress, rest, restrain, scotch, seal, silence, sojourn, stall, staunch, stay, stem, stymie, suspend, tarry, terminate.

antonyms advance, continue, start.

n bar, block, break, bung, cessation, check, conclusion, control, depot, destination, discontinuation, end, finish, halt, hindrance, impediment, plug, rest, sojourn, stage, standstill, station, stay, stop-over, stoppage, termination, terminus, ventage, visit.

antonyms continuation, start.

interj avast, cease, cut it out, desist, easy, give over, halt, hang on, hold it, hold on, hold your horses, lay off, leave it out, refrain, stop it, wait, wait a minute, whoa.

stop-gap *n* expedient, improvisation, makeshift, resort, shift, substitute.

adj emergency, expediential, impromptu, improvised, makeshift, provisional, rough-and-ready, temporary.

antonyms finished, permanent.

stoppage *n* abeyance, arrest, blockage, check, close, closure, curtailment, cut-off, deduction, desistance, discontinuance, halt, hartal, hindrance, interruption, lay-off, obstruction, occlusion, shut-down, sit-in, standstill, stasis, stopping, strike, walk-out.

antonyms continuation, start.

stopper *n* bung, cork, plug, stopple.

store *v* accumulate, cupboard, deposit, garner, hive, hoard, husband, keep, lay aside, lay by, lay in lavender, lay up, put aside, reserve, salt away, save, stash, stock, stockpile, treasure.

antonym use.

n abundance, accumulation, bank, cache, cupboard, database, depository, emporium, esteem, fund, hoard, keeping, lot, market, mart, memory, mine, outlet, panary, plenty, plethora, provision, quantity, repository, reserve, reservoir, shop, stock, stockpile, storehouse, storeroom, supermarket, supply, value, warehouse, wealth.

antonym scarcity.

storehouse *n* armoury, arsenal, barn, cellar, depository, depot, elevator, entrepot, etape, fund, garderobe, garner, granary, hold, larder, pantry, repertory, repository, silo, treasury, vault, warehouse.

storey *n* deck, etage, flight, floor, level, stage, stratum, tier.

storm *n* agitation, anger, assault, attack, blast, blitz, blitzkrieg, blizzard, clamour, commotion, cyclone, disturbance, dust-devil, furore, gale, gust, haboob, hubbub, hurricane, offensive, onset, onslaught, outbreak, outburst, outcry, paroxysm, passion, roar, row, rumpus, rush, sandstorm, squall, stir, strife, tempest, tornado, tumult, turmoil, violence, whirlwind.

antonym calm.

v assail, assault, beset, bluster, charge, complain, expugn, flounce, fly, fume, rage, rampage, rant, rave, rush, scold, stalk, stamp, stomp, thunder.

stormy *adj* blustering, blustery, boisterous, choppy, dirty, foul, gustful, gusty, inclement, oragious, raging, rough, squally, tempestuous, turbulent, wild, windy.

antonym calm.

story *n* account, ancedote, article, chronicle, episode, fable, fairy-tale, falsehood, feature, fib, fiction, historiette, history, legend, lie, Märchen, myth, narration, narrative, news, novel, plot, recital, record, relation, report, romance, scoop, spiel, tale, untruth, version, yarn.

storyteller *n* anecdotist, author, bard, chronicler, clype, fabulist, fibber, liar, narrator, novelist, raconteur, raconteuse, romancer, tell-tale.

stout *adj* able-bodied, athletic, beefy, big, bold, brave, brawny, bulky, burly, chopping, corpulent, courageous, dauntless, doughty, embonpoint, enduring, fat, fearless, fleshy, gallant, hardy, heavy, hulking, husky, intrepid, lion-hearted, lusty, manly, muscular, obese, overweight, plucky, plump, portly, resolute, robust, rotund, stalwart, strapping, strong, sturdy, substantial, thick, tough, tubby, valiant, valorous, vigorous.

antonyms slim, timid, weak.

stove *n* calefactor, chauffer, cockle, cooker, furnace, grill, heater, kiln, oven, range.

stow *v* bundle, cram, deposit, dump, jam, load, pack, secrete, sling, stash, store, stuff, tuck.

antonym unload.

straggle *v* amble, dilly-dally, drift, lag, loiter, ramble, range, roam, rove, scatter, spread, stray, string out, trail, wander.

straggly *adj* aimless, disorganised, drifting, irregular, loose, rambling, random, spreading, straggling, straying, strung out, untidy.

antonyms grouped, organised, tidy.

straight *adj* accurate, aligned, arranged, authentic, balanced, blunt, bourgeois, candid, consecutive, conservative, continuous, conventional, decent, direct, downright, equitable, erect, even, fair, forthright, frank, honest, honourable, horizontal, just, law-abiding, level, near, neat, non-stop, normal, orderly, organised, orthodox, outright, perpendicular, plain, plumb, point-blank, pure, reliable, respectable, right, running, settled, shipshape, short, smooth, solid, square, straightforward, successive, sustained, through, tidy, traditional, true, trustworthy, unadulterated, undeviating, undiluted, uninterrupted, unmixed, unqualified, unrelieved, unswerving, upright, vertical.

antonyms circuitous, dilute, dishonest, evasive, indirect, roundabout.

adv candidly, directly, frankly, honestly, outspokenly, point-blank, upright.

straightaway *adv* at once, directly, immediately, instanter, instantly, now, right away, straightway, there and then, this minute, tout de suite.

antonym eventually.

straighten *v* arrange, neaten, order, untwist.

antonyms bend, twist.

straighten out clear up, correct, disentangle, rectify, regularise, resolve, settle, sort out, unfankle, unsnarl, work out.

antonym muddle.

straightforward *adj* candid, clear-cut, direct, easy, elementary, forthright, genuine, guileless, honest, open, open-and-shut, penny-plain, routine, simple, sincere, truthful, uncomplicated, undemanding.

antonyms complicated, devious, evasive.

strain[1] *v* compress, distend, drive, embrace, endeavour, exert, express, extend, fatigue, filter, injure, labour, overtax, overwork, percolate, pull, purify, restrain, retch, riddle, screen, seep, separate, sieve, sift, sprain, squeeze, stretch, strive, struggle, tauten, tax, tear, tighten, tire, tug, twist, weaken, wrench, wrest, wrick.

n anxiety, burden, effort, exertion, force, height, injury, key, pitch, pressure, pull, sprain, stress, struggle, tautness, tension, wrench.

strain² *n* ancestry, blood, descent, extraction, family, humour, lineage, manner, pedigree, race, spirit, stem, stock, streak, style, suggestion, suspicion, temper, tendency, tone, trace, trait, vein, way.

strained *adj* artificial, awkward, constrained, difficult, embarrassed, epitonic, false, forced, laboured, self-conscious, stiff, tense, uncomfortable, uneasy, unnatural, unrelaxed.

antonym natural.

strains *n* air, lay, measure, melody, song, theme, tune.

strait *n* channel, gat, gut, kyle, narrows, sound.

straitened *adj* difficult, distressed, embarrassed, impoverished, limited, poor, reduced, restricted.

antonyms easy, well-off.

strait-laced *adj* moralistic, narrow, narrow-minded, old-maidish, prim, proper, prudish, puritanical, strict, stuffy, upright, Victorian.

antonyms broad-minded, easy-going.

straits *n* crisis, difficulty, dilemma, distress, embarrassment, emergency, extremity, hardship, hole, mess, perplexity, plight, poverty, predicament.

strand *n* fibre, fibril, fibrilla, filament, length, lock, rope, string, thread, tress, twist.

stranded *adj* abandoned, aground, ashore, beached, grounded, helpless, high and dry, homeless, in the lurch, marooned, penniless, shipwrecked, wrecked.

strange *adj* abnormal, alien, astonishing, awkward, bewildered, bizarre, curious, disorientated, disoriented, eccentric, eerie, exceptional, exotic, extraordinary, fantastic(al), ferly, foreign, frain, fremd, fremit, funny, irregular, lost, marvellous, mystifying, new, novel, odd, out-of-the-way, peculiar, perplexing, queer, rare, remarkable, remote, singular, sinister, unaccountable, unacquainted, uncanny, unco, uncomfortable, uncommon, unexplained, unexplored, unfamiliar, unheard of, unknown, untried, unversed, weird, wonderful.

antonyms comfortable, common, familiar, ordinary.

strangeness *n* abnormalism, abnormality, abnormity, bizarreness, bizarrerie, eccentricity, eeriness, exoticness, extraordinariness, fantasticality, fantasticalness, irregularity, oddity, oddness, peculiarity, queerness, singularity, uncanniness.

antonym ordinariness.

stranger *n* alien, foreigner, fraim, fremd, fremit, guest, incomer, newcomer, non-member, outlander, unknown, visitor.

antonyms local, native.

strangle *n* asphyxiate, choke, constrict, gag, garrotte, inhibit, jugulate, repress, smother, stifle, strangulate, suffocate, suppress, throttle.

strap *n* belt, leash, selvagee, thong, tie, vitta.

v beat, belt, bind, buckle, fasten, flog, lash, scourge, secure, tie, truss, whip.

strapping *adj* beefy, big, brawny, burly, hefty, hulking, hunky, husky, powerful, robust, stalwart, strong, sturdy, well-built.

antonym puny.

stratagem *n* artifice, device, dodge, feint, fetch, intrigue, manoeuvre, plan, plot, ploy, ruse, ruse de guerre, scheme, subterfuge, trick, wile.

strategic *adj* calculated, cardinal, critical, crucial, decisive, deliberate, diplomatic, important, key, planned, politic, strategetical, vital.

antonym unimportant.

strategy *n* approach, design, manoeuvring, plan, planning, policy, procedure, programme, scheme, way.

stratum *n* bed, bracket, caste, category, class, grade, group, layer, level, lode, rank, region, seam, station, stratification, table, tier, vein.

stray *v* deviate, digress, diverge, drift, err, get lost, meander, ramble, range, roam, rove, straggle, wander (off).

adj abandoned, accidental, chance, erratic, forwandered, freak, homeless, lost, odd, random, roaming, scattered, vagrant.

streak *n* band, dash, element, freak, layer, line, slash, smear, strain, strip, stripe, stroke, touch, trace, vein.

v band, dart, daub, flash, fleck, fly, gallop, hurtle, slash, smear, speed, sprint, striate, stripe, sweep, tear, whistle, whizz, zoom.

streaked *adj* banded, barred, brinded, brindle(d), flecked, fleckered, lined, streaky, striate, veiny.

stream *n* beck, brook, burn, course, creek, current, drift, flow, freshet, ghyll, gill, gush, outpouring, rill, rillet, river, rivulet, run, runnel, rush, surge, tide, torrent, tributary.

v cascade, course, emit, flood, flow, glide, gush, issue, pour, run, shed, spill, spout, surge, well out.

streamer *n* banner, ensign, flag, gonfalon, gonfanon, pennant, pennon, plume, ribbon, standard.

streamlined *adj* efficient, graceful, modernised, organised, rationalised, sleek, slick, smooth, smooth-running, superior, time-saving, up-to-the-minute, well-run.

antonyms clumsy, inefficient, old-fashioned.

street *n* avenue, boulevard, carriageway, corso, crescent, drive, gate, highway, lane, prospect, road, roadway, row, terrace, thoroughfare.

strength *n* advantage, anchor, asset, backbone, brawn, brawniness, cogency, concentration, courage, effectiveness, efficacy, energy, firmness, foison, force, fortitude, fushion, health, intensity, lustiness, mainstay, might, muscle, potency, power, resolution, robustness, security, sinew, spirit, stamina, stoutness, sturdiness, thew, toughness, vehemence, vigour, virtue.

antonyms timidness, weakness.

strengthen *v* afforce, bolster, brace, buttress, confirm, consolidate, corroborate, edify, encourage, enhance, establish, fortify, harden, hearten, heighten, increase, intensify, invigorate, justify, nerve, nourish, reinforce, rejuvenate, restore, steel, stiffen, substantiate, support, toughen.

antonym weaken.

strenuous *adj* active, arduous, bold, demanding, determined, eager, earnest, energetic, exhausting, hard, Herculean, laborious, persistent, resolute, spirited, strong, taxing, tireless, toilful, toilsome, tough, uphill, urgent, vigorous, warm, zealous.

antonyms easy, effortless.

stress *n* accent, accentuation, anxiety, beat, burden, emphasis, emphaticalness, force, hassle, importance, oppression, pressure, significance, strain, tautness, tension, trauma, urgency, weight, worry.

antonym relaxation.

v accentuate, belabour, emphasise, repeat, strain, tauten, underline, underscore.

antonym relax.

stretch *n* area, bit, distance, exaggeration, expanse, extensibility, extension, extent, period, reach, run, space, spell, spread, stint, strain, sweep, term, time, tract.

v cover, distend, elongate, expand, extend, inflate, lengthen, pull, rack, reach, spread, strain, swell, tauten, tighten, unfold, unroll.

antonyms relax, squeeze.

stretch one's legs exercise, go for a walk, move about, promenade, stroll, take a breather, take a walk, take the air.

stretch out hold out, lie down, porrect, put out, reach, relax, stretch forth.

antonym draw back.

strew *v* bespread, besprinkle, bestrew, disperse, litter, scatter, spread, sprinkle, toss.

antonym gather.

stricken *adj* affected, afflicted, expunged, hit, injured, smitten, struck, wounded.

antonym unaffected.

strict *adj* absolute, accurate, austere, authoritarian, close, complete, exact, faithful, firm, harsh, meticulous, no-nonsense, particular, perfect, precise, religious, restricted, rigid, rigorous, scrupulous, severe, stern, stringent, thoroughgoing, total, true, unsparing, utter, Victorian.

antonyms easy-going, flexible, mild.

strictness *n* accuracy, austerity, authoritarianism, exactness, firmness, harshness, martinetism, meticulousness, rigidity, rigidness, rigorousness, rigour, scrupulousness, severity, sternness, stringency, stringentness.

antonyms flexibility, mildness.

stricture *n* animadversion, blame, censure, criticism, flak, rebuke, reproof.

antonym praise.

strident *adj* cacophonous, clamorous, clashing, discordant, grating, harsh, jangling, jarring, loud, rasping, raucous, screeching, shrill, stridulant, stridulous, unmusical, vociferous.

antonyms quiet, sweet.

strife *n* animosity, battle, bickering, brigue, colluctation, combat, conflict, contention, contest, contestation, controversy, discord, dissension, friction, quarrel, rivalry, row, squabbling, struggle, warfare, wrangling.

antonym peace.

strike *n* attack, buffet, hartal, hit, mutiny, raid, refusal, stoppage, thump, walk-out, wallop, work-to-rule.

v achieve, affect, afflict, arrange, assail, assault, assume, attack, attain, bang, beat, bop, box, buff, buffet, cancel, chastise, clap, clash, clobber, clout, clump, cob, coin, collide with, cuff, dart, dash, delete, devastate, discover, dismantle, douse, down tools, drive, dunt, effect, encounter, find, force, hammer, hit, impel, impress, interpose, invade, knock, mutiny, penetrate, pierce, pound, print, punish, ratify, reach, register, remove, revolt, seem, shoot, slap, slat, smack, smite, sock, stamp, stumble across, stumble upon, surrender, swap, swipe, swop, thrust, thump, touch, trap, turn up, uncover, unearth, walk out, wallop, whack, wham, work to rule, zap.

strike down afflict, assassinate, destroy, kill, murder, ruin, slay, smite.

strike out cancel, cross out, delete, efface, erase, excise, expunge, remove, score off, score out, strike off, strike through.

antonym add.

striking *adj* arresting, astonishing, conspicuous, dazzling, distingue(e), extraordinary, forcible, foudroyant, frappant, impressive, memorable, noticeable, outstanding, salient, stunning, wonderful.

antonym unimpressive.

string *n* bunch, chain, cord, fibre, file, line, number, procession, queue, row, sequence, series, strand, succession, train, twine.

v festoon, hang, link, loop, sling, stretch, suspend, thread, tie up.

string along[1] accompany, agree, assent, collaborate, co-operate, go along.

antonym dissent.

string along[2] bluff, deceive, dupe, fool, hoax, humbug, play (someone) false, play fast and loose with, put one over on, take (someone) for a ride.

string out disperse, extend, fan out, lengthen, protract, space out, spread out, straggle, stretch out, wander.

antonyms gather, shorten.

stringent *adj* binding, demanding, exacting, flexible, inflexible, mild, rigid, rigorous, severe, strict, tight, tough.

strings *n* catches, conditions, limitations, obligations, prerequisites, provisos, qualifications, requirements, restrictions, stipulations.

stringy *adj* chewy, fibrous, gristly, ropy, sinewy, tough, wiry.

antonym tender.

strip[1] *v* bare, clear, defoliate, denude, deprive, despoil, devest, disadorn, disembellish, disgarnish, disinvest, disleaf, disleave, dismantle, displenish, disrobe, divest, doff, empty, excoriate, excorticate, expose, gut, husk, lay bare, loot, peel, pillage, plunder, ransack, rob, sack, skin, spoil, unclothe, uncover, undress, widow.

antonyms cover, provide.

strip[2] *n* band, belt, bit, fillet, lath, list, piece, ribbon, sash, screed, shred, slat, slip, spline, strake, strap, swathe, tape, thong, tongue, vitta.

stripe *n* band, bar, belt, chevron, flash, fleck, striation, vitta.

striped *adj* banded, barred, streaky, striated, stripy, vittate.

stripling *n* adolescent, boy, fledgling, hobbledehoy, lad, shaver, teenager, youngling, youngster, young'un, youth.

strive *v* attempt, compete, contend, endeavour, fight, labour, push oneself, strain, struggle, toil, try, work.

stroke *n* accomplishnment, achievement, apoplexy, attack, blow, clap, collapse, effleurage, feat, fit, flourish, hit, knock, move, movement, pat, rap, seizure, shock, swap, swop, thump.

v caress, clap, fondle, pat, pet, rub.

stroll *v* amble, da(c)ker, dander, dawdle, mosey, promenade, ramble, saunter, stooge, toddle, wander.

n airing, bummel, constitutional, dawdle, excursion, promenade, ramble, saunter, toddle, turn, walk.

stroller *n* dawdler, flâneur, rambler, saunterer, walker, wanderer.

strong *adj* acute, aggressive, athletic, beefy, biting, bold, brave, brawny, bright, brilliant, burly, capable, clear, clear-cut, cogent, compelling, competent, concentrated, convincing, courageous, dazzling, dedicated, deep, deep-rooted, determined, distinct, drastic, durable, eager, effective, efficient, emphasised, excelling, extreme, fast-moving, fervent, fervid, fierce, firm, forceful, forcible, formidable, glaring, great, grievous, gross, hale, hard, hard-nosed, hard-wearing, hardy, heady, healthy, hearty, heavy-duty, Herculean, highly-flavoured, highly-seasoned, hot, intemperate, intense, intoxicating, keen, loud, lusty, marked, muscular, nappy, numerous, offensive, overpowering, persuasive, petrous, piquant, pithy, plucky, pollent, potent, powerful, pungent, pure, rank, redoubtable, reinforced, resilient, resolute, resourceful, robust, self-assertive, severe, sharp, sinewy, sound, spicy, stalwart, stark, staunch, steadfast, sthenic, stout, stouthearted, strapping, stressed, sturdy, substantial, telling, tenacious, thewy, tough, trenchant, undiluted, unmistakable, unseemly, unyielding, urgent, vehement, violent, virile, vivid, weighty, well-armed, well-built, well-established, well-founded, well-knit, well-protected, well-set, well-versed, zealous.

antonyms mild, weak.

strong point advantage, aptitude, asset, bag, bent, forte, gift, long suit, metier, speciality, specialty, strength, strong suit, talent, thing.

strongarm *adj* aggressive, bullying, coercive, forceful, intimidatory, oppressive, physical, terror, threatening, thuggish, violent.

antonym gentle.

stronghold *n* bastion, bulwark, castle, centre, citadel, fastness, fort, fortress, hedgehog, keep, redoubt, refuge.

strong-minded *adj* determined, firm, independent, iron-willed, resolute, steadfast, strong-willed, tenacious, unbending, uncompromising, unwavering.

antonym weak-willed.

stroppy *adj* awkward, bad-tempered, bloody-minded, cantankerous, difficult, obstreperous, perverse, quarrelsome, refractory, rowdy, unco-operative, unhelpful.

antonyms co-operative, sweet-tempered.

structural *adj* configurational, constructional, design, formational, organisational, tectonic.

structure *n* arrangement, building, compages, configuration, conformation, construction, contexture, design, edifice, erection, fabric, form, formation, make-up, organisation, pile, set-up.

v arrange, assemble, build, construct, design, form, organise, shape.

struggle *v* agonise, battle, compete, contend, fight, grapple, labour, scuffle, strain, strive, toil, work, wrestle.

antonyms give in, rest.

n agon, agony, battle, brush, clash, combat, conflict, contest, effort, encounter, exertion, grind, hostilities, labour, luctation, pains, scramble, skirmish, strife, toil, tussle, work.

antonyms ease, submission.

strut *v* brank, cock, parade, peacock, prance, stalk, swagger.

stub *n* butt, counterfoil, dog-end, doup, end, fag-end, remnant, snub, stump, tail, tail-end.

stubborn *adj* bull-headed, contumacious, cross-grained, difficult, dogged, dour, fixed, headstrong, inflexible, intractable, intransigent, mulish, obdurate, obstinate, opinionated, persistent, pertinacious, pig-headed, recalcitrant, refractory, rigid, self-willed, stiff, stiff-necked, tenacious, unbending, unmanageable, unshakable, unyielding, wilful.

antonym compliant.

stubby *adj* bristling, bristly, chunky, dumpy, knobbly, knubbly, knubby, nubbly, nubby, prickly, rough, short, squat, stocky, stubbly, stumpy, thickset.

antonyms long, tall, thin.

stuck *adj* baffled, beaten, cemented, fast, fastened, firm, fixed, glued, joined, nonplussed, stumped, stymied.

antonym loose.

stuck on crazy about, dotty about, enthusiastic about, infatuated with, keen on, mad on, nuts on, obsessed with, wild about.

antonym indifferent to.

stuck-up *adj* arrogant, big-headed, conceited, condescending, exclusive, haughty, high and mighty, hoity-toity, overweening, patronising, prideful, proud, snobbish, snooty, swollen-headed, toffee-nosed, uppish, uppity.

antonym humble.

studded *adj* bejewelled, bespangled, dotted, flecked, ornamented, scattered, set, spangled, speckled, spotted, sprinkled.

student *n* apprentice, bajan, bejant, bookman, chela, co-ed, collegianer, contemplator, disciple, fresher, freshman, learner, observer, pupil, scholar, seminarist, soph, sophomore, undergraduate, undergraduette.

studied *adj* calculated, conscious, deliberate, forced, intentional, over-elaborate, planned, premeditated, purposeful, unnatural, voulu, wilful.

antonyms natural, unplanned.

studio *n* atelier, school, workroom, workshop.

studious *adj* academic, assiduous, attentive, bookish, careful, diligent, eager, earnest, hard-working, heedful, intellectual, intent, meditative, reflective, scholarly, sedulous, serious, solicitous, thoughtful.

antonym lazy.

study *v* analyse, cogitate, con, consider, contemplate, cram, deliberate, dig, examine, investigate, learn, lucubrate, meditate, mug up, peruse, ponder, pore over, read, read up, research, scan, scrutinise, survey, swot.

n analysis, application, attention, cogitation, consideration, contemplation, cramming, critique, examination, inclination, inquiry, inspection, interest, investigation, learning, lessons, lucubration, memoir, monograph, prolusion, reading, report, research, reverie, review, scrutiny, survey, swotting, thesis, thought, zeal.

stuff *v* binge, bombast, compress, cram, crowd, fill, force, gobble, gorge, gormandise, guzzle, jam, load, overindulge, pack, pad, push, ram, sate, satiate, shove, squeeze, steeve, stodge, stow, trig, wedge.

antonyms nibble, unload.

n belongings, clobber, cloth, effects, equipment, essence, fabric, furniture, gear, goods, impedimenta, junk, kit, luggage, material, materials, materiel, matter, objects, paraphernalia, pith, possessions, provisions, quintessence, staple, substance, tackle, textile, things, trappings.

stuffing *n* bombast, farce, farcing, filler, force-meat, kapok, packing, quilting, wadding.

stuffy *adj* airless, close, conventional, deadly, dreary, dull, fetid, fogram, fogyish, frowsty, frowzy, fuggy, fusty, heavy, humourless, muggy, musty, old-fashioned, oppressive, poking, poky, pompous, priggish, prim, staid, stale, stifling, stilted, stodgy, strait-laced, suffocating, sultry, uninteresting, unventilated, Victorian.

antonyms airy, informal, interesting, modern.

stultify *v* benumb, blunt, dull, hebetate, invalidate, negate, nullify, numb, smother, stifle, stupefy, suppress, thwart.

antonyms prove, sharpen.

stultifying *adj* dulling, hebetant, hebetating, numbing, stupefying.

antonym electrifying.

stumble *v* blunder, fall, falter, flounder, fluff, hesitate, lurch, reel, slip, stagger, stammer, stutter, titubate, trip.

stumble on blunder upon, chance upon, come across, discover, encounter, find, happen upon, light upon.

stumbling-block *n* bar, barrier, crux, difficulty, hindrance, hurdle, impediment, obstacle, obstruction, pons asinorum, snag.

antonym boost.

stump *v* baffle, bamboozle, bewilder, clomp, clump, confound, confuse, defeat, dumbfound, flummox, foil, lumber, mystify, nonplus, outwit, perplex, plod, puzzle, stamp, stomp, stop, stymie, trudge.

antonym assist.

stump up contribute, cough up, donate, fork out, hand over, pay, pay out, pay up, shell out.

antonym receive.

stumped *adj* baffled, bamboozled, floored, flummoxed, nonplussed, perplexed, stuck, stymied.

stumpy *adj* chunky, dumpy, dwarf, dwarfish, heavy, short, squat, stocky, stubby, thick, thickset.

antonyms long, tall, thin.

stun *v* amaze, astonish, astound, bedeafen, bewilder, confound, confuse, daze, deafen, dumbfound, flabbergast, overcome, overpower, shock, stagger, stupefy.

stung *adj* angered, bitten, exasperated, goaded, hurt, incensed, irked, needled, nettled, peeved, piqued, resentful, roused, wounded.

antonym soothed.

stunned *adj* astounded, dazed, devastated, dumbfounded, flabbergasted, floored, numb, shocked, staggered, stupefied.

antonym indifferent.

stunner *n* beauty, charmer, dazzler, dish, dolly, eye-catcher, eyeful, femme fatale, good-looker, heart-throb, honey, knock-out, looker, lovely, peach, sensation, siren, smasher, stotter, wow.

antonym dog.

stunning *adj* beautiful, brilliant, dazing, dazzling, devastating, gorgeous, great, heavenly, impressive, lovely, marvellous, ravishing, remarkable, sensational, smashing, spectacular, stotting, striking, wonderful.

antonyms poor, ugly.

stunt[1] *n* act, campaign, deed, enterprise, exploit, feat, feature, gest(e), performance, tour de force, trick, turn.

stunt[2] *v* arrest, check, dwarf, hamper, hinder, impede, restrict, slow, stop.

antonym promote.

stunted *adj* diminutive, dwarfed, dwarfish, little, runtish, runty, small, tiny, undersized.

antonyms large, sturdy.

stupefaction *n* amaze, amazement, astonishment, awe, bafflement, bewilderment, wonder, wonderment.

stupefy *v* amaze, astound, baffle, benumb, bewilder, confound, daze, drowse, dumbfound, hocus, numb, shock, stagger, stun.

stupendous *adj* amazing, astounding, breathtaking, colossal, enormous, fabulous, fantastic, gigantic, huge, marvellous, mind-blowing, mind-boggling, overwhelming, phenomenal, prodigious, staggering, stunning, superb, tremendous, vast, wonderful.

antonym unimpressive.

stupid *adj* anserine, asinine, beef-brained, beef-witted, blockish, Boeotian, boobyish, boring, bovine, brainless, chuckle-headed, clueless, crackbrained, cretinous, cuckoo, damfool, dazed, deficient, dense, dilly, dim, doltish, donnart, donnered, dopey, dovie, dozy, drippy, dull, dumb, fat-witted, foolish, fozy, futile, gaumless, glaikit, gormless, groggy, gullible, half-baked, half-witted, hammer-headed, idiotic, ill-advised, imbecilic, inane, indiscreet, insensate, insensible, insulse, irrelevant, irresponsible, laughable, looby, ludicrous, lumpen, lurdan, meaningless, mindless, moronic, naïve, nonsensical, obtuse, opaque, pointless, puerile, punch-drunk, rash, semiconscious, senseless, short-sighted, simple, simple-minded, slow, slow-witted, sluggish, stolid, stunned, stupefied, thick, thick-headed, thick-witted, trivial, unintelligent, unthinking, vacuous, vapid, witless, wooden-headed.

antonyms alert, clever.

stupidity *n* absurdity, asininity, betise, brainlessness, crassitude, crassness, denseness, dimness, dopiness, doziness, dullness, dumbness, duncery, fatuity, fatuousness, feeble-mindedness, folly, foolhardiness, foolishness, futility, goosery, idiocy, imbecility, impracticality, inaneness, inanity, indiscretion, ineptitude, insipience, irresponsibility, ludicrousness, lunacy, madness, naïvete, naivety, obtuseness, oscitancy, pointlessness, puerility, rashness, senselessness, silliness, simplicity, slowness, thick-headedness, thickness, vapidity.

antonyms alertness, cleverness.

stupor *n* coma, daze, inertia, insensibility, kef, lethargy, numbness, stupefaction, torpor, trance, unconsciousness, wonder.

antonym alertness.

sturdy *adj* athletic, brawny, determined, durable, firm, flourishing, hardy, hearty, husky, lusty, muscular, obstinate, powerful, resolute, robust, secure, solid, stalwart, staunch, steadfast, stout, strong, substantial, vigorous, well-built, well-made.

antonyms decrepit, puny.

stutter *v* falter, hesitate, mumble, splutter, stammer, stumble.

style *n* affluence, appearance, approach, bon ton, category, chic, comfort, cosmopolitanism, custom, cut, dash, design, diction, dressiness, dress-sense, ease, elan, elegance, expression, fashion, fashionableness, flair, flamboyance, form, genre, grace, grandeur, hand, haut ton, kind, luxury, manner, method, mode, panache, pattern, phraseology, phrasing, pizzazz, polish, rage, refinement, savoir-faire, smartness, sophistication, sort, spirit, strain, stylishness, taste, technique, tenor, tone, treatment, trend, type, urbanity, variety, vein, vogue, way, wording.

antonym inelegance.

v adapt, address, arrange, call, christen, create, cut, denominate, design, designate, dress, dub, entitle, fashion, label, name, shape, tailor, term, title.

stylish *adj* a la mode, chic, chichi, classy, dapper, dressy, fashionable, groovy, in vogue, modish, natty, polished, smart, snappy, snazzy, trendy, urbane, voguish.

antonym unstylish.

stylus *n* gnomon, graphium, graver, hand, index, needle, pen, pointer, probe, style.

stymie *v* baffle, balk, bamboozle, confound, defeat, flummox, foil, frustrate, hinder, mystify, nonplus, puzzle, snooker, stump, thwart.

antonym assist.

suave *adj* affable, agreeable, bland, charming, civilised, courteous, diplomatic, gracious, obliging, pleasing, polite, smooth, smooth-tongued, soft-spoken, sophisticated, unctuous, urbane, worldly.

antonym unsophisticated.

suavity *n* blandness, charm, sophistication, unctuosity, unctuousness, urbanity.

antonym coarseness.

subaquatic *adj* demersal, subaqua, subaqueous, submarine, submersed, undersea, underwater.

subconscious *adj* hidden, inner, innermost, intuitive, latent, repressed, subliminal, suppressed, unconscious.

antonym conscious.

n id, super-ego, unconscious, underself.

subdue *v* allay, break, check, conquer, control, crush, damp, dampen, daunt, defeat, discipline, humble, master, mellow, moderate, overcome, overpower, overrun, quell, quieten, reduce, repress, soften, soft-pedal, subact, subject, suppress, tame, trample, vanquish.

antonym arouse.

subdued *adj* abated, chastened, crestfallen, dejected, dim, downcast, grave, hushed, low-key, muted, quiet, repentant, repressed, restrained, sad, serious, shaded, sober, soft, solemn, sombre, subfusc, subtle, unobtrusive.

antonyms aroused, lively.

subject *n* affair, business, case, chapter, citizen, client, dependant, ground, issue, liegeman, matter, mind, national, object, participant, patient, point, question, subordinate, substance, theme, topic, vassal, victim.

antonym master.

adj answerable, captive, cognisable, conditional, contingent, dependent, disposed, enslaved, exposed, heteronomous, inferior, liable, obedient, open, prone, satellite, subjugated, submissive, subordinate, subservient, susceptible, vulnerable.

antonyms free, insusceptible, superior.

v expose, lay open, subdue, submit, subordinate, treat.

subjection *n* bondage, captivity, chains, crushing, defeat, domination, enslavement, mastery, oppression, quelling, servitude, shackles, slavery, subduing, subjugation, thraldom, thrall, vassalage.

subjective biased, emotional, idiosyncratic, individual, instinctive, introspective, intuitive, personal, prejudiced.

antonym objective.

subjugate *v* conquer, crush, defeat, enslave, enthrall, master, overcome, overpower, overthrow, quell, reduce, subdue, suppress, tame, thrall, vanquish.

antonym free.

sublimate *v* channel, divert, elevate, exalt, heighten, purify, redirect, refine, sublime, transfer, transmute, turn.

antonym let out.

sublime *adj* Dantean, Dantesque, elevated, eminent, empyreal, empyrean, exalted, glorious, grand, great, high, imposing, lofty, magnificent, majestic, noble, transcendent.

antonym lowly.

submerge *v* deluge, demerge, dip, drown, duck, dunk, engulf, flood, immerse, implunge, inundate, overflow, overwhelm, plunge, sink, submerse, swamp.

antonym surface.

submerged *adj* concealed, demersal, demersed, drowned, hidden, immersed, inundated, obscured, subaquatic, subaqueous, submarine, submersed, sunk, sunken, swamped, undersea, underwater, unseen.

submission *n* acquiescence, argument, assent, capitulation, compliance, contention, deference, docility, entry, meekness, obedience, passivity, presentation, proposal, resignation, resignedness, submissiveness, submitting, suggestion, surrender, tendering, tractability, yielding.

antonym intractability.

submissive *adj* abject, accommodating, acquiescent, amenable, biddable, bootlicking, complaisant, compliant, deferential, docile, dutiful, humble, ingratiating, malleable, meek, obedient, obeisant, obsequious, passive, patient, pliant, resigned, subdued, subservient, supine, tractable, uncomplaining, unresisting, yielding.

antonym intractable.

submit *v* accede, acquiesce, advance, agree, argue, assert, bend, bow, capitulate, claim, commit, comply, contend, defer, endure, knuckle under, move, present, proffer, propose, propound, put, refer, state, stoop, succumb, suggest, surrender, table, tender, tolerate, volunteer, yield.

antonym struggle.

subnormal *adj* cretinous, ESN, feeble-minded, imbecilic, inferior, low, moronic, retarded, slow, unteachable.

antonym gifted.

subordinate *adj* ancillary, auxiliary, dependent, inferior, junior, lesser, lower, menial, minor, secondary, servient, subject, subservient, subsidiary, supplementary.

antonym superior.

n adjunct, aide, assistant, attendant, dependant, inferior, junior, second, second banana, stooge, sub, subaltern, underdog, underling, underman, under-workman, weakling.

antonym superior.

subordination *n* inferiority, servitude, subjection, submission, subservience.

antonym superiority.

subscribe *v* acquiesce, advocate, agree, approve, consent, contribute, cough up, countenance, donate, endorse, fork out, give, offer, pledge, promise, shell out, support.

subscription *n* abonnement, contribution, donation, dues, fee, gift, offering, payment.

subsequent *adj* after, consequent, consequential, ensuing, following, later, postliminary, postliminous, resulting, succeeding.

antonym previous.

subsequently *adv* after, afterwards, consequently, later.

antonym previously.

subservient *adj* abject, accessory, ancillary, auxiliary, bootlicking, conducive, cringing, deferential, dough-faced, helpful, inferior, instrumental, obsequious, serviceable, servile, slavish, subject, submissive, subordinate, subsidiary, sycophantic, truckling, useful.

antonyms domineering, rebellious, unhelpful.

subside *v* abate, collapse, decline, decrease, descend, diminish, drop, dwindle, ease, ebb, fall, lessen, lower, moderate, quieten, recede, settle, sink, slacken, slake, wane.

antonym increase.

subsidence *n* abatement, decline, decrease, de-escalation, descent, detumescence, diminution, ebb, lessening, settlement, settling, sinking, slackening.

antonym increase.

subsidiary *adj* adjective, aiding, ancillary, assistant, auxiliary, branch, contributory, co-operative, helpful, lesser, minor, secondary, serviceable, subordinate, subservient, succursal, supplemental, supplementary, useful.

antonym chief.

n affiliate, branch, division, offshoot, part, section.

subsidise *v* aid, back, finance, fund, promote, sponsor, support, underwrite.

subsidy *n* aid, allowance, assistance, backing, contribution, finance, grant, help, sponsorship, subvention, support.

subsist *v* continue, endure, exist, hold out, inhere, last, live, remain, survive.

subsistence *n* aliment, existence, food, keep, livelihood, living, maintenance, nourishment, prog, provision, rations, support, survival, sustenance, upkeep, victuals.

substance *n* actuality, affluence, assets, body, burden, concreteness, consistence, element, entity, essence, estate, fabric, force, foundation, gist, gravamen, ground, hypostasis, import, material, matter, meaning, means, nitty-gritty, pith, property, reality, resources, significance, solidity, stuff, subject, subject-matter, texture, theme, wealth.

substandard *adj* damaged, imperfect, inadequate, inferior, poor, second-rate, shoddy, tawdry, unacceptable.

antonym first-rate.

substantial *adj* actual, ample, big, bulky, considerable, corporeal, durable, enduring, essential, existent, firm, full-bodied, generous, goodly, hefty, important, large, massive, material, positive, real, significant, sizable, solid, sound, stout, strong, sturdy, tidy, true, valid, weighty, well-built, worthwhile.

antonyms insignificant, small.

substantially *adv* essentially, largely, materially, significantly, to all intents and purposes.

antonym slightly.

substantiate *v* affirm, authenticate, confirm, corroborate, embody, establish, prove, support, validate, verify.

antonym disprove.

substitute *v* change, commute, exchange, interchange, replace, subrogate, swap, switch.

n agent, alternate, depute, deputy, equivalent, ersatz, locum, locum tenens, makeshift, proxy, relief, replacement, replacer, reserve, stand-by, stop-gap, sub, succedaneum, supply, surrogate, temp, vicar.

adj acting, additional, alternative, ersatz, proxy, replacement, reserve, second, surrogate, temporary, vicarious.

substitute for act for, cover for, deputise, double for, fill in for, relieve, stand in for, sub.

substitution *n* change, exchange, interchange, replacement, swap, swapping, switch, switching.

subterfuge *n* artifice, deception, deviousness, dodge, duplicity, evasion, excuse, expedient, machination, manoeuvre, ploy, pretence, pretext, quibble, ruse, scheme, shift, stall, stratagem, trick.

antonyms honesty, openness.

subtle *adj* artful, astute, crafty, cunning, deep, delicate, designing, devious, discriminating, elusive, faint, fine-drawn, fine-spun, impalpable, implied, indirect, ingenious, insinuated, intriguing, keen, Machiavellian, nice, obstruse, over-refined, penetrating, profound, rarefied, refined, scheming, shrewd, slight, sly, sophisticated, tenuous, understated, wily.

antonyms open, unsubtle.

subtlety *n* acumen, acuteness, artfulness, astuteness, cleverness, craftiness, cunning, delicacy, deviousness, discernment, discrimination, finesse, guile, intricacy, nicety, openness, penetration, refinement, sagacity, skill, slyness, sophistication, unsubtlety, wiliness.

subtract *v* debit, deduct, detract, diminish, remove, withdraw.

antonyms add, add to.

suburbs *n* banlieue, commuter belt, dormitory, environs, exurbia, faubourg, neighbourhood, outskirts, precincts, purlieus, stockbroker belt, suburbia, villadom.

antonyms centre, heart.

subversive *adj* destructive, disruptive, incendiary, inflammatory, insurrectionary, overthrowing, perversive, riotous, seditious, treasonous, underground, undermining.

antonym loyal.

n deviationist, dissident, fifth columnist, freedom fighter, insurrectionary, quisling, saboteur, seditionary, seditionist, terrorist, traitor.

subvert *v* confound, contaminate, corrupt, debase, demolish, demoralise, deprave, destroy, disrupt, invalidate, overturn, pervert, poison, raze, ruin, sabotage, undermine, upset, vitiate, wreck.

antonyms boost, uphold.

subway *n* metro, tube, underground.

succeed *v* arrive, ensue, fadge, flourish, follow, make good, make it, prosper, result, supervene, thrive, triumph, work.

antonyms fail, precede.

succeed to accede, come into, enter upon, inherit, replace, supersede, take over.

antonyms abdicate, precede.

succeeding *adj* coming, ensuing, following, later, next, subsequent, successive, to come.

antonym previous.

success *n* ascendancy, bestseller, celebrity, eminence, fame, fortune, happiness, hit, luck, prosperity, sensation, somebody, star, triumph, VIP, well-doing, winner.

antonym failure.

successful *adj* acknowledged, bestselling, booming, efficacious, favourable, flourishing, fortunate, fruitful, lucky, lucrative, moneymaking, paying, profitable, prosperous, rewarding, satisfactory, satisfying, soaraway, thriven, thriving, top, unbeaten, victorious, wealthy, well-doing.

antonym unsuccessful.

successfully *adv* beautifully, famously, fine, great, swimmingly, victoriously, well.

antonym unsuccessfully.

succession *n* accession, assumption, chain, concatenation, continuation, course, cycle, descendants, descent, elevation, flow, inheritance, line, lineage, order, procession, progression, race, run, sequence, series, train.

successive *adj* consecutive, following, in succession, sequent, succeeding.

succinct *adj* brief, compact, compendious, concise, condensed, gnomic, laconic, pithy, short, summary, terse.

antonym wordy.

succour *v* aid, assist, befriend, comfort, encourage, foster, help, help out, nurse, relieve, support.

antonym undermine.

n aid, assistance, comfort, help, helping hand, ministrations, relief, support.

succulent *adj* fleshy, juicy, luscious, lush, mellow, moist, mouthwatering, rich, sappy.

antonym dry.

succumb *v* capitulate, collapse, deteriorate, die, fall, give in, knuckle under, submit, surrender, yield.

antonym overcome.

suck *v* absorb, drain, draw in, extract, imbibe.

sucker *n* butt, cat's-paw, dupe, fool, mark, mug, patsy, pushover, sap, stooge, victim.

sucking-up *n* arse-licking, bootlicking, currying favour, fawning, flattering, ingratiating, toadying, truckling.

sudden *adj* abrupt, hasty, hurried, impulsive, prompt, quick, rapid, rash, snap, startling, subitaneous, swift, unexpected, unforeseen, unusual.

antonym slow.

suddenness *n* abruptness, haste, hastiness, hurriedness, impulsiveness.

antonym slowness.

sue *v* apply, beg, beseech, charge, entreat, indict, petition, plead, prosecute, solicit, summon, supplicate.

suffer *v* ache, agonise, allow, bear, brook, deteriorate, endure, experience, feel, grieve, hurt, let, permit, sorrow, support, sustain, tolerate, undergo.

suffering *n* ache, affliction, agony, anguish, discomfort, distress, hardship, martyrdom, misery, ordeal, pain, pangs, torment, torture.

suffice *v* answer, content, do, measure up, satisfy, serve.

sufficiency *n* adequacy, adequateness, competence, conceit, enough, enow, plenty, quantum sufficit, satiety, sufficience.

antonym insufficiency.

sufficient *adj* adequate, competent, effective, enough, satisfactory, sufficing, well-off, well-to-do.

antonyms insufficient, poor.

suffocate *v* asphyxiate, choke, smother, stifle, strangle, throttle.

suffuse *v* bathe, colour, cover, flood, imbue, infuse, mantle, permeate, pervade, redden, steep, transfuse.

suggest *v* advise, advocate, connote, evoke, hint, imply, indicate, inkle, innuendo, insinuate, intimate, move, propose, recommend.

antonyms demonstrate, order.

suggestion *n* breath, hint, incitement, indication, innuendo, insinuation, intimation, motion, plan, proposal, proposition, recommendation, suspicion, temptation, trace, whisper.

antonyms demonstration, order.

suggestive *adj* bawdy, blue, evocative, expressive, immodest, improper, indecent, indelicate, indicative, insinuating, meaning, off-colour, page-three, provocative, prurient, racy, redolent, reminiscent, ribald, risque, rude, smutty, spicy, titillating, unseemly.

antonyms clean, unevocative.

suicide *n* felo de se, hara-kiri, kamikaze, self-destruction, self-immolation, self-murder, self-slaughter, suttee.

suit *v* accommodate, adapt, adjust, agree, answer, become, befit, correspond, do, fashion, fit, gee, gratify, harmonise, match, modify, please, proportion, satisfy, tailor, tally.

antonyms clash, displease.

n. action, addresses, appeal, attentions, case, cause, clothing, costume, courtship, dress, ensemble, entreaty, get-up, habit, invocation, kind, lawsuit, outfit, petition, prayer, proceeding, prosecution, request, rig-out, series, trial, type.

suitability *n* appositeness, appropriateness, aptness, fitness, fittingness, opportuneness, rightness, timeliness.

antonym unsuitability.

suitable *adj* acceptable, accordant, adequate, applicable, apposite, appropriate, apt, becoming, befitting, competent, conformable, congenial, congruent, consonant, convenient, correspondent, due, fit, fitting, opportune, pertinent, proper, relevant, right, satisfactory, seemly, square, suited, well-becoming, well-beseeming.

antonym unsuitable.

suitably *adv* acceptably, accordingly, appropriately, fitly, fittingly, properly, quite.

antonym unsuitably.

suite *n* apartment, attendants, collection, entourage, escort, followers, furniture, household, retainers, retinue, rooms, sequence, series, servants, set, train.

suitor *n* admirer, beau, follower, pretendant, swain, wooer, young man.

sulk *v* boody, brood, grouch, grump, mope, pet, pout.

sulky *adj* aloof, churlish, cross, disgruntled, grouty, ill-humoured, moody, morose, perverse, pettish, petulant, put out, resentful, sullen.

antonym cheerful.

sullen *adj* baleful, brooding, cheerless, cross, dark, dismal, dull, farouche, gloomy, glowering, glum, heavy, lumpish, malignant, moody, morose, obstinate, perverse, silent, sombre, sour, stubborn, sulky, surly, unsociable.

antonym cheerful.

sullenness *n* brooding, glowering, glumness, heaviness, moodiness, moroseness, sourness, sulkiness, surliness.

antonym cheerfulness.

sully *v* befoul, besmirch, blemish, contaminate, darken, defile, dirty, disgrace, dishonour, distain, mar, pollute, spoil, spot, stain, taint, tarnish.

antonyms cleanse, honour.

sultry *adj* close, come-hither, erotic, hot, humid, indecent, lurid, muggy, oppressive, passionate, provocative, seductive, sensual, sexy, sticky, stifling, stuffy, sweltering, torrid, voluptuous.

antonyms cold, cool.

sum *n* aggregate, amount, completion, culmination, entirety, height, quantity, reckoning, result, score, substance, sum total, summary, tally, total, totality, whole.

sum up close, conclude, perorate, precis, recapitulate, review, summarise.

summarily *adv* abruptly, arbitrarily, expeditiously, forthwith, hastily, immediately, peremptorily, promptly, speedily, swiftly.

summarise *v* abbreviate, abridge, condense, encapsulate, epitomise, outline, precis, review, shorten, sum up.

antonym expand (on).

summary *n* abridgement, abstract, compendium, digest, epitome, essence, extract, outline, precis, recapitulation, resume, review, rundown, summation, summing-up, synopsis.

adj arbitrary, brief, compact, compendious, concise, condensed, cursory, expeditious, hasty, laconic, perfunctory, pithy, short, succinct.

antonym lengthy.

summer-house *n* belvedere, gazebo, pavilion.

summit *n* acme, apex, apogee, crown, culmination, head, height, high noon, peak, pinnacle, point, top, vertex, zenith.

antonyms bottom, nadir.

summon *v* accite, arouse, assemble, beckon, bid, call, cite, convene, convoke, gather, hist, invite, invoke, mobilise, muster, preconise, rally, rouse.

antonym dismiss.

sumptuous *adj* costly, dear, expensive, extravagant, gorgeous, grand, lavish, luxurious, magnificent, opulent, plush, posh, princely, rich, ritzy, splendid, superb.

antonym mean.

sun *n* daystar, star, sun-disc, sunlight, sunshine.

v bake, bask, brown, insolate, sunbathe, tan.

sunbathe *v* bake, bask, brown, insolate, take the sun, tan.

sunburnt *adj* blistered, bronzed, brown, burnt, peeling, red, ruddy, scarlet, tanned, weather-beaten.

antonym pale.

sunder *v* chop, cleave, cut, dissever, dissunder, divide, part, separate, sever, split.

antonym join.

sundry *adj* a few, assorted, different, divers, miscellaneous, separate, several, some, varied, various.

sunk *adj* done for, doomed, finished, lost, ruined, up the creek, up the spout.

sunken *adj* buried, concave, depressed, drawn, emaciated, gaunt, haggard, hollow, hollowed, immersed, lower, recessed, submerged.

sunless *adj* bleak, cheerless, cloudy, dark, depressing, dismal, dreary, gloomy, grey, hazy, overcast, sombre.

antonym sunny.

sunny *adj* beaming, blithe, bright, brilliant, buoyant, cheerful, cheery, clear, cloudless, fine, genial, happy, joyful, light-hearted, luminous, optimistic, pleasant, radiant, smiling, summery, sun-bright, sunlit, sunshiny.

antonym gloomy.

sunrise *n* aurora, cock-crow, crack of dawn, dawn, daybreak, daylight, dayspring, sun-up.

sunset *n* crepuscule, dusk, evening, eventide, gloaming, nightfall, sundown, twilight.

super *adj* excellent, glorious, incomparable, magnificent, marvellous, matchless, outstanding, peerless, sensational, smashing, superb, terrific, top-notch, wizard, wonderful.

antonym poor.

superannuated *adj* aged, antiquated, decrepit, fogram, moribund, obsolete, old, past it, pensioned off, put out to grass, retired, senile, superannuate.

antonym young.

superb *adj* admirable, breathtaking, choice, clipping, excellent, exquisite, fine, first-rate, gorgeous, grand, magnificent, marvellous, splendid, superior, unrivalled.

antonym poor.

supercilious *adj* arrogant, condescending, contemptuous, disdainful, haughty, highty-tighty, hoity-toity, imperious, insolent, lofty, lordly, overbearing, patronising, proud, scornful, snooty, snotty, snouty, stuck-up, toffee-nosed, uppish, uppity, upstage, vainglorious.

antonym humble.

superficial *adj* apparent, casual, cosmetic, cursory, desultory, empty, empty-headed, evident, exterior, external, frivolous, hasty, hurried, lightweight, nodding, ostensible, outward, passing, perfunctory, peripheral, seeming, shallow, silly, sketchy, skin-deep, slapdash, slight, surface, trivial, unanalytical, unreflective.

antonym detailed.

superficially *adv* apparently, externally, ostensibly, seemingly.

antonym in depth.

superfluity *n* excess, exuberance, glut, perissology, pleonasm, plethora, postiche, redundancy, superabundance, surfeit, surplus.

antonym lack.

superfluous *adj* de trop, excess, excessive, extra, needless, otiose, pleonastic(al), postiche, redundant, remaining, residuary, spare, superabundant, supererogatory, supernumerary, surplus, uncalled-for, unnecessary, unneeded, unneedful, unwanted.

antonym necessary.

superhuman *adj* divine, great, herculean, heroic, immense, paranormal, phenomenal, preternatural, prodigious, stupendous, supernatural, valiant.

antonyms average, ordinary.

superintend *v* administer, control, direct, guide, inspect, manage, overlook, oversee, run, steer, supervise.

superintendence *n* administration, care, charge, control, direction, government, guidance, inspection, management, supervision, surveillance.

superintendent *n* administrator, chief, conductor, controller, curator, director, gaffer, governor, inspector, manager, overseer, supervisor.

superior *adj* admirable, airy, better, choice, condescending, de luxe, disdainful, distinguished, excellent, exceptional, exclusive, fine, first-class, first-rate, good, grander, greater, haughty, high-class, higher, highty-tighty, hoity-toity, lofty, lordly, par excellence, patronising, predominant, preferred, pretentious, prevailing, respectable, snobbish, snooty, snotty, snouty, stuck-up, supercilious, superordinate, surpassing, top-flight, top-notch, transcendent, unrivalled, upper, uppish, uppity, upstage, worthy.

antonyms humble, inferior.

n boss, chief, director, foreman, gaffer, higher-up, manager, principal, senior, supervisor.

antonyms inferior, junior.

superiority *n* advantage, ascendancy, edge, excellence, lead, predominance, pre-eminence, preponderance, prevalence, supremacy, vis major.

antonym inferiority.

superlative *adj* consummate, crack, excellent, greatest, highest, magnificent, matchless, nonpareil, outstanding, peerless, supreme, surpassing, transcendent, unbeatable, unbeaten, unparalleled, unrivalled, unsurpassed.

antonym poor.

superman *n* colossus, giant, Übermensch.

supernatural *adj* abnormal, dark, ghostly, hidden, hyperphysical, metaphysical, miraculous, mysterious, mystic, occult, paranormal, phantom, preternatural, psychic, spectral, spiritual, superlunary, supersensible, supersensory, uncanny, unearthly, unnatural.

antonym natural.

supernumerary *adj* excess, excessive, extra, extraordinary, redundant, spare, superfluous, surplus.

antonym necessary.

supersede *v* annul, displace, oust, overrule, remove, replace, succeed, supplant, supplement, suspend, usurp.

superstition *n* Aberglaube, delusion, fable, fallacy, illusion, myth, old wives' tale, voodooism.

superstitious *adj* delusive, fallacious, false, fetishistic, groundless, illusory, voodooistic.

supervise *v* administer, conduct, control, direct, general, handle, inspect, keep tabs on, manage, oversee, preside over, run, superintend.

supervision *n* administration, auspices, care, charge, control, direction, guidance, instruction, leading-strings, management, oversight, stewardship, superintendence, surveillance.

supervisor *n* administrator, boss, chief, foreman, gaffer, inspector, manager, overseer, steward, superintendent.

supervisory *adj* administrative, directorial, executive, managerial, overseeing, superintendent.

supine *adj* apathetic, bored, careless, flat, heedless, horizontal, idle, inactive, incurious, indifferent, indolent, inert, languid, lazy, lethargic, listless, negligent, passive, prostrate, recumbent, resigned, slothful, sluggish, spineless, spiritless, torpid, uninterested, unresisting.

antonyms alert, upright.

supplant *v* displace, dispossess, oust, overthrow, remove, replace, supersede, topple, undermine, unseat.

supple *adj* bending, double-jointed, elastic, flexible, limber, lithe, loose-limbed, plastic, pliable, pliant, whippy, willowish, willowy.

antonym rigid.

supplement *n* addendum, addition, appendix, codicil, complement, extra, insert, postscript, pull-out, rider, sequel, supplemental, supplementary, suppletion.

v add, add to, augment, complement, eke, eke out, extend, fill up, reinforce, supply, top up.

antonym deplete.

supplementary *adj* accompanying, additional, ancillary, auxiliary, complementary, extra, secondary, supplemental, suppletive, suppletory.

antonym core.

suppliant *adj* begging, beseeching, craving, entreating, imploring, importunate, supplicating.

n applicant, petitioner, pleader, postulant, suitor, supplicant.

supplication *n* appeal, entreaty, invocation, orison, petition, plea, pleading, prayer, request, rogation, solicitation, suit, supplicat.

supplicatory *adj* begging, beseeching, imploring, imprecatory, petitioning, precative, precatory, supplicating.

supplier *n* dealer, hawker, Italian warehouseman, pedlar, provider, purveyor, retailer, seller, shop-keeper, sutler, vendor, vivandier, vivandière, wholesaler.

supplies *n* equipment, food, foodstuffs, materials, materiel, necessities, provender, provisions, rations, stores, victuals, vittles.

supply *v* afford, contribute, endow, equip, fill, furnish, give, grant, minister, outfit, produce, provide, purvey, replenish, satisfy, stock, store, victual, yield.

antonym take.

n cache, fund, hoard, materials, necessities, provender, provisions, quantity, rations, reserve, reservoir, service, source, stake, stock, stockpile, store, stores.

antonym lack.

support *v* adminiculate, advocate, aid, appui, appuy, assist, authenticate, back, bear, bolster, brace, brook, buttress, carry, champion, cherish, confirm, corroborate, countenance, crutch, defend, document, endorse, endure, finance, foster, fund, help, hold, keep, maintain, nourish, promote, prop, rally round, reinforce, second, stand (for), stay, stomach, strengthen, strut, submit, subsidise, substantiate, succour, suffer, sustain, take (someone's) part, thole, tolerate, underpin, underwrite, uphold, verify.

antonyms contradict, oppose.

n abutment, adminicle, aid, aidance, approval, appui, assistance, back, backbone, backer, backing, backstays, backstop, blessing, brace, championship, comfort, comforter, crutch, encouragement, foundation, friendship, fulcrum, furtherance, help, jockstrap, keep, lining, livelihood, loper, loyalty, mainstay, maintenance, patronage, pillar, post, prop, protection, relief, second, sheet-anchor, shore, stanchion, stay, stiffener, subsistence, succour, supporter, supportment, supporture, sustenanace, sustenance, underpinning, upkeep.

antonym opposition.

supporter *n* adherent, advocate, ally, apologist, bottle-holder, champion, co-worker, defender, fan, follower, friend, heeler, helper, patron, seconder, sponsor, upholder, well-wisher.

antonym opponent.

supportive *adj* attentive, caring, encouraging, helpful, reassuring, sympathetic, understanding.

antonym discouraging.

suppose *v* assume, believe, calculate, conceive, conclude, conjecture, consider, expect, fancy, guess, hypothesise, hypothetise, imagine, infer, judge, opine, posit, postulate, presume, presuppose, pretend, surmise, think.

antonym know.

supposed *adj* accepted, alleged, assumed, conjectured, hypothetical, imagined, presumed, presupposed, professed, putative, reported, reputed, rumoured.

antonym known.

supposed to expected to, intended to, meant to, obliged to, required to.

supposedly *adv* allegedly, assumedly, avowedly, hypothetically, ostensibly, presumably, professedly, purportedly, theoretically.

antonym really.

supposition *n* assumption, conjecture, doubt, guess, guesstimate, guesswork, hypothesis, idea, notion, opinion, postulate, presumption, speculation, surmise, theory.

antonym knowledge.

suppress *v* censor, check, conceal, conquer, contain, crush, extinguish, muffle, muzzle, overpower, overthrow, quash, quell, repress, restrain, silence, smother, snuff out, squelch, stamp out, stifle, stop, strangle, subdue, submerge, vote down, withhold.

antonyms encourage, incite.

suppression *n* censorship, check, clampdown, crackdown, crushing, dissolution, elimination, extinction, inhibition, prohibition, quashing, quelling, smothering, termination.

antonyms encouragement, incitement.

suppurate *v* discharge, fester, gather, matter, maturate, ooze, weep.

suppuration *n* diapyesis, festering, mattering, pus, pussiness.

supremacy *n* ascendancy, dominance, domination, dominion, hegemony, lordship, mastery, paramountcy, predominance, pre-eminence, primacy, sovereignty, sway.

supreme *adj* cardinal, chief, consummate, crowning, culminating, extreme, final, first, foremost, greatest, head, highest, incomparable, leading, matchless, nonpareil, paramount, peerless, predominant, pre-eminent, prevailing, prime, principal, second-to-none, sovereign, superlative, surpassing, top, transcendent, ultimate, unbeatable, unbeaten, unsurpassed, utmost, world-beating.

antonyms lowly, poor, slight.

sure *adj* accurate, assured, banker, bound, certain, clear, confident, convinced, decided, definite, dependable, effective, fast, firm, fixed, foolproof, guaranteed, honest, indisputable, ineluctable, inescapable, inevitable, infallible, irrevocable, persuaded, positive, precise, reliable, safe, satisfied, secure, solid, stable, steadfast, steady, sure-fire, trustworthy, trusty, undeniable, undoubted, unerring, unfailing, unmistakable, unswerving, unwavering.

antonyms doubtful, unsure.

surely *adv* assuredly, certainly, confidently, definitely, doubtlessly, firmly, indubitably, inevitably, inexorably, safely, undoubtedly, unquestionably.

surety *n* bail, bond, bondsman, certainty, deposit, guarantee, guarantor, hostage, indemnity, insurance, mortgagor, pledge, safety, security, sponsor, warrant, warranty.

surface *n* covering, day, exterior, façade, face, facet, grass, outside, plane, side, skin, superficies, top, veneer, working-surface, worktop.

antonym interior.

adj apparent, exterior, external, outer, outside, outward, superficial.

antonym interior.

v appear, come to light, emerge, materialise, rise, transpire.

antonyms disappear, sink.

surfeit *n* bellyful, excess, glut, overindulgence, plethora, satiety, superabundance, superfluity.

antonym lack.

v cram, fill, glut, gorge, overcloy, overfeed, overfill, satiate, stuff.

surge *v* billow, eddy, gush, heave, rise, roll, rush, seethe, swell, swirl, tower, undulate.

n access, billow, breaker, efflux, flood, flow, gurgitation, gush, intensification, outpouring, roller, rush, swell, uprush, upsurge, wave.

surly *adj* bearish, brusque, chuffy, churlish, crabbed, cross, crusty, curmudgeonly, grouchy, gruff, grum, gurly, ill-natured, morose, perverse, sulky, sullen, testy, uncivil, ungracious.

antonym pleasant.

surmise *v* assume, conclude, conjecture, consider, deduce, fancy, guess, imagine, infer, opine, presume, speculate, suppose, suspect.

antonym know.

n assumption, conclusion, conjecture, deduction, guess, hypothesis, idea, inference, notion, opinion, possibility, presumption, speculation, supposition, suspicion, thought.

antonym certainty.

surmount *v* conquer, exceed, get over, master, overcome, surpass, triumph over, vanquish.

surpass *v* beat, best, ding, eclipse, exceed, excel, outdo, outshine, outstrip, override, overshadow, surmount, top, tower above, transcend.

surpassing *adj* exceptional, extraordinary, incomparable, inimitable, matchless, outstanding, phenomenal, rare, supreme, transcendent, unrivalled, unsurpassed.

antonym poor.

surplus *n* balance, excess, overplus, remainder, residue, superabundance, superfluity, surfeit, surplusage.

antonym lack.

adj excess, extra, odd, redundant, remaining, spare, superfluous, unused.

antonym essential.

surprise *v* amaze, astonish, astound, bewilder, confuse, disconcert, dismay, flabbergast, nonplus, stagger, startle, stun.

n amazement, astonishment, bewilderment, bombshell, dismay, eye-opener, incredulity, jolt, revelation, shock, start, stupefaction, wonder.

antonym composure.

surprised *adj* amazed, astonished, confounded, disconcerted, incredulous, nonplussed, open-mouthed, shocked, speechless, staggered, startled, thunderstruck.

antonyms composed, unsurprised.

surprising *adj* amazing, astonishing, astounding, extraordinary, incredible, marvellous, remarkable, staggering, startling, stunning, unexpected, unlooked-for, unusual, unwonted, wonderful.

antonyms expected, unsurprising.

surrender *v* abandon, capitulate, cede, concede, forego, give in, give up, quit, relinquish, remise, renounce, resign, submit, succumb, waive, yield.

antonym fight on.

n appeasement, capitulation, decheance, delivery, Munich, relinquishment, remise, rendition, renunciation, resignation, submission, white flag, yielding.

surreptitious *adj* behind-door, clandestine, covert, fraudulent, furtive, secret, sly, sneaking, stealthy, unauthorised, underhand, veiled.

antonym open.

surrogate *n* deputy, proxy, replacement, representative, stand-in, substitute.

surround *v* begird, besiege, compass, embosom, encase, encincture, encircle, enclose, encompass, envelop, environ, girdle, invest, ring.

surrounding *adj* adjacent, adjoining, ambient, bordering, circumambient, circumjacent, encircling, enclosing, environing, environmental, nearby, neighbouring.

surroundings *n* ambience, background, entourage, environment, environs, locale, location, milieu, neighbourhood, setting, vicinity.

surveillance *n* care, charge, check, control, direction, guardianship, inspection, monitoring, observation, regulation, scrutiny, stewardship, superintendence, supervision, vigilance, watch.

survey *v* appraise, assess, consider, contemplate, estimate, examine, inspect, measure, observe, peruse, plan, plot, prospect, reconnoitre, research, review, scan, scrutinise, study, supervise, surview, triangulate, view.

n appraisal, assessment, conspectus, examination, geodesy, inquiry, inspection, measurement, overview, perusal, review, sample, scrutiny, study, triangulation.

surveying *n* geodesy, geodetics, measurement, triangulation.

surveyor *n* assessor, examiner, geodesist, inspector.

survive *v* endure, exist, last, last out, live, live out, live through, outlast, outlive, ride, stay, subsist, weather, withstand.

antonym succumb.

susceptibility *n* defencelessness, liability, openness, predisposition, proclivity, proneness, propensity, responsiveness, sensitivity, suggestibility, tendency, vulnerability, weakness.

antonyms impregnability, resistance.

susceptible *adj* defenceless, disposed, given, impressible, impressionable, inclined, liable, open, predisposed, pregnable, prone, receptive, responsive, sensitive, subject, suggestible, tender, vulnerable.

antonyms impregnable, resistant.

suspect *v* believe, call in question, conclude, conjecture, consider, distrust, doubt, fancy, feel, guess, infer, mistrust, opine, speculate, suppose, surmise.

adj debatable, dodgy, doubtful, dubious, fishy, questionable, suspicious, unauthoritative, unreliable.

antonyms acceptable, innocent, straightforward.

suspend *v* adjourn, append, arrest, attach, cease, dangle, debar, defer, delay, disbar, discontinue, dismiss, expel, freeze, hang, hold off, interrupt, postpone, shelve, sideline, stay, swing, unfrock, withhold.

antonyms continue, expedite, reinstate, restore.

suspended *adj* abeyant, dangling, hanging, pendent, pending, pensile, put on ice, shelved.

suspense *n* anticipation, anxiety, apprehension, doubt, excitement, expectancy, expectation, incertitude, indecision, insecurity, irresolution, tension, uncertainty, wavering.

antonyms certainty, knowledge.

suspension *n* abeyance, abeyancy, adjournment, break, cessation, deferment, deferral, delay, diapause, disbarment, discontinuation, dormancy, intermission, interruption, moratorium, postponement, remission, respite, standstill, stay.

antonyms continuation, reinstatement, restoration.

suspicion *n* apprehension, chariness, conjecture, distrust, doubt, glimmer, guess, hint, hunch, idea, impression, intuition, jealousy, misgiving, mistrust, notion, presentiment, qualm, scepticism, shade, shadow, soupçon, strain, streak, suggestion, supposition, surmise, suspiciousness, tinge, touch, trace, wariness.

antonym trust.

suspicious *adj* apprehensive, chary, distrustful, dodgy, doubtful, dubious, fishy, incredulous, irregular, jealous, louche, mistrustful, peculiar, queer, questionable, sceptical, shady, suspect, suspecting, unbelieving, uneasy, wary.

antonyms innocent, trustful, unexceptionable.

sustain *v* aid, approve, assist, bear, carry, comfort, confirm, continue, endorse, endure, experience, feel, foster, help, hold, keep going, maintain, nourish, nurture, prolong, protract, provide for, ratify, relieve, sanction, stay, suffer, support, survive, sustenate, undergo, uphold, validate, verify, withstand.

sustained *adj* constant, continuous, long-drawn-out, non-stop, perpetual, prolonged, protracted, steady, unremitting.

antonyms broken, intermittent, interrupted, occasional, spasmodic.

sustenance *n* aliment, board, comestibles, commons, eatables, edibles, etape, fare, food, freshments, livelihood, maintenance, nourishment, nutriment, pabulum, provender, provisions, rations, refection, subsistence, support, viands, victuals.

svelte *adj* elegant, graceful, lissom, lithe, polished, shapely, slender, slinky, smooth, sophisticated, streamlined, sylphlike, urbane, willowy.

antonyms bulky, ungainly.

swagger *v* bluster, boast, brag, brank, bully, cock, crow, gasconade, hector, parade, prance, roist, roister, strut, swank.

n arrogance, bluster, boastfulness, boasting, braggadocio, display, fanfaronade, gasconade, gasconism, ostentation, rodomontade, show, showing off, swank, vainglory.

antonyms diffidence, modesty, restraint.

swaggerer *n* attitudiniser, blusterer, boaster, braggadocio, braggart, fanfaron, gascon, gasconader, loudmouth, peacock, poser, poseur, poseuse, posturer, rodomontader, roister, roisterer, scaramouch, show-off, strutter, swank, swashbuckler, whiffler.

swallow *v* absorb, accept, assimilate, believe, buy, consume, devour, down, drink, eat, englut, engulf, gulp, imbibe, ingest, ingurgitate, knock back, quaff, stifle, suppress, swig, swill, wash down.

swallow up absorb, consume, deplete, dissipate, drain, eat up, engulf, envelop, exhaust, gobble up, guzzle, ingurgitate, overrun, overwhelm, use up, waste.

swamp *n* bog, dismal, everglades, fen, marsh, mire, morass, moss, quagmire, quicksands, slough, vlei.

v beset, besiege, capsise, deluge, drench, engulf, flood, inundate, overload, overwhelm, saturate, sink, submerge, waterlog.

swampy *adj* boggy, fenny, marish, marshy, miry, mushy, paludal, quaggy, soggy, squelchy, uliginous, waterlogged, wet.

antonyms arid, dehydrated, dry.

swank *v* attitudinise, boast, parade, posture, preen oneself, show off, strut, swagger.

n boastfulness, conceit, conceitedness, display, ostentation, pretentiousness, self-advertisement, show, showing-off, swagger, vainglory.

antonyms modesty, restraint.

swanky *adj* de luxe, epideictic, exclusive, expensive, fancy, fashionable, flash, flashy, glamorous, grand, lavish, luxurious, ostentatious, plush, plushy, posh, pretentious, rich, ritzy, showy, smart, stylish, sumptuous, swish.

antonyms discreet, unobtrusive.

swap, swop *v* bandy, barter, exchange, interchange, substitute, switch, trade, traffic, transpose.

swarm *n* army, bevy, concourse, crowd, drove, flock, herd, horde, host, mass, mob, multitude, myriad, shoal, throng.

v congregate, crowd, flock, flood, mass, stream, throng.

swarm with abound, bristle, crawl, hotch, teem.

swarthy *adj* black, brown, dark, dark-complexioned, dark-skinned, dusky, swart, swarth, tawny.

antonyms fair, pale.

swashbuckling *adj* adventurous, bold, daredevil, dashing, exciting, flamboyant, gallant, lusty, mettlesome, rip-roaring, robust, roisterous, spirited, swaggering.

antonyms tame, unadventurous, unexciting.

swastika *n* fylfot, gammadion, gammation, Hakenkreuz.

swathe *v* bandage, bind, cloak, drape, enshroud, envelop, enwrap, fold, furl, lap, sheathe, shroud, swaddle, wind, wrap.

antonyms unwind, unwrap.

sway *v* affect, bend, control, direct, divert, dominate, fluctuate, govern, guide, incline, induce, influence, lean, lurch, oscillate, overrule, persuade, rock, roll, swerve, swing, titter, veer, wave.

n ascendency, authority, cloud, command, control, dominion, government, hegemony, influence, jurisdiction, leadership, power, predominance, preponderance, rule, sovereignty, sweep, swerve, swing.

swear[1] *v* affirm, assert, asseverate, attest, avow, declare, depose, insist, promise, testify, vow, warrant.

swear[2] *v* blaspheme, blind, curse, cuss, eff, imprecate, maledict, take the Lord's name in vain, turn the air blue.

swearing *n* bad language, billingsgate, blasphemy, coprolalia, cursing, cussing, effing and blinding, expletives, foul language, imprecations, maledictions, profanity.

swear-word *n* blasphemy, curse, expletive, four-letter word, imprecation, oath, obscenity, profanity.

sweat *n* agitation, anxiety, chore, dew, diaphoresis, distress, drudgery, effort, exudation, fag, flap, hidrosis, labour, panic, perspiration, strain, sudation, sudor, worry.

v agonise, chafe, exude, fret, glow, perspirate, perspire, swelter, worry.

sweaty *adj* clammy, damp, glowing, moist, perspiring, sticky, sudorous, sweating.

antonyms cool, dry.

sweep *v* brush, career, clean, clear, dust, flounce, fly, glance, glide, hurtle, pass, remove, sail, scud, skim, tear, whisk, zoom.

n arc, bend, clearance, compass, curve, expanse, extent, gesture, impetus, move, movement, onrush, range, scope, span, stretch, stroke, swing, vista.

sweeping *adj* across-the-board, all-embracing, all-inclusive, blanket, broad, comprehensive, exaggerated, extensive, far-reaching, global, indiscriminate, overdrawn, oversimplified, overstated, radical, simplistic, thoroughgoing, unanalytical, unqualified, wholesale, wide, wide-ranging.

sweepstake *n* draw, lottery, sweep, sweepstakes.

sweet[1] *adj* affectionate, agreeable, amabile, amiable, appealing, aromatic, attractive, balmy, beautiful, beloved, benign, charming, cherished, clean, cloying, darling, dear, dearest, delightful, dulcet, engaging, euphonic, euphonious, fair, fragrant, fresh, gentle, gracious, harmonious, honeyed, icky, kin, lovable, luscious, mellow, melodious, melting, mild, musical, new, perfumed, pet, precious, pure, redolent, saccharine, sickly, silver-toned, silvery, soft, suave, sugary, sweetened, sweet-smelling, sweet-sounding, sweet-tempered, syrupy, taking, tender, toothsome, treasured, tuneful, unselfish, wholesome, winning, winsome.

antonyms acid, bitter, cacophonous, discordant, malodorous, salty, sour, unpleasant.

n afters, dessert, pudding, second course, sweet course.

sweet[2] *n* bonbon, candy, comfit, confect, confection, confectionery, sweetie, sweetmeat.

sweeten *v* alleviate, appease, cushion, dulcify, edulcorate, honey, mellow, mollify, pacify, soften, soothe, sugar, sugar-coat, take the sting out of, temper.

antonyms aggravate, embitter, jaundice.

sweetheart *n* admirer, beau, beloved, betrothed, boyfriend, darling, dear, dona, Dulcinea, flame, follower, girlfriend, inamorata, inamorato, lady-love, leman, love, lover, Romeo, steady, suitor, swain, sweetie, truelove, valentine.

sweetness *n* amiability, balminess, charm, dulcitude, euphony, fragrance, freshness, harmony, kindness, love, loveliness, lusciousness, mellowness, suavity, succulence, sugariness, sweet temper, syrup, tenderness, winsomeness.

antonyms acidity, bitterness, cacophony, nastiness, saltness, sourness.

sweet-smelling *adj* ambrosial, aromatic, balmy, fragrant, odoriferous, odorous, perfumed, redolent, sweet-scented.

antonyms fetid, malodorous.

swell[1] *v* aggravate, augment, balloon, belly, billow, blab, bloat, boll, bulb, bulge, dilate, distend, enhance, enlarge, expand, extend, fatten, grow, heave, heighten, hove, increase, intensify, intumesce, louden, mount, protrude, reach a crescendo, rise, strout, surge, tumefy, volume.

antonyms contract, dwindle, shrink.

n billow, bore, bulge, distension, eagre, enlargement, loudening, rise, surge, swelling, undulation, wave.

swell[2] *n* adept, beau, bigwig, blade, cockscomb, dandy, dude, fop, nob, popinjay, toff.

antonyms down-and-out, scarecrow, tramp.

adj de luxe, dude, exclusive, fashionable, flashy, grand, posh, ritzy, smart, stylish, swanky.

antonyms seedy, shabby.

swelling *n* blister, boll, botch, bruise, bulb, bulge, bump, dilation, distension, emphysema, enlargement, gall, gathering, gout, inflammation, intumescence, lump, oedema, protuberance, puffiness, tuber, tubercle, tumescence, tumour, venter.

sweltering *adj* airless, baking, broiling, burning, hot, humid, oppressive, perspiring, scorching, steamy, stifling, suffocating, sultry, sweating, torrid, tropical.

antonyms airy, breezy, chilly, cold, cool, fresh.

swerve *v* bend, carve, deflect, deviate, diverge, incline, sheer, shift, skew, stray, sway, swing, turn, veer, wander, warp, wind.

swift *adj* abrupt, agile, expeditious, express, fast, fleet, fleet-footed, flying, hurried, light-heeled, light-legged, limber, nimble, nimble-footed, nippy, precipitate, prompt, quick, rapid, ready, short, spanking, speedy, sudden, winged.

antonyms slow, sluggish, tardy.

swiftly *adj* at full tilt, double-quick, expeditiously, express, fast, hotfoot, hurriedly, instantly, posthaste, promptly, quickly, rapidly, speedily.

antonyms slowly, tardily.

swiftness *n* alacrity, celerity, dispatch, expedition, fleetness, immediacy, immediateness, instantaneity, promptness, quickness, rapidity, readiness, speed, speediness, suddenness, velocity.

antonyms delay, slowness, tardiness.

swill *v* consume, drain, drink, gulp, guzzle, imbibe, knock back, quaff, swallow, swig, toss off.

n hogwash, mash, mush, offal, pigswill, refuse, scourings, slops, waste.

swill out cleanse, drench, flush, rinse, sluice, wash down, wash out.

swimming-pool *n* Jacuzzi®, leisure pool, lido, swimming-bath, swimming-pond.

swimsuit *n* bathers, bathing-costume, bathing-dress, bathing-suit, bikini, cossie, maillot, swimming costume, swimwear, trunks.

swindle *v* bamboozle, bilk, bunko, cheat, chicane, chouse, con, deceive, defraud, diddle, do, dupe, finagle, financier, fleece, grift, gyp, hand someone a lemon, hornswoggle, overcharge, ramp, rip off, rook, sell smoke, sell someone a pup, skelder, trick.

n chicanery, con, deceit, deception, double-dealing, fakery, fiddle, fraud, gold-brick, grift, gyp, imposition, knavery, racket, rip-off, roguery, scam, sharp practice, shenanigans, skin-game, swizz, swizzle, trickery.

swindler *n* charlatan, cheat, chicaner, con man, escroc, fraud, fraudster, grifter, impostor, jackman, knave, mountebank, rascal, rogue, rook, shark, sharper, slicker, spieler, trickster.

swine *n* beast, boar, boor, brute, cad, heel, pig, reptile, rotter, scoundrel.

swing *v* arrange, brandish, control, dangle, fix, fluctuate, hang, hurl, influence, librate, oscillate, pendulate, rock, suspend, sway, swerve, vary, veer, vibrate, wave, whirl.

n fluctuation, impetus, libration, motion, oscillation, rhythm, scope, stroke, sway, swaying, sweep, sweeping, vibration, waving.

swing round curve, gyrate, pivot, revolve, rotate, spin, swivel, turn, twirl, wheel.

swingeing *adj* Draconian, drastic, excessive, exorbitant, extortionate, harsh, heavy, huge, oppressive, punishing, severe, stringent, thumping.

antonym mild.

swinging *adj* contemporary, dynamic, fashionable, fast, groovy, hip, jet-setting, lively, modern, stylish, toney, trendy, up-to-date, up-to-the-minute, with it.

antonyms old-fashioned, square.

swipe *v* appropriate, clip, filch, half-inch, hit, lift, pilfer, pinch, purloin, slap, slosh, snaffle, snitch, sock, steal, strike, thwack, wallop, whack.

n blow, clip, clout, cuff, gobble, gowff, slap, smack, thwack, wallop, whack.

swirl *v* agitate, boil, churn, eddy, purl, scud, spin, surge, swish, twirl, twist, wheel, whirl.

swish[1] *v* birch, brandish, flog, flourish, lash, rustle, swing, swirl, swoosh, thrash, twirl, wave, whip, whirl, whisk, whistle, whiz(z), whoosh.

swish[2] *adj* de luxe, dude, elegant, exclusive, fashionable, flash, grand, plush, posh, ritzy, smart, sumptuous, swanky, swell.

antonyms seedy, shabby.

switch[1] *v* change, change course, change direction, chop and change, deflect, deviate, divert, exchange, interchange, put, rearrange, replace, shift, shunt, substitute, swap, trade, turn, veer.

n about-turn, alteration, change, change of direction, exchange, interchange, shift, substitution, swap.

switch off inactivate, put off, turn off.

switch[2] *v* birch, flog, jerk, lash, swish, twitch, wave, whip, whisk.

n birch, cane, jerk, rod, whip, whisk.

swivel *v* gyrate, pirouette, pivot, revolve, rotate, spin, swing round, turn, twirl, wheel.

swollen *adj* bloated, bolled, bulbous, distended, dropsical, emphysematous, enlarged, inflamed, intumescent, oedematose, oedematous, puffed up, puffy, tumescent, tumid, turgid, ventricose, ventricous.

antonyms contracted, emaciated, shrunken.

swoop *v* descend, dive, drop, fall, lunge, pounce, rush, stoop, sweep.

n attack, descent, drop, lunge, onslaught, plunge, pounce, rush, stoop, sweep.

swop *see* **swap**.

sword *n* bilbo, blade, broadsword, claymore, cutlass, foil, gladius, machete, rapier, sabre, schiavone, scimitar.

sworn *adj* attested, confirmed, devoted, eternal, implacable, inveterate, relentless.

swot *v* bone up, burn the midnight oil, con, cram, dig, learn, lucubrate, memorise, mug up, pore over, revise, study, work.

n bluestocking, bookworm, crammer, dig, worker.

antonym idler.

sybarite *n* bon vivant, epicure, epicurean, hedonist, one of the idle rich, parasite, playboy, pleasurer, pleasure-seeker, sensualist, voluptuary.

antonyms ascetic, toiler.

sybaritic *adj* easy, epicurean, hedonistic, Lucullan, luxurious, parasitic, pleasure-loving, pleasure-seeking, self-indulgent, sensual, voluptuous.

antonym ascetic.

sycophancy *n* adulation, arse-licking, backscratching, bootlicking, cringing, fawning, flattery, grovelling, kowtowing, obsequiousness, servility, slavishness, toadyism, truckling.

sycophant *n* arse-licker, backscratcher, bootlicker, cringer, fawner, flatterer, flunky, groveller, hanger-on, lickspittle, parasite, slave, sponger, toad-eater, toady, truckler, yes-man.

sycophantic *adj* arse-licking, backscratching, bootlicking, cringing, fawning, flattering, grovelling, ingratiating, obsequious, parasitical, servile, slavish, slimy, smarmy, timeserving, toad-eating, toadying, truckling, unctuous.

syllabus *n* course, curriculum, plan, programme, schedule, table.

syllogism *n* argument, deduction, epicheirema, proposition.

sylph-like *adj* elegant, graceful, lithe, slender, slight, slim, streamlined, svelte, willowy.
antonyms bulky, plump.

symbiotic *adj* commensal, co-operative, emphytic, endophytic, epizoan, epizoic, epizootic, interactive, interdependent, synergetic.

symbol *n* badge, character, emblem, figure, grammalogue, ideogram, ideograph, image, logo, logogram, logograph, mandala, mark, representation, rune, sign, token, type.

symbolic *adj* allegorical, allusive, aniconic, emblematic, figurative, metaphorical, representative, ritual, significant, symbolical, token, typical.

symbolise *v* allude to, betoken, connote, denote, emblem, emblematise, emblemise, exemplify, mean, personate, personify, represent, signify, typify.

symmetrical *adj* balanced, corresponding, isometric, parallel, proportional, regular, well-balanced, well-proportioned, well-rounded.
antonyms asymmetrical, irregular.

symmetry *n* agreement, balance, correspondence, evenness, form, harmony, isometry, order, parallelism, proportion, regularity.
antonyms asymmetry, irregularity.

sympathetic *adj* affectionate, agreeable, appreciative, caring, comforting, commiserating, companionable, compassionate, compatible, concerned, congenial, consoling, empathetic, empathic, exorable, feeling, friendly, interested, kind, kindly, like-minded, pitying, responsive, supportive, tender, understanding, warm, warm-hearted, well-intentioned.
antonyms antipathetic, callous, indifferent, unsympathetic.

sympathetically *adv* appreciatively, comfortingly, compassionately, consolingly, feelingly, kindly, pityingly, responsively, sensitively, supportively, understandingly, warm-heartedly, warmly.

sympathise *v* agree, commiserate, condole, empathise, feel for, identify with, pity, rap, respond to, side with, understand.
antonyms disapprove, dismiss, disregard, ignore, oppose.

sympathiser *n* adherent, admirer, backer, condoler, fan, fellow-traveller, friend in need, partisan, supporter, well-wisher.
antonyms enemy, opponent.

sympathy *n* affinity, agreement, comfort, commiseration, compassion, condolement, condolence, condolences, congeniality, correspondence, empathy, fellow-feeling, harmony, pity, rapport, responsiveness, tenderness, thoughtfulness, understanding, warmth.
antonyms callousness, disharmony, incompatibility, indifference.

symptom *n* concomitant, diagnostic, evidence, expression, feature, indication, manifestation, mark, note, sign, syndrome, token, warning.

symptomatic *adj* associated, characteristic, indicative, suggestive, typical.

syndicate *n* alliance, bloc, cartel, combination, combine, group, ring.

synonymous *adj* co-extensive, comparable, corresponding, equal, equivalent, exchangeable, identical, identified, interchangeable, parallel, similar, substitutable, tantamount, the same.
antonyms antonymous, dissimilar, opposite.

synopsis *n* abridgement, abstract, aperçu, compendium, condensation, conspectus, digest, epitome, outline, precis, recapitulation, resume, review, run-down, sketch, summary, summation.

synthesis *n* alloy, amalgam, amalgamation, blend, coalescence, combination, composite, compound, fusion, integration, pastiche, unification, union, welding.

synthesise *v* amalgamate, blend, coalesce, combine, compound, fuse, integrate, manufacture, merge, unify, unite, weld.
antonyms analyse, resolve, separate.

synthetic *adj* artificial, bogus, ersatz, fake, imitation, man-made, manufactured, mock, pseud, pseudo, put-on, sham, simulated.
antonyms genuine, real.

syphilis *n* clap, French pox, gonorrhoea, pip, pox, venereal disease.

system *n* arrangement, classification, co-ordination, logic, method, methodicalness, methodology, mode, modus operandi, orderliness, organisation, plan, practice, procedure, process, regularity, routine, rule, scheme, set-up, structure, systematisation, tabulation, taxis, taxonomy, technique, theory, usage.

systematic *adj* businesslike, efficient, habitual, intentional, logical, methodical, ordered, orderly, organised, planned, precise, standardised, systematical, systematised, well-ordered, well-planned.
antonyms disorderly, inefficient, unsystematic.

systematise *v* arrange, classify, dispose, make uniform, methodise, order, organise, rationalise, regiment, regulate, schematise, standardise, tabulate.

T

tab *n* docket, flag, flap, label, marker, sticker, tag, ticket.

tabby *adj* banded, brindled, mottled, streaked, striped, stripy, variegated, wavy.

table *n* agenda, altar, bench, board, catalogue, chart, counter, diagram, diet, digest, fare, flat, flatland, food, graph, index, inventory, list, mahogany, paradigm, plain, plan, plateau, record, register, roll, schedule, slab, spread, stall, stand, syllabus, synopsis, tableland, victuals.

v postpone, propose, put forward, submit, suggest.

tableau *n* diorama, picture, portrayal, representation, scene, spectacle, tableau vivant, vignette.

taboo *adj* accursed, anathema, banned, forbidden, inviolable, outlawed, prohibited, proscribed, sacrosanct, unacceptable, unmentionable, unthinkable, verboten.

antonym acceptable.

n anathema, ban, curse, disapproval, interdict, interdiction, prohibition, proscription, restriction.

tabulate *v* arrange, catalogue, categorise, chart, classify, codify, index, list, order, range, sort, systematise, table, tabularise.

tacit *adj* implicit, implied, inferred, silent, ulterior, undeclared, understood, unexpressed, unprofessed, unspoken, unstated, unuttered, unvoiced, voiceless, wordless.

antonyms explicit, express, spoken, stated.

taciturn *adj* aloof, antisocial, cold, distant, dumb, mute, pauciloquent, quiet, reserved, reticent, saturnine, silent, tight-lipped, uncommunicative, unconversable, unforthcoming, withdrawn.

antonyms communicative, forthcoming, sociable, talkative.

tack *n* approach, attack, bearing, course, direction, drawing-pin, heading, line, loop, method, nail, path, pin, plan, procedure, route, staple, stitch, tactic, thumb-tack, tin-tack, way.

v add, affix, annex, append, attach, baste, fasten, fix, join, nail, pin, staple, stitch, tag.

tackle[1] *n* accoutrements, apparatus, equipment, gear, harness, implements, outfit, paraphernalia, rig, rigging, tackling, tools, trappings.

v harness.

tackle[2] *n* attack, block, challenge, interception, intervention, stop.

v attempt, begin, block, challenge, clutch, confront, deal with, embark upon, encounter, engage in, essay, face up to, grab, grapple with, grasp, halt, intercept, seize, set about, stop, take on, throw, try, undertake, wade into.

antonyms avoid, side-step.

tacky *adj* adhesive, cheap, gimcrack, gluey, gummy, messy, nasty, scruffy, seedy, shabby, shoddy, sleazy, sticky, tasteless, tatty, tawdry, vulgar, wet.

tact *n* address, adroitness, consideration, delicacy, diplomacy, discernment, discretion, finesse, grace, judgement, perception, prudence, savoir-faire, sensitivity, skill, thoughtfulness, understanding.

antonyms clumsiness, indiscretion, tactlessness.

tactful *adj* careful, considerate, delicate, diplomatic, discerning, discreet, graceful, judicious, perceptive, polished, polite, politic, prudent, sensitive, skilful, subtle, thoughtful, understanding.

antonym tactless.

tactic *n* approach, course, device, line, manoeuvre, means, method, move, ploy, policy, ruse, scheme, shift, stratagem, subterfuge, tack, trick, way.

tactical *adj* adroit, artful, calculated, clever, cunning, diplomatic, judicious, politic, prudent, shrewd, skilful, smart, strategic.

antonym impolitic.

tactician *n* brain, campaigner, co-ordinator, director, mastermind, orchestrator, planner, politician, strategist.

tactics *n* approach, campaign, game plan, line of attack, manoeuvres, moves, plan, plan of campaign, plans, ploys, policy, procedure, shifts, stratagems, strategy.

tactless *adj* blundering, boorish, careless, clumsy, discourteous, gauche, hurtful, ill-timed, impolite, impolitic, imprudent, inappropriate, inconsiderate, indelicate, indiscreet, inept, insensitive, maladroit, rough, rude, thoughtless, uncivil, undiplomatic, unfeeling, unkind, unsubtle.

antonym tactful.

tactlessness *n* bad timing, boorishness, clumsiness, discourtesy, gaucherie, impoliteness, indelicacy, indiscretion, ineptitude, insensitivity, maladdress, maladroitness, rudeness, thoughtlessness.

antonym tact.

tag[1] *n* aglet, aiglet, aiguillette, appellation, dag, designation, docket, epithet, flap, identification, label, mark, marker, name, note, slip, sticker, tab, tally, ticket.

v add, adjoin, affix, annex, append, call, christen, designate, dub, earmark, fasten, identify, label, mark, name, nickname, style, tack, term, ticket.

tag along accompany, attend, dog, follow, hang round, shadow, tail, trail.

tag[2] *n* dictum, fadaise, gnome, gobbet, maxim, moral, motto, proverb, quotation, quote, remnant, saw, saying.

tail *n* appendage, backside, behind, bottom, bum, buttocks, conclusion, croup, detective, empennage, end, extremity, file, follower, fud, line, posterior, queue, rear, rear end, retinue, rump, scut, suite, tailback, tailpiece, tailplane, train.

v dog, follow, keep with, shadow, spy on, stalk, track, trail.

tail off decrease, die, die out, drop, dwindle, fade, fail, fall away, peter out, tail away, taper off, wane.

antonyms grow, increase.

tailless *adj* acaudal, acaudate, anurous, ecaudate, excaudate, Manx.

tailor *n* clothier, costumer, costumier, couturier, couturière, darzi, dressmaker, modiste, outfitter, seamstress, whipcat, whip-stitch.

v accommodate, adapt, adjust, alter, convert, cut, fashion, fit, modify, mould, shape, style, suit, trim.

tailor-made *adj* bespoke, custom-built, custom-made, fitted, ideal, made-to-measure, perfect, right, suitable, suited.

antonyms ill-adapted, unsuitable.

taint *v* adulterate, besmirch, blacken, blemish, blight, blot, brand, contaminate, corrupt, damage, defile, deprave, dirty, disgrace, dishonour, envenom, foul, infect, muddy, poison, pollute, ruin, shame, smear, smirch, soil, spoil, stain, stigmatise, sully, tarnish, vitiate.

n blemish, blot, contagion, contamination, corruption, defect, disgrace, dishonour, fault, flaw, infamy, infection, obloquy, odium, opprobium, pollution, shame, smear, smirch, spot, stain, stigma.

take *v* abduct, abide, abstract, accept, accommodate, accompany, acquire, adopt, appropriate, arrest, ascertain, assume, attract, bear, believe, betake, bewitch, blight, book, brave, bring, brook, buy, call for, captivate, capture, carry, cart, catch, charm, clutch, conduct, consider, consume, contain, convey, convoy, deduct, deem, delight, demand, derive, detract, do, drink, eat, effect, eliminate, enchant, endure, engage, ensnare, entrap, escort, execute, fascinate, ferry, fetch, filch, gather, glean, grasp, grip, guide, haul, have, have room for, hire, hold, imbibe, ingest, inhale, lead, lease, make, measure, misappropriate, necessitate, need, nick, observe, obtain, operate, perceive, perform, photograph, pick, pinch, please, pocket, portray, presume, purchase, purloin, receive, regard, remove, rent, require, reserve, secure, seize, select, stand, steal, stomach, strike, subtract, succeed, suffer, swallow, swipe, thole, tolerate, tote, transport, undergo, understand, undertake, usher, weather, win, withstand, work.

n catch, gate, haul, income, proceeds, profits, receipts, return, revenue, takings, yield.

take aback astonish, astound, bewilder, disconcert, dismay, flabbergast, floor, nonplus, stagger, startle, stun, surprise, upset.

take apart analyse, disassemble, dismantle, resolve, take down, take to pieces.

take back deny, disavow, disclaim, eat one's words, recant, reclaim, regain, renounce, repossess, repudiate, retract, unsay, withdraw.

take down deflate, demolish, disassemble, dismantle, humble, humiliate, level, lower, minute, mortify, note, put down, raze, record, reduce, set down, strike, transcribe, unstep, write.

take effect be effective, become operative, begin, come into force, work.

take heart brighten up, buck up, cheer up, perk up, rally, revive.

antonym despond.

take in absorb, accommodate, admit, annex, appreciate, assimilate, bamboozle, bilk, bluff, cheat, comprehend, comprise, con, contain, cover, cozen, deceive, digest, do, dupe, embrace, enclose, encompass, fool, furl, grasp, gull, hoodwink, imagine, include, incorporate, kid, mislead, realise, receive, shelter, subdue, swindle, tighten, trick, understand.

take issue call in question, challenge, disagree, dispute, object, oppose, quarrel, question, take exception.

take it ill be miffed, be offended, miff, object, protest, take the huff.

take off beat it, bloom, burgeon, caricature, decamp, depart, disappear, discard, divest, doff, drop, expand, flourish, go, imitate, lampoon, leave, mimic, mock, parody, remove, satirise, scarper, send up, soar, spoof, strip, take wing, travesty, vamoose.

take offence be miffed, miff, sulk, take it ill, take the huff.

take on accept, acquire, assume, complain, contend with, employ, engage, enlist, enrol, face, fight, grieve, hire, lament, oppose, retain, tackle, undertake, vie with.

take part associate oneself, be instrumental, be involved, join, partake, participate, play a part, share, take a hand.

take pity on feel compassion for, forgive, give quarter, have mercy on, melt, pardon, pity, relent, reprieve, show mercy, spare.

take place befall, betide, come about, come off, come to pass, fall, happen, occur.

take stock appraise, assess, estimate, size up, survey, weigh up.

take the plunge commit oneself, cross the Rubicon, decide, pop the question.

take to task blame, censure, criticise, lecture, rebuke, reprimand, reproach, reprove, scold, tell off, tick off, upbraid.

antonyms commend, praise.

take up absorb, accept, adopt, affect, arrest, assume, begin, borrow, carry on, consume, continue, cover, engage in, engross, fasten, fill, interrupt, lift, monopolise, occupy, proceed, raise, recommence, restart, resume, secure, start, use up.

take-off *n* burlesque, caricature, imitation, lampoon, mickey-take, mimicry, parody, spoof, travesty.

takeover *n* amalgamation, coalition, combination, coup, incorporation, merger.

taking *adj* alluring, appealing, attractive, beguiling, captivating, catching, charming, compelling, delightful, enchanting, engaging, fascinating, fetching, intriguing, pleasing, prepossessing, winning, winsome.

antonyms repellent, repulsive, unattractive.

n agitation, alarm, coil, commotion, consternation, flap, fuss, panic, passion, pother, state, sweat, tiz-woz, tizzy, turmoil, wax.

takings *n* earnings, emoluments, gain, gate, haul, income, pickings, proceeds, profits, receipts, returns, revenue, take, yield.

tale *n* account, anecdote, fable, fabrication, falsehood, fib, fiction, legend, lie, Märchen, Munchausen, myth, narration, narrative, old wives' tale, relation, report, rigmarole, romance, rumour, saga, spiel, story, superstition, tall story, tradition, untruth, yarn.

talent *n* ability, aptitude, bent, capacity, endowment, faculty, feel, flair, forte, genius, gift, knack, long suit, nous, parts, power, strength.

antonyms inability, ineptitude, weakness.

talented *adj* able, accomplished, adept, adroit, apt, artistic, brilliant, capable, clever, deft, gifted, ingenious, inspired, well-endowed.

antonyms clumsy, inept, maladroit.

talisman *n* abraxas, amulet, charm, fetish, juju, mascot, periapt, phylactery, telesm.

talk *v* articulate, blab, blether, chat, chatter, chinwag, commune, communicate, confabulate, confer, converse, crack, gab, gossip, grass, inform, jaw, natter, negotiate, palaver, parley, prate, prattle, rap, say, sing, speak, squeak, squeal, utter, verbalise, witter.

n address, argot, bavardage, blather, blether, causerie, chat, chatter, chinwag, chitchat, clash, claver, colloquy, conclave, confab, confabulation, conference, consultation, conversation, crack, dialect, dialogue, discourse, discussion, disquisition, dissertation, gab, gossip, gup, harangue, hearsay, jargon, jaw, jawing, language, lecture, lingo, meeting, natter, negotiation, oration, palabra, palaver, parley, patois, rap, rumour, seminar, sermon, slang, speech, spiel, symposium, tittle-tattle, utterance, words.

talk big bluster, boast, brag, crow, exaggerate, swank, vaunt.

talk into bring round, coax, convince, encourage, overrule, persuade, sway, win over.

antonym dissuade.

talk out of caution, deter, discourage, dissuade, expostulate, head off, protest, put off, remonstrate, urge against.

talkative *adj* chatty, communicative, conversational, conversative, effusive, expansive, forthcoming, gabby, garrulous, gossipy, long-tongued, long-winded, loquacious, prating, prolix, unreserved, verbose, vocal, voluble, wordy.

antonyms pauciloquent, reserved, taciturn.

talker *n* chatterbox, communicator, conversationalist, lecturer, orator, speaker, speech-maker.

talking-to *n* criticism, dressing-down, earful, jaw, jawbation, lecture, rebuke, reprimand, reproach, reproof, row, scolding, slating, telling-off, ticking-off, wigging.

antonyms commendation, congratulation, praise.

tall *adj* absurd, big, dubious, elevated, embellished, exaggerated, far-fetched, giant, grandiloquent, great, high, implausible, improbable, incredible, lanky, leggy, lofty, overblown, preposterous, remarkable, soaring, steep, topless, towering, unbelievable, unlikely.

antonyms low, reasonable, short, small.

tallness *n* altitude, height, loftiness, procerity, stature.

tally *v* accord, agree, coincide, compute, concur, conform, correspond, figure, fit, harmonise, jibe, mark, match, parallel, reckon, record, register, square, suit, tie in, total.

antonyms differ, disagree.

n account, count, counterfoil, counterpart, credit, duplicate, label, mark, match, mate, notch, reckoning, record, score, stub, tab, tag, tick, total.

tame *adj* amenable, anaemic, biddable, bland, bloodless, boring, broken, compliant, cultivated, disciplined, docile, domesticated, dull, feeble, flat, gentle, humdrum, insipid, lifeless, manageable, meek, obedient, prosaic, spiritless, subdued, submissive, tedious, tractable, unadventurous, unenterprising, unexciting, uninspired, uninspiring, uninteresting, unresisting, vapid, wearisome.

antonyms exciting, rebellious, unmanageable, wild.

v break in, bridle, calm, conquer, curb, discipline, domesticate, enslave, gentle, house-train, humble, master, mellow, mitigate, mute, pacify, quell, repress, soften, subdue, subjugate, suppress, temper, train.

tamper *v* alter, bribe, cook, corrupt, damage, fiddle, fix, influence, interfere, intrude, juggle, manipulate, meddle, mess, rig, tinker.

tang *n* aroma, bite, flavour, hint, kick, overtone, piquancy, pungency, reek, savour, scent, smack, smell, suggestion, taste, tinge, touch, trace, whiff.

tangible *adj* actual, concrete, corporeal, definite, discernible, evident, manifest, material, objective, observable, palpable, perceptible, physical, positive, real, sensible, solid, substantial, tactile, touchable.

antonym intangible.

tangle *n* burble, coil, complication, confusion, convolution, embroglio, embroilment, entanglement, fankle, fix, imbroglio, jam, jumble, jungle, knot, labyrinth, mass, mat, maze, mesh mess, mix-up, muddle, raffle, snarl, snarl-up, twist, web.

v catch, coil, confuse, convolve, embroil, enmesh, ensnare, entangle, entrap, hamper, implicate, interlace, interlock, intertwine, intertwist, interweave, involve, jam, knot, mat, mesh, muddle, snarl, trap, twist.

antonym disentangle.

tangled *adj* complex, complicated, confused, convoluted, dishevelled, entangled, intricate, involved, jumbled, knotted, knotty, matted, messy, mixed-up, scrambled, snarled, tortuous, tousled, twisted.

antonyms clear, free.

tangy *adj* biting, bitter, fresh, gamy, piquant, pungent, savoury, sharp, spicy, strong, tart.

antonym insipid.

tank[1] *n* aquarium, basin, cistern, container, reservoir, vat.

tank[2] *n* armoured car, armoured vehicle, panzer.

tantalise *v* baffle, bait, balk, disappoint, entice, frustrate, lead on, play upon, provoke, taunt, tease, thwart, titillate, torment, torture.

antonym satisfy.

tantamount *adj* as good as, commensurate, equal, equivalent, synonymous, the same as, virtually.

tantrum *n* bate, fit, flare-up, fury, hysterics, outburst, paddy, paroxysm, rage, scene, storm, temper, wax.

tap[1] *v* beat, chap, drum, knock, pat, rap, strike, tat, touch.

n beat, chap, knock, pat, rap, rat-tat, touch.

tap[2] *n* bug, bung, faucet, plug, receiver, spigot, spile, spout, stop-cock, stopper, valve.

v bleed, broach, bug, drain, exploit, milk, mine, open, pierce, quarry, siphon, unplug, use, utilise, wiretap.

tape *n* band, binding, magnetic tape, riband, ribbon, strip, tape-measure.

v assess, bind, measure, record, seal, secure, stick, tape-record, video, wrap.

taper[2] *v* attenuate, decrease, die away, die out, dwindle, fade, lessen, narrow, peter out, reduce, slim, subside, tail off, thin, wane, weaken.

antonyms increase, swell, widen.

taper[2] *n* bougie, candle, spill, wax-light, wick.

tardily *adv* at the eleventh hour, at the last minute, belatedly, late, late in the day, slowly, sluggishly, unpunctually.

antonyms promptly, punctually.

tardiness *n* belatedness, dawdling, delay, dilatoriness, lateness, procrastination, slowness, sluggishness, unpunctuality.

antonyms promptness, punctuality.

tardy *adj* backward, behindhand, belated, dawdling, delayed, dilatory, eleventh-hour, lag, last-minute, late, loitering, overdue, procrastinating, retarded, slack, slow, sluggish, unpunctual.

antonyms prompt, punctual.

target *n* aim, ambition, bull's-eye, butt, destination, end, goal, intention, jack, mark, object, objective, prey, prick, purpose, quarry, scapegoat, victim.

tariff *n* assessment, bill of fare, charges, customs, duty, excise, impost, levy, menu, price list, rate, schedule, tax, toll.

tarnish *v* befoul, blacken, blemish, blot, darken, dim, discolour, dislustre, dull, mar, rust, soil, spoil, spot, stain, sully, taint.

antonyms brighten, enhance, polish up.

n blackening, blemish, blot, discoloration, film, patina, rust, spot, stain, taint.

antonyms brightness, polish.

tarry *v* abide, bide, dally, dawdle, delay, dwell, lag, linger, loiter, pause, remain, rest, sojourn, stay, stop, wait.

tart[1] *n* pastry, pie, quiche, tartlet.

tart[2] *adj* acerb, acerbic, acid, acidulous, acrimonious, astringent, barbed, biting, bitter, caustic, cutting, incisive, piquant, pungent, sardonic, scathing, sharp, short, sour, tangy, trenchant, vinegary.

tart[3] *n* broad, call girl, drab, fallen woman, fille de joie, fille publique, floosie, harlot, hooker, prostitute, slut, street-walker, strumpet, trollop, whore.

task *n* assignment, aufgabe, burden, business, charge, chore, darg, duty, employment, enterprise, exercise, imposition, job, job of work, labour, mission, occupation, pensum, toil, undertaking, work.

v burden, charge, commit, encumber, entrust, exhaust, load, lumber, oppress, overload, push, saddle, strain, tax, test, weary.

taste *n* appetite, appreciation, bent, bit, bite, choice, correctness, cultivation, culture, dash, decorum, delicacy, desire, discernment, discretion, discrimination, drop, elegance, experience, fancy, finesse, flavour, fondness, gout, grace, gustation, inclination, judgement, leaning, liking, morsel, mouthful, nibble, nicety, nip, palate, partiality, penchant, perception, polish, politeness, predilection, preference, propriety, refinement, relish, restraint, sample, sapor, savour, sensitivity, sip, smack, smatch, soupçon, spoonful, style, swallow, tact, tactfulness, tang, tastefulness, titbit, touch.

v assay, degust, degustate, differentiate, discern, distinguish, encounter, experience, feel, know, meet, nibble, perceive, relish, sample, savour, sip, smack, test, try, undergo.

tasteful *adj* aesthetic, artistic, beautiful, charming, comme il faut, correct, cultivated, cultured, delicate, discreet, discriminating, elegant, exquisite, fastidious, graceful, handsome, harmonious, judicious, polished, refined, restrained, smart, stylish, well-judged.

antonym tasteless.

tasteless *adj* barbaric, bland, boring, cheap, coarse, crass, crude, dilute, dull, flashy, flat, flavourless, garish, gaudy, graceless, gross, improper, inartistic, indecorous, indelicate, indiscreet, inelegant, inharmonious, insipid, low, mild, naff, rude, stale, tacky, tactless, tame, tatty, tawdry, thin, uncouth, undiscriminating, uninspired, uninteresting, unseemly, untasteful, vapid, vulgar, watered-down, watery, weak, wearish.

antonym tasteful.

tasting *n* assay, assessment, gustation, sampling, testing, trial.

tasty *adj* appetising, delectable, delicious, flavorous, flavourful, flavoursome, gusty, luscious, mouthwatering, palatable, piquant, sapid, saporous, savoury, scrumptious, succulent, toothsome, yummy.

antonyms disgusting, insipid, tasteless.

tattered *adj* duddie, frayed, in shreds, lacerated, ragged, raggy, rent, ripped, tatty, threadbare, torn.

antonyms neat, trim.

tatters *n* duddery, duds, flitters, rags, ribbons, shreds.

tattle *v* babble, blab, blather, blether, chat, chatter, clash, claver, gab, gash, gossip, jabber, natter, prate, prattle, talk, tittle-tattle, yak, yap.

n babble, blather, blether, chat, chatter, chitchat, clash, claver, gossip, hearsay, jabber, prattle, rumour, talk, tittle-tattle, yak, yap.

tattler *n* busybody, gossip, newsmonger, quidnunc, rumour-monger, scandalmonger, talebearer, tale-teller, tell-tale.

taunt *v* bait, chiack, deride, fleer, flout, flyte, gibe, insult, jeer, mock, provoke, reproach, revile, rib, ridicule, sneer, tease, torment, twit.

n barb, catcall, censure, cut, derision, dig, fling, gibe, insult, jeer, poke, provocation, reproach, ridicule, sarcasm, sneer, teasing.

taut *adj* contracted, rigid, strained, stressed, stretched, tense, tensed, tight, tightened, unrelaxed.

antonyms loose, relaxed, slack.

tautological *adj* iterative, otiose, pleonastic, redundant, repetitious, repetitive, superfluous, truistic.

antonyms economical, succinct.

tautology *n* duplication, iteration, otioseness, perissology, pleonasm, redundancy, repetition, repetitiousness, repetitiveness, superfluity.

antonyms economy, succinctness.

tavern *n* alehouse, bar, boozer, bush, dive, doggery, fonda, hostelry, inn, joint, local, pub, public house, roadhouse, tap-house.

tawdry *adj* brummagem, cheap, cheap-jack, flashy, garish, gaudy, gimcrack, gingerbread, glittering, meretricious, pinchbeck, plastic, raffish, showy, tacky, tasteless, tatty, tinsel, tinselly, vulgar.

antonyms excellent, fine, superior.

tawny *adj* fawn, fulvid, fulvous, golden, sandy, tan, xanthous, yellow.

tax *n* agistment, assessment, burden, charge, contribution, customs, demand, drain, duty, excise, geld, imposition, impost, levy, load, octroi, pressure, rate, scat, scot, strain, tariff, tithe, toll, tribute, weight.

v accuse, arraign, assess, blame, burden, censure, charge, demand, drain, enervate, exact, exhaust, extract, geld, impeach, impose, impugn, incriminate, load, overburden, overtax, push, rate, reproach, sap, strain, stretch, task, tithe, try, weaken, weary.

taxi *n* cab, fiacre, hackney-coach, hansom-cab, taxicab.

taxing *adj* burdensome, demanding, draining, enervating, exacting, exhausting, heavy, onerous, punishing, stressful, tiring, tough, trying, wearing, wearisome.

antonyms easy, gentle, mild.

teach *v* accustom, advise, coach, counsel, demonstrate, direct, discipline, drill, edify, educate, enlighten, ground, guide, impart, implant, inculcate, inform, instil, instruct, school, show, train, tutor, verse.

teacher *n* abecedarian, coach, dominie, don, educator, guide, guru, instructor, khodja, kindergartener, kindergärtner, lecturer, luminary, maharishi, master, mentor, mistress, pedagogue, professor, pundit, school-marm, schoolmaster, schoolmistress, school-teacher, trainer, tutor, usher.

teaching *n* didactics, doctrine, dogma, education, gospel, grounding, indoctrination, instruction, pedagoguism, pedagogy, precept, principle, schooling, tenet, training, tuition.

team *n* band, body, bunch, company, crew, écurie, équipe, gang, group, line-up, pair, set, shift, side, span, squad, stable, troupe, yoke.

v combine, couple, join, link, match, yoke.

team up band together, combine, co-operate, join, unite.

teamwork *n* collaboration, co-operation, co-ordination, esprit de corps, fellowship, joint effort, team spirit.

antonyms disharmony, disunity.

tear *v* belt, bolt, career, charge, claw, dart, dash, dilacerate, divide, drag, fly, gallop, gash, grab, hurry, lacerate, mangle, mutilate, pluck, pull, race, rend, rip, rive, run, rupture, rush, scratch, seize, sever, shoot, shred, snag, snatch, speed, split, sprint, sunder, wrench, wrest, yank, zoom.

n hole, laceration, rent, rip, run, rupture, scratch, snag, split.

tearaway *n* daredevil, delinquent, good-for-nothing, hoodlum, hooligan, hothead, madcap, rascal, rough, roughneck, rowdy, ruffian, tityre-tu, tough.

tearful *adj* blubbering, crying, distressing, dolorous, emotional, lachrymose, lamentable, maudlin, mournful, pathetic, pitiable, pitiful, poignant, sad, sobbing, sorrowful, upsetting, weeping, weepy, whimpering, woeful.

tears *n* blubbering, crying, distress, lamentation, mourning, pain, regret, sadness, sobbing, sorrow, wailing, water-drops, waterworks, weeping, whimpering, woe.

tease *v* aggravate, annoy, badger, bait, banter, bedevil, chaff, chiack, chip, gibe, goad, grig, guy, irritate, josh, mock, needle, pester, plague, provoke, rag, rib, ridicule, take a rise out of, tantalise, taunt, torment, twit, vex, worry.

technique *n* address, adroitness, approach, art, artistry, course, craft, craftsmanship, delivery, executancy, execution, expertise, facility, fashion, knack, know-how, manner, means, method, mode, modus operandi, performance, procedure, proficiency, skill, style, system, touch, way.

tedious *adj* annoying, banal, boring, deadly, drab, draggy, dreary, dreich, dull, fatiguing, humdrum, irksome, laborious, lifeless, long-drawn-out, longsome, long-spun, monotonous, prosaic, prosy, soporific, tiring, unexciting, uninteresting, vapid, wearisome.

antonyms exciting, interesting.

tedium *n* banality, boredom, drabness, dreariness, dullness, ennui, lifelessness, monotony, prosiness, routine, sameness, tediousness, vapidity.

teem *v* abound, bear, brim, bristle, burst, increase, multiply, overflow, overspill, produce, proliferate, pullulate, swarm.

antonyms lack, want.

teeming *adj* abundant, alive, brimful, brimming, bristling, bursting, chock-a-block, chock-full, crawling, fruitful, full, numerous, overflowing, packed, pregnant, proliferating, pullulating, replete, swarming, thick.

antonyms lacking, rare, sparse.

teenage *adj* adolescent, immature, juvenile, pubescent, teen, young, youthful.

teenager *n* adolescent, bobbysoxer, boy, girl, juvenile, minor, youth.

teeny *adj* diminutive, microscopic, miniature, minuscule, minute, teensy-weensy, teeny-weeny, tichy, tiny, tottie, wee.

teeter *v* balance, lurch, pitch, pivot, rock, seesaw, stagger, sway, titubate, totter, tremble, waver, wobble.

teetotaller *n* abstainer, nephalist, non-drinker, Rechabite, water-drinker.

telegram *n* cable, telegraph, telemessage, telex, wire.

telegraph *n* cable, radiotelegraph, telegram, teleprinter, telex, wire.

v cable, send, signal, telex, transmit, wire.

telepathy *n* clairvoyance, ESP, mind-reading, sixth sense, thought transference.

telephone *n* blower, dog and bone, handset, line, phone.

v buzz, call, call up, contact, dial, get in touch, get on the blower, give someone a tinkle, phone, ring (up).

telescope *v* abbreviate, abridge, compress, concertina, condense, contract, crush, curtail, cut, reduce, shorten, shrink, squash, trim, truncate.

television *n* boob tube, goggle-box, idiot box, receiver, set, small screen, telly, the box, the tube, TV, TV set.

tell *v* acquaint, announce, apprise, authorise, bid, calculate, chronicle, command, communicate, comprehend, compute, confess, count, depict, describe, differentiate, direct, discern, disclose, discover, discriminate, distinguish, divulge, enjoin, enumerate, express, foresee, identify, impart, inform, instruct, mention, militate, narrate, notify, number, order, portray, predict, proclaim, reckon, recount, register, rehearse, relate, report, require, reveal, say, see, speak, state, summon, tally, understand, utter, weigh.

tell off bawl out, berate, censure, chide, dress down, lecture, objurgate, rebuke, reprimand, reproach, reprove, scold, take to task, tear off a strip, tick off, upbraid.

telling-off *n* bawling-out, castigation, dressing-down, jawbation, jawing, jobation, lecture, rebuke, reprimand, reproach, reproof, row, scolding, tongue-lashing.

temerity *n* assurance, audacity, boldness, brass neck, chutzpah, daring, effrontery, forwardness, gall, heedlessness, impudence, impulsiveness, intrepidity, nerve, pluck, rashness, recklessness.

antonym caution.

temper *n* anger, annoyance, attitude, bait, calm, calmness, character, composure, constitution, cool, coolness, disposition, equanimity, fury, heat, humour, ill-humour, irascibility, irritability, irritation, mind, moderation, mood, nature, paddy, passion, peevishness, pet, petulance, rage, resentment, sang-froid, self-control, surliness, taking, tantrum, temperament, tenor, tranquillity, vein, wax, wrath.

v abate, admix, allay, anneal, assuage, calm, harden, indurate, lessen, mitigate, moderate, modify, mollify, palliate, restrain, soften, soothe, strengthen, toughen.

temperament *n* anger, bent, character, complexion, constitution, crasis, disposition, excitability, explosiveness, hot-headedness, humour, impatience, make-up, mettle, moodiness, moods, nature, outlook, personality, petulance, quality, soul, spirit, stamp, temper, tendencies, tendency, volatility.

temperamental *adj* capricious, congenital, constitutional, emotional, erratic, excitable, explosive, fiery, highly-strung, hot-headed, hypersensitive, impatient, inborn, inconsistent, ingrained, inherent, innate, irritable, mercurial, moody, natural, neurotic, over-emotional, passionate, petulant, sensitive, touchy, undependable, unpredictable, unreliable, volatile, volcanic.

antonyms calm, serene, steady.

temperance *n* abstemiousness, abstinence, continence, discretion, forbearance, moderation, prohibition, restraint, self-abnegation, self-control, self-denial, self-discipline, self-restraint, sobriety, teetotalism.

antonyms excess, intemperance.

temperate *adj* abstemious, abstinent, agreeable, balanced, balmy, calm, clement, composed, continent, controlled, cool, dispassionate, equable, even-tempered, fair, gentle, mild, moderate, pleasant, reasonable, restrained, sensible, sober, soft, stable.

antonyms excessive, extreme, intemperate.

tempest *n* bourasque, commotion, cyclone, disturbance, ferment, furore, gale, hurricane, squall, storm, tornado, tumult, typhoon, upheaval, uproar.

tempestuous *adj* agitated, blustery, boisterous, breezy, emotional, excited, feverish, furious, gusty, heated, hysterical, impassioned, intense, passionate, raging, squally, stormy, troubled, tumultuous, turbulent, uncontrolled, violent, wild, windy.

antonyms calm, quiet.

temple *n* church, delubrum, fane, gompa, haffet, joss-house, mandir(a), masjid, monopteron, monopteros, mosque, pagoda, sanctuary, shrine, tabernacle, vihara, wat.

tempo *n* beat, cadence, measure, metre, pace, pulse, rate, rhythm, speed, time, velocity.

temporal *adj* carnal, civil, earthly, evanescent, fleeting, fleshly, fugacious, fugitive, impermanent, lay, material, momentary, mortal, mundane, passing, profane, secular, short-lived, sublunary, temporary, terrestrial, transient, transitory, unspiritual, worldly.

antonym spiritual.

temporarily *adv* briefly, fleetingly, for the nonce, for the time being, in the interim, momentarily, pro tem, transiently, transitorily.

antonym permanently.

temporary *adj* brief, ephemeral, evanescent, fleeting, fugacious, fugitive, impermanent, interim, makeshift, momentary, passing, pro tem, pro tempore, provisional, short-lived, stop-gap, transient, transitory.

antonyms everlasting, permanent.

temporise *v* delay, equivocate, hang back, hum and haw, pause, play for time, procrastinate, stall, tergiversate.

tempt *v* allure, attract, bait, coax, dare, decoy, draw, enamour, entice, incite, inveigle, invite, lure, provoke, risk, seduce, tantalise, test, try, woo.

antonyms discourage, dissuade.

temptation *n* allurement, appeal, attraction, attractiveness, bait, blandishments, coaxing, come-on, decoy, draw, enticement, fascination, forbidden fruit, inducement, invitation, lure, persuasion, pull, seduction, snare.

tempting *adj* alluring, appetising, attractive, enticing, inviting, lickerish, liquorish, mouthwatering, seductive, tantalising, temptatious.

antonyms unattractive, uninviting.

temptress *n* Circe, coquette, Delilah, enchantress, femme fatale, flirt, seductress, siren, sorceress, vamp.

tenable *adj* arguable, believable, credible, defendable, defensible, justifiable, maintainable, plausible, rational, reasonable, sound, supportable, viable.

antonyms indefensible, unjustifiable, untenable.

tenacious *adj* adamant, adhesive, backboned, clinging, coherent, cohesive, determined, dogged, fast, firm, forceful, gluey, glutinous, inflexible, intransigent, mucilaginous, obdurate, obstinate, persistent, pertinacious, resolute, retentive, single-minded, solid, staunch, steadfast, sticky, strong, strong-willed, stubborn, sure, tight, tough, unshakeable, unswerving, unwavering, unyielding, viscous.

antonyms loose, slack, weak.

tenacity *n* adhesiveness, application, clinginess, coherence, cohesiveness, determination, diligence, doggedness, fastness, firmness, force, forcefulness, indomitability, inflexibility, intransigence, obduracy, obstinacy, perseverance, persistence, pertinacity, power, resoluteness, resolution, resolve, retention, retentiveness, single-mindedness, solidity, solidness, staunchness, steadfastness, stickiness, strength, stubbornness, toughness, viscosity.

antonyms looseness, slackness, weakness.

tenancy *n* holding, incumbency, lease, leasehold, occupancy, occupation, possession, renting, residence, tenure.

tenant *n* gavelman, inhabitant, landholder, leaseholder, lessee, occupant, occupier, renter, resident.

tend[1] *v* affect, aim, bear, bend, conduce, contribute, go, gravitate, head, incline, influence, lead, lean, move, point, trend, verge.

tend[2] *v* attend, comfort, control, cultivate, feed, guard, handle, keep, maintain, manage, minister to, nurse, nurture, protect, serve, succour.

antonym neglect.

tendency *n* bearing, bent, bias, conatus, course, direction, disposition, drift, drive, heading, inclination, leaning, liability, movement, partiality, penchant, predilection, predisposition, proclivity, proneness, propensity, purport, readiness, susceptibility, tenor, thrust, trend, turning.

tender[1] *adj* aching, acute, affectionate, affettuoso, amoroso, amorous, benevolent, breakable, bruised, callow, caring, chary, compassionate, complicated, considerate, dangerous, delicate, difficult, emotional, evocative, feeble, fond, fragile, frail, gentle, green, humane, immature, impressionable, inexperienced, inflamed, irritated, kind, loving, merciful, moving, new, painful, pathetic, pitiful, poignant, raw, risky, romantic, scrupulous, sensitive, sentimental, smarting, soft, soft-hearted, sore, sympathetic, tender-hearted, ticklish, touching, touchy, tricky, vulnerable, warm, warm-hearted, weak, young, youthful.

antonyms callous, chewy, hard, harsh, rough, severe, tough.

tender[2] *v* advance, extend, give, offer, present, proffer, propose, submit, suggest, volunteer.

n bid, currency, estimate, medium, money, offer, payment, proffer, proposal, proposition, specie, submission, suggestion.

tender-hearted *adj* affectionate, benevolent, benign, caring, compassionate, considerate, feeling, fond, gentle, humane, kind, kind-hearted, kindly, loving, merciful, mild, pitying, responsive, sensitive, sentimental, soft-hearted, sympathetic, warm, warm-hearted.

antonyms callous, cruel, hard-hearted, unfeeling.

tenderness *n* ache, aching, affection, amorousness, attachment, benevolence, bruising, callowness, care, compassion, consideration, delicateness, devotion, discomfort, feebleness, fondness, fragility, frailness, gentleness, greenness, humaneness, humanity, immaturity, impressionableness, inexperience, inflammation, irritation, kindness, liking, love, loving-kindness, mercy, newness, pain, painfulness, pity, rawness, sensitiveness, sensitivity, sentimentality, soft-heartedness, softness, soreness, sweetness, sympathy, tender-heartedness, vulnerability, warm-heartedness, warmth, weakness, youth, youthfulness.

antonyms cruelty, hardness, harshness.

tenet *n* article of faith, belief, canon, conviction, credo, creed, doctrine, dogma, maxim, opinion, precept, presumption, principle, rule, teaching, thesis, view.

tenor *n* aim, burden, course, direction, drift, essence, evolution, gist, intent, meaning, path, point, purport, purpose, sense, spirit, substance, tendency, theme, trend, way.

tense *adj* anxious, apprehensive, edgy, electric, exciting, fidgety, jittery, jumpy, moving, nerve-racking, nervous, overwrought, restless, rigid, strained, stressful, stretched, strung up, taut, tight, uneasy, uptight, worrying.

antonyms calm, lax, loose, relaxed.

v brace, contract, strain, stretch, tauten, tighten.

antonyms loosen, relax.

tension *n* anxiety, apprehension, edginess, hostility, nervousness, pressure, restlessness, rigidity, stiffness, strain, straining, stress, stretching, suspense, tautness, tightness, tone, unease, worry.

antonyms calm(ness), laxness, looseness, relaxation.

tent *n* big top, canvas, marquee, marquise, tabernacle, tepee, wigwam, y(o)urt.

tentative *adj* cautious, conjectural, diffident, doubtful, experimental, faltering, hesitant, indefinite, peirastic, provisional, speculative, timid, uncertain, unconfirmed, undecided, unformulated, unsettled, unsure.

antonyms conclusive, decisive, definite, final.

tenuous *adj* attenuated, delicate, doubtful, dubious, fine, flimsy, gossamer, insignificant, insubstantial, nebulous, questionable, rarefied, shaky, sketchy, slender, slight, slim, thin, weak.

antonyms significant, strong, substantial.

tenure *n* habitation, holding, incumbency, occupancy, occupation, possession, proprietorship, residence, tenancy, term, time.

tepid *adj* apathetic, cool, half-hearted, indifferent, lew, lukewarm, unenthusiastic, warmish.

antonyms animated, cold, hot, passionate.

tergiversation *n* apostasy, defection, desertion, equivocation, fencing, hedging, prevarication, shilly-shallying, vacillation, wavering.

term¹ *n* appellation, denomination, designation, epithet, epitheton, expression, locution, name, phrase, title, word.

v call, denominate, designate, dub, entitle, label, name, style, tag, title.

term² *n* bound, boundary, close, conclusion, confine, course, culmination, duration, end, finish, fruition, half, interval, limit, period, season, session, space, span, spell, terminus, time, while.

terminal *adj* bounding, concluding, deadly, desinent, desinential, extreme, fatal, final, incurable, killing, last, lethal, limiting, mortal, ultimate, utmost.

antonym initial.

n boundary, depot, end, extremity, limit, termination, terminus.

terminate *v* abort, cease, close, complete, conclude, cut off, discontinue, drop, end, expire, finish, issue, lapse, result, stop, wind up.

antonyms begin, initiate, start.

termination *n* abortion, cessation, close, completion, conclusion, consequence, dénouement, discontinuation, effect, end, ending, expiry, finale, finis, finish, issue, result, wind-up.

antonyms beginning, initiation, start.

terminology *n* argot, cant, jargon, language, lingo, nomenclature, patois, phraseology, terms, vocabulary, words.

terminus *n* boundary, close, depot, destination, end, extremity, furthermost point, garage, goal, limit, station, target, termination.

terms *n* agreement, charges, compromise, conditions, fees, footing, language, particulars, payment, phraseology, position, premises, price, provisions, provisos, qualifications, rates, relations, relationship, specifications, standing, status, stipulations, terminology, understanding.

terrain *n* country, countryside, ground, land, landscape, territory, topography.

terrestrial *adj* earthly, global, mundane, subastral, sublunary, tellurian, terrene, worldly.

antonyms cosmic, empyreal, heavenly.

terrible *adj* abhorrent, appalling, awful, bad, beastly, dangerous, desperate, dire, disgusting, distressing, dread, dreaded, dreadful, extreme, fearful, foul, frightful, god-awful, gruesome, harrowing, hateful, hideous, horrendous, horrible, horrid, horrific, horrifying, loathsome, monstrous, obnoxious, odious, offensive, outrageous, poor, repulsive, revolting, rotten, serious, severe, shocking, unpleasant, vile.

antonyms great, pleasant, superb, wonderful.

terribly *adv* awfully, decidedly, desperately, exceedingly, extremely, frightfully, gravely, greatly, much, seriously, shockingly, thoroughly, very.

terrific *adj* ace, amazing, awesome, awful, breathtaking, brilliant, dreadful, enormous, excellent, excessive, extreme, fabulous, fantastic, fearful, fierce, fine, gigantic, great, harsh, horrific, huge, intense, magnificent, marvellous, monstrous, outstanding, prodigious, sensational, severe, smashing, stupendous, super, superb, terrible, tremendous, wonderful.

terrified *adj* alarmed, appalled, awed, dismayed, frightened, horrified, horror-struck, intimidated, panic-stricken, petrified, scared.

terrify *v* affright, alarm, appal, awe, dismay, frighten, horrify, intimidate, petrify, scare, shock, terrorise.

territorial *adj* area, district, domainal, geographical, localised, regional, sectional, topographic, zonal.

territory *n* area, bailiwick, country, dependency, district, domain, jurisdiction, land, park, preserve, province, region, sector, state, terrain, tract, zone.

terror *n* affright, alarm, anxiety, awe, blue funk, bogeyman, bugbear, consternation, devil, dismay, dread, fear, fiend, fright, horror, intimidation, monster, panic, rascal, rogue, scourge, shock, tearaway.

terrorise *v* alarm, appal, awe, browbeat, bully, coerce, dismay, frighten, horrify, intimidate, menace, oppress, petrify, scare, shock, strongarm, terrify, threaten.

terse *adj* abrupt, aphoristic, brief, brusque, clipped, compact, concise, condensed, crisp, curt, economical, elliptical, epigrammatic, gnomic, incisive, laconic, neat, pithy, sententious, short, snappy, succinct.

antonyms long-winded, prolix, repetitious.

test *v* analyse, assay, assess, check, examine, experiment, investigate, prove, screen, try, verify.

n analysis, assessment, attempt, catechism, check, evaluation, examination, hurdle, investigation, moment of truth, ordeal, pons asinorum, probation, proof, shibboleth, trial, try-out.

testament *n* attestation, demonstration, devise, earnest, evidence, exemplification, proof, testimony, tribute, will, witness.

testicles *n* balls, bollocks, gonads, goolies, knackers, nuts, pills, stones.

testify *v* affirm, assert, asseverate, attest, avow, certify, corroborate, declare, depone, depose, evince, show, state, swear, vouch, witness.

testimonial *n* certificate, character, commendation, credential, endorsement, gift, memorial, plug, recommendation, reference, tribute.

testimony *n* affidavit, affirmation, asseveration, attestation, avowal, confirmation, corroboration, declaration, demonstration, deposition, evidence, indication, information, manifestation, profession, proof, statement, submission, support, verification, witness.

testy *adj* bad-tempered, cantankerous, captious, carnaptious, crabbed, cross, crusty, fretful, grumpy, impatient, inflammable, irascible, irritable, peevish, peppery, petulant, quarrelsome, quick-tempered, short-tempered, snappish, snappy, splenetic, sullen, tetchy, touchy, waspish.

antonyms even-tempered, good-humoured.

tether *n* bond, chain, cord, fastening, fetter, halter, lead, leash, line, restraint, rope, shackle.

v bind, chain, fasten, fetter, lash, leash, manacle, picket, restrain, rope, secure, shackle, tie.

text *n* argument, body, contents, lection, libretto, matter, motif, paragraph, passage, reader, reading, script, sentence, source, subject, textbook, theme, topic, verse, wordage, wording, words.

texture *n* character, composition, consistency, constitution, fabric, feel, grain, quality, structure, surface, tissue, weave, weftage, woof.

thankful *adj* appreciative, beholden, contented, grateful, indebted, obliged, pleased, relieved.

antonyms thankless, unappreciative, ungrateful.

thankless *adj* fruitless, unappreciated, ungrateful, unprofitable, unrecognised, unrequited, unrewarding, useless.

antonym rewarding.

thanks *n* acknowledgement, appreciation, credit, grace, gratefulness, gratitude, recognition, thank-offering, thanksgiving.

interj cheers, danke (schön), gracias, gramercy, grand merci, grazie, merci, merci beaucoup, merci bien, ta.

thanks to as a result of, because of, by reason of, due to, in consequence of, on account of, owing to, through.

thaw *v* defreeze, defrost, dissolve, liquefy, melt, soften, unbend, uncongeal, unfreeze, unthaw, warm.

antonym freeze.

the end beyond endurance, enough, insufferable, intolerable, the final blow, the last straw, the limit, the worst, too much, unbearable, unendurable.

the limit enough, it, the end, the final blow, the last straw, the worst.

the masses hoi polloi, the admass, the common people, the commonalty, the crowd, the majority, the many, the multitude, the people, the plebs, the proles, the proletariat, the rank and file.

theatre *n* amphitheatre, auditorium, hall, lyceum, odeon, opera house, penny gaff, playhouse.

theatrical *adj* affected, artificial, ceremonious, dramatic, dramaturgic, exaggerated, extravagant, hammy, histrionic, mannered, melodramatic, ostentatious, overdone, pompous, scenic, showy, stagy, stilted, theatric, Thespian, unreal.

theft *n* abstraction, blag, embezzlement, fraud, heist, kleptomania, larceny, pilfering, plunderage, purloining, rip-off, robbery, stealing, thievery, thieving.

thematic *adj* conceptual, notional, taxonomic, classificatory.

theme *n* argument, burden, composition, dissertation, essay, exercise, idea, keynote, leitmotiv, lemma, matter, motif, mythos, paper, subject, subject-matter, text, thesis, topic, topos.

theological *adj* divine, doctrinal, ecclesiastical, hierological, religious.

theorem *n* deduction, dictum, formula, hypothesis, postulate, principle, proposition, rule, statement, thesis.

theoretical *adj* abstract, academic, conjectural, doctrinaire, doctrinal, hypothetical, ideal, impractical, on paper, pure, speculative.

antonyms applied, concrete, practical.

theorise *v* conjecture, formulate, guess, hypothesise, postulate, project, propound, speculate, suppose.

theory *n* abstraction, assumption, conjecture, guess, hypothesis, ism, philosophy, plan, postulation, presumption, proposal, scheme, speculation, supposition, surmise, system, thesis.

antonyms certainty, practice.

therapeutic *adj* ameliorative, analeptic, beneficial, corrective, curative, good, healing, recuperative, remedial, restorative, salubrious, salutary, sanative, tonic.

antonym harmful.

therapy *n* cure, healing, prophylaxis, tonic, treatment.

therefore *adv* accordingly, as a result, consequently, ergo, for that reason, hence, so, then, thence, thus.

thesaurus *n* dictionary, encyclopedia, lexicon, repository, storehouse, synonymicon, synonymy, treasury, vocabulary, wordbook.

thesis *n* argument, assumption, composition, contention, disquisition, dissertation, essay, hypothesis, idea, monograph, opinion, paper, postulate, premiss, proposal, proposition, statement, subject, supposition, surmise, theme, theory, topic, tract, tractate, treatise, view.

thick *adj* abundant, brainless, brimming, bristling, broad, bulky, bursting, chock-a-block, chock-full, chummy, close, clotted, coagulated, compact, concentrated, condensed, confidential, covered, crass, crawling, crowded, decided, deep, dense, devoted, dim-witted, distinct, distorted, dopey, dull, excessive, familiar, fat, foggy, frequent, friendly, full, gross, guttural, heavy, hoarse, husky, impenetrable, inarticulate, indistinct, insensitive, inseparable, intimate, marked, matey, moronic, muffled, numerous, obtuse, opaque, packed, pally, pronounced, replete, rich, slow, slow-witted, solid, soupy, squabbish, strong, stupid, substantial, swarming, teeming, thick-headed, throaty, turbid, wide.

antonyms brainy, clever, slender, slight, slim, thin, watery.

n centre, focus, heart, hub, middle, midst.

thicken *v* cake, clot, coagulate, condense, congeal, deepen, gel, incrassate, inspissate, jell, set.

antonym thin.

thicket *n* bosket, brake, clump, coppice, copse, covert, dead-finish, greave, grove, macchie, maquis, spinney, wood, woodland.

thickhead *n* blockhead, bonehead, chump, clot, dimwit, dolt, dope, dullard, dummy, dunce, dunderhead, fathead, fool, idiot, imbecile, moron, nitwit, numskull, pinhead, thick, twit.

thick-headed *adj* asinine, blockheaded, brainless, dense, dim-witted, doltish, dopey, dull-witted, idiotic, imbecilic, moronic, obtuse, slow, slow-witted, stupid, thick.

antonyms brainy, clever, intelligent, sharp.

thickness *n* body, breadth, bulk, bulkiness, density, diameter, layer, ply, sheet, spissitude, stratum, viscosity, width.

antonym thinness.

thickset *adj* beefy, brawny, bulky, burly, dense, heavy, muscular, nuggety, powerful, solid, squabbish, squabby, squat, stocky, strong, stubby, sturdy, thick, well-built.

antonym lanky.

thick-skinned *adj* callous, case-hardened, hard-boiled, hardened, impervious, insensitive, inured, obdurate, pachydermatous, stolid, tough, unfeeling.

antonym thin-skinned.

thief *n* abactor, Autolycus, bandit, burglar, cheat, cracksman, crook, cut-purse, embezzler, filcher, hoister, house-breaker, kleptomaniac, ladrone, land-rat, larcener, larcenist, latron, mugger, pickpocket, pilferer, plunderer, prigger, purloiner, robber, shop-lifter, snatch-purse, St Nicholas's clerk, stealer, swindler.

thieve *v* abstract, cheat, embezzle, filch, half-inch, heist, knock off, lift, misappropriate, nick, peculate, pilfer, pinch, plunder, poach, purloin, rip off, rob, steal, swindle, swipe.

thieving *n* banditry, burglary, crookedness, embezzlement, larceny, mugging, peculation, pilferage, pilfering, piracy, plundering, robbery, shop-lifting, stealing, theft, thievery.

thievish *adj* crooked, dishonest, fraudulent, furacious, larcenous, light-fingered, piratical, predatory, rapacious, sticky-fingered, thieving.

thin *adj* attenuate, attenuated, bony, deficient, delicate, diaphanous, dilute, diluted, emaciated, feeble, filmy, fine, fine-drawn, flimsy, gaunt, gossamer, inadequate, insubstantial, insufficient, lanky, lean, light, meagre, narrow, poor, rarefied, runny, scant, scanty, scarce, scattered, scragged, scraggy, scrawny, see-through, shallow, sheer, skeletal, skimpy, skinny, slender, slight, slim, spare, sparse, spindly, superficial, tenuous, translucent, transparent, unconvincing, undernourished, underweight, unsubstantial, washy, watery, weak, wishy-washy, wispy.

antonyms broad, dense, fat, solid, strong, thick.

v attenuate, decrassify, dilute, diminish, emaciate, extenuate, prune, rarefy, reduce, refine, trim, water down, weaken, weed out.

thing *n* act, action, affair, apparatus, article, aspect, attitude, being, body, circumstance, concept, contrivance, creature, deed, detail, device, dislike, entity, event, eventuality, facet, fact, factor, feat, feature, fetish, fixation, gadget, hang-up, happening, idée fixe, implement, incident, instrument, item, liking, machine, mania, matter, means, mechanism, monomania, object, obsession, occurrence, part, particular, phenomenon, phobia, point, portion, possession, preoccupation, problem, proceeding, quirk, something, statement, substance, thought, tool.

things *n* baggage, belongings, bits and pieces, clobber, clothes, effects, equipment, gear, goods, impedimenta, junk, luggage, odds and ends, paraphernalia, possessions, stuff, traps, utensils.

think *v* anticipate, be under the impression, believe, brood, calculate, cerebrate, cogitate, conceive, conclude, consider, contemplate, deem, deliberate, design, determine, envisage, esteem, estimate, expect, foresee, hold, ideate, imagine, intellectualise, judge, meditate, mull over, muse, ponder, presume, purpose, ratiocinate, reason, recall, reckon, recollect, reflect, regard, remember, revolve, ruminate, suppose, surmise.

n assessment, cogitation, consideration, contemplation, deliberation, meditation, reflection.

think much of admire, esteem, prize, rate, respect, set store by, think highly of, value.

antonym abominate.

think over chew over, consider, contemplate, meditate, mull over, ponder, reflect upon, ruminate, weigh up.

think up conceive, concoct, contrive, create, design, devise, dream up, imagine, improvise, invent, visualise.

thinkable *adj* cogitable, conceivable, feasible, imaginable, likely, possible, reasonable, supposable.

antonym unthinkable.

thinker *n* brain, ideologist, imaginist, intellect, mastermind, philosopher, sage, theorist.

thinking *n* assessment, cogitation, conclusions, conjecture, idea, judgement, opinion, outlook, philosophy, position, ratiocination, reasoning, theory, thoughts, view.

adj analytical, cerebral, contemplative, cultured, dianoetic, intelligent, meditative, philosophical, ratiocinative, rational, reasoning, reflective, sophisticated, thoughtful.

thin-skinned *adj* hypersensitive, irascible, irritable, sensitive, snappish, soft, susceptible, tender, testy, touchy, vulnerable.

antonym thick-skinned.

third-rate *adj* bad, cheap and nasty, cheap-jack, duff, indifferent, inferior, low-grade, mediocre, poor, ropy, shoddy.

thirst *n* appetite, craving, desire, drought, drouth, drouthiness, dryness, eagerness, hankering, hunger, hydromania, keenness, longing, lust, passion, thirstiness, yearning, yen.

thirsty *adj* adry, appetitive, arid, athirst, avid, burning, craving, dehydrated, desirous, drouthy, dry, dying, eager, greedy, hankering, hungry, hydropic, itching, longing, lusting, parched, thirsting, yearning.

thorn *n* acantha, affliction, annoyance, bane, barb, bother, curse, doorn, irritant, irritation, nuisance, pest, plague, prickle, scourge, spike, spine, torment, torture, trouble.

thorny *adj* acanthous, awkward, barbed, bristly, difficult, fraught, harassing, hard, irksome, pointed, prickly, problematic, sharp, spiky, spinous, spiny, sticky, ticklish, tough, troublesome, trying, unpleasant, upsetting, vexatious, vexed, worrying.

thorough *adj* absolute, all-embracing, all-inclusive, arrant, assiduous, careful, complete, comprehensive, conscientious, deep-seated, downright, efficient, entire, exhaustive, full, in-depth, intensive, meticulous, out-and-out, painstaking, perfect, pure, root-and-branch, scrupulous, sheer, sweeping, thoroughgoing, total, unmitigated, unqualified, utter.

antonyms careless, haphazard, partial.

thoroughfare *n* access, avenue, boulevard, concourse, highway, motorway, passage, passageway, road, roadway, street, turnpike, way.

thoroughly *adv* à fond, absolutely, assiduously, carefully, completely, comprehensively, conscientiously, downright, efficiently, entirely, every inch, exhaustively, fully, inside out, intensively, meticulously, painstakingly, perfectly, point-device (-devise), quite, root and branch, scrupulously, sweepingly, totally, utterly, with a fine-tooth comb.

antonyms carelessly, haphazardly, partially.

though *conj* albeit, allowing, although, even if, granted, howbeit, notwithstanding, while.

adv all the same, even so, for all that, however, in spite of that, nevertheless, nonetheless, notwithstanding, still, yet.

thought *n* aim, anticipation, anxiety, aspiration, assessment, attention, attentiveness, belief, brainwork, care, cerebration, cogitation, compassion, concept, conception, concern, conclusion, conjecture, considerateness, consideration, contemplation, conviction, dash, deliberation, design, dream, estimation, excogitation, expectation, heed, hope, idea, intention, introspection, jot, judgement, kindness, little, meditation, mentation, muse, musing, notion, object, opinion, plan, prospect, purpose, reflection, regard, resolution, rumination, scrutiny, solicitude, study, sympathy, thinking, thoughtfulness, touch, trifle, view, whisker.

thoughtful *adj* absorbed, abstracted, astute, attentive, canny, careful, caring, cautious, circumspect, considerate, contemplative, deliberate, deliberative, discreet, heedful, helpful, introspective, kind, kindly, meditative, mindful, musing, pensieroso, pensive, prudent, rapt, reflective, ruminative, serious, solicitous, studious, thinking, unselfish, wary, wistful.

antonym thoughtless.

thoughtless *adj* absent-minded, careless, étourdi(e), foolish, heedless, ill-considered, impolite, imprudent, inadvertent, inattentive, inconsiderate, indiscreet, injudicious, insensitive, mindless, neglectful, negligent, rash, reckless, regardless, remiss, rude, selfish, silly, stupid, tactless, uncaring, undiplomatic, unkind, unmindful, unobservant, unreflecting, unthinking.

antonym thoughtful.

thraldom *n* bondage, enslavement, serfdom, servitude, slavery, subjection, subjugation, vassalage, ville(i)nage.

antonym freedom.

thrash *v* beat, belt, bethump, bethwack, birch, cane, chastise, clobber, crush, defeat, drub, flagellate, flail, flog, hammer, heave, horse-whip, jerk, lam, lambaste, larrup, lather, lay into, leather, maul, overwhelm, paste, plunge, punish, quilt, rout, scourge, slaughter, spank, squirm, swish, tan, thresh, toss, towel, trim, trounce, wallop, whale, whap, whip, writhe.

thrash out debate, discuss, negotiate, resolve, settle, solve.

thrashing *n* beating, belting, caning, chastisement, defeat, dressing, drubbing, flogging, hammering, hiding, laldie, lamming, lashing, leathering, mauling, pasting, punishment, quilting, rout, strap-oil, tanning, trouncing, whaling, whipping, whopping.

thread *n* cotton, course, direction, drift, fibre, filament, film, fimbria, line, motif, plot, story-line, strain, strand, string, tenor, theme, yarn.

v ease, inch, meander, pass, string, weave, wind.

threadbare *adj* clichéd, cliché-ridden, commonplace, conventional, corny, down-at-heel, frayed, hackneyed, moth-eaten, old, overused, overworn, ragged, scruffy, shabby, stale, stereotyped, stock, tattered, tatty, tired, trite, used, well-worn, worn, worn-out.

antonyms fresh, luxurious, new, plush.

thread-like *adj* fibriform, fibrillar(y), fibrillate(d), filaceous, filamentary, filamentous, filiform, filose, fine, slender, stringy, thin, thready.

threat *n* commination, danger, foreboding, foreshadowing, frighteners, hazard, menace, omen, peril, portent, presage, risk, sabre-rattling, warning.

threaten *v* browbeat, bully, comminate, cow, endanger, forebode, foreshadow, impend, imperil, intimidate, jeopardise, menace, portend, presage, pressurise, terrorise, warn.

threatening *adj* baleful, bullying, cautionary, comminatory, Damoclean, grim, inauspicious, intimidatory, menacing, minacious, minatory, ominous, sinister, terrorising, warning.

threesome *n* trey, triad, trilogy, trine, trinity, trio, triple, triplet, triplex, triptych, triumvirate, triune, troika.

threshold *n* beginning, brink, dawn, door, door-sill, door-stead, doorstep, doorway, entrance, inception, minimum, opening, outset, sill, start, starting-point, verge.

thrift *n* carefulness, conservation, economy, frugality, husbandry, parsimony, prudence, saving, thriftiness.

antonyms profligacy, waste.

thriftless *adj* dissipative, extravagant, improvident, imprudent, lavish, prodigal, profligate, spendthrift, unthrifty, wasteful.

antonym thrifty.

thrifty *adj* careful, conserving, economical, frugal, parsimonious, provident, prudent, saving, sparing.

antonyms prodigal, profligate, thriftless, wasteful.

thrill *n* adventure, buzz, charge, flutter, fluttering, frisson, glow, kick, pleasure, quiver, sensation, shudder, stimulation, throb, tingle, titillation, tremble, tremor, vibration.

v arouse, electrify, excite, flush, flutter, glow, move, quake, quiver, send, shake, shudder, stimulate, stir, throb, tingle, titillate, tremble, vibrate, wow.

thrilling *adj* electrifying, exciting, exhilarating, gripping, hair-raising, heart-stirring, quaking, rip-roaring, riveting, rousing, sensational, shaking, shivering, shuddering, soul-stirring, stimulating, stirring, trembling, vibrating.

thrive *v* advance, bloom, blossom, boom, burgeon, develop, flourish, gain, grow, increase, profit, prosper, succeed, wax.

antonyms die, fail, languish, stagnate.

thriving *adj* affluent, blooming, blossoming, booming, burgeoning, comfortable, developing, flourishing, growing, healthy, prosperous, successful, wealthy, well.

antonyms ailing, dying, failing, languishing, stagnating.

throat *n* craw, fauces, gorge, gullet, halse, oesophagus, the Red Lane, thropple, throttle, weasand, windpipe.

throaty *adj* deep, gruff, guttural, hoarse, husky, low, rasping, raucous, thick.

throb *v* beat, palpitate, pound, pulsate, pulse, thump, vibrate.

n beat, palpitation, pounding, pulsating, pulsation, pulse, thump, thumping, vibration, vibrato.

throe *n* convulsion, fit, pain, pang, paroxysm, seizure, spasm, stab.

throes *n* agony, anguish, death-agony, distress, pain, suffering, torture, travail.

throng *n* assemblage, bevy, concourse, congregation, crowd, crush, flock, herd, horde, host, jam, mass, mob, multitude, pack, press, swarm.

v bunch, congregate, converge, cram, crowd, fill, flock, herd, jam, mill around, pack, press, swarm.

throttle *v* asphyxiate, choke, control, gag, garrotte, inhibit, silence, smother, stifle, strangle, strangulate, suppress.

through *prep* as a result of, because of, between, by, by means of, by reason of, by virtue of, by way of, during, in, in and out of, in consequence of, in the middle of, past, thanks to, throughout, using, via.

adj completed, direct, done, ended, express, finished, non-stop, terminated.

through and through altogether, completely, entirely, from top to bottom, fully, thoroughly, to the core, totally, unreservedly, utterly, wholly.

throughout *adv* everywhere, extensively, ubiquitously, widely.

throw *v* astonish, baffle, bemuse, bring down, cast, chuck, confound, confuse, defeat, discomfit, disconcert, dislodge, dumbfound, elance, execute, fell, fling, floor, heave, hurl, jaculate, launch, lob, overturn, perform, perplex, pitch, produce, project, propel, put, send, shy, sling, slug, toss, unhorse, unsaddle, unseat, upset, whang.

n attempt, cast, chance, essay, fling, gamble, hazard, heave, lob, pitch, projection, put, shy, sling, spill, toss, try, venture, wager.

throw away blow, blue, cast off, discard, dispense with, dispose of, ditch, dump, fritter away, jettison, lose, reject, scrap, squander, waste.

antonyms keep, preserve, rescue, salvage.

throw dust in the eyes of con, confuse, cozen, deceive, delude, dupe, fool, have on, hoodwink, mislead, take in.

throw off abandon, cast off, confuse, discard, disconcert, disturb, doff, drop, shake off, throw, unsaddle, unseat, unsettle, upset.

throw out confuse, diffuse, discard, disconcert, dismiss, disseminate, disturb, ditch, dump, egurgitate, eject, emit, evict, expel, give off, jettison, radiate, reject, scrap, throw, turf out, turn down, unhouse, unsettle, upset, utter.

throw over abandon, chuck, desert, discard, drop, finish with, forsake, jilt, leave, quit, reject.

throw up abandon, chuck, disgorge, egurgitate, give up, heave, jack in, leave, produce, puke, quit, regurgitate, relinquish, renounce, resign, retch, reveal, spew, vomit.

throwaway *adj* careless, casual, cheap, disposable, offhand, passing, undramatic, unemphatic.

thrust *v* bear, butt, drive, force, impel, intrude, jab, jam, lunge, pierce, plunge, poke, press, prod, propel, push, ram, shove, stab, stick, urge, wedge.

n drive, flanconade, impetus, lunge, momentum, poke, prod, prog, push, shove, stab, stoccado.

thud *n* clonk, clump, clunk, crash, knock, smack, thump, thwack, wallop, wham.

v bash, clonk, clump, clunk, crash, knock, smack, thump, thunder, thwack, wallop, wham.

thug *n* animal, assassin, bandit, bangster, bruiser, bully-boy, cut-throat, gangster, goon, gorilla, heavy, highbinder, hood, hoodlum, hooligan, killer, mugger, murderer, phansigar, robber, ruffian, tough.

thumb one's nose at cock a snook at, deride, flout, guy, jeer at, laugh at, mock, ridicule, scoff.

thumb through browse through, flick through, flip through, glance at, leaf through, peruse, riffle through, scan, skim.

thumbnail *adj* brief, compact, concise, miniature, pithy, quick, short, small, succinct.

thumbs down disapproval, negation, no, rebuff, refusal, rejection, turn-down.

antonym thumbs up.

thumbs up acceptance, affirmation, approval, encouragement, go-ahead, green light, OK, sanction, yes.

antonym thumbs down.

thump *n* bang, blow, box, clout, clunk, crash, cuff, knock, rap, smack, thud, thwack, wallop, whack.

v bang, batter, beat, belabour, box, clout, crash, cuff, daud, ding, dunt, dush, hit, knock, lambaste, pound, rap, smack, strike, thrash, throb, thud, thwack, wallop, whack.

thumping *adj* big, colossal, enormous, excessive, exorbitant, gargantuan, gigantic, great, huge, immense, impressive, mammoth, massive, monumental, terrific, thundering, titanic, towering, tremendous, whooping.

antonyms insignificant, petty, piddling, trivial.

thunder *n* boom, booming, clap, cracking, crash, crashing, detonation, explosion, pealing, roll, rumble, rumbling.

v bark, bellow, blast, boom, clap, crack, crash, curse, declaim, denounce, detonate, explode, fulminate, inveigh, peal, rail, resound, reverberate, roar, rumble, shout, threaten, yell.

thundering *adj* enormous, excessive, great, monumental, remarkable, tremendous, unmitigated.

thunderous *adj* booming, deafening, ear-splitting, loud, noisy, resounding, reverberating, roaring, stentorian, tumultuous.

thunderstruck *adj* agape, aghast, amazed, astonished, astounded, dazed, dumbfounded, flabbergasted, floored, flummoxed, nonplussed, open-mouthed, paralysed, petrified, shocked, staggered, stunned.

thus *adv* accordingly, as follows, consequently, ergo, hence, in this way, like so, like this, so, then, therefore, thuswise.

thwack *v* bash, beat, buffet, clout, cuff, flog, hit, slap, smack, thump, wallop, whack.

n bash, blow, buffet, cloud, cuff, slap, smack, thump, wallop, whack.

thwart *v* baffle, balk, check, defeat, foil, frustrate, hinder, impede, obstruct, oppose, outwit, prevent, spite, stonker, stop, stymie, transverse, traverse.

antonyms abet, aid, assist.

tic *n* jerk, spasm, tic douloureux, twitch.

tick *n* clack, click, clicking, dash, flash, instant, jiffy, mark, minute, moment, sec, second, shake, stroke, tap, tapping, tick-tick, tick-tock, trice, twinkling.

v beat, choose, clack, click, indicate, mark (off), select, tally, tap.

tick off bawl out, berate, censure, chide, haul over the coals, keelhaul, lecture, rebuke, reprimand, reproach, reprove, scold, take to task, tear off a strip, tell off, upbraid.

antonym praise.

ticket *n* card, certificate, coupon, docket, label, marker, pass, slip, sticker, tab, tag, tessera, token, voucher.

tickle *v* amuse, cheer, delight, divert, enchant, entertain, excite, gratify, please, thrill, titillate.

ticklish *adj* awkward, critical, delicate, difficult, dodgy, hazardous, nice, precarious, risky, sensitive, thorny, touchy, tricky, uncertain, unstable, unsteady.

antonyms easy, straightforward.

tide *n* course, current, direction, drift, ebb, flow, flux, movement, stream, tendency, tenor, trend.

tidings *n* advice, bulletin, communication, dope, gen, greetings, information, intelligence, message, news, report, word.

tidy *adj* ample, businesslike, clean, cleanly, considerable, fair, generous, good, goodly, handsome, healthy, large, largish, methodical, neat, ordered, orderly, respectable, shipshape, siz(e)able, spick, spick-and-span, spruce, substantial, systematic, trim, uncluttered, well-groomed, well-kept.

antonyms disorganised, untidy.

v arrange, clean, fettle, groom, neaten, order, spruce up, straighten.

tie *v* attach, bind, confine, connect, draw, equal, fasten, hamper, hinder, hold, interlace, join, knot, lash, ligature, limit, link, match, moor, oblige, restrain, restrict, rope, secure, strap, tether, truss, unite.

n affiliation, allegiance, band, bond, commitment, connection, contest, copula, cord, dead heat, deadlock, draw, duty, encumbrance, fastening, fetter, fixture, game, hindrance, joint, kinship, knot, liaison, ligature, limitation, link, match, obligation, relationship, restraint, restriction, rope, stalemate, string.

tie up attach, bind, conclude, end, engage, engross, finish off, lash, ligate, moor, occupy, pinion, restrain, rope, secure, settle, terminate, tether, truss, wind up, wrap up.

tie-in *n* affiliation, association, connection, co-ordination, hook-up, liaison, link, relation, relationship, tie-up.

tier *n* band, belt, echelon, floor, gradin(e), layer, level, line, rank, row, stage, storey, stratification, stratum, zone.

tiff *n* barney, difference, disagreement, dispute, falling-out, huff, ill-humour, pet, quarrel, row, scrap, set-to, spat, squabble, sulk, tantrum, temper, words.

tight[1] *adj* close, close-fitting, compact, competent, constricted, cramped, dangerous, difficult, even, evenly-balanced, fast, firm, fixed, grasping, harsh, hazardous, hermetic, impervious, inflexible, mean, miserly, narrow, near, niggardly, parsimonious, penurious, perilous, precarious, precise, problematic, proof, rigid, rigorous, sealed, secure, severe, snug, sound, sparing, stern, sticky, stiff, stingy, stretched, strict, stringent, taut, tense, ticklish, tight-fisted, tough, tricky, trig, troublesome, uncompromising, unyielding, watertight, well-matched, worrisome.

antonyms lax, loose, slack.

tight[2] *adj* blotto, drunk, half cut, half-seas-over, in one's cups, inebriated, intoxicated, pickled, pie-eyed, pissed, plastered, smashed, sozzled, stewed, stoned, three sheets in the wind, tiddly, tipsy, under the influence.

antonym sober.

tighten *v* close, constrict, constringe, cramp, crush, fasten, fix, narrow, rigidify, screw, secure, squeeze, stiffen, stretch, tauten, tense.

antonyms loosen, relax.

tight-fisted *adj* cheese-paring, close, close-fisted, grasping, mean, mingy, miserly, niggardly, parsimonious, penny-pinching, penurious, sparing, stingy, tight.

antonym generous.

tight-lipped *adj* close-lipped, close-mouthed, mum, mute, quiet, reserved, reticent, secretive, silent, taciturn, uncommunicative, unforthcoming.

antonyms garrulous, talkative.

till *v* cultivate, dig, dress, plough, work.

tilt *v* attack, cant, clash, contend, duel, encounter, fight, heel, incline, joust, lean, list, overthrow, pitch, slant, slope, spar, tip.

n angle, cant, clash, combat, duel, encounter, fight, inclination, incline, joust, list, lists, pitch, set-to, slant, slope, thrust, tournament, tourney.

timber *n* beams, boarding, boards, forest, logs, planking, planks, trees, wood.

timbre *n* colour, klang, resonance, ring, tonality, tone, voice quality.

time *n* age, beat, chronology, date, day, duration, epoch, era, generation, heyday, hour, instance, interval, juncture, life, lifespan, lifetime, measure, metre, occasion, peak, period, point, rhythm, season, space, span, spell, stage, stretch, tempo, term, tide, while.

v clock, control, count, judge, measure, meter, regulate, schedule, set.

time and again frequently, many times, often, on many occasions, over and over again, recurrently, repeatedly, time after time.

time-honoured *adj* accustomed, age-old, ancient, conventional, customary, established, fixed, historic, long-established, old, traditional, usual, venerable.

timeless *adj* abiding, ageless, amaranthine, ceaseless, changeless, deathless, endless, enduring, eternal, everlasting, immortal, immutable, imperishable, indestructible, lasting, permanent, perpetual, persistent, undying.

timely *adj* appropriate, convenient, judicious, opportune, prompt, propitious, punctual, seasonable, suitable, tempestive, well-timed.

antonyms ill-timed, inappropriate, unfavourable.

timetable *n* agenda, calendar, curriculum, diary, list, listing, programme, roster, rota, schedule.

time-worn *adj* aged, ancient, broken-down, bromidic, cliché'd, dated, decrepit, dog-eared, hackneyed, hoary, lined, old hat, out of date, outworn, passé, ragged, ruined, run-down, shabby, stale, stock, threadbare, tired, trite, weathered, well-worn, worn, wrinkled.

antonyms fresh, new.

timid *adj* afraid, apprehensive, bashful, cowardly, coy, diffident, faint-hearted, fearful, hen-hearted, irresolute, modest, mousy, nervous, pavid, pusillanimous, retiring, shrinking, shy, spineless, timorous.

antonyms audacious, bold, brave.

timorous *adj* afraid, apprehensive, aspen, bashful, cowardly, coy, diffident, faint-hearted, fearful, inadventurous, irresolute, modest, mousy, nervous, pusillanimous, retiring, shrinking, shy, tentative, timid, trembling.

antonyms assertive, assured, bold.

tincture *n* aroma, colour, dash, flavour, hint, hue, seasoning, shade, smack, stain, suggestion, tinct, tinge, tint, touch, trace.

v colour, dye, flavour, imbue, infuse, permeate, scent, season, stain, suffuse, tinge, tint.

tinge *n* bit, cast, colour, dash, drop, dye, flavour, pinch, shade, smack, smatch, smattering, sprinkling, stain, suggestion, tinct, tincture, tint, touch, trace, wash.

v colour, dye, encolour, imbue, shade, stain, suffuse, tint.

tingle *v* dindle, itch, prickle, ring, sting, thrill, throb, tickle, vibrate.

n frisson, gooseflesh, goose-pimples, itch, itching, pins and needles, prickling, quiver, shiver, stinging, thrill, tickle, tickling.

tinker *v* dabble, fiddle, meddle, monkey, play, potter, putter, toy, trifle.

n botcher, bungler, diddicoy, fixer, itinerant, mender.

tinsel *adj* brummagem, cheap, clinquant, flashy, gaudy, gimcrack, meretricious, ostentatious, pinchbeck, plastic, sham, showy, specious, superficial, tawdry, trashy.

n artificiality, clinquant, display, flamboyance, frippery, garishness, gaudiness, glitter, insignificance, meaninglessness, ostentation, pinchbeck, pretension, sham, show, spangle, triviality, worthlessness.

tint *n* cast, colour, dye, hint, hue, rinse, shade, stain, streak, suggestion, tinct, tincture, tinge, tone, touch, trace, wash.

v affect, colour, dye, influence, rinse, stain, streak, taint, tincture, tinge.

tiny *adj* diminutive, dwarfish, infinitesimal, insignificant, itsy-bitsy, Lilliputian, little, microscopic, mini, miniature, minute, negligible, petite, pint-size(d), pocket, puny, pygmy, slight, small, teensy, teentsy, teeny, teeny-weeny, tiddl(e)y, tottie, totty, trifling, wee, weeny.

antonyms big, immense.

tip[1] *n* acme, apex, cap, crown, end, extremity, ferrule, head, nib, peak, pinnacle, point, summit, top.

v cap, crown, finish, pinnacle, poll, pollard, prune, surmount, top.

tip[2] *v* cant, capsize, ditch, dump, empty, heel, incline, lean, list, overturn, pour out, slant, spill, tilt, topple over, unload, up-end, upset.

n bing, coup, dump, midden, refuse-heap, rubbish-heap, slag-heap.

tip[3] *n* baksheesh, clue, forecast, gen, gift, gratuity, hint, information, inside information, lagniappe, perquisite, pointer, pourboire, refresher, suggestion, tip-off, warning, word, word of advice, wrinkle.

v advise, caution, forewarn, inform, remunerate, reward, suggest, tell, warn.

tipple *v* bib, drink, imbibe, indulge, quaff, swig, tope.

n alcohol, booze, drink, liquor, poison, wet.

tippler *n* bibber, boozer, dipso(maniac), drinker, drunk, drunkard, inebriate, lush, soak, sot, sponge, toper, wine-bag.

tipsy *adj* a peg too low, a pip out, cockeyed, corny, drunk, elevated, fuddled, happy, mellow, merry, moony, moppy, mops and brooms, nappy, pixil(l)ated, rocky, screwed, screwy, slewed, sprung, squiff(y), tiddled, tiddley, tiddly, tight, totty, wet, woozy.

antonym sober.

tirade *n* abuse, denunciation, diatribe, fulmination, harangue, invective, lecture, outburst, philippic, rant.

tire *v* annoy, betoil, bore, cook, drain, droop, enervate, exasperate, exhaust, fag, fail, fatigue, flag, harass, irk, irritate, jade, knacker, sink, weary.

antonyms energise, enliven, exhilarate, invigorate, refresh.

tired *adj* all in, awearied, aweary, beat, bone-weary, bushed, clapped-out, clichéd, conventional, corny, dead-beat, disjaskit, dog-tired, drained, drooping, drowsy, enervated, épuisé(e), exhausted, fagged, familiar, fatigued, flagging, forfairn, forfough(t)en, forjeskit, hackneyed, jaded, knackered, old, outworn, shagged, shattered, sleepy, spent, stale, stock, threadbare, trite, weary, well-worn, whacked, worn out.

antonyms active, energetic, fresh, lively, rested.

tireless *adj* determined, diligent, energetic, indefatigable, industrious, resolute, sedulous, unflagging, untiring, unwearied, vigorous.

antonyms tired, unenthusiastic, weak.

tiresome *adj* annoying, boring, bothersome, dull, exasperating, fatiguing, flat, irksome, irritating, laborious, monotonous, pesky, tedious, troublesome, trying, uninteresting, vexatious, wearing, wearisome.

antonyms easy, interesting, stimulating.

tiring *adj* arduous, demanding, draining, enervating, enervative, exacting, exhausting, fagging, fatiguing, laborious, strenuous, tough, wearing, wearying.

tiro *n* apprentice, beginner, catechumen, freshman, greenhorn, initiate, learner, neophyte, novice, novitiate, pupil, starter, student, tenderfoot, trainee.

antonyms old hand, veteran.

tissue *n* accumulation, agglomeration, collection, combination, concatenation, conglomeration, fabric, fabrication, gauze, mass, mesh, network, pack, paper, series, structure, stuff, texture, tissue-paper, web.

tit for tat a Roland for an Oliver, counterblow, counterbuff, countercharge, lex talionis, measure for measure, quid pro quo, requital, retaliation, revenge, talion.

titan *n* Atlas, colossus, giant, Hercules, leviathan, superman.

titanic *adj* Brobdingnagian, colossal, cyclopean, enormous, giant, gigantic, herculean, huge, immense, jumbo, mammoth, massive, mighty, monstrous, monumental, mountainous, prodigious, stupendous, towering, vast.

antonyms insignificant, small.

titbit *n* appetiser, bonne bouche, dainty, delicacy, goody, morsel, scrap, snack, tidbit, treat.

tithe *n* assessment, duty, impost, levy, rent, tariff, tax, tenth, toll, tribute.

v assess, charge, give, hand over, levy, pay, rate, take in, tax.

titillate *v* arouse, captivate, excite, interest, intrigue, provoke, stimulate, tantalise, tease, thrill, tickle, turn on.

titillating *adj* arousing, captivating, exciting, interesting, intriguing, lewd, lurid, provocative, sensational, stimulating, suggestive, teasing, thrilling.

titivate *v* doll up, make up, prank, preen, primp, prink, refurbish, smarten up, tart up, touch up.

title *n* appellation, caption, championship, claim, crown, denomination, designation, entitlement, epithet, handle, heading, inscription, label, laurels, legend, letter-head, moniker, name, nickname, nom de plume, ownership, prerogative, privilege, pseudonym, right, sobriquet, style, term.

v call, christen, designate, dub, entitle, label, name, style, term.

titter *v* chortle, chuckle, giggle, laugh, mock, snigger, tee-hee.

tittle-tattle *n* babble, blather, blether, cackle, chatter, chitchat, clishmaclaver, gossip, hearsay, jaw, natter, prattle, rumour, twaddle, ya(c)k, yackety-yak.

v babble, blather, blether, cackle, chat, chatter, chitchat, gossip, jaw, natter, prattle, tell tales, witter, ya(c)k, yackety-yak.

titular *adj* formal, honorary, nominal, puppet, putative, so-called, token.

to a fault excessively, immoderately, in the extreme, needlessly, out of all proportion, over the top, overly, overmuch, preposterously, ridiculously, to extremes, unduly.

to a man bar none, every one, nem con, one and all, unanimously, without exception.

to a turn correctly, exactly, perfectly, precisely, to perfection.

to all intents and purposes as good as, practically, pretty much, pretty well, virtually.

to be reckoned with consequential, considerable, formidable, important, influential, powerful, significant, strong, weighty.

to the full completely, entirely, fully, thoroughly, to the utmost, utterly.

to the hilt absolutely, completely, entirely, fully, totally, wholly.

to the letter accurately, exactly, literally, literatim, precisely, spot on, strictly, word for word.

to the point applicable, apposite, appropriate, apropos, apt, brief, fitting, germane, pertinent, pithy, pointed, relevant, short, suitable, terse.

antonym irrelevant.

toady *n* arse-licker, bootlicker, clawback, crawler, creep, fawner, flatterer, flunky, groveller, hanger-on, jackal, Jenkins, lackey, lick-platter, lickspittle, lick-spittle, minion, nark, parasite, pick-thank, running dog, spaniel, sucker, sycophant, toad-eater, truckler, tuft-hunter, yes-man.

v bootlick, bow and scrape, butter up, crawl, creep, cringe, curry favour, fawn, flatter, grovel, kiss the feet, kowtow, suck up, truckle.

toast[1] *v* broil, brown, grill, heat, roast, warm.

toast[2] *n* compliment, darling, drink, favourite, grace cup, health, hero, heroine, pledge, salutation, salute, tribute, wassail.

to-do *n* agitation, bother, brouhaha, bustle, commotion, disturbance, excitement, flap, flurry, furore, fuss, hoo-ha, performance, pother, quarrel, ruction, rumpus, stew, stir, stramash, tumult, turmoil, unrest, uproar.

together *adv* all at once, arranged, as one, as one man, at the same time, cheek by jowl, closely, collectively, concurrently, consecutively, contemporaneously, continuously, en masse, fixed, hand in glove, hand in hand, in a body, in a row, in concert, in co-operation, in fere, in mass, in succession, in unison, jointly, mutually, on end, ordered, organised, pari passu, settled, shoulder to shoulder, side by side, simultaneously, sorted out, straight, successively.

antonym separately.

adj calm, commonsensical, composed, cool, down-to-earth, level-headed, sensible, stable, well-adjusted, well-balanced, well-organised.

toil *n* application, donkey-work, drudgery, effort, elbow grease, exertion, graft, industry, labor improbus, labour, pains, slog, sweat, travail, yakka.

v drudge, graft, grind, grub, labour, persevere, plug away, slave, slog, strive, struggle, sweat, tew, work.

toiler *n* donkey, drudge, grafter, labourer, menial, navvy, slave, slogger, struggler, workaholic, worker, workhorse, workman.

antonyms idler, loafer, shirker.

toilet *n* ablutions, bathing, bathroom, bog, can, closet, comfort station, convenience, dressing, gents', grooming, john, karsey, kazi, ladies', latrine, lavatory, loo, outhouse, powder-room, privy, reredorter, rest-room, smallest room, thunder-box, toilette, urinal, washroom, water closet, WC.

toilsome *adj* arduous, backbreaking, burdensome, difficult, fatiguing, hard, herculean, laborious, painful, severe, strenuous, taxing, tedious, tiresome, tough, uphill, wearisome.

token *n* badge, clue, demonstration, earnest, evidence, expression, index, indication, keepsake, manifestation, mark, memento, memorial, note, pledge, proof, remembrance, reminder, representation, sign, souvenir, symbol, tessera, testimony, voucher, warning.

adj emblematic, hollow, inconsiderable, minimal, nominal, perfunctory, superficial, symbolic.

tolerable *adj* acceptable, adequate, all right, allowable, average, bearable, endurable, fair, fair to middling, indifferent, liv(e)able, mediocre, middling, not bad, OK, ordinary, passable, run-of-the-mill, so-so, sufferable, supportable, unexceptional.

antonym intolerable.

tolerance *n* allowance, broad-mindedness, charity, endurance, fluctuation, forbearance, fortitude, hardiness, hardness, indulgence, lenity, magnanimity, open-mindedness, patience, permissiveness, play, resilience, resistance, rope, stamina, sufferance, swing, sympathy, toughness, variation.

antonyms bigotry, intolerance, narrow-mindedness, prejudice.

tolerant *adj* biddable, broad-minded, catholic, charitable, complaisant, compliant, easy-going, fair, forbearing, indulgent, kind-hearted, latitudinarian, lax, lenient, liberal, long-suffering, magnanimous, open-minded, patient, permissive, soft, sympathetic, understanding, unprejudiced.

antonyms biased, bigoted, intolerant, prejudiced, unsympathetic.

tolerate *v* abear, abide, accept, admit, allow, bear, brook, condone, connive at, countenance, endure, indulge, permit, pocket, put up with, receive, sanction, stand, stomach, suffer, swallow, take, thole, turn a blind eye to, undergo, wear, wink at.

toleration *n* acceptance, allowance, condonation, connivance, endurance, indulgence, permissiveness, sanction, sufferance, tholing, wearing.

toll[1] *v* announce, call, chime, clang, knell, peal, ring, send, signal, sound, strike, summon, warn.

toll[2] *n* assessment, charge, cost, customs, damage, demand, duty, fee, impost, inroad, levy, loss, payment, penalty, rate, tariff, tax, tithe, tribute.

tomb *n* burial-place, catacomb, cenotaph, crypt, dolmen, grave, mastaba, mausoleum, sepulchre, sepulture, speos, vault.

tomboy *n* gamine, gilp(e)y, hempy, hoyden, minx, randie, randy, romp.

tombstone *n* gravestone, headstone, marker, memorial, monument, stone.

tome *n* book, opus, volume, work.

tomfoolery *n* balderdash, baloney, bilge, bosh, buffoonery, bunk, bunkum, childishness, claptrap, clowning, foolishness, hogwash, hooey, horseplay, idiocy, inanity, larking about, larks, messing about, messing on, nonsense, poppycock, rot, rubbish, shenanigans, silliness, skylarking, stupidity, tommyrot, tosh, trash, twaddle.

tone *n* accent, air, approach, aspect, attitude, cast, character, colour, drift, effect, emphasis, feel, force, frame, grain, harmony, hue, inflection, intonation, klang, manner, modulation, mood, note, pitch, quality, shade, spirit, strength, stress, style, temper, tenor, timbre, tinge, tint, tonality, vein, volume.

v blend, harmonise, intone, match, sound, suit.

tone down alleviate, assuage, dampen, dim, mitigate, moderate, modulate, palliate, play down, reduce, restrain, soften, soft-pedal, subdue, temper.

tone up brighten, freshen, invigorate, limber up, shape up, sharpen up, touch up, trim, tune up.

tongue *n* argot, articulation, clack, clapper, dialect, discourse, idiom, language, languet(te), lath, lingo, parlance, patois, red rag, speech, talk, utterance, vernacular, voice.

tongue-tied *adj* dumb, dumbstruck, inarticulate, mute, silent, speechless, voiceless.

antonyms garrulous, talkative, voluble.

tonic *n* analeptic, boost, bracer, cordial, fillip, inspiration, livener, pick-me-up, refresher, restorative, roborant, shot in the arm, stimulant.

too[1] *adv* also, as well, besides, further, in addition, into the bargain, likewise, moreover, to boot, what's more.

too[2] *adv* excessively, exorbitantly, extremely, immoderately, inordinately, over, overly, ridiculously, to excess, to extremes, unduly, unreasonably, very.

tool *n* agency, agent, apparatus, appliance, cat's-paw, contraption, contrivance, creature, device, dupe, flunkey, front, gadget, hireling, implement, instrument, intermediary, jackal, lackey, machine, means, medium, minion, pawn, puppet, stooge, toady, utensil, vehicle, weapon, widget.

v chase, cut, decorate, fashion, machine, ornament, shape, work.

tooth *n* cog, denticle, denticulation, dentil, fang, incisor, jag, masticator, molar, prong, tush, tusk.

toothless *adj* edentate, edentulous, fangless, gummy, powerless.

toothsome *adj* agreeable, ambrosial, appetising, dainty, delectable, delicious, flavoursome, luscious, mouthwatering, nice, palatable, sapid, savoury, scrumptious, sweet, tasty, tempting, yummy.

antonyms disagreeable, unpleasant.

top *n* acme, apex, apogee, cacumen, cap, cop, cork, cover, crest, crown, culmen, culmination, head, height, high point, lead, lid, meridian, peak, pinnacle, stopper, summit, upside, vertex, zenith.

antonyms base, bottom, nadir.

adj best, chief, crack, crowning, culminating, dominant, elite, finest, first, foremost, greatest, head, highest, lead, leading, pre-eminent, prime, principal, ruling, sovereign, superior, topmost, upmost, upper, uppermost.

v ascend, beat, best, better, cap, climb, command, cover, crest, crown, decorate, eclipse, exceed, excel, finish, finish off, garnish, head, lead, outdo, outshine, outstrip, roof, rule, scale, surmount, surpass, tip, transcend.

topic *n* issue, lemma, matter, motif, point, question, subject, subject-matter, talking-point, text, theme, thesis.

topical *adj* contemporary, current, familiar, newsworthy, popular, relevant, up-to-date, up-to-the-minute.

topmost *adj* apical, dominant, foremost, highest, leading, loftiest, maximum, paramount, principal, supreme, top, upper, uppermost.

antonyms bottom, bottommost, lowest.

topple *v* capsize, collapse, oust, overbalance, overthrow, overturn, totter, tumble, unseat, upset.

topsy-turvy *adj* arsy-versy, backside-foremost, chaotic, confused, disarranged, disorderly, disorganised, inside-out, jumbled, messy, mixed-up, untidy, upside-down.

antonyms ordered, tidy.

torch *n* brand, cresset, firebrand, flambeau, flashlight, lampad, link.

torment *v* afflict, agitate, agonise, annoy, bedevil, bother, chivvy, crucify, devil, distort, distress, excruciate, harass, harrow, harry, hound, irritate, nag, pain, persecute, pester, plague, provoke, rack, tease, torture, trouble, vex, worry, wrack.

n affliction, agony, angst, anguish, annoyance, bane, bother, distress, harassment, hassle, hell, irritation, misery, nag, nagging, nuisance, pain, persecution, pest, plague, provocation, scourge, suffering, torture, trouble, vexation, worry.

torn *adj* cut, dithering, divided, havering, irresolute, lacerated, ragged, rent, ripped, slit, split, swithering, uncertain, undecided, unsure, vacillating, wavering.

tornado *n* cyclone, gale, hurricane, monsoon, squall, storm, tempest, twister, typhoon, whirlwind.

torpid *adj* apathetic, benumbed, dormant, drowsy, dull, fainéant, hebetudinous, inactive, indolent, inert, lackadaisical, languid, languorous, lazy, lethargic, listless, lymphatic, motionless, numb, passive, slothful, slow, slow-moving, sluggish, somnolent, stagnant, supine.

antonyms active, lively, vigorous.

torpor *n* accidie, acedia, apathy, dormancy, drowsiness, dullness, hebetude, inactivity, inanition, indolence, inertia, inertness, languor, laziness, lethargy, listlessness, numbness, passivity, sloth, sluggishness, somnolence, stagnancy, stupidity, stupor, torpidity.

antonyms activity, animation, vigour.

torrent *n* barrage, cascade, deluge, downpour, effusion, flood, flow, gush, outburst, rush, spate, stream, tide, volley.

torrid *adj* ardent, arid, blistering, boiling, broiling, burning, dried, dry, emotional, erotic, fervent, fiery, hot, intense, parched, parching, passionate, scorched, scorching, sexy, sizzling, steamy, stifling, sultry, sweltering, tropical.

antonym arctic.

tortuous *adj* ambagious, ambiguous, bent, Byzantine, circuitous, complicated, convoluted, crooked, cunning, curved, deceptive, devious, indirect, involved, mazy, meandering, misleading, roundabout, serpentine, sinuous, tricky, twisted, twisting, winding, zigzag.

antonyms straight, straightforward.

torture *v* afflict, agonise, crucify, distress, excruciate, harrow, lacerate, martyr, martyrise, pain, persecute, rack, torment, wrack.

n affliction, agony, anguish, distress, gyp, hell, laceration, martyrdom, misery, pain, pang(s), persecution, rack, suffering, torment.

toss *v* agitate, cant, cast, chuck, disturb, fling, flip, heave, hurl, jiggle, joggle, jolt, labour, launch, lob, lurch, pitch, project, propel, rock, roll, shake, shy, sling, thrash, throw, tumble, wallow, welter, wriggle, writhe.

n cast, chuck, fling, lob, pitch, shy, sling, throw.

tot *n* baby, bairn, child, dram, finger, infant, measure, mite, nip, shot, slug, snifter, toddler, toothful, wean.

tot up add (up), calculate, compute, count (up), reckon, sum, tally, total.

total *n* aggregate, all, amount, ensemble, entirety, lot, mass, sum, totality, whole.

adj absolute, all-out, complete, comprehensive, consummate, downright, entire, full, gross, integral, out-and-out, outright, perfect, root-and-branch, sheer, sweeping, thorough, thoroughgoing, unconditional, undisputed, undivided, unmitigated, unqualified, utter, whole, whole-hog.

antonyms limited, partial, restricted.

v add (up), amount to, come to, count (up), reach, reckon, sum (up), tot up.

totalitarian *adj* authoritarian, despotic, dictatorial, monocratic, monolithic, omnipotent, one-party, oppressive, tyrannous, undemocratic.

antonym democratic.

totality *n* aggregate, all, completeness, cosmos, entireness, entirety, everything, fullness, pleroma, sum, total, universe, whole, wholeness.

totally *adv* absolutely, completely, comprehensively, consummately, entirely, fully, perfectly, quite, thoroughly, unconditionally, undisputedly, undividedly, unmitigatedly, utterly, wholeheartedly, wholly.

antonym partially.

totter *v* daddle, daidle, falter, lurch, quiver, reel, rock, shake, stagger, stumble, sway, teeter, titter, tremble, waver.

touch *n* ability, acquaintance, adroitness, approach, art, artistry, awareness, bit, blow, brush, caress, characteristic, command, communication, contact, correspondence, dash, deftness, detail, direction, drop, effect, facility, familiarity, feel, feeling, flair, fondling, hand, handiwork, handling, hint, hit, influence, intimation, jot, knack, manner, mastery, method, palpation, pat, pinch, push, skill, smack, smattering, soupçon, speck, spot, stroke, style, suggestion, suspicion, tactility, tap, taste, technique, tig, tincture, tinge, trace, trademark, understanding, virtuosity, way, whiff.

v abut, adjoin, affect, attain, border, brush, caress, cheat, compare with, concern, consume, contact, converge, disturb, drink, eat, equal, feel, finger, fondle, graze, handle, hit, hold a candle to, impress, influence, inspire, interest, mark, match, meet, melt, move, palp, palpate, parallel, pat, pertain to, push, reach, regard, rival, soften, stir, strike, stroke, tap, tat, tinge, upset, use, utilise.

touch off actuate, arouse, begin, cause, fire, foment, ignite, inflame, initiate, light, provoke, set off, spark off, trigger (off).

touch on allude to, broach, cover, deal with, mention, refer to, remark on, speak of.

touch up arouse, brush up, enhance, finish off, fondle, improve, patch up, perfect, polish up, renovate, retouch, revamp, round off, stimulate, titivate.

touch-and-go *adj* close, critical, dangerous, dodgy, hairy, hazardous, near, nerve-racking, offhand, parlous, perilous, precarious, risky, sticky, tricky.

touched *adj* affected, barmy, batty, bonkers, crazy, cuckoo, daft, disturbed, dotty, eccentric, impressed, mad, melted, moved, nuts, nutty, softened, stirred, swayed, upset.

touchiness *n* bad temper, captiousness, crabbedness, grouchiness, grumpiness, irascibility, irritability, peevishness, pettishness, petulance, surliness, testiness, tetchiness.

touching *adj* affecting, emotional, emotive, haptic, heartbreaking, libant, melting, moving, pathetic, piteous, pitiable, pitiful, poignant, sad, stirring, tender.

touchstone *n* bench-mark, criterion, gauge, measure, norm, proof, standard, yardstick.

touchy *adj* bad-tempered, captious, crabbed, cross, feisty, grouchy, grumpy, huffy, irascible, irritable, miffy, peevish, pettish, petulant, querulous, quick-tempered, sensitive, snippety, snuffy, sore, splenetic, surly, testy, tetchy, thin-skinned.

antonyms calm, imperturbable, serene, unflappable.

tough *adj* adamant, arduous, bad, baffling, brawny, butch, callous, cohesive, difficult, durable, exacting, exhausting, firm, fit, hard, hard-bitten, hard-boiled, hardened, hard-nosed, hardy, herculean, inflexible, intractable, irksome, knotty, laborious, lamentable, leathery, merciless, obdurate, obstinate, perplexing, pugnacious, puzzling, refractory, regrettable, resilient, resistant, resolute, rigid, rough, ruffianly, rugged, ruthless, seasoned, severe, solid, stalwart, stern, stiff, stout, strapping, strenuous, strict, strong, stubborn, sturdy, tenacious, thorny, troublesome, unbending, unforgiving, unfortunate, unlucky, unyielding, uphill, vicious, vigorous, violent.

antonyms brittle, delicate, fragile, liberal, soft, tender, vulnerable, weak.

n bravo, bruiser, brute, bully, bully-boy, bully-rook, droog, gorilla, hooligan, rough, roughneck, rowdy, ruffian, thug, yob, yobbo.

toughness *n* arduousness, callousness, difficulty, durability, firmness, fitness, grit, hardiness, hardness, inflexibility, intractability, laboriousness, obduracy, obstinacy, pugnacity, resilience, resistance, rigidity, roughness, ruggedness, ruthlessness, severity, solidity, sternness, stiffness, strength, strenuousness, strictness, sturdiness, tenacity, viciousness.

antonyms fragility, liberality, softness, vulnerability, weakness.

tour *n* circuit, course, drive, excursion, expedition, jaunt, journey, outing, peregrination, progress, ride, round, trip.

v drive, explore, journey, ride, sightsee, travel, visit.

tourist *n* emmet, excursionist, globe-trotter, grockle, holidaymaker, journeyer, rubber-neck, sightseer, sojourner, traveller, tripper, voyager.

tournament *n* championship, competition, contest, event, joust, lists, match, meeting, series, tourney.

tourniquet *n* garrot.

tousled *adj* disarranged, dishevelled, disordered, messed up, ruffled, rumpled, tangled, tumbled.

tow *v* drag, draw, haul, lug, pull, tote, trail, transport, trawl, tug, yank.

towards *prep* a little short of, about, almost, approaching, close to, coming up to, concerning, for, getting on for, in the direction of, in the vicinity of, just before, nearing, nearly, on the way to, regarding, to, -wards, with regard to, with respect to.

tower *n* barbican, bastille, bastion, belfry, castle, citadel, column, donjon, fort, fortification, fortress, keep, minar, minaret, mirador, obelisk, pillar, refuge, skyscraper, steeple, stronghold, turret.

v ascend, dominate, exceed, loom, mount, overlook, overtop, rear, rise, soar, surpass, top, transcend, uprise.

towering *adj* burning, colossal, elevated, excessive, extraordinary, extreme, fiery, gigantic, great, high, immoderate, imposing, impressive, inordinate, intemperate, intense, lofty, magnificent, mighty, monumental, outstanding, overpowering, paramount, passionate, prodigious, soaring, sublime, superior, supreme, surpassing, tall, transcendent, vehement, violent.

antonyms minor, small, trivial.

town *n* borough, bourg, burg, burgh, city, metropolis, municipality, settlement, township.

antonym country.

town-dweller *n* burgher, citizen, oppidan, townsman, towny, urbanite.

antonyms country-dweller, rustic.

toxic *adj* baneful, deadly, harmful, lethal, morbific, noxious, pernicious, pestilential, poisonous, septic, unhealthy.

antonym harmless.

toy *n* bauble, doll, game, gewgaw, kickshaw(s), knick-knack, plaything, trifle, trinket.

v dally, fiddle, flirt, play, potter, putter, sport, tinker, trifle, wanton.

trace *n* bit, dash, drop, evidence, footmark, footprint, footstep, hint, indication, iota, jot, mark, path, record, relic, remains, remnant, scintilla, shadow, sign, smack, soupçon, spoor, spot, suggestion, survival, suspicion, tincture, tinge, token, touch, track, trail, trifle, vestige, whiff.

v ascertain, chart, copy, delineate, depict, detect, determine, discover, draw, find, follow, map, mark, outline, pursue, record, seek, shadow, show, sketch, stalk, track, trail, traverse, unearth, write.

track *n* course, drift, footmark, footprint, footstep, line, mark, orbit, path, pathway, piste, rail, rails, ridgeway, road, scent, sequence, slot, spoor, tack, trace, trail, train, trajectory, wake, wavelength, way.

v chase, dog, follow, hunt, pursue, shadow, spoor, stalk, tail, trace, trail, travel, traverse.

track down apprehend, capture, catch, dig up, discover, expose, ferret out, find, hunt down, locate, run to earth, sniff out, trace, unearth.

tract[1] *n* area, district, estate, expanse, extent, lot, plot, quarter, region, section, stretch, territory, zone.

tract[2] *n* booklet, brochure, discourse, disquisition, dissertation, essay, homily, leaflet, monograph, pamphlet, sermon, tractate, treatise.

tractable *adj* amenable, biddable, complaisant, compliant, controllable, docile, ductile, fictile, governable, malleable, manageable, obedient, persuadable, plastic, pliable, pliant, submissive, tame, tractile, willing, workable, yielding.

antonyms headstrong, intractable, obstinate, refractory, stubborn, unruly, wilful.

traction *n* adhesion, drag, draught, drawing, friction, grip, haulage, propulsion, pull, pulling, purchase, resistance.

trade *n* avocation, barter, business, calling, clientele, commerce, commodities, craft, custom, customers, deal, dealing, employment, exchange, interchange, job, line, market, métier, occupation, patrons, profession, public, pursuit, shopkeeping, skill, swap, traffic, transactions, truck.

v bargain, barter, commerce, deal, do business, exchange, peddle, swap, switch, traffic, transact, truck.

trademark *n* badge, brand, crest, emblem, hallmark, identification, idiograph, insignia, label, logo, logotype, name, sign, symbol.

trader *n* barrow-boy, barterer, broker, buyer, dealer, marketer, merchandiser, merchant, seller, sutler.

tradesman *n* artisan, craftsman, dealer, journeyman, mechanic, merchant, retailer, seller, shopkeeper, shopman, vendor, workman.

tradition *n* convention, custom, customs, folklore, habit, institution, lore, praxis, ritual, usage, usance, way, wony.

traditional *adj* accustomed, ancestral, conventional, customary, established, fixed, folk, historic, long-established, new, old, oral, time-honoured, tralaticious, transmitted, unconventional, unwritten, usual.

traduce *v* abuse, asperse, blacken, calumniate, decry, defame, denigrate, deprecate, depreciate, detract, disparage, knock, malign, misrepresent, revile, run down, slag, slander, smear, vilify.

traducer *n* abuser, asperser, calumniator, defamer, denigrator, deprecator, detractor, disparager, knocker, mud-slinger, slanderer, smearer, vilifier.

traffic *n* barter, business, commerce, communication, dealing, dealings, doings, exchange, freight, intercourse, movement, passengers, peddling, relations, toing and froing, trade, transport, transportation, truck, vehicles.

v bargain, barter, deal, do business, exchange, intrigue, market, merchandise, peddle, trade, truck.

trafficker *n* broker, dealer, merchant, monger, peddler, trader.

tragedy *n* adversity, affliction, blow, calamity, catastrophe, disaster, misfortune, unhappiness.

antonyms prosperity, success, triumph.

tragic *adj* anguished, appalling, awful, calamitous, catastrophic, deadly, dire, disastrous, doleful, dreadful, fatal, grievous, heartbreaking, heart-rending, ill-fated, ill-starred, lamentable, miserable, mournful, pathetic, pitiable, ruinous, sad, shocking, sorrowful, thespian, unfortunate, unhappy, woeful, wretched.

antonyms comic, successful, triumphant.

trail *v* chase, dangle, dawdle, drag, draw, droop, extend, follow, hang, haul, hunt, lag, linger, loiter, pull, pursue, shadow, stalk, straggle, stream, sweep, tail, tow, trace, track, traipse.

n abature, appendage, drag, footpath, footprints, footsteps, mark, marks, path, road, route, scent, spoor, stream, tail, trace, track, train, wake, way.

trail away decrease, die away, diminish, disappear, dwindle, fade (away), fall away, lessen, peter out, shrink, sink, subside, tail off, taper off, trail off, weaken.

train *v* aim, coach, direct, discipline, drill, educate, excercise, focus, guide, improve, instruct, lesson, level, point, prepare, rear, rehearse, school, teach, tutor.

n appendage, attendants, caravan, chain, choo-choo, column, concatenation, convoy, cortege, course, court, entourage, file, followers, following, household, lure, order, process, procession, progression, retinue, sequence, series, set, staff, string, succession, suite, tail, trail.

trainer *n* coach, drill-master, handler, instructor, teacher, tutor, walker.

training *n* coaching, discipline, dressage, education, exercise, grounding, guidance, instruction, manège, practice, preparation, schooling, teaching, tuition, tutelage, upbringing, working-out.

traipse *v* plod, slouch, trail, tramp, trudge.

n plod, slog, tramp, trek, trudge.

trait *n* attribute, characteristic, feature, idiosyncrasy, lineament, mannerism, peculiarity, quality, quirk, thew.

traitor *n* apostate, back-stabber, betrayer, deceiver, defector, deserter, double-crosser, fifth columnist, informer, Judas, miscreant, nithing, proditor, quisling, rebel, renegade, turncoat.

traitorous *adj* apostate, dishonourable, disloyal, double-crossing, double-dealing, faithless, false, perfidious, proditorious, renegade, seditious, treacherous, treasonable, unfaithful, untrue.

antonyms faithful, loyal, patriotic.

trajectory *n* course, flight, line, path, route, track, trail.

trammel *n* bar, block, bond, chain, check, clog, curb, fetter, hamper, handicap, hindrance, impediment, obstacle, rein, shackle, stumbling-block.

v bar, block, capture, catch, check, clog, curb, enmesh, ensnare, entrammel, entrap, fetter, hamper, handicap, hinder, impede, inhibit, net, pinion, restrain, restrict, shackle, snag, tie.

tramp *v* crush, footslog, hike, march, plod, ramble, range, roam, rove, slog, stamp, stomp, stump, toil, traipse, trample, tread, trek, trudge, walk, yomp.

n clochard, derelict, dosser, down-and-out, drifter, drummer, footfall, footstep, hike, hobo, march, piker, plod, ramble, slog, stamp, toe-rag(ger), tread, trek, vagabond, vagrant, weary willie.

trample *v* crush, flatten, hurt, infringe, insult, squash, stamp, tread, violate.

trance *n* abstraction, catalepsy, daze, dream, ecstasy, muse, rapture, reverie, spell, stupefaction, stupor, unconsciousness.

tranquil *adj* at peace, calm, composed, cool, disimpassioned, dispassionate, pacific, peaceful, placid, quiet, reposeful, restful, sedate, serene, still, undisturbed, unexcited, unperturbed, unruffled, untroubled.

antonyms agitated, disturbed, noisy, troubled.

tranquillise *v* calm, compose, lull, narcotise, opiate, pacify, quell, quiet, relax, sedate, soothe.

antonyms agitate, disturb, upset.

tranquilliser *n* barbiturate, bromide, downer, narcotic, opiate, opium, sedative.

tranquillity *n* ataraxia, ataraxy, calm, calmness, composure, coolness, equanimity, hush, imperturbability, peace, peacefulness, placidity, quiet, quietness, quietude, repose, rest, restfulness, sedateness, serenity, silence, stillness.

antonyms agitation, disturbance, noise.

transact *v* accomplish, carry on, carry out, conclude, conduct, discharge, dispatch, do, enact, execute, handle, manage, negotiate, perform, prosecute, settle.

transaction *n* action, affair, arrangement, bargain, business, coup, deal, deed, enterprise, event, execution, matter, negotiation, occurrence, proceeding, undertaking.

transactions *n* affairs, annals, concerns, doings, goings-on, minutes, proceedings, record.

transcend *v* eclipse, exceed, excel, outdo, outrival, outshine, outstrip, overleap, overstep, overtop, surmount, surpass.

transcendence *n* ascendancy, excellence, greatness, incomparability, matchlessness, paramoun(t)cy, predominance, pre-eminence, sublimity, superiority, supremacy, transcendency.

transcendent *adj* consummate, exceeding, extraordinary, foremost, incomparable, matchless, peerless, pre-eminent, sublime, superior, transcendental, unequalled, unique, unparalleled, unrivalled, unsurpassed.

transcribe *v* copy, engross, exemplify, interpret, note, record, render, reproduce, rewrite, take down, tape, tape-record, transfer, translate, transliterate.

transcript *n* carbon, copy, duplicate, manuscript, note, notes, record, recording, reproduction, tenor, transcription, translation, transliteration, version.

transfer *v* carry, cede, change, consign, convey, decal, decant, demise, displace, grant, hand over, move, relocate, remove, second, shift, translate, transmit, transplant, transport, transpose.

n change, changeover, crossover, decantation, displacement, handover, move, relocation, removal, shift, switch, switch-over, transference, translation, transmission, transposition, virement.

transfigure *v* alter, apotheosise, change, convert, exalt, glorify, idealise, metamorphose, transform, translate, transmute.

transfix *v* engross, fascinate, fix, hold, hypnotise, impale, mesmerise, paralyse, petrify, pierce, puncture, skewer, spear, spellbind, spike, spit, stick, stun, transpierce.

antonym bore.

transform *v* alter, change, convert, metamorphose, reconstruct, remodel, renew, revolutionise, transfigure, translate, transmogrify, transmute, transverse.

antonym preserve.

transformation *n* alteration, change, conversion, metamorphosis, metanoia, metastasis, renewal, revolution, sea-change, transfiguration, translation, transmogrification, transmutation.

antonym preservation.

transfuse *v* imbue, instil, permeate, pervade, suffuse, transfer.

transgress *v* breach, break, contravene, defy, disobey, encroach, err, exceed, infringe, lapse, misbehave, offend, overstep, sin, trespass, violate.

antonym obey.

transgression *n* breach, contravention, crime, debt, encroachment, error, fault, infraction, infringement, iniquity, lapse, misbehaviour, misdeed, misdemeanour, offence, peccadillo, peccancy, sin, trespass, violation, wrong, wrongdoing.

transgressor *n* criminal, culprit, debtor, delinquent, evil-doer, felon, lawbreaker, malefactor, miscreant, offender, sinner, trespasser, villain, wrong-doer.

transience *n* brevity, briefness, caducity, deciduousness, ephemerality, evanescence, fleetingness, fugacity, fugitiveness, impermanence, shortness, transitoriness.

antonym permanence.

transient *adj* brief, caducous, deciduous, ephemeral, evanescent, fleeting, flying, fugacious, fugitive, impermanent, momentary, passing, short, short-lived, short-term, temporary, transitory.

antonym permanent.

transit *n* alteration, carriage, cartage, carting, change, changeover, conversion, conveyance, crossing, haulage, motion, movement, passage, portage, shift, shipment, transfer, transition, transport, transportation, travel, traverse.

transition *n* alteration, change, changeover, conversion, development, evolution, flux, metabasis, metamorphosis, metastasis, passage, passing, progress, progression, shift, transformation, transit, transmutation, upheaval.

antonyms beginning, end.

transitional *adj* changing, developmental, fluid, intermediate, metabatic, passing, provisional, temporary, transition, transitionary, unsettled.

antonyms final, initial.

transitory *adj* brief, deciduous, ephemeral, evanescent, fleeting, flying, fugacious, fugitive, impermanent, momentary, passing, short, short-lived, short-term, temporary, transient, vanishing.

antonym lasting.

translate *v* alter, carry, change, construe, convert, convey, decipher, decode, do, do up, elucidate, enrapture, explain, improve, interpret, metamorphose, move, paraphrase, remove, render, renovate, send, simplify, spell out, transcribe, transfer, transfigure, transform, transliterate, transmogrify, transmute, transplant, transport, transpose, turn.

translation *n* alteration, change, conversion, conveyance, crib, decoding, elucidation, explanation, gloss, interpretation, metamorphosis, metaphrase, metaphrasis, move, paraphrase, removal, rendering, rendition, rephrasing, rewording, simplification, transcription, transference, transfiguration, transformation, transliteration, transmutation, transposition, version.

translator *n* dragoman, exegete, exegetist, glossarist, glossator, glosser, interpreter, linguist, metaphrast, paraphraser, paraphrast.

translucent *adj* clear, diaphanous, limpid, lucent, pellucid, translucid, transparent.

antonym opaque.

transmigration *n* metempsychosis, Pythagoreanism, rebirth, reincarnation, transformation.

transmission *n* broadcast, broadcasting, carriage, communication, conveyance, diffusion, dispatch, dissemination, passage, programme, relaying, remission, sending, shipment, show, showing, signal, spread, trajection, transfer, transference, transit, transport, transportation.

antonym reception.

transmit *v* bear, broadcast, carry, communicate, convey, diffuse, dispatch, disseminate, forward, impart, network, radio, relay, remit, send, spread, traject, transfer, transport.

antonym receive.

transmute *v* alter, change, convert, metamorphose, remake, transfigure, transform, translate, transmogrify, transverse.

antonym retain.

transparency[1] *n* apparentness, candidness, clarity, clearness, diaphanousness, directness, distinctness, explicitness, filminess, forthrightness, frankness, gauziness, limpidity, limpidness, obviousness, openness, patentness, pellucidity, pellucidness, perspicuousness, plainness, sheerness, straightforwardness, translucence, translucency, translucidity, transparence, unambiguousness, visibility, water.

antonyms ambiguity, opacity, unclearness.

transparency[2] *n* photograph, picture, plate, slide.

transparent *adj* apparent, candid, clear, crystalline, diaphanous, dioptric, direct, distinct, easy, evident, explicit, filmy, forthright, frank, gauzy, hyaline, hyaloid, ingenuous, limpid, lucent, lucid, manifest, obvious, open, patent, pellucid, perspicuous, plain, plain-spoken, recognisable, see-through, sheer, straight, straightforward, translucent, transpicuous, unambiguous, understandable, undisguised, unequivocal, visible.

antonyms ambiguous, opaque, unclear.

transpire *v* appear, arise, befall, betide, chance, come out, come to light, emerge, happen, leak out, occur, take place, turn up.

transplant *v* displace, pot on, relocate, remove, repot, resettle, shift, transfer, uproot.

antonym leave.

transport *v* banish, bear, bring, captivate, carry, carry away, convey, delight, deport, ecstasise, electrify, enchant, enrapture, entrance, exile, fetch, haul, move, ravish, remove, run, ship, spellbind, take, transfer, waft.

antonyms bore, leave.

n bliss, carriage, cartage, carting, conveyance, delight, ecstasy, enchantment, euphoria, happiness, haulage, heaven, rapture, ravishment, removal, shipment, shipping, transference, transportation, vehicle, waterage.

antonym boredom.

transportation *n* carriage, cartage, carting, conveyance, haulage, postage, transfer, transport, transportal.

transpose *v* alter, change, exchange, interchange, metathesise, move, rearrange, relocate, reorder, shift, substitute, swap, switch, transfer.

antonym leave.

transverse *adj* cross, crossways, crosswise, diagonal, oblique, transversal.

transvestism *n* cross-dressing, drag, eonism, travesty.

trap *n* ambush, artifice, bunker, danger, deception, device, gin, hazard, net, noose, pitfall, ruse, snare, spring, springe, springle, strategem, subterfuge, toils, trap-door, trepan, trick, trickery, wile.

v ambush, beguile, benet, catch, corner, deceive, dupe, enmesh, ensnare, entrap, illaqueate, inveigle, lime, snare, take, tangle, trepan, trick.

trapped *adj* ambushed, beguiled, caught, cornered, deceived, duped, ensnared, illaqueated, inveigled, netted, snared, stuck, surrounded, trepanned, tricked.

antonym free.

trapper *n* backwoodsman, frontiersman, hunter, huntsman, voyageur.

trappings *n* accompaniments, accoutrements, adornments, clothes, decorations, dress, equipment, finery, fittings, fixtures, fripperies, furnishings, gear, housings, livery, ornaments, panoply, paraphernalia, raiment, things, trimmings.

trash *n* balderdash, draff, dreck, dregs, drivel, dross, garbage, hogwash, inanity, junk, kitsch, litter, nonsense, offscourings, offscum, refuse, riddlings, rot, rubbish, scoria, sullage, sweepings, trashery, tripe, trumpery, twaddle, waste.

antonym sense.

trashy *adj* brummagem, catchpenny, cheap, cheap-jack, flimsy, grotty, inferior, kitschy, meretricious, pinchbeck, rubbishy, shabby, shoddy, tawdry, third-rate, tinsel, worthless.

antonym first-rate.

trauma *n* agony, anguish, damage, disturbance, hurt, injury, jolt, lesion, ordeal, pain, scar, shock, strain, suffering, torture, upheaval, upset, wound.

antonyms healing, relaxation.

traumatic *adj* agonising, damaging, distressing, disturbing, frightening, hurtful, injurious, painful, scarring, shocking, unpleasant, upsetting, wounding.

antonyms healing, relaxed, relaxing.

travail *n* birth-pangs, childbirth, distress, drudgery, effort, exertion, grind, hardship, labour, labour pains, pain, slavery, slog, strain, stress, suffering, sweat, tears, throes, toil, tribulation.

antonym rest.

travel *v* carry, commute, cross, excursionise, go, hump the bluey, journey, locomote, move, peregrinate, proceed, progress, ramble, roam, rove, tour, traverse, trek, voyage, walk, wander, wayfare, wend.

antonym stay.

traveller *n* agent, drummer, excursionist, explorer, globetrotter, gypsy, hiker, holiday-maker, itinerant, journeyer, migrant, nomad, passenger, peregrinator, rep, representative, salesman, saleswoman, tinker, tourist, tripper, vagrant, viator, voyager, wanderer, wayfarer.

travelling *adj* itinerant, migrant, migratory, mobile, movable, moving, multivagrant, nomadic, on the move, peripatetic, roaming, roving, touring, vagrant, viatorial, wandering, wayfaring.

antonyms fixed, stay-at-home.

travels *n* excursion, expedition, globetrotting, journey, passage, peregrination, ramble, tour, travel, trip, voyage, walk, wanderings, wayfare.

travel-worn *adj* footsore, jet-lagged, saddle-sore, travel-weary, waygone, wayworn, weary.

antonym fresh.

traverse *v* balk, bridge, check, consider, contradict, contravene, counter, counteract, cover, cross, deny, dispute, examine, eye, frustrate, hinder, impede, inspect, investigate, move, negotiate, obstruct, oppose, peregrinate, ply, range, review, roam, scan, scrutinise, span, study, swing, thwart, turn, wander.

antonyms aid, confirm.

travesty *n* apology, botch, burlesque, caricature, distortion, lampoon, mockery, parody, perversion, send-up, sham, take-off.

v burlesque, caricature, deride, distort, lampoon, mock, parody, pervert, pillory, ridicule, send up, sham, spoof, take off.

treacherous *adj* dangerous, deceitful, deceptive, disloyal, double-crossing, double-dealing, double-hearted, double-tongued, duplicitous, faithless, false, hazardous, icy, perfidious, perilous, precarious, proditorious, proditory, Punic, recreant, risky, slippery, slippy, traitorous, treasonable, tricky, unfaithful, unreliable, unsafe, unstable, untrue, untrustworthy.

antonyms dependable, loyal.

treacherously *adv* deceitfully, disloyally, faithlessly, falsely, perfidiously.

antonym loyally.

treachery *n* betrayal, disloyalty, double-cross, double-dealing, duplicity, faithlessness, falseness, infidelity, Judas-kiss, laesa majestas, Medism, perfidiousness, perfidy, Punic faith, Punica fides, trahison, treason.

antonyms dependability, loyalty.

tread *v* crush, hike, march, oppress, pace, pad, plod, press, quell, repress, squash, stamp, step, stride, subdue, subjugate, suppress, tramp, trample, trudge, walk, walk on.

n footfall, footstep, gait, pace, step, stride, walk.

tread on someone's toes affront, annoy, bruise, discommode, disgruntle, hurt, inconvenience, infringe, injure, irk, offend, upset, vex.

antonym soothe.

treason *n* disaffection, disloyalty, duplicity, laesa majestas, lese-majesty, mutiny, perfidy, sedition, subversion, trahison, traitorousness, treachery.

antonym loyalty.

treasonable *adj* disloyal, false, insurrectionary, mutinous, perfidious, seditious, subversive, traitorous, treacherous.

antonym loyal.

treasure *n* cash, darling, ewe-lamb, flower, fortune, funds, gem, gold, jewel, jewels, money, nonpareil, paragon, pearl, precious, pride and joy, prize, riches, valuables, wealth.

v adore, cherish, esteem, idolise, love, preserve, prize, revere, value, venerate, worship.

antonym disparage.

treasurer *n* bursar, cashier, purser, quaestor.

treasury *n* assets, bank, cache, capital, chrestomathy, coffers, corpus, exchequer, finances, fisc, funds, hoard, money, Parnassus, repository, resources, revenues, store, storehouse, thesaurus, vault.

treat *n* banquet, celebration, delight, enjoyment, entertainment, excursion, feast, fun, gift, gratification, joy, outing, party, pleasure, refreshment, satisfaction, surprise, thrill, wayzgoose.

antonym drag.

v attend to, bargain, care for, confer, consider, contain, deal with, discourse upon, discuss, doctor, entertain, feast, give, handle, manage, medicament, medicate, medicine, negotiate, nurse, parley, provide, regale, regard, stand, use.

treatise *n* disquisition, dissertation, essay, exposition, monograph, pamphlet, pandect, paper, prolegomena, prolusion, study, thesis, tract, tractate, work, writing.

treatment *n* care, conduct, cure, deal, dealing, discussion, handling, healing, management, manipulation, medication, medicine, prescript, reception, regimen, remedy, surgery, therapeutics, therapy, usage, use.

treble *adj* high, high-pitched, piping, sharp, shrill, threefold, triple.

antonym deep.

treaty *n* agreement, alliance, bargain, bond, compact, concordat, contract, convention, covenant, entente, negotiation, pact.

tree *n* arbor, bush, conifer, cross, evergreen, frutex, gallows, pollard, sampling, seedling, shrub.

trek *n* expedition, footslog, hike, journey, march, migration, odyssey, safari, slog, tramp, walk.

v footslog, hike, journey, march, migrate, plod, range, roam, rove, slog, traipse, tramp, trudge, yomp.

tremble *v* heave, oscillate, quake, quiver, rock, shake, shiver, shudder, teeter, totter, vibrate, wobble.

n heart-quake, oscillation, quake, quiver, shake, shiver, shudder, tremblement, tremor, vibration.

antonym steadiness.

trembling *n* heart-quake, oscillation, quaking, quavering, quivering, rocking, shakes, shaking, shivering, shuddering, tremblement, trepidation, vibration.

antonym steadiness.

tremendous *adj* ace, amazing, appalling, awe-inspiring, awesome, awful, colossal, deafening, dreadful, enormous, excellent, exceptional, extraordinary, fabulous, fantastic, fearful, formidable, frightful, gargantuan, gigantic, great, hell of a, herculean, huge, immense, incredible, mammoth, marvellous, monstrous, prodigious, sensational, spectacular, stupendous, super, terrible, terrific, titanic, towering, vast, whopping, wonderful.

antonyms boring, dreadful, run-of-the-mill, tiny.

tremor *n* agitation, earthquake, quake, quaking, quaver, quavering, quiver, quivering, shake, shaking, shiver, shock, thrill, tremble, trembling, trepidation, trillo, vibration, wobble.

antonym steadiness.

tremulous *adj* afraid, agitated, agog, anxious, aspen, dithery, excited, fearful, frightened, jittery, jumpy, nervous, quavering, quivering, quivery, scared, shaking, shivering, timid, trembling, trembly, tremulant, trepid, trepidant, vibrating, wavering.

antonyms calm, firm.

trench *n* channel, cut, ditch, drain, earthwork, entrenchment, excavation, fosse, furrow, grip, gullet, gutter, pit, rill, sap, trough, waterway.

trenchant *adj* acerbic, acid, acidulous, acute, astringent, biting, caustic, clear, clear-cut, cogent, crisp, cutting, distinct, driving, effective, effectual, emphatic, energetic, explicit, forceful, forthright, hurtful, incisive, keen, mordant, penetrating, piquant, pointed, potent, powerful, pungent, sarcastic, scratching, severe, sharp, strong, tart, unequivocal, vigorous.

antonym woolly.

trend *n* bias, course, crazed, current, dernier cri, direction, drift, fad, fashion, flow, inclination, leaning, look, mode, rage, style, tendency, thing, vogue.

trendy *adj* fashionable, funky, groovy, hip, in, latest, modish, stylish, up to the minute, voguish, with it.

antonym unfashionable.

trepidation *n* agitation, alarm, anxiety, apprehension, butterflies, cold sweat, consternation, dismay, disquiet, disturbance, dread, emotion, excitement, fear, fright, jitters, misgivings, nervousness, palpitation, perturbation, qualms, quivering, shaking, trembling, tremor, unease, uneasiness, worry.

antonym calm.

trespass *v* encroach, err, infringe, injure, intrude, invade, obtrude, offend, poach, sin, transgress, violate, wrong.

antonyms keep to, obey.

n breach, contravention, crime, debt, delinquency, encroachment, error, evil-doing, fault, infraction, infringement, iniquity, injury, intrusion, invasion, misbehaviour, misconduct, misdeed, misdemeanour, offence, poaching, sin, transgression, wrong-doing.

trespasser *n* criminal, debtor, delinquent, evil-doer, infringer, interloper, intruder, invader, malefactor, offender, poacher, sinner, transgressor, wrong-doer.

tress *n* braid, bunch, curl, lock, pigtail, plait, queue, ringlet, tail.

trial *n* adversity, affliction, assay, attempt, audition, bane, bother, burden, check, contest, crack, distress, effort, endeavour, examination, experience, experiment, go, grief, hardship, hassle, hearing, irritation, litigation, load, misery, nuisance, ordeal, pain, pest, plague, probation, proof, shot, sorrow, stab, suffering, taster, temptation, test, testing, tribulation, tribunal, trouble, try, trying, unhappiness, venture, vexation, whack, woe, worry, wretchedness.

antonyms happiness, rest.

adj dry, dummy, experimental, exploratory, pilot, probationary, provisional, testing.

triangular *adj* cuneiform, three-cornered, three-sided, trigonal, trigonic, trigonous, trilateral.

tribal *adj* class, ethnic, family, gentilitial, gentilitian, gentilitious, group, narrow, native, parochial, primitive, savage, sectarian, sectional, uncivilised, uncultured.

tribe *n* blood, branch, caste, clan, class, division, dynasty, family, gens, group, house, ilk, nation, people, phratry, race, seed, sept, stock.

tribulation *n* adversity, affliction, blow, burden, care, curse, distress, grief, heartache, misery, misfortune, ordeal, pain, reverse, sorrow, suffering, travail, trial, trouble, unhappiness, vexation, woe, worry, wretchedness.

antonyms happiness, rest.

tribunal *n* bar, bench, court, examination, hearing, inquisition, trial.

tribute *n* accolade, acknowledgement, annates, applause, charge, commendation, compliment, contribution, cornage, credit, customs, duty, encomium, esteem, eulogy, excise, first-fruits, gavel, gift, gratitude, homage, honour, horngeld, impost, laudation, offering, panegyric, payment, praise, ransom, recognition, respect, subsidy, tax, testimonial, testimony, toll.

antonym blame.

trice *n* flash, instant, jiff, jiffy, minute, moment, sec, second, shake, tick, twinkling, whiff.

trick *n* antic, art, artifice, cantrip, caper, characteristic, chicane, command, con, craft, deceit, deception, device, dodge, dog-trick, expedient, expertise, feat, feint, foible, fraud, frolic, gag, gambol, gift, gimmick, habit, hang, hoax, idiosyncrasy, imposition, imposture, jape, joke, josh, knack, know-how, legerdemain, leg-pull, mannerism, manoeuvre, peculiarity, ploy, practical joke, practice, prank, put-on, quirk, quiz, rig, ruse, secret, shot, skill, sleight, spell, stall, stratagem, stunt, subterfuge, swindle, technique, toy, trait, trap, trinket, turn, wile.

adj artificial, bogus, counterfeit, ersatz, fake, false, feigned, forged, imitation, mock, pretend, sham.

antonym genuine.

v bamboozle, beguile, cheat, con, cozen, deceive, defraud, delude, diddle, dupe, fool, gull, hoax, hocus-pocus, hoodwink, hornswoggle, illude, lead on, mislead, outwit, pull a fast one on, pull someone's leg, sell, swindle, trap.

trick out adorn, array, attire, bedeck, bedizen, decorate, do up, doll up, dress up, ornament, prank, prink, spruce up, tart up, trick up.

trickery *n* cheating, chicanery, con, conveyance, deceit, deception, dishonesty, dodgery, double-dealing, dupery, flim-flam, fraud, funny business, guile, hanky-panky, hoax, hocus-pocus, imposture, jiggery-pokery, jugglery, monkey business, pretence, shennanigans, skulduggery, sleight, sleight-of-hand, swindling, trickstering.

antonym honesty.

trickle *v* dribble, drip, drop, exude, filter, gutter, leak, ooze, percolate, run, seep.

antonyms gush, stream.

n drib, dribble, driblet, dribs and drabs, drip, seepage.

antonyms gush, stream.

trickster *n* cheat, con man, cozener, deceiver, diddler, fraud, hoaxer, impostor, joker, pretender, quiz, quizzer, swindler, tregetour, tricker.

tricky *adj* artful, complicated, crafty, cunning, deceitful, deceptive, delicate, devious, difficult, foxy, Gordian, knotty, legerdemain, problematic, risky, scheming, slippery, sly, sticky, subtle, thorny, ticklish, touch-and-go, trickish, tricksome, tricksy, wily.

antonyms easy, honest.

trifle *n* bagatelle, bauble, bit, concetto, dash, drop, falderal, finicality, foolishness, gewgaw, jot, knick-knack, little, nonsense, nothing, pinch, plaything, spot, touch, toy, trace, trinket, triviality, whigmaleerie, whim-wham.

v coquet, dabble, dally, dawdle, faddle, fiddle-faddle, flirt, fool, fribble, fritter, frivol, idle, meddle, niggle, palter, play, play with, sport, toy, wanton, waste.

trifler *n* dallier, dilettante, fribbler, futilitarian, good-for-nothing, idler, layabout, loafer, ne'er-do-well, piddler, waster.

trifles *n* inessentials, minor considerations, minutiae, nugae, trivia, trivialities.

antonym essentials.

trifling *adj* empty, footling, foozling, fribbling, fribblish, frivolous, idle, inconsiderable, insignificant, minuscule, negligible, nugatory, paltry, petty, piddling, piffling, puny, shallow, silly, slight, small, tiny, trivial, unimportant, valueless, worthless.

antonym important.

n desipience, fiddling, fooling, footling, frivolity, piddling, piffling, whifflery.

trigger *v* activate, actuate, cause, elicit, generate, initiate, produce, prompt, provoke, set off, spark off, start.

n catch, goad, lever, release, spur, stimulus, switch.

trill *v* cheep, chirp, chirrup, sing, tweet, twitter, warble, whistle.

trim *adj* clean-limbed, compact, dapper, natty, neat, orderly, shipshape, slender, slim, smart, smirk, soigné, spick-and-span, spruce, streamlined, svelte, trig, well-dressed, well-groomed, willowy.

antonym scruffy.

v adjust, adorn, arrange, array, balance, barb, barber, beautify, bedeck, clip, crop, curtail, cut, decorate, distribute, dock, dress, dub, embellish, embroider, garnish, lop, order, ornament, pare, prepare, prune, settle, shave, shear, tidy, trick.

n adornment, array, attire, border, clipping, condition, crop, cut, decoration, disposition, dress, edging, embellishment, equipment, fettle, fitness, fittings, form, frill, fringe, garnish, gear, health, humour, nick, order, ornament, ornamentation, piping, pruning, repair, shape, shave, shearing, situation, state, temper, trappings, trimming.

trimmer *n* time-server, vicar of Bray, weathercock.

trimming *n* adornment, border, braid, decoration, edging, embellishment, falbala, fimbriation, frill, fringe, frou-frou, furbelow, garnish, ornamentation, passament, passementerie, piping, trim.

trimmings *n* accessories, accompaniments, additions, appurtenances, clippings, cuttings, ends, extras, frills, garnish, ornaments, paraphernalia, parings, remnants, shavings, trappings.

trinity *n* threefoldness, threesome, triad, trilogy, trio, tripersonality, triple, triplet, triumvirate, triune, triunity, troika.

trinket *n* bagatelle, bauble, bibelot, bijou, doodad, fairing, gewgaw, gimcrack, kickshaws, knick-knack, nothing, ornament, toy, trifle, trinkum-trankum, whigmaleerie, whim-wham.

trio *n* terzetto, threesome, triad, trilogy, trine, trinity, triple, triplet, triptych, triumvirate, triune.

trip *n* blunder, boob, errand, error, excursion, expedition, fall, faux pas, foray, indiscretion, jaunt, journey, lapse, misstep, outing, ramble, run, skip, slip, step, stumble, tour, travel, voyage.

v activate, blunder, boob, caper, confuse, dance, disconcert, engage, err, fall, flip, flit, frisk, gambol, go, hop, lapse, miscalculate, misstep, pull, ramble, release, set off, skip, slip, slip up, spring, stumble, switch on, throw, tilt up, tip up, tour, trap, travel, tumble, unsettle, voyage.

tripe *n* balderdash, balls, blah, bosh, bullshit, bunkum, claptrap, drivel, garbage, guff, hogwash, inanity, nonsense, poppycock, rot, rubbish, tosh, trash, trumpery, twaddle.

antonym sense.

triple *adj* ternal, three-branched, threefold, three-ply, three-way, treble, trigeminal, trinal, trinary, tripartite, triplex, triplicate, triploid.

n threefoldness, threesome, triad, trilogy, trine, trinity, trio, triplet, triplicity, triumvirate, triune, triunity.

v treble, triplicate.

triplet *n* tercet, terzetta, threesome, triad, trilling, trilogy, trin, trine, trinity, trio, triple, triplicity, tripling, triumvirate, triune, troika.

tripper *n* emmet, excursionist, grockle, holiday-maker, sightseer, tourist, voyager.

trite *adj* banal, bromidic, cliché'd, common, commonplace, corny, dull, hack, hackneyed, Mickey Mouse, ordinary, overworn, pedestrian, rinky-dink, routine, run-of-the-mill, stale, stereotyped, stock, threadbare, tired, uninspired, unoriginal, well-trodden, well-worn, worn, worn out.

antonym original.

triumph *n* accomplishment, achievement, ascendancy, attainment, conquest, coup, elation, exultation, feat, happiness, hit, joy, jubilation, masterstroke, mastery, pride, rejoicing, sensation, smash, smash-hit, success, tour de force, victory, walk-away, walk-over, win.

antonym disaster.

v best, celebrate, crow, defeat, dominate, exult, gloat, glory, have the last laugh, humble, humiliate, jubilate, overcome, overwhelm, prevail, prosper, rejoice, revel, subdue, succeed, swagger, vanquish, win.

antonym fail.

triumphant *adj* boastful, celebratory, cock-a-hoop, conquering, dominant, elated, epinikian, exultant, gloating, glorious, joyful, jubilant, proud, rejoicing, successful, swaggering, triumphal, undefeated, victorious, winning.

antonyms defeated, humble.

trivia *n* details, irrelevancies, minutiae, nugae, pap, trifles, trivialities.

antonym essentials.

trivial *adj* commonplace, dinky, everyday, frivolous, incidental, inconsequential, inconsiderable, insignificant, little, meaningless, Mickey Mouse, minor, negligible, nugatory, paltry, pettifogging, petty, piddling, piffling, puny, slight, small, snippety, trifling, trite, unimportant, valueless, worthless.

antonym significant.

trivialise *v* belittle, depreciate, devalue, minimise, play down, scoff at, underestimate, underplay, undervalue.

antonym exalt.

triviality *n* detail, frivolity, futility, inconsequence, inconsequentiality, insignificance, littleness, meaninglessness, minor matter, negligibility, nothing, nugatoriness, paltriness, pettiness, slightness, smallness, technicality, trifle, triteness, unimportance, valuelessness, worthlessness.

antonyms essential, importance.

troop *n* assemblage, band, body, bunch, company, contingent, crew, crowd, division, drove, flock, gang, gathering, group, herd, horde, multitude, pack, squad, squadron, swarm, team, throng, trip, unit.

v crowd, flock, go, march, pack, parade, stream, swarm, throng, traipse, turn.

troops *n* army, men, military, servicemen, soldiers, soldiery.

trophy *n* award, booty, cup, laurels, memento, memorial, prize, souvenir, spoils.

tropical *adj* equatorial, hot, humid, lush, luxuriant, steamy, stifling, sultry, sweltering, torrid.

antonyms arctic, cold, cool, temperate.

trot *v* bustle, canter, jog, lope, pace, run, scamper, scurry, scuttle.

n canter, jog, jog-trot, lope, run.

trot out adduce, bring forward, bring up, drag up, exhibit, recite, rehearse, reiterate, relate, repeat.

troubadour *n* balladeer, cantabank, jongleur, minnesinger, minstrel, poet, singer, trouvère, trouveur.

trouble *n* affliction, agitation, ailment, annoyance, anxiety, attention, bother, care, commotion, complaint, concern, danger, defect, difficulty, dilemma, disability, discontent, discord, disease, disorder, disquiet, dissatisfaction, distress, disturbance, effort, exertion, failure, grief, heartache, illness, inconvenience, irritation, labour, malfunction, mess, misfortune, nuisance, pain, pains, pest, pickle, predicament, problem, row, scrape, shtook, solicitude, sorrow, spot, strife, struggle, suffering, thought, torment, travail, trial, tribulation, tumult, uneasiness, unrest, upheaval, upset, vexation, woe, work, worry.

antonyms calm, peace.

v afflict, agitate, annoy, bother, burden, discomfort, discommode, discompose, disconcert, disquiet, distress, disturb, fash, fret, grieve, harass, incommode, inconvenience, molest, muddy, pain, perplex, perturb, pester, plague, sadden, torment, upset, vex, worry.

antonyms help, reassure.

troublemaker *n* agent provocateur, agitator, bell-wether, bolshevik, bovver boy, firebrand, heller, incendiary, instigator, meddler, mischief-maker, rabble-rouser, ringleader, stirrer, tub-thumper.

antonym peace-maker.

troublesome *adj* annoying, arduous, bothersome, burdensome, demanding, difficult, disorderly, fashious, harassing, hard, importunate, inconvenient, insubordinate, irksome, irritating, laborious, oppressive, pestilential, plaguesome, plaguey, poxy, rebellious, recalcitrant, refractory, rowdy, spiny, taxing, thorny, tiresome, tricky, trying, turbulent, unco-operative, undisciplined, unruly, upsetting, vexatious, violent, wearisome, worrisome, worrying.

antonyms easy, helpful, polite.

trough *n* back, channel, conduit, crib, depression, ditch, duct, flume, furrow, gully, gutter, hollow, manger, trench, tub.

trounce *v* beat, best, censure, clobber, crush, drub, hammer, lick, overwhelm, paste, punish, rebuke, rout, slaughter, thrash, whale, whitewash.

troupe *n* band, cast, company, group, set, troop.

trouper *n* actor, artiste, entertainer, old hand, performer, player, Roscius, theatrical, thespian, veteran.

trousers *n* bags, bloomers, breeches, breeks, culottes, denims, ducks, dungarees, flannels, indescribables, inexpressibles, jeans, knickerbockers, lederhosen, Levis"trade", pantaloons, pants, pedal-pushers, plus-fours, shorts, slacks, trews, trunk-breeches, trunk-hose, unmentionables, unutterables.

truancy *n* absence, dodging, malingering, shirking, skiving.

antonyms attendance, effort.

truant *n* absentee, deserter, dodger, hookey, malingerer, runaway, shirker, skiver, wag.

adj absent, malingering, missing, runaway, skiving.

v desert, dodge, malinger, play truant, shirk, skive, skive off.

truce *n* armistice, break, cease-fire, cessation, intermission, interval, let-up, lull, moratorium, peace, respite, rest, stay, suspension, treaty, Truce of God.

antonym hostilities.

truck[1] *n* business, commerce, communication, connection, contact, dealings, exchange, intercourse, relations, trade, traffic.

truck[2] *n* barrow, bogie, camion, cart, drag, float, hand-cart, lorry, trailer, trolley, van, wag(g)on, water-cart, water-wagon, wheelbarrow.

truculent *adj* aggressive, antagonistic, bad-tempered, bellicose, belligerent, combative, contentious, cross, defiant, fierce, hostile, ill-tempered, obstreperous, pugnacious, quarrelsome, savage, scrappy, sullen, violent.

antonyms co-operative, good-natured.

trudge *v* clump, footslog, hike, labour, lumber, march, mush, plod, slog, stump, traipse, tramp, trek, walk.

n footslog, haul, hike, march, mush, slog, traipse, tramp, trek, walk.

true *adj* absolute, accurate, actual, apod(e)ictic, authentic, bona fide, confirmed, conformable, constant, correct, corrected, dedicated, devoted, dutiful, exact, factual, faithful, fast, firm, genuine, honest, honourable, legitimate, loyal, natural, perfect, precise, proper, pure, real, right, rightful, sincere, sooth, spot-on, square, staunch, steady, true-blue, true-born, true-hearted, trustworthy, trusty, truthful, typical, unerring, unswerving, upright, valid, veracious, veridical, veritable.

antonyms faithless, false, inaccurate.

adv accurately, correctly, exactly, faithfully, honestly, perfectly, precisely, properly, rightly, truly, truthfully, unerringly, veraciously, veritably.

antonyms falsely, inaccurately.

true-blue *adj* card-carrying, committed, confirmed, constant, dedicated, devoted, dyed-in-the-wool, faithful, loyal, orthodox, staunch, true, trusty, uncompromising, unwavering.

antonyms superficial, wavering.

truism *n* axiom, bromide, cliché, commonplace, platitude, saw, truth, verity.

truly *adv* accurately, authentically, constantly, correctly, devotedly, dutifully, en verité, exactly, exceptionally, extremely, factually, faithfully, fegs, firmly, genuinely, greatly, honestly, honourably, in good sooth, in reality, in truth, indeed, indubitably, legitimately, loyally, precisely, properly, really, rightly, sincerely, soothly, staunchly, steadfastly, steadily, truthfully, undeniably, veraciously, verily, veritably, very.

antonyms faithlessly, falsely, incorrectly, slightly.

trump up *v* concoct, contrive, cook up, create, devise, fabricate, fake, invent, make up.

trumped-up *adj* concocted, contrived, cooked-up, fabricated, fake, faked, false, falsified, invented, made-up, phoney, spurious, untrue.

antonym genuine.

trumpery *adj* brummagem, cheap, flashy, grotty, meretricious, nasty, pinchbeck, rubbishy, shabby, shoddy, tawdry, trashy, trifling, useless, valueless, worthless.

antonym first-rate.

trumpet *n* bellow, blare, blast, bray, bugle, call, clarion, cry, honk, horn, roar.

v advertise, announce, bellow, blare, blast, bray, broadcast, call, extol, honk, preconise, proclaim, publish, roar, shout, tout.

truncate *v* abbreviate, clip, crop, curtail, cut, cut short, lop, maim, pare, prune, shorten, trim.

antonym lengthen.

truncheon *n* baton, club, cosh, cudgel, knobkerrie, life-preserver, night-stick, shillela(g)h, staff.

trunk[1] *n* bin, box, case, chest, coffer, crate, Gladstone bag, kist, locker, portmanteau, suitcase.

trunk[2] *n* body, bole, frame, shaft, stalk, stem, stock, torso, tube.

trunk[3] *n* nose, proboscis, snout.

truss *v* bind, bundle, fasten, hogtie, pack, pinion, secure, strap, tether, tie.

antonym untie.

n bale, bandage, beam, binding, brace, bundle, buttress, joist, prop, shore, stanchion, stay, strut, support.

trust *n* affiance, assurance, belief, care, certainty, certitude, charge, confidence, conviction, credence, credit, custody, duty, expectation, faith, fidelity, guard, guardianship, hope, obligation, protection, reliance, responsibility, safekeeping, trusteeship, uberrima fides.

antonym mistrust.

v assign, assume, bank on, believe, command, commit, confide, consign, count on, credit, delegate, depend on, entrust, expect, give, hope, imagine, presume, rely on, suppose, surmise, swear by.

antonym mistrust.

trustee *n* administrator, agent, custodian, depositary, executor, executrix, fiduciary, guardian, keeper.

trusting *adj* confiding, credulous, gullible, innocent, naïve, optimistic, simple, trustful, unguarded, unquestioning, unsuspecting, unsuspicious, unwary.

antonyms cautious, distrustful.

trustworthy *adj* authentic, dependable, ethical, four-square, honest, honourable, level-headed, mature, principled, reliable, responsible, righteous, sensible, steadfast, true, trusty, truthful, upright.

antonym unreliable.

trusty *adj* dependable, faithful, firm, honest, loyal, reliable, responsible, solid, staunch, steady, straightforward, strong, supportive, true, trustworthy, upright.

antonym unreliable.

truth *n* accuracy, actuality, axiom, candour, certainty, constancy, dedication, devotion, dutifulness, exactness, fact, facts, factuality, factualness, faith, faithfulness, fidelity, frankness, genuineness, historicity, honesty, integrity, law, legitimacy, loyalty, maxim, naturalism, precision, realism, reality, sooth, truism, truthfulness, uprightness, validity, veracity, verdicality, verity.

antonym falsehood.

truthful *adj* accurate, candid, correct, exact, faithful, forthright, frank, honest, literal, naturalistic, plain-spoken, precise, realistic, reliable, sincere, sooth, soothfast, soothful, straight, straightforward, true, trustworthy, veracious, veridicous, verist, veristic, veritable.

antonym untruthful.

truthfulness *n* candour, frankness, honesty, openness, righteousness, sincerity, straightness, uprightness, veracity, verism.

antonym untruthfulness.

try *v* adjudge, adjudicate, afflict, aim, annoy, appraise, attempt, catechise, endeavour, essay, evaluate, examine, experiment, hear, inconvenience, inspect, investigate, irk, irritate, pain, plague, prove, sample, seek, strain, stress, strive, struggle, taste, tax, test, tire, trouble, undertake, upset, venture, vex, wear out, weary.

n appraisal, attempt, bash, crack, effort, endeavour, essay, evaluation, experiment, fling, go, inspection, sample, shot, stab, taste, taster, test, trial, whack.

try out appraise, check out, evaluate, inspect, sample, taste, test, try on.

trying *adj* aggravating, annoying, arduous, bothersome, difficult, distressing, exasperating, fatiguing, hard, irksome, irritating, searching, severe, stressful, taxing, testing, tiresome, tough, troublesome, upsetting, vexing, wearisome.

antonym calming.

tub *n* back, barrel, basin, bath, bathtub, bucket, butt, cask, hogshead, keeve, keg, kid, kit, pail, puncheon, stand, tun, vat.

tubby *adj* buxom, chubby, corpulent, fat, obese, overweight, paunchy, plump, podgy, portly, pudgy, roly-poly, stout, well-upholstered.

antonym slim.

tube *n* channel, conduit, cylinder, duct, hose, inlet, main, outlet, pipe, shaft, spout, trunk, vas.

tuberculosis *n* consumption, phthisis, TB.

tubular *adj* pipelike, pipy, tubate, tubelike, tubiform, tubulate, tubulous, vasiform.

tuck[1] *v* cram, crease, fold, gather, insert, push, stuff.

n crease, fold, gather, pinch, pleat, pucker.

tuck[2] *n* comestibles, eats, food, grub, nosh, prog, scoff, victuals, vittles.

tuck in devour, dine, eat, eat up, fall to, feast, gobble, gorge, scoff, sup.

tuft *n* beard, bunch, clump, cluster, collection, crest, dag, daglock, dollop, floccule, flocculus, floccus, flock, knot, shock, tassle, topknot, truss, tussock.

tug *v* drag, draw, haul, heave, jerk, jigger, lug, pluck, pull, tow, wrench, yank.

n drag, haul, heave, jerk, pluck, pull, tow, traction, wrench, yank.

tuition *n* education, instruction, lessons, pedagogics, pedagogy, schooling, teaching, training, tutelage, tutoring.

tumble *v* disorder, drop, fall, flop, jumble, overthrow, pitch, plummet, roll, rumple, stumble, topple, toss, trip up.

n collapse, drop, fall, flop, plunge, roll, spill, stumble, toss, trip.

tumbledown *adj* broken-down, crumbling, crumbly, decrepit, dilapidated, disintegrating, ramshackle, rickety, ruined, ruinous, shaky, tottering.

antonym well-kept.

tumbler[1] *n* acrobat, contortionist, gymnast, voltigeur.

tumbler[2] *n* beaker, cup, drinking-glass, glass, goblet, mug, schooner.

tumid *adj* affected, bloated, bombastic, bulbous, bulging, distended, enlarged, euphuistic, flowery, fulsome, fustian, grandiloquent, grandiose, high-flown, inflated, magniloquent, oro(ro)tund, overblown, pompous, pretentious, protuberant, puffed up, puffy, sesquipedalian, stilted, swollen, tumescent, turgid.

antonyms flat, simple.

tumour *n* cancer, carcinoma, growth, lump, lymphoma, melanoma, myeloma, neoplasm, sarcoma, swelling, tubercle, tubercule, tuberculoma, tuberculum.

tumult *n* ado, affray, agitation, altercation, bedlam, brattle, brawl, brouhaha, bustle, clamour, coil, commotion, deray, din, disorder, disturbance, Donnybrook, émeute, excitement, fracas, hubbub, hullabaloo, outbreak, pandemonium, quarrel, racket, riot, rookery, rout, row, ruction, ruffle, stir, stramash, strife, turmoil, unrest, upheaval, uproar.

antonym calm.

tumultuous *adj* agitated, boisterous, clamorous, confused, disorderly, disturbed, excited, fierce, hectic, irregular, lawless, noisy, obstreperous, passionate, raging, restless, riotous, rowdy, rumbustious, stormy, tempestuous, troubled, turbulent, unrestrained, unruly, uproarious, violent, vociferous, wild.

antonym calm.

tune *n* agreement, air, attitude, concert, concord, consonance, demeanour, disposition, euphony, frame of mind, harmony, melisma, melody, mood, motif, pitch, song, strain, sympathy, temper, theme, unison.

v adapt, adjust, attune, harmonise, pitch, regulate, set, synchronise, temper.

tuneful *adj* canorous, catchy, euphonious, harmonious, mellifluous, mellow, melodic, melodious, musical, pleasant, sonorous.

antonym tuneless.

tuneless *adj* atonal, cacophonous, clashing, discordant, dissonant, harsh, horrisonant, unmelodic, unmelodious, unmusical.

antonym tuneful.

tunnel *n* burrow, channel, chimney, drift, flue, gallery, hole, passage, passageway, sap, shaft, subway, underpass.

v burrow, dig, excavate, mine, penetrate, sap, undermine.

turbid *adj* clouded, cloudy, confused, dense, dim, disordered, feculent, foggy, foul, fuzzy, hazy, impure, incoherent, muddled, muddy, murky, opaque, roily, thick, unclear, unsettled.

antonym clear.

turbulence *n* agitation, boiling, chaos, commotion, confusion, disorder, disruption, instability, pandemonium, roughness, storm, tumult, turmoil, unrest, upheaval.

antonym calm.

turbulent *adj* agitated, anarchic, blustery, boiling, boisterous, choppy, confused, disordered, disorderly, foaming, furious, insubordinate, lawless, mutinous, obstreperous, raging, rebellious, refractory, riotous, rough, rowdy, seditious, stormy, tempestuous, tumultuous, unbridled, undisciplined, ungovernable, unruly, unsettled, unstable, uproarious, violent, wild.

antonym calm.

turf *n* clod, divot, glebe, grass, green, sod, sward.

turf out banish, bounce, chuck out, discharge, dismiss, dispossess, eject, elbow, evict, expel, fire, fling out, give the elbow to, kick out, oust, sack, throw out, turn out.

turgid *adj* affected, bloated, bombastic, bulging, congested, dilated, distended, extravagant, flowery, fulsome, fustian, grandiloquent, grandiose, high-flown, inflated, magniloquent, oro(ro)tund, ostentatious, overblown, pompous, pretentious, protuberant, puffy, sesquipedalian, stilted, swollen, tumescent, tumid, windy.

antonyms flat, simple.

turmoil *n* agitation, bedlam, brouhaha, bustle, chaos, combustion, commotion, confusion, disorder, disquiet, disturbance, Donnybrook, dust, émeute, ferment, flurry, hubbub, hubbuboo, noise, pandemonium, pother, pudder, rookery, rout, row, ruffle, stir, stour, stramash, strife, tracasserie, trouble, tumult, turbulence, uproar, violence, welter.

antonym calm.

turn *v* adapt, alter, apostatise, appeal, apply, approach, become, caracol, change, circle, construct, convert, corner, curdle, defect, deliver, depend, desert, divert, double, execute, fashion, fit, form, frame, go, gyrate, hang, hinge, infatuate, influence, issue, look, make, metamorphose, mould, move, mutate, nauseate, negotiate, pass, perform, persuade, pivot, prejudice, remodel, renege, resort, retract, return, reverse, revolve, roll, rotate, shape, shift, sicken, sour, spin, spoil, swerve, switch, swivel, taint, transfigure, transform, translate, transmute, twirl, twist, upset, veer, wheel, whirl, write.

n act, action, airing, aptitude, bend, bent, bias, bout, caracol, cast, chance, change, circle, circuit, constitutional, crack, crankle, crisis, culmination, curve, cycle, deed, departure, deviation, direction, distortion, drift, drive, excursion, exigency, fashion, favour, fling, form, format, fright, gesture, go, guise, gyration, heading, innings, jaunt, make-up, manner, mode, mould, occasion, opportunity, outing, performance, performer, period, pivot, promenade, reversal, revolution, ride, rotation, round, saunter, scare, service, shape, shift, shock, shot, spell, spin, start, stint, stroll, style, succession, surprise, swing, tendency, time, trend, trick, try, turning, twist, uey, U-turn, vicissitude, walk, warp, way, whack, whirl.

turn away avert, deflect, depart, deviate, discharge, dismiss.

antonym accept.

turn back beat off, do a uey, drive back, drive off, force back, go back, rebuff, repel, repulse, resist, retrace one's steps, return, revert.

antonyms go on, stay.

turn down decline, diminish, fold, invert, lessen, lower, muffle, mute, quieten, rebuff, refuse, reject, repudiate, soften, spurn.

antonyms accept, turn up.

turn in deliver, enter, give back, give up, go to bed, hand in, hand over, hit the sack, register, retire, return, submit, surrender, tender.

antonyms get up, give out, keep.

turn inside out evaginate, evert, extravert, introvert.

turn of events affair, galère, happening, incident, occurrence, outcome, phenomenon, result.

turn of phrase diction, expression, idiom, locution, metaphor, phraseology, saying, style.

turn off alienate, bore, branch off, cut out, depart from, deviate, discourage, disenchant, disgust, dismiss, displease, divert, irritate, kill, leave, nauseate, offend, put off, put out, quit, repel, shut, shut down, sicken, stop, switch off, turn out, unplug.

antonym turn on.

turn on activate, arouse, assail, assault, attack, attract, balance, depend, energise, excite, expose, fall on, hang, hinge, ignite, inform, initiate, introduce, pivot, please, rest, round on, rouse, show, start, start up, stimulate, switch on, thrill, titillate, trip, turn against, work up.

antonym turn off.

turn out accoutre, apparel, appear, assemble, attend, attire, banish, become, cashier, clean out, clear, clothe, come, come about, crop up, deport, develop, discharge, dishome, dishouse, dismiss, displant, dispossess, dress, drive out, drum out, emerge, empty, end up, eventuate, evict, evolve, expel, fabricate, finish, fire, fit, gather, go, happen, kick out, make, manufacture, muster, oust, outfit, process, produce, result, sack, show up, switch off, throw out, transpire, turf out, turn off, turn up, unplug, unseat.

antonyms stay away, turn on.

turn over activate, assign, break up, capsize, commend, commit, consider, contemplate, crank, deliberate, deliver, dig, examine, give over, give up, hand over, keel over, mull over, overturn, pass on, plough, ponder, reflect on, render, reverse, revolve, rob, ruminate, start up, surrender, switch on, think about, think over, transfer, upend, upset, yield.

antonym stand firm.

turn over a new leaf amend, begin anew, change, change one's ways, improve, mend one's ways, pull one's socks up, reform.

antonym persist.

turn tail escape, flee, hightail it, make off, retreat, run away, run for it, run off, scarper, skedaddle, take off, take to one's heels, vamoose.

antonym stand firm.

turn up amplify, appear, arrive, attend, boost, come, crop up, dig up, disclose, discover, disgust, enhanse, expose, find, increase, intensify, invert, pop up, raise, reveal, show, show up, transpire, unearth.

antonyms stay away, turn down.

turncoat *n* apostate, backslider, blackleg, defector, deserter, fink, rat, recreant, renegade, renegate, scab, seceder, tergiversator, traitor.

turning *n* bend, crossroads, curve, flexure, fork, junction, turn, turn-off.

turning-point *n* change, climacteric, crisis, crossroads, crux, cusp, moment of truth, watershed.

turn-out *n* array, assemblage, assembly, attendance, attire, audience, company, congregation, costume, crowd, dress, equipage, equipment, gate, gear, get-up, number, outfit, output, outturn, product, production, productivity, rig-out, team, throng, turnover, volume, yield.

turnover *n* business, change, flow, income, movement, output, outturn, production, productivity, profits, replacement, volume, yield.

turpitude *n* badness, baseness, corruption, corruptness, criminality, degeneracy, depravity, evil, flagitiousness, foulness, immorality, iniquity, nefariousness, rascality, sinfulness, viciousness, vileness, villainy, wickedness.

antonym honour.

tussle *v* battle, brawl, compete, contend, fight, grapple, scramble, scrap, scuffle, struggle, vie, wrestle.

n battle, bout, brawl, competition, conflict, contention, contest, dust-up, fight, fracas, fray, mêlée, punch-up, race, scramble, scrap, scrimmage, scrum, scuffle, set-to, struggle.

tutelage *n* aegis, care, charge, custody, education, eye, guardianship, guidance, instruction, patronage, preparation, protection, schooling, teaching, tuition, vigilance, wardship.

tutor *n* coach, director of studies, educator, governor, guardian, guide, guru, instructor, lecturer, master, mentor, preceptor, répétiteur, supervisor, teacher.

v coach, control, direct, discipline, drill, edify, educate, guide, instruct, lecture, school, supervise, teach, train.

tutorial *n* class, lesson, seminar, teach-in.

adj coaching, didactic, educative, educatory, guiding, instructional, teaching.

twaddle *n* balderdash, balls, blather, blether, bunk, bunkum, chatter, claptrap, drivel, fadaise, gabble, garbage, gobbledegook, gossip, guff, havers, hogwash, hot air, inanity, nonsense, piffle, poppycock, rigmarole, rot, rubbish, stuff, tattle, tosh, trash, trumpery, waffle.

antonym sense.

tweak *v, n* jerk, nip, pull, punch, snatch, squeeze, tug, twist, twitch.

twee *adj* affected, bijou, cute, cutesy, dainty, kitschy, precious, pretty, quaint, sentimental, sweet.

tweezers *n* forceps, pincers, tongs, vulsella.

twiddle *v* adjust, fiddle, finger, jiggle, juggle, swivel, turn, twirl, twist, wiggle.

twig[1] *n* branch, offshoot, ramulus, shoot, spray, spring, stick, wattle, whip, withe, withy.

twig[2] *v* catch on, comprehend, cotton on, fathom, get, grasp, rumble, savvy, see, tumble to, understand.

twilight *n* crepuscle, crepuscule, decline, demi-jour, dimness, dusk, ebb, evening, eventide, gloaming, half-light, sundown, sunset.

adj crepuscular, darkening, declining, dim, dying, ebbing, evening, final, last, shadowy.

twin *n* clone, corollary, counterpart, doppelgänger, double, duplicate, fellow, gemel, likeness, lookalike, match, mate, ringer.

adj balancing, corresponding, didymous, double, dual, duplicate, geminate, geminous, identical, matched, matching, paired, parallel, symmetrical, twofold.

v combine, couple, join, link, match, pair, yoke.

twine *n* cord, string, twist, yarn.

v bend, braid, coil, curl, encircle, entwine, interlace, interweave, knit, loop, meander, plait, snake, spiral, splice, surround, tie, twist, weave, wind, wrap, wreathe, wriggle, zigzag.

twinge *n* bite, gripe, pain, pang, pinch, prick, qualm, spasm, stab, stitch, throb, throe, tweak, twist, twitch.

twinkle *v* blink, coruscate, flash, flicker, gleam, glint, glisten, glitter, scintillate, shimmer, shine, sparkle, vibrate, wink.

n amusement, blink, coruscation, flash, flicker, gleam, glimmer, glistening, glitter, glittering, light, quiver, scintillation, shimmer, shine, spark, sparkle, wink.

twinkling *adj* blinking, bright, coruscating, flashing, flickering, gleaming, glimmering, glistening, glittering, nitid, polished, scintillating, shimmering, shining, sparkling, winking.

n flash, instant, jiff, jiffy, mo, moment, no time, sec, second, shake, tick, trice, twinkle, two shakes.

twirl *v* birl, coil, gyrate, gyre, pirouette, pivot, revolve, rotate, spin, swivel, turn, twiddle, twist, wheel, whirl, wind.

n coil, convulution, gyration, gyre, helix, pirouette, revolution, rotation, spin, spiral, turn, twiddle, twist, wheel, whirl, whorl.

twirling *adj* gyral, gyratory, pirouetting, pivotal, pivoting, revolving, rotating, rotatory, spinning, swivelling, whirling.

twist *v* alter, change, coil, contort, corkscrew, crankle, crinkle, crisp, curl, distort, encircle, entangle, entwine, garble, intertwine, misquote, misrepresent, pervert, pivot, revolve, rick, screw, spin, sprain, squirm, strain, swivel, turn, tweak, twine, warp, weave, wigwag, wind, wrap, wreathe, wrench, wrest, wrick, wriggle, wring, writhe.

n aberration, arc, bend, bent, braid, break, change, characteristic, coil, confusion, contortion, convolution, crankle, curl, curlicue, curve, defect, deformation, development, distortion, eccentricity, entanglement, fault, flaw, foible, hank, idiosyncrasy, imperfection, intortion, jerk, kink, knot, meander, mess, mix-up, nuance, oddity, peculiarity, plug, proclivity, pull, quid, quirk, revelation, roll, screw, slant, snarl, spin, sprain, squiggle, surprise, swivel, tangle, tortion, trait, turn, twine, undulation, variation, warp, wind, wrench, wrest, zigzag.

twist someone's arm bulldoze, bully, coerce, dragoon, force, intimidate, lean on, persuade, pressurise.

twisted *adj* bent, biased, bitter, coiled, contorted, convoluted, curled, deformed, deviant, devious, distorted, garbled, intertwined, intorted, jaundiced, misshapen, perverse, perverted, quirky, thrawn, torqued, tortile, tortuous, unnatural, warped, wound, woven, wry.

antonyms straight, straightforward.

twister *n* blackguard, cheat, con man, crook, deceiver, fraud, phoney, rogue, rotter, scoundrel, swindler, trickster.

twit[1] *v* banter, berate, blame, censure, chiack, deride, jeer, mock, rib, scorn, taunt, tease, upbraid.

twit[2] *n* ass, blockhead, buffoon, chump, clot, clown, dope, fool, halfwit, idiot, muggins, nerd, nincompoop, ninny, nitwit, noodle, nurd, silly ass, simpleton, twerp.

twitch *v* blink, flutter, jerk, jump, pinch, pluck, pull, snatch, tug, tweak, vellicate, yank.

n blink, convulsion, flutter, jerk, jump, pluck, pull, spasmytic, subsultus, tremor, tweak, twinge, vellication.

twitter *v* chatter, cheep, chirp, chirrup, giggle, prattle, simper, sing, snigger, titter, trill, tweet, warble, whistle.

n agitation, anxiety, call, chatter, cheeping, chirping, chirruping, cry, dither, excitement, flurry, fluster, flutter, nervousness, song, tizz, tizzy, trill, tweeting, warble.

two-faced *adj* deceitful, deceiving, devious, dissembling, double-dealing, double-tongued, duplicitous, false, hypocritical, insincere, Janus-faced, lying, mendacious, perfidious, treacherous, untrustworthy.

antonyms candid, frank, honest.

tycoon *n* baron, big cheese, big noise, big shot, capitalist, captain of industry, Croesus, Dives, entrepreneur, fat cat, financier, gold-bug, industrialist, magnate, mogul, nabob, plutocrat, potentate, supremo.

type[1] *n* archetype, breed, category, class, classification, description, designation, emblem, embodiment, epitome, essence, example, exemplar, form, genre, group, ilk, insignia, kidney, kind, mark, model, order, original, paradigm, pattern, personification, prototype, quintessence, sort, species, specimen, stamp, standard, strain, subdivision, variety.

type[2] *n* case, characters, face, font, fount, lettering, print, printing.

typhoon *n* baguio, cordonazo, cyclone, hurricane, squall, storm, tempest, tornado, twister, whirlwind, willy-willy.

typical *adj* archetypal, average, characteristic, classic, conventional, distinctive, essential, illustrative, indicative, model, normal, orthodox, quintessential, representative, standard, stock, symptomatic, usual, vintage.

antonyms atypical, untypical.

typify *v* characterise, embody, encapsulate, epitomise, exemplify, illustrate, incarnate, personify, represent, symbolise.

tyrannical *adj* absolute, arbitrary, authoritarian, autocratic, coercive, despotic, dictatorial, domineering, high-handed, imperious, inexorable, iron-handed, magisterial, Neronian, oppressive, overbearing, overpowering, overweening, peremptory, ruthless, severe, tyrannous, unjust, unreasonable.

antonyms liberal, tolerant.

tyrannise *v* browbeat, bully, coerce, crush, dictate, domineer, enslave, intimidate, lord it, oppress, subjugate, terrorise.

tyranny *n* absolutism, authoritarianism, autocracy, coercion, despotism, dictatorship, harshness, high-handedness, imperiousness, injustice, liberticide, monocracy, oppression, peremptoriness, relentlessness, ruthlessness.

antonyms democracy, liberality.

tyrant *n* absolutist, authoritarian, autocrat, bully, despot, dictator, Hitler, liberticide, martinet, monarch, oppressor, satrap, slave-driver, sovereign, taskmaster.

tyro *see* **tiro.**

U

ubiquitous *adj* all-over, common, commonly-encountered, ever-present, everywhere, frequent, global, omnipresent, pervasive, universal.

antonym rare.

ubiquity *n* commonness, frequency, omnipresence, pervasiveness, popularity, prevalence, universality.

antonym rarity.

ugliness *n* danger, deformity, disgrace, enormity, evil, frightfulness, heinousness, hideosity, hideousness, homeliness, horridness, horror, menace, monstrosity, monstrousness, nastiness, offensiveness, plainness, repulsiveness, unattractiveness, unloveliness, unpleasantness, unsightliness, vileness.

antonyms beauty, charm, goodness, pleasantness.

ugly *adj* angry, bad-tempered, dangerous, dark, disagreeable, disgusting, distasteful, evil, evil-favoured, forbidding, frightful, hagged, haggish, hard-favoured, hard-featured, hideous, homely, horrid, ill-faced, ill-favoured, ill-looking, malevolent, menacing, misshapen, monstrous, nasty, objectionable, offensive, ominous, plain, repugnant, repulsive, revolting, shocking, sinister, spiteful, sullen, surly, terrible, threatening, truculent, unattractive, unlovely, unpleasant, unprepossessing, unsightly, vile.

antonyms beautiful, charming, good, pretty.

ulcer *n* abscess, canker, fester, impostume, noma, sore, ulceration.

ulterior *adj* concealed, covert, hidden, personal, private, secondary, secret, selfish, undisclosed, unexpressed.

antonyms declared, overt.

ultimate *adj* basic, conclusive, consummate, decisive, elemental, end, eventual, extreme, final, fundamental, furthest, greatest, highest, last, maximum, paramount, perfect, primary, radical, remotest, superlative, supreme, terminal, topmost, utmost.

n consummation, culmination, daddy of them all, dinger, epitome, extreme, granddaddy, greatest, height, peak, perfection, summit.

ultimately *adv* after all, at last, basically, eventually, finally, fundamentally, in origin, in the end, originally, primarily, sooner or later.

ultra *adj* avant-garde, excessive, extravagant, extreme, fanatical, immoderate, rabid, radical, revolutionary, way-out.

ultra- *adv* especially, exceptionally, excessively, extra, extraordinarily, extremely, remarkably, unusually.

ululate *v* cry, holler, hoot, howl, keen, lament, moan, mourn, scream, screech, sob, wail, weep.

umbrage *n* anger, chagrin, disgruntlement, displeasure, grudge, high dudgeon, huff, indignation, offence, pique, resentment, sulks.

umbrella *n* aegis, agency, brolly, bumbershoot, chatta, cover, en tout cas, gamp, mush, mushroom, parasol, patronage, protection, sunshade, umbel.

umpire *n* adjudicator, arbiter, arbitrator, daysman, judge, linesman, mediator, moderator, ref, referee.

v adjudicate, arbitrate, call, control, judge, moderate, ref, referee.

umpteen *adj* a good many, a thousand, considerable, countless, innumerable, millions, n, numerous, plenty, uncounted.

antonym few.

unabashed *adj* blatant, bold, brazen, composed, confident, unawed, unblushing, unconcerned, undaunted, undismayed, unembarrassed.

antonyms abashed, sheepish.

unable *adj* impotent, inadequate, incapable, incompetent, ineffectual, powerless, unequipped, unfit, unfitted, unqualified.

antonym able.

unabridged *adj* complete, entire, full, full-length, uncondensed, uncut, unexpurgated, unshortened, whole.

antonym abridged.

unacceptable *adj* before the pale, disagreeable, displeasing, distasteful, improper, inadmissible, insupportable, objectionable, offensive, ugly, undesirable, unpleasant, unsatisfactory, unwelcome.

antonym acceptable.

unaccommodating *adj* disobliging, inflexible, intransigent, obstinate, perverse, rigid, stubborn, unbending, uncomplaisant, uncompromising, unco-operative, unyielding.

antonyms flexible, obliging.

unaccompanied *adj* a cappella, alone, lone, solo, unattended, unescorted.

antonym accompanied.

unaccountable *adj* astonishing, baffling, extraordinary, impenetrable, incomprehensible, inexplicable, inscrutable, mysterious, odd, peculiar, puzzling, singular, strange, uncommon, unexplainable, unfathomable, unheard-of, unintelligible, unusual, unwonted.

antonyms accountable, explicable.

unaccustomed *adj* different, green, inexperienced, new, remarkable, special, strange, surprising, unacquainted, uncommon, unexpected, unfamiliar, unpractised, unprecedented, unused, unusual, unwonted.

antonyms accustomed, customary.

unacquainted *adj* ignorant, strange, unaccustomed, unfamiliar.

unadorned *adj* austere, outright, plain, restrained, severe, simple, stark, straightforward, undecorated, unembellished, unornamented, unvarnished.

antonyms decorated, embellished, ornate.

unaffected[1] *adj* aloof, impervious, naïf, natural, proof, spontaneous, unaltered, unchanged, unimpressed, unmoved, unresponsive, untouched.

antonyms affected, unnatural.

unaffected[2] *adj* artless, blasé, genuine, honest, indifferent, ingenuous, naive, plain, simple, sincere, straightforward, unassuming, unconcerned, unpretentious, unsophisticated, unspoilt, unstudied.

antonyms affected, impressed, moved.

unafraid *adj* confident, daring, dauntless, fearless, imperturbable, intrepid, unshakeable.

antonym afraid.

unalterable *adj* final, fixed, immutable, inflexible, invariable, permanent, rigid, steadfast, unchangeable, unchanging, unyielding.

antonyms alterable, flexible.

unanimity *n* accord, agreement, chorus, concert, concord, concurrence, consensus, consent, correspondence, harmony, like-mindedness, unison, unity.

antonyms disagreement, disunity.

unanimous *adj* agreed, common, concerted, concordant, harmonious, in accord, in agreement, joint, united.

antonyms disunited, split.

unanimously *adv* at one man, by common consent, conjointly, in concert, nem con, unopposed, without exception, without opposition.

unanswerable *adj* absolute, conclusive, final, incontestable, incontrovertible, indisputable, irrefragable, irrefutable, unarguable, undeniable.

antonyms answerable, refutable.

unappetising *adj* disagreeable, distasteful, insipid, off-putting, tasteless, unappealing, unattractive, unexciting, uninteresting, uninviting, unpalatable, unpleasant, unsavoury.

antonym appetising.

unapproachable *adj* aloof, distant, forbidding, formidable, frigid, godforsaken, inaccessible, remote, reserved, stand-offish, unbending, unfriendly, un-get-at-able, unreachable, unsociable, withdrawn.

antonym approachable.

unapt *adj* inapplicable, inapposite, inappropriate, inapt, malapropos, unfit, unfitted, unseasonable, unsuitable, unsuited, untimely.

antonym apt.

unarmed *adj* assailable, defenceless, exposed, helpless, inerm, open, pregnable, unarmoured, unprotected, vulnerable, weak, weaponless.

antonym armed.

unashamed *adj* impenitent, open, shameless, unabashed, unconcealed, undisguised, unrepentant.

unasked *adj* gratuitous, spontaneous, unbidden, undemanded, undesired, uninvited, unprompted, unrequested, unsolicited, unsought, unwanted, voluntary.

antonyms invited, solicited.

unassailable *adj* absolute, conclusive, impregnable, incontestable, incontrovertible, indisputable, invincible, inviolable, invulnerable, irrefutable, positive, proven, sacrosanct, secure, sound, undeniable, well-armed, well-fortified.

antonym assailable.

unassertive *adj* backward, bashful, diffident, meek, mousy, quiet, retiring, self-effacing, shy, timid, timorous, unassuming.

antonym assertive.

unassuming *adj* diffident, humble, meek, modest, natural, quiet, restrained, retiring, self-effacing, simple, unassertive, unobtrusive, unostentatious, unpresuming, unpretentious.

antonyms assuming, presumptuous, pretentious.

unattached *adj* autonomous, available, fancy-free, footloose, free, independent, non-aligned, single, unaffilated, uncommitted, unengaged, unmarried, unspoken for.

antonyms attached, committed, engaged.

unattended *adj* abandoned, alone, disregarded, ignored, unaccompanied, unescorted, unguarded, unsupervised, unwatched.

antonyms attended, escorted.

unattractive *adj* disagreeable, disgusting, distasteful, homely, ill-favoured, objectionable, offensive, off-putting, plain, repellent, ugly, unappealing, unappetising, uncomely, undesirable, unexciting, uninviting, unlovely, unpalatable, unpleasant, unprepossessing, unsavoury, unsightly, unwelcome.

antonym attractive.

unauthorised *adj* illegal, illicit, irregular, unlawful, unofficial, unsanctioned, unwarranted.

antonym authorised.

unavailing *adj* abortive, barren, bootless, fruitless, futile, idle, ineffective, ineffectual, inefficacious, pointless, unproductive, unprofitable, unsuccessful, useless, vain.

antonyms productive, successful.

unavoidable *adj* certain, compulsory, fated, ineluctable, inescapable, inevitable, inexorable, mandatory, necessary, obligatory.

antonym avoidable.

unaware *adj* blind, deaf, forgetful, heedless, ignorant, incognisant, oblivious, unconscious, unenlightened, uninformed, unknowing, unmindful, unsuspecting, unsuspicious.

antonym aware.

unawares *adv* aback, abruptly, accidentally, by surprise, imperceptibly, inadvertently, insidiously, mistakenly, off guard, on the hop, suddenly, unconsciously, unexpectedly, unintentionally, unknowingly, unprepared, unthinkingly, unwittingly.

unbalanced *adj* asymmetrical, biased, crazy, demented, deranged, disturbed, dysharmonic, eccentric, erratic, inequitable, insane, irrational, irregular, lopsided, lunatic, mad, off-balance, off-centre, one-sided, partial, partisan, prejudiced, shaky, touched, unequal, uneven, unfair, unhinged, unjust, unsound, unstable, unsteady, wobbly.

antonym balanced.

unbearable *adj* insufferable, insupportable, intolerable, outrageous, unacceptable, unendurable, unspeakable.

antonyms acceptable, bearable.

unbeatable *adj* indomitable, invincible, matchless, nonpareil, supreme, unconquerable, unstoppable, unsurpassable.

antonyms inferior, weak.

unbeaten *adj* supreme, triumphant, unbowed, unconquered, undefeated, unsubdued, unsurpassed, unvanquished, victorious, winning.

antonyms defeated, vanquished.

unbecoming *adj* discreditable, dishonourable, ill-suited, improper, inappropriate, incongruous, indecorous, indelicate, offensive, tasteless, unattractive, unbefitting, unfit, unflattering, unmaidenly, unmeet, unseemly, unsightly, unsuitable, unsuited.

antonyms becoming, seemly.

unbelief *n* agnosticism, atheism, disbelief, distrust, doubt, incredulity, scepticism.

antonyms belief, faith.

unbelievable *adj* astonishing, far-fetched, implausible, impossible, improbable, inconceivable, incredible, outlandish, preposterous, questionable, staggering, unconvincing, unimaginable, unlikely, unthinkable.

antonyms believable, credible.

unbeliever *n* agnostic, atheist, disbeliever, doubter, doubting Thomas, infidel, nullifidian, sceptic.

antonyms believer, supporter.

unbelieving *adj* disbelieving, distrustful, doubtful, doubting, dubious, incredulous, nullifidian, sceptical, suspicious, unconvinced, unpersuaded.

antonyms credulous, trustful.

unbend *v* loosen up, relax, straighten, thaw, unbutton, uncoil, uncurl, unfreeze.

antonyms stiffen, withdraw.

unbending *adj* aloof, distant, firm, forbidding, formal, formidable, hard-line, inflexible, intransigent, reserved, resolute, Rhadamanthine, rigid, severe, stiff, strict, stubborn, tough, uncompromising, unyielding.

antonyms approachable, friendly, relaxed.

unbiased *adj* disinterested, dispassionate, equitable, even-handed, fair, fair-minded, impartial, independent, just, neutral, objective, open-minded, uncoloured, uninfluenced, unprejudiced.

antonym biased.

unbidden *adj* free, spontaneous, unasked, unforced, uninvited, unprompted, unsolicited, unwanted, unwelcome, voluntary, willing.

antonyms invited, solicited.

unbind *v* free, liberate, loose, loosen, release, unchain, undo, unfasten, unfetter, unloose, unloosen, unshackle, untie, unyoke.

antonyms bind, restrain.

unblemished *adj* clear, flawless, immaculate, irreproachable, perfect, pure, spotless, unflawed, unimpeachable, unspotted, unstained, unsullied, untarnished.

antonyms blemished, flawed, imperfect.

unblinking *adj* assured, calm, composed, cool, emotionless, fearless, impassive, imperturbable, steady, unafraid, unemotional, unfaltering, unflinching, unshrinking, unwavering.

antonyms cowed, faithful, fearful.

unblushing *adj* amoral, blatant, bold, brazen, conscience-proof, immodest, shameless, unabashed, unashamed, unembarrassed.

antonyms abashed, ashamed.

unborn *adj* awaited, coming, embryonic, expected, foetal, future, hereafter, in utero, later, subsequent, succeeding.

unbosom *v* admit, bare, confess, confide, disburden, disclose, divulge, lay bare, let out, pour out, reveal, tell, unburden, uncover.

antonyms conceal, suppress.

unbounded *adj* absolute, boundless, endless, immeasurable, infinite, lavish, limitless, prodigal, unbridled, unchecked, unconstrained, uncontrolled, unlimited, unrestrained, vast.

antonym limited.

unbreakable *adj* armoured, durable, indestructible, infrangible, lasting, permanent, proof, resistant, rugged, shatter-proof, solid, strong, tough, toughened.

antonyms breakable, fragile.

unbridled *adj* excessive, immoderate, intemperate, licentious, profligate, rampant, riotous, unchecked, unconstrained, uncontrolled, uncurbed, ungovernable, ungoverned, unrestrained, unruly, violent, wanton.

unbroken *adj* ceaseless, complete, constant, continuous, endless, entire, incessant, intact, integral, perpetual, progressive, serried, solid, successive, total, unbowed, unceasing, undivided, unimpaired, uninterrupted, unremitting, unsubdued, untamed, whole.

antonyms cowed, fitful, intermittent.

unburden *v* confess, confide, disburden, discharge, disclose, discumber, disencumber, empty, lay bare, lighten, offload, pour out, relieve, reveal, tell all, unbosom, unload.
antonyms conceal, hide, suppress.

uncalled-for *adj* gratuitous, inappropriate, needless, undeserved, unheeded, unjust, unjustified, unmerited, unnecessary, unprovoked, unwanted, unwarranted, unwelcome.
antonym timely.

uncanny *adj* astonishing, astounding, bizarre, creepy, eerie, eldritch, exceptional, extraordinary, fantastic, incredible, inspired, miraculous, mysterious, preternatural, prodigious, queer, remarkable, scary, singular, spooky, strange, supernatural, unaccountable, unco, unearthly, unerring, unheard-of, unnatural, unusual, weird.

uncaring *adj* callous, inconsiderate, indifferent, negligent, unconcerned, unfeeling, uninterested, unmoved, unresponsive, unsympathetic.
antonyms concerned, solicitous.

unceasing *adj* ceaseless, constant, continual, continuing, continuous, endless, incessant, never-ending, non-stop, perpetual, persistent, relentless, unbroken, unending, unfailing, uninterrupted, unrelenting, unremitting.
antonyms intermittent, spasmodic.

uncertain *adj* ambiguous, ambivalent, chancy, changeable, conjectural, dicky, dithery, doubtful, dubious, erratic, fitful, hazardous, hazy, hesitant, iffy, in the lap of the gods, incalculable, inconstant, indefinite, indeterminate, indistinct, insecure, irregular, irresolute, on the knees of the gods, precarious, problematic, questionable, risky, shaky, slippy, speculative, unclear, unconfirmed, undecided, undetermined, unfixed, unforeseeable, unpredictable, unreliable, unresolved, unsettled, unsure, vacillating, vague, variable, wavering.
antonym certain.

uncertainty *n* ambiguity, bewilderment, confusion, diffidence, dilemma, doubt, dubiety, hesitancy, hesitation, incalculability, inconclusiveness, indecision, insecurity, irresolution, misgiving, peradventure, perplexity, puzzlement, qualm, quandary, risk, scepticism, unpredictability, vagueness.
antonym certainty.

unchallengeable *adj* absolute, conclusive, final, impregnable, inappellable, incontestable, incontrovertible, indisputable, irrefragable, irrefutable.
antonyms contestable, inconclusive.

unchangeable *adj* changeless, eternal, final, immutable, intransmutable, irreversible, permanent, unchanging.
antonym changeable.

unchanging *adj* abiding, changeless, constant, continuing, enduring, eternal, fixed, immutable, imperishable, lasting, permanent, perpetual, phaseless, steadfast, steady, unchanged, unfading, unvarying.
antonyms changeable, changing.

uncharitable *adj* callous, captious, cruel, hard-hearted, hypercritical, inhumane, insensitive, mean, merciless, pitiless, stingy, unchristian, unfeeling, unforgiving, unfriendly, ungenerous, unkind, unsympathetic.
antonym charitable.

uncharted *adj* foreign, mysterious, new, novel, strange, undiscovered, unexplored, unfamiliar, unknown, unplumbed, virgin.
antonyms familiar, well-known.

unchaste *adj* defiled, depraved, dishonest, dissolute, fallen, immodest, immoral, impure, lewd, licentious, loose, promiscuous, wanton.
antonym chaste.

uncivil *adj* abrupt, bad-mannered, bearish, boorish, brusque, churlish, curt, discourteous, disrespectful, gruff, ill-bred, ill-mannered, impolite, rude, surly, uncouth, ungracious, unmannerly.
antonym civil.

uncivilised *adj* antisocial, barbarian, barbaric, barbarous, boorish, brutish, churlish, coarse, gross, heathenish, ill-bred, illiterate, philistine, primitive, savage, tramontane, uncouth, uncultivated, uncultured, uneducated, unpolished, unsophisticated, untamed, vulgar, wild.
antonym civilised.

unclassifiable *adj* doubtful, elusive, etypic(al), ill-defined, indefinable, indefinite, indescribable, indeterminate, indistinct, uncertain, unconformable, undefinable, unidentifiable, vague.
antonyms conformable, definable, identifiable.

unclean *adj* contaminated, corrupt, defiled, dirty, evil, filthy, foul, impure, insalubrious, nasty, polluted, soiled, spotted, stained, sullied, tainted, unhygienic, unwholesome.
antonym clean.

unclear *adj* ambiguous, as clear as mud, dim, doubtful, dubious, equivocal, hazy, indefinite, indiscernible, indistinguishable, multivocal, obscure, uncertain, vague.
antonym clear.

unclothed *adj* bare, disrobed, en cuerpo, in one's birthday suit, in the altogether, in the buff, naked, nude, stark naked, starkers, stripped, unclad, undressed.
antonyms clothed, dressed.

uncomfortable *adj* awkward, bleak, confused, conscience-stricken, cramped, disagreeable, discomfited, discomfortable, discomposed, disquieted, distressed, disturbed, embarrassed, hard, ill-fitting, incommodious, irritating, painful, poky, self-conscious, sheepish, troubled, troublesome, uneasy.
antonyms comfortable, easy.

uncommitted *adj* available, fancy-free, floating, free, neutral, non-aligned, non-partisan, unattached, undecided, uninvolved.
antonym committed.

uncommon *adj* abnormal, atypical, bizarre, curious, distinctive, exceptional, extraordinary, incomparable, infrequent, inimitable, notable, noteworthy, novel, odd, outstanding, peculiar, queer, rare, recherché, remarkable, scarce, singular, special, strange, superior, unfamiliar, unparalleled, unprecedented, unusual, unwonted.

antonym common.

uncommonly *adv* abnormally, exceptionally, extremely, infrequently, occasionally, outstandingly, particularly, peculiarly, rarely, remarkably, seldom, singularly, strangely, unusually, very.

antonyms commonly, frequently.

uncommunicative *adj* brief, close, curt, guarded, laconic, reserved, reticent, retiring, secretive, short, shy, silent, taciturn, tight-lipped, unforthcoming, unresponsive, unsociable, withdrawn.

antonym communicative.

uncompromising *adj* decided, die-hard, firm, hard-core, hard-line, hardshell, inexorable, inflexible, intransigent, obdurate, obstinate, rigid, steadfast, strict, stubborn, tough, unaccommodating, unbending, unyielding.

antonyms flexible, open-minded.

unconcealable *adj* clear, insistent, insuppressible, irrepressible, manifest, obvious, plain, uncontrollable, undistinguishable.

unconcealed *adj* admitted, apparent, blatant, conspicuous, evident, frank, ill-concealed, manifest, naked, noticeable, obvious, open, overt, patent, self-confessed, unashamed, undistinguished, visible.

antonyms hidden, secret.

unconcern *n* aloofness, apathy, callousness, detachment, indifference, insouciance, jauntiness, negligence, nonchalance, pococurantism, remoteness, uninterestedness.

antonym concern.

unconcerned *adj* aloof, apathetic, blithe, callous, carefree, careless, complacent, composed, cool, detached, dispassionate, distant, easy, incurious, indifferent, insouciant, joco, nonchalant, oblivious, pococurante, relaxed, serene, uncaring, uninterested, uninvolved, unmoved, unperturbed, unruffled, unsympathetic, untroubled, unworried.

antonym concerned.

unconditional *adj* absolute, categorical, complete, downright, entire, full, implicit, out-and-out, outright, plenary, positive, thoroughgoing, total, unequivocal, unlimited, unqualified, unreserved, unrestricted, utter, whole-hearted.

antonym conditional.

unconformity *n* disconformity, discontinuity, irregularity, unconformability.

antonym conformability.

uncongenial *adj* antagonistic, antipathetic, disagreeable, discordant, displeasing, distasteful, incompatible, unappealing, unattractive, uninviting, unpleasant, unsavoury, unsuited, unsympathetic.

antonym congenial.

unconnected *adj* detached, disconnected, disjointed, divided, illogical, incoherent, independent, irrational, irrelevant, off-line, separate, unattached, unrelated.

antonyms connected, relevant.

unconquerable *adj* enduring, indomitable, ingrained, insuperable, insurmountable, inveterate, invincible, irrepressible, irresistible, overpowering, unbeatable, undefeatable, unyielding.

antonyms weak, yielding.

unconscionable *adj* amoral, criminal, excessive, exorbitant, extravagant, extreme, immoderate, inordinate, outrageous, preposterous, unethical, unjustifiable, unpardonable, unprincipled, unreasonable, unscrupulous, unwarrantable.

unconscious *adj* accidental, automatic, blind to, comatose, concussed, deaf to, heedless, ignorant, inadvertent, innate, insensible, instinctive, involuntary, knocked out, latent, oblivious, out, out cold, out for the count, reflex, repressed, senseless, stunned, subconscious, subliminal, suppressed, unaware, unintended, unintentional, unknowing, unmindful, unsuspecting, unwitting.

antonym conscious.

unconstraint *n* abandon, freedom, laissez-aller, laissez-faire, liberality, openness, relaxation, unreserve, unrestraint.

uncontrollable *adj* frantic, furious, intractable, irrepressible, irresistible, irrestrainable, mad, masterless, recalcitrant, refractory, strong, ungovernable, unmanageable, unruly, violent, wild.

antonyms controllable, manageable.

uncontrolled *adj* boisterous, furious, masterless, rampant, riotous, unbridled, unchecked, uncurbed, undisciplined, ungoverned, unhindered, unrestrained, unruly, untrammelled, violent, wild.

antonyms contained, controlled.

unconventional *adj* abnormal, alternative, atypical, bizarre, bohemian, different, eccentric, freakish, idiosyncratic, individual, individualistic, informal, irregular, nonconforming, odd, offbeat, original, spacy, unconformable, unorthodox, unusual, way-out, wayward.

antonym conventional.

unconvincing *adj* doubtful, dubious, feeble, fishy, flimsy, implausible, improbable, inconclusive, lame, questionable, specious, suspect, tall, thin, unlikely, unpersuasive, weak.

antonyms convincing, plausible.

unco-ordinated *adj* awkward, bumbling, clodhopping, clumsy, desultory, diffuse, disjointed, disorganised, graceless, inept, lumbering, maladroit, unconcerted, ungainly, ungraceful.

antonyms concerted, graceful, systematic.

uncouth *adj* awkward, barbarian, barbaric, boorish, clownish, clumsy, coarse, crude, gauche, gawky, graceless, gross, ill-mannered, loutish, lubberly, oafish, rough, rude, rustic, uncivilised, uncultivated, ungainly, unrefined, unseemly, vulgar.

antonyms polished, polite, refined, urbane.

uncover *v* bare, detect, disclose, discover, dismask, disrobe, divulge, exhume, expose, leak, lift the lid off, open, reveal, show, strip, unearth, unmask, unveil, unwrap.

antonyms conceal, cover, suppress.

uncritical *adj* accepting, credulous, indiscriminate, naïve, non-judgemental, superficial, trusting, undiscerning, undiscriminating, unexacting, unfussy, unscholarly, unselective, unthinking.

antonyms critical, discriminating, sceptical.

unctuous *adj* fawning, glib, greasy, gushing, ingratiating, insincere, obsequious, oily, pietistic, plausible, religiose, sanctimonious, slick, smarmy, smooth, suave, sycophantic.

uncultivated *adj* fallow, incult, natural, rough, uncultured, wild.

antonym cultivated.

uncultured *adj* awkward, boorish, coarse, crude, hick, raw, rustic, uncivilised, uncouth, uncultivated, unrefined, unsophisticated.

antonym cultured.

undaunted *adj* bold, brave, courageous, dauntless, fearless, gallant, indomitable, intrepid, resolute, steadfast, unbowed, undashed, undeterred, undiscouraged, undismayed, unfaltering, unflinching, unperturbed, unshrinking.

antonyms cowed, timorous.

undecided *adj* ambivalent, debatable, dithering, doubtful, dubious, hesitant, in two minds, indefinite, irresolute, moot, open, pending, swithering, tentative, torn, uncertain, uncommitted, unconcluded, undetermined, unfixed, unsettled, unsure, vague, vexed, wavering.

antonyms certain, decided, definite.

undecorated *adj* austere, classical, functional, inornate, plain, severe, simple, stark, unadorned, unembellished, unornamented.

antonyms decorated, ornate.

undefended *adj* defenceless, exposed, expugnable, inerm, naked, open, pregnable, unarmed, unfortified, unguarded, unprotected, vulnerable.

antonyms armed, defended, fortified.

undefiled *adj* chaste, clean, clear, flawless, immaculate, intact, intemerate, inviolate, pure, sinless, spotless, unblemished, unsoiled, unspotted, unstained, unsullied, virginal.

undefined *adj* formless, hazy, ill-defined, imprecise, indefinite, indeterminate, indistinct, inexact, nebulous, shadowy, tenuous, unclear, unexplained, unspecified, vague, woolly.

antonyms definite, precise.

undemonstrative *adj* aloof, cold, contained, cool, distant, formal, impassive, phlegmatic, reserved, restrained, reticent, stiff, stolid, unbending, uncommunicative, unemotional, unresponsive, withdrawn.

antonym demonstrative.

undeniable *adj* certain, clear, evident, incontestable, incontrovertible, indisputable, indubitable, irrefragable, irrefutable, manifest, obvious, patent, proven, sound, sure, unassailable, undoubted, unmistakable, unquestionable.

undependable *adj* capricious, changeable, erratic, fair-weather, fickle, inconsistent, inconstant, irresponsible, mercurial, treacherous, uncertain, unpredictable, unreliable, unstable, untrustworthy, variable.

antonyms dependable, reliable.

under *prep* belonging to, below, beneath, governed by, included in, inferior to, junior to, lead by, less than, lower than, secondary to, subject to, subordinate to, subservient to, underneath.

adv below, beneath, down, downward, less, lower.

under an obligation beholden, bound, duty-bound, grateful, honour-bound, in debt to, in honour bound, indebted, obligated, obliged, thankful.

under the weather ailing, below par, groggy, hung over, ill, indisposed, mops and brooms, nauseous, off-colour, out of sorts, peelie-wally, poorly, queer, seedy, sick, squeamish, the worse for wear.

under way afoot, begun, going, in motion, in operation, in progress, launched, moving, on the go, on the move, started.

underclothes *n* frillies, lingerie, smalls, underclothing, undergarments, underlinen, underwear, undies, unmentionables.

undercover *adj* clandestine, concealed, confidential, covert, furtive, hidden, hush-hush, intelligence, private, secret, spy, stealthy, surreptitious, underground.

antonyms open, unconcealed.

undercurrent *n* atmosphere, aura, cross-current, drift, eddy, feeling, flavour, hint, movement, murmur, overtone, rip, riptide, sense, suggestion, tendency, tenor, tide, tinge, trend, underflow, undertone, undertow, vibes, vibrations.

undercut *v* excavate, gouge out, hollow out, mine, sacrifice, scoop out, underbid, undercharge, undermine, underprice, undersell.

underestimate *v* belittle, dismiss, fail to appreciate, minimise, miscalculate, misprise, sell short, underrate, undervalue.

antonyms exaggerate, overestimate.

undergo *v* bear, brook, endure, experience, run the gauntlet, stand, submit to, suffer, sustain, weather, withstand.

underground *adj* alternative, avant-garde, buried, clandestine, concealed, covered, covert, experimental, hidden, hypogeal, hypogean, hypogene, hypogeous, radical, revolutionary, secret, subterranean, subversive, surreptitious, undercover.

n métro, subway, tube.

undergrowth *n* bracken, brambles, briars, brush, brushwood, firth, frith, ground cover, scrub, underbrush.

underhand *adj* clandestine, crafty, crooked, deceitful, deceptive, devious, dishonest, dishonourable, fraudulent, furtive, immoral, improper, shady, shifty, sly, sneaky, stealthy, surreptitious, treacherous, underhanded, unethical, unscrupulous.

antonym above board.

underline *v* accentuate, emphasise, highlight, italicise, labour, mark, point up, press, reiterate, stress, underscore, urge.

antonyms play down, soft-pedal.

underling *n* flunkey, hireling, inferior, lackey, menial, minion, nobody, nonentity, retainer, servant, slave, subordinate, understrapper, weakling.

antonyms boss, leader, master.

underlying *adj* basal, basic, concealed, elementary, essential, fundamental, hidden, intrinsic, latent, lurking, primary, prime, root, subjacent, substratal, substructural, veiled.

undermine *v* debilitate, disable, erode, excavate, impair, mar, mine, sabotage, sap, subvert, threaten, tunnel, undercut, vitiate, weaken, wear away.

antonyms fortify, strengthen.

underprivileged *adj* deprived, destitute, disadvantaged, impecunious, impoverished, needy, poor, poverty-stricken.

antonyms affluent, fortunate, privileged.

underrate *v* belittle, depreciate, discount, dismiss, disparage, misprise, underestimate, undervalue.

antonyms exaggerate, overrate.

undersell *v* cut, depreciate, disparage, mark down, play down, reduce, slash, undercharge, undercut, understate.

undersized *adj* achondroplastic, atrophied, dwarfed, dwarfish, miniature, minute, puny, pygmy, runtish, runty, small, stunted, tiny, underdeveloped, underweight.

antonyms big, oversized, overweight.

understand *v* accept, appreciate, apprehend, assume, believe, commiserate, comprehend, conceive, conclude, cotton on, discern, fathom, follow, gather, get, get the message, get the picture, grasp, hear, know, learn, penetrate, perceive, presume, realise, recognise, savvy, see, see daylight, suppose, sympathise, think, tolerate, tumble, twig.

antonym misunderstand.

understanding *n* accord, agreement, appreciation, awareness, belief, comprehension, conclusion, discernment, estimation, grasp, idea, impression, insight, intellect, intellection, intelligence, interpretation, judgement, knowledge, notion, opinion, pact, penetration, perception, reading, sense, view, viewpoint, wisdom.

adj accepting, compassionate, considerate, discerning, forbearing, forgiving, kind, kindly, loving, patient, perceptive, responsive, sensitive, sympathetic, tender, tolerant.

antonyms impatient, insensitive, intolerant, unsympathetic.

understate *v* belittle, dismiss, make light of, make little of, minimise, play down, soft-pedal, underplay, undersell.

understatement *n* dismissal, litotes, meiosis, minimisation, restraint, underplaying.

understood *adj* accepted, assumed, axiomatic, implicit, implied, inferred, presumed, tacit, unspoken, unstated, unwritten.

understudy *n* alternate, deputy, double, fill-in, replacement, reserve, stand-in, substitute.

undertake *v* accept, agree, assume, attempt, bargain, begin, commence, contract, covenant, embark on, endeavour, engage, guarantee, pledge, promise, shoulder, stipulate, tackle, try.

undertaker *n* funeral director, funeral furnisher, mortician.

undertaking *n* adventure, affair, assurance, attempt, business, commitment, effort, emprise, endeavour, enterprise, game, operation, pledge, project, promise, task, venture, vow, word.

undertone *n* atmosphere, current, feeling, flavour, hint, murmur, suggestion, tinge, touch, trace, undercurrent, undervoice, whisper.

undervalue *v* depreciate, discount, dismiss, disparage, disprize, minimise, misjudge, misprice, misprise, underestimate, underrate.

antonyms exaggerate, overrate.

underwater *adj* subaquatic, subaqueous, submarine, submerged, sunken, undersea.

underwear *n* frillies, lingerie, smalls, underclothes, underclothing, undergarments, underlinen, undies, unmentionables.

underweight *adj* emaciated, half-starved, puny, skinny, thin, undernourished, undersized.

antonym overweight.

underworld *n* Avernus, criminal fraternity, gangland, gangsterland, Hades, hell, nether world, the Inferno.

underwrite *v* approve, authorise, back, consent, countenance, countersign, endorse, finance, fund, guarantee, initial, insure, okay, sanction, sign, sponsor, subscribe, subsidise, validate.

undesirable *adj* disagreeable, disliked, disreputable, distasteful, dreaded, objectionable, obnoxious, offensive, repugnant, unacceptable, unattractive, unpleasant, unpopular, unsavoury, unsuitable, unwanted, unwelcome, unwished-for.

antonym desirable.

undeveloped *adj* dwarfed, embryonic, immature, inchoate, latent, potential, primordial, stunted, unformed.

antonyms developed, mature.

undignified *adj* foolish, improper, inappropriate, indecorous, inelegant, infra dig, petty, unbecoming, ungentlemanly, unladylike, unrefined, unseemly, unsuitable.

antonym dignified.

undisciplined *adj* disobedient, disorganised, obstreperous, uncontrolled, unpredictable, unreliable, unrestrained, unruly, unschooled, unsteady, unsystematic, untrained, wayward, wild, wilful.

antonym disciplined.

undisguised *adj* apparent, blatant, confessed, evident, explicit, frank, genuine, ill-concealed, manifest, naked, obvious, open, out-and-out, outright, overt, patent, stark, thoroughgoing, transparent, unadorned, unashamed, unconcealed, unmistakable, utter, whole-hearted.

antonyms concealed, hidden, secret.

undisguisedly *adj* blatantly, frankly, obviously, openly, outright, overtly, patently, transparently, unreservedly.

antonym secretly.

undisputed *adj* accepted, acknowledged, certain, conclusive, incontestable, incontrovertible, indisputable, irrefragable, irrefutable, recognised, sure, unchallenged, uncontested, undeniable, undoubted, unequivocal, unmistakable, unquestioned.

antonyms dubious, uncertain.

undistinguished *adj* banal, commonplace, everyday, indifferent, inferior, mediocre, ordinary, pedestrian, prosaic, run-of-the-mill, so-so, unexceptional, unexciting, unimpressive, unremarkable.

antonyms distinguished, exceptional.

undisturbed *adj* calm, collected, composed, equable, even, motionless, placid, quiet, serene, tranquil, unaffected, unconcerned, uninterrupted, unperturbed, unruffled, untouched, untroubled.

antonyms disturbed, interrupted.

undivided *adj* combined, complete, concentrated, concerted, entire, exclusive, full, individuate, solid, thorough, tight-knit, unanimous, unbroken, united, whole, whole-hearted.

undo *v* annul, cancel, defeat, destroy, disengage, dislink, invalidate, loose, loosen, mar, neutralise, nullify, offset, open, overturn, quash, reverse, ruin, separate, shatter, spoil, subvert, unbutton, undermine, unfasten, unlink, unlock, unloose, unloosen, untie, unwind, unwrap, upset, vitiate, wreck.

antonym fasten.

undoing *n* besetting sin, blight, collapse, curse, defeat, destruction, disgrace, downfall, hamartia, humiliation, misfortune, overthrow, overturn, reversal, ruin, ruination, shame, tragic fault, trouble, weakness.

undomesticated *adj* ferae naturae, feral, natural, savage, uncivilised, unhouseproud, unhousewifely, unmaternal, unmotherly, unpractical, untamed, wild.

antonyms domesticated, home-loving, tame.

undone[1] *adj* betrayed, destroyed, lost, ruined.

undone[2] *adj* forgotten, incomplete, left, neglected, omitted, outstanding, unaccomplished, uncompleted, unfinished, unfulfilled, unperformed.

antonyms accomplished, complete, done.

undone[3] *adj* loose, open, unbraced, unbuttoned, unfastened, unlaced, unlocked, untied.

antonyms fastened, secured.

undoubted *adj* acknowledged, certain, definite, evident, incontrovertible, indisputable, indubitable, obvious, patent, sure, unchallenged, undisputed, unquestionable, unquestioned.

undoubtedly *adv* assuredly, certainly, definitely, doubtless, indubitably, of course, surely, undeniably, unmistakably, unquestionably.

undreamed-of *adj* astonishing, inconceivable, incredible, miraculous, undreamt, unexpected, unforeseen, unheard-of, unhoped-for, unimagined, unsuspected.

undress *v* disrobe, divest, peel off, remove, shed, strip, take off.

n déshabillé, disarray, dishabille, nakedness, nudity.

undressed *adj* disrobed, en cuerpo, naked, nude, stark naked, starkers, stripped, unclad, unclothed.

undue *adj* disproportionate, excessive, extravagant, extreme, immoderate, improper, inordinate, intemperate, needless, overmuch, supererogatory, uncalled-for, undeserved, unnecessary, unreasonable, unseemly, unwarranted.

antonym reasonable.

undulate *v* billow, heave, ripple, rise and fall, roll, surge, swell, wave.

undulating *adj* billowing, flexuose, flexuous, rippling, rolling, sinuous, undate, undulant, wavy.

antonym flat.

unduly *adv* disproportionately, excessively, extravagantly, immoderately, inordinately, over, overly, overmuch, too, unjustifiably, unnecessarily, unreasonably.

antonym reasonably.

undutiful *adj* careless, defaulting, delinquent, disloyal, neglectful, negligent, remiss, slack, unfilial.

antonym dutiful.

undutifulness *n* default, defection, delinquency, dereliction, desertion, disloyalty, incivism, neglect, negligence, remissness.

antonyms dutifulness, loyalty.

undying *adj* abiding, constant, continuing, deathless, eternal, everlasting, immortal, imperishable, indestructible, inextinguishable, infinite, lasting, perennial, permanent, perpetual, sempiternal, undiminished, unending, unfading.

antonyms impermanent, inconstant.

unearth *v* detect, dig up, discover, disinter, dredge up, excavate, exhume, expose, ferret out, find, reveal, uncover.

unearthly *adj* abnormal, eerie, eldritch, ethereal, extraordinary, ghostly, haunted, heavenly, nightmarish, other-worldly, phantom, preternatural, spectral, spine-chilling, strange, sublime, supernatural, uncanny, ungodly, unreasonable, weird.

uneasiness *n* agitation, alarm, anxiety, apprehension, apprehensiveness, dis-ease, disquiet, doubt, dysphoria, inquietude, misgiving, nervousness, perturbation, qualms, suspicion, unease, worry.

antonyms calm, composure.

uneasy *adj* agitated, anxious, apprehensive, awkward, constrained, discomposed, disquieting, disturbed, disturbing, edgy, impatient, insecure, jittery, nervous, niggling, on edge, perturbed, precarious, restive, restless, shaky, strained, tense, troubled, troubling, uncomfortable, unquiet, unsettled, unstable, upset, upsetting, worried, worrying.

antonyms calm, composed.

uneconomic *adj* loss-making, non-profit-making, uncommercial, unprofitable.

antonyms economic, profitable.

uneducated *adj* benighted, ignorant, illiterate, low-brow, philistine, uncultivated, uncultured, uninstructed, unlessoned, unlettered, unread, unschooled, untaught.

antonym educated.

unembellished *adj* austere, bald, bare, functional, modest, plain, severe, simple, stark, unadorned, undecorated, unelaborated, unornamented, unvarnished.

antonyms embellished, ornate.

unemotional *adj* apathetic, cold, cool, dispassionate, impassive, indifferent, laid-back, low-key, objective, passionless, phlegmatic, reserved, undemonstrative, unexcitable, unfeeling, unimpassioned, unresponsive.

antonyms emotional, excitable.

unemphatic *adj* down-beat, played-down, soft-pedalled, underplayed, understated, unobtrusive, unostentatious.

unemployed *adj* idle, jobless, on the dole, out of work, redundant, resting, unoccupied, workless.

antonym employed.

unending *adj* ceaseless, constant, continual, endless, eternal, everlasting, incessant, interminable, never-ending, perpetual, unceasing, undying, unrelenting, unremitting.

antonyms intermittent, transient.

unendurable *adj* insufferable, insupportable, intolerable, overwhelming, shattering, unbearable.

antonyms bearable, endurable.

unenthusiastic *adj* apathetic, blasé, bored, cool, half-hearted, indifferent, laodicean, lukewarm, neutral, nonchalant, unimpressed, uninterested, unmoved, unresponsive.

antonym enthusiastic.

unenviable *adj* disagreeable, painful, thankless, uncomfortable, uncongenial, undesirable, unpalatable, unpleasant, unsavoury.

antonyms desirable, enviable.

unequal *adj* asymmetrical, different, differing, disparate, disproportionate, dissimilar, ill-equipped, ill-matched, inadequate, incapable, incompetent, insufficient, irregular, unbalanced, uneven, unlike, unmatched, variable, varying.

antonym equal.

unequalled *adj* exceptional, incomparable, inimitable, matchless, nonpareil, paramount, peerless, pre-eminent, supreme, surpassing, transcendent, unmatched, unparalleled, unrivalled, unsurpassed.

unequivocal *adj* absolute, certain, clear, clear-cut, crystal-clear, decisive, definite, direct, distinct, evident, explicit, express, incontrovertible, indubitable, manifest, plain, positive, straight, unambiguous, uncontestable, unmistakable.

antonyms ambiguous, vague.

unerring *adj* accurate, certain, dead, exact, faultless, impeccable, infallible, perfect, sure, uncanny, unfailing.

antonym fallible.

unerringly *adv* accurately, bang, dead, infallibly, unfailingly.

unethical *adj* dirty, discreditable, dishonest, dishonourable, disreputable, illegal, illicit, immoral, improper, shady, underhand, unfair, unprincipled, unprofessional, unscrupulous, wrong.

antonym ethical.

uneven *adj* accidented, asymmetrical, broken, bumpy, changeable, desultory, disparate, erratic, fitful, fluctuating, ill-matched, inconsistent, intermittent, irregular, jerky, lopsided, notchy, odd, one-sided, patchy, rough, spasmodic, unbalanced, unequal, unfair, unsteady, variable.

antonym even.

uneventful *adj* boring, commonplace, dull, humdrum, monotonous, ordinary, quiet, routine, tame, tedious, unexceptional, unexciting, uninteresting, unmemorable, unremarkable, unvaried.

antonyms eventful, memorable.

unexampled *adj* incomparable, never before seen, novel, unequalled, unheard-of, unique, unmatched, unparalleled, unprecedented.

unexceptional *adj* average, commonplace, conventional, indifferent, insignificant, mediocre, normal, ordinary, pedestrian, run-of-the-mill, typical, undistinguished, unimpressive, unmemorable, unremarkable, usual.

antonyms exceptional, impressive.

unexcitable *adj* calm, composed, contained, cool, dispassionate, easy-going, impassive, imperturbable, laid-back, passionless, phlegmatic, relaxed, self-possessed, serene, unimpassioned.

antonym excitable.

unexpected *adj* abrupt, accidental, amazing, astonishing, chance, fortuitous, startling, sudden, surprising, unaccustomed, unanticipated, unforeseen, unlooked-for, unpredictable, unusual, unwonted.

antonyms expected, normal, predictable.

unexpectedly *adv* abruptly, by chance, ex improviso, fortuitously, out of the blue, suddenly, surprisingly, unpredictably, without warning.

unexpressive *adj* blank, dead-pan, emotionless, expressionless, immobile, impassive, inexpressive, inscrutable, vacant.

antonyms expressive, mobile.

unfading *adj* abiding, durable, enduring, fadeless, fast, immarcescible, imperishable, lasting, undying, unfailing.

antonyms changeable, transient.

unfailing *adj* certain, constant, dependable, faithful, infallible, loyal, reliable, staunch, steadfast, steady, sure, true, undying, unfading.

antonyms fickle, impermanent, transient.

unfair *adj* arbitrary, biased, bigoted, crooked, discriminatory, dishonest, dishonourable, inequitable, one-sided, partial, partisan, prejudiced, uncalled-for, undeserved, unethical, unjust, unmerited, unprincipled, unscrupulous, unsporting, unwarranted, wrongful.

antonym fair.

unfairness *n* bias, bigotry, discrimination, inequity, injustice, maldistribution, one-sidedness, partiality, partisanship, prejudice.

antonyms equity, fairness.

unfaithful *adj* adulterous, deceitful, dishonest, disloyal, faithless, false, false-hearted, fickle, godless, inconstant, perfidious, recreant, traitorous, treacherous, treasonable, two-timing, unbelieving, unchaste, unreliable, untrue, untrustworthy.

antonyms faithful, loyal.

unfaltering *adj* constant, firm, fixed, indefatigable, pertinacious, resolute, steadfast, steady, tireless, unfailing, unflagging, unflinching, unswerving, untiring, unwavering.

antonyms faltering, uncertain, wavering.

unfamiliar *adj* alien, curious, different, foreign, new, novel, out-of-the-way, strange, unaccustomed, unacquainted, uncharted, uncommon, unconversant, unexplored, unknown, unpractised, unskilled, unusual, unversed.

antonyms customary, familiar.

unfashionable *adj* antiquated, dated, démodé, demoded, dismoded, fogram, obsolete, old hat, old-fashioned, out, out of date, outmoded, passé, square, unpopular.

antonym fashionable.

unfasten *v* detach, disconnect, loosen, open, separate, uncouple, undo, unlace, unlock, unloose, unloosen, untie.

antonym fasten.

unfathomable *adj* abstruse, baffling, bottomless, deep, esoteric, fathomless, hidden, immeasurable, impenetrable, incomprehensible, indecipherable, inexplicable, mysterious, profound, unknowable, unplumbed, unsounded.

antonyms comprehensible, explicable, penetrable.

unfavourable *adj* adverse, bad, contrary, critical, disadvantageous, discouraging, hostile, ill-suited, inauspicious, infelicitous, inimical, inopportune, low, negative, ominous, poor, threatening, uncomplimentary, unfortunate, unfriendly, unlucky, unpromising, unpropitious, unseasonable, unsuited, untimely, untoward.

antonym favourable.

unfeeling *adj* apathetic, callous, cold, cruel, hard, hardened, hard-hearted, harsh, heartless, inhuman, insensitive, pitiless, soulless, stony, uncaring, unsympathetic.

antonym concerned.

unfeigned *adj* frank, genuine, heartfelt, natural, pure, real, sincere, spontaneous, unaffected, unforced, whole-hearted.

antonyms feigned, insincere, pretended.

unfettered *adj* free, unbridled, unchecked, unconfined, unconstrained, unhampered, unhindered, uninhibited, unrestrained, unshackled, untrammelled.

antonyms constrained, fettered.

unfinished *adj* bare, crude, deficient, half-done, imperfect, incomplete, incondite, lacking, natural, raw, rough, rude, sketchy, unaccomplished, uncompleted, undone, unfulfilled, unpolished, unrefined, wanting.

antonyms finished, polished, refined.

unfit *adj* debilitated, decrepit, feeble, flabby, flaccid, hypotonic, ill-adapted, ill-equipped, inadequate, inappropriate, incapable, incompetent, ineffective, ineligible, unequal, unhealthy, unprepared, unqualified, unsuitable, unsuited, untrained, useless.

antonyms competent, fit, suitable.

unflagging *adj* constant, fixed, indefatigable, never-failing, persevering, persistent, single-minded, staunch, steady, tireless, unceasing, undeviating, unfailing, unfaltering, unremitting, unswerving, untiring.

antonyms faltering, inconstant.

unflappable *adj* calm, collected, composed, cool, equable, impassive, imperturbable, level-headed, phlegmatic, self-possessed, unexcitable, unruffled, unworried.

antonyms excitable, nervous, temperamental.

unflattering *adj* blunt, candid, critical, honest, outspoken, unbecoming, uncomplimentary, unfavourable, unprepossessing.

antonyms complimentary, flattering.

unflinching *adj* bold, constant, determined, firm, fixed, resolute, stalwart, staunch, steadfast, steady, sure, unblinking, unfaltering, unshaken, unshrinking, unswerving, unwavering.

antonyms cowed, scared.

unfold *v* clarify, describe, develop, disclose, disentangle, divulge, elaborate, evolve, expand, explain, flatten, grow, illustrate, mature, open, present, reveal, show, spread, straighten, stretch out, uncoil, uncover, undo, unfurl, unravel, unroll, unwrap.

antonyms fold, suppress, withhold, wrap.

unforeseen *adj* abrupt, accidental, fortuitous, startling, sudden, surprise, surprising, unanticipated, unavoidable, unexpected, unheralded, unlooked-for, unpredicted.

antonyms expected, predictable.

unforgettable *adj* exceptional, extraordinary, historic, impressive, memorable, momentous, notable, noteworthy.

antonyms unexceptional, unmemorable.

unforgivable *adj* deplorable, disgraceful, indefensible, inexcusable, reprehensible, shameful, unconscionable, unjustifiable, unpardonable, unwarrantable.

antonyms forgivable, venial.

unforgiven *adj* unabsolved, unredeemed, unregenerate, unrepentant, unshrived, unshriven.

antonyms absolved, forgiven.

unfortunate *adj* adverse, calamitous, cursed, deplorable, disadventurous, disastrous, doomed, hapless, hopeless, ill-advised, ill-fated, ill-starred, ill-timed, inappropriate, infelicitous, inopportune, lamentable, luckless, poor, regrettable, ruinous, star-crossed, tactless, unbecoming, unfavourable, unhappy, unlucky, unprosperous, unsuccessful, unsuitable, untimely, untoward, wretched.

antonym fortunate.

unfortunately *adv* miserabile dictu, regrettably, sad to relate, sad to say, sadly, unhappily, unluckily, worse luck.

antonym fortunately.

unfounded *adj* baseless, fabricated, false, gratuitous, groundless, idle, spurious, trumped-up, unjustified, unmerited, unproven, unsubstantiated, unsupported.

antonym justified.

unfrequented *adj* deserted, desolate, god-forsaken, isolated, lone, lonely, remote, secluded, sequestered, solitary, uninhabited, unvisited.

antonyms busy, crowded, populous.

unfriendly *adj* alien, aloof, antagonistic, chilly, cold, critical, disagreeable, distant, hostile, ill-disposed, inauspicious, inhospitable, inimical, quarrelsome, sour, stand-offish, surly, unapproachable, unbending, uncongenial, unfavourable, unneighbourly, unsociable, unwelcoming.

antonyms agreeable, amiable, friendly.

unfrock *v* degrade, demote, depose, disfrock, disgown, dismiss, suspend.

antonyms reinstate, restore.

unfruitful *adj* arid, barren, exhausted, fruitless, impoverished, infecund, infertile, infructuous, sterile, unproductive, unprofitable, unprolific, unrewarding.

antonym fruitful.

ungainly *adj* awkward, clumsy, gangling, gauche, gawky, inelegant, loutish, lubberly, lumbering, slouching, unco-ordinated, uncouth, unwieldy.

antonyms elegant, graceful.

ungirded *adj* discinct, unbelted, ungirt, unprepared, unready.

ungodly *adj* blasphemous, corrupt, depraved, dreadful, godless, horrendous, immoral, impious, intolerable, irreligious, outrageous, profane, sinful, unearthly, unreasonable, unseasonable, unseemly, unsocial, vile, wicked.

ungovernable *adj* disorderly, masterless, rebellious, refractory, uncontrollable, ungoverned, unmanageable, unrestrainable, unruly, wild.

ungracious *adj* bad-mannered, boorish, churlish, discourteous, disrespectful, graceless, ill-bred, impolite, offhand, rude, uncivil, unmannerly.

antonyms gracious, polite.

ungrateful *adj* heedless, ill-mannered, ingrate, selfish, thankless, unappreciative, ungracious, unmindful.

antonym grateful.

unguarded[1] *adj* careless, foolhardy, foolish, heedless, ill-considered, impolitic, imprudent, incautious, indiscreet, rash, thoughtless, uncircumspect, undiplomatic, unheeding, unthinking, unwary.

antonyms cautious, guarded.

unguarded[2] *adj* defenceless, exposed, pregnable, undefended, unpatrolled, unprotected, vulnerable.

antonyms guarded, protected.

unhandy *adj* awkward, bungling, cack-handed, clumsy, cumbersome, fumbling, heavy-handed, ill-contrived, incompetent, inconvenient, inept, inexpert, maladroit, unco-ordinated, unskilful, unwieldy.

antonyms adroit, deft, handy.

unhappy *adj* awkward, blue, clumsy, contentless, crestfallen, cursed, dejected, depressed, despondent, disconsolate, dismal, dispirited, down, downcast, gauche, gloomy, hapless, ill-advised, ill-chosen, ill-fated, ill-omened, ill-timed, inappropriate, inapt, inept, infelicitous, injudicious, long-faced, luckless, lugubrious, malapropos, melancholy, miserable, mournful, sad, sorrowful, sorry, tactless, uneasy, unfortunate, unlucky, unsuitable, wretched.

antonyms fortunate, happy.

unharmed *adj* intact, safe, scot-free, sound, undamaged, unhurt, unimpaired, uninjured, unscarred, unscathed, untouched, whole.

antonyms damaged, harmed, impaired.

unhealthy *adj* ailing, bad, baneful, corrupt, corrupting, degrading, deleterious, delicate, demoralising, detrimental, epinosic, feeble, frail, harmful, infirm, insalubrious, insalutary, insanitary, invalid, morbid, noisome, noxious, polluted, poorly, sick, sickly, undesirable, unhygienic, unsound, unwell, unwholesome, weak.

antonyms healthy, hygienic, robust, salubrious.

unheard-of *adj* disgraceful, extreme, inconceivable, new, novel, obscure, offensive, out of the question, outrageous, preposterous, shocking, singular, unacceptable, unbelievable, undiscovered, undreamed-of, unexampled, unfamiliar, unimaginable, unique, unknown, unprecedented, unregarded, unremarked, unsung, unthinkable, unthought-of, unusual.

antonyms famous, normal, usual.

unheeded *adj* disobeyed, disregarded, forgotten, ignored, neglected, overlooked, unnoticed, unobserved, unremarked.

antonyms heeded, noted, observed.

unheralded *adj* surprise, unadvertised, unannounced, unexpected, unforeseen, unnoticed, unproclaimed, unpublicised, unrecognised, unsung.

antonyms advertised, publicised, trumpeted.

unhesitating *adj* automatic, immediate, implicit, instant, instantaneous, prompt, ready, resolute, spontaneous, steadfast, unfaltering, unquestioning, unreserved, unswerving, unwavering, whole-hearted.

antonyms hesitant, tentative, uncertain.

unhinge *v* confuse, craze, derange, disorder, distract, drive mad, madden, unbalance, unnerve, unsettle, upset.

unholy *adj* appalling, base, corrupt, depraved, dishonest, evil, heinous, immoral, iniquitous, irreligious, outrageous, profane, shocking, sinful, taboo, unconscionable, unearthly, ungodly, unnatural, unreasonable, vile, wicked.

antonyms godly, holy, pious, reasonable.

unhoped-for *adj* incredible, surprising, unanticipated, unbelievable, undreamed-of, unexpected, unforeseen, unimaginable, unlooked-for.

unhurried *adj* calm, deliberate, easy, easy-going, laid-back, leisurely, relaxed, sedate, slow.

antonyms hasty, hurried.

unicorn *n* monoceros.

unidentified *adj* anonymous, incognito, mysterious, nameless, unclaimed, unclassified, unfamiliar, unknown, unmarked, unnamed, unrecognised, unspecified.

antonyms identified, known, named.

unification *n* alliance, amalgamation, coalescence, coalition, combination, confederation, enosis, federation, fusion, incorporation, merger, union, uniting.

antonyms separation, split.

uniform *n* costume, dress, garb, gear, habit, insignia, livery, outfit, regalia, regimentals, rig, robes, suit.

adj alike, consistent, constant, equable, equal, even, homochromous, homogeneous, homomorphic, homomorphous, identical, like, monochrome, montonous, of a piece, regular, same, selfsame, similar, smooth, unbroken, unchanging, undeviating, unvarying.

antonyms changing, colourful, varied.

uniformity *n* constancy, drabness, dullness, evenness, flatness, homogeneity, homomorphism, invariability, monotony, regularity, sameness, similarity, similitude, tedium.

antonyms difference, dissimilarity, variation.

unify *v* amalgamate, bind, combine, confederate, consolidate, federate, fuse, join, marry, merge, unite, weld.

antonyms separate, split.

unifying *adj* combinatory, consolidative, esemplastic, henotic, reconciling, unific, uniting.

antonym divisive.

unimaginable *adj* fantastic, impossible, inconceivable, incredible, indescribable, ineffable, mind-boggling, unbelievable, undreamed-of, unheard-of, unhoped-for, unknowable, unthinkable.

unimaginative *adj* banal, barren, blinkered, commonplace, derivative, dry, dull, hackneyed, lifeless, matter-of-fact, myopic, ordinary, pedestrian, predictable, prosaic, routine, short-sighted, tame, uncreative, uninspired, unoriginal.

antonyms imaginative, original.

unimpeachable *adj* blameless, faultless, immaculate, impeccable, irreproachable, perfect, spotless, unassailable, unblemished, unchallengeable, unexceptionable, unquestionable.

antonyms blameworthy, faulty.

unimpeded *adj* all-round, clear, free, open, unblocked, unchecked, unconstrained, unhampered, unhindered, uninhibited, unrestrained, untrammelled.

antonyms hampered, impeded.

unimportant *adj* immaterial, inconsequential, insignificant, irrelevant, low-ranking, Mickey Mouse, minor, minuscule, negligible, nugatory, off the map, paltry, paravail, petty, slight, small-time, trifling, trivial, worthless.

antonym important.

unimpressive *adj* average, commonplace, dull, indifferent, mediocre, undistinguished, unexceptional, uninteresting, unremarkable, unspectacular.

antonyms impressive, memorable, notable.

uninhibited *adj* abandoned, candid, emancipated, frank, free, informal, instinctive, liberated, natural, open, relaxed, spontaneous, unbridled, unchecked, unconstrained, uncontrolled, uncurbed, unrepressed, unreserved, unrestrained, unrestricted, unselfconscious.

antonyms constrained, inhibited, repressed.

uninspired *adj* boring, commonplace, dull, humdrum, indifferent, ordinary, pedestrian, prosaic, stale, stock, trite, undistinguished, unexciting, unimaginative, uninspiring, uninteresting, unoriginal.

antonyms inspired, original.

unintelligent *adj* brainless, dense, dull, dumb, empty-headed, fatuous, foolish, gormless, half-witted, obtuse, silly, slow, stupid, thick, unreasoning, unthinking.

antonym intelligent.

unintelligible *adj* double Dutch, garbled, illegible, inapprehensible, inarticulate, incoherent, incomprehensible, indecipherable, indistinct, jumbled, meaningless, muddled, unfathomable.

antonym intelligible.

unintentional *adj* accidental, fortuitous, inadvertent, involuntary, unconscious, undeliberate, unintended, unpremeditated, unthinking, unwitting.

antonyms deliberate, intentional.

uninterested *adj* apathetic, blasé, bored, distant, impassive, incurious, indifferent, listless, pococurante, unconcerned, unenthusiastic, uninvolved, unresponsive.

antonyms concerned, enthusiastic, interested, responsive.

uninteresting *adj* boring, commonplace, corny, drab, dreary, dry, dull, flat, humdrum, monotonous, tame, tedious, tiresome, uneventful, unexciting, unimpressive, uninspiring, wearisome.

antonyms exciting, interesting.

uninterrupted *adj* constant, continual, continuous, non-stop, peaceful, prolonged, quiet, steady, sustained, unbroken, undisturbed, unending.

antonyms broken, intermittent.

uninvited *adj* unasked, unbidden, unsolicited, unsought, unwanted, unwelcome.

antonyms invited, solicited.

uninviting *adj* disagreeable, distasteful, offensive, off-putting, repellent, repulsive, unappealing, unappetising, unattractive, undesirable, unpleasant, unsavoury, unwelcoming.

antonyms inviting, welcome.

uninvolved *adj* disengaged, fancy-free, footloose, free, heart-free, heart-whole, independent, unattached, uncommitted, unengaged, unhampered, unhindered, untrammelled.

antonyms attached, committed.

union *n* accord, agreement, alliance, amalgam, amalgamation, Anschluss, association, blend, Bund, coalition, coition, coitus, combination, compact, concord, concrescence, concurrence, confederacy, confederation, conjugation, conjunction, copulation, couplement, coupling, enosis, federation, fusion, harmony, intercourse, junction, juncture, league, marriage, matrimony, mixture, symphysis, synthesis, unanimity, unison, uniting, unity, wedlock.

antonyms alienation, disunity, estrangement, separation.

unique *adj* incomparable, inimitable, lone, matchless, nonpareil, one-off, only, peerless, single, singular, sole, solitary, sui generis, unequalled, unexampled, unmatched, unparalleled, unprecedented, unrivalled.

antonym commonplace.

unison *n* accord, accordance, aggreement, concert, concord, co-operation, harmony, homophony, monophony, unanimity, unity.

antonyms disharmony, polyphony.

unit *n* ace, assembly, component, constituent, detachment, element, entity, Gestalt, group, item, measure, measurement, member, module, monad, monas, one, part, piece, portion, quantity, section, segment, system, whole.

unite *v* accrete, ally, amalgamate, associate, band, blend, coadunate, coalesce, combine, confederate, conglutinate, conjoin, conjugate, consolidate, cooperate, couple, fay, fuse, incorporate, join, join forces, league, link, marry, merge, pool, splice, unify, wed.

antonyms separate, sever.

united *adj* affiliated, agreed, allied, collective, combined, concerted, concordant, conjoined, conjoint, conjunctive, corporate, in accord, in agreement, leagued, like-minded, one, pooled, unanimous, unified.

antonyms differing, disunited, separated, unco-ordinated.

unity *n* accord, agreement, community, concord, concurrence, consensus, entity, harmony, integrity, oneness, peace, singleness, solidarity, unanimity, unification, union, wholeness.

antonyms disagreement, disunity.

universal *adj* across-the-board, all-embracing, all-inclusive, all-round, catholic, common, ecumenic, ecumenical, entire, general, global, omnipresent, total, ubiquitous, unlimited, whole, widespread, worldwide.

universality *n* all-inclusiveness, commonness, completeness, comprehensiveness, entirety, generalisation, generality, predominance, prevalence, totality, ubiquity.

universally *adv* always, everywhere, invariably, ubiquitously, uniformly.

universe *n* cosmos, creation, firmament, heavens, macrocosm, nature, world.

university *n* academia, academy, Athenaeum, college, institute, multiversity, varsity.

unjust *adj* biased, gratuitous, groundless, inequitable, one-sided, partial, partisan, prejudiced, undeserved, unethical, unfair, unjustified, unmerited, wrong, wrongful.

antonym just.

unjustifiable *adj* excessive, immoderate, indefensible, inexcusable, outrageous, steep, unacceptable, unforgivable, unjust, unpardonable, unreasonable, unwarrantable, wrong.

antonym justifiable.

unkempt *adj* bedraggled, blowsy, disarranged, dishevelled, disordered, frowsy, mal soigné, messy, mop-headed, ratty, rumpled, scruffy, shabby, shaggy, slatternly, sloppy, slovenly, sluttish, tousled, uncombed, ungroomed, untidy.

antonyms neat, tidy.

unkind *adj* callous, cruel, disobliging, hard-hearted, harsh, inconsiderate, inhuman, inhumane, insensitive, malevolent, malicious, mean, nasty, spiteful, thoughtless, unamiable, uncaring, uncharitable, unchristian, unfeeling, unfriendly, unsympathetic.

antonyms considerate, kind.

unkindness *n* callousness, cruelty, disobligingness, hard-heartedness, harshness, ill-turn, inhumanity, insensitivity, maliciousness, meanness, spite, uncharitableness, unfriendliness.

antonyms friendship, kindness.

unknowable *adj* in the lap of the gods, incalculable, incognisable, infinite, on the knees of the gods, unascertainable, unfathomable, unforeseeable, unimaginable, unpredictable, untold.

unknown *adj* alien, anonymous, concealed, dark, foreign, hidden, humble, incognito, mysterious, nameless, new, obscure, secret, strange, uncharted, undisclosed, undiscovered, undistinguished, unexplored, unfamiliar, unheard-of, unidentified, unnamed, unrecognised, unsung, untold.

antonyms familiar, known.

unladylike *adj* boyish, coarse, hoydenish, ill-bred, impolite, indelicate, inelegant, rough, rude, tomboyish, uncivil, unfeminine, ungracious, unmannerly, unrefined, unseemly.

antonyms ladylike, seemly.

unlawful *adj* actionable, banned, criminal, forbidden, illegal, illegitimate, illicit, outlawed, prohibited, unauthorised, unconstitutional, unlicensed, unsanctioned.

antonym lawful.

unleash *v* free, loose, release, unloose, untether, untie.

antonym restrain.

unlettered *adj* ignorant, illiterate, uneducated, unlearned, unlessoned, unschooled, untaught, untutored.

antonym educated.

unlike *adj* contrasted, different, difform, disparate, dissimilar, distinct, divergent, diverse, ill-matched, incompatible, opposed, opposite, unequal, unrelated.

antonyms related, similar.

unlikely *adj* doubtful, dubious, faint, implausible, improbable, incredible, questionable, remote, slight, suspect, suspicious, tall, unbelievable, unconvincing, unexpected, unimaginable.

antonyms likely, plausible.

unlikeness *n* contrast, difference, disparity, dissemblance, dissimilarity, divergence, diversity, incompatibility.

antonym similarity.

unlimited *adj* absolute, all-encompassing, boundless, complete, countless, endless, extensive, full, great, illimitable, immeasurable, immense, incalculable, infinite, limitless, total, unbounded, uncircumscribed, unconditional, unconstrained, unfettered, unhampered, unqualified, unrestricted, vast.

antonyms circumscribed, limited.

unload *v* disburden, discharge, discumber, disencumber, disload, dump, empty, offload, relieve, unburden, unpack.

unlock *v* bare, disengage, free, open, release, unbar, unbolt, undo, unfasten, unlatch.

antonyms fasten, lock.

unlooked-for *adj* chance, fortuitous, fortunate, lucky, surprise, surprising, unanticipated, undreamed-of, unexpected, unforeseen, unhoped-for, unpredicted, unthought-of.

antonyms expected, predictable.

unloved *adj* detested, disliked, forsaken, hated, loveless, neglected, rejected, spurned, uncared-for, uncherished, unpopular, unwanted.

antonyms beloved, loved.

unlucky *adj* cursed, disastrous, doomed, hapless, ill-fated, ill-omened, ill-starred, inauspicious, infaust, jinxed, left-handed, luckless, mischanceful, miserable, ominous, unfavourable, unfortunate, unhappy, unsuccessful, untimely, wretched.

antonym lucky.

unman *v* daunt, demoralise, discourage, disman, dispirit, effeminate, effeminise, emasculate, emolliate, enervate, enfeeble, evirate, intimidate, unnerve, weaken.

antonyms brace, nerve, steel.

unmanageable *adj* awkward, bulky, cumbersome, difficult, disorderly, fractious, inconvenient, intractable, obstreperous, recalcitrant, refractory, stroppy, uncontrollable, unco-operative, unhandy, unruly, unwieldy, wild.

antonyms docile, manageable.

unmanly *adj* chicken-hearted, cowardly, craven, dishonourable, effeminate, epicene, feeble, ignoble, namby-pamby, sissy, soft, weak, weak-kneed, weedy, wet, womanish, yellow.

antonym manly.

unmannerly *adj* badly-behaved, bad-mannered, boorish, discourteous, disrespectful, graceless, ill-bred, ill-mannered, impolite, low-bred, rude, uncivil, uncouth, ungracious.

antonym polite.

unmarried *adj* available, bachelor, celibate, fancy-free, footloose, maiden, single, unattached, unwed, unwedded, virgin.

antonym married.

unmask *v* bare, detect, disclose, discover, dismask, expose, reveal, show, uncloak, uncover, unveil.

unmatched *adj* beyond compare, consummate, incomparable, matchless, nonpareil, paramount, peerless, supreme, unequalled, unexampled, unparalleled, unrivalled, unsurpassed.

unmentionable *adj* abominable, disgraceful, disreputable, immodest, indecent, innominable, nefandous, scandalous, shameful, shocking, taboo, unnameable, unspeakable, unutterable.

unmerciful *adj* brutal, callous, cruel, hard, heartless, implacable, merciless, pitiless, relentless, remorseless, ruthless, sadistic, uncaring, unfeeling, unrelenting, unsparing.

antonym merciful.

unmethodical *adj* confused, desultory, disorderly, haphazard, illogical, immethodical, irregular, muddled, random, unco-ordinated, unorganised, unsystematic.

antonym methodical.

unmindful *adj* blind, careless, deaf, forgetful, heedless, inattentive, indifferent, lax, neglectful, negligent, oblivious, regardless, remiss, slack, unaware, unconscious, unheeding.

antonyms aware, heedful, mindful.

unmistakable *adj* certain, clear, conspicuous, crystal-clear, decided, distinct, evident, explicit, glaring, indisputable, manifest, obvious, palpable, patent, plain, positive, pronounced, sure, unambiguous, undeniable, undisputed, unequivocal, unquestionable.

antonyms ambiguous, unclear.

unmitigated *adj* absolute, arrant, complete, consummate, downright, grim, harsh, intense, oppressive, out-and-out, outright, perfect, persistent, pure, rank, relentless, sheer, thorough, thoroughgoing, unabated, unalleviated, unbroken, undiminished, unmodified, unqualified, unredeemed, unrelenting, unrelieved, unremitting, utter.

unmoved *adj* adamant, cold, determined, dispassionate, dry-eyed, fast, firm, impassive, indifferent, inflexible, obdurate, phlegmatic, resolute, resolved, steadfast, steady, unaffected, unchanged, undeviating, unfeeling, unimpressed, unresponsive, unshaken, untouched, unwavering.

antonyms affected, moved, shaken.

unnatural *adj* aberrant, abnormal, absonant, affected, anomalous, artificial, assumed, bizarre, brutal, callous, cataphysical, cold-blooded, contrived, cruel, disnatured, evil, extraordinary, factitious, false, feigned, fiendish, forced, freakish, heartless, inhuman, insincere, irregular, laboured, mannered, monstrous, odd, outlandish, perverse, perverted, phoney, queer, ruthless, sadistic, savage, self-conscious, stagy, stiff, stilted, strained, strange, studied, supernatural, theatrical, unaccountable, uncanny, unfeeling, unspontaneous, unusual, wicked.

antonyms acceptable, natural, normal.

unnecessary *adj* dispensable, expendable, inessential, needless, non-essential, otiose, pleonastic, redundant, supererogatory, superfluous, supernumerary, tautological, uncalled-for, unjustified, unneeded, useless.

antonyms indispensable, necessary.

unnerve *adj* confound, daunt, demoralise, disconcert, discourage, dishearten, dismay, dispirit, fluster, frighten, intimidate, rattle, scare, shake, unhinge, unman, upset, worry.

antonyms brace, nerve, steel.

unnoticed *adj* disregarded, ignored, neglected, overlooked, passed over, unconsidered, undiscovered, unheeded, unobserved, unperceived, unrecognised, unrecorded, unremarked, unseen.

antonyms noted, remarked.

unobtrusive *adj* humble, inconspicuous, low-key, meek, modest, quiet, restrained, retiring, self-effacing, subdued, unassertive, unassuming, unemphatic, unnoticeable, unostentatious, unpretentious.

antonyms obtrusive, ostentatious.

unobtrusively *adv* inconspicuously, modestly, on the q.t., on the quiet, quietly, surreptitiously, unostentatiously.

antonyms obtrusively, ostentatiously.

unoccupied *adj* désoevré, disengaged, empty, free, idle, inactive, jobless, unemployed, uninhabited, untenanted, vacant, workless.

antonyms busy, occupied.

unofficial *adj* backyard, confidential, illegal, informal, personal, private, ulterior, unauthorised, unconfirmed, undeclared, wildcat.

antonym official.

unoriginal *adj* cliché-ridden, copied, cribbed, derivative, derived, second-hand, stale, trite, unimaginative, uninspired.

antonyms imaginative, original.

unorthodox *adj* abnormal, alternative, fringe, heterodox, irregular, nonconformist, unconventional, unusual, unwonted.

antonyms conventional, orthodox.

unpaid *adj* due, free, honorary, outstanding, overdue, owing, payable, unremunerative, unsalaried, unsettled, voluntary.

antonym paid.

unpalatable *adj* bitter, disagreeable, displeasing, distasteful, inedible, insipid, offensive, repugnant, unappetising, unattractive, uneatable, unenviable, unpleasant, unrelished, unsavoury.

antonyms palatable, pleasant.

unparalleled *adj* consummate, exceptional, incomparable, matchless, peerless, rare, singular, superlative, supreme, surpassing, unequalled, unexampled, unique, unmatched, unprecedented, unrivalled, unsurpassed.

unpardonable *adj* deplorable, disgraceful, indefensible, inexcusable, irremissible, outrageous, scandalous, shameful, shocking, unconscionable, unforgivable.

antonyms forgivable, understandable.

unperturbed *adj* calm, collected, composed, cool, impassive, placid, poised, self-possessed, serene, tranquil, undisturbed, unexcited, unflinching, unflustered, unruffled, untroubled, unworried.

antonyms anxious, perturbed.

unpleasant *adj* abhorrent, bad, disagreeable, displeasing, distasteful, god-awful, ill-natured, irksome, nasty, objectionable, obnoxious, poxy, repulsive, rocky, sticky, traumatic, troublesome, unattractive, unpalatable.

antonym pleasant.

unpleasantness *n* annoyance, bother, embarrassment, esclandre, furore, fuss, ill-feeling, nastiness, scandal, trouble, upset.

unpolished *adj* coarse, crude, home-bred, rough, rough and ready, rude, sketchy, uncivilised, uncouth, uncultivated, uncultured, unfashioned, unfinished, unrefined, unsophisticated, unworked, vulgar.

antonyms finished, polished, refined.

unpopular *adj* avoided, detested, disliked, hated, neglected, rejected, shunned, undesirable, unfashionable, unloved, unsought-after, unwanted, unwelcome.

antonyms fashionable, popular.

unprecedented *adj* abnormal, exceptional, extraordinary, freakish, new, novel, original, remarkable, revolutionary, singular, unexampled, unheard-of, unknown, unparalleled, unrivalled, unusual.

unpredictable *adj* chance, changeable, doubtful, erratic, fickle, fluky, iffy, in the lap of the gods, inconstant, on the knees of the gods, random, scatty, unforeseeable, unreliable, unstable, variable.

antonym predictable.

unprejudiced *adj* balanced, detached, dispassionate, enlightened, even-handed, fair,

fair-minded, impartial, just, non-partisan, objective, open-minded, unbiased, uncoloured.
antonyms narrow-minded, prejudiced.

unpremeditated *adj* extempore, fortuitous, impromptu, impulsive, offhand, off-the-cuff, spontaneous, spur-of-the-moment, unintentional, unplanned, unprepared, unrehearsed.
antonym premeditated.

unprepared *adj* ad-lib, extemporaneous, half-baked, ill-considered, improvised, incomplete, napping, off-the-cuff, spontaneous, surprised, unawares, unfinished, ungirded, unplanned, unready, unrehearsed, unsuspecting.
antonyms prepared, ready.

unpretentious *adj* homely, honest, humble, modest, natural, penny-plain, plain, simple, straightforward, unaffected, unassuming, unimposing, unobtrusive, unostentatious, unpretending, unsophisticated, unspoiled.
antonym pretentious.

unprincipled *adj* amoral, corrupt, crooked, deceitful, devious, discreditable, dishonest, dishonourable, immoral, underhand, unethical, unprofessional, unscrupulous.
antonym ethical.

unproductive *adj* arid, barren, bootless, dry, fruitless, futile, idle, ineffective, inefficacious, infertile, otiose, sterile, unavailing, unfruitful, unprofitable, unprolific, unremunerative, unrewarding, useless, vain, valueless, worthless.
antonyms fertile, productive.

unprofessional *adj* amateur, amateurish, improper, inadmissible, incompetent, inefficient, inexperienced, inexpert, lax, negligent, unacceptable, unbecoming, unethical, unfitting, unprincipled, unseemly, unskilled, untrained, unworthy.
antonyms professional, skilful.

unpromising *adj* adverse, depressing, discouraging, dispiriting, doubtful, gloomy, inauspicious, ominous, unfavourable, unpropitious.
antonym promising.

unprotected *adj* defenceless, exposed, helpless, inerm, liable, naked, open, pregnable, unarmed, unattended, undefended, unfortified, unguarded, unsheltered, unshielded, unvaccinated, vulnerable.
antonyms immune, protected, safe.

unprovable *adj* indemonstrable, indeterminable, unascertainable, undemonstrable, unverifiable.
antonym verifiable.

unqualified *adj* absolute, categorical, complete, consummate, downright, ill-equipped, incapable, incompetent, ineligible, out-and-out, outright, thorough, thoroughgoing, total, uncertificated, unconditional, unfit, unmitigated, unmixed, unprepared, unreserved, unrestricted, untrained, utter, whole-hearted.
antonyms conditional, tentative.

unquestionable *adj* absolute, certain, clear, conclusive, definite, faultless, flawless, incontestable, incontrovertible, indisputable, indubitable, irrefutable, manifest, obvious, patent, self-evident, sure, unchallenged, undeniable, unequivocal, unmistakable.
antonyms dubious, questionable.

unquestioning *adj* implicit, questionless, unconditional, unhesitating, unqualified, whole-hearted.
antonym doubtful.

unravel *v* disentangle, explain, extricate, figure out, free, interpret, penetrate, puzzle out, ravel out, resolve, separate, solve, sort out, undo, unknot, untangle, unwind, work out.
antonyms complicate, tangle.

unreal *adj* academic, artificial, chimerical, fabulous, fairy-tale, fake, false, fanciful, fantastic, fictitious, hypothetical, illusory, imaginary, immaterial, impalpable, insincere, insubstantial, intangible, made-up, make-believe, mock, moonshiny, mythical, nebulous, ostensible, phantasmagorical, pretended, seeming, sham, storybook, synthetic, vaporous, visionary.
antonyms genuine, real.

unrealistic *adj* half-baked, idealistic, impracticable, impractical, improbable, quixotic, romantic, starry-eyed, theoretical, unworkable.
antonyms pragmatic, realistic.

unreasonable *adj* absurd, arbitrary, biased, blinkered, capricious, cussed, erratic, excessive, exorbitant, extortionate, extravagant, far-fetched, foolish, froward, headstrong, illogical, immoderate, inconsistent, irrational, mad, nonsensical, opinionated, perverse, preposterous, quirky, senseless, silly, steep, stupid, thrawn, uncalled-for, undue, unfair, unjust, unjustifiable, unjustified, unwarranted.
antonyms moderate, rational, reasonable.

unrecognisable *adj* altered, changed, disguised, incognisable, incognito, unidentifiable, unknowable.

unrefined *adj* boorish, coarse, crude, imperfect, inelegant, raw, rude, uncultivated, uncultured, unfinished, unperfected, unpolished, unpurified, unsophisticated, untreated, vulgar.
antonyms finished, refined.

unregenerate *adj* abandoned, hardened, impenitent, incorrigible, intractable, obdurate, obstinate, persistent, recalcitrant, refractory, shameless, sinful, stubborn, unconverted, unreformed, unrepentant, wicked.
antonyms reformed, repentant.

unrelated *adj* different, disparate, dissimilar, distinct, extraneous, inapplicable, inappropriate, irrelevant, unassociated, unconnected, unlike.
antonyms related, similar.

unrelenting *adj* ceaseless, constant, continual, continuous, cruel, endless, implacable, incessant, inexorable, insistent, intransigent, merciless, perpetual, pitiless, relentless, remorseless, ruthless, steady, stern, tough, unabated, unalleviated, unbroken, unceasing, uncompromising, unmerciful, unremitting, unsparing.
antonyms intermittent, spasmodic.

unreliable *adj* deceptive, delusive, disreputable, erroneous, fair-weather, fallible, false, implausible, inaccurate, inauthentic, irresponsible, mistaken, specious, uncertain, unconvincing, undependable, unsound, unstable, untrustworthy.

antonym reliable.

unremitting *adj* assiduous, ceaseless, conscientious, constant, continual, continuous, diligent, incessant, indefatigable, perpetual, relentless, remorseless, sedulous, tireless, unabated, unbroken, unceasing, unrelenting.

antonym spasmodic.

unrepentant *adj* callous, hardened, impenitent, incorrigible, obdurate, shameless, unabashed, unashamed, unregenerate, unremorseful, unrepenting.

antonyms penitent, repentant.

unreserved *adj* absolute, candid, complete, demonstrative, direct, entire, extrovert, forthright, frank, free, full, open, open-hearted, outgoing, outspoken, total, unconditional, unhesitating, uninhibited, unlimited, unqualified, unrestrained, whole-hearted.

antonyms inhibited, tentative.

unreservedly *adv* completely, entirely, outright, plump, unhesitatingly, utterly, whole-heartedly.

unresisting *adj* docile, like a lamb to the slaughter, meek, obedient, passive, submissive.

antonyms protesting, resisting.

unresolved *adj* doubtful, indefinite, moot, pending, problematical, unanswered, undecided, undetermined, unsettled, unsolved, up in the air, vague, vexed.

antonyms definite, determined.

unresponsive *adj* aloof, apathetic, cool, echoless, indifferent, unaffected, uninterested, unmoved, unsympathetic.

antonyms responsive, sympathetic.

unrest *n* agitation, anxiety, apprehension, disaffection, discontent, discord, disquiet, dissatisfaction, dissension, distress, perturbation, protest, rebellion, restlessness, sedition, strife, tumult, turmoil, unease, uneasiness, worry.

antonyms calm, peace.

unrestrained *adj* abandoned, boisterous, free, immoderate, inordinate, intemperate, irrepressible, natural, rampant, unbounded, unbridled, unchecked, unconstrained, uncontrolled, unhindered, uninhibited, unrepressed, unreserved, uproarious.

antonym inhibited.

unrestricted *adj* absolute, all-round, clear, free, free-for-all, free-wheeling, open, public, unbounded, uncircumscribed, unconditional, unhindered, unimpeded, unlimited, unobstructed, unopposed, unregulated.

antonyms limited, restricted.

unripe *adj* green, immature, undeveloped, unready, unripened.

antonyms mature, ripe.

unrivalled *adj* incomparable, inimitable, matchless, nonpareil, peerless, superlative, supreme, surpassing, unequalled, unexcelled, unmatched, unparalleled, unsurpassed, without equal.

unruffled *adj* calm, collected, composed, cool, even, imperturbable, level, peaceful, placid, serene, smooth, tranquil, unbroken, undisturbed, unflustered, unmoved, unperturbed, untroubled.

antonyms anxious, troubled.

unruly *adj* camstairy, disobedient, disorderly, fractious, headstrong, insubordinate, intractable, lawless, mutinous, obstreperous, rebellious, refractory, riotous, rowdy, ruleless, turbulent, uncontrollable, ungovernable, unmanageable, wayward, wild, wilful.

antonym manageable.

unsafe *adj* dangerous, exposed, hazardous, insecure, parlous, perilous, precarious, risky, threatening, treacherous, uncertain, unreliable, unsound, unstable, vulnerable.

antonyms safe, secure.

unsaid *adj* undeclared, unexpressed, unmentioned, unpronounced, unspoken, unstated, unuttered, unvoiced.

antonym spoken.

unsaleable *adj* invendible, unmarketable, unsellable.

antonyms marketable, saleable.

unsatisfactory *adj* deficient, disappointing, displeasing, dissatisfying, frustrating, inadequate, inferior, insufficient, leaving a lot to be desired, mediocre, poor, rocky, thwarting, unacceptable, unsatisfying, unsuitable, unworthy, weak.

antonym satisfactory.

unsavoury *adj* disagreeable, distasteful, nasty, nauseating, objectionable, obnoxious, offensive, repellent, repugnant, repulsive, revolting, sickening, sordid, squalid, unappetising, unattractive, undesirable, unpalatable, unpleasant.

antonyms palatable, pleasant.

unscathed *adj* intact, safe, scot-free, sound, unharmed, unhurt, uninjured, unmarked, unscarred, unscratched, untouched, whole.

antonyms harmed, injured.

unscrupulous *adj* corrupt, crooked, cynical, discreditable, dishonest, dishonourable, immoral, improper, ruthless, shameless, unethical, unprincipled.

antonym scrupulous.

unseasonable *adj* ill-timed, inappropriate, inopportune, intempestive, malapropos, mistimed, unsuitable, untimely.

antonyms seasonable, timely.

unseasoned *adj* green, unmatured, unprepared, unprimed, untempered, untreated.

unseat *v* depose, dethrone, discharge, dishorse, dismiss, dismount, displace, disseat, oust, overthrow, remove, throw, topple, unhorse, unsaddle.

unseemly *adj* discreditable, disreputable, improper, inappropriate, indecorous, indelicate, shocking, unbecoming, unbefitting, undignified, undue, ungentlemanly, unladylike, unrefined, unsuitable.

antonyms decorous, seemly.

unseen *adj* concealed, hidden, invisible, lurking, obscure, overlooked, undetected, unnoticed, unobserved, unobtrusive, unperceived, veiled.

antonyms observed, visible.

unselfish *adj* altruistic, charitable, dedicated, devoted, disinterested, generous, humanitarian, kind, liberal, magnanimous, noble, philanthropic, self-denying, selfless, self-sacrificing, single-eyed, ungrudging, unstinting.

antonym selfish.

unsentimental *adj* cynical, hard as nails, hard-headed, level-headed, practical, pragmatic, realistic, shrewd, tough.

antonyms sentimental, soft.

unsettle *v* agitate, bother, confuse, destabilise, discompose, disconcert, disorder, disturb, fluster, flutter, perturb, rattle, ruffle, shake, throw, trouble, unbalance, upset.

antonyms compose, settle.

unsettled *adj* agitated, anxious, changeable, changing, confused, debatable, disorderly, disoriented, disturbed, doubtful, due, edgy, flustered, iffy, inconstant, insecure, moot, open, outstanding, overdue, owing, payable, pending, perturbed, problematical, restive, restless, shaken, shaky, tense, troubled, uncertain, undecided, undetermined, uneasy, unnerved, unpredictable, unresolved, unstable, unsteady, upset, variable.

antonyms certain, composed, settled.

unshakable *adj* absolute, adamant, constant, determined, firm, fixed, immovable, resolute, stable, staunch, steadfast, sure, unassailable, unswerving, unwavering, well-founded.

antonym insecure.

unsheathe *v* dissheathe, draw, evaginate, expose, reveal, uncover.

antonyms retract, sheathe.

unshod *adj* barefooted, discalced, shoeless.

antonym shod.

unsightly *adj* disagreeable, displeasing, hideous, horrid, off-putting, repellent, repugnant, repulsive, revolting, ugly, unattractive, unpleasant, unprepossessing.

antonym pleasing.

unskilful *adj* amateurish, awkward, bungling, clumsy, fumbling, gauche, incompetent, inept, inexperienced, inexpert, maladroit, unapt, uneducated, unhandy, unpractised, unprofessional, unqualified, unskilled, untalented, untaught, untrained.

antonyms skilful, skilled.

unsociable *adj* aloof, chilly, cold, distant, farouche, hostile, inconversable, inhospitable, introverted, reclusive, reserved, retiring, stand-offish, taciturn, uncommunicative, uncongenial, unforthcoming, unfriendly, unneighbourly, unsocial, withdrawn.

antonyms friendly, sociable.

unsolicited *adj* gratuitous, spontaneous, unasked, uncalled-for, unforced, uninvited, unrequested, unsought, unwanted, unwelcome, voluntary.

antonyms invited, solicited.

unsophisticated *adj* artless, childlike, funky, guileless, hick, homespun, inexperienced, ingenuous, innocent, naïve, natural, plain, simple, small-town, straightforward, unaffected, uncomplicated, uninvolved, unpretentious, unrefined, unspecialised, unspoilt, untutored, unworldly.

antonyms complex, pretentious, sophisticated.

unsound *adj* ailing, defective, delicate, deranged, dicky, diseased, erroneous, fallacious, fallible, false, faulty, flawed, frail, ill, ill-founded, illogical, insecure, invalid, shaky, specious, unbalanced, unhealthy, unhinged, unreliable, unsafe, unstable, unsteady, unwell, weak, wobbly.

antonyms safe, sound.

unsparing *adj* abundant, bountiful, generous, hard, harsh, implacable, inexorable, lavish, liberal, merciless, munificent, open-handed, plenteous, prodigal, profuse, relentless, rigorous, ruthless, scathing, severe, stern, stringent, uncompromising, unforgiving, ungrudging, unmerciful, unstinting.

antonyms forgiving, mean, sparing.

unspeakable *adj* abhorrent, abominable, appalling, dreadful, evil, execrable, frightful, heinous, horrible, inconceivable, indescribable, ineffable, inexpressible, loathsome, monstrous, nefandous, odious, overwhelming, repellent, shocking, unbelievable, unimaginable, unutterable, wonderful.

unspectacular *adj* boring, dull, methodical, ordinary, plodding, systematic, unexciting, unimpressive, unremarkable.

unspoilt *adj* artless, innocent, intact, natural, perfect, preserved, scatheless, unaffected, unaltered, unassuming, unblemished, unchanged, undamaged, unharmed, unimpaired, unscathed, unsophisticated, unspoiled, unstudied, untouched, wholesome.

antonyms affected, spoilt.

unspoken *adj* assumed, implicit, implied, inferred, mute, silent, speechless, tacit, undeclared, understood, unexpressed, unsaid, unstated, unuttered, voiceless, wordless.

antonym explicit.

unstable *adj* astable, capricious, changeable, erratic, fitful, fluctuating, inconsistent, inconstant, insecure, irrational, labile, precarious, rickety, risky, shaky, shoogly, slippy, ticklish, tottering, unpredictable, unsettled, unsteady, untrustworthy, vacillating, variable, volatile, wobbly.

antonyms stable, steady.

unsteady *adj* changeable, dicky, erratic, flickering, flighty, fluctuating, frail, inconstant, infirm, insecure, irregular, precarious, reeling, rickety, shaky, shoogly, skittish, tittupy, tottering, totty, treacherous, tremulous, unreliable, unsafe, unstable, unsteeled, vacillating, variable, volatile, wavering, wobbly.

antonyms firm, steady.

unstinting *adj* abounding, abundant, ample, bountiful, full, generous, large, lavish, liberal, munificent, plentiful, prodigal, profuse, ungrudging, unsparing.

antonyms grudging, mean.

unsubstantial *adj* airy, chimerical, dreamlike, erroneous, fanciful, flimsy, fragile, frail, ill-founded, illusory, imaginary, immaterial, impalpable, inadequate, insubstantial, light, slight, superficial, tenuous, thin, unsound, unsupported, vaporous, visionary, weak.

antonyms real, valid.

unsubstantiated *adj* debatable, dubious, questionable, unattested, unconfirmed, uncorroborated, unestablished, unproved, unproven, unsupported, unverified.

antonyms proved, proven.

unsuccessful *adj* abortive, bootless, failed, foiled, fruitless, frustrated, futile, ill-fated, inadequate, ineffective, ineffectual, losing, luckless, manqué, otiose, sterile, thwarted, unavailing, unfortunate, unlucky, unproductive, unsatisfactory, useless, vain.

antonyms effective, successful.

unsuitable *adj* improper, inapposite, inappropriate, inapt, incompatible, incongruous, inconsistent, indecorous, ineligible, infelicitous, malapropos, unacceptable, unbecoming, unbefitting, unfitting, unlikely, unseasonable, unseemly, unsuited.

antonyms seemly, suitable.

unsullied *adj* clean, immaculate, intact, perfect, pristine, pure, spotless, stainless, unblackened, unblemished, uncorrupted, undefiled, unsoiled, unspoiled, unspotted, unstained, untarnished, untouched.

antonyms dirty, stained.

unsung *adj* anonymous, disregarded, forgotten, neglected, obscure, overlooked, unacknowledged, uncelebrated, unhailed, unhonoured, unknown, unnamed, unrecognised, unrenowned.

antonyms famous, renowned.

unsure *adj* agnostic, distrustful, doubtful, dubious, hesitant, insecure, irresolute, mistrustful, sceptical, suspicious, tentative, uncertain, unconvinced, undecided, unpersuaded.

antonyms resolute, sure.

unsurpassed *adj* consummate, exceptional, incomparable, matchless, nonpareil, paramount, peerless, sublime, superlative, supreme, surpassing, transcendent, unequalled, unexcelled, unparalleled, unrivalled.

unsuspecting *adj* childlike, confiding, credulous, green, gullible, inexperienced, ingenuous, innocent, naïve, trustful, trusting, unconscious, uncritical, unsuspicious, unwary, unwitting.

antonyms conscious, knowing.

unswerving *adj* constant, dedicated, devoted, direct, firm, fixed, immovable, resolute, single-minded, staunch, steadfast, steady, sure, true, undeviating, unfaltering, unflagging, untiring, unwavering.

antonyms irresolute, tentative.

unsympathetic *adj* antagonistic, antipathetic, apathetic, callous, cold, compassionless, cruel, hard, hard as nails, hard-hearted, harsh, heartless, indifferent, inhuman, insensitive, soulless, stony, uncharitable, uncompassionate, unconcerned, unfeeling, unkind, unmoved, unpitying, unresponsive.

antonyms compassionate, sympathetic.

unsystematic *adj* chaotic, confused, desultory, disorderly, disorganised, haphazard, illogical, indiscriminate, irregular, jumbled, muddled, random, shambolic, slapdash, sloppy, unco-ordinated, unmethodical, unorganised, unplanned, untidy.

antonyms logical, systematic.

untamed *adj* barbarous, ferae naturae, feral, fierce, haggard, savage, unbroken, undomesticated, unmellowed, untameable, wild.

antonyms domesticated, tame.

untangle *v* disentangle, explain, extricate, ravel out, resolve, solve, undo, unravel, unsnarl.

antonyms complicate, tangle.

untarnished *adj* bright, burnished, clean, glowing, immaculate, impeccable, intact, polished, pristine, pure, shining, spotless, stainless, unblemished, unimpeachable, unsoiled, unspoilt, unspotted, unstained, unsullied.

antonyms blemished, tarnished.

untenable *adj* fallacious, flawed, illogical, indefensible, insupportable, rocky, shaky, unmaintainable, unreasonable, unsound, unsustainable.

antonyms sound, tenable.

unthinkable *adj* absurd, illogical, implausible, impossible, improbable, incogitable, inconceivable, incredible, insupportable, outrageous, preposterous, shocking, unbelievable, unheard-of, unimaginable, unlikely, unreasonable.

unthinking *adj* automatic, careless, heedless, impulsive, inadvertent, incautious, inconsiderate, indiscreet, insensitive, instinctive, mechanical, negligent, oblivious, rash, rude, selfish, senseless, tactless, thoughtless, unconscious, undiplomatic, unguarded, vacant, witless.

antonyms conscious, deliberate, witting.

untidy *adj* bedraggled, chaotic, cluttered, dishevelled, disorderly, higgledy-piggledy, jumbled, littered, messy, muddled, ratty, raunchy, rumpled, scruffy, shambolic, slatternly, slipshod, sloppy, slovenly, sluttish, topsy-turvy, unkempt, unsystematic.

antonyms systematic, tidy.

untie *v* free, loosen, release, unbind, undo, unfasten, unknot, unlace, unloose, unloosen, untether.

antonyms fasten, tie.

untimely *adj* awkward, early, ill-timed, inappropriate, inauspicious, inconvenient, inopportune, intempestive, malapropos, mistimed, premature, unfortunate, unseasonable, unsuitable.

antonyms opportune, timely.

untiring *adj* constant, dedicated, determined, devoted, dogged, incessant, indefatigable, patient, persevering, persistent, staunch, steady, tenacious, tireless, unfailing, unfaltering, unflagging, unremitting, unwearied.

antonym inconstant.

untold *adj* boundless, countless, hidden, incalculable, indescribable, inexhaustible, inexpressible, infinite, innumerable, measureless, myriad, numberless, private, secret, uncountable, uncounted, undisclosed, undreamed-of, unimaginable, unknown, unnumbered, unpublished, unreckoned, unrecounted, unrelated, unrevealed, unthinkable, unutterable.

untouched *adj* indifferent, intact, safe, scatheless, unaffected, unaltered, unconcerned, undamaged, unharmed, unhurt, unimpaired, unimpressed, uninjured, unmoved, unscathed, unstirred.

antonyms affected, impaired, moved.

untoward *adj* adverse, annoying, awkward, contrary, disastrous, ill-timed, improper, inappropriate, inauspicious, inconvenient, indecorous, inimical, inopportune, irritating, ominous, troublesome, unbecoming, unexpected, unfavourable, unfitting, unfortunate, unlucky, unpropitious, unseemly, unsuitable, untimely, vexatious, worrying.

antonyms auspicious, suitable.

untrained *adj* amateur, green, inexperienced, inexpert, raw, uneducated, unpractised, unprofessional, unqualified, unschooled, unskilled, untaught, untutored.

antonyms expert, trained.

untried *adj* experimental, exploratory, innovative, innovatory, new, novel, unestablished, unproved, untested.

antonyms proven, tested.

untroubled *adj* calm, composed, cool, impassive, peaceful, placid, serene, steady, tranquil, unconcerned, undisturbed, unexcited, unflappable, unflustered, unperturbed, unruffled, unstirred, unworried.

antonyms anxious, troubled.

untrue *adj* deceitful, deceptive, deviant, dishonest, disloyal, distorted, erroneous, faithless, fallacious, false, forsworn, fraudulent, inaccurate, inauthentic, inconstant, incorrect, lying, mendacious, misleading, mistaken, perfidious, sham, specious, spurious, traitorous, treacherous, two-faced, unfaithful, untrustworthy, untruthful, wrong.

antonyms honest, true.

untrustworthy *adj* capricious, deceitful, devious, dishonest, disloyal, dubious, duplicitous, fair-weather, faithless, false, fickle, fly-by-night, shady, slippery, treacherous, tricky, two-faced, undependable, unfaithful, unreliable, unsafe, untrue, untrusty.

antonyms reliable, trustworthy.

untruth *n* deceit, deceitfulness, duplicity, fabrication, falsehood, falsification, falsism, falsity, fib, fiction, inexactitude, invention, inveracity, lie, lying, mendacity, perjury, prevarication, story, tale, trick, truthlessness, untruthfulness, whopper.

antonym truth.

untruthful *adj* crooked, deceitful, deceptive, dishonest, dissembling, false, hypocritical, lying, mendacious, untrustworthy, unveracious.

antonym truthful.

untwine *v* disentwine, uncoil, unravel, untwist, unwind.

antonyms twine, wind.

untwist *v* detort, ravel out, uncoil, unravel, untwine, unwind.

antonym twist.

untutored *adj* artless, ignorant, illiterate, inexperienced, inexpert, simple, uneducated, unlearned, unlessoned, unpractised, unrefined, unschooled, unsophisticated, untrained, unversed.

antonyms educated, trained.

unused *adj* available, extra, fresh, idle, intact, left, left-over, new, pristine, remaining, unaccustomed, unconsumed, unemployed, unexploited, unfamiliar, untouched, unutilised.

unusual *adj* abnormal, anomalous, atypical, bizarre, curious, different, eccentric, exceptional, extraordinary, odd, phenomenal, queer, rare, remarkable, singular, strange, surprising, uncommon, unconventional, unexpected, unfamiliar, unwonted.

antonyms normal, usual.

unutterable *adj* egregious, extreme, indescribable, ineffable, nefandous, overwhelming, unimaginable, unspeakable.

unvarnished *adj* bare, candid, frank, honest, naked, plain, pure, sheer, simple, sincere, stark, straightforward, unadorned, undisguised, unembellished.

antonyms disguised, embellished.

unveil *v* bare, disclose, discover, disenshroud, divulge, expose, reveal, uncover, unfold, unshroud.

antonyms cover, hide.

unwanted *adj* de trop, extra, otiose, outcast, rejected, superfluous, surplus, unasked, undesired, uninvited, unnecessary, unneeded, unrequired, unsolicited, unwelcome, useless.

antonyms necessary, needed, wanted.

unwarranted *adj* baseless, gratuitous, groundless, indefensible, inexcusable, uncalled-for, unjust, unjustified, unprovoked, unreasonable, vain, wrong.

antonyms justifiable, warranted.

unwary *adj* careless, credulous, hasty, heedless, imprudent, incautious, indiscreet, rash, reckless, thoughtless, unchary, uncircumspect, unguarded, unthinking, unwatchful.

antonyms cautious, wary.

unwavering *adj* consistent, dedicated, determined, resolute, single-minded, staunch, steadfast, steady, sturdy, tenacious, undeviating, unfaltering, unflagging, unquestioning, unshakable, unshaken, unswerving, untiring.

antonyms fickle, wavering.

unwelcome *adj* disagreeable, displeasing, distasteful, excluded, rejected, thankless, unacceptable, undesirable, uninvited, unpalatable, unpleasant, unpopular, unwanted, upsetting, worrying.

antonyms desirable, welcome.

unwell *adj* ailing, ill, indisposed, mops and brooms, nohow, nohowish, off-colour, poorly, sick, sickly, unhealthy.

antonyms healthy, well.

unwholesome *adj* anaemic, bad, corrupting, degrading, deleterious, demoralising, depraving, epinosic, evil, harmful, immoral, innutritious, insalubrious, insalutary, insanitary, junk, noxious, pale, pallid, pasty, perverting, poisonous, sickly, tainted, unhealthy, unhygienic, wan, wicked.

antonyms salubrious, wholesome.

unwieldy *adj* awkward, bulky, burdensome, clumsy, cumbersome, cumbrous, gangling, hefty, hulking, inconvenient, massive, ponderous, ungainly, unhandy, unmanageable, weighty.

antonyms dainty, neat, petite.

unwilling *adj* averse, disinclined, grudging, indisposed, laggard, loath, loathful, opposed, reluctant, resistant, slow, unenthusiastic.

antonyms enthusiastic, willing.

unwillingness *n* backwardness, disinclination, hesitancy, indisposition, lack of enthusiasm, loathfulness, nolition, reluctance, slowness.

antonyms enthusiasm, willingness.

unwind *v* calm down, detort, disentangle, quieten down, relax, slacken, uncoil, undo, unravel, unreel, unroll, unswathe, untwine, untwist, unwrap, wind down.

antonyms twist, wind.

unwise *adj* foolhardy, foolish, ill-advised, ill-considered, ill-judged, impolitic, improvident, imprudent, inadvisable, indiscreet, inexpedient, injudicious, irresponsible, rash, reckless, senseless, short-sighted, silly, stupid, thoughtless, unintelligent.

antonyms prudent, wise.

unwitting *adj* accidental, chance, ignorant, inadvertent, innocent, involuntary, unaware, unconscious, unintended, unintentional, unknowing, unmeant, unplanned, unsuspecting, unthinking.

antonyms conscious, deliberate, knowing, witting.

unwonted *adj* atypical, exceptional, extraordinary, infrequent, peculiar, rare, singular, strange, unaccustomed, uncommon, uncustomary, unexpected, unfamiliar, unheard-of, unusual.

antonyms usual, wonted.

unworldly *adj* abstract, celestial, ethereal, extramundane, extra-physical, extra-terrestrial, green, idealistic, impractical, inexperienced, innocent, metaphysical, naïve, otherworldly, religious, spiritual, transcendental, unearthly, unsophisticated, visionary.

antonyms materialistic, practical, worldly.

unworried *adj* collected, composed, downbeat, unabashed, undismayed, unperturbed, unruffled, untroubled.

antonym anxious.

unworthy *adj* base, contemptible, degrading, desertless, discreditable, disgraceful, dishonourable, disreputable, ignoble, improper, inappropriate, ineligible, inferior, shameful, unbecoming, unbefitting, undeserving, unfitting, unprofessional, unseemly, unsuitable, unsuited.

antonyms commendable, worthy.

unwritten *adj* accepted, conventional, customary, implicit, oral, recognised, tacit, traditional, understood, unformulated, unrecorded, verbal, vocal, word-of-mouth.

antonyms recorded, written.

unyielding *adj* adamant, determined, firm, hardline, immovable, implacable, inexorable, inflexible, intractable, intransigent, obdurate, obstinate, relentless, resolute, rigid, solid, staunch, steadfast, stubborn, tough, unbending, uncompromising, unrelenting, unwavering.

antonyms flexible, yielding.

up to one's eyes busy, engaged, inundated, overwhelmed, preoccupied, tied up.

antonyms free, idle.

up to scratch acceptable, adequate, capable, comme il faut, competent, OK, satisfactory, sufficient.

antonym unsatisfactory.

up-and-coming ambitious, assertive, eager, enterprising, go-getting, promising, pushing.

upbeat *adj* bright, bullish, buoyant, cheerful, cheery, encouraging, favourable, forward-looking, heartening, hopeful, optimistic, positive, promising, rosy.

antonyms down-beat, gloomy.

upbraid *v* admonish, berate, blame, carpet, castigate, censure, chide, condemn, criticise, dress down, jaw, lecture, rate, rebuke, reprimand, reproach, reprove, scold, take to task, tell off, tick off.

antonyms commend, praise.

upbringing *n* breeding, bringing-up, care, cultivation, education, instruction, nurture, parenting, raising, rearing, tending, training.

update *v* amend, correct, modernise, renew, renovate, revamp, revise.

upgrade *v* advance, ameliorate, better, elevate, embourgeoise, enhance, gentilise, gentrify, improve, promote, raise.

antonyms degrade, downgrade.

upgrading *n* advancement, amelioration, betterment, elevation, embourgeoisement, enhancement, gentrification, improvement, promotion.

upheaval *n* cataclysm, chaos, confusion, disorder, disruption, disturbance, earthquake, eruption, overthrow, revolution, shake-up, turmoil, upset.

uphill *adj* acclivious, acclivitous, arduous, ascending, climbing, difficult, exhausting, gruelling, hard, laborious, mounting, punishing, rising, strenuous, taxing, tough, upward, wearisome.

antonyms downhill, easy.

uphold *v* advocate, aid, back, champion, countenance, defend, encourage, endorse, fortify, hold to, justify, maintain, promote, stand by, stengthen, support, sustain, vindicate.

upkeep *n* care, conservation, expenditure, expenses, keep, maintenance, oncosts, operating costs, outgoing, outlay, overheads, preservation, repair, running, running costs, subsistence, support, sustenance.

antonym neglect.

uplift *v* advance, ameliorate, better, boost, civilise, cultivate, edify, elate, elevate, enlighten, exalt, heave, hoist, improve, inspire, lift, raise, refine, upgrade.

n advancement, betterment, boost, cultivation, edification, enhancement, enlightenment, enrichment, improvement, lift, refinement.

upper *adj* elevated, eminent, exalted, greater, high, higher, important, loftier, senior, superior, top, topmost, uppermost.

antonyms inferior, junior, lower.

upper hand advantage, ascendancy, control, dominance, domination, dominion, edge, mastery, superiority, supremacy, sway.

upper-class *adj* aristocratic, blue-blooded, educated, élite, exclusive, gentle, high-born, high-class, noble, patrician, swanky, top-drawer, tweedy, well-born, well-bred.

antonyms humble, working-class.

uppermost *adj* chief, dominant, first, foremost, greatest, highest, leading, loftiest, main, paramount, predominant, pre-eminent, primary, principal, prominent, supreme, top, topmost, upmost.

antonyms bottommost, lowest.

uppish *adj* affected, arrogant, assuming, big-headed, bumptious, cocky, conceited, hoity-toity, impertinent, overweening, presumptuous, self-important, snobbish, stuck-up, supercilious, swanky, toffee-nosed, uppity.

antonyms diffident, unassertive.

upright *adj* arrect, bluff, conscientious, erect, ethical, faithful, four-square, good, high-minded, honest, honourable, incorruptible, just, noble, perpendicular, principled, righteous, straight, straightforward, true, trustworthy, unimpeachable, upstanding, vertical, virtuous.

antonyms dishonest, flat, horizontal, prone, supine.

uprising *n* inqilab, insurgence, insurgency, insurrection, mutiny, putsch, rebellion, revolt, revolution, rising, sedition, upheaval.

uproar *n* brawl, brouhaha, clamour, commotion, confusion, din, disorder, furore, hubbub, hullabaloo, hurly-burly, katzenjammer, noise, outcry, pandemonium, racket, rammy, randan, riot, ruckus, ruction, rumpus, stramash, tumult, turbulence, turmoil.

uproarious *adj* boisterous, clamorous, confused, convulsive, deafening, disorderly, gleeful, hilarious, hysterical, killing, loud, noisy, rib-tickling, riotous, rip-roaring, roistering, rollicking, rowdy, rowdy-dowdy, side-splitting, tempestuous, tumultuous, turbulent, unrestrained, wild.

antonym sedate.

uproot *v* deracinate, destroy, disorient, displace, disroot, eliminate, eradicate, exile, exterminate, extirpate, grub up, remove, rip up, root out, weed out, wipe out.

upset *v* agitate, bother, capsize, change, conquer, defeat, destabilise, discombobulate, discompose, disconcert, dismay, disorder, disorganise, disquiet, distress, disturb, fluster, grieve, hip, overcome, overset, overthrow, overturn, perturb, ruffle, shake, spill, spoil, tip, topple, trouble, unnerve, unsteady.

n agitation, bother, bug, complaint, defeat, disorder, disruption, disturbance, illness, indisposition, malady, purl, reverse, shake-up, shock, sickness, surprise, trouble, upheaval, worry.

adj agitated, bothered, capsized, chaotic, choked, confused, disconcerted, dismayed, disordered, disquieted, distressed, disturbed, frantic, gippy, grieved, hurt, ill, messed up, muddled, overturned, overwrought, pained, poorly, qualmish, queasy, ruffled, shattered, sick, spilled, toppled, topsy-turvy, troubled, tumbled, worried.

upshot *n* conclusion, consequence, culmination, end, event, finale, finish, issue, outcome, pay-off, result.

upside down at sixes and sevens, chaotic, confused, disordered, higgledy-piggledy, inverted, jumbled, muddled, overturned, topsy-turvy, upset, upturned, wrong side up.

antonym shipshape.

upstanding *adj* erect, ethical, firm, four-square, good, hardy, healthy, hearty, honest, honourable, incorruptible, lusty, moral, principled, robust, stalwart, strong, sturdy, true, trustworthy, upright, vigorous.

antonyms puny, untrustworthy.

upstart *n* arriviste, mushroom, nobody, nouveau riche, parvenu, social climber.

uptight *adj* anxious, edgy, hung-up, irritated, nervy, prickly, tense, uneasy.

antonyms calm, cool, relaxed.

up-to-date *adj* à la mode, all the rage, contemporary, current, fashionable, in, latest, modern, modish, newest, now, popular, smart, stylish, swinging, trendy, up-to-the-minute, vogue, voguish, with it.

antonym old-fashioned.

upturn *n* advancement, amelioration, boost, improvement, increase, recovery, revival, rise, upsurge, upswing.

antonyms downturn, drop, setback.

urban *adj* built-up, burghal, city, civic, inner-city, metropolitan, municipal, oppidan, town, urbanised.

antonyms country, rural, rustic.

urbane *adj* bland, civil, civilised, cosmopolitan, courteous, cultivated, cultured, debonair, easy, elegant, mannerly, polished, refined, smooth, sophisticated, suave, well-bred, well-mannered.

antonyms gauche, uncouth.

urbanity *n* blandness, charm, civility, courtesy, cultivation, culture, ease, elegance, eutrapelia, grace, mannerliness, polish, refinement, smoothness, sophistication, suavity, worldliness.

antonyms awkwardness, gaucheness.

urchin *n* brat, gamin, gutter-snipe, kid, mudlark, ragamuffin, street Arab, tatterdemalion, waif.

urge *v* advise, advocate, beg, beseech, champion, compel, constrain, counsel, drive, emphasise, encourage, entreat, exhort, force, goad, hasten, hist, impel, implore, incite, induce, instigate, nag, plead, press, propel, push, recommend, solicit, spur, stimulate, support, underline, underscore.

antonyms deter, dissuade.

n compulsion, desire, drive, eagerness, fancy, impulse, inclination, itch, libido, longing, wish, yearning, yen.

antonym disinclination.

urgency *n* exigence, exigency, extremity, gravity, hurry, imperativeness, importance, importunity, instancy, necessity, need, pressure, seriousness, stress.

urgent *adj* clamorous, cogent, compelling, critical, crucial, eager, earnest, emergent, exigent, immediate, imperative, important, importunate, insistent, instant, intense, persistent, persuasive, pressing, top-priority.

urinal *n* gents, pissoir.

urinate *v* ease oneself, leak, make water, micturate, pass water, pee, piddle, piss, relieve oneself, spend a penny, stale, tinkle, wee, wee-wee.

urination *n* emiction, Jimmy, micturition, run-off.

urine *n* pee, piddle, piss, stale, water.

usable *adj* available, current, exploitable, functional, operating, operational, practical, serviceable, utilisable, valid, working.

antonyms unusable, useless.

usage *n* application, control, convention, custom, employment, etiquette, form, habit, handling, management, method, mode, operation, practice, procedure, protocol, régime, regulation, routine, rule, running, tradition, treatment, use, wont.

use *v* apply, bring, consume, employ, enjoy, exercise, exhaust, expend, exploit, handle, manipulate, misuse, operate, ply, practise, spend, treat, usufruct, utilise, waste, wield, work.

n advantage, application, avail, benefit, call, cause, custom, employment, end, enjoyment, exercise, good, habit, handling, help, meaning, mileage, necessity, need, object, occasion, operation, point, practice, profit, purpose, reason, service, treatment, usage, usefulness, usufruct, utility, value, way, wont, worth.

use up absorb, consume, deplete, devour, drain, eat into, exhaust, finish, fritter, sap, squander, swallow, waste.

used *adj* accustomed, cast-off, dog-eared, familiar, hand-me-down, nearly new, reach-me-down, second-hand, shop-soiled, soiled, worn.

antonyms fresh, new, unused.

useful *adj* advantageous, all-purpose, beneficial, convenient, effective, fruitful, general-purpose, handy, helpful, practical, productive, profitable, salutary, serviceable, valuable, worthwhile.

antonym useless.

useless *adj* bootless, clapped-out disadvantageous, effectless, feckless, fruitless, futile, hopeless, idle, impractical, incompetent, ineffective, ineffectual, inefficient, inept, naff, of no use, pointless, profitless, shiftless, spastic, stupid, unavailing, unproductive, unworkable, vain, valueless, weak, worthless.

antonym useful.

uselessness *n* futility, hopelessness, idleness, impracticality, incompetence, ineffectiveness, ineffectuality, ineptitude, inutility.

antonyms effectiveness, usefulness.

usher *n* attendant, doorkeeper, escort, guide, huissier, usherette.

v conduct, direct, escort, guide, lead, pilot, shepherd, steer.

usher in announce, herald, inaugurate, initiate, introduce, launch, precede, ring in.

usual *adj* accepted, accustomed, common, constant, conventional, customary, everyday, expected, familiar, fixed, general, habitual, nomic, normal, ordinary, recognised, regular, routine, standard, stock, typical, unexceptional, wonted.

antonyms unheard-of, unusual.

usually *adv* as a rule, by and large, chiefly, commonly, customarily, generally, generally speaking, habitually, in the main, mainly, mostly, normally, on the whole, ordinarily, regularly, routinely, traditionally, typically.

antonym exceptionally.

usurer *n* extortionist, gombeen-man, loan-shark, money-lender, note-shaver, Shylock.

usurp *v* annex, appropriate, arrogate, assume, commandeer, seize, steal, take, take over, wrest.

usury *n* extortion, gombeen, interest, loan-sharking, money-lending, usance.

utensil *n* apparatus, contrivance, device, gadget, gismo, implement, instrument, tool.

utilise *v* adapt, appropriate, employ, exploit, make use of, put to use, resort to, take advantage of, turn to account, use.

utilitarian *adj* convenient, down-to-earth, effective, efficient, functional, lowly, practical, pragmatic, sensible, serviceable, unpretentious, useful.

antonyms decorative, impractical.

utilitarianism *n* eudaemonism.

utility *n* advantage, advantageousness, avail, benefit, convenience, efficacy, expedience, fitness, point, practicality, profit, satisfactoriness, service, serviceableness, use, usefulness, value.

antonym inutility.

utmost *adj* extreme, farthest, final, first, greatest, highest, last, maximum, outermost, paramount, remotest, supreme, ultimate, uttermost.

n best, hardest, maximum, most, uttermost.

Utopia *n* bliss, Eden, Elysium, Erewhon, Garden of Eden, heaven, heaven on earth, paradise, seventh heaven, Shangri-la.

Utopian *adj* airy, chimerical, dream, Elysian, fanciful, fantastic, ideal, idealistic, illusory, imaginary, impractical, perfect, romantic, unworkable, visionary, wishful.

utter[1] *adj* absolute, arrant, complete, consummate, dead, downright, entire, out-and-out, perfect, sheer, stark, thorough, thoroughgoing, total, unalleviated, unmitigated, unqualified.

utter[2] *v* articulate, declare, deliver, divulge, enounce, enunciate, express, proclaim, promulgate, pronounce, publish, reveal, say, sound, speak, state, tell, tongue, verbalise, vocalise, voice.

utterance *n* announcement, articulation, comment, declaration, delivery, ejaculation, expression, gift of tongues, glossolalia, illocution, opinion, pronouncement, remark, speaking with tongues, speech, statement, verbalisation, vocalisation, vociferation.

utterly *adv* absolutely, completely, dead, diametrically, entirely, extremely, fully, perfectly, thoroughly, totally, wholly.

U-turn *n* about-turn, backtrack, enantiodromia, reversal, tergiversation, uey, volte-face.

V

vacancy *n* accommodation, emptiness, gap, job, opening, opportunity, place, position, post, room, situation, space, vacuity, vacuousness, vacuum, void.

vacant *adj* absent, absent-minded, abstracted, available, blank, disengaged, dreaming, dreamy, empty, expressionless, free, idle, inane, inattentive, incurious, thoughtless, to let, unemployed, unengaged, unfilled, unoccupied, untenanted, unthinking, vacuous, void.

antonyms engaged, occupied.

vacate *v* abandon, depart, evacuate, leave, quit, withdraw.

vacillate *v* fluctuate, haver, hesitate, oscillate, shilly-shally, shuffle, sway, swither, temporise, tergiversate, waver.

vacillating *adj* hesitant, irresolute, oscillating, shilly-shallying, shuffling, swithering, temporising, uncertain, unresolved, wavering.

antonyms resolute, unhesitating.

vacillation *n* fluctuation, hesitancy, hesitation, inconstancy, indecision, indecisiveness, irresolution, shilly-shallying, temporisation, tergiversation, unsteadiness, wavering.

vacuity *n* apathy, blankness, emptiness, inanity, incognisance, incomprehension, incuriosity, nothingness, space, vacuousness, vacuum, void.

vacuous *adj* apathetic, blank, empty, idle, inane, incurious, stupid, uncomprehending, unfilled, unintelligent, vacant, void.

vacuum *n* chasm, emptiness, gap, nothingness, space, vacuity, void.

vagabond *n* beggar, bum, down-and-out, hobo, itinerant, land-louper, migrant, nomad, outcast, palliard, rascal, rover, runabout, runagate, tramp, vagrant, wanderer, wayfarer.

vagary *n* caprice, crotchet, fancy, fegary, humour, megrim, notion, prank, quirk, whim, whimsy.

vagrant *n* beggar, bum, gangrel, hobo, itinerant, land-louper, rolling stone, stroller, tramp, wanderer.

adj footloose, homeless, itinerant, nomadic, roaming, rootless, roving, shiftless, travelling, vagabond, wandering.

vague *adj* amorphous, blurred, dim, doubtful, evasive, fuzzy, generalised, hazy, ill-defined, imprecise, indefinite, indeterminate, indistinct, inexact, lax, loose, misty, nebulous, obscure, shadowy, uncertain, unclear, undefined, undetermined, unknown, unspecific, unspecified, woolly.

antonyms certain, clear, definite.

vaguely *adv* absent-mindedly, dimly, faintly, imprecisely, inexactly, obscurely, slightly, vacantly.

vagueness *n* ambiguity, amorphousness, dimness, faintness, fuzziness, haziness, imprecision, inexactitude, looseness, obscurity, uncertainty, woolliness.

antonyms clarity, precision.

vain *adj* abortive, affected, arrogant, baseless, bigheaded, conceited, egotistical, empty, fruitless, futile, groundless, hollow, idle, inflated, mindless, narcissistic, nugatory, ostentatious, overweening, peacockish, pointless, pretentious, proud, purposeless, self-important, self-satisfied, senseless, stuck-up, swaggering, swanky, swollen-headed, time-wasting, trifling, trivial, unavailing, unimportant, unproductive, unprofitable, unsubstantial, useless, vainglorious, vaporous, worthless.

antonyms modest, self-effacing.

valediction *n* adieu, farewell, godspeed, goodbye, leave-taking, send-off, vale.

antonyms greeting, welcome.

valet *n* body servant, gentleman's gentleman, man, man-servant, valet de chambre.

valetudinarian *adj* delicate, feeble, frail, hypochondriac, infirm, invalid, neurotic, sickly, weakly.

antonym stoical.

valiant *adj* bold, brave, courageous, dauntless, doughty, fearless, gallant, heroic, indomitable, intrepid, plucky, redoubtable, stalwart, staunch, stout, stout-hearted, valorous, worthy.

antonym cowardly.

valid *adj* approved, authentic, binding, bona fide, cogent, conclusive, convincing, efficacious, efficient, genuine, good, just, lawful, legal, legitimate, logical, official, potent, powerful, proper, rational, reliable, sound, substantial, telling, weighty, well-founded, well-grounded.

antonym invalid.

validate *v* attest, authenticate, authorise, certify, confirm, corroborate, endorse, legalise, ratify, substantiate, underwrite.

validity *n* authority, cogency, force, foundation, grounds, justifiability, lawfulness, legality, legitimacy, logic, point, power, soundness, strength, substance, weight.

antonym invalidity.

valley *n* clough, coomb, cwm, dale, dean, dell, den, depression, dingle, glen, graben, griff, gulch, hollow, hope, slade, strath, vale.

valorous *adj* bold, brave, courageous, dauntless, doughty, fearless, gallant, hardy, heroic, intrepid, lion-hearted, mettlesome, plucky, redoubtable, stalwart, valiant.

antonyms cowardly, weak.

valour *n* boldness, bravery, courage, derring-do, doughtiness, fearlessness, fortitude, gallantry, hardiness, heroism, intrepidity, lion-heartedness, mettle, spirit.

antonyms cowardice, weakness.

valuable *adj* advantageous, beneficial, blue-chip, cherished, costly, dear, esteemed, estimable, expensive, fruitful, handy, helpful, high-priced, important, invaluable, precious, prizable, prized, productive, profitable, serviceable, treasured, useful, valued, worthwhile, worthy.

antonyms useless, valueless.

valuation *n* appraisement, assessment, computation, estimate, evaluation, survey.

value *n* account, advantage, avail, benefit, cost, desirability, equivalent, good, help, importance, merit, price, profit, rate, significance, use, usefulness, utility, worth.

v account, appraise, appreciate, apprize, assess, cherish, compute, esteem, estimate, evaluate, hold dear, price, prize, rate, regard, respect, survey, treasure.

antonyms disregard, neglect, undervalue.

valued *adj* beloved, cherished, dear, esteemed, highly regarded, loved, prized, respected, treasured.

values *n* ethics, morals, principles, standards.

vamoose *v* absquatulate, clear off, decamp, disappear, do a bunk, make oneself scarce, quit, scarper, scram, skedaddle, vanish.

vanish *v* dematerialise, depart, die out, disappear, disperse, dissolve, evanesce, evaporate, exit, fade, fizzle out, melt, peter out.

antonyms appear, materialise.

vanity *n* affectation, airs, arrogance, bigheadedness, conceit, conceitedness, egotism, emptiness, frivolity, fruitlessness, fume, futility, hollowness, idleness, inanity, narcissism, ostentation, peacockery, pointlessness, pretension, pride, self-admiration, self-conceit, self-love, self-satisfaction, swollen-headedness, triviality, unreality, unsubstantiality, uselessness, vainglory, worthlessness.

antonyms modesty, worth.

vanquish *v* beat, confound, conquer, crush, defeat, humble, master, overcome, overpower, overwhelm, quell, reduce, repress, rout, subdue, subjugate, triumph over.

vapid *adj* banal, bland, bloodless, boring, colourless, dead, dull, flat, flavourless, insipid, jejune, lifeless, limp, stale, tame, tasteless, tedious, tiresome, trite, uninspiring, uninteresting, watery, weak, wishy-washy.

antonyms interesting, vigorous.

vaporous *adj* brumous, chimerical, fanciful, flimsy, foggy, fumous, fumy, gaseous, insubstantial, misty, steamy, vain.

antonym substantial.

vapour *n* breath, brume, damp, dampness, exhalation, fog, fumes, halitus, haze, miasm, miasma, mist, reek, roke, smoke, steam.

variable *adj* capricious, chameleonic, changeable, fickle, fitful, flexible, fluctuating, inconstant, mercurial, moonish, mutable, protean, shifting, temperamental, unpredictable, unstable, unsteady, vacillating, varying, versiform, wavering.

antonym invariable.

n factor, parameter.

variance *n* difference, disagreement, discord, discrepancy, disharmony, dissension, dissent, divergence, division, inconsistency, quarrelling, strife, variation.

antonyms agreement, harmony.

variant *adj* alternative, derived, deviant, different, divergent, exceptional, modified.

antonyms normal, standard, usual.

n alternative, development, deviant, modification, rogue, sport, variation.

variation *n* alteration, change, departure, deviation, difference, discrepancy, diversification, diversity, elaboration, inflection, innovation, modification, modulation, novelty, variety.

antonyms monotony, similitude, uniformity.

varied *adj* accidented, assorted, different, diverse, heterogeneous, manifold, miscellaneous, mixed, motley, multifarious, sundry, various.

antonyms similar, uniform.

variegated *adj* diversified, freaked, jaspé, many-coloured, motley, mottled, multicoloured, parti-coloured, pied, poikilitic, polychrome, streaked, varicoloured, veined, versicoloured.

antonyms monochrome, plain.

variety *n* array, assortment, brand, breed, category, change, class, collection, difference, discrepancy, diversification, diversity, intermixture, kind, make, manifoldness, many-sidedness, medley, miscellany, mixture, multifariousness, multiplicity, olio, olla-podrida, order, pot-pourri, range, sort, species, strain, type, variation.

antonyms monotony, similitude, uniformity.

various *adj* assorted, different, differing, disparate, distinct, divers, diverse, diversified, heterogeneous, many, many-sided, miscellaneous, multifarous, omnifarous, several, sundry, varied, variegated, varying.

varnish *n* coating, glaze, gloss, japan, lac, lacquer, polish, resin, shellac.

vary *v* alter, alternate, change, depart, differ, disagree, diverge, diversify, fluctuate, inflect, intermix, modify, modulate, permutate, reorder, transform.

vase *n* amphora, container, ewer, hydria, jar, jug, pitcher, urn, vessel.

vassal *n* bondman, bondservant, bondsman, galloglass, liege, liegeman, retainer, serf, slave, subject, thrall, villein.

vassalage *n* bondage, dependence, serfdom, servitude, slavery, subjection, subjugation, thraldom, villeinage.

vast *adj* astronomical, boundless, capacious, colossal, cyclopean, enormous, extensive, far-flung, fathomless, gigantic, great, huge, illimitable, immeasurable, immense, limitless, mammoth, massive, measureless, monstrous, monumental, never-ending, prodigious, stupendous, sweeping, tremendous, unboudned, unlimited, vasty, voluminous, wide.

vat *n* container, keeve, kier, tank, tub.

vault[1] *v* bound, clear, hurdle, jump, leap, leap-frog, spring.

vault[2] *n* arch, camera, cavern, cellar, concave, crypt, depository, mausoleum, repository, roof, span, strongroom, tomb, undercroft, wine-cellar.

vaunt *v* blazon, boast, brag, crow, exult in, flaunt, parade, show off, trumpet.

antonyms belittle, minimise.

veer *v* change, sheer, shift, swerve, tack, turn, wheel.

vegetables *n* greens, greenstuff, legumes.

vegetarian *adj* grass-eating, herbivorous, Pythagorean, vegan.

vegetate *v* degenerate, deteriorate, go to seed, idle, languish, moulder, rust, rusticate, stagnate.

vehemence *n* animation, ardour, eagerness, earnestness, emphasis, energy, enthusiasm, fervency, fervour, fire, force, forcefulness, heat, impetuosity, intensity, keenness, passion, urgency, verve, vigour, violence, warmth, zeal.

antonym indifference.

vehement *adj* animated, ardent, eager, earnest, emphatic, enthusiastic, fervent, fervid, fierce, forceful, forcible, heated, impassioned, impetuous, intense, passionate, powerful, strong, urgent, violent, zealous.

antonyms apathetic, indifferent.

vehicle *n* apparatus, channel, conveyance, means, mechanism, medium, organ.

veil *v* cloak, conceal, cover, dim, disguise, dissemble, dissimulate, hide, mantle, mask, obscure, screen, shade, shadow, shield.

antonyms expose, uncover.

n blind, cloak, cover, curtain, disguise, film, humeral, integument, mask, screen, shade, shroud, velum.

vein *n* blood vessel, course, current, dash, frame of mind, hint, humour, lode, mode, mood, note, seam, strain, stratum, streak, stripe, style, temper, tenor, thread, tone, trait.

veined *adj* freaked, jaspé, marbled, mottled, streaked, variegated.

velocity *n* celerity, fleetness, impetus, pace, quickness, rapidity, rate, speed, swiftness.

venal *adj* bent, bribable, buyable, corrupt, corruptible, grafting, mercenary, purchasable, simoniacal.

antonym incorruptible.

vendetta *n* bad blood, bitterness, blood-feud, enmity, feud, quarrel, rivalry.

veneer *n* appearance, coating, façade, front, gloss, guise, layer, mask, pretence, semblance, show, surface.

venerable *adj* aged, august, dignified, esteemed, grave, honoured, respected, revered, reverenced, reverend, sage, sedate, venerated, wise, worshipful.

venerate *v* adore, esteem, hallow, honour, respect, revere, reverence, worship.

antonyms anathematise, disregard, execrate.

veneration *n* adoration, awe, deference, devotion, dulia, esteem, hyperdulia, latria, respect, reverence, worship.

vengeance *n* avengement, lex talionis, reprisal, requital, retaliation, retribution, revanche, revenge, talion, tit for tat.

antonym forgiveness.

vengeful *adj* avenging, implacable, punitive, rancorous, relentless, retaliatory, retributive, revanchist, revengeful, spiteful, unforgiving, vindictive.

antonym forgiving.

venial *adj* excusable, forgivable, insignificant, minor, negligible, pardonable, slight, trifling, trivial.

antonyms mortal, unforgivable, unpardonable.

venom *n* acrimony, bane, bitterness, gall, grudge, hate, hatred, ill-will, malevolence, malice, maliciousness, malignity, poison, rancour, spite, spitefulness, spleen, toxin, venin, vindictiveness, virulence, virus, vitrio.

venomous *adj* baleful, baneful, envenomed, hostile, malicious, malign, malignant, mephitic, noxious, poison, poisonous, rancorous, savage, spiteful, toxic, vicious, vindictive, virulent, vitriolic.

vent *n* aperture, blowhole, duct, hole, opening, orifice, outlet, passage, spiracle, split.

v air, discharge, emit, express, let fly, release, unloose, utter, voice.

ventilate *v* air, broadcast, debate, discuss, examine, expound, express.

antonym suppress.

venture *v* advance, adventure, chance, dare, endanger, hazard, imperil, jeopardise, make bold, presume, put forward, risk, speculate, stake, suggest, take the liberty, volunteer, wager.

n adventure, chance, endeavour, enterprise, fling, gamble, hazard, operation, project, risk, speculation, undertaking.

venturesome *adj* adventurous, audacious, bold, courageous, daredevil, daring, dauntless, doughty, enterprising, fearless, intrepid, plucky, spirited.

antonyms pusillanimous, unenterprising.

veracious *adj* accurate, credible, dependable, exact, factual, faithful, frank, genuine, honest, reliable, straightforward, true, trustworthy, truthful, veridical.

antonym untruthful.

veracity *n* accuracy, candour, credibility, exactitude, frankness, honesty, integrity, precision, probity, rectitude, trustworthiness, truth, truthfulness, verity.

antonym untruthfulness.

verbal *adj* lexical, oral, spoken, unwritten, verbatim, word-of-mouth.

verbatim *adv* exactly, literally, precisely, to the letter, (verbatim et) literatim, word for word.

verbiage *n* circumlocution, periphrasis, perissology, pleonasm, prolixity, repetition, verbosity.

antonyms economy, succinctness.

verbose *adj* ambagious, circumlocutory, diffuse, garrulous, long-winded, loquacious, multiloquent, periphrastic, phrasy, pleonastic, prolix, windy, wordy.

antonyms economical, laconic, succinct.

verbosity *n* garrulity, logorrhoea, long-windedness, loquaciousness, loquacity, multiloquy, prolixity, verbiage, verboseness, windiness, wordiness.

antonyms economy, succinctness.

verdant *adj* fresh, graminaceous, gramineous, grassy, green, leafy, lush, virid, viridescent.

verdict *n* adjudication, assessment, conclusion, decision, finding, judgement, opinion, sentence.

verdure *n* foliage, grass, greenery, greenness, greenth, herbage, leafage, meadows, pasture, verdancy, vert, viridescence, viridity.

verge *n* border, boundary, brim, brink, edge, edging, extreme, limit, lip, margin, roadside, threshold.

verge on approach, border on, come close to, near.

verification *n* attestation, authentication, checking, confirmation, corroboration, proof, substantiation, validation.

verify *v* attest, authenticate, check, confirm, corroborate, prove, substantiate, support, testify, validate.

antonyms discredit, invalidate.

verisimilitude *n* authenticity, colour, credibility, likeliness, plausibility, realism, resemblance, ring of truth, semblance.

antonym implausibility.

verity *n* actuality, authenticity, factuality, soundness, truth, truthfulness, validity, veracity.

antonym untruth.

vernacular *adj* colloquial, common, endemic, indigenous, informal, local, mother, native, popular, vulgar.

n argot, cant, dialect, idiom, jargon, language, lingo, parlance, patois, speech, tongue.

versatile *adj* adaptable, adjustable, all-round, flexible, functional, general-purpose, handy, many-sided, multifaceted, multipurpose, protean, Renaissance, resourceful, variable.

antonym inflexible.

verse *n* canto, doggerel, elegaics, fit, iambics, jingle, poesy, poetastery, poetry, rhyme, stanza, stave, strophe, verse-making, verse-mongering, versicle, versification.

versed *adj* accomplished, acquainted, au fait, competent, conversant, experienced, familiar, knowledgeable, learned, practised, proficient, qualified, seasoned, skilled.

versifier *n* poet, poetaster, poetess, poeticule, rhymer, rhymester, rhymist, verse-maker, verse-monger, verser, verse-smith, versificator.

version *n* account, adaptation, design, form, interpretation, kind, model, paraphrase, portrayal, reading, rendering, rendition, style, translation, type, variant.

vertex *n* acme, apex, apogee, crown, culmination, extremity, height, peak, pinnacle, summit, top, zenith.

antonym nadir.

vertical *adj* erect, on end, perpendicular, upright, upstanding.

antonym horizontal.

vertigo *n* dizziness, giddiness, light-headedness, megrim.

verve *n* animation, brio, dash, élan, energy, enthusiasm, force, gusto, life, liveliness, pizzazz, punch, relish, sparkle, spirit, vigour, vim, vitality, vivacity, zeal, zip.

antonym apathy.

very *adv* absolutely, acutely, awfully, decidedly, deeply, dogged, dooms, eminently, exceeding(ly), excessively, extremely, fell, gey, greatly, highly, jolly, noticeably, particularly, passing, rattling, really, remarkably, superlatively, surpassingly, terribly, truly, uncommonly, unusually, wonderfully.

antonyms hardly, scarcely, slightly.

adj actual, appropriate, bare, exact, express, identical, mere, perfect, plain, precise, pure, real, same, selfsame, sheer, simple, unqualified, utter.

vessel *n* barque, boat, canister, container, craft, holder, jar, pot, receptacle, ship, utensil.

vestibule *n* anteroom, entrance, entrance-hall, entrance-way, foyer, hall, lobby, porch, portico.

vestige *n* evidence, glimmer, hint, indication, print, relic, remainder, remains, remnant, residue, scrap, sign, suspicion, token, trace, track, whiff.

vestigial *adj* functionless, imperfect, incomplete, reduced, rudimentary, surviving, undeveloped.

vet[1] *v* appraise, audit, check, examine, inspect, investigate, review, scan, scrutinise, survey.

vet[2] *n* dog-leech, farrier, hippiatrist, horse-doctor, horse-leech, veterinarian, veterinary, veterinary surgeon.

veteran *n* master, old hand, old soldier, old stager, old-timer, pastmaster, pro, trouper, war-horse.

antonyms novice, recruit.

adj adept, battle-scarred, experienced, expert, long-serving, masterly, old, practised, professional, proficient, seasoned.

antonyms inexperienced, raw.

veto *v* ban, blackball, disallow, forbid, interdict, kill, negative, prohibit, reject, rule out, turn down.

antonyms approve, sanction.

n ban, embargo, interdict, prohibition, rejection, thumbs down.

antonyms approval, assent.

vex *v* afflict, aggravate, agitate, annoy, bother, bug, chagrin, deave, displease, distress, disturb, exasperate, fret, gall, get (to), harass, hump, irritate, molest, needle, nettle, offend, peeve, perplex, pester, pique, plague, provoke, rile, spite, tease, torment, trouble, upset, worry.

antonym soothe.

vexation *n* aggravation, anger, annoyance, bore, bother, chagrin, difficulty, displeasure, dissatisfaction, exasperation, frustration, fury, headache, irritant, misfortune, nuisance, pique, problem, trouble, upset, worry.

vexatious *adj* afflicting, aggravating, annoying, bothersome, burdensome, disagreeable, disappointing, distressing, doggone, exasperating, fashious, harassing, infuriating, irksome, irritating, nagging, pesky, pestful, pestiferous, pestilent, plaguesome, plagu(e)y, provoking, teasing, tormenting, troublesome, trying, unpleasant, upsetting, worrisome, worrying.

antonyms pleasant, soothing.

vexed *adj* afflicted, aggravated, agitated, annoyed, bedevilled, bored, bothered, chagrined, confused, contested, controversial, deaved, displeased, disputed, distressed, disturbed, exasperated, harassed, irritated, miffed, moot, nettled, peeved, perplexed, provoked, put out, riled, ruffled, tormented, troubled, upset, worried.

viable *adj* achievable, applicable, feasible, operable, possible, practicable, usable, workable.

antonyms impossible, unworkable.

vibes *n* ambience, atmosphere, aura, emanation, emotions, feel, feelings, reaction, response, vibrations.

vibrant *adj* alive, animated, bright, colourful, dynamic, electric, electrifying, jazzy, oscillating, palpitating, peppy, pulsating, quivering, responsive, sensitive, sparkling, spirited, trembling, vivacious, vivid.

vibrate *v* dinnle, dirl, fluctuate, judder, oscillate, pendulate, pulsate, pulse, quiver, resonate, reverberate, shake, shimmy, shiver, shudder, sway, swing, throb, tremble, undulate.

vibration *n* diadrom, fremitus, frisson, judder, juddering, oscillation, pulsation, pulse, quiver, resonance, reverberation, shaking, shudder, throb, throbbing, trembling, tremor.

vicarious *adj* acting, commissioned, delegated, deputed, empathetic, indirect, second-hand, substituted, surrogate.

vice *n* bad habit, besetting sin, blemish, corruption, defect, degeneracy, depravity, evil, evil-doing, failing, fault, hamartia, immorality, imperfection, iniquity, profligacy, shortcoming, sin, venality, weakness, wickedness.

antonym virtue.

vicinity *n* area, circumjacency, district, environs, locality, neighbourhood, precincts, propinquity, proximity, purlieus, vicinage.

vicious *adj* abhorrent, atrocious, backbiting, bad, barbarous, bitchy, brutal, catty, corrupt, cruel, dangerous, debased, defamatory, depraved, diabolical, fiendish, foul, heinous, immoral, infamous, malicious, mean, monstrous, nasty, perverted, profligate, rancorous, savage, sinful, slanderous, spiteful, unprincipled, venomous, vile, vindictive, violent, virulent, vitriolic, wicked, worthless, wrong.

antonyms gentle, good, virtuous.

viciousness *n* badness, bitchiness, brutality, corruption, cruelty, depravity, ferocity, immorality, malice, profligacy, rancour, savagery, sinfulness, spite, spitefulness, venom, virulence, wickedness.

antonyms gentleness, goodness, virtue.

vicissitude *n* alteration, alternation, change, deviation, divergence, fluctuation, mutation, revolution, shift, turn, twist, variation.

victim *n* casualty, dupe, fall guy, fatality, gull, innocent, mark, martyr, patsy, sacrifice, scapegoat, sitting target, sucker, sufferer.

victimise *v* bully, cheat, deceive, defraud, discriminate against, dupe, exploit, fool, gull, hoodwink, oppress, persecute, pick on, prey on, swindle, use.

victor *n* champ, champion, conqueror, first, prize-winner, subjugator, top dog, vanquisher, victor ludorum, victrix, winner.

antonyms loser, vanquished.

victorious *adj* champion, conquering, first, prize-winning, successful, top, triumphant, unbeaten, winning.

antonyms losing, unsuccessful.

victory *n* conquest, laurels, mastery, palm, prize, subjugation, success, superiority, triumph, vanquishment, win.

antonyms defeat, loss.

victuals *n* aliment, bread, comestibles, eatables, eats, edibles, food, grub, meat, nosh, provisions, rations, stores, supplies, sustenance, viands, vittles.

vie *v* compete, contend, contest, corrival, fight, rival, strive, struggle.

view *n* aspect, attitude, belief, contemplation, conviction, display, estimation, examination, feeling, glimpse, impression, inspection, judgement, landscape, look, notion, opinion, outlook, panorama, perception, perspective, picture, prospect, scan, scene, scrutiny, sentiment, sight, spectacle, survey, viewing, vision, vista.

v behold, consider, contemplate, deem, examine, explore, eye, inspect, judge, observe, perceive, read, regard, scan, speculate, survey, watch, witness.

viewer *n* looker-in, observer, onlooker, spectator, watcher.

viewpoint *n* angle, Anschauung, attitude, feeling, opinion, perspective, position, slant, stance, standpoint.

vigil *n* lookout, pernoctation, sleeplessness, stake-out, wake, wakefulness, watch.

vigilance *n* alertness, attentiveness, carefulness, caution, circumspection, guardedness, observation, wakefulness, watchfulness.

vigilant *adj* alert, Argus-eyed, attentive, careful, cautious, circumspect, guarded, on one's guard, on one's toes, on the alert, on the lookout, on the qui vive, sleepless, unsleeping, wakeful, watchful, wide-awake.

antonyms careless, forgetful, lax, negligent.

vigorous *adj* active, brisk, dynamic, effective, efficient, energetic, enterprising, flourishing, forceful, forcible, full-blooded, hale, hardy, healthy, hearty, intense, lively, lusty, mettlesome, powerful, red-blooded, robust, sound, spanking, spirited, stout, strenuous, strong, virile, vital, zippy.

antonyms feeble, lethargic, weak.

vigorously *adv* briskly, eagerly, energetically, forcefully, hard, heartily, lustily, powerfully, strenuously, strongly.

antonyms feebly, weakly.

vigour *n* activity, animation, dash, dynamism, energy, force, forcefulness, gusto, health, liveliness, might, oomph, pep, potency, power, punch, robustness, snap, soundness, spirit, stamina, strength, verve, vim, virility, vitality, zip.

antonyms impotence, sluggishness, weakness.

vile *adj* abandoned, abject, appalling, bad, base, coarse, contemptible, corrupt, debased, degenerate, degrading, depraved, despicable, disgraceful, disgusting, earthly, evil, foul, horrid, humiliating, ignoble, impure, loathsome, low, mean, miserable, nasty, nauseating, nefarious, noxious, offensive, perverted, repellent, repugnant, repulsive, revolting, scabbed, scabby, scandalous, scurvy, shocking, sickening, sinful, ugly, vicious, vulgar, wicked, worthless, wretched.

vileness *n* baseness, coarseness, corruption, degeneracy, depravity, dreadfulness, enormity, evil, foulness, meanness, noxiousness, offensiveness, outrage, profanity, ugliness, wickedness.

vilification *n* abuse, aspersion, calumniation, calumny, contumely, criticism, defamation, denigration, disparagement, invective, mud-slinging, revilement, scurrility, vituperation.

vilify *v* abuse, asperse, bad-mouth, berate, calumniate, criticise, debase, decry, defame, denigrate, denounce, disparage, malign, revile, slander, smear, stigmatise, traduce, vilipend, vituperate.

antonyms adore, compliment, eulogise, glorify.

village *n* clachan, community, dorp, hamlet, kampong, kraal, pueblo, settlement, township.

villain *n* anti-hero, baddy, blackguard, bravo, caitiff, criminal, devil, evil-doer, heavy, knave, libertine, malefactor, miscreant, profligate, rapscallion, rascal, reprobate, rogue, scoundrel, wretch.

antonyms angel, goody, hero, heroine.

villainous *adj* atrocious, bad, base, blackguardly, criminal, cruel, debased, degenerate, depraved, detestable, diabolical, disgraceful, evil, fiendish, hateful, heinous, ignoble, infamous, inhuman, malevolent, mean, nefarious, opprobrious, outrageous, ruffianly, scoundrelly, sinful, terrible, thievish, vicious, vile, wicked.

antonyms angelic, good, heroic.

villainy *n* atrocity, badness, baseness, crime, criminality, delinquency, depravity, devilry, iniquity, knavery, rascality, roguery, sin, turpitude, vice, viciousness, wickedness.

vindicate *v* absolve, acquit, advocate, assert, clear, defend, establish, exculpate, excuse, exonerate, justify, maintain, rehabilitate, support, uphold, verify.

antonyms accuse, convict.

vindication *n* apology, assertion, defence, exculpation, excuse, exoneration, extenuation, justification, maintenance, plea, rehabilitation, substantiation, support, verification.

antonyms accusation, conviction.

vindictive *adj* implacable, malevolent, malicious, malignant, merciless, punitive, rancorous, relentless, resentful, retributive, revengeful, spiteful, unforgiving, unrelenting, vengeful, venomous.

antonyms charitable, forgiving, merciful.

vintage *n* collection, crop, epoch, era, generation, harvest, origin, period, year.

adj best, choice, classic, fine, mature, old, prime, quintessential, rare, ripe, select, superior, venerable, veteran.

violate *v* abuse, assault, befoul, break, contravene, debauch, defile, desecrate, dishonour, disobey, disregard, flout, infract, infringe, invade, outrage, pollute, profane, rape, ravish, transgress.

antonyms obey, observe, uphold.

violation *n* abuse, breach, contravention, defilement, desecration, disruption, encroachment, infraction, infringement, offence, profanation, rapine, sacrilege, spoliation, transgression, trespass.

antonyms obedience, observance.

violence *n* abandon, acuteness, bestiality, bloodshed, bloodthirstiness, boisterousness, brutality, conflict, cruelty, destructiveness, ferocity, fervour, fierceness, fighting, force, frenzy, fury, harshness, hostilities, intensity, murderousness, passion, power, roughness, savagery, severity, sharpness, storminess, terrorism, thuggery, tumult, turbulence, vehemence, wildness.

antonyms passivity, peacefulness.

violent *adj* acute, agonising, berserk, biting, bloodthirsty, blustery, boisterous, brutal, cruel, destructive, devastating, excruciating, extreme, fiery, forceful, forcible, furious, harsh, headstrong, homicidal, hot-headed, impetuous, intemperate, intense, maddened, maniacal, murderous, outrageous, painful, passionate, peracute, powerful, raging, riotous, rough, ruinous, savage, severe, sharp, strong, tempestuous, tumultuous, turbulent, uncontrollable, ungovernable, unrestrained, vehement, vicious, wild.

antonyms calm, gentle, moderate, passive, peaceful.

VIP *n* big cheese, big name, big noise, big shot, bigwig, celebrity, dignitary, headliner, heavyweight, lion, luminary, notable, personage, somebody, star.

antonyms nobody, nonentity.

virago *n* battle-axe, dragon, fury, gorgon, harridan, hell-cat, randy, scold, shrew, tartar, termagant, vixen, Xanthippe.

virgin *n* bachelor, celibate, damsel, girl, maid, maiden, spinster, vestal, virgo intacta.

adj chaste, fresh, immaculate, intact, maidenly, modest, new, pristine, pure, snowy, spotless, stainless, uncorrupted, undefiled, unsullied, untouched, unused, vestal, virginal.

virginal *adj* celibate, chaste, fresh, immaculate, maidenly, pristine, pure, snowy, spotless, stainless, uncorrupted, undefiled, undisturbed, untouched, vestal, virgin, white.

virginity *n* chasteness, chastity, maidenhead, maidenhood, purity, virtue.

virile *adj* forceful, husky, lusty, macho, male, man-like, manly, masculine, potent, red-blooded, robust, rugged, strong, vigorous.

antonyms effeminate, impotent, weak.

virility *n* huskiness, machismo, manhood, manliness, masculinity, potency, ruggedness, vigour.

antonyms effeminacy, impotence, weakness.

virtual *adj* effective, essential, implicit, implied, indirect, potential, practical, tacit.

antonym actual.

virtually *adv* almost, as good as, effectively, effectually, in effect, in essence, nearly, practically, to all intents and purposes.

virtue *n* advantage, asset, attribute, chastity, credit, excellence, goodness, high-mindedness, honour, incorruptibility, innocence, integrity, justice, merit, morality, plus, probity, purity, quality, rectitude, redeeming feature, righteousness, strength, uprightness, virginity, worth, worthiness.

antonym vice.

virtuosity *n* bravura, brilliance, éclat, expertise, finesse, finish, flair, mastery, panache, polish, skill, wizardry.

virtuoso *n* ace, artist, crackerjack, dabster, genius, maestro, magician, master, prodigy, whiz, wizard.

adj bravura, brilliant, crackerjack, dazzling, expert, masterly, wizard.

virtuous *adj* blameless, celibate, chaste, clean-living, continent, ethical, excellent, exemplary, good, high-principled, honest, honourable, incorruptible, innocent, irreproachable, moral, praiseworthy, pure, righteous, spotless, squeaky-clean, unimpeachable, upright, virginal, worthy.

antonyms bad, dishonest, immoral, vicious, wicked.

virulence *n* acrimony, antagonism, bitterness, deadliness, harmfulness, hatred, hostility, hurtfulness, infectiousness, malevolence, malice, malignancy, poison, rancour, resentment, spite, spleen, toxicity, venom, viciousness, vindictiveness, virulency, vitriol.

virulent *adj* acrimonious, baneful, bitter, deadly, envenomed, hostile, infective, injurious, lethal, malevolent, malicious, malignant, noxious, pernicious, poisonous, rancorous, resentful, septic, spiteful, splenetic, toxic, venomous, vicious, vindictive, vitriolic.

viscera *n* bowels, chitterlings, entrails, gralloch, harigal(d)s, ha(r)slet, innards, insides, intestines, vitals.

viscous *adj* adhesive, clammy, gelatinous, gluey, glutinous, gooey, gummy, mucilaginous, mucous, sticky, syrupy, tacky, tenacious, thick, treacly, viscid.

antonyms runny, thin, watery.

visible *adj* apparent, aspectable, clear, conspicuous, detectable, discernible, discoverable, distinguishable, evident, manifest, noticeable, observable, obvious, open, palpable, patent, perceivable, perceptible, plain, unconcealed, undisguised, unmistakable.

antonym invisible.

vision *n* aisling, apparition, chimera, concept, conception, construct, daydream, delusion, discernment, dream, eyes, eyesight, fantasy, far-sightedness, foresight, ghost, hallucination, idea, ideal, illusion, image, imagination, insight, intuition, mirage, penetration, perception, phantasm, phantasma, phantom, picture, prescience, revelation, seeing, sight, spectacle, spectre, view, wraith.

visionary *adj* chimerical, delusory, dreaming, dreamy, fanciful, fantastic, ideal, idealised, idealistic, illusory, imaginary, impractical, moonshiny, prophetic, quixotic, romantic, speculative, starry-eyed, unreal, unrealistic, unworkable, utopian.

n daydreamer, Don Quixote, dreamer, enthusiast, fantasist, idealist, mystic, prophet, rainbow-chaser, romantic, seer, theorist, utopian, zealot.

antonym pragmatist.

visit *v* afflict, assail, attack, befall, call in, call on, drop in on, haunt, inspect, look in, look up, pop in, punish, see, smite, stay at, stay with, stop by, take in, trouble.

n call, excursion, sojourn, stay, stop.

visitation *n* appearance, bane, blight, calamity, cataclysm, catastrophe, disaster, examination, infliction, inspection, manifestation, nemesis, ordeal, punishment, retribution, scourge, trial, visit.

visitor *n* caller, company, emmet, grockle, guest, holidaymaker, tourist, visitant.

vista *n* enfilade, panorama, perspective, prospect, view.

visual *adj* discernible, observable, ocular, optic, optical, perceptible, specular, visible.

visualise *v* conceive, envisage, ideate, imagine, picture.

vital *adj* alive, animate, animated, animating, basic, cardinal, critical, crucial, decisive, dynamic, energetic, essential, forceful, fundamental, generative, imperative, important, indispensable, invigorating, key, life-giving, life-or-death, live, lively, living, necessary, quickening, requisite, significant, spirited, urgent, vibrant, vigorous, vivacious, zestful.

antonyms inessential, peripheral, unimportant.

vitality *n* animation, energy, exuberance, foison, go, life, liveliness, lustiness, oomph, pep, robustness, sparkle, stamina, strength, vigour, vim, vivaciousness, vivacity.

vitiate *v* blemish, blight, contaminate, corrupt, debase, defile, deprave, deteriorate, devalue, harm, impair, injure, invalidate, mar, nullify, pervert, pollute, ruin, spoil, sully, taint, undermine.

antonym purify.

vitriolic *adj* acerbic, acid, bitchy, biting, bitter, caustic, destructive, envenomed, malicious, sardonic, scathing, venomous, vicious, virulent, withering.

vituperate *v* abuse, berate, blame, castigate, censure, denounce, rate, reproach, revile, slag, slam, slang, slate, upbraid, vilify.

antonyms applaud, eulogise, extol, praise.

vituperation *n* abuse, blame, castigation, censure, contumely, diatribe, fault-finding, flak, invective, objurgation, obloquy, phillipic, rebuke, reprimand, reproach, revilement, scurrility, stick, vilification.

antonyms acclaim, eulogy, praise.

vituperative *adj* abusive, belittling, calumniatory, censorious, defamatory, denunciatory, derogatory, fulminatory, harsh, insulting, malign, objurgatory, opprobrious, sardonic, scornful, scurrilous, withering.

antonym laudatory.

vivacious *adj* animated, bubbling, bubbly, cheerful, chipper, ebullient, effervescent, frisky, frolicsome, gay, high-spirited, jolly, light-hearted, lively, merry, scintillating, sparkling, spirited, sportive, sprightly, vital.

antonym languid.

vivacity *n* animation, brio, bubbliness, ebullience, effervescence, energy, friskiness, gaiety, high spirits, jollity, life, liveliness, pep, quickness, sparkle, spirit, sprightliness.

antonym languor.

vivid *adj* active, animated, bright, brilliant, clear, colourful, distinct, dramatic, dynamic, eidetic, energetic, expressive, flamboyant, glowing, graphic, highly-coloured, intense, lifelike, lively, memorable, powerful, quick, realistic, rich, sharp, spirited, stirring, striking, strong, telling, vibrant, vigorous.

antonyms dull, lifeless.

vividness *n* brightness, brilliancy, clarity, distinctness, glow, immediacy, intensity, life, liveliness, lucidity, radiance, realism, refulgence, resplendence, sharpness, sprightliness, strength.

antonyms dullness, lifelessness.

vixen *n* beldam, bitch, fury, harpy, harridan, hell-cat, scold, shrew, spitfire, termagant, virago, Xanthippe.

vocabulary *n* dictionary, glossary, idiom, idioticon, language, lexicon, lexis, nomenclature, thesaurus, word-book, words.

vocal *adj* articulate, clamorous, eloquent, expressive, forthright, frank, free-spoken, noisy, oral, outspoken, plain-spoken, said, shrill, spoken, strident, uttered, vociferous, voiced.

antonyms inarticulate, quiet.

vocation *n* bag, business, calling, career, employment, job, métier, mission, niche, office, post, profession, pursuit, role, trade, work.

vociferous *adj* clamant, clamorous, loud, loud-mouthed, noisy, obstreperous, ranting, shouting, shrill, stentorian, strident, thundering, uproarious, vehement, vocal.

antonyms quiet, silent.

vogue *n* acceptance, craze, currency, custom, day, dernier cri, fashion, fashionableness, favour, haut ton, last word, mode, popularity, prevalence, style, the latest, the rage, the thing, trend, usage, use.

adj current, fashionable, in, modish, now, popular, prevalent, stylish, trendy, up-to-the-minute, voguish, with it.

voice *n* agency, articulation, decision, expression, inflection, instrument, intonation, language, medium, mouthpiece, organ, part, say, sound, speech, spokesman, spokesperson, spokeswoman, tone, utterance, vehicle, view, vote, will, wish, words.

v air, articulate, assert, bruit, convey, declare, disclose, divulge, enunciate, express, say, speak of, utter, ventilate.

void *adj* bare, blank, cancelled, clear, dead, drained, emptied, empty, free, inane, ineffective, ineffectual, inoperative, invalid, nugatory, null, tenantless, unenforceable, unfilled, unoccupied, useless, vacant, vain, worthless.

antonyms full, valid.

n blank, blankness, cavity, chasm, emptiness, gap, hiatus, hollow, lack, opening, space, vacuity, vacuum, want.

v abnegate, annul, cancel, defecate, discharge, drain, eject, elimate, emit, empty, evacuate, invalidate, nullify, rescind.

antonyms fill, validate.

volatile *adj* airy, changeable, erratic, explosive, fickle, flighty, gay, giddy, hot-headed, hot-tempered, inconstant, lively, mercurial, sprightly, temperamental, unsettled, unstable, unsteady, variable, volcanic.

antonyms constant, steady.

volition *n* choice, choosing, determination, discretion, election, option, preference, purpose, resolution, taste, velleity, will.

volley *n* barrage, blast, bombardment, burst, cannonade, discharge, enfilade, explosion, fusillade, hail, salvo, shower.

voluble *adj* articulate, fluent, forthcoming, garrulous, glib, loquacious, talkative.

antonym pauciloquent.

volume *n* aggregate, amount, amplitude, bigness, body, book, bulk, capacity, compass, dimensions, fascic(u)le, heft, mass, part, publication, quantity, tome, total, treatise.

voluminous *adj* abounding, ample, big, billowing, bulky, capacious, cavernous, commodious, copious, full, large, massive, prolific, roomy, vast.

antonyms scanty, slight.

voluntarily *adv* by choice, consciously, deliberately, freely, intentionally, of one's own accord, of one's own free will, on one's own initiative, purposely, spontaneously, willingly.

antonyms involuntarily, unwillingly.

voluntary *adj* conscious, deliberate, discretional, free, gratuitous, honorary, intended, intentional, optional, purposeful, purposive, spontaneous, unconstrained, unforced, unpaid, volunteer, wilful, willing.

antonyms compulsory, forced, involuntary, unwilling.

volunteer *v* advance, communicate, extend, offer, present, proffer, propose, put forward, step forward, suggest, tender.

voluptuary *n* bon vivant, debauchee, epicurean, hedonist, libertine, playboy, pleasure-seeker, profligate, sensualist, sybarite.

antonym ascetic.

voluptuous *adj* ample, buxom, curvaceous, effeminate, enticing, epicurean, erotic, goluptious, hedonistic, licentious, luscious, luxurious, pleasure-loving, provocative, seductive, self-indulgent, sensual, shapely, sybaritic.

antonym ascetic.

voluptuousness *n* buxomness, carnality, curvaceousness, licentiousness, lusciousness, opulence, seductiveness, sensuality, shapeliness.

antonym asceticism.

vomit *v* barf, boak, boke, bring up, cat, chunder, disgorge, egurgitate, eject, emit, heave, posset, puke, regurgitate, retch, sick up, spew out, spew up, throw up.

vomiting *n* chundering, egurgitation, ejection, emesis, emission, puking, regurgitation, retching, sickness, spewing.

voracious *adj* acquisitive, avid, devouring, edacious, gluttonous, greedy, hungry, insatiable, omnivorous, pantophagous, prodigious, rapacious, ravening, ravenous, uncontrolled, unquenchable.

voracity *n* acquisitiveness, avidity, eagerness, edacity, greed, hunger, pantophagy, rapacity, ravenousness.

vortex *n* eddy, maelstrom, whirl, whirlpool, whirlwind.

votary *n* addict, adherent, aficionado, believer, devotee, disciple, follower, monk.

vote *n* ballot, election, franchise, plebiscite, poll, referendum, show of hands, suffrage.

v ballot, choose, declare, elect, judge, opt, plump for, pronounce, propose, recommend, return, suggest.

voucher *n* certificate, check, coupon, ticket, token, warrant.

vouch for affirm, assert, asseverate, attest to, avouch, back, certify, confirm, endorse, guarantee, support, swear to, uphold.

vouchsafe *v* accord, bestow, cede, confer, deign, grant, impart, yield.

vow *v* affirm, avouch, bename, consecrate, dedicate, devote, maintain, pledge, profess, promise, swear.

n avouchment, oath, pledge, promise, troth.

voyage *n* crossing, cruise, expedition, journey, passage, peregrination, travels, trip.

vulgar *adj* banausic, blue, boorish, cheap and nasty, coarse, common, crude, dirty, flashy, gaudy, general, gross, ill-bred, impolite, improper, indecent, indecorous, indelicate, low, low-life, low-lived, low-minded, low-thoughted, naff, nasty, native, naughty, ordinary, pandemian, plebby, plebeian, ribald, risqué, rude, suggestive, tacky, tasteless, tawdry, uncouth, unmannerly, unrefined, vernacular.

antonyms correct, decent, elegant, noble, polite, refined.

vulgarian *n* arriviste, barbarian, boor, nouveau riche, parvenu, philistine, upstart.

vulgarity *n* coarseness, crudeness, crudity, dirtiness, gaudiness, grossness, indecency, indecorum, indelicacy, ribaldry, rudeness, suggestiveness, tastelessness, tawdriness.

antonyms decency, politeness.

W

wacky *adj* crazy, daft, eccentric, erratic, goofy, irrational, loony, loopy, nutty, odd, screwy, silly, unpredictable, wild, zany.

antonym sensible.

wad *n* ball, block, bundle, chunk, hump, hunk, mass, pledget, plug, roll.

wadding *n* cotton-wool, filler, lining, packing, padding, stuffing.

waddle *v* rock, shuffle, sway, toddle, totter, wiggle, wobble.

waffle *v* blather, fudge, jabber, prate, prattle, prevaricate, rabbit on, spout, witter on.

n blather, gobbledegook, guff, jabber, nonsense, padding, prating, prattle, prolixity, verbiage, verbosity, wordiness.

waft *v* bear, carry, convey, drift, float, ride, transmit, transport, whiffle, winnow.

n breath, breeze, current, draught, puff, scent, whiff.

wag[1] *v* bob, bobble, flutter, jiggle, nod, oscillate, pendulate, quiver, rock, shake, stir, vibrate, waggle, wave, wiggle.

n bob, bobble, flutter, jiggle, nod, oscillation, quiver, shake, toss, vibration, waggle, wave, wiggle.

wag[2] *n* banterer, card, clown, comedian, comic, droll, fool, humorist, jester, joker, wit.

wage *n* allowance, compensation, earnings, emolument, fee, guerdon, hire, pay, payment, penny-fee, recompense, remuneration, reward, salary, screw, stipend, wage-packet, wages.

v carry on, conduct, engage in, practise, prosecute, pursue, undertake.

wager *n* bet, flutter, gage, gamble, hazard, pledge, punt, speculation, stake, venture.

v bet, chance, gamble, hazard, lay, lay odds, pledge, punt, risk, speculate, stake, venture.

waggish *adj* amusing, arch, bantering, comical, droll, espiègle, facetious, frolicsome, funny, humorous, impish, jesting, jocose, jocular, merry, mischievous, playful, puckish, risible, roguish, sportive, witty.

antonyms grave, serious, staid.

waggle *v* bobble, flutter, jiggle, oscillate, shake, wag, wave, wiggle, wobble.

n bobble, flutter, jiggle, oscillation, shake, wag, wave, wiggle, wobble.

wagon *n* buggy, carriage, cart, dray, float, train, truck, tumbrel, van.

waif *n* foundling, orphan, stray, wastrel.

wail *v* bemoan, bewail, complain, cry, deplore, grieve, howl, keen, lament, mewl, moan, ululate, weep, yammer, yowl.

n caterwaul, complaint, cry, grief, howl, keen, lament, lamentation, moan, ululation, weeping, yowl.

wait *v* abide, dally, delay, hang fire, hesitate, hold back, hover, linger, loiter, mark time, pause, remain, rest, stay, tarry.

antonyms depart, go, leave.

n delay, halt, hesitation, hiatus, hold-up, interval, pause, rest, stay.

waive *v* abandon, defer, disclaim, forgo, postpone, relinquish, remit, renounce, resign, surrender.

antonyms claim, maintain.

waiver *n* abandonment, abdication, deferral, disclaimer, postponement, relinquishment, remission, renunciation, resignation, surrender.

wake[1] *v* activate, animate, arise, arouse, awake, awaken, bestir, enliven, excite, fire, galvanise, get up, kindle, provoke, quicken, rise, rouse, stimulate, stir, unbed.

antonyms relax, sleep.

n death-watch, funeral, pernoctation, vigil, watch.

wake[2] *n* aftermath, backwash, path, rear, track, trail, train, wash, waves.

wakeful *adj* alert, alive, attentive, heedful, insomniac, observant, restless, sleepless, unblinking, unsleeping, vigilant, wary, watchful.

antonyms inattentive, sleepy, unwary.

waken *v* activate, animate, arouse, awake, awaken, enliven, fire, galvanise, get up, ignite, kindle, quicken, rouse, stimulate, stir, whet.

walk *v* accompany, advance, amble, convoy, escort, go by Shanks's pony, hike, hoof it, march, move, pace, pedestrianise, perambulate, plod, promenade, saunter, step, stride, stroll, take, traipse, tramp, tread, trek, trog, trudge.

n aisle, alley, ambulatory, avenue, carriage, constitutional, esplanade, footpath, frescade, gait, hike, lane, mall, march, pace, path, pathway, pavement, pawn, perambulation, promenade, ramble, saunter, sidewalk, step, stride, stroll, trail, traipse, tramp, trek, trudge, turn.

walk of life activity, area, arena, calling, career, course, field, line, métier, profession, pursuit, sphere, trade, vocation.

walker *n* ambulator, backpacker, footslogger, hiker, pedestrian, rambler, wayfarer.

walk-out *n* industrial action, protest, rebellion, revolt, stoppage, strike.

walk-over *n* child's play, cinch, doddle, picnic, piece of cake, pushover, snap, walk-away.

walkway *n* ambulatory, esplanade, footpath, lane, path, pathway, pavement, promenade, sidewalk.

wall *n* bailey, barricade, barrier, block, breastwork, bulk-head, bulwark, dike, divider, dyke, embankment, enclosure, fence, fortification, hedge, impediment, membrane, obstacle, obstruction, palisade, panel, parapet, partition, rampart, screen, septum, stockade.

wallet *n* bill-fold, case, holder, note-case, pochette, pocket-book, pouch, purse.

wallop *v* batter, beat, belt, best, buffet, clobber, crush, defeat, drub, hammer, hit, lambaste, lick, paste, pound, pummel, punch, rout, slug, smack, strike, swat, swipe, thrash, thump, thwack, trounce, vanquish, whack, worst.

n bash, belt, blow, haymaker, hit, kick, punch, slug, smack, swat, swipe, thump, thwack, whack.

wallow *v* bask, delight, enjoy, flounder, glory, indulge, lie, lurch, luxuriate, relish, revel, roll, splash, stagger, stumble, tumble, wade, welter.

wan *adj* anaemic, ashen, bleak, bloodless, cadaverous, colourless, dim, discoloured, faint, feeble, ghastly, livid, lurid, mournful, pale, pallid, pasty, sickly, waxen, weak, weary, whey-faced, white.

wand *n* baton, mace, rod, sceptre, sprig, staff, stick, twig, verge, withe, withy.

wander *v* aberrate, babble, cruise, depart, deviate, digress, divagate, diverge, drift, err, hump the bluey, lapse, meander, mill around, peregrinate, ramble, range, rave, roam, rove, saunter, squander, straggle, stravaig, stray, stroll, swerve, traipse, veer, wilder.

n cruise, excursion, meander, peregrination, ramble, saunter, stroll, traipse.

wanderer *n* drifter, gypsy, itinerant, nomad, rambler, ranger, rolling stone, rover, strag, straggler, stray, stroller, traveller, vagabond, vagrant, voyager.

wandering *n* aberration, deviation, digression, divagation, divergence, drift(ing), evagation, journey(ing), meander(ing), odyssey, peregrination, travels, walkabout.

adj aberrant, circumforaneous, drifting, homeless, itinerant, migratory, nomadic, peregrinatory, peripatetic, rambling, rootless, roving, strolling, travelling, vagabond, vagrant, voyaging, wayfaring.

wane *v* abate, atrophy, contract, decline, decrease, dim, diminish, droop, drop, dwindle, ebb, fade, fail, lessen, shrink, sink, subside, taper off, weaken, wither.

antonyms increase, wax.

n abatement, atrophy, contraction, decay, decline, decrease, diminution, drop, dwindling, ebb, fading, failure, fall, lessening, sinking, subsidence, tapering off, weakening.

antonym increase.

wangle *v* arrange, contrive, engineer, fiddle, finagle, fix, flam, manage, manipulate, manoeuvre, pull off, scheme, work, work the oracle.

want *v* call for, covet, crave, demand, desiderate, desire, fancy, hanker after, hunger for, lack, long for, miss, need, pine for, require, thirst for, wish, yearn for, yen.

n absence, appetite, besoin, craving, dearth, default, deficiency, demand, desideratum, desire, destitution, famine, fancy, hankering, hunger, indigence, insufficiency, lack, longing, necessity, need, neediness, paucity, pauperism, penury, poverty, privation, requirement, scantiness, scarcity, shortage, thirst, wish, yearning, yen.

antonyms abundance, plenty, riches.

wanting *adj* absent, defective, deficient, disappointing, faulty, imperfect, inadequate, incomplete, inferior, insufficient, lacking, less, missing, patchy, poor, short, shy, sketchy, substandard, unsatisfactory, unsound.

antonyms adequate, sufficient.

wanton *adj* abandoned, arbitrary, careless, coltish, cruel, dissipated, dissolute, evil, extravagant, fast, gratuitous, groundless, heedless, immoderate, immoral, intemperate, lavish, lecherous, lewd, libertine, libidinous, licentious, loose, lubricious, lustful, malevolent, malicious, motiveless, needless, outrageous, promiscuous, rakish, rash, reckless, senseless, shameless, spiteful, uncalled-for, unchaste, unjustifiable, unjustified, unprovoked, unrestrained, vicious, wicked, wild, wilful.

n Casanova, debauchee, Don Juan, gammerstang, giglet, giglot, gillet, gillflirt, harlot, jillet, jillflirt, lecher, libertine, mort, profligate, prostitute, rake, roué, slut, strumpet, tart, trollop, voluptuary, whore.

war *n* battle, bloodshed, combat, conflict, contention, contest, enmity, fighting, hostilities, hostility, jihad, strife, struggle, ultima ratio regum, warfare.

antonym peace.

v battle, clash, combat, contend, contest, fight, skirmish, strive, struggle, take up arms, wage war.

war cry battle cry, rallying-cry, slogan, war-song, war-whoop, watchword.

warble *v* chirp, chirrup, quaver, sing, trill, twitter, yodel.

n call, chirp, chirrup, cry, quaver, song, trill, twitter.

ward *n* apartment, area, care, charge, cubicle, custody, dependant, district, division, guardianship, keeping, minor, precinct, protection, protégé, pupil, quarter, room, safe-keeping, vigil, watch, zone.

ward off avert, avoid, beat off, block, deflect, disperse, evade, fend off, forestall, parry, repel, repulse, stave off, thwart, turn aside, turn away.

warden *n* administrator, captain, caretaker, castellan, châtelaine, concierge, curator, custodian, guardian, janitor, keeper, ranger, steward, superintendent, warder, watchman.

warder *n* custodian, gaoler, guard, jailer, keeper, prison officer, screw, turnkey, wardress.

wardrobe *n* apparel, attire, closet, clothes, cupboard, garderobe, outfit.

warehouse *n* depository, depot, entrepot, freightshed, godown, hong, repository, stockroom, store, storehouse.

wares *n* commodities, goods, lines, manufactures, merchandise, produce, products, stock, stuff, vendibles.

warfare *n* arms, battle, blows, combat, conflict, contention, contest, discord, fighting, hostilities, passage of arms, strife, struggle, war.

antonyms harmony, peace.

warily *adv* apprehensively, cagily, carefully, cautiously, charily, circumspectly, distrustfully, gingerly, guardedly, hesitantly, leerily, suspiciously, uneasily, vigilantly, watchfully.

antonyms heedlessly, recklessly, thoughtlessly, unwarily.

wariness *n* alertness, apprehension, attention, caginess, care, carefulness, caution, circumspection, discretion, distrust, foresight, heedfulness, hesitancy, mindfulness, prudence, suspicion, unease, vigilance, watchfulness.

antonyms heedlessness, recklessness, thoughtlessness.

warlike *adj* aggressive, antagonistic, bellicose, belligerent, bloodthirsty, combative, hawkish, hostile, inimical, jingoistic, martial, militaristic, military, pugnacious, sabre-rattling, truculent, unfriendly.

antonym peaceable.

warlock *n* conjurer, demon, enchanter, magician, magus, necromancer, sorcerer, witch, wizard.

warm *adj* affable, affectionate, amiable, amorous, animated, ardent, balmy, calid, cheerful, cordial, dangerous, disagreeable, earnest, effusive, emotional, enthusiastic, excited, fervent, friendly, genial, glowing, happy, hazardous, hearty, heated, hospitable, impassioned, incalescent, intense, irascible, irritable, keen, kindly, lively, loving, lukewarm, passionate, perilous, pleasant, quick, sensitive, short, spirited, stormy, sunny, tender, tepid, thermal, touchy, tricky, uncomfortable, unpleasant, vehement, vigorous, violent, zealous.

antonyms cool, indifferent, unfriendly.

v animate, awaken, excite, heat, heat up, interest, melt, mull, put some life into, reheat, rouse, stimulate, stir, thaw, turn on.

antonym cool.

warm-blooded *adj* ardent, earnest, emotional, enthusiastic, excitable, fervent, homothermic, homothermous, hot-blooded, idiothermous, impetuous, lively, passionate, rash, red-blooded, spirited, vivacious.

warm-hearted *adj* affectionate, ardent, compassionate, cordial, generous, genial, kind-hearted, kindly, loving, sympathetic, tender, tender-hearted.

antonyms cold, unsympathetic.

warmth *n* affability, affection, amorousness, animation, ardour, calidity, cheerfulness, cordiality, eagerness, earnestness, effusiveness, empressement, enthusiasm, excitement, fervency, fervour, fire, happiness, heartiness, heat, hospitableness, hotness, intensity, kindliness, love, passion, spirit, tenderness, transport, vehemence, vigour, violence, warmness, zeal, zest.

antonyms coldness, coolness, unfriendliness.

warn *v* admonish, advise, alert, apprise, caution, counsel, forewarn, inform, notify, put on one's guard, tip off.

warning *n* admonishment, admonition, advance notice, advice, alarm, alert, augury, caution, caveat, forenotice, foretoken, forewarning, griffin, hint, larum, larum-bell, lesson, monition, notice, notification, omen, premonition, presage, prodrome, sign, signal, siren, threat, tip, tip-off, token, vigia, word, word to the wise.

adj admonitory, aposematic, cautionary, in terrorem, monitive, monitory, ominous, premonitory, prodromal, prodromic, threatening.

warp *v* bend, contort, deform, deviate, distort, kink, misshape, pervert, twist.

antonym straighten.

n bend, bent, bias, contortion, deformation, deviation, distortion, irregularity, kink, perversion, quirk, turn, twist.

warrant *n* authorisation, authority, commission, guarantee, licence, permission, permit, pledge, sanction, security, voucher, warranty.

v affirm, answer for, approve, assure, attest, authorise, avouch, be bound, call for, certify, commission, declare, demand, empower, entitle, excuse, guarantee, justify, license, necessitate, permit, pledge, require, sanction, secure, underwrite, uphold, vouch for.

warrantable *adj* accountable, allowable, defensible, excusable, justifiable, lawful, legal, necessary, permissible, proper, reasonable, right.

antonyms indefensible, unjustifiable, unwarrantable.

warranty *n* assurance, authorisation, bond, certificate, contract, covenant, guarantee, justification, pledge.

warring *adj* at daggers drawn, at war, belligerent, combatant, conflicting, contending, embattled, fighting, hostile, opposed, opposing.

warrior *n* champion, combatant, fighter, fighting man, gallo(w)glass, ghazi, man-at-arms, soldier, wardog, war-horse.

wart *n* excrescence, growth, lump, protuberance, verruca.

wary *adj* alert, apprehensive, attentive, cagey, careful, cautious, chary, circumspect, distrustful, guarded, hawk-eyed, heedful, leery, on one's guard, on the lookout, on the qui vive, prudent, suspicious, vigilant, watchful, wide-awake.

antonyms careless, foolhardy, heedless, reckless, unwary.

wash[1] *v* bath, bathe, clean, cleanse, launder, moisten, rinse, scrub, shampoo, shower, sluice, swill, wet.

n a lick and a promise, ablution, bath, bathe, cleaning, cleansing, coat, coating, ebb and flow, film, flow, laundering, layer, overlay, rinse, roll, screen, scrub, shampoo, shower, souse, stain, suffusion, surge, sweep, swell, washing, wave.

wash one's hands abandon, abdicate responsibility, give up on, have nothing to do with, leave to one's own devices.

wash[2] *v* bear examination, bear scrutiny, carry weight, hold up, hold water, pass muster, stand up, stick.

washed-out *adj* all in, blanched, bleached, colourless, dead on one's feet, dog-tired, drained, drawn, etiolated, exhausted, faded, fatigued, flat, haggard, knackered, lacklustre, mat, pale, pallid, peelie-wally, spent, tired-out, wan, weary, worn-out.

wash-out *n* disappointment, disaster, dud, failure, fiasco, flop, incompetent, lead balloon, lemon, loser, mess.

antonyms success, triumph, winner.

waspish *adj* bad-tempered, bitchy, cantankerous, captious, crabbed, crabby, cross, crotchety, fretful, grouchy, grumpy, ill-tempered, irascible, irritable, peevish, peppery, pettish, petulant, prickly, snappish, splenetic, testy, touchy, waxy.

waste *v* atrophy, blow, consume, corrode, crumble, debilitate, decay, decline, deplete, despoil, destroy, devastate, disable, dissipate, drain, dwindle, eat away, ebb, emaciate, enfeeble, exhaust, fade, fritter away, gnaw, lavish, lay waste, misspend, misuse, perish, pillage, prodigalise, rape, ravage, raze, rig, ruin, sack, sink, spend, spoil, squander, tabefy, throw away, undermine, wane, wanton, wear out, wither.

n debris, desert, desolation, destruction, devastation, dissipation, dregs, dross, effluent, expenditure, extravagance, garbage, havoc, leavings, leftovers, litter, loss, misapplication, misuse, mullock, offal, offscouring(s), prodigality, ravage, recrement, refuse, rubbish, ruin, scrap, slops, solitude, spoilage, squandering, sweepings, trash, void, wastefulness, wasteland, wild, wilderness.

adj bare, barren, desolate, devastated, dismal, dreary, empty, extra, left-over, superfluous, supernumerary, uncultivated, uninhabited, unproductive, unprofitable, unused, unwanted, useless, wild, worthless.

wasted *adj* abandoned, atrophied, cadaverous, debauched, depleted, dissipated, dissolute, emaciated, exhausted, finished, gaunt, profligate, shrivelled, shrunken, spent, tabescent, tabid, wanton, war-worn, washed-out, withered.

antonyms healthy, robust.

wasteful *adj* dissipative, extravagant, improvident, lavish, prodigal, profligate, ruinous, spendthrift, thriftless, uneconomical, unthrifty.

antonyms economical, frugal, thrifty.

wasteland *n* barrenness, desert, solitude, void, waste, wilderness, wild(s).

waster *n* drone, good-for-nothing, idler, layabout, loafer, lounger, malingerer, ne'er-do-well, profligate, shirker, skiver, spendthrift, wastrel.

antonym worker.

wasting *n* atrophy, degeneration, dystrophy, emaciation, marasmus, tubefaction, tubes, tubescence.

adj destroying, devastating, dystrophic, emaciating, enfeebling, marasmic, tubescent, tubetic, tubid.

antonym strengthening.

watch[1] *v* attend, contemplate, eye, gaze at, guard, keep, keep an eye open, look, look after, look at, look on, look out, mark, mind, note, observe, ogle, pay attention, peer at, protect, regard, see, spectate, stare at, superintend, take care of, take heed, tend, view, wait.

n alertness, attention, eye, heed, inspection, lookout, notice, observation, pernoctation, supervision, surveillance, vigil, vigilance, wake, watchfulness.

watch out have a care, keep a weather eye open, keep one's eyes open, keep one's eyes peeled, keep one's eyes skinned, mind oneself.

watch over defend, guard, keep an eye on, look after, mind, preserve, protect, shelter, shield, stand guard over, tend.

watch[2] *n* chronometer, clock, ticker, tick-tick, tick-tock, timepiece, wristwatch.

watch-dog *n* custodian, guard dog, guardian, house-dog, inspector, monitor, ombudsman, protector, scrutineer, vigilante.

watcher *n* Argus, looker-on, lookout, member of the audience, observer, onlooker, peeping Tom, spectator, spy, viewer, voyeur, witness.

watchful *adj* alert, attentive, cautious, circumspect, guarded, heedful, observant, on one's guard, on the lookout, on the qui vive, on the watch, suspicious, unmistaking, vigilant, wary, wide awake.

antonym inattentive.

watchfulness *n* alertness, attention, attentiveness, caution, cautiousness, circumspection, heedfulness, suspicion, suspiciousness, vigilance, wariness.

antonym inattention.

watchman *n* caretaker, custodian, guard, security guard, security man, sentry, wakeman.

watchword *n* battle-cry, buzz-word, byword, catch phrase, catchword, countersign, magic word, maxim, motto, password, rallying-cry, shibboleth, signal, slogan.

water *n* Adam's ale, Adam's wine, aqua, lake, ocean, rain, river, saliva, sea, stream, sweat, tears, urine.

v adulterate, damp, dampen, dilute, douse, drench, drink, flood, hose, irrigate, moisten, soak, souse, spray, sprinkle, thin, water down, weaken.

antonyms dry out, purify, strengthen.

water down adulterate, dilute, mitigate, mix, qualify, soften, thin, tone down, water, weaken.

antonyms purify, strengthen.

water-closet *n* bog, cludge, convenience, gents', head, john, ladies', lav, lavatory, loo, powder-room, privy, public convenience, toilet, urinal, wash-room, WC.

watercourse *n* arroyo, channel, ditch, khor, river, stream, wadi, water-channel.

water-diviner *n* dowser, water-finder.

waterfall *n* cascade, cataract, chute, fall, force, lash, lin(n), torrent.

water-power *n* white coal.

waterproof *adj* coated, damp-proof, impermeable, impervious, proofed, rubberised, water-repellent, water-resistant.

antonym leaky.

watertight *adj* airtight, firm, flawless, foolproof, hermetic, impregnable, incontrovertible, sound, unassailable, waterproof.

antonyms leaky, unsound.

watery *adj* adulterated, aqueous, damp, dilute, diluted, flavourless, fluid, humid, hydatoid, insipid, liquid, marshy, moist, poor, rheumy, runny, soggy, squelchy, tasteless, tear-filled, tearful, thin, washy, watered-down, waterish, weak, weepy, wet, wishy-washy.

antonyms solid, strong.

wave[1] *v* beckon, brandish, direct, flap, flourish, flutter, gesticulate, gesture, indicate, oscillate, quiver, ripple, shake, sign, signal, stir, sway, swing, undulate, waft, wag, waver, weave, wield.

wave[2] *n* billow, breaker, comber, current, drift, flood, ground swell, movement, outbreak, rash, ripple, roller, rush, stream, surge, sweep, swell, tendency, tidal wave, trend, tsunami, undulation, unevenness, upsurge, water-wave, wavelet, white horse.

waver *v* blow hot and cold, dither, falter, flicker, fluctuate, haver, hesitate, hum and haw, quiver, reel, rock, seesaw, shake, shilly-shally, sway, swither, totter, tremble, undulate, vacillate, vary, waffle, wave, weave, wobble.

antonyms decide, stand.

waverer *n* ditherer, doubter, haverer, invertebrate, shilly-shallier, wobbler.

wavering *adj* dithering, dithery, doubtful, doubting, havering, hesitant, in two minds, shilly-shallying.

antonym determined.

wavy *adj* curly, curvy, flamboyanat, ridged, ridgy, rippled, ripply, sinuate(d), sinuous, undate, undulate, undulated, winding, wrinkled, zigzag.

antonyms flat, smooth.

wax *v* become, develop, dilate, enlarge, expand, fill out, grow, increase, magnify, mount, rise, swell.

antonym wane.

waxen *adj* anaemic, ashen, bloodless, colourless, ghastly, livid, pale, pallid, wan, white, whitish.

antonym ruddy.

waxy *adj* ceraceous, cereous, impressible, impressionable, pallid, pasty, soft, waxen.

way *n* access, advance, aim, ambition, approach, aspect, avenue, channel, characteristic, choice, circumstance, condition, conduct, course, custom, demand, desire, detail, direction, distance, elbow-room, fashion, feature, fettle, gate, goal, habit, headway, highway, idiosyncrasy, journey, lane, length, manner, march, means, method, mode, movement, nature, opening, particular, passage, path, pathway, personality, plan, pleasure, point, practice, procedure, process, progress, respect, road, room, route, scheme, sense, shape, situation, space, state, status, street, stretch, style, system, technique, thoroughfare, track, trail, trait, usage, will, wish, wont.

way of life life-style, modus vivendi.

wayfarer *n* bird of passage, dusty-foot, globetrotter, gypsy, itinerant, journeyer, nomad, piepowder, rover, traveller, trekker, viator, voyager, walker, wanderer.

antonyms resident, stay-at-home.

wayfaring *adj* drifting, itinerant, journeying, multivagant, nomadic, peripatetic, rambling, roving, travelling, viatorial, voyaging, walking, wandering.

antonyms resident, stay-at-home.

waylay *v* accost, ambush, attack, buttonhole, catch, hold up, intercept, lie in wait for, seize, set upon, surprise.

way-out *adj* advanced, amazing, avant-garde, bizarre, crazy, eccentric, excellent, experimental, fantastic, far-out, freaky, great, marvellous, off-beat, outlandish, progressive, satisfying, tremendous, unconventional, unorthodox, unusual, weird, wild, wonderful.

antonym ordinary.

ways and means capability, capacity, capital, cash, funds, methods, procedure, reserves, resources, tools, way, wherewithal.

wayward *adj* capricious, changeable, contrary, contumacious, cross-grained, disobedient, erratic, fickle, flighty, froward, headstrong, inconstant, incorrigible, insubordinate, intractable, mulish, obdurate, obstinate, perverse, rebellious, refractory, self-willed, stubborn, undependable, ungovernable, unmanageable, unpredictable, unruly, uppity, wilful.

antonyms complaisant, good-natured.

weak *adj* anaemic, asthenic, atonic, cowardly, debile, debilitated, decrepit, defenceless, deficient, delicate, diluted, disturbant, dull, effete, enervated, exhausted, exposed, faint, faulty, feeble, fibreless, flimsy, fragile, frail, helpless, hollow, imperceptible, impotent, inadequate, inconclusive, indecisive, ineffective, ineffectual, infirm, insipid, invalid, irresolute, lacking, lame, languid, low, milk-and-water, muffled, namby-pamby, pathetic, poor, powerless, puny, quiet, runny, shaky, shallow, sickly, slight, small, soft, spent, spineless, substandard, tasteless, tender, thin, timorous, toothless, unconvincing, under-strength, unguarded, unprotected, unresisting, unsafe, unsatisfactory, unsound, unsteady, unstressed, untenable, vulnerable, wanting, wasted, watery, weak-hearted, weak-kneed, weakly, weak-minded, weak-spirited, wishy-washy.

antonym strong.

weaken *v* abate, adulterate, craze, cut, debase, debilitate, depress, dilute, diminish, disinvigorate, droop, dwindle, ease up, effeminate, effeminise, emasculate, enervate, enfeeble, eunuchise, fade, fail, flag, give way, impair, invalidate, lessen, lower, mitigate, moderate, reduce, sap, soften up, temper, thin, tire, undermine, wane, water down.

antonym strengthen.

weakening *n* abatement, dilution, diminishment, dwindling, easing, fading, failing, flagging, labefactation, labefaction, lessening, lowering, moderation, reduction, waning.

antonym strengthening.

weakling *n* coward, doormat, drip, milksop, milquetoast, mouse, sissy, softling, underdog, underling, wally, weed, wet, wimp, windlestraw, wraith.

antonyms hero, stalwart.

weakness *n* Achilles' heel, asthenia, atonicity, atony, blemish, debility, decrepitude, defect, deficiency, enervation, enfeeblement, faible, failing, faintness, fault, feebleness, flaw, foible, fondness, fragility, frailty, imperfection, impotence, inclination, infirmity, irresolution, lack, liking, passion, penchant, powerlessness, predilection, proclivity, proneness, shortcoming, soft spot, soft underbelly, underbelly, vulnerability, weakpoint, weediness.

antonyms dislike, strength.

weak-willed *adj* complaisant, compliant, faint-hearted, irresolute, persuadable, persuasible, pliable, pusillanimous, spineless, submissive, weak-hearted, weak-kneed, weak-minded.

antonym strong-willed.

weal *n* cicatrice, cicatrix, contusion, mark, ridge, scar, streak, stripe, wale, welt, wheal, wound.

wealth *n* abundance, affluence, assets, bounty, capital, cash, copiousness, cornucopia, estate, fortune, fullness, funds, golden calf, goods, klondike, lucre, mammon, means, money, opulence, pelf, plenitude, plenty, possessions, profusion, property, prosperity, resources, riches, richness, store, substance.

antonym poverty.

wealthy *adj* affluent, comfortable, easy, filthy rich, flush, living in clover, loaded, moneyed, opulent, prosperous, rich, rolling in it, well-heeled, well-off, well-to-do.

antonym poor.

wear *v* abrade, accept, allow, annoy, bear, bear up, believe, brook, carry, consume, corrode, countenance, deteriorate, display, don, drain, dress in, endure, enervate, erode, exasperate, exhibit, fall for, fatigue, fly, fray, grind, harass, have on, hold up, irk, last, permit, pester, put on, put up with, rub, show, sport, stand for, stand up, stomach, swallow, take, tax, tolerate, undermine, use, vex, waste, weaken, weary.

n abrasion, apparel, attire, attrition, clothes, corrosion, costume, damage, depreciation, deterioration, dress, durability, employment, erosion, friction, garb, garments, gear, habit, mileage, outfit, service, things, use, usefulness, utility, wear and tear.

wear down abrade, chip away at, consume, corrode, diminish, erode, grind down, lessen, macerate, overcome, reduce, rub away, undermine.

wear off abate, abrade, decrease, diminish, disappear, dwindle, ebb, efface, fade, lessen, peter out, rub away, subside, wane, weaken.

antonym increase.

wear out consume, deteriorate, enervate, erode, exhaust, fag out, fatigue, fray, impair, knacker, prostrate, rub through, sap, tire (out), tucker (out), use up, wear through, weary.

antonyms refresh, replenish.

weariness *n* drowsiness, enervation, ennui, exhaustion, fatigue, languor, lassitude, lethargy, listlessness, prostration, sleepiness, tiredness.

antonym freshness.

wearing *adj* abradant, abrasive, exasperating, exhausting, fatiguing, irksome, oppressive, taxing, tiresome, tiring, trying, wearisome.

antonym refreshing.

wearisome *adj* annoying, boring, bothersome, burdensome, dreary, dull, ennuying, exasperating, exhausting, fatiguing, humdrum, irksome, monotonous, oppressive, pestilential, prolix, prosaic, protracted, tedious, troublesome, trying, vexatious, weariful, wearing.

antonym refreshing.

weary *adj* all in, arduous, awearied, aweary, beat, bored, browned-off, dead beat, dead on one's feet, discontented, dog-tired, drained, drooping, drowsy, enervated, enervative, ennuied, ennuyé, exhausted, fagged, fatigued, fed up, flagging, impatient, indifferent, irksome, jaded, knackered, laborious, sick, sick and tired, sleepy, spent, taxing, tired, tiresome, tiring, wayworn, wearied, wearing, wearisome, whacked, worn out.

antonyms excited, fresh, lively.

v annoy, betoil, bore, bug, burden, debilitate, drain, droop, enervate, ennui, exasperate, fade, fag, fail, fatigue, irk, irritate, jade, plague, sap, sicken, tax, tire, tire out, wear out.

wearying *adj* ennuying, exhausting, fatiguing, taxing, tiring, trying, wearing, wearisome.

antonym refreshing.

weather *n* climate, conditions, rainfall, temperature.

v brave, come through, endure, expose, harden, live through, overcome, pull through, resist, ride out, rise above, season, stand, stick out, suffer, surmount, survive, toughen, weather out, withstand.

antonym succumb.

weave *v* blend, braid, build, construct, contrive, create, criss-cross, entwine, fabricate, fuse, incorporate, intercross, interdigitate, interlace, intermingle, intertwine, introduce, knit, make, mat, merge, plait, put together, spin, twist, unite, wind, zigzag.

weaver *n* brabener, wabster, webster.

web *n* interlacing, lattice, mesh, mesh-work, net, netting, network, palama, screen, snare, tangle, tela, texture, toils, trap, weave, webbing, weft.

wed *v* ally, blend, coalesce, combine, commingle, dedicate, espouse, fuse, get hitched, interweave, join, jump the broomstick, link, marry, merge, splice, tie the knot, unify, unite, wive, yoke.

antonym divorce.

wedding *n* bridal, espousals, marriage, matrimony, nuptials.

antonym divorce.

adj bridal, epithalamial, epithalamic, hymeneal, hymenean, marriage, matrimonial, nuptial.

wedge *n* block, chock, chunk, cleat, lump, wodge.

v block, cram, crowd, force, jam, lodge, pack, push, ram, squeeze, stuff, thrust.

antonyms dislodge, space out, take out.

wedlock *n* holy matrimony, marriage, matrimony, union.

wee *adj* diminutive, insignificant, itsy-bitsy, Lilliputian, little, microscopic, midget, miniature, minuscule, minute, negligible, small, teeny, teeny-weeny, tiny, weeny.

antonym large.

weed *v* hoe.

weed out eliminate, eradicate, extirpate, get rid of, purge, remove, root out.

antonyms add, fix, infiltrate.

weedy *adj* feeble, frail, ineffectual, insipid, lanky, namby-pamby, puny, skinny, thin, undersized, ungainly, weak, weak-kneed, wet, white-shoe, wimpish.

antonym strong.

week *n* hebdomad, sennight.

weekly *adv* by the week, every week, hebdomadally, once a week.

adj hebdomadal, hebdomadary.

weep *v* bemoan, bewail, blub, blubber, boo-hoo, bubble, complain, cry, drip, exude, greet, keen, lament, leak, moan, mourn, ooze, pipe, pipe one's eye, pour forth, pour out, rain, snivel, sob, tune one's pipes, ululate, whimper, whinge.

antonym rejoice.

n blub, bubble, cry, greet, lament, moan, snivel, sob.

weepie *n* melodrama, sob-stuff, tear-jerker.

weepy *adj* blubbering, crying, labile, lachrymose, sobbing, tearful, teary, weeping.

antonym dry-eyed.

weigh *v* bear down, burden, carry weight, consider, contemplate, count, deliberate, evaluate, examine, give thought to, impress, matter, meditate on, mull over, oppress, ponder, ponderate, prey, reflect on, study, tell, think over.

antonyms cut no ice, hearten.

weigh down afflict, bear down, burden, depress, get down, load, oppress, overburden, overload, press down, trouble, weigh upon, worry.

antonyms hearten, lighten, refresh.

weigh up assess, chew over, cogitate, consider, contemplate, deliberate, discuss, examine, mull over, perpend, ponder, ruminate on, think over.

weight *n* authority, avoirdupois, ballast, burden, clout, consequence, consideration, efficacy, emphasis, force, gravity, heaviness, heft, impact, import, importance, impressiveness, influence, load, mass, millstone, moment, onus, oppression, persuasiveness, ponderance, ponderancy, poundage, power, preponderance, pressure, significance, strain, substance, tonnage, value.

antonym lightness.

v ballast, bias, burden, charge, encumber, freight, handicap, hold down, impede, keep down, load, oppress, overburden, slant, unbalance, weigh down.

antonym lighten.

weightless *adj* airy, imponderous, insubstantial, light, unsubstantial.

antonym heavy.

weighty *adj* backbreaking, burdensome, consequential, considerable, critical, crucial, crushing, cumbersome, demanding, dense, difficult, exacting, forcible, grave, heavy, hefty, important, leading, massive, momentous, onerous, oppressive, ponderous, portentous, respected, revered, serious, significant, solemn, substantial, taxing, worrisome, worrying.

antonyms trivial, unimportant.

weir *n* dam, fence, garth, lash, wear.

weird *adj* bizarre, creepy, eerie, eldritch, freakish, ghostly, grotesque, mysterious, odd, outlandish, preternatural, queer, spooky, strange, superlunar, supernatural, uncanny, unco, unearthly, unnatural, witching.

antonym normal.

weirdo *n* crackpot, crank, cure, eccentric, freak, fruitcake, loony, nut, nutcase, nutter, oddball, queer fish, weirdie.

welcome *adj* able, acceptable, accepted, agreeable, allowed, appreciated, delightful, desirable, entitled, free, gratifying, permitted, pleasant, pleasing, refreshing.

antonym unwelcome.

n acceptance, greeting, hospitality, reception, red carpet, salaam, salutation.

v accept, approve of, embrace, greet, hail, meet, receive, roll out the red carpet for.

antonyms reject, snub.

weld *v* bind, bond, cement, connect, fuse, join, link, seal, solder, unite.

antonym separate.

n bond, joint, seal, seam.

welfare *n* advantage, benefit, good, happiness, heal, health, interest, profit, prosperity, success, weal, well-being.

antonym harm.

well[1] *n* bore, cavity, fount, fountain, hole, lift-shaft, mine, pit, pool, repository, shaft, source, spring, waterhole, well-spring.

v brim over, flood, flow, gush, jet, ooze, pour, rise, run, seep, spout, spring, spurt, stream, surge, swell, trickle.

well[2] *adv* ably, abundantly, accurately, adeptly, adequately, admirably, agreeably, amply, approvingly, attentively, capitally, carefully, clearly, closely, comfortably, completely, conscientiously, considerably, correctly, deeply, easily, effectively, efficiently, expertly, fairly, famously, favourably, fittingly, flourishingly, fully, glowingly, graciously, greatly, happily, heartily, highly, intimately, justly, kindly, nicely, personally, pleasantly, possibly, proficiently, profoundly, properly, prosperously, readily, rightly, satisfactorily, skilfully, smoothly, splendidly, substantially, successfully, sufficiently, suitably, thoroughly, warmly.

antonym badly.

adj A1, able-bodied, advisable, agreeable, bright, fine, fit, fitting, flourishing, fortunate, good, great, hale, happy, healthy, hearty, in fine fettle, in good health, lucky, on the top of the world, pleasing, profitable, proper, prudent, right, robust, satisfactory, sound, strong, thriving, up to par, useful.

antonyms bad, ill.

well done! brava, bravo, euge.

well-balanced *adj* graceful, harmonious, judicious, level-headed, nutritious, proportional, rational, reasonable, sane, sensible, sober, sound, symmetrical, together, well-adjusted, well-proportioned.

antonym unbalanced.

well-being *n* comfort, contentment, good, happiness, prosperity, weal, welfare.

antonyms discomfort, harm.

well-bred *adj* aristocratic, blue-blooded, civil, courteous, courtly, cultivated, cultured, gallant, genteel, gentle, gentlemanly, highborn, ladylike, mannerly, noble, patrician, polished, polite, refined, titled, upper-crust, urbane, well-born, well-brought-up, well-mannered.

antonym ill-bred.

well-deserved *adj* appropriate, condign, deserved, due, just, justified, meet, merited, rightful.

antonym undeserved.

well-disposed *adj* agreeable, amicable, favourable, friendly, sympathetic, well-aimed, well-arranged, well-minded, well-placed.

antonym ill-disposed.

well-dressed *adj* dapper, natty, neat, smart, spruce, tidy, trim, well-groomed.

antonym scruffy.

well-equipped *adj* well-appointed, well-found.

well-known *adj* celebrated, famed, familiar, famous, illustrious, notable, noted, popular, renowned.

antonym unknown.

well-off *adj* affluent, comfortable, flourishing, flush, fortunate, in the money, loaded, lucky, moneyed, prosperous, rich, successful, thriving, warm, wealthy, well-heeled, well-to-do.

antonym poor.

well-thought-of *adj* admired, esteemed, highly regarded, honoured, reputable, respected, revered, venerated, weighty.

antonym despised.

well-to-do *adj* affluent, comfortable, flush, loaded, moneyed, prosperous, rich, warm, wealthy, well-heeled, well-off.

antonym poor.

well-wisher *n* fan, supporter, sympathiser, well-willer.

well-worn *adj* bromidic, commonplace, hackneyed, overused, stale, stereotyped, threadbare, timeworn, tired, trite.

antonym original.

welsh *v* cheat, defraud, diddle, do, swindle, welch.

welt *n* cicatrice, cicatrix, contusion, mark, ridge, scar, streak, stripe, wale, weal, wheal.

welter *v* billow, flounder, heave, lie, pitch, roll, splash, stumble, toss, tumble, wade, wallow, writhe.

n confusion, hotchpotch, jumble, mess, mish-mash, mixter-maxter, muddle, tangle, web.

wend one's way go, hike, meander, move, plod, proceed, progress, travel, trudge, walk, wander.

antonym stay.

werewolf *n* lycanthrope, lycanthropist, werwolf.

western *adj* Hesperian, occidental.

antonym eastern.

n horse opera, spaghetti western.

wet *adj* boggy, clammy, damp, dank, drenched, dripping, drizzling, effete, feeble, foolish, humid, ineffectual, irresolute, misty, moist, moistened, namby-pamby, pouring, raining, rainy, saturated, showery, silly, sloppy, soaked, soaking, sodden, soft, soggy, sopping, soppy, soused, spineless, spongy, teeming, timorous, waterlogged, watery, weak, weedy, white-shoe, wimpish, wimpy.

antonyms dry, resolute, strong.

n clamminess, condensation, damp, dampness, drip, drizzle, humidity, liquid, milksop, milquetoast, moisture, rain, rains, sap, water, weakling, weed, wetness, wimp.

antonym dryness.

v bedabble, bedew, bedrench, damp, dampen, dip, douse, drench, humidify, imbue, irrigate, moisten, saturate, sluice, soak, splash, spray, sprinkle, steep, water.

antonym dry.

wet behind the ears callow, green, immature, inexperienced, innocent, naïve, new, raw, untrained.

antonym experienced.

wetness *n* clamminess, condensation, damp, dampness, dankness, humidity, liquid, moisture, soddenness, sogginess, water, wet.

antonym dryness.

wet-nurse *n* amah.

whack *v* bang, bash, beat, belabour, belt, biff, box, buffet, clobber, clout, cuff, hit, lambaste, rap, slap, slug, smack, sock, strike, thrash, thump, thwack, wallop, whale, whang.

n allotment, attempt, bang, bash, belt, biff, bit, blow, box, buffet, clout, crack, cuff, cut, go, hit, part, portion, quota, rap, share, shot, slap, slug, smack, sock, stab, stroke, thump, thwack, try, turn, wallop, wham, whang.

wham *n* bang, bash, blow, clout, concussion, hit, impact, slam, smack, splat, thump, thwack, wallop, whack, whang.

wharf *n* dock, dockyard, jetty, landing-stage, marina, pier, quay, quayside.

what's-its-name *n* dingus, doodad, jigamaree, jiggumbob, thingumajig, thingumbob, thingummy, what-d'ye-call-it, whatsit, what-you-may-call-it.

wheedle *v* cajole, charm, coax, court, draw, entice, flatter, importune, inveigle, persuade, whilly, whillywha(w).

antonym force.

wheel *n* birl, circle, gyration, pivot, revolution, roll, rotation, spin, turn, twirl, whirl.

v birl, circle, gyrate, orbit, pirouette, revolve, roll, rotate, spin, swing, swivel, turn, twirl, whirl.

wheelbarrow *n* ball-barrow, barrow, hand-cart, monotroch.

wheeze[1] *v* cough, gasp, hiss, rasp, whiss, whistle, whiz(z).

n cough, gasp, hiss, rasp, whistle, whiz(z).

wheeze[2] *n* anecdote, catch-phrase, chestnut, crack, expedient, gag, idea, joke, one-liner, plan, ploy, practical joke, prank, ruse, scheme, story, stunt, trick, wrinkle.

whereabouts *n* location, place, position, site, situation, vicinity.

wherewithal *n* capital, cash, funds, means, money, necessary, readies, resources, supplies.

whet *v* acuminate, arouse, awaken, file, grind, hone, incite, increase, kindle, pique, provoke, quicken, rouse, sharpen, stimulate, stir, strop, titillate.

antonyms blunt, dampen.

whiff *n* aroma, blast, breath, draught, gale, gust, hint, niff, odour, pong, puff, reek, scent, smell, sniff, stench, stink.

whim *n* caprice, chimera, conceit, concetto, crank, craze, crotchet, fad, fancy, fizgig, flam, freak, humour, impulse, maggot, notion, quirk, sport, urge, vagary, whims(e)y.

whimper *v* blub, blubber, cry, girn, grizzle, mewl, moan, pule, snivel, sob, weep, whine, whinge.

n girn, moan, snivel, sob, whine.

whimsical *adj* capricious, chimeric(al), crotchety, curious, dotty, droll, eccentric, fanciful, fantastic(al), freakish, funny, Gilbertian, maggoty, mischievous, odd, peculiar, playful, quaint, queer, singular, unusual, waggish, weird, whimmy.

antonym sensible.

whine *n* beef, belly-ache, complaint, cry, girn, gripe, grouch, grouse, grumble, moan, sob, wail, whimper.

v beef, belly-ache, carp, complain, cry, girn, gripe, grizzle, grouch, grouse, grumble, kvetch, moan, sob, wail, whimper, whinge.

whinge *v* beef, belly-ache, carp, complain, gripe, grouse, grumble, kvetch, moan.

n beef, belly-ache, complaint, gripe, grouse, grumble, moan.

whip *v* agitate, beat, best, birch, cane, castigate, clobber, compel, conquer, dart, dash, defeat, dive, drive, drub, flagellate, flash, flit, flog, flounce, fly, foment, goad, hammer, hound, incite, instigate, jambok, jerk, knout, k(o)urbash, lash, leather, lick, outdo, overcome, overpower, overwhelm, paddle, prick, prod, produce, provoke, pull, punish, push, quirt, remove, rout, rush, scourge, shoot, sjambok, snatch, spank, spur, stir, strap, switch, tan, tear, thrash, trounce, urge, whale, whisk, whop, worst.

n birch, bullwhip, cane, cat, cat-o'-nine-tails, crop, flagellum, horsewhip, jambok, knout, k(o)urbash, lash, paddle, quirt, rawhide, riding-crop, scourge, sjambok, switch, thong.

whip up agitate, arouse, excite, foment, incite, inflame, instigate, kindle, provoke, psych up, stir up, work up.

antonyms dampen, deter.

whippersnapper *n* hobbledehoy, nipper, shaver, whiffet.

whipping *n* beating, belting, birching, caning, castigation, flagellation, flogging, hiding, lashing, leathering, paddling, punishment, quilting, spanking, tanning, thrashing.

whirl *v* birl, circle, gyrate, gyre, pirouette, pivot, reel, revolve, roll, rotate, spin, swirl, swivel, turn, twirl, twist, wheel.

n agitation, birl, bustle, circle, commotion, confusion, daze, dither, flurry, giddiness, gyration, gyre, hubbub, hubbuboo, hurly-burly, merry-go-round, pirouette, reel, revolution, roll, rotation, round, series, spin, stir, succession, swirl, tumult, turn, twirl, twist, uproar, vortex, wheel, whorl.

antonym calm.

whirling *adj* birling, gyral, gyrating, gyratory, pirouetting, pivoting, reeling, revolving, rotating, spinning, turning, twirling, vertiginous, vortical, vorticular, vorticuse, vortiginous, wheeling.

antonym stationary.

whirlpool *n* maelstrom, vortex, weel.

whirlwind *n* cyclone, dust-devil, tornado, vortex, waterspout.

adj hasty, headlong, impetuous, impulsive, lightning, precipitate, quick, rapid, rash, short, speedy, split-second, swift.

antonyms deliberate, slow.

whisk *v* beat, brush, dart, dash, flick, fly, grab, hasten, hurry, race, rush, scoot, shoot, speed, sweep, swipe, tear, twitch, whip, wipe.

n beater, brush, swizzle-stick.

whisker *n* bristle, hair, hair's breadth, vibrissa.

whisk(e)y *n* barley-bree, bourbon, John Barleycorn, malt, mountain dew, peat-reek, rye, Scotch, usquebaugh.

whisper *v* breathe, buzz, divulge, gossip, hint, hiss, insinuate, intimate, murmur, rustle, sigh, sough, susurrate, tittle.

antonym shout.

n breath, buzz, gossip, hint, hiss, innuendo, insinuation, murmur, report, rumour, rustle, shadow, sigh, sighing, soughing, soupçon, suggestion, suspicion, susurration, susurrus, swish, tinge, trace, underbreath, undertone, whiff, word.

antonym roar.

whistle *n* call, cheep, chirp, hooter, siren, song, warble.

v call, cheep, chirp, pipe, siffle, sing, warble, wheeze, whiss.

whit *n* atom, bit, crumb, damn, dash, drop, fragment, grain, hoot, iota, jot, little, mite, modicum, particle, piece, pinch, scrap, shred, speck, tittle, trace.

antonym lot.

white *adj* ashen, auspicious, bloodless, bright, canescent, Caucasian, clean, colourless, dealbate, favourable, ghastly, grey, grizzled, hoar, hoary, honest, immaculate, innocent, pale, pallid, pasty, pure, purified, reliable, silver, snowy, spotless, stainless, unblemished, unsullied, wan, waxen, whey-faced.

antonyms black, dark, dishonest, ruddy, unclean, unreliable.

n albumen, gub, gubbah, honkie, whitey.

white-collar *adj* clerical, executive, non-manual, office, professional, salaried.

antonyms blue-collar, manual.

whiten *v* blanch, bleach, blench, decolour, etiolate, fade, pale, whitewash.

antonyms blacken, colour, darken.

whitewash[1] *n* camouflage, concealment, cover-up, deception, extenuation.

antonym exposure.

v camouflage, conceal, cover up, euphemise, extenuate, gloss over, make light of, suppress.

antonym expose.

whitewash[2] *v* beat, best, clobber, crush, drub, hammer, lick, paste, thrash, trounce, whale.

whitlow *n* paronychia.

whittle *v* carve, consume, cut, destroy, diminish, eat away, erode, hew, pare, reduce, scrape, shape, shave, trim, undermine, wear away.

whole *adj* better, complete, cured, entire, faultless, fit, flawless, full, good, hale, healed, healthy, in one piece, intact, integral, integrate, inviolate, mint, perfect, recovered, robust, sound, strong, total, unabbreviated, unabridged, unbroken, uncut, undamaged, undivided, unedited, unexpurgated, unharmed, unhurt, unimpaired, uninjured, unmutilated, unscathed, untouched, well.

antonyms damaged, ill, partial.

n aggregate, all, ensemble, entirety, entity, everything, fullness, Gestalt, lot, piece, total, totality, unit, unity.

antonym part.

whole-hearted *adj* committed, complete, dedicated, determined, devoted, earnest, emphatic, enthusiastic, genuine, heartfelt, hearty, passionate, real, sincere, true, unfeigned, unqualified, unreserved, unstinting, warm, whole-souled, zealous.

antonym half-hearted.

wholesale *adj* broad, comprehensive, extensive, far-reaching, indiscriminate, mass, massive, sweeping, total, wide-ranging.

antonym partial.

adv comprehensively, en bloc, extensively, indiscriminately, massively, totally.

antonym partially.

wholesome *adj* advantageous, beneficial, clean, decent, edifying, exemplary, good, healthful, health-giving, healthy, helpful, honourable, hygienic, improving, innocent, invigorating, moral, nice, nourishing, nutritious, propitious, pure, respectable, righteous, salubrious, salutary, sanitary, squeaky-clean, uplifting, virtuous, worthy.

antonym unwholesome.

wholly *adv* absolutely, all, altogether, completely, comprehensively, entirely, exclusively, fully, in toto, only, perfectly, solely, thoroughly, through and through, totally, utterly.

antonym partly.

whoop *v, n* cheer, cry, holler, hoop, hoot, hurrah, roar, scream, shout, shriek, yell.

whooping-cough *n* pertussis.

whopper *n* colossus, cracker, fable, fabrication, fairy story, falsehood, giant, lie, monster, plumper, tall story, untruth.

whopping *adj* big, enormous, extraordinary, giant, gigantic, great, huge, large, mammoth, massive, mighty, monstrous, monumental, prodigious, staggering, tremendous, whacking.

antonym tiny.

whore *n* brass, broad, call girl, courtesan, demimondaine, demirep, drab, fallen woman, fille de joie, harlot, hooker, hustler, loon, loose fish, lorette, Paphian, prostitute, scarlet woman, strange woman, street-walker, strumpet, succubus, tart, tramp, trollop, waistcoateer, wench, woman of the town, working girl.

whorehouse *n* bagnio, bawdy-house, bordello, brothel, cat-house, house of ill repute, knocking-shop, stew.

whorl *n* coil, convolution, corkscrew, helix, spiral, turn, twist, vortex.

wicked *adj* abandoned, abominable, acute, agonising, amoral, arch, atrocious, awful, bad, black-hearted, bothersome, corrupt, debased, depraved, destructive, devilish, difficult, dissolute, distressing, dreadful, egregious, evil, facinorous, fearful, fiendish, fierce, flagitious, foul, galling, guilty, harmful, heinous, immoral, impious, impish, incorrigible, inexpiable, iniquitous, injurious, intense, irreligious, mighty, mischievous, nasty, naughty, nefarious, nefast, offensive, painful, piacular, rascal-like, rascally, roguish, scandalous, severe, shameful, sinful, spiteful, terrible, troublesome, trying, ungodly, unpleasant, unprincipled, unrighteous, vicious, vile, villainous, worthless.

antonyms good, harmless, modest, upright.

wickedness *n* abomination, amorality, atrocity, corruption, corruptness, depravity, devilishness, dissoluteness, enormity, evil, facinorousness, fiendishness, foulness, heinousness, immorality, impiety, iniquity, pravity, reprobacy, shamefulness, sin, sinfulness, unrighteousness, vileness, villainy.

antonym uprightness.

wickerwork *n* basket-work, wattle, wattle-work.

wide *adj* ample, away, baggy, broad, capacious, catholic, commodious, comprehensive, diffuse, dilated, distant, distended, encyclopaedic, expanded, expansive, extensive, far-reaching, full, general, immense, inclusive, large, latitudinous, loose, off, off-course, off-target, outspread, outstretched, remote, roomy, spacious, sweeping, vast.

antonyms limited, narrow.

adv aside, astray, off course, off target, off the mark, out.

antonym on target.

wide-awake *adj* alert, astute, aware, conscious, fully awake, heedful, keen, observant, on one's toes, on the alert, on the ball, on the qui vive, quick-witted, roused, sharp, vigilant, wakened, wary, watchful.

antonym asleep.

widely *adv* extensively, generally, ubiquitously, universally.

widen *v* broaden, dilate, distend, enlarge, expand, extend, open out, splay, spread, stretch.

antonym narrow.

wide-open *adj* defenceless, expansive, exposed, gaping, indeterminate, open, outspread, outstretched, splayed, spread, susceptible, uncertain, unfortified, unpredictable, unprotected, unsettled, vulnerable, wide.

antonyms closed, narrow.

widespread *adj* broad, common, epidemic, extensive, far-flung, far-reaching, general, pervasive, popular, prevailing, prevalent, rife, sweeping, universal, unlimited, wholesale.

antonyms limited, uncommon.

widowed *adj* bereaved, viduous.

widowhood *n* viduage, viduity.

width *n* amplitude, beam, breadth, compass, diameter, extent, girth, measure, range, reach, scope, span, thickness, wideness.

wield *v* apply, brandish, command, control, employ, exercise, exert, flourish, handle, have, hold, maintain, manage, manipulate, ply, possess, swing, use, utilise, wave, weave.

wife *n* better half, bride, consort, dutch, helpmate, helpmeet, little woman, mate, missis, missus, old lady, old woman, partner, rib, spouse, woman.

antonym husband.

wifely *adj* uxorial.

wig *n* caxon, dalmahoy, gizz, Gregorian, hairpiece, jas(e)y, jazy, jiz, merkin, peruke, postiche, tie-wig, toupee.

wiggle *v, n* jerk, jiggle, shake, shimmy, squirm, twist, twitch, wag, waggle, wriggle, writhe.

wild *adj* agrest(i)al, barbaric, barbarous, berserk, blustery, boisterous, brutish, chaotic, chimeric(al), choppy, crazed, crazy, daft, delirious, demented, desert, deserted, desolate, dishevelled, disordered, disorderly, eager, empty, enthusiastic, excited, extravagant, fantastic, ferae naturae, feral, feralised, ferine, ferocious, fierce, flighty, foolhardy, foolish, frantic, free, frenzied, furious, giddy, god-forsaken, howling, hysterical, ill-considered, impetuous, impracticable, imprudent, inaccurate, indigenous, intense, irrational, lawless, mad, madcap, maniacal, native, natural, noisy, nuts, outrageous, potty, preposterous, primitive, rabid, raging, rash, raving, reckless, riotous, rough, rowdy, rude, savage, self-willed, tempestuous, tousled, trackless, turbulent, unbridled, unbroken, uncheated, uncivilised, uncontrollable, uncontrolled, uncultivated, undisciplined, undomesticated, unfettered, ungovernable, uninhabited, unjustified, unkempt, unmanageable, unpopulated, unpruned, unrestrained, unruly, unsubstantiated, untamed, untidy, uproarious, violent, virgin, wayward, woolly.

antonyms civilised, peaceful, sane, sensible, tame, unenthusiastic.

wilderness *n* clutter, confusion, congeries, desert, jumble, jungle, mass, maze, muddle, tangle, waste, wasteland, welter, wild, wild-land.

wildlife *n* animals, fauna.

wilds *n* back-veld, desert, outback, the back of beyond, the boondocks, the middle of nowhere, the sticks, wasteland, wilderness.

wile *n* artfulness, artifice, cheating, chicanery, contrivance, craft, craftiness, cunning, deceit, device, dodge, expedient, fraud, guile, hanky-panky, imposition, lure, manoeuvre, ploy, ruse, slyness, stratagem, subterfuge, trick, trickery.

antonym guilelessness.

wilful *adj* adamant, bloody-minded, bull-headed, conscious, deliberate, determined, dogged, froward, headstrong, inflexible, intended, intentional, intractable, intransigent, mulish, obdurate, obstinate, persistent, perverse, pig-headed, purposeful, refractory, self-willed, stubborn, thrawn, uncompromising, unyielding, volitional, voluntary.

antonyms complaisant, good-natured.

will *n* aim, attitude, choice, command, decision, declaration, decree, desire, determination, discretion, disposition, fancy, feeling, inclination, intention, mind, option, pleasure, preference, prerogative, purpose, resolution, resolve, testament, velleity, volition, will power, wish, wishes.

v bequeath, bid, cause, choose, command, confer, decree, desire, determine, devise, direct, dispose of, elect, give, leave, opt, ordain, order, pass on, resolve, transfer, want, wish.

willing *adj* agreeable, amenable, biddable, compliant, consenting, content, desirous, disposed, eager, enthusiastic, favourable, game, happy, inclined, nothing lo(a)th, pleased, prepared, ready, so-minded, volitient, willing-hearted.

antonym unwilling.

willingly *adv* by choice, cheerfully, eagerly, freely, gladly, happily, nothing lo(a)th, readily, unhesitatingly, voluntarily.

antonym unwillingly.

willingness *n* agreeableness, agreement, complaisance, compliance, consent, desire, disposition, enthusiasm, favour, inclination, volition, will, wish.

antonym unwillingness.

will-o'-the-wisp *n* fatuous fire, fen-fire, friar's lantern, ignis fatuus, wisp.

willowy *adj* graceful, gracile, limber, lissom, lithe, lithesome, slender, slim, supple, svelte, sylph-like.

antonym buxom.

will-power *n* determination, drive, grit, resolution, resolve, self-command, self-control, self-discipline, self-mastery, single-mindedness.

willy-nilly *adv* compulsorily, necessarily, nolens volens, of necessity, perforce.

wilt *v* atrophy, diminish, droop, dwindle, ebb, fade, fail, flag, flop, languish, melt away, sag, shrivel, sink, wane, weaken, wither.

antonym perk up.

wily *adj* arch, artful, astute, cagey, crafty, crooked, cunning, deceitful, deceptive, designing, fly, foxy, guileful, intriguing, long-headed, Machiavellian, scheming, sharp, shifty, shrewd, sly, streetwise, tricky, underhand, versute, wileful.

antonym guileless.

wimp *n* clot, clown, drip, fool, jerk, marshmallow, milksop, milquetoast, nebbich, neb(b)ish, nyaff, sap, softy, wally, wet.

win *v* accomplish, achieve, acquire, attain, bag, capture, catch, collect, come away with, conquer, earn, gain, get, net, obtain, overcome, pick up, prevail, procure, receive, secure, succeed, sweep the board, triumph.

antonym lose.

n conquest, mastery, success, triumph, victory.

antonym defeat.

win over allure, attract, carry, charm, convert, convince, disarm, dissuade, induce, influence, persuade, prevail upon, sway, talk round.

wince *v* blench, cower, cringe, draw back, flinch, funk, jerk, quail, recoil, shrink, start.

n cringe, flinch, jerk, start.

wind[1] *n* air, air-current, babble, blast, blather, bluster, boasting, breath, breeze, clue, current, cyclone, draught, flatulence, flatus, gab, gale, gas, gregale, gust, harmattan, hint, hot air, humbug, hurricane, idle talk, inkling, intimation, khamsin, levanter, libeccio, mistral, monsoon, notice, puff, report, respiration, rumour, scirocco, sirocco, suggestion, talk, tidings, tornado, warning, whisper, williwaw, windiness, zephyr.

wind[2] *v* bend, coil, curl, curve, deviate, encircle, furl, loop, meander, ramble, reel, roll, serpent, serpentine, serpentinise, snake, spiral, turn, twine, twist, wreath, zigzag.

n bend, curve, meander, turn, twist, zigzag.

wind down decline, diminish, dwindle, lessen, quieten down, reduce, relax, slacken off, slow, slow down, subside, unwind.

antonyms increase, tense.

wind up close, close down, coil, conclude, crank up, end, end one's days, end up, excite, finalise, find oneself, finish, finish up, hoist, liquidate, raise, settle, terminate, tighten, work up, wrap up.

antonym begin.

wind-bag *n* big-mouth, blether, boaster, bore, braggart, gas-bag, gossip, rodomontader.

winded *adj* breathless, out of breath, out of puff, panting, pooped, puffed, puffed out.

antonym fresh.

windfall *n* bonanza, find, godsend, jackpot, manna, pennies from heaven, stroke of luck, treasure-trove.

windiness *n* borborygmus, breeziness, flatulence, flatulency, gassiness, gustiness, storminess, ventosity.

antonym calm.

winding *adj* anfractuous, bending, circuitous, convoluted, crooked, curving, flexuose, flexuous, indirect, meandering, meandrous, roundabout, serpentine, sinuate(d), sinuous, spiral, tortuous, turning, twisting.

antonym straight.

window *n* dormer, dormer-window, fenestella, fenestra, fenestral, glass, light, loop-light, lucarne, opening, oriel, oriel-window, pane, rosace, rose-window, skylight, ventana.

windpipe *n* pharynx, throat, trachea, weasand.

wind-sock *n* drogue, wind-cone, wind-sleeve.

windy *adj* afraid, blowy, blustering, blustery, boastful, boisterous, bombastic, breezy, changeable, chicken, conceited, cowardly, diffuse, empty, fearful, flatulent, flatuous, frightened, garrulous, gusty, long-winded, loquacious, meandering, nervous, pompous, prolix, rambling, scared, squally, stormy, tempestuous, thrasonic, timid, turgid, ventose, verbose, wild, windswept, wordy.

antonyms calm, fearless, modest.

wine *n* champagne, claret, plonk, port, rosé, vin, vin ordinaire, vinho verde, vino, vintage.

wine-glass *n* flute, glass, goblet, schooner.

wine-grower *n* vigneron, viniculturist, viticulturist.

wine-growing *n* viniculture, viticulture.

wing *n* adjunct, annexe, arm, branch, circle, clique, coterie, extension, faction, flank, group, grouping, mudguard, pinion, protection, section, segment, set, side.

v clip, fleet, flit, fly, glide, hasten, hit, hurry, move, nick, pass, race, soar, speed, travel, wound, zoom.

wink *v* bat, blink, flash, flicker, flutter, gleam, glimmer, glint, nictate, nictitate, pink, sparkle, twinkle.

n blink, flash, flutter, gleam, glimmering, glint, hint, instant, jiffy, moment, nictation, nictitation, second, sparkle, split second, twinkle, twinkling.

winner *n* champ, champion, conqueror, corker, cracker, daisy, dinger, first, humdinger, master, vanquisher, victor, world-beater, wow.

antonym loser.

winning *adj* alluring, amiable, attractive, bewitching, captivating, charming, conquering, delectable, delightful, disarming, enchanting, endearing, engaging, fascinating, fetching, lovely, on top, pleasing, prepossessing, successful, sweet, taking, triumphant, unbeaten, undefeated, victorious, winsome.

antonyms losing, unappealing.

winnings *n* booty, gains, motser, motza, prize(s), proceeds, profits, spoils, takings, velvet.

antonym losses.

winnow *v* comb, cull, diffuse, divide, fan, part, screen, select, separate, sift, waft.

winsome *adj* agreeable, alluring, amiable, attractive, bewitching, captivating, charming, cheerful, comely, delectable, disarming, enchanting, endearing, engaging, fair, fascinating, fetching, graceful, pleasant, pleasing, prepossessing, pretty, sweet, taking, winning.

antonym unattractive.

wintry *adj* algid, bleak, brumous, cheerless, chilly, cold, desolate, dismal, freezing, frore, frosty, frozen, gelid, harsh, hibernal, hiemal, icy, rimy, Siberian, snowy, winterly.

antonym summery.

wipe *v* absterge, brush, clean, clear, deterge, dicht, dry, dust, erase, mop, remove, rub, sponge, swab, take away, take off.

n brush, dicht, lick, rub, swab.

wipe out abolish, annihilate, blot out, destroy, efface, eradicate, erase, expunge, exterminate, extirpate, massacre, obliterate, put paid to, raze.

antonym establish.

wire-pulling *n* clout, conspiring, influence, intrigue, Machiavellianism, manipulation, plotting, pull, scheming.

wiry *adj* bristly, lean, sinewy, stiff, strong, tough, withy.

antonym puny.

wisdom *n* anthroposophy, astuteness, circumspection, comprehension, discernment, enlightenment, erudition, foresight, gnosis, intelligence, judgement, judiciousness, knowledge, learning, penetration, prudence, reason, sagacity, sapience, sence, sophia, understanding.

antonym folly.

wise *adj* aware, clever, discerning, enlightened, erudite, informed, intelligent, judicious, knowing, long-headed, long-sighted, perceptive, politic, prudent, rational, reasonable, sagacious, sage, sapient, sensible, shrewd, sound, understanding, well-advised, well-informed.

antonym foolish.

wiseacre *n* clever dick, smart Alec(k), smartypants, wise guy, wiseling.

wisecrack *n* barb, funny, gag, jest, jibe, joke, one-liner, quip, witticism.

wish *v* ask, aspire, bid, command, covet, crave, desiderate, desire, direct, greet, hanker, hope, hunger, instruct, long, need, order, require, thirst, want, whim, yearn, yen.

antonyms dislike, fear.

n aspiration, bidding, command, desire, hankering, hope, hunger, inclination, intention, liking, order, request, thirst, urge, velleity, voice, want, whim, will, yearning, yen.

antonyms dislike, fear.

wishbone *n* furcula, merry-thought.

wishy-washy *adj* bland, feeble, flat, ineffective, ineffectual, insipid, jejune, namby-pamby, tasteless, thin, vapid, watered-down, watery, weak, wersh.

antonym strong.

wisp *n* jag, lock, piece, shred, snippet, strand, thread, twist.

wispy *adj* attenuate, attenuated, delicate, diaphanous, ethereal, faint, fine, flimsy, flyaway, fragile, frail, gossamer, insubstantial, light, thin, unsubstantial.

antonym substantial.

wistful *adj* contemplative, disconsolate, dreaming, dreamy, forlorn, longing, meditative, melancholy, mournful, musing, pensive, reflective, sad, soulful, thoughtful, wishful, yearning.

wit *n* acumen, badinage, banter, brains, card, cleverness, comedian, common sense, comprehension, conceit, discernment, drollery, epigrammatist, eutrapelia, facetiousness, farceur, fun, homme d'esprit, humorist, humour, ingenuity, insight, intellect, intelligence, jocularity, joker, judgement, levity, merum sal, mind, nous, perception, pleasantry, punster, quipster, raillery, reason, repartee, sense, smeddum, understanding, wag, wisdom, wit-cracker, wordplay.

antonyms seriousness, stupidity.

witch *n* enchantress, galdregon, gyre-carline, hag, hex, lamia, magician, necromancer, occultist, pythoness, reim-kennar, sorceress, sortileger, weird, wise woman, witch-wife.

witchcraft *n* black magic, conjuration, divination, enchantment, glamour, goety, incantation, invultuation, magic, myalism, necromancy, occultism, pishogue, sorcery, sortilege, sortilegy, spell, the black art, the occult, voodoo, witchery, witching, wizardry.

witch-doctor *n* angek(k)ok, magician, medicine-man, shaman.

witch-hunt *n* hounding, hue and cry, McCarthyism.

with it fashionable, groovy, hep, hip, in, modern, modish, progressive, trendy, up-to-date, up-to-the-minute, vogue.

antonym out-of-date.

withdraw *v* abjure, absent oneself, back out, depart, disavow, disclaim, disengage, disenrol, disinvest, draw back, draw out, drop out, extract, fall back, go, go away, hive off, leave, pull back, pull out, recall, recant, remove, repair, rescind, retire, retract, retreat, revoke, secede, subduct, subtract, take away, take back, take off, unsay, waive.

antonyms advance, deposit, persist.

withdrawal *n* abjuration, departure, disavowal, disclaimer, disengagement, disinvestment, Dunkirk, exit, exodus, extraction, recall, recantation, removal, repudiation, rescission, retirement, retraction, retreat, revocation, secession, waiver, withdrawment.

antonyms advance, deposit, persistence.

withdrawn *adj* aloof, detached, distant, hidden, introvert, isolated, out-of-the-way, private, quiet, remote, reserved, retiring, secluded, shrinking, shy, silent, solitary, taciturn, uncommunicative, unforthcoming, unsociable.

antonym outgoing.

wither *v* abash, blast, blight, decay, decline, desiccate, disintegrate, droop, dry, fade, humiliate, languish, miff, mortify, perish, put down, shame, shrink, shrivel, snub, wane, waste, welt, wilt.

antonyms boost, thrive.

wither away decrease, die, die off, disappear, dwindle, fade away, miff, shrink, shrivel, wilt.

withering *adj* deadly, death-dealing, destructive, devastating, humiliating, killing, mortifying, murderous, scathing, scornful, searing, slaughterous, snubbing, wounding.

antonym supportive.

withhold *v* check, conceal, deduct, detain, hide, keen, keep back, refuse, repress, reserve, resist, restrain, retain, sit on, suppress, suspend.

antonyms accord, give.

without delay at once, immediately, pronto, quick-stick(s), right away, straight away, straightway, there and then, tout de suite.

without doubt certainly, doubtless, no doubt, questionless, unquestionably.

without fail conscientiously, constantly, dependably, faithfully, like clockwork, predictably, punctually, regularly, reliably, religiously, unfailingly, without exception.

antonyms unpredictably, unreliably.

withstand *v* bear, brave, combat, confront, cope with, defy, endure, face, grapple with, hold off, hold one's ground, hold out, last out, oppose, put up with, resist, stand, stand fast, stand one's ground, stand up to, survive, take, take on, thwart, tolerate, weather.

antonyms collapse, yield.

witless *adj* crazy, cretinous, daft, dull, empty-headed, foolish, gormless, half-witted, idiotic, imbecilic, inane, moronic, obtuse, senseless, silly, stupid.

antonym intelligent.

witness *n* attestant, beholder, bystander, corroborator, deponent, eye-witness, looker-on, observer, onlooker, spectator, testifier, viewer, vouchee, voucher, watcher, witnesser.

v attend, attest, bear out, bear witness, confirm, corroborate, countersign, depone, depose, endorse, look on, mark, note, notice, observe, perceive, see, sign, testify, view, watch.

wits *n* acumen, astuteness, brains, cleverness, comprehension, faculties, gumption, ingenuity, intelligence, judgement, marbles, mother-wit, nous, reason, sense, understanding.

antonym stupidity.

witticism *n* bon mot, epigram, jeu d'esprit, mot, one-liner, pleasantry, pun, quip, repartee, riposte, sally.

witty *adj* amusing, brilliant, clever, comic, droll, epigrammatic, facetious, fanciful, funny, humorous, ingenious, jocular, lively, original, piquant, salty, sparkling, waggish, whimsical.

antonyms dull, unamusing.

wizard[1] *n* conjurer, enchanter, mage, magician, magus, necromancer, occultist, reim-kennar, shaman, sorcerer, sortileger, thaumaturge, warlock, witch.

wizard[2] *n* ace, adept, dabster, deacon, expert, genius, hotshot, maestro, master, prodigy, star, virtuoso, whiz.

antonym duffer.

adj ace, brilliant, enjoyable, fab, fantastic, good, great, marvellous, sensational, smashing, super, superb, terrif, terrific, tiptop, top-hole, topping, tremendous, wonderful.

antonym rotten.

wizardry *n* black magic, conjuration, divination, enchantment, glamour, goety, incantation, invultuation, magic, myalism, necromancy, occultism, pishogue, sorcery, sortilege, sortilegy, the black art, the occult, voodoo, warlockry, witchcraft, witchery, witching.

wizened *adj* dried up, gnarled, lined, sere, shrivelled, shrunken, thin, weazen, weazened, withered, wizen, worn, wrinkled.

antonyms plump, smooth.

wobble *v* dither, dodder, fluctuate, haver, heave, hesitate, oscillate, quake, rock, seesaw, shake, shilly-shally, shoggle, sway, swither, teeter, totter, tremble, vacillate, vibrate, waver.

n oscillation, quaking, rock, shake, tremble, tremor, unsteadiness, vibration.

wobbly *adj* doddering, doddery, rickety, shaky, shoogly, teetering, tottering, unbalanced, uneven, unsafe, unstable, unsteady, wonky.

antonym stable.

woe *n* adversity, affliction, agony, anguish, burden, curse, dejection, depression, disaster, distress, dole, dolour, dule, gloom, grief, hardship, heartache, heartbreak, melancholy, misery, misfortune, pain, sadness, sorrow, suffering, tears, trial, tribulation, trouble, unhappiness, wretchedness.

antonym joy.

woebegone *adj* blue, crestfallen, dejected, disconsolate, dispirited, doleful, down in the mouth, downcast, downhearted, forlorn, gloomy, grief-stricken, hangdog, long-faced, lugubrious, miserable, mournful, sad, sorrowful, tearful, tear-stained, troubled, wretched.

antonym joyful.

woeful *adj* agonising, appalling, awful, bad, calamitous, catastrophic, cruel, deplorable, disappointing, disastrous, disconsolate, disgraceful, distressing, doleful, dreadful, feeble, gloomy, grieving, grievous, heartbreaking, heart-rending, hopeless, inadequate, lamentable, lousy, mean, miserable, mournful, paltry, pathetic, piteous, pitiable, pitiful, plaintive, poor, rotten, sad, shocking, sorrowful, sorry, terrible, tragic, unhappy, woesome, wretched.

antonym joyful.

wolf *n* Casanova, dallier, Don Juan, ladies' man, lady-killer, lecher, Lothario, philanderer, Romeo, seducer, womaniser.

wolf down bolt, cram, devour, gobble, gorge, gormandise, gulp, pack away, put away, scoff, shift, stuff.

antonym nibble.

wolf-man *n* lycanthrope, lycanthropist, werewolf.

woman *n* bimbo, bint, bird, bride, broad, chambermaid, char, charwoman, chick, dame, daughter, domestic, fair, female, feme, femme, Frau, gimmer, girl, girlfriend, handmaiden, housekeeper, kept woman, lady, lady-in-waiting, ladylove, lass, lassie, maid, maiden, maidservant, mate, miss, mistress, mort, old lady, partner, piece, placket, she, sheila, spouse, sweetheart, vrouw, wife, woman-body.

antonym man.

womanhood *n* muliebrity, woman, womankind, womenfolk(s), womenkind.

womaniser *n* Casanova, dallier, Don Juan, ladies' man, lady-killer, lecher, Lothario, philanderer, Romeo, seducer, wolf.

womanising *n* dalliance, lechery, philandering, venery, wenching, whoring.

womanly *adj* female, feminine, ladylike, matronly, motherly, weak, womanish.

antonym manly.

womb *n* matrix, uterus.

women *n* distaff side, muliebrity, muslin, womanhood, womankind, womenfolk(s), womenkind.

wonder *n* admiration, amaze, amazement, astonishment, awe, bewilderment, curiosity, fascination, marvel, miracle, nonpareil, phenomenon, portent, prodigy, rarity, sight, spectacle, stupefaction, surprise, wonderment, wunderkind.

antonyms disinterest, ordinariness.

v ask oneself, boggle, conjecture, doubt, gape, gaup, gawk, inquire, marvel, meditate, ponder, puzzle, query, question, speculate, stare, think.

wonderful *adj* ace, admirable, amazing, astonishing, astounding, awe-inspiring, awesome, brilliant, épatant, excellent, extraordinary, fab, fabulous, fantastic, great, incredible, magnificent, marvellous, miraculous, mirific(al), odd, oustanding, peculiar, phenomenal, remarkable, sensational, smashing, staggering, startling, strange, stupendous, super, superb, surprising, terrif, terrific, tiptop, top-hole, topping, tremendous, unheard-of, wizard, wondrous.

antonyms ordinary, rotten.

wonders *n* curiosities, magic, marvels, mirabilia, miracles, phenomena, prodigies, sights.

wonky *adj* amiss, askew, awry, groggy, infirm, shaky, skew-whiff, squint, unsound, unsteady, weak, wobbly, wrong.

antonyms stable, straight.

wont *adj* accustomed, given, habituated, used.

n custom, habit, practice, routine, rule, use, way.

wonted *adj* accustomed, common, conventional, customary, daily, familiar, frequent, habitual, normal, regular, routine, usual.

antonym unwonted.

woo *v* chase, court, cultivate, importune, look for, pay court to, pursue, seek, seek the hand of.

wood[1] *n* hyle, lumber, planks, timber.

wood[2] *n* bosk, coppice, copse, forest, grove, hanger, holt, hurst, plantation, thicket, trees, underwood, woodland, woods.

wooded *adj* bosky, forested, nemorous, silvan, timbered, tree-covered, woody.

antonym open.

wooden *adj* awkward, blank, clumsy, colourless, deadpan, dense, dim, dim-witted, dull, dull-witted, emotionless, empty, expressionless, gauche, gawky, glassy, graceless, inelegant, inflexible, lifeless, ligneous, maladroit, muffled, oaken, obstinate, obtuse, rigid, slow, spiritless, stiff, stupid, thick, timber, treen, unbending, unemotional, ungainly, unresponsive, unyielding, vacant, woody, xyloid.

antonyms bright, lively.

woodland *n* boscage, forest, frith (firth), wood(s).

woody *adj* bosky, forested, ligneous, sylvan, tree-covered, wooded, wooden, xyloid.

antonym open.

wool *n* down, fleece, floccus, fluff, hair, yarn.

woolly *adj* blurred, clouded, confused, fleecy, floccose, flocculent, foggy, frizzy, fuzzy, hairy, hazy, ill-defined, indefinite, indistinct, lanate, laniferous, lanigerous, lanose, muddled, nappy, nebulous, shaggy, ulotrichous, unclear, vague, woolled, woollen, woolly-haired.

n cardigan, guernsey, jersey, jumper, pullover, sweater.

woozy *adj* befuddled, bemused, blurred, confused, dazed, dizzy, fuddled, nauseated, pickled, pixil(l)ated, rocky, tipsy, unsteady, vague, wobbly, woolly.

antonyms alert, sober.

word *n* account, advice, affirmation, assertion, assurance, bidding, bulletin, chat, colloquy, command, commandment, comment, communication, communiqué, confab, confabulation, consultation, conversation, countersign, declaration, decree, dicky-bird, discussion, dispatch, edict, expression, firman, go-ahead, green light, guarantee, hatti-sherif, hint, information, intelligence, interlocution, intimation, lexigram, locution, mandate, message, news, notice, oath, order, palabra, parole, password, pledge, promise, remark, report, rescript, rumour, sign, signal, slogan, talk, term, tête-à-tête, tidings, ukase, undertaking, utterance, vocable, vow, war-cry, watch-word, will.

v couch, explain, express, phrase, put, say, write.

wordiness *n* bafflegab, logorrhoea, perissology, verbal diarrhoea, verbiage, wordage.

wording *n* choice of words, diction, language, phraseology, phrasing, style, terminology, verbiage, wordage, words.

word-lover *n* logodaedalus, philologist, philologue, verbalist, verbarian, vocabularian, wordsmith.

word-perfect *adj* accurate, exact, faithful, letter-perfect, spot-on.

antonym inaccurate.

word-play *n* paronomasia, punning, puns, repartee, wit, witticisms.

words *n* altercation, argument, barney, bickering, contention, disagreement, dispute, libretto, lyrics, quarrel, row, run-in, set-to, squabble, text.

wordy *adj* diffuse, discursive, garrulous, longiloquent, long-winded, loquacious, phrasy, pleonastic, prolix, rambling, verbose, windy.

antonyms concise, laconic.

work *n* achievement, art, assignment, book, business, calling, chore, commission, composition, craft, creation, darg, deed, doings, drudgery, duty, effort, elbow grease, employ, employment, exertion, graft, grind, handiwork, industry, job, labour, line, livelihood, métier, occupation, oeuvre, office, opus, ouvrage, performance, piece, play, poem, production, profession, pursuit, service, skill, slog, stint, sweat, task, toil, trade, travail, undertaking, workload, workmanship.

antonyms hobby, play, rest.

v accomplish, achieve, act, arrange, beaver, bring about, bring off, cause, contrive, control, convulse, create, cultivate, dig, direct, drive, drudge, effect, encompass, execute, exploit, farm, fashion, fiddle, fix, force, form, function, go, graft, handle, implement, knead, labour, make, manage, manipulate, manoeuvre, mould, move, operate, peg away, perform, ply, process, progress, pull off, run, shape, slave, slog, sweat, swing, till, toil, twitch, use, wield, writhe.

antonyms fail, play, rest.

work on butter up, cajole, coax, dissuade, influence, inveigle, persuade, soft-soap, sweet-talk, talk round, wheedle.

work out accomplish, achieve, add up to, amount to, arrange, attain, calculate, clear up, come out, come to, construct, contrive, develop, devise, drill, effect, elaborate, evolve, excogitate, exercise, exhaust, expiate, figure out, flourish, form, formulate, go, happen, pan out, plan, practise, prosper, put together, puzzle out, reach, resolve, result, solve, succeed, train, turn out, warm up, win, worry out.

work up agitate, animate, arouse, elaborate, enkindle, excite, expand, foment, generate, incite, increase, inflame, instigate, move, rouse, spur, stir up, wind up.

workable *adj* doable, effectible, feasible, possible, practicable, practical, realistic, viable.

antonym unworkable.

workaday *adj* common, commonplace, dull, everyday, familiar, humdrum, labouring, mundane, ordinary, practical, prosaic, routine, run-of-the-mill, toiling, work-day, working.

antonym exciting.

worker *n* artisan, craftsman, employee, hand, labourer, proletarian, staffer, tradesman, work-girl, workhorse, working man, working woman, workman, work-woman.

antonym idler.

workforce *n* employees, hands, labour, labour force, personnel, shop-floor, staff, workers, workfolk(s), work-people.

working *n* action, functioning, manner, method, operation, routine, running.

adj active, employed, functioning, going, labouring, operational, operative, running.

antonyms idle, inoperative, retired, unemployed.

workings *n* diggings, excavations, mine, pit, quarry, shaft.

workman *n* artificer, artisan, craftsman, employee, hand, journeyman, labourer, mechanic, navvy, operative, tradesman, worker.

workmanlike *adj* adept, careful, efficient, expert, masterly, painstaking, professional, proficient, satisfactory, skilful, skilled, thorough, workmanly.

antonym amateurish.

workmanship *n* art, artistry, craft, craftsmanship, execution, expertise, facture, finish, handicraft, handiwork, manufacture, skill, technique, work.

work-mate *n* associate, colleague, co-worker, fellow-worker, work-fellow, yoke-fellow, yoke-mate.

works[1] *n* factory, foundry, mill, plant, shop, workshop.

works[2] *n* actions, acts, books, canon, deeds, doings, oeuvre, output, plays, poetry, productions, writings.

works[3] *n* action, gearing, guts, innards, insides, machinery, mechanism, movement, parts, workings.

workshop *n* atelier, class, discussion group, factory, mill, plant, school, seminar, shop, studio, symposium, workroom, works.

world *n* age, area, class, creation, days, division, domain, earth, environment, epoch, era, existence, field, globe, human race, humanity, humankind, kingdom, life, man, mankind, men, nature, people, period, planet, province, public, realm, society, sphere, star, system, terrene, times, universe, Welt.

worldly *adj* ambitious, avaricious, blasé, carnal, cosmopolitan, covetous, earthly, experienced, fleshly, grasping, greedy, knowing, lay, materialistic, mondain, mundane, physical, politic, profane, secular, selfish, sophisticated, sublunary, temporal, terrene, terrestrial, unspiritual, urbane, worldly-minded, worldly-wise.

antonym unworldly.

worldwide *adj* catholic, general, global, international, mondial, pandemic, ubiquitous, universal.

antonym local.

worn *adj* attrite, bromidic, careworn, cliché'd, drawn, exhausted, fatigued, frayed, hackneyed, haggard, jaded, lined, pinched, played-out, ragged, shabby, shiny, spent, tattered, tatty, threadbare, tired, trite, wearied, weary, wizened, woe-wearied, woe-worn, worn-out.

antonyms fresh, new.

worn out all in, clapped out, clapped-out, dead on one's feet, decrepit, dog-tired, done, done in, épuisé(e), exhausted, fatigued, finished, fit to drop, forswunk, frayed, jiggered, knackered, moth-eaten, on its last legs, played-out, prostrate, ragged, shabby, spent, tattered, tatty, threadbare, tired, tired out, used, useless, warby, weary, worn, zonked.

antonym fresh.

worried *adj* afraid, agonised, anxious, apprehensive, bothered, concerned, distracted, distraught, distressed, disturbed, fearful, frabbit, fretful, frightened, ill at ease, nervous, on edge, overwrought, perturbed, strained, tense, tormented, troubled, uneasy, unquiet, upset.

antonyms calm, unconcerned, unworried.

worrisome *adj* agonising, anxious, apprehensive, bothersome, disquieting, distressing, disturbing, fretful, frightening, insecure, irksome, jittery, nail-biting, nervous, perturbing, troublesome, uneasy, upsetting, vexing, worrying.

antonyms calm, reassuring, unworried.

worry *v* agonise, annoy, attack, badger, bite, bother, brood, deave, disquiet, distress, disturb, faze, feeze, frab, fret, get one's knickers in a twist, gnaw at, go for, harass, harry, hassle, hector, importune, irritate, kill, lacerate, nag, perturb, pester, plague, savage, tantalise, tear, tease, torment, trouble, unsettle, upset, vex.

antonyms comfort, reassure.

n agitation, annoyance, anxiety, apprehension, care, concern, disturbance, fear, irritation, misery, misgiving, perplexity, pest, plague, problem, stew, tew, tizz, tizzy, torment, trial, trouble, unease, vexation, woe, worriment.

antonyms comfort, reassurance.

worrying *adj* anxious, disquieting, distressing, disturbing, harassing, nail-biting, perturbing, troublesome, trying, uneasy, unsettling, upsetting, worrisome.

antonym reassuring.

worsen *v* aggravate, damage, decay, decline, degenerate, deteriorate, disimprove, exacerbate, go downhill, pejorate, retrogress, sink, take a turn for the worse.

antonym improve.

worsening *n* decay, decline, degeneration, deterioration, exacerbation, pejoration, retrogression.

antonym improvement.

worship *v* adore, adulate, deify, exalt, glorify, honour, idolatrise, idolise, kanticoy, laud, love, misworship, praise, pray to, respect, revere, reverence, venerate.

antonym despise.

n adoration, adulation, allotheism, deification, devotion(s), dulia, exaltation, glorification, glory, homage, honour, hyperdulia, image-worship, knee-drill, latria, latry, laudation, love, misdevotion, misworship, monolatry, praise, prayer(s), puja, regard, respect, reverence, will-worship.

antonym vilification.

worst *v* beat, best, conquer, crush, defeat, drub, master, overcome, overpower, overthrow, subdue, subjugate, vanquish, whitewash.

worth *n* aid, assistance, avail, benefit, cost, credit, desert(s), excellence, goodness, help, importance, merit, price, quality, rate, significance, use, usefulness, utility, value, virtue, worthiness.

antonym worthlessness.

worthless *adj* abandoned, abject, base, beggarly, Brummagem, contemptible, depraved, despicable, draffish, draffy, futile, good-for-nothing, grotty, ignoble, ineffectual, insignificant, littleworth, meaningless, miserable, naff, no use, no-account, no-good, nugatory, paltry, pointless, poor, rubbishy, scabbed, scabby, screwy, stramineous, trashy, trifling, trivial, unavailing, unimportant, unusable, useless, valueless, vaurien, vile, wretched.

antonym valuable.

worthwhile *adj* beneficial, constructive, furthersome, gainful, good, helpful, justifiable, productive, profitable, useful, utile, valuable, worthy.

antonym useless.

worthy *adj* admirable, appropriate, commendable, creditable, decent, dependable, deserving, estimable, excellent, fit, good, honest, honourable, laudable, meritorious, praiseworthy, reliable, reputable, respectable, righteous, suitable, upright, valuable, virtuous, worthwhile.

antonyms disreputable, unworthy.

n big cheese, big noise, big pot, big shot, big-wig, dignitary, luminary, name, notable, personage.

wound *n* anguish, cut, damage, distress, gash, grief, harm, heartbreak, hurt, injury, insult, laceration, lesion, offence, pain, pang, scar, shock, slash, slight, torment, torture, trauma.

v annoy, bless, cut, cut to the quick, damage, distress, gash, grieve, harm, hit, hurt, injure, irritate, lacerate, mortify, offend, pain, pierce, pip, shock, slash, sting, traumatise, wing, wring someone's withers.

wraith *n* apparition, ghost, larva, lemur, phantom, revenant, shade, spectre, spirit, spook.

wrangle *n* altercation, argument, argy-bargy, barney, bickering, brawl, clash, contest, controversy, dispute, quarrel, row, set-to, slanging match, squabble, tiff, tussle.

antonym agreement.

v altercate, argue, argufy, bicker, brawl, contend, digladiate, disagree, dispute, ergotise, fall out, fight, quarrel, row, scrap, squabble.

antonym agree.

wrap *v* absorb, bind, bundle up, cloak, cocoon, cover, encase, enclose, enfold, envelop, fold, hap, immerse, muffle, pack, package, roll up, sheathe, shroud, surround, swathe, wind.

antonym unwrap.

n cape, cloak, mantle, pelisse, robe, shawl, stole.

wrap up[1] bring to a close, complete, conclude, end, finish off, pack up, package, parcel, round off, terminate, wind up.

antonym begin.

wrap up[2] be quiet, hold one's tongue, hold one's wheesht, put a sock in it, shoosh, shut it, shut one's cakehole, shut one's face, shut one's mouth, shut one's trap, shut up, wheesht.

wrapper *n* cover, dust-jacket, envelope, jacket, packaging, paper, sheath, sleeve, wrapping.

wrapping *n* blister card, blister pack, bubble pack, carton, case, cellophane®, envelope, Jiffybag®, packaging, paper, silver-paper, swathe, tinfoil, wrappage.

wrath *n* anger, bitterness, choler, displeasure, exasperation, fury, indignation, ire, irritation, passion, rage, resentment, spleen, temper.

antonyms calm, pleasure.

wrathful *adj* angry, bitter, displeased, enraged, furibund, furious, gusty, in a paddy, incensed, indignant, infuriated, irate, ireful, on the warpath, raging, waxy, wrathy, wroth.

antonyms calm, pleased.

wreak *v* bestow, bring about, carry out, cause, create, effect, execute, exercise, express, inflict, perpetrate, unleash, vent, visit, work.

wreath *n* anadem, band, chaplet, coronet, crown, festoon, garland, lei, loop, ring.

wreathe *v* adorn, coil, crown, encircle, enfold, entwine, envelop, enwrap, festoon, intertwine, interweave, surround, swathe, twine, twist, wind, wrap, writhe.

wreck *v* break, crab, demolish, destroy, devastate, mar, play havoc with, ravage, ruin, shatter, smash, spoil, torpedo, write off.

antonyms repair, save.

n derelict, desolation, destruction, devastation, disruption, hulk, mess, overthrow, ruin, ruination, shipwreck, undoing, write-off.

wreckage *n* debris, flotsam, fragments, pieces, remains, rubble, ruin, waveson, wrack.

wrench *v* distort, force, jerk, pull, rax, rick, rip, sprain, strain, tear, tug, twist, wrest, wring, yank.

n ache, blow, jerk, monkey-wrench, pain, pang, pliers, pull, sadness, shock, sorrow, spanner, sprain, tear, tug, twist, upheaval, uprooting.

wrest *v* extract, force, pervert, pull, seize, strain, take, twist, win, wrench, wring.

wrestle *v* battle, combat, contend, contest, fight, grapple, scuffle, strive, struggle, tussle, vie.

wretch *n* blackguard, cad, caitiff, cullion, cur, good-for-nothing, insect, miscreant, no-good, outcast, pilgarlick, profligate, rapscallion, rascal, rascallion, rat, rogue, rotter, ruffian, scoundrel, swine, vagabond, villain, wight, worm.

wretched *adj* abject, base, broken-hearted, caitiff, calamitous, cheerless, comfortless, contemptible, crestfallen, dejected, deplorable, depressed, despicable, disconsolate, distressed, doggone, doleful, downcast, forlorn, gloomy, grotty, hapless, hopeless, inferior, low, low-down, mean, melancholy, miserable, paltry, pathetic, pesky, pitiable, pitiful, poor, ratty, scurvy, shabby, shameful, sorry, unfortunate, unhappy, vile, woebegone, woeful, worthless.

antonyms excellent, happy.

wriggle *v* crawl, dodge, edge, extricate, jerk, jiggle, manoeuvre, scriggle, sidle, slink, snake, sneak, squiggle, squirm, talk one's way out, turn, twist, wag, waggle, wiggle, worm, writhe, zigzag.

n jerk, jiggle, squirm, turn, twist, twitch, wag, waggle, wiggle.

wring *v* coerce, distress, exact, extort, extract, force, hurt, lacerate, mangle, pain, pierce, rack, rend, screw, squeeze, stab, tear, torture, twist, wound, wrench, wrest.

wrinkle *n* corrugation, crease, crinkle, crow's-foot, crumple, fold, furrow, gather, line, pucker, rumple, wimple.

v corrugate, crease, crinkle, crumple, fold, furrow, gather, line, pucker, rivel, ruck, rumple, runkle, shrivel.

wrinkled *adj* creased, crinkled, crinkly, crumpled, furrowed, puckered, ridged, rivelled, rugate, rugose, rugous, rumpled, wrinkly.

antonym smooth.

writ *n* court order, decree, subpoena, summons.

write *v* compose, copy, correspond, create, draft, draw up, indite, inscribe, jot down, pen, record, screeve, scribble, scribe, set down, take down, tell, transcribe.

write off cancel, crash, cross out, destroy, disregard, scrub, smash up, wreck.

writer *n* amanuensis, author, authoress, clerk, columnist, copyist, crime writer, detectivist, dialogist, diarist, diatribist, dramatist, dramaturg, dramaturgist, elegiast, elegist, encomiast, epigrammatist, epistler, epistolarian, epistoler, epistolist, epitapher, epitaphist, epitomist, essayist, farceur, fictionist, hack, librettist, littérateur, man of letters, memoirist, novelist, panegyrist, paper-stainer, pen, penman, penny-a-liner, penpusher, penwoman, periodicalist, playwright, prosaist, proseman, proser, prose-writer, quill-driver, scribbler, scribe, secretary, wordsmith, writeress.

writhe *v* coil, contort, jerk, squirm, struggle, thrash, thresh, toss, twist, wiggle, wreathe, wriggle.

writing *n* autography, belles-lettres, book, calligraphy, chirography, composition, document, exaration, hand, handwriting, letter, letters, literature, opus, penmanship, print, publication, scrawl, scribble, script, work.

written *adj* documental, documentary, drawn up, recorded, set down, transcribed.

antonyms unwritten, verbal.

wrong *adj* abusive, amis, askew, awry, bad, blameworthy, criminal, crooked, defective, dishonest, dishonourable, erroneous, evil, fallacious, false, faulty, felonious, funny, illegal, illicit, immoral, improper, in error, in the wrong, inaccurate, inappropriate, inapt, incongruous, incorrect, indecorous, infelicitous, iniquitous, inner, inside, inverse, malapropos, misinformed, mistaken, off base, off beam, off target, opposite, out, out of commission, out of order, reprehensible, reverse, sinful, unacceptable, unbecoming, unconventional, under, undesirable, unethical, unfair, unfitting, unhappy, unjust, unlawful, unseemly, unsound, unsuitable, untrue, wicked, wide of the mark, wrongful, wrongous.

antonym right.

adv amiss, askew, astray, awry, badly, erroneously, faultily, improperly, inaccurately, incorrectly, mistakenly, wrongly.

antonym right.

n abuse, crime, error, grievance, immorality, inequity, infraction, infringement, iniquity, injury, injustice, misdeed, offence, sin, sinfulness, transgression, trespass, unfairness, wickedness, wrong-doing.

antonym right.

v abuse, cheat, discredit, dishonour, harm, hurt, ill-treat, ill-use, impose on, injure, malign, maltreat, misrepresent, mistreat, oppress, traduce.

wrong-doer *n* criminal, culprit, delinquent, evil-doer, felon, law-breaker, malefactor, miscreant, offender, sinner, transgressor, trespasser.

wrong-doing *n* crime, delinquency, error, evil, fault, felony, immorality, iniquity, maleficence, mischief, misdeed, offence, sin, sinfulness, transgression, wickedness.

wrongful *adj* blameworthy, criminal, dishonest, dishonourable, evil, felonious, illegal, illegitimate, illicit, immoral, improper, reprehensible, unethical, unfair, unjust, unlawful, wicked, wrong, wrongous.

antonym rightful.

wrongly *adv* badly, by mistake, erroneously, in error, inaccurately, incorrectly, mistakenly.

antonym rightly.

wrought *adj* beaten, decorative, fashioned, hammered, made, manufactured, ornamental, ornamented, ornate, shaped.

wry *adj* askew, aslant, awry, contorted, crooked, deformed, distorted, droll, dry, ironic, mocking, pawky, perverse, sarcastic, sardonic, thrawn, twisted, uneven, warped.

antonym straight.

XYZ

xenophobia *n* ethnocentrism, racialism, racism, xenophoby.

antonym xenomania.

xenophobic *adj* ethnocentrist, parochial, racialist, racist.

ya(c)k *v* blather, chatter, gab, gossip, jabber, jaw, prattle, run on, tattle, twattle, witter on, yap, yatter.

n blah, blather, chat, chinwag, confab, gossip, hot air, jaw, prattle, twattle, ya(c)kety-ya(c)k, yatter.

yank *v, n* haul, heave, jerk, pull, snatch, tug, wrench.

yap *v* babble, blather, chatter, go on, gossip, jabber, jaw, prattle, talk, tattle, twattle, ya(c)k, yammer, yatter, yelp, yip.

yard *n* court, court-yard, garden, garth, Hof, hypaethron, quad, quadrangle.

yardstick *n* benchmark, comparison, criterion, gauge, measure, standard, touchstone.

yarn[1] *n* abb, fibre, fingering, gimp, lisle, thread.

yarn[2] *n* anecdote, cock-and-bull story, fable, fabrication, story, tale, tall story.

yawn *v* gape, ga(u)nt, open, split.

yawning *adj* cavernous, gaping, hiant, huge, vast, wide, wide-open.

antonym narrow.

yearly *adj* annual, per annum, per year.

adv annually, every year, once a year.

yearn for ache for, covet, crave, desire, hanker for, hunger for, itch for, languish for, long for, lust for, pant for, pine for, want, wish for, yen for.

antonym dislike.

yell *v* bawl, bellow, holler, hollo, howl, roar, scream, screech, shout, shriek, squawl, squeal, whoop, yelp, yowl.

antonym whisper.

n bellow, cry, holler, hollo, howl, roar, scream, screech, shriek, squawl, whoop, yelp.

antonym whisper.

yellow *adj* flavescent, flaxen, fulvid, fulvous, gold, golden, lemon, primrose, saffron, vitellary, vitelline, xanthic, xanthochroic, xanthomelanous, xanthous.

yelp *v* bark, bay, cry, yap, yell, yip, yowl.

n bark, cry, yap, yell, yip, yowl.

yen *n* craving, desire, hankering, hunger, itch, longing, lust, passion, thing, yearning.

antonym dislike.

yes *interj* absolutely, affirmative, agreed, aye, quite, right, uh-huh, yea, yeah, yep.

antonym no.

yes-man *n* arse-licker, bootlicker, crawler, creature, lackey, minion, sycophant, toad-eater, toady.

yesterday's *adj* bygone, hesternal, passé, past, stale.

antonym tomorrow's.

yield[1] *v* abandon, abdicate, accede, acquiesce, admit defeat, agree, allow, bow, capitulate, cave in, cede, comply, concede, consent, cry quits, give, give in, give way, go along with, grant, knuckle under, part with, permit, relinquish, resign, resign oneself, submit, succumb, surrender, throw in the towel.

antonym withstand.

yield[2] *v* afford, bear, bring forth, bring in, earn, fructify, fructuate, fruit, furnish, generate, give, net, pay, produce, provide, return, supply.

n crop, earnings, harvest, income, output, proceeds, produce, product, profit, return, revenue, takings.

yielding *adj* accommodating, acquiescent, amenable, biddable, complaisant, compliant, docile, easy, elastic, flexible, obedient, obliging, pliable, pliant, quaggy, resilient, soft, spongy, springy, submissive, supple, tractable, unresisting.

antonyms obstinate, solid.

yobbo *n* apache, corner-boy, hoodlum, hooligan, keelie, lager lout, loafer, lout, rough, rowdy, ruffian, thug, tough, yahoo, yob.

yoke *n* bond, bondage, burden, chain, coupling, enslavement, helotry, ligament, link, oppression, serfdom, service, servility, servitude, slavery, subjugation, thraldom, tie, vassalage.

v bracket, connect, couple, enslave, harness, hitch, inspan, join, link, tie, unite.

antonym unhitch.

yokel *n* boor, bucolic, bumpkin, clodhopper, cornball, country cousin, hick, hillbilly, jake, joskin, peasant, rustic.

antonyms sophisticate, towny.

young *adj* adolescent, baby, callow, cub, early, fledgling, green, growing, immature, infant, junior, juvenile, little, new, recent, unblown, unfledged, youthful.

antonym old.

n babies, brood, chicks, cubs, family, fledglings, issue, litter, little ones, offspring, progeny, quiverful.

antonym parents.

youngster *n* boy, girl, juvenile, kid, lad, laddie, lass, lassie, nipper, shaver, teenybopper, urchin, young pup, youth.

antonym oldie.

youth *n* adolescence, adolescent, boy, boyhood, colt, ephebe, ephebus, girlhood, halflin(g), hobbledehoy, immaturity, juvenescence, juvenile, kid, lad, salad days, shaveling, springal(d), stripling, swain, teenager, the young, young man, young people, young shaver, younger generation, youngster, younker.

antonyms old age, oldie.

youthful *adj* active, boyish, childish, ephebic, fresh, girlish, immature, inexperienced, juvenescent, juvenile, lively, pubescent, puerile, sprightly, spry, vigorous, vivacious, well-preserved, young.

antonyms aged, languorous.

youthfulness *n* freshness, juvenileness, juvenility, liveliness, sprightliness, spryness, vigour, vivaciousness, vivacity.

antonyms agedness, languor.

yowl *v* bay, caterwaul, cry, howl, screech, squall, ululate, wail, yell, yelp.

n cry, howl, screech, wail, yell, yelp.

yucky *adj* beastly, dirty, disgusting, filthy, foul, grotty, horrible, messy, mucky, revolting, saccharine, sentimental, sickly, unpleasant.

antonym nice.

zany *adj* amusing, clownish, comical, crazy, daft, droll, eccentric, funny, goofy, kooky, loony, madcap, nutty, screwy, wacky.

antonym serious.

n buffoon, card, clown, comedian, cure, droll, fool, jester, joker, kook, laugh, merry-andrew, nut, nutcase, nutter, screwball, wag.

zeal *n* ardour, dedication, devotion, eagerness, earnestness, enthusiasm, fanaticism, fervency, fervour, fire, gusto, keenness, militancy, passion, spirit, verve, warmth, zelotypia, zest.

antonym apathy.

zealot *n* bigot, devotee, enthusiast, extremist, fanatic, fiend, freak, maniac, militant.

zealous *adj* ardent, burning, devoted, eager, earnest, enthusiastic, fanatical, fervent, fervid, fired, gung-ho, impassioned, keen, militant, passionate, rabid, spirited.

antonym apathetic.

zenith *n* acme, apex, apogee, climax, culmination, height, high point, meridian, peak, pinnacle, summit, top, vertex.

antonym nadir.

zero *n* bottom, cipher, duck, goose-egg, love, nadir, naught, nil, nothing, nought.

zero in on aim for, concentrate on, converge on, direct at, fix on, focus on, head for, home in on, level at, pinpoint, train on.

zest *n* appetite, charm, delectation, élan, enjoyment, flavour, gusto, interest, joie de vivre, keenness, kick, peel, piquancy, pungency, relish, rind, savour, smack, spice, tang, taste, zeal, zing.

antonym apathy.

zigzag *v* meander, snake, wind, yaw.

adj meandering, serpentine, sinuous, zigzagging, zigzaggy.

antonym straight.

zing *n* animation, brio, dash, élan, energy, go, joie de vivre, life, liveliness, oomph, pizazz, sparkle, spirit, vigour, vitality, zest, zip.

antonym listlessness.

zip *n* brio, drive, élan, energy, enthusiasm, get-up-and-go, go, gusto, life, liveliness, oomph, pep, pizzazz, punch, sparkle, spirit, verve, vigour, vim, vitality, zest, zing.

antonym listlessness.

v dash, flash, fly, gallop, hurry, race, rush, scoot, shoot, speed, tear, whiz, whoosh, zoom.

zone *n* area, belt, district, region, section, sector, sphere, stratum, territory, tract, zona, zonule, zonulet.

zoo *n* animal park, aquarium, aviary, menagerie, safari park, zoological gardens.

zoom *v* buzz, dash, dive, flash, fly, gallop, hare, hurtle, pelt, race, rush, scoot, shoot, speed, streak, tear, whirl, whiz, whoosh, zip.

Appendices

Appendix I: classified word lists

Appendix II: words listed by suffix

Appendix I

Classified word-lists

air and space vehicles

aerobus
aerodrome
aerodyne
aerohydroplane
aeroplane
aerostat
air-ambulance
air-bus
airship
all-wing aeroplane
amphibian
autogiro
balloon
biplane
blimp
bomber
cable-car
camel
canard
chopper
comsat
convertiplane
crate
delta-wing
dirigible
dive bomber
fan-jet
fighter
fire-balloon
flying boat
flying saucer
flying wing
glider
gondola
gyrocopter
gyroplane
helibus
helicopter
hoverbus
hovercar
hovercraft
hovertrain
hydro-aeroplane
hydrofoil
hydroplane
intercepter
jet
jetliner
jetplane
lem
microlight
module
monoplane
multiplane
plane
rocket
rocket-plane
runabout
sailplane
satellite
seaplane
space platform
space probe
space shuttle
spacecraft
spaceship
spitfire
sputnik
step-rocket
stol
strato-cruiser
stratotanker
swingtail cargo aircraft
swing-wing
tanker
taube
téléférique
tow-plane
tractor
triplane
troop-carrier
tube
tug
turbojet
turbo-jet
twoseater
UFO
warplane
zeppelin

alphabets, writing systems

Chalcidian alphabet
cuneiform
Cyrillic
devanagari
estrang(h)elo
finger-alphabet
futhark
Glagol
Glossic
Greek
Gurmukhi
hieroglyphs
hiragana
ideograph
kana
katakana
Kufic
linear A
linear B
logograph
nagari
naskhi
og(h)am
pictograph
Roman
runic
syllabary

anatomical

abductor
acromion
adductor
alvine
ancon
astragalus
atlas
aural
auricular
axilla
biceps
blade-bone
bone
brachial
bregma
buccal
calcaneum
calcaneus
capitate
cardiac
carpal
carpus
cartilage
cephalic
cerebral
cholecyst
clavicle
coccyx
c(o)eliac
collar-bone
concha
coracoid
crural
cuboid
cuneiform
deltoid
dental
derm
derma
dermal
dermic
diaphragm
diencephalon
digital
diploe
diverticulum
dorsal
dorsolumbar
dorsum
duodenal
duodenum
dura mater
earlap
elbow
enarthrosis
encephalic
encephalon
endocardiac
endocardial
endocardium
endocrinal
endocrine
epencephalic
epencephalon
epidermal
epidermic
epidermis
epididymis
epigastric
epigastrium
epiglottic
epiglottis
epithelium
eponychium
erythrocyte
ethmoid
extensor
Fallopian tubes
false rib
femur
fenestra ovalis
fenestra rotunda
fibula
flexor
floating rib
fontanel(le)
fonticulus
foramen magnum
forearm
forebrain
forefinger
foreskin
fourchette
fr(a)enum
frontal
funiculus
funny bone
gastric
gastrocnemius
gena
genal
genial
genitalia
genu
gingival
glabella
glabellar
gladiolus
glossa
glossal
glottal
glottic
glottis
glut(a)eus
gnathal
gnathic
gonion
gracilis
gremial
gristle

anatomical *(contd.)*
groin
gula
gular
gullet
guttural
h(a)emal
haematic
hallux
ham
hamate
hamstring
helix
hepatic
hind-brain
hindhead
hip-bone
hip-girdle
hock
huckle-bone
humeral
humerus
hyoid
hypogastrium
hypothalamus
iliac
ilium
incus
inguinal
innominate
innominate bone
intercostal
ischium
jugular
labial
lachrymal
lacrimal
leucocyte
ligament
lumbar
lumbrical
lunate
luz
malar
malleolus
malleus
mamillar(y)
mammary
mandible
mandibular
manubrium
marriage-bone
mastoid
maxilla
maxillary
membral
mental
merrythought
metacarpal
metatarsal
mons veneris
mount of Venus
muscle
nasal
nates
navicular
neural
obturators
occipital
occiput
occlusal
occlusion
occlusor
ocular
odontic
(o)esophagus
omentum
omohyoid
omoplate
optical
orbicularis
orbit(a)
origin
os innominatum
oscheal
oscular
ossicle
otic
otolith
palatal
palatine
palpebral
parasphenoid
parietal
paroccipital
parotid
patella
patellar
pecten
pectoral
pedal
pelvic girdle
pelvis
periotic
perone
phalanges
pisiform
plantar
popliteal
poplitic
prefrontal
premaxilla
premaxillary
pronator
prootic
prosencephalon
psoas
pubis
pudenda
pulmonary
quadriceps
radius
renal
rhomboid
rib
rictal
sacrocostal
sacrum
sartorius
scaphoid
scapula
sesamoid
shoulder-blade
shoulder-bone
skull
soleus
spade-bone
sphenoid
spine
splinter-bone
stapes
sternum
stirrup-bone
supinator
sural
talus
tarsal
temporal
tendon
thigh-bone
tibia
trapezium
trapezius
trapezoid
triceps
triquetral
turbinal
tympanic
ulna
umbilicus
unguis
urachus
uterus
uvula
vagus
vas deferens
velum
vermis
vertebra
vertebrae
vertex
vesica
voice-box
vomer
vulva
windpipe
wisdom tooth
womb
wrist
xiphisternum
xiphoid
zygapophysis
zygoma
zygomatic

architecture and building

abacus
abutment
acrolith
acroter
acroterial
acroterion
acroterium
alcove
annulet
anta
antefix
araeostyle
architrave
ashlar
ashler
astragal
baguette
bandelet
banderol(e)
barge-board
barge-couple
barge-stones
battlement
bellcote
bema
bratticing
canephor
canton
cartouche
caryatid
Catherine-wheel
cavetto
centering
cinque-foil
concha
corbeil
corbel
corner-stone
corona
cradling
crenel
crocket
crossette
cruck
cul-de-four
dado
decorated
demi-bastion
demi-lune
dentil
diaconicon
diaper
diastyle
diglyph
dimension work
dinette
dipteros
distyle
ditriglyph
dodecastyle
dog-leg(ged)
dogtooth
dome
domed
domical
donjon
Doric
dormer
double-glazing
doucine
drawbridge
drawing-room
dreamhole
dressing
drip
dripstone
dromic
dromos
drum
dry-stone
duplex
Early English
eaves
echinus
egg-and-anchor
egg-and-dart
egg-and-tongue
egg-box
el
elevation
Elizabethan
embattlement
embrasure
emplection
encarpus
engage

architecture and building *(contd.)*
engaged
engrail
enneastyle
entresol
epaule
epaulement
epistyle
eustyle
exedra
extrados
eye-catcher
façade
fan tracery
fan vaulting
fanlight
fascia
fastigium
feathering
fenestella
fenestra
fenestral
fenestration
festoon
fillet
finial
flamboyant
flèche
Flemish bond
fletton
fleuron
foliation
fornicate
fortalice
French sash/window
frieze
fronton
furring
fusarol(e)
fust
gable
gablet
galilee
gambrel roof
gargoyle
gatehouse
glacis
glyph
gopura(m)
gorgerin
Gothic
gradin(e)
griff(e)
groin
groundplan
groundsel
guilloche
gutta
hagioscope
half-timbered
hammer-beam
hammer-brace
hance
hanging buttress
harling
haunch
haute époque
headstone
heart
helix
herringbone
hexastyle
hip
hip-knob
holderbat
hood-mould(ing)
hypostyle
imbrex
imbricate
imbrication
imperial
impost
impostume
intercolumniation
intrados
jamb
javelin
jerkinhead
knosp
lierne
linen-fold
linen-scroll
lintel
mansard(-roof)
mascaron
merlon
metope
modillion
monostyle
mullion
muntin(g)
mutule
Norman
oeil-de-boeuf
ogee
opisthodomos
oriel
out-wall
ovolo
ox-eye
pagoda
pantile
parget
patera
paternoster
patten
pediment
Persian
pilaster
pineapple
pinnacle
plafond
platband
plateresque
plinth
poppy-head
predella
propylaeum
propylon
prostyle
pylon
quatrefeuille
quatrefoil
queen-post
quirk
rear-arch
reglet
regula
rere-arch
retrochoir
reredos
revet
rocaille
rococo
Romanesque
rood-loft
rood-screen
rood-steeple
rood-tower
roof
roof-tree
rosace
rose
rosette
rotunda
roughcast
sacristy
skew-back
socle
soffit
solidum
spandrel
strap-work
stria
string-course
subbasal
surbase
swag
systyle
tabernacle-work
table
telamon
terrazzo
tierceron
tondino
toroid
torsel
torus
trabeation
tracery
triforium
trumeau
tympanum
vault
vaultage
vaulted
vaulting
Venetian mosaic
vermiculate(d)
vice
vitrail
vitrailled
Vitruvian
volute
voussoir
wainscot
wall-plate
water-joint
water-table
weathering
xystus

art

abstract
abstraction
action painting
anaglyph
anastasis
anastatic
anthemion
aquarelle
bas relief
Bauhaus
camaieu
cire perdue
dadaism
decal
decoupage
Der Blaue Reiter
diaglyph
Die Brücke
diptych
dry-point
duotone
écorché
enamel
encaustic
engraving
etch
etchant
faience
fashion-plate
Fauve
Fauvism
fête champêtre
figurine
filigree
flambé
flannelgraph
Flemish
flesh-tint
Florentine
free-hand
fresco
fret
frit
futurism
futurist
gadroon
genre
gesso
glyptics
glyptography
Gobelin
gouache
graphic
graphics
graphium
graticulation
gravure
grecque
grisaille
gumption
hachure
hatch
hatching
haut relief
herm(a)
historiated
hound's-tooth
intaglio
linocut
literalism
litho
lithochromatic(s)
lithochromy
lithograph
lithoprint
lost wax
mandorla
meander
monotint

art *(contd.)*
monotype
morbidezza
Parian
paysage
phylactery
pietra-dura
piqué
pochoir
pompier
putto
quattrocento
relievo
repoussage
repoussé
reserved
retroussage
rilievo
sculp(t)
scumble
sea-piece
seascape
secco
serigraph
statuary
stipple
stylus
surrealism
symbolism
tachism(e)
tempera
tenebrism
tessellated
tessera
tondo
trecento
triptych
ukiyo-e
velatura
Venetian mosaic
Venetian red
verditer
verism
vermiculate(d)
versal
vitrail
vitraillist
vitrifacture
vitrine
vitro-di-trina
volute
vorticism
woodblock
wood-carving
woodcut
wood-engraving
xoanon
zoomorphic

canonical hours

compline
lauds
matins
none
orthros
prime
sext
terce
undern
vespers

cattle breeds

Africander
Alderney
Angus
Ankole
Ayrshire
Blonde d'Aquitaine
Brahman
Brown Swiss
cattabu
cattalo
Charol(l)ais
Chianina
Chillingham
Devon
dexter
Durham
Friesian
Galloway
Guernsey
Hereford
Highland
Holstein
Jersey
Latvian
Limousin
Luing
Red Poll
Romagnola
Santa Gertrudis
short-horn
Simmenthal(er)
Teeswater
Ukrainian
Welsh Black

cheeses

Amsterdam
Bel Paese
Blarney
Bleu d'Auvergne
Blue Vinny
Boursin
Brie
brynza
Caboc
Caerphilly
Camembert
Carré
Cheddar
Cheshire
Chevrotin
Colwick
Coulommiers
crowdie
Danish blue
Derby
Dolcelatte
Dorset Blue
double Gloucester
Dunlop
Edam
Emmental
Emment(h)al(er)
Esrom
ewe-cheese
Feta
Fynbo
Gammelost
G(j)etost
Gloucester
Gorgonzola
Gouda
Grana
Grevé
Gruyère
Handkäse
Havarti
Herrgårdsost
Herve
Huntsman
Hushållsost
Islay
Jarlsberg
Killarney
Kryddost
Lancashire
Leicester
Limburg(er)
Lymeswold®
mouse-trap
mozzarella
Munster
Mysost
Neufchâtel
Parmesan
Petit Suisse
pipo creme
Pont-l'Évêque
Port(-du-)Salut
Prästost
Provolone
Pultost
Raclette
Red Windsor
Reggiano
ricotta
Romadur
Roquefort
sage Derby
Saint-Paulin
Samsø
sapsago
Stilton
stracchino
Tilsit(er)
Vacherin
Wensleydale
Wexford

chemical elements

actinium
aluminium
americium
antimony
argon
arsenic
astatine
barium
berkelium
beryllium
bismuth
boron
bromine
cadmium
caesium
calcium
californium
carbon
cerium
chlorine
chromium
cobalt
copper
curium
dysprosium
einsteinium
erbium
europium
fermium
fluorine
francium
gadolinium
gallium
germanium
gold
hafnium
hahnium
helium
holmium
hydrogen
indium
iodine
iridium
iron
krypton
lanthanum
lawrencium
lead
lithium
lutetium
magnesium
manganese
mendelevium
mercury
molybdenum
neodymium
neon
neptunium
nickel
niobium
nitrogen
nobelium
osmium
oxygen
palladium
phosphorus
platinum
plutonium
polonium
potassium
praseodymium
promethium
protoactinium
radium
radon
rhenium
rhodium
rubidium
ruthenium
rutherfordium
samarium
scandium
selenium
silicon
silver
sodium
strontium
sulphur
tantalum

chemical elements *(contd.)*

technetium
tellurium
terbium
thallium
thorium
thulium
tin
titanium
tungsten
uranium
vanadium
xenon
ytterbium
yttrium
zinc
zirconium

cloths, fabrics

abaca
abb
alamode
alepine
alpaca
American cloth
angora
armozine
armure
arrasene
astrakhan
atlas
baft
bagging
Balbriggan
baldachin
balzarine
barathea
barege
barracan
batiste
batting
bayadère
bearskin
beaver
beige
bengaline
Binca®
blanket
blanketing
blonde(e)-lace
bobbinet
bobbin-lace
bombasine
bone-lace
botany
bouclé
bo(u)lting cloth
box-cloth
broadcloth
brocade
brocatel(le)
broché
Brussels lace
buckram
buckskin
budge
buff
bunting
Burberry
burlap
burnet
burrel
butter-cloth
butter-muslin
byssus
caddis
calamanco
calico
cambric
cameline
camlet
candlewick
canvas
carmelite
carpeting
casement-cloth
cashmere
cassimere
catgut
(cavalry) twill
challis
chamois
chantilly (lace)
charmeuse
cheesecloth
Dacron®
damask
damassin
delaine
denim
devil's dust
dhoti
d(h)urrie
diamanté
diaper
dimity
doe-skin
doily
domett
dornick
dowlas
drab
drabbet
Dralon®
drap-de-Berry
dreadnought
drill
droguet
drugget
duchesse lace
duck
duffel
dungaree
dupion
durant
Dutch carpet
duvetyn
ecru
éolienne
façonné
faille
far(r)andine
fearnought
felt
ferret
filet
flannel
flannelette
foulard
foulé
frieze
frocking
fustian
gaberdine
galatea
galloon
gambroon
gauze
genappe
georgette
gingham
Gobelin(s)
gold-cloth
gold-lace
grass cloth
grenadine
grogram
grosgrain
guipure
gunny
gurrah
habit-cloth
haircloth
harn
Hessian
hodden
holland
homespun
Honiton
hopsack
horsehair
huckaback
humhum
jaconet
Jaeger®
jamdani
jean
jeanette
jersey
kalamkari
karakul
kente cloth
kersey
kerseymere
khaddar
khaki
kid
kidskin
kilt
kincob
kip-skin
lamé
lampas
lawn
leather
leather-cloth
leatherette
leghorn
leno
levant
Lincoln-green
linen
linsey
linsey-woolsey
llama
lockram
loden
longcloth
lovat
Lurex®
lustre
lustring
lutestring
Lycra®
mac(k)intosh
madras
mantling
marcella
marocain
maroquin
marquisette
mazarine
Mechlin
medley
melton
merino
Mexican
mignonette
mohair
moire
moleskin
monk's cloth
moreen
morocco
mourning-stuff
mousseline
mousseline-de-laine
mousseline-de-soie
Moygashel®
mull
mulmul(l)
mungo
musk-rat
muslin
muslinet
musquash
nacarat
nainsook
nankeen
ninon
nitro-silk
nun's-veiling
nylon
oilcloth
organdie
organza
organzine
orleans
osnaburg
orris
ottoman
overcoating
paduasoy
paisley
panne
paper-cloth
paper-muslin
par(r)amatta
peau-de-soie
penistone
percale
percaline
perse
petersham
piña-cloth
pin-stripe
piqué
plaid
plush
point-lace
polycotton
poplin

cloths, fabrics *(contd.)*
poplinette
prunella
purple
quilting
rabanna
ratine (ratteen)
raven('s)-duck
rep (repp)
roan
russel
russel-cord
russet
sackcloth
sacking
sagathy
sail-cloth
samite
sarsenet
satara
sateen
satin
satinette
satin-sheeting
saxony
say
scarlet
schappe
scrim
seersucker
sendal
serge
shagreen
shalloon
shammy(-leather)
shantung
sharkskin
sheepskin
Shetland wool
shoddy
Sicilian
sicilienne
silesia
silk
slipper satin
soneri
split
sponge-cloth
spun silk
stammel
strouding
suede
suedette
suiting
surah
surat
swansdown
swan-skin
tabaret
tabbinet
tabby
taffeta
tamin(e)
tamise
tammy
tarlatan
tarpaulin
tartan
tat
Tattersall (check)
T-cloth
tentage
tent-cloth
terry
Terylene®
thibet
thickset
thrown-silk
thunder-and-lightning
ticken
tick(ing)
tiffany
toile
toilinet(te)
torchon lace
towelling
tram
tricot
troll(e)y
tulle
tusser(-silk)
tweed
union
Valenciennes
veiling
Velcro®
velour(s)
veloutine
velveret
velvet
velveteen
velveting
vicuña
voile
wadmal
waistcoating
watchet
waterwork
waxcloth
webbing
whipcord
wigan
wild silk
wincey
winceyette
wire gauze
woolsey
worcester
worsted
zanella
zephyr

coins, currencies

agora
antoninianus
as
asper
aureus
baht
balboa
bawbee
bekah
belga
bezant
bit
bod(d)le
bolivar
boliviano
bonnet-piece
broad(piece)
buck
cardecu(e)
Carolus
cash
cent
centavo
centime
chiao
colon
conto
cordoba
couter
crown
crusado
cruzeiro
dam
daric
deaner
décime
denarius
denier
Deutschmark
didrachm(a)
dime
dinar
dirham
doit
dollar
double
doubloon
drachma
ducat
dupondius
duro
eagle
écu
eighteen-penny piece
ekuele
escudo
farthing
fen
fifty-pence piece
fifty-penny piece
five-pence piece
five-penny piece
florin
forint
franc
geordie
gerah
gourde
groat
groschen
guinea
gulden
haler
half-crown
half-dollar
halfpenny
half-sovereign
heller
jacobus
jane
jiao
jitney
joe
joey
jo(h)annes
kina
knife-money
koban(g)
kopeck
koruna
kreutzer
krona
krone
Krugerrand
kwacha
kyat
lek
lempira
leone
lepton
leu
lev
lilangeni
lion
lira
litre
livre
louis
louis-d'or
mag
maik
make
manch
mancus
maravedi
mark
markka
mawpus
merk
metical
mil
millième
millime
milreis
mina
mite
mna
mohur
moidore
mopus
naira
napoleon
(naya) paisa
(new) cedi
ngwee
nickel
nicker
obang
obol
obolus
öre
øre
Paduan
pagoda
pänga
paolo
para
pataca
patrick
paul
peseta
pesewa
peso
pfennig
piastre
picayune
pice
piece of eight
pine-tree money
pistareen

coins, currencies *(contd.)*
pistole
pistolet
plack
portague
portcullis
pound
pula
punt
qintar
quetzal
quid
rag
rand
real
red
red cent
reichsmark
reis
renminbi
rial
rider
riel
ringgit
rix-dollar
riyal
rose-noble
r(o)uble
royal
ruddock
ruddy
rupee
rupiah
ryal
saw-buck
sceat(t)
schilling
scudo
semis
semuncia
sen
sequin
sesterce
sestertium
sextans
shekel
shilling
silverling
sixpence
skilling
smacker
sol
soldo
solidus
sou
sovereign
spade-guinea
spur-royal
stater
sterling
stiver
sucre
sword-dollar
sycee
tael
taka
talent
tanner
tenner
tenpence
ten-pence piece
ten-penny piece
tester(n)
testo(o)n
testril(l)
tetradrachm
thaler
thick'un
thin'un
three-farthings
three-halfpence
threepence
threepenny bit/piece
tical
tick(e)y
tizzy
toman
turner
twenty-pence piece
twenty-penny piece
two bits
twopence
two-pence piece
two-penny piece
unicorn
ure
vellon
wakiki
wampum
won
xerafin
yen
yuan
zack
zaire
zecchino
zimbi
zloty
zuz
zwanziger

collective nouns
building of rooks
cast of hawks
cete of badgers
charm of goldfinches
chattering of choughs
clamour of rooks
clowder of cats
company of widgeon
covert of coots
covey of partridges
down of hares
drift of swine
drove of cattle
dule of doves
exaltation of larks
fall of woodcock
fesnyng of ferrets
gaggle of geese
gam of whales
gang of elks
grist of bees
husk of hares
kindle of kittens
leap of leopards
leash of bucks
murder of crows
murmuration of starlings
muster of peacocks
mute of hounds
nide of pheasants
pace of asses
pod of seals
pride of lions
school of porpoises
siege of herons
skein of geese
skulk of foxes
sloth of bears
sounder of boars
spring of teals
stand of plovers
stud of mares
team of ducks
tok of capercailzies
troop of kangaroos
unkindness of ravens
walk of snipe
watch of nightingales

collectors, enthusiasts
abolitionist
ailurophile
antiquary
antivaccinationist
antivivisectionist
arachnologist
arctophile
audiophil(e)
balletomane
bibliolatrist
bibliomane
bibliopegist
bibliophagist
bibliophile
bibliophilist
bicameralist
campanologist
canophilist
cartophile
cartophilist
cheirographist
coleopterist
conservationist
cynophilist
Dantophilist
deltiologist
discophile
dog-fancier
ecclesiologist
egger
entomologist
environmentalist
ephemerist
epicure
ex-librist
feminist
Francophile
Gallophile
gastronome
gemmologist
Germanophil(e)
gourmet
herpetologist
hippophile
homoeopathist
iconophilist
incunabulist
Kremlinologist
lepidopterist
medallist
miscegenationist
monarchist
myrmecologist
negrophile
negrophilist
notaphilist
numismatist
oenophile
oenophilist
ophiophilist
orchidomaniac
ornithologist
orthoepist
orthographist
ostreiculturist
pangrammatist
Panhellenist
panislamist
Pan-Slavist
paragrammatist
paroemographer
perfectionist
philanthrope
philatelist
philhellene
phillumenist
philogynist
philologist
philologue
prohibitionist
pteridophilist
reincarnationist
Russophile
Russophilist
scripophile
scripophilist
sericulturist
Sinophile
Slavophile
spelaeologist
steganographist
stegophilist
supernaturalist
tege(s)tologist
timbrologist
timbromaniac
timbrophilist
tulipomane
tulipomaniac
Turcophile
ufologist
ultramontanist
vexillologist
virtuoso
vulcanologist
xenophile
zoophile
zoophilist

colours
anthochlore
anthocyan(in)
anthoxanthin
aquamarine
argent
aurora
avocado
badious

colours *(contd.)*
Berlin blue
beryl
biscuit
black
blae
blood-red
blue
bottle-green
brick-red
buff
caesious
canary
caramel
carmine
carnation
celadon
celeste
cerise
cerulean
cervine
champagne
charcoal
cobalt-blue
coral
cyan
dove
drab
dun
Dutch pink
dwale
eau de Nil
ebony
emerald
fawn
feldgrau
ferrugin(e)ous
filemot
flame
flavescent
flaxen
flesh-colour
fulvous
fuscous
ginger
glaucous
gold
golden
green
greige (grège)
grey (gray)
gridelin
griseous
grizzle(d)
gules
guly
hoar
horse-flesh
hyacinth
hyacinthine
ianthine
icterine
icteritious
incarnadine
indigo
isabel
isabella
isabelline
jacinth
khaki
lake
lateritious
lemon
lilac
lovat
lurid
luteolous
luteous
lutescent
magenta
mahogany
maize
mandarin(e)
maroon
mauve
mazarine
miniate
minium
modena
morel
mouse-colour(ed)
mous(e)y
mulberry
murrey
nacarat
Naples-yellow
nattier blue
Nile green
nut-brown
ochroleucous
off-white
orange
oxblood
Oxford blue
palatinate
pansy
peach
peach-bloom
peacock
peacock-blue
perse
philomot
piceous
pink
plum
plumbeous
pompadour
ponceau
pongee
porphyry
porraceous
puce
purple
purpure
pyrrhous
red
reseda
roan
rose
rose-coloured
rose-pink
rose-red
rosy
rubicund
rubied
rubiginous
rubineous
rubious
ruby
ruby-red
ruddy
rufescent
rufous
russet
rust-coloured
rusty
sable
saffron
sage
salmon
sand
sapphire
saxe blue
scarlet
sepia
siena
silver
sky
slate
smalt
straw
tan
taupe
tawny
tenné
Titian
tomato
tusser
Tyrian
ultramarine
vermeil
vermilion
vinous
violet
virescent
vitellary
vitreous
watchet
white
wine
xanthic
xanthous
yellow

confections, dishes, foods
andouillette
angels-on-horseback
battalia pie
bir(i)yani
blanquette
Bombay duck
borsch(t)
bouillabaisse
bubble-and-squeak
bummalo
burgoo
calzone
cannelloni
carbon(n)ade
carpet-bag (steak)
cassoulet
cecils
charlotte russe
chilli con carné
chocolate vermicelli
chop-suey
chorizo
chowder
chow-mein
cockaleekie
colcannon
consommé
Danish pastry
dariole
devil
devil's food cake
devils-on-horseback
Devonshire cream
diet-bread
dika-bread
dimsum
dough-boy
doughnut
dragée
drammock
drisheen
duff
dumpling
dunderfunk
Eccles cake
éclair
Edinburgh rock
egg custard
enchilada
eryngo
escalope
escargot
espangole
faggot
fancy-bread
farle
fedelini
felafel
fettuc(c)ine
feuilleté
fishball
fishcake
fishfinger
flan
flapjack
floater
flummery
foie gras
fondant
fondue
forcemeat
fortune cookie
fraise
frankfurter
French bread
French dressing
French fry
French stick
French toast
fricandeau
fricassee
friedcake
fritter
fritto misto
friture
froise
fruit cocktail
fruit salad
fruitcake
frumenty
fu yung
fudge
fumado
galantine
game chips
garam masala
garbanzo

confections, dishes, foods *(contd.)*
Garibaldi biscuit
gateau
gazpacho
gefilte fish
Genoa cake
ghee
ginger nut
gingerbread
gingersnap
gnocchi
gofer
goulash
graham bread
graham crackers
grits
gruel
guacamole
gumdrop
gundy
haberdine
haggis
halva(h)
hamburger
hard sauce
hardbake
hardtack
hoe-cake
hominy
hoosh
hot dog
hot-cross-bun
hotpot
howtowdie
humbug
hummus
hundreds-and-thousands
hyson
jemmy
kedgeree
knish
lardy-cake
latke
laverbread
linguini
matelote
millefeuille(s)
minestrone
mous(s)aka
na(a)n
navarin
nuoc mam
olla-podrida
opsonium
paella
pakora
panada
panettone
pastrami
pavlova
pem(m)ican
pep(p)eroni
pesto
pettitoes
pilaff
pilau
pinole
piri-piri
pirozhki
pizza
ploughman's lunch
plum-duff
plum-porridge
plum-pudding
poi
polenta
polony
popover
pop(p)adum
porterhouse(-steak)
pot-au-feu
prairie-oyster
profiterole
prosciutto
pumpernickel
queen of puddings
queen's pudding
quenelle
quiche
raclette
ragout
ramekin
ratatouille
ravioli
remoulade
rijst(t)afel
rillettes
risotto
rissole
roly-poly pudding
Sachertorte
salmagundi
salmi(s)
saltimbocca
sambal
samosa
sashimi
sauce hollandaise
sauerkraut
scampi
schnitzel
sch(t)chi
Scotch woodcock
shashlik
shepherd's pie
smørbrød
smörgåsbord
soufflé
spaghetti (alla) bolognese
spotted dick
spring roll
stovies
stroganoff
succotash
sukiyaki
summer pudding
sundae
sup(p)awn
sushi
syllabub
Tabasco®
tabbouleh
tablet
taco
tagliarini
tamal(e)
tandoori
tapioca
taramasalata
tempura
timbale
toad-in-the-hole
torte
tortellini
tortilla
trifle
tsamba
turtle-soup
tutti-frutti
tzimmes
velouté sauce
vermicelli
vichyssoise
vienna loaf
vienna steak
vindaloo
vol-au-vent
wafer
waffle
warden pie
wastel-bread
water-biscuit
water-gruel
welsh rabbit (rarebit)
white sauce
white-pot
white-pudding
Wiener schnitzel
Wimpy®
wine-biscuit
wonder
Worcestershire sauce
wurst
yoghurt
Yorkshire pudding
zabaglione
Zwieback

dances

allemande
beguine
belly-dance
bergamask
black bottom
bolero
bossa nova
bourree
branle
breakdown
bunny-hug
cachucha
cakewalk
canary
cancan
carioca
carmagnole
carol
cha-cha
chaconne
Charleston
cinque-pace
Circassian circle
clogdance
conga
coranto
corroboree
cotill(i)on
country-dance
courant
cracovienne
csárdás (czardas)
dos-à-dos (dosi-do)
dump
écossaise
egg-dance
fading
fado
fandango
farruca
figure-dance
flamenco
fling
flip-flap(-flop)
forlana
fox-trot
galliard
gallopade
galop
gavotte
gigue
gopak
habanera
haka
halling
haymaker
hey (hay)
hey-de-guy
Highland fling
hoedown
hoolachan
hula-hula
jig
jitterbug
jive
John Canoe
joncanoe
jota
juba
kathek
kazatzke
kolo
lancers
loure
malagueña
mambo
matachin
maxixe
mazurka
minuet
Moresco
morris-dance
musette
onestep
Paduan
paso doble
passacaglia
passepied
passy-measure
Paul Jones
pavan(e)
pericon
petronella
planxty
polacca
polka
polo
polonaise
poule
poussette
quadrille
quickstep
redowa

dances *(contd.)*
reel
r(h)umba
rigadoon
ring-dance
romaika
ronggeng
roundel
roundelay
roundle
rumba
salsa
saltarello
samba
sand-dance
saraband
sardana
schottische
sequidilla
shimmy(-shake)
siciliano
spring
square-dance
stomp
strathspey
sword-dance
tamborin
tango
tap-dance
tarantella
the twist
toe-dance
tripudium
turkey-trot
two-step
Tyrolienne
valeta
valse
varsovienne
volta
waltz
war dance
zapateado
ziganka

dog breeds
affenpinscher
badger-dog
basenji
basset(-hound)
Bedlington (terrier)
Blenheim spaniel
boar-hound
Border terrier
borzoi
Boston terrier
Briard
Brussels griffon
bull mastiff
bulldog
bull-terrier
cairn terrier
Cavalier King Charles spaniel
chihuahua
chow
clumber spaniel
coach-dog
cocker spaniel
collie
corgi
dachshund
Dalmatian
Dandie Dinmont
Dane
deerhound
dhole
dingo
Doberman(n) pinscher
elkhound
Eskimo dog
foxhound
fox-terrier
German police dog
German Shepherd dog
Great Dane
greyhound
griffon
harlequin
(Irish) water-spaniel
Jack Russell
keeshond
King Charles spaniel
Labrador
laika
lhasa apso
lurcher
lyam-hound
malemute
Maltese
mastiff
peke
Pekin(g)ese
pinscher
pointer
Pomeranian
poodle
pug
pug-dog
retriever
Rottweiler
saluki
Samoyed(e)
sausage-dog
schipperke
schnauzer
Scotch-terrier
Sealyham
setter
sheltie
Shetland sheepdog
shih tzu
shough
Skye (terrier)
spaniel
Spartan
spitz
St Bernard
staghound
Sussex spaniel
talbot
teckel
terrier
vizsla
volpino
warragal
water-dog
Weimaraner
whippet
wire-hair(ed terrier)
wolf-dog
wolf-hound
Yorkshire terrier
zorro

drinks, alcoholic
absinth(e)
aguardiente
akvavit
amontillado
anisette
apple-jack
aqua-mirabilis
aquavit
aqua-vitae
arak
Armagnac
arrack
audit ale
ava
bacharach
badminton
barley-bree
Beaujolais
Beaune
Benedictine
bingo
bishop
black velvet
bloody Mary
blue ruin
bourbon
brandy-pawnee
bride-ale
Bristol-milk
bucellas
bumbo
burgundy
Calvados
Campari
canary
catawba
Chablis
chain-lightning
Chambertin
Champagne
Chardonnay
Chartreuse
cherry brandy
cherry-bounce
Chianti
chicha
cider
claret
claret-cup
cobbler
cobbler's punch
Cognac
Cointreau®
cold-without
Constantia
cool-tankard
cooper
cordial
corn-brandy
daiquiri
demerara
dog's-nose
dop
Drambuie®
eau de vie
eau des creoles
egg-flap
eggnog
enzian
espumoso
fine
fino
flip
four-ale
geneva
genevrette
geropiga
gimlet
gin
gin and it
gin-fizz
ginger wine
ginsling
glogg
glühwein
gooseberry wine
grappa
Graves
grog
haoma
heavy wet
herb-beer
hermitage
hippocras
hock
hollands
hoo(t)ch
it
Johannisberger
John Barleycorn
John Collins
kaoliang
kava
kefir
kir
kirsch
kirschwasser
k(o)umiss
kümmel
kvass
London particular
madeira
malmsley
manzanilla
maraschino
marc brandy
Marcobrunner
margarita
Marsala
Martini®
Médoc
metheglin
mirabelle
mobbie
Moselle
mountain
mountain dew
muscat
muscatel
negus
Nipa
noyau
oenomel
Old Tom
oloroso
olykoek

drinks, alcoholic *(contd.)*

Orvieto
ouzo
pastis
peach-brandy
Pernod®
perry
persico(t)
Peter-see-me
pils(e)ner
Pinot
plottie
pombe
port
pot(h)een
pousse-café
pulque
punch
purl
quetsch
ratafia
resinata
retsina
Rhine-wine
Riesling
Rioja
rosé
Rudesheimer
Rüdesheimer
rum
rumbo
rumfustian
rum-punch
rum-shrub
rye
rye-whisky
sack
sack-posset
sake
samshoo
sangaree
sangria
Sauterne(s)
Sauvignon
schiedam
schnapps
Scotch
shandy
sherry
sherry-cobbler
shrub
sidecar
Sillery
skokiaan
sling
slivovitz
sloe-gin
small beer
small-ale
sour
spruce-beer
St Julien
Steinberger
stengah
stinger
stingo
swipes
swizzle
tafia
Tarragona
tent
tequil(l)a
tipper
toddy
Tokay
Tom Collins
Tom-and-Jerry
twankay
twopenny
usquebaugh
vermouth
vin blanc
vin ordinaire
vin rosé
vinho verde
vodka
wassail
water-brose
whisk(e)y
whisky toddy
white wine
white-ale
Xeres
zythum

French Revolutionary calendar

Brumaire
Floréal
Frimaire
Fructidor
Germinal
Messidor
Nivôse
Pluviôse
Prairial
Thermidor
Vendémiaire
Ventôse

furniture, furnishings

andiron
banquette
basket-chair
basketwork
bergama
bergamot
bolster
bonheur-du-jour
box-bed
bracket clock
brise-soleil
buffet
buhl
bureau
cabriolet
camp-bed
canterbury
chair-bed
chaise-longue
chesterfield
cheval-glass
chiffonier
coaster
coffee-table
commode
continental quilt
credence (table/shelf)
credenza
davenport
day-bed
desk
deuddarn
dinner-table
dinner-wagon
divan
dos-à-dos
drape
drawer
drawing-table
draw-leaf table
dresser
dressing-table
dumb-waiter
easy-chair
elbow-chair
electrolier
encoignure
escritoire
étagere
faldstool
fauteuil
fender
fender-stool
festoon-blind
fire-dog
fireguard
firescreen
four-poster
gasalier
girandole
girnel
guéridon
hallstand
hassock
hearth-rug
highboy
high-chair
hip-bath
humpty
jardinière
lectern
looking-glass
lounge
lounger
love-seat
lowboy
lug-chair
mirror
mobile
ottoman
overmantel
pelmet
pembroke (table)
picture rail
piecrust table
pier-glass
pier-table
plaque
plenishings
pouf(fe)
prie-dieu
pulpit
pulvinar
radiator
rocking chair
sag-bag
scatter rug/cushion
sconce
secretaire
settee
settle
settle-bed
sideboard
side-table
sofa
sofa-bed
sofa-table
squab
standard lamp
studio couch
swivel-chair
table
tallboy
tapestry
tatami
teapoy
tea-service
tea-set
tea-table
tea-tray
tea-trolley
tent-bed
tête-à-tête
toilet-table
toilet(te)
torchère
tridarn
tringle
umbrella-stand
Vanitory®
vanity unit
vargueño
veilleuse
vis-à-vis
vitrine
wall-unit
wardrobe
washhand-stand
wash-stand
water bed
Welsh dresser
whatnot
writing-desk
writing-table

garments, vestments

aba
abaya
abba
abolla
achkan
acton
Afghan
alb
alpargata
amice
anorak
antigropelo(e)s
ascot
babouche
babushka
balaclava
Balbriggan
balibuntal
balmoral
bandan(n)a
bania(n)
barret
basher

garments, vestments *(contd.)*
bashlyk
basinet
basque
basquine
bathing-costume
bauchle
beanie
bearskin
beaver
bed-jacket
bedsocks
beetle-crushers
belcher
benjamin
benny
Bermuda shorts
Bermudas
bertha
bikini
billycock
biretta
blanket
blouson
blucher
boa
boater
bobbysock
bodice
body stocking
body-warmer
bolero
bomber jacket
bongrace
bonnet
bonnet-rouge
boob-tube
bootee
bottine
box-coat
bow-tie
bra
brassière
breeches
breeks
breton
broad-brim
brogue(s)
buckskins
buff
buffalo-robe
buff-coat
buff-jerkin
bumfreezer
Burberry
burdash
burk(h)a
burnous(e)
busby
bush jacket
bush shirt
buskin
bustle
bustle
bycoket
caftan
cagoul(e)
calamanco
calash
calceamentum
calotte
calyptra
camiknickers
camise
camisole
capa
cape
capel(l)ine
capote
capuche
capuchin
carcanet
car-coat
cardigan
cardinal
carmagnole
cashmere
casque
cassock
casuals
catsuit
caul
cere-cloth
cerement
chadar
chaparajos
chapeau
chapeau-bras
chaperone
chapka
chaplet
chaps
chasuble
cimar
collar of esses
corset
corslet
cummerbund
cymar
dalmahoy
Dalmatic
dashiki
décolletage
derby
diadem
diaper
dick(e)y
dinner-gown
dinner-jacket
dirndl
dishabille
dittos
divided skirt
djellaba(h)
djibbah
dog-collar
Dolly Varden
dolman
donkey jacket
doublet
drainpipes
drapesuit
drawers
dreadnought
dress uniform
dress-coat
dress-improver
dressing-gown
dressing-jacket
dressing-sack
dress-shirt
dress-suit
dress-tie
duffel coat
dungarees
earmuffs
encolpion
epaulet(te)
ephod
epitrachelion
espadrille
Eton collar
Eton jacket
Etons
evening dress
evening-dress
exomis
faldetta
falling band
fannel(l)
fanon
farthingale
fascinator
fatigues
fedora
ferronnière
fez
fibula
fichu
filibeg
fillet
finnesko
flat-cap
flip-flop
fob
fontange
fore-and-after
fraise
French knickers
frock
frock-coat
frog
frontlet
fustanella
gaberdine
gaiter
galligaskins
galoshes
gamash
gambeson
garibaldi
gauchos
gay deceivers
gee-string (G-string)
geneva bands
geta
gibus
gi(e)
gilet
girandole
gizz
grego
gremial
g-suit
guernsey
gumboot
gum(shoe)
habergeon
hacqueton
haik
hair-net
hair-piece
half-boot
hat
hatband
hatpin
hattock
hauberk
havelock
headcloth
head-hugger
headsquare
hejab
hennin
himation
hip-huggers
hipsters
hogger
Homburg
hood
hotpants
housecoat
hug-me-tight
humeral veil
hummel
hunting cap
ihram
indescribables
jabot
jacket
Jap-silk
jeans
jersey
jiz
jubbah (djibbah)
jumper
jump-suit
jupon
kabaya
kaffiyeh
kaftan
kagoul
kalpak
kalyptra
kamees
kamik
kanzu
kell
kerchief
k(h)anga
k(h)urta
Kilmarnock
Kilmarnock cowl
kimono
kirtle
kiss-me
kiss-me-quick
knickerbockers
knickers
lammy
lava-lava
lederhosen
leggings
leghorn
leg-warmers
leotard
Levis®
liberty bodice
lingerie
loden
lounger
lounge-suit
lungi

garments, vestments *(contd.)*
mac(k)
mackinaw
mac(k)intosh
madras
manta
manteau
mantilla
mantle
mantlet
manto
matinee
matinee jacket/coat
maud
mazarine
mazarine hood
middy (blouse)
mink
mitre
mitt
mitten
mob
mob-cap
mode
modius
mohair
moleskins
monkey-jacket
monteith
montero
montero-cap
morning-dress
morning-gown
mortar-board
Mother Hubbard
mourning-cloak
mousquetaire
moz(z)etta
muff
muffin-cap
muffler
mutch
muu-muu
netherstock
newmarket
nightingale
Nithsdale
Norfolk jacket
nubia
obi
omophorion
orarion
orarium
overcoat
overgarment
Oxonian
paduasoy
paenula
pagri
paletot
pall
palla
pallium
paludament
pantable
pantalets
pantaloons
panties
pantihose
pantof(f)le
panton
pantoufle
pants
pants suit
pareu
pea-coat
pea-jacket
pearlies
pectoral
pedal-pushers
pelerine
pelisse
pencil skirt
penitentials
peplos
peplum
petasos
petersham
petticoat
petticoat
petticoat-breeches
ph(a)elonion
Phrygian cap
picture-hat
pierrot
pilch
pileus
pill-box
pinafore
pinafore-dress
pinafore-skirt
pinner
piupiu
pixie-hood
plaid
plimsoll
plus-fours
plushes
pneumonia-blouse
poke-bonnet
polonaise
polo-neck
poncho
pontificals
pos(h)teen
powdering-gown
pressure-helmet
pressure-suit
pressure-waistcoat
princess(e)
pumps
puttee
rabato
raglan
raincoat
rami(e)
Ramil(l)ie(s)
ra-ra skirt
rat-catcher
rational
rationals
rebater
rebato
redingote
reefer
reefing-jacket
riding-breeches
riding-cloak
riding-clothes
riding-coat
riding-glove
riding-habit
riding-hood
riding-robe
riding-skirt
riding-suit
robe
robe-de-chambre
rochet
roll-neck sweater
roll-on
rompers
romper-suit
roquelaure
ruff
rug-gown
sabot
sack
sack-coat
safari jacket
safari suit
sagum
sailor-hat
sakkos
salopette
samfoo
sanbenito
sandal
sarafan
sari
sarong
sash
sayon
scapular
scarf
scarpetto
schema
scotch bonnet
screen
sea-boots
sealskin
semmit
separates
shalwar
shako
shaps
shauchle
shawl
shawl-waistcoat
shell suit
shift
shirt
shirt dress
shirtwaist
shirtwaister
shoe
shooting-jacket
short-clothes
short-coats
shortgown
shorts
shovel-hat
silk-hat
silly-how
singlet
siren suit
skeleton suit
skin-tights
skirt
skullcap
slacks
slicker
sling-back
slip
slip-over
slipper(s)
slipslop
sloppy Joe
slop(s)
slouch(-hat)
small-clothes
smalls
smicket
smock
smock-frock
smoking cap
smoking jacket
sneaker(s)
snood
snow-boots
snow-shoe(s)
sock
sola(r) topi/helmet
solitaire
solleret
sombrero
sontag
soubise
soutane
sou'-wester
space-suit
spat
spattee
spatterdash
spencer
sphendone
sponge-bags
sporran
sports jacket
sports shirt
start-up
stays
steenkirk
steeple-crown
steeple-hat
stephane
step-in
Stetson
sticharion
stock
stockinet(te)
stockingette
stocking(s)
stola
stole
stomacher
stovepipe (hat)
strait-jacket
strait-waistcoat
straw (hat)
string vest
string-tie
strip
stuff-gown
subfusc
subucula
succinctorium
sun-bonnet
sundown
sun-dress
sunhat
sunsuit
superhumeral

garments, vestments *(contd.)*
surcingle
surcoat
surplice
surtout
suspender-belt
suspenders
swaddling-band/cloth/clothes
swagger-coat
swallow-tail
sweat band
sweat suit
sweater
sweat-shirt
swimming costume
swimsuit
swimwear
sword-belt
tabard
taglioni
tail-coat
tails
taj
talar
talaria
tall hat
tallith
talma
tam
Tam O'Shanter
tammy
tanga
tank top
tarboosh
tarpaulin
tasse
tawdry-lace
tea-gown
Teddy suit
tee-shirt
ten-gallon hat
terai
thrum-cap
tiar(a)
tie
tights
tile(-hat)
tippet
toga
tonnag
top-boots
topcoat
topee
topi
topper
tops
toque
toreador pants
tournure
tower
toy
tozie
track shoe
track suit
trenchard
trench-coat
trencher-cap
trews
tricorn(e)
trilby
trollopee
trot-cozy
trouser suit
trousers
trouse(s)
trunk-breeches
trunk-hose
trunks
truss(es)
trusty
T-shirt
tube-skirt
tunic
tunicle
tuque
turban
turtle-neck
tuxedo
twin-set
ugly
ulster
ulsterette
undercoat
underpants
undershorts
undervest
upper-stock
Vandyke (collar)
vareuse
veil
veld(-)schoen
vest
victorine
visite
vitta
volet
waistcloth
waistcoat
wam(p)us
war bonnet
warm
watch cap
watch chain
Watteau bodice
weeper
wellie
wellington
wet-suit
whisk
white tie
wide-awake
wig
wimple
windcheater
windjammer
wing collar
winkle-pickers
woggle
wrap
wraparound
wrapover
wrapper
wrap-rascal
wristlet
wylie-coat
yarmulka
yashmak
Y-fronts
zamarra
zoot suit
zoster
zucchetto

heraldry
abatement
addorsed
affrontee
Albany Herald
allusive
annulet
armorist
assurgent
augmentation
baton-sinister
bendlet
bend-sinister
bendwise
bendy
bezant
bicorporate
billet
bordure
botoné
brisure
caboched
cabré
cadency
canting
canton
catherine-wheel
champ
chequy
chevron
chevrony
chief
coupé
debased
debruised
declinant
delf
device
dexter
difference
dimidiate
dismembered
displayed
dormant
double
doubling
dragonné
dwale
eightfoil
embattled
emblaze
emblazon
emblazoner
emblazonment
emblazonry
enarched
enarmed
engouled
engrail
engrailed
engrailment
enveloped
escrol(l)
escutcheon
extendant
fess(e)
fesse-point
fetterlock
field
fimbriate
fitché(e)
flanch
flanched
flotant
fracted
fret
fructed
fur
fusil
gale
gamb
garb(e)
gemel
gerbe
golp(e)
gorged
grieced
g(u)ardant
gules
gyron
gyronny
hatchment
haurient
herisson
honour-point
impale
impalement
increscent
inescutcheon
interfretted
invected
jessant
langued
lioncel
lis
lozenge
lozengy
manche
mantling
martlet
mascle
mascled
masculy
moline
morné
morned
mounted
mullet
naiant
naissant
nombril
nowed
nowy
opinicus
or
orle
palewise
pall
passant
patonce
patté(e)
pean
percussant
pheon
pile
point
pommelé
pommelled

heraldry *(contd.)*
pommetty
portate
portcullis
posé
potencé
potent
primrose
quarter
quartering
quarterly
queue
ragged staff
raguled
raguly
rampant
raping
rebate
regardant
respect
respectant
roundel
rustre
saltire
sans nombre
satyral
scarp
segreant
sej(e)ant
semé(e)
square-pierced
statant
tenné
trangle
tressure
trippant
umbrated
undee
undifferenced
unguled
urinant
vair
vairé
verdoy
vert
voided
vol
volant
vorant
vuln
vulned
waved
weel
wivern
woodwose
(wood-house)

herbs, spices

amaracus
basil thyme
caraway seeds
cardamom
cassia
cayenne
chervil
chilli
chive
cinnamon
cloves
coriander
cum(m)in
dill
dittany
endive
eyebright
fennel
fenugreek
finoc(c)hio
galega
garlic
gentian
ginger
groundsel
hellebore
henbane
horehound
horseradish
Hyoscyamus
hyssop
isatis
juniper
lemon thyme
liquorice
lovage
lungwort
mace
marjoram
mint
motherwort
mustard
myrrh
nutmeg
oregano
orpine
paprika
parsley
peppermint
purslane
rampion
rape
rosemary
rue
saffron
sage
savory
stacte
tarragon
thyme
turmeric
vanilla
verbena
watercress
wintergreen
wormwood
woundwort
yerba

jewels, gems

agate
amber
amethyst
aquamarine
asteria
balas ruby
baroque
beryl
bloodstone
brilliant
cairngorm
cameo
carbuncle
chalcedony
chrysolite
coral
cornelian
crystal
diamond
draconites
dumortierite
emerald
fire-opal
garnet
girasol(e)
grossular(ite)
heliodor
hyacinth
hyalite
hydrophane
intaglio
jacinth
jade
jango(o)n
jasper
jet
lapis lazuli
ligure
marcasite
marquise
Mocha stone
moonstone
morganite
mother-of-pearl
nacre
olivet
olivine
onyx
opal
oriental amethyst
paragon
pearl
peridot(e)
pyreneite
pyrope
Rhinestone
rhodolite
rose
rose-cut
rose-diamond
ruby
sapphire
sard
sardine
sardonyx
smaragd
topaz
tourmaline
turquoise
water-sapphire
wood-opal
yu
yu-stone
zircon

Jewish calendar

Ab
Abib
Adar
Adar Sheni
Elul
Hes(h)van
Iy(y)ar
Kislev
Nisan
S(h)ebat
Sivan
Tammuz
Tebet(h)
Tis(h)ri
Veadar

languages

Aeolic
Afghan
Afrikaans
Akkadian
Albanian
Alemannic
Algonki(a)n
Altaic
Ameslan
Amharic
Anatolian
Anglo-Saxon
Arabic
Aramaic
Armenian
Armoric
Aryan
Assyrian
Attic
Austric
Austroasiatic
Austronesian
Avestan
Bahasa Indonesia
Balinese
Baltoslav(on)ic
Baluch(i)
Bantu
Basque
Basuto
Bengali
Berber
Bohemian
bohunk
Breton
Brezonek
British
Brythonic
Bulgarian
Bulgaric
Burmese
B(y)elorussian
Cajun
Carib
Catalan
Celtic
Chaldaic
Cherokee
Chinese
Choctaw
Circassian
Cornish
creole
Croat(ian)
Cushitic
Czech
Danish
Dardic
Doric

languages *(contd.)*
Dravidian
Dutch
Early English
Efik
English
Erse
Eskimo
Esperanto
Est(h)onian
Ethiopic
Etruscan
Euskarian
Fanti
Farsi
Finnish
Finno-Ugric (-Ugrian)
Flemish
Franglais
French
Frisian
Gadhelic (Goidelic)
Gaelic
Gaulish
Geëz (Giz)
Gentoo
Georgian
German
Germanic
Greek
Guaraní
Gujarat(h)i
Gullah
Hausa
Hawaiian
Hebrew
Hellenic
Herero
High German
Hindi
Hindustani
Hittite
Hottentot
Hungarian
Icelandic
Idiom Neutral
Ido
I(g)bo
Indian
Indic
Indo-European
Indo-Germanic
In(n)uit
Interlingua
Ionic
Iranian
Iraqi
Irish
Iroquoian
Italian
Italic
Japanese
Kalmuck
Kanarese
Kannada
Karen
Kennick
Khmer
Koine
Kolarian
Kuo-yü
Kurdish
Ladin
Ladino
Lallans
Landsmaal
Langue d'oc
Langue d'oil
Langue d'oui
Laplandish
Lapp
Lappish
Latin
Latvian
Lettic
Lettish
lingua franca
lingua geral
Lithuanian
Low German
Magyar
Malagasy
Malay
Malayala(a)m
Maltese
Manchu
Mandaean
Mandarin
Mandingo
Manx
Maori
Marathi
Median
Melanesian
Mexican
Micmac
Middle English
Moeso-gothic
Mohawk
Mohican
Mon
Mongolian
Moto
Munda
Nahuatl
Navaho
Neo
Newspeak
Norwegian
Novial
Nynorsk
Old English
Old Norse
Oriya
Oscan
Ostyak
Pali
Papiamento
Pawnee
Pehlevi
Pekin(g)ese
Pennsylvania Dutch
Persian
Persic
Phoenician
Pictish
pig Latin
Pilipino
Platt-Deutsch
Polabian
Polish
Portuguese
Prakrit
Provençal
Provinçal
Prussian
Punic
Punjabi
Pushtu
Quechua
Rabbinic
Rhaetic
Rhaeto-Romance
Rhaeto-Romanic
Rock English
rogues' Latin
Romaic
Romance
Romanes
Romanic
Roman(n)y
Romans(c)h
Rumanian
Russian
Russniak
Ruthenian
Sakai
Samnite
Samoyed(e)
Sanskrit
Saxon
Scots
Scythian
Semitic
Serb(ian)
Serbo-Croat(ian)
Shan
Shona
Siamese
Sinhalese
Siouan
Slavonic
Slovak
Slovenian
Somali
Sorbian
Sorbish
Spanish
Sudanic
Sumerian
Suomi
Swahili
Swedish
Swiss
Syriac
Taal
Tagálog
Taino
Tamil
Tataric
Telugu
Teutonic
Thai
Tibetan
Tocharian
Tswana
Tuareg
Tungus(ian)
Tupi
Turki
Turkish
Twi
Ugrian
Ugro-finnic
Ukrainian
Umbrian
Uralic
Urdu
Uzbeg
Vaudois
Vietnamese
Volapük
Volga-Baltic
Volscian
Welsh
Wendic
Wendish
West-Saxon
Wolof
Xhosa
Yakut
Yiddish
Yoruba
Zulu

legal
abate
abatement
absolvitor
abstract of title
acceptilation
accession
accessory
accessory after the fact
accessory before the fact
Acts of Adjournal
(ad) avizandum
adeem
adhere
adjudication
adminicle
administrator
afforce
alienee
alienor
allenarly
allodial
amicus curiae
amove
appointer
apprize
apprizer
assumpsit
attorn
back-bond
bairn's-part
capias
certiorari
chaud-mellé
cognosce
cognovit
compear
compulsitor
copyhold
cross-examine
decree absolute
decree nisi
decreet
decretals

legal *(contd.)*
decretist
dedimus
deed
deed of accession
defalcate
defeasance
defeasanced
defeasible
defendant
defender
deforce
deforcement
deforciant
delapidation
delate
delation
delator
delict
demurrer
deodand
detainer
detinue
devastavit
devest
diet
dimissory
disapply
disbar
disbench
discovert
discoverture
disentail
disgavel
disinherison
dispone
disponee
disposition
disseise
disseisin
disseisor
distinguish
distrain
distrainee
distrainer
distrainment
distrainor
distraint
distress
distringas
dittay
dole
donatary
droit
droit du Seigneur
duplicand
duply
dying declaration
easement
ejectment
embracer
embracery
emendals
emphyteusis
en ventre sa mère
enfeoff
enfeoffment
enjoin
enlevé
enlevement
entry
eric
escheat
escrow (escroll)
escuage
esnecy
esrepe
essoin
estate
estop
estoppel
estover
estray
estreat
estrepement
examination
excamb
excambion
excambium
executry
exemplify
expromission
extend
extent
extinguishment
extract
extradition
facile
facility
factorise
faldage
felo de se
felony
feme
feme covert
feme sole
feoff
feoffee
feoffer (feoffor)
feoffment
feu
feuar
fief
filacer
fire-bote
fiscal
folio
force and fear
force majeure
foreclose
foreclosure
forinsec
forisfamiliate
forjudge
frankalmoign
free-bench
frontager
fugitation
fungibles
garnishee
garnisheement
garnisher
gavelkind
gavelman
granter (grantor)
grassum
hamesucken
hedge-bote
hide
homologation
horning
house-bote
hypothec
hypothecary
hypothecate
hypothecation
improbation
indenture
indict
indictment
induciae
infangthief
infeft
inquirendo
institorial
insucken
interlocutor
interplead
interpleader
interpose
irrepleviable
irreplevisable
ish
John Doe and
 Richard Roe
joinder
jointure
jus primae noctis
laches
law-agent
law-burrows
legitim
lenocinium
letters of administration
lien
life-rent
malfeasance
mens rea
mesne
messuage
misdemeanant
misfeasance
misfeasor
misprision
mittimus
mora
mortmain
multiplepoinding
nolle prosequi
nolo contendere
non-access
nonage
non-compearance
non-entry
nonsuit
non-user
notour
novalia
noverint
novodamus
noxal
obligant
obligation
obligor
obreption
onus probandi
ouster
outfangthief
overt act
owelty
oyer
pactum nudum
Pandect
panel
pernancy
personalty
pickery
plaint
plaintiff
porteous roll
portioner
practic
prima facie
privy
prorogate
pupil
quadruply
realty
recaption
recusation
reddendo
relator
relaxation
remise
replevin
replevy
repone
reprobator
res gestae
retour
retroact
retroactive
reverser
right of drip
rout
scutage
stillicide
supersedeas
supplicavit
surrebut
surrebuttal
surrebutter
surrejoin
surrejoinder
terminer
tolt
tort
tortfeasor
tortious
udal
udaller
ultimus haeres
unlaw
uses
usucapient
usucapion (usucaption)
usucapt
usucaptible
usufruct
usufructuary
ultimogeniture
vacatur
venire (facias)
venter
venue
vert
vest
vested
visne
voidable

legal *(contd.)*
voir dire
volunteer
wage
waive
waste
watch
watching brief
water-privilege
wit

minerals

adularia
aegirine
aegirite
alabandine
almandine
alum-shale
alum-slate
alum-stone
alunite
amazonite
amazon-stone
amianthus
amosite
amphibole
analcime
anatase
andesine
aplite
argil
arkose
asbestos
asparagus-stone
asphalt(um)
aventurine
baetyl
balas
Barbados earth
barilla
baryta
barytes
basalt
Bath stone
bath-brick
bezoar
bitter-earth
bitter-spar
bitumen
blackjack
blacklead
blaes
blende
bloodstone
blue ground
blue John
blue vitriol
bluestone
Bologna phosphorus
borane
borax
borazon
boride
bornite
boulder-clay
breccia
Bristol-brick
Bristol-diamond
brown spar
brownstone
buhrstone
cacholong
caen-stone
cairngorm
calamine
calc-sinter
calcspar
calc-tuff
caliche
calp
Carborundum®
cat's-eye
cat-silver
cauk
celestine
cement-stone
ceruse
chalcedony
chalcedonyx
chalk
chert
Chile saltpetre
china clay
china stone
chrome-alum
chrome-spinel
chrysoberyl
chrysocolla
chrysoprase
chrysotile
cinnabar
cinnamon-stone
cipollino
corundum
cryolite
cymophane
dacite
dendrite
Derbyshire spar
diabase
diallage
dialogite
diaspore
diatomite
dice-coal
diopside
dioptase
diorite
dogger
dogtooth-spar
dolerite
dolomite
dopplerite
dropstone
dunite
dyscrasite
dysodyle
eagle-stone
earthflax
earthwax
eclogite
electric calamine
elvan
emery
encrinite
enhydrite
enhydros
epidiorite
epidosite
epidote
epistilbite
epsomite
erinite
erionite
erubescite
erythrite
euclase
eucrite
eudialyte
eutaxite
euxenite
fahlerz
fahlore
fakes
fayalite
fel(d)spar
felsite
felstone
flint
fluorite
fluorspar
franklinite
French chalk
fuchsite
fulgurite
fuller's earth
gabbro
gadolinite
gahnite
galena
galenite
gangue
gan(n)ister
garnet-rock
gibbsite
glance
glauberite
glauconite
glimmer
gmelinite
gneiss
goldstone
goslarite
gossan
göthite
granite
granitite
granodiorite
granophyre
granulite
graphic granite
graphite
green earth
greenockite
greensand
greenstone
greisen
greywacke
gummite
gypsum
haematite
hälleflinta
halloysite
harmotome
hatchettite
haüyne
heavy spar
hedyphane
hemimorphite
hepatite
hercynite
(h)essonite
heulandite
hiddenite
honey-stone
hornblende
hornfels
hornstone
horseflesh ore
humite
hyacinth
hyalophane
hypersthene
ice-spar
ice-stone
idocrase
ironstone
jacinth
keratophyre
kermes
kermesite
kieselguhr
knotenschiefer
kunkur
kupferschiefer
lamprophyre
lapis lazuli
lepidomelane
limestone
lithomarge
marlstone
meerschaum
mellite
mica
microlite
microlith
mispickel
morion
moss-agate
mundic
nail-head-spar
needle-tin
nepheline
nickel-bloom
nickel-ochre
Norway saltpetre
nosean
noselite
obsidian
omphacite
onyx
onyx-marble
ophiolite
orthoclase
orthophyre
ottrelite
ozokerite
peacock-ore
pencil-ore
pencil-stone
peperino
periclase
pericline
petuntse
piedmontite
pipeclay
pipestone
plagioclose
pleonaste
porphyry
potstone
prase
protogine

minerals *(contd.)*
pyrites
quartz
realgar
rock-oil
rubicelle
ruby-spinel
rutile
saltpetre
sandstone
sanidine
sapphire
sapphire-quartz
sapphirine
sard
sardonyx
satin-spar
satin-stone
scaglia
scawtite
schalstein
schiller-spar
schist
schorl
serpentine
serpentine(-rock)
shale
shell-limestone
shell-marl
silica
silver-glance
sinter
slate
soapstone
spar
speiss-cobalt
spelter
sphene
spiegeleisen
spinel
spinel-ruby
spodumene
stinkstone
strontian(ite)
sunstone
surturbrand
swinestone
sylvine
tabular spar
tachylyte
talc
talc-schist
terne
terpene
terpineol
terra alba
terracotta
terra-japonica
terramara
terra-rossa
terra-sigillata
terts
thulia
tiger(s)-eye
till
tin-stone
toad-stone
tombac
touchstone
tourmaline
trass
travertin(e)
tripoli
troutstone
tufa
tuff
Turkey hone
Turkey stone
turquoise
tutty
uinta(h)ite
umber
Uralian emerald
uralite
uraninite
uranite
uvarovite
vanadinite
variolite
variscite
veinstone
veinstuff
Venice talc
verd-antique
vesuvianite
vitrain
vivianite
vulpinite
wacke
wad(d)
wallsend
wavellite
Wernerite
whet-slate
whewellite
whinstone
white pyrites
willemite
witherite
wolfram
wollastonite
wood-coal
wulfenite
wurtzite
zaratite
zarnich
zeolite
zeuxite
zinkenite
zircon
zoisite
zorgite

musical instruments

aeolian harp
aerophone
alpenhorn
alphorn
althorn
alto
Amati
American organ
apollonicon
archlute
arpeggione
atabal
autoharp
balalaika
bandore
bandura
banjulele
baryton(e)
bass clarinet
bass drum
bass fiddle
bass horn
bass tuba
bass viol
basset horn
bazooka
bombard
bombardon
bongo (drum)
bouzouki
buccina
bugle
buglet
bull fiddle
calliope
castanets
celeste
cello
cembalo
chair-organ
chalumeau
chamber organ
chikara
Chinese pavilion
chitarrone
chordophone
cinema-organ
cithara
cither(n)
citole
cittern
clarichord
clarinet
clarino
clarion
clarsach
clave
clavichord
cornet
cornettino
crwth
cymbal
cymbalo
decachord
dichord
didgeridoo
digitorium
double bass
drum
dulcimer
Dulcitone®
dumb-piano
echo
electric guitar
electric organ
euphonium
fagotto
fife
fipple-flute
flageolet
flügel
flügelhorn
flute
flûte-à-bec
flutina
French horn
gamelan
German flute
gimbard
gittern
glass harmonica
glockenspiel
grand piano
gu
guiro
guitar
gusla
Hammerklavier
hand-horn
hand-organ
harmonica
harmonicon
harmoniphone
harmonium
harp
harpsichord
hautboy
heckelphone
heptachord
horn
hornpipe
humstrum
hunting-horn
hurdy-gurdy
idiophone
jingling Johnny
kantele
kazoo
kent-bugle
keyboard(s)
keybugle
klavier
koto
krummhorn
Kuh-horn
langsp(i)el
lituus
lur(e)
lyra-viol
lyre
mandola
mandolin(e)
mandora
manzello
maraca
marimba
marimbaphone
marine trumpet
melodeon
metallophone
mirliton
monochord
Moog synthesizer
mouth-harp
mouth-organ
mridangam
musette
musical glasses
naker
nose-flute
nun's-fiddle
oboe
oboe d'amore
oboe di caccia
ocarina
octachord
octave-flute
ophicleide
organ-harmonium

musical instruments *(contd.)*
orpharion
orpheorion
pandora
panharmonicon
Pan-pipes
Pan's pipes
pantaleon
pianette
pianino
piano
piano-accordion
pianoforte
Pianola®
piano-organ
piffero
pipe
pipeless organ
pipe-organ
player piano
polyphon(e)
poogye
posaune
psaltery
pyrophone
quena
quint(e)
racket(t)
rebec(k)
regal
rote
sackbut
salpinx
sambuca
sancho
sang
santir
sarangi
sarod
sarrusophone
sausage-bassoon
saxhorn
saxophone
seraphine
serinette
serpent
s(h)amisen
shawm
side-drum
sitar
small-pipes
sourdeline
sousaphone
spinet(te)
squeeze-box
squiffer
steel drum
sticcado
stock-and-horn
strad
Stradivari(us)
string bass
sultana
symphonion
symphony
synthesiser
syrinx
tabla
tabor
tabo(u)rin
tabret
tambour
tamboura
tambourine
tam-tam
testudo
tetrachord
theatre organ
theorbo
timbal
timbrel
timpano
tin whistle
traps
triangle
trichord
tromba marina
trombone
trump
trumpet
trumpet marine
tuba
tubular bells
tympan
uillean pipes
ukulele
vibraharp
vibraphone
vielle
vihuela
vina
viol
viola
viola da braccio
(viola da) gamba
viola da gamba
viola da spalla
viola d'amore
violin
violoncello
violone
virginal(s)
vocalion
waldflute
waldhorn
Welsh harp
xylophone
xylorimba
zambomba
zampogna
zanze
zel
zeze
zinke
zither
zufolo

parliaments

Althing (Iceland)
Cortes (Spain
Portugal)
Dáil (Ireland)
d(o)uma (Russia)
ecclesia (Athens)
eduskunta (Finland)
Folketing (Denmark)
House of Commons (UK)
House of Keys (Isle of Man)
House of Lords (UK)
Knesset (Israel)
Lagt(h)ing (Norway)
Lagting (Norway)
Landst(h)ing (Denmark)
Landtag (Germany)
Løgting (Faroes)
Lok Sabha (India)
Majlis (Iran)
Odelst(h)ing (Norway)
Oireachtas (Ireland)
Parliament (UK)
Pnyx (Athens)
Porte (Turkey)
Rajya Sabha (India)
Reichsrat(h) (Austria)
Reichstag (Germany)
Rigsdag (Denmark)
Riksdag (Sweden)
Seanad (Ireland)
Senate (Rome
USA
etc.)
Skupshtina (Yugoslavia)
Sobranje (Bulgaria)
Stort(h)ing (Norway)
Tynwald (Isle of Man)
witenagemot (England)

prosody

Alcaic
alexandrine
amphibrach
amphibrachic
amphimacer
Anacreontic
anacrusis
anacrustic
anapaest
anapaestic
antibacchius
antispast
antispastic
antistrophe
Archilochian
arsis
Asclepiad
asynartete
atonic
bacchius
catalectic
choliamb
choree
choriamb
cinquain
cretic
dactyl
decastich
decasyllabic
decasyllable
dipody
dispondaic
dispondee
distich
disyllable
ditrochean
ditrochee
dizain
dochmiac
dochmius
dodecasyllabic
dodecasyllable
dolichurus
duan
ectasis
ecthlipsis
elide
elision
enjamb(e)ment
envoy
epic
epirrhema
epistrophe
epitrite
epode
epopee
epopoeia
epos
epyllion
extrametrical
eye-rhyme
false quantity
feminine caesura
feminine ending
feminine rhyme
fifteener
free verse
galliambic
g(h)azal
glyconic
gradus
haiku
head-rhyme
hendecasyllabic
hendecasyllable
hephthemimer
heptameter
heptapody
heptasyllabic
heterostrophic
heterostrophy
hexameter
hexametric(al)
hexapody
hexastich
Hudibrastic
huitain
hypercatalectic
hypercatalexis
hypermetrical
iamb
iambus
ictus
Ionic
irrational
kyrielle
laisse
Leonine
limerick
limma
linked verse
logaoedic
long-measure
macaronic(s)
masculine ending
masculine rhyme
meliboean
miurus
monometer
monorhyme
monostich
monostrophic

prosody *(contd.)*
mora
outride
oxytone
pantoum
pentameter
pentastich
penthemimer
Pherecratean
Pherecratic
Pindaric
poulters' measure
proceleusmatic
pyrrhic
Pythian
quatorzain
quatrain
reported verses
rhopalic
rhyme-royal
rich rhyme
riding-rhyme
rime riche
rime suffisante
rondeau
rondel
rove-over
rubaiyat
run-on
Sapphics
scazon
semeion
senarius
septenarius
sestina
spondee
strophe
synaphe(i)a
tetrameter
tetrapody
tetrasemic
tetrastich
thesis
tirade
tribrach
trimeter
tripody
triseme
trochee
villanelle
virelay

ranks in armed forces

able seaman
acting sub-lieutenant
admiral
admiral of the fleet
air chief marshal
air commandant
air commodore
air vice marshal
aircraftman
air-marshal
brigadier
captain
chief officer
chief petty officer
chief technician
colonel
commandant
commander
commodore
corporal
field marshal
first officer
fleet chief petty officer
flight lieutenant
flight officer
flight sergeant
flying
officer
general
group captain
group officer
junior seaman
junior technician
lance-corporal
lance-jack
lance-sergeant
leading aircraftman
leading seaman
lieutenant
lieutenant-colonel
lieutenant-commander
lieutenant-general
major
major-general
marshal
marshal of the Royal
Air Force
master-at-arms
midshipman
ordinary seaman
petty officer
pilot officer
post-captain
private
purser
quartermaster
quartermaster-general
quartermaster-sergeant
quartermistress
rear-admiral
risaldar
ritt-master
second lieutenant
second officer
senior aircraftman
sergeant
sergeant-major
squadron leader
squadron officer
staff sergeant
sub-lieutenant
superintendent
third officer
vice admiral
warrant officer
wing commander
wing officer

rhetoric

abscission
alliteration
amoebaean
anacoluthia
anacoluthon
anadiplosis
anaphora
anaphoric
anastrophe
antimetabole
antimetathesis
antiphrasis
antiphrastic(al)
antithesis
antithetic(al)
antonomasia
aporia
asteism
asyndeton
auxesis
catachresis
chiasmus
climax
diallage
diegesis
dissimile
double entendre
dramatic irony
dysphemism
ecbole
echoic
ecphonesis
ellipsis
enallage
enantiosis
enumeration
epanadiplosis
epanalepsis
epanaphora
epanodos
epanorthosis
epexegesis
epiphonema
epizeuxis
erotema
erotetic
figure
flower
head-rhyme
hendiadys
holophrase
hypallage
hyperbaton
hyperbole
hypobole
hypostrophe
hypotyposis
hysteron-proteron
increment
irony
litotes
meiosis
metalepsis
metaphor
metonym
metonymy
mixed metaphor
onomatopoeia
oxymoron
parabole
paral(e)ipsis
parenthesis
prolepsis
simile
syllepsis
symploce
synchoresis
synchysis
synecdoche
synoeciosis
trope
vicious circle
zeugma

titles of rulers

abuna
adelantado
ag(h)a
alderman
amir
amman
amtman
ard-ri(gh)
atabeg
atabek
ataman
atheling
ayatollah
Ban
beglerbeg
begum
bey
boyar
burgrave
caboceer
cacique
caliph
caudillo
Cid
Dan
Dauphin
Dauphine
Dauphiness
dey
diadochus
doge
duce
duke
ealdorman
elector
emir
emperor
empress
ethnarch
exarch
gospodar
Graf
Gräfin
grave
Great Mogul
harmost
heptarch
hospodar
huzoor
imperator
Inca
infanta
infante
jarl
kaid
kaiser
kalif
khan
khedive
king
kinglet
kingling
landgrave
landgravine

titles of rulers *(contd.)*
maharaja(h)
maharani
mandarin
marchesa
marchese
marchioness
margrave
margravine
marquess
marquis
marquise
mikado
Mirza
Monseigneur
monsieur
Monsignor
Monsignore
mormaor
mpret
nabob
naik
nawab
nizam
nomarch
omrah
padishah
palatine
palsgrave
pasha
pendragon
pentarch
pharaoh
prince
prince-bishop
prince-imperial
princess
raja(h)
rajpramukh
rana
rani
Rhinegrave
Rhinegravine
sachem
sagamore
satrap
shah
sheik(h)
sherif
shogun
sirdar
sovereign
stad(t)holder
starosta
suba(h)dar
sultan
suzerain
taoiseach
theocrat
toiseach
toparch
tsar
tuchun
voivode
waldgrave

tools
about-sledge
aiguille
auger
auger-bit
awl
boaster
bodkin
bolster
bradawl
broach
bucksaw
burin
burr
buzz-saw
card
caschrom
caulking-iron
celt
centre-bit
chaser
chisel
chopper
clamp
cleaver
cold-chisel
cradle-scythe
crosscut-saw
crown-saw
diamond-drill
dibble
dividers
dolly
drawing-knife
draw-knife
drill
drove
els(h)in
extirpator
fillister
float
forceps
forfex
fork
fraise
frame-saw
fretsaw
gad
gang-saw
gavelock
gimlet
gouge
grapnel
grapple
graver
gurlet
hacksaw
hammer
handsaw
hawk
hay fork
hay knife
helve-hammer
hod
hoe
holing-axe
jackhammer
jack-plane
jointer
laster
level
levelling-rod
levelling-staff
loy
mace
madge
maker
mall
mallet
mattock
maul
monkey
moon-knife
mortar
muller
oliver
oustiti
pachymeter
pad-saw
palstave
panel saw
panga
paper-cutter
paper-knife
pattle
pecker
peel
pestle
pick
pickaxe
pincers
pinch
pinking-shears
piolet
pitchfork
plane
planer
plessor
plexor
pliers
plough
plow
plugger
plumb
plumb-line
plumb-rule
plummet
pocket-knife
pointel
pricker
priest
priming-iron
priming-wire
probang
probe
probing-scissors
prod
prog
pruning-bill
pruning-hook
pruning-knife
pruning-shears
prunt
punch
puncheon
punty
quadrant
quannet
rabble
rake
raspatory
reed-knife
repositor
retractor
ricker
rickstick
riddle
riffle
ripper
ripping-saw
ripple
rip-saw
risp
router
rule
ruler
sash-tool
saw
sax
scalpel
scauper
scissors
scoop
scooper
scorper
scraper
screwdriver
screwjack
screw-wrench
scribe(r)
scutch(er)
scythe
seam-set
serving-mallet
shave
shears
shovel
sickle
slane
slate-axe
slater
slicker
smoother
snap
snarling-iron
snarling-rod
snips
soldering-bolt
soldering-iron
spade
spanner
spider
spokeshave
spud
squeegee
stadda
stake
stapler
stapling-machine
steel
stithy
stone-hammer
stretching-iron
strickle
strigil
stubble-rake
style
stylet
swage
swingle(-hand)
switch
tedder
tenon-saw
threshel
thresher
thrust-hoe
tint-tool

tools *(contd.)*
tongs
trepan
trowel
T-square
turfing-iron
turf-spade
turning-saw
tweezers
twist drill
upright
van
vice
vulsella
waster
whip-saw
widener
wimble
wood-shears
wortle
xyster
Y-level

units of measurement

acre
ampere
angstrom
anker
ardeb
are
arpent
arroba
arshin
as
bar
barleycorn
barn
barrel
bath
baud
becquerel
bel
bigha
bit
Board of Trade Unit/BTU
board-foot
boll
bolt
braccio
bushel
butt
cab
cable
calorie
candela
candle
candy
carat
catty
cell
cental
centner
chain
chalder
chaldron
ch(o)enix
chopin
chronon
clove
co(o)mb
cor
cord
coss
coulomb
cran
crith
cubit
cumec
curie
cusec
cyathus
daraf
Debye (unit)
degree
demy
dessiatine
digit
dirham
dra(ch)m
dyne
ell
em
en
epha(h)
erg
farad
faraday
fathom
fermium
firkin
firlot
foot
fother
fou
furlong
gal
gallon
gerah
gilbert
gill
grain
gram(me)
hectare
henry
hertz
hin
hogshead
homer
hoppus foot
hundredweight
inch
joule
kaneh
kantar
kelvin
k(h)at
kilderkin
kin
knot
league
leaguer
li
liang
liard
ligne
link
lippy
lire
lisp(o)und
litre
log
lux
maneh
maund
metre
mho
micrometre
micron
mile
mil(l)
mina
minim
minute
mna
modius
mole
morgen
muid
mutchkin
nail
neper
nepit
newton
nit (information)
nit (luminance)
noggin
obol
oersted
ohm
oke
omer
ounce
oxgang
parasang
pascal
peck
perch
picul
pin
pint
pipe
poise
pole
pood
pound
poundal
quart
quarter
quartern
quintal
quire
radian
ream
rem
rod
rood
rote
rotolo
run(d)let
rutherford
sabin
s(a)eculum
sazhen
scruple
second
seer
semuncia
shekel
shippound
siemens
sievert
sone
span
square
stadium
steradian
stere
stilb
stoke(s)
stone
tael
talent
tare
tesla
therm
tical
tierce
tod
toise
tola
ton
tonne
tonneau
tor
truss
tun
vara
verst
virgate
volt
watt
weber
wey
yard
yardland
yojan

vehicles

aerotrain
air-car
amtrack
araba
arba
aroba
barouche
Bath chair
berlin(e)
bicycle
biga
bobsled
bobsleigh
bogie
boneshaker
brake
britzka
brougham
brute
bubble-car
buckboard
buckcart
buck-wagon
buggy
bus
cab
caboose
cabriolet
caisson
calash
camper
car
caravan
caravanette

vehicles *(contd.)*
caroche
car(r)iole
carry-all
catafalque
chair
chaise
chaise-cart
chapel cart
charabanc
chariot
clarence
coach
coaler
convertible
conveyance
cycle
dandy-cart
dandy-horse
dennet
désobligeante
dhooly
diesel
diligence
dilly
Dodgem(s)®
dog-cart
dogcart
dolly
doolie
dormitory-car
drag
dray
dros(h)ky
duck
ekka
fiacre
fly
fork-lift truck
four-in-hand
gharri
gig
glass-coach
go-kart
Green Goddess
gyrocar
gyrodyne
hack
hackery
hackney-carriage/coach
hatchback
herdic
honey-cart
honey-wag(g)on
HUMV
hurley-hacket
ice-yacht
inside-car
jeep
jingle
jinricksha(w)
jitney
juggernaut
kago
kajawah
kart
kibitka
landau
landaulet(te)
limousine
litter
lorry
mail-cart
minibus
monorail
motor caravan
motor-bicycle
motor-bike
motor-bus
motor-car
motor-coach
motor-cycle
motor-lorry
motor-scooter
norimon
omnibus
outside-car
palanquin (palankeen)
palki
pantechnicon
pedal cycle
pedicab
people mover
phaeton
pick-up
pill-box
pincers
post-chaise
prairie schooner
pulka
quad
quadriga
rail-bus
rail-car
rail-motor
ricksha(w)
roadster
rockaway
runabout
safety bicycle
saloon-car
saloon-carriage
samlor
scooter
sedan
sedan-chair
shandry(dan)
shooting-brake
sidecar
single-decker
skateboard
ski-bob
sled
sledge
sleeper
sleeping-car
sleeping-carriage
sleeping-coach
sleigh
slip-carriage
slip-coach
slipe
snowmobile
snow-plough
sociable
solo
speedster
spider
spring-carriage
spring-cart
squad car
stage-coach
stage-wagon
stanhope
station-wagon
steam-car
steam-carriage
steamer
steam-roller
stillage
stone boat
straddle carrier
street-car
sulky
surrey
tally-ho
tandem
tank
tank-car
tank-engine
tanker
tank-wagon
tarantas(s)
tartana
tax(ed)-cart
taxi
taxicab
T-cart
telega
telpher
tender
thoroughbrace
through-train
tilbury
tim-whisk(e)y
tin Lizzie
tip
tip-cart
tipper
toboggan
tonga
tourer
touring-car
tractor
trailer
train
tram
tramway-car
transporter
transport-rider
trap
tricar
tricycle
trike
triplet
trishaw
troika
trolley
trolley-bus
trolley-car
troop-carrier
truck
tube
tumble-car(t)
tumbrel
turbocar
two-decker
twoseater
two-wheeler
velocipede
vettura
victoria
village cart
vis-à-vis
volante
wag(g)on
wagonette
wagon-lit
wain
water-cart
water-wagon
weasel
wheelbarrow
wheel-chair
whisk(e)y
Whitechapel cart

vessels, ships
argosy
barca
barque
barquentine
bateau
bawley
Berthon-boat
bilander
billyboy
bireme
birlinn
boat
bomb-ketch
bomb-vessel
brig
brigantine
Bucentaur
budgerow
bum-boat
buss
butty
cabin cruiser
caique
canal-boat
canoe
caravel
Carley float
carrack
casco
cat
catamaran
catboat
clipper
coaler
coaster
cob(b)le
cockboat
cockleshell
cog
collier
commodore
coracle
corocore
corvette
cot
crare
crayer
currach
cutter
dandy
deep-sinker
deepwaterman
destroyer
d(h)ow
dinghy

vessels, ships *(contd.)*
diving-bell
dogger
drake
dreadnought
dredger
drog(h)er
dromond
dugout
East-Indiaman
E-boat
faltboat
felucca
flatboat
floating battery
flyboat
flying bridge
fore-and-after
frigate
frigatoon
funny
gabbart
galleass
galleon
galley
gal(l)iot
gallivat
gay-you
geordie
gondola
grab
hatch boat
herringer
hooker
hovercraft
hoy
hydrofoil
hydroplane
hydrovane
ice-boat
Indiaman
iron-clad
jigger
jollyboat
junk
kayak
ketch
koff
laker
landing-craft
lapstreak
launch
liberty-ship
lighter
line-of-battle-ship
liner
long-boat
longship
lorcha
lugger
lymphad
mackinaw
masoolah
merchantman
mistico
monitor
monkey-boat
monohull
monoxylon
montaria
motor-boat
motor-launch
motor-ship
motoscafo
mud-boat
mudscow
multihull
nacelle
nuggar
outrigger
packet
packet-boat
packet-ship
pair-oar
patamar
pedalo
penteconter
periagua
peter-boat
pink
pinkie
pinky
pinnace
piragua
pirogue
pleasure-boat
pocket battleship
polacca
polacre
pontoon
powerboat
praam
pra(h)u
pram
privateer
puffer
pulwar
punt
puteli
quadrireme
quinquereme
randan
razee
river-boat
river-craft
row-barge
row-boat
rowing-boat
saic
sail-boat
sailing-boat
sailing-ship
salmon-coble
sampan
schooner
schuit
scooter
scow
scull
sculler
sea-boat
seaplane-carrier
settee
shallop
ship
ship-of-the-line
shore-boat
show-boat
skiff
sloop
sloop-of-war
smack
smuggler
snow
speed-boat
speedster
square rigger
steamboat
steamer
steam-launch
steam-packet
steamship
steam-tug
steam-vessel
steam-yacht
stern-wheeler
stew-can
sub
submarine
super-Dreadnought
supertanker
surface-craft
surf-board
surf-boat
surf-canoe
surfing-board
swamp boat
tanker
tartane(e)
tender
tern
three-decker
three-master
tilt-boat
torpedo-boat
torpedo-boat destroyer
track-boat
tracker
trader
train ferry
tramp
transport-ship
trawler
trek-schuit
triaconter
trimaran
trireme
troop-carrier
trooper
troop-ship
tub
tug
tug-boat
turbine-steamer
turret-ship
two-decker
two-master
U-boat
umiak
vaporetto
vedette(-boat)
vessel
wager-boat
warship
water-bus
well-boat
well-smack
whaleboat
whaler
wherry
whiff
windjammer
xebec
yacht
yawl
zabra
zulu

weapons, armour

A-bomb
ack-ack
aerodart
ailette
air rifle
amusette
an(e)lace
arbalest
arblast
Archibald
Archie
arcubalist
armet
arquebus(e)
baldric(k)
ballista
ballistic missile
bandolier
basilisk
baton gun
bazooka
beaver
bill
Biscayan
blackjack
blowgun
blowpipe
bludgeon
blunderbuss
boarding-pike
bodkin
Bofors gun
bolas
bomb
bombard
boomerang
bowie knife
brassard
breastplate
breech-loader
Bren (gun)
bricole
brigandine
broadsword
brown Bess
brown bill
buckler
buckshot
bulldog
bullet
bundook
Bungalore torpedo
burganet
byrnie
caltrop
cannon
carbine
carronade
casque
cataphract
catapult
chain-armour
chain-mail
chamfrain

weapons, armour *(contd.)*
Chassepot
chausses
cheval-de-frise
chokebore
claymore
cluster-bomb
coal-box
co(e)horn
Colt
Congreve
corium
dag
dagger
dah
Damascus blade
Damascus sword
demi-cannon
demi-culverin
demi-lance
depth-bomb
depth-charge
dirk
dragoon
elephant gun
épée
escopette
Exocet®
express rifle
falchion
falconet
field gun
fire-arm
fire-arrow
firebomb
firelock
firepot
fission bomb
flail
flame-thrower
flick-knife
flintlock
foil
fougade
fougasse
four-pounder
fusee
fusil
Garand rifle
gatling-gun
gavelock
genouillère
gisarme
gladius
gorget
grapeshot
greave
Greek fire
grenade
gun
habergeon
hackbut
hacqueton
hailshot
halberd
half-pike
hand-grenade
hand-gun
han(d)jar
handstaff
harquebus
hauberk
H-bomb
heaume
helm
helmet
hielaman
howitzer
jack
jamb(e)
jazerant
jesserant
Jethart staff
kalashnikov
katana
kirpan
kris
lamboys
lame
lance
Lochaber-axe
Long Tom
machete
machine-gun
mangonel
martel
Martini (-Henry)
matchlock
Mauser
Maxim(-gun)
mesail
Mills bomb
Mills grenade
mine
mine-thrower
mini-rocket launcher
minnie
mitrailleur
mitrailleuse
morgenstern
morglay
morning-star
mor(r)ion
mortar
musket
musketoon
nulla-nulla
oerlikon
panga
partisan
Patriot
pauldron
pavis(e)
peasecod-cuirass
pederero
pelican
pelta
perrier
petrary
petronel
pickelhaube
pike
pilum
pistol
pistolet
placket
plastron
plate-armour
pocket-pistol
poitrel
pole-ax(e)
poleyn
pompom
poniard
potgun
quarter-staff
queen's-arm
rapier
rerebrace
rest
revolver
rifle
rifle-grenade
sabaton
sabre
saker
sallet
saloon-pistol
saloon-rifle
sap
sarbacane
schiavone
schläger
scimitar
scorpion
Scud
scutum
serpentine
sharp
shell
shield
shillela(g)h
shortsword
shotgun
shrapnel
siege-artillery
siege-gun
siege-piece
singlestick
six-gun
six-shooter
skean(dhu)
sling
slung-shot
small-arm
small-sword
smoke-ball
smoke-bomb
snickersnee
spadroon
sparth(e)
spear
spear gun
splint-armour
spontoon
spring-gun
squid
steel
sten gun
Sterling
stern-chaser
stiletto
stone axe
stone-bow
stylet
submachine-gun
sumpit(an)
switch-blade (knife)
swivel-gun
sword
sword bayonet
sword-cane
sword-stick
tace
targe
target
taslet
tasse
tasset
testudo
three-pounder
threshel
throw-stick
time-bomb
toc emma
toggle-iron
tomahawk
Tomahawk
tomboc
tommy-gun
tormentum
torpedo
tortoise
trecento
trench-mortar
trident
truncheon
tuille
tuillette
tulwar
turret-gun
twibill
vambrace
vamplate
V-bomb
visor
vou(l)ge
war-wolf
waster
water-cannon
water-pistol
Welsh hook
white-arm
Winchester (rifle)
wind-gun
wo(o)mera(ng)
yatag(h)an
zumbooruk

wine-bottle sizes
baby
balthasar
jeroboam
magnum
Methuselah
nebuchadnezzar
nip
rehoboam
salmanazar

zodiac signs
Aquarius
Aries
Cancer
Capricorn
Gemini
Leo
Libra
Pisces
Sagittarius
Scorpio
Taurus
Virgo

Appendix II

Words listed by suffix

-ast

chiliast
diaskeuast
dicast
dikast
dynast
ecclesiast
ecdysiast
elegiast
encomiast
enthusiast
fantast
gymnasiast
gymnast
Hesychast
hypochondriast
iconoclast
idoloclast
metaphrast
orgiast
paederast
pancratiast
paraphrast
peltast
phantasiast
pleonast
scholiast
utopiast

-aster

criticaster
grammaticaster
medicaster
philosophaster
poetaster
politicaster
theologaster

-cide

aborticide
acaricide
algicide
aphicide
aphidicide
bacillicide
bactericide
biocide
deicide
ecocide
ethnocide
feticide
filicide
foeticide
fratricide
fungicide
genocide
germicide
giganticide
herbicide
homicide
infanticide
insecticide
larvicide
liberticide
matricide
menticide
molluscicide
ovicide
parasiticide
parasuicide
parricide
patricide
pesticide
prolicide
regicide
rodenticide
sororicide
spermicide
suicide
taeniacide
trypanocide
tyrannicide
uxoricide
vaticide
verbicide
vermicide
viricide
viticide
vulpicide
weedicide

-cracy

aristocracy
autocracy
bureaucracy
chrysocracy
cottonocracy
democracy
demonocracy
despotocracy
dollarocracy
doulocracy
dulocracy
ergatocracy
Eurocracy
gerontocracy
gynaecocracy
hagiocracy
hierocracy
isocracy
kakistocracy
meritocracy
millocracy
mobocracy
monocracy
nomocracy
ochlocracy
pantisocracy
pedantocracy
physiocracy
plantocracy
plutocracy
plutodemocracy
pornocracy
ptochocracy
slavocracy
snobocracy
squattocracy
stratocracy
technocracy
thalassocracy
thalattocracy
theocracy
timocracy.

-crat

aristocrat
autocrat
bureaucrat
cosmocrat
democrat
hierocrat
meritocrat
millocrat
mobocrat
monocrat
ochlocrat
pantisocrat
pedantocrat
physiocrat
plutocrat
slavocrat
stratocrat
technocrat
theocrat.

-cratic

aristocratic
autocratic
bureaucratic
cosmocratic
democratic
Eurocratic
gerontocratic
gynaecocratic
hierocratic
isocratic
meritocratic
mobocratic
monocratic
ochlocratic
pancratic
pantisocratic
pedantocratic
physiocratic
plutocratic
stratocratic
technocratic
theocratic
timocratic
undemocratic

-cultural

acculturral
agricultural
arboricultural
crinicultural
cultural
floricultural
horticultural
piscicultural
subcultural
vinicultural
vocicultural

-culture

agriculture
apiculture
aquaculture
aquiculture
arboriculture
aviculture
culture
electroculture
floriculture
horticulture
mariculture
monoculture
ostreiculture
pisciculture
pomiculture
self-culture
sericiculture
sericulture
silviculture
stirpiculture
subculture
sylviculture
viniculture
viticulture
water-culture
zooculture

-cyte

athrocyte
cyte
erythrocyte
fibrocyte
gonocyte
granulocyte
haemocyte
leucocyte
lymphocyte
macrocyte
microcyte
oocyte

-cyte *(contd.)*
phagocyte
poikilocyte
spermatocyte
thrombocyte
thymocyte

-dom

Anglo-Saxondom
apedom
archdukedom
attorneydom
babeldom
babudom
bachelordom
beadledom
beggardom
birthdom
bishopdom
boredom
Bumbledom
chiefdom
Christendom
clerkdom
cockneydom
crippledom
cuckoldom
czardom
demirepdom
devildom
Dogberrydom
dolldom
dufferdom
dukedom
duncedom
earldom
enthraldom
fairydom
fandom
filmdom
flunkeydom
fogydom
freedom
fresherdom
Greekdom
gypsydom
halidom
heathendom
heirdom
hobbledehoydom
hobodom
junkerdom
kaiserdom
kingdom
kitchendom
leechdom
liegedom
mandom
martyrdom
masterdom
newspaperdom
niggerdom
noodledom
noveldom
officialdom
overfreedom
penny-wisdom
popedom
princedom
puppydom
puzzledom
Quakerdom
queendom
queerdom
rascaldom
rebeldom
sachemdom
saintdom
savagedom
Saxondom
scoundreldom
serfdom
sheikdom
sheikhdom
sheriffdom
Slavdom
spinsterdom
squiredom
stardom
subkingdom
swelldom
thanedom
thraldom
thralldom
topsyturvydom
tsardom
underkingdom
unwisdom
villadom
whoredom
wisdom
Yankeedom

-ferous

aluminiferous
amentiferous
antenniferous
argentiferous
auriferous
bacciferous
balsamiferous
bulbiferous
calciferous
carboniferous
celliferous
celluliferous
cheliferous
cobaltiferous
conchiferous
coniferous
coralliferous
corniferous
cruciferous
culmiferous
cupriferous
cupuliferous
diamantiferous
diamondiferous
doloriferous
dorsiferous
ferriferous
flagelliferous
flammiferous
floriferous
foraminiferous
fossiliferous
frondiferous
fructiferous
frugiferous
furciferous
garnetiferous
gemmiferous
glandiferous
glanduliferous
globuliferous
glumiferous
granuliferous
guaniferous
gummiferous
guttiferous
lactiferous
laniferous
laticiferous
lethiferous
luciferous
luminiferous
mammaliferous
mammiferous
manganiferous
manniferous
margaritiferous
melliferous
metalliferous
morbiferous
mortiferous
moschiferous
muciferous
nectariferous
nickeliferous
nubiferous
nuciferous
odoriferous
oleiferous
omniferous
ossiferous
oviferous
ovuliferous
ozoniferous
papilliferous
papuliferous
Permo-Carboniferous
pestiferous
petaliferous
petroliferous
piliferous
platiniferous
plumbiferous
polliniferous
pomiferous
poriferous
proliferous
pyritiferous
quartziferous
reptiliferous
resiniferous
rotiferous
sacchariferous
saliferous
salutiferous
sanguiferous
sebiferous
seminiferous
septiferous
siliciferous
soboliferous
somniferous
soporiferous
spiniferous
spinuliferous
splendiferous
staminiferous
stanniferous
stelliferous
stigmatiferous
stoloniferous
strombuliferous
styliferous
sudoriferous
tentaculiferous
thuriferous
titaniferous
tuberiferous
umbelliferous
umbriferous
unfossiliferous
uriniferous
vitiferous
vociferous
yttriferous
zinciferous
zinkiferous

-gamy

allogamy
apogamy
autogamy
bigamy
chalazogamy
chasmogamy
cleistogamy
clistogamy
cryptogamy
deuterogamy
dichogamy
digamy
endogamy
exogamy
geitonogamy
hercogamy
herkogamy
heterogamy
homogamy
hypergamy
isogamy
misogamy
monogamy
oogamy
pangamy
pantagamy
plasmogamy
plastogamy
polygamy
porogamy
siphonogamy
syngamy
trigamy
xenogamy
zoogamy

-genesis

abiogenesis
agamogenesis
anthropogenesis
autogenesis
biogenesis
blastogenesis
carcinogenesis
chondrogenesis
cytogenesis
diagenesis

-genesis *(contd.)*
diplogenesis
dynamogenesis
ectogenesis
electrogenesis
embryogenesis
epeirogenesis
epigenesis
gametogenesis
gamogenesis
haematogenesis
heterogenesis
histogenesis
homogenesis
hylogenesis
hypnogenesis
merogenesis
metagenesis
monogenesis
morphogenesis
mythogenesis
neogenesis
noogenesis
ontogenesis
oogenesis
organogenesis
orogenesis
orthogenesis
osteogenesis
paedogenesis
palingenesis
pangenesis
paragenesis
parthenogenesis
pathogenesis
perigenesis
petrogenesis
phylogenesis
phytogenesis
polygenesis
psychogenesis
pyogenesis
schizogenesis
spermatogenesis
sporogenesis
syngenesis
thermogenesis
xenogenesis

-genic
aesthesiogenic
allergenic
androgenic
anthropogenic
antigenic
biogenic
blastogenic
carcinogenic
cariogenic
cryogenic
dysgenic
ectogenic
electrogenic
endogenic
epeirogenic
erogenic
erotogenic
eugenic
genic
glycogenic
hallucinogenic
histogenic
hypnogenic
hysterogenic
iatrogenic
lactogenic
lysigenic
mammogenic
mutagenic
myogenic
neurogenic
odontogenic
oestrogenic
oncogenic
ontogenic
orogenic
orthogenic
osteogenic
pathogenic
photogenic
phytogenic
polygenic
psychogenic
pyogenic
pyrogenic
pythogenic
radiogenic
rhizogenic
saprogenic
schizogenic
somatogenic
spermatogenic
telegenic
teratogenic
thermogenic
tumorgenic
tumorigenic
visiogenic
zoogenic
zymogenic

-gon
chiliagon
decagon
dodecagon
endecagon
enneagon
hendecagon
heptagon
hexagon
isogon
nonagon
octagon
pentagon
perigon
polygon
tetragon
trigon

-gram
aerogram
anagram
anemogram
angiogram
audiogram
ballistocardiogram
barogram
cablegram
calligram
cardiogram
cartogram
centigram
centimetre-gram
chromatogram
chromogram
chronogram
cryptogram
dactylogram
decagram
decigram
dendrogram
diagram
echogram
electrocardiogram
electroencephalogram
encephalogram
engram
epigram
ergogram
ferrogram
harmonogram
hectogram
hexagram
hierogram
histogram
hologram
ideogram
indicator-diagram
isogram
kilogram
lexigram
lipogram
logogram
lymphogram
marconigram
marigram
meteorogram
microgram
monogram
myogram
nanogram
nephogram
neurogram
nomogram
organogram
oscillogram
pangram
paragram
parallelogram
pentagram
phonogram
photogram
phraseogram
pictogram
program
psychogram
pyelogram
radiogram
radiotelegram
röntgenogram
scintigram
seismogram
sialogram
skiagram
sociogram
spectrogram
spectroheliogram
sphenogram
sphygmogram
steganogram
stereogram
tachogram
telegram
tephigram
tetragram
thermogram
tomogram
trigram

-graph
Addressograph®
aerograph
airgraph
allograph
anemograph
apograph
audiograph
autograph
autoradiograph
ballistocardiograph
bar-graph
barograph
biograph
cardiograph
cathodograph
cerograph
chirograph
choreograph
chromatograph
chromolithograph
chromoxylograph
chronograph
cinematograph
coronagraph
coronograph
cryptograph
cyclograph
cymagraph
cymograph
diagraph
Dictograph®
digraph
dynamograph
eidograph
electrocardiograph
electroencephalograph
electrograph
electromyograph
ellipsograph
encephalograph
epigraph
ergograph
evaporograph
flannelgraph
glyphograph
harmonograph
hectograph
helicograph
heliograph
hierograph
hodograph
holograph
homograph
hydrograph
hyetograph
hyetometrograph
hygrograph
ideograph
idiograph
jellygraph

-graph *(contd.)*
keraunograph
kinematograph
kinetograph
kymograph
lithograph
logograph
magnetograph
marconigraph
marigraph
meteorograph
micrograph
microphotograph
microseismograph
mimeograph
monograph
myograph
nephograph
nomograph
odograph
odontograph
oleograph
opisthograph
orthograph
oscillograph
pantograph
paragraph
pentagraph
phonautograph
phonograph
photograph
photolithograph
photomicrograph
phototelegraph
photozincograph
phraseograph
pictograph
planigraph
plethysmograph
polygraph
pseudograph
psychograph
pyrophotograph
radioautograph
radiograph
radiometeorograph
radiotelegraph
rotograph
seismograph
selenograph
serigraph
shadowgraph
skiagraph
spectrograph
spectroheliograph
sphygmograph
spirograph
steganograph
stenograph
stereograph
Stevengraph
stylograph
syngraph
tachograph
tachygraph
Telautograph®
telegraph
telephotograph
thermograph
thermometrograph
tomograph
torsiograph
trigraph
vectograph
vibrograph
xylograph
zincograph

-graphical
autobiographical
bathygraphical
bathyorographical
bibliographical
biobibliographical
biogeographical
biographical
cacographical
calligraphical
cartographical
cerographical
chorographical
cinematographical
climatographical
cosmographical
geographical
glossographical
graphical
hagiographical
hierographical
historiographical
hydrographical
hyetographical
hygrographical
ichnographical
ideographical
lexicographical
lexigraphical
lithographical
logographical
monographical
myographical
oceanographical
oreographical
orographical
orthographical
palaeographical
palaeontographical
pantographical
paragraphical
pasigraphical
petrographical
photographical
physiographical
prosopographical
pseudepigraphical
psychobiographical
psychographical
pterylographical
seismographical
selenographical
spectrographical
stenographical
stereographical
stratigraphical
tachygraphical
topographical
typographical
xylographical
zincographical
zoogeographical
zoographical

-graphy
aerography
ampelography
angiography
anthropogeography
anthropography
areography
autobiography
autography
autoradiography
autotypography
ballistocardiography
bibliography
biogeography
biography
brachygraphy
cacography
calligraphy
cardiography
cartography
cathodography
ceramography
cerography
chalcography
chartography
cheirography
chirography
cholangiography
choregraphy
choreography
chorography
chromatography
chromolithography
chromotypography
chromoxylography
chronography
cinematography
cinemicrography
climatography
cometography
cosmography
cryptography
crystallography
dactyliography
dactylography
demography
dermatography
dermography
discography
dittography
doxography
echocardiography
ectypography
electrocardiography
electroencephalography
electrography
electromyography
electrophotography
encephalography
enigmatography
epigraphy
epistolography
ethnography
ferrography
filmography
geography
glossography
glyphography
glyptography
hagiography
haplography
heliography
heresiography
hierography
historiography
holography
horography
hydrography
hyetography
hymnography
hypsography
ichnography
ichthyography
iconography
ideography
lexicography
lexigraphy
lipography
lithography
logography
lymphography
mammography
metallography
microcosmography
micrography
microphotography
mimography
monography
morphography
myography
mythography
nomography
nosography
oceanography
odontography
oleography
opisthography
orchesography
oreography
organography
orography
orthography
osteography
palaeogeography
palaeography
palaeontography
pantography
paroemiography
pasigraphy
pathography
petrography
phonography
photography
photolithography
photomicrography
phototelegraphy
photoxylography
photozincography
physiography
phytogeography
phytography
pictography
polarography
polygraphy
pornography
prosopography
pseudepigraphy
pseudography
psychobiography
psychography
pterylography

-graphy *(contd.)*
pyelography
pyrography
pyrophotography
radiography
radiotelegraphy
reprography
rhyparography
röntgenography
scenography
scintigraphy
seismography
selenography
serigraphy
sialography
snobography
spectrography
sphygmography
steganography
stenography
stereography
stratigraphy
stylography
symbolography
tachygraphy
technography
telautography
telegraphy
telephotography
thalassography
thanatography
thaumatography
thermography
tomography
topography
typography
ultrasonography
uranography
urography
ventriculography
xerography
xeroradiography
xylography
xylopyrography
xylotypography
zincography
zoogeography
zoography

-hedron

chiliahedron
decahedron
dihedron
dodecahedron
enneahedron
hemihedron
hexahedron
holohedron
icosahedron
icositetrahedron
leucitohedron
octahedron
octohedron
pentahedron
polyhedron
pyritohedron
rhombohedron
scalenohedron
tetrahedron
tetrakishexahedron
trapezohedron
triakisoctahedron
trihedron
trisoctahedron

-hood

adulthood
angelhood
apehood
apprenticehood
babyhood
bachelorhood
beadlehood
beasthood
bountihood
boyhood
brotherhood
cathood
childhood
Christhood
companionhood
cousinhood
cubhood
deaconhood
dollhood
drearihood
elfhood
fairyhood
falsehood
fatherhood
flapperhood
flesh-hood
gawkihood
gentlehood
gentlemanhood
gianthood
girlhood
godhood
hardihood
high-priesthood
hobbledehoyhood
hoghood
hoydenhood
idlehood
invalidhood
jealoushood
kinghood
kinglihood
knighthood
ladyhood
likelihood
livelihood
lustihood
maidenhood
maidhood
manhood
masterhood
matronhood
misshood
monkhood
motherhood
nationhood
needy-hood
neighbourhood
novicehood
nunhood
old-maidhood
orphanhood
pagehood
parenthood
popehood
priesthood
princehood
prophethood
puppyhood
queenhood
sainthood
selfhood
serfhood
sisterhood
spinsterhood
squirehood
statehood
swinehood
tabbyhood
thanehood
thinghood
traitorhood
unlikelihood
virginhood
waiterhood
widowerhood
widowhood
wifehood
wivehood
womanhood
youthhood

-iac

ammoniac
amnesiac
anaphrodisiac
anglomaniac
Anglophobiac
antaphrodisiac
anthomaniac
aphasiac
aphrodisiac
archgenethliac
bacchiac
bibliomaniac
cardiac
celiac
Cluniac
coeliac
coprolaliac
demoniac
dextrocardiac
Dionysiac
dipsomaniac
dochmiac
dysthymiac
egomaniac
elegiac
endocardiac
erotomaniac
etheromaniac
Genesiac
genethliac
haemophiliac
hebephreniac
heliac
hypochondriac
iliac
insomniac
intracardiac
Isiac
kleptomaniac
maniac
megalomaniac
melancholiac
melomaniac
monomaniac
morphinomaniac
mythomaniac
necrophiliac
neurastheniac
nymphomaniac
opsomaniac
orchidomaniac
paedophiliac
Pandemoniac
paradisiac
paranoiac
paraphiliac
paroemiac
pericardiac
phrenesiac
pyromaniac
sacroiliac
scopophiliac
scoriac
simoniac
symposiac
Syriac
theomaniac
theriac
timbromaniac
toxiphobiac
zodiac
zygocardiac

-iatric

chemiatric
chemopsychiatric
geriatric
hippiatric
kinesiatric
paediatric
psychiatric
psychogeriatric

-iatry

chemopsychiatry
geriatry
hippiatry
neuropsychiatry
orthopsychiatry
paediatry
podiatry
psychiatry

-ician

academician
acoustician
aeroelastician
aesthetician
arithmetician
audiometrician
beautician
biometrician
clinician
cosmetician
diagnostician
dialectician
dietician
econometrician
ekistician

-ician *(contd.)*
electrician
geometrician
geopolitician
geriatrician
informatician
linguistician
logician
logistician
magician
magnetician
mathematician
mechanician
metaphysician
metrician
mortician
musician
obstetrician
optician
paediatrician
patrician
Paulician
phonetician
physician
politician
practician
psychogeriatrician
psychometrician
rhetorician
rubrician
statistician
systematician
tactician
technician
theoretician

-ics
acoustics
acrobatics
aerobatics
aerobics
aerodynamics
aeronautics
aerostatics
aesthetics
agogics
agonistics
ambisonics
apologetics
aquabatics
aquanautics
astrodynamics
astronautics
astrophysics
athletics
atmospherics
autonomics
avionics
axiomatics
ballistics
bioastronautics
biodynamics
bioethics
biomathematics
biomechanics
biometrics
bionics
bionomics
biophysics
biorhythmics
biosystematics
cacogenics
calisthenics
callisthenics
catacoustics
catallactics
cataphonics
catechetics
catoptrics
ceroplastics
chemotherapeutics
chrematistics
chromatics
civics
cliometrics
conics
cosmonautics
cosmopolitics
cryogenics
cryonics
cryophysics
cybernetics
cytogenetics
deontics
dermatoglyphics
diacoustics
diagnostics
dialectics
dianetics
didactics
dietetics
dioptrics
dogmatics
dramatics
dynamics
dysgenics
eclectics
econometrics
economics
ecumenics
ekistics
electrodynamics
electrokinetics
electromechanics
electronics
electrostatics
electrotechnics
electrotherapeutics
electrothermics
energetics
entoptics
environics
epigenetics
epistemics
epizootics
ergonomics
ethics
ethnolinguistics
eudaemonics
eudemonics
eugenics
eurhythmics
euthenics
exegetics
floristics
fluidics
forensics
genetics
geodetics
geodynamics
geophysics
geopolitics
geoponics
geostatics
geotectonics
geriatrics
gerontotherapeutics
glyptics
gnomonics
gnotobiotics
graphemics
graphics
gyrostatics
halieutics
haptics
harmonics
hedonics
hermeneutics
hermetics
hippiatrics
histrionics
homiletics
hydraulics
hydrodynamics
hydrokinetics
hydromagnetics
hydromechanics
hydroponics
hydrostatics
hydrotherapeutics
hygienics
hypersonics
hysterics
informatics
irenics
isagogics
isometrics
kinematics
kinesics
kinetics
linguistics
lithochromatics
liturgics
logistics
loxodromics
macrobiotics
macroeconomics
magnetics
magneto-hydrodynamics
magneto-optics
maieutics
mathematics
mechanics
melodics
metalinguistics
metamathematics
metaphysics
metapsychics
meteoritics
microeconomics
microelectronics
microphysics
mnemotechnics
mole-electronics
monostrophics
morphemics
morphophonemics
nautics
nucleonics
numismatics
obstetrics
olympics
onomastics
optics
optoelectronics
orchestics
orthodontics
orthodromics
orthogenics
orthopaedics
orthopedics
orthoptics
orthotics
paedeutics
paediatrics
paedodontics
paideutics
pantopragmatics
paralinguistics
party-politics
pataphysics
patristics
pedagogics
peptics
periodontics
pharmaceutics
pharmacodynamics
pharmacokinetics
phelloplastics
phonemics
phonetics
phonics
phonocamptics
phonotactics
photics
photochromics
photoelectronics
phototherapeutics
photovoltaics
psionics physics
physiotherapeutics
plastics
pneumatics
pneumodynamics
polemics
politico-economics
politics
power-politics
problematics
prosthetics
prosthodontics
psionics
psychics
psychodynamics
psychogeriatrics
psycholinguistics
psychometrics
psychonomics
psychophysics
psychosomatics
psychotherapeutics
pyrotechnics
quadraphonics
quadrophonics
radionics
radiophonics
radiotherapeutics
rhythmics
robotics
semantics
semeiotics
semiotics
Semitics

-ics *(contd.)*
sferics
significs
sociolinguistics
sonics
sophistics
spherics
sphragistics
statics
stereoptics
strategics
stylistics
subatomics
subtropics
syllabics
symbolics
synectics
systematics
tactics
technics
tectonics
telearchics
thaumaturgics
theatrics
therapeutics
thermionics
thermodynamics
thermotics
toponymics
toreutics
transonics
transsonics
ultrasonics
vitrics
zoiatrics
zootechnics
zymotechnics

-iform

aciform
acinaciform
aciniform
aeriform
alphabetiform
amoebiform
anguiform
anguilliform
antenniform
asbestiform
auriform
aviform
bacciform
bacilliform
biform
bursiform
cactiform
calcariform
calceiform
calyciform
cambiform
campaniform
campodeiform
cancriform
capriform
cauliform
cerebriform
cirriform
claviform
clypeiform
cobriform
cochleariform
coliform
colubriform
conchiform
coniform
coralliform
cordiform
corniform
corolliform
cotyliform
crateriform
cribriform
cristiform
cruciform
cteniform
cubiform
cucumiform
culiciform
cultriform
cumuliform
cuneiform
curviform
cyathiform
cylindriform
cymbiform
cystiform
deiform
dendriform
dentiform
digitiform
dolabriform
elytriform
ensiform
equisetiform
eruciform
falciform
fibriform
filiform
flabelliform
flagelliform
floriform
fringilliform
fungiform
fusiform
gangliform
gasiform
glandiform
granitiform
granuliform
hydatidiform
incisiform
infundibuliform
insectiform
janiform
jelliform
lamelliform
lanciform
lapilliform
larviform
lentiform
limaciform
linguiform
lumbriciform
lyriform
malleiform
mamilliform
mammiform
maniform
medusiform
mitriform
monadiform
moniliform
morbilliform
multiform
mummiform
muriform
mytiliform
napiform
natiform
naupliiform
nubiform
omniform
oviform
paliform
panduriform
papilliform
patelliform
pelviform
penicilliform
penniform
perciform
phialiform
piliform
pisciform
pisiform
placentiform
planuliform
plexiform
poculiform
proteiform
pulvilliform
pyriform
quadriform
radiciform
raduliform
raniform
reniform
restiform
retiform
sacciform
sagittiform
salpiform
scalariform
scalpelliform
scalpriform
scoleciform
scolopendriform
scutiform
scyphiform
securiform
septiform
serpentiform
spiniform
spongiform
squamiform
stalactiform
stalactitiform
stelliform
stratiform
strigiform
strobiliform
strombuliform
styliform
tauriform
tectiform
telescopiform
thalliform
triform
tuberiform
tubiform
tympaniform
umbraculiform
unciform
unguiform
uniform
vaporiform
variform
vasculiform
vasiform
vermiform
verruciform
versiform
villiform
viperiform
vitriform
vulviform
ypsiliform
zeolitiform

-ism

abnormalism
abolitionism
aboriginalism
absenteeism
absolutism
academicalism
academicism
accidentalism
achromatism
acosmism
acrobatism
acrotism
actinism
activism
Adamitism
adiaphorism
adoptianism
Adoptionism
adventurism
aeroembolism
aerotropism
aestheticism
Africanism
ageism
agnosticism
agrarianism
Albigensianism
albinism
albinoism
alcoholism
algorism
alienism
allelomorphism
allotropism
alpinism
altruism
amateurism
Americanism
ametabolism
amoralism
amorism
amorphism
anabaptism
anabolism
anachronism
anagrammatism
anarchism
anastigmatism
androdioecism
andromonoecism
aneurism
Anglicanism

-ism *(contd.)*
anglicism
Anglo-Catholicism
aniconism
animalism
animatism
animism
annihilationism
antagonism
anthropomorphism
anthropomorphitism
anthropopathism
anthropophuism
anthropopsychism
antichristianism
anticivism
anticlericalism
antidisestablish-
mentarianism
anti-federalism
anti-Gallicanism
anti-Jacobinism
antinomianism
antiochianism
antiquarianism
anti-Semitism
antisepticism
antisocialism
antitheism
antitrinitarianism
antivaccinationism
antivivisectionism
anythingarianism
apheliotropism
aphorism
apism
aplanatism
apochromatism
apogeotropism
apoliticism
Apollinarianism
apostolicism
apriorism
Arabism
Aramaism
Arcadianism
archaicism
archaism
Arianism
aristocratism
Aristotelianism
Aristotelism
Arminianism
asceticism
asepticism
Asiaticism
aspheterism
asteism
asterism
astigmatism
asynchronism
asystolism
atavism
atheism
athleticism
Atlanticism
atomism
atonalism
atropism
Atticism
attorneyism
Augustinianism
Australianism
authorism
authoritarianism
autism
autochthonism
autoeroticism
autoerotism
automatism
automobilism
automorphism
autotheism
avant-gardism
Averrhoism
Averroism
Baalism
Baathism
Ba'athism
Babbitism
Babeeism
babelism
Babiism
Babism
babuism
bacchanalianism
bachelorism
Baconianism
Bahaism
bantingism
baptism
barbarism
bashawism
bastardism
bathmism
bedlamism
behaviourism
Benthamism
Bergsonism
Berkeleianism
bestialism
betacism
biblicism
bibliophilism
bilateralism
bilingualism
bimetallism
bipedalism
blackguardism
blepharism
bogeyism
bogyism
Bohemianism
bolshevism
Bonapartism
bonism
boobyism
Boswellism
botulism
Bourbonism
bowdlerism
bradyseism
braggartism
Brahmanism
Brahminism
Braidism
Briticism
Britishism
Brownism
bruxism
Buchmanism
Buddhism
bullyism
Burschenism
Byronism
Byzantinism
cabalism
cabbalism
Caesarism
caesaropapism
caffeinism
caffeism
Calvinism
cambism
Camorrism
cannibalism
capitalism
Carbonarism
careerism
Carlism
Carlylism
carnalism
Cartesianism
casualism
catabolism
catastrophism
catechism
catechumenism
Catharism
catheterism
catholicism
causationism
cauterism
cavalierism
Celticism
centenarianism
centralism
centripetalism
centrism
cerebralism
ceremonialism
chaldaism
characterism
charism
charlatanism
chartism
Chasidism
Chassidism
Chaucerism
chauvinism
chemism
chemotropism
chloralism
Christianism
chromaticism
churchism
Ciceronianism
cicisbeism
cinchonism
civism
cladism
classicism
clericalism
cliquism
clubbism
coalitionism
Cobdenism
cocainism
cockneyism
coenobitism
collectivism
collegialism
colloquialism
colonialism
commensalism
commercialism
communalism
communism
compatriotism
comstockism
Comtism
conacreism
conceptualism
concettism
concretism
confessionalism
confrontationism
Confucianism
Congregationalism
conservatism
consortism
constitutionalism
constructionism
constructivism
consubstantialism
consumerism
contact-metamorphism
continentalism
contortionism
contrabandism
conventionalism
conversationism
convictism
copyism
corporatism
corporealism
corybantism
cosmeticism
cosmism
cosmopolitanism
cosmopolitism
cosmotheism
cottierism
Couéism
courtierism
creatianism
creationism
cretinism
cretism
criticism
cronyism
crotalism
cubism
cultism
curialism
cyclicism
cynicism
czarism
Dadaism
Daltonism
dandyism
Darwinism
deaf-mutism
decimalism
defeatism
deism
demagogism
demagoguism
demoniacism
demonianism
demonism
denominationalism
departmentalism
descriptivism

-ism *(contd.)*
despotism
deteriorism
determinism
deviationism
devilism
diabolism
diachronism
diageotropism
diaheliotropism
dialecticism
diamagnetism
diaphototropism
diastrophism
diatropism
dichroism
dichromatism
dichromism
diclinism
dicrotism
didacticism
diffusionism
dilettanteism
dilettantism
dimerism
dimorphism
dioecism
diorism
diothelism
diphysitism
dirigism
dissenterism
dissolutionism
disyllabism
ditheism
ditheletism
dithelism
dithelitism
divisionism
Docetism
doctrinairism
doctrinarianism
Dogberryism
dogmatism
do-goodism
dolichocephalism
donatism
donnism
do-nothingism
Doricism
Dorism
dowdyism
draconism
dragonism
dramaticism
drudgism
druidism
dualism
dudism
dufferism
dunderheadism
dynamism
dyotheletism
dyothelism
dysphemism
ebionism
ebionitism
echoism
eclecticism
ecumenicalism
ecumenicism
ecumenism
Edwardianism
egalitarianism
egoism
egotheism
egotism
electromagnetism
electromerism
elementalism
elitism
Elizabethanism
embolism
emotionalism
empiricism
enantiomorphism
Encratism
encyclopaedism
endemism
Englishism
entrism
environmentalism
eonism
epicism
Epicureanism
epicurism
epiphenomenalism
epiphytism
epipolism
episcopalianism
episcopalism
equalitarianism
equestrianism
Erastianism
eremitism
erethism
ergotism
eroticism
erotism
erythrism
escapism
esotericism
esoterism
Essenism
essentialism
etacism
etherism
ethicism
ethnicism
ethnocentrism
eudaemonism
eugenism
euhemerism
eumerism
eunuchism
eunuchoidism
euphemism
euphuism
Eurocommunism
Europeanism
evangelicalism
evangelicism
evangelism
evolutionism
exclusionism
exclusivism
exhibitionism
existentialism
ex-librism
exorcism
exotericism
exoticism
expansionism
experientialism
experimentalism
expressionism
extensionalism
externalism
extremism
Fabianism
factionalism
faddism
fairyism
fakirism
falangism
familism
fanaticism
fantasticism
faradism
fascism
fatalism
Fauvism
favism
favouritism
Febronianism
federalism
femininism
feminism
Fenianism
fetichism
fetishism
feudalism
feuilletonism
fideism
fifth-monarchism
filibusterism
finalism
fissiparism
flagellantism
flunkeyism
fogyism
formalism
fortuitism
Fourierism
fractionalism
Froebelism
functionalism
fundamentalism
fusionism
futurism
gaelicism
Galenism
Gallicanism
gallicism
galvanism
gamotropism
ganderism
gangsterism
Gargantuism
gargarism
gargoylism
Gasconism
Gaullism
generationism
Genevanism
genteelism
gentilism
geocentricism
geomagnetism
geophagism
geotropism
Germanism
giantism
gigantism
Girondism
Gnosticism
Gongorism
gormandism
Gothicism
gourmandism
gradualism
Graecism
grammaticism
Grangerism
Grecism
gregarianism
griffinism
Grobianism
Grundyism
gynandrism
gynandromorphism
gynodioecism
gynomonoecism
gypsyism
gyromagnetism
haptotropism
Hasidism
Hassidism
heathenism
Hebraicism
Hebrewism
hectorism
hedonism
Hegelianism
hegemonism
heliotropism
Hellenism
helotism
hemihedrism
hemimorphism
henotheism
hermaphroditism
heroism
hetaerism
hetairism
heterochronism
heteroecism
heteromorphism
heterostylism
heterothallism
heurism
Hibernianism
Hibernicism
hidalgoism
hierarchism
highbrowism
High-Churchism
Hildebrandism
Hinduism
Hippocratism
hispanicism
historicism
historism
histrionicism
histrionism
Hitlerism
Hobbesianism
Hobbianism
Hobbism
hobbledehoyism
hobbyism
hobgoblinism
hoboism
holism

-ism (contd.)
holohedrism
holometabolism
holophytism
homeomorphism
homoeomorphism
homoeroticism
homoerotism
homomorphism
homothallism
hooliganism
hoydenism
humanism
humanitarianism
Humism
humoralism
hybridism
hydrargyrism
hydrotropism
hylicism
hylism
hylomorphism
hylopathism
hylotheism
hylozoism
hyperadrenalism
hyperbolism
hypercriticism
hyperthyroidism
hyphenism
hypnotism
hypochondriacism
hypocorism
hypognathism
hypothyroidism
Ibsenism
iconomaticism
iconophilism
idealism
idiotism
idolism
illuminism
illusionism
imagism
immanentism
immaterialism
immediatism
immersionism
immobilism
immoralism
imperialism
impossibilism
impressionism
incendiarism
incivism
incorporealism
indeterminism
indifferentism
individualism
industrialism
infallibilism
infantilism
inflationism
Infralapsarianism
inquilinism
inspirationism
institutionalism
instrumentalism
insularism
insurrectionism
intellectualism
interactionism
internationalism
interventionism
intimism
intransigentism
intuitionalism
intuitionism
intuitivism
invalidism
iodism
Ionism
iotacism
irenicism
Irishism
irrationalism
irredentism
Irvingism
Islamism
ism
Ismailism
isochronism
isodimorphism
isolationism
isomerism
isomorphism
isotropism
itacism
Italianism
italicism
Jacobinism
Jacobitism
Jainism
Jansenism
Jesuitism
jingoism
jockeyism
Johnsonianism
Johnsonism
journalism
Judaism
junkerism
kaiserism
Kantianism
Kantism
karaism
katabolism
Kelticism
Keynesianism
klephtism
know-nothingism
Krishnaism
labdacism
labialism
labourism
laconicism
laconism
ladyism
Lamaism
Lamarckianism
Lamarckism
lambdacism
landlordism
Laodiceanism
larrikinism
lathyrism
Latinism
latitudinarianism
laxism
leftism
legalism
leggism
Leibnitzianism
Leibnizianism
Leninism
lesbianism
liberalism
liberationism
libertarianism
libertinism
lichenism
lionism
lipogrammatism
Listerism
literalism
literaryism
localism
Lollardism
Londonism
Low-Churchism
Luddism
luminarism
Lutheranism
Lutherism
lyricism
lyrism
Lysenkoism
macarism
Machiavellianism
Machiavellism
Magianism
Magism
magnetism
Magyarism
Mahdiism
Mahdism
maidism
malapropism
Malthusianism
mammonism
Manichaeanism
Manichaeism
Manicheanism
Manicheism
mannerism
Maoism
Marcionitism
Marinism
martialism
martinetism
Marxianism
Marxism
masochism
materialism
mathematicism
matriarchalism
maudlinism
Mazdaism
Mazdeism
McCarthyism
mechanism
mediaevalism
medievalism
Medism
melanism
meliorism
memoirism
Mendelism
mentalism
mephitism
mercantilism
mercenarism
mercurialism
merism
merycism
mescalism
mesmerism
mesocephalism
mesomerism
Messianism
metabolism
metachronism
metamerism
metamorphism
metasomatism
metempiricism
meteorism
methodism
metopism
Micawberism
Michurinism
micro-organism
microseism
militarism
millenarianism
millenarism
millennianism
millenniarism
Miltonism
minimalism
minimism
misoneism
Mithraicism
Mithraism
mithridatism
modalism
moderatism
modernism
Mohammedanism
Mohammedism
Molinism
monachism
monadism
monarchianism
monarchism
monasticism
monergism
monetarism
mongolism
mongrelism
monism
monkeyism
monochromatism
monoecism
monogenism
monolingualism
monometallism
monophysitism
monorchism
monosyllabism
monotheism
monotheletism
monothelism
monothelitism
Monroeism
Montanism
moralism
Moravianism
Morisonianism
Mormonism
morphinism
mosaicism
Mosaism
Moslemism

-ism *(contd.)*
mountebankism
multiracialism
Munichism
municipalism
Muslimism
mutism
mutualism
myalism
mysticism
mythicism
mythism
namby-pambyism
nanism
Napoleonism
narcissism
narcotism
nationalism
nativism
naturalism
naturism
navalism
Nazaritism
Naziism
Nazism
necessarianism
necessitarianism
necrophilism
negativism
negroism
negrophilism
neoclassicism
neocolonialism
Neo-Darwinism
Neofascism
Neohellenism
Neo-Impressionism
Neo-Kantianism
Neo-Lamarckism
neologism
Neo-Malthusianism
neo-Nazism
neonomianism
neopaganism
neoplasticism
Neo-Plasticism
Neoplatonism
Neopythagoreanism
neoterism
neovitalism
nephalism
Nestorianism
neuroticism
neutralism
newspaperism
nicotinism
Nietzscheanism
niggerism
nihilism
noctambulism
Noetianism
nomadism
nominalism
nomism
northernism
notaphilism
nothingarianism
nothingism
Novatianism
novelism
nudism
nyctitropism
obeahism
obeism
obiism
objectivism
obscurantism
obsoletism
Occamism
occasionalism
Occidentalism
occultism
Ockhamism
odism
odylism
oecumenicalism
oecumenicism
oecumenism
officialism
old-maidism
onanism
oneirocriticism
onirocriticism
Ophism
Ophitism
opportunism
optimism
Orangeism
Orangism
organicism
organism
Orientalism
Origenism
Orleanism
orphanism
Orphism
orthognathism
orthotropism
ostracism
ostrichism
Owenism
pacificism
pacifism
Paddyism
paedobaptism
paedomorphism
paganism
palaeomagnetism
palladianism
paludism
panaesthetism
Pan-Africanism
Pan-Americanism
Pan-Arabism
panchromatism
pancosmism
panderism
panegoism
Pan-Germanism
Panhellenism
panislamism
panlogism
panpsychism
pansexualism
Pan-Slavism
pansophism
panspermatism
panspermism
Pantagruelism
pantheism
papalism
papism
parabaptism
parachronism
paragnathism
paraheliotropism
parallelism
paralogism
paramagnetism
paramorphism
parapsychism
parasitism
Parkinsonism
parliamentarism
Parnassianism
Parnellism
parochialism
Parseeism
Parsiism
Parsism
partialism
particularism
partyism
passivism
pasteurism
pastoralism
paternalism
patrialism
patriarchalism
patriarchism
patriotism
Patripassianism
patristicism
Paulinism
pauperism
pedagogism
pedagoguism
pedanticism
pedantism
pedestrianism
Pelagianism
pelmanism
pelorism
pennalism
penny-a-linerism
pentadactylism
pentamerism
pentaprism
peonism
perfectibilism
perfectionism
peripateticism
perpetualism
Persism
personalism
perspectivism
pessimism
petalism
Petrarchianism
Petrarchism
Petrinism
phaeism
phagocytism
phalansterianism
phalansterism
phallicism
phallism
pharisaism
phariseeism
phenakism
phenomenalism
phenomenism
philhellenism
philistinism
philosophism
phobism
phoneticism
phonetism
phosphorism
photism
photochromism
photoperiodism
phototropism
physicalism
physicism
physitheism
pianism
pietism
piezomagnetism
Pindarism
Pittism
plagiarism
plagiotropism
Platonicism
Platonism
plebeianism
pleiotropism
pleochroism
pleomorphism
plumbism
pluralism
Plutonism
Plymouthism
pococuranteism
pococurantism
poeticism
pointillism
polonism
polychroism
polycrotism
polydactylism
polygenism
polymastism
polymerism
polymorphism
polynomialism
polysyllabicism
polysyllabism
polysyllogism
polysyntheticism
polysynthetism
polytheism
Pooterism
populism
porism
Porphyrogenitism
positivism
possibilism
Post-Impressionism
post-millennialism
Poujadism
Powellism
practicalism
pragmatism
precisianism
predestinarianism
predeterminism
preferentialism
preformationism
prelatism
premillenarianism
premillennialism
Pre-Raphaelism
Pre-Raphaelitism

-ism *(contd.)*
Presbyterianism
presentationism
preternaturalism
prettyism
priapism
priggism
primitivism
primordialism
probabiliorism
probabilism
prochronism
professionalism
prognathism
progressionism
progressism
progressivism
prohibitionism
proletarianism
propagandism
prophetism
prosaicism
prosaism
proselytism
prostatism
prosyllogism
protectionism
Protestantism
proverbialism
provincialism
prudentialism
Prussianism
psellism
psephism
pseudo-archaism
pseudoclassicism
pseudomorphism
psilanthropism
psychism
psychologism
psychopannychism
psychoticism
ptyalism
puerilism
pugilism
puppyism
purism
puritanism
Puseyism
pyrrhonism
Pythagoreanism
Pythagorism
Quakerism
quattrocentism
quietism
quixotism
rabbinism
Rabelaisianism
racemism
Rachmanism
racialism
racism
radicalism
Ramism
ranterism
rascalism
rationalism
reactionarism
realism
rebaptism
Rebeccaism
Rechabitism
recidivism
red-tapism
reductionism
reformism
regalism
regionalism
reincarnationism
relationism
relativism
religionism
Rembrandtism
representationalism
representationism
republicanism
restitutionism
restorationism
resurrectionism
reunionism
revanchism
revisionism
revivalism
revolutionism
rheotropism
rheumatism
rhopalism
rhotacism
Ribbonism
rigorism
ritualism
Romanism
romanticism
Rosicrucianism
Rosminianism
Rotarianism
routinism
rowdyism
royalism
ruffianism
ruralism
Russianism
Russophilism
Sabaism
Sabbatarianism
sabbatism
Sabellianism
Sabianism
sacerdotalism
sacramentalism
sacramentarianism
Sadduceeism
Sadducism
sadism
sado-masochism
saintism
Saint-Simonianism
Saint-Simonism
Saivism
Saktism
salvationism
Samaritanism
sanitarianism
sansculottism
sapphism
saprophytism
Saracenism
satanism
saturnism
Saxonism
scepticism
schematism
scholasticism
scientism
sciolism
Scotism
Scotticism
scoundrelism
scribism
scripturalism
scripturism
secessionism
sectarianism
sectionalism
secularism
self-criticism
self-hypnotism
selfism
semi-Arianism
semi-barbarism
Semi-Pelagianism
Semitism
sensationalism
sensationism
sensism
sensualism
sensuism
sentimentalism
separatism
serialism
servilism
servo-mechanism
sesquipedalianism
sexism
sexualism
Shaivism
shakerism
Shaktism
shamanism
shamateurism
Shiism
Shintoism
Shivaism
shunamitism
sigmatism
Sikhism
simplism
sinapism
sinecurism
singularism
Sinicism
Sinophilism
Sivaism
Slavism
snobbism
socialism
Socinianism
sociologism
Sofism
solarism
solecism
sol-faism
solidarism
solidism
solifidianism
solipsism
somatism
somnambulism
somniloquism
sophism
southernism
sovietism
specialism
speciesism
Spencerianism
Spinozism
spiritism
spiritualism
spoonerism
spread-eagleism
Stahlianism
Stahlism
Stakhanovism
Stalinism
stand-pattism
statism
stercoranism
stereoisomerism
stereotropism
stibialism
stigmatism
stoicism
strabism
structuralism
strychninism
strychnism
Stundism
subjectivism
sublapsarianism
subordinationism
substantialism
suburbanism
suffragism
Sufiism
Sufism
suggestionism
supernationalism
supernaturalism
superrealism
Supralapsarianism
supremacism
suprematism
surrealism
sutteeism
Swadeshism
swarajism
Swedenborgianism
swingism
sybaritism
sybotism
syllabism
syllogism
symbolism
symphilism
synaposematism
synchronism
syncretism
syndactylism
syndicalism
synecdochism
synergism
synoecism
syntheticism
Syriacism
Syrianism
systematism
tachism
tactism
Tammanyism
tantalism
Tantrism
Taoism
tarantism
Tartuffism

-ism *(contd.)*
Tartufism
tautochronism
tautologism
tautomerism
teetotalism
teleologism
tenebrism
teratism
terminism
territorialism
terrorism
tetramerism
tetratheism
Teutonicism
Teutonism
textualism
thanatism
Thatcherism
thaumaturgism
theanthropism
theatricalism
theatricism
theism
theomorphism
Theopaschitism
theophilanthropism
theosophism
therianthropism
theriomorphism
thermotropism
thigmotropism
Thomism
thrombo-embolism
thuggism
tigerism
Timonism
Titanism
Titoism
toadyism
tokenism
Toryism
totalitarianism
totemism
tourism
tractarianism
trade-unionism
traditionalism
Traducianism
traitorism
transcendentalism
transformism
transmigrationism
transsexualism
transvestism
transvestitism
traumatism
trialism
tribadism
tribalism
trichroism
trichromatism
tricrotism
triliteralism
trimorphism
Trinitarianism
trinomialism
tripersonalism
tritheism
triticism
trituberculism
trivialism
troglodytism
troilism
trophotropism
tropism
Trotskyism
truism
tsarism
tuism
Turcophilism
tutiorism
tutorism
tychism
ultra-Conservatism
ultraism
ultramontanism
undenominationalism
unicameralism
unidealism
uniformitarianism
unilateralism
unionism
unitarianism
universalism
unrealism
unsectarianism
unsocialism
untruism
uranism
utilitarianism
utopianism
utopism
Utraquism
vagabondism
Valentinianism
valetudinarianism
vampirism
vandalism
Vansittartism
Vaticanism
Vedism
veganism
vegetarianism
ventriloquism
verbalism
verism
vernacularism
Victorianism
vigilantism
vikingism
virilism
virtualism
vitalism
viviparism
vocalism
vocationalism
volcanism
Voltaireanism
Voltairianism
Voltairism
voltaism
voltinism
voluntarism
voluntaryism
voodooism
vorticism
voyeurism
vulcanism
vulgarism
vulpinism
vulturism
Wagnerianism
Wagnerism
Wahabiism
Wahabism
welfarism
werewolfism
Wertherism
werwolfism
Wesleyanism
westernism
Whiggism
whiteboyism
wholism
witticism
Wodenism
Wolfianism
xanthochroism
Yankeeism
yogism
zanyism
Zarathustrianism
Zarathustrism
zealotism
Zionism
Zoilism
zoism
Zolaism
zombiism
zoomagnetism
zoomorphism
zoophilism
zootheism
Zoroastrianism
Zwinglianism
zygodactylism
zygomorphism

-itis
adenitis
antiaditis
aortitis
appendicitis
arteritis
arthritis
balanitis
blepharitis
bronchitis
bursitis
carditis
cellulitis
cephalitis
ceratitis
cerebritis
cholecystitis
colitis
conchitis
conjunctivitis
crystallitis
cystitis
dermatitis
diaphragmatitis
diphtheritis
diverticulitis
duodenitis
encephalitis
endocarditis
endometritis
enteritis
fibrositis
gastritis
gastroenteritis
gingivitis
glossitis
hamarthritis
hepatitis
hysteritis
ileitis
iritis
keratitis
labyrinthitis
laminitis
laryngitis
lymphangitis
mastitis
mastoiditis
meningitis
metritis
myelitis
myocarditis
myositis
myringitis
nephritis
neuritis
onychitis
oophoritis
ophthalmitis
orchitis
osteitis
osteo-arthritis
osteomyelitis
otitis
ovaritis
panarthritis
pancreatitis
panophthalmitis
papillitis
parotiditis
parotitis
pericarditis
perigastritis
perihepatitis
perinephritis
perineuritis
periostitis
peritonitis
perityphlitis
pharyngitis
phlebitis
phrenitis
pleuritis
pneumonitis
poliomyelitis
polyneuritis
proctitis
prostatitis
pyelitis
pyelonephritis
rachitis
rectitis
retinitis
rhachitis
rhinitis
rhinopharyngitis
salpingitis
scleritis
sclerotitis
sinuitis
sinusitis
splenitis
spondylitis
staphylitis

-itis *(contd.)*
stomatitis
strumitis
synovitis
syringitis
tendonitis
tenosynovitis
thrombo-phlebitis
thyroiditis
tonsilitis
tonsillitis
tracheitis
trachitis
tympanitis
typhlitis
ulitis
ureteritis
urethritis
uteritis
uveitis
uvulitis
vaginitis
valvulitis
vulvitis

-latrous

bibliolatrous
heliolatrous
ichthyolatrous
idolatrous
litholatrous
Mariolatrous
Maryolatrous
monolatrous
ophiolatrous
zoolatrous

-latry

angelolatry
anthropolatry
astrolatry
autolatry
bardolatry
bibliolatry
Christolatry
cosmolatry
demonolatry
dendrolatry
ecclesiolatry
epeolatry
geolatry
hagiolatry
heliolatry
hierolatry
ichthyolatry
iconolatry
idolatry
litholatry
lordolatry
Mariolatry
Maryolatry
monolatry
necrolatry
ophiolatry
physiolatry
plutolatry
pyrolatry
symbololatry
thaumatolatry
theriolatry
zoolatry

-logical

aerobiological
aerological
aetiological
agrobiological
agrological
agrostological
algological
alogical
amphibological
analogical
anthropological
arachnological
archaeological
astrological
atheological
audiological
autecological
axiological
bacteriological
batological
battological
biological
bryological
campanological
carcinological
cartological
chorological
Christological
chronological
climatological
codicological
conchological
cosmological
craniological
cryobiological
cryptological
cytological
demonological
dendrological
deontological
dermatological
dysteleological
ecclesiological
ecological
Egyptological
electrophysiological
embryological
entomological
epidemiological
epistemological
eschatological
ethnological
ethological
etymological
futurological
gastrological
gemmological
gemological
genealogical
genethlialogical
geochronological
geological
geomorphological
gerontological
glaciological
glossological
gnotobiological
graphological
gynaecological
hagiological
helminthological
hepaticological
herpetological
histological
histopathological
homological
horological
hydrobiological
hydrological
ichthyological
ideological
illogical
immunological
laryngological
limnological
lithological
logical
malacological
mammalogical
martyrological
metapsychological
meteorological
micrological
mineralogical
monological
morphological
musicological
mycological
myological
myrmecological
mythological
necrological
neological
nephological
nephrological
neurological
nomological
nosological
nostological
oceanological
odontological
oenological
ontological
ophiological
ophthalmological
oreological
ornithological
orological
osteological
paedological
palaeontological
palaeozoological
palynological
parapsychological
pathological
pedological
penological
pestological
petrological
phaenological
phenological
phenomenological
philological
phonological
phraseological
phrenological
phycological
physiological
phytological
phytopathological
pneumatological
poenological
pomological
posological
potamological
protozoological
psephological
psychobiological
psychological
radiological
reflexological
rheumatological
rhinological
scatological
sedimentological
seismological
selenological
serological
Sinological
sociobiological
sociological
somatological
soteriological
Sovietological
spectrological
spelaeological
stoechiological
stoicheiological
stoichiological
synecological
tautological
technological
teleological
teratological
terminological
theological
topological
toxicological
traumatological
trichological
tropological
typological
unlogical
untheological
urological
virological
volcanological
vulcanological
zoological
zoophytological
zymological

-logous

analogous
antilogous
dendrologous
heterologous
homologous
isologous
tautologous

-logue

aeglogue
analogue
apologue
catalogue

-logue *(contd.)*
collogue
decalogue
dialogue
duologue
eclogue
epilogue
grammalogue
homologue
idealogue
ideologue
isologue
monologue
philologue
prologue
Sinologue
theologue
travelogue
trialogue

-logy

acarology
aerobiology
aerolithology
aerology
aetiology
agriology
agrobiology
agrology
agrostology
algology
amphibology
anaesthesiology
analogy
andrology
anemology
angelology
anthology
anthropobiology
anthropology
antilogy
apology
arachnology
archaeology
archeology
archology
aristology
Assyriology
astacology
astrogeology
astrology
atheology
atmology
audiology
autecology
autology
axiology
bacteriology
balneology
batology
battology
bibliology
bioecology
biology
biotechnology
brachylogy
bryology
bumpology
cacology
caliology
campanology
carcinology
cardiology
carphology
cartology
cetology
characterology
cheirology
chirology
choreology
chorology
Christology
chronobiology
chronology
cine-biology
climatology
codicology
cometology
conchology
coprology
cosmetology
cosmology
craniology
criminology
cryobiology
cryptology
cytology
dactyliology
dactylology
deltiology
demology
demonology
dendrochronology
dendrology
deontology
dermatology
diabology
diabolology
dialectology
diplomatology
dittology
docimology
dogmatology
dosiology
dosology
doxology
dyslogy
dysteleology
ecclesiology
eccrinology
ecology
edaphology
Egyptology
electrobiology
electrology
electrophysiology
electrotechnology
elogy
embryology
emmenology
endemiology
endocrinology
entomology
enzymology
epidemiology
epistemology
escapology
eschatology
ethnology
ethnomusicology
ethology
Etruscology
etymology
euchology
eulogy
exobiology
festilogy
festology
folk-etymology
futurology
gastroenterology
gastrology
gemmology
gemology
genealogy
genethlialogy
geochronology
geology
geomorphology
gerontology
gigantology
glaciology
glossology
glottology
gnomonology
gnoseology
gnosiology
gnotobiology
graphology
gynaecology
haematology
hagiology
hamartiology
haplology
heliology
helminthology
heortology
hepaticology
hepatology
heresiology
herpetology
heterology
hierology
hippology
histiology
histology
histopathology
historiology
homology
hoplology
horology
hydrobiology
hydrogeology
hydrology
hydrometeorology
hyetology
hygrology
hymnology
hypnology
ichnology
ichthyology
iconology
ideology
immunology
insectology
irenology
kidology
kinesiology
koniology
Kremlinology
laryngology
lepidopterology
lexicology
lichenology
limacology
limnology
lithology
liturgiology
macrology
malacology
malariology
mammalogy
Mariology
martyrology
Maryology
Mayology
menology
metapsychology
meteorology
methodology
microbiology
microclimatology
micrology
micro-meteorology
microtechnology
mineralogy
misology
monadology
monology
morphology
muscology
museology
musicology
mycetology
mycology
myology
myrmecology
mythology
necrology
nematology
neology
nephology
nephrology
neurobiology
neurohypnology
neurology
neuropathology
neurophysiology
neuroradiology
neurypnology
nomology
noology
nosology
nostology
numerology
numismatology
oceanology
odonatology
odontology
oenology
olfactology
oncology
oneirology
onirology
ontology
oology
ophiology
ophthalmology
optology
orchidology
oreology
ornithology
orology

-logy *(contd.)*
orthopterology
oryctology
osteology
otolaryngology
otology
otorhinolaryngology
ourology
paedology
palaeanthropology
palaeethnology
palaeichthyology
palaeoclimatology
palaeolimnology
palaeontology
palaeopedology
palaeophytology
palaeozoology
palillogy
palynology
pantheology
papyrology
paradoxology
paralogy
parapsychology
parasitology
paroemiology
pathology
patrology
pedology
pelology
penology
pentalogy
periodontology
perissology
pestology
petrology
phaenology
pharmacology
pharyngology
phenology
phenomenology
philology
phonology
photobiology
photogeology
phraseology
phrenology
phycology
physiology
phytology
phytopathology
planetology
plutology
pneumatology
podology
poenology
pomology
ponerology
posology
potamology
primatology
proctology
protistology
protozoology
psephology
pseudology
psychobiology
psychology
psychopathology
psychophysiology
pteridology
pyramidology
pyretology
pyroballogy
radiobiology
radiology
reflexology
rheology
rheumatology
rhinology
röntgenology
sarcology
satanology
scatology
Scientology
sedimentology
seismology
selenology
selenomorphology
semasiology
semeiology
semiology
serology
sexology
sindonology
Sinology
sitiology
sitology
skatology
sociobiology
sociology
somatology
soteriology
spectrology
spelaeology
sphagnology
sphygmology
spongology
stichology
stoechiology
stoicheiology
stoichiology
stomatology
storiology
symbology
symbolology
symptomatology
synchronology
synecology
synoecology
syphilology
systematology
tautology
technology
teleology
teratology
terminology
terotechnology
tetralogy
thanatology
theology
thermology
therology
thremmatology
timbrology
tocology
tokology
topology
toxicology
traumatology
tribology
trichology
trilogy
trophology
tropology
typhlology
typology
ufology
uranology
urbanology
urinology
urology
venereology
vexillology
victimology
vinology
virology
volcanology
vulcanology
xylology
zoopathology
zoophytology
zoopsychology
zymology

-lysis

analysis
atmolysis
autocatalysis
autolysis
bacteriolysis
catalysis
cryptanalysis
cytolysis
dialysis
electroanalysis
electrolysis
haematolysis
haemodialysis
haemolysis
histolysis
hydrolysis
hypno-analysis
leucocytolysis
microanalysis
narco-analysis
neurolysis
paralysis
photolysis
plasmolysis
pneumatolysis
proteolysis
psephoanalysis
psychoanalysis
pyrolysis
radiolysis
thermolysis
uranalysis
urinalysis
zincolysis
zymolysis

-lytic

analytic
anxiolytic
autocatalytic
autolytic
bacteriolytic
catalytic
dialytic
electrolytic
haemolytic
histolytic
hydrolytic
paralytic
photolytic
plasmolytic
pneumatolytic
proteolytic
psychoanalytic
pyrolytic
sympatholytic
tachylytic
thermolytic
unanalytic

-mancy

aeromancy
axinomancy
belomancy
bibliomancy
botanomancy
capnomancy
cartomancy
ceromancy
cheiromancy
chiromancy
cleromancy
coscinomancy
crithomancy
crystallomancy
dactyliomancy
gastromancy
geomancy
gyromancy
hieromancy
hydromancy
lampadomancy
lithomancy
myomancy
necromancy
nigromancy
oenomancy
omphalomancy
oneiromancy
oniromancy
onychomancy
ornithomancy
pyromancy
rhabdomancy
scapulimancy
spodomancy
tephromancy
theomancy
zoomancy

-mania

acronymania
anglomania
anthomania
arithmomania
balletomania
bibliomania
Celtomania
demonomania
dipsomania
egomania
eleutheromania
erotomania

-mania *(contd.)*
etheromania
flagellomania
francomania
gallomania
graphomania
hydromania
hypomania
hysteromania
kleptomania
megalomania
melomania
methomania
metromania
monomania
morphinomania
mythomania
nostomania
nymphomania
oenomania
opsomania
orchidomania
petalomania
phyllomania
potichomania
pteridomania
pyromania
squandermania
technomania
theatromania
theomania
timbromania
toxicomania
trichotillomania
tulipomania
typomania
xenomania

-mantic
cheiromantic
chiromantic
geomantic
hydromantic
myomantic
necromantic
ornithomantic
pyromantic
scapulimantic
spodomantic
theomantic
zoomantic

-mathic
chrestomathic
philomathic
polymathic

-mathy
chrestomathy
opsimathy
philomathy
polymathy

-meter
absorptiometer
acceierometer
acidimeter
actinometer
aerometer
alcoholometer
alkalimeter
altimeter
ammeter
anemometer
araeometer
areometer
arithmometer
atmometer
audiometer
auxanometer
auxometer
barometer
bathometer
bathymeter
bolometer
bomb-calorimeter
calorimeter
cathetometer
centimeter
chlorimeter
chlorometer
chronometer
clinometer
colorimeter
Comptometer®
coulombmeter
coulometer
craniometer
cryometer
cyanometer
cyclometer
decelerometer
declinometer
dendrometer
densimeter
densitometer
diagometer
diameter
diaphanometer
diffractometer
dimeter
dose-meter
dosimeter
drosometer
dynamometer
effusiometer
electrodynamometer
electrometer
endosmometer
ergometer
eriometer
evaporimeter
extensimeter
extensometer
fathometer
flowmeter
fluorimeter
fluorometer
focimeter
galactometer
galvanometer
gas-meter
gasometer
geometer
geothermometer
goniometer
gradiometer
gravimeter
harmonometer
heliometer
heptameter
hexameter
hodometer
hydrometer
hyetometer
hygrometer
hypsometer
iconometer
inclinometer
interferometer
isoperimeter
katathermometer
konimeter
kryometer
lactometer
luxmeter
lysimeter
machmeter
magnetometer
manometer
mekometer
meter
micrometer
microseismometer
mileometer
milometer
monometer
nephelometer
Nilometer
nitrometer
octameter
odometer
oenometer
ohmmeter
ombrometer
oncometer
ophthalmometer
opisometer
opsiometer
optometer
osmometer
oximeter
pachymeter
parameter
passimeter
pedometer
pelvimeter
pentameter
perimeter
permeameter
phonmeter
phonometer
photometer
piezometer
planimeter
planometer
plessimeter
pleximeter
pluviometer
pneumatometer
polarimeter
potentiometer
potometer
psychometer
psychrometer
pulsimeter
pulsometer
pycnometer
pyknometer
pyrheliometer
pyrometer
quantometer
radiogoniometer
radiometer
radiotelemeter
refractometer
rheometer
rhythmometer
saccharimeter
saccharometer
salimeter
salinometer
scintillometer
sclerometer
seismometer
semi-diameter
semiperimeter
sensitometer
slot-meter
solarimeter
spectrophotometer
speedometer
spherometer
sphygmomanometer
sphygmometer
spirometer
stactometer
stalagmometer
stereometer
strabismometer
strabometer
swingometer
sympiesometer
tacheometer
tachometer
tachymeter
taseometer
tasimeter
taximeter
telemeter
tellurometer
tetrameter
thermometer
Tintometer®
tonometer
torque-meter
tribometer
trigonometer
trimeter
trocheameter
trochometer
tromometer
udometer
urinometer
vaporimeter
variometer
viameter
vibrometer
viscometer
viscosimeter
voltameter
voltmeter
volumenometer
volumeter
volumometer
water-barometer
water-meter
water-thermometer
wattmeter
wavemeter

-meter *(contd.)*
weatherometer
xylometer
zymometer
zymosimeter

-metry
acidimetry
aerometry
alcoholometry
alkalimetry
anemometry
anthropometry
araeometry
asymmetry
barometry
bathymetry
biometry
bolometry
calorimetry
chlorimetry
chlorometry
chronometry
clinometry
colorimetry
coulometry
craniometry
densimetry
densitometry
dissymmetry
dosimetry
dynamometry
electrometry
galvanometry
gasometry
geometry
goniometry
gravimetry
hodometry
horometry
hydrometry
hygrometry
hypsometry
iconometry
interferometry
isometry
isoperimetry
micrometry
microseismometry
nephelometry
noometry
odometry
ophthalmometry
optometry
pelvimetry
perimetry
photometry
planimetry
plessimetry
pleximetry
polarimetry
pseudosymmetry
psychometry
psychrometry
pyrometry
saccharimetry
seismometry
sociometry
spectrometry
spectrophotometry
spirometry
stalagmometry
stereometry
stichometry
stoechiometry
stoicheiometry
stoichiometry
symmetry
tacheometry
tachometry
tachymetry
telemetry
tensiometry
thermometry
trigonometry
unsymmetry
uranometry
viscometry
viscosimetry
zoometry

-monger
balladmonger
barber-monger
borough-monger
carpetmonger
cheese-monger
costardmonger
costermonger
fellmonger
fishmonger
flesh-monger
gossip-monger
ironmonger
lawmonger
love-monger
maxim-monger
meal-monger
miracle-monger
mystery-monger
newsmonger
panic-monger
peace-monger
pearmonger
peltmonger
phrasemonger
place-monger
prayer-monger
relic-monger
scandalmonger
scaremonger
sensation-monger
species-monger
starmonger
state-monger
system-monger
verse-monger
warmonger
whoremonger
wit-monger
wonder-monger

-morphic
actinomorphic
allelomorphic
allotriomorphic
anamorphic
anthropomorphic
automorphic
biomorphic
dimorphic
ectomorphic
enantiomorphic
endomorphic
ergatomorphic
gynandromorphic
hemimorphic
heteromorphic
homeomorphic
homoeomorphic
homomorphic
hylomorphic
idiomorphic
isodimorphic
isomorphic
lagomorphic
mesomorphic
metamorphic
monomorphic
morphic
ophiomorphic
ornithomorphic
paedomorphic
paramorphic
perimorphic
pleomorphic
polymorphic
protomorphic
pseudomorphic
tetramorphic
theomorphic
theriomorphic
trimorphic
xenomorphic
xeromorphic
zoomorphic
zygomorphic

-morphous
amorphous
anamorphous
anthropomorphous
dimorphous
enantiomorphous
gynandromorphous
heteromorphous
homeomorphous
homoeomorphous
homomorphous
isodimorphous
isomorphous
lagomorphous
mesomorphous
monomorphous
ophiomorphous
perimorphous
pleomorphous
polymorphous
pseudomorphous
rhizomorphous
tauromorphous
theriomorphous
trimorphous
xeromorphous
zygomorphous

-onym
acronym
anonym
antonym
autonym
cryptonym
eponym
exonym
heteronym
homonym
metonym
paronym
polyonym
pseudonym
synonym
tautonym
toponym
trionym

-onymic
acronymic
Hieronymic
homonymic
matronymic
metonymic
metronymic
patronymic
polyonymic
synonymic
toponymic

-osis
abiosis
acidosis
actinobacillosis
actinomycosis
aerobiosis
aeroneurosis
alkalosis
amaurosis
amitosis
anabiosis
anadiplosis
anaerobiosis
anamorphosis
anaplerosis
anastomosis
anchylosis
ankylosis
anthracosis
anthropomorphosis
antibiosis
apodosis
aponeurosis
apotheosis
arteriosclerosis
arthrosis
asbestosis
aspergillosis
ateleiosis
atherosclerosis
athetosis
autohypnosis
avitaminosis
bacteriosis
bagassosis
bilharziosis
biocoenosis
bromhidrosis
bromidrosis
brucellosis
byssinosis

-osis *(contd.)*
carcinomatosis
carcinosis
chlorosis
cirrhosis
coccidiosis
cyanosis
cyclosis
dermatosis
diarthrosis
diorthosis
diverticulosis
dulosis
ecchymosis
enantiosis
enarthrosis
endometriosis
endosmosis
enosis
enteroptosis
epanadiplosis
epanorthosis
exosmosis
exostosis
fibrosis
fluorosis
furunculosis
gliomatosis
gnotobiosis
gomphosis
gummosis
haematosis
halitosis
hallucinosis
heliosis
heterosis
hidrosis
homeosis
homoeosis
homomorphosis
homozygosis
hydronephrosis
hyperhidrosis
hyperidrosis
hyperinosis
hypersarcosis
hypervitaminosis
hypinosis
hypnosis
hypotyposis
ichthyosis
kenosis
keratosis
ketosis
kurtosis
kyllosis
kyphosis
leishmaniosis
leptospirosis
leucocytosis
limosis
lipomatosis
listeriosis
lordosis
madarosis
marmarosis
meiosis
melanosis
metachrosis
metamorphosis
metempsychosis
miosis
mitosis
molybdosis
mononucleosis
monosis
morphosis
mucoviscidosis
mycosis
mycotoxicosis
myosis
myxomatosis
narcohypnosis
narcosis
necrobiosis
necrosis
nephroptosis
nephrosis
neurosis
onychocryptosis
ornithosis
osmidrosis
osmosis
osteoarthrosis
osteoporosis
otosclerosis
paedomorphosis
parabiosis
paraphimosis
parapsychosis
parasitosis
pediculosis
phagocytosis
phimosis
pholidosis
phytosis
pneumoconiosis
pneumokoniosis
pneumonokoniosis
pneumonoultramicroscopic-
silicovolcanoconiosis
pollenosis
polyposis
porosis
proptosis
psilosis
psittacosis
psychoneurosis
psychosis
pterylosis
ptilosis
ptosis
pyrosis
resinosis
salmonellosis
sarcoidosis
sarcomatosis
sclerosis
scoliosis
self-hypnosis
siderosis
silicosis
sorosis
spirillosis
spirochaetosis
spondylosis
steatosis
stegnosis
stenosis
strongylosis
sycosis
symbiosis
symptosis
synarthrosis
synchondrosis
syndesmosis
synoeciosis
synostosis
syntenosis
syssarcosis
thanatosis
theriomorphosis
thrombosis
thylosis
thyrotoxicosis
torulosis
toxoplasmosis
trichinosis
trichophytosis
trichosis
trophobiosis
trophoneurosis
tuberculosis
tylosis
ulosis
urosis
virosis
visceroptosis
xerosis
zoonosis
zygosis
zymosis

-path

allopath
homeopath
homoeopath
kinesipath
naturopath
neuropath
osteopath
psychopath
sociopath
telepath

-pathic

allopathic
anthropopathic
antipathic
empathic
homoeopathic
hydropathic
idiopathic
kinesipathic
naturopathic
neuropathic
osteopathic
protopathic
psychopathic
sociopathic
telepathic

-pathy

allopathy
anthropopathy
antipathy
apathy
cardiomyopathy
dyspathy
empathy
enantiopathy
homeopathy
homoeopathy
hydropathy
idiopathy
kinesipathy
myocardiopathy
naturopathy
neuropathy
nostopathy
osteopathy
psychopathy
sociopathy
sympathy
telepathy
theopathy
zoopathy

-phage

bacteriophage
macrophage
ostreophage
xylophage

-phagous

anthropophagous
autophagous
carpophagous
coprophagous
creophagous
endophagous
entomophagous
exophagous
geophagous
hippophagous
hylophagous
ichthyophagous
lithophagous
mallophagous
meliphagous
monophagous
myrmecophagous
necrophagous
omophagous
ophiophagous
ostreophagous
pantophagous
phyllophagous
phytophagous
polyphagous
rhizophagous
saprophagous
sarcophagous
scatophagous
theophagous
toxicophagous
toxiphagous
xylophagous
zoophagous

-phagy

anthropophagy
autophagy
coprophagy
dysphagy
endophagy
entomophagy
exophagy

-phagy *(contd.)*
geophagy
hippophagy
ichthyophagy
monophagy
mycophagy
omophagy
ostreophagy
pantophagy
polyphagy
sarcophagy
scatophagy
theophagy
xerophagy

-phile
ailurophile
arctophile
audiophile
bibliophile
cartophile
discophile
francophile
gallophile
Germanophile
gerontophile
halophile
hippophile
homophile
iodophile
logophile
Lusophile
lyophile
myrmecophile
necrophile
negrophile
oenophile
ombrophile
paedophile
psammophile
Russophile
scripophile
Sinophile
Slavophile
spermophile
thermophile
Turcophile
xenophile
zoophile

-philia
ailurophilia
anglophilia
canophilia
coprophilia
ephebophilia
Germanophilia
gerontophilia
haemophilia
necrophilia
neophilia
paedophilia
paraphilia
scopophilia
scoptophilia
zoophilia

-philist
bibliophilist
canophilist
cartophilist
Dantophilist
iconophilist
negrophilist
notaphilist
oenophilist
ophiophilist
pteridophilist
Russophilist
scripophilist
stegophilist
timbrophilist
zoophilist

-phily
acarophily
anemophily
bibliophily
cartophily
entomophily
halophily
hydrophily
myrmecophily
necrophily
notaphily
oenophily
ornithophily
photophily
scripophily
Sinophily
symphily
timbrophily
toxophily
xerophily

-phobe
ailurophobe
anglophobe
francophobe
gallophobe
Germanophobe
gerontophobe
hippophobe
hygrophobe
lyophobe
negrophobe
ombrophobe
photophobe
Russophobe
Slavophobe
Turcophobe
xenophobe

-phobia
acrophobia
aerophobia
agoraphobia
aichmophobia
ailurophobia
algophobia
anemophobia
anglophobia
anthropophobia
arachnophobia
arithmophobia
astraphobia
astrapophobia
bathophobia
bibliophobia
canophobia
claustrophobia
clinophobia
cynophobia
dromophobia
dysmorphophobia
ecophobia
ergophobia
euphobia
francophobia
gallophobia
gerontophobia
graphophobia
gynophobia
hierophobia
homophobia
hydrophobia
hypsophobia
kenophobia
monophobia
mysophobia
necrophobia,
negrophobia
neophobia
nosophobia
nyctophobia
ochlophobia
ophthalmophobia
panophobia
pantophobia
pathophobia
phagophobia
phengophobia
phonophobia
photophobia
Russophobia
satanophobia
scopophobia
sitiophobia
sitophobia
symmetrophobia
syphilophobia
taphephobia
taphophobia
technophobia
thanatophobia
theophobia
toxicophobia
toxiphobia
triskaidecaphobia
triskaidekaphobia
xenophobia
zelophobia
zoophobia

-phobic
aerophobic
agoraphobic
anglophobic
claustrophobic
heliophobic
hydrophobic
lyophobic
monophobic
phobic
photophobic

-phone
aerophone
allophone
anglophone
Ansaphone®
audiphone
chordophone
detectophone
diaphone
dictaphone
diphone
earphone
Entryphone®
francophone
geophone
gramophone
harmoniphone
headphone
heckelphone
homophone
hydrophone
idiophone
interphone
kaleidophone
megaphone
metallophone
microphone
monotelephone
optophone
phone
photophone
Picturephone®
polyphone
pyrophone
radiogramophone
radiophone
radiotelephone
sarrusophone
saxophone
sousaphone
speakerphone
sphygmophone
stentorphone
telephone
theatrophone
triphone
vibraphone
videophone
videotelephone
viewphone
xylophone

-phonic
acrophonic
allophonic
anglophonic
antiphonic
aphonic
cacophonic
cataphonic
chordophonic
dodecaphonic
dysphonic
euphonic
gramophonic
homophonic

-phonic *(contd.)*
microphonic
monophonic
paraphonic
photophonic
quadraphonic
quadrophonic
radiophonic
stentorophonic
stereophonic
symphonic
telephonic
xylophonic

-phony
acrophony
antiphony
aphony
autophony
cacophony
colophony
dodecaphony
euphony
gramophony
homophony
laryngophony
monophony
photophony
polyphony
quadraphony
quadrophony
radiophony
radiotelephony
stereophony
symphony
tautophony
telephony

-phorous
discophorous
Eriophorous
galactophorous
hypophosphorous
mastigophorous
necrophorous
odontophorous
phosphorous
pyrophorous
rhynchophorous
sporophorous

-phyte
aerophyte
bryophyte
cormophyte
dermatophyte
ectophyte
endophyte
entophyte
epiphyte
gametophyte
geophyte
halophyte
heliophyte
heliosciophyte
holophyte
hydrophyte
hygrophyte
hylophyte
lithophyte
mesophyte
microphyte
neophyte
oophyte
osteophyte
phanerophyte
phreatophyte
protophyte
psammophyte
pteridophyte
saprophyte
schizophyte
spermaphyte
spermatophyte
spermophyte
sporophyte
thallophyte
tropophyte
xerophyte
zoophyte
zygophyte

-saurus
Allosaurus
Ankylosaurus
Apatosaurus
Atlantosaurus
brachiosaurus
brontosaurus
Ceteosaurus
Dolichosaurus
Ichthyosaurus
megalosaurus
Plesiosaurus
Stegosaurus
Teleosaurus
Titanosaurus
tyrannosaurus

-scope
aethrioscope
auriscope
baroscope
bathyscope
benthoscope
bioscope
bronchoscope
chromoscope
chronoscope
colposcope
cryoscope
cystoscope
dichrooscope
dichroscope
dipleidoscope
ebullioscope
electroscope
endoscope
engiscope
engyscope
epidiascope
episcope
fluoroscope
galvanoscope
gastroscope
gyroscope
hagioscope
helioscope
hodoscope
horoscope
hydroscope
hygroscope
iconoscope
iriscope
kaleidoscope
kinetoscope
koniscope
lactoscope
laparoscope
laryngoscope
lychnoscope
megascope
microscope
mutoscope
myringoscope
myrioscope
nephoscope
opeidoscope
ophthalmoscope
oscilloscope
otoscope
pantoscope
periscope
pharyngoscope
phenakistoscope
phonendoscope
polariscope
poroscope
praxinoscope
proctoscope
pseudoscope
pyroscope
radarscope
radioscope
rhinoscope
scintilloscope
scope
seismoscope
sigmoidoscope
somascope
spectrohelioscope
spectroscope
sphygmoscope
spinthariscope
statoscope
stereofluoroscope
stereoscope
stethoscope
stroboscope
tachistoscope
teinoscope
telescope
thermoscope
triniscope
ultramicroscope
vectorscope
Vertoscope®
vitascope

-scopic
autoscopic
bronchoscopic
cryoscopic
deuteroscopic
dichrooscopic
dichroscopic
ebullioscopic
electroscopic
endoscopic
gyroscopic
hagioscopic
helioscopic
horoscopic
hygroscopic
kaleidoscopic
laryngoscopic
macroscopic
megascopic
metoposcopic
microscopic
necroscopic
ophthalmoscopic
orthoscopic
pantoscopic
periscopic
poroscopic
rhinoscopic
seismoscopic
spectroscopic
stethoscopic
stroboscopic
submicroscopic
tachistoscopic
telescopic
thermoscopic
ultramicroscopic
zooscopic

-scopy
autoscopy
bronchoscopy
colposcopy
cranioscopy
cryoscopy
cystoscopy
dactyloscopy
deuteroscopy
ebullioscopy
endoscopy
episcopy
fluoroscopy
foetoscopy
hepatoscopy
hieroscopy
horoscopy
laparoscopy
laryngoscopy
metoposcopy
microscopy
necroscopy
omoplatoscopy
oneiroscopy
oniroscopy
ophthalmoscopy
ornithoscopy
ouroscopy
peritoneoscopy
pharyngoscopy
poroscopy
proctoscopy
radioscopy
retinoscopy
rhinoscopy
röntgenoscopy
skiascopy
spectroscopy
stereoscopy

-scopy *(contd.)*
stethoscopy
telescopy
tracheoscopy
ultramicroscopy
urinoscopy
uroscopy
zooscopy

-ship
abbotship
accountantship
acquaintanceship
administratorship
admiralship
advisership
aedileship
airmanship
aldermanship
amateurship
ambassadorship
apostleship
apprenticeship
archonship
assessorship
associateship
attorneyship
auditorship
augurship
authorship
bachelorship
bailieship
baillieship
bardship
barristership
bashawship
batsmanship
beadleship
bedellship
bedelship
benchership
bondmanship
brinkmanship
bursarship
bushmanship
butlership
cadetship
Caesarship
candidateship
captainship
cardinalship
catechumenship
censorship
chairmanship
chamberlainship
championship
chancellorship
chaplainship
chelaship
chiefship
chieftainship
citizenship
clanship
clerkship
clientship
clownship
coadjutorship
colleagueship
collectorship
colonelship
commandantship
commandership
commissaryship
commissionership
committeeship
companionship
compotationship
comradeship
conductorship
confessorship
connoisseurship
conservatorship
constableship
consulship
controllership
copartnership
co-rivalship
corporalship
counsellorship
countship
courtship
cousinship
cowardship
craftmanship
craftsmanship
creatorship
creatureship
curateship
curatorship
custodianship
deaconship
dealership
deanship
demyship
denizenship
devilship
dictatorship
directorship
discipleship
disfellowship
doctorship
dogeship
dogship
dollarship
donship
draftsmanship
dukeship
editorship
eldership
electorship
emperorship
endship
ensignship
entrepreneurship
envoyship
executorship
factorship
fathership
fellowship
foxship
freshmanship
friendship
gamesmanship
generalship
gentlemanship
giantship
gladiatorship
goddess-ship
godship
good-fellowship
governor-generalship
governorship
grandeeship
guardianship
guideship
hardship
headship
hectorship
heirship
heraldship
heroship
hership
hetmanship
horsemanship
hostess-ship
housewifeship
huntsmanship
inspectorship
interpretership
interrelationship
janitorship
jockeyship
judgeship
justiceship
kaisership
keepership
kindredship
kingship
kinship
knaveship
ladyship
lairdship
land-ownership
laureateship
leadership
lectorship
lectureship
legateship
legislatorship
librarianship
lieutenant-
commandership
lieutenant-generalship
lieutenant-governorship
lieutenantship
lifemanship
logship
lordship
ludship
mageship
major-generalship
majorship
managership
marshalship
mastership
matronship
mayorship
mediatorship
membership
Messiahship
milk-kinship
minorship
mistress-ship
moderatorship
monitorship
multi-ownership
musicianship
noviceship
nunship
oarsmanship
one-upmanship
overlordship
ownership
partisanship
partnership
pastorship
patroonship
peatship
pendragonship
penmanship
physicianship
poetship
popeship
possessorship
postmastership
praetorship
preachership
precentorship
prefectship
prelateship
premiership
prenticeship
presbytership
presidentship
pretendership
priestship
primateship
primogenitureship
principalship
priorship
probationership
proconsulship
proctorship
procuratorship
professorship
progenitorship
prolocutorship
prophetship
proprietorship
prosectorship
protectorship
provostship
pursership
quaestorship
queenship
rajahship
rajaship
rangership
readership
recordership
rectorship
regentship
registrarship
relationship
residentiaryship
residentship
retainership
rivalship
rogueship
rulership
sachemship
saintship
salesmanship
scholarship
school-friendship
schoolmastership
scrivenership
seamanship
secretaryship
seigniorship
sempstress-ship
senatorship
seneschalship

-ship *(contd.)*
serfship
sergeantship
serjeantship
servantship
servitorship
sextonship
sheriffship
showmanship
sibship
sizarship
soldiership
solicitorship
sonship
speakership
spectatorship
spinstership
sponsorship
sportsmanship
squireship
statesmanship
stewardship
studentship
subahship
subdeaconship
subeditorship
subinspectorship
subjectship
successorship
suffraganship
sultanship
superintendentship
superiorship
supervisorship
suretyship
surgeonship
surrogateship
surveyorship
survivorship
swordsmanship
teachership
tellership
tenantship
thaneship
thwartship
tide-waitership
township
traineeship
traitorship
treasurership
treeship
tribuneship
truantship
trusteeship
tutorship
twinship
umpireship
uncleship
under-clerkship
undergraduateship
under-secretaryship
unfriendship
ushership
vaivodeship
vergership
vicarship
vice-chairmanship
vice-chancellorship
vice-consulship
viceroyship
virtuosoship
viscountship
viziership
vizirship
voivodeship
waivodeship
wardenship
wardship
watermanship
Whigship
workmanship
worship
wranglership
writership
yachtsmanship

-sophy

anthroposophy
gastrosophy
gymnosophy
pansophy
philosophy
sciosophy
theosophy

-stat

aerostat
antistat
appestat
bacteriostat
barostat
chemostat
coccidiostat
coelostat
cryostat
gyrostat
haemostat
heliostat
humidistat
hydrostat
hygrostat
klinostat
pyrostat
rheostat
siderostat
thermostat

-therapy

actinotherapy
aromatherapy
balneotherapy
chemotherapy
cryotherapy
curietherapy
electrotherapy
heliotherapy
hydrotherapy
hypnotherapy
immunotherapy
kinesitherapy
musicotherapy
narcotherapy
opotherapy
organotherapy
pelotherapy
phototherapy
physiotherapy
psychotherapy
pyretotherapy
radiotherapy
röntgenotherapy
serotherapy
serum-therapy
zootherapy

-tomy

adenectomy
adenoidectomy
anatomy
anthropotomy
appendectomy
appendicectomy
arteriotomy
autotomy
cephalotomy
cholecystectomy
cholecystotomy
colotomy
cordotomy
craniectomy
craniotomy
cystotomy
dichotomy
duodenectomy
embryotomy
encephalotomy
enterectomy
enterostomy
enterotomy
gastrectomy
gastrotomy
gingivectomy
glossectomy
hepatectomy
herniotomy
hysterectomy
hysterotomy
iridectomy
iridotomy
keratotomy
laparotomy
laryngectomy
laryngotomy
leucotomy
lipectomy
lithotomy
lobectomy
lobotomy
lumpectomy
mastectomy
meniscectomy
microtomy
myringotomy
necrotomy
nephrectomy
nephrotomy
neurectomy
neuroanatomy
neurotomy
oophorectomy
orchidectomy
orchiectomy
osteotomy
ovariotomy
patellectomy
pharyngotomy
phlebotomy
phytotomy
pleurotomy
pneumonectomy
pogonotomy
prostatectomy
rhytidectomy
salpingectomy
sclerotomy
splenectomy
stapedectomy
stereotomy
strabotomy
sympathectomy
symphyseotomy
symphysiotomy
syringotomy
tenotomy
tetrachotomy
thymectomy
tonsilectomy
tonsillectomy
tonsillotomy
tonsilotomy
topectomy
tracheotomy
trichotomy
tubectomy
ultramicrotomy
uterectomy
uterotomy
varicotomy
vasectomy
zootomy

-urgy

chemurgy
dramaturgy
electrometallurgy
hierurgy
hydrometallurgy
liturgy
metallurgy
micrurgy
theurgy
zymurgy

-vorous

apivorous
baccivorous
carnivorous
fructivorous
frugivorous
graminivorous
granivorous
herbivorous
insectivorous
lignivorous
mellivorous
myristicivorous
nucivorous
omnivorous
ossivorous
piscivorous
radicivorous
ranivorous
sanguinivorous
sanguivorous
vermivorous